American Musicological Society
Music Library Association Reprint Series

Dover Publications, Inc., New York, in cooperation with the American Musicological Society and the Music Library Association, has undertaken to bring back into print a select list of scholarly musical works long unavailable to the researcher, student, and performer. A distinguished Committee representing both these professional organizations has been appointed to plan and supervise the series, which will include facsimile editions of indispensable historical, theoretical and bibliographical studies as well as important collections of music and translations of basic texts. To make the reprints more useful and to bring them up to date, new introductions, supplementary indexes and bibliographies, etc., will be prepared by qualified specialists.

Sir John Hawkins, *A General History of the Science and Practice of Music*

W. H., A. F., and A. E. Hill, *Antonio Stradivari, His Life and Work*

Curt Sachs, *Real-Lexikon der Musikinstrumente*, new revised, enlarged edition

The Complete Works of Franz Schubert (19 volumes), the Breitkopf & Härtel Critical Edition of 1884-1897 *(Franz Schubert's Werke. Kritisch durchgesehene Gesammtausgabe.)*

Charles Read Baskervill, *The Elizabethan Jig and Related Song Drama*

George Ashdown Audsley, *The Art of Organ-Building,* corrected edition

Emanuel Winternitz, *Musical Autographs from Monteverdi to Hindemith,* corrected edition

William Chappell, *Popular Music of the Olden Time,* 1859 edition

F. T. Arnold, *The Art of Accompaniment from a Thorough-Bass as Practised in the 17th and 18th Centuries*

The Breitkopf Thematic Catalogue, 1762-1787, with new introduction and indexes by B. S. Brook

Otto Kinkeldey, *Orgel und Klavier in der Musik des 16. Jahrhunderts*

Andreas Ornithoparcus, *Musice active micrologus,* together with John Dowland's translation, *A. O. his Micrologus, or Introduction, Containing the Art of Singing*

O. G. T. Sonneck, *Early Concert-life in America (1731-1800)*

Giambattista Mancini, *Practical Reflections on the Figurative Art of Singing* (translated by Pietro Buzzi)

Denis Stevens, *Thomas Tomkins, 1572-1656*

Thoinot Arbeau, *Orchesography* (translated by Mary Stewart Evans)

Edmond vander Straeten, *La Musique aux Pays-Bas avant le XIXᵉ siècle*

Frits Noske, *La Mélodie française de Berlioz à Duparc* (translated by Rita Benton)

Board of Music Trade, *Complete Catalogue of Sheet Music and Musical Works* (1870)

A
GENERAL HISTORY
of the
SCIENCE AND PRACTICE
of
MUSIC

by

SIR JOHN HAWKINS

With a New Introduction by
CHARLES CUDWORTH
Curator, Pendlebury Library of Music
University Music School, Cambridge, England

In Two Volumes

Volume I

DOVER PUBLICATIONS, INC.
NEW YORK   NEW YORK

Published in Canada by General Publishing Company, Ltd., 30 Lesmill Road, Don Mills, Toronto.
Ontario.

Published in the United Kingdom by Constable
and Company, Ltd., 10 Orange Street, London
WC 2.

This new Dover edition, first published in 1963,
is an unabridged republication of the edition published by J. Alfred Novello in 1853.

In the 1853 edition, the portraits and other full-
page illustrations appeared as a separate volume; in
this Dover edition, all these illustrations are re-
produced in appropriate places within the two-volume
text.

This Dover edition also contains a new Introduc-
tion especially prepared for this edition by Charles
Cudworth, Curator, Pendlebury Library of Music,
University Music School, Cambridge, England.

Library of Congress Catalog Card Number: 63-4484

Manufactured in the United States of America

Dover Publications, Inc.
180 Varick Street
New York 14, N.Y.

Introduction to Dover Edition

This twentieth-century edition of Sir John Hawkins' famous *General History of the Science and Practice of Music* is a reprint of the 1853 edition. That edition contained an anonymous but painstaking biography of the author, so it is not really necessary for me to recount again the story of his life, but rather to call the reader's attention to the abiding interest and musicological value of Hawkins' *History.*

Musicologists (and their predecessors, the musical antiquarians) have long realised the value of Hawkins' *History.* Inevitably, of course, it has been compared with the rival history by Dr. Burney; the comparison began in the momentous year of 1776, when both histories of music were first offered to the reading public. Partisanship was strong then and has been so ever since, but the truth is that the two histories of music are complementary rather than competitive; we cannot do without either of them, and the wise musicologist and perspicacious reader make equal use of both. Yet competitive they always have been, from the beginning. This was largely Burney's fault. For all his outward charm and social graciousness, Charles Burney could be an unscrupulous rival and an unforgiving enemy. He obviously rushed his own first volume through the press in order to bring it out before Sir John could issue his five monumental volumes; having beaten his rival by a very short head, and thus getting an option on the market, Burney proceeded to start a malicious whispering campaign in order to denigrate his rival's history in the eyes of the public and above all in the already prejudiced minds of the musical

profession. The result was that Sir John's volumes stood in unsold piles on the booksellers' counters, whilst Burney's, brought out on the instalment plan, sold well and brought their author an ever-increasing reputation. Burney's charming literary style, high professional status, engaging manners and wide acceptance in cultivated London society stood him in excellent stead, and gave him a marked advantage over Sir John, who was not exactly an easy writer, nor the most popular or ingratiating of men; as Dr. Johnson proclaimed in an unfortunate, if unforgettable phrase: "Hawkins is a most *unclubbable* man!" Yet Sir John was a very worthy man; born in humble circumstances, he had risen, at first by sheer hard work, and later by a fortunate marriage, from being a mere lawyer's clerk to a quite enviable position as a wealthy magistrate and knight of the shire. He was also an indefatigable literary man, and to do him justice, a sincere lover of music and especially of old music, or "ancient" music, as he and his contemporaries thought of it. For him, "modern" music had taken a wrong path, after the death of the great Mr. Handel. Hawkins, like Avison before him, found little to admire in the easy-going, Galante "modern" music of his time, and was particularly scathing on the subject of the new symphonies of the Mannheim School: "the general uproar of a modern symphony or overture neither engages attention, nor interrupts conversation" (*History,* Conclusion, p. 919). His *History,* significantly enough, ends with the death of Geminiani, the last of the great Italian violinist-composers of the Late Baroque Era.

Poor Sir John! His memory has come down to posterity with Burney's smears and Dr. Johnson's unfortunate label firmly attached to it, and in spite of the undeniable fact that when Johnson himself wanted a trustworthy friend to appoint as his own executor, it was to Hawkins that he turned. But in some ways it was Sir John's own fault that he gained none of Burney's easy popularity. It wasn't only Johnson who found Hawkins "unclubbable" or at least difficult. Many of his contemporaries dubbed him contumacious, to say the least, although oddly enough that most precious of male blue-stockings, his neighbour Horace Walpole, surprises us by declaring that Hawkins was "a very honest, moral man," although even he added that Hawkins was "obstinate and contentious." But we are not concerned so much with Hawkins' personal character as with his qualities as a musical historian and writer. Burney was undoubtedly the better stylist; Sir John's style was dogged and persevering rather than ingratiating or vivid, although he could occasionally come out with shrewdly dry and penetrating comments, such as "Many persons, in the total absence of thought, flatter themselves that they are merry," or, apropos of late-eighteenth-century taste in music, "Who now remembers, or rather does not affect to forget, the music that pleased him last year?" And discerning musicologists of all ages have always found in him an invaluable storehouse of information, certainly equal to Burney's own, and sometimes even superior. Hawkins' dogged pertinacity in ploughing through the driest and mustiest tomes of musical learning and reducing them to readable synopses was appreciated even by his rival Burney, who did not scruple to borrow as heavily from Hawkins as Handel did from Telemann and with as little acknowledgement. And Sir John's love of older music gave him a much readier sympathy with earlier composers than the modernistic and sometimes rather narrowly fashionable Burney could command. Burney's viewpoint was always that of the up-to-the-minute late-eighteenth-century professional musician, ever ready to applaud the latest thing, but generally scornful of anything which seemed to him old-fashioned, "irregular" or merely crude. Burney could see little

merit in the old madrigalists whose music Sir John had loved and sung at those gatherings of lowly amateurs which he had frequented in his own humble youth.

As musical historians, both Burney and Hawkins were pioneers, exploring practically unknown territory as far as the British reading public was concerned. Little had been written in English on the history of music, and even less published, when the two men began their herculean labours. And what labours they were! Before they could even begin to write, each man had to accumulate his own source materials, a task vast enough in itself to daunt the most courageous of modern musical scholars, spoiled as we are by easy access to great libraries and the casual handiness of the microfilm. Burney even went abroad and scoured the Continent for materials, thus going one better than Sir John. Burney's *History* is better arranged, too; Sir John, for all his strict legal training, obviously found it difficult to maintain control over his vast array of facts, and he did little to help his readers, not even providing headings for his twenty books and their 197 attendant chapters. Perhaps he ought really to have compiled a dictionary of music, just as his friend Johnson compiled a dictionary of words; many of his accounts of composers and performers are really dictionary articles, rather than chapters in a general history. But the facts they contain are invaluable and often cannot be found elsewhere and, let us admit it, now that modern editors have provided us with adequate indexes to Hawkins' work, we should be very badly off without the *History* when we ourselves have to compile our own dictionary articles. This is especially true of the early eighteenth century, that period which Hawkins himself knew and remembered, when men like Handel and Pepusch and Geminiani and Greene had walked the streets of London. And although, unlike Burney, Hawkins was rarely epigrammatical, and although he could never quite match Burney's exquisite prose, nevertheless he too could convey unforgettable pictures to his readers—as, for example, in that fascinating glimpse he gives of Handel's organ playing, in Book XX, p. 912, that passage which concludes: "Such in general was the manner of his performance; but who shall describe its effects on his enraptured auditory? Silence, the truest applause, succeeded the instant that he addressed himself to the instrument, and that so profound, that it checked respiration, and seemed to controul the functions of nature, while the magic of his touch kept the attentions of his hearers awake only to those enchanting sounds to which it gave utterance." Which informs us of many things, and not least that eighteenth-century audiences were not always as noisy and inattentive as they are often said to have been—they too could be quiet, when great music was to be heard. But sometimes Hawkins can shake us with his own severely critical point of view, as when he states so uncompromisingly, of Handel's now-idolised Op. 6 Concertos: "But as to these twelve Concertos, they appear to have been made in a hurry,

and in this issue fell very short of answering the expectations that were formed of them, and inclined men to think that the composition of music merely instrumental, and of many parts, was not Handel's greatest excellence." (Book XX, p. 890).

Yes, I can recommend Hawkins to you; I turn to him myself, again and again, and I am rarely disappointed. I have had considerable cause to thank those Victorian editors who saw fit to reprint him, rather than Burney, in the middle of the nineteenth century, and I am delighted to know that their reprint is to be reprinted yet again, in a newer and even more useful format. Long life to Hawkins' *History;* its author may have been "unclubbable," but as a musical historian, he is quite indispensable.

Cambridge
1962

CHARLES CUDWORTH

List of Portraits in Volume One

SIR JOHN HAWKINS.

From an Original Picture by I.Roberts, in the Music School, Oxford.

LIFE OF
SIR JOHN HAWKINS,

COMPILED FROM

ORIGINAL SOURCES.

SIR JOHN HAWKINS, the friend and executor of Dr. Johnson, and a descendant of the Sir John Hawkins who commanded the Victory, and one of the four divisions of the fleet, as vice-admiral, at the destruction of the Spanish armada, was born in 1719. His father, an architect and surveyor, at first brought his son up to his own profession, but eventually bound him to an attorney, 'a hard taskmaster and a penurious housekeeper.' At the expiration of the usual term, the clerk became a solicitor, and by unremitting assiduity, united to the most inflexible probity, he, unfriended, established himself in a respectable business, while by his character and acquirements he gained admission into the company of men eminent for their accomplishments and intellectual attainments. He was an original member of the Madrigal Society, and at the age of thirty was selected by Mr. (afterwards Dr.) Johnson as one of the nine who formed his Thursday-evening Club in Ivy-lane; a most flattering distinction, which confirmed his literary habits, and powerfully influenced his future pursuits when, not many years after, he relinquished his profession.

In 1753, Mr. Hawkins married Sidney, the second daughter of Peter Storer, Esq., with whom he received an independent fortune, which was greatly augmented in 1759 by the death of his wife's brother. He then retired from all professional avocations, giving up his business to his clerk, Mr. Clark, who subsequently became chamberlain of the city of London. With this increase of wealth is connected an anecdote of far too honorable a nature to be omitted here. The brother of Mrs. Hawkins made a will, giving her the whole of his fortune, except a legacy of £500 to a sister from whom he had become alienated, and communicated the fact to Mr. and Mrs. Hawkins, who, by representing the injustice of this act, and by adding entreaty to argument, prevailed on him to make a more equitable distribution of his property, and an equal division was the consequence. 'We lost by this (says Miss Hawkins, her father's biographer) more than £1,000 a-year; but our gain is inestimable, and we can ride through a manor gone from us with exultation.'

Upon retiring from the law, Mr. Hawkins purchased a **house** at Twickenham, intending to dedicate his future life to literary labour and the enjoyment of select society. But in 1771 he was inserted in the commission of the peace for the county of Middlesex, and immediately became a most active magistrate. Here his independent spirit and charitable disposition were manifested. Acting as a magistrate, he at first refused the customary fees; but finding that this generous mode of proceeding rather increased the litigious disposition of the people in his neighbourhood, he altered his plan, took what was his due, but kept the amount in a separate purse, and at fixed periods consigned it to the clergyman of his parish, to be distributed at his discretion.

Being about this time led, by the defective state of the Highways, to consider the laws respecting them, and their deficiencies, he determined to revise them, and accordingly drew up a scheme for an Act of Parliament, to consolidate the several former statutes, and to add such other regulations as appeared to him necessary. His ideas on this subject he published in 1763, in an 8vo. volume entituled 'Observations on the state of Highways, and on the Laws for amending and keeping them in repair;' subjoining a draught of the Act before-mentioned. This very bill was afterwards introduced into the House of Commons, and passing through the usual forms, became the Act under which all the Highways in the kingdom were for many years regulated, and which forms the nucleus of the statutes now in force.

Some time after this, a cause as important in its nature, if not so extensive in its influence, induced him again to exert himself in the service of the public. The Corporation of London, finding it necessary to rebuild the gaol of Newgate, at an expense, according to their own estimates, of £40,000, had applied to Parliament, by a bill brought in by their own members, to throw the onus of two-thirds of the outlay on the County of Middlesex. This the Magistrates of the County thought fit to resist, and accordingly a vigorous opposition was commenced under the conduct of Mr. Hawkins, who drew a petition accompanied by a case, which was printed and distributed among the members of both Houses of Parliament. This memorial became the subject of a day's discussion in the House of Lords, and in the Commons produced such an effect, that the City of London, by their own members, moved for leave to withdraw the bill.

He was, in 1765, elected chairman of the Middlesex quarter-sessions.

Not long after this event, the rector and officers of the parish of St. Andrew's, Holborn, in which he was then a resident, solicited his assistance in opposing an attempt of the Corporation of London, to carry out a design which was fraught with injury to their interests. The City had projected opening a street from Blackfriars-bridge (then lately built) across the bottom of Holborn-hill, and as much farther northward as they might think proper. In the execution of this scheme, they had contemplated, among other changes, the bestowal of the Fleet prison (an intolerable nuisance) on their neighbours, the parishioners of St. Andrew's, by its removal to the spot on which Ely House then stood. They had accordingly entered into a treaty with the then bishop of Ely, and were exerting all their influence to drive a bill through the House of Commons, which should confirm that contract, and enable the bishop to alienate the inheritance. The inhabitants of the neighbourhood, together with the earl of Winchelsea, the ground landlord, reasonably alarmed at this project, determined to oppose it throughout, and to this end applied to Mr. Hawkins for his aid. He accordingly drew two petitions, one in behalf of the rector and churchwardens, and the other in that of lord Winchelsea, with a case for each, containing the reasons on which they rested their opposition. These, like his previous endeavours, were successful, and the application of the City of London failed. For this assistance, the parish not content with returning him their thanks, determined to expend £30 in the purchase of a silver cup to be presented to him, a resolution which was shortly afterwards carried into effect. During this time his literary reputation had become so highly established, that the University of Oxford, meditating a re-publication of Sir Thomas Hanmer's Shakespeare, in 6 vols. 4to, with additional notes, applied to him to furnish them. This he accordingly did, and on the issue of the work, received from the University a copy as a present—a favor the more to be esteemed as but six copies of the impression were thus given. Of these the King received one, the Queen another, the King of Denmark a third, and Mr. Hawkins a fourth. To whom the other two were presented is now not known. In 1770, a charge was delivered by him, in his capacity of Chairman of the Quarter Sessions, to the grand jury of Middlesex, which, at their general request, was printed and published. During the years of which we have been speaking, popular discontent had occasionally risen high, and in the execution of his duty as a magistrate Mr. Hawkins had more than once been called into service of great personal danger; but his was not a character to shrink from peril in a good cause, and when the riots at Brentford broke out, as they did with great violence on various occasions, he and some of his brethren presenting themselves on the spot, effectually suppressed the tumult by their resolute demeanour.

When, too, the rising of the Spitalfields weavers took place, the Middlesex magistrates, and he at their head, attended at Moorfields, the scene of the disturbances, with a party of the Guards, and succeeded by their firmness and conduct in dispersing the mob, and repressing an outbreak which at one time seemed to threaten formidable results.

Having thus, on many occasions, given proofs of his courage, loyalty, and ability, he in 1772 received from his Majesty, George III., the honor of knighthood.

A fresh edition of Shakespeare being contemplated by Dr. Johnson and Mr. Stevens in 1773, he was, for the second time, requested to furnish notes to that author, which he accordingly did.

In 1775, the year in which it was determined to commence the disastrous American war, it being thought proper to carry up an address from the county of Middlesex to the King on the occasion, the magistrates, at his instance, voted one which he drew up, and had the honor of presenting to his Majesty in the October of that year.

It may not be out of place to notice here, an assertion made by Boswell in his Life of Johnson, vol. i. p. 168, that 'upon occasion of presenting an address to the King, he (Hawkins) accepted the *usual* offer of knighthood.' Without remarking on the spirit which has evidently actuated Boswell whenever he has spoken of Sir John, it is enough to state that no address whatever was presented in 1772 (the year in which he was knighted), or for some years previously; and, moreover, that there is strong reason to believe that the address of 1775, mentioned above (which was presented exactly three years *after* the date of his knighthood), was the only one in which he ever was concerned. Be this last as it may, the fact above mentioned sufficiently disproves the allegation. Even, however, if the honor had been attained as Boswell describes, it would have mattered little; for that he was not unworthy of it may be gathered from the fact, that the Earl of Rochford (then one of the Secretaries of State), when presenting him to the King for knighthood, took occasion to describe him as the best magistrate in the kingdom.

In the memorable year 1780, an order from the Privy Council having been issued through the Secretary of State's office, requiring the Middlesex magistrates to assemble for the preservation of the public peace, he and some others met early in the morning of Monday, the 5th of June, and continued sitting at Hicks's Hall, their Sessions House, till late in the evening. On the following day they did likewise; but at night, instead of returning to their own homes, they determined to form parties of two each, and thus to distribute themselves in those places where mischief was to be apprehended. This resolution was taken in consequence of the prevalence of a report that the mob intended to attack the houses of Lord North and of other members of the Administration, and also that of Lord Mansfield. As Sir John had long been honored with the friendship of the latter, he fixed upon him as the object of his attention, and accordingly proceeded to his house, accompanied by a brother magistrate who resided in the neighbourhood. On their arrival they found Lord Mansfield writing to the Secretary of War for a party of the Guards, and the interval between the despatch of the application and the arrival of the troops was spent in conferences with his Lordship and the Archbishop of York (his neighbour), on the plan to be adopted. On Lord Mansfield's asking Sir John his intentions, he answered that his design was to place the men behind the piers which divided the windows, and to hold them in readiness to fire on the mob directly the demonstrations of the rioters rendered such an act necessary. To this, however, Lord Mansfield objected, from a dislike to bloodshed, and on the arrival of the troops, declined to take them into the house, sending them to the vestry at Bloomsbury, to remain there, in readiness to act, if their services should be required. As it appeared he did not wish to retain the magistrates, they retired, having arranged that Sir John should remain at the house of his colleague in Southampton-row, close by, till 12 P.M., at which time he intended, if all remained quiet, to return to his own home, as his Lordship would still have one magistrate in his immediate vicinity in case of any emergency. In Southampton-row he accordingly staid till past midnight, when, no disturbance having occurred at Lord Mansfield's, and a messenger arriving from Northumberland House to say that it was beset, and that the Duke had sent for Sir John, he proceeded thither.* On his arrival there, he found that a considerable mob was assembled in front of the house, but that no assault had yet been attempted. Proper precautions were immediately taken for its defence, and in order that the projected measures might be duly carried out, in the event of an outbreak, the Duke pressed Sir John to stay there the remainder of the night, which he accordingly consented to do. He was, however, very near paying dearly for his conduct, for, notwithstanding the lateness of the hour at which he entered Northumberland House, he had been recognised by the mob, who were heard to menace him with their vengeance. This threat they evidently intended to carry out, for on his return to his house in Queen's-square, Westminster, he discovered that it had been marked with a red cross, the symbol by which during that period the rioters devoted property to destruction. Being, fortunately for him, fully aware of the meaning of the sign, he immediately saw the necessity of erasing it. This, however, was no easy matter, for, from the crowds of people who had assembled in all parts of the town, there was great danger of any attempt to efface it being at once discovered. Placing himself, however, with his back against the wall, in the careless way in which an indifferent spectator might be supposed to stand,

* It was afterwards discovered that there had been an error in the message which he received. It had really been sent from Lord North's, in Downing-street, and not the Duke of Northumberland's. The similarity in the names probably originated the mistake, which might be farther confirmed by the fact that the Duke, as Lord Lieutenant of the county, was a likely object of attack, at a time when every magistrate was favored with the detestation of the populace.

he passed his hand, in which was a handkerchief, behind him, and thus succeeded in totally obliterating the ill-omened symbol. Fortunately, his having done so was unnoticed; the mark was not renewed, and his house escaped the destruction which, the following night, overtook all others similarly distinguished.

When these tumults had in some measure subsided, it became necessary to bring to trial many persons who, by their participation in them, had become involved in the guilt of high treason; and it was therefore imperative that the grand jury of Middlesex, to whom the indictments were to be presented, should be instructed in the state of the law as bearing upon the offence in question. A message, at the instance of the Attorney-General, was accordingly sent to Sir John, desiring him to deliver, at the then ensuing session, a charge to the grand jury, explanatory of the duties required of them. This desire, at the moment it was made, was sufficiently embarrassing, for he was away from home, and consequently at a distance from the books he wished to consult; and, moreover, he had but forty-eight hours in which to prepare his address. Notwithstanding these disadvantages, he, however, constructed a charge which on its delivery was highly commended, and which the grand jury, after passing a vote of thanks to him for its 'learning and eloquence,' desired to have printed and published.

But to return to the narrative of his youth; from which this digression has been made in order to relate uninterruptedly the incidents of his magisterial career. Very early in life he cultivated music as the solace of his severer occupations—the recreation of his leisure hours. It was the society of the eminent that young Hawkins courted, and in the practice of the classical music of his day that he took delight. Immyns, and through him Dr. Pepusch, were his earliest musical associates. His daughter records an interesting anecdote of his acquaintance with Handel. She says :—

"Were I to attempt enumerating my father's musical friendships, I should copy, a second time, the greater part of the last volume of his History of Music; I will, however, record what I have heard and known of those between whom and himself this powerful union subsisted. Handel had done him the honor frequently to try his new productions in his young ear; and my father calling on him one morning to pay him a visit of respect, he made him sit down, and listen to the air of *See the conquering Hero comes*, concluding with the question, 'How do you like it?' my father answering, 'Not so well as some things I have heard of yours;' he rejoined, 'Nor I neither; but, young man, you will live to see that a greater favorite with the people than my other fine things.'

He was an original member of the 'Madrigal Society,' founded by the former in 1741. With Stanley he engaged in 1742, in the joint publication of some Canzonets of which Hawkins furnished the greater portion of the words, while Stanley composed the music.

Young men, accomplished in music, frequently find it an excellent introduction to company which otherwise they would hardly reach, and a recommendation to patrons by whom their legal or mercantile abilities might be overlooked. And so young Hawkins found: his Canzonets were sung and encored at Vauxhall, Ranelagh, and other places. The author of 'Who'll buy a heart?' was enquired after: amongst others, a Mr. Hare, a brewer, and musical amateur, who had often met Hawkins at Mr. Stanley's, invited him to his house. At Mr. Hare's he met his future father-in-law, Mr. Storer, who being a practitioner in a high grade of the law, but declining into years, found in the young amateur of music, first a valuable assistant, and afterwards a welcome husband for his daughter, and sharer of his opulence.

Some time previous to the publication of the Canzonets mentioned above, he had been well known in the literary world as the author of various contributions to the 'Gentleman's Magazine,' and other periodicals of similar description. These, being mostly anonymous, are now, of course, not easily traced. This much, however, is known: that they were not confined to any one subject, but embraced many different topics, and that they comprised both prose and poetry. A copy of verses to Mr. John Stanley, inserted in the *Daily Advertiser* for Feb. 21, 1741, and bearing date Feb. 19, 1740, is supposed to have been the earliest of his productions now known. But it was not only to the lighter occupation of literature that his attention was directed; for when, in the eventful year of 1745, the young Pretender published his manifesto, an answer to it, written by Mr. Hawkins, was widely circulated and read; and a series of papers on the same subject, furnished to the magazines and newspapers of the day, attested his attachment to the House of Hanover. His conduct, indeed, at this critical period, attracted the notice of the Duke of Newcastle, who wished to bring him into public life—'which attempt,' says a friend and contemporary of Sir John's, in writing to his son, 'was frustrated by your father's predilection for a studious life, and from a reserved disposition.' Nor was this the only occasion on which the honor was offered him, for in the same letter, dated Feb. 4, 1796, the correspondent, Mr. T. Gwatkin, of Eign, near Hereford, says—'When the noise was 'loud about Wilkes and liberty, Sir John's conduct as 'a magistrate, and his subsequent charges, met with 'the approbation of the Duke of Northumberland, the 'Lord Lieutenant for the county of Middlesex, who 'wished to introduce him into Parliament. I strongly 'urged him to accept the offer: my arguments made some 'impression; but he was then deeply engaged in the 'History of Music; besides he was, as I could easily 'collect from repeated conversations—although both from 'habit and theoretical reasoning entirely attached to the 'House of Hanover—jealous of his own personal in- 'dependence. If, merely from personal interest, he could 'have been returned for a county or city, I believe he 'would have had no objection; but although he was a

'friend to the Administration, he did not choose to come 'into Parliament under the auspices of any minister. 'An offer was made him of placing you and your brother 'upon the foundation of King's Scholars at Westminster, 'and I pressed him to accept it, from the examples of 'Lord Mansfield and other great men who were upon 'the foundation, yet from the same principle of inde- 'pendence he rejected it.'

This letter, which certainly gives great insight into Sir John's character, would not have been quoted so much at length, did it not furnish the best possible refutation of the stigma cast upon him by Boswell—that, in his intercourse with Johnson, he betrayed an unworthy spirit of subserviency. Of this, however, it will be requisite to speak hereafter.

The motive that induced him to decline the offer of the presentation, was the feeling that the intention of the founder would be violated, if those who were in a position to pay for the education of their children, placed them on a foundation designed exclusively for 'poor scholars.'

In 1760, being in possession of some authentic and interesting documents relating to the author, he published an edition of Walton's 'Complete Angler,' with the second part by Cotton. To the original work he added notes, and wrote a life of Walton appending one of Cotton by the well-known Mr. W. Oldys: and that no means of making the work attractive might be neglected, he embellished it with cuts, designed by Wade, and engraved by Ryland, which are even at this time, when art has so much advanced, remarkable for their elegance. Of this work, three editions were sold off before the year 1784, when he published a fourth. For this, he had revised the life of Walton, and the notes throughout the work, and made large additions to both, while he re-wrote the life of Cotton in order to compress it, retaining, however, every fact respecting him mentioned in the former impressions, and subjoining several more. After his death, a fifth edition was published by his eldest son, who inserted the last corrections and additions found in Sir John's papers.

About the year 1770, the Academy of Ancient Music finding that, owing to the increase in the number of places of public amusement, and the consequent enlarged demands for eminent performers, their subscription of two guineas and a half was not sufficient to carry out the plan they had adopted, were obliged to solicit farther assistance. To this end Mr. Hawkins, then a member, drew up and published a pamphlet entitled 'An Account of the institution and progress of the 'Academy of Ancient Music, with a comparative view of 'the Music of the past and present times.' This was published in octavo in 1770, but without any author's name.

Hawkins had long been a member of all the best concerts in London; and when circumstances permitted him to make his own house a central point of assembly, the first musical men of the day flocked with pleasure to Austin Friars. Drs. Cooke and Boyce were among his intimate friends; and Bartleman, then a boy, his protegé. He collected all the standard compositions of his own day, and of former times, and purchased, after the death of their owner, Dr. Pepusch's invaluable collection of theoretical treatises.* The idea of becoming the historian of the art he cultivated with so much ardour, is said to have been first suggested to him by the celebrated Horace Walpole: and when the inheritance of his brother-in-law rendered him independent of any involuntary labour, he seriously applied himself to the task. Of itself it was no easy one, and the multiplied demands which the duties of an active and presiding magistrate made upon his time considerably prolonged its duration. In this, as in all his other literary labours, his daughter, together with his sons, afforded the assistance of amanuensis, collator, and corrector of the press. In collecting his materials Sir John Hawkins was indefatigable—

' Nil actum reputans, si quid superesset agendum.'

He corresponded with every one from whom information could be hoped, and amongst others with Dr. Gostling, of Canterbury,† from whose collections and recollections he obtained much curious matter that no other person could have furnished. Correspondence led to personal intimacy, and Sir John visited Mr. Gostling at Canterbury in 1772 and the following year. He also, in 1772, resided a considerable time in Oxford, making extracts from MSS. in the Bodleian and other libraries, and accompanied by an artist from London to copy the portraits in the Music School.

In 1776 he published, in 5 vols. 4to, his 'History of Music,' a work upon which he had been engaged for the space of sixteen years. Three years before, he had obtained permission to dedicate his book to George III.; and he now presented it to his Majesty at Buckingham House, during a long audience granted for the purpose. The King, no doubt, appreciated the work as it deserved, and the University of Oxford showed their estimation of it by offering to confer on the author the degree of Doctor in Law, which he had reasons for declining; but that learned body paid him the compliment of requesting his portrait, which now hangs in the Music School.

In this delightful book, authorities have been consulted and brought together from various libraries and museums, with a diligence in research, and a solicitude almost affectionate in their collection and arrangement, forming together a mass of the most curious and entertaining

information upon a subject the most enchanting. No pains have been spared to render the work complete. It bears evidence of being a labour of love; of being one of those tasks, which are none to the compiler,—but a delight. The evident pleasure he takes in his work, reflects itself upon the reader; rendering it light and agreeable,—nothing wearisome, however long and minute. There is evidence of toil, but the perusal is not toilsome; for the author's toil is so willingly undertaken, and so enjoyingly pursued, that the effect upon the reader is unalloyed enjoyment. No amount of care has been deemed too much; and the reader feels grateful for being spared the trouble of seeking, while he luxuriously profits by the result. He sits in his arm-chair, comfortably ruminating the stores of knowledge which have been culled for him from various wide-spread sources, by patient, worthy Sir John; who,—the beauty of it is,—has evidently had as much gratification in gathering the materials for the feast, as the reader finds from the feast itself. Besides the information contained in the book, there is abundance of amusing reading. It was a favorite with Charles Lamb, who, though no musical authority, was an eminent literary one, of unsurpassed refined taste and high judgment. In the shape of notes, there is a fund of anecdote, and a large amount of incidental miscellaneous matter, scattered through the work, that pleasantly relieve the graver main theme. Anything entertaining, that can by possibility be linked on to the subject of music, is easily and chattily introduced; as though the author and his reader were indulging in a cheerful gossip by the way. We have, in quaint succession, such things as that romantic love-passage of Giuffredo Rudello, the troubadour poet; or that wondrous account of the Moorish Admirable Crichton, Alpharabius,—which is like a page out of the 'Arabian Nights;' or that naïve detail of bluff King Harry's fancy for my Lord Cardinal's minstrels, and of his setting off with them for a certain nobleman's house where was a shrine to which he had vowed a pilgrimage, and where he spent the night in dancing to the sound of the minstrels' playing.

Sir John had no prototype of his great work. The design, as the execution, was entirely his own; and when the large extent, and various nature of his materials are considered, the plan will be allowed to have been devised with considerable ability.

It is not an unusual, and at first sight appears not an unreasonable prejudice, to suppose that, in order to qualify a man to write upon any art, he should be a professor of, or at least have been regularly educated to, the art of which he treats. A lawyer seems as little qualified to write a history of Music, as a composer would be to expound the nature of Uses and Trusts, or a violin player to explain the principles of Architectural beauty. To write on the practical department of an art certainly requires experience and information which an artist alone can acquire; and had Sir John Hawkins published a new book of instructions for the organ or violoncello, he would probably have subjected himself to being deservedly ac-

---

* This collection, when his History of Music was published, Sir John gave to the British Museum, and thus preserved it from the fate which attended the rest of his library.

† The Rev. William Gostling, Minor Canon of Canterbury Cathedral, was the son of that Mr. Gostling for whom Purcell wrote his celebrated anthem, ' They that go down to the sea in ships,' and of whom Charles II. said, ' You may talk of your nightingales and sky-larks, but I have a Gosling shall beat them all.' Combining his own knowledge to the information derived from his father, Mr. Gostling was a living depository of musical history and anecdote back nearly to the middle of the seventeenth century.

cused of presumption. The theory of an art, even, can hardly be satisfactorily explained, except by one who has that intimate familiarity with its practice and its nomenclature which is rarely, if ever, attained by an amateur. But with the historian the case is different: it is to be presumed that a man who voluntarily dedicates years of labour to collect from all quarters the scattered records of an art, must be, on the one hand, himself attached to it, and familiar with its practice, in a degree amply sufficient to secure him against the danger of misinterpreting any technical or conventional phrases; while, on the other hand, the habits of research, the knowledge of languages, and the various literary acquirements requisite for the historian, are but seldom to be found united in the mere artist. Captain Cook used to say that the best weatherglass in the world would be made by the amalgamation (or, as he called it, stewing down together) of a sailor and a shepherd: for the one spent his whole life in studying the prognostics of wind and rain, and the other those of sunshine and rain. So the beau ideal of a his-

torian of music would be found in a man who united in his own person the composer, performer, linguist, and philosopher, together with the leisure *and* studious habits of the man of letters. But if we cannot find this phœnix, if we must rest contented either with the artist or the student, the balance of qualification is highly in favour of the latter. Sir John Hawkins, however, was made to feel the weight of the prejudice we have alluded to: in immediate competition with his History of Music, another work under the same title was published by Dr. Burney. The public did not even compare the respective merits of the works: they eagerly purchased the professor's history, while that of the amateur was left unasked for, or sneered at, on the publisher's counter.

The fate of the work, however, was decided at last, like that of many more important things, by a trifle, a word, a pun. A pun condemned Sir John Hawkins's sixteen years' labour to long obscurity and oblivion. Some wag wrote the following catch, which Dr. Callcott set to music :—

N.B.—Leave out the Bars between ╬ ╬ till the 3rd Voice comes in, then go on.

I. W. CALLCOTT, B.M.

Burn his history was straightway in every one's mouth; and the bookseller, if he did not literally follow the advice, actually '*wasted*,' as the term is, or sold for waste paper some hundred copies, and buried the rest of

the impression in the profoundest depths of a damp cellar, as an article never likely to be called for; so that now hardly a copy can be procured undamaged by damp and mildew. It has been for some time, however, rising—is rising—and the more it is read and known, the more it will rise in public estimation and demand.

It may not, however, be generally known that Burney's History, which was more successful at the time, was not begun till many years after this, nor till its author had been allowed constant and unrestrained access to the materials collected by Sir John for his work. Moreover, the first volume only of Burney's History was published simultaneously with Sir John's complete work, while the remaining three followed at intervals of two years between each volume.

The unfair competition, all things considered, of Dr. Burney, and the prejudices it engendered, rendered it scarcely surprising that Sir John's History of Music did not even furnish a pair of carriage horses to its author; who had often declared that if, in a pecuniary point of view, he obtained that trifling reward of his sixteen years' labour he should be well satisfied.

Which of the rival histories is intrinsically the better, and consequently the more calculated to secure an enduring meed of approbation, has been carefully considered; and the result is, the re-production of Sir John Hawkins's valuable work. The great progress which has been made in the art since that period, as well as the consequent increase in the number of accomplished musicians, formed the turning-point in favor of this decision.

When it is considered that the science of Music is one that has pervaded all time, and been to a greater or less extent the common property of all nations, it is evident that one who could hope to succeed in recording its history, must bring to his undertaking a competent knowledge of both ancient and modern languages; an acquaintance with history critically exact with regard to its periods and their peculiarities; and a familiarity with blackletter and obsolete signs and abbreviations, sufficient to discover and decipher any documents relating to the art which might be recorded in them. To this were to be added a careful assiduity—which, unscared by its details, and undeterred by its intricacies, should follow the art in its progress through centuries extending from Jubal down to Handel;—a laborious zeal, which might know neither fatigue nor rest, in investigating not only the properties of the science itself, but likewise all circumstances respecting the subject which might in any way, however remotely, relate to it;—a keen, discriminating action, which should unhesitatingly and accurately determine authenticities and affix dates;—and, finally, a judicious method, which should first arrange and systematize the knowledge acquired, and then present it in the clearest form to the contemplation of the world. Sir John Hawkins united in himself most of these qualities in an eminent degree.

In the month of December, 1783, Dr. Johnson, with whom he had for many years been on terms of great friendship, sent for him, and imparting to him that he had discovered in himself symptoms of dropsy, declared his desire of making a will, and his wish that Sir John should be one of his executors. On his consenting, the Doctor entered into an account of his circumstances, and mentioned the disposition he intended to make of his effects. Of this matter Boswell has thought fit to say 'that by assiduous attendance upon Johnson in his last illness, he (Hawkins) obtained the post of one of his executors.'

Now the impression created by this statement on the mind of a person not acquainted with the facts would be, firstly, that up to the period mentioned, the acquaintance between the Doctor and Sir John had been slight, and secondly, that the attention paid by the latter to his dying friend proceeded from an unworthy motive. With regard, then, to the former portion of the insinuation, it may be sufficient to state that the acquaintance between them had subsisted for more than thirty years, and that up to a comparatively recent period, there were those living who had been in the habit of frequently meeting Johnson at Hawkins's house, and who could testify to the closeness of their intimacy. To the latter, we have the whole tenor of Sir John's life to oppose; and it is not very probable that he, who from a scruple which the world may consider overstrained, but must admit to be honorable, had used, and successfully used, all his energies to dissuade another who was bent on enriching him, from carrying his intentions into effect; who had, from a spirit of independence, twice declined a seat in Parliament, then a much greater object of ambition than now; and who, as a matter of conscience, had preferred defraying the expense of his sons' education at one public school to accepting a free presentation for them to another;—it is not likely, we say, that the man who had acted in this way, would stoop to the moral degradation imputed to him. To these general facts, indeed, his vindication might well be left; but there are others of a more particular nature. In the first place, then, the conversation in which Dr. Johnson engaged Sir John to be his executor, took place in December, 1783; and about the middle of 1784 he was 'so well recovered from all his ailments' that 'both himself and his friends hoped that he had some years to live.' Thus it appears that, far from the appointment being the effect of anything that occurred in his last illness, it in fact, preceded it; for although the will was not executed till December, 1784, all the arrangements had been made the year before. In the second place, it is established by the testimony of one of Sir John's sons, that Johnson had for many years been accustomed to consult him on all important matters, and more especially those connected with business; and in the third, it can be stated on the same authority, that 'the office had been wholly unsolicited by words or actions.'

To take, however, Boswell's assertion as it stands— if it really be the case that Johnson was moved to select Sir John as he describes, it argues a weakness on the great Doctor's part which Boswell, as his friend, would have done well to conceal; a weakness, by the way, the supposition of which is far from being borne out by his choice of the co-executors, Dr. William Scott (afterwards

Lord Stowell) and Sir Joshua Reynolds. If it be not so, and Johnson, in the full enjoyment of his usual strength of mind, deliberately preferred Hawkins to Boswell, [and *hinc illæ lacrymæ*] the inference is obvious that he selected the person in whom he had the greatest confidence. Neither is Boswell's assertion correct, that in consequence of his appointment as an executor, the booksellers of London employed him to publish an edition of Johnson's works and to write his life. The fact is, that a number of slanders and calumnies had been propagated against Johnson during his life, and he was apprehensive that many more would be circulated after his decease. With this impression on his mind, he frequently, in the many interviews which took place between the friends during the last year of his life, committed *in express terms*, 'the care of his fame' to Sir John. It was, therefore, to this injunction, and not to a contract with the booksellers, that the life of Johnson and edition of his works, published by Hawkins in 1787, owed its existence.

He had scarce entered upon his task when his own library, that dearest pride and most cherished worldly good of a literary man——a labour which it had been the toil and delight of more than thirty years to collect, and which comprised among its books, prints and drawings, many articles that no money could replace——was destroyed by fire, at the time his house in Queen Square, Westminster, was burnt down. The blow was a severe one, but the sufferer was never heard to murmur or complain, and as soon as he was settled in another habitation, he sought in renewed study the solace of his misfortune.

In 1787 he closed his literary career, by publishing his life of Johnson and edition of his works. Immediately on its appearance, it was virulently attacked by Boswell and others; but the author was repeatedly accosted in the streets by utter strangers, who thanked him for the amusement and information he afforded them. No one can doubt that there existed, at the time of its publication, many causes, totally irrespective of the merits of the book, which may account for its being so violently decried. In the first place, he who undertakes to give to the world accounts of his contemporaries invariably runs the risk of incurring great animosity: and the more candidly and impartially he performs his task, the greater is his danger in this respect; for while the friends of the deceased consider that his virtues and amiable qualities are not sufficiently enlarged upon, those who disliked him, on the other hand, determine that his failings have been too much glossed over. This was eminently the case with Johnson: there can be no question that his strong sense, his wonderful acquirements, and his gigantic intellect, had excited the unbounded admiration and secured the enduring love of many; but it is equally certain that his dictatorial spirit and his boorish manner, under which some had personally smarted, had created him enemies in an equal proportion. With Hawkins's work, then, both parties were dissatisfied—the one, that the representation given of him fell so far short of their

extravagant idea of his perfection, the other that it exceeded what they considered his deserts. Again, there were, no doubt, others who had pleased their imaginations with the hope, that the slight acquaintance they might have with Johnson, would induce the writer of his life to hand them down to posterity as the friends of the great Lexicographer, and who, having travelled through the biography without attaining the 'wished-for consummation' of seeing their 'names in print,' were not inclined to view with very favorable eyes the labours of his historian. Another, and the not least bitter class, was composed of those who, sufficiently aware of the extent of Johnson's reputation, had conceived the design of profiting by his celebrity. Of these projected biographers the number was not small, and it cannot be supposed that they could be other than hostile to a work which, by superseding the necessity for a second, defeated their hope of fame or emolument, whichever might be their object.

Before concluding this narration, it may be allowable to remark, that while few persons have been, both during life and after death, so rancorously attacked as Sir John Hawkins, none have come out of an ordeal so severe as that to which his reputation has been exposed, more thoroughly unscathed than he has done. Some of the most probable causes of his being so virulently assailed, have been stated above: but there are doubtless others; and the one which drew upon him the enmity of Stevens is too important to be omitted. It appears that an inexplicable coolness had arisen between Garrick and Hawkins, who had formerly been on very intimate terms, and on some accidental circumstances leading the latter to investigate the source of this, it was discovered, on irrefragable evidence, that Stevens had made mischief between the two. With this he was taxed by Sir John; and unable, to refute the impeachment, was by him ejected from his house. This, Stevens was not likely to forgive; more especially as he must have been conscious that he had been detected in another act of most disgraceful nature. A day or two before the intended presentation of the address of 1775, mentioned above, he had called on Sir John. A manuscript copy of the address lay on the table in the room into which he was shown. This after his departure was missed and was never found again. On the publication of the *St. James's Chronicle*, the paper with which Stevens was connected, a copy of the missing address was found inserted, with an account of its presentation. Now it so happened that, owing to some accident, the reception of the address by the king had been postponed, and that at the time the public were reading this account, the address had not yet been presented at all. The address too, only existed in manuscript, and in Sir John's possession: under these circumstances there can be no doubt that Stevens had purloined the copy, trusting that the address would be presented at the time proposed, which was anterior to the publication of his paper, and that on its appearance in the *St. James's Chronicle*, it would be supposed that he had received it from some person about the Court. The accidental delay had however defeated this hypothesis; and, with the other circumstances, fixed the guilt of the theft upon him.

As another instance of Mr. Stevens's mode of procedure, the following is subjoined :—

9, Bridge-street, Westminster, April 3, 1853.

MY DEAR SIR,—I enclose you the anecdote which I promised. Any information in relation to your edition of Hawkins that I am able to afford, shall be cheerfully contributed in aid of so spirited and useful a publication.

Most truly yours, W. AYRTON.

To Mr. J. Alfred Novello.

Hawkins's History and George Stevens.

" When Hawkins's History of Music was ready for printing, Stevens—who contributed to it *much* of the literary portion—that is, the literary facts and the result of his research—went to Thomas Payne (' Old, honest Tom Payne, of the Mews-gate'), and strongly recommended him to purchase the work, at the price of 500 guineas, extolling it as exhibiting great learning, and abounding in interesting detail.

" The week after the work appeared, a letter was published in the *St. James's Evening Post*, attacking it with great violence. Stevens, in Payne's shop, entered on the subject of the letter, condemning in strong terms the injustice and violence of the critique. Shortly after, a second attack appeared in the same journal, and Stevens, at his usual—almost daily—visit to the Mews-gate, where many of the literati used to assemble and converse, again expressed his surprise and disgust at the continuance of such wanton hostility, saying, ' It is a most unfair and most malignant enemy who writes in the *St. James's Evening Post*.' ' Yes,' said Mr. Payne, ' it is most malignant and unjust; and I have the best proofs, Mr. Stevens, that you are the author of those letters, and I never wish to see your face again in this place !'

" Stevens never after repeated his visits; but wishing to meet, as usual, his friend, the Rev. Mr. Cracherode, used to walk on the side opposite Payne's shop at the time when Cracherode generally called there, in order to enjoy his almost daily literary chat with him.*

" The foregoing I had from Mr. Thomas Payne, who succeeded his father in the business, which he removed to Pall Mall. The account was given to me, in nearly the same words, by Mr. Evans, bookseller in Pall Mall, who had been a shopman of the elder Payne; and this has been confirmed by Mr. Henry Foss, who, on the death of the second T. Payne, carried on the business, in partnership with Mr. John Thomas Payne, in Pall Mall.

" I have a clear recollection of Sir J. Hawkins, who was a constant *dropper-in* at my father's house, James-street, Buckingham-gate. He was generally thought somewhat austere; but to me, as a child, he was gentle and kind. After the destruction, by fire, of his house in Queen-square, Westminster, and of his curious library, he resided in the Broad Sanctuary, close to the Abbey; which house was recently pulled down, to make way for the improvements in that quarter.

" W. A."

* Mr. Cracherode (qy. Dr. ?) lived at No. 24, Queen-square, Westminster, and at Clapham; was a man of large fortune, and possessed one of the finest libraries then existing, which, at his death, was purchased by the British Museum, for £14,000.

All this was surely sufficient to make Stevens rejoice in the opportunity of assailing Hawkins, and to induce him to use any means to injure one who had such just reason to regard him with contempt.

Where Boswell and Stevens led, others have been found to follow; but it may be remarked that their assaults consist more of violent expressions of opinion, than of records of facts calculated to affect his personal or literary fame.

The terms of friendship, indeed, on which he stood with those who were the best men of the day, both as regards high character and literary attainment, form the surest criterion of the estimation in which he was held by those persons whose good opinion was most to be valued.

Sir John Hawkins had always been a pious man : as advancing years brought him nearer and nearer to the event which no care can avoid, he became more and more attentive to the duties of religion, and to devotional and theological studies, to which he latterly dedicated every hour which some imperative duty did not claim.

On the morning of the 14th of May, 1789, he was attacked, while away from home, by a paralytic affection : he immediately returned and was carried up to bed, but rallied so far in the course of the day as to get up again to receive an old friend who had promised to visit him in the evening : he was however again seized, and was compelled to return to his bed from which he never again rose, for his malady becoming aggravated by apoplectic symptoms, put a period to his life on the 21st of May, just one week from the date of his first attack.

He left behind him—to use the words of Chalmers— ' A high reputation for abilities and integrity, united with the well-earned character of an active and resolute magistrate, an affectionate husband and father, a firm and zealous friend, a loyal subject, and a sincere Christian, and rich in the friendship and esteem of very many of the first characters for rank, worth, and abilities, of the age in which he lived.'

He was buried in the cloisters of Westminster Abbey, in the North Walk, under a stone which, by his express direction, bears no more than the following inscription :—

J. H.

OBIIT XXI MAII, MDCCLXXXIX,

Ætatis LXX.

His wife, who survived him four years, is buried in the same grave.

He left two sons, John Sidney and Henry, and one daughter, Letitia Matilda; all, but especially the latter, well known in the literary world. Miss Hawkins's novels evince talent; while the cause of virtue, usefulness, and right feeling has never found a more zealous, and but seldom, very seldom, a more efficient advocate.

By this summary of the circumstances which marked Sir John Hawkins's life, one of the great ends of Biography is achieved : serving to stimulate men by a worthy example; and showing, that, however contemporaneous meanness, envy, or detraction, may cause full justice to be delayed, it cannot prevent eventual honor from accruing to one who steadfastly maintains his virtuous integrity. It supplies a pregnant instance of the unfailing comfort of conscious rectitude, beneath unfounded aspersion and venomous assault. It inspires a consoling reliance upon ultimate equitable estimate, however long deferred. It furnishes a sustaining monition, that patient desert, whatever may be the amount of injurious misapprehension it chances temporarily to encounter, is sure in the end to triumph, and to secure to itself a genuine though tardily-yielded acknowledgement. The paltry malice, and base tricks, of such men as Boswell and Stevens, in their endeavour to degrade an honorable gentleman in the eyes of the world,—to obtain an undervaluing and false opinion of him,—and to procure the failure of his productions, would not have been recorded here; were it not that there are times when such candour of revelation is absolutely needful. No

occasion could be more fitting than this, when relating Sir John's biography, and re-printing his great work. Not only was it requisite in justification,—to rescue a worthy, honest name from unmerited imputation, and to reclaim his literary efforts from unfair slight; but it was proper, in order to show how uniformly the machinations of such insidious maligners, after a period of apparent success in prevailing against the object of their attack, are sure to recoil upon their devisers' own heads, when the verdict of the world shall at last adjudge the cause, in a clearer knowledge of the truth.

Posterity awards honoring repute and distinction to Sir John Hawkins, as an excellent upright man, in his private character; and testifies value for his literary capacity, by giving the palm to his admirable History over the one which claims to be its rival,—a fact proved from the present demand for this re-print of the work here offered to the Public.

ANNOUNCEMENT.

In the present age, when public attention is so extensively directed towards the study and practice of Music, it has been thought that a new edition of Sir John Hawkins's valuable History of the Science and Practice of Music would prove peculiarly acceptable, as being by far the best history of the Art extant.

The whole of the original Text has been printed in its integrity, together with the Illustrations of Instruments (for which more than 200 Woodcuts have been engraved), the Musical Examples, and the Fac-similes of Old Manuscripts.

The form adopted, super-royal 8vo., has the advantage of bringing much more matter under the eye at one view, and in point of economy the 2722 pages of the Quarto are comprised in 1016 pages. The paging has been continued from the beginning to the end, as more simple for reference, and to enable those who like such information in one volume, to bind it in that form; but provision has been made, by adding a second title after page 486, to divide the work into two volumes, an arrangement which may generally be preferable.

The Medallion Portraits of Musical Composers, which were in the Quarto edition, have been printed in a separate volume; these may be purchased optionally, and thus decrease the price of the History to those with whom economy must be a consideration. They consist of upwards of sixty portraits, printed from the original copperplates engraved for the 1776 edition; to which has been added a portrait of Sir John Hawkins himself from the painting in the Oxford Music School, through the courtesy of the surviving members of his family. All the additional manuscript notes which adorn the Author's own copy left to the British Museum, are inserted (by permission of the authorities) in the edition now presented to the public: it may therefore be considered what a new edition edited by Sir John Hawkins himself would have

been; the additions in text or notes are distinguished by being printed in italics.

To ensure the careful reproduction of matter of such varied character, the assistance of many correctors has been secured. The general correction of the press was confided to Mrs. Cowden Clarke, but the pages also passed under the eye of the musician, the mathematician, and the classical linguist. In these departments, various portions have had the care of Mr. Edward Holmes, Mr. Josiah Pittman, Mr. W. H. Monk, and Mr. Burford G. H. Gibsone, with occasional suggestions from other well-wishers; and the whole work, such advantage as might be derived from the Publisher's printing experience.

There has been added a Memoir of the Author, compiled from original sources, which will be read with interest; but it is anticipated that the most valuable addition to the book will be found in the carefully-made general and other Indexes. The large subject of a History of Music, embracing heterogeneous matter and the result of wide research, makes it a storehouse to which a definite clue is required in giving ready access. The Indexes have been going on cotemporaneously with the printing of the book; and Mrs. Cowden Clarke's experience derived from her Concordance to Shakespeare, fitted her especially for the task of their compilation. A table of parallel books, chapters, and pages has been added, to render the new Indexes available for those who possess the Quarto edition.

In concluding these brief but necessary words of explanation, the warmest thanks are offered to the editorial friends above specified, as also to those kind supporters who have subscribed for the work during its periodical issue by the Public's, and their obedient servant,

THE PUBLISHER.

69, *Dean Street, Soho, London.*
August, 1853.

AUTHOR'S DEDICATION AND PREFACE.

To GEORGE THE THIRD, King of Great Britain, &c., a Prince not more distinguished by his patronage of those elegant arts which exalt humanity and administer to the imaginative faculties the purest delights, than honoured and beloved for his regal and private virtues, the following History is, with all due reverence and gratitude, dedicated by him who esteems it equally an honour and a felicity to subscribe himself His Majesty's faithful and devoted subject and servant, THE AUTHOR.

A HISTORY OF MUSIC by any but a professor of the science, may possibly be looked on as a bold understaking; and it may appear not a little strange that one, who is perhaps better known to the world as occupying a public station than as a writer, should choose to be the author of a work of this kind, and for which the course of his studies can hardly be supposed to have in any degree qualified him.

In justification of the attempt, and to account for this seeming inconsistency, the reader is to know, that the author having entertained an early love of music, and having in his more advanced age not only become sensible of its worth, but arrived at a full conviction that it was intended by the Almighty for the delight and edification of his rational creatures, had formed a design of some such work as this many years ago, but saw reason to defer the execution thereof to a future period.

About the year 1759, he found himself in a situation that left his employments, his studies, and his amusements in a great measure to his own choice; and having in a course of years been as industrious in making collections for the purpose as could well consist with the exercise of a laborious profession, he, with a copious fund of materials, began the work: but before any considerable progress could be made therein, he was interrupted by a call to preside in the magistracy of the county of his residence, which, though unsolicited on his part, he could not decline without betraying an indifference to the interests of society, and the preservation of public order, or such an aversion to the occupations of an active life, as in few cases is excusable, and in many reproachful.

Determining, however, to avail himself of those intervals of leisure which the stated recesses from the exercise of his office afforded, and which seemed too precious to be wasted either in sloth and indolence, or those fashionable recreations and amusements, to which he was ever disposed to prefer the pursuit of literature, he re-assumed his work; and with the blessing of health, scarcely interrupted for a series of years, has been able to present it to the world in the condition in which it now comes forth.

What the reader is to expect from it, and as the fruit of many years study and labour, is the history of a science deservedly ranked among those, which, in contradistinction to the manual arts, and others of lower importance, have long been dignified with the characteristic of liberal; and as the utility of Music is presupposed in the very attempt to trace its progress, an enumeration of its various excellencies will scarcely be thought necessary; the rather perhaps as its praises, and the power it exercises over the human mind, have been celebrated by the ablest panegyrists.

Farther than the circumstances attending the peculiar situation of the author and the work may be allowed to entitle him to it, the favour or indulgence, or whatever else it is the practice of writers to crave of the public, is not here sued for, either on the ground of want of leisure, inadvertence, or other pretences; for this reason, that there can be no valid excuse for a publication wittingly imperfect; and it is but a sorry compliment that an author makes to his reader, when he tenders him a work less worthy regard than it was in his power to make it.

To be short, the ensuing volumes are the produce of sixteen years labour, and are compiled from materials which were not collected in double that time. The motives to the undertaking were genuine, and the prosecution of it has been as animated as the love of the art, and a total blindness to lucrative views, could render it. And perhaps the best excuse the author can make for the defects and errors that may be found to have escaped him, must be drawn from the novelty of his subject, the variety of his matter, and the necessity he was under of marking out himself the road which he was to travel.

It may perhaps be objected that music is a mere recreation, and an amusement for vacant hours, conducing but little to the benefit of mankind, and therefore to be numbered among those vanities which it is wisdom to contemn. To this it may be answered, that, as a source of intellectual pleasure, music has greatly the advantage of most other recreations; and as to the other branch of the objection, let it be remembered that all our desires, all our pursuits, our occupations, and enjoyments are vain. What are stately palaces, beautiful and extensive gardens, costly furniture, sculptures, and pictures, but vanities? and yet there are few men so vain as that they had rather be without than possess them. Nay, if these be denied us, where are we to seek for amusements,—for relief from the cares, the anxieties and troubles of life; how support ourselves in solitude, or under the pressure of affliction,—or how preserve that equanimity, which is necessary to keep us in good humour with ourselves and mankind? As to the abuses of this excellent gift, enough it is presumed is said in the ensuing work by way of caution against them, and even to demonstrate that as there is no science or faculty whatever that more improves the tempers of men, rendering them grave, discreet, mild, and placid, so is there none that affords greater scope for folly, impertinence, and affectation.

The end proposed in this undertaking is the investigation of the principles, and a deduction of the progress of a science, which, though intimately connected with civil life, has scarce ever been so well understood by the generality, as to be thought a fit subject, not to say of criticism, but of sober discussion: instead of exercising the powers of reason, it has in general engaged only that faculty of the mind, which, for want of a better word to express it by, we call Taste; and which alone, and without some principle to direct and controul it, must ever be deemed a capricious arbiter. Another end of this work is the settling music upon somewhat like a footing of equality with those, which, for other reasons than that, like music, they contribute to the delight of mankind, are termed the sister arts; to reprobate the vulgar notion that its ultimate end is merely to excite mirth; and, above all, to demonstrate that its principles are founded in certain general and universal laws, into which all that we discover in the material world, of harmony, symmetry, proportion, and order, seems to be resolvable.

The method pursued for these purposes will be found to consist in an explanation of fundamental doctrines, and a narration of important events and historical facts, in a chronological series, with such occasional remarks and evidences, as might serve to illustrate the one and authenticate the other. With these are intermixed a variety of musical compositions, tending as well to exemplify that diversity of style which is common both to music and speech or written language, as to manifest the gradual improvements in the art of combining musical sounds. The materials which have furnished this intelligence must necessarily be supposed to be very miscellaneous in their nature, and abundant in quantity: to speak alone of the treatises for the purpose, the author may with no less propriety than truth assert, that the selection of them was an exercise of deep skill, the result of much erudition, and the effect of great labour, as having been for a great part of his life the employment of that excellent theorist in the science, Dr. Pepusch. These have been accumulating and encreasing for a series of years past: for others of a different kind, recourse has been had to the Bodleian library and the college libraries in both universities; to that in the music-school at Oxford; to the British Museum, and to the public libraries and repositories of records and public papers in London and Westminster; and, for the purpose of ascertaining facts by dates, to cemeteries and other places of sepulture; and to him that shall object that these sources are inadequate to the end of such an undertaking as this, it may be answered, that he knows not the riches of this country.

A correspondence with learned foreigners, and such communications from abroad as suit with the liberal sentiments and disposition of the present age, together with a great variety of oral intelligence respecting persons and facts yet remembered, have contributed in some degree to the melioration of the work, and to justify the title it bears of a General History; which yet it may be thought would have been more properly its due, had the plan of the work been more extensive, and comprehended the state of music in countries where the approaches to refinement have yet been but small.

It must be confessed that in some instances, particularly in the discussion of the first principles of morality, and the origin of human manners, the researches of learned men have been extended to nations, or tribes of people, among whom the simple dictates of nature seemed to be the only rule of action; but the subjects here treated of are science, and the scientific practice of music: now the best music of barbarians is said to be hideous and astonishing sounds.* Of what importance then can it be to enquire into a practice that has not its foundation in science or system, or to know what are the sounds that most delight a Hottentot, a wild American, or even a more refined Chinese?

For the style, it will be found to be uniformly narratory; as little encumbered with technical terms, and as free from didactic forms of speech, as could consist with the design of explaining doctrines and systems; and it may also be said that care has been taken not to degrade the work by the use of fantastical phrases and modes of expression, that, comparatively speaking, were invented yesterday, and will die to-morrow; these make no part of any language, they conduce nothing to information, and are in truth nonsense sublimated.

For the insertions of biographical memoirs and characters of eminent musicians, it may be given as a reason, that, having benefited mankind by their studies, it is but just that their memories should live: Cicero, after Demosthenes, says that "bona fama propria possessio defunctorum;" and for bestowing it on men of this faculty, we have the authority of that scripture which exhorts us to praise "such as found out musical tunes, and recited verses in writing."† Besides which it may be observed, that in various instances the lives of the professors of arts are in some sort a history of the arts themselves. For digressions from his subject, the insertion of anecdotes that have but a remote relation to it, or that describe ancient modes or customs of living, the author has less to say; these must be left to the judgment of his readers, who cannot be supposed to be unanimous in their opinions about them.

It remains now that due acknowledgment be made of the assistance with which the author has been favoured and honoured in the course of his work; but as this cannot be done without an enumeration of names, for which he has obtained no permission, he is necessitated to declare his sense of the obligation in general terms, with this exception, that having need of assistance in the correction of the music plates, he was in sundry instances eased of that trouble by the kind offices of one, who is both an honour to his profession and his country, Dr. William Boyce; and of the difficulty of decyphering, as it were, and rendering in modern characters the compositions of greatest antiquity amongst those which he found it necessary to insert, by the learning and ingenuity of Dr. Cooke, of Westminster Abbey, Mr. Marmaduke Overend, organist of Isleworth in Middlesex, and Mr. John Stafford Smith, of the royal chapel.

* Characteristics, vol. I. page 242. † Ecclesiasticus, chap. xliv. verse 5.

Hatton Garden,
26th Aug., 1776.

PRELIMINARY DISCOURSE.

The powers of the imagination, with great appearance of reason, are said to hold a middle place between the organs of bodily sense and the faculties of moral perception; the subjects on which they are severally exercised are common to the senses of seeing and hearing, the office of which is simply perception; all pleasure thence arising being referred to the imagination.

The arts which administer to the imaginative faculty the greatest delight, are confessedly poetry, painting, and music, the two former exhibiting to the mind by their respective media, either natural or artificial,* the resemblances of whatever in the works of nature is comprehended under the general division of great, new, and beautiful; the latter as operating upon the mind by the power of that harmony which results from the concord of sounds, and exciting in the mind those ideas which correspond with our tenderest and most delightful affections.

These, it must be observed, constitute one source of pleasure; but each of the above arts may in a different degree be said to afford another, namely, that which consists in a comparison of the images by them severally and occasionally excited in the mind, with their architypes; thus, for instance, in poetry, in comparing a description with the thing described; in painting, a landscape and the scene represented by it, or a portrait and its original; and in music, where imitation is intended, as in the songs of birds, or in the expression of those various inflexions of the voice which accompany passion or exclamation, weeping, laughing, and other of the human affections, the sound and the thing signified.

It is easy to discover that the pleasures above described are of two distinct kinds,—the one original and absolute, the other relative; for the one we can give no reason other than the will of God, who in the formation of the universe and the organization of our bodies, has established such a relation as is discoverable between man and his works; the other is to be accounted for by that love of truth which is implanted in the human mind.† In poetry and painting therefore we speak, and with propriety, of absolute and relative beauty; as also of music merely imitative; for as to harmony, it is evident that

the attribute of relation belongs not to it, as will appear by a comparison of each with the others.‡

With regard to poetry, it may be said to resemble painting in many respects, as in the description of external objects, and the works of nature; and so far it must be considered as an imitative art; but its greatest excellence seems to be its power of exhibiting the internal constitution of man, and of making us acquainted with characters, manners, and sentiments, and working upon the passions of terror, pity, and various others. Painting is professedly an imitative art; for, setting aside the harmony of colouring, and the delineation of beautiful forms, the pleasure we receive from it, great as it is, consists in the truth of the representation.

But in music there is little beyond itself to which we need, or indeed can, refer to heighten its charms. If we investigate the principles of harmony, we learn that they are general and universal; and of harmony itself, that the proportions in which it consists are to be found in those material forms, which are beheld with the greatest pleasure, the sphere, the cube, and the cone, for instance, and constitute what we call symmetry, beauty, and regularity; but the imagination receives no additional delight; our reason is exercised in the operation, and that faculty alone is thereby gratified. In short, there are few things in nature which music is capable of imitating, and those are of a kind so uninteresting, that we may venture to pronounce, that as its principles are founded in geometrical truth, and seem to result from some general and universal law of nature, so its excellence is intrinsic, absolute, and inherent, and, in short, resolvable only into His will, who has ordered all things in number, weight, and measure.§

Seeing therefore that music has its foundation in nature,

---

* The natural media seem to consist only in colour and figure, and refer solely to painting: the artificial are words, which are symbols by compact of ideas, as are also, in a limited sense, musical sounds, including in the term the accident of time or duration.

† In this sentiment liberty has been taken to differ from Mr. Harris, who with his usual accuracy, has analysed this principle of the human mind in the following note on a passage in the second of his Three celebrated Treatises :—

'That there is an eminent delight in this very recognition itself, abstract 'from any thing pleasing in the subject recognised, is evident from 'hence—that, in all the mimetic arts, we can be highly charmed with 'imitations, at whose originals in nature we are shocked and terrified. 'Such, for instance, as dead bodies, wild beasts, and the like.

'The cause assigned for this, seems to be of the following kind: we 'have a joy, not only in the sanity and perfection, but also in the just and 'natural energies of our several limbs and faculties. And hence, among 'others, the joy in reasoning, as being the energy of that principal faculty, 'our intellect or understanding. This joy extends, not only to the wise, 'but to the multitude. For all men have an aversion to ignorance and 'error; and in some degree, however moderate, are glad to learn and to 'inform themselves.

'Hence therefore the delight arising from these imitations; as we are 'enabled in each of them to exercise the reasoning faculty; and, by com-'paring the copy with the architype in our minds, to infer that this 'is such a thing, and that another; a fact remarkable among children, 'even in their first and earliest days.'

‡ Nevertheless there have not been wanting those, who, not contemplating the intrinsic excellence of harmony, have resolved the efficacy of music into the power of imitation; and to gratify such, subjects have been introduced into practice, that to injudicious ears have afforded no small delight; such, for instance, as the noise of thunder, the roaring of the winds, the shouts and acclamations of multitudes, the wailings of grief and anguish in the human mind; the song of the cuckow, the whooting of the screech-owl, the cackling of the hen, the notes of singing-birds, not excepting those of the lark and nightingale. Attempts also have been made to imitate motion by musical sounds; and some have undertaken in like manner to relate histories, and to describe the various seasons of the year. Thus, for example, Froberger, organist to the emperor Ferdinand III. is said to have in an allemand represented the passage of Count Thurn over the Rhine, and the danger he and his army were in, by twenty-six cataracts or falls in notes. See page 627. Kuhnau, another celebrated musician, composed six sonatas, entitled Biblische Historien, wherein, as it is said, is a lively representation in musical notes of David manfully combating Goliah. Page 663, in note. Buxtehude of Lubec also composed suites of lessons for the harpsichord, representing the nature of the planets. Page 851. Vivaldi, in two books of concertos has striven to describe the four seasons of the year. Page 837. Geminiani has translated a whole episode of Tasso's Jerusalem into musical notes. Page 916. And Mr. Handel himself, in his Israel in Egypt, has undertaken to represent two of the ten plagues of Egypt by notes, intended to imitate the buzzing of flies and the hopping of frogs.

But these powers of imitation, admitting them to exist in all the various instances above enumerated, constitute but a very small part of the excellence of music; wherefore we cannot but applaud that shrewd answer of Agesilaus, king of Sparta, recorded in Plutarch, to one who requested him to hear a man sing that could imitate the nightingale, 'I have heard the nightingale herself.' The truth is, that imitation belongs more properly to the arts of poetry and painting than to music; for which reason Mr. Harris has not scrupled to pronounce of musical imitation, that at best it is but an imperfect thing. See his Discourse on Music, Painting, and Poetry, page 69.

§ Wisdom, xi. 20.

and that reason recognizes what the sense approves, what wonder is it, that in all ages, and even by the least enlightened of mankind, its efficacy should be acknowledged; or that, as well by those who are capable of reason and reflection, as those who seek for no other gratifications than what are obvious to the senses, it should be considered as a genuine and natural source of delight? The wonder is, that less of that curiosity, which leads men to enquire into the history and progress of arts, and their gradual advances towards perfection, has been exercised in the instance now before us, than in any other of equal importance.

If we take a view of those authors who have written on music, we shall find them comprehended under three classes, consisting of those who have resolved the principles of the science into certain mathematical proportions; of others who have treated it systematically, and with a view to practice; and of a third, who, considering sound as a branch of physics, have from various phenomena explained the manner in which it is generated and communicated to the auditory faculty. But to whom we are indebted for the gradual improvements of the art, at what periods it flourished, what checks and obstructions it has at times met with, who have been its patrons or its enemies, what have been the characteristics of its most eminent professors, few are able to tell. Nor has the knowledge of its precepts been communicated in such a manner as to enable any but such as have devoted themselves to the study of the science to understand them. Hence it is that men of learning have been betrayed into numberless errors respecting music; and when they have presumed to talk about it, have discovered the grossest ignorance. When Strada, in the person of Claudian, recites the fable of the Nightingale and the Lyrist, how does his invention labour to describe the contest, and how does he err in the confusion of the terms melody and harmony; and in giving to music either attributes that belong not to it, or which are its least excellence! and what is his whole poem but a vain attempt to excite ideas for which no correspondent words are to be found in any language? Nor does he, who talks of the genius of the world, of the first beauty, and of universal harmony, symmetry, and order, the sublime author of the Characteristics, discover much knowledge of his subject, when after asserting with the utmost confidence that the ancients were acquainted with parts and symphony, he makes it the test of a good judge in music 'that he understand a fiddle.'*

Sir William Temple speaking of music in his Essay upon the ancient and modern Learning, has betrayed his ignorance of the subject in a comparison of the modern music with the ancient; wherein, notwithstanding that Palestrina, Bird, and Gibbons lived in the same century with himself, and that the writings of Shakespeare and the Paradise Lost were then extant, he scruples not to assert that 'the science is wholly lost in the world, and 'that in the room of music and poetry we have nothing 'left but fiddling and rhyming.'

Mr. Dryden, in those two admirable poems, Alexander's Feast, and his lesser Ode for St. Cecilia's day, and in his Elegy on the death of Purcell, with great judgment gives to the several instruments mentioned by him their proper attributes; and recurring perhaps to the numerous common places in his memory respecting music, has described its effects in adequate terms; but when in the prefaces to his operas he speaks of recitative, of song, and the comparative merit of the Italian, the French, and the English composers, his notions are so vague and indeterminate, as to convince us that he was not master of his subject, and does little else than talk by rote.

* Vide Characteristics, Vol. III., page 263, in note 269.

Mr. Addison, in those singularly humorous papers in the Spectator, intended to ridicule the Italian opera, is necessitated to speak of music, but he does it in such terms as plainly indicate that he had no judgment of his own to direct him. In the paper, Numb. 18, the highest encomium he can vouchsafe music is, that it is an agreeable entertainment; and a little after he complains of our fondness for the foreign music, not caring whether it be Italian, French, or High Dutch, by which latter we may suppose the author meant the music of Mynheer Hendel, as he calls him.

In another paper, viz. Numb. 29, the same person delivers these sentiments at large respecting Recitative:—
'However the *Italian* method of acting in *Recitativo* 'might appear at first hearing, I cannot but think it more 'just than that which prevailed in our *English* Opera 'before this innovation; the Transition from an air to 'Recitative Musick being more natural than the passing 'from a Song to plain and ordinary Speaking, which was 'the common Method in *Purcell's* operas.

'The only Fault I find in our present Practice, is the 'making use of the *Italian Recitativo* with *English* words.

'To go to the Bottom of this Matter, I must observe that 'the Tone, or, as the *French* call it, the Accent of every 'Nation in their ordinary Speech is altogether different 'from that of every other People, as we may see even in 'the Welsh and Scotch, who border so near upon us. By 'the Tone or Accent I do not mean the Pronunciation of 'each particular Word, but the Sound of the whole Sen-'tence. Thus it is very common for an English gentle-'man, when he hears a French Tragedy, to complain that 'the Actors all of them speak in a Tone; and therefore he 'very wisely prefers his own countrymen, not considering 'that a Foreigner complains of the same Tone in an 'English Actor.

'For this Reason, the Recitative Music in every Lan-'guage should be as different as the Tone or Accent of 'each Language; for otherwise what may properly ex-'press a Passion in one Language, will not do it in 'another. Every one that has been long in Italy knows 'very well that the Cadences in the Recitativo bear a 'remote Affinity to the Tone of their Voices in ordinary 'Conversation; or, to speak more properly, are only the 'Accents of their Language made more Musical and 'Tuneful.

'Thus the Notes of Interrogation or Admiration in the 'Italian Musick (if one may so call them), which re-'semble their Accents in Discourse on such Occasions, 'are not unlike the ordinary Tones of an English Voice 'when we are angry; insomuch that I have often seen our 'Audiences extremely mistaken as to what has been 'doing upon the Stage, and expecting to see the Hero 'knock down his Messenger when he has been asking 'him a question; or fancying that he quarrels with his 'Friend when he only bids him Good-morrow.

'For this reason the Italian artists cannot agree with 'our English musicians in admiring Purcell's Composi-'tions, and thinking his Tunes so wonderfully adapted 'to his words, because both Nations do not always ex-'press the same Passions by the same Sounds.

'I am therefore humbly of opinion that an English 'Composer should not follow the Italian Recitative too 'servilely, but make use of many gentle Deviations from 'it in Compliance with his own Native Language. He 'may copy out of it all the lulling Softness and Dying 'Falls (as Shakespeare calls them), but should still re-'member that he ought to accommodate himself to an 'English Audience, and by humouring the Tone of our 'Voices in ordinary Conversation, have the same Regard 'to the Accent of his own Language, as those Persons 'had to theirs whom he professes to imitate. It is ob-

'served that several of the singing Birds of our own
Country learn to sweeten their Voices, and mellow the
'Harshness of their natural Notes by practising under
'those that come from warmer Climates. In the same
'manner I would allow the Italian Opera to lend our
'English Musick as much as may grace and soften it, but
'never entirely to annihilate and destroy it. Let the
'Infusion be as strong as you please, but still let the
'Subject Matter of it be English.

'A Composer should fit his Musick to the Genius of
'the People, and consider that the Delicacy of Hearing
'and Taste of Harmony has been formed upon those
'Sounds which every Country abounds with. In short,
'that musick is of a relative Nature, and what is Harmony
'to one Ear may be Dissonance to another.'

Whoever reflects on these sentiments must be inclined
to question as well the goodness of the author's ear as his
knowledge of subject. The principle on which his reasoning is founded, is clearly that the powers of music are
local; deriving their efficacy from habit, custom, and
whatever else we are to understand by the genius of
a people; a position as repugnant to reason and experience as that which concludes his disquisition, viz.,
that 'what is harmony to one ear may be dissonance to
'another;' whence as a corollary it must necessarily follow,
that the same harmony or the same succession of sounds
may produce different effects on different persons; and
that one may be excited to mirth by an air that has
drawn tears from another.

A late writer, in a strain of criticism not less erroneous
than affectedly refined, forgetting the energy of harmony,
independent of the adventitious circumstances of loudness
or softness that accompany the utterance of it; or perhaps not knowing that certain modulations or combinations of sounds have a necessary tendency to inspire
grand and sublime sentiments, such, for instance, as we
hear in the Exaltabo of Palestrina, the Hosanna of
Gibbons, the opening of the first concerto of Corelli, and
many of Mr. Handel's anthems, ascribes to the *bursts*, as
he calls them, of Boranello,* and the symphonies of
Yeomelli† the power of dilating, agitating, and rousing
the soul like the paintings of Timomachus and Aristides,‡
whose works by the way no man living ever saw, and of
whose very names we should be ignorant, did they not
occur, the one in Pliny, the other in some of the epigrams
in the Greek Anthologia.

In a manner widely different do those poets and philosophers treat music, who, being susceptible of its charms,
and considering it as worthy the most abstract speculation, have made themselves acquainted with its principles.
Milton, whenever he speaks of the subject, and there are
many passages in the Paradise Lost and his other poems
where he has taken occasion to introduce it, besides
expressing an enthusiastic fondness for music, talks the
language of a master.

His ideas of the joint efficacy of music and poetry, and
of the nature of harmony, are manifested in the following
well-known passage :—

And ever against eating cares
Lap me in soft Lydian aires;
Married to immortal verse,
Such as the meeting soul may pierce
In notes, with many a winding bout
Of linked sweetness long drawn out,
With wanton heed, and giddy cunning,
The melting voice through mazes running;
Untwisting all the chains, that tye
The hidden soul of harmony.

* i. e. Buranello, a disciple of Lotti.
† Nicola Iomelli, a celebrated composer now living at Naples.
‡ See an Inquiry into the Beauties of Painting by Daniel Webb, Esq.
8vo. 1769, page 167.

Cathedral music and choral service he describes in
terms that sufficiently declare his abilities to judge of it,
and its effects on his own mind :—

There let the pealing organ blow,
To the full-voic'd choir below,
In service high, and anthems clear,
As may with sweetness through mine ear
Dissolve me into extasies,
And bring all heav'n before mine eyes.

The following sonnet, addressed to his friend Mr.
Henry Lawes, points out one of the great excellencies in
the composition of music to words :—

Harry, whose tuneful and well-measur'd song
First taught our English music how to span
Words with just note and accent, not to scan
With Midas' ears, committing short and long;
Thy worth and skill exempt thee from the throng,
With praise enough for envy to look wan;
To after-age thou shalt be writ the man,
That with smooth air could humour best our tongue.
Thou honour'st verse, and verse must lend her wing
To honour thee, the priest of Phœbus' choir,
That tun'st their happiest lines in hymn or story.
Dante shall give Fame leave to set thee higher
Than his Casella, whom he woo'd to sing,
Met in the milder shades of Purgatory.

His sonnet to Mr. Lawrence Hyde conveys his sense of
the delights of a musical evening :—

Lawrence, of virtuous father virtuous son,
Now that the fields are dank, and ways are mire,
Where shall we sometimes meet, and by the fire
Help waste a sullen day; what may be won
From the hard season gaining? time will run
On smoother, till Favonius re-inspire
The frozen earth; and clothe in fresh attire
The lilie and the rose, that neither sow'd nor spun.
What neat repast shall feast us, light and choice,
Of Attic taste, with wine; whence we may rise
To hear the lute well toucht, or artful voice
Warble immortal notes and Tuscan air?
He, who of those delights can judge, and spare
To interpose them oft is not unwise.

And in his tractate on Education, he recommends the
practice of music in terms that bespeak his skill in the
science. 'The interim of unsweating themselves regu-
'larly, and convenient rest before meat, may both with
'profit and delight be taken up in recreating and com-
'posing their travail'd spirits with the solemn and divine
'harmonies of musick heard or learnt; either while the
'skilful organist plies his grave and fancied descant, in
'lofty fugues, or the whole symphony with artful and un-
'imaginable touches adorn and grace the well studied
'chords of some choice composer; sometimes the lute, or
'soft organ-stop waiting on elegant voices either to
'religious, martial, or civil ditties: which, if wise men and
'prophets be not extremely out, have a great power over
'dispositions and manners, to smooth and make them
'gentle from rustic harshness and distempered passions.'

Lord Bacon, in his Natural History, has given a great
variety of experiments touching music, that shew him to
have been not barely a philosopher, an enquirer into the
phenomena of sound, but a master of the science of harmony, and very intimately acquainted with the precepts
of musical composition.

That we have so few instances of this kind is greatly to
be wondered at, seeing that in poetry and painting the
case is far otherwise: in the course of a classical education
men acquire not only a taste of the beauties of the Greek
and Roman poets, but a nice and discriminating faculty,
that enables them to discern their excellencies and defects;
and in painting, an attentive perusal of the works of
eminent artists, aided by a sound judgment, will go near

to form the character of a connoisseur, and render the possessor of it susceptible of all that delight which the art is capable of affording; and this we see exemplified in numberless instances, where persons unskilled in the practice of painting become enabled to distinguish hands, to compare styles, and to mark the beauties of composition, character, drawing, and colouring, with a degree of accuracy and precision equal to that of masters. But few, except the masters of the science, are possessed of knowledge sufficient to enable them to discourse with propriety on music; nor indeed do many attend to that which is its greatest excellence, its influence on the human mind, or those irresistable charms which render the passions subservient to the power of well modulated sounds, and inspire the mind with the most exalted sentiments. One admires a fine voice, another a delicate touch, another what he calls a brilliant finger; and many are pleased with that music which appears most difficult in the execution, and in judging of their own feelings, mistake wonder for delight.

To remove the numberless prejudices respecting music, which those only entertain who are ignorant of the science, or are mistaken in its nature and end; to point out its various excellencies, and to assert its dignity, as a science worthy the exercise of our rational as well as audible faculties, the only effectual way seems to be to investigate its principles, as founded in general and invariable laws, and to trace the improvements therein which have resulted from the accumulated studies and experience of a long succession of ages, such a detail is necessary to reduce the science to a certainty, and to furnish a ground for criticism; and may be considered as a branch of literary history, of the deficiency whereof Lord Bacon has declared his sentiments in the following emphatical terms:

'History is Natural, Civil, Ecclesiastical, and Literary, 'whereof the three first I allow as extant, the fourth I 'note as deficient. For no man hath propounded to him- 'self the general state of learning to be described and 'represented from age to age, as many have done the 'works of nature, and the state civil and ecclesiastical; 'without which the history of the world seemeth to 'me to be as the statue of Polyphemus with his eye out, 'that part being wanting which doth most shew the spirit 'and life of the person. And yet I am not ignorant, that 'in divers particular sciences, as of the jurisconsults, the 'mathematicians, the rhetoricians, the philosophers, there 'are set down some small memorials of the schools, 'authors, and books; and so likewise some barren relations 'touching the invention of arts or usages.

'But a just story of learning, containing the antiquities 'and originals, of knowledges and their sects, their inven- 'tions, their traditions, their diverse administrations and 'managings, their flourishings, their oppositions, decays, 'depressions, oblivions, removes, with the causes and 'occasions of them, and all other events concerning 'learning, throughout the ages of the world, I may truly 'affirm to be wanting.'*

If anything can be necessary to enforce arguments so weighty as are contained in the above passage; it must be instances of error, resulting from the want of that intelligence which it is the business of history to communicate; and it is greatly to be lamented that music affords more examples of this kind than perhaps any science whatever: for, not to remark on those uncertain and contradictory accounts which are given of the discovery of the consonances, some writers attributing it to Pythagoras, others to Diocles, that relation of the fact which has gained most credit with mankind, as deriving its authority from the Pythagorean school, is demonstrably

false and erroneous.† Again, as to the invention of symphoniac harmony, or, as we now call it, music in parts, many ascribe it to the ancients, and say that it was in use among the Greeks, though no evidence of the fact can be drawn from their writings now extant. Others assert it to be a modern improvement, but to whom it is due no one has yet been able to discover.

As to the modern system, there is the irrefragable evidence of his own writings extant, though not in print, that it was settled by Guido Aretinus, a Benedictine monk of the monastery of Pomposa in Tuscany, who flourished about the year 1028; yet this fact, which is also related as an important event in the Annales Ecclesiastici of Cardinal Baronius, has been rendered doubtful by an assertion of a writer now living, Signor Martinelli, that one of the same name and place, Fra Guittone d'Arezzo, an Italian poet of great eminence, and who lived about two hundred years after, adjusted that musical scale by which we now sing ;‡ and further that the same Fra Guittone was the inventor of counterpoint. Again, those who give the invention of the modern system, and the application thereto of the syllables used in solmisation to the true author, ascribe also to him the invention of music in consonance, and also of the Clavicembalum or harpsichord; whereas the harpsichord is an improvement of the Clavicitherium, an instrument known in England in Gower's time by the name of the Citole, from Cistella, a little chest. Another writer asserts, on what authority we are not told, that counterpoint, which implies music in consonance, was invented by John of Dunstable, who flourished anno 1400; and another, § mistaking the name, attributes it to St. Dunstan, archbishop of Canterbury. Mr. Marpourg of Berlin, a person now living, has taken up this relation, groundless as it is, and in a book of his writing, entitled 'Traité de la Fugue et du Counterpoint,' has done little less than assert that St. Dunstan invented counterpoint, by reducing into order the rules for composition in four parts, and not a few give credit to his testimony.||

Again we are told, that whereas the Greeks signified the several sounds in their scale by the letters of their alphabet, or by characters derived from them, Guido invented a more compendious method of notation by points stationed on a stave of five lines, and occupying both the lines and the spaces. This assertion is true but in part; for the stave, and that of many lines, was in use near half a century before Guido was born; and all that can be ascribed to him is the placing points as well in the spaces

---

* Of the advancement of Learning, book II.

† Vide infra, page 10, et seq.

‡ 'Fra Guittone d'Arezzo, celebre per i suoi scritta sopra la musica, 'inventore del contrappunto, e dal quale furono fissati i tuoni, che pre- 'sentemente si cantano.' Lettere familiari e critiche di Vincenzio Martinelli, Londra, 1758. Prefazione, page viii. This person had undertaken to write a history of music. See his letters above cited, page 164, containing an apology for his not having published it.
Of this Fra Guittone an account may be seen in the Istoria della Volgar Poesia of Crescimbeni, lib. II. page 84. He flourished about 1250, and is celebrated among the best of the ancient Tuscan poets. In the same work, lib. III. page 176, is a sonnet of his writing; and in Mr. Baretti's History of the Italian Tongue, prefixed to his Italian library, page ix. is a fable of Fra Guittone, which Baretti says may be taken for a composition of yesterday.

§ Wolfgang Caspar Printz, in his History of Music, written in the German language, and published at Dresden in the year 1690, who has given a relation purporting that 'In the year of our Lord, 940, Dunstan, otherwise Dunstaphus, an Englishman, being very young, betook him- 'self to the study of music, and thereby acquired immortal fame. He 'was the first that composed songs of different parts, that is to say, Bass, 'Tenor, Descant, and Vagant or Alt,' page 104, sect. 23. The whole relation is an error, arising from a mistaken sense of a passage in the Præceptiones Musices Poeticæ of Johannes Nucius, a writer on music in the year 1613. Vide infra, page 176 in note, 274 in note, 651 in note.

|| 'Dunstan, Archevêque de Canterbory, qui vivoit dans le dixième 'siècle, a toûjours eu l'honneur d'avoir commencé, ainsi que d'avoir 'frayé le chemin aux autres. Il redigea en ordre les regles de la com- 'position à quartre parties, et par là donna une nouvelle époque á la 'musique.' Partie II. page vi.

as on the lines, which it must be owned is an ingenious and useful contrivance.

To assist the memory and facilitate the practice of solmisation, it is also said that Guido made use of the left hand, giving to the top of the thumb the note ΓAM UT, to the joint below it A RE, to the next B MI, and so on, placing the highest note of his system, E LA, at the extremity of the hand, viz., the tip of the middle finger; but nothing of this kind is to be found, or indeed is mentioned, or even hinted at, in any of his writings, and we may therefore conclude that the whole is an invention of some other person.

Little less confusion attends the relations extant respecting the invention of the Cantus Mensurabilis, and those marks or characters used to signify the several lengths or durations of notes. The vulgar tale is, that John de Muris, a Norman, and a doctor of the Sorbonne about the year 1330, invented eight musical characters, namely, the Maxima, or as we call it, the Large, the Long, the Breve, Semibreve, Minim, Semiminim or Crotchet, Chroma or Quaver, and the Semichroma, assigning to each a several length in respect of time or duration.* Now upon the face of the relation there is great reason to conclude, that in the original institution of the Cantus Mensurabilis, the semibreve was the shortest note; but there is undeniable evidence that as well the minim as the notes in succession after it, were of comparatively late invention.

But this is not all; De Muris was not a Norman, but an Englishman: he was not the inventor of the Cantus Mensurabilis: not he, but a person of the name of Franco, a scholastic, as he is called, of Liege, about the middle of the eleventh century invented certain characters to signify the duration of sounds,† that is to say, the four first above mentioned.

Another prevailing error respecting music has got possession of the minds of many people, viz., that those singularly sweet and pathetic melodies with which the Scots music abounds, were introduced into it by David Rizzio, an Italian musician, and a favourite of Mary, queen of Scots; the reverse is the truth of the matter, and that by the testimony of the Italians themselves; the Scots tunes are the genuine produce of Scotland; those of greatest merit among them are compositions of a king of that country; and of these some of the most celebrated madrigals of one of the greatest of the Italian composers are avowed imitations.‡

Again, few are sufficiently acquainted with the history of the science, and in particular how long the several musical instruments now known by us have been in use, to prevent being imposed on by pretended new inventions: the harp of Æolus, as it is called, on which so much has been lately said and written, was constructed by Kircher above a century ago, and is accurately described in his Musurgia; as is also the perpendicular harpsichord, and an instrument so contrived as to produce sound by the friction of wheels, from which the modern lyrichord is manifestly taken. The new system, as it is called, of the flute abec, proposed about forty years ago by the younger Stanesby, is in truth the old and original system of that instrument, and is to be found in Mersennus; and the clarinet, an instrument unknown in England till within these last twenty years, was invented by John Christopher Denner, a wind musical instrument maker of Leipsic above a century ago.§

Farther, it has for the honour of this our native country been said of Purcell, that his music was very different from the Italian; that it was entirely English, that it was masculine. ‖ Against the two first of these assertions we have his own testimony in the preface to one of his works, wherein he says that he has endeavoured at a just imitation of the most famed Italian masters, with a view, as he adds, to bring the gravity and seriousness of that sort of music into vogue.¶ As to the third, the judicious peruser of his compositions will find that they are ever suited to the occasion, and are equally calculated to excite tender, and robust or manly affections.

Lastly, of the many who at this time profess to love music, few are acquainted with the characters, and even the names of those many eminent persons celebrated for their skill and great attainments in the science, and who flourished under the patronage of the greatest potentates, previous to the commencement of the present century; and, with respect to those of our own country, it is true there is scarce a boy in any of the choirs in the kingdom but knows that Tallis and Bird composed anthems, and Child, Batten, Rogers, and Aldrich services; but of their compositions at large, and in what particulars they excelled, even their teachers are ignorant.

Under a thorough conviction of the benefits that must result from the kind of intelligence here recommended, attempts have been made at different periods to trace the rise and progress of music in a course of historical narration; and let it not be deemed an invidious office, if those defects in the attempts of others are pointed out, which alone can justify the present undertaking.

In the Menagiana, tome I. page 303, mention is made of a canon of Tours of the name of Ouvard, who wrote a history of music: Mattheson, in his Volkommenen Capellmeister, takes notice of this work, and says that it comes down to the end of the seventeenth century, and is perhaps extant in MS. in some library at Paris. But the first attempt of this kind in print is a treatise of Johannes Albertus Bannius, 'De Musicæ origine, progressu et 'deniquè studio bene instituendo,' published in 1637, in octavo.

Next to this, in point of time, is the History of Music of Wolfgang Caspar Printz, chapel-master and director of the choir of the church of Sorau, printed at Dresden in the year 1690, in a small quarto volume, with the title of 'Historiche Beschreibung der Edelen Singund Kling- 'kunst.' Neither of the two latter works can be considered as a history of the science; the first of them is a very small volume, and the other not a large one, containing little more than a list of writers on music disposed in chronological order.

The appendix of Dr. Wallis to his edition of Ptolemy, published in 1682, though not a history of the science, contains many historical particulars respecting music, besides that in sundry instances it renders intelligible the doctrines of the ancient writers. It is written with great accuracy and perspicuity, and abounds with instances of that acuteness and penetration for which the author is celebrated.

In 1683, the Sieur Gabriel Guillaume Nivers, organist of the chapel of Lewis XIV. published 'Dissertation 'sur le Chant Gregorien,' a small octavo volume, but in effect a history of ecclesiastical music, with a relation of the many corruptions it has undergone. In it are many curious passages relating to the subject, extracted from the fathers and the ritualists, with the observations of the author, who appears to have been a learned man in his profession.

---

* Nicola Vicentino, a writer of the sixteenth century, with some degree of ingenuity, attempts to shew that these characters are but different modifications of the round and square b, which had been introduced into Guido's scale for another purpose.

† Vide infra, pages 217, 221, 253.

‡ Vide infra, page 563.

§ Vide infra, page 651.

‖ Granger's Biographical History of England, as it is called, vol. II., part II., class X. tit. MUSICIANS, art. HENRICUS PURCELL.

¶ Vide infra, page 744.

In 1695 Gio. Andrea Angelini Bontempi, of Perugia, published in a thin volume a work of some merit, entitled 'Historia Musica.' Berardi mentions a work of one Pietro Arragona, a Florentine, entitled 'Istoria Armonica,' but Brossard doubts the existence of it.*

A history of the pontifical chapel, and of the college of singers thereto belonging, is contained in a work entitled 'Osservazioni per ben regolare il Coro de i Cantori della 'Cappella Pontificia, tanto nelle Funzioni ordinarie, che 'straordinarie,' by Andrea Adami da Bolsena, Maestro della Cappella Pontificia, published at Rome in 1711, in a quarto volume. In this book are many curious particulars.

There is also extant in two volumes duodecimo, but divided into four, a book entitled 'Histoire de la Musique 'et de ses Effets,' printed first at Paris in 1715, and afterwards at Amsterdam in 1725. The materials for this publication were certain papers found in the study of the Abbé Bourdelot, and others of his nephew Bonnet Bourdelot, physician to the king of France, the letters of the Abbé Raguenet and others, on the comparative merits of the Italian and French opera and music, together with sundry other papers on the same subject. The publisher was　　　　　　Bonnet, a nephew of the Abbé Bourdelot; and the best that can be said of the work is, that the whole is a confused jumble of intelligence and controversy; and, saving that it contains some curious memoirs of Lully, and a few other of the French musicians, has very little claim to attention.

About the year 1730, Mr. Peter Prelleur, an able musician and organist, published a work entitled 'The 'modern Music-master, containing an introduction to 'singing, and instructions for most of the instruments in 'use.' At the end of this book is a brief history of music, in which are sundry particulars worth noting: it has no name to it, but was nevertheless compiled by the above person.

John Godfrey Walther, a professor of music, and organist of the church of St. Peter and Paul at Weimar, published in 1732 a musical Lexicon or Bibliotheque, wherein is a great variety of information respecting music and musicians of all countries and ages. Mattheson of Hamburg, in his 'Critica Musica,' his 'Orchestre,' and a work entitled 'Volkommenen Capellmeister,' i. e. the perfect Chapelmaster, has brought together many particulars of the like kind; but the want of method renders these compositions, in an historical view, of little use.

In the year 1740, an ingenious young man of the name of Grassineau,† published a Dictionary of Music in one octavo volume, with a recommendation of the work by Dr. Pepusch, Dr. Greene, and Mr. Galliard. The book had the appearance of a learned work, and all men wondered who the author could be : it seems he had been an amanuensis of the former of these persons. The foundation of this dictionary is a translation of that of Sebastian Brossard; the additions include all the musical articles contained in the two volumes of Chambers's Dictionary, with perhaps a few hints and emendations furnished by Dr. Pepusch. The book nevertheless abounds with errors, and, though a useful and entertaining publication, is not to be relied on.

In 1756, Fr. Wilhelm Marpourg, a musician of Berlin, published in a thin quarto volume, 'Traité de la Fugue et 'du Contrepoint,' the second part whereof is a brief history of counterpoint and fugue. The same person is also the author of a work entitled 'Critische Einleitung in die 'Geschichte und Lehrsake der alten und neuen Musick,' printed at Berlin in 1759. It is part of a larger work, and the remainder is not yet published.

The 'Storia della Musica' of Padre Martini of Bologna, of which as yet only two volumes have been published, and those at the distance of thirteen years from each other, is a learned and curious work ; but the great study and labour bestowed by the author in compiling it, make us despair of ever seeing it completed.

The 'Histoire generale, critique, et philologique de la 'Musique,' of Mons. De Blainville, printed at Paris in 1767, in a thin quarto volume, has very little pretence to the title it bears: like some other works of the kind, it is diffuse where it ought to be succinct, and brief where one would wish to find it copious.

A character very different is due to a work in two volumes, quarto, entitled 'De Cantu et Musica sacra, 'a prima Ecclesiæ Ætate usque ad præsens Tempus; 'Auctore Martino Gerberto, Monasterii et Congregationis 'Sancti Blasii in Silva Nigra Abbate, Sacrique Romani 'Imperii Princeps. Typis San-Blasianis, 1774.' In this most valuable work the author has with great learning, judgment, and candour, given the history of ecclesiastical music ; and the author of the present work felicitates himself on finding his sentiments on the subject, particularly of the church composers, and the corruptions of the church style, confirmed by the testimony of so able a writer. He is farther happy to see that without any communication with this illustrious dignitary, and without having perused his book, by the help of materials, which this country alone has furnished, he has been able to pursue a similar track of narration, and to relate and authenticate many facts contained therein.‡

At the beginning of this present year 1776, the musical world were favoured with the first volume of a work entitled 'A General History of Music from the earliest 'Ages to the present Period, with a Dissertation on the 'Music of the Ancients, by Charles Burney, Mus. D., 'F. R. S.' The author in the proposals for his subscription has given assurances of the publication of a second, which we doubt not he will make good.

From those who have thus taken upon them to trace the rise and progress of music in a course of historical deduction, we pass to others who appear to have made collections for the like purpose, but were defeated in their intentions of benefiting the science by their labours.

And first Anthony Wood, who himself was a proficient in music, and entertained an enthusiastic fondness for the art, had it seems meditated a history of musicians, a work which his curiosity and unwearied industry rendered him very fit for : to this end he made a collection of memoirs, which is extant, in his own hand-writing, among the manuscripts in the Ashmolean Museum ; and in the printed catalogue thereof is thus numbered and described: '8568. 106. Some materials toward a history of the lives 'and compositions of all English musicians; drawn up 'according to alphabetical order in 210 pages by A. W.' Of these materials he seems to have availed himself in the Fasti Oxonienses, wherein are contained a great number of memoirs of eminent English musicians, equally curious and satisfactory, the perusal whereof in the original MS. has contributed to render this work somewhat less imperfect than it must have been without such information as they afford.

Dr. Henry Aldrich, dean of Christ Church, an excellent scholar, and of such skill in music, that he holds a place among the most eminent of our English church musicians, had formed a design of a history of music on a most extensive plan. His papers in the library of Christ Church college, Oxford, have been carefully perused : among them are a great number of loose notes, hints, and memo-

---

* Catalogue of writers on music at the end of his 'Dictionnaire de 'Musique,' octavo, page 369.

† See an account of him page 30, in the notes.

‡ The fact is, that the fifth volume of this work was printed off in July in the present year, and the former ones in succession in the years preceding, and the two volumes of the Abbot Gerbert's work came to hand in the month immediately following.

randa relating to music and the professors of the science; in the collection whereof he seems to have pursued the course recommended by Brossard in the catalogue of writers on music at the end of his Dictionnaire de Musique, page 367; but among a great multitude of papers in his own hand-writing, there are none to be found from whence it can with certainty be concluded that he had made any progress in the work.

Nicola Francesco Haym, a musician, and a man of some literature, published, above forty years ago, proposals containing the plan of a history of music written by himself, but, meeting with little encouragement, he desisted from his design of printing it.

Much intelligence respecting music might have been hoped for from the abilities and industry of Ashmole, Dr. Hooke, and Sir William Petty, the two former of whom had been choristers, the one in the cathedral of Litchfield, the other of Christ Church, Oxford: the last of the three was professor of music at Gresham college; but these persons abandoning the faculty in which they had been instituted, betook themselves to studies of a different kind: Ashmole, at first a solicitor in Chancery, became an antiquary, a herald, a virtuoso, a naturalist, and an Hermetic philosopher: Hooke took to the study of natural philosophy, mechanics, and architecture, and attained to great skill in all:* and Petty, choosing the better part, laid the foundation of an immense estate by a various exertion of his very great talents, and was successively a physician, a mathematician, a mechanic, a projector, a contractor with the government, and an improver of land.

Enough it is presumed has been said to prove the utility, and even the necessity, in order to a competent knowledge of the science, of a History of Music, in the deduction whereof the first object that presents itself to view is the system of the ancient Greeks, adjusted, it must be confessed, with great art and ingenuity, but labouring under many defects, which, if we are not greatly deceived, are remedied in that of the moderns. Of the origin of this system we have such authentic intelligence as leaves little room to doubt that it was invented by Pythagoras, a name sufficiently known and revered, and the subsequent deduction of the progress of the science, involving in it the names and improvements of men well known, such as Philolaus, Archytas of Tarentum, Aristoxenus, Euclid, Nicomachus, Ptolemy, and many

others, may truly be called history, as being founded in truth; and the utility and certainty of their relations will teach us to distinguish between fact and fable.

It is much to be lamented that the greater part of what we believe touching music, is founded on no better authority than the fictions of poets and mythologists, whose relations are in most instances merely typical and figurative; such must the stories of Orpheus and Amphion appear to be, as having no foundation in truth, but being calculated solely for the purpose of moral instruction.

And with regard to facts themselves, a distinction is to be made between such as are in their own nature interesting, and those that tend only to gratify an idle curiosity: to instance in the latter, what satisfaction does the mind receive from the recital of the names of those who are said to have increased the chords of the primitive lyre from four to seven, Chorebus, Hyagnis, and Terpander; or when we are told that Olympus invented the enarmonic genus, as also the Harmatian mood; or that Eumolpus and Melampus were excellent musicians, and Pronomus, Antigenides, and Lamia celebrated players on the flute? In all these instances, where there are no circumstances that constitute a character, and familiarize to us the person spoken of, we naturally enquire who he is; and, for want of farther information, become indifferent as to what is recorded of him.

Mr. Wollaston has a remark upon the nature of fame that seems to illustrate the above observation, and indeed goes far beyond the case here put, inasmuch as the persons by him spoken of, are become wellknown characters: his words are these: 'When it is said that 'Julius Cæsar subdued Gaul, beat Pompey, changed the 'Roman commonwealth into a monarchy, &c. it is the 'same thing as to say, the conquerer of Pompey was 'Cæsar; that is, Cæsar and the conqueror of Pompey are 'the same thing; and Cæsar is as much known by one 'designation as the other. The amount then is only 'this: that the conqueror of Pompey conquered Pompey; 'or somebody conquered Pompey; or rather, since 'Pompey is as little known as Cæsar, somebody con-'quered somebody.'†

That memorials of persons, who at this distance of time must appear thus indifferent to us, should be transmitted down to posterity, together with those events that make a part of musical history, is not to be wondered at; and Plutarch could never have recorded the facts mentioned by him in his Dialogue on Music, had he not also given the names of those persons to whom they are severally ascribed; and if they now appear uninteresting we may reject them. But the case is far otherwise with respect to what is told us of the marvellous power and efficacy of the ancient music. Aristoxenus expressly asserts that the foundation of ingenuous manners, and a regular and decent discharge of the offices of civil life, are laid in a musical education; and Plutarch, speaking of the education of Achilles, and relating that the most wise Chiron was careful to instruct him in music, says, that whoever shall in his youth addict himself to the study of music, if he be properly instructed therein, shall not fail to applaud and practise that which is noble and generous, and detest and shun their contraries: music teaching those that pursue it to observe decorum, temperance, and regularity; for which reason he adds, that in those cities which were governed by the best laws, the greatest care was taken that their youth should be taught music. Plato, in his treatise De Legibus, lib. II., insists largely on the utility of this practice; and Polybius, lib. IV., cap. iii., scruples not to attribute the misfortunes of the Cynetheans, a people of Arcadia, and that general corruption of their

---

* It is said by Anthony Wood of Dr. Hooke, that, being at Westminster-school, he lodged and dieted in the house of Mr. Busby, the master, and that there, of his own accord, he learned to play twenty lessons on the organ, and invented thirty several ways of flying. Athen. Oxon. vol. II. col. 1039. The latter of these facts must stand on the authority of the relator, or rather his authors, Dr. Busby and the great Dr. Wilkins of Wadham college; but the former is rendered highly probable by the following anecdote respecting Dr. Busby, the communication whereof we owe to Dr. Wetenhall, one of Busby's scholars, and afterwards bishop of Cork and Ross, viz.: that 'the first 'organ he ever saw or heard was in his, Dr. Busby's house; and that the 'same was kept for sacred use, and that even when it was interdicted.' Dedication of a treatise entitled 'Of Gifts and Offices in the public 'Worship of God, by Edward Wetenhall, D.D., Chanter of Christ 'Church, Dublin, 8vo. 1679.' That he was also eminently skilled in architecture, may be inferred from an assertion of Dr. Ward, in his life of Sir Christopher Wren, among the Gresham professors, viz.: that he greatly assisted Sir Christopher in re-building the public edifices. Wood goes so far as to say that Hooke designed New Bedlam, Montague-house, the College of Physicians, and the pillar on Fish-street Hill; but the erection of the latter of these edifices is ascribed to Sir Christopher Wren. As to Montague-house and the College of Physicians, there are in Moxon's Mechanic Exercises, under the head of Bricklayer's Work, intimations that they were both designed by Hooke; and Strype, in his edition of Stowe's Survey of London, speaking of Aske's hospital at Hoxton, says it was built after a modern design of Dr. Hooke.

Of this latter person it may be said, that he was perhaps one of the greatest proficients in the art of thriving of his time: by places, by projects, and by grants, some to himself, and others to his wife, he acquired estates, real and personal, to the annual amount of £15,000, to the accumulation of which wealth we may well suppose that the virtue of parsimony contributed not a little, and the rather as he suffered a natural daughter of his to be an actress on the stage under Sir William D'Avenant at the Duke's theatre in Dorset-Garden.

† Religion of Nature delineated, page 117.

manners, by him described, to the neglect of the discipline and exercise of music; which he says the ancient Arcadians were so industrious to cultivate, that they incorporated it into, and made it the very essence of, their government; obliging not their children only, but the young men till they attained the age of thirty, to persist in the study and practice of it. Innumerable also are the passages in the ancient writers on harmonics wherein the power of determining the minds of men to virtue or vice is ascribed to music with as little doubt of its efficacy in this respect, as if the human mind was possessed of no such power as the will, or was totally divested of those passions, inclinations, and habits, which constitute a moral character.

Now, forasmuch as we at this day are incapable of discovering any such power as is here attributed to mere musical sounds, we seem to be warranted in withholding our assent to these relations, till the evidence on which they are grounded becomes more particular and explicit; or it shall be shown that they are not, what some men conceive them to be, hyperbolical forms of speech, in which the literal is as far from the true sense, as it is in the stories of the effects of music on inanimate beings. If indeed by music we are to understand musical sounds jointly operating with poetry, for this reason that music is ever spoken of by the ancients as inseparably united with poetry; and farther, because we are told that the ancient poets, for instance, Demodocus, Thaletas of Crete, Pindar, and others, not only composed the words, but also the music to their odes and pœans, and sang them to the lyre; a degree of efficacy must be allowed it, proportioned to the advantages which it could not but derive from such an union.* But here a difficulty will arise, which, though it does not destroy the credit of these reports, as they stand on the footing of other historical facts, would incline us to suspect that the music here spoken of was of a kind very different from what it is in general conceived to be, and that for the following reason.

We know by experience that there is no necessary connection between music and poetry; and such as are competent judges of either, know also that though the powers of each are in some instances concurrent, each is a separate and distinct language. The poet affects the passions by images excited in the mind, or by the forcible impression of moral sentiments; the musician by sounds either simple and harmonical only in succession, or combined: these the mind, from its particular constitution, supposing it endued with that sense which is the perfection of the auditory faculty, without referring to any other subject or medium, recognizes as the language of nature; and the affections of joy, grief, and a thousand nameless sensations, become subservient to their call.

As the powers of music and poetry are thus different, it necessarily follows that they may exist independently of each other; and the instances are as numerous of poets incapable of articulating musical sounds, as of musicians unpossessed of a talent for poetry.

If then the poets of the ancients were only such as to the harmony of their verse, were capable of joining that of music, by composing musical airs, and also singing them, and that to an audience grounded and well instructed in music, what can we suppose the music of their odes to have been? Perhaps little else than bare recitation; not in true musical intervals, but with such inflections of the voice as accompany speech when calculated to make a forcible impression on the hearers.

As to the relations of the effects of music in former ages on the passions of men, and of its provoking them to acts of desperation, it may be said that they afford no greater proofs of its influence on the passions than modern history is capable of furnishing.† But there are

---

* Quintilian has elegantly expressed his sense of the joint efficacy of music and poetry in the following passage: 'Namque et voce et 'modulatione grandia elatè, jucunda dulciter, moderata leniter canit, 'totâque arte consentit cum eorum, quæ dicuntur, affectibus.' Inst. Orat. lib. I. cap. x.

But, notwithstanding this observation, which, as far as it goes, must be allowed to be just, the powers of music will be found inadequate to the expression of many of those sentiments in poetry which are comprehended in the ideas of the beautiful and the sublime; such, for instance, as these:—

Where glowing embers round the room
Teach light to counterfeit a gloom.

Where I may oft outwatch the bear,
With thrice great Hermes, and unsphere
The spirit of Plato to unfold
What worlds or what vast regions hold
The immortal mind.

Sentiments that defy the utmost powers of music to suit them with correspondent sounds.

Nor will it be found that the melody or the cadence of sounds are either of them so peculiarly appropriated to particular passions or descriptions, as to rank the faculty of expression among the principal excellencies of music. And in proof of this assertion some examples might be given that would stagger an infidel in these matters. The late Dr. Brown, when he had written his ode entitled the Cure of Saul, for the music to it made a selection from the works of the most celebrated composers, of such favourite movements as he thought would best express the sense of the words; in particular he took the saraband in the eighth sonata of Corelli's second opera for a solo air; and that most divine movement in Purcell's 'O give thanks,' 'Remember me, O Lord,' for a chorus; and any stranger would have thought that the music had been originally composed to the words: the music to that admired song in Samson, 'Return, O God of hosts,' was taken from an Italian cantata of Mr. Handel, composed in his youth; as was also the music to the other, 'Then long eternity,' in the same oratorio: farther, the chorus in Alexander's Feast, 'Let old Timotheus yield the prize,' saving the addition of one of the interior parts, was originally an Italian trio; as was also that in the Il Penseroso, 'These pleasures melancholy give.' Finally, a great part of the music to Mr. Dryden's lesser ode for St. Cecilia's Day was originally composed by Mr. Handel for an opera entitled Alceste, written by Dr. Smollet, but never performed.

---

† Vide infra, pages 118, 119; and Plutarch relates that Antigenides, the tibicinist, playing before Alexander the Great, in a measure of time distinguished by the name of the Harmatian mood, enflamed the hero to such a degree, that, leaping from his seat, and drawing his sword, he in a frenzy of courage assailed those who were nearest him. In Orat II. De Fortun. vel Virtut. Alexandr. Magn.

To these instances may be opposed the following, which modern history affords. The first is related of Ericus, king of Denmark, surnamed the Good, who reigned about 1130, and is to the following purport. When Ericus was returned into his kingdom, and held the yearly assembly, he was greatly pleased with the industry both of his soldiers and artificers. Among other of his attendants was a musician, who asserted that by the power of his art he was able to excite in men whatsoever affections he thought proper; and to make the sad cheerful, the cheerful sad, the angry placid, and such as were pleased discontented, and even drive them into a raging madness; and the more he insisted on his abilities the greater was the king's desire to try them. The artist now began to repent his having thus magnified his talent, foreseeing the danger of making such experiments on a king, and he was afraid that if he failed in the performance of what he had undertaken, he should be esteemed a liar; he therefore entreated all who had any influence over the king to endeavour to divert him from his intention to make proof of his art; but all without effect, for the more desirous he was to evade the trial of his skill, the more the king insisted on it. When the musician perceived that he could not be excused, he begged that all weapons capable of doing mischief might be removed, and took care that some persons should be placed out of the hearing of the Cithara, who might be called in to his assistance, and were, if necessity required it, to snatch the instrument from his hands, and break it on his head. Every thing being thus prepared, the citharist began to make proof of his art on the king, who sat with some few about him in an open hall; first, by a grave mode, he threw a certain melancholy into the minds of the auditors; but, changing it into one more cheerful, he converted their sadness into mirth that almost incited his hearers to dancing; then varying his modulation, on the sudden he inspired the king with fury and indignation, which he continued to work up in him till it was easy to see he was approaching to frenzy. The sign was then given for those who were in waiting to enter; they first broke the Cithara according to their directions, and then seized on the king; but such was his strength, that he killed some of them with his fist; being afterwards overwhelmed with several beds, his fury became pacified, and, recovering his reason, he was grievously afflicted that he had turned his wrath against his friends. Saxo Grammaticus, in Hist. Danicæ, edit. Basil. lib. XII. page 113. The same author adds, that he broke open the doors of a chamber, and, snatching up a sword, ran four men through the body; and that when he returned to his senses he made a pilgrimage to Jerusalem as an expiation of his crime. Olaus Magnus, who tells the same story, says that he afterwards died in the island of Cyprus. Vide Olaus Magnus, in Hist. Gent. Sept. lib. XV. cap. xxviii. and Krantzius, in Chron. Regn. Daniæ, Sueciæ, et Norvegiæ.

Hieronymus Magius gives the following relation of a fact recent in memory in the year 1564: Cardinal Hippolyto de Medicis, being a legate in the army at Pannonia, the troops being about to engage, upon sounding the alarm by the trumpets and drums, was so enflamed with a martial ardour, that, girding on his sword, he mounted his horse, and could not be restrained from charging the enemy at the head of those

others that stagger human belief, and leave us in doubt whether to give or refuse credit to them; such, for instance, are the stories of the cure of diseases, namely, the sciatica, epilepsy, fevers, the bites of vipers, and even pestilences, by the power of harmony.

What an implicit assent has been given to the reports of the sovereign efficacy of music in the cure of the frenzy occasioned by the bite of the Tarantula! Baglivi, an eminent physician, a native of Apulia, the country where the Tarantula, a kind of spider, is produced, has given the natural history of this supposed noxious insect, and a variety of cases of persons rendered frantic by its bite, and restored to sanity and the use of their reason; and in Kircher's Musurgia we have the very air or tune by which the cure is said to be effected. Sir Thomas Brown, that industrious exploder of vulgar errors, has let this, perhaps the most egregious of any that he has animadverted on, pass as a fact not to be controverted; and Dr. Mead has strengthened the belief of it by his reasoning on the nature of poisons. After all the whole comes out to be a fable, an imposture calculated to deceive the credulous, and serve the ends of designing people inhabiting the country.*

The natural tendency of these reflections is to draw on a comparison of the ancient with modern music; which latter, as it pretends to no such miraculous powers, has been thought by the ignorant to be so greatly inferior to the former, as scarce to deserve the name. In like manner do they judge of the characters of men, and the state of human manners at remote periods, when they compare the events of ancient history, the actions of heroes, and the wisdom of legislators, with those of modern times, inferring from thence a depravity in mankind, of which not the least trace is discernible.

This mistaken notion seems to be but the necessary consequence of that system of education which directs the attention of young minds to the discoveries and transactions of the more early times; assigning, as the rule of civil policy, and the standard of moral perfection and excellence in arts, the conduct, the lives, and works of men whose greatest achievements are only wonderful as they were rare; whose valour was brutality, and whose policy was in general fraud, or at best craft; and whose inventions and discoveries have in numberless instances been superseded by those of later times. To these, which we may call classical prejudices, we are to impute those numerous and reiterated complaints which we meet with of the degeneracy of modern times; and when they are once imbibed, complaints of the declension of some arts, and of the loss of others, as also of the corruption of manners, appear to be but of course. Whether, therefore, our reverence for antiquity has not been carried too far both as to matters of science and morality, comprehending in the latter the virtue of justice, and the qualities of personal courage, general benevolence, and refined humanity, of which the examples are not less numerous and conspicuous in modern than in ancient history, is a question well worthy consideration.†

whose duty it was to make the onset. Var. Lect. seu Miscell. Venet. 1564, lib. IV. cap. xiii.

And, lastly, it is related, that at the celebration of the marriage of the duke of Joyeuse, a gentleman was so transported with the music of Claude le Jeune, performed at that solemnity, that he seized his sword, and swore that, unless prevented, he must fight with some one present; but that a sudden change in the music calmed him. Bayle, art. GOUDIMEL, in not. Vide infra, page 434.

* Vide infra, page 639, in note.

† In a book, which few readers at this day think worth looking into, Dr. Hakewill's Apologie for the Power and Providence of God, are the following sentiments touching the reverence due to antiquity: ' Antiquity ' I unfeignedly honour and reverence; but why I should reverence the ' rust and refuse, the dross and dregs, the warts and wens thereof, I am ' yet to seek.——As in the little, so in the great world, reason will tell ' you that old age or antiquity is to be accounted by the farther distance ' from the beginning, and the nearer approach to the end; and as grey

Of the loss of many arts, that contribute as well to the benefit as delight of mankind, much has been said; and there is extant a large volume, written in Latin by Guido Pancirollus, a lawyer of Padua, entitled ' De rebus memo-' rabilibus deperditis et noviter inventis,' which has not escaped censure for the mistakes and peurilities with which it abounds, the tendency thereof being to shew that many arts known to the ancients are either totally lost, or so greatly depraved, that they can scarcely be said to have an existence among us.‡ In this book, which has proved a plentiful source of intelligence to such as have laboured to depreciate all modern attainments, it is roundly asserted of music, which was anciently a science, that there are not the least footsteps remaining: and farther, that the Cardinal of Ferrara, by whom it is supposed is meant Hippolyto de Este, the patron of Vicentino, took great pains to recover it, but all to no purpose.§

Such as seem to have adopted the opinion of Pancirollus with respect to music, for example, Dr. Pepusch, and

' beards are for wisdom and judgment to be preferred before young green ' heads, because they have more experience in affairs; so likewise for the ' same cause the present times are to be preferred before the infancy or ' youth of the world, we having the history and practice of former ages ' to inform us, which they wanted.——In disgracing the present times ' you disgrace antiquity properly so called.' Book V. page 133.

Farther to this purpose the learned and sagacious Sir Thomas Brown delivers his sentiments in the following terms: ' The mortalest enemy ' unto knowledge, and that which hath done the greatest execution upon ' truth, hath been a peremptory adhesion unto authority; and more ' especially the establishing of our belief upon the dictates of antiquity. ' For, (as every capacity may observe) most men of ages present, so ' superstitiously do look upon ages past, that the authorities of the one ' exceed the reasons of the other: whose persons indeed being far ' removed from our times, their works, which seldom with us pass ' uncontroled, either by contemporaries, or immediate successors, are ' now become out of the distance of envies: and the farther removed ' from present times, are conceived to approach the nearer unto truth ' itself. Now hereby methinks we manifestly delude ourselves, and ' widely walk out of the track of truth.

' For, first, men hereby impose a thraldom on their times, which the ' ingenuity of no age should endure, or indeed the presumption of any ' did ever yet enjoin. Thus Hippocrates, about two thousand years ago, ' conceived it no injustice either to examine or refute the doctrines of ' his predecessors: Galen the like, and Aristotle the most of any. Yet ' did not any of these conceive themselves infallible, or set down their ' dictates as verities irrefragable; but when they either deliver their ' own inventions, or reject other men's opinions, they proceed with ' judgment and ingenuity: establishing their assertions, not only with ' great solidity, but submitting them also unto the correction of future ' discovery.

' Secondly, men that adore times past, consider not that those times ' were once present, that is, as our own are at this instant; and we ' ourselves unto those to come, as they unto us at present: as we rely ' on them, even so will those on us, and magnify us hereafter, who ' at present condemn ourselves. Which very absurdity is daily com-' mitted amongst us, even in the esteem and censure of our own times. ' And, to speak impartially, old men, from whom we should expect the ' greatest example of wisdom, do most exceed in this point of folly; ' commending the dayes of their youth, which they scarce remember, at ' least well understood not; extolling those times their younger years ' have heard their fathers condemn, and condemning those times the ' gray heads of their posterity shall commend. And thus is it the ' humour of many heads to extol the dayes of their fore-fathers, and ' declaim against the wickedness of times present. Which, notwith-' standing they cannot handsomely do, without the borrowed help and ' satyrs of times past, condemning the vices of their own times, by the ' expressions of vices in times which they commend; which cannot but ' argue the community of vice in both. Horace, therefore, Juvenal, ' and Persius were no prophets, although their lines did seem to ' indigitate and point at our times. There is a certain list of vices ' committed in all ages, and declaimed against by all authors, which will ' last as long as humane nature; which, digested into common places, ' may serve for any theme, and never be out of date until Dooms day.' Enquiries into Vulgar and Common Errours, Book I. Chap. vi.

‡ Of the many instances of arts or inventions lost, or in a state of depravity at this time, there are very few, if any, of which evidence can be found, or at least that have not been succeeded by others tending to the same purpose, and of far greater utility. To instance in a few particulars, instead of the papyrus of the ancients, prepared from the leaves of a certain bullrush, we have the paper of the moderns; in the room of their specular stones, glass; and of clepsydræ, instruments that measured time by the dropping of water, or the falling of sand, clocks and watches. As to the art of staining or painting glass, which ceased to be practised about the Reformation, and has almost ever since been deplored as a lost invention, it is effected by chemical means, and is at this day in as great perfection as ever. Vide Chambers's Dict. voce GLASS. Anecdotes of Painting in England by Mr. Horace Walpole, vol. II. page 15.

§ A like attempt was made in France in the year 1570, by the establishment of an academy under the direction of Jean Antoine Baïf a few of his disciples, have asserted as an instance in support of it, that the chromatic and enarmonic genera are now neither practised nor accurately known. Farther they add, that of the various modes of the ancients, only two are remaining, viz., those which answer to the keys A and C; for, say they, the ancients took the tones and semitones in order as they naturally arise in the diapason system, and, without any dislocation of either, considered the progression from any fundamental chord as a mode or key, and formed their melodies accordingly.

With regard to the enarmonic genus, it will in the ensuing work be shewn that the ancients themselves suffered it to grow into disuse by reason of its intricacy; and therefore it cannot so properly be said to have been lost, as that it is rejected, and the rather as we are assured that Salinas and others have accurately determined it:* of the chromatic as much seems to have been retained as is necessary to the perfection of the diatonic; and as to the modes, it will also be shewn that there never was, nor can there in nature be more, or any other than the two abovementioned; and consequently that in this respect music has sustained no injury at all.

The loss of arts is a plausible topic of declamation, but the possibility of such a calamity by other means than a second deluge, or the interposition of any less powerful agent than God himself, is a matter of doubt; and when appearances every where around us favour the opinion of our improvement not only in literature, but in the sciences and all the manual arts, it is wonderful that the contrary notion should ever have got footing among mankind.

As to the general prejudices in behalf of antiquity, it has been hinted above that a reason for them is to be found in that implicit belief which the course of modern education disposes us to entertain of the superior virtue, wisdom, and ingenuity of those, who in all these instances we are taught to look on as patterns the most worthy of imitation; but it can never be deemed an excuse for some writers for complimenting nations less enlightened than ourselves with the possession or enjoyment of arts which it is pretended we have lost; as they do when they magnify the attainments of nations comparatively barbarous, and making those countries on which the beams of knowledge can scarcely be said to have yet dawned the theatres of virtue and the schools of science, recommend them as fit exemplars for our imitation.

Of this class of authors, Sir William Temple and Isaac Vossius seem to be the chief; the one a statesman retired from business, an ingenious writer, but possessed of little learning, other than what he acquired in his later years, and which it is suspected was not drawn from the purest sources; the other a man of great erudition, but little judgment, the weakness whereof he manifested in a childish credulity, and a disposition to believe things incredible. These men, upon little better evidence than the reports of travellers, and the relations of missionaries, who might have purposes of their own to serve, have celebrated the policy, the morality, and the learning of the Chinese, and done little less than proposed them as examples of all that is excellent in human nature.†

The topics insisted on by Sir William Temple, in that part of his Essay on Heroic Virtue, where he takes occasion to speak of the Chinese, are their wisdom, their knowledge, their wit, their learning, ingenuity, and civility, on which he bestows the most extravagant encomiums.

Vossius is more particular, and says that ' the Chinese ' deplore the loss of their music, the superior merit ' whereof may be inferred from the relics of it yet re- ' maining, which are so excellent, that for their perfection ' in the art, the Chinese may impose silence on all ' Europe.' Farther he says of their pantomimes, or theatrical representations by mute persons, in which the sentiments are expressed by gesticulations, and even nods, that 'these declare their skill in the rythmus, which ' is the soul of music.'‡ Elsewhere he takes occasion to celebrate this people for their skill on the tibia, and bestows on their performance the following enthusiastic encomium: 'The tibia, by far to be preferred to the ' stringed instruments of every kind, is now silenced, so ' that, excepting the Chinese, who alone excel on it, ' scarce any are to be found that are able to please even ' an ordinary hearer.'§

Another writer is more particular, and gives us for history this nonsense; that Fou-Hi, the first of the emperors and legislators of China, delivered the precepts of music, and having invented fishing, composed a song for those who exercised the art; and to banish all impurity from the heart, made a lyre with strings of silk; and farther that Chin-Nong, a succeeding emperor, celebrated the fertility of the earth in songs of his own composing, and made a beautiful lyre and a guitar enriched with precious stones, which produced a noble harmony, curbed the passions, and elevated many to virtue and heavenly truth.‖

These are the opinions of men who have acquired no small reputation in the world of letters; and therefore that error might not derive a sanction from authority, it seemed necessary to enquire into the evidence in support of them; of what sort it is, the passage above cited may serve to show. It remains now to make the comparison above proposed of the modern with the ancient music.

The method hitherto pursued by those writers who have attempted to draw a parallel between the ancient and modern music, has been to bring together into one point of view the testimonies in favour of the former, and to strengthen them by their own suffrages, which upon examination will be found to amount to just nothing; for these testimonies being no more than verbal declarations or descriptions, every reader is at liberty to supply them by ideas of his own; ideas which can only have been excited by that music which he has actually heard,

---

and Joachim Theobalde de Courville, but through envy, as it is said, the design failed. Mersennus in Quest. et Explic. in Genesin. art. XV. pag. 1683. Walth. Musicalisches Lexicon, voce ACADEMIE ROYALE DE MUSIQUE.

* Vide infra, page 39.

† As an instance of their superior skill in the science of medicine, he says that their physicians pretend that they are able, not only to tell by the pulse how many hours or days a sick man can last, but how many years a man in perfect seeming health may live, in case of no accident or violence. Essay of Heroic Virtue, sect. II.

The following summary of Chinese knowledge may serve to show how well they are entitled to the exaggerated encomiums of such writers. They carry their history back to many ages before the time of the creation. Hearne's Duct. Historic. vol. I. page 16. Their notion of an eclipse is, that there is in heaven a dragon of an immense bigness, ready at all times to eat up the sun or moon, which he likes best; when

an eclipse of either happens, they suppose he has got the planet between his teeth, and, to make him quit his hold, they beat drums and brass kettles. Le Comte's Memoirs of China, edit. 1738, page 70, 488. In the judgment of Cassini, and other great astronomers, they err in their accounts of sundry conjunctions of the planets; in some of them not less than five hundred years. Jenkin on the Reasonableness and Certainty of the Christian Religion, vol. I. page 339. They are so little skilled in mechanics, that they took a watch, brought into their country by a Jesuit, for an animal. They are strangers to the use of etters as the elements of words; and have even at this day no alphabet. Ibid. Moreover they pretend to be the inventors of music, notwithstanding that in the opinion of Father Le Comte they have nothing among them that deserves the name. See his Memoirs, page 214.

Of their propensity to fraud and deceit in their dealings, there are abundant examples in Le Comte and Lord Anson's voyage; and of their morality and civil policy, which are so highly extolled, any one may judge, when he is told that in Pekin and other large cities there is an officer, whose duty it is every morning to destroy the numerous infants that have been exposed in the streets in the preceding night. Mod. Univ. Hist. fol. vol. I. page 175.

‡ De poemat. cant. et virib. Rythmi, page 95.

§ Ibid, page 107.

‖ Extraits des Hist. Chinois, published by Mons. Goguet, page 567, 572. Dissert. on the Union, &c. of Poetry and Music, page 167.

or at least perused and contemplated. An instance borrowed from the practice of some critics in painting, may possibly illustrate this sentiment : the works of Apelles, Parrhasius, Zeuxis, and Protogenes, together with those of other artists less known, such as Bularchus, Euphranor, Timanthes, Polygnotus, Polycletes, and Aristides, all famous painters, have been celebrated in terms of high applause by Aristotle, Philostratus, Pliny, and the poets ; and those who attend to their descriptions of them, associate to each subject ideas of excellence as perfect as their imaginations can suggest, which can only be derived from such works of later artists as they have seen ; in like manner as we assist the descriptions of Helen in Homer, and of Eve in Milton, with ideas of female beauty, grace, and elegance, drawn from our own observation :* the result of such a comparison in the case of painting, has frequently been a determination to the prejudice of modern artists ; and the works of Raphael, Domenichino, and Guido have been condemned as not answering to those characters of sublime and beautiful, which are given to the productions of the ancient artists.† In like manner to speak of music, we can form ideas of the perfection of harmony and melody, and of the general effect resulting from the artful combination of musical sounds, from that music alone which we have actually heard ; and when we read of the music of Timotheus or Antigenides, we must either resemble it to that of the most excellent of the modern artists, or forbear to judge about it ; and if in the comparison such critics as Isaac Vossius, Sir William Temple, and some others, reject the music of the moderns as unworthy of attention or notice, how egregiously are they deceived, and what do they but forego the substance for the shadow ?

Other writers have taken a different course, and endeavoured to prove the inferiority of the modern music to the ancient, by a comparison of the powers of each in depriving men of the exercise of their rational faculties, and by impelling them to acts of violence. To these it may be said, that, admitting such a power in music, it seems to be common in some degree to that of all ages and countries, even the most savage ; but the fact is, that these effects are adventitious, and in all the instances produced will be found to have followed from some predisposition of the mind of the hearer, or peculiar coincidence of circumstances, for that in truth music pretends not to the power of working miracles, nor is it the more to be esteemed for exciting men to frenzy. Those who contemplate it in a philosophical and rational manner, and attend to its genuine operation on the human affections, are abundantly satisfied of its efficacy, when they discover that it has a tendency to exhilarate the mind, to calm the passions, to assuage the pangs of affliction,‡ to

assist devotion, and to inspire the mind with the most noble and exalted sentiments.

Others, despairing of the evidence of facts, have recourse to argument, contending that the same superiority with respect to music is to be yielded to the ancients as we allow them in the arts that afford delight to the imagination ; poetry, eloquence, and sculpture, for instance, of which, say they, their works bear luculent testimony. To this it may be answered, that the evidence of works or productions now existing is irrefragable, but in a question of this kind there is no reasoning by analogy ; and farther, that in the case of music, proof of the superiority of the ancients is not only wanting, but the weight of the argument lies on the other side ; for where are those productions of the ancients that must decide the question ? Lost, it will be said, in the general wreck of literature and the arts. If so, they cease to be evidence. Appeal we then to those remaining monuments that exhibit to us the forms of their instruments, of which the lyre and the tibia are the most celebrated ; and that these are greatly excelled by the instruments of the moderns will not bear a question. As to the lyre, considered as a musical instrument, it is a very artless invention, consisting merely of a few chords of equal length but unequal tensions, in such a situation, and so disposed, as, without any contrivance, to prolong or reverberate the sound, to vibrate in the empty air. The tibia, allowing it the perfection to which the flute of the moderns is arrived, could at best be but an imperfect instrument ;§ and yet we are told it was in such estimation among the ancients, that at Corinth the sum of three, some say seven, talents was given by Ismenias, a musician, for a flute.

But a weightier argument in favour of modern music, at least so far as regards the improvements in theory and practice that necessarily result from the investigation of new principles and the discovery of new combinations, may be drawn from the natural course and order of things, which is ever towards perfection, as is seen in other sciences, physics and mathematics, for instance ; so that of music it may be said, that the discoveries of one age have served but as a foundation for improvements in the next ; the consequence whereof is, that the fund of harmony is ever increasing. What advantages must accrue to music from this circumstance, may be discerned if we inquire a little into those powers which are chiefly exercised in practical composition. The art of invention is made one of the heads among the precepts of rhetoric, to which music in this and sundry instances bears a near

---

* Mr. Harris to this purpose has given his sentiments in the following judicious observation : 'When we read in Milton of Eve, that

    'Grace was in all her steps, heav'n in her eye,
    'In ev'ry gesture dignity and love ;

'we have an image not of that Eve which Milton conceived, but of such 'an Eve only as every one by his own proper genius is able to represent 'from reflecting on those ideas which he has annexed to those several 'sounds. The greater part in the mean time have never perhaps 'bestowed one accurate thought upon what Grace, Heaven, Love, and 'Dignity mean ; or ever enriched the mind with ideas of beauty, or 'asked whence they are to be acquired, and by what proportions they 'are constituted. On the contrary, when we view Eve as painted by an 'able painter, we labour under no such difficulty ; because we have 'exhibited before us the better conceptions of an artist, the genuine 'ideas of perhaps a Titian or a Raphael.' Disc. on Music, Painting, and Poetry, page 77, in not.

† Vide Inquiry into the Beauties of Painting, by Daniel Webb, Esq. passim.

‡ To this purpose we meet in Procopius with the following affecting relation, viz : that Gelimer, king of the Vandals, being at war with the emperor Justinian, and having been driven to the mountains by Belisarius, his general, and reduced to great straits, was advised in a letter by a friend of his named Pharas to make terms with the enemy ; but in the greatness of his spirit disdaining submission, he returned

this answer : 'Quod mihi consilium dedisti, magnam habeo tibi gratiam, 'ut etiam hosti injusto serviam ; id verò mihi intolerandum videtur. 'Si Deus faveret, repetere, pœnas ab eo vellem, qui à me nunquam nec 'facto violatus nec verbo, bello, cujus nulla est causa legitima, prætex- 'tum præbuit, meque in hunc statum redegit, accito, nescio unde, 'immissoque Belisario. Non improbabile esse sciat, passurum ipsum, 'tanquam hominem ac principem, eorum aliquid, unde abhorrit. 'Nequit ultra progredi stylus, auferente mentem calamitate, quæ me 'circumvenit. Vale, amice Phara, et mihi quod te oro, citharam, panem 'unum ac spongiam mitte.' Procopius Cæsariensis de Bello Vandalico, vol. I. lib. II. cap. vi. page 240, edit. Paris, 1662, which we thus render : I esteem it a great kindness that you vouchsafe me your advice, recommending a submission to my enemy, unjust as he has been to me, but the thought thereof is intolerable. If it please God I am prepared to suffer the worst from him, who having never been injured by me, has found a pretext for a war, for which no justifiable reason can be assigned ; and has let loose upon me Belisarius, who has reduced me to this extremity. Let him know that he is a man, and, though a prince, that he is not beyond the reach of misfortune. I can proceed no farther, the calamities which surround me depriving me of my reason. Farewell my friend Pharas, and send to me a harp, a loaf of bread, and a sponge. The historian adds, that the harp was to console him in his affliction, the loaf to satisfy his hunger, he not having seen bread for a long time, and the sponge to dry up his tears.

§ The imperfection of the flute consists in the impossibility of attempering its tones, there being no rule or canon by which it can be tuned ; to which we may add, that the tones in the upper octave are as dissimilar, in respect of sound, as those of the human voice in those persons who have what is called the falsetto. In the flute abec the difference is discernible in the double shake, which is made on a note that divides the two systems of the natural and artificial tones.

resemblance; the end of persuasion, or affecting the passions, being common to both. This faculty consists in the enumeration of common places, which are revolved over in the mind, and requires both an ample store of knowledge in the subject upon which it is exercised, and a power of applying that knowledge as occasion may require. It differs from memory in this respect, that whereas memory does but recall to the mind the images or remembrance of things as they were first perceived, the faculty of invention divides complex ideas into those whereof they are composed, and recommends them again after different fashions, thereby creating variety of new objects and conceptions. Now, the greater the fund of knowledge above spoken of is, the greater is the source from whence the invention of the artist or composer is supplied; and the benefits thereof are seen in new combinations and phrases, capable of variety and permutation without end. And thus much must serve at present touching the comparative merits of the ancient and modern music.

In tracing the progress of music, it will be observed, that it naturally divides itself into the two branches of speculation and practice, and that each of these requires a distinct and separate consideration.* Of the dignity and importance of the former, Ptolemy, lib. I. cap ii. has delivered his sentiments to the following purpose: 'It is 'in all things the business of contemplation and science 'to show that the works of nature, well regulated as they 'are, were constituted according to reason, and to answer 'some end; and that nothing has been done by her 'without consideration, or as it were by chance; more 'especially in those that are deemed the finest of her 'works, as participating of reason in the greatest degree, 'the senses of sight and hearing.' And Sir Isaac Newton, speaking of the examination of those ratios that afford pleasure to the eye in architectural designs, says it tends to exemplify the simplicity in all the works of the Creator. And farther he gives it as his opinion, 'that 'some general laws of the Creator prevail with respect to 'the agreeable or unpleasing affections of all our senses.'† By practical music we are to understand the art of composition as founded in the laws of harmony, and deriving its grace, elegance, and power of affecting the passions from the genius and invention of the artist or composer; in the exercise of which faculty it may be observed, that the precepts for combining and associating sounds are as it were the syntax of his art, and are drawn out of it, as the rules of grammar are from speech.‡

In musical history the several events most worthy of attention seem to be those of the first establishment of a system, the introduction of music into the church service, the rise of dramatic music; under these several heads all that intelligence which to us is the most interesting may be comprehended. As touching the first, it is certain that we owe it to the Greeks, and there is nothing that at this distance of time can be superadded to the relations of the ancient writers on the subject; nor can it be safe to deviate, either in respect of form or manner, from the ac-

counts from them transmitted to us of the original constitution of the lyre, or of the invention and successive progress of a musical scale; much less can we be warranted in speaking of the ancient practice, and the more abstruse parts of the science, namely, the genera and the modes, in any other terms than themselves make use of. Were a liberty to do otherwise allowed, the same mischief would follow that attends the multiplication of the copies of a manuscript, or a translation through the medium of divers languages, where a new sense may be imposed upon the text by different transcribers and translators in succession, till the meaning of the original becomes totally obscured.

Vitruvius, in his treatise De Architectura, has a chapter on music, wherein he laments the want of words in the Roman language equivalent to the Greek musical terms; the same difficulty is experienced in a greater or less degree by all who take occasion to speak of the ancient music, whether of the Hebrews or the Greeks. The English translators of the Bible were necessitated to render the words כנור Kinnor and צונב Gnugab, by harp and organ; and a translator of musical appellatives will in many instances be reduced to as great difficulty as the Laplander, who in rendering a passage in the Canticles, 'He looketh forth at the windows, shewing himself at the lattice,' could find no nearer a resemblance to a lattice than a snow-shoe, a thing like a racket used in the game of tennis, and translated it accordingly.

The complaint of Vitruvius above mentioned furnishes an occasion of enquiry into the state of music among the Romans; and this will appear, even in their most flourishing condition, to have been, both in theory and practice, very low, there being no author to be found till after the destruction of the commonwealth who has written on the subject; and of those that lived in the time of Augustus and afterwards, the number is so small, and, if we except Boetius, their writings are so inconsiderable, as scarce to deserve notice. Vitruvius wrote not professedly on music; all that he says of it is contained in the third, fourth, and fifth chapters of the third book of his treatise De Architectura; wherein laying down the rules for the construction of theatres, he speaks of harmony in general terms, and afterwards of certain hollow vessels disposed in niches for the purpose of reverberating the voice of the singers or actors; and thence takes occasion to mention the genera of the ancients, which he illustrates by a scale or diagram, composed, as he says, by Aristoxenus himself, though it does not occur in the valuable edition of that author published by Meibomius. In the same work, lib. X. cap. ii. entitled De Hydraulicis, he describes the hydraulic organ of the ancients, but in such terms, that no one has been able satisfactorily to ascertain either its figure or the use of its parts.

Of Censorinus, Macrobius, Martianus Cappella, and Cassiodorus, it was never pretended that they had made any new discoveries, or contributed in the least to the improvement of music. Boetius indeed with great industry and judgment, collected the sense of the ancient Greek writers on Harmonics, and from the several works of Aristoxenus, Euclid, Nicomachus, Alypius, Ptolemy, and others whose discourses are now lost, compiled his most excellent treatise De Musica. In this he delivers the doctrines of the author above mentioned, illustrated by numerical calculations and diagrams of his own invention; therein manifesting a thorough knowledge of the subject. Hence, and because of his great accuracy and precision, this work of Boetius, notwithstanding it contains little that can be said to be new, has ever been looked upon as a valuable repository of musical erudition.§

---

* There are but few instances of musicians that have been eminently distinguished for skill both in the theory and practice of music, Zarlino, Tartini, and Rameau excepted. The two branches of the science have certainly no connection with each other, as may be gathered from the following sentiment of an ingenious writer on the subject: 'The delights 'of practical music enter the ear without acquainting the understanding 'from what proportions they arise, or even so much as that proportion 'is the cause of them: this the philosopher observes from reason and 'experience, and the mechanic must be taught, for the framing 'instruments; but the practiser has no necessity to study, except he 'desires the learning as well as the pleasure of his art.' Proposal to perform Music in perfect and mathematical Proportions, by Tho. Salmon, 4to. Lond. 1688.

† Vide infra, page 410, in note.

‡ 'The art by which language should be regulated, viz. Grammar, is of 'much later invention than languages themselves, being adapted to what 'was already in being, rather than the rule of making it so.' Bishop Wilkins's Essay towards a real Character, page 19.

§ The works of Boetius were published in a folio volume at Venice, in the year 1499, and at Basil by Glareanus, in 1570. In the treatise De Musica are sundry diagrams invented by the editor, which tend greatly to the illustration of his author.

Long before the time of Boetius, the enarmonic and chromatic genera had grown into disuse; the diatonic genus only remaining, the musical characters were greatly reduced in number; and the notation of music became so simple, that the Romans were able to represent the whole series of sounds contained in the system of a double octave, or the bisdiapason, by fifteen characters; rejecting therefore the characters used by the Greeks for the purpose, they assumed the first fifteen letters of their own alphabet; and this is the only improvement or innovation in music that we know of that can be ascribed to the Romans.

As to the practice of music, it seems to have been carried to no very great degree of perfection by the Romans; the tibia and the lyre seem to have been the only instruments in use among them; and on these there were no performers of such distinguished merit as to render them worthy the notice of posterity, which perhaps is the reason that the names of but few of them are recorded.

Caspar Bartholinus has written a treatise ' De Tibiis ' veterum et earum antiquo usu,' in which he has brought together a great variety of intelligence respecting the flutes of the ancients : in this tract is a chapter entitled ' Tibia in Ludis Spectaculis atque Comediis,' wherein the author takes occasion to speak of the tibiæ pares et impares, and also of the tibiæ dextræ et sinistræ, used in the representation of the comedies of Terence, which he illustrates by plates representing the forms of them severally, as also the manner of inflating them, taken from coins and other authentic memorials. In particular he gives an engraving from a manuscript in the Vatican library, of a scene in an ancient comedy, in which a tibicinist is delineated standing on the stage, and blowing on two equal flutes : what relation his music has to the action we are to seek. He also gives from a marble at Rome the figure of a man with an inflected horn near him, thus inscribed, M. IULIUS VICTOR EX COLLEGIO LITICINUM CORNICINUM.

It appears from a passage in Valerius Maximus, that there was at Rome a college of tibicinists or players on the flute, who we may suppose were favoured with some special privileges and immunities. These seem to have been a distinct order of musicians from the former, at least there are sundry inscriptions in Gruter purporting that there was at Rome a college comprehending both tibicinists and fidicinists ; which latter seem to have been no other than lyrists, a kind of musicians of less account among the Romans than the players on their favourite instrument the flute. Valerius Maximus, lib. II. cap. v. relates of the tibicinists that they were wont to play on their instrument in the forum, with their heads covered, and in party-coloured garments.

That the tibicinists were greatly indulged by the Romans, may be inferred from the nature of their office, which required their attendance at triumphs, at sacrifices, and indeed all public solemnities ; at least the sense of their importance and usefulness to the state is the only reason that can be suggested for their intemperance, and that insolence for which they were remarkable, and which both Livy and Valerius Maximus have recorded in a narration to the following purpose. ' The censors had ' refused to permit the tibicines to eat in the temple of ' Jupiter, a privilege which they claimed as founded on ' ancient custom ; whereupon the tibicines withdrew to ' Tibur, a town in the neighbourhood of Rome, now ' Tivoli. As the tibicines were necesssary attendants on ' the sacrifices, the magistrates were at a loss how to per- ' form those solemnities in their absence ; the senate ' therefore sent embassadors to the Tiburtines, requesting ' them to deliver them up as officers of the state who had

' fled from their duty : at first persuasions were tried, but ' these proving ineffectual, the Tiburtines had recourse to ' stratagem ; they appointed a public feast, and inviting ' the tibicines to assist at it, plied them with wine till they ' became intoxicated, and, while they were asleep, put ' them into carts, which conveyed them to Rome. The ' next day, having in some degree recovered their reason, ' the tibicines were prevailed on to stay in the city, and ' were not only restored to the privilege of eating in the ' temple, but were permitted annually to celebrate the ' day of their return, though attended with circumstances ' so infamous to their office, by processions in which the ' most licentious excesses were allowed.' *

The secession of the tibicinists was in the consulate of Caius Junius Bubulcus and Quintus Æmilius Barbula : that is to say in the year of the world 3640, three hundred and eight years before Christ ; and serves to shew the extreme licentiousness of Roman manners at that period, as also the low state of their music, when the best instruments they could find to celebrate the praises of their deities were a few sorry pipes, little better than those which now serve as playthings for children.

But, leaving the tibicines and their pipes to their admirers, if we proceed to enquire into the state of music among the Romans at any given period of their history, we shall find that, as a science, they held it in small estimation. And to this fact Cornelius Nepos bears the fullest testimony ; for, relating in his life of Epaminondas that he could dance, play on the harp and flute, he adds, that in Greece these accomplishments were greatly esteemed, but by the Romans they were little regarded. And Cicero, in his Tusculan Questions, lib. I. cap. i. to the same purpose, observes that the ancient Romans, addicting themselves to the study of ethics and politics, left music and the politer arts to the Greeks. Farther we may venture to assert, that neither their religious solemnities, nor their triumphs, their shows or theatrical representations, splendid as they were, contributed in the least to the improvement of music either in theory or practice : to say the truth, they seemed scarcely to have considered it as a subject of speculation ; and it was not until it received a sanction from the primitive fathers of the church. that the science began to recover its ancient dignity.

The introduction of music into the service of the church affords ample scope for reflection, and comprehends in its history a great part of what we know of modern music. All that need be mentioned in this place respecting that important event is, that after the example of the Jews, and upon the authority of sundry passages in scripture, and more especially in compliance with the exhortation of St. Paul in his Epistles, St. Basil, St. Ambrose, and St. Chrysostom about the middle of the fourth century instituted antiphonal singing in their respective churches of Cesarea in Cappadocia, Milan, and Constantinople. St. Ambrose, who must be supposed to have been eminently skilled in the science, prescribed a formula of singing in a series of melodies called the ecclesiastical tones, apparently borrowed from the modes of the ancient Greeks ; these, as constituted by him, were in number only four, and are meant when we speak of the Cantus Ambrosianus ; but St. Gregory, near two centuries after, increased them to eight. The same father drew up a number of precepts respecting the limits of the melodies, the fundamental note, and the succession of tones and semitones in each ; and, with a view to the establishment of a settled and uniform musical science, that would apply to all the several offices at that time used in divine worship, founded and endowed a school for the instruction of youth in the

* Livy, lib. IX. cap. xxx. See also Valerius Maximus, lib. II. cap. v. The same story is related by Ovid, Fasti, lib. VI., who adds that the thirteenth day of June was celebrated as the anniversary.

rudiments of music, as contained in this formula, which was distinguished by the appellation of the Cantus Ecclesiasticus, and in later times by that of the Cantus Gregorianus.

Before this time music had ceased to be a subject of speculation: Ptolemy was the last of the philosophers that had written professedly on it; and though it may be said that his three books of Harmonics, as also those of Aristoxenus, Euclid, Nichomachus, Aristides Quintilianus, and others, being extant, music was in a way of improvement from the studies of men no less disposed to think and reflect than themselves; yet the fact is, that among the Romans the science not only had made no progress at all, but even before the dissolution of the commonwealth, with them it seemed to be extinct. Nor let the supposition be thought groundless, that during some of the succeeding ages the books, the very repositories of what we call musical science, might be lost; the history of the lower empire furnishing an instance, the more remarkable, as it relates to their own, the Roman civil law, which proves at least the possibility of such a misfortune.*

To these causes, and the zeal of the fathers above mentioned, and more especially of St. Gregory, to disseminate its precepts, it is to be ascribed that the cultivation of music became the peculiar care of the clergy. But here a distinction is to be noted between the study and practice of the science; for we find that at the time of the institution of the Cantus Ambrosianus, an order of clergy was also established, whose employment it was to perform such parts of the service as were required to be sung. These were called Psalmistæ; and though by Bellarmine and a few other writers they are confounded with the Lectors, yet were they by the canonists accounted a separate and distinct order. The reason for their institution was, that whereas in the apostolical age the whole congregation sang in divine service, and great confusion and disorder followed therefrom, it was found necessary to settle what the church calls a regular and decent song, which, as it was framed by rule, and founded in the principles of harmony, required skill in the performance; and accordingly we find a canon of the council of Laodicea held as early as the beginning of the fourth century, forbidding all except the canonical singers, that is to say, those who were stationed in the Ambo, where the singing-desk was placed, and who sang out of a book or parchment, to join in the psalms, hymns, and other parts of musical divine service. We may well suppose that this order of men were endowed with all the requisites for the discharge of their function, and that the peculiar form which the council of Carthage directs to be used for the ordination of Psalmistæ or singers,† was in effect a recognition of their skill and abilities.

The order of men above mentioned can be considered in no other view than as mere practical musicians, the principal object of whose attention was to make themselves acquainted with the songs of the church, and to utter them with that decency and gravity, and in such a manner as tended most to edification. From the frequent repetition of the same offices it must be supposed that in general they sang by rote; at least we have no better reason to assign than that they must have so done, for the establishment of a school by St. Gregory for the instruction of youth in the Cantus Ecclesiasticus, as reformed by himself, and for that sedulous attention to their improvement in it which he manifested in sundry instances.

At the same time that we applaud the zeal of this father of the church, we cannot but wonder at that of his predecessors, which is not more apparent in their commendations of music, as associated with religious worship, than in their severe censures of that which was calculated for private recreation. As to the songs of the stage in the ages immediately succeeding the Christian era, we know little more of them than in general that they were suited to the corrupt manners of the times; and these, by reason of their lewdness, and perhaps impiety of sentiment, might be a just subject of reprehension; but against the music, the sounds to which they were uttered, or the particular instruments that assisted the voice in singing them, an objection can scarce be thought of; and yet so frequent and so bitter are the invectives of the primitive fathers, namely, Clemens Alexandrinus, Tertullian, St. Cyprian, Lactantius, Epiphanius, Gregory Nazianzen, and of St. Basil, St. Augustine, and St. Chrysostom, who were lovers and promoters of the practice of music, against wicked measures and effeminate melodies, the noise of flutes, cymbals, harps, and other instruments of deceit, seducing the hearers to intemperance, and even idolatry, that if credit be given to their opinions of the nature and tendency of secular music, we must be inclined to believe, as they in good earnest profess to have done, that it was an invention of the Devil.

The cultivation of music as a science was the employment of a set of men, in whom all the learning of the times may then be said to have centered; these were the regular clergy, of such of whom as flourished in the eleventh century afterwards, it must in justice be said, that what they wanted in knowledge, they made up in industry; and that those frequent barbarisms which occur in their writings, were in no small degree atoned for by the clearness and precision ‡ with which on every occasion they delivered their sentiments. Nor was the conciseness and method of the monkish treatises on music a less recommendation of them than their perspicuity: they consisted either of such maxims as were deemed of greatest importance in the study of the science, or of familiar colloquies between a master and his disciple, in which in an orderly course of gradation, first the elements, and then the precepts of the art were delivered and illustrated. To enumerate the instances of this kind which have occurred in the course of this work, would be an endless task; let it suffice to say that the Histoire Litteraire de France, and the Memoirs of Bale, Pits, and the Bibliotheca of Tanner abound with references to a variety of manuscript tracts deposited in the public and other libraries, that abundantly prove the mode of musical instruction to have been such as is above described.

Before the period above spoken of, music had for very good reasons been admitted into the number of the liberal sciences; and accordingly in the scholastic division of the arts into the trivium and quadrivium, it held a place in the latter: nevertheless, till the Greek literature began to revive in Europe, saving the summary of harmonics contained in the treatise De Musica of Boetius, the students in that faculty had scarce any source of intelligence; and to this it must be attributed that in none of the many tracts written by the monks of those times, and afterwards by the professors or scholastics as they were called, do we meet with any of those profound disquisitions on harmony and the proportions which resolve the principles of music into geometry · nor any of those nice calculations and comparisons of ratios, or subtile distinctions between the consonances of one kind and those of another, which abound in the writings of the ancient Greeks; so that were we to judge from the many

* See the relation of the discovery of the Litera Pisana at page 180.

† See page 106, in note.

‡ These qualities seem to be but the necessary result of the old scholastic method of institution, in which logic made a considerable part, and are in no instance more manifest than in the ancient forms of judicial proceedings, such as writs and pleadings; of which Sir Matthew Hale, in his History of the law, chap. 7, remarks that they were very short, but very clear and conspicuous, orderly digested, pithy, clear, and rational. The same may be said in general of the more ancient statutes.

discourses written during that dark period, and bearing the titles of Micrologus, Metrologus, and others of the like import, we should conclude that the science of harmonics had scarce any existence among mankind. Nor could any great advantage result from the writings of Boetius, seeing that there wanted light to read by; and this was not obtained till Franchinus introduced it, by procuring translations of those authors from whose writings Boetius had compiled his work.

That the studies of the monkish musicians must have been confined to the Cantus Gregorianus is evident from this consideration, that they were strangers to music of every other kind; an assertion which will be the more readily credited when we are told that till the middle of the eleventh century rythmic or mensurable music was not known. Their method of teaching it was by the monochord, without which they had no method of determining the progression of tones and semitones in the octave, nor consequently of measuring by the voice any of the intervals contained in it.

The reformation of the scale by Guido Aretinus, and more especially his invention of a method of singing by certain syllables adapted to the notes, facilitated the practice of singing to such a degree, that, as himself relates, the boys of his monastery were rendered capable in a month's time of singing in a regular and orderly succession the several intervals with the utmost accuracy and precision.* We are told, though not by himself, that he also by an ingenious contrivance transferred the notes of his scale to the left hand, making a several joint of each of the fingers the position of a note. Whether this invention is to be ascribed to him or not, it is pretty certain that it followed soon after the reformation of the scale, and that it gave rise to a distinction of music into manual and tonal, the first comprehending the precepts of singing by the syllables, the other the Cantus Ecclesiasticus, as instituted in the formula of St. Gregory.

At this time the world were strangers to what we call rythmic music, the practice of singing, and thereby of associating music with poetry, which till then had universally prevailed, rendering any such invention unnecessary. Nevertheless, there were some writers who had entertained an idea of transferring the prosody of poetry to music; and a few scattered hints of this kind, which occur in the writings of St. Augustine and our countryman Bede on the subject of metre, suggested the formation of a system of metrical laws, such as would not only enable music to subsist of itself, but aid the powers of melody with that force and energy which it is observed to derive from the regular commixture and interchange of long and short quantities.

This improvement was effected in the institution of what is called the Cantus Mensurabilis; a branch of musical science which subjected the duration of musical sounds to rule and measure, by assigning to those of the slowest progression certain given portions of time, and to the next in succession a less, in a regular gradation, and which taught a method of signifying by characters, varying in form and colour, the radical notes, with their several ramifications, terminating in those of the smallest value, i. e. of the shortest duration.

An invention of this kind was all that could then be thought wanting to the perfection of instrumental music; and from this period we may observe that it began to flourish: it is true that the state of the mechanic arts was then very low, and that the instruments in common use were so rudely constructed, as to be scarcely capable of yielding musical sounds. Bartholomeus, in his book De Proprietatibus Rerum, in an enumeration of the musical instruments of his time, has described the flute as made of the boughs of an elder-tree hollowed; and an instrument

called the Symphonia, as made of a hollow tree, closed in leather on either side, which he says is beaten of minstrels with sticks, and that 'by accord of hyghe and lowe thereof comyth full swete notes.' And again, describing the Psalterium or Sawtrie, he says it differs from the harp, for that it is made of an hollow tree, and that 'the sowne comyth upward, the strynges being smytte downwarde; whereas in the harpe the hollownesse of the tre is byneathe.' These descriptions, and others of the like kind which are elsewhere to be met with, are evidence of the inartificial construction of musical instruments in those days, and leave it a question what kind of harp or other instrument that could be on which King Alfred had attained to such a degree of excellence as to rival the musicians of his time.

Nevertheless it appears that there were certain instruments, perhaps not in common use, better calculated to produce melody than those above-mentioned, namely, those of the viol kind; the specific difference between which and other stringed instruments is, that in the former the sound is produced by the action of a plectrum or bow of hair on the strings : of these the mention is not only express, but frequent in Chaucer, by the names of the Fithel, Getron, Ribible, and other appellations, clearly synonymous : the invention of this class of instruments is by some, who make the viol the prototype of it, ascribed to the French; but there are other writers who derive the viol itself from the Arabian Rebab, from whence perhaps Ribible and Rebec, the use whereof it is said the Christians learned from the Saracens in the time of the Crusades; but it is more probable, by reason of its antiquity, that it was brought into Spain by the Moors.

To ascertain the degree of perfection to which the practice of instrumental music had attained at any period before the sixteenth century, would be very difficult. The Provençal songs, as being mere vocal compositions, afford no ground on which a conjecture might be formed : and as to their popular tunes, the airs of the Musars and Violers, besides that they seem to have been mere melodies, for the most part the effusions of fancy, and not regulated by harmonical precepts, the impression of them can hardly be supposed to have been either deep or lasting, and this may be the chief reason that the knowledge of them has not reached posterity.

That the practice of instrumental music was become familiar with such persons of both sexes as had received the benefit of a good education, is clearly intimated by the old poets. Not only the Squire, but the Clerk, Absolon, in Chaucer, are by him described, the one as floyting, i. e. fluting all the day, the other as playing songs on a small Ribible, and elsewhere on the Geterne;† and in the Confessio Amantis of Gower, fol. 178, b. is a plain intimation that the Citole, an instrument nearly resembling the virginal, was in his time the recreation of well educated young women.‡

We are also told by Boccace, in his Account of the Plague at Florence in 1348, that the ladies and gentlemen who retired from that city, and are relators of the several stories contained in his Decameron, among other recreations in the intervals of their discourses, intermixed music; and that sundry of the persons whose names he mentions played on the lute and the viol. They also danced to the music of the Cornamusa or bagpipe, an instrument which we may infer to have been held in but ordinary estimation from this circumstance, that it is put into the hands of Tindarus, a domestic of one of the ladies; besides that Chaucer in characterising his Miller says,

'A baggepipe well couth he blowe and soune.'

---

* Vide infra, page 164.

† See the character of the Squire among the Prologues to the Canterbury Tales, as also the Miller's Tale passim.

‡ Vide infra, page 206.

Of vocal concerts, as they stood about the year 1550, or perhaps earlier, a judgment may be formed from the madrigals of that time, which abound with all the graces of harmony. Concerts of instruments alone seem to be of later invention, at least there is no clear evidence of the form in which they existed, other than treatises and compositions for concerts of viols called Fantasias, few whereof were published till thirty years after.*

Gio. Maria Artusi, an ecclesiastic of Bologna, and a writer on music about the year 1600, describes the concerts of his time as abounding in sweetness of harmony, and consisting of cornets, trumpets, violins, viols, harps, lutes, flutes, and harpsichords : these, as also organs, regals, and guitars, are enumerated in the catalogue of instruments prefixed to the opera, L'Orfeo, composed by Claudio Monteverde, and represented at Mantua in 1607. Tom Coryat speaks also of a performance at Venice, chiefly of instrumental music, which he protests he would have travelled a hundred miles on foot to hear, but without any such particular description as can enable us to compare it with the concerts of more modern times.

As touching the theory of the science, it has above been said to have consisted in manual, tonal, and mensurable music, with this farther remark, that, as it was included in the very nature of their profession, and besides required some degree of literature, the great cultivators of it were the regular clergy. These men contented themselves with that small portion of knowledge which was to be attained by the perusal of Boetius, Cassiodorus, Guido, and a few others, who wrote in the Latin tongue ; the little they knew they freely communicated ; and it was not till the beginning of the fourteenth century that men began to suspect that the science was capable of farther improvement.

About this time Johannes De Muris improved the Cantus Mensurabilis, by reducing it to form and demonstrating that the measures thereof, like the ratios of the consonances, were founded in number and proportion : from the rules laid down by him in a treatise entitled Practica Mensurabilis Cantûs, are derived the distinctions of duple and triple proportion, as they respect the duration of sounds, with all the various modifications thereof. On this tract Prosdocimus Beldimandis wrote a commentary, and farther illustrated the doctrines contained therein in sundry discourses on the subjects of plain and mensurable music. It appears that both these persons were philosophers at large, and eminently skilled in the mathematics ; and the liberal manner in which they wrote on music, treating it as a subject of deep speculation, was an inducement with many learned men, who lived under no ecclesiastical rule, to enter into an investigation of its principles. Some of these assumed the character of professors of the science, and undertook by public lectures to disseminate its principles. The most eminent of these persons were Marchettus of Padua, Johannes Tinctor, Gulielmus Garnerius, and Antonius Suarcialupus, to whom we may add Politian, whose skill in music is manifested in a discourse De Musica, contained in his Panepistemon or Prælectiones, extant in print. But notwithstanding the pains thus taken to revive the science, the improvement of it went on very slowly ; whatever advances were made in the practice, the theoretical topics of disquisition were soon exhausted, and the science of harmonics may be said to have been for some ages at a stand.

At length the beams of learning began to dawn on the

western empire : the city of Constantinople had been the seat of literature for some ages, but the sack of it by the Turks in the year 1453, had driven a great number of learned Greeks thence, who bringing with them an immense treasure of manuscripts, took refuge in Italy. Being settled there, they opened their stores, took possession of the public schools, and became the professors and teachers of the mathematical and other sciences, and indeed of philosophy, eloquence, and literature in general, in all the great cities. Of the many valuable books of Harmonics that are known to have been written by the mathematicians and other ancient Greeks, some have escaped that fate which learning is sure to experience from the ravages of conquest,† and the contents of these being made public, the principles of the science began to be known and understood by many, who till then were scarcely sensible that it had any principles at all.

This communication of intelligence was very propitious to music, as it determined many persons to the study of the science of harmony. The tonal laws and the Cantus Mensurabilis were left to those whose duty it was to understand them ; the ratios of sounds, and the nature of consonance were considered as essentials in music, and the investigation of these was the chief pursuit of such as were sensible of the value of that kind of learning.

Of the many who had profited in this new science, as it may be called, one was Franchinus Gaffurius, a native of Lodi, who having quitted the tuition of a Carmelite monk, who had been his instructor, became soon distinguished for skill in those theoretic principles, the knowledge whereof he had derived from an attendance on the Greek teachers. And having procured copies of the treatises on harmonics of Aristides Quintilianus, Ptolemy, Manuel Bryennius, and Bacchius senior, he caused them to be translated into Latin ; and, besides discharging the duty of a public professor of music in the several cities of Italy, became the revivor of musical erudition ; and that as well posterity, as those of his own time, might profit by his labours, he digested the substance of his lectures into distinct treatises, and gave them to the world.

The writings of Franchinus, as they were replete with learning drawn from the genuine source of antiquity, and contained the clearest demonstrations of the principles of harmony, were so generally studied, that music began now to assume the character of a secular profession. The precepts therein delivered afforded a greater latitude to the inventive faculty than the tonal laws allowed of ; and emancipating the science from the bondage thereof, many who had no relation to the church set themselves to frame compositions for its service, in which the powers both of harmony and melody were united. And hence we may at least with a show of probability date the origin of an office that yet subsists in the choral establishments of Italy, namely, that of Maestro di Cappella ; the duty whereof seems uniformly to have been not only that the person appointed to it should as precentor regulate the choir, but also adapt to music the offices performed both on ordinary and solemn occasions. Of the dignity and importance of the office of Maestro di Capella a judgment may be formed from this circumstance, that the persons elected to it for some centuries past appear to have been of distinguished eminence ;‡ and of its necessity and utility no stronger argument can be offered, than that

* The earliest of which we can speak with certainty, is a treatise in folio by Thomas à Santa Maria, a Spanish Dominican, published at Valladolid in 1570, entitled 'Arte de tanner fantasia para tecla, viguela, 'y todo instrumendo de tres o quatro ordenes,' which carries the antiquity of concerts for Viols, and those compositions called Fantasias, back to that time, but leaves us at a loss as to other instrumental concerts.

† Laurus Quirinus of Venice was told by Cardinal Ruthen that upwards of one hundred and twenty thousand volumes were destroyed. Hody, de Græcis illustr. lib. II. cap. i.

‡ Andrea Adami Bolsena, in the historical preface to his 'Osservazioni 'per ben regolare il Coro de i Cantori della Capella Pontificia,' asserts that anciently in the college of pontifical singers the maestro di cappella was a bishop.

among the Germans, to whom the knowledge of music was very soon communicated after its revival in Italy, the office was recognized by the appointment of a director of the choir in the principal churches of all the provinces and cities. The same sense of the importance of this office appears to have been entertained by the protestants, who at the time of the Reformation we find to have been no less sedulous in the cultivation of music with a view to religious worship, than the church that had established it. It is true that Calvin was for some time in doubt whether to adopt the solemn choral service, or that plain metrical psalmody which is recommended by St. Paul to the Colossians, as an incentive to such mirth as was consistent with the Christian profession, and at length determined on the latter.

But Luther, who was excellently skilled in music, considered it not merely as a relief under trouble and anxiety, but as the voice of praise, and as having a tendency to excite and encourage devout affections, besides that he had translated into the German language the Te Deum, and composed sundry hymns, as also tunes to some of the German psalms,* he, with the approbation of Melancthon, received into his church a solemn service, which included anthems, hymns, and certain sweet motetæ, of which he speaks very feelingly, and of music in general he gives his opinion in these words: 'Scimus musicam dæmonibus etiam invisam et intolerabilem esse.'† That the office of a chapel-master was recognized by the protestants in the manner above mentioned is hardly to be doubted, seeing that it was exercised at Bavaria by Ludovicus Senfelius, a disciple of Henry Isaac, and an intimate friend and correspondent of Luther,‡ and subsists in Germany to this day.

For the reasons above assigned, we may without scruple attribute to Franchinus a share of that merit which is ascribed to the revivers of Literature in the fifteenth century; and the rather as his writings, and the several translations of ancient treatises on harmonics which he procured to be made, furnished the students in the science with such a copious fund of information, as enabled them not only to reason justly on its principles, but to extend the narrow bounds of harmony, and lay a foundation for those improvements which it has been the felicity of later times to experience. And it is not a groundless supposition that the reputation of his writings was a powerful incentive to the publication of those numerous discourses on music of which the ensuing work contains a detail. Indeed so general was the propensity in the professors of the science in Italy, and in Germany more especially, to the compilation of musical institutes, dialogues, and discourses in various forms, that the science was for some time rather hurt by the repetition of the same precepts, than benefited by any intelligence that could in strictness be said to be new. The writings of Zarlino and Salinas are replete with erudition; the same, though in a less eminent degree, may be said of those of Glareanus and the elder Galilei; but of the generality of the Introductions, the Enchiridions, and the Erotomata published in Italy and Germany from about the year 1550 to the middle of the next century, the perspicuity of them is their best praise.

* Melchior Adamus, in his life of Luther, has inserted a letter from him to Spalatinus, written anno 1524, wherein he says he is looking out for poets to translate the whole of the Psalms into the German tongue, and requests of Spalatinus his assistance therein. This was some years before Marot translated the Psalms into French.

† In an epistle to Senfelius, Musicus, cited by Dr. Wetenhall from Sethus Calvisius, in his Gifts and Offices in the public worship of God, page 434, but without reference to any work of Calvisius. This epistle, wherever it is, and the above cited passage, are also noticed by Butler in his Principles of Music, page 115. Dr. Wetenhall applies this passage to the music of our church, and on the authority thereof pronounces it to be such as no Devil can stand against.

‡ Some motetts of his composition are extant in the Dodecachordon of Glareanus.

As the revival of the theory of music is to be ascribed to the Italians, so also are those improvements in the practice of it that have brought it to the state of perfection in which we behold it at this day. It is true that in the practice of particular instruments the masters of other countries have been eminently distinguished, as, namely, those of Germany for skill on the organ; the French for the lute and harpsichord; and we are indebted for many valuable discoveries touching the nature and properties of sound, of consonance and dissonance, the method of constructing the various kinds of musical instruments, and, above all, for a nice and accurate investigation of the principles of harmonics, to the learning and industry of Mersennus, a Frenchman; but in the science of composition the musicians of Italy have uniformly been the instructors of all Europe.

To relate the subsequent instances of improvement in music, or to enumerate the many persons of distinguished eminence that have excelled in the theory and practice thereof, would be to anticipate that information, which it is the end of history to communicate; and to animadvert on the numberless defects of the ancient music, may seem unnecessary, seeing that as well the paucity as the structure of the ancient instruments affords abundant evidence of a great disproportion between their practice and their theory; it is nevertheless worthy of remark, that they who were so skilful and accurate in the invention of characters and symbols, the types not only of things, but of images or ideas, as the Greeks are allowed to have been, have, in the instance of music, manifested a great want of that faculty, inasmuch as there is not to be found in any of the characters in the ancient musical notation, the least analogy or relation between the sign and the sound or thing signified; a perfection so obvious in the practice of the moderns, that we contemplate it with astonishment, there being no possible arrangement or disposition of musical sounds, nor no series or succession of equal or unequal, similar or dissimilar measures, but may with the greatest accuracy be described by the stave of Guido, and the forms of notes with their adjuncts, as directed by the rules of the Cantus Mensurabilis; insomuch that the modern system of notation, comprehending in it the types or symbols of things, and not of notions or ideas, may be said to possess all the advantages of a real character.

To celebrate formally the praises of music in a work, the design whereof is to display its excellencies, may seem unnecessary; and the rather, as it has from the infancy of the world, with historians, orators, and poets, been a subject of panegyric: besides the power and effect of musical sounds to assuage grief and awaken the mind to the enjoyment of its faculties, is acknowledged by the most intelligent of mankind; and, were it necessary, to prove that the love of music is implanted in us, and not the effect of refinement, examples thereof might be produced from the practice of those, who, from their particular situation of country, or circumstances of life, are presumed to approach nearly to that state in which the natural and genuine suggestions of the will are supposed to be most clearly discernible. To say nothing of the Turks, who are avowed enemies of literature, or of the Chinese, who, as has been shewn, notwithstanding all that is asserted of them, are so circumstanced, as seemingly never to be able to attain to any degree of excellence, nations the most savage and barbarous profess to admit music into their solemnities, such as they are, their rejoicings, their triumphs for victories, the meetings of their tribes, their feasts and their marriages; and to use it for their recreation and private solace.§ St. Chry-

§ Father Lafitau, in his Mœurs des Sauvages, tome II. page 213, et seq. has given a full description of the festal solemnities, accompanied with music, of the Iroquois, Hurons, and other tribes of American savages;

sostom, in his Homily on psalm xli. estimates the importance of music by its universality, and, in a strain of simplicity, corresponding with the manners of the times in which he lived, says that human nature is so delighted with canticles and poems, that by them infants at the breast when they are froward or in pain, are lulled to rest; that travellers in the heat of noon, driving their beasts, such as are occupied in rural labours, as treading or pressing grapes, or bringing home the vintage; and even mariners labouring at the oar, as also women at their distaff, deceive the time, and mitigate the severity of their labour by songs adapted to their several employments or peculiar conditions. Clearchus relates that at Lesbos the people had a song which they sung while they were grinding corn, and for that reason called ἐπιμύλιον; and Thales affirms that he had heard a female slave of that country singing it, turning a mill: it began ' Mole pistrinum mole, nam et Pittacus molit rex magnæ ' Mitylenæ,' and alluded to the practice of that king, who was used to grind corn with a hand-mill, esteeming it a healthy exercise.

Other writers go farther, and affect to discern the principles of music not only in the songs, but the occupations and exercises of artificers and even labourers; one of these in a vein of enthusiasm, perhaps more humorous and singular than persuasive, says, ' What shall I speak ' of that pettie and counterfeit music which carters make ' with their whips, hempknockers with their beetels, ' spinners with their wheels, barbers with their sizzers, ' smithes with their hammers? where methinkes the ' master-smith with his treble hammer sings deskant ' whilest the greater buz upon the plainsong: who doth ' not straitwaies imagin upon musick when he hears his ' maids either at the woolhurdle or the milking pail? good ' God, what distinct intention and remission is there of ' their strokes? what orderly dividing of their straines? ' what artificial pitching of their stops?'*

and in the Royal Commentaries of Peru, book II. chap. xiv. the author, Garcilasso de la Vega, besides informing us that their fabulous songs were innumerable, and carried in them the evidence of a savage spirit, speaks thus particularly of their music: ' In musick they arrived to a ' certain harmony, in which the Indians of Colla did more particularly ' excell, having been the inventors of a certain pipe made of canes glued ' together, every one of which having a different note of higher and lower, ' in the manner of organs, made a pleasing musick by the dissonancy of ' sounds, the treble, tenor and basse exactly corresponding and answering ' each to other; with these pipes they often plaid in concert, and made ' tolerable musick, though they wanted the quavers, semiquavers, aires, ' and many voices, which perfect the harmony amongst us. They had ' also other pipes, which were flutes with four or five stops, like the pipes ' of shepherds; with these they played not in consort, but singly, and ' tuned them to sonnets, which they composed in metre, the subject of ' which was love, and the passions which arise from the favours or dis- ' pleasures of a mistress. These musicians were Indians trained up in ' that art for divertisement of the Incas, and the Curacas, who were his ' nobles, which, as rustical and barbarous as it was, it was not common, ' but acquired with great industry and study.

' Every song was set to its proper tune; for two songs of different sub- ' jects could not correspond with the same aire, by reason that the music ' which the gallant made on his flute, was designed to express the satis- ' faction or discontent of his mind, which were not so intelligible perhaps ' by the words, as by the melancholy or chearfulness of the tune which he ' plaid. A certain Spaniard one night late encountered an Indian woman ' in the streets of Cozco, and would have brought her back to his lodgings; ' but she cryed out, " For God's sake, Sir, let me go, for that pipe which " you hear in yonder tower calls me with great passion, and I cannot " refuse the summons, for love constrains me to go, that I may be his wife, " and he my husband."

' The songs which they composed of their wars and grand atchievements ' were never set to the aires of their flutes, being too grave and serious to ' be intermixed with the pleasures and softnesses of love; for those were ' onely sung at their principal festivals, when they commemorated their ' victories or triumphs. When I came from Peru, which was in the year ' 1560, there were then five Indians residing at Cozco, who were great ' masters on the flute, and could play readily by book any tune that was ' laid before them; they belonged to one Juan Rodriguez, who lived at a ' village called Labos, not far from the city: and now at this time, being ' the year 1602, 'tis reported that the Indians are so well improved in ' musick, that it was a common thing for a man to sound divers kinds of ' instruments; but vocal musick was not so usual in my time, perhaps ' because they did not much practise their voices, though the mongrils, ' or such as came of a mixture of Spanish and Indian blood, had the ' faculty to sing with a tunable and a sweet voice.'

* The Praise of Musicke, 8vo. printed anno 1586, at Oxford, for Joseph

But besides the pleasure that men derive from music, this satisfaction arises from the study of it, that its principles are founded in the very frame and constitution of the universe, and are as clearly demonstrable as mathematical truth and certainty can render them; and in this respect music may be said to have an advantage over many sciences and faculties in the pursuit whereof the attention of mankind has at different periods been deeply engaged. To say nothing of school divinity, which, happily for the world, has given place to rational theology, what can be said of law in general, other than that it is mere human invention? a fabric of science erected it is true on the basis of a few uncontrovertible principles of morality, and of that which we call natural justice, but so accommodated to particular circumstances, to the genius, situation, temper, and capacities of those who are the objects of it, as that what is permitted and encouraged in one country, poligamy, for instance, shall be punished in another. In some constitutions a difference of sex shall aggravate the guilt of the same offence; and custom and usage shall preserve the inheritance of the parent for the benefit of the eldest of his male descendants with the same pretence to justice as the law of nature and reason distributes it among them all. Finally, what shall we say to that system of jurisprudence, which, being allowed to be imperfect, craves the aid of equity to regulate its operation, and mitigate its rigours? or of those glosses and comments which in the civil and canon law are of little less authority than the laws themselves?

As to medicine, setting aside the knowledge of the human frame, and the uses of its constituent parts, a noble subject of speculation it must be confessed, the wiser part of men, rejecting theory as vain and delusive, resolve the whole of the science into observation and practice; thereby confessing that its principles are either very few, or so void of certainty, as not with safety to be relied on.

Of other liberal arts, such as grammar, logic, and rhetoric, it must be allowed that they are of singular use; but, as being the mere inventions of men, and at best auxiliaries to other arts or faculties, they are in their nature subordinate, and in that respect do but resemble the art of memory, which all men know to be founded on principles not existing in nature, but assumed by ourselves; widely differing from those which are the basis as well of musical as mathematical science.

From this view of the comparative excellence of music, and its pre-eminence over many other sciences and faculties, we become convinced of the stability of its principles, and are therefore at a loss for the reasons why, in these later times at least, novelty in music should be its best recommendation; or that the love of variety should so possess the generality of hearers, as almost to leave it a question whether or no it has any principles at all.

To satisfy these doubts, it may be sufficient to observe that the principles of harmony allow, as it is fit they should, great scope for the exercise of the invention; and though they pretend to skill in the arts without being in some degree or other possessed of it, yet as all the imaginative arts presuppose a disposition in mankind to receive their impressions, all claim a right, and many the ability, to judge of works of invention and fancy.

The epic poet, trusting that the mind of his reader is co-extensive with his own, endeavours to excite in him the ideas of sublimity and beauty; the dramatic writer hopes to move the affections of his audience to terror and pity by the representation of actions, the reflection on which

Barnes, but conjectured to have been written by Dr. John Case, page 76. Of this person there is a curious account in Athen. Oxon. col. 299. Thomas Ravenscroft, in the Apologie prefixed to his discourse on the true charactering of music, published in 1614, cites it as a work of Dr. Case, whom he styles a ' Mæcenas of musicke.'

inspired his mind with those passions; and the painter, giving form to those ideas of grace, greatness, and character which occupy his mind, or selecting the beauties of nature, and transferring them to canvas, or at other times contenting himself with simple imitation, in all these exercises of imagination and art, expects from the judgment of the well-informed connoisseur the approbation of his work.

Now in the several instances above adduced, notwithstanding the concessions made to them, we may discern in the generality of men the want of that sense to which the appeal is made; for, with respect to the epic poem, few are endowed with an imagination sufficiently capacious to discover its beauties; and as to dramatic representation, the most favourite of all public entertainments, although all men pretend to be judges of nature, and the cant of theatres has persuaded most that they are so, few are acquainted with her operations in the various instances exhibited on the stage, or know with any kind of certainty in what manner the actor is to speak, what tones or inflections of the voice are appropriated to different passions, or what are the proper gesticulations to express or accompany the sentiment which he is to utter. How many individuals among those numerous audiences, who for a series of years past have affected to admire our great dramatic poet, may we suppose capable of discerning his sense, delivered in a style of dialogue very little resembling that of the present day, or of relishing those high philosophical sentiments with which his compositions and those of Milton abound?* The answer must be, very few. Even humour, a talent which lies level with the observation of the many, is not alike intelligible to all; and some are disgusted with those delineations of low manners, however just and natural, that afford delight to others, as exhibiting to view the human mind in the simplicity of nature, and free from those restraints which are imposed on it by education and refinement.

The painter, in like manner, submitting his work to the public censure, shall find for one that will applaud the grandeur of the design, the fineness of the composition, or the correctness of the drawing, a hundred that would have dispensed with all these excellencies for a greater glare of colouring, and attitudes suited to their own ideas of grace and elegance.

The case is the same in sculpture and architecture; to speak of the first :—In Roubiliac's statue of Mr. Handel at Vauxhall, few are struck with the ease and gracefulness of the attitude, the dignity of the figure, the artful disposition of the drapery, or the manly plumpness and rotundity of the limbs, but all admire how naturally the slipper depends from the left foot. In works of architecture we look for elegance joined with stability; for symmetry, harmony of parts, and a judicious and beautiful arrangement of pleasing forms; but to these a vulgar eye is blind; whatever is great or massy, it rejects as heavy and clumsy. Such judges as these prefer for its lightness a Chinese to a Palladian bridge; and are pleased with a diagonal view of the towers at the west end of St. Paul's cathedral, for the same reason as they are with a bird cage.

Finally, with respect to music, it must necessarily be, that the operation of its intrinsic powers can extend no

* The masque of Comus, written for the entertainment of a noble family, and a company of chosen spectators, which within these few years was introduced on the public stage, may seem to contradict this observation, for this reason, that although the sentiments contained in it are well known to be drawn from the Platonic, the sublimest of all philosophy; and the imagery has an immediate and uniform reference to the fictions of mythology, it afforded great entertainment to the upper gallery; and the performance gave rise to sundry meetings for the purpose of drinking and singing, some of which were dignified with the name of Comus's Court. Nevertheless it may be supposed that the mirth of the enchanter and his crew were more sensibly felt by the multitude than the charms of divine philosophy, which the author endeavours to display, or the reliance on divine providence, which it is the end of the poem to inculcate.

farther than to those whom nature has endowed with the faculty which it is calculated to delight; and that a privation of that sense, which, superadded to the hearing, is ultimately affected by the harmony of musical sounds, must disable many, and, as some compute, not fewer than nine out of ten, from receiving that gratification in music which others experience. Such hearers as these are insensible of its charms, which yet they labour to persuade themselves are very powerful; but finding little effect from them, they seek for that gratification in novelty which novelty will not afford; and hence arises that incessant demand for variety which has induced some to imagine that music is in its very nature as mutable as fashion itself. It may be sufficient in this place to have pointed out the reasons or causes of this erroneous opinion of the nature and end of music, the effects and operation thereof will be the subject of future disquisition.

In the interim it must be confessed that there is somewhat humiliating in a discrimination of mankind, that tends to exclude the greater number of them from the enjoyment of those elegant and refined pleasures which the works of genius and invention afford; but this condition of human nature is capable of proof, and is justified by that partial dispensation of those faculties and endowments which we are taught to consider as blessings, and which no one without impiety can censure. Seeing this to be the case, it may be asked how it comes to pass that a sense of what is true, just, elegant, and beautiful in any of the above-mentioned arts, exists as it does at this day? or that there are any works of genius which men with one common consent profess to applaud and admire as the standards of perfection? To this it may be answered, that although the right of private judgment is in some degree exercised by all, it is controuled by the few; and it is the uniform testimony of men of discernment alone that stamps a character on the productions of genius, and consigns them either to oblivion or immortality.

It is beside the purpose of the present discourse to enter into a minute investigation of any particular branch of the science of which this work is the history; what is here proposed is the communication of that intelligence which seemed but the prerequisite to the understanding of what will be hereafter said on the subject. This was the inducement to the above observations on Taste, and the motives that influence it; and this must be the apology for a further examen, a pretty free one it may be said, of those musical entertainments, and that kind of musical performance which the public are at present most diposed to favour.

The present great source of musical delight throughout Europe is the opera, or, as the French call it, the musical tragedy, concerning which it is to be known, that, if regard be due to the opinions of some writers, who are yet no friends to this entertainment, it is a revival of the old Roman tragedy; and it seems that the inventors of the modern recitative, Jacopo Peri and Guilio Caccini, wished to have it thought so; forasmuch as they professed in this species of musical intonation to imitate the practice of the ancients, remarking with great accuracy the several modes of pronunciation, and the notes and accents proper to express grief, joy, and the other affections of the human mind; but by what exemplars they regulated their imitation we are no where told: and it is to be conjectured that those general directions for pronunciation, which are to be found in many discourses on the subject of oratory, were the chief sources whence their intelligence was derived.

In what other respects the musical representations of the ancients and moderns bear a resemblance to each other it is not necessary here to enquire; it may suffice to say of the modern opera, that by the sober and judicious part of mankind it has ever been considered as the mere offspring of luxury; and those who have examined it with a critical eye, scruple not to pronounce that it is of all entertainments the most unnatural and absurd. To descend to particulars in proof of this assertion, would be but to repeat arguments which have already been urged, with little success it is true, but with great force of reason, aided by all the powers of wit and humour.

The principal objections against the opera are summed up by an author, who, though a professed lover of music, has shown his candour in describing the genuine effect of representations of this kind on an unprejudiced ear. The person here spoken of is Mons. St. Evremond, and the following are his sentiments :—

' I am no great admirer of comedies in music,* such as ' now-a days are in request. I confess I am not dis- ' pleased with their magnificence; the machines have ' something that is surprising; the musick, in some ' places, is charming, the whole together is wonderful: ' but it must be granted me also, that this wonderful is ' very tedious; for where the mind has so little to do, ' there the senses must of necessity languish. After the ' first pleasure that surprize gives us, the eyes are taken ' up, and at length grow weary of being continally fixed ' upon the same object. In the beginning of the consorts ' we observe the justness of the concords; and amidst all ' the varieties that unite to make the sweetness of the ' harmony, nothing escapes us. But 'tis not long before ' the instruments stun us, and the musick is nothing else to ' our ears but a confused sound that suffers nothing to be ' distinguished. Now how is it possible to avoid being tired ' with the Recitativo, which has neither the charm of ' singing, nor the agreeable energy of speech? The soul ' fatigued by a long attention, wherein it finds nothing to ' affect it, seeks some relief within itself; and the mind, ' which in vain expected to be entertained with the show, ' either gives way to idle musing, or is dissatisfied that it ' has nothing to employ it. In a word the fatigue is so ' universal, that every one wishes himself out of the house, ' and the only comfort that is left to the poor spectators, ' is the hopes that the show will soon be over.

' The reason why, commonly, I soon grow weary at ' operas is, that I never yet saw any which appeared not ' to me despicable, both as to the contrivance of the ' subject, and the poetry. Now it is in vain to charm ' the ears, or gratify the eyes, if the mind be not satisfied; ' for my soul being in better intelligence with my mind ' than with my senses, struggles against the impressions ' which it may receive, or at least does not give an ' agreeable consent to them, without which even the most ' delightful objects can never afford me any great pleasure. ' An extravagance, set off with music, dances, machines, ' and fine scenes, is a pompous piece of folly, but 'tis still ' a folly. Tho' the embroidery is rich, yet the ground it ' is wrought upon is such wretched stuff, that it offends ' the sight.

' There is another thing in operas so contrary to nature, ' that I cannot be reconciled to it, and that is the singing ' of the whole piece, from beginning to end, as if the ' persons represented were ridiculously matched, and had ' agreed to treat in musick both the most common, and ' most important affairs of life. Is it to be imagined that ' a master calls his servant, or sends him on an errand, ' singing; that one friend imparts a secret to another, ' singing; that men deliberate in council singing; that ' orders in time of battle are given singing; and that men ' are melodiously kill'd with swords and darts. This is

<hr>

* The word COMEDIE in French comprehends every kind of theatrical representation; a truer designation of an opera is the term Tragedie en Musique; those of Lully are in general so called in the title-page; and it is plain by the context that the author means not the comic but the tragic opera.

' the downright way to lose the life of representation, ' which without doubt is preferable to that of harmony; ' for harmony ought to be no more than a bare attendant, ' and the great masters of the stage have introduced it as ' pleasing, not as necessary, after they have perform'd all ' that relates to the subject and discourse. Nevertheless ' our thoughts run more upon the musician than the hero ' in the opera; Luigi, Cavallo, and Cesti, are still present ' to our imagination. The mind not being able to conceive ' a hero that sings, thinks of the composer that set the ' song; and I don't question but that in the operas at the ' Palace Royal, Baptist is a hundred times more thought ' of than Theseus or Cadmus.' †

The same author, speaking of recitative, particularly that of the Venetian opera, says that it is neither singing nor reciting,‡ but somewhat unknown to the ancients, which may be defined to be an aukward use of music and speech. §

It may perhaps be said that music owes much of its late improvement to the theatre, and to that emulation which it has a tendency to excite, as well in composers as performers; but who will pretend to say what direction the studies of the most eminent musicians of late years would have taken, had they been left to themselves; it being most certain that every one of that character has two tastes, the one for himself, and the other for the public? Purcell has given a plain indication of his own, in a declaration that the gravity and seriousness of the

<hr>

† Works of Mons. St. Evremond, vol. II. page 84, in a letter to Villiers, duke of Buckingham.

‡ This remark upon examination will be found to be but too true, notwithstanding the arguments in favour of recitative, which amount in substance to this, that it is a kind of prose in music, that its beauty consists in coming near nature, and in improving the natural accents of words by more pathetic or emphatical tones. Preface to the opera of Semele by Mr. Congreve. Mr. Hughes to the same purpose, delivers these as his sentiments: ' The recitative style in composition is founded on that ' variety of accent which pleases in the pronunciation of a good orator, ' with as little deviation from it as possible, The different tones of the ' voice in astonishment, joy, sorrow, rage, tenderness, in affirmations, ' apostrophes, interrogations, and all other varieties of speech, make ' a sort of natural music which is very agreeable; and this is what is ' intended to be imitated, with some helps, by the composer, but without ' approaching to what we call a tune or air; so that it is but a kind of ' improved elocution.' Preface to Mr. Hughes's Cantatas in the first volume of his Poems.

Upon these several passages it may be remarked, that in the expression of the passions nature doth not offer musical sounds to the human ear: for though the natural tones of grief and joy, the two passions which are most effectually expressed by music, approach nearer to musical precision than any other, yet still they are inconcinnous and unmusical. Farther, that the sounds of the voice in speech are immusical is asserted by Lord Bacon in the following passage: ' All sounds ' are either musical sounds, which we call tones, whereunto there may ' be a harmony; which sounds are ever equal, as singing, the sounds of ' stringed and wind instrments, the ringing of bells, &c.; or immusical ' sounds, which are ever unequal; such as the voice in speaking, all ' whisperings, all voices of beasts and birds, except they be singing birds, ' all percussions of stones, wood, parchment, skins, as in drums, and ' infinite others.' Nat. Hist. cent. II. sect. 101.

The conclusion from these premises must be, that musical sounds do not imitate common speech; and therefore that recitative can in no degree be said to be an improvement of elocution.

But admitting the contrary to be the case, and that the sounds of speech were equally musical with those employed in recitative, the inflexions of the voice are too minute to fall in with the division of the scale, allowing even the enarmonic diesis, or the comma, the smallest of all sensible intervals, to make a part of it; and of this opinion is Mons. Duclos, who, in the Encyclopedia, art. DECLAMATION DES ANCIENS, for this reason denies the possibility of a notation for speech.

Upon the whole, the beauties of the recitative style in music consist not in the power of imitating the tones, much less the various inflexions of the voice in speech, but in the varieties of accent and melody, which follow from its not being subject to metrical laws: In short, what has been said and insisted on in this discourse of music in general, may be applied to recitative, viz., that its mimetic powers are very inconsiderable, and that whatever charms it possesses are absolute and inherent.

§ These observations of St. Evremond respect the musical tragedy, but the Italians have also a musical comedy called a Burletta, which has been lately introduced into England, and given rise to the distinction in the advertisements for subscriptions of first, second, &c. serious man or woman. This entertainment affords additional proof how little music, as such, is able to support itself: in the tragic opera it borrows aid from the tumidity of the poetry; in the comic, from the powers of ridicule, to which music has not the least relation.

Italian music were by him thought worthy of imitation : * the studies of Stradella, Scarlatti, and Bononcini for their own delight were not songs or airs calculated to astonish the hearers with the tricks of the singer, but cantatas and duets, in which the sweetness of the melody, and the just expression of fine poetical sentiments, were their chief praise ; or madrigals for four or more voices, wherein the various excellencies of melody and harmony were united, so as to leave a lasting impression on the mind. The same may be said of Mr. Handel, who, to go no farther, has given a specimen of the style he most affected in a volume of lessons for the harpsichord, with which no one will say that any modern compositions of the kind can stand in competition. These, as they were made for the practice of an illustrious personage, as happy in an exquisite taste and correct judgment as a fine hand, may be supposed to be, and were in fact compositions *con amore*. In other instances this great musician compounded the matter with the public, alternately pursuing the suggestions of his fancy, and gratifying a taste which he held in contempt.†

Whoever is curious to know what that taste could be, to which so great a master as Mr. Handel was compelled occasionally to conform, in prejudice to his own, will find it to have been no other than that which is common to every promiscuous auditory, with whom it is a notion that the right, as some may think, the ability to judge, to applaud and condemn, is purchased by the price of admittance ; a taste that leads all who possess it to prefer light and trivial airs, and such as are easily retained in memory, to the finest harmony and modulation ; and to be better pleased with the licentious excesses of a singer, than the true and just intonation of the sweetest and most pathetic melodies, adorned with all the graces and elegancies that art can suggest. Such critics as these, in their judgment of instrumental performance, uniformly determine in favour of whatever is most difficult in the execution, and, like the spectators of a rope-dance, are never more delighted than when the artist is in such a situation as to render it doubtful whether he shall incur or escape disgrace.

To such a propensity as this, the gratifications whereof are of necessity but momentary, leaving no impression upon the mind, we may refer the ardent thirst of novelty in music, and that almost general reprobation of whatever is old, against the sense of the poet :—

> Now, good Cesario, but that piece of song,
> That old and antique song we had last night,
> Methought it did relieve my passion much ;
> More than light airs, and recollected terms
> Of these most brisk and giddy-paced times.
> TWELFTH NIGHT, Act II. Scene iv.

But to account for it is in no small degree difficult : to justify it, it is said that there is a natural vicissitude of things, and that it were vain to expect that music should be permanent in a world where change seems to predominate.

But it may here be observed, that there are certain laws of nature that are immutable and independent on time and place, the precepts of morality and axioms in physics for instance ; there never was since the creation a time when there did not exist an irreconcileable difference between truth and falsehood ; or when two things, each

equal to the same third, were unequal one to the other ; or, to carry the argument farther, when consonance and dissonance were not as essentially distinguished from each other, both in their ratios and by their effects, as they are at this day ; or when certain interchanges of colours, or forms and arrangements of bodies were less pleasing to the eye than the same are now ; from whence it should seem that there are some subjects on which this principal of mutation does not operate : and, to speak of music alone, that, to justify the love of that novelty which seems capable of recommending almost any production, some other reasons must be resorted to than those above.

But, declining all farther research into the reason or causes of this principle, let us attend to its effects ; and these are visible in the almost total ignorance which prevails of the merits of most of the many excellent artists who flourished in the ages preceding our own : of Tye, of Redford, Shephard, Douland, Weelkes, Wilbye, Est, Bateman, Hilton, and Brewer, we know little more than their names ; these men composed volumes which are now dispersed and irretrievably lost, yet did their compositions suggest those ideas of the power and efficacy of music, and those descriptions of its manifold charms that occur in the verses of our best poets. To say that these and the compositions of their successors Blow, Purcell, Humphrey, Wise, Weldon, and others, were admired merely because they were new, is begging a question that will be best decided by a comparison, which some of the greatest among the professors of the art at this day would shrink from.

Upwards of two hundred years have elapsed since the anthem of Dr. Tye, ' I will exalt thee,' was composed ; and near as long a time since Tallis composed the motett ' O sacrum convivium,' which is now sung as an anthem to the words ' I call and cry to thee, O Lord ;' and it is comparatively but a few years since Geminiani was heard to exclaim in a rapture that the author of it was inspired.‡ Amidst all the varieties of composition in canon, which the learning and ingenuity of the ablest musicians have produced, that of Bird, composed in the reign of his mistress Elizabeth, is considered as a model of perfection. Dr. Blow's song, ' Go, perjured man,' was composed at the command of king Charles the Second, and Purcell's ' Sing ' all ye Muses,' in the reign of his successor ; but no man has as yet been bold enough to attempt to rival either of these compositions. Nor is there any of the vocal kind, consisting of recitative and air, which can stand a competition with those two cantatas, for so we may venture to call them, ' From rosy bowers,' and ' From silent shades.'

Of poetry, painting, and sculpture, it has been observed that they have at different periods flourished and declined ; and that there have been times when each of those arts has been at greater perfection than now, is to be attributed to that vicissitude of things which gave rise to the present enquiry, and is implied in an observation of Lord Bacon, that in the youth of a state arms do flourish, in its middle age learning, and in its decline mechanical arts and merchandise.§ And if this observation on the various

---

* It is worth remarking that the poets, who of all writers seem the most sensible of the efficacy of music, appear uniformly to consider it as an intellectual, and consequently, a serious pleasure, engaging not only the attention of the ear, but the powers and faculties of the soul. To this end, and not for the purpose of exciting mirth, it is in numberless instances introduced by Shakespeare ; and among the poems of Milton is one entitled ' At a solemn Music.'

† An intimate friend of Mr. Handel, looking over the score of an opera newly composed by him, observed of some of the songs that they were excellent. ' You may think so,' says Mr. Handel, ' but it is not to them, but to these,' turning to others of a vulgar cast, ' that I trust for the success of the opera.'

‡ To this testimony we may add that of a foreigner respecting the church-music of queen Elizabeth's days, thus recorded by Strype in his Annals of the Reformation, vol. II. page 314 :—
' In her (the queen's) passing, (I say) she visited Canterbury ; how ' magnificently she was received and entertained here by archbishop ' Parker, I have related elsewhere. This I only add, that while she ' was here, the French ambassador came to her. Who hearing the ' excellent music in the cathedral church, extolled it up to the sky, ' and brake out into these words : "O God, I think no prince beside ' in all Europe ever heard the like, no not our Holy Father the Pope " himself." A young gentleman that stood by him replied, " Ah, do you " compare our queen to the knave of Rome, or rather prefer him before " her ?" Whereat the ambassador was highly angred, and told it to some ' of the councillors. They bade him be quiet, and take it patiently, ' for the boys, said they, with us do so call him and the Roman Anti-' christ too.'

§ Essay of Vicissitude of Things.

fates of poetry, painting, and sculpture be true, why is it to be assumed of music that it is continually improving, or that every innovation in it must be for the better? That the music of the church has degenerated and been greatly corrupted by an intermixture of the theatric style, has long been a subject of complaint; the Abbat Gerbert laments this and other innovations in terms the most affecting; * and indeed the evidence of this corruption must be apparent to every one that reflects on the style and structure of those compositions for the church that are now most celebrated abroad, even those of Pergolesi, his masses, for instance, and those of Iomelli and Perez, have nothing that distinguishes them but the want of action and scenic decoration, from dramatic represent-ations : like them they abound in symphony and the accompaniment of various instruments, no regard is paid to the sense of the words, or care taken to suit it with correspondent sounds; the clauses Kyrie Eleison and Christe Eleison, and Miserere mei and Amen are uttered in dancing metres; and the former not seldom in that of a minuet or a jig. Even the funeral service of Perez, lately published in London, so far as regards the measures of the several airs, and the instrumental aids to the voice-parts, differs as far from a sacred and solemn composure as a burletta does from an opera or musical tragedy.

From these premises it may be allowed to follow, that a retrospect to the musical productions of past ages is no such absurdity, as that a curious enquirer need decline it. No man scruples to do the like in painting; the con-noisseurs are as free in remarking the excellencies of Raphael, Titian, Domenichino, and Guido, as in com-paring succeeding artists with them; and very con-siderable benefits are found to result from this practice : our present ignorance with respect to music may betray us into a confusion of times and characters, but it is to be avoided by an attention to those particular circumstances that mark the several periods of its progress, its perfection and its decline.

Of the monkish music, that is to say the Cantus Ecclesiasticus, little can be said, other than that it was solemn and devout : after the introduction into the church of music in consonance, great skill and learning were exercised in the composition of motetts; but the elaborate contexture, and, above all, the affectation of musical and arithmetical subtilities in these compositions, as they con-duced but little to the ends of divine worship, subjected them to censure, and gave rise to a style, which, for its simplicity and grandeur many look up to as the perfection of ecclesiastical harmony; and they are not a few who think that at the end of the sixteenth century the Romish church-music was at its height, as also that with us of the reformed church its most flourishing state was during the reign of Elizabeth; though others postpone it to the time of Charles II. grounding their opinion on the anthems of Blow, Humphrey, and Purcell, who received their first notions of fine melody from the works of Carissimi, Cesti, Stradella, and others of the Italians.

For the perfection of vocal harmony we must refer to a period of about fifty years, commencing at the year 1560, during which were composed madrigals for private recreation in abundance, that are the models of excellence in their kind; and in this species of music the composers of our own country appear to be inferior to none. The improvement of melody is undoubtedly owing to the drama; and its union with harmony and an assemblage of all the graces and elegancies of both we may behold in the madrigals of Stradella and Bononcini, and the chorusses and anthems of Handel; and among the com-positions for private practice in the duets of Steffani and Handel. As to the harmony of instruments, it is the

* De Cantu et Musica Sacra. tom. II. page 375.

least praise that can be bestowed on the works of Corelli, Geminiani, and Martini, to say that through all the vicissitudes and fluctuations of caprice and fancy, they retain their primitive power of engaging the affections, and recommending themselves to all sober and judicious hearers.†

To music of such acknowledged excellence as this, the preference of another kind, merely on the score of its novelty, is surely absurd; at least the arguments in favour of it seem to be no better than those of Mr. Bayes in behalf of what he calls the new way of dramatic writing; which however were not found to be of such strength as to withstand the force of that ridicule, which which was very seasonably employed in restoring the people to their wits.

The performance on the organ is for the most part un-premeditated, as the term Voluntary, which is appro-priated to that instrument, imports; we may therefore look on this practice as extemporary composition; and it is not enough to be regretted how much the applauses be-stowed on the mere powers of execution have contributed to degrade it. Bird and Blow, as organists, are celebrated not so much for an exquisite hand, as for their skill, and that fulness of harmony which distinguished their per-formance, and which this noble instrument alone is cal-culated to exhibit.‡ The canzones of Frescobaldi, Kerl, Krieger, and Thiel, and above all, the fugues of Mr. Handel, including those in his lessons, shew us what is the true organ style, and leave us to lament that the idea of a voluntary on the organ is lost in those Capriccios on a single stop, which, as well in our parochial as cathedral service, follow the psalms. As to what is called a con-certo on the organ, it is a kind of composition consisting chiefly of solo passages, contrived to display what in modern musical phrase is termed a brilliant finger; and which, if attended to, will, amidst the clamour of the ac-companiment, in fact be found instead of four, to consist of but two parts.

But of all the abuses of instrumental performance, none is more injurious to music than the practice of single instruments, exemplified in solos and solo concertos, ori-ginally intended for private recreation, but which are now considered as an essential part of a musical entertainment. Music composed for a single instrument, as consisting of the mere melody of one part, is less complicated than that which is contrived for many : and melody is ever more pleasing to an unlearned ear than the harmony of different parts. The uniformity of a minuet, consisting of a deter-mined number of bars, the emphasis of each whereof returns in an orderly succession of measures or times, corresponds with some ideas of metrical regularity which are common to all minds, and affords a reason for that

† Of the instrumental music of the present day, notwithstanding the learning and abilities of many composers, the characteristics of it are noise without harmony, exemplified in the frittering of passages into notes, requiring such an instantaneous utterance, that thirty-two of them are frequently heard in the time which it would take moderately to count four; and of this cast are the Symphonies, Periodical Overtures, Quartettos, Quintettos, and the rest of the trash daily obtruded on the world.

Of solos for the violin, an elegant species of composition, as is evident in those most excellent ones of Corelli and Geminiani, and in many of those of Le Clair, Carbonelli, Festing, and Tartini, few have of late been published that will bear twice hearing; in general, the sole end of them is to display the powers of execution in prejudice to those talents which are an artist's greatest praise.

The lessons for the harpsichord of Mr. Handel, abounding with fugues of the finest contexture, and the most pathetic airs, are an inexhaustible fund of delight; those of the present time have no other tendency than to degrade an instrument invented for the elegant recreation of the youthful of the other sex, and to render it what at best it now appears to be, and may as truly as emphatically be termed, a tinkling cymbal.

‡ Old Mr. Arthur Bedford, chaplain to Aske's Hospital at Hoxton, and who died not many years ago, was acquainted with Dr. Blow, and says of him that he was reckoned the greatest master in the world for playing most gravely and seriously in his voluntaries. The Great Abuse of Musick, by Arthur Bedford, M.A. Lond. 8vo. 1711, page 248.

delight which the ear receives from the pulsatile instruments. Hence it is easy to account for the obtrusion of such compositions on the public ear as furnish opportunities of displaying mere manual proficiency in the artist; a solo or a concerto on the violin, the violoncello, the hautboy, or some other such instrument, does this, and gives scope for that exercise of a wild and exuberant fancy which distinguishes, or rather disgraces, the instrumental performance of this day.

The first essays of this kind were solos for the violin, the design whereof was to affect the hearer by the tone of the instrument, and those graces of expression which are its known characteristic; but it was no sooner found that the merit of these compositions was estimated by the difficulty of performing them, than the plaudits of the auditory became an irresistible temptation to every kind of extravagance. These have been succeeded by compositions of a like kind, but framed with a very different view, Solos and Concertos, containing passages that carried the melody beyond the utmost limits of the scale, indeed so high on the instrument, that the notes could not be distinctly articulated, in violation of a rule that Lord Bacon has laid down, that the mean tones of all instruments, as being the most sweet, are to be preferred to those at either extremity of either the voice or instrument.* The last improvement of licentious practice has been the imitation of tones dissimilar to those of the violin, the flute, for instance, and those that resemble the whistling of birds; and the same tricks are played with the violoncello. To what farther lengths these extravagances will be carried, time only can discover.

Amidst that stupor of the auditory faculties, which leads to the admiration of whatever is wild and irregular in music, a judicious hearer is necessitated to seek for delight in those compositions, which, as owing their present existence solely to their merit, must, like the writings of the classic authors, be looked on as the standards of per-

* Nat. Hist. cent. II. sect. 173. The Sylva Sylvarum, or Natural History of Lord Bacon, contains a great variety of experiments and observations tending to explain the propertes of sound and the nature of harmony. The following judicious remark may serve as a specimen of the author's skill in his subject, and at the same time shew his sentiments of harmony, and in what he conceived the perfection thereof to consist. 'The sweetest and best harmony is, when every part or instrument is not 'heard by itself, but a conflation of them all; which requireth to stand 'some distance off, even as it is in the mixture of perfumes, or the taking 'of the smells of several flowers in the air.' Cent. III. sect. 225.

fection; in the grave and solemn strains of the most celebrated composers for the church, including those of our own country, who in the opinion of the best judges are inferior to none; † or in the gayer and more elegant compositions, as well instrumental as vocal, of others contrived for the recreation and solace, in private assemblies and select companies, of persons competently skilled in the science.

How far remote that period may be when music of this kind shall become the object of the public choice, no one can pretend to tell. To speak of music for instruments, the modern refinements in practice, and the late improvements in the powers of execution have placed it beyond the reach of view: and it affords but small satisfaction to a lover of the art to reflect that the world is in possession of such instrumental compositions as those of Corelli, Bononcini, Geminiani, and Handel, when not one principal performer in ten has any relish of their excellencies, or can be prevailed on to execute them but with such a degree of unfeeling rapidity as to destroy their effect, and utterly to defeat the intention of the author. In such kind of performance, wherein not the least regard is paid to harmony or expression, we seek in vain for that most excellent attribute of music, its power to move the passions, without which this divine science must be considered in no better a view than as the means of recreation to a gaping crowd, insensible of its charms, and ignorant of its worth.

† Such music as this has been the delight of the wisest men in all ages. Luther, who was so great an admirer of music, that he scrupled not as a science, to rank it next to theology, which is styled the queen of the sciences, was often used to be recreated with the singing of motetts. Bishop Williams, while he was lord keeper, chose to retain the deanery of Westminster for the sake of the choral service performed there: 'He was loathe,' says the historian, 'to stir from the seat where he had 'the command of such exquisite music.' And in a more particular manner the same person speaks of the love which that great prelate bore to music, for, says he, 'that God might be praised with a cheerful noise in 'his sanctuary, he procured the sweetest music both for the organ and 'voices of all parts that ever was heard in an English quire. In those 'days that abbey and the Jerusalem Chamber, where he gave entertain-'ment, were the volaries of the choicest singers that the land had bred.' Life of the Lord Keeper Williams, by Hackett, Bishop of Litchfield and Coventry, page 62, 46. Milton has been very explicit in declaring what kind of music delighted him most, in the verses entitled 'At a solemn music.' Dr. Busby the master of Westminster-school had an organ, and music of the most solemn kind in his house at the time when choral service was throughout the kingdom forbidden to be performed. Vide ante, page xxi. in note.

A

GENERAL HISTORY

OF THE

SCIENCE AND PRACTICE OF MUSIC.

BOOK I.   CHAP. I.

THERE is scarce any consideration that affords greater occasion to lament the inevitable vicissitude of things, than the obscurity in which it involves, not only the history and the real characters, but even the discoveries of men. When we consider the various pursuits of mankind, that some respect merely the interest of individuals, and terminate with themselves, while others have for their object the investigation of truth, the attainment and communication of knowledge, or the improvement of useful arts; we applaud the latter, and reckon upon the advantages that posterity must derive from them: but this it seems is in some degree a fallacious hope; and, notwithstanding the present improved state of learning in the world, we have reason to deplore the want of what is lost to us, at the same time that we rejoice in that portion of knowledge which we possess.

Whoever is inclined to try the truth of this observation on the subject of the present work, if he does not see cause to acquiesce in it, will at least be under great difficulties to satisfy himself how it comes to pass, that seeing what miraculous effects have been ascribed to the music of the ancients, we know so little concerning it, as not only to be ignorant of the use and application of most of their instruments, but even in a great measure of their system itself.

To say that in the general deluge of learning, when the irruptions of barbarous nations into civilized countries, the seats and nurseries of science, became frequent, music, as holding no sympathy with minds actuated by ambition and the lust of empire, was necessarily overwhelmed, is not solving the difficulty; for though barbarism might check, as it did, the growth of this as well as other arts, the utter extirpation of it seems to have been as much then, as it is now, impossible. That conquest did not produce the same effect on the other arts is certain; the architecture, the sculpture, and the poetry of ancient Greece and Rome, though they withdrew for a time, were yet not lost, but after a retirement of some centuries appeared again. But what became of their music is still a question: the

Pyramids, the Pantheon, the Hercules of Glycon, the Grecian Venus, the writings of Homer, of Plato, of Aristotle, and other ancients, are still in being; but who ever saw, or where are deposited, the compositions of Terpander, Timotheus, or Phrynis? Did the music of these, and many other men whom we read of, consist of mere Energy, in the extemporary prolation, of solitary or accordant sounds; or had they, in those very early ages, any method of notation, whereby their ideas of sound, like those of other sensible objects, were rendered capable of communication? It is hard to conceive that they had not, when we reflect on the very great antiquity of the invention of letters; and yet before the time of Alypius, who lived A. C. 115, there are no remaining evidences of any such thing.

The writers in that famous controversy set on foot by Sir William Temple, towards the close of the last century, about the comparative excellence of the ancient and modern learning, at least those who sided with the ancients, seem not to have been aware of the difficulty they had to encounter, when they undertook, as some of them did, to maintain the superiority of the ancient over the modern music, a difficulty arising not more from the supposed weight on the other side of the argument, than from the want of sufficient Data on their own. In the comparison of ancient with modern music, it was reasonable to expect that the advocates for the former should at least have been able to define it; but Sir William Temple, who contends for its superiority, makes no scruple to confess his utter incapacity to judge about it: 'What,' says he, 'are become of the charms of music, by which 'men and beasts, fishes, fowls, and serpents were so 'frequently enchanted, and their very natures changed; 'by which the passions of men are raised to the greatest 'height and violence; and then so suddenly appeased, 'so as they might be justly said to be turned into 'lions or lambs, into wolves or into harts, by the 'powers and charms of this admirable art? 'Tis 'agreed of all the learned that the science of music, 'so admired by the ancients, is wholly lost in the 'world, and that what we have now is made up of 'certain notes that fell into the fancy or observation

Mersennus says that by means of his friends Naudè and Gaffarel, he had obtained from Rome, and other parts of Italy, drawings of sundry ancient instruments from coins and marbles; among many which he has given, are these of the lyre; the first is apparently a part of a tortoise shell, the other is part of the head with the horns of a bull.

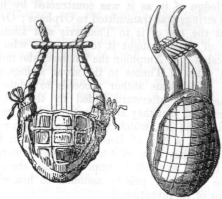

The above-cited authors mention also a *Plectrum*, of about a span in length, made of the lower joint of a goat's leg; the use whereof was to touch the strings of the lyre, as appeared to Galilei by several ancient bass-reliefs and other sculptures discovered at Rome in his time.

Kircher has prefixed as a frontispiece to the second tome of the Musurgia, a representation of a statue in the Matthei garden near Rome, of Apollo standing on a circular pedestal, whereon are carved in basso relievo a great variety of ancient musical instruments. But the most perfect representation of the lyre is the instrument in the hand of the above statue, which is of the form in which the lyre is most usually delineated. Vide Musurg. tom. I. pag. 536. *

The pipe, the original and most simple of wind instruments, is said to have been formed of the shank-bone of a crane, and the invention thereof is ascribed to Apollo, Pan, Orpheus, Linus, and many others. Marsyas, or as others say, Silenus, was the

* Isaac Vossius, a bigotted admirer of the ancients, de Poemat. cant. et virib. Rythm. pag. 97, contends that hardly any of these remaining monuments of antiquity are in such a state as to warrant any opinion touching the form of the ancient lyre. He speaks indeed of two statues of Apollo in the garden of his Britannic majesty at London, in the year 1673, (probably the Privy Garden behind the then palace of Whitehall) each holding a lyre; and as neither of these instruments was then in the least mutilated, he considers them as true and perfect representations of the ancient cythara or lyre, in two forms, and has thus delineated and described them :—

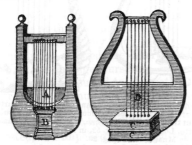

A   The bridge over which the chords are stretched.
B   The chordotonum, from which the chords proceed.
C C The echei, made of brass, and affixed to the bridge to encrease the
     sound.
D   The bridge as in the former figure.

first that joined pipes of different lengths together with wax; but Virgil says,

Pan primos calamos cera conjungere plures
    Instituit.†

forming thereby an instrument, to which Isidore, bishop of Seville, gives the name of Pandorium, and others that of Syringa and which is frequently represented in collections of antiquities.‡

As to the instruments of the pulsatile kind, such as are the Drum, and many others, they can hardly be ranked in the number of musical instruments; inasmuch as the sounds they produce are not reducible to any system, though the measure and duration or succession of those sounds is; which is no more than may be said of many sounds, which yet are not deemed musical.

Such are the accounts that are left us of the invention of the instruments above-mentioned, which it is necessary to make the basis of an enquiry into the origin of a system, rather than the Harp, the Organ, and many others mentioned in sacred writ, whose invention was earlier than the times above referred to, because their respective forms are known even at this time of day to a tolerable degree of precision: a lyre consisting of strings extended over the concave of a shell, or a pipe with a few equidistant perforations in it, are instruments we can easily conceive of; and indeed the many remaining monuments of antiquity leave us in very little doubt about them; but there is no medium through which we can deduce the figure or construction of any of the instruments mentioned either in the Pentateuch, or the less ancient parts of sacred history; and doubtless the translators of those passages of the Old Testament, where the names of musical instruments occur, after due deliberation on the context, found themselves reduced to the necessity of rendering those names by such terms as would go the nearest to excite a correspondent idea in their readers: so that they would be grossly mistaken who should imagine that the organ, handled by those of whom Jubal is said to have been the father,§ any way resembled the instrument now known among us by that name.

Those accounts which give the invention of the lyre to Mercury, agree also in ascribing to him a system adapted to it; though with respect to the nature of that system, as also to the number of strings of which the lyre consisted, there is a great diversity of opinions; and indeed the settling the first of these questions would go near to determine the other. Boetius inclines to the opinion that the lyre of Mercury had only four strings; and adds, that the first and the fourth made a diapason; that the middle distance was a tone, and the extremes a diapente.‖

Zarlino, following Boetius, adopts his notion of a tetrachord, and is more particular in the explanation of it;¶ his words are as follows :—'From the first ' string to the second was a diatessaron or a fourth;

† Eclog II. ver. 32.
‡ Vide Mersen. de Instrum. Harmon. lib. II. pag. 73.
§ Genesis, chap. iv. ver. 21.
‖ De Musica, lib. I. cap. 20. Bontempi, 48.
¶ Istitutioni Harmoniche, pag. 72.

'from the second to the third was a tone; and from
'the third to the fourth was a diatessaron; so that the
'first with the second, and the third with the fourth,
'contained a diatessaron; the first with the third,
'and the second with the fourth, a diapente or fifth.'
Admitting all which, it is clear that the first and
fourth strings must have constituted a diapason.

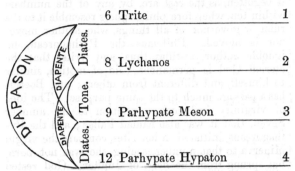

It is to be observed that the above diagram is used
by Boetius, and is adopted by Zarlino, Kircher, and
many other writers;* but that though the application of the letters C G F C in one edition of
Boetius, is plainly intended to shew that the strings
immediately below them were supposed to correspond with those notes in our system, yet the authors
who follow Boetius have not ventured to make use
of them; and indeed there is great reason to reject
them; for in the earlier editions of Boetius de Musica,
the diagram above given is without letters. It seems
as if Glareanus, who assisted in the publication of the
Basil edition of that author, in 1570, thought he
should make the system more intelligible by the
addition of those letters; but there is no ground to
suppose that the Mercurian lyre, admitting it to consist of four strings, was so constructed.

Bontempi, an author of great credit, relying on
Nicomachus, suspects the relation of Boetius, as to
the number of the strings of the Mercurian lyre; and
farther doubts whether the system of a diapason, as
it is above made out, did really belong to it or not;
and indeed his suspicions seem to be well grounded;
for, speaking of this system, he says that none of the
Greek writers say anything about it, and that the
notion of its formation seems to be founded on a discovery made by Pythagoras, who lived about 500
years before Christ, of which a very particular relation will be given in its proper place; and farther to
shew how questionable this notion is, he quotes the
very words of Nicomachus before cited, concluding
with a modest interposition of his own opinion, which
is that the lyre of Mercury had *three* strings only,
and was thus constituted :—†

```
                                    G
Interval of a tone.
                                    F
Interval of a hemitone.
                                    E
```

However, notwithstanding the reasons of the above

* Vide Boetius de Musica, lib. I. cap. 20. Kircher, Musurgia universalis, tom. I. lib. ii. cap. 6. Zarlino Istit. Harmon. pag. 73. 75.
† Hist. Music. pag. 49.

author, the received opinion seems to have been that
the lyre consisted of four strings, tuned to certain
concordant intervals, which intervals were undoubtedly at first adjusted by the ear; but nevertheless
had their foundation in principles which the inventor
was not aware of, though what that tuning was, is
another subject of controversy. Succeeding musicians
are said to have given a name to each of these four
strings, which names, though they are not expressive
of the intervals, are to be adopted in our inquiry
after a system: to the first or most grave was given
the name of Hypate, or principal; the second was
called Parhypate, viz., next to Hypate; the third was
called Paranete, and the fourth Nete, which signifies
lowest; it is observable here, that it seems to have
been the practice of the ancients to give the more
grave tones the uppermost place in the scale, contrary to the moderns, by whom we are to understand
all who succeeded the grand reformation of music by
Guido, in the eleventh century, of which there will
be abundant occasion to speak hereafter.

The several names above-mentioned, exhibit the
lyre in a very simple state, viz., as consisting of four
strings, having names from whence neither terms nor
intervals can be inferred.

```
┌─────────HYPATE─────────┐
│────────PARHYPATE───────│
│────────PARANETE────────│
└──────────NETE──────────┘
```

Those who speak of the lyre in the manner above-
mentioned, seem to imagine that its compass included
two diatessarons or fourths, which being conjoined,
extended to a seventh, differing from that of Boetius,
in that his diatessarons, being separated by a tone,
took in the extent of an octave, and thereby formed
a diapason. They proceed to relate farther, that
Chorebus, the son of Atys, king of Lydia, added
a fifth string, which he placed between Parhypate
and Paranete, calling it, from its middle situation,
Mese; that Hyagnis, a Phrygian, added a sixth, which
he placed between Mese and Parhypate; this string
he called Lychanos, a word signifying the *indicial*
finger, viz., that on the left hand, next the thumb:
and lastly say these writers, Terpander added a
seventh string, which he placed between Mese and
Paranete, and called Paramese: the lyre, thus improved, included a septenary, or system of seven
terms, disposed in the following order :—

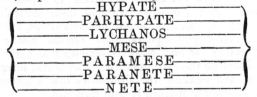

CHAP. II.

THE system above exhibited was the Heptachord
Synemmenon of the Greeks; it consisted of two
tetrachords or fourths, conjoined, that is to say, the
middle term was the end of the one, and the beginning of the other; and as the last string was added

To refute this error it is necessary in some sort to adopt it, and proceed after Bontempi to describe what he calls the first addition to the system of Terpander. His words are nearly these:—

'To the lyre of seven strings, forming a conjunct 'tetrachord, were added two tetrachords; the most grave 'was joined to that tetrachord, which for its gravest, 'or, to use the modern method of position, its lowest 'sound, had Hypate, and the most acute tetrachord 'was joined to that which for its most acute sound, 'had Nete: the acuter of these two additional tetra-'chords, from its situation named hyperboleon, pro-'ceeded from Nete by three other terms, viz., Trite, 'Paranete, and Nete, to each whereof was given the 'epithet Hyperboleon, to distinguish them from the 'sounds denoted by the same names in the primitive 'septenary. The other of the additional tetrachords, 'which began from Mese, was called Synemmenon 'or conjunct, and proceeded likewise by the same 'terms of Trite, Paranete, and Nete; and each of 'these had, for the reason just given, the epithet of 'Synemmenon, as in the following figure appears:'—

ADDITION I. to the SYSTEM of TERPANDER.

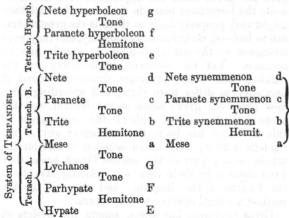

It is observable in the above scheme, that between the Synemmenon tetrachord and that marked B, which was originally a part of the system of Terpander, there is not the least difference: the interval of a hemitone between a and b being common to both; of what use then this auxiliary tetrachord was, or how it became necessary to distinguish it by the epithet Synemmenon or conjoined, from that which as yet had never been disjoined, is hard to conceive; the only addition therefore that we consider is that of the Hyperboleon tetrachord, which increasd the number of terms to ten, as above is shown: how-ever, after all, as the lyre thus limited to the compass of a musical tenth, reaching from E to g, was not commensurate in general to the human voice, a farther extension of it was found necessary; and another tetrachord was added to this, which began at Hypate in the former system, and proceeded by a repetition of the same terms as that did, with the addition of hypaton. This addition begat also a dis-tinction in the terms of the tetrachord, to which it had been joined; which, to shew their relation to the Mese, had each of them the adjunct of meson, and the

tetrachord to which they belonged was thence called the tetrachord meson. This last addition of the te-trachord Hypaton increased the number of terms to thirteen, in which were included four conjunct tetra-chords, the Mese being the seventh from each ex-treme, and carried the system down to B; though to show that hypate Hypaton was a hemitone below Parhypate or C, the Italians generally denote it by the character ♭.

ADDITION II. to the SYSTEM OF TERPANDER.

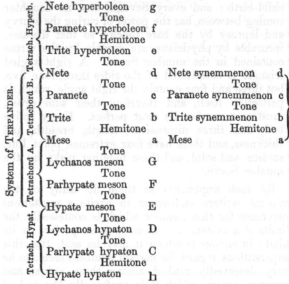

In this diagram also the synemmenon Tetrachord is inserted: we forbear to repeat the reasons against connecting it with the system of Terpander, with which it seems absolutely incompatible, and shall hereafter endeavour to shew when and how the in-vention of it became necessary, and what particular ends it seems calculated to answer. In order to this it must be observed, that the system, improved even to the degree above related, wanted much of perfection: it is evident that the lower sound Hypate hypaton, or as we should now call it, B♮, was a hemitone below C, and that b, which in the order of succession upwards was the eighth term, was a whole tone below the term next above it, consequently it was a hemi-tone short of a complete musical octave or diapason; to remedy this defect, as also for divers other reasons, Pythagoras is said to have reverted to the primitive system of a septenary, and with admirable sagacity, by interposing a tone in the middle of the double tetra-chord, to have formed the system of a Diapason or Octochord.

But before we proceed to relate the particulars of this and other improvements of Pythagoras in music, and the wonderful discovery made by him of the proportions of musical sounds, it may be proper to take notice of two variations in the septenary, intro-duced by a philosopher, and a disciple of Pythagoras, named Philolaus; the one whereof, for ought we can discover, seems to have been but very inconsiderable, that is to say, no more than an alteration of the term

Mese, which, because that sound was a third distant from Nete, he called Trite; the other consisted in an extension of the diatessaron included between the Mese and Nete to a diapente, by the insertion of a trihemitone between Paramese, or as he termed it, Trite and Paranete; by which the system, though it laboured under the inconvenience of an Hiatus, comprehended the interval of a diapason, the extreme terms whereof formed a consonance much more grateful to the ear than any of those contained in that of Terpander. Nicomachus speaks more than once of Philolaus, and says that he was the first who called that Trite, which before was called Paramese, as being a diatessaron distant from Nete. But although it is certain that he was a contemporary of Pythagoras, we must suppose that this improvement of his to be prior to that of Pythagoras above hinted at; for the latter adopted the appellation of Trite, though by restoring the ancient name Paramese, which he gave to the inserted tone, he altered the situation of it, as will be shown hereafter.

SYSTEM OF PHILOLAUS.

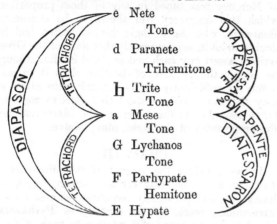

The gradual improvements of this system from the time of Terpander to that of Philolaus having been severally enumerated, and its imperfection noted, we are now to speak of those made by Pythagoras. His regulation of the octave by the insertion of a tone has been just hinted, and it will be necessary to be more particular; but previous to this it is requisite to mention that discovery of his, which though merely accidental, enabled him to investigate the ratios of the consonances, and to demonstrate that the foundations of musical harmony lay deeper than had ever before his time been imagined.

Of the manner of this discovery Nicomachus has given a relation, which Mr. Stanley has inserted in his History of Philosophy in nearly the following terms:—

'Pythagoras being in an intense thought whether 'he might invent any instrumental help to the ear, 'solid and infallible, such as the sight hath by a 'compass and a rule, and by a Dioptre; or the touch, 'or by a balance, or by the invention of measures; 'as he passed by a smith's shop by a happy chance 'he heard the iron hammers striking on the anvil, 'and rendering sounds most consonant to one another 'in all combinations except one. He observed in

'them these three concords, the diapason, the diapente, 'and the diatessaron; but that which was between 'the diatessaron and the diapente he found to be 'a discord in itself, though otherwise useful for the 'making up of the greater of them, the diapente. 'Apprehending this came to him from God, as 'a most happy thing, he hastened into the shop, and 'by various trials finding the difference of the sounds 'to be according to the weight of the hammers, and 'not according to the force of those who struck, nor 'according to the fashion of the hammers, nor according to the turning of the iron which was in 'beating out: having taken exactly the weight of the 'hammers, he went straightway home, and to one 'beam fastened to the walls, cross from one corner 'of the room to the other, lest any difference might 'arise from thence, or be suspected to arise from the 'properties of several beams, tying four strings of 'the same substance, length, and twist, upon each of 'them he hung a several weight, fastening it at the 'lower end, and making the length of the strings 'altogether equal; then striking the strings by two 'at a time interchangeably, he found out the afore- 'said concords, each in its own combination; for 'that which was stretched by the greatest weight, 'in respect of that which was stretched by the least 'weight, he found to sound a Diapason. The greatest 'weight was of twelve pounds, the least of six; thence 'he determined that the diapason did consist in 'double proportion, which the weights themselves 'did shew. Next he found that the greatest to the 'least but one, which was of eight pounds, sounded 'a Diapente; whence he inferred this to consist in 'the proportion called Sesquialtera, in which pro- 'portion the weights were to one another; but unto 'that which was less than itself in weight, yet greater 'than the rest, being of nine pounds, he found it to 'sound a Diatessaron; and discovered that, propor- 'tionably to the weights, this concord was Sesqui- 'tertia; which string of nine pounds is naturally 'Sesquialtera to the least; for nine to six is so, viz., 'Sesquialtera, as the least but one, which is eight, 'was to that which had the weight six, in proportion 'Sesquitertia; and twelve to eight is Sesquialtera; 'and that which is in the middle, between Diapente 'and Diatessaron, whereby Diapente exceeds Dia- 'tessaron, is confirmed to be in Sesquioctava propor- 'tion, in which nine is to eight. The system of both 'was called Diapason,* that is both of the Diapente 'and Diatessaron joined together, as duple proportion 'is compounded of Sesquialtera and Sesquitertia; 'such as are twelve, eight, six, or on the contrary, 'of Diatessaron and Diapente, as duple proportion is 'compounded of Sesquitertia and Sesquialtera, as 'twelve, nine, six, being taken in that order.

'Applying both his hand and ear to the weights 'which he had hung on, and by them confirming the 'proportion of the relations, he ingeniously trans- 'ferred the common result of the strings upon the 'cross beam to the bridge of an instrument, which he 'called Χορδοτονο, *Chordotonos*; and for stretching 'them proportionably to the weights, he invented

* i. e. per omnes.

'pegs, by the turning whereof he distended or
'relaxed them at pleasure. Making use of this
'foundation as an infallible rule, he extended the
'experiment to many kinds of instruments, as well
'pipes and flutes, as those which have strings ; * and
'he found that this conclusion made by numbers was
'consonant without variation in all. That sound
'which proceeded from the number six he named
'Hypate ; that from eight Mese, being Sesquitertia
'to the other ; that from nine Paramese, it being one
'tone more acute, and sesquioctave to the Mese ; that
'from twelve he termed Nete ; and supplying the
'middle spaces with proportionable sounds, according
'to the diatonic genus, he so ordered the octochord
'with convenient numbers. Duple, Sesquialtera, Ses-
'quitertia, and the difference of the two last, Sesqui-
'octava.

'Thus by a kind of natural necessity he found the
'progress from the lowest to the highest, according
'to the diatonic genus ; and from thence he proceeded
'to declare the chromatic and enharmonic kinds.'†
Hist. of Philosophy, pag. 387. folio edit. 1701.

* This seems difficult to conceive, for the turning of pipes and flutes
is regulated by the size and distance of the apertures for the emission of
the wind or breath ; and to these the proportions of six, eight, nine,
twelve, are in no way whatever applicable.

† The result of this discovery is, that consonancy is founded on
geometrical principles, the contemplation whereof, and the making them
the test of beauty and harmony, is a pleasure separate and distinct from
that which we receive by the senses. This geometrical relation of the
consonances has been farther illustrated by Archimedes, who has demonstrated that the proportions of certain solid bodies are the same with
those of the musical consonances ; to speak first of the diapason.

By a corollary from the thirty-fourth proposition of Archimedes it is
shewn, that the proportion of the octave is as the whole superficies of
a right cylinder described about a sphere, is to the whole superficies of an
equilateral cylinder inscribed, that is to say, as 2 is to 1. For the circumscribed is to the spheric superficies as 12 is to 8 ; but the spheric is to
the inscribed as 8 is to 6 ; therefore the circumscribed is to the inscribed
as 12 is to 6, or 2 to 1. Vide Theorems selected out of Archimedes by
Andrew Taquet, printed at the end of Whiston's Euclid.

As to the diatessaron, the proportion of it is precisely the same with
that which subsists between the superficies of a sphere and the whole
superficies of a square cylinder inscribed therein, viz., 4 to 3. Ibid.
Prop. xxxiv.

But which is admirable, the sesquialteral proportion of the diapente,
and of the same interval continued, is demonstrated by Tacquet himself,
by a sphere, a right cylinder, and an equilateral cone thus disposed :—

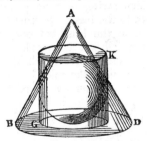

His words are these : 'An equilateral cone circumscribed about a
'sphere, and a right cylinder in like manner circumscribed about the
'same sphere, and the same sphere itself continue the same proportion ;
'to wit, the sesquialteral, as well as in respect of the solidity as of the
'whole superficies.

'For by 32 of this book, the right cylinder G K encompassing the
'sphere, is to the sphere, as well in respect of solidity, as of the whole
'superficies, as 3 is to 2, or as 6 to 4. But by the foregoing, the equilateral
'cone B A D circumscribed about the sphere, is to the sphere, in both the
'said respects, as 9 is to 4. Therefore the same cone is to the cylinder,
'both in respect of solidity and surface, as nine is to six ; wherefore
'these three bodies, a cone, a cylinder, and sphere, are betwixt them
'selves as the numbers 9, 6, 4 ; and consequently continue the sesqui-
'alteral proportion.' Q. E. D. Prop. xlv. at the conclusion of the
'Theorems of Archimedes by Tacquet.

Farther the same author shows, that the same sesquialteral proportion
holds betwixt an equilateral cone and cylinder circumscribed about the
same sphere, in respect of their whole surfaces, their simple surfaces,
their solidities, altitudes, and bases.

Archimedes was so delighted with the thirty-second of his propositions,
above referred to, that he left it in charge to his friends to erect on his

Other writers attribute the discovery of the consonances to another, named Diocles ; who, say they,
passing by a potter's shop, chanced to strike his
stick against some empty vessels which were standing
there ; that observing the sounds of grave and acute
resulting from the strokes on vessels of different magnitudes, he investigated the proportions of music,
and found them to be as above related ; ‡ notwithstanding which testimony, the uniform opinion of
mankind has been, that we owe this invention to
Pythagoras ; the result whereof may be conceived
by means of the following diagram :—

It is observable that there is nothing in this
account to authorise the supposition that the lyre
of Mercury was tuned in any of those proportions
which this discovery had shewn to be consonant.
Bontempi, who, as we have hinted before, had his
doubts about it, says expressly that none of the Greek
writers assert any such matter ; and Zarlino, though
he adopts the relation of Boetius, does it in such
a way as sufficiently shews it stuck with him : we
may therefore justly suspect that Boetius went too
far in assigning to the strings of the Mercurian lyre
the proportions of six, eight, nine, twelve.

CHAP. III.

IF we consider the amount of this discovery, it
will appear to be, that certain sounds, which the
human ear had previously recognised as grateful and
harmonious, were, by the sagacity of Pythagoras,
found to have a wonderful relation to each other in
certain proportions ; that those proportions do really
subsist between the musical concords above-mentioned
is demonstrated by Ptolemy, and will be shown hereafter ; but then it has been by experiments of a
different kind from that of strings distended by
hammers or other weights in the proportion of six,
eight, nine, twelve, and such as prove a most
egregious error in those said to be made by Pythagoras ; so that though his title to the discovery
of the proportions above-mentioned is not contested ;
yet that it was the result of the experiment above
related to have been made by him, is demonstrably
false.

For suppose, as will be shown hereafter, that the
sounds of four strings, in every other respect alike,
and in length as these numbers, six, eight, nine,
twelve, will make the intervals above-mentioned, viz.,
a fourth, fifth, and octave ; yet let weights in these
proportions be hung to strings of equal length and
thickness, and the intervals between the sounds pro-

tomb a sphere included in a cylinder, and Tacquet seems to have been
little less pleased with his improvement on it, for he has given the figure
referred to in the demonstration of it, in the title page of his Theorems
selected from Archimedes.

‡ Vincent. Galilei, Dial. della Musica, pag. 127.

duced by strings thus distended will be far different from those above-mentioned.

It is said that we owe the detection of this error to the penetration and industry of Galileo Galilei, whose merits as well as sufferings are sufficiently known. He was the son of a noble Florentine named Vincentio Galilei, the author of a most learned and valuable work, intitled Dialogo della Musica antica e moderna, printed at Florence in 1581 and 1602; and also of a tract, intitled Discorso intorno all' Opere del Zarlino; and of his father, who was an admirable performer on the lute, learned both the theory and practice of music; in the latter whereof he is said to have been such a proficient, as to be able to perform to a great degree of excellence on a variety of instruments; however, notwithstanding this his propensity to music, his chief pursuits were natural philosophy and the mathematics. The inquisitiveness of his temper leading him to the making experiments, in the course thereof he made many noble discoveries; that of the telescope seems to be universally attributed to him; his first essay towards an instrument for viewing the planets was an organ pipe with glasses fixed therein; and it was he that first investigated those laws of pendulums, which Mr. Huygens afterwards improved into a regular and consistent theory.

In a work of the younger Galilei, intitled Discorsi e Dimostrazioni Matematiche intorno, à due nuove Scienze, attenenti alla Mecanica, ed i Movimenti locali, is contained a detection of that error, which it is here proposed to refute.

It is true some writers refer this discovery to Vincentio Galilei; and first Bontempi says, that in his discourse on the works of Zarlino, he affirms, that in order ' to find the consonances by weights hung ' to chords, the weight to produce the diapason ' ought to be in quadruple proportion; that to pro- ' duce the diapente ought to be in dupla sesquiquarta; ' for the diatessaron in sesquisettima partientenono ' and for the tone in sesquisettima partiente 64.' *

Malcolm also, speaking of the discovery of the consonances by Pythagoras, makes use of these words: ' But we have found an error in this account, which ' Vincenzo Galileo, in his Dialogues of the ancient ' and modern Music, is, for what I know, the first ' who observes; and from him Meibomius repeats it ' in his notes upon Nicomachus.'†

Here it may be observed, that this author Malcolm has himself been guilty of two mistakes; for first, it is not in his notes on Nicomachus, but in those on Gaudentius that Meibomius mentions the error now under consideration: and farther, in the passage of Meibomius, which Malcolm meant to refer to, the discovery is not ascribed to Vincentio Galilei, but to Galileo Galilei his son. To take the whole together, Gaudentius, speaking of the experiment of Pythagoras, and asserting, that if two equal chords be distended by weights in the same proportion to each other as the terms of the ratio, containing any interval, those chords when struck will give that interval. Meibomius upon this passage remarks in the following words: ' Mirandum sane, hanc experientiam, tot

' gravissimorum auctorum adsertione confirmatam, ' nostro primum seculo deprehensam esse falsam. ' Inventionis gloriam debemus nobilissimo mathema- ' tico Galileo Galilei, quem vide pag. 100. Tractatus ' qui inscribitur: Discorsi e Dimostrazioni Matem- ' atiche intorno à due nuove Scienze.'‡

But notwithstanding Bontempi has given from the elder Galilei a passage which seems to lead to a discovery of the error of Pythagoras, yet he himself acquiesces in the opinion of Meibomius, that the honour of a formal refutation of it is due to the younger, and is contained in the passage above referred to, which translated is as follows :—

' I stood a long time in doubt concerning the forms ' of consonance, not thinking the reasons commonly ' brought by the learned authors who have hitherto ' wrote of music sufficiently demonstrative. They ' tell us that the diapason, that is the octave, is con- ' tained by the double; and that the diapente, which ' we call the fifth, is contained by the sesquialter: ' for if a string, stretched upon the monochord, be ' sounded open, and afterwards placing a bridge ' under the midst of it, its half only be sounded, you ' will hear an eighth; and if the bridge be placed ' under one third of the string, and you then strike ' the two thirds open, it will sound a fifth, to that of ' the whole string struck when open; whereupon ' they infer that the eighth is contained between ' two and one, and the fifth between three and two. ' But I do not think we can conclude from hence ' that the double and sesquialteral can naturally ' assign the forms of the diapason and diapente; and ' my reason for it is this: there are three ways by ' which we may sharpen the tone of a string, viz., by ' shortening it, by stretching it, or by making it ' thinner: if now, retaining the same tension and ' thickness, we would hear an eighth, we must make ' it shorter by half; i. e., we must first sound the ' whole string, and then its half. But if, keeping the ' same length and thickness, we would have it rise to ' an eighth from its present tone, by stretching it, or ' screwing it higher, it is not sufficient to stretch it ' with a double, but with four times the force: thus, ' if at first it was distended by a weight, suppose of ' one pound, we must hang a four pound weight to ' it, in order to raise its tone to an eighth. And ' lastly, if, keeping the same length and tension, we ' would have a string to sound an eighth, this string ' must be but one fourth of the thickness of that ' which it must sound an eighth to.§ And this that ' I say of the eighth, I would have understood of all ' other musical intervals. To give an instance of the ' fifth, if we would produce it by tension, and in order ' thereto hang to the grave string a four-pound ' weight; we must hang to the acute, not one of six, ' which yet is in sesquialteral proportion to four, viz.,

---

* Hist. Music, pag. 54.   † Malcolm on Music, pag. 503.

‡ Meibom. Not. in Gaudent. pag. 37.

§ Isaac Vossius says that in this passage the author has erred, and with his usual temerity asserts, that cæteris paribus, the thicker the chord, the acuter the sound. De Poemat. Cant. et Viribus Rythmi, pag. 113. And this, even though he confesses that both Des Cartes and Mersennus were of opinion with Galilei in this respect. The only appeal in such a case as this must be to experiment, and whoever will make one for the purpose will find the converse of this proposition to be true, and that, as Galilei has said, chords comparatively thin render acute, and not grave sounds.

'three to two, but one of nine pounds. And to pro-
'duce the above intervals by strings of the same
'length, but different thickness, the proportion
'between the grave and the acute string must be
'that of nine to four. These things being really so
'in fact, I saw no reason why these sage philosophers
'should rather constitute the form of the eighth
'double than quadruple, and that of the fifth rather
'in sesquialtera than in double sesquiquarta, &c.' *
Discorsi e Dimostrazioni Matematiche del Galileo
Galilei, pag. 75.

To give yet farther weight to the above objection,
it may be necessary here briefly to explain a doctrine
yet unknown to the ancients, viz., that of pendulums,
between the vibrations whereof, and those of musical
chords, there is an exact coincidence.

Sound is produced by the tremulation of the air,
excited by the insensible vibrations of some elastic,
sonorous body ; and it has been manifested by repeated experiments, that of musical sounds the acute
are produced by swift, and the grave by comparatively
slow vibrations.† A chord distended by a weight or
otherwise, is, with respect to the vibrations made
between its two extremities, to be considered as
a double pendulum, ‡ and as subject to the same laws.

The proportions between the lengths of pendulums,
and the number of vibrations made by them, are in
an inverse duplicate ratio ; so that if the length be
quadrupled, the vibrations will be subdupled ; on the
contrary, if the length be subquadupled, the vibrations will be dupled.§

The same proportions hold also with respect to
a chord, but with this difference, that in the case of
pendulums the ratios are inverse, the greater length
giving the fewer vibrations ; whereas in that of
chords they are direct, the greater tension giving
the greater number of vibrations : thus if the tensive
power be as one, if that be quadrupled, the number
of vibrations is dupled ; and the sound produced by
the greater power will be duple in acumen to that
produced by the lesser. In a word, the same ratios
that subsist between the vibrations of pendulums and
their respective lengths, are to be found inversely
between the vibrations of chords and the powers that
distend them : what those ratios are, so far as they

respect the acuteness or gravity of sound, will shortly
be made appear.

In order to apply the doctrine of tensive powers
to the question in debate, it is necessary to state the
ratios of the several consonances, and those are demonstrated to be as follows, viz., that of the diapente
3 to 2, and of the diatessaron 4 to 3, that of the diapason 2 to 1, and that of the tone 9 to 8 ; or in other
words, a chord being divided into five parts, the sound
produced at three of these parts will be a diapente
to that produced at two ; if divided into seven parts,
four of them will sound a diatessaron against the remaining three ; and if divided into three parts, two
of them make a diapason against the other one :
farther, if the chord be divided into seventeen parts,
nine of them on one side will sound a sesquioctave
tone to the eight remaining on the other. These are
principles in harmonics which we may safely assume,
and the demonstrations may be seen in Ptolemy's
description of the nature and use of the Harmonic
Canon. ‖

It is equally certain, and is deducible from the
doctrine of pendulums, that if two chords, of equal
lengths, A B be so distended as that their vibrations shall be as three to two, that is, that A shall
make three vibrations while B is making two, the
consonance produced by striking them together will
be a diapente.

If the vibrations be as four to three, the consonance
will be a diatessaron.

If the vibrations be as two to one, the consonance
will be a diapason ; and lastly—

If the vibrations be as nine to eight, the interval
will be a sesquioctave tone.

We are now to enquire what are the degrees of
tensive power requisite to produce the vibrations
above-mentioned ; and here we must recur to the
principle above laid down, that the squares of the
vibrations of equal chords are to each other as their
respective tensions : if then we suppose a given sound
to be the effect of a tension by a weight of six pounds,
and would know the weight necessary to produce the
diapente, which has a ratio to its unison of 3 to 2,
we must take the square of those numbers 9 to 4,
and seek a number that bears the same ratio to six,
as nine does to four, and this can be no whole number,
but is thirteen and a half.

By the same rule we adjust the weight for the
diatessaron, 4 to 3, which numbers squared are sixteen and nine, and as 16 is to 9, so is $10\frac{2}{3}$ to 6.

For the diapason 2 to 1, which numbers squared
are 4 to 1, the weight must be twenty-four ; so as 4
is to 1, so is 24 to 6.

The several weights above adjusted, have a reference to the unison expressed in the scheme of Pythagoras, by the number six, supposed to result from
a tension of six pounds. But the sesquioctave tone,
as it is the difference between the diapente and diatessaron, takes its ratio from the sound expressed by

---

* The reason of these sage philosophers for doing thus, notwithstanding
that Galilei could not discover it, seems to be very obvious ; they constituted the form of the eighth double because they found it to arise
from the division of a chord into two equal parts ; and the fifth they
found to arise from the division of a chord into five parts, three whereof
struck against the remaining two produced that interval ; therefore they
assigned to it the sesquialtera proportion, 3 to 2. And certainly there
needs no better reason for the Pythagorean constitution of the consonances, than that it is founded in the actual division of a chord ; and
had the followers of Pythagoras rested the matter there, their tenets
would have escaped reprehension.

But they say of him that he produced the consonances by chords of
equal length and thickness, distended by weights of six, eight, nine,
and twelve pounds ; Galilei has shewn that this could not be ; and from
the principles laid down by writers since his time, as also by experiments,
it most evidently appears, that to produce the consonances, from chords
thus conditioned, weights must be used of a very different proportion
from those said to have been taken by Pythagoras.

As to the proportions, there can be no boubt but that they are as
above-stated : but the error chargeable on the Pythagoreans is the
making the discovery of them the result of an experiment, which must
have produced, instead of consonances, dissonances of the most offensive
kind.

† Treatise on the natural Grounds and Principles of Harmony, by
William Holder. Passim.

‡ Ibid. xi. 43.

§ Ibid. 16.

‖ Mersennus recommends for the purpose of making these experiments,
the use of two chords rather than one, for this reason, that where one
only is taken, only one sound can be heard at a time ; whereas when two
are used, both sounds are heard at the same instant, and thereby the
consonance is perceived. Harmonie universelle, Traitè des Instrumens,
Prop. v.

the number eight, as the diapente does from that expressed by nine ; in order then to adjust the weight for this interval, we must square those numbers ; and as 81 is to 64, so is $13\frac{1}{2}$ to $10\frac{2}{3}$.

Whoever is disposed to prove the truth of these positions, and doubts the certainty of numerical calculation, may have recourse to experiment ; in which, however, this caution is to be observed, that in the making it the utmost degree of accuracy is necessary ; for it should seem that one of the authors above-cited failed in an attempt of this sort, which is not to be wondered at, if we consider the nature of the subject.

The author here meant is Bontempi ; who, after citing the authority of Vincentio and Galileo Galilei, adds, that, ' prompted by curiosity, he made an ex-' periment by hanging weights to strings of equal ' lengths and thickness, the result whereof was, that ' the first and second strings, having weights of 12 ' and 9, produced not the diatessaron, but the trihemi-' tone ; the first and third 12, 8, not the diapente but ' the ditone ; the first and fourth, 12, 6, not the dia-' pason but the tritone ; the second and the third, 9, 8, ' not the tone, but the defective or incomplete hemi-' tone ; the second and fourth, 9, 6, not the diapente, ' but the semiditone ; and the third and fourth, 8, 6, ' not the diatessaron, but the distended or excessive ' tone, as the following figure demonstrates :—*

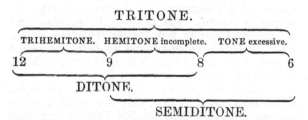

TRITONE.

| TRIHEMITONE. | HEMITONE incomplete. | TONE excessive. |
| 12 | 9 | 8 | 6 |

DITONE.

SEMIDITONE.

But that the proportions of a diatessaron tone and diatessaron would result from an experiment made by strings of several lengths of twelve, nine, eight, six ; or rather by a division of the monochord, according to that rule, is demonstrable. This invention of Pythagoras, as it regarded only the proportions or ratios of sounds, was applicable to no one system in

particular ; however it produced a discovery, which enabled him at once to supply a defect in even the improved system of Terpander, and lay a foundation for that more enlarged one, which is distinguished by his name, and has never since his time been capable of any substantial improvement. We are here to remember that the diapason or octave had been found to consist in duple proportion, or in the ratio of 12 to 6 ; and that the interval between the diatessaron twelve, nine, and that other eight, six, viz., nine, eight, was a complete tone, or sesquioctave ratio. Pythagoras, in consequence of this discovery recurring to the ancient septenary, found that its extremes were discordant, and that there wanted but little to produce that supremely sweet concord the diapason, which the means above had enabled him to investigate. Observing farther that in the septenary the interval between Mese and Paramese was but a hemitone, he immediately interposed between them a whole tone, and thereby completed the diapason.

It must be confessed that some authors have in general terms ascribed the addition of an eighth string to the heptachord lyre to others ; Boetius gives it to Licaon, and Pliny to Simonides ; but Nicomachus, from whom the following relation is taken, does most expressly attribute it to Pythagoras.

History has also transmitted to us the bare names of sundry persons, by whom at different times the strings of the lyre are said to have been encreased to eighteen in number ; as Theophrastus, who added a ninth ; Hestius, who added a tenth, and so on ;† but as to the ratio subsisting between them, or any system to which they could be said to be adapted, there is a total silence. Indeed we have the greatest reason to think that these additions were not made in any ratio whatever, but served only to increase the variety of sounds‡. That innovations were made in the heptachord is certain ; and when we are informed that Timotheus, for his presumption in adding to the strings of the ancient lyre, had a fine imposed on him by the magistracy, we may fairly conclude that those innovations tended rather to the corruption than the improvement of music.

But the case is different with respect to him of whom we are now speaking ; the system of Pythagoras had its foundation in nature : the improvement of an instrument was not his care ; he was a philosopher and a musician in the genuine sense of the word, and proposed nothing less than the establishment of a theory to which the practice of succeeding ages should be accommodated. His motives for attempting it, and in what manner he effected this great purpose, shall now be given in the words of his learned biographer :—

' Pythagoras, lest the middle sound by conjunction ' being compared to the two extremes, should render ' the diatessaron concent both to the Nete and ' the Hypate ; and that we might have a greater ' variety, the two extremes making the fullest con-' cord each to other, that is to say, a diapason, which

* Egli è cosa da restar confuso, e formare un cumulo di maraviglie, che questo sperimento, confermato da gravissimi autori, e tenuto tanti secoli per vero sia stato finalmente scoperto esser falso da Galileo Galilei, sicome riferisce ne' suoi Discorsi e Dimostrazioni Mathematiche, e Vincenzo Galilei nel discorso intorno all' opere del Zarlino afferma, che per ritrovare co' pesi attaccati alle corde le consonanze de Martelli ; per la diapason debbono costituirsi i pesi in quadrupla proportione ; per la diapente, in dupla sesquiquarta ; per la diatessaron, in sesqui 7 partiente 9 ; e pe'l tuono, in sesqui 7 partiente 64. E noi, spinti dalla curiosità messo in opera questo sperimento co' pesi de Martelli, habbiamo ritrovato che il primo ed il secondo 12, 9, partoriscono non la diatessaron : ma il triemituono ; il primo ed il terzo, 12, 8, non la diapente : ma il ditone ; il primo e'l quarto 12, 6, non la diapason ; ma il tritone ; il secondo e'l terzo 9, 8, non il tuono : ma l'hemituono rimesso o mancante ; il secondo e'l quarto 9, 6, non la diapente : ma il semiditono ; ed il terzo e'l quarto 8, 6, non la diatessaron : ma il tuono disteso overo eccedente, sicome la ottoposta figura dimostra. Bontempi, pa. 54.

Ptolemy observes, that it is extremely difficult to find chords perfectly equal in respect of crassitude, density, and other qualities that determine their several sounds ; and farther he says, that the same chord distended by the same weight,, will at different times yield different sounds. Ptolem. Harmonicor. lib. I. cap. 8. Ex vers. Wallis. Mersenn. Harm. universelle. Traité des Instrumens, Prop. iv. So that the success of experiments for investigating the consonances, by the means of weights hung to chords, must be very precarious, and is little to be depended on.

† Boetius de Musica, lib. ii., cap. 20. Vincen. Galilei, Dial. della Musica, pag. 116.

‡ Nicom. lib. ii. Boet. lib. i., cap. 20. Bont. pag. 71.

'consists in duple proportion, inserted an eighth
'sound between the Mese and the Paramese, placing
'it from the Mese a whole tone, and from the Para-
'mese a semitone ; so that what was formerly the
'Paramese in the heptachord, is still the third from
'the Nete, both in name and place ; but that now
'inserted is the fourth from the Nete, and hath a
concent to it of diatessaron, which before the Mese
had to the Hypate : but the tone between them,
that is the Mese, and the tone inserted, called the
'Paramese, instead of the former, to whichsoever
'tetrachord it be added, whether to that which is
'at the Hypate, being the lower, or to that of the
'Nete, being the higher, will render the concord of
'diapente ; which is either way a system, consisting
'both of the tetrachord itself, and of the additional
'tone : and as the diapente proportion, viz., sesqui-
'altera, is found to be a system of sesquitertia and
'sesquioctava, the tone therefore is sesquioctava.
'Thus the interval of four chords, and of five, and
'of both conjoined together, called diapason, with
'the tone inserted between the two tetrachords,
'completed the octochord."*

SYSTEM OF PYTHAGORAS.

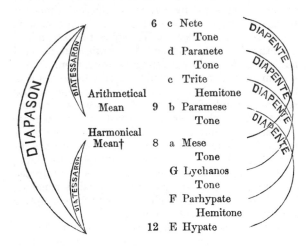

It remains now to enquire what this variation of
and addition to the septenary led to. Pythagoras
immediately after he had adjusted his system of the
octochord in the manner above related, transferred to
it the additions which had been made to that of Terpander ; and first he connected with it the tetrachord
hypaton, which carried the system down to B, and
placing at the other extremity the hyperboleon
tetrachord, he continued it up to a a, as is here
shewn.

---

* Stanl. Hist. of Philosophy, pag. 386, from Nicom. lib. i.

† The difference between the arithmetical and harmonical division of
the diapason is explained in a subsequent chapter. But as this division
is frequently occurring, it may not be improper here to remark in general
that the numbers 12, 9, 6, express the arithmetical, and 12, 8, 6, the
harmonical division.

GREAT SYSTEM OF PYTHAGORAS.

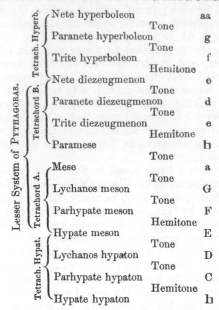

In consequence of the separation of the system of
the octochord above noted, we see that in the above
diagram the tetrachord B is separated from the
tetrachord A by a whole tone : this disunion of the
one diatessaron from the other, gave rise to the
epithet of Diezeugmenon or disjunct, whereby the
former of the two tetrachords is distinguished : we
are therefore now to look for the invention of that
other tetrachord, which hitherto has been represented
as part of a system, to which it could never with any
propriety be applied.

No one in the least acquainted with the principles
of harmony need be told, that that relation which
modern musicians denominate a Tritonus, can have
no place in any regular series of progression, either
ascending or descending ; for of the effects of sounds
produced at the same instant we are not now speaking : that such a relation immediately arose from the
separation of the Diezeugmenon and Meson tetrachords, will appear by observing that in the progression
upwards through the Meson tetrachord, beginning
at Parhypate Meson, and proceeding to Paramese,
that interval which should be a diatessaron, and consist of two tones and a hemitone, will contain three
tones, and have for its ultimate sound what in this
place is to be considered as an excessive fourth.‡
The consequence of this was, that the lower sound
could never be used as a fundamental ; and so far the
system must be said to have been imperfect. To
remedy this defect in part, collateral or auxiliary
tetrachord was with great ingenuity constituted, in
which the sounds followed in the order of hemitone,
tone, and tone, a succession which a true and perfect
diatessaron requires.

---

‡ Some writers have given the name of Tritonus to the defective fifth,
♭ f, for this reason, that it is an interval compounded of hemitone, tone,
tone, and hemitone, the sum whereof is three tones. But in this they
are mistaken, for the ratios of the tritonus or excessive fourth, and the
semidiapente or defective fifth are different, the one being 45 to 32, the
other 64 to 45. Vide Mersennus Harmonic, De Dissonantiis, pag. 75.
Holder on the natural Grounds and Principles of Harmony, pag. 128.

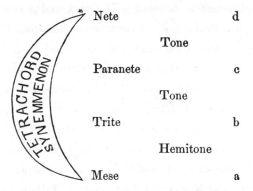

Nete	d
Tone	
Paranete	c
Tone	
Trite	b
Hemitone	
Mese	a

The intervals that compose this system will appear upon comparison to be precisely the same with those of the tetrachord B, in the conjunct system; whereas between the tetrachord B. in the disjunct system, and that at present under consideration, this difference is apparent; in the former the distance between a and b is a whole tone, in the latter it is a hemitone: if therefore this question should be asked, Wherein did the merit of the improvements made by Pythagoras to the ancient system consist? the answer would be, first, in the invention of the disjunct system, and the consequent completion of the octochord; next in the introduction of the octochord into the system of Terpander; and lastly, in such a disposition of the disjunct tetrachord as was yet consistent with the re-admission of that part of the system which it seems to exclude whenever the perfection of the harmony should require it. After what has been said it will be needless to add that this collateral tetrachord was distinguished by the epithet of Synemmenon or conjunct. With these improvements the Pythagorean system assumed the following form:—

ADDITION to the GREAT SYSTEM of PYTHAGORAS.

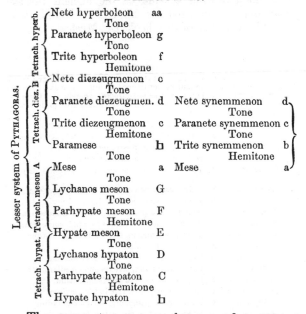

Nete hyperboleon	aa		
Tone			
Paranete hyperboleon	g		
Tono			
Trite hyperboleon	f		
Hemitone			
Nete diezeugmenon	c		
Tone			
Paranete diezeugmen.	d	Nete synemmenon	d
Tone		Tone	
Trite diezeugmenon	c	Paranete synemmenon	c
Hemitone		Tone	
Paramese	h	Trite synemmenon	b
Tone		Hemitone	
Mese	a	Mese	a
Tone			
Lychanos meson	G		
Tone			
Parhypate meson	F		
Hemitone			
Hypate meson	E		
Tone			
Lychanos hypaton	D		
Tono			
Parhypate hypaton	C		
Hemitone			
Hypate hypaton	h		

There were two reasons that seemed to suggest

a still farther improvement; the one was that by the separation of the Diezeugmenon and Meson tetrachords there followed an unequal division of the system; for, ascending from Mese to Nete Hyperboleon, the distance was a complete Octave; whereas descending to Hypate Hypaton it was only a Seventh: from hence arose another inconvenience, a false relation between Hypate Hypaton and Parhypate Meson, which though to appearance a fifth, was in truth an interval of only two tones and two hemitones, constituting together the very discordant relation of a defective fifth. To supply this defect nothing more was required than the addition of a tone at the lower extremity of the system. Pythagoras accordingly placed another chord at the distance of a tone below Hypate Hypaton, which he named Proslambanomenos, a word signifying additional or supernumerary, it not being includablc in the division of the system by tetrachords; and thus was completed that system of a Bisdiapason or double octave, which the Italians distinguished by the several appellations of Systema immutabile, Systema diatonico, Systema Pitagorico, and Systema massimo.

IMMUTABLE SYSTEM OF PYTHAGORAS.

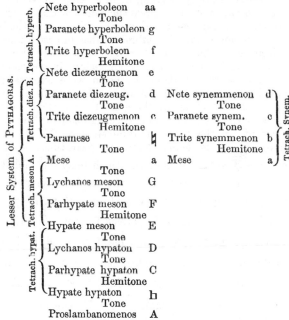

Nete hyperboleon	aa		
Tone			
Paranete hyperboleon	g		
Tone			
Trite hyperboleon	f		
Hemitone			
Nete diezeugmenon	e		
Tone			
Paranete diezeug.	d	Nete synemmenon	d
Tone		Tone	
Trite diezeugmenon	c	Parhypate synem.	c
Hemitone		Tone	
Paramese	♮	Trite synemmenon	b
Tone		Hemitone	
Mese	a	Mese	a
Tone			
Lychanos meson	G		
Tono			
Parhypate meson	F		
Hemitone			
Hypate meson	E		
Tone			
Lychanos hypaton	D		
Tone			
Parhypate hypaton	C		
Hemitone			
Hypate hypaton	h		
Tone			
Proslambanomenos	A		

Here it is to be observed, that although in this and the preceding scale the Synemmenon tetrachord is given at large, yet the generality of writers either insert it entire in its place, immediately above the Meson tetrachord. placing the Diezeugmenon tetrachord above it, as Kircher in his Musurgia, tom. I. lib. III. cap. xiii. or else following perhaps the example of Guido, whose reformation of the scale might suggest this latter method as the most concise, they have borrowed from the synemmenon tetrachord one only of its terms, Trite, and inserted it immediately after Mese, with Paramese next above it; thereby leaving it to the imagination to select which of the two sounds the nature of the progression might require; however, the better to explain its construction and use, it was here thought proper to exhibit the synemmenon tetrachord in that detached situation which seems most agreeable to its original formation.*

CHAP. IV.

But here it may very naturally be asked what were the marks or characters whereby the ancients expressed the different positions or powers of their musical sounds? An answer to this question may be produced from an author of undoubted credit, Boetius, and also Alypius, an ancient Greek, of whose writings we shall have occasion to speak more particularly, and these inform us that the only characters in use among the Greeks to denote the sounds in music, were the letters of their alphabet, a kind of Brachygraphy totally devoid of analogy or resemblance between the sign and the thing signified. Boetius de Musica, lib. IV., cap. iii., gives an account of the ancient method of notation in the following words:—'The ancient musicians, to avoid the 'necessity of always writing them at length, invented 'certain characters to express the names of the chords 'in their several genera and modes; this short method 'was the more eagerly embraced, that in case a mu'sician should be inclined to adapt music to any poem, 'he might, by means of these characters, in the same 'manner as the words of the poem were expressed 'by letters, express the music, and transmit it to 'posterity. Out of all these modes we shall only 'specify the Lydian.' This description of the sounds consisted in the different application of the Greek letters to each of them; Boetius proceeds thus:—'To express Proslambanomenos, which may be called 'Acquisitus, was used Z imperfect, and tau lying ⊢. 'Hypate hypaton, Γ reversed and Γ right ꓕΓ. 'Parhypate hypaton, B imperfect Γ supine, B/L. Hy'paton enarmonios, V supine and Γ reversed, having 'a stroke ʼ/V. Hypaton chromatice, V, having a line 'and Γ reversed, having two lines V/ꓕ. Hypaton dia'tonos, φ Greek, and digamma φ/F. Hypate meson C 'and C, C/C. Parhypate meson P and C supine P/C. 'Meson enarmonios, Π Greek and C reversed. Π/Ɔ. Me'son chromatice, Π having a stroke, and C reversed, 'having a stroke through the middle. Meson 'diatonos, M Greek and Π drawn open M/ꓶ. Mese, 'I and Λ lying, I/<. Trite synemmenon, Θ and Λ 'supine Θ/V. Synemmenon enarmonios, H Greek and 'Λ lying, with a stroke through the middle </H. 'Synemmenon chromatice, H Greek and Λ reversed 'with a stroke. Synemmenon diatonos, Γ and 'N N/Γ. Nete synemmenon, Ω supine and Z, ω/Z. Para'mese, Z and Γ Greek lying ⊏/Z. Trite diezeugmenon, 'E square and Γ supine E/L. Diezeugmenon enarmo'nios, Δ and Γ Greek lying reversed Λ/⊐. Diezeug'menon chromatice, Δ with a stroke, and Π Greek lying 'reversed with an angular line. Diezeugmenon 'diatonos, Ω square and Z, ω/Z. Nete diezeugmenon, φ 'lying and N inverted draw open Θ/N. Trite hyperbo'leon, Γ looking downwards to the right, and half Λ 'to the left L/\. Hyperboleon enarmonios, T supine 'and half A to the right supine. Hyperboleon 'chromatice, T supine, having a line and half A to the 'right supine, having a line drawn backward. 'Hyperboleon, diatonos M Greek having an acute, 'and Γ having an acute M′/ꓶ. Nete hyperboleon, I hav'ing an acute, and A lying having an acute also I′/>.†

Here it is to be remarked, that although the above passage of Boetius is given, not from any of the printed copies of his works, but from a very ancient manuscript, which Mr. Selden collated, and is prefixed to Meibomius's version of Alypius: there occur in it some instances of disagreement between the verbal description of the character and the character itself; some of these Meibomius in his notes has remarked, and others have escaped him; nevertheless it was not thought advisable to vary the representation which Boetius has given, and therefore the following scheme of the ancient musical characters is inserted, as he has delivered it in lib. IV. cap. iii. of his book De Musica.

* Mersenn. Harmon. lib. vi. De Generibus et Modis, pag. 100.

† Boetius as he goes along gives the Latin signification of the Greek names, which it was thought proper to omit in order to make room for an extract from Kircher to the same purpose, wherein the Latin are opposed to the Greek names in the order in which they arise in the several tetrachords:—

	aa	Nete hyperboleon, sive ultima acutarum.
Tetrachordon	g	Paranete hyperboleon, sive secunda acutarum.
Neton	f	Trite hyperboleon, sive tertia acutarum.
	e	Nete, sive ultima disjunctarum.
Tetrachordon	d	Paranete diezeugmenon, sive secunda disjunctarum.
Diezeugm.	c	Trite diezeugmenon, sive tertia disjunctarum.
	b	Paramese, sive vicina mediis.
Tetrachordon	d	Nete synemmenon, sive ultima conjunctarum.
Synemmen.	c	Paranete synemmenon, sive secunda conjunctarum.
	b	Trite synemmenon, sive tertia conjunctarum.
	a	Mese, id est media.
Tetrachordon	G	Lychanos meson, sive index mediarum.
Meson	F	Parhypate meson, sive secunda mediarum.
	E	Hypate meson, sive gravis mediarum.
Tetrachordon	D	Lychanos hypaton, sive index gravium.
Hypaton	C	Parhypate hypaton, sive secunda gravium
	B	Hypate hypaton, sive gravis gravium.
	A	Proslambanomenos, sive vox assumpta.

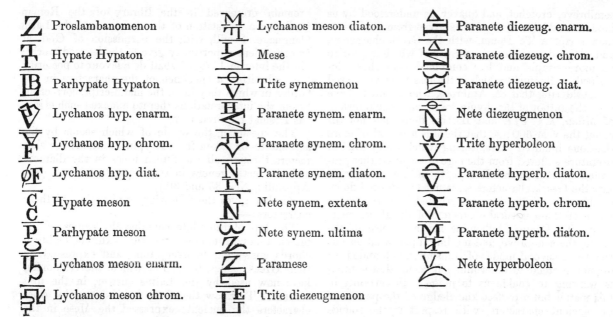

Proslambanomenon	Lychanos meson diaton.	Paranete diezeug. enarm.
Hypate Hypaton	Mese	Paranete diezeug. chrom.
Parhypate Hypaton	Trite synemmenon	Paranete diezeug. diat.
Lychanos hyp. enarm.	Paranete synem. enarm.	Nete diezeugmenon
Lychanos hyp. chrom.	Paranete synem. chrom.	Trite hyperboleon
Lychanos hyp. diat.	Paranete synem. diaton.	Paranete hyperb. diaton.
Hypate meson	Nete synem. extenta	Paranete hyperb. chrom.
Parhypate meson	Nete synem. ultima	Paranete hyperb. diaton.
Lychanos meson enarm.	Paramese	Nete hyperboleon
Lychanos meson chrom.	Trite diezeugmenon	

There is this remarkable difference between the method of notation practised by the ancients, and that now in use, that the characters used by the former were arbitrary, totally destitute of analogy, and no way expressive of those essential properties of sound, gravity and acuteness; which is the more to be wondered at, seeing that in the writings of the ancients the terms Acumen and Gravitas are perpetually occuring, whereas the modern scale is so adjusted, that those sounds, which in their own nature are comparatively grave or acute, have such a situation in it, as does most precisely distinguish them according to their several degrees of each; so that the graver sounds have the lowest, and the acuter the highest place in our scale. But here it may be asked, does this distinction of high and low properly belong to sound, or do we not borrow those epithets from the scale in which we see them so posited? It should seem that we do not; for if we attend to the formation of sounds by the animal organs, we shall find that the more grave are produced from the lower part of the larynx, as the more acute are from the higher; so that the difference between the one and the other seems to be more than ideal, and to have its foundation in nature: the modern musicians seem however to pay a greater regard to this diversity than is either requisite or proper; for where is the necessity that in a vocal composition such a sentiment as this, ' They that go down to the sea in ships,' &c. should be expressed by such sounds, as for the degree of gravity few voices can reach? much less can we see the reasonableness of that precept which directs that the words Hell, Heaven, are invariably to be expressed, the one by a very grave, and the other by a very acute sound. Those who affect to be severely critical on the compositions of this later age, allow no greater merit to this sort of analogy than is due to a pun, and their censure seems to be no more than the error will warrant.

The description above given of the ancient musical characters, is derived, through Boetius, from Alypius, the most copious and intelligible of all the Greek writers on this branch of music: his authority, so far as it goes, has been implicitly acquiesced in; and indeed from his testimony there can lye no appeal. The reader will naturally expect to be informed of the method by which the ancients denoted the different degrees in the length or duration of their musical sounds; but it seems they were strangers to music merely instrumental: the lyre, and other instruments in use among them, was applied in aid of the voice; and the ode, or hymn, or pean, or whatever else the musician sang, determined by its measure, and the feet of the verse the length of the sound adapted to it, and took away the necessity for such marks or characters of distinction in this respect as are used by the moderns. Nor need we any farther proof of this assertion, than the absolute silence of the Greek writers as to any method of denoting what we now understand by the Time or measure of sounds. It is true that those among the learned who have undertaken a translation of some few remaining fragments of ancient music into modern notes, have, in particular instances, ventured to render the characters in the original by notes of different lengths; but it is to be presumed they were determined so to do rather by the cadence of the verse, than by any rythmical designation observable in any of those characters. Mr. Chilmead, the publisher of the Oxford edition of Aratus, and of Eratosthenes de Astris, in octavo, 1672, has given at the end of it three hymns or odes of a Greek poet named Dionysius, with the ancient musical characters, which he has rendered by semibreves only; but Kircher, in his Musurgia, tom. I. pag. 541. from a manuscript in the library of the monastery of St. Salvator, near the gate of Messina, in Sicily, has inserted an ancient fragment of Pindar, with the musical notes, which he has explained by the different signs of a breve, semibreve, crotchet, and quaver, as understood by us moderns. Meibomius also has given from an ancient manuscript a Te Deum, with the Greek characters, and in modern notes, the former of which appear to be more simple and less combined than those described by Boetius; which is the less to be wondered at considering that St. Ambrose, who is said to have been the author of that hymn,* was consecrated bishop of Milan, A. C. 374, and Boetius flourished not till about the year 500; so that there is a period of more than one hundred years, during which every kind of literature suffered from the rage of conquest that prevailed throughout all Europe, to induce a suspicion that the Greek characters were not transmitted down to the time of Boetius uncorrupted. In the translation of these musical characters of the above-mentioned Te Deum, Meibomius has made use of the breve, the semibreve, and minim : upon what authority those several modes of translation is founded we do not pretend to determine; it seems that nothing is wanting to enable us to judge with certainty in this matter but a perfect knowledge of the powers of the ancient characters, with respect to the sounds which they were intended to signify; and concerning these Kircher seems to have entertained no kind of doubt : he had access to two manuscripts of great antiquity, and his judgment of their authority, and the use that may be made of them, he has given in the following words :—' The ancient musical ' characters were no way similar to those of the ' moderns; for they were certain letters, not indeed ' the pure Greek ones, but those sometimes right, ' sometimes inverted, and at others mutilated and ' compounded in various manners, each of which ' characters answered to one of the chords in the ' musical system. I laid my hands on two manu- ' scripts, which by God's mercy, were preserved ' from the injuries of time, the one in the Vatican ' library, the other in ours of the Roman college : ' the author is Alypius; he, in order to give the ' harmonical characters of the ancients in great per- ' fection, has exhibited with wonderful care every ' tone in the Octodecachord, according to the different ' genera. He keeps a twofold order in these several ' characters; the first as they were used in the Can- ' tus; the second as adapted to instruments, differing ' from the former almost after the same manner as at ' this day the notes of vocal music do from those ' characters called by us the Tablature, which are ' used only in instrumental music. Several writers, ' not understanding this order of Alypius, have con- ' sidered this twofold series as a single one : among ' these are Liardus, and Solomon de Caux, who has ' followed him, both of whom have given to the ' world most false and corrupted specimens of ancient ' music. Alypius wrote an entire volume on the ' musical characters or notes, which, together with ' other manuscripts of the old Greek musicians,

' remain preserved in the library of the Roman ' college; a translation of this volume into the Latin ' language, I will, with the permission of God, at ' a convenient opportunity give to the learned world; ' in the interim I trust I shall do a favour to posterity ' by exhibiting a specimen of the characters in the ' order in which they lie in the manuscript, correcting ' from the interpretations thereto annexed such errors ' as I found required it.'†

The specimen, the whole of which seems by his account to be taken from Alypius, contains the characters through all the fifteen tones in the diatonic and chromatic genera in two separate tables. (See Appendix, Nos. 35 and 36.)

Kircher gives the following explanation of these characters :—

The top of the plate contains the names of the fifteen tones or modes : the side exhibits eighteen chords, answering to every tone, and expressed by their Greek names, to each of which, the Guidonian keys now used by the Latins answer, in the first column. To know therefore, for instance, by what characters the ancients expressed the Mese in the Phrygian tone, we must look in the side for the chord Mese, and on the top for Tonus Phrygius, and where they meet we shall find the character sought for, and so for the rest.

Having exhibited this key to the ancient characters, Kircher gives the fragment of Pindar above-mentioned in the Greek notes, and also in those of the modern scale, as is represented. (See Appendix, No. 37.)

And the tables (35 and 36) given from him seem to have been his authority for rendering the ancient characters in modern notes, as shewn in 37. By way of illustration he adds, that the Chorus vocalis contains the characters written over each word; and that the Chorus instrumentalis, which is nothing else but the antistrophe to the former, was played according to the strophe, on the cythara or the pipe. As the characters agree with those of Alypius, he says he has no doubt about their meaning; and as to the time, he is clear that it was given by the measures of the syllables, and not by the characters.

The several variations of the system of music have been traced with as much accuracy as the nature of the subject will allow of : the improvements made by Terpander and others, more especially Pythagoras, have been distinctly enumerated, we are therefore now to proceed in our narration.

Pythagoras having, as has been related, investigated the proportion of sounds, and extended the narrow limits of the ancient system, and also demonstrated, not merely the affinity of sounds, but that a harmony, analogous to that of music, was to be found in other subjects wherein number and proportion were concerned; and that the coincidences of sounds were

---

* The Te Deum is commonly styled the Song of St. Ambrose, and it is said that it was composed jointly by him and St. Augustine, upon occasion of the baptism of the latter by St. Ambrose. Alliance of Divine Offices, by Hamon L'Estrange, folio, 1690, pag. 79. But archbishop Usher ascribes it to Nicetius, and supposes it not to have been composed till about the year 500, which was long after the time of Ambrose and Augustine. Ibid.

† It seems by this that Alypius had not been published in Kircher's time; and though he here promises to give the world a translation of it, there is no other extant than that very correct one of Meibomius. Kircher expresses a confidence that by publishing these characters he should confer an obligation on the learned world, but the manner in which he has done it, furnished a ground of censure to Meibomius, which he delivers in very bitter terms in the preface to his edition of the Greek writers.

a physical demonstration of those proportions which arithmetic and the higher geometry had till then enabled mankind only to speculate, it followed that music from thenceforth became a subject of philosophical contemplation. Aristotle, by several passages in his writings now extant, appears to have considered it in this view : it is even said that he wrote a treatise professedly on the subject of music, but that it is now lost.

Fabricius has given a catalogue of sundry writers, as namely, Jades, Lasus Hermionensis, Mintanor, Diocles, Hagiopolites, Agatho, and many others, whose works are lost; and in the writings of Aristoxenus, Nicomachus, Ptolemy, Porphyry, Manuel Bryennius, and other ancient authors, we meet with the names of Philolaus, Eratosthenes, Archytas of Tarentum, and Didymus of Alexandria, who seem mostly to have been philosophers; but as they are also enumerated among the scriptores perditi, nothing can be said about them. In those early times the principles of learning were very slowly disseminated among mankind, and it does not appear, that from the time of Pythagoras, to that of Aristoxenus, which included a period of near three hundred years, the music of the ancients underwent any very considerable alteration, unless we except that new arrangement and subdivision of the parts of the great system, which constituted the Genera, and those dissimilar progressions from every sound to its diapason, which are distinguished by the name of Modes. Of these it is necessary now to speak; and first of the Genera.

Till the time of Pythagoras, the progression of sounds was in that order, which as well the modern as the ancient writers term the diatonic, as proceding by tones, a progression from the unison to its fourth by two tones and a hemitone, which we should now express by the syllables DO, RE, MI, FA, confessedly very natural and extremely grateful to the ear; though it seems not so much so as to hinder succeeding musicians from seeking after other kinds of progression; and accordingly by a different division of the integral parts of each of the tetrachords, they formed another series of progression, to which, from the flexibility of its nature, they gave the epithet of Chromatic, from Chroma, a word signifying colour; and to this they added another, which was termed enharmonic; besides this they invented a subvariation of each progression, and to distinguish the one from the other, they made use of the common logical term genus, by which we are to understand, as Kircher tells us, tom. I. lib. III. cap. xiii. a certain constitution of those sounds that compose a diatessaron, or musical fourth; or, in other words, a certain relation which the four chords of any given tetrachord bear to each other. The Genera are elsewhere defined, certain kinds of modulation arising from the different disposition of the sounds in a tetrachord: every Cantus or composition, says Aristoxenus,* is either Diatonic, Chromatic, or Enharmonic; or it may be mixed, and include a community of the genera. Aristoxenus, for aught now discoverable,

is the first that has written professedly, though obscurely, on this part of music. Ptolemy, as he is in general the most accurate and methodical of all the ancient writers, so is he more copious in his explanation of the Genera. Nicomachus has mentioned them, but in a very superficial manner; and as to the latter authors, we are not to wonder if they have contented themselves with the bare enumeration of them; since before the times in which the greater number of them wrote, the Diatonic was the only one of the three genera in common use. Nor does it any where appear, that even of the five Species, into which that Genus was divided, any more than one, namely, the syntonous or intense of Ptolemy, was in general estimation. It must be confessed that no part of the musical science has so much divided the writers on it as this of the genera; Ptolemy has exhibited no fewer than five different systems of generical harmony, and, after all, the doctrine on this subject is almost inscrutable : however, the substance of what these and other authors have related concerning the nature of it, is here, as in its proper place, referred to the consideration of such as are desirous to know the essential difference between the music of this and the more early ages.

But before this doctrine of the Genera can be rendered to any degree intelligible, it is necessary to observe, that hitherto we have spoken only of the more common and obvious musical intervals, the tone and hemitone; for the system of Pythagoras is formed of these only; and a more minute division of it was not till after his time thought on, nevertheless it is to be noted, that in order to the completion of his system, it was found requisite to institute a method of calculation that should as it were resolve the intervals into their elements, and adjust the ratios of such sounds as were not determinable by the division of a chord in the manner herein beforementioned. That division was sufficient, and it answered to the greatest degree of mathematic exactness for ascertaining the ratios of the diatessaron, the diapente, and the tone : and, agreeable to what has been already laid down concerning the investigation of the consonances by Pythagoras, it will most evidently appear upon experiment, that if a chord be divided into twelve equal parts, six of those parts will give an octave to that sound which would have been produced by the same chord, if struck before such division; from whence it appears, that the ratio subsisting between the unison and its octave is duple : again, that eight parts of the twelve will give a diatessaron, which bears to the unison six a ratio of 4 to 3; and that nine parts, according to the same division; will produce the diapente, which bears to the unison six a ratio of 3 to 2; and lastly, that the sound produced at the ninth part will be distant from that at the eighth, and so reciprocally; a tone, in the ratio of 9 to 8, called a Sesquioctave, and often the Diezeuctic tone, which furnished the ear at least with a common measure for the greater intervals.

But we are to note, that the system of Pythagoras was not completed, till, by the very artful contrivance

* Lib. II. pag. 44. ex Vers. Meibom.

of two tetrachords, to be used alternately, as the nature of the melody might require, a division of the tone between a and ♮ was effected. By this an interval of a Hemitone was introduced into the system, with which no one section of the chord, supposing it to be divided into twelve parts, would by any means coincide: with great ingenuity therefore did Euclid invent that famous division the Sectio Canonis, by means whereof not only the positions of the several sounds on a supposed chord are precisely ascertained, but a method is suggested for bringing out those larger numbers, which alone can shew the ratios of the smaller intervals, and which therefore make a part of every representation that succeeding writers have given of the immutable system.

The Sectio Canonis of Euclid is a kind of appendix to his Isagoge, or Introductio Harmonica, containing twenty theorems in harmonics. Nevertheless the title of Sectio Canonis was by him given to the following scheme of a supposed chord, divided for the purpose of demonstrating the ratios of the several intervals thereby discriminated, which scheme is inserted at the end of his work.

SECTIO CANONIS OF EUCLID.

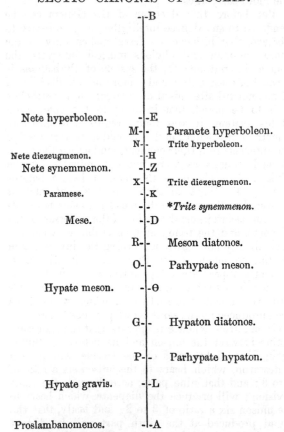

Nete hyperboleon.	‑E
M‑	Paranete hyperboleon.
N‑	Trite hyperboleon.
Nete diezeugmenon.	‑H
Nete synemmenon.	‑Z
X‑	Trite diezeugmenon.
Paramese.	‑K
	Trite synemmenon.
Mese.	‑D
R‑	Meson diatonos.
O‑	Parhypate meson.
Hypate meson.	‑Θ
G‑	Hypaton diatonos.
P‑	Parhypate hypaton.
Hypate gravis.	‑L
Proslambanomenos.	‑A

The foregoing canon or scheme of a division is introduced by a series of theorems, preparatory to an explanation of it, which explanation is contained in Theorems XIX and XX; the first of these refers to the immoveable sounds, that is to say, Proslambanomenos, and the other sounds to the left of the line,

and the latter to the moveable, which are Parhypate, and the rest on the right thereof; the sum of which two species composed the great or immutable system.

Theorem XIX directs the adjustment of the canon for the Stabiles or immoveable sounds, and that in the manner following:—

'Let the length of the canon be A B, and let it be 'divided into four equal parts at G D E, therefore 'B A, as it will be the gravest sound, will be the 'sonus bombus. Farther, A B is supertertius of G B, 'therefore G B will sound a diatessaron to A B, 'towards the acumen, and A B is Proslambanomenos; 'wherefore G B will be Hypaton Diatonos. Again, 'because A B is duple of B D, the former will sound 'a diapason to the latter, and B D will be Mese. 'Again, because A B is quadruple of E B, E B will 'be Nete Hyperboleon; therefore G B is divided 'twofold in Z, and G B will be duple of Z B, so as 'G B will sound to Z B the interval of a diapason, 'wherefore Z B is Nete Synemmenon. Cut off from 'D B a third part D H, and D B will be sesquialtera 'to H B, so as for this reason D B will sound to H B 'the interval of a diapente, therefore H B will be 'Nete diezeugmenon. Farther, make H Θ equal to 'H B, therefore Θ B will sound a diapason to H B, 'so that Θ B will be Hypate meson. Again, take the 'third part of Θ B, Θ K, and then Θ B will be 'sesquialtera to K B, so that K B will be Paramese. 'Lastly, cut off L K equal to K B, and then L B will 'be Hypate the most grave, and thus all the immove- 'able sounds will be taken in the canon.'

Theorem XX contains the following directions respecting the Mobiles or moveable sounds:—

'Divide E B into eight parts, of which make E M 'equal to one, so as M B may be superoctave of E B. 'And again, divide M B into eight equal parts, and 'make one of them equal to N M, therefore N B will 'be a tone more grave than B M, and M B will be a 'tone graver than B E; so as N B will be Trite 'hyperboleon, and M B will be Paranete hyperboleon 'diatonos. Farther, divide N B into three parts, and 'make N X equal to one of them, so as X B will be 'supertertius of N B, and the diatessaron will be pro- 'duced towards the grave, and X B will be Trite 'diezeugmenon. Again, taking half of X B, make X O 'equal to it, so as for this reason O B will give a 'diapente to X B, wherefore O B will be Parhypate 'meson; then make O P equal to O B,* so as P B 'will be Parhypate hypaton. Lastly, take the fourth 'part of G B, G R, and R B will be Meson diatonos.'

CHAP. V.

The Sectio Canonis of Euclid, in the judgment of the most eminent writers on harmonics, was the first essay towards a determination of the ratios by the supposed division of a chord; and, assuming the proportions of the diapason, diapente, diatessaron,

* In the Canon O P is not equal to O B but to O X, and Meibomius, with all his care, has made a mistake, which the following page, to go no farther, furnishes the means of rectifying; for observe, that in the Canon of Aristides Quintilianus, which has the numbers to it, Trite diezeug- menon, marked X in that of Euclid, is 3888, and Parhypate hypaton marked P in that of Euclid also, is 7776, which is just double the former number, the consequence whereof is evident.

diezeuctic tone, and limma, as laid down by the Pythagoreans, the division will be found to answer to the ratios: yet this does not appear by a bare inspection, but can only be proved by an actual admeasurement of the several intervals contained in the canon. Now as whatever is geometrically divisible, is also divisible by numbers, succeeding writers in assigning the ratios of the intervals have taken the aid of the latter, and have applied the numbers to each of the sounds, as they result from a division of the canon. How they are brought out will hereafter be made appear.

But here it is necessary to add, that the Sectio Canonis of Euclid, perfect in its kind as it may seem, is supposed to have received some improvement from Aristides Quintilianus, at least with respect to the manner of dividing it; for this we have the testimony of Meibomius, who speaks of a canon of Aristides, which had been once extant, but was perished, or at least was wanting in all the copies of his work: and which he his editor had happily restored. The following is a representation of the Canon, with the numbers annexed:—

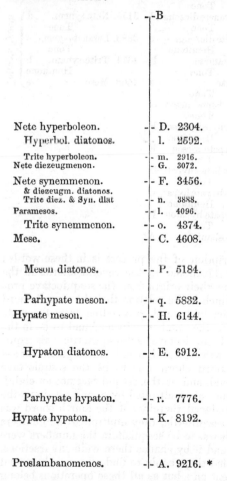

	-B	
Nete hyperboleon.	D.	2304.
Hyperbol. diatonos.	l.	2592.
Trite hyperboleon.	m.	2916.
Nete diezeugmenon.	G.	3072.
Nete synemmenon.	F.	3456.
& diezeugm. diatonos.		
Trite diez. & Syn. diat	n.	3888.
Paramesos.	l.	4096.
Trite synemmenon.	o.	4374.
Mese.	C.	4608.
Meson diatonos.	P.	5184.
Parhypate meson.	q.	5832.
Hypate meson.	H.	6144.
Hypaton diatonos.	E.	6912.
Parhypate hypaton.	r.	7776.
Hypate hypaton.	K.	8192.
Proslambanomenos.	A.	9216. *

It does not appear whether the numbers were originally part of the canon, or whether they were inserted by Meibomius. However, from several passages in Ptolemy, particularly in Book I. Chap. 10, where he demonstrates the ratio of the limma, we meet with the number 2048, which is the half of 4096, 1944, the half of 3888, and others, which shew the antiquity of this method of numerical division.

The following is an explanation of the canon as given by Meibomius, in his notes on Aristides Quintilianus, page 312, et seq.;—

'The standing sounds are first set down in the 'division of the canon, and after them the moveable 'ones; we have marked the standing sounds by 'capital letters, and to these are added the moveable 'ones. The Hypaton diatonos and the rest are 'marked by the small letters. They are thus to be 'taken:—

'I. Proslambanomenos, A B, which is the whole 'length of the chord or line.

'II. Mese, C B, half thereof.

'III. Nete hyperboleon, D B, the fourth part of 'the whole chord.

'IV. Hypaton diatonos, E B, three fourths thereof.

'V. Nete synemmenon, F B, the said three fourths, 'E B, divided into two equal parts.

'VI. Nete diezeugmenon, G B, two thirds of half 'the chord, that is one third of the whole chord; 'but this may be perceived by multiplying an half 'by two thirds, thus, $\frac{1}{2}$ $\frac{2}{3}$ | $\frac{1}{3}$.

'VII. Hypate meson, H B, two thirds of the whole 'chord, or the two thirds, G B, of the half chord 'twice set off, which chord therefore we take in the 'opening of the dividers, and set off twice.

'VIII. Paramesos, I B, (one third I H, being 'taken out of the two thirds H B of the whole chord) 'is two thirds of two thirds of the whole.

'IX. Pypate hypaton, K B; two thirds I B of the 'two thirds H B twice set off.

'In order to assume the lesser intervals, the fol'lowing method must be made use of:—

'I. The 4th part D B of the whole chord being 'divided into eight equal parts, I set off l below 'D equal to one of those parts, and l B will be 'Paranete hyperboleon.

'II. Trite hyperboleon m B is assumed in the 'same manner, viz., by dividing the line l B into 'eight equal parts, and taking l m equal to one of 'them out of l A.

'III. Trite diezeugmenon, and the following 'moveable sounds, are easily to be assumed in the 'same manner.'

Besides the foregoing explanation of the canon, Meibomius has given the following, which he calls a

---

* The division of Euclid agrees with that of Aristides as to the manner of obtaining the standing, but differs as to some of the moveable chords, for Euclid finds the Trite diezeugmenon, by setting off towards the grave a diatessaron from the Trite hyperboleon; he next finds the Parhypate meson, by setting off towards the grave a diapente from the Trite diezeugmenon, which might be easier found by setting down a diapason from the Trite hyperboleon. He also finds the Parhypate hypaton by making O P equal to O X, that is by setting off a diapason towards the grave from the Trite diezeugmenon, for he had made O X equal to half X B, and consequently twice O X O P must be equal to X B. And lastly, he finds the Meson diatonos by setting off a diatessaron towards the acute from the Hypaton diatonos, whereas all the four sounds, as well as the other moveable ones, are found in Aristides, by a division into eight parts, that is by setting off sesquioctave tones. It seems, however, upon the whole, that Aristides followed the division of Euclid, but neither of these can answer to the Aristoxenian principles, for this reason, that the Sectio Canonis both of Euclid and Aristides refer to those arithmetic and harmonic ratios, which are discernable in the proportions of Pythagoras, whereas Aristoxenus rejected the criterion of ratios, and maintained that the measure of intervals was determinable by the sense of hearing only.

Notable Theorem, and says of it that it is very useful in facilitating the section of the canon.

'The difference between two lines that are to each 'other in a sesquitertia ratio, being divided into two 'equally, will give the eighth part of the greater line.

'A B is sesquitertia to D E; C B is the excess of 'A B above D E, C B divided into two equally will 'exhibit the eighth part of A B.

'We shall see the same in the section of our canon. 'Let the line G B be divided into eight equal parts, 'I say the part G D thereof will contain two eighth 'parts; so that this need only be divided into two 'equally, as appears by this following demonstration; 'for as G B is sesquitertia to D B, that is as 4 to 3, 'if G B be divided into twice four parts, that is 'eighths, D B will contain six of those eighths, and 'consequently D G two eighths, and its half will 'contain one eighth. Also if F B is to be divided 'into eight equal parts, its part F l need be divided 'only into two equally, in order to have one eighth 'part, which I set off from F to n, to find the excess 'of the tone above F B. The same method may be 'used in the following ones.

'Moreover, the Meson diatonos, and the other two 'moveable chords may also be obtained by the follow-'ing method, namely, Meson diatonos, by setting off 'the part l B, twice from B; Parhypate meson, by 'setting off the part m B, twice; Parhypate hypaton, 'by setting off the part n B, twice.

'But whatsoever is here shown in lines may, by 'the ingenuity of the intelligent reader, be easily 'applied in finding out the numbers.'

The canon of Aristides Quintilianus, with the numbers affixed, supposes the whole chord to contain 9216 parts, and being struck open, to produce the most grave sound of the system, viz., A; the interval then of a tone at ♮, the next sound in succession, as being in the proportion of 8 to 9 to A, will require that the chord be stopped at 8192; and, supposing it to answer, we may with the utmost propriety say, that the ratio of a tone is as 9216 is to 8192, or in other words, that ♮ is produced at 8192 of those parts whereof the chord A contains 9216; and these two numbers will be found to bear the same proportion to each other as those of 9 and 8. Again, for the diapason a, the number is 4608, which is just the half of 9216, as 6 is the half of 12; for the diatessaron D, the number is 6912, which is three fourths of 9216; and for the diapente E, the number is 6144, which is two thirds of 9216. Hence it appears that the numbers thus taken for the tone, or for the consonances of the diatessaron, and the diapente, or their replicates, as often as it may be thought necessary by the reiteration of an octave, or any less system, to extend that of the bisdiapason, answer in like manner to the ratios of 9 to 8, 6 to 12, 12 to 9, and 12 to 8, in the primitive system.

These proportions we are told will be the result of an actual division of a string, which whoever is desirous of making the experiment, is hereby enabled to try; though, by the way, it is said by Meibomius that for this purpose one of two ells in length will be found necessary. Nevertheless, by the help of the principles already laid down, namely, that the diapason has a ratio of 2 to 1, the diapente of 3 to 2, the diatessaron of 4 to 3, and the tone of 9 to 8, which are to be considered as data that all harmonical writers agree in, it is very easy, by means of arithmetic alone, to bring out the numbers corresponding to the intervals, in the diatonic bisdiapason. Bontempi has given a very particular relation of the process in an account of the method taken by the ancients for that purpose; and immediately after, an exhibition of that system with the proper numbers in the following scale:—

Tetrach. hyperb.	2304. Nete hyperb.	aa			
	Tone				
	2592. Paranete hyperb.	g			
	Tone				
	2916. Trite hyperb.	f			
	Hemitone				
Tetrach. diez.	3072. Nete diezeug.	e			
	Tone				
	3456. Paranete diezeug.	d	3456. Nete synem.	d	
	Tone		Tone		
	3888. Trite diezeug.	c	3888. Paranete synem.	c	
	Hemitone		Tone		Tetrach. Synem.
	4096. Paramese	♮	4374. Trite synem.	b	
	Tone		Hemitone		
Tetrach. meson.	4608. Mese	a	4608. Mese	a	
	Tone				
	5184. Lychanos meson	G			
	Tone				
	5832. Parhypate meson	F			
	Hemitone				
Tetrach. hypat.	6144. Hypate meson	E			
	Tone				
	6912. Lychanos hypat.	D			
	Tone				
	7776. Parhypate hypat.	C			
	Hemitone				
	8192. Hypate hypaton	♮			
	Tone				
	9216. Proslambano.	A*			

His description of the process is in these words: 'The numbers affixed to the several chords in the 'system draw their origin from the sesquioctave pro-'portion, which is the relation that the second chord 'bears to the first; and, proceeding from the acute 'to the grave, the numbers will be found to be in the 'ratio of subsesquioctave, subsesquitertia, subsesqui-'altera, and subduple. But to be more particular:—

'As the third chord was to be the sesquioctave 'of the second, and as the second had not an eighth 'part, the ancients multiplied by 8, and set down the 'number produced thereby: if the fourth chord was 'to be the sesquitertia, they multiplied the numbers 'by 3; If it was to be sesquialtera the numbers were 'doubled; and if by chance there were any fractions, 'they doubled them again to find even numbers, and 'so they went on: but as all these operations belong 'to arithmetic, and of course must be known, there 'is no necessity to explain them farther.

'However, as all this is different from any practice

* Bontemp. 97.

'in the modern music, in order that those who are not
'perfectly versed in arithmetic may understand the
'foundation of this science, it will be amiss here to
'explain it. You must then know, that as harmonic
'music was subordinate to arithmetic, the ancients
'shewed only the intervals by numbers arising from
'the measures they had found out by experiments
'upon the monochord.

'When they wanted therefore to demonstrate in
'the constitution of the system what chord was either
'double, or sesquialtera, or sesquitertia, or sesqui-
'octave to another by arithmetical numbers, they
'used multiplication, or the doubling of the numbers,
'in order that they might rise by degrees one above
'the other. They began from the most acute chord,
'which is the Nete hyperboleon, going on as far as
'the Trite synemmenon; which operation is demon-
'strated by the following columns of numbers :—

	1	2	3	4	5	6
aa	8	64	192	576	1152	2304
g	9	72	216	648	1296	2592
f		81	243	729	1458	2916
e			256	768	1536	3072
d			288	864	1728	3456
c			324	972	1944	3888
♮				1024	2048	4096
b					2187	4374*

'The method which they used in these multipli-
'cations and reduplications was this; as g was to be
'sesquioctave of aa, and f sesquioctave of g; and as
'g had not an eighth part, to find it they multiplied
'aa and g by 8; from which multiplication the
'numbers of the second order were produced, and
'they put down 81 sesquioctave of 72. As e was to
'be sesquitertia of aa, and had not a third part, they
'multiplied all the second order by 3; from which
'multiplication was produced the third order, and
'there came out the number 256, sesquitertia of 192;
'in like manner d was found to be sesquitertia of g,
'and c of f.

'As ♮ was to be sesquitertia of e, and had not a
'third part, they multiplied all the third order by 3,
'from which was produced the fourth order, and
'there came out 1024, sesquitertia of 768; as b was
'to be sesquialtera of f, there came out fractions, to
'avoid which all the fourth order was doubled, and
'so the fifth order was produced; and there was the
'number 2187, sesquialtera of 1458.

'In a word, give me leave to repeat again this
'operation, with common explications for those who
'are quite unacquainted with the rules of arithmetic;
'by multiplying eight times 8 they had 64 for aa;
'by multiplying nine times 8 they had 72 for g; and
'adding to 72 the number nine, they had 81 for f.

'The sesquitertia, which is nothing but the pro-
'portion 4 to 3, constituting the diatessaron from e
'to aa, was produced by giving to aa three times 64,
'which made 192, and to e four times 64, which made
'256.

'That of d to g was produced by giving to g three
'times the number 72, which made 216; and to d
'four times the same, which made 288.

'That of c to f was produced by giving to g three
'times 81, which made 243; and to c four times the
'same, which made 324.

'That of ♮ to e was produced by giving to e three
'times 256, which made 768; and to ♮ four times
'the same, which made 1024.

'The sesquialtera, which is nothing but the pro-
'portion 3 to 2, constituting the diapente from b to f,
'was produced by giving to f twice 729, which made
'1458; and to b three times the same, which made
'2187.

'Finally, in order that this kind of numbers might
'do for the chords of the chromatic and enharmonic
'genera; to avoid fractions they doubled all the fifth
'order, and thereby brought out the sixth; so that
'the second order is the produce of the first multi-
'plied by 8; the third order is the produce of the
'second multiplied by 3; the fourth order is the
'produce of the third multiplied by 3; the fifth
'order is double the fourth, and the sixth double
'the fifth; and the numbers of the sixth order are
'the same as those of the tetrachords Hyperboleon,
'Diezeugmenon, and Synemmenon, in the foregoing
'scale.

'There is besides these the Mese, the number of
'which is 4608, which is the double of 2304, the
'number of the Nete hyperboleon, because there is
'between the one and the other chord the interval of
'a diapason.

'The number 5184 of the Lychanos meson is twice
'the number 2592 of the Paranete hyperboleon, be-
'cause there is between them the same interval of
'the diapason; and so the following numbers towards
'the grave are double to the numbers belonging to
'the acute chords, following from the Paranete hyper-
'boleon in succession; because there is between them
'all, in their respective degrees, the usual interval of
'the diapason. As the sounds of the diatonic genus
'have their numbers, so likewise have the sounds of
'the other genera numbers, which are peculiar to
'them, except the Nete hyperboleon, the Nete die-
'zeugmenon, the Nete synemmenon, the Paramese,
'the Mese, the Hypate meson, the Hypate hypaton,
'and the Proslambanomenos, whose numbers are
'common to all the genera, as their sounds are
'fixed. Every thing relating to them may be seen
'in their respective systems.'

It is to be remembered, that it was for the purpose
of explaining the doctrine of the genera that the foregoing enquiry into the proportions of the intervals
was entered into; this enquiry respected the diatonic
series only, and the proportions thereby ascertained
are the diapason, diapente, diatessaron, and tone;
besides these, another interval, namely, that whereby
the diatessaron exceeds the ditone, and which is
generally supposed to be a semitone, for now we
shall use the appellation given to it by the Latin
writers, has been adjusted, and in general shewn to
have a ratio of 256 to 243.

But here it is necessary to mention, that the ratio
of this interval was a subject of great controversy
with the ancient musicians. What were the sentiments of Pythagoras about it we are nowhere told;

though if it be true that he constituted the diatessaron in the ratio of 4 to 3, and made each of the tones contained in it sesquioctave, it will follow as a consequence, that the interval necessary to complete that system must have been in the ratio of 256 to 243 : this is certain, that Boetius, and the rest of the followers of Pythagoras, deny the possibility that it can consist in any other : but this is a method of deduction by numerical calculation, and the appeal is made to our reason, which, in a question of this nature, say some, has nothing to do.

The first who asserted this doctrine, and he has done it in terms the most explicit, was Aristoxenus, the disciple and successor of Aristotle; he taught that as the ear is the ultimate judge of consonance, we are able by the sense of hearing alone to determine the measure both of the consonants and dissonants, and that both are to be measured or estimated, not by ratios but by intervals.* The method he took was this, he considered the diapason as consisting of the two systems of a diatessaron and diapente; it was easy to discover the difference between the two to be a tone, which was soon found, allowing the ear to be the judge, to be divisible into semitones. These two latter intervals being once recognized by the ear, became a common measure, and enabled him to determine the magnitude of any interval whatever, which he did by various additions to, and subductions from, those above mentioned; in like manner as is practised by the singers of our times, who by an instantaneous effort of the voice, are able not only to utter a fourth, a fifth, a greater or lesser third, a tone, a semitone, and the rest, but by habit and practice are rendered capable of separating and combining these intervals at pleasure, without the assistance of any arithmetical process or computation.

It must be confessed that there seems to be a kind of retrogradation in a process which directs the admeasurement of a part by the whole, rather than of the whole by a part, as this evidently does; but notwithstanding this seeming irregularity, the adherents to the former method are very numerous.

The principles on which these two very different methods of judging are founded, became the subject of great contention; and might perhaps give rise to another question, as extensive in its latitude, as important in its consequences, namely, whether the understanding or the imagination be the ultimate judge of harmony and beauty; or, in other words, what are the peculiar offices of reason and sense in subjects common to them both. The consequence of this diversity of opinions, so far as it related to music, was that, from the time of Aristoxenus the musicians of earlier times, according as they adhered to the one or the other of these opinions, were denominate either Pythagoreans or Aristoxeneans, by which appellations the two sects continued for a long time to be as much distinguished as those of the Peripatetics and Stoics were by their respective names.†

* Wallis Appendix de Veterum Harmonica, Quarto, pag. 290.
† Porphyrii in Ptolemæi Harmonica Commentarius, Edit. Wallisii, pag. 189.

But it seems that as well against the one as the other of the positions maintained by the two parties, there lay strong objections; for as to that of Pythagoras, that reason, and not the hearing, is to determine of consonance and dissonance, it was erroneous in this respect, it accommodated harmonical proportions to incongruous intervals; and as to Aristoxenus, he, by rejecting reason, and referring all to sense, rendered the very fundamentals of the harmonical science incapable of demonstration. The several offices of reason and sense, by which we are here to understand the sense of hearing, are very accurately discriminated by Ptolemy, who undertook the task of reviewing this controversy; and the method he took to reconcile these two militant positions will be shewn at large in that extract from his treatise, which we mean hereafter to exhibit in its proper place; the only question at present to be discussed, is that relating to the measure of the diatessaron. That it exceeded two of those tones, one whereof constituted the difference between the diapente and diatessaron, was agreed by both parties; but the measure of this excess was the point in debate: the Pythagoreans asserted it to be an interval in the ratio of 256 to 243, to which, for want of a better, they gave the name of Limma; the Aristoxeneans, on the other hand, contended that it was neither more nor less than a semitone. The question then became, Whether is the system of a diatessaron compounded of two tones and a limma, or of two tones and a semitone?

Ptolemy has entered into a very minute examination of this question; and though he professes to be, as he certainly is, an impartial arbiter between the two sects, and is very free in his censures on each; yet has he most irrefragably demonstrated the Pythagorean tenet to be the true one. The method he has taken to do it may be seen in the first book of his Harmonics, chap. x., but the following process will enable any one to judge of the force of his reasoning.

Let the number 1536, which it is said is the smallest that will serve the purpose, be taken, and after that 1728, its sesquioctave, to express a tone; and again, the sesquioctave of 1728, which is 1944, for another tone; the numbers 1536 and 1944 will then stand for the ditone. The diatessaron is sesquitertian, or as 4 to 3, it is therefore necessary to seek a number that shall contain four of those parts, of which 1536 is three, and this can be no other than 2048; so that the interval whereby the diatessaron exceeds the ditone, is in the ratio of 2048 to 1944; or, in smaller numbers, as 256 to 243. But to judge of the magnitude of this interval, let the sesquioctave of 1944, 2187 be taken for a third tone; it will then remain to enquire the difference between the two ratios 2187 to 2048, and 2048 to 1944, and the former will be found the greater; for 2187 exceeds 2048 by more than a fifteenth, and by less than a fourteenth part; whereas 2048 exceeds 1944 by more than a nineteenth, and by less than an eighteenth; and consequently that which, together with the ditone completes the diatessaron, is the lesser part of the third tone.

Salinas calls this demonstration of Ptolemy an excellent one, as most undoubtedly it is, and in his Treatise de Musica, lib. II., cap. xx., exhibits it in the following diagram :—

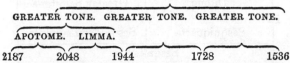

DIATESSARON.

GREATER TONE.   GREATER TONE.   GREATER TONE.

APOTOME.   LIMMA.

2187   2048   1944   1728   1536

To this lesser part of the third tone 2048 to 1944, or in lesser numbers, 256 to 243, was given the name of the Limma of Pythagoras; though some writers, and those of the Pythagorean sect, scrupled not to term it a Diesis. The greater part of the tone resulting from the above division was termed Apotome, a word signifying the residue of what remains of a line after part has been cut off.

Salinas, lib. II. cap xx., remarks, that both the theoretic and practical musicians among the moderns are deceived in thinking that the Apotome of the ancients is that interval, which, in such musical instruments as the organ, and others of the like kind, is found between ♮ and ♭; or, in other words, that the interval between ♮ and ♭ is greater than that between ♮ and c, and than that between ♭ and a; when, says he, the thing is quite the reverse, and may be proved by the ear.

Farther, lib. II. cap. x., he observes of the Limma, that as Pythagoras had divided the diapason into two diatessarons and a sesquioctave tone, he discovered that the diatessaron was capable of a like method of division, namely, into two continued tones, and that interval which remained after a subtraction of the ditone from the diatessaron. And this which he calls a semitone, is that which Ptolemy calls the semitone accepted and best known; and of which Plato in Timeus makes mention; when having followed the same proportion, he says that all the duple ratios were to be filled up with a sesquitertias and a sesquioctave, and all the sesquitertias with sesquioctaves, and the interval 256 to 243. He adds, that Cicero mentions this semitone in his book de Universitate, as does Boetius in all his divisions; and that there were none of the ancients to whom it was not known, for that all the Philosophers embraced the Pythagorean traditions of music. The same author adds, that the Pythagorean Limma was esteemed by the Greeks, particularly Bacchius and Bryennius, to be irrational; and that Plato himself dared not to call it a proportion, for the reason, as he conceives, that it was not superparticular.

Hitherto we have spoken of the tone in general terms, and as an interval in a sesquioctave ratio, such as constitutes the difference between the diatessaron and diapente, and it is said that the Pythagoreans acknowledged no other;[*] it is nevertheless necessary to mention that there is a lesser interval, to which the appellation of tone is also given; the ratio whereof is that of 10 to 9. It is not sufficiently clear who it was that first discovered it, but, from

several passages in the harmonics of Ptolemy,[†] it should seem that Didymus, an ancient musician, whom he frequently takes occasion to mention, was the first that adjusted its ratio.

Dr. Wallis, who seems to have founded his opinion on that of Salinas, and certainly entertained the clearest conceptions of the subject, has demonstrated very plainly how both the greater and lesser tone are produced; for assuming the diapente to be in the ratio of 3 to 2, or which is the same, the numbers being doubled, 6 to 4; by the interposition of the arithmetical mean 5, he shows it to contain two intervals, the one in the ratio of 6 to 5, the other in that of 5 to 4.[‡]

DIAPENTE.		
Semiditone		Ditone
6	5	4
Sesquialtera.		

The latter of these, which constituted the ditone or greater third, subtracted from the diapente, left that interval in the ratio of 6 to 5, which by the Greeks was called a Trihemitone, and by the Latins a deficient, or *semi* ditone, but by the moderns a lesser or flat third.

The consideration of the semiditone will be hereafter resumed; but as to the ditone it had a superparticular ratio, and consequently would not, any more than the diapente, admit of an equal division.[§] In order therefore to come at one that should be the nearest to equality, Dr. Wallis doubled the terms 5, 4, and thereby produced the numbers 10, 8, which have the same ratio. Nothing then was wanting but the interposition of the arithmetical mean 9,

DITONE.		
Greater Tone.		Lesser Tone.
8	9	10
Sesquioctave		Sesquinonal
Sesquiquarta.		

and a division was effected which produced the greater or sesquioctave tone, 9 to 8, and the lesser or sesquinonal tone, 10 to 9.[‖]

CHAP. VI.

HAVING thus adjusted the proportions of the greater and lesser tone, it follows next in order to consider the several divisions of each, the first and most obvious whereof is that of the semitone; but here two things are to be remarked, the one that the adjunct *semi*, though it may seem to express, as it does in most instances, the half of any given quantity, yet in musical

---

* Salinas de Musica, lib. II., cap. 17. Boet. lib. IV., cap. 5.

† Lib. II., cap. 13, 14. Salinas, lib. II , cap. 17.
‡ Wallis, Append. de Vet. Harm. quarto, pag. 322.
§ That a superparticular is incapable of an equal division is clearly demonstrated by Boetius, lib. III., cap. 1, and must be considered as a first principle in harmonics. Vide Macrobius in Somnium Scipionis, lib. II., cap. 1.
‖ Wallis Append. de Vet. Harm. quarto, pag. 323. Salinas de Musica, lib. II., cap. 17.

language has a signification the same with deficient or incomplete : the other is that although as the lesser is always contained in the greater, and consequently the tone comprehends the semitone and more, yet the semitone is not, nor can be found in, or at least cannot be extracted from, or produced by any possible division of the tone. The Aristoxeneans, who asserted that the diatessaron consisted of two tones and a half, had no other way of defining the half tone, than by taking the ditone out of the diatessaron, and the residue they pronounced to be a hemitone, as it nearly is ; and the Pythagoreans, who professed the admeasurement and determination of intervals by ratios, and not by the ear, were necessitated to proceed in the same way ; for after Pythagoras had adjusted the diezeutic tone, and found its ratio to be sesquioctave, or as 9 to 8, it nowhere appears that he or any of his followers proceeded to a division of that interval into semitones, and indeed it is not in the nature of the thing possible to effect any such division of it by equal parts. Ptolemy, who, so far as regards the method of defining the intervals by their ratios, must be said to have been a Pythagorean, has had recourse to this method of subtracting a lesser interval from a greater for adjusting the proportion of the Limma ; for after having assumed that the ratio of the diatessaron was sesquitertia, answering to the numbers 8 and 6, or which is the same, 4 to 3, he measures out three sesquioctave tones, 1536, 1728, 1944, 2187, and subtracts from them the diatessaron 2048 to 1536, and thereby leaves a ratio of 2187 to 2048, which is that of the apotome ; the limma 2048 to 1944, then remains an adjunct to the two sesquioctave tones 1728 to 1536, and 1944 to 1728 ; and the ratio of 2048 to 1536 is 8 to 6, or 4 to 3 ; and would we know the ratio of 2048 to 1944, it will be found to be 256 to 243, for eight times 256 is 2048, and eight times 243 is 1944.*

And Didymus, who after he had discovered the necessity of a distinction of tones into the greater and lesser, and found that it required an interval different in magnitude from the limma, to complete the diatessaron, had no way to ascertain the ratio of that interval, but by first adjusting that of the ditone ; in the doing whereof he also determined that of the semitone, for so are we necessitated to call the interval by which the diatessaron is found to exceed the ditone. With respect to this interval, which in the judgment of Salinas, is of such importance, that he seems to think it the hinge on which the knowledge of all instrumental harmony turns ; it seems clearly to have taken place of the limma, immediately after the discrimination of the greater and lesser tone : and there is reason to think it was investigated by Didymus in the following manner. First he considered the ratio of the diatessaron to be, as has been shewn, sesquitertian, or as 8 to 6 ; or, which is the same, those numbers being doubled, 16 to 12. The ditone he had demonstrated to be in sesquiquarta proportion, as 5 to 4. It remained then to find out a number that should contain 5 of these parts, of

which 12 contained four, and this could be no other than 15, and these being set down, demonstrated the ratio of the semitone to be 16 to 15.

DIATESSARON.			
Ditone		Greater Semitone	
12	15		16
Sesquiquarta		Sesquidecimaquinta	
Sesquitertia.			†

This interval is also the difference between the semiditone 6 to 5, and the sesquioctave tone 9 to 8, which, multiplying the extreme numbers by 3, is thus demonstrated :—

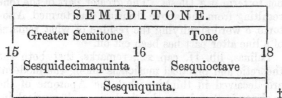

SEMIDITONE.			
Greater Semitone		Tone	
15	16		18
Sesquidecimaquinta		Sesquioctave	
Sesquiquinta.			‡

But it seems that this interval, so very accurately adjusted, did not answer all the combinations of which the greater and lesser tones were capable ; nor was it adapted to any division of the system, other than that which distinguishes the diatonic genus. These considerations gave rise to the invention of the lesser semitone, an interval so peculiarly appropriated to the chromatic genus, that Salinus and Mersennus scruple not to call it the Chromatic Diesis ; the measure of it is the difference between the ditone and semiditone, the former whereof is demonstrated to be in sesquiquarta proportion, or as 5 to 4 ; or, which is the same, each of those numbers being multiplied by 5, 25 to 20. The semiditone is sesquiquinta, that is to say, as 6 to 5 ; or multiplying each of those numbers by four, as 24 to 20 ; from a comparison therefore of the semiditone with the ditone, it will appear that the difference between them is an interval of 25 to 24, the ratio sought, and which is the measure of the lesser semitone.

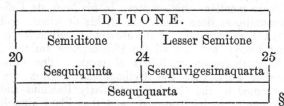

DITONE.			
Semiditone		Lesser Semitone	
20	24		25
Sesquiquinta		Sesquivigesimaquarta	
Sesquiquarta			§

Salinas remarks that this lesser semitone of 25 to 24, and the greater one of 16 to 15, compose the sesquinonal or lesser, and not the sesquioctave or greater tone, between which and the former he demonstrates the difference to be a comma, or an interval in the ratio of 81 to 80.

Salinas, Mersennus, and other writers, chiefly moderns, speak of a mean semitone in the ratio of

---

* See the preceding demonstration of the ratio of the Pythagorean limma.

† This and most of the diagrams for demonstrating the other intervals are taken from Salinas, who, it is to be remarked, differs from many other writers in the order of the numbers of ratios, placing the smallest first.
‡ Salinas, lib. II. cap. xviii.
§ Salinas, de Musica, lib. II. cap. 20

135 to 128, which with that greater one of 16 to 15, completes the sesquioctave tone ; and of another in the ratio of 27 to 25, which added to the lesser semitone 25 to 24, also makes up the greater or sesquioctave tone.* Salinas ascribes the invention of this latter to Ludovicus Follianus, a very ingenious musician of the sixteenth century, of whom an account will be hereafter given ; but he says it is unfit for harmony : and indeed it does not appear to have ever been admitted into practice. Salinas de Musica, lib. III., cap. 7.

We are now to speak of the Diesis, as being an interval less in quantity than a semitone : though it is to be remembered that the word as it imports indefinitely a Particle,† is of very loose signification, and is used to express a great variety of dissimilar intervals. Aristotle calls dieses the Elements of song, as letters are of speech ; but in this the moderns differ from him. Others of the Greek writers, and Vitruvius, a Latin, after them, make the diesis to be a quarter of a tone, and Salinas less. The Pythagoreans use the word Diesis and Limma indiscriminately to express the interval 256 to 243. In the subsequent division of the tone into lesser parts, the name of diesis has been given sometimes to one, and at others to other parts arising from that division ; and hence those different definitions which we meet with of this interval ; but the general opinion touching it is that it is less than a semitone, and more than a comma. We will consider it in all its variety of significations.

Boetius, in the third book of his treatise de Musica, has related at large the method taken by Philolaus the Pythagorean for dividing the tone into nine parts, called commas, of which we shall speak more particularly hereafter ; according to this division, two commas make a diaschisma, and two diaschismata a diesis. This is one of the senses in which the term diesis is used, but it is not easy to discover the use of this interval, for it does not seem to be adapted either to the tetrachord composed of sesquioctave tones, or that later one of Didymus, which supposes a distinction of a greater and lesser tone ; so that in this instance the term seems to be restrained to its primitive signification, and to import nothing more than a particle ; and Salinas seems to concur in this sense of the word when he says that in each of the genera of melodies the least interval is called a diesis.

In other instances we are to understand by it such an interval as, together with others, will complete the system of a diatessaron. There are required to form a diatessaron, or tetrachord in each of the genera, tones, semitones, and dieses. In the diatonic genus the diesis is clearly that, be it either a semitone, a limma, or any other interval, which, together with two tones is necessary to complete the tetrachord. If with the Pythagoreans we suppose the two tones to be sesquioctave, it will follow that the diesis and the limma 256 to 243 are one and the same interval ; on the other hand, if with Didymus we assign to the two tones, the different ratios of 10 to 9, and 9 to 8, the interval necessary to complete the diatessaron will be 16 to 15 ; or the difference between the ditone in the ratio of 5 to 4, and the diatessaron above demonstrated. In short, this suppletory interval, whatever it be, is the only one in the diatonic genus, to which the appellation of diesis is ever given.

To the chromatic genus belong two intervals of different magnitudes, and the term diesis is common to both ; the first of these is that of 25 to 24, mentioned above, and shewn to be the difference between the ditone and semiditone, and is what Salinas has appropriated to the chromatic genus. Gaudentius mentions also another species of diesis that occurs in this genus, in quantity the third part of a tone,‡ in which he has followed Aristoxenus ; but as all the divisions of the Aristoxeneans were regulated by the ear, and supposed a division of the tone into equal parts, which parts being equal, must necessarily be irrational, it would be in vain to seek a numerical ratio for the third part of a tone.

We are now to speak of that other diesis incident to the enarmonic genus, to which the term, in the opinion of most writers, seems to be appropriated ; § for whereas the other diesis obtained that name, only as being the smallest interval required in each genus, this other is the smallest that any kind of musical progression will possibly admit of. Aristides Quintilianus says, a diesis is as it were a dissolution of the voice.‖

According to Boetius, who must everywhere be understood to speak the sense of the Pythagoreans, the two dieses contained in the tetrachord of the enarmonic genus must have been unequal, for he makes them to arise from an arithmetical division of the limma, 256 to 243. ¶

Ptolemy has exhibited,** as he has done in each of the other genera, a table of the enarmonic genus, according to five different musicians, all of whom, excepting Aristoxenus, make the dieses to be unequal, those of Ptolemy are 24 to 23, and 46 to 45.

Salinas uses but one enarmonic diesis, which he makes to be the difference between the greater semitone 16 to 15, and the lesser 25 to 24.

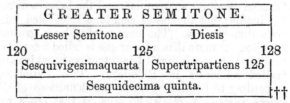

GREATER SEMITONE.	
Lesser Semitone	Diesis
120 125	128
Sesquivigesimaquarta	Supertripartiens 125
Sesquidecima quinta.	††

Which numbers are thus produced, 15 and 16 each multiplied by 8 will give 120, and 128, for the greater semitone ; we are then to seek for a number that bears the same ratio to 120, as 25 does to 24, which can be no other than 125, so that the ratio of the diesis will stand 125 to 128.

Brossard has applied the term diesis to those signs

* Salinas, lib. II. cap. 20, lib. III. cap. 7. Mersen. Harmonic. lib. V. De Dissonantiis, pag. 7.

† Macrob. in Somn. Scipion. lib. II. cap. 1

‡ Ex Vers. Meibom. pag. 5.
§ Boetius lib. II. cap. 23, has given dieses only to the enarmonic.
‖ Ex Vers. Meibom. pag. 13.
¶ Boetius, lib. IV. cap. 5.
** Lib. II. cap. 14.
†† Salinas, lib II. cap. 21.

or characters used by the moderns to denote the several degrees by which a sound may be elevated or depressed above or beneath its natural situation; for the doing whereof he seems to have had no better authority than that of the practitioners of his time, who perhaps are the only persons entitled to an excuse for having given to the sign the name of the thing signified. He professes to follow Kircher, when he says that there are three sorts of dieses, namely, the lesser enarmonic or simple diesis, containing two commas or about a quarter of a tone; the chromatic or double diesis, containing a lesser semitone, or nearly four commas, and the greater enarmonic diesis, containing nearly three fourths of a tone, or from six to seven commas; but this definition is by much too loose to satisfy a speculative musician.

These are all the intervals that are requisite in the constitution of a tetrachord in any of the three genera: it may not be improper however to mention a division of the tone, invented perhaps rather as an essay towards a temperature, than as necessary to the perfection of the genera; namely, that ascribed by Boetius, and others to Philolaus, by which the tone was made to consist of nine parts or commas.

The account of this matter given by Boetius is long, and rather perplexed; but Glareanus,* who has been at the pains of extracting from it the history of this division, speaks of it thus: 'A tone in a ses- 'quioctave ratio is divided into a greater and lesser 'semitone; the greater was by the Greeks called an 'apotome, the lesser a limma or diesis, and the 'difference between these two was a comma. The 'diesis was again divided into diaschismata, of which 'it contained two; and the comma into schismata, 'two whereof made the comma.' The passage, to give it at length, is thus:—

'It is demonstrated by musicians, for good reasons, 'that a tone cannot be divided into two equal parts, 'because no superparticular ratio, such as is that of a 'tone, is capable of such a division as Divus Severinus 'Boetius fully shews in his third book, chap. i., a 'tone which is in a sesquioctave ratio is divided into 'a greater and lesser semitone. The Greeks call the 'greater semitone an apotome, and the lesser a diesis 'or limma; but the lesser semitone is divided into 'two diaschismata. The excess whereby a greater 'semitone is more than a lesser one is called a comma, 'and this comma is divided into two parts, which are 'called schismata by Philolaus. This Philolaus, 'according to Boetius, gives us the definitions of all 'those parts. A diesis, he says, is that space by 'which a sesquialteral ratio or diatessaron exceeds 'two tones; and a comma is that space whereby 'a sesquioctave ratio is greater than two dieses, that 'is than two lesser semitones. A schisma is that 'half of a comma, and a diaschisma is the half of a 'diesis, that is of a lesser semitone; from which 'definitions and the following scheme you may easily 'find out into how many diaschismata, and the other 'smaller spaces, a tone may be divided, for the same 'Boetius shews that it can be done many ways in his

* Dodecachordon, lib. I. cap. x.

'treatise, lib. III. cap. viii., from whence we have 'taken these descriptions. It is to be observed that 'the name of diesis is proper in this place; but when, 'as the ancients have done, we give it to the enar- 'monic diaschisma, it is improper :—

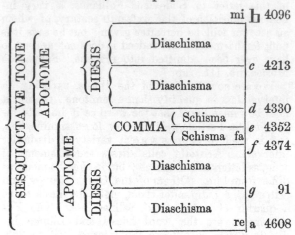

'Let a ♮ be a tone, ♮ d, or f a, a lesser semitone, 'or as the Greeks call it, as Boetius witnesseth lib. II, 'cap. xxvii., a limma or diesis, ♮ f, or d a, a greater 'semitone, called by the Greeks an apotome, ♮ c and 'c d, also f g and g a, diaschismata, or the halves of 'a diesis, d f a comma, whose halves d e and e f are 'schismata; but it is necessary for our purpose 'to observe this, let a be Mese, or a la mi re, f 'Trite synemmenon or fa in b fa ♮ mi ♮ Paramese 'or mi in b fa ♮ mi, therefore the note re in a la mi 're is distant from fa in b fa ♮ mi by a lesser 'hemitone, and from mi in the same key by a tone; 'from whence it follows, that the two notes in b fa '♮ mi, which seem to be of the same key, are farther 'distant from each other than from the extremes or 'neighbouring keys above and below, viz., mi from c 'sol fa ut, and fa from a la mi re, for mi and fa are 'separated from each other by a greater semitone, and 'from the extremes on either side by only a lesser 'semitone, for which reason this theory is not to be 'despised. We must not omit what the same Seve- 'rinus tells us in lib. III., cap. xiv. and xv., to wit, 'that a lesser semitone is not altogether four commas, 'but somewhat more than three; and that a greater 'semitone is not five commas, but somewhat more 'than four; from whence it comes to pass that a tone 'exceeds eight commas, but does not quite make up 'nine.'

This of Philolaus is generally deemed the true division of the tone, and may serve to prove the truth of that position, which all the theoretic writers on music seem to agree in, namely, that the sesqui- octave tone, as being in a superparticular ratio, is incapable of an equal division. But unfortunately the numbers made use of by Glareanus do not answer to the division, for those for the diesis or limma ♮ d 4330, 4096 have no such ratio as 256 to 243, which is what the limma requires, and that other f a, has, and it seems that in his assertion that ♮ and b are farther distant from each other than from c and a, respectively, he is mistaken. This is noticed by Salinas, who insists that the converse of the proposition is the truth. De Musica, lib. II. cap. xx.*

As to the comma, it appears by the foregoing calculation to be in the ratio of 4374 to 4330. Nevertheless, Salinas, for the purpose of accommodating it to practice, has assumed for the comma an interval in the ratio of 81 to 80, which is different from that of Glareanus and Boetius, but is clearly shewn by Salinas to be the difference between the greater and lesser tone. Ptolemy looked upon this latter comma as an insensible interval, and thought that therefore it was a thing indifferent whether the sesquioctave or sesquinonal tone held the acutest situation in the diatonic tetrachord; but Salinas asserts, that though it is the least, it is yet one of the sensible intervals, and that by means of an instrument which he himself caused to be made at Rome, he was enabled to distinguish, and by his ear to judge, of the difference between the one and the other of the tones.

Mersennus says that the Pythagoreans had another comma, which was in the ratio of 531441 to 524288, and was between sesqui $\frac{1}{73}$ and sesqui $\frac{1}{74}$; and that Christopher Mondore, in a book inscribed by him to Margaret, the sister of Henry III. of France, speaks of another between sesqui $\frac{1}{86}$, and sesqui $\frac{1}{87}$.† As to the first, though he does not mention it, it is clear that he took the ratio of it from Salinas, who in the nineteenth and thirty-first chapters of his fourth book speaks very particularly of the Pythagorean comma, and says that it is the difference whereby the apotome exceeds the limma.

We have now investigated in a regular progression the ratios of the several intervals of the greater and lesser tone, the greater and lesser semitone, the apotome and limma, the diesis, and the comma; and thereby resolved the tetrachord into its elements. It may be worth while to observe the singular beauties that arise in the course of this deduction, and how wonderfully the lesser intervals spring out of the greater; for the difference between

The { Diapente and Diatessaron } is - - a sesquioctave tone.

The { Ditone and Greater tone } is - - a sesquinonal tone.

The { Semiditone and greater tone, and also between the diatessaron and ditone, } is a greater semitone.

The { Lesser tone and greater semitone, and also between the ditone and semiditone, } is a lesser semitone.

The { Greater tone and Lesser tone } is - - a comma.

The { Greater semitone and Lesser semitone } is - an enarmonic diesis.

Salinas remarks much to the same purpose on the regular order of the simple consonances in these words. ' It seems worthy of the greatest observa-' tion, that the differences of the simple consonances, ' each above that which is the next under it, are ' found to be in the proportions which the first square ' numbers hereunderwritten bear to those that are the

' next less to them : to instance in the diapason, the ' excess above the diapente is the diatessaron, which ' is found in the ratio between the first square num-' ber 4, and its next less number 3. The excess of ' the diapente above the diatessaron is the greater ' tone, which is found in the ratio between the num-' bers 9 and 8. Again, that of the diatessaron above ' the ditone is the greater semitone, found in the ratio ' 16 to 15; farther, the excess of the ditone above the ' semiditone is the lesser semitone 25 to 24. All ' these will appear more clearly in the following dis-' position of the numbers :—

A					
B	C	A	A	B	C
2	3	4	Diapason	Diapente	Diatessaron
6	8	9	Diapente	Diatessaron	Tone Major
12	15	16	Diatessaron	Ditone	Semitone majus
20	24	25	Ditone	Semiditone	Semitone minus

' In the above disposition, the last numbers are ' square, the first longilateral, and the middle ones ' less than those that are square by unity, but greater ' than the longilateral ones by as many units as there ' are numbers of squares above them. The greatest ' ratios are those between the longilaterals and the ' squares, the lesser between the longilaterals and ' middle numbers, and the least or differences those ' between the squares and the middle ones. Of the ' ratios the greatest are marked A, the lesser B, and ' the least C.' ‡

Observations of this kind are perpetually occurring in the course of harmonical calculations; and it cannot but be a matter of astonishment to an intelligent mind to find, that those combinations of musical sounds which afford delight to the sense of hearing, have such a relation among themselves, and are disposed with such order and regularity, that they approve themselves also to the understanding, and exhibit to the mind a new species of beauty, such as is observable in theorems, and will for ever result from design, regularity, truth, and order. It is said that the senses are arbitrary, and that too in so great a degree, as to give occasion to a well-known axiom that precludes all dispute about them; but that of hearing seems to be an exception; for what the ear recognises to be grateful, the understanding approves as true. To enquire farther into the reasons why the sense is delighted with harmony and consonance, would be vain, since all beyond what we are able to discover by numerical calculation is resolvable into the will of Him who has ordered all things in number, weight, and measure.

The genera, as has been mentioned, were three; the diatonic, the chromatic, and the enharmonic. We are farther to understand a subdivision of these into species. Gaudentius expressly says, ' The ' species or colours of the genera are many,'§ and an author of much greater authority, Aristoxenus, has particularly enumerated them. According to him the diatonic genus had two species, the soft and the

* See his sentiment of it pag. 25 of the present work.
† Harmonicor. lib. V. Dissonantiis, pag. 88.

‡ De Musica, lib. II. cap. xx.
§ Ex Vers. Meibom. pag. 5.

intense ; the chromatic three, the soft, the hemiolian,* and the tonic ;† as to the enharmonic, it had no subdivision. Indeed, the representations of the genera and their species, as well by diagrams as in words, are almost as numerous as the writers on music. Monsieur Brossard has exhibited a view of the Aristoxenean division, taken as he says, from

Vitruvius ; and the same is to be met with in an English dictionary of music, published in the year 1740, by James Grassineau.‡

But this representation is not near so particular and accurate, as the Aristoxenean Synopsis of the Genera given by Dr. Wallis in the Appendix to his edition of Ptolemy, and here inserted :—

	Enharmonic Genus	Chromatic Genus			Diatonic Genus		
		Soft	Hemiolian	Toniac	Soft	Intense	
30	Nete	Nete	Nete	Nete	Nete	Nete	30
24						12	24
			21	18	15		
18	24	22				Paranete / Lichanos	18
15					Paranete / Lichanos		15
12				Paranete / Lichanos		12	12
9		Paranete / Lichanos	Paranete / Lichanos	6	9		9
6	Paranete / Lichanos 3	4	4½ Trite	Trite	Trite	Trite	6
3	Trite Parhypate 3	Trite Parhypate 4	Parhypate 4½	Parhypate 6	Parhypate 6	Parhypate 6	3

In order to understand this scheme, we must suppose the tetrachord hypaton, though any other would have served the purpose as well, divided into thirty equal parts : in the primitive division of this system, according to the diatonic genus, the stations of the two intermediate sounds parhypate and lichanos, for it is to be noted that those at the extremities termed stabiles, or immovables, were at 6 and 18 ; that is to say, the first interval in the tetrachord was 6 parts, and each of the other two 12, making together 30 ; so that the second interval was the double of the first, and the third equal to the second, answering precisely to the hemitone, tone, and tone ; this is spoken of the intense diatonic, for it is that species which the ancients are supposed to have meant whenever they spoke of the diatonic generally.

The soft diatonic has for its first interval 6, for its second 9, or a hemitone and a quadrantal diesis, or three fourths of a tone, and for its third 15, viz., a tone and a quadrantal diesis.

We are now to speak of the chromatic genus, the first species whereof, the tonic, had for its first inter-

val 6, or a hemitone ; for its second also 6, and for its third 18, a trihemitone, or tone and a half.

In the hemiolian chromatic, called also the sesquialteral,§ the first and also the second interval was 4½, which is a hemiolian or sesquialteral diesis ; and the third 21, or a tone, a hemitone, and a quadrantal diesis.

* This is but another name for sesquialtera, as Andreas Ornithoparcus asserts in his Micrologus, lib. II. on the authority of Aulus Gellius. It signifies a whole and its half, consequently the sesquialtera ratio in its smallest numbers is 3 to 2.

† Vide Wall. Append. de veter. Harm. quarto, pag. 299.

‡ At the time when the above book was published the world were surprised ; no such person as James Grassineau being known to it as possessed of any great share of musical erudition, and the work offered to the public appeared to be the result of great study and skill in the science. But the wonder ceased when it came to be known that the basis of Grassineau's book was the Dictionaire de Musique of Monsieur Sebastian Brossard, of Strasburg ; though, to do him justice, Grassineau in his preface ingenuously confesses he had made a liberal use of it. For the rest of it he stood indebted to Dr. Pepusch, and perhaps, in a small degree to the other masters, Dr. Greene and Mr. Galliard, who have joined in the recommendation of it.

Grassineau was an ingenious young man ; he understood the Latin and French languages, the latter very well, and knew a little of music ; he had been clerk to Mr. Godfrey, the chemist in Southampton Street, Covent Garden, but being out of employ, he became the amanuensis of Dr. Pepusch, and translated for him into English some of the Greek harmonicians from the Latin version of Meibomius. The Doctor having no farther occasion for him, recommended it to him to translate Brossard's dictionary above-mentioned, which he undertook and completed, the Doctor furnishing him with many new articles, and with additional matter for the enlargement of those contained in Brossard ; and Grassineau's dictionary would have been an inestimable present to the musical world, had due care been taken in the correction of it, but it abounds with errors, and the author is not now living to correct them in a new edition.

Although the dictionary of Brossard, and this of Grassineau, contain a great variety of useful knowledge, it is to be wished that it had been communicated to the world in some better form than that of a dictionary ; for to speak of the latter, some of the articles contained in it are complete treatises.

§ Vide previous note in this page.

The soft chromatic makes the first and also the second interval a triental diesis, or third part of a tone, by assigning to parypate and lichanos, the stations of 4 and 18 ; and gives to the third twenty-two twelfths of a tone, or, which is the same, twenty-two thirtieths of the whole tetrachord, which amount to a tone, a hemitone, and a triental diesis.

In the enharmonic genus, which, in the opinion of most authors, had no division into species, the first and second intervals, being terminated by 3 and 6, were each quadrantal dieses, or three twelfths of a tone, and the last a ditone. Of the diesis in this genus it is said by Aristoxenus and others, that it is the smallest interval that the human voice is capable of expressing ; and it is farther to be remarked, that it is ever termed the enarmonic diesis, as being appropriated to the enarmonic genus.

Euclid's account of the genera is not much different from this of Aristoxenus. The diatonic, he says, proceeds from the acute to the grave by a tone, a tone, and a hemitone ; and, on the contrary, from the grave to the acute by a hemitone, a tone, and a tone. The chromatic from the acute to the grave by a trihemitone, a hemitone, and a hemitone : and contrarywise, from the grave to the acute by a hemitone, a hemitone, and a trihemitone. The enharmonic progression, he says, is a descent to the grave by a ditone, a diesis, and a diesis ; and an ascent to the acumen by a diesis, a diesis, and a ditone. He speaks of a commixture of the genera, as namely, the diatonic with the chromatic, the diatonic with the enarmonic, and the chromatic with the enarmonic.

He exhibits the bisdiapason according to each of the genera, enumerating the several sounds as they occur, from Proslambanomenos to Nete hyperboleon, and observes that some of them are termed Stantes or standing sounds, and others Mobiles or moveable ; the meaning of which is no more than that the extreme sounds of each tetrachord are immoveable, and that the difference between the genera consists in those several mutations of the intervals, which are made by assigning different positions to the two intermediate sounds.

Colour he defines to be a particular division of a genus ; and, agreeable to what is said by Aristoxenus, he says that of the enarmonic there is one only ; of the chromatic three ; and of the diatonic two. He says farther, that the enharmonic progression is by a diesis, a diesis, and incomposite ditone ; that the chromatic colours or species are the soft, proceeding by two dieses, each being the third part of a tone, and an incomposite interval equal to a tone, and its third part ; and the sesquialteral, proceeding by a diesis in a sesquialteral ratio to that in the enarmonic, another such diesis, and an incomposite interval consisting of seven dieses, each equal to a fourth part of a tone ; and the tonic by a hemitone, a hemitone, and a trihemitone. Of the diatonic he says there are two species, namely, the soft and the intense, by some called also the syntonous ; the former proceeding by a hemitone, an interval of three quadrantal dieses, and by another of five such dieses ; and the latter by a common division, with its genus, namely, a tone, a tone, and a hemitone.

And here it is to be observed, that these several definitions of the genera are taken from some one or other of their respective species ; thus, that of the tonic chromatic is the same by which the genus itself is defined ; and the definition of the syntonous or intense diatonic is what is used to denote the genus itself. From hence it should seem that of the species some were deemed spurious, or at least that some kind of pre-eminence among them, unknown to us, occasioned this distinction ; which amounts to no less than saying that the soft chromatic is more truly the chromatic than either of the other two species of that genus ; and that the intense or syntonous diatonic is more truly the diatonic than the soft diatonic : as to the enarmonic, it cannot in strictness be said to have had any colour or species, for it admits of no specific division.

To demonstrate the intervals in each species by numbers, Euclid supposes a division of the tone into twelve parts. To the hemitone he gives six, to the quadrantal diesis three, and to the triental diesis four ; and to the whole diatessaron he assigns thirty. In the application of these parts to the several species, he says first, that the intervals in the soft chromatic are four, four, and twenty-two ; in the sesquialteral four and a half, four and a half, and twenty-one ; and in the tonic six, six, and eighteen ; in the soft diatonic six, nine, and fifteen ; and in the syntonous six. twelve, and twelve.

CHAP. VII.

ARISTIDES Quintilianus, who, in the judgment of Dr. Wallis,[*] seems in this respect to have been an Aristoxenean, speaks of the genera and their species in the following manner :—' Genus is a certain di-
' vision of the tetrachord. There are three genera
' of modulation, namely, the harmonic, chromatic,
' and diatonic ; the difference between them consists
' in the distances of their respective intervals. The
' harmonic is that genus which abounds in the least
' intervals, and takes its name from adjoining together.
' The diatonic is so called because it proceeds by, or
' abounds in, tones. The chromatic is so termed,
' because, as that which is between white and black
' is called Colour, so also that which holds the middle
' place between the two former genera as this does,
' is named Chroma. The enarmonic is sung by a
' diesis, diesis, and an incomposite ditone towards the
' acute ; and contrarywise towards the grave. The
' chromatic towards the acute by a hemitone, a hemi-
' tone, and trihemitone ; and contrarywise towards
' the grave. The diatonic by a hemitone, a tone,
' and tone towards the acute : and contrarywise to-
' wards the grave. The diatonic is the most natural
' of all, because it may be sung by every one, even
' by such as are unlearned. The most artificial is
' the chromatic, for only learned men can modulate
' it ; but the most accurate is the enharmonic : it is
' approved of by only the most skilful musicians ;
' for those who are otherwise look on the diesis as
' an interval which can by no means be sung, and to

---

[*] Append. de veter. Harm. pag. 318.

'these, by reason of the debility of their faculties,
'the use of this genus is impossible. Each of the
'genera may be modulated both by consecutive
'sounds and by leaps. Moreover, modulation is
'either direct or straightforward, reverting or turn-
'ing back, or circumcurrent, running up and down:
'the direct is that which stretches towards the acute
'from the grave; the reverting that which is contrary
'to the former; and the circumcurrent is that which
'is changeable, as when we elevate by conjunction,
'and remit by disjunction. Again, some of the
'genera are divided into species, others not. The
'enarmonic, because it consists of the smallest
'dieses, is indivisible. The chromatic may be
'divided into as many rational intervals as are
'found between the hemitone and enarmonic diesis;
'the third, namely the diatonic, into as many rational
'intervals as are found between the hemitone and
'tone; there are therefore three species of the chro-
'matic, and two of the diatonic. And, to sum up
'the whole, these added to the enarmonic make six
'species of modulation; the first is distinguished by
'quadrantal dieses, and is called the enarmonic;
'the second by triental dieses, and is called the soft
'chromatic; the third by dieses that are sesquialteral
'to those in the enarmonic, and is therefore called
'the sesquialteral chromatic. The fourth has a pe-
'culiar constitution of two hemitones, it is called
'the tonic chromatic: the fifth consists of an hemi-
'tone and three dieses, and the five remaining ones,
'and is called the soft diatonic: the sixth has an
'hemitone, tone, and tone, and is called the intense
'diatonic. But that what we have said may be
'made clear, we shall make the division in the
'numbers. Let the tetrachord be supposed to con-
'sist of sixty units, the division of the enarmonic
'is 6, 6, 48, by a quadrantal diesis, a quadrantal
'diesis, and a ditone. The division of the soft chro-
'matic 8, 8, 44, by a triental diesis, a triental diesis,
'and a trihemitone and triental diesis. The division
'of the sesquialteral chromatic is 9, 9, 42, by a
'sesquialteral diesis, a sesquialteral diesis, and a tri-
'hemitone and quadrantal diesis. The division of
'the tonic chromatic is 12, 12, 36, by an hemitone,
'an hemitone, and a trihemitone. That of the soft
'diatonic is 12, 18, 30, by a hemitone, and three
'quadrantal dieses, and five quadrantal dieses. That
'of the intense diatonic is 12, 24, 24, by a hemitone,
'a tone, and a tone.'*

It is observable in this division of Aristides Quintilianus, that the numbers made use of by him are
double those used by Euclid; the reason is, that the
two dieses in the sesquialteral chromatic are not so
well defined by four parts and a half of thirty, as by
9 of 60; and it is evident that preserving the proportions, whether we take the number 30 or 60 for
the gross content of the tetrachord, the matter is
just the same.

Ptolemy, the most copious, and one of the most
accurate of all the ancient harmonicians, has treated

* Aristides Quintilianus ex vers. Meib. pag 18, et seq., in which passage it is observable that he sometimes uses the term αρμονια, and
others εναρμονια, to signify the enarmonic genus.

very largely of the genera; and has, for the reason
above given, adopted the number 60 for the measure
of the tetrachord; he has represented the Aristoxenean constitution of the six species by the following
proportions:—

Acute	48	44	42	36	30	24
Mean	6	8	9	12	18	24
Grave	6	8	9	12	12	12
	60	60	60	60	60	60
	Enar-monic	Chro-matic soft	Chro-matic sesqui-alteral	Chro-matic tonic	Dia-tonic soft	Dia-tonic intense

In which proportions he agrees both with Euclid
and Aristides Quintilianus; though, for the purpose
of ascertaining them, he has preferred the numbers
of the latter to those used by Euclid.

In chapter xiv. of his second book, Ptolemy has
given the genera, with each of their several species,
according to the five different musicians, namely,
Archytas,† Aristoxenus, Eratosthenes,‡ Didymus,
and himself. The sum of his account, omitting the
division of Aristoxenus, for that is given above, is as
follows:—

Archytas
$$\text{Enharmonic } \tfrac{28}{27} \times \tfrac{36}{35} \times \tfrac{5}{4} = \tfrac{4}{3}$$
$$\text{Chromatic } \tfrac{28}{27} \times \tfrac{243}{224} \times \tfrac{32}{27} = \tfrac{4}{3}$$
$$\text{Diatonic } \tfrac{28}{27} \times \tfrac{8}{7} \times \tfrac{9}{8} = \tfrac{4}{3}$$

Eratosthenes
$$\text{Enarmonic } \tfrac{40}{39} \times \tfrac{39}{38} \times \tfrac{19}{15} = \tfrac{4}{3}$$
$$\text{Chromatic } \tfrac{20}{19} \times \tfrac{19}{18} \times \tfrac{6}{5} = \tfrac{4}{3}$$
$$\text{Diatonic } \tfrac{256}{243} \times \tfrac{9}{8} \times \tfrac{9}{8} = \tfrac{4}{3}$$

Didymus
$$\text{Enharmonic } \tfrac{32}{31} \times \tfrac{31}{30} \times \tfrac{5}{4} = \tfrac{4}{3}$$
$$\text{Chromatic } \tfrac{16}{15} \times \tfrac{25}{24} \times \tfrac{6}{5} = \tfrac{4}{3}$$
$$\text{Diatonic } \tfrac{16}{15} \times \tfrac{10}{9} \times \tfrac{9}{8} = \tfrac{4}{3}$$

In his own division Ptolemy supposes five species
of the diatonic genus, which, together with the enharmonic, and two species of the chromatic, he thus
defines:—

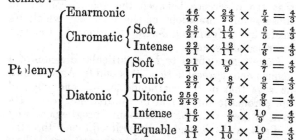

Ptolemy
$$\text{Enarmonic } \tfrac{46}{45} \times \tfrac{24}{23} \times \tfrac{5}{4} = \tfrac{4}{3}$$
Chromatic
$$\text{Soft } \tfrac{28}{27} \times \tfrac{15}{14} \times \tfrac{6}{5} = \tfrac{4}{3}$$
$$\text{Intense } \tfrac{22}{21} \times \tfrac{12}{11} \times \tfrac{7}{6} = \tfrac{4}{3}$$
Diatonic
$$\text{Soft } \tfrac{21}{20} \times \tfrac{10}{9} \times \tfrac{8}{7} = \tfrac{4}{3}$$
$$\text{Tonic } \tfrac{28}{27} \times \tfrac{8}{7} \times \tfrac{9}{8} = \tfrac{4}{3}$$
$$\text{Ditonic } \tfrac{256}{243} \times \tfrac{9}{8} \times \tfrac{9}{8} = \tfrac{4}{3}$$
$$\text{Intense } \tfrac{16}{15} \times \tfrac{9}{8} \times \tfrac{10}{9} = \tfrac{4}{3}$$
$$\text{Equable } \tfrac{12}{11} \times \tfrac{11}{10} \times \tfrac{10}{9} = \tfrac{4}{3}$$

† There were two of this name, the one of Tarentum, a Pythagorean,
famous, as Aulus Gellius and others relate, for having constructed an
automaton in the form of a pigeon, which had the power of flying to
a considerable distance; the other a musician of Mitylene. They are
both mentioned by Diogenes Laertius, but it is not certain which of the
two was the author of the division here given.

‡ Erathosthenes, a Cyrenean philosopher, and a disciple of Aristo and
Callimachus, was librarian at Alexandria to Ptolemy Evergetes. He
was for his great learning esteemed a second Plato. An astronomical
discourse of his is extant in the Oxford edition of Aratus; prefixed to
which is an account of many other books of his writing now lost. He
is said to have lived to the age of eighty-two; and, according to Helvicus,
flourished about the Olympiad cxxxviii. that is to say, about two hundred
and thirty years before Christ.
The above-mentioned edition of Aratus is a book not unworthy the
notice of a learned musician, as containing a short but curious dissertation De Musicâ antiquâ Græcâ, by the editor Mr. Edmund Chilmead.
Aratus was an eminent astronomer and poet, contemporary with Eratosthenes; and in the Oxford publication is an astronomical poem, which
it seems St. Paul alludes to in his speech at Athens, Acts xvii. ver. 28.
'As certain of your own poets have said.' Aratus was a Cilician, and
a countryman of the Apostle. Vide Bentley's Sermons at Boyle's
Lecture, Sermon II.

Martianus Capella gives this explanation of the genera :—' The enarmonic abounds in small intervals, ' the diatonic in tones.　The chromatic consists wholly ' of semitones, and is called chromatic, as partaking of ' the nature of both the others ; for the same reason ' as we call that affection colour which is included ' between the extremes of white and black.　The ' enarmonic is modulated towards the acumen, or, as ' we should now say, ascends by a diesis, diesis, and ' an incomposite ditone ; the, chromatic by a semi- ' tone, semitone, and an incomposite trihemitone : ' and the diatonic, content with larger intervals, ' proceeds by a semitone, tone, and tone : we now ' chiefly use the diatonic.'　He says farther,—' The ' possible divisions of the tetrachord are innumerable, ' but there are six noted ones, one of the enarmonic, ' three of the chromatic, and two of the diatonic. ' The first of the chromatic is the soft, the second ' is the hemiolian, and the third the tonian.　The ' divisions of the diatonic are two, the one soft and ' the other robust.　The enarmonic is distinguished ' by the quadrantal diesis, the soft chromatic by the ' triental diesis, and the hemiolian chromatic by the ' hemiolian diesis, which is equal to an enarmonic ' diesis and a half, or three eighths of a tone.'*　In ' all this Capella is but a copier of Aristides Quin- ' tilianus ; and, in the judgment of his editor Mei- ' bomius, and others, he is both a servile and an ' injudicious one.'

Boetius † has treated the subject of the genera in a manner less satisfactory than could have been ex- pected from so scientific a musician : he mentions nothing of the species, but contents himself with an exhibition of the enarmonic, the chromatic, and diatonic, in three several diagrams, which are here given.　He says that the diatonic is somewhat hard, but that the chromatic departs from that natural in- tension, and becomes somewhat more soft ; and that the enarmonic is yet better constituted through the five tetrachords.　The diatonic progression, he says, is by a semitone, tone, and tone ; and that it is called diatonic, as proceeding by tones.　He adds that the chromatic, which takes its name from the word Chroma, signifying colour, is, as it were, the first change or in- flexion from that kind of intension preserved in the diatonic : and is sung by a semitone, a semitone, and three semitones ;‡ and that the enarmonic, which in his judgment is the most perfect of all the genera, is sung by a diesis and a ditone ; a diesis, he says, is the half of a semitone.　The following is his division of the tetrachord in each of the three genera :—

DIATONIC		
Semitone	Tone	Tone

* De Nuptiis Philologiæ et Mercurii, lib. IX. De Generibus Tetra- chordorum.

† Lib. I. cap. xxi.

‡ In a diagram of Glareanus, representing Boetius's division of the chromatic, the last interval is thus defined :—' tria semitonia incom- posita,' which epithet, as Boetius himself explains it, is not meant to signify that the semitones are incomplete, but that the interval con- stituted by them is to be considered as an integer, and uncompounded like the tone, without regard to its constituent parts.　De Mus. lib. I. cap. xxiii.

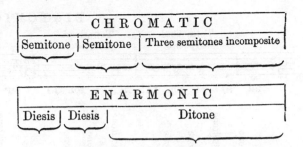

He is somewhat more particular in his fourth book, chap. v., and again in the seventh chapter, for in the chromatic tetrachord he makes the semitones to be, the one a greater and the other a lesser ; and the trihemitone he makes to consist of one greater and two lesser semitones.

TETRACHORD.

	Nete hyperboleon		Nete hyperboleon		Ncte hyperboleon
	2304		2304		2304
Tone		Three Hemitones, one greater and two lesser		Ditone	
	2592				
	Paranete hyp.				
			2736		
Tone		Hemitone greater	Paranete hyp.		
	2916		2916		2916
Hemitone lesser	Trite hyperb.	Hemitone lesser	Trite hyperb.	Diesis Diesis	Paranete hyp.
					Trite hyperb.
	3072		3072		3072
	Nete diezeug. DIATONIC		Nete diezeug. CHROMATIC		Nete diezeug. ENARMONIC

(Left margin: DIATESSARON.　Ratio Sesquitertia)

It is somewhat remarkable that this author has said nothing of the colours or species of the genera, about which so much is to be met with in Ptolemy and other writers, except towards the conclusion of his work, where he professes to deliver the sentiments of Aristoxenus and Archytas on this head ; but he seems rather to reprehend than adopt their opinions, for which it seems difficult to assign any reason, other than that he was, as his writings abundantly prove, a most strenuous assertor of the doctrines of Pythagoras.

Mersennus§ has given a scale of the succession of sounds in each of the three genera, as near as it could be done, in the characters of modern notation, which is here inserted, and may serve to shew how ill the division of the tetrachord in the chromatic and enar- monic genera agree with the notions at this time entertained of harmony, and the natural progression of musical sounds.

§ Harmonic. De Generibus et Modis, pag. 97.

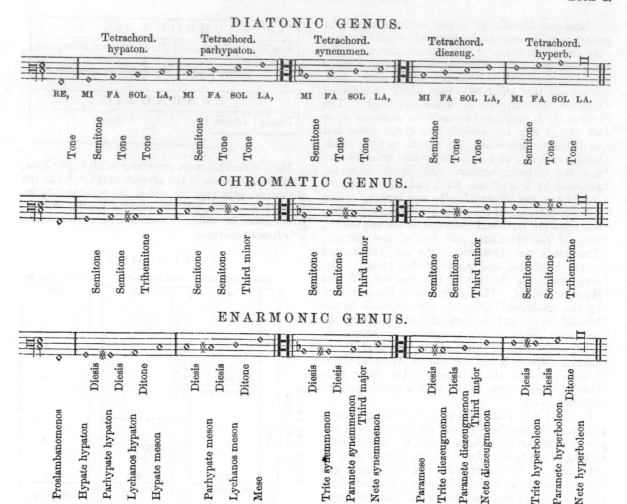

Other authors there are, particularly Franchinus, Vicentino, Vincentio Galilei, and Zarlino, that profess to treat of the genera; but it is to be noted that all their intelligence is derived from the same source, namely, the writings of Aristoxenus, Euclid, Aristides Quintilianus, and more especially Ptolemy; and therefore we find no other variation among them than what seems necessarily to arise from their different conceptions of the subject. Boetius himself can in this respect be considered no otherwise than as a modern; and he himself does not pretend to an investigation of the genera, but contents himself with a bare repetition of what is to be found in the writings of the ancients respecting them: and when it is considered that in his time only the diatonic genus was in use, the other genera having been rejected for their intricacy, and other reasons, long before, it must appear next to impossible that he could contribute much to the explanation of this most abstruse part of the science; and the excessive caution with which he delivers his sentiments touching them, is a kind of proof of the difficulties he had to encounter.

If this was the case with Boetius, how little is to be expected from the writers of later times. In short, for information as to the doctrine of the genera, we are under an indispensible necessity of recurring to the ancients; and it will be much safer to acquiesce in their relations, defective and obscure as they are, than to trust to the glosses of modern authors, who in general are more likely to mislead than direct us: for this reason it has been thought proper to reject an infinitude of schemes, diagrams, and explanations, which the fertile inventions of the moderns have produced to exemplify the constitution of the chromatic and enarmonic genera, and that from a thorough persuasion that many of them are erroneous.

But it seems the considerations above suggested were not sufficient to deter a writer, who flourished in the sixteenth century, who, to say the least of him, appears to have been one of the ablest theorists of modern times, from attempting to develope the doctrine of the genera, and deliver it free from those difficulties.

The author here meant is Franciscus Salinas, a Spaniard by birth, and who, under all the disadvantages of incurable blindness, applied himself with the most astonishing patience and perseverance to the study of the theory of music; and in many respects the success of his researches has been equal to the degree of his resolution. His system of the genera is much too copious to be inserted here; it is therefore referred to a part of this work reserved for an account of him and his writings.

Kircher has given a compendious view of the genera,* together with the proportions of their component intervals, in the tetrachord of each genus, by the help whereof we are enabled to form an idea of those various progressions that constitute the difference between the one and the other of them. But though he professes to have in his possession, and to have perused the manuscripts of Aristoxenus, Archytas, Didymus, Eratosthenes, and others,† he gives the preference to Ptolemy in respect to his division of the genera, and apparently follows the elder Galilei, not indeed in the order, but in the method of representation. According to him the species of the diatonic genus are five, namely, the ditonic or Pythagorean, the soft, the syntonous, the toniac, and the equable. The following is his definition and representation of them severally in their order, with his remarks on each:—

DITONIC or PYTHAGOREAN DIATONIC I.

'The Pythagorean or ditonic diatonic consists in a 'progression from the grave to the acute, through the 'tetrachord, by the interval of a lesser semitone, and 'two tones, each in the ratio of 8 to 9; and con- 'trarywise from the acute to the grave by two tones 'and a lesser semitone, as in the following example:—

TETRACHORD
6144 ——————————————Hypate meson
Sesquioctave tone, 8 to 9
6912 ——————————————Lychanos hypaton
Sesquioctave tone, 8 to 9
7776 ——————————————Parypate hypaton
Lesser semitone, 243 to 256
8192 ——————————————Hypate hypaton

'This kind of progression is said to have been held 'in great estimation by the philosophers, particularly 'Plato and Aristotle, as having a conformity with the 'composition of the world and with nature itself.

SOFT DIATONIC II.

'The second or soft species of the diatonic genus 'proceeds from the grave to the acute by an interval, 'in the ratio of 20 to 21; the other intervals have 'a ratio, the one of 9 to 10, and the other of 7 to 8, 'as is here represented:—

TETRACHORD
63 ——————————————Hypate meson
Sesquiseptima, 7 to 8
72 ——————————————Lychanos hypaton
Sesquinona, 9 to 10
80 ——————————————Parypate hypaton
Sesquivigesima, 20 to 21
84 ——————————————Hypate hypaton

* Musurg. tom. I. lib. III. cap. xiii.

† Meibomius questions the truth of this assertion, upon the supposition that Archytas, Didymus, and Eratosthenes are to be reckoned among the scriptores perditi. It is true that, excepting a small astronomical tract of Eratosthenes, there is nothing of the writing of either of them in print. But it is said that in the library of St. Mark, at Venice, there are even now a great number of Greek manuscripts that were brought into Italy upon the sacking of Constantinople, and among them it is not impossible that some tracts of the above-named writers might be found.

SYNTONOUS DIATONIC III.

'The third species, distinguished by the epithets 'syntonum incitatum, or hastened, proceeds from the 'grave to the acute by an interval in the ratio of 15 'to 16, or greater semitone, a greater tone 8 to 9, and 'a lesser 9 to 10; and descends from the acute to the 'grave by the same intervals.

Greater terms.
TETRACHORD { Sesquitertia. { Sesquiquart. { Sesquiquint. {
36 ——————————————Hypate meson
Sesquinona, 9 to 10 tone minor
40 ——————————————Lychanos hypaton
Sesquioctave, 8 to 9 tone major
45 ——————————————Parypate hypaton
Sesquiquindecima, 15 to 16 greater semit.
48 ——————————————Hypate hypaton

TONIAC DIATONIC IV.

'The toniac, the fourth species of the diatonic 'genus, supposes such a disposition of the tetrachord 'as the first and second chords shall include an inter- 'val of 27 to 28; next an interval of 7 to 8, and 'lastly one of 8 to 9. Thus adjusted it will ascend 'from the grave to the acute, and on the contrary 'descend from the acute to the grave, as in the 'example :—

Greater terms.
TETRACHORD {
168 ——————————————Hypate meson
Sesquioctave, 8 to 9
189 ——————————————Lychanos hypaton
Sesquiseptima, 7 to 8
216 ——————————————Parypate hypaton
Sesquivigesimaseptima, 27 to 28
224 ——————————————Hypate hypaton

EQUABLE DIATONIC V.

'The fifth and last species of this genus is the 'equable, proceeding in arithmetical progression from 'the grave to the acute, by the ratios of 11 to 12, 10 'to 11, and 9 to 10; and contrarywise from the 'acute to the grave :—

TETRACHORD DIATESSARON {
9 ——————————————Hypate meson
Sesquinona
10 ——————————————Lychanos hypaton
Sesquidecima
11 ——————————————Parypate hypaton
Sesquiundecima
12 ——————————————Hypate hypaton

'Ptolemy, whose fondness for analogies has already 'been remarked, resembles the tetrachord thus con- 'stituted to Theology and Politics.'

The chromatic genus, in the opinion of this author had three species, the ancient, the soft, and the syntonous, thus severally described by him :—

ANCIENT CHROMATIC I.

'This species proceeded by two semitones, and 'a trihemitone, that is to say, it ascended from the 'grave to the acute, by a lesser semitone; then by an 'interval somewhat greater, as being in the ratio of

'81 to 76; and lastly by an incomplete trihemitone, 'in the ratio of 19 to 16 :—

TETRACHORD DIATESSARON

6144 ——————————— Hypate meson
   Trihemitone, 16 to 19
7296 ——————————— Lychanos hypaton
   Semitone, 76 to 81
7776 ——————————— Parypate hypaton
   Lesser semitone, 243 to 256
8192 ——————————— Hypate hypaton

SOFT CHROMATIC II.

'The chromatic molle was so disposed, as that the 'lowest chord and the next to it had a ratio of 27 to '28, the second and third 14 to 15, and the third and 'fourth 5 to 6 :—

TETRACHORD

105 ——————————— Hypate meson
   Sesquiquinta, 5 to 6
126 ——————————— Lychanos hypaton
   Sesquiquartadecima, 14 to 15
135 ——————————— Parypate hypaton
   Sesquivigesimaseptima, 27 to 28
140 ——————————— Hypate hypaton

SYNTONOUS CHROMATIC III.

'In the chromatic syntonum the first and second 'chords, reckoning from the lowest, were distant by 'an interval in the proportion of 22 to 21, the second 'was removed from the third by an interval in the 'proportion of 12 to 11, and the third from the fourth 'by one of a sesquisexta proportion, which is as 6 to '7, as here is shewn :—

TETRACHORD

66 ——————————— Hypate meson
   Sesquisexta, 6 to 7
77 ——————————— Lychanos hypaton
   Sesquiundecima, 11 to 12
84 ——————————— Parypate hypaton
   Sesquivigesima prima, 21 to 22
88 ——————————— Hypate hypaton

'Of this genus it is said by Macrobius that it was 'deemed to be of an effeminate nature, and that it had 'a tendency to enervate the mind;* for which reason 'the ancients very seldom used it; Ptolemy resembles 'this tetrachord to œconomics.'

The enarmonic, the third and last in order of the genera, seems to have been originally simple or undivided into species; but the refinements of Ptolemy led to a variation in the order of the enarmonic progression, which formed that species distinguished by his name, so that it may be said the enarmonic contained two species, the ancient and the Ptolemaic. Kircher thus defines it :—

ANCIENT ENARMONIC I.

'In this species the tetrachord ascended by two 'dieses, and an incomplete ditone, the several ra-'tios whereof were as denoted by the following 'numbers :—

* Vide Macrob. in Somn. Scipion. Lib. II. cap. iv.

TETRACHORD

6144 ——————————— Hypate meson
   Ditone
7776 ——————————— Lychanos hypaton
   Diesis
7984 ——————————— Parypate hypaton
   Diesis
8192 ——————————— Hypate hypaton

ENARMONIC OF PTOLEMY II.

'The Ptolemaic enarmonic, which was scarce 'formed before both the chromatic and enarmonic 'grew into dis-esteem, ascended from the most grave 'to the next chord by an interval in the ratio of 45 'to 46, thence by one of 23 to 24, and lastly by one 'of 4 to 5, which is said to be a true enharmonic 'ditone :—

TETRACHORD

276 ——————————— Hypate meson
   Sesquiquarta, 4 to 5
345 ——————————— Lychanos hypaton
   Sesquivigesima tertia 23 to 24
360 ——————————— Parypate hypaton
   Sesquiquadragesimaquinta, 45 to 46
368 ——————————— Hypate hypaton

Dr. Wallis has treated this subject of the genera in a manner worthy of that penetration and sagacity for which he is admired. It has been mentioned, that of all the ancients Ptolemy has entered the most minutely into a discussion of this doctrine; he has delivered the sentiments of many writers, which but for him we should scarcely have known, and has adjusted the species in such a way as to leave it a doubt whether even Aristoxenus or he be the nearest the truth: Dr. Wallis published an edition of this valuable author, with a translation and notes of his own; to this work he has added an appendix, wherein is contained a very elaborate and judicious disquisition on the nature of the ancient music, and a comparison of the ancient system with that of the moderns. In this he has taken great pains to explain, as far as it was possible, the genera: the enarmonic and chromatic he gives up, and speaks of as irrecoverably lost; but of the diatonic genus he expresses himself with great clearness and precision; for, after defining, as he does very accurately, the several species of the diatonic, he says, that one only of them is now in practice; and, as touching the question which of them that one is, he gives the opinions of several musicians, together with his own; and lastly shows how very small and inconsiderable must have been the difference between those divisions that distinguish the species of the diatonic genus. His words are nearly these :—

'It now remains to discuss one point, which we 'have referred to this place, the genera and their 'colours or species. We have before said that for 'many years only one of them all has been received 'in practice, and this is by all allowed to be the 'diatonic; the enarmonic and all the chromatics, and 'the other diatonics, being laid aside. But it is 'matter of dispute whether it is the intense diatonic 'of Aristoxenus, or the ditonic diatonic of Ptolemy,

'or the intense diatonic of the same Ptolemy; that
'is to say, when we sing a diatessaron from MI or LA
'in the grave towards the acute in the syllables FA
'SOL LA, which express so many intervals, to ascertain
'the degree of magnitude which each of these in-
'tervals contains. The first opinion is that of Aris-
'toxenus, who, when he made the diatessaron to
'consist of two tones and a half, would have the
'greatest sound FA, to be a hemitone, and the other
'two SOL LA, to be whole tones, which is the intense
'diatonic of this author.* And in this manner
'speak all musicians even to this day, at least when
'they do not profess to speak with nicety. But
'those who enter more minutely into the matter,
'will have what is understood by a hemitone to be,
'not exactly the half of, but somewhat a little less
'than a tone; and this is demonstrated by Euclid,
'who in other respects was an Aristoxenean, though
'I do not know whether he was the first that did
'it. Euclid, I say, admitting the principles of the
'Pythagoreans in estimating the intervals of sounds
'by ratios; and admitting also that a tone is in
'a sesquioctave ratio, in his harmonic introduction
'treats of the tones and hemitones in the same
'manner as do the Aristoxeneans; yet in his section
'of the canon he shews that what remains after
'subtracting two tones from a diatessaron is less than
'a hemitone, and is called a limma, which is in the
'ratio of $\frac{256}{243}$; for if a diatessaron contains two tones
'and a half, then a diapason, which is two diatessarons
'and one tone, must contain six tones; but a diapason,
'which has a duple ratio, is less than six tones, for
'a sesquioctave ratio six times compounded is more
'than duple;† a diapason therefore is less than six
'tones, and a diatessaron less than two tones and
'a half.

CHAP. VIII.

'THE next opinion is that of those, who, instead
'of a tone, tone, and hemitone, substitute a tone,
'tone, and limma. And these, if at any time they
'call it a hemitone, would yet have us understand
'them to mean a limma, which differs very little from
'a hemitone, and therefore they will have the syl-
'lable LA to express a limma, and the syllables SOL LA
'two tones, that is $\frac{256}{243} \times \frac{4}{3} \times \frac{9}{8} = \frac{4}{3}$, and this is the
'ditonic diatonic of Ptolemy, but which was shewn
'by Euclid before Ptolemy; and it was also the
'diatonic of Eratosthenes, as has been said above;
'and these have been the sentiments of musicians
'almost as low as to our own times. Ptolemy
'himself, though he has given other kinds of diatonic
'genera, does not reject this; and the rest who have
'spoken of this matter in a different way, did it
'more out of compliance with custom, than that they
'adhered to any contrary opinion of their own, as
'Ptolemy himself tells us, lib. I. cap. xvi. And
'thus Boetius divides the tetrachord, and after him
'Guido Aretinus, Faber Stapulensis, Glareanus, and
'others; it is true, however, that, about the begin-

'ning of the sixteenth century, Zarlino, and also
'Kepler, resumed the intense diatonic of Ptolemy,
'and attempted to bring it into practice;‡ but for
'this they were censured by the elder Galileo. §

'The third opinion, therefore, is that of those
'who, following Ptolemy, substituted in the place of
'a hemitone or limma, a sesquidecimaquinta ratio
'$\frac{16}{15}$, which they also call a hemitone; and for the
'tones, both which the others had made to be in the
'ratio $\frac{9}{8}$, one they made to be in the ratio $\frac{10}{9}$, so
'that they compounded the diatessaron by the ratios
'$\frac{16}{15} \times \frac{9}{8} \times \frac{10}{9} = \frac{4}{3}$, expressing by the syllable FA the
'ratio $\frac{16}{15}$, by SOL that of $\frac{9}{8}$, and by LA $\frac{10}{9}$,|| which
'is the intense diatonic of Ptolemy, and the diatonic
'of Didymus, except that he, changing the order,
'has $\frac{16}{15} \times \frac{10}{9} \times \frac{9}{8} = \frac{4}{3}$.

'And as they called $\frac{16}{15}$ a greater hemitone, they
'made the lesser $\frac{25}{24}$, which with $\frac{16}{15}$ completes the
'lesser tone, as $\frac{16}{15} \times \frac{25}{24} \times = \frac{10}{9}$, and is the difference,
'as they say, between the greater and the lesser
'third. Mersennus adds two other hemitones, one
'in the ratio $\frac{135}{128}$, which with $\frac{16}{15}$ completes $\frac{9}{8}$ the
'greater tone, and the other $\frac{27}{25}$, which with $\frac{25}{24}$ also
'makes up $\frac{9}{8}$ the greater tone.'¶

The above is an impartial state of the several
opinions that at different times have prevailed among
the moderns, touching the preference of one or other
of the species of the diatonic genus to the rest.
Dr. Wallis is certainly right in saying, that to the
time of Boetius, and so on to the end of the sixteenth
century, the ditonic diatonic of Ptolemy prevailed,
for so much appears by the writings of those several
authors; and as to the latter part of his assertion, it
is confirmed by the present practice, which is to
consider the tetrachord as consisting of a sesquidecimaquinta ratio, a tone major, and a tone minor,
and to this method of division he gives the preference; but he closes his relation with a remark
that shews of how very little importance all enquiries
are, which tend to adjust differences too minute for
a determination by the senses, and cognizable only
by the understanding, and that, too, not till after
a laborious investigation. His words are these :—

'But as those species which we have mentioned
'differ so very little from one another, that the nicest
'ear can scarcely, if at all, distinguish them, since the
'ratio $\frac{16}{15}$ from the ratio of a limma $\frac{256}{243}$, as also the
'ratio of a greater tone $\frac{9}{8}$ from $\frac{10}{9}$ differ only by the
'ratio $\frac{81}{80}$, which is so small that the ear can with
'difficulty discriminate between the one and the
'other of the two tones; we must therefore judge
'not so much by our senses, which opinion ought

---

* See the Synopsis, p. 30, of Dr. Wallis's Appendix, herein-before
given.

† This is excellently demonstrated by Boetius, lib. III. cap. i.

‡ Dr. Wallis has a little mistaken Kepler in this place : it was not the
intense diatonic of Ptolemy, but of Didymus $\frac{16}{15} \times \frac{10}{9} \times \frac{9}{8} = \frac{4}{3}$ that
he was for resuming. Joann. Keplerus Harm. Mundi, lib. III. cap. vii.

§ Galileo did not contend for the ditonic division of the diatonic, but
for the intense of Aristoxenus, defined in his synopsis of the genera
herein before given; the reason whereof was, that he was a lutenist, and
the performers on that instrument unanimously prefer the Aristoxenean
division.

|| It may be proper to remark, that in this and other instances of sol-
misation that occur in the passage now quoting, Dr. Wallis uses the
method of solmisation by the tetrachords, in which the syllables UT RE
are rejected, and which took place about the year 1650. See Clifford's
Collection of Divine Services and Anthems, printed in the year 1664.

¶ Append. de Vet. Harm. 317, et seq.

'most to be regarded, because the senses would 'without any difficulty admit any of them, but 'reason greatly favours the last.'*

There is yet another writer, with whose sentiments, and a few observations thereon, we shall conclude our account of the genera; this was Dr. John Christopher Pepusch, a man of no small eminence in his profession, and who for many years enjoyed, at least in England, the reputation of being the ablest theorist of his time. In a letter to Mr. Abraham de Moivre, printed in the Philosophical Transactions of the year 1746, No. 481, he proposes to throw some light upon the obscure subject of the ancient species of music; and after premising that, according to Euclid, the ancient scale must have been composed of tones major and limmas, without the intervention of tones minor, which in numbers are thus to be expressed, $\frac{9}{8} \frac{256}{243} \frac{9}{8} \frac{9}{8} \frac{256}{243} \frac{9}{8} \frac{9}{8}$, he proceeds in these words:—'It was usual among the Greeks to 'consider a descending as well as an ascending scale, 'the former proceeding from acute to grave pre-'cisely by the same intervals as the latter did from 'grave to acute. The first sound in each was the 'proslambanomenos. The not distinguishing these 'two scales, has led several learned moderns to sup-'pose that the Greeks in some centuries took the 'proslambanomenos to be the lowest note in their 'system, and in other centuries to be the highest; but 'the truth of the matter is, that the proslambano-'menos was the lowest or highest note according as 'they considered the ascending or descending scale. 'The distinction of these is conducive to the variety 'and perfection of melody; but I never yet met 'with above one piece of music where the composer 'appeared to have any intelligence of this kind. 'The composition is about one hundred and fifty 'or more years old, for four voices, and the words 'are,—'Vobis datum est noscere mysterium regni "Dei, cæteris autem in parabolis; ut videntes non "videant, et audientes non intelligant.' By the 'choice of the words the author seems to allude to 'his having performed something not commonly 'understood.' The doctor then exhibits an octave of the ascending and descending scales of the diatonic genus of the ancients, with the names of their several sounds, as also the corresponding modern letters, in the following form:—

A		Proslambanomenos	$\frac{8}{9}$	g
B	$\frac{9}{8}$	Hypate hypaton	$\frac{243}{256}$	f
C	$\frac{256}{243}$	Parhypate hypaton	$\frac{8}{9}$	e
D	$\frac{9}{8}$	Lychanos hypaton	$\frac{8}{9}$	d
E	$\frac{9}{8}$	Hypate meson	$\frac{243}{256}$	c
F	$\frac{256}{243}$	Parhypate meson	$\frac{8}{9}$	b
G	$\frac{9}{8}$	Lychanos meson	$\frac{8}{9}$	a
a	$\frac{9}{8}$	Mese		G

He observes, that in the octave above given, the Proslambanomenos, Hypate hypaton, Hypate meson, and Mese, were called Stabiles, from their remaining fixed throughout all the genera and species; and

* Append. de Vet. Harm. 318.

that the other four, being the Parhypate hypaton, Lychanos hypaton, Parhypate meson, and Lychanos meson, were called Mobiles, because they varied according to the different species and varieties of music.

He then proceeds to determine the question what the genera and species were, in this manner:—'By 'genus and species was understood a division of the 'diatessaron, containing four sounds, into three in-'tervals. The Greeks constituted three genera, 'known by the names of Enarmonic, Chromatic, 'and Diatonic. The chromatic was subdivided into 'three species, and the diatonic into two. The three 'chromatic species were, the chromaticum molle, the 'sesquialterum, and the toniæum. The two diatonic 'species were, the diatonicum molle, and the inten-'sum; so that they had six species in all. Some of 'these are in use among the moderns, but others are 'as yet unknown in theory or practice.

'I now proceed to define all these species by 'determining the intervals of which they severally 'consisted, beginning by the diatonicum intensum as 'the most easy and familiar.

'The diatonicum intensum was composed of two 'tones and a semitone; but, to speak exactly, it con-'sists of a semitone major, a tone minor, and a tone 'major. This is in daily practice, and we find it 'accurately defined by Didymus in Ptolemy's Har-'monics, published by Dr. Wallis.†

'The next species is the diatonicum molle, as yet 'undiscovered, as far as appears to me, by any 'modern author. Its component intervals are the 'semitone major, an interval composed of two semi-'tones minor, and the complement of these two to 'the fourth, being an interval equal to a tone major 'and an enarmonic diesis.

'The third species is the chromaticum toniæum, 'its component intervals are a semitone major suc-'ceeded by another semitone major, and lastly, the 'complement of these two to the fourth, commonly 'called a superfluous tone.

'The fourth species is the chromaticum sesqui-'alterum, which is constituted by the progression of 'a semitone major, a semitone minor, and a third 'minor. This is mentioned by Ptolemy as the

† Dr. Wallis has remarked in the passage above cited, that it had long been a matter of controversy whether the system of the moderns corresponded with the intense diatonic of Aristoxenus, the ditonic diatonic of Ptolemy, or rather Pythagoras, or the intense of Ptolemy; and though he seems to incline to the opinion of Zarlino, that the music now in use is no other than the intense diatonic of Ptolemy, it is far from clear that the moderns have gone farther than barely to admit in theory and in a course of numerical calculation the latter as the most eligible. Salinas, lib. III. cap. xiii. contends for an equality of tones, and for the consequent necessity of distributing throughout the diapason system those intervals by which the greater tones exceed the lesser.

Bontempi, Hist. Mus. 188. says that that temperament which makes the intervals irrrational, is to be looked upon as a divine thing, and asserts that nowhere in Italy, nor indeed in Europe, does the practice of discriminating between the greater and lesser tone prevail in the tuning of the organ, and that the organ of St. Mark's chapel at Venice, where he himself sang for seven years, continued to be tuned without regard to this distinction, notwithstanding what Zarlino had written and the efforts he made to get it varied.

The practice has long been in tuning the organ, and such like instruments, to make the fifths as flat and the thirds as sharp as the ear will bear, which necessarily induces an inequality in the tones.

Lastly, Dr. Smith, in his Harmonics, second edition, pag. 33, asserts that since the invention of a temperament, the ancient systems of ditonic diatonic, intense diatonic, &c., have justly been laid aside. So that after so many opinions to the contrary, it may very well be doubted whether the diatonicum intensum is in daily practice or not.

'chromatic of Didymus.* Examples among the 'moderns are frequent.

'The fifth species is the chromaticum molle. Its 'intervals are two subsequent semitones minor, and 'the complements of these two to the fourth, that is 'an interval compounded of a third minor and an 'enarmonic diesis. This species I never met with 'among the moderns.

'The sixth and last species is the enarmonic. 'Salinas and others have determined this accurately.† 'Its intervals are the semitone minor, the enarmonic 'diesis, and the third major.

'Examples of four of these species may be found 'in modern practice. But I do not know of any 'theorist who ever yet determined what the chro-'maticum toniæum of the ancients was; nor have 'any of them perceived the analogy between the 'chromaticum sesquialterum and our modern chro-'matic. The enarmonic, so much admired by the 'ancients, has been little in use among our musicians 'as yet. As to the diatonicum intensum, it is too 'obvious to be mistaken.'

The above-cited letter is very far from being what the title of it indicates, an explanation of the various genera and species of music among the ancients. To say the best of it, it contains very little more than is to be met with in almost every writer on the subject of ancient music, except that seemingly notable discovery, that the ancients made use of both an ascending and descending scale, the consideration whereof will be presently resumed. As to the six species above enumerated, the doctor says four are in modern practice, but of these four he has thought proper to mention only two, namely, the diatonicum intensum, and the chromaticum ses-quialterum; and it is to be wished that he had referred to a few of those examples of the four, which he says are to be found; or at least that he

had mentioned the authors in whose works the latter two of them occur; and the rather, because Dr. Wallis asserts that the enarmonic, all the chromatics, and all but one of the diatonics, for many years, he might have said centuries, have been laid aside.

As to his assertion that the Greeks made use of both an ascending and descending scale, it is to be remarked, that there are no notices of any such dis-tinction in the writings of any of the Greek har-monicians. The ground of it is a composition about one hundred and fifty years old, in the year 1746, to the words of a verse in the gospel of St. Mark,‡ so obscure, if we consider them as referring to the music, that they serve more to excite, than allay curiosity; and Dr. Pepusch could not have wished for a fairer opportunity of displaying his learning and ingenuity than the solution of this musical enigma afforded him. Nay, had he condescended to give this composition in the state he found it, or had he barely referred to it, the world would have been sensible of the obligation. The only excuse that can be alledged for that incommunicative dis-position which the whole of this letter betrays, is, that the author of it subsisted for many years by teaching the precepts of his art to young students, and it was not his interest to divulge them. How far the composition above-mentioned, which is not yet two hundred years old, is an evidence of the practice of the ancient Greeks, will not here be in-quired into; but it may gratify the curiosity of the reader to be told that the author of it was Costanzo Porta, a Franciscan monk, and chapel-master in the church of St. Mark, at Ancona, and that it is pub-lished at the end of a book printed at Venice in 1600, entitled, 'L'Artusi, overo delle Imperfettioni della moderna Musica,' written by Giovanni Maria Artusi, an ecclesiastic of Bologna, of whom a particular account will hereafter be given. As to the com-position, it is for four voices, and is as follows :—

* Lib. II. cap. xiv.

† Salinas de Musica, lib. III. cap. viii.

‡ Chap. iv. ver. 9.

Vo - bis da - tum est   no - sce Mis - te - - ri - um no -

Vo - bis da - tum est   no - sce Mis - te - - ri - um, no - - sce Mis - te - ri -

Vo - bis da - tum est   no - sce Mis

Vo - bis da - tum est no - sce Mis - te - ri - um, no - sce Mis - te - ri - um,

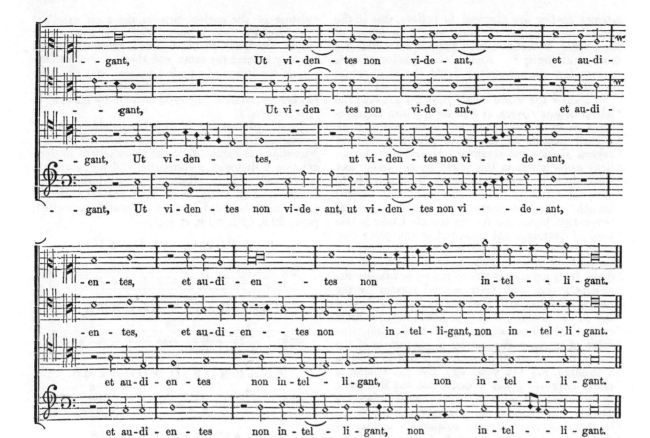

Artusi observes upon this composition, which, the better to shew the contrivance of it, is here given in score, that it is a motet for four voices, and that it may be sung two ways, that is to say, first, as the cliffs direct that are placed nearest to the notes, and afterwards turning the top of the book downwards, from the right to the left; taking the extreme cliff for a guide in naming the notes; the consequence whereof will be, that the base will become the soprano, the tenor the contralto, the contralto the tenor, and the soprano the base. Besides this, he says that the second time of singing it, b must be assumed for ♯, and in other instances FA for MI. He concludes with a remark upon the words of this motet, that they indicate that it is not given to every one to understand compositions of this kind.

Upon the example above adduced the remark is obvious, that it falls short of proving the use of both an ascending and descending scale by the Greek harmonicians. In a word, it is evidence of nothing more than the antiquity of a kind of composition, of which it is probable Costanzo Porta might be the inventor, namely that, where the parts are so contrived as to be sung as well backwards as forwards. In this he has been followed by Pedro Cerone, and other Spanish musicians, and by our own countryman Elway Bevin, and others, who seem to have thought that the merit of a musical composition consisted more in the intricacy of its construction than in its aptitude to produce the genuine and natural effects of fine harmony and melody on the mind of an unprejudiced hearer.

From the foregoing representations of the genera, the reasons for the early preference of the diatonic to the chromatic and enarmonic are clearly deducible; but notwithstanding these and the consequent rejection of the latter two by Guido and all his followers, the ingenuity of a few speculative musicians has betrayed them into an opinion that they are yet actually existing, and that with the addition of a few intervals, occasionally to be interposed among those that constitute the diapason, both the chromatic and enarmonic genera may be brought into practice.

The first of these bold assertors was Don Nicola Vicentino, an author of whom farther mention will hereafter be made. In a work entitled 'L'Antica Musica ridotta alla Moderna Prattica,' published by him at Rome in 1555, we find not only the tetrachord divided in such a manner as seemingly to answer the generical division of the ancients, but compositions actually exhibited, not only in one and the other of the genera, but in each of them severally, and in all of them conjunctly, and this with such a degree of persuasion on his part that he had accurately defined them, as seems to set all doubt at defiance.

It is true that little less than this was to be expected from an author who professes in the very title of his book to reduce the ancient music to modern practice, but that he has succeeded in his attempt so few are disposed to believe, that in the general estimation of the most skilful professors of the science, Vicentino's book has not its fellow for musical absurdity.* And of the justice of this censure few can entertain a doubt, that shall peruse the following account of himself and of his studies :—

'To shew the world that I have not grudged the 'labour of many years, as well for my own improve-'ment, as to be useful to others, in the present work 'I shall publish all the three genera with their 'several species and commixtures, and other inven-'tions never given to the world by any body; and 'shall shew in how many ways it is possible to 'compose variously in the sharp and flat modes: 'though at present there are some professors of 'music that blame me for the trouble I take in this 'kind of learning, not considering the pains that 'many celebrated philosophers have taken to explain 'the doctrine of harmonics; nevertheless I shall not 'desist from my endeavours to reduce to practice the 'ancient genera with their several species by the 'means of voices and instruments; and if I shall 'fail in the attempt, I shall at least give such hints 'to men of genius as may tend to the improve-'ment of music. We see by a comparison of the 'music that we use at present, with that in practice 'a hundred, nay ten years ago, that the science is 'much improved; and I doubt not but that these 'improvements of mine will appear strange in com-'parison with those of our posterity, and the reason 'is, that improvements are continually making of 'things already invented, but the invention and be-'ginning of every thing is difficult; therefore I re-'joice that God has so far favoured me, that in these 'days for his honour and glory I am able to shew 'my honourable face among the professors of music. 'It is true that I have studied hard for many years; 'and as the divine goodness was pleased to enlighten 'me, I began this work in the fortieth year of my 'age, in the year 1550, the jubilee year, in the 'happy reign of Pope Julius the Third; since that 'I have gone on, and by continual study have en-'deavoured to enlarge it, and to compose according 'to the precepts therein contained, as likewise to 'teach the same to many others, who have made 'some progress therein, and particularly in this 'illustrious town of Ferrara, where I dwell at pre-'sent, to the inhabitants whereof I have explained 'both the theory and practice of the art; and many 'lords and gentlemen who have heard the sweetness 'of this harmony have been charmed therewith, and 'have taken pains to learn the same with exquisite 'diligence, because it really comprehends what the 'ancient writers shew. As to the diatonic genus, it 'was in use in the music sung at public festivals, and 'in common places, but the chromatic and enarmonic 'were reserved for the private diversion of lords and 'princes, who had more refined ears than the vulgar, 'and were used in celebrating the praises of great 'persons and heroes. And, not to detract from the

'virtues of the ancient princes, the most excellent 'prince of Ferrara, Alfonso d'Este, after having very 'much countenanced me, has with great favour and 'facility learned the same, and thereby shown to the 'world the image of a perfect prince; and he, as he 'has a most worthy name of eternal glory in arms, 'so has he acquired immortal honours by his skill in 'the sciences.'†

In the prosecution of this his notable design of accommodating the ancient music to modern practice, Vicentino has exhibited in the characters of modern notation a diatonic, a chromatic, and an enarmonic fourth and fifth in all their various forms. The following is an example of their several varieties, taken from the third book of his work above-cited, pages 59 a, 59 b, 62 b, et seq. :—

DIATONIC FOURTHS.

CHROMATIC FOURTHS.

ENARMONIC FOURTHS.

DIATONIC FIFTHS.

CHROMATIC FIFTHS.

ENARMONIC FIFTHS.

Having thus adjusted the several intervals of a fourth and fifth in each of the three genera, the author proceeds to exhibit certain compositions of his own in each of them; and first we have a motet composed by himself, and sung, as he says, in his

* This is remarked by Gio Battista Doni, in his treatise entitled De Præstantia Musicæ veteris. Florent. 1647, and numberless other writers. Kircher, however, seems to entertain a different opinion of it; his sentiments are given at length in a subsequent page of this chapter.

† Libro primo, cap. iv.

church on the day of the resurrection, as a specimen of the true chromatic :—

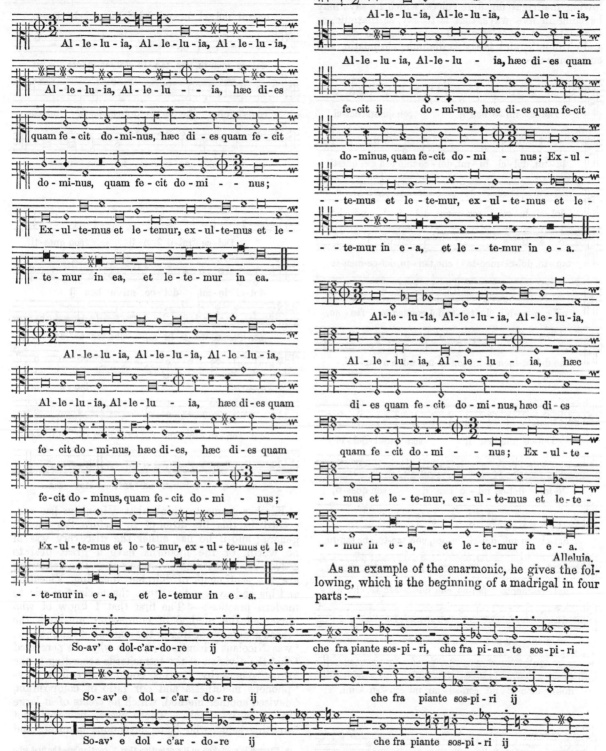

As an example of the enarmonic, he gives the following, which is the beginning of a madrigal in four parts :—

NOTE.—Vicentino has not been particular in explaining the use of the points over many of the notes in this and the following examples of the enarmonic; but from the practice of Salinas and other writers it is presumed that the point is intended to denote the enarmonic diesis as defined in the foregoing representations of that genus.

And as a proof of the practicability of uniting all the genera in one composition, he exhibits the following madrigal for four voices, which he says may be sung in five ways, that is to say, as diatonic, as chromatic, as chromatic and enarmonic, as diatonic and chromatic, and lastly as diatonic, chromatic, and enarmonic :—

Dol-ce mi-o ben ij　　　son questi dol-ci

lu-mi, dol-ci lu-mi, dol-ce mio ben son questi

dol-ci lu-mi　　son questi, dol-ci lu-mi che

tan-to, dol-ce-men-te　　che tan-to, dol-ce-men-te

mi con-su-mi, che tan-to dol-ce-men-te　　fan-no,

che dol-ce-men-te mi con-su-mi, mi con-su-mi.

Dol-ce mio ben ij　　　son questi dol-ci

lu-mi, dol-ce mi-o ben ij　　　son ques-ti,

dol-ci lu-mi, dol-ci lu-mi, che tan-to, che tan-to,

dol-ce-mente　　fan-no, che dol-cemen-te, che dol-

- - ce-mente mi con-su-mi, mi con-su-mi, fan-no che

dol-ce-men-te mi con-su-mi, mi con-su-mi.

Dol-ce mi-o ben son questi dol-ci lu-

- - mi, dol-ce mio ben son ques-ti dol-ci lu-mi, son

ques-ti dol-ci lu-mi, dol-ci lu-mi che tan-to

dol-ce-men-te, che tan-to dol-ce-mente　　mi

con-su-mi,　che tan-to dol-cemen-te　　mi con-

- - su-mi　dol-ce-men-te, mi con-su-mi.

Dol-ce mi-o ben ij　　　son ques-ti

dol-ci lu-mi,　dol-ce mi-o ben ij

son ques-ti dol-ci lu-mi　　che tan-to dol-ce -

- - men-te　　　　fan - no, che

mi con-su-mi, che dol-ce-men-te　mi con -

- - su-mi,　mi con-su-mi.　Hay - me.

Kircher seems to think that Vicentino has succeeded in this his attempt to restore the ancient genera ; and if he has, either the discovery was of no worth, or the moderns have a great deal to answer for in their not adopting it. The following are the sentiments of Kircher touching Vicentino and his endeavours to reduce the ancient music to modern practice :—'The first that I know of who 'invented the method of composing music in the 'three genera, according to the manner of the ancients, 'was Nicolaus Vicentinus ;* who when he perceived 'that the division of the tetrachords according to the 'three genera by Boetius could not suit a poly-'phonous melothesia and our ratio of composition, 'devised another method, which he treats of at large 'in an entire book. There were, however, not 'wanting some, who being strenuous admirers and

* Kircher is mistaken in his assertion that Vicentino was the first who attempted the revival of the ancient genera ; for it seems that Giovanni Spataro, of Bologna, in the year 1512, made an attempt of that kind, but without success. Storia della Musica di Giambatista Martini, tom. I. pag. 126, in not.
But notwithstanding the discouragements the two writers above-mentioned met with, Domenico Mazzochi, of Rome, about the year 1600, attempted a composition in all the three genera, entitled Planctus Matris Euryalis, which is printed in the Musurgia, tom. I. pag 660.

'defenders of ancient music, cavilled at him wrong-
'fully and undeservedly for having changed the
'genera that had been wisely instituted by the
'ancients, and put in their stead I know not what
'spurious genera; but those who shall examine
'more closely into the affair will be obliged to con-
'fess that Vicentinus had very good reason for what
'he did, and that no other chromatic enarmonic
'polyphonous melothesia could be made than as he
'taught.'*

This declaration of Kircher is not easily to be
reconciled with those positive assertions of his in the
Musurgia, that the ancients were strangers to polyphonous music; and the examples above given are
all of that kind.

But waving this consideration, whoever will be at
the pains of examining these several compositions,
will find it a matter of great difficulty to reconcile
them with the accounts that are given of the manner
of dividing the tetrachord in the several genera; he
will not be able easily to discover the chromatic interval of three incomposite semitones; much less
will he be able to make out the enarmonic diesis;
and much greater will be his difficulty to persuade
himself, or any one else, that either of the above
compositions can stand the test of an ear capable of
distinguishing between harmony and discord.

But all wonder at this attempt of Vicentino must
cease, when it is known that he contended with some
of the greatest musicians, his contemporaries, that the
modern or Guidonian system was not simply of the
diatonic kind, but compounded of all the three genera.
He has himself, in the forty-third chapter of his
fourth book, given a most curious relation of a dispute between him and a reverend father on this
subject, which produced a wager, the decision
whereof was referred to two very skilful professors,
who gave judgment against him. An account of this
dispute is contained in a subsequent chapter of the
present work.

CHAP. IX.

It does not anywhere appear that the music which
gave rise to the controversy between Vicentino and
his opponents, was any other than what is in use at
this day; which that it is the true diatonic of the
ancients is more than probable; though, whether it
be the diatonicum Pythagoricum, or the diatonicum
intensum of Aristoxenus, of Didymus, or of Ptolemy,
has been thought a matter of some difficulty to
ascertain, but is of little consequence in practice.

But we are not to understand by this that the
music now in use is so purely and simply diatonic,
as in no degree to participate of either the enarmonic
or chromatic genus, for there is in the modern scale
such a commixture of tones and semitones as may
serve to warrant a supposition that it partakes in
some measure of the ancient chromatic; and that it
does so, several eminent writers have asserted, and
seems to be the general opinion. Monsieur Brossard
says, that after the division of the tone between the

Mese and Paramese of the ancients, which answer to
our A and ♭, into two semitones, it was thought
that the other tones might be divided in like manner;
and that therefore the moderns have introduced the
chromatic chords of the ancient scale, and thereby
divided the tones major in each tetrachord into two
semitones : this, he adds, was effected by raising the
lowest chord a semitone by means of this character,
✕, which was placed immediately before the note
so to be raised, or on its place immediately after
the cliff. Again he says, that it having been found
that the tones minor terminating the tetrachords
upwards were no less capable of such division than
the tones major, they added the chromatic chords to
the system, and in like manner divided the tones
minor, so that the octave then became composed of
thirteen sounds and twelve intervals, eight of which
sounds are diatonic or natural, distinguished in the
following scheme by white notes thus, ◊ and five
chromatic by black ones thus, ◆ with the sharp sign,
which Brossard calls a double diesis prefixed to each
of the notes so elevated :—

This, though a plausible, is a mistaken account of
the matter; for first it is to be observed, this introduction of the semitones into the system, was not for
the purpose of a progression of sounds different from
that in the diatonic genus : on the contrary, nothing
more was intended by it than to render it subservient
to the diatonic progression; or, in other words, to
institute a progression in the diatonic series from any
given chord in the diapason, and we see the design of
this improvement in its effects.

For, to assume the language of the moderns, if we
take the key of E, in which no fewer than four of the
sharp signatures are necessary, it is evident to demonstration that in the system of the diapason the tones
and semitones will arise precisely in the same order
as they do in the key of C, where not one of those
signatures are necessary, and the same, mutatis
mutandis, may be said of all the other keys with the
greater third; and the like will be found in those
with the lesser third, comparing them with that of
A, the prototype of them all.‡

From hence it follows, that the use of the above
signatures has no effect either in the intension or
remission of the intervals; but the same remain, notwithstanding the application of them the same as in
the diatonic genus.

It is true, that since the invention of polyphonous
or symphoniacal music, a species of harmony of
which the ancients seem to have been totally
ignorant; among the various combinations that may
occasionally occur in a variety of parts, some may
arise that shall nearly answer to the chromatic intervals, and it shall sometimes happen that a given
note shall have for its accompaniment those sounds
that constitute a chromatic tetrachord; and of this
opinion are some of the most skilful modern organists,

* Musurg. tom. I. pag. 637.

† Dictionaire de Musique, Article Systema.
‡ See this demonstrated in the next book.

who are inclined to think that they sometimes use the chromatic intervals, without knowing that they do so.* But the question in debate can only be determined by a comparison of the melody of the moderns with that of the ancients; and in that of the moderns we meet with no such progression as that which is characterised by three incomposite semitones and two semitones, which is the least precise division of the tetrachord that any of the ancients have given us.

Our countryman Morley gives his opinion of the matter in the following words:—'The music which 'we now use is neither just diatonic, nor right 'chromatic. Diatonicum is that which is now in use, 'and riseth throughout the scale by a whole note, a 'whole note, and a lesser or half note. A whole note 'is that which the Latins call Integer Tonus, and 'is that distance which is betwixt any two notes, 'except *mi* and *fa*; for betwixt *mi* and *fa* is not a 'full halfe note, but is lesse than halfe a note by a 'comma, and therefore called the lesser halfe note, in 'this manner :—

'Chromaticum is that which riseth by semitonium 'minus, or the less halfe note, the greater halfe note, 'and three halfe notes thus :—

'The greater halfe note betwixt *fa* and *mi* in b '*fa* ♮ *mi*. Enarmonicum is that which riseth by 'diesis, diesis (diesis is the halfe of the lesse halfe 'note) and ditonus; but in our musicke I can give no 'example of it, because we have no halfe of a lesse 'semitonum; but those who would shew it set down 'this example

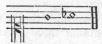

'of enarmonicum, and mark the diesis thus ✕ as it 'were the halfe of the apotome or greater halfe note, 'which is marked thus ✳. This sign of the more 'halfe note we now-a-daies confound with our b 'square, or signe of *mi* in ♮ *mi*, and with good 'reason; for when *mi* is sung in b *fa* ♮ *mi*, it is in 'that habitude to *a la mi re*, as the double diesis 'maketh F *fa ut* sharpe to E *la mi*, for in both 'places the distance is a whole note; but of this 'enough: and by this which is already set downe, it 'may evidentlie appeare that this kind of musick 'which is usual now-a-daies, is not fully and in 'every respect the ancient diatonicum; for if you 'begin any four notes, singing *ut, re, mi, fa*, you 'shall not find either a flat in E *la mi*, or a sharp in 'F *fa ut*; so that it must needes follow that it is 'neither just diatonicum nor right chromaticum.

* It is also said, that in passages of notes in succession the chromatic intervals sometimes occur. The following not uncommon passage is said to be an example of the hemiolian or sesquialtera chromatic :—

'Likewise by that which is said it appeareth this 'point, which our organists use—

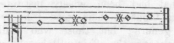

'is not right chromatica, but a bastard point, patched 'up of halfe chromaticke and half diatonick. Lastlie, 'it appeareth by that which is said, that those vir-'ginals which our unlearned musytians cal cromatica '(and some also grammatica) be not right chromatica, 'but half enharmonica; and that al the chromatica 'may be expressed uppon our common virginals ex-'cept this :—

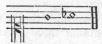

'for if you would thinke that the sharpe in g *sol re* '*ut* would serve that turne by experiment, you shall 'find that it is more than halfe a quarter of a note too 'low.' †

From hence we may conclude in general, that the system as it stands at present, is not adapted to the chromatic genus; and were there a possibility, which no one can admit, of rendering the chromatic tolerable to a modern ear, the revival of it would require what has often been attempted in vain, a new and a better temperament of the system than the present.

From the several hypotheses above stated, and the different methods of dividing the tetrachord in each genus, it clearly appears that among the most ancient of the Greek harmonicians there was a great diversity of opinions with respect to the constitution of the genera. And it also appears that both the chromatic and enarmonic gave way to the diatonic, as being the most natural, and best adapted to the general sense of harmony; indeed it is very difficult to account for the invention and practice of the former two, or to persuade ourselves that they could ever be rendered grateful to a judicious ear. And after all that has been said of the enarmonic and chromatic, it is highly probable that they were subservient to oratory, or in short that they were modes of speaking and not of singing, the intervals in which they consist not being in any of the ratios which are recognized by the ear as consonant.

Another subject in harmonics, no less involved in obscurity, is the doctrine of the Modes, Moods, or Tones, for so they are indiscriminately termed by such as have professed to treat of them. The appellation of Moods has indeed been given to the various kinds of metrical combination, used as well in music as poetry, and were the word Tone less equivocal than Mode, it might with propriety be substituted in the place of the former. Euclid has given no fewer than four senses in which the word Tone is accepted;‡ whereas that of Mode or Mood is capable of but two; and when it is said that these appellations refer to subjects so very different from each other as sound

† Plaine and easie Introduction to Practicall Musicke. Annotations on Part I.
‡ Introd. Harmon. ex. vers. Meibom. pag. 19. et vide Meib. in loc. citat.

and duration, that is to say tone and time, there can be little doubt which of the two is to be preferred.

To consider the term Mode in that which is conceived to be its most eligible sense, it signifies a certain series or progression of sounds. Seven in number at least are necessary to determine the nature of the progression; and the distinction of one mode from another arises from that chord in the system from whence it is made to commence; in this respect the term Mode is strictly synonymous with the word Key, which at this day is so well understood as to need no explanation.

As to the number of the modes, there has subsisted a great variety of opinions, some reckoning thirteen, others fifteen, others twelve, and others but seven; and, to speak with precision, it is as illimitable as the number of sounds. The sounds that compose any given series, with respect to the degree of acumen or gravity assigned to each, are capable of an innumerable variety; for as a point or a line may be removed to places more or less distant from each other ad infinitum; in like manner a series of sounds may be infinitely varied, as well with respect to the degree of acumen or gravity, as the position of each in the system;* we are therefore not to wonder at the diversity of opinions in this respect, or that while some limit the modes to seven, others contend for more than double that number.

At what time the modes were first invented does no where clearly appear. Bontempi professes himself at a loss to fix it;† but Aristides Quintilianus intimates that they were known so early as the time of Pythagoras;‡ and considering the improvements he made, and that it was he who perfected the great or immutable system, it might naturally be supposed that he was the inventor of them; but the contrary of this is to be inferred from a passage in Ptolemy, who says that the ancients supposed only three modes, the Dorian, the Phrygian, and the Lydian,§ denominations that do but ill agree with the supposition that any of them were invented by Pythagoras, who it is well known was a Samian. But farther, Aristides Quintilianus, in the passage above referred to, has given the characteristical letters of all the fifteen modes according to Pythagoras; so that admitting him to have been the inventor of the additional twelve, the institution of the three primitive modes is referred backwards to a period anterior to that in which the system is said to have been perfected.

Euclid relates that Aristoxenus fixed the number of the modes at thirteen, that is say, 1. The Hypermixolydian or Hyperphrygian. 2. The acuter Mixolydian, called also the Hyperiastian. 3. The graver Mixolydian, called also the Hyperdorian. 4. The acuter Lydian. 5. The graver Lydian, called also the Æolian. 6. The acuter Phrygian. 7. The graver Phrygian, called also the Iastian. 8. The Dorian. 9. The acuter Hypolydian. 10. The graver Hypolydian, called also the Hypoœolian. 11. The

acuter Hypophrygian. 12. The graver Hypophrygian, called also the Hypoiastian. 13. The Hypodorian.‖ The most grave of these was the Hypodorian; the rest followed in a succession towards the acute, exceeding each other respectively by a hemitone; and between the two extreme modes was the interval of a diapason.¶

The better opinion however seems to be, that there are in nature but seven, and as touching the diversity between them, it is thus accounted for. The Proslambanomenos of the hypodorian, the gravest of all the modes, was, in the judgment of the ancients, the most grave sound that the human voice could utter, or that the hearing could distinctly form a judgment of; they made the Proslambanomenos of the hypoiastian or graver hypophrygian to be acuter by a hemitone than that of the hypodorian; and consequently the Hypate of the one more acute by a hemitone than the Hypate of the other, and so on for the rest; so that the Proslambanomenos of the hypoiastian was in the middle, or a mean between the Proslambanomenos of the hypodorian and its Hypate hypaton. The Proslambanomenos of the acuter hypophrygian was still more acute by a hemitone, and consequently more acute by a whole tone than the hypodorian, and therefore it coincided with the Hypate hypaton of that mode, as is thus represented by Ptolemy, lib. II. cap. xi.**

ACUTE

Tone	Hypermixolydian
	Mixolydian
Limma	
	Lydian
Tone	
	Phrygian
Tone	
	Dorian
Limma	
	Hypolydian
Tone	
	Hypophrygian
Tone	
	Hypodorian

GRAVE

Those who contended for fifteen modes, among whom Alypius is to be reckoned, to the thirteen above enumerated, added two others in the acute, which they termed the Hyperlydian and Hyperæolian.††

But against this practice of increasing the modes by hemitones, Ptolemy argues most strongly in the eleventh chapter, and also in the four preceding chapters of the second book of his Harmonics: and indeed were it to prevail, the modes might be multiplied without end, and to no purpose. Notwithstanding this, Martianus Capella contends for fifteen and Glareanus for twelve modes; but it is to

---

* Wallis, Append. de Vet. Harm. pag. 312.
† Histor. Mus. pag. 136.
‡ Lib. I. pag. 28, ex. vers. Meibom.
§ Harmonicor. lib. II. cap. vi. x. ex vers. Wallis.

‖ Euclid. Introd. Harm. pag. xx.
¶ Wallis. Append. de Vet. Harm. pag. 312.
** Ibid. pag. 313.
†† Wallis. Append. pag. 312.

be observed, that both these latter writers are, in respect of the Greek harmonicians, considered as mere moderns; and besides these there are certain other objections to their testimony, which will be mentioned in their proper place.

As to the two additional modes mentioned by Alypius, they seem to have been added to the former thirteen, more with a view to regularity in the names and positions of the modes, than to any particular use; and perhaps there is no assignable period of time during which it may with truth be said, that more than thirteen were admitted into practice.

Ptolemy however rejects as spurious six of the thirteen allowed by the Aristoxeneans, and this in consequence of the position he had advanced, that it was not lawful to encrease the modes, by a hemitone. It is by no means necessary to give his reasons at large for limiting the number to seven, as his doctrine contains in it a demonstration that the encrease of them beyond that number was rather a corruption than an improvement of the harmonic science. As to the three primitive modes, the Dorian, the Phrygian, and the Lydian, each of them was situated at the distance of a sesquioctave tone from that next to it,* and therefore the two extremes were distant from each other two such tones; or, in other words, the Phrygian mode was more acute than the Dorian by one tone, and the Lydian more acute than the Phrygian by one tone; consequently the Lydian was more acute than the Dorian by two tones.

To these three modes Ptolemy added four others, making together seven, which, as he demonstrates, are all that nature can admit of. As to the Hypermixolydian, mentioned by him in the tenth chapter of his second book, it is evidently a repetition of the hypodorian.

MIXOLYDIAN

LYDIAN

PHRYGIAN

DORIAN

HYPOLYDIAN

HYPOPHRYGIAN

HYPODORIAN†

The above is the order in which they are given by Euclid, Gaudentius, Bacchius, and Ptolemy himself, though the latter, in the eleventh chapter of his second book, has varied it by placing the Dorian first, and in consequence thereof transposing all the rest; but this was for a reason which a closer view of the subject will make it unnecessary to explain.

Having proceeded thus far in the endeavour to distinguish between the legitimate and the spurious modes, it may now be proper to enter upon a more particular investigation of their natures, and see if it be not possible, notwithstanding that great diversity of opinion that has prevailed in the world, to draw from those valuable sources of intelligence the ancient harmonic writers, such a doctrine as may

afford some degree of satisfaction to a modern enquirer. It must be confessed that this has been attempted by several writers of distinguished abilities, and that the success of their labours has not answered the expectations of the world. The Italians, particularly Franchinus, or as he is also called, Gaffurius, Zaccone, Zarlino, Galilei, and others, have been at infinite pains to explain the modes of the ancients, but to little purpose. Kircher has also undertaken to exhibit them; but notwithstanding his great erudition and a seeming certainty in all he advances, his testimony is greatly to be suspected; and, if we may believe Meibomius, whenever he professes to explain the doctrines of the ancients, he is scarcely intitled to any degree of credit. The reason why these have failed in their attempts is obvious, for it was not till after most of them wrote, that any accurate edition of the Greek harmonicians was given to the world: so lately as the time when Morley published his Introduction, that is to say in the reign of queen Elizabeth, it was doubted whether the writings of some of the most valuable of them were extant even in manuscript; and it seemed to be the opinion that they had perished in that general wreck of literature which has left us just enough to guess at the greatness of our loss.

To the several writers above-mentioned we may add Glareanus of Basil, a contemporary and intimate friend of Erasmus; but he confesses that he had never seen the Harmonics of Ptolemy, nor indeed the writings of any of the Greek Harmonicians, and that for what he knew of them he was indebted to Boetius and Franchinus. From the perusal of these authors he entertained an opinion that the number of the modes was neither more nor less than twelve; and, confounding the ancient with the modern, or, as they are denominated, the ecclesiastical modes, which, as originally instituted by St. Ambrose, were only four in number, but were afterwards by St. Gregory, about the year 600, encreased to eight, he adopted the distinction of authentic and plagal modes, and left the subject more perplexed than he found it.

To say the truth, very few of the modern writers in the account they give of the modes are to be depended on; and among the ancients, so great is the diversity of opinions, as well with respect to the nature as the number of them, that it requires a great deal of attention to understand the designation of each, and to discriminate between the genuine and those that are spurious. In general it is to be observed that the modes answer to the species of diapason, which in nature are seven and no more, each terminating or having its final chord in a regular succession above that of the mode next preceding: for instance, the Dorian, which had its situation in the middle of the lyre or system, had for its final note hypate meson or E; the Hypolydian, the next in situation towards the grave, had for its final chord parhypate meson or F; and the Hypophrygian, the next in situation towards the grave to the Hypolydian, had for its final chord lychanos hypaton or G; so that the differences between the modes in succession, with respect to their degrees of gravity,

---

* Wallis. Append. pag. 312.
† Called also the Locrensian. Euclid Introd. Harm. pag. 16.

corresponded with the order of the tones and semitones in the diatonic series. But it seems that those of the ancient harmonicians, who contended for a greater number of modes than seven, effected an encrease of them by making the final chord of each in succession, a semitone more acute than that of the next preceding mode : and against this practice of augmenting the modes by semitones Ptolemy has expressly written in the eleventh chapter of the second book of his Harmonics, and that with such force of reason and argument, as cannot fail to convince every one that reads and understands him, to which end nothing can so much conduce as the attentive perusal of that learned Appendix to his Harmonics of Dr. Wallis, so often cited in the course of this work.

Besides this Appendix, the world is happy in the possession of a discourse entitled, An Explanation of the Modes or Tones in the ancient Græcian Music, by Sir Francis Haskins Eyles Stiles, Bart., F. R. S., and published in the Philosophical Transactions for the year 1760; and by the assistance of these two valuable tracts it is hoped that this abstruse part of musical science may be rendered to a great degree intelligible.

CHAP. X.

To conceive aright of the nature of the modes, it must be understood, that as there are in nature three different kinds of diatessaron, and also four different kinds of diapente; and as the diapason is composed of these two systems, it follows that there are in nature seven species of diapason.* The difference among these several systems arises altogether from the different position of the semitone in each species. To explain this difference in the language of the ancient writers would be very difficult, as the terms used by them are not so well calculated to express the place of the semitone as those syllables invented by the moderns for that sole purpose, the practice whereof is termed solmization. We must therefore so far transgress against chronological order, as, in conformity to the practice of Dr. Wallis, to assume these syllables for the purpose of distinguishing the several species of diatessaron, diapente, and diapason, reserving a particular account of their invention and use to its proper place.

To begin with the diatessaron; it contains four chords and three intervals : its species are also three : the first is said to be that which has LA, the characteristical ratio or sound of the diatessaron, as MI is of the diapente and diapason, in the first or more acute place ; the second which hath it in the second, and the third which hath it in the third.†

Euclid defines these several species by the appellatives that denote their situation on the lyre, viz., Βαρυπυκνοι Barypyknoi, Μεσοπυκνοι Mesopyknoi, and Οξυπυκνοι Oxypyknoi,‡ meaning by the first the series from Hypaton hypaton to Hypate meson,

which we sing in ascending from the grave to the acute by the syllables FA, SOL, LA; by the second, the series from Parhypate hypaton to Parhypate meson, SOL, LA, FA; and by the third, that from Lychanos hypaton to Lychanos meson, FA, SOL, LA.§ As to the other series here under exhibited from Hypate meson to Mese, it is inserted to shew that the diatessaron is capable of but three mutations ; for this latter will be found to be precisely the same as, or in truth but a bare repetition of, the first,‖ as is evident in the following scales, in which the extreme or grave sound from which we ascend, is distinguished by a difference of character; the syllables being ever intended to express the intervals or ratios, and not the chords themselves.

SPECIES of the DIATESSARON III.

Mese	a la			la
	G sol		sol	sol
	F fa	fa	fa	fa
Hypate meson	E la	la	la	la	LA
	D sol	sol	sol	SOL	1
	C fa	fa	FA	3
Hypate hypaton	B MI	MI	2
	1

The above is the tetrachord hypaton of the great system; but as a diapente contains five chords and four intervals, to explain the nature of the several species included in that system a greater series is required; it is therefore necessary for this purpose to make use of those two tetrachords between which the diezeuctic tone may be properly interposed ; and these can be no other than the tetrachord Meson, and the tetrachord Diezeugmenon. It has been just said that the characteristic syllable of the diapente is MI, and this will be found to occur in the first, second, third, and fourth places of the following example of the possible variations in that system, the consequence whereof is, that the first species is to be sung FA, SOL, LA, MI, the second SOL, LA, MI, FA, the third LA, MI, FA, SOL, and the fourth MI, FA, SOL, LA, as in the following scales :—

SPECIES of the DIAPENTE IV.

Nete diezeugmenon	e la			la
	d sol		sol	sol
	c fa|	fa	fa	fa
Paramese	b mi	mi	mi	mi	mi
Mese	a la	la	la	la	LA
	G sol	sol	sol	SOL	4
	F fa	fa	FA	3
Hypate meson	E LA	LA	2
	1

These are all the mutations of which the diapente is capable ; that an additional series, namely, that from ♮ to f, was not inserted as a proof of it, agreeable to what was done in respect to the next preceding diagram, was because between ♮ and f the diazeuctic tone marked by the syllable MI does no where occur : or, in other words, that series is a semidiapente or false fifth, containing only three tones, which is less by a semitone, or, to speak with

* Vide Ptolem. Harm. lib. II. cap. ix. ex vers. Wallis. Wallis. Append. de Vet. Harm. pag. 310. Euclid. Introd. Harm. pag. 15. ex vers. Meibom. Kirch. Musurg. tom. I. cap. xv. xvi.
† Wall. Append. de Vet. Harm. pag. 310.
‡ Introd. Harm. pag. 15, ex vers. Meib.

§ Wallis. Append. de Vet. Harm. pag. 310.
‖ Ibid.

precision, a limma, than a true diapente. As for example :

    ♭ Semitone c Tone d Tone e Semitone f

and were another series to be added, it must begin from MI or ♭; now the diazeuctic tone is the interval between a and ♭, and consequently is out of the pentachord.*

To distinguish the seven species of diapason, two conjunct diapasons are required; for example, from Proslambanomenos to Nete hyperboleon, to be sung by the syllables LA, MI, FA, SOL, LA, MI, FA, SOL, LA, FA, SOL, LA,† in which series will be found all the seven species of the diapason; and that there are no more will appear by a repetition of the experiment made in the case of the diatessaron; for were we to proceed farther, and after the seventh begin from a or LA, the succession of syllables would be in precisely the same order as in the first series, which is a demonstration that those two species are the same.‡

SPECIES of the DIAPASON VII.

From hence it appears, that to exhibit all the various species of diapason, a less system than the disdiapason would have been insufficient; for though the same sounds, as to power, return after the single diapason, yet all the species are not to be found therein. Ptolemy defines a system to be a consonance of consonances; adding, that a system is called perfect, as it contains all the consonances with their and every of their species; ‖ for that whole can only be said to be perfect, which contains all the parts. According therefore to the first definition, the diapason is a system, as is also the diapason and diatessaron, the diapason and diapente, and the disdiapason; for every of these is composed of two or more consonances; but, according to the second definition, the only perfect system is the disdiapason; for that, which no less system can do, it contains six consonances, namely, the diatessaron 1, diapente 2, diapason 3, diapason and diatessaron 4, diapason and diapente 5, and disdiapason 6;¶ and nature admits of no other.

The above scales declare the specific difference between the several kinds of diatessaron, diapente, and diapason, by shewing the place of the semitone in each.

Salinas,** by a discrimination of the greater and lesser tone, has increased the number of combinations of the diatessaron to six in this manner :—

---

* Wallis. Append. de Vet. Harm. pag. 311.
† Ibid.
‡ Ibid.
§ Ibid.
‖ Lib. II. cap. iv.
¶ Vide Euclid. Introd. Harm. ex vers. Meib.
** Lib. IV. cap. iii.

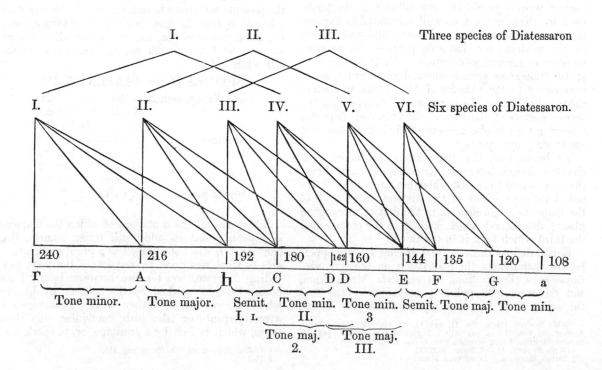

According to which, each of the diatessarons is made to consist of a hemitone, tone, and tone; yet out of the above six combinations, we see that these intervals do not occur twice in the same order.

Besides these, Salinas has shewn the following six other species of diatessaron; in his opinion not less true than those above exhibited :—

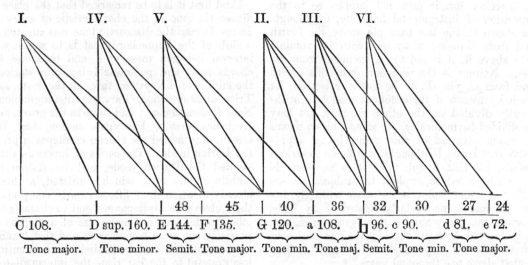

	I.	IV.	V.		II.	III.			VI.	
			48	45	40	36	32	30	27	24
C 108.		D sup. 160.	E 144.	F 135.	G 120.	a 108.	♮ 96.	c 90.	d 81.	e 72.
Tone major.		Tone minor.	Semit.	Tone major.	Tone min.	Tone maj.	Semit.	Tone min.	Tone major.	

It seems however that he has considered that as a diatessaron, which in truth is only nominally so, namely, the Tritonus between F and ♮;* the situation whereof, in respect to the others in the above diagram, seems to have suggested to him a motive for inserting from Bede an account of a very curious method of divination, formerly practised, which is here, with some small variation, translated from Salinas :—

'It is very credible that this disposition gave 'rise to that well-known game, the design whereof 'is to divine when three men placed in order have 'distributed among themselves three lots of different 'magnitudes, which of those lots each person has 'received; which must be done after six manners, 'and those the same by which the diatessaron is 'divided, and its intervals placed in order as we 'have shewn, that is to say, each lot may be twice 'placed in each of the three situations; for the three 'men answer to the three places, the first to the 'grave, the second to the mean, and the third to the 'acute; and the three lots of different magnitudes to 'the three intervals also of different quantity; the 'greater to the greater tone, the middle to the lesser 'tone, and the least to the semitone. This method 'of divination is performed by the help of twenty-'four little stones, of which the diviner himself 'gives one to the first, two to the second, and three 'to the third, with this injunction, that he who has 'received the greatest lot, do take up out of the 'remaining eighteen stones as many as were at first 'distributed to him; he who has the lot in the middle 'degree of magnitude, twice as many as he has; and 'he that has the least lot, four times as many as he 'also has. By this means the diviner will be able to 'know from the number of stones remaining, which 'of the things each person has; for if the distri-'bution be made after the first manner, there will

* Salinas De Musica, lib. IV. cap. iii.

'be one left; if after the second two, if after the 'third three, if after the fourth five, if after the fifth 'six; and, lastly, if after the sixth seven; for there 'can never four remain, for which a twofold reason 'may be assigned; the one from the disposal of the 'instituent, who from the truth of the thing, though 'perhaps the reason thereof was not known by him, 'was impelled to constitute the game in this manner.

"Haud equidem sine mente reor, sine numine divûm."

'The other taken from the constant and settled 'order of the harmonical ratio; but four cannot 'possibly remain, because the first and third persons 'having received an uneven number of stones, either 'of them must, if he have the greatest lot, take up 'an uneven number also; as by the injunction of the 'instituent, he was to take up as many stones as 'were at first distributed to him; and an uneven 'number being taken out of an even one, the re-'mainder must necessarily be uneven; but as each 'of them may have the greatest lot twice, there 'must be four uneven remainders of stones out of 'the six changes: as to the second, he can have it 'only twice; because as he has an even number, and 'takes up a number equal thereto, there must an 'even number remain; for the others must also take 'up even numbers, as they are enjoined to take up 'twice, and four times as many as they had received; 'and the greatest lot may fall to the second person 'in two cases, for either the first may have the 'middling, and the third the smallest, and then the 'remainder will be two; or contrarywise, and then 'there will remain six; and as the greatest lot can-'not come three times to the second, it is plain that 'the third even number, which is four, cannot by any 'means be left. But the other reason taken from 'the harmonical ratio, is much truer and stronger; 'for as it is shewn in the seven sounds of a diapason 'from C to c, that a diatessaron may be produced 'towards the acute from six of them, that is to say,

'the first, second, third, fifth, sixth, and seventh, the
'fourth being passed over because the diatessaron
'cannot be produced therefrom; so also in this play
'the number four is passed over as having no con-
'cern therein; but it does not happen so in the
'composition of instrumental harmony, for though,
'as is shewn in the last example above, the fourth
'sound from C makes a tritone, with its nominal
'fourth above it, it is not to be excluded from the
'series. Neither is the diapason from this fourth
'sound from C, viz., F, to be totally rejected; for
'though by reason of the tritone it cannot be arith-
'metically divided as the other six may, yet may
'it be divided harmonically. I should by no means
'have made mention of this game, being appre-
'hensive that I may be thought to trifle on so serious
'an affair, but that I look upon it as an example
'very much suited to explain the subject we are
'treating of; and I did it the more willingly, be-
'cause I found it particularly treated of by Bede,
'surnamed the Venerable, a most grave man, and
'deeply learned both in theology and secular arts,
'from whence we may conjecture that it has been
'invented above one thousand years." *

But, to return from this digression, notwithstanding the species of diapason are manifestly seven, the
modes seem originally to have been but three in

* The passage on which this assertion is grounded, has eluded a cursory search among the writings of Bede; nevertheless it may possibly be
found in some one or other of those numerous little tracts on arithmetic,
music, and other of the sciences, contained in his voluminous works,
many whereof as yet exist only in manuscript. The description given by
Salinas of this method of divination is in nearly these words:—

Ab hac etiam dispositione credendum est, ortum habuisse lusum illum
notissimum, cujus propositum est, tribus hominibus ordine dispositis, tres
res diversæ magnitudinis inter se distribuentibus, quam quis eorum
acceperit, divinare. Quod sex modis fieri, necesse est: atque eisdem,
quibus diatessaron dividitur, et eodem ordine dispositis, quo tria ipsius
intervalla, tribus in locis bis singula in singulis ostendimus collocari.
Tribus enim locis respondent tres homines: primus gravissimo, secundus
medio, tertius acutissimo. Et tres res diversæ magnitudinis, tribus
intervallis etiam variæ quantitatis, maxima tono majori, media minori,
minima semitonio. Conficetur autem hic lusus 24 lapillis, ex quibus
primo unum, secundo duos, tertio tres divinaturus ipse tradit; ea lege,
ut ex 18 reliquis, qui rem maximam accipiet, tot, quot habet: qui
mediam, bis totidem: qui minimam, totidem quater assumat: quo ex
eorum, qui supererunt numero, quæ cuique obvenerit, possit cognoscere.
Nam si primo modo fiet distributio, relinquetur unus: si fiet secundo,
duo: si tertio, tres: si quatuor, quinque: si quinto, sex: et si denique
sexto, septem. Neque quatuor unquam poterunt superesse, cujus duplex
ratio potest assignari. Altera, ex arbitrio instituentis ab ipsa rei veritate
forsitan illi non cognita ad lusum sic instituendum impulsi,

'Haud equidem sine mente reor, sine numine divûm.'

Altera ex æterna rationis harmonice dispositione desumpta. Quod autem
ad instituendum attinet, quatuor id circo remanere non possunt, quoniam
primus, et tertius lapillos impares susceperunt: et cum ex lege tot, quot
habent, accipere teneantur, si maximam habebunt, assument impares:
quibus ex paribus sublatis, impares relinqui necesse est, quod alterutri
bis evenire continget, unde quater impares restabunt. Et cum secundus
etiam bis maximam possit accipere, quoniam habet pares, totidem
assumptis relinquentur pares: nam reliquos necesse est pares assumere,
cum duplicare, et quadruplicare lapillos, quos habent, teneantur. Quod
bis evenire continget; aut enim primus mediam habebit, et tertius minimam, et restabunt duo; aut contra, et restabunt sex. Et cum maxima
secundo ter evenire nequeat, constat, tertiam parem, qui quatuor est,
nullo modo posse relinqui. Sed multo verior, et fortior est, quæ ex
ratione harmonica desumitur. Nam quemadmodum in septem sonis
diapason ostensum est, à sex illorum diatessaron in acutem protrahi
posse, qui sunt primus, secundus, tertius, quintus, sextus, septimus: et
quartum præteriri neque in eo reperiri potest: sic etiam in lusu ipso
præteritur quarta dictio, quæ occisa est; quod non ita evenit in harmoniæ
instrumentalis compositione. Quandoquidem (ut dictum est) significat
tritonum, quod à quarto sono inter septem sonos diapason invenitur, cum
à sex aliis omnibus, diatessaron inveniatur. Unde etiam in septem diapason speciebus, quæ à septem sonis oriuntur, sex arithmeticè dividi possunt;
una verò nequaquam, quæ a C cum prima sit, progrediendo in acutum,
erit quarta. Hujus autem lusus neutiquam ego mentionem fecissem, ne
in re tam seria ludere velle viderer, nisi ad rem, qua de agimus, faciliùs
explicandam, aptissimum esset exemplum Quod eò libentius feci,
quoniam eum comperi ex professo traditum á Beda, cognomento Venerabili, viro gravissimo et in divinis literis, ac secularibus disciplinis erudi-
tissimo. Unde conjectari licet, ante mille annos excogitatum fuisse.
Salinas de Musica, lib. IV. cap. v.

number, namely, the Dorian, the Phrygian, and the
Lydian: † the first proceeding from E to e, the
second from D to d, and the third from C to c, ‡ how
these are generated shall be made appear.

And first it is to be remarked that the place of the
diazeuctic tone is the characteristic of every mode.
In the Dorian the diazeuctic tone was situated in the
middle of the heptachord, that is to say, it was the
interval between mese or a, and paramese ♭, the
chords mese and paramese being thus stationed in
the middle of the system, three in the acute, namely,
Trite diezeugmenon, Paranete diezeugmenon, and
Nete diezeugmenon; and three in the grave, namely,
Lychanos meson, Parhypate meson, and Hypate
meson, determined the species of diapason proper to
the Dorian mode. The series of intervals that constituted the Dorian mode, had its station in the
middle of the lyre, which consisted, as has been
already mentioned, of fifteen chords, comprehending
the system of a disdiapason; and to characterise the
other modes, authors make use of a diapason with
precisely the same boundaries; and that because the
extreme chords, both in remission and intention, are
less grateful to the ear than the intermediate ones.
Ptolemy takes notice of this, saying, that the ear is
delighted to exercise itself in the middle melodies: §
and he therefore advises, for the investigation of the
modes, the taking the diapason as nearly as may be
from the middle of the lyre. ‖

The Dorian mese being thus settled at a, and the
position of the diazeuctic tone thereby determined,
a method is suggested for discovering the constitution
of the other six modes, namely, the Mixolydian,
Lydian, Phrygian, Hypolydian, Hypophrygian, and
Hypodorian, making together with the Dorian, seven,
and answering to the species of the diapason; all
above which number, according to the express declaration of Ptolemy, are to be rejected as spurious.¶

But in order to render this constitution intelligible,
it is necessary to take notice of a distinction made
by Ptolemy, lib. II. cap. xi. between the natural, or,
which is the same, the Dorian Mese and the modal
Mese; as also between every chord in the lyre or
great system, and its corresponding sound in each of
the modes, which he has noted by the use of the two different terms Positions and Powers. In the Dorian mode
these coincided, as for example, the Mese of the lyre,
that is to say the Mese in position, was also the Mese
in power, the Proslambanomenos in position was also
the Proslambanomenos in power, and so of the rest.**

But in the other modes the case was far otherwise;
to instance, in the Phrygian, there the Mese in
position was the Lychanos meson in Power, and the
Proslambanomenos in position the Paranete hyperboleon in power. In the Lydian the Mese in position

† Ptolem. Harm. lib. II. cap. vi. Wallis Append. de Vet. Harm. p. 312.
‡ Vide Kirch. Musurg. tom. I. cap. xvi.
§ Harmonicor. lib. II. cap. xi.
‖ Ibid. lib. II. cap. xi.
¶ Lib. II. cap. viii. ix. xi. ex. vers. Wallis.
** Vide Sir Francis Stiles on the Modes, pag. 702.
By the Mese in power is to be understood not the actual Mese or the
middle chord of the septenary, but that which marks the position of the
diazeuctic tone which varies in each mode. In the Dorian, for instance,
it holds the middle or fourth, in the Phrygian the third, and in the
Lydian the second place, reckoning from the acute towards the grave. See
the diagram of the species of diapason in the seven Ptolemaic modes
hereafter inserted.

was the Parhypate meson in power, and the Proslambanomenos in position was the Trite hyperboleon in power; and to the rule for transposition of the Mese the other intervals were in like manner subject.

From this distinction between the real, and the nominal or potential Mese, followed, as above is noted, a change in the name of every other chord on the lyre, which change was regulated by that relation which the several chords in each mode bore to their respective Meses, and the term Mese not implying any thing like what we call the Pitch of the sound, but only the place of the diazeuctic tone in the lyre, this change of the name became not only proper, but absolutely necessary: nor is it any thing more than is practised at this day, when by the introduction of a new cliff, we give a new name, not only to One, but a series of sounds, without disturbing the order of succession, or assigning to them other powers than nature has established.

The following scale taken from the notes of Dr. Wallis on the eleventh chapter of the second book of the Harmonics of Ptolemy, exhibits the position on the lyre, of each of the modal Meses:—

aa Nete hyperboleon
g Paranete hyperboleon
f Trite hyperboleon
e Nete diezeugmenon
d Paranete diezeugmenon
c Trite diezeugmenon
♮ Paramese
a Mese
G Lychanos meson
F Parhypate meson
E Hypate meson
D Lychanos hypaton
C Parypate hypaton
♮ Hypate hypaton
A Proslambanomenos *

d	Paranete diezeugmenon	Mixolydian	
c	Trite diezeugmenon	Lydian	
♮	Paramese	Phrygian	
a	Mese	Dorian	MESE
G	Lychanos meson	Hypolydian	
F	Parhypate meson	Hypophrygian	
E	Hypate meson	Hypodorian	

Now that diversity of stations for the Mese above represented, necessarily implies the dislocation of the diazeuctic tone for every mode; and from the rules in the tenth chapter of the second book of Ptolemy, for taking the modes, it follows by necessary consequence that in the Mixolydian mode the diazeuctic tone must be the first interval, reckoning from acute to grave; in the Lydian the second, in the Phrygian the third, in the Dorian the fourth, in the Hypolydian the fifth, in the Hypophrygian the sixth, and in the Hypodorian the last.†

The situation of the Mese, and consequently of the diazeuctic tone being thus adjusted, the component

* Ptolem. Harmonic. ex vers. Wallis, pag. 137, in not.

† Sir Francis Stiles on the Modes, pag. 709. And see the diagram of the seven Ptolemaic modes hereinafter inserted.

intervals of the diapason above and below it, follow of course as they arise in the order of nature; and we are enabled to say not only that the species of diapason answering to the several modes in their order are as follow:—

Mixolydian			B to b
Lydian			C to c
Phrygian			D to d
Dorian	from		E to e
Hypolydian			F to f
Hypophrygian			G to g
Hypodorian			A to a, or a to aa‡

But that the following is the order in which the tones and semitones occur in each series, proceeding from grave to acute:—

Mixolydian—Semitone, tone, tone, semitone, tone, tone, tone.

Lydian—Tone, tone, semitone, tone, tone, tone, semitone.

Phrygian—Tone, semitone, tone, tone, tone, semitone, tone.

Dorian—Semitone, tone, tone, tone, semitone, tone, tone.

Hypolydian—Tone, tone, tone, semitone, tone, tone, semitone.

Hypophrygian—Tone, tone, semitone, tone, tone, semitone, tone.

Hypodorian—Tone, semitone, tone, tone, semitone, tone, tone.§

And this, according to Ptolemy, is the constitution of the seven modes of the ancients.

‡ Sir F. S. on the Modes, 708.   Kirch. Musurg. tom. I. cap. xvi.

§ Upon the constitution of the first of the above modes a great difficulty arises, namely, how to reconcile it to the rules of harmonical progression, for it is expressly said by Kircher and also by Sir Francis Stiles, in his Discourse on the Modes, pag. 407, and may be inferred from what Ptolemy says concerning them in his Harmonics, lib. II. cap. x. that the Mixolydian answers to the species of diapason from Hypate hypaton to Paramese, that is to say, from ♮ to ♮, and that the semitones in it are the first and fourth intervals in that series; now if this be the case, as most clearly it is, the interval between the chord ♮ and the chord Parypate meson or F, must be a semidiapente, which is a false relation, arising from two inconcinnous chords, and consequently is unfit for musical practice.

Again, in the Hypolydian, from Parhypate meson to Trite hyperboleon, or F to f, a tritone occurs between F and ♮, which is a false relation, and renders this species equally with the former unfit for musical practice.

Dr. Wallis seems to have been aware of this difficulty, and has attempted to solve it in a diagram of his, containing a comparative view of the ancient modes with the several keys of the moderns, by prefixing the flat sign b, to Hypate hypaton; agreeable to what he says in another place, that in the Mixolydian mi is placed in E la mi, and to get rid of the tritone in the latter case he prefixes a second flat in E la mi, excluding thereby mi from thence, and placing it in A la mi re.

Sir Francis Styles has done the same, and farther both these writers have made use of the acute sign ♯ for similar purposes. In all which instances it is supposed they are justified by the practice of the ancients; for it is to be noted that they had a particular turning for every key, which could be for no other purpose than that of dislocating the intervals from their respective stations in the several species of diapason, and might probably reduce them to that arrangement observable in the keys of the moderns, which, after all that can be said about them, are finally resolvable into two.

BOOK II.   CHAP. XI.

In the foregoing enquiry touching the modes, endeavours have been used to demonstrate the coincidence between the seven genuine modes and the seven species of diapason. But supposing the relation between them to be made out, a question yet

remains, namely, whether the progression in each of the modes was in the order prescribed by nature or not. In what order of succession the tones and semitones arise in each species of the diapason has already been declared; and it seems from the repre-

sentation above given of the species, that as the keys
of the moderns are ultimately reducible to two, DO
MI, and RE FA, so the seven modes of the ancients by
the dislocation of the Mese for each, and that consequent new tuning of the diapason for each, which
is mentioned by Ptolemy in the eleventh chapter of
his second book, are by such dislocation of the Mese
and a new tuning reduced to two. To this purpose
Dr. Wallis seems uniformly to express himself, and
particularly in this his description of the modes taken
from Ptolemy :—

'Ptolemy, in the eleventh chapter of his second
'book, and elsewhere, makes the Dorian the first of
'the modes, which, as having for its Mese and
'Paramese the Mese and Paramese both in position,
'and power, or, to speak with the moderns, having
'its *mi* in ♮, may be said to be situated in the midst
'of them all; he therefore constitutes the Dorian
'mode so as that between the real and assumed names
'of all the chords, there is throughout a perfect coin-
'cidence : and to this mode answers that key of the
'moderns in which no signature is placed at the head
'of the stave to denote either flat or sharp.

'Secondly he takes a mode more acute than the
'former by a diatessaron, which therefore has for its
'Mese a chord also more acute by a diatessaron,
'namely the Paranete diezeugmenon of the Dorian,
'and consequently its Paramese, which is our *mi*,
'must answer to the Nete diezeugmenon, that is as
'we speak, *mi* is placed in E *la mi*, and this he calls
'the Mixolydian. The moderns for a similar pur-
'pose place a flat on B *fa*, and thereby exclude *mi*.

'And from hence he elsewhere, lib. II. cap. vi.
'concludes, that there is no necessity for that which
'the ancients called the conjunct system, namely, the
'system from Proslambanomenos to Nete synem-
'menon, since that is sufficiently supplied by the
'change made in Mese from the Dorian to the Mixo-
'lydian mode; for here follows after the two conjunct
'tetrachords in the Dorian, from Hypate hypaton to
'the Mese, that is from B *mi* to A *la mi re*, a third in
'the Mixolydian from its Hypate Meson, which is the
'Mese in the Dorian to its Mese, that is from A *la
'mi re* to D *la sol re*; so that there are three con-
'junct tetrachords from B *mi*, the Hypate hypaton
'of the Dorian, to D *la sol re*, the Mese of the
'Mixolydian.

'Thirdly, as another diatessaron above that in the
'acute, could not be taken without exceeding that
'diapason in the midst whereof the Mese of the
'Dorian was placed, Ptolemy assumes in the room
'thereof a diapente towards the grave, which may
'answer to a diatessaron taken towards the acute, in
'as much as the sounds so taken, differing from each
'other by a diapason, may in a manner be accounted
'the same. The Mese therefore of this new mode
'must be graver by a diapente than that of the
'Mixolydian; that is to say, it is the Lychanos
'hypaton of the Mixolydian, or, which is the same,
'the Lychanos meson of the Dorian, and consequently
'its Paramese will be the Mese of the Dorian; that
'is as we should say, *mi* in A *la mi re*. This is
'what Ptolemy calls the Hypolydian mode, to denote

'which we put besides the flat placed before in B *fa*
'*b mi*, a second flat in E *la mi*, to exclude *mi* from
'thence, and thereby *mi* is removed into A *la mi re*.

'Fourthly, as he could not from hence towards
'the grave, take either a diapente or diatessaron,
'without going beyond the above diapason, Ptolemy
'takes a mode more acute than the Hypolydian by
'a diatessaron, which he calls the Lydian, the Mese
'whereof is the Paranete diezeugmenon, and its
'Paramese the Nete diezeugmenon of the Hypo-
'lydian; which latter is also the Paranete diezeug-
'menon of the Dorian, that is as we speak, *mi* in D
'*la sol re*. We, to denote this mode, besides the
'two flats already set in b and e, put a third in A *la
'mi re*, whereby we exclude *mi* from thence, and
'transfer it to D *la sol re*.

'Fifthly, as the Mixolydian was taken from the
'Dorian, and made a diatessaron more acute, so is the
'Hypodorian to be taken from the same Dorian
'towards the grave, and made more grave than that
'by a diatessaron : the Mese therefore of the Hy-
'podorian is the Hypate meson of the Dorian; and
'its Paramese, which is our *mi*, is the Parhypate
'meson of the Dorian, that is as we speak, *mi* in F
'*fa ut*. We, to denote this mode, leaving out all
'the flats, place an acute signature or sharp in F *fa
'ut*, which would otherwise be elevated by a hemi-
'tone only, and called *fa*, but it is now called *mi*, and
'elevated by a whole tone above the next note under
'it; by reason whereof the next note in the acute
'will be distant only a hemitone from that next
'under it, and be called *fa*, and *mi* will return in
'a perfect diapason in the F *fa ut* next above it.

'Sixthly, as another diatessaron towards the grave
'cannot be assumed from the Hypodorian thus
'situated, without exceeding the limits of the above
'diapason, he takes the Phrygian mode a diapente
'more acute, which is the same thing in effect, since
'between any series in the fifth above and in the
'fourth below, the distance is precisely a diapason;
'the Mese therefore of this mode is the Nete die-
'zeugmenon of the Hypodorian, that is the Paramese
'of the Dorian, and consequently its Paramese is the
'Trite diezeugmenon of the Dorian, that is as we
'speak, *mi* in c *fa ut*; to denote which, besides the
'sharp placed before in F *fa ut*, we put another
'sharp in C *fa ut*, which would otherwise be
'elevated by only an hemitone above the next note
'under it, but is now elevated by a whole tone; and
'as before it would have been called *fa*, it must now
'be called *mi*; and from hence to g *sol re ut* is now
'only a hemitone, which is therefore to be called *fa*,
'*mi* returning either in cc *sol fa* above, or in c *fa ut*
'below.

'Seventhly and lastly, the Hypophrygian is taken
'from the Phrygian, as above defined, and is distant
'therefrom by a diatessaron towards the grave. Its
'Mese therefore is the Hypate meson of the Phrygian,
'that is to say the Parhypate meson of the Dorian,
'consequently its Paramese, which is our *mi*, is the
'Lychanos meson of the Dorian. That is as we
'speak, *mi* in G *sol re ut*, to express which, the rest
'standing as above, we place a third sharp in G *sol*

' re ut, which otherwise, by reason that F fa ut was
' made sharp before, would be elevated by only a
' hemitone, and called fa, is now elevated by a whole
' tone and called mi, and therefore A la mi re, distant
' from G sol re ut by a hemitone, is called fa, and
' mi returns in g sol re ut above, or in Γ ut below.

'The modes being thus determined, we gather
' from thence that the Mixolydian mode is distant
' from the Lydian as in Ptolemy, lib. II. cap. x. by
' a limma, or not to speak so nicely, by a hemitone,
' the Lydian from the Phrygian by a tone, the
' Phrygian from the Dorian by a tone, the Dorian
' from the Hypolydian by a limma, the Hypolydian
' from the Hypophrygian by a tone, and the Hypo-
' phrygian from the Hypodorian also by a tone.

' From these premises Ptolemy concludes, not only
' that the seven modes above enumerated are all that
' are necessary, but even that there is not in nature
' room for any more, by reason that all the chords in
' the diapason are by this disposition occupied : for
' since all the chords, from the Hypate meson to the
' Paranete diezeugmenon inclusively, are the Mese of
' some mode, there is no one of them remaining to
' be made the mese of any intermediate mode : for
' example, the Mese in power of the Hypodorian is
' in position the Hypate meson, and the Mese in
' power of the Hypophrygian is the Parhypate meson ;
' and as there is no chord lying between these two
' there is none left, nor can be found to be the Mese
' of any intermediate mode, or which, as Aristoxenus
' supposes, may with propriety be called the graver
' Hypophrygian or Hypoiastian ; and what has been
' said of the Mese may with equal reason be said of
' the Paramese, which is our mi.' *

Thus far Dr. Wallis, who has undoubtedly delivered, though in very concise terms, the sense of
his author ; nevertheless as the whole of the arguments for restraining the number of modes to seven
is contained in the eleventh chapter of the second
book of Ptolemy, and Sir Francis Stiles has bestowed
his pains in an English version thereof, it may not
be amiss to give it as translated by him, and his
words are as follow :—

'Now these being the modes which we have
' established, it is plain, that a certain sound of the
' diapason is appropriated to the Mese in power,
' of each, by reason of their being equal in number
' to the species. For a diapason being selected out
' of the middle parts of the perfect system, that
' is the parts from Hypate meson in position to Nete
' diezeugmenon, because the voice is most pleased
' to be exercised about the middle melodies, seldom
' running to the extremes, because of the difficulty
' and constraint in immoderate intensions, and re-
' missions, the Mese in power of the Mixolydian will
' be fitted to the place of Paranete diezeugmenon,
' that the tone may in this diapason make the first
' species ; that of the Lydian, to the place of Trite
' diezeugmenon, according to the second species ;
' that of the Phrygian, to the place of Paramese,
' according to the third species ; that of the Dorian,
' to the place of the Mese, making the fourth and

' middle species of the diapason ; that of the Hy-
' polydian, to the place of Lychanos meson, accord-
' ing to the fifth species ; that of the Hypophrygian.
' to the place of Parhypate meson, according to the
' sixth species ; and that of the Hypodorian, to the
' place of Hypate meson, according to the seventh
' species ; that so it may be possible in the alterations
' required for the modes, to keep some of the sounds
' of the system unmoved, for preserving the mag-
' nitude of the voice, meaning the pitch of the
' diapason ; it being impossible for the same powers,
' in different modes to fall upon the places of the
' same sounds. But should we admit more modes
' than these, as they do who augment their excesses
' by hemitones, the Meses of two modes must of
' necessity be applied to the place of one sound ; so
' that in INTERCHANGING THE TUNINGS of those two
' modes, the whole system in each must be removed,
' not preserving any one of the preceding tensions
' in common, by which to regulate the proper pitch
' of the voice. For the Mese in power of the Hypo-
' dorian for instance, being fixed to Hypate meson
' by position, and that of the Hypophrygian to
' Parhypate meson, the mode taken between these
' two, and called by them the graver Hypophrygian,
' to distinguish it from the other acuter one, must
' have its Mese either in Hypate, as the Hypodorian,
' or in Parhypate, as the acuter Hypophrygian ;
' which being the case, when we interchange the
' tuning of two such modes, which use one common
' sound, this sound is indeed altered an hemitone in
' pitch by intension or remission ; but having the
' same power in each of the modes, viz., that of the
' Mese, all the rest of the sounds are intended or
' remitted in like manner, for the sake of preserving
' the ratios to the Mese, the same with those taken
' before the mutation, according to the genus common
' to both modes ; so that this mode is not to be
' held different in species from the former, but the
' Hypodorian again, or the same Hypophrygian, only
' somewhat acuter or graver in pitch, that these
' seven modes therefore are sufficient, and such as
' the ratios require, be it thus far declared.' †

Dr. Wallis continues his argument, and with
a degree of perspicuity that leaves no room to doubt
but that he is right in his opinion, shows that the
modes of the ancients were no other than the seven
species of diapason : for, as a consequence of what
he had before laid down, he asserts that the syllable
mi, to speak, as he says, with the moderns, has
occupied all the chords by the modes now determined,
since in the Hypodorian, mi is found in F, and also
in f, which is a diapason distant therefrom. In the
Hypophrygian it is found in G, and therefore also
in Γ and in g, which are each a diapason distant
therefrom. In the Hypophrygian it is found in
a, and therefore in A and aa, each distant a diapason
therefrom. In the Dorian it is found in ♭, and
therefrom in ♭ and ♭♭. In the Phrygian mi is
found in c, and also in C and cc. In the Lydian it
is found in d, and therefore in D and dd. And
lastly, in the Mixolydian it is found in e, and con-

sequently in E and ee; from all which it is evident that there can no one chord remain whereon to place *mi* for any other mode, which would not coincide with some one of these above specified.*

Nothing need be added to illustrate this account of the modes but an observation, that instead of g and c for the respective places of *mi* in the Hypo-

phrygian and Phrygian modes, their true positions will be found to be in g♯ and c♯ and their replicates.

The following scheme is exhibited by Dr. Wallis to show the correspondence between the several keys as they arise in the modern system, and the modes of the ancients:—

By which it should seem that the key of A with the lesser third answers to the Dorian; D with the lesser third to the Mixolydian; G with the lesser third to the Hypolydian; C with the lesser third to the Lydian; E with the lesser third to the Hypodorian; B with the lesser third to the Phrygian, and F♯ with the lesser third to the Hypophrygian.

These are the sentiments of those who taught that the modes were coincident with the species of diapason. Another opinion however prevailed, namely, that the word Mode or tone signified not so properly any determinate Succession of sounds, as the Place of a sound; and indeed this is one of the definitions given by Euclid of the word Tone or Mode;‡ or, in other words, the difference between one tone and another consisted in the Tension, or, as we should say, the Pitch of the system.§ The occasion of this diversity of opinion seems to be this, Aristoxenus the father of that sect which rejected the measure by ratios, and computed it by intervals, in his treatise on Harmonics, book the second, divides the science into seven parts, 1. Of sounds   2. Of intervals 3. Of genera.   4. Of systems.   5. Of tones.   6. of mutations.   7. of melopoeïa.‖   Now had he considered the species of diapason to have been the same as, or even connected with, the modes, it had been natural for him to have placed them under the fifth division, that is to say, of tones, or at least under the sixth, of mutations. instead of which we find them ranged under the fourth, namely, that of systems; and even there it is not expressly said, though from their denominations, and other circumstances it might well be inferred, that the species of diapason had a relation to the modes.¶   The silence of Aristoxenus, and indeed of all his followers, in this respect, has created a difficulty in admitting a connexion between the species of diapason and the modes, and has led some to suspect that they were distinct; though after all that can be said, if the modes were not the same with the species, it is extremely hard to conceive what they could be; for a definition of a mode, according to the Aristoxeneans,

does by no means answer to the effects ascribed by the ancient writers, such as Plutarch and others, to the modes; for instance, can it be said of the Dorian that it was grave and solemn, or of the Phrygian that it was warlike, or that the Lydian was soft and effeminate, when the difference between them consisted only in a different degree of intension or remission; or, in other words, a difference in respect of their acumen or gravity? On the other hand, the keys of the moderns, which, as already has been shewn, answers to the modes of the ancients, have each their characteristic, arising from the different measures of their component intervals; those with the minor third are all calculated to excite the mournful affections; and yet amongst these a difference is easily noted : the funereal melancholy of that of F is very distinguishable from the cloying sweetness of that of A; between those with the greater third a diversity is also apparent, for neither is the martial ardour of the key D at all allied to the hilarity that distinguishes the key E, nor the plaintive softness of E b to the masculine energy of B b; but surely no such diversity could exist, if the sole difference among them lay in the Pitch, without regard to their component intervals.

This difficulty, whether greater or less, seems however to be now removed by the industry and ingenuity of the above-named Sir Francis Stiles, who in the discourse so often above-cited, namely, his Explanation of the Modes or Tones in the ancient Græcian Music, has reconciled the two doctrines, and suggested a method for demonstrating that to adjust the pitch of any given mode is also to adjust the succession of its intervals, the consequence whereof is a discovery that the two doctrines, though seemingly repugnant, are in reality one and the same. The reasonings of this very able and accurate writer are so very close and scientific, that it is not easy to deliver his sense in other terms than his own; however it may not be amiss to give a short statement of his arguments.

The two doctrines which he has undertaken thus to reconcile, he distinguishes by the epithets of Harmonic and Musical; the former of these, which he says had the Aristoxeneans for its friends, taught that the difference between one mode and another,

---

* Append. de Vet. Harm. 315.
† Ptolem. Harmonic. ex vers. Wallis, pag. 137, in not.
‡ Introd. Harm. pag. 19, ex vers. Meibom.
§ Sir Francis Stiles on the Modes, pag. 698.
‖ Lib. II. pag. xxxv. et seq. ex vers. Meibom.
¶ Vide Sir Francis Stiles on the Modes, pag. 704.

lay in the tension or pitch of the system; the latter, and which Ptolemy with great force of reasoning contends for, teaches that this difference consisted in the manner of dividing an octave, or, as the ancients express it, in the different species of diapason: the task which this writer has undertaken is, to shew that between these two definitions of a musical mode there is a perfect agreement and coincidence.

In order to demonstrate this he shews, pag. 701, from Bacchius, pag. 12, edit. Meibom. that the Mixolydian mode was the most acute, the Lydian graver by a hemitone, the Phrygian graver than the Lydian by a tone, the Dorian graver than the Phrygian by a tone, the Hypolydian graver than the Dorian by a hemitone, the Hypophrygian graver than the Hypolydian by a tone, and the Hypodorian graver than the Hypophrygian by a tone.* He adds, ' that as the Guidonian scale answers to the system ' of the ancients in its natural situation, which was ' in the Dorian mode, and our A _la mi re_ conse-' quently answers to the pitch of the Dorian Mese, ' we have a plain direction for finding the absolute ' pitch of the Meses for all the seven in our modern ' notes, and they will be found to stand thus:—

Mixolydian Mese in	-	-	d
Lydian in	-	-	c✕
Phrygian in	-	-	b
Dorian in	-	-	a
Hypolydian in	-	-	g✕
Hypophrygian in	-	-	f✕
Hypodorian in	-	-	e †

But to understand this doctrine as delivered by the ancients, the same author says it will be necessary to examine how the Meses of the seven modes were stationed upon the lyre; and in order to that, to consider the structure of the instrument; this he explains in the following words:—The lyre, after ' its last enlargement, consisted of fifteen strings, ' which took in the compass of a disdiapason or ' double octave; these strings were called by the ' same names as the fifteen sounds of the system, and ' when tuned for the Dorian mode corresponded ' exactly with them. Indeed there can be no doubt ' but that the theory of the system had been origi-' nally drawn from the practic of the lyre in this ' mode, which was the favourite one of the Greeks, ' as the lyre was also their favourite instrument. In ' this mode then the Mese of the system was placed ' in the Mese of the lyre, but in every one of the ' rest it was applied to a different string, and every ' sound in the system transposed accordingly. Hence ' arose the distinction between a sound in Power and ' a sound in Position; for when the system was ' transposed from the Dorian to any other mode, ' suppose for instance the Phrygian, the Mese of the ' lyre, though still Mese in position, acquired in this ' case the power of the Lychanos meson; and the

' Paramese of the lyre, though still Paramese in ' position, acquired the power of the Mese. In these ' transpositions, one or more of the strings always ' required _new tunings,_ to preserve the relations of ' the system; but notwithstanding this alteration of ' their pitch they retained their old names when ' spoken of, in respect to their positions only; for the ' name implied not any particular pitch of the string, ' but only its place upon the lyre in the numerical ' order, reckoning the Proslambanomenos for the ' first.' ‡

These are the sentiments of the above-cited author, with respect to the Harmonic doctrine: the Musical has been already explained; or if any thing should be wanting, the scale hereinafter inserted, shewing the position of the Mese, and the succession of chords in each of the modes in a comparative position with those in the natural system, will render it sufficiently intelligible.

CHAP. XII.

It now remains to shew the method by which this author proposes to reconcile the two doctrines. He says that by the Harmonic doctrine we are told the pitch of the system for each mode; and by the Musical, in what part of the system to take the species of diapason, and that by combining the two directions we gain the following plain canon for finding any mode required:—§

CANON.

' First pitch the system for the mode, as ' directed by the harmonic doctrine; then select ' from it the diapason, directed by the musical; ' and we have the characteristic species of the ' mode in its true pitch.' ||

To make this more plainly appear, he has annexed a diagram of the species of diapason, which is here also exhibited, and which he says will shew at what pitch of the Guidonian scale each sound of the diapason is brought out by the canon for each of the seven modes; and that as in the construction of this diagram the directions of the canon have been strictly pursued, so it will appear that the result of it is in all respects conformable to the principles of both doctrines. ' Thus,' continues he, ' in the Dorian, for in-' stance, it will be seen that the Mese is placed in A ' _la mi re,_ and that the rest of the sounds exhibited ' in that diapason, are placed at the proper distances, ' for preserving the order of the system as required ' by the harmonic doctrine. It will also be seen that ' the diapason selected lies between Hypate meson ' and Nete diezeugmenon; that the semitones are the ' first interval in the grave, and third in the acute; ' and that the Diazeuctic tone is in the fourth interval, ' reckoning from the acute. All which circumstances ' were also required by the musical doctrine for this ' mode; and in the rest of the modes all the cir-' cumstances required by each doctrine will in like ' manner be found to obtain: So that no objection

---

* Sir F. S. on the Modes, 701.

† Ibid. Dr. Wallis, in his edition of Ptolemy, pag. 137, assigns c, g, and f natural, for the positions of the Lydian, Hypolydian, and Hypophrygian Mese; but Sir Francis Stiles, for reasons mentioned in his discourse, pag. 703, places them in c✕, g✕, and f✕.

‡ Sir Francis Stiles on the Modes, pag. 702.
§ Ibid, 710.　|| Ibid.

'can well be raised to the principles on which the 'diagram has been framed, by the favourers of either 'doctrine separately : and the very coincidence of 'the two doctrines therein might furnish a probable 'argument in justification of the manner in which 'I have combined them in the canon.' *

Here follows the diagram of the seven species of diapason above-mentioned :—

* Ibid. 711.

SPECIES OF THE DIAPASON IN THE SEVEN MODES ADMITTED BY PTOLEMY.

Mode	Sequence of notes (high → low)
HYPODORIAN	Nete hyperb. (e), Paran. Hyperb. (d), Trite hyperb. (c), Nete diezeug. (b), Paran. diez. (a), Trite diezeug. (g), Paramese (f*) — Diaz. tone — Mese (e)
HYPOPHRYGIAN	Paran. hyperb. (e), Trite hyperb. (d), Nete diezeug. (c*), Paran. diez. (b), Trite diezeug. (a), Paramese (g) — Diaz. tone — Mese (g), Lich. mese (f*), (e)
HYPOLYDIAN	Trite hyperb. (e), Nete diezeug. (d*), Paranete diez. (c*), Trite diezeug. (b), Paramese (a*) — Diaz. tone — Mese (g*), Lich. mes. (f*), Parhyp. mes. (e)
DORIAN	Nete diezeug. (e), Paranete diez. (d), Trite diezeug. (c), Paramese (b) — Diaz. tone — Mese (a), Lich. mes. (g), Parhyp. mes. (f), Hyp. mes. (e)
PHRYGIAN	Paranete diez. (e), Trite diezeug. (d), Paramese (c*) — Diaz. tone — Mese (b), Lich. meson (a), Parhyp. mes. (g), Hyp. meson (f*), Lich. hyp. (e)
LYDIAN	Trite diez. (e), Paramese (d*) — Diaz. tone — Mese. (c*), Lich. meson (b), Parhyp. meson (a), Hypat. meson (g*), Lich. meson (f*), Parhyp. hyp. (e)
MIXOLYDIAN	Paramese (e) — Diaz. tone — Mese (d), Lich. meson (c), Parhyp. meson (b♭), Hypat. meson (a), Lich. hypaton (g), Parhyp. hyp. (f), Hypat. hyp. (e)

By the help of the above diagram it is no very difficult matter to ascertain, beyond the possibility of doubt, the situations of the different modes with respect to each other ; or, in other words, to demonstrate that six of them were but so many transpositions from the Dorian, which occupies the middle station : whether after such transposition the intervals remained the same or not, is a subject of dispute.

With regard to this question it may be observed, that throughout the whole of Ptolemy's treatise, nothing is to be met with that leads to a comparison between the modes of the ancients and the keys of the moderns ; for it seems that with the former the characteristic of each mode was the position of the diazeuctic tone, and the consequent arrangement of the tones and semitones corresponding with the several species of diapason, to which they respectively answer. But the keys of the moderns are distinguished by the final chord, and therefore unless they could be placed in a state of opposition to each other, it is very difficult to demonstrate that this or that key answers to this or that of the ancient modes, or unless a several tuning of the lyre for each mode be supposed, to ascertain the constituent intervals of the latter. Sir Francis Stiles seems to have been aware of this difficulty, for though in page 708 of his discourse, he has given a diagram in which the Mixolydian mode is made to answer to the series from ♮ to ♮, and the others in succession, to the succeeding species, he means nothing more by this than to compare them severally with a species of diapason selected from the middle of the lyre, without regard to the fundamental chord or key-note.

Neither does the diagram of the seven species of diapason, given by him and above inserted, afford any intelligence of this kind ; and but for a hint that he has dropped at the close of his discourse, that the Hypodorian answers exactly to our A mi la, with a minor third, and the Lydian to our A mi la, with a major third,* we should be totally at a loss with respect to his sentiments touching the affinity between the ancient modes and the modern keys.

That there was some such affinity between the one and the other is beyond a doubt ; † and we see Dr. Wallis's opinion of the matter in the diagram above inserted from his notes on the eleventh chapter, lib. II. of his author, containing a comparative view of the keys with the modes. And though it is to be

feared that there is not that precise agreement between them which he has stated, there is good ground to suppose that, as in the keys, the succession of intervals is in the order which the sense approves, so the succession in the modes could not but have been in some degree also grateful to the ear.

This supposition is founded on a passage in the eleventh chapter of the second book of Ptolemy, importing no less than that each of the modes required a peculiar tuning, and these tunings have been severally investigated, and are given by Sir Francis Stiles ; for what purpose, then, it may be asked, but to render the intervals grateful to the sense, was a new tuning of the lyre for every mode necessary ; and what could that terminate in, but two constitutions, in the one whereof the interval between the fundamental chord and its third was a semiditone, and in the other a ditone ; and when the lyre was so tuned, what became of the seven species of diapason ? The answer to this latter demand is, that as there seem to be in nature but the two species above mentioned, proceeding, as will presently be shewn, from A and C respectively, the remaining five were rejected, and considered as subjects of mere speculation.

But before we proceed to refute the opinion of those who without knowing, or even suspecting, that the tuning of the lyre was different in each mode, contend, that there are in nature seven, not merely nominal, but real modes, it is but just to state the reasons on which it is founded.

And first it is said on the authority of those ancient writers who define a mode to be a given species of diapason, that as there are in nature seven such species, so are there seven modes, in each whereof the succession of tones and semitones must be in that order which nature has established, or as they arise in the scale, without interposing any of those signatures to denote remission or intension, which are used for that purpose by the moderns. They say farther that none of the species were at any time rejected by the ancients as unfit for practice ; and from thence take occasion to lament the depravity of the modern system, which admits of no other diversity of modes or keys than what arises from the difference between the major and the minor third ; for, say they, and they say truly, the modern system admits in fact of but two, namely A and C ; the first the protoype of the flat, as the latter is of the sharp keys, all the rest being respectively resolvable into one or the other of these.‡

---

* The anonymous author of a Letter to Mr. Avison, who by the way was the late reverend and learned Dr. Jortin, had in that letter blamed Sanadon and Cerceau for affirming, in their Observations on Horace, that the Dorian mode answered exactly to our A mi la with a major third, and the Phrygian to our A mi la with a major third : from hence Sir Francis Stiles takes occasion to give the above as his opinion of the matter. In which, after all, it seems that he is mistaken, and that the author of the letter was in the right : his words are these, and they are well worth noting :—

'Sanadon and Cerceau in their observations on Horace, Carm. v. 9.

    'Sonante mixtum tibiis carmen lyra,
    'Hac Dorium, illis barbarum.

'affirm that the Modus Dorius answered exactly to our A mi la with 'a minor third, and the Modus Phrygius to our A mi la with a major 'third : but surely this is a musical error, and a dream from the ivory 'gate. Two modes, with the same tonic note, the one neither acuter nor 'graver than the other, make no part of the old system of modes.'

This is very true ; and the reason of Sir Francis Stiles for asserting the contrary was that he had deceived himself into a different opinion by placing the acute signs to f c and g in the Lydian, thereby giving to that series the appearance of the key of A⛬. But upon his own principles the Lydian answers to our key of C fa ut with the major third,

    Tone, tone, semitone, tone, tone, tone, semitone
      DO   RE   MI   FA   SOL   RE   MI

For though the acute signs require that the final chord be A, the succession of intervals is that proper to the diapason C c.

† Sethus Calvisius seems to have been of this opinion in the following passage cited by Butler in his Principles of Music, pag 86. in not :—'In 'hoc chorali cantu, diligentissime considerct huic Arti deditus, qui sint 'ubique ; Modulationis progressus, quod Exordium, et quis Finis : ut 'cognoscat ad quem modum referatur. Inde enim tam primarium illius 'Modi clausulam, quam Secundariam, eruere, et convenientibus locis 'annotare, et inserere poterit.' Calvis, c. 17, and Butler himself adds that this is the general sentiment of musicians. Notwithstanding that Cælius Rhodoginus out of Cassiodorus distinguishes the modes by their several effects. Ibid.

‡ In the Dissertation sur le Chant Gregorien of Monsieur Nivers, Paris 1688, chap. xii. it is said that the eight ecclesiastical tones, which all men know have their foundation in the ancient modes, are reducible to four, and in strictness to two, as being no otherwise essentially distinguished than by the greater and lesser third ; and the same may be inferred from a well-known discourse, entitled a Treatise on Harmony, containing the chief rules for composing in two, three, and four parts, which though at first printed in 1730 by one of his disciples, was indisputably the work of Dr. Pepusch, and was afterwards published by him with additions, and examples in notes. In this tract is a chapter on transposition, in which the reader is referred to a plate at the end of the work, containing a table of the keys, with their characteristics, and a stave of musical lines, with certain letters inscribed thereon, which, for the purpose of resolving any transposed or factitious key into its natural tone by the annihilation of the flat or sharp signatures, he is directed to cut off and apply to the above-mentioned table, by means whereof it may be discovered that all the flat keys are transpositions from that of A, and all the sharp from that of C. This is a process so merely mechanical, that no one can be the wiser for having performed it, and

But what, if after all, the ear will not recognise any other succesion of intervals than is found in the constitution of the keys A and C? The consequence is rather calculated to disguise than explain the true method of reducing a transposition to its natural key. But in a small tract, entitled, Elements ou Principes de Musique mis dans un novel Ordre, par M. Loulie, printed at Amsterdam, in 1698, we meet with a notable rule or canon for this purpose, which fully answers the design of its invention. This author premises that the dieses, or what we should call the sharps, placed at the begining of the musical stave, arise by fifths, beginning from F, that is to say, C G D A E, and that the B mols or flats arise by fourths, begining from B in this order, E A D G C. The rule or canon which he deduces from hence is this: In keys which are determined by sharp signatures, call the last sharp SI; or as any but a Frenchman would say MI, and place or suppose such a cliff at the head of the stave as in a regular course of solmisation, will make it so. To give an instance of the key of E with the major third:—

Here the attentive peruser will observe that the interval between the third and fourth, and also between the seventh and eighth notes, is a semitone; and that to make the last sharp D, MI, the tenor cliff must be placed on the first line of the stave, and when this is done as here it is—

DO   RE   MI   FA   SOL   RE   MI   FA

the progression of tones and semitones will be exactly in the same order as in the key of C, from which this of E is therefore said to be a transposition.

The canon farther directs in the keys with the flat signatures, to call the last of the flats FA, and to place or suppose a cliff accordingly, and to shew the effect of the rule in an instance of that kind, the following example is given of the key of F with the minor third:—

Here the intervals between the second and third, and also between the fifth and sixth notes, are semitones: and to make the last flat, which is D, FA, it is necessary to place the bass cliff on the fourth line of the stave, which annihilates the flat signatures, and demonstrates that the above key of F is a transposition from that of A with the minor third:—

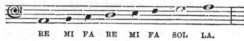

RE   MI   FA   RE   MI   FA   SOL   LA.

Another rule for the above purpose, and which indeed Dr. Pepusch would communicate to his favorite disciples, is, in the case of keys with the sharp signatures, to call the last sharp B, and count the lines and spaces upwards or downwards till the station of a cliff is found; and the placing that cliff accordingly annihilates the sharps, and bespeaks the natural key. In keys with the flat signatures the rule directs to call the last flat F, and count as before.

But amongst the keys with flat signatures, a diversity is to be noted, that is to say, between those with a major and those with a minor third; for in the former the process must be repeated, as in this of A b with the major third:—

In this instance the rule directs to call the last flat, which is the key-note, F; and to count on to the place of a cliff: in doing this the cliff will fall on the first line, and make the key-note F; by which it should seem that the key of A b with the major third is a transposition from F also with a major third.

But as there is in the key of F a flat on b, it is necessary to repeat the process, and see what key this of F is a transposition from; and this by the above rule is to be done by calling the flat b F, and proceeding as before directed:—

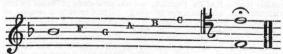

and this key of F will appear to be a transposition from that of C, and by consequence that of A b, from which that of F is transposed, must be a transposition from the key of C also.

then seems to be that there are in nature no other. Now if it be true that the sense of hearing is averse to those modulations that have no relation to any fundamental chord, and that it expects, nay longs for some one sound that shall at stated periods determine the nature of the progression, there is an end of the question. In short, a single experiment of the effect of the Mixolydian mode, which answers to the series from ♮ to ♮, in its natural order, and gives to the diapente a semitone less than its true content, will offend the ear, and convince any impartial enquirer that the existence of seven modes is, in the sense contended for, nominal·and not real.*

But notwithstanding the uniformity of keys in the modern system, there is a diversity among them worth noting, arising from that surd quantity in the diapason system, which it has been the labour of ages to attemper and distribute among the several intervals that compose it, so as not to be discoverable; the consequences of which temperament is such a diversity in the several keys, as gives to each a several effect; so that upon the whole it seems that the modern constitution of the modes or keys is liable to no objection, save the want of such a division of the intervals as seems to be inconsistent with the principles of harmonics, and the established order of nature.

The several effects of the modern keys are discoverable in the tendency which each has to excite a peculiar temper or disposition of mind; for, not to mention that soothing kind of melancholy which is felt on the hearing music in keys with the minor third, and the gaiety and hilarity excited by that in keys with the greater third,† each key in the two several species is possessed of this power in a different degree, and a person endowed with a fine ear will be

* Vide ante, pag. 59, and Dr. Wallis asserts that there are passages in Ptolemy which plainly indicate that the ancients had a several tuning for every mode, which could not have been necessary had they followed the above order. Farther, to this purpose Malcolm expresses himself in the following remarkable passages:—'If every song kept in one mode, there 'was need for no more than one diatonic series; and by occasional 'changing the tune of certain chords these transpositions of every mode 'to every chord may be easily performed; and I have spoken already of 'the way to find what chords are to be altered in their tuning to effect 'this, by the various signatures of ♯ and ♭: But if we suppose that in 'the course of any song a new species is brought in, this can only be 'effected by having more chords than in the fixed system, so as from any 'chord of that, any order or species of octave may be found. On Music, 'pag, 536.
'If this be the true nature and use of the tones, I shall only observe 'here, that according to the notions we have at present of the principles 'and rules of melody, most of these modes are imperfect and incapable 'of good melody, because they want some of those we reckon the essen 'tial and natural notes of a tone mode or key, of which we reckon only 'two species, viz., that from C and A, or the Parhypate hypaton and 'Proslambanomenos of the ancient fixed system. Ibid.
'Again, if the essential difference of the modes consists only in the 'gravity or acuteness of the whole octave, then we must suppose there 'is one species or concinnous division of the octave, which being applied 'to all the chords of the system, makes them true fundamentals for 'a certain series of successive notes. These applications may be made in 'the manner already mentioned, by changing the tune of certain chords 'in some cases, but more universally by adding new chords to the system, 'as the artificial or sharp and flat notes of the modern scale. But in 'this case, again, where we suppose they admitted only one concinnous 'species, we must suppose it to be corresponding to the octave a, of what 'we call the natural scale; because they all state the order of the systema 'immutatum in the diagram, so as it answers to that octave.' Ibid 537.

† Dr. Jortin has discovered a new characteristic for these two species of keys; he calls one the male, the other the female: the thought is ingenious, and is thus expressed by him in a letter published at the end of the latter editions of Avison's Remarks on Musical Expression:—'By 'making use of the major and minor third we have two real and distinct 'tones, a major and a minor, which may be said to divide music, as nature 'seems to have intended, into male and female. The first hath strength, 'the second hath softness; and sweetness belongs to them both.'

variously affected by the keys A and F, each with the lesser, as also by those of C and E with the greater third.

Effects like these, but to a degree of extravagance that exceeds the bounds of credibility, are ascribed to the modes of the ancients : that the Dorian was grave and solemn, and the Lydian mild and soothing,* may be believed, but who can credit the relation, though of Cicero himself, and after him Boetius,† that by an air in the Phrygian mode played on a solitary pipe (one of the ancient tibiæ) a drunken young man, of Tauromenium, was excited to burn down the house wherein a harlot had been shut up by his rival, and that Pythagoras brought him to his reason, by directing the tibicenist to play a spondeus in a different mode ? Or that not the fumes of wine or a disturbed imagination, rather than the flute of Timotheus, played on in the Phrygian mode, provoked Alexander to set fire to Persepolis.

CHAP XIII.

HAVING thus collected into one point of view the sentiments of the ablest writers on those two most important desiderata in the ancient music, the genera and the modes, in order to trace the successive improvements of the science, it is necessary to recur to those only genuine sources of intelligence, the writings of the Greek harmonicians. And here we cannot but applaud the ingenuity and industry of those learned men, their remote successors, who from ancient manuscripts, dispersed throughout the world, have been able to settle the text of their several works ; and who with a great degree of accuracy have given them to the public, together with Latin versions, illustrated with their own learned annotations.

Those whom we are most obliged to in this respect are, Marcus Meibomius, a German ; and our countryman Dr. John Wallis : the former of these has given to the world seven of the ancient Greek writers, namely, Aristoxenus, Euclid, Nicomachus, Alypius, Gaudentius, Bacchius Seniori, and Aristides Quintilianus ; as also a Discourse on Music, which makes the ninth book of Martianus Capella's Latin work, entitled De Nuptiis Philologiæ et Mercurii ; and the latter a complete translation of the harmonics of Ptolemy, with notes, and a most valuable appendix ; as also translations of Porphyry and Manuel Bryennius in like manner.

Concerning these writers, it is to be observed that the Greeks are by far of the greatest authority ; and that their division of music into several branches, as being more scientific than that of the Latin writers, is entitled to the preference. The most ample of these is the division of Aristides Quintilianus, which is thus analyzed by his editor Meibomius, in his notes on that author, pag. 207 :—

Musicæ
- Theoretica : (alia est pars) cujus rursus partes duæ,
  - Physica : quæ dividitur in
    - Arithmeticum.
    - Physicam, generi cognominem.
  - Artificialis : quæ dividitur in
    - Harmonicam.
    - Rythmicam.
    - Metricam.
- Practica : (alia) cujus item partes duæ,
  - Usualis : cujus partes
    - Melopœia.
    - Rhythmopœia.
    - Poësis.
  - Enarrativa : cujus partes
    - Organica.
    - Odica.
    - Hypocritica.

Nevertheless, the most general is that threefold division of music into Harmonica, Rhythmica, and Metrica ; the two latter of which, as they relate chiefly to poetry, are but superficially treated of by the harmonic writers. Upon this division of music it is observable that the more ancient writers were very careful in the titles of their several treatises : such of them as confined their discourses to the elementary part of the science, as namely, Aristoxenus, Euclid, Nicomachus, Gaudentius, Ptolemy, and Bryennius, call the several treatises written by them Harmonica ; whereas Aristides, Bacchius, and Martianus Capella entitle theirs Musica ; as does Boetius, although he was a strict Phythagorean. Porphyry indeed, who professes nothing more than to be a commentator on the harmonics of Ptolemy, institutes another mode of division, and, without distinguishing the speculative part of the science from the practical, divides it into six general heads, namely, Harmonica, Rythmica, Metrica, Organica, Poetica, and Hypocritica ; Rythmica he applies to dancing, Metrica to the enunciative, and Poetica to verses.‡ The branch of the science, which has been

---

* Milton adopts these characteristics of the Dorian and Lydian modes :

———— Anon they move
In perfect phalanx to the Dorian mood
Of flutes and soft recorders ; such as rais'd
To height of noblest temper heroes old
Arming to battle.   PARADISE LOST, B. I. line 549.

And ever against eating cares
Lap me in soft Lydian airs.   L'ALLEGRO.

And Dryden describes the Lydian by its effects, in these words :

Softly sweet in Lydian measures
Soon he sooth'd his soul to pleasures. ALEXANDER'S FEAST.

From which passage it is to be suspected that the poet thought with Cornelius Agrippa and some others, that the epithet Lydian referred to the measure, whereas it clearly relates to the harmony, but Dryden knew little about music.

† De Musica, lib. I. cap, i.

‡ Malcolm has taken notice of this division, but prefers to it that of Quintilian, upon whose analysis he has given the following concise and perspicuous commentary :—'Aristides considers music in the largest 'sense of the word, and divides it into *contemplative* and *active*. The 'first he says is either *natural* or *artificial* ; the *natural* is *arithmetical*, 'because it considers the proportion of numbers ; or *physical*, which 'disputes of everything in nature ; the *artificial* is divided into *har-*'*monica*, *rythmica* (comprehending the dumb motions) and *metrica* : the '*active*, which is the application of the *artificial*, is either, *enunciative* '(as in oratory) *organical*, (or instrumental performance) *odical* (for 'voice and singing of poems) *hypocritical* (in the motions of the

most largely treated by the ancients, is the Harmonica, as will appear by the extracts hereinafter given from their works.

From the relation hereinbefore given of the invention of, and successive improvements made in, music, a very accurate judgment may be formed of the nature of the ancient system, which, together with the ratios of the consonances, and the doctrine of the genera and the modes, constituted the whole of the harmonical science as it stood about the year of the world 3500. After which Aristoxenus, Euclid, Nicomachus, and other Greek writers, made it a subject of Philosophical enquiry, and composed those treatises on harmonics which are severally ascribed to them, and of which, as also of their respective authors, a full account will hereafter be given. What was the state of the science previous to the era above-mentioned, can only be learned from those particulars relating to music, which are to be met with in the several accounts extant of the life and doctrines of Pythagoras, who, for any thing that can now be collected to the contrary, seems indisputably intitled to the appellation of the Father of Music.

Pythagoras, according to the testimony of the generality of writers, was born about the third year of the fifty-third Olympiad, which answers to the year of the world 3384, and to about 560 years before the birth of our Saviour; and although he was of that class of philosophers called the Italic sect, he is supposed to have been a native of Samos, and in consequence of this opinion is usually stiled the Samian sage or philosopher. His father, named Mnesarchus, is reported to have been a merchant, or, as some say, an engraver of rings. Of his travels into various parts of the world for the acquiring of knowledge; of the wonders related of him, or of his doctrines in general, it is needless to give an account in this place. It seems to be agreed that he left not any thing behind him of his writing, and all that is to be known of his doctrines is grounded on the testimony of his disciples, who were very many, and were drawn to hear him from the most distant parts of Greece and Italy. Of these Nicomachus was one, who because he himself has written on the science of harmonics, may well be supposed to understand the doctrines of his master; from him therefore, as also from others, as namely, Ptolemy, Macrobius, and Porphyry, who, though they lived many years after Pythagoras, were of his sect, we may with some degree of confidence determine as to the tenets of his school. A summary of these is given by his learned biographer Stanley, in the passages here cited; and first as to those respecting music in general, he gives them in these words:—

'The Pythagoreans define music an apt com-
'position of contraries, and an union of many, and
'consent of differents; for it not only co-ordinates
'rythms and modulation, but all manner of systems.
'Its end is to unite and aptly conjoin. God is the

'reconciler of things discordant, and this is his
'chiefest work, according to music and medicine,
'to reconcile enmities. In music, say they, consists
'the agreement of all things, and aristocracy of the
'universe. For what is harmony in the world, 'in
'a city is good goverment; in a family, temperance.'

'Of many sects, saith Ptolemy, that were con-
'versant about harmony, the most eminent were
'two, the Pythagoric and Aristoxenean; Pythagoras
'dijudicated it by reason, Aristoxenus by sense.
'The Pythagoreans, not crediting the relation of
'hearing, in all those things wherein it is requisite,
'adapted reasons to the differences of sounds, con-
'trary to those which are perceived by the senses;
'so that by this criterion (reason) they gave occasion
'of calumny to such as were of a different opinion.

'Hence the Pythagoreans named that which we
'now call harmonic Canonic, not from the canon or
'instrument, as some imagine, but from rectitude;
'since reason finds out that which is right by using
'harmonical canons or rules even of all sorts of in-
'struments framed by harmonical rules, pipes, flutes,
'and the like. They call the exercise Canonic, which
'although it be not canonic, yet is so termed, because
'it is made according to the reasons and theorems of
'canonics; the instrument therefore seems to be
'rather denominated from its canonic affection. A
'canonic in general is a harmonic who is conversant
'by ratiocination about that which consists of har-
'mony. Musicians and harmonics differ; musicians
'are those harmonics who begin from sense, but
'canonics are Pythagoreans, who are also called
'harmonics; both sorts are termed by a general
'name musicians.' *

As touching the human voice, the same author delivers the following as the Pythagorean tenets:—

'They who were of the Pythagorean school said
'that there are (as of one genus) two species. One
'they properly named Continuous, and the other
'Diastematic (intermissive) framing the appellations
'from the accidents pertaining to each. The Dia-
'stematic they conceived to be that which is sung
'and rests upon every note, and manifests the muta-
'tion which is in all its parts, which is inconfused
'and divided, and disjoined by the magnitudes,
'which are in the several sounds as coacerved, but
'not commixt, the parts of the voice being applied
'mutually to one another, which may easily be
'separated and distinguished, and are not destroyed
'together; such is the musical kind of voice, which
'to the knowing manifests all sounds of what magni-
'tude every one participates: For if a man use it
'not after this manner, he is not said to sing but to
'speak.†

'Human voice having in this manner two parts,
'they conceived that there are two places, which
'each in passing possesseth. The place of con-
'tinuous voice, which is by nature infinite in magni-
'tude, receiveth its proper term from that wherewith
'the speaker began until he ends, that is the place
'from the begining of his speech to his conclusive
'silence. So that the variety thereof is in our power,

'pantomimes). To what purpose some add hydraulical I do not under-
'stand, for this is but a species of the organical, in which water is someway
'used, for producing or modifying the sound. The musical faculties, as
'they call them, are *Melopœia*, which gives rules for the tones of the
'voice or instrument; *Rythmopœia*, for motions; and *Poesis* for making
'of verse.' Treatise of Music, Edinb. 1721, pag. 455.

* Hist. of Philos. by Thomas Stanley, Esq. folio edit. 1701, pag. 385.
† Ibid.

'but the place of diastematic voice is not in our
'power, but natural; and this likewise is bound by
'different effects. The beginning is that which is
'first heard, the end that which is last pronounced;
'for from hence we begin to perceive the magnitudes
'of sounds, and their mutual commutations, from
'whence first our hearing seems to operate; whereas
'it is possible there may be some more obscure
'sounds perfected in nature which we cannot perceive
'or hear: as for instance, in things weighed there
'are some bodies which seem to have no weight, as
'straws, bran, and the like; but when as by appo-
'sition of such bodies some beginning of ponderosity
'appears, then we say they first come within the
'compass of static. So when a low sound increaseth
'by degrees, that which first of all may be perceived
'by the ear, we make the beginning of the place
'which musical voice requireth.'*

These were the sentiments of the Pythagoreans,
with respect to music in general, and of voice in
particular. Farther, they maintained an opinion
which numbers, especially the poets, have adopted,
and which seems to prevail even at this day, namely,
that music, and that of a kind far surpassing mortal
conception, is produced by the motion of the spheres
in their several orbits. The sum of this doctrine
is comprised in the following account collected by
Stanley from Nicomachus, Macrobius, Pliny, and
Porphyry:—

'The names of sounds in all probability were
'derived from the seven stars, which move circularly
'in the heavens, and compass the earth. The cir-
'cumagitation of these bodies must of necessity cause
'a sound; for air being struck, from the intervention
'of the blow, sends forth a noise. Nature herself
'constraining that the violent collision of two bodies
'should end in sound.'

'Now, say the Pythagoreans, all bodies which are
'carried round with noise, one yielding and gently
'receding to the other, must necessarily cause sounds
'different from each other, in the magnitude and
'swiftness of voice and in place, which (according to
'the reason of their proper sounds, or their swiftness,
'or the orbs of repressions, in which the impetuous
'transportation of each is performed) are either more
'fluctuating, or, on the contrary, more reluctant.
'But these three differences of magnitude, celerity,
'and local distance, are manifestly existent in the
'planets, which are constantly with sound circum-
'agitated through the ætherial diffusion; whence
'every one is called ἀςὴρ, as void of στάσις, station,
'and ἀεὶ ϧεῶν, always in course, whence God and
'Æther are called Θεὸς and Αἰθὴρ.'†

'Moreover the sound which is made by striking
'the air, induceth into the ear something sweet and
'musical, or harsh and discordant: for if a certain
'observation of numbers moderate the blow, it effects
'a harmony consonant to itself; but if it be teme-
'rarious, not governed by measures, there proceeds
'a troubled unpleasant noise, which offends the ear.
'Now in heaven nothing is produced casually, no-
'thing temerarious; but all things there proceed

'according to divine rules and settled proportions:
'whence irrefragably is inferred, that the sounds
'which proceed from the conversion of the celestial
'spheres are musical. For sound necessarily proceeds
'from motion, and the proportion which is in all
'divine things causeth the harmony of this sound.
'This Pythagoras, first of all the Greeks, conceived
'in his mind; and understood that the spheres
'sounded something concordant, because of the
'necessity of proportion, which never forsakes ce-
'lestial beings.'‡

'From the motion of Saturn, which is the highest
'and farthest from us, the gravest sound in the
'diapason concord is called Hypate, because ὑπατον
'signifieth highest; but from the lunary, which is
'the lowest, and nearest the earth, Neate; for νεατον
'signifieth lowest. From those which are next these,
'viz., from the motion of Jupiter who is under
'Saturn, Parypate; and of Venus, who is above the
'moon, Paraneate. Again, from the middle, which
'is the sun's motion, the fourth from each part Mese,
'which is distant by a diatessaron, in the heptachord
'from both extremes, according to the ancient way;
'as the sun is the fourth from each extreme of the
'seven planets, being in the midst. Again, from
'those which are nearest the sun on each side from
'Mars, who is placed betwixt Jupiter and the sun,
'Hypermese, which is likewise termed Lichanus;
'and from Mercury, who is placed betwixt Venus
'and the sun, Paramese.'§

'Pythagoras, by musical proportion, calleth that
'a tone, by how much the moon is distant from the
'earth: from the moon to Mercury the half of that
'space, and from Mercury to Venus almost as much;
'from Venus to the sun, sesquiple; from the sun
'to Mars, a tone, that is as far as the moon is from
'the earth: from Mars to Jupiter, half, and from
'Jupiter to Saturn, half, and thence to the zodiac
'sesquiple. Thus there are made seven tones, which
'they call a diapason harmony, that is an universal
'concent, in which Saturn moves in the Doric mood,
'Jupiter in the Phrygian, and in the rest the like.'‖

'Those sounds which the seven planets, and the
'sphere of fixed stars, and that which is above
'us, termed by them Antichton, make, Pythagoras
'affirmed to be the nine Muses; but the composition
'and symphony, and as it were connexion of them
'all, whereof, as being eternal and unbegotten, each
'is a part and portion, he named Mnemosyne.'¶

That the above notion of the music of the spheres
was first entertained by Pythagoras, seems to be
agreed by most writers. The reception it has met
with has been different, according as the temper of
the times, or the different opinions of men have
contributed to favour or explode it. Cicero mentions
it in such a way as shews him inclined to adopt it,
as does also Boetius, lib. I. cap. ii. Macrobius, in
his Commentary on the Somnium Scipionis, lib. II.
cap. iii. speaks of it as a divine and heavenly notion.
Valesius, on the contrary, treats it as an ill-grounded
conceit. Sacr. Philosoph. cap. xxvi. &c. pag. 446.
edit. 1588. Notwithstanding which it has ever been

---

* Ibid.   † Ibid. 386.

‡ Ibid.   § Ibid.   ‖ Ibid.   ¶ Ibid.

favoured by the poets: Milton, who was a great admirer of music, while at college composed and read in the public school, a small tract De Sphærarum Concentu, which with a translation thereof is published in Peck's Memoirs of him. Mr. Fenton, in his notes on Waller, suggests that Pythagoras might possibly have grounded his opinion of the music of the spheres upon a passage in the book of Job, the reasons for this conjecture are very ingenious, and will be best given in his own words, which are these :—

' Pythagoras was the first that advanced this doc- ' trine of the music of the spheres, which he probably ' grounded on that text in Job, understood literally, ' "When the morning stars sang together," &c. ' chap. xxix. ver. 7. For since he studied twelve ' years in Babylon, under the direction of the learned ' impostor Zoroastres, who is allowed to have been ' a servant to one of the prophets, we may reasonably ' conclude that he was conversant in the Jewish ' writings, of which the book of Job was ever ' esteemed of most authentic antiquity. Jamblicus ' ingenuously confesseth that none but Pythagoras ' ever perceived this celestial harmony; and as it ' seems to be a native of imagination, the poets have ' appropriated it to their own province, and our ' admirable Milton employs it very happily in the ' fifth book of his Paradise Lost :—

> That day, as other solemn days, they spent
> In song and dance about the sacred hill :
> Mystical dance ! which yonder starry sphere
> Of planets and of fix'd, in all her wheels
> Resembles nearest, mazes intricate,
> Eccentric, intervolv'd, yet regular
> Then most, when most irregular they seem ;
> And in their motions harmony divine
> So smooths her charming tones, that God's own ear
> Listens delighted——*

Censorinus suggests a notable reason why this heavenly music is inaudible to mortal ears, viz., its loudness, which he says is so great as to cause deafness. De Die Natal. cap. xi. which Butler has thus ridiculed :—

> Her voice, the music of the spheres,
> So loud it deafens mortal ears,
> As wise philosophers have thought,
> And that's the cause we hear it not.
> HUDIBRAS, Part II. Cant. i. line 617.

After all, whether the above opinion be philosophically true or not, the conception is undoubtedly very noble and poetical, and as such it appears in the passage above-cited from the Paradise Lost, and in this other of Milton, equally beautiful and sublime :—

> Ring out, ye chrystal spheres,
> Once bless our human ears,
>   If ye have power to touch our senses so ;
> And let your silver chime
> Move in melodious time,
>   And let the base of heav'n's deep organ blow.
> HYMN ON THE NATIVITY.

Touching the division of the diapason, the following is the doctrine of the Pythagoreans :—

' The diatonic genus seems naturally to have these ' degrees and progresses, hemitone, tone and tone, ' (half note, whole note and whole note); this is the ' system diatessaron, consisting of two tones, and that ' which is called a hemitone ; and then, another tone ' being inserted, diapente is made, being a system of ' three tones and a hemitone. Then in order after ' this, there being another hemitone, tone and tone, ' they make another diatessaron, that is to say, ' another Sesquitertia : so that in the ancienter ' heptachord, all fourths from the lowest, sound a ' diatessaron one to another, the hemitone taking ' the first, second, and third place, according to the ' progression in the tetrachord. But in the Pytha- ' goric octochord, which is by a conjunction a system ' of the tetrachord and the pentachord, and that either ' jointly of two tetrachords, or disjointly of two tetra- ' chords separated from one another by a tone, the ' procession will begin from the lowest, so that every ' fifth sound will make diapente, the hemitone passing ' into four places, the first, the second, the third, and ' the fourth.'†

It appears also that Pythagoras instituted the canon of the Monochord, and proceeded to a subdivision of the diatessaron and diapente into tones and semitones, and thereby laid the foundation for the famous Sectio Canonis, which Euclid afterwards adjusted, and is given in his Introduction, as also in a foregoing chapter of this work. Duris, an author cited by Porphyry, mentions a brazen tablet, set up in the Temple of Juno by Arimnestus, the son of Pythagoras, near two cubits in diameter, on which was engraven a musical canon, which was afterwards taken away by Simon, a Thracian, who arrogated the canon to himself, and published it as his own. ‡

Stanley speaks farther of Pythagoras in these words : ' Pythagoras, saith Censorinus, asserted that ' this whole world is made according to musical pro- ' portion, and that the seven planets betwixt heaven ' and the earth, which govern the nativities of mortals, ' have an harmonious motion, and intervals corres- ' pondent to musical diastemes ; and render various ' sounds, according to their several heights, so con- ' sonant that they make most sweet melody ; but to ' us inaudible, by reason of the greatness of the noise, ' which the narrow passage of our ears is not capable ' to receive. For, as Eratosthenes collected that the ' largest circumference of the earth is 252000 stadia, ' so Pythagoras declared how many stadia there are ' betwixt the earth and every star. In this measure ' of the world we are to understand the Italick sta- ' dium, which consists of 625 feet, for there are others ' of a different length, as the Olympic of 600 feet, the ' Pythic of 500. From the Earth, therefore, to the ' Moon Pythagoras conceived it to be about 126000 ' stadia ; and that distance, (according to musical ' proportion) is a tone. From the Moon to Mercury,

---

* One of the earliest editors of Milton has the following note on this passage, which Dr. Newton has retained :—
' There is a text in Job xxxviii. 37. that seems to favour the opinion of the Pythagoreans, concerning the musical motion of the spheres,

' though our translation differs therein from other versions. "Con- ' centum cæli quis dormire faciet ?" Who shall lay asleep, or still the ' concert of the heaven ? But this is to be understood metaphorically ' of the wonderful proportions observed by the heavenly bodies in their ' various motions.'—HUME.

The above is the vulgate translation ; that of Beza is less to this purpose, as is also that of Tremelius.

† Stanl. Hist. of Philos. pag. 387.

‡ Ibid 388, 366.

'who is called στιλβων, half as much, as it were
'a hemitone. From thence to Phosphorus, which is
'the star Venus, almost as much, that is another
'hemitone: from thence to the Sun twice as much,
'as it were a tone and an half. Thus the Sun is
'distant from the Earth three tones and a half, which
'is called Diapente; from the moon two and a half,
'which is Diatessaron. From the Sun to Mars, who
'is called Πυρόεις, there is the same interval as from
'the Earth to the Moon, which makes a tone. From
'thence to Jupiter, who is called Φαεϑων, half as
'much, which makes a hemitone. From thence to
'the supreme heaven, where the signs are, a hemitone
'also; so that the diasteme from the supreme heaven
'to the Sun is Diatessaron, that is two tones and a
'half: from the supreme heaven to the top of the
'earth six tones, a diapason concord. Moreover
'he referred to other stars many things which the
'masters of music treat of, and shewed that all
'this world is enarmonic.'* Thus Censorinus: 'but
'Pliny, delivering his opinion of Pythagoras, reckons
'seven tones from the earth to the supreme heaven;
'for whereas Censorinus accounts but a hemitone from
'Saturn to the zodiac, Pliny makes it Sesquiple.'†

Stanley represents the intervals of the spheres in
the following diagram :—

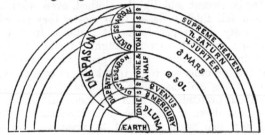

* These positions of the Pythagoreans, that the universe is framed
according to musical proportion, and that all this world is enarmonic,
refer to the general frame and contexture of the whole. But there are
arguments in favour of music, deducible from the properties and affections of matter, discoverable in its several parts: in short, it may be said
in other words, that the whole world is in tune, inasmuch as there are
few bodies but are sonorous. The skin of an animal may be tuned to
any given note, as is observable in the drum: a cable distended by a
sufficient power is as much a musical chord as a lute string or one of
wire. And Strada somewhere mentions six great guns in a fortification
at Groningen, which from the sounds uttered by them in their explosion,
had the names of UT, RE, MI, FA, SOL, LA. The percussion of all metals,
of stones, nay of timber, or of the trunks of trees when felled, produces
a musical sound: hollow vessels, as well of wood, as earth and metal,
when struck do the same. Of this fact the Indian Gong, as it is called,
is a surprising instance; it is an instrument of brass, or some other
factitious metal, in form like a sieve, and about two feet in diameter.
The late duke of Argyle had one in his observatory at Whitton, near
Twickenham, in Middlesex, which being suspended edgeways by a cord,
and struck with a stick muffled at the end, many times, till the quickest
vibrations it could make were excited, yielded not only a clear musical
sound, but the whole harmony of a diapason, namely, the unison third,
fifth, and octave, so clearly and distinctly, that each was obvious to the
ear. This instrument is mentioned by Capt. Dampier in one of his
voyages, and is thus described by him :—
   'In the sultan's mosque [at Mindanao] there is a great drum with but
'one head, called a Gong, which is instead of a clock. This gong is
'beaten at twelve o'clock, at three, six, and nine, a man being appointed
'for that service. He has a stick as big as a man's arm, with a great
'knob at the end bigger than a man's fist, made with cotton, bound fast
'with small cords; with this he strikes the gong as hard as he can about
'twenty strokes, beginning to strike leisurely the first five or six strokes,
'then he strikes faster, and at last strikes as fast as he can; and then he
'strikes again slower and slower so many strokes: thus he rises and falls
'three times a-day, and then leaves off till three hours after.' Dampier's
Voyages, vol. I. pag. 388.
   Glass, and many other bodies, affected by the voice, or the vibrations
of chords, return the same sound that agitate them. It is credibly reported
of old Smith, the organ-maker, that he could not tune a certain pipe in
St. Paul's organ till he had broken a pane of glass in the sash that
incloses it.

† Stanl. Life of Pythag. pag. 393.

CHAP. XIV.

In what manner Pythagoras discovered the consonances, and adjusted the system, has already been
mentioned. The particulars of his life are related
by Jamblichus and other authors; and a summary
of his doctrines is contained in the account given
of him by the learned Stanley, in his history of
Philosophy. Pythagoras lived to the age of eighty,
or, according to some writers, ninety years. The
manner of his death, which all agree was a violent
one, is as variously reported; some say, that being
with others at the house of his friend Milo, one who
had been refused admittance among them set it on
fire, and that Pythagoras, running to escape the
flames, was overtaken and killed, together with
forty of his disciples, among whom was Archytas of
Tarentum.‡ Others say that he fled to the Temple
of the Muses at Metapontum, and died for want of
food, having lived forty days without eating.§ He
had for one of his disciples Philolaus, a Crotonian
(although he is classed among those of Tarentum,
his followers) whose system of a septenary is herein-
before inserted; and who was also the inventor of
that division of the sesquioctave tone into commas,
which Boetius has recognized, and is approved of
even at this day. This Philolaus is said to have
been the first that asserted the circular motion of the
earth, and to have written of the doctrines of the
Pythagorean school. One of his books was purchased by Plato of his relations, at forty Alexandrian
Minæ, an immense price.‖

Among many tenets of the Pythagoreans, one was
that there is a general and universal concent or
harmony in the parts of the universe, and that
the principles of music pervade the whole material
world; for which reason they say that the whole
world is enarmonic. And in the comparison they
assert that those proportions into which the consonances in music are resolvable, are also to be found
in those material forms, which from the symmetry
of their parts excite pleasure in the beholder. The
effect of this principle is in nothing so discoverable
as in the works of the architects of ancient times,
in which the proportions of 2 to 1, answering to the
diapason; of 3 to 2, or Sesquialtera, 4 to 3, or
Sesquitertia, are perpetually resulting from a comparison between the longitude and latitude of the
whole or constituent parts, such as porticos, pedi-
ments, halls, vestibules, and apertures of all kinds,
of every regular edifice.

At a time when philosophy had derived very
little assistance from experiment, such general conclusions as these, and that the universe was founded
on harmonic principles, had little to recommend
them but the bare probability that they might be
well grounded; but how great must have been the
astonishment of a Pythagorean or a Platonist, could
he have been a witness to those improvements which
a more cultivated philosophy has produced! And
how would he who exulted in the discovery that the

‡ Stanley in the Life of Pythagoras, chap. xix.
§ Ibid.
‖ Ibid. pag. 436.

consonances had a ratio of 12. 9. 8. 6, have been pleased to hear the consonances at the same instant in a sonorous body; or been transported to find, by the help of a prism, a similar coincidence of proportions among colours, and that the principles of harmony pervaded as well the objects of sight as hearing? For Sir Isaac Newton happily discovered, that the breadths of the seven primary colours in the sun's image, produced by the refraction of his rays through a prism, are proportional to the seven differences of the lengths of the eight musical strings, D, E, F, G, A, B, C, d, when the intervals of their sounds are T, H, t; T, t, H, T.*

The earliest of the harmonic writers, whose works are now extant, was ARISTOXENUS; he was the son of a musician of Tarentum, in Italy, called also Spintharus. Aristoxenus studied music first under his father at Mantinea, and made a considerable proficiency therein: he had also diverse other tutors, namely, Lamprius, Erythræus, Xenophilus the Pythagorean, and lastly Aristotle, whom, as some say, he greatly reviled after his death, for having left his school to Theophrastus, which Aristoxenus expected to have had, he being greatly applauded by his hearers: though others on the contrary assert, that he always mentioned Aristotle with great respect. He lived in the time of Alexander the Great, viz., about the hundred and eleventh Olympiad, which answers nearly to A.M. 3610. There are extant of his writing Elements of Harmonics, in three books. He is said to have written on music, philosophy, history, and other branches of learning, books to the number of four hundred and fifty-three, and to have expressly treated on the other parts of music, namely, the Rythmic, the Metric, and the Organic; but that above-mentioned is the only work of his now remaining.

Touching the elements of Aristoxenus, there is great diversity of opinions: Cicero, who, as being a philosopher, we may suppose to have studied the work with some degree of attention, in his Treatise de Finibus, lib. V. 19. pronounces of it that it is utterly unintelligible. Meibomius, on the other hand, speaks of it as a most valuable relique of antiquity, and scruples not to style the author the Prince of Musicians. And the principal end of Euclid's Introduction is to reduce the principles of the Aristoxeneans into form. Notwithstanding all this, a very learned writer, namely, Sir Francis Stiles, of whom mention has already been made, hesitates not to say, that the whole three books of harmonics ascribed to Aristoxenus are spurious. On what authority this assertion is grounded he has forborne to mention; however, as the work is recognized by Ptolemy, and is constantly appealed to by him, as the test of the Aristoxenean doctrine, its authenticity will at this day hardly bear a question.

In the first book of the Elements of Harmonics of Aristoxenus, is contained that explanation of the genera, and also of their colours or species, which has already been given from him. The rest of that book consists of some general definitions of terms, particularly those of Sound, Interval, and System, which, though in some respects arbitrary, all the subsequent writers seem to have acquiesced in.

In his second book we meet with an assertion of the author, which at this day must doubtless appear unintelligible, namely, that music has a tendency to improve or corrupt the morals. This notion, strange as it may seem, runs through the writings of all the ancient philosophers, as well those who did not, as those that did, profess to teach music. Plutarch insists very largely on it; and it is well known what effects the Spartans attributed to it, when they made it an essential in the institution of their youth. Aristophanes, in his comedy of The Clouds, puts into the mouth of Justice, whom he represents as engaged in a contest with Injustice, a speech so very pertinent to this subject, that it is here inserted at length, as Mr. Theobald has translated it:—'I'll tell 'you then what was the discipline of old, whilst 'I flourished, had liberty to preach up temperance 'to mankind, and was supported in it by the laws; 'then it was not permitted for the youth to speech it 'in public, but every morning the young people of 'each borough went to their music school, marched 'with a grave composed countenance through the 'streets, decent and lightly clothed, even when the 'snow fell thick. Before their master they sat with 'modesty, in proper ranks, at distance from each 'other; there they were taught to sing in lofty 'strains some hymn to the great and formidable 'Pallas, or other canto of that kind, in concert with 'the strong and masculine music of their country, 'without pretending to alter the tones that had been 'derived down to them by their forefathers. And 'if any one were observed to wanton it in his 'performance, and sing in an effeminate key, like 'those that now sing your corrupted airs of Phrynis, 'he was immediately chastised as one that depraved 'and ruined music. You would not then have seen 'a single instance of one that should dare commit 'the least immodesty, or discover ought that honesty 'enjoined him to hide: they were so scrupulously 'nice in this respect, that they never forgot to sweep 'up the sand on which they had sat. None then 'assumed the lawless minion, or defiled himself with 'wanton glances; none were suffered to eat what 'was an incentive to luxury, or injured modesty: 'radishes were banished from their meals; the anise 'and rock-parsley that are proper for old constitu-'tions, were forbid them, and they were strangers 'to high and seasoned dishes: they sat with gravity 'at table, never encouraged an indecent posture, 'or the tossing of their legs lazily up and down.'†

---

* Vide Smith's Harmonics, pag. 31, in a note. And Sir Isaac Newton's Optics, book I. part ii. prop. 3. pag. 91 of the quarto edition.

† Polybius in his fourth book, chap. iii. has given a description of the ancient Arcadian discipline of youth, nearly corresponding with that of the Spartans above cited, in a passage, which, as it is often alluded to by the writers on music, is here inserted in the words of his elegant translator Mr. Hampton:—

'All men know that Arcadia is almost the only country in which 'children, even from their most tender age, are taught to sing in 'measure the songs and hymns that are composed in honour of their 'gods and heroes: and that afterwards when they have learned the 'music of Timotheus and Philoxenus, they assemble once in every year 'in the public theatres, at the feast of Bacchus, and there dance with 'emulation to the sound of flutes, and celebrate according to their 'proper age, the children those that are called the puerile, and the

It has already been said that this philosopher did by no means acquiesce in the opinion of Pythagoras and his followers, that the understanding is the ultimate judge of intervals ; and that in every system there must be found a mathematical coincidence before such system can be said to be harmonical : this position Aristoxenus and all of his school denied. The philosopher himself, in this second book of his Elements, expressly asserts, that ' by the hearing we ' judge of the magnitude of an interval, and by the ' understanding we consider its several powers.' And again he says, ' that the nature of melody is best ' discovered by the perception of sense, and is re- ' tained by memory ; and that there is no other way ' of arriving at the knowledge of music ;' and though, he says, ' others affirm that it is by the study of ' instruments that we attain this knowledge ;' this, he says, is talking wildly, ' for that as it is not necessary ' for him who writes an Iambic to attend to the ' arithmetical proportions of the feet of which it is ' composed, so it is not necessary for him who writes ' a Phrygian Cantus to attend to the ratios of the ' sounds proper thereto.' The meaning of this passage is very obvious, and may be farther illus- trated by a comparison of music with painting, the practice whereof is so little connected with the theory of the art, that it requires not the least skill in the former to make a painter. The laws of vision, or the theory of light and colours, never suggest themselves to him who is about to design a picture, whether it be history, landscape, or portrait : the common places in his mind are ideas of effect and harmony, drawn solely from experience and observa- tion ; and in like manner the musical composer adverts to those harmonies or melodies, those com- binations, which from their effect alone he has found to be the most grateful, without recurring to the ratios that subsist among them.

Aristoxenus then proceeds to a general division of music into seven parts, which he makes to be, 1. The Genera. 2. Intervals. 3. Sounds. 4. Sys- tems. 5. Tones or Modes. 6. Mutations. And 7. Melopœia ; and in this method he is followed by Aristides, Nicomachus, and most other ancient writers.

The remainder of the above-mentioned work, the Elements of Aristoxenus, is taken up with a dis- cussion of the several parts of music according to the order which he had prescribed to himself. But it must be owned, so great is the obscurity in which his doctrines are involved, that very little instruction is to be obtained from the most attentive perusal of him ; nor will the truth of this assertion be ques- tioned, when the reader is told that Cicero himself has pronounced his work unintelligible.* The use, however, proposed to be made of it is occasionally to refer to such parts of it as are least liable to this censure, and this will be done as often as it shall appear necessary.

The next in order of time of the writers on music is EUCLID, the author of the Elements of Geometry. He lived about the year of the world 3617, and wrote an Introduction to Harmonics, which he begins with some necessary definitions, particularly of the words Acumen and Gravitas, térms that frequently occur in the writings of the ancient harmonicians : the first of these he makes to be the effect of intension or raising, and the other of remission or falling the voice. He then proceeds to treat of the genera and the modes ; what he has said of each is herein-before mentioned. His Isagoge or Introduction is a very small tract, and little remains to be said of it, except that it contains the famous Sectio Canonis, a geo- metrical division of a chord for the purpose of ascertaining the ratios of the consonances, herein- before inserted. In this, and also in his opinion touching the diatessaron and diapente, namely, that the former is less than two tones and a hemitone, and the latter less than three tones and a hemitone, he is a Pythagorean, but in other respects he is apparently a follower of Aristoxenus.† The fundamental prin- ciple of Euclid's preliminary discourse to the Sectio Canonis is, that every concord arises either from a multiple or superparticular ratio ; the other ne- cessary premises are, 1. That a multiple ratio twice compounded, that is multiplied by two, makes the total a multiple ratio. 2. That if any ratio twice compounded makes the total multiple, that ratio is itself multiple. 3. A superparticular ratio admits of neither one nor more geometrical mean proportionals. 4. From the second and third propositions it follows, that a ratio not multiple, being twice compounded, the total is a ratio neither multiple nor superpar- ticular. Again, from the second it follows that if any ratio twice composed make not a multiple ratio, itself is not multiple. 5. The multiple ratio, 2 to 1, which is that of the diapason, and is the least of the kind and the most simple, is composed of the two greatest superparticular ratios 3 to 2, and 4 to 3, and cannot be composed of any other two that are super- particular.‡

The foregoing account of the nature and design of Euclid's division is contained in a series of theorems prefixed to the Sectio Canonis, and are reduced to a kind of Summary by Malcolm, who appears to have been extremely well versed in the mathematical part of music.

† Wallis. Append. de Vet. Harm. pag. 307.

‡ Malcolm on Music, pag. 508.

The above terms were used by the old arithmetical writers before the invention of fractional arithmetic, since which they have in a great measure been laid aside. What is to be understood by those kinds of musical proportion to which they are severally applied, will hereafter be shewn ; however it may here be necessary to give a short explanation of terms, and such a one follows :—

Multiple proportion is when the antecedent being divided by the con- sequent, the quotient is more than unity ; as 25 being divided by 5, it gives 5 for the quotient, which is the multiple proportion.

Superparticular proportion is when one number or quantity contains another one, and an aliquot part, whose radical or least number is one ; so that the number which is so contained in the greater, is said to be to it in a superparticular proportion.

To these may be added superpartient proportion, which is when one number or quantity contains another once, and some number of aliquot parts remaining, as one $\frac{2}{3}$, one $\frac{3}{4}$, &c.

' young men the manly games. And even in their private feasts and ' meetings they are never known to employ any hired bands of music ' for their entertainment, but each man is himself obliged to sing in turn. ' For though they may without shame or censure disown all knowledge ' of every other science, they dare not, on the other hand, dissemble or ' deny that they are skilled in music, since the laws require that every ' one should be instructed in it : nor can they, on the other hand, refuse ' to give some proofs of their skill when asked, because such refusal ' would be esteemed dishonourable. They are taught also to perform in ' order all the military steps and motions to the sound of instruments ; ' and this is likewise practised every year in the theatres, at the public ' charge, and in sight of all the citizens.' Hampton's Polybius, pag. 359.

* De Finibus, lib. V. 19.

It was not till the time of Meibomius that the world was possessed of a genuine and accurate edition of the Isagoge of Euclid; it seems that a MS. copy of a Treatise on Harmonics in the Vatican had written in it 'Incerti Introductio Harmonica;' and that some person has written therein the name of Cleonidas, and some other, with as little reason, Pappus Alexandrinus. Of this MS. Georgius Valla, a physician of Placentia, published at Venice, in 1498, a Latin translation, with the title of Cleonidæ Harmonicum Introductorium; which after all appears to be a brief compendium of Euclid, Aristides Quintilianus, and Manuel Bryennius, of very little worth: and as to Cleonidas, the reader is as much to seek for who he was, and where he lived, as he would have been had Valla never made the above translation.

DIDYMUS of Alexandria, an author to be reckoned among the scriptores perditi, inasmuch as nothing of his writing is now extant, must nevertheless be mentioned in this place: he flourished about the year of the world 4000, and is said to have first discovered and ascertained the difference between the greater and lesser tone. Ptolemy takes frequent occasion to mention him, and has given his division of the diatessaron in each of the three genera.

CHAP. XV.

MARCUS VITRUVIUS POLLIO, the architect, has usually been ranked among the writers on music; not so much because he appears to have been skilled in the art, but for those chapters in his work De Architectura, in ten books, written in Latin, and dedicated to the emperor Augustus, in which he treats of it. He flourished in the time of Julius Cæsar, to whom he says he became known by his skill in his profession, which it is agreed was superlatively great; though, to consider him as a writer, it is remarked that his style is poor and vulgar. In some editions of his work, particularly that of Florence, 1496, and in another published at Venice the year after, by some unaccountable mistake he is called Lucius, whereas his true name was Marcus, and so by common consent he is called. In the fifth book of the above-mentioned treatise, chap. iii. entitled De Theatro, he takes occasion to treat of sound, particularly that of the human voice, and of the methods practised by the ancients in the construction of their theatres, to render it more audible and musical: the various contrivances for this purpose will doubtless appear strange to modern apprehension, and give an idea of a theatre very different from any that can be conceived without it. His words are as follow:—' The ancient architects having made very 'diligent researches into the nature of the voice, 'regulated the ascending gradations of their theatres 'accordingly, and sought, by mathematical canons 'and musical ratios, how to render the voice from the 'stage more clear and grateful to the ears of the 'audience.' Chap. iv. harmony, he says, is a musical literature, very obscure and difficult to such as understand not the Greek language; and, if we are desirous to explain it we must necessarily use Greek words,

some whereof have no Latin appellations; wherefore, says he, 'I shall explain it as clearly as I am 'able from the writings of Aristoxenus, whose dia-'gram I shall give, and shall define the sounds so as 'that whoever diligently attends may easily conceive 'them.' He then proceeds, 'For the changes of the 'voices, some are acute and others grave. The genera 'of modulations are three; the first, named in Greek 'Harmonica, the second Chroma, the third Diatonon; 'the harmonic genus is grave and solemn in its 'effect; the chromatic has a greater degree of 'sweetness, arising from the delicate quickness and 'frequency of its transitions; the diatonic, as it is 'the most natural, is the most easy.' He then proceeds to describe the genera in a more particular manner. Chap. v. intitled De Theatri Vasis, he speaks of the methods of assisting the voice in the manner following:—' Let vessels of brass be con-'structed agreeably to our mathematical researches, 'in proportion to the dimensions of the theatre, and 'in such manner, that when they shall be touched 'they may emit such sounds as shall be to each 'other a diatessaron, diapente, and so on in order, 'to a disdiapason; and let these be disposed among 'the seats, in cells made for that purpose, in a musical 'ratio, so as not to touch any wall, having round 'them a vacant place, with a space overhead. They 'must be placed inversely: and, in the part that 'fronts the stage, have wedges put under them, at 'least an half foot high; and let there be apertures 'left before these cells, opposite to the lower beds; 'these openings must be two feet long, and half a foot 'high, but in what places in particular they are to 'be fixed is thus explained. If the theatre be not 'very large, then let the places designed for the 'vases be marked quite across, about half way up 'its height, and let thirteen cells be made therein, 'having twelve equal intervals between them. In 'each of these, at the extremes or corners, let there 'be placed one vase, whose echo shall answer to 'Nete hyperboleon; then on each side next the 'corners place another, answering to the diatessaron 'of Nete synemmenon. In the third pair of cells, 'reckoning, as before, from the angles, place the 'diatessaron of Nete parameson; in the fourth pair 'that of Nete synemmenon; in the fifth the dia-'tessaron of Mese; in the sixth the diatessaron of 'Hypate meson; and in the middle the diatessaron 'of Hypate hypaton. In this ratio, the voice, which 'is sent out from the stage as from a centre, undu-'lating over the whole, will strike the cavities of 'every vase, and the concords agreeing with each of 'them, will thereby return clearer and increased; but 'if the size of the theatre be larger, then let its height 'be divided into four parts, and let there be made 'three rows of cells across the whole, one whereof is 'designed for Harmonia, another for Chroma, and the 'other for Diatonos. In the first or lower row, which 'is for Harmonia, let the vases be placed in the same 'manner as is above directed for the lesser theatre; but 'in the middle row let those be placed in the corners 'whose sounds answers to the Chromaticon hyperbo-leon; in the pair next to the corners the diatessaron,

'to the Chromaticon diezeugmenon; in the third the
'diatessaron to the Chromaticon synemmenon; in the
'fourth the diatessaron to the Chromaticon meson; in
'the fifth the diatessaron to the Chromaticon hypaton;
'and in the sixth the diatessaron to the Chromaticon
'Parameson; for the Chromaticon hyperboleon dia-
'pente has an agreement of consonancy with the
'Chromaticon meson diatessaron. But in the middle
'cell nothing need be placed, by reason that in the
'chromatic genus of symphony no other quality of
'sounds can have any concordance. As to the upper
'division or row of cells, let vases be placed in the
'extreme corners thereof, which answers to the sounds
'Diatonon hyperboleon; in the next pair to them the
'diatessaron to Diatonon diezeugmenon; in the third
'the diatessaron to Diatonon synemmenon; in the
'fourth the Diatessaron to Diatonon meson; in the
'fifth the diatessaron to Diatonon hypaton; in the
'sixth the diatessaron to Proslambenomenos: the
'diapason to Diatonon hypaton has an agreement of
'symphony with the diapente. But if any one would
'easily arrive at perfection in these things, let him
'carefully inspect the diagram at the latter end of the
'book which Aristoxenus composed with great care
'and skill, concerning the divisions of modulations,*
'from which, if any one will attend to his reasoning,
'he will the more readily be able to effect the con-
'structions of theatres according to the nature of the
'voice, and to the delight of the hearers.' Thus far
Vitruvius.

We are too little acquainted with the nature of the
ancient drama to be able to account particularly for
the effects of this singular invention : to suppose that
in their theatrical representations the actors barely
pronounced their speeches, accompanying their utterance with correspondent gesticulations, and a proper
emphasis, as is practised in our times, would render
it of no use; for the vases so particularly described
and adjusted by this author, are evidently calculated
to reverberate, not the tones used in ordinary speech,
which have no musical ratio, but sounds absolutely
musical: and on the other hand, that the actor
should, instead of the lesser inflexions of the voice
proper to discourse, make use of the consonances
diatessaron, diapente, and diapason, and consequently
sing, as well the familiar speeches proper to comedy,
as those of the more sublime and exalted kind which
distinguish tragedy, is utterly impossible for us to
conceive.

If it was for the purpose of reverberating the music
used in the dramatic representations of the ancient
Romans, that this disposition of hollow vessels, directed by Vitruvius, was practised, we may fairly
pronounce that the end was not worthy of the means;
for however excellent the musical theory of the
ancients might be, yet in the number and perfection
of their instruments they were greatly behind the
moderns; and were it a question, we need look no
farther for a proof of the fact than the comedies of
Terence, where we are told that the music performed
at the acting of each of them was composed by

Flaccus, a freed-man of Claudius; and that it was
played in some instances, as at the Andria, tibiis
paribus, dextris et sinistris; and in others, tibiis
paribus generally; and at the Phormio tibiis impa-
ribus, that is to say, by flutes or pipes right-handed
and left-handed, in pairs, or of unequal lengths. This
was not at a time when the ancient music was in its
infancy : the system had been adjusted many ages
before; and we may look on this refinement mentioned by Vitruvius as the last that the art was
thought capable of. It is not here meant to anticipate
a comparison, which will come more properly hereafter; but let any one take a view of the ancient
music at the period above referred to, with even the
advantage of this improvement drawn from the
doctrine of Phonics, and compare it with that of
modern times; let him reflect on the several improvements which distinguish the modern from the
ancient music, such as the multiplication of parts, the
introduction of instruments, some to extend the compass of sounds, others to increase the variety of tones,
and others more forcibly to impress the time and
measure, as the drum and other instruments of the
pulsatile kind are manifestly calculated to do; the
use of a greater and lesser chorus; that enchanting
kind of symphony, known only to the moderns,
called thorough bass; and those very artful species
of composition, fugue and canon. Let this comparison be made, and the preference assigned to that
æra which has the best claim to it.

Although this work of Vitruvius is professedly
written on the subject of architecture, it is of a very
miscellaneous nature, and treats of matters very little
allied to that art, as namely, the construction of the
balista, the catapulta, and other warlike engines;
clocks and dials, and the nature of colours. In chap.
xi. lib. X. intitled De Hydraulicis, he undertakes to
describe an instrument called the hydraulic or water-
organ, but so imperfectly has he described it, that to
understand his meaning has given infinite trouble
and vexation to many a learned enquirer.†

For the existence of this strange instrument we
have not only the testimony of Vitruvius, but the
following passage in Claudian, which cannot by any
kind of construction be referred to any other :—

Vel qui magna levi detrudens murmura tactu,
Innumeras voces segetis modulatur ahenæ;
Intonat erranti digito, penitusque trabali
Vecte laborantes in carmina concitat undas.

It is said by some that the hydraulic organ was
invented by Hero, of Alexandria; others assert that
Ctesibus, about the year of the world 3782, invented
an instrument that produced music by the compression of water on the air; and that this instrument,
which answers precisely to the hydraulic organ, was
improved by Archimedes and Vitruvius, the latter of
whom has given a very particular description of it.

Ctesibus the inventor of it was a native of Alexandria, and the son of a barber. He was endowed

---

* This diagram is inserted in Grassineau's Dictionary, article
GENERA.

† Mersennus, speaking of this machine, says it is much more complex
than the common pneumatic organ, and that he has laboured to describe
a thing very obscure, and the meaning of which he could not come at,
though assisted by the commentary of Daniel Barbaro. De Instrumentis
Harmonicis, pag. 138. He farther says that Politian in his Panepistemon
has in vain attempted to explain it.

with an excellent genius for mechanic inventions, which he soon discovered in the contrivance of a looking-glass for his father's shop, so hung as that it might be easily pulled down or raised higher by means of a hidden rope. The manner of this invention is thus related by Vitruvius. He put a wooden tube under a beam where he had fastened some pullies, over which a rope went that made an angle in ascending and descending into the tube, which was hollow, so that a little leaden ball might run along it, which ball, in passing and repassing in this narrow cavity, by violent motion expelled the air that was inclosed, and forced it against that without; these oppositions and concussions made an audible and distinct sound, something like the voice. He therefore on this principle, invented engines which received motion from the force of water inclosed, and others that depended upon the power of the circle or lever; and many ingenious inventions, particularly clocks that move by water. To set these engines at work he bored a plate of gold or a precious stone, and chose such kind of materials, as not being subject to wear by constant passing of the water, or liable to contract filth and obstruct its passage; this being done, the water, which ran through the small hole, raised a piece of cork, or little ship inverted, which workmen call Tympanum, upon which was a rule and some wheels equally divided, whose teeth moving one another made these wheels turn very leisurely. He also made other rules and wheels, divided after the same manner, which by one single motion in turning round produced divers effects; made several small images move round about pyramids, threw up stones like eggs, made trumpets sound, and performed several other things not essential to clockwork. Vitruvius de Architectura, lib. IX. cap. viii.

But to return: The following is the description given by Vitruvius of the hydraulic organ:—

'Autem quas habeant ratiocinationes, quam bre- 'vissimè proxime que attingere potero: et scriptura 'consequi, non prætermittam. De materia compacta 'basi area in ea ex ære fabricata collocatur. Supra 'basin eriguntur regulæ dextra ac sinistra scalari 'forma compactæ: quibus includuntur ærei modioli 'fundulis ambulationibus ex torno subtiliter subactis 'habentibus infixos in media ferreos ancones; et 'verticulis cum vectibus conjunctos pellibusque lana- 'tis involutos. Item in summa planitie foramina cir- 'citer digitorum ternum, quibus foraminibus proximè 'in verticulis collocati ærei delphini, pendentia habent 'catenis cymbalia ex ore in fra foramina modiorum 'celata. Intra aream: quo loci aqua sustinetur in 'est in id genus uti infundibulum inversum: quem 'super traxilli alti circiter digitorum ternum sup- 'positi librant spatium imum. Ima inter labra phi- 'gæos et aræ fundum. Supra autem cerviculum ejus 'coagmenta arcula sustinet caput machinæ quæ Grecè 'Canon Musicus appellatur: in cujus longitudine si 'canalis tetrachordos est fiunt quatuor. Si exachordos 'sex. Si octochordos octo. Singulis autem canalibus 'singula epithonia sunt inclusa manubriis ferreis 'collocata. Quæ manubria cum torquentur ex arca 'patefaciunt nares in canales. Ex canalibus autem

'canon habet ordinata in transverso foramina res- 'pondentia in naribus; quæ sunt in tabula summa: 'quæ tabula Græcè Pinas dicitur. Inter tabulam 'et canona regulæ sunt interpositæ ad eundem modum 'foratæ ex oleo subactæ: ut faciliter impellantur: 'et rursus introrsus reducantur: quæ obturant ea 'foramina: plinthidesque appellantur. Quarum itus 'et reditus alias obturat: alias operit terebrationes. 'Hæ regulæ habent ferrea choragia fixa et juncta 'cum pinnis quarum tactus motiones efficit. Regu- 'larum continentur supra tabulam foramina quæ 'ex canalibus habent egressum spiritus sunt annuli 'agglutinati: quibus lingulæ omnium includuntur 'organorum. E modiolis autem fistulæ sunt conti- 'nentes conjunctæ ligneis cervicibus: pertinentesque 'ad nares: quæ sunt in arcula: in quibus axes sunt 'ex torno subacti: et ibi collocati. Qui cum recipit 'arcula animam spiritum non patientur obturantes 'foramina rursus redire. Ita cum vectes extolluntur 'ancones educunt fundos modiolorum ad imum. Del- 'phinique qui sunt in verticulis inclusi calcantes 'in eos cymbala replent spatia modiolorum: atque 'ancones extollentes fundos intra modiolos vehementi 'pulsus cerebritate: et obturantes foramina cymbalis 'superiora. Aera qui est ibi clausus pressionibus 'coactum in fistulas cogunt: per quas in ligna 'concurrit: et per ejus cervices in arcam. Motione 'vero vectium vehementiores spiritus frequens com- 'pressus epithoniorum aperturisinfluit,et replet animæ 'canales itaque cum pinæ manibus tactæ propellunt 'et reducunt continenter regulas alterius obturant 'foramina alterius aperiendo ex musicis artibus multi- 'plicibus modulorum varietatibus sonantes excitant 'voces.* Quantum potui niti, ut obscura res, per 'scripturam dilucidè pronunciaretur; contendi. Sed 'hæc non est facilis ratio: neque omnibus expedita 'ad intelligendum præter eos, qui in his generibus 'habent exercitationem. Quod si qui parum intel- 'lexerint e scriptis cum ipsam rem cognoscent: pro- 'fectò invenient curiose et subtiliter omnia ordinata.'†

This description, which to every modern reader must appear unintelligible, Kircher has not only undertaken to explain, but the strength of his imagination co-operating with his love of antiquity, and his desire to inform the world, he has exhibited in the Musurgia an instrument which no one can contemplate seriously; and, after all, he leaves it a question whether it was an automaton, acted upon by that air, which by the pumping of water was forced through the several pipes, or whether the hand of a skilful musician, sitting at the front of it, with the quantity of some tons of water in a reservoir under him, was not necessary to produce that music which the bigoted admirers of antiquity ascribe to this instrument, and affect to be so fond of. Isaac Vossius, in his treatise De Poematum Cantu et Viribus Rythmi, pag. 100, has given a representation of the hydraulic organ, no way resembling that of Kircher, but which he yet says is almost exactly conformable to the words of Vitruvius; after which follows a description thereof in words not less

* Vitruvius de Architectura, lib. X. cap. xi.
† Ibid. cap. xii.

obscure than those of Vitruvius and Kircher: neither one nor the other of the diagrams will bear the test of an impartial examination, or is worthy to be inserted in any work intended to convey information to a sober enquirer after truth; but the confidence with which Vossius speaks of his discovery will make it necessary to give his delineation of the hydraulic organ, together with a description of it in his own words.

Kircher indeed, after all the pains he had taken, has the modesty to confess the inferiority of the ancient hydraulic to the modern organ; for he says that if the former be compared to the latter it must seem a very insignificant work, for, adds he, ' I can-'not perceive what harmony a disposition of four, 'five, six, or eight pipes could produce, and I very 'much wonder how Nero should be so exceedingly 'affected by so small and poor an hydraulic, for 'Vitruvius testifies that when his life and empire were 'both in danger, and every thing at the last hazard 'by a sedition of his generals and soldiers, he did not 'relinquish his great care and affection, or desire 'thereof. We may from hence easily form a judg-'ment what great pleasure he must have taken in our 'modern organs, not composed of four, five, six, 'or eight pipes, but such as our greater organs of 'Germany, consisting of eleven hundred and fifty-two 'double pipes, animated by the help of twenty-four 'different registers; or had he seen our automata, or 'engines of this kind which move of their own 'accord without the help of any hand. Certainly 'these most enlightened ages have invented several 'things to which the inventions of the ancients can 'in no manner be compared.'*

Of a very different opinion is the before-cited Vossius, who declares himself not ashamed to assert, not only that the tibiæ alone of the ancients are by very far to be preferred to all the instruments of his age, but that, if we except the pipes of the organs, commonly used in churches, it will be found that scarce any others are worthy to be called by the name of tibiæ. And he adds, 'even those very 'organs which now please so much, can by no means 'be compared to the ancient hydraulics. And the 'modern Organarii, to speak after the manner of the 'ancients, are not in reality Organarii, but Ascaulæ 'or Utricularii, that is to say, Bag-pipers, for by 'that name were those called who furnish wind to 'the tibiæ by the means of bags or wallets, and 'bellows, as is done in churches.' He farther says that 'those are ridiculous who suppose the above 'appellations to belong to those mendicants who 'go about the streets with a Cornamusa, and with 'their arms force out continued and unpleasing 'sounds.' No, says this sagacious writer, 'the 'Ascaulæ or Utricularii did not in the least differ 'from our modern organists; and the ancient Or-'ganarii were those only who played on the hydraulic 'organ, and they were so called from Organum, a 'brazen vessel, constructed like a round altar, out of 'which the air by the help of the incumbent water is 'pressed with great force, which yet flows equally

'into the tibiæ.'† After remarking on the bad success of many who had attempted to find out the meaning of Vitruvius in his description of this instrument, and to restore it to practice, he says very confidently that he himself has done it, and accordingly exhibits it in the following form:—

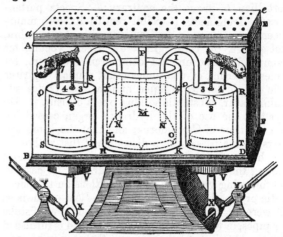

And describes it in these words: 'fiat basis lignea 'A B C D E F, et in ea constituatur ara rotunda 'G H I K ex ære fabricata et torno fideliter expolita. 'Fiat quoque clibanus seu hemisphærium æreum 'L M N O, quam exactissime huic adaptatum. Sit 'vero in medio perforatus hic clibanus, et insertum 'habeat tubum et ipsum æreum et utrinque apertum 'M P. Habeat quoque clibanus alterum foramen, cui 'insertus sit siphon N I Q, cujus nares pertingunt ad 'modiolum æreum Q R S T. Siphon hic habeat 'assarium seu platysmation ad N. Modiolo vero 'Q R S T aptetur embolus V cui affixa sit regula 'firmiter admodum compacta V X, ita ut à vecte 'X Y Z embolus V commode moveri possit. Mo-'diolus autem Q R S T habeat in superiori superficie 'aliud foramen 3, 4, cum platysmatio per quod aër 'ingredi possit. Iste vero ingredietur cum vectis 'X Y Z in Z attollitur. Quando vero idem de-'primitur, platysmation hoc clauditur, et ingressus 'aër per siphonem Q I N, aperto platysmatio ad N, 'exprimitur in clibanum L M N O, unde per tubum 'M P influit in arcam A a C c E e, cujus afflatu 'tibiæ animantur. Clibano vero L M N O, quamvis 'magni sit ponderes, veluti æneo, quo tamen fortius 'subjectum premat aërem et fidelius ne effluat cus-'todiat, superinfunditur aqua, puta ad f f, vel altius 'si fortiores velimus efficere sonos. Fiat itaque ex 'continua vectis agitatione, ut attollatur tandem 'clibanus L M N O, immoto interim perstante tubo 'M P, et siphone N I Q, et notandum simulac 'vehementia ingressi spiritus attollitur clibanus, tum 'quoque æqualem fieri compressionem aëris qui in 'arca continetur. Licet enim effluente per tibias 'aëre clibanus descendat, idemque rursus agitatione 'vectis attollatur, quamdiu tamen clibanus suspensus 'et à fundo separatus manet, tandiu propter æquali-'tatem prementis ponderis, æqualis etiam manet, in-'clusi aëris constipatio, ipsaque clibani et superinfusæ 'aquæ inconstans et mobilis altitudo efficit æqualitatem 'flatus, quo tibiæ aspirantur.'*

The same author affects to be very merry with those who have asserted that this organ was mounted only with six or eight tibiæ, and cites the foregoing verses of Claudian, and the following exclamation of Tertullian, to prove the contrary:—' Specta porten-'tosam Archimedis (Ctesibii rectius dixisset) muni-'ficentiam : organum hydraulicum dico, tot membra, 'tot partes, tot compagines, tot itinera vocum, tot 'compendia sonorum, tot commercia modorum, tot 'acies tibiarum, et una moles erunt omnia. Spiritus 'ille qui de tormento aquæ anhelat, per partes ad-'ministratur, substantia solidus, opera divisus.'† He says that the use of the hydraulic organ ceased be-fore the time of Cassiodorus; and that the same ap-pears from a passage in a discourse of that author on the hundred-and-fiftieth Psalm, wherein, without making the least mention of the hydraulic, he bestows the following very high commendations on the pneu-matic organ, then in common use :—' An organ is as 'it were a tower composed of several different fistulæ 'or pipes, in which the most copious sound is furnished 'by the blowing of bellows : and that it may be com-'posed of a graceful modulation, it is constructed with 'certain wooden tongues in the inner part, which 'being skilfully pressed down by the fingers of the 'master, produce a great sounding and most sweet 'cantilena.'‡

He notwithstanding asserts that the hydraulic organ continued in use lower down than the time of Cassiodorus; for that in the French annals of a certain anonymous writer, he is informed that in the year 826, a certain Venetian, called Georgius, or rather Gregorius, constructed a hydraulic organ for Lewis the Pious, at Aix la Chapelle, and that after the manner of the ancients.§ He elsewhere says that the hydraulic organ of Daniel Barbaro, described in his Commentary on Vitruvius, is with great reason ex-ploded by all;‖ and that those who in his time had in their writings concerning music, inserted the con-struction of the Vitruvian organ, while they de-preciate the inventions of the ancients, may serve as an example to shew how customary a thing it is for men to despise what they themselves do not under-stand. This passage is manifestly intended as a censure on Kircher's description of the hydraulic organ, and proves nothing but the extreme bigotry

of Vossius.¶ As to the hydraulic organs of modern Italy of which Grassineau says there are several in the grottos of vineyards, particularly one belonging to the family d'Este, near the Tiber, described by Baptista Porta, he says they are very different, and no way resemble the ancient hydraulic organ. These perhaps will be found to be nothing more than the common organ played on by a barrel, which by a very easy contrivance is set in motion by a small stream of water : and that these for more than a century past have been in use in various parts of Italy there is additional evidence. In a book supposed to be written by one Dr. Thomas Powell, a canon of St. David's, entitled Human Industry, or a History of the Manual Arts, it is said that Pope Sylvester II. made an organ which was played on by warm water ; and that such hydraulics, frequent in Italy, are sounded with cold water. Oldy's British Librarian, No. I. pag. 51. And in an old English comedy of Webster, printed in 1623, intitled the Devil's Law-Case, Romelia, a wealthy merchant of Naples, speaking of the greatness of his income says,

—————————— My factors' wives
Weare shaperoones of velvet ; and my scriveners,
Meerely through my employment, grow so rich
They build their palaces and belvidears
With *musical water-workes.*

Comedy, which in general exhibits a very just repre-sentation of contemporary manners and characters, is, in cases of this sort, authority : and the poet, in the passage above-cited, would hardly have pointed out this instance of Italian profusion, had he not had some example in his eye to warrant it.

CHAP. XVI.

But to return to the ancient hydraulic organ, a hundred questions might be asked touching the use and application of its several parts, as also what system it was adapted to ; and particularly whether those who have undertaken to delineate it with such exactness, have not formed an idea of it from the organ of our own times, and done a violence to historical truth by incorporating two instruments, which cannot possibly exist in a state of union. And after all that can be said in favour of it, the censure of Kircher above-cited, must undoubtedly appear to be very just, and may serve to show what

---

* De Poemat. pag. 101.

In the cabinet of Christina, queen of Sweden, was formerly a beautiful and large medallion of Valentinian ; having on the reverse one of these hydraulic organs, with two men, one on the right, the other on the left side thereof, seeming to pump the water which plays it, and to listen to the sound of it. It had only eight pipes, and those were placed on a round pedestal ; the inscription PLACEA SPETRI.

† Ibid. pag. 105. In English thus : Behold the wonderful munificence of Archimedes ! (he should have said of Ctesibius) I mean the hydraulic organ ; so many numbers, so many parts, so many joinings, so many roads or passages for the voices, such a compendium of sounds, such an intercourse of modes, such troops of tibiæ, and all composing one great whole ! The spirit or air which is breathed out from this engine of water, is administered through the parts, solid in substance, but divided in operation.

‡ Organum itaque est quasi turris diversis fistulis fabricata, quibus flatu follium vox copiosissima destinatur, et ut eam modulatio decora componat, linguis quibusdam ligneis ab interiore parte construitur, quas disciplinabiliter magistrorum digiti reprimentes grandisonem efficiunt et suavissimum cantilenam. De Poemat. pag. 106.

§ De Poemat. 106.

‖ Ibid pag. 99.

¶ The enthusiastic attachmemt to antiquity of this author is strongly evinced by the sentiments he entertains of the energy of the ancient Tibia, which he scruples not to prefer to every instrument of modern invention. His words are these :—' As to what belongs to the cantus of 'the Tibia which is blown upon by the mouth, I think it may be truly 'said that the tibicinists know no more concerning that instrument than 'the ancient shepherds, and perhaps not so much. This most excellent 'art is banished among the mendicants ; and the Tibia, which was by 'far preferred to all stringed instruments, and to all other instruments 'of music, is now silenced to such a degree, that, if you except the 'Chinese alone, who excel in this part, you will find none in this age 'that can even please a moderate ear ; and the very name of the Tibia 'is justly despised by the European nations. That the Tibia was 'formerly held in greater esteem, and accounted sweeter than the lyre, 'is not only evinced by Aristotle, in his problems, but also by the very 'punishment of Marsyas. How great the care and diligence of the 'ancients was in improving this instrument, sufficiently appears from 'what both Theophrastus and Pliny have written concerning the reeds of 'the lake Orchomenius. It was not sufficient that they were cut at 'certain periods of years, when the lake became dry ; unless they 'were also macerated by the sun, rain, and frost, and afterwards softened 'by long use ; and, remaining without any defect, satisfied the wish of 'the artists. He who reads and considers these things, will the less 'wonder that sometimes Tibiæ have been sold for seven talents, as 'Lucian testifies.' Vossius De Poemat. 107.

little reason there is to lament the loss of many inventions of the ancients, particularly those in which the knowledge of mechanics is any way concerned. The hydraulic organ is one of those ancient inventions mentioned by Pancirollus as now lost,* a misfortune which at this day we lament perhaps with as little reason as we should have for saying that the loss of the ancient Clepsydræ † is not amply compensated by the invention of clocks and watches. With respect to this instrument, it cannot so properly be said to be lost, as to have given way to one of a more artificial construction, and nobler in its effects, as unquestionably the modern organ is. It is remarkable that those who would infer the debility of the later ages, from the few remaining monuments of ancient ingenuity, generally confine themselves to poesy, sculpture, and other arts, which owe their perfection rather to adventitious circumstances, than to the vigorous exertion of the powers of invention : but, with respect to instruments, machines, and engines of various kinds, it is not in the nature of things possible but that mankind must continue to improve as long as the world shall last.

NICOMACHUS GERASENUS, so called from his having been born in Gerasa, a city of Arabia, lived about A. C. 60. He was a philosopher, and wrote an Introduction to Harmony, at the request, as it should seem by the beginning of it, of some learned female contemporary. He was a follower of Pythagoras : and it is by this work alone that we know how, and by what means, his master discovered the consonances. He begins his work with an address to his female friend, whom he styles the most virtuous of women ; and reflects with some concern on the difference in sentiment of the several writers on the elements of harmony. He excuses his inability to reconcile them by reason of the long journeys he is obliged to take, and his want of leisure, which he prays the gods to vouchsafe him, and promises to complete a work which he has in contemplation, of which what he now gives seems to be but a part. Professing to follow the Pythagoreans, he considers the human voice as emitting sounds, which are either commensurable by intervals, as when we are said to *sing* ; or incommensurable, as when we converse by speech. In this latter use of the voice, he says, we are not obliged by any rule ; but in the former we are bound to an observance of those intervals and magnitudes in which harmony does consist.

The sounds and their names, continues this author, are probably taken from the seven planets in the heavens which surround this earth ; for it is said that all bodies which are carried round with any great degree of velocity, must necessarily, and by reason of their magnitude, and the celerity of their motions, cause a sound, which sound will vary in proportion to the degrees of magnitude in each, the celerity of their motions, or the repression of the orb wherein they act. These differences, he says, are manifest in the planets, which perpetually turn round, and produce their proper sounds : for example, the motion of Saturn, the planet most distant from us, produces a sound the most grave, in which it resembles the consonance diapason ; as does Hypate, which signifies the same as principal. To the motion of the moon, the lowest of the planets, and nearest the earth, we apply the most acute term, called Nete, for Neaton is the same as low.

He then proceeds to declare the supposed analogy between the rest of the planets and the intermediate chords, as mentioned in the foregoing account of Pythagoras. But here it may be proper to take notice that the ancient writers were not unanimous in opinion that the graver sounds were produced by the bodies of greatest magnitude : Cicero, in particular, is by Glareanus‡ said to have maintained that the lesser bodies produce the graver sounds, and the greater the more acute. And from this dictum of Cicero, Glareanus has been at the pains of forming a diagram, intended to represent this fanciful coincidence of revolutions and harmonies, which is given in a subsequent page of this work.

In the Somnium Scipionis, which is what Glareanus means when he refers to Cicero de Republica, lib. VI. is a great deal concerning the music of the spheres in general ; and Macrobius, in his commentary on that fragment, has made the most of it. Nevertheless the general sentiment of mankind seems till very lately§ to have been that the whole doctrine is to be regarded as a poetical fiction ; and as to the fact, that it has no foundation in reason or philosophy.

But to return to our author Nicomachus, and his opinion of the harmony of the planets : it is true, says he, that it is inaudible to our ears, but to our reason it is clear.

Nicomachus proceeds to define the terms made use of by him, distinguishing, as others of the ancients do, between sound and noise. Speaking of instruments, he says they are of two kinds, viz., such as are blown, as are the flute, trumpet, organ, and the like ; or such as are strung, to wit, the lute, lyre, and harp ; of the latter kind are also the monochord, by many called the Pandora,‖ and by

---

* Guido Pancirollus De Rerum memorabilium sive deperditarum, lib. I. cap. ii.

† Clepsydra, an hour-glass made with water. The use of Clepsydræ was very ancient, and among the Romans there were several sorts of them ; in general they resembled a sand hour-glass, which is composed of two vessels, so joined at top and bottom, as that which is contained in the upper may run into the under of them. The Clepsydræ contained water, which passing through a small hole, imperceptibly raised a piece of cork with an index fixed thereto that pointed to the hours marked on the under glass. They were all subject to two inconveniences : the first was that which Plutarch takes notice of, to wit, that the water passed through with more or less difficulty, according as the air was more or less thick, cold, or hot, for that hindered the hours from being equal ; the other was, that the water ran faster at first, when the vessel from whence the water came was full, than at last.

These Clepsydræ were chiefly used in a city called Achanta, beyond the Nile. In this city there was a huge vessel of this kind, into which three hundred and sixty-five priests daily brought water from the Nile, which running out of the vessel again, declared the hours. The use of the Clepsydra was to tell the hour in the night, or in cloudy weather when it could not be found by the sun-dial.

‡ Dodecachordon, lib. II. cap. xiii.

§ See a subsequent note, in the present book, containing the sentiments of Dr. Gregory and Mr. Maclaurin on this subject.

‖ An appellative from which the English word Bandore seems clearly to be derived. Meibomius gives the following note on this passage :—

'Φανδρρς. [Phandourous.] Hesychius speaks of it thus : "Pandura ' or Panduris is a musical instrument ; Pandurus he who plays on ' that instrument." Monochords were also by some called Phanduras. ' Nicomachus here says the same, and seems as if he approved of the ' practice. These instruments are various ; Pollux, lib. IV. cap. ix. ' says, "The monochord was invented by the Arabians, and the trichord

the Pythagoreans the Canon, and also the Trigon or triangular dulcimer. He also mentions crooked and other flutes made of the box-tree, of which he proposes to speak again. Of the stringed species he says those with the greater tensions express the more acute sounds; on the contrary, those with the lesser give the more languid and grave; and in instruments that are blown, the more hollow and long, the more languid and grave are their sounds. He then proceeds to relate how Pythagoras discovered the consonances, and to give that account of his system which Stanley has taken into his life of that philosopher, and is inserted in the foregoing part of this work, together with some remarks, the result of late experiments, which in some degree, though not essentially, weaken the credit of the relation.

But without enquiring farther into the weight of the hammers, and other circumstances attending the discovery of the consonances, we may very safely credit Nicomachus, so far as to believe that Pythagoras, by the means of chords of different lengths, did discover them; that the philosopher to the sound produced by the first number six, gave the name Hypate; to eight he gave Mese, which is sesquitertian thereto; to nine Paramese, which is a tone more acute, and therefore sesquioctave of the last; and to the last number, twelve, he gave the name Nete; and afterwards filled up the intermediate spaces with sounds in the succession proper to the diatonic genus, and thereby completed the system of eight chords. The diatonic genus, as this author describes it, is a natural progression to the system of a diatessaron by a semitone, tone, and tone; and to a diapente by three tones and a semitone. This is the manner in which it is said the ancient system was adjusted and extended to that of a complete octave, an improvement so much the more to be valued, as we are told that in the ancient or primitive lyre, all the sounds from the lowest were fourths to each other;* whereas in the Pythagorean lyre, composed of a tetrachord and pentachord conjoined; or, which is the same, of two tetrachords disjoined by an intervening tone, we have a continued progression of sounds.

Nicomachus proceeds to relate that the magnitude of the scale in the diatonic genus is two diapasons, for that the voice cannot easily extend itself either upwards or downwards beyond this limit; and for this reason, to the ancient lyre formed of seven strings, by the conjunction of two tetrachords, each extending from Hypate to Mese, and thence to Nete, were adjoined two tetrachords at the outward extremity of the former; that which began at Nete was called Hyperboleon, signifying excellent. This tetrachord, he says, consists of three

adjoined sounds, whose names are worthy to be remembered; as first, Trite hyperboleon, then Paranete hyperboleon, and lastly, Nete hyperboleon. The other tetrachord was joined to the chord Hypate, and was thence called Hypaton; and each of the three adjoined sounds had the addition of Hypaton to distinguish it from the chord of the same denomination in the lower of the two primitive tetrachords; thus Hypate hypaton, Parhypate hypaton, Diatonos hypaton, or Lychanos hypaton, for it matters not which it is called; and this system from Hypate hypaton to Mese is seven chords, making two conjoint tetrachords; and that from Hypate hypaton to Nete is thirteen; so that Mese having the middle place, and conjoining two systems of a septenary each, reckoning either upwards from Hypate hypaton, or downwards from Nete hyperboleon, each system contained seven chords.

From this it is evident that the additional tetrachords were originally adapted to the system of Terpander, which did not separate Mese from Trite by a whole tone, as that of Pythagoras did. What advantages could be derived from this addition it is not easy to say; nor is it conceivable that that system could be reducible to practice which gave to a nominal diapason four tones and three hemitones, instead of five tones and two hemitones.

But the addition of the new tetrachords to the two disjunct tetrachords of Pythagoras was very natural, and made way for what this author next proceeds to mention, the tetrachord synemmenon, which took place in the middle of that interval of a tone, by which Pythagoras had divided the two primitive tetrachords. The design of introducing this tetrachord synemmenon, which placed Trite but a hemitone distant from Mese, was manifestly to give to Parhypate meson what it wanted before, a perfect diatessaron for its nominal fourth; and this opinion of its use is maintained by all who have written on the subject of music.

The author then proceeds to a verbal enumeration of the several chords, which by the disjunction made by Pythagoras, and the addition of Proslambanomenos, it appears were encreased to fifteen, with their respective tonical distances: it has already been mentioned, that, contrary to the method now in use, the ancients gave the most grave sounds the uppermost place in their scale; he therefore begins with Proslambanomenos and reckons downwards to Nete hyperboleon.

He gives the same kind of enumeration of the several sounds that compose the tetrachord synemmenon, having first Trite synemmenon at the distance of a hemitone from Mese, then after a tone Paranete synemmenon, and after another tone Nete synemmenon of the same tenor and sound as Paranete diezeugmenon.

Mese
    Hemitone
Trite
    Tone
Paranete
    Tone
Nete

"by the Assyrians, who gave it the name of Pandura." He justly says 'that Pandura was an Assyrian word. But the most learned of the 'Hebrews do not seem sufficiently to understand the signification of it; 'they explain it by a twig or rod, whip, thong of leather, as appears 'from Buxtorf in the Talmudical Lexicon, from Talmud Hierosol. 'I imagine the true origin of this appellation to be this, the instrument 'was mounted or stretched with thongs of bull's hides, in the same 'manner as the pentachord of the Scythians, concerning which the 'same Pollux speaks thus:—"The pentachord is an invention of the "Scythians, it was stretched or mounted with thongs made of the raw "hides of oxen, but their plectra were the jaw bones of she-goats."

  * Nicomach. Harmonic. Manual. pag. 5, ex vers. Meibom.

So that there exist five tetrachords, Hypaton, Meson, Synemmenon, Diezeugmenon, and Hyperboleon; though it is to be remembered that the third of these is but auxiliary, and whenever it is used it is only in the room of the fourth, for reasons before given; and in these tetrachords there are two disjunctions and three conjunctions; the disjunctions are between Nete synemmenon and Nete diezeugmenon, and between Proslambanomenos and Hypate hypaton : the conjunctions are between Hypaton and Meson, and, which is the same, Meson and Synemmenon, and between Diezeugmenon and Hyperboleon.

We must understand that the foregoing is a representation of the tetrachords as they are divided in the diatonic genus, the characteristic whereof is a progression by a hemitone, tone, and tone; for as to the other genera, the chromatic and enharmonic, this author professes not to deliver his sentiments, but promises to give them at large, together with a regular progression in all the three in his Commentaries, a work he often speaks of, as having undertaken it for the information of his learned correspondent : he also engages to give the testimonies of the ancients, the most learned and eloquent of men on this subject, and an exposition of Pythagoras's section of the canon, not as Eratosthenes or Thrasyllus badly understand it, but according to Locrus Timæus, the follower of Plato, although nothing of his on the subject is remaining at this day; however he has given an idea of the genera in the following words :—' The first ' and most simple of consonances is the diatessaron. ' The diatonic tetrachord proceeds by a hemitone, tone, ' and tone, or four sounds and three intervals; and ' it is called diatonic, as proceeding chiefly by tones. ' The chromatic progression in the tetrachord is by ' a hemitone, hemitone, and an incomposite trihemi- ' tone, and therefore, though not constituted as the ' other, it contains an equal number of intervals. ' The enharmonic progression is by a diesis, which ' is half a hemitone, another diesis, also half a hemi- ' tone, and the remainder is an incomposite ditone; ' and these latter are also equal to a hemitone and ' two tones. Amongst these it is impossible to adapt ' sound to sound, for it is plain that the difference of ' the genera does not consist in an interchange of the ' four sounds, but only of the two intermediate ones; ' in the chromatic the third sound is changed from ' the diatonic, but the second is the same, and it ' has the same sound as the enharmonic; and in ' the enharmonic the two intermediate sounds are ' changed, with respect to the diatonic, so as the ' enharmonic is opposite to the diatonic, and the ' chromatic is in the middle between them both; for ' it differs only a hemitone from the diatonic, whence ' it is called chromatic, from Chroma, a word sig- ' nifying a disposition flexible and easy to be changed : ' in opposition to this we call the extremes of each ' tetrachord Stantes, or standing sounds, to denote ' their immovable position. This then is the system ' of the diapason, whether from Mese to Proslam- ' banomenos, or from Mese to Nete hyperboleon; ' and as the diatessaron is two tones and a hemitone,

' and the diapente three tones and a hemitone, the ' diapason should seem to be six whole tones; but in ' truth it is only five tones and two hemitones, which ' hemitones are not strictly complete; and therefore ' the diapason is somewhat less than six complete ' whole tones :* and with this agree the words of ' Philolaus when he says that harmony hath five ' superoctaves and two dieses; now a diesis is the ' half of a hemitone, and there is another hemitone ' required to make up the number six.'

His second book Nicomachus begins with an account of the invention of the lyre of Mercury, already related, and which has been adopted by almost every succeeding writer on music, adding that some among the ancients ascribed it to Cadmus the son of Agenor. He proceeds to state the proportions, which he does in a way not easily reconcileable with the practice of the moderns : he then reconsiders the supposed relation between the sounds in the harmonical septenary and the motions of the planets; and endeavours to account for these different denominations, which it seems were given them in his days. He says that the chord Hypate is applied to Saturn, as the chief of the planets, and Nete to Luna, as the least. Mese is Sol, Parhypate is attributed to Jove, Paramese not to Mercury but to Venus, by a perverse order, says his editor, unless there is an error in the manuscript. Paramese to Mars, Trite to Venus, Luna or the Moon is said to be acute, as it answers to Nete; and Saturn grave as is Hypate. Those that reckon contrarywise, applying Hypate to the Moon, and Nete to Saturn, do it, because say they the graver sounds are produced from the lower and more profound parts of the body, and therefore are properly adapted to the lower orbs; whereas the acute sounds are formed in the higher parts, and do therefore more naturally resemble the more remote of the heavenly bodies :—

Saturn	-	-	-	-	Nete
Jupiter	-	-	-	-	Paranete
Mars	-	-	-	-	Paramese
Sol	-	-	-	-	Mese
Venus	-	-	-	-	Lichanos
Mercury	-	-	-	-	Parhypate
Luna	-	-	-	-	Hypate

Nicomachus then proceeds to enumerate the several persons who added to the system of the diapason, completed as it was by Pythagoras; but as he expressly says the additional chords were not adjusted in any precise ratio, and as their names have already been given, it seems needless to be more particular about them. Speaking of the great system, viz., that of the disdiapason, he cites Ptolemy, to show that it must necessarily consist of fifteen chords; but as it is certain that Nichomachus lived A. c. 60, and that Claudius Ptolemæus flourished about one hundred and forty years after the commencement of the Christian Æra, there arises an anachronism, which is not to be accounted for but upon a supposition that the manuscript is corrupted. From divers passages in this author, and others to be met with in the Greek

* This is demonstrated by Ptolemy, lib I. cap. xi. of his Harmonics, and also by Boetius, lib V. cap. xiii.

writers, it is evident that the ancients were not wholly unacquainted with the doctrine of the vibrations of chords : they had observed that the acute sounds were produced by quick, and the grave by slow motions, and that the consonances arose from a coincidence of both ; but it no where appears that they made any use of the coincidences in adjusting the ratios of the consonances ; on the contrary, they seem to have referred the whole to the ratio of lengths and tensions by weights, and a division of the monochord ; and in this respect it is unquestionably true that the speculative part of music has received considerable advantages from those improvements in natural philosophy which in the latter ages have been made. The inquisitive and acurate Galileo was the first that investigated the laws of pendulums : he found out that all the vibrations of the same string, the longer and the shorter, were made in equal time, that between the length of a chord and the number of its vibrations, there subsists a duplicate proportion of length to velocity ; and that the length quadrupled will subduple the velocity of the vibrations, and the length subquadrupled will duple the vibrations ; for the proportion holds reciprocally : adding to the length will diminish, and shortening it will encrease the frequency of vibrations. These, and numbers of other discoveries, the result of repeated experiments, have been found of great use, as they were soon after the making of them applied to the measure of time, and other most valuable purposes.

Having given an extract which contains in substance almost the whole of what Nicomachus has given us on the subject of harmony, it remains to observe that his work is manifestly incomplete : it appears from his own words to have been written while he was upon a journey, and for the particular information of the lady to whom he has, in terms of the greatest respect, inscribed it ; and is no other than what he himself with great modesty entitles it, a Manual ; it is however to be esteemed a very valuable fragment, as it is by much the most clear and intelligible of the works of the Greek writers now remaining. Boetius, in his treatise De Musica, cites divers passages from Nicomachus that are not to be found in this discourse of his, from whence it is highly probable that he had seen those commentaries which are promised in it, or some other tract, of which at this distance of time no account can be given.

CHAP. XVII.

Plutarch is also to be numbered among the ancient writers on music, for in his Symposiacs is a discourse on that subject, which is much celebrated by Meibomius, Doni, and others. A passage in the French translation, by Amyot, of the works of that philosopher, has given rise to a controversy concerning the genuineness of this tract, the merits of which will hereafter be considered. This discourse contains in it more of the history of the ancient music and musicians than is to be met with anywhere else, for which reason it is here meant to give a copious extract from it. It is written in dialogue ;

the speakers are Onesicrates, Soterichus, and Lysias. The latter of these, in answer to a request of Onesicrates, gives a relation of the origin and progress of the science, in substance as follows :—

' According to the assertion of Heraclides, in a ' Compendium of Music, said to have been written by ' him, Amphion, the son of Jupiter and Antiope, was ' the inventor of the harp and of Lyric poesy ; and ' in the same age Linus the Eubean composed elegies : ' Anthes of Anthedon in Bœotia was the first author ' of hymns, and Pierius of Pieria of verses in honour ' of the Muses ; Philamon the Delphian also wrote ' a poem, celebrating the nativity of Latona, Diana, ' and Apollo ; and was the original institutor of ' dancing about the temple of Delphos. Thamyris, ' of Thracian extraction, had the finest voice, and ' was the best singer of his time, for which reason he ' is by the poets feigned to have contended with the ' Muses ; he wrought into a poem the war of the ' Titans against the gods. Demodocus the Corcyrean ' wrote in verse the history of the destruction of ' Troy, and the nuptials of Vulcan and Venus. To ' him succeeded Phemius of Ithaca, who composed ' a poem on the return of those who came back with ' Agamemnon from the siege of Troy ; and besides ' that these poems were severally written by the ' persons above-named, they were also set to musical ' notes by their respective authors. The same ' Heraclides also writes that Terpander was the ' institutor of those laws by which the metre of verses, ' and consequently the musical measure, were re- ' gulated ; and according to these rules he set musical ' notes both to his own and Homer's words, and sung ' them at the public games to the music of the lyre. ' Clonas, an epic and elegiac poet, taking Terpander ' for his example, constituted rules which should ' adjust and govern the tuning and melody of flutes ' or pipes, and such-like wind-instruments ; and in ' this he was followed by Polymnestes the Colo- ' phonian.

' Timotheus is said to have made lyric preludes to ' his epic poems, and to have first introduced the ' dithyrambic, a measure adapted to songs in the ' praise of Bacchus, which songs required a violent ' motion of the body, and a certain irregularity in the ' measure.

' Farther of Terpander, one of the most ancient of ' musicians, he is recorded to have been four times ' a victor at the Pythian games.

' Alexander the historian says, that Olympus ' brought into Greece the practice of touching the ' strings of the lyre with a quill ; for before his time ' they were touched by the fingers : and that Hyagnis ' was the first that sang to the pipe, and Marsyas his ' son the next, and that both these were prior to ' Olympus. He farther says that Terpander imitated ' Homer in his verses, and Orpheus in his music ; ' but that Orpheus imitated no one. That Clonas, ' who was some time later than Terpander, was, as ' the Arcadians affirm, a native of Tegea, a city of ' Arcadia ; though others contend that he was born ' in Thebes ; and that after Terpander and Clonas ' flourished Archilochus : yet some writers affirm

'that Ardalus the Troezenian taught wind-music
'before Clonas.

'The music appropriated to the lyre under the
'regulations of Terpander continued without any
'variation, till Phrynis became famous, who altered
'both the ancient rules, and the form of the instru-
'ment to which they were adapted.'

Having thus discoursed concerning the ancient
musicians, and stringed and wind-instruments in
general, Lysias proceeds, and confining himself to
the instruments of the latter kind, speaks to this
effect :—

'Olympus, a Phrygian, and a player on the flute,
'invented a certain measure in honour of Apollo,
'which he called Polycephalus or of many heads.
'This Olympus, as it is said, was descended from the
'first Olympus, the son of Marsyas, who being
'taught by his father to play on the flute, first
'brought into Greece the laws of harmony. Others
'ascribe the invention of the Polycephalus to Crates,
'the disciple of Olympus. The same Olympus was
'the author of the Harmatian mood, as Glaucus
'testifies in his treatise of the ancient poets, and as
'some think of the Orthian mood also.* There was
'also another mood in use among the ancients, termed
'Cradias, which Hipponax the Mimnermian greatly
'delighted in. Sacadas of Argos, being himself a
'good poet, composed the music to several odes and
'elegies, and became thrice a victor at the Pythian
'games. It is said that this Sacadas, in conjunction
'with Polymnestes, invented three of the moods, the
'Dorian, the Phrygian, and the Lydian; and that
'the former composed a strophe, the music whereof
'was a commixture of all the three. The original
'constitution of the modes was undoubtedly by
'Terpander, at Sparta; but it was much improved
'by Thales the Gortynian, Xenedamus the Cytherian,
'Xenocritus the Locrian, and Polymnestes the Colo-
'phonian.

'Aristoxenus ascribes to Olympus the invention of
'the enarmonic genus; for before his time there
'were no other than the diatonic and chromatic
'genera.

'As to the measures of time, they were in-
'vented at different periods and by different persons.
'Terpander, amongst other improvements which he
'made in music, introduced those grave and decent
'measures which are its greatest ornament; after
'him, besides those of Terpander, which he did not
'reject, Polymnestes brought into use other measures
'of his own; as did also Thales and Sacadas, who,
'though of fertile inventions, kept within the bounds
'of decorum. Other improvements were also made
'by Stesichorus and Alcmas, who nevertheless re-

'ceded not from the ancient forms; but Crexus,
'Timotheus, and Philoxenus, and others of the same
'age, affecting novelty, departed from the plainness
'and majesty of the ancient music.'

Another of the interlocutors in this dialogue of
Plutarch, Soterichus by name, who is represented
as one not only skilled in the science but eminently
learned, speaks of the invention and progress of
music to this effect :—

'Music was not the invention of any mortal,
'but we owe it to the god Apollo. The flute was
'invented neither by Marsyas, nor Olympus, nor
'Hyagnis, but Apollo invented both that and the
'lyre, and, in a word, all manner of vocal and
'instrumental music. This is manifest from the
'dances and sacrifices which were solemnized in
'honour of Apollo. His statue, placed in the tem-
'ple of Delos, holds in his right hand a bow, and
'at his left the Graces stand with each a musical
'instrument in her hand, one bearing a lyre, another
'a flute, and another a shepherd's pipe; and this
'statue is reported to be as ancient as the time of
'Hercules. The youth also that carries the temple
'laurel into Delphos is attended by one playing
'on the flute; and the sacred presents of the Hyper-
'boreans were sent of old to Delos, attended by
'flutes, pipes, and lyres; and some have asserted
'that the God himself played on the flute. Venerable
'therefore is music, as being the invention of Gods;
'but the artists of these later times, contemning
'its ancient majesty, have introduced an effeminate
'kind of melody, mere sound without energy. The
'Lydian mode, at first instituted, was very doleful,
'and suited only to lamentations; wherefore Plato
'in his Republic utterly rejects it. Aristoxenus
'in the first book of his Harmonics relates that
'Olympus sung an elegy in that mode on the death
'of Python; though some attribute the invention of
'the Lydian mode to Menalippides, and others to
'Torebus. Pindar asserts that it was first used at
'the nuptials of Niobe; Aristoxenus, that it was
'invented by Sappho, and that the tragedians learned
'it of her, and conjoined it with the Dorian; but
'this is denied by those who say that Pythocleides
'the player on the flute, and also Lysis the Athenian,
'invented this conjunction of the Dorian with the
'Lydian mode. As to the softer Lydian, which was
'of a nature contrary to the Lydian properly so
'called, and more resembling the Ionian, it is said
'to have been invented by Damon the Athenian.
'Plato deservedly rejected these effeminate modes,
'and made choice of the Dorian, as more suitable
'to warlike tempers; not that we are to suppose him
'ignorant of what Aristoxenus has said in his second
'book, that in a wary and circumspect government
'advantages might be derived from the use of the
'other modes; for Plato attributed much to music,
'as having been a hearer of Draco the Athenian,
'and Metellus of Agrigentum; but it was the con-
'sideration of its superior dignity and majesty that
'induced him to prefer the Dorian mode. He knew
'moreover that Alcmas, Pindar, Simonides, and
'Bacchylides, had composed several Parthenioi in

---

* These moods, the Harmation and Orthian, were unquestionably
moods of time. The former, if we may trust the English translator of
Plutarch's Dialogue on Music, as it stands in the first volume of his
Morals, Lond. 1684, was the measure termed Zarlino, La Curule, in
which it is supposed was sung the story of Hector's death, and of the
dragging him in a chariot round the walls of Troy: of the Orthian mood
the same translator gives the following description:—'This mood con-
'sisted of swift and loud notes, and was used to inflame the courage of
'soldiers going to battle, and is mentioned by Homer in the seventh
'book of the Iliad, and described by Eustathius. This mood Arion
'made use of when he flung himself into the sea, as Aulus Gellius
'writes, lib. XVI. cap. xix. the time of it was two down and four up.'
Meibomius on Aristides.

'the Dorian mode; and that supplications and hymns
'to the Gods, tragical lamentations, and sometimes
'love-verses were also composed in it; but he con-
'tented himself with such songs as were made in
'honour of Mars and Minerva, or those other that
'were usually sung at the solemn offerings called
'Spondalia. The Lydian and Ionian modes were
'chiefly used by the tragedians, and with these also
'Plato was well acquainted. As to the instruments
'of the ancients, they were in general of a narrow
'compass; the lyre used by Olympus and Terpander,
'and their followers, had but three chords, which
'is not to be imputed to ignorance in them, for those
'musicians who made use of more were greatly their
'inferiors both in skill and practice.

'The chromatic genus was formerly used by those
'who played on the lyre, but by the tragedians never.
'It is certainly of greater antiquity than the enar-
'monic; yet the preference given to the diatonic and
'enarmonic was not owing to ignorance, but was the
'effect of judgment. Telephanes of Megara was
'so great an enemy to the syrinx or reed-pipe, that
'he would never suffer it to be joined to the tibia;
'or that other pipe made of wood, generally of the
'lote-tree, and for that reason he forbore to go to
'the Pythian games. In short, if a man is to be
'deemed ignorant of that which he makes no use of,
'there would be found a great number of ignorant
'persons in this age; for we see that the admirers
'of the Dorian mode make no use of the Anti-
'genidian method of composition : and other musi-
'cians refuse to imitate Timotheus, being bewitched
'with the trifles and idle poems of Polyeides.

'If we compare antiquity with the present times,
'we shall find that formerly there was great variety
'in music, and that the diversities of measure were
'then more esteemed than now. We are now
'lovers of learning, they were lovers of time and
'measure; plain it is therefore that the ancients did
'not because of their ignorance, but in consequence
'of their judgment, refrain from broken measures;
'and if Plato preferred the Dorian to the other modes,
'it was only because he was the better musician; and
'that he was eminently skilled in the science appears
'from what he has said concerning the procreation of
'the soul in his Timæus.

'Aristotle, who was a disciple of Plato, thus
'labours to convince the world of the majesty and
'divine nature of music: "Harmony, saith he,
"descended from heaven, and is of a divine, noble,
"and angelic nature; being fourfold as to its efficacy,
"it has two mediums, the one arithmetical, the other
"harmonical. As for its members, its dimensions,
"and excesses of intervals, they are best discovered
"by number and equality of measure, the whole
"system being contained in two tetrachords."

'The ancient Greeks were very careful to have
'their children thoroughly instructed in the principles
'of music, for they deemed it of great use in forming
'their minds, and exciting in them a love of decency,
'sobriety, and virtue : they also found it a powerful
'incentive to valour, and accordingly made use of
'pipes or flutes when they advanced to battle : the

'Lacedemonians and the Cretans did the same; and
'in our times the trumpet succeeding the pipe, as
'being more sonorous, is used for the same purpose.
'The Argives indeed at their wrestling matches made
'use of fifes called Schenia, which sort of exercise
'was at first instituted in honour of Danaus, but
'afterwards was consecrated to Jupiter Schenius or
'the Mighty; and at this day it is the custom to use
'fifes at the games called Pentathla, which consist of
'cuffing, running, dancing, hurling the ball, and
'wrestling. But among the ancients, music in the
'theatres was never known; for either they employed
'it in the education of their youth, or confined it
'within the walls of their temples; but now our
'musicians study only compositions for the stage.

'If it should be demanded, Is music ever to remain
'the same, and is there not room for new inventions?
'The answer is that new inventions are allowed, so
'as they be grave and decent; the ancients them-
'selves were continually adding to and improving
'their music. Even the whole Mixolydian mode was
'a new invention; such also were the Orthian and
'Trochean songs; and, if we may believe Pindar,
'Terpander was the inventor of the Scolian song, and
'Archilocus of the iambic and divers other measures,
'which the tragedians took from him, and Crexus
'from them. The Hypolydian mode was the inven-
'tion of Polymnestes, who also was the first that
'taught the manner of alternately soft and loud.
'Olympus, besides that he regulated in a great
'measure the ancient Greek music, found out and
'introduced the enarmonic genus, and also the Pro-
'sodiac, the Chorian, and the Bacchian measures; all
'of which it is manifest were of ancient invention.
'But Lasus Hermionensis* applying these measures
'to his dithyrambic compositions, and making use of an
'instrument with many holes, by an addition of tones
'and hemitones made an absolute innovation in the
'ancient music. In like manner Menalippides, the
'lyric poet, Philoxenus, and Timotheus, all forsook
'the ancient method. The latter, until the time of
'Terpander, of Antissa, used a lyre with only seven
'strings, but afterwards he added to that number.
'The wind-instruments also received a great alter-
'ation; and in general the plainness and simplicity
'of the ancient music was lost in that affected variety
'which these and other musicians introduced.

'In ancient times, when Poetry held the precedency
'of the other arts, the musicians who played on wind-
'instruments were retained with salaries by the poets,
'to assist those who taught the actors, till Menalip-
'pides appeared, after which that practice ceased.

'Pherecrates, the comic poet, introduces Music in
'the habit of a woman with her face torn and bruised;
'and also Justice, the latter of whom, demanding the
'reason of her appearing in that condition, is thus
'answered by Music :—†

* Lasus Charbini, from Hermione, a city of Achaia, lived about the
58th Olympiad, in the time of Darius Hystaspes: some reckon him
among the seven wise men, in the room of Periander. He was the first
who wrote a book concerning music, and brought the dithyrambics into
the games and exercises, where he was a judge or moderator, deciding
contentious disputations. This Lasus was a musician of great fame, and
is mentioned by Plutarch as the first who changed any thing in the
ancient music. Meibom. on Aristoxenus, from Suidas.

† This Pherecrates, the comic poet, lived in the time of Alexander the

" It is my part to speak and yours to hear, there-
" fore attend to my complaints. I have suffered
" much, and have long been oppressed by that beast
" Menalippides, who dragged me from the fountain
" of Parnassus, and has tormented me with twelve
" strings : to complete my miseries, Cinesian, the
" Athenian, a pretender to poetry, composed such
" horrid strophes and mangled verses, that I, tortured
" with the pain of his dithyrambics, was so distorted
" that you would have sworn that my right side was
" my left : nor did my misfortunes end here, for
" Phrynis, in whose brains is a whirlwind, racked me
" with small wires, from which he produced twelve
" tiresome harmonies. But him I blame not so much,
" because he soon repented of his errors, as I do
" Timotheus, who has thus furrowed my face, and
" ploughed my cheeks; and Pyrrias, the Milesian,
" who, as I walked the streets, met me, and with his
" twelve strings bound and left me helpless on the
" earth."

' That virtuous manners are in a great measure the
' effect of a well-grounded musical education, Aris-
' toxenus has made apparent. He mentions Telesias,
' the Theban, a contemporary of his, who being a
' youth, had been taught the noblest excellencies of
' music, and had studied the best Lyric poets, and
' withal played to perfection on the flute; but being
' past the prime of his age, he became infatuated with
' the corrupted music of the theatres, and the inno-
' vations of Philoxenus and Timotheus; and when he
' laboured to compose verses, both in the manner of
' Pindar and of Philoxenus, he could succeed only in
' the former, and this proceeded from the truth and
' exactness of his education; therefore if it be the aim
' of any one to excel in music, let him imitate the
' ancients; let him also study the other sciences, and
' make philosophy his tutor, which will enable him
' to judge of what is decent and useful in music.

' The genera of music are three, the diatonic, the
' chromatic, and enarmonic; and it concerns an under-
' standing artist to know which of these three kinds
' is the most proper for any given subject of poetry.

' In musical instruction the way has sometimes

Great, and attended him, as we are told, in his expeditions, [Suid. in
Pherecrates] and was contemporary with Aristophanes, Plato, Eupolis
and Phrynicus, all comic writers [Id. in Plato]. Phrynis, who played on
the lyre, was the son of Cabon [Id. in Phrynis], and scholar of Aristo-
cleides, who pretended to be of the family of Terpander, and was a
favourite with Hiero, king of Sicily, as some accounts tell us, which
would throw him back near one hundred and fifty years in time before
our poet Pherecrates : but if we may believe Plutarch, he should have
been a contemporary with the poet at least, if he personally contended
the music prize with Timotheus, with whose playing we are told Alexander's spirit was so raised and animated to war. [Suid in Timotheus.]
But may it not be said that Timotheus did contend the prize against
some piece formerly composed by Phrynis, as the dramatic poets sometimes contested the priority against a play of some deceased poet? If so,
Phrynis then might have lived as early as the period mentioned by
Suidas.

It is true indeed Plutarch, where he gives us this point of history,
does not mention Phrynis by name, but distinguishes him only as the
son of Cabon, and by his nickname Ιωνοκαμπτης, Ionocamptes;
which sarcastical addition he obtained, because by his effeminate modulations he had corrupted the old music in the like manner as the Ionic
movements had debauched the old masculine dances. Jul. Pollux,
lib. IV. cap. ix. § 66.

The same Phrynis is likewise rallied by Aristophanes [in Nubibus,
v. 967] and others of the comic poets, for the levity of his compositions,
and for overdoing every thing in his performance. He was marked out,
even to infamy, for his innovations in music; for his soft and affected
modulations, which were so abhorrent from the simplicity of the ancient
music; for his intermingling and confounding the modes; and for
debasing the science to parasitism and servile offices.

' been for the tutor first to consider the genius and
' inclination of the learner, and then to instruct him
' in such parts of the science as he should discover
' most affection for; but the more prudent sort, as
' the Lacedemonians of old, the Mantinæans, and
' Pellenians, rejected this method.'

Here the discourse of Soterichus grows very
obscure, and has a reference to terms of which a
modern can entertain no idea. Farther on he resumes
the consideration of the genera, which he speaks of
to this effect :—

' Now then, there being three genera of harmony,
' equal in the quantity of systems or intervals, and
' number of tetrachords, we find not that the ancients
' disputed about any of them except the enarmonic,
' and as to that they differed only about the interval
' called the diapason.'

The speaker, by whom all this while we are to
understand Soterichus, then proceeds to shew that a
mere musician is an incompotent judge of music in
general; and to this purpose he asserts that Pythagoras rejected the judgment of music by the senses,
and maintained that the whole system was included
in the diapason. He adds, that the later musicians
had totally exploded the most noble of the modes;
that they made hardly the least account of the enarmonic intervals, and were grown so ignorant as to
believe that the enarmonic diesis did not fall within
the apprehension of sense.

He then enumerates the advantages that accrue
from the use of music, and cites Homer to prove its
effects on Achilles in the height of his fury against
Agamemnon : he speaks also of a sedition among the
Lacedemonians, which Terpander appeased by the
power of his music; and a pestilence among the same
people, which Thales, the Cretan, stopped by the
same means.

Onesicrates, who hitherto appears to have acted
the part of a moderator in this colloquy, after bestowing his commendations both on Lysias and
Soterichus, addresses them in these terms :—

' But for all this, my most honoured friends, you
' seem to have forgotten the chief of all music.
' Pythagoras, Archytas, Plato, and many others of
' the ancient philosopers maintain that there could be
' no motion of the spheres without music, since that
' the supreme Deity constituted all things harmo-
' niously; but now it would be unseasonable to enter
' upon a discourse on that subject.'

And so singing a hymn to the Gods and the
Muses, Onesicrates dismisses the company.

Thus ends the Dialogue of Plutarch on music,
which, though a celebrated work of antiquity, is in
the judgment of some persons rendered still more
valuable by the passage from Pherecrates, which he
has introduced into it. The least that can be said of
which is, that without a comment it is next to impossible to understand it : the following remarks,
which were communicated to the late Dr. Pepusch
by a learned but anonymous correspondent of his,
may go near to render it in some degree intelligible :—

' The poet, speaking of the successive abuses of
' music, mentions first Phrynis, and afterwards Timo-

' theus ; so that Phrynis should seem to have led the
' way to the abuses which Timotheus is reprehended
' for, or rather gave into, to the prejudice of music ;
' and it is probable he did so, from a speech of Agis
' made to Leonidas, which is transmitted to us by
' Plutarch in the life of Agis.

' What we want the explanation of, is that passage
' of Pherecrates which relates to the five strings and
' the twelve harmonies.

' From the time of Terpander, and upwards, we
' know that the lyre had seven strings, and those
' adjusted to the number of the seven planets, and as
' some suppose to their motions also. For though
' Euphorion in Athenæus is made to say, that the use
' of the instruments with many strings was of very
' great antiquity, yet the lyre was reckoned complete,
' and to have attained the full measure of perfect
' harmony when it had seven strings ; because, as
' Aristotle observed, the harmonies consisted in the
' number of chords, and because that was the number
' of old used.

' And therefore when Timotheus added four
' strings to the former seven, that innovation was so
' offensive to the Lacædemonians, that he was formally
' prosecuted for the presumption ; and it was one of
' the causes for which they were said to have banished
' him their state. The edict by which they did so,
' still extant, is transmitted to us as a curiosity by
' Boetius ; * some however have said that Timotheus
' cleared himself from this sentence by producing a
' very ancient statue of Apollo found at Lacedæmon,
' holding a lyre with nine strings.† But if he
' avoided this sentence of banishment, he did not
' wholly escape censure ; for Pausanias, who wrote
' as early as Athenæus, tells us where the Lacedæ-
' monians hung up his lyre publicly, having punished
' him for superadding four strings, in compositions
' for that instrument, to the ancient seven ; and
' Plutarch likewise tells us that before this, when the
' above-mentioned Phrynis was playing on the lyre
' at some public solemnity, one of the Ephori, Ec-
' prepes by name, taking up a knife, asked him on
' which side he should cut off the strings that ex-
' ceeded the number of nine.‡

' But though these innovations of Timotheus were

' said to be so offensive to the Lacedæmonians, it was
' not the first time of their having been put in practice ;
' for Phrynis had before done the like, and been
' punished, as we shall find, in the same manner.

' These accounts therefore go thus far towards an
' explanation of one part of the passage before us ;
' that as to the five strings, we may be pretty certain
' that the lyre of Phrynis was not confined to that
' number, nay we have particular testimonies that
' Phrynis himself was noted for playing on the lyre
' with more than seven strings ; the system of the
' lyre, from the time of Terpander to that of Phrynis,
' had continued altogether simple and plain, but
' Phrynis beginning to subvert this simplicity by
' adding two strings to his instrument, we are told
' by Plutarch, in more than one passage, that Ecprepes
' the magistrate cut off two of his nine strings.' §

' The next thing therefore to be enquired into, is
' what the poet could mean by playing twelve har-
' monies on five strings ?

' Perhaps by Harmonies we are to understand
' Modes ; and if so, Phrynis may be ridiculed for
' such a volubility of hand, and such an affectation of
' variety, that he extracted a dozen tones from five
' strings only, or that he played over the whole
' twelve modes within that compass. For besides
' the seven principal modes, it is said that Aristoxenus
' by converting five species of the diapason, intro-
' duced five other secondary modes ; and that the
' intermingling of the modes is the sense of ἁρμονίας
' here, seems plain from another passage in Plutarch,||
' where he says, " That it was not allowed to compose
" for the lyre formerly, as in his time, nor to inter-
" mingle the modes ἁρμονίας and measures of time,
" for they observed one and the same cast peculiar to
" each distinct mode, which had therefore a name to
" distinguish it by ; they were called Νομοί or rules
" and limitations, because the composers might not
" transgress or alter the form of time and measure
" appointed to each one in particular."

' For we are certain that both the Athenians and
' Lacedæmonians had their laws by which the
' particular species of music were designed to be
' preserved distinct and unconfused ; and their hymns,
' threni, pæans, and dithyrambs kept each to their
' several sort of ode ; and so the composers for the
' lyre were not permitted to blend one melody with
' another, but they who transgressed were censured
' and fined for it.'

It has already been mentioned that the genuineness
of this dialogue has been questioned, some writers
affirming it to be a spurious production, and others
contending it to be a genuine work of Plutarch,
worthy of himself, and in merit not inferior to the
best of the treatises contained in the Symposiacs.
It is therefore necessary to take a view of the controversy, and to state the arguments of the contending
parties in support of their several opinions. It seems
that the original ground of this dispute was a note
prefixed to Amyot's French translation of this dialogue in the following words : ' Ce traité n' appartient

---

* Boetius, in his treatise De Musica, Lib. I. cap. i. has given it in the
original Greek ; and the author of a book lately published, entitled
Principles and Power of Harmony, has given the following translation
of it :—

Whereas Timotheus, the Milesian, coming to our city, has deformed
the ancient music ; and laying aside the use of the seven-stringed lyre,
and introducing a multiplicity of notes, endeavours to corrupt the ears
of our youth by means of these his novel and complicated conceits,
which he calls chromatic, by him employed in the room of our established,
orderly, and simple music ; and whereas, &c. It therefore seemeth good
to us the King and Ephori, after having cut off the superfluous strings
of his lyre, and leaving only seven thereon, to banish the said Timotheus
out of our dominions, that every one beholding the wholesome severity
of this city, may be deterred from bringing in amongst us any unbecoming customs, &c. *Infra page* 118.

† Casaub. ad Athenæum, lib. VIII. cap. xi.

‡ This fact is alluded to by Agis king of Sparta, in a speech of his to
Leonidas, thus recorded by Plutarch :—

' And you that use to praise Ecprepes, who being Ephore, cut off two
' of the nine strnigs from the instrument of Phrynis the musician, and
' to commend those who did afterwards imitate him in cutting the strings
' of Timotheus's harp, with what face can you blame me for designing to
' cut off superfluity and luxury from the commonwealth ? Do you think
' those men were so concerned only about a fiddle-string, or intended
' any thing else than by checking the voluptuousness of music, to keep
' out a way of living which might destroy the harmony of the city ?
' Plutarch in Vitâ Agidis.'

§ Vide the last preceding note, and Plutarch in Laconic. Institutio.
|| De Musica.

'point, ou bien peu à la musique de plusieurs voix
'accordées & entrelacées ensemble, qui est aujourd'hui
'en usage ; ains à la façon ancienne, qui consistoit en
'la convenance du chant avec le sens & la mesure de
'la lettre, & la bonne grace du geste ; & le style ne
'semble point être de Plutarque.'

Amyot's translation bears date in 1610; notwithstanding which, Fabricius, in his catalogue of
the writings of Plutarch, has mentioned this discourse without suggesting the least doubt of its
authenticity.* But a dispute having arisen in the
French Academy of Inscriptions and Belles Lettres,
on the question, whether the ancients were acquainted with music in consonance or not, this
tract of Plutarch, in which there is not the slightest
mention of any such practice, was urged in proof
that they were strangers to it. While a doubt remained of the genuineness of this discourse, its
authority could not be deemed conclusive ; those
who maintained the affirmative of the principal
question, therefore insisted on the objection raised
by Amyot ; and this produced an enquiry into the
ground of it, or, in other words, whether Plutarch
was really the author of that discourse on music
which is generally ascribed to him, or not : this
enquiry is contained in three papers written by
Monsieur Burette, and inserted in the Memoirs of
the above-mentioned Academy, tome onzieme, Amst.
1736, with the following titles, Examen du Traité
de Plutarque sur la Musique—Observations touchant
l'Histoire litteraire du Dialogue De Plutarque sur la
Musique—Analyse du Dialogue de Plutarque sur la
Musique, the publication whereof has put an end to
a question, which but for Amyot had probably never
been started.

Meibomius, in the general preface to his edition
of the musical writers, and Doni, are lavish in their
commendations of this treatise : the latter of them,
in his discourse De Præstantia Musicæ Veteris,
pag. 65, calls it a golden little work ; but whether it
merits such an encomium must be left to the judgment of such as can truly say they understand it.
As to the historical part, it is undoubtedly curious,
except in some instances, that seem to approach too
near that species of history which we term fabulous,
to merit any great share of attention ; but as to that
other wherein the author professes to explain the
nature of the ancient music, it is to be feared he is
much too obscure for modern comprehension. The
particulars most worthy of observation in this work
of Plutarch are, the perpetual propensity to innovation, which the musicians in all ages seem to have
discovered, and the extreme rigour with which those
in authority have endeavoured to guard against such
innovations : the famous decree of the Ephori against
Timotheus just mentioned, which some how or other
was recovered by Boetius, and is inserted in a preceding note,† is a proof that the state thought itself
concerned in preserving the integrity of the ancient
music ; and if it had so great an influence over the
manners of the Spartan youth, as in the above trea-

tise is suggested, it was doubtless an object worthy
of their attention.

CHAP. XVIII.

ARISTIDES QUINTILIANUS is supposed to have
flourished, A. C. 110. This is certain, that he wrote
after Cicero, for from his books De Republica he
has abridged all the arguments that Cicero had
advanced against music, and has opposed them to
what he urged in behalf of it in his oration for
Roscius. It is farther clear that Aristides must
have been prior to Ptolemy, for he speaks of Aristoxenus who admitted of thirteen modes, and of
those who after him allowed of fifteen, but he takes
no notice of Ptolemy who restrained the number of
them to seven. His treatise De Musica consists
of three books. The first contains an ample discussion of the doctrine of the modes : speaking of
the diagram by which the situation and relation of
them is explained, he says it may be delineated in
the form of wings, to manifest the difference of
the tones among themselves ; but he has given no
representation of it.

All that has been hitherto said of the modes is to
be understood of melody, for there is another and
to us a more intelligible sense of the word, namely
that, where it is applied to the proportions of time,
or the succession and different duration of sounds,
of which whether they are melodious, or such as
arise from the simple percussion of bodies, the modes
of time, for by that appellation we choose to distinguish them from the modes of tone, are as so
many different measures. The effect of the various
metrical combinations of sounds is undoubtedly what
the ancients, more particularly this author, meant by
the word Rythmus. Of time he says there are two
kinds, the one simple and indivisible, resembling
a point in geometry ; the other composite, and that
of different measures, namely, duple, treble, and
quadruple.‡ The rythmic genera he makes to be
three in number, namely, the equal, the sesquialteral,
and the duple ; others he says add the supertertian :
these are constituted from the magnitude of the
times ; for one compared to itself begets a ratio of
equality, two to one is duple, three to two is sesquialteral, and four to three supertertian : He speaks
of the elation and position of some part of the body,
the hand or foot perhaps, as necessary to the rythmus,
probably as a measure ; and this corresponds with
the practice of the moderns in the measuring of time
by the tactus or beat. The remainder of the first
book of this work of Quintilian contains a very
laborious investigation of measures, with all their
various inflexions and combinations, in which the
author discovers a profound knowledge.

The second book treats of music as a means to

---

* Biblioth. Græc. lib IV. cap. xi. pag. 364, N. 124.

† *A translation on page 80, the original infra* 118.

‡ This passage in Aristides Quintilianus has drawn on him a severe
censure from the late Dr. Pemberton, the Gresham professor of physic,
who says that he here endeavours to make out four different measures
of time in verse also. This, says the Dr., is talking nonsense. But,
adds he, this writer is apt to amuse himself with fanciful resemblances ;
and having first imagined I know not what analogy between these four
measures of time, and the four dieses, into which a tone was considered
as divisable, he must needs try at making out the like in relation to
words. Observations on Poetry especially the Epic. Lond. 1738. page 110.

regulate the external behaviour, as that of philosophy is to improve the mind. Music, he says, by its harmony polishes the manners, and its rythmus renders the body more agreeable; for youth being impatient of mere admonition, and capable of instruction by words alone, require such a discipline as without disturbing the rational part of their natures shall familiarly and by degrees instruct them: he adds that it is easily perceived that all boys are prompt to sing and ready for brisk motions, and that it is not in the power of their governors to hinder them from the pleasure which they take in exercises of this sort. In human things, continues this author, there is no action performed without music; it is certain that divine worship is rendered more solemn by it, particular feasts and public conventions of cities rejoice with it, wars and voyages are excited by it, the most difficult and laborious works are rendered easy and delightful by it, and we are excited to the use of music by divers causes. Nor are its effects confined to the human species; irrational animals are affected by it, as is plain from the use which is made of pipes by shepherds, and horns by goatherds. Of the use of music in war, as practised by the ancients, he has the following passage:—'Numa has said, that by music he corrected 'and refined the manners of the people, which before 'were rough and fierce: to that end he used it 'at feasts and sacrifices. In the wars where it is 'and will be used, is there any need to say how 'the Pyrrhic music is a help to martial discipline? 'certainly it is plain to every one, and that to issue 'commands by words in time of action would intro-'duce great confusion, and might be dangerous by 'their being made known to the enemies, if they 'were such as use the same language. To the 'trumpet, that martial instrument, a particular cantus 'or melody is appropriated, which varies according 'to the occasion of sounding it, so as for the attack 'by the van or either wing, or for a retreat, or 'whether to form in this or that particular figure, 'a different cantus is requisite; and all this is so 'skilfully contrived, as to be unintelligible to the 'enemy, though at the same time by the army it 'is plainly understood.'

Thus much of this author is intelligible enough to a reader of this time; but when he speaks, as he does immediately after, of the efficacy of music in quieting tumults and appeasing an incensed multitude, it must be owned his reasoning is not so clear: as little can we conceive any power in music over the irascent and concupiscent affections of the mind, which he asserts are absolutely under its dominion. The remainder of this second book consists of a chain of very abstruse reasoning on the nature of the human soul, no way applicable to any conception that we at this time are able to form of music, and much too refined to admit of a place in a work, in which it is proposed not to teach, but to deliver a history of, the science.

The third book contains a relation of some experiments made with strings, distended by weights in given proportions, for finding out the ratios of con-sonances; a method which this author seems to approve; and to recommend this practice, he cites the authority of Pythagoras, who he says, when he departed this life, exhorted his disciples to strike the monochord, and thereby rather inform their understandings than trust to their ears in the measure of intervals. He speaks also of an instrument for the demonstration of the consonances, called a helicon, which was of a square form, and on which were stretched, with an equal tension, four strings.* For the reason above given, it seems no way necessary to follow this author through that series of geometrical reasoning, which he has applied for the investigation of his subject in the succeeding pages of his book, wherefore a passage relating to the tetrachords, remarkable enough in its kind, shall conclude this extract from his very learned but abstruse work. 'The tetrachords are agreed to be five in number, 'and each has a relation to one or other of the 'senses; the tetrachord hypaton resembles the touch, 'which is affected in new-born infants, when they 'are impelled by the cold to cry. The tetrachord 'meson is like the taste, which is necessary to the 'preservation of life, and hath a similitude to the 'touch. The third, called synemmenon, is compared 'to the smell, because this sense is allied to the taste; 'and many, as the sons of art say, have been restored 'to life by odours. The fourth tetrachord, termed 'diezeugmenon, is compared to the hearing, because 'the ears are so remote from the other organs of 'sense, and are disjoined from each other. The 'tetrachord hyperboleon is like the sight, as it is the 'most acute of the systems, as the sight is of the 'senses.' Farther, this author tells us that 'the five 'tetrachords do in like manner answer to the five 'primary elements, that is to say, hypaton to the 'earth, as the most grave; meson to the water, as 'nearest the earth; synemmenon to the air, which 'passes through the water remaining in the profun-'dities of the sea and the caverns of the earth, and 'is necessary for the respiration of animals, which 'could not live without it; diezeugmenon to the fire, 'the motion whereof, as tending upwards, is against 'nature; lastly, the tetrachord hyperboleon answers 'to the æther, as being supreme and above the rest.' There are, he says, also analogies between the three several systems of diapente and the senses; but we hasten to dismiss this fanciful doctrine. Moreover, adds he, 'in discoursing of the human soul, systems 'are 'not improperly compared to the virtues. Hypaton 'and meson are to be attributed to temperance, the 'efficacy whereof is double, and consists in an ab-'stinence from unlawful pleasures, resembling the 'most grave of these two systems: as also in a mo-'derate use of lawful enjoyments, not improperly 'signified by the tetrachord meson; but the tetra-'chord synemmenon is to be attributed to justice, 'which being joined with temperance, exerts itself 'in the discharge of public duties, and in acts of 'private beneficence: the diezeugmenon has the 'resemblance of fortitude, which virtue delivers the 'soul from the dominion of the body; lastly, the

---

* See it in a subsequent chapter of this second book.

'hyperboleon emulates the nature of prudence, for 'that tetrachord is the end of the acumen, and 'this virtue is the extremity of goodness. Again, 'these virtues may be assimilated to the three systems 'of diapente; * the two first, justice and temperance, 'which are always placed together as being a check 'to the concupiscent part of the mind, resemble the 'first of these systems; fortitude may be compared 'to the second, as that virtue denotes the irascent 'part and refers to each of our two natures; and 'prudence to the third, as declaring the rational 'essence. Add to this, that the two species of 'diapason answer to the twofold division of the mind; 'the first resembling the irrational, and the second 'the rational part thereof.'

It has been remarked of Quintilian that he is extremely fond of analogies, vide pag. 81, in a note; and the above passages are a proof that this charge against him is not ill-grounded.

ALYPIUS, the next in succession of the authors now remaining to him above cited, or, as some suppose, a contemporary of his, as flourishing about A.C. 115,† compiled a work, entitled an Introduction to Music, which seems to be little else than a set of tables explaining the order of the sounds as they arise in the several modes of their respective genera in the ancient method of notation. The musical characters used by the ancients were arbitrary; they were nothing more than the Greek capitals mutilated, inverted, and variously contorted, and are estimated at no fewer than twelve hundred and forty. A specimen of them is herein-before inserted in two plates from Kircher. (Appendix, Nos. 35 and 36.)

MANUEL BRYENNIUS, another of the Greek writers on music, is supposed to have flourished under the elder Palæologus, viz., about the year of Christ 120. He wrote three books on harmonics, the first whereof is a kind of commentary on Euclid, as the second and third are on Ptolemy.‡ He professes to have studied perspicuity for the sake of young men, but has given very little more than is to be found in one or other of the above authors. Meibomius had given the public expectations of a translation of this work, but not living to complete it, Dr. Wallis undertook it, and it now makes a part of the third volume of his works, published at Oxford in three volumes in folio, 1699.

BACCHIUS SENIOR was a follower of Aristoxenus; Fabricius supposes him to have been tutor to the emperor Marcus Antoninus, and consequently to have lived about A.C. 140.§ He wrote in Greek a very short introduction to music in dialogue, which, with a Latin translation thereof, Meibomius has published. It seems it was first published in the original by Mersennus, in his Commentary on the six first chapters of Genesis; and that afterwards he published a translation of it in French, which Meibomius, in the preface to his edition of the ancient musical authors, censures as being grossly erroneous.

GAUDENTIUS, the philosopher, according to Fabricius,‖ seems to have written before Ptolemy, and treading in the steps of Aristoxenus, composed an introduction to harmonics, which Cassiodorus commends as an elegant little work; though he does not pretend to say who he was, or where he lived; however upon his authority Cassiodorus relates that Pythagoras found out the original precepts of the art by the sound of hammers and the percussion of extended chords; and indeed as to this matter Gaudentius is very explicit. For his work in general, excepting a few definitions and a representation of the musical characters in the method of Alypius, it is little more than an abridgement of Aristoxenus, and that so very short and obscure, that little advantage can be derived from the perusal of it.

CLAUDIUS PTOLEMEUS was an Egyptian, born at Pelusium; not one of the Ptolemies, kings of Egypt, with some one of whom he has been confounded; nor the same with Ptolemy, the mathematician and astronomer, who, as Plutarch relates in his life of Galba, was the constant companion of that emperor, and was also attendant on the emperor Otho, in Spain, and foretold that he should survive Nero, as Tacitus tells us, lib. I. cap. xxii. The Ptolemy here spoken of flourished in the reign of the emperor Marcus Aurelius Antoninus, as Suidas testifies; and also himself in his Magnæ Syntaxis, where he says that he drew up his astronomical observations at Alexandria, for which reason he is by Suidas and others called Alexandrinus, in the second year of Antoninus Pius, which answers to the year of Christ 139.¶ He was the author of a treatise on harmonics in three books, a work much more copious than any of those above-mentioned; and it must be allowed that he of all the ancient writers seems to have entered the most deeply into the subject of harmonics. In the first chapter of his first book, he assigns the criteria of harmony, which he makes to be sense and reason: the former of these, he says, finds out what is nearly allied to truth, and approves of what is accurate, as the latter finds out what is accurate and approves of what is nearly allied to truth. Chap. iii. speaking of the causes of acuteness and gravity, he takes occasion to compare the wind-pipe to a flute; and to remark as a subject of wonder, that power or faculty which enables a singer readily and instantaneously to hit such degrees of dilatation and contraction as are necessary to produce sounds, grave or acute, in any given proportion.

In the sixth chapter of the same book he condemns the method of the Pythagoreans, and in the ninth that of the Aristoxeneans, in the adjusting of the consonances, but thinks the former the less erroneous of the two: the Pythagoreans, he says, not sufficiently attending to the ear, often gave harmonic proportions to incongruous sounds; on the contrary, the Aristoxeneans, ascribing all to the ear, applied numbers, the images of reason, not to the differences of sound, but to their intervals. To correct the errors of these two very different methods, he contrived an instru-

---

* The varieties or different systems of diapente are four, and therefore it may be questioned why in this place the author has limited them to three.

† Fabr. Biblioth. Græc. lib. III. cap. x.

‡ Ibid.

§ Ibid.

‖ Biblioth. Græc. lib. III. cap. x.

¶ Ibid. cap. xiv.

ment very simple and inartificial in its construction, but of singular use in the adjusting of ratios, which, though in truth but a monochord, as consisting of one string only, he with great propriety called the Harmonic Canon, by which appellation it is constantly distinguished in the writings of succeeding authors. His description of the instrument and its use, as also the reasons that led him to the invention, are contained in the eighth chapter of the same first book, and are to the following effect :—'We omit to explain 'what is proposed, by the means of pipes or flutes, or 'by weights affixed to strings, because they cannot 'make the necessary demonstrations with sufficient 'accuracy, but would rather occasion controversy; 'for in pipes and flutes, as also in the breath which is 'injected into them, there is great disorder ; and as 'to strings with weights affixed to them, besides that 'of a number of such strings, we can hardly be sure 'that they are exactly equal in size, it is almost im-'possible to accommodate the ratios of the weights 'to the sounds intended to be produced by them; 'for with the same degree of tension two strings of 'different thickness would produce sounds differently 'grave or acute : and farther, which is more to the 'present purpose, a string, at first of an equal length 'to others, by the affixing to it a greater weight than 'is affixed to the rest, becomes a longer string, from 'whence arises another difference of sound besides 'what might be deduced from the ratio of weight 'alone. The like will happen in sounds produced 'from hammers or quoits of unequal weights ; and 'we may observe the same in some vessels that are 'first empty, and afterwards filled ; and certainly it 'is difficult in all these cases to provide against the 'diversity of matter and figure in each ; but in the 'canon, as I term it, the chord most readily and 'accurately demonstrates the ratios of the several 'consonances :'—

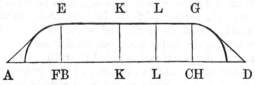

A B C D The line of the canon.

A E G D The chord.

A E, G D The ligament or place where it is fastened.

E B, G C Perpendiculars of the immoveable magades or bridges.

K K, L L The moveable magades.

B K, L C The canon or rule divided.

Suppose A B C D to be a right line, at each end thereof apply magades or little bridges, equal in height, and having surfaces as nearly spherical as possible ; as suppose the surface B, E to be described round the center F, and the surface C, G round the center H. Let then the points E, G be taken in the middle or bisection of these curved superficies, the magades being so placed as that lines E, F, and G, H, drawn from the said bisections E and G, may be perpendicular to the right line A B, C D. Now

if from the points A D a chord be strained over the middle points E and G of the said curved superficies, the part E G will be parallel to the right line A B, C D, because of the equal height of the magades, and will have its limits at E and G. Transfer then the line E G to the line A B C D, and having first bisected the whole length at K, and the half of that distance at L, place under the chord other magades, which must be very thin, and somewhat higher, but in every other respect like the former, so that both the intermediate magades may be straight with the middle of the external ones ; now if the part of the chord E K be found equitonal to K G, and the part K L to L G, then are we convinced that the chord is equable and perfect as to its constitution and make, and consequently fit for the experiment; but if it should not prove so, the trial is to be transferred to another part, or even to a new chord, till we obtain this condition of equability under the circumstances of similar moveable magades, and a similar length and tension of the parts of the chord. This being done and the chord divided according to the proportions of the consonances, we shall by the application of the moveable magades prove by our ears the rations of corresponding sounds ; for giving to the distance E K four of such parts whereof K G is three, the sounds on both sides will produce the consonance diatessaron, and have a sesquitertian ratio ; and giving to E K three parts whereof K G is two, the sounds on both sides will make the consonance diapente, which is in sesquialteral ratio. Again, if the whole length be so divided as that E K may be two parts and K G one of them, it shall be the unison diapason, which consists in a duple ratio. If it be so that E K be eight parts whereof K G is three, it will be the consonance diapason and diatessaron, in the ratio of eight to three ; farther if it be divided so as that E K be three parts and K G one of them, it will be diapente and diapason, in a triple ratio ; and lastly if it be so divided as that E K be four and K G one, it will be the unison disdiapason in a quadruple ratio.

RATIOS.	THE PROOF.				CONSONANCES.
$\frac{4}{1}$	E	4	K	1	G Disdiapason
$\frac{3}{1}$	E	3	K	1	G Diapason and diapente
$\frac{8}{3}$	E	8	K	3	G Diapason and diatessaron
$\frac{2}{1}$	E	2	K	1	G Diapason
$\frac{3}{2}$	E	3	K	2	G Diapente
$\frac{4}{3}$	E	4	K	3	G Diatessaron
	E	1	K	1	G

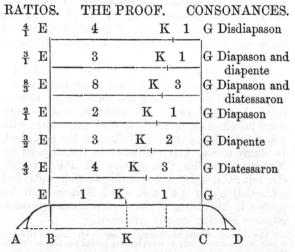

How the monochord of Pythagoras was constructed, or in what manner he divided it, we are no where told : it seems difficult to conceive that for producing the consonances it could be divided in any other manner than this of Ptolemy, and yet this author censures the followers of Pythagoras for not knowing how to reason about the consonances, which one would think they could not fail to do from principles so clear as those deducible from experiments on the monochord. But as to the Aristoxeneans, he censures them for rejecting the reasonings of the Pythagoreans, at the same time that they would not endeavour to find out better. To understand these and other invectives against this sect, it is to be observed that they measured the intervals by the ear as our practical musicians do now, that is to say, the greater by fourths or fifths, and the less by tones and semitones ; thus to ascertain the measure of an octave, they applied that of a diatessaron or fourth above the unison, and another below the octave, and between the approximating extremities of these two intervals they found the distance of a tone, which furnished a common measure for the less intervals of a fourth, a fifth, and the rest ; and enabled them to say that a tone is the difference between the diatessaron and the diapente : this Ptolemy calls remitting one question to another, and he adds that the ear, when it would judge of a tone needs not the help of a comparison of it with the diatessaron or any other consonance, and yet adds he, ‘ if we would ‘ ask of the Aristoxeneans what is the ratio of a tone, ‘ they will say, perhaps, that it is two of those in- ‘ tervals, that is to say, hemitones, of which the dia- ‘ tessaron contains five, and in like manner that the ‘ diatessaron is five, of those of which the diapason is ‘ twelve, and so of the rest, till at last they come to ‘ say that the ratio of a tone is two, which is not de- ‘ fining those ratios.'

Ptolemy, lib. I. cap. x. farther denies the assertion of the Aristoxeneans, that the diatessaron contains two tones and a half, and the diapente three and a half ; as also that the diapason consists of six tones, as the several contents of those two systems of two and a half, and three and a half, supposing this estimation of them to be just, would make undoubtedly six ; but by his division of the monochord, he clearly demonstrates that the term by which the diatessaron exceeds the diatone, and which he calls a limma, is less than a hemitone, in the same proportion as 1944 bears to 2048, a difference however much too small for the ear to distinguish. His demonstration of this proposition is given in a preceding chapter of this work.

To enter into a discussion of that very abstruse subject, the division of the diapason, would require a much more minute investigation of the doctrine of ratios than is requisite in this place ; it must however be observed, that supposing the ear alone to determine the precise limits of any system, that of the diatessaron for example, and that such system were transferred to the monochord, a repetition of the system so transferred would fail to produce a series of systems consonant in the extremities. Thus let a given sound be, as we should now call it G, and let the monochord be divided by a bridge according to

the rules above prescribed, so as to give its fourth C ; and let a tone, D, be set on by another bridge in like manner, and after that another fourth, which would terminate at G, and would seem to make what we should call a diapason : we should find upon taking away the intermediate bridges at C and D, that the interval from G to G would be more than a diapason ; and that were this method of ascertaining the terms of the consonances repeated through a series of octaves, the dissonance would be increased in proportion to the number of repetitions. Ptolemy has taken another method, chap. xi. of this his first book, and by an accumulation of sesquioctave tones has clearly demonstrated that six such exceed the consonance diapason. This deficiency, if it may be so called, in the intervals of which the diapason is compounded, and the difference between tuning by the ear and by numbers, has suggested to mathematicians what is called a temperament, which proposes a certain number of integral parts for the limit of the diapason, and the division of the amount of the several limmas that occur in the progression to it, in such a manner as to make the consonances contained in it as nearly perfect as possible.

The remainder of Ptolemy's first book treats of the genera. Chap. xii. exhibits the division of Aristoxenus, which he condemns ; and chap. xiii. that of Archytas of Tarentum, whom he censures for defining the genera by the interjacent intervals rather than by the ratios of the sounds among themselves, and charges him with rashness and want of thought.

The use and application of the genera is at this day so little understood, that we are greatly at a loss to account for any other division of the tetrachord than that which characterizes the diatonic genus : Nor does it seem possible, with the utmost strength of the imagination, to conceive how a series of sounds so extremely ungrateful to the ear as those of which the chromatic and enarmonic genera are said to be formed, could ever be received as music in the sense in which that word is now understood.

CHAP. XIX.

In the first Chapter of his second book, Ptolemy undertakes to shew by what means the ratios of the several genera may be received by the sense, in the course of which demonstration he points out the different offices of sense, or the ear, and reason, in the admeasurement of intervals, by which it should seem that the former is previously to adjust the consonances, and that these being transferred to the canon, become a subject of calculation ; and this position of his is undoubtedly true ; for the determination of the senses in all subjects where harmony or symmetry are concerned is arbitrary, and it is the business of reason, assisted by numbers, to enquire whether this determination has any foundation in nature or not ; and if it has not, we pronounce it fantastical and capricious ; for example, we perceive by the ear a consonance between the unison and its octave, and we are conscious of the harmony resulting from those two sounds ; but little are we aware of the wonderful relation that subsists between them, or that if an experiment be made by suspending weights to the chords that produce it, whose lengths are by the laws of harmony required to be in the proportion of 2 to 1, that the shorter would make two vibrations to one of the longer, and that the vibrations would exactly coincide in that relation as long as both chords should continue in motion. Again with respect to the forms of bodies, when we prefer that of a sphere to one less regular, we never attend to the properties of a sphere, but reason will demonstrate a perfection in that figure which is not to be found in an irregular polygon.

In the second chapter of his second book he describes an instrument or diagram called the Helicon, invented as it should seem by himself, for demonstrating the consonances, so simple in its construction that its very figure seems to speak for itself, and to render a verbal explanation, though he has given a very long one of it, unnecessary. It is of this form:—

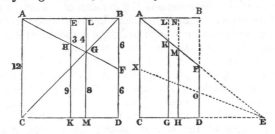

The side of the square A C 12 shews the diapason: the half of B D, that is to say B F or F D 6 the unison. The line G M 8, terminated by the diagonal B C, the diatessaron. The line E K divides the quadrangle equally, and H K 9, terminated by the line A F, shews the diapente. The lines L G and E H are in the ratio of 4 to 3, which is that of the diatessaron; and lastly the lines H K 9 and G M 8 shew the sesquioctave tone.

To this diagram Ptolemy has added another not less easy to be comprehended than the former, in which the lines B D, N H, L G, and A C, are supposed to be chords of equal lengths but bisected by the line A F in the direction A E : this line may be supposed to be a bridge, or subductorium, stopping the four chords at A K M F, and thereby giving the proportions 12 9 8 6 ; which proportions will also result from a subductorium placed in the direction X E, for X C will be duple of O D, and the two intermediate chords sesquialtera and sesquitertia, and with respect to each other, sesquioctave ; in all agreeing with the ratios in the former diagram.

In the ninth chapter of book II. Ptolemy takes occasion to say that there are only seven tones or modes, for that there are but seven species of diapason ; a position that will be easily granted him by the moderns who suppose the word, tone or mode, when applied to sound, to answer to what we term the key or fundamental note. What he says farther concerning the modes has already been mentioned in a preceding chapter of this book.

Chapter xii. the same author speaks of the monochord ; and here he proposes, but not for the purpose

of experiments, a different method of dividing it, not, says he, according to one tone or mode only, but according to all the tones together ; by which one would imagine he meant somewhat like a temperament of its imperfections, and a design to render it an instrument not of speculation but practice ; and indeed besides exhibiting it in a form more adapted to practice, and more resembling a musical instrument than its primitive one :—*

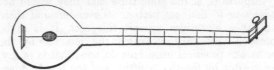

He speaks, though not very intelligibly, of the manner of performing on it, and recommends, to conceal its defects, the conjunction with it, either of a pipe or the voice. A little after, he speaks of Didymus a musician, who endeavoured to correct this instrument by a different application of the magades ; but for the greater imperfections he says Didymus was not able to find out a cure. Towards the close of this second book he exhibits a short scheme of the three genera, according to five musicians, namely, Archytas, Aristoxenus, Eratosthenes, the same Didymus, and himself ; and a little farther on, tables of the section of the canon in all the seven modes according to the several genera.

In the third book chap. iv. he speaks in general of the faculty of harmony, and of mathematical reasoning as applied to it ; the use whereof he says is to contemplate and adjust the ratios. In the next ensuing chapter he proceeds, in the manner of Quintilian, to state the analogy of music with the affections of the human mind, the system of the universe, and in short with every other subject in which number, proportion, or coincidence are concerned. In the course of this his reasoning, he mentions that Pythagoras advised his disciples at their rising in the morning to use music, whereby that perturbation which is apt to affect the mind at the awakening from sleep, might be prevented, and the mind be reduced to its wonted state of composure : besides which he says, that it seems the Gods themselves are to be invoked with hymns and melody, such as that of flutes or Egyptian trigons, to shew that we invite them to hear and be propitious to our prayers.

Upon a very careful review of this work of Ptolemy, it will appear that the doctrines contained in it, so far as they are capable of being rendered intelligible, are of singular use in the determination of ratios, and his very accurate division of the monochord carries demonstration with it. It was doubtless for this reason that our countryman Dr. Wallis, a man to whom the learned world are under high obligations, undertook the publication of it from a manuscript in the Bodleian library, in the original Greek, with a Latin translation of his own, together with copious notes, and an appendix by way of commentary,

* There is very little doubt but that the instrument here delineated is the pandura of the Arabians, mentioned in a note of Meibomius on a passage in Nicomachus, for among the Arabian and Turkish instruments described by Mersennus are many in this form.

which the Doctor was the better qualified to give, as it abundantly appears, as well by divers other of his writings in the Philosophical Transactions, as the work we are now speaking of, that he was very profoundly skilled in the science of music. How far he is to be depended on when he undertakes to render the ancient modes in modern characters seems very questionable, for were the Doctor's opinion right in that matter, all that controversy which has subsisted for these many centuries, not only touching the specific differences between them, but even as to their number, must necessarily have ended ages ago; whereas, even at this day, the ablest writers on the subject do not hesitate at saying that the doctrine of the modes is absolutely inscrutable; and perhaps it is for this reason only that so many have imagined that with them we have lost the most valuable part of the art; but on the contrary it is worth remarking that the Doctor, though he was perhaps the ablest geometer of his time, and had all the prejudices in favour of the ancients that a man conversant with the best of their writers could be supposed to entertain, never intimates any such matter; nay, so far is he from adjudging a preference to the ancient music over that of the moderns, that he scruples not to ascribe the relations that are given of the effects of the former to the ignorance of mankind in the earlier ages, the want of refinement, the charms of novelty, and other probable causes. Dr. Wallis gave two editions of this work of Ptolemy, the one published in quarto at Oxford in 1682; another, as also the commentary of Porphyry, and a treatise of Manuel Bryennius, makes part of the third volume of his works, published in three volumes in folio, 1699.

CENSORINUS, a most famous grammarian, lived at Rome about A.C. 238,* and wrote a book entitled De Die Natali. It was published by Erycius Puteanus, at Louvain, in 1628, who styles it Doctrinæ rarioris Thesaurus; and it is by others also much celebrated for the great light it has thrown on learning. It is a very small work, consisting of only twenty-four chapters; the tenth is concerning music; and the subsequent chapters, as far as the thirteenth inclusive, relate to the same subject.

He professes to relate things not known even to musicians themselves. He defines music to be the science of well modulating, and to consist in the voice or sound. He says that sound is emitted at one time graver, at others acuter; that all simple sounds, in what manner soever emitted, are called phthongoi; and the difference, whereby one sound is either more grave or more acute than another, is called diastema.

The rest of his discourse on music is here given in his own words:—'Many diastemata may be placed 'in order between the lowest and the highest sound, 'some whereof are greater, as the tone, and others 'less, as the hemitone; or a diastem may consist of 'two, three, or more tones. To produce concordant 'effects, sounds are not joined together capriciously, 'but according to rule. Symphony is a sweet concent 'of sounds. The simple or primitive symphonies 'are three, of which the rest consist; the first, having

'a diastem of two tones, and a hemitone, is called a 'diatessaron; the second, containing three tones and 'a hemitone, is called a diapente; the third is the 'diapason, and consists of the two former, for it is 'constituted either of six tones, as Aristoxenus and 'other musicians assert, or of five tones and two 'hemitones, as Pythagoras and the geometricians say, 'who demonstrate that two hemitones do not com-'plete the tone; wherefore this interval, improperly 'called by Plato a hemitone, is truly and properly a 'diesis or limma.

'But to make it appear that sounds, which are 'neither sensible to the eyes, nor to the touch or 'feeling, have measures, I shall relate the wonderful 'comment of Pythagoras, who, by searching into the 'secrets of nature, found that the sounds of the 'musicians agreed to the ratio of numbers; for he 'distended chords equally thick and equally long, by 'different weights, these being frequently struck, and 'their sounds not proving concordant, he changed 'the weights; and having frequently tried them one 'after another, he at length discovered that two 'chords struck together produced a diatessaron; 'when their weights being compared together, bore 'the same ratio to each other as three does to four, 'which the Greeks call επιτριτος, epitritos, and the 'Latins supertertium. He at the same time found 'that the symphony, which they call diapente, was 'produced when the weights were in a sesquialtera 'proportion, namely, that of 2 to 3, which they called 'hemiolium. But when one of the chords was 'stretched with a weight duple to that of the other, 'it sounded a diapason.

'He also tried if these proportions would answer 'in the tibiæ, and found that they did; for he pre-'pared four tibiæ of equal cavity or bore, but unequal 'in length; for example, the first was six inches 'long, the second eight, the third nine, and the 'fourth twelve; these being blown into, and each 'compared with the others, he found that the first 'and second produced the symphony of the diates-'saron, the first and third a diapente, and the first 'and fourth the diapason: but there was the difference 'between the nature of the chords and that of the 'tibiæ, that the tibiæ became graver in proportion 'to the increase of their lengths, while the chords 'became acuter by an additional augmentation of 'their weights; the proportion however was the 'same each way.

'These things being explained, though perhaps 'obscurely, yet as clearly as I was able, I return to 'shew what Pythagoras thought concerning the 'number of the days appertaining to the partus. First, 'he says there are in general two kinds of birth, the 'one lesser, of seven months, which comes forth from 'the womb on the two hundred and tenth day after 'conception; the other greater, of nine months, which 'is delivered on the two hundred and seventy-fourth 'day.' Censorinus then goes on to relate from Plato that in the work of conception there are four periods, the first of six days, the second of eight, which two numbers are the ratio of the diatessaron; the third of nine, which answers to the diapente, and the

* Fabricius. Biblioth. Lat. tom. I. pag. 537.

fourth, at the end whereof the fœtus is formed, of twelve, answering to the diapason in duple proportion. After this he proceeds to declare the relations of the above numbers in these words :—

'These four numbers, six, eight, nine, and twelve, 'being added together, make up thirty-five; nor is 'the number six undeservedly deemed to relate to 'the birth, for the Greeks call it τελειος, teleios, and 'we perfectum, because its three parts, a sixth, 'a third, and a half, that is one, two, three, make up 'itself; but as the first stage in the conception is 'completed in this number six, so the former number 'thirty-five being multiplied by this latter six, the 'product is two hundred and ten, which is the 'number of days required to maturate the first 'kind of birth. As to the other or greater kind, 'it is contained under a greater number, namely, 'seven, as indeed is also the whole of human life, 'as Solon writes: the practice of the Jews, and the 'ritual books of the Etruscans, seem likewise to 'indicate the predominancy of the number seven 'over the life of man; and Hippocrates, and other 'physicians, in the diseases of the body account the 'seventh as a critical day; therefore as the origin of 'the other birth is six days, so that of this greater 'birth is seven; and as in the former the members 'of the infant are formed in thirty-five days, so here 'it is done in almost forty, and for this reason, forty 'days are a period very remarkable; for instance, 'a pregnant woman did not go into the temple till 'after the fortieth day; after the birth women are 'indisposed for forty days; infants for the most part 'are in a morbid state for forty days; these forty 'days, multiplied by the seven initial ones, make 'two hundred and eighty, or forty weeks: but 'because the birth comes forth on the first day of 'the fortieth week, six days are to be subtracted, 'which reduces the number of days to two hundred 'and seventy-four, which number very exactly cor-'responds to the quadrangular aspect of the Chal-'deans; for as the sun passes through the zodiac 'in three hundred and sixty-five days and some 'hours; if the fourth part of this number, namely, 'ninety-one days and some hours, be deducted there-'from, the remainder will be somewhat short of two 'hundred and seventy-five days, by which time the 'sun will arrive at that place where the quadrature 'has an aspect to the beginning of conception. But 'let no man wonder how the human mind is able to 'discover the secrets of human nature in this respect, 'for the frequent experience of physicians enables 'them to do it.

'It is not to be doubted but that music has an 'effect on our birth; for whether it consists in the 'voice or sound only, as Socrates asserts, or, as 'Aristoxenus says, in the voice and the motion of 'the body, or of both these and the emotion of 'the mind, as Theophrastus thinks, it has certainly 'somewhat in it of divine, and has a great influence 'on the mind. If it had not been grateful to the 'immortal Gods, scenical games would never have 'been instituted to appease them; neither would 'the tibiæ accompany our supplications in the holy

'temples. Triumphs would not have been celebrated 'with the tibia; the cithara or lyre would not have 'been attributed to Apollo, nor the tibia, nor the 'rest of that kind of instruments to the Muses; 'neither would it have been permitted to those who 'play on the tibia, by whom the deities are appeased, 'to exhibit public shows or plays, and to eat in the 'Capitol, or during the lesser Quinquatria,* that 'is on the ides of June; to range about the city, 'drunk, and disguised in what garments they pleased. 'Human minds, and those that are divine, though 'Epicurus cries out against it, acknowledge their 'nature by songs. Lastly, symphony is made use 'of by the commanders of ships to encourage the 'sailors, and enable them to bear up under the 'labours and dangers of a voyage; and while the 'legions are engaged in battle the fear of death is 'dispelled by the trumpet; wherefore Pythagoras, 'that he might imbue his soul with its own divinity, 'before he went to sleep and after he awaked was 'accustomed, as is reported, to sing to the cithara; 'and Asclepiades the physician relieved the dis-'turbed minds of frenetics by symphony. Etophilus, 'a physician also, says that the pulses of the veins 'are moved by musical rhythmi; so that both the 'body and the mind are subject to the power of 'harmony, and doubtless music is not a stranger 'at our birth.

'To these things we may add what Pythagoras 'taught, namely, that this whole world was con-'structed according to musical ratio, and that the 'seven planets which move between the heavens and 'the earth, and predominate at the birth of mortals, 'have a rythmical motion and distances adapted to 'musical intervals, and emit sounds, every one dif-'ferent in proportion to its height, which sounds are 'so concordant as to produce a most sweet melody, 'though inaudible to us by reason of the greatness 'of the sounds, which the narrow passages of our 'ears are not capable of admitting.' Then follows the passage declaring the Pythagorean estimate of the distances of the planets and their supposed harmonical ratio, herein-before cited from him.†

Censorinus concludes his Discourse on Music with saying that Pythagoras compared many other things which musicians treat of to the other stars, and de-monstrated that the whole world is constituted in harmony. Agreeably to this he says Dorylaus writes that this world is the instrument of God: and others, that as there are seven wandering planets, which have regular motions, they may fitly be resembled to a dance.‡

---

* A feast in honour of Minerva.

† See it in page 65, with a diagram.

‡ The general opinion of the learned in former ages, touching the harmony of the spheres, has been mentioned in a preceding page, but there appears a disposition in the modern philosophers to revive the notion. It seems that Dr. Gregory thought it well founded; and Mr. Maclaurin, in conformity with his opinion, Phil. Discov. of Newton, pag. 35, explains it thus:—'If we should suppose musical 'chords extended from the sun to each planet; that all these chords 'might become unison, it would be requisite to encrease or diminish 'their tensions in the same proportions as would be sufficient to render 'the gravities of the planets equal; and from the similitude of these '(proportions the celebrated doctrine of the harmony of the spheres 'is supposed to have been derived.'

The author of a book lately published, entitled Principles and Power of Harmony, has added his suffrage in support of the opinion. 'Certain,

PORPHYRIUS, a very learned Greek philosopher, of the Platonic sect, and who wrote a commentary on the Harmonics of Ptolemy, lived about the end of the third century. His preceptors in philosophy were Plotinus and Amolius; he was a bitter enemy to the Christian religion, which perhaps is the reason why St. Jerome will have him to be a Jew; but Eunapius affirms that he was a native of Tyre, and that his true name was Malchus, which in the Syrian language signifies a king; and that Longinus the Sophist, who taught him rhetoric, gave him the name of Porphyrius, in allusion to the purple usually worn by kings. Besides the commentary on Ptolemy he wrote the lives of divers philosophers, of which only a fragment, containing the life of Pythagoras, is now remaining; a treatise of abstinence from flesh, an explication of the categories of Aristotle, and a treatise, containing fifteen books, against the Christian religion, which he once professed, as St. Augustine, Socrates, and others assert: this latter was answered by Methodius, bishop of Tyre, and afterwards by Eusebius. He died about the end of the reign of Dioclesian, and in 388 his books were burned.

With regard to his commentary, it is evidently imperfect; for whereas the treatise of Ptolemy, is divided into three books, the second whereof contains fifteen chapters, Porphyry's commentary is continued no farther than to the end of chapter seven of that book, concluding with the series of sounds through each of the three genera. He seems to have been a virulent opposer of the Aristoxeneans, and like his author adheres in general to the tenets of Pythagoras. Porphyry has given a description of the harmonic canon much more intelligible than that of Ptolemy, and has delineated it in the following form:—

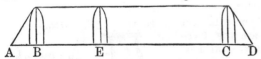

By which it appears that a chord, A D, strained over the immoveable magades B and C, which are nothing more than two parallelograms, with a semicircular arch at the top of each, together with a moveable bridge of the same form E, but somewhat higher, will be sufficient for the demonstration of the consonances, and this indeed is the representation which Dr. Wallis in his notes on Ptolemy has thought proper to give of it.

Dr. Wallis has contented himself with publishing a bare version of this author, without the addition of

'says he, as this harmonic coincidence is now become, till Sir Isaac
'Newton demonstrated the laws of gravitation in relation to the planets,
'it must have passed for the dream of an Utopian philosopher.' Pag. 146.
  The same author, pag. 145, agreeably to what Censorinus above asserts, says that 'there are traces of the harmonic principle scattered up and 'down, sufficient to make us look on it as one of the great and reigning 'principles of the inanimate world.' Some of these have hereinbefore been pointed out. Vide pag. 65, in note. To the instances there mentioned, the following may not improperly be added. The web of a spider formed of threads is of an hexangular figure, and each of the threads that divide the whole into six triangles, may be considered as a beam intended to give firmness and stability to the fabric; from one to the other of these beams the insect conducts lines in a parallel direction, which, supposing them to be ten in number, do, in consequence of their different lengths, constitute a perfect decachord. Kircher, who made this discovery, says, that were these lines or chords capable of sustaining a force sufficient to make them vibrate, it must necessarily follow from the ratios of their lengths, that between the sound of the outer and the innermost, the interval would be a diapason and semiditone; and that the rest of the chords, in proportion to their lengths, would produce the other consonances. Musurg. tom. I, pag. 441.

notes, except a few such short ones as he thought necessary to correct a vicious reading, or explain a difficult passage.

The works of the several authors above-named declare very fully the ancient Greek theory; their practice may in a great measure be judged of from the forms of the ancient instruments, and of these it may be thought necessary in this place to give some account.

The general division of musical instruments is into three classes, the pulsatile, tensile, and inflatile; and to this purpose Cardinal Bellarmine, in his Exposition of the CLth psalm, verse 3, says: ' Tria sunt instru-' mentorum genera, vox, flatus, et pulsus; omnium ' meminit hoc loco propheta.'

Of the first are the drum, the sistrum, and bells. Of the second, the lute, the harp, the clavicymbalum, and viols of all kinds. Of the third are the trumpet, flutes, and pipes, whether single or collected together, as in the organ.

And Kircher, in his Musurgia, preface to book VI., has this passage:—' Omnia instrumenta musica ad ' tria genera, ut plurium revocantur: Prioris generis ' dicuntur εγχορδα sive εντατά, quæ nervis, seu ' chordis constant quæque plectris, aut digitis in har-' monicos motus incitantur, ut sunt Testudines, ' Psalteria, Lyræ, Sambucæ, Pandoræ, Barbita, ' Nablia, Pectides, Clavicymbala, aliaque hujus ' generis innumera. Secundi generis sunt εμφυσωμενα, ' ωνευματικα, vel εμπνευςα, quæ inflata, seu spiritu, ' incitata sonum edunt ut Fistulæ, Tibiæ, Cornua, ' Litui, Tubæ, Buccinæ, Classica. Tertii generis ' sunt κρυςα, sive pulsatilia uti sunt Tympana, Sistra, ' Cymbala, Campanæ, &c.'

This division is adopted by a late writer, Franciscus Blanchinus of Verona, in a very learned and curious dissertation on the musical instruments of the ancients; * which upon the authority of ancient medals, intaglias, bass-reliefs, and other sculptures of great antiquity, exhibits the forms of a great variety of musical instruments in use among the ancient Greeks and Romans, many whereof are mentioned, or alluded to, by the Latin poets, in such terms as contain little less than a precise designation of their respective forms. He has deviated a little from the order prescribed by the above division of musical instruments into classes, by beginning with the inflatile species instead of the tensile; nevertheless his dissertation is very curious and satisfactory, and contains in it a detail to the fol- Fig. 1. Fig. 2. lowing effect:—

One of the most simple musical instruments of the ancients is the Calamus pastoralis, made of an oaten reed; it is mentioned by Virgil and many others of the Latin poets, and by Martianus Capella. See the form of it fig. 1.

Other writers mention an instrument of very great antiquity by the name of Ossea tibia, a pipe made of the leg-bone of a crane. Fig. 2.

* De tribus Generibus Instrumentorum Musicæ veterum Organicæ, Dissertatio; Romæ, 1742.

The Syringa or pipe of Pan is described by Virgil, and the use of it by Lucretius, lib. V.

Et supra calamos unco percurrere labro.

Fig. 3.

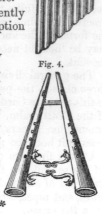

The figure of it occurs so frequently on medals, that a particular description of it is unnecessary. Fig. 3.

Fig. 4.

The Tibiæ pares, mentioned by Terence to have been played on, the one with the right, and the other with the left hand, are diversely represented in Mersennus De Instrumentis harmonicis, pag. 7, and in the Dissertation of Blanchinus now citing; in the former they are yoked together towards the bottom, and at the top, as fig. 4. In the latter they are much slenderer, and are not joined. Fig. 5.*

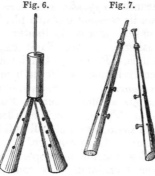

The author last mentioned speaks also of other pipes, namely, the Tibiæ bifores, fig. 6, the Tibiæ gemine, fig. 7, instruments used in theatrical representations; the latter of these seem to be the Tibiæ impares of Terence : he also describes the Tibiæ utriculariæ, or bag-pipes, fig. 8, anciently the entertainment of shepherds and other rustics.

Fig. 6.   Fig. 7.

The Horn, fig. 9, was anciently used at funeral solemnities; it is alluded to by Statius. Theb. lib. VI.

Fig. 8.   Fig. 9.

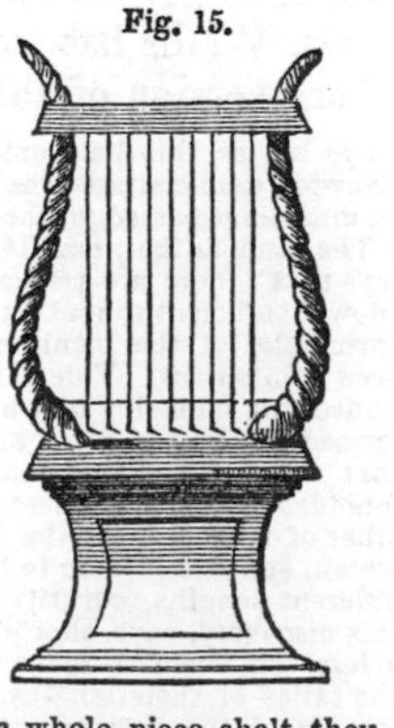

* The tibiæ of the ancients, and especially those mentioned in the titles of Terence's comedies, have been the subject of much learned enquiry. Caspar Bartholinus the anatomist has written a whole volume De Tibiis Veterum. Ælius Donatus, a Latin grammarian, and the preceptor of St. Jerome, says that the tone of the tibiæ dextræ was grave, and adapted to the serious parts of the comedy; and that that of the tibiæ sinistræ, and also of the tibiæ sarranæ, or Tyrian pipes, was light and cheerful. 'Dextræ tibiæ sua gravitate seriam comedæ dic-'tionem pronunciabant. Sinistræ et sarranæ hoc est Tyriæ acuminis 'suavitate jocum in comedia ostendebant. Ubi autem dextrâ et sinistrâ 'acta fabula inscribebatur mistim jocos et gravitatem denunciabat.' Donat. Fragm. de Traged. & Comed. The abbé du Bos says that this passage explains that other in Pliny, where it is said that the ancients to make left-handed pipes, took the bottom of that very reed, the top whereof they had before used for the right-handed. The sense of this passage is manifest; but it does not strictly agree with what Donatus says, unless it can be supposed that, contrary to the order of nature, the reeds were small at bottom, and grew tapering upwards.

The ancient Buccina or horn-trumpet, fig. 10, is mentioned by Ovid, Vegetius, Macrobius, and others.

Fig. 10.

The Tuba communis, seu recta, so called in contradistinction to the Tuba ductilis, is of very ancient original; it was formerly, as now, made of silver or brass, of the form fig. 11. Blanchinus hesitates not to

Fig. 11.

assert that the two trumpets of silver which God commanded Moses to make in the wilderness were of this form.† It seems that the trumpet has retained this figure without the least external diversity, so low down as the year 1520; for in a very curious picture at Windsor, supposed to be of Mabuse, representing the interview between Ardres and Guisnes, of Henry VIII. and Francis I. are trumpets precisely corresponding in figure with the Tuba recta above referred to.

Of the instruments of the second class, comprehending the tensile species, the Monochord is the most simple. This instrument is mentioned by Aristides Quintilianus, and other ancient writers, but we have no authentic designation of it prior to the time of Ptolemy, it nevertheless is capable of so many forms, that any instrument of one string only answers to the name; for which reason some have not scrupled to represent the monochord like the bow of Diana.

Figures 12 and 13, are the Lyre of three and four chords, ascribed to Mercury, by Nicomachus, Macrobius, Boetius, and a number of other writers, the forms whereof are here given from ancient sculptures in and about Rome, referred to by Blanchinus; as are also those figures 14 and 15, representing the one a Lyre with seven chords, and the other one with nine.

Fig. 12.   Fig. 13.

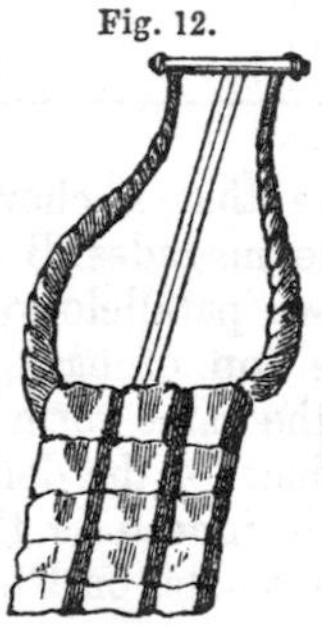

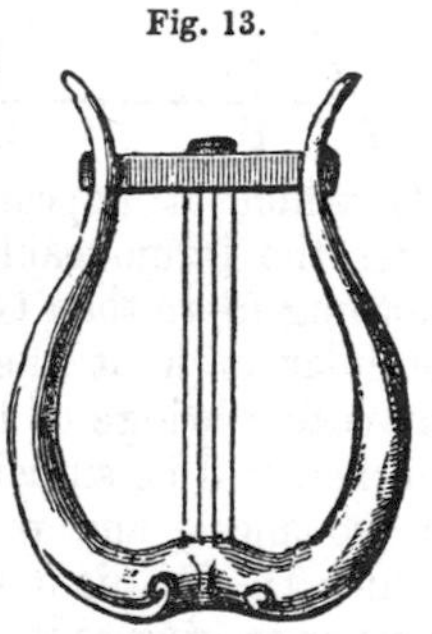

Fig. 14. 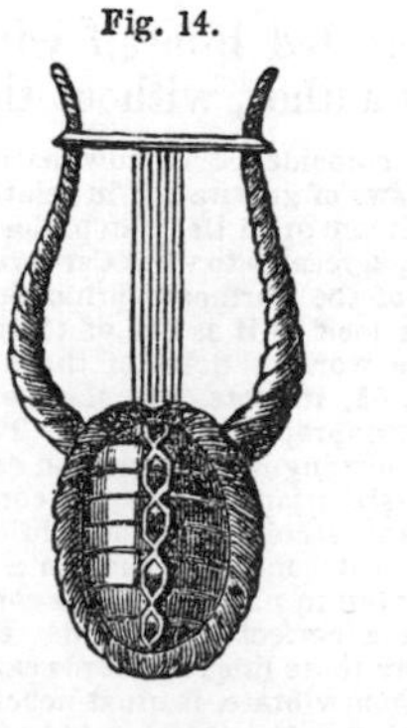   Fig. 15.

† 'Make thee two trumpets of silver; of a whole piece shalt thou 'make them, that thou mayest use them for the calling of the assembly, 'and for the journeying of the camps. Numbers, chap. x. verse 2.

Fig. 16 is the Lyre of Amphion, and 17 the plectrum, with which not only this, but every species

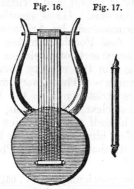

Fig. 16.   Fig. 17.

Fig. 18.

of the lyre was struck, as may be collected from the following passage in Ovid :—

> Instructamque fidem gemmis et dentibus Indis
> Sustinet à lævâ : tenuit manus altera plectrum.
> Artificis status ipse fuit, tum stamina docto
> Pollice sollicitat : quorum dulcedine captus
> Pana jubet Tmolus citheræ submittere cannus.
>
> Met. lib. xi. l. 167.*

Figures 19 and 20 are other forms of the Lyre in a state of improvement.

Fig. 19.   Fig. 20.

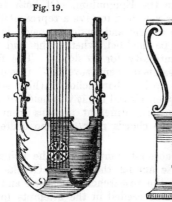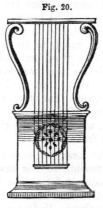

* It is very probable that the use of the bow, with which the viol species of instruments is sounded, was borrowed from a practice of the ancients. Of the many kinds of lyre among them, it seems that they had one, in which the fingers of one hand were employed in stopping the strings, at the instant that they were stricken with a stick held in the other.

Virgil intimates a practice somewhat like this in the following passage of the Æneid :—

> Nec non Threïcus longa cum veste sacerdos
> Obloquitur numeris septem discrimina vocum :
> Jamque eadem digitis, jam pectine pulsat eburno.
>
> Lib. VI. l. 645.

> The Thracian bard, surrounded by the rest,
> There stands conspicuous in his flowing vest,
> His flying fingers, and harmonious quill,
> Strike sev'n distinguish'd notes, and sev'n at once they fill.
>
> Dryden's translation, book VI. l. 877.

From which it at least appears, that the instrument was placed in a horizontal position, and that the strings were struck, not by the fingers, but with a plectrum, which might be a quill or a bow, or almost any other thing fit for the purpose.

Plato, in his treatise de Legibus VII. 794. Ed. Serr. advises to train up children to use the right and the left hand indifferently. In some things, says he, we can do it very well, as when we use the lyre with the left hand and the stick with the right. Dr. Jortin says it may be collected from this, that the fingers of the left hand were occupied in some manner upon the strings, else barely to hold a lyre shewed no very free use of the left hand ; and it appears from Ptolemy, II. 12, that they used both hands at once in playing upon the lyre, and that the fingers of the left were employed, not in stopping, but in striking the string.

But see the figure of an ancient statue, representing Apollo playing on

Figures 21, 22, are two different representations of the Lyra triplex, the one from Blanchinus, the other from a writer of far less respectable authority ; concerning this instrument it is necessary to be somewhat particular.

Fig. 21.   Fig. 22.

Athenæus lib. VIV. cap. xv. describes an instrument of a very singular construction, being a lyre in the form of a tripod, an invention, as it is said, of Pythagoras Zacynthius. This person is mentioned by Aristoxenus, in his Elements, page 36 ; and Meibomius, in a note on the passage, says, on the authority of Diogenes Laertius, that he was the author of Arcana Philosophiæ, and adds, that it was from him that the proverbial saying, ipse dixit, had its rise ; with respect to the instrument, it is exhibited in two forms (see above), the first taken from a sarcophagus at Rome, referred to by Blanchinus, the other from an engraving in the Histoire de la Musique, of Monsieur de Blainville, for which it is to be suspected he had no other authority than the bare verbal description of Athenæus, who has said, that it comprehended three distinct sets of chords, adjusted to the three most ancient of the modes, the Dorian, the Phrygian, and the Lydian.

The Trigon, an instrument mentioned by Nichomachus, among those which were adjusted by Pythagoras, after he had discovered and settled the ratios of the consonances. It was used at feasts, and it is said, was played on by women, and struck either with a quill, or beaten with little rods of different lengths and weights, to occasion a diversity in the sounds. The figure 23 is taken from an ancient Roman anaglyph, mentioned by Blanchinus. Figure 24 is also a Trigon, described by the same author ; figure 25 is the reverse of an ancient medal, and shews the manner of playing on it.

Fig. 23.

Fig. 24.   Fig. 25.

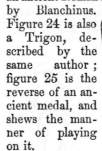

The Cymbals

the lyre, fig. 18, which seems very clearly to evince the practice above spoken of.

Upon this relic of antiquity, a drawing whereof was found in the collection of the late Mr. N. Haym, it is observable that the lyre is of a form very nearly resembling the violin, as having a body, and also a neck, which is held in the left hand ; the instrument in the right, undoubtedly answers to the modern bow, with this difference, that its use was percussion and not friction, which latter is a modern and noble improvement ; the position of the instrument deserves to be remarked, as it corresponds exactly with the viol di braccio.

Fig. 26.

of Bacchus, figure 26, were two small brass vessels, somewhat in the form of a shield, which being struck together by the hands, gave a sound. The well-known statue of the dancing faun has one of these in each hand.

Fig. 27.

The Tympanum leve, figure 27, an instrument yet known by the name of the Tambouret, and frequently used in dancing, was also used to sing to; it is distinguished by Catullus, Ovid, Suetonius, St. Augustine, and Isidore, of Sevil, from the great brazen drum, properly so called, this above-mentioned, was covered with the skin of some animal, and was struck either with a short twig or with the hand, as fig. 28.

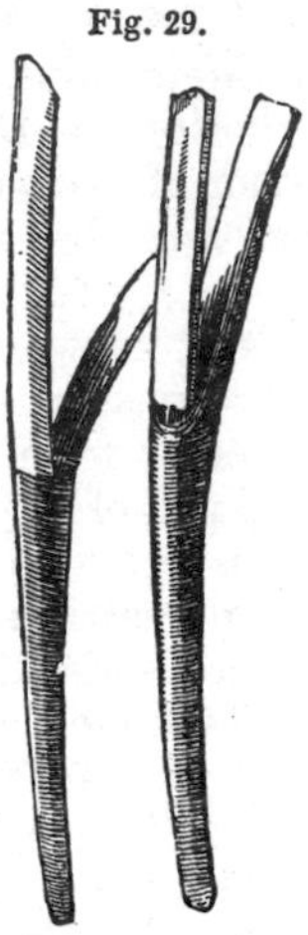

Crotala, figure 29. These were instruments also of the pulsatile kind. The Crotalum was made of a reed, divided into two by a slit from the top, extending half way downwards: the sides thus divided being struck one against the other with different motions of the hands, produced a sound like that which the stork makes with her bill, wherefore the ancients gave that bird the epithet of Crotalistria, *i.e.,* Player upon the Crotalum;* and Aristophanes calls a great talker a Crotalum.

Fig. 28.   Fig. 29.

* Pausanias relates, that Hercules did not kill the Stymphalides with his arrows, but that he frighted, and drove them away with the noise of the crotala, the consequence whereof, supposing the relation to be true, is, that the crotalum must be a very ancient instrument. Ovid joins the crotalum with the cymbals.

    Cymbala cum crotalis prurientiaque arma Priapo
        Ponit, et adducit tympana pulsa manu.

It appears by an ancient poem, entitled Copa, by some ascribed to Virgil, that those who played with the crotala danced at the same time. It farther appears, that in these dances, which were chiefly of women, such a variety of wanton gesticulations and indecent attitudes and postures were practised, that Clemens Alexandrinus says, that the use of these instruments ought to be banished from the festivals of all Christians. And the same might have been said of the cymbals. See figures 30 and 31.

Fig. 30.   Fig. 31.

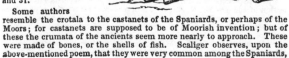

Some authors resemble the crotala to the castanets of the Spaniards, or perhaps of the Moors; for castanets are supposed to be of Moorish invention; but of these the crumata of the ancients seem more nearly to approach. These were made of bones, or the shells of fish. Scaliger observes, upon the above-mentioned poem, that they were very common among the Spaniards,

Mention is made by some writers on music, of an instrument of forty chords, called, from the name of its inventor, the Epigonium. Epigonius was a native of Ambracia, a city of Epirus, and a citizen of Sicyon, a town of Peloponnesus. He is mentioned together with Lasus Hermionensis, by Aristoxenus, in his Elements, pag. 3. And Porphyry makes him the head of one of those many sects of musicians that formerly subsisted, giving him the priority even of Aristoxenus, in these words :—'There were many 'sects, some indeed before Aristoxenus, as the Epi-'gonians, Damonians, Eratocleans, Agenorians, and 'some others; which he himself makes mention of; 'but there were some after him, which others have 'described, as the Archestratians, Agonians, Philis-'cians, and Hermippians.'

Julius Pollux, in his Onomasticum, lib. IV. cap. ix. speaking of the instruments invented by certain nations, says, that the Epigonium obtained its name from Epigonius, who was the first that struck the chords of musical instruments without a plectrum.† The same author adds, that the Epigonium had forty chords, as the Simicum had thirty-five. Athenæus, lib. IV. speaks to the same purpose.

As to the Simicum, nothing more is known about it, than that it contained thirty-five chords. Vincentio Galilei, with good reason, supposes it to be somewhat more ancient than the Epigonium. Of both these instruments he has ventured to give a representation, in his dialogue on ancient and modern music; but it is very much to be doubted, whether he had any authority from antiquity for so doing. The form which he has assigned them severally, resembles nearly that of an upright harpsichord, which seems to indicate, that when played on, it was held between the legs of the musician, different perhaps from the harp, with the grave chords near and the acute remote from him.

The foregoing account comprehends the principal instruments in use among the ancient Greeks and Romans, so far as the researches of learned and inquisitive men have succeeded in the attempts to recover them; their forms seem to be thereby ascertained beyond the possibility of a doubt, and these it may be said, declare the state of the ancient musical practice, much more satisfactorily than all the hyperbolical relations extant, of its efficacy and influence over the human passions; and leave it an un-

especially the inhabitants of the province of Bœtica [Andalusia] about Cadiz, to which Martial alludes.

        Nec de Gadibus improbis puellæ
        Vibrabunt sine fine prurientes
        Lascivos docili tremore lumbos.   Lib. V. epigr. lxxix.

The same poet elsewhere speaks of the crumata in these words :—

        Edere lascivos ad Bœtica crusmata gestus,
        Ed Gaditanis ludere docta modis.   Lib. VI. epigr. lxxi.

From which two passages, it appears clearly, that the above censure of Clemens Alexandrinus was well grounded.

† Plutarch in his dialogue before cited, relates that Olympus introduced the plectrum into Greece, which it is supposed was then deemed a useful invention. Certainly the lyre was originally touched by the fingers, and all that can be meant here, is, that Epigonius recurred to the primitive method, and played on his instrument, as the harp is now played on with the fingers; between which, and the touch of a plectrum or quill, the difference is very wide, as may be discovered by a comparison of the lute or harp with the harpsichord.

questionable fact, that the discoveries of Pythagoras, and the improvements made by the Greeks, his successors, terminated in a theory, admirable in speculation it is true, but to which such instruments were adapted, as would have disgraced any performance, even in the least enlightened period, since the invention of that species of harmony, which has been the delight of later ages.

BOOK III.   CHAP. XX.

The gradual declension of learning which had begun before the time of Porphyry, the last of the Greek musical writers, and above all, the ravages of war, and the then embroiled state of the whole civilized world, put an end to all farther improvements in the science of harmonics; nor do we find, that after this time it was made a subject of philosophical enquiry: the succeeding writers were chiefly Latins, who, as they were for the most part followers of the Greeks, contributed but very little to its advancement; and, for reasons which will hereafter be given, the cultivation of music became the care of the clergy; an order of men, in whom the little of learning then left, in a few ages after the establishment of christianity, centered.

But before we proceed farther to trace the progress of the science, it is proper to remark, that the writings of the Greeks not only leave us in great uncertainty as to the state of music in other countries, but that they do not exclude the possibility of its having arrived at a great degree of perfection, even before that discovery of the consonances, which is by all of them allowed to be the very basis of the Greek system. For let it be remembered, that Pythagoras is supposed to have lived so late as A. M. 3384, which is about 560 years before the birth of Christ; and that long before his time, such effects were ascribed to music, as well by the sacred as profane historians, as are utterly inconsistent with the supposition, that it was then in its infancy. It were endless to enumerate the many passages in sacred writ, declaring the power of music: the story of David and Saul, and the effects attributed to the harp; but more especially the frequent mention of instruments with ten strings, would lead us to think, that the art had arrived to a state of greater perfection than the writers above-mentioned suppose. Here then arises a question, the solution whereof is attended with great difficulty; namely, whether the Jews, not to mention the various other nations, that had subsisted for many ages, previous to the times from whence we begin our account, in a state of very improved civilization, had not a musical theory? or is it to be conceived, that mankind, with whose frame and structure, with whose organs and faculties, harmony is shewn to be connatural, could remain for so many centuries in an almost total ignorance of its nature and principles?

To this it is answered, that the knowledge of the state and condition of past times, is deducible, with any degree of certainty, only from history; that the information communicated by the means of writing, must depend on an infinite variety of circumstances, such as a disposition in men of ability to communicate that information which is derived from a long course of study, the permanency of language, a faithful and uncorrupt transmission of facts, and an absence of all those accidents, that in the course of events hinder the propagation of knowledge; and wherever these fail, the progress of human intelligence must necessarily be intercepted. To obstructions arising from one or other of these causes, is to be imputed that impenetrable obscurity in which the events of the earlier ages lie involved; an obscurity so intense, that no one presumes to trace the origin of any of the arts, and a vast chasm is supplied by the mythologists, the poets, and that species of history which we distinguish from what is truly authentic and worthy of credit by the epithet of fabulous; even antiquity itself, which stamps a value on some sort of evidence, will in many cases diminish the credit of an historian; and mankind have not yet settled what degree of assent is due to the testimony of the most ancient of all profane historians, the venerable Herodotus.

Admitting as a fact, that Egypt in the infancy of the world, was as well the seat of learning as of empire; and admitting also the learning of the Persian Magi, the Indian Brachmans, and other people of the east, not to mention the Phœnicians and the Chinese, to be as great as some pretend, who have magnified it to a degree that exceeds the bounds of moderate credulity; nevertheless, the more sober researchers into antiquity, have contented themselves with a retrospect limited by the time when philosophy began to flourish in Greece; and it is only on the writers of that country that we can depend.

An investigation of the Jewish theory would be a fruitless attempt, but of their practice we are enabled to form some judgment, by the several passages in the Old Testament that declare the names and number of the Hebrew instruments, and mention the frequent use of them in sacrifices, and other religious solemnities; but it is to be observed, that the correspondence of the names of their instruments, with the names of those in use in modern times, is a circumstance from which no argument in their favour can be drawn, for a reason herein before given.

Mersennus, and after him Kircher, whose elaborate researches into the more abstruse parts of ancient literature, render him in some particulars a respectable authority, have exhibited the forms of many of the ancient Jewish musical instruments: the latter of these authors professes to have gone to the fountain head for his intelligence; and the result of an attentive perusal of as many of the Rabbinical writers and commentators on the Talmud as he could lay his hands on, he has given to the public in the Musurgia, tom. I. pag. 47. How far the authorities adduced by him will warrant such a precise designation of their respective forms, as verges in some instances too near our own times, is left to the decision of those who shall have curiosity enough to peruse them; but lest it should be said that the subject is too important to be passed over in silence, the substance of what he has delivered on this head is here given.

He says that the author of a treatise entitled Schilte Haggiborim, *i. e.* the Shield of the Mighty, who he elsewhere makes to be Rabbi Hannase, treats very accurately on the musical instruments of the Hebrews, and reckons that they were thirty-six in number, and of the pulsatile kind, and that David was skilled in the use of them all. Kircher however does not seem to acquiesce altogether in the first of these opinions, for he proceeds to a description de instrumentis Hebreorum Polychordis sive Neghinoth; these it seems, according to his author abovenamed, were of wood, long and round, consisting of three strings made of the intestines of beasts; the instruments had holes bored underneath them; and, to make them sound, the strings were rubbed with a bow composed of the hairs of a horse's tail, well extended and compacted together. Kircher speaks particularly of the Psaltery, or Nablium, the Cythara, or, which is the same thing, the Assur, Nevel, Chinnor, the Machul, and the Minnin. He says that no one has rightly described the Psaltery of David, and that some have thought that the word rather denoted certain genera of harmony, or modulations of the voice, than any kind of instrument: that according to Josephus it had twelve sounds, and was played on with the fingers; that Hilarius, Didymus, Basilius, and Euthymius call it the straitest of all musical instruments — that Augustine says it was carried in the hand of the player, and had a shell or concave piece of wood on it that caused the strings to resound—that Hieronymus describes this instrument as having ten strings, and resembling in its form a square shield—that Hilarus will have it to be the same with the Nablium. Kircher himself is certain that it was a stringed instrument, and cites Suidas to prove that the word Psalterium is derived from Psallo, to strike the chords with the ends of the fingers. He farther says, that many writers suppose it to have had a triangular form, and to resemble the harp of David, as commonly painted in pictures of him; and that some are express in the opinion that the Psalterium and the Nablium, as being struck with the fingers of both hands, were one and the same instrument; and to this purpose he cites the following passage from Ovid :—

Disce etiam duplici genialia Naulia palmâ
Verrere : conveniunt dulcibus illa modis.
                              Art. Amat. lib. III. l. 327.

The Nevel, notwithstanding the resemblance between its name and that of the Nablium, and the confusion which Kircher has created by using them promiscuously, clearly appears to have been a different instrument; for he says it was in the form of a trapezium; and the Nablium, which he has taken great pains to prove to be the same with the Psalterium, he shows to have been of a square form. Of the Assur, he only says that it had ten chords;

the Chinnor he supposes to have had thirty-two, the Machul six, and the Minnin three or four; and that in their form they resembled, the one the Viol and the other the Chelys. To give a clearer idea, he has exhibited, from an old book in the Vatican library, several figures representing the Psalterium, figure 32; the Chinnor, figure 33; the Machul, figure 34; the Minnin, fig. 35; and the Nevel, figure 36.*

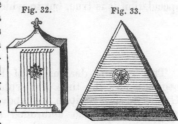

Fig. 32.   Fig. 33.

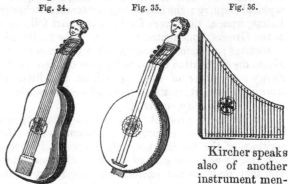

Fig. 34.   Fig. 35.   Fig. 36.

Kircher speaks also of another instrument mentioned by Rabbi Hannase, who it seems was the author of the book before cited, Schilte Haggiborim, and also in the Targum, called Haghniugab, consisting of six strings, and resembling the greater Chelys or Viol di Gamba, differing from it only in the number of its chords: he says it is often confounded with the Machul.

He next proceeds to treat of the pulsatile instruments of the Hebrews, in contradistinction to those of the fidicinal or stringed kind; and first he speaks of the Thoph or Tympanum, figure 37, an instrument of Egyptian original, and used by the priests of that country in their public worship. He relates on the authority of Rabbi Hannase that it had the likeness of a ship; and that by the Greeks it was also called Cymbalum, from cymba, a boat: he adds that it was covered with the skin of an animal, and was beat on with a pestle or rod of iron or brass.

Fig. 37.

He proceeds to say that though the Machul is ranked among the fidicinal or stringed instruments, this name was given to an instrument of a very different form, and of the pulsatile kind; nay, he adds that Rabbi Hannase asserts that it was precisely the same with the Sistrum of the Egyptians, or the Krousma of the Greeks; and that it was of a circular

* The truth of this representation, so far as it relates to the Machul and Minnin, is strongly to be suspected; they both seem to require the aid of the hair bow, a kind of plectrum to which the ancients seem to have been absolute strangers. Besides their near resemblance to the lute and viol, instruments which it is supposed had their origin in Provence, is a strong argument against their antiquity.

form, made of iron, brass, silver, or gold, with little bells hung round it. Kircher corrects this description, and instead of little bells, supposes a number of iron rings, strung as it were on a rod or bar in a lateral position that went across the circle. He says that a handle was affixed to it, by means whereof the instrument was flung backwards and forwards, and emitted a kind of melancholy murmur, arising from the collision of the rings. as well against each other as against the sides, the circle, and the bar on which they moved, figure 38. He adds, that the Thoph, or rather Sistrum of the Hebrews was thus constructed, and that the virgins every where made use of it in the dances of the Sistri, as we read in the books of Exodus and Judges, that Mary, the sister of Moses, and the daughter of Jephtha, did: and he farther says, that according to accounts which he has received from credible witnesses, the Syrians in his time preserved the use of the Sistrum in Palestine.*

Fig. 38.

Fig. 39.

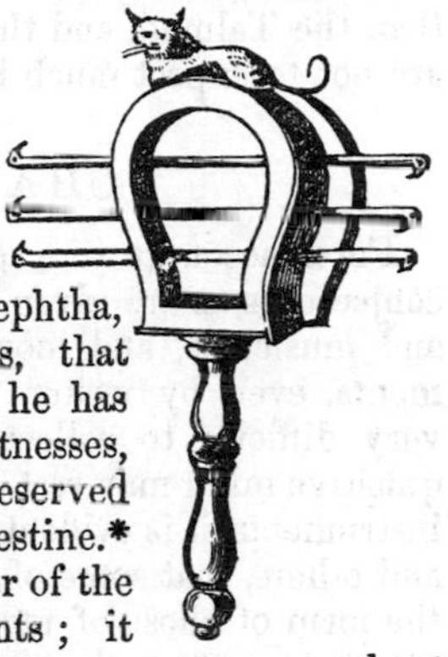

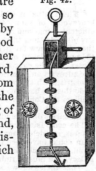

Gnets Berusim was another of the Hebrew pulsatile instruments; it seems by Kircher that there was some controversy about the form of it, but that Rabbi Hannase represents it as nothing more than a piece of fir in shape like a mortar. He says there belonged to it a pestle of the same wood, with a knob at each end, and in the middle thereof a place for the hand to grasp it: that those that beat on the instrument held it in the left hand and struck with the right on the edge and in the middle, using the knobs alternately. Figures 40, 41. Kircher compares this instrument to the Crotalum already described, but seemingly with little propriety; and to the Gnaccari of the Italians, of which word, considered as a technical term, it is hard to find the meaning.

Fig. 40.   **Fig. 41.**

Minagnghinim was the name of another of the Hebrew pulsatile instruments, which, according to Rabbi Hannase, was a certain square table of wood, having a handle so fitted as conveniently to be held by it. On the table were balls of wood or brass, through which was put either an iron chain or an hempen chord, and this was stretched from the bottom to the top of the table. When the instrument was shaken, the striking of the balls occasioned a very clear sound, which might be heard at a great distance. See the representation which Kircher gives of it, figure 42.

Fig. 42.

Magraphe Tamid, another of the pulsatile instruments of the Hebrews, is conjectured by Kircher to have been used for convoking the priests and Levites together into the temple: it is said to have emitted prodigious sound; and though Rabbi Hannase says no one can describe the form of it, Kircher thinks it must have been like one of our largest bells.

We are now to declare what instruments of the pneumatic kind were in use amongst the ancient Hebrews; and first we meet with the Masrakitha, which consisted of pipes of various sizes, fitted into a kind of wooden chest, open at the top, but at the bottom stopped with wood covered with a skin; by means of a pipe fixed to the chest, wind was conveyed into it from the lips: the pipes were of lengths proportioned musically to each other, and the melody was varied at pleasure by the stopping and unstopping with the fingers the apertures at the upper extremity. Kircher thinks it differed but little from the instrument which Pan is constantly represented as playing on; there seems however to be a difference in the manner of using it. See fig. 43.

Fig. 43.

Of the Sampunia, derived, as Kircher conjectures, from the Greek Symphonia, as also of the preceding instrument, mention is made, as Kircher asserts, in the Chaldaic of the book of Daniel, chap. iii. He says also that it is described in the Schilte Haggiborim, as consisting of a round belly, made of the skin of a ram or wether, into which two pipes were inserted, one to fill the belly with wind, the other to emit the sound; the lower pipe had holes in it, and was played on by the fingers. In short, it seems to have been neither more nor less than the Cornamusa, or common bag-pipe; and Kircher says that in Italy, even in his days, it was known by the name of the Zampugna.

The Hebrews had also an instrument, described in the Schilte Haggiborim, called Macraphe d'Aruchin, consisting of several orders of pipes, which were supplied with wind by means of bellows; it had keys, and would at this time without hesitation be called an organ. See fig. 44.†

Fig. 44.

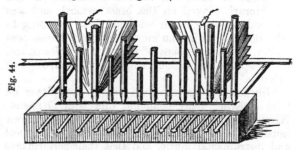

---

* The invention of the Sistrum is not to be ascribed to the Jews: it is generally supposed to be of Egyptian original. There are some forms of it, as that in particular, figure 39, which bears on it a figure of one of those many brute animals to which this superstitious and idolatrous people paid divine honours.

† This instrument is delineated by Kircher, but the figure of it above referred to, is taken from the Musica Historica of Wolfgang Gaspar Printz, written in the German language, and printed at Dresden in 4to. anno. 1690, who cites the Collectaneis Philologicis of Johannes Schütterus, to justify his deviations from Kircher, in the form of some of the instruments described in the Musurgia. But it is to be feared, that his author has erred in giving to the Machul and Minnin above described, the hair bow, of which not the least trace is to be found in the writings of any of the ancients.

Of Fistulæ it seems the Hebrews had sundry kinds; they were chiefly the horns or bones of animals, straight or contorted, as nature fashioned them: the representations of sundry kinds of them, in figures 45, 46, 47, 48, are taken from Kircher.

Fig. 45.   Fig. 46.

Fig. 47.   Fig. 48.

In the account which Blanchinus has given of the Jewish musical instruments, he mentions a mallet of wood used by them in their worship, and which at certain times is beaten by the people on the beams, seats, and other parts of the synagogue, in commemoration of the tumult preceding the Crucifixion, or, as the modern Jews say, at the hanging of Haman, figure 49. Instruments of this kind, and which produce noise rather than sound, are improperly classed among instruments of music.

Fig. 49.

Of the Hebrew musicians no very satisfactory account can be given. This of Kircher, extracted from the Rabbinical writers, is, perhaps, the best that can be expected: 'Asaph, according to the 'opinion of the interpreters, was the composer of 'certain psalms; he is said also to have been a singer, 'and to have sung to the cymbals of brass, and to 'have praised the Lord, and ministred in the sight 'of the ark.

'Eman Ezraita, the singer, the son of Joel, of the 'children of Caath, was most skilful in the cymbal, 'and was in a manner equal in knowledge and 'wisdom to Ethan; he is the supposed author of the 'Psalm, beginning Domine Deus salutis meæ, which, 'because he gave it to be sung by the sons of Coreh, 'he inscribed both with his own and their name.

'Ethan of Ezrachus, the son of Assaia, the son 'of Merari, played on the brass cymbal, and was 'endued with so much wisdom, that, according to 'the Book of Kings, no mortal, except Solomon, was 'wiser. The three sons of Coreh, Asir, Elcana, and 'Abiasaph, were famous singers and composers of 'Psalms.'

'Idithus was an excellent singer, and player on 'the cythara; many confound him with Orpheus.' Kircher supposes, that he and the other Hebrew musicians were inspired with the knowledge of vocal and instrumental music, and that their performance was equal to their skill. He says, he doubts not but that there were many other men, especially in the time of king Solomon, who were well skilled in divine music, for that the most excellent music was fittest for the wisest of mortals, and that of the

Hebrews must have been more efficacious in exciting the affections than that of the Greeks, or of later times, but of what kind in particular it was, and by what characters expressed, he says, its antiquity prevents us from knowing.*

A much later writer than him above cited, and who is now living, Giambatista Martini, of Bologna, has entered very deeply into the music of the Hebrews; and it were to be wished, that he had been able to give a more satisfactory account of it than is to be found in his very learned work, the Storia della Musica, now publishing, but of which, as yet [in this year, 1771] the public are in possession of only one volume. Having few other sources of intelligence than the Talmud, and the writing of the Rabbins, we are not to expect much information in this particular.

CHAP. XXI.

From accounts so vague, and so abounding with conjectures, as are given of the ancient Hebrew music and musicians, and more especially of their instruments, even by writers of the best authority, it is very difficult to collect any thing whereon an inquisitive mind may rest. With regard to the Hebrew instruments, it is evident from the accounts of Kircher, and others, that some of them approach so nearly to the form of those of more modern times, as to give reason to suspect the authenticity of the representation: others appear to have been so very inartificially constructed, that we scarce credit the relation given of their effects. It is clear, that Kircher and Schütterus had from the Rabbinical writers little more than the bare names of many of the instruments described by them; yet, have they both, in some instances, ventured to represent them by forms of a comparatively late invention. Who does not see, that the Minnin, as represented by the former, and the lute, are one and the same instrument? and what difference can be discerned between the Machul and the Spanish Guitar? or can we believe, that the Macraphe d' Aruchin, and such rude essays towards melody as the Gnets Berusim, the Sistrum, or the Minagnghinim, could subsist among the same people, in any given period of civilization?

As to Martini's account, it speaks for itself; it is extracted from the sacred writings, which, at this distance of time, even with the assistance of the most

* The confusion of Idithus with Orpheus, suggests a remark on the endeavours of some, to establish the identity of eminent persons of different names and countries, and perhaps of different ages, upon hardly any other ground, than some one particular in their history common to them both: how far it is possible to extend a hypothesis of this kind, the present bishop of Gloucester has shewn in his Divine Legation of Moses. In the course of that work, the author has thought it necessary to controvert an assertion of Sir Isaac Newton; namely, that Osiris and Sesostris, both kings of Egypt, were one and the same person; in order to do this, he has undertaken to prove that the British king Arthur and William the Conqueror were not two distinct beings, but identically one person; and, as far as the method of reasoning usual in such kind of arguments will serve him, he has established his proposition. The conclusion from this correspondence of such a variety of circumstances, is much stronger in favour of the identity of Arthur and William, than could have been imagined, and yet, it has no other effect on the mind, than to discredit this method of reasoning, which is fraught with fallacy, and must terminate in scepticism.

What then can we say to the opinion of those, who confound the Hebrew musician Idithus with the ancient Orpheus; what rather can we think of him, who has attempted to show that this latter, and the royal prophet David, were one and the same person. See the Life of David, by Dr. Delany.

learned comments, fall short of affording that satisfaction, which is to be wished for in an enquiry of this kind.

Under these disadvantages, which even an enquiry into the instruments of the Hebrews lies under, an attempt to explain their musical theory must seem hopeless. Nor is it possible to conceive any thing like a system, to which such instruments as the Thoph, or the Gnets Berusim could be adapted : if the strokes of the pestle against a mortar, like those of the latter, be reducible to measure ; yet, surely the rattling of a chain, like the music of the Minagnghinim, is not ; or what if they were, would the sounds produced in either case make music ? To speak freely on this matter, whatever advantages this people might derive from the instructions of an inspired law-giver, and the occasional interpositions of the Almighty, it no where appears that their attainments in literature were very great : or that they excelled in any of those arts that attend the refinement of human manners ; the figure they made among the neighbouring nations appears to have been very inconsiderable ; and with respect to their music, there is but too much reason to suppose it was very barbarous. The only historical relation that seems to stand in the way of this opinion, is, that of the effects wrought by the music of David on the mind of Saul, a man of a haughty irascible temper, not easily susceptible of the emotions of pity or complacency, and, at the time when David exercised his art on him, under the power of a demon, or, at best, in a frenzy.

Kircher has taken upon him to relate the whole process of the dispossession of Saul, by David, and has done it as circumstantially as if he had been present at the time ; his reasoning is very curious, and it is here given in his own words :—

‘ That we may be the better able to resolve this ‘ question, how David freed Saul from the evil spirit, ‘ I shall first quote the words of the Holy Scripture, ‘ as found in the first book of Samuel, chap. xvi. ver. ‘ 23.’ “ And it came to pass when the evil spirit from “ God was upon Saul, that David took an harp, “ and played with his hand : so Saul was refreshed, “ and was well, and the evil spirit departed from him.” ‘ The passage in the holy text informs us very clearly, ‘ that the evil spirit, whatsoever it was, was driven ‘ away by music ; but how that came to pass is ‘ differently explained. The Rabbins on this place ‘ say, that when David cured Saul, he played on ‘ a cythara of ten strings ; they say also, that David ‘ knew that star, by which it was necessary the music ‘ should be regulated, in order to effect the cure : ‘ thus Rabbi Abenezra. But Picus of Mirandola says, ‘ that music sets the spirits in motion, and thereby ‘ produces the like effects on the mind, as a medicine ‘ does on the body ; from whence it may seem, that ‘ the comment of Abenezra is vain and trifling, and ‘ that David regarded not the aspects of the stars ; ‘ but trusting to the power of his instrument, struck ‘ it with his hand as his fancy suggested.

‘ And we, rejecting such astrological fictions, assert, ‘ that David freed Saul, not with herbs, potions, or ‘ other medicaments, as some maintain, but by the

‘ sole force and efficacy of music. In order to de‘ monstrate which, let it be observed, that those appli‘ cations which unlock the pores, remove obstructions, ‘ dispel vapours and cheer the heart, are best calculated ‘ to cure madness, and allay the fury of the mind ; ‘ now music produces these effects, for as it consists ‘ in sounds, generated by the motion of the air, it ‘ follows that it will attenuate the spirits, which by ‘ that motion are rendered warmer, and more quick ‘ in their action, and so dissipate at length the ‘ melancholy humour. On the contrary, where it is ‘ necessary to relax the spirits, and prevent the ‘ wounding or affecting the membranes of the brain ; ‘ in that case, it is proper to use slow progressions of ‘ sound, that those spirits and biting vapours, which ‘ ascend thither from the stomach, spleen, and hypo‘ condria, may be quietly dismissed. Therefore, the ‘ music of David might appease Saul, in either of ‘ these two ways of attenuation or dismission : by the ‘ one, he might have expelled the melancholy from ‘ the cells of the brain, or he might by the other have ‘ dissolved it, and sent it off in thin vapours, by in‘ sensible perspiration. In either case, when the ‘ melancholy had left him, he could not be mad ‘ until the return of it, he being terrestial, and as it ‘ were, destitute of action, unless moved thereto by ‘ the vital spirits, which had led him here and there ; ‘ but they had left him, when for the sake of the har‘ mony they had flown to the ears, abandoning, as ‘ I may say, their rule over him. And though, upon ‘ the cessation of the harmony they might return, yet, ‘ the patient having been elevated, and rendered ‘ cheerful, the melancholy might have acquired a ‘ more favourable habit. From all which, it is mani‘ fest, that this effect proceeded not from any casual ‘ sound of the cythara, but from the great art and ex‘ cellent skill of David in playing on it ; for, as he ‘ had a consummate and penetrating judgment, and ‘ was always in the presence of Saul, as being his ‘ armour-bearer, he must have been perfectly ac‘ quainted with the inclination and bent of his mind, ‘ and to what passions it was most subject : hence, ‘ without doubt, he being enabled, not so much by ‘ his own skill, as impelled by a divine instinct, knew ‘ so dexterously, and with sounds suited to the humour ‘ and distemper of the king, to touch the cythara, or ‘ indeed any other instrument ; for, as has been ‘ mentioned, he was skilled in the use of no fewer ‘ than thirty-six, of different kinds. It might be, ‘ that at the instant we are speaking of, he recited ‘ some certain rhythmi, proper for his purpose, and ‘ which Saul might delight to hear ; or, that by the ‘ power of metrical dancing, joined to the melody of ‘ the instrument, he wrought this effect : for Saul was ‘ apt to be affected in this manner, by the music and ‘ dancing of his armour-bearer ; as he was a youth of ‘ a very beautiful aspect, these roused up the spirits, ‘ and the words, which were rhythmically joined to ‘ the harmony, tickling the hearing, lifted up the ‘ mind, as from a dark prison, into the high region ‘ of light, whereby the gloomy spirits which oppressed ‘ the heart were dissipated, and room was left for ‘ it to dilate itself, which dilation was naturally 'followed by tranquillity and gladness.' Musurgia, 'tom. II. pag. 214, et seq.

Whoever will be at the pains of turning to the original from whence this very circumstantial relation is taken, will think it hardly possible for any one to compress more nonsense into an equal number of words than this passage contains, for which no better apology can be made than that Kircher, though a man of great learning, boundless curiosity, and indefatigable industry, was less happy in forming conclusions than in relating facts; his talents were calculated for the attainment of knowledge, but they did not qualify him for disquisition; in short he was no reasoner. With regard to the dispossession of Saul, supposing music to have been in any great degree of perfection among the Hebrews in his time, there is nothing incredible in it; and besides it has the evidence of sacred history to support it: it would therefore have argued more wisdom in the jesuit to have admitted the fact, without pretending to account for it, than by so ridiculous a theory as he has endeavoured to establish, to render the narration itself doubtful.

After this censure above passed on the music of the Hebrews, it would argue an unreasonable prejudice against them, were it not admitted that their poetry carries with it the signatures of a most exalted sublimity: to select instances from the prophets might be deemed unfair, as there are good reasons to believe that something more than mere human genius dictated those very energetic compositions; but if we look into those of their writings which the canon of our church has not adopted, we shall find great reason to admire their poetical abilities. It is true that the boldness of their figures, and those abrupt transitions, which distinguish the oriental compositions from those of most other countries, are not so well relished by a people with whom the false refinements on life and manners have taken place of the original simplicity of nature; but in the more regular and less enthusiastic spirit of expression, we feel and admire their excellence. Not to mention the numberless instances of this sort that occur in the Psalms, there is one poem among them, which for its truly elegiac simplicity, pathetic expression of the woes of captivity, and the lamentations for the sufferings of an afflicted people, has perhaps not its fellow in any of the dead or living languages. The poem here meant is the CXXXVIIth Psalm.*

From the manner in which it appears the ancients treated music, we may observe that they reasoned very abstractedly about it; the measure of intervals, either by their ratios, or by their ear, was in their judgment a very important branch of the science, and we are not to wonder at that close connection, which in the writings of the Pythagoreans at least,

is discoverable between the three sciences, music, arithmetic, and geometry. In this view it may perhaps be said that the study of music had an influence on the minds and tempers of men, as we say that the study of the mathematics has a tendency to induce a habit of thinking, to invigorate the powers of the understanding, and to detect the fallacy of specious and delusive reasoning, but in what other way it could affect the manners, or indeed the mind, unless in that very obvious one of an address to the passions, which we at this day are all sensible of, is utterly impossible to determine.

And indeed the investigation of proportions and the properties of numbers may be said to be very different from the art of combining sounds, so as to excite that pleasure which we ascribe to music; and perhaps it may not be too much to say that the understanding has little to do with it, nay, some have carried this matter so far as to question whether the delight we receive from music does not partake more of the sensual than the intellectual kind;† however this at least may be said, that it is some faculty, very different from the understanding, that enables us to perceive the effects of harmony, and to distinguish between consonant and dissonant sounds, and in this respect, the affinity between music, and that other art, which for more reasons than all are aware of, has ever been deemed its sister, is very remarkable. That painting has its foundation in mathematical principles, is certain, nay, that there is a harmony between colours, analogous to that of sounds, is demonstrable; now the laws of optics, the doctrine of light and colours, and the principles of perspective, connected as they are with geometry, all of which painting has more or less to do with, are things so different from the representation of corporeal objects, from the selection and artful arrangement of beautiful forms, from the expressions of character and passion as they appear in the human countenance, and, lastly, from that creative faculty in which we suppose the perfection of painting to consist, that we scruple not to say that a man may be an excellent painter with a slender knowledge of the mathematics; and the examples of the most eminent professors of the art, are a proof of the assertion.

But the reason why the ancient writers treated the subject in this manner is, that they used the word Harmony to express relation and coincidence in general; nay, so extensively was this appellation used, that many authors of treatises on this subject have thought it previously necessary to a discussion of music in its three most obvious divisions of rythmic, metric, and harmonic, to treat of mundane, humane, and political music; the three last of which species, if at all intitled to the name of music,‡ must

---

* It has already been mentioned, page 93, that among the Jews the chief use of music was in sacrifices and other religious ceremonies. To this may be added that it also accompanied the celebration of the funereal rites. When Jesus approached the Ruler's house, in order to revive his daughter, we are told by the Evangelist, Matthew, chap ix., v. 23., that he saw "the Minstrels and People making a noise." Dr. Hammond, in a very learned note on this passage, informs us that the custom of having music at funerals came to the latter Jews from the Gentiles.

† This metaphysical question is discussed and determined in the negative, i. e. that music is an intellectual pleasure, by the ingenious Mr. John Norris, of Bemerton. See his Miscellanies, pag. 309, 12mo.

‡ Aristoxenus's division is rhythmic, metric, organic, lib. II. That of Boetius, mundane, humane, and instrumental. By the first is to be understood the harmony of the spheres, before spoken of; by the second, the harmony subsisting between the body and the rational soul as united together, each being actuated by the other: and also that other kind of harmony, consent, relation, or whatever else it may be called, between the parts of the body, with respect to each; and again between those

owe it to a metaphor, and that a very bold one: Aristides Quintilianus uses another method of division, which it must be confessed is the more natural of the two, and says that music is of two kinds, the contemplative and the active; the first of these he subdivides into natural and artificial; which latter he again divides into the harmonic, the rhythmic, and the metric; the active he divides into the usual and the enunciative; the usual, containing melopœia, rhythmopœia, and poesia; and the enunciative the organic, the odiac, the hypocritic.*

Thus we see that the ancients, when they treated of music, used the word Harmony in a sense very different from that in which it is understood at this day; for there is doubtless a harmony between sounds emitted in succession, which is discernible as long as the impression of those already struck remains uneffaced; yet we choose to distinguish this kind of relation by the word Melody, and that of Harmony is appropriated to the coincidence of different sounds produced at the same instant: if it be asked why the ancients used the word Harmony in a sense so very restrained, as is above represented, the answer is easy, if that position be true which many writers have advanced, namely, that their music was solitary, and that they were utter strangers to symphoniac harmony. This the admirers of antiquity will by no means allow; and, to say the truth, there are very few questions which have more divided the learned world than this. In order that the reader may be able to form a judgment on a matter of so great curiosity, the authorities on both sides shall now be produced, and submitted to his consideration.

To avoid confusion, it will be necessary first to reduce the proposition to the form of a question, which, to take it in the sense in which it has generally been discussed, seems to be, Whether the ancients had the knowledge of music in symphony or consonance, or not?

The advocates for the affirmative are Franchinus, or, as he is frequently named, Gaffurius, Zarlino, Gio. Battista Doni, Isaac Vossius, and Zaccaria

Tevo, all, excepting Vossius, musicians, and he confessedly a man of learning, but a great bigot, and of little judgment: the sum of their arguments is, that it appears by the writings of the ancients that their skill in harmony was very profound, and that they reasoned upon it with all the accuracy and precision which became philosophers; that the very first discoveries of the nature of musical consonance, namely, those made by Pythagoras, tended much more naturally to establish a theory of harmony than of mere melody or harmony in succession, that supposing Pythagoras never to have lived, it could not have happened, but that the innumerable coincidences of sounds produced by the voice or by the percussion of different bodies at the same instant, which must necessarily occur in the course of a very few years, could not fail to suggest a trial of the effects of concordant sounds uttered together, or at one and the same point of time; that those passages of sacred writ that mention commemoration of remarkable events, or the celebration of public festivals, as that of the dedication of Solomon's temple, with a great number of voices and instruments, hardly allow of the supposition that the music upon these occasions was unisonous.

All this it may be said is mere conjecture, let us therefore see what farther evidence there is to countenance the belief that the ancients were acquainted with the use of different parts in music; Aristotle in his treatise concerning the world, lib. V. has this question, 'If the world is made of contrary 'principles, how comes it that it was not long ago 'dissolved?' In answer to this he shows that its beauty, perfection, and duration are owing to the admirable mixture and temperament of its parts, and the general order and harmony of nature. In his illustration of this argument he introduces music, concerning which he has this passage: Μϑσικὴ δὲ ὀξεῖς ἅμα κ̀ βαρεῖς, μακρυς τε κ̀ βραχεῖς φθόγγϑς μίξασα, ἐν διαφόραις φωναῖς, μίαν ἀπετέλεσεν ἁρμονίαν. 'Music, by a mixture of acute and grave, and of 'long and short sounds of different voices, yields an 'absolute or perfect concentus or concert.'—Again, lib. VI. explaining the harmony of the celestial motions, he says, that 'though each orb has a motion 'proper to itself, yet is it such a motion as tends to 'one general end, proceeding from a principle com- 'mon to all the orbs, which produce, by the concord 'arising from their motions, a choir in the heavens:' and he pursues the comparison in these words: Καθάπερ δὲ ἐν χορῶ κορυφαῖϑ καταρξαντες, συνεπηχεῖ πᾶς ὁ χορὸς ἀνδρῶν ἔθ' ὅτε κ̀ γυναικων ἐν διαφόραις φωναις ὀξυτέραις κ̀ βαρυτέραις μιαν ἁρμονίαν ἐμμελῆ κεραννύντων.

Seneca, in his Epistles, has this passage. 'Do you 'not see of how many voices the chorus consists, 'yet they make but one sound? In it some are acute, 'others grave, and others in a mean between both; 'women are joined with men, and pipes are also 'interposed among them, yet is each single voice 'concealed, and it is the whole that is manifest.'†

---

affections of the human mind, which, opposed to, or counterbalancing each other, and aided by reason, produce a kind of moral harmony, the effects whereof are visible in an orderly and well-regulated conduct.

To these Kircher and others have added musica politica, which, say they, consists in that harmonical proportion, which in every well-regulated government subsists between the three several orders of the people, the high, the low, and the middle state.

Kircher, whose inventive faculty never fails him, has given scales demonstrating each of these supposed kinds of harmony; but whoever would be farther informed as to the nature of mundane music, as it is above called, or is desirous of knowing to what extravagant lengths the human imagination may be led, may consult the writings of our country-man Dr. Robert Fludd, or de Fluctibus, a physician, and a Rosicrusian philosopher; and who, though highly esteemed for his learning by Selden, was perhaps one of the greatest mystics that ever lived. In a work of his entitled, Utriusque Cosmi majoris scilicet et minoris metaphysica, physica, atque technica Historia, printed at Oppenheim 1617, folio, is one book intitled De Musica mundana, wherein the author exhibits the form of what he calls Monochordum mundanum, an instrument representing a monochord, with the string screwed up by a hand that issues from the clouds. Fludd supposes the sound of the chord, when open, to answer to terra or the earth, and to correspond with the note gamut in the scale of music: from thence he ascends by tones and semitones, in regular order, to water, and the other elements, through the planets, and so to the empyræan, answering to g g in the ratio of the disdiapason.

Mersennus has thought this diagram worthy of a place in his Latin work; and, to say the truth, most of the plates in this and other of Fludd's works, and by the way they abound with them, are to the last degree curious and diverting. There will be farther occasion to speak of this extraordinary man, Fludd, in the course of this work.

* See the Analysis of Quintilian, in chap. xviii. of the next preceding book.

† 'Non vides quam multorum vocibus chorus constet? unus tamen ex 'omnibus sonus redditur. Aliqua illic acuta est, aliqua gravis, aliqua 'media. Accedunt viris feminæ, interponuntur tibiæ, singulorum 'latent voces, omnium apparent.' Seneca Epist. 84.

Cassiodorus has the following passage, which may seem somewhat stronger : ' Symphony is the adjust-' ment of a grave sound to an acute, or an acute to ' a grave sound, making a melody.'

From the several passages above-cited it appears, that the ancients were acquainted with symphonetic music of a certain kind, and that they employed therein voices differing in degrees of acuteness and gravity ; and thus far the affirmative of the question in debate may seem to be proved.

But in support of the negative we have the authorities of Glareanus, Salinas, Bottrigari, Artusi, Cerone, Kircher, Meibomius, Kepler, Bontempi, our countrymen Morley, Wallis, and others, a numerous band, who infer an absolute ignorance among the ancients of harmony produced by different and concordant sounds, affecting the sense at the same instant, from the general silence of their writers about it, for the exceeding skill and accuracy with which they discussed the other parts of music, leave no room to imagine but that they would have treated this in the same manner had they been acquainted with it : what discoveries accident might produce in that long series of years prior to the time of Pythagoras no one can say ; history mentions none, nor does it pretend that even he made any use of his discovery, other than to calculate the ratios of sounds, regulate the system, and improve the melody of his time.

That voices and instruments, to a very great number, were employed at public solemnities is not denied, but it is by no means a consequence that therefore the music produced by them consisted of different parts ; at this day among the reformed churches singing by a thousand different voices of men, women, and children, in divine worship is no very unusual thing ; and yet the result of all this variety of sound is hardly ever any thing more than mere melody, and that of the simplest and most artless kind. Thus much in answer to the arguments founded on the improbability that the ancients could be ignorant of symphonetic harmony, in the sense wherein at this day the term is understood.

With respect to the several passages above-cited, they seem each to admit of an answer ; to the first, produced from Aristotle, it is said that the word Symphony, by which we should understand the harmony of different sounds uttered at one given instant, is used by him to express two different kind of consonance, symphony and antiphony ; the first, according to him, is the consonance of the unison, the other of the octave. In his Problems, § xix. prob. 16. he asks why symphony is not as agreeable as antiphony ? the answer is, because in symphony the one voice being altogether like the other, they eclipse each other ; the symphony can therefore in this place signify nothing but unisonous or integral harmony : and he elsewhere explains it to be so, by calling that species of consonance, Omophony ; as to Antiphony, it is clear that he means by it the harmony of an octave, for he constantly uses the word in that sense ; and lest there should any doubt remain about it, he says that it is the consonance between sounds produced by the different voices of a boy and a man, that are as Nete and Hypate ; and that those sounds form

a precise octave is evident from all the representations of the ancient system that have ever been given. The sum of Aristotle's testimony is, that in his time there was a commixture of sounds, which produced a concinnous harmony : no doubt there was, but what is meant by that concinnous harmony his own words sufficiently explain.

As to Seneca, it must be confessed that the vox media must imply two extremes ; but what if in the chorus which he speaks of, the shrill tibiæ were a disdiapason above the voices of the men, and that the women sung, as they ever do, an octave above them, would not these different sounds produce harmony ? Certainly they would ; but of what kind ? Why the very kind described by him, such as seems to make but one sound, which can be said of no harmony but that of the unison or octave.

Lastly, as to Cassiodorus, his words are ' Sym-' phonia est temperamentum sonitus gravis ad acutum ' vel acuti ad gravem, modulamen efficiens, sive in ' voce, sive in percussione, sive in flatu : ' * as to the word Temperamentum, it can mean only an adjustment ; and Modulamen was never yet applied to sounds but as they followed each other in succession : to modulate is to pass, to proceed from one key or series to another ; the very idea of modulation is motion : the amount then of this definition is, that the attemperament or adjustment of a grave to an acute sound, or of an acute to a grave one, constitutes such a kind of symphony as nothing will answer to but melody ; which is above shewn to be not instantaneous, but successive symphony or consonance.

There is yet another argument to the purpose. The ancients did not reckon the third and sixth among the consonances ; this is taken notice of by a very celebrated Italian writer, Giov. Maria Artusi, of Bologna, who, though he has written expressly on the imperfections of modern music, scruples not therefore, and because the third and sixth are the beauty of symphoniac music, to pronounce that the ancients must have been unacquainted with the harmony of music in parts, in the sense in which the term is now understood : † and an author whom we shall presently have occasion to cite more at large, says expressly that they acknowledge no other consonances than the diapason, diapente, and diatessaron, and such as were composed of them ; ‡ nor does it any where appear that they were in the least acquainted with the use of discords, or with the pleasing effects produced by the preparation and resolution of the dissonances ; and if none of these were admitted into the ancient system, let any one judge of its fitness for composition in different parts.

In Morley's Introduction is a passage from whence his opinion on this question may be collected ; and, as he was one of the most learned musicians that this nation ever produced, some deference is due to it ; speaking of Descant, § he uses these words : ' When ' descant did begin, by whom, and where it was in-

* M. Aur. Cassiodor. Opera. De Musica.
† Artusi delle Imperfettioni della Moderna Musica. Ragionam. primo, Cart. 14.
‡ Musurg. tom. I. pag. 540.
§ Descant, as used by this author, has two significations ; the one answers precisely to music in consonance, the other will be explained hereafter.

' vented, is uncertaine ; for it is a great controversie
' amongst the learned if it were knowne to the
' antiquitie, or no ; and divers do bring arguments to
' prove, and others to disprove the antiquitie of it ; and
' for disproving of it, they say that in all the workes
' of them who have written of musicke before Fran-
· chinus, there is no mention of any more parts then
' one ; and that if any did sing to the harpe (which
' was their most usual instrument) they sung the same
' which they plaied. But those who would affirme
' that the ancients knew it, saie, That if they did not
' know it, to what ende served all those long and
' tedious discourses and disputations of the conso-
' nantes, wherein the moste part of their workes are
' consumed ; but whether they knew it or not, this
' I will say, that they had it not in halfe that variety
' wherein we now have it, though we read of much
' more strange effects of their musicke then of ours.'
Annotations on Morley's Introduction, part II.

CHAP. XXII.

THE suffrage of Kircher, in a question of this
nature, will be thought to carry some weight : this
author, whose learning and skill in the science are
universally acknowledged, possessed every advantage
that could lead to satisfaction in a question of this
nature, as namely, a profound skill in languages, an
extensive correspondence, and an inquisitive disposition ; and for the purpose had been indulged
with the liberty of access to the most celebrated
repositories of literature, and the use of the most
valuable manuscripts there to be met with ; and who,
to sum up all, was at once a philosopher, an antiquary,
an historian, a scholar, and a musician, has given his
opinion very much at large in nearly the following
words :—

' It has for some time been a question among
musicians whether the ancients made use of several
parts in their harmony or not : in order to determine
which, we are to consider their polyodia as threefold, natural, artificial, and unisonous ; I call that
' natural which is not regulated by any certain rules
' or precepts, but is performed by an extemporary and
' arbitrary symphony of many voices, intermixing
' acute and grave sounds together ; such as we observe
' even at this time, happens amongst a company of
' sailors or reapers, and such people, who no sooner
' hear any certain melody begun by any one of them,
' than some other immediately invent a bass or tenor,
' and thus is produced an harmony extemporary, and
' not confined by any certain laws, and which is very
' rude and imperfect, as it is almost always unison,
' containing nothing of harmony, except in the closes,
' and therefore of no worth ; that the Greeks had
' such a kind of music none can doubt. But the
' question is not concerning this kind of polyodia,
' but whether they had compositions for several
' voices, framed according to the rules of art. I have
' taken great pains to be satisfied in this matter ; and
' as in none of the Greek and Latin writers I have
' met with, any mention is made of this kind of music,
' it seems to me that either they were ignorant of it,

' or that they did not make use of it, as imagining
' perhaps that it interrupted the melody, and took
' away from the energy of the words ; as to the term
' Harmonici concentus, it is only to be understood of
' the agreement between the voice and the sound of
' the instrument.

' Those who attempt to prove from Euclid that the
' ancients did compose music in really different parts,
' do not seem to understand his meaning ; for when
' he mentions the four parts of a song, ἀγωγὴ, τονὴ,
' πεττεία, πλοκὴ, he does not thereby mean the four
' polyodical parts of cantus, altus, tenor, and bass,
' but so many different affections of the voice, certain
' harmonical figures or tropes, whereby the song
' acquired a particular beauty and grace ; for what
' else can the word Ἀγωγὴ mean than a certain transi-
' tion of the voice from some given sound to another
' that is related to it. Τονὴ signifies a certain stay or
' dwelling on a sound ; Πλοκὴ, or implication, is a
' particular species or colour of the Ἀγωγὴ, as Πεττεία.
' frisking or playing on, is of Τονὴ : what the Ἀγωγὴ
' is to Τονὴ, such is the Πλοκὴ to the Πεττεία.

' Some imagine that the ancients had a polyodical
' instrumental music from the diversity of their pipes ;
' and are of opinion that at least an organical or
' instrumental harmony or symphony, regulated by
' art, was in use among the ancients, because their
' authors make mention of certain pipes, some of
' which were termed Παρθενιοι, or fit for girls ; some
' Παιδικοι, or fit for boys ; some Τελιοι, as being in a
' mean between the acute and grave sounds ; and
' others Ὑπερτελιοι, as agreeing with the grave. The
' better to clear up this doubt, we must consider the
' organical polyodia as twofold, natural and artificial ;
' and both these I make no doubt were in use as well
' as the vocal polyodia ; for it is very probable that
' such as played on those pipes, becoming skilful by
' such practice, invented certain symphonies adapted
' to their purpose, and which they played on their
' public festivals, distributing themselves into certain
' chorusses. Symphonies of this sort are at this time
' to be heard among the country people, who, though
' ignorant of the musical art, exhibit a symphony,
' such a one as it is, on their flutes and pipes of
' different sizes, and this merely through the judgment
' of their ear ; and it is also probable that the ancient
' Hebrews by this means alone became enabled to
' celebrate the praises of God on so many Cornua,
' Fistulæ, Litui, Tubæ, Buccinæ, as they are said to
' have been used at once in their temple ; and I
' remember to have heard the Mahometan slaves in
' the island of Malta exhibit symphonies of this kind.
' An affection therefore of the polyodia is implanted
' in the nature of man ; and I doubt not but that the
' ancients knew and practised it in the manner above
' related : but though I have taken great pains in my
' researches, I could never find the least sign of their
' having any artificial organical Melothesia of many
' parts ; which, had they been acquainted with it,
' they would doubtless have mentioned, it being so
' remarkable a thing. What Boetius, Ptolemy, and
' others speak concerning harmony, is to be under-
' stood only as to a single voice, to which an instru-

'ment was joined; add to this that the ancients
'acknowledged no other concords than the diapason,
'the diapente, and the diatessaron, and such as were
'composed of them; for they did not reckon as now,
'the ditone, semiditone, and hexachord among the
'consonances. It therefore follows that the ancient
'Greeks acknowledged nothing more than the Mo-
'nodia, adapted, it must be confessed, with much care
'and the greatest art to the sound of the lyre or the
'tibia; so that nothing was deficient either in the
'variety of the modulation, the sweetness of the
'singing, the justness of the pronunciation, or the
'gracefulness of the body in all its gestures and
'motions: and I imagine that the lyre of many
'strings was sounded in a harmonical concentus to
'the voice, in no other manner than is used in our
'days.' *

Dr. Wallis has given his opinion on this important
question in terms that seem decisive; for speaking
of the music of the ancients he makes use of these
words :—

'We are to consider that their music, even after it
'came to some good degree of perfection, was much
'more plain and simple than ours now-a-days. They
'had not concerts of two, three, four, or more parts
'or voices, but one single voice, or single instrument
'a-part, which to a rude ear is much more taking
'than more compounded music; for that is at a pitch
'not above their capacity, whereas this other con-
'founds it with a great noise, but nothing distinguish-
'able to their capacity.' † And again in the same
paper he says: 'I do not find among the ancients
'any footsteps of what we call several parts or voices
'(as bass, treble, mean, &c. sung in concert), answering
'to each other to complete the music.' And in the
Appendix to his edition of Ptolemy, pag. 317, he
expresses himself on the same subject to this purpose :—'But that agreement which we find in the
'modern music, of parts (as they term it) or of two,
'three, four, or more voices (singing together sounds
'which are heard altogether), was entirely unknown
'to the ancients, as far as I can see.'

From the several passages above-cited, it appears
that the question, whether the ancients were acquainted with music in consonance or not, has been
frequently and not unsuccessfully agitated, and that the
arguments for the negative seem to preponderate.
Nevertheless the author of a book lately published,
entitled 'Principles and Power of Harmony,' after
taking notice that Dr. Wallis, and some others, maintained that the ancients were strangers to symphoniac
music, has, upon the strength of a single passage in
Plato, been hardy enough to assert the contrary: his
words are these :—

'The strongest passage which I have met with in
'relation to this long-disputed point, is in Plato; a
'passage which I have never seen quoted, and which
'I shall translate : " Young men should be taught to
"sing to the lyre, on account of the clearness and
"precision of the sounds, so that they may learn to
"render tone for tone. But to make use of different

"simultaneous notes, and all the variety belonging to
"the lyre, this sounding one kind of melody, and the
"poet another—to mix a few notes with many, swift
"with slow, grave with acute, consonant with dis-
"sonant, &c. must not be thought of, as the time
"allotted for this part of education is too short for
"such a work." Plat. 895. I am sensible that
'objections may be made to some parts of this trans-
'lation, as of the words πυκνοτης, μανοτης, and
'αντιφωνοις, but I have not designedly disguised
'what I took to be the true sense of them, after due
'consideration. It appears then upon the whole, that
'the ancients were acquainted with music in parts,
'but did not generally make use of it.' ‡

Whoever will be at the pains of comparing the
discourse of Dr. Wallis, above-cited, and his appendix
to Ptolemy, with the several paragraphs in the
Principles and Power of Harmony, relating to the
question in debate, and calculated, as the author professes, to vindicate the Greek music, will discover in
the one the modesty of a philosopher, and in the
other the arrogance of a dogmatist.

Opinions delivered in terms so positive, and indeed
so contemptuous, as this latter writer has chosen to
make use of, § are an affront to the understandings of
mankind, who are not to be supposed ready to
acquiesce in the notions of others merely because
they are propagated with an unbecoming confidence:
and as to the judgment of this author on the question
in debate, the least that can be said of it is, that it is
founded in mistake and ignorance of his subject; for,
first, it is very strange, seeing how much the powers
of harmony exceed those of mere melody, that the
ancients, when once they had found themselves in
possession of so valuable an improvement as symphoniac music, should ever forego it. The moderns
in this respect were wiser than their teachers, for no
sooner did they discover the excellence of music in
parts than they studied to improve it, and have cultivated it with great care ever since. Secondly, this
writer, in support of his opinion, has been driven to
the necessity of translating those words of his author
which he thinks make most for his purpose, in a
manner which he confesses is liable to objections, and
into such English phrase as, in the opinion of many,

---

* Musurg. tom. I. pag. 537, et seq.
† Abridgment of Philosoph. Transactions by Lowthorp and Jones,
vol. I. pag. 618.

‡ Principles and Power of Harmony, p. 133. The speech in the
original, containing the passage of which it is pretended that above is
a translation, is here given at length, as it stands in the edition of Plato,
by Marsilius Ficinus; which is what this author appears to have made
use of :—Τετων τοίνυν δεῖ χάριν τοῖς φθόγγοις τῆς λύρας
προσχρῆσθαι, σαφηνείας ἕνεκα τῶν χορδῶν, τόν τε κιθαριςὴν
ἠ τὸν παιδευόμενον, ἀποδιδόντας πρόσχορδα τὰ φθέγματα
τοῖς φθέγμασι· τὴν δ' ἑτεροφωνίαν ἠ ποικιλίαν τῆς λύρας,
ἄλλα μὲν μέλη τῶν χορδῶν ἱειςῶν, ἄλλα δὲ τε τὴν μελῳδίαν
ξυνθέντος ποιητε· ἠ δὴ ἠ πυκνότητα μανότητι, ἠ τάχος
βραδυτῆτι, ἠ ὀξύτητα βαρύτητι, σύμφωνον ἠ ἀντίφωνον
παρεχομένες, ἠ τῶν ρυθμῶν, ὡσαύτως παντοδαπὰ ποικίλ-
ματα προσαρμόττοντας τοῖσι φθόγγοις τῆς λύρας· πάντα εν
τὰ τοιαῦτα μὴ προσφέρειν τοῖς μέλλεσιν ἐν τρισὶν ἔτεσι τὸ
τῆς μεσικῆς χρήσιμον ἐκλήψεσθαι διὰ τάχες· τὰ γὰρ ἐναντία,
ἄλληλα ταράττοντα δυσμαθίαν παρέχει· δεῖ δὲ ὅτι μάλιςα
εὐμαθεῖς εἶναι τες νέες.

§ As where he insinuates a resemblance between those who doubt the
truth of his assertions and the most ignorant of mankind, in these
words : 'If all these circumstances are not sufficient to gain our belief,
'merely because we moderns have not the same musical power, then
'have the Kamschatcans a right to decide that it is impossible to foretel
'an eclipse, or to represent all the elements of speech by about twenty-
'four marks.'

is not intelligible.   Thirdly and lastly, this very passage of Plato, upon which he lays so much stress, was discovered about fifty years ago, and adduced for the very purpose for which he has cited it, by Mons. l'Abbé Fraguier, a member of the Academy of Inscriptions and Belles Lettres, and occasioned a controversy, the result whereof will presently be related.

Monsieur Fraguier had entertained a high opinion of the Greek music, and a belief that the ancients were acquainted with music in consonance; in support of which latter opinion he produced to the academy the passage above-cited, which is to be found in Plato de Legibus, lib. VII.* He also produced for the same purpose a passage in Cicero de Republica, and another from Macrobius, both which are given in the note subjoined.†

The arguments deduced by Mons. Fraguier from these several passages, were learnedly refuted by Mons. Burette, a member also of the academy: and as to the interpretations which Mons. Fraguier had put upon them, the same Mons. Burette demonstrated that they were forced and unwarranted, either by the context or the practice of the ancients.

The substance of these arguments is contained in a paper or memoir entitled Examen d'un Passage de Platon sur la Musique, which may be seen in the History of the Academy of Inscriptions, tom. III. pag. 118.   This question was farther prosecuted by the same parties, as appears by sundry papers in the subsequent volumes of the History and Memoirs of the above Academy; and in the course of the controversy the passages above-cited from Aristotle, Seneca, Cassiodorus, and others, were severally insisted on.   As to those from Cicero and Macrobius, and this from Horace,

> Sonante mistum tibiis carmen lyra,
> Hac Dorium, illis Barbarum.
>
> Ad Mecænat. Epod. ix.

which had formerly been adduced for the same purpose, they went but a very little way towards proving the affirmative of the question in debate.   Mons. Burette took all these into consideration; he admits, that the ancients made use of the octave and the fifteenth, the former in a manner resembling the drone of a bag-pipe; and he allows that they might accidentally, and without any rule, use the fourth and fifth; but this is the farthest advance he will allow the ancients to have made towards the practice of symphoniac music; for as to the imperfect consonances and the dissonances, he says they were ignorant of the use and application of all of them in harmony: and finally he demonstrates, by a variety of arguments, that the ancients were absolute strangers to music in parts.‡

Martini, in his Storia della Musica, vol. I. pag. 172, has given an abridgement of this controversy, as it lies dispersed in the several volumes of the Memoirs of the Academy of Inscriptions, and acquiesces in the opinion of Mons. Burette, who, upon the whole, appears to have so much the advantage of his opponents, that it is highly probable this dispute will never be revived.

To speak of the ancient Greek music in general, those who reflect on it will be inclined to acquiese in the opinion of Dr. Wallis, who says, he takes it for granted, ' that much of the reports concerning the ' great effects of music in former times, beyond what ' is to be found in latter ages, is highly hyperbolical, ' and next door to fabulous; and therefore, he adds, ' great abatements must be allowed to the elogies of ' their music.'   Certainly many of the relations of the effects of music are either fabulous or to be interpreted allegorically, as this in Horace:—

> Silvestres homines sacer interpresque Deorum,
> Cædibus & victu fœdo deterruit Orpheus;
> Dictus ob hoc lenire tigres rabidosque leones.
> Dictus & Amphion, Thebanæ conditor Arcis,
> Saxa movere sono testudinis, & prece blanda.
> Ducere quo vellet.
>
> ARTE POETICA, lib. II. l. 391.

> The wood-born race of men, when Orpheus tam'd,
> From acorns and from mutual blood reclaim'd,
> This priest divine was fabled to assuage
> The tiger's fierceness, and the lion's rage.
> Thus rose the Theban wall; Amphion's lyre
> And soothing voice the list'ning stones inspire.
>
> FRANCIS.

Hyperbolical expressions of the power and efficacy of music signify but little; for these convey nothing more than the ideas of the relator: and every man speaks in the highest terms he can invent of that, whatever it be, that has administered to him the greatest delight.   How has the poet, in the Prolusions of Strada, laboured in describing the contest between the nightingale and the lutenist! and what does that celebrated poem contain, but a profusion of words without a meaning?

To conclude, every one that understands music is enabled to judge of the utmost effects of a single pipe, by hearing the flute, or any other single stop, finely touched on the organ: and as to the lyre, whether of three, four, seven, or ten strings, it is impossible but that it must have been greatly inferior to the harp, the lute, and many other instruments in use among the moderns.

Having taken a view of the state of music in the

---

* In Stephens's edition it is pag. 812, and in that of Marsilius Ficinus 895.

† ' Ut in fidibus, ac tibiis atque cantu ipso, ac vocibus concentus est ' quidam tenendus ex distinctis sonis, quem immutatum ac discrepantem ' aures eruditæ ferre non possunt; isque concentus ex dissimilimarum ' vocum moderatione concors tamen efficitur et congruens: sic ex sum- ' mis, et infimis, et mediis interjectis ordinibus, ut sonis, moderata ' ratione civitas, consensu dissimilimorum concinit; et quæ harmonia a ' musicis dicitur in cantu, ea est in civitate concordia.' Cicer. lib. ii. de Repub. Fragm. pag. 527, tom. III.

' Vides quam multorum vocibus chorus constet una tamen ex omnibus ' redditur.   Aliqua est illic acuta, aliqua gravis, aliqua media: accedunt ' viris feminæ: interponuntur fistula.   Ita singulorum illic latent voces, ' omnium apparent, et fit concentus ex dissonis.'—Macrob. Saturnalior Proœm.

‡ The learned Dr. Jortin, who, with the character of a very worthy man and a profound scholar, possessed that of a learned musician, has delivered his sentiments on this question in the following terms:—' One ' would think that an ancient musician, who was well acquainted with ' concords and discords, who had an instrument of many strings or many ' keys to play upon, and two hands and ten fingers to make use of, would ' try experiments, and would fall into something like counterpoint and ' composition in parts.   In speculation nothing seems more probable, ' and it seemed more than probable to our skilful musician Dr. Pepusch; ' when I once conversed with him upon the subject; but in fact it doth ' not appear that the ancients had this kind of composition, or rather it ' appears that they had not; and it is certain, that a man shall overlook ' discoveries which stand at his elbow, and in a manner intrude them- ' selves upon him.' Letter to Mr. Avison, published in the second edition of his Essay on Musical Expression, pag. 36.

earlier ages of the world, and traced the ancient system from its rudiments to its perfection, and thereby brought it down to nearly the close of the third century, we shall proceed to relate the several subsequent improvements that have from time to time been made of it, in the order in which they occurred; and shew to whom we owe that system, which for its excellence is now universally adopted by the civilized world.

We have seen that hitherto the science of music, as being a subject of very abstracted speculation, and as having a near affinity with arithmetic and geometry, had been studied and taught by such only as were eminent for their skill in those sciences: of these the far greater number were Greeks, who, in the general estimation of mankind, held the rank of philosophers. The accounts hereafter given of the Latin writers, such as Martianus Capella, Macrobius, Cassiodorus, and others, will shew how little the Romans contributed to the improvement of music; and in general their writings are very little more than abridgements of, or short commentaries on the works of Nicomachus, Euclid, Aristides Quintilianus, Aristoxenus, and others of the ancient Greeks. As to Boetius, of whom we shall speak hereafter, it is clear that his intention was only to restore to those barbarous times in which he lived, the knowledge of the true principles of harmony, and to demonstrate, by the force of mathematical reasoning, the proportions and various relations to each other, of sounds; in the doing whereof he evidently shews himself to have been a Pythagorean. As this was the design of his treatise De Musica, we are not to wonder that the author has said so little of the changes that music underwent among the Latins, or that he does but just hint at the disuse of the enarmonic and chromatic genera, and the introduction of the Roman characters in the room of the Greek.

It must however be admitted, that for one improvement of the system we are indebted to the Latins, namely, the application of the Roman capital letters to the several sounds that compose the scale, whereby they got rid of that perplexed method of notation invented by the Greeks: we have seen, by the treatise of Alypius, written professedly to explain the Greek musical characters, to what an amazing number they amounted, 1240 at the lowest computation; and after all, they were no better than so many arbitrary marks or signs placed on a line over the words of the song, and, having no real inherent or analogical signification, must have been an intolerable burthen on the memory. These the Latins rejected, and in their stead introduced the letters of their own alphabet, A, B, C, D, E, F, G, H, I, K, L, M, N, O, P, fifteen in number, and sufficient to express every sound contained in the disdiapason. If it be asked, how could this small number serve the purpose of more than 1200? the answer is, that this amazing multiplicity of characters arose from the necessity of distinguishing each sound with respect to the genus, and also the mode in which it was used; and before this innovation of the Romans, we are assured, that both the enarmonic and chromatic genera were

grown out of use, and that the diatonic genus, on account of its sweetness and conformity to nature, was retained amongst them: and as to the modes, there is great reason to suspect, that even at the time when Ptolemy wrote, the doctrine of them was but ill understood; fifteen characters, we know, are at this time sufficient to denote all the sounds in a diatonic disdiapason, and consequently must have been so then.

It has already been observed, that the science of harmony was anciently a subject of philosophical enquiry; and it is manifest, from the account herein before given of them and their writings, that the Greeks treated it as a subject of very abstract speculation, and that they neither attended to the physical properties of sound, nor concerned themselves with the practice of music, whether vocal or instrumental. Ptolemy was one of the last of the Greek harmonicians; and from his time it may be observed, that the cultivation of music became the care of a set of men, who, then, at least, made no pretensions to the character of philosophers. This may be accounted for either by the decline of philosophy about this period, or by the not improbable supposition, that the subject itself was exhausted, and that nothing remained but an improvement in practice on that foundation which the ancient writers, by their theory, had so well laid. But whatever may have been the cause, it is certain, that after the establishment of Christianity the cultivation of music became the concern of the church: to this the Christians were probably excited by the example of the Jews, among whom music made a considerable part of divine worship, and the countenance given to it in the writings of St. Paul. Nor is it to be wondered at by those who consider the effects of music, its influence on the passions, and its power to inspire sentiments of the most devout and affecting kind, if it easily found admittance into the worship of the primitive Christians: as to the state of it in the three first centuries, we are very much at a loss; yet it should seem from the information of St. Augustine, that in his time it had arrived at some degree of perfection; possibly it had been cultivating, both in the Eastern and Western empire, from the first propagation of Christianity. The great number of men who were drawn off from secular pursuits by their religious profession, amidst the barbarism of the times, thought themselves laudably employed in the study of a science which was found to be subservient to religion: while some were engaged in the oppugning heretical opinions, others were taken up in composing forms of devotions, framing liturgies; and others in adapting suitable melodies to such psalms and hymns as had been received into the service of the church, and which made a very considerable part of the divine offices: all which is the more probable, as the progress of human learning was then in a great measure at a stand.

But as the introduction of music into the service of the church seems to be a new æra, it is necessary to be a little more particular, and relate the opinions of the most authentic writers, as well as to the reception it at first met with, as its subsequent progress among the converts to Christianity. If among the accounts to be given of these matters, some should carry the appearance of improbability, or should even verge towards the regions of fable, let it be remembered, that very little credit would be due to history, were the writer to suppress every relation against the credibility whereof there lay an objection. History does not propose to transmit barely matters of real fact, or opinions absolutely irrefragable; falsehood and error may very innocently be propagated, nay, the general belief of falsehood, or the existence of any erroneous opinion, may be considered as facts; and then it becomes the duty of a historian to relate them. Whoever is conversant with the ecclesiastical historians must allow that the superstition of some, and the enthusiasm of others of them, have somewhat abated the reverence due to their testimony. But notwithstanding this, the characters of Eusebius, Socrates, Sozomen, Theodoret, and Evagrius, for veracity and good intelligence, stand so high in the opinion of all sober and impartial men, that it is impossible to withhold our assent from the far greater part of what they have written on this subject.

The advocates for the high antiquity of church-music urge the authority of St. Paul in its favour, who, in his Epistle to the Ephesians, charges them to speak to themselves in psalms, and hymns, and spiritual songs, singing and making melody in their hearts to the Lord; * and who exhorts the Colossians to teach and admonish one another in psalms, hymns, and spiritual songs.† Cardinal Bona is one of these; and he scruples not to assert, on the authority of these two passages, that songs and hymns were, from the very establishment of the church, sung in the assemblies of the faithful. Johannes Damascenus goes farther back; and relates, that at the funeral of the Blessed Virgin, which was celebrated at Gethsemane, the apostles, assisted by angels, continued singing her requiem for three whole days incessantly. The same author, speaking of the ancient hymn called the Trisagion, dates its original from a miracle that was performed in the time of Proclus, the archbishop: his account is, that the people of Constantinople being terrified with some portentous signs that had appeared, made solemn processions and applications to the Almighty, beseeching him to avert the calamities that seemed to threaten their city, in the midst whereof a boy was caught from among them, and taken up to heaven; who, upon his return, related, that he had been taught by angels to sing the hymn, in Greek,

Αγιος ο Θεος, αγιος ισχυρος, αγιος αθανατος, ελεησον ημας.

Holy God, holy and strong, holy and immortal, have mercy upon us.

The truth of this relation is questioned by some, who yet credit a vision of St. Ignatius; of which Socrates, the ecclesiastical historian, gives the following account: ' St. Ignatius, the third bishop of ' Antioch, in Syria, after the apostle Peter, who also ' conversed familiarly with the apostles, saw the ' blessed spirits above singing hymns to the Sacred

' Trinity alternately, which method of singing, says ' the same historian, Ignatius taught to his church; ' and this, together with an account of the miracle ' which gave rise to it, was communicated to all the ' churches of the East.' ‡ Nicephorus, St. Chrysostom, Amalarius, and sundry others. acquiesce in this account of the origin of antiphonal singing; as do our countrymen, Hooker, Hammond, Beveridge, and Dr. Comber.

By the Apostolical Constitutions, said to have been, if not compiled by the apostles themselves, at least collected by Clement, a disciple of theirs, the order of divine worship is prescribed; wherein it is expressly required, that after the reading of the two lessons, one of the presbyters should sing a psalm or hymn of David; and that the people should join in singing at the end of each verse. It would be too little to say of this collection, that the authority of it is doubted, since it is agreed, that it did not appear in the world till the fourth century; and the opinions of authors are, that either it is so interpolated as to deserve no credit, or that the whole of it is an absolute forgery.

Hitherto, then, the high antiquity of church-music stands on no better a foundation than tradition, backed with written evidence of such a kind as to have scarce a pretence to authenticity: there are, however, accounts to be met with among the writers of ecclesiastical history, that go near to fix it at about the middle of the fourth century.

In short, the æra from whence we may reasonably date the introduction of music into the service of the church, is that period during which Leontius governed the church of Antioch; that is to say, between the years of Christ 347 and 356, when Flavianus and Diodorus, afterwards bishops, the one of Antioch and the other of Tarsus, divided the choristers into two parts, and made them sing the Psalms of David alternately, Theodoret. Hist. Eccl. lib. II. cap. xxiv.; a practice, says the same author, which began first at Antioch, and afterwards spread itself to the end of the world. Valesius acquiesces in this account, and professes to wonder whence Socrates had the story of Ignatius's vision, Vales. in Socrat. lib. VI. cap. viii. The occasion of antiphonal singing seems to have been this: Flavianus and Diodorus, although then laymen, but engaged in a monastic life, were in great repute for their sanctity; and Leontius, their bishop, was an avowed Arian, whom they zealously opposed: in order to draw off the people from an attendance on the bishop, who, in the opinion of Flavianus and Diodorus, was a preacher of heresy, they set up a separate assembly for religious worship, in which they introduced antiphonal singing, which so captivated the people, that the bishop, to call them back again, made use of it also in his church. Flavianus, it seems, had a high opinion of the efficacy of this kind of music; for it is reported, that the city of Antioch having, by a popular sedition, incurred the displeasure of the Emperor Theodosius, sent Flavianus to appease him, and implore forgiveness; who, upon his first audience,

---

* Chap. v. verse 19.   † Chap. iii. verse 16.   ‡ Hist. Eccles. lib. VI. cap. viii.

though in the imperial palace, directed the usual church-service to be sung before him: the emperor melted into pity, wept, and the city was restored to his favour. Other instances are to be met with in history, that show the fondness of the people of Antioch for this kind of music; and which favour the supposition, that amongst them it took its rise.

Antioch was the metropolis of Syria; the example of its inhabitants was soon followed by the other churches of the East; and in a very few ages after its introduction into the divine service, the practice of singing in churches not only received the sanction of public authority, but those were forbidden to join in it who were ignorant of music. For at the council of Laodicea, held between the years of Christ, 360 and 370, a canon was made, by which it was ordained, That none but the canons, or singing men of the church, which ascend the Ambo,* or singing-desk, and sing out of the parchment, [so the words are] should presume to sing in the church. Balsamon seems to think that the fathers intended nothing more than to forbid the setting or giving out the hymn or psalm by the laity: but the reason assigned by Baronius for the making of this canon, shews that it was meant to exclude them totally from singing in the church-service; for he says that when the people and the clergy sang promiscuously, the former, for want of skill, destroyed the harmony, and occasioned such a discord as was very inconsistent with the order and decency requisite in divine worship. Zonanus confirms this account, and adds, that these canonical singers were reckoned a part of the clergy.† Balsamon, in his scholia on this canon, says, that before the Laodicean council, the laity were wont, in contempt of the clergy, to sing, in a very rude and inartificial manner, hymns and songs of their own invention; to obviate which practice, it was ordained by this canon that none should sing but those whose office it was. Our learned countryman, Bingham, declares himself of the same opinion in his Antiquities of the Christian Church, book III. chap. vii. and adds, that from the time of the council of Laodicea the psalmistæ, or singers, were called κανονικοι ψαλται, or canonical singers, though he is inclined to think the provision in the canon only temporary.

CHAP. XXIII.

GREAT stress is also laid on the patronage given to church-music by St. Basil, St. Ambrose, and St. Chrysostom; as to the first, he had part of his education at Antioch, where he was a continual spectator of that pompous worship which prevailed there. He

was first made a deacon by Meletius, and afterwards, that is to say about the year 371, was promoted to the bishopric of Cæsarea in Cappadocia, his own country; and in this exalted station he contracted such a love for church-music, as drove him to the necessity of apologizing for it.‡ In his epistle to the Neocæsarian clergy, still extant, he justifies the practice, saying, that the new method of singing, at which they were so offended, was now become common in the Christian church, the people rising before day and going to church, where, having made their confessions and prayers, they proceeded to the singing of psalms: and he adds, that in his holy exercise, the choir being divided into two parts, mutually answered each other, the precentor beginning, and the rest following him. He farther tells them, that if to do thus be a fault, they must blame many pious and good men in Egypt, Lybia, Palestine, Arabia, Phœnicia, and Syria, and sundry other places. To this they urged that the practice was otherwise in the time of their bishop Gregory Thaumaturgus; in answer to which Basil tells them, that neither was the Litany used in his time; and that in objecting to music, while they admitted the Litany, they strained at a gnat and swallowed a camel.

St. Chrysostom, whose primitive name was John, was a native of Antioch, and received his education there, he was ordained a deacon by Meletius, and presbyter by Flavianus; and having been accustomed to the pompous service introduced by the latter into the Church of Antioch, he conceived a fondness for it. When he became bishop of Constantinople, which was about A. C. 380, he found occasion to introduce music among his people: the manner of his doing it is thus related: The Arians in that city were grown very insolent: they held conventicles at a small distance without the walls; but on Saturdays and Sundays, which were set apart for the public assemblies, they were wont to come within the city, where, dividing themselves into several companies, they walked about the porticos, singing such words as these: 'Where are they who affirm three to be one power?' and hymns composed in defence of their tenets, adding petulant reflexions on the orthodox;§ this they continued for the greatest part

---

* The Ambo was what we now call the reading-desk, a place made on purpose for the readers and singers, and such of the clergy as ministered in the first service called Missa Catechumenorum. It had the name of Ambo, not as Walafridus Strabo imagines, 'ab ambiendo,' because it surrounded them that were in it, but from αναβαινειν, because it was a place of eminency, to which they went up by degrees or steps. Bingham's Antiquities of the Christian Church, book VIII. chap. v. § 4.

† It seems they were one of the many orders in the primitive church, and that they received ordination at the hands, not of the bishop or choriepiscopus, but of a presbyter, using this form of words, prescribed by the canon of the fourth council of Carthage: 'See that thou believe 'in thy heart what thou singest with thy mouth; and approve in thy 'works what thou believest in thy heart.' Bingh. Antiq. book III. chap. vii. § 4.

‡ Vales. in Socrat. lib. IV. cap. xxvi.

§ It seems that the orthodox could in their turns not only be petulant, but industrious in provoking their enemies to wrath, as may be collected from the following relation of Theodoret:—

'Publia, the deaconess, a woman admired and celebrated for her 'piety, was the mother of the famous John, who for many years was first 'presbyter of the church of the Antioch, and though often and unanimously 'elected to the apostolic throne, refused that dignity. She, and a chorus 'of consecrated virgins with her, spent great part of their time in singing 'anthems and divine songs; and once when the emperor [Julian] had 'occasion to pass by them, they sung psalms chosen purposely to expose 'and ridicule the extravagancies of heathenism and idolatry, singing 'them with an exalted voice; and among the rest they applied, very 'properly to the occasion, the hundred and fifteenth, from the fourth to 'the eighth verse, "Their idols are silver and gold, even the work of "men's hands, &c." "Let those that make them be like unto them, and "also all such as put their trust in them." This so disturbed the empe- 'ror, that he commanded silence should be kept whenever he came by 'that place, but to so little purpose, that upon his returning, at the 'motion of Publia they gave him another welcome in these words:— "Let God arise, and let his enemies be scattered." And now his anger 'was raised so high, that he ordered the chantress to be brought before 'him, and had her beat on the face till her cheeks were stained with 'blood; which efforts of the tyrant's unmanly passion the aged good 'woman received with pleasure, went home, and, as often as an oppor- 'tunity offered, entertained him still with the very same sort of dis- 'agreeable compositions.' Hist. Eccles.

of the night; in the morning they marched through the heart of the city, singing in the same manner, and so proceeded to the place of their assembly. In opposition to these people, St. Chrysostom caused hymns to be sung in the night; and to give his performance a pomp and solemnity, which the other wanted, he procured crosses of silver to be made at the charge of the empress Eudoxia, which, with lighted torches thereon, were borne in a procession, at which Briso, the empress's eunuch, officiated as precentor; this was the occasion of a great tumult, in which Briso received a wound in the forehead with a stone, and some on both sides were slain.* This was followed by a sedition, which ended in the expulsion of the Arians. This manner of singing, thus introduced by them, was, as Sozomen relates,† used in Constantinople from that time forwards; however, in a short time it was performed in such an unseemly way as gave great offence; for the singers, affecting strange gestures and boisterous clamours, converted the church into a mere theatre; for which Chrysostom reproved them, by telling his people that their rude voices and disorderly behaviour were very improper for a place of worship, in which all things were to be done with reverence to that Being who observes the behaviour of every one there.

St. Ambrose, who had entertained a singular veneration for St. Basil, like him was a great lover of the church-service: it is true he was not originally an ecclesiastic, but having been unexpectedly elected bishop of Milan, he applied himself to the duties of the episcopal function. Justina, whom the emperor Valentinian had married, proving an Arian, commenced a prosecution against Ambrose and the orthodox; during which the people watched all night in the church, and Ambrose appointed that psalms and hymns should be sung there after the manner of the oriental churches, lest the people should pine away with the tediousness of sorrow; and from this event, which happened about 374, we may date the introduction of singing into western churches.

But the zeal of St. Ambrose to promote this practice, is in nothing more conspicuous than in his endeavours to reduce it into form and method; as a proof whereof, it is said that he, jointly with St. Augustine, upon occasion of the conversion and baptism of the latter, composed the hymn Te Deum laudamus, which even now makes a part of the liturgy of our church, and caused it to be sung in his church at Milan; but this has been discovered to be a mistake:‡ this however is certain, that he instituted that method of singing, known by the name of the Cantus Ambrosianus, or Ambrosian

* Socrat. Hist. Eccles. lib. VI. cap. viii.

† Hist. Eccles. lib. VIII. cap. viii.

‡ The very learned Dr. Usher, upon the authority of two ancient manuscripts, asserts the Te Deum to have been made by a bishop of Triers, named Nicetius or Nicettus, and that not till about the year 500, which was almost a century after the death both of St. Ambrose and St. Augustine. L'Estrange's Alliance of Divine Offices, 79. The Benedictines, who published the works of St. Ambrose, judge him not to have been the author of it; and Dr. Cave, though at one time he was of a different judgment, and bishop Stillingfleet, concur in the opinion that the Te Deum was not the composition of St. Ambrose, or of him and St. Augustine jointly. Bingham's Antiquities of the Christian Church, book XIV. chap. ii. § 9.

Chant, a name, for ought that now appears, not applicable to any determined series of notes, but invented to express in general a method of singing agreeable to some rule given or taught by him. This method, whatever it was, is said to have had a reference to the modes of the ancients, or rather to those of Ptolemy, which we have shewn to have been precisely coincident with the seven species of the diapason; but St. Ambrose conceiving all above four to be superfluous, reduced them to that number, retaining only the Dorian, the Phrygian, the Lydian, and the Mixolydian, § which names he rejected, choosing rather to distinguish them by epithets of number, as protos, deuteros, tritos, tetrartos. His design in this was to introduce a kind of melody founded on the rules of art, and yet so plain and simple in its nature, that not only those whose immediate duty it was to perform the divine service, but even the whole congregation might sing it; accordingly in the Romish countries the people now join with the choir in chanting the divine offices; and if we may credit the relations of travellers in this respect, this distinguished simplicity of the Ambrosian Chant is even at this day to be remarked in the service of the church of Milan, where it was first instituted.

A particular account of the ecclesiastical modes, as originally constituted by St. Ambrose, with the subsequent improvement of them by Gregory the Great, is reserved for another place: in the interim it is to be noted that the ecclesiastical modes are also called tropes, but more frequently tones; which latter appellation was first given to them by Martianus Capella, as we are informed by Sir Henry Spelman, in his Glossary, voce FRIGDORÆ. The following scheme represents the progression in each:—

d	e	f	g
c	d	e	f
h	c	d	e
a	h	c	d
G	a	h	c
F	G	a	h
E	F	G	a
D	E	F	G

And this was the original institution of what are called, in contradistinction to the modes or moods of the ancients, the ecclesiastical modes or tones. These of St. Ambrose, however well calculated for use and practice, were yet found to be too much restrained, and not to admit of all that variety of modulation which the several offices in the church-service seemed to require; and accordingly St. Gregory, surnamed the Great, the first pope of that name, with the assistance of the most learned and skilful in the music of that day, set about an amendment of the Cantus Ambrosianus, and instituted what became known to later times by the name of the Cantus Gregorianus, or, the Gregorian Chant: but as this was not till near two hundred and thirty years after the time of St. Ambrose, the account of this, and the other improve-

§ Sir Henry Spelman in his Glossary, voce FRIGDORÆ, in the place of the Mixolydian puts the Æolian.

ments made in music by St. Gregory, must be referred to another place.

With respect to the music of the primitive church, though it consisted in the singing of psalms and hymns, yet was it performed in sundry different manners, that is to say, sometimes the psalms were sung by one person alone, the rest hearing with attention; sometimes they were sung by the whole assembly; sometimes alternately, the congregation being for that purpose divided into separate choirs; and, lastly, by one person, who repeated the first part of the verse, the rest joining in the close thereof.*

Of the four different methods of singing above enumerated, the second and third were very properly distinguished by the names of symphony and antiphony, and the latter was sometimes called responsaria;† and in this, it seems, women were allowed to join, notwithstanding the apostle's injunction on them to keep silence.

The method of singing in the last place above mentioned, clearly suggests the origin of the office of precentor of a choir, whose duty, even at this day, it is to govern the choir, and see that the choral service be reverently and justly performed.

It farther appears, that almost from the time when music was first introduced into the service of the church, it was of two kinds, and consisted in a gentle inflection of the voice, which they termed plain-song, and a more artificial and elaborate kind of music, adapted to the hymns and solemn offices contained in its ritual; and this distinction has been maintained through all the succeeding ages, even to this time.

Besides the reverend fathers of the church abovementioned, we are told, and indeed it appears from many passages in his writings, that SAINT AUGUSTINE was a passionate lover of music; this which follows, taken from his Confessions, lib. IX. cap. vi. is the most commonly produced as an evidence of his approbation of music in the church-service, though, it must be owned, he lived to recant it: 'How abundantly 'did I weep before God, to hear those hymns of 'thine; being touched to the very quick, by the 'voices of thy sweet church song. The voices flowed 'into my ears, and thy truth pleasingly distilled into 'my heart; which caused the affections of my de- 'votion to overflow, and my tears to run over; and 'happy did I find myself therein.' From hence there is little reason to doubt, that he enjoined the use of it to the clergy of his diocese. He wrote a treatise De Musica, in six books, chiefly, indeed, on the subject of metre and the laws of versification, but interspersed with such observations on the nature of the consonances, as shew him to have been very well skilled in the science of music.

It is not necessary to enter into a particular character, either of St. Augustine or of this his work:

* Bingham's Antiq. book XIV. chap. i.

† In this distinction between symphoniac and antiphonal psalmody, we may discern the origin of the two different methods of singing practised in the Romish and Lutheran churches, and of those that follow the rule of Calvin, and others of the reformers: in the former the singing is antiphonal, in the latter it is a plain metrical psalmody, in which all join; so that for each practice the authority of the primitive church may be appealed to.

those who are acquainted with ecclesiastical history need not be told, that he was a man of great learning, for the time he lived in, of lively parts, and of exemplary piety. To such, however, whose curiosity is greater than their reading, the following short account of this eminent father of the church may not be unpleasing:—

He was born at Thagaste, a city of Numidia, on the 13th of November, 354. His father, a burgess of that city, was called Patricius; and his mother, Monica, who being a woman of great virtue, instructed him in the principles of the Christian religion. In his early youth he was in the rank of the catechumens, and falling dangerously ill, earnestly desired to be baptized; but the violence of the distemper ceasing, his baptism was delayed. His father, who was not yet baptized, made him study at Thagaste, Madaura, and afterwards at Carthage. St. Augustine, having read Cicero's books of philosophy, began to entertain a love for wisdom, and applied himself to the study of the Holy Scriptures; nevertheless, he suffered himself to be seduced by the Manicheans. At the age of nineteen, he returned to Thagaste, and taught grammar, and also frequented the bar: he afterwards taught rhetoric at Carthage, with applause. The insolence of the scholars at Carthage made him take a resolution to go to Rome, though against his mother's will. Here also he had many scholars; but disliking them, he quitted Rome, and settled at Milan, and was chosen public professor of rhetoric in that city. Here he had opportunities of hearing the sermons of St. Ambrose, which, together with the study of St. Paul's Epistles, and the conversion of two of his friends, determined him to retract his errors, and quit the sect of the Manicheans: this was in the thirty-second year of his age. In the vacation of the year 386, he retired to the house of a friend of his, named Verecundus, where he seriously applied himself to the study of the Christian religion, in order to prepare himself for baptism, which he received at Easter, in the year 387. Soon after this, his mother came to see him at Milan, and invite him back to Carthage; but at Ostia, whither he went to embark, in order to his return, she died. He arrived in Africa about the end of the year 388, and having obtained a garden-plot without the walls of the city of Hippo, he associated himself with eleven other persons of eminent sanctity, who distinguished themselves by wearing leathern girdles, and lived there in a monastic way for the space of three years, exercising themselves in fasting, prayer, study, and meditation, day and night: from hence sprang up the Augustine friars, or eremites of St. Augustine, being the first order of mendicants; those of St. Jerome, the Carmelites, and others, being but branches of this of St. Augustine. About this time, or as some say before, Valerius, bishop of Hippo, against his will ordained him priest: nevertheless, he continued to reside in his little monastery, with his brethren, who, renouncing all property, possessed their goods in common. Valerius, who had appointed St. Augustine to preach in his place, allowed him to do it in his presence, contrary to the custom of the churches in

Africa. He explained the creed, in a general council of Africa, held in 393. Two years after, Valerius, fearing he might be preferred to be bishop of another church, appointed him his coadjutor or colleague, and caused him to be ordained bishop of Hippo, by Megalius, bishop of Calame, then primate of Numidia. St. Augustine died the 28th day of August, 430, aged seventy-six years, having had the misfortune to see his country invaded by the Vandals, and the city where he was bishop besieged for seven months.

The works of St. Augustine make ten tomes; the best edition of them is that of Maurin, printed at Antwerp, in 1700; they are but little read at this time, except by the clergy of the Greek church and in the Spanish universities; our booksellers in London receive frequent commisions for them, and indeed for most of the fathers, from Russia, and also from Spain.

About this time flourished AMBROSIUS AURELIUS THEODOSIUS MACROBIUS, an author whose name appears in almost every catalogue of musical writers extant; but whose works scarcely entitle him to a place among them. He lived in the time of Theodosius the younger, who was proclaimed emperor of the East, anno 402. He was a man of singular dignity, and held the office of chamberlain to the emperor. Fabricius makes it a question whether he was Christian or a Pagan. His works are a commentary on the Somnium Scipionis of Cicero, in two books, and Saturnalia Convivia, in seven books; in both which he takes occasion to treat of music, and more especially the harmony of the spheres. The chief of what he says concerning music in general is contained in his Commentary on the Somnium Scipionis, and is taken from Nicomachus, and others of the followers of Pythagoras. Martini mentions also a discourse on mundane music of his, which was translated into Italian by Ercole Bottrigari, with notes; but he speaks of it as a manuscript, and by the list of the works of Macrobius, it does not appear to have ever been printed.

Of such writers as Macrobius, and a few other of the Latins who will shortly be mentioned, that have written not professedly on music, but have briefly or transiently taken notice of it in the course of a work written with some other view than to explain it, little is to be said. There is nevertheless a Greek writer of this class, who lived some considerable time before Macrobius, and indeed was prior to Porphyry, the last of the Greek musical writers that deserves to be taken notice of, not so much because he has contributed to the improvement of the science, as because in a voluminous work of his there are interspersed a great variety of curious particulars relating to it, not to be found elsewhere. The author here meant is Athenæus the grammarian, called, by way of eminence, the Grecian Varro; he was born at Naucratis in Egypt, and flourished in the third century; of many works that he wrote, one only remains, intitled The Deipnosophists, that is to say, the Sophists at Table, where he introduces a number of learned men of all professions, who converse upon various subjects at the table of a Roman citizen

named Larensius. In this work there are many very pleasant stories, and an infinite variety of facts, citations, and allusions, which make the reading of it extremely delightful. The little that he has said of music lies scattered up and down in this work, which, with the Latin translation of it, makes a large folio volume.

In his fourth book, pag. 174, he gives the names of the supposed inventors of the ancient musical instruments, and, among others, of Ctesibus, and of the hydraulic organ constructed by him; and it is supposed that this is the most ancient and authentic account of that instrument now extant. He says, pag. 175, that the Barbiton or lyre, or, as Mersennus will have it, the viol, was the invention of Anacreon; and the Monaulon, or single pipe, of the Egyptian Osiris.

Elsewhere, viz., in his fourteenth book, he speaks of the power of music, and of the fondness which the Arcadians, above all other people, entertained for it: and in the same book, pag. 637, he describes that strange instrument, invented by Pythagoras Zacynthius, called the tripod lyre, corresponding in every particular with the description of it hereinbefore given from Blanchinus; to which may be added, that Athenæus expressly says that the three several sets of chords between the legs, were in their tuning adjusted to the three primitive modes, the Dorian, the Lydian, and the Phrygian.

Of this learned, curious, and most entertaining work, the best edition is that of Dalechamp, with the Greek original and Latin translation in opposite columns. To this are added the animadversions of Isaac Casaubon, which are very curious, and make another volume. In these it is said that the Musicorum διαγςάμματα, or Tablatura, i. e., the art of writing or noting down of music, was invented by Stratonicus of Rhodes. Is. Casaub. Animadvers. in Athenæum, lib. VIII. cap. xii.

MARTIANUS MINEUS FELIX CAPELLA was born, as Cassiodorus testifies, at Madaura, a town in Africa, situated between the countries of Getulia and Numidia, lived at Rome under Leo the Thracian, viz., about the year of Christ 457; he was the author of a work intitled, De Nuptiis Philologiæ et Mercurii, the style whereof, in the opinion of some, is harsh, and rather barbarous, though others, and Fabricius in particular, who terms it a delightful fable,* think it in nowise deserves such a character: this work, which consists of prose and verse intermixed, is in fact a treatise on the seven liberal sciences, and consequently includes a discourse on music, which makes the ninth book thereof, and is introduced in the following manner: the author supposes the marriage of Philologia, a virgin, to Mercury, and that Venus and the other deities, as also Orpheus, Amphion, and Arion, are assembled to honour the solemnity; the Sciences, who, to render the work as poetical as may be, are represented as persons, also attend, among whom is Harmonia, described as having her head decked with variety of ornaments, and bearing symbols of the faculty over which she is feigned to

---

* Biblioth. Lat. Art. CAPELLA.

preside. She is made to exhibit the power of sounds by such melody as Jupiter himself commends, which is succeeded by a request of Apollo and Minerva to unfold the mysteries of harmony. She first craves leave to relate that she formerly was an inhabitant of the earth, and that through the inspirations of Pythagoras, Aristoxenus, and others, she had taught men the use of the lyre and the pipe; and by the singing of birds, the whistling of the winds, and the murmuring of water-falls, had instructed even the artless shepherds in the rudiments of melody. That by the power of her art she had cured diseases, quieted seditions, and composed and attempered the irregular affections of mankind; notwithstanding all which, she had been contemned and reviled by those sons of earth, and had therefore sought the heavens, where she found the motions of the orbs regulated by her own principles. She then proceeds to explain the precepts of harmony in a short discourse, which, if we consider the substance and method rather than the style of it, must be allowed to be a very elegant composition, and by much the most intelligible of any ancient treatise on the science of music now extant.

Capella concludes this ninth book of his treatise De Nuptiis thus: 'When Harmonia had run over ' these things concerning songs, and the sweetness of ' verse, in a manner both august and persuasive, to ' the gods and heroes, who were very intent, she de- ' cently withdrew; then Jupiter rose up, and Cymesis ' modulating in divine symphonies, came to the ' chamber of the virgin, to the great delight of all.'

The above discourse of Martianus Capella is mani- festly taken from Aristides Quintilianus, of which, to say the truth, it is very little more than an abridg- ment, but it is such a one as renders it in some respects preferable to the original; for neither is it so prolix as Quintilian's treatise, nor does it partake of that obscurity which discourages so many from the study of his work; and when it is said, as it has been by some, that the style of Capella is barbarous, this must be taken as the opinion of grammarians, who, without regarding the intrinsic merit of any work, estimate it by certain rules of classical elegance, which they themselves have established as the test of perfection. It is by these men, and for this reason, and perhaps because he had not the good fortune to be born at Rome, that Capella is termed a semi-barbarian, and his writings reprobated as unworthy the perusal of men of science.* But, notwithstanding these opinions, one of the best gram- marians of the present age, the learned and ingenious

author of Hermes, or a Philosophical Inquiry con- cerning Universal Grammar, has forborne to pass a censure of barbarity on the style of this author: his sentiment of him is, that he was rather a philo- logist than a philosopher; a testimony that leaves him a better character than some of those deserve who have been so liberal in their censures of him. It has been said above, that Fabricius has given to the treatise De Nuptiis the character of a delightful fable; and Gregory of Tours delivers his opinion of it at large in the following words: 'In gram- ' maticis docent legere, in dialecticis altercationum ' propositiones advertere, in rhetoricis persuadere, in ' geometricis terrarum linearumque mensuras col- ' ligere, in astrologicis cursus siderum contemplari, ' in arithmeticis numerorum partes colligere, in har- ' moniis sonorum modulationes suavium accentuum ' carminibus concrepare.' Hence it may seem that Mr. Malcolm was rather too hasty in condemning this work; and that in pronouncing of its author as he has done in his Treatise on Music, pag. 498, that he was but a sorry copier from Aristides, he has done him injustice. Of Capella's work, De Nuptiis Philologiæ et Mercurii, there have been many edi- tions; that of Meibomius is the most useful to a musician; but there is a very good one, with corrections and notes, by Grotius, in octavo, published in 1559, when he was but fourteen years of age.

CHAP. XXIV.

THE several works hereinbefore enumerated con- tain the whole of what, in the strict sense of the term, we are to understand by the ancient system of music; and as many of them appear to be of very great antiquity, we are to esteem it a singular instance of good fortune that they are yet remaining; that they are so, is owing to the care and industry of very many learned men, who, from public li- braries, and other repositories, have sought out the most correct manuscripts of the respective authors, and given them to the world in print; As to Aris- toxenus, the first in the list of the harmonical writers, it is doubtful whether his Elements ever appeared in print, till near the middle of the seventeenth century, inasmuch as Morley, who lived in the reign of our queen Elizabeth, and was a very learned and inquisitive man in all matters relating to musical science, professes never to have seen the Elements of Aristoxenus; Euclid indeed had been published in the year 1498, in a Latin translation of Georgius Valla, of Placentia, but under the name of Cleonidas, It was also, in 1557, published at Paris in Greek, with a new Latin translation by Johannes Pena, mathematician to the French king, but in a very incorrect manner; other editions were also published of it, in which the errors of the former were multi- plied. At length, with the assistance of our country- men Selden, and Gerard Langbaine, Marcus Mei- bomius, a man well acquainted with the science, and well skilled in Greek literature, published it, to- gether with Aristoxenus Nicomachus, Alypias, Gau- dentius, Bacchius Senior, Aristides Quintilianus,

---

* The learned bishop of Avranches is somewhat less severe in his censure. He gives the following character of Capella and his work:— 'Martianus Capella has given the name of satire to his work because it ' is written in verse and prose, and the profitable and entertaining parts ' are agreeably interwoven. His design is to treat of the arts, which ' have the appellation of liberal; and these he represents by certain ' allegorical personages, with attributes proper to each. The principal ' action in this fable is the marriage of Mercury and Philology, a feigned ' being, intended to signify the love of literature. The artifice of this ' allegory is not very subtle, and as to the style it is barbarism itself; ' and for the figures, they are unpardonably bold and extravagant; ' besides all which it is so obscure as hardly to be intelligible; otherwise ' it is learned, and full of notions not common. Some write that the ' author was an African; if he was not, his harsh and forced style would ' induce one to believe he was of that country. The time he lived in is ' unknown; it only appears that he was more ancient than Justinian.' Huetius de l'Origine des Romains.

and the ninth book of the fable de Nuptiis Philologiæ et Mercurii of Martianus Capella, with a Latin translation of the first seven of the above-named writers, a general preface replete with excellent learning, and copious notes on them all.

Besides the general preface, Meibomius has given a particular one to each author as they stand in his edition, which prefaces, as they contain a variety of particulars relating to the respective authors and their works, and are otherwise curious, are well worthy of attention. The Manual of Nicomachus was first published and translated into Latin by Meibomius, who gives the author a very great character, and with great ingenuity fixes the time when he lived; for he observes that Nicomachus in the course of his work mentions Thrasyllus, who he says he thinks to be the same with one of that name mentioned frequently by Suetonius in Augustus and Tiberius, and by the old commentator on Juvenal, Sat. VI. as a famous mathematician, and from hence he infers that he lived after the time of Augustus.

To the Isagoge of Alypius the preface is but very short, but in that to Gaudentius, which follows it next in order Meibomius cites a passage from Cassiodorus, a Latin writer on music, who flourished in the fifth century, and will presently be spoken of, from whence he thinks the age when Alypius lived may in some measure be learned. He observes also that it appears from the same passage of Cassiodorus that Gaudentius had been translated into Latin by a Roman, a friend of his, named Mutianus;[*] the whole passage, to give it together as it stands in Cassiodorus, is in these words : 'Gratissima ergo nimis utilisque cog-'nitio, quæ et sensum nostrum ad superna erigit, et 'aures modulatione permulcet : quam apud Græcos 'Alypius, Euclydes, Ptolemæus, et cæteri probabili 'institutione, docuerunt. Apud Latinos autem vir 'magnificus Albinus librum de hac re, compendio, 'sub brevitate conscripsit, quem in bibliotheca Romæ 'non habuisse atque studiosè legisse retinemus. Qui 'si forte gentili incursione sublatus est, habetis hic 'Gaudentium Mutiani Latinum : quem si solicita 'intensione legitis, hujus scientiæ vobis atria patefacit. 'Fertur etiam latio sermone et Apuleium Madauren-'sam instituta hujus operis efficisse, scripsit etiam et 'pater Augustinus de Musica sex libros, in quibus 'humanam vocem, rhythmicos sonos, et harmoniam 'modulabilem in longis syllabis atque brevibus 'naturaliter habere monstravit. Censorinus quoque 'de accentibus voci nostræ ad necessariæ subtiliter 'disputavit, pertinere dicens ad musicam disciplinam : 'quem vobis inter cæteros transcriptum reliqui.' Cassiod. de Musica.

Gaudentius is published from a manuscript, which the editor procured of his friends Selden and Langbaine, who collated it for him, with two others which had been presented to the Bodleian library, the one by Sir Henry Savil, and the other by William, Earl of Pembroke, formerly chancellor of the university of Oxford. It seems that our countryman Chilmead had undertaken to publish an edition of Gaudentius, but being informed that Meibomius had entertained

a design of giving it to the world, he generously sent him his papers, and remitted the care of publishing them to him.

Bacchius Senior was first published in the original Greek, and with a French translation by Mersennus, in a commentary on certain chapters in the book of Genesis, written by him to explain the music of the ancient Hebrews and Greeks, intitled ' Questiones et ' Explicatio in sex priora capita Geneseos, quibus ' etiam Græcorum et Hebræorum Musica instauratur.' Of this translation Meibomius, in his general preface, speaks in very severe terms ; he says he did not know that any such was extant, till he was informed thereof by his friend Ismael Bullialdus ; he says that he then had it brought to him from Paris by the courier, and that if he had seen it before he had published his notes on that author, they would have been made much fuller by observations on his errors. However the only error that Meibomius here charges Mersennus with, is that of having confounded the Stantes with the Mobiles in his representation of the Systema maximum.

Aristides Quintilianus is taken from a manuscript which Meibomius frequently mentions as belonging to Joseph Scaliger, in which was contained Alypius, Nicomachus, Aristoxenus, Aristides, and Bacchius. This manuscript was deposited in the library of Leyden, and communicated to him by Daniel Heinsius, together with two manuscripts of Martianus Capella.

With the assistance of the several manuscripts above-mentioned, and a correspondence with the most learned men of his time, namely, Selden, Langbaine, Salmasius, Leo Allatius, and many others, Meibomius completed his edition of the ancient musical authors, and published it at Amsterdam in the year 1652, with a dedication to Christina, queen of Sweden.

With respect to the other Greek writers, namely, Ptolemy, Manuel Bryennius, and Porphyry, the former of these was published, together with Porphyry's Commentary, by Antonius Gogavinus, at Venice, with a Latin version in 1562, but, as it should seem from Dr. Wallis's censure of it, in a very inaccurate manner : Meibomius somewhere says that he had intended to publish both Porphyry and Manuel Bryennius, but he not having done it, Dr. Wallis undertook it, and has given it to the world in the third volume of his works. Most of the manuscripts that were made use of for the above publications, had been carried to Constantinople upon the erection of the eastern empire, to preserve them from the ravages of the northern invaders : and as that city continued to be the seat of learning for some centuries, they, together with an immense collection of Greek and Latin manuscripts, containing the works of the most valuable of the Greek and Roman writers, were preserved there with great care. But the taking and sacking of Constantinople by the Turks, in the year 1453, was followed by an emigration of learning and learned men, who, escaping from the destruction that threatened them, settled chiefly in Italy, and became the revivers of literature in the western parts of Europe.

[*] Mutianus also translated the Homilies of St. Chrysostom. Fabr. Biblioth. Græc. lib. III. cap. x.

These men upon their removal from Constantinople brought with them into Italy an immense treasure of learning, consisting of ancient manuscripts in all the several branches thereof, which they disseminated by lectures in the public schools : many of these manuscripts have at different periods been printed and dispersed throughout Europe, and others of them remain unpublished, either in public libraries, or in the collections of princes and other great persons.*

These men are also said to have introduced into Italy the knowledge of ancient music, which they could no otherwise do than by public lectures, and by giving to the world copies of the several treatises of the Greek harmonicians, hereinbefore particularly mentioned ; and the effects of these their labours to cultivate that kind of knowledge were made apparent by Gaffurius, or Franchinus, as he is otherwise called, who, before the end of the fifteenth century, published those several works of his, which have justly entitled him to the appellation of the Father of Music among the moderns.

Before the migration of learning from the East, all that was known of the ancient music in the western parts of Europe was contained in the writings of Censorinus, Macrobius, Martianus Capella, Boetius, Cassiodorus, and a few other Latin writers, who, as Meibomius says of Capella, might very justly be termed Pedarians, inasmuch as they were strict followers of the ancient harmonicians ; or else in the works of a very learned and excellent man, to whom this censure cannot be extended, namely, Boetius, of whom, and of whose inestimable work De Musica a very particular account will shortly be given ; in the interim it will be necessary to mention some innovations that had been made in music subsequent to Ptolemy, and before Boetius, of whom we are about to speak ; and first it is to be noted that in this interval, if not before the commencement of it, the genera, at least in practice, were reduced to one, namely, the diatonic : and next it is to be remarked, that the method of notation used by the ancients, the explanation whereof is almost the sole purpose of Alypius's book, was totally changed by the Romans, who to the great system, which consisted, as has been shewn, of a bisdiapason, containing fifteen sounds, applied as many letters of their own alphabet ; so that assigning to Proslambanomenos the letter A, the system terminated at P. It does not appear that at this time, nor indeed till a long time after, any marks or characters had been invented to denote the length or duration of musical sounds ; nor, notwithstanding

all that has been said about the rhythmus of the ancients, does it in the least appear that they had any rule for determining the length of the sounds, other than that which constituted the measure of the verses† to which those sounds were severally applied ; which consideration leaves it in some sort a question whether among the ancients there was any such thing as merely instrumental music.

In this method of notation by the first fifteen letters of the Latin alphabet, a modern will discover a great defect ; for, being in a lineal position, they by their situation inferred no diversity between grave and acute, whereas in the stave of the moderns the characters by a judicious analogy are made to express, according to their different situations in the stave, all the differences of the acute and grave from one extremity of the system to the other.

ANITIUS MANLIUS TORQUATUS SEVERINUS BOETIUS,† was the most considerable of all the Latin writers on music ; indeed his treatise on the subject supplied for some centuries the want of those Greek manuscripts which were supposed to have been lost ; for this reason, as also on account of his superior eminence in literature, he merits to be very particularly spoken of. He was by birth a Roman, descended of an ancient family, many of whom had been senators, and some advanced to the dignity of the consulate : the time of his birth is related to have been about that period in the Roman history when Augustulus, whose fears had induced him to a resignation of the empire, was banished, and Odoacer, king of the Herulians, began to reign in Italy, viz., in the year of Christ 476, or somewhat after. The father of Boetius dying while he was yet an infant. his relations undertook the care of his education and the direction of his studies ; his excellent parts were soon discovered, and, as well to enrich his mind with the study of philosophy, as to perfect himself in the Greek language, he was sent to Athens. Returning young to Rome, he was soon distinguished for his learning and virtue, and promoted to the principal dignities in the state, and at length to the consulate. Living in great affluence and splendour, he addicted himself to the study of theology, mathematics, ethics, and logic ; and how great a master he became in each of these branches of learning appears from those works of his now extant. The great offices which he bore in the state, and his consummate wisdom and inflexible integrity, procured him such a share in the public councils, as proved in the end his destruction ; for as

---

* The manuscripts relating to music which Kircher procured access to for the purpose of compiling his Musurgia, are by him said to be extant in the library of the Roman College ; and he speaks of one huge tome in particular, in which he says are the several works of Aristides Quintilianus, Bryennius, Plutarch, Aristotle, Callimachus, Aristoxenus, Alypius, Ptolemy, Euclid, Nicomachus, Boetius, Martianus Capella, Valla, and some others. In the account of the late discoveries in the ruins of Herculaneum, given by the Abbé Winckelman, mention is made of an ancient Greek treatise on music found there, written by one Philodemus, an author who has escaped the researches of the industrious Fabricius. Nevertheless, a philosopher of that name occurs among the Locrians, in Stanley's list of the Pythagorean School. Hist. of Philosophy, Pythagoras, chap. xxiv. This manuscript the antiquaries employed by the King of Naples on music, though it is burned to a crust, have begun to unroll ; but the condition of it, and the nature of the process made use of for developing it, render it almost impossible that the world can ever be the better for its contents. See the Letter of the Abbé Winckelman to Count Bruhl on this subject.

† In the Chronology of Sir Isaac Newton, pag. 14, is the following passage :—' In the year 1035 [before Christ] the Idæi Dactyli [a people ' supposed to have come from Numidia, vide Heyl. Cosm. pag. 555. edit. ' 1703] find out iron in mount Ida in Crete, and work it into armour and ' iron tools, and thereby give a beginning to the trades of smiths and ' armourers in Europe ; and by singing and dancing in their armour, ' and keeping time by striking upon one another's armours with their ' swords, they bring in music and poetry, and at the same time they ' nurse up the Cretan Jupiter in a cave of the same mountain, dancing ' about him in their armour.'
The origin of metrical numbers, and of the rhythmus, as it is called, is by some referred to this event ; but admitting this as a fact, it does not ascertain the time when the characters declaring the length or duration of sounds were first invented ; and the truth is that these are, comparatively speaking, a modern improvement in music.

* *The name of this eminent person is sometimes written Boethius. Hoffman, in his lexicon, determines in favour of Boetius, and it is to be noted, that in the edition of the works of Boetius, printed at Venice in 1499, the same reading is uniformly adhered to.*

he ever employed his interest in the king for the protection and encouragement of deserving men, so he exerted his utmost efforts in the detection of fraud. the repressing of violence, and the defence of the state against invaders. At this time Theodoric the Goth had attempted to ravage the Campania; and it was owing to the vigilance and resolution of Boetius that that country was preserved from destruction. At length, having murdered Odoacer, Theodoric became king of Italy, where he governed thirty-three years with prudence and moderation, during which time Boetius possessed a large share of his esteem and confidence. It happened about this time that Justin, the emperor of the East, upon his succeeding to Anastasius, made an edict condemning all the Arians, except the Goths, to perpetual banishment from the eastern empire: in this edict Hormisda, bishop of Rome, and also the senate concurred; but Theodoric, who, as being a Goth, was an Arian, was extremely troubled at it, and conceived an aversion against the senate for the share they had borne in this proscription. Of this disposition in the king, three men of profligate lives and desperate fortunes, Gaudentius, Opilio, and Basilius, took advantage; for having entertained a secret desire of revenge against Boetius, for having been instrumental in the dismission of the latter from a lucrative employment under the king, they accused him of several crimes, such as the stifling a charge, the end whereof was to involve the whole senate in the guilt of treason; and an attempt, by dethroning the king, to restore the liberty of Italy; and, lastly, they suggested that, to acquire the honours he was in possession of, Boetius had had recourse to magical arts.

Boetius was at this time at a great distance from Rome; however Theodoric transmitted the complaint to the senate, enforcing it with a suggestion that the safety, as well of the people as the prince, was rendered very precarious by this supposed design to exterminate the Goths: the senate perhaps fearing the resentment of the king, and having nothing to hope from the success of an enterprize, which, supposing it ever to have been meditated, was now rendered abortive, without summoning him to his defence, condemned Boetius to death. The king however, apprehending some bad consequence from the execution of a sentence so flagrantly unjust, mitigated it to banishment. The place of his exile was Ticinum, now the city of Pavia, in Italy: being in that place separated from his relations, who had not been permitted to follow him into his retirement, he endeavoured to derive from philosophy those comforts which that alone was capable of affording to one in his forlorn situation, sequestered from his friends, in the power of his enemies, and at the mercy of a capricious tyrant; and accordingly he there composed that valuable discourse, entitled De Consolatione Philosophiæ. To give a more particular account of this book would be needless, it being well known in the learned world: one remarkable circumstance relating to it is, that, by those under affliction it has in various times been applied to, as the means of fortifying their minds and re-

conciling them to the dispensations of Providence, almost as constantly as the scriptures themselves. Our Saxon king Alfred, whose reign, though happy upon the whole, was attended with great vicissitudes of fortune, had recourse to this book of Boetius, at a time when his distresses compelled him to seek retirement; and, that he might the better impress upon his mind the noble sentiments inculcated in it, he made a complete translation of it into the Saxon language, which, within these few years, has been given to the world in its proper character: Chaucer made a translation of it into English, which is printed among his works, and is alluded to in these verses of his :—

> Adam Scrivener, yf ever it the befalle
> Boece or Troiles for to write new,
> Under thy longe lockes thou muft have the fcalle:
> But after my makynge thou write more true;
> So ofte a daye I mote thy werke renewe,
> It to correcte, and eke to rubbe and fcrape,
> And al is thorow thy negligence and rape.

And Camden relates, that queen Elizabeth, during the time of her confinement by her sister Mary, to mitigate her grief, read and afterwards translated it into very elegant English.

It is more than probable that Boetius would have ended his exile by a natural death, had it not been for an event that happened about two years after the pronouncing his sentence; for, in the year 524, Justin, the emperor, thought fit to promulgate an edict against the Arians, whereby he commanded, without excepting the Goths, as he had done lately, on another occasion, that all bishops who maintained that heresy should be deposed, and their churches consecrated after the true Christian form. To avert this decree, Theodoric sent an embassy to the emperor, which, to render it the more splendid and respectable, consisted of the bishop or pope himself, who at that time was John the Second, the immediate successor of Hormisda, and four others, of the consular and patrician orders, who were instructed to solicit with the emperor the repeal of this decree, with threats, in case of a refusal, that the king would destroy Italy with fire and sword. Upon the arrival of the ambassadors at Constantinople, the emperor very artfully contrived to receive them in such a manner as naturally tended to detach them from their master, and make them slight the business they were sent to negociate, and he succeeded accordingly; for as soon as they approached the city, the emperor, the clergy, and a great number of the people, went in procession to meet them. In their way to the church, the upper hand of the emperor was given to the bishop; and upon their arrival there, the holy father, to shew his gratitude for the honour done him of sitting on the right of the imperial throne, celebrated the day of the Resurrection after the Roman use, and crowned Justin emperor. Of the insufferable pride and arrogance of this John so many instances are related, that no one who reads them can lament the fate which afterwards befel him, viz., that he died in a dungeon. It is recorded, that upon his arrival at Corinth, in his way to Constantinople, great enquiry was made for a gentle horse for him to ride on ; upon which, a nobleman of that city sent him one that, for the goodness of its temper, had been reserved for the use of his lady ; the bishop accepted the favour, and, after travelling as far as he thought fit, returned the beast to the owner : but behold what followed, the sagacious animal, conscious of the merit of having once borne the successor of St. Peter, refused ever after to let the lady mount him ; upon which the husband sent him again to the Pope, with a request that he would accept of that which was no longer of any use to the owner. This event, it is to be noted, is recorded as a miracle ; but if we allow it the credit due to one, it will reflect but little honour on the worker of it, since the utmost it proves is, that the Pope had the power of communicating to a horse a quality which had rendered the primitive possessor of it to the last degree odious.

It is not easy to see how, with any degree of propriety, or consistent with justice, the misbehaviour of the ambassadors could be imputed to Boetius, who, all this while, was confined to the place of his exile, and seemed to be employing his time in a way much more suited to his circumstances and character than in the abetting the misguided and malevolent zeal of either of two enthusiastic princes ; nevertheless, we are told, that Theodoric no sooner heard of the behaviour of John and his colleagues, than he began to meditate the death of Boetius : he however suppressed his resentment, till he had received a formal complaint from his people of the infidelity of those trusted by him. Immediately on his arrival, he committed the bishop to close confinement, wherein he shortly after ended his days. Had his revenge stopped here, his conduct might have escaped censure, but he completed the ruin of his character by sentencing Boetius to death, who, together with Symmachus, the father of his wife, was beheaded in prison on the tenth of the kalends of November, 525. In order to palliate the cruelty of the king, it has been insinuated, that the treachery of his ambassadors was a kind of evidence that the conspiracy had a foundation in truth ; and that fact once established, the intimacy which had subsisted for several years between Boetius and the bishop, before the banishment of the former, furnished a ground for suspicion that he was at least not ignorant of it. It is farther said, that, as if he believed the conspiracy to be real, the king sent to Boetius, in prison, offers of pardon, if he would disclose the whole treason ; but the protestations which he made upon that occasion of his innocence, afford the strongest evidence that could be given that he was not privy to it.

But the causes of this severe resolution of Theodoric are elsewhere to be sought for : he was arrived at the age of seventy-two, and for some years had been infected with the vices usually imputed to old age : he had reigned more than thirty-three years ; and though the mildness and prudence of his government, and that paternal tenderness with which he had ruled his people, were greater than could be expected from a prince who had made his way to dominion by the murder of the rightful sovereign, the dis-

appointments he had met with, the insults that had been offered him, one particularly in the person of his sister, who had received some indignities from the African Vandals, the contempt that had been shewn him in this late embassy, and, above all, his utter inability to resent these injuries in the way he most desired, these misfortunes concurring, deprived him of that equanimity of temper which had been the characteristic of his reign : in short, he grew jealous, timid, vindictive, and cruel ; and after this, nothing he did was to be wondered at.* But to return to Boetius.

The extensive learning and eloquence of this great man are conspicuous in his works ; and his singular merits have been celebrated by the ablest writers that have lived since the restoration of learning. His first wife, for he was twice married, was named Helpes, a Sicilian lady of great beauty and fortune, but more eminently distinguished by the endowments of her mind, and her inviolable affection for so excellent a man. She had a genius for poetry, and wrote with a degree of judgment and correctness not common to her sex. He desired much to have issue by her ; but she dying young, he embalmed her memory in the following elegant verses :—

Helpes dicta fui, Siculæ regionis alumna,
    Quam procùl à patria, conjugis egit amor.
Quo sine, mœsta dies, nox anxia, flebilis hora
    Nec solum caro, sed spiritus unus erat.
Lux mea non clausa est, tali remanente marito,
    Majorique animæ, parte superstes ero.
Porticibus sacris tam nunc peregrina quiesco,
    Judicis eterni testificata thronum.
Ne qua manus bustum violet, nisi fortè jugalis,
    Hæc iterum cupiat jungere membra suis.
Ut Thalami cumuliq ; comes, nec morte revellar.
    Et socios vitæ nectat uterque cinis.

His other wife, Rusticiana, was the daughter of Quintus Aurelius Menius Symmachus, a chief of the senate, and consul in the year 485 : with her he received a considerable accession to his fortune. He had several children by her ; two of whom arrived to the dignity of the consulate. His conjugal tenderness was very exemplary ; and it may be truly said, that, for his public and private virtues, he was one of the great ornaments of that degenerate age in which it was his misfortune to be born.

The tomb of Boetius is to be seen in the church of St. Augustine, at Pavia, near the steps of the chancel, with the following epitaph :—

Mœonia et Latia lingua clarissimus, et qui
Consul eram, hic perii, missus in exilium ;
Et quia mors rapuit? Probitas me vexit ad auras,
Et nunc fama viget maxima vivit opus.

Many ages after his death the emperor Otho the Third enclosed his bones, then lying neglected

* Procopius relates that he was frighted to death ; the following is his account of that strange accident :—
'Symmachus and his son-in-law, Boetius, just men and great relievers 'of the poor, senators and consuls, had many enemies, by whose false 'accusations Theodoric, being persuaded that they plotted against him, 'put them to death, and confiscated their estates. Not long after, his 'waiters set before him at supper the head of a great fish, which seemed 'to him to be the head of Symmachus, lately murthered ; and with his 'teeth sticking out, and fierce glaring eyes, to threaten him. Being 'frighted, he grew chill, went to bed lamenting what he had done to 'Symmachus and Boetius, and soon after died.' De Bello Gothico, lib. I.

amongst the rubbish, in a marble chest; upon which occasion Gerbert, an eminent scholar of that time, and who was afterwards advanced to the papal chair by the name of Sylvester the Second, did honour to his memory in the following lines :—

> Roma potens, dum jura suo declarat in orbe,
> Tu pater, et patriæ lumen, Severine Boeti,
> Consulis officio, rerum disponis habenas,
> Infundis lumen studiis, et cedere nescis
> Græcorum ingeniis, sed mens divina coercet
> Imperium mundi. Gladio bacchante Gothorum
> Libertas Romana perit : tu consul et exul,
> Insignes titulos præclara morte relinquis,
> Tunc decus Imperii, summas qui prægravat artes,
> Tertius Otho sua dignum te judicat aula ;
> Æternumque tui statuit monumenta laboris,
> Et bene promeritum, meritis exornat honestis.

The writings of Boetius, the titles whereof are given below,* seem to have been collected with great care : an edition of them was printed at Venice, in one volume in folio, 1499. In 1570, Glareanus, of Basil, collated that with several manuscripts, and published it, with a few various readings in the margin. To render his author more intelligible, the editor has inserted sundry diagrams of his own ; but has been careful not to confound them with the original ones of Boetius.

But before these, or indeed the doctrines of Boetius, can be rendered intelligible, it is necessary first to state the general drift and tendency of the author, in his treatise De Musica ; and next to explain the several terms made use of by him in the demonstration of the proportions of the consonances and other intervals, as also the proportions themselves, distinguishing between the several species of arithmetical, geometrical, and harmonical proportion.

The design of Boetius in the above-mentioned treatise was, by the aid of arithmetic, to demonstrate those ratios which those of the Pythagorean school had asserted subsisted between the consonances. These ratios are either of equality, as 1 : 1, 2 : 2, 8 : 8, or of inequality, as 4 : 2, because the first contains the latter once, with a remainder : and of these ratios, or proportions of inequality, there are five kinds, as, namely, multiplex, superparticular, superpartient, multiplex superparticular, and multiplex superpartient ; all which will hereafter be explained.

* In Porphyrium à Victorino translatum, lib. II. In Porphyrium à se Latinum factum, lib. V. In Prædicamenta Aristotelis, lib. IV. In librum de Interpretatione Commentaria minora, lib. II. In eundem de Interpretatione Commentaria majora, lib. VI. Analyticorum priorum Aristotelis, Anitio Manlio Severino Boethio interprete, lib. II. Analyticorum posteriorum Aristotelis, Anitio Manlio Severino Boethio interprete, lib. II. Introductio ad categoricos Syllogismos, lib. I. De Syllogismo categorico, lib. II. De Syllogismo hypothetico, lib. II. De Divisione, lib. I. De Diffinitione, lib. I. Topicorum Aristotelis, Anitio Manlio Severino, interprete, lib. VIII. Elenchorum Sophisticorum Aristotelis, Anitio Manlio Severino Boethio interprete, lib. II. In Topica Cironis, lib. VI. De Differentiis Topicis, lib. IV. De Consolatione Philosophiæ, luculentissimis Johannis Murmelli (partim etiam Rodolphi Agricolæ) Commentariis illustrati, lib. V. De Sancta Trinitate, cum Gilberti episopi Pictaviensis, cognemento porretæ doctissimi olim viri commentariis, jam primum ex vetustissimo scripto codice in lucem editis, lib. IV. Quorum primus continet excelientem & piam doctrinam, de Trinitate & Unitate Dei : quomodo Trinita sit Unus Deus, & non Tres Dii, lib. I. Secundus tractat Questionem An Pater, & Filius, & Spiritus Sanctus substantialiter prædicentur, lib. I. Tertius complectitur Hebdomaden : An omne quod sit, bonum sit, lib. I. Quartus evidenter & piè docet, in Christo duas esse Naturas, & unam Personam, adversus Eutychen & Nestorium, lib. I. De Unitate & Uno, lib. I. De Disciplina Scholarium, lib. I. De Arithtica, lib. II. De Musica, lib. V. De Geometria, lib. II.

These terms are made use of by Euclid, and others of the Greek writers, and were adopted by Boetius, and through him have been continued down to the Italian writers, in whose works they are perpetually occurring ; and though the modern arithmeticians have rejected them, and substituted in their places, as a much shorter and more intelligible method of designation, the numbers that constitute the several proportions, it is necessary to the understanding of the ancient writers, that the terms used by them should also be understood.

Another thing necessary to be known, in order to the understanding not only of Boetius and his followers, but all who have written on those abstruse parts of music the ancient modes, the ecclesiastical tones, and their divisions into authentic and plagal, is the nature of the three different kinds of proportion, namely, arithmetical, geometrical, and harmonical ; an explanation whereof, as also of the several kinds of proportion of inequality can hardly be given in terms more accurate, precise, and intelligible, than those of Dr. Holder, in his treatise on the Natural Grounds and Principles of Harmony, chap. v. wherein, after premising that all harmonic bodies and sounds fall under numerical calculations, he speaks thus of proportion in general :—

'We may compare (i. e. amongst themselves) 'either (1) magnitudes (so they be of the same 'kind) ; or (2) the gravitations, velocities, durations, 'sounds, &c. from thence arising ; or, farther, the 'numbers themselves, by which the things compared 'are explicated ; and if these shall be unequal, we 'may then consider either, first, how much one of 'them exceeds the other ; or, secondly, after what 'manner one of them stands related to the other, 'as to the quotient of the antecedent (or former 'term) divided by the consequent (or latter term) 'which quotient doth expound, denominate, or shew, 'how many times, or how much of a time or times, 'one of them doth contain the other : and this by 'the Greeks is called λογος, ratio, as they are wont 'to call the similitude or equality of ratios αναλογια, 'analogie, proportion, or proportionality ; but custom, 'and the sense assisting, will render any over-curious 'application of these terms unnecessary.

From these two considerations last mentioned, the same author says, there are wont to be deduced three sorts of proportion, arithmetical, geometrical, and a mixed proportion, resulting from these two, called harmonical. These are thus explained by him :—

'1. Arithmetical, when three or more numbers 'in progression have the same difference ; as 2, 4, '6, 8, &c. or discontinued, as 2, 4, 6 ; 14, 16, 18.'

'2. Geometrical, when three or more numbers 'have the same ration, as 2, 4, 8, 16, 32 ; or discontinued, as 2, 4 ; 64, 128.'

'Lastly, Harmonical, (partaking of both the other) 'when three numbers are so ordered, that there be 'the same ration of the greatest to the least, as there 'is of the difference of the two greater to the difference of the two less numbers, as in these three 'terms, 3, 4, 6, the ration of 6 to 3, (being the 'greatest and least terms) is duple ; so is 2, the

'difference of 6 and 4 (the two greater numbers) to
'1, the difference of 4 and 3 (the two less numbers)
'duple also. This is proportion harmonical, which
'diapason, 6 to 3, bears to diapente, 6 to 4, and
'diatessaron, 4 to 3, as its mean proportionals.'

'Now for the kinds of rations most properly
'so called; *i. e.* geometrical: first observe, that in
'all rations, the former term or number, (whether
'greater or less) is always called the antecedent;
'and the other following number, is called the con-
'sequent. If therefore, the antecedent be the greater
'term, then the ration is either multiplex, super-
'particular, superpartient, or (what is compounded of
'these) multiplex superparticular, or multiplex super-
'partient.'

'1. Multiplex; as duple, 4 to 2; triple, 6 to 2;
'quadruple, 8 to 2.'

'2. Superparticular; as 3 to 2, 4 to 3, 5 to 4;
'exceeding but by one aliquot part, and in their
'radical, or least numbers, always but by one; and
'these rations are termed sesquialtera, sesquitertia,
'(or supertertia) sesquiquarta, or (superquarta) &c.
'Note, that numbers exceeding more than by one,
'and but by one aliquot part, may yet be super-
'particular, if they be not expressed in their radical,
'*i. e.* least numbers, as 12 to 8, hath the same ration
'as 3 to 2; *i. e.* superparticular; though it seem not
'so till it be reduced by the greatest common divisor
'to its radical numbers, 3 to 2. And the common
'divisor, (*i. e.* the number by which both the terms
'may severally be divided) is often the difference
'between the two numbers; as in 12 to 8, the dif-
'ference is 4, which is the common divisor. Divide
'12 by 4, the quotient is 3; divide 8 by 4, the
'quotient is 2; so the radical is 3 to 2. Thus also,
'15 to 10, divided by the difference, 5, gives 3 to 2;
'yet in 16 to 10, 2 is the common divisor, and gives
'8 to 5, being superpartient. But in all super-
'particular rations, whose terms are thus made larger
'by being multiplied, the difference between the
'terms is always the greatest common divisor; as in
'the foregoing examples.'

'The third kind of ration is superpartient, exceed-
'ing by more than one, as 5 to 3; which is called
'superbipartiens tertias, (or tria) containing 3 and
'$\frac{2}{3}$ 8 to 5, supertripartiens quintas, 5 and $\frac{3}{5}$.'

'The fourth is multiplex superparticular, as 9 to
'4, which is duple, and sesquiquarta; 13 to 4, which
'is triple and sesquiquarta.'

'The fifth and last is multiplex superpartient, as
'11 to 4; duple, and supertripartiens quartas.'*

'When the antecedent is less than the consequent,
'viz., when a less is compared to a greater; then the
'same terms serve to express the rations, only pre-
'fixing sub to them; as, submultiplex, subsuper-
'particular, (or subparticular) subsuperpartient, (or
'subpartient) &c. 4 to 2 is duple; 2 to 4 is subduple,
'4 to 3 is sesquitertia; 3 to 4 is subsesquitertia, 5 to

'3 is superbipartiens tertias; 3 to 5 is subsuper-
'bipartiens tertias, &c.'

The same author proceeds to find how the habitudes of rations are found in these words:—

'All the habitudes of rations to each other, are
'found by multiplication or division of their terms,
'by which any ration is added to or subtracted from
'another: and there may be use of progression of
'rations or proportions, and of finding a medium,
'or mediety, between the terms of any ration: but
'the main work is done by addition and subtraction
'of rations, which, though they are not performed
'like addition and subtraction of simple numbers in
'arithmetic, but upon algebraic grounds, yet the
'praxis is most easy.'

'One ration is added to another ration, by mul-
'tiplying the two antecedent terms together, *i. e.* the
'antecedent of one of the rations, by the antecedent
'of the other. (For the more ease, they should be
'reduced into their least numbers or terms); and
'then the two consequent terms, in like manner.
'The ration of the product of the antecedents to
'that of the product of the consequents, is equal to
'the other two, added or joined together. Thus,
'for example, add the ration of 8 to 6; *i. e.* (in
'radical numbers) 4 to 3, to the ratio of 12 to 10
'*i. e.* 6 to 5; the product will be 24 and 4— | —3
'15, *i. e.* 8 to 5; you may set them thus, |
'and multiply 4 by 6, they make 24; 6— | —5
'which set at the bottom; then multiply ————
'3 by 5, they make 15; which likewise   24   15
'set under, and you have 24 to 15: which is a ration
'compounded of the other two, and equal to them
'both. Reduce these products, 24 and 15, to their
'least radical numbers, which is by dividing as far
'as you can find a common divisor to them both
'(which is here done by 3), and that brings them to
'the ration of 8 to 5. By this you see that a third
'minor, 6 to 5, added to a fourth, 4 to 3, makes
'a sixth minor, 8 to 5. If more rations are to be
'added, set them all under each other, and multiply
'the first antecedent by the second, and that product
'by the third; and again that product by the fourth,
'and so on; and in like manner the consequents.'

'This operation depends upon the fifth proposition
'of the eighth book of Euclid; where he shows
'that the ration of plain numbers is compounded of
'their sides. See these diagrams:—'

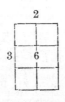

'Now compound these sides. Take for the ante-
'cedents, 4, the greater side of the greater plane,
'and 3, the greater side of the less plane, and they
'multiplied give 12. Then take the remaining two
'numbers, 3 and 2, being the less sides of the planes
'(for consequents), and they give 6. So the sides of
'4 and 3, and of 3 and 2, compounded (by multiplying

* The above terms were used by the ancient geometers and arithmeticians; and therefore, for the understanding of such, and of Boetius in
particular, it is very necessary that their meaning should be ascertained:
but the manner now is to express the proportions by the numbers themselves, rather than by the terms; and briefly to say, as 31 is to 7, or as
7 is to 31, rather than to say, quadrupla superbipartiens septimas, or
subquadrupla supertri partiens septimas. Vide Harris's Lex. Tech.
vol. I. PROPORTION.

' the antecedent terms by themselves and the con-
' sequents by themselves) make 12 to 6 ; *i. e.* 2 to 1,
' which being applied, amounts to this ; ratio sesqui-
' altera 3 to 2, added to ration sesquitertia, 4 to 3,
' makes duple ration, 2 to 1. Therefore, diapente
' added to diatessaron, makes diapason.'

' Subtraction of one ration from another greater,
' is performed in like manner, by multiplying the
' terms ; but this is done not laterally, as in addition,
' but crosswise ; by multiplying the antecedent of
' the former (*i. e.* of the greater) by the consequent
' of the latter, which produceth a new antecedent ;
' and the consequent of the former by the antecedent
' of the latter, which gives a new consequent ; and
' therefore, it is usually done by an oblique de-
' cussation of the lines. For example, if
' 4 3   you would take 6 to 5 out of 4 to 3, you
'   may set them down thus : Then 4, mul-
' **X**   tiplied by 5, makes 20 ; and 3, by 6, gives
' 6 5   18; so 20 to 18, *i. e.* 10 to 9, is the re-
' 20 18   mainder. That is, subtract a third minor
' 10 9   out of a fourth, and there will remain a
'   tone minor.

' Multiplication of ratios is the same with their
' addition ; only it is not wont to be of divers rations,
' but of the same, being taken twice, thrice, or oftener,
' as you please. And as before, in addition, you added
' divers rations, by multiplying them ; so here, in mul-
' tiplication, you add the same ration to itself, after
' the same manner, viz., by multiplying the terms of
' the same ratio by themselves ; *i. e.* the antecedent
' by itself, and the consequent by itself, (which in
' other words, is to multiply the same by 2) and will
' in the operation be to square the ration first pro-
' pounded (or give the second ordinal power ; the
' ration first given being the first power or side) and
' to this product, if the simple ration shall again be
' added, (after the same manner as before) the aggre-
' gate will be the triple of the ration first given ; or
' the product of that ration, multiplied by 3, viz., the
' cube, or third ordinal power. Its biquadrate, or
' fourth power, proceeds from multiplying it by 4 ;
' and so successively in order, as far as you please
' you may advance the powers. For instance, the
' duple ration, 2 to 1, being added to itself, dupled
' or multiplied by 2, produceth 4 to 1, (the ration
' quadruple) ; and if to this, the first again be added,
' (which is equivalent to multiplying that said first
' by 3), there will arise the ration octuple, or 8 to 1.
' Whence the ration, 2 to 1, being taken for a root,
' its duple 4 to 1, will be the square ; its triple, 8 to 1,
' the cube thereof, &c. as hath been said above. And
' to use another instance ; to duple the ration of 3 to 2,
' it must be thus squared :—3 by 3 gives 9 ; 2 by 2
' gives 4, so the duple or square of 3 to 2 is 9 to 4.
' Again, 9 by 3 is 27, and 4 by 2 is 8 ; so the cubic
' ration of 3 to 2 is 27 to 8. Again, to find the
' fourth power or biquadrate, (*i. e.* squared square,)
' 27 by 3 is 81, 8 by 2 is sixteen ; so 81 to 16 is the
' ration of 3 to 2 quadrupled ; as it is dupled by the
' square, tripled by the cube, &c. To apply this
' instance to our present purpose, 3 to 2 is the ration
' of diapente, or a fifth in harmony ; 9 to 4 is the

' ratio of twice diapente, (or a ninth, viz., diapason,
' with tone major ;) 27 to 8 is the ration of thrice
' diapente, or three fifths, which is diapason, with
' sixth major, viz., 13 major ; the ration of 81 to 16
' makes four fifths, *i. e.* disdiapason, with two tones
' major, *i. e.* a seventeenth major, and a comma of 81
' to 80.'

' To divide any ration, the contrary way must be
' taken ; and by extracting of these roots respectively,
' division by their indices will be performed, E. gr.
' to divide it by 2, is to take the square root of it ;
' by 3, the cube root ; by 4 the biquadratic, &c.
' Thus, to divide 9 to 4 by 2, the square root of 9
' is 3, the square root of 4 is 2 ; then 3 to 2 is a
' ration just half so much as 9 to 4 '

CHAP. XXV.

THE nature of proportion being thus explained,
without a competent knowledge whereof it would be
in vain to attempt the reading of Boetius, it remains
to give such an account of his treatise De Musica
as is consistent with a general history of the science,
and may be sufficient to invite the studious inquirer
to an attentive perusal of this most valuable work.
Here therefore follow, in regular order, the titles of
the several chapters contained in the five books of
Boetius's treatise De Musica, with an abridgment of
such of them as seem most worthy of remark.

Chap. i. Musicam naturaliter nobis esse conjunc-
tam, et mores vel honestare vel evertere.

Boetius in this chapter observes, that the sensitive
power of perception is natural to all living creatures,
but that knowledge is attained by contemplation.
All mortals, he says, are endued with sight, but whether the perception be effected by the coming of the
object to the sight, or by rays sent forth to it, is a
doubt. When any one, continues he, beholds a triangle or a square, he readily acknowledges what he
discovers by his eyes, but he must be a mathematician to investigate the nature of a triangle or a
square. Having established this proposition, he
applies it to the other liberal arts, and to music in
particular ; which he undertakes to shew is connected with morality, inasmuch as it disposes the
mind to good or evil actions ; to this purpose he
expresses himself in these terms : ' The power or
' faculty of hearing enables us not only to form a
' judgment of sounds, and to discover their differ-
' ences, but to receive delight, if they are sweet and
' adapted to each other ; whence it comes to pass that,
' as there are four mathematical sciences,* the rest

* The four mathematical arts are arithmetic, geometry, music, and
astronomy ; these were anciently termed the quadrivium, or fourfold
way to knowledge ; the other three, grammar, rhetoric, and logic, completing the number of the seven liberal sciences, were termed the
trivium or threefold way to eloquence. Vide Du Cange, voce QUA-
DRIVIUM.
    This scholastic division is recognized in an ancient monumental
inscription in Westminster Abbey, in memory of Gilbert Crispin, who
died abbot of Westminster in 1117.

Mitis eras justus prudens fortis moderatus
Doctus quadrivio nec minus in trivio.
                    Widmore's Hist. of Westminster Abbey.

    And these are the arts understood in the academical degrees of bachelor
and master of arts, for the ancient course of scholastic institution required a proficiency in each. The satire, as it is called, of Martianus
Capella, De Nuptiis Philologiæ et Mercurii, is a treatise on the seven

labour at the investigation of truth; but this, besides
'that it requires speculation, is connected with mo-
'rality; for there is nothing that more peculiarly
distinguishes human nature, than that disposition
observable in mankind to be one way affected by
sweet, and another by contrary sounds; and this
'affection is not peculiar to particular tempers or
'certain ages, but is common to all; and infants,
'young, and even old men, are by a natural instinct
'rendered susceptible of pleasure or disgust from
'consonant or discordant sounds. From hence we
'may discern that it was not without reason that
'Plato said, that the soul of the world was conjoined
'with musical proportion: and such is the effect of
'music on the human manners, that a lascivious mind
'is delighted with lascivious modes, and a sober mind
'is more disposed to sobriety by those of a contrary
'kind: and hence it is that the musical modes, for
'instance the Lydian and Phrygian, take their names
'from the tempers or distinguishing characteristics
'of those nations that respectively delight in them:
'for it cannot be that things, in their nature soft,
'should agree with such as are harsh, or contrary-
'wise; for it is similitude that conciliates love;
'wherefore Plato held that the greatest caution was
'to be taken not to suffer any change in a well-
'moraled music, there being no corruption of man-
'ners in a republic so great as that which follows a
'gradual declination from a prudent and modest
'music; for, whatever corruptions are made in music,
'the minds of the hearers will immediately suffer the
'same, it being certain that there is no way to
'the affections more open than that of hearing: and
'these effects of music are discernible among different
'nations, for the more fierce, as the Getæ, are de-
'lighted with the harder modes, and the more gentle
'and civilized with such as are moderate; although
'in these days few of the latter are to be found.'

Boetius then proceeds to relate that the Lacedæmonians, sensible of the great advantages resulting to
a state from a sober, modest, and well-regulated
music, invited, by a great reward, Taletas the Cretan
to settle among them, and instruct their youth in
music. And he relates that the Spartans were so
jealous of innovations in their music, that, for adding
only a single chord to those he found, they banished
Timotheus from Sparta by a decree; which, however
he could come by so great a curiosity, he gives in the
original Greek, and is as follows:—ΕΠΕΙ ΔΕ ΤΙΜΟ-
ΘΕΟΣ Ο ΜΙΛΕΣΙΟΣ ΠΑΡΑΓΙΜΕΝΟΣ ΕΝ ΤΑΝ
ΑΜΕΤΕΡΑΝ ΠΟΛΙΝ, ΤΑΝ ΠΑΛΑΙΑΝ ΜΟΛΠΗΝ
ΑΤΙΜΑΣΑΣ. ΚΑΙ ΤΑΝ ΔΙΑ ΠΑΝ ΕΠΤΑ ΧΟΡΔΑΝ
ΚΙΘΑΡΙΖΕΙ, ΑΠΟΣΤΡΕΦΟΜΕΝΟΣ ΠΟΛΥΦΩΝΙΑΝ
ΕΙΣΑΓΩΝ, ΛΥΜΑΙΝΕΤΑΙ ΤΑΣ ΑΚΟΑΣ ΤΩΝ
ΝΕΩΝ ΔΙΑ ΤΕ ΤΑΣ ΠΟΛΥΧΟΡΔΑΣ, ΚΑΙ ΤΑΣ
ΚΑΙΝΟΤΑΤΑΣ ΤΟΥΤΩΝ ΜΕΛΕΟΣ ΑΓΕΝΝΕ ΚΑΙ
ΠΟΙΚΙΛΑΝ ΑΝΤΙΑΠΛΟΑΝ, ΚΑΙ ΤΕΤΑΓΜΕΝΑΝ
ΑΜΦΙΑΥΙΑΝ ΜΟΛΠΗΝ ΕΠΙ ΧΡΩΜΑΤΟΣ ΣΥ-
ΝΕΙΣΤΑΜΕΝ ΤΟΥΤΟΥ ΜΕΛΕΟΣ, ΔΙΑΣΤΑΣΙΝ.

liberal sciences: Cassiodorus, who lived about half a century after him,
wrote also De septem Disciplinis; and others of the learned in like manner have written professedly on them all. Farther, of Joannes Basingus
sive Basingstockius, who flourished in 1252, it is on the authority
of Matthew Paris, who knew him, related that he was, 'Vir quidem in
trivis et quadrivis experientissimus.' Tauner's Bibliotheca 431.

ΑΝΤΙ ΓΑΡ ΕΝΑΡΜΟΝΙΩ ΠΟΙΑΝ ΑΝΤΙΣΤΡΕΦΟΝ
ΑΜΟΙΒΑΝ. ΠΑΡΑΚΑΛΑΘΕΙΣ ΔΕ ΕΝ ΤΟΝ ΑΓΩ-
ΝΑ ΤΑΣ ΕΛΕΥΣΙΝΙΑΣ ΔΑΜΑΤΡΟΣ ΑΙΧΟΣ ΔΙΕ-
ΦΗΜΙΣΑΤΟ ΤΑΝ ΤΩ ΜΥΘΩ ΚΙΔΝΗΣΙΝ: ΤΑΝ
ΓΑΡ ΣΕΜΕΛΑ ΟΔΥΝΑΝ ΟΥΚ ΕΝΔΕΚΑΤΟΣ ΝΕΟΣ
ΔΙΔΑΧΗΝ ΕΔΙΔΑΞΕ. ΕΙΤΑ ΠΕΡΙ ΤΟΥΤΟΝ ΤΟΝ
ΒΑΣΙΔΕΑΝ ΚΑΙ ΤΟΥ ΡΗΤΟΡΟΣ ΜΕΜΨΑΤΑΙ ΤΙ-
ΜΟΘΕΟΝ, ΕΠΑΝΑΤΙΘΕΤΑΙ ΔΕ ΚΑΙ ΤΑΝ ΕΝΔΕΚΑ
ΧΟΡΔΑ ΕΚΤΑΝΩΝ ΤΑΣ ΠΕΡΙΑΣΤΑΣ ΕΠΙΛΕΙ-
ΠΟΜΕΝΟΣ ΤΑΝ ΕΠΤΑΧΟΡΔΟΝ ΑΣΤΟΣ. ΤΟ ΓΑΡ
ΠΟΛΙΟΣ ΒΑΡΟΣ ΑΠΤΟΝ ΤΕΤΑΡ ΒΗΤΑΙ ΕΣ ΤΑΝ
ΣΠΑΡΤΑΝ ΕΠΙΦΕΡΕΙΝ: ΤΙΘΩΝ ΜΗ ΚΑΛΩΝ ΝΗ-
ΤΩΝ ΜΗΠΟΤΕ ΤΑΡΑΤΤΗΤΑΙ ΚΛΕΟΣ ΑΓΟΡΩΝ.*

He then proceeds to declare the power of music in
these words:—'It is well known that many wonderful
'effects have been wrought by the power of music
'over the mind; oftentimes a song has repressed
'anger; and who is ignorant that a certain drunken
'young man of Taurominium being incited to violence
'by the sound of the Phrygian mode, was by the
'singing of a spondeus appeased; for when a harlot
'was shut up in the house of his rival, and the young
'man, raging with madness, would have set the house
'on fire, Pythagoras, who, agreeable to his nightly
'custom, was employed in observing the motions of
'the celestial bodies, as soon as he was informed that
'the young man had been incited to this outrage by
'the Phrygian mode, and found that he would not
'desist from his wicked attempt, though his friends
'repeated their admonitions to him for that purpose,
'ordered them to change the mode, and thereby
'attempered the disposition of the raging youth to
'a most tranquil state of mind. Cicero relates the
'same story in different words, but in nearly the same
'manner:—" When (says he) certain drunken men
" stirred up, as is often the case, by the sound of the
" tibia, would have broke open the doors of a modest
" woman, Pythagoras is said to have admonished the
" tibicinist to play a spondeus, which he had no sooner
" done than the lustfulness of these men was appeased
" by the slowness of the mode and the gravity of the
" performer." But to gather some similar examples
'in few words, Terpander and Arion of Methymne,
'the next city in Lesbos to Mitylene for grandeur,
'cured the Lesbians and Ionians of most grievous
'diseases by the means of music; Hismenias, the
'Theban, by his music is reported to have freed from
'their torments divers Beotians, who were sorely
'afflicted with sciatic pains.† Empedocles also, when
'a certain person in a fury would have attacked his
'guest, for having accused and procured the con-
'demnation of his father, is said to have diverted him
'by a particular mode in music, and by that means to
'have appeased the anger of the young man. And
'so well was the power of music known to the ancient
'philosophers, that the Pythagoreans, when they had

* *Translation, see pag. 80, note.*

† There are many relations in history of the efficacy of music in the
cure of bodily diseases. It is reported that Thales, the Cretan, being by
the advice of the Oracle called to Sparta, cured a raging pestilence by
the power of music alone. The assertion of Boetius with respect to the
Sciatica seems to be founded on a passage in Aulus Gellius, lib. IV. chap.
xiii. who reports that persons afflicted with that disease were eased of
their pains by certain gentle modulations of the tibia; and that by the
same means many had been cured who had been bitten by serpents and
other venemous creatures.

'a mind to refresh themselves by sleep after the
'labours and cares of the day, made use of certain
'songs to procure them an easy and quiet rest; and
'when they awaked they also dispelled the dulness
'and confusion occasioned by sleep by others, know-
'ing full well that the mind and the body were con-
'joined in a musical fitness, and that whatever affects
'the body, will also produce a similar effect on the
'mind; which observation it is reported Democritus,
'whom his fellow-citizens had confined, supposing
'him mad, made to Hippocrates, the physician, who
'had been sent for to cure him. To what purpose
'then are all these things? We cannot doubt but
'that our body and mind are in manner constituted
'in the same proportions by which harmonical modu-
'lations are joined and compacted, as the following
'argument shall shew; for hence it is that even
'infants are delighted with a sweet, or disgusted with
'a harsh song: every age and either sex are affected
'by music, and though they are different in their
'actions, yet do they agree in their love of music.
'Nay, such as are under the influence of sorrow, even
'modulate their complaints, which is chiefly the case
'with women, who, by the sweetness of their songs,
'find means to alleviate their sorrows;* and it was
'for this reason that the ancients had a custom for the
'tibia to precede in their funeral processions. Pa-
'pinius Statius testifies as much in the following
'verse:—

    'Cornu grave mugit adunco,
    'Tibia cui teneros suetum producere manes.

'And though a man cannot sing sweetly, yet while
'he sings to himself he draws forth an innate sweet-
'ness from his heart. Is it not manifest that the
'sound of the trumpet fires the minds of the com-
'batants, and impels them to battle; why then is it
'not probable that a person may be incited to fury
'and anger from a peaceful state of mind? There is
'no doubt but that a mode may restrain anger or
'other inordinate desires; for what is the reason that
'when a person receives into his ears any song with
'pleasure, that he should not also be spontaneously
'converted to it, or that the body should not form or
'fashion some motion similar to what he hears: from
'all these things it is clear beyond doubt that music
'is naturally joined to us, and that if we would we
'cannot deprive ourselves of it; wherefore the power
'of the mind is to be exerted, that what is implanted
'in us by nature should also be comprehended by
'science. For as in sight it is not sufficient for
'learned men barely to behold colours and forms,
'unless they also investigate their properties; so also
'is it not sufficient to be delighted with musical songs,
'unless we also learn by what proportion of voices or
'sounds they are joined together.'

Cap. ii. Tres esse musicas, in quibus de vi musicæ
narratur.

The three kinds of music here meant are, mundane,
humane, and instrumental; and of each of these
mention has been made in a preceding page.

* Modern history furnishes a curious fact to prove the truth of this
observation; for it is related of the princess of Navarre, mother of Henry
IV. of France, that at the instant when she was delivered of him she sung
a song in the Bearnois language. Life of Henry le Grand by the Bishop
of Rodez.

Cap. iii. De vocibus ac de musicæ elementis.—
Cap. iv. De speciebus inequalitatis.—Cap. v. Quæ
inequalitatis species consonantiis aptentur.—Cap. vi.
Cur multiplicitas, et superparticularitas consonantiis
deputentur.—Cap. vii. Quæ proportiones quibus consonantiis musicis aptentur.—Cap. viii. Quid sit sonus,
quid intervallum, quid concinentia.—Cap. ix. Non
omne judicium dandum esse sensibus, sed amplius
rationi esse credendum, in quo de sensuum fallacia.

It is the business of this chapter to show, that
though the first principles of harmony are taken from
the sense of hearing, for this reason, that were it
otherwise there could be no dispute about sounds;
yet, in this case, the sense is not the sole arbiter.
Boetius to this purpose expresses himself very rationally in the following terms:—'Hearing is as it were
'but a monitor, but the last perfection and power of
'judging about it depends upon reason. What need
'is there for many words to point out the error which
'the senses are liable to, since we know that neither
'is the same power of perception given to every one
'alike, nor is it always equal in the same man; on the
'other hand, it is vain to commit the examination of
'truth to an uncertain judgment. The Pythagoreans
'for this reason took as it were a middle way; for
'though they did not make the hearing the sole
'arbiter, yet did they search after and try some
'things by the ears only: they measured the con-
'sonants themselves by the ears, but the distances by
'which these consonants differed from each other they
'did not trust to the ears, the judgment whereof is
'inaccurate, but committed them to the examination
'of reason, thereby making the sense subservient to
'reason, which acted as a judge and a master. For
'though the momenta of all arts, and of life itself,
'depend upon our senses, yet no sure judgment can
'be formed concerning them, no comprehension of
'the truth can exist, if the decision of reason be
'wanting; for the senses themselves are equally de-
'ceived in things that are very great or very little:
'and with respect to that of hearing, it with great
'difficulty perceives those intervals which are very
'small, and is deafened by those which are very great.'

Cap. x. Quemadmodum Pythagoras proportiones
consonantiarum investigaverit.—Cap. xi. Quibus
modis variè à Pythagora proportiones consonantiarum
perpensæ sint.

The account delivered in the two preceding chapters, and which is mentioned in almost every treatise
on the subject of music extant, is evidently taken from
Nicomachus, whose relation of this supposed discovery of Pythagoras is hereinbefore given at length.

Cap. xii. De divisione vocum, earumque explana-
tione.—Cap. xiii. Quod infinitatem vocum humana
natura finierit.—Cap. xiv. Quis sit modus audiendi.—
Cap. xv. De ordine theorematum, id est speculati-
onum.—Cap. xvi. De consonantiis proportionum, et
tono et semitonio.—Cap. xvii. In quibis primis
numeris semitonium constet.—Cap. xviii. Diatessaron
a diapente tono distare.—Cap. xix. Diapason quinque
tonis, et duobus semitoniis jungi.—Cap. xx. De ad-
ditione chordarum, earumque nominibus.

The substance of this chapter has already been
given.

Cap. xxi. De generibus cantilenarum.—Cap. xxii. De ordine chordarum nominibusque in tribus generibus.—Cap. xxiii. Quæ sint inter voces in singulis generibus proportiones.

These three chapters give a brief and but a very superficial account of the genera.

Cap. xxiv. Quid sit synaphe.—Cap. xxv. Quid sit diezeuxis.

In these two chapters the difference between the conjunct and disjunct tetrachords is explained.

Cap xxvi. Quibus nominibus nervos appellaverit Albinus.

Albinus is said by Cassiodorus to have been a great man, and to have written a brief discourse on music, which he himself had seen and attentively perused in one of the public libraries at Rome; and Cassiodorus seems to prophecy that some time or other it would be taken away in an incursion of the Barbarians: it has accordingly sustained that fate; for Meibomius, in his preface to Gaudentius, speaks of that manuscript as irrecoverably lost.

Cap. xxvii. Qui nervi quibus syderibus comparentur.

The substance of this chapter is for the most part an extract from Cicero de Repub. lib. VI. and is a declaration of the supposed analogy between the planets and the sounds in the septenary.

Cap. xxviii. Quæ sit natura consonantiarum.—Cap. xxix. Ubi consonantiæ reperiuntur.—Cap. xxx. Quemadmodum Plato dicat fieri consonantias.—Cap. xxxi. Quid contra Platonem Nicomachus sentiat.—Cap. xxxii. Quæ consonantia quam merito præcedat.—Cap. xxxiii. Quo sint modo accipienda quæ dicta sunt.—Cap. xxxiv. Quid sit musicus.

In this, which is a very curious chapter, the author observes that the theoretic branch of every science is more honourable than the practical, for 'that prac-'tice attends like a servant, but reason commands 'like a mistress; and unless the head executes what 'reason dictates, its labour is vain.' He adds, 'the 'speculations of reason borrow no aid of the exe-'cutive part; but contrarywise, the operations of 'the hand without the guidance of reason are of no 'avail;'—that the greatness of the merit and glory 'of reason may be collected from this; corporeal 'artists in music receive their appellations, not from 'the science itself, but rather from the instruments, 'as the citharist from the cithara; the tibicen, or 'player on the pipe, from the tibia; but he only is 'the true musician, who, weighing every thing in 'the balance of reason, professes the science of music, 'not in the slavery of execution, but in the authority 'of speculation. In like manner he says those who 'are employed in the erection of public structures, 'or in the operations of war, receive no praise except 'what is due to industry and obedience; but to 'those by whose skill and conduct buildings are 'erected, or victory achieved, the honours of inscrip-'tions and triumphs are decreed.' He then proceeds to declare that three faculties are employed in the musical art; one which is exercised in the playing on instruments, another that of the poet, which directs the composition of verses, and a third which

judges of the former two; and touching these, and that which he makes the principal question in this chapter, he delivers his opinion thus: 'As to the 'first, the performance of instruments, it is evident 'that the artists obey as servants, and as to poets, 'they are not led to verse so much by reason as by 'a certain instinct which we call genius. But that 'which assumes to itself the power of judging of 'these two, that can examine into rhythmus, songs, 'and their verse, as it is the exercise of reason and 'judgment, is most properly to be accounted music; 'and he only is a musician who has the faculty of 'judging according to speculation and the approved 'ratios of sounds, of the modes, genera, and rhythmi 'of songs, and their various commixtures, and of the 'verses of the poets.'

Lib. II. cap. i. Proemium.—Cap. ii. Quid Pythagoras esse philosophiam constituerit.—Cap. iii. De differentiis quantitatis, et quæ cuique disciplinæ sit deputata.—Cap. iv. De Relatæ quantitatis differentiis.—Cap. v. Cur multiplicitas antecellat.—Cap. vi. Qui sint quadrati numeri deque his speculatio.—Cap. vii. Omnem inequalitatem ex equalitate procedere, ejusque demonstratio.—Cap. viii. Regula quotlibet continuas proportiones superparticulares inveniendi.—Cap. ix. De proportione numerorum qui ab alias metiunter.—Cap. x. Quæ ex multiplicibus et superparticularibus multiplicitates siant.—Cap. xi. Qui superparticulares quos multiplices efficiant.

The nine foregoing chapters contain demonstrations of the five several species of proportion of inequality; of these an explanation may be seen in that extract from Dr. Holder's Treatise on the Natural Grounds and Principles of Harmony, hereinbefore inserted, with a view to facilitate the study of Boetius, and to render this very abstruse part of his work intelligible.

Cap. xii. De arithmetica, geometrica, harmonica, medietate.

The three several kinds of proportionality, that is to say, arithmetical, geometrical, and harmonical, are also explained in the extract from Dr. Holder's book above referred to.

Cap. xiii. De continuis medietatibus et disjunctis.—Cap. xiv. Cur ita appellatæ sint digestæ superius medietates.—Cap. xv. Quemadmodum ab æqualitate supradictæ processerant medietates.—Cap. xvi. Quemadmodum inter duos terminos supradictæ medietates vicissim collocentur.—Cap. xvii. De consonantiarum modo secundum Nicomachum.—Cap. xviii. De ordine consonantiarum sententia Eubulidis et Hippasi.

Two ancient musicians, of whose writings we have nothing now remaining.

Cap. xix. Sententia Nicomachi quæ quibus consonantiis apponantur.—Cap. xx. Quid oporteat præmitti, ut diapason in multiplici genere demonstretur—Cap. xxi. Demonstratio per impossibile, diapason in multiplici genere esse.—Cap. xxii. Demonstratio per impossibile, diapente, diatessaron, et tonum in superparticulari esse.—Cap. xxiii. Demonstratio diapente et diatessaron in maximis superparticularibus collocari.—Cap. xxiv. Diapente in sesquialtera, diatessaron, in sesquitertia esse, tonum in sesquioctava.—Cap. xxv. Diapason ac diapente in tripla proportione esse; bisdiapason in quadrupla.—Cap. xxvi. Diatessaron ac diapason non esse consonantiam, secundum Pythagoricos.

The two last of the foregoing chapters have an immediate connection with each other; in the first it is demonstrated that the diapason and diapente conjoined, making together the consonant interval of a twelfth, are in triple proportion; and that the disdiapason is in quadruple proportion, the ratios whereof are severally 3 to 1 and 4 to 1; but with respect to the diapason and diatessaron conjoined, the ratio whereof is 8 to 3, the interval arising from such conjunction is clearly demonstrated by Boetius to be dissonant: from hence arises an evident discrimination between the diatessaron and the other perfect consonances; for whereas not only they but their replicates are consonant, this of the diatessaron is simply a consonance itself, its replicates being dissonant. It is true that the modern musicians do not reckon the diatessaron in the number of the consonances; and whether it be a concord or a discord has been a matter of controversy; nevertheless it is certain that among the ancients it was always looked upon as a consonance, and that with so good reason, that Lord Verulam* professes to entertain the same opinion; and yet after all, the imperfection which Boetius has pointed out in this chapter, seems to suggest a very good reason for distinguishing between the diatessaron and those other intervals, which, whether taken singly, or in conjunction with the diapason, are consonant.

Cap. xxvii. De semitonio in quibus minimis numeris constet.

The arguments in this chapter are of such a kind, that it behoves every musician to be master of them. The ratios of the limma and apotome have already been demonstrated in those larger numbers which Ptolemy had made choice of for the purpose. In this chapter Boetius gives the ratio of the limma in the smallest numbers in which it can possibly consist, that is to say, 256 to 243; and as this is the most usual designation of the Pythagorean limma, or the interval, which, being added to two sesquioctave tones, completes the interval of a diatessaron, it is a matter of some consequence to know how these numbers are brought out; and this will best be declared in the words of Boetius himself, which are as follow:—

' The semitones seem to be so called not that they
' are exactly the halves of tones, but because they are
' not whole tones. The interval which we now call
' a semitone was by the ancients called a limma, or
' diesis; and it is thus found: if from the sesquitertia proportion, which is the diatessaron, two sesquioctave ratios be taken away, there will be left
' an interval, called a semitone. To prove this, let
' us find out two consecutive tones; but because these, as has been said, are constituted in sesquioctave proportion, we cannot find two such, until
' that multiple from whence they are derived be first

* Nat. Hist. Cent. II. Numb. 107.

' found: let therefore unity be first set down, and
' then 8, which is its octuple: from this we derive
' one multiple; but because we want to find two,
' multiply 8 by 8, to produce 64, which will be a
' second multiple, from which we may bring out two
' sesquioctave ratios; for if 8, which is the eighth
' part of 64, be added thereto, the sum will be 72;
' and if the eighth part of this, which is 9, be added
' to it, the sum will be 81; and these will be the two
' consecutive tones, in their lowest terms. Thus, set
' down 64, 72, 81 :—

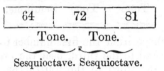

64	72	81

Tone.   Tone.

Sesquioctave. Sesquioctave.

' We are now therefore to seek a sesquitertia to 64;
' but it is found not to have a third part: wherefore,
' all these numbers must be multiplied by 3, and all
' remain in the same proportion as they were in
' before this multiplication by 3. Then three times
' 64 makes 192, to which if we add its third part, 64,
' the sum will be 256; which gives the sesquitertia
' ratio, containing the diatessaron. Then set down
' the two sesquioctaves to 192, in their proper order,
' that is, three times 72, which is 216, and three times
' 81, which is that 243: these two being set between
' the terms of the sesquitertia, the whole will stand
' thus :—

Tone   Tone   Semit.

192	216	243	256

Diatessaron.

' In this disposition of the numbers, the first con-
' stitutes a diatessaron with the last, and the first with
' the second, and also the second with the third, do
' each constitute a tone; therefore the remaining in-
' tervals 243 and 256, is a semitone in its least terms.'

Cap. xxviii. Demonstrationes non esse, 243, ad 256, toni medictatem.

That the limma in the ratio 256 to 243 is less than a true semitone, has been already demonstrated in the course of this work.

Cap. xxix. De majore parte toni in quibus minimis numeris constet.

The apotome has no place in the system, nor can it in any way be considered as a musical interval; in short, it is nothing more than that portion of a sesquioctave tone that remains after the limma has been taken therefrom. For this reason, its ratio is a matter of mere curiosity; and it seems from this chapter of Boetius, that the smallest numbers in which it can be found to consist, are those which Ptolemy makes use of, that is to say, 2187 to 2048.

Cap. xxx. Quibus proportionibus diapente, diapason, constent, et quoniam diapason sex tonis non constet.

The demonstrations contained in this chapter are levelled against the Aristoxeneans, and declare so fully the sentiments of the Pythagoreans, with respect to the measure of the consonant intervals, that they are worthy of particular attention, and cannot be better given than in the words of Boetius himself.

  ‘ The diapente consists of three tones and a semi-
‘ tone, that is, of a diatessaron and a tone : for let the
‘ numbers 192, 216, 243, 256, comprehended in the
‘ above scheme, be set down thus :—

DIATESSARON.

192	216	243	256

Tone   Tone   Semitone.

  ‘ In this disposition, the first number to the second and the second to the third, bear the proportions of ‘ tones, and the third to the fourth that of a lesser ‘ semitone, has been shown above. If then for the ‘ purpose of ascertaining the contents of the diapente, ‘ 32 be added to 256, the sum will be 288, which is ‘ another sesquioctave tone ; for 32 is the eighth part ‘ of 256, and 256 to 288, is 8 to 9. The extreme ‘ numbers will then be 192 to 288, which is sesqui-
‘ altera, the ratio of the diapente :—

192	288

DIAPENTE
Sesquialtera.

  ‘ Finally, by comparing the first number with the ‘ second, the second with the third, and the fourth ‘ with the fifth, i. e., 288, it will plainly appear, first, ‘ that in the diapente are three tones, and a lesser ‘ semitone. If then the diatessaron consists of two ‘ tones and a lesser semitone, and the diapente of three ‘ tones and a lesser semitone ; and if the diatessaron ‘ and diapente make up together the diapason, it will ‘ follow, that in the diapason are five tones and two ‘ lesser semitones, which joined together do not make ‘ up a full and complete tone, and therefore that the ‘ diapason does not consist of six tones, as Aristoxenus ‘ maintained, which also will evidently appear when

‘ these intervals are properly disposed in numbers.
‘ For let six octuples be thus produced :—

     1, 8, 64, 512, 4096, 32768, 262144.

‘ From this last number six tones, constituted in ‘ sesquioctave proportion, may be set down, with the ‘ octuple terms and their several eighth parts, in the ‘ order following :—

Octuples.

     1, 8, 64, 512, 4096, 32768, 262144.

Sesquioctaves.	Eighth parts.
262144	32768
294912	36864
331776	41472
373248	46656
419904	52488
472392	59049
531441	

  ‘ The nature of the above disposition is this : the ‘ first line contains the octuple numbers ; and the ‘ sesquioctave proportions in the first column are de-
‘ duced from the last of them. The numbers con-
‘ tained in the second column are the eighth parts of ‘ those to which they are respectively opposite ; and ‘ if each of these be added to the number against it, ‘ the sum will be the number of the next sesquioctave, ‘ in succession. Thus, if to the number 262144 ‘ 32768 be added, the sum will be 294912 ; and the ‘ rest are found in the same manner. And were the ‘ last number, 531441, duple to the first, 262144, ‘ then would the diapason truly consist of six tones ; ‘ but here it is found to be more ; for the duple of ‘ 292144 is 524288, and the number of the sixth tone ‘ is 531441. Hence it appears, that the consonant ‘ diapason is less than six tones ; and the excess of ‘ the six tones above the diapason is called a comma, ‘ which in its lowest terms is 52428 to 531441 :—

7153	
524288	531441

COMMA, or the inter-
val by which six tones
exceed a diapason. *

Six Octuples.

1	8	64	512	4096	32768	262144
	9	72	576	4608	36864	294912
			648	5184	41472	331776
			729	5832	46656	373248
				6561	52488	419904
					59049	472392
						531441

All the diagonals are ninefold.

The numbers in the up-
per row make six octuples,
and those placed under
them are sesquioctaves to
each other in succession.

In the third book Boetius continues his controversy with the Aristoxeneans, who, as they assert, that the diatessaron contains two tones and an half, and the diapente three tones and an half, must be supposed to believe that the tone is capable of a division into two equal parts, contrary to that maxim of Euclid, that ‘ inter superparticulare non cadit medium,’ a superparticular ration cannot have a mediety. And Boe-

tius, in the first chapter of his third book, with great clearness and precision demonstrates, that no such division of the tone can be made, as that which Aristoxenus and his followers contend for.

Lib. III. cap. i. Adversus Aristoxenum demonstratio,

* This is called the Pythagorean comma, and is taken notice of by Mersennus, vide Harmonicor. de Dissonantiis, pag. 88. It is less than that of 81 to 80, called the comma majus, or schisma, and which is the difference between the greater and lesser tone.

superparticularem proportionem dividi in æqua non posse, atque ideo nec tonum.—Cap. ii. Ex sesquitertia proportione sublatis duobus tonis, toni dimidium non relinqui.—Cap. iii. Adversum Aristoxenum demonstrationes, diatessaron consonantiam ex duobus tonis et semitonio non constare, nec diapason sex tonis.—Cap. iv. Diapason consonantiam à sex tonis commate excedi, et qui sit minimus numerus commatis.—Cap. v. Quemadmodum Philolaus, tonum dividat.

Pythagoras found out the tone by the difference of a fourth and fifth, subtracting one from the other; Philolaus, who was of his school, proceeded farther, and effected a division of the tone into commas. The manner of his doing it is thus related by Boetius:—

' Philolaus the Pythagorean tried to divide the tone, ' by taking the original of the tone from that number ' which among the Pythagoreans was esteemed very ' honourable : for as the number 3 is the first uneven ' number, that multiplied by 3 will give 9, which ' being multiplied by 3 will necessarily produce 27, ' which is distant from the number 24 by a tone, and ' preserves the same difference of 3; for 3 is the ' eighth part of 24, and being added thereto com- ' pletes the cube of the number 3, viz., 27. Philolaus ' therefore divided this into two parts; one whereof ' was greater than the half, which he called the apo- ' tome; and the other less, which he termed the ' diesis, and those that came after him denominated ' a lesser semitone; and their difference he termed ' a comma. The diesis he supposes to consist of 13 ' unities, because he supposed that to be the difference ' between 243 and 256, and because the number 13 ' consisted of 9, 3, and unity; which unity he con- ' sidered as a punctum. 3 he considered as the first ' uneven number, and 9 as the first uneven square : ' for this reason, when he fixed the diesis or semitone ' at 13, he made the remaining part of the number 27, ' containing 14 unities to be the apotome. But be- ' cause unity is the difference between 13 and 14, he ' imagined unity ought to be assigned to the place of ' the comma; but the whole tone he made to be 27 ' unities, that number being the difference between ' 216 and 243, which are distant from each other by ' a tone.'

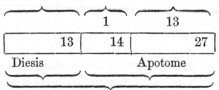

Cap. vi. Tonum ex duobus semitoniis ac commate constare.—Cap. vii. Demonstratio, tonum duobus semitoniis commate distare. — Cap. viii. De minoribus semitonii intervallis. — Cap. ix. De toni partibus per consonantias sumendis.—Cap. x. Regula sumendi semitonii.—Cap. xi. Demonstratio Archytæ, superparticularem in equa dividi non posse; ejusque reprehensio.

It seems by this chapter, that this Archytas, who it is supposed was he of Tarentum, mentioned in the account herein before given of the genera and their

species, was a Pythagorean. He it seems had undertaken to demonstrate that proposition of the Pythagorean school, that a superparticular ratio cannot be divided into two equally; but Boetius says he has done it in a loose manner, and for this he reprehends him. It may be inferred from this chapter, that some of the writings of Archytas on music were in being in the time of Boetius; but that there are none now remaining is agreed by all.

Cap. xii. In qua numerorum proportione sit comma, et quoniam in ea quæ major sit quam 75 ad 74 minor quam, 74 ad 73.—Cap. xiii. Quod semitonium minus majus quidem sit quam 20 ad 19, minus quam 19½ ad 18½.—Cap. xiv. Semitonium minus, majus quidem esse tribus comatibus; minus vero quatuor. — Cap. xv. Apotome majorem esse quam 4 commata, minorem quam 5. Tonem majorem quam 8, minorem quam 9.—Cap. xvi. Superius dictorum per numeros demonstratio.

Lib. IV. cap. i. Vocum differentias in quantitate consistere.—Cap. ii. Diversæ de intervallis speculationes.

This, as its title imports, is a chapter of a miscellaneous kind. Among other things, it contains a demonstration somewhat different from that which he had given before, that six sesquioctave tones are greater than a duple interval. That they are so will appear upon a bare inspection of the following diagram :—

Six sesquioctave proportions greater than a duple interval.						
Sesqui-octave.	Sesqui-octave.	Sesqui-octave.	Sesqui-octave.	Sesqui-octave.	Sesqui-octave.	Sesqui-octave.
A	B	C	D	E	G	K
262144.	294912.	331776.	373248.	419904.	472392.	531441.

The number A 262144. is half the underwritten number; and therefore the diapason is deficient of the number K by 7153.

The duple interval reaches to 524288.

Cap. iii. Musicarum per Græcus ac Latinas literas notarum nuncupatio.

In this chapter are contained some of the principal characters used by the Greeks in their musical notation. It seems, that at the time when Glareanus published his edition of Boetius, they had been corrupted, which, considering they were arbitrary, or at best that they were the letters of the Greek alphabet reduced to a state of deformity, is not to be wondered at. Meibomius had the good fortune to get intelligence of an ancient manuscript here in England, in which this chapter was found, in a state of great purity. He had interest enough with Mr. Selden to get him to collate his own by it : and the whole is very correctly published, and prefixed to the Isagoge of Alypius, in his edition of the ancient musical authors.

Cap. iv. Monochordi regularis partitio in genere diatonico.—Cap. v. Monochordi netarum hyperboleon per tria genera partitio.—Cap. vi. Ratio superius digestæ descriptionis.—Cap. vii. Monochordi netarum diezeugmenon per tria genera partitio.—Cap. viii. Monochordi netarum synemmenon per tria genera partitio.—Cap. ix. Monochordi meson per tria genera partitio. — Cap. x. Monochordi hypaton per tria genera partitio, et totius dispositio descriptionis.—Cap. xi. Ratio superius dispositæ descriptionis.—Cap. xii. De stantibus et mobilibus vocibus. —Cap. xiii. De consonantiarum speciebus.—Cap. xiv. De modorum exordiis, in quo dispositio notarum per singulos modos ac voces.—Cap. xv. Descriptio continens modorum ordinem ac differentias.— Cap. xvi. Superius dispositæ modorum descriptiones. —Cap. xvii. Ratio superius dispositæ modorum descriptionis.—Cap. xviii. Quemadmodum indubitanter musicæ consonantiæ aure dijudicari possint.

Lib. V. Proemium.

In this Boetius gives the form of the monochord, little differing from that of Ptolemy and Porphyry herein before described.

Cap. i. De vi harmonicæ, et quæ sint ejus instrumenta judicii, et quo nam usque sensibus oporteat credi.—Cap. ii. Quid sit harmonica regula, vel quam intentionem harmonici Pythagorici, vel Aristoxenus, vel Ptolemæus esse dixere.—Cap. iii. In quo Aristoxenus, vel Pythagorici, vel Ptolemæus gravitatem atque acumen constare posuerint.—Cap. iv. De sonorum differentiis Ptolemæi sententia.—Cap. v. Quæ voces enharmoniæ sunt aptæ.—Cap. vi. Quem numerum proportionum Pythagorici statuunt.—Cap. vii. Quod reprehendat Ptolemæus Pythagoricos in numero proportionum. — Cap. viii. Demonstratio secundum Ptolemæum diapason et diatessaron consonantiæ.— Cap. ix. Quæ sit proprietas diapason consonantiæ.— Cap. x. Quibus modis Ptolemæus consonantias statuat. —Cap. xi. Quæ sunt equisonæ, vel quæ consonæ, vel quæ emmelis. — Cap. xii. Quemadmodum Aristoxenus intervallum consideret.—Cap. xiii. Descriptio octochordi, qua ostenditur diapason consonantiam minorum esse sex tonis. — Cap. xiv. Diatessaron consonantiam tetrachordo contineri.—Cap. xv. Quomodo Aristoxenus vel tonum dividat vel genera ejusque divisionis dispositio. — Cap. xvi. Quomodo Archytas tetrachordo dividat, eorumque descriptio. —Cap. xvii. Quemadmodum Ptolemæus et Aristoxeni et Archytæ, tetrachordorum divisiones reprehendat.—Cap. xviii. Quemadmodum tetrachordorum divisionem fieri dicat oportere.

CHAP. XXVI.

From the foregoing extracts a judgment may be formed, not only of the work from which they are made, but also of the manner in which the ancients, more especially the followers of Pythagoras, thought of music. Well might they deem it a subject of philosophical speculation, when such abstruse reasoning was employed about it. To speak of Boetius in particular, it is clear that he was upon the whole a Pythagorean, though he has not spared to detect many of the errors imputed to that sect; and his work is so truly theoretic, that in reading him we never think of practice: the mention of instruments, nor of the voice, as employed in singing, never occurs; no allusions to the music of his time, but all abstracted speculation, tending doubtless to the per-

fection of the art, but seemingly little connected with it. Here then the twofold nature of music is apparent: it has its foundation in number and proportion; like geometry, it affords that kind of pleasure to the mind which results from the contemplation of order, of regularity, of truth, the love whereof is connatural with human nature; like that too, its principles are applicable to use and practice. View it in another light, and if it be possible, consider music as mechanical, as an arbitrary constitution, as having no foundation in reason: but how exquisite is the pleasure it affords! how subservient are the passions to its influence! and how much is the wisdom and goodness of God manifested in that relation which, in the case of music, he has established between the cause and the effect!

That Boetius is an obscure writer must be allowed; the very terms used by him, and his names for the proportions, though they are the common language of the ancient arithmeticians, are difficult to be understood at this time. Guido, who lived about five hundred years after him, scruples not to say, that 'his work is fit only for philosophers.' It was, nevertheless, held in great estimation for many centuries, and to this its reputation many causes co-operated; to which may be added that the Greek language was little understood, even by the learned, for a much longer period than that above mentioned; and to those few that were masters of it, all that treasure of musical erudition contained in the writings of Aristoxenus, Euclid, Nicomachus, Ptolemy, and the rest of the Greek harmonicians, was inaccessible. So late as the time of our queen Elizabeth, it was doubted whether the writings of some of them were any where extant in the world.*

For these reasons, we are not to wonder that the Treatise de Musica of Boetius was for many ages looked upon as the grand repository of harmonical science.. To go no farther than our own country for proofs, the writings of all who treated on the subject before the beginning of the fourteenth century, and whose names are preserved in the collections of Leland, Bale, Pits, and Tanner, are but so many commentaries on him: nay, an admission to the first degree in music, in the universities of Oxford and Cambridge, was but a kind of manuduction to the study of his writings;† and in the latter the exercise for a doctor's degree was generally a lecture on Boetius.‡

And, to come nearer to our own times, Salinas and Zarlino have pursued the same train of reasoning that Boetius first introduced. If it be asked how has this contributed to the improvement of music, the answer is not easy. if the question refers to the practice of it; since what Mersennus and others have said is very true, that in the division of sounds we are determined wholly by the ear, and not by ratios; and therefore the makers and tuners of instruments are in

---

* Morley, in the Peroratio to his Introduction.

† Wood, in the Fasti. Oxon. pag. 58, says, of bachelors of music, that they were such who were admitted to the reading any of the musical books of Boetius; and in his account of John Mendus, a secular priest, who, anno 1535, supplicated for that decree. he says, he obtained it with the privilege of reading Boetius. Fasti. Oxon. pag. 56.

‡ Athen. Oxon. passim.

fact, though they know it not, Aristoxeneans; but if by Music we are to understand the Theory of the science, this method of treating it has contributed greatly to its improvement. This is enough to satisfy such as are aware of the importance of theory in every science : those whose minds are too illiberal to conceive any thing beyond practice and mere manual operation or energy, might perhaps demand, What has theory, what have the ratios of numbers to do with an art, the end whereof is to move the passions, and not convince the understanding ; were these considered, or even understood, by the ablest professors of the science ; did Palestrina, Stradella, did Corelli adjust their harmonies by the monochord, or consult Euclid or Ptolemy when they composed respectively their motets, madrigals, and concertos ; or is it necessary in the performance of them that the singers, or any of those who perform on an instrument, the tuning whereof is not adjusted to their hands, perpetually bear in mind the true harmonic canon, and be aware of the difference between the greater and lesser tone, and the greater and lesser semitone ; and that what in common practice is called a semitone, is in fact an interval in the ratio of 256 to 243, and unless so prolated is a dissonance ? And after all it may perhaps be argued that this kind of knowledge adds nothing to the pleasure we receive from music.

To such as are disposed to reason in this manner it may be said, We all know that the dog who treads the spit-wheel ; or, to go higher, the labourer that drives a wedge, or adds the strength of his arms to a lever, are ignorant of all but the effects of their labour ; but we also know that the ignorance of the brute and of the uninstructed rational in this respect afford no reason why others are to remain ignorant too ; much less does it prove it fruitless and vain for men of a philosophical and liberal turn of mind to attempt an investigation of the principles upon which these machines act.*

Farther, as a motive to the study of the ratios and coincidences of harmonic intervals, it may be said that the noblest of our faculties are exercised in it ; and that the pleasure arising from the contemplation of that truth and certainty which are found in them, is little inferior to what we receive from hearing the most excellent music. And to this purpose the learned and ingenious Dr. Holder expresses himself in a passage which is inserted in a note subjoined.†

* The reader will find this argument much better enforced by the learned and ingenious author of a treatise intitled Hermes or a Philosophical Inquiry concerning Universal Grammar. Here it was necessary to vary it, in order to adapt it to the present subject ; but the author applies it to that of speech ; the whole passage is very beautiful, and is as follows :—' Methinks I hear some objector, demanding with an air of ' pleasantry and ridicule—Is there no speaking then without all this ' trouble ? Do we not talk every one of us, as well unlearned as learned, ' as well poor peasants as profound philosophers ? We may answer by ' interrogating on our part—Do not those same poor peasants use the ' lever and the wedge, and many other instruments, with much habitual ' readiness ? And yet have they any conception of those geometrical ' principles from which those machines derive their efficacy and force ? ' And is the ignorance of these peasants a reason for others to remain ' ignorant, or to render the subject a less becoming enquiry ? Think of ' animals and vegetables that occur every day—of time, of place, and of ' motion—of light, of colours, and of gravitation—of our senses and intellects by which we perceive every thing else—That they are, we all ' know and are perfectly satisfied—What they are, is a subject of much ' obscurity and doubt ; were we to reject this last question because we ' are certain of the first, we should banish all philosophy at once out of ' the world.' Hermes, pag. 293.

† ' And in searching, stating, and comparing the rations of those in-

After all, we ought not to estimate the works of learned men by the consideration of their immediate utility : to investigate is one thing ; to apply, another ; and the love of science includes in it a degree of enthusiasm, which whoever is without, will want the strongest motive to emulation and improvement that the mind is susceptible of. Is it to be conceived that those who are employed in mathematical researches attend to the consequences of their own discoveries, or that their pursuits are not extended beyond the prospect of bare utility ? In short, no considerable progress, no improvement in any science can be expected, unless it be beloved for its own sake : as well might we expect the continuation of our species from principles of reason and duty, abstracted from that passion which holds the animal world in subjection, and to which human nature itself owes its existence.‡

Taking this for granted, the merit of Boetius will appear to consist in the having communicated to the world such a knowledge of the fundamental principles of the ancient music, as is absolutely necessary to the right understanding even of our own system : and this too at a period when there was little or no ground to hope for any other intelligence, and therefore Morley has done him but justice in the eulogium which he has given of him in the following words :—
' Boetius being by birth noble, and most excellent ' well versed in divinity, philosophy, law, mathematicks, poetry, and matters of estate, did notwithstanding write more of musick than of all the other ' mathematical sciences, so that it may be justly said, ' that if it had not beene for him the knowledge of ' musicke had not yet come into our westerne part of ' the world. The Greek tongue lying as it were dead

' tervals of sounds by which harmony is made, there is found so much ' variety and certainty, and facility of calculation, that the contemplation ' of them may seem not much less delightful than the very hearing the ' good music itself, which springs from this fountain ; and those who ' have already an affection for music cannot but find it improved and ' much enhanced by this pleasant and recreating chase, as I may call it, ' in the large field of harmonic rations and proportion, where they will ' find, to their great pleasure and satisfaction, the hidden causes of harmony (hidden to most, even to practitioners themselves) so amply ' discovered and laid plain before them.' Natural Grounds and Principles of Harmony, chap. v.

‡ For the farther illustration of this proposition, viz., that knowledge is an object worthy to be pursued for its own sake, we must be indebted to the author above-cited, who to this purpose thus expresses himself:—
' But a graver objector now accosts us. What (says he) is the utility, ' whence the profit, where the gain ? Every science whatever (we may ' answer) has its use. Arithmetic is excellent for gauging of liquors ; ' geometry for measuring of estates ; astronomy for making of almanacks ; and grammar perhaps for drawing of bonds and conveyances.
' Thus much for the sordid—If the liberal ask for something better than ' this, we may answer, and assure them from the best authorities, that ' every exercise of the mind upon theorems of science, like generous and ' manly exercise of the body, tends to call forth and strengthen nature's ' original vigour. Be the subject itself immediately lucrative or not, the ' nerves of reason are braced by the mere employ, and we become abler ' actors in the drama of life, whether our part be of the busier, or of the ' sedater kind.
' Perhaps too there is a pleasure even in science itself, distinct from ' any end to which it may be farther conducive. Are not health and ' strength of body desirable for their own sakes, though we happen not to ' be fated either for porters or draymen ? And have not health and ' strength of mind their intrinsic worth also, though not condemned to ' the low drudgery of sordid emolument ? Why should there not be a ' good (could we have the grace to recognize it) in the mere energy of our ' intellect, as much as in energies of lower degree ? The sportsman believes there is good in his chase ; the man of gaiety, in his intrigue ; ' even the glutton in his meal. We may justly ask of these, why they ' pursue such things ; but if they answer they pursue them because they ' are good, 'twould be folly to ask them farther, why they pursue what is ' good. It might well in such case be replied on their behalf (how ' strange soever it may at first appear) that if there was not something ' good, which was in no respect useful, even things useful themselves could ' not possibly have existence. For this is in fact no more than to assert, ' that some things are ends, some things are means ; and that if there ' were no ends, there could be of course no means.' Hermes, pag. 294.

' under the barbarisme of the Gothes and Hunnes, and
' musicke buried in the bowels of the Greeke works
' of Ptolemæus and Aristoxenus, the one of which
' as yet hath never come to light, but lies in written
' copies in some bibliothekes of Italy, the other hath
' been set out in print ; but the copies are every
' where so scant and hard to come by, that many
' doubt if he have been set out or no.' *

Other improvements were reserved for a more enlightened age, when the study of physics began to be
cultivated, when the hypotheses of the ancients were
brought to the test of experiment ; and the doctrine
of pendulums became another medium for demonstrating the truth of those ratios which the ancient
harmonicians had investigated merely by the power
of numbers.

To the reasons above adduced in favour of the
writings of Boetius, another may be added, which
every learned reader will acquiesce in, namely, that
he was the last of the Latin writers whose works have
any pretence to purity, or to entitle them to the
epithet of classical.

It must however be confessed that the treatise De
Musica of Boetius is but part of a much larger discourse which he intended on that subject : most
authors speak of it as of a fragment, and the very
abrupt manner in which it concludes shews that he
had not put the finishing hand to it. The whole of
the five books extant are little more than an investigation of the ratio of the consonances, the nature
of the several kinds of proportionality, and a declaration of the opinions of the several sects with
respect to the division of the monochord and the
general laws of harmony : these are, it is true, the
foundations of the science, but there remained a great
deal more to be said in order to render this work of
Boetius complete ; and that it was his design to
make it so, there is not the least reason to doubt.

The desiderata of the ancient music seem to be the
genera and the modes, and to these may be added the
measure of sounds in respect of their duration, or, in
other words, the laws of metre. It is to be observed
that music was originally vocal, and in that species
of it the voice was employed, not in the bare utterance
of inarticulate sounds, but of poetry, to the words
whereof correspondent sounds in an harmonical ratio
were adopted, and therefore the duration of those
sounds might be, and probably was determined by
the measure of the verse, yet both were subject to
metrical laws, which had been largely discussed
before the time of Boetius, and these it became a
writer like him to have reduced to some standard.

Had Boetius lived to complete his work, it is
more than probable that he would have entered into
a discussion of the modes of the ancients, and not left
it a question, as it is at this day, whether they regarded only the situation of the final or dominant
note in respect of the scale, or whether they consisted
in the different position of the tones and semitones in
the system of a diapason. For the same reason we
may conclude that, had not his untimely death prevented it, Boetius would have treated very largely

* See the Peroratio to his Introduction, towards the end.

on the ecclesiastical tones : he was a Christian, and,
though not an enthusiast, a devout man ; music had
been introduced into the church-service for above a
century before the time when he lived ; St. Ambrose
had established the chant which is distinguished by
his name, and the ecclesiastical tones, then but four
in number, were evidently derived from the modes of
the ancients.

These are but conjectures, and may perhaps be
thought to include rather what was to be wished than
expected from a writer of so philosophical a turn as
Boetius ; we have nevertheless great reason to lament
his silence in these particulars, and must impute the
present darkness in which the science is unhappily
involved, to the want of that information which he of
all men of his time seems to have been the most able
to communicate.

MAGNUS AURELIUS CASSIODORUS, senator, a christian, born at Brutium, on the confines of Calabria,
flourished about the middle of the sixth century. He
had a very liberal education considering the growing
barbarism of the age he lived in, and by his wisdom,
learning, and eloquence, recommended himself to
the protection of the Gothic kings Theodoric and
Athalaric, Amalasuentha the daughter of the former,
Theodohadus her husband, and Vitiges his successor.
Theodoric appointed him to the government of
Sicily, in which province he gave such proofs of his
abilities, that in the year 490 he made him his chancellor, and admitted him to his councils. After
having filled several important and honourable posts
in the state, he was advanced to the consulate, the
duties of which office he discharged without any
colleague in the year 514. He was continued in the
same degree of confidence and favour by Athalaric,
who succeeded Theodoric about the year 526 ; but in
the year 537, being dismissed from all his employments by Vitiges, he betook himself to a religious
life. Trithemius says he became a monk, and afterwards abbot of the monastery of Ravenna ; after
which it seems he retired to the monastery of Viviers,
in the extreme parts of Calabria, which he had built
and endowed himself. In his retirement from the
business of the world he led the life of a scholar, a
philosopher, and a Christian, amusing himself at
intervals in the invention and framing of mechanical
curiosities, such as sun-dials, water hour-glasses, perpetual lamps, &c. He collected a very noble and
curious library, and wrote many books himself, particularly Commentaries on the Psalms, Canticles, the
Acts of the Apostles, the Epistles of St. Paul, and
the Apocalypse, and a Chronology : farther he framed,
or drew into one body, the tripartite history of
Socrates, Sozomen, and Theodoret, translated by
Epiphanius, the scholastic. He wrote also Institutionem Divinarum Lectionum, in two books, which
Du Pin says abounds with fine remarks on the Holy
Scriptures, and a treatise De Ratione Animæ, which
the same writer also highly commends. There are
extant of his, twelve books of Letters, ten of which
are written in the names of Theodoric and Athalaric,
he being it seems secretary to them both ; the other
two are in his own name, and they all abound with a

variety of curious and interesting particulars. He was also the author of a treatise De septem Disciplinis, or of the Arts of Grammar, Rhetoric, Logic, Arithmetic, Geometry, Music, and Astronomy ; * what he says of music is contained in one chapter or section of four quarto pages ; in this he is very brief, referring very often to Gaudentius, Censorinus, and other writers. His general division of music is into three parts, harmonic, rhythmic, and metric. His division of instrumental music is also into three parts, namely, percussional, tensile, and inflatile, agreeing in this respect with other writers of the best authority.

One thing worthy of remark in the treatise of Cassiodorus De Musica is, that he makes the consonances to be six, namely, the diatessaron, diapente, diapason, diapason and diatessaron, or eleventh, diapason and diapente, or twelfth, and, lastly, the disdiapason ; in which he manifestly differs from Boetius, whom he must have known and been intimate with, for Boetius has bestowed a whole chapter in demonstrating that the diapason cum diatessaron is not a consonant but a dissonant. Cassiodorus makes the number of the modes, or, as he calls them the tones, to be fifteen ; from which circumstance, as also because he here prefers the word Tone to Mode, it may be concluded that he writes after Martianus Capella.

Cassiodorus died at his monastery of Viviers, about the year 560, aged above ninety. Father Simon has given a very high character of his theological writings ; they, together with his other works, have been several times printed, but the best edition of them is that of Rohan, in the year 1679, in two volumes folio, with the notes and dissertations of Johannes Garetius, a Benedictine monk.†

The several improvements of music hereinbefore

enumerated, regarded chiefly the theory of the science, those that followed were for the most part confined to practice : among the latter none have a greater title to our attention than those made about the end of the sixth century, by St. Gregory the Great, the first pope of that name, a man not more remarkable for his virtues than for his learning and profound skill in the science of music.

The first improvement of music made by this father consisted in the invention of that kind of notation by the Roman letters, which is used at this day. It is true that before his time the use of the Greek characters had been rejected ; and as the enarmonic and chromatic genera, with all the various species of the latter, had given way to the diatonic genus, the first fifteen letters of the Roman alphabet had even before the time of Boetius been found sufficient to denote all the several sounds in the perfect system ; and accordingly we find in his treatise De Musica all the sounds from Proslambanomenos to Nete hyperboleon characterised by the Roman letters, from A to P inclusive ; but Gregory reflecting that the sounds after Lychanos meson were but a repetition of those before it, and that every septenary in progression was precisely the same, reduced the number of letters to seven, which were A, B, C, D, E, F, G ; but, to distinguish the second septenary from the first, the second was denoted by the small, and not the capital, Roman letters ; and when it became necessary to extend the system farther, the small letters were doubled thus, aa, bb, cc, dd, ee, ff, gg.

But the encreasing the number of tones from four to eight, and the institution of what is called the Gregorian Chant, or plain song, is the improvement for which of all others this father is most celebrated. It has already been mentioned that St. Ambrose when he introduced singing into the church-service, selected from the ancient modes four, which he appropriated to the several offices : farther it is to be observed, that to these modes the appellation of Tones was given, probably on the authority of Martianus Capella, who, as Sir Henry Spelman remarks, was the first that substituted the term Tones in the room of Modes. But we are much at a loss to discover more of the nature of the tones instituted by St. Ambrose, than that they consisted in certain progressions, corresponding with different species of the diapason ; and that under some kind of regulation, of which we are now ignorant, the divine offices were alternately chanted, and this by the express institution of St. Ambrose himself, who all agree was the first that introduced the practice of alternate or antiphonal singing, at least into the western church ; but it was such a kind of recitation as in his own opinion came nearer to the tone of reading than singing.‡

Cardinal Bona§ cites Theodoret, lib. IV. to prove that the method of singing introduced by St. Ambrose was alternate ; and proceeds to relate that as the vigour of the clerical discipline, and the majesty of

* This arrangement of the liberal sciences had been made before the time of Cassiodorus, as appears by the fable De Nuptiis Philologiæ et Mercurii of Martianus Capella, which contains a seperate discourse on each of them. This division comprehends both the trivium and the quadrivium described in a preceding page. Mosheim censures the professors, or scholastics, as they were called, of that day, for teaching the sciences in a barbarous and illiberal manner.
'The whole circle of sciences was composed of what they called the ' seven liberal arts, viz., grammar, rhetoric, logic, arithmetic, music, ' geometry, and astronomy ; the three former of which they distinguished ' by the title of trivium, and the four latter by that of quadrivium. ' Nothing can be conceived more wretchedly barbarous than the manner ' in which these sciences were taught, as we may easily perceive from ' Alcuin's treatise concerning them ; and the dissertations of St. Augustin ' on the same subject, which were in the highest repute at this time. ' In the greatest part of the schools the public teachers ventured no ' farther than the trivium, and confined their instructions to grammar, ' rhetoric, and logic ; they, however, who, after passing the trivium, and ' also the quadrivium were desirous of rising yet higher in their literary ' pursuits, were exhorted to apply themselves to the study of Cassiodorus ' and Boethius, as if the progress of human knowledge was bounded by ' the discoveries of those two learned writers.' Ecclesiast. Hist. Cent. VIII. part ii. cap. 1.

† Upon the writings of the Latins the remark is obvious, that they added nothing to musical science ; and indeed their inferiority to the Greeks, both in philosophy and the more elegant arts, seems to be allowed by the best judges of ancient literature.
Indeed in their practice of music they seem to have somewhat improved on that of their predecessors, as is evident from Vitruvius's description of the hydraulic organ, an instrument which Sidonius Apollinaris takes notice of in one of his epistles, where he speaks of the amusements of Theodoric, and particularly adds that he was wont to be entertained with the music of the hydraulic organ while he sat at dinner : and it is in the history of the period in which Boetius and Cassiodorus flourished, that we meet with the first intimation of such a profession as that of a teacher of music. The following is an epitaph in the epistles of the same Sidonius Apollinaris on one of this profession :—

Orator Dialecticus Poeta
Tractator, Geometra, Musicus
Psalmorum Modulator, Phonascus
Instructas docuit sonare classes.   Lib. IV. pag. 143.

‡ Vossius De Scientiis mathematicis, cap. xxi. § II.
§ De Rebus Liturgicis.

the Christian religion eminently shone forth in the ecclesiastical song, the Roman pontiffs and the bishops of other churches took care that the clerks from their tender years should learn the rudiments of singing under proper masters ; and that accordingly a music-school was instituted at Rome by pope Hilary, or, as others contend, by Gregory the Great, to whom also we are indebted for restoring the ecclesiastical song to a better form ; for though the practice of singing was from the very foundation of the Christian church used at Rome, yet are we ignorant of what kind the ecclesiastical modes were, before the time of Gregory, or what was the discipline of the singers. In fact the whole service seems to have been of a very irregular kind, for we are told that in the primitive church the people sang each as his inclination led him, with hardly any other restriction than that what they sang should be to the praise of God. Indeed some certain offices, such as the Lord's Prayer and the Apostles' Creed, had been used in the church-service almost from the first establishment of Christianity ;* but these were too few in number to prevent the introduction of hymns and spiritual songs at the pleasure of the heresiarchs, who began to be very numerous about the middle of the sixth century, and that to a degree which called aloud for reformation. The evil increasing, the emperor Theodosius requested the then pope, Damasus, to frame such a service as should consist with the solemnity and decency of divine worship; the pope readily assented, and employed for this purpose a presbyter named Hieronymus, a man of learning, gravity, and discretion, who formed a new ritual, into which he introduced the Epistles, Gospels, and the Psalms,† with the Gloria Patri and Alleluiah ; and these, together with certain hymns which he thought proper to retain, made up the whole of the service.

It is very doubtful whether any thing like an antiphonary existed at this time, or indeed whether St. Ambrose did any thing more than institute the tones, leaving it to the singers, under the regulations thereby prescribed, to adapt such musical sounds to the several offices as they should from time to time think fit ; and to this the confusion that had arisen in the church-service was in a great measure owing. What methods were taken by Gregory to remedy this evil will be related in the following account of him.

CHAP. XXVII.

GREGORY THE FIRST, surnamed the Great, was born at Rome of an illustrious family, about the year 550. He studied with great success, and his quality and merit so recommended him, that the emperor Justin the younger made him prefect of that city. After he had held this high office for some time, he discovered that it made him too fond of the world, and thereupon he retired to a convent which he had founded in his own house at Rome; but he was soon called out of this retirement by pope Pelagius II., who, in

582, made him one of his deacons, and sent him to Constantinople, there to reside in the court of the emperor Tiberius, in quality of his nuncio or surrogate, though his immediate business there was to solicit succours against the Lombards. Upon the death of Tiberius in 586, Gregory returned to Rome, and was there employed as secretary to Pelagius ; but at length he obtained of him leave to retire again to his monastery, the government whereof he had formerly bestowed on an ecclesiastic named Valentius, whom for his great merit he had taken from a monastery in the country. Here he thought to indulge himself in the pleasures of a studious and contemplative life, but was soon drawn from his retirement by a contagious disease, which at that time raged with such violence, that eight hundred persons died of it in one hour.‡ To avert this calamity Gregory quitted his retreat, came forth into the city, and instituted litanies § and a sevenfold procession, consisting of several orders of the people, upon whose arrival at the great church it is said the distemper ceased. Of this disease Pelagius himself died, and by the joint suffrage of the clergy, the senate, and people of Rome, Gregory was chosen for his successor ; but he was so little disposed to accept this dignity, that he got himself secretly conveyed out of the city in a basket, thereby deceiving the guards that were set at the gates to hinder his escape, and went and hid himself in a cave in the middle of a wood ; but being discovered, he was prevailed on to return, and was consecrated on the third of September, 590, and was the first of the popes that used the style 'Servus servorum Dei.' He was of a very infirm and weakly constitution, but had a vigorous mind, and discharged the duties of his station with equanimity and firmness. He possessed a great share of learning, and was so well skilled in the tempers and dispositions of mankind, that he made even the private interests and ambitious views of princes subservient to the ends of religion. One of the greatest events which by his prudence and good management he brought about during his pontificate, was the conversion of the English to Christianity, which, as related by Bede, makes one of the prettiest stories in our history. But what gives him a title to a place in this work is his having effected a reformation in the music of the church.‖

---

‡ One of the symptoms of this disease was a violent sneezing, which was looked upon as mortal, and upon this occasion gave rise to the ejaculation 'God bless you !' in favour of such as were suddenly taken with that convulsion. Isaacson's Chronology, anno. 590.

§ *The word Litany, taken in its larger sense, includes public prayers of all kinds, but in its limited signification it denotes that kind of prayer attended with Rogations which was formerly used in the church to deprecate impending judgments. Of these Mamercus, bishop of Vienna about the year 450, and Sidonius bishop of Averna, are said to have been the institutors, but some writers refer the first use of them to the time of St. Basil. The Litany instituted by St. Gregory was that named Litania Septiformis, which, as Hooker asserts, contains the flower of the former litanies, and with this, the Litany now used in our church very nearly corresponds. Confer. Bingh. Antiq. Book XIII, chap. 1. Sec. æl. Hook. Eccl. Pol. Book V. Sec. 41. Lestrange's Alliance of Divine Offices, Annot. on Chap. IV.*

‖ Johannes Diaconus, who wrote the life of this pope, says that he imitated the most wise Solomon in this respect ; and that he with infinite labour and great ingenuity composed an antiphonary ; and other writers add a gradual also, not in the way of compilation, or by collecting the offices therein contained, but that he dictated or pointed, and actually neumatized the musical cantus both to the antiphonary and gradual. Neuma is a word possibly derived from the Greek $\pi\nu\epsilon\nu\mu\alpha$, and, as explained by Sir Henry Spelman, signifies an aggregation of as many

---

* Nivers sur le Chant Gregorien, chap. i.
† Ibid. Damasus is said to have first introduced the Psalms into the service. Platina in Damasus, Isaacs. Chron. anno 371.

Maimbourg in his Histoire du Pontificat de St. Gregoire has collected from Johannes Diaconus and others, all that he could find on this subject. The account given by him is as follows :—

' He especially applied himself to regulate the ' office and the singing of the church, to which ' end he composed his antiphonary—nothing can be ' more admirable than what he did on this occasion. ' Though he had upon his hands all the affairs of ' the universal church, and was still more burthened ' with distempers than with that multitude of business ' which he was necessarily to take care of in all parts ' of the world, yet he took time to examine with what ' tunes the psalms, hymns, oraisons, verses, responses, ' canticles, lessons, epistles, the gospel, the prefaces, ' and the Lord's Prayer were to be sung; what were ' the tones, measures, notes, moods, most suitable to ' the majesty of the church, and most proper to inspire ' devotion ; and he formed that ecclesiastical music so ' grave and edifying, which at present is called the ' Gregorian music. He moreover instituted an aca- ' demy of singers for all the clerks to the deaconship ' exclusively, because the deacons were only to be ' employed in preaching the Gospel and the dis- ' tributing the alms of the church to the poor ; and ' he would have the singers to perfect themselves in ' the art of true singing according to the notes of his ' music, and to bring their voices to sing sweetly and ' devoutly ; which, according to St. Isidore, is not to ' be obtained but by fasting and abstinence : for, says ' he, the ancients fasted the day before they were to ' sing, and lived for their ordinary diet upon pulse, ' to make their voices clearer and finer ; whence it is ' that the heathens called those singers bean-eaters.*
' * * * * * However, St. Gregory took care to ' instruct them himself, as much a pope as he was, ' and to teach them to sing well. Johannes Diaconus ' says, that in his time, this pope's bed was preserved ' with great veneration, in the palace of St. John of ' Lateran, in which he sang, though sick, to teach the ' singers ; as also the whip, wherewith he threatened ' the young clerks and the singing boys, when they ' were out, and failed in the notes.'

The account given by Johannes Diaconus is some- what more particular than that of Maimbourg, and is to this effect :—' Gregory instituted a singing school, ' and built two houses for the habitation of the scho- ' lars, and endowed them with ample revenues ; one ' of these houses was near the stairs of the church of ' St. Peter, and the other near the Lateran palace. ' For many ages after his death, the bed on which he ' modulated as he lay, and the whip which he used ' to terrify the younger scholars, were preserved with ' a becoming veneration, together with the authentic ' antiphonary, above said to have been compiled by ' him.'†

Other additions to and improvements of the service are attributed to St. Gregory. It is said, that he added the prayers, particularly this, ' Diesque nostros in pace disponas,' and the Kyrie Eleeson, and the Alleluia, both which he took from the Greek liturgy ; and that he introduced many hymns, and adopted the responsaria to the lessons and gospels : nay, some have gone so far as to assert that he invented the stave. Kircher speaks of a MS. eight hundred years old, which he had seen, containing music, written on a stave of eight lines ; but Vincentio Galilei, in his Dialogo della Musica, shews that it was in use before Gregory's time :‡ this is a matter of some uncertainty ; but the merit of substituting the Roman letters in the room of the Greek characters, the reformation of the antiphonary, the foundation and endowment of seminaries for the study of music, and the intro- duction of four additional tones, are certainly his due ; and these are the chief particulars which historians have insisted on, to shew Gregory's affection for music. The augmentation of the tones must doubtless be considered as a great improve- ment ; the tones, as they stood adjusted by St. Ambrose, were only four, and are defined by a series of eight sounds, in the natural or diatonic order of progression, ascending from D, from E, from F, and from G, in the grave, to the same sounds in the acute.

But before the nature of this improvement can be understood, it must be premised, that although the ecclesiastical tones, consisting merely of a varied succession of tones and semitones, in a gradual ascent from the lower note to its octave, answer exactly to the several keys, as they are called by modern musicians ; yet in this respect they differ ; for in modern compositions the key-note is the principal, and the whole of the harmony has a relation to it ; but the modes of the church suppose another note, to which that of the key seems to be but subordinate, which is termed the Dominant, as prevailing, and being most frequently heard of any in the tone ; the other, from whence the series ascends, is called the Final.§

Farther, to understand the nature and use of this distinction between the dominant and final note of every tone, it is to be observed, that at the intro- duction of music into the service of the Christian church, it was the intent of the fathers that the whole should be sung, and no part thereof said or uttered in the tone or manner of ordinary reading or praying.

' Romana Ecclesia modulatur constituit ; eique cum nonnullis prædiis duo ' habitacula ; scilicet, alterum sub gradibus Basilicæ B. Petri Apostoli, ' alterum verò sub Lateranensis Ecclesiæ Patriarchii domibus fabricavit ; ' ubi usque hodie lectus ejus, in quo recubans modulabatur, et flagellam ' ipsius, quo pueris minabatur veneratione congrua, cum authentico ' antiphonario reservatur.' Johann. Diacon. in Vita Greg. lib. II. cap. vi. Johannes Diaconus flourished about the year 880 ; so that these relics might have been two hundred and seventy years old at the time when he wrote the life of Gregory.

‡ It is worthy of remark, that the musical stave has varied in its limits since it was first invented. By the passage in Galilei above re- ferred to, it seems to have been originally contrived to include the system of a diapason, as containing eight lines ; on which only, and not in the spaces, the points or notes were originally placed. Guido Aretinus, by making use of the spaces, reduced it to five lines. After his time, that is to say in the thirteenth century, the stave was finally settled at four lines, in consequence, it is supposed, of that correction of the antiphonary of the Cistercian order, which St. Bernard undertook and perfected some years before ; and this number has ever since been found sufficient for the notation of the Cantus Gregorianus.

§ Niv. sur le Chant Gregorien, chap. xii.

sounds as may be uttered in one single respiration. Spelm. Gloss. voce NEUMA : and in this sense it is used by Guido himself, Franchinus, and other writers.
* ' Pridie quam cantandum erat cibis abstinebant psallentes, legumine in causâ vocis assidue utebantur, unde et cantores apud gentiles Fabarii dicti sunt.' Isid. de Eccl. Offic. lib. II. cap. xii.
† ' Deinde in domo Domini (Divus Gregorius) more sapientissimi Salamonis propter musicæ compunctionem dulcedinis, antiphonarium centonem cantorum studiosissimus nimis utiliter compilavit. Scholam ' quoque cantorum, quæ hactenus ejusdem institutionibus in Sancta

It seemed therefore necessary, in the institution of a musical service, so to connect the several parts of it as to keep it within the bounds of the human voice; and this could only be done by restraining it to some one certain sound, as a medium for adjusting the limits of each tone, and which should pervade the whole of the service, as well the psalms and those portions of scripture that were ordinarily read to the people, as the hymns, canticles, spiritual songs, and other parts thereof, which, in their own nature, were proper to be sung.

Hence it will appear, that in each of the tones it was necessary not only that the concords, as, namely, the fourth, the fifth, and the octave, should be well defined; but that the key-note should so predominate as that the singers should never be in danger of missing the pitch, or departing from the mode in which the service should be directed to be sung; this distinction, therefore, between the dominant and final, must have existed at the early time of instituting the Cantus Ambrosianus, and the same prevails at this day.

The characteristics of the four primitive modes were these: in each of them the diatessaron was placed above the diapente, which is but one of the two kinds of division of which the diapason is susceptible. Gregory was aware of this, and interposed four other tones between the four instituted by St. Ambrose, in which the diapente held the uppermost place in the diapason: in short, the tones of St. Ambrose arise from the arithmetical, and those of St. Gregory from the harmonical, division of the diapason.* The addition of the four new tones gave rise to a distinction which all the writers on the subject have adopted; and accordingly those of the first class have the epithet of Authentic, and the latter that of Plagal: the following diagram may serve to shew the difference between the one and the other of them:—

	1	3	5	7	
Diatessaron.	d c **h** a	e d c **h**	f e d c	g f e d	
Diapente.	G F E D C **h** A	a G F E D C **h**	**h** a G F E D C	c **h** a G F E D	Diatessaron. Diapente.
	2	4	6	8	

Occasion has already been taken to remark, that

* We have no authentic formula of the tones in musical characters more ancient than what is to be found in the writings of Franchinus: there is indeed one in MS. in the British Museum, which was part of the Cotton library, Nero, A. xii. 13, beginning 'Si vis scire artem musicam;' but the notes, which were written in red ink, are effaced by time.

there are three different species of diatessaron, and four of diapente; and that from the conjunction of these two, there arise seven species of diapason. Authors have differed in their manner of characterising these several systems, as may be seen in Bontempi, who calls the comparison of them anunprofitable operation. † That of Gaffurius seems best to correspond with the notions of those who have written professedly on the Cantus Gregorianus, particularly of Erculeo, who, in his treatise, intitled Il Canto Ecclesiastico, has thus defined them:—

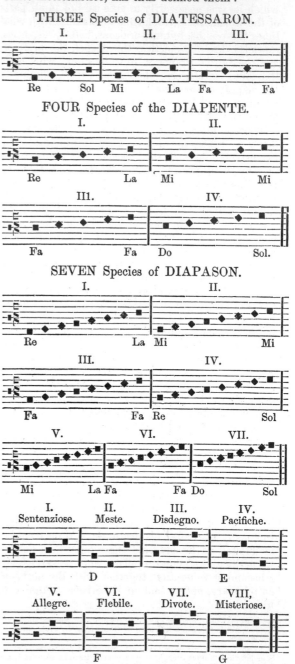

THREE Species of DIATESSARON.

FOUR Species of the DIAPENTE.

SEVEN Species of DIAPASON.

It now remains to show how the tones correspond with the seven species of diapason; and this will

† Hist. Mus. pag. 177.

most clearly appear from the description which Gaffurius has given of them in his Practica Musicæ utriusque Cantus, lib. I. wherein he says,

'The first tone is formed of the first species of 'diapente, between D SOL RE and A LA MI RE, and 'the first species of diatessaron from the same A LA 'MI RE to D LA SOL RE in the acute, constituting the 'fourth species of diapason, D d.

'The second is formed of the same species of 'diapente and diatessaron; but so disposed as to form 'the first species of diapason, A a.

'The third is formed of the second species of 'diapente, between E LA MI, grave, and ♮ MI; and 'the second species of diatessaron from the same ♮ 'MI, to E LA MI, acute, constituting the fifth species 'of diapason, E e.

'The fourth is formed of the same species of 'diapente and diatessaron; but so disposed as to form 'the second species of diapason, ♮♮.

'The fifth is formed of the third species of dia-'pente, between F FA UT, grave, and C SOL FA UT; 'and the third species of diatessaron, from the same 'C SOL FA UT to F FA UT, acute; constituting the 'sixth species of diapason, F f.

'The sixth is formed of the same species of dia-'pente and diatessaron; but so disposed as to form 'the third species of diapason, C c.

'The seventh is formed of the fourth species of 'diapente, between G SOL RE UT, grave, and D LA 'SOL RE; and the first species of diatessaron from 'the same D LA SOL RE, to G SOL RE UT, acute; 'constituting the seventh species of diapason, G g.

'The eighth is formed of the same species of 'diapente and diatessaron; but so disposed as to 'form the fourth species of diapason, D d, which is 'the characteristic of the first tone: but the dominant 'of the one being A, and that of the other G, there 'is an essential difference between them.'

Hence it appears, that the difference between the Authentic and Plagal modes, arises from the different division of the diapason in each; the Authentics being divided in harmonical, and the Plagals in arithmetical proportion. The nature of these is fully explained in the treatise De Musica of Boetius, lib. II. cap. xii.; and by Dr. Holder, in his treatise of the Natural Grounds and Principles of Harmony, chap. v.*

From the principles laid down by the latter of these writers,† it will follow, that taking the numbers 12, 9, 8, 6, to express the proportion of the diapason, and its component intervals, the diatessaron and diapente; when the division of the diapason is thus, 12, 9, 6, or A D a, giving to the diatessaron the lowest position, the proportion is arithmetical: When it is 12, 8, 6, or A E a, in which the diapente holds the lowest place, it is harmonical.‡

* See an extract from it, supra, chap. xxiv.   † Vide Hold. pag. 86.

‡ Malcolm, in his Treatise of Musick, pag. 162, says that the arithmetical division puts the 5th next the lesser extreme, and the harmonical next the greater, as in the numbers 6, 8, 9, 12, as they certainly do. Again he says, page 563, that the harmonical division places the 5th lowest, which is also true; hence it appears that he looks upon the lesser extreme to be the lowest position, but in this he errs; for if six parts give a, a twelve must give the octave below it, i. e. A. Bontempi is also grossly erroneous in pages 70 and 173, et seq. of his history, and has made strange confusion, by giving the smaller number to the graves, and the larger to the acutes, and in the consequent misapplication of the adverbs sotto and sopra.

Having adjusted the number and limits of the tones, Gregory proceeded to the invention of a Cantus, such as he thought would be consistent with the gravity and dignity of the service to which it was to be applied. A plain unisonous kind of melody, frequently inflected to the concords of its key, seemed to him the fittest for this purpose; and having prescribed a rule to himself, as well as to others, he proceeded to apply to the divine offices that kind of Cantilena which prevails in the Roman church even at this day; and which is known in Italy by the name of Canto Fermo, in France by that of Plain Chant, and in Germany and most other countries by that of the Cantus Gregorianus. Cardinal Bona gives this description of it :—' The cantus insti-'tuted by Saint Gregory was plain and unisonous, 'proceeding by certain limits and bounds of tones, 'which the musicians term Modes or Tropes, and 'define by the octonary number, according to the 'natural disposition of the diatonic genus.'

Considering that the right understanding of the ecclesiastical tones is essential to the regular performance of choral service, it is not to be wondered at, that almost every writer on music, who professes to treat the subject at large, has taken them under his consideration; and though it may seem, that after they were first established and promulgated through the church, they ceased to be an object worthy the attention of theorists in musical science, yet there is no assignable period in which it was not necessary to review them, and purge them from those errors which the levity and inattention of the singers were from time to time introducing; for, for near a century after Gregory's time, innovations of this kind were so frequent, that it seemed hardly possible to preserve the Cantus Gregorianus in any degree of purity; and, therefore, the court of Rome was continually troubled with applications from the princes of Europe, expressing their fears that the Cantus Gregorianus was in danger of being lost, and praying its interposition in order to its restoration.

A more particular account of these applications, and the success they met with, will shortly follow; they are mentioned in this place to shew that the Cantus Gregorianus was esteemed a matter of great importance in divine worship, and to account in some measure for the numerous tracts that are extant in the world concerning it.

CHAP. XXVIII.

IN the earlier ages the treatises written with a view to preserve the integrity of the ecclesiastical tones, were composed in monasteries: Guido Aretinus, a Benedictine monk, in a tract entitled Micrologus, a very particular account whereof will hereafter be given, has bestowed three chapters on the explanation of the modes or tropes, which are no other than the eight ecclesiastic tones. Many other discourses on the same subject are also extant in manuscript; and in print they are innumerable.

Of manuscripts none can pretend to greater authority than the Micrologus of Guido Aretinus, the twelfth, thirteenth, and fourteenth chapters whereof contain a general description of the eight ecclesiastical modes, tropes, or tones, but without any distinction of their respective finals and dominants. In a manuscript in the library of Baliol college, containing the Micrologus of Guido, and several other musical tracts, is a dialogue beginning with these words, 'Quid est Musica?' in which the tones are treated with a somewhat less degree of obscurity; but this also is defective in that it contains no Formula to ascertain the relation between the Dominant and the Final in each of them. But the manuscript of greatest value and curiosity, in respect of its copiousness and perspicuity, of any now extant, is one on vellum with the following title, 'Hunc Librum vocitatum Musi-'cam Guidonis scripsit Dominus Johannes Wylde, 'quondam exempti Monasterii Sancta Crucis de 'Waltham Præcentor,' the property of Mr. West now president of the Royal Society, and which formerly belonged to Tallis, as appears by his handwriting on a blank leaf thereof.* In this book, of which a more particular account will be given hereafter, are contained a great number of discourses on the subject of music, composed by sundry persons, as namely, the above-mentioned Johannes Wylde,   Kendale, Johannes Torkesey, Thomas Walsyngham, Lyonell Power,   Chilston, and others; and among these are several short tracts on the tones or tropes as they are called. The first in the book, which seems to have been not barely copied, but composed by Wylde, is on the subject of what he calls Guidonian music. It is divided into two parts, the one treating of Manual, *i. e.*, elementary music, from the figure of the left hand, which Guido is said to have made use of for explaining his system; and the other of Tonal music, containing the doctrine of the ecclesiastical tones.

In the thirteenth chapter of this second part of Wylde's tract it is said that all the tones are produced from the seven species of diapason; but as there are eight of the former, and only seven of the latter, the author first takes upon him to explain how the eighth tone was generated: he says that Ptolemy considered the seventh species as produced from the third, and thought that the fourth was also capable of producing another tone, which he added to the seven, making thereby an eighth: he adds, that he disposed one after another, the fifteen letters, which comprehended the bisdiapason; constituting A for the first note thereof, and P for the last; and having drawn seven semicircles, which pointed out seven species or tones, he added the eighth, extending from the middle letter ♭ or H to the last letter P, which was the only eighth that wanted a semicircle; pointing out thereby the fourth species, which has its mediation in G, in which the eighth tone is terminated: and this, says he, Boetius asserted to be

the eighth mode or tone which Ptolemy superadded. The same author observes that though the species are Eight, yet the genera of tones are in truth but Four, each being divided into authentic and plagal; and that each genus is by some writers termed a Maniera, which appellation he rejects, as coming from the French. He says that no cantus in any of the tones can with propriety exceed the limits of a tenth; and so indeed do all the writers on this subject.†

In the same manuscript are several other tracts, one in particular composed by a certain monk of Sherborne, in metre, tending to explain the precepts of what was then called tonal music.

Many other manuscripts on this subject there are, which, by the assistance of the printed catalogues may be found; but as a comparison of the several definitions therein contained, might introduce a degree of confusion which no diligent enquirer would wish to encounter, it is safest to rely on those authors who have written since the invention of printing, and whose works have stood the test of ages.

Of these Gaffurius, as he is of the greatest antiquity, so is he of unquestionable authority. In his book intitled Practica Musicæ utriusque Cantus, printed in the year 1502, he has entered into a large discussion of the ecclesiastical tones, and has exhibited them severally in the following forms:—

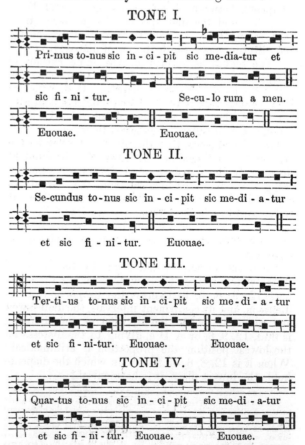

TONE I.

Pri-mus to-nus sic in-ci-pit sic me-dia-tur et sic fi-ni-tur.   Se-cu-lo rum a men.

Euouae.   Euouae.

TONE II.

Se-cundus to-nus sic in-ci-pit sic me-di-a-tur et sic fi-ni-tur.   Euouae.

TONE III.

Ter-ti-us to-nus sic in-ci-pit sic me-di-a-tur et sic fi-ni-tur. Euouae.   Euouae.

TONE IV.

Quar-tus to-nus sic in-ci-pit sic me-di-a-tur et sic fi-ni-tur. Euouae.   Euouae.

† This rule must be understood as referring only to that unisonous cantus which is used in the intonation of the psalms and other parts of the service, and not to that of the antiphons and hymns; for to these

TONE V.

Quintus to-nus sic in - ci-pit   sic me-di - a-tur

et sic fi - ni - tur.   Euouae.

TONE VI.

Sex-tus to-nus sic in-ci-pit   sic me-di - a - tur

et sic fi - ni - tur.

TONE VII.

Vel sic.

Sep-timus   to - nus sic   in - ci - pit.

et sic me-di-a-tur   et sic fi - ni - tur.

Euouae.   Euouae.   Euouae.

TONE VIII.

Vel sic solennis.

Oc-tavus   tonus sic   in-ci-pit sic medi - a-tur

et sic fi - ni - tur.   Euouae.

a double, triple, and frequently a quadruple cantus is adapted; and in these the interior parts have often anomalous initials and finals; and in the extreme parts the ambit of the grave and acute sounds will often necessarily exceed the interval of a tenth.

The above characters exhibit the essential parts of each of the tones, that is to say, the beginning, the mediation, and the close, which is generally contained in the Euouae, a word, or rather a compages of letters, that requires but little explanation, being nothing more than the vowels contained in the words Seculorum Amen; and which whenever it occurs, as it does almost in every page of the antiphonary, is meant as a direction for singing those words to the notes of the Euouae.

From Gaffurius the tones have been continued down to this time, through all the books that have been written on the subject of music at large, in almost every country in Europe. Of those written professedly on the ecclesiastical tones, there are two that merit a particular attention, the one entitled Armonia Gregoriana, by Gerolamo Cantone, Master of the Novices, and vicar of the convent of St. Francis, at Turin, published in 1678, oblong quarto. The other has the title of Il Canto Ecclesiastico, the author D. Marzio Erculeo, printed at Modena in 1686, in small folio.

The first of these books contains the rudiments of singing, and the most important rules for the Canto Fermo, which for the most part are comprised in short memorial verses. The author has given a brief designation of the eight tones, but in his twenty-second chapter, entitled De' Toni Misti, he has assumed a licence which seems unwarranted by any precedent, at least in ancient practice, of combining together the first and second, the third and fourth, the fifth and sixth, and the seventh and eighth tones, and thereby exceeded the limits prescribed by the ancient writers, who all concur in restraining the canto fermo to the ambit of a tenth.

The latter of these books gives very ample directions for the singing of all the offices in the Roman service, and a representation of the tones in the following order :—

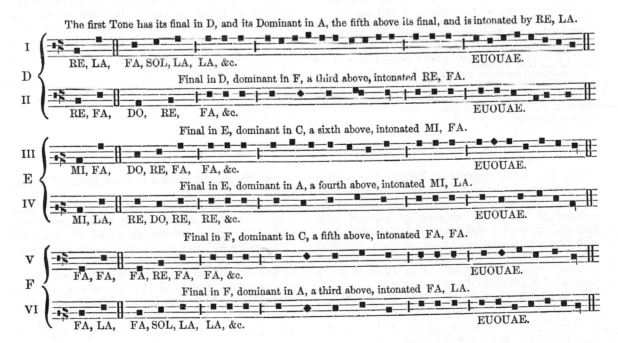

The first Tone has its final in D, and its Dominant in A, the fifth above its final, and is intonated by RE, LA.

I { RE, LA,   FA, SOL, LA, LA, &c.   EUOUAE.

D {

Final in D, dominant in F, a third above, intonated RE, FA.

II { RE, FA,   DO, RE,   FA, &c.   EUOUAE.

Final in E, dominant in C, a sixth above, intonated MI, FA.

III { MI, FA,   DO, RE, FA, FA, &c.   EUOUAE.

E {

Final in E, dominant in A, a fourth above, intonated MI, LA.

IV { MI, LA,   RE, DO, RE, RE, &c.   EUOUAE.

Final in F, dominant in C, a fifth above, intonated FA, FA.

V { FA, FA,   FA, RE, FA, FA, &c.   EUOUAE.

F {

Final in F, dominant in A, a third above, intonated FA, LA.

VI { FA, LA,   FA, SOL, LA, LA, &c.   EUOUAE.

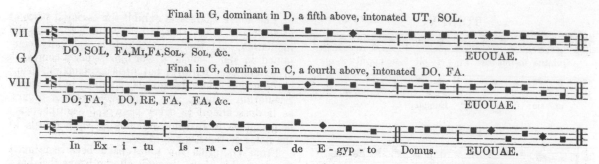

There is also another tone used in the Romish service, called by some of the writers on the Cantus Gregorianus, Il Tuono Pellegrino, *i. e.*, the Wandering Tone ; and by others Tuono Misto, or mixed ; the manner in which it is intonated appears by the last stave above.

The writers on the Cantus Gregorianus have assigned to each of the eight ecclesiastical tones a peculiar character, supposing that each is calculated to excite different affections of the mind : this notion is to the last degree fanciful, as will appear from what Bontempi and Kircher severally say touching the power and efficacy of each.* Erculeo has distinguished them in the manner represented at the end of his scheme of the species of diatessaron, diapente, and diapason, herein before inserted.†

The consequence of these and other publications of the same import, was that the doctrine of the Cantus Gregorianus was rendered so perspicuous, and the forms of the tones so well established, that they became familiar even to children ; but the stability they had acquired was not so great, but that about the beginning of the seventeenth century the levity and wantonness of the singers gave reason to fear the corruption of them.‡ It was about this time that the theatric style of music began to be formed, in the performance whereof Castrati, and others with flexible and extensive voices, were principally employed ;

* Vide Bontempt. pag. 241. Kirch. Musurg. lib. VIII. pag. 142.

† Doctor Pepusch, in his short Introduction to Harmony, pag. 65, has remarked of the key E that it differs from all others, as in truth it does ; for it has for its second a semitone, for which reason, and because of certain peculiarities in the modulation of it, and which render it very solemn, he says it is as it were appropriated to church-music, and called by the Italians Tuono di Chiesa.

This assertion of the Doctor may possibly be well grounded, but it is to be remarked that no such distinction occurs in the writings of Guido or Franchinus, or any of the other authors who have been consulted in the course of this work, for the purpose of explaining the Cantus Gregorianus, and the nature of the ecclesiastical tones.

‡ Erculeo, pag. 52.

these singers, for very obvious reasons, made use of divisions and all the other usual artifices to excite applause ; and these were so grateful to the ears of the vulgar, that the singers employed in the choral service became infected with the like passion, and so mutilated and distorted the Cantus Gregorianus, that the dignity and simplicity of it was almost lost. This gave occasion in the year 1683 to an excellent French musician, Guillaume Gabriel Nivers, organist of the chapel of Lewis XIV. and master of music to his queen,§ to publish a book entitled Dissertation sur le Chant Gregorien. In the composition of this learned and judicious work, the author appears to have derived great assistance from the writings of Amalarius Fortunatus and St. Bernard, and from Cardinal Bona's book De Rebus Liturgicis, Durandus's Rationale Divinorum Officiorum, and, above all, from a more modern author, named Peytat, who wrote a history of the chapel of the king of France, a book abounding with a great variety of curious particulars.

Nivers succeeded so well in his endeavours to reform the cantus ecclesiasticus, that he was employed by the king to correct the Roman antiphonary, for the use of the churches in France ; and the editions of that great volume since his time, bear testimony to the skill and industry which he must have exercised in so laborious and important a reformation. In short, he has not only reduced the tones to the standard of primitive purity, but has given such directions for the performance of the Cantus Gregorianus, and guarded so well against innovations in it, that there is very little reason to fear the loss of this precious relic of antiquity.

§ Nivers was also organist of the church of St. Sulpice, in Paris. He was the author of a book, entitled, Traité de la Composition de Musique, printed at Amsterdam, in octavo, 1697, and of some motets and pieces for the organ, which are also in print.

BOOK IV.   CHAP. XXIX.

The first eight chapters of Nivers's Dissertation sur le Chant Gregorien, contain a history of the primitive institution of it, and a vindication of the practice of antiphonal singing in general, from Socrates, Theodoret, and other ecclesiastical writers, with answers to the objections of such as either denied its authority or had contributed to the increase of those errors in the practice of it, which it is the purpose of his book to detect and reform.

In the ninth chapter the author enumerates the several characters necessary in the notation of it, and describes them thus :—

'Twelve characters are sufficient for the plain-'song ; the first consists of four lines, upon which, 'and in the spaces between them, all the notes are 'situate ; the fifth line, which certain innovaters have 'added, is useless and embarrassing.

'The second character is the key of C sol ut fa 'or else by the method of the si ; the key of C sol 'ut made thus ♮ or thus ♯ cannot be situate but on

'the first, the second, or the third, and never or very
'rarely on the fourth, because the key on the second
'line with a b soft commonly in B, has altogether
'the same effect as the same key on the fourth line
'without b soft; for it is always said the note on
'this fourth line is always sung UT, and the other
'notes consecutively in order. This is to be under-
'stood of the song, but not of the organ or other
'instruments.

'The third character is the key of F UT FA, made
'thus ▦▦ or thus ▦§ which is generally situated
'on the second line, and sometime, but very rarely,
'upon the first.

'The fourth and fifth characters are the two notes,
'the long and the breve, made thus ■ ♦, but as the
'number of characters necessary in it is one of the
'grand questions relating to the cantus, we defer
'speaking of it till in the next chapter, to confute
'the opinion of those who admit but one of them,
'namely, the long.*

'The sixth and seventh characters are the two
'bars; the great and the less, made thus ▦▦
'which are used to denote the place where all the
'choir together ought to take breath and make a little
'pause. These are the same in a song as stops are
'to words, wherefore we always at two points or
'a colon, and sometimes at commas, put a great bar
'to make the song complete, answering to a full
'stop. The principal use of the lesser bar is to
'give time for the whole choir together to draw
'breath, to the end that none of the singers may
'go on faster than the rest, and that the uniformity
'of the cantus may be preserved by all, and in all
'with an equal measure. At the end of every piece
'there are put two great bars to mark the end of the
'song; these bars are the most efficacious contrivance
'that can be thought on to remedy all the cacophonies
'and contrarieties in the voices of the singers, who,
'without them, could not guess when to rest; but
'the abuse of these bars is become almost general,
'for the markers or writers of notes and the printers
'imagine there must be one at every word; so that
'if there are four, five, six, or seven monosyllables
'following one another, they put as many bars as
'there are notes, as if all the notes were not of
'themselves as well separated, without bars, as the
'words are. St. Bernard speaks of this confusion

'in these words: "What sort of liberty is this
"which introduces the confusion of uncertainty, &c."
'And in effect this confusion of bars is of no service,
'since all the notes are of themselves as distinct as
'the words; and all these bars are not only useless
'and embarrassing, but they yet (which is remark-
'able) destroy the benefit of their institution, because
'the singers, no longer knowing where to repose
'themselves, some stop while others advance, which
'occasions the greatest disorders in the song; and
'the excess of bars puts the song again into its
'former abuse, when it had no bars, which we see in
'the more ancient manuscripts.

'The eighth character is the guidon, made upon
'the line, or in the space thus ▦▦† or thus ⫟⫟
'to mark where the following note will be situate
'in the other line.

'The ninth character is the bemol, made thus in
'a space, but rarely on a line ♭▦ which is always
'marked in B, and very rarely in E.

'The tenth is the point • between two short notes:
'the use of it is to augment the precedent one, and
'diminish that following it, to observe a certain
'regulated measure, for example, that of two times.
'Sometimes the point is also put between a long
'note and a short one; and in such case it only
'augments the long note with the half of its own
'value, so that the point and the following breve
'considered together complete the just measure of
'a long note.

'The eleventh character is the bond or joining,
'made thus ⌣, or thus ⌢, which serves to tie two
'or more notes, or long ones and breves on one and
'the same syllable, to keep the regulated measure.

'The last character is the diesis, made thus ⚹, or
'thus ×; the use of it is to soften the following note,
'or that above or under which it is placed; the
'dieses are rarely marked in the plain-song, because
'the voice itself naturally leads to it.‡

---

* Nivers, in the subsequent chapter, undertakes the discussion of
a question which it seems had subsisted for a long time, namely, how
many characters or marks of time were necessary in the cantus ecclesiasticus? He contends that not more than two, namely, the long and
the breve, are admissable into it; for this he cites the acts of the council
of Rheims in 1564, in which it was decreed that the cantus should contain but one note on a syllable, and that the quantities of each should be
observed in the notation. He seems to think that this was the very
reformation intended by the council of Trent, in that decree of it which
is mentioned by Father Paul, pag. 559. of his history, to have been made
in 1562, against over-curious and wanton singing. He also cites Rabanus
Maurus to prove that all clerks should perfectly understand the nature
of the accents, and accommodate their notation to it. Farther he asserts,
on the authority of Radulphus, that in the gradual of the blessed Gregory
at Rome there are but few notes, and that there is reason to believe that
many characters in those of an hundred years after him have no warrant
for their admission.

In the course of this disquisition Nivers seems not to be in the least
aware of a reformation of the cantus ecclesiasticus made by Palestrina
and Francesco Suriano, about the year 1580, which consisted in the
reduction of the characters to three, namely, the long, the breve, and
the semibreve; and is expressly mentioned by Marzio Erculeo, in his
Discourse on the Cantus Ecclesiasticus above-cited.

† This is the form of the guidon in ancient missals, and other books
written or printed with musical notes: it is an indication of the first
note in a succeeding stave, and is that note in a smaller character. This
kind of guidon is now disused, and has given place to that other above
described.

‡ The following directions of Nivers contain the principal rules to be
observed in the performance of the cantus ecclesiasticus:—
'To begin to sing or intonate an anthem, or any other part of the
'office whatsoever, the rule is to attend particularly to the dominant of
'the choir, which ought to be regulated according to the voices which
'compose it; for it would be acting quite contrary to nature and reason
'to pretend to establish the same dominant for the low, the middle, and
'the highest voices.
'To arrive at a perfect knowledge of these things, it ought to be
'known that the whole song consists in eight modes or tones, which may
'be reduced to four by their finals, and even to two, by only the difference
'of the greater third and the lesser third.
'The uneven tones, which are only so termed, as being distinguished
'by the odd numbers 1, 3, 5, 7, are called authentics or principals: the
'others are named plagals or dependents, because they have one and the
'same final each with their authentic, and thus the first and second have
'one and the same final, so the third and fourth, the fifth and sixth, the
'seventh and eighth; all their difference consists only in the extent,
'which in the authentics is above, and in the plagals below.
'Every tone has two essential chords, called the final and the domi-
'nant, upon which all sorts of songs turn and are founded. The final is
'that by which the tone ought for the most part to begin, but always to
'end. The dominant is that which rules or prevails the oftenest in the
'song, and upon which the tenor of the psalms, oraisons, and all that is
'to be sung straight forward, or nearly straight forward, is made.
'Wherefore this dominant ought to be a little higher than the middle
'of the natural voice, and not lower, because that in all the tones the
'extent of the notes is greater below than above the dominant; but it is
'not a small difficulty to take it just and in a good pitch.
'For the common and ordinary voices they put the dominant of the
'choir in A of the organ; I mean the organs which have the tone of the

Having thus explained the characters, Nivers, in his twelfth book, proceeds to a discrimination of the tones by the finals and dominants of each in their respective order, in the words following :—

'The first has its final in D, and its dominant in 'A, the fifth to its final ; RE LA.'

'The second has its final in D, and its dominant in 'F, a third to its final ; RE FA.'

'The third has its final in E, and its dominant in 'C, a sixth to its final ; MI UT.'*

'The fourth has its final in E, and its dominant in 'A, a fourth to its final ; MI LA.'

'The fifth has its final in F, and its dominant in 'C, a fifth to its final ; UT SOL, or else FA UT with B '♮, not ♭.'

'The sixth has its final in F, and its dominant in 'A, a third to its final ; UT MI, or else FA LA, with B '♮, not ♭.'

'The seventh has its final in G, and its dominant 'in A, a fifth to its final ; SOL RE.'

'The eighth has its final in G, and its dominant in 'C, a fourth to its final ; SOL UT.'

The dissertation of Nivers contains also Formulæ Cantus Ordinarii Officii Divini. These he has given in Latin, together with the musical notes : they contain directions for singing the oraisons and responses, and for reading the prophets, the epistles, and gospels, and for the intonation of the psalms. There are also several litanies and antiphons, and that famous lamentation of the Virgin, in monkish rhyme :—

　　　Stabat mater dolorosa
　　　Juxta crucem lachrymosa.

The formula of the tones intitled Tabula tonorum, is also given in musical characters, and contains the following examples :—

Intonatio, Tractus Notarum, Mediatio, Tractus Terminatio.

Dix-it　Dominus Domi-no me-o:　Se-de　à dextris me - is.

'king's chapel, which all the famous organs of Paris and elsewhere have, 'wherefore this tone is called the tone of the chapel, to distinguish it 'from the tone of the king's chamber, which is a semitone higher, and 'so commonly are, or ought to be, the organs in nunneries ; the nuns 'having generally an extent of voice higher by an octave than the 'common voices of men.

'For the low voices they put the dominant in G of the organ.

'For the high voices they put the dominant in B of the organ.

'For the voices of religious women they put the dominant in C, or even 'in D of the organ, according to the quality of the voices.

'The first thing therefore that ought to be known is the dominant of 'the choir, which is only a generical sound, or tone if you will, and not 'fixed to any note or degree, that is to any rule or interval on which this 'dominant can be placed.

'The second thing to be observed is the mode or tone of the anthem 'which is to be sung, and to regulate the dominant of the anthem to the 'unison of the dominant of the choir which performs it, and then to 'proceed from this dominant regularly, and pass through all the degrees 'as far as the note by which the anthem ought to begin ; for example, if 'I would intonate the first anthem of the Feast of the Holy Sacrament, "Sacerdos in æternum," I sing slowly the dominant of this anthem, 'which is LA, to the unison of the dominant of the choir, and descend 'by degrees to the final of the anthem, by which it begins, singing LA, 'SOL, FA, MI, RE, to find the just tone of the first note of the said anthem, "Sacerdos in æternum," and after the same manner in other anthems 'and tones. But one should not be ignorant of the essential chords of 'every tone.'

It should seem by these several tracts of Erculeo and Nivers, and other authors who might be named, that the doctrine of the tones is now so well established, that there is not the least reason to fear any corruption of them. In England the little book entitled A pious Association, published for the instruction of persons of the Romish persuasion in the true church plain-song, contains a formula of the eight tones, exactly corresponding with that of Nivers above given ; and it farther appears, that in the seminaries throughout Italy it is taught to children in a way that admits of no variation. In short, its principles seem to be as well understood as those of arithmetic, or any other mathematical science.

* According to the French method of solmization ; but Erculeo makes it LA.

Intonatio, Tractus Notarum, Mediatio, Tractus Terminatio.

Dix-it　Dominus Domi-no me-o:　Se-de　à dextris me - is.

To facilitate the remembrance of the formula of each of the tones, and particularly to impress upon the minds of children the finals and dominants that characterise them, memorial verses have been composed, of which the following are a specimen :—

Primus habet tonus F SOL LA, sextus et idem :
Ut RE FA octavus : sit tertius, atque secundus :
LA SOL LA quartus : dant UT MI SOL tibi quintum :
Septimus at tonus FA MI FA SOL tibi monstrat.

Septimus et sextus, dant FA MI RE MI quoque primus.
Quintus et octavus, dant FA SOL FA sicque secundus.
SOL FA MI RE FA tertius, RE UT RE MI reque quartus.

Primus cum quarto dant A LA MI RE, quoque sextus
E FA UT secundus : C SOL FA UT tertius tibi notat,
Cum eo quintus, octavusque signat ibidem :
Septimus in D LA SOL RE suum ponit EUOUAE.

By the foregoing deduction of the nature of the Cantus Gregorianus, nothing more is intended than to explain its original form, for it will be observed that none of the authors above-cited presume to make any additions to, or amendments of it ; on the contrary they labour to represent it in its purity, and to preserve it from corruption. This was evidently the design of Nivers ; and his book, which is of the controversial kind, is calculated to correct certain abuses in the service that arose from the wantonness and levity of the singers, and were peculiar to his time ; but the Cantus Gregorianus suffered greatly from corruptions that were the effect of ignorance, and which took place within a century after its institution ; and these corruptions, their nature, and causes, and the methods taken to remove them by the several princes of Europe, especially those of Germany, France, and England, make a very considerable part in the History of Music, and therefore require to be particularly mentioned ; and if the foregoing digression may seem to deviate from the rule which chronology prescribes in the relation of events, let it be remembered that in this case a strict adherence to it would have been absurd ; for who can understand a relation of the several corruptions of the Cantus Gregorianus, who is not first made sensible of its nature and application ; in short, who has not a clear conception of the thing itself, in its original state of purity and perfection.

That the Cantus Gregorianus became corrupt in a short time after its institution, may be gathered from the ecclesiastical and other writers, from the seventh century downwards. Saint Bernard, in a preface to the antiphonary of the Cistertians, has enumerated many abuses, disorders, and irregularities which had crept into the church-service before his time, and this even at Rome itself : he speaks of the singers of his time as ignorant and obstinate to a degree that is scarce to be credited ; for he represents them as confounding the rules, and preferring error to truth : and referring to an Antiphon, ' Nos qui ' vivimus,' the proper termination whereof is in D, he adds, that those unjust prevaricators, the singers of his time, would terminate it in G, and assert with an oath or wager, that it was of the eighth tone.

Sir Henry Spelman (whom Gerard Vossius has followed, in an account given by him of this matter)* upon the authority of an anonymous commentator on Hugo Reutlingensis, relates that the Cantus Gregorianus was very much corrupted by the Germans. The words of the author thus referred to are, 'Certain ' Germans, and particularly the clergy of the order of ' St. Benedict, who had learned perfectly and by ' heart the musical cantus, not only theoretically, but ' also by practice and exercise, leaving out the keys ' and lines which are required in the musical Neuma,† ' note or character, began to note them down simply ' in their books ; and after that, their successors sang ' in the same manner, and taught their scholars, not ' theoretically, but by frequent practice and long ' exercise ; which cantus thus learned by practice, ' became various in different places, wherefore it was ' then termed practice, usus,‡ and not music. In this ' cantus however the scholars afterwards began to ' differ in many things from their masters, and the ' masters from their scholars ; from which difference, ' and the ignorance of the theory, the practice was ' said to be confused, which confused practice being ' despised, almost all the Germans, who were hitherto ' miserably seduced by that cantus, are returned to ' the true art.'

These corruptions, according to the author above-cited, seem to have been peculiar to Germany ; but there were others of an earlier date which prevailed in France and also in Britain, for the latter of which countries Gregory seems to have entertained such a degree of affection, as makes it highly probable that the inhabitants of it were some of the first people to whom the knowledge of the Cantus Gregorianus was communicated, and that they became Christians and singers at one and the same period.

The history of the conversion of the Saxon inhabitants of this island to christianity in the year 585, is related by all our historians, particularly by Bede, whose account of it, as exhibiting a very natural representation of the simplicity of manners which then prevailed, is here inserted :—

' It is reported that merchants arriving at Rome, ' when on a certain day many things were to be sold ' in the market-place, abundance of people resorted ' thither to buy, and Gregory himself with the rest, ' where, among other things, boys were set to sale ' for slaves, their bodies white, their countenance ' beautiful, and their hair very fine : having viewed ' them, he asked as is said, from what country or ' nation they were brought, and was told from the ' island of Britain, whose inhabitants were of such ' a presence.§ He again enquired whether those ' islanders were Christians, or still involved in the ' errors of paganism, and was informed that they ' were pagans. Then fetching deep sighs from the ' bottom of his heart, " Alas ! what pity, said he, that " the author of darkness is possessed of men of such " fair countenances, and that being remarkable for " such graceful aspects, their minds should be void " of inward grace." He therefore again asked what ' was the name of that nation, and was answered, that ' they were called Angles : " Right, said he, for they " have an angelical face, and it becomes such to be co-" heirs with the angels in heaven. What is the name," ' proceeded he, "of the province from which they are " brought ? " ' It was replied, that the natives of ' that province were called Deiri,‖ " Truly Deiri, " said he, withdrawn from wrath and called to the " mercy of Christ. How is the king of that province " called ? " They told him his name was Elle ; and ' he, alluding to the name, said, " Hallelujah, the " praise of God the creator must be sung in those " parts." Then repairing to the bishop of the Roman ' and apostolical see (for he was not himself then ' made pope) he entreated him to send some ministers ' of the word into Britain, to the nation of the English, ' by whom it might be converted to Christ.' ¶

The above relation is very characteristic of the humanity and simplicity of the reverend father. Fuller, who labours hard to make all mankind as merry as himself, thinks that in his ready application of the answers of the merchants to his purpose, his wit kept pace with his benevolence, and having a mind to try whether he could not be as witty as the father, he has given the whole conversation a dramatic turn, by putting it into the form of a dialogue.**

The sight of these children, and the knowledge which Gregory thereby acquired of this country and its inhabitants, were the motives for sending Augustine the monk hither, with whom, as we are expressly told by Johannes Diaconus, who wrote the Life of St. Gregory, singers were also sent (Augustine then going to Britain), and afterwards

---

* Voce Frigdoræ. Sed vide Ger. Voss. De Scientiis Mathematicis, cap. xxi. § 12.

† This word, which Sir Henry Spelman has elsewhere said is synonymous with the noun Note, has two significations ; that which Gaffurius has given of it is its primitive and true one ; and he says it is an aggregation of as many sounds or notes as may be conveniently uttered in one single respiration. Vide Spelman's Gloss. voce NEUMA ; and Gaffurius, Pract. Mus. lib. I. cap. viii. Probably it is derived from the Greek Πνευμα.

‡ For which reason, the terms Salisbury use, Hereford use, the use of Bangor, York, Lincoln, are taken to describe the ritual of those several cathedrals in the preface to the book of Common Prayer.

§ William Thorn, a monk, of St. Augustine's Canterbury, says there were three of these boys : 'Vidit in foro Romano tres pueros Anglicos lactei candoris.' Decem Scriptores, pag. 1757.

‖ i. e. of Deirham, or Durham.

¶ Bed. Hist. Ecclesiast. lib. II. cap. i.

** Church Hist. of Britain, Cent. VI. book II.

dispersed through the west, who thoroughly instructed the barbarians in the Roman institution. The same author proceeds to relate that after the death of these men* the modulation of the western churches became very corrupt, and continued so till pope Vitalianus the First, who introduced the organ into the choral service, sent John, a famous Roman singer, together with Theodore, afterwards archbishop of Canterbury, by the way of France into Britain, who corrected the abuses that had crept into the church-service of this, as it should seem, favourite people.

Farther he says, that afterwards the Gregorian chant became again corrupt, particularly in France, for which reason Charlemagne sent two clerks to

* The names of the singers who came into Britain with Augustine are no where particularly mentioned. We learn however from Bede that the church song was at first only known in Kent; that afterwards, that is to say about the year 620, when Paulinus became bishop of the Northumbrians, a deacon of his, named James, had rendered himself very famous for his skill in the church song; and that Wilfrid, a succeeding bishop of the same see, about the year 664 invited out of Kent Eddi, surnamed Stephen, for the purpose of teaching the same in the several churches of the Northumbrians. Farther, Bede gives a particular account of John the singer above-mentioned, whom he styles archchanter or precentor of the church of the holy apostle Peter, and abbot of the monastery of St. Martin, and elsewhere singer of the apostolic see: he says he was sent into Britain by pope Agatho, that he might teach the method of singing throughout the year, as it was practised at St. Peter's at Rome; and that he settled in a monastery which Ecgfrid king of the Northumbrians had founded at the mouth of the river Wire. He farther says that John did as he had been commanded by the pope, teaching the singers of this monastery the order and manner of singing and reading aloud, and committing to writing all that was required throughout the whole course of the year for celebrating festivals, all which were in Bede's time observed in that monastery, and transcribed by many others elsewhere; he says farther that the said John did not only teach the brethren of that monastery, but that such as had skill in singing resorted from almost all the monasteries of the same province to hear him.

The reverend Mr. Johnson, late of Cranbrook in Kent, has given a summary of this relation, with his own sentiments thereon, in a book which hardly any one now looks into, but which abounds with a great variety of curious learning, his Collection of Ecclesiastical Laws; in the general preface to which he says, upon the authority of Bede, that pope Agatho, above eighty years after Augustine's coming over, sent John, the precentor of St. Peter's church in Rome, to instruct the monks of Wirmuth in the annual course of singing; and that he did accordingly teach them the order and rite of singing and reading in the celebration of feasts through the circle of the whole year, and that he wrote down and left behind him whatever was requisite to this purpose. And that the sum of what he taught them consisted in new tunes or modes of music, some variations of habit, gesture, and perhaps of the series of performing religious offices according as the fashions had been altered at Rome since Augustine's coming hither—that he taught them viva voce, and what he wrote down concerned only the celebration of the festivals —that John was sent to one monastery only, and is not said to have taught any but the Northumbrians.—That upon Theodore's first coming to Canterbury, which was ten or twelve years before this, the Roman way of singing was well known in Kent, and then began to be taught in other churches—that Wilfred soon after invited Eddi, otherwise called Stephen, out of Kent into the North, to teach his practice there. But thirty-five years before Theodore's arrival, James, the Kentish deacon, had been left at York by Paulinus when he retired to Rochester, on purpose to teach them the way of singing used by the Romans and the Kentish. The same author adds as a conjecture of his own, that it is probable that neither of these Kentish singing-masters went farther than Hexham, however not to Wirmuth.

The same Collection contains a decree of the Roman council, which as it relates to music, and was made to reform an abuse of it that prevailed about this time, it may not be improper here to mention. By this act it is decreed that bishops, and all whosoever that profess the religious life of the ecclesiastical order, do not use weapons, nor keep musicians of the female sex, nor any musical concerts whatsoever, nor do allow of any buffooneries or plays in their presence.

Of James, the deacon of Paulinus above-mentioned, he says that he lived to his [Bede's] time. If so, and considering that Paulinus was bishop of Northumbria, in which province Bede's monastery was situate, it is more than probable that Bede and James were intimately acquainted.

Bede also mentions as living in the time of Theodore, Putta, a man of great simplicity in his manners, extremely well versed in ecclesiastical discipline, and remarkably skilful in church-music, and who, on account of these his excellencies, was preferred to the see of Rochester. Mention will be made of this person hereafter, in the interim it is to be observed, that the testimony of Bede is of great weight in all matters that relate to church discipline, and that hardly any man of his time was better acquainted with the music of the church than himself: in a summary of his own life, at the end of his Ecclesiastical History, he mentions his being a priest of the monastery of Wiremouth, the very monastery where John the precentor settled upon his arrival in Britain; and that he there applied himself to the meditation of scripture, the observance of regular discipline, and the daily care of singing in the church; and that he always delighted in learning, teaching, and writing.

Rome with a request to Adrian, the then pope, that they might be instructed in the rudiments of the genuine Roman song; these brought back the metropolis of Metz to its original purity of singing, and that city communicated its example to all France. The same author adds that the death of these two men produced the same effect, though in a less degree, in France, as that of the others had done in Britain; wherefore the king wrote again to Adrian, who sent him two singers, who found that the church of Metz had deviated a little from the true rule of singing, but the other churches a great deal. The same author adds, that this diversity was remarkable in his time, for that the rest of the French and all the German churches were then as much inferior in the purity of their choral service to that of Metz, as the latter were to the Roman; but for the present he says these men reduced the church of Metz to order.

Monsieur Nivers, from Peytat, a modern writer, and a countryman of his, who it seems wrote an ecclesiastical history of the chapel of the king of France, cites the following passage :—

Pope Stephen II. being constrained to seek to Pepin king of France for protection of the holy see against the Lombards, arrived in that kingdom so soon after Pepin's ascent to the throne, as to perform the ceremony of his consecration in the abbey-church of St. Denys. From Rome the pope had brought with him chaplains and singers, who first made it their business to instruct the choir of St. Denys in the Roman office; and afterwards, for the pope made a considerable stay in France, assisted in communicating the knowledge of it to the other churches in that kingdom. At that time the chapel of Pepin consisted of the very flower of the clergy, and, with the assistance of the Romans, not only the plainchant but the use of instruments was spread throughout the realm. This reformation it is true did not last long, for upon the death of Pepin, his son Charlemagne found the choral service in as great disorder as ever, which, says the monk of St. Cibard of Angoulesme, was the reason that induced this emperor to apply to Adrian for assistance from Rome.

CHAP. XXX.

THE account given of this matter by another ancient writer, a monk of St. Gal, is that the pope sent to France, at the request of the emperor Charlemagne, twelve excellent singers, answering to the number of the apostles, whose instructions were to reform the music of the French churches, and regulate the service, so as that there might be an uniformity in this respect throughout the kingdom; but that these men, jealous of the glory of France, in their way thither plotted to corrupt and diversify the plain-chant in such a manner as to increase the confusion in which it was involved, and thereby render the people for ever incapable of performing it correctly. As soon as they arrived in France, where they were received with great honour, they were, by order of the emperor, dispersed to different parts of the kingdom ; but how well they answered the purpose of sending for them, the event soon showed ; for every man teaching a different chant for the true one of St. Gregory, which they were sent for to restore to its original purity and propagate, the confusion was greater than ever.*

The emperor it seems was too well skilled in music for this deceit to pass upon him unnoticed : he had, in the life-time of his father, heard the true Roman chant at Treves, where he had passed the Christmas, and at Metz also he had been present when it was sung in its perfection ; but after the arrival of these people, spending part of that festival at Paris and the rest at Tours, he was surprised to hear a melody different from that which before he had so much admired ; his disappointment excited in him a curiosity to hear the service as it was performed in the other churches ; but among the singers he found such a disagreement, that he complained to the pope of the behaviour of those whom he had sent ; the pope recalled them to Rome, and condemned some of them to banishment, and the rest to perpetual imprisonment. After this it was that Adrian sent to France the two singers who reformed the French church-music, as above is related.

None of the historians who relate the transactions of this period, except Baronius, assign the reason of the emperor's application to pope Adrian for assistance in the reformation of choral music in his kingdom of France. It seems that that pope had established the use of the Cantus Gregorianus by the decree of a council, which he had summoned for that purpose, and that his zeal to render it universal was the effect of a miracle, which, if we may believe the writers of those times, had then lately been wrought in its favour. It is said, that after the death of Gregory the method of singing instituted by him began to decline, and the Ambrosian cantus to revive. Adrian had entertained an opinion of the superior excellence of the former, and was determined to establish the use of it throughout the church ; for this purpose he summoned a council above-mentioned, who being unable to determine the preference between the one and the other of the offices, referred the decision of the matter to God, and a miracle announced that the preference was due to the Gregorian office.

Durandus has given a very circumstantial relation of this extraordinary event in the following words :—†

'We read in the life of St. Eugenius that till his 'time the Ambrosian office was more used by the 'church than the Gregorian : pope Adrian summoned 'a council, by which it was decreed that the Gregorian 'ought to be universally observed. Moreover St. 'Eugenius coming to a certain council, summoned for 'this purpose, and finding that it had been already 'dissolved three days, he persuaded the lord pope to 'recall all the prelates who had been present thereat. 'The council, therefore, being reassembled, it was the 'unanimous opinion of all the fathers, that the Am-

'brosian and Gregorian missals should be laid upon 'the altar of St. Peter, the apostle, secured by the 'seals of most of the bishops, and the doors of the 'church shut, and that all persons present should 'spend the night in prayer that God would show by 'some sign which of these missals he chose to have 'used by the church ; and this was done in every 'respect. Accordingly, in the morning, when they 'entered the church they found the Gregorian missal 'torn to pieces, and scattered here and there, but 'they found the Ambrosian only open upon the altar, 'in the same place where it had been laid. By which 'sign they were taught from heaven that the Gregorian 'office ought to be dispersed throughout the whole 'world, and that the Ambrosian should be observed 'only in that church in which it was first instituted. 'And this regulation prevails to the present day ; for 'in the time of the emperor Charles, the Ambrosian 'office was very much laid aside, and the Gregorian, 'by the imperial authority, was brought into common 'use. Ambrose instituted many things according to 'the ritual of the Greeks.' Gulielm. Durandus Rationale Divinorum Officiorum. Lugd. 1574, lib. II. cap. ii. numb. 5.

The historians of the time take notice, that in the year 787 a violent contest arose between the Roman and French singers, concerning the true method of singing divine service, which was carried on with so much heat and bitterness, that neither side could be made to yield. At length, the matter was brought before the emperor ; who, after hearing the reasons and arguments of each party, determined in favour of the Roman practice, by declaring, that the French singers had corrupted the Cantus Gregorianus. Baronius has related the transaction at length in these words :—

'In the ancient chronicle of Charles king of France, 'which Pithoeus published, these things then done at 'Rome are recorded. The most pious king Charles 'returned, and celebrated Easter at Rome with the 'apostolical lord. Behold a contention arose, during 'the time of the paschal feast, between the Roman 'and French singers : the French said that they sang 'better and more gracefully than the Romans ; the 'Romans said they performed the ecclesiastical cantus 'more learnedly, as they had been taught by St. 'Gregory, the pope ; and that the French sang 'corruptly, and debased and ruined the true cantilena. 'This contention came before the emperor Charles ; 'and the Gauls relying on his favour, violently ex-'claimed against the Roman singers ; and the Romans, 'upon the authority of their great learning, affirmed 'that the Gauls were fools and rustics, and as un-'learned as brute beasts, and preferred the learning 'of St. Gregory to their rusticity : and the altercation 'ceasing on neither side, the emperor said to his 'singers, "Tell me plainly, which is the purer, and "which the better, the living fountain, or its rivulets "running at a distance." They all, with one voice, 'answered the fountain ; as the head and origin is 'the purer, and the rivulets, the farther they depart 'from the fountain, are by so much the more muddy, 'foul, and corrupted with impurities. "Then, said

* Vid. Niv. sur le Chant. Greg. chap. iv. pag. 33.
† Afterwards pope : the second of that name. Du Pin, Hist. Eccl. vol. III. pag. 6.

"the emperor, return ye to the fountain of St.
"Gregory, for ye have manifestly corrupted the
"ecclesiastical cantus."

'The emperor, therefore, soon after desired sing-
'ers of pope Adrian, who might reform the French
'singing; and he sent to him Theodore and Bene-
'dict, two of the most learned singers of the Roman
'church, who had been taught by St. Gregory; and
'he sent by them the antiphonary of St. Gregory,
'which he had marked with the Roman note. The
'emperor returning into France, sent a singer of the
'city of Metz, with orders that the masters of schools
'throughout all the provinces of France should de-
'liver their antiphonaries to them to be corrected, and
'that they should learn to sing of them. Upon this,
'the antiphonaries of the French were corrected, which
'every one had corrupted, by adding or diminish-
'ing according to his own fancy, and all the singers
'of France learned the Roman note; except that the
'French, who, with their voices, which are naturally
'barbarous, could not perfectly express the delicate
'or tremulous, or divided sounds, in music, but broke
'the sounds in their throats, rather than expressed
'them: but the greatest singing school was that in the
'city of Metz; and as much as the Roman school
'excels the Metensian in the practice of singing, by
', so much does the Metensian excel the other schools
'of France. In like manner, the aforesaid Roman
'singers instructed the singers of the French in the
'art of instrumental music: and the emperor Charles
'again brought with him from Rome into France,
'masters of grammar and mathematics, and ordered
'the study of letters to be every where pursued; for
'before his time, there was no attention paid to the
'liberal arts in Gaul. This account is given of these
'affairs in that chronicle. Moreover, there is an
'ordinance of Charles the Great himself concerning
'the performance of the Roman music in Gaul, in
'these words: "That the monks fully and regularly
"perform the Roman singing in the nocturnal stated
"service, according to what our father king Pepin,
"of blessed memory, decreed should be done, when
"he introduced the Gallican singing for the sake of
"unanimity in the Apostolic See, and the peaceful
"concord of the Holy Church." *

The zeal which this prince discovered through the
course of a long reign, in favour of the church, and
for the re-establishment of ecclesiastical discipline,
has procured him a place among those ecclesiastical
writers enumerated in Du Pin's voluminous history.
It was the good fortune of this emperor to have in
his service a secretary, named Eginhart, a man not
more eminent for his knowledge of the world, than
celebrated for his skill in the literature of those times.
To him we are indebted for a life of this great prince,
one of the most curious and entertaining works of the
kind at this day extant: in this are recorded, not
only the great events of Charlemagne's reign, but the
particulars of his life and character, a very exact
description of his person, his studies, his recreations,
and, in short, all that can gratify curiosity, or tend to
exhibit a lively portrait of a great man. Not to

enter into a minute detail of his wars and negociations,
or the other important transactions during his government, let this short sketch of his personal and mental
endowments, and his labours to restore the service of
the church to its original purity, suffice, as having a
more immediate relation to the subject of this work.

CHARLEMAGNE was born in the year of Christ 769,
at Ingelheim, a town in the neighbourhood of the city
of Liege, in Germany. His father was Pepin, king
of France, surnamed the Little, by reason of the low-
ness of his stature; who, upon his decease, made a
partition of his dominions between his two sons,
bequeathing to Charlemagne, the elder, France, Burgundy, and Aquitain, and to Carloman, Austria,
Soissons, and other territories; but Carloman surviving his father a very short time, Charlemagne
became the heir of all his dominions, and at length
emperor of the West.

The stature and person of Charlemagne are very
particularly taken notice of and described by the
writers of his history, by which it appears, that he
was as much above the ordinary size of men, as his
father Pepin was below it. Turpin, the archbishop
of Rheims, relates, that he was eight feet high, that
his face was a span and an half long, and his forehead
one foot in breadth, and that his body and limbs were
well proportioned. He had a great propensity to
learning, having had some of the most celebrated
scholars of the age in which he was born, for his
tutors; and it is to the honour of this country that
Alcuin, an Englishman, and a disciple of Bede, surnamed the Venerable, was his instructor in rhetoric,
logic, astronomy, and the other liberal sciences; †
notwithstanding which, there is a very curious particular recorded of him, namely, that he never could,
though he took infinite pains for the purpose, acquire
the manual art of writing or delineating the letters of
the alphabet; ‡ so that whatever books or collections
are ascribed to him, must be supposed either to have
been dictated by him, or written by others under his
immediate inspection: indeed, the works attributed
to him are of such a kind as necessarily to imply the
assistance of others, and that they are to be deemed
his in no other sense than as they received his sanction
or approbation; for they are chiefly either capitularies,
as they are called, relating to ecclesiastical matters, as
the government of the church, the order of divine
service, the observance of rites and ceremonies, and
the regulation of the several orders of the clergy; or
they are letters to the several princes and popes, his
contemporaries, and to bishops, abbots, and other
ecclesiastical persons.§ Two works in particular are
ascribed to him, and the opinion that they were of his
composition is generally acquiesced in; these are
letters written in his name to Elipandus, bishop of

---

* Baron. Annal. Ecclesiast. tom. IX. pag 415.

† Alcuin was well versed in the liberal sciences, particularly in music,
as appears by a tract of his on the use of the Psalms, and by the preface
to Cassiodorus De septem Disciplinis, first printed in Garetius's edition
of that author, and which is expressly said by Du Pin, Fabricius, and
others, to have been written by Alcuin. It was at the instance of Alcuin
that Charlemange, in the year 790, founded the university of Paris.

‡ Tentabat et scribere, tabulasque et codicellos ad hoc in lectulo sub
cervicalibus circumferre solebat, et cum vacuum tempus esset, manum
effingendis literis assuefacerit. Sed parum prospere successit labor
praeposterus ac sero inchoatus. Eginhart De Vita Caroli Magni, cap. xxv.
edit. Besselii.

§ Du Pin, Nouv. Biblioth. de Auteurs Ecclesiast. Siec. VIII.

Toledo, and other bishops of Spain, on certain points of doctrine; and four books against the worship of images: and it is with a view to these, and some other compositions that passed for his, that Sigebert, Du Pin, and others, give him a place among the ecclesiastical writers of the eighth century.

The zeal of this emperor to introduce the Cantus Gregorianus into his dominions, and to preserve it in a state of purity, has drawn upon him an imputation of severity; and upon the authority of that single passage in the Rationale of Durandus, above-cited, he is censured as having forced it upon the French with great cruelty. But there is nothing either in his relation of the supposed miracle in its favour, or in that of Baronius touching the contention at Rome, which will warrant this charge; for in that dispute at which Eugenius was present, it does not appear that he at all intermeddled; and in the other, the question which he put to his own clergy, is manifestly an appeal to reason, and no way indicates a disposition to coercive measures. 'Tell me,' said the emperor, 'which is the purer, the living fountain, or 'its rivulets?' They answered, 'the former.' Then said the emperor, 'Return ye to the fountain of St. 'Gregory; for in the rivulets the ecclesiastical cantus 'is corrupted.' Eginhart has mentioned in general that Charlemagne laboured to rectify the disorderly manner of singing in the church; * but he mentions no circumstances of bloodshed, or cruelty, to enforce a reformation: and the fact is, that several churches in his dominions, particularly those of Milan and Corbetta, were suffered to retain either the Ambrosian or a worse use, notwithstanding his wishes and efforts to the contrary.† In short, it seems that his behaviour upon this occasion was that of a wise man, or, at least, of one whose zeal had a sufficient allay of discretion;‡ and that he was possessed of a very

* Eginhart, De Vita Caroli Magni, cap. xxvi. edit. Besselii.

† Mosh. Eccl. Hist. 8vo. vol. II. pag. 98.
The notes of Besselius and others upon this passage of Eginhart [Legendi atque psallendi disciplinam diligentissime emendavit] are very curious, as they declare what were the abuses in singing which Charlemagne laboured to reform. Quantum veteres sono vocum distincto studuerint, vel illud argumento est, quod *phonasco* sedulam dederint operam, teste etiam *in Augusto* Sueton. cap. lxxxiv. Cæterum de *missaticis cantionibus et officio Ambrosiano* à Carolo correctis, prolixe Sigebertus, ad an. 774 & 790. Gobelin. Person. *ætat.* 6. *Cosmodrom.* cap. xl. p. 193. *Guliel. Durandus,* lib. V. *Rational. Divin. Offic.* cap. ii. Frid. Lindenbrogius *Glossar. L L. Antiq.* fol. 1369, & Goldast. *in Ekkebardi Junioris casus,* pag. 114. *tom. I. Rer. Alamannic.* Besselius. Carolus dissonantia cantus inter Romanos & Francos offensus,-eum conciliare & emendare omnibus viribus studuit; ideo a papa cantores Romanos sibi mitti petiit, qui Francos vera psallendi ratione imbuerent. Horum duos accepit, ex quibus unum palatio suo præfecit, alterum Metas misit, qui etiam ejus urbis incolas ita in canendi scientia erudivit, ut sicut Roma inter omnes cantu, sic Metæ inter Francos emineret, & seminarium quasi cantorum Cisalpinorum esset. Ab hac igitur urbe cantilena ecclesiastica Germanice tunc temporis *mete* dicebatur, quia hic præcipue cantus excolebatur, cujus denominationis vestigia adhuc hodie in vulgari locutione, *die Früh mette singen,* deprehenduntur. Horisonus maxime majorum nostrorum erat cantus, quem Monach. Egolism. in Vita Karoli M. ita describit: *Tremulas vel vinnulos, seu collisibiles, seu secabiles voces in cantu non poterant perfecte exprimere Franci, naturali voce barbarica frangentes in gutture voces potius, quam experimentes.* Clarius Ekkchard. Minim. in vit. Notkeri, cap. viii. *Alpina siquidem corpora,* ait, *vocum suarum tonitruis altisone perstrepentia, susceptæ modulationis dulcedinum proprie non resultant, quia bibuli gutturis barbara grossitas, dum inflexionibus et repercussionibus et diaphonarium diphtongis mitem nititur edere cantilenam, naturali quodam fragore, quasi plaustra per gradus confuse sonantia, rigidas voces jactat, sicque audientium animos, quos mulcere debuerant, tales exasperando magis ac obstrependo conturbant.* Nemo hæc opinor, mirabitur, qui fragmenta antiquæ Germanorum linguæ legit, ex quibus satis æstimari potest, quam difficilis fuerit Teutonicæ linguæ pronuntiatio, ac proin modulatio. Schmincke.

‡ His behaviour in this respect seems to have been widely different from that of Alphonsus, king of Spain, who, in the year 1080, banished the Gothic Liturgy out of his kingdom, and introduced the Roman

considerable portion of this latter quality, and entertained a mild and forgiving disposition towards those who had offended him, may be inferred from that very pretty story related by Mr. Addison, in the Spectator, No. 181, of the princess Imma, his daughter, and his secretary Eginhart, and her ingenious device, by carrying him on her back through the snow, to prevent the discovery of an amour which terminated in their marriage.

The purity to which the Gregorian chant was restored by the zeal of Charlemagne, subsisted no longer in France than to the time of Lewis the Debonnaire, his son and immediate heir, who succeeded to the empire of the West in 814; for in his reign the music of the church was again corrupted to that degree, that the Gregorian chant subsisted only in the memory of certain Romans, who had been accustomed to the singing it; for neither were there in France or at Rome, any books wherein it had been written. This strange circumstance is related by Amalarius Fortunatus, a principal ecclesiastic in the chapel of Lewis the Debonnaire, who himself was sent by Lewis to request of Gregory IV. then pope, a sufficient number of singers, to instruct the people; by whom the pope sent to the emperor for answer, that he could not comply with his request, for that the last of those men remaining at Rome had been sent into France with Walla, who had formerly been ambassador from Charlemagne on the same errand. The words of Amalarius, in the preface to his book De Ordine Antiphonarii, are these: 'When I had been a long while affected 'with anxiety, on account of the difference among 'the singers of antiphons in our province, and did 'not know what should be rejected and what retained, 'it pleased him who is bountiful to all, to ease me 'of my scruples; for there having been found in the 'monastery of Corbie, in Picardy, four books, three 'whereof contained the nocturnal, and the other the 'diurnal, office, I strove to make all the sail I could 'out of this sea of error, and to make a port of 'quiet; for when I was sent to Rome by the holy 'and most christian emperor, to the holy and most 'reverend father Gregory, concerning these books, 'it pleased his holiness to give me the following

office, though miracles were pleaded in favour of the former. Talent. ann. 1080. col. I. and vide Mariana, in his history of Spain, book IX. pag. 152. The circumstances of this extraordinary event, and the miracles that preceded it, are more particularly related by other historians, who speak to this purpose:—Alexander II. had proceeded so far in the year 1068, as to persuade the inhabitants of Arragon into his measures, and to conquer the aversion which the Catalonians had discovered for the Roman worship. But the honour of finishing this difficult work, and bringing it to perfection was reserved for Gregory VII. who, without interruption, exhorted, threatened, admonished, and intreated Sancius and Alphonso, the kings of Arragon and Castile, until, fatigued with the importunity of this restless pontiff, they consented to abolish the Gothic service in their churches, and to introduce the Roman in its place; Sancius was the first who submitted to this innovation, and in the year 1080 his example was followed by Alphonso. The methods which the nobles of Castile employed to decide the matter were very extraordinary. First, they chose two champions, who were to determine the controversy by single combat, one fighting for the Roman liturgy, the other for the Gothic. The fiery trial was next made use of to terminate the dispute; the Roman and Gothic liturgies were committed to the flames, which, as the story goes, consumed the former, while the latter remained unblemished and entire. Thus were the Gothic rites crowned with a double victory, which however was not sufficient to maintain them against the authority of the pope, and the influence of the queen Constantia, who determined Alphonso in favour of the Roman service. Vide Bona De Rebus Liturg. lib. I. cap. ix. pag. 216. Le Brun, loc. citat. pag. 292. Jo. de Ferreras, Hist. de l'Espagne, tom. III. pag. 237. 241. 246. Mosh. Eccl. Hist. vol. II. pag. 341.

'answer: "I have no singers of antiphons, whom "I can send to my son and lord the emperor; the "only remaining ones that we had, were sent from "hence into France with Walla, who was here on "an embassy." By means of these books, I dis-'covered a great difference between the antiphons of 'our singers and those formerly in use; the books 'contained a multitude of responsaria and antiphons, 'which they could not sing: among them I found 'one of those which were ordained by the apostolic 'Adrian. I knew that these books were older than 'that which remained in the Roman city, and though 'in some respects better instituted, yet they stood in 'need of some corrections, which, by the assistance 'of the Roman book, might be made of them: 'I therefore took the middle way, and corrected 'one by the other.' Notwithstanding this labour of Amalarius to reform the antiphonary, Nivers asserts, that the corruptions of music were then so great, that it was very difficult to say where the Gregorian Chant lay;* and, after all, the corrections of it by Amalarius Fortunatus were very ill received, as will appear by the following account of him.

Symphosius Amalarius, or, as he is called by most writers, Amalarius Fortunatus, was a deacon of Metz, and, as some ancient manuscripts assert, also an abbot. There seems to have been another of the latter name, archbishop of Treves, with whom he is often confounded; they both flourished about the middle of the ninth century. This of whom it is meant here to speak was a great ritualist, and wrote four books on the ancient ecclesiastical offices, which he dedicated to Lewis the Debonnaire, by whom he seems to have been greatly favoured. In these books he gives mystical reasons for those rites and ceremonies in divine worship, which wiser men look on as mere human inventions. To give a specimen of his manner of treating this subject, speaking of the habits of the priests, he says, 'The 'priest's vest signifies the right management of the 'voice; his albe, the subduing of the passions; his 'shoes, upright walking; his cope, good works; 'his stole, the yoke of Jesus Christ; the surplice, 'readiness to serve his neighbour; his handkerchief, 'good thoughts; and the pallium, preaching.†

But the book of Amalarius Fortunatus which more immediately relates to choral service, or the music of the church, is intitled, De Ordine Antiphonarii. In this he vindicates the disposition of the anthems, responses, and psalms, which he had made in the antiphonary, for the use of the churches in France. It seems, that in this and other of his works, he had censured the usage of the church of Lyons: this drew on him the resentment of two very able men, Agobard, archbishop of that city, and Florus, a deacon of the same church; the former of these wrote three treatises against his book of offices, and his correction of the antiphonary; and the latter accused him, in the councils of Quierci and Thionville, of maintaining erroneous opinions touching the moral and mystical significations of the ceremonies, and of insisting too strenuously on the use of the Roman ritual, which, notwithstanding its authority, had never been generally acquiesced in.

Agobard himself had corrected the antiphonary of his own church; and the treatises which he wrote against Amalarius, were not only a defence of those corrections, but a censure of his adversary. He says, that the poetical compositions of vain and fantastical men are not to be admitted into divine service, the whole of which ought to be taken from the scriptures: he complains, that the clergy spent more time in the practice of singing than in the study of the holy scriptures, and the discharge of their duty in the ministry of the gospel.

The writings of Amalarius upon the offices had given rise to many very captious questions; and to this in particular, Whether it be lawful to spit immediately after receiving the eucharist? His opinion on this point of theology is contained in one of his letters, wherein, after premising that he himself was very much troubled with phlegm, he holds it lawful to spit, when the communicant can no longer forbear that evacuation.‡

From the time of the attack on him by Agobard, and Florus, his deacon, we hear no more of Amalarius Fortunatus; and there is good reason to believe, that immediately after it, his memory sank into oblivion.

Before we dismiss this subject of the Cantus Gregorianus, it may not be improper to mention, that it has ever been held in such high estimation, that the most celebrated musicians in every age since its first institution, have occasionally exercised themselves in composing harmonies upon it; and numberless are the antiphons, hymns, misereres, and other offices, which have one or other of the ecclesiastical tones for

---

* The true causes of the first corruptions of the Cantus Gregorianus are plainly pointed out by the interpreter of Hugo Reutlingensis, who, in the passage cited by Sir Henry Spelman, ascribes it to the disuse of the stave, the cliffs, and other characters, necessary in the notation of music. To the same purpose Nivers relates, that they were not marked by notes, but by little points and irregular characters; which account is confirmed by some manuscripts, in which the corrupt method of notation above hinted at does most evidently appear. Martini of Bologna has exhibited some curious examples of this kind, and has with no less ingenuity than industry, from characters the most barbarous that can be conceived, and which were intended to express the initial clauses, and also the euouae of sundry antiphons, as used in particular churches, extracted a meaning, and reconciled them to the true method of notation.

† An opinion something like this, touching the mystical signification of habits and the manner of wearing them, seems to have been entertained by the common-law judges in the reign of king James, as appears by a solemn decree or rule, made by all the judges of the courts at Westminster, on the fourth day of June, 1635, for the purpose of appointing what robes they should thenceforth wear, upon ordinary and special occasions. In this decree mention is made of the scarlet casting-hood, which is by the decree directed to be put above the tippet, for which it is given as a reason that 'justice Walmesley and justice Warburton, and 'all the judges before, did wear them in that manner, and did declare, "that by wearing the hood on the right side and above the tippet, was "signified mere temporal dignity; and by the tippet on the left side only, "the judges did resemble priests." Dugd. Origines Juridiciales, pag. 102.

The author from whom the above passage is cited, craves leave to

mention a word or two concerning the collar of S S worn by the chief justices and chief baron, some orders of knights, the kings at arms, and others. Touching this badge of distinction, he, upon the authority of Georgius Wicelius, relates, that it has a reference to two brethren, Roman senators, named Simplicius and Faustinus, who suffered martyrdom under the emperor Dioclesian; and gives the following description of it from his author:—'It was the custom of those persons (the society 'of St. Simplicius) to wear about their necks silver collars, composed of 'double S S, which noted the name of St. Simplicius. Between these 'double S S the collar contained twelve small plates of silver, in which 'were engraved the twelve articles of the creed, together with a single 'trefoyle. The image of St. Simplicius hung at the collar, and from it 'seven plates, representing the seven gifts of the Holy Ghost.'

Dugdale adds, 'that the reason of wearing this chain was in regard 'that these two brethren were martyred, by tying a stone with a chain 'about their necks, and casting their bodies into the river Tiber.'

‡ Du Pin. Nouv. Biblioth. des Aut. Ecclesiast. Siec. IX.

their fundamental harmony. In a collection of madrigals, intitled Musica Divina, published by Pietro Phalesio, at Antwerp, in 1595, is one composed by Gianetto Palestina, beginning 'Vestiva 'i Colli,' in five parts, which is evidently a praxis on the fourth tone; and in 1694, Giov. Paolo Colonna, of Bologna, published certain of the psalms, for eight voices, 'Ad ritum ecclesiasticæ musices concinendi.'

CHAP. XXXI.

It is highly probable that from the time of its original institution the cantus ecclesiasticus pervaded the whole of the service; but this at least is certain, that after the final improvement of it by St. Gregory, all the accounts of the Romish ritual, and the manner of celebrating divine service in the western church, lead to the belief that, excepting the epistles and gospels, and certain portions of scripture, and the passional or martyrology, the whole of the service, nay that even the prayers and penitential offices, were sung. Among the canons of Elfric, made anno 957,* is the following :—

. 'Now it concerns mass - priests and all God's 'servants to keep their churches employed with 'divine service. Let them sing therein the seven 'tide-songs that are appointed them, as the synod 'earnestly requires, viz., the uht-song, the prime- 'song, the undern-song, the midday-song,† the noon- 'song, the even-song, the seventh [or night] song.' Can. xix. What these severally are, may be seen in a collection of ecclesiastical laws by the reverend and learned Mr. Johnson of Cranbrook, who has bestowed a note on the passage.

The twenty-first of the same canons is in these words :—' The priest shall have the furniture for his 'ghostly work before he be ordained, that is the holy 'books, the psalter and the pistol-book, gospel-book, 'and mass-book, the song-book, and the hand-book, 'the kalendar, the pasconal,‡ the penetential, and the 'lesson-book. It is necessary that the mass-priest 'have these books; and he cannot be without them 'if he will rightly exercise his function, and duly in- 'form the people that belongeth to him.'

These injunctions may seem to regard the celebration of mass, as well on festivals as on ordinary occasions, in cathedral and other churches; nevertheless the practice of singing, by which in this place nothing can possibly be understood but the Cantus Gregorianus, was not restrained either to the solemn choral service, or to that in parish-churches,

but in short it was used in the lesser offices. In the English-Saxon homily for the birth day of St. Gregory, the people are told that it was one of the injunctions of that father that the litany should be sung, and upon certain occasions to the number of seven times a-day. Among the ecclesiastical laws of king Canute, who reigned from 1016 to 1035, is one whereby the people are required to learn the Lord's prayer and the creed, because, says the law, 'Christ 'himself first *sang* pater-noster, and taught that 'prayer to his disciples.' Mrs. Elstob in her preface to the translation of the above homily, pag. 36, has inserted this law, and on the words Ꝺɲıꝛꞇ ꝛeaʟꝼ ꝛanᵹe Paꞇeɲ Noꝛꞇeɲ has the following note :— 'Singing the service was so much in practice in these 'times, [*i. e.* about the sixth century, when Austin the 'monk was sent by Gregory into Britain] that we find 'the same word ꝛınᵹan to signify both to pray and 'sing, as in the present instance.'

Farther, among the canons of Elfric above-cited is one containing directions for visiting the sick, wherein that rule of St. James, 'And they shall pray over 'him,' is expressed in these words, ᵹ hi him oꝼeɲ ꝛınᵹon that is, 'they shall sing over them.' The passage above-cited is part of the thirty-first of Elfric's canons, and is in truth a paraphrase on the words of St. James in his General Epistle, chap. v. ver. 13, 14, and, to give it at length, is as follows :— 'If any of you be afflicted, let him pray for himself 'with an even mind, and praise his Lord. If any be 'sick among you, let him fetch the mass-priests of the 'congregation, and let them sing over him, and pray 'for him and anoint him with oil in the name of the 'Lord. And the prayer of faith shall heal the sick, 'and the Lord shall raise him up; and if he be in 'sins, they shall be forgiven him : confess your sins 'among yourselves, and pray for yourselves among 'yourselves, that ye be healed.'

The several passages above-cited, as they show in some measure the ancient manner of celebrating divine service, and prove that almost the whole of it, particularly the lesser offices, was sung to musical notes; so do they account for that care and assiduity with which the study of music appears to have been cultivated in the several monasteries, schools, and universities throughout Europe, more especially in France and England. That the knowledge of music was confined to the clergy, and that monks and presbyters were the authors of most of the treatises on music now extant, is not so well accounted for by the general course of their lives, and the opportunities they had for study, as by this consideration, it was their profession; and to sing was their employment, and in a great measure their livelihood.§ The works of Chaucer and other old poets abound with allusions to the practice of singing divine service, and with evidences that a knowledge of the rudiments of singing was essential in every cleric, indeed little less so than for such a one to be able to read. In the Vision of Pierce Plowman, Sloth, in the character of a priest,

---

* Elfric is supposed to have been archbishop of York about the time above-mentioned, and Wulfin, to whom they are directed, bishop of one of the ancient sees of Dorchester or Shirburn, but which of the two is rather uncertain. This, as also some other collections of ecclesiastical laws here cited, are to be found in Sir Henry Spelman's Councils; but the extracts above given are from Mr. Johnson's valuable and useful work, which in some respects is preferable to the former.

† Midday-song was certainly at twelve o'clock, which we call noon; and the canon above mentions both a midday and a noon-song; this noon was the hora nona with the Latins, and our three o'clock. In the Shepherd's Almanac noon is midday, high noon three. Vide Johnson's Canons, title King Edgar's Laws Ecclesiastical, in a note on law V.
High noon is expressly mentioned in the old ballad of Chevy-Chase—
And long before highe noone they had
An hundrede fat buckes flaine ;

‡ *i. e.* The Passional or Martyrology.

§ The statutes of All-Souls college, in Oxford, which are but declaratory of the usage of ancient times, require that those elected to fellowships should be 'bene nati, bene vestiti, et mediocritur docti in plano cantu.'

among other instances of laziness and ignorance, confesses that he cannot perfectly repeat his Pater-noster as the priest singeth it ; and that though he had been in orders above thirty years, he can neither sol-fa, nor sing, nor read the lives of saints : the whole of his speech, which is exceedingly humourous and characteristic, is here inserted :—

> Than came Sloth, all beflaberd, with two flimy eyne,
> I muft fit faid the leg, or els I muft nedes nap,
> I mai not ftond ne ftoupe, ne without my ftole knele,
> Wer I brought a bed, but if my talend it made,
> Should no ringing do me rife, or I were ripe to dine,
> He began benedicite with a belke, and on his breaft knoked
> And rafkled and rored, and rut at the laft.
> Awak, reuk quod Repentaunce, and rape thee to the fhrift.
> If I fhould die by this day, me lyft not to looke :
> I can not perfitly my pater nofter, as the prieft it fingeth,
> But I can rimes of Robenhod, and Randal of Chefter,
> But of our Lord or our Lady, I lerne nothing at all ;
> I have made vows xl, and forgotten hem on the morow ;
> I performed never penance, as the prieft me hight,
> Ne right fory for my finnes, yet was I never ;
> And if I bid any beades, but it be of wrathe
> That I tel with my tong, is two mile from my hart ;
> I am occupied every day, holy day and other
> With idle tales at the ale, and other while in churches.
> God's peyne and his paffion, ful felde I thinke thereon,
> I vifited never feble men, ne fettred folk in pittes,
> I have lever hear an harlotry, or a fommers game
> Or leffinges to laugh at, and belye my neighboures,
> Than al that ever Marke made, Mathew, Jhon, and Lucas,
> And vigiles and fafting daies, all thefe I let paffe,
> And lie in bed in Lent, and my lemman in mine armes
> Till mattens and maffe be done, and than go I to the freres,
> Com I to 'Ite miffa eft,' * I hold me ferved ;
> I am not fhriven fometime, but if fickenes it make.
> Not twife in two year, and than up gueffe I thrive me.
> I have been prieft and perfon paffing thirty winter,
> Yet can I neither folfe nor fing, ne faindtes lives read,
> But I can finde in a fielde, or a furlong, an hare,
> Better than in Beatus vir, or in Beati omnes
> Conftrue one claufe, and ken it to my parifhens.
> I can hold loue daies, and heare a revenes rekening,
> And in cannon and in decretals I cannot read a line
> Yf I bugge and borrow ought, but if it be tailed
> I forget it as fonne, and if men me it afke
> Six fithes or feven, I forfake it with othes,
> And thus tene I true men, ten hundred times,
> And my fervauntes falary fometimes is behind,
> Ruth is to hear the rekening, when we fhal mak account ;
> So with wicked wil and with wrath my workmen I pai.
> Yf any man do me benefite, or helpe me at nede
> I am unkind againft his curtefi, and cannot underftand it,
> For I have and have had fome deale haukes maners.
> I am not lured with love, but if ought be under the thombe
> That kindnefs that mine even chriften, kid me ferther
> Sixe fithes I Sloth, have forgotten it fithe.
> In fpech and in fparing of fpence, I fpilt many a time
> Both flefh and fifh, and many other vitailes,
> Both bread and ale, butter, milke, and chefe,
> For Slouth in my fervice til it mighte ferve no man.
> I ran about in youth, and gave me not to learning,
> And ever fith have ben a beggar for my foule flouth.†

The foregoing account, as it relates solely to the Cantus Gregorianus, must be supposed to contain only the history of the choral music of the western church ; for it is to be remembered that antiphonal singing was introduced by the Greek fathers, and was first practised in the churches of the East ; and

* *i. e.* See an explanation of these words in a subsequent note. The meaning of the above passage is, 'If I come before the instant the 'people are dismissed from mass, I hold it sufficient.'

† Vision of Pierce Plowman, Passus quintus.

that the cantus of the Greek church, whatever it was, was not near so well cultivated and refined as that of the Roman ; this consideration, together with the short duration of the eastern empire, may serve to show how little is to be expected from an enquiry into the nature of the ancient Greek choral music. Vossius says in general, that the Greek church made use of modulations different from those of the western ; ‡ but for a formula of them we are very much to seek. As to the method of notation made use of by the Greeks in after-times, it did not in the least resemble that of the Latins, and was widely different from that of the ancient Greeks. Mont-faucon, in his Palœographia Græca, lib. V. cap. iii. gives a curious specimen of Greek musical notation from a manuscript of the eleventh century. (See Appendix, No. 38.)

Dr. Wallis had once in his hands a manuscript, which upon examination proved to be a Greek ritual ; it had formerly been part of the famous library founded at Buda by Matthæus Corvinus, king of Hungary, in 1485. In 1529 the city of Buda was taken by the Turks, and in 1686 retaken, after a long siege, by the forces of the emperor Leopold.

A description of this manuscript, and a general account of its contents is extant in a letter of Dr. Wallis to some person, probably the owner of it, who seems to have referred to the Doctor as being well skilled in music ; the doctor's opinion of it may be seen in the copy of his letter inserted at length at the bottom of the page. § It has lately been

‡ Ger. Voss. De Scientiis Mathematicis, cap. xxi. § 12.

§ 'Sir, I have seen and cursorily perused that ancient Greek manu-'script which is said to have been found in Buda, at the taking of that 'place from the Turks in the present war between the German emperor 'and the Turk.
'It is elegantly written in a small Greek hand, and is judged to be at 'least three hundred years old. The form of the letter is much different 'from that of those which we now use, and not easy to be read by those 'who are not acquainted with the Greek hand used in the manuscripts 'of that age.
'It bears, after the first three leaves, this title Αρχη συν Θεω αγίω 'της παπαδικης Τεκνης, which I take to intimate thus much:— 'Here begins, with the assistance of the sacred Deity, the patriarchal 'art ; for I take παπας then to signify as much as pope or patriarch, 'which is farther thus explained :—ακολθίαι ψαλλόμεναί εν Κον-'ςαντινοπολει, συντιθεισαι ταρα των κατα χαιρϫς ευρισκ-'ομενων εν αυτη ποιητων παλαιων τε και νεων. That is, the 'order of services in Constantinople composed by poets, such as from 'time to time have been there found, as well ancient as modern ; so that 'it seems to be a pandect or general collection of all the musical church-'services there used, as well the more ancient, as those which were 'then more modern ; after which it thus follows :—ων η αρχη σημοι-'δια και αι τϫτων φωναι, beginning with the musical notes and 'their sounds.
'After which title we have accordingly for about five leaves, an account 'of the musical notes then in use, their figures, names, and signifi-'cations ; without which the rest of the book would not be intelligible, 'and even as it is, it will require some sagacity and study, to find out 'the full import of it, and to be able to compare it with our modern 'music.
'The rest of the book consists of anthems, church-services for par-'ticular times, and other compositions, according to the music of that 'age, near a thousand I guess of one sort or other, or perhaps more.
'The whole consists of four hundred and thirteen leaves, close written 'on both sides in a small Greek hand, in the shape or form of what we 'would now call a very large octavo, on a sort of thick paper used in the 'eastern countries at that time.
'There is for the most part about twenty-eight lines in each page, 'that is fourteen lines of Greek text, according to which it is to be sung ; 'not such as those which we now use, nor like those of the more ancient 'Greeks, which they called of which Meibomius gives us 'a large account out of Alypius. But a new sort of notes, later than 'those of the ancient Greeks, but before those of Guido Aretinus, which 'we now use ; and commonly two or three compositions in one leaf, with 'the author's name for the most part.
'I do not find in it any footsteps of what is now common in our present 'music ; I mean compositions in two, three, four, or more parts ; all 'these, for ought I find, being only single compositions.

discovered that the MS. abovementioned was the property of Mr. Humfrey Wanley, as appears by a letter of his to Dr. Arthur Charlett, inserted also in the note, in which he offers to part with it to the university of Oxford. It is to be conjectured that the university declined purchasing it, and that Mr. Wanley disposed of it to the earl of Oxford, for in the printed Catalogue of the Harleian manuscripts in the British Museum, No. 1613, is the following article :—

‘ Codex chartaceus in 8vo, ut ajunt, majori, diversis ‘ manibus scriptus, et Græcorum more compactus; ‘ quem Dño Henrico Worslejo in Terra Sancta pere- ‘ grinanti dono dedet Notara (Νοταρᾶ an Νοταρίος ;) ‘ tunc Metropolita Cæsariensis; qui exinde, de mor- ‘ tuo doctissimo suo avunculo, factus est Patriarcha ‘ Hierosolymitanus ; adhuc, ni fallor, superstes. In ‘ illo habentur varia Ecclesiæ Grecæ Officia, Cantica, ‘ &c. Græcè descripta, Notulisq; Græcis Musicalibus ‘ insignita. Non iis dico, quæ priscis seculis apud ‘ Ethnicos Poetas et Philosophos in usu fuerunt; ‘ quarum etiamnum nonnullæ restant quasi e Nau- ‘ fragio Tabulæ : sed alterius planè formæ, quas ante ‘ plurima secula introductas adhuc retinet hodierna ‘ Græcorum Ecclesia.’

Mr. Wanley has inserted the rubrics in the order in which they occur ; these are to be considered as

‘ That which renders it most valuable is this ; we have of the more ‘ ancient Greek musicians seven published by Marcus Meibomius in the ‘ year 1652, Aristoxenus, Euclid, Nicomachus, Alypius, Gaudentius, ‘ Bacchius, and Aristides Quintilianus, before that of Martianus Capella ‘ in Latin. I have since published Ptolemy's Harmonics in the year 1682, ‘ and I have now caused to be printed Porphyry's Commentary on Ptolemy ‘ and Bryennius, which are both finished some while since, and they will ‘ thereby come abroad as soon as some other things are finished which are ‘ to bear them company. All these, except Martianus Capella, in Greek ‘ and Latin, and these are thought to be all the Greek musicians now ‘ extant.

‘ But all those concern only the theoretical part of music, of the prac- ‘ tical part of it, that is, musical compositions of the ancient Greeks, it ‘ hath been thought till that, there was not one extant at this day, ‘ whereby we have been at a loss what kind of compositions theirs were, ‘ and how theirs did agree or disagree with what we now have, and it is ‘ a surprise to light at once upon so many of them.

‘ 'Tis true that all those are more modern than those of Aristoxenus, ‘ Euclid, Nicomachus, and others of the more ancient Greeks, being all ‘ since the times of Christianity, and such as were used in the Greek ‘ church of Constantinople : but they are much more ancient than any ‘ were thought to be extant.   Your's,
                                                        ‘ JOHN WALLIS.’

Copy of Mr. Wanley's letter to Dr. Charlett.

‘ Honoured Sir,   London, June 13, 1698.
‘ I cannot forbear sending you word of the good fortune I have lately ‘ had to compass a Greek manuscript, which contains the art of singing, ‘ with the names, powers, and characters of their musical notes in great ‘ variety. And a collection of anthems, hymns, &c. set to their musick ‘ by the best masters of Constantinople, as intended and used to be sung ‘ in their churches upon all the chief festivals of the year. It has like- ‘ wise the musical part of their common liturgy with the notes ; and ‘ both these, not only of the later music of the said masters, but very ‘ often the more antient too, used before their times The names of ‘ these masters prefixed to their compositions, are about threescore in ‘ number, some of which I here set down : [Here follows a long list of ‘ Greek names, which it is needless to insert, as the MS. is yet in being ‘ and accessible.]

‘ I believe many of their names, and much more their works, might ‘ have been long enough unknown to us without the help of this book. ‘ Here is likewise a sprinkling of the music used in the churches of ‘ Anatolia, Thessalonica, Thebes, and Rhodes, besides that piece called ‘ Περσικὸν, and other tracts.

‘ The MS. was taken from the Turks in plundering Buda, about the ‘ year 1686, and was afterwards bought by an English gentleman for 4l. ‘ but I lying here at great charges, cannot afford to sell it so cheap. It ‘ is about 300 years old, fairly written upon cotton paper, taking up above ‘ four hundred leaves in a large 8vo.

‘ The book ought to be placed in the publick library ; and if, Sir, you ‘ are willing to think that the university will consider me for it, I will ‘ bring it along with me the next week : If not, I can be courted to part ‘ with it here upon my own terms.
‘ For the Rev. Dr. Charlett,   I am reverend and honoured Sir,
‘ Master of University college   Your most faithful and obedient servant,
‘ in Oxford.   HUMFREY WANLEY.’

so many distinct heads, and give occasion for an explanation of many difficult words made use of in them, and also in the offices ;* in which he discovers great learning and sagacity.

* To give a few instances. 295. Τροπάριον. Vox generica, et Canticis in Ecclesia Græca receptis communis : MODULUM semper vertit, et ANTIPHONAS Latinorum quadantenus respondere observat Goarus. Du Cang.

In Ecclesia Orientali, canebantur certis diebus certi CANONES, quos in TROPARIA dividebant plerumque 30, et nonnumquam plura : excepto uno MAGNO CANONE, qui 250 complectebatur. Suicer. ex Triodio.

CANONES in ODAS dividuntur ; ODÆ in TROPARIA, ex quibus componuntur. Singula namque Troparia continent aut plura aut pauciora, cum eorum Numerus determinatus non sit. Troparia quandoque Libera ac Vaga relinquunter : quandoque primis Litteris quasi Annulis in Verbis veluti Catenula inseruntur, quam Acrostichida autores vocant. Du Cang. ex Allatio de Georgiis.

378. Ἀντίφονον, Fœmineum ANTIPHONA à Neutrio ANTIPHONUM discrimen apud nos obtinet maximum : quamvis ab uno Græco vocabulo, utrumque fuerint Latini mutuati : ANTIPHONA namque est Sententia vel Modulus cuilibet Psalmo decantato adjunctus, et quasi EP OPPOSITO RESPONDENS, inquit Honorius Solitarius, lib. ii. cap. 17. ANTIPHONUM autem ut hic usurpatur Psalmi sunt plures Versus, ad quorum singulos, una et eadem sit semper ab altero Choro Responsio : et propter hanc Unam et Reciprocam Sententiam semper illatam, ἀντίφονον, quasi VOX OPPOSITA, seu Vocis oppositio vocatur. Ejus forma qualis sit, ex his Mysallibus Antiphonis (i. e. Liturgia S. Chrysostomi) fol. 105, et seq. positis innotescit. Extat enim ibi Psalmus ἀγαθὸν τὸ ἐξομολογεισθαι τω κυρίω cujus singulis versibus respondet αντιφωνων Ταῖς πρεσβείαις τῆς Θεοτόκε ᷉ καὶ τὰ εξῆς, illis sæplus OPPONENDUM. Quamvis fatear rem potius in adversum sensum trahendam . cum enim Psalmus ipse vocatur αντιφωνον, ejus Versus sunt qui uni et eidem dicto, i. e. resumpto (εφυμνιω ejus frequentius repetito) OPPONUNTUR. Ut certe, quia mutua et utriusque Chori ad invicem Responsio : et voces jam auditæ, rursum vel ex toto, vel ex parte, iterantur prout quoque in Latinis RESPONSORIIS contingit) ἀντίφωνον appellatur. Unde, tum propter Vocis Significationem, tum propter Compositionis formam, Latine RESPONSORIUM congrue reddi posset. Vetat tamen Usus loquendi antiquus, ut Missæ Introitum alio quam ANTIPHONI vel ANTIPHONÆ Nomine dicatur, &c. Goar.

428. Τρισάγιον, TRISANCTUM, Hymni genus, cujus hæc erant Verba, Ἅγιος ὁ Θεὸς, ἅγιος ἰσχυρὸς, ἅγιος ἀθάνατος, ἐλεησον, ἡμᾶς in quo ἅγιος ὁ Θεὸς referebatur ad Deum Patrem; ἅγιος ἰσχυρὸς ad Deum Filium; ἅγιος ἀθάνατος ad Spiritum sanctum. Vocatur etiam τρισαγιος ὑμνολογια, χερββικος ὕμνος, ἀγγελων ὑμνολογια, τρισαγιος αινος αγγελων Ὑμνωδια et τρισαγια φωνη. Anno enim Theodosii Junioris quinto (vel trigesimo secundum Cedrenum, &c.) magno existente Terræ Motu, et Muris corruentibus, quia Amalechitæ intra Urbem inhabitarent, et adversus Hymnum hunc Blasphemias proloquerentur : Preces et Supplicationes in Campo Tribunalis, Theodosius cum Proclo Patriarcha instituit. Cum vero κύριε ἐλέησον clamarent Horis aliquot continuis, Adolescentulus quidam inconspectu omnium in aërem sublatus est, audivitque Angelos clamantes, Ἁγιος ὁ δεὸς, ἅγιος ἰσχυρὸς, ἅγιος ἀθάνατος, ἐλεησον ἡμᾶς. Quod cum mox demissus narrâsset, omnes eodem modo TRISAGIUM canere cœperunt, et cessavit Terræ Motus. Huic Hymno Imperator Anastasius post illa ἅγιος ἀθάνατος addi voluit ο ϛαυροϑεις ὑπὲρ ημεν, verum id cum magno Malo et suo, et Constantinopolitanórum.— Observandum tandem discrimen quod est inter το Τρισάγιον et ΙΤΜΝΙΟΝ ΕΡΙΝΙCΙΟΝ, in quo similiter Ἅγιος canebatur, hunc in modum, ἅγιος, ἅγιος, ἅγιος κύριος σαβαωθ —Ergo τρισάγιον initio Liturgiæ ante Epistolæ Lectionem canebatur. Hymnus vero CHERUBICUS et ἐπινίκιος, post Catechumenorum et Pœnitentium dimissionem. Τρισάγιον quoque usurpabant pro Sacrosancta Trinitate. Suicer.

441. Χορός, proprie notat Canentium atque Saltantium collectam Multitudinem, notum est in Ecclesia hodie Psalmodiam retineri, et quidem CHORO, quibusdam in Locis, bifariam diviso. Improprie notat Multitudinem amice conspirantium in doctrina, &c. Suicer.

Χορός, dividebantur χοροὶ in δεξιόν, DEXTRUM, et ἀρίςερον, SINISTRUM. Triodium in Sabbato Sancto αρχεται ἀνθις μετὰ μελβς ὁ δεξιὸς ἤλβς ὁ πρᾶτος χορός, in quo quidem DEXTRO ac PRIMO CHORO consistit Sacerdos qui sacræ Liturgiæ præest. Du Cang.

The practice of dividing the chorus into two parts, and disposing the singers on both sides of the choir, seems best of any method to correspond with the intention of antiphonal or responsive singing. But it is to be remarked that in the Romish service there are many offices composed for four, and even eight choirs as they are termed. These are in fact not distinct choirs, but rather so many smaller chorusses, singing alternately with each other, and together at stated intervals ; and these are also divided according to the choral order, and stationed on both sides of the choir. In our English service-books the two different sides are distinguished by the names of the officers that superintend them respectively ; for instance, as the seat of the Dean is on the right, those on that side are directed when to sing by the word Decani ; and as the station of the præcentor or chanter is on the left, those on that side are directed by the word Cantoris. *The Dean and the Precentor are the*

But as a mere verbal description of this MS. would fail to convey an adequate idea of the character in which it is written, or of the musical notes, which are the principal object of the present enquiry, the initial and final pages of the volume are given in that kind of transcript which the curious distinguish by the appellation of facsimile. (Appendix, Nos. 39, 40.)

It is very clear from that letter that Dr. Wallis looked upon manuscripts of this kind as a very great curiosity; and this judgment of his is founded upon an opinion which he says prevailed at the time of giving it, that there was no such thing as an ancient Greek musical composition extant.

The causes of this scarcity of Greek ritual music are to be sought in the history of that church. It has already been related that choral service was first introduced by the Greek fathers, and that as the pomp and splendour of the Greek worship was very great, and calculated to engage the affections of the people, the greater part of the offices were sung. The consequence thereof was, that the clerks employed for that purpose were of little less estimation than those that exercised the sacerdotal function. This appears from a passage in the liturgy of St. Mark, wherein is a prayer for priests, deacons, and singers.* We may hence conclude that a ritual of some kind or other subsisted in that very early age; and it is very probable that that kind of melody which St. Ambrose instituted in his church at Milan, was no other than what was used by St. Basil and Chrysostom in their several churches in Asia, since it is apparently founded on the ancient Greek modes. The music of the Greek church might in all probability continue to flourish until the translation of the imperial seat from the East to the West; and as after that important event that church lost the protection of an emperor, and was left in a great measure to shift for itself, its splendour, its magnificence and discipline declined apace, and it was not the authority of a patriarch that was sufficient to support it.

But the ruin of the Greek church was completed in the taking and sacking of Constantinople by the Turks in the year 1453, when their libraries and public repositories of archives and manuscripts were destroyed, and the inhabitants driven to seek shelter in the neighbouring islands, and such other places as their conquerors would permit them to abide in.

From that time the Greek Christians, excepting those who inhabit the empire of Russia, have lived in a state of the most absolute subjection to the enemies of true religion and literature, and this to so great a degree, that the exercise of public worship is not permitted them but upon conditions so truly humiliating, as to excite the compassion of many who have been spectators of it. Maundrel in his Journey from Aleppo to Jerusalem, mentions his visiting a Greek church at a village called Bellulca, where he saw an altar of no better materials than dirt, and a crucifix of two bits of lath fastened cross-wise together.†

A modern traveller, Dr. Frederic Hasselquist, who visited the Levant in the year 1749, indeed mentions that in the church at Bethlehem he saw an organ, but it seems that it belonged to the Latin convent: as to the Greek Christians he represents them as living in a state of absolute poverty and dejection in almost all the places that he visited.

Laying all these circumstances together, it will cease to be a wonder that so few vestiges of the Greek church-music are now remaining, whatever others there are may possibly be found in the Russian ritual; but as no one can say how far that may have deviated from the primitive one, it is to be feared that an enquiry of this kind would elude the utmost efforts of industry.‡

CHAP. XXXII.

Isidore, bishop of Seville, is frequently ranked among the writers on music, for this reason, as it seems, that he was the author of Originum, sive Etymologiarum, a kind of epitome of all arts and sciences, in which are several chapters with the following titles, as Cap. i. De Musica et ejus Nomine. Cap. ii. De Inventoribus ejus. Cap. iii. Quid sit

---

officers of the greatest dignity in all choral establishments, but there are others which usage and successive endowments have authorised and the canon law recognises; for which reason a brief delineation of Cathedral Polity as it subsists in England and elsewhere may seem but a necessary adjunct to this note. The Bishop is properly the head of the church, having the Presbyters who are variously termed Canons or Prebendaries, though their offices in the choir are but ill-defined by the canonists, are his council, and were anciently ten in number. In the choral functions the Precentor presided till about the middle of the sixth century, but afterwards when endowments began to be made of cathedral and collegiate churches, it was thought unfit that he who was at most but one of the Choir should govern as well as direct the rest; this made the office of Dean necessary, which being a term borrowed from the military discipline and derived from Decanus, and that from δεκὰς, ten, imports a right of presiding over ten subordi-'nates; these in their corporate capacity are stiled Dean and Chapter.—The Dean is then to be considered as Arch-presbyter and head of the choir, as the Bishop is of the church; next to him in legal order follows the Precentor formerly stiled Primicerius and in later times Chanter; then the Canons, and after them Minor Canons, who are also Presbyters, and with the Lay Vicars are conjectured to hold the place of the ancient Psalmistæ or Canonical Singers, who in a Canon of the Council of Laodicea are described as singing out of the Parchment; lastly Choristers or Singing Children. Vide Bp. Wetenhall, of Gifts and Offices, page 522 et seq.

442. Κανονάρχης. Præfectus Canonum, qui Monachos ad psallendos in Vigiliis Canones excitabat. Suicer.

509. Πρωτοψάλτης, Primicerius Cantorum; qui dictus etiam δομέσικος τῶν ψαλῶν. Verum non habebat Ecclesiæ Proto-Psaltas, sed Domesticos Cantorum; cum Proto-Psaltæ propriè essent Cleri Palatini, &c. Du Cang.

* See a collection of the principal liturgies used in the celebration of the holy eucharist, by Dr. Thomas Brett, pag. 34.

† 'Being informed that here were several Christian inhabitants in 'this place, we went to visit their church, which we found so poor and 'pitiful a structure, that here Christianity seemed to be brought to its 'humblest state, and Christ to be laid again in a manger. It was only 'a room of about four or five yards square, walled with dirt, having 'nothing but the uneven ground for its pavement; and for its ceiling 'only some rude traves laid athwart it, and covered with bushes to keep 'out the weather. On the east side was an altar built of the same 'materials with the wall; only it was paved at top with pot-sherds and 'slates, to give it the face of a table. In the middle of the altar stood 'a small cross composed of two laths nailed together in the middle: 'on each side of which ensign were fastened to the wall two or three old 'prints, representing our blessed Lord and the blessed Virgin, &c., the 'venerable presents of some itinerant friars, that had passed this way. 'On the south side was a piece of plank supported by a post, which we 'understood was the reading-desk, just by which was a little hole 'commodiously broke through the wall to give light to the reader. 'A very mean habitation this for the God of heaven! but yet held in 'great esteem and reverence by the poor people; who not only come 'with all devotion hither themselves, but also deposit here whatever is 'most valuable to them in order to derive upon it a blessing. When we 'were there the whole room was hanged about with bags of silk-worms' 'eggs; to the end that by remaining in so holy a place, they might 'attract a benediction and a virtue of encreasing.' Maundrell's Journey from Aleppo to Jerusalem, pag. 7.

‡ A gentleman, who has lately obliged the world with an account of the Greek church, in Russia, speaking of the ritual of the Russians, takes notice that the music of their service books is written on a stave of five lines, from which he rightly infers that the ecclesiastical tones as sung by them are either corrupted, or have widely deviated from their original institution. The Rites and Ceremonies of the Greek Church in Russia, by Dr. John Glen King, pag. 43, in not.

Musica. Cap. iv. De tribus Partibus Musicæ. Cap.
v. De triformi Musicæ Divisione. Cap. vi. De prima
Divisione Musicæ harmonica. Cap. vii. De secunda
Divisione organica. Cap. viii. De tertia Divisione
rythmica. Cap. ix. De Musicis Numeris; and also
a Treatise on the Ecclesiastical Offices, in both of
which there are many things relating to music, and
in the former especially, many etymologies of musical
terms, and names of musical instruments. His father
was Severianus, a son of Theodoric king of Italy;
he succeeded his brother Leander in the bishopric
of Seville about the year 595, and governed that
church near forty years : he was very learned in all
subjects, more especially in geometry, music, and
astrology; his book on the Offices contains the principal points of discipline and ecclesiastical polity.
Mosheim in his chronological tables makes him the
principal compiler of the Mosarabic liturgy, which
is the ancient liturgy of Spain. He died in the
year 636, and has a place in the calendar of Romish
saints.

Of the introduction of music into the church-
service, of the institution of the four tones by St.
Ambrose, and of the extension of that number to
eight by St. Gregory, mention has been made;
we are now to speak of another very considerable
improvement of church music, namely, the introduction of that noble instrument the organ, which
we are told took place about the middle of the
seventh century. Authors in general ascribe the
introduction of organs into churches to pope Vitalianus, who, as Du Pin, Platina, and others relate, was
advanced to the pontificate in A. C. 663 : the enemies
of church music, among whom the Magdeburg commentators are to be numbered, invidiously insinuate
that it was in the year 666 that organs were first
used in churches,* from whence they infer the unlawfulness of this innovation, as commencing from an
era that corresponds with the number of the beast
in the Apocalypse : but the wit of this sarcasm is
founded on a supposition that, upon enquiry, will
appear to be false ·in fact; for though it is uncon-
troverted that Vitalianus introduced the organ into
the service of the Romish church, yet the use of
instruments in churches was much earlier; for we
are told that St. Ambrose joined instruments of
music with the public service in the cathedral church
of Milan, which example of his was so well approved
of, that by degrees it became the general practice of
other churches, and has since obtained in almost all
the Christian world besides. Nay, the antiquity of
instrumental church-music is still higher, if we may
credit the testimony of Justin Martyr and Eusebius,
the latter of whom lived fifty, and the former two
hundred years before the time of St. Ambrose. But
to return :—

Sigebert relates that in the year 766 the emperor
Constantine† sent an organ as a present to Pepin,

then king of France, though the annals of Metz
refer to the year 757; from hence some with good
reason date the first introduction of the organ into
that kingdom, but it was not till about the year 826
that organs became common in Europe.

Whoever is acquainted with the exquisite mechanism of this instrument, and considers the very
low state of the manual arts at that time, will hardly
be persuaded that the organ of the eighth century
bore any very near resemblance to that now in use.
Zarlino, in his Sopplimenti Musicali, libro VIII.
pag. 290, has bestowed great pains in a disquisition
on the structure of the ancient organ ; the occasion
of it he says was this: a lady of quality, Madonna
Laura d'Este, in the year 1571, required of Zarlino,
by his friend Francesco Viola, his sentiments of the
organ in general, and whether he took the modern
and the ancient instrument of that name to be alike
or different : in giving his opinion on this question
he attempts a description of the hydraulic organ from
Vitruvius, which he leaves just as he found it ; he
then cites a Greek epigram of Julian the Apostate,
who lived about the year 364, in which an organ is
described. A translation of this epigram in the
following words is to be found in Mersennus, lib. III.
De Organis, pag. 113 :—

Quam cerno, alterius naturæ est fistula : nempe
Altera produxit fortasse hæc œnea tellus.
Horrendum stridet, nec nostris illa movetur
Flatibus, et missus taurino e carcere ventus
Subtus agit læves calamos, perque ima vagatur.
Mox aliquis velox digitis, insignis et arte
Adstat, concordes calamis pulsatque tabellas :
Ast illæ subito exiliunt, et carmina miscent.

As to the organ of the moderns, he says the common opinion is that it was first used in Greece, and
from thence introduced into Hungary, and afterwards
into Bavaria; but this he refutes, as he does also the
supposed antiquity of an organ in the cathedral
church of Munich, pretended to be the most ancient
in the world, with pipes of one entire piece of box,
equal in magnitude to those of the modern church
organ : he then speaks of the sommiero of an organ
in his possession that belonged to a church of the
nuns in the most ancient city of Grado, the seat of
a patriarch before the sacking of it by Pepo the
patriarch of Aquileia, in the year 580. This sommiero he describes as being about two feet long, and
a fourth of that measure broad, and containing only
thirty pipes and fifteen keys, but without any stop;
the pipes he says were ranged in two orders, each
containing fifteen, but whether they were tuned in
the unison or octave, as also whether they were of
wood or metal, he says is hard to guess : he says
farther that this instrument had bellows in the back
part, such as are to be seen in the modern regali, and
exhibits a draft of this instrument in the following
form :—

---

* Isaacson on very good authority fixes it at 660.

† Surnamed Copronymus, because he is said to have defiled the font
at his baptism. Mosh. vol. II. pag. 92, in not.
Other writers speak particularly, and say that the first use of organs in

the western church was at Acon. Isaacs. Chron. Anno Christi 826.
Church Story : but see Bingh. Antiqu. Vol. I· 314, a citation from Thomas
Aquinas, shewing that they were not in use in his time, viz., 1250.

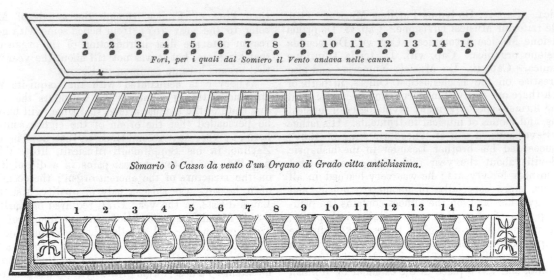

Fori, per i quali dal Somiero il Vento andava nelle canne.

Sòmario ò Cassa da vento d'un Organo di Grado citta antichissima.

Zarlino speaks also of an ancient organ in the church of St. Anthony of Padua, of a convenient bigness. which had many orders of pipes, but no stops; and both these instruments he makes to be much more ancient than that of Munich in Bavaria; concerning the accounts of which he seems to be dissatisfied; for as to the pipes, he says there are no boxtrees, except such as grow in the country of Prester John, of a size sufficient to make pipes of one piece so large as those are said to be; and that, after such were found, an organ so constructed as that a single pipe should require a whole tree, is not easily to be conceived of.

He farther takes some pains to shew the error of those who imagine that the organ mentioned by Dante, in the ninth canto of his Purgatory, was different in many respects from that of the ancients. The passage in Dante is an imitation of Lucan, lib. III. 'Tunc rupes tarpeia sonat:'—

> Non ruggio sì, nè si mostrò si acra
> Tarpeia, come tolto le fu il buono
> Metello, donde poi rimase macra.
> Io mi rivolsi attento al primo tuono,
> E, *Te Deum laudamus*, mi parea
> Udir in voce mista al dolce suono.
> Tale imagine appunto mi rendea
> Ciò ch' l' udiva, qual prender si suole
> Quando a cantar con organi si stea:
> Che or si or no s'intendon le parole.

But upon the whole, he is clearly of opinion that the hydraulic organ of Vitruvius, that other mentioned in the epigram of Julian above-cited, the Bavarian organ, and that in the city of Grado, were essentially the same with the organ of his time.*

That choral music had its rise in the church of Antioch, the metropolis of Syria, and that from thence it spread through Greece, and was afterwards brought into Italy, the several testimonies above adduced sufficiently shew: from thence it made its way into France, Britain, Spain, and Germany, and at length was received throughout Christendom. As

'may conjecture what they can; for that it is sufficient that he has given 'the practice of his own age, which, he says, by far surpasses any thing 'that the ancients have left behind on this subject.' Harm. Univer. lib. VI. pag. 387.

The monument above spoken of has been recovered. Probably it is extant in some one or other of the collections of the antiquities, published since the time of Mersennus, but the following representation of it was found among the papers of Nicola Francesco Haym, the author of Il Tesoro Britannico delle Medaglie Antiche, and as it corresponds exactly with the description of it by Mersennus, it is here inserted:—

L. APISIUS C. F. SCAPTIA CAPITOLINUS EX TESTAMENTO FIERI MONUMEN. JUSSIT ARBITRATU HEREDUM MEMORUM SIBI ET SUIS;

The same author takes occasion to mention an organ described in an epistle to Dardanus, in the fourth volume of the works of St. Jerome, which, from the many barbarisms that appear in it, he says, ought not to be attributed to that excellent man. This organ, he says, is represented as having twelve pair of bellows and fifteen pipes, and a windchest, made of two elephant skins; and as yielding a sound as loud as thunder, which might be heard at more than a thousand paces distance. Mersennus adds, that in the same epistle mention is made of an organ at Jerusalem, which was heard at the mount of Olives. He says, there are many other instruments described in the same epistle; but he remarks, that if the elephant skins above mentioned were sewed together, and were fitted by bellows, the instrument was more properly a cornamusa, or bagpipe, than an organ.

To this account of organs of a singular construction, the following may be added of some less ancient. Fuller, in his Worthies of Denbighshire, pag. 33, mentions an organ with golden pipes. Leander Alberti, in his Description of Italy, says, he saw one, in the court of the duke of Mantua, of alabaster; and another at Venice, made all of glass; and Pope Sylvester the Second made an organ that was played on by warm water. See Oldys's British Librarian, No. 1. pag. 51.

---

* Mersennus seems to carry the antiquity of the organ farther back than Zarlino has done in the passage above cited, and to think that not only the hydraulic but the pneumatic organ, was in use among the Romans, though he has left it to the antiquaries to ascertain the precise time; for speaking of the epigram made in its praise by the emperor Julian, and which is inserted in his (Mersennus's) Latin work, he relates 'that the Sieur Naudè had sent him from the Matthei gardens at Rome, 'the form of a little cabinet of an organ, with bellows like those made use 'of to kindle a fire, and a representation of a man placed behind the 'cabinet blowing the bellows, and of a woman touching the keys.' He says, 'that on the bottom of the cabinet was the following inscription:— 'L. APISIUS C. F. SCAPTIA CAPITOLINUS EX TESTAMENTO 'FIERI MONUMEN. JUSSIT ARBITRATU HEREDUM ME-'ORUM SIBI ET SUIS; concerning which, he adds, the antiquarians

to the time and manner of its introduction into Britain, history has ascertained it beyond a possibility of doubt; for we are expressly told, that at the time when Austin the monk arrived here, charged with a commission to convert the inhabitants of Britain to Christianity, singers attended him : and so watchful were the Roman pontiffs over its progress in this island, that in little more than half a century, one of the most excellent chanters that Rome afforded was sent hither, by Agatho, to reform such abuses as in that short period he might find to have crept into it. That it was received with great eagerness by the people of this country, there are many reasons for thinking; for, first, their fondness for music of all kinds was remarkably great; Giraldus Cambrensis asserts, almost in positive terms, that the natives of Wales and the northern parts of Great Britain were born musicians.

Besides this, there are proofs in history that, in a very short time after its first planting amongst us, music was observed to flourish; and that, in short, it loved the soil, and therefore could not fail to grow.

It was in the cathedral church of Canterbury that the choral service was first introduced; and till the arrival of Theodore, and his settlement in that see, the practice of it seems to have been confined to the churches of Kent; but after that, it spread over the whole kingdom. The clergy made music their study, they became proficients in it, and, differing perhaps in that respect from those of other countries, they disseminated the knowledge of it among the laity. Hollinshed, after Bede, describes the progress of singing in churches in these words :—

' Also, whereas before-time there was in a manner ' no singing in the Englishe churches, except it were ' in Kent, now they began in every church to use ' singing of divine service, after the ryte of the church ' of Rome. The archbishop Theodore, finding the ' church of Rochester void by the death of the last ' bishop, named Damian, he ordeyned one Putta, ' a simple man in worldly matters, but well instructed ' in ecclesiastical discipline, and namely well seene in ' song, and musicke to be used in the church, after ' the manner as he had learned of Pope Gregories ' disciples.' *

After this, viz., in 677, Ethelred, king of the Mercians, invaded the kingdom of Kent with a great army, destroying the country before him, and amongst other places the city of Rochester; the cathedral church thereof was also spoiled and defaced, and Putta driven from his residence; upon which, as the same historian relates, ' he wente unto Scroulfe, the bishop ' of Mercia, and there obteyning of him a small cure, ' and a portion of ground, remayned in that country; ' not once labouring to restore his church of Rochester ' to the former state, but went aboute in Mercia to ' teach song, and instruct such as would learne ' musicke, wheresoever he was required, or could get ' entertainment.'†

* First volume of the Chronicles of England, Scotland, and Ireland, pag. 178, col. ii. edit. 1577.

† Ibid. pag. 181.

CHAP. XXXIII.

The several improvements herein before enumerated, related solely to that branch of music which those who affect to use the terms of the ancients, called the Melopœia; what related to the measures of time, which, has been shewn, were regulated solely by the metrical laws, as they stood connected with poetry, or, to use another ancient term, the rhythmopœia was suffered to remain without innovation till the beginning of the fourteenth century, as it is said, when John De Muris, a doctor of the Sorbonne, and a native of England, though the generality of writers suppose him to have been a Norman, invented characters to signify the different lengths of sounds, and, in short, instituted a system of metrical music.

It has already been mentioned, that till within these few years it was a dispute among the writers on music, whether the ancients, by whom we are to understand the Greek harmonicians and their followers, were acquainted with music in consonance, or not : the several arguments of each party have been stated, and, upon a comparison of one with the other, it does most clearly come out, that music in consonance, though as to us it be of great antiquity, is, with respect to those of whom we are now speaking, a modern improvement.

In fixing the æra of this invention, those who deny that it was known to the ancients are almost unanimous in ascribing it, as indeed they do the invention of the polyplectral species of instruments, which are those adapted to the performance of it, to Guido Aretinus. Kircher was the first propagator of this opinion,‡ which he confesses is founded on a bare hint of Guido; but in this he is mistaken, both in his opinion and in the fact which he assigns as a reason for it; for neither in the Micrologus nor in the other tract of Guido, intitled, Argumentum novi Cantus inveniendi, of both which a very particular account will be given hereafter, is there the least intimation of a claim to either of the above inventions.

Not to insist farther on this mistake, the fact is, that symphoniac music was known in the eighth century, and that Bede does very particularly mention a well-known species of it, termed Descant : and this alone might suffice to show that music in consonance, though unknown to the ancient Greeks, was yet in use and practice before the time of Guido, who flourished not till the beginning of the eleventh century; for what are we to understand by the word Descant, but music in consonance?

But lest a doubt should remain touching the nature of the practice which the word Descant is intended to signify, let us attend to a very particular description of it, contained in an ancient manuscript, formerly part of the Cotton library, but which was destroyed by the accident of fire which happened some years ago, 23 Oct., 1731. at Ashburnham-house, where it was deposited. The passage above mentioned may be thus translated. §

‡ Musurg. tom. I. pag. 215.

§ From a copy made for the use of Dr. Pepusch. Vide Mr. Castley's catalogue.

'If two or three descant upon a plain-song, they 'must use their best endeavours to begin and proceed 'by different concordances; for if one of them should 'concur with another, and sing the same concord to 'the plain-song, then ought they immediately to 'constitute another. If you would descant under 'the plain-song, in the duple, [i. e. octave] in the 'sixth, the fifth, the third, the twelfth, or in the 'fifteenth, you ought to proceed in the same manner 'as you would were you to descant above the plain-'song; whoever sings above it must be experienced 'in the grave sounds, their nature and situation; for 'on this the goodness of the harmony in a great 'measure depends. Another method of descanting 'is practised, which, if it be well pronounced, will, 'though easy, appear very artificial, and several will 'seem to descant on the plain-song, when in reality 'one only shall descant, and the others modulate the 'plain-song in different concordances: it is this, let 'there be four or five singers, and let one begin the 'plain-song in the tenor; let the second pitch his 'voice in the fifth above, the third in the eighth, 'and the fourth, if there be four besides him who 'sings the tenor or plain-song, in the twelfth, and 'all begin and continue in these concordances to the 'end; only let those who sing in the eighth and 'twelfth break and flower the notes in such manner 'as may best grace the measure; and note well, that 'whosoever sings the tenor must pronounce the notes 'full in their measure, and that he who descants 'must avoid the perfect, and take only the imperfect 'concords, namely, the third, sixth, and tenth, both 'ascending and descending; and thus a person who 'is skilled in the practice of descant, and having 'a proper ductility of voice, may make great melody 'with others, singing according to the above direc-'tions; and for this kind of singing four persons are 'sufficient, provided there be one to descant con-'tinually, in a twelfth above the plain-song.'

Morley, in his Introduction, pag. 70, speaking of the word Descant, indeed says, that 'it is a word 'usurped of the musitions in divers significations;' yet he adds, 'that it is generally taken for singing 'a part extempore, on a playne-song; so that when 'a man talketh of a descanter, it must be one that 'can extempore sing a part upon a playne-song.'

The practice of descant, in whichsoever of these two senses the word is accepted, may reasonably be supposed to have taken its rise from the choral service, which, whether we consider it in its primitive state, as introduced by St. Ambrose, or as improved by pope Gregory, consisted either of that plain and simple melody, which is understood when we speak of the Ambrosian or Gregorian chant, or of com-positions of the hymnal kind, differing from the former, in that they were not subject to the tonic laws which at different periods had been laid down by those fathers of the church.

Continual practice and observation suggested to those whose duty obliged them to a constant and regular attendance at divine service, the idea of a polyphonous harmony; by means whereof, without disturbing the melody, the ear might be gratified with a variety of concordant sounds, uttered by a number of voices; and indeed little less than a discovery of this nature was to be expected from the introduction of music into the church, consider-ing the great number of persons whose duty it became to study and practise it; considering also, the great difference, in respect of acuteness and gravity, between the voices of men and boys; and, above all, that nice discriminating sense of harmony and discord, resulting from an attention to the sound of that noble instrument the organ. Platina has fixed the æra when the organ was first introduced into churches at the year 660, and gives the honour of it to Vitalianus; and in less than half a century afterwards, we discover the advantages arising from it, in that which is the subject of the present en-quiry, the invention of a kind of music consisting of a variety of parts, called descant, the nature whereof is explained above, and is mentioned by Bede, who flourished at the beginning of the eighth century, and not only was extremely well skilled in the science of music, but spent the far greater part of his life in the study and practice of it.

An Italian writer of good authority,* whose pre-judices, if he had any, did not lead him to favour the moderns, has gone farther, and ascribed the use of the term to our countryman; and there is extant, in the Cambriæ Descriptio of Giraldus Cambrensis, a relation of a practice that prevailed in his time among the inhabitants of this country, not incon-sistent with the supposition that either Bede himself, or some of the brethren of the monastery where he resided, might be the inventors of music in consonance.

The relation of Giraldus Cambrensis above re-ferred to is to the following effect :—

'In the northern parts of Britain, beyond the 'Humber and on the borders of Yorkshire, the 'people there inhabiting, make use of a kind of 'symphoniac harmony in singing, but with only two 'differences or varieties of tones or voices. In this 'kind of modulation, one person [submurmurante] 'sings the under part in a low voice, while another 'sings the upper in a voice equally soft and pleasing. 'This they do, not so much by heart as by a habit, 'which long practice has rendered almost natural; 'and this method of singing is become so prevalent 'amongst these people, that hardly any melody is 'accustomed to be uttered simply, or otherwise than 'variously, or in this twofold manner.'†

* Gio. Bat. Doni, in his treatise De Generi e de Modi della Musica, pag. 97.
† In musico modulamine non unformiter ut alibi, sed multipliciter multisque modis et modulis cantilenas emittunt, adeò ut in turba canentium, sicut huic genti mos est, quot videas capita, tot audias car-mina discrimináque vocum, varia in unam denique sub B. Mollis dulcedine blanda consonantiam et organicam convenientia melodiam. In borealibus quoque majoris Britanniæ partibus trans Humbrum, Eboracique finibus Anglorum populi qui partes illas inhabitant simili canendo symphoniaca utuntur harmonia: binis tamen solummodo tonorum differentiis et vocum modulando varietatibus, una inferius sub murmurante altera verò supernè demulcente pariter et delectante. Nec arte tantùm sed usu longævo et quasi in naturam mora diutina jam converso, hæc vel illa sibi gens hanc specialitatem comparavit Qui adeò apud utramque invaluit et altas jam radices posuit, ut nihil hic simpliciter, ubi multipliciter ut apud priores, vel saltem dupliciter ut apud sequentes, mellitè proferri consueverit. Pueris etiam (quòd magis admirandum) et ferè infantibus, (cum primum à fletibus in cantus erumpunt) eandem modulationem obseruantibus. Angli verò quoniam non generaliter omnes sed boreales solùm hujusmodi vocum utuntur

As this method of singing seems by the account above given of it to have been subservient to the laws of harmony, an enquiry into its origin may lead to a discovery when and where music in consonance was first practised. The author above cited would insinuate that the inhabitants of this country might receive it from the Dacians, or Norwegians; but he has not shewn, nor is there the least reason to think that any such practice prevailed among either of those people; and till evidence to that purpose shall be produced, we may surely suspend our belief, and refer the honour of the invention to those who are admitted to have been in possession of the practice. It will be remembered, that in the foregoing pages it has been related that the monastery of Weirmouth, in the kingdom of Northumbria, was famous for the residence of John the arch-chanter, and other the most skilful musicians in Britain. It is therefore not improbable that symphoniac music might have its rise there, and from thence it might have been disseminated among the common people inhabiting that part of the kingdom; nay, it is next to impossible that a practice so very delightful, and to a certain degree so easily attainable, could be confined within the walls of a cloister.

It is true, that the reasons above adduced will warrant nothing more than a bare conjecture that music in consonance had its rise in this island; but it may be worth considering whether any better evidence than that it was known and practised in England so early as the eighth century, can be produced to the contrary.

But without pursuing an enquiry touching the particular country where symphoniac music had its rise, enough has been said to ascertain, within a few years, the time of its origin; it remains to account for the error of those writers who ascribe the invention of it to Guido.

Besides the application of the syllables UT, RE, MI, FA, SOL, LA, to the first six notes of the septenary, it is universally allowed, that he improved, if not invented the stave; and that if he was not the first who made use of points placed upon one or other of the lines to signify certain notes, he was the first that placed points in the spaces between the lines, and by the invention of the keys or cliffs, compressed as it were, the whole system of the double diapason into the narrow limits of a few lines.

After he had thus adjusted the stave, and had either invented or adopted, it matters not which, the method of notation by points instead of letters, it was but a consequence that the notation of music of more parts than one should be by points placed one under another: and as in his time, the respective notes contained in the several parts, being regulated by one common measure, viz., that of the feet or syllables to which they were to be sung, they stood in need of no other kind of discrimination than what arose from their different situations on the same stave, or on different staves, and, by consequence, the points

must have been placed in a vertical situation, and in opposition to each other; and this method of notation suggested for music of more than one part the name of Counterpoint, a term in the opinion of some favouring of the barbarity of the age in which it was invented, but which is too expressive of the idea intended to be conveyed by it to be quarrelled with.

What has been said above respecting the improvement of Guido, will furnish a rule for judging of the credibility of the assertion which it is here proposed to refute, namely, that he was the inventor of polyphonous or symphoniac music, and lead to the source of that, which by this time, cannot but be thought an error. The writers who maintain this position, and they are not a few, have mistaken the sign for the thing signified, that is to say, Counterpoint, for Music in Consonance, the thing characterised by counterpoint. The fact in short is, that music in consonance was in use before Guido's time; he invented the method of notation, calculated to define it, called Counterpoint: this is the whole relating to the invention now under consideration that can be ascribed to him; and it must have been the effect of strange inattention that a different opinion has prevailed so long in the world.

Towards the end of the eighth century flourished BEDE, well known to the world by the epithet of VENERABLE. He was born about the year 672, and was educated in the monastery situate at Weirmouth, near the mouth of the river Tyne, in the bishopric of Durham. He studied with incredible diligence, and, in the opinion of the famous Alcuin, was, for learning, humility, and piety, a pattern for all other monks. He wrote an Ecclesiastical History of Britain, at the end whereof are some memoirs of his own life, from which it appears that he was very assiduous in acquiring a knowledge of music, and punctual in the performance of choral duty in the church of his monastery. He had the good fortune to be very intimately acquainted with some of the singers whom pope Agatho had sent into Britain to teach the method of singing, as it was practised at Rome; and was, in a word, one of the greatest men of his time. He died in the year 735. His works have been many times printed, and in the latter editions make eight volumes in folio; the last is that of Cologne, in 1688. The first volume contains a great number of small tracts on arithmetic, grammar, rhetoric, astronomy, chronology, music, the means of measuring time, and other subjects. On that of music, in particular, there is a tract intitled De Musica Theorica; and another, De Musica Quadrata, Mensurata, seu Practica.* It is said, that he had no fewer than six hundred pupils; and that Alcuin, the preceptor to Charlemagne, was one of them. There is a well written life of him in the Biographia Britannica, and an accurate catalogue of his works in the Bibliotheca Britannico-Hibernica of bishop Tanner.

NOTGERUS, or NOTKER, surnamed LE BEGUE, a monk of St. Gal, flourished about the year 845, under the emperor Lotharius, son of Lewis the Pious. Among other things, he is famed for his book De

---

modulationibus, credo quòd a Dacis et Norwagiensibus qui partes illas insulæ frequentiùs occupare ac diutiùs obtinere solebant, sicut loquendi affinitatem, sic canendi proprietatem contraxerunt. Cambriæ Descriptio cap. xiii.

* Vide Tan. Biblioth. pag. 89, in not. col. ii.

Musica et Symphonia. He is supposed to have been the inventor of the Sequentiæ, which are those parts of the office in which the people answer to the priest, and which pope Nicolas I. ordained to be sung at mass. He died in 912. Innocent III. had taken order for his canonization, but his design was never carried into execution. There was another of the name, bishop of Liege : Trithemius has confounded them together.

RABANUS MAURUS, is reckoned in the number of those who have written on music. He was born at Mentz, in 788, and bred up in the monastery of Fulda. He studied at Tours, under Alcuin, and returning to his monastery, was chosen abbot thereof, in 822. Having enjoyed that dignity twenty years, he laid it down to please the monks, who said he applied himself too much to study, and too little to the affairs of the monastery. He retired to Mount St. Pierre ; and was at last chosen archbishop of Mentz, in 847. In a treatise of the universe, consisting of twenty-two books, which he wrote and sent to Lewis le Debonnaire,* he has comprised an infinite number of common places, amongst which, it is supposed, are many relating to music, since Brossard has ranked him in his second class of writers on that subject. In a commentary of his upon the liturgy, he expatiates on the sacrifice, as it is called of the mass,† which latter word he supposes to be derived from the ' Ite ' missa est,' Go, ye are dismissed, the form used for the dismission of the catechumens, and to signify that the service was ended.

WALAFRIDUS STRABO, so surnamed because he squinted, was first a monk of Fulda, and afterwards abbot of Richenou, in the diocese of Constance. He is reckoned among the musical writers, and had been a disciple of Rabanus Maurus. He flourished about the year 842, and wrote De Officiis Divinis, the twenty-fifth chapter of which tract is intitled De Hymnis & Cantilenis eorumque incrementis, &c.‡ The Benedictines, compilers of the Histoire Litteraire de la France, have discovered that there was another of his name, dean of the abbey of St. Gal, in the preceding century, with whom he is often confounded. Hist. Lit. de la France, tom. IV. pag. 59, in not.

BRISTAN, or BRICSTAN, a native of England, a Benedictine monk, and precentor in the monastery of Croyland, is celebrated by Pits as an excellent mathematician, poet, and musician.§ Ingulphus, pag.

867, speaks thus of him : ' Bristanus, quondam cantor ' monasterii, musicus peritissimus et poeta facundis- ' simus.' He lived about 870, at the time when, in one of the invasions of the Danes, his monastery was burned, and the monks slain : he had, however, the good fortune to escape, and composed certain elegiac verses, wherein he relates the cruelties exercised by the invaders, the sufferings of his brethren, and the misfortunes attending this disastrous event.

As it is proposed in this work to give an account as well of practical as theoretical musicians, there will need little apology for inserting in this place a few particulars of our own king ALFRED, who is celebrated by Bale, and other writers, for his skill in music, and his performance on the harp : that he was very sedulous in his endeavours to promote the study of music in his kingdom, we are told by Sir John Spelman, in his life of this great monarch, pag. 135 ; and particularly that he procured to be sent from France one Grimbald,‖ a man very skilful in music, of a singular good life, great learning, and who besides was an excellent churchman. Sir John Spelman adds, that the king first came to the knowledge of this person by his courtesy, he having made very much of him in his childhood, at Rheims, when he was in his passage towards Rome.

Again, the same author relates, that among the rest of his attendants, he is noted, Solomon like, to have provided himself of musicians, not common, or such as knew but the practic part ; but men skilful in the art itself, whose skill and service yet farther improved with his own instruction, and so ordered the manner of their service as best befitted the royalty of a king. Spelm. Life of Alfred, pag. 199.

That he himself was also a considerable proficient on the harp, were other evidences wanting, the well-known story related by Ingulphus, William of Malmesbury, and succeeding historians, of his entering the Danish camp, disguised like a harper or minstrel, is a proof.

The substance of which relation is, that being desirous to know the strength and circumstances of the Danish army, then in Somersetshire, he disguised himself like a minstrel, and taking with him a harp, and one only confidant, he went into the Danish camp, the privilege of his disguise intitling him to free admittance every where, even into the king's tent ; and there, for many days, he so employed himself as that, while he entertained his enemies with his mirth and music, he obtained the fullest satisfaction touching their ability to resist the attack on them, which he had for some time been meditating. This was in the year 378.¶

---

* Du Pin. Nouv. Biblioth. des Auteurs Eccles. siec. ix.

† As the word Mass will frequently occur in the course of this work, the following note of the translator of Du Pin's Bibliotheque, vol. VI. pag. 3, may serve for an explanation of that rite :—
' The word Missa, or Mass, is an old Latin word, and signifies gene- ' rally the whole service of the church, but more especially the holy ' sacrament of Christ's body and blood. It was called Missa, or Di- ' missio, because no man was suffered to remain in the church that ' could not or would not receive the sacrament ; and therefore such ' persons as had a mind to see and hear, but not receive, were all, with- ' out exception, dismissed by the deacon, after the sermon was ended, ' with these words, " Ite, missa est ; Go, ye are dismissed : " and if any ' delayed, they were urged to depart by the deacons and exorcists, saying ' aloud, " Si quis non communicet det locum ; Whoever will not receive, ' " let him go out." The Roman church puts a different sense upon this ' word Mass, understanding by it that solemn service wherein they do ' pretend to offer unto God the body and blood of his Son, as a pro- ' pitiatory sacrifice for the sins, both of the quick and dead. Isidore ' here takes it in the first sense, calling it Ordo Precum, i. e. the Form of ' Prayers. But Du Pin, by joining it with the word Canon, (a word of ' a much later use, and which signifies, in the Roman church, the rule ' or form of celebrating their mass) seems to bring it over to the latter, ' but against the sense of St. Isidore of Seville.'

‡ Vide Du Pin. Biblioth. cent. ix. cap. xiii.

§ Pits. De Reb. Angl. pag. 167. Tann. 124.

‖ Of this Grimbald very honourable mention is made in the Histoire de la France, tom. V. pag. 694. Alfred had written to Eulk, archbishop of Rheims, intreating him to send to England a person skilled in the liberal sciences, particularly music. The archbishop wrote the king a long letter in answer, recommending Grimbald, a monk of St. Bertin, the person above mentioned. This was about the year 880 ; and had Grimbald been a much greater man than he was, the French would have been bound in gratitude to have spared him to us ; for a few years before, they had from us Alcuin, the tutor of Charlemagne. It appears that Grimbald behaved very well whilst he was here. In the chronicle of Nic. Harpsfield are the heads of a speech of his, in a synod at London, before king Alfred and archbishop Æthelred, wherein he discoursed gravely and wisely of the primitive dignity of human nature, and of its corruption by the fall of Adam. The whole is said to be in the Annals of Winchester. Vide Spelm. Life of Alfred, pag. 135, in not.

¶ Vide Spelman's Life of Alfred, pag. 63.

HUCBALD, HUGBALDUS, or HUBALDUS, for by all these names is he called, is spoken of as the most celebrated doctor in France at the close of the ninth century. He was a Benedictine monk, of the abbey of St. Amand, in the diocese of Tournay, and flourished about the year 880, under Charles the Bald. He is celebrated for his profound skill in the learning of those days, and particularly for his excellence in poetry and music.* He is said to have invented a division of the monochord, by means whereof music might be learned without the help of a master; and to have invented certain signs, independent of lines and letters, to mark the sounds in the octave. Martini, who sometimes calls him Ubaldo, has given a specimen of this his method of punctuation from a manuscript of his, intitled De Harmonica Institutione, in the following form:—

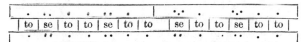

Which he renders thus in modern characters:—

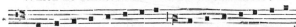

The authors of the Histoire Litteraire de la France also speak in general terms of a method of musical punctuation invented by him, doubtless the same with that above; and add, that he composed and noted offices in honour of many of the saints. He died at the age of ninety, in the year 930, and was buried in the church of St. Peter, in his own abbey. The merits of Hucbald, his learning and virtues, were celebrated by many of his surviving friends, in epitaphs, and other metrical compositions; the two which follow are extant in the work above-cited, and are here inserted, not so much on account of their elegance, as to shew the degree of estimation in which he stood with his contemporaries:—

EPITAPH I.

Dormit in hac tumba simplex sine felle Columba
Doctor, flos, & honos tam cleri quàm monachorum
Hucbaldus, famam cujus per climata mundi
Edita sanctorum modulamina, gestaque clamant.
Hic Cyrici membra pretiosa, reperta Nivernis.
Nostris invexit oris, scripsitque triumphum.

EPITAPH II.

Præcluis orator sudans opobalsama cosmo
Archas mellifluus rhetor super æthera notus,
En Huncbalde pater salve per secla verenter
Tu lampas monachis, tu flos & doxa peritis:
Te plebs æternùm lugens sibi deflet ademtum.
Vige juge, sophista, vale, Theophile care.
Ediderat stylo examussim certamen honesto
Matris Julitæ, Cirici prolisque venustæ,
Ceu doctor, celeber gnavus per cuncta magister.
Laudetur, vigeat, quod quæso legatur, ametur.
Hæc quisquis legis, requiem dic det Deus illi,
Palmam cum superis gestet super astra choreis
Gloria pauper hæc peregit, metra clienter.

* Hist. Litteraire de la France, tom. VI. pag. 210.
Sigebert, Trithemius, and others, mention a poem of Hugbald's composing, and of a very singular kind. It is an encomium on Baldness, in heroic verse, inscribed to the emperor Charles the Bald, in which every word begins with the initial letter of the emperor's name, as in the following line:—
        Carmina clarisona clavis cantate Camenæ.

† Storia della Musica, pag. 183.

The above Hucbald is usually styled Hucbald de Saint Amand; notwithstanding which he is sometimes confounded with two other writers of the same name, the one a monk of Orbais, the other a clerk in the church of Liege, neither of whom seem to stand in any degree of competition with him.‡

AURELIANUS, a clerk in the church of Rheims, lived in the year 890, under the emperor Arnulphus, and on to the reign of Lewis IV. He was in great estimation for his learning, and author of a treatise on the tones, intitled, Tonarius regularis, which he composed for the use of his church, and inscribed to Bernard, the precentor of the choir. He is placed by Trithemius among the ecclesiastical writers.§

CHAP. XXXIV.

WE are now arrived at a period, namely the commencement of the tenth century, when learning began to flourish throughout Europe. In France, particularly, not only mathematics, but the arts of painting, sculpture, and architecture, were cultivated with great assiduity. The abbies of Corbie, of Rheims, and Cluni, were the great seminaries of that country, and produced a succession of men eminent in all faculties; the former of these was so famous for musical institution, that young monks from England were usually sent thither to be taught the true method of singing in divine service. Letald, Remi de Auxerre, Notker le Begue, Wigeric bishop of Metz, and Hucbald de St. Amand, before-mentioned, were all skilled in music, and are some of the most celebrated names that occur in the literary history of those times.‖

ODO, abbot of Cluni, in the province of Burgundy, a Frenchman of noble descent, also flourished in this age, that is to say, about the year 920. He is highly celebrated by the writers of those times, for his learning, his piety, and his zeal to reform the manners of the clergy. The authors of the Histoire Litteraire de la France speak of him as one of the great luminaries of that kingdom. As to his skill in music, they represent him as surpassing most of his cotemporaries: they speak also of a manuscript of his, which is no other than the Enchiridion, mentioned by Gerard Vossius, and commended by Guido himself, beginning 'Quid est musica?' as a great curiosity, and being extant only in the Vatican library, and in that of the queen of Sweden; nevertheless, it is to be found in the library of Baliol college, and makes part of a volume, that contains the Micrologus, and other tracts of Guido, with some others on the subject of music, of great value; and Martini refers to another, in the conventual library at Cesana, near Ravenna, in Italy.

The Enchiridion of Odo is in the form of a dialogue between a teacher and his disciple: it begins with directions for the making and dividing of the monochord, and contains a general definition of the consonances, the method of notation by the Roman letters, as instituted by Gregory, a formula of the

‡ Storia della Musica, pag. 214.
§ Vossius De Scientiis Mathem. cap. ix. § 6.
‖ Hist. Litteraire de la France, tom. VI. pag 71.

tones, and concludes with general directions for antiphonal singing.

It is to be remarked, that all the tracts written about this time, which profess to teach the knowledge of music, and there are innumerable of them extant, begin, as this does, with directions for making and dividing the monochord : the reason of this is, that the method of ascertaining the places of the semitones in the diapason, by the syllables, was not then discovered ; and hardly any instrument then in use, excepting the organ, would answer the end of impressing upon the memory of a child, the difference between the greater and lesser intervals ; the teachers of music therefore invariably directed their pupils to find out the intervals themselves, and lay the foundation of their studies in the knowledge of the monochord.

SILVESTER, the second pope of that name, is justly celebrated as one of the great ornaments of the tenth century. He was a monk of Aurillac, in the province of Auvergne, a monastery which had been founded at the latter end of the preceding age. His pursuits were so various, and his excellence in all branches of learning so great, that it is difficult to say in what class of learned men he merits most to be placed ; or whether we should consider him as a divine, a mathematician, or a philosopher at large. It is certain that he wrote upon geometry, particularly on the quadrature of the circle, on astronomy, logic, and rhetoric ; that he was deeply skilled in the science of music, as a proof whereof it is said that he made some considerable improvements of the organ, on which he was an excellent proficient : William of Malmesbury speaks, with admiration, of an improvement made by him in the hydraulic organ.* He was born of obscure parents, in the neighbourhood of Aurillac : his name of baptism was Gerbert, or Girbirt : his great merit, and a disposition to communicate to the world the discoveries he made in the course of his studies, facilitated his promotion to the highest dignities of the church ; for he was successively archbishop of Rheims and Ravenna, and at last pope. While he was archbishop of Rheims, he had the misfortune to see that city sustain a close siege, which obliged him to seek refuge in the court of the emperor Otho III. who had been his disciple. During his residence there, he invented an instrument for the measuring of time by the motion of the polar star, which some writers have confounded with the astrolabe. By the interest of his patron Otho, in the year 998, he was promoted to the archbishopric of Ravenna, and the following year to the papacy on the death of Gregory V., which he held but four years, for he died in 1003.

Mosheim has bestowed an eulogium on Gerbert as characteristic of the age in which he lived, as of the person he means to celebrate. He relates that he derived his learning in a great measure from the Arabians, among whom at that time there were many very considerable men ; though it is remarkable that we meet with the name of but one writer on music of that country, viz., Alfarabius, who is barely mentioned in a note in the life of Hai Ebn Yokdhan, an ingenious fiction translated from the original Arabic by Simon Ockley, 8vo. 1708. A treatise of his on music is referred to in the Margarita Philosophica of Gregorius Reischius, printed at Basil in 1517. Mosheim speaks thus of the state of learning in Gerbert's time :—

' It was not however to the fecundity of his genius ' alone that Gerbert was indebted for the knowledge ' with which he now began to enlighten the European ' provinces ; he had derived a part of his erudition, ' particularly in physic, mathematics, and philosophy, ' from the writings and instructions of the Arabians, ' who were settled in Spain. Thither he had repaired ' in pursuit of knowledge, and had spent some time in ' the seminaries of learning at Cordova and Seville, ' with a view to hear the Arabian doctors ; and it ' was, perhaps, by his example, that the Europeans ' were directed and engaged to have recourse to this ' source of instruction in after times. For it is undeniably ' certain, that, from the time of Gerbert, such ' of the Europeans as were ambitious of making any ' considerable progress in physic, arithmetic, geometry, ' or philosophy, entertained the most eager and ' impatient desire of receiving instruction either from ' the academical lessons, or from the writings of the ' Arabian philosophers, who had founded schools in ' several parts of Spain and Italy. Hence it was that ' the most celebrated productions of these doctors ' were translated into Latin, their tenets and systems ' adopted with zeal in the European schools, and that ' numbers went over to Spain and Italy to receive ' instruction from the mouths of these famous teachers, ' which were supposed to utter nothing but the deepest ' mysteries of wisdom and knowledge. However ' excessive this veneration for the Arabian doctors ' may have been, it must be owned nevertheless that ' all the knowledge, whether of physic, astronomy, ' philosophy, or mathematics, which flourished in ' Europe from the tenth century, was originally ' derived from them, and that the Spanish Saracens ' in a more particular manner may be looked upon as ' the fathers of European philosophy.' Mosh. Eccles. Hist. vol II. pag. 199.

The diligence with which Gerbert pursued his studies, and his proficiency in so many various branches of learning, raised in the vulgar a suspicion of his being addicted to magic, which Platina has without hesitation adopted ; for he says he obtained the papacy by ill arts, and that he left his monastery to follow the devil. He however allows him the merit of a sincere repentance, but mentions some prodigies at his death, which few can believe on the authority of such a writer. Naudeus has written a justification of a great number of learned men who have undergone the same censure, and has included Silvester among them ; but long before his time a certain poet had done him that good office in the following epigram :—

---

* Said to have been played on by warm water. See the History of the Manual Arts, by Dr. Thomas Powell, octavo, 1661, abridged in Oldys's British Librarian, No. I. pag. 51.

Ne mirare Magum fatui quod inertia vulgi
  Me (veri minime gnara) fuisse putat.
Archimedis studium quod eram sophiæque sequutus
  Tum, cum magna fuit gloria scire nihil.
Credebant Magicum esse rudes, sed busta loquuntur
  Quam pius, integer & religiosus eram.

The following epitaph bespeaks his character, and
is an epitome of his history :—

Iste locus mundi Silvestri membra sepulti
  Venturo Domino conferet ad sonitum.
Quem dederat mundo celebrem doctissima virgo.
  Atque caput mundi culmina Romulea.
Primum Gerbertus meruit Francigena sede
  Remensis populi metropolim patriæ.
Inde Ravennatis meruit conscendere summum
  Ecclesiæ regimen nobile, sicque potens
Post annum Romam mutato nomine sumsit,
  Ut toto pastor fieret orbe novus.
Cui nimium placuit sociali mente fidelis.
  Obtulit hoc Cæsar tertius Otho sibi.
Tempus uterque comit clara virtute sophiæ ;
  Gaudet, et omne seclum frangitur omne reum
Clavigeri instar erat cælorum sede potitus,
  Terna suffectus cui vice pastor erat.
Iste vicem Petri postquam suscepit, abegit
  Lustrali spatio sæcula morte sui.
Obriguit mundus discussa pace triumphus
  Ecclesiæ mutans, dedidicit requiem.
Sergius hunc loculum miti pietate sacerdos,
  Successorque suus comsit amore sui.
Quisquis ad hunc tumulum devexa lumina vertis,
  Omnipotens Domine, dic, misere sui.

Berno, abbot of Richenou, in the diocese of Constance, who flourished about the year 1008, is celebrated as a poet, rhetor, musician, philosopher, and
divine. He was the author of several treatises on
music, particularly of one De Instrumentis Musicalibus, beginning with the words 'Musicam non
'esse contempnendum!' which he dedicated to
Aribon, archbishop of Mentz. He also wrote De
Mensura Monochordi : but the most celebrated of his
works is a treatise De Musica seu Tonis, which he
wrote and dedicated to Pelegrinus, archbishop of
Cologne, beginning 'Vero mundi isti advenæ et
Peregrino :' this latter tract is part of the Baliol
manuscript, and follows the Enchiridion of Odo,
above referred to : it contains a summary of the
doctrines delivered by Boetius, an explanation of the
ecclesiastical tones, intermixed with frequent exhortations to piety, and the application of music to
religious purposes. He was highly favoured by the
emperor Henry II. for his great learning and piety,
and succeeded so well in his endeavours to promote
learning, that his abbey of Richenou was as famous
in his time as those of St. Gal and Cluni, then the
most celebrated in France. He died in 1048, and
was interred in the church of his monastery, which
but a short time before he had dedicated to St. Mark.

From the account hereinbefore given of the rise
and progress of choral service, and of the institution
of the ecclesiastical tones, modes, tropes, or whatever
else they may be termed, it is clear that before the
eleventh century they were in number eight, besides
which, the actual existence at this day of manuscripts,
such as those of Aurelianus, Odo of Cluni, and this of

Berno above-mentioned, in which not only eight
tones are spoken of, but a formula of each is given in
words at length, are indisputable evidence of the fact.
A learned gentleman, Dr. King, the author of a book
lately published, intitled the Rites and Ceremonies of
the Greek Church in Russia, has intimated, pag. 43,
that the addition of the four plagal tones, as they
are called, to the four authentic of St. Ambrose, is
by some ascribed to Guido Aretinus, who, by the
way, in his Micrologus lays not the least claim to
this improvement, but speaks of the eight ecclesiastical tones as an ancient establishment. We are
therefore necessitated to conclude that the contrary
opinion is without foundation, and the rather, as no
writer of authority among the many that have been
consulted in the course of this work, has intimated
the least doubt but that the Cantus Gregorianus
consisted of eight tones.

Through all the variations that attended music,
the ancient system of a bisdiapason, constituted of
tetrachords, retained its authority; we do not find
that even in the time of Boetius the system itself
had received any alteration; the Latins it is true
had rejected the ancient Greek characters, and introduced the Roman capital letters in their stead ; and
pope Gregory reduced those letters to the first seven
of the Roman alphabet, which, by repeating them
in each septenary, he made to serve the purpose of
a great number, calling the first series graves, the
second acutes, and the third, distinguished by double
small letters, super-acutes; but the tetrachord system,
said to be immutable, as also the Greek names
anciently appropriated to the several chords, continued in use till the close of the tenth century, soon
after which such a reformation of the ancient scale
was made, as was thought worthy of commemoration,
not only by chronologers, but by the gravest historians. The person to whose ingenuity and industry
we owe this inestimable improvement was an ecclesiastic, Guido Aretinus, a Benedictine monk. The
relation given by Cardinal Baronius of this event
is to the following effect ; viz : That in the pontificate of Benedict VIII. Guido Aretinus, a monk,
and an excellent musician, to the admiration of all,
invented a method of teaching music, so that a boy
in a few months* might learn what no man, though
of great ingenuity, could before that attain in several
years.—That the fame of this invention procured
him the favour of the pope, who invited him to
Rome, as did afterwards John XX. his successor.—
That in the thirty-fourth year of his age he composed
a treatise, which he called Micrologus, and dedicated
to Theodald, bishop of Arezzo. Annal. Eccl. tom.
XI. pag. 73, et seq.

To this account Baronius has subjoined the epistle
from Guido to a friend of his, Michael of Pomposa, beginning 'Clarissimo atque dulcissimo fratri Michaëli,'
containing the history of his invention, and of
his invitation to Rome and reception by the pope ;
the particulars whereof are referred to an extract
from the epistle itself, which is given in a subsequent

* Guido in the prologue to the Micrologus says, in the space of one
month, 'unius mensis spatium.'

page of this work.* General accounts of the reformation of the scale made by Guido are to be met with in almost every treatise on the subject composed since his time ; yet among these some improvements are attributed to him, as namely the invention of the stave, and of the figure of a hand, to explain his method of notation, to the merit whereof, if we are to judge from his own writings, he does not appear to have made the least claim.

It has been related that the method of notation among the Greeks was by the letters of their alphabet, as also that the Latins in their stead made use of the Roman capital letters, A, B, C, D, E, F, G, and so on to P, as is mentioned by Boetius in his fourth book ; and that afterwards Gregory rejected all but the first seven, which he made to serve for the whole scale, distinguishing the grave series by the capitals and the acute by the small letters. Their manner of singing was from A to B, a tone ; from B to C, a semitone ; from C to D, a tone ; from D to E, a tone ; from E to F, a semitone ; from F to G, a tone ; so that, to speak of the diapason only, the seven capital letters served to express, ascending and descending, either gradually or by leaps, the seven notes ;† but so difficult was it according to this method to know and to hit precisely the place of the two semitones, that before the pupils were able to acquire a knowledge of the Canto Fermo, ten years were usually consumed. Guido studied with great diligence to remove this obstruction ; and the current account of this invention is, that being at vespers, and singing the hymn to St. John, ' Ut queant laxis,' it by chance came into his head to apply, as being of easy pronunciation, certain syllables of that hymn to as many sounds in a regular succession, and thereby

he removed those difficulties that had a long time retarded the improvements of practical music.

UT queant laxis REsonare fibris
MIra gestorum FAmuli tuorum
SOLve polluti LAbii reatum.

Sancte Joannes.‡

This is the substance of what is related by Gaffurius, Glareanus, Vicentino, Galilei, Zarlino, Kircher, Mersennus, Bontempi, and other writers, touching the invention of the syllables ; but the scale, as it stood in the time of Guido, was not adapted for the reception of six syllables, and therefore the application which he made of them does necessarily imply some previous improvement of the scale, either actually made by him, or which he had at that time under consideration. It is pretty certain that this improvement could be no other than the converting the ancient tetrachords into hexachords, which, to begin with the tetrachord Hypaton, he effected in this manner : that tetrachord was terminated in the grave by Hypate hypaton, or ♮ ; for though the Proslambanomenos A, carried the system a tone lower, it was always considered, as its name imports to be, acquisitus, supernumerary, or redundant ; the addition therefore of a tone below A immediately converted the tetrachord Hypaton into a hexachord, and drove the semitone into a situation that divided the hexachord into two equal parts. To this additional tone Guido, as some say, in honour of the Greeks, the fathers of music, or, as others suggest, to perpetuate the memory of his invention, and thereby acquire honour to himself, affixed the Greek gamma Γ, which fortunately for such a supposition, was the initial letter of his name.§

By this constitution the position of the semitone was clearly pointed out to every theorist ; but the thing in pursuit was a method of hitting it in practice, the want whereof rendered the singing extempore so very difficult, that few could attain to it without great labour ; but the accidental hearing of the hymn above-mentioned suggested to Guido a thought that the six syllables therein contained might be so fitted to the six sounds in his newly-formed hexachord, as to furnish a rule for this purpose ; accordingly he

---

* By the epistle above referred to, it appears, that Baronius has been guilty of an error in saying that Guido was invited to Rome both by Benedict and John ; for it was from John only that he received this mark of favour. Neither does he clearly distinguish between the Argumentum novi Cantus inveniendi and the Micrologus ; the former contained his method of singing by the syllables, and procured him a general reputation, and the favour of Benedict : the latter, his reformation of the scale, and, as Guido himself expressly says, was composed in the thirty-fourth year of his age, John XX. being then pope. Besides this, he adds, that the Micrologus was written at the monastery of Pomposa, whither he retired not, till after his interview with the pope.

† Zarlino has been guilty of a gross mistake in asserting, as he does in his Institutions, part ii. chap. 30. that Guido first made use of the method of notation by the capital and small Roman letters : the current opinion is, that Gregory introduced it ; but supposing that matter doubtful, there is sufficient evidence to prove that the practice in question prevailed before Guido's time ; for the Enchiridion of Odo, abbot of Cluni, contains directions for dividing the monochord, and marking the first septenary with the capital, and the second with the small Roman letters ; and Vincentio Galilei, in his Dialogo della Musica, pag. 96, has given the following specimen of Canto Fermo :—

d   c   ♮   c   d   e   d   c   ♮   a   ♮   c   d   a   G   F   G   G
Sit nomen Do - mi - ni be - ne - dictum in sæ - cu - la

F   G   a   G   F   F   G   F   E   F   G   F   E   D   C   D
Adju - to - rium nostrum in no   - - mine Do - mi - ni

Sit nomen Do - mi - ni be - ne - dictum in sæ - cu - la

Ad - ju - to - ri - um nostrum in no - - mi - ne Do - mi - ni.

which he asserts was composed many years before Guido was born.

The perusal of the Enchiridion of Otho has furnished the means of refuting a vulgar error, namely, that Guido, to perpetuate the memory of his reformation of the scale, prefixed to it the Greek Γ, the initial letter of his name ; the contrary of this is manifest in the directions of Odo for dividing the monochord, in which he assumes that very character.

‡ The words of the above hymn were composed by Paulus Diaconus, Paul, a deacon of the church of Aquilea, about the year 770, and in the reign of Charlemagne, as Possevin relates. Dr. Wallis, from Alstedius, in the room of Adonic, Sancte Joannes, has inserted O Pater Alme. Brossard, and others after him say, that Angelo Berardi has very prettily comprised the six syllables in this line.

UT RElevet MIserum FAtum SOLitosque LAbores.

But Gerard Vossius, De quatuor Artibus Popularibus, pag. 93, without taking notice of Berardi, says it is only part of the following verse composed by some person who lived after Guido :—

Cur adhibes tristi numeros cantumque labori?
UT RElevet MIserum FAtum SOLitosque LAbores.

§ Meibomius denies that Guido extended the ancient Greek system either upwards or downwards, or that he even made any addition to the tetrachord Hypaton ; for he asserts, with an unwarrantable degree of confidence, that though the Proslambanomenos was generally understood as the lowest sound in the ancient system, yet that the Greeks in truth recognized another, which was a tone below it, but that as it prolated a confused and undistinguishable sound, it was neglected. He says that when Guido determined to reassume this tone, he was necessitated to mark it with the Grecian gamma, Γ ; for that otherwise, as he has given the Latin G to its diapason Lychanos meson, he must either have introduced a strange character, or doubled the letter G, which latter method could not please him so well. Meibomius also says that the Greek system proceeded even farther in the acutes than that of Guido ; but the truth of this assertion will be best judged of by a comparison of the ancient system with that of Guido, as they stand opposed to each other in a subsequent page of this volume.

made the experiment, and applying the syllable UT to the first note of the hexachord, and the rest to the others in succession, he gave to every note an articulate sound.

The view of Guido in this contrivance was to impress upon the minds of learners an idea of the powers of the several sounds, as they stood related to the first sound in the hexachord; for he saw that from an habitual application of the syllables to their respective notes, it must follow that the former would become a common measure for the five intervals included within the limits of the hexachord, and that in a short time the idea of association between the syllables and the notes would become so strong as to make it almost impossible to misapply them.

Finding that this invention was likely to succeed, he added two tones to the tetrachord Meson, thereby making that also a hexachord, and to this also he applied the syllables.

Lastly, he made a like addition of two tones to the tetrachord Synemmenon, and thereby formed a third hexachord.

The several combinations and conjunctions of these tetrachords for the purpose of ascertaining the intervals in any given system, exceeding the limits of the hexachord, will be hereafter explained; the result of the invention was clearly this, that in a regular succession of six sounds in their natural order, beginning either from Γ, from C, or from F, taking in B b, the progression with respect to the tones and semitone in each was precisely the same: and supposing the learner to have acquired by constant practice a habit of expressing with his voice the interval G C, which is an exact fourth, by the syllables UT FA, the two sounds proper to the interval G C would become a kind of tune, which he must necessarily apply to UT FA, wherever those syllables should occur; and in what other situation they occur the above constitution of the different hexachords shows; for as in the hexachord from G to E the syllables UT FA express the fourth G C, so in that from C to A do they express a fourth C F, and in the hexachord from F to D the fourth F B b.

The introduction of B b to avoid the Tritonus has been related at large; and here it may be proper to add that the exceeding discordancy or hardness of B ♭, when taken as a fourth, gave occasion to the epithet soft, which for the sake of distinction was given to B b; for this reason the hexachord from F is called the molle or soft hexachord, as that from G is called durum or hard; these appellatives begot another, namely, that of the natural hexachord, which is given to the hexachord from C. The method of singing each is termed a property in singing, and is thus described in the following distich :—

C Naturum dat, f b molle nunc tibi signat,
g quoque b durum tu semper habes caniturum.*

The intervals thus adjusted in the several hexachords, became alike commensurable in each by the syllables; and UT MI would as truly express the ditone C E or F A as G B, to which they were originally adapted : the same may be said of every

other interval in each of the hexachords, and their exact uniformity is visible in this, that the semitone has the same situation in them all, and divides them into two equal parts.

CHAP. XXXV.

THE writers on music, as has been mentioned above, have also attributed to Guido another very considerable improvement of the musical scale, which they suppose to be coeval with the formation of the hexachords, namely, the Stave, consisting of parallel lines in a horizontal position, such as is now used in the writing of music : in this they seem to have been mistaken, for all the examples made use of by him to illustrate his doctrine, are given in the Roman capital and small letters, agreeably to the method of St. Gregory. Besides which it is demonstrable that the stave was of a much earlier invention than this opinion supposes. The proof of this assertion is to be found in the Dialogo della Musica of Vincentio Galilei, pag. 37, which contains a diagram of musical punctuation on a stave consisting of no less than seven lines, which he says was in use long before the time of Guido.†

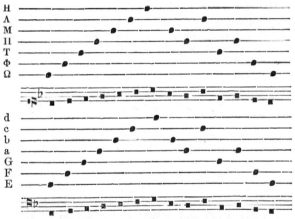

And immediately after he exhibits an example of notation on a stave of ten lines, concerning which he thus expresses himself : ‘ Eccovi l’ essempio d’ una ‘ Cantilena tra le altre, che mi sono capitate in mano, ‘ la quale mi fu gia da un gentiluomo nostro Fioren- ‘ tino donata, ritrovata da lui in un antichissimo suo ‘ libro : ed è delle pui intere, è meglio conservata d’ ‘ altra che io abbia mai veduta.’

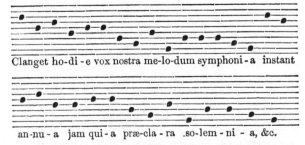

Clanget ho-di-e vox nostra me-lo-dum symphoni-a instant

an-nu-a jam qui-a præ-cla-ra .so-lem-ni-a, &c.

† By an unaccountable accident the examples here referred to, are in some copies of Galilei's book defective, as giving only the stave, and not the points ; but they are here supplied from Martini, who has rendered them into the characters of modern notation. Vid. Stor. della Musica, pag. 185.

* Morley in the Annotations on Book I, of his Introduction to Practicall Musicke.

Clanget ho-di-e vox nostra me-lodum sympho-ni-a instant

an-nu-a jam qui-a præcla-ra so-lem-ni-a.

To these examples of lineal punctuation another may be adduced from the Musurgia, tome I. pag. 213, wherein the points are placed on a stave of eight lines. We owe this discovery to Kircher, who relates that being on a voyage to Malta he went to visit the library of S. Salvator in Messana, which is well furnished with Greek manuscripts; and that one of the monks there produced to him a manuscript book of hymns, which had been written about seven hundred years, in which was contained the following :—

Παρθέ σι η μέ γα χαρέ θωσ δό τε δ ωτόρ εαω ν μητερ απομο σύνης

Kircher mentions that while he was writing the Musurgia, he received from a friend of his, the reverend abbot Didacus De Franchis, an extract from a very ancient antiphonary in the monastery of Vallombrosa, containing an example of interlineary punctuation in the following form :—

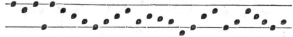

In which he says the points correspond with the notes of a well-known antiphon, beginning with the words 'Salve Regina.'

These evidences sufficiently prove that the stave is more ancient than is generally supposed; for it is agreed that the Micrologus was written between the years 1020 and 1030; and a period of seven hundred years before the publication of the Musurgia, in 1650, will carry the use of the stave back to the year 950, which is more than forty years before Guido was born, and show the error of those who ascribe the invention of the stave to him.

Indeed Guido has intimated that in his method of notation, points may be placed as well in the spaces as on the lines; and for this, as also for the consequent reduction of the stave from eight to five, or rather, for the purpose of ecclesiastical notation, to four lines, posterity are undoubtedly obliged to him.

It will be remembered that the ancient Greek scale was composed of tetrachords, and that it exhibits a succession of chords from Proslambanomenos, or A, to Nete hyperboleon, or aa. As to the Proslambanomenos, it was termed Acquisitus or Assumed, and therefore made no part of the tetrachord Hypaton. In prosecution of his scheme of converting the tetrachords into hexachords, with respect to the lowest tetrachord in the scale, Guido had nothing more to do than to add to it a single chord, to

which he affixed the Greek letter Γ, and this he termed the durum hexachord, to distinguish it from that other beginning at F, in which B is flat, and which therefore is called the molle hexachord : but of this, and also of the natural hexachord beginning at C, mention is made before.

The hexachords, constituted in the manner above described, with the additional improvement of the stave, and before they were incorporated into the scale assumed the following form :—

DURUM HEXACHORD.
G A B C D E

UT RE MI FA SOL LA

NATURAL HEXACHORD.
C D E F G A

UT RE MI FA SOL LA

MOLLE HEXACHORD.
F G A B♭ C D

UT RE MI FA SOL LA

The power or situation in the scale, of each of these points, is signified by the letters respectively placed above them : but the intention of the stave was to supersede the literal scheme of notation; it may therefore be said, supposing the letters away, that each hexachord is but a repetition of the other two, and that the power of each point in all the three is similar : but the case is far otherwise; for by a contrivance, which shows the admirable sagacity of the inventor, the stave of four lines is rendered capable of expressing every one of the three different hexachords which the reformed musical scale requires.

To manifest this diversity Guido invented certain characters called Cliffs, in number three, whereof the first was Γ, the other two were the letters C and F : the first of these indicated a progression of sounds from the lowest note in the scale upwards to E : the second denotes a series from C to A, and the third another series from F through B♭ to D : these cliffs, which were also termed claves or keys, were placed by Guido on the lower line at the head of his stave. It is evident from hence, that by the application of the characters Γ, C, F, the power of the six points used to denote the hexachord, were, without the least change of their situation in respect of the stave, made capable of a threefold variety, and consequently required different denominations.

That Guido invented some method for ascertaining the initial chords of each of the hexachords is certain, but that he made use of the letters, or cliffs, Γ, C, F, for that purpose, is rather conjecture than fact. Indeed the contrary seems to be clear from his own words, and that his method of discriminating the hexachords was not by the cliffs, but by making those lines of the stave, which were their proper stations, of a different colour from the rest. In the Micrologus we meet with these verses :—

> Quasdam lineas signamus variis coloribus
> Ut quo loco sit sonus mox discernat oculus ;
> Ordine tertiæ vocis splendens crocus radiat,
> Sexta ejus, sed affinis flavo rubet minio.

To understand which, it is necessary to observe that the third and sixth notes here mentioned are the third and sixth from A ; for Γ, as has been frequently said, was an assumed chord : Hypo-Proslambanomenos is the appellation given to it even by modern musicians, and for some ages after its introduction it was not in strictness considered as part of the scale. That this is Guido's meaning is clear from the following passage in the Micrologus : 'We make ' use of two colours, viz., yellow and red, which ' furnish a very useful rule for finding the tone and ' letter of the monochord to which every Neuma and ' note belongs. There are seven letters in the mono-' chord, and wheresoever you see yellow it is the ' third, and wherever red it is the sixth letter.' The third and sixth letters here mentioned are most evidently the third and sixth from A, the first of the seven letters on the monochord, that is to say C and F, which are the stations of two of the cliffs ; and the above citations incontestibly prove that to indicate the key of C, Guido made use of a yellow, and for that of F, a red line.*

Hitherto we have considered the hexachords as the integral parts of Guido's system, and as independent of each other ; but their use, and indeed the ingenuity and excellence of his invention, can only be discerned in that methodical arrangement of them by means whereof they are made to coincide with the great or immutable system : this, as has been shewn, was comprehended in the Hypaton, Meson, Diezeugmenon, and Hyperboleon tetrachords ; for the tetrachord to which they gave the name Synemmenon was merely auxiliary, as being suited to that kind of progression only, which leads through what we now call b flat. The system of Guido, supposing it to terminate as that of the ancients did at aa, and exclusive of the chord Γ added by him, to contain the bisdiapason, includes five hexachords differently constituted, the molle hexachord being auxiliary, and answering to the tetrachord synemmenon, which five hexachords respectively have their commencement from Γ, from C, from F, from G, and from C : but he found it capable of extension, and by adding four chords above aa, and a consequent repetition of the molle and durum hexachords from f and from g, he carried it up to ee, beyond which it was so seldom extended, as to give occasion to a proverbial exclamation, by which even at this day we reprehend the use of hyperbolical modes of speech, viz., 'that ' was a note above e la.' By this addition of chords the hexachords were increased to seven, that is to say, so many as are necessary for the conjugation of the system included within Γ and ee.

But between the tetrachords of the ancients, and the hexachords of Guido, this difference is most ap-

parent : the former were simply measures of the diatessaron system ; they succeeded each other in an orderly progression through the whole bisdiapason : the hexachord is also, at least in the opinion of the moderns, the measure of a system ; but their collateral situation, and the being made as it were to grow the one out of the other, varies the nature of their progression, and points out, in the compass of twenty-two notes, seven gradations or deductions, for so they are termed by the monkish writers, of six notes, each beginning at a different place in the diapason, and yet in all other respects precisely the same. Add to this that the hexachords with the syllables thus adapted to them, become as it were, so many different conjugations, by which we are able to measure and try the musical truth of the several intervals of which they are composed.

The chords contained in the enlarged system of Guido, are twenty-two in number, reckoning b in the acutes, and bb in the super-acutes : otherwise in strictness they are but twenty, seeing that b and ♮ can never occur in one and the same hexachord : for the designation of them two staves of five lines each are necessary ; and in that conjoint position which the ascending scale requires, the hexachords will have this appearance :—†

† The representations of Guido's system are many and various ; for he not having exhibited it by way of diagram, succeeding writers have thought themselves at liberty to exercise their several inventions in schemes and figures to explain it. Franchinus, and others after him, have enclosed each column of syllables, as they apply to Γ, and the letters above it, in two parallel lines, with a point at bottom, exactly like an organ pipe ; but as there is not the least analogy to warrant this form, others have rejected it. Peter Aron and others have placed the hexachords in a collateral situation, resembling the tables of the decalogue. Bontempi makes use of the following scheme of the hexachords to represent their mutations, and dependence on each other. Hist. Mus. pag. 183 :—

1536	ee	-	-	-	la
1728	dd	-	-	-	la sol
1944	cc	-	-	-	sol fa
2048	♮♮	-	-	-	mi
2187	bb	-	-	-	fa
2304	aa	-	-	la mi re
2592	g	-	-	sol re ut
2916	f	-	-	fa ut
3972	e	-	-	- la mi
3456	d	-	-	la sol re
3888	c	-	-	sol fa ut
4096	♮	-	-	mi
4374	b	-	-	fa
4608	a	-	- la mi re
5184	G	-	-	sol re ut
5832	F	-	-	fa ut
6144	E	-	la mi
6912	D	-	-	sol re
7776	C	-	-	fa ut
8192	♮	-	mi
9216	A	-	-	- re
10368	Γ	-	-	ut

It may seem strange, as Guido has characterised the durum hexachord by the key Γ, that that of F should be the first that occurs in the scale ; but the reason of this is, that the placing of F on the fourth line of the stave, does as much determine the series as Γ on the first would have done ; the same reason may serve for postponing the cliff C to F. As to g, it occurs as soon as is necessary, and not before ; and here it may be remarked that g is situated on the third line above C, as C is on the third line above F. Farther, a stave of five lines, with the cliff F on the fourth, is supposed to signify the five lower lines of the scale. One with C on the third, the five above F inclusive, and one with g on the second, the five above C. All this will most clearly appear from the two foregoing schemes, which exhibit an example of ingenuity and sagacity that has stood the test of ages, and is worthy the admiration of all men.

Many have thought Guido's scheme defective in that it gives no syllable to F. Dr. Wallis was of this opinion, and says what a wonder it is that he did not apply to it the syllable SA, from the first word of the Adonic verse Sancte JOANNES? Mersennus, Harmonie Universelle, pag. 183, seems to have thought much in the same manner, by his adding the syllable SI, which is used by the French at this day. The original introduction of this syllable is by him and other writers attributed to one Le Maire, a French musician, who says he laboured for thirty years in vain to bring it into practice ; but that he was no sooner dead than all the musicians of his country made use of it. Notwithstanding which

* See an example of this kind in a subsequent page of this book.

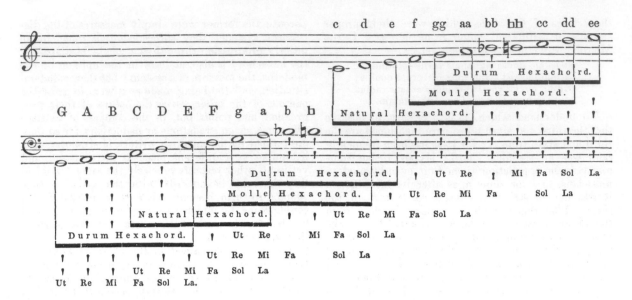

The above scheme is intended to shew the situation of the notes on the lines and spaces, and the relation which the hexachords bear each to the others: another compounded of two schemes, the one of Bontempi, and the other of Doctor Wallis, contains the reformed scale of Guido in a collateral situation with that of the ancients. (See Appendix, No. 56.)

To the lower chord the moderns have given the name Hypo-Proslambanomenos; the number assigned to it may, by the rule herein before given, be easily

found, it being nine of those parts of which 9216 is eight, and shews the ratio of Γ to A to be sesquioctave, in the proportion of 9 to 8. The same rule will also suggest the means of bringing out the numbers proper to the notes added to the scale by Guido, which are those from aa upwards; for, to begin with bb, it is in a subduplicate ratio to b, its number therefore will be the half of 4374, that is to say 2187. The next note ♭♭ having the same ratio to ♭, will in like manner require the subduplicate of 4096, which is 2048.

From the foregoing disposition of the tetrachords we learn the true names of the several sounds that compose the system; for it is observable that though in fact each septenary contained in it is but a repetition of the former, and that therefore the generical name of each chord is repeated, yet their specific differences in respect of situation are admirably distinguished by the different names assigned to each: thus, for instance, the lower chord is Γ UT, or GAMUT, but its replicate is for a very obvious reason termed g SOL RE UT; the replicates of A RE are a LA MI RE, those of C FA UT are c SOL FA UT and c SOL FA; those of D SOL RE, d LA SOL RE, and d LA SOL; and here it is to be remarked that as well the recision as the addition of a syllable expresses the situation of a note; for the last of the seven hexachords cuts off a syllable from the names of the three upper chords, leaving to the uppermost one only, e la, as may be seen in the example.

As a farther improvement of his system, and to facilitate the practice of solmisation, for so we are to call the conjugation of any given cantilena by means of the syllables UT, RE, MI, FA, SOL, LA, most authors relate that he made use of the left hand, calling the top of the thumb Γ, and applying the names of the rest of the notes to the joints of each finger, giving to the top of the middle finger, as being the highest situation, the note e LA, as in the following page is shewn:—

the general opinion is that the syllable SI was introduced into the scale by Ericius Puteanus of Dort, who lived about the year 1580, and wrote a treatise on music entitled Musathena.

This is in substance the account which Mons. Brossard has given of the introduction of the syllable SI; but another writer, Mons. Bourdelot, has given a very different account of this matter; for he relates that about the year 1675 a certain Cordelier introduced the syllable SI into the scale. He seems however to doubt the fact, as being founded only on tradition; and goes on to relate that the abbé de la Louette, master of the choir of the cathedral church of Paris, had assured him that the syllable in question was invented, or perhaps a second time brought into practice, by one Metru, a famous singing-master in Paris about the year 1676. Bourdelot adds that Le Moine, an excellent lutenist, of sixty years practice, had assured him that he knew Metru very well, and that he introduced the syllable SI; and that he remembered also a Cordelier of the convent of Ave Maria, who had made some variation in the ancient scale about the latter end of the last century. For these reasons Bonet inclines to think that the honour of the invention might be due to the Cordelier, but that the merit of reviving it is to be ascribed to Metru. But whichsoever of the above relations is true, it is pretty certain that both Mersennus and Brossard are mistaken in what they say respecting the invention of the syllable SI by Le Maire.

The same author, Bourdelot, insinuates, that notwithstanding the use of the syllable SI is much approved of by the French musicians, yet in Italy they disdain to make use of it, as being the invention of a Frenchman. Histoire de la Musique et de ses Effets, par Bourdelot, Amsterd. 1725, tom. I. pag. 17.

It seems that the musicians of other countries have been aware of the necessity of a seventh syllable in order to get rid of the difficulties which the mutations, as they are called, are attended with in the practice of singing; for in the Porque de la Musica of Andrea Lorente of Alcala, published in 1672, we find the syllable BI applied to ♭ in the progression from C to c.

And here it may not be improper to observe, that the Italians at this day make use of the syllable DO instead of UT, as being more easy of pronunciation: this variation may be traced back to the year 1678, and is to be found in a treatise herein before cited, entitled Armonia Gregoriani, written by Gerolamo Cantone, and printed at Turin in that year.

Mersennus, Harm. Univers. pag. 183, intimates that for expressing the semitone between A and B♭, some of the musicians of his country made use of the syllable ZA, that of SI being appropriated to B ♮; but this distinction seems not to prevail at this day. Mons. Loulié, the author of Elements ou Principes de Musique, printed at Amsterdam, 1698, rejecting the syllable ZA, has retained only SI; and this method of solmization is practised throughout France.

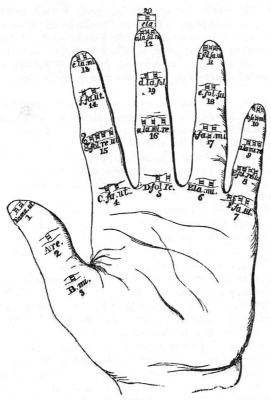

But to warrant this opinion there seems to be no better authority than bare tradition; for in no part of Guido's writings does the mention of the hand occur; nay, it seems from a passage in the manuscript of Waltham Holy Cross, herein before cited, that the hand was an invention posterior in time to that when Guido is supposed to have lived; * its use was to instruct boys in the names and respective situations of the notes of his scale; and for choosing the left hand rather than the right this notable reason is given, 'that it being nearest the heart, the instruction 'derived from thence is likely to make the deeper 'impression on the minds of learners.'

As to the precise time when he lived, authors are very much divided. Zaccone and others assert it to have been about the year of Christ 960; Baronius, that it was about 1022; Alstedius, and after him Bontempi, place him under pope Leo IX. and the emperor Henry III. in the year 1049; but Sigebert testifies that he flourished in the time of the emperor Conrade the younger, and that 1028 was the precise year when the reformation of Guido took place; and for this opinion we have also the authority of Trithemius.† But Guido has decided this question in a relation given by him of his invitation to Rome by John the XX., and he it is agreed began his pontificate in the year 1024.

CHAP. XXXVI.

Some account of Guido is to be gathered from his writings, particularly an epistle from him to his friend Michael, a monk of Pomposa, and the tract to which that is an introduction, entitled Argumentum novi Cantus inveniendi: from these, and some scattered passages to be met with in ancient manuscripts, the following memoirs are collected:—

He was a native of Arezzo, a city in Tuscany, and having been taught the practice of music in his youth, and probably retained as a chorister in the service of the Benedictine monastery founded in that city, he became a monk professed, and a brother of the order of St. Benedict: the state of learning was in those times very low, and the ecclesiastics had very few subjects for study, if we except theological controversy, church history, logic, and astrology, which was looked on by them as the most considerable of the mathematical sciences: these engaged the attention of such members of those fraternities as were endued with the most active, not to say contentious, spirits; while the exercises of devotion, the contemplating the lives of saints, and the qualifying themselves for the due discharge of the choral duty, employed those of a more ascetic and ingenuous turn of mind. Vossius makes Guido to have been at first a monk in the monastery of St. Leufred in Normandy; ‡ but this is by a mistake, which will be accounted for hereafter; so that the only places of his settlement, of which we can speak with certainty, are the Benedictine monastery of Arezzo, the city where he was born, and that of Pomposa in the duchy of Ferrara.

In this retirement he seems to have devoted himself to the study of music, particularly the system of the ancients, and above all to reform their method of notation. The difficulties that attended the instruction of youth in the church-offices were so great, that, as he himself says, ten years were generally consumed barely in acquiring the knowledge of the plain-song; and this consideration induced him to labour after some amendment, some method that might facilitate instruction, and enable those employed in the choral office to perform the duties of it in a correct and decent manner. If we may credit those legendary accounts that are extant in old monkish manuscripts, we should believe he was assisted in his pious intention by immediate communications from heaven: some speak of the invention of the syllables as the effect of inspiration; and Guido himself seem to have been of the same opinion, by his saying it was revealed to him by the Lord; or as some interpret his words, in a dream; but graver historians say, that being at vespers in the chapel of his monastery it happened that one of the offices appointed for that day was the above-mentioned hymn to St. John Baptist, written by Paulus Diaconus, and that the hearing thereof suggested this notable improvement.

We must suppose that the converting the tetrachords into hexachords had been the subject of frequent contemplation with Guido, and that a method of discriminating the tones and semitones was the one thing wanting to complete his invention. During the performance of the hymn he remarked the iteration of the words, and the frequent returns of UT, RE, MI, FA, SOL, LA: he observed likewise

* Kircher, in the Musurgia, tome I. pag. 115, says this expressly.
† De Viris illustr. ord. Bened. lib. II. cap. 74.
‡ De Scient. Mathem. cap. xxii. § 7.

a dissimilarity between the closeness of the syllable MI, and the broad open sound of FA, which he thought could not fail to impress upon the mind a lasting idea of their congruity, and immediately conceived a thought of applying these six syllables to his new formed hexachord.

Struck with the discovery, he retired to his study, and having perfected his system, began to introduce it into practice : the persons to whom he communicated it were the brethren of his own monastery, from whom it met with but a cold reception, which in the Epistle to his friend, above-mentioned, he ascribes undoubtedly to its true cause, envy; however, his interest with the abbot, and his employment in the chapel, gave him an opportunity of trying the efficacy of his method on the boys who were training up for the choral service, and it exceeded the most sanguine expectation.

The fame of Guido's invention soon spread abroad, and his method of instruction was adopted by the clergy of other countries : we are told by Kircher that Hermannus, bishop of Hamburg, and Elvericus, bishop of Osnabrug, made use of it; and by the authors of the Histoire Litteraire de la France,* that it was received in that country, and taught in all the monasteries in the kingdom. It is certain that the reputation of his great skill in music had excited in the pope a desire to see and converse with him, of which, and of his going to Rome for that purpose, and the reception he met with from the pontiff, himself has given a circumstantial account of in the epistle before cited.

The particulars of this relation are very curious, and as we have his own authority, there is no room to doubt the truth of it. It seems that John XX. or, as some writers compute, the nineteenth pope of that name, having heard of the fame of Guido's school, and conceiving a desire to see him, sent three messengers to invite him to Rome; upon their arrival it was resolved by the brethren of the monastery that he should go thither attended by Grimaldo the abbot, and Peter the chief of the canons of the church of Arezzo. Arriving at Rome he was presented to the holy father, and by him received with great kindness. The pope had several conversations with him, in all which he interrogated him as to his knowledge in music; and upon sight of an antiphonary which Guido had brought with him, marked with the syllables agreeable to his new invention, the pope looked on it as a kind of prodigy, and ruminating on the doctrines delivered by Guido, would not stir from his seat till he had learned perfectly to sing off a verse; upon which he declared that he could not have believed the efficacy of the method if he had not been convinced by the experiment he had himself made of it. The pope would have detained him at Rome, but labouring under a bodily disorder, and fearing an injury to his health from the air of the place, and the heats of the summer, which was then approaching, Guido left that city upon a promise to revisit it, and explain to his holiness the principles of his new system.

On his return homewards he made a visit to the abbot of Pomposa, a town in the duchy of Ferrara, who was very earnest to have Guido settle in the monastery of that place, to which invitation it seems he yielded, being, as he says, desirous of rendering so great a monastery still more famous by his studies there.

Here it was that he composed a tract on music, intitled Micrologus, i. e. a short discourse, which he dedicated to Theodald, bishop of Arezzo, and finished, as he himself at the end of it tells us, under the pontificate of John XX. and in the thirty-fourth year of his age. Vossius speaks also of another musical treatise written by him, and dedicated to the same person.

Divers others mention also his being engaged in the controversy with Berenger about the Eucharist, particularly Mersennus and Vossius; the latter of whom, who, by the manner in which he has spoken of Guido elsewhere, can hardly be supposed to have mistaken another person for him, says expressly that in the year 1070, namely, in the time of Gregory VII. flourished Guido, or Guidmundus, by country an Aretine, first a monk of the monastery of St. Leufred, and afterwards a cardinal of the church of Rome, and archbishop of Aversa; that while he was a monk he wrote two books on music to the bishop Theodald, the first in prose, the other partly in heroic verse, and partly in rythmical trochaics; and that he is the same who wrote against Berengarius three books concerning the body and blood of our Lord in the sacrament of the Eucharist.† Trithemius refers him to the year 1030, and Sigebert to 1028, which latter speaks also of the musical notes found out by him.

Du Pin, who in his Ecclesiastical History has given an account of Berenger and his errors, has enumerated the several authors that have written against him; among these he mentions Guimond or Guitmond, bishop of Aversa, as one who, in opposition to Berenger, maintained the real presence of the body and blood of Jesus Christ in the Eucharist. Nay, he goes so far as to cite several books of his writing in the controversy with Berenger, as namely, a treatise De Veritate Eucharistiæ, wherein he charges him with maintaining, among other errors, the nullity of infant baptism, and the lawfulness of promiscuous embraces.

Supposing this to be true, and Guimond and Guido to be one and the same person, the generality of writers have done his memory an injury in representing Guido as simply a monk, who was not only a dignitary of the church, but an archbishop, and a member of the sacred college. But it seems that Vossius and those whom he has followed are mistaken in these particulars : Bayle has detected this error, and has set the matter right, by relating that Guido and Guitmond were nearly contemporaries, but that it was the latter who was the monk of St. Leufred, in the diocese of Evreux in Normandy, afterwards bishop of Aversa in Italy, and at length a cardinal, and who wrote three books De Veritate Corporis et Sanguinis Christi in Eucharistia adversus Beren-

---

* Tom. VII. pag. 143, 144.

† De Scientiis Mathem. cap. xxii. § 7.

garium, which, he adds, have been printed separately, and in the Bibliotheca Patrum.*

Most of the authors who have taken occasion to mention Guido, speak of the Micrologus as containing the sum of his doctrine: what are the contents of the Micrologus will hereafter be related; but it is in a small tract, intitled Argumentum novi Cantus inveniendi, that his declaration of the use of the syllables, with their several mutations, and, in short, his whole doctrine of solmisation, is to be found. This tract makes part of an epistle to a very dear and intimate friend of Guido, whom he addresses thus: 'Beatissimo atque dulcissimo fratri Michaëli;'† and at whose request the tract itself seems to have been composed. In this epistle, after lamenting very pathetically the exceeding envy that his fame had excited, and the opposition that his method of instruction met with, he relates the motives of his journey to Rome, and the reception he met with there, and then proceeds to an explanation of his doctrine.

It seems that in the time of Guido, musical instruments were either scarce or ill tuned, and that the only method of acquiring a true knowledge of the intervals was by means of the monochord; for both in the Micrologus, and in this shorter work, of which we are now speaking, the author gives directions how to construct and divide properly this instrument; but upon the whole he seems to condemn the use of it, comparing those who depend on it to blind men; for this reason he discovers to his friend a method of finding out an unknown cantus, which he says he tried on the boys under his care, who thereby became able to sing in no greater a space of time than three days what they could not have mastered by any other method in less than many weeks: and this method is no other than the applying the syllables to the hexachords in the manner before directed. But here perhaps it may be fitting that he should speak for himself, and the following is a translation of his own words:—

'I have known many acute philosophers, not only 'Italians, but French, Germans, and even Greeks 'themselves, who, though they have been sought out 'for as masters in this art, have trusted to this rule, 'the monochord alone; but yet I cannot say that 'I think either musicians or singers can be made by 'the help of it. A singer ought to find out and re- 'tain in memory the elevations and depressions of 'notes, with their several diversities and properties; 'and this by our method you may attain to do, and 'also be able to communicate the means of doing it 'to others; for if you commit to memory any Neuma, 'so as that it may immediately occur to you when 'you find it in any cantus, then you will directly and 'without hesitation be able to sound it: and this 'Neuma, whatever it be, being retained in your 'memory, may with ease be applied to any new

'cantus of the same kind. The following is what 'I made use of in teaching the boys:—

UT queant laxis REsonare fibris
MIra gestorum FAmuli tuorum,
SOLve polluti LAbii reatum
Sancte Joannes.‡

‡ Martini, in his Storia della Musica, vol. I. pag. 180, from a manuscript in his possession, written in praise of Guido, and, as he conjectures, in the sixteenth century, has given the notes to this hymn in the Gregorian characters in the following order:—

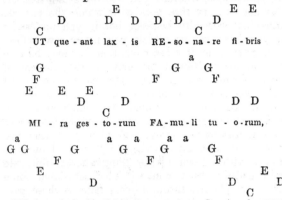

which he has rendered thus in modern characters:—

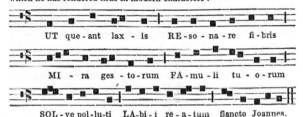

Pedro Cerone and Berardi, the one in his treatise De la Musica, lib. II. cap. 44, and the other in his Miscellanea Musicale, part II. pag. 55 give it in this form:—

which they both render thus:—

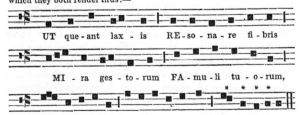

[This last Bar does not appear to be a faithful rendering.—ED.]

Berardi adds, that the method of notation by the letters of Gregory, as in the above example, was used in his time in Hungary, and other parts of Germany. He also cites a passage from the Practica Musica of Herman Finek, or Fink, to prove that these were the notes which Guido applied to the hymn 'Ut queant laxis.' Fink has asserted this fact on the authority of Albertus Magnus, who wrote on music, and lived in the thirteenth century.

* Art. ARETIN [Guy] in not. Vide also Hist. Litter. de France, tom. VIII. Guitmond Evêque d'Averse, pag. 561, where this error is taken notice of, and rectified.

† The copy inserted in Baronius reads, 'Charissimo atque dulcissimo,' &c.

'In the above symphony you see six different
'particles, which are to be applied to as many
'different notes; and whenever the singer is able
'to apply these to such of the six notes as they
'properly belong to, he will be able to sing his
'devotions with ease. When you hear any Neuma,
'examine in your own mind which of these particles
'does best agree with its ending, so as that the final
'note of the Neuma, and the principal particles may
'be equisonous, whereby you will be certain that the
'Neuma ends in that note with which the particle
'agreeing therewith begins: but if you undertake
'any written cantus which you never saw before,
'you must sing it often over, that you may be able
'to end every Neuma properly, so that the end of
'each Neuma may in the same manner be joined
'with the beginning of the particle which begins
'by the same note in which the Neuma ends. By
'this method you will presently be able to sing any
'new cantus by the notes; and when you hear any
'that is not noted, you will soon perceive how it is
'to be written down, in the doing whereof this rule
'will greatly assist you. I have set down some
'short symphonies through every note of these par-
'ticles, and when you shall carefully have looked
'them over, you will be glad to find out the depres-
'sions and elevations of every note in order in the
'beginnings of these particles: but if you should
'have a mind to attemperate certain particles of
'different symphonies by connexion, you may by
'a very short and easy rule learn all the difficult and
'manifold varieties of Neumas; but these cannot all
'be so well explained by letter, and would be more
'plainly opened in a familiar colloquy.

A
F Alme rector mores nobis sacrato; Summe pater ser-
D
A
F vis tuis miserere; Salus nostra honor noster esto Deus.
D
A
F Deus, judex justus fortis, et patiens: Tibi totus ser-
D
A
F vit mundus uni, Deus. Stabunt justi ante dominum
D
A
F Semper læti: Domino laudes omnis creatura dicat.*

He then proceeds thus: 'In writing we have
'twenty-three letters, but in every cantus we have
'only seven notes; for as there are seven days in
'a week, so are there seven notes in music, for all
'that are added above are the same, and are sung
'alike through the whole, differing in nothing but
'that they are sounded doubly higher. We say
'there are seven grave and seven acute, and that the
'second order of seven letters is written different
'from the other in this manner :—

a	h	c	d	e	f	g
A	B	C	D	E	F	G

* It is supposed that the above are the initial sentences of some
hymns or other offices anciently used in the church, and which were
part of the choral service. Guido has intimated that these examples
can hardly be rendered intelligible without a verbal explanation; but
it is conjectured by the letters D F A, that they are to be sung in the
first of the ecclesiastical tones, that having A for its dominant, and D
for its final.

Towards the end of this tract Guido directs the
manner of constructing and dividing the monochord,
which because he has done it more at large in the
Micrologus, we forbear to speak of here; the rest
of the epistle is taken up with a short disquisition
on the ecclesiastical tones, at the close whereof he
recommends the perusal of his Micrologus, and also
a Manual, written with great perspicuity by the
most reverend abbot Obdo,† from whose example
he owns he has somewhat deviated, choosing, as he
says, to follow Boetius, though he gives it as his
opinion that his work is fitter for Philosophers than
Singers.

The Micrologus, though, as its title imports,
a short discourse, is considerably longer than the
former tract. The title of it, as given by some
transcriber of his manuscript, is, Micrologus, id est
brevis Sermo in Musica, editus a Domine Guidone
piissimo Monacho et peritissimo Musico.

In this tract, too, the author complains very feelingly of the envy of the times, and the malignity
of his detractors.

In the dedication of the Micrologus to Theodald,
the bishop of Arezzo, his diocesan, Guido confesses
the goodness of his patron in vouchsafing to become
his associate in the study of the Holy Scriptures,
which he attributes to a desire to comfort and support
him under the weight of his bodily and mental
infirmities, and acknowledges, that if his endeavours
are productive of any good to mankind, the merit
of it is due to his patron, and not to him. He says
that when music was employed in the service of the
church, he laboured in the art not in vain, seeing
that his discoveries in it were made public by the
authority, and under the protection of his patron,
who as he had regulated the church of St. Donatus,
over which it was his office to preside, so had he
rendered the servants thereof, by those privileges
by him conferred on them, respectable amongst the
clergy. He adds, that it is matter of surprise to him
to find that the boys of the church of Arezzo should,
in the art of modulation, excel the old men of other
churches; and professes to explain the rules of the
art for the honour of their house, not in the manner
of the philosophers, but so as to be a service to
their church, and a help to their boys, for that the
art had a long time lain hid, and, though very
difficult, had never been sufficiently explained.

The dedication is followed by a prologue, in which
the author attributes to the grace of God the success
of his endeavours to facilitate the practice of music;
which success he says was so great, that the boys
taught by his rules, and exercised therein for the
space of a month, were able to sing at first sight,
and without hesitation, music they had never heard
before, in such a manner as to surprise most people.

It appears, as well from the epistle to his friend
Michael, as from the Micrologus, that in the opinion
of Guido the only way of coming at a knowledge
of the intervals so as to sing them truly, was by
means of the monochord; for which reason, though

† Odo of Cluni, of whom, and also of his Enchiridion, see an account
in chap. 34. of this work.

he condemns the use of it for any other purpose than the bare initiation of learners in the rudiments of singing, he constantly recommends the study of it to young people. In the very beginning of the Micrologus he says, 'Whoever desires to be 'acquainted with our exercise, must learn such songs 'as are set down in our notes, and practise his hand 'in the use of the monochord, and often meditate 'on our rules, until he is perfect in the power and 'nature of the notes, and is able to sing well at first 'sight; for the notes, which are the foundation of 'this art, are best to be discerned in the monochord, 'by which also we are taught how art, imitating 'nature, has distinguished them.'

Guido proposes that the monochord shall contain twenty-one notes, concerning the disposition whereof he speaks thus :—

'First set down Γ Greek, which is added by the 'moderns, then let follow the first seven letters of 'the alphabet, in capitals, in this manner, A, B, 'C, D, E, F, G; and after these the same seven 'letters in the smaller characters; the first series 'denotes the graver, and the latter the acuter sounds. 'Nevertheless, among the smaller letters we insert 'occasionally b or ♮, the one character being round, 'the other square, thus a, b, ♮, c, d, e, f, g; to 'these add the tetrachord of superacutes, in which 'b is doubled in the same manner, aa, bb, ♮♮, cc, 'dd, ee. These letters make in all twenty-two, 'Γ, A, B, C, D, E, F, G, a, b, ♮, c, d, e, f, g, aa, bb, '♮♮, cc, dd, ee, the disposition whereof has hitherto 'been so perplexed as not to be intelligible, but it 'shall here be made most clear and plain, even 'to boys.'

For the division of the monochord he gives the following directions :—

'Gamma Γ being placed at one extremity of the 'monochord, divide the space between that and the 'end of the chord into nine parts, and at the end 'of the first ninth part place A, from whence the 'ancients fixed their beginning; then from A divide 'the space to the end of the chord into nine parts, 'and in the same manner place B; then returning to 'Γ; divide the whole space to the end into four parts, 'and at the end of the first fourth part place C. In 'the same manner as from Γ you found C, by a division 'of four parts, you will from A find D; from B, E; 'from C, F; from D, G; from E, a acute; from F, 'b round; the rest that follow are easily found by 'a bisection of the remaining parts of the line in the 'manner above directed, as for example, in the middle 'between B and the end place ♮. In like manner 'from C you will find a new c; from D a new d; 'from E another e; from F another f; and from G 'another g; and the rest in the same manner, pro-'ceeding upwards or downwards, ad infinitum, un-'less the precepts of the art should by their authority 'restrain it. Out of the many and divers divisions of 'the monochord, I have set down this in particular, it 'being easily to be understood, and when once under-'stood is hardly to be forgotten.—Here follows 'another method of dividing the monochord, which,

'though not so easily to be retained, is more ex-'peditiously performed. Divide the whole into nine 'parts, the first part will terminate in A, the second 'is vacant; the third in D, the fourth vacant; the 'fifth a, the sixth d, the seventh aa, the rest vacant. 'Again, divide from A to the end into nine parts; 'the first part will terminate in B, the second will 'be vacant, the third E, the fourth vacant, the fifth '♮, the sixth e, the seventh ♮♮, the rest vacant : 'again, divide the whole from Γ to the end into four 'parts, the first will terminate in C, the second in G, 'the third in g, and the fourth finishes. Divide 'from C to the end likewise into four parts, the first 'part will end in F, the second in c, the third in cc, 'and the fourth finishes. Divide from F into four 'parts, the first will end in b round, the second in f : 'divide from b round into four parts, in the second 'you will find bb round, the rest are vacant. Divide 'from aa into four parts, the first will be dd, the rest 'are vacant. For the disposition of the notes these 'two methods of division are sufficient; the first is 'the more easy to be remembered, the second the 'more expeditious.'

Upon this division of the monochord he observes, that there appears a greater distance between some of the notes, as Γ, A, and A, B, than between others, as B, C : he says the greater distance is called a tone, and the lesser a semitone, from semis an half; that a ditone is an interval consisting of two tones, as C, D, E, and that that is called a semi-ditone which contains only a tone and half, as from D to F. He says that when between any two notes there occur in any order whatever, two tones and a semitone, as from A to D, from B to E, and from C to F, the extreme sounds make a diatessaron, but that a diapente is greater by a tone; as when between any two notes there occur three tones and a semitone, as from A to E, or from C to G. He reckons up six consonances, that is to say, the tone, semitone, ditone, semiditone, diatessaron, and diapente, to which number he says may also be added the dia-pason as a seventh; but that as it is seldom intro-duced, it is not so commonly ranked among them.*

In the seventh chapter of the Micrologus the author treats of the affinity of notes, or, in other words, of the consonances; those of the diatessaron and dia-pente he explains by the following figure :—

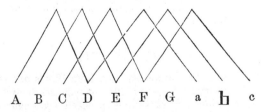

A   B   C   D   E   F   G   a   ♮   c

In the eighth he shews the affinity between b and ♮, and distinguishes between the diatessaron and diapente in this diagram :—

* The manuscript must certainly be erroneous in this place, for the semitone can in no sense whatever be deemed a consonance; and as to the diapason, it is so far from being seldom introduced, that it is the most usual and perfect of all the consonances.

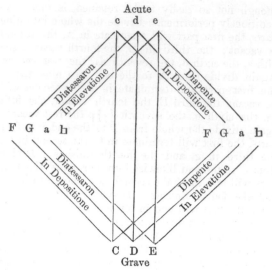

In the twelfth and thirteenth chapters he speaks of the division of the four modes into eight, and says that as there are eight parts of speech, and eight forms of blessedness, *i. e.* beatitudes, so ought there to be eight modes in music. In the fourteenth chapter he treats more particularly of the modes, which he calls Tropes, and of the effects of music: of these he says their properties are so different, that in the same manner as a person accustomed to different countries is able out of several men placed before him, to say 'this is a Spaniard, this an Italian, 'this a German, and this other a Frenchman;' so may one that is skilled in music by their diversities distinguish the tropes. Farther he ascribes to the tropes different properties; for 'one person,' says he, 'delights in the broken leaps of the second authentic; 'another in the softness of the third plagal; a third 'shall be delighted with the garrulity of the fourth 'authentic, and another shall approve the mellifluous 'sweetness of the fourth plagal.' As to the power of music, he says it is so great as to cure many diseases of the human body; he cites a relation of a frantic person who was restored to reason by the music of Asclepiades the physician; and mentions also that a certain other person was by the sound of the lyre, so stirred up to lust, that he attempted to force into the chamber of a young woman with intent to violate her chastity, but that the musician, immediately changing the mode, caused him to desist from his purpose.

CHAP. XXXVII.

According to Guido, cap. xv. four things are required in every cantus,—sounds, consonances, neumas, and distinctions: from sounds proceed consonances, from consonances neumas, and from neumas distinctions: this it seems was the ancient scholastic division of vocal music, and it is adopted by all the monkish writers on the art. A Neuma is the smallest particle of a cantus, and is elsewhere said to signify as many notes as can be sung in one respiration. By distinctions the author seems to mean nothing more

than the different measures of time, which, for aught that any where appears to the contrary, were regulated solely by the metre of the verse to which the notes were sung. Speaking of neumas, he says they may be reciprocated or return by the same steps as they proceeded by; and adds that a cantus is said to be metrical when it scans truly, which, if it be right, it will do even if sung by itself. Neumas, he says, should correspond to neumas, and distinctions to distinctions, according to the perfectly sweet method of Ambrosius. Farther he says that the resemblance between metres and songs is not small, for that neumas answer to feet, and distinctions to verses; the neuma answers to the dactyl, spondee, or iambic; the distinction to the tetrameter, the pentameter, or the hexameter, and the like. He adds, 'Every cantus 'should agree with the subject to which it is adapted, 'whether it be grave, tranquil, jocund, or exulting; 'and that towards the end of every distinction the 'notes should be thinly disposed, that being the place 'of respiration; for we see that when race-horses 'approach the end of the course they abate their 'speed, and move as if wearied.'

Cap. xvi. he treats of the manifold variety of sounds and neumas, and says that it ought not to seem wonderful that such a variety should arise from so few notes, since from a few letters syllables are formed, which, though not innumerable, do yet produce an infinite number of parts. 'How many kinds 'of metre' adds he, 'arise out of a few feet, and by 'how many varieties is each capable of diversifica- 'tion? but this he says is the province of the gram- 'marians.' He proceeds to show what different neumas may be formed from the six consonances; he assumes that every neuma, or, as we should now say, every passage, must necessarily either ascend or descend; an ascending neuma he terms Arsis, a descending, Thesis; these he says may be conjoined: and farther he says that by means of a total or partial elevation or depression of any neuma, different combinations may be formed, and a great variety of melody produced.

In cap. xvii. he lays it down as a rule, that as whatever is spoken may be written, so there can be no cantus formed but what may be designed by letters; and here he exhibits a rule for a kind of extemporaneous musical composition, which must doubtless appear very strange to a modern: he says in singing no sound can be uttered but by means of one or other of the five vowels, and that from their changes a sweet concord will ensue; he therefore first directs the placing the letters of the monochord, and the vowels under them in this order:—

Γ A B C D E F g a ♮ c d e f g a
a e i o u a e i o u a e i o u a

And, to exemplify their use, recommends the taking some such known sentence as this:—

Sancte Joannes, meritorum tuorum copias, nequeo digne canere.

In this example the vowels determine the music; for as in the above scheme the power of each sound is transferred to its correspondent vowel, the succession of the vowels will exhibit a series of sounds to which every syllable may be sung :—

It is clear from the connection between the vowels and the letters of the monochord, that the diapente here made use of is taken from among the acutes ; because in the disposition above made, the vowel a answers to Γ ; but had he chosen the graves for an example, the progression of the cantus had been precisely the same ; for as d is to c, so is A to Γ, and as f is to c, so is C to Γ ; as g is to c, so is D to Γ, and so of the rest.

This it must be confessed is but a fortuitous kind of melody ; it seems however to have suited well enough with the simplicity of the times, which affords us no reason to believe that the art of composing music was arrived at any great degree of perfection. By the rule here given the above cantus may easily be rendered into modern notes, in which it will have this appearance :—

Sanc - te   Jo - an - nes, me - ri - to - rum   tu - o - rum

co - pi - as, ne - que - o   dig - ne   ca - ne - re.

The eighteenth chapter of the Micrologus is an explanation of the Diaphonia, by which term we are to understand those precepts that teach the use of the organ, and its application to vocal melody ; concerning which Guido says, that supposing the singer to utter any given sound, as for instance A, if the organ proceed to the acutes, the A may be doubled, as A D a, in which case it will sound from A to D, a diatessaron, from D to a, diapente, and from A to a, a diapason : he farther says, that these three kinds, when uttered by the organ, commix together with great sweetness, and that the apt copulation of notes is called Symphony. He gives this which follows as an example of the diaphonia :—

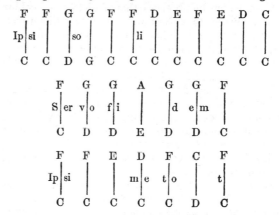

And adds that a cantus may be doubled by the organ, and the organ itself in the diapason, as much as the organist pleases. He says that having made the doubling of sounds sufficiently clear, he will explain the method of adapting grave sounds to a cantus, in the doing whereof he premises that the Diaphonia admits not of the semitone nor diapente, but that it accepts of the tone, ditone, semiditone,

and diatessaron, among which consonances the diatessaron holds the principal place. Of the modes, which he calls Tropes, he says that some are fit, some more fit, and others most fit, for the Diaphonia ; and these degrees of fitness seem to bear a proportion to the number of concordant intervals in each. As an instance of the highest degree of this kind of perfection, he mentions the third and fourth tones, which he says follow kindly and sweetly, with a tone, ditone, and diatessaron.

In the nineteenth chapter are contained sundry examples to illustrate the precepts delivered in the chapter preceding, among which are the following :—

F	F	G	G	F	F	D	E	F	E	D	C
Ip	si		so			li					
C	C	D	G	C	C	C	C	C	C	C	C

F	G	G	A	G	G	F
S	er	v	o	f	i		d	e	m	
C	D	D	E	D	D	C

F	F	E	D	F	C	F
Ip	si			m	e	t	o		t	
C	C	C	C	C	D	C

The several precepts contained in the Micrologus, together with the examples above given, may serve to shew the inartificial contexture of the music in those early days : they farther tend to confirm those accounts which carry the antiquity of the organ back to a time, when, from the uncultivated state of the mechanic arts, it would hardly be supposed that an instrument so wonderfully constructed could have been fabricated.*

After delivering the precepts of the Diaphonia, the author from Boetius relates the discovery of the consonances by Pythagoras. He exhorts such as mean to become excellent in music to take the monochord for their guide, and repeats his instructions for making and dividing it.

A little farther on he resumes the consideration of the tones, and is somewhat precise in ascertaining their respective limits, and distinguishing between the authentic and the plagal. He says that the same antiphon may be sung in different sounds without changing the harmony : or, in other words, that it may be so transposed, as that the sounds may bear the

* The state of the mechanic arts, so far as they relate to the constructing and making the several utensils and conveniences for domestic life, would, were it possible to come at it, afford great satisfaction to a curious enquirer, as it would enable him, by a comparison of two very remote periods, to estimate the degree of perfection at which we are now arrived. Few of those persons, who are curious enough to attend to the manual operations of our English artificers, are ignorant that they work with an amazing degree of truth and accuracy. A very curious book, now extant, called the Book of St. Alban's, written by dame Julyans Bernes, prioress of the nunnery of Sopwell, near St. Alban's, describes the method of making an angling rod in the year 1496 ; and gives us to understand that the mechanics of that time thought the neatest method of hollowing a stick for that purpose was the burning it through with a hot spit ; and it is not unlikely but that four hundred years before that, an organ-pipe was perforated in no better a manner ; and if we suppose the same want of neatness in the various other parts of that complicated machine of which we are now speaking, we may fairly conclude that both the organ and the music of the eleventh century were equally rude and inartificial.

same relation to each other as if not transposed. He says that the second letter, by which we are to understand ♭, is rejected as ignoble, and unfit to be the principal of any tone: the reason of this is, that its fifth is defective, as being less than a true diapente by a semitone.

The residue of this tract, the Micrologus, consists of miscellaneous reflections on the use and efficacy of music: towards the close of it is the following tetrastic.

Quasdam lineas signamus variis coloribus
Ut quo loco sit sonus mox discernat oculus;
Ordine tertiæ vocis splendens crôcus radiat,
Sexta ejus, sed affinis flavo rubet minio.

Upon which he observes, that if a letter and colour be not affixed to a Neuma, it will be 'like a well without a rope.' These verses are an absolute enigma, and it would be a vain attempt to explain them, did not a passage in another part of this author's writings afford some intimation that by the red line he intended to denote the F, and by the yellow the C cliff: however we are not to look on this method of distinguishing the cliffs by lines of different colours as the invention of Guido, since it appears to have been in use so early as the year 900, which is at least an hundred years before the time when he wrote.

He seems to close his tract with an assurance that he has made the rules clear, and laid open to singers the regular and perfect manner of singing in a method unknown to former times. But he immediately resumes his subject in these words, 'Temporibus nostris 'super omnes homines fatui sunt cantores;' and goes on to explain some particulars that are before but obscurely treated of; in the doing whereof Guido takes occasion to represent the woful state of music, and the deplorable ignorance of singers at the time when he wrote; the whole is curious, and will be best understood if given in his own words, which are nearly these:—

' In these our times no set of men are so infatuated ' as singers; in every other art we improve, and in ' time attain to a greater degree of knowledge than ' we derived from our teachers: thus by reading ' over the simple psalter, boys are enabled to read ' other books; the countryman by use and exercise ' acquires the knowledge of agriculture; he who has ' pruned one vine, planted one shrub, or loaded one ' ass, is able not only to do the same again, but to do ' it better; but, miserable disciples of singers, they, ' though they should practise every day for an hun-' dred years, would never be able to sing even one ' little antiphon themselves, nor without the help of ' a master, but lose as much time in attaining to sing, as would have enabled them fully to understand the divine writ. And what is more to be lamented is, that many clerks of the religious orders, and ' monks too, neglect the psalms, the nocturnals and ' vigils, and other lessons of piety, by which we are ' led to everlasting glory, while they with a most ' foolish and assiduous labour prosecute the art of ' singing, which they are never able to attain. Who ' then can refrain from tears to see such an evil ' creep into the church? from whence such discord

' ensues, that we are unable to celebrate the divine ' offices. Nor is this all, for this ignorance of their ' duty begets reproach, from whence proceeds con-' tention; scarce the scholar with the master can ' agree, and much less one fellow scholar with another. ' Neither is there any uniformity of music at this ' day in the churches; for there are as many kinds ' of antiphons as there are masters; insomuch that ' no one can say as heretofore, this is the antiphon ' of Gregory, or Leo, or Albert, or any other; but ' every one either varies these, or forms others at his ' pleasure. It ought not therefore to give offence if I ' contend with the corruptions of the times, and en-' deavour to render the practice of music conformable ' to the rules of the art: and as all these corruptions ' have arisen from the ignorance of musicians, I must ' earnestly request that no one will presume to make ' antiphons, unless he be well skilled in the art of ' forming them according to the known and established ' rules of music; it being most certain that he who is ' not the disciple of truth will be a teacher of error. ' And for these reasons I intend, with the help of ' God, to note down a book of antiphons, by means ' whereof any assiduous person may attain to sing ' truly, and without hesitation; and if any one doubts ' the efficacy of our method, let him come and see ' what our little boys can do, who labouring under ' their ignorance, as not being able to read the com-' mon psalter, are yet capable of singing the music to ' it, and can without the help of a master sing the ' notes, though they cannot pronounce the words.'

The letters of Gregory, he says, 'are so disposed, ' that if a note be repeated ever so often it will always ' have the same character; but the better to distin-' guish the order of notes, lines are drawn near to ' each other, and notes are placed on these lines, and ' also on the spaces between the lines.' He adds, 'we ' make use of two colours, yellow and red, by means ' whereof I give a rule very useful and convenient ' for finding out the tone and the letter of the mono-' chord, to which any given neuma is to be referred. ' There are seven letters in the monochord; and ' wherever you see the yellow it is the sign of the ' third letter, and wherever red it denotes the sixth, ' whether the colours are drawn in the lines or over ' them.'

This is the passage above hinted at as containing a solution of the enigmatical tetrastic at the latter end of the Micrologus: the author has said that the letters of the monochord are seven; it is supposed that he means to exclude Γ from the number, as the chord of which that letter is a sign is assumed; if so, the letters must be A, B, C, D, E, F, G, and then the yellow line will denote the place of C, and the red that of F. Father Martini, who had an opportunity of consulting a greater variety of missals and other manuscripts than are to be found in this country, makes no scruple to assert that this is Guido's meaning, and produces divers fragments from ancient books of the church-offices, which have both a yellow and a red line, the first ever with the letter C, and the other with F, in the usual place of the cliff.

The examples of the use of the yellow and red lines

produced by Martini are very many, but as the lines do all stand single, and as upon, above, and below them divers characters are placed, which bear not the least resemblance to the points used by Guido and his successors, it may be questioned whether this variety of colors was not originally adapted to a method of notation in use before his time, notwithstanding that it coincides so well with the stave. But Kircher, in the Musurgia, tome I. pag. 555, has reduced this question to a certainty; and, notwithstanding the general opinion, that before the time of Guido the only method of notation in use was by the Roman capital and small letters, which St. Gregory introduced, Martini proves that the notators, as they are called, of that time, made use of certain marks in this form ((Π ʋ .. ✓:* and as to lines of different colours, Kircher relates that he had found in the monastery of Vallombrosa sundry very ancient books, written for the use of the choir there, before the time of Guido ; and that the method of notation in those books was by a red line, with certain notes or points placed in different situations above and below, according to the intervals intended to be marked by them.† Nivers speaks also to the same purpose ; for enquiring into the causes of the corruption of the Cantus Gregorianus, he assigns for one, the uncertainty of the method of notation before the time of Guido ; for he says till his reformation of the scale, the characters were only small points, commas, accents, and certain little oblique strokes, occasionally interposed ; which great variety of minute figures he says was very difficult to comprehend, still more to retain, and impossible to reduce to practice without the assistance of a master.   In proof of this assertion he waives the authority of Kircher, who has mentioned the same fact, and says that he engaged in an exact and laborious research among the most ancient manuscripts in the library of the king of France, and in that of St. Germain De Prez, and others.   Nay, he says that he had caused the Vatican to be searched, and had received from thence, memoirs and extracts from manuscript antiphonaries, and graduals, many of which were above nine hundred years old, in which these characters appear.   He farther says, that in this method of notation, by points and other marks, it was impossible to ascertain the difference between the tone and semitone, which is in effect saying that the whole contrivance was inartificial, productive of error, and of very little worth.   Dissertation sur le Chant Gregorien, chap. vi.   Specimens of this method of notation, taken from Martini, vol. I. pag. 184, are inserted in the Appendix, No. 42.‡

* Stor. della Musica, pag. 183.

† What Guido has said respecting the stations of the cliffs, and the practice of distinguishing them by red and yellow lines, is confirmed by the specimens from Martini (Appendix, 42.); but it may here be remarked that they were also distinguished by lines of a different thickness from the others in the stave, as appears by an example, taken from the Lexicon Diplomaticum of Johannes Ludolphus Walther, fol. Ulm. 1756. (See Appendix, No. 41.

‡ There has lately been discovered in the library of Bennet college in Cambridge, a manuscript containing examples of the method of notation by irregular points above spoken of ; and a learned and ingenious gentleman of that college has furnished this work with the following article from the catalogue of that collection :—

473. N. xxxviii. Codex membranaceous minoris formæ, ante Conquisitionem exaratus. Hymni (sive ut sæpius in hoc Codice nominantur

From what has been said some idea may be formed of the nature and tendency of the Micrologus, and other tracts of Guido.   Whether he was the author of any other than have been mentioned, is not easy to determine ; but it seems that those from which the foregoing extracts are taken, contain as much of his doctrine as he thought communicable by writing ; for it is to be remarked that he frequently takes occasion to say that some particulars of it are not to be understood but by a familiar conversation, and it is to be feared that most of his readers must entertain the same opinion.

It no where appears that any of his works were ever printed, except that Baronius, in his Annales Ecclesiastici, tom. XI. pag. 73, has given at length the epistle from him to his friend Michael of Pomposa, and that to Theodald, bishop of Arezzo, prefixed to the Micrologus, and yet the writers on music speak of the Micrologus as of a book in the hands of every one.   Martini cites several manuscripts of Guido, as namely, two in the Ambrosian library at Milan, the one written about the twelfth century, the other less ancient : another among the archives of the chapter of Pistoja, a city in Tuscany ; and a third in the Mediceo-Laurenziano library at Florence, of the fifteenth century: these are clearly the Micrologus. Of the Epistle to Michael of Pomposa, together with the Argumentum novi Cantus inveniendi, he mentions only one, which he says is somewhere at Ratisbon §.

Of the several tracts above-mentioned, the last excepted, a manuscript is extant in the library of Baliol college in Oxford.   Several fragments of the two first, in one volume, are also among the Harleian manuscripts now in the British Museum, Numb. 3199, but so very much mutilated, that they afford but small satisfaction to a curious enquirer.   The Baliol manuscript contains also the Enchiridion of Odo, which Guido, at the close of the Argumentum novi Cantus inveniendi, highly commends ; as also the tract of Berno abbot of Richenou before mentioned.

The above particulars of the life and labours of Guido, which have indeed the merit of being immediately collected from his own writings, are possibly all that we shall ever be able to learn about him ; for by a kind of fatality, very difficult to account for, his memory lives only in his inventions, and though there is scarce a dictionary, not to mention the innumerable tracts that direct the practice of vocal music, but mention him as having taken the syllables UT, RE, MI, FA, SOL, LA from a hymn of St. John the Baptist, and applied them to certain notes in the scale of music, yet no one author of credit, if we except cardinal Baronius, and he seems more desirous of recording the Invention, than perpetuating the Memory of its author, has thought him worthy of a more honourable testimony than is every day given by the writers of Bibiotheques, Memoirs, and Anecdotes, to any scribbling professor of the Belles Lettres.

This supineness, or ignorance, or whatever else it

Tropi) recitandi diebus Dominicis et festis inter sacra celebranda cum notis musicis.
The last specimen in this plate is inserted from the manuscript thus described.

§ Storia della Musica, passim, et pag. 457, GUIDO.

may deserve to be called, with respect to Guido and his improvements, has been the source of many mistakes, as namely, that he was the inventor of music in consonance, and of the organ and harpsichord; and that he was the first that introduced the practice of descant in singing. In the course of the present work some of these inventions have been, and the others severally will be, fixed at periods very remote from that in which Guido lived: at present it shall suffice to refute them by saying, that as to the organ, it was invented long before;* and farther, Guido himself in his Micrologus frequently mentions the organ as an instrument in common use in his time. As to the harpsichord, the name of it, or of the spinnet, of which it is manifestly but an improvement, does not once occur in the writings of the monkish musicians who wrote after Guido, nor in the works of Chaucer, who seems to have occasionally mentioned all the various instruments in use in his time. Gower indeed speaks of an instrument called the citole, in these verses :—

> He taughte hir till fhe was certeyne
> Of harpe, citole, and of riote,
> With many a tewne, and many a note.
> Confessio Amantis, fol. 178, b.

And by an ancient list of the domestic establishment of Edward III. it appears that he had in his service a musician called a cyteller, or cysteller: the citole or cistole, derived from cistella, a little chest, might probably be an instrument resembling a box with strings on the top or belly, which by the application of the tastatura or key-board, borrowed

* Vide ante page 147.

from the organ, and jacks, became a spinnet. But as to the harpsichord, the earliest description of it which, after a careful research, could be found, is that of Ottomarus Luscinius, in his Musurgia, published at Strasburg, in 1536. As to descant, it was the invention, as some imagine, of Bede, and he lived under the Saxon heptarchy, about the year 673; and lastly, whether the common use of the organ and the practice of descant, do not pre-suppose music in consonance, is submitted to the judgment of all who profess to know any thing of the science.

As Guido made no pretensions to great learning, or skill in philosophy, but seems indeed to have been absorbed in the study of his psalter and the church offices, no one of the many writers who have occasionally mentioned him, has entered into the particulars either of his character or his institution; but his reformation of the scale, his improvement of the stave, and the method of notation invented by him, which has introduced into the world a kind of universal character,† bespeak his merit more than the most laboured encomium could do, and have procured him a reputation that must in all probability endure as long as the love of music shall subsist.

† It is literally true, that for the purpose of representing musical sounds by writing, the system of Guido is an universal character; and every day's experience informs us that men of different countries, and who speak different languages, and therefore are incapable of verbal communication, have yet the same idea of the power of the musical characters, which they discover by their readiness in performing compositions that they have never studied. And this consideration has induced some men to assert that the scale of music might be made to serve the purpose of an alphabet. Bishop Wilkins first started this notion, and it is very ingeniously prosecuted in his tract entitled The secret and swift Messenger, chap. xviii. and by Mr. Oldys in the life of Peter Bales, the famous penman, in the Biographia Britannica.

BOOK V. CHAP. XXXVIII.

The system of Guido, and the method invented by him for facilitating the practice of vocal melody, was received with universal applause, and in general adopted throughout Europe. The clergy, no doubt, favoured it as coming from one of their own order; and indeed they continued to be the only cultivators of music in general for many centuries after his time. The people of England have long been celebrated for their love of cathedral music; not only in Italy, Germany, and France, but here also, the offices were multiplied in proportion to the improvements made in music; and a great emulation arose, among different fraternities, which should excel in the composition of music to particular antiphons, hymns, and other parts of divine service. It farther appears, that about the middle of the eleventh century, the order of worship was not so settled but that a latitude was left for every cathedral church to establish each a formulary for itself, which in time was called its Use: of this practice there are the plainest intimations in the preface to the Common Prayer of queen Elizabeth,‡ And we elsewhere learn, that

‡ 'And where heretofore there hath beene great diversitie in saying 'and singing in churches within this realme; some following Salisburie 'use, some Hereford use, some the use of Bangor, some of Yorke, and 'some of Lyncolne. Now from henceforth all the whole realme shall 'have but one use.' Upon which passage it is to be noted that in the

of the several uses which had obtained in this kingdom, that of Sarum, established anno 1077, was the most followed; and that hence arose the adage 'Secundum usum Sarum.'§

Of the origin of the use of Sarum there are several relations, none of which do great honour to its inventor Osmund, bishop of that see. Bale, of whom indeed it may be said, that almost all his writings are libels, has given this account of him, and the occasion of framing it :—'Ofmundus was 'a man of great adventure and policye in hys tyme, 'not only concernynge robberyes, but alfo the flaughter 'of men in the warres of kyng Wyllyam Conquerour: 'whereupon he was firft the grande captayne of Saye, 'in Normandy, and afterwards earle of Dorfet, and 'alfo hygh-chauncellour of Englande. As Herman, 'the byfhop of Salifbury, was dead, he gaue over all, 'and fucceeded him in that byfhopryck, to lyue, as it 'were, in a fecuryte or eafe in hys lattre age; for than 'was the church become Jefabel's pleafaunt and eafy 'cowch. His cautels were not fo fyne in the other

northern parts, the use of the archiepiscopal church of York prevailed; in South Wales, that of Hereford; in North Wales, that of Bangor; and in other places, the use of other of the principal sees, particularly that of Lincoln. Ayliffe's Parergon, pag. 356. Burn's Eccl. Law, vol. II. pag. 278.

§ Vid. Fuller's Worthies in Wilts, pag. 146.

'kynde for deſtruċtyon of bodyes; but they were alſo
'as good in thys, for deſtruċtyon of ſowles. To
'obſcure the glory of the goſpel preachynge, and
'augment the filthyneſſe of ydolatry, he praċtyſed
'an ordynary of popyſh ceremonyes, the whyche he
'entytled a Conſuetudynary, or uſual boke of the
'churche. Hys fyrſt occaſyon was thys: a great
'battayle chaunced at Glaſtenburye, whyls he was
'byſhop, betweene Turſtinus, the abbot, and hys
'monkes, wherein ſome of them were ſlayne, and
'ſome ſore wounded, as is ſayd afore. The cauſe of
'that battayle was thys: Turſtinus contempnynge
'their quere ſervyce, than called the uſe of Saint
'Gregory, compelled hys monkes to the uſe of one
'Wyllyam, a monke of Fiſcan, in Normandy. Upon
'thys, Oſmundus devyſed that ordynary called the
'Uſe of Sarum, whyche was afterwards received in
'a manner of all Englande, Irelande, and Wales.
'Every Syr Sander Slyngeſby had a boke at hys belte
'thereof, called hys Portaſſe, contaynynge many ſuper-
'ſtycyouſe fables and lyes, the teſtament of Chryſt ſet
'at nought. For thys aċte was that brothel byſhop
'made a popyſh god at Saliſbury.'*

Fox, a writer not quite ſo bitter as the former,
gives the following account of the matter :—

'A great contention chanced at Glayſtenbure, be-
'tweene Thurſtanus, the abbat, and his convent, in
'the daies of William Conqueror, which Thurſtanus
'the ſaid William had brought out of Normandy,
'from the abbey of Cadonum, and placed him abbat
'of Glaſtenburye. The cauſe of this contentious bat-
'tell was, for that Thurſtanus contemning their quier
'ſervice, then called the Uſe of S. Gregory, compelled
'his monkes to the uſe of one William, a monke of
'Fiſcan, in Normandy: whereupon came ſtrife and
'contentions amongſt them; firſt in words, then from
'words to blowes, after blowes, then to armour. The
'abbat, with his gard of harneſt men, fell upon the
'monks, and drave them to the ſteps of the high altar,
'where two were ſlain, eight were wounded with
'ſhafts, ſwords, and pikes. The monks, then driven
'to ſuch a ſtrait and narrow ſhift, were compelled to
'defend themſelves with formes and candleſticks, where-
'with they did wound certaine of the ſouldiers. One
'monk there was, an aged man, who, inſtead of his
'ſhield, took an image of the crucifix in his armes
'for his defence; which image was wounded in the
'breaſt by one of the bowmen, whereby the monk
'was ſaved. My ſtory addeth more, that the ſtriker,
'incontinent upon the ſame, fell mad; which ſavoreth
'of ſome monkiſh addition, beſides the text. This
'matter being brought before the king, the abbat was
'ſent again to Cadonum, and the monkes, by the
'commandement of the king, were ſcattered in far
'countries. Thus, by the occaſion hereof, Oſmundus,
'biſhop of Saliſbury, deviſed that ordinary which is
'called the Uſe of Sarum, and was afterwards received,
'in a manner through all England, Ireland, and Wales.†

* The ſecond Part, or Contynuacyon of the Engliſh Votaryes, fol. 39. b.

† It appears from Lyndwood, not only that the use of Sarum prevailed almoſt throughout the province of Canterbury, but that in respect thereof the bishop of that diocese claimed, by ancient usage and custom, to

'And thus much for this matter, done in the time of
'this king William.'‡

As to the formulary itself, we meet with one called
the Use of Sarum, translated into English by Miles
Coverdale, bishop of Exeter, in the Acts and Monuments of Fox, vol. III. pag. 3, which in truth is but
a partial representation of the subject; for the Use
of Sarum not only regulated the form and order of
celebrating the mass, but prescribed the rule and
office for all the sacerdotal functions; and these are
contained in separate and distinct volumes, as the
Missal itself, printed by Richard Hamillon, anno
1554; the Manual, by Francis Regnault, at Paris,
anno 1530; Hymns, with the notes, by John Kyngston and Henry Sutton, Lond. 1555; the Primer, and
other compilations: all which are expressly said to
be 'ad usum ecclesiæ Sarisburiensis.' Sir Henry
Spelman seems to have followed Fox rather implicity
in the explanation which he gives of the Use of Sarum
in his Glossary, pag. 501.

It is no easy matter, at this distance of time, to
assign the reasons for that authority and independence
of the church of Salisbury which the framing a liturgy,
to call it no more. for its own proper use, and especially
the admiſſion of that liturgy into other cathedrals,
supposes: but this is certain, that the church of
Sarum was distinguished by divers customs and
usages peculiar to itself, and that it adopted others
which the practice of other churches had given a
sanction to: among the latter was one ſo remarkable
as to have been the subject of much learned enquiry.§

The usage here particularly alluded to, is that of
electing a Bishop from among the choristers of the

execute the office of precentor, and to govern the choir, whenever the
archbishop of Canterbury performed divine service in the presence of
the college of bishops. 'Quasi tota provincia [Cantuariensis] hunc usum
'sequitur;' and adds, as one reason of it, 'Episcopus namque Sarum
'in collegio episcoporum est præcentor, et temporibus quibus archi-
'episcopus Cantuariensis solenniter celebrat divina, præsente collegio
'episcoporum, chorum in divinis officiis regere debet, de observantiâ et
'consuetudine antiquâ.' Provinciale, tit. De Feriis, cap. ult. [Anglicanæ
Ecclesiæ] Ver. Usum Sarum. Gibs. Cod. pag. 294. And an instance
of the actual exercise of the office of precentor or chanter at a public
solemnity, by a bishop of Salisbury, occurs in an account of the christen-
ing of prince Arthur in the Collectanea of Leland, vol. III. pag. 208.
and is thus related :—'The bishop of Ely was deken, and rede the
'gospel. The bishop of Rochester bar the crosse, and redde th' epistoll.
'The bishop of Saresbury was channter, and beganne the office of the
'masse.' *The Bishop of Salisbury officiated as Precentor or Chanter at
the Coronation of King George III. and his Queen. The Precentor's fee of
old on the coronation day was a mark of gold. Strype's Stow, book VI.
pag. 13.*

‡ Acts and Monuments, Lond. 1640, vol. I. pag. 238.

§ See a tract entitled Episcopus Puerorum in Die Innocentium, or
a Discovery of an ancient Custom in the Church of Sarum, of making
an anniversary Bishop among the Choristers; it was written at the
instance of bishop Montague by John Gregory of Christ Church, Oxon,
and is among his Posthuma, or second part of his works, published in
1684.

In this tract, which abounds with a great variety of curious learning,
the author takes occasion to remark, that the observance of Innocent's
Day is very ancient in the Christian church; and that in a runic wooden
calendar, a kind of almanac, from which the log or clog, mentioned in
Dr. Plot's History of Staffordshire, is derived, this and other holydays
are distinguished by certain hieroglyphics: for an instance to the purpose, the holyday here spoken of was signified by a drawn sword, to
denote the slaughter of that day. That of SS. Simon and Jude by a ship,
because they were fishers. The festival of St. George, by a horse,
alluding to his soldier's profession. The day of St. Gregory which is
the twelfth of March, this author says was thus symbolized :—'They
'set you down in a picture a school-master holding a rod and ferula in
'his hands. It is, adds he, because at that time, as being about the
'beginning of the spring, they use to send their children first to school.
'And some, he says, are so superstitiously given, as upon this night to
'have their children asked the question in their sleep, whether they have
'a mind to book or no; and if they say yes they count it for a very good
'presage, but if the children answer nothing, or nothing to that purpose,
'they put them over to the plough.'

cathedral of Sarum, on the anniversary of St. Nicholas, being the sixth day of December; who was invested with great authority, and had the state of a diocesan bishop from the time of his election until Innocent's Day, as it is called, the twenty-eighth of the same month. It seems, that the original design of this singular institution was to do honour to the memory of St. Nicholas, bishop of Myra, in Lycia; who, even in his infancy, was remarkable for his piety, and, in the language of St. Paul to Timothy, is said to have known the scriptures of a child. Ribadeneyra has given his life at large; but the following extract from the English Festival,* contains as much about him as any reasonable man can be expected to believe. ' It is fayed, that hys fader hyght Epiphanius, ' and his moder, Joanna, &c. And whan he was born, ' &c. they made hym Chryften, and called hym Nycolas, ' that is a mannes name; but he kepeth the name of ' a chyld; for he chose to kepe vertues, meknes, and ' symplenes, and without malyce. Also we rede, ' whyle he lay in hys cradel, he fafted Wednefday and ' Fryday: these days he would fouke but ones of the ' day, and therewyth held hym plefed. Thus he lyved ' all his lyf in vertues, with thys chyldes name; and ' therefore chyldren don hym worfhip before all other ' faynts.†

That St. Nicholas was the patron of young scholars is elsewhere noted; and by the statutes of St. Paul's school, founded by dean Colet, it is required that the children there educated, 'shall, every Childermas ' Day, come to Paulis churche, and hear the chylde- ' byshop sermon, and after be at the hygh-masse, and ' each of them offer a i. d. to the childe-byshop, and ' with them the maisters and surveiours of the scole.‡

The ceremonies attending the investiture of the Episcopus Puerorum are prescribed by the statutes of the church of Sarum, which contain a title, De Episcopo Choristarum; and also by the Processional. From these it appears, that he was to bear the name and maintain the state of a bishop, habited, with

* In St Nicholas, fol. 55.
† A circumstance is related of this bishop Nicholas, which does not very well agree with the above account of his meek and placid temper; for at the Council of Nice, this same bishop, upon some dispute that arose between them, is said to have given the heretic Arius a box on the ear. Bayle, vol. II. pag. 530, in not.

‡ By this statute, which with the rest is printed as an Appendix to Dr. Knight's life of dean Colet, it should seem, that at the cathedral of St. Paul also they had an Episcopus Puerorum; for besides the mention of the sermon, the statute directs, that an offering be made to the childe byshop. Indeed Strype says, 'that almost every parish had its saint 'Nicholas.' Memorials Ecclesiastical under Queen Mary, pag. 206. In the book of the household establishment of Henry Algernon Percy, earl of Northumberland, compiled anno 1512, and lately printed, are the following entries:—' Item, My lord usith and accustomyth yerely, when 'his lordship is at home, to yef unto the barne-bishop of Beverlay, when 'he comith to my lord in Christmas hally-dayes, when my lord kepith 'his hous at Lekynfield, xxs. Item, my lord useth and accustomyth to 'gif yearly, when his lordship is at home, to the barne-bishop of Yorke, 'when he comes over to my lord in Christynmasse hally-dayes, as he is 'accustomed yearly, xxs.' Hence it appears that there were formerly two other barne, i.e. bearn, or infant-bishops in this kingdom, the one of Beverly, the other of York. And Dr Percy, the learned editor of the above book, in a note on the two articles here cited, from an ancient MS. communicated to him, has given an inventory of the splendid robes and ornaments of one of these little dignitaries. Farther, there is reason to suppose that the custom above-spoken of prevailed, as well in foreign cathedrals, as in those of England, for the writer above-cited, [Mr. Gregory] on the authority of Molanus, speaks of a chorister-bishop in the church of Cambray, who disposed of a prebend which fell void in the month or year of his episcopate, in favour of his master. Some of these customs that relate to the church are more general than is imagined, that of obliging travellers, who enter a cathedral with spurs on, to pay a small fine, called spur-money, to the choristers, upon pain of being locked into the church, prevails almost throughout Europe.

a crosier or pastoral-staff in his hand, and a mitre on his head. His fellows, the rest of the children of the choir, were to take upon them the style and office of prebendaries, and yield to the bishop canonical obedience; and, farther, the same service as the very bishop himself, with his dean and prebendaries, had they been to officiate, were to have performed, the very same, mass excepted, was done by the chorister and his canons, upon the eve and the holiday. The use of Sarum required also, that upon the eve of Innocent's day, the chorister-bishop, with his fellows, should go in solemn procession to the altar of the Holy Trinity, in copes, and with burning tapers in their hands; and that, during the procession, three of the boys should sing certain hymns, mentioned in the rubric. The procession was made through the great door at the west end of the church, in such order, that the dean and canons went foremost, the chaplain next, and the bishop, with his little pre- bendaries, last; agreeable to that rule in the ordering of all processions, which assigns the rearward station to the most honourable. In the choir was a seat or throne for the bishop: and as to the rest of the children, they were disposed on each side of the choir, upon the uppermost ascent. And so careful was the church to prevent any disorder which the rude curiosity of the multitude might occasion in the celebration of this singular ceremony, that their statutes forbid all persons whatsoever, under pain of the greater excommunication, to interrupt or press upon the children, either in the procession or during any part of the service directed by the rubric; or any way to hinder or interrupt them in the execution or performance of what it concerned them to do. Farther it appears, that this infant-bishop did, to a certain limit, receive to his own use, rents, capons, and other emoluments of the church.

In case the little bishop died within the month, his exequies were solemnized with great pomp: and he was interred, like other bishops, with all his orna- ments. The memory of this custom is preserved, not only in the ritual books of the cathedral church of Salisbury, but by a monument in the same church, with the sepulchral effigies of a chorister-bishop, sup- posed to have died in the exercise of his pontifical office, and to have been interred with the solemnities above noted.

Such as is related in the foregoing was the Use of Sarum, which appears to have been no other than a certain mode of divine service, the ritual whereof, as also the several offices required in it, lie dispersed in the several books before enumerated. Whether the forms of devotion, or any thing else contained in these volumes, were so superlatively excellent, or of such importance to religion, as to justify the shedding of blood in order to extend the use of them, is left to the determination of those whom it may concern to enquire. It seems, however, that contentions of a like nature with this were very fre- quent in the early ages of Christianity; which were not less distinguished by the general ignorance that then prevailed, than by a want of urbanity in all ranks and orders of men. That general decorum, the effect of long civilization, which is now observable in all the different countries of Europe, renders us unwilling to credit a fact, which nevertheless every person conversant in ecclesiastical history is acquainted with, and believes; namely, that the true time for celebrating Easter was the ground of a controversy that subsisted for some centuries, and occasioned great slaughter on both sides. The relation above given of the fray at Glastonbury, is not less reproachful to human nature, in any of the different views that may be taken of it; for if we consider the persons, they were men devoted to a religious life; if the place, it was the choir of a cathedral; and if the time, it was that of divine service. And yet we find that contentions of this kind were frequent; for at York, in 1190, there arose another: and Fox, who seems to exult in the remembrance of it, for no other reason than that both parties were, what at that time they could scarce choose but be, papists, has given the following ludicrous account of it :—

' The next yeere then enfued, which was 1190, in ' the beginning of which year, upon Twelfe even, fell ' a foule northerne brawle, which turned well neere to ' a fray, betweene the archbifhop new elected, of the ' church of Yorke, and his company on the one fide, ' and Henry, dean of the faid church, with his catho- ' like partakers on the other fide, upon occafion as ' followeth: Gaufridus or Geoffry, fonne to king Henry ' the fecond, and brother to king Richard, whom the ' king had elected a little before to the archbifhopricke ' of Yorke, upon the even of Epiphany, which we call ' Twelfe Day, was difpofed to hear even-fong with all ' folemnity in the cathedral church, having with him ' Hamon the chanter, with divers canons of the church, ' who tarrying fomething long, belike in adorning and ' attiring himfelfe, in the meane while Henry the deane, ' and Bucardus the treafurer, difdaining to tarry his ' comming, with a bold courage luftily began their holy ' evensong with finging their pfalmes, ruffling of defcant, ' and merry piping of organs; thus this catholike even- ' fong with as much devotion begun, as to God's high ' fervice proceeding, was now almoft halfe complete, ' when as at length, they being in the middeft of their ' mirth, commeth in the new elect with his traine and ' gardenians, all full of wrath and indignation, for that ' they durft be fo bold, not waiting for him, to begin ' God's fervice, and fo eftfoones commanded the quier ' to ftay and hold their peace: the chanter likewife by ' vertue of his office commandeth the fame; but the ' deane and treafurer on the other fide willed them to ' proceed, and fo they fung on and would not ftint. ' Thus the one halfe crying againft the other, the whole ' quier was in a rore: their finging was turned to fcold- ' ing, their chanting to chiding, and if inftead of the ' organs they had had a drum, I doubt they would have ' folefaed by the ears together.

' At laft through the authority of the archbifhop, ' and of the chanter, the quier began to furceafe and ' give filence. Then the new elect, not contented with ' what had beene fung before, with certaine of the ' quier began the evenfong new againe. The treafurer ' upon the fame caufed, by virtue of his office, the

' candles to be put out, whereby the evenfong having ' no power further to proceed, was ftopped forthwith: ' for like as without the light and beames of the funne ' there is nothing but darkneffe in all the world, even ' fo you muft underftand the pope's church can fee to ' doe nothing without candle-light, albeit the funne doe ' fhine never fo cleere and bright. This being fo, the ' archbifhop, thus difappointed on every fide of his ' purpofe, made a grievous plaint, declaring to the ' clergie and to the people what the deane and treafurer ' had done, and fo upon the fame, fufpended both them ' and the church from all divine fervice, till they fhould ' make to him due fatisfaction for their trefpaffe.

' The next day, which was the day of Epiphany, ' when all the people of the citie were affembled in the ' cathedral church, as their manner was, namely, in ' fuch feafts devoutly to hear divine fervice, as they call ' it, of the church, there was alfo prefent the archbifhop ' and the chanter, with the refidue of the clergie, look- ' ing when the deane and treasurer would come and ' fubmit themfelves, making fatisfaction for their crime. ' But they ftill continuing in their ftoutneffe, refufed fo ' to do, exclaiming and uttering contemptuous words ' againft the archbifhop and his partakers; which when ' the people heard, they in a great rage would have ' fallen upon them: but the archbifhop would not ' fuffer that. The deane then, and his fellowes, per- ' ceiving the ftir of the people, for feare, like pretie ' men, were faine to flee; fome to the tombe of S. ' William of York, fome ranne into the deane's houfe, ' and there fhrouded themfelves, whom the archbifhop ' then accurfed. And fo for that day the people re- ' turned home without any fervice.' *

In the year 1050 flourished HERMANNUS CONTRAC- TUS, so surnamed because of a contraction in his limbs, whom Vossius styles Comes Herengensis, a monk also of the monastery of St. Gal. He excelled in mathematics, and wrote two books of music, and one of the monochord.

MICHAEL PSELLUS, a Greek, and a most learned philosopher and physician, flourished about the year 1060, and during the reign of the emperor Constantinus Ducas, to whose son Michael he was preceptor. His works are but little known; for indeed few of his manuscripts have been printed. What intitles him to a place here, is a book of his, printed at Paris, in 1557, with this title, Michael Psellus de Arithmetica, Musica, Geometrica, et proclus de Sphæra, Elia Vineto Santone interprete. The name of this author has a place in almost every list of ancient musical writers to be met with; an honour which he seems to have but little claim to; for he has given no more on the subject of music than is contained in twenty pages of a loosely printed small octavo volume.

The several improvements of Guido hereinbefore enumerated, respected only the harmony of sounds, the

* Acts and Monuments, vol. I. pag. 305.
Gervase of Canterbury relates, that upon the second coronation of Richard I. after his release from captivity and return from the Holy Land, there was a like contention between the monks and clerks who assisted at that ceremony. ' Facta est autem altercatio inter monachos ' et clericos dum utrique Christus vincit cantarent.' X. Script. 1588. It is very probable that ' Christus vincit' was the beginning of a hymn composed in Palestine, after one of Richard's great victories. This contention was in 1194, four years after that above-mentioned.

reformation of the scale, and the means of rendering the practice of music more easily attainable; in a word, they all related to that branch of the musical science which among the ancients was distinguished by the name of Melopoeia; with the other, namely, the Rythmopoeia, it does not appear that he meddled at all. We nowhere in his writings meet with any thing that indicates a necessary diversity in the length or duration of the sounds, in order to constitute a regular cantus, nor consequently with any system or method of notation, calculated to express that difference of times or measures which is founded in nature, and is obvious to sense. If we judge from the Micrologus and other writings of that early period, it will seem, that in vocal music these were regulated solely by the cadence of the syllables: and that the instrumental music of those times was, in this respect, under no regulation at all.

Of the nature of the ancient rythmopoeia it is very difficult to form any other than a general idea. Isaac Vossius, who had bestowed great pains in his endeavours to restore it, at length gives it up as irretrievable. From him, however, we learn the nature and properties, or characteristics, of the several feet which occur in the composition of the different kinds of verse; and as to the rythmus, he describes it to the following effect :—

'Rythmus is the principal part of verse; but the 'term is differently understood by writers on the 'subject: with some, foot, metre, and rythmus, are 'considered as one and the same thing; and many 'attribute to metre that which belongs to rythmus. 'All the ancient Greeks assert, that rythmus is the 'basis or pace of verse; and others define it by saying, 'that it is a system or collection of feet, whose times 'bear to each other a certain ratio or proportion. 'The word Metre has a more limited signification, as 'relating solely to the quantity and measure of sylla-'bles. Varro calls metre, or feet, the substance or 'materials, and rythmus the rule of verse; and Plato, 'and many others, say, that none can be either a poet 'or a musician to whom the nature of the rythmus is 'unknown.'

After this general explanation of the rythmus, the same author, Vossius, enlarges upon its efficacy; indeed, he resolves the whole of its influence over the human mind into that which at best is but a part of music. The following are his sentiments on this matter :—*

'I cannot sufficiently admire those who have 'treated on music in this and the past age, and have 'endeavoured diligently to explain every other part, 'yet have written nothing concerning rythmus, or if 'they have, that they have written so that they seem 'entirely ignorant of the subject: the whole of them 'have been employed in symphoniurgia, or counter-'point, as they term it; neglecting that which is the 'principal in every cantus, and regarding nothing but 'to please the ear. Far be it from me to censure any 'of those who labour to improve music; but I cannot 'approve their consulting only the hearing, and neg-'lecting that which alone can afford pleasure to the

'faculties of the soul; for as unity does not make 'number, so neither can sound alone, considered by 'itself, have any power, or if it has any, it is so small 'and trifling that it entirely escapes the sense. Can 'the collision of stones or pieces of wood, or even the 'percussion of a single chord, without number or 'rythmus, have any efficacy in moving the affections, 'when we feel nothing but an empty sound? and 'though we compound many sounds that are har-'monical and concordant, yet we effect nothing; 'such an harmony of sounds may indeed please the 'ear, but as to the delight, it is no more than if we 'uttered unknown words, or such as have no sig-'nification. To affect the mind, it is necessary that 'the sound should indicate somewhat which the mind 'or intellect can comprehend; for a sound void of all 'meaning can excite no affections, since pleasure 'proceeds from perception, and we can neither love 'nor hate that which we are unacquainted with.'†

These are the sentiments of the above author on the rythmic faculty in general. With respect to the force and efficacy of numbers, and the use and application of particular feet, as the means of exciting different passions, he thus expresses himself :—

'If you would have the sound to be of any effect, 'you must endeavour to animate the cantus with 'such motions as may excite the images of the things 'you intend to express; in which if you succeed, 'you will find no difficulty in leading the affections 'whither you please: but in order to this, the musical 'feet are to be properly applied. The pyrrichius and 'tribrachys are adapted to express light and voluble 'motions, such as the dances of satyrs; the spondeus, 'and the still graver molussus, represent the grave 'and slow motions; soft and tender sentiments are 'excited by the trochæus, and sometimes by the 'amphibrachys, as that also has a broken and effemi-'nate pace; the iambus is vehement and angry; the 'anapæstus is almost of the same nature, as it inti-'mates warlike motions. If you would express any 'thing cheerful and pleasant, the dactylus is to be 'called in, which represents a kind of dancing 'motion; to express any thing hard or refractory, 'the antispastus will help you; if you would have 'numbers to excite fury and madness, not only the 'anapæstus is at hand, but also the fourth pæon, 'which is still more powerful. In a word, whether 'you consider the simple or the compounded feet, 'you will in all of them find a peculiar force and 'efficacy; nor can any thing be imagined which may 'not be represented in the multiplicity of their 'motions.'‡

But notwithstanding the peculiar force and efficacy which this author would persuade us are inherent in the several metrical feet, he says, that it is now more than a thousand years since the power of exciting the affections by music has ceased; and that the knowledge and use of the rythmus is lost, which alone is capable of producing those effects which historians ascribe to music in general. This misfortune is by him attributed to that alteration in respect of its

* De Poematum Cantu et Viribus Rythmi, pag. 5, et seq.

† De Poematum Cantu et Viribus Rythmi, pag. 72.
‡ Ibid, pag. 74.

pronunciation, which the Greek, in common with other languages, has undergone ; and to the introduction of a new prosody, concerning which he thus expresses himself :—

'There remains to be considered prosody, the 'ratio of accents, which was not only the chief but 'nearly the sole cause of the destruction of the musical 'and poetical art ; for with regard to the change 'made in the letters and diphthongs, the cantus of 'verse might have still subsisted entire, had not 'a new prosody entirely changed the ancient pro-'nunciation ; for while the affairs of Greece flourished, 'the ratio of prosody, and the accents, was quite 'different from what it was afterwards, not only the 'ancient grammarians testified, but even the term 'itself shows that prosody was employed about the 'cantus of words ; and hence it may be easily collected, 'that it was formerly the province of musicians, and 'not of grammarians, to affix to poems the prosodical 'notes or characters.   But as all speech is, as it were, 'a certain cantus, this term was transferred to the 'pronunciation of all words whatsoever, and the 'grammarians, at length, seized the opportunity of 'accommodating the musical accents to their own use, 'to show the times and quantities of syllables.   The 'first grammarian that thus usurped the accents, if 'we may depend on Apollonius Arcadius, and other 'Greek writers, was Aristophanes the grammarian, 'about the time of Ptolemy Philopater, and Epiphanes. 'His scholar Aristarchus, following the footsteps of 'his master, increased the number of accents ; and 'Dionysius the Thracian, a hearer of Aristarchus, 'prosecuted the same study, as did also those who 'succeeded him in the school of Alexandria.   The 'ancient ratio of speaking remained till the times of 'the emperors Antonius and Commodus   How recent 'the custom, of affixing the accents to writing is, 'appears from this, that none are to be found on any 'marbles or coins, or in books of any kind, that are 'ancienter than a thousand years ; and during that 'period which intervened between the time of Aris-'tophanes the grammarian, and the commencement 'of that above-mentioned, namely, for the space of 'eight or nine centuries, the marks for the accents 'were applied by the grammarians to no other use 'than the instructing youth in the metrical art.*

CHAP. XXXIX.

WHAT marks or signatures were used by the ancient Greeks to express the different quantities of musical sounds, independent of the verse, or whether they had any at all, is not now known.   Those characters contained in the introduction of Alypius are evidently of another kind, as representing simply the several sounds in the great system, as they stand distinguished from each other by their several degrees of acuteness and gravity.   Neither are we capable of understanding those scattered passages relating to the rythmus which are to be met with in Aristides Quintilianus, and other of the Greek harmonicians, published by Meibomius ; nor do Porphyry, Manuel

* De Poematum Cantu et Viribus Rythmi, pag. 17.

Bryennius, or any other of their commentators, afford the means of explaining them : Ptolemy himself is silent on this head, and Dr. Wallis professes to know but little of the matter.   In a word, if we may credit Vossius and a few others, who have either written professedly on, or occasionally adverted to, this subject, the rythmopoeia of the ancients is irrecoverably lost, and the numbers of modern poetry retain very little of that force and energy which are generally attributed to the compositions of the ancients : but, after all, it will be found very difficult to assign a period during which it can be said either that the common people were insensible of the efficacy of numbers, or that the learned had not some system by which they were to be regulated.   Something like a metrical code subsisted in the writings of St. Austin and Bede, and, not to enquire minutely into the structure of the Runic poetry, or the songs of the bards, about which so much has been written, it is agreed that they were framed to regular measures.   From all which it is certain, that at the period now speaking of, and long before, the public ear was conscious of a species of metrical harmony arising from a regular arrangement and interchange of long and short quantities ; and that metre was considered as the basis of poetry in its least cultivated state.   The want of this metrical harmony was not discernible in vocal music, because the sounds, in respect of their duration or continuance, were subservient to the verse, or as it may be said in other words, because the measure or cadence of the verse was communicated or transferred to the music.   But this was an advantage peculiar to vocal music ; as to instrumental, it was destitute of all extrinsic aid : in short, it was mere symphony, and as such was necessarily liable to the objection of a too great uniformity.   From all which it is evident, that a system of metrical notation, which should give to mere melody the energy and force of metre, was wanting to the perfection of modern music.

Happily the world is now in possession of a system fully adequate to this end, and capable of denoting all the possible combinations of long and short quantities.   The general opinion is, that the author of this improvement was Johannes de Muris, a doctor of the Sorbonne, about the year 1330, and considerably learned in the faculty of music ; and this opinion has, for a series of years, been so implicitly acquiesced in, that not only no one has ventured to question the truth of it, but scarce a single writer on the subject of music since his time, has forborne to assert, in terms the most explicit, that Johannes de Muris was the inventor of the Cantus Mensurabilis ; that is to say, that kind of music, whether vocal or instrumental, which, in respect of the length or duration of its component sounds, is subject to rule and measure ; or, in other words, that he invented the several characters for distinguishing between the quantities of long and short, as they relate to musical sounds.   Against an opinion so well established as this seems to be, nothing can with propriety be opposed but fact ; nor can it be expected that the authority of such men as Zarlino, Bontempi, Mersennus, and Kircher, should yield to an assertion that tends to deprive a learned man of the honour of an ingenious discovery, unless it can be clearly proved to have been made and recognized before. Whether the evidence now to be adduced to prove that the Cantus Mensurabilis existed above two centuries before the time of De Muris, be less than sufficient for that purpose is submitted to the judgment of the candid and impartial enquirer.

And first it is to be remarked, that in the writings of some of the most ancient authors on music, the name of Franco occurs, particularly in the Practica Musicæ utriusque Cantus of Gaffurius, lib. II. cap. iv. where he is mentioned as having written on the characters used to signify the different lengths of notes, but without any circumstances that might lead to the period in which he lived. Passages also occur in sundry manuscript treatises now extant, which will hereafter be given at length, that speak him to have been deeply skilled in music, and which, with respect to the order of time, postpone the improvements of De Muris to certain very important ones, made by Franco. Farther, there is now extant a manuscript mentioned by Morley, in the Annotations on his Introduction, as old as the year 1326, which is no other than a commentary by one Robert de Handlo, on the subject of mensurable music.*

Authors are not agreed as to the precise time of De Muris's supposed invention, some fixing at 1330, others at 1333; but to take it at the soonest, De Handlo's Commentary was extant four years before; and how long it was written before that, no one can tell: it might have been many years. And still backwarder than that, must have been the time when those rules or maxims of Franco were framed, on which the treatise of De Handlo is professedly a commentary.

But all the difficulties touching the point of priority between these two writers, Franco and De Muris, have been removed by the care and industry of those learned Benedictines, the authors and compilers of the Histoire Litteraire de la France, who, in the eighth volume of that valuable work, have fixed the time when Franco flourished to the latter end of the eleventh century. They term him a scholastic of Liege; for as the first seminaries of learning in France were denominated schools, so the first teachers there, were called scholastics, and their style of address was Magister; and after distinguishing with great accuracy between him and three others of the same name, his contemporaries, they relate, that he lived at least to the year 1083. They say, that he wrote on music, particularly on plain chant; and that some of his treatises are yet to be found in the libraries of France. They farther say, that in that of the abbey De Lira, in Normandy, is a manuscript in folio, intitled, Ars Magistri Franconis de Musica Mensurabili. They mention also another manuscript in the Bodleian library, in six chapters, intitled, Magistri Franconis Musica; and another by the same author, contained in the same volume, intitled, Compendium de Discantu, tribus capitibus.

These assertions, grounded on the testimony of sundry writers, whose names are cited for the purpose in the above work, preclude all doubt as to the merits of the question, and leave an obscure, though a learned writer, in possession of the honour of an invention, which, for want of the necessary intelligence, has for more than four hundred years been ascribed to another.

The same authors speak of Franco as a person profoundly skilled in the learning of his time; particularly in geometry, astronomy, and other branches of mathematical science, and in high esteem for the sanctity of his life and manners.

In the year 1074, under William the Conqueror, flourished in England OSBERN, a monk of Canterbury, and precentor in the choir of that cathedral:† he was greatly favoured by Lanfranc archbishop of that see. Trithemius, Bale, and Pits speak of him as a man profoundly skilled in the science of music. He left behind him a treatise De Re Musica; some add, that he wrote another on the consonances, but the general opinion is, that this and the former are one and the same work. Bale, who places him above a century backwarder than other writers do, making him to have been familiar with Dunstan, who was archbishop of Canterbury in 963, insinuates that Guido did but follow him in many of the improvements made by him in music: His words are, ‘ Ofbernus, a monke of Canterbury, practyfed newe ‘ poyntes of mufyk; and his example in Italy folowed ‘ Guido Aretinus, to make,’ as this candid writer asserts, ‘ the veneraycyon of ydolles more pleafaunt.’§

---

† In tracing the progress of choral music in this country, it is worthy of remark that as it was first established in the cathedral of Canterbury, where the first of the Roman singers settled on the conversion of the English to christianity; so that choir for a series of years produced a succession of men distinguished for their excellence in it. Among these Theodore, the archbishop, and Adrian, the abbot, his friend and coadjutor, are particularly noted; the former was of Tarsus, St. Paul's country, the latter an African by birth, and died in 708. Bede Hist. Eccl. lib. IV. cap. i. He was entombed in the above cathedral with this epitaph. Weever's Funeral Monuments, pag. 251.

Qui legis has apices, Adriani pignora, dices
Hoc sita sarcophago sua nostro gloria pago,
Hic decus abbatum, patrie lux, vir probitatum
Subvenit à cœlo si corde rogetur anhelo.

St. Aldhelm, abbot of Malmesbury, and afterwards bishop of Shireburn, received at Canterbury, from Theodore and Adrian, his knowledge of the Greek language, and was by them instructed in vocal and instrumental music. Camden [Brit. in Wilts. 104.] relates that he was the first of the Saxons that ever wrote in Latin; and that taught the method of composing Latin verse. An acrostic of his composition, in that language, is preserved in Pits's account of him. Bishop Nicholson [Engl. Hist. lib. xli.] speaks of St. Aldhelm's hymns and other musical composures, and laments that they are lost. Of this person many fabulous stories are told; and Bayle, who takes every occasion in his way to ridicule a virtue which some would suspect he did not possess, [Art. St. Francis] makes himself merry with the means he is said to have used to preserve the dominion of reason over his appetite. But Bede, who very probably was acquainted with him [Hist. Eccl. lib. V. cap. xix.] gives him the character of a learned and elegant writer; and Camden celebrates him for the sanctity of his life.

Fuller, in his Worthies of Wiltshire, 147, in his quaint manner, relates of him, that coming to Rome to be consecrated bishop of Sherburn, he reproved pope Sergius his fatherhood, for being a father indeed to a base child, then newly born. And that returning home he lived in great esteem until the day of his death, which happened anno Domini, 709.' See more of him in Leland, Pits, and Tanner.

St. Dunstan is not less celebrated for his skill in music, than for his learning in the other sciences. Pits styles him ‘ Vir Græcè Latinèque ‘doctus, et omnibus artibus liberalibus egregiè instructus, musicus ‘præsertim insignis, et statuarius non contemnendus:' and, by an egregious mistake of Dunstable for Dunstan, Mattheson of Hamburg has made him the inventor of music in parts, which some writers, particularly Johannes Nucius, in a tract entitled Præceptiones Musices Poeticæ, seu de Compositione Cantus, quarto, 1613, with little foundation, have ascribed to John of Dunstable, a musician who flourished in the fifteenth century, and will be spoken of in his place.

§ The seconde Part, or Contynuacyon of the English Votaryes, fol. 13, b.

---

* Morl. Annot. on his Introd. part I. where it is expressly said, that Franco first divided the breve into semibreves, and that one *Robert de Haulo, i. e. Handlo,* made as it were commentaries upon his rules.

Well might Fuller give this man the name of bilious Bale, who, though a protestant bishop, and a great pretender to sanctity, had not the least tincture of charity or moderation.

Under the emperor Henry III. in the diocese of Spires, lived GULIELMUS ABBAS HIRSAUGIENSIS.* He was esteemed the most learned man of his time in all Germany : he excelled in music, and wrote on the tones ; he also wrote three books of philosophical and astronomical institutions, and one De Horologia. There are extant of his writing Letters to Anselm, archbishop of Canterbury. He died in 1091, with the reputation of having wrought many miracles.†

Of the writings of the several authors above enumerated, as they exist only in manuscript, no particular account can be given, nor are we able to form a judgment of their manner of treating music, otherwise than by the help of those few tracts which we know of, and which are deposited in collections accessible to every learned enquirer, and of these the chief are the Enchiridion of Odo ; the Epistle from Berno to Pelegrinus, archbishop of Cologne ; the Argumentum novi Cantus inveniendi ; and the Micrologus and Epistle of Guido. The censure which Guido passes upon the treatise De Musica of Boetius, namely, that it is a work fitter for philosophers than singers, may serve to shew that the writers of those times meddled very little with the philosophy of the science : as to that branch of it, Boetius, who had thoroughly studied the ancients, was their oracle ; and the monkish writers who succeeded him, looking upon music as subservient to the ends of religion, treated it altogether in a practical way, and united their efforts to preserve the music of the church in that state of purity from which it had so often and so widely deviated.

But how ineffectual all their endeavours were, appears from the writings of St. BERNARD, or, as he is otherwise called, St. Bernard the abbot. This man lived about the beginning of the twelfth century : his employments in the church having given him opportunities of remarking the great disorder and confusion of their music, arising, among other causes, from the manuscript multiplication of copies, he resolved to correct the antiphonary of his own order ; and to prove the necessity of such a work, wrote a treatise entitled De Cantu seu Correctione Antiphonarii, containing a plan for the reformation of the Cistercian antiphonary, and an enumeration of all the errors that had crept into the holy offices, with directions for restoring them to their original elegance and purity.

Whatever was the cause of it, the reformation intended by St. Bernard did not take effect, so as to prevent future corruptions of the Cantus Gregorianus. The tract however is extant in the fourth tome of his works. Authors speak of it as an admirable composition, and seem to say that we owe to it all that with any certainty can now be said to be known touching the subject ; part of it is as follows :—

' The song which the churches belonging to the

* Hirsaugia was an abbey in Germany.
† Voss. de Scient. Mathem. cap. xxxv. § xii., cap. lx. § ix., cap. lxxi. § vii.

' Cistercian order have been accustomed to sing, ' although grave and full of variety, is overclouded ' with error and absurdity, and yet the authority of ' the order has given its errors a kind of sanction. ' But because it ill becomes men who profess to live ' together agreeably to the rule of their order, to sing ' the praises of God in an irregular manner, with the ' consent of the brethren I have corrected their song, ' by removing from it all that filth of falsity which ' foolish people had brought into it, and have regulated ' it so that it will be found more commodious for ' singing and notation than the song of other churches ; ' wherefore let none wonder or be offended if he shall ' hear the song in somewhat another form than he ' has been accustomed to, or that he finds it altered ' in many respects ; for in those places where any ' alterations occur, either the progression was irre- ' gular, or the composition itself perverted. That ' you may wonder at, and detest the folly of those ' who departing from the rules of melody, have taken ' the liberty to vary the method of singing, look into ' the antiphon, Nos qui vivimus, as it is commonly ' sung, and although its termination should be pro- ' perly in D, yet these unjust prevaricators conclude ' it in G, and assert with an oath or wager that it ' belongs to the eighth tone. What musician, I pray ' you, can be able to hear with patience any one at- ' tribute to the eighth tone, that which has for its ' natural and proper final the note D ?

' Moreover, there are many songs which are two- ' fold, and irregular ; and that they ascend and descend ' contrary to rule is allowed by the very teachers of ' this error ; but they say it is done by a kind of ' musical licence : what sort of licence is this, which ' walking in the region of dissimilitude, introduces ' confusion and uncertainty, the mother of presumption ' and the refuge of error ? I say what is this liberty ' which joins opposites, and goes beyond natural ' land-marks ; and which as it imposes an inelegance ' on the composition, offers an insult to nature ; since ' it is as clear as the day that that song is badly and ' irregularly constituted, which is either so depressed ' that it cannot be heard, or so elevated that it cannot ' be rightly sung ?

' So that if we have performed a work that is ' singular or different from the practice of the singers ' of antiphons, we have yet this comfort, that reason ' has induced us to this difference, whereas chance, or ' somewhat else as bad, not reason, has made them to ' differ among themselves ; and this difference of ' theirs is so great, that no two provinces sing the ' same antiphon alike : for to instance, in the co- ' provincial churches, take the antiphonary used at ' Rheims and compare it with that of Beauvais, or ' Amiens, or Soissons, which are almost at your doors, ' and see if they are the same, or even like each other.'

From the very great character given of St. Bernard, it should seem that his learning and judgment were not inferior to his zeal : the epistle above-cited, and his endeavours for a reformation of the abuses in church-music, show him to have been well skilled in the science ; and it is but justice to his memory to say that he was one of the truest votaries of, and strongest advocates for music, of any whom that age produced. The accounts extant of him speak him to have been born of noble and pious parents, at the village of Fontaines in Burgundy, in the year 1091. At the age of twenty-three he took the habit of a religious at Citeaux, from whence he was sent to the new-founded abbey of Clairvaux, of which he was the first abbot. The fame of his learning and sanctity occasioned such a resort to this house, that in a very short time no fewer than seven hundred novices became resident in it. His authority in the church was so great, that he was a common arbiter of the differences between the pope, the bishops, and the princes of those contentious times. By his advice Innocent II. was acknowledged sovereign pontiff, and by his management Victor the anti-pope, was induced to make a voluntary abdication of the pontificate, whereby an end was put to a schism in the church.

It was in the time of St. Bernard that Peter Abaelard flourished, a man not more famous for his theological writings, than remarkable for his unhappy amour with Heloissa, or Eloisa, of whom more will be said hereafter : he had advanced certain positions that were deemed heretical, and St. Bernard instituted and conducted a process against him, which ended in their condemnation. The story of Abaelard and Heloissa is well known, but the character of Abaelard is not generally understood ; and indeed his history is so connected with that of St. Bernard, that it would savour of affectation to decline giving an account of him in this place.

PETER ABAELARD was born in a town called Palais, three leagues from Nantes ; having a great inclination to the study of philosophy from his youth, he left the place of his nativity, and after having studied at several schools, settled at Paris, and took for his master William of Champeaux, archdeacon of Paris, and the most celebrated professor of that time. Here a difference arose between Abaelard and the professor, upon which he left him ; and, first at Melun, and afterwards at Corbeil, set up for himself, and, in emulation of his master, taught publicly in the schools ; but his infirmities soon obliged him to seek the restoration of his health in his native air. Upon his recovery he returned to Paris, and finding that William of Champeaux had been promoted to a canonry of the church of St. Victor, and that he continued to profess in that city, he entered into a disputation with him, but was foiled, and quitted Paris. After this Abaelard studied divinity at Laon, under Anselm, canon and dean of that city ; and meaning to emulate his master, he there gave lectures in theology, but was silenced by an order which Anselm had procured for that purpose. From Laon, he removed to Paris, and there for some time remained in peace, explaining the holy scriptures, and by his labours, besides a considerable sum of money, acquired great reputation.

It happened that a canon of the church of Paris, named Fulbert, had a niece, a very beautiful young woman, and of fine parts, whom he had brought up from her infancy, her name was Heloissa. To assist her in her studies this wise uncle and guardian retained Abaelard, a handsome young man, and pos-

sessed of all those advantages which the study of the classics, and a genius for poetry, may be supposed to give him ; and, to mend the matter, took him to board in his house, investing him with so much power over the person of his fair pupil, that though she was twenty-two years of age, he was at liberty to correct her ; and by the actual use of the lash compel her to attend to his instructions ; the consequence of this engagement was, the pregnancy of Heloissa, and the flight of the two lovers into Abaelard's own country, where Heloissa was delivered of a son, who was baptized by the name of Astrolabius. To appease Fulbert, Abaelard brought back his niece to Paris and married her ; but as Abaelard was a priest, and had acquired a canonry in the church, which was not tenable by a husband, and complete reparation could not be made to Heloissa for the injury she had sustained without avoiding this preferment, the marriage was at her own request kept a secret, and she, to remove all suspicion, put on the habit of a nun, and retired to the monastery of Argenteüil. But all this would not pacify her uncle and other relations ; they seized and punished Abaelard by an amputation of those parts with which he had offended. Upon this he took a resolution to embrace a monastic life, and Heloissa was easily persuaded to sequester herself from the world ; they both became professed at the same time, he at St. Denys, and she at Argenteüil.

The letters from Abaelard to Heloissa after their retirement, extant in the original Latin, have been celebrated for their elegance and tenderness ; as to the Epistle from Eloisa of Mr. Pope, it is confessedly a creature of his own imagination, and though a very fine composition, the world perhaps might have done very well without it. With the licence allowed to poets, he has deviated a little from historical truth in suppressing the circumstance of Abaelard's subsequent marriage to his mistress, with a view to make her love to him the more refined, as not resulting from legal obligation : it may be that the supposition on which this argument is founded is fallacious, and the conclusion arising from it unwarranted by experience. But it is to be feared that by the reading this animated poem, fewer people have been made to think honourably and reverentially of the passion of love, than have become advocates for that fascinating species of it, which frequently terminates in concubinage, and which it is the drift of this epistle, if not to recommend, to justify.

But to leave this disquisition, and return to Abaelard : his disgrace, though it sank deeply into his mind, had less effect on his reputation than was to have been expected. He was a divine, and professed to teach the theology, such as it was, of those times ; persons of distinction resorted to St. Denys, and entreated of him lectures in their own houses. The abbot and religious of that monastery had lain themselves open to the censures and reproaches of Abaelard by their disorderly course of living, they made use of the importunity of the people to become his auditors as a pretext for sending him from amongst them. He set up a school in the town, and drew so many to hear him, that the place was not sufficient to lodge, nor the country about it to feed them.

Here he composed sundry theological treatises, one in particular on the Trinity, for which he was convened before a council held at Soissons; the book was condemned to the flames, and the author sentenced to a perpetual residence within the walls of a monastery: after a few days confinement in the monastery of St. Medard at Soissons, he was sent back to his own of St. Denys: there he advanced that St. Denys of France was not the Areopagite; and by maintaining that proposition, incurred the enmity of the abbot and his religious brethren. Not thinking himself safe among them, he made his escape from that place in the night, and fled into the territories of Theobald, count of Champagne, and at Troyes, with the leave of the bishop, built a chapel in a field that had been given to him by the proprietor for that purpose. No sooner was he settled in this place, than he was followed by a great number of scholars, who for the convenience of hearing his lectures built cells around his dwelling: they also built a church for him, which was dedicated to the Holy Trinity, and by Abaelard called Paraclete. His enemies, exasperated at this establishment, and the prospect it afforded him of a quiet retreat from the tumult of the times, instigated St. Norbert and St. Bernard to arraign him on the two articles of faith and manners before the ecclesiastical judges. The duke of Bretagne, in pity to Abaelard, had offered him the abbacy of St. Gildas, of Ruis, in the diocese of Nantes, and in order to avert the consequences of so formidable an accusation, he accepted it; and the abbot of St. Denys having expelled the nuns from Argenteüil, he bestowed on Heloissa, their prioress, the church of Paraclete with its dependencies; which donation was confirmed by the bishop of Troyes, and pope Innocent II. in 1131. But these endeavours of Abaelard did not avert the malice of his persecutors: Bernard had carefully read over two of his books, and selected from thence certain propositions, which seemed to bespeak their author at once an Arian, a Pelagian, and a Nestorian; and upon these he grounded his charge of heresy; Abaelard affecting rather to meet than decline it, procured Bernard to be convened before a council at Sens, in order, if he was able, to make it good; but his resolution failed him, and rather than abide the sentence of the council, he chose to appeal to Rome. The bishops in the council nevertheless proceeded to examine, and were unanimous in condemning his opinions; the pope was easily wrought upon to concur with them; he enjoined Abaelard a perpetual silence, and declared that the abettors of his doctrines deserved excommunication. Abaelard wrote a very submissive apology, disowning the bad sense that had been put upon his propositions, and set out for Rome in order to back it, but was stopped at Cluni by the venerable Peter, abbot of that monastery, his intimate friend; there he remained for some time, during which he found means to procure a reconciliation with St. Bernard. At length he was sent to the monastery of St. Marcellus, at Chalons upon the Soane, and,

overwhelmed with affliction, expired there in the year 1142, and in the sixty-third of his age.

Of this calamitous event Peter of Cluni gave Heloissa intelligence in a very pathetic letter, now extant: she had formerly requested of Abaelard, that whenever he died his body should be sent to Paraclete for interment; this charitable office Peter performed accordingly, and with the body sent an absolution of Abaelard 'ab omnibus peccatis suis.' *

Soon after Abaelard's death Peter made a visit to Paraclete, probably to console Heloissa: in a letter to him she acknowledges this act of friendship, and the honour he had done her of celebrating mass in the chapel of that monastery. She also commends to his care her son Astrolabius, then at the abbey of Cluni, and conjures him, by the love of God, to procure for him, either from the archbishop of Paris, or some other bishop, a prebend in the church.

The works of Abaelard were printed at Paris in 1616. His genius for poetry, and a few slight particulars that afford but a colour for such a supposition, induced the anonymous author of the History of Abaelard and Heloissa, published in Holland 1693, to ascribe to him the famous romance of the Rose; and to assert, that in the character of Beauty he has exhibited a picture of his Heloissa; but Bayle has made it sufficiently clear that that romance, excepting the conclusion, was written by William de Loris, and that John de Meun put the finishing hand to it. A collection of the letters of Abaelard and Heloissa, in octavo, was published from a manuscript in the Bodleian library, in the year 1718, by Mr. Rawlinson. As to the letters commonly imputed to them, and of which we have an English translation by Mr. Hughes, they were first published in French at the Hague in 1693; and in the opinion of Mr. Hughes himself are rather a paraphrase on, than a translation from, the original Latin. Even the celebrated Epistle of Mr. Pope, the most laboured and pathetic of all his juvenile compositions, falls far short of inspiring sentiments in any degree similar to those that breathe through the genuine epistles of this most eloquent and accomplished woman; nor does it seem possible to express that exquisite tenderness, that refined delicacy, that exalted piety, or that pungent contrition, which distinguishes these compositions, in any words but her own.†

* For a fuller account of him see Du Pin Biblioth. Eccies. Cent. XII. and the articles ABAELARD, HELOISE, FOULQUES, and FULBERT, in Bayle.

† The profession of Abaelard, the condition of the monastic life to which he had devoted himself, and, above all, the course of his studies, naturally lead to an opinion that, notwithstanding his disastrous amour with Heloissa, the general tenour of his conduct was in other respects at least blameless, but on the contrary he appears to have been a man of a loose and profligate life. In a letter from one of his friends, Foulques, prior of Deuil, to him, he is charged with such a propensity to the conversation of lewd women, as reduced him to the want of even food and raiment. Bayle, art. FOULQUES, in not.

To say the truth, the theology of the schools, as taught in Abaelard's time, was merely scientific, and had as little tendency to regulate the manners of those who studied it as geometry, or any other of the mathematical sciences; and this is evident from the licentiousness of the clergy at this and the earlier periods of christianity, and the extreme rancour and bitterness which they discovered in all kinds of controversy.

Of the latter, the persecution of Abaelard by St. Bernard, and other his adversaries, is a proof, and for the former we have the testimony of the most credible and impartial of the ecclesiastical writers. Mosheim among other proofs of the degeneracy and licentiousness of the clergy in the tenth century, mentions the example of Theophylact, a Grecian patriarch, and on the authority of Fleury's Histoire Ecclesiastique,

But to return to St. Bernard; his labours for preserving the music of the church in its original purity, have deservedly intitled him to the character of one of its greatest patrons: the particulars of his life, which appears to have been a very busy one, are too numerous to be here inserted; but the ecclesiastical historians speak of him as one of the most shining lights of the age in which he lived. They speak also of another St. Bernard, at one time official, and afterwards abbot of the church of Pisa, a disciple of the former, and at last pope by the name of Eugenius III.

The works of St. Bernard the abbot are extant; the best edition of them is that of Mabillon, in two volumes, folio. Du Pin says that in his writings he did not affect the method of the scholastics of his time, but rather followed the manner of the preceding authors; for which reason he is deemed the last of the fathers. He died 1153, and left near one hundred and sixty monasteries of his order, which owed their foundation to his zeal and industry.

CHAP. XL.

THE establishment of schools and other seminaries of learning in France, particularly in Normandy, already mentioned in the course of this work, began now to be productive of great advantages to letters in general, for notwithstanding that the beginning of the twelfth century gave birth to a kind of new science, termed scholastic divinity, of which Peter Lombard Gilbert de la Poree and Abaelard are said to be the inventors, a new and more rational division of the sciences than is included in the Trivium and Quadrivium, was projected and took effect about this time.* In that division theology had no place, but was termed the queen of sciences; it was now added to the other seven, and assumed a form and character very different from what it had heretofore borne. It consisted no longer in those doctrines, which, without the least order or connection were deduced from passages in the holy scriptures, and were founded on the opinions of the fathers and primitive doctors;

lib. IV. pag. 97, relates the following curious particulars of him:—'This 'exemplary prelate, says he, who sold every ecclesiastical benefice as 'soon as it became vacant, had in his stable above two thousand hunting 'horses, which he fed with pignuts, pistachios, dates, dried grapes, figs 'steeped in the most exquisite wines, to all which he added the richest 'perfumes. One Holy Thursday he was celebrating high-mass, his 'groom brought him the joyful news that one of his favourite mares 'had foaled, upon which he threw down the liturgy, left the church, and 'ran in raptures to the stable, where having expressed his joy at that 'grand event, he returned to the altar to finish the divine service, which 'he had left interrupted during his absence.' Translation of Mosheim's Ecclesiastical History, by Dr. Maclane, octavo, 1768, vol. II. pag. 201, in not.

* It seems notwithstanding, that the distinctions of Trivium and Quadrivium subsisted as late as the time of Henry VIII. when it is probable they ceased; for Skelton, in that libel of his on cardinal Wolsey, entitled Why come ye not to Court? thus satirizes him for his ignorance of the seven liberal sciences:—

> He was parde,
> No doctour of diuinitie,
> Nor doctour of the law,
> Nor of none other faw,
> But a pore maifter of arte,
> God wot had little part
> Of the quadrivials,
> Nor yet of trivials,
> Nor of philofophye,
> Nor of philology.

but was that philosophical or scholastic theology, which with the deepest abstraction pretended to trace divine truth to its first principles, and to pursue it from thence through all its various connections and branches. Into this system of divinity were introduced all the subtleties of logic and metaphysics, till the whole became a science of mere sophistry, and chicane, and unintelligible jargon, conducing neither to the real improvement of the rational faculties, or the promotion of religion or moral virtue. This system of divinity, such as it was, was however honoured with the name of a science, and added to the former seven; to this number were added jurisprudence and physic, taken in that limited sense in which the word is yet used; not as comprehending the study of nature and her operations; and hence arose the three professions of divinity, law, and physic. That the second of these was thus honoured, was owing in a great measure to an accident, the discovery, in the year 1137, of the original manuscript of the Pandects of Justinian, which had been lost for five hundred years, and was then recovered, of which fortunate event, to go no farther for evidence of it, Mr. Seldon gives the following account:—'The em-'perors from Justinian, who died 565, until Lo-'tharius II. in the year 1125, so much neglected the 'body of the civil law, that all that time none ever 'professed it. But when the emperor Lotharius II. 'took Amalfi, he there found an old copy of the Pan-'dects or Digests, which as a precious monument he 'gave to the Pisans, by reason whereof it was called 'Litera Pisana; from whence it hath been translated to 'Florence, &c., and is never brought forth but with 'torch-light, or other reverence.' Annotations on Fortescue de Laudibus, pag. 18, 19.

No sooner was the civil law placed in the number of the sciences, and considered as an important branch of academical learning, than the Roman pontiffs and their zealous adherents, judged it not only expedient, but also highly necessary, that the canon law should have the same privilege. There were not wanting before this time, certain collections of the canons or laws of the church; but these collections were so destitute of order and method, and were so defective, both in respect to matter and form, that they could not be conveniently explained in the schools, or be made use of as systems of ecclesiastical polity. Hence it was that Gratian, a Benedictine monk belonging to the convent of St. Felix and Nabor at Bolonia, by birth a Tuscan, composed, about the year 1130, for the use of the schools, an abridgment or epitome of canon law, drawn from the letters of the pontiffs, decrees of councils, and writings of the ancient doctors. Pope Eugenius III. was extremely satisfied with this work, which was also received with the highest applause by the doctors and professors of Bolonia, and was unanimously adopted as the text they were to follow in their public lectures. The professors at Paris were the first that followed the example of those of Bolonia, which in process of time was imitated by the greatest part of the European colleges. But notwithstanding the encomiums bestowed upon this performance which was commonly called the Decretal of Gratian, and was intitled by the author himself, the reunion or coalition of the jarring canons, several most learned and eminent writers of the Romish communion acknowledge it to be full of errors and defects of various kinds. However as the main design of this abridgment of the canons was to support the despotism, and to extend the authority of the Roman pontiffs, its innumerable defects were overlooked, its merits exaggerated, and, what is still more surprising, it enjoys at this day, in an age of light and liberty, that high degree of veneration and authority which was inconsiderately, though more excusably lavished upon it in an age of tyranny, superstition, and darkness.

Such among the Latins as were ambitious of making a figure in the republic of letters, applied themselves with the utmost zeal and diligence to the study of philosophy. Philosophy, taken in its most extensive and general meaning, comprehended, according to the method universally received towards the middle of this century, four classes, it was divided into theoretical, practical, mechanical, and logical. The first class comprehended theology, mathematics, and natural philosophy; in the second class were ranked ethics, œconomics, and politics; the third contained the arts more immediately subservient to the purposes of life, such as navigation, agriculture, hunting, &c. The fourth was divided into grammar and composition, the latter of which was farther subdivided into rhetoric, dialectic, and sophistry; and under the term dialectic was comprehended that part of metaphysics, which treats of general notions; this division was almost universally adopted: some indeed were for separating grammar and mechanics from philosophy, a notion highly condemned by others, who under the general term philosophy comprehended the whole circle of the sciences.

This new arrangement of the sciences can hardly be said to comprehend music, as it would be too much to suppose it included in the general division of mathematics; for notwithstanding its intimate connection with both arithmetic and geometry, it is very certain that at the time of which we are now speaking, it was cultivated with a view merely to practice, and the rendering the choral service to the utmost degree pompous and solemn; and there is no other head in the above division under which it could with propriety be arranged. We are told that in the time of Odo, abbot of Cluni, lectures were publicly read in the university of Paris on those parts of St. Augustine's writings that treat of music and the metre of verses; this fact is slightly mentioned in the Menagiana, tom. II. But the authors of the Histoire Litteraire de la France are more particular, for they say that in the tenth century music began to be cultivated in France with singular industry and attention; and that those great masters Remi d'Auxerre, Hucbald de St. Amand, Gerbert, and Abbon, gave lectures on music in the public schools. But it seems that the subjects principally treated on in these their lectures had very little

connection with the theory of music. In short, their view in this method of institution was to render familiar the precepts of tonal and rythmical music; to lay down rules for the management of the voice, and to facilitate and improve the practice of plain chant, which Charlemagne with so much difficulty had established in that part of his dominions.*

The reformation of the scale by Guido Aretinus, and the other improvements made by him, as also the invention of the Cantus Mensurabilis by Franco, were so many new accessions to musical science. It is very remarkable that the Cantus Mensurabilis, which was all that was wanting to render the system complete, was added by Franco, within sixty years after the improvement of it by Guido, and this, as it associated metrical with harmonical combinations, was productive of infinite variety, and afforded ample scope, not only for disquisition, but for the exercise of the powers of invention in musical composition.

But notwithstanding these and other advantages which the science derived from the labours of Guido and Franco, it is much to be questioned whether the improvements by them severally made, and especially those of the former, were in general embraced with that degree of ardour which the authors of the Histoire Litteraire de la France seem in many places of their work to intimate; at least it may be said that in this country it was some considerable time, perhaps near a century, before the method of notation, by points, commas, and such other marks as have hereinbefore been described, gave place to that invented by Guido; and for this assertion there is at least probable evidence in a manuscript now in the Bodleian library, thus described in the catalogue of Bodleian manuscripts, which makes part of the Catalogi Librorum manuscriptorum, printed at Oxford 1697, viz., No. 2558, 63. 'Codex elegan-'tissime scriptus qui Troparion appellatur: continet 'quippe tropos, sive hymnos sacros, viz., Alleluja. 'tractus, modulamina prosas per anni circulum in 'festos et dies Dominicos: omnia notis musicis anti-'quis superscripta.'

The precise antiquity of this manuscript is now very difficult to be ascertained, and the rather as it appears to be written by different persons in a variety of hands and characters. There are three specimens of its contents, which for the particular purpose of inserting them, have with all possible exactness been traced off from the book itself. (See Appendix, No. 44.)

But upon a comparison of the character in which the words of these specimens are written, with many other ancient manuscripts, it seems clearly to be that of the twelfth century; and if so, it proves that the ancient method of notation was retained near a century after the time when Guido flourished.

It is farther to be observed, that the improvements

* The labours of Charlemagne to this end were not merely the effects of his zeal, for he entertained a great love for music, and was himself skilled in it. In the university of Paris, founded by him, and in other parts of his dominions, he endowed schools for the study and practice of music; at church he always sang his part in the choral service, and he exhorted other princes to do the same. He was very desirous also that his daughters should attain a proficiency in singing, and to that end had masters to instruct them three hours every day.

of Guido and Franco were at first received only by the Latin church, and that it was many centuries before they were acquiesced in by that of the Greeks: an inference to this purpose might possibly be drawn from a passage in the letter of Dr. Wallis above-cited, in which, after giving his opinion of the Greek ritual therein mentioned, he conjectures it to be at least three hundred years old; but it is a matter beyond a doubt that the ancient method of notation above spoken of, was retained by the Greek church so low down as to near the middle of the seventeenth century. In the library of Jesus college, Oxon, is a manuscript with this title in a modern character, perhaps the handwriting of some librarian who had the custody of it, viz., 'Meletius Monachus de Mu-'sica Ecclesiastica, cum variorum Poetarum sacrorum 'Canticis,' purporting to be the precepts of choral service, and a collection of offices used in the Greek church, in Greek characters, with such musical notes as are above-mentioned. As to Meletius, he appears clearly to be the writer and not the composer, either of the poetry or the music of these hymns; for besides that the colophon of the manuscript indicates most clearly that it was written and corrected with the hand of Meletius himself, the names of the several persons who composed the tunes or melodies as they occur in the course of the book, are regularly sub-joined to each.

The name of Meletius appears in the catalogue of the Medicæan library; and tom. III. pag. 167 thereof he is styled 'Monachus Monasterii SS. Trini-'tatis apud Tiberiopolim in Phrygia Majore, incertæ 'Ætatis;' notwithstanding which the time of his writing this manuscript is by himself, and in his own handwriting, most precisely ascertained, as hereafter will be made to appear.

As to the contents of the book, it may suffice to say in general that it is a transcript of a great variety of hymns, psalms, and other offices, that is to say, the words in black, and the musical notes in red charac-ters. In a leaf preceding the title is a portrait of an ecclesiastic, probably that of Meletius himself.

Then follows the transcriber's title, which is in red characters, and is to this effect, 'Instructions for 'Singing in the Church, collected from the ancient 'and modern Musicians;' these instructions seem to presuppose a knowledge of the rudiments of music in the reader, and for the most part are meant to declare what melodies are proper to the several offices as they occur in the course of the service, and to ascertain the number of syllables to each note. We have given a specimen of a hymn (See Appendix, No. 43), the words whereof have a close resemblance to those in the Harleian MS. above spoken of, as will appear by a comparison one with the other.

To the offices are subjoined the names of the per-sons who severally composed the melodies; among these the following most frequently occur, Joannes Lampadarius, Manuel Chrisaphus, Joasaph Kuku-zelus, Johannes Kukuzeli, Demetrius Redestes, Johannes Damascenus,* Poletikes, Johannes Lascares,

Georgius Stauropulus, Arsenius Monachus, probably he that was afterwards patriarch of Constantinople under Theodore Lascares the younger, in 1255, Elias Chrysaphes, Theodulus, Gerasimus, Agalleanus, An-thimus, Xachialus, Clemens Monachus, Agioretes.

The specimen given from the above-mentioned curious manuscript is inserted with a view to deter-mine a very important question, namely, what were the musical characters in use among the modern Greeks: if any circumstance is wanting to complete the evidence that they were those above represented, it can only be the age in which Meletius lived: but this is ascertained by the colophon of the MS. which is to this effect :—' This book was wrote and corrected 'by me Meletius, a monk and presbyter, in the year of our Lord 1635.' †

JOHANNES SARISBURIENSIS, a very learned and polite scholar of the twelfth century, has a place in Walther's Catalogue of musical writers: he was a

---

* Johannes Damascenus is celebrated by Du Pin as a subtle divine, a clear and methodical writer, and able compiler. The account given of him by this author in his Bibliotheque, cent. VIII. contains not the least intimation that he was better acquainted with music than others of his profession; nevertheless a very learned and excellent musician of this century, Mattheson of Hamburg, in his Volkommenon Capellmeister, Hamburg, 1739, pag. 26, asserts that he was not only very well skilled in it, but that he obtained the appellation of Μελωδὸς, Melodos, by reason of his excellent singing, and also for his having composed those fine melodies to which the Psalms are usually sung in the eastern churches. He flourished in the eighth century; and in the account which Du Pin has given of him, some of the most remarkable par-ticulars are, that he being counsellor of state to the caliph of the Saracens, who resided at Damascus, and having discovered a zeal for image-worship, the emperor Leo Isauricus, a great enemy to images, procured a person to counterfeit the writing of Damascenus in a letter to the caliph, purporting no less than a design to betray the city of Damascus into the hands of Leo, which wrought such an effect, that Damascenus was sentenced to lose his right hand, which was cut off accordingly, and exposed on a gibbet to the view of all the citizens. Du Pin adds, that if we believe the author of St. John Damascene's life, his hand was reunited to his arm by a miracle, for that as soon as it was cut off he begged it of the caliph, and immediately retiring to his dwelling, applied it to the wrist from whence it had been cut, and pros-trating himself before an image of the Virgin, besought her to unite it to his arm, which petition she granted. As soon as he had received the benefit of this miracle, he retired from the court of the caliph to the monastery of St. Sabas at Jerusalem, and applied himself to the study of music, and very probably to the composition of those very melodies which have rendered his name so famous. He died about the year 750, having some few years before been ordained priest by the patriarch of Jerusalem.

† It is highly probable that this method of notation continued to be practised by the modern Greeks till within these few years; at least it seems to have been in use at the time of publishing a tract entitled Balliofergus, or a Commentary upon the foundation, Founders, and Affaires of Balliol College, Oxon, by Henry Savage, Master of the said College, quarto, Oxford, 1668, in which, pag. 121, is the following article :—

'Nathaniel Conopius was a Cretan born, and trained up in the Greek 'church; he became Πρωτοσύνκελλος, or Primore, to the aforesaid 'Cyrill, patriarch of Constantinople; upon the strangling of whom by the 'vizir, the Grand Signeur of the Turks being not then returned from the 'siege of Babylon, he fled over, and came into England, addressing himself 'with credentials from the English agent in Constantinople to the lord 'archbishop of Canterbury, Laud, who allowed him maintenance in this 'college, where he took on himself the degree of bachelor of divinity 'about anno 1642. And lastly, being returned home, he became bishop 'of Smyrna. He spoke and wrote the genuine Greek, for which he was 'had in great veneration in his country, others using the vulgar only; 'which must be understood of prose too, for poetical Greek he had not, 'but what he learned here. As for his writing, I have seen a great book 'of musick, as he said of his own composing; for his skill wherein his 'countrymen, in their letters to him, stiled him μσσικώτατον; but 'the notes are such as are not in use with, or understood by, any of the 'western churches.'

The author from whom the above account is taken was personally intimate with Conopius, and adds that he had often heard him sing a melody, which, in the book above-cited he has rendered in modern musical characters. Wood has taken notice of this person, Athen. Oxon. 1140, and relates that while he continued in Baliol college he made the drink for his own use called coffee, and usually drank it every morning, being the first, as the ancients of the house had informed him, that was ever drank in Oxon. Wood, in the account of his life written by himself, pag. 65, 80, says that in 1650, a Jew, named Cirques Jobson, born near Mount Libanus, opened a coffee-house in Oxford, between Edmund hall and Queen's college corner, and that after remaining there some time, he removed to London, and sold it in Southampton-buildings, Holborn, and was living there in 1671. More of Conopius may be seen in the Epistles of Gerard John Vossius, part II. pag. 145.

native of England, being born, as his name imports, at Salisbury, and about the year 1110. At the age of seventeen he went into France, and some years afterwards was honoured with a commission from the king his master, to reside near Pope Eugenius, and attend to the interests of his country; being returned to England he received great marks of friendship and esteem from Becket, then lord chancellor, and became an assistant to him in the discharge of that office. It is said that Becket took the advice of Johannes Sarisburiensis about the education of the king's eldest son, and many young noble English lords, whom he had undertaken to instruct in learning and good manners; and that he committed to him the care of his domestic concerns whilst he was abroad in Guienne with king Henry II. Upon Becket's promotion to the see of Canterbury, Sarisburiensis went to reside with him in his diocese, and retained such a sense of his obligation to him, that when that prelate was murdered, he intercepted a blow which one of the assassins aimed at the head of his master, and received a wound on his arm, so great, that after a twelvemonth's attendance on him, his surgeons despaired of healing it; at length however he was cured, and in the year 1179, at the earnest entreaty of the province, was made bishop of Chartres, upon which he went to reside there, and lived an example of that modesty and virtue which he had preached and recommended in his writings. He enjoyed this dignity but three years, for he died 1182, and was interred in the church of Notre Dame da Josaphat. Leland professes to discover in him ' Omnem scientiæ orbem;' and Bale, Cent. III. No. 1., celebrates him as an excellent Greek and Latin scholar, musician, mathematician, philosopher, and divine. Among other books he composed a treatise in Latin, entitled Polycraticus, sive de Nugis Curialium et Vestigiis Philosophorum, the sixth chapter of the first book whereof is entitled De Musica et Instrumentis, et Modis et Fructu eorum, and is a brief but very ingenious dissertation on the subject; and as to the book in general, notwithstanding the censure of Lipsius, who calls it a patch-work, containing many pieces of purple, intermixed with fragments of a better age, it may be truly said that it is a learned, curious, and very entertaining work; and of this opinion Du Pin seems to be in the following character which he has given of it:—' This is an excellent book ' relating to the employments, the duties, the virtues, ' and vices of great men, and especially of princes and ' great lords, and contains a great many moral ' thoughts, sentences, fine passages of authors, ex-' amples, apologues, pieces of history, and common ' topics.' * It was first printed by Constantine Frandinus, at Paris, in 1513, in a small octavo size.

CHAP. XLI.

Conradus, a monk of the abbey of Hirsaugia, in Germany, and therefore surnamed Hirsaurgiensis, flourished about 1140, under the emperor Conrade III., whom the historians and chronologers place between Conrade II. and Frederick Barbarossa. He was a philosopher, rhetorician, musician, and poet; and, among other things, was author of a book on music and the tones.†

Adamus Dorensis, Adam of Dore, Door, or Dowr, from the British Dûr, the site of an abbey in Herefordshire, is much celebrated for his learning, and particularly for his skill in the science of music. The following is the sum of the account which Bale, Pits, and other biographical writers give of him :—' Adam ' of Dore, a man of great note, was educated in the ' abbey of Dore, and very profitably spent his younger ' years in the study of the liberal sciences. He was ' a lover of poetry, philosophy, and music, attaining ' to great perfection in all ; to these accomplishments ' he added piety, and strict regularity of life, and ' made such proficiency in all kinds of virtue, that for ' his great merit he was elected abbot of the monas-' tery of Dore. In his time there were great conten-' tions between the seculars and the monks; upon ' which occasion Sylvester Girald, a learned man, ' and of great eminence among the clergy, ‡ wrote a ' book entitled Speculum Ecclesiæ, in which he ' charged the regulars with avarice and lust, not ' sparing even the Cistertian monks. Adam, to vin-' dicate the honour of the religious, and especially ' those of his own order, wrote a book against the ' Speculum of Girald ; he wrote also a Treatise on ' the Elements of Music, and some other things, par-' ticularly satires, bitter ones enough, against Simon ' Ashe, a canon of Hereford, Sylvester Girald's advo-' cate and friend. This Adam flourished in 1200, ' under King John.' §

Albertus Magnus was born about the year of Christ 1200: a man illustrious by his birth, but more for his deep and extensive learning ; he was descended from the dukes of Schawben, and taught at Paris and Cologne ; Thomas Aquinas was his disciple. In 1260 he was elected bishop of Ratisbon, but at the end of three years resigned his bishopric, and returned to his cell at Cologne. In 1274 he assisted at the council of Lyons, in quality of ambassador from the emperor. He left many monuments of his genius and learning, and has treated the subjects of arithmetic, geometry, astronomy, perspective, or optics, and music, in a manner worthy of admiration. It is said that he had the secret of transmutation, and that by means of that art he discharged all the debts of his bishopric of Ratisbon within the three years that he continued to hold it. Some have gone farther, and charged him with being a magician ; as a proof whereof they relate that he had formed a machine in the shape of a man, which he resorted to as an oracle for the explanation of all difficulties that occurred to him : they say that he wrought thirty years without interruption in forging this wonderful figure, which Naudeus calls the Androis of Albertus, and that the several parts of it were formed under particular aspects and constellations ; but that Thomas

---

* Bibl. des Auteurs Eccl. cent. XII.

† Vossius, de Scient. Math. cap. lx. § 10.
‡ Otherwise called Giraldus Cambrensis. Tann. Bibl. in Art. He was the author of the tract entitled Cambriæ Descriptio, cited in book IV. chap. 33.
§ Tann. Biblioth. Gibson's view of the churches of Door and Hom Lacy, Lond. quarto, pag. 15.

Aquinas, the disciple of Albertus, not being able to bear its everlasting tittle-tattle, broke it to pieces, and that too in his master's house. The general ignorance of mankind at different periods has exposed many a learned man to an imputation of the like sort; pope Sylvester II., Robert Grosthead,* bishop of Lincoln, and Roger Bacon, if we may believe some writers, had each a brazen head of his own making, which they consulted upon all difficulties. Naudeus has exposed the folly of this notion in an elaborate apology for these and other great men whose memories have been thus injured; and though he admits that Albertus might possibly have in his possession a head, or statue of a man, so ingeniously contrived, as that the air which was blown into it might receive the modifications requisite to form a human voice; he denies that any magical power whatever was necessary for the construction of it. Albertus died at Cologne in the year 1280; his body was interred in the choir of the church of the Dominican convent there, and was found entire in the time of the emperor Charles V. Although his learning and abilities had acquired him the epithet of Great, it is related that he was in his person so very little a man, that when upon his arrival at Rome he kissed the feet of the pope, his holiness, after he had risen up, thinking he was yet on his knees, commanded him to stand. The number of books which he wrote is prodigious, for they amount to twenty-one volumes in folio.†

GREGORY of Bridlington, a canon regular of the order of St. Augustine, precentor of the church of his monastery of Bridlington, and afterwards prior thereof, flourished about the year 1217. He wrote a Treatise De Arte Musices, in three books, and is mentioned by bishop Tanner as a man of learning and abilities.

GUALTERUS ODINGTONUS, otherwise Walter of Evesham, a writer of great skill in the science of music, was a Benedictine monk, he flourished in the reign of our Henry III. about the year 1240. Bishop Tanner, on the authority of Pits, Bale, and Leland, gives him the character of a very learned man; and Fuller has celebrated him among the worthies of Worcestershire. Tanner‡ refers to a manuscript treatise of his in the library of Christ Church college Cambridge intitled De Speculatione Musices, in six books, beginning 'Plura quam digna de musicæ specula;' and in a manuscript collection of tracts in the Cotton library, Tiberius, B. IX. tract 3, is a treatise of the notes or musical characters, and their different properties, in which the long, the large, the breve, the semibreve, and the minim,

are particularly characterised; at the end of this treatise we have these words, 'Hæc Odyngtonus,' plainly intimating that the writer, whoever he was, looked upon Gualterus Odingtonus as the author of it; but there is great reason to suspect that it is not genuine, for the initial sentence does not agree with that of the tract De Speculatione Musices, as given by Tanner; and it is expressly asserted by Morley that the minim was invented by Philippus de Vitriaco, a famous composer of motets, who must have lived long after Walter. Mr. Stephens, the translator and continuator of Dugdale's Monasticon, in his catalogue of English learned men of the order of St. Benedict, gives the following account of this person:—

'Walter, monk of Evesham, a man of facetious 'wit, who applying himself to literature, lest he 'should sink under the labour of the day, the watch-'ing at night, and continual observance of regular 'discipline, used at spare hours to divert himself 'with the decent and commendable diversion of 'musick, to render himself the more chearful for 'other duties; whether at length this drew him off 'from other studies I know not, but there appears 'no other work of his than a piece intitled Of the 'Speculation of Musick. He flourished in 1240.'

VINCENTIUS, archbishop of Beauvois, in France, about the year 1250, was in great repute. He was a native of Burgundy, and treated of the science of music in his Doctrinale.

ROGER BACON, a monk of the Franciscan order, born at Ilchester, in Somersetshire, in 1214, the great luminary of the thirteenth century, a celebrated mathematician and philosopher, as appears by his voluminous writings in almost all branches of science, and the testimony of the learned in every age, wrote a treatise De Valore Musices. He died about the year 1292. He was greatly favoured by Robert Grosthead, bishop of Lincoln, and underwent the common fate of learned men in those times, of being accounted by the vulgar a magician. The story of friar Bacon's brazen head is well known, and is too silly to merit a refutation. There is an excellent life of him in the Biographia Britannica, written, as it is said, by Dr. Campbell.

SIMON TAILLER, a Dominican and a Scotsman, mentioned by Tanner, flourished about the year 1240. He wrote De Cantu Ecclesiastico reformando, De Tenore Musicali, and two other tracts, the one intitled Tetrachordum, and the other Pentachordum.

JOHANNES PEDIASIMUS, a native of Bulgaria, a lawyer by profession, and keeper of the patriarchal seal there, is reckoned in the number of musical writers. He flourished about the year 1300, and wrote a Compendium of Geometry and a book of the dimensions of the earth; the first is in the library of the most christian king, the latter, and also a Treatise on the Science of Music, in that of the city of Augsburg in Germany.§

Pope JOHN XXII. has a place among the writers on music, but for what reason it is somewhat difficult to shew; Du Pin, who speaks of him among the

---

* '———of the great clerk Grosteft
'I rede, howe busy that he was
'Upon the clergie an head of bras
'To forge, and make it for to telle
'Of such things as befelle:
'And seven yeres besineffe
'He laide, but for the lacheffe
'Of half a minute of an houre,
'Fro firft he began to laboure,
'He lofte all that he had do.'
         Gower. Confessio Amantis, fol. lxiv.

† Bayle, in art.
‡ Bibliotheca, pag. 558.

§ Vossius, De Scient. Mathem. cap. liv. § 16.

ecclesiastical writers of the fourteenth century, says he was ingenious, and well versed in the sciences;[*] but by the catalogue of his works in the chronological table for that period, it seems that his chief excellence was his skill in the canon law; nevertheless he is taken notice of by Brossard and Walther, as having written on music; and in the Micrologus of Andreas Ornithoparcus, who wrote about the year 1535, a treatise of music of his writing is frequently referred to; and in the second chapter of the first book of the Micrologus, where the author professes to distinguish between a musician and a singer, he cites a passage from pope John XXII. to this effect: ' To whom shall I compare a cantor ' better than a drunkard (which indeed goeth home) ' but by what path he cannot tell? A musician to ' a cantor is as a prætor to a cryer.' And in the seventh chapter of the same book he cites him to explain the meaning of the word Tone: ' A tone, ' says he, is the distance of one voyce from another ' by a perfect sound, sounding strongly, so called ' à tonando, that is thundering; for tonare [as ' Johannes Pontifex XXII. cap. viii. saith] signifieth ' to thunder powerfully.'

The same author, lib. I. cap. iii. on the authority of Franchinus, though the passage as referred to by him is not to be found, asserts that pope John and Guido, after Boetius, are to be looked on as the most excellent musicians.

It is said that John was the son of a shoemaker of Cahors, and that on account of his excellence in literature Charles II., king of Naples, appointed him preceptor to his son; that from thence he rose to the purple, and at length to the papacy, being elected thereto anno 1316.

The particulars herein before enumerated respecting the progress of music from the time of its introduction into the church-service to about the middle of the thirteenth century; as also the accounts herein before given of the most eminent writers on music during that period, are sufficient to shew, not only that a knowledge of the principles of harmony and the rudiments of singing were deemed a necessary part of the clerical institution, but also that the clergy were by much the most able proficients, as well in instrumental as vocal music, for this very obvious reason, that in those times to sing was as much the duty of a clerk, or as we should now call him, a clergyman, as at this day it is for such a one to read: nevertheless it cannot be supposed but that music, to a certain degree, was known also to the laity; and that the mirth, good humour, and gaity of the common people, especially the youthful of both sexes, discovered itself in the singing of such songs and ballads as suited with their conceptions and characters, and are the natural effusions of mirth and pleasantry in every age and country. But of these it is not easy to give a full and satisfactory account; the histories of those times being little more than brief and cursory relations of public events, or partial representations of the actions and characters of princes and other great men, who had recommended them-

selves to the clergy by their munificence; seldom descending to particulars, and affording very little of that kind of intelligence from whence the manners, the humours, and particular customs of any given age or people are to be collected or inferred. Of these the histories contained in that valuable collection entitled the Decem Scriptores, not to mention the rhyming Chronicles of Robert of Gloucester, Peter Langtoft, and others, are instances.

An enquiry into the origin of those rhyming chronicles, of which the two histories last abovementioned are a specimen, will lead us to that source from whence, in all probability, the songs and ballads of succeeding times were deduced: so early as the time of Charlemagne, who lived in the eighth century, that species of rhyming Latin poetry called Leonine verse, was the admiration and delight of men of letters; but subsequent to his time, that is to say about the end of the tenth century, there sprang up in Provence certain professions of men called Troubadours, or Trouverres, Jongleours, Cantadours, Violars, and Musars, in whom the faculties both of music and poetry seemed to concentre: the first of these were so denominated from the art which they professed of inventing or finding out, as well subjects and sentiments as rhymes, constituting what at that time was deemed poetry. The Jongleours are supposed to have taken their name from some musical instrument on which they played, probably of a name resembling in its sound that by which their profession was distinguished. The Cantadours, called also Chanterres, were clearly singers of songs and ballads, as were also the Musars; and the Violars were as certainly players on the viol, an instrument of greater antiquity than is generally imagined.

Of the ancient writers of romance a history is extant in the lives of the Provençal poets, written in French by Johannes Nostradamus;[†] but a much more satisfactory account of them is contained in the translation thereof into Italian, with great additions thereto, by Gio. Mario de Crescimbeni, and by him published with the title of Commentari intorno all' Istoria della volgare Poesia. Of the origin of these, and particularly of the Jongleurs or Jugleurs, with the rest of the class above-mentioned, he gives a very curious relation in the fifth book, cap. v. of his work above-mentioned, to the following effect:—

' After having remarked that from Provence the ' Italians derived not only the origin and art of ' writing romances, but also the very subjects on ' which they were founded, it will not be disagreeable ' to the reader, before we proceed to speak of our

_____
[*] Biblioth. des Auteurs ecclesiastique, cent. XIV.

[†] The lives of the Provençal poets were written by an ecclesiastic of the noble family of Cibo in Genoa, who is distinguished by the fantastical name of the Monk of the Golden Islands, and lived about the year 1248; another person, an ecclesiastic also, named Ugo di Sancesario, and a native of Provence, who flourished about the year 1435, compiled the lives of the poets of his country. From the collections made by these two persons, Johannes Nostradamus, the younger brother of Michael Nostradamus the astrologer and pretended prophet, compiled and published at Lyons, in 1575, the lives of the ancient poets of Provence. This book Giovannio Mario de Crescimbeni translated into Italian, and published with the addition of many new lives, and a commentary containing historical notes and critical observations, in the year 1710. A very good judge of Italian literature, Mr. Baretti, says of this work of Crescimbeni that a true poet will find it a book very delightful to read. Italian Library, pag. 192.

' own, to say somewhat of the romance writers, as
' well of France in general, as of Provence, par-
' ticularly as to their exercises and manner of living.
' It is not known precisely who were the romance
' writers of Provence, for authors that mention them
' speak only in general ; nor have we seen any ro-
' mances with the author's name, other than that of
' the Rose, begun by William de Lorry, and finished
' by John de Meun, as may be seen in a very old
' copy on parchment in the library of Cardinal
' Ottoboni.

' Some of their romances however may be met with
' in many of the famous Italian libraries ; and besides
' that of the Round Table, and that of Turpin, Du
' Cange, Huetius, and Fauchet, before them mention
' several, such as Garilla, Locran, Tristram, Launcelot
' of the Lake, Bertram, Sangreale, Merlin, Arthur,
' Perceval, Perceforest, Triel Ulespieghe, Rinaldo,
' and Roncisvalle, that very likely have been the
' foundation of many of those written by our Italians.

' These romances no doubt were sung, and perhaps
' Rossi, after Malatesta Porta, was not mistaken when
' he thought that the romance singers were used to
' sell their works on a stage as they were singing ;
' for in those times there was in vogue a famous art
' in France called Arte de Giuglari : these juglers,
' who were men of a comical turn, full of jests and
' arch sayings, and went about singing their verses
' in courts, and in the houses of noblemen, with a viol
' and a harp, or some other instrument, had besides
' a particular dress like that of our Pierrots in com-
' mon plays, not adapted to the quality of the subject
' they were singing (like the ancient rhapsodists, who,
' when they sung the Odyssey, were dressed in blue,
' because they celebrated Ulysses's heroes that were
' his companions in his voyages ; and when they re-
' peated the Illiad they appeared generally in red, to
' give an idea of the vast quantity of blood spilt at
' the siege of Troy) but for the sake of entertaining
' and pleasing in a burlesque manner their protectors
' and masters, for which reason they were called
' Juglers, quasi Joculatores, as the learned Menage
' very rightly conjectures.

' Many of the Provençal poets were used to practice
' the same art, and also our Italians, who composed
' verses in that language ; for we read in the Vatican
' manuscripts, that Elias de Bariols, a Genoese, to-
' gether with one Olivieri, went to the court of count
' Amsos de Provence as juglers, and thence passed
' into Sicily. Ugo della Penno, and Guglielmo della
' Torre, exercised the same profession in Lombardy ;
' and cardinal Peter de Veilac, whenever he went to
' visit a king or a baron, which happened very often,
' was always accompanied by juglers, who sang the
' songs called in those places Serventesi. Besides
' those enumerated by Nostradamus, Alessandro
' Velutello reckons up many others, who travelled
' about and subsisted by the profession of minstrelsy,
' the nature whereof is described by Andrew Du
' Chesne, in his notes on the works of Alain Chartier,*

* Alain Chartier was born in 1386, and died about 1458. Crescimb.
in loc. cit.

' where he cites from a romance written in the year
' 1230, the following lines :—

' Quand les tables ostées furent,
' C'il Juggleur in pies esturent,
' S'ont vielles et harpes prises,
' Chansons, sons, vers, et reprises.
' Et de gestes chanté nos ont.

When the tables were taken away,
The juglers stood up,
Took their lyres, and harps ;
Songs, tunes, verses, and catches,
And exploits they sang to us.

' It is not our intention to enquire what sort of
' music they made use of, but however, in order to
' satisfy the reader's curiosity, we shall say that it
' must have been very simple and plain, not to say
' rough, as may be seen by a manuscript in the Vatican
' library, in characters of the fourteenth century,
' where there are written the songs of divers Pro-
' vençal poets, with the music.   We have copied the
' following example, which is the song of Theobald,
' king of Navarre, who flourished about the year 1235,
' no less celebrated among monarchs than poets, by
' the honourable praises bestowed on him by Dante
' in his Inferno, cant. xxii :—

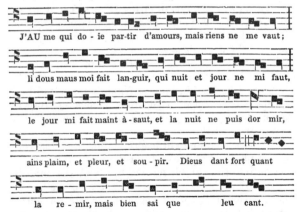

J'AU me qui do - ie par-tir d'amours, mais riens ne me vaut;

li dous maus moi fait lan-guir, qui nuit et jour ne mi faut,

le jour mi fait maint à - saut, et la nuit ne puis dor mir,

ains plaim, et pleur, et sou - pir. Dieus dant fort quant

la re - mir, mais bien sai que leu cant.

The Provençal poets were not only the inventors
and composers of metrical romances, songs, ballads
and rhymes, to so great a number, and of such a
kind, as to raise an emulation in most countries of
Europe to imitate them ; but, if we may credit the
Italian writers, the best poets of Italy, namely Petrarch and Dante, owed much of their excellence to
their imitation of the Provençals ; and it is farther
said that the greater part of the novels of Boccace are
taken from Provençal or ancient French romances.*

The Glossary of Du Cange contains a very great
number of curious particulars relating to the Troubadours, Jongleurs, Cantadours, Violars, and Musars, of
Provence ; and it appears that in the French language all these arts were comprehended under the
general denomination of Menestraudie, Menestraudise,
Jonglerie.†

* The same may be supposed of the Heptameron of Margaret queen
of Navarre, a work of the same kind with the Decameron, and containing
a great number of entertaining stories.   A general account of it is given
by Bayle, in the article NAVARRE.

† ' On peut comprendre sous le nom de JONGLERIE tout ce qui appar-
' tient aux anciens chansonniers Provencaux, Normands, Picards, &c.
' Le corps de la Jonglerie etoit formé des Trouveres, ou Troubadours, qui

The learned Dr. Percy, in his Essay on the ancient English Minstrels, has given a very curious and satisfactory account of these fathers of modern poetry and popular music; and although he agrees that the several professions above enumerated were included under the general name of Minstrel, in the notes on that Essay, pag. xlii., he has with great accuracy assigned to each its distinct and peculiar office.

In the work of Crescimbeni above-cited the name of our own king Richard I., surnamed Coeur de Lion, occurs as a Provençal poet, and a composer of verses, professedly in imitation of that species of poetry which is the subject of the present enquiry. It is true that the very learned and accurate bishop Tanner, from whom we might have expected some account of this fact, has in his Bibliotheca omitted the mention of Richard as a writer; and it is probable that Rymer, the compiler of the Fædera, a man of deep research, though of all critics that ever wrote, one of the most wild and absurd, is the first of our countrymen that have in earnest asserted Richard's claim to that character. The account which he gives of it is, that Richard and his brother Geoffrey, who by the way is also ranked among the poets of that time, had formerly lived much in the courts of several princes in and about Provence, and so came to take delight in their language, their poetry, then called the Gay Science, and their poets, which began not long before his time to be in great vogue in the world.*

But before he proceeds to the proof of the fact, that Richard was a composer of verses, Rymer takes upon him to refute a charge of Roger Hoveden, importing nothing less than that Richard was but a vain pretender to poetry, and that whatever reputation he had acquired of that sort, he had bought with his money. The words of the historian are 'Hic ad 'augmentum et famam sui nominis, emendicata car-'mina, et rithmos adulatorios comparabat, et de 'regno Francorum cantores et joculatores allexerat 'ut de illo canerent in plateis et dicebatur ubique 'quod non erat talis in orbe.' 'Richard to raise 'himself a name, went about begging and buying 'verses and flattering rhymes; and by rewards en-'ticed over from France, singers and jesters to sing 'of him in the streets. And it was everywhere 'given out that there was not the like of him in the 'world again.'

Rymer observes upon this passage, first, that the assertion contained in it that the songsters and jesters were brought from France is most false; for that France had no pretensions thereabouts in those days, those countries being fiefs of the empire: more particularly he adds that Frederic the First had enfeoffed Raimond Beringer of the country of Provence, For-

calquiers, and places adjacent, as not long after Frederic II. installed William prince of Orange, king of Arles and Viennes, which family had formerly possessed Provence.† Again he observes, that about the same time that the Provençal poetry began to flourish, the heresy of the Albingenses sprang up; and that Raimond count of Tholouse was the protector of the Albingenses, and also a great favourer of these poets; and that all the princes that were in league together to support the Albingenses against France and the pope, encouraged and patronized these poets, and amongst the rest a king of Arragon, who lost his life in the quarrel, at a battle where Simon Mountfort commanded as chief of the crusade.‡

The argument which Rymer makes use of to invalidate the testimony of the monk, is a weapon of such a form, that we know not which end to take it by: he means to say, that if Richard was a favourer of the heresy of the Albingenses, it could not but draw upon him the resentment of the clergy, and that therefore Roger Hoveden, in revenge for the encouragement which he had shewn to the enemies of the church, endeavoured to deprive him of the reputation of a poet. But as this is only negative evidence of Richard's title to a place among the Provençal poets, Rymer goes farther, and introduces from a manuscript in the possession of Signor Redi, the testimony of Guilhem Briton, an ancient bard, in these verses:—

> Coblas a tiera faire adroitement,
> Pou vos oillez enten dompna gentilz.

> Stanzas he trimly could invent
> Upon the eyes of lady gent.§

But, to remove all doubts about the fact, Rymer cites the following stanza, part of a song written by Richard himself while a prisoner in Austria:—

> Or sachan ben mos homs, et mos barons
> Anglez, Normans, Peytavins, et Gascons,
> Qu' yeu non ay ja si paure compagnon,
> Que per aver lou laissess en preson.

> Know ye, my men, my barons all,
> In England and in Normandy,
> In Poictiers and in Gascony,
> I no companion held so small,
> To let him thus in durance lie. ‖

Having thus far proved his point, our author is disposed to indulge that inclination to mirth and pleasantry, which seems to have dictated those two curious works of his, the Short View of Tragedy, and the Tragedies of the last Age considered; and upon the stanza above written, as facetiously as pertinently remarks, that our king Richard had not the expedient of the French king, St. Lewis, who, taken prisoner by the Saracens, pawned the eucharist, body for body, to the infidels for his ransom.¶

He concludes his account of this matter with saying, that which hereafter will appear to be true, viz., that a manuscript with king Richard's poetry, and many other of the Provençal poets, were in the custody of Signor Redi, librarian to the great duke of Tuscany.

'composoient les chansons, et parmi lesquels il y avoit des *Improvisateurs*, 'comme on en trouve en *Italie*: des *Chanteours* ou *Chanteres*, qui exe-'cutoient ou chanteoient ces compositions: des *Conteurs* qui faisoient, 'en vers ou en prose contes, les recits, les histoires: des *Jongleurs* ou '*Menestrels* qui accompagnoient de leurs instrumens. L'art de ces 'chantres, ou chansonniers, etoit nommé la Science Gaie. *Gay Saber.*' Pref. Anthologie Franç. 1765, octavo, pag. 17.

Fauchet, to much the same purpose, has the following passage:— 'Bientôt apres la division de ce grand empire François en tant de petits 'royaumes, duchez, et comtez, au lieu des poetes commencerent a se 'faire cognoistre les *Trouverres*, et *Chanterres*, *Conteours*, et Jugleours: 'qui sont Trouveurs, Chantres, Conteurs, JONGLEURS, ou JUGLEURS, 'c'est à dire MENESTRIERS chantans avec la viole.'

* Short View of Tragedy, pag. 66.

† Short View of Trag. pag. 68.   ‡ Ibid. pag. 69.   § Ibid. pag. 74.
‖ Ibid.   ¶ Ibid. pag. 75.

To these evidences may be added the testimony of Crescimbeni, who in his Commentari della Volgar Poesia, vol. II. part I. pag. 103, says, that Richard, being struck with the sweetness of that tongue, set himself to compose a sonnet in it, which he sent to the princess Stephanetta, wife of Hugh de Baux, and daughter of Gisbert, the second count of Provence. He says afterwards, in a chapter expressly written on this king, that residing in the court of Raimond Berlinghieri, count of Provence, he fell in love with the princess Leonora, one of the prince's four daughters, whom Richard afterwards married : that he employed himself in rhyming in that language, and when he was prisoner composed certain sonnets, which he sent to Beatrix, countess of Provence, sister of Leonora, and in which he complains of his barons for letting him lie in captivity.

Crescimbeni goes on to relate that there are poems of king Richard in the library of St. Lorenzo, at Florence, ' in uno de codici Provenzali,' and others, ' nel No. 3204, della Vaticana.' The perusal of this passage excited the curiosity of a gentleman, to whom the literary world is under great obligations ; Mr. Walpole procured both these repositories to be searched. In the Vatican was found a poem by Richauts de Verbeil, and another by Richauts de Terascon, but nothing that could with any degree of propriety be ascribed to Richard I., king of England. In the Laurentine library were found the verses above spoken of, which as a very singular and valuable curiosity, Mr. Walpole has given to the world in the first volume of his Catalogue of royal and noble Authors ; they are as follow :—

Reis Rizard.

Ja nus hom pris non dira sa raison
Adreitament se com hom dolent non
Mas per conort pot il faire chanson
Pro adamis, mas povre son li don
Onta j avron, se por ma reezon
Soi fai dos yver pris.

Or Sanchon ben mi hom e mi baron
Engles, Norman, Pettavin et Gascon,
Qe ge navoie si povre compagnon
Qeu laissasse por aver en preison
Ge nol di pas, por nulla retraison
Mas anquar soige pris.

Jan sai eu de ver certanament
Com mort ne pris na amie ne parent
Quant il me laissent por or ni por argent
Mal mes de mi, ma perz mes por ma gent
Qapres ma mort n auron reperzhament
Tan longament soi pris.

Nom merveille seu ai le cor dolent
Qe messen her met ma terra en torment
No li menbra del nostre segrament
Qe nos feimes an dos communelment
Bem sai de ver qe gaire longament
Non serai eu sa pris.

Mi compagnon cui j amoi e cui j am
Cil de chaill e cil de persarain
De lor chanzon qil non sont pas certain
Unca vers els non oi cor fals ni vain
Sil me guertoient il feron qe vilain
Tan com ge soie pris.

Or sachent ben Enjevin e Torain
E il bachaliers qi son legier e sain
Qen gombre soie pris en autrui main
Il ma juvassen mas il no ve un grain
De belles armes sont ora voit li plain
Per zo qe ge soi pris.

Contessa soit votre prez sobrain
Sal deus e garde cel per cui me clam
Et per cui ge soi pris :
Ge nol di pas por cela de certrain
La mere loys.

CHAP XLII.

Besides that Richard was endued with the poetical faculty, it is recorded of him that he was skilled in music. In the Theatre of Honour and Knighthood, translated from the French of Mons. Favine, and printed at London in 1623, tom. II. pag. 48, is a curious relation of Richard's deliverance from captivity by the assistance of Blondel de Nesle, a rhymer or minstrel, whom he had trained up in his court, and who by singing a song known to them both, discovered his master imprisoned in a castle belonging to the duke of Austria. This story is taken from the Recueil de l'Origine de la Langue et Poesie Francoise, Ryme, et Romans, &c. of president Fauchet, Paris 1581 : but Favine,* from Matthew Paris, and other historiographers, and from an ancient manuscript of old poesies, has given as well a relation of the causes and manner of his captivity, as of his deliverance from it. The whole is curious and entertaining, and is here given in the words of the old English translator :—

' Richard saved himself by a more prosperous
' wind, with one named Guillaume de l'Estang, and
' a boy that understood the Germaine tongue, tra-
' vayling three dayes and nights without receiving
' any sustenance, or tarrying in any place. But
' hunger pressing them extremely, they came to
' lodge in a towne being neere to the river of Dan-
' ubie, named Gynatia in Austria, as saith Mathew
' Paris, but according to the histories of Germanie,
' which I have red, it is called Erdbourg, where then
' remained Leopold, duke of Austria,† to welcome
' Richard thither, like him falne out of a feaver into
' a farre worse disease. Being come to his inne, he
' sent his boy to make provision for him in the
' market, where the boy shewing his purse to be full

* This book of Favine abounds with a great variety of curious particulars relative to chivalry and manners in general. Ashmole appears to have derived great assistance from it in the compiling his History of the Order of the Garter.

† The causes of Leopold's enmity to Richard are variously related, but the author now citing assigns the following as the first occasion of their quarrel :—
' Richard, at his return endured ten thousand afflictions, whereof
' briefly behold the subject. In the yeare one thousand one hundred
' fourescore and twelve, Leopold duke of Austria came into the Holy
' Land, to beare armes there as other Christian princes did. At his
' arrival the marshall of his campe, having marked out a lodging for
' the duke his maister, planted downe his tent and his ensigne on it.
' A Norman, being a follower of king Richard, maintained that the
' lodging place belonged to him. From words they fell to blowes, and
' Richard, without understanding the reasons of the parties, caused the
' duke of Austria's tent and ensigne to be pull'd downe and hurl'd upon
' a heape into a ditch of mire. The duke made complaint to Richard,
' to have reparation of this offence, but he payed him with derision ;
' whereupon, the duke seeing he was despised, desired God to doe
' reason for him, and then he would remit the injurie.'

'of bezans,* and buying very exquisite victuals; he
'was stayed by the inhabitants of the towne to
'understand further of his condition. Having cer-
'tefied them that he belonged to a wealthie merchant,
'who would arrive there within three dayes; they
'permitted him to depart. Richard being heerof
'advertised, and much distasted in his health by so
'many hard sufferances on the seas, and perillous
'passages on the waves, concluded to repose there
'some few dayes in the towne, during which time
'the boy alwayes made their provision of food.
'But by ill accident, on the day of St. Thomas the
'Apostle, the boy being in the market, chaunced
'(through neglect) to have king Richard's gloves
'tuckt under his girdle: the magistrate of the towne
'observing it, tooke the boy and gave him torment
'to make him confesse whose gloves they were.
'The power of punishment, and threates to have
'his tongue cut out of his head, compelled him to
'tell the trueth. So in short while after, the duke
'of Austria hearing the tydings, engirt the inne
'where Richard was with a band of armed men, and
'Richard, with his sword in his hand yielded him-
'selfe to the duke, which kept him strongly environed
'with well-armed souldiours, who watched him night
'and day, with their swords readie drawne. This
'is the affirmation of Mathew Paris, concerning the
'surprizall of king Richard.

'But I have read an ancient manuscript of old
'poesies, written about those very times, which re-
'porteth this historie otherwise; saying that Richard
'being in his inne, disguised himselfe like a servant
'cooke, larding his meate, broching it, and then
'turning it at the fire himselfe: in which time, one
'of the duke of Austrieas followers, being then in
'the inne, came accidentally into the kitchin, who
'tooke knowledge of this royall cooke; not by his
'face, which he purposely disfigured with the soyling
'of the kitchin; but by a ring of gold, which very
'unadvisedly he wore on his finger. This man ran
'immediately and advertised the duke his maister
'that the king of England was within the compasse
'of his power, and upon this advertisement Richard
'was arrested.

'In the yeare following, namely, one thousand
'one hundred fourescore and thirteene, the duke
'sold king Richard to the emperor Henry, for the
'sum of threescore thousand pounds of silver, the
'pounds answering the weight and order observed at
'Cologne; with which sum Leopold towred the
'wals of the citie of Vienna in Austria, and bought
'the duchie of Styria, Neopurg, and the counties of
'Lins and Wels, of the Bishops of Passau and of
'Wirtspourg. So speaketh the Latin chronicle of
'Otho of Austria, bishop of Frisinghen, for these

'perticularities were forgotten by Mathew Paris,
'who further saith, That in the same yeere of
'fourescore and thirteene, the third holy day after
'Palme-Sunday, Leopold led Richard prisoner to
'the emperor, who sent him under sure guard to the
'Tribales. "Retrudi eum præcepit in Triballis,
"à quo carcere nullus ante dies istos exiuit, qui
"ibidem intrauit: de quo Aristoteles libro quinto.
"Bonum est mactare patrem in Triballis; Et alibi."

"Sunt loca, sunt gentes, quibus est mactare parentes.'

'The Englishmen were more than a whole yeare,
'without hearing any tydings of their king, or in
'what place he was kept prisoner. He had trained
'up in his court a rimer or minstrill called Blondell
'de Nesle, who (so saith the manuscript of old
'poesies, and an auncient manuscript French chron-
'icle) being so long without the sight of his lord,
'his life seemed wearisome to him, and he became
'much confounded with melancholy. Knowne it
'was, that he came backe from the Holy Land,
'but none could tell in what countrey he arrived.
'Whereupon this Blondel resolving to make search
'for him in many countries, but he would heare
'some newes of him; after expence of divers dayes
'in travaile, he came to a towne (by good hap) neere
'to the castell where his maister king Richard was
'kept. Of his host he demanded to whom the
'castell appertained, and the host told him it be-
'longed to the duke of Austria. Then he enquired
'whether any prisoners were therein detained or no;
'for alwayes he made such secret questionings where-
'soever he came, and the hoste gave answer that
'there was one onely prisoner, but he knew not
'what he was, and yet he had bin detained there
'more than the space of a yeare. When Blondel
'heard this, he wrought such meanes, that he became
'acquainted with them of the castell, as minstrells
'doe easily win acquaintance any where; but see
'the king he could not, neither understand that it
'was he. One day he sat directly before a window
'of the castell where king Richard was kept prisoner,
'and began to sing a song in French, which king
'Richard and Blondel had sometime composed to-
'gether. [When king Richard heard the song, he
'knew it was Blondel that sung it; and when Blondel
'paused at halfe of the song, the king entreated him
'to sing the rest.†] Thus Blondel won knowledge
'of the king his maister; and returning home into
'England, made the barons of the countrie acquainted
'where the king was.'

Fauchet, in his relation of this extraordinary event,
says that he had met with a narrative of it in
a French Chronicle written in the time of Philip
the August, about the year 1200.

It is generally said that the ransom of Richard
was one hundred thousand marks. but Matthew
Paris asserts that it was a hundred and forty thousand
marks of silver, Cologne weight, a sum so very great,

---

* Bezans, bezants, or besans, are pieces of gold coin. Guillim thus
explains the term:—'A beisaunte, or as some call them, a talent, is
'taken for a massive plate or bullion of gold, containing, according to
'Leigh, of troy weight 104 lb. and two ounces, and is in value 3750 lb.
'sterling, and had for the most part no similitude or representation upon
'it, as some hold, but only fashioned round and smooth, as if it were
'fitted and prepared to receive some kind of stampe. But others are of
'opinion that they were stamped, and that they were called bezants, or
'rather bizants, of Bizantium, the place where they were anciently
'coined.' Display of Heraldry, Lond. 1632, pag. 33. From the exceeding
magnitude of this coin it is certain that Favine means only to say in
general that the boy's purse was well stored with money.

† Dr. Percy has given the passage from Fauchet in his own words,
which are these:—'Et quant Blondelle ôt dicte la moite de la Chanson,
'le roi Richart se prist à dire l'autre moitie et l'acheva:' and renders the
last clause of the sentence thus:—'BEGAN THE OTHER HALF AND
'COMPLETED IT.' Essay on English Minstrels, pag. xxx.

that to raise it, the English were obliged to sell their church plate, even to the very chalices.*

The foregoing account contains incontestible evidence that Richard was of the class of poets, for the reasons above given termed Provençal, and of these the minstrels appear to be the genuine offspring. The nature of their profession is learnedly treated on by Dr. Percy in his Essay on the ancient Minstrels, prefixed to the Reliques of English Poetry. The most generally received opinion of them is that they were players on musical instruments, and those chiefly of the stringed kind, such as the harp, the cittern, and others; but the word Minstrel, in the larger acceptation of it, signifies a musician in general. Dr. Cowel in his Law Dictionary thus explains it; 'a musician, a fidler, a piper:' and in the old poem of Lydgate, entitled the Daunce of Machabree or of Death, in the Appendix to Sir William Dugdale's History of St. Paul's Cathedral, pag. 265, col. i. he is said to be a minstrel, who can both note, *i. e.* sing, and pipe.

Dr. Percy has asserted, with great appearance of truth, that the employment of the Anglo-Saxon bards was to sing to the harp the praises of their patrons, and other distinguished persons. Nay, it is farther clear from a passage in the Ecclesiastical History of Bede, relating to the poet Cædmon, cited by him in the notes on the Essay on the ancient English Minstrels, pag. 50, that to sing to the Harp at festivals even by the guests themselves, was so customary, that such as were incapable of doing it were frequently necessitated to retire.† And that

the employment of the ancient Minstrels also was to sing panegyrical songs and verses on their benefactors, is farther clear from the explanation of the word Minstrel in that learned work the Law Dictionary of Dr. Cowel, who concludes the article with saying, it was usual with these minstrels, not only to divert princes and the nobility with sports, but also with musical instruments, and with flattering songs in the praise of them and their ancestors, which may be seen in these verses :—

Principis a facie, cytharæ celeberrimus arte
Assurgit mimus, ars musica quem decoravit
Hic ergo chorda resonante subintulit ista :
Inclite rex regum, probitatis stemmate vernans,
Quem vigor et virtus extollit in æthera famæ,
Indole virtutis qui vinces facta parentis.
Major ut Atrides, patrem Neptunius Heros
Ægea, Pelides excedit Pelea, Jason
Esona, nec prolem pudor est evincere patrem ;
Corde gigas, agnus facie Laertius astu,
Consilio Nestor, &c.

The history of this country affords a remarkable instance of favour shewn to this vagabond profession of a minstrel. The privileges which they are possessed of are of such a kind, as to entitle them to the countenance of the legislature, and, what must appear very remarkable, to the protection of the law ; for although minstrels, in common with fencers, bearwards, and common players of interludes, are in the law deemed rogues and vagabonds, there is a special provision in all the statutes that declare them to be so, in favour of common fiddlers and Minstrels, through-

---

* Robert of Gloucester thus speaks of the means used to raise this sum :—

The hundred thoufend marc were ipaid biuore hond
And wel narwe igadered in Engelond,
Nor broches, and ringes zimmes alfo,
And the calis of the weud me foolde ther to
And grey monckes that new come, and pouere tho were
Zeue al her welle there to of one zere.
CHRON. 489.

The distress which this occasioned gave rise to a scholastic question, namely, what substance, silver and gold being wanting, was proper to contain the wine in the eucharist: and we find in Lyndwood, lib. I. de Summa Trinitate et Fide Catholica, cap. II. pag. 9, § doceant. verb. In Calice, that it was thereupon concluded to make use of chalices of latten. The objections against vessels formed of other substances savour of the divinity of those times ; glass was too brittle, wood was spongy, alchymy, aurichalcum, a factitious metal, vulgarly ochamy, as when we say an ochamy spoon, was subject to rusting, and copper had a tendency to provoke vomiting. Fuller, who in this instance is more merry than wise, laughs at this decision, and calls it deep divinity. The question was of importance, and respected no less than a sacred rite and the health of the people.

This usage continued till about the year 1443, when, to take the words of Fuller, for there is no provincial constitution to that purpose extant, 'the land being more replenished with silver, John Stafford archbishop 'of Canterbury enknotted that priest in the greater excommunication 'who should consecrate poculum stanneum.' Vide Fuller's History of the Holy War, book III. chap. xiii.

† The passage cited by Dr. Percy from Bede, and more especially the Anglo-Saxon version thereof by king Alfred, are abundant evidence of the facts which they are cited to prove. As it does not appear from either of the quotations who the poet Cædmon was, nor what are the particulars of the story in which he is mentioned, the same are here given at large in the language of a modern translator of Bede's History, a person, as is conjectured, of the Romish communion. 'In the monas-'tery of the abbess Hilda, [situated in a place called Streaneshalh 'supposed to be somewhere in the north of England] there resided 'a brother, particularly remarkable for the grace of God, who was wont 'to make pious and religious verses, so that whatsoever was interpreted 'to him out of holy writ, he soon after put the same into poetical 'expressions of much sweetness and compunction, in his own, that is, 'the English language. By his verses the minds of many were often 'excited to despise the world and to aspire to the heavenly life. Others 'after him attempted in the English nation to compose religious poems, 'but none could ever compare with him ; for he did not learn the art of 'poetising of men, but through the divine assistance ; for which reason

'he never could compose any trivial or vain poem, but only these that 'relate to religion, and suited his religious tongue; for having lived in 'a secular habit till well advanced in years, he had never learnt any 'thing of versifying ; for which reason being sometimes at entertainments, 'when it was agreed for the more mirth, that all present should sing in 'their turns ; when he saw the instrument come towards him, he rose 'up from table and returned home. Having done so at a certain time, 'and going out of the house where the entertainment was, to the stable, 'the care of horses falling to him that night, and composing himself 'there to rest at the proper time, a person appeared to him in his sleep, 'and saluted him by his name, said, "Cedmon, sing some song to me;" 'he answered, "I cannot sing ; for that was the reason why I left the "entertainment and retired to this place, because I could not sing." 'The other who talked to him, replied, "However you shall sing." "What shall I sing?" rejoined he, "Sing the beginning of creatures," 'said the other. Hereupon he presently began to sing verses to the 'praise of God, which he had never heard, the purport whereof was 'thus :—"We are now to praise the Maker of the heavenly kingdom, "the power of the Creator and his council, the deeds of the Father of "glory: how he, being the eternal God, became the author of all "miracles, who first, as almighty preserver of the human race, created "heaven for the sons of men as the roof the house, and next the earth." 'This is the sense, but not the words in order as he sung them in his 'sleep: for verses, though never so well composed, cannot be literally 'translated out of cne language into another without losing much of 'their beauty and loftiness. Awaking from his sleep, he remembered 'all that he had sung in his dream, and soon added much more to the 'same effect in divine verses. Coming in the morning to the steward 'that he was under, he acquainted him with the gift he had received ; 'and being conducted to the abbess, he was ordered, in the presence of 'many learned men, to tell his dream and repeat the verses, that they 'might give all their judgment what it was, and whence it proceeded 'that he said : They all concluded that an heavenly grace had been con-'ferred on him by our Lord. They expounded to him a passage in holy 'writ, either historical or doctrinal, ordering him, if he could, to put the 'same into verse. Having undertaken it, he went away, and returning 'the next morning, gave it to them composed into most excellent 'verse ; whereupon the abbess, embracing the grace of God in the man, 'instructed him to quit the secular habit, and take upon him the mo-'nastical life ; which being accordingly done, she associated him to the 'rest of the brethren in the monastery, and ordered that he should be 'taught the whole series of the sacred history.' Bede, Hist. Eccl. lib. IV. cap. xxiv.

A poetical paraphrase of the book of Genesis and certain scripture stories was published by Francis Junius at Amsterdam, in 1655, in quarto, from a manuscript of archbishop Usher. This Cædmon is supposed by Tanner, and many other writers, to be the Cædmon mentioned by Bede; but Dr. Hickes seems to entertain some doubt of it.

out the county of Chester, of which the following is the history :—

In the statute of 17 Geo. II. cap. 5, is the following proviso :—' Provided always that this act, or any ' thing therein contained, or any authority thereby ' given, shall not in anywise extend to disinherit, ' prejudice, or hinder the heirs or assigns of John ' Dutton, of Dutton, late of the county of Chester, ' esquire, for, touching, or concerning the liberty, ' privilege, pre-eminence or authority, jurisdiction or ' inheritance, which they, their heirs or assigns now ' lawfully use, or have, or lawfully may or ought to use ' within the county palatine of Chester, and county of ' Chester, or either of them, by reason of any ancient ' charters of any kings of this land, or by reason of ' any prescription or lawful usage or title whatsoever.'

This right which the parliament of Great Britain has shown itself so tender of infringing, is founded on an event, of which the following relation is to be met with in the Historical Antiquities of Cheshire, collected by Sir Peter Leycester, Bart., part II. chap. vi. and is mentioned in a book intitled Ancient Tenures of Land made public, by Thomas Blount, Esq. octavo, 1679, pag. 156, et seq.

'In the time of king John, Randle the third, surnamed ' Blundevil, earl of Chester, having many conflicts ' with the Welsh, was at last distressed by them, and ' forced to retreat to the castle of Rothelent in Flint- ' shire, where they besieged him, who presently sent ' to his constable of Chester, Roger Lacy, surnamed ' Hell, for his fierce spirit, that he would come with ' all speed, and bring what forces he could for his ' relief. Roger having gathered a tumultuous rout of ' Fiddlers, Players, Cobblers, and debauched persons, ' both men and women, out of the city of Chester (for ' it was then the fair there) marched immediately with ' them towards the earl.* The Welsh perceiving a ' great multitude coming, raised the siege and fled. ' The earl coming back with his constable to Chester, ' gave him power over all the Fiddlers and Shoe- ' makers of Chester, in reward and memory of his ' service. The constable retained to himself and his ' heirs the authority and donation of the Shoemakers, ' but John his son conferred the authority over the ' profligates of both sexes on his steward, which then ' was Dutton of Dutton, by this his deed.

" Sciant præsentes et futuri, quod ego Johannes, " Constabularius Cestriæ, dedi et concessi, et hac " præsenti carta mea confirmavi Hugoni de Dutton, " et hæredibus suis, magistratum omnium leccatorum " et meretricum totius Cestershiriæ, sicut liberius " illum magistratum teneo de comite ; salvo jure meo " mihi et hæredibus meis. Hiis testibus," &c.

Blount goes on to observe, that though this original grant makes no mention of giving rule over Fiddlers and Minstrels, yet that an ancient custom has now reduced it only to the minstrelsy ; for probably the rout, which the constable brought to the rescue of the

earl, were debauched persons, drinking with their sweethearts in the fair, the fiddlers that attended them, and such loose persons as he could get.

He proceeds to relate, that Anno 14 Hen. VII. a Quo Warranto was brought against Laurence Dutton, of Dutton, esq. to shew why he claimed all the minstrels of Cheshire and the city of Chester, to appear before him at Chester yearly, on the feast of St. John Baptist, and to give him at the said feast, ' Quatuor legenas vini et unam lanceam,' i. e. four flaggons of wine and a lance ; and also every minstrel then to pay him four pence half-penny ; and why he claimed from every harlot in Cheshire, and the city of Chester ' (officium suum exercente)' four pence yearly at the said feast, &c. whereunto he pleaded prescription.

And farther, that ' the heirs of this Hugh de Dutton ' enjoy the same power and authority over the min- ' strelsy of Cheshire, even to this day, and keep a ' court every year upon the feast of St. John Baptist, ' at Chester, being the fair day, where all the Minstrels ' of the county and city do attend and play before the ' lord of Dutton upon their several instruments ; he ' or his deputy then riding through the city thus ' attended, to the Church of St. John, many gentlemen ' of the county accompanying him, and one walking ' before him in a " surcoat of his arms depicted upon " taffata ;" and after divine service ended, hold his ' court in the city ; where he or his steward renews ' the old licences granted to the Minstrels, and gives ' such new ones as he thinks fit, under the hand and ' seal of himself or his steward, none presuming to ' exercise that faculty there without it. But now this ' dominion or privilege is by a daughter and heir of ' Thomas Dutton, devolved to the lord of Gerrard, ' of Gerrard's Bromley in Staffordshire.'

He adds, that whereas by the statute of 39 Eliz. Fiddlers are declared to be Rogues ; yet by a special proviso therein, those in Cheshire, licensed by Dutton of Dutton, are exempted from that infamous title, in respect of this his ancient custom and privilege.

Another writer† derives this privilege from a higher source, for among many instances of favour shown to the abbey of St. Werburg in Chester, by Leofric earl of Chester, in the time of Edward the Confessor, he mentions the grant of a fair on the festival of that saint, to be holden for three days ; to whose HONOUR he likewise granted, that whatsoever Thief or Malefactor came to the solemnity, should not be attached while he continued in the same fair, except he committed any new offence there.

Which special privilege, says the same writer, 'as in ' tract of time it drew an extraordinary confluence of ' loose people thither at that season, so happened it ' to be of singular advantage to one of the succeeding ' earles. For being at Rodelent castle in Wales, and ' there besieged by a power of the Welsh, at such ' a time he was relieved rather by their number than ' strength, under the conduct of Robert de Lacy, ' constable of Chester, who with pipers and other ' sorts of Minstrels drew them forth, and marching ' towards the castle, put the Welsh to such terror that

---

* It seems that this earl had rendered himself famous by his prowess, and that his exploits were celebrated in rhymes and songs down to the time of Richard II. for in the Visions of Pierce Plowman, Passus quintus, Sloth says of himself :—

I cannot perfitly my Pater-noster as the prift it fingeth,
But I con rimes of Robenhod and Randal of Chefter.

† Daniel King in his Vale Royal of England illustrated, part II. pag. 29.

'they presently fled. In memory of which notable
'exploit, that famous meeting of such Minstrels hath
'been duly continued to every Midsummer fair, at
'which time the heir of Hugh de Dutton, accompanied
'with diverse gentlemen, having a pennon of his arms
'borne before him by one of the principal Minstrels,
'who also weareth his surcoat, first rideth up to the
'east gate of the city, and there causing proclamation
'to be made that all the Musicians and Minstrels
'within the county-palatine of Chester do approach
'and play before him. Presently so attended he
'rideth to St. John's church, and having heard solemn
'service, proceedeth to the place for keeping of his
'court, where the steward having called every
'Minstrel, impanelleth a jury, and giveth his charge.
'First, to enquire of any treason against the king or
'prince (as earl of Chester); secondly, whether any
'man of that profession hath " exercised his instru-
'ment " without licence from the lord of that court,
'or what misdemeanour he is guilty of. And thirdly,
'whether they have heard any language amongst
'their fellows, tending to the dishonour of their lord
'and patron (the heir of Dutton) which privilege was
'anciently so granted by John de Lacy, constable of
'Chester, son and heir to the before specified Roger,
'unto Hugh de Dutton and his heirs, by a special
'charter in these words, viz., " Magisterium omnia
" leccatorum et meretricum totius Cestrishire," and
'hath been thus exercised time out of mind.'

Another instance of favour to Minstrels, and of
privileges enjoyed by them, occurs in Dr. Plot's
History of Staffordshire, chap. X. § 69, where the
author taking occasion to mention Tutbury-castle, a
seat of the ancient earls and dukes of Lancaster, is
led to speak of Minstrels appertaining to the honour
of Tutbury, and of their king, with his several
officers; of whom, and of the savage sport commonly
known by the name of the Tutbury Bull-running, he
gives the following accurate account :—

'During the time of which ancient earls and dukes
'of Lancaster, who were ever of the blood royal,
'great men in their times, had their abode, and kept
'a liberal hospitality here, at their honour of Tut-
'bury, there could not but be a general concourse of
'people from all parts hither, for whose diversion all
'sorts of musicians were permitted likewise to come
'to pay their services; amongst whom (being nu-
'merous) some quarrels and disorders now and then
'arising, it was found necessary after a while they
'should be brought under rules; diverse laws being
'made for the better regulating of them, and a
'governor appointed them by the name of a king,
'who had several officers under him, to see to the
'execution of those laws; full power being granted
'to them to apprehend and arrest any such Minstrels
'appertaining to the said honour, as should refuse to
'do their services in due manner, and to constrain
'them to do them; as appears by the charter granted
'to the said king of the Minstrels by John of Gaunt,
'king of Castile and Leon, and duke of Lancaster,
'bearing date the 22nd of August in the 4 year of the
'raigne of king Richard the second, entituled Carta
'le Roy de Ministralx, which being written in old

'French, I have here translated, and annexed it to
'this discourse, for the more universal notoriety of
'the thing, and for satisfaction how the power of the
'king of the Minstrels and his officers is founded;
'which take as follows :—

" John, by the grace of God, king of Castile and
" Leon, duke of Lancaster, to all them who shall
" see or hear these our letters, greeting. Know ye,
" we have ordained, constituded, and assigned to our
" well-beloved the King of the Minstrels in our
" honor of Tutbury, who is, or for the time shall be,
" to apprehend and arrest all the Minstrels in our
" said honor and franchise, that refuse to doe the
" service and Minstrelsy as appertain to them to
" do from ancient times at Tutbury aforesaid, yearly
" on the day of the Assumption of our Lady; giving
" and granting to the said King of the Minstrels for
" the time being, full power and commandement to
" make them reasonably to justify and to constrain
" them to doe their services and Minstrelsies in
" manner as belongeth to them, and as it hath been
" there, and of ancient times accustomed. In witness
" of which thing we have caused these our letters to
" be made patents. Given under our privy seal, at
" our castle of Tutbury, the 22nd day of Aug. in the
" fourth year of the raigne of the most sweet king
" Richard the second."

'Upon this, in process of time, the defaulters
'being many, and the amercements by the officers
'perhaps not sometimes over reasonable, concerning
'which, and other matters, controversies frequently
'arising, it was at last found necessary that a court
'should be erected to hear plaints, and determine
'controversies between party and party, before the
'steward of the honor; which is held there to this
'day on the morrow after the Assumption, being
'the 16th of August, on which day they now also
'doe all the services mentioned in the abovesaid
'grant; and have the bull due to them anciently
'from the prior of Tutbury, now from the earle
'of Devon, whereas they had it formerly on the
'Assumption of our Lady, as appears by an In-
'speximus of king Henry the sixth, relating to the
'customs of Tutbury, where, amongst others, this
'of the bull is mentioned in these words: " Item
" est ibidem quædam consuetudo quod histriones ve-
" nientes ad matutinas in festo Assumptionis beatæ
" Mariæ, habebunt unum taurum de priore de Tutte-
" bury, si ipsum capere possunt citra aquam Dove
" propinquiorem Tuttebury; vel prior dabit eis xld.
" pro qua quidem consuetudine dabuntur domino ad
" dictum festum annuatim xxd." i. e. that there is
'a certain custom belonging to the honor of Tutbury,
'that the minstrells who came to mattins there on
'the feast of the Assumption of the blessed Virgin,
'shall have a bull given them by the prior of
'Tutbury, if they can take him on this side the
'river Dove, which is next Tutbury; or else the
'prior shall give them xld. for the enjoyment of
'which custom they shall give to the lord at the
'said feast yearly, xxd.

'Thus I say the services of the Minstrels were
'performed and bull enjoyed anciently on the feast

'of the Assumption; but now they are done and
'had in the manner following : on the court day,
'or morrow of the Assumption, being the 16th of
'August, what time all the Minstrells within the
'honor come first to the bailiff's house of the manor
'of Tutbury, who is now the earl of Devonshire,
'where the steward for the court to be holden
'for the king, as duke of Lancaster (who is now the
'duke of Ormond) or his deputy, meeting them,
'they all go from thence to the parish church of
'Tutbury, two and two together, music playing
'before them, the King of the Minstrells for the year
'past, walking between the steward and bailiff, or
'their deputies; the four stewards or under officers
'of the said King of the Minstrells, each with
'a white wand in their hands, immediately following
'them, and then the rest of the company in order.
'Being come to the church, the vicar reads them
'divine service, chusing psalms and lessons suitable
'to the occasion: the psalms when I was there, an.
'1680, being the 98. 149. 150: the first lesson 2
'Chron. 5; and the second the 5 chap. of the Epistle
'to the Ephesians, to the 22 verse. For which
'service every Minstrell offered one penny, as a due
'always paid to the vicar of the church of Tutbury
'upon this solemnity.

' Service being ended, they proceed in like manner
'as before, from the church to the castle-hall or
'court, where the steward or his deputy taketh his
'place, assisted by the bailiff or his deputy, the King
'of the Minstrells sitting between them, who is to
'oversee that every Minstrell dwelling within the
'honor and making default, shall be presented and
'amerced: which that he may the better do, an
'O Yes is then made by one of the officers, being
'a Minstrell, 3 times, giving notice, by direction
'from the steward, to all manner of Minstrells dwell-
'ing within the honor of Tutbury, viz., within the
'counties of Stafford, Darby, Nottingham, Leicester,
'and Warwick, owing suit and service to his ma-
'jesty's Court of Musick, here holden as this day,
'that every man draw near and give his attendance,
'upon pain and peril that may otherwise ensue; and
'that if any man will be assigned* of suit or plea,
'he or they should come in, and they should be
'heard. Then all the musicians being called over
'by a court-roll, two juries are impanelled, out of
'24 of the sufficientest of them, 12 for Staffordshire,
'and twelve for the other counties; whose names
'being delivered in court to the steward, and called
'over, and appearing to be full juries, the foreman
'of each is first sworn, and then the residue, as is
'usual in other courts, upon the holy evangelists.

'Then, to move them the better to mind their
'duties to the king, and their own good, the steward
'proceeds to give them their charge; first commend-
'ing to their consideration the Original of all Musick,
'both Wind and String Musick; the antiquity and
'excellency of both; setting forth the force of it upon
'the affections by diverse examples; how the use of
'it has always been allowed, as is plain from holy

'writ, in praising and glorifying God; and the skill
'in it always esteemed so considerable, that it is still
'accounted in the schools one of the liberal arts, and
'allowed in all godly christian commonwealths;
'where by the way he commonly takes notice of the
'statute, which reckons some musicians amongst
'vagabonds and rogues; giving them to understand
'that such societies as theirs, thus legally founded
'and governed by laws, are by no means intended by
'that statute, for which reason the Minstrells belong-
'ing to the manor of Dutton, in the county palatine
'of Chester, are expressly excepted in that act. Ex-
'horting them upon this account to preserve their
'reputation; to be very careful to make choice of
'such men to be officers amongst them as fear God,
'are of good life and conversation, and have know-
'ledge and skill in the practice of their art. Which
'charge being ended, the jurors proceed to the elec-
'tion of the said officers, the king being to be chosen
'out of the four stewards of the preceding year, and
'one year out of Staffordshire, and the other out of
'Darbyshire, interchangeably; and the four stewards,
'two of them out of Staffordshire, and two out of
'Darbyshire, three being chosen by the jurors, and
'the fourth by him that keeps the court, and the
'deputy steward or clerk.

'The jurors departing the court for this purpose,
'leave the steward with his assistants still in their
'places, who in the mean time make themselves merry
'with a banquet, and a Noise† of musicians playing
'to them, the old king still sitting between the
'steward and bailiff as before; but returning again
'after a competent time, they present first their
'chiefest officer by the name of their King; then the
'old king arising from his place, delivereth him a
'little white wand in token of his sovereignty, and
'then taking up a cup filled with wine, drinketh to
'him, wishing him all joy and prosperity in his office.
'In the like manner do the old stewards to the new,
'and then the old king riseth, and the new taketh his
'place, and so do the new stewards of the old, who
'have full power and authority, by virtue of the
'king's steward's warrant, directed from the said
'court, to levy and distrain in any city, town cor-
'porate, or in any place within the king's dominions,
'all such fines and amercements as are inflicted by
'the said juries that day upon any Minstrells, for his
'or their offences, committed in the breach of any of
'their ancient orders, made for the good rule and
'government of the said society. For which said
'fines and amercements so distrained, or otherwise
'peaceably collected, the said stewards are account-
'able at every audit; one moiety of them going to
'the king's majesty, and the other the said stewards
'have for their own use.

'The election, &c. being thus concluded, the court
'riseth, and all persons then repair to another fair
'room within the castle, where a plentiful dinner is
'prepared for them, which being ended, the Minstrells

---

* This word should be essoined, for so it is in Blount, and is nonsense otherwise. In this place it means respited.

† It seems that a company of musicians is termed a Noise; this we learn from a passage in the Second Part of Henry IV., Act II., Sce. IV., where mention is made of Sneak's Noise, i. e. a company of Musicians of which one named Sneak was the Master; it may be inferred that a Noise of Musicians is not a sarcastic, but a technical term.

'went anciently to the abbey-gate, now to a little
'barn by the town side, in expectance of the bull to
'be turned forth to them, which was formerly done,
'according to the custom above-mentioned, by the
'prior of Tutbury, now by the earl of Devonshire;
'which bull, as soon as his horns are cut off, his Ears
'cropt, his Taile cut by the stumple, all his Body
'smeared over with Soap, and his nose blown full of
'beaten pepper; in short, being made·as mad as 'tis
'possible for him to be, after solemn Proclamation
'made by the Steward, that all manner of persons
'give way to the Bull, none being to come near him
'by 40 foot, any way to hinder the Minstrells, but to
'attend his or their own safeties, every one at his own
'peril: he is then forthwith turned out to them
'(anciently by the prior), now by the lord Devon-
'shire, or his deputy, to be taken by them and none
'other, within the county of Stafford, between the
'time of his being turned out to them, and the setting
'of the sun of the same day; which if they cannot
'do, but the Bull escapes from them untaken, and
'gets over the river into Darbyshire, he remains still
'my lord Devonshire's bull: but if the said Minstrells
'can take him, and hold him so long as to cut off but
'some small matter of his Hair, and bring the same
'to the Mercat Cross, in token they have taken him.
'the said Bull is then brought to the Bailiff's house
'in Tutbury, and there collered and roap'd, and so
'brought to the Bull-Ring in the High-street, and
'there baited with doggs: the first course being
'allotted for the King; the second for the Honour
'of the Towne; and the third for the King of the
'Minstrells, which after it is done the said Minstrells
'are to have him for their owne, and may sell, or
'kill, and divide him amongst them, according as
'they shall think good.

'And thus this Rustic Sport, which they call the
'Bull-running, should be annually performed by the
'Minstrells only, but now-a-days they are assisted by
'the promiscuous multitude, that flock hither in great
'numbers, and are much pleased with it; though
'sometimes through the emulation in point of Man-
'hood, that has been long cherished between the
'Staffordshire and Darbyshire men, perhaps as much
'mischief may have been done in the trial between
'them, as in the Jeu de Taureau, or Bull-fighting,
'practised at Valentia, Madrid, and many other
'places in Spain, whence perhaps this our custom of
'Bull-running might be derived, and set up here by
'John of Gaunt, who was king of Castile and Leon,
'and lord of the Honor of Tutbury; for why might
'not we receive this sport from the Spanyards as well
'as they from the Romans, and the Romans from the
'Greeks? wherein I am the more confirmed, for that
'the Ταυροκατα ψίων ἡμέραι amongst the Thessalians,
'who first instituted this Game, and of whom Julius
'Cæsar learned it, and brought it to Rome, were
'celebrated much about the same time of the year our
'Bull-running is, viz., Pridie Ides Augusti, on the
'12th of August; which perhaps John of Gaunt, in
'honour of the Assumption of our Lady, being but
'three days after, might remove to the 15th, as after
'ages did (that all the solemnity and court might be

'kept on the same day, to avoid further trouble) to
'the 16th of August.'

The foregoing account of the modern usage in the
exercise of this barbarous sport, is founded on the
observation of the relater, Dr. Plot, whose curiosity
it seems led him to be present at it in the year 1680:
how it was anciently performed appears by an extract from the Coucher-book of the honour of Tutbury, which is given at large in Blount's Collection
of ancient Tenures before cited.*

CHAP. XLIII.

Such were the exercises and privileges of the
minstrels in this country; and it will be found that
the Provençal troubadours, jongleurs, musars, and
violars, from whom they clearly appear to have
sprung, possessed at least an equal share of favour and
protection under the princes and other great personages who professed to patronize them. The Provençals
are to be considered as the fathers of modern poesy
and music, and to deduce in a regular order the
history of each, especially the latter, it is necessary
to advert to those very circumstantial accounts that
are extant of them, and the nature of their profession
in the several authors who speak of them. It should
seem that among them there were many men of great
eminence; the first that occurs in the history of them
given by Crescimbeni is Giuffredo Rudello, concerning whom it is related that he was very intimate with
Geoffrey, the brother of Richard the First; and that
while he was with him, hearing from certain pilgrims,
who were returned from the Holy Land, of a countess
of Tripoli, a lady much celebrated, but the story says
not for what, he determined to make her a visit; in
order to which he put on the habit of a pilgrim, and
began his voyage. In his way to Tripoli he became
sick, and before he could land was almost dead. The
countess being informed of his arrival, went on board
the ship that brought him, just time enough to see him
alive: she took him by the hand, and strove to comfort him. The poet was but just sensible; he opened
his eyes, said that having seen her he was satisfied,
and died. The countess, as a testimony of her
gratitude for this visit, which probably cost poor
Geoffrey his life, erected for him a splendid tomb of
porphyry, and inscribed on it his epitaph in Arabic
verse: besides this she caused his poems to be collected,
and curiously copied and illuminated with letters of
gold.† She was soon afterwards seized with a deep
melancholy, and became a nun.

* In the collection of ancient ballads, known by the name of
Robin Hood's Garland, is a very apt allusion to the Tutbury feast or
bull-running, in the following passage:—
'This battle was fought near Tutbury town
'When the bag-pipers baited the bull,
'I am king of the fiddlers, and swear 'tis a truth,
'And call him that doubts it a gull;
'For I saw them fighting, and fiddl'd the while,
'And Clorinda sung Hey derry down:
'The bumpkins are beaten, put up thy sword Bob,
'And now let's dance into the town.
'Before we came to it we heard a great shouting,
'And all that were in it look'd madly;
'For some were a bull-back, some dancing a morrice.
'And some singing Arthur a Bradley.'
Song I.
† Comment. della Volgar Poesia, vol. II. part I. pag. 11.

A canzone, which he wrote while he was upon this romantic voyage, is yet extant; it is as follows:—

> Irat, et dolent me' en partray
>   S' yeu non vey est' amour deluench,
> E non say qu' ouras la veyray
>   Car son trop nostras terras luench.
>
> Dieu que fes tout quant ven e vay,
>   E forma quest' amour luench,
> My don poder al cor, car hay
>   Esper, vezer l' amour de luench.
>
> Segnour, tenes my per veray
>   L' amour qu' ay vers ella de luench,
> Car per un ben que m' en esbay
>   Hai mille mals, tant soy de luench.
>
> Ja d' autr' amours non jauziray,
>   S' yeu non iau dest' amour de luench
> Qu' na plus bella non en say,
>   En luec que sia, ny pres, ni luench.*

Which Rymer has thus translated:—

> Sad and heavy should I part,
>   But for this love so far away;
> Not knowing what my ways may thwart,
>   My native land so far away.
>
> Thou that of all things maker art,
>   And form'st this love so far away;
> Give body's strength, then shan't I start
>   From seeing her so far away.
>
> How true a love to pure desert,
>   My love to her so far away!
> Eas'd once, a thousand times I smart,
>   Whilst, ah! she is so far away.
>
> None other love, none other dart
>   I feel, but her's so far away,
> But fairer never touch'd an heart,
>   Than her's that is so far away.†

The emperor Frederic I., or, as he is otherwise called, Frederic Barbarossa, is also celebrated for his poetical talents, of which the following madrigal in the Provençal dialect is given as a specimen:—

> Plas my cavallier Frances
>   E la dama Catallana
> E l' onrar del Gynoes
>   E la cour de Kastellana:
> Lou kantar Provensalles,
>   E la danza Triuyzana.
> E lou corps Aragonnes,
>   Et la perla Julliana,
> Las mans e kara d' Angles,
>   E lou donzel de Thuscana.‡

Which Rymer says is current every where, and is thus translated by himself:—

> I like in France the chivalry,
>   The Catalonian lass for me;
> The Genoese for working well;
>   But for a court commend Castile:
> For song no countrey to Provance,
>   And Treves must carry't for a dance.
> The finest shapes in Arragon,
>   In Juliers they speak in tune,
> The English for an hand and face,
>   For boys, troth, Tuscany's the place.§

Concerning this prince, it is related, that he was of an invincible courage, of which he gave many signal instances in the wars against the Turks, commenced by the Christians for the recovery of the Holy Land. He was elected emperor in the year 1153, and having reigned about thirty-eight years, was drowned as he was bathing in the Cydnus, a river in Asia Minor, issuing out of Mount Taurus, esteemed one of the coldest in the world ‖

ARNALDO DANIELLO, another of the Provençals flourished about the year 1189, and is greatly celebrated by Nostradamus and his commentator Crescimbeni: he composed many comedies and tragedies. It is said that Petrach has imitated him in many places; and that Daniello not only was a writer of sonnets, madrigals, and other verses, but that he composed the music to many of them. As a proof whereof the following passages are cited:—

> Ma canzon prec qe non vus sia en nois   versi]¶
>   Gar si volez grazir lo son, e 'l mos [cioè la musica, ei
>   Pauc prez Arnaut cui qe plaz, o que tire.

Which Crescimbeni thus translates,—

> Mia canzon, prego, non vi sia in noia
>   Che se gradir volete il suono, e 'l motto;
>   Cui piaccia, o nó, apprezza poco Arnaldo.

And this other,—

> Ges per maltrag qem sofri
> De ben amar non destoli
> Si tot me son endesert
> Per lei faz lo son el rima.

Thus translated by Crescimbeni,—

> Già per mal tratto ch' io soffersi
> Di ben amar non mi distolsi
> Si tosto, ch' io mi sono in solitudine,
> Per lei faccio lo suono, e la rima.**

One proof of Arnaldo Daniello's reputation as a poet is, that Petrarch taking occasion to mention Arnaldo di Maraviglia, another of the Provençals, styles him ' Il men famoso Arnaldo,' meaning thereby to give the former a higher rank in the class of poets.

Many others, as namely, Guglielmo Adimaro, Folchetto da Marsiglia, Raimondo di Miravalle, Anselmo Faidit, Arnaldo di Maraviglia, Ugo Brunetto, Pietro Raimondo il Prode, Ponzio di Bruello, Rambaldo d' Oranges, Salvarico di Malleone, an English gentleman, Bonifazio Calvi, Percivalle Doria, Giraldo di Bornello, Alberto di Sisterone, Bernardo Rascasso, Pietro de Bonifazi, and others, to the amount of some hundreds in number, occur in the catalogue of Provençal poets, an epithet which was given to them, not because they were of that country, for they were of many countries, but because they cultivated that species of poetry which had its rise in Provence: nor were they less distinguished by their different ranks and conditions in life, than by the respective places of their nativity. Some were men of quality, such as counts and barons, others knights, some lawyers, some soldiers, others merchants, nay some were mechanics, and even pilgrims.

All these were favoured with the protection, and

---

* Comment. della Volgar Poesia, vol. II. part I. pag. 12.
† Short View of Trag. pag. 72.
‡ Comm. della Volgar Poesia, vol. II. part I. pag. 15.
§ Short View of Tragedy, pag. 75.

‖ It is remarkable that Alexander the Great by bathing in this river contracted that illness of which his physician Philip cured him.
¶ Crescimb.
** Comment. della volgar Poesia, vol. II. part I. pag. 25.

many of them were maintained in the court of Raimondo Berlinghieri, or Beringhieri, for the orthography of his name is a matter of question.* This prince, who was the son of Idelfonso king of Arragon, was himself an excellent poet, of great liberality, and a patron of learning and ingenious men. The following is the account given of him by Nostradamus :—

'Raimondo Berlinghieri count of Provence and of
'Folcachiero, son of Idelfonso, king of Arragon, was
'a descendant of the family of Berlinghieri of Arragon.
'He was a good Provençal poet, a lover of learned
'men, and of those in particular that could write in
'the Provençal manner; a prince of great gentleness
'and benignity, and withal so fortunate, that while he
'held the crown, which he succeeded to on the death
'of his father, he conquered many countries, and
'that more by his prudence than by the force of his
'arms. He married Beatrice, the daughter of Thomas
'count of Savoy, a very wise, beautiful, and virtuous
'princess, in praise of whom many of the Provençal
'poets composed songs and sonnets, in recompence
'for which she presented them with arms, rich
'habiliments, and money. By this lady the count had
'four daughters, beautiful, wise, and virtuous, all of
'whom were married to kings and sovereign princes,
'by means of a discreet man named Romeo, who
'governed the palace of Raimondo a long time : the
'first of these ladies, named Margarita, was married
'to Lewis king of France; the second, named
'Eleonora, to Henry the Third, or, as others write,
'to Edward king of England; the third, named
'Sanchia, was married to that Richard king of Eng-
'land, who was afterwards king of the Romans; and
'the last, named Beatrice, who by her father's will
'was declared heiress of Provence, was married to
'Charles of Anjou, afterwards king of Naples and
'Sicily.'† It is said of Raimondo, that besides many
'other instances of favour to the poets of his time and
'country, he exempted them from the payment of
'all taxes, and other impositions of a like nature.‡
'He died at the age of forty-seven, in the year of our
'Lord 1245.

The above is the substance of the account given by Nostradamus, and other writers, of this extraordinary personage; and hitherto we may consider him as a shining example of those virtues which contribute to adorn an elevated station; but his character is not free from blemish, and he is not less remarkable in history for his munificence than his ingratitude; of which the following curious story, related by Velu-tello. and by Crescimbeni, inserted in his annotations on the life of Raimondo Berlinghieri by Nostradamus, may serve as an instance :—§

'The liberality of Raimondo, for which he is so
'celebrated, had reduced him to the necessity of
'mortgaging his revenues; and at a time when his
'finances were in great disorder, a pilgrim, the above-
'named Romeo, who had travelled from the extremity
'of the West, and had visited the church of St. James
'of Compostella, arrived at his court; and having by
'his discreet behaviour acquired the esteem and con-
'fidence of Raimondo, the latter consulted him on
'the state of his affairs, and particularly touching
'the means of disencumbering his revenues. The
'result of many conferences on this important subject
'was, a promise on the part of the pilgrim to reform
'his household, reduce the expenses of his govern-
'ment, and deliver the count from the hands of
'usurers, and other persons who had incumbrances
'on his estates and revenues. The count listened very
'attentively to this proposal, and finally committed
'to Romeo the care of his most important concerns,
'and even the superintendence of his house and
'family; and in the discharge of his engagements
'Romeo effected more than he had promised. It has
'already been mentioned that Raimondo had no other
'issue than the four daughters above-named, and it
'was by the exquisite prudence and good manage-
'ment of this stranger that they were married to so
'many sovereign princes. The particulars of a con-
'versation between the count and Romeo, touching
'the marriage of these ladies, is recorded, and show
'him to have been of singular discretion, an able
'negociator, and, in short, a man thoroughly skilled
'in the affairs of the world : for, with respect to the
'eldest daughter Margarita, he proposed to the count
'the marriage of her to Lewis the Good, king of
'France, and effected it by raising for her a much
'larger portion than Raimond ever intended to give
'her, or his circumstances would bear : the reason
'which Romeo gave for this is worth recording;
"If," said he to the count, "your eldest daughter be
"married to Lewis, such an alliance cannot fail to
"facilitate the marriage of the rest;" and the event
'showed how good a judge he was in such matters.

'The barons and other great persons about the
'count could neither behold the services nor the
'success of Romeo without envy; they insinuated
'to the count that he had embezzled the public
'treasure. Raimond attended to their suggestions,
'and called him to a strict account of his admi-
'nistration, which when he had rendered, Romeo
'addressed the count in these pathetic terms: 'Count,
"I have served you a long time, and have increased
"your little revenue to a great one; you have lis-
"tened to the bad counsel of your barons, and have
"been deficient in gratitude towards me; I came
"into your court a poor man, and lived honestly
"with you; return me the little Mule, the Staff, and

---

* Fontanini mentions particularly no fewer than five of the name; the person here spoken of is the last of them. Della Eloquenza Italiana, pag. 60.

† Both Nostradamus and his commentator Crescimbeni have betrayed a most gross ignorance of history in this passage: it is very true that Raimond had four daughters, and that they were married to four kings: the poet Dante says :—

> Quattro figlie hebbe et ciascuna reina
> Ramondo Beringhieri——

> Four lovely daughters, each of them a queen,
> Had Ramond Beringher.———

But neither of them fell to the lot of Richard; his queen was Berengaria or Berenguella, daughter of Sancho of Navarre, and, as Mr. Walpole observes, no princess of Provence. As to the four ladies, they were thus disposed of:—Margaret was married to Lewis king of France, Eleanor to our Henry III, Sanchia to Richard king of the Romans, and nephew to Richard king of England; and Beatrice to Charles king of Naples and Sicily.

‡ It seems that these men were as well knights as poets, for which reason their patron and they have been resembled to king Arthur and his knights of the Round Table. Fontan. della Eloqu. Ital. pag. 63.

§ Comment. della volgar Poesia, vol. II. part I. pag. 78.

" the Pouch, which I brought with me hither, and
" never more expect any service from me."*

'Conscious of the justness of this reproach,
'Raimondo desired that what had past might be
'forgotten, and intreated Romeo to lay aside his
'resolution of quitting his court; but the spirit of
'this honest man was too great to brook such treat-
'ment; he departed as he came, and was never more
'heard of.'

Few of the many authors who have taken occasion
to mention this remarkable story, have forborne to
blame Raimondo for his ingratitude to a man who
had merited not only his protection, but the highest
marks of his favour. The poet Dante has censured
him for it, and borne his testimony to the deserts of
the person thus injured by him, by placing him in
paradise; and considering how easy it was to have
done it, it was almost a wonder that he did not place
his master in a less delightful situation.

The passage in Dante is as follows:—

   E dentro à la presente Margarita
     Luce la luce di Romeo; di cui
     Fu l' opra grande, e bella mal gradita.
   Mai Provenzali, che fer contra lui,
     Non hanno riso: e però mal camina,
     Qual si fa danno del ben fare altrui.
   Quattro figlie hebbe, e ciascuna reina,
     Ramondo Beringhieri; e ciò gli feci
     Romeo persona humile e peregrina:
   E poi 'l mosser le parole biece
     A' dimandar ragione à questo giusto;
     Che gli assegno sette, e cinque per dieci:
   Indi partissi povero, e vetusto:
     E se 'l mondo sapesse 'l cor, ch' egli hebbe
     Mendicando sua vita à frustro à frustro;
   Assai lo loda, e più lo loderebbe.†

Many are the stories related of the Provençal
poets; and there is great reason to suspect that the
history of them abounds with fables. The collection
of their lives by Nostradamus is far from being
a book of the highest authority, and, but for the
Commentary of Crescimbeni, would be of little value:
the labours of these men have nevertheless contributed to throw some light on a very dark part of
literary history, and have furnished some particulars
which better writers than themselves seem not to
have been aware of.

From such a source of poetical fiction as the
country of Provence appears to have been, nothing
less could be expected than a vast profusion of
romances, tales, poems of various kinds, songs, and
other works of invention: it has already been mentioned that some of the first and best of the Italian
poets did but improve on the hints which they had
received from the Provençals. Mr. Dryden is of

opinion that the celebrated story of Gualterus, marquis of Saluzzo, and Griselda, is of the invention of
Petrarch; but whether it be not originally a Provençal tale, may admit of doubt: for first Mr.
Dryden's assertion in the preface to his Fables,
namely, that the tale of Grizzild was the invention
of Petrarch, is founded on a mistake; for it is the
last story in the Decameron, and was translated by
Petrarch into Latin, but not till he had received it
from his friend Boccace. This appears clearly from
a letter of Petrarch to Boccace, extant in the Latin
works of the former, and which has been lately
reprinted as an appendix to a modern English version
of this beautiful story by Mr. Ogle: this ingenious
gentleman has taken great pains to trace the origin
of the Clerk of Oxford's tale, for in that form the
story of Griselda comes to the mere English reader;
and every one that views his preface must concur in
opinion with him, that it is of higher antiquity than
even the time of Boccace; and is one of those
Provençal tales which he is supposed to have amplified and adorned with his usual powers of wit and
elegance. This latter part of Mr. Dryden's assertion,
which is 'that the tale of Grizzild came to Chaucer
from Boccace,' is not less true than the former; for
it was from Petrarch, and that immediately, that
Chaucer received the story which is the subject of
the present inquiry. In the Clerk of Oxenford's
Prologue is this passage:—

   I woll you tell a tale, whiche that I
   Lerned at Padow, of a worthy clerke,
   As preued is by his wordes and his werke.
   He is now deed, and nailed in his chefte,
   I praye to God fende his foule good refte.
   Fraunces Petrarke, the Laureat poete,
   Hight this clerke, whofe rhetorike fwete
   Enlumined all Italie of poetrie,
   As Liuian did of philofophie,
   Or lawe, or other arte perticulere;
   But deth, that woll not fuffre us dwellen here,
   But as it were the twinkling of an eye,
   Hem both hath flaine, and al we fhal dye.

This is decisive evidence that Chaucer took the
tale from Petrarch, and not from Boccace: it is
certain that Petrarch was so delighted with it, that
he got it by heart, and was used to repeat it to his
friends. In the Latin letter above referred to, he
mentions his having shewn it to a friend abroad;
Chaucer is said to have attended the duke of Clarence
upon the ceremony of his marriage with the daughter of the duke of Milan; and Paulus Jovius expressly says that Petrarch was present upon that
occasion:† might not therefore Chaucer at this time
receive, and that from Petrarch himself, that narrative
which is the foundation of the Clerk of Oxenford's
tale?

To be short, the Provençals were the fathers of
modern poesy, and if we consider that a great number of their compositions were calculated to be sung,
as the appellation of Canzoni, by which they are
distinguished, imports; and, if we consider farther
the several occupations of their Musars and Violars,
it cannot be supposed but that they were also pro-

---

* 'Conte, io ti ho servito gran tempo, e messoti il piccolo stato in
'grande; e di ciò, per falso consiglio de' tuoi baroni, sei contro a me
'poco grato. Io venni in tua corte povero Romeo, e onestamente sono
'del tuo vivuto: fammi dare il mi muletto, e il mio bordone, e scarsella,
'com' io ci venni, e quetoti ogni servigio.' Crescimb 79, from Velutello.
Landino relates the same story, adding, that at his departure Romeo
uttered these words, 'Povero venni, e povero me ne parto; Poor I came,
'and poor I go.' Ibid. 78.
  Fontenelle was so affected with the story of this injured man, that he
intended to have written it at length, but was prevented. Near thirty
pages of it may however be seen in the Paris edition of his works,
published in 1758, tome VIII. It is entitled Histoire du Romieu de
Provence.
  † Paradiso, canto VI.

† See the letter prefixed to the Clerk of Oxford's Tale modernized by
George Ogle, Esq., quarto, 1739, pag. vii.

ficients in music; nay, we find that many of their poets were also musicians; and of Arnaldo Daniello it is expressly said, and proved by a passage above-cited from his works, that he was a composer of music, and adapted musical notes to many songs of his own writing.

These particulars afford sufficient reason to believe that the Provençals were as well musicians as poets; but to speak of them as musicians, there are farther evidences extant that they were not only singers and players on the viol, the harp, the lute, and other instruments, but composers of musical tunes, in such characters as were used in those times. Crescimbeni speaks of a manuscript in the Vatican library, in the characters of the fourteenth century, in which were written a great number of Canzoni of the Provençal poets, together with the musical notes; one of these, composed by Theobald king of Navarre, of whom it is said that he was equally celebrated both as a prince and a poet, is given at page 186 of this work; and may be deemed a great curiosity, as being perhaps the most ancient song with the musical notes of any extant, since the invention of that method of notation so justly ascribed to Guido and Franco of Liege.

CHAP. XLIV.

One of the most obvious divisions of the music of later times, is that which distinguishes between religious and civil or secular music; or, in other words, the music of the church and that of the common people : the former was cultivated by the ecclesiastics, and the latter chiefly by the laity, who at no time can be supposed to have been so insensible of its charms, as not to make it an auxiliary to festivity, and an innocent incentive to mirth and pleasantry. Not only in the palaces of the nobility : at weddings, banquets, and other solemnities, may we conceive music to have made a part of the entertainment; but the natural intercommunity of persons in a lower station, especially the youthful of both sexes, does necessarily presuppose it to have been in frequent use among them also. Farther, we learn that music in those times made a considerable part of the entertainment of such as frequented taverns and houses of low resort. Behold a picture of his own times in the following verses of Chaucer :—

> In Flaunders whilom there was a company
> Of yonge folk, that haunted foly,
> As hafard, riot, ftewes, and tauernes,
> Where as with harpes, lutes, and geternes,
> Thei dauncen and plaien at dice night and day,
> And eten alfo, over that her might may
> Through which they don the deuil facrifice
> Within the deuils temple, in curfed wife
> By fuperfluite abhominable,
> Her othes ben fo great and fo dampnable,
> That it is grifly for to here hem fwere,
> Our bliffed lordes body they al to tere
> Hem thought Jews rent him not inough,
> And eche of hem at others finne lough.
> And right anon comen in tomblefteres,
> Fetis and fmale and yonge foiteres,
> Singers with harpes, baudes, and waferers,
> Whiche that ben verely the deuils officers.
> Pardoner's Tale.

These were the divertisements of the idle and the profligate; but the passage above-cited may serve to shew that the music of Lutes, of Harps, and Citterns, even in those days was usual in taverns. As to the music of the court, it was clearly such as the Provençals used; and as to the persons employed in the performance of it, they had no other denomination than that of minstrels. We are told by Stow that the priory of St. Bartholomew, in Smithfield, was founded about the year 1103, by Rahere,* a pleasant, witty gentleman, and therefore in his time called the king's minstrel. Weever, in his Funeral Monuments, pag. 433. Dugdale, in his Monasticon, vol. II. fol. 166, 167, gives this further account of him :—'That he was born of mean parentage, and 'that when he attained to the flower of his youth he 'frequented the houses of the nobles and princes; 'but not content herewith, would often repair to 'court, and spend the whole day in sights, banquets, 'and other trifles, where by sport and flattery he 'would wheedle the hearts of the great lords to him, 'and sometimes would thrust himself into the pre-'sence of the king, where he would be very officious 'to obtain his royal favour; and that by these 'artifices he gained the manor of Aiot, in Hertford-'shire, with which he endowed his hospital.'† In the Pleasaunt History of Thomas, of Reading, quarto, 1662, to which perhaps no more credit is due than to mere oral tradition, he is also mentioned, with this additional circumstance, that he was a great musician, and kept a company of minstrels, i. e., fiddlers, who played with silver bows.

These particulars it is true, as they respect the œconomy of courts, and the recreations and amusements of the higher ranks of men in cities and places of great resort, contain but a partial representation of the manners of the people in general; and leave us

---

* The curious in matters of antiquity may possibly be pleased to know that a monument of this extraordinary person, not in the least defaced, is yet remaining in the parish church of St. Bartholomew, in Smithfield. This monument was probably erected by Bolton, the last prior of that house, a man remarkable for the great sums of money which he expended in building, (for he built Canonbury, vulgarly Canbury, house near Islington, and repaired and enlarged the priory at his own charge) and indeed for general munificence. He was parson of Harrow, in the county of Middlesex, which parish is situated on the highest hill in the county, and has a church, which king Charles the Second, alluding to one of the topics in the Romish controversy, with a pun, was used to call the Visible church. Hall relates that Bolton, from certain signs and conjunctions of the planets which he had observed, prognosticated a deluge, which would probably drown the whole county, and that therefore he builded him a house at Harrow-on-the-Hill, and furnished it with provision of all things necessary for the space of two months: but this story is refuted by Stow in his Survey, with an assertion that he builded no house at Harrow save a Dove-house. One particular more of prior Bolton: we meet with a direct allusion to him in the following passage in the New Inn, a comedy of Ben Jonson :—

'Or prior Bolton with his Bolt and Ton.'

The host is debating with himself on a rebus for the sign of his inn, and having determined on one, the Light Heart, intimates that it is as good a device as that of the Bolt and Ton, which had been used to bespeak the name of prior Bolton. This rebus was till of late a very common sign to inns and ale-houses in and about London; from whence by the way the celebrity of this man may be inferred; the device was a tun pierced by an arrow, the feathers thereof appearing above the bung-hole, and the barb beneath. The wit of this rebus is not intelligible unless it be known that the word Bolt is precisely synonymous with Arrow. Chaucer in the Miller's Tale uses this simile :—

Winfyng fhe was as is a iolie colt,
Long as a maft and upright as a bolt.

Shakespeare somewhere speaks of the arrows of Cupid, and by a metonymy calls them Bird-bolts. The proverbial expression, "A fool's bolt is soon shot," is in the mouth of every one; and in common speech we say bolt-upright.

† Vide Chauncey's History of Hertfordshire, pag. 322.

at a loss to guess how far music made a part in the ordinary amusements of the people in country towns and villages. But here it is to be observed that at the period of which we are now speaking, namely, that between the beginning of the twelfth, and the middle of the thirteenth century, this country, not to mention others, abounded with monasteries, and other religious houses; and although these seminaries were originally founded and endowed for the purpose of promoting religion and learning, it was not with an equal degree of ardour that the inhabitants of them strove to answer the ends of so laudable an institution. Had the temptations to the monastic life been of such a kind as to affect only the devout, or those who preferred the practice of religion and the study of improvement to every other pursuit, all had been well; but the mischief was that they drew in the young, the gay, and the amorous: and such as thought of nothing so little as counting their rosary, or conning their psalter; can it be supposed that in such a monastery as that of St. Alban, Glastonbury, Croyland, Bermondsey, Chertsey, and many others, in which perhaps half the brethren were under thirty years of age, that the Scriptures, the Fathers, or the Schoolmen, were the books chiefly studied? or that the charms of a village beauty might not frequently direct their attention to those authors who teach the shortest way to a female heart, and have reduced the passion of love to a system?

The manners of the people at this time were in general very coarse, and from the nature of the civil constitution of this country, many of the females were in a state of absolute bondage: a connection with a damsel of this stamp hardly deserved the name of an Amour; it was an intimacy contracted without thought or reflection. But between the daughter of a Villain, and the heiress of an Esquire or Franklein, the difference was very great; these latter may be supposed to have entertained sentiments suitable to their rank; and to engage the affections of such as these, the arts of address, and all the blandishments of love were in a great measure necessary. The wife of the carpenter Osney, of whom Chaucer has given the following lively description,—

Faire was this yong wife, and there withal
As any wifele her bodie gentle and small,
A feinte fhe weared, barred all with filke,
A barme cloth, as white as morowe milke;
Upon her lendes, full of many a gore,
Whit was her fmock, and embrouded all bifore,
And eke behinde on her colere about,
Of cole blacke filke, within and eke without;
The tapes of her white volipere
Were of the fame fute of her colore,
Her filet brode of filke, and fet full hye
And fickerly, fhe had a likerous iye;
Full fmall ipulled were her browes two,
And tho were bent, and black as any flo.
She was moche more blifsfull for to fee
Then is the newe Perienet tree,
And fofter than the woll is of a weather,
And by her girdel hong a purfe of leather,
Taffed with filke, and perled with latoun,*
In all this worlde, to feken up and doun,
There nis no man fo wife, that couth thence
So gaie a popelote, or fo gaie a wenche;

* i. e. Tasselled with silk, and having an edging of brass or tinsel lace. Perl is the edge or extremity of lace.

Full brighter was the fhinyng of her hewe,
Than in the toure the Noble forged newe.
But of her fong, it was fo loud and yerne,
As any fwalowe fittynge on a berne:
Thereto fhe couthe fkippe, and make a game
As any kidde or calfe folowyng his dame;
Her mouth was fwete, as braket or the meth,
Or horde of apples, lying in haie or heth;
Winfyng fhe was, as is a iolie colt,
Long as a mafte, and upright as a bolt.
A brooche fhe bare on her lowe colere,
As brode as the boffe of a bucklere;
Her fhoes were laced on her legges hie
She was a primrofe and piggefnie,
For any lorde to liggen in his bedde,
Or yet for any good yoman to wedde.—MILLER'S TALE.

is courted with songs to the music of a gay sautrie, on which her lover Nicholas the scholar of Oxford

- - - - made on nightes melodie
So fwetely that all the chamber rong,
And *Angelus ad Virginem* he fong,
And after that he fong the kynges note,
Full oft bleffed was his mery throte.—Ibid.

Her other lover, Absolon, the parish-clerk sung to the music of his geterne and his ribible, or fiddle. His picture is admirably drawn, and his manner of courtship thus represented by Chaucer :—

A merie childe he was, fo God me faue,
Well coud he let blood, clippe and fhaue,
And make a charter of lond, and acquittaunce;
In twentie maner could he trippe and daunce,
After the fchole of Oxenforde tho,
And with his legges caften to and fro
And plaie fonges on a fmale ribible; †
Therto he fong fometyme a loude quinible. ‡
And as well coud he plaie on a geterne,
In all the toune nas brewhoufe ne tauerne
That he ne vifited with his folas,
There any gaie tapftere was.   *   *   *
This Abfolon that was ioily and gaie,
Goeth with a cenfer on a Sondaie,
Cenfyng the wiues of the parifhe fafte,
And many a louely look on hem he cafte,
And namely on this carpenters wife
To look on her hym thought a merie life,
She was fo propre, and fwete as licorous;
I dare well faine if fhe had been a mous,
And he a catte, he would have her hent anon.
This parifhe clerke, this ioily Abfolon,
Hath in his harte foch a loue longying,
That of no wife he tooke none offeryng,
For curtefie he faied he would none.
The moone, when it was night, bright fhone,

† RIBIBLE is by Mr. Urry, in his Glossary to Chaucer, from Speght, a former editor, rendered a fiddle or gittern. It seem that Rebeb is a Moorish word, signifying an instrument with two strings, played on with a bow. The Moors brought it into Spain, whence it passed into Italy, and obtained the appellation of Ribeca; from whence the English Rebec, which Phillips, and others after him, render a fiddle with three strings. The Rebeb or Rebab is mentioned in Shaw's Travels as a Turkish or Moorish instrument now in use; and is probably an improvement on the Arabian Pandura, described by Mersennus, and previously mentioned in this work, pag. 86.

‡ Mr. Urry, on the same authority, makes this word synonymous with treble. This signification is to be doubted; the word may rather mean a high part, such as in madrigals and motets is usually distinguished by the word quintus, which in general lies above the tenor, and is sometimes between that and the contratenor; and at others between the contratenor and the superius or treble; and from the word quintus quinible may possibly be derived; and this is the more probable, for that in an ancient manuscript treatise on descant, of which an account will hereafter be given, the accords for the quatribil sight are enumerated; and quatribil will hardly be thought a wider deviation from its radical term than quinible is from quintus. Stow records an endowment by the will of a citizen of London, dated in 1492, for a canable to sing a twelvemonth after his decease in the church of St. Sepulchre; and conjectures that by Canable we are to understand a singing priest. Surv. of London. with Additions by Strype, book III. pag. 241. And quere if Canable in this place may not mean Quinible, i. e. a priest with a voice of a high pitch?

> And Abfolon his Geterne* hath itake,
> For paramours he thought for to wake,
> And foorth he goeth, jelous and amerous,
> Till he came to the carpenter's hous
> A little after the cockes had icrow,
> And dreffed him by a fhot windowe
> That was upon the carpenter's wall;
> He fingeth in his voice gentle and fmall,
> Now dere ladie, if thy will be
> I praie you that ye would rewe on me.
> Full well accordyng to his Geternyng,
>   This carpentere awoke and heard him fyng.—Ibid.

His manner of courtship, and the arts he made use of to gain the favour of his mistress, are farther related in the following lines :—

> Fro daie to daie, this ioily Abfolon
> So woeth her, that hym was wo bygon ;
> He waketh all the night, and all the daie.
> He kembeth his lockes brode, and made him gaie ;
> He woeth her by meanes and brocage,
> And fwore that he would been her owne page.
> He Singeth brokkyng as a nightingale.
> He sent her piment, methe, and fpiced ale,
> And wafres piping hotte out of the glede,
> And for fhe was of toun, he profered her mede ;
> For fome folke wolle be wonne for richeffe,
> And fome for ftrokes, and fome with gentleneffe.—Ibid.

If so many arts were necessary to win the heart of the youthful wife of a carpenter, what may we suppose were practised to obtain the affections of females in a higher station of life? Who were qualified to compose verses, songs, and sonnets, but young men endowed with a competent share of learning? and who were so likely to compose musical tunes as those who had the means of acquiring the rudiments of the science in those fraternities of which they were severally members, and in which they were then only taught? Even the satires and bobbing rhymes, as Camden calls them, of those days, though they were levelled at the vices of the clergy, were written by clergymen. Lydgate was a monk of Bury, and Walter de Mapes, of whom Camden relates that in the time of king Henry the Second he filled all England with his merriments, was archdeacon of Oxford. He in truth was not so much a satirist on the vices of other men, as an apologist for his own, and these by his own confession were intemperance and lewdness; which he attempts to excuse in certain Latin verses, which may be found in the book entitled Remains concerning Britain.

From these particulars, and indeed from the general ignorance of the laity, we may fairly conclude that the knowledge of music was in a great measure confined to the clergy; and that they for the most part were the authors and composers of those Songs and Ballads with the tunes adapted to them, which were the ordinary amusements of the common people; and these were as various in their kinds as the genius, temper, and qualifications of their authors. Some were nothing more than the legends of saints, in such kind of metre as that in which the Chronicles of Robert of Gloucester and of Peter Langtoft and others are written; others were metrical romances; others were songs of piety and devotion, but of such a kind, as is hard to conceive of at this time. And here it is to be noted, that as the Psalms were not then translated into the vulgar tongue, the common people wanted much of that comfort and solace, which they administred to our great grandmothers; and that in those times the principal exercises of a devout heart were the singing such songs as are above-mentioned. These had frequently for their subject the sufferings of the primitive christians, or the virtues of some particular saint, but much oftner an exhortation from Christ himself, represented in the pangs of his crucifixion, adjuring his hearers by the nails which fastened his hands and feet, by the crown of thorns on his head, by the wound in his side, and all the calamitous circumstances of his passion, to pity and love him. Of the compositions of this kind the following is an authentic specimen :—

> Wofully arayd
> My blod man for the ran,
> Yt may not be nayed,
> My body bloo and wan,
>   Wofully arayd.
>
> Behold me I pray the
>   With all thy hool refon
> And be not fo hard hartyd,
>   For thys enchefon ;
> Syth I for thy fowls fake,
>   Was flayn in gode fefon,
> Begyld and betrayd
>   By Judas fals trefon.
>
> Unkyndly entretyd
> With fharp cord fore frettyd,
> The Jewes me thretyd,
>   They mowed they gyrned ;
> They fcorned me,
> Condemned to deth,
> As thou mayft fee,
>   Wofully arayd.
>
> Thus nayked am I nayled,
>   O man for thy fake,
> I love thee then love me,
>   Why flepift thou ? awake,
> Remember my tender hart rote
>   For the brake.
>
>   What payns
>   My vaynes
> Conftraynd to crake,
> Thus tuggyd to and fro,
> Thus wrappyed all in woo,
>   In most cruel wyfe,
> Like a lambe offeryd in facrifice,
>   Wofully arayd.
>
> Of fharpe thorn I have worne
> A croune on my hed
>   So payned,
>   So ftrayned,
> So rewfully red,
>   Thus bobbid,
>   Thus robbid,
> Thus for thy lone dede
>   Enfaynd,
>   Not deynyd
> My blod for to fhed.
>
> My feet and hands fore,
> The fturdy nayls bore,
> What might I fuffer more
> Than I have done O man for the !
>   Cum when ye lyft,
>   Welcum to me ;
> My bloud man for the ranne,
>   My body bloo and wanne,
>   Wofully arayd.†

---

* It is intimated by Speght and Urry, in the Glossary to Chaucer, that by the word Gitterne is meant a fiddle; but more probably it is a corruption of Cittern, a very different instrument.

† Skelton, in his poem entitled the Crown of Laurell, alludes to this

CHAP. XLV.

IN a manuscript, of which a full account will be given hereafter, as ancient as the year 1326, mention is made of ballads and roundelays; these were no other than popular songs, and we find that Chaucer himself composed many such. Stow collected his ballads, and they were published for the first time in an edition of Chaucer printed by John Kyngston in 1561; * they are of various kinds, some moral, others descriptive, and others satirical.

One John Shirley, who lived about 1440, made a large collection, consisting of many volumes of compositions of this kind by Chaucer, Lydgate, and other writers. Stowe had once in his possession one 'of these volumes, entitled 'A Boke cleped the ab- 'stracte brevyaire, compyled of diverse balades, 'roundels, virilays,† tragedyes, envoys, complaints, 'moralities, storyes practysed, and eke devysed and 'ymagined, as it sheweth here followyng, collected 'by John Shirley,'‡ which is yet extant, and remains part of the Ashmolean collection of manuscripts; and the late Mr. Ames had in his possession a folio volume of ballads in manuscript, composed by one John Lucas, about the year 1450, which is probably yet in being.

There are hardly any of the tunes of these ancient ballads but must be supposed to be irretrievably lost. One indeed to that in Chaucer's works, beginning, 'I have a lady,' is to be found in a vellum manu- script, formerly in the hands of Dr. Robert Fairfax, mentioned in Morley's Catalogue, who lived about 1500, and which afterwards became part of the col- lection of Mr. Ralph Thoresby, and is mentioned in the list of his curiosities, at the end of his History of Leeds; the tune was composed by Cornysh, who lived temp. Hen. VIII., but then the ballad itself is not so old as is pretended, for in the Life of Chaucer, prefixed to Urry's edition, it is proved to have been written after his death.

Nor, which is much to be lamented, have we any dance-tunes so ancient as the year 1400. The oldest country-dance-tune now extant being that known by the name of Sellenger's, i. e. St. Leger's Round, which may be traced back to nearly the time of Hen. VIII., for Bird wrought it into a virginal-lesson for lady Nevil :§ that they must have had such sort of musical compositions, and those regular ones, long before, is in the highest degree probable, since it is certain that the measures of time were invented and reduced to rule at least before the year 1340, which

is more than half a century earlier, and consequently that the musicians of that time had the same means of composing them as we have now.

The most ancient English song with the musical notes perhaps any where extant, is now in the British Museum, concerning which Mr. Wanley, who was as good a musician as he was a judicious collector, has given this account in that part of the Catalogue of the Harleian Manuscripts, which he himself drew up.||

'*Antiphona* PERSPICE XP'TICOLA, *Miniatis Lit-* 'teris scripta; supra quam, tot Syllabis, nigro '*Atramento seu communi, cernuntur Verba An-* 'glica, cum Notis Musicis, à quatuor Cantoribus '*seriatim atq; simul Canenda. Hoc genus Con-* '*trapunctionis sive Compositionis,* CANONEM *vocant* '*Musici moderni; Anglicè (cum verba, sicut in* '*præsenti Cantico, sint omnino ludicra)* A CATCH; '*vetustioribus verò, uti ex præsenti Codice videre* '*est, nuncupabatur* ROTA. Hanc ROTAM *cantare* 'possunt quatuor Socij; a paucioribus autem quam 'a Tribus, vel Saltem Duobus, non debet dici, preter 'eos qui dicunt PEDEM. Canitur autem sic; Tacen- 'tibus ceteris, unus inchoat cum hijs qui tenent 'PEDEM, et cum venerit ad primam Notam post 'Crucem, inchoat alius; et sic de ceteris, &c. *fol. 9. b.*

'*Notandum etiam, hoc ludicræ Cantionis apud* '*Anglos, Regulis quoque Musices quodam modo* '*astrictæ, avitâ in super Linguâ exhibitæ, Exem-* '*plar esse omnium quæ adhuc mihi videre contiget* '*Antiquissimum.*

The following is an exact copy of the song above described, with the directions for singing it :—

CANON in the UNISON,
From an ancient MS. in the British Museum.

SUMER is i cumen in,   Lhude sing Cuccu,
Per-spi-ce chris-ti-co-la   *que dig-na-ci-o,*

groweth seed and bloweth mead, and springth the wde nu,
ce-li-eus a-gri-co-la pro vi-tis vi-ci-o,

Sing Cuccu, Awe bleteth after lomb, lhouth after calve cu,
Fi-li-o, nonparcens ex-po-su-it mor-tis ex-i-ci-o,

Bul-luc sterteth, Bucke vert-eth, mu-rie sing cuc-cu,
Qui cap-ti-vos, Se-mi-vi-vos, a sup-pli-ci-o,

Cuccu cuccu, wel sings thu cuccu, ne swik thu naver nu.
Vi-te donat, et secum co-ro-nat in ce-li so-li-o.

|| The number of the manuscript, as it stands in the printed catalogue, is 978. The volume contains divers tracts on music, and other subjects; and the song above spoken of is numbered 5, that is to say, it has the fifth place in vol. 978.

---

song in a manner that seems to indicate that it was of his writing. See his poems, 12mo. 1736, pag. 54.

* This is the edition referred to in all the quotations from Chaucer that occur in the course of this work.

† Roundel and Virilay are words nearly synonymous; both are supposed to signify a rustic song or ballad, as in truth they do, but with this difference, the roundel ever begins and ends with the same sentence, the virilay is under no such restriction.

‡ Vid. Tann. Biblioth. pag. 668.

§ The knowledge of this fact is derived from a curious manuscript volume yet extant, containing a great number of lessons all composed by Bird: the book is in the handwriting of John Baldwine, of Windsor, and appears to have been finished anno 1591; it is very richly bound, and has these words, 'My Layde Nevell's booke' impressed in gold letters on the covers, and the family arms depicted on one of the blank leaves. The first lesson in it is entitled Lady Nevel's Grownde; from all which par- ticulars it is to be supposed that the book itself was a present from Bird himself to lady Nevil, who perhaps might have been his scholar.

Hanc rotam cantare possunt quatuor socii, A paucioribus autem quam a tribus, vel saltem duobus, non debet dici, præter eos qui dicunt pedem. Canitur autem sic; Tacentibus cæteris unus inchoat cum hijs qui tenent pedem, et cum venerit ad primam notam post crucem, inchoat alius; et sic de ceteris. Singuli vero repausent ad pausaciones scriptas, et non alibi, spacio unius longæ notæ.

Pes {

Hoc repetit unus quoties opus est, faciens pausacionem in fine.

Sing cuccu nu, sing cuccu.

Hoc dicit alius pausans in medio et non in fine, sed immediate repetens principium.

Sing cuccu, sing cuccu nu.

It is to be noted that in the Harleian MS. the stave on which the above composition is written consists of red lines, and that the Latin words above given are of the same colour, as are also the directions for singing the Pes, as it is called. Du Cange voce Rota, remarks that this word sometimes signifies a hymn. The words 'Hanc rotam cantare possunt,' &c. may therefore be supposed to refer to the Latin 'Perspice Christicola,' and not to the English 'Sumer 'is icumen in,' &c. which latter stand in need of an explanation, and are probably to be thus rendered:—

Summer is a-coming in,
Loud sing cuckow.
Groweth seed,
And bloweth mead; *
And spring'th the wood new.
Ewe bleateth after lamb,
Loweth after calf cow:
Bullock starteth,
Buck verteth,†
Merry sing cuckow,
Well sing'st thou cuckow,
Nor cease to sing [or labour thy song] nu [now].‡

As to the music, it is clearly of that species of composition known by the name of canon in the Unison. It is calculated for four voices, with the addition of two for the Pes, as it is called, which is a kind of ground, and is the basis of the harmony. Mr. Wanley has not ventured precisely to ascertain the antiquity of this venerable musical relic, but the following observations will go near to fix it to about the middle of the fifteenth century. It has already been shown that the primitive form of polyphonous or symphoniac music was counterpoint, *i. e.* that kind of composition which consisted in the opposition of note to note: the invention of the cantus mensurabilis made no alteration in this respect, for though it introduced a diversity in the measures of the notes as they stood related to each other, the correspondence of long and short quantities was exact and uniform in the several parts.

To counterpoint succeeded the cantus figuratus, in which it is well known that the correspondence, in respect of time, is not between note and note, but rather between the greater measures; or, to speak with the moderns, between bar and bar, in each part; and this appears to have been the invention of John Dunstable, who wrote on the cantus mensurabilis, and died in 1455, and will be spoken of in his place.§ Now the composition above given is evidently of the figurate kind, and it follows from the premises, that it could not have existed before the time when John of Dunstable appears to have lived. The structure of it will be best understood by the following score in the more modern method of notation:—

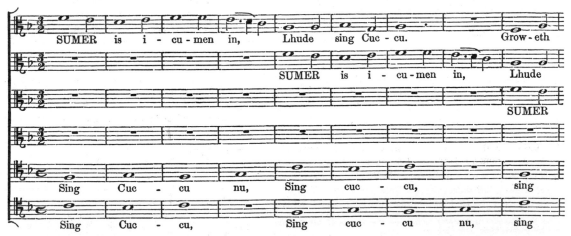

* The flowers in the meadow.
† Goeth to vert, *i. e.*, to harbour among the fern.
‡ It is observable that the most ancient species of musical imitation is the song of the cuckow, which must appear to be a natural and very obvious subject for it. Innumerable are the instances that might be produced to this purpose; a very fine madrigal in three parts, composed by Thomas Weelkes, organist of Chichester cathedral about the year 1600, beginning 'The Nightingale the Organ of Delight,' has in it the cuckow's song. Another of the same kind, not less excellent, in four parts, beginning, 'Thirsis sleepest thou?' occurs in the Madrigals of John Bennet, published in 1599. Vivaldi's cuckow concerto is well known, as is also that of Lampe, composed about thirty years ago. The song of the cuckow is in truth but one interval, that is to say a minor third, terminated in the scale by a LA MI RE acute, and C SOL FA. Vide Kirch. Musurg. tom I. Iconism. III., nevertheless, in all the instances above referred to, it is defined by the interval of a major third.
§ This assertion is grounded on the authority of a book intitled Præceptiones Musices Poeticæ, seu de Compositione Cantus, written by Johannes Nucius, printed in 1613, wherein, to give it at length,

is the following remarkable passage, intended by the author as an answer to the question, 'Quem dicimus poeticum musicum?':—
'Qui non solum precepta musicæ apprimè intelligit, et juxta ea rectè,
'ac bene modulatur, sed qui proprii ingenii penetralia tentans, novas
'cantilenas cudit, et flexibiles sonos pio verborum pondere textibus
'aptat. Talem artificem Glareanus symphonetæ appellatione describit.
'Sicut Phonasci nomine cantorem insinuat. Porrò tales artifices claru-
'erunt, primum circa annum Christi 1400, aut certè paulò post. Dunx-
'tapli Anglus à quo primum figuralem musicam inventam tradunt.'
Thomas Ravenscroft, the author of A brief Discourse of the true but neglected Use of characterising the Degrees in measurable Music, quarto, 1614, asserts that John of Dunstable was the first that invented musical composition, in which, taking the above-cited passage for his authority, he appears most grossly to have erred. Musical composition must certainly be as ancient as the invention of characters to denote it; nay, it may be conjectured that counterpoint was known and practised before the time spoken of, but as to figurate music, we are at a loss for evidence of its existence before the time of Dunstable, and in truth it is the invention of figurate music only that is ascribed to him by Nucius.

The history of music, so far as regards the use and practice of it, is so nearly connected with that of civil life, as in a regular deduction of it to require the greatest degree of attention to the customs and modes of living peculiar to different periods : a knowledge of these is not to be derived from history, properly so called, which has to do chiefly with great events ; and were it not for the accurate and lively representation of the manners of the old Italians, and the not less ancient English, contained in the writings of Boccace and Chaucer, the inquisitive part of mankind would be much at a loss for the characteristics of the fourteenth century. Happily these authors have furnished the means of investigating this subject, and from them we are enabled to frame an idea of the manners, the amusements, the conversation, garb, and many other particulars of their contemporaries.

The Decameron of Boccace, and the Canterbury Tales of Chaucer, appear each to have been composed with a view to convey instruction and delight, at a time when the world stood greatly in need of the former ; and by examples drawn from feigned history, to represent the consequences of virtue and vice ; and in this respect it may be said that the authors of both these works appear to have had the same common end in view, but in the prosecution of this design each appears to have pursued a different method. Boccace, a native of Italy, and a near neighbour to that country where all the powers of wit and invention had been exerted for upwards of two centuries in fictions of the most pleasing kind, had opportunities of selecting from a great variety such as were fittest for his purpose. Chaucer, perhaps not over solicitous to explore those regions of fancy, contented himself with what was laid before him, and preferred the labour of refining the metal to that of digging the ore.

Farther, we may observe that besides the ends of instruction and delight, which each of these great masters of the science of human life proposed, they meant also to exhibit a view of the manners of their respective countries, Italy and England, with this difference, that the former has illustrated his subject by a series of conversations of persons of the most refined understanding, whereas the latter, without being at the pains attending such a method of selection, has feigned an assemblage of persons of different ranks, the most various and artful that can be imagined, and with an amazing propriety has made each of them the type of a peculiar character.

To begin with Boccace. A plague which happened in the city of Florence, in the year of our Lord 1348, suggests to him the fiction that seven ladies, discreet, nobly descended, and perfectly accomplished ; the youngest not less than eighteen, nor the eldest exceeding twenty-eight years of age ; their names Pampinea, Fiammetta, Philomena, Emilia, Lauretta, Neiphile, and Eliza, meet together at a church, and, after their devotions ended, enter into discourse upon the calamities of the times : to avoid the infection they agree to retire a small distance from the town, to live in common, and spend part of the summer in contemplating the beauties of nature, and in the ingenious and delightful conversation of each other ;

but foreseeing the inconveniences that must have followed from the want of companions of the other sex, they add to their number Pamphilo, Philostrate, and Dioneo, three well-bred young gentlemen, the admirers and honourable lovers of three of these accomplished ladies. They retire to a spacious and well furnished villa. Pampinea is elected their queen for one day, with power to appoint her successor ; different offices are assigned to their attendants ; wines, and other necessaries, chess-boards, backgammon-tables, cards, dice, books, and musical instruments are provided ; the heat of the season excluding the recreations of riding, walking, dancing, and many others, for some part of the day, they agree to devote the middle of it to the telling of stories in rotation : the conversations of this kind take up ten days, each is the narrator of ten novels. Such is the structure of the Decameron.

The highest sense of virtue, of honour, and religion, and the most exact attention to the forms of civility, are observable in the behaviour of these ladies and gentlemen ; nevertheless many of the stories told by them are of such a kind as to excite our wonder that well-bred men could relate, or modest women hear them ; from whence this inference may be fairly drawn, that although nature may be said to be ever the same, yet human manners are perpetually changing ; particular virtues and vices predominate at different periods, chastity of sentiment and purity of expression are the characteristics of the age we live in.

But to pursue more closely the present purpose, we find from the novels of Boccace that Music made a considerable part in the entertainment of all ranks of people. In the introduction we are told that on the first day after they had completed the arrangement of this little community, when dinner was over, as they all could dance, and some both play and sing well, the queen ordered in the musical instruments, and commanded Dioneo to take a lute, and Fiammetta ' una vivola,' a viol, to the music whereof they danced, and afterwards sang. And at the end of the first Giornata we are told that Lauretta danced, Emilia singing to her, and Dioneo playing upon the lute : the canzone, or song, which is a very elegant composition, is given at length. At the end of the third Giornata, Dioneo, by whom we are to understand Boccace himself, and Fiammetta, under whom is shadowed his mistress, the natural daughter of Robert king of Naples, sing together the story of Guiglielmo and the lady of Vergiu, while Philomena and Pamphilo play at chess ; and at the end of the seventh Giornata the same persons are represented singing together the story of Palamon and Arcite, after which the whole company dance to the music, ' della Cor-' namusa,' of a bagpipe, played on by Tindarus, a domestic of one of the ladies, and therefore a fit person to perform on so homely an instrument.

These representations, fictitious as they undoubtedly are, may nevertheless serve to ascertain the antiquity of those musical instruments, the Lute, the Viol, and the Cornamusa, or Bagpipe ; they also prove to some degree the antiquity of that kind of measured dance, which was originally invented to display all the graces and elegancies of a beautiful form, and is at this day esteemed one of the requisites in a polite education.

CHAP. XLVI.

It remains now to speak of our ancient English poet, and from that copious fund of intelligence and pleasantry the Canterbury Tales, to select such particulars as will best illustrate the subject now under consideration. The narrative supposes that twenty-nine persons of both sexes, of professions and employments as different as invention could suggest, together with Chaucer himself, making in all thirty, sat out from the Tabarde inn in Southwark * on a pilgrimage to the shrine of St. Thomas Becket in the cathedral church of Canterbury, and that this motley company consisted of a knight, a 'squire his son, and his yeoman or servant; a prioress, a nun, and three priests her attendants; a monk, a friar, a merchant, a clerk of Oxford, a serjeant at law, a franklin or gentleman, a haberdasher, a carpenter, a weaver, a dyer, a tapiser or maker of tapestry, a cook, a shipman or master of a trading vessel, a doctor of physic, the wife of a weaver of Bath, a parson, a plowman, or, as we should now call such a one, a farmer, a miller, a manciple, a reeve, a summoner, a pardoner, and Chaucer himself, who was a courtier, a scholar, and a poet. The characters of these, drawn with such skill, and painted in such lively colours, that the persons represented by them seem to pass in review before us, precede, and are therefore called the Prologues to, the Tales. After the prologues follows a relation of the conversation of the pilgrims at their supper, in which the host desires to make one of the company, which being assented to, he proposes that in the way to Canterbury each should tell two tales, and on their return the same number; and he that recounts the best shall be treated with a supper by his companions. To this they assent, and early in the morning set out, taking the host for their guide. They halt at St. Thomas's Watering, a place well known near Southwark, and the host proposes drawing cuts to determine who shall tell the first tale; the lot falls upon the knight, as having drawn the shortest, and making a brief apology (wherein his discretion and courtesy are remarkable) he begins by a recital of the knightly story of Palamon and Arcite.†

* This inn was formerly the lodging of the abbot of Hyde near Winchester, the sign was a Tabarde, a word signifying a short jacket, or sleeveless coat, whole before, open on both sides, with a square collar and hanging sleeves. Stow's Survey, lib. IV. chap. 1. From the wearing of this garment some of those on the foundation at Queen's college in Oxford are called Taberdarii. The servants of their respective masters at the great call of serjeants in the year 1736, walked in coats of this form, and of a violet colour, in the procession from the Middle Temple hall to Westminster. It was anciently the proper habit of a servant, and there cannot be a clearer proof of it than that all the knaves in a pack of cards are dressed in it. A few years ago the sign of this inn was the Talbot or beagle, an evidence that the signification of the word Tabarde was at least unknown to its then owner. The host in Chaucer's time was Henry Bailie, a merry fellow, the humour of whose character, which is admirably drawn by the poet, is greatly heightened by the circumstance of his having a shrew for his wife. It is with great justice that Mr. Dryden remarks that from that precise and judicious enumeration of circumstances contained in this and the other characters of Chaucer, 'he was enabled to form an idea of the humours, the features, and the 'very dress of the pilgrims, as distinctly as if he had supped with them 'at the Tabarde in Southwark.'

† It is very remarkable that Cowley could never relish the humour

In the prologues the following particulars relating to music are observable; and first in that of the 'squire it appears that

> He coude fonges make and wel endite,
> Jufte, and eke daunce, portray, and wel write.

And that the prioress,

> - - - - - called dame Eglentine,
> Ful wel fhe fong the fervice devine,

Of the Frere it is said that

> - - - certainly he had a mery note,
> Wel coude he finge and plain on a Rote.

And that

> In harping whan he had fong
> His eyen twinkeled in his hed aright,
> As done the fterres in a frofty night.

From the character of the clerk of Oxenforde we learn that the Fiddle was an instrument in use in the time of Chaucer.

> For him was leuer to haue at his beddes heed
> Twenty bookes cladde with blacke or reed,
> Of Ariftotle and of his philofophie,
> Than robes riche, or fiddell, or gay fautrie.

And of the miller the author relates that

> A baggepipe well couth he blowe and foune.

In the Cook's Tale is an intimation that the apprentice therein mentioned could sing and hop, i. e. dance, and play on the Getron and Ribible; and in the romaunt of the Rose is the following passage:—

> There mighteft thou se thefe Flutours,
> Minftrals, and eke Joglours,
> That well to fing did her paine,
> Some fong fonges of Loraine,
> For in Loraine her notes be
> Ful fweter than in this countre.—Fol. 119, b.

From the passages above-cited we learn that the son of a knight, educated in a manner suitable to his birth, might be supposed to be able to read, write, dance, pourtray, and make verses. That in convents the nuns sang the service to the musical notes. That the Lute, the Rote, the Fiddle, the Sautrie, the Bagpipe, the Getron, the Ribible, and the Flute, were instruments in common use: Speght supposes the appellative Rote to signify a musical instrument used in Wales, mistaking the word, as Mr. Urry suspects, for Crota, a crowd; but Dr. Johnson in his Dictionary, makes it to mean a Harp, and cites the following passage from Spenser:—

> Worthy of great Phæbus rote,
> The triumphs of Phlegrean Jove he wrote,
> That all the gods admired his lofty note.

But in the Confessio Amantis of Gower is the following passage:—

> He taught hir, till fhe was certene
> Of Harpe, Citole,‡ and of Riote,
> With many a tewne, and many a note.—Fol. 178, b.

of Chaucer. Dryden relates the fact, and gives his authority for it in these words:—'I have often heard the late earl of Leicester say that 'Mr. Cowley himself was of opinion that Chaucer was a dry old 'fashioned wit, not worth receiving; and that having read him over at 'my lord's request, he declared he had no taste of him.' Pref. to Dryden's Fables.

This fact is as difficult to account for as another of a similar kind; Mr. Handel made no secret of declaring himself totally insensible to the excellencies of Purcell's compositions.

‡ Citole, in the passage above-cited from Gower is derived from Cistella, a little chest, and probably means a dulcimer, which is in truth no other than a little chest or box with strings on the lid or top.

Upon which it is observable that the words Harpe and Riote, or Rote, occur in the same line, which circumstance imports at least a doubt, whether in strictness of speech they can be said to be synonymous. The word Sautrie is clearly a corruption of Psaltery, a kind of harp; Getron or Getern has the same signification with Cittern; and Ribible or Rebible, is said by Speght and Urry to mean a Fiddle, and sometimes a Getern. The names of certain other instruments, not so easy to explain, are alluded to in the following list of musicians attending king Edw. III. extracted from a manuscript-roll of the officers of his household, communicated by the late Mr. Hardinge of the House of Commons :—*

Mynstrells.	Trompetters	-	-	5
	Cytelers†	-	-	1
	Pypers	-	-	5
	Tabrete	-	-	1
	Mabrcrs	-	-	1
	Clarions	-	-	2
	Fedeler	-	-	1
	Wayghtes ‡	-	-	3

As to the organ, it was clearly used in churches, long before the time of Chaucer: he mentions it in the tale of the Nun's Priest; and what is somewhat remarkable, with epithet of merry,—

His voice was merier than the mery Orgon
On maffe daies, that in the churches gon.

Other particulars occur in the prologues, which as they relate to modes of life, are characteristic of the times, and tend to elucidate the subject of the present enquiry; as that at Stratford, near Bow in Middlesex, was a school for girls, wherein the French language, but very different from that of Paris was taught, and that at meals, not to wet the fingers deep in the sauce was one sign of a polite female education. And here it may not be improper to remark that before the time of king James the First, a fork was an implement unknown in this country. Tom Coriate the traveller learned the use of it in Italy, and one which he brought with him from thence was here esteemed a great curiosity.§ But to return to Chaucer: al-

though forbidden by the canon law to the clergy, it appears from him that the monks were lovers of hunting, and kept greyhounds—that serjeants at law, were as early as the time of Edward the Third, occasionally judges of assize, and that the most eminent of them were industrious in collecting Doomes, i. e. judicial determinations, which by the way did not receive the appellation of Reports till the time of Plowden, who flourished in the reign of Elizabeth, before which persons were employed at the expense of our kings to attend the courts at Westminster, and take short notes of their decisions for the use of the public : || a series of these is now extant, and known to the profession of the law by the name of Year-books — that the houses of country gentlemen abounded with the choicest viands—that a haberdasher, a carpenter, a weaver, a dyer, and a maker of tapestry, were in the rank of such citizens as hoped to become aldermen of London; and that their wives claimed to be called Madam—That cooks were great cheats, and would dress the same meat more than once—That the masters of ships were pirates, and made but little conscience of stealing wine out of the vessels of their chapmen when the latter wore asleep —That physicians made astrology a part of their study—That the weaving of woollen cloth was a very profitable trade, and that the neighbourhood of Bath was one of the seats of that manufacture—That a pilgrimage to Rome, nay to Jerusalem, was not an extravagant undertaking for the wife of a weaver—That the mercenary sort of clergy were accustomed to flock to London, in order to procure chauntries in the cathedral of St. Paul ¶—That at the Temple the members were not more than thirty,** twelve of whom

* Of the several instruments above-mentioned it seems that the harp was the most esteemed. It is well known that king Alfred himself played on the harp: and we are told by Walter Hemingford in his Chronicle, published by Dr. Thomas Gale, in the Hist. Brit. et Ang. otherwise called the XV. Scriptores, vol. III. p. 591, that Edward I. while he was prince of Wales, and in the Holy Land, was attended by a Citharedus or harper; and it is probable that he had contracted a love for this instrument in some of those expeditions into Wales, which he undertook in the life-time of his father Hen. III. The same author relates that it was this harper that killed the assassin who stabbed Edward with a poisoned knife at Ptolemais. The manner of it is thus described by him :—'After the prince had received the wound he wrested 'the knife from the assassin, and ran it into his belly: his servant [the 'harper] alarmed by the noise of the struggle, rushed into the room, and 'with a stool beat out his brains.' See also Fuller's Hist. of the Holy War, book IV. chap. 29.

† From CITOLE, above explained.

‡ 'WAYGHTES or WAITS,' are Hautbois. Butler, Principles of Music, ag. 93. It is remarkable of this noun that it has no singular number; for we never say a Wait, or the Wait, but the Waits. In the Etymologicum of Junius the word is used to signify the players on these instruments, and is thus explained :—['WAITS, lyricines, tibicines, ci-'tharædi, f. à verb, to wait, quia sc. magistratus et alios in pompis instar 'stipatorum, sequunter, vel à G. guet, vigilia, guetter, quia noctu ex-'cubias agunt quæ eandem agnoscunt originem ac nostrum watch, 'vigiliæ.' Skin.

§ 'Here I wil mention a thing that might have been spoken of before in discourse of the first Italian towne. I observed a custome in all those Italian cities and townes through the which I passed, that is not used in any other country that I saw in my travels, neither doe I thinke that any other nation of Christendome doth use it, but only Italy.

'The Italian, and also most strangers that are commorant in Italy, doe 'alwaies at their meales use a little forke when they cut their meate. 'For while with their knife, which they hold in one hand, they cut the 'meate out of the dish, they fasten their forke, which they hold in their 'other hand, upon the same dish, so that whatsoever he be that sitting 'in the company of any others at meale, should unadvisedly touch the 'dish of meate with his fingers from which all at the table doe cut, he 'will give occasion of offence unto the company, as having transgressed 'the lawes of good manners, insomuch that for his error he shall be at 'the least brow-beaten, if not reprehended in wordes. This forme of 'feeding I understand is generally used in all places of Italy, their forks 'being for the most part made of yron or steele, and some of silver, but 'those are used only by gontlemen. The reason of this their curiosity is, 'because the Italian cannot by any meanes indure to have his dish 'touched with fingers, seeing all mens fingers are not alike cleane. 'Hereupon I myselfe thought good to imitate the Italian fashion by this 'forked cutting of meato, not only while I was in Italy, but also in 'Germany, and oftentimes in England since I came home; being once 'quipped for that frequent using of my forke by a certain learned gentle-'man, a familiar friend of mine, one M. Laurence Whitaker, who in his 'merry humour doubted not to call me at table Furcifer, only for using 'a forke at feeding, but for no other cause.' Coriate's Crudities, pag. 90.

|| Pref. to 3d. Rep.

¶ Besides such clerks as held chauntries in the nature of benefices, there were others who were mere itinerants, wandering about the kingdom, and seeking employment by singing mass for the souls of the founders. Fuller says that the ordinary price for a mass sung by one of these clerks was four pence; but that if they dealt in the gross, it was forty marks for two thousand. Worthies in Essex, pag. 339.

** This account of the number of members in one of the principal inns of court must appear strange in comparison with the state of those seminaries at this time, unless we suppose, as perhaps we ought, that Chaucer means by the persons to whom the manciple is servant, Benchers, and not those of a less standing. In the reign of Henry the Sixth the students in each of the inns of court were computed at two hundred; and these bear but a small proportion to their numbers at this day. The reason given by Fortescue for the smallness of their number in his time is very curious, and is but one of a thousand facts which might be brought to prove the vast increase of wealth in this country. His words are these :—'In these greater innes there can no student be maintained 'for lesse expenses by the year then twenty markes, and if he have 'a servant to waite upon him, as most of them have, then so much the 'greater will his charges be. Now, by reason of this charges, the 'children onely of noblemen do study the lawes in those innes, for the

were qualified to be stewards to any peer of the realm —That their manciple was a rogue, and had cunning enough to cheat them all—That stewards grew rich by lending their lords their own money. The summoner, an officer whose duty it is to execute the process of the ecclesiastical court, is a character now grown obsolete; from that which Chaucer has given of one, we however learn that they were a sort of men who throve by the incontinence of the common people, that they affected to speak Latin, that is to say, to utter a few of those cant phrases which occur in the practice of the consistory, and other ecclesiastical courts; and that they would for a small fee suffer a good fellow to have his concubine for a twelvemonth. That they were of counsel with all the lewd women in the diocese, and made the vulgar believe that the pains of hell were not more to be feared than the curse of the archdeacon.*

These several particulars, extracted from the prologues to the Tales, exhibit, as far as they go, a lively and accurate representation of the manners of the people of England in Chaucer's time; but these are few in comparison with the facts and circumstances to the same purpose which are to be met with in the tales themselves; nor are the portraits of the principal agents in the tales, and which accidentally occur therein, less exact than those contained in the prologues. The scholar Nicholas, in the Miller's Tale, is an instance of this kind; for see how the poet has described him.

He represents him as young, amorous, and learned; not a member of any college, for there were but few at Oxford in Chaucer's time, but living 'at his friends finding and his rent,' and lodging in the house of a carpenter, an old man, who had a very young and beautiful wife. In the house of this man the scholar had a chamber, which he decked with sweet herbs; he is supposed to study astronomy, or rather astrology; his chamber is furnished with books great and small, among which is the Almagist, a treatise said to be written by Ptolemy; an Asterlagour, or Astrolabe, an instrument used for taking the altitude of the sun and stars. He has also a set of Augrim Stones,† a kind of pebbles at that time made use of

in numeral computation, and to which counters afterwards succeeded, and above all lay his musical instrument.

His rival Absolon, the parish clerk, is of another cast, a spruce fellow, that sung, danced, and played on the Fiddle; that was great with all the tapsters and brew-house girls in the town, and 'visited them 'with his solace.' His ingenuity and learning qualified him to let blood, clip hair, shave, and make a charter of land, or an acquittance. His employment in the church obliged him to assist the parish priest in the performance of divine service; and it appears to have been his duty on holidays to go round the church with a censer in his hand, conformable to the practice of the times, 'censing the wives of the parish.' But nothing can be more picturesque than the description of his person and dress. His hair shone like gold, and strutted broad like a fan; his complexion red, and his eyes grey as a goose; and the upper leathers of his shoes were carved to resemble the windows of St. Paul's cathedral; his stockings were red, and his kertle or upper coat of light watchet, that is to say sky-colour, not tied here and there, merely to keep it close, but thick set with points,‡ more for ornament than use; all which gay habiliments were covered with a white surplice.

The Reve's Tale contains the characters of Denyse Simkin, the proud miller of Trompington, and his prouder wife: from the poet's description of them it appears that the husband, as a fashion not inconsistent

metic. Glossary to Chaucer. Gower's definition of the science of arithmetic seems to favour this opinion:—

> Of arithmetic the matere
> Is that of whiche a man may lere,
> What Algorifme in nombre amounteth
> Whan that the wise man accounteth
> After the formel propretee
> Of Algorifmes a, b, c;
> By which multiplicacion
> Is made, and the diminucion
> Of fommes, by the experience
> Of this arte, and of this fcience.
>
> Confessio Amantis, fol. 141. b.

But in a book entitled Arithmetick, or the Ground of Arts, written by Robert Record, doctor in physic, and dedicated to king Edw. VI., afterwards augmented by the famous Dr. John Dee, and republished in 1590 and 1648, 8vo., the word, as also another of the same signification, viz., Arsemetrick, is thus explained:—' Both names are corruptly written, ' Arsemetrick for Arithmetick, as the Greeks call it, and Augrime for ' Algorisme, as the Arabians sound it, which doth betoken the science of 'numbering.' Pag. 8. Augrim stones seem to have been the origin of counters, the use whereof in numerical calculation was continued down to the time of publishing the above book, for the author, pag. 9, says 'the art of arithmetic may be wrought diversely with pen or with coun-'ters:' the powers of these counters were determined by their situation in the higher or lower of six rows or lines; but in this respect there was a difference, the merchants observing one rule, and the auditors of public accounts another.

‡ POINTS were anciently a necessary article in the dress, at least of men; in the ancient comedies and other old books we meet with frequent mention of them; to describe them exactly, they were bits of string about eight inches in length, consisting of three strands of cotton yarn, of various colours, twisted together, and tagged at both ends with bits of tin plate; their use was to tie together the garments worn on different parts of the body, particularly the breeches or hose, as they were called, hence the phrase 'to untruss a point.' With the leather doublet or jerkin buttons were introduced, and these in process of time rendered points useless; nevertheless they continued to be made till of very late years, and that for a particular purpose. On Ascension-day it is the custom of the inhabitants of parishes with their officers to perambulate in order to perpetuate the memory of their boundaries, and to impress the remembrance thereof on the minds of young persons, especially boys; to invite boys therefore to attend this business, some little gratuities were found necessary, accordingly it was the custom at the commencement of the procession to distribute to each a willow wand, and at the end thereof a handful of the points above spoken of; which were looked on by them as honorary rewards long after they ceased to be useful, and were called tags.

'poor and common sort of the people are not able to bear so great charges 'for the exhibition of their children. And marchant men can seldom 'find it in their hearts to hinder their merchandise with so great yearly 'expenses. And thus it falleth out that there is scant any man found 'within the realm skilful and cunning in the lawes, except he be a 'gentleman born, and come of a noble stock. Wherefore they more then 'any other kind of men have a speciall regard to their nobility, and to 'the preservation of their honor and fame. And, to speak uprightly, 'there is in these greater innes, yea, and in the lesser too, beside the 'study of the laws, as it were an university or school of all commendable 'qualities requisite for noblemen. There they learn to sing, and to 'exercise themselves in all kinde of harmony. There also they practice 'dauncing, and other noblemen's pastimes, as they use to do, which are 'brought up in the king's house. On the working dayes most of them 'apply themselves to the study of the law; and on the holie daies to the 'study of holy scripture; and out of the time of divine service to the 'reading of chronicles. For there indeed are virtues studied, and vices 'exiled; so that, for the endowment of vertue, and abandoning of vice, 'knights and barons, with other states, and noblemen of the realm, place 'their children in those innes, though they desire not to have them 'learned in the lawes, nor to live by the practice thereof, but onely upon 'their father's allowance.' De Laudibus Legum Angliæ, cap. 49. Mulcaster's Translation.

* Some of these Prologues, modernized, as it is said, by Mr. Betterton, are printed in the Miscellany of Mr. Pope, in two volumes 12mo. Mr. Fenton, suspecting that they were indeed Pope's, requested of him the sight of Betterton's manuscript, but could never obtain it.

† Augrim is supposed by Mr. Urry to be a corruption of Algorithm, by which he says is meant the sum of the principal rules of common arith-

with his vocation, wore both a sword and a dagger. As to his wife, she is said to have been the daughter of the parson of the town, who on her marriage gave her 'full many a pan of brass;' and because of her birth and her education, for she is said to have been 'fostered in a nunnery,' she was insolent to her neighbours, and assumed the style of Madam. The business which drew the scholars John and Alein to the mill of Simkin, bespeaks the difference which a long succession of years has made in a college life; for the rents of college estates were formerly paid, not in money, but in corn, which it was the business of the manciple to get ground and made into bread. During the sickness of the manciple of Soller's hall at Cambridge, two scholars, with a sack of corn laid on the back of a horse, armed each with a sword and buckler, set out for the mill at Trompington, a neighbouring village. The miller contrives to steal their corn, and the scholars take ample vengeance on him.

From the several passages above-cited and referred to, a judgment may be formed, and that with some degree of exactness, of the manners of the common people of this country; those of the higher orders of men are to be sought for elsewhere. Persons acquainted with the ancient constitution of England, need not be told that it was originally calculated as well for conquest as defence; and that before the introduction of trade and manufactures, every subject was a soldier: this, and the want of that intercourse between the inhabitants of one part of the kingdom and another, which nothing but an improved state of civilization can promote, rendered the common people a terror to each other: and as to the barons, the ancient and true nobility, it might in the strictest sense of a well known maxim in law, be said that the house of each was his castle. The many romances and books of chivalry extant in the world, although abounding in absurdities, contain a very true representation of civil life throughout Europe; and the Forest, the Castle, the Moat, and the Drawbridge, if not the Dungeon,* had their existence long before they became the subjects of poetical description.

It is true the pomp and splendour of the ancient nobility appeared to greater advantage than it would have done, had not the condition of the common people been such as to put it out of the power of any of their own order to rival their superiors; but to the immense possessions of the latter such power was annexed, as must seem tremendous to one who judges of the English constitution by the appearance which it wears at this day. To be short, all the lands in this kingdom were holden either mediately or immediately of the crown, by services strictly military. The king had the power of calling forth his barons, and they their tenants, and these latter their dependents also, to battle; and to levy on them money

and other requisites for the carrying on either offensive or defensive war. At this time we see but little of those pecuniary emoluments arising from the relation between the lord and his tenant, which were then the principal sources of splendour and magnificence in the nobility, and men of large estates; or, in other words, it seems that anciently personal service was accepted in lieu of rent. But here the power and influence attendant on the feudal system breaks forth; the lord was entitled to the wardship of the heir of his freehold tenant under the age of twenty-one, and to the profits of all his estates without account. Nor was this all, he had the power of marrying his ward to whom he pleased; and where the inheritance descended to daughters, the marrying of them to any person above the degree of a villain, was as much the right of the lord as his castle or mansion; and had it been the fate of the four beautiful daughters of the great duke of Marlborough to have lived before the making the statute of king Charles the Second for abolishing tenures in capite, and to have survived their father, being under age, not one of them could have been married without the licence of the king, or perhaps his minister.

A system of civil policy, like that above described could not fail to influence the minds of the people; and in consequence of that jealousy which it had a tendency to excite, they lived in a state of hostility: a dispute about boundaries, the right of hunting, or pursuing beasts of chace, would frequently beget a quarrel, in which whole families, with all their dependants immediately became parties; and the thirst of revenge descended from father to son, so as to seem attached to the inheritance. Many of the old songs and ballads now extant are histories of the wars of contending families; the song of the battle of Otterburn, and the old ballad of Chevy-Chace, with many others in Dr. Percy's collection, are instances of this kind, and were these wanting, a curious history of the Gwedir family, lately published by the learned and ingenious Mr. Barrington, would sufficiently show what a deadly enmity prevailed in those barbarous times among the great men of this kingdom.

It has already been hinted that under the ancient constitution the generality of women lived in a state of bondage; and how near that state approaches to bondage, in which a woman is denied the liberty of choosing the man she likes for a husband, every one is able to see; most of the laws made to preserve their persons from violence were the effects of modern refinement, and sprang from that courtesy which attended the knightly exercise of Arms, concerning the origin of which, as it contributed to attemper the almost natural ferocity of the people, and reflect a lustre on the female character, it may not be improper here to enquire.

CHAP. XLVII.

WHETHER chivalry had its rise from those frequent expeditions for the recovery of the Holy Land, which

---

* When the servants of great families were formerly much more numerous than now, some place of confinement for such as were unruly seems to have been necessary: and it is an indisputable fact that anciently in the houses of the principal nobility, putting them in the stocks was the punishment for drunkenness, insolence, and other offences: the knowledge of this practice will account for the treatment of Kent in king Lear, who by the command of Cornwall is set in the stocks. Within the memory of some persons now living the stocks were used for the above purpose at Sion house, near Isleworth, in Middlesex.

authors mean when they speak of the crusades, or whether crusading was the offspring of chivalry, is a matter of controversy; but whatever be the fact, it is certain that for some time they had a mutual dependence on each other; the military orders of religious were instituted for the sole purposes of guarding the holy sepulchre, and protecting the persons of pilgrims to Jerusalem from violence. During the continuance of the Holy War, as it was called, and for some centuries after, incredible numbers of persons of all conditions flocked from every part of Europe to Jerusalem on pilgrimage; and supposing these vast troops to include, as in fact they did, the sons and daughters of the principal families, it might be truly said that the flower of all Europe were at the mercy not only of the enemies of the Christian faith, but of pirates and land-robbers. Injuries offered to the persons of beautiful and distressed damsels in those perilous expeditions, called forth the resentment of their brave countrymen or fellow Christians, and induced great numbers of young men to engage in their defence, and, well mounted and completely armed, to ride forth in search of adventures. To what length some were hurried by their attention to these calls of humanity, we may in some measure learn from that vast profusion of fabulous compositions, the romances of the eleventh and succeeding centuries, which, though abounding with incredible relations, had their foundation in the manners of the times in which they were written,*

* It is observable that the ancient romances abound with particular descriptions of the shields, devices, and impressions of the combatants at tilts and tournaments; and it is notorious that throughout Europe families are distinguished by what is called their coat armour. The heralds, for the honour of their profession, contend that this method of distinction had its origin in that assignment of a certain badge or cognizance, which Jacob, Genesis, chap xlix. seems to make to his twelve sons, when he resembles Judah to a lion's whelp, and says Zabulon shall be a haven for ships, Isachar an ass, Dan a serpent, &c. Dame Juliana Bernes, who wrote the book of St. Alban's, asserts that Japhet bore arms, and therefore styles him gentlemanly Japhet. But in fact the practice is not to be traced farther back than to the time of the crusades. Sir William Dugdale gave Mr. Siderfin, a barrister of the Inner Temple in the time of Charles the Second, and the collector of the Reports which bear his name, the following account of the origin of coat armour, viz., 'When Richard I. with a great number of his subjects, 'made a voyage to Jerusalem in order to recover it from the Turks, the 'commanders in that expedition distinguished themselves by certain 'devices depicted on their shields; but this invention not being found 'sufficient to answer the end, they made use of silk coats, with their 'devices or arms painted on the back and breast, which silk coats were 'worn over the armour, and from these came the coat which the heralds 'now wear, and hence the term Coat of Arms; and from this time, 'nothing interposing to prevent it, arms became hereditary, descending 'to all the sons, in the nature of Gavelkind.' Vide 1 Inst. 140. From whence by the way it should seem that women are not entitled to the distinction of coat armour, though it is the practice of the heralds to blazon arms for unmarried ladies in a lozenge.

The origin of Supporters is thus accounted for: when the exercises of tilts and tournaments were in use, it was the practice of princes by proclamation to invite, upon particular solemnities, knights, and other persons of martial dispositions, from all parts of Christendom, to make proof of their skill and courage in those conflicts; for which purpose a plain was usually chosen, lists marked out, and barriers erected. Within the lists were pitched the tents of the combatants, and some time before the exercises began, shields were severally placed at the doors of their tents, with their arms and other devices depicted thereon; and as these attracted the eyes of the spectators to view and contemplate them, it was thought an addition to the pomp and splendour of the ceremony that the shields should be supported, and the 'squires or pages of the knights were thought the properest persons for this employment. Fancy, which was ever at work upon these occasions, suggested the thought of dressing these persons in emblematical garbs, suited to the circumstances of those whom they attended. Some of these supporters were made to represent savages, or green Men, seemingly naked, but with green leaves on their heads, and about their loins; some appearing like saracens, with looks that threatened destruction to their beholders; others were habited like palmers or pilgrims, and some were angels. A little stretch of invention led them to assume the figure of lions, griffins, and a world of other forms, and hence the use of supporters became common.

Here it may be observed that the bad success of the holy war had ren-

Particular instances of that knightly bravery which chivalry inspired, are not now to be expected, and we have no other evidence than the testimony of the sage writers of romance to induce a belief that Giants were the owners of Castles, that Dwarfs were their porters, or that they kept beautiful damsels imprisoned in their dungeons: nevertheless it is certain that the exercise of arms had a tendency to excite a kind of emulation in the brave and youthful, which was productive of good consequences, for it gave rise to that quality which we term Courtesy, and is but a particular modification of humanity: it inspired sentiments of honour and generosity, and taught the candidates for the favour of ladies to recommend themselves by the knightly virtues of courage and constancy.

Milton has in a few words described those offsprings of chivalry, tilts and tournaments, in the following lines:—

> Where throngs of knights and barons bold
> In weeds of peace high triumphs hold,
> With store of ladies, whose bright eyes
> Rain influence, and judge the prize
> Of wit, or arms, while both contend
> To win her grace, whom all commend.
> L'ALLEGRO.

From the institution of exercises of this and the like kind, and from the sentiments which they are calculated to inspire, is to be dated the introduction of women on the theatre of life, and the assigning to them those parts which nature has enabled them to act with propriety: and from this time they are to be considered as parties in the common and innocent amusements of life, present at public festivities, and joining in the social and domestic recreations of music and dancing.

These indulgences it must be confessed were the prerogative of ladies, and could not in their nature extend to the lower rank of women: the refinement of the times left these latter in much the same state as it found them: household œconomy, and an attention to the means of thriving, were the distinguishing characteristics of the wives and daughters of farmers, mechanics, and others of that class of life. In a poem intitled the Northern Mother's Blessing to her Daughter, written, as it is said, nine years before the death of Chaucer, which contains a curious representation of the manners of the common people, are a great number of excellent precepts for forming the character of a good housewife, among which are the following:—

> My doughter gif thou be a wife, wifely thou werke,
> Looke euer thou loue God and the holy kirke,
> Go to kirke when thou may, and let for no rayne,
> And then fhall thou fare the bet, when thou God has fayn:
> Full well may they thriue
> That feruen God in their liue,
> My leue dere child.

dered the name of a saracen a terror to all Christendom, and the sign of the saracen's head one of the most common for inns of any in England, is a picture of a giant with great whiskers, and eyes glowing with fire, in short, he is represented in the act of blaspheming. The reason of this may be collected from the following curious anecdote, perhaps first communicated to writing by Mr. Selden:—' When our countrymen came 'home from fighting with the saracens, and were beaten by them, they pictured them with huge big terrible faces (as you still see the sign of the saracen's head is), when in truth they were like other men. But this they did to save their own credits.' Table-talk, Tit. War.

When thou fits in the kirke thy bedes fhalt thou bid ;
Therein make no ianglin with friend ne fib.
Laugh not to fcorne nodir old ne young,
Be of good bering, and haue a good tongue ;
  For after thy bering
    So fhall thy name fpring,
      My, &c,

Gif any man with worfhip defire to wed thee,
Wifely him anfwere, fcorne him not what he bee,
And tell it to thy friends, and hide thou it nought ;
Sit not by him, nor ftand not that fin mow be wrought.
  For gif a flaunder be once rayfed,
    It is not fo fone ftilled,
      My, &c.

What man that fhall wed the fore God with a ring,
Looke thou loue him beft of any earthly thing ;
And meekly him anfwere, and not too fnatching,
So may thou flake his yre and be his darling :
  Faire words flaken yre,
    Suffer and haue thy defire.
      My, &c.

When thou goes by the gate, go not too faft ;
Ne bridle not with thy hede, ne thy fhoulders caft,
Be not of many words, ne fweare not to gret,
All euill vices my doughter thou foryet ;
  For gif thou have an euill name,
    It will turne the to grame,*
      My, &c.

Goe not oft to the towne as it were a gaze,
Fro one houfe to odir for to feeke the maze,
Ne go not to market, thy barrell to fill ;
Ne ufe not the tauerne thy worfhip to fpill :
  For who the tauern ufis,
    His thrift he refufes,
      My, &c.

Gif thou be in place where good drink is on loft,
Wheder that thou ferue, or thou fit fofte ;
Mefurely take thou, and get the no blame ;
Gif thou be drunken it turnes the to fhame.
  Who fo loues meafure and fkill,
    He fhall ofte haue his will,
      My, &c.

Go not to the wraftling, ne fhoting the cock,
As it were a ftrumpet or a giglot.†
Be at home doughter, and thy things tend,
For thine owne profit at the latter end.
  Mery is owne thing to fee,
    My dere doughter I tell it thee,
      My, &c.

Hufewifely fhall thou go on the werk-day :
Pride, reft, and idlenes, put hem cleane away.
And after on the holy day well clad fhalt thou be :
The haliday to worfhip, God will loue the
  More for worfhip of our Lord,
    Than for pride of the world,
      My, &c.

Look to thy meyny, and let them not be ydell :
Thy hufbond out, looke who does much or litell,
And he that does well quite him his meede ;
And gif he doe amiffe amend thou him bidde,
And gif the work be great, and the time ftrait,
Set to thy hond, and make a hufwife's brayd,
  For they will do better gif thou by them ftond :
    The worke is foner done, there as is mony hond,
      My, &c.

And looke what thy men doon, and about hem wend.
At euery deede done be at the tone end :
And gif thou finde any fault, foone it amend ;
Eft will they do the better and thou be neare hand.
  Mikell him behoues to doe,
    A good houfe that will looke to,
      My, &c.

* GRAME, sorrow, vexation, Iɲam, furor. URRY.
† GIGLOT, lascivus, petulans, libidinosus, venereus. JUNIUS.

Looke all thing be well when they worke leauen,
And take thy keyes to the when it is euen ;
Looke all thing be well, and let for no fhame,
And gif thou fo do thou gets thee the lafs blame ;
  Truft no man bett thyfelfe,
    Whileft thou art in thy helth.
      My, &c.

Sit not at euen too long at gaze with the cup
For to waffell and drinke all uppe ;
So to bed betimes at morne rife beliue,
And fo may thou better learne to thriue ;
  He that woll a good houfe keepe
    Muft ofte-times breake a fleepe,
      My, &c.

Gif it betide daughter thy friend fro the fall,
And God fend the children that for bread will call,
And thou haue mickle neede, helpe little or none,
Thou muft then care and fpare hard as the ftone,
  For euill that may betide,
    A man before fhould dread,
  My, &c.

Take heede to thy children which thou haft borne
And wait wel to thy doughters that they be not forlone ;
And put hem betime to their mariage,
And giue them of thy good when they be of age,
  For maydens bene louely,
    But they ben untrufty,
      My, &c.

Gif thou loue thy children hold thou hem lowe,
And gif any of hem mifdo, banne hem not ne blow,
But take a good fmart rod, and beat hem arowe,
Till they cry mercy, and their gilts bee know,
  For gif thou loue thy children wele,
    Spare not the yard neuer a deale,
      My, &c.‡

The foregoing stanzas exhibit a very lively picture of the manners of this country, so far as respects the conduct and behaviour of a class of people, who at the time when they were written, occupied a station some degrees removed above the lowest; and seem to presuppose that women of this rank stood in need of admonitions against incontinence and drunkenness, vices at this day not imputable to the wives of farmers or tradesmen. It is much to be lamented that the means of recovering the characteristics of past ages are so few, as every one must find who undertakes to delineate them. The chronicles and history of this country, like those of most others, are in general the annals of public events; and a history of local manners is wanting in every country that has made the least progress towards a state of civilization. One of the best of those very few good sentiments contained in the writings of the late lord Bolingbroke is this, 'History is philosophy teaching by example.' And men would be less at a loss than they are how to act in many situations, could it be known what conduct had heretofore been pursued in similar instances. Mankind are possessed with a sort of curiosity, which leads them to a retrospect on past times, and men of speculative natures are not content to know that a nation has subsisted for ages under a regular form of government, and a system of laws calculated to promote virtue and restrain vice, but they wish for that intelligence which would enable

‡ The poem from which the above stanzas are taken was printed, together with the stately tragedy of Guistard and Sismond, and a short copy of verses entitled 'The Way to Thrift,' by Robert Robinson, for Robert Dexter, in 1597 ; and in the title-page all the three are said to be 'of great antiquitie, and to have been long reserved in manuscript in the 'studie of a Northfolke gentleman.'

them to represent to their minds the images of past transactions with the same degree of exactness as is required in painting. With what view but this are collections formed of antiquities, of various kinds of medals, of marbles, inscriptions, delineations of ancient structures, even in a state of ruin, warlike instruments, furniture, and domestic utensils. Why are these so eagerly sought after but to supply that defect which history in general labours under ?

Some of our English writers seem to have been sensible of the usefulness of this kind of information, and have gratified the curiosity of their readers by descending to such particulars as the garb, and the recreations of the people of this country. In the description of the island of Britain, borrowed, as it is supposed, from Leland, by William Harrison, and prefixed to Hollinshed's Chronicle, is a very entertaining account of the ancient manner of living in England. Stowe is very particular with respect to London, and spends a whole chapter in describing their sports and pastimes. Hall, in his Chronicle, has gone so far as to describe the habits of both sexes worn at several periods in this country. Some few particulars relating to the manners of the English, according to their several classes, are contained in that curious little book of Sir Thomas Smith, De Republica Anglorum ; others are to be met with in the Intinerary of Fynes Moryson, and others to the last degree entertaining in that part of the Intinerary of Paul Hentzner, published by the honourable Mr. Walpole in 1757, with the title of a Journey into England in 1589.

These it is presumed are the books from which a curious enquirer into the customs and manners of our forefathers would hope for information ; but there is extant another, which though a great deal is contained in it, few have been tempted to look into ; it is that entitled De Proprietatibus Rerum, of Bartholomæus, written originally in Latin, and translated into English by John Trevisa, in the year 1398. Of the author and translator the following is an account :—

The author Bartholomæus, surnamed Glantville, was a Franciscan friar, and descended of the noble family of the earls of Suffolk, The book, De Proprietatibus Rerum, was written about the year 1366. Trevisa was vicar of the parish of Berkeley, in the year 1398, and favoured by the then Earl of Berekeley, as appears by the following note at the end of this his translation, which fixes also the time of making it.*

' Endlefs grace, blyffe, thankyng, and prayfyng unto
' our Lorde God omnipotent be giuen, by whoos ayde
' and helpe this tranflacyon was ended at Berkeleye
' the fyxte daye of Feuerer, the yere of our Lord
' M.ccclxxxxviii. the yere of the reyne of kynge
' Rycharde the feconde, after the conquefte of Englonde
' xxii. The yere of my lordes aege fyre Thomas lorde of
' Berkeleye that made me to make this tranflacyon xlvii.'

It seems that the book in the original Latin was printed at Haerlem in 1485 ; but as to the translation, it remained extant in written copies till the time of

Caxton, who first printed it in English, as appears by the Proem of a subsequent impression of it by Wynken de Worde, some time before the year 1500.

It was again printed in 1535 by Thomas Berthelet ; and in 1582, one Stephen Batman, a professor of divinity, as he styles himself, published it with the title of Batman upon Bartholome his booke De Proprietatibus Rerum, with additions. Like many other compilations of those early times, it is of a very miscellaneous nature, and seems to contain the whole of the author's reading on the subjects of theology, ethics, natural history, medicine, astronomy, geography, and other mathematical sciences. What renders it worthy of notice in this place is, that almost the whole of the last book is on the subject of music, and contains, besides a brief treatise on the science, an account of the instruments in use at the time when it was written. This treatise is the more to be valued, as it is indisputably the most ancient of any yet published in the English language on the subject of music, for which reason the whole of it is inserted verbatim in a subsequent part of this work.

The sixth book contains twenty-seven chapters, among which are these with the following titles : De Puero, De Puella, De Ancilla, De Viro, De Patre, De Servis, De Proprietatibus Servi mali, De Proprietatibus boni Servi, De Bono Domino ; these several chapters furnish the characteristics of childhood, youth, and mature age, at the time when this author wrote. And though it is true that this sixth book has little to do with music, and the mention of songs and carols does but occasionally occur in it ; nevertheless the style of this author is, in respect to his antiquity, so venerable, his arrangement of the different classes of life so just, and the picture exhibited by him of ancient manners in this country so lively, and to all appearance true, that a short digression from the purposed work to that of Bartholomeus, will carry its own apology to every inquisitive and curious observer of human life and manners.

Of children he says, that when a child has passed the age of seven years, he is ' fette to lernynge, and ' compellid to take lernynge and chaftyfynge.'†   At

---

* Vid. Tann. Biblioth. Brit. pag. 326. The same Trevisa translated also out of Latin into English the Bible, and the Polychronicon of Ranalph Higden. Ibid. pag. 720.

† In the infancy of literature the correction of children, in order to make them diligent and obedient, seems to have been carried to great excess in this and other countries ; in the poem above-cited, the daughter is exhorted in the education of her children ' not to be sparing of the ' yard,' i. e., not to refrain from beating them with a stick with which cloth is measured ; and it is probably owing to Mr. Locke's Treatise on Education that a milder and more rational method of institution prevails at this day : it seems as if men thought that no proficiency could be made in learning without stripes. When Heloissa was committed to the tuition of Abaelard, he was invested by her uncle with the power of correcting her, though she was then twenty-two years of age. The lady Jane Gray complained very feelingly to Ascham of the pinches, nippes, and bobbes, and other nameless severities which she underwent from her parents in order to quicken her diligence in learning. See a letter of Robert Ascham to his friend Sturmius, in the Epistles of the former, and the Scholemaster of Ascham. Tusser, the author of the Five hundred Points of Husbandry, speaks of his ' toozed ears and bobbed lips,' and other hardships which he sustained in the course of his education ; and mentions with a kind of horror the severity of Udal, the master of Eton school, who gave him at once fifty-three stripes for that which was either none, or at most a very small fault. The cruelty of this man elsewhere appears to have been so great as to afford a reason to many of the boys for running away from the school, as is related by Ascham in his Scholemaster. Even so late as the reign of Charles II. the correction of a young gentleman in the course of his exercises was very common, as appears from the caution which the duke of Newcastle gives to the teachers of the art of horsemanship, not to ' revile their ' pupils with harsh language, nor to throw stones at them,' which, says he ' many masters do, and for that purpose carry them in their pockets.'

that age he says they are 'plyaunt of body, able and
' lyghte to moeuynge, wytty to lerne carolles, and
' wythoute befyneffe, and drede noo perylles more
' thane betynge with a rodde; and they loue an apple
' more than golde.' Farther that they 'loue playes,
' game, and vanytee, and forfake worthynes; and of
' contrarite, for mooft worthy they repute leeft worthy,
' other not worthy, and defire thynges that is to theym
' contrary and greuous; and fette more of the ymage
' of a chylde than of thymage of a man; and make
' forrowe and woo, and wepe more for the loffe of an
' apple than for the loffe of theyr heritage; and the
' goodneffe that is done for theym they lete it paffe out
' of mynde. They defire all thynges that they fe, and
' praye and afke wyth voyce and wyth honde. They
' loue talkynge and counfeylle of fuch children as they
' ben, and voyde company of olde men. They kepe no
' counfeylle, but they telle all that they here: fodenly
' they laugh, and fodenly they wepe: alwaye they
' crye, jangle, and jape, uneth they ben ftylle whyle
' they flepe. Whan they ben waffhe of fylthe, anone
' they defoyle themfelfe ayen; whan the moder waffh-
' ith and kometh them they kick and fpraul, and put
' wyth fete and wyth hondes, and wythftondyth wyth
' al theyr myghte, for they thynke oonly on wombe-
' joy, and knowe not the mefure of their wombes:
' they defire to drynke alwaye uneth they are oute of
' bedde, when they crie for mete an oue.

In the sixth chapter a damsel is thus described:—

[*De Puella.*] 'A mayde, chylde, and a damoyfel
' is callyd *Puella*, as it were Clene and Pure as the
' blacke of the eye. Amonge all thynges that ben
' louyd in a mayden, chaftyte and clenneffe ben louyd
' moft. Men byhoue to take hede of maydens, for
' they ben hote and moyfte of complexyon, and tendre,
' fmale, plyaunt, and fayr of difpofycyon of body.
' Shamfafte, ferdefull, and mery, touchynge with affec-
' cyon, delycate in clothynge, for, as *Senica* fayth,
' that femely clothynge byfemyth to them well that
' ben chafte damoyfels. *Puella* is a name of aege of
' foundnes wythout wem, and alfo of honefte. And
' for a woman is more meker than a man, and more
' enuyous, and more laughynge and louynge, and males*
' of foule is more in a woman than in a man; and fhe
' is of feble kynde, and fhe makyth more lefynges, and
' is more fhamefaft, and more flowe in werkynge, and
' in meuynge, than is a man.

' [*De Ancilla.*] 'A feruant-woman is ordeyned to
' lern the wyues rule as it is put to offyce, aud werke
' of traueyle and of defoyle, and is fedde wyth grete
' mete and fimple, and clothed in foule clothes, and
' kepte lowe under the yocke of thraldom and of fer-
' uage; and yf fhe conceyue a chylde, fhe is yeue in
' thralle, or it be born, and take from the moders
' wombe to feruage. Alfo yf a feruying-woman be of
' bond condycyon fhe is not fuffred to take an hufband
' at her owne wylle: and he that weddyth her, yf he
' be fre afore, he is made bonde after the contracte.
' A bonde-feruaunte-woman is boute and folde lyke
' a beeft; and yf a bonde-feruaunt-man or woman is

*　* Malice.

' made fre, and afterwarde unkynde, he fhall be callyd
' and brought ayen into charge of bondage and
' of thraldom. Alfo a bonde feruant fuffrith many
' wronges, and is bete wyth roddes, and conftreyned,
' and holde lowe wyth dyuerfe and contrary charges
' and trauelles; amonges wretchydnes and woo, uneth
' he is fuffred to refte or to take brethe; and therefore
' amonge all wretchydnes and woo the condycyon of
' bondage and thraldom is moft wretchid. It is oo
' proprite of bonde-feruynge-wymmen, and of them
' that ben of bonde condycyon, to grutche and to be
' rebell and unbuxom to theyr lordes and ladies. And
' whan they ben not holde lowe wyth drede, their
' hertes fwelle, and wer ftoute and proude ayenft the
' commaundmentes of their foueraynes, as it farid of
' *Agar,* a woman of Egypt, feruaunt of *Saira,* for fhe
' fawe that fhe had conceyued, and was wyth chyld,
' and dyfpleyfed her owne lady, and wolde not amende
' her; but then her lady putte her to be fcourged, and
' bete her, and foo it is writ that *Saira* chaftyfed her
' and bete her, &c. Pryde makyth bonde-men and
' wymmem meke and lowe: and goodly loue makyth
' theim prowde, and ftoute, and dyfpiteous; and fo it
' is fayd there it is wrytte, he that nouryffhyth his
' feruant delycatly, he fhall fynde hym rebell at thende.

[*De Viro.*] 'A man is callyd *Vir* in Latyn, and
' hath that name of mighte and uertue, and ftrengthe,
' for in myghte, and in ftrengthe a man paffyth a
' woman. A man is the hede of a woman, as the
' Appoftle fayth, therefore a man is bounde to rule his
' wife, as the heed hath cure and rule of the body.
' And a man is callyd *Maritus,* as it were wardynge
' and defendyng the moder, for he taketh warde and
' kepynge of his wyfe, that is moder of the chyldren,
' and is callyd *Sponfus* alfo, and hath that name of
' *Spondeè,* for he byhotyth and oblygith himfelf; for in
' the contracte of weddinge he plighteth his trouth to
' lede his lyfe wyth hys wyfe, wythout departynge,
' and to paye her dettes, and to kepe and loue her afore
' all other. A man hath foo grete loue to his wyfe,
' that becaufe hereof he auentryth hymfelf to perylles,
' and fettyth her loue afore his moders loue: for he
' dwellyth with his wyfe, and forfakyth his moder and
' his fader, for foo fayth God, a man fhall forfake fader
' and moder, and abyde wyth his wyfe.

' Afore weddynge the fpoufe thynkyth to wynne the
' loue of her that he wowyth, with yefte, and certefyeth
' of his wyll wyth lettres and meffengers, and wyth
' diuerfe prefents, and yeuyeth many yeftes and moche
' good and catayle, and promyfeth moche more; and
' to playfe her puttyth hym to diuerfe playes and games
' among gaderyng of men; and ufe ofte dedes of armes
' of myght and of mayftry; and makyth hym gay and
' femely in dyuerfe clothynge and araye; and all that
' he is prayed to giue thereto for her loue he yeuyeth,
' and dooth anone with all his myght, and denyeth no
' peticyon that is made in her name, and for her loue.
' He fpekyth to her pleyfauntly, and byholdeth her
' cheer in the face wyth pleyfynge and glad cheer, and
' wyth a fharp eye, and affentyth to her at lafte, and
' tellith openly his wyll in prefence of her frendes, and
' fpoufith her with a rynge, and takyth her to wyfe,

' and yeueth her yeftes in token of contract of weddynge,
' and makyth her chartres and dedes of graunt, and of
' yeftes; and makyth reuels, and feeftes, and fpoufayles,
' and yeuyth many good yeftes to frendes and giftes,
' and comfortyth and gladdith his giftes with fonges
' and pypes, and other mynftralfye of mufyke; and
' afterwarde he bringeth her to the pryuitees of his
' chambre, and makyth her felow at borde and at bedd;
' and thene he makyth her lady of money, and of his
' hous meyny.　Thene he hath caufe to her as his
' owne, and takyth the charge and keepynge of her,
' and fpecyally louyingly auyfeth her yf fhe doe amys,
' and takyth of her berynge and gooynge, of fpekynge
' and lokynge; of her paffynge and ayencomynge, and
' entrynge.　Noo man hath more welth than he that
' hath a gode woman to his wyfe, and no man hath
' more woo than he that hath an euyll wyfe, cryenge
' and janglynge, chydynge and fkoldynge, dronklewe
' and unftedfafte, and contrary to hym: coftlewe,
' ftowte, and gaye, enuyous, noyful, lepynge ouer
' londes, moch fufpycyous, and wrathful.

' In a good fpoufe and wyfe byhoueth thife condy-
' cyons, that fhe be befye and deuote in Goddys feruyfe;
' meke and feruyfeable to her hufbonde, and fayre
' fpekynge and goodly to her meyny; merycable and
' good to wretches that ben nedy, eafy and peafyable
' to her neyghbours, ready waar and wife in thynges
' that fhold be auoyed, ryghtfull and pacyent in fuf-
' frynge, befy and dilygente in her doinge, manerly in
' clothyinge, fobre in mouyng, waar in fpekynge,
' chafte in lokynge, honefte in beringe, fadde in goynge,
' fhamfafte amonge the people, mery and gladde amonge
' men wyth her hufbonde, and chafte in pryuyte.
' Such a wyfe is worthy to be prayfed that entendyth
' more to pleyfe her hufbonde wyth her homely word,
' than with her gayly pinchynge and nycetees, and
' defyreth more with vertues than with fayr and gay
' clothes.　She ufyth the goodnes of matrymony more
' bycaufe of chyldren than of flefhly lykynge, and
' more lykynge in chyldren of grace than of kynde.'

BOOK VI.　CHAP. XLVIII.

The description given by Bartholomæus of the several states and conditions of life, refer to the relations of father, mother, son, daughter, and female servant, and the duties resulting from each, adapted to the manners of the fourteenth century, which, though comparatively rude and unpolished, were not so very coarse and sordid as not to admit of those recreations and amusements, which are common to all ages and countries, and are indeed as necessary for the preservation of mental as corporeal sanity, and among these are to be reckoned music and dancing.

Mention has already been made in general terms of those songs and ballads which were the entertainment of the common people; and examples of poetical compositions, suited to the mouths of the vulgar, will occur in their place.

These it may be said are very homely representations of ancient manners: it is true they are, but they are representatives of the manners of homely and uninstructed people, the better sort of both sexes entertaining formerly, as now, very different sentiments; and what respect and civilities were anciently thought due to women of rank and character, may be learned from the feigned conversations between knights and their ladies, with which the old romances abound. Nay, such was the respect paid to the chastity of women, that the church lent its aid to qualify men for its protection; and over and above the engagements which the law of arms required as the condition of knighthood, most of the candidates for that honour, that of the Bath in particular, were obliged to fast, to watch, to pray, and to receive the sacrament, to render them susceptible of it; and their investiture was attended with ceremonies which had their foundation in Gothic barbarism and Romish superstition. How long the idea of sanctity of life and manners continued to make a part of the knightly character, may be inferred from Caxton's recommend-

ation of his Boke of the Ordre of Chyvalry or Knighthood, translated out of French, and imprinted by him, wherein are these words:—' O ye knights
' of Englond! where is the cuftom and ufage of noble
' chyvalry that was ufed in thofe dayes?　What do you
' now, but go to the baynes, [baths,] and play at dyfe?
' and fome not well aduifed, ufe not honeft and good
' rule, agayn all order of knighthood.　Leue this, leue
' it, and rede the noble volumes of Saynt Greal,* of
' Lancelot, of Galaad, of Triftram, of Perfeforeft, of
' Percyual, of Gawayne, and many mo: There fhall
' ye fee manhode, curtoys, and gentlenes; and loke in

* The noble volume thus entitled is said to be no other than the romance of Sir Launcelot of the Lake, and King Arthur and his Knights. See the Supplement to the translator's preface to Jarvis's Don Quixote, where it is also said that St. Greaal was the name given to a famous relic of the holy blood, pretended to have been collected into a vessel by Joseph of Arimathea, and that the ignorance of the times led men to the belief that it was the name of a knight. Huetius, in his Treatise on the Origin of Romances, says that Kyrie Eleison [Lord have mercy on us] and Paralipomenon [the title of the two books of Chronicles] and another eminent writer adds the word Deuteronomy, were in like manner taken for the names of saints or holy men. Other instances to this purpose might be produced, but this that follows of St. Veronica, a holy young woman said to have been possessed of a handkerchief with the impression of Christ's face on it, surpasses all of the kind. Misson, in his Description of the Chapel of the Holy Handkerchief [Le Saint Suaire] at Turin, giving an account of this inestimable relic, relates the story of it in these words:—' It is a pretended veil, or handkerchief which was ' presented (says the tradition) to our Saviour as he was carrying his ' cross (according to St. John) by a maid named Veronica.　They pretend ' that Jesus Christ wiped his face with it, and gave it back to her who ' had presented him with it; and that the face of Jesus Christ remained ' imprinted upon it with some colour.　This is the holy handkerchief, ' Sudarium; and as for Veronica, the devout virgin, 'tis a pretty diverting ' stroke of ignorance: with these words Vera Icon, that is to say, a true ' image or representation (viz., of the face of Jesus Christ) those curious ' doctors have made Veronica, and afterwards they took a fancy that ' Veronica was the name of the pretended young woman supposed by ' themselves to have presented her handkerchief to our Saviour.　The ' Sudarium was carried from Chamberry in the year 1532, the chapel ' where it was at Chamberry having been accidentally burnt.　There are ' five or six more at Rome and other places.　See Reifkius de Imagini- ' bus Christi, and Bede de Locis sanctis.'　Misson's new voyage to Italy, London, 1714, vol. II. part II. pag. 388.　The famous story of the eleven thousand virgins is as void of foundation in historical truth as that above related.　It arose thus: some blunderer seeing in a calendar upon the twelfth of the calends of November, Undecimilla, Virgo & Martyr, read Undecim mille; and of course Virgines & Martyres.　Undecimilla, a diminutive of Undecima, was undoubtedly the name of a woman, probably the eleventh child of her parents, who might have been a martyr.　Vide Pref. to Castley's Catalogue of the Manuscripts of the King's Library, pag. xvii.

'latter dayes of the noble actes fyth the conquefte, as
'in king Richard's days, Cuer de Lion: Edward I. and
'III. and his noble fonnes: Sir Robert Knolles, &c.
'Rede, Froiffart. Alfo behold that victorious and
'noble king, Harry the Fifth, &c.'

But to reassume the proposed discrimination between the manners of the higher and lower orders of
the people. It is certain that the courtesy and
urbanity of the one was at least equal in degree to
the rudeness and incivility of the other; for, not to
recur to the compositions of the Provençal poets,
Boccace himself is in his poetical compositions the
standard of purity and elegance. He it is said was
the inventor of the Ottava Rima, of which a modern
writer asserts that it is the noblest concatenation of
verses the Italians have; and the sonnets, and other
poetical compositions interspersed throughout the
Decameron, may serve to shew what a degree of refinement prevailed in the conversations of the better
sort at that early period. If farther proofs were
wanting, the whole of the compositions of Petrarch
might be brought in support of this assertion. The
sonnets of this elegant and polite lover are not more
remarkable for their merit as poetical compositions,
than for charity and purity of sentiment: and much
of that esteem and respect with which women have
long been treated, is owing to those elegant models
of courtship contained in the addresses of Petrarch to
his beloved Laura, which have been followed, not
only by numberless of his own countrymen, but by
some of the best poets of this nation, as namely, the
earl of Surrey, Sir Thomas Wiat, Sir Edward Dyer,
Vere, earl of Oxford, Spenser, Shakespeare, and
others.

A few enquiries touching the recreation of dancing,
will lead us back to the subject of this history, from
which it is to be feared the foregoing disquisition
may be thought a digression; and here it is to be
observed, that even at the times now spoken of,
dancing was the diversion of all ranks of people;
though to ascertain the particular mode of this exercise, and how it differed from that now in use, is a
matter of great difficulty. The art of Orchesography,
or denoting the several steps and motions in dancing
by characters, is a modern invention of a French
master, Mons. Beauchamp, who lived in the time of
Lewis XIV., though it has been improved and perfected by another, namely, Mons. Feuillet: * and of
the several kinds of dance in fashion in the days of
queen Elizabeth, we know little more than the names,
such as the Galliard, the Pavan,† the Coranto, and
some others. Sir Thomas Elyot, in his book called
the Governor, says in general, that dancing by persons
of both sexes is a mystical representation of matrimony,

these are his words: 'It is diligently to be noted that
'the company of man and woman in dancing, they
'both observing one number and time in their
'movings, was not begun without a special consider-
'ation, as well for the conjunction of those two per-
'sonnes, as for the imitation of sundry vertues which
'be by them represented.‡

'And forasmuch as by the joyning of a man and
'woman in dauncing may be signified matrimony,
'I could in declaring the dignitie and comoditie of
'that sacrament make intier volumes if it were not
'so commonly knowen to al men, that almost every
'frier lymitour caryeth it written in his bosome.'§

And elsewhere he says, 'In every daunce of
'a most ancient custome ther daunced together a man
'and a woman, holding each other by the hand or
'by the arme, which betokeneth concord. Now it
'behoveth the dauncers, and also the beholders of
'them, to know al qualities incident to a man, and
'also al qualities to a woman likewise appertaining.'‖

A little farther he speaks of a dance called the
Braule, by which he would have his reader understand a kind of dancing, the motions and gesticulations whereof are calculated to express something
like altercation between the parties: whether this
term has any relation to that of the Bransle of
Poitiers, which occurs in Morley's Introduction, may
be a matter of some question: Minshew and Skinner
derive it from the verb Bransler, Vibrare, to brand-
ish; the former explains the word Braule, by saying
it is a kind of dance. Phillips is more particular,
calling it 'a kind of dance in which several persons
'danced together in a ring, holding one another by
'the hand.'

Over and above this particular specification of one
of the old dances, Sir Thomas Elyot mentions some
other kinds, as Bargenettes, Pavyons, Turgyons,¶
and Roundes, concerning which he says, 'that as for
'the special names, they were taken as they be now,
'either of the names of the first inventours, or of
'the measure and number that they do conteine; or
'of the first words of the dittie which the song
'comprehendeth, whereoff the daunce was made.
'In every of the said daunces there was a continuitie
'of moving the foote and body, expressing some
'pleasaunt or profitable affects or motions of the
'mind.'**

This account carries the present enquiry no farther
back than to somewhat before the author's time, who
flourished under Henry the Eighth, and whose book
is dedicated to that monarch; and therefore what

---

‡ Pag. 69. a.
§ Ibid.
‖ Ibid. 69. b.
¶ Of the word Bargenett there is no explanation to be met with in
any of our lexicographers, and yet in the collection of poems entitled
England's Helicon, is one called the Barginet of Antimachus. Skinner
has Bargaret, Tripudium Pastoritium, a dance used by shepherds, from
the French Berger a shepherd. For Turgyon no signification is to be
found.

The Pavan, from Pavo, a peacock, is a grave and majestic dance; the
method of performing it was anciently by gentlemen, dressed with a cap
and sword; by those of the long robe in their gowns; by princes in their
mantles; and by ladies in gowns with long trains, the motion whereof
in the dance resembled that of a peacock's tail. This dance is supposed
to have been invented by the Spaniards. Grassineau says its tablature on
the score is given in the Orchesographia of Thoinet Arbeau. Every
Pavan has its Galliard, a lighter kind of air, made out of the former.

** Ibid. 68. b.

---

* Furetiere, in his Dictionary, ascribes this invention to one Thoinet
Arbeau, a Frenchman, mentioned by Walther in his Musical Lexicon,
pag 43, to have published in 1558, a book with the title of Orcheso-
graphie. Furetiere confesses he never could get a sight of the book; but
Mr. Weaver, the dancing-master, who had perused it, says that it treats
on dancing in general, beating the drum, and playing on the fife; and
contains nothing to the purpose of the Orchesography here spoken of.
Feuillet's book was translated into English, and published by Mr. Weaver
about the beginning of this century. Vide Weaver's Essay towards an
History of Dancing, 12mo. pag. 171.

† See an explanation of these two words in the opposite note. The
Coranto is of French original, and is well understood to mean a kind of
dance resembling running.

kind of dances were in use during the preceding century cannot at this distance of time be ascertained.

It is highly probable that in this period the Morrice Dance was introduced into this and other countries; it is indisputable that this dance was the invention of the Moors, for to dance a Morisco is a term that occurs in some of our old English writers. The lexicographers say it is derived from the Pyrrhic dance of the ancients, in which the motions of combatants are imitated. All who are acquainted with history know, that about the year 700 the Moors being invited by count Julian, whose daughter Cava, Roderic king of Spain had forced, made a conquest of that country; that they mixed with the natives, built the city of Granada, and were hardly expelled in the year 1609. During their continuance in Spain, notwithstanding the hatred which the natives bore them, they intermarried with them, and corrupted the blood of the whole kingdom: many of their customs remain yet unabrogated; and of their recreations, the dance now spoken of is one. The practice of dancing with an instrument called the Castanet, formed of two shells of the chesnut, is so truly of Moorish original, that at this day a puppet-show is hardly complete without a dance of a Moor to the time of a pair of Castanets, which he rattles in each hand. Nay, the use of them was taught in the dancing-schools of London till the beginning of the present century; and that particular dance called the Saraband is supposed to require, as a thing of necessity, the music, if it may be called so, of this artless instrument.*

But to return to the Morrice Dance, there are few country places in this kingdom where it is not known; it is a dance of young men in their shirts, with bells at their feet, and ribbons of various colours tied round their arms, and slung across their shoulders. Some writers, Shakespeare in particular, mention a Hobby-horse and a Maid Marian, as necessary in this recreation. Sir William Temple speaks of a pamphlet in the library of the earl of Leicester, which gave an account of a set of morrice-dancers in king James's reign, composed of ten men or twelve men, for the ambiguity of his expression renders it impossible to say which of the two numbers is meant, who went about the country: that they danced a Maid Marian, with a tabor and pipe, and that their ages one with another made up twelve hundred years.† It seems by this relation, which the author has given with his usual inaccuracy of style and sentiment, that these men were natives of Herefordshire.

It seems that about the year 1400 the common country dance was not so intricate and mazy as now. Some of the ancient writers, speaking of the Roundelay or Roundel, as a kind of air appropriated to dancing, which term seems to indicate little more

than dancing in a circle with the hands joined. Stowe intimates that before his time the common people were used to recreate themselves abroad, and in the open air, and laments the use of those diversions which were followed within doors, and out of the reach of the public eye; and while dancing was practised in fields and other open places, it seems to have been no reproach to men of grave professions to join in this recreation, unless credit be given to that bitter satire against it contained in the Stultifera Navis, or the Ship of Fools, written in Dutch by Sebastian Brant, a lawyer, about the middle of the fifteenth century, afterwards translated into Latin by James Locher, and thence into English by Alexander Barclay, in which the author thus exclaims against it :—

' What els is daunſing, but even a nurcery,
' Or els a bayte to purchaſe and mayntayne
' In yonge heartes the vile ſinne of ribawdry,
' Them fettring therin, as in a deadly chayne ?
' And to ſay truth, in wordes cleare and playne,
' Generous people have all their whole pleaſaunce
' Their vice to noriſhe by this unthrifty daunce.

' Then it in the earth no game is more damnable :
' It ſemeth no peace, but battayle openly ;
' They that it uſe of mindes ſeme unſtable,
' As mad folk running with clamour ſhout and cry.
' What place is voide of this furious folly ?
' None, ſo that I doubt within a while
' Theſe fooles the holy church ſhall defile.

' Of people what ſort or order may we find,
' Riche or poore, hye or lowe of name,
' But by their fooliſhness and wanton minde,
' Of eche ſorte ſome are geven unto the ſame.
' The prieſtes and clerkes to daunce have no ſhame ;
' The frere or monke in his frocke and cowle,
' Muſt daunce in his doctor, leping to play the foole.

' To it comes children, maydes, and wives,
' And flatering yonge men to ſee to haue their pray,
' The hande in hande great falſhode oft contrives,
' The old quean alſo this madneſs will aſſay ;
' And the olde dotarde, though he ſcantly may,
' For age and lamenes ſtyrre eyther foote or hande,
' Yet playeth he the foole with other in the bande. ‡

' Do away with your daunces yc people much unwiſe,
' Defiſt your fooliſhe pleaſure of travayle :
' It is methinke an unwyſe uſe and gyfe
' To take ſuche labour and payne without avayle.

The same author censures as foolish and ridiculous the custom of going about the streets with harps, lutes, and other instruments by night; and blames

---

* 'I remember, said an old beau of the last age (speaking of his mother as one of the most accomplished women of her time) 'that when 'Hamet Ben Hadgi, the Morocco ambassador, was in England, my 'mother danced a saraband before him with a pair of Castanets in each 'hand; and that his excellency was so delighted with her performance, 'that as soon as she had done he ran to her, took her in his arms, and 'kissed her, protesting that she had half persuaded him that he was in 'his own country.'

† Miscel. part III. pag. 277.

‡ It seems that the recreation of dancing was in ancient times practised by men of the gravest professions. It is not many years since the Judges, in compliance with ancient custom, danced annually on Candlemas-day in the hall of Serjeant's Inn, Chancery-lane. Dugdale, speaking of the revels at Lincoln's Inn, gives the following account of them :—
'And that nothing might be wanting for their encouragement in this 'excellent study [the law] they have very anciently had Dancings for 'their recreations and delight, commonly called revels, allowed at certain 'seasons; and that by special order of the society, as appeareth in '9 Hen. VI. viz., that there should be four revels that year, and no 'more; one at the feast of All-hallown, another at the feast of St. Erken-'wald; the third at the feast of the Purification of our Lady; and the 'fourth at Midsummer-day, one person yearly elected of the society 'being made choice of for director in those pastimes, called the master 'of the revels. Which sports were long before then used.' And again he says, 'Nor were these exercises of dancing merely permitted, but 'thought very necessary, as it seems, and much conducing to the 'making of gentlemen more fit for their books at other times; for by an 'order made 6th Feb. 7 Jac. it appears that the under barristers were by 'decimation put out of commons for example's sake, because the whole 'bar offended by not dancing on Candlemas-day preceding, according to 'the ancient order of this society when the judges were present; with 'this that if the like fault were committed afterwards they should be 'fined or disbarred.' Dugd. Orig. Jurid. cap. 64.

young men for singing songs under the windows of their lemans : in short, the practice here meant is that of serenading, which is yet common in Spain, and other parts of Europe, and is allowed by him, even in his time, to have been more frequent abroad than in this country. The verses are very humourous and descriptive, and are as follows :—

'The furies fearful, fprong of the floudes of hell,
'Bereft thefe uagabondes in their minds, fo
'That by no meane can they abide ne dwell
'Within their houfes, but out they nede muft go ;
'More wildly wandring then either bucke or doe.
'Some with their harpes, another with their lute,
'Another with his bagpipe, or a foolifhe flute.

'Then meafure they their fonges of melody
'Before the doores of their lemman deare ;
'Howling with their foolifhe fonge and cry,
'So that their lemman may their great folly heare :

'But yet moreover thefe fooles are fo unwife,
'That in colde winter they ufe the fame madnes.
'When all the houfes are lade with fnowe and yfe,
'O madmen amafed unftable, and witlefs !
'What pleafure take you in this your foolifhnefs ?
'What joy haue ye to wander thus by night,
'Sauc that ill doers alway hate the light ?

'But foolifhe youth doth not alone this ufe,
'Come of lowe birth, and fimple of degree,
'But alfo ftates themfelves therein abufe,
'With fome yonge fooles of the fpiritualtie :
'The foolifhe pipe without all gravitie
'Doth eche degree call to his frantic game ;
'The darknes of night expelleth feare of fhame.

'One barketh, another bleateth like a fhepe ;
'Some rore, fome countre, fome their ballades fayne
'Another from finging geveth himfelf to wepe ;
'When his foveraigne lady hath of him difdayne,
'Or fhutteth him out : and to be fhort and playne,
'Who that of this fort beft can play the knave,
'Looketh of the other the mayftery to have.

'When it is night, and eche fhould drawe to reft,
'Many of our fooles great payne and watching take
'To proue mayftryes, and fee who can drinke beft,
'Eyther at the tauerne of wine or the ale ftake,
'Eyther all night watcheth for their lemmans fake,
'Standing in corners like as it were a fpye,
'Whether that the wether be whot, colde, wet, or dry.'

The passages above-cited are irrefragable evidence, not only that dancing was a favourite recreation with all ranks of people at the period now spoken of, but that even then it was subject to rule and measure : and here a great difficulty would be found to attend our researches, supposing music to have continued in that state in which most writers on the subject have left it : for notwithstanding the great deal which Vossius and other writers have said concerning the Rythmus of the ancients, there is very little reason to think that they had any method of denoting by characters the length or duration of sounds ; the consequence whereof seems to be that the dancing of ancient times must have wanted of that perfection which it derives from its correspondence with mensurable music. Nay if credit be given to the accounts of those writers who ascribe the invention of the Cantus Mensurabilis to Johannes de Muris, we shall be at a loss to account for the practice of regular dancing before the commencement of the fourteenth century ; but if the Cantus Mensurabilis be attributed to Franco, the scholastic of Liege, who flourished in

the eleventh century, the antiquity of regular dancing is removed near three hundred years farther back. This historical fact merits the attention of every curious enquirer into the history and progress of music, not only as it carries with it a refutation not of a vulgar, but of a general and universal error, but because without the knowledge of it the idea of dancing to regular measures before the year 1330, is utterly inconceivable.*

CHAP. XLIX.

THE æra of the invention of mensurable music is so precisely determined by the account herein before given of Franco, that it is needless to oppose the evidence of his being the author of it to the ill-grounded testimony of those writers who give the honor of this great and last improvement to De Muris : nevertheless the regard due to historical truth requires that an account should be given of him and his writings, and the order of chronology determines this as the proper place for it.

JOHANNES DE MURIS was a doctor of the Sorbonne, and flourished in the fourteenth century. Mersennus styles him ' Canonicus et Decanus Ecclesiæ Paris-' iensis.'† The general opinion is, that he was a native of Normandy ; but bishop Tanner has ranked him among the English writers ; in this he has followed Pits,‡ who expressly asserts that he was an Englishman ; and though the Oxford antiquary, following the French writers, says that he was a Frenchman of Paris,§ the evidence of his being a native of England is stronger than even Pits or Tanner themselves were aware of ; for in a very ancient manuscript, which it no where appears that either of them had ever seen, and of which a very copious account will hereafter be given, are the following verses :—

'Ihon de Muris, variis floruitque figuris,
'Anglia cantorum nomen gignit plurimorum.

Monsieur Bourdelot, the author of the Histoire de la Musique ct sos Effets, in four tomes, printed at Paris in 1715, and at Amsterdam in 1725, has grossly erred in saying of De Muris, that he lived in 1553 ; for it was more than two hundred years before that time, that is to say in 1330, that we are told by writers of the greatest authority he flourished. To shew his mistake in some degree we need only appeal to Franchinus, who in his Practica Musicæ, printed in 1502, lib. II., besides that he gives the several characters of which De Muris is said to have been the inventor, cap. 13, expressly quotes him by name, as he does also Prosdocimus Beldemandis, his commentator, cap. 4. Glareanus also in his Dodeca-chordon, published at Basil in 1540, has a chapter De Notarum Figuris, and has given compositions

* Franco is supposed to have invented the Cantus Mensurabilis about the year 1060 ; and it is certain that Guido reformed the scale about the year 1028. It is very remarkable that two such considerable improvements in music should be made so nearly together as that the difference in point of time between the one and the other should be less than forty years.
† Harmonic. lib. I. prop. xxv. pag. 8.
‡ Append. 872.
§ Athen. Oxon. 407.

of sundry musicians of that day, in notes of different lengths, that could not have existed, if we suppose that De Muris invented these characters, and consequently that they were not known till 1553.

By the account which Bishop Tanner gives of him in his Bibliotheca, it appears that De Muris was a man of very extensive knowledge; and in particular that he was deeply skilled in the mathematics. Indeed the very titles of his books seem to indicate a propensity in the author to the more abstruse parts of learning. His treatise on the Quadrature of the Circle, shews him to have been a geometer; and that on the Alphonsine Tables, an astronomer.*

The tracts on music written by De Muris exist only in manuscript, and appear by Bishop Tanner's account to have been four, namely, one beginning 'Quoniam Musica est de sono relato ad numeros.' 2. Another intitled, 'Artem componendi (metiendi) 'fistulas organorum secundum Guidonem,' beginning 'Cognita consonantia in chordis.' 3. Another with this title 'Sufficientiam musicæ organicæ editam, '(ita habet MS.) à mag. Johanne de Muris, musico 'sapientissimo, et totius orbis subtillissimo experto,' beginning 'Princeps philosophorum Aristoteles.' 4. Another entitled 'Compositionem consonantiarum 'in symbolis secundum Boetium,' beginning 'Omne 'instrumentum musicæ.'† Besides these Mersennus mentions a tract of his entitled Speculum Musicæ, which he had seen in the French king's library, and attentively perused.‡ And Martini has given a short note of the title of another in the words following: 'De Muris Mag. Joan. de Normandia alias Paris-'iensis Practica Mensurabilis Cantus, cum exposit. Prosdocimi de Beldemandis.' Patav. MS. an. 1404.

The manuscripts of De Muris above-mentioned to be in the Bodleian library, have been carefully perused with a view to ascertain precisely the improvements made by him in mensurable music, but they appear to contain very little to that purpose. Nevertheless, from the title of the tract last-mentioned, there can be scarce a doubt but that it is in that that he explains the nature and use of the character used in mensurable music; and there are yet extant divers manuscripts written by monks, chanters, and precentors in the choirs of ancient cathedrals and abbey-churches, mostly with the title of Metrologus, that sufficiently explain the nature of the Cantus Mensurabilis, though none so clearly and accurately as the Practica Musicæ utriusque Cantus of Franchinus. But besides that many of them attribute to De Muris this improvement, they ascribe to him the invention of characters which there is great reason to believe were

not made use of till many years after his decease. In a tract entitled Regulæ Magistri Joannes de Muris, contained among many others in a manuscript collection of musical tracts, herein-before referred to by the appellation of the Manuscript of Waltham Holy Cross, mention is made of the following characters—the Long, the Breve, the Semibreve, the Minim, and the Simple, which can be no other than the Crotchet, inasmuch as two simples are there made equivalent to a minim, and the simple is said to be indivisible, and to be accounted as unity.

Thomas de Walsyngham,§ the author of one of the tracts contained in the above manuscript, and who it is conjectured flourished about the year 1400, makes the number of the characters to be five, namely, the Large, Long, Breve, Semibreve, and Minim. But he adds, that 'of late a New character 'has been introduced, called a Crotchet, which would 'be of no use, would musicians remember that beyond 'the minim no subdivision ought to be made.'

Indeed a strange fatality seems to have attended all the enquiries concerning the particulars of De Muris's improvements; for first no writer has yet mentioned in which of the several tracts, of which he was confessedly the author, they are to be found; secondly, there is a diversity of opinions with respect to the number of characters said to be invented by him. Nay, Mersennus goes so far as to say he had read the manuscripts of Johannes de Muris, which are in the library of the king of France, but never found that he invented any of the characters in modern use.

That these mistaken opinions respecting De Muris and his improvements in music should ever have obtained, is no other way to be accounted for than by the ignorance of the times, and that inevitable obscurity which was dispelled by the revival of literature and the invention of printing. But the greatest of all wonders is, that they should have been adopted by men of the first degree of eminence for learning, and propagated through a succession of ages. The truth is, that in historical matters the authority of the first relator is in general too implicitly acquiesed in; and it is but of late years that authors have learned to be particular as to dates and times, and to cite authorities in support of the facts related by them.

Franchinus indeed may be remarked as an exception to this rule; and whoever peruses his works will find his care in this respect equal to the modesty and diffidence with which he every where delivers his opinion. Now it is worthy of note that throughout his writings the name of De Muris occurs but in very few places; that he ranks him with Marchettus of Padua, Anselmus of Parma, Tinctor, and other writers on the Cantus Mensurabilis; and that he is as far from giving the honour of that invention to De Muris as to Prosdocimus Beldemandis, his commentator. Neither do the authors who wrote

---

* The Alphonsine Tables derive their name from Alphonsus, surnamed the Wise, king of Leon and Castile about the year 1260; a man possessed of so great a share of wisdom, learning, and other great qualities, that we are unwilling to credit Lipsius when he relates, as he does, that having read the Bible fourteen times through, and deeply considered the fabric of the universe, he uttered this impious sentiment:— 'That if God had advised with him in the creation, he would have 'given him good counsel' As to the tables that bear his name, they are founded on the calculations of the ablest astronomers and mathematicians of his time, employed by him for that purpose, and were completed at an expence of not less than four hundred thousand crowns.

† These are all in the Bodleian library, and may easily be found by the help of the printed catalogue, and the references to them in the article MURIS, in Tanner's Bibliotheca.

‡ Harmonic. lib. I. prop. xxv. pag. 8. Harm. univ. part II. pag. 11.

§ The name of this person does not occur in any catalogue of English writers on music. Bishop Tanner mentions two of that name, the one an historian, the other precentor of the abbey-church of St. Alban; that the latter of these was the author of the above-mentioned treatise is very probable. Tanner, pag. 752, in not.

immediately after Franchinus, as namely, Peter Aron, Glareanus, Jacobus Faber Stapulensis, Ottomarus Luscinius, or any other writer of the German or Italian schools before the year 1555, as far as can be collected from an attentive perusal of their works, assert, or even intimate, that the characters now used to denote the length or duration of sounds in music were contrived by Johannes De Muris; and the declaration of Mersennus above-cited may almost be said to be evidence of the contrary. Upon this state of facts a question naturally arises, to what mistaken representation is it owing that the honour of this important improvement in music is ascribed to one who had no title to it, and that not by one, but many writers? for Zarlino, Berardi, and all the Italians, Kircher, Brossard, and Bourdelot relate it with a degree of confidence that seems to exclude all doubt.

An answer to this question is at hand, which upon the face of it has the appearance of probability. In short, this erroneous opinion seems to have been originally entertained and propagated by an author whose character as a musician has held the world in suspense for two centuries; and it seems hardly yet determined whether his ingenuity or his absurdity be the greater. The person here meant is Don Nicola Vicentino, a Roman musician, hereinbefore spoken of, as having attempted to restore the ancient genera, who flourished about the year 1492, and in 1555 published at Rome, in folio, a work entitled L'Antica Musica Ridotta alla moderna Prattica, con la Dichiaratione, et con gli Essempi de i tre Generi, con la loro Spetie, which contains the following relation:—

'After the invention of the hand by Guido, and the 'introduction of the stave with lines, the method to 'express the sounds was by points placed on those 'lines; from whence it became a usual form of com- 'mendation of a cantus for more voices than one, to 'say, "Questo e' un bel contrapunto," "this is a fine "counterpoint;" plainly indicating that the notes 'were placed against each other, and consequently 'that they were of equal measures. But Giovanni de 'Muris, grandissimo Filosofo in the university of 'Paris, found out the method of distinguishing by 'eight characters the notes which we now place on 'the lines and spaces, and also invented those charac- 'ters the circle and semicircle, traversed and un- 'traversed, together with the numbers, as also the 'written marks for pauses or rests; all which were 'added to his invention of the eight characters. 'Others added the round b to e la mi in their com- 'positions, and likewise the mark of four strokes, 'described in this manner ⅏; and so from time to 'time one added one thing, and another another, as 'happened a little while ago, when in the organ to 'the third a la mi re above g sol re ut, a fifth was 'formed in e la mi with a round b, or, as you may 'call it, e la mi flat:* and from those characters '♮ and b, and also this ⅏, many others have been

* This is a very curious anecdote, for it goes near to ascertain the time when many of the transposed keys could not have existed. The author is however mistaken in making e la mi b the fifth to a la mi re, for it is an interval consisting of but three tones. He had better have called it the fourth to b fa, which it truly is.

'invented of great advantage to music, for I am of 'opinion that the characters ♮ and b were the first 'principles upon which were invented the eight 'musical figures now treating of; for John De Muris 'being desirous of distinguishing those several figures 'the Large, Long, Breve, Semibreve, Minim, Semi- 'minim, or Crotchet, Chroma, or Quaver, and Semi- 'chroma, was necessitated to seek such forms as 'seemed to him fittest for the purpose, and by the 'help of these to frame such other characters as could 'be best adapted to musical practice; and to me it 'seems that none could be found so well suited to his 'intention as these two of ♮ and b.

'For first it is to be observed that the breve ◻ is 'derived from ♮, and so also are the large and the 'long; the breve being but ♮ without legs, and the 'large and the long being the same ♮ with one leg, 'with this only difference, that the large ▰ exceeds 'considerably in magnitude the long ▰ . From the 'other of the two characters above-mentioned, viz., b, 'was formed the semibreve O, or ⊙, by cutting off the 'leg. After the philosopher had so far adjusted the 'form of the characters, he assigned them their proper 'names; and first to that note which was simply the ♮ 'without the legs, he gave the name of Breve, thereby 'meaning to express only the shortness of its propor- 'tion in comparison with the figure from whence, as 'has been shewn, it was derived.

'It seems that the breve and the semibreve were 'the roots from whence the several other notes of 'addition and diminution sprang; and seeing that a 'greater variety was wanting, De Muris, for the 'avoiding a multiplicity of characters, as it were gave 'back the leg of the breve, and placing it on the right 'side ▰ , called it a long, giving to it twice the 'value or time of the breve. Farther, he added to 'the long half its breadth ▰ , and called it a large, 'at the same time assigning to it the value of two 'longs.

'From those several characters arose the invention 'of various tyings and bindings, and other com- 'binations, called by modern writers, Ligatures, some 'in a square or horizontal position, and others in a 'direction oblique, and both ascending and descend- 'ing, as the progression of the sounds required; but 'of these it is not here intended to treat.

'Having spoken sufficiently of the origin and use of 'the Breve, the Long, and the Large, it remains to 'account for the invention of the Minim, the Semi- 'minim, Chroma, and Semichroma, which, as have 'already been mentioned, were generated from the 'b round. As to the semibreve, it is clearly the b 'round without a leg; and the minim is no other 'than the semibreve with a stroke, proceeding not 'from either side, but from the middle of the figure 'thus ♢, in order that no confusion might arise from 'its similitude to b. And to this character was 'assigned half the value of the semibreve. From the 'same figure diversified by blackness, and by marks 'added to the leg, the philosopher formed three other 'characters of different values, the first was the semi- 'minim ♩, in value, as its name imports, half the

'minim; and which is no other than the minim
'blackened. To the leg of this semiminim he added
'a little stroke thus ⌡, and thereby reduced it to half
'its value, and called the character thus varied a
'Chroma: he proceeded still farther, and by the
'addition of a little stroke to the chroma formed the
'Semichroma ⌡.' *

Kircher delivers the above as his opinion also, for
after relating the manner of Guido's improvement of
the scale, he expresses himself to the following
purpose:—

'And these were the elements of the figurate
'music of Guido, which, like all other inventions, in
'their infancy, had something I know not what of
'rude and unpolished about it, while, instead of notes,
'points only, without any certain measure or propor-
'tion of time were used, which was the case till about
'two hundred years after, when Joannes de Muris
'resuming the invention of Guido, completed the
'musical art, for from ♮ and b, by which characters
'Guido was accustomed to distinguish certain notes
'in his system, he produced those characters, whereof
'each was double to the preceding one, as to the
'measure of its time; the first note produced from b
'he called the minim, and the same blackened the
'semiminim; the latter character with a tail he
'called Fusa, and that with two tails Semifusa; so
'that there proceeded from b only four different
'species of character, namely, the minim, semiminim,
'fusa, and semifusa; † and from b hard or square ♮
'he formed the remaining notes of a longer time,
'except that from ♮ defective, and wanting both
'tails, he formed the breve, and from b round the
'semibreve.' ‡

After such a testimony as this of Kircher, it may
be unnecessary to add that the modern writers seem
to be as unanimously agreed in attributing the invention of all the characters used to denote the measure
of sounds to De Muris, as they are in ascribing the
reformation of the ancient Greek scale to Guido
Aretinus. But in this they are greatly mistaken,
and the account herein-before given of Franco is
undeniable evidence of the countrary.

Morley, who was a man of learning in his profession, and a diligent researcher into such matters of
antiquity as were any way related to it, has in the
annotations on the first book of his Plain and easie
Introduction to practicall Musicke, given a short
history of the art of signifying the length or duration
of sounds by written characters, which, as it is
curious, is here given in his own words: 'There
'were in old time foure maners of pricking [writing

* The writers on the Cantus Mensurabilis seem to have been hard put
to it to find names for their characters. Franchinus and his followers
call the semiminim Fusa, which in the barbarous Latin signifies a Spindle. Litt. We at this day call it a crotchet, but that name seems more
properly to belong to the quaver, by reason of its curved tail, the word
crotchet being, as Butler says, Princ. of Mus. pag. 28, derived from the
French Croc, a crook. The word Chroma, which in the Greek signifies
Colour, is properly enough given to those characters that are not evacuated, but coloured either black or red; and if so, it is in strictness
common to all the characters under the minim, and cannot be appropriated to the quaver.

† Isaac Vossius censures the terms Maximæ, Longæ, Breves, Semibreves, Minimæ, Semiminimæ, Fusæ, and Semifusæ, as barbarous.
De Poem. Cant. et Virib. Rythmi, pag. 128.

‡ Musurg. tom. I. pag. 556.

'of music], one al blacke, which they termed blacke
'Full, another which we use now, which they called
'blacke Void; the third all red, which they called
'red Ful, the fourth red, as ours is blacke, which they
'called redde Void; al which you may perceive
'thus:—

[PRINTED IN BLACK.]   [PRINTED IN RED.]

'But if a white note (which they called blacke
'voide) happened amongst blacke full, it was di-
'minished of halfe the value; so that a minime was
'but a crotchet, and a semibriefe, a minime, &c. If
'a redde full note were found in blacke pricking, it
'was diminished of a fourth part; so that a semi-
'briefe was but three crotchettes, and a red minime
'was but a crotchette: and thus you may perceive
'that they used their red pricking in al respects as
'we use our blacke noweadaies. But that order of
'pricking is gone out of use now, so that wee use the
'blacke voides as they used their blacke fulles, and
'the blacke fulles as they used the red fulles. The
'redde is gone almost quite out of memorie, so
'that none use it, and fewe knowe what it meaneth,
'Nor doe we pricke anye blacke notes amongst
'white, except a semibriefe thus ▭ in which
'case the semibriefe so blacke is a minime and a
'pricke (though some would have it sung in tripla
'maner, and stand for ⅔ of a semibriefe), and the
'blacke minime a crotchet, as indeede it is. If more
'blacke semibriefes or briefes bee togither, then is
'there some proportion; and most commonly either
'Tripla or Hemiolia, which is nothing but a rounde
'common tripla or sesquialtera. As for the number
'of the formes of notes, there were within these two
'hundred yeares but foure knowne or used of the
'musytions: those were the Longe, Briefe, Semi-
'briefe, and Minime. The minime they esteemed
'the least or shortest note singable, and therefore
'indivisible. Their long was in three maners, that
'is, either simple, double, or triple; a simple long
'was a square form, having a tail on the right side,
'hanging downe or ascending; a double long was so
'formed as some at this daie frame their larges, that
'is as it were compact of two longs. The triple was
'bigger in quantitie than the double; of their value
'we shall speake hereafter. The semibriefe was at
'the first framed like a triangle thus ◢, as it were the
'halfe of a briefe, divided by a diameter thus ◪; but
'that figure not being comly, or easie to make, it
'grew afterward to the figure of a rhombe or loseng
'thus ◆, which forme it still retaineth. The minime
'was formed as it is now, but the taile of it they ever
'made ascending, and called it Signum Minimitatis
'in their Ciceronian Latine. The invention of the
'minime they ascribe to a certaine priest (for who he
'was I know not) in Navarre, or what countrie else
'it was which they tearmed Navernia; but the first
'who used it was one Philippus De Vitriaco, whose
'motetes for some time were of al others best esteemed
'and most used in the chuch. Who invented the

'crotchet, quaver, and semiquaver, is uncertaine.
'Some attribute the invention of the crotchet to the
'afore-named Philip, but it is not to be found in his
'workes; and before the saide Philip the smallest
'note used was a semibriefe, which the authors of
'that time made of two sortes, more and less; for
'one Francho divided the briefe, either in three equal
'partes (terming them semibriefes) or in two unequal
'partes, the greater whereof was called the more
'semibriefe (and was in value equal to the imperfect
'briefe): the other was called the less semibriefe, as
'being but halfe of the other aforesaid. This Francho
'is the most ancient of all those whose workes of
'practical music have come to my handes: one
'Roberto De Haulo hath made as it were commen-
'taries upon his rules and termed them Additions.
'Amongst the rest, when Francho setteth downe that
'a square body having a taile coming downe on the
'right side is a long, he saith thus: "Si tractum
"habeat à parte dextra ascendente, erecta vocatur ut

"hic; ponuntur enim iste longæ erectæ
"ad differentiam longarum quæ sunt rectæ et vocantur
"erectæ quod ubicunque inveniuntur per semitonium
"eriguntur," that is, "if it have a taile on the righte
"side going upwards, it is called erect or raised

"thus: for these raised longes be put
"for difference from others which be right, and are
"raised because wheresoveer they be found, they be
"raised halfe a note higher;" a thing which I be-
'lieve neither he himselfe, nor any other ever saw in
'practice. The like observation he giveth of the
'briefe, if it have a taile on the left side going
'upward. The large, long, briefe, semibriefe, and
'minime (saith Glareanus) have these seventy yeares
'been in use; so that reckoning downeward from
'Glareanus his time, which was about fiftie years
'ago, we shal find that the greatest antiquitie of our
'pricked song is not above 130 years old.' *

The account above-given from Morley is extremely
curious, and coincides with the opinion that De Muris
was not the inventor of the characters for notes of
different lengths; and lest the truth of it should be
doubted, recourse has been had to those testimonies
on which it is founded; and these are evidently the
writings of ecclesiastics and others, who treated on
this part of musical science in the ages preceding
the time when Morley wrote. A valuable collection
of tracts of this kind in a large volume, was extant
in the Cotton library in the year 1731, when a fire
which happened at Ashburnham-house in Westminster, where it was then deposited, consumed many
of the manuscripts, and did great damage to this
and divers other valuable remains of antiquity. It
fortuned however that before that accident a copy
had been taken of this volume by Dr. Pepusch, which
is now extant,† and it appears to contain some of the

tracts expressly referred to by Morley, and by means
thereof we are able not only to clear up many difficulties that must necessarily attend an enquiry into
the state of music during that long interval between
the time of Guido, and the end of the fifteenth century,
when Franchinus flourished, but to establish the
authority of Morley's testimony in this respect beyond
the possibility of a doubt.

The manuscript above-mentioned contains several
treatises, and first that of Roberto De Haulo, as
Morley calls him, though by the way his true name
was Handlo,‡ which he says is a kind of commentary
on the rules of Franco, and are termed Additions.

It is now near four hundred and fifty years since
this copy was made, as appears by an inscription at
the end of it, inporting that it was finished on Friday
next before the feast of Pentecost, a.c. 1326.

Of this writer, Robertus De Handlo, no account
can be found, except in the Bibliotheca of bishop
Tanner, taken from the manuscript above-mentioned.
It is however worth observing that the above date,
1326, carries the supposed invention of De Muris
somewhat farther backward than the time at which
most writers have fixed it.

But, to proceed, in a tract of an uncertain author,
part of the Cotton manuscript above spoken of,
mention is made of red notes, and the reader is
referred to the motetts of Philippus De Vitriaco for
instances of notes of different colours.

Morley says that 'the antient musytions esteemed
'the minime the shortest note singable;' this is in
a great measure confirmed by a passage above-cited
from Thomas De Walsyngham, and is expressly said
by Franchinus. Morley farther says that the invention of the minim is ascribed to a certain priest in
Navarre, for so he translates Navernia; but that the
first who used it was Philippus De Vitriaco; and
that some attribute the invention of the crotchet to
the aforesaid Philip, but it is not found in his works.
To this purpose the following passage, which Morley
evidently alludes to, may be seen in the copy of the
above-cited manuscript: *Figura verò minimæ est
corpus oblongum ad modum losongæ gerens tractum
rooto supra capite qui tractus signum minitantis
dicitur, ut hic* *De minina verò* Magister
Franco *mentionem in sua arte non facit sed tantum de longis et brevibus, ac semibrevibus, Minima
autem in Naverina inventa erat, et à* Philippo De
Vitriaco,§ *qui fuit filos. totius mundi musicorum
approbata et usitata; qui autem dicunt prædictum
Philippum crochatum sive semiminimam aut drag-*

---

* Morl. Introd. Annotations on the first part.

† Dr. Smith, in his Catalogue of the Cotton library, pag. 24, has
given the title of the tracts contained in the volume; and Mr. Castley,
in the Appendix to his catalogue of the king's library, pag. 314, has
given the following note concerning it:—'Tiberius, B. IX. burnt to
'a crust. Dr. Pepusch has copies of the 3, 4, and 5th tracts.' It seems
by Dr. Pepusch's copy that the musical tracts were at least seven in
number; they make together two hundred and ten folio pages.

‡ De Handlo is a proper surname: by the Chronica Series, at the
end of Dugdale's Origines Juridiciales, it appears that Nicholas de
Handlo was a justice of the court of Common Pleas, and a justice
itinerant. Ann. 1256.

§ It seems that this Philip was much celebrated. In a poem printed
among Skelton's works, 12mo. 1736, entitled A Treatise betwene Trouth
and Informacion, said to be written by William Cornishe, chapelman to
the most famose and noble kyng Henry VII., is the following stanza:—

I affayde theis tunes, methought them not fwete,
The concordes were nothynge muficall,
I called mafters of mufike cunyng and difcrete;
And the firft prynciple, whofe name was Tuballe,
Guido, Boice, John de Murris, Vitryaco, and them al
I prayed them of helpe of this combrous fonge,
Priked with force and lettred with wronge.

mam fecisse aut eis concessisse, errant, ut in notis suis manifeste apparet.

Each of the several measures above-enumerated, that is to say, the large, long, breve, semibreve, and minim, had then, as now, their correspondent pauses or rests ; these were contrived to give time for the singers to take breath ; besides this they contributed to introduce a variety of neumas or points ; the difference occasioned thereby is obvious.

But besides the characters invented to denote the measures of time which were simple and distinct, there were certain combinations of them used by the ancient musicians, known by the name of Ligatures ; of the invention whereof no satisfactory account is any where given. The earliest explanation of their nature and use seems to be that text of Franco, upon which the additions of Robertus De Handlo are a comment. Farther back than to these rules and maxims, or, as his commentator styles them, the Rubric, probably from the red character in which they might have been written, to distinguish the text from the comment, it would be in vain to look for the doctrine of the ligatures, they were most probably of his own invention, and seem to be coeval with mensurable music.

Upon the whole it seems to be clear that Franco, and not De Muris, is intitled to the merit of having invented the more essential characters, by which the measures of time are adjusted, with their respective pauses or rests ; and it detracts very little from the merit of this improvement to say that the lesser measures were invented by others, since the least attention to his principles must have naturally suggested such a subdivision of the greater characters as could not but terminate in the production of the lesser. We have seen this kind of subdivision carried much farther than either Franco, Vitriaco, or any of their followers, thought necessary ; and were any one to extend it to a still more minute division than we know of at present, the merit of such a refinement would hardly insure immortality to its author.

CHAP. L.

The rules of Franco, and the additions of his commentator, shew that the ligatures were in use as early at least as the year 1236. By another tract, of an anonymous author, written, as it is presumed at a small distance of time after the former, and of which an account will be given hereafter, it appears that this invention of the ligatures was succeeded by another variety in the method of notation, namely, evacuated, or, as Morley calls them, void characters, concerning which it is laid down as a rule, that every full or perfect character, if it be evacuated, receives a diminution, and loses a third part of its value, as for instance, the perfect semibreve ✦, which when full is equal in value to three minims, is when evacuated ◇ reduced to the value of two ; and the same rule holds with respect to the breve, the long, and the large, and also to the punctum or semiminim.

Other modes of diminution are here also mentioned, as the cutting off the half of either a full or an evacuated character, as here ▶ ◁, by which they are respectively reduced to half their primitive value. Another kind of diminution consisted in the use of red instead of black ink, which it seems at that time was a liquid not always at hand, as appears by this passage of the author : 'The diversities of time may 'be noted by red characters, when you have where-'withal to make red characters, and these also it is allowed to evacuate.'

The signs of augmentation are here also described, as first that of a point after a note, which at this day is used to encrease its value by one half. Another sign of augmentation, now disused, was a stroke drawn from any given character upwards, as here ↓, where a minim is augmented so as to be equal in value to a semibreve.

It appears very clearly from this little tract, and also from numberless passages in others, written about the same time and after, that in music in consonance, the part of all others the most regarded, and to which the rest seem to have been adapted, was the tenor, from the verb teneo, to hold. This was the part which contained the melody, and to this the other parts were but auxiliary.

Those who consider how very easily all the measures of time, with their several combinations, are expressed by the modern method of notation, will perhaps wonder to find that the Cantus Mensurabilis makes so considerable a part of the musical treatises written about this time ; and that such a diversity of opinions should subsist about it as are to be found among the writers of the fourteenth century. The true reason of all this confusion is, that the invention was new, it was received with great approbation, and immediately spread throughout Europe ; the utility of it was universally acknowledged, and men were fond of refining upon, and improving a contrivance so simple and ingenious ; but they carried their refinements too far, and we are now convinced that the greater part of what has been written on the subject since the time of De Muris might very well have been spared.

As to the ligatures, they are totally disused ; every conjunction of notes formerly described by them being now much more intelligibly expressed by separate characters conjoined by a circular stroke over them, and to this improvement the invention of bars has not a little contributed. The doctrine of the ligatures can therefore no farther be of use than to enable a modern to decypher as it were, an ancient composition, and whether any of those composed at this early period be worthy of that labour may admit of a question. If it should be thought otherwise, enough about the ligatures to answer this purpose is to be found in Morley, and other writers his contemporaries.

It may however not be improper to exhibit a general view of the simple and unligated characters of those times, and to explain the terms Perfection and Imperfection as they relate to time, which latter cannot be better done than from the manuscript treatise last above-cited.

It is to be observed that in mensurable music

perfection is ascribed to the Ternary, and imperfection to the Binary number, whether the terms be applied to longs, breves, or semibreves; for as to the minim, it is simple, and incapable of this distinction. The reason the ternary number is said to be perfect is that it has a beginning, a middle, and an end. If a compounded whole contains two equal parts, it is said to be imperfect, if three it is perfect: two minims make an imperfect, and three minims a perfect semibreve, and so of the larger measures; and this rule is general.

With respect to the unligated characters, though few in number, their different adjuncts and various modifications rendered their respective values so precarious, that whole volumes have been written to explain their nature and use. Indeed, towards the end of the sixteenth century much of this kind of learning was become obsolete, and the modes of time with their several diversities were reduced within an intelligible compass. In order however to understand the language of these writers, it may be necessary to explain the terms used by them, and exhibit a general view of mensurable music in this its infant state.

And first with respect to the terms, the most essential were Mode, Time, and Prolation; and to each of these, as applied to the subject now under consideration, a secondary sense was affixed widely different from its primitive meaning. In the first place the word Mode was made to signify that kind of progression wherein the greater characters of time were measured by the next lesser, as larges by longs, or longs by breves. Where the admeasurement was of breves by semibreves it was called Time; perhaps for this reason, that in musical speech Semibreve and Time are convertible terms, it being formerly, as usual, to say for instance a pause of two or more Times, as of so many semibreves;* and lastly, if the admeasurement was of semibreves by minims, it was called Prolation.† Vide Morley, pag. 12. Franch. Pract. Mus. lib. II. cap. iii. ix.

To each of those, that is to say Mode, Time, and Prolation, was annexed the epithet of Perfect or Imperfect, according as the progression was of the ternary or binary kind; and amongst these such interchanges and commixtures were allowed, that in a cantus of four parts the progression was frequently alternative, that is to say, in the bass and contra-tenor binary, and in the tenor and altus ternary, or otherwise in the bass and contra-tenor ternary, and in the tenor and altus binary.

This practice may be illustrated by a very familiar image; a cantus of four parts may be resembled to a tree, and the similitude will hold, if we suppose the fundamental or bass part to answer to the root, or rather the bole or stem, the tenor to the branches, the contra-tenor to the lesser ramifications, and the altus to the leaves. We must farther suppose the bass part to consist of the greater simple measures, which are those called longs, the tenor of breves, the contra-tenor of semibreves, and the altus of minims. In this situation of the parts, the first admeasurement, viz., that which is made by the breaking of the longs into breves, acquires the name of mode; the second, in which the breves are measured by semibreves, is called time; and the third, in which the semibreves are broken into minims, is termed prolation, of which it seems there were two kinds, the greater and the lesser; in the former the division into minims was by three, in the latter by two, answering to perfection and imperfection in the greater measures of the long, the breve, and the semibreve.

As to the modes themselves, they were of two kinds, the greater and the lesser; in the one the large was measured by longs, in the other the long was measured by breves.‡ There were also certain arbitrary marks or characters invented for distinguishing the modes, such as these O ⊙ C; but concerning their use and application there was such a diversity of opinions that Morley himself professes almost to doubt the certainty of those rules, which, being a child, he had learned with respect to the measures of the Large and the Long.§ And farther he says that though all that had written on the modes agree in the number and form of degrees, as he calls them, yet should his reader hardly find two of them tell one tale for the signs to know them. For time and prolation he says there was no controversy, but that the difficulty rested in the modes;|| for this reason he has bestowed great pains to explain the several characters used to distinguish them, and rejecting such as he deemed mere innovations, has reduced the matter to a tolerable degree of certainty.

For first he mentions an ancient method of denoting the degrees, which, because it naturally leads to an illustration of the subject, is here given in his own words: 'The auncient musitians' (by whom

* Glareanus, in his Dodechachordon, lib. III. cap. viii pag. 203, and Ornithoparcus in his Micrologus, translated by John Douland, pag. 46, say that time is measured by a semibreve. Morley, Introd. pag. 9, calls a time a stroke, and gives examples of semibreves for whole strokes or times. Nevertheless he adds that there is a more stroke, comprehending the time of a breve, but that the less stroke seems the most usual. Butler says the principal time-note is the semibreve, by whose time the time of all notes is known; and that it is measured by tactus, or the stroke of the hand. Princ. of Music, lib. I. cap. ii. § iv. And in a note on the above passage he speaks thus:—'As in former time, when the 'semibreve and minim were the least notes, the breve was the measure-'note, or principal time-note (by which being measured by the stroke of 'the hand, the just time of all other notes was known) so since the in-'venting of the smaller notes (the breve growing by little and little out 'of use) the semibreve became the measure-note in his stead; as now 'in quick time the minim beginneth to encroach upon the semibreve.

'The time-stroke of the breve Listenius termeth Tactus major, and of 'the semibreve tactus minor, the which he doth thus define:—"Tactus "major est, cùm brevis tactu mensuratur: Minor est, cùm semibrevis "sub tactum cadit integrum." But now the semibreve time is our 'major tactus, and the minim-time our Tactus minor.

'The Tactus major of Listenius, which gives a breve to a stroke, is 'the time that is meant in the canons of fugues, as "fuga in unisono, "post duo tempora: i. e. post 4 semibrevia." Ib. pag. 28.

† Prolation, from the Latin Prolatio, a speaking, uttering, or pronouncing, in the language of musicians, signifies generally singing as opposed to pausing or resting. But in the sense in which it is here used it is supposed to mean singing by the notes that most frequently occur, viz., Minims; for Listenius remarks that the notes invented since the Minim served rather for instrumental than vocal music. Vide Butl. pag. 28. Andreas Ornithoparcus in his Micrologus, lib. II. cap. iv. thus explains the term:—'Prolation is the essential quantitie of semibreves; 'or it is the setting of two or three minims against one semibreve; and 'it is twofold, to wit, the greater, which is a semibreve measured by

'three minims, or the comprehending of three minims in one semibreve, 'and the lesser, wherein the semibreve is measured by two minims only.' Grassineau, notwithstanding he had Brossard before him, betrays great ignorance in calling prolation the art of shaking or making several inflexions of the voice on the same note or syllable, a practice unknown to the ancients, and not introduced till the middle of the last century.

‡ Morl. Introd. pag. 12, 13.
§ Annotat. on book I. pag. 12. ver. 16.
|| Ibid.

we understand those who lived within about three hundred years preceding the time when Morley wrote) 'did commonlie sette downe a particular 'signe for every degree of music in the song; so 'that they having no more degrees than three, that 'is the two modes and time, (prolation not being in-'vented,) they set down three signs for them: so 'that if the great moode were perfect it was signified 'by a whole circle, which is a perfect figure, and if 'imperfect by a halfe circle. Therefore wheresoever 'these signs O 33 were set before any songe, there 'was the great moode perfect signified by the circle, 'the small moode perfect signified by the first figure 'of three, and time perfect by the last. If the song 'were marked thus C 33, then was the great moode 'unperfect, and the small moode and time perfect. 'But if the first figure were a figure of two thus C '23, then were both moodes unperfect, and time 'perfect. If it were thus C 22, then were all un-'perfect. But, if in all the songe there were no large, 'then did they set downe the signes of such notes as 'were in the songe, so that if the circle or semicircle 'were set before one onelie cifer, as O 2, then did it 'signifie the lesse moode, and by that reason that 'circle now last sette downe with the binarie cifer 'following it, signified the lesse moode perfect, and 'time unperfect. If thus C 2, then was the lesse 'moode unperfect, and time perfect. If thus C 3, 'then was both the lesse moode and time unperfect, 'and so of others. But since the prolation was in-'vented, they have set a pointe in the circle or halfe-'circle, to shew the More prolation, which notwith-'standing altereth nothing in the moode nor time. 'But these are little used now at this present.'

The above-cited passage is taken from the annota-tions on the first book of Morley's Introduction.* His account of the characters used to distinguish the several modes is contained in the text,† and by that it appears that in his time, and long before, the Great Mode Perfect, which, as he says, gave to the large three longs, was thus signified O 3. The Great Mode Imperfect, which gave to the large only two longs, thus C 3. The lesser mode which measured the longs by breves, was also either perfect or imperfect: the sign of the former, wherein the long contained three breves, was this O 2; that of the latter, wherein the long contained only two breves, was this C 2. As to Time, which was the measure of breves by semibreves, that also was of two kinds, perfect and imperfect: perfect time, which was when the breve contained three semibreves, had for signs these marks O 3. C 3. O. Imperfect time, which divided the breve into semibreves, had these O 2. C 2. C. As to Prolation, that of the More, wherein the semibreve contained three minims, its signs were a circle or half circle with a point thus ⊙ ℂ. Prolation of the less, which was when the semibreve was but two minims, was signified by the same characters without a point, as thus O C.

From all which the same author deduces the following position, 'that the number doth signifie 'the mode, the circle, the time, and the presence or 'absence of the poynt the prolation.'‡

So much as above is adduced for the explanation of the degrees and the signs or marks by which they were anciently distinguished, seems absolutely necessary to be known, in order to the understanding a very elaborate and methodical representation of all the various measures of time, with their several com-binations contained in a collection of tracts already mentioned by the name of the Cotton manuscript, and frequently referred to in the course of this en-quiry concerning the doctrine and practice of men-surable music. A more particular account of this invaluable manuscript, with a number of copious ex-tracts therefrom, is inserted in that part of this work wherein the aid of such intelligence as it abounds with seems most necessary.

It is true that for this purpose recourse might have been had to the printed works of Franchinus, Glareanus, and other ancient writers, who have written on the subject, and whose authority in this respect is unquestionable. But to this it is answered, that not only Glareanus, but Franchinus, who on account of his antiquity is justly deemed the Father of our present music, represent the Cantus Men-surabilis as in a state of maturity: and our business here is not so much to explain the principles of the science, as to trace its progress, and mark the several gradations through which it is arrived to that state of perfection in which we now behold it.

If this be allowed, it will follow that in a regular deduction of the several improvements from time to time made in music, the earliest accounts are the best: and, setting aside other evidences, when it has been mentioned that the MS. above referred to abounds with frequent commendations of learned and skilful musicians, such as Guido, Boetius, Johannes De Muris, and others now less known, but who are notwithstanding highly celebrated by its author, while the names of Franchinus and Glareanus do not once occur in it: when all this is considered, the point of precedence in respect of antiquity, which is all that is now contended for, will appear to be in a manner settled, and we shall be driven to allow that in this particular the testimony of these writers is of less authority than the manuscript here spoken of.

For this reason the following types, as being of very great antiquity, are here inserted as a specimen of the method which the ancient writers made use of, to represent the several degrees of measures, and the order in which they are generated. The author, whoever he was, has given them the name of musical trees, and although Doni in his treatise De Præstantia Musicæ Veteris§ in ridicule of diagrams in this form, terms them cauli-flowers, they seem very well to answer the end of their invention:—

Perfect Mode, Perfect Time, Greater Prolation.

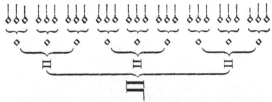

§ Pag. 16, where the author is unwarrantably severe in his censure of rhythmical music, and the characters used to denote it.

Perfect Mode, Perfect Time, Lesser Prolation.

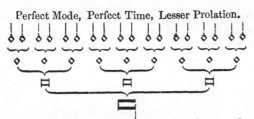

The several other species of mode, time, and prolation, are represented in like manner, mutatis mutandis; and the last or most minute division of the greater quantity in the Cantus Mensurabilis is exhibited in a scheme that gives to the triple long no fewer than eighty-one minims, and may be easily conceived, of, by means of the two foregoing examples.

None of the several modal characters described by Morley, are annexed to any of the foregoing types; nor do any of those marks or signs, invented to denote the time and prolation, occur among them; but the author has in a subsequent paragraph given an explanation of them, which coincides very nearly with that of Morley. The augmentation of measures, by placing a point after a breve or other character, is also here mentioned, as are likewise sundry methods of diminution, whereby a perfect measure is rendered imperfect; and amongst the rest the diminution by red characters, which he says are used in motets, and frequently in those of Philippus de Vitriaco, for three reasons, namely, to signify a change in the mode, the time, or the prolation. As to the Pauses or Rests, the marks or characters made use of by the ancient writers to denote them, correspond exactly with those which we meet with in the works of other writers on the subject of mensurable music.

The foregoing pages contain an account of the invention of, and the successive improvements made in, the Cantus Mensurabilis, which, as it is collected from the writings of sundry authors extant only in manuscript, and whose works were probably composed for the instruction of particular fraternities in different countries, and at different times, and consequently had never received the sanction of public approbation, is necessarily incumbered with difficulties: the truth of the matter is, that this branch of musical science had not acquired any great degree of stability till towards the close of the fourteenth century; for this reason the farther consideration of mensurable music, and such a representation of the measures of time, with their several modifications as corresponds with the modern practice, is referred to that part of the present work, where only it can with propriety be inserted.

In order to judge of the effects of this invention, and of the improvements which by the introduction of the Cantus Mensurabilis were made in music, it will be necessary to take a view of the state of the science in the ages next preceding the time of this discovery; and though some of those writers, who had the good fortune to live in a more enlightened age, have affected to treat the learning of those times with contempt; and, overlooking the ingenuity of such men as Guido, Franco, De Handlo, De Muris,

Vitriaco, Tinctor, and many others, have reproached them with barbarism, and the want of classical elegance in their writings, perhaps there are some who consider philology rather as subservient to the ends of science, than as science itself; and who may think knowledge of more importance to mankind than the form in which it is communicated; such men may be inclined to excuse the want of that elegance which is the result of refinement, and may be pleased to contemplate the progress of scientific improvement, without attending to the structure of periods, or bringing a Monkish style to the test of Ciceronian purity.

The first considerable improvement after the regulation of the tones by Gregory the Great, and the establishment of the chant known by his name, was the invention of Polyphonous music, exemplified at first in that extemporaneous kind of harmony, which was anciently signified by the term Descant.*

Guido, besides new modelling the scale, and converting the ancient tetrachords into hexachords, found out a method of placing the points in the spaces, as well as on the lines. This, together with the cliffs, rendered the stave of five lines nearly commensurate to the whole system, and suggested the idea of written descant, for the notation whereof nothing more was required than an opposition of point to point; and to music written according to this method of notation, the monks, very soon after its invention, gave the name of Contrapunctum, Contrapunto, or Counterpoint; appellations, in the opinion of many, so strongly favouring of the barbarism of the times in which they were first introduced, as not to be atoned for by their precision.

From hence it will pretty clearly appear that counterpoint, that is to say the method of describing descant by such characters as we now use, was the invention of Guido. But it does by no means follow that he was the inventor of symphoniac music; on the contrary it has been shewn that it was in use among the northern inhabitants of this kingdom, and that so early as the eighth century, and that Bede had given it the name of Descant.

To the evidences already mentioned in support of this assertion, it may here be added, that the invention and use of the organ amounts to little less than a proof that symphoniac music was known long before Guido's time. The fact stands thus: the organ, not to reassume the enquiry as to the time of its invention, was added to church music by pope Vitalianus, who, as some say, was advanced to the papacy anno 655, though others postpone it to the year 663. Those of the first class fix the æra of the introduction of the organ into the choral service precisely at 660, the others by consequence somewhat later. And Guido

* If we allow for the difference between written and extemporary music it will appear that the modern acceptation of the word Descant differs very little from that of the eighth century. See ante, Book IV, page 150. For a learned musical lexicographer thus explains it:—

DISCANTO [Ital.] DISCANTUS [Lat.] quasi BISCANTUS, *i* e., diversus cantus, not only because this part being the highest of many admits of the most coloratures, divisions, graces, and variations of any, but because the earlier writers among the moderns used to call a figurate song, in contradistinction to Canto-fermo or Plain-song, Discantum; and what we now call the composing of figurate music, discanture. Walth. Lex. in Art.

himself, besides frequently mentioning the organ in the Micrologus, recommends the use of it in common with the monochord, for tuning the voice to the several intervals contained in the septenary.

It is true when we speak of the organ we are to understand that there are two kinds of instrument distinguishable by that name; the one, for the smallness of its size, and simplicity of its construction, called the Portative, the other the Positive, or immoveable organ; both of these are very accurately described by Ottomarus Luscinius, in his Musurgia, printed at Strasburg, in 1536. As to the first, its use was principally to assist the voice in ascertaining the several sounds contained in the system, and occasionally to facilitate the learning of any Cantus. The other is that noble instrument, to the harmony whereof the solemn choral service has ever since its invention been sung, and which is now degraded to the accompaniment of discordant voices in the promiscuous performance of metrical psalmody in parochial worship.

Guido might possibly mean that the former of these was proper to tune the voice by; but he goes on farther, and speaks of the organ in general terms, as an instrument to which the hymns, antiphons, and other offices were daily sung in cathedral and conventual churches, and other places of religious worship. Now let him mean either the one or the other of the above-mentioned instruments, it is scarce credible that during so long a period as that between 800 and 1020, during all which the world was in possession of the organ, neither curiosity nor accident should lead to the discovery of music in consonance. Is it to be supposed that this noble instrument, so constructed as to produce the greatest variety of harmony and fine modulation, was played on by one finger only? was the organist, who must be supposed to be well skilled in the nature of consonance, never tempted by curiosity to try its effect on the instrument the object of his studies, and perhaps the only one, if we except the harp, then known, on which an experiment of this kind could possibly be made? did no accident or mistake, or lastly, did not the mere tuning the instrument from time to time, as occasion required, or, if that was not his duty, the bare trying if it were in tune or no, teach him experimentally that the diatessaron, diapente, and diapason, to say nothing of the other consonances, are as grateful to the audible as their harmonical coincidences are to the reasoning faculties?

Perhaps it may be objected that this argument will carry the use of symphoniac music back to those times in which it is asserted no such thing was known; for it may be asked, does not the hydraulic organ mentioned by Vitruvius as necessarily presuppose music in consonance, as that in use at the time of Guido's writing the Micrologus? In answer to this it is said, that the hydraulic organ is an instrument so very ill defined, that we are incapable of forming to ourselves any idea of its frame, its construction, or its use. Kircher has wrested Vitruvius's description of it, so as to make it resemble the modern organ, and has even exhibited the form of it in the

Musurgia; but who does not see that the instrument thus accurately delineated by him is a creature of his own imagination? and does he not deny its aptitude for symphoniac music by saying as he does in the strongest and most express terms, that after a most painful and laborious research he had never been able to find the slightest vestiges of symphoniac harmony in either the theory or practice of the ancients?

CHAP. LI.

IT now remains to take a view of music as it stood immediately after this last improvement of Guido. Descant, in the original sense of the word, was extemporaneous song, a mere energy; for as soon as uttered it was lost: it no where appears that before the time of Guido any method of notation had been thought of, capable of fixing it, or that the stave of eight lines, mentioned by Vincentio Galilei, or that other of Kircher, on both which the points were situated on the lines, and not in the spaces, was ever used for the notation of more than the simple melody of one part; whereas the stave of Guido, wherein the spaces were rendered as useful as the lines, not only brought the melody into a narrower compass, but for the purpose of singing written descant enabled him, by means of the cliffs, to separate and so discriminate the several parts, as to make the practice of music in consonance, a matter of small difficulty.

The word Score is of modern invention, and it is not easy to find a synonyma to it in the monkish writers on music: nevertheless the method of writing in score must have been practised as well with them as by us, since no man could know what he was about, that in framing a Cantus did not dispose the several parts regularly, the lowest at bottom, and the others in due order above it. In Guido's time there was no diversity in the length of the notes, the necessary consequence whereof was, that the points in each stave were placed in opposition to those in the others; and a cantus thus framed was no less properly than emphatically called Counterpoint.

It is needless to say that before the invention of the Cantus Mensurabilis this was the only kind of music in consonance; where it was adapted to words the metre was regulated by the cadence of the syllables, and where it was calculated solely for instruments, the notes in opposition were of equal length, adjusted by the simple radical measures, out of which all the different modifications of common and triple time, as we now call them, are known to spring. But this kind of equality subsisted only between the integral parts of the Cantus, as they stood opposed to each other in consonance, and the radical measures were not less obvious then than they are now. The whole of the Rythmopoieia was founded in the distinction between long and short quantities, and a foot, consisting solely of either, is essentially different from one in which they are combined; in one case the Arsis and Thesis are equal; in the other they have a ratio of two to one. From hence there is reason to conclude that the primitive counterpoint, as being subject to different general measures, was of two forms, answering precisely to the common and triple time of the moderns. The former of these may thus be conceived of :—

And the latter thus :—

But although these were all the varieties in respect to time or measure, which it was originally capable of, counterpoint was even then susceptible of various forms, and admitted of an almost endless diversity of combinations, arising as well from a difference in the motion or progression of the sounds, as in the succession of consonances. The combinations, in a series of those eight sounds which constitute the diapason, are estimated at no fewer than 40,320. And in the case of a cantus in consonance these allow of a multiplication by the number of the additional parts to the amount of four. Hence it is that in a cantus thus constituted, the iteration of the same precise melody and harmony is an event so extremely fortuitous, that we estimate the chance of its happening, at nothing.

Another source of variety is discernible in the different motions which may be assigned to the several parts of a cantus in consonance, which, as they stand opposed to each other, may be in either of the following forms :—

VARIOUS PROCESSES OF HARMONY.

Direct Motion.	Direct Motion by conjunct Degrees.	Direct Motion by disjunct Degrees.	Oblique Motion by conjunct Degrees.	Oblique Motion by disjunct Degrees.	Contrary Motion.	Motion by leaps.
1	2	3	4	5	6	7

These observations may serve as a general explanation of the nature of counterpoint, of which it will appear there are several kinds; for the thorough understanding whereof it is necessary to be remembered that the basis of all counterpoint is simple melody, to which the concords placed in the order of point against point are but auxiliary. The foundation on which the harmonical superstructure is erected is termed by the ancient Italian writers Canto Fermo, of which the following is an example :—

R℞, Ec - - ce appare - bit Domi - - nus.*

As to counterpoint, notwithstanding the several divisions of it into Contrapunctus simplex, Contrapunctus diminutus sive floridus, Contrapunctus coloratus, Contrapunctus fugatus, and many other kinds, it is in truth that species of harmony only, in which the notes contained in the Canto Fermo, and each of the other parts, are of equal lengths, as here :—

CONTRAPUNCTUS SIMPLEX.

This kind of symphoniac harmony was doubtless very grateful to the hearers as long as it retained the charm of novelty, and when adapted to words, was not liable to any objection arising from its want of metrical variety; but in music merely instrumental, the uniformity of its cadence, and the unvaried iteration of the same measures, could not at length fail to produce satiety and disgust. For it is not in the bare affinity or congruity of sounds, though ever so well adjusted, combined, or uttered, that the ear can long find satisfaction : this is experienced by those who study that branch of musical science known by the name of continued or thorough bass, the private practice whereof, whether it be on the organ, harpsichord, arch-lute, or any other instrument adapted for the purpose, in a short time becomes irksome. But the invention of the different measures for time, together with the pauses or rests, and also of the ligatures, gave rise to another species, in which the rigorous opposition of point to point was dispensed with; and this relaxation of a rule which, while it was observed, held the invention in fetters, gave rise to those other species of harmony above-enumerated, improperly called counterpoint.

The Contrapunctus diminutus was evidently the first improvement of the Contrapunctus simplex, in which it is observable that the notes opposed in the Canto Fermo are more in number, and consequently less in value, than the latter of this species. The following, though not a very ancient composition, may serve as an example :—

* From a MS. cited by Martini, supposed to have been written in the thirteenth century. Storia della Musica, tom. I. pag. 187.

CONTRAPUNCTUS DIMINUTUS sive FLORIDUS.

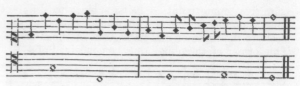

This was followed by the introduction of little points, imitations, colligations of notes, and responsive passages, not so elegant in their structure and contrivance as, but somewhat resembling, the fugue of modern times.

The rudiments of this species are discernible in the following Kyrie, said to have been composed about the year 1473 :—*

CANTO FIGURATO.

Ky - ri - e   e — — — — — — — — — — — — — — — ley - son.

Ky - ri - e   e — — — — — — — — — — — — — — leyson.

Ky - ri - e   e — lei - son,   Ky - ri - e   e — — — leison.

Ky - ri - e   e — — lei - son,   Kyri-e — — — leison.

To this latter kind of music were given the epithets of Figurate, Coloured, and many others of the like import. The Italians to this day call it Canto Figurato, and oppose it to Contrapunto or counterpoint. Other countries have relaxed the signification of the word Descant, and have given that name to counterpoint; and the two kinds are now distinguished by the appellations of Plain and Figurate descant.

From hence it appears that the word Descant, considered as a noun, has acquired a secondary signification; and that it is now used to denote any kind of musical composition of more parts than one; and as to the verb formed from it, it has, like many others, acquired a metaphorical sense, as in the following passage :—

'And Descant on mine own deformity.'
Shakespeare, Rich. III.

But neither can its original meaning be understood, nor the propriety and elegance of the above figure be discerned, without a clear and precise idea of the nature of descant, properly so called.

If we compute the distance in respect of time between the last improvement of the Cantus Ecclesiasticus by St. Gregory, and the invention of the Cantus Mensurabilis by Franco, it will be found to include nearly five hundred years; and although that period produced a great number of writers on the subject of music whose names and works have herein

before been mentioned in chronological order, it does not appear that the least effort was made by any of them towards such an improvement as that of Franco, which is the more to be wondered at as the ratio of accents, which is what we are to understand by the term Prosody, was understood to a tolerable degree of exactness, even after the general declension of literature; and long before the commencement of that period was deemed, as it is now, a necessary part of grammar. St. Austin has written a treatise on the various measures of the ancient verse, and our countryman Bede has written a discourse De Metrica Ratione; but it seems that neither of them ever thought of applying the ratio of long and short measures to music, abstracted from verse.

Neither can it be reasonably inferred from any thing that Isaac Vossius has said in his treatise De Poematum Cantu et Viribus Rythmi, admitting all that he has advanced in it to be true, that the Rythmopoieia of the ancients had any immediate relation to Music: it should rather seem by his own testimony to refer solely to the Poetry of the ancients, and to be as much a branch of grammar as prosody is at this day. This however is certain that the ancient method of notation appears to be calculated for no other end than barely to signify the diversities of sounds in respect of their acuteness and gravity. Nor do any of the fragments of ancient music now extant

* Martini, Storia della Musica, tom. I. pag. 188.

furnish any means of ascertaining the respective lengths of the sounds, other than the metre of the verses to which they are adapted. It may perhaps be urged as a reason for the practice of adjusting the measures of the music by those of the verse, rather than the measures of the verse by those of the music, that the distinction of long and short times or quantities could not with propriety be referred to music: but this is to suppose that music merely instrumental has no force or efficacy save what arises from affinity of sound; the contrary whereof is at this day so manifest, that it would be ridiculous to question it: nay the strokes on an anvil have a metrical ratio, and the most uniform monotony may be so broken into various quantities, and these may again be so combined as to form a distinct species capable of producing wonderful effects.

If this should be doubted, let it be considered that the Drum, which has no other claim to a place among the pulsatile musical instruments, than that it is capable of expressing the various measures and modifications of time, owes all its energy to that which in poetry would be called Metre, which is nothing more than a regular and orderly commixture of long and short quantities; but who can hear these uttered by the instrument now speaking of, who can attend to that artful interchange of measures, which it is calculated to express, and that in a regular subjection to metrical laws, without feeling that he is acted upon like a mere machine?

With the utmost propriety therefore does our great dramatic poet style this instrument the Spirit-stirring drum; and with no less policy do those act who trust to its efficacy in the hour of battle, and use it as the means of exciting that passion which the most eloquent oration imaginable would fail to inspire.*

* It seems that the old English march of the foot was formerly in high estimation, as well abroad as with us; its characteristic is dignity and gravity, in which respect it differs greatly from the French, which, as it is given by Mersennus, is brisk and alert. Sir Roger Williams, a gallant Low-country soldier of queen Elizabeth's time, and who has therefore a place among the worthies of Lloyd and Winstanley, had once a conversation on this subject with marshal Biron, a French general. The marshal observed that the English march being beaten by the drum was slow, heavy, and sluggish: 'That may be true,' answered Sir Roger, 'but slow as it is, it has traversed your master's 'country from one end to the other.' This bon mot is recorded in one of those little entertaining books, written by Crouch the bookseller in the Poultry, and published about the end of the last century, under the fictitious name of Robert Burton; the book here referred to is entitled Admirable Curiosities, Rarities, and Wonders in England, Scotland, and Ireland; the story is to be met with in pag. 5, of it, but where else is not said.

Notwithstanding the many late alterations in the discipline and exercise of our troops, and the introduction of fifes and other instruments into our martial music, it is said that the old English march is still in use with the foot. Mr. Walpole has been very happy in discovering a manuscript on parchment, purporting to be a warrant of Charles I., directing the revival of the march agreeably to the form thereto subjoined in musical notes signed by his majesty, and countersigned by the earl of Arundel and Surrey, the then earl marshal. This curious manuscript was found by the present earl of Huntingdon in an old chest, and as the parchment has at one corner the arms of his lordship's predecessor, then living, Mr. Walpole thinks it probable that the order was sent to all lords lieutenants of counties.

The following is a copy of the warrant, and of the musical notes of the march, taken from the Catalogue of Royal and Noble Authors, vol. I. pag. 201:—

    'CHARLES REX,
'Whereas the ancient custome of nations hath ever bene to use one 'certaine and constant forme of march in the warres, whereby to be dis-'tinguished one from another. And the march of this our English 'nation, so famous in all the honourable atchievements and glorious 'warres of this our kingdome in forraigne parts [being by the appro-'bation of strangers themselves confest and acknowledged the best of all 'marches] was through the negligence and carelessness of drummers, 'and by long discontinuance so altered and changed from the ancient 'gravitie and majestie thereof, as it was in danger utterly to have bene

It may be remembered that in the foregoing deduction of the improvements made in music, counterpoint was mentioned as the last that preceded the invention of the Cantus Mensurabilis. To shew the importance of this last, it was necessary to state the defects in that species of harmony which admitted of no metrical variety. It was also necessary in the next place to shew that although the Rythmopoieia of the ancients has long ceased to be understood, yet that the rudiments of it subsist even now in the prosody of the grammarians. Seeing then that the art of combining long and short quantities, and the subjecting them to metrical laws was at all times known, it may be asked wherein did the merit of Franco's invention consist? The answer is, in the transferring of metre from poetry or verse to mere sound; and in the invention of a system of notation, by means whereof all the possible modifications of time are definable, and that to the utmost degree of exactness.

But the merit of Franco's invention, and the subsequent improvement of it by De Muris and other writers, are best to be judged of by their consequences, which were the union of the Melopoieia with the Rythmopoieia, or, in other words, Melody and Metre; and from hence sprang all those various species of counterpoint, which are included under the general

'lost and forgotten. It pleased our late deare brother prince Henry to 'revive and rectifie the same by ordayning an establishment of one 'certaine measure, which was beaten in his presence at Greenwich, 'anno 1610. In confirmation whereof wee are graciously pleased, at the 'instance and humble sute of our right trusty and right well-beloved 'cousin and counsellour Edward viscount Wimbledon, to set down and 'ordaine this present establishment hereunder expressed. Willing and 'commanding all drummers within our kingdome of England and prin-'cipalitie of Wales exactly and precisely to observe the same, as well in 'this our kingdome, as abroad in the service of any forraigne prince or 'state, without any addition or alteration whatsoever. To the end that 'so ancient, famous, and commendable a custome may be preserved as a 'patterne and precedent to all posteritie. Given at our palace of West-'minster the seventh day of February, in the seventh yeare of our raigne, 'of England, Scotland, France, and Ireland.

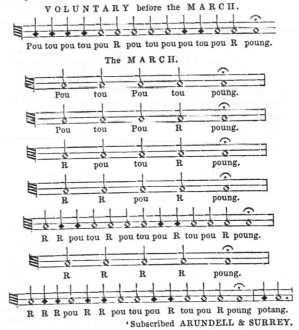

VOLUNTARY before the MARCH.

Pou tou pou tou pou R pou tou pou pou tou pou R poung.

The MARCH.

Pou   tou   Pou   tou   poung.

Pou   tou   Pou   R   poung.

R   pou   tou   R   poung.

R   R   pou   R   poung.

R R pou tou R pou tou pou R tou pou R poung.

R   R   R   R   poung.

R R R pou R R pou tou pou R tou pou R poung potang.

'Subscribed ARUNDELL & SURREY,

'This is a true copie of the original, signed by his Majestie
                                    'ED. NORGATE, Windsor.'

appellation of Canto Figurato. The first and most obvious improvement of counterpoint, which, as has been already shewn, was originally simple, and consisted in a strict opposition of note to note, is visible in that which is termed Contrapunctus iminutus sive floridus, wherein the notes in one part, the plain-song for instance, are opposed by others of a less value, but corresponding to the former in the general measure of its constituent sounds, of which kind of composition an example has herein before been given. The subsequent improvements on this invention have been shewn to be, the Canto Figurato, Canon, and other kinds of symphoniacal composition, all which are evidently the offspring of the Cantus Mensurabilis, an invention so much the more to be valued, as it has rendered that fund of harmonical and metrical combination almost infinite in its extent, which else must long ago have been exhausted.

If we take a view of music in the state in which Guido left it, it will be found to have derived all its power and efficacy from the coincidence of sounds, and that those sounds being regulated by even and uniform measures, though they might be grateful to the ear, which is delighted with harmony even in cases where it refers to nothing beyond itself, must necessarily fail of producing those effects which follow from their being subjected to metrical regulations.

Proofs abundant of these effects might be adduced from the compositions of the last century, as namely, Carissimi, Stradella, Gasparini, and others of the Italians, and our own Purcell, but were these wanting, and no evidence subsisted of the benefits which have resulted to music from the union of harmony and metre, those of Handel are an irrefragable testimony of the fact, the force and energy of whose most studied works is resolvable into a judicious selection of measures calculated to sooth or animate, to attemper or inflame, in short to do with the human mind whatever he meant to do.

Having thus explained the nature of the Cantus Mensurabilis, and also of Descant, the knowledge whereof is absolutely necessary to the understanding the writers who succeeded John De Muris, it remains to give an account of a number of valuable tracts, composed, as it is conceived, subsequent to the time when he lived and of the final establishment of an harmonical and metrical theory by Franchinus.

Mention has been made in the course of this work of a manuscript, to which, for the want of another title, that of the Cotton MS. has been given, and also of another, for distinction-sake called the manuscript of Waltham Holy Cross. The former of these is now rendered useless by the fire that happened at Ashburnham-house. But before this disastrous event a copy thereof, not so complete as could be wished, as wanting many of the diagrams and examples in notes occasionally inserted by way of illustration, had been procured and made at the expense of the late Dr. Pepusch. As to the other manuscript, that of Waltham Holy Cross, it formerly belonged to some person who was so much a friend to learning as to oblige Dr. Pepusch with permission to copy it, and his copy thereof is extant. The original is now

the property of Mr. West, the president of the Royal Society, who, actuated by the same generous spirit as the former owner, has vouchsafed the use of it for the furtherance of this work. These assistances afford the means of giving an account of a number of curious tracts on the subject of music, which hardly any of the writers on that science seem ever to have seen, and which perhaps are now no where else to be found.

The first of these manuscripts contains tracts by different authors, most of whom seem to have been well skilled in the less abstruse parts of the science. The compiler of this work is unknown, but the time when it was completed appears by the following note at the conclusion of the first tract :—

'Finito libro reddatur gloria Christo. Expliciunt 'Regulæ cum additionibus: finitæ die Veneris proximo 'ante Pentecost, anno domini millesimo tricentisimo 'vicesimo sexto, et cætera, Amen.'

Of the first tract, which bears the title of 'Regulæ 'cum maximis magistri Franconis, cum additioni- 'bus aliorum Musicorum, compilatæ à Roberto de 'Handlo,' some mention has already been made ; and as to Franco, the author of the Rules and Maxims, an account of him, of his country, and the age in which he lived, has also been given.[*] Of his commentator De Handlo, bishop Tanner has taken some notice in his Bibliotheca ; but as his account refers solely to the manuscript now before us, the original whereof it is probable he had seen, it seems that he was unable to say more of him than appears upon the face of this his work.

As to the commentary, it is written in dialogue ; the speakers are Franco himself and De Handlo, and other occasional interlocutors. The subject of it is the art of denoting the time or duration of musical sounds by characters, and there is little reason to doubt but that it contains the substance of what Johannes De Muris taught concerning that matter. It consists of thirteen divisions or Rubrics, as the author terms them, from their being in red characters, the titles whereof with the substance of each are as follow :—

Rubric I. Of the Long, Breve, and Semibreve, and of the manner of dividing them.

Rubric II. Of the Long, the Semi-long,[†] and their value, and of the Double Long.

Rubric III. How to distinguish the Long from the Semi-long, and the Breve from the Semibreve ; and of the Pauses corresponding with each ; and of the equality of the Breve and the Breve altera.

Rubric IV. Of Semibreves, and their equality and inequality, and of the division of the Modes [of time] and how many ought to be assumed.

Under this head the author mentions one Petrus De Cruce as a composer of motetts ; the names of Petrus Le Visor, and Johannes De Garlandia also occur as interlocutors in the dialogue.

---

[*] Supra, pag. 176, to which may be added that in the Index of Authors, at the end of Martini's first volume, is the following article : 'FRAN- 'CONUS Parisiensis. Ars Cantus Mensurabilis. Codex Ambrosianus 'signat D. 5, in fol.' which is probably no other than a copy of the tracts there ascribed to him.

[†] This is but another name for the breve.

Rubric V. Of the Longs which exceed in value a double Long.

This rubric exhibits a species of notation unknown to us at this day, namely, a single character encreased in its value by the encrease of its magnitude. A practice which will be best understood from the author's own words, which are these :—' A figure 'having three quadrangles in· it is called a triple 'long, that is to say a note of three perfections ; if 'it has four, it is called quadruple, that is a note of 'four perfections ; and so on to nine, but no farther. 'See the figures of all the longs as they appear here :—

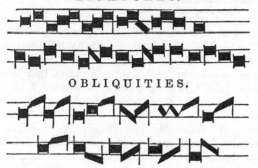

Rubric VI. Of the beginnings of Ligatures and Obliquities, and in what manner they are found.

A Ligature is here defined to be a mass of figures, either in a right or an oblique direction ; and an Obliquity is said to be a solid union or connexion of two ascending or descending notes in one. Here follow examples, from the author, of each :—

LIGATURES.

OBLIQUITIES.

Of ligatures, and also of obliquities, some are here said to be with propriety, others without propriety, and others with an opposite propriety ; these species are severally known by their beginnings. The matter of this rubric, and the commentary on it are of very little import.

It is farther said that no additional mark or character is to be made at the end of an ascending obliquity, except a Plica, a word which in this place signifies that perpendicular stroke which is the termination of such characters as the long.

Rubric VII. To know the terminations of the ligatures. The beginnings and terminations of ligatures, and also of obliquities, declare the nature of the time, whether it be perfect or imperfect ; or, as we should now say, duple or triple.

Rubric VIII. Teaches also to know the terminations of the ligatures.

Rubric IX. Concerning the Conjunctions of semibreves, and of the figures or ligatures with which such semibreves may be joined.

Here we meet with the name of Admetus de Aureliana, who, as also the singers of Navernia, the name of a country which puzzled Morley, and which probably means Navarre, are said to have conjoined Minoratas and Minims together.

Rubric X. How the Plicas are formed in ligatures and obliquities, and in what manner a plicated long becomes an erect long.

Rubric XI. Concerning the value of the Plicas.

Rubric XII. Concerning the Pauses.

The pauses are here said to be six in number, the first of three times, the second of two, and the third of one. The fourth is of two third parts, and the fifth one third part of one time. As to the sixth it is said to be of no time, and that it is better called an immeasurable pause, and that the use of it is to shew that the last note but one must be held out, although but a breve or semibreve. The characters of the pauses are also thus described : a pause of three times covers three spaces, or the value of three, namely, two and two halves, A ; a pause of two times covers two spaces or one entire space, and two halves, B ; a pause of one time covers one space or two halves, C ; a pause of two perfections of one time covers only two parts of one time, D ; a pause of the third part of one time covers the third part of one space E ; a pause, which is said to be immeasurable F, is called the end of the punctums, and covers four spaces, their five forms appear here :—

In this rubric the colloquium is between Franco, Jacobus de Navernia, and the above-named Johannes de Garlandia.

Rubric XIII. How the Measures or Modes of time are formed.

Here it is laid down that there are five modes of time used by the moderns, the first consisting of all perfect longs, as the following motet :—

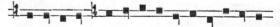

In Bethleem

The second mode consists of a breve, a long, and a breve, as in this example :—

The third of a long, two breves and a long, as in this motet : only it is to be observed that to this mode belongs a pause of three times, a long going before :—

Quid mi - ra - ris par-tum vir - gi - ne - um.

The fourth mode is of two breves, a long, and two breves, as here :—

Ro-su - la primu - la sal-ve Jes-se vir-gu-la.

and to it belongs a pause of three times. After this designation of the fourth mode there occurs a caution, which will doubtless appear somewhat singular, namely, that care must be taken that in the singing the notes be not expressed in a lascivious manner. The fifth mode consists of breves and semibreves of both kinds, that is to say, perfect and imperfect, as appears in the following example :—

Ag-mi - na fi - de - li-um Ka-te - ri - na,

novum me-los prome-re, Re-gi-na Regni glo - ri - e,

So - la sal-ve sin-gu - la-ris gratie.

From this mode, it is said, proceed a great number of melodies or airs, the names whereof can scarcely be rendered in English, as namely, Hockets, * Rundelli, Balladea, Coreæ, Cantusfracti, Estampetæ, Florituræ. It seems that these five modes may be mixed or used interchangeably, in which respect they agree with the modes in use at this day. The whole of the explanation of this last rubric comes from the mouth of De Handlo, the author of the tract, which he concludes with words to this purpose : ' Every mode of measures, and every measure of ' cantus is included in the above five modes and ' rules, and maxims for their use and application ' might be given without end ; nevertheless attend ' to the instructions contained in this small volume. ' All that now hear me are singers, therefore pray ' fervently to God for the life of the writer. Amen.'

CHAP. LII.

To the tract of De Handlo, the next in order that occurs is a discourse by an anonymous author, entitled ' Tractatus diversarum Figurarum per quas dulcis ' Modis discantantur,'† to appearance a compendium of the doctrine of De Muris, containing in the beginning of it a remarkable eulogium on him by the name of Egidius de Muris, or de Morino, viz., that he, as it pleased God, most carefully, and to his great glory, searched into and improved the musical art. So that the characters, namely, the double Long, Long, Breve, Semibreve, Minim, are now made manifest.

Herein also are treated of the pauses or rests, which, as well as the characters to denote the length or duration of the several notes, are said to be of his invention ; also of the several methods of augmentation in the value of the notes by a point, and diminution by a variation of the character in respect of colour, that is to say, either by making it black or red, full or void, or by making it with a tail or without, are here enumerated. Next follow certain precepts, tending to facilitate the practice of descant, whereby it appears that the tenor being in one mode

of measure or time, the descant may be another ; this may be conceived, if it be understood that the metres coincide in the general division of them, otherwise it seems to be absolutely impossible.

The use of red characters is but barely hinted at in the tract now citing : indeed the author does no more than intimate that where it is necessary to diminish the value of notes by a third part, making those imperfect which else would be perfect, it may be done either by evacuating them, or making them red, ' when the writer has wherewithal to do so.'

This kind of alteration in the value by a change in the colour of notes, occurs frequently in old compositions, and is mentioned by most authors, who when they speak of the diversity of colours mention black full and black void, and red full and red void : Nevertheless in a very curious ancient poem, entitled A Treatise betweene Trouth and Information, printed at the end of Skelton's works, there is the following passage, whereby it may seem that Vert or Green, was also used among musicians to note a diversity of character :—

In mufyke I have lerned iiii colors as this,
    Blake, ful blake, Verte, and in lykewyfe redde ;
By thefe colors many fubtill alteracions there is,
    That wil begile one tho in conying he be well fped.

The author of this poem was William Cornysh, of the royal chapel in the reign of Henry VII., a man so eminent for his skill in music, that Morley has assigned him a place in his catalogue of English musicians, an honour, which, to judge of him by many of his compositions now extant, he seems to have well deserved ; and these considerations do naturally induce a suspicion, if not a belief, that notwithstanding the silence of other writers in this respect, Green characters might sometimes be made use of in musical notation.

But a little reflection on the passage will suggest an emendation that renders it consistent with what others have said on the subject. In short, if we read and point it thus :—

In mufyke I have lerned iiii colors ; as this,
    Blake ful, blake *voide*, and in lykewife redde,

it is perfectly intelligible and is sound musical doctrine.

The next in order of the tracts contained in the Cotton manuscript is a very copious, elaborate, and methodical discourse on the science of music in general, by an unknown author. The initial words of it are ' Pro aliquali notitia de musica habenda :' it begins with the etymology of the word music, which he says is derived either from the Muses, or from the Greek word Moys, signifying water, because without water or moisture no sweetness of sound can subsist.‡ Boetius's division of music into mun-

---

* An explanation of this strange word will be met with in a subsequent page.

† This tract contains most evidently a summary of the improvements of De Muris on the Cantus Mensurabilis, but by an unaccountable mistake he is here called Egidius instead of Johannes, a name which does not once occur in any of the authors that have been consulted in the course of this work. We must therefore look on the character above given of Giles, to be intended for John, De Muris. It seems that Mr. Casley, by a mistake of a different kind, looked upon this tract as having been written by Giles De Muris. See his Catalogue, pag. 320 ; but Dr. Pepusch's copy, for the original has been resorted to and appears to be not legible, contains the following rubric title of the tract in question : ' Alius Tractatulus de Musica incerto Authore.'

‡ That there is such a Greek word as Moys does not any where appear. Kircher, who adopts this far-fetched etymology of the word Music, says that it is an Hebrew appellation, Musurg. tom. I. pag. 44., but in this he elsewhere contradicts himself, by asserting that it is an ancient Egyptian or Coptic word ; and this is rather to be credited because it is said in scripture that Moses, or as he is also called, Moyses, was so named because he was taken out of the water. Exod. chap. ii. ver. 10., and it is remarkable that this name was given him, not by his Hebrew parents, but by Pharaoh's daughter, an Egyptian princess.

The meaning of the above passage is very obscure, unless it be known that the ancient Egyptian litui or pipes were made of the reeds and papyrus growing on the banks of the river Nile, or in other marshy places ; wherefore it is said that without water, the efficient cause of

dane, humane, and instrumental, is here adopted. The first, says this author, results from the orderly effects of the elements, the seasons, and the planets. The second is evident in the constitution and union of the soul and body. And the third is produced by the human voice, or the action of human organs on certain instruments. He next proceeds to give directions for the making of a monochord, which as they differ but little from those of Guido, it is not necessary here to repeat. It is however worth observing, that he recommends for that purpose some instrument emitting sound as a Viol [Vielle, Fr.] a circumstance that in some sort ascertains the antiquity of that instrument, of which there are now so many species, and which is probably of French invention.

He next proceeds to explain the nature of the consonances, in which it is evident that he follows Boetius. Indeed we may conclude that his intelligence is derived from the Latin writers only, and not from the Greeks; not only because the Greek language was very little understood, even among the learned of those times, but also because this author himself has shewn his ignorance of it in a definition given by him of the word Ditone, which says he, is compounded of Dia, a word signifying Two, and Tonos, a Tone, whereas it is well known that it is a composition of Dis, twice, and Tonas; and that the Greek preposition Dia, answers to the English by, wherefore we say Diapason, by all; Diapente, by five; Diatessaron, by four.

After ascertaining the difference between b and ♮, he proceeds to a brief explication of the genera of the ancients, the characters of the three he thus discriminates: the Chromatic as soft, and conducing to lasciviousness; the Enarmonic as hard and disgusting; and the Diatonic as modest and natural; and it is to this genus that the division of the monochord by tones and semitones is adapted.

What immediately follows seems to be little less than an abridgement of Boetius, whose work De Musica, the author seems to have studied very diligently.

In the next place he treats of the plain cantus as distinguished from the Cantus Mensurabilis, which he makes to consist of five parts, namely, first the Characters, with their names; second, the Lines and spaces; third, the Properties; fourth, the Mutations; and fifth, the eight Tropes or Modes. As to the first, he says they are no other than the seven Latin letters A, B, C, D, E, F, G, which also are called Keys, because as a key opens a lock, these open the melody of music, although Γ Greek is placed before A, to signify that music was invented by the Greeks. He then relates, that six names for the notes were given by Guido to these seven letters, UT, RE, MI, FA, SOL, LA; and that he placed a tone between UT and RE, a semitone between MI and FA, a tone between FA and SOL, and a tone between SOL and LA, that the

progression might be according to the diatonic genus. But because there are more letters used in the division of the monochord than there are notes or syllables; for no one can ascend above LA, nor descend below UT, without a repetition of the syllables, seven deductions were constituted, which appoint the place of the syllable UT, and direct the application of the rest in an orderly succession. The place of UT is either at C, F, or g; the deductions he says might be infinitely multiplied, but seven are sufficient for the human voice. It is well known that every repetition of the letters in the musical scale is signified by a change, not of the letter, but of the character; for this reason the author of the tract now before us observes, that immediately after C we are to take the smaller Roman letters; and in the third series we are to use other characters having the same powers; we now double the former thus aa, bb, ♭♭, cc, dd, ee, but he has chosen to express them by Gothic characters, The first series are termed Graves, the second Acutes, and the last Superacutes.

Having thus explained the names and characters of the musical notes, the author proceeds to shew the use of the lines and spaces, which he does in very few words; but as sufficient has been said on that subject by Guido himself, and the substance of his doctrine is contained in an abstract of his own work herein-before given, what this author has said upon it is here purposely omitted. He mentions, though without ascribing it to Guido, the invention of the hand for the instruction of boys, and, taking the left for an example, he directs the placing UT at the end of the thumb, and the other notes in the places following :—

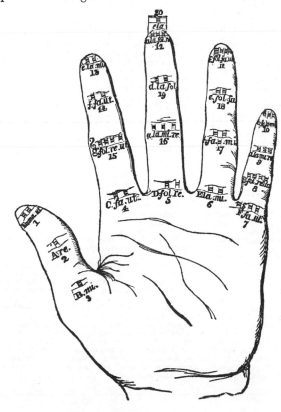

He next proceeds to treat of the Proprieties, meaning thereby not those of the Cantus Mensurabilis, but of the Monochord; and these he defines to be certain affections, from which every cantus takes the denomination of Hard or Soft, according as it is determined by one or other of these characters ♮, or b; or Natural, which is when the Cantus is contained within such a limit, namely, that of a hexachord, as that neither the ♮ hard, nor b soft, can possibly occur: to render this intelligible he adds, that every cantus which begins in b is by sung by ♮ hard in F, by b soft, and in C by nature.*

The author then goes on to explain the mutations, which are necessary, when the six syllables are too few to express the whole Cantus; or, in other words, when the cantus requires a conjunction of another hexachord, by certain diagrams of a circular form, supposed to be taken from a tract intitled De Quatuor Principalium,† mentioned in the preceding note, and which diagrams, to the number of nineteen, Morley has given with his own improvements; but the whole is a poor contrivance, and so much inferior to that most ingenious one, representing the three hexa-

* To explain this matter a little more fully, we must borrow the assistance of our countryman Morley, who in the instructions to Philomathes, his imaginary pupil, tells him that 'there be three principal keys, containing the three natures or proprieties of singing.' Which position of his occasions the following short dialogue:—
'Phi. Which be the three properties of singing? Mast. b Quarre, 'Properchant, and b Molle. Phi. What is b Quarre? Mast. It is a 'property of singing wherein mi is alwaies sung in b fa ♮ mi, and is 'alwaies when you sing ut in gamut. Phi. What is Properchant? 'Mast. It is a property of singing wherein you may sing either fa or 'mi, in b fa ♮ mi, according as it shall be marked b or thus, ♮, and is 'when the ut is in C fa ut. Phi. What if there be no marke? Mast. 'There it is supposed to be sharpe ♮. Phi. What is b Molle? Mast. It 'is a propertie of singing, wherein fa must always be sung in b fa ♮ 'mi, and is when the ut is in F fa ut.'
Upon this passage the following is the note of the author:—
"A propertie of singing is nothing else but the
"difference of plain-songs caused by the note in
"b fa ♯ mi having the halfe note either above or
"belowe it. And it may plainly be seen that
"those three properties have not bin devised for
"prickt-song; for you shal find no song included
"in so smal bounds as to touch no b. And there-
"fore these plain songs which were so conteined
"were called naturall, because every key of their
"six notes stood invariable the one to the other,
"howsoever the notes were named; as from
"d sol re to e la mi, was alwaies a whole note,
"whether one did sing sol la, or re mi, and so-forth of others. If the
"b had the semitonium under it, then was it noted b, and was termed
"b molle or soft; if above it, then was it noted thus ♮, and termed
"b Quadratum, or b quarre. In an olde treatise, called Tractatus
"quatuor Principalium, I find these rules and verses, 'Omne ut inci-
"piens in C cantatur per naturum. In F per b molle. In g per ♮
"quadratum,' that is every ut beginning in C is sung by properchant,
"in F by b molle or flat; in g by the square ♮ or sharpe. The verses
"be these.
"C. naturum dat F b molle nunc tibi signat, g quoque
"b durum tu semper habes caniturum.
"Which if they were no truer in substance than they be fine in words,
"and right in quantitie of syllables, were not much worth."

† † This tract, the title whereof is Quatuor, Principalia Artis Musicæ, and, as it is elsewhere described, De quatuor Principiis Artis Musicæ, is by Wood, Hist. et Antiq. Oxon. ii. 5, and in the Oxford Catalogue of Manuscripts, ascribed to one Thomas Teuksbury, a Franciscan of Bristol; for what reason bishop Tanner says he does not clearly see; but upon looking into the manuscript, there appears at least a colour for Wood's assertion, for the name Tho. de Tewkesbury is written on the outer leaf of it. It is true, as Tanner says, Biblioth. pag. 707, the name Johannes de Tewkesbury is written on a loose leaf; but it is manifest that he was not the author of it, and no such person as Johannes de Tewkesbury occurs in any of the catalogues of the old English musicians; besides this, in the Catalogue of the Bodleian manuscripts, the tract above-mentioned is ascribed to Tho. de Teukesbury. Nevertheless bishop Tanner asserts that it was written by one John Hamboys, an eminent musician, and a doctor in that faculty, who flourished about the year 1470, and is mentioned by Holinshed among the famous writers of Edward the Fourth's time. The reason he gives is this: it appears from Pits, pag. 662, that Hamboys was the author of a work entitled Summam Artis Musicæ, the initial sentence whereof, as Tanner reports, is this: 'Quemadmodum inter Tritico,' and the Quatuor Principalia Musicæ has precisely the same beginning.

chords, and directing the method of conjoining them in plate IV. at the end of Dr. Pepusch's Short Introduction to Harmony, that the not inserting the circular diagrams in this place will hardly be regretted.

Of the Tropes or Modes, though he includes them in the general division of his subject, the author has said nothing in this place. But he proceeds to an explanation of the nature of mensurable music, which, after Franco, he defines to be a cantus measured by long and short times. In this part of his discourse there will be little need to follow him closely, as a more distinct account of the modes or ecclesiastical tones has already been given from Franchinus.

His first position is that all quantity is either continuous or discrete; and from hence he takes occasion to observe that the minim is the beginning of measured time, in like manner as unity is the beginning of number; and adds, that time is as well the measure of a sound prolated or uttered, as of its contrary, a sound omitted.

The comparison which the author makes between the minim and the unit, induces a presumption, to call it no more, that in his time the minim was the smallest quantity in use. But he explains the matter very fully, by asserting that the minim was invented by Philippus de Vitriaco, who he says was a man very famous in his time, and approved of by all the world; and that the semiminim was then also known, though Vitriaco would never make use of it in any of his works, looking upon it as an innovation.

From hence it is manifest, notwithstanding that formal relation to the contrary, which is given by Vicentino, that De Muris was not the inventor of the characters for the lesser quantities from the breve downwards; nay it is most apparent in the rules of Franco, and the commentary thereon by De Handlo, that even the breve was made use of by the former; and it is highly probable that that character, together with the semibreve, for that also is to be found in his rules, was invented by him at the same time with the large and the long.

And here it may not be improper, once for all, to observe, that the necessary consequence of the introduction of these lesser quantities into the Cantus Mensurabilis was a diminution in value of the larger; and we are expressly told by the author now citing, some pages forwarder in his work, not only that at the time when Franco wrote, to say nothing of the minim, neither the imperfect mode, nor the imperfect time were known, but that the breve and the long, which seem to be put as examples for the rest of the notes, were then pronounced as quick as now they are in the imperfect time, so that the introduction of the imperfect time accelerated the pronunciation of the several notes, by subtracting from each one third part of its value. The invention of the minim, and the other subordinate characters, was attended with similar consequences; so that if we measure a time, or, as we now call it, a bar, by pauses, as Franchinus directs, it will be found that in triple, for that is what is to be understood by perfect time, the crotchet has taken the place of the minim, which before had taken place of the semibreve, and so progressively backwards. All which considered, it is clear that though by the invention of the minim, crotchet, quaver, and other notes of a still less value, the modern music is comparatively much more quick than the ancient, the ancient music was not uttered so slowly as the characters, which most frequently occur in it, seem to indicate.

We meet here also with directions concerning the use and application of the Plica, as it is called, which is nothing more than that stroke, which, drawn from the body of a breve, makes it a long, as thus ■ ■, and is at this day called the tail of a note; but it seems that the due placing this was formerly a matter of some nicety, the reason whereof may be that it prevented confusion among the characters, and that fair, curious, and correct writing was then a matter of more consequence than it has been at any time since the invention of printing, a fact, which all who have been conversant with manuscripts, or have been accustomed to the perusal of ancient deeds or charters, well know to be true.

Franco's definition of the Plica is, that it is a mark of distinction between a grave and an acute character; but surely the best distinction of a character in this respect is its situation in the stave. Others term it an Inflexion of a note; but neither is this an adequate definition, nor indeed does the subject seem to be worth one; all that need here be said about it is, that ascending, the Plica of the long was drawn upwards on the right side of the note thus ■, descending, it was drawn downwards thus ■.

Our author next proceeds to a description of the ligatures, taking notice of that threefold distinction of them into those with Propriety, those without Propriety, and those with an opposite Propriety, the nature of which division is explained by Robert De Handlo, adding, as his own judgment, that every descending ligature having a stroke descending from the left side of the first note, is said to be with Propriety, if the ligature has no stroke, it is said to be without Propriety; likewise every ascending ligature, without a stroke on either side, is said to be without propriety; and lastly, every ligature, whether ascending or descending, having a stroke ascending from the first note, is said to be with an opposite Propriety. To this he opposes the rule of Franco, which agrees but ill with this definition, but declines attempting to reconcile the difference, for the reason, that, whether true or false, the rule of Franco is grown out of use.

CHAP. LIII.

The several measures of time, called, rather improperly, the Modes or Moods, and the methods of distinguishing the one from the other, are now so well adjusted, that their respective characters speak for themselves; but it seems that for some time after the invention of the Cantus Mensurabilis, these, as being regulated by certain laws, the reason whereof is not very apparent, were the subject of great speculation, as appears by the author now before us; for, after mentioning the modes of the plain cantus to be eight, as undoubtedly they are, being the same with the eight ecclesiastical tones, and to consist in a certain progression of grave and acute sounds, he proceeds to speak of other modes, namely, those of time, or which refer solely to the Cantus Mensurabilis; and a mode in this sense of the word he defines to be a representation of a long sound measured by short times. As to the number of these modes, he says it had been a matter of controversy, that Franco had limited it to five; but that the more modern writers, and the practice of the singers in the Roman church had extended it to six.

To give a general idea of these six modes of time, it is sufficient to say, that the first consisted of a long and a breve ¶ ¶ ¶ ■; the second of a breve and a long ■ ■ ¶ ¶; the third of one long and two breves ¶ ¶ ¶ ¶ ¶; the fourth of two breves and one long ¶ ¶ ¶ ¶ ¶; the fifth, of a progression by longs only ¶ ¶ ¶ ¶ ¶; and the sixth of breves and semibreves interchanged, in the following order: ■ ■ ■ ◆ ◆ ◆ ■ ◆ ◆ ◆ ◆ ◆

But notwithstanding this variety of six, and a greater that might be formed, the author now citing observes, that the modes are reducible to two, namely, the Perfect and the Imperfect, most exactly agreeing with the present theory of mensurable music, according to which it is well known that all the possible diversities of measure are comprehended within the general division of duple and triple time; the first whereof being regulated by a measure of two, answering precisely to the old imperfect mode, and the other as exactly corresponding with the perfect mode, the measure whereof is the number three.

Next follow some remarks tending to an explanation of the Ligatures, so obscurely worded that it would answer no purpose to transcribe it; and indeed, after reflecting that Morley lived at a time when this method of notation was practised; and that he, speaking of the ancient writers on the ligatures, says, that 'scarce any two of them tell the same tale,' there is very little ground to hope for more information from any of them than is to be met with in his own valuable work.

The author then goes on to shew that mensurable music proceeds by a gradation from unity to the binary, and from thence to the ternary number, and that within the numbers two and three, all mensurable music is comprehended. To explain this, it may be necessary to mention that where the progression is duple, as when the semibreve contains two minims only, it is said to be Imperfect; and where it is triple, the semibreve containing three minims, it is called Perfect: and this is the author's meaning when he lays it down as a rule that where a compounded whole contains two equal parts it is called imperfect; if three, it is called perfect; the reason of which distinction is founded in an opinion of a certain perfection inherent in the number three, which, as well among the learned as the illiterate has long prevailed. And it seems that this attribute of perfection was applicable in three ways, to the Mode, the Time, and the

Prolation : to the Mode, when the greater measure, the long for example, contained three breves ; to the Time, when the breve, which by Franchinus and other authors is also called a time, contained three semibreves ; and to the Prolation, when the semibreve contained three minims ; though it is to be remarked, that it is more usual to apply the epithet of Greater and Lesser than Perfect and Imperfect to Prolation ; but this distinction of perfection and imperfection, with its various modifications, will be more clearly understood from a perusal of the musical trees, as they are called, herein before inserted, than by any verbal description.

It appears also from the work now citing, that the point, by which at this day we augment any given note half its length in value, was in use so early as the period now speaking of. Its original and genuine uses, according to this author, were two, namely, Perfection and Division ; the first is retained by the moderns, the latter seems to have been better supplied by the invention of bars.

The placing a point after a note is called Augmentation ; but it appears by this author and others, that among the old musicians there was a practice called Diminution, to which we at this day are strangers, which consisted in rendering a perfect note imperfect. Of this our author gives many instances, which seem to establish the following position as a general rule, that is to say, a perfect note consisting necessarily of three units, is made imperfect, or to consist of only two, by placing a note of the next less value immediately before it, as in this case ■ ■, where by placing a breve before a perfect long, the long is diminished one third part of its value, and thereby made imperfect ; and the same rule holds for the other characters.

Other methods of diminution are here also mentioned, but the practice is now become not only obsolete, but so totally unnecessary, the modern system of notation being abundantly sufficient for expressing every possible combination of measures, that it would be lost time to enquire farther about it.

In the former part of the tract now citing, the author had given a general idea of the consonances in almost the very words of Boetius, whom he appears to have studied very attentively ; but proposing to himself to treat of the practice of descant, which we have already shewn to be in effect composition, and consequently to require a practical knowledge of the use and application of the consonances, he takes occasion in his Rules for Descant, which immediately follow his explanation of the Cantus Mensurabilis, to resume the consideration of the nature of the several intervals that compose the great system. These he divides into consonances and dissonances, and the former again into perfect and imperfect ; the Perfect consonances he makes to be four, namely, the diapason, diapente, diatessaron, and tone, and gives it as a reason for calling them perfect, that the ratio between each of them and its unison is simple and uncompounded, and by these and no other the monochord is divided. The Imperfect consonances he makes also to be four, viz., the semiditone, ditone, semitone

with a diapente, and a tone with a diapente, which he says are called Imperfect, being commensurable by simple proportions, but arising out of the others by such various additions and subtractions as are necessary for their production.

The reason given by this author for reckoning the tone among the consonances, is certainly an inadequate one, since no man ever yet considered the second as any other than a discord, and that so very offensive in its nature, as to excite a sensation even of pain at the hearing it. Of the perfect consonances he makes the diatessaron to be the principal, at the same time that he admits it is not a concord by itself, or, in other words, that it is only a concord when the harmony consists of more than two parts ; to which position the modern practice of using it as a discord in compositions of two parts only, is perfectly agreeable. *

Boetius has by numbers demonstrated the singular properties of this consonance, and shewn that it can only under particular circumstances be received as a concord. His reasoning is very clear and decisive about it ; nevertheless many, not knowing perhaps that the contrary had ever been proved, have ranked the diatessaron among the perfect concords, and that without any restriction whatsoever. †

But whatever may be urged to the contrary, it is certain that the diatessaron is not a perfect consonance ; for wherever a sound is a perfect consonance with its unison, the replicate of that sound will also be a consonance, as is the case with the diapente and diapason, whose replicates are not less grateful to the ear than are the radical sounds themselves ; on the contrary, the replicate of the diatessaron is so far from being a consonance, that the ear will hardly endure it. They that are curious may see this imperfection of the diatessaron demonstrated by numbers in the treatise De Musica of Boetius, lib. II. cap. xxvi ‡. But to return to our author.

It is to be remarked that in this place he has not reckoned the unison among the consonances, as all the moderns do ; the reason whereof is, that a sound and its unison are so perfectly one and the same,

* Vide Dr. Pepusch's Short Introduction to Harmony, second edition, pag. 39. 41. In the course of the controversy between Mons. Burette and Mons. Fraguier, mentioned in chap. XXII. the former asserts that in order to render the fourth a concord it must be taken with the sixth. Mem. de l'Academie Royale des Inscriptions, &c. tome xi.

† Lord Bacon professes to be of opinion with the ancients, that the diatessaron is to be numbered among the consonances. Nat. Hist. Cent. II. No. 107. But it is to be remarked that he ranks it among the semi-perfect consonances, viz., the third and sixth ; and Butler, who calls the rejection of this ancient concord a novel fancy, notwithstanding the authority of Sethus Calvisius, whom he cites, leaves it a question whether the diatessaron be a primary or secondary concord, and after all inclines to the latter opinion. Principles of Music, pag. 53, et seq.

The late Dr. Atterbury, bishop of Rochester, who it is supposed had learned a little of music from Dr. Aldrich, affected to think with the ancients that the diatessaron was a perfect consonance. He drew up a small tract on the subject of music, wherein he complains in very affecting terms of the injuries which the diatessaron has sustained from modern musicians, by being degraded from its rightful situation among the concords, and concludes with as ardent wishes and prayers for its restoration, as he could have offered up for that of his master. A MS. of the tract above-mentioned was formerly in the hands of Mr. Tonson the bookseller ; it appeared to be a very futile performance, written probably while the author was at college, extremely rhetorical and declamatory, abounding with figures, but destitute of argument.

‡ It is to be supposed that Salinas was not aware of this demonstration of Boetius, since he mentions a Resurrexit for two voices in the famous mass of Jodocus Pratensis, intitled, but for what reason is not known, L'Homme armè, so often celebrated by Glareanus, and other writers, wherein the composer has taken the diatessaron, which, says Salinas, he would never have done had he judged it to be a dissonant. De Musica, lib. II. cap. 21.

that they admit of no comparison; and, according to Boetius, consonancy is a concordance of dissimilar sounds.

Having explained the nature of concords, he proceeds to give directions for the practice of descant; and first he supposes a plain-song to descant on, to which plain-song he gives the name of Tenor, à teneo, to hold, for it holds or sustains the air, the point, the substance, or meaning of the whole Cantus; and every part superadded to it, is considered merely as its auxiliary: and in this disposition of parts, which was constantly and uniformly practised by the old musicians, there appears to be great propriety. Lord Verulam's remark that the extreme sounds, not only of all instruments, but of the human voice, are less pleasing to the ear than those that hold a middle situation, is indisputably true; what therefore can be more rational than that the Air, to borrow a word from the moderns, of a musical composition, should be prolated, not only by sounds the most audible, but also the most grateful to the ear.*

After premising that the perfect concordances are the unison, the fifth, eighth, twelfth, and fifteenth, he says that the Descantus or upper part must begin and also conclude with a perfect concord; that where the plain-song is situated among the grave sounds, the Descantus may begin in the twelfth or fifteenth, otherwise in the eighth or twelfth; and if the plain-song lies chiefly among the acutes, the descant may be in the fifth or eighth. Again, the descant beginning on one or other of the above concords, the descanter is to proceed to the nearest concords, avoiding to take two perfect concords of the same kind consecutively, and so to order his harmony, that when the plain-song ascends the descant shall descend, and vice versa. Farther, if two or more sing upon a plain-song, they must use their best endeavours to avoid taking the same concords. These, as far as they go, are the authors' rules for descant; and to them succeed others more particular, which, as they are peculiarly adapted to, and are descriptive of the practice of descant, are here given in nearly his own words:—

'Let there be four or five men, and the first of ' them begin the plain-song in the tenor; let the ' second begin in the fifth, the third in the eighth, ' and the fourth in the twelfth; and let all continue ' the plain-song in these concords to the end, observ- ' ing this, that those who sing in the eighth and ' twelfth do Break and Flower the notes in such ' manner as best to grace the melody. But note well ' that he who sings the Tenor must utter the notes full ' and distinctly, and that he who descants must take ' only the imperfect concords, namely, the third, sixth, ' and tenth, and must proceed by these ascending ' and descending, as to him shall seem most expedient ' and pleasing to the ear.' The author adds, that observing these rules each of the singers will appear to descant, when in truth only one does so, the rest

simply modulating on the fundamental melody of the tenor or plain-song.

To give weight to the above precept, which requires the person who sings the tenor to utter the notes fully and distinctly, the author adds, that it is the practice of the Roman palace, and indeed of the French and all other choirs, where the service is skilfully performed, for the tenor, which is to regulate and govern the Descantus, to be audibly and firmly pronounced, lest the descanter should be led to take dissonances instead of concords.

From this and many other passages in this work, wherein the singer is cautioned against the use of discords, and more especially as nothing occurs in it concerning their preparation and resolution, without which every one knows they are intolerable, there is good reason to infer that the use of discords in musical composition was unknown at the time when this author wrote, which at the latest has been shewn to be anno 1326. But the particular æra of this improvement will be the subject of future enquiry.

Whoever shall attentively peruse the foregoing passages, and reflect on the nature and end of musical composition, in fact will find it extremely difficult to conceive it possible for five, or four, or even three persons, thus extemporaneously, and without any other assistance than a written paper, which each is supposed to have before him, containing the melody upon which he is to sing, to produce a succession of such sounds as shall be grateful to the ear, and consequently consistent with the laws of harmony. As difficult also is it to discern the possibility of avoiding the frequent repetition of the same concords, the taking whereof in consecution is by the rule above laid down expressly forbidden.

This is certain, that notwithstanding the generality of the practice of extempore descant, and the effects ascribed to it, so long ago as the reign of queen Elizabeth it was a matter of doubt with one of the greatest masters of that time, whether, supposing three or more persons to sing extempore on a plain-song, the result of their joint endeavours could possibly be any other than discord and confusion.

Having thus explained the nature of extempore descant, the author proceeds to treat of Polyphonous or Symphoniac music at large; and here it is necessary to be observed, that although the precepts of descant, as given by him, do in general refer to that kind of musical composition, which is understood by the word Counterpoint; yet, from the directions which he gives for Flowering or breaking the notes, and from sundry passages that occur in his work, where he speaks of a Conjunction, and in others of a Conglutination of notes in one and the same part, there is ground to imagine that even so early as the time of composing this tract the studies of musicians were not confined to counterpoint, but that they had some idea of Canto Figurato. And this opinion is rendered to the highest degree probable by the concluding pages of his work, which contain an explanation of the nature and use of Hockets.

It must be confessed that at this day the word Hocket is not very intelligible; its etymology does

---

* It seems that the contrary practice, namely, that of giving the air to the Soprano, or upper part, had its rise in the theatre, and followed the introduction of Castrati into musical performances; since that it has been adopted by the composers of instrumental music, and it is now universally the rule to give the principal melody to the first violin.

not occur on perusal, and none of our dictionaries, either general or technical, furnish us with a definition of it. We must therefore be content with such an explanation of this barbarous term as is only to be met with in the authors that use it; the earliest of these is De Handlo, who, in his twelfth rubric, without professing to define the term, says, that 'Hockets are formed by the combination of notes and pauses.' The author of the tract now citing has this passage : 'One descant is simply prolated, 'that is without fractions or divisions; another is 'copulated or flowered; and another is Truncatus or 'mangled, and such as this last are termed Hockets;' the meaning whereof in other words seems to be, that one descant is simple, even, and corresponding in length of notes with the plain-song; another copulated, and consisting of certain bundles or Compages of notes, coinciding with the plain-song only in respect of the general measure by which it is regulated; and another consisting of notes and pauses intermixed; and a combination of notes and pauses thus formed is called a Hocket. And elsewhere he says a truncation [Truncatio, Lat.] is a Cantus, prolated in a maimed or mangled manner by expressed [rectæ] notes, and by omitted notes, which can mean only pauses; and that a truncation is the same as a hocket, as an example whereof he gives the following :—

Upon which he remarks that a hocket may be formed upon any given tenor or plain-song, so that while one sings, the other or others may be silent; but yet there must be a general equivalence in the times or measures, as also a concordance between the prolated notes of the several parts.

The author next proceeds to speak of the organ as an instrument necessary in the Cantus Ecclesiasticus, the antiquity whereof he confesses himself at a loss to ascertain. He says it is of Greek invention, for that in the year 797 an organ was sent by Constantine king of the Greeks to Pepin, emperor of France, at which time he says the Cantus Mensurabilis was unknown. He says that this improvement of music was made by slow degrees, and that Franco was the first approved author who wrote on it.

CHAP. LIV.

THE next succeeding tract in the Cotton manuscript, beginning 'Cognita modulatione Melorum 'secundum viam octo Troporum,' by an anonymous author, is altogether as it should seem on the Cantus Mensurabilis ; and by this it clearly appears, that as among the ancient musicians there were eight tones, modes, or tropes of melody, or, in other words, eight ecclesiastical tones, so were there eight modes of time in use among them ; and this, notwithstanding it is said in the former tract that Franco had limited the number to five ; but for this the same reason may be given as for extending it to six, against the precept of Franco, to wit, that it was the practice of the singers in the Roman palace.*

The author speaks of one Magister Leoninus as a celebrated musician of the time, and also of a person named Perotinus,† whom he surnames the Great whenever he takes occasion to mention him.

The tract now citing goes on to say of Leoninus, before-mentioned, that he was a most excellent organist, and that he made a great book of the Organum for the Gradual and the Antiphonam, in order to improve the divine service ; and that it was in use till the time of Perotinus ; but that the latter, who was an excellent descanter, indeed a better than Leoninus himself, abbreviated it, and made better points or subjects for descant or fugue, and made also many excellent quadruples and triples. The same author says that the compositions of Perotinus Magnus were used till the time of Robertus de Sabilone, in the choir of the greater church of the Blessed Virgin at Paris. Mention is here also made of Peter, a most excellent notator, and John, dictus Primarius, Thomas de Sancto Juliano, a Parisian, and others deeply skilled in the Cantus Mensurabilis. These for the most part are celebrated as excellent notators ; but the same author mentions some others as famous for their skill in descant, and other parts of practical music, as namely, Theobaldus Gallicus, Simon de Sacalia, and Joannes de Franconus of Picardy. He says farther that there were in England men who sang very delightfully, as Johannes Filius Dei, one Makeblite of Winchester, and another named Blakismet, probably Blacksmith, a singer in the palace of our lord Henry the last. He speaks of the Spaniards, and those of Pampeluna, and of the English and French in general, as excelling in music.

The author, after an explanation of the modes of time, the nature of the ligatures, and other particulars, of which an account has already been given, proceeds to relate what must be thought a matter of some curiosity, namely, that the stave of five lines, which was, as indeed appears from old musical manuscripts, for some purposes reduced to a less number, was frequently made to consist of lines of different colours. As this seems to coincide with a passage in the Micrologus of Guido, it is worthy of remark.

The passage in the author now citing is very curious, and is here given in a translation of his own words :—' Some notators were accustomed in the 'Cantus Ecclesiasticus always to rule Four lines of 'the same colour between two of writing, or above 'one line of writing ; but the ancients were not ac'customed to have more than three lines of different 'colours, and others two of different colours ; and 'others one of one colour, their lines were ruled with

---

* Vide supra, pag. 235.

† In bishop Tanner's Bibliotheca, and also in the Fasti Oxon, vol. I. col. 23, is an article for Robert Perrot, born at Haroldston in the county of Pembroke, a doctor of music, and organist of Magdalen college in Oxford, the composer of the music to various sacred hymns ; and there would be little doubt that he was the person here meant, but that he is said to have died in 1550. However it is to be observed that the Cotton manuscript contains a number of treatises on music by different authors ; and though the first carries evidence on the face of it, that it was composed so early as 1326, it does not follow that the others are of as great antiquity. Nay there is no reason to suppose that that now under consideration is so ancient as that the person mentioned by Tanner might not be the Perotinus Magnus above celebrated.

'some hard metal, as in the Cartumensian and other
'books, but such books are not used among the or-
'ganists in France, in Spain and Arragon, in Pam-
'pelone, or England, nor many other places, accord-
'ing to what fully appears in their books, but they
'used Red or Black lines drawn with ink. At the
'beginning of a cantus they placed a sign, as, F or c
'or g ; and in some parts d. Also some of the an-
'cients made use of points instead of notes. Observe
'that organists in their books make use of five lines,
'but in the tenors of descants are used only four, be-
'cause the tenor was always used to be taken from
'the ecclesiastical cantus, noted by four lines, &c.'*

Farther on the author speaks of a method of notation by the letters of the alphabet, which is no
other than that introduced by St. Gregory ; the examples he gives are of letters in the old Gothic character, and such are to be seen in the Storia della
Musica of Padre Martini, vol. I. pag. 178 ; but he
says that the method of notation in use in his time
was by points, either round or square, sometimes
with a tail and sometimes without.

Having treated thus largely of the Cantus Mensurabilis, he proceeds to an explanation of the harmonical concordances, in which as he does but abridge
Boetius, it is needless to follow him.

He then proceeds to relate that the word Organum
is used in various senses, for that it sometimes signifies
the instrument itself, and at other times that kind of
choral accompaniment which comprehends the whole
harmony, and is treated of in the Micrologus of
Guido. He speaks also of the Organum Simplex, or
pure organ, a term which frequently occurs in the
monkish musical writers, and which seems to mean
the unisonous accompaniment of the tenor or other
single voice in the versicles of the service. The precepts for the Organum or general accompaniment are
manifestly taken from Guido, and the examples are
in letters like those in the Micrologus.

Next follow the rudiments of descant, of which
sufficient has been said already.

Speaking of the Triples, Quadruples, and Copulæ,
terms that in this place relate to the Cantus Mensurabilis, he digresses to descant ; and, speaking of the
concords, says that although the ditone and semiditone are not reckoned among the perfect concords,
yet that among the best organists in some countries,
as in England, in the country called Westcontre, they
are used as such.

And here it is to be observed, that for the first
time we meet with the mention of Discords ; for the
author now citing says, that many good organists and
makers of hymns and antiphons put discords in the
room of concords, without any rule or consideration,
except that the discord of a tone or second be taken
before a perfect concord. He adds, that this practice
was much in use with the organists of Lombardy.

A little farther on he speaks of the works of Perotinus Magnus, in six volumes, which he says contain
the colours and beauties of the whole musical art.

The author of the above-cited tract appears to have

been deeply skilled, at least in the practical part of
music, and to have been better acquainted with the
general state of it, than most of the writers in those
dark times. It should seem by his manner of speaking of England and of the West Contre, which very
probably he mistook for the North country, which
abounded with good singers and musicians. that he
was a foreigner ; and his styling Pepin Emperor of
France, at the instant that he calls Constantine King
of the Greeks, is a ground for conjecture that he was
a Frenchman.

What follow in the Cotton manuscripts are rather
detached pieces or extracts from some larger works,
than complete treatises themselves : the first of these,
beginning 'Sequitur de Sineminis,' is a short discourse, chiefly on the use and application of the
Synemmenon tetrachord, in which it is to be remarked that the author takes occasion to mention
the use of a cross between F and G, corresponding
most exactly to that acute signature which is used at
this day to prevent the tritonus or defective fifth
between ♮ and f.

The next, beginning 'Est autem unisonus,' treats
very briefly of the consonances. of descant, and of
solmisation, the practice whereof is illustrated by the
figure of a hand, with the syllables placed on the
several joints, as represented by other authors, together with examples in notes to explain the doctrine.

The last tract, beginning 'Cum in isto tractatu,'
which is chiefly on the Cantus Mensurabilis, contains
little worthy of observation except the words 'Hæc
Odyngtonus,' at the end of it, to account for which is
a matter of great difficulty.

Odingtonus [Gualterus,] Odendunus, et Gualteriu
Eoveshamensis, or Walter of Evesham, was a monk
of Evesham, in the county of Worcester, and a very
able astronomer and musician.† He wrote De Speculatione Musices, lib. VI., and the manuscript is in the
library of Christ Church college, Cambridge. The
titles of the several books are as follow :—

'Prima pars est de inæqualitate numerorum et
'eorum habitudine. Secunda de inæqualitate sono-
'rum sub portione numerali et ratione concordiarum.
'Tertia de compositione instrumentorum musicorum,
'et de . . . . Quarta de inaequalitate temporum in
'pedibus, quibus metra et rhythmi decurrunt. Quinta
'de harmonia simplici, i.e. de plano cantu. Sexta et
'ultima de harmonia multiplici, i.e. de organo et ejus
'speciebus, necnon de compositione et figuratione.'‡

Now it is observable that not one of the six books
professes to treat of the Cantus Mensurabilis ; on the
contrary, the title of the fourth is 'De inaequalitate
'temporum in pedibus, quibus metra et rhythmi de-
'currunt ;' terms that ceased to be made use of after
the invention of the Cantus Mensurabilis. This is
enough to excite a suspicion that Odyngtonus was
not the author of the tract in question ; but the time
when he lived is not to be reconciled to the supposition that he knew aught of its contents.

In short he flourished about the beginning of the
thirteenth century : his name occurs as a witness to

---

* The number of lines for the Cantus Ecclesiasticus was settled at
four in the thirteenth century. Stor. della Musica, pag. 399, in not.

† Vide supra, pag. 184.

‡ Tann. Biblioth. 558, in not.

a charter of Stephen Langton, archbishop of Canterbury, in the year 1220. It is said that Walter of Evesham, a monk of Canterbury, was elected archbishop of Canterbury 12 Hen. III. A. D. 1228, but that the pope vacated the election.* The conclusion deducible from these premises is obvious.

A few loose notes of the different kinds of metre conclude the collection of tracts above-cited by the name of the Cotton Manuscript, of which perhaps there is no copy extant other than that made use of in this work. It contains 210 folio pages, written in a legible hand; and as the original from whence it was taken is rendered useless, it may possibly hereafter be given up to the public, and deposited in the British Museum.

Another manuscript volume, little less curious than that above-mentioned, has been frequently referred to in the course of this work by the name of the manuscript of Waltham Holy Cross. The title whereof is contained in the following inscription on the first leaf thereof: 'Hunc librum vocitatum Mu- 'sicam Guidonis, scripsit dominus Johannes Wylde, 'quondam exempti monasterii sanctæ Crucis de 'Waltham precentor.' And then follows this, which imports no less than a curse on any who should by stealing or defacing the book deprive the monastery of the fruit of his labours :—

'Quem quidem librum, aut hunc titulum, qui 'malitiosé abstulerit aut deleverit, anathema sit.' †

Notwithstanding which, upon the suppression of the monastery, violent hands were laid on it, and it became the property of Tallis, as appears by his name of his own handwriting in the last leaf; and there is little reason to suspect that he felt the effects of the anathema.

Of this religious foundation, the monastery of Waltham Holy Cross, in Essex, which in truth was nothing less than a mitred abbey, possessed of great privileges, and a very extensive jurisdiction in the counties of Hertford and Essex, in which last it was situated, a history is given in the Monasticon of Sir William Dugdale; and some farther particulars relating to it may be found in the History of Waltham Abbey, by Dr. Fuller, at the end of his Church History. Here it may suffice to say, that the church and buildings belonging to it were very spacious and magnificent; and here, as in most abbeys and conventual churches, where the endowment would admit of it, choral service was duly performed, the conduct whereof was the peculiar duty of a well-known officer called the precentor.

At what time the above-mentioned John Wylde lived does no where appear, but there is reason to conjecture that it was about the year 1400.

Upon the title of this manuscript, Musicam Gui-

* Tann. in loc. citat.

† Admonitions of this kind are frequently to be met with in manuscripts that formerly belonged to religious houses. That mentioned in pag. 234 of this work, as containing the tract De quatuor Principalia, &c. now in the Bodleian library, had been given to a convent of friars minors in 1388; and the last leaf of it is thus inscribed: 'Ad informa- 'tionem scire volentibus principia artis musice: istum libellum vocatur 'Quatuor Principalia Musice. Frater Johannes de Tewkesbury contulit 'communitati fratrum mynorum Oxoniâ auctoritate et assensu fratris 'Thomæ de Kyngusbury tunc ministri Angliâ, viz Anno Domini '1388. Ita qui non alienatur à prædictâ communitate fratrum sub 'penâ sacrilegii.'

donis, it is to be observed that it is not the work of Guido himself, but a collection of the precepts contained in the Micrologus, and other of his writings, and that therefore the appellation which Wylde has given to it, importing it to be Guidonian music, is very proper.

The manuscript begins 'Quia juxta sapientissimum 'Salomonem dura est, ut inferius emulatio,' which are the first words to the preface of the book, in which the compiler complains of the envy of some persons, but resolves notwithstanding to deliver the precepts of Boetius, Macrobius, and Guido, from whom he professes to have taken the greatest part of his work; meaning, as he says, to deliver not their words, but their sentiments. He distinguishes music into Manual and Tonal, the first so-called from the Hand, to the joints whereof the notes of the Gamut or scale are usually applied. The Tonal he says is so called, as treating particularly of the Tones. Upon the use of the hand he observes that the Gamut is adapted to the hands of boys, that they may always carry, as it were, the scale about them; and adds that the left hand is used rather than the right, because it is the nearest the heart.

The tract now citing contains twenty-two chapters with an introduction, declaring the pre-requisites to the right understanding the scale of Guido, as namely, the succession of the letters and syllables in the first or grave series, with the distinction between ♮ and b. Then follows the scale itself, called the Gamma, answering to Guido's division of the monochord, which is followed by the figure of a hand, with the notes and syllables disposed in order on the several joints thereof, as has already been represented.

In the first chapter the author treats of the invention of music, of those who introduced it into the church, and of the etymology of the word Music. Upon the authority of the book of Genesis he asserts that Tubal Cain invented music; and, borrowing from the relation of Pythagoras, he interposes a fiction of his own, saying that he found out the proportions by the sound of hammers used by his brother, who, according to him, was a worker in iron. He says that St. Ambrose, and after him pope Gregory, introduced into the church the modulations of Graduals, Antiphons, and Hymns. As to the etymology of the word Music, he says, as do many others, that it is derived from the word Moys, signifying water.

In Chap. II. the author speaks of the power of music, and cites a passage from Macrobius's Commentary on the Somnium Scipionis of Cicero, to shew that it banishes care, persuades to clemency, and heals the diseases of the body. He adds that the angels themselves are delighted with devout songs, and that therefore it is not to be wondered that the fathers have introduced into the church this alone of the seven liberal sciences.

In Chap. III. it is said that the ancient Greeks noted the musical sounds with certain characters, as appears by the table in Boetius, but that the Latins afterwards changed them for those simple letters, which in the calendar are made use of to denote the seven days of the week, as A, B, C, D, E, F, G; and that they assumed only seven letters, because, as Virgil says, there are only seven differences of sounds; and nature herself witnesses that the eighth is no other than the replicate of the first, with this difference, that the one is grave and the other acute.

Chap. IV. contains the reasons why the Greek Γ was prefixed by the Latins to the scale, and why that letter rather than any other. The reasons given by the author seem to be of his own invention; and he seems to have forgot that Guido was the first that made use of that character.

The reasons contained in Chap. V. for the repetition of the letters to the number nineteen, are not less inconclusive than those contained in the former chapter, and are therefore not worth enumerating.

Chap VI. assigns a reason why the letters are differently described in the monochord, that is to say, some greater, some lesser, some square, some round, and some doubled. The following are the author's words :—

' As the foundation is more worthy and solid than
' the rest of the edifice, so in the musical fabric the
' letters that are placed in the bottom are not im-
' properly made larger and stronger than those which
' follow, it is therefore that they should be made
' square, as every thing that is square stands the
' firmest.* The other septenary ought to be made
' less, for as we begin from the bottom, the higher we
' ascend by regular steps, the more subtle or acute
' does the sound become : roundness then best suits
' in its nature with these seven letters, for that
' which is round is more easily moved about ; and the
' sounds which are placed between the grave and
' superacute are the most easy for the voice of the
' singer to move in, seeing he can readily pass from
' the one to the other freely and at his pleasure ; the
' four remaining letters are formed double, and as it
' were with two bellies, because they are formed to
' make a bisdiapason with the grave, that is a double
' diapason.'

In Chap. VII. we meet with the names of Guido the Younger, and Guido the Elder, by the latter of whom the author certainly means Guido Aretinus,

* This method of illustration by reasons drawn from a subject foreign to that to which they are applied, is not unusual with the authors who wrote before the revival of literature. Bracton, an eminent civil and common lawyer of the thirteenth century, speaking of the right to the inheritance of land, and the course of lineal descent, says that it is ever downwards, that is to say, from father to son, and for it gives this notable reason: ' Quod quasi ponderosum quiddam jure naturæ descendit, nam ' omne grave fertur deorsum.' De Legibus lib II. cap. 29, et vide Coke's Reports, part III. fol. 40, Ratcliff's case. In a life of Æsop, the reputed author of the fables that go under his name, supposed to be written by a Greek monk named Maximus Planudes, who lived about the year 1317, is a curious specimen of physiological ratiocination, somewhat resembling the former. A gardener proposed this question to Xanthus, a philosopher, the master of Æsop : ' What is the reason that ' the herbs which I plant grow not so fast as those which the earth pro-' duces spontaneously ?' The philosopher resolved it into the divine Providence; but the gardener not being satisfied with this answer, Xanthus, unable to give a better, refers him to his slave Æsop, who bespeaks the gardener thus :—' A widow with children marries a second ' husband, who hath children also : to the children by her former husband ' she stands in the relation of mother; but to those of her second hus-' band, the issue of his former marriage, she is no more than step-mother, ' the consequence whereof is, that she is less affectionate to them than to ' the children of her husband. In like manner,' continues Æsop to the gardener, ' the earth, to those things which she produces spontaneously ' is a mother, but to those which thou plantest she is a step-mother. The ' one she nourishes, and the other she slights.' The gardener was as much the wiser for this answer as those who enquire why the great letters are the lowest in the scale, or why land descends rather than ascends, are made, by the answers severally given to those demands.

for he cites the Sapphic verse, ' Ut queant laxis,' &c. from whence the syllables UT, RE, MI, FA, SOL, LA, are universally allowed to have been taken ; who is meant by Guido the Younger will be shewn hereafter.

In Chap. VIII. he speaks of the six syllables, and the notes adapted to them, and seems to blame Guido for not giving a seventh to the last note of the septenary. It has already been mentioned that Dr. Wallis and others have lamented that Guido did not take the first syllable of the last line of the verse ' Sancte Johannes ; ' and the author here cited seems to intimate that he might have done so ; but it evidently appears that he was not in earnest, for see his words : ' The author seems here blameable for ' not marking the seventh with a syllable, especially ' as there are so many particles in that verse ; he ' might have assigned the first syllable of the last line ' to the seventh note thus, Sancte Joannes, as this ' syllable is as different from all the rest as the ' seventh sound is. What fault, I pray you, did the ' last line commit, that its first syllable should not be ' disposed of to the seventh note, as all the other first ' syllables were assigned to the rest of the notes ? ' But fair and soft, because a semitone always occurs ' in the seventh step, which semitone is contained ' under these two notes, FA and MI ; for when the ' semitone returns to the seventh step, in the sixth ' you will have MI, and in the seventh FA. But if ' the eighth step, a tritone intervening, makes the ' semitone, all the syllables of the notes are expended ; ' therefore whether you will or no, unless you make ' false music, the semitone, to wit MI, returns in the ' seventh, if the disposition be elevated ; but if it be ' remitted it will give FA, which nevertheless makes ' a semitone under it ; therefore these two notes, on ' whose account these names were particularly insti-' tuted, will have as many notes above as below, ' marked with their proper syllables, for MI has under ' it two, RE and UT ; and FA has two above, SOL ' and LA.'

Chap. IX. treats of the Mutations, which are changes of the syllables, occasioned by the going out of one hexachord into another ; concerning which the author with great simplicity observes, that as the cutters out of leather or cloth, when the stuff runs short, are obliged to piece it to make it longer ; so when either in the intension or remission of the scale the notes exceed the syllables, there is a necessity for repeating the latter. What follows on this head will best be given in the author's own words, which are these :—' We must substitute for that which is de-' ficient such a note as may supply the defect by ' proceeding farther : hence it is that with the note ' LA, which cannot of itself proceed any higher, you ' will always find such a note as can at least ascend ' four steps, LA, MI, FA, SOL, LA. In the same manner ' the note UT, which of itself can nowhere descend, ' will have a collateral, which may at least be de-' pressed four notes, UT, FA, MI, RE, UT, the Greek Γ ' and d superacute are excepted ; the first whereof ' has neither the power nor the necessity of being ' remitted, nor the other that of ascending ; for which ' reason UT and LA can never have the same stations.'

The nine succeeding chapters relate chiefly to the mutations, and the use of the square and round or soft b, which, as it is sufficiently understood at this day, it is needless to enlarge upon.

Chap. XIX. treats of the Keys, by which are to be understood in this place nothing more than the characters F C g prefixed to the head of the stave: he says these letters are called keys, for that as a key opens an entrance to that which is locked up, so the letters give an entrance to the knowledge of the whole cantus, to which they are prefixed; and that without them the singer would find it impossible to avoid sometimes prolating a tone for a semitone, and vice versa, or to distinguish one conjunction from another. At the end of this chapter he censures the practice of certain unskilful notators or writers of music, who he says were used to forge adulterate and illegitimate keys, as by putting D grave under F, a acute under c, and e acute under g, making thereby as many keys as lines.

Chap. XX. demonstrates that b round and ♮ square are not to be computed among the keys. This demonstration is effected in a manner curious and diverting, namely by the supposition of a combat between these two characters, a relation whereof, with the various success of the combatants, is here given in the author's own words: 'Observe that 'b round and ♮ square are not to be computed 'among the keys; first, because they wander through 'an empty breadth of space, without any certainty 'of a line; next because they can never be placed 'in any line without the support of another key, for 'it is necessary that another key should be prefixed 'to the line. Moreover as ♮ square never appears, 'unless b round come before it; and b soft ought 'not to be set down unless we are to sing by it: can 'any thing of its coming be expected if it be not 'immediately prefixed to the beginning of a line of 'another key, as it is never to be sung without 'a key? Likewise, as they are mutually overthrown 'by each other, and each is made accidental, who 'can pronounce them legitimate keys? for unless 'b round comes in and gives the first blow as 'a challenge, ♮ square would never furnish matter 'for the beginning of a combat; but as soon as it 'appears it entirely overthrows its adversary b round, 'which only makes a soft resistance. But sometimes 'it happens that b round, though lying prostrate, 'recovering new strength, rises up stronger, and 'throws down ♮ square, who was triumphing after 'his victory.' For the reasons deducible from this artless allegory, which it is probable the author of it, a simple illiterate monk, thought a notable effort of his invention, and because ♮ square and b round are not stable or permanent, he pronounces that they cannot with propriety be termed keys.

In Chap. XXI. the author gives the reason why the notes are placed alternately on the lines and spaces of the stave: but first, to prove the necessity of the lines, he shrewdly observes, that without them no certain progression could be observed by the voice. 'Would not,' he asks, 'in that case the notes 'seem to shew like small birds flying through the 'empty immensity of air?' Farther he says, that were they placed on the lines only, no less confusion would arise, for that the multitude of lines would confound the sight, since a cantus may sometimes include a compass of ten notes. He says, which is true, that in order to distinguish between each series of notes, the grave, the acute, and the superacute, any one given note, which in the grave is placed on a line, will in the acute fall on a space, and that in the superacute it will fall on a line again. He adds, that in a simple cantus no more lines are used than four, to which are assigned five spaces,* for this reason, that the ancient musicians, by whom he must be understood to mean those after the time of Gregory, never permitted any tone to exceed the compass of a diapason; so that every tone had as many notes as there were tones. He says farther that the modern musicians would sometimes extend a cantus to a tenth note; but that nevertheless it did not run through ten notes, but that the tenth, which might be either the highest or the lowest, was only occasionally touched. He adds that when this is the case, the key or letter should be changed for a short time; or, in other words, that one letter may be substituted for another on the same line. Upon this passage is a marginal note, signifying that it is better in such a case to add a line than to transpose the letter or cliff, which is the practice at this day.

To this chapter the author subjoins a cantus for the reader to exercise himself, in which he says he will find six verses applied, two for the grave, two for the acute, and two for the superacute. The cantus is without musical characters, and is in the words following :—

For the graves,
    Hâc puer, arte scies gravium mutamina vocum,
    Quæ quibus appropries nomina, quemve locum.

For the acutes,
    Reddit versutas versuta b mollis acuta,
    Quas male dum mutas, mollia quadra putas.

For the superacutes,
    Gutturis arterias cruciat vox alta b mollis;
    Difficiles collis reddit ubique vias.

Chap. XXII. contains what is called a cantus of the second tone, in which the mutations of the four grave letters C, D, E, F, are contained; it is with musical notes, but they are utterly inexplicable.

CHAP. LV.

Upon the above twenty-two chapters, which constitute the first part or distinction, as it is termed, of the first tract, it is observable that they contain, as they profess to do, the precepts of Manual music; and that this first part is a very full and perspicuous commentary on so much of the Micrologus as relates to that subject.

The second part or distinction, intitled Of Tonal Music, contains thirty-one chapters. In the first

* That is to say three between the lines, one at top, and another at bottom. Martini says that the number of lines to denote the tones was settled at four in the thirteenth century. Stor. dell. Mus. pag. 399, in not.

whereof is an intimation of the person in the seventh chapter of the former part, distinguished by the appellation of Guido Minor; he says that he was surnamed Augensis, and that by his care and industry the cantus of the Cistertian order had been regularly corrected. He cites a little book written by the same Guido Minor for a definition of the consonances.

In Chap. II. he defines the semitone in a quotation from Macrobius, demonstrating it to be no other than the Pythagorean limma.

Chap. III. treats of the Tone, a word which the author says has two significations, namely, a Maniera, a term synonymous with ecclesiastical tone, or an interval in a sesquioctave ratio.

From these two intervals, namely, the tone and semitone, the author asserts that all the concords are generated, and the whole fabric of music arises; in which respect, says this learned writer, 'They, that 'is to say, the tone and semitone, may be very aptly 'compared to Leah and Rachael, of whom it is re-'lated in the book of Genesis that they built up the 'house of Israel.' It would be doing injustice to this ingenious argument to give it in any other words than those of the author. Here they are, and it is hoped the reader will edify by them :—

—— 'For as Jacob was first joined in marriage 'to Leah, and afterwards to Rachael, thus sound, the 'element of music, first produces a tone, and after-'wards a semitone, and is in some sense married to 'them. The semitone, from which the symphony of 'all music principally is generated, as it tempers the 'rigour and asperity of the tones, may aptly be 'assigned to Rachael, who chiefly captivated the 'heart of Jacob, as she had a beautiful face and 'graceful aspect. Moreover a semitone is made up 'of four parts, and, unless a tritone intervenes, is 'always in the fourth step; so also Rachael is re-'corded to have had four sons, two of her own, and 'two by her handmaid. "Enter in, says she, to my "handmaid, that she may bring forth upon my knees, "that I may at least have children from her." The 'tone rendering a rigid and harsh sound, but fre-'quently presenting itself, agrees with Leah, who 'was blear-eyed, and was married to Jacob against 'his will; but fruitful in the number of her children. 'The proportion of the tone is superoctave; Leah 'had also eight sons, namely, six natural sons, and 'two adopted, that were born of her handmaid: but 'the ninth part, which is less than the rest or others, 'may aptly be compared to Dinah, the daughter of 'Leah, who bore afterwards eight sons. When Leah 'had four sons she ceased bearing children, and the 'adopted ones followed: when four steps of the notes 'are made, a semitone follows, which is divided into 'two sorts, as has been said; these may be compared 'to the following sons, the two natural ones, which 'Leah had afterwards, and also the two adopted ones. 'Then follow Joseph and Benjamin, the natural sons 'of Rachael.'

Chap. IV. treats of the ditone.

Chap. V. Of the semiditone and its species, which are clearly two.

Chapters VI. VII. and VIII. treat respectively of the diatessaron, diapente, and diapason, with their

several species, which have already been very fully explained.

Chap. IX. shews how the seven species of diapason are generated.

Chap. X. contains a Cantilena, as it is said, of Guido Aretinus, including as well the dissonances as the consonances. It is a kind of praxis on the intervals that constitute the scale, such as are frequently to be met with in the musical tracts of the monkish writers, and in those written by the German musicians for the instruction of youth about the time of Luther;* but as to this, whether it be of Guido or not, it is highly venerable in respect of its antiquity, as being in all probability one of the oldest compositions of the kind in the world :——

TER ter - ni sunt mo-di, quibus omnis can-ti-le-na contex-i-tur, sci-li-cet, U-ni-sonus, Semi-to-nium, Tonus, Semiditonus, Ditonus, Dyatessaron, Dyapente, Semitonium cum Dyapente. Ad hæc Tonus Dyapason si quem de-lectet, e-jus hunc modum es-se ag-nos-cat qu-umque tam paucis clausulis to-ta armo-ni-a forma-tur, u-ti-lis -si-mum est e-as al-tæ me-mo-ri-æ commendare, Nec pri-us ab hu-jus mo-di stu-di-o qui-es-ce-re, donec vocum intervallis agnatis Armo-ni-æ to-ti-us fa-cil-li-me que-as comprehendere no-ti-ti-am. Tonus. Se-mi-to-ni-us. Di-to-nus. Se-mi-di-to-nus. Dya-tes- - -sa-ron. Dyapente. Dy-a-pason. et intente et re-mis-se pa-ri-ter con-so-nan-ti-a.

* Many such are extant in print; they are in easy Latin, and resemble in size and form the common Latin Accidence. The sense that the reformers entertained of the great importance of a musical education, may be inferred from the pains they took to disseminate the rudiments of plain and mensurable music, and to render the practice of singing familiar to children; and there cannot be the least doubt but that the singing and getting by heart such a Cantilena as is here given, was as frequent an exercise for a child as the declension of a noun, or the conjugation of a verb.

Chap. XI. treats of the nature of b round, of which enough has been said already.

Of Chap. XII. there is nothing more than the title, purporting that the chapter is an explanation of a certain Formula or diagram which was never inserted.

Chap. XIII. treats of the species of diapason, and shews how the eight tones arise therefrom. This chapter is very intricate and obscure; and as it contains a far less satisfactory account of the subject than has already been given from Franchinus, and other writers of unquestioned authority, the substance of it is here omitted.

Chap. XIV. treats of the four Manieras, and farther of the eight tones. Maniera, as this author asserts, is a term taken from the French, and seems to be synonymous with Mode; a little lower he says that a Maniera is the property of a cantus, or that rule whereby we determine the final note of any cantus. In short, he uses Maniera to express the Genus, and Tone the Species of the ecclesiastical modes or tones. In this chapter he complains of the levity of the moderns in making use of b soft, and introducing feigned music,* which in his time he complains had been greatly multiplied.

Chap. XV. concerns only the finals of the several manieras and tones.

Chap. XVI. contains certain curious observations on the terms Authentic and Plagal, as applied to the tones; these are as follow:—

——‘Some tones are called authentic, and some ‘plagal; for in every maniera the first is called ‘authentic, the second plagal. The first, third, fifth, ‘and seventh are termed authentic from the word ‘Authority; because they are accounted more worthy ‘than their plagals: they are collected by the uneven ‘numbers, which among the philosophers were called ‘masculine, because they do not admit of being di-‘vided equally into two parts: thus man cannot be ‘easily turned aside or diverted from his purpose; ‘but an even number, because it may be divided into ‘two equally, is by them not unaptly called woman, ‘because she sometimes weeps, sometimes laughs, and ‘soon yields and gives way in the time of temptation. ‘Hence it is that the second, fourth, sixth, and eighth ‘tones are ascribed to the even number, because the ‘feminine sex is coupled in marriage to the mas-‘culine sex: they are called collateral or plagal, that ‘is, provincials to the authentics. And that you may ‘the sooner learn the properties and natures of each ‘of the tones, those songs are called authentic which ‘ascend more freely and higher from their final letter, ‘running more wantonly by leaps and various bend-‘ings backwards and forwards; in the same manner ‘as it becomes men to exercise their strength in ‘wrestling and other sports, and to be employed in ‘their necessary affairs and occupations in remote ‘parts, until they return back to the final letter by ‘which they are to be finished, as to their own house

‘or home, after the completion of their affairs. But ‘the plagal or collateral songs are those which do not ‘mount up so as to produce the higher parts, but turn ‘aside into the lower, in the region under the letter ‘by which they are to be terminated, and make their ‘stops or delays and circuits about the final letter, ‘sometimes below and sometimes above; as a woman ‘that is ti●d to a husband does not usually go far from ‘her home, and run about, but is orderly and decently ‘employed in taking care of her family and domestic ‘concerns.’

Chap. XVII. assigns the reasons why the final notes are included between D grave and c acute; but the author means to be understood that the double, triple, and quadruple cantus, which are vocal compositions of two, three and four parts, are not restrained to this rule, for in such no more is required than that the under part be subservient to it. It appears that of the final notes, by which, to mention it once for all, the terminations of the several tones are meant, four are grave, and three only acute: for this inequality the author gives a notable reason, namely, that by reason of the load of carnal infirmities that weigh them down, fewer men are found to have grave and rude, than acute and sweet voices.

Chap. XVIII. the author shews from Guido, and other teachers of the musical art, that the compass of a diapason is sufficient for any cantus. Notwithstanding which he says some contend that ten, and even eleven notes are necessary. This notion the author condemns, and says that the unison and its octave resemble the walls of a city, and that the ninth, which is placed above the octave, and the tenth, stationed under the unison, answer to the pallisado or ditch; and that as it is customary to walk about on the walls, and in the city itself, but not in the ditch, or by the pallisado, it becomes all who profess to travel in the path of perfection, to accommodate themselves to this practice, which he says is both modest and decent.†

The following chapters, which are fifteen in number, exhibit a precise designation of the eight ecclesiastical tones; but as these have been very fully explained from Gaffurius, and other writers of acknowledged authority, it is unnecessary to lengthen this account of Wylde's tract by an explanation of them from him.

There is very little doubt but that Wylde was an excellent practical singer, as indeed his office of precentor of so large a choir as that of Waltham required he should be. His book is very properly called a System of Guidonian Music, for it extends no farther than an illustration of those precepts which Guido Aretinus taught: hardly a passage occurs in it to intimate that he was in the least acquainted with the writings of the Greeks, excepting that where he cites Ptolemy by the name of Tholomæus. The truth of the matter is, that at the time when Wylde wrote, the writings of Aristoxenus, Euclid, Nicomachus, and the other Greek harmonicians, were at Constantinople, or Byzantium

---

* Described by Franchinus, Pract. Mus. lib. III. cap. xiii, De fictæ Musicæ contrapuncto, and by Andreas Ornithoparcus, in his Micrologus, lib. I. cap. x. the latter calls it that kind of music termed by the Greeks Synemmenon, or a song that abounds with conjunctions; but it had been better to have called it music transposed from its natural key by b round, the characteristic of the synemmenon tetrachord, in which case B b, E b, or A b, might be made finals, as they now frequently are, but it seems that the old musicians abhorred the practice.

† He gives an example of a double cantus at the beginning of Chapter I, which clearly shews that by a double cantus we are to understand one in two parts.

as it was called, which was then the seat of literature. How and by whom they were brought into Italy, and the doctrines contained in them diffused throughout Europe, will in due time be related.

The tract immediately following that of Wylde in the manuscript of Waltham Holy Cross is entitled 'De octo Tonis ubi nascuntur et oriuntur aut efficiuntur.'

This is a short discourse, contained in two pages of the manuscript, tending to shew the analogy between the seven planets and the chords included in the musical septenary. The doctrine of the music of the spheres, and the opinion on which it is founded, has been mentioned in the account herein before given of Pythagoras. Those who first advanced it have not been content with supposing that the celestial orbs must in their several revolutions produce an harmony of concordant sounds; but they go farther, and pretend to assign the very intervals arising from the motion of each. This the author now citing has done, and perhaps following Pliny, who asserts it to be the doctrine of Pythagoras, he says that in the motion of the Earth Γ is made, in that of the moon A, Mercury B, Venus C, the Sun D, Mars E, Jupiter F, and Saturn g. And that here the musical measure is truly formed.

Next follows a very short tract, with the name Kendale at the conclusion of it. It contains little more than the Gamma, vulgarly called the Gamut, or Guidonian scale, and some mystical verses on the power of harmony, said to be written by a woman of the name of Magdalen. It should seem that Kendale was no more than barely the transcriber of this tract, for the rubric at the beginning ascribes it to a certain monk of Sherborne, who professes to have taken it from St. Mary Magdalen.

'Monachus quidam de Sherborne talem Musicam profert de Sancta Maria Magdelene.'

Next follows a tract entitled 'De Origine et Effectu Musicæ,' in four sections, the initial words whereof are 'Musica est scientia recte canendi, sive 'scientia de numero relato ad sonum,' wherein the author, after defining music to be the science of number applied to sound, gives his reader the choice of two etymologies for the word music. The one from the Muses, the other from the word Moys, signifying water, which he will have to be Greek. He then proceeds, but rather abruptly, to censure those who through ignorance prolate semitones for tones, in these words: 'Many now-a-days, when they ascend 'from RE by MI, FA, SOL, scarce make a semitone 'between FA and SOL; moreover, when they pro'nounce SOL, FA, SOL, or RE, UT, RE, prolate a semi'tone for a tone; and thus they confound the dia'tonic genus, and pervert the plain-song. Yet these 'may be held in some measure excusable, as not 'knowing in what genus our plain-song is consti'tuted; and being asked for what reason they thus 'pronounce a semitone for a tone, they alledge they 'do it upon the authority of the singers in the chapels 'of princes, who, say they, would not sing so without 'reason, as they are the best singers. So that being 'thus deceived by the footsteps of others, they one

'after another follow in all the same errors. There 'are others who will have it that this method of sing'ing is sweeter and more pleasing to the ear, and 'therefore that method being as it were good, should 'be made use of. To these Boetius answers, saying 'all credit is not to be given to the ears, but some 'also to reason, for the hearing may be deceived. 'So also is it said in the treatise De quatuor Princi'palium, cap. lvi., and as a proof thereof, it is farther 'said that those who follow hunting are more de'lighted with the barking of the dogs in the woods, 'than with hearing the office of God in the church. 'Reason, however, which is never deceived, shews 'the contrary.'

Sect. II. entitled De tribus Generibus melorum, treats of the three genera of melody, but contains nothing that has not been better said by others.

Sect. III. entitled Inventores Artis Musicæ equeformis, contains an account of the inventors of the musical art, by much too curious to be given in any other than the author's own words, which are these:—

'There was a certain smith, Thubal by name, 'who regulated the consonances by the weights of 'three hammers striking upon one anvil. Pythagoras 'hearing that sound, and entering the house of the 'smith, found the proportion of the hammers, and 'that they rendered to each other a wonderful con'sonance. When Thubal heard and knew that God 'would destroy the world, he made two pillars, the 'one of brick and the other of brass, and wrote on 'each of them the equiformal musical art, or plain 'cantus; that if the world should be destroyed by fire, 'the pillar of brick might remain, as being able to 'withstand the fire; or if it were to be destroyed by 'water, the brazen pillar might remain till the deluge 'was subsided. After the deluge king Cyrus, who 'was king over the Assyrians, and Enchiridias, and 'Constantinus, and after these Boetius, beginning 'with the proportion of numbers, demonstrated the 'consonances, as appears by looking into the treatise 'of the latter, De Musica. Afterwards came Guido 'the monk, who was the inventor of the Gamma, 'which is called the Monochord. He first placed 'the notes in the spaces between the lines, as is 'shewn in the beginning of this book. Afterwards 'Guido de Sancto Mauro, and after these Guido 'Major and Guido Minor. After these Franco, 'who shewed the alterations, perfections, and im'perfections of the figures in the Cantus Men'surabilis, as also the certitude of the beginnings 'Then Philippus Vitriaco, who invented that figure 'called the Least Prolation, in Navarre. Afterward 'St. Augustine and St. Gregory, who instituted 'the equiformal cantus throughout all the churches 'After these Isidorus the etymologist, and Joanne 'De Muris, who wrote ingenious rules concerning 'the measure and the figuration of the cantus, from 'whence these verses:—

' Per Thubal inventa musarum sunt elementa.
' Atque collumellis nobis exempta gemellis.
' Et post diluvium tunc subscriptus perhibetur :
' Philosophus princeps pater Hermes hic Trismegistus
' Invenit Musas quas dedit et docuit

' Pictagoras tum per martellas fabricantum,
' Antea confusas numerantur tetrarde musas.
' Quem Musis generat medium concordia vera
' Qui tropus ex parte Boicius edidit.
' Unum composuit ad gamma vetus tetrachordum.
' Et dici meruit fuisse Guido monochordum
' Gregorius musas primo carnalitur usas,
' Usu sanctarum mutavit Basilicarum.
' Ast Augustinus formam fert psalmodizandi,
' Atque chori regimen Bernardus Monachus offert,
' Ethimologiarum statuit coadjutor Isidorus
' Pausas juncturas, facturas, atque figuras ;
' Mensuraturam formavit Franco notarum,
' Et John De Muris, variis floruitque figuris.
' Anglia cantorum nomen gignit plurimorum.'*

Sect. IV. entitled De Musicæ instrumentali et ejus Inventoribus, gives first a very superficial account of the inventors of some particular instruments, among whom two of the nine Muses, namely, Euterpe and Terpsichore, are mentioned ; the first as having invented the Tuba, [trumpet] and the other the Psalterium. This must appear to every one little better than a mere fable ; but the author closes this account with a positive assertion that the Tympanum, or drum, was the invention of Petrus de Sancta Cruce.

In this chapter the author takes occasion to mention what he terms the Cantus Coronatus, called also the Cantus Fractus, which he defines to be a cantus tied to no degrees or steps, but which may ascend and descend by the perfect or imperfect consonances indifferently. This seems to be the reason for calling it the Cantus Fractus. That for calling it Cantus Coronatus is that it may be crowned, namely, that it may be sung with a Faburden, of which hereafter.

What follows next is a very brief and immethodical enumeration of the measures of verse, the names of the characters used in the Cantus Mensurabilis, and of the consonances and dissonances, with other matters of a miscellaneous nature : among these are mentioned certain kinds of melody, namely Roundellas, Balladas, Carollas, and Springas ; but these the author says are fantastic and frivolous, adding, that no good musical writer has ever thought it worth while to explain their texture.

The next in order of succession to the treatise De Origine et Effectu Musicæ, is a tract entitled Speculum Psallentium, in which is contained the Formula of St. Gregory for singing the offices, together with certain verses of St. Augustine to the same purpose, and others of St. Bernard on the office of a precentor ; the formula of St. Gregory is as follows :—

' Uniformity is necessary in all things. The metre
' with the pauses must be observed by all in psalmo-
' dizing ; not by drawing out, but by keeping up
' the voice to the end of the verse, according to the
' time. Let not one chorus begin a verse of a psalm
' before the other has ended that preceding it. Let
' the pauses be observed at one and the same time
' by all ; and let all finish as it were with one voice ;

' and, reassuming breath, begin together as one mouth ;
' and let each chorus attend to its cantor, that, accord-
' ing to the precept of the blessed apostle Paul, we
' may all honour the Lord with one voice. And, as
' it is said the angels are continually singing with
' one voice, Holy, Holy, Holy ; so ought we to do
' without any remission, which argues a want of
' devotion : whence these verses of St. Augustine
' for the form of singing Psalms :—

' Tedia nulla chori tibi sint, assiste labori,
' Hora sit ire foras postquam compleveris horas,
' Egressum nobis ostendunt perniciosum
' Dyna, Chaim, Corius, Judas, Esau, Semeyque,
' Psallite devotè, distinctè metra tenete,
' Vocibus estote concordes, vana canete,
' Nam vox frustratur, si mens hic inde vagatur,
' Vox sæpe quassatur, si mens vana meditatur.
' Non vox, sed votum ; non musica, sed cor
' Non clamor, sed amor sonat in aure Dei.
' Dicendis horis adsit vox cordis, et oris,
' Nunquam posterior versus prius incipiatur,
' Ni suus anterior perfecto fine fruatur.'

The verses of St. Bernard have the general title of Versus Sancti Bernardi ; they consist of three divisions, the first is entituled—

' De Regimene Chori et Officio Precentoris.

' Cantor corde chorum roga, cantum lauda sonorum,
' Concors Psalmodia, simul ascultanda sophia ;
' Præcurrat nullus, nec post alium trahat ullus,
' Sed simul incipere, simul et finem retinere,
' Nulli tractabunt nimis, aut festive sonabunt,
' Vive sed et munda cantabunt voce rotunda
' Versus in medio, bona pausa sit ordine dicto,
' Ultima certetur, brevior quam circa sonetur.
' Ultima dimissa tibi syllaba sit quasi scissa,
' Ars tum excipiat si scandens ultima fiat,
' Tunc producatur monosyllaba, sique sequatur,
' Barbara (si sequitur producta) sonans reperitur.

' Detestatio contra perverse psallentes.

' Qui psalmos resecant qui verba recissa volutant
' Non magis illi ferent quam si male lingue tacerent
' Hi sunt qui psalmos corrumpunt nequiter almos.
' Quos sacra scriptura damnat, reprobant quoque jura
' Janglers, cum Japers, Nappers, Galpers quoque Dralbers
' Momlers, Forskippers, Ourenners, sic Ourhippers,
' Fragmina verborum TUTTIVILLUS colligit horum.

' De septem misteriis septem horarum canonicarum.

' Hinc est septenis domino cur psallimus horis ;
' Prima flagris cedit, adducit tertia morti,
' Sexta legit solem sed nona videt morientem,
' Vespera deponit, stravit completa sepultum ;
' Virium nox media devicta morte revelat
' Si cupis intentam psallendi reddere vocem,
' Crebro crucem pingas, in terram lumina figas,
' Observate preces, et ne manus aut caput aut pes
' Sit motus, pariter animi cum corpore pungas.' †

---

* The three last lines of the above verses are additional evidence in favour of two positions that have been uniformly insisted on in the course of this work, to wit, that Franco, and not De Muris, was the inventor of the Cantus Mensurabilis, and that De Muris was not a Frenchman, but a native of England.

† The above verses, as they are descriptive of the state of church-music, and the manner of singing the choral offices in the time of St. Bernard, who lived in the twelfth century, are matter of great curiosity. They may be said to consist of three parts or divisions : the first is an exhortation to the precentor to govern the choir with resolution, and to encourage those who sing to sing the cantus audibly, not wantonly, with a clear round voice. The second part, entitled Detestatio contra perverse Psallentes, is an execration on such as in their singing corrupt the Psalms and other offices. And it seems by the context that the performance of the choral service was not confined to the clerks and officers of the choir, but that a lewd rabble of lay singers bore a part in it, and were the authors of the abuses above complained of. These men are

The next tract has for its title Metrologus, which any one would take to mean a discourse on metre; but the author explains it by the words Brevis Sermo, which had certainly been better expressed by the word Micrologus, a title very commonly given to a short discourse on any subject whatever. Guido's treatise bearing that name has been mentioned largely in its place; and an author named Andreas Ornithoparcus has given the same title to a musical tract of his writing, which was translated into English by our countryman Douland, the lutenist, and published in the year 1609.

This author says of music, that it is so called as having been invented by the Muses, for which he cites Isidore.

Under the head De Inventoribus Artis Musice, he explodes the opinion that Pythagoras invented the consonances; for he roundly asserts, as indeed one of the authors before-cited has done, that Tubal first discovered them. The following are his words:—

'The master of history [i e. Moses] says that 'Tubal was the father of those that played on the 'cithra and other instruments; not that he was the 'inventor of those instruments, for they were invented 'long after; but that he was the inventor of music, 'that is of the consonances. As the pastoral life was 'rendered delightful by his brother, so he, working 'in the smith's art, and delighted with the sound of 'the hammers, by means of their weights carefully 'investigated the proportions and consonances arising 'from them. And because he had heard that Adam 'had prophesied of the two tokens, he, lest this art, 'which he had invented, should be lost, wrote and 'engraved the whole of it on two pillars, one of 'which was made of marble, that it might not be 'washed away by the deluge, and the other of brick, 'which could not be dissolved by fire: and Josephus 'says that the marble one is still extant in the land 'of Syria. So that the Greeks are greatly mistaken

distinguished by the strange appellations of Janglers, Japers, Nappers, Galpers, Dralbers, Momlers, Forskippers, Ourenners, and Ourhippers, for the signification whereof St. Bernard, the author, refers to a writer named Tuttivillus; but as his work is not now to be found, it remains to see what assistance can be derived from lexicographers and etymologists towards ascertaining the meaning of these very strange terms.

And first Janglers seems to be a corruption of Jongleours, a word which has already been shewn to be synonymous with minstrels. Japers are clearly players, Hisriones. Skinner, Voce JAPE. Nappers are supposed to be drinkers, from NAPPE, the Saxon term for a cup. Benson's Saxon Vocabulary. For Galpers it is difficult to find any other meaning than Gulpers, i. e. such as swallow large quantities of liquor, from the verb GULP; and for this sense we have the authority of the vision of Pierce Plowman, in the following passage, taken from the Passus Quintus of that satire:—

> There was laughing and louring, and let go the cuppe,
> And so sitten they to even song, and songen other while
> Till Gloton had igalped a gallon and a gill.

Dralbers may probably be from the word Drab. Momlers may signify Talkers, Praters in the time of divine service, from the verb MUMBLE, to talk, which see in Skinner. Forskippers may be Fair skippers, i. e. dancers at fairs. For Ourenners and Ourhippers no signification can be guessed at; nor does it seem possible to ascertain, with any degree of precision, the meaning of any of the above words, without the assistance of the book from which they were taken: and supposing none of the above interpretations to hold, there is nothing to rest on but conjecture; and one of the most probable that can be offered seems to be this, that the above are cant terms, invented to denote some of the lowest class of minstrels, whose knowledge of music had procured them occasional employment in the church.

The third division of these verses of St. Bernard is entitled 'De septem Misteriis, septem Horarum canonicarum,' and gives directions to singers to cross themselves, and perform other superstitious acts at the canonical hours.

'in ascribing the invention of this art to Pythagoras, 'the philosopher.'

What follows is chiefly taken from the Micrologus of Guido de Sancto Mauro: that the author means Guido Aretinus there cannot be the least doubt, for some whole chapters of the Micrologus are in this tract inserted verbatim.

Next follow memorial verses for ascertaining the dominants and finals of the ecclesiastical tones; a relation of the discovery of the consonances by Pythagoras; remarks on the difference between the graves, the acutes, and superacutes, and on the distinction between the authentic and plagal modes, manifestly taken from the Micrologus; for it is here said, as it is there also, that there are eight tones, as there are eight Parts of Speech, and eight Forms of Blessedness.

CHAP. LVI.

NEXT follows a tract with this strange title, 'Distinctio inter Colores musicales et Armorum Heroum,' the intent whereof seems to be to demonstrate the analogy between music and coat armour. The author's own words will best show how well he has succeeded in his argument; they are as follow:—

'The most perfect number is sixteen, because it 'may always be divided into two equal parts, as 16, '8, 4, 2. There are six natural colours, from which 'all the other colours are compounded. First, the 'colour black, secondly white, thirdly red or ruddy, 'fourthly purple, fifthly green, sixthly fire-red. The 'colour black is in arms called sable; white, silver; 'red, gules; green, vert; fire-red, or; thus called in 'cantus in order as they stand—

In Music		In Arms
'Black is the worst		Sable is the best and most [benign]
'White better than black		Silver second
'Red better than white		Gules third
'Purple better than red		Azure fourth
'Green better than purple		Vert fifth
'Fire-red better than green		Gold sixth

In Arms		In Music
'Fire-red is the worst colour		Gold is the first and most [benign]
'White	- bottor	Silver second
'Red	- better	Gules third
'Purple	- better	Azure fourth
'Green	- better	Green fifth
'Black	- better	Sable worst

'The musical colours are six; the principal of 'which is gold, the second silver, the third red, the 'fourth purple, the fifth green, the sixth black; an 'equal proportion always falls to the principal colour, 'which is therefore called the foundation of all the 'colours; and it is called the principal proportion, 'because all the unequal proportions may be produced 'from it.' This to the intelligent reader must appear to be little better than stark nonsense, as is indeed almost the whole tract, which therefore we hasten to have done with.

This fanciful contrast of the colours in arms with those in music, is succeeded by the figures of a triangle and a shield thus disposed:—'

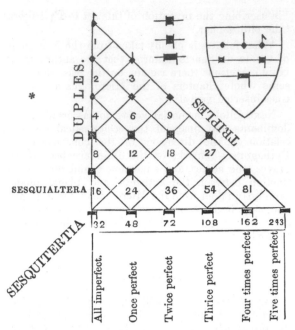

The next tract in order has for its title 'Declaratio 'trianguli superius positi et figure de tribus primis 'figuris quadratis et earum specibus, ac etiam scuti 'per Magistrum Johannem Torkesey;' which declaration translated is in the following words :—

'In order to attain a perfect knowledge of men- 'surable music, we should know that to praise God, 'three and one, there are three species of square 'characters, from whence are formed six species of 'simple notes. In the greatest square consists only 'one species, which is called a large ; and from the 'mediation of that square there are made two species, 'namely, a breve and a long ; from the upper square 'are made three species, namely, the semibreve, 'minim, and simple ; from what has been said it 'appears that no more species could be conveniently 'assigned. All these are found in the small figure of 'the three squares, and in the shield of the six simple 'notes.'

The author then goes on with an explanation of the above six species of notes, and their attributes of perfection and imperfection, wherein nothing is observable, except that the smallest note, which is in value half the minim, is by him called a Simple ; its

* Notwithstanding the explanation which immediately follows the two foregoing figures, it seems necessary to mention in this place, that the first column of numbers contains a series of duple ratios, which are called imperfect, the attribute of perfection being by all musical writers ascribed to the number 3. The next series of numbers which have a diagonal progression from right to left, are triple ratios, and are therefore said to be perfect : the others in succession are also said to be once, twice, thrice, and so on, perfect, in respect of their distance from the column of duples ; for example, the number 24, being but once removed from 8, is said to be once perfect ; whereas 36, which is twice removed from 4, is said to be twice perfect ; and so of the rest.
The first line of numbers below the base of the triangle is a series of numbers in sesquialtera proportion, as 32. 48. 72. 108. 162. 243. in which each succeeding number contains the whole and a half of the former. Those in a diagonal progression from left to right are in sesquitertia proportion, as to take one line only for an example, 32. 24. 18 : in which order each preceding number contains four of those equal parts, three of which compose the succeeding ones, for instance, 24 is three fourths of 32, and 18 has the same ratio to 24.
As to the shield it is a poor conceit, and contains nothing more than the six characters used in the Cantus Mensurabilis, which might have been disposed in any other form ; and as to the representation of the three first square figures, it speaks for itself.

value is a crotchet, but its character that of a modern quaver.

A table of the ratios of the consonances and dissonances, with their several differences, follows next in order, after which occur a few miscellaneous observations on descant, among which is this rule :—

' It is to be known that no one ought to make two 'concordances the one after the other.'

This, though a well-known rule in composition, is worthy of remark, and the antiquity of it may be inferred from its occurring in this place.

The above explanation of the shield and triangle, with the several matters above-enumerated, subsequent thereto, are followed by a tract entitled Regule Magistri Johannis De Muris, which, though it seems to carry the appearance of a tract written by De Muris himself, is in truth but an abridgment of his doctrine touching the Cantus Mensurabilis, together with that of the ligatures, which most writers seem to agree were an improvement on the original invention.

The rules contained in this discourse are not only to be met with in most of the tracts before cited, but in every book that professes to treat of mensurable music. We however learn from it that originally the minim was not, as now, evacuated, or open at the top, as appears by this author's definition of it :—
' A minim is a quadrangular character resembling a 'semibreve with a stroke ascending from the upper 'angle as here ————— and the simple or 'crotchet is characterised thus : —————

To these rules succeed others of an author hereinbefore named, Thomas Walsyngham, of the same import with those of De Muris, in which nothing material occurs, save that the author complains, that whereas there are but five species of character, namely, the Large, Long, Breve, Semibreve, and Minim, the musicians of his time had added a sixth, namely, the Crotchet, which he says would be of no use, would they but observe that beyond the minim there is no right of making a division.

Here it may not be amiss to observe, that neither of the names Johannes Torkesey, nor Thomas Walsyngham occur in Leland, Bale, or Pits, or in any other of the authors who profess to record the names and works of the ancient English writers. It is true that bishop Tanner, in his Bibliotheca, pag. 752, has taken notice of the latter, but without any particular intimation that he was the author of the tract above ascribed to him : and it is farther to be noted that not one of the tracts contained in this manuscript of Waltham Holy Cross is mentioned or referred to in any printed catalogue of manuscripts now extant.

Next follow two tracts on the subject of descant, the first by one Lyonel Power, an author whose name occurs in the catalogue at the end of Morley's Introduction, the other by one Chilston, of whom no account can be given. As to the tracts themselves, they are probably extant only in manuscript. They are of great antiquity ; for the style and orthography of them both, render it probable that the authors were among the first writers in the English language on this subject ; at least if we compare their respective works with the prose works of Chaucer and Lydgate, we shall find very little reason to think they were written a great while after the time when the latter of those authors lived.

Power tells his reader that 'his tretis is contynued 'upon the gamme for hem that wil be syngers, or 'makers, or techers ;' and as to what he says of descant it is here given in his own words :—

'For the ferst thing of alle ye must kno how many 'cordis of discant ther be. As olde men sayen, and 'as men syng now-a-dayes, ther be nine ; but whoso 'wil syng mannerli and musikili, he may not lepe to 'the fyfteenth in no maner of discant ; for it longith 'to no manny's voys, and so ther be but eyght 'accordis after the discant now usid. And whosover 'wil be a maker, he may use no mo than eyght, and 'so ther be but eyght fro unison unto the thyrteenth. 'But for the quatribil syghte ther be nyne accordis of 'discant, the unison, thyrd, fyfth, syxth, eyghth, tenth, 'twelfth, thyrteenth, and fyfteenth, of the whech 'nyne accordis, fyve be perfyte and fower be im- 'perfyte. The fyve perfyte be the unison, fyfth, 'eyghth, twelfth, and fyfteenth ; the fower imperfyte 'be the thyrd, syxth, tenth, and thyrteenth : also 'thou maist ascende and descende wyth all maner of 'cordis excepte two accordis perfyte of one kynde, as 'two unisons, two fyfths, two eyghths, two twelfths, 'two fyfteenths, wyth none of these thou maist neyther 'ascende, neyther descende ; but thou must consette 'these accordis togeder, and medele* hem wel, as 'I shall enforme the. Ferst thou shall medele wyth 'a thyrd a fyfth, wyth a syxth an eyghth, wyth an 'eyghth a tenth, wyth a tenth a twelfth, wyth a 'thyrteenth a fyfteenth ; under the whech nyne 'accordis three syghtis be conteynyd, the mene 'syght, the trebil syght, and the quatribil syght : 'and others also of the nyne accordis how thou shalt 'hem ymagyne betwene the playn-song and the dis- 'cant here folloeth the ensample. First, to en- 'forme a chylde in hys counterpoynt, he must 'ymagyne hys unison the eyghth note fro the playn- 'song, benethe hys thyrd ; the syxth note benethe 'hys fyfth ; the fowerth benethe hys syxth ; the 'thyrd note benethe hys eyghth, even wyth the 'playne-song ; hys tenth the thyrd note above, hys 'twelfth the fyfth note above, hys thyrteenth the 'syxth above, hys fyfteenth the eyghth note above 'the playne-song.'

The conclusion of this discourse on the practice of descant is in these words :—

'But who wil kenne his gamme well, and the 'imaginacions therof, and of hys acordis, and sette 'his perfyte acordis wyth his imperfyte accordis, as 'I have rehersed in thys tretise afore, he may not 'faile of his counterpoynt in short tyme.'

The latter of the two tracts on descant above- mentioned, viz., that with the name of Chilston, is also part of the manuscript of Waltham Holy Cross : it immediately follows that of Lyonel Power, and is probably of little less antiquity. There is no

i e. Mingle.

possibility of abridging a discourse of this kind, and therefore the most material parts of it are here given in the words of the author. The following is the introduction :—

'Her followth a litil tretise according to the ferst 'tretise of the syght of descant, and also for the 'syght of conter, and for the syght of the contirtenor, 'and of Faburdon.'

To explain the sight of descant the author first enumerates the nine accords mentioned in the former tract ; distinguishing them into perfect and imperfect, and then proceeds to give the rules in the following words :—

'Also it is to wete that ther be three degreis of 'descant, the quatreble sighte, and the treble sighte, 'and the mene sighte. The mene begynneth in 'a fifth above the plain-song in vois, and with the 'plain-song in sighte. The trebil begynneth in an 'eyghth above in voise, and with the plaine-song in 'sighte. The quatreble begynnyth in a twilfth above 'in voise, and wyth the playne-song in sighte. To 'the mene longith properli five accordis, scil. unyson. 'thyrd, fyfthe, syxthe, and eyghth. To the treble 'song longith properli fyve accordis, scil. fyfthe, 'syxthe, eyghth, tenth, and twelfthe. To the qua- 'treble longith properli five accordis, scil. eyghth, 'tenth, twelfth, thyrteenth, and fyfteenth. Further- 'more it is to wete that of al the cords of descant 'sume be above the playne-song, and sume benethe, 'and sume wyth the playne-song. And so the dis- 'canter of the mene shal begyne hys descant wyth 'the plain-song in sighte, and a fyfthe above in voise ; 'and so he shal ende it in a fyfthe, havyng next 'afore a thyrd, yf the plain-song descende and ende 'downward, as FA, MI, MI, RE, RE, UT ; the second 'above in sight is a sixth above in voise ; the thyrde 'benethe in sighte is a thyrd above in voise ; the 'fowerth above in sighte is an eyghth above in 'voise ; the syxth above in sight is a tenth above 'in voise, the wheche tenth the descanter of the 'mene may syng yf the plain-song go low ; never- 'thelesse ther long no mo acordis to the mene but 'fyve, as it is aforsaide.'

The above are the rules of descant, as they respect that part of the harmony, by this and other authors called the Mene. He proceeds next to give the rules for the treble descant, and after that for the quadrible.

By these latter we learn that the mean descant must be sung by a man, and the quadrible by a child.

Afterwards follow these general directions :—

'Also yt is to knowe when thou settist a perfite 'note ayenst a FA, thou must make that perfite note 'a FA, as MI, FA, SOL, LA ; also it is fayre and meri 'singing many imperfite cordis togeder, as for to 'sing three or fower or five thyrds together, a fyfth 'or a unyson next aftir. Also as many syxts next 'aftir an eyghth ; also as many tenths nexte aftir 'a twelfth ; also as many thirteenths next aftir 'a fyfteenth : this maner of syngyng is mery to the 'synger, and to the herer.'

And concerning the practice of Faburden, men- tioned in the title of his tract, the author above-cited has these words :—

'For the leest processe of sightis natural and most
'in use is expedient to declare the sight of Faburdun,
'the whech hath but two sightis, a thyrd above the
'plain-song in sight, the wheche is a syxt fro the
'treble in voice; and even wyth the plain-song in
'sight, the wheche is an eyghth from the treble in
'voise. These two acordis of the Faburden must
'rewle be the mene of the plain-song, for whan he
'shal begin his Faburdun he must attende to the
'plain-song, and sette hys sight evyn wyth the plain-
'song, and his voice in a fyfth benethe the plain-song;
'and after that, whether the plain-song ascende or
'descende, to sette his sight alwey both in reule and
'space above the plain-song in a thyrd; and after
'that the plain-song haunteth hys course eyther in
'acutes, fro g sol re ut above, to G sol re ut
'benethe, to close dunward in sight, evyn upon the
'plain-song, upon one of these keyes, D la sol re,
'C sol fa ut, A la mi re. or G sol re ut benethe.
'And yf the plain-song haunt hys course from G
'sol re ut benethe, downe towarde A re conveny-
'ently, than to see before wher he may close wyth
'two or three or fower thyrds before, eyther in F
'fa ut benethe, or D sol re, or C fa ut, or A re,
'and al these closis gladli to be sunge and closid at
'the laste ende of a word : and as ofte as he wil, to
'touche the plain-songe and void the fro excepte
'twies togedir, for that may not be; inasmoche as
'the plain-song sight is an eyghth to the treble, and
'a fyfth to the mene, and so to every degree he is
'a perfite corde; and two perfite acordis of one
'nature may not be sung togedir in no degree of
'descant.'

The foregoing treatise on descant of Chilston is
immediately followed by another of the same author
on proportion, which is thus introduced :—

'Now passid al maner sightis of descant, and with
'hem wel replesshid, that natural appetide not satu-
'rate sufficientli, but ferventli desirith mo musical
'conclusions, as now in special of proporcions, and of
'them to have plein informacion, of the whech after
'myn understonding ye shall have open declaracion.
'But forasmoche as the namys of hem be more con-
'venientli and compendiusli set in Latin than in
'English, therefore the namys of hem shal stonde
'stille in Latin, and as brievely as I can declare the
'naturis of them in English. First ye shal under-
'stond that proporcion is a comparison of two
'thinges be encheson of numbir or of quantitie, like
'or unlike eyther to other; so that proporcion is
'seid in two maner of wyse, scilicet, Equalitatis, and
'Inequalitatis. Proporcion of Equalitie is when two
'evyn thinges be likenyd, either sette togedir in
'comparison, as 2 to 2, or 4 to 4, and so of others.
'Proporcion of Inequalitie is when the more thinge
'is sette in comparison to the lasse, or the lasse to
'the more, as 2 to 4, or 4 to 2, or 3 to 5, or 5 to 3;
'and thys proportion of inequalitie hath five species
'or naturis or keendys, whois namys be these in
'general : 1. Multiplex; 2. Superparticularis; 3. Su-
'perpartiens; 4. Multiplex superparticularis; 5. Mul-
'tiplex superpartiens. The first spece of every
'keende of inequalitie is callid Multiplex, that is to

'sey manifold, and is whan the more nombre con-
'teynyth the lasse manyfolde, as twies 1 ; and that is
'callid in special, Dupla, id est, tweyfold, as 2 to 1,
'or 4 to 2, or 6 to 3, and so forthe endlesli. Yf the
'more numbir conteyne thries the lasse, than it is
'callid in special, Tripla, as 3 to 1, 6 to 2, 9 to 3 ;
'yf it be four times the lasse conteinid in the more,
'than it is Quadrupla, as 4 to 1, 8 to 2, 12 to 3, and
'so forthe. Quindupla, Sexdupla, Sepdupla, Ocdupla,
'and so upward endlesli. As for other keendis, ye
'shall understond that there be two manere of parties,
'one is callid Aliquota, and another is callid Non
'aliquota. Pars Aliquota is whan that partie be ony
'maner of multiplicacion yeldeth his hole, as whan
'betwene his hole and him is proporcion Multiplex,
'as a unite is Pars Aliquota of every numbir ; for be
'multiplicacion of that, every numbir wexeth tweyne :
'or dualite is Pars Aliquota of every evyn numbir ;
'and thus this partie shal be namyd in special after
'the numbre on whom he is multiplied and yeldeth
'his hole; for if he yeldeth his hole be multiplicacion
'of 2, it is callid Altera, one halfe ; and yf he yeldeth
'his hole be multiplicacion of three, it is called Tertia,
'in the third part ; Sequitur exemplum, two is the
'thirde part of 6, and 3 of 9, and 4 of 12 ; and yf he
'yeldeth his multiplicacion be 4, than it is called
'Quarta, as 2 for 8, for 4 tymys 2 is 8 ; and if it
'yeldith his hole be multiplicacion of 5, than it is
'callid Quinta, and of 6 Sexta, and so forth endlesli.
'Pars non aliquota is whan that partie be no maner
'of multiplicacion may yelde his hole, as 2 is a parte
'of 5 ; but he is non aliquota, for howsoever he be
'multiplied he makith not evyn 5, for yf ye take him
'twies he makith but 4 ; and if ye take him thries
'he passith and makith 6. Proportio superparticu-
'laris is whan the more numbir conteynyth the lasse ;
'and moreover a party of him that is Aliquota, and
'aftir the special name of that Parties shal that pro-
'porcion be namid in special, as betwene 6 and 4 is
'Proporcion sesquialtera ; Ses in Greek, Totum in
'Latin, al in Englishe, so Sesquialtera is for to sey al
'and a halfe, for the more numbir conteynyth al the
'lasse, and halfe thereof more over. Between 8 and
'6 is proportion Sesquitercia, for the more numbir
'conteynyth the lasse, and hys thyrd part over. Be-
'twene 10 and 8 is sesquiquarta, betwene 12 and 10
'is sesquiquinta, betwene 14 and 12 is sesquisexta, et
'sic infinitè. Proporcio superparciens is whan the
'more numbir conteynyth the lasse ; and moreover
'the whech excesse eyther * superplus is not Pars
'aliquota of the lasse numbir, as betwene 5 and 3.
'But than thou must loke to that excesse whan the
'more number passith the lasse, and devyde it into
'sweche parties that be aliquota ; and loke how many
'there be thereof, and what is her special namys, and
'whether they be thyrde, fowerth, or fyfthe, and so
'forthe. And yf ther be two parties aliquote, than
'thou shalt sey in special Superbiparciens ; and yf
'ther be three, supertriparciens ; and yf ther be four,
'superquartiparciens, and so forthe. And ferther-
'more tho parties that be tercie, than thou shalt sey
'alwey at last ende, Tercias ; and yf ther be four

---

* Eyther for or, in this and many other places through this quotation.

'Quartas, and so forth endlesli. Sequitur exemplum,
'betwene 5 and 3 is proporcion Superbiparciens ter-
'tias, for the more number conteynyth the lasse, and
'two parties over that be tercie; but they both
'togedir be not pars aliquota of the lasse number;
'betwene 7 and 5 is Superbiparciens quintas; be-
'twene 7 and 3 is Dupla sesquitercias; betwene 9
'and 5 is Superquartiparciens quintas; betwene 10
'and 6 is Superbiparciens tercias: and loke ye take
'goode hede that ye devyde the excesse into the
'grettest partyes aliquotas that ye may, as here, in
'this last ensample, 4 is devyded into 2 dualities, that
'beene tercie of six. And take this for a general
'rewle, that the same proportion that is betwene
'twoe smale numberis, the same is betwene her
'doubles and treblis, and quatrebils, and quiniblis,
'and so forth endlesly. Sequitur exemplum, the
'same proporcion that is betwene 5 and 3, is betwene
'10 and 6; betwene 20 and 12; betwene 40 and 24;
'betwene 80 and 48, and so forth endlesli. Multi-
'plex superparticularis is when the more numbir
'conteynythe the lasse, and a partye of him that is
'aliquota; as 5 and 2 is dupla sesquialtera, and so is
'10 and 4; and so is 20 and 8; but 7 and 3 is dupla
'sesquitercia, and so is 14 and 6. Multiplex super-
'parciens is when the more numbir conteynyth the
'lasse, and the parties that be over aliquote. But
'thei alle togedir be not one parte aliquota, as 8 and
'3 is dupla superbiparciens tercias, and so is 16
'and 6, 32 and 12.

'Here folowyth a breve tretise of proporcions, and
'of their denominacions, with a litil table folwing :—

'The proporcion betwene 1 and 1, 2 and 2, 3 and
'3, and so in more numbir, is callid evyn proporcion,
'for every parcell be himselfe is evyn in nombir, and
'the same.

'Betwene 8 and 4 is callid dowble proporcion, for
'the more nombir conteynyth twice the lasse. Be-
'twene 5 and 4 is Sesquiquarta, for the more numbir
'conteynyth the lasse, and the fourthe parte of him
'over. Betwene 5 and 3 is Superbiparciens tercias,
'for the more numbir conteynythe the lasse, and 2 par-
'ties over, of the whech eche be himselfe, is the thyrde
'parte of the lasse. Betwene 14 and 4 is dupla ses-
'quialtera, for the more numbir conteynyth thries the
'lesse, and the halfe over.* Betwene 8 and 3 is dupla
'superbiparciens tercias, for the more numbir con-
'teynyth twies the lasse, and his two parties over;
'of the whech Pars aliquota is not made be the lesse
'numbir, but ech be himselfe is the thyrde parte of
'the lesse numbir. Betwene 3 and 2 is Sesquialtera,
'for the more numbir conteynyth the lesse, and the
'halfe of him over; betwene 4 and 3 is Sesquitercia,
'for the more numbir conteynyth the lasse, and thries
'one parte over, the whech is the thyrde parte of the
'lesse numbir. Betwene 6 and 2 is Tripla, for the
'more numbir conteynyth thries the lesse numbir.
'Betwene 6 and 3 is Dupla, for the more numbir con-
'teynyth twies the lasse. Betwene 3 and 1 is Tripla,
'ut supra. Betwene 5 and 2 is Dupla Sesquialtera,
'for the more numbir conteynyth twies the lesse, and
'the halfe parti of him over. Betwene 6 and 5 is

* Quere, if not Triple sesquialtera, for the reason above.

'Sesquiquinta, for the more numbir conteynyth thries
'the lasse, and his fifth part over. Betwene 7 and
'2 is Tripla Sesquialtera, for the more numbir con-
'teynyth thries the lasse, and halfe him over. Be-
'twene 7 and 3 is Sesquitercia, ut supra. Betwene
'8 and 5 is Supertriparciens quintas, for the more
'numbir conteynyth the lasse, and three parties over,
'of the whech pars aliquota is not made. Betwene
'9 and 2 is Quadrupla Sesquialtera, for the more
'numbir conteynyth the lesse, [four times] and his
'halfe over.'

Then follow two tables of the proportions in
figures, in no respect different from those that are to
be met with in Salinas, Zarlino, Mersennus, Kircher,
and other writers, for which reason they are not
here inserted.

'Thus over passid the reulis of proporcions, and
'of their denominacions, now shal ye understonde
'that as proporcion is a comparison betwene diverse
'quantiteis or their numbris, so is Proporcionalitas
'a comparison eyther a likeness be 2 proporcions
'and 3 diverse quantiteis atte last, the whech
'quantiteis or numbris been callid the termis of
'that proporcionalite; and whan the ferst terme
'passith the seconde than it is callid the ferst ex-
'cesse; and whan the seconde terme passith the
'thyrd, than it is callid the seconde excesse : so ther
'be 3 maner of proporcionalities, sc. Geometrica,
'Arithmetica, and Armonica. Proporcionalitas Geo-
'metrica is when the same proporcion is betwene
'the ferst terme and the seconde, that is betwene the
'second and the thyrde; whan al the proporcions be
'like, as betwene 8, 4, 2, is Proporcionalitas Geo-
'metrica ; for proporcion dupla is the ferst, and so is
'the seconde ; 9 to 6, 6 to 4 Sesquialtera ; 16 to 12,
'12 to 9 Sesquitercia ; 25 to 20, 20 to 16 Sesqui-
'quarta ; 36 to 30, 30 to 25 Sesquiquinta, and so forth
'upward, encresing the numbir of difference be one.
'The numbir of difference and the excesse is all one.
'Whan the ferst numbir eyther terme passith the
'seconde, eyther the seconde the thyrde, than after
'the lasse excesse or difference shall that proporcion
'be callid bothe the ferst and the seconde, as 9, 6, 4 ;
'the lasse difference is 2, and aliquota that is namyd
'be 2, is callid the seconde or altera : put than to
'the excesse or difference one unite more, and that is
'the more difference, and the tweyne proporcions be
'than bothe callid Sesquialtera. Than take the most
'numbir of the three termys, and increse a numbir
'above what the more difference that was before,
'than hast thou 9 and 12, whois difference is 3.
'Encrese than the more numbir be 3, and one unite,
'scil. be 4, than hast thou 16. So here be 3, 9, 12,
'16, in proporcionalite Geometrica, wherof bothe
'proporcions be called Sesquitercia, after the lesse
'difference. Werk thus forthe endlesli, and thou
'shal finde the same Sesquisexta, Sesquiseptima,
'Sesquioctava, Sesquinona, Sesquidecima, Sesqui-
'undecima.

'Another general reule to fynde this proporcion-
'alite that is callid Geometrica is this, take whech
'2 numbris that thou wilt that be immediate, and
'that one that passith the other be one unite, mul-

'tiplie the one be the other, and every eche be him-
'selfe, and thou shalt have 3 termys in proporcion-
'alite Geometrica, and eyther proporcion shal be
'namyd in general, Superparticularis, be the lasse
'numbir of the 2, that thou toke ferst. Exemplum,
'as 3, 4 ; multiplye 3 be himselfe, and it makith 9 ;
'multiply 3 be 4, and it makith 12 ; multiplye 4 be
'himselfe and it makith 16 ; than thus thou hast 3,
'9, 12, 16, in proporcionalite Geometrica, and thus
'thou shalt finde the same, what 2 numbris immediate
'that ever thou take.

　'And take this for a general reule in this maner
'proporcionalite, that the medil terme multiplied be
'himselfe is neyther mo ne lesse then the two ex-
'tremyteis be, eche multiplied be other : exemplum,
'12 multiplied be himselfe is 12 tymes 12, that is 144,
'and so is 9 tymes 16, or 16 tymes 9, that is al one.
'And this reule faylith never of this maner propor-
'cionalite in no maner of keende of proporcion, asay
'whoso wil. Proporcionalitas Arithmetica is whan
'the difference or the excesse be like 1, whan the
'more numbir passith the seconde as moche as the
'seconde passith the thyrde, and so forthe, yf ther be
'mo termys than 3, exemplum 6, 4, 2. The ferst
'excesse or difference is 2 between 6 and 4, and thus
'the seconde betwene 4 and 2. Proporcionalitas
'Armonica is whan there is the same proporcion be-
'twene the ferst excesse or difference and the seconde
'that is betwene the ferst terme and the thyrd, ex-
'emplum, 12, 8, 6. Here the firste difference
'betwene 12 and 8 is 4 ; the seconde betwene 8 and
'6 is 2 ; than the same proporcion is betwene 4 and 2
'that is betwene 12 and 6, for eyther is proporcion
'dupla. These 3 proporcionalites Boys * callith
'Medietates, i. e. Midlis, and thei have these namis,
'Geometrica, Arithmetica, Armonica. As for the
'maner of tretting of these 3 sciences, Gemetrye
'tretith of lengthe, and brede of londe ; Arithmeticke
'of morenesse and lassnesse of numbir ; Musike of
'the highness and louness of voyse. Than whan
'thou biddest me yefe the a midle betwene 2 num-
'bris, I may aske the what maner of midle thou wilt
'have, and after that shal be the diversite of myn
'answer ; for the numbris may be referrid to lengthe
'and brede of erth, or of other mesore that longith
'to Geometrie ; eyther thei may be considered as
'they be numbir in himselfe, and so they long
'to Arithmetike ; eyther thei may be referrid to
'lengthe and shortnesse and mesure of musical in-
'strumentis, the whech cause highnesse and lownesse
'of voyse, and so thei long to Armonye and to
'craft of musike : Exemplum of the ferst, i. e.,
'Gemetrye : of 9 and 4 yf thou aske me whech is
'the medle by Gemetrye, I sey 6 for this skille ;
'yf there were a place of 9 fote long and 4 fote
'brode be Gemetrye, that wer 36 fote square : than
'yf thou bade me yeve the a bodi, or another
'place that wer evyn square, that is callid Quadratum
'equilaterum, wherein wer neythir more space ne
'lesse than is in the former place that was ferst
'assigned, than must thou abate of the lengthe of the
'former place, and eke as moche his brede, so that it

* Boetius.

'be no lengir than it is brode, that must be by pro-
'porcion, so that the same proporcion be betwene the
'lenthe of the former bodi and a syde of the seconde
'that is betwene the same syde and the brede of the
'ferst bodi ; and then hast thou the medil betwene
'the lengthe and the bredth of the ferst bodi or place ;
'and be that medle a place 4 square that is evyn
'thereto, as in this ensample that was ferst assignyd,
'9 and 4 and 6 is the medil, and as many fote is in
'a bodi or a place that is evyn 4 square 6 fote, as in
'that that is 9 fote longe and 4 fote brode, viz., 36 in
'bothe. The seconde proporcionalite is opin whan
'it is callid the medil be Arithmetike, the whech
'trettyth of morenesse and lassenesse of numbir, in
'as moche as the more numbir passith the seconde
'be as moche as the seconde passith the thirde.
'Neyther more ne lesse passith 12, 9, than 9 passyth
'6, and therefore 9 is Medium Arithmeticum. The
'thirde proporcionalite is callid Armonica, or a medil
'be armonye for this skille. Dyapason, that is pro-
'porcion dupla, is the most perfite acorde aftir the
'unison : betwene the extremyteis of the dyapason,
'i. e. the trebil and the tenor, wil be yeven a mydle
'that is callid the Mene, the whech is callid Dyapente,
'i. e. Sesquialtera to the tenor and dyatessaron, i. e.
'Sesquitercia to the trebil, therefore that maner of
'mydle is callid Medietas Armonica. Sequitur exem-
'plum : a pipe of 6 fote long, with his competent
'bredth, is a tenor in dyapason to a pipe of 3 fote
'with his competent brede ; than is a pipe of 4 fote
'the mene to hem tweyne, dyatessaron to the one
'and dyapente to the other. As thou shalt fynde
'more pleynli in the makyng of the monocorde,
'that is called the Instrument of Plain-song, the
'whech monocorde is the ferst trettyse in the begyn-
'nyng of this boke, but this sufficith for knowleeg of
'proporcions.'

CHAP. LVII.

THE two foregoing manuscripts, that is to say, that
in the Cotton library, and the other called the Manuscript of Waltham Holy Cross, above-mentioned to
be the property of Mr. West, are such valuable
treasures of recondite learning, that they would
justify a copious dissertation on the several tracts
contained in them ; in the course whereof it might
be demonstrated, that without the assistances which
they afford, it had been extremely difficult to have
traced the history of music through a period of three
hundred years, the darkest in which literature of
most kinds can be said to have been involved. But
as a minute examen of each would too much interrupt
the course of this work, some general remarks on
them in their order, must suffice.

And first of De Handlo's Commentary on the
rules and maxims of Franco. The time when it
was compiled appears to be a little before the feast
of Pentecost, 1326 ; but it is observable that the
memorandum at the end, which thus fixes the time,
refers solely to De Handlo's tract, and how long the
rules of Franco had existed before the commentary,
is clearly ascertained by the account herein before
given of him and his improvement.

It must be confessed that to carry the invention of the Cantus Mensurabilis so far back as the eleventh century, is in effect to deprive De Muris of the honour of that discovery, and to contradict those many authors who have ascribed it to him; but here let it be remembered, that not one of those who give to De Muris the honour of inventing the Cantus Mensurabilis, has referred to the authority on which their several assertions are founded. Vicentino seems to have been the first of the Italians that speak of De Muris as the inventor of notes of different lengths; and he seems to affect to say more of the matter than it was possible for him to know, considering that he lived near two hundred years after him; for he not only relates the fact, but assigns the motives to, and even the progress of the invention, in terms that destroy the credibility of his relation. As to the other writers that mention De Muris as the inventor of the Cantus Mensurabilis, as namely, Doni, Berardi, Kircher, Mersennus, and many others, they seem to have taken the fact for granted, and have therefore forborne the trouble of such a research as was necessary to settle so important a question; the consequence whereof is, that the evidence of De Muris's claim rests solely on tradition and a series of vague reports, propagated with more zeal than knowledge, through a period of four hundred years.

In opposition to this evidence stands, first, the fact of Franco's having written on the subject of the Cantus Mensurabilis in the eleventh century. Next, the commentary of De Handlo on his rules, extant in the year 1326, which is some years earlier than the pretended invention of De Muris. Next a passage in the succeeding tract entitled Tractatus diversarum Figurarum, given at large in its place, and importing that an ingenious method of notation invented by certain ancient masters in the art of music, had been improved by De Muris; so that the characters of the double long, the long, breve, semibreve, and minim, are now made manifest to every one. And lastly, the following passage in the tract 'Pro aliquali notitia 'de Musica habenda,' in the Cotton manuscript, '————non enim erat musica tunc mensurata, sed 'paulatim crescebat ad mensuram, usque ad tempus 'Franconis, QUI ERAT MUSICÆ MENSURABILIS PRIMUS 'AUCTOR APPROBATUS.'

These evidences may perhaps be deemed decisive of the question, By whom was the Cantus Mensurabilis invented? but others are yet behind: in the manuscript of Waltham Holy Cross are certain verses, in which Franco and De Muris are mentioned together; the former as the Inventor, and the other as the Improver, of the Cantus Mensurabilis :—

Pausas juncturas, facturas, atque figuras;
Mensuratarum formavit Franco notarum,
Et John De Muris, variis floruitque figuris
Anglia cantorum nomen gignit plurimorum.

The premises duly weighed and considered, the conclusion seems most clearly to be, that the opinion so long entertained, and so confidently propagated, namely, that the characters which now, and for several centuries past have been used to signify the different lengths of musical notes, were invented by Johannes

De Muris, is no better than an ill-grounded conjecture, a mere legendary report, and is deservedly to be ranked among those vulgar errors, which it is one of the ends of true history to detect and refute.

The tract beginning 'Pro aliquali notitia de mu-'sica habenda,' contains a great variety of musical learning, extracted chiefly from Boetius and Guido Aretinus; for it is to be noted that the writers of this period carried their researches no farther back than the time of the former, for this obvious reason, that the Greek language was then but little understood, which is in some measure proved by the manner in which this author uses the Greek terms; we are nevertheless indebted to him for the names of many eminent musicians who flourished in or about his time, as also for the honour he has done this country in ranking several persons by name, in different parts of England, among some of the best practical musicians of the age. It is farther to be remarked on this tract, that by the trebles and quadruples, which Perotinus and Leoninus are by him said to have made, we are to understand compositions in three and four parts, and that he has positively asserted of the Cantus Mensurabilis that Franco was the first approved author that wrote on it.

Of the manuscript of Waltham Holy Cross it is to be remarked, that it appears to be a collection of Wylde's making, and that there is reason to believe that the first treatise, consisting of two parts, the one on manual, and the other on tonal music, was composed by Wylde himself. In the latter of these we meet with the term Double Cantus, and an example thereof in the margin, by which is to be understood a cantus of two parts.

Wylde's tract comprehends the precepts of practical music, and may be considered as a compendium of that kind of knowledge which was necessary to qualify an ecclesiastic in that very essential part of his function, the performance of choral service. His relation of the combat between ♮ square and ♭ round, though it seems to have been but a drawn battle, can no more be read with a serious countenance than his learned argument tending to prove the resemblance of Leah and Rachel to the tone and semitone, and that the sons of Jacob were produced in much the same manner as the musical consonances.

Of the treatise De octo Tonis nothing requires to be said save that it contains a very imperfect state of that fanciful doctrine touching the Music of the Spheres, which very few of the many authors that mention it believe a word about. And as to the offering of the monk of Sherborne, notwithstanding his having received it of St. Mary Magdalen, it appears to have been a present hardly worth his acceptance.

The Treatise De Origine et Effectu Musicæ is remarkable for a certain simplicity of style and sentiment, corresponding exactly with the ignorance of the age in which it may be supposed to have been written. Indeed it would be difficult to produce stronger evidence of monkisk ignorance, at least in history, than is contained in this tract, where the author, confounding profane with sacred history, relates that Thubal kept a smith's shop, and that Pythagoras adjusted the consonances by the sound of his hammers. The two pillars which he speaks of are mentioned by various authors, and Josephus in particular, who says that one of them was remaining in his time; but no one except this author has ventured to assert that the precepts of music were engraven on either of them. His want of accuracy in the chronology of his history would incline an attentive reader to think that Cyrus, king of the Assyrians, lived within a few years after the deluge; and as to king Enchiridias, he has neither told us when he reigned, nor whether his kingdom was on earth or in the moon. Notwithstanding all these evidences of gross ignorance, he seems entitled to credit when he relates facts of a more recent date, to the knowledge of which he may be supposed to have arrived by authentic tradition; and among these may be reckoned that contained in the verses at the conclusion of the third chapter of his treatise, which give to England the honour of having produced Johannes De Muris, the greatest musician of his time.

But besides this relation, which gives credit to the testimony of bishop Tanner and other writers, who assert also that De Muris was a native of England, this tract furnishes the means of ascertaining, to a tolerable degree of certainty, the time when every line in the manuscript of Waltham Holy Cross was written; at least it has fixed a certain year, before which the manuscript cannot be supposed to have existed; nay, it goes farther, and demonstrates that this, namely, the treatise De Origine et Effectu Musicæ, was composed after the year 1451. The proof of this assertion is as follows: towards the end of the first chapter, and in several other places, the author cites a tract entitled De quatuor Principalium, which by the way is frequently referred to by Morley in the annotations on his Introduction. This treatise, which is now in the Bodleian library, is ascribed to an old author named Thomas de Tewksbury, a Franciscan friar of Bristol, who lived about the year 1388. But bishop Tanner has shewn this to be an error, and that the tract, the proper title whereof is Quatuor Principalia Artis Musicæ, was written by Johannes Hamboys, doctor of music, in the year 1451. But to return to the treatise De Origine et Effectu Musicæ.

In the third chapter, in which the author speaks of the supposed inventor of music, and of some who have improved it, he mentions Guido the monk as the composer of the Gamma, and also Guido de Sancto Mauro, who, as he relates, lived after him: besides these two, who will presently be shewn to be one and the same person, he speaks of Guido Major and Guido Minor. That Guido de Sancto Mauro is no other than Guido Aretinus is demonstrably certain; for the subsequent tract, entitled Metrologus, contains several whole chapters, which, though said to be 'secundum Guidonem de Sancto Mauro,' are taken verbatim from the Micrologus of Guido Aretinus; and as to Guido Major and Guido Minor, they are clearly Guido Aretinus, and that other Guido, surnamed Augensis, mentioned by Wylde in the first chapter of the second part of his treatise, to have corrected the cantus of the Cistercian order.

But here it is to be remarked, that Wylde's tract contains two designations of Guido Minor, which are utterly inconsistent with each other, there being no ecclesiastic or other person surnamed Augensis, mentioned in history as the corrector of the Cistercian cantus. On the contrary, we are told that St. Bernard the abbot, who was of the monastery of Clairvaux, and lived about the year 1120, was the person that corrected the Cistercian cantus, or rather antiphonary. On the other hand, Berno, abbot of Rickhow, or Rickenow, in the diocese of Constance, and therefore surnamed Augensis, Augia being the Latin name of the place, wrote several treatises on music, of which some account has herein before been given. And he does not make the least pretence to the having improved the Cistercian antiphonary; so that upon the whole it seems as if Wylde had confounded the two names together, and that by Guido Minor we are to understand St. Bernard the abbot.

The Speculum Psallentium contains a few general directions for singing the divine offices; the verses of St. Augustine are to the same purpose, and those of St. Bernard a satire on disorderly singers, who are described in such barbarous Latin as it seems impossible to translate.

Of the Metrologus little need be said, it being scarce any thing more than a compendium of the Micrologus of Guido Aretinus, with some remarks of the author's own, tending very little to the illustration of the subject. That it should be entitled Metrologus is not to be accounted for, seeing there is scarce anything relating to the Cantus Mensurabilis to be found in it.

The tract entitled Distinctio inter Colores musicales et Armorum Heroum, is a work of some curiosity, not so much on account of its merit, for it has not the least pretence to any, but its absurdity; for the author attempts to establish an analogy between music, the princples whereof are interwoven in the very constitution of nature, and those of heraldry, which are arbitrary, and can scarce be said to have any foundation at all: this may in some measure be accounted for from the high estimation in which the science of Coat Armour, as it is called, was formerly held. Most of the authors who have formerly written on it, as namely, dame Juliana Barnes, Sir John Ferne, Leigh, Boswell, and others, term it a divine and heavenly knowledge; but the wiser moderns regard it as a study of very little importance to the welfare of mankind in general. Morley had seen this notable work, and has given his sentiments of heraldical, or rather, as he terms it, alcumistical music, in the annotations on the first part of his Introduction.

The declaration of the triangle and the shield by John Torkesey has some merit, for though the shield be a whimsical device, the triangle, which shews how the perfect or triple and imperfect or duple proportions are generated, is an ingenious diagram. Zarlino and many other authors have adopted it; and Morley has improved on it in a scheme intitled a table containing all the usual proportions.

The treatise entitled Regule Magistri Johannes De Muris, can hardly be perused without a wish that the author had given some intimation touching the work from which these rules are extracted; not that there is any reason to doubt their authenticity, but that the world might be in possession of some better evidence than tradition, that he was the author of that improvement in music which is so generally ascribed to him.

The treatise of the accords by Lionel Power, as it contains the rudiments of extempore descant, must be deemed a great curiosity, were it only because it is an undeniable evidence of the existence of such a practice: but it is valuable in another respect; it is a kind of musical syntax, and contains the laws of harmonical combination adapted to the state of music, perhaps as far back as the time of Henry IV. There are no other memorials of this author than the catalogue of musicians at the end of Morley's Introduction, in which only his christian and surname occur.

As to Chilston, he seems to have been the author of three distinct treatises; the first on descant, the second on Faburden, and the third on the proportions; and each of these subjects requires to be distinctly considered.

The precepts of descant, although the practice is now become antiquated, so far as they are consistent with the laws of harmony, and the rules of an orderly modulation, are of general use; since they are applicable, as well to the most studied compositions, as to extempore practice; and accordingly we see them exemplified in many instances, particularly in the works of Tallis, Bird, Bull, and others, and in a book published in 1591, entitled 'Divers and sundrie 'Wayes of two Parts in one, to the number of fortie, 'upon one playn-song, by John Farmer.' In these the office of the plain-song is to sustain, while that part which is termed the Descantus breaks; or, as some of the authors above-cited term it, flowers the melody according to the will and pleasure of the composer.

But as to extempore descant, it seems difficult to assign any reason for the prevalence of it, other than that it was an exercise for the invention of young musical students, or that it furnished those a little above the rank of common people with the means of forming a kind of music somewhat more pleasing than the dry and inartificial melodies of those days; for as to its general contexture, it was unquestionably very coarse.

Morley, who in his second dialogue professes to teach his scholar the art of descant, but in a way calculated for written practice, has, in the annotations on that part of his work, given his sense at large on this practice of extempore descant in the following words:—

'As for singing upon a plain-song, it hath byn in 'times past in England (as every man knoweth) and 'is at this day in other places, the greatest part of 'the usual musicke which in any churches is sung, 'which indeed causeth me to marvel how men ac- 'quainted with musicke can delight to hear suche 'confusion, as of force must bee amongste so many 'singing extempore. But some have stood in an

'opinion, which to me seemeth not very probable, 'that is that men accustomed to descanting will sing 'together upon a plain-song without singing eyther 'false chords, or forbidden descant one to another, 'which till I see I will ever think unpossible. For 'though they should all be moste excellent men, and 'every one of their lessons by itself never so well 'framed for the ground, yet is it unpossible for them 'to be true one to another, except one man shoulde 'cause all the reste to sing the same which he sung 'before them: and so indeed (if he have studied the 'canon beforehand) they shall agree without errors, 'else shall they never do it.'*

These are the sentiments of Morley with respect to the practice of descant or extempore singing on a given plain-song, a practice which seems to have obtained, not so much on the score of its intrinsic worth, as because it was an evidence of such a degree of readiness in singing as few persons ever arrive at; and that this was the case is evident from the preference which the old writers give to written descant, which they termed Prick-song, in regard that the harmony was written or pricked down; whereas in the other, which obtained the name of Plain-song, it rested in the will of the singer. Besides many other reasons for this preference, one was that the former was used in the holy offices, whereas the latter was almost confined to private meetings and societies, and was considered as an incentive to mirth and pleasantry; and the different use and application of these two kinds of vocal harmony, induced a sort of competition between the favourers of the one and the other. Such persons as were religiously disposed contended for the honour of prick-song, that it was pleasing to God; and as far as this reason can be supposed to weigh, it must be admitted that they had the best of the argument.

Of the different sentiments that formerly prevailed, touching the comparative excellence of Prick-song and Plain-song, somewhat may be gathered from an interlude published about the latter end of the reign of king Henry VII. by John Rastall, brother-in-law of Sir Thomas More, with the following title, 'A new 'interlude, and a mery of the nature of the iiii ele- 'ments, declarynge many proper poynts of phylofophy 'naturall, and of dyvers flraunge landys, and of dyvers 'ftraunge effects and caufes, whiche interlude, yf the 'hole matter be playde, wyl conteyne the fpace of an 'houre and a halfe, &c.'† The speakers in this

---

* The difference between written and extempore descant, as above stated, is obvious; and unless it be admitted it will be very difficult to conceive it possible that children of tender years could arrive at any degree of proficiency in the practice of descant, which yet they are supposed to be capable of. In a book containing an account of the household establishment of Edward IV., entitled Liber niger Domus Regis, it is required of the master of the grammar-school to instruct the king's Henchmen, and the children of the chapel, 'after they cane 'their Descante, and other men and children of the court disposed to learn 'it, the science of gramere.' Now it can hardly be conceived that a child educated in music, but of such tender age as to be unripe for grammatical instruction, could be acquainted with the practice of *extempore* descant, or that he could know more of music than was necessary to enable him to sing the Descantus or the written part assigned him; and therefore it seems that by the expression, 'after they cane their descante,' &c., nothing more is meant than that after they are become capable of singing, perhaps at sight, they shall be taught the rudiments of grammar.

† At the end of the Dramatis Personæ is this note:—'Alfo if ye 'lyft ye may brynge in a dyfgyfynge.' Percy's Essay on ancient Songs and Ballads. Rel. of Ancient English Poetry, vol, I. p. 132, in not.

interlude are the Messengere [or prologue] Nature naturate, Humanyte, Studious Desire, Sensuall Appetyte, the Taverner, Experyence, Ygnoraunce, between whom and Humanyte is the following dialogue :—

Humanyte.   Prick-fong may not be difpyfed,
For therewith God is well plefyd,
Honoured, prayfd, and fervyd
In the church oft tymes among.

Ygnorance.   Is God well pleafyd troweft thou thereby?
Nay, nay, for there is no reason why,
For is it not as good to fay playnly
Gyf me a fpade,
As gyf me a fpa ve, va, ve, va, ve, vade?
But yf thou wilt have a fong that is gode,
I have one of Robinhode,
The beft that ever was made.

Human.   Then a felefhyp, let us here it.

Ygn.   But there is a borden thou muft bere,
Or ellys it wyll not be.

Human.   Then begyn and care not for,
Downe, downe, downe, &c.

By means of the several passages above-cited some idea may be formed of the nature of extempore descant, and the degree of estimation in which it stood about the middle of the sixteenth century; a kind of vocal harmony of great antiquity, but of which it must now be said that there are not the smallest remains now left amongst us.

As to Faburden, a species of descant mentioned by Chilston, and which seems not to fall within any of the above rules, Morley thus explains it.

'It is also to be understood, that when men did 'sing upon their plain-songs, he who sung the ground 'would sing it a sixth under the true pitche, and 'sometimes would breake some notes in division; 'which they did for the more formall comming to 'their closes; but every close (by the close in this 'place you must understand the note which served 'for the last syllable of every verse in their hymnes) 'he must sing in that tune as it standeth, or then in 'the eighth below. And this kind of singing was 'called in Italy Falso Bordone, and in England 'Faburden, whereof here is an example; first the 'plain-song and then the Faburden :—

Conditor alme syderum.

'And though this be prickt a third above the 'plain-song, yet was it alwaies sung under the plain-song.'*

The treatise of Musical Proportions is a very learned work; and as it is a summary of those principles on which the treatise De Musica of Boetius is founded, and affords the means of judging of the nature of the ancient arithmetic, so different from that of modern times, it merits to be read with great attention.

The two manuscripts from which the foregoing extracts are severally made, appear to have been held in great estimation. The latter of them was formerly the property of Tallis, as appears by the name Thomas Tallis, written in the last leaf thereof. And it evidently appears that Morley had perused

* Brossard says of Faburden that it is the burden or ground-bass of a song, not framed according to the rules of harmony, but preserving the same order of motion as the upper part, as is often practised in singing the Psalms and other parts of the divine offices. The Italians, he says, give this name to a certain harmony produced by the accompaniments of several sixths following one another, which make fourths between the two higher parts, because the intermediate part is obliged to make tierces with the bass, as in this example :—

He adds, that some are of opinion that the MI in the middle part marked A should be proceeded by a B MOL, and made FA, to avoid the false relation of a tritone with the FA in the bass, marked B; though others pretend that on many occasions this dissonance has its beauty, and examples of both these methods occur in eminent authors. Diction. de Musique, in Voce FALSO BORDONE.

them both very attentively, previous to the writing of his Introduction to Music. That passage thereof wherein he cites Robert de Haulo, and those other wherein he mentions Philippus de Vitriaco and the singers of Navernia, plainly shew that he had perused the Cotton manuscript. As to the other, as it was in the hands of his friend Tallis, very little proof is necessary to induce a belief that he made a very liberal use of that also; but the express mention of the treatise De Quatuor Principalium, his ridicule of that heraldical musician who undertakes to shew the analogy between music and coat armour, and, above all his explanation of the terms Geometrical, Harmonical, and Arithmetical proportion, in his annotations on the first part of his Introduction, are proofs irrefragable that he had availed himself of Wylde's labours, and made a due use of the manuscript of Waltham Holy Cross.

The Cotton manuscript, and that of Waltham Holy Cross, which seem to contain all of music that can be supposed to have been known at the time of writing them, make but a very inconsiderable part of those which appear to have been written in that period which occurred between the time of Guido and the invention of printing; and innumerable are those who, in the printed accounts of ancient English writers in particular, are said to have written on various branches of the science. That the greater number of these authors were monks is not to be wondered at, for not only their profession obliged them to the practice of music, but their sequestered manner of life gave them leisure and opportunities of studying it to great advantage.

To entertain an adequate idea of the monastic life

in this country, during the three centuries preceding the Reformation, it is in some measure necessary that we should guard against the reports that were raised to justify that event ; as that religious houses were the retreats of sloth and ignorance, and that very little benefit accrued to mankind from the joint efforts of the whole body of the regular clergy of this kingdom.

This must appear very improbable to such as are acquainted with the state of learning at the time now spoken of, since it is not only certain that all that was to be known in those days of inevitable ignorance was known to them ; but that it was part of the regimen of every religious house to assign to the brethren employments suitable to their several abilities ; and that while some were employed in offices respecting the œconomy of the house, and the improvements and expenditure of its revenues, some in manual occupations, such as binding books, and making garments, others were treading the mazes of logic, multiplying the glosses on the civil, and enlarging the pale of the canon law, or refining on the scholastic subtilties of Peter Lombard, Aquinas, and Scotus. Another class of those engaged in literary pursuits were such whose abilities qualified them to become authors in form, and these were taken up in the composing of tracts on various subjects, as their several inclinations led them. Nor must those be forgotten who laboured in the copying of music, in the transcribing and illuminating of Missals, Antiphonaries, Graduals, and other collections of offices used in the church-service,* the beauty and neatness

whereof are known only to those who have made it their business to collect or peruse them. Some of these in the public libraries and private collections are, for fine drawing and colouring, as well of a great variety of scripture histories, as of the numberless illuminations with which they abound, the objects of admiration, even among artists themselves ; and as to the character in which they are written, there are no productions of modern times that can stand in competition with it, in respect either of beauty, neatness, or stability : others were employed in writing the ledger books of their respective houses, and in composing histories and chronicles of the times. Many undertook the transcribing of the fathers ; and others, even in those times of supposed ignorance and indolence, the classics. John Whethamstead, abbot of St. Albans, caused above eighty books to be transcribed during his abbacy, and fifty-eight were copied by the care of one abbot of Glastonbury. Indeed if we may believe some writers, others were less laudably employed in the forging of deeds and ancient charters, in order to fortify the right of their confreres to such manors, lands, &c. as they happened to hold under a litigious or disputable title ; these men were both antiquaries and lawyers ; they were scriveners, or, to go a step higher, perhaps conveyancers, they made wills and charters of land, and gave legal counsel to the neighbouring farmers and others.

The benefits that accrued to learning from the

* The number of books necessary for the performance of divine service in the several churches was so great, that the writing of them must have afforded employment for many thousand persons. By the provincial constitutions of Archbishop Winchelsey, made at Merton, A.D. 1305. Const. 4. it is required that in every church throughout the province of Canterbury there should be found a Legend, an Antiphonary, a Grail or Gradual, a Psalter, a Troper, an Ordinal, a Missal and a Manual. And as there are but three dioceses in this kingdom, which are not within the province of Canterbury, this law was obligatory upon almost the whole of the realm ; as to the religious houses they can hardly be supposed to have stood in need of any injunction of this sort. Besides that the writing of service-books was a constant, it appears also to have been a lucrative employment. Sir Henry Spelman says that two Antiphonaries cost the little monastery of Crabhuse in Norfolk, twenty-six marks, in the year 1424 ; which, he adds, was equal to fifty-two pounds, according to the value of money in his age. Gloss. Voce ANTIPHONARUM. And it is elsewhere said that the common price of a mass-book was five marks, the vicar's yearly revenue. Johnson's Ecclesiastical Laws. Winchel. in not.
To understand this constitution it may be necessary to explain the terms made use of in it : a Legend or Lectionary contained all the lessons, whether out of the scriptures or other books that were directed to be read in the course of the year. The Antiphonary contained all the invitatories, responsories, collects, and whatever else was said or sung in the choir, except the lessons. In the Grail or Gradual was contained all that was sung by the choir at high-mass, as namely, the tracts, sequences, hallelujahs, the creed, offertory, and Trisagium, as also the office for sprinkling the holy water. Johnson, ibid. Among the furniture given to the chapel of Trinity-college, Oxford, by the founder, mention is made of ' four Grayles of parchment lyned with gold.' Warton's Observations on Spencer, Vol. II. p. 244. The Troper contained the sequences, which were devotions used after the Epistle. Johnson, ibid. There is now extant in the Bodleian library a very curious manuscript of this kind, with musical notes, which the catalogue, page 135, No. 2558, calls a Troparion ; an extract from it is given in the Appendix to this work No. 44, and referred to in chap. 40, book V. The Ordinal contained directions for the performance of the divine offices, and is conjectured to be the same with the Pye, which the preface to queen Elizabeth's liturgy mentions as being very intricate and difficult to turn. The Missal was the whole mass-book used by the priest, and the Manual was the ritual, containing the rites, directions to the priests, and prayers used in the administration of baptism and other sacraments ; the blessing of holy-water, and, as Lyndewode adds, the whole service used in processions. Johnson, ibid. Vide Lyndw. Prov lib. III. tit. 27, edit. 1679.
Johnson conjectures the Ordinal to be the same with the Pye mentioned in queen Elizabeth's liturgy, the words are : ' Moreover, the number ' and hardness of the rules called the Pye, and the manifold chaungings ' of the service, was the cause that to turne the booke only, was so hard

' and intricate a matter, that many times there was more business to find ' out what should be read, then to reade it when it was found out.'
Bishop Sparrow has attempted to explain this strange word, and supposes it to be derived from the Greek word Πιναξ, Pinax, a table or order how things should be digested or performed ; but he adds the Latin word is Pica, which he imagines came from the ignorance of friars, who have thrust many barbarous words into liturgies. Farther he supposes it might come from Littera Picata, a great black letter at the beginning of some new order in the prayer ; for that among printers the term Pica letter is used. See his answer to liturgical demands in his Rationale of the Common Prayer. And to the same purpose Hamon L'Estrange in his Alliance of Divine Offices, page 24, thus speaks :—
' Pica, or in English the Pye, I observe used by three several sorts of men, ' first by the quondam Popish clergy here in England before the Reform- ' ation, who called their ordinal or directory Ad usum Sarum (devised ' for the more speedy finding out the order of reading their several ' services appointed for several occasions at several times) the Pye. ' Secondly, by printers, who call the letters wherewith they print books ' and treatises in party colours, the Pica letters. Thirdly, by officers of ' civil courts, who call their callenders or alphabetical catalogues, di- ' recting to the names and things contained in the rolls and records of ' their courts, the Pyes. Whence it gained this denomination is difficult ' to determine, whether from the bird Pica, variegated with diverse ' colours, or whether from the word Πιναξ, contracted into Πι, which ' denoteth a table, the Pye in the directory being nothing else but a table ' of rules, directing to the proper service for every day, I cannot say : ' from one of these probably derived it was.'
These authorities seem to justify Johnson in his opinion that the words Ordinal and Pye are synonymous, to which it may be added that bishop Gibson explains the latter by saying that it means a table for finding out the service belonging to each day. Codex 299, in not.
Such immense numbers of these service-books, and indeed other manuscripts on vellum and parchment, were seized to the king's use, and dispersed throughout the realm upon the dissolution of monasteries, that they became as common as waste paper ; and it is notorious that the common and ordinary binding of old printed books was originally the leaves of such manuscripts as are now spoken of : such as remain yet entire are still sought after as matters of great curiosity ; but none are more ready to purchase an ancient vellum manuscript than the gold-beaters, who make use of them in the beating of gold into leaves, in the doing whereof a leaf of gold is placed between two of vellum. These artificers may be said to entertain a reverence for antiquity, for they prefer the more to the less ancient manuscripts, and for so doing give this notable reason, that the former are less greasy than the latter.
The use of the several books above enumerated, and many others of the like kind, as namely, Antiphoners, Missals, Grailes, Processionals, Manuals, Legends, Pies, Portuasses, Primers Latin and English, Couchers, Journals, Ordinals and other books, hereto before used for service of the church, other than such as shall be set forth by the king's majesty, is abolished by a statute of 3 and 4 Edw: VI. chap 10.

labours of these men must have been very great, since it is well known that before the invention of printing the only method of multiplying copies of books was by writing; and for the purpose of diffusing knowledge in the several faculties, the writers of manuscripts, though very slowly, did the business of printers; and the value that was set on their manual operations is only to be judged of by that extreme care and caution which men of learning were wont to exert over their collections of books. In those days the loan of a book was attended with the same ceremonies as a mortgage; and a scholar would hardly be prevailed upon to oblige his friend with the perusal of a book without a formal obligation to return it at an appointed day.*

BOOK VII.　CHAP. LVIII.

THE censures of monkish ignorance and dissoluteness, so frequent in the works of modern writers are become almost proverbial expressions; and were we to credit them, we should believe that neither learning of any kind, nor regularity, nor œconomy had the least countenance among them. Objections of this kind are generally made by men less knowing than those they thus condemn; such as speak of the study of musty records, and researches into antiquity, with contempt; men of no curiosity, and who are willing to take all things upon trust, and who palliate their ignorance by affecting to despise that of which they are ignorant. That the world is under great obligations to the regular clergy is evinced by the numerous volumes yet extant, the works of monks; and that the strictest order and regularity was observed among them, will appear from the following general detail of the monastic institution, and of the rule and order observed in the greater abbeys and religious houses in this kingdom.

The officers in abbeys were either supreme, as the abbot; or obediential, as all others under him. The abbot had lodgings by himself, with all offices thereunto belonging, the rest took precedency according to the statutes of their convents.

Immediately next under the abbot was the prior; though by the way, in some convents, which had no abbots, the prior was principal, as the president in some Oxford foundations; and being installed priors, some voted as barons in parliament, as the priors of Canterbury and Coventry; but where the abbot was supreme, the person termed prior was his subordinate, and in his absence, in mitred abbeys, by courtesy was saluted as the lord prior; there was also a sub-prior, who assisted the prior when he was resident, and acted in his stead when absent.

The greater officers under these were generally six in number, as in the monastery of Croyland; and this order prevailed in most of the larger foundations; they are thus enumerated:—

1. Magister operis, or master of the fabric; who probably looked after the buildings, and took care to keep them in good repair.

2. Eleemosynarius, or the almoner; who had the oversight of the alms of the house, which were every day distributed at the gate to the poor, and who divided the alms upon the founder's day, and at other obits and anniversaries, and in some places provided for the maintenance and education of the choristers.

3. Pitantiarius; who had the care of the pietances, which were allowances upon particular occasions, over and above the common provisions.

4. Sacrista, or the sexton; who took care of the vessels, books, and vestments belonging to the church; looked after and accounted for the oblations at the great altar, and other altars and images in the church, and such legacies as were given either to the fabric or utensils; he likewise provided bread and wine for the sacrament, and took care of burying the dead.

5. Camerarius, or the chamberlain; who had the chief care of the dormitory, and provided beds and bedding for the monks, razors and towels for shaving them, and part of, if not all their clothing.

6. Cellerarius, or the cellarer; who was to procure provisions for the monks, and all strangers resorting to the convent; viz., all sorts of flesh, fish, fowl, wine, bread, corn, malt for their ale and beer, oatmeal, salt, &c., as likewise wood for firing, and all utensils for the kitchen. Fuller says that these officers affected secular gallantry, and wore swords like lay gentlemen.

Besides these were also—

Thesaurarius, or the burser; who received all the common rents and revenues of the monastery, and paid all the common expences.

Precentor, or the chanter; who had the chief care of the choir-service, and not only presided over the singing men, organist, and choristers, but provided books for them, paid them their salaries, and repaired the organ: he had also the custody of the seal, and kept the liber diurnalis, or chapter-book, and provided parchment and ink for the writers, and colours for the limners of books for the library.

Hostilarius, or hospitalarius; whose business it was to see strangers well entertained, and to provide firing, napkins, towels, and such like necessaries for them.

Infirmarius; who had the care of the infirmary, and of the sick monks, who were carried thither, and was to provide them physic, and all necessaries whilst

* In Selden's Dissertation on Fleta is given a copy of an instrument of this kind, made anno 1277, acknowledging the receipt of a well-known law-book, entitled Breton, in the words following:—

'Universis præsentes literas inspecturis R. de Scardeburgh Archidiaconus salutem in Domino sempiternam. Noveritis me recipisse et habuisse ex causa commodati librum quem dominus Henricus de Breton composuit, à venerabili patre Domino R. Dei gratia Bathoniensi Episcopo per manum Magistri, Thomæ Beke, Archidiaconi Dorset, quem eidem restituere teneor in festo sancti Joh' Baptiste, an. Dom. MCCLXXVIII. In cujus rei testimonium præsentibus sigillum meum appensum, Datæ Dover die Veneris post purific' Virginis Gloriosæ. anno MCCLXXVII.'

The following less ancient instances of the same kind, occur in the catalogue of the Harleian manuscripts, No. 378. Sir Simonds D'Ewes' bond of £100 for borrowing Sir Thomas Cotton's book of Saxon Charters (viz. Augustus II.) which was not executed since Sir Thomas refused to lend it. Eight other instances are in the same manuscripts.

living, and to wash and prepare their bodies for burial when dead.

Refectionarius; who looked after the hall, providing table-cloths, napkins, towels, dishes, plates, spoons, and all other necessaries for it, and even servants to attend there; he had likewise the keeping of the cups, salts, ewers, and all the silver utensils whatsoever belonging to the house, except the church plate.

There was likewise Coquinarius, Gardinarius, and Portarius, 'et in cœnobiis, quæ jus archiaconale in 'prædiis et ecclesiis suis obtinuerunt, erat monachus 'qui archidiaconi titulo et munere insignitus est.'

The offices belonging to an abbey were generally these :—

The hall, or refectionary, and, adjoining thereto, the locutorium, or parlour, where leave was given for the monks to discourse, who were enjoined silence elsewhere.

Oriolium, or the oriol, was the next room, the use whereof was for monks who were rather distempered than diseased, to dine therein.

Dormitorium, the dormitory, where they all slept together.

Lavatorium, generally called the landry, where the clothes of the monks were washed, and where also at a conduit they washed their hands.

Scriptorium, a room where the Chartularius was busied in writing, especially in the transcribing of these books—1. Ordinals, containing the rubric of their missal, and directory of their priests in service. 2. Consuetudinals, presenting the ancient customs of their convents. 3. Troparics. 4. Collectaries, wherein the ecclesiastical collects were fairly written. This was the ordinary business of the Chartularius and his assistant monks, but they also employed themselves in transcribing the fathers and classics, and in recording historical events.

Adjoining to the Scriptorium was the Library, which in most abbeys was well furnished with a variety of choice manuscripts.

The Kitchen, with larder and pantry adjoining.

The abbey church consisted of—1. Cloisters, consecrated ground, as appears by the solemn sepultures therein. 2. Navis ecclesiæ, or the body of the church. 3. Gradatorium, the ascent by steps out of the former into the choir. 4. Presbyterium, or the choir; on the right side whereof was the stall of the abbot, with his moiety of monks, and on the left that of the prior, with his: and these alternately chanted the responsals in the service. 5. Vestiarium, or the vestry, where their copes, surplices, and other habiliments were deposited. 6. Vaulta, a vault, being an arched room over part of the church, which in some abbeys, as St. Albans, was used to enlarge their dormitory, where the monks had twelve beds for their repose.

Concamuratio, being an arched room betwixt the east end of the church and the high altar, so that in procession they might surround the same, founding their practice on David's expression—'and so will 'I compass thine altar, O Lord.'*

* The want of this in the new cathedral of St. Paul is not to be imputed to Sir Christopher Wren as an omission, but to the disuse of processions in our reformed church, which has rendered such a provision unnecessary.

To the church belonged also, Cerarium, a repository for wax candles. Campanile, the steeple. Polyandrium, the church-yard. The remaining rooms of an abbey stood at a distance from the main structure, and were as follow :—

Eleëmosynaria, the almonry, vulgarly the ambry, a building near or within the abbey, wherein poor and impotent persons were relieved and maintained by the charity of the house.

Sanctuarium, or the sanctuary, wherein debtors taking refuge from their creditors, malefactors from the judge, lived in all security.

At a distance stood the stables, which were under the care and management of the Stallarius, or master of the horse, and the Provendarius, who, as his name imports, laid in provender for the horses; these were of four kinds, namely,—1. Manni, geldings for the saddle of the larger size. 2. Runcini, runts, small nags. 3. Summarii, sumpter-horses. 4. Averii, cart or plough horses.†

Besides the buildings above-mentioned, there was a prison for incorrigible monks. The ordinary punishment for small offences was carrying the lanthorn, but contumacious monks were by the abbot committed to prison.

Other buildings there were, such as Vaccisterium, the cow-house, Porcarium, the swine-stye, &c.

Granges were farms at a distance, kept and stocked by the abbey, and so called à grana gerendo, the overseer whereof was commonly called the Prior of the grange: these were sometimes many miles from the monastery. In female foundations of nunneries there was a correspondency of all the same essential officers and offices.

Besides there were a number of inferior officers in abbeys, whose employments can only be guessed at by the barbarous appellations used to distinguish them; such were—1. Coltonarius [cutler]. 2. Cupparius. 3. Potagiarius. 4. Scutellarius Aulæ. 5. Salsarius. 6. Portarius. 7. Carectarius Cellerarii. 8. Pelliparius [parchment provider]. 9. Brasinarius [malster].‡

If in the admirable construction of that edifice proof of his skill and sagacity were wanting, the following recent one in another public work of his might be adduced, though known to few :—

About seven years ago, when the houses on London-bridge were taken down in order to make a footway on each side thereof, it was found that the tower of St. Magnus church, through which was an entrance into the church from the west, projected so far westward as to reduce passengers on the east side of the bridge to the necessity of going round it. Upon this it became a subject of consultation, whether it were advisable or not to cut through the tower an arch which should continue the footway from the bridge up Fish-street-hill, and prevent the trouble and danger of going about. The thought was bold, for the tower was heavy, and besides contained a peal of large bells; however it was at length resolved on : upon pulling down the houses, the south side of the tower appeared to be a plain superficies of the roughest materials that masons use, and upon this the city surveyor had drawn such an arch as he meant to cut through from south to north; but as soon as the workmen began to execute his design, by breaking through the exterior surface, they, to the joy and admiration of every one, found a passage and an arch ready formed to their hands by the original designer of the edifice, who, with a sagacity and penetration peculiar to himself, had foreseen the probability of taking down the houses on the bridge, and the consequent necessity of such a provision for the convenience and safety of passengers as that above-mentioned.

† This was the four-fold division of the horses of William the two-and-twentieth abbot of St. Alban's, who lost an hundred horses in one year.

‡ The offices aforesaid in smaller abbeys were but one room, but in the greater monasteries each was a distinct structure, with all under offices attendant thereupon. Thus the Firmorie in the priory of Canterbury had a refectory, a kitchen, a dortour distributed into several chambers, and a private chapel for the devotions of the sick; their almonry also was ac-

Different orders were bound to the observance of different canonical constitutions; however, the rule of the ancient Benedictines, with some small variations, prevailed through most monasteries, and was in general as follows:—

i. Let monks praise God seven times a-day, that is to say,—
1. At cock-crowing. 2. Mattins, which were performed at the first hour, or six o'clock. 3. The third hour, or nine o'clock. 4. The sixth hour, or twelve o'clock. 5. The ninth hour, or three o'clock. 6. Vespers, the twelfth hour, or six o'clock in the afternoon. 7. Seven o'clock at night, when the completory was sung.*

The first or early prayers were at two o'clock in the morning, when the monks, who went to bed at eight at night, had slept six hours, which were judged sufficient for nature. It was no fault for the greater haste, to come without shoes, or with unwashen hands, if sprinkled at their entrance with holy water: and there is nothing expressly said to the contrary, but that they might go to bed again; but a flat prohibition after mattins; when to return to bed was accounted a petty apostacy.

ii. Let all at the sign given, leave off their work and repair presently to prayers.†

iii. Let those who are absent in public employment be reputed present in prayer.‡

iv. Let no monk go alone, but always two together.§

v. From Easter to Whitsunday let them dine always at twelve, and sup at six o'clock.||

vi. Let them at other times fast on Wednesdays and Fridays till three o'clock in the afternoon.¶

vii. Let them fast every day in Lent till six o'clock at night.**

viii. Let no monk speak a word in the refectory when they are at their meals.

ix. Let them listen to the lecturer reading scripture to them whilst they feed themselves.

x. Let the septimarians dine by themselves after the rest.††

xi. Let such who are absent about business observe the same hours of prayer.‡‡

xii. Let none, being from home about business, and hoping to return at night, presume 'foris mandicare,' to eat abroad.§§

xiii. Let the completory be solemnly sung about seven o'clock at night.||||

xiv. Let none speak a word after the completory ended, but hasten to their beds.¶¶

xv. Let the monks sleep in beds singly by themselves, but all if possible in one room.

xvi. Let them sleep in their clothes, girt with their girdles, but not having their knives by their sides for fear of hurting themselves in their sleep.

xvii. Let not the youth lie by themselves, but mingled with their seniors.

xviii. Let not the candle in the dormitory go out all night.***

xix. Let infants incapable of excommunication be corrected with rods.†††

xx. Let offenders in small faults, whereof the abbot is sole judge, be only sequestered from the table.‡‡‡

xxi. Let offenders in greater faults be suspended from table and prayers.§§§

xxii. Let none converse with any excommunicated under the pain of excommunication.|||| ||

xxiii. Let incorrigible offenders be expelled the monastery.

xxiv. Let an expelled brother, being readmitted on promise of amendment, be set last in order.¶¶¶

xxv. Let every monk have 2 coats and 2 cowls, &c.****

xxvi. Let every monk have his table-book, knife, needle, and handkerchief.

xxvii. Let the bed of every monk have a mat, blanket, rug, and pillow.††††

commodated with all the aforesaid appurtenances, and had many distinct manors consigned only to its maintenance.

To many abbeys there appertained also cells, which in some instances were so remote, that the mother abbey was in England, and the cell beyond the seas. Some of these were richly endowed, as that of Wyndham, in Norfolk, which though but a cell annexed to St. Alban's, yet was able at the dissolution to expend of its own revenues seventy-two pounds per annum. These were colonies, into which the abbeys discharged their superfluous members, and whither the rest retired when infections were feared at home.

* These were the stated times of public prayer in religious houses; but besides these, occasional ejaculations by christians, as well of the laity as the clergy, were customary till near the end of the last century. Howel, in one of his letters says, 'I knock thrice at heaven-gate; in the 'morning, in the evening, and at night; besides prayers at meals, and 'some other occasional ejaculations; upon the putting on of a clean 'shirt, washing of my hands, and at lighting of candles; and this he adds 'he was able to do in seven languages.' Familiar Letters, vol. II. sect. vi. letter 32, and this practice is recommended by Cosins, bishop of Durham, in a book of devotions published by him.

† This in England, commonly called the ringing-island, was done with tolling a bell, but in other countries with loud strokes; and the canon was so strict, that it provided 'scriptores literam non integrent;' that writers having begun to frame and flourish a text letter, were not to finish it, but to leave off in the middle.

‡ At the end of prayers there was a particular commemoration made of them that were absent, and they by name recommended to divine protection.

§ That they might mutually have both testem honestatis, and monitorem pietatis, in imitation of Christ's sending his disciples to preach two and two before his face.

|| The primitive church forbad fasting for those fifty days, that Christians might be cheerful for the memory of Christ's resurrection. 'Immunitate jejunandi à die Paschæ Pentecosten usque gaudemus;' and therefore more modern is the custom of fasting on Ascension eve.

¶ So making but one meal a day, but the twelve days in Christmas were excepted in this canon.

** Stamping a character of more abstinence on that time; for though the whole of a monk's life ought to be a Lent, yet this most especially, wherein they were to abate of their wonted sleep and diet, and add to their daily devotion: yet so that they might not lessen their daily fare without leave from the abbot.

†† These were weekly officers, such as the lecturer, servitors at the table, cook, who could not be present at the public refection, but like the bible-clerks in the Queen's-college, Cambridge, waited on the fellows at dinner, and had a table by themselves.

‡‡ Be it by sea or land, in ship, house, or field, they were to fall down on their knees and briefly keep time with the convent in their devotions.

§§ This canon was afterwards so dispensed with by the abbot on several occasions, that it was frustrate in effect when monks became common guests at laymen's tables.

|||| Completory, so called, because it ended the duties of the day. This service was concluded with that versicle of the Psalmist, 'Set a watch, O 'Lord, before my mouth, and keep the door of my lips.'

¶¶ They might express themselves by signs, and in some cases whisper, but so softly, that a third might not overhear. This silence was so obstinately observed by some of them, that they would not speak, though assaulted by thieves, to make a discovery in their own defence.

*** In case any should fall suddenly sick, that this standing candle might be a stock of light to recruit the rest.

††† Such were all accounted under the age of fifteen years, of whom were many in monasteries.

‡‡‡ As coming to dinner after grace said, breaking the earthen ewer wherein they washed their hands; being out of tune in setting the psalm; taking any by the hand; receiving letters from, or talking with a friend, without leave of the abbot, &c. [From the table] such were to eat by themselves, and three hours after the rest, until they had made satisfaction.

§§§ Viz., theft, &c., this in effect amounted to the greater excommunication, and had all the penalties thereof.

|||| || Yet herein his keeper, deputed by the abbot, was excepted. [Converse] Either to eat or speak with him; he might not so much as bless him or his meat, if carried by him: yet to avoid scandal he might rise up, bow, or bare his head to him, in case the other did first salute him with silent gesture.

¶¶¶ He was to lose his former seniority, and begin at the bottom. Whosoever quitted the convent thrice, or was thrice expelled for misdemeanors, might not any more be received.

**** Not to wear at once, except in winter, but for exchange whilst one was washed. And when new clothes were delivered them their old ones were given to the poor.

†††† The abbot also every Saturday was to visit their beds, to see if they had not shuffled into it some softer matter than was allowed of; or purloined meat or dainties to eat in private.

xxviii. Let the abbot be chosen by the merits of his life and learning.

xxix. Let him never dine alone; but when guests are wanting call some brethren unto his table.*

xxx. Let the cellarer be a discreet man to give all their meat in due season.

xxxi. Let none be excused from the office of cook, but take his turn in his week.†

xxxii. Let the cook each Saturday when he goeth out of his office leave the linen and vessels clean and sound to his successor.‡

xxxiii. Let the porter be a grave person to discharge his trust with discretion.§

From this view of the constitution and discipline of religious houses, it is clear that they had a tendency to promote learning and good manners among their own members; but besides this they were productive of much good to the public, seeing that they were also schools of learning and education, for every convent had one person or more appointed for this purpose; and all the neighbours that desired it, might have their children instructed in grammar and church music without any expence to them. In the nunneries also, young women were taught needle-work, and to read English, and Latin if they desired it; and not only the daughters of the lower class of people, but even those of the nobility and gentry, were educated in these seminaries. Farther, monasteries were in effect great hospitals, many poor people being fed therein every day; they were also houses of entertainment, for almost all travellers: even the nobility and gentry, when upon a journey, took up their abode at one religious house or another, there being at that time but few inns in this country. In these, also, the nobility and gentry provided for their children and impoverished friends, by making the former monks and nuns, and in time priors and prioresses, abbots and abbesses,‖ and by procuring for the latter corodies and pensions.¶

* Such as were relieved by his hospitality are by canonical critics sorted into four ranks:—
1. Convivæ, guests living in or near the city where the convent stood.
2. Hospites, strangers, coming from distant parts of the country.
3. Peregrini, pilgrims of another nation, and generally travelling for devotion.
4. Mendici, boggars, who received alms without at the gate.

† The abbot and the cellarer in great convents were excepted, but this was only anciently. This was the rule in poor monasteries, with an exception of the abbot and the cellarer; in the larger were cooks and under cooks, lay persons.

‡ Upon pain to receive twenty-five claps on the hand for every default of this kind; harder was that rule which enjoined that the cook might not taste what he dressed for others. Understand it thus, though he might eat his own pittance or dimensum, yet he must meddle with no more, lest the tasting should tempt him to gluttony and excess.

§ Whose age might make him resident in his place. [Discharge his trust] In listening to no secular news, and if hearing it not to report it again; in carrying the keys every night to the abbot, and letting none in or out without his permission.

‖ Mary, the daughter of King Edward I., and also thirteen noblemen's daughters, were at one time nuns at Ambresbury. Angl. Sacr. vol. I. pag. 208. And Ralph, earl of Westmoreland, having twenty children, made three of his daughters nuns. Six sons of Henry, lord of Harley, were monks. Angl. Sacr. vol. I. pag. 205. Bridget, the fourth daughter of Edward IV., was a nun at Dartford, in Kent.

¶ A Corody, à conradendo, from eating together, is an allowance of meat, drink, and clothing, due to the king from an abbey, or other house of religion, for the reasonable sustenance of such of his servants as he should bestow it on. Termes de la Ley. Cowel's Interp. in Voce, et vide Mon. Angl. vol. II. pag. 933. Burn. Reform. vol. I. pag. 223. Collier's Eccl. Hist. vol. II. pag. 165. In Plowden's Commentaries, in the case of Throckmerton versus Tracey, is an allusion, but without a particular reference, to a case which nevertheless seems to have received a legal decision, arising upon this question, viz., Whether under a grant of a corody to a man and his servant, the grantee might bring to sit at mess with the abbot and convent, a person infected with the leprosy or other noisome disease. Vide Finch's NOMOTEXNIA, fol. 15. b. Finch

Notwithstanding these and other advantages resulting to the public from monastic foundations, it must be confessed that the mischiefs arising from them were very great, for it appears that they were very injurious to the parochial clergy, with whom indeed they seemed to live in a state of perpetual hostility, by accumulating prebends and benefices, and by procuring the appropriation of churches, which they did in this way, first they obtained the advowson, and then found means to get the appropriation also. Bishop Kennet says that at one time above one half of the parochial churches in England were in the hands or power of cathedral churches and monasteries. Case of Appropriations, pag. 18, 19. And where their endeavours to get the appropriation failed, they frequently got a pension out of it. They were farther injurious to the secular clergy by the many exemptions which they had from episcopal jurisdiction, and the payment of tythes.

The public also were sufferers by religious houses in these respects, they drew off a great number of persons, who otherwise would have been brought up to arms, to labour, or the exercise of the manual arts.** The inhabitants of them busied themselves with secular employments, for they were great farmers, and even brewers and tanners, concerning which latter employment of theirs, Fuller thus humorously expresses himself:—'Though the monks themselves 'were too fine-nosed to dabble in tan-fats, yet they 'kept others bred in that trade to follow their work; 'these convents having bark of their own woods, 'hides of the cattle of their own breeding and kill-'ing, and, which was the main, a large stock of 'money to buy at the best hand, and to allow such 'chapmen as they sold to, a long day of payment, 'easily eat out such who were bred up in that 'vocation. Whereupon in the one-and-twentieth of 'king Henry VIII. a statute was made that no priest 'either regular or secular should on heavy penalties 'hereafter meddle with such mechanic employments.'

Sanctuaries, of which there were many, as at Westminster, Croyland, St. Burien's, St. John of Beverley, and other places, were an intolerable grievance on the public. Stowe, in his Chronicle, pag. 443. complains of them in these words: 'Unthrifts riot, 'and run in debt upon the boldness of these places; 'yea and rich men run thither with poor men's 'goods, where they build; there they spend, and 'bid their creditors go whistle them; men's wives 'run thither with their husband's plate, and say 'they dare not abide with their husbands for beating 'them; thieves bring thither their stolen goods, 'and live thereon; there they devise robberies; 'nightly they steal out, they rob and reave, and kill, 'and come in again as though those places gave 'them not only a safeguard for the harm they have 'done, but a licence to do more.'

Add to all these, other mischiefs, the inevitable

of Law, 56. A pension was an annual allowance in money from an abbey to one of the king's chaplains for his better maintenance, until provided with a benefice. Cowel, voce CORODY.

** It is said that in the ninth century there were in this kingdom more monks than military men; and to this bad policy some have scrupled not to attribute the success of the Danes in their several invasions.

consequences of those prohibitions and restraints imposed on the clergy, as well secular as regular.*

Undoubtedly these evils co-operating with motives of a political nature, were the causes of that reformation, for which even at this distance of time we have abundant reason to be thankful: it cannot be denied that some of the principal agents in that revolution were actuated by the noblest of all motives, namely, zeal for the honor of God; and whether the objections against it, that it was effected by unjustifiable means, such as corruption, subornation, and the invasion of corporate rights, sanctified by law and usage: whether all or any of these are admissable in a subject of so important a nature as the advancement of learning, and the exercise of true religion, is a question that has already been discussed by those who were best able to decide upon it, and will hardly ever again become a subject of controversy.

CHAP. LIX.

THE accounts herein before given of the gradual improvement of music, and the several extracts from manuscripts, herein before contained, may serve to shew the state of the science in this country in or about the fifteenth century; and it remains now to speak of its application, or, in other words, to take a view of the practice of it amongst us. And first it will appear that as it was become essential to the performance of divine service, it was used in all cathedral and collegiate churches, and that the clergy were very zealous to promote it. Of the introduction of the organ into the choral service by pope Vitalianus, in the year 660, mention has already been made; and for the early use of that instrument in this kingdom we have the testimony of Sir Henry Spelman [in his Glossary, voce Organum] who, upon the authority of the book of Ramsey, relates that on the death of king Edgar the choir of monks and their organs were turned into lamentations.

Farther, William of Malmesbury relates that St. Dunstan, in the reign of the same king, gave many great bells and organs to the churches of the West;† which latter he so describes, as that they appear to have been very little different from those now in use, viz., 'Organa ubi per æreas fistulas musicis 'mensuris elaboratas dudum conceptas follis vomit

'anxius auras.'‡ And it is elsewhere said that they had brass pipes and bellows.§ The same writer mentions that the organ at Malmesbury had the following distich inscribed on brass, declaring who was the donor of it :—

Organa do sancto præsul Dunstanus Aldelmo
Perdat hic æternum, qui vult hinc tollere, regnum.‖

Fuller, in his Worthies of Denbighshire, pag. 33, mentions a famous organ, formerly at Wrexham in that county, a matter of great curiosity, in respect that the instrument was erected, not in a cathedral, but in a parochial church : he speaks also of an improvement of the organ by one Bernard, a Venetian, of whom he asserts, on the authority of Sabellicus, that he was absolutely the best musician in the world.

With respect to abbey and conventual churches, we meet with few express foundations of canons, minor canons, and choristers; and it may therefore well be supposed that the choral duty in each of these was performed by members of their own body, and by children educated by themselves; but in cathedral churches we meet with very ample endowments, as well for vicars, or minor canons, clerks, choristers, and lay singers, as for a dean, and canons or prebendaries. As to the value and extent of these endowments in the metropolitical churches of Canterbury and York, and the cathedrals of Durham, Winchester, London, Ely, Salisbury, Exeter, Norwich, Lincoln, and many others, we are greatly at a loss, for they, having been refounded by Henry VIII., the ancient foundations were absorbed in the modern, and it is of the latter only that there are any authentic memorials now remaining; of those that retain their original constitution the following are some of the principal :—

Hereford, the cathedral rebuilt in the time of William the Conqueror, and by the contributions of benefactors endowed so as to maintain a bishop, dean, two archdeacons, a chancellor, treasurer, twenty-eight prebendaries, twelve priest-vicars, four lay clerks, seven choristers, and other officers. In aid of this foundation Richard II. incorporated the vicars-choral, endowing them with lands for their better support; and they exist now as a body distinct in some respects from the dean and chapter.¶

Of the original endowment of the cathedral of St. Paul, little is now to be known. We learn however from Dugdale that considerable grants of land and benefactions in money were made for its support by divers persons at different times, as also for the maintenance of its members, so early as the time of Edward the Confessor. Of the minor canons the following is the history. They were twelve in number, and had anciently their habitation in and about the church-yard; but at length by the bounty of well-disposed persons, they became enabled to meet and dine together in a common hall or refectory, on the north side of the church. In the year 1363 Robert de Keteryngham, rector of St. Gregory's,

---

* And yet it seems that the licentiousness of the regulars was not general throughout this kingdom, even in the most corrupt state of clerical manners, for lord Herbert of Cherbury relates, that upon the visitation of religious houses it was found that some societies behaved so well, that their lives were not only exempt from notorious faults, but their spare time was bestowed in writing books, painting, carving, graving, and the like exercises: and in the preamble to the statute of 27 Hen. VIII. cap. 28, is this remarkable declaration, 'In the greater 'monasteries, thanks be to God, religion is right well observed and 'kept up.'

† It has elsewhere, viz., pag. 176, of this work, been remarked that Dunstan was well skilled in music. There is a tradition that his harp made music of itself, thus humorously related by Fuller in his Church History, pag. 128 :—

St. Dunstan's harp fast by the wall
    Upon a pin did hang—a ;
The harp itself with lye and all,
    Untouch'd by hand, did twang—a.

This might have happened, supposing two strings tuned in the unison, and the wind to have blown hard against the instrument, and this accident might suggest the invention of the instrument described by Kircher in the Musurgia, tom. II. pag. 352, and lately given to the world as a new discovery, by the name of the harp of Æolus.

‡ Gul. Malmesb. lib. V. de Pontif. inter xv. Script Galei, pag. 366.
§ Gul. Malmesb. in Vitâ Aldhelmi, pag. 33.
‖ Cul. Malmesb. de Pontif. lib. V. pag. 366.
¶ Tanner's Notitia Monastica, pag. 171, 179.

with licence of king Edward III. granted to the dean and chapter certain messuages and lands of the yearly value of vi. l. xiii. s. iv. d. to the end that the minor canons should sing divine service daily in the church of St. Paul, for the good estate of the king, and queen Philippa his consort, and all their children during their lives, and also for their souls after their decease. Richard II. by his letters patent in the eighteenth year of his reign, incorporated them by the style of the college of the twelve petty canons of St. Paul's church, and augmented their maintenance by a grant to them of divers lands and rents; and 24 Henry VI. the church of St. Gregory was appropriated to them.*

At Wells also is a college of vicars, founded originally for the maintenance of thirteen chantry priests, who officiated in the cathedral. In 1347 Radulphus de Salopia, bishop of Bath and Wells, erected a college for the vicars of the cathedral church, got them incorporated, and augmented their revenues with certain lands of his own.†

The ancient foundation of Litchfield cathedral appears to have been a bishop, dean, precentor, chancellor, treasurer, four archdeacons, twenty-seven prebendaries, five priest-vicars, seven lay-clerks or singing-men, eight choristers, and other officers and servants.‡

Many collegiate churches had also endowments for the performance of choral service, as that of South-well, in Nottinghamshire; Beverley in Yorkshire; Arundel in Sussex, now dissolved; Westminster, which by the way has been successively an abbey, a cathedral, and a collegiate church.

Some of the colleges in Oxford have also endowments of this kind, as namely, New college, for ten chaplains, three clerks, and sixteen choristers; Magdalen college, for four chaplains, eight clerks, and sixteen choristers; All-Souls, for chaplains, clerks, and choristers indefinitely; *there also was an institution of some kind or other of chaplains, clerks, choristers at St. John's college, Oxon: but the same was annulled in 1577, the college estate being impaired. Sir W. Paddy, Physician to James I., refounded the choir.* In the college at Ipswich, founded by Cardinal Wolsey, was a provision for a dean, twelve secular canons, and eight choristers; but the college was suppressed, and great part of the endowment alienated upon the disgrace of the founder.

In some free chapels§ also were endowments for choral service, as in that of St. George at Windsor, now indeed a collegiate church, in which are a dean, twelve canons or prebendaries, thirteen vicars or minor canons, four clerks, six choristers, and twenty-six poor alms knights, besides other officers.

' The kynge's college of our Lady by Etone besyde

'Wyndesore,' was founded by king Henry VI. anno regni 19, for a provost, ten priests, four clerks, six choristers, twenty-five poor grammar-scholars, with a master to teach them, and twenty-five poor old men; and though some of its endowment was taken away by king Edward IV., yet it still continues (being particularly excepted in the acts of dissolution) in a flourishing estate, with some small alteration in the number of the foundation, which now consists of a provost, seven fellows, two schoolmasters, two conducts, one organist, seven clerks, seventy king's scholars, ten choristers, besides officers and servants belonging to the college.‖

The chapel of St. Stephen, near the great hall at Westminster, first built by king Stephen, and afterwards rebuilt by Edward III. in the year 1347, was by the latter ordained to be a collegiate church, and therein were established a dean, twelve canons secular, who had their residence in Canon, vulgarly, Channel-row, Westminster, thirteen vicars, four clerks, six chorists, two servitors, a verger, and a keeper of the chapel. The same king endowed this chapel or collegiate church with manors, lands, &c. to a very great value: it was surrendered to Edward VI., and the chapel is now the place in which the House of Commons sit.¶‖

As to small endowments for the maintenance of singing men with stipends, they were formerly very many.

At Christ-church, London, was one for five singing men, with a yearly salary of eight pounds each.** There was also another called Poultney college, from the founder Sir John Poultney, annexed to the parish church of St. Lawrence, in Candlewick, now Canon-street, London, with an endowment for a master, or warden, thirteen priests, and four choristers, who had stalls, and performed divine service in the chapel of Jesus, adjoining to the church of St. Lawrence aforesaid.†† At Leadenhall Sir Simon Eyre, who had been some time mayor of London, erected a beautiful and large chapel, and bequeathed to the company of Drapers three thousand marks, upon condition to establish and endow perpetually, a master or warden, five secular priests, six clerks and two choristers, to sing daily service by note in this chapel; and also three schoolmasters and an usher, viz., one master, with an usher, for grammar, another master for writing, and the other for singing. The master's salary to be ten pounds per annum, every other priest's eight pounds, every clerk's five pounds six shillings and eight pence, and every chorister's five marks; but it seems this endowment never took effect.‡‡ In the church of St. Michael Royal, London, which had been new built by the famous Sir Richard Whittington, several times lord mayor of London, was founded by him, and finished by his executors A.D. 1424, a college dedicated to the Holy Ghost and the Virgin Mary, for a master and four fellows, all to be masters of arts; besides clerks, choristers, &c.§§ In the church of St. Mary at Warwick was an endowment by Roger, earl of

---

* The minor canons of the cathedral church of St. Paul have now a college, situate on the south side of the church-yard, and near thereto is a place called Paul's Bakehouse Court, from whence it may be inferred that the members of that church lived together, that the rents arising from their estates situate in the neighbourhood of London were paid in corn, which was made into bread by their own servants, and baked at or near the place above-mentioned.

† Tann. 477.   ‡ Ibid. 485.

§ Free chapels were places of religious worship exempt from all jurisdiction of the ordinary, in which respect they differed from chantries, which were ever united to some cathedral, collegiate, or parochial church.

‖ Tann. 33.

¶ Newcourt's Repertorium, vol. I. pag. 745.   ** Ibid. vol. I. pag. 319.

†† Tann. Notit. pag. 319.   ‡‡ Ibid. pag. 325.   §§ Ibid.

Warwick, about the year 1123, for a dean and secular canons ; this foundation was considerably augmented by the succeeding earls, so that at the time of the dissolution it consisted of a dean, five prebendaries or canons, ten priest-vicars, and six choristers.*

One thing very remarkable in all these foundations, except that of Eton, is that they afforded no provision for an organist.† That excellent musician Dr. Benjamin Rogers, who was very well versed in the history of his own profession, once took notice of this to Anthony Wood : and, considering that the use of organs in divine service is almost coeval with choral singing itself, to account for it is somewhat difficult ; it seems however not improbable that in most cathedral, and other foundations for the performance of divine service, the duty of organist was discharged by some one or other of the vicars choral. In the statutes of Canterbury cathedral provision is made for players on sackbuts and cornets, which on solemn occasions might probably be joined to, or used in aid of the organ.‡

The foregoing notices refer solely to that kind of music which was used in the divine offices ; but over and above the several musical confraternities formerly subsisting in different parts of this kingdom, a set of men, called stipendiary priests, derived a subsistence from the singing of masses, in chantries endowed for that purpose, for the souls of the founders.§ In the cathedral church of St. Paul were no fewer of these than forty-seven ; and in the church of St. Saviour, Southwark, was a chantry, with an endowment for a mass to be sung weekly on every Friday throughout the year, for the soul of the poet Gower, the author of the Confessio Amantis. The common price for a mass was four pence, or for two thousand forty marks, which it seems could be only the mode of payment where the service was occasional, since

the endowment must be supposed to have in a great measure ascertained the stipend, and this was sometimes so considerable, as to occasion as much solicitation for a chantry as for some other ecclesiastical benefices. Chaucer mentions it to the credit of his parson, that he did not flock to St. Paul's to get a chantry. These superstitious foundations survived the fate of the monasteries but a very short time, for they, together with free chapels, were granted to Henry VIII. by the parliament in 1545, and were dissolved by the statute of 1 Edw. VI. chap. 14.

Such was the nature of the monastic institution, and such the state of ecclesiastical music among us, in the ages preceding the Reformation, in which indeed there seems to be nothing peculiar to thi country, for the same system of ecclesiastical policy prevailed in general throughout Christendom. In Italy, in Germany, in France, and in England, the government of abbeys and monasteries was by the same officers, and the discipline of religious house: in each country very nearly the same, saving the difference arising from the rule, as it was called, of their respective orders, as of St. Augustine, St. Benedict, and others, which each house professed to follow. This uniformity was but the effect of that authority which, as supreme head of the church, the pope was acknowledged to be invested with, and which was constantly exerted in the making and promulging decretals, constitutions, canons, and bulls, and all that variety of laws, by whatsoever name they are called, which make up the Corpus Juris Canonici : add to these the acts of provincial councils, and ecclesiastical synods, the ultimate view whereof seems to have been the establishment of a general uniformity of regimen and discipline in all monastic foundations, as far as was consistent with their several professions.

In aid of these, the ritualists, who are here to be considered as commentators on that body of laws above referred to, have with great precision not only enumerated the several orders in the church,‖ but have also prescribed the duty of every person employed in the sacred offices. In consequence whereof we find that the power and authority of an abbot, a prior, a dean, were in every respect the same in all countries where the papal authority was submitted

---

* Tann. Notit. pag. 570.

† *The first instance we have found of a stipendiary organist, is that of one Leonard Fitz Simon, mentioned by Mr. Warton in his life of Sir Thomas Pope, as being organist of Trinity College, Oxon: about 1580, at a salary of 20s. a year.*

‡ There have been but very few foundations of colleges since the dissolution of monasteries, except those of Henry VIII. In the only one that can now be recollected, that of Dulwich, founded by Alleyn the player, in the reign of James I., provision is made by the statutes that the children there educated should be taught prick-song ; and for that purpose, and for performing the service of the chapel, one of the fellows is required to be a skilful organist. Of this worthy man, Mr. Edward Alleyn, the honour of his profession, there is a well-written life, the work of the late Mr. Oldys, in the Biographia Britannica. In his time it said that there were no fewer than nineteen playhouses in London, Prynne's Histrio-mastix, pag. 492, which are two more than are enumerated in the Preface to Dodsley's collection of old plays ; the two omitted in Dodsley's account are said by Prynne to have been, the one in Bishopsgate-street, and the other on Ludgate-hill. The situation of the former of these may possibly be yet ascertained ; Fuller, Worthies in London, pag. 223, says that Alleyn was born in the parish of Bishopsgate, near Devonshire-house, where now is the sign of the Pie. Now it may be proved, by incontestible evidence, that the Magpie alehouse, situate on the east side of Bishopsgate-street, between Houndsditch and Devonshire-street, with the adjacent houses, are part of the estate with which Alleyn endowed his college, and they are now actually held under leases granted by the college. It is therefore to be supposed, as the Pie was the place of his birth, and continued to be part of his estate to the time of his death ; that it was also his dwelling during his life ; and if so, where was the playhouse in Bishopsgate-street so likely to be as at the Magpie? Add to this that the very house, now in being, is unquestionably as old as the time of James I., for the fire never reached Bishopsgate; it fronts the street, and the garden behind it was probably the site of the playhouse.

§ This superstitious service was usually performed at some particular altar, but oftener in a small chapel, of which there were many in all the cathedral and collegiate, and in some parish churches in this kingdom. Vide Godolphin's Repertorium Canonicum, pag. 329. Fuller's Church History, book VI. pag. 350. Weever's Funeral Monuments, pag. 733.

‖ Besides the orders of bishops, priests, and deacons, there are both in the Romish and Greek churches others of an inferior degree, though as to their number there appears to be a great diversity of sentiments. Baronius asserts it to be five, viz., subdeacons, acolythists, exorcists, readers, and ostarii, or doorkeepers ; others make them a much greater number, including therein psalmistæ, or singers, and the inferior officers employed in and about the church. The duty of each may in general be inferred from their names, except that of the acolythists, which appears to have been originally nothing more than to light the candles of the church, and to attend the ministers with wine for the eucharist. Bishop Hall has exhibited a very lively picture of an acolythist in the exercise of his office in the following lines :—

' To see a lasie dumbe Acolithite
' Armed against a devout flyes despight
' Which at th'hy altar doth the chalice vaile,
' With a broad flie-flappe of a peacocke's tayle,
' The whiles the likerous priest spits every trice
' With longing for his morning sacrifice.'
                    Virgidemiarum, edit. 1602, pag. 100.

And yet, notwithstanding the seeming insignificance of this order, we meet with an endowment, perhaps the only one ever known in this kingdom, at Arundel, in Sussex, for a master and twelve secular canons, three deacons, three subdeacons, two acolites, seven choristers, two sacrists, and other officers ; but it was suppressed at the time of the general dissolution of other religious houses.

to; and the same may be said of the duties of the canons or prebendaries, the precentor, the chorists, and other officers in all cathedral churches. One very remarkable instance of that uniformity in government, discipline, and practice, is that of the episcopus puerorum, mentioned in a preceding chapter of this volume, which is there shown to be common to France and England, and probably prevailed throughout the western church; for the traces of it are yet remaining in the reformed churches, as in Holland, and many parts of Germany.

The rule of bestowing on minor canons, or vicars choral, livings within a small distance of a cathedral church, is generally observed by deans and their chapters throughout this kingdom, and by those of other countries.*

CHAP. LX.

HAVING treated thus largely of ecclesiastical, it remains now to pursue the history of secular music, and to give an account of the origin of such of the instruments now in use as have not already been spoken of. What kind of music, and more particularly what instruments were in use among the common people, and served for the amusement of the several classes of the laity before the year 1300, is very difficult to discover: it appears however that so early as the year 679, the bishops and other ecclesiastics were used to be entertained at the places of their ordinary residence with music; and, as it should seem, of the symphoniac kind; and that by women too, for in the Roman council, held on British affairs anno 679, is the following decree :—'We also 'ordain and decree that bishops, and all whosoever 'profess the religious life of the ecclesiastical order, 'do not use weapons, nor keep musicians of the

'Female sex, nor any musical concerts whatsoever;†
'nor do allow of any buffooneries or plays in their 'presence. For the discipline of the holy church 'permits not her faithful priests to use any of these 'things, but charges them to be employed in divine 'offices, in making provision for the poor, and for 'the benefit of the church. Especially let lessons 'out of the divine oracles be always read for the 'edification of the churches, that the minds of the 'hearers may be fed with the divine word, even at 'the very time of their bodily repast.'

Of instruments in common use, it is indisputable that the triangular harp is by far of the greatest antiquity. Vincentio Galilei ascribes the invention of it to the Irish; but Mr. Selden speaks of a coin of Cunobeline, which he seems to have seen with the figure on the reverse of Apollo with a harp,‡ which at once shews it to have been in use twenty-four years before the birth of Christ, and furnishes some ground to suppose that it was first constructed by those who were confessedly the most expert in the use of it, the ancient British bards.

The above account of the harp leads to an enquiry into the antiquity of another instrument, namely, the Cruth or Crowth, formerly in common use in the principality of Wales. In the Collectanea of Leland, vol. v. pag. — amongst some Latin words, for which the author gives the Saxon appellations, Liticen is rendered a **Cruth.**§

The instrument here spoken of is of the fidicinal kind, somewhat resembling a violin, twenty-two inches in length, and an inch and half in thickness. It has six strings, supported by a bridge, and is played on with a bow; the bridge differs from that of a violin in that it is flat, and not convex on the top, a circumstance from which it is to be inferred that the strings are to be struck at the same time, so as to afford a succession of concords. The bridge is not placed at right angles with the sides of the instrument, but in an oblique direction; and, which is farther to be remarked, one of the feet of the bridge goes through one of the sound holes, which are circular, and rests on the inside of the back; the other foot, which is proportionably shorter, resting on the belly before the other sound-hole.

Of the strings, the four first are conducted from the bridge down the finger-board, as those of a violin, but the fifth and sixth, which are about an inch longer than the others, leave the small end of the

---

* In the tales of Bonaventure des Periers, valet de chambre to Margaret queen of Navarre, is the following pleasant story, which proves at least that this was the usage in France :—

In the church of St. Hilary, at Poitiers, was a singing man with a very fine counter-tenor voice; he had served in the choir a long time, and began to look to his chapter for preferment; to this end he made frequent applications to the canons severally, and received from them the most favourable answers, and promises of the first benefice that should become vacant, but when any fell he had the mortification to see some other person preferred to it. Finding himself thus frequently disappointed, he thought of an expedient to make his good masters the canons ashamed of themselves; he got together a few crowns, and affecting still to court them, he invited them to a dinner at his house; they accepted his invitation, but, considering the slender circumstances of the man, sent in provisions of their own for the entertainment, which he received with seeming reluctance, but nevertheless took care to have served up to them: in short, he set before his guests a dish of an uncommon magnitude, containing flesh, some salt and some fresh, fowl, some roast and some boiled, fish, roots, pulse, herbs, and soups of all kinds; in a word, all the provisions that had been sent in. No man being able to eat of this strange mess, each began to hope that his own provision would be set on the table, but the singing man gave them to understand that all was before them; and perceiving their disgust, he thus addressed them :—' My masters,' said he, ' the dish that I proposed for your entertainment displeases ye, are ' not the ingredients good in their kind that compose it? Are not capons, ' are not pigeons and wild-fowl, are not trout, carp, and tench, are not ' soups, the richest that can be made, excellent food? True, you say, ' they are so separately, but they are naught being mixed and jumbled together. Even so are you my worthy friends; every one of ye separately has for these ten years promised me his favour and patronage, each has flattered me with the hopes of his assistance in procuring for me such a benefice in the church, such a provision for the remainder of my life, as my services in the choir intitle me to. What have ye done ' for me in all this time? and how much better in your collective capacity ' are ye than this nauseous mixture of viands which ye now despise?' Here he ended his reproaches, and ordering the table to be covered with such fare as was fit to entertain them with, they dined, and left him with an assurance that he should soon be provided for, which shortly after he was, to his great satisfaction.

† Those of the clergy who entertained a real love for music, were by this decree and a subsequent canon totally restrained from the practice of it for their recreation; the decree forbids social harmony; and by the fifty-eighth of king Edgar's canons, made anno 960, is an express charge, ' That no priest be a common rhymer, nor play on any musical instrument ' by himself or with any other men, but be wise and reverent as become 'his order.' Vide Johnson's Ecclesiastical Laws, tit. Canons made in King Edgar's Reign. As to the decree of the concil of 679, above mentioned, it is confined to the singing of females at private meetings; but it seems that before that time girls were used to sing in the churches; for by a canon of a council held in France anno 614, it is expressly forbidden.

‡ Notes on Drayton's Polyolbion, Song VI.

§ Carpentier, in his Supplement to the Glossary of Du Cange, lately published, gives the word Lituicenes, which he explains, players on wind instruments. This appellative is not formed of Liticen, but of Lituus, which is a wind instrument, and therefore he is right. Walther, in his Musical Lexicon, for Lituus gives Tubam curvam, and supposes it to mean the Chalameau, which see in Mersennus; but more probably it is the cornet, to which the Lituus of the Jews in Kircher bears a near resemblance.

neck about an inch to the right. The whole six are wound up either by wooden pegs in the form of the letter T, or by iron pins, which are turned with a wrest like those of a harp or spinnet. The figure, together with the tuning of this singular instrument, is here given :—

Tuning of the Cruth.

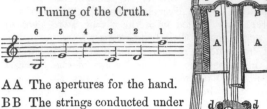

AA The apertures for the hand.

BB The strings conducted under the end board.

c c The pegs.

d d The sound-holes.

Of the tuning it is to be remarked that the sixth and fifth strings are the unison and octave of G, the fourth and third the same of C, and the second and first the same of D; so that the second pair of strings are a fourth, and the third a fifth to the first.

Touching the antiquity of the cruth, it must be confessed there is but little written evidence to carry it farther back than to the time of Leland; nevertheless the opinion of its high antiquity is so strong among the inhabitants of the country where it is used, as to afford a probable ground of conjecture that the cruth might be the prototype of the whole fidicinal species of musical instruments.

Another kind of evidence of its antiquity, but which tends also to prove that the cruth was not peculiar to Wales, arises from a discovery lately made, and communicated to the Society of Antiquarians, respecting the abbey church of Melross in Scotland, supposed to have been built about the time of Edward II. It seems that among the outside ornaments of that church, there is the figure of the instrument now under consideration very little different from the representation above given of it.

The word Cruth is pronounced in English crowth, and corruptly crowd: a player on the cruth was called a Crowther or Crowder, and so also is a common fiddler to this day; and hence undoubtedly Crowther or Crowder, a common surname.

Butler, with his usual humour, has characterized a common fiddler, and given him the name of Crowdero, in the following passage :—

> I'th' head of all this warlike rabble,
> Crowdero march'd, expert and able.
> Instead of trumpet and of drum,
> That makes the warrior's stomach come,
> Whose noise whets valour sharp, like beer
> By thunder turn'd to vinegar;
> (For if a trumpet sound, or drum beat,
> Who has not a month's mind to combat?)
> A squeaking engine he apply'd
> Unto his neck, on north-east side,

> Just where the hangman does dispose,
> To special friends, the knot or noose:
> For 'tis great grace, when statesmen straight
> Dispatch a friend, let others wait.
> His warped ear hung o'er the strings,
> Which was but souse to chitterlings;
> For guts, some write, ere they are sodden,
> Are fit for musick, or for pudden:
> From whence men borrow ev'ry kind
> Of minstrelsy, by string or wind.
> His grisly beard was long and thick,
> With which he strung his fiddle-stick,
> For he to horse-tail scorn'd to owe,
> For what on his own chin did grow.
> 　　　　　　Hud. part I. canto II. v. 105.

Upon which passage it may be questioned why the poet has chose to make the North-East side the position of the instrument; the answer may be this: that of the four cardinal points the east is the principal, it being from thence that the day first appears; supposing then the face to be turned to the east, and in such a case as this, cæteris paribus, any circumstance is a motive for preference, the left is the north side, and in this situation the instrument being applied to the neck, will have a north-east direction.

The instrument above spoken of is now so little used in Wales, that there is at present but one person in the whole principality who can play on it, his name is John Morgan, of Newburgh, in the island of Anglesey; and, as he is now near sixty years of age, there is reason to fear the succession of performers on the cruth is nearly at an end.

The period which has been filled up with the account of the ancient jougleours, violars, and minstrels, and more especially the extracts from Chaucer, and other old poets, furnish the names of sundry other instruments, as namely, the Lute, the Getron or Cittern, the Flute, the Fiddle, and the Cornamusa, or Bagpipe, which it is certain were all known, and in common use before the year 1400.

The book herein before cited by the title of Bartholomæus de Proprietatibus Rerum, furnishes the names of sundry other instruments, with a description of their several forms and uses, and contains besides, a brief discourse on the science of music in general. As translated into English by Trevisa, it is, for many reasons to be looked on as a great curiosity; for not to mention the great variety of learning contained in it, the language, style, and sentiment are such, as render it to a very great degree instructive and entertaining. Numberless words and phrases, not taken notice of by any of our lexicographers, and which are now either become totally obsolete, or are retained only in particular parts of this kingdom, are here to be met with, the knowledge whereof would greatly facilitate the understanding of the earlier writers. In short, to speak of the translation of Bartholomæus by Trevisa, it is a work that merits the attention of every lover of antiquity, every proficient in English literature. The latter part of the nineteenth and last book is wholly on music, and is unquestionably the most ancient treatise on the subject in the English language extant in print. The latter of these reasons would alone justify the insertion of it in this place.

A short account of Bartholomæus, and of this his work, together with some extracts from it, has been given in a foregoing chapter: here follows the proem to it, a singular specimen of old English poetry :—

Eternal lawde to God, gretteſt of myght
Be hertely yeue of euery creature,
Whyche of his goodneſſe ſendyth grace
To ſondry folke as bleſſyd auenture,
Whoſe ſpyryte of counſell comforteth full ſure,
All ſuche as luſte to ſeeke for ſapience,
And makyth them wyſe by grete intelligence.

As thus where men full naturally deſire
Of ſundry thynges and meruels for to knowe,
Of erthe, of ayre, of water, and of fire,
Of erbe and tree whych groweth both hyge and lowe,
And other thynges as nature hath them ſowe,
Of thyſe the knowlege comyth by Goddis grace,
And of all thynge that reaſon may them brace.

Whan I beholde the thynges naturall,
Gadryd by grace ſent from the Holy Ghoſt,
Briefly compyled in bokes ſpecyall,
As Bartholomewe ſheweth and eke declaryth moſt,
Than I rejoyce, remembrynge euery coſte,
How ſome countree hath grete commodite,
Some rote, ſome frute, ſome ſtoon of hyghe degree.

Prayſed be God, which hath ſo well enduyd
The auctor wyth grace de Proprietatibus
To ſe ſo many naturall thynges renewd,
Whych in his boke he hath compyled thus,
Where thrugh by redynge we may comforte us,
And wyth conceytes dyuers fede our mynde,
As bokes empryntid ſhewyth ryght as we fynde.

By Wyken de Worde, which thrugh his dyligence
Emprentyd hath at prayer and deſyre
Of Roger Thorney, mercer, and from thens
This mocion ſprange to ſette the hertes on fyre
Of ſuche a loue to rede in euery ſhire,
Dyuers maters in voydynge ydylneſſe,
Eyke as this boke hath ſhewed to you expreſſe,

And many an other wonderful conceyte
Shewyth Bartholowe de Proprietatibus,
Whyche beſyed hymſelfe to take the ſwete receyte
Of holſom cunnynge, his tyme diſpendynge thus,
Geuynge example of vertue gloryous,
Bokes to cheryſh, and make in ſondry wiſe
Vertue to folowe and idleneſſe to diſpyſe.

For in this worlde, to rekon euery thynge
Pleſure to man there is none comparable,
As is to rede and underſtondynge
In bokes of wyſdome they ben ſo delectable,
Whiche ſowne to vertue and ben profytable ;
And all that loue ſuche vertue ben full glade
Bokes to renewe and cauſe theym to be made.

And alſo of your charyte call to remembraunce
The ſoul of William Caxton, firſt prynter of this boke
In Laten tonge at Coleyn hymſelf to auaunce
That euery well diſpoſyd man may thereon loke ;
And John Tate the yonger joye mote he broke
Whiche late hathe in Englonde doo make this paper thynne
That now in our Englyſh this boke is printed inne.

That yong and olde thrugh plente may reioyſe
To gyue theym ſelf to good occupacion,
And ben experte as ſhewyth the comyn voyce,
To voyde alle vyce and defamacyon,
For idylneſſe all vertue put adowne,
Than rede and ſtudie in bokes vertuoſe,
So ſhall thy name in heuen be glorioſe.

For yf one thyng myght laſt a M. yere,
Full ſone comyth aege that frettyth all away ;
But like as Phebus wyth hys bemes clere
The mone repeyreth as bryght as ony day,
Whan ſhe is waſtyd ryght ſo may we ſay
Thiſe bokes old and blinde, whan we renewe
By goodly pryntyng they ben bryht of hewe.

Then all that cauſe the good contynuaunce,
And helpe ſuche werke in furtheryng to their mizt
Ben to be ſette in good remembraunce,
For ſuche deſerue reward of God all myght,
They put aſyde both wyked thought and ſyght,
And cauſe full often ryghte good gouernaunce,
Wrouten whyche ſynne wold hym ſelf auaunce.

Now gloryous God that regneſt one in thre,
And thre in one, graunt vertue myght and grace
Unto the prynter of this werke, that he
May be rewarded in thy heavenly place ;
And whan the worlde ſhall come before thy face,
There to receyve according to deſert
Of grace and mercy make hym then expert.

Batman, who, as is above said, in 1582 published an edition of the book De Proprietatibus Rerum, took great liberties with Trevisa's translation, by accommodating the language of it to his own time, a very unwarrantable practice in the editor of any ancient book ; he may however be said in some respects to have made amends for this his error, by the additions of his own which he has occasionally made to several sections of his author. Here follows that part of the nineteenth book above referred to, taken verbatim from the edition of Wynken de Wordo, with the additions of Stephen Batman, distinguished as they occur:—

De Muſica.

' As arte of nombres and meſures ſeruyth to diuinite,
' ſo doth the arte of melody for muſyk ; by the whyche
' accorde and melody is knowe in ſowne, and in ſonge
' is nedeful to know myſtyk meanynge of holy writte ;
' for it is ſayd that the worlde is compownyd and made
' in a certayne and proporcion of armeny, as Yſyder*
' ſayth libro tertio.
' And it is ſaid that heuen gooth aboute wyth conſo-
' nancye and acorde of melody. For muſyk meuyth
' affeccions, and excyteth the wyttes to dyuerſe diſpo-
' ſycyons. Alſo in bataylle the noyſe of the trompe
' comfortyth werryours, and the more ſtronge that the
' trompynge is, the more ſtronge and bolde men ben to
' fyghte : and comfortyth ſhypmen to ſuffre alle the
' dyſeaſes and trauelle. And comforte of voys pleaſyth
' and comfortyth the hert, and inwyttes in all dyſeaſe
' and traueylle of werks and weryneſſe. And muſyk
' abatyth mayſtry of euyl ſpyrytes in mankynde, as we
' rede of Dauid that delyuered Saul of an unclene ſpy-
' ryte by crafte of melodye. And muſyk excyteth and
' comfortyth beſtis and ſerpentes, foules and delphines
' to take hede therto ; and ſo veynes and ſynewes of
' the body and puls therof ; and ſo all the lymmnes of
' the body ben ſocied togyder by vertue of armenye as
' Iſider ſayth. Of Muſyk ben thre partyes, Armonica,
' Rethmica, and Metrica. Armonica dyſtyngueth grete
' and ſmalle in ſownes, and hyghe and lowe, and pro-
' porcyonall chaungyng of voys and of ſowne. And
' Armonia is ſwete accorde of ſonge, and cometh of
' due proporcyon in dyuerſe voyces, other blaſtes towch-
' ynge and ſmytynge ſownes : for, as Iſider ſayth, ſowne
' comyth of voys, as of mouthe and jowes ; other of
' blaſte, as of trompes and pypes ; other of touchinge
' and ſmytynge of cymbale and harpe ; and other
' ſuche that ſowneth wyth ſmytynge and ſtrokes.

* Isidore, bishop of Sevil.

'Voys comyth to one accorde, as *Hugucyon** fayth,
'for in all melodye nedyth many voys, other fownes,
'and that accordyng; for one voys pleafyth not fo
'moche as the voys and fonge of the Gnokken, and† yf
'many dyfcordith, the voys plefith not; for of fuche
'dyfcorde comyth not fonge, but howlynge other
'yellynge; but in many voyces accordynge in one is
'proporcyon of armony and melodye other fwete
'fymphonia. And fo *Ifyder* fayth that fymphonia is
'temperate modulacyon, accordynge in fownes highe
'and lowe. And by this armony hyghe voys accor-
'dyth, fo that yf one difcordyth it greueth the herynge;
'and fuche accordynge of voys hyghte Euphonia, that is
'fwetneffe of voys, and hyghte alfo Melodya, and hath
'that name of fwetneffe and of Mel, that is Honey;
'and the contrary is called *Dyaphonia*, fowle voys and
'dyfcordyng. To make melodye of armony nedyth
'diaftema, diefis, tonus, iperludius, podorius, arfis,
'thefis, and fwete voys and temperate fowne. Diaf-
'tema is a couenable fpace of two voyces, other of
'moo, acordynge. Diefis is the fpace and doynge of
'melodye, and chaungynge out of one fowne in to
'another. Tonus is the fharpneffe of voys, and is
'difference and quantitie of armony, and ftandyth in
'accent and tenor of voys. And muficyons maketh
'thereof fyftene partyes. *Iperludius* is the lafte thereof
'and mooft fharpeft; and *Podorius* is mooft heavy of
'alle, as *Ifyder* fayth. *Arfis* is rerynge of voys, and is
'the beginning of fonge. *Thefis* is fettynge, and is the
'ende, as *Ifyder* fayth; and fo fonge is the bendynge of
'the voys, for fome paffeth ftreighte, as he fayth, and
'is to fore fonge. And euery uoys is fowne, and not
'ayen warde; for fowne is the objecte of herynge, for
'all that is perceyued by herynge is called fowne, as
'breking of trees, fmytyng togyder of ftones, hurlynge
'and rufhyng of waues and of wynde, chytterynge of
'byrdes, lowynge of beeftys, voys and gronynge of
'men, and fmytynge of organes. And a voys is
'properly the fowne that comyth of the mouthe of
'a beeft; and fowne comyth of ayre fmytte ayenft an
'harde body; and the fmytynge is fooner feen than the
'fowne is herde, and the lyghtnyng is fooner feen than
'the thondre is herde. A voys is mooft thyne ayre,
'fmytte wyth the wrefte of the tongue; and fome voys
'fygnyfyeth and tokenyth by kynde, as chytterynge of
'byrdes and gronyng of fyke men. And fome tokenyth
'at wylle, as the voys of a man that is ordeyned, and
'there fhape by hefte of reafon to telle out certain
'wordes. The voys berith forthe the worde, and the
'worde that is in the thoughte maye not come oute
'but by helpe of the voys that it oute bryngeth. And
'fo fyrft the inwytte gendrith a worde in the thoughte,
'and puttyth it afterwarde out at the mouthe by the
'voyce; and fo the worde that is gendryd and con-
'teyned by inwytte, comyth oute by the voys as it
'were by an inftrumente, and is knowe. The voyce
'that is dyfpofyd to fonge and melodye hath thife
'proprytees, as *Ifyder* fayth. Voyces he fayth ben

'fmalle, fubtill, thicke, clere, fharpe, and fhylle. In
'fubtyll voys the fpyryte is not ftrong, as in chyldren
'and in wymmen; and in other that haue not grete
'fynews, ftronge and thycke; for of fmalle ftrynges
'comyth fmalle voys and fubtyll. The voyces ben
'fatte and thyck whan moche fpyryte comyth out, as
'the voys of a man. The voys is clere that fownyth
'well, and ryngeth wythout any holloweffe. Sharpe
'voyces ben full hyghe, fhylle voyces ben lowde, and
'drawth a longe, and fylleth foone all the place, as the
'noyce of trumpes. The harde voys is hofe, and alfo
'the harde voys is grymme and gryfely whan the fowne
'therof is vyolente, and as the fowne of thondre, and
'of a felde bete with grete malles. The rough voys is
'hofe and fparplyd by fmalle, and is ftuffyd and dureth
'not longe, as the fowne of erthen veffell. Voys
'*uniuolenta*‡ is *neffhe*§ and plyaunt. That name *uni-*
'*uolenta*, of *Viuo*,|| that is a lytyll belle nefhly bende.
'The perfyghte voys is hyghe, fwete, and ftronge and
'clere; hyghe to be well herde, clere to fylle the eeres;
'fwete to pleyfe, and not to fere the herynge, and to
'comfort the hertes to take hede thereto. Yf ought
'herof faylyth, the voys is not perfyghte, as *Yfyder*
'fayth. Here ouer is armonia of organes, that comyth
'of blafte whan certayn inftrumentes ben craftely made
'and duly blowe, and yeuyth by quantyte of the blafte
'craftly, dyuers by dyuerfite of organes and inftru-
'mentes, as it fareth of organes, trompes, and pipes,
'and other fuche that yeuyth dyuerfe fownes and noyce.
'*Organum* is a generall name of all inftrumentes of
'mufyk, and is netheleffe fpecyally a propryte to the
'inftrument that is made of many pipes, and blowe
'wyth belowes. And now holy chyrche ufeth oonly
'this inftrument of mufyk, in profes, fequences, and
'ympnes; and forfakyth for men's ufe of mynftralfye
'all other inftrumentes of mufyk.¶

'The *Turenes* founde fyrfte the trompe. *Virgil*
'fpekyth of them, and fayth that the voys of the
'trompe of *Turene* lowyth in the ayre.** Men in olde
'tyme ufyd trompes in battayle to fere and affraye
'theyr enmyes, and to comforte theyre owne knyghtes
'and fyghtynge men; and to comforte horfe of werre
'to fyghte and to refe and fmyte in the batayle; and
'tokenyth worfhip wyth vyctory in the fyghtynge,
'and to call them ayen that begyn to fle. And ufyd
'alfo trompettes in feeftys to call the people togider,
'and for befineffe in prayfynge of God. And for
'cryenge of welthe of joye the *Hebrewes* were
'commaunded to blowe trompettes in batayle, in the
'begynnynge of the newe mone, and to crye and
'warne the comynge of the Jubile, the yere of grace
'with noyce of trompes, and to crye and refte to all
'men. As *Ifyder* fayth *libro xviii*.°

'A trompe is properly an inftrument ordeyned for
'men that fyghteth in batayle, to crye and to warne
'of the fygnes of batayle. And where the cryers
'voys maye not be herde for noyfe, the noyfe of the
'trompe fholde be herde and knowen. And *Tuba*
'hath that name as it were *Tona*, that is holowe

'wythin, and full fmothe for to take the more brethe,
'and is rounde wythout, and ftreyghte atte the tromp-
'ers mouth, and brode and large at the other ende;
'and the tromper with his honde putteth it to his
'mouth, and the trompe is rulyd upwarde and down-
'warde, and holde forth ryght; and is dyuerfe of
'noyfe, as *Yfyder* fayth. For it is fomtime blowe to
'araye bataylles, and fomtyme for that batoylles fholde
'fmyte togyder, and fometyme for the chafe, and to
'take men in to the hofte.

De Buccina.

'*Buccina* hath the name as it were *vociva parua*,
'and is a trompe of horne, of tree, eyther of braffe,
'and was blowen ayenft enmyes in old tyme; for as
'*Ifyder* fayth, *libro decimo octavo*, the wylde *Panems*
'were fomtyme gaderyd to al manere doynge wyth
'the blowynge of fuche a manere trompe, and foo
'*Buccina* was properly a token to wylde men. *Perfius*
'fpekyth herof, and fayth that Buccina made the olde
'*Qwyrites* araye themfelft, namely, in armoure. The
'voys of fuche a trompe, hyght *Buccinium* as he fayth,
'and the *Hebrewes* ufed trompes of horne, namely in
'*Kalendus*, in remembraunce of the delyueraunce of
'*Yfaac*, whanne an hornyd wetther was offryd and
'made oblacion of in his ftede, as the Gloc.* fayth
'fuper *Genefis*.†

De Tibia.

'*Tibia* is a pype, and hath that name for it was
'fyrfte made of legges of hartes, yonge and olde, as
'men trowe; and the noyfe of pypes was called *Other*,
'as *Hugucion* fayth. This name *Tibia* comyth of
'*Tibium*, that is a rufhe, other a rede, and therof
'comyth this name *Tibicen* a pype. And was fom-
'tyme an inftrument of doole and lamentacyon, whyche
'men dyde ufe in office and fepultures of deed men, as
'the Gloc. fayth fuper *Math. ix.* and thereby the fonge
'was fonge of doole and of lamentacyon.

De Calamo.

'*Calamus* hath that name of thys worde *Calando*,
'fowning; and is the generall name of pypes. A pype
'hyghte *Fiftula*, for voyce comyth therof. For voyce
'hyghte *Fest* in *Grewe*,§ and fend, *Iftola*|| in *Grewe*.
'And foo the pype hyghte *Fiftula*, as it were *fendyng*
'oute voyce other fowne. Hunters ufeth this inftru-
'ment, for hartes louyth the noyfe therof. But whyle
'the harte taketh hede and likynge in the pypynge of
'an hunter, another hunter whyche he hath no know-
'lege of, comyth and fhoteth at the harte and fleeth
'hym. Pypyng begyleth byrdes and foules, therefore
'it is fayd "the pype fyngeth fwetely whyle the fowler
'begyleth the byrde."¶ And fhepe louyth pypynge,
'therfore fhepeherdes ufyth pipes whan they walk wyth
'theyr fhepe. Therefore one whyche was callyd *Pan*
'was callyd God of hirdes, for he joyned dyuerfe redes,
'and arayed them to fonge flyghly and craftely. *Virgil*

'fpekyth therof, and fayth that *Pan* ordeyned fyrft to
'join [in one horne]** *Pan* hath cure of fhepe and of
'fhepherdes. And the fame inftrument of pypes hyghte
'*Pan donum*, for *Pan* was fynder therof as *Yfyder* fayth.
'And wyth pipes watchynge men pleyfeth fuche men
'as reftyth in beddes, and makyth theym flepe the
'fooner and more fwetly by melodye of pypes.††

De Sambuca.

'*Sambuca* is the Ellerne tree brotyll, and the bowes
'therof ben holowe, and voyde and fmothe; and of
'thofe fame bowes ben pipes made, and alfo fome
'maner fymphony, as *Yfyder* fayth.

De Symphonia.

'The *Symphonye* is an inftrument of mufyke, and is
'made of an holowe tree, clofyd in lether in eyther
'fyde, and mynftralles betyth it wyth ftyckes; and by
'accorde of hyghe and lowe therof comyth full fwete
'notes, as *Ifyder* fayth. Neuertheleffe the accorde ot
'all fownes hyghte *Symphonia*, is lyke wife as the
'accorde of dyuerfe voys hyghte *Chorus*, as the Gloc.
'fayth fuper *Luc.*

De Armonya.

'*Armonya Rithinica* is a fownynge melodye, and
'comyth of fmyttyng of ftrynges, and of tynklyng
'other ryngynge of metalle. And dyuerfe inftrumentes
'fcruyth to this manere armonye, as *Tabour*, and *Tym-
'bre*, *Harpe*, and *Sawtry*, and *Nakyres*, and alfo *Siftrum*.

De Tympano.

'*Tympanum* is layed ftreyghte to the tree in the one
'fide, and half a tabour other halfe a fymphony, and
'fhape as a fyfue,‡‡ and beten wyth a ftycke; ryght as
'a tabour, as *Ifyder* fayth, and maketh the better
'melody yf there is a pype therwyth.

De Cithara.

'The harpe hyghte *Cithara*, and was fyrft founde
'of *Appollin*, as the *Grekes* wene; and the harpe is
'like to a mannys brefte, for lyke wyfe as the voyce
'comyth of the brefte, foo the notes cometh of the
'harpe, and hath therfore that name *Cithara*, for the
'brefte is callyd *Thorica thieurim*. And afterwarde
'fome and fome,§§ came forth many manere inftru-
'mentes therof, and hadde that name *Cithara*, as the
'harpe, and fawtry, and other fuche.
'And fome ben foure cornerde, and fome thre
'cornerde; the ftrynges ben many, and fpecyall
'manere therof is dyuerfe.
'Men in olde tyme callyd the harpe *Fidicula*, and
'alfo *Fidicen*, for the ftrynges therof accordyth as well
'as fome men accordyth in Fey.|||| And the harpe had
'feuen ftrynges, and foo *Virgil* fayth *libro feptimo*. Of
'fowne ben feuen *Difcrimina*¶¶ of voys, and ben as the

---

* *i. e.* The gloss or commentary.

† Batman, in a note on the trompe and buccina, says that the warnings in battle were 'the Onfet, the Alarum, and Retrate,' and adds, 'Some 'used the greate wilke shell in steed of a trumpet, some hornes of 'beastes, and some the thigh bones of a man, as do the Indians. In 'civil discords the flute, the fieft, and the cornet, made winding like the 'rammes horne.'

‡ Fos. Batm.   § *i. e.* Greek. || Stolia. Batm.

¶ 'Fistula dulce canit, volucrem dum decipit auceps.' Caton. Dist. lib. I.

** 'With wax manye pipes in one.' Batm. on the authority of this passage: 'Pan primos calamos cerâ conjungere plures.'

†† Addition of Batman. 'Pan, called the god of shepheardes: he is 'thought to be Demogorgon's son, and is thus described; in his forehead 'he hath hornes like the sunbeames, a long beard, his face red like the 'cleer air; in his brest the star Nebris, the nether part of his body rough, 'his feet like a goate, and alway is imagined to laugh. He was wor-'shipped, especiallye in Arcadia. When there grew betwixt Phœbus and 'Pan a contention whether of them two should be judged the best 'musition; Midas preferring the bagpipe, not respecting better skill, was 'given for his reward a paire of asse eares.'

‡‡ *i. e.* A sieve.   §§ At different times. |||| Faith.

¶¶ 'Septem sunt soni, septem discrimina vocum.'

'nexte ftrynge therto. And ftrynges ben feuen, for
'the fulleth alle the note. Other for heuen fownyth
'in feuen meuyngs. A ftrynge hyghte *Corda*, and
'hathe the fame name of corde the herte; for as the
'puls of the herte is in the brefte, foo the puls of the
'ftrynges is in the harpe. *Mercurius* founde up fyrfte
'fuche ftrynges, for he ftrenyd fyrfte ftrynges, and
'made them to fowne, as *Yfyder* fayth.

'The more drye the ftrynges ben ftreyned the more
'they fowne. And the wrefte hyghte *Plectrum*.

De Pfalterio.

'The Sawtry highte *Pfalterium*, and hath that name
'of *Pfallendo*, fyngynge; for the confonant anfweryth
'to the note therof in fyngynge. The harpe is lyke to
'the fawtry in fowne. But this is the dyuerfytee and
'difcorde bytwene the harpe and the fawtry; in the
'fawtry is an holowe tree, and of that fame tree the
'fowne comyth upwarde, and the ftrynges ben fmytte
'dounwarde, and fownyth upwarde; and in the harpe
'the holowneffe of the tre is bynethe. The *Hebrewes*
'callyth the fawtry *Decacordes*, an inftrument hauinge
'ten ftringes, by numbre of the ten heftes or com-
'maundementes. Stringes for the fawtry ben befte
'made of laton, or elles thofe ben goode that ben
'made of fyluer.

De Lira.

'*Lira* hath that name of dyuerfytee of fowne; for
'the *Lira* geueth dyuerfe fownes, as *Ifyder* fayth. And
'fome people fuppofe that *Mercurius* fyrfte founde up
'this inftrument *Lira* in this wife. The river *Nylus*
'was flowen and aryfen, and afterward was aualyd
'and wythdrawen ayen in to his propre channelle.
'And lefte in the felde many dyuerfe beeftys, and alfo
'a fnaylle; and whan the fnaylle was roftyd the
'fynewes left, and were ftreyned in the fnaylles houfe.
'And *Mercurius* fmote the fynewes, and of theym came
'a fowne. And *Mercurius* made a *Lira* to the lykneffe
'of the fnaylles houfe, and gave the fame *Lira* to one
'that was namyd *Orpheus*, whiche was mooft befy
'abowtte fuch thinges; and fo it was fayd that by the
'fame crafte, not oonly wylde beeftys drewe to fonge
'and melodye, but moreouer ftones and alfo wodes.
'And fyngers in fables don meane that thys forfayd
'inftrument *Lira* is fette amonge fterres for loue of
'ftudy and prayfynge of fong, as *Ifyder* fayth.

De Cymbalis.

'*Cymbales* ben inftrumentes of mufyk, and ben fmytte
'togider, and fowneth and ryngeth.*

De Siftro.

'*Siftrum* is an inftrument of mufyk, and hath the
'name of a lady that firfte brought it up; for it is
'proued that *Ifis*, quene of *Egypte*, was the firft fynder
'of *Siftrum*: and *Juuenalis* fpekyth therof and fayth,
'*Ifis et irato feriat mea lumina fiftro.* And wymmen
'ufyth this inftrument, for a woman was the fyrfte
'fynder therof. Therfore among the *Amazones* the
'hofte of wymmen is callyd to bataylle with the
'inftrument *Siftrum*.†

---

* Addition of Batman. 'Compaffed like a hoope; on the upper com-
paffe, under a certain holownes hangeth halfe bells five or feaven.
† Addition of Batman. 'An inftrument like a horn, used in battaile
'infteed of a trumpet, also a brazen timbrell.'

De Tintinabulo.

'*Tintinabuluz* is a belle, other at *Campernole*; and
'hath the name of *Tiniendo*, tynklynge or ryngynge.
'A belle hathe this propryte, that whyle he prouffyteth
'to other in fowninge, he is waftyd ofte by fmytynge.
'Thyfe inftrumentes, and many other feruyth to mufyk
'that treatyth of voyfe and of fownes, and knoweth
'neuertheleffe dyfpofycyon of kyndly thynges, and pro-
'porcyon of nombres, as *Boicius* fayth; and fettyth
'enfample of the nombre of twelue in comparyfon to
'fyxe, and to other nombres that ben bytwene, and
'fayth in this wyfe. Here we fyndeth all the accordes
'of mufyk, from eyghte to fyxe, nyne to twelue, makyth
'the proporcyon *Sefquitercia*, and makyth togydre the
'confonancy *Dyapente*; and twelue to fyxe makyth
'dowble proporcyon, and fyngyth the accorde *Dia-*
'*pafon*. Eyghte to nyne in comparyfon ben meane,
'and makyth *Epogdonus*, whych is callyd *Tonus* in
'melody of mufyk, and is comin mefure of alle the
'fownes. And foo it is too underftonde that bytwene
'*Dyatefferon* and *Dyapente* tonus is dyuerfyte of ac-
'cordes; as bytwene the proporcyons *Sexquitercia* and
'*Sexquialtera* oonly *Epogdolis* is dyuerfyte, *huc ufque*
'*Boicius in fecundo Arfmetrice*‡ *capitulo ultimo.*

'And the melodye of mufyk is nempnyd and callyd
'by names of the nombres. *Dyatefferon*, *Dyapente*,
'and *Dyapafon* haue names of the nombres whyche
'precedeth and gooth tofore in the begynnynge of
'thofe fayd names. And the proporcyon of theyr
'fownes is founde and had in thofe fame nombres, and
'is not founde, nother had, in none other nombres.

'For ye fhall underftonde that the fowne and the
'accorde in *Diapafon*, is of proporcyon of the dowble
'nombre; and the melodye of *Dyateffraon* dooth come
'of *Epitrica collimie* that is *Sexquitercia proporcio*,

* * * * * * *

Quid fit numerus fefquialterus.

'The nombre *Sexqualterus* conteyneth other halfe
'the leffe nombre, as thre conteyneth tweyne and the
'halfe deale of two, that is one: fo nyne conteyneth
'fyxe and the halfe deale, that is thre. And fo twelue
'to eyghte, and fyftene to ten, and fo of other. Thife
'wordes ben in themfelfe deepe and full myftyk, derk
'to underftondynge. But to them that ben wyfe and
'cunnyng in arfmetrik and in mufyk, they ben more
'clerer than moche lyghte; and ben derke and alle un-
'knowen to them whyche ben uncunnynge, and haue
'no ufage in arfmetrik. Therfore he that woll knowe
'the forfayde wordes and proporcyons of nombres of
'voys and fownes, fhall not dyfpyfe to afke counfeylle,
'and to defyre to haue knowlege by thofe whyche ben
'wyfer, and that haue more cunnyng in gemetry and
'mufyk. And *Ifyder* fayth that in termes and figures
'and accordes of mufyk is fo grete, that the felfe man
'ftondeth not perfyghte there withoute, for perfyghte
'mufyk comprehendyth alle thynges. Alfo reuolue and
'confydre herof in thy minde, that mufyk and armonye
'unyeth and accordyth dyuerfe thynges and contrary;
'and makyth the hye fowne to accorde wyth the lowe,
'and the lowe wyth the hyghe: and accordyth con-

---

‡ Arithmetic.

'trary wylles and defyres, and refreynyith and abatyth
'intencyons and thoughtes, and amendyth and com-
'fortyth feble wyttes of felyuge, and cryeth namely,
'and warnyth us of the unytee of the exemplar of
'God in contrary werkynges; and dyuerfly mani-
'fefteth and fheweth that erthly thynges may be joyned
'in accorde to heuenly thynges; and caufeth and maketh
'gladde and joyful hertes, more gladde and joyful, and
'fory hertes and elenge, more fory and elenge: for as
'*Auftin* fayth by a preuy and fecrete lykneffe of pro-
'pryte of the foule and of armonye, melodye con-
'fourmyth itfelfe to the affeccyons and defires of the
'foule. And therfore auctores meanyth that inftru-
'mentes of mufyk makyth the gladde more gladde,
'and the fory more fory. Loke other proprytees of
'armonye tofore in this fame boke, whereas other
'wordes of *Ifyder* ben rehercyd and fpoken of.'

To this brief but very curious discourse of Bartholomæus, his editor Batman has added a supplement, containing his own sentiments and those of
sundry other writers on the subject. This supplement may be considered as a commentary on his
author, but is too long to be here inserted.

CHAP. LXI.

THE foregoing extract may well be considered as a
supplement to the several tracts contained in the
Cotton manuscript and that of Waltham Holy Cross,
of the contents whereof a copious relation has herein
before been given; forasmuch as these treat in general on the nature of the consonances, the rudiments
of song, the Cantus Gregorianus, and its application
to the choral offices, the Cantus Mensurabilis, and the
precepts of extemporary descant, and this of Bartholomæus contains such a particular account of the
various instruments in use at the time of writing it,
which, to mention it again, was about the year 1366,
as it would be in vain to seek for in any manuscript
or printed book of equal antiquity, as yet known to
be extant.

It is true that in the account which he has given
of the inventors of the several instruments described
by him, Bartholomæus seems to have founded his
opinion on vulgar tradition; and indeed in some
respects he is contradicted by authors whose good
fortune it was to live in more enlightened times, and
from whose testimony there can lie no appeal. But
rejecting his relation as fabulous in this respect,
enough will be left in this little work of his to engage
the attention of a curious enquirer into the history
and progress of music; as it is from such accounts
as this alone that we are enabled to form an estimate
of the state of musical practice at any given period.

The several descriptions given by this author of
the ancient trumpet made of a Horn, or of a Tree;
of the Tibia, formed of the leg-bone of a hart; as also
of the Fistula, seem to refer to the practice of the
Hebrews and ancient Greeks; but nothing can be
less artificial than the Sambuca, a kind of pipe, made,
as he relates, of the branch of an Elder Tree; or that
other instrument described by him in the chapter De

Symphonia, made of an 'holowe tree, closyd in lether
'in eyther syde, whych mynstralles betyth wyth
'styckes;' or of the Tympanum, 'layed streyghte to
'the tree, in shape as a syve, having halfe a tabour
'and halfe a symphony;' and which 'being beten
'with a stycke, makyth the better melodie yf there is
'a pype therwyth.'

These, and other particulars remarkable in the
above-mentioned tract of Bartholomæus, bespeak, as
strongly as words can do, the very low and abject
state of instrumental music in his time; and were it
not for the proofs contained in other authors, that the
organ, the harp, the lute, and other instruments of a
more elegant structure were in use at that time, would
induce a suspicion that instrumental music was then
scarcely known. But to what degrees of improvement
these rude essays towards the establishment of an
instrumental practice were carried in the space of
about fourscore years, may be collected from the Liber
Niger Domus Regis, before cited, in which is contained an account of the several musicians retained by
Edward IV. as well for his private amusement, as for
the service of his chapel, with their duties. Batman,
in the additions made by him, seems to have discharged, as far as he was able, the duty of a commentator: and has given such an eulogium on the science
of music as might be expected from a man of great
reading and little skill, and such the author appears
to have been. The account of the household establishment of Edward IV. above-mentioned, is contained
in the following words:—

'MINSTRELLES thirteene, thereof one is virger, which
'directeth them all festyvall dayes in their statyones of
'blowings and pypyngs to such offyces as the officeres
'might be warned to prepare for the king's meats and
'soupers; to be more redyere in all services and due
'tyme; and all thes sytyng in the hall together, whereof
'some be trompets, some with the shalmes and smalle
'pypes, and some are strange mene coming to this court
'at fyve feastes of the year, and then take their wages of
'houshold after iiij. d. ob. by daye, after as they have
'byne presente in courte,* and then to avoyd aftere the
'next morrowe aftere the feaste, besydes theare other re-
'wards yearly in the king's exchequer, and clothinge
'with the householde, wintere and somere for eiche of
'thom xxs., and they take nightelye amongeste them all
'iiij galanes ale; and for wintere seasone thre candles
'waxe, vj candles pich, iiij talesheids;† lodging suffy-
'tyente by the herbengere for them and theire horses
'nightelye to the courte. Aulso having into courte ij ser-
'vants to bear their trompets, pypes, and other instru-
'ments, and torche for wintere nightes whilest they blowe
'to suppore of the chaundry; and alway two of thes per-
'sones to contynewe stylle in courte at wages by the
'cheque rolle whiles they be presente iiij. ob. dayly, to
'warne the king's ridynge houshold when he goethe to

* *i. e.* According to the time, &c.

† TALSHIDE or TALWOOD [Taliatura] is firewood cleft and cut into
billets of a certain length. By a statute of 7 Edward VI. cap. 7. every
Talshide marked j, being round-bodied, shall contain sixteen inches of
assize in compass, &c. Cowel, in voce.
By the book of the earl of Northumberland's household establishment
it appears that the liveries of wood were of so may *Shides* for each room,
and of so many faggots for brewing and baking.
The distinction seems to have consisted in this, that Talshides or
Talesheides were the larger timber, split and cut into a proper length for
burning upon hearths in the apartments. And that faggots were made,
as they now are, of the lops and branches of the trees.
Tal or *tale* prefixed to shides or sheides, perhaps is derived from the
French word taillè, cut.

'horsbacke as oft as it shall require, and that his hous-
'hold meny maye followe the more redyere aftere by the
'blowinge of their trompets. Yf any of thes two min-
'strelles be lete bloode in courte, he taketh two loves,
'ij messe of great meate, one galone ale. They part
'not at no tyme with the rewards given to the houshold.
'Also when it pleasethe the kinge to have ij mynstrelles
'continuinge in courte, they will not in no wise that thes
'mynstrelles be so famylliere to aske rewards.

'A wayte, that nightely from Mychelmas to Shreve
'Thorsdaye pipethe watche within this courte fowere
'tymes; in the somere nightes iij tymes, and makethe
'Bon Gayte at every chambere, doare, and offyce, as
'well for feare of pyckeres and pillers. He eatethe in
'the halle with mynstrelles, and takethe lyverey at nighte
'a loffe, a galone of alle, and for somere nightes ij candles
'piche, a bushel of coles; and for wintere nightes halfe
'a loffe of bread, a galone of alle, iiij candles piche, a
'bushel of coles; daylye whilste he is presente in courte
'for his wages in cheque roale allowed iiij. d. ob. or else
'iij. d. by the discresshon of the steuarde and tressorore,
'and that aftere his cominge and deservinge : * also
'cloathinge with the houshold yeomen or mynstrelles
'lyke to the wages that he takethe; and he be sycke he
'taketh twoe loves, ij messe of great meate, one galone
'alle. Also he partethe with the houshold of general
'gyfts, and hathe his beddinge carried by the comptrol-
'leres assygment; and under this yeoman to be a groome
'watere. Yf he can excuse the yeoman in his absence,
'then he takethe rewarde, clotheinge, meat, and all other
'things lyke to other grooms of houshold. Also this
'yeoman-waighte, at the making of knightes of the Bathe,
'for his attendance upon them by nighte-time, in watch-
'inge in the chappelle, hathe to his fee all the watchinge-
'clothing that the knight shall wear uppon him.

'Deane of the chappelle, caled the king's Cheefe
'Chaplene, syttinge in the hall, and served after a bar-
'rone service, begynninge the chappell bourd, havinge
'one chappelene, and one gentleman eatyinge in the
'halle, and lyverey to his chambere for all daye and
'nighte iij loaves, ij messe of great meate, a picher of
'wyne, two gallones of ale ; and for wintere seasone one
'torche, one picher, ij candles waxe, iij candles pich, iij
'talesheids, lyttere, and rushes all the year of the serjante
'usher of the hall and chambere, and the dutyes of the
'king's charges; and all the offerings of wexe in Candle-
'mas-daye of the hole housholde by the king's gyffe, with
'the fees of the beene sat uppe in the feastes of the yeare
'when it is brente into a shasmonde. Also this deane is
'yearly clothing with the houshold for winter and somere,
'or else in moneyes of the comptyng-house viij markes,
'and carradge for his competente hernes in the offyce of
'vesterye, by oversyght of the comptrolere, and keepynge
'in all within this courte iiij persones; and when himself
'is out of court his chamberlene eatethe with the cham-
'berlenes in the halle. The deane come agayne, he must
'have lodginge suffytyente for his horses by the herben-
'ger, and for his other servants in the toune or contrey;
'also he hathe all the swoords that all the knightes of the
'Bathe offere to Gode in the king's chapelle, as ofte as
'any shall be made. This dean is curate of confesshon
'of houshold.

     *   *   *   *   *

'This deane hath all correctyones of chappelmen, in
'moribus et scientia; except in some cases to the stuard
'and comptyng-house; he nor non of the chappell part-
'ethe with the houshold of noe general gyffs excepte
'vestire.

    'Chaplenes, and clerkes of the chappelle xxiiij.

'by the deane's electtyone or denomenatyone, endowed
'with virtues morrolle and specikatyve, as of the muscke,
"shewinge in descante, clean voyced, well releshed in
"pronounsynge. Eloquent in readinge, suffytyente in
"organes playinge,'' and modestial in all other havour,
'syttynge in the hall togethere at the deane's boarde,
'also lodginge togethere within the courte in one cham-
'bere, or else nighe thertoo. And every eiche of them
'beinge in courte, for his dayly wages allowed in the
'cheque rolle, vij. ob. And for every eiche of them
'clothinge in wintere and somere, or else of the comp-
'tyng-house xs., and lyvery to their chamberes nightely
'amongste them all ij loves of breade, j picher of wyne,
'vj galones of ale. And for wintere lyvery from Alhol-
'lontyde till Estere, amongest them all ij candles waxe,
'xij candles pich, viij talsheids. Thei parte not with any
'tythes of houshold at noe tyme, but yf it be given unto
'the chappelle alone. Also they pay for their carriadge
'of beddinge and harnesse, taking all the year for their
'chambere, lyttere and rushes of the serjante usher of the
'hall; and havinge into this courte for every eiche of
'these chaplenes, being preeste, one servante ; and for
'every twoe gentlemen clerkes of the chappelle, one
'honeste servante, and lyverye suffytyente for their
'horses and their servantes nighe to the towne. The
'king's good grace avauncethe thes people by prebends
'churches of his patremonye, or by his highness reco-
'mendatorye, and other free chappelles or hospitalles.
'Oore Lady Masse preestes and the gospelleres are
'assigned by the deane ; and if any of thes be let bloode
'in courte, he taketh dayly ij loves, one messe of great
'meate, one messe of roste, one galone of ale : and when
'the chappelle syng mattenes over nighte, called Black
'Mattynes, then they have allowed spice and wine.

'Yeomen of the chappelle, twoe, called Pisteleres,†
'growinge from the chilrene of the chappelle by succes-
'syone of age; and aftere the change of their voyses, and
'by the deane's denomenatyon, and after theire conninge
'and virtue : thes twoe yeomen eatynge in the halle at
'the chapelle board, take dayly when they be presente in
'court abyding the nighte, for their wages alowed in the
'cheque roles iij. d. and clothinge playne with the yeo-
'men of houshold, and carryadge for their competente
'beddynge with the children of the chappelle; or else
'eiche of them at rewarde liij. s. iiij. d. by the yeare,
'aftere the discresyon of stuard and tresorore.

'Children of the chappelle viij, founden by the
'king's privie cofferes for all that longethe to their appe-
'relle by the hands and oversyghte of the deane, or by
'the Master of Songe assigned to teache them, which
'mastere is appointed by the deane, chosen one of the
'nomber of the felowshipe of chappelle after rehearsed,
'and to drawe them to other schooles after the form of
'Sacotte,‡ as well as in Songe in Orgaines and other.
'Thes childrene eate in the hall dayly at the chappell
'boarde, nexte the yeomane of vestery ; taking amongeste
'them for lyverye daylye for brekefaste and all nighte,
'two loves, one messe of great meate, ij galones ale ; and
'for wintere seasone iiij candles piche, iij talsheids, and
'lyttere for their pallets of the serjante usher, and car-
'ryadge of the king's coste for the competente beddynge
'by the oversyghte of the comptrollere. And amongeste
'them all to have one servante into the court to trusse
'and bear their harnesse and lyverey in court. And that
'day the king's chapelle removeth every of thes children
'then present receaveth iiij. d. at the green clothe of the
'comptyng-house for horshire dayly, as long as they be
'jurneinge. And when any of these children comene to

---

* *i. e.* According to his attendance and deserts. The word *after* is here to be taken in the sense above given of it.

† Epistellers, readers of the epistles. We read also of Gospellers in this and other chapel establishments.

† Of this word no explanation is given by any of the lexicographers.

' xviij yeares of age, and their voyces change, ne cannot
' be preferred in this chapelle, the nombere being full,
' then yf they will assente " the kinge assynethe them to
' a colledge or Oxford or Cambridge of his foundatione,
' there to be at fynding and studye bothe suffytyently,
' tylle the kinge may otherwise advaunse them.*

' CLERKE OF THE KING'S CLOSETE keepethe the stuff of
' the closete, arrayeng and makinge redye the aulteres,
' takinge upe the traverse, bering the cushones and car-
' petts, and fytethe all other things necessarye therto.
' He helpethe the chaplenes to saye masse ; and yf the
' clarks lefe torche, tapore, mortere of waxe,† or such
' other goinge of the tresorore of houshold, his charge in
' any parte, then he to answere thearfore as the judges of
' the green clothe will awarde. Also he eatethe in the
' hall with the serjante of the vestery by the chappelle,
' and takinge for his lyverye at nighte a galone ale, and
' for wintere lyvereye ij candles piche, a talesheid, rushes
' for the clossete, and lytere for his bede, of the serjante
' ushere ; and dayly for his wages in courte by the cheque
' roule iij. d. ob. and clothing for wintere and somere with
' the houshold, or else xx s. and at every eiche of the iiij
' feasts in the year receavinge of the great spicery a
' towelle of worke, contayning iiij elles, for the king's
' houselynge, and that is the clerk's fee anon the king is
' housled. He partethe not with the gyfts of houshold,
' but and he be sycke in courte, he taketh ij loves, j messe
' of great mette, one galone ale, and lyverey of the her-
' bengere ; and for the cariage of the closete is assyned
' one sompter horse, and one somptere man, of the treso-
' rore's charge, by the comptrollore his oversyght ; the
' chamberlene is this clark's auditore and apposore.‡

' MASTER OF THE GRAMERE SCHOLE, " quem necessarium
" est in poeta, atque in regulis positive gramatice expe-
" ditum fore, quibus audiencium animos cum diligentia
" instruit ac infermet." The king's henxemene the chil-
' dren of the chappelle aftere they cane their descante, the
' clarks of the Armorye§ with other mene and childrene
' of the courte, disposed to learn in this syence ; which
' master amonge yf he be preeste, muste synge our Lady
' Masse in the king's chappelle, or clse amonge to reade
' the gospell, and to be at the greate processyone ; this to
' bee by the deane's assygnacyone ; takinge his meate in
' the halle, and lyvereye at nighte a galone of ale ; and
' for wintere lyvereye one candle pich, a talesheid, or one
' faggote ; and for his dayly wages allowed in the cheque
' role, whilest he is presente in courte, iiij. d. ob. and
' clothinge with the housholde for winter and somere, or
' else xx. s. cariage for his competente beddynge and
' bokes with the childrene of the chapelle, by comptrole-
' mente, not partynge with noe gyftes of housholde, but
' abydinge the king's avauncement after his demerits ;
' and lyverye for his horses by the king's herbengere ;
' and to have in his court one honeste servante.'‖

Of minstrels in general, and of the nature of their
employment, an account has already been given, as
also of the method practised to keep up a succession
of them in the king's palace. By the above provision

---

* This seems to be a more formal establishment of the kind than any
that we know of in these times or before, but it seems to have been
founded in ancient usage ; for we have it from Selden that it was the old
way ' when the king had his house, there were canons to sing service in
' his chapel ; ' so at Westminster, in St. Stephen's-chapel, where the
House of Commons sits ; from which canons the street called Canon-row
has its name. Table-Talk, tit. King of England, § 4.

† MORTER à Mortarium, a light or taper set in churches, to burn possibly over the graves or shrines of the dead. Cowel.

‡ The word apposer signifies an examiner. In the court of Exchequer
is an officer called the foreign apposer. Cowel in art. In the office of
confirmation, in the first liturgy of Edw. VI. the rubric directs the bishop,
or such as he shall appoint, to appose the child ; and anciently a bishop's
examining chaplain was called the bishop's poser.

§ i. e. Almonry.

‖ Vide Catal. Libror. MSS. Biblioth. Harl. Numb. 293.

---

it appears that the minstrel's was not altogether a
vagabond profession ; but many of those that followed
it were retainers to the court, and seem to have been
no other than musicians, players on instruments of
divers kinds. Dr. Percy, in his Reliques of ancient
English Poetry, has obliged the world with an essay
on the ancient English minstrels, in which he has
placed in one point of view a great number of curious
particulars that tend to illustrate this subject.

And here it may be observed, that the order and
œconomy in the families of the ancient nobility bore
a very near resemblance to that of the royal household, of which there cannot be clearer evidence than
the liberal allowances for minstrels ; and also chapels,
with singing-men, children, and proper officers for
the performance of divine service in such families.
In that of the ancient earls of Northumberland was
an express establishment for minstrels, and also a
chapel ; an account fo the latter will hereafter be
given from the household-book of Henry, the fifth earl
of Northumberland ; that relating to the minstrels,
contained in the same book, is as follows :—

Sect. V.

' Of the noumbre of all my lord's servaunts in his chequir-
' roul daily abidynge in his houschold.

*   *   *   *   *

' MYNSTRALS iij, viz., a tabret, a luyte, and a rebecc.'

Sect. XLIV. 2.

' Rewardes to be given to strangers, as players, myn-
' straills, or any other, &c.

' Furst, my lorde usith and accustomyth to gyf to the
' KING'S JUGLER, if he have wone, when they custome to
' come unto hym yerely, vi. s. viij. d.

' Item, My lorde usith and accustomyth to gyf yerely
' to the king's or queene's Barwarde, if they have one,
' when they custom to com unto hym yerely, vi. s. viij. d.

' Item, My lorde usith and accustomyth to gyf yerely
' to every erlis MYNSTRELLIS, when they custome to come
' to hym yerely, iij. s. iiij. d. And if they come to my
' lorde seldome ones in ij or iij yeres, than vj. s. viij. d.

' Item, My lord usith and accustomyth to gyf yerely
' to an erls MYNSTRALL, if he be his speciall lorde, frende,
' or kynsman, if they come yerely to his lordschip, ...
' And if they come to my lord seldome ones in ij or iij
' yeares, vj. s. viij. d.

*   *   *   *   *

' Item, My lorde usith and accustomyth to gyf yerely
' a dooke's or erlis TRUMPETTS, if they cum vj together to
' his lordshipp, viz., if they come yerely vj. s. viij. d
' And if they come but in ij or iij yeres, than x. s.

' Item, My lorde usith and accustomyth to gyf yerely,
' his lordschip is at home, to gyf to iij the kyng's SHAMES,
' whether they com to my lorde yerely x. s.

Sect. XLIV. 3.

' Rewards to his lordship's servaunts, &c.

' Item, My lord usith and accustomith to gyf yerly,
' when his lordschipp is at home, to his MYNSTRAILLS that
' be daly in his houshold, as his tabret, lute, ande rebeke,
' upon New Yeres-day in the mornynge, when they doo
' play at my lordis chambre doure, for his lordschipe and
' my lady xx. s. viz., xiij. s. iiij. d. for my lord, and
' vi. s. viij. d. for my lady, if sche be at my lords fynd-
' ynge and not at hir owen ; and for playing at my lordis
' sone and heir chaumbre doure, the lord Percy, ij. s.
' And for playinge at the chaumbre doures of my lords
' yonger sonnes, my yonge maisters, after viiij. d. the
' pece for every of them.—xxiij. s. iiij. d.'

*   *   *   *   *

T

This establishment, though no older than about the third year of the reign of Henry VIII. is not to be considered as a novel institution; on the contrary it appears to be a recognition of that rule and order which had been observed in the family for ages preceding; and that minstrels were formerly persons of some consideration, at least in the northern parts of the kingdom, may be inferred from an inscription still legible on a pillar in the ancient church of St. Mary, at Beverley, in Yorkshire. It seems that to the expense of erecting this fabric the nobility and gentry of the town and its neighbourhood were voluntary contributors: one of the pillars that support it was built by the minstrels, in memory whereof the capital is decorated with the figures of five men, carved in stone, dressed in short coats; one of these bears in his hand an instrument of a rude form, but somewhat resembling a lute, and under this sculpture are these words in ancient characters, 𝕿𝖍𝖞𝖘 𝖕𝖞𝖑𝖑𝖆𝖗 𝖒𝖆𝖉𝖊 𝖙𝖍𝖊 𝕸𝖞𝖓𝖘𝖙𝖗𝖑𝖑𝖘.

The chapel establishment of this noble family was perhaps less ancient, and might have been borrowed from that of Edward the Fourth, contained in the foregoing account of his household; it was nevertheless very noble, and will be given in a subsequent part of this work.*

John of Dunstable, so called from the town of that name in the county of Bedford, where he was born, seems to have been a very learned man, and an excellent musician. He flourished about the year 1400, and was the author of a tract De Mensurabilis Musica. Gaffurius, in his Practica Musicæ, lib. II. cap. vii. has cited him by the name of Donstable, and has produced an example from a hymn of his composition, beginning 'Veni sancte spiritus,' to explain a passage in that work. Morley has named him in his catalogue of English practitioners; and he elsewhere appears to have been a very considerable man in his time.† He is said to have died in 1455, and to have been buried in the parish church of St. Stephen, Walbrook, in London. In Fuller's Worthies, Bedfordshire, 116, is the following epitaph on him:—

Clauditur hoc tumulo qui cœlum pectore clausit,
Dunstable I, juris astrorum conscius ille,
Judice novit *hieramis* abscondita pandere cœli;
Hic vir erat tua laus, tua lux, tua musica princeps,
Quique tuas dulces per mundum sparserat *artes*
Anno Mil. C. quater, semel L. tria jungito Christi
Pridie natale sidus transmigrat ad astra
Suscipiant proprium civem cœli sibi cives.

And in Fuller are also these verses, written, as it is said, by John Whethamsted, abbot of St. Alban's.

Musicus hic Michalus alter, novus et Ptolomæus
Junior ac Atlas supportans robore cœlos,
Pausat sub cinere; melior vir muliere,
Nunquam natus erat; vitii quia labe carebat,
Et virtutis opes possedit unicus omnes.
Perpetuis annis celebretur fama Johannis
Dunstable; in pace requiescat et hic sine fine.

Fuller, who seeks all occasions to be witty, speaking of these two compositions, uses these words: 'What is true of the bills of some unconscionable 'tradesmen, if ever paid overpaid, may be said of 'these hyperbolical epitaphs: if ever believed over 'believed, yea one may safely cut off a third in any 'part of it, and the remainder will amount to make 'him a most admirable person. Let none say that 'these might be two distinct persons; seeing besides 'the concurrence of time and place, it would bankrupt 'the exchequer of nature to afford two such persons, 'one Phœnix at once being as much as any one will 'believe.' Morley, in his Introduction, pag. 178, has convicted this author of no less a crime than the interposing two rests, each of a long, between two syllables of the same word. The passage is as follows: 'We must also take heed of separating any 'part of a word from another by a rest, as some 'Dunces have not slacked to do; yea one, whose 'name is Johannes Dunstable, an ancient English 'author, hath not onlie divided the sentence, but in 'the verie middle of a word hath made two long 'rests thus, in a song of four parts upon these words: '"Nesciens virgo mater virum":—

Ip-sum re-gem An-ge-lo-rum   so-la vir-go lac-ta-bat

'for these be his owne notes and words, which is one 'of the greatest absurdities which I have seene committed in the dyttying of musicke.' The passage cited by Morley is certainly absurd enough; but that he was betrayed into an illiberal reflection on his author's supposed want of understanding by the tempting harmony of Dunce and Dunstable will hardly be doubted.

Franchinus, or as he is otherwise called Gaffurius, frequently cites a writer on music named Marchettus: this author was of Padua; he lived about the year 1400, and wrote a treatise entitled Luci-

* Besides the Minstrels that were retainers to great houses, there appear to be others of a vagrant class. The following note to that purpose is taken from the Appendix to Hearne's Liber Scaccarii, Numb. XII. pag. 598, Lond. 1771:—
'The fraternity of the Holy Crosse in Abingdon, in H. 6. tyme, being 'there were nowe the hospitall is, did every yeare keep a feast, and then 'they used to have twelve priestes to sing a dirige, for which they had 'given them fourpence a piece. They had also twelve minstrels, some 'from Coventre, and some from Maydenhith, who had two shillings and 'three-pence a-peece, besides theyre dyet and horse meat; this was in 'the raigne of H. 6. Observe that in those dayes they payd there myn-'strells better than theyre priestes.'

† Johannes Nucius, in his Præceptiones Musices Poeticæ, printed in 1613, expressly asserts that he was the inventor of musical composition. If by this we are to understand composition of music in more parts than one, there is an end of a question that has long divided the learned, namely, whether symphoniac music be an ancient or modern invention. That it had its origin in the practice of extemporary descant, mentioned in the account hereinbefore given of Bede, and of the singing of the Northumbrians, his countrymen, described by Giraldus Cambrensis, is more than probable, but the precise time when written descant first came into use is no where ascertained. The works of Franchinus contain

sundry examples of music in parts, but before his time we meet with nothing of the kind. Morley takes notice of this in the annotations on the second part of his Introduction, and says, 'In all the workes of them 'who have written of musicke before Franchinus, there is no mention of 'any more parts than one; and if any did sing to the harpe, they sung 'the same which they plaied.' A modern German writer, Francis Lustig, in his Musikkunde has mistaken the sense of Nucius in the passage above-cited, by ascribing the invention of music in parts to St. Dunstan, archbishop of Canterbury, instead of John of Dunstable, who, as above is shewn, had no title to the merit of it.

darium in Arte Musice plane, and another De Musica mensurata.

PROSDOCIMUS DE BELDEMANDIS, of Padua, flourished about the year 1403. He wrote several tracts on plain and mensurable music, and was engaged in a controversary with Marchettus; but he is most frequently mentioned as the commentator of De Muris, on whose treatise entitled Practica Mensurabilis Cantus, he wrote a learned exposition. Besides being an excellent musician, he is celebrated as a philosopher and astrologer: the latter character he owed to a tract De Sphæra of his writing.

JOHANNES TINCTOR, a doctor of the civil law, archdeacon of Naples, and chanter in the chapel of the king of Sicily, lived about this time, but somewhat prior to Franchinus, who cites him in several parts of his works. He wrote much on music, particularly on the measures of time, on the tones, and a tract entitled De Arte Contrapuncti.*

ANTONIUS SUARCIALUPUS, a Florentine, about the year 1430, excelled so greatly in music, that numbers came from remote parts to hear his harmony. He published some things in this art, but the particulars are not known. The senate of Florence in honour of his memory, caused a marble statue of him to be erected near the great doors of the cathedral church.†

ANGELUS POLITIANUS, a person better known in the learned world as one of the revivers of literature in the fifteenth century, than for his skill in the science, was nevertheless a writer on, and passionate admirer of music. His Panepistemon, or Prælectiones, contains a discourse De Musica naturali, mundana, et artificiali. Glareanus mentions him in two or three places of his Dodecachordon, as having misapprehended the doctrine of the ancient modes. Indeed he has not stuck to charge him with an error, which stares the reader even of the title-page of the Dodecachordon in the face; for in a catalogue of fourteen modes, which form the title page of that work, the Hyperphrygian mode, with the letter F prefixed occurs, with this note under it, 'Hyperlydius Politiani; sed est error.' He flourished about the year 1460, and acquired such a reputation for learning and eloquence, that Laurence de Medicis committed to his care the education of his children, of whom John, afterwards pope Leo the tenth, was one. The place of his residence was a mountain in Tuscany, to which in honor of him, the appellation of Mons Politianus, by the Italians corrupted into Monte Pulciano, was given. Though an ecclesiastic and a dignitary of the church, for it seems he was a canon, he is represented by Mons. Varillas as a man of loose morals, as a proof whereof he relates the following story : 'Ange Politien, a native of Florence, who ' passed for the finest wit of his time in Italy, met ' with a fate which punished his criminal love. ' Being professor of eloquence at Florence, he un- ' happily became enamoured of one of his young ' scholars who was of an illustrious family, but ' whom he could neither corrupt by his great pre- ' sents, nor by the force of his eloquence. The

* Walth. Mus. Lex.
† Voss. De Scient. Mathem. cap. lx. sect. 14.

' vexation he conceived at this disappointment was ' so great as to throw him into a burning fever ; ' and in the violence of the fit he made two couplets ' of a song upon the object with which he was trans- ' ported. He had no sooner done this than he raised ' himself from his bed, took his lute, and accompanied ' it with his voice, in an air so tender and affecting, ' that he expired in singing the second couplet.' Mons. Balzac gives a different account of his death. He says that as he was singing to the lute, on the top of the stair-case, some verses which he had formerly made on a young woman with whom he was then in love, the instrument fell out of his hand, and he himself fell down the stairs and broke his neck.

Bayle has refuted both these stories, and assigned good reasons to induce a belief that the sole cause of Politian's untimely death, was the grief he had conceived for the decay of the house of Medicis, to which he had great obligations.

CHAP. LXII.

THE several writers herein before enumerated, and mentioned to have lived after the time of Boetius, were of liberal professions, being either ecclesiastics, lawyers, physicians, or general scholars : nevertheless there was a certain uniformity in their manner of treating the subject of music, that seemed to preclude all theoretic improvement. Boetius had collected and wrought into his work the principal doctrines of the ancients; he had given a general view of the several opinions that had prevailed amongst them, and had adopted such as he thought had the most solid foundation in reason and experiment. The accuracy with which he wrote, and his reputation as a philosopher and a man of learning, induced an almost implicit acquiescence in his authority.

This was one reason why the succeeding writers looked no farther backward than to the time of Boetius for their intelligence in harmonics; but there was another, which, had their inclination been ever so strong to trace the principles of the science to their source, must have checked it, and that was a general ignorance throughout the western empire of the Greek language. The consequence hereof was, that of the many treatises on music which were written between the end of the sixth, and the beginning of the twelfth century, if we except such as treated of the scale as reformed by Guido, the ecclesiastical tones, and the Cantus Mensurabilis, the far greater part were but so many commentaries on the five books De Musica of Boetius : and this almost impossibility of farther explaining the theory of the science was so universally acknowledged, that of the candidates for academical honours, the principal qualifications required were a competent knowledge of his doctrines.

But though all improvements in the Theory of music may seem to have been at a stand during this period of five centuries, or a longer, for it may be extended backward to the time of Ptolemy, it is sufficiently clear that it fared otherwise with the Practice. Guido, who does not appear to have ever read the

Greek writers, effected a very important reformation of the scale; and, by an invention perfectly new, facilitated the practice of singing with truth and certainty. Some add that he was also the inventor of music in consonance; but of this the evidence is not so clear as to preclude all doubt. Franco invented, and De Muris and others perfected, the Cantus Mensurabilis; and these improvements were of a nature so important, that they extended themselves to every country where the practice of music prevailed, and in short pervaded the whole civilized world.

As to the science of harmonics, it had retreated to that part of the world, which, upon the irruption of the Goths into Europe, became the seat of literature, Constantinople; thither we may reasonably suppose the several works of Aristoxenus, Euclid, and other ancient harmonicians, perhaps the only remaining books on the subject that escaped the wreck of learning, were carried; and these were the foundation of that constitution, which we are expressly told came from the East, the ecclesiastical tones. It does not indeed appear that the science received any considerable improvement from this recess, since of the few books written during it, the greater part are abridgments, or at best but commentaries on the more ancient writers; and of this the treatises of Marcianus Capella, Censorinus, Porphyry, and Manuel Bryennius, are a proof, and indeed the almost impossibility of any such improvement after Ptolemy is apparent; for before his time the enarmonic and chromatic genera were grown into disuse, and only one species of the diatonic genus remained: nay, it is evident from the whole tenor of his writings, and the pains he has taken to explain them, that the doctrine both of the genera and of the modes was involved in great obscurity: if this was the case in the time of Ptolemy, who is said to have lived about the year 139, and the practice of music had undergone so great a change as arose from the reduction of the genera with their several species to one or two at most, and the loss of the modes, all that the ancients had taught became mere history; and the utmost that could be expected from a set of men who lived at the distance of some centuries from the latest of them, was that they should barely understand their doctrines.

All Theoretic improvement being thus at a stand, we are not to wonder if the endeavours of mankind were directed to the establishment and cultivation of a new Practice; and that these endeavours were vigorously exerted, we need no other proof than the zeal of the ancient Greek fathers to introduce music into the service of the church, the institution of the ecclesiastical tones, the reformation of the scale, and the invention of the Cantus Mensurabilis.

The migration of learning from the east to the west, is an event too important to have escaped the notice of historians. Some have asserted that the foundation of the musical practice now in use was laid by certain Greeks, who, upon the sacking of Constantinople by the Turks under Mahomet the Great, in 1453, * retired from that scene of horror

and desolation, and settled at Rome, and other cities of Italy. To this purpose Mons. Bourdelot, the author of Histoire Musique et ses Effets, in four small tomes, relates that certain ingenious Greeks who had escaped from the sacking of Constantinople, brought the polite arts, and particularly music, into Italy: for this assertion no authority is cited, and though recognized by the late reverend and learned Dr. Brown, it seems to rest solely on the credit of an author, who, by a strange abuse of the appellation, has called that a history, which is at best but an injudicious collection of unauthenticated anecdotes and trifling memoirs.

To ascertain precisely the circumstances attending the revival of learning in Europe, recourse must be had to the writings of such men as have given a particular relation of that great event; and by these it will appear, that before the taking of Constantinople divers learned Greeks settled in Italy, and became public teachers of the Greek language; and that Dante, Boccace, and Petrarch, all of whom flourished in the fourteenth century, availed themselves of their instructions, and co-operated with them in their endeavours to make it generally understood. The most eminent of these were Leontius Pilatus, Emanuel Chrysoloras, Theodorus Gaza, Georgius Trapezuntius, and cardinal Bessarion. To these, at the distance of an hundred years, succeeded Joannes Argyropylus, Demetrius Chalcondyles, and many others, whose lives and labours have been sufficiently celebrated.[†]

It no where appears that any of these men were skilled in music; on the contrary, they seem in general to have been grammarians, historians, and divines, fraught with that kind of erudition which became men who professed to be the restorers of ancient learning. Nor have we any reason to believe that the practice of music had so far flourished in the eastern part of the world, as to qualify any of them to become public teachers of the science. It is true that music had been introduced by St. Basil, Chrysostom, and others of the Greek fathers, into the service of the church, and that the emperor Constantine had sent an organ as a present to Pepin king of France; but it is as true that all the great improvements in the art were made at home. Pope Gregory improved upon the Ambrosian chant, and established the eight ecclesiastical tones; Guido reformed the scale, and Franco invented the Cantus Mensurabilis; and the very term Contrapunto bespeaks it to have sprung from Italy.

From these premises it seems highly probable that it was not a Practice more refined than that in general use, nor an improved Theory which these persons brought from Constantinople, but that the introduction of the ancient Greek harmonicians, together with

* This important event gave rise to a proverbial expression, usually applied to persons that suddenly became rich: 'He hath been at the sacking of Constantinople.' Sir Paul Rycaut's History of the Turks, vol. I. pag. 236.

† Bayle has given a particular account of some of the most eminent of them, as namely cardinal Bessarion, and a few others; but a summary of their lives, and a history of that important æra is contained in a valuable work of Dr. Humphrey Hody, lately published by Dr. Samuel Jebb, entitled 'De Græcis illustribus Linguæ Græcæ Literarumque Humaniorum 'Instauratoribus.' The names of the persons chiefly celebrated in this work, besides those above-mentioned, are Nicolaus Secundinus, Joannes Andronicus Callistus, Tranquillus Andronicus, Georgius Christonymus, Joannes Polo, Constantinus Lascaris, Michael Marulius, Manilius Rhallus, Marcus Musurus, Angelus Calabrus, Nicolaus Sophianus, Georgius Alexander, Joannes Moschus, Demetrius Moschus, Emanuel Adramyttenus, Zacharias Caliergus, Nicolaus Blastus, Aristobulus Apostolius, Demetrius Ducas, Nicetas Phaustus, Justinus Corcyraeus, Nicolaus Petrus, Antonius Eparchas, Matthaeus Avarius, Hermodorus Zacynthius.

such a knowledge of the language as enabled the professors of music in Italy and other countries to understand and profit by their writings, is the ground of that obligation which music in particular owes them.

The probability of this conjecture will farther appear when we reflect on the opinion which the Italians entertain of the rise and progress of music in Europe, and that is, that Guido for the practice, and Franchinus for the theory, were the fathers of modern music. How well founded that opinion is with respect to the latter of these two, will appear from the account of him which will shortly hereafter be given, and from the following view of the state of music in those countries, that made the greatest advances as well in scientific as literary improvements.

It seems that before the time of Franchinus the teachers of music in Italy were the monks, and the Provençal musars, violars, &c., the former may be supposed to have taught, as well as they were able, the general principles of harmony, as also the method of singing the divine offices, and the latter the use of instruments: it seems also that about the middle of the fifteenth century the Jews were great professors of music, for by a law of Venice, made in the year 1443, it appears that one of their chief employments at that time was the teaching children to sing; and they are thereby expressly forbidden to continue it, under severe penalties.

In France it is observable, that after the introduction of Guido's system into that kingdom, the progress of music was remarkably slow; one improvement however seems to have had its rise in that country, namely, Fauxbourdon, or what we in England were used to term Faburden, the hint whereof was probably taken from the Cornamusa or bagpipe; and of this kind of accompanyment the French were so extremely fond, that they rejected the thought of any other; nay, they persisted in their attachment to it after the science had arrived to a considerable degree of perfection in Italy and other parts of Europe.

In Germany the improvements in music kept nearly an even pace with those in Italy. Indeed they were but very few; they consisted solely in the formation of new melodies subject to the tonic laws, adapted to the hymns, and other church offices, which were innumerable; but the disgusting uniformity of these left very little room for the exercise of the inventive faculty:* the Germans indeed appear to have attained to great perfection in the use of the organ so early as the year 1480; for we are told that in that year a German, named Bernhard, invented the Pedal; from whence it should seem that he had entertained conceptions of a fuller harmony than could be produced from that instrument by the touch of the fingers alone. This fact seems to agree but ill with Morley's opinion, that before the time of Franchinus there was no such

thing as music in parts; but, notwithstanding this conjecture of his, the evidence that music in consonance, of some kind or other, was known at least as far back, in point of time, as the invention of the organ, is too strong to be resisted; and indeed the form and mechanism of the instrument do little less than demonstrate it. How and in what manner the organ was used in the accompanyment of divine service it is very difficult to say; some intimations of its general use are nevertheless contained in the Micrologus of Guido, and these lead to an opinion that although the singing of the church offices was unisonous, allowing for the difference between the voices of the boys and men employed therein, yet that the accompanyment thereof might be symphoniac, and contain in it those consonances which no musician could possibly be ignorant of in theory, and which in practice it must have been impossible to avoid.

Of Franchinus, of whom such frequent mention has been made in the course of this work, of his labours to cultivate the science of harmony, and of the several valuable treatises by him compiled from the writings of the ancient Greeks, then lately introduced into Italy, the following is an account, extracted immediately from his own works, and those of contemporary authors.

Franchinus Gaffurius, surnamed Laudensis, from Lodi, a town in the Milanese, where he was born, was a professor of, and a very learned and elaborate writer on music, of the fifteenth century. He was born on the fourteenth day of January, in the year 1451, and was the son of one Betino, of the town of Bergamo, a soldier by profession, and Catherina Fixaraga his wife. We are told that while he was yet a boy he was initiated into the service of the church; from whence perhaps nothing more is to be inferred than that he assisted in the choral service. His youth was spent in a close application to learning; and upon his attainment of the sacerdotal dignity, he addicted himself with the greatest assiduity to the study of music. His first tutor was Johannes Godendach, a Carmelite; having acquired under him a knowledge of the rudiments of the science, he left the place of his nativity, and went to his father then at Mantua, and in the service of the marquis Ludovico Gonzaga. Here for two years he closely applied himself day and night to study, during which time he composed many tracts on the theory and practice of music. From Mantua he moved to Verona, and commenced professor of music: there, though he taught publicly for a number of years, he found leisure and opportunity for the making large collections relative to that science, and composed a work intitled Musicæ Institutionis Collocutiones, which does not appear to have ever been printed, unless, as is hereafter suggested, it might be published under a different title. The great reputation he had acquired at Verona procured him an invitation from Prospero Adorni to settle at Genoa: his stay there was but short, for about a year after his removal thither, his patron being expelled by Baptista Campofragoso and Giovanni Galeazzo, dukes of Milan,

* Bourdelot relates that the intercourse between the French and Italians during the reigns of Charles VIII., Lewis XII., and Francis I., and afterwards in the time of Queen Catherine de Medicis, who was in every respect an Italian, contributed greatly to refine the French music; and brought it to a near resemblance with that of Italy; but that many of the churches in France had gone so far as to constitute bands of musicians to add to the solemnity, but that after some years they were dismissed. The chapter of Paris entertained a dislike of them; and by certain capitulary resolutions made in the year 1646, ordained that the Fauxbourdon should be revived; and of this kind of harmony, simple and limited as it is, the French are even at this day remarkably fond.

he fixed his residence at Naples; in that city he found many musicians who were held in great estimation, namely, Johannis Tinctor, Gulielmus Garnerius, Bernardus Hycart, and others, and by the advice of his friend and townsman Philipinus Bononius, who then held a considerable employment in that city, Franchinus maintained a public disputation against them. Here he is said to have written his Theoricum Opus Musicæ Discipline, a most ingenious work; but the pestilence breaking out in the city, which, to complete its calamity, was engaged in a bloody war with the Turks, who had ravaged the country of Apulia, and taken the city of Otranto; he returned to Lodi, and took up his abode at Monticello, in the territory of Cremona, being invited to settle there by Carolo Pallavicini, the bishop of that city. During his stay there, which was three years, he taught music to the youth of the place, and began his Practica Musicæ utriusque Cantus, which was printed first at Milan, in 1496, again at Brescia in 1497, and last at Venice in 1512. Being prevailed on by the entreaties of the inhabitants of Bergamo, and the offer of a large stipend, he removed thither; but a war breaking out between them and the duke of Milan, he was necessitated to return home. There he stayed not long, for Romanus Barnus, a canon of Lodi, a man of great power, as he exercised the pastoral authority in the absence of the archbishop of Milan, incited by the fame of his learning and abilities as a public instructor, in the year 1484 invited him to settle there; and such are we told was the high esteem in which he was held by the greatest men there, that by the free consent of the chief of the palace, and without any rival, he was placed at the head of the choir of the cathedral church of Milan. How much he improved music there by study and by his lectures, the number of his disciples, and the suffrage of the citizens are said to have afforded an ample testimony: besides the two works above-mentioned, he wrote also a treatise entitled Angelicum ac divinum Opus Musicæ Franchini Gafurii Laudensis Regii Musici, Ecclesiæque Mediolanensis Phonasci: Materna Lingua scriptum. From several circumstances attending its publication, particularly that of its being written in the Italian language, there is great reason to believe that this is no other than the Musicæ Institutionis Collocutiones, mentioned above; and that it contains in substance the lectures which he read to his scholars in the course of his employment as public professor. Last of all, and in the forty-ninth year of his age, he wrote a treatise De Harmonia Musicorum Instrumentorum, at the end whereof is an eulogium on Franchinus and his writings by Pantaleone Meleguli of Lodi, from which this account is for the most part taken. Besides the pains he took in composing the works above-mentioned, not being acquainted, as we may imagine, with the Greek language, he at a great expense procured to be translated into Latin the harmonical treatises of many of the more ancient writers, namely, Aristides Quintilianus, Manuel Bryennius, Ptolemy, and Bacchius Senior. The author above-cited, who seems to have been well acquainted

with him, and to manifest an excusable partiality for his memory, has borne a very honourable testimony to his character; for, besides applauding him for the services he had done the science of music by his great learning and indefatigable industry, he is very explicit in declaring him to have been a virtuous and good man. The time of his death is no where precisely ascertained; but in his latter years he became engaged in a controversy with Giovanni Spataro, professor of music at Bologna; and it appears that the apology of Franchinus against this his adversary was written and published in the year 1520, so that he must have lived at least to the age of seventy.

After having said thus much, it may not be amiss to give a more particular account of the writings of so considerable a man as Gaffurius; and first of the Theorica: it is dedicated to the famous Ludovico Sforza, governor of Milan, the same probably with him of that name mentioned by Philip de Comines; it is divided into five books, and was printed first at Naples in 1480, and again at Milan, in 1492.

It is very clear that the doctrines taught in this work, the Theorica Musicæ of Franchinus, are the same with those delivered by Boetius. Indeed the greater part appears to be an abridgement of Boetius de Musica, with an addition of Guido's method of solmisation; for which reason, and because copious extracts from this latter work have been already given, and Guido's invention has been explained in his own words, it is thought unnecessary to be more particular in the present account of it.

The treatise entitled Practica Musicæ utriusque Cantus, so called because the purpose of it is to declare the nature of both the plain and mensurable cantus, is of a kind as different from the former as its title imports it to be. For, without entering at all into the theory of the science, the author with great perspicuity teaches the elements of music, and the practice of singing, agreeable to the method invented by Guido, the rules of the Cantus Mensurabilis, the nature of counterpoint, and, lastly, the proportions as they refer to mensurable music; and this in a manner that shews him to have been a thorough master of his subject. But perhaps there is no part of the Practica Musicæ more curious than that formula of the Ecclesiastical Tones contained in the first book of it, and which is inserted in the former part of this work.*

In the first chapter of the second book of this work of Franchinus, the author treats of the several kinds of metre in the words following:—

'The poets and musicians in times past, maturely

---

* The extract above referred to contains perhaps the most ancient and authentic formula of the tones extant, and must therefore be deemed a great curiosity. Rousseau says of plain-chant in general, that it is a precious relique of antiquity: this might be said supposing the tones to be no older than the time of St. Ambrose; but it is certain that if they are not the modes of the ancient Greeks, and consequently more ancient by a thousand years, they resemble them so nearly, that they may well be taken for the same, and therefore are an object of still greater veneration. With respect to their use at present, it is true that they make no part of divine service in the churches of the Reformed, but in that of Rome they are still preserved, and are daily to be heard in England in the chapels of the ambassadors from Roman Catholic princes. From all which considerations it cannot but be wished that the integrity of them may be preserved; and to this end nothing can be more conducive than an authentic designation of them severally, and such that hereinbefore given is supposed to be.

'considering the time of every word, placed a long
'or a short mark over each, whereby each syllable
'was denoted to be either long or short; wherefore
'over a short syllable they affixed a measure of one
'time, and over a long one the quantity of two
'times; whence it is clear that the short syllable
'was found out before the long, as Diomedes the
'grammarian testifies, for one was prior to two.
'They account a syllable to be short, either in its
'own nature, or in respect to its position; they also
'make some syllables to be common; as when they
'are naturally short and a liquid follows a mute, as
'in "tenebræ patris." This appears as well among
'the Greek as the Latin poets; and these syllables
'are indifferently measured, that is to say, they are
'sometimes short, and at other times long; and thus
'they constructed every kind of verse by a mixture
'of different feet, and these feet were made up of
'different times; for the Dactyl, that I may mention
'the quantities of some of them, contained three
'syllables, the first whereof was long, and the other
'two short, as "armiger, principis;" it therefore
'consisted of four times. The Spondee has also four
'times, but disposed into two long syllables, as
"fælix, æstas." The Iambus, called the quick foot,
'has three times, drawn out on two syllables, the
'one long and the other short, as Musa. The Ana-
'pestus, by the Greeks called also Antidactylus,
'because it is the reverse of the Dactyl, consists of
'three syllables, the two first whereof are short, and
'the last long, as "pietas, erato." The Pyrrhichius
'of two short syllables, as "Miser, pater." The
'Tribrachus contains three short syllables, as "Do-
'minus." The Amphibrachus has also three, the first
'short, the second long, and the third short, as
"Carina." The Creticus, or Amphiacrus, consists
'likewise of three syllables; the first long, the second
'short, and the third long, as "insulæ." The Bac-
'chius also has three syllables, the first short, and the
'other two long, as "Achates et Ulixes." The
'Proceleumaticus, agreeing chiefly with Lyric verse,
'has four short syllables, as "avicula." The Dis-
'pondeus was composed of eight times and four long
'syllables, as "Oratores." The Coriambus consisted
'also of four syllables, the first long, the two follow-
'ing short, and the last long, as "armipotens." The
'Biiambus had four syllables, the first short, the
'second long, the third short, and the fourth long,
'as "Propinquitas." The Epitritus, or Hippius, as it
'is called by Diomedes, was fourfold; the first kind
'consisted of four syllables, the first whereof was
'short, the other three long; and it comprehended
'seven times, as "sacerdotes." The second Epitri-
'tus had four syllables, the second whereof was short,
'and all the rest long, as "conditores." The third
'Epitritus contained four syllables, the third whereof
'was short and all the rest long, as "Demosthenes."
'The fourth Epitritus was formed also of four sylla-
'bles, the last whereof was short, and the three first
'long, as "Fesceninus." Some of these are supposed
'to be simple, as the Spondeus and Iambus, and
'others compound, as the Dispondeus and Biiambus.
'Diomedes and Aristides, in the first book, and St.

'Augustine, have explained them all. Musicians
'have invented certain characters with fit and proper
'names, by means whereof, the diversity of measured
'times being previously understood, they are able to
'form any Cantus, in the same manner as verse is
'made from different feet. Philosophers think that
'the measure of short time ought to be adjusted by
'the equable motions of the pulse, comparing the
'Arsis and Thesis with the Diastole and Stole. In
'the measure of every pulse the Diastole signifies
'dilatation, and the Stole contraction.
'The poets have an Arsis and Thesis, that is an
'elevation and deposition of their feet according to
'the passions; and they use these in reciting, that
'the verse may strike the ear and soften the mind.
'The connexion of the words is regulated according
'to the nature of the verse; so that the very texture
'of the verse will introduce such numbers as are
'proper to it. Rythmus, in the opinion of Quin-
'tilian, consists in the measures of times; and I con-
'ceive time to be the measure of syllables. But Bede,
'in his treatise concerning figures and metres, has
'interpreted Rythmus to be a modulated composition,
'not formed in any metrical ratio but to be deter-
'mined by the ear, in the same manner as we judge
'of the verses of the common poets. Yet we some-
'times meet with Rythmi not regulated by any art,
'but proceeding from the sound or modulation itself;
'these the common poets form naturally, whereas the
'Rythmi of the learned are constructed by the rules
'of art. The Greeks assert that Rythmus consists
'in the Arsis and Thesis, and that sort of time
'which some call vacant or free. Aristoxenus says
'it is time divided numerically; and, according to
'Nicomachus, it is a regulated composition of times;
'but it is not our business to prescribe rules and
'canons, for we leave to the poets that which pro-
'perly belongs to them; yet it were to be wished
'that they who make verses had good ears, whereby
'they might attain a metrical elegance in poetry.'

CHAP. LXIII.

IN the second chapter Franchinus treats of the
characters used to denote the different measures of
time in the words following:—
'The measure of time is the disposition of the
'quantity of each character. Every commensurable
'description is denoted either by characters or pauses;
'the Greeks in their Rythmus used the following,
'viz., for the breve ▬, for the long of two times
'∿, for that of three times V, for that of four
'times W, for that of five times V. To express
'the Arsis they added a point to each character,
'thus ∿., V.. The Thesis was understood by
'the simple character, without any such addition.
'As to the consonant intentions, such as the diates-
'saronic, diapentic, diapasonic, and the rest, they
'were expressed by certain characters, which I pur-
'posely omit, as being foreign to the present practice.

'The musicians of this day express the measure of
'one time by a square filled up ▰; that of two,
'called a long, by a square with a stroke on the
'right side, either ascending or descending, which
'stroke was four times as long as one side of the
'square. Some however, because of the deformity
'arising from the too great length of the stroke,
'made it equal in length to only three times the side
'of the square, and others made it but twice, thus
'⌐. The long of three times was expressed also
'by a square and a stroke, but with this diversity,
'one third of its body was white or open, thus ◳
'or thus ◳. The long of four times was signified
'by a full quadrangle with a stroke, the body where-
'of was double in length to its height ▰; and this
'was called a double long. The triple long had
'a square of triple extension ▰▭, and contained six
'times. There were also characters that comprehended
'in them several longs, each of which was distin-
'guished by a single stroke thus ▰▥. Those
'that came afterwards, subverting the order of these
'characters, described the marks open, having many
'short squares in one body, thus ▭▥. They
'also marked the long conjoined with the breve, and
'the breve with the long, in one and the same figure
'thus ▭▭. But as these latter characters are
'now disused, we will leave them, and speak con-
'cerning those by which the fashion and practice of
'those latter days may be known to one.'

The third chapter treats of what the author calls
the five essential characters, in the following words:—

'A character is a mark used to signify either the
'continuance or the privation of sound; for tacitur-
'nity may as well be the subject of measure as sound
'itself. The measures of taciturnity are called pauses,
'and of these some are short and others long.

'Musicians have ascribed to the breve the character
'of a square ☐, which they call also a time, as it
'expresses the measure of one time. The long they
'signified by a square, having on the right side
'a stroke either upwards or downwards, in length
'equal to four times the side of the square, thus ▱;
'it was called also the double breve; but the writers
'of music for the most part make this stroke without
'regard to any proportion. Again they divided the
'square of the breves diagonally into two equal parts,
'in this manner ◺, and joined to it another triangle,
'they turned the angles upwards and downwards
'thus ◊ and called the character thus formed a semi-
'breve, and gave to it half the quantity of the breve.*
'Lastly, those of latter days gave the measure of
'one time to a semibreve, comprehending in it the
'Diastole and the Systole;† and as the Diastole and

'Systole, or Arsis and Thesis, which are the least
'measure of the pulse, are considered as the measure
'of one time, so also is the semibreve, which, in
'respect of its measure, coincides exactly with the
'measure of the pulse; and as they considered the
'measure of the Diastole or Systole, or of the Arsis
'or Thesis as the measure of the shortest duration
'in metrical sound, they gave to the character which
'denoted it, the name of Minim, and described it by
'a semibreve, with a stroke proceeding either up-
'wards or downwards from one of its angles thus
'◊ or thus ◊.

'The short character, consisting of one time, and
'the long of two times, are termed the elementary
'characters of measurable sound, and their quantities
'answer to the just and concinnous intervals, or rather
'the integral parts of a tone; for according to Aris-
'tides and Anselm, the tone is capable of a division
'into four of these diesis, which are termed enar-
'monic, and answerable to this division the long is
'divided into four semibreves, and the breve into
'four minims, as if one proceeded from each angle of
'the breve: therefore as everything arises or is pro-
'duced from the Minimum, or least of his own kind;
'and number, for instance, takes its increase from
'unity, as being the least, and to which all number
'is ultimately resolvable; and as every line is gene-
'rated and encreased by, and again reduced to a
'point; so every measure of musical time is pro-
'duced from, and may again be reduced to a minim,
'as being the least measure.

'Lastly, musicians have invented another cha-
'racter, the double long, which is used in the tenor
'part of motetts, and is equal in quantity to four
'short times or breves. It exceeds the other
'characters, both in respect of its quantity, and
'the dimension of its figure, this they call the
'Maxima or Large, and describe it thus ▰. This
character is aptly enough compared to the chord
'Proslambanomenos, the most grave of the perfect
'system; and the rest of the characters may with
'equal propriety be compared to other chords, as
'having the same relation to different parts of the
'system as those bear to each other; and in this
'method of comparison the minim will be found
'to correspond with the tone, the semibreve to the
'diatessaron, and the large to the bisdiapason.'

In the fourth chapter Franchinus proceeds to
explain the more minute characters in these words:—

'Posterity subdivided the character of the minim,
'first into two equal parts, containing that measure
'of time called the greater semiminim, which Pros-
'docimus describes in a twofold way; for taking his

* Franchinus, in his Angelicum et divinum Opus, tract III. cap. i.
resembles this character to a grain of barley. And here it may be noted
that his account of the invention of the characters used in mensurable
music is much more probable than that of Vicentino, pag. 219, of this
work, which though ingenious is fanciful.

† This observation of Franchinus is worthy of remembrance, for not-

withstanding what he says a few lines above, and the remark of Listenius
in the note pag. 223, of this work, we are here taught to consider the
semibreve, or tactus minor, as the measure of a time, or as we should
now say, of a bar, consisting of two pulses or strokes, the one down, the
other up. The use of the observation is this, fugues written in canon
have always a direction to shew at what distance of time the replicate is
to follow the guide or principal, such as fuga in Hypodiapente post
tempus. Butl. Princ. of Mus. 76, fuga in unisono post duo tempora, ib. 77,
et vide Zarl. Istit. Harm. Parte III. cap. lv. now unless the value of a
time be previously ascertained, a canon is no rule for the singing of a
fugue: and that the practice corresponds with the observation of Franchinus here remarked on, may be seen in sundry examples to the purpose,
in the Prattica di Musica of Lodovico Zacoone, libro II. fol. 113.

'notion of a minim from Tinctor, he first describes
'the semi-minim by the figure of a minim having the
'end of its stem turned off to the right, with a kind
'of crooked tail, thus ♪; and the lesser semiminim, in

'quantity half the greater, with two such turns, thus ♪.
'Secondly, keeping precisely to the form of the minim,
'he makes the body full black, thus ↓, and divides
'this last character into two equal parts, by giving
'to it the same turn of the stem as before had been
'given to the minim, thus ♪, and this they called the
'lesser semiminim. The former characters, viz,, those
'with the open or white body, are called by Pros-
'docimus, the minims of Tinctor, drawn into duple
'or quadruple proportion ; but others, whose ex-
'ample we choose rather to follow, call these charac-
'ters of subdivision with a single turn of the stem,
'seminims, as being a kind of disjunct or separated
'minims ; and again they call the parts of these
'seminims, from the smallness of their measure
'and quantity, semiminimims ; so that the seminim
'follows the minim as a greater semitone does a
'tone, and the semiminimim looks back upon the
'minim as a lesser semitone does on the tone.

'There is yet a third, the most diminished particle
'of a minim, and which the same Prosdocimus would
'have to be called the minim of Tinctor in an octuple
'proportion ; others the lesser semiminim ; and others
'a comma, which we think would more properly be
'called a diesis, the name given to the least harmo-
'nical particle in the division of a tone : this many
'describe by a full semiminim, having a crooked tail
'turned towards the right, and a crooked stroke pro-

'ceeding from its angle underneath, in this manner ♪;

'but as the appearance of this character among the
'other diminutions is very deformed, we have ex-
'pressed it by a crooked stem drawn from its summit,
'and turned towards the left in this manner ♪, to
'denote its inferiority in respect of that character
'which it resembles, and which is turned to the right.
'There are some who describe the measures of time
'by characters variously different from those above
'enumerated, as Franco, Philippus de Caserta, Johan-
'nes de Muris, and Anselmus of Parma, which last
'draws a long Plica, or winding stroke ascending,
'and also a short one, both having tails on either side.
'Again, the same Anselmus makes a greater, a lesser,
'and a mean breve ; the greater he has expressed by
'a square, with a stroke descending on the left side,
'in this manner ⊐ ; the lesser by a square with a
'stroke ascending from the left side thus ⊔ ; and
'the mean by a square without any stroke, thus ⊓.
'Likewise the greater semibreve he describes with
'two strokes, the one ascending and the other descend-
'ing, both on the right side, thus ⊐ ; the lesser
'semibreve by a square with two strokes on the left
'side, thus ⊔ , and the mean semibreve by a square
'with a stroke drawn through it both upwards and
'downwards in this manner ⊟ and by a like
'method he signifies the rest of the measures ; but

'these latter characters later musicians have chose
'rather to reject than approve.'

The fifth chapter of the same book contains an
explanation of the ligatures, of which enough has
been said in the foregoing part of this work.

In the sixth chapter, De Pausis, Franchinus thus
explains the characters by which the rests are described :—

'A pause is a character used to denote a stop made
'in singing according to the rules of art. The pause
'was invented to give a necessary relief to the voice,
'and a sweetness to the melody ; for as a preacher
'of the divine word, or an orator in his discourse
'finds it necessary oftentimes to relieve his auditors
'by the recital of some pleasantry, thereby to make
'them more favourable and attentive, so a singer
'intermixing certain pauses with his notes, engages
'the attention of his hearers to the remaining parts
'of his song. The character of a pause is a certain
'line or stroke drawn through a space or spaces, or
'part of a space, not added to any note, but entirely
'separated from every other character. The ancients
'had four pauses in their songs, which, because they
'were the measures of omitted notes, assumed the
'respective names of those notes, as the pause of a
'Minim, of a Semibreve, of a Breve, and of a Long.
'The breve pause is a stroke comprehending two
'such intervals ; the pause of three times, whose ex-
'tremities include four lines, occupies three entire
'spaces ; this they call a perfect long, because it passes
'over in silence three equal proper times, which are
'called Breves, for in the quantities of characters of
'this kind the ternary number is esteemed perfect.'

The characters of the several pauses of a perfect
long, an imperfect long, a breve, semibreve, minim,
semiminim or crotchet, and semiminimim or quaver,
are thus described by Franchinus, and are in truth
the same with those now in use.

Long   Long   Breve   Semibreve   Minim   Semi-   Semi-
perfect   imperfect   minim   minimim

By the first of which characters is to be understood
a measure of quantity different in its nature from the
second ; for it is to be observed that in the writings
of all who have treated on the Cantus Mensurabilis,
the attribute of Perfection is ascribed to those numbers only which are called Ternary, as including a
progression by three ; the reasons for which, whether
good or bad it matters not, are as follow :—

'The Ternary number in the quantities of this
'kind is esteemed perfect, first, because the Binary
'number is ever accounted feminine, whereas this,
'which is the first uneven number, is said to be mas-
'culine ; and by the alternate coupling of these two
'the rest of these numbers are produced. Secondly,
'it is composed both of Aliquot and Aliquant parts.
'Thirdly, there is a relation between the numbers
'1, 2, 3, as they follow in the natural order, which, as
'St. Augustine testifies, is not to be found between
'any others ; for, not to mention that between them
'no number can intervene, 3 is made up of the two
'numbers preceding, which cannot be said of 4 or 5,
'nor of those that follow them. Fourthly, there is a

'threefold equality in the number 3, for its begin-
'ning, middle, and end are precisely the same; and by
'means thereof we discern the Divine Trinity in the
'supreme God. Lastly, there is a perfection in the
'number 3, arising from this property, if you multi-
'ply 3 by 2, or 2 by 3, the product will be six, which
'mathematicians pronounce to be a perfect number
'in respect of its aliquot parts.'

The third book of the treatise De Practica contains
the elements of counterpoint with the distinctions of
the several species, and examples of each in two,
three, and four parts. The fourth chapter, entitled
'Quæ et ubi in Contrapuncto admittendæ sint discor-

'dantiæ,' though it be a proof that discords were
admitted into musical composition so early as the
author's time, shews yet that they were taken very
cautiously, that is to say, they never exceeded the
length of a semibreve; and this restriction, for which
he cites Dunstable, and other writers, may well be
acquiesced in, seeing that the art of preparing and
resolving discords seems to have been unknown at
this time.

In chap. XI. De Compositione diversarum Partium
Contrapuncti, are several examples in four parts, viz.,
Cantus, Contra-tenor, Tenor, and Baritonans, one
whereof is as follows :— *

CANTUS   TENOR   BARITONANS   CONTRATENOR

Upon these examples it is observable that the
musical characters from their dissimilarity seem not
to have been printed upon letter-press types, but on
wooden blocks, in which the lines, cliffs, and notes
had been first cut or engraved.

The fourth book is altogether on the subject of the
proportions, not as they refer to consonance, but as
they relate to mensurable music; and though the
various species of proportion have already been explained, it seems necessary here to recapitulate what
has been said on that head, in order to give an idea
of the general view and design of the author in this
last book of his treatise De Practica.

Proportion is the ratio that two terms bear to each
other, as two numbers, two lines, two sounds, &c.; as
if we were to compare UT below with SOL above, or
any other two sounds at different parts of the scale.
In general there are two kinds of proportion.

The first is of Equality, and is when two terms are
equal, the one containing neither more or less than

the other, as 1 1, 2 2, 8 8; the two sounds in this
proportion are said to be unisons, that is having the
same degree of gravity and acuteness.

The other is of Inequality, as when of two terms
one is larger than the other, i. e. contains more parts,
as 4, 2; because the first contains the latter once and
something left, this therefore must be inequality. Of
this proportion there are five species, which the
Italians call Generi.

First, Moltiplice or Multiple is when the larger
number contains the small one twice, as 4, 2. If this
greater term do contain the less but twice, as 4, 2; 6, 3;
16, 8; &c. it is called Proporzione Dupla, if three
times Tripla, if four Quadrupla, and so on to infinity.

The second proportion of inequality is Proporzione
del Genere superparticulare, and is that wherein the
greater term contains the less once, and an aliquot or
exact part of the lesser remains, as 3, 2; if the number
remaining be exactly half the less number, the proportion is called Sesquialteral; if a third part of the
less as 4, 3, Sesquiterza, and so on, adding to Sesqui
the ordinal number of the less term.

The third proportion of inequality is called Proporzione del Genere superparziente, in which the
greater term contains the less once, and two, three,
four, or more parts of the less remaining; or as
Zarlino says, 2, 3, 4, or more units, &c. This proportion is distinguished by the words Bi, Tri, Quadri,
&c. between Super and Parziente; thus the proportion of 5, 3, is called Superbiparziente Terza, because
5 contains 3 once and two units remain, which are
two parts of 3; that of 7, 4, Supertriparziente Quarta,
by reason 7 contains 4 once, and three parts of 4
remain, and so of others.

The fourth and fifth kinds of proportion of inequality are compounded of the multiple and one of those
above described. †

Morley, in the following table, has very clearly
shewn how the most usual proportions in music are
generated :—

---

* In the composition of music in symphony, it is to be noted that the
number of parts can never in strictness exceed four; and that where any
composition is said to be of more, some of the parts must necessarily
pause while others sing.

The most usual names for the several parts of a vocal composition are
base, tenor, counter-tenor, and cantus; where it is for five voices, another
part called the medius or mean is interposed between the counter-tenor
and the cantus. In three parts, where there is no cantus, the upper part
is generally the counter-tenor, which in that case assumes the name of
Altus; but these which are the general rules observed in the arrangement of parts allow of many variations. Franchinus, in the example
above-cited, has given the name of Baritonans to one of the parts; this
is a term signifying that kind of base, which for the extent of its compass
may be considered as partaking of the nature both of the base and tenor.
In compositions for instruments, and sometimes in those for voices, the
cantus is called the Treble, which several terms are thus explained by
Butler in his Principles of Music, lib. I. chap. iii. in not.

The Base is so called because it is the basis or foundation of the song.

The Tenor, from teneo to hold, consisted anciently of long holding
notes, containing the ditty or plain-song, upon which the other parts
were wont to descant in sundry sorts of figures.

The Counter-tenor is so named, as answering the tenor, though commonly in higher notes; or it may be thus explained, Counter-tenor quasi
Counterfeit-tenor, from its near affinity to the tenor.

Cantus seems to be an arbitrary term, for which no reason or etymology
is assigned by any of the writers on music.

The Treble has clearly its name from the third or upper septenary of
notes in the scale, which are ever those of the treble or cantus part.

The term Baritonans answers precisely to the French Contre-basse, an
appellation very proper for a part, which as it is said above, seems to bear
the same affinity to the base as the counter-tenor does to the tenor.

---

† Vide Brossard, Dictionaire de Musique, in art.

The triangular proportion diagram (reading from apex downward):

Decupla

Nonupla — Quintupla

Octupla — Quadrupla sesquialtra — Tripla sesquitertia

Septupla — Quadrupla — Tripla — Dupla sesquialtra

Sextupla — Tripla sesquialtra — Dupla sesquitertia — Dupla superbi-partiens tertias — Dupla sesquiquarta — Dupla

Quintupla — Tripla — Dupla sesquiquarta — Super-quadri-partiens quintas — Superbi-partiens septimas

Quadrupla — Dupla sesquialtra — Dupla — Superti-partiens quartas — Dupla — Superti-partiens quintas — Superbi-partiens septimas

Tripla — Dupla — Superbi-partiens tertias — Sesquialtra — Sesquiquinta — Superti-partiens quintas — Sesquiseptima — Superti partiens septimas

Dupla — Sesquialtra — Sesquitertia — Superti-partiens quartas — Sesquiquarta — Sesquiquinta — Sesquisexta — Sesquiseptima — Superbi-partiens septimas — Sesquioctavus — Sesquinona

C	C	¢	C	C	O	CC	C	C	O	C
1	2	3	4	5	6	7	8	9	10
2	4	6	8	10	12	14	16	18	20
3	6	9	12	15	18	21	24	27	30
4	8	12	16	20	24	28	32	36	40
5	10	15	20	25	30	35	40	45	50
6	12	18	24	30	36	42	48	54	60
7	14	21	28	35	42	49	56	63	70
8	16	24	32	40	48	56	64	72	80
9	18	27	36	45	54	63	72	81	90
10	20	30	40	50	60	70	80	90	100

and has explained its use and reference to the purposes of musical calculation in the following terms:—

'As for the use of this table, when you would know 'what proportion any one number hath to another, 'finde out the two numbers in the table, then looke 'upwarde to the triangle inclosing those numbers, 'and in the angle of concourse, that is where your 'two lynes meete togither, there is the proportion of 'your two numbers written: as for example, let your 'two numbers be 18 and 24; looke upward, and in 'the top of the tryangle covering the two lynes which 'inclose those numbers, you will find written Sesqui-'tertia; so likewise 24 and 42 you finde in the angle 'of concourse written super tripartiens quartas, and 'so of others.'

There is reason to think that this ingenious and most useful diagram was the invention of Morley himself; since neither in Franchinus, Peter Aron,

Glareanus, Zarlino, nor many other ancient writers, who have been consulted for the purpose, is it to be found. Indeed in the Theorica of Franchinus we meet with that deduction of numbers which forms the basis of the triangle, and nothing more, but that work Morley declares he had never seen:* it is

* For this we have his own word in a passage which proves, though he takes frequent occasion to cite Franchinus, yet that he had the misfortune to be a stranger to the most valuable of his works, as also to some particulars relating to ancient music, which he would have been glad to have known. These are Morley's own words: 'And though Friar 'Zaccone out of Franchinus affirme that the Greekes didde sing by 'certaine letters signifying both the time that the note is to be holden in 'length, and also the heighth and lownesse of the same: yet because 'I find no such matter in Franchinus his Harmonia Instrumentorum '(for his Theorica nor Practica I have not seene, nor understand not 'his arguments) I knowe not what to saie to it.' [Annotations on the 'first part of the Introduction to Practical Music.]

The passage above alluded to by Morley is to be found in the Prattica di Musica of Zacconi, lib. I. cap. 15, but it contains no reference to any particular work of Franchinus, nevertheless it is clear that he must have had his eye on the second chapter of the second book of the Practica Musicæ utriusque Cantus, in which are exhibited the characters used to denote the measures or times which constituted the rythmus of the

highly probable however that he found these numbers in some other old author; and as to the several triangles produced therefrom, he may well be supposed to have taken the hint of drawing them from that diagram in the manuscript of Waltham Holy Cross, inserted in page 248 of this work, in which a series of duple, triple, sesquialteral, and sesquitertian proportions is deduced from certain numbers there assumed.

CHAP. LXIV.

THE use of the several proportions contained in the foregoing diagram, so far as they regard music, was originally to ascertain the ratios of the consonances, and for that purpose they are applied by Euclid in the Sectio Canonis; for instance, the diapason is by him demonstrated to be in duple, which is a species of Multiplex proportion; the diatessaron in superparticular, that is to say Sesquitertia proportion, 4 to 3; the diapente also in superparticular, that is to say Sesquialtera proportion, 3 to 2; and lastly, the Diezeuctic tone also in superparticular, that is to say Sesquioctave proportion, 9 to 8. All which proportions were investigated by the division of the monochord, and are now farther demonstrable by the vibrations of pendulums of proportionable lengths.

That the Cantus Mensurabilis had also a foundation in numerical proportion is evident, for not only it consisted in a combination of long and short quantities, but each had a numerical ratio to the other; for instance, to the Large the Long was in duple, and the Breve in quadruple proportion; this was in the imperfect mode, but in the perfect, where the division was by three, the Long was to the Large in triple, and the Breve in nonuple proportion.

There does not seem to have been any original necessity for transferring the ratios from consonance to measures, or at least of retaining more than the duple and triple proportions, with those others generated by them, since we have found by experience that all mensurable music is resolvable into either the one or the other of these two; but no sooner were they adjusted, and a due discrimination made between the attributes of perfection and imperfection as they related to time, then the writers on mensurable music set themselves to find out all the varieties of proportion which the radical numbers are capable of producing. How these proportions could possibly be applied to practice, or what advantage music could derive from them, supposing them practicable, is one of the hardest things to be conceived of in the whole science. Morley, in the first part of his Introduction, pag. 27, has undertaken to declare the use of the most simple of them, namely the Duple, Triple, Quadruple, Sesquialtera, and Sesquitertia, which he thus explains in the following dialogue:—

Greeks. See them in pag. 279, of this work. But Zaccone seems to be mistaken in supposing that these characters signified as well the melodial distances as the quantity of the notes, for Franchinus intimates nothing like it, on the contrary he says expressly, that these latter were denoted by certain characters, which he purposely omits; and what these characters were may be seen in Boetius de Musica, lib. IV. cap. iii. and in book I. chap. iv. of this work.

'PHILOMATHES. What is proportion?

'MASTER. It is the comparing of numbers placed 'perpendicularly one over an other.

'PHI. This I knewe before; but what is that to 'musicke?

'MA. Indeede wee do not in musicke consider 'the numbers by themselves; but set them for a sign 'to signifie the altering of our notes in the time.

'PHI. Proceede then to the declaration of pro-'portion.

'MA. Proportion is either of equality or une-'quality. Proportion of equalitie is the comparing 'of two equal quantities togither, in which because 'there is no difference, we will speak no more at this 'time. Proportion of inequalitie is when two things 'of unequal quantitie are compared togither, and is 'either of them more or less inæqualitie. Proportion 'of the more inequalitie is when a greater number is 'set over and compared to a lesser, and in musicke 'doth always signifie diminution. Proportion of the 'lesse inequalitie is where a lesser number is set 'over and compared to a greater, as $\frac{2}{3}$, and in 'musicke doth alwaies signifie augmentation.

'PHI. How many kinds of proportions do you 'commonly use in musicke, for I am persuaded it is 'a matter impossible to sing them all, especially those 'which be termed superparcients?

'MA. You saie true, although there be no pro-'portion so harde but might be made in musicke; 'but the hardenesse of singing them hath caused 'them to be left out, and therefore there be but five 'in most common use with us, Dupla, Tripla, Qua-'drupla, Sesquialtera, and Sesquitertia.

'PHI. What is Dupla proportion in musicke?

'MA. It is that which taketh halfe the value of 'every note and rest from it, so that two notes of one 'kinde doe but answere to the value of one; and it 'is knowen when the upper number containeth the 'lower twise, thus $\frac{2}{1}$, $\frac{4}{2}$, $\frac{6}{3}$, $\frac{8}{4}$, $\frac{12}{6}$, &c. * * *

'PHI. What is Tripla proportion in musicke?

'MA. It is that which diminisheth the value of 'the notes to one third part; for three briefes are set 'for one, and three semibreves for one, and is knowen 'when two numbers are set before the song, whereof 'the one contayneth the other thrise, thus $\frac{3}{1}$, $\frac{6}{2}$, $\frac{9}{3}$, &c.

'PHI. Proceed now to quadrupla.

'MA. Quadrupla is proportion diminishing the 'value of the notes to the quarter of that which they 'were before; and it is perceived in singing when 'a number is set before the song, comprehending 'another four times, as $\frac{4}{1}$, $\frac{8}{2}$, $\frac{12}{3}$, &c. * * * Quintupla 'and Sextupla I have not seen used by any strangers 'in their songs so far as I remember, but here we use 'them, but not as they use their other proportions, 'for we call that Sextupla where wee make six black 'minyms to the semibreve, and Quintupla when we 'have but five, &c., but that is more by custom than 'by reason. * * *

'PHI. Come then to Sesquialtera: what is it?

'MA. It is when three notes are sung to two of 'the same kinde, and is knowne by a number con-'taining another once and his halfe, $\frac{3}{2}$, $\frac{6}{4}$, $\frac{9}{6}$. * *

'Sesquitertia is when four notes are sung to three of

'the same kinde, and is knowen by a number set
'before him, contayning another once and his third
'part, thus, $\frac{4}{3}$, $\frac{8}{6}$, $\frac{12}{9}$. And these shall suffice at this
'time, for knowing these, the rest are easily learned.
'But if a man would ingulphe himselfe to learne to
'sing, and set down all them which Franchinis
'Gaufurius hath set downe in his booke De Pro-
'portionibus Musicis, he should find it a matter not
'only hard but almost impossible.'

It is evident from the passages above-cited, that
whatever might have been the number of the proportions formerly in use, they were in Morley's time
reduced to five, and that he himself doubted whether
many of those contained in the Practica Musice
utriusque Cantus et Franchinus, could possibly be
sung; and farther there is great reason to think
that in this opinion he was not singular.

To give a short account of the contents of Franchinus's fourth book, it contains fifteen chapters,
entitled as follow :—

The first chapter of this book treats of proportion
in general, with the division thereof into discrete
and continuous, rational and irrational. In this discrimination of its several kinds, Franchinus professes
to follow Euclid, and other of the ancient writers on
the subject; referring also to a writer on proportion,
but little known, named Johannes Marlianus. In
the subsequent chapters are contained a great variety
of short musical compositions calculated to illustrate
the several proportions treated of in each: some in
two parts, viz., tenor and cantus; others in three,
viz., tenor, contratenor and cantus. The duples,
triples, and quadruples may in general be conceived
of from what Morley has said concerning them; and
so might the others, if this explanation, which, mutatis mutandis, runs through them all, were at this
day intelligible, namely, that a certain number of the
latter notes in each, are equivalent in quantity and
measure of time to a less number of precedent ones,
apparently of an equal value. To give an instance
in sextuple proportion, these are the author's words:

'Sextupla proportio quinta multiplicis generis species
'fit quum maior sequentiam notularum numeros ad
'minorem præcedentium relatus: eum in se com-
'præhendit sexies præcise: et æquiualet ei in quan-
'titate et temporis mensura ut vi. ad. i. et xii. ad ii.
'et xviii. ad. iii. sex enim notulæ secundum hanc
'dispositionem uni sibi consimili æquivalent et coæ-
'quantur: ita ut singulæ quæque ipsarum sex
'diminuantur de quinque sextis partibus sui quan-
'titatiui valoris: describitur enim in notulis hoc
'modo $\frac{6}{1}$ $\frac{12}{2}$ $\frac{18}{3}$ quod hoc monstratur exemplo :—'*

CANTUS.

TENOR.

* Pract. Mus. lib. IV. cap. iii.

Franchinus is not sufficiently clear to a modern apprehension with
respect to the manner in which the proportions are to be sung; but with
the assistance of Morley, and by the help of that rule, which in his
Annotations on pag. 31 of the first part of his Introduction he lays down
as infallible, namely, that 'in all musical proportions the upper number
signifieth the semibreve, and the lower the stroke;' or, in other words,
because the division may be into less notes than semibreves, and the
notes divided may be less in quantity than a stroke or breve; and that
other in pag. 28, of the Introduction, to wit, 'that the upper number
'signifieth the progression, and the under the measure,' it is discoverable
that in duple proportion two notes in one part are to be sung to one in
the other, in triple three, in quadruple four, and in quintuple five. Of
the two former kinds he has given examples in the twenty-eighth and
subsequent pages of his Introduction; and of the two latter the following
occur, pag. 91 of the same work :—

QUADRUPLA.

QUINTUPLA.

As to that other work of Franchinus, entitled Angelicum ac divinum Opus musice, the epithets

Sesquialtera and Sesquitertia are thus represented by him:—

SESQUIALTERA.

given to it might induce a suspicion that it was a posthumous publication by some friend of the

SESQUITERTIA.

Upon the former whereof he remarks as follows:—

'Here they set downe certaine observations, which they termed In-'ductions as here you see in the first two barres sesquialtera perfect: 'that they called the induction to nine to two, which is quadruple ses-'quialtera. In the third barre you have broken sesquialtera, and the 'rest to the end is quadrupla sesquialtera, or, as they termed it, nine to 'two; and every proportion whole is called the induction to that which 'it maketh, being broken. As tripla being broken in the more prolation 'wil make nonupla, and so is tripla the induction to nonupla. Or in the 'less prolation wil make sextupla, and so is the induction to sextupla.'

The general method of reconciling dissimilar proportions, and reducing them to practice, is exhibited by Morley in the following composition of Alessandro Striggio, being the latter part of the thirtieth song of the second book of his madrigals for six voices to the words 'All' acqua 'sagra.' Introd. pag. 35 :—

author, rather than that he gave it to the world himself; but the dedication of this book to Simone Crotto, a patrician of Milan, excludes the possibility of doubt that it was published by Franchinus, and gives occasion to remark how much the manners of the fifteenth century are exceeded by those of the present time, in which should an author of the first degree of eminence in any faculty or science give to a work of his own the character of Angelic or Divine, he would be more censured for his vanity than admired for his learning or ingenuity.

The difference here noted carries with it no imputation of excessive vanity in Franchinus, as it is in a great measure accounted for by the practice of the age he lived in; but it may serve to shew that the refinements of literature have a necessary effect on the tempers and conduct of men, and that learning and urbanity generally improve together.

To give a particular account of this work would in effect be to recapitulate the substance of what has already been cited from the writings of the ancient harmonicians, more especially Boetius, of whom, as he was a Latin writer, Franchinus has made considerable use, as indeed have all the musical writers;

Upon which Morley makes the following comment : ' Herein you have ' one poynt handled first in the ordinary moode through all the parts, ' then in Tripla through all the parts, and lastly, in proportions, no part ' like unto another, for the treble conteyneth diminution in the Quadruple ' proportion. The second treble or Sextus hath Tripla prickt all in black ' notes. Your Altus or meane conteyneth diminution in Dupla pro- ' portion. The Tenor goeth through with his Tripla (which was begone ' before) to the ende. The Quintus is Sesquialtera to the breefe, which ' hath this sign 𝄴 3/2 set before it. But if the sign were taken away, ' then woulde three minyms make a whole stroke, whereas now three ' semibriefs make but one stroke. The Base is the ordinary moode, ' wherein is no difficulty.'

It seems not very easy to reconcile proportions so dissimilar as are contained in the examples above given, in respect that the Arsis and Thesis in the several parts do not coincide, unless, which probably was the method of singing them, in the beating one bar was marked by a down, and the other by an up stroke.

But after all it is extremely difficult to account for this capricious interchange of proportions in the same Cantus, or to assign any good reason for retaining them. In the one example produced by Morley, from Alessandro Striggio, and given above, we are more struck with the quaintness of the contrivance, than pleased with the effect. In short, the multiplicity of proportions seems to have been the abuse of music; and this the same author seems to allow in the course of his work, and to censure where he says, that ' being a childe he had heard him greatly ' commended who coulde upon a plaine song sing hard proportions, and ' that he who could bring in manifest of them was accounted the jollyest ' fellowe.' Introd. pag. 119.

So much for the use of different proportions in different parts. The terms by which they were anciently characterised come next to be considered; and here we shall find that the terms Multiplex, Superparticular, and Superpartient, with their several compounds, are better supplied by those characters called the Inductions; for the former do but declare the nature of the proportions, which is a mere speculative consideration, whereas the latter denote the proportions themselves. To conceive justly of these it is necessary to premise that the measure of a modern bar in duple time is a semibreve, and that all the triples have a supposed ratio to this measure. If the progression be by Minims, the radical number is the number of minims contained in the bar of duple time, and the upper the number of progression, as in this instance 3/2, which denotes that species of triple in which three minims are contained in the bar. If the progression be by Crotchets, the radical gives the number of crotchets in a bar of duple time, and the upper the number of progression, as 3/4, signifying that three crotchets are contained in a bar. If the progression be by Quavers, eight are contained in a bar of duple time, and 3/8 is the signature of a movement wherein three quavers make a bar.

The above observations are intended to shew that our want of an accurate knowledge of the ancient proportions of time is a misfortune that may very well be submitted to, since it is but a consequence of improvements that have superseded the necessity of any concern about them; it being incontrovertible that there is not any kind of proportion or measure that the invention can suggest as proper for music, which is not to be expressed by the characters now in use. These, and the division of time by bars, have rendered useless all the learning of the ligatures, all the distinctions of mood, time, and prolation; all the various methods of augmentation and diminution by black full and black void, red full and red void characters, and, in a word, all the doctrine of proportions as applied to time, which Franchinus and numberless authors before him had laboured to teach and establish.

for as to the Greeks, it is well known that till the revival of learning in Europe, their language was understood but by very few: Franchinus himself was unable to read the Greek authors in the original, and for that reason, as has been already mentioned, he procured translations of them to be made at his own expense. There are however many things in this work of Franchinus that deserve to be mentioned.

It was printed at Milan in the year 1508; and from the language, which is the Italian of that day, and the style and manner in which this book is written, there can be no doubt but that it is the same in substance, perhaps nearly so in words, with those lectures which we are told he read at Cremona, Lodi, and elsewhere. Indeed the frontispiece to the book, which represents him in the act of lecturing, seems to indicate no less.

The work, as it now appears, differs in nothing from an institute on the harmonical science: it begins with an explanation of the five kinds of proportion of greater inequality, namely, multiple, superparticular, superpartient, multiple superparticular, and multiple superpartient.

The author then proceeds to declare the nature of the consonances, and exhibits the ancient system, consisting of a double diapason, with his own observations on it. He then endeavours, by the help of Ptolemy and Manuel Bryennius, but chiefly of Boetius, to explain the doctrine of the three genera; in the doing whereof he professes only to give the sentiments of the above, and a few less considerable writers. He also shews the difference between arithmetical, geometrical, and harmonical proportionality.

After declaring the nature of Guido's reformation of the scale, the use of the syllables, the cliffs, and the order in which the mutations arise, he proceeds to demonstrate the ratios of the diatessaron, diapente, and diapason, and thereby leads to an enquiry concerning the modes of the ancients, which, agreeable to Ptolemy, he makes to be eight.

The ecclesiastical tones come next under his consideration; and of these he gives an explanation not near so copious, but to the same effect with that contained in the Practica Musicæ utriusque Cantus already given at length.

The same may be said of that part of this work, wherein the measures of time are treated on; a brief account of them, and of the ligatures, and also of the pauses or rests, is here given, but for more ample information the author refers his reader to his former work.

The fourth part of this tract contains the doctrine of counterpoint.

In the fifth and last part the proportions of greater and lesser inequality are very accurately discussed; these are solely applicable to the Cantus Mensurabilis, but, as for reasons herein before given, the use of intricate proportions has long been exploded, and the simple ones have been found to be better characterized by numbers than by the terms formerly used for that purpose, a particular account of the contents of this last book seems to be no way necessary.

CHAP. LXV.

Of the work De Harmonia Musicorum Instrumentorum, little more need be said than that it was printed at Milan in 1518, and is dedicated to Johannes Grolerius, questor or treasurer of Milan to Francis I. king of France. It is a general exhibition of the doctrines contained in the writings of the Greek harmonicians, at least of such of them as may be supposed to have come to the hands of its author; for some of them it is not pretended that he ever saw; and for the sense of those with which he appears to have been best acquainted, he seems to have been beholden to Boetius, who in many respects is to be considered both as a translator and a commentator on the Greek writers. In this work of Franchinus the nature of the perfect or immutable system is explained, as are also, as well as the author was able, the genera of the ancients, and the proportions of the consonances. He considers also the division of the tone, and the dimension of the tetrachord, and shews the several species of diatessaron, diapente, and diapason; and demonstrates, as Boetius has also done, that six sesqui octave tones exceed the diapason by a comma. He next explains the nature of arithmetical, geometrical, and harmonical proportionality, and shews wherein they differ from each other. In the fourth and last book he treats on the modes of the ancients, in the doing whereof he apparently follows Ptolemy, and speaks of the Dorian as the most excellent.

Notwithstanding the great reputation which Franchinus had acquired by his writings, and the general acquiescence of his contemporaries in the precepts from time to time delivered by him, a professor of Bologna, Giovanni Spataro by name, in the year 1531 made a furious attack upon him in a book entitled Tractato di Musica, wherein he takes upon him an examination of Franchinus's treatise De Practica, and charges him with gross ignorance in that part of musical science in which Franchinus was confessedly better skilled than any professor of his time, the Cantus Mensurabilis. Spataro speaks of his preceptor Bartholomeo Ramis, a Spaniard, who had read lectures at Bologna, which were published in 1482, with the title of De Musica tractatus, sive Musica practica, as a man of profound erudition; and cites him as authority for almost everything he advances. He speaks of Franco, who by a mistake he makes to have been a professor of Cologne instead of Liege, as the unquestionable inventor of the Cantus Mensurabilis, scarcely mentioning John De Muris in the course of his work; and speaks of Marchettus of Padua as an author against whose judgment there can lie no appeal.

The principal grounds of dispute between Spataro and Franchinus were the values of the several characters that constitute the Cantus Mensurabilis and the ratios of the consonances, which the former in some of his writings had ventured to discuss. Spataro was the author also of a tract entitled Utile et breve Regule di Canto, in which also he is pretty free in his censures of Franchinus and his writings: and besides these it should seem by Franchinus's defence of himself, published in 1520, that Spataro had written

to him several letters from Bologna, in which the charge of ignorance and vanity was strongly enforced. * In the management of this dispute, which seems to have had for its object nothing less than the ruin of Franchinus as a public professor, it is supposed that Spataro had the assistance of some persons who envied the reputation of his adversary no less than himself did: this may be collected from the title of Franchinus's defence, which is, Apologii Franchini Gafurii Musici adversus Joannem Spatarium et complices Musicos Bononienses, and seems to be confirmed by the dedication of the Tractato di Musica to Peter Aron of Florence, a writer of some note, and who will be mentioned hereafter, and an epistle from Aron to him, which immediately follows the dedication of the above-mentioned work. To speak in the mildest terms of Spataro's book it is from beginning to end a libel on his adversary, who was a man of learning and integrity; and nothing but the manners of the age in which he lived, in which the style of controversy was in general as coarse as envy and malice could dictate, can excuse the terms he has chosen to make use of; and, to say the truth, the defence of Franchinus stands in need of some such apology, for he has not scrupled to retort the charge of ignorance and arrogance in terms that indicate a radical contempt of his opponent.

The chronology of this controversy is no otherwise to be ascertained than by the apology of Franchinus, which is dated the twentieth day of April, 1520, at which time the author was turned of seventy years of age, and the letters therein mentioned, one whereof bears date February, and the other March, 1519; whereas Spataro's book appears to have been published in 1531: so that it is highly probable that Spataro's book, as it is not referred to in the apology of Franchinus, was not published till after the decease of the latter; yet it may be supposed to contain the substance of Spataro's letters, inasmuch as it includes the whole of the objections which Franchinus in his apology has refuted.

It would be too much to give this controversy at large, the merits of it appear by Franchinus's apology, wherein he has very candidly stated the objections of his opponent, and given an answer to the most weighty of them in the following terms.

‘ You Spartarius, who are used to speak ill of others,
‘ have given occasion to be spoken against yourself,
‘ by falling with such madness on my lucubrations,
‘ though your attack has turned out to my honour.
‘ Your ignorance is scarce worth reprehension; but
‘ you are grown so insolent, that unless your petulance
‘ be chastised, you will prefer yourself before all
‘ others, and impute my silence to fear and ignorance.
‘ I shall now make public your folly which I have so
‘ long concealed; not with the bitterness it merits
‘ but with my accustomed modesty. How could you
‘ think to reach Parnassus, who understand not Latin?
‘ You who are not above the vulgar class, profess not
‘ only music, but also philosophy and mathematics, and
‘ the liberal arts, and yet you have desired me to write

---

* Morley, Introd. pag. 92, says that Spataro wrote a great book on the manner of singing sesquialtera proportion.

' to you in our mother tongue. Could no one else
' declare war against me but you, who are void of all
' learning, who infect the minds of your pupils, and
' pervert the art itself? But though my knowledge
' be small, yet I have sufficient to detect your errors,
' and likewise those of your master Bartholomeo
' Ramis.

' When therefore in your fourteenth description
' you speak of the sesquioctave 9 to 8 as divided into
' nine minute parts arithmetically, which you begged
' from a mathematician, you should know that a
' division merely arithmetical is not accounted of by
' musicians, because it does not contain concinnous,
' perfect intervals; and your mathematician might
' have marked down that sesquioctave more clearly,
' had he given the superparticular proportions in this
' manner, 81, 80, 79, 78, 76, 75, 74, 73, 72, for the
' two extremes 81 and 72 constitute the sesquioctave.
' But when you quote the authority of Marchettus of
' Padua you seem to despise Bartholomeo Ramis,
' your master, whom you extol as invincible; for he
' in the first book of his Practica, after Guido esteems
' Marchettus (who is also accounted by Joannes Car-
' thusinus as wanting a rod) not worth even four
' Marcheta,* and reproves him as erroneous. But
' I imagine that you only dreamt that Marchettus di-
' vided the tone into nine dieses; for if the diesis be
' the half of the lesser semitone, as Boetius and all mu-
' sicians esteem it, the tone would contain four lesser
' semitones, and the half of a semitone, a thing never
' heard of. This division of the Tone is not admitted
' by musicians; and if you think that the tone contains
' nine commas, as some imagine, the contrary is
' proved by Boetius. Anselmus's division of the
' system into greater and lesser semitones is no more
' the chromatic, as Marchettus intimates, than that
' of the tetrachord given by your mathematician;
' for in the chromatic tetrachord the two graver
' intervals do not make up a tone according to
' Boetius, but are of what I call the mixt genus.
' Do not think that any proportions of numbers are
' congruous to musical intervals, except the chords
' answer the natural intervals.

' In your sixteenth description, spun out to the
' length of four sheets, you ostentatiously insist on
' many very unnecessary things; for you endeavour
' to prove that this mediation 6, 5, 3, is harmonical,
' because the chords marked by these numbers when
' touched together produce consonance. This is
' readily granted, for the extreme terms sound the
' diapason; the two greater sound the lesser third,
' which is greater than the semitone by a comma, 80 to
' 81; and the two lesser the greater sixth, diminished
' by a comma. These three chords will indeed pro-
' duce consonance, but not that most sweet mediation
' of these, 6, 4, 3, which Pythagoras, Plato, and Aris-
' totle extol as the most concinnous mediation possible.

' But in your seventh babbling description you bring
' this mediation, 1, 2, 3, as truly harmonical, having
' the diapente towards the grave, and the diapason in
' the acute, which I do not admit; for the extremes
' bear not a due proportion to each other. Again the

* A coin of Venice, of small value.

' duple 2, 1, above the sesquialtera having no harmo-
' nical mediation, cannot be as sweet as 6, 4, 3. I add
' that this happens on account of the equality of the
' differences (and therefore of the intervals) for the
' sesquialteral space towards the grave is equal to the
' duple immediately following it towards the acute,
' as appears from the thirty-seventh chapter of the
' second book De Harmonia Musicorum Instrumen-
' torum; neither is it equal in sweetness to this me-
' diation of the triple, for this is truly harmonical, but
' yours is not. You moreover blame Pythagoras for
' not introducing the Sesquiquarta and Sesquiquinta
' as concinnous in his system; but these are distant
' from the entire and proper intervals, namely, the
' ditone and semiditone, by a comma, and he made
' use of none but entire intervals in his mediations.
' Socrates, and the divine Plato, who also heard Draco
' the Athenian, and Metellus the Agrigentine, fol-
' lowed him: Guido himself described the eccle-
' siastical cantus diatonically; and before him the
' popes Ignatius, Basilius, Hilarius, Ambrose, Gela-
' sius, Gregory, used that modulation.

' You seem to imitate your master Ramis (who is
' as impure as yourself) in petulance and ingratitude,
' for if he borrowed the Sesquiquarta and Sesqui-
' quinta, as you assert, from Ptolemy, he must be
' a plagiary in not quoting him; and you who
' profited by the studies of Gaffurius, yet ungrate-
' fully and enviously attack Gaffurius. How can
' youth studying music profit by the erudition of
' thy master? who described his very obscure and
' confused scale by these eight syllables, " Psal li tur
' per vo ces is tas," wherein the natural lesser semi-
' tone is marked by a various and dissimilar denomi-
' nation; but he frighted and repenting, laid that
' aside, and was forced to return to the diatonic scale
' of Guido, in which he has introduced the mixt
' genus, filled up with as it were chromatic, though
' false condensations, as appears in the course of his
' practical treatise.

' In your eighteenth and last description you attack
' me for having in the third chapter of the fourth
' book De Harmonia ascribed the chord Nete Synem-
' menon to the acute extreme of the Dorian mode,
' when the tetrachord of the conjuncts is not admitted
' in any figure of intervals. This Nete Synemmenon
' might be called Paranete Diezeugmenon, as they are
' both in the same place, so that there is not any ne-
' cessity for the tetrachord of the conjuncts in the
' production of this tetrachord. Your Ramis, in his
' practical treatise, constitutes the fourth species of
' the diapason from D SOL RE to d SOL RE, mediated
' in G; whereby he makes the first ecclesiastical
' tone, for the Dorian is the fourth species of the
' diapason, become plagal from an authentic, and
' subverts the sacred modulation. You attack me
' for saying that Ptolemy constituted his eighth or
' hypermixolydian mode in similar intervals with the
' hypodorian, asserting that he made them of different
' diapentes and diatessarons; but you ought to know
' that the hypermixolydian differs from the hypodo-
' rian not formally, but in acumen only; being acuter
' by a diapason. But do not think that this is the

'eighth ecclesiastical tone which is plagal, for the
'contrary is shewn in lib. I. cap. vii. of our Practica.

'In your two first detractory descriptions you
'object against some things, in themselves not ma-
'terial, in our book De Harmonia Musicorum In-
'strumentorum. I shall first answer that dated at
'Bologna, the last day of February, 1519. We say
'that the terms tetrachord and quadrichord are in-
'differently used, for each comprehends four chords.
'But the most ancient tetrachord of Mercury sounded
'the diapason between the two extremes, as in these
'numbers 6, 8, 9, 12. Neither think that by the
'term Tetrachord is always meant the consonance
'diatessaron, for every space containing four chords
'is called a tetrachord or quadrichord; and even the
'tritone contained under four chords, from Parhypate
'meson to Paramese is a tetrachord, though it exceeds
'the diatessaron. Johannes Cocleus Noricus, the
'Phonascus of Nuremberg, gave the name of Tetra-
'chordum to his book of music, as being divided
'into four parts. Samius Lichaon, who added the
'eighth chord to the musical system, is imagined by
'most people to be Pythagoras himself.

'I do not forget your babbling when you assert
'that the Duple and the Sesqualtera conjoined pro-
'duce the Sesquitertia in this order, 4, 2, 3, making
'the Duple in 4, 2, and the Sesqualtera in 2, 3; but
'in this you are wrong, for 2, 3, is here Subses-
'quialtera.

'In your letter, dated the fifteenth of October,
'you say you will not answer the questions I pro-
'posed to you, which were, whether consonance is
'not a mixture of acute and grave sounds sweetly
'and uniformly approaching the ear; and in what
'manner that mixture is made, whether by the con-
'junction, or by the adherence of the one to the
'other: and again, which conduces most to con-
'sonance, the grave or the acute, and which of
'the two predominates. You moreover write that
'Laurentius Gazius, a monk of Cremona, and well
'skilled in music, came to you to discourse con-
'cerning the canon of your master, and that Boetius
'was only an interpreter, and not an author in music;
'in this opinion you are mistaken, for he was the
'most celebrated lawyer, philosopher, mathematician,
'orator, poet, astronomer, and musician of his age,
'as his almost innumerable works declare. And
'Cassiodorus bears witness of his musical erudition
'in the epistle of the emperor Theodoric to Boetius
'himself, to this purpose: "When the king of
"the Franks, induced by the fame of our banquet,
"earnestly requested a Cithæraedist from us, the only
"reason why we promised to comply, was because
"we knew you were well skilled in the musical art."

After a very severe censure on a Canticum of
Bartholomeo Ramis, produced by him in a lecture
which he publicly read at Bologna, Franchinus concludes with saying, that 'the precepts delivered by
'him will, if not perverted, appear to be founded in
'truth and reason; and that though his adversary
'Spataro should grow mad with rage, the works of
'Gaffurius, and the fame of his patron Grolerius
'will live for ever.'

Pietro Aron, a Florentine, and a canon of Rimini,

of the order of Jerusalem, and the patron of Spataro,
was the author of Libri tres de Institutione harmonica, printed at Bologna, 1516; Tratto della
Natura e Cognitione di tutti gli Tuoni di Canto
figurato, Vinegia 1525. Lucidario in Musica di
alcune Oppenioni antiche et moderne, Vinegia 1545.
Toscanello de la Musica, Vinegia 1523, 1529. Nova-
mente Stampato con la gionta, 1539. Compendiolo
di molti dubbi Segreti et Sentenze intorno al Canto
Fermo et Figurato, Milano 15—. The first of these
was originally written in the Italian language, and
is only extant in a Latin translation of Johannes
Antonius Flaminius Forocorneliensis, an intimate
friend of the author.

The work entitled Toscanello is divided into two
books; the first contains an eulogium on music, and
an account of the inventors of it, drawn from the
ancient poets and mythologists. In this definition
of music the author recognizes the division of it
by Boetius and others into mundane, humane, and
instrumental music. After briefly distinguishing
between vocal and instrumental music, he by a very
abrupt transition proceeds to an explanation of the
Cantus Mensurabilis and the ligatures, in which he
does but repeat what had been much better said by
Franchinus and others before him.

The second book treats of the intervals and the
consonances, and in a very superficial manner, of the
genera of the ancients. From thence the author
proceeds to a declaration of counterpoint, for the
composition whereof he delivers ten precepts; these
are succeeded by a brief explanation of the several
kinds of proportion, of greater and lesser inequality,
and of arithmetical, geometrical, and harmonical
proportionality; the remainder of the book consists
of directions for dividing the monochord according
to the rule of Guido Aretinus, with a chapter intitled De la Participatione et Modo da cordare
l' Instrumento.

In the course of his work he highly commends
as a theorist Bartholomeo Ramis, the preceptor of
Spataro, styling him 'Musico dignissimo, veramente
'da ogni dotto venerato;' and as practical musicians
he celebrates Iodocus Pratensis by the name of
Josquino, Obreth, Busnois, Ocheghen, and Duffai.
To these in other places he adds Giovanni Mouton,
Richafort, Pierazzon de Larve, Allessandro Agricola,
and some others, of whom he says they were the
most famous men in their faculty.

The edition of the Toscanello of 1539 has an
appendix, which the author intitles 'Aggiunta del
'Toscanello, à complacenza de gli Amici fatta,' containing directions for the intonation of the Psalms,
and the singing of certain offices on particular
festivals.

The writings of Peter Aron contain nothing
original or new; for it is to be observed that Boetius
and Franchinus had nearly exhausted the subject of
musical science, and that few of the publications subsequent to those of the latter contain anything worthy
of notice, such as treat of music in that general and
extensive way in which Kircher, Zarlino, and Mersennus have considered it.

The ten precepts of counterpoint, which constitute

the twenty-first and nine following chapters of the second book of the Toscanello, seem to carry in them the appearance of novelty, but they are in truth extracted from the writings of Franchinus, though the author has studiously avoided the mention of his name. They are in effect nothing more than brief directions for adjusting the parts in an orderly succession, and with proper intervals between each, in a composition of many parts. Morley appears to have studied Peter Aron, and has given the substance of his precepts, very much improved and enlarged, in the third part of his Introduction.

The above restriction of the precepts of music to the number of ten, is not the only instance of the kind that we meet with in the works of writers on the science: Andreas Ornithoparcus, of Meyning, has discovered as great a regard for this number, founded perhaps in a reverence for the Decalogue, as Peter Aron has done; for in his Micrologus, printed at Cologne in 1535, he has limited the precepts for the decent and orderly singing of divine service to ten, though they might with great propriety have been encreased to double that number.

CHAP. LXVI.

About the same time with Franchinus and Peter Aron flourished John Hamboys, of whom bishop Tanner in his Bibliotheca gives the following account:—

'John Hamboys, a most celebrated musician, and 'a doctor in that faculty. Bale calls him a man of 'great erudition; and adds, that being educated in 'the liberal sciences, he in his riper years applied 'himself to music with great assiduity. He wrote 'Summam Artis Musicæ, lib. i. beginning "Quemad-"modum inter Triticum." The MS. book in the 'Bodleian library, Digby 90, which has for its title 'Quatuor Principalia Musicæ, lib. iv. completed at 'Oxford, 1451, has the same beginning. Wrongfully 'therefore in the catalogues, and by A. Wood, is it 'assigned to Thomas of Teukesbury.'

Hamboys was the author also of certain musical compositions, entitled Cantionum artificialium diversi Generis, and is said to have flourished anno 1470. Bal. viii. 40. Pits, pag. 662.

In Holinshed's Chronicle, vol. II. pag. 1355, is an enumeration of the most eminent men for learning during the reign of Edward IV.[*] in which the author

* It is highly probable from the establishment of his chapel, and the provision therein made for a succession of singers, that this prince was a lover of music, and a favourer of musicians; and it seems that Hamboys, though very eminent, was not the only celebrated musician of his time; for in Weever's Funeral Monuments, pag. 422, is the following inscription on a tomb, formerly in the old church of St. Dunstan in the East:—

Clausus in hoc tumulo Gulielmus Payne requiescit,
Quem sacer edituum fouerat iste locus.
Clarum cui virtus, ars et cui musica nomen
Eduardi quarti regis in ede dabat.
Si tibi sit pietas, tumuli si cura, viator,
Hoc optes illi quod cupis ipse tibi,
Ob. 1508.

Another musician of the same surname is noted by an inscription in the parish church of Lambeth in Surrey, in these words:—

Of your charity pray for the foul of Sir Ambrofe Payne, parfon of Lambeth, and bachelour of mufick, and chapleyn to the lords cardynals Boufar and Morton, who departed May the xxviii.
A.D. 1528.

includes John Hamboys, an excellent musician, adding, that for his notable cunning therein he was made doctor of music.

There is reason to suppose that Hamboys was the first person on whom the degree of doctor in music was conferred by either of the universities in this kingdom, at least there is no positive evidence to the contrary; and as to the antiquity of degrees in music, although the registers of the universities do not ascertain it, academical honours in this faculty may be traced up to the year 1463, for it appears that in that year Henry Habington was admitted to the degree of bachelor of music at Cambridge; and that in the same year Thomas Saintwix, doctor in music, was made master of King's College in the same university.[†]

Such as are concerned for the honour of the science will look upon this as a remarkable æra. And if we consider the low estimation in which music is held by persons unacquainted with its principles, it must appear somewhat extraordinary to see it ranked with those arts which entitle their professors not merely to the character of learned men, but to the highest literary honours. How and for what reasons music came to be thus distinguished, will appear by the following short deduction of its progress between the year 1300, and the time now spoken of.

As to the Cantus Gregorianus and the tonal laws, they were a mere matter of practice, and related solely to the celebration of the divine offices, but the principles of the science were a subject of very abstruse speculation, and in that view music had a place among the liberal arts. This discrimination between the liberal and manual or popular arts is at least as ancient as the fourth century, for St. Augustine himself takes notice of it, and these two admitted a distinction into the Trivium and Quadrivium, which already in the course of this work has been noted: in the former were included grammar, rhetoric, and logic; in the latter arithmetic, music, geometry, and astronomy. Du Cange explains these terms by saying that the Trivium signified the threefold way to eloquence, and the Quadrivium the fourfold way to knowledge. In what a barbarous manner the sciences were taught may be in some degree inferred from a treatise on them by the famous Alcuin, the preceptor of Charlemagne, and that other of Cassiodorus, entitled De septem Disciplinis. In the greater part of the schools the public teachers ventured no farther than the Trivium, confining their instructions to grammar, rhetoric, and logic; but those of their disciples who had passed both the Trivium and Quadrivium were referred to the study of Cassiodorus and Boetius. It is easy to discover from this account of the method of academical institution, the

† It is conjectured that about this time music was arrived at great perfection in this country; to this purpose we meet with the following remarkable passage in the Moriæ Encomium of Erasmus, Basil edition. pag. 101:—'Natura ut singulis mortalibus suam, ita singulis nationibus, 'ac penè civitatibus communem quandam insevisse Philautium: atque 'hinc fieri Britanni præter alia, formam, musicam, et lautas mensas 'proprie sibi vindicent.' Viz., As nature has implanted self-love in the minds of all mortals, so has she dispensed to every country and nation a certain tincture of the same affection. Hence it is that the English challenge the prerogative of having the most handsome women, of the being most accomplished in the skill of music, and of keeping the best tables.

track in which the students of music were necessitated to walk: utterly ignorant of the language in which the precepts of harmony were originally delivered, and incapable of viewing them otherwise than through the medium of a Latin version, they studied Marcianus Capella, Macrobius, Cassiodorus, Boetius, Guido Aretinus, and those numberless authors who had written on the tones and the Cantus Mensurabilis; and in these their pursuits the students in the English universities of Oxford and Cambridge, for it nowhere appears to have been the practice in other countries, were rewarded with the academical degrees of bachelor and doctor.*

In the Fasti, at the end of the Athen. Oxon. vol. I. which commences at 1500, mention is frequently

* The statutes of the two universities prescribe the exercises for degrees in this and the other faculties, but they leave us at a loss for the regimen of students in the pursuit of them. It is however certain that formerly a course of study subjected the candidates for academical honours to a greater degree of hardship than we at this day are aware of. In a sermon of Maister Thomas Leuer, preached at Poules Cross the xiij day of December, anno 1550, is a description of college discipline, that in this age of refinement would make a student shudder: these are the author's words: 'There were [in the time of Hen. VIII.] in houses 'belonginge to the universitie of Cambridge twoo hundrede studentes 'of dyvinitye, many very well learned, whyche be now all cleane gone, 'house and man; yong towarde scolars, and old fatherly doctors, not 'one of them left: one hundred also of another sort, that having rich 'frends, or being beneficed, did live of themselves in ostles and innes, 'be either gone away, or elles faine to crepe intoo colleges, and put poor 'men from bare livynges. Those both be all gone, and a small number 'of poor dilygent students now remainyng only in colleges, be not able 'to tarry and continue their study in the universitie for lack of exhibition and helpe. There be divers there which rise daily betwixt iiij. 'and fyve of the clock in the mornynge, and from fyve until syxe of the 'clocke use common prayer, with an exhortation of God's word, in a 'common chapell, and from syxe untoo ten use ever eyther private 'study or commune lectures. At ten of the clocke they go to dinner, 'where as they be contente with a penie peice of befe amongst iiij, 'havinge a few potage made of the brothe of the same beefe, with salt 'and oatmeal, and nothing elles. After this slender dyner they be either 'teachinge or learninge until v. of the clocke in the evyning, when as 'they have a supper not muche better then their dinner, immediately 'after the which they go either to reasoning in problemes, or unto some 'other studie, until it be nyne or tenne of the clocke, and there beyinge 'without fire, are faine to walke or runne up and downe halfe a houre to 'get a hete on their fete when they go to bed.'

The late learned Mr. Wise of Oxford, was of opinion that degrees in music are more ancient than the time above-mentioned. His sentiments on the subject, and also touching the antiquity of degrees in general, are contained in a letter to a friend of his, from which the following passage is extracted:—

'England, in the time of the Saxons, through means of its frequent 'intercourses with Rome, and its neighbourhood to France, seems to 'have arrived at as great a pitch of excellence in all good arts as any 'other nation of the Christian world during that dark period of time. 'This appears from several remains of poetry in Saxon and Latin, from 'some buildings, jewels, and vast numbers of fair manuscripts written 'by the Saxons, and illuminated in as fair a manner as the taste of that 'age would admit of. Amongst other arts, music does not seem to have 'been one of the least studied amongst them, several specimens of their 'skill in church-music remaining to this day, particularly a fair manuscript, formerly belonging to the church of Winchester, now in the 'Bodleian library, called a Troparion, written in the reign of king 'Ethelred the West-Saxon.

'His brother and immediate successor, Alfred the Great, as he is 'reported by historians to have been excellent in all sorts of learning, 'and a very great proficient in civil as well as military arts, so is he particularly recorded for his skill in music, by which means he obtained a 'great victory over the Danes.

'It is therefore not to be wondered at, that upon restoring the Muses 'to their ancient seat at Oxford, he should appoint amongst the rest of 'the liberal arts a professor of music, as we expressly read he did, anno '886. [Annals of Hyde, quoted by Harpsfield] namely, John, the monk 'of St. David's.

'As to the origin of degrees in general in the universities, though 'nothing certain appears upon record, yet they seem from the very nature 'of them, to be almost, if not quite, as old as the universties themselves; 'it being necessary, even in the infancy of an university, to keep up the 'face and form of it, by distinguishing the proficients in each science 'according to the difference of their abilities and time spent in study, as 'it is now to divide school-boys into forms or classes.

'Our university, like others, being founded in the faculty of arts, 'degrees were accordingly given in logic, geometry, and each particular 'one, and in process of time in all of them together, the degree of master 'of arts being the highest in esteem in the university. But when the faculties of 'law and physic came into esteem in the world, and at length into the 'university, I don't mention divinity, because that was always cultivated 'here, then the lesser arts began to decline in their credit, as being less 'gainful; and degrees in most of them were entirely dropt, as logic, 'arithmetic, geometry, and astronomy; rhetoric indeed maintained its 'ground till the beginning of the sixteenth century, and grammar '(because nobody was allowed to teach it unless graduated in one of the 'universities) held it a good while longer; but music has maintained its 'credit to this time, and with this remarkable advantage over the rest of 'its sister arts, that whereas the only degrees of them were bachelor, or 'at most master, music, for what reason I am at present at a loss, gives 'the title of doctor.'

Bachelor is a word of uncertain etymology, it not being known what was its original sense. Junius derives it from Βακηλος, foolish. Menage from Bas Chevalier, a knight of the lowest rank. Spelman from Baculus, a staff. Cujas from Buccella, an allowance of provision. The most probable derivation of it seems to be from Bacca Laurus, the berry of a laurel or bay; bachelors being young and of good hopes, like laurels in the berry. In Latin Baccalaureus. Johns. Dict. in art. Vide Ayliffe's ancient and present State of the University of Oxford, vol. II. pag. 195.

By the statutes of the university of Oxford, it is required of every proceeder to the degree of bachelor in music, that he employ seven years in the study or practice of that faculty, and at the end of that term produce a testimonial of his having so done, under the hands of credible witnesses; and that previous to the supplication for his grace towards this degree, he compose a song of five parts, and perform the same publicly in the music-school, with vocal and instrumental music, first causing to be affixed on each of the doors of the great gates of the schools a Programma, giving three days notice of the day and hour of each performance. Of a bachelor, proceeding to the degree of doctor, it is required that he shall study five years after the taking his bachelor's degree; and produce the like proof of his having so done, as is requisite in the case of a bachelor. and farther, shall compose a song in six or eight parts, and publicly perform the same 'tam vocibus quam instrumentis etiam musicis,' on some day to be appointed for that purpose, previously notifying the day and hour of performance in the manner before prescribed. Such exercise to be performed in the presence of Dr. Heyther's professor of music. This being done, the candidate shall supplicate for his grace in the convocation-house, which being granted by both the Savilian professors, or by some master of arts deputed by them for that purpose, he shall be presented to his degree.

The statutes of the university of Oxford, do in like manner prescribe the exercises for degrees in the other faculties, but in terms at this day so little understood, that an attempt to explain them in this place may to some be not unacceptable. In Title VI. Sect. 2, De Exercitiis præstandis pro Gradu Bacculaurei in Artibus, the exercises required are Disputationes in Parvisiis: on this term the following are the sentiments of glossographers:—

Before the schools were erected the young students held their disputations in Parvisiis, in the porch of St. Mary's church. There they sate, vis-a-vis, one over against the other. This might be expressed in the Norman French of those times perhaps by Par-Vis, and this again in barbarous Latin would be rendered by in Parvisiis.

In Skinner's Lexicon the word Parvis is said to signify in Norman French a church-porch; and he quotes Spelman, as deriving it from the word Paradisus. Perhaps, says he, because the porch was, with respect to the church itself, what Paradise is to Heaven. This reason is harsh and whimsical; the word Parvis seems rather to be a corruption of a barbarous Latin word Pervisus, from Perviso, to look through, because people looked through the porch into the church. Or if, as is frequently the case, one porch was opposite to the other, then at the porch people might be said to look through the church. Pervisus then, or Parvis is literally speaking the place of looking-through.

Chaucer, in the Prologues to the Canterbury Tales, characterizing the Sergeant at Law, says,—

A ſergeant of lawe, ware and wiſe,
That often had ben at the perviſe.

And in the Glossary at the end of Urry's edition, the word Pervise is thus explained: 'Parvis, Fr. contracted from *Paradis*, Παράδεισος, 'Τόπος εη ῶ περιπάτοι. Hesych. *Locus porticibus et deambulatoriis 'circundatus.* A Portico or court before a church. *Fr. Gl.* in *Paradisus*. 'The place before the church of *Notre Dame* at *Paris*, called *Parvis*, RR. '7151, was anciently called *Paradis*. Men. Fr. in *Parvis*, *Spelman* says 'in *Parvœ*, &c. that our lawyers used formerly to walk in such a place to 'meet their clients, and not for law exercises, as *Blount* and others write, 'being perhaps led into that mistake by that passage, Prol. 312; and 'others, considering the context more than the sense of the word *Pervise*, 'explain it a bar.'

Another writer says of this word that it signifies the nether part of a church, set apart for the teaching of children in it, and that thence it is called the Parvis, à parvis pueris ibi edoctis; adding that this sense of it explains the following story in Matthew Paris, Hist. Angl. in Hen. III. pag. 798:—

'In the reign of king Hen. III. the pope's collector met a poor priest 'with a vessel of holy water, and a sprinkler, and a loaf of bread that he 'had gotten at a place for sprinkling some of his water; for he used to 'go abroad, and bestow his holy water, and receive of the people what 'they gave him, as the reputed value thereof. The pope's collector 'asked him what he might get in one year in that way? The priest 'answered about twenty shillings; to which the collector presently replied, then there belongs as due out of it, as the tenths, two shillings to 'my receipt yearly, and obliges him to pay it accordingly. Upon which 'now comes the passage, "Cogebatur ille pauperculus, multis diebus "scholas exercens, venditis in Parvisio libellis, vitam famelicam pro-"telare pro illâ substantiâ persolvenda." *i. e.* The poor priest, to enable 'him to pay that imposition, and to get a sort of livelihood, was constrained to take up the trade of selling little books at the school in the 'Parvise. And hence it is, as some think, that the French call the '*Proanos, le Parvis.*' History of Churches in England, by Thomas Staveley, octavo, 1712, pag. 157. For more on this subject consult the Glossary to Dr. Wats's edition of Matthew Paris, and that of Somner to

made of admission to bachelors' degrees in the several faculties, and of the privilege thereby acquired of reading publicly on certain books in each of them respectively, for instance, in divinity the graduate was allowed to read the Master of the Sentences; in civil law, the Institutes of Justinian; in canon law, the Decretals; in physic, Hippocrates; in arts, the Logic of Aristotle; and in music, Boetius: thus, to give an instance of the latter, Henry Parker, of Magdalen-hall, in 1502, John Mason, and John Sherman, in 1508, John Wendon, and John Clawsey, in 1509, John Dygon, a Benedictine monk, in 1512, and Thomas Mendus, a secular chaplain, in 1534, were severally admitted to the degree of bachelor of music; and of such it is said in the Fasti, Col. 5, and again Col. 69, that they were thereby admitted to the reading of any of the musical books of Boetius, which at that time were almost the only ones from whence any knowledge of the principles of the science could be derived.

The efforts of Franchinus for the improvement of music are related in the foregoing account of him and his writings, and the advantages which accrued from his labours may in some measure be deduced from thence as a necessary consequence; but the disseminating his precepts by writing through the learned world, was not all that he did towards the advancement of the science, for besides this he laid a foundation for endless disquisition, by procuring copies of the works of the ancient Greek harmonicians, the masters of Boetius himself, and by causing translations of them to be made for the use of the many that were absolutely ignorant of the language and character in which they were written. But the operation of these his labours for the advancement of the science must necessarily have been very slow, and will hardly account for those amazing improvements in the art of practical composition which appear in the works of Iodocus Pratensis, Orlando de Lasso, Philippo de Monte, Andrian Willaert, and in short, of the musicians in almost every country in Europe to whom the benefit of his instructions had extended. These are only to be accounted for by that part of his history which declares him to have been a public professor of the science, and to have taught publicly in some of the principal cities of Italy. This he did to crowded auditories, at a time when the inhabitants of Europe were grown impatient of their ignorance: when the popes and secular princes of Italy were giving great encouragement to learning. This disposition co-operating with the labours of the studious and industrious in the several faculties, brought about a reformation in literature, the effects whereof are felt at this day. Not to mention the arts of painting and sculpture, which were now improving apace, it may

the X Scriptores, voce TRIFORIUM, and Selden in his notes on Fortescue De Laudibus.

In the statutes of the university of Oxford, Tit. VI. Sect. 3. 'De 'disputationes in Parviso, tum habendis, tum frequentandis,' we meet with the term Disputationes in Augustinensibus: these, in the academical style of speaking, were disputations with the Augustine monks, who had acquired great reputation for exercises of this kind, and had formerly a monastery at Oxford, the site whereof was afterwards purchased for the purpose of erecting Wadham College. With them the students held disputations at the place, and in the manner above related. Some traces of this practice yet remain in the university exercises; and the common phrase of young scholars, 'answering Augustine's' or 'doing Austin's,' has a direct allusion to it.

suffice to say, that at this time men began to think and reason justly on literary subjects; and that they did so in music was owing to the discoveries of Franchinus, and his zeal to cultivate the science; for no sooner were his writings made public than they were spread over Europe, and the precepts contained in them inculcated with the utmost diligence in the many schools, universities, and other public seminaries throughout Italy, France, Germany, and England; and the benefits resulting from his labours were manifested, not only by an immense number of treatises on music, which appeared in the world in the age next succeeding that in which he flourished, but in the musical compositions of the sixteenth century, formed after his precepts, and which became the models of musical perfection. Of these latter it will be time enough to speak hereafter: of the authors that immediately succeeded him, and the improvements made by them, it is necessary to say something in this place.

The first writer on music of any note after Franchinus and Peter Aron seems to have been JACOBUS FABER STAPULENSIS, who flourished about the year 1503. Among other works, he has left behind him four books on music, entitled Elementa Musicalia, printed at Paris in 1496 and 1551, a thin folio. In the beginning of this work he celebrates his two masters in the science, Jacobus Labinius, and Jacobus Turbelinus. Josephus Blancanus held it in such estimation, that he recommends to students that they begin with the study of it above all other things; and that after reading it, they proceed to Boetius, Aristoxenus, Ptolemy, and Euclid. Salinas speaks very differently of the Elementa Musicalia, for he says it discovers that the author knew more of the other parts of mathematics than of music; he however commends the author for having treated the subject with a degree of perspicuity equal to that of Euclid in his Elements of Geometry. He adds, that he does not seem to have read Ptolemy, or any other of the Greek writers, but is entirely a Boetian, and does nothing more than demonstrate what he has laid down. This is certainly a very favourable censure; Salinas might truly have called the book a partial abridgment of Boetius, for such it must appear to every attentive peruser of it. Faber was of Picardy; his name, in the language of his own country, was Jacques Le Fevre D'Estaples; he was a doctor of the Sorbonne, and beloved by Erasmus. Bayle relates that he was once in the hands of the inquisitors, but was delivered by the queen of Navarre. Buchanan has celebrated his learning in the following elegant epitaph:—

Qui studiis primus lucem intulit omnibus, artes
Edoctum cunctas hæc tegit urna Fabrum.
Heu! tenebræ tantum potuere extinguere lumen?
Si non in tenebris lux tamen ista micet.

The improvements made by Franchinus were followed by another of very considerable import, namely, the invention of Fugue, from the Latin Fuga, a chace, a species of symphoniac composition, in which a certain air, point, or subject is propounded by one part and prosecuted by another.

Zarlino resembles it to an echo; and it is not improbable that the accidental reverberation of some passage or particle of a musical tune might have originally suggested the idea of composition in fugue. The merit of this invention cannot, at this distance of time, be ascribed to any one musician in preference to another, but the antiquity of it may, with great appearance of probability, be fixed to about the beginning of the sixteenth century: this opinion is grounded on the following observations.

Franchinus, the most ancient of the musical writers who have expressly treated on composition in symphony, seems to have been an absolute stranger to this species of it, for his precepts relate solely to counterpoint, the terms fugue or canon never once occurring in any part of his writings; and the last of his tracts, viz., that De Harmonia Musicorum Instrumentorum, as already has been remarked, was published in 1518. On the other hand, in the Dode-cachordon of Glareanus of Basil we meet with fugues to a very great number, and indeed with a canon of a very extraordinary contrivance, composed by Iodocus Pratensis, for the practice of his master Lewis XII. king of France.

But to draw a little nearer towards a conclusion, there is extant a book entitled Micrologus, written by Andreas Ornithoparcus of Meyning, a master of arts, and a professor of music in several universities in Germany. This book was first published at Cologne in 1535, and contains, lib. II. cap vii. a definition and an example of canon to the following purpose :—

'A canon is an imaginary rule, drawing that part 'of the song which is not set down out of that 'which is set down. Or it is a rule which doth 'wittily discover the secrets of a song. Now we 'use canons either to shew art, or to make shorter 'work, or to try others cunning, thus :—

Comparing therefore the date of Franchinus's last treatise with that of the Micrologus, the interval between the publication of the one and the other of them appears to be seventeen years, a very short period for so considerable an improvement in the practice of musical composition.

It is natural to suppose that the first essays of this kind were fugues in two parts; and a fugue thus constructed was called two parts in one, for this reason, that the melody of each might be found in the other. In the framing of these parts, two things were necessary to be attended to, namely, the distance of time or number of measures at which the reply was to follow the principal subject, and the interval between the first note in each : with respect to the latter of these particulars, if the reply was precisely in the same notes with the subject, the composition was called a fugue in the unison ; and if in any other series of concordant intervals, as namely, the fourth or fifth above or below, it was denominated accordingly, as hereafter will be shewn. The primitive method of noting fugues appears by the following examples of two parts in one, contained in an ancient manuscript on vellum, of one Robert Johnson, a priest, the antiquity whereof may be traced back to near the beginning of the sixteenth century ; the first of these is evidently a fugue in the unison, of two parts in one, and the latter a fugue of two parts in one in the eleventh, or diapason cum diatessaron,*

* In compositions of this kind it seems to have been the ancient practice to frame them on a given plain-song, and that in general was some well-known melody of a psalm or hymn.

The plain-song on which this fugue is composed is taken from the notes of an ancient hymn, O Lux beata Trinitas, which seems to have been a very popular melody before the time of king Henry VIII. In Skelton's poem, entitled, The Bouge of Court, Riot is characterized as a rude, disorderly fellow, and one that could upon occasion sing it.

'Counter he coulde O Lux upon a potte,'

And Bird, whose excellence in this kind of composition is well known, made a great number of canons, on this very plain song.

A practice similar to this, of composing songs and divisions for instruments on a ground-base, prevailed for many years ; and it was not become quite obsolete in the time of Corelli, whose twelfth solo is a division on a well-known melody, known in England by the name of

as will appear by comparing the latter with the former part of each respectively.

Two parts in one, in one voyce, A mynnym after another.

The other part.

O LUX

Two parts in one, An eleventh above another.

Farinel's Ground; as is also the twelfth of Vivaldi's Suonate da Camera, Opera prima.

That Purcell was very fond of this kind of composition, appears throughout the Orpheus Britannicus, and elsewhere in his works, as well for the church as the theatre. In the year 1667 a book was published in Latin and English, by Christopher Simpson, a famous violist, entitled 'Chelys minuritionum artificio exornata,' or, the Division Viol, containing a great variety of old grounds, with divisions thereon : these were the constant exercises of practitioners, as well on the violin as the viol, till the time that Corelli's music was first introduced into England, before which he was looked on as an excellent performer who could play the country-dance tune of Old Sir Simon the king, with the divisions.

This which immediately follows is the resolution of a canon of two parts in one, composed by Bird, on the same plain song as the former, with this difference, that the reply is in longer notes than the principal, for which reason, it is called a fugue by diminution. Of these two kinds as also of fugue of four parts in two, and of three in one, the succeeding are examples :—

WILLIAM BIRD.

WILLIAM BIRD.

WILLIAM BIRD.

Of the foregoing canons of Bird it may be remarked, that as the former examples of two parts in one are studies on the well-known plain-song of O Lux, so this is an exercise on a plain-song of Miserere, for the origin whereof we are to seek: the celebrity of it may however be inferred from this circumstance, that Dr. John Bull, who was exquisitely skilled in canon, made a variety of compositions on it, some whereof will hereafter be inserted. But we are told by Morley that Bird and Alphonso Ferabosco made canons, each to the number of forty, and his friend Mr. George Waterhouse above a thousand, upon the same plain song of Miserere, and it is probable that this of Bird is one of the number. The passage is curious, and is as follows: 'If you thinke to imploy 'anie time in making of parts on a plain-song, 'I would counsell you diligentlie to peruse those ' waies which my loving maister (never without 'reverence to be named of musitians) M. Bird and 'M. Alphonso, in a virtuous contention in love between 'themselves, made upon the plain-song of Miserere; 'but a contention as I said in love, which caused 'them strive everie one to surmount another without 'malice, envie or backbiting: but by great labour, 'studie, and paines each making other censure of that

'which they had done. Which contention of theirs, 'speciallie without envie, caused them both become 'more excellent in that kind, and winne such a name, 'and gaine such credite, as will never perish so long 'as musicke indureth. Therefore there is no waie 'readier to cause you become perfect than to contend 'with some one or other, not in malice (for so is 'your contention upon passion not for love of vertue) 'but in love shewing your adversarie your worke, 'and not scorning to bee corrected of him, and to 'amende your fault, if hee speake with reason: but 'of this enough. To return to M. Bird and M. 'Alphonso, though either of them made to the num- 'ber of fortie waies, and could have made infinite 'more at their pleasure, yet hath one manne, my 'friend and fellow, M. George Waterhouse,* upon 'the same plain-song of Miserere for varietie sur- 'passed all who ever laboured in that kinde of studie.

* Of this person, so excellent in music as he is above said to have been, as far as appears after a diligent research and enquiry, there is not a single composition remaining. All that can be learned concerning him is, that he was first of Lincoln, and afterwards of the chapel to queen Elizabeth, and that having spent several years in the study and practice of music, in the year 1592 he supplicated at Oxford for the degree of bachelor, but Wood was not able to discover that he was admitted to it. Fasti, Anno 1592. By the entry in the cheque-book of the chapel royal, it appears that he died the eighteenth day of February, 1601,

'For hee hath already made a thousand waies (yea,
'and though I shoulde talk of halfe as manie more,
'I should not be far wide of the truth) everie one
'different and several from another. But because
'I do hope very shortlie that the same shall be
'published for the benefite of the worlde, and his
'owne perpetual glorie, I will cease to speake anie
'more of them, but onlie to admonish you, that
'whoso will be excellent must both spende much
'time in practice, and looke over the doings of
'other men.'

Touching these exercises, it is to be observed, that
they are calculated to facilitate the practice of composing in fugue, by exhibiting the many various
ways in which the point may be brought in; or, in
other words, how the replicate may be made to
correspond with, or answer, the principal. The
utility of this kind of study may be in some measure
inferred from a variety of essays in it by Bird, Bull,
and others, yet to be met with in ancient collections
of music; and to a still greater degree from a little
book entitled 'Divers and sundrie waies of two
'parts in one to the number of fortie upon one
'playn-song; sometimes placing the ground above
'and two parts benethe, and otherwise the ground
'benethe, and two parts above. Or againe, otherwise
'the ground sometimes in the middest betweene both.
'Likewise other conceites, which are plainlie set
'downe for the profite of those which would attaine
'unto knowledge, by John Farmer, imprinted at
'London, 1591,' small octavo.

Elway Bevin, a disciple of Tallis, a gentleman
extraordinary of the royal chapel in 1605, and
organist of the cathedral church of Bristol, published
in the year 1631, a book, which, though entitled
a Brief Introduction of Music and Descant, is in
truth a treatise on canon, and contains a manifold
variety of fugues of two, three, and more parts in
one, upon one plain-song most skilfully and ingeniously constructed; but of him, and also of this
his work, an account will be given hereafter.

Fugues in the unison were also called rounds,
from the circular progression of the melody; and
this term suggested the method of writing them in
a circular form, of which the following canon of
Clemens Non Papa, musician to the emperor Charles
V. with the resolution thereof in modern characters,
is an example :—

CANON IN THE UNISON, FOR FIVE VOICES.

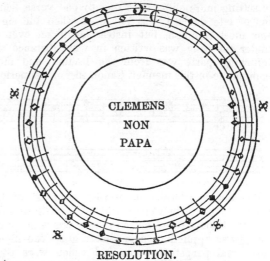

RESOLUTION.

A fugue written in one line, whether in a circle or
otherwise, with directions for the other parts to
follow, is called a Canon. Morley ascribes the invention of this compendious method of writing to the
Italian and French musicians; his account of it is
curious, and is here given in his own words : 'The
'Frenchmen and Italians have used a waie, that
'though there were four or five partes in one, yet
'might it be perceived and sung at the first; and the
'manner thereof is this. Of how manie parts the
'canon is, so manie cliefes do they set at the beginning
'of the verse; still causing that which standeth nearest
'unto the musick serve for the leading parte; the
'next towards the left hand for the next following
'parte, and so consequentlie to the last. But if
'betweene anie two cliefes you finde rests, those
'belong to that part which the cliefe standing next
'unto them on the left side, signifieth.

EXAMPLE.

'Here be two parts in one in the Diapason cum dia-
'tessaron, or, as we tearme it, in the eleventh above;
'where you see first a C sol fa ut cliefe standing on
'the lowest rule, and after it three minime rests.
'Then standing the F fa ut cliefe on the fourth rule
'from below; and because that standeth neerest to the

'notes, the base (which that cliefe representeth) must
'begin, resting a minim rest after the plain-song, and
'the treble three minim rests. And least you should
'misse in reckoning your pauses or rests, the note
'whereupon the following part must begin is marked
'with this sign ?. It is true that one of those two,

'the sign or the rests is superfluous; but the order 'of setting more cliffes than one to one verse being 'but of late devised, was not used when the signe 'was most common, but instead of them, over or 'under the song was written in what distance the 'following parte was from the leading, and most 'commonlie in this manner, Canon in,* or * superiore 'or interiore. But to shun the labour of writing 'those words, the cliffes and rests have been devised, 'shewing the same thinge. And to the intent you 'may the better conceive it, here is another example 'wherein the treble beginneth, and the meane fol-'loweth within a semibreve after, in the Hypodia-'pente or fifth below':—

The above relation of Morley accounts for the origin of the term Canon, which in truth signifies no more than a rule; but no sooner was it invented, than it was applied to perpetual fugue, even in the score; and perpetual fugue and canon were then, and now are, looked on as convertible terms; than which it seems nothing can be more improper, for when a fugue is once scored it ceases to be a canon.

From fugues in the unison, or of many parts in one, musicians proceeded to the invention of such as gave the answer to the subject, at a prescribed distance of time, in some concordant interval, as namely, the fourth, fifth, or eighth, either above or below; and to distinguish between the one and the other the Greek prepositions Epi and Hypo were added to the names of the consonances in which the parts were to follow; for instance, where the reply was above the principal, it was said to be in the epidiatessaron, epidiapente, or epidiapason; when it was below, it was called hypodiatessaron, hypo-diapente, hypodiapason;* adding in either case, where the number of parts required it, a farther direction: for an example of one of these kinds we have that celebrated composition of our countryman William Bird, to the words 'Non nobis Domine,' which in the manner of speaking above described would be called a canon of three parts, viz., in the hypodiatessaron et diapason, post tempus, and in the Musurgia, tom. I. page 389, is a canon of four parts in the hypodiapente, diapason, et hypodiapason cum diapente, composed by Emilio Rossi, chapel-master of Loretto, remarkable for the elegance of its con-texture, the resolution whereof is here inserted:

EMILIO ROSSI.

CHAP. LXVII.

SOON after its invention farther improvements were made in this species of composition, by the con-trivance of fugues, that sung both backward and forward, or, in musical phrase, recte et retro; and of others that sung per Arsin and Thesin, that is to say, so as that one part ascended while the other descended. Of the former kind the following canon of Dr. John Bull, with the resolution thereof in the present method of notation, is an example:—

* These are the most general forms of canon, but Morley, pag. 172, says a canon may be made in any distance, comprehended within the reach of the voice.

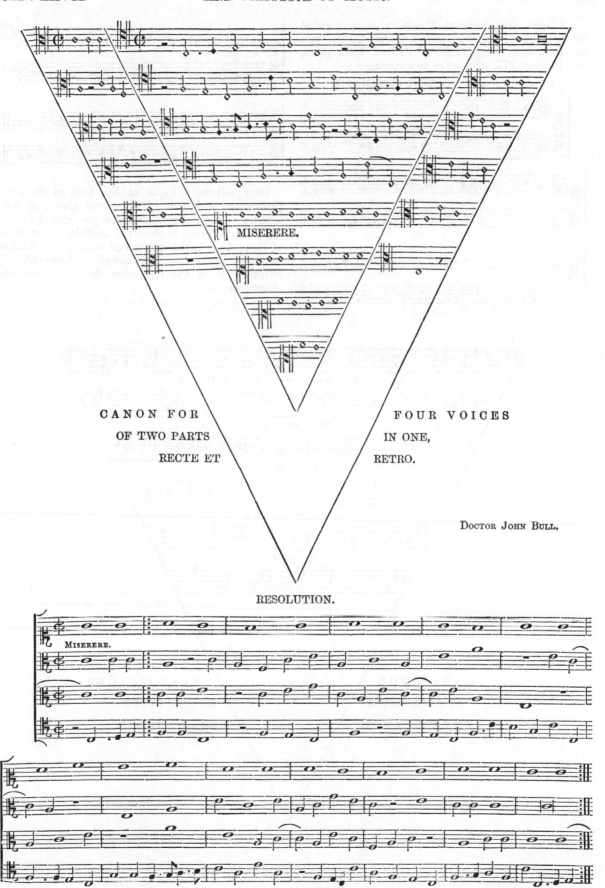

CANON FOR   FOUR VOICES

OF TWO PARTS   IN ONE,

RECTE ET   RETRO.

DOCTOR JOHN BULL.

RESOLUTION.

Of fugue per Arsin et Thesin, or, as it is called by the Italians, per Muovimenti contrarii, this from the Istitutione Harmoniche of Zarlino, terza parte, cap. lv. pag. 277, may serve as a specimen :—

FUGA PER MUOVIMENTI CONTRARII.

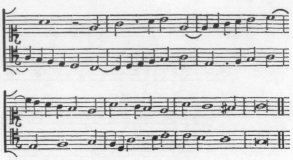

Here follows a fugue of Dr. Bull on the same plain-song with that of his above given, of both kinds, viz., recte et retro, and also per arsin et thesin; the canon whereof, to shew the artificial construction of its parts, is in the manuscript whence it was taken exhibited in the form of a triangle, and immediately following it, is the resolution thereof in modern characters :—

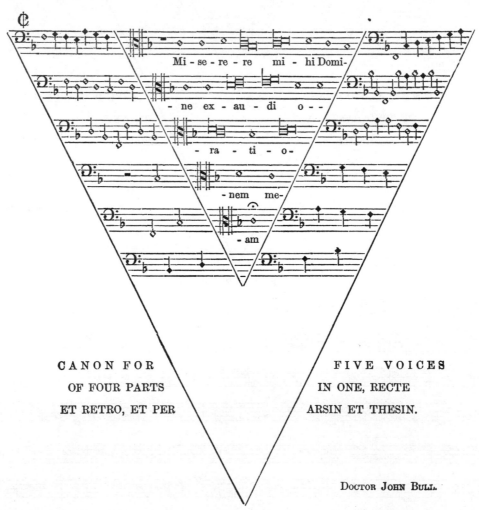

CANON FOR   FIVE VOICES

OF FOUR PARTS   IN ONE, RECTE

ET RETRO, ET PER   ARSIN ET THESIN.

DOCTOR JOHN BULL.

RESOLUTION.

This and the former by the same author, in the manuscript from which they were taken, are given in a triangular form, with a view to exhibit the singularity of their contexture, and the mutual relation and various progressions of the several sounds; and that figure is here preserved in both instances: but lest this representation should appear too enigmatical, the resolution of each canon in score is above given.

Morley, in the second part of his Introduction, pag. 103, has given a fugue of Bird's composing, of two parts in one, per Arsin et Thesin, with the point reverted, note for note, of which he says, 'that 'whoever shall go about to make such another upon 'a common knowne plaine-song or hymne, shall 'find more difficultie than he looked for; and that 'although he shoulde assaie twentie several hymnes 'or plain-songs for finding of one to his purpose, 'he doubts if he should anie waie goe beyonde the 'excellencie of that which he speaks of, for which 'reason he has given it in this form :—

WILLIAM BIRD.*

Butler is lavish in his commendations of this fugue; indeed his words are a sort of comment on it, and as they are calculated to point out and unfold its excellencies, they are here given from his Principles of Music, lib. I. cap. iii. sect. 4. in his own words :—

'The fifth and last observation is, that all sorts of

* The several examples of canon by Dr. Bull and Bird, above given, are not in print, and it may therefore be expected that their authenticity should be ascertained: with respect to the former, they are taken from a very curious MS. formerly in the library of Dr. Pepusch, in an outer leaf whereof is written 'Ex Dono Willi Theed;' this Mr. Theed was many years a member of the academy of ancient music; and very well skilled in the science. The book contains, among many other compositions of the like nature, the above canons of Dr. Bull, and also that of Clemens Non Papa, with the several resolutions thereof in the form above inserted.

As to the examples ascribed to Bird, they are taken from a MS. also once part of Dr. Pepusch's library, in the hand-writing of Mr. Galliard: the fugues upon O Lux and Miserere are written in canon with the usual sign for the parts to follow: the resolutions are clearly the studies of Mr. Galliard, who it seems thought himself warranted in the insertion of flat and sharp signatures in many instances, though no such appear in the canons themselves. Both these manuscripts are now in the collection of the author of this work.

It is necessary here to remark that these several exemplars of fugue and canon are adduced with a view solely to investigate and explain the nature of these intricate species of composition, for which purpose the resolutions alone in the latter instances will be thought sufficient.

'fugues (reports and reverts of the same, and of 'divers points in the same, and divers canons, and in 'the same and divers parts) are sometimes most 'elegantly intermedled, as in that inimitable lesson 'of Mr. Bird's, containing two parts in one upon 'a plain-song, wherein the first part beginneth with 'a point, and then reverteth it note for note in 'a fourth or eleventh; and the second part first 'reverteth the point in the fourth as the first did, 'and then reporteth it in the unison; before the end 'whereof, the first part having rested three minims 'after his revert, singeth a second point, and re-'verteth it in the eighth; and the second first re-'verteth the point in a fourth, and then reporteth 'it in a fourth: lastly, the first singeth a third point, 'and reverteth it in the fifth, and then reporteth it 'in an unison, and so closeth with some annexed 'notes; and the second first reverteth it in a fifth, 'and then reporteth it in an unison, and so closeth 'with a second revert; where, to make up the full 'harmony, unto these three parts is added a fourth, 'which very musically toucheth still upon the points 'reported and reverted.

But here a distinction is to be noted between perpetual fugues, such as those above given, in which every note in the one part has its answer in the other part; and that other transitory kind of fugue, in which the point only, whatever it be, is repeated in the succeeding parts; in this case the intermediate notes are composed ad placitum, for which reason the former kind of fugue is termed by Zarlino and other Italian writers, Fuga legata, and the other Fuga sciolta, that is to say, strict or constrained, and free or licentious fugue.

The Italians also give to the leading part of a fugue and its replicate or answer, the appellations of Guida and Consequenza; Morley, and others after him, distinguish them by the names of principal and reply: and with the appearance of reason it is said that the notes in each should sol-fa alike; that is to say, the intervals in each part ought to be precisely the same with respect to the succession of the tones and semitones; nevertheless, this rule is not strictly adhered to, a spurious kind of fugue having, in the very infancy of this invention sprung up, known by the name of Fuga in nomine, as being to appearance and nominally only, fugue, and not that species of composition in the strict sense of musical language.

Zarlino and other Italian writers speak of a kind of fugue called Contrapunto doppio, double counterpoint, which supposes the notes in each part to be of equal time, but that the subject of the principal and the reply shall be different in respect of the point, being yet in harmony with each other: the exact opposition of note to note in this kind of composition was, soon after its invention, dispensed with, and the principal and its reply made to consist of notes of different lengths or times; after which it obtained the name of double descant, the terms descant and counterpoint being always used in opposition to each other. Sethus Calvisius includes both under the comprehensive name Harmonia Gemina; and to fugues of this kind, where a third point or subject is introduced, he gives the name of Ter-gemina. Morley has given examples of each at the end of the second part of his Introduction.

From the foregoing explanation of the nature of canon it must appear to be a very elaborate species of musical composition, and in which perhaps, substance, that is to say, fine air and melody is made to give place to form; just as we see in those fanciful poetical conceits, acrostics, anagrams, chronograms, &c. where the sense and spirit of the composition is ever subservient to its form; but the comparison does not hold throughout, for the musical compositions above spoken of derive an advantage of a peculiar kind from those restraints to which they are subjected; for in the first place the harmony is thereby rendered more close, compact, and full; nor does this harmony arise merely from the concordance of sounds in the several parts, but each distinct part produces a succession of harmony in itself, the laws of fugue or canon being such as generally to exclude those dissonant intervals which take away from the sweetness or melody of the point. In the next place the ear is gratified by the successive repetition of the point of a fugue through all its parts; and the mind receives the same pleasure in tracing the exact resemblance of the several parts each to the other, as it does in comparing a picture or statue with its archetype; the truth of this observation must be apparent to those who are aware of the scholastic distinction of beauty into absolute and relative.

The general directions for singing of fugue when written in canon are such as these: Fuga in tertia superiore post tempus.—Fuga in Hypodiapente, post tempus.—Fuga 5 vocum in tertia superiore, post tempus.—Fuga in Unisono post duo tempora, et per contrarium motum. But many musicians have been less explicit, as choosing to give them an enigmatical form, and leaving it to the peruser to exercise his patience in the investigation of that harmony which might easily have been rendered obvious. Morley, pag. 173 of his Introduction, has given an enigmatical canon of Iodocus Pratensis; and he there refers to others in the Introductions of Raselius and Sethus Calvisus: he has also given a canon of his own invention in the figure of a cross, with its resolution; but there is one in that form infinitely more curious in a work entitled El Melopeo y Maestro, written by Pedro Cerone, of Bergamo, master of the royal chapel of Naples, published in 1613.*

It now remains to speak of a species of fugue in the unison, wherein for particular reasons the strict rules of harmony are frequently dispensed with, namely, the catch or round, which Butler, after Calvisus thus defines: 'A catch is also a kind of 'fuga,' when upon a certain rest the parts do follow 'one another round in the unison. In which concise 'harmony there is much variety of pleasing conceits, 'the composers whereof assume unto themselves 'a special licence of breaking Priscian's head, in 'unlawful taking of discords, and in special con-

* In this voluminous work are contained a great number of musical conceits, which whoever has a mind to divert himself with them, will find in the twenty-second book, entitled 'Que es los enigmas musicalis.'

'secutions of unisons and eighths, when they help to 'the melody of a part.'†

This, though the sentiment of both Calvisus and Butler, is by no means a true definition of a catch; and indeed the term itself seems to indicate a thing very different from that which they have described, for whence can come the appellation but from the verb Catch? yet is there nothing in the passage above-cited to this purpose. A catch, in the musical sense of the word, is a fugue in the unison, wherein, to humour some conceit in the words, the melody is broken, and the sense interrupted in one part, and caught again or supplied by another: an instance of this may be remarked in the well-known catch 'Let's 'lead good honest lives,' ascribed to Purcell, though in truth composed many years before his time, by Cranford, a singing-man of St. Paul's, to words of a very different import. See a collection of catches and rounds, entitled Catch that Catch can, or the Musical Companion, printed for old John Playford, Lond. 1677, oblong quarto; in this both the words and the music catch, as they do also in another elegant composition of this kind, 'Come here's the 'good health, &c,' by Dr. Cæsar, and ' Jack thou'rt 'a toper,' both printed by Pearson in 1710.

Butler refers to three examples of this kind of song in Calvisus; but the truth of the matter is, that it

† To say the truth, notwithstanding the severe restrictions to which it is subject, canon does in many respects afford a great latitude for invention. Kircher relates, that in the writing of his Musurgia, more especially that part which treats of canon, he was assisted by Pietro Francesco Valentini of Rome, who gave him the following:—

Canon Polymorphus.

of which he thus speaks: Musurg. Univ. tom. I. lib. V. cap. xix. 'This wonderful canon contains ten times, one pause, and seventeen 'notes; it may sung by two, three, four, or five voices, more than two 'thousand ways; nay, by combining the parts, this variety may be in-'finitely extended. The second voice is retrograde to the first, the third 'is inverse of the first, or proceeds by contrary motion to it; the fourth 'is retrograde to the third, as may be seen hereunder:—

second voice.

third voice.

fourth voice

Kircher adds that the same musician proposed another canon, which he called Nodus Salomonis, which may be sung by ninety-six voices, namely twenty-four in each part, treble, counter-tenor, tenor, and bass, and yet there are only four notes in the canon; but it is to be observed, that to introduce a regular variety of harmony, some of the ninety-six voices are to sing all longs, some all breves, some semibreves, some minims, some semi-minims. See the relation at length in the Musurgia, tom. I. pag. 403, et seq., with the disposition of the several parts in their order.

Kircher, in the Musurgia, tom. I. page 408, says he afterwards found out that the same canon might be sung by five hundred and twelve voices, or, which is the same thing, distributed into one hundred and twenty-eight choirs; and afterwards proceeds to shew how it may be sung by twelve million two hundred thousand voices, nay, by an infinite number; and then says, in Corollary iii. that this place of the Apocalypse is made clear, viz., chap. xiv. 'And I heard the voice of harpers harping 'with their harps, and they sung as it were a new song, &c., and no man 'could learn that song but the one hundred and forty-four thousand 'which were redeemed from the earth.' Kircher asserts that this passage in scripture may be interpreted literally, and then shews that the canon above described may be so disposed as to be sung by one hundred and forty-four thousand voices. Musurg. tom. I. pag. 414.

was known in England long before his time. Of this the catch 'Sumer is icumen in,' is evidence ; and it has been said, with some shew of probability, that the English were the inventors of it. Dr. Tudway, formerly music professor in the university of Cambridge, and who for many years was employed in collecting music books for Edward earl of Oxford, has asserted it in positive terms in a letter to a son of his, yet extant in manuscript ; and it may with no less degree of certainty be said, that as this kind of music seems to correspond with the native humour and freedom of English manners, there are more examples of it here to be found than in any other country whatsoever. The following specimens of rounds or catches in three, four, and five parts, may suffice to give an idea of the nature of this species of composition : others will hereafter be inserted, as occasion shall require. As touching the first, it may be deemed a matter of some curiosity. In Shakespeare's play of Twelfth Night, Act II. Scene iii. Sir Toby and Sir Andrew agree to sing a catch : Sir Toby proposes that it shall be 'Thou knave,' upon which follows this dialogue :—*

CLOWN. Hold thy peace thou knave? knight, I shall be constrain'd in't to call thee knave, knight.

SIR AND. 'Tis not the first time I have constrain'd one to call me knave. Begin, fool ; it begins 'Hold 'thy peace.'

CLOWN. I shall never begin if I hold my peace.

SIR AND. Good I'faith : come begin. [They sing a catch.]

The above conversation has a plain allusion to the first of the catches here inserted, 'Hold thy peace,' the humour of which consists in this, that each of the three persons that sing calls, and is called, knave in turn :—

CANON IN THE UNISON.   A 3 Voc.

CANON IN THE UNISON.   A 3 Voc.

* That the songs occasionally introduced in Shakespeare's plays were such as were familiar in his time, is clearly shewn by Dr. Percy, in his Reliques of Ancient English Poetry, who has been so fortunate as to recover many of them ; the above may be added to the number. as may also this alluded to in the same scene of Twelfth Night, by the words Three merry men be wee.'

The Wisemen were but seven ; nor more shall be for me.
The Muses were but nine. The worthies three times three.   [are we.
    And three merry boyes, and three merry boyes, and three merry boyes
The Vertues they are sev'n, and three the greater be.
The Cæsars they were twelve, and the fatal sisters three.   [are we.
    And three merry girles, and three merry girles, and three merry girles

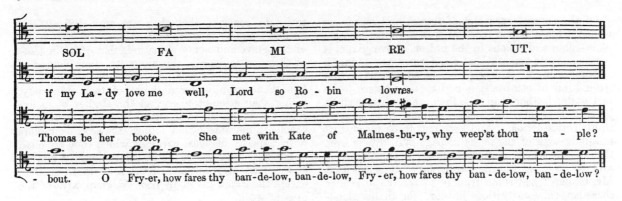

SOL   FA   MI   RE   UT.

if my La - dy love me well, Lord so Ro - bin lowres.

Thomas be her boote, She met with Kate of Malmes - bu - ry, why weep'st thou ma - ple?

- bout. O Fry - er, how fares thy ban - de - low, ban - de - low, Fry - er, how fares thy ban - de - low, ban - de - low?

CANON IN THE UNISON.   A 5 Voc.

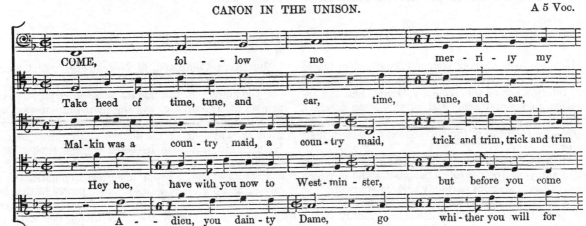

COME,   fol - - low   me   mer - ri - ly my

Take heed of time, tune, and   ear,   time,   tune, and ear,

Mal - kin was a coun - try maid, a coun - try maid,   trick and trim, trick and trim

Hey hoe,   have with you now to West - min - ster,   but before you come

A - - dieu, you dain - ty Dame,   go   whi - ther you will for

mates,   let all a - - gree,   and make no faults.

and then with-out all   doubt   we need not fear   to sing this catch through - out.

as she might be,   she would needs to the court She said,   to sell milk and fir - men - ty.

there,   be - - cause the way is   far, some pret - ty talk   let's hear.

me,   you are the ve - ry   same   I took you for to be.

CANON IN THE UNISON.   A 5 Voc.

HOW should we sing well   and   not be wea - ry,

and   not be wea - - ry, Since we lack mo - ney to

make us mer - - ry,   to make us mer - ry,

Since we lack mo - ney to make us mer - ry,

Since we lack mo - ney to make us mer - ry.

x

Of the several examples of fugues and rounds, or to adopt the common mode of speech, of fugues on a plain-song, and canons in the unison, above given, it is necessary to remark that the former are adduced, as being some of the most ancient specimens of that strict kind of composition perhaps any where to be met with : farther than this, they are studies, perhaps juvenile ones, of Bird, and are alluded to by Morley in his Introduction. And here it is to be noted, that the plain-song of the fugue in page 295, differs from that of the others, and from its serpentine figure is said to be ' per naturam synophe.' It seems that Mr. Galliard had some trouble to resolve or render these several compositions in score, for in his manu-

script he remarks that they are very difficult and curious : and it is more than conjectured that many of the grave and acute signatures that occur in some of them, were inserted by him with some degree of hesitation ; it was nevertheless thought proper to retain them, even under a doubt of their propriety, rather than attempt to correct the studies of so excellent a judge of harmony. As to the rounds or canons in the unison that follow, they are exemplars of that species of vocal harmony which they are cited to explain : they are of the sixteenth century, and we know of no compositions of the kind more ancient, except the canon given in book V. chap. xlv. of the present work.

BOOK VIII.   CHAP. LXVIII.

HAVING in a regular course of succession traced the several improvements in music, including therein the reformation of the scale by Guido, and the invention of counterpoint, and of the canto figurato, with all the various modifications of fugue and canon, it remains to speak of the succeeding writers in their order.

ALANIUS VARENIUS, of Montaubon, in Tholouse, about the year 1503, wrote Dialogues, some of which treat of the science of harmony and its elements.

LUDOVICUS CÆLIUS RHODIGINUS flourished about the year 1510 ; he wrote nothing professedly on the subject of music, yet in his work De Antiquarum Lectionem, in thirty books, are interspersed many things relating thereto, particularly in lib. V. cap. 23, 25, 26. Kircher, in the Musurgia, tom. I. pag. 27, cites from him a relation to the following effect, viz. : That he, Cælius Rhodiginus, being at Rome, saw a parrot, which had been purchased by Cardinal Ascanius, at the price of an hundred golden crowns, which parrot did most articulately, and as a man would, repeat in words the Creed of the Christian faith. Cælius Rhodiginus was tutor to Julius Cæsar Scaliger, and died in 1525, of grief, as it is said, for the fate of the battle of Pavia, in which his patron Francis the First, from whom he had great expectations, was taken prisoner. He is taxed with having borrowed some things from Erasmus, without making the usual acknowledgments.

GREGORIUS REISCHIUS, of Friburg, was the author of a work entitled Margarita Philosophica,* i. e. the Philosophical Pearl, a work comprehending not only a distinct and separate discourse on each of the seven liberal sciences, in which, by the way, judicial astrology is considered as a branch of astronomy, but a treatise on physics, or natural philosophy, metaphysics, and ethics, in all twelve books ; that on music is taken chiefly from Boetius, yet it seems to owe some part of its merit to the improvements of Franchinus. The Margarita Philosophica is a thick quarto ; it was printed at Basil in 1517, and in France six years after ; the latter edition was revised and corrected by Orontius Finæus, of the college of Navarre. †

* This book, the Margarita Philosophica, is frequently mentioned in a work entitled Il Musico Testore, by Zaccaria Tevo, printed at Venice in 1706, in which many passages are cited from it verbatim.

† Bayle ORONCE FINE.

JOHANNES COCHLEUS, of Nuremberg, was famous about the year 1525, for his Polemical writings. He was the author of Rudimenta Musicæ et Geometria, printed at Nuremberg, and the tutor of Glareanus, as the latter mentions in his Dodecachordon, a doctor in divinity, and dean of the church of Francfort on the Maine. He was born in 1503, but the time of his death is uncertain, some writers making it in 1552, and others sooner. From his great reputation, as a scholar and divine, it is more than probable that he was one of the learned foreigners consulted touching the divorce of Henry the Eighth, for the name of Johannes Cochlæus occurs in the list of them. Peter Aron, in his Toscanello, celebrates him by the title of Phonascus of Nuremberg.

LUDOVICUS FOLIANUS, of Modena, published at Venice, in 1529, in folio, a book intitled Musica Theoretica; it is written in Latin, and divided into three sections, the first contains an investigation of those proportions of greater and lesser inequality necessary to be understood by musicians ; the second treats of the consonances, where, by the way, it is to be observed that the author discriminates with remarkable accuracy between the greater and lesser tone ; and by insisting, as he does in this section De Utilitate Toni majoris et minoris, plainly discovers that he was not a Pythagorean, which is much to be wondered at, seeing that the substance of his book appears for the most part to have been taken from Boetius, who all men know was a strict adherer to the doctrines of Pythagoras. It is therefore said, and with great appearance of reason, that it is to Folianus that the introduction into practice of the intense or syntonous diatonic, in preference to the ditonic diatonic, is to be attributed. This particular will appear to be more worthy of remark, when it is known, that about the middle of the sixteenth century it became a matter of controversy which of those two species of the diatonic genus was best accommodated to practice. Zarlino contended for the intense or syntonous diatonic of Ptolemy, or rather Didymus, for he it was that first distinguished between the greater and lesser tone. Vincentio Galilei, on the other hand, preferred that division of Aristoxenus, which, though irrational according to the judgment of the ear, gave to the tetrachord two tones and a half. In the course of the dispute, which was conducted with great warmth on both sides, Galilei takes great pains to inform his reader that Zarlino was not the first that discovered the supposed excellence of that division which he preferred, for that Ludovico Fogliano, sixty or seventy years before, had done the same ;* and in the table or index to his book, article Lodovico Fogliano, which contains a summary of his arguments on this head, he speaks thus : 'Lodovico Fogliano fu il primo ' che considerasse che il diatonico che si canta hoggi, ' non era il ditoneo, ma il syntono ;' which assertion contains a solution of a doubt which Dr. Wallis en-

tertained, namely, whether Zarlino or some more ancient writer first introduced the syntonous or intense diatonic into practice.†

The third section of Folianus's book is principally on the division of the Monochord, in which he undertakes to shew the necessity of setting off D, and also of Bb twice.

Many of the divisions, particularly in the first chapter of the second section, are exemplified by cuts, which as they shew the method of using the Monochord, with the ratios of the consonances, and are in other respects curious, are here inserted.

* Dial. della Musica antica e moderna, pag. 112.

† Append. de Veter. Harmon. quarto, pag. 318.

Johannes Froschius, a doctor of divinity, and prior of the Carmelites at Augsburg, was the author of Opusculum Rerum Musicalium, printed at Strasburg in 1535, a thin folio, and a very methodical and concise book, but it contains little that can be said to be original.

Andreas Ornithoparcus, a master of arts in the university of Meyning, was the author of a very learned and instructive treatise on music, intitled Micrologus, printed at Cologne in 1535, in oblong quarto. It is written in Latin, and was translated into English by our countryman John Douland, the celebrated lutenist, and published by him in 1609. This work contains the substance of a course of lectures which Ornithoparcus had publicly read in the universities of Tubingen, Heidelberg, and Mentz. It is divided into four books, the contents whereof are as follow.

The first book is dedicated to the governors of the state of Lunenburg. The first three chapters contain a general division of music into mundane, humane, and instrumental, according to Boetius, which the author again divides into organical, harmonical, speculative, active, mensural, and plain music, and also the rudiments of singing by the hexachords, according to the introductory or scale of Guido. In his explanation whereof he relates that the Ambrosians distinguished the stations of the cliffs by lines of different colours, that is to say, they gave to F FA UT a red, to C SOL FA UT a blue, and to bb a sky-coloured line ; but that the Gregorians, as he calls them, whom the church of Rome follow, mark all the lines with

one colour, and describe each of the keys by its first letter, or some character derived from it.

In the fourth chapter he limits the number of tones to eight ; and, speaking of the ambit or compass of each, says there are granted but ten notes wherein each tone may have his course ; and for this assertion he cites the authority of St. Bernard, but adds, that the licentious ranging of modern musicians hath added an eleventh to each.

The fifth and sixth chapters contain the rules for solfaing by the hexachords, and for the mutations.

In the seventh chapter he speaks of the consonant and dissonant intervals, and cites Ambrosius Nolanus and Erasmus to shew, that as the disdiapason is the natural compass of man's voice, all music should be confined to that interval.

In the eighth and ninth chapters he teaches to divide, and recommends the use of the Monochord, by the help whereof he says any one may by himself learn any song, though never so weighty.

Chapter X. is intitled De Musica ficta, which he thus defines : 'Fained musicke is that which the 'Greeks call Synemmenon, a song made beyond the 'regular compass of the scale ; or it is a song which 'is full of conjunctions.'

By these conjunctions are to be understood conjunctions of the natural and molle hexachords by the chord Synemmenon, characterized by b ; and in this chapter are discernible the rudiments of transposition, a practice which seems to have been originally suggested by that of substituting the round, in the place of the square b, from which station it was first removed into the place of E LA MI, and has since been made to occupy various other situations ; * as has also the acute signature ✗, which although at first invented to perfect the interval between ♮ MI and F FA UT, which is a semidiapente or imperfect fifth, it is well known is now made to occupy the place of G SOL RE UT, C SOL FA UT, and other chords.

The eleventh chapter treats of transposition, which the author says is twofold, that is to say, of the song and of the key, but in truth both are transpositions of the song, which may be transposed either by an actual removal of the notes to some other line or space than that in which they stand, or by the removal of the cliff to some other line, thereby giving by elevation or depression to each note a different power.

The ecclesiastical tones are the subject of the twelfth and thirteenth chapters of the first book : in these are contained rules for the intonation of the Psalms, in which the author takes occasion to cite a treatise of Pontifex, i. e. pope John XXII., who it seems wrote on music, and an author named Michael Galliculo de Muris, a most learned man, author of certain rules of the true order of singing.

In treating of the tones Ornithoparcus follows for

---

* That the use of the tetrachord synemmenon, or rather of its characteristic b round, was to avoid the tritonus or superfluous fourth between F FA UT and b MI, must appear upon reflection, but this author has made it apparent in the following, which is the fourth of his rules for ficta music.

'Marking FA in b FA ♯ MI, or in any other place, if the song from 'that shall make an immediate rising to a fourth, a fifth, or an eighth, 'even there FA must necessarily be marked to eschew a tritone, a semi-'diapente, or a semidiapason, and in usual and forbidden moods, as 'appeareth in the example underwritten :—

An Exercise of Ficta Musicke.

the most part St. Bernard and Franchinus; his formula of the eight tones, as also of the Peregrine or wandering tone, differs but very little from that of Franchinus in his Practica Musicæ, herein before exhibited.

In the thirteenth and last chapter of this book the author shews that divers men are delighted with divers modes, an observation that Guido had made before in the thirteenth chapter of his Micrologus, and to this purpose he says: 'Some are delighted 'with the crabbed and courtly wandering of the 'first tone; others do affect the hoarse gravity of 'the second; others take pleasure in the severe, and 'as it were disdainful stalking of the third; others 'are drawn with the flattering sound of the fourth; 'others are moved with the modest wantonness of the 'fifth; others are led with the lamenting voice of the 'sixth; others do willingly hear the warlike leapings 'of the seventh; others do love the decent, and as it 'were matronal-like carriage of the eighth.'

The second book is dedicated to the author's 'worthy and kind friend George Brachius, a most 'skilful musician, and chief doctor of the Duke of 'Wittenberg his chappell.'

In the second chapter of this book the author explains the nature of mensural music, and the figures used therein: these he says were anciently five, but that those of after ages have drawn out others for quickness sake; those described by him are eight in number, viz., the large, long, breve, semibreve, minim, crotchet, quaver, and semiquaver; but it is worthy of notice that he gives to the semibreve two forms, the one resembling a lozenge, agreeable to the character of the semibreve now or lately in use, the other that of an equilateral triangle or half lozenge.

The third chapter contains an explanation of the ligatures from Franchinus, but much too concise to be intelligible.

The fourth chapter treats of mood, time, and prolation, of which three terms the following is his definition: 'The degrees of music, by which we 'know the value of the principal figures, are three, to 'wit, mood, time, and prolation. Neither doth any 'of them deale upon all notes, but each onely with 'certaine notes that belong to each. As mood dealeth 'with larges and longs, time with breefes, prolation 'with semibreefes.' This general definition is followed by one more particular, which is here given in the translator's own words:—

'A Moode (as Franchinus saith in the second 'booke, cap. 7. of his Pract.) is the measure of longs 'in larges, or of breefes in longs. Or it is the 'beginning of the quantitie of larges and longs, 'measuring them either by the number of two, or the number of three.

'Time is a breefe which contains in it two or three 'semibreefes. Or it is the measuring of two or three 'semibreefes in one breefe. And it is twofold, to 'wit, perfect: and this is a breefe measured with 'three semibreefes. Whose signe is the number of 'three joined with a circle or a semicircle, or a 'perfect circle set without a number, thus O 3. C 3. O.

'The imperfect is wherein a breefe is measured only 'by two semibreefes. Which is knowne by the num- 'ber of two joyned with a perfect circle, or a semi- 'circle, or a semicircle without a number, thus O 2. 'C 2.

'Wherefore prolation is the essential quantitie of 'semibreefes; or it is the setting of two or three 'minims against one semibreefe; and it is twofold, 'to wit, the greater (which is a semibreefe measured 'by three minims, or the comprehending of three 'minims in one semibreefe) whose signe is a point 'inclosed in a signe thus, ⊙ ⊖. The lesser pro- 'lation is a semibreefe measured with two minims 'onely, whose signe is the absence of a pricke. For 'Franchinus saith, they carry with them the imper- 'fecting of the figure when the signes are wanting.'

In the course of this explanation the author takes occasion to mention the extrinsical and intrinsical signs in mensural music; the former he says are the circle, the number, and the point. As to the circle, when entire it originally denoted perfection, as it was called, or a progression by three, or in what we now call triple time. When the circle was discontinued, or cut through by a perpendicular or oblique stroke, it signified imperfection, or a progression by two, or, as we should say, in duple time; when the circle had a point in the centre it signified a quicker progression in the proportions of perfect and imperfect, according as the circle was either entire or mutilated, as above. As to the figures 3 and 2, used as extrinsic signs, they seem intended only to distinguish the greater mood, which gave three longs to the large, from the lesser, which gave three breves to the long; but the propriety of this distinction is not easy to be discovered. As these characters are now out of use, and are supplied by others of modern invention, it is not necessary to be very inquisitive about them;* it is however very certain that the musicians, from the beginning of the sixteenth century, downwards, seem to betray an universal ignorance of their original use and intention; and since the commencement of that period, we nowhere find the circle used to denote perfect or triple time; on the contrary, the character for the several species of it are intended to bespeak the relation which the intended progression in triple time bears to common or imperfect time; for instance $\frac{3}{2}$ is a progression by three of these notes, two whereof would make a bar or measure of duple time, that is to say, minims; $\frac{3}{4}$ and $\frac{3}{8}$ are progressions in triple time by crotchets and quavers; and this observation will

* It may not be improper here to take notice, that notwithstanding the complaints of Morley of the confusion in which the Cantus Mensurabilis was involved, and his absolute despair of restoring the characters anciently used in it, an author, who lived a few years after him, Thomas Ravenscroft, a bachelor of music, published a book with this title, viz.: 'A breefe discourse of the true (but neglected) use of charact'ring the 'degrees by their perfection, imperfection, and diminution in mensurable 'musicke, against the common practice and custom of these times. 'Examples whereof are exprest in the harmony of 4 vovces, concerning 'the pleasure of 5 usual recreations, 1 hunting, 2 hawking, 3 dauncing, '4 drinking, 5 enamouring.' London, 1614, quarto.

The author has discovered, as well in the apology and the preface to this book, as in the discourse itself, a great share of musical erudition; but the arguments severally contained in them failed to convince the world that the revival of an obsolete practice, which from its intricacy and inutility had insensibly grown into disuse, could in any way tend to the perfection of the science; and experience has shewn that that method of charactering the degrees, which, as he contends is the only true one, is not essential in the notation of music.

serve to explain various other signatures not here mentioned. As to these other numbers $\frac{6}{8}$ $\frac{12}{8}$, the denominator in each having a duple ratio, they are clearly the characteristics of common time; but though the entire circle is no longer used as a characteristic of time, yet the discontinued or mutilated circle is in daily practice. Some ignorant writers on music, from its resemblance to the letter C, suppose to be the initial of the word Common; adding, that where a perpendicular stroke is drawn through it, it signifies a quick, and where it is inverted a still quicker succession of notes.* *But this appropriation of the epithet* COMMON *to duple time is unwarrantable, for in truth duple time is no more common than triple, the one occurring as often in musical compositions as the other.*

The intrinsic signs used in music are no other than the rests which correspond with the measures of notes, and that alteration of the value of notes, which consists in a variety of colour, as black full, black void, red full, and red void, mentioned by Morley and other writers.

The sixth chapter treats of Tact, thus defined by the author: 'Tact is a successive motion in singing, 'directing the equality of the measure. Or it is a 'certain motion made by the hand of the chief singer 'according to the nature of the marks, which motion 'directs a song according to measure.

'Tact is threefold, the greater, the lesser, and the 'proportionate; the greater is a measure made by 'a slow, and as it were reciprocal motion; the writers 'call this tact the whole or total tact; and because it 'is the true tact of all songs, it comprehends in his 'motion a semibreefe not diminished, or a breefe 'diminished, in a duple. The lesser tact is the half 'of the greater, which they call a semi-tact, because 'it measures by its motion a semibreefe diminished 'in a duple; this is allowed of only by the unlearned. 'The proportionate is that whereby three semibreefes 'are uttered against one, as in a triple, or against two, 'as in a sesquialtera.'

In the seventh chapter the author takes occcasion to define the word Canon in these words :—

'A canon is an imaginary rule, drawing that part 'of the song which is not set downe, out of that part 'which is set downe. Or it is a rule which doth 'wittily discover the secrets of a song. Now we use 'canons either to shew art, or to make shorter worke, 'or to try others cunning.'

From this, which is an excellent definition of the term, we may learn that it is very improperly applied to that kind of perpetual fugue which is generally understood by the word Canon; for it is a certain compendious rule for writing down a composition of that kind on a single stave, and for singing it accordingly; and hence it seems to be a solecism to say a canon in score; for when once the composition is scored, the rule or canon for singing it does not apply to it.

As in the former chapter the author had mentioned augmentation of the value of notes by a point in the signature, and other marks or directions, in this, which is the eighth of the second book, he speaks of diminution, which he also calls Syncopation, and divides into virgular, the sign whereof is the circle mutilated, or having a perpendicular or oblique stroke, as before is mentioned; and numeral, signified by figures. In this chapter the author takes occasion to mention a man living in his time, and hired to be organist in the castle of Prague, of whom, to use his own words, he thus speaks : 'Who though he knew 'not, that I may conceale his greater faults, how to 'distinguish a perfect time from an imperfect, yet 'gives out publickly that he is writing the very 'depth of music, and is not ashamed to say that 'Franchinus (a most famous writer, one whom he 'never so much as tasted of) is not worth the reading, 'but fit to be scoffed at and scorned by him. Foolish, 'bragging, ridiculous rashnes, grosse madnes ! which 'therefore only doth snarle at the learned, because it 'knows not the means how to emulate it. I pray 'God the wolfe may fall into the toiles, and hereafter 'commit no more such outrage, nor like the crow 'brag of borrowed feathers, for he must need be 'counted a dotard that prescribes that to others the 'elements whereof himself never saw.'

The ninth, tenth, and eleventh chapters treat of rests, and of the alteration of notes by the addition of a point; and of imperfection by the note, the rest, and the colour, that is to say, the subtraction of a third part from a given note agreeable to the rule in mensural music, that perfection consists in a ternary, and imperfection in a binary progression of time.

The twelfth chapter speaks of a kind of alteration by a secondary singing of a note for the perfecting of the number 3. These four chapters refer to a method of notation which is now happily superseded by the rejection of ligatures and the insertion of bars.

The subject of the thirteenth chapter is proportion, in the explanation whereof he follows Euclid, Boetius, and Franchinus. Speaking of proportion in general, he says it is either of equality or inequality; but that because the dissimilitude and not the similitude of voice doth make harmony, so music considers only the proportion of inequality. And this he says is two-fold, to wit, the proportion of the greater and of the lesser inequality : the proportion of the greater inequality is the relation of the greater number to the less, as 4 to 2, 6 to 3 ; the proportion of the lesser inequality is contrarily the comparison of a less number to the greater, as of 2 to 4, of 3 to 6.

Of the proportions of the greater inequality, he says, as indeed do all the writers on the subject, that it is of five kinds, namely, multiplex, superparticular, superpartiens, multiplex superparticular, and multiplex superpartiens, the latter two compounded of the former three, which are simple.

To these he says are opposed five other kinds of proportions, to wit, those of the lesser inequality, having the same names with those of the greater inequality, save that they follow the preposition submultiplex, &c.

---

* This supposition seems in some measure to be warranted by the practice of Corelli, who throughout his works has characterized those movements, where the crotchets are in effect quavers, by a semicircle, with a perpendicular stroke drawn through it; and Geminiani has done the same. See the sonatas of Corelli, passim, and the last movement in his ninth solo, and the second and third operas of Geminiani, passim, in the edition published by himself in score.

CHAP. LXIX.

As the subject of proportion has already been treated of, this brief account of the author's sentiments concerning it may suffice in this place, the rather as it is a subject, about which not only arithmeticians and musicians, but all mathematicians are agreed. But under this head of proportion there is one observation touching duple proportion, which will be best given in his own words. 'Duple proportion, 'the first kind of the multiplex, is when the greater 'number, being in relation with the less, doth com-'prehend it in itselfe twice, as 4 to 2, 8 to 4; but 'musically, when two notes are uttered against one, 'which is like them both in nature and kind. The 'signe of this some say is the number 2; others 'because proportion is a relation not of one thing 'but of two, affirm that one number is to be set 'under another thus $\frac{2}{1} \frac{4}{2} \frac{6}{3}$, and make no doubt but in 'all the rest this order is to be kept.

'I would not have you ignorant that the duple 'proportion, and all the other of the multiplex kind, are 'marked by certain canons, saying thus, Decrescit in 'duplo, in triplo, and so forth. Which thing, because 'it is done either to encrease men's diligence, or to 'try their cunning, we mislike not. There be that 'consider the whole proportion in figures, which are 'turned to the left hand-ward, with signs and crookes, 'saying that this C is the duple of this ◯, and this '⌠ of ⌡; and in rests, that this ▐ is the duple of 'this ⌐ I think only upon this reason that Fran-'chinus, Pract. lib. II. cap. iv. saith that the right 'side is greater and perfecter than the left, and the 'left weaker than the right, against which opinion 'neither myself am. For Valerius Probus, a most 'learned grammarian, in his interpretation of the 'Roman letters, saith that the letter C, which hath 'the form of a semicircle, signifies Caius, the man; 'and being turned, signifies Caia, the woman; and 'Fabius Quintilianus, in approving of Probus his 'opinion, saith Caius is shewed by the letter C, 'which being turned signifies a woman; and being 'that men are more perfect than women, the per-'fection of the one is declared by turning the semi-'circle to the right hand, and the weakness of the 'other by turning it to the left.*

Book III. is dedicated to Philip Surus of Milten-burg, 'a sharp-witted man, a master of art, and a 'most cunning musician, chapel-master to the count 'palatine the duke of Bavaria.'

The first chapter contains the praise of accent, which is delivered in the following fanciful allegory.

'Accent hath great affinity with Concent, for they 'be brothers, because Sonus or Sound (the king of

* Lib. II. cap. xiii.
This passage is not to be understood unless the adjectives right and left are taken in the sense in which the terms dexter and sinister are used by the heralds in the blazoning of coat-armour, in the bearing whereof the dexter is opposed to the left side of the spectator.
The above observation of the author seems to suggest a reason for a practice in writing country-dances, which it would otherwise be difficult to account for, namely, that of distinguishing the men and women by these characters ⊙⊙⊙⊙, which are evidently founded in the ideas of perfection and imperfection above alluded to, though signified by an entire and a mutilated figure; the circle, which is a perfect figure, de-noting the man, and the semicircle, which is imperfect, the woman.

'ecclesiastical harmony) is father to them both, and 'begat the one upon Grammar, the other upon 'Music; whom after the father had seen to be of 'excellent gifts both of body and wit, and the one 'not to yeeld to the other is any kind of knowledge; 'and further, that himselfe (now growing in yeeres) 'could not live long, he began to think which he 'should leave his kingdom unto, beholding some time 'the one, some time the other, and the fashions of 'both. The Accent was elder by yeares, grave, 'eloquent, but severe, therefore to the people less 'pleasing. The Concent was merry, frolicke, lively, 'acceptable to all, desiring more to be loved than to 'be feared, by which he easily wonne unto him all 'men's minds, which the father noting, was daily more 'and more troubled in making his choyce, for the 'Accent was more frugal, the other more pleasing to 'the people. Appointing therefore a certaine day, 'and calling together the peers of his realme, to wit, 'singers, poets, orators, morall philosophers, besides 'ecclesiastical governors, which in that function held 'place next to the king; before these king Sonus is 'said to have made this oration: "My noble peers, "which have undergone many dangers of warre by "land and sea, and yet by my conduct have carried "the prize throughout the whole world; behold the "whole world is under our rule; wee have no enemy, "all things may goe prosperously with you, only upon "me death encreaseth, and life fadeth; my body is "weakned with labor, my soul consumed with care, "I expect nothing sooner than death. Wherefore "I purpose to appoint one of my sonnes lord over "you, him I say whom you shall by your common "voyces choose, that he may defend this kingdome, "which hath been purchased with your blood, from "the wrong and invasion of our enemies."

'When he had thus said, the nobles began to con-'sult, and by companies to handle concerning the 'point of the common safety, yet to disagree, and 'some to choose the one, some the other, for the 'orators and poets would have the Accent, the musi-'tians and the moralists chose the Concent. But the 'papal prelates, who had the royalties in their hands, 'looking more deeply into the matter, enacted that 'neither of them should be refused, but that the king-'dome should be divided betwixt them, whose opinion 'the king allowed, and so divided the kingdome, 'that Concentus might be chiefe ruler over all things 'that are to be sung (as hymnes, sequences, antiphones, 'responsories, introitus, tropes, and the like), and 'Accent over all things which are read, as gospels, 'lectures, epistles, orations, prophesies; for the func-'of the papal kingdom are not duely performed with-'out Concent: so these matters being settled, each 'part departed with their king, concluding that both 'Concent and Accent should be especially honoured 'by those ecclesiasticall persons. Which thing Leo 'the Tenth, and Maximilian the most famous Roman 'emperor, both chiefe lights of good arts, and espe-'cially of musicke, did by general consent of the 'fathers and princes, approve, endowe with privi-'ledges, and condemned all gainsayers as guilty of 'high treason, the one for their bodily, the other for

'their spiritual life. Hence was it that I marking
'how many of those priests which (by the leave of
'the learned) I will say doe reade those things they
'have to read so wildly, so monstrously, so faultily,
'that they doe not onely hinder the devotion of the
'faithful, but also even provoke them to laughter and
'scorning with their ill reading, resolved after the
'doctrine of concent, to explaine the rules of accent,
'inasmuch as it belongeth to a musitian, that together
'with concent accent might also, as true heire in this
'ecclesiastical kingdome be established. Desiring
'that the praise of the highest king, to whom all
'honour and reverence is due, might duely be per-
'formed.'

Accent, as this author explains it, belongs to churchmen, and is a melody pronouncing regularly the
syllables of any word, according as the natural accent
of them requires.

According to the rules laid down by him, it seems
that in the reading the holy scriptures the ancient
practice was to utter the words with an uniform tone
of voice, with scarce any inflexion of it at all; which
manner of reading, at least of the prayers, is at this
day observed even in protestant churches. Nevertheless he directs that the final syllable, whatever it
be, should be uttered in a note, sometimes a fourth,
and at others a fifth lower than the ordinary intonation of the preceding syllables, except in the case of
interrogatory clauses, when the tone of the final syllable is to be elevated; and to this he adds a few
other exceptions. It seems by this author that there
was a method of accenting the epistles, the gospels,
and the prophecies, concerning which last he speaks
in these words : 'There are two ways for accenting
'prophesies, for some are read, after the manner of
'epistles, as on the feast daies of our Lady, the Epi-
'phany, Christmas, and the like, and those keep the
'accent of epistles ; some are sung according to the
'manner of morning lessons, as in Christ's night, and
'in the Ember fasts, and these keep the accent of
'those lessons. But I would not have you ignorant
'that in accenting, oftentimes the manner and cus-
'tome of the country and place is kept, as in the
'great church of Magdeburg ; Tu autem Domine is
'read with the middle syllable long, by reason of the
'custome of that church ; whereas other nations doe
'make it short according to the rule. Therefore let
'the reader pardon me if our writings doe sometime
'contrary the diocese wherein they live. Which
'though it be in some few things, yet in the most
'they agree. For I was drawne by my own expe-
'rience, not by any precepts, to write this booke.
'And if I may speake without vain-glory, for that
'cause have I seen many parts of the world, and in
'them divers churches, both metropolitane and cathe-
'drall, not without great impeachment of my state,
'that thereby I might profit those that shall live after
'me. In which travaile of mine I have seen the five
'kingdomes of Pannonia, Sarmatia, Boemia, Den-
'marke, and of both the Germanies, 63 diocesses,
'cities 340, infinit fashions of divers people, besides
'sayled over the two seas, to wit, the Balticke, and
'the great ocean, not to heape riches, but increase

'my knowledge. All which I would have thus taken
'that the reader may know that this booke is more
'out of my experience than any precepts.'

The fourth book is dedicated 'to the worthy and
'industrious master Arnold Schlick, a most exquisite
'musician, organist to the count Palatine,' and declares the principles of counterpoint : to this end the
author enumerates the concords and discords ; and,
contrary to the sentiments of the more learned among
musicians, reckons the diatessaron in the latter class.
Of the concords he says, 'Some be simple or primarie,
'as the unison, third, fifth, and sixth ; others are re-
'peated or secondary, and are equisonous with their
'primitives, as proceeding of a duple dimension ; for
'an eighth doth agree in sound with an unison, a
'tenth with a third, a twelfth with a fifth, and a
'thirteenth with a sixth ; others are tripled, to wit, a
'fifteenth, which is equal to the sound of an unison
'and an eighth ; a seventeenth, which is equal to a
'third and a tenth ; and a nineteenth, which is equal
'to a fifth and a twelfth ; a twentieth, which is equal
'to a sixth and a thirteenth, and so forth. Of con-
'cords also, some be perfect, some imperfect ; the
'perfect are those, which being grounded upon cer-
'tain proportions, are to be proved by the help of
'numbers ; the imperfect, as not being probable, yet
'placed among the perfects, make an unison sound.'*

Touching the fourth, he says, 'It may be used as
'a concord in two cases ; first, when being shut be-
'twixt two eighths it hath a fifth below, because if
'the fifth be above, the concord is of no force, by that
'reason of Aristotle, whereby in his problems he
'shews that the deeper discordant sounds are more
'perceived than the higher. Secondly, when the
'tenor and meane do go by one or more sixths, then
'that voice which is middling shall alwayes keep a
'fourth under the cantus, and a third above the
'tenor.'

Speaking of the parts of a song in the fifth chapter, he says, 'They are many, to wit, the treble, tenor,
'high tenor, melody, concordant, vagrant, contra-
'tenor, base, yea and more than these.' Of the discantus he says in general 'That it is a song made of
'divers voyces, for it is called Discantus, quasi diver-
'sus cantus, that is as it were another song, but we,
'because Discantus is a part of a song severed from
'the rest, will describe it thus, Discantus is the
'uppermost part of each song, or it is an harmony to
'be song with a child's voyce.' Of the other parts
he speaks thus : 'A tenor is the middle voyce of each
'song ; or, as Gafforus writes, lib. III. cap. v. it is
'the foundation to the relation of every song, so called
''à tenendo, of holding, because it doth hold the con-
''sonance of all the parts in itselfe in some respect.'
'The Bassus, or rather Basis, is the lowest part of
'each song, or it is an harmony to be sung with a
'deepe voice, which is called Baritonus, a vari, which
'is low, by changing V into B, because it holdeth
'the lower part of the song. The high tenor is the
'uppermost part save one of a song, or it is the grace

* Ornithoparcus has not distinguished with sufficient clearness between
the perfect and imperfect concords, though the reason of the distinction
is properly assigned by him ; the imperfect concords are the third and
sixth, with their replicates,

'of the base, for most commonly it graceth the base, 'making a double concord with it. The other parts 'every student may describe by himselfe.'

The rules or special precepts of counterpoint laid down by this author, are so very limited and mechanical, that at this time of day, when the laws of harmony have been extended, and the number of allowable combinations so multiplied as to afford ample scope for the most inventive genius, they can hardly be thought of any use.

The eighth chapter has this title ' Of the divers 'fashions of singing, and of the ten precepts for 'singing,' and is here given in the words of the translator.

' Every man lives after his owne humour, neither 'are all men governed by the same lawes; and divers 'nations have divers fashions, and differ in habite, 'diet, studies, speech, and song. Hence is it that the 'English do carroll; the French sing; the Spaniards 'weepe; the Italians which dwell about the coasts of 'Janua caper with their voyces, the other barke; but 'the Germanes, which I am ashamed to utter, doe 'howle like wolves. Now because it is better to 'breake friendship than to determine any thing 'against truth, I am forced by truth to say that 'which the love of my countrey forbids me to pub-'lish. Germany nourisheth many cantors but few 'musicians. For very few, excepting those which 'are or have been in the chapels of princes, do truely 'know the art of singing. For those magistrates to 'whom this charge is given, do appoint for the govern-'ment of the service youth cantors, whom they chuse 'by the shrilnesse of their voyce, not for their cun-'ning in the art, thinking that God is pleased with 'bellowing and braying, of whom we read in the 'scripture that he rejoyceth more in sweetness than 'in noyse, more in the affection than in the voyce. 'For when Salomon in the Canticles writeth that the 'voyce of the church doth sound in the eares of 'Christ, hee doth presently adjoyne the cause, because 'it is sweet. Therefore well did Baptista Mantuan '(that modern Virgil) inveigh every puffed up igno-'rant bellowing cantor, saying,

"Cur tantis delubra boum mugitibus imples,
"Tu ne Deum tali credis placare tumultu."

'Whom the prophet ordained should be praised in 'cymbals, not simply, but well sounding.

' Of the ten precepts necessary for every singer.

' Being that divers men doe diversly abuse them-'selves in God's praise, some by moving their body 'undecently, some by gaping unseemely, some by 'changing the vowels, I thought good to teach all 'cantors certain precepts by which they may err 'lesse.

' 1. When you desire to sing any thing, above all 'things marke the tone and his repercussion. For 'he that sings a song without knowing the tone, doth 'like him that makes a syllogisme without moode 'and figure.

' 2. Let him diligently marke the scale under 'which the song runneth, least he make a flat of 'a sharpe, or a sharpe of a flat.

' 3. Let every singer conforme his voyce to the 'words, that as much as he can he make the concent 'sad when the words are sad, and merry when they 'are merry. Wherein I cannot but wonder at the 'Saxons, the most gallant people of all Germany '(by whose furtherance I was both brought up and 'drawne to write of musicke) in that they use in their 'funerals an high, merrie, and jocunde concent, for 'no other cause I thinke, than that either they hold 'death to be the greatest good that can befall a man '(as Valerius, in his fifth book, writes of Cleobis and 'Biton, two brothers) or in that they believe that the 'soules (as it is in Macrobius his second booke De 'Somnio Scip.) after this body doe returne to the 'original sweetness of music, that is to heaven, which 'if it be the cause, we may judge them to be valiant 'in contemning death, and worthy desirers of the 'glory to come.

' 4. Above all things keepe the equality of measure, 'for to sing without law and measure is an offence to 'God himselfe, who hath made all things well in 'number, weight, and measure. Wherefore I would 'have the Easterly Franci (my countrymen) to fol-'low the best manner, and not as before they have 'done, sometime long, sometime to make short the 'notes in plain-song, but take example of the noble 'church of Herbipolis, their head, wherein they sing 'excellently. Which would also much profit and 'honour the church of Prage, because in it also they 'make the notes sometimes longer, sometime shorter 'than they should. Neither must this be omitted, 'which that love which we owe to the dead doth 'require, whose vigils (for so are they commonly 'called) are performed with such confusion, hast, and 'mockery (I know not what fury possesseth the 'mindes of those to whom this charge is put over) 'that neither one voyce can be distinguished from 'another, nor one syllable from another, nor one verse 'sometimes throughout a whole Psalme from ano-'ther; an impious fashion, to be punished with the 'severest correction. Think you that God is pleased 'with such howling, such noise, such mumbling, in 'which is no devotion, no expressing of words, no 'articulating of syllables ?

' 5. The songs of authentical tones must be timed 'deepe of the subjugall tones, high of the neutrall 'meanly, for these goe deep, those high, the other 'both high and low.

' 6. The changing of vowels is a signe of an 'unlearned singer. Now though divers people do 'diversely offend in this kinde, yet doth not the 'multitude of offenders take away the fault. Here 'I would have the Francks to take heed they pro-'nounce not u for o, as they are wont saying nuster 'for noster. The country churchmen are also to 'be censured for pronouncing Aremus instead of 'Oremus. In like sort doe all the Renenses, from 'Spyre to Confluentia, change the vowel i into the 'dipthong ei, saying Mareia for Maria. The West-'phalians for the vowel a pronounce a and e together, 'to wit, Aebste for Abste. The lower Saxons, and 'all the Suevians, for the vowel e read e and i, saying 'Deius for Deus. They of Lower Germany do all

'expresse u and e instead of the vowel u. Which
'errours, though the German speech doth often re-
'quire, yet doth the Latin tongue, which hath the
'affinitie with ours, exceedingly abhorre them.

'7. Let a singer take heed least he begin too loud,
'braying like an asse; or when he hath begun with
'an uneven height, disgrace the song. For God is
'not pleased with loud cryes, but with lovely sounds;
'it is not saith our Erasmus the noyse of the lips,
'but the ardent desire of the heart, which like the
'loudest voyce doth pierce God's eares. Moses spake
'not, yet heard these words, "Why dost thou cry
"unto me?" But why the Saxons, and those that
'dwell upon the Balticke coast, should so delight in
'such clamouring, there is no reason, but either
'because they have a deafe God, or because they
'thinke he is gone to the south side of heaven, and
'therefore cannot so easily heare both the easterlings
'and the southerlings.

'8. Let every singer discerne the difference of
'one holiday from another, least on a sleight holiday
'he either make too solemne service, or too sleight
'on a great.

'9. The uncomely gaping of the mouth, and un-
'graceful motion of the body is a signe of a mad
'singer.

'10. Above all things let the singer study to
'please God, and not men (saith Guido) there are
'foolish singers who contemne the devotion they
'should seeke after, and affect the wantonesse which
'they should shun, because they intend their singing
'to men not to God, seeking for a little worldly
'fame, that so they may lose the eternal glory,
'pleasing men that thereby they may displease God,
'imparting to others that devotion which themselves
'want, seeking the favour of the creature, con-
'temning the love of the creatour. To whom is due
'all honour, and reverence, and service. To whom
'I doe devote myself and all that is mine; to him
'will I sing as long as I have being, for he hath
'raised mee (poore wretch) from the earth, and from
'the meanest basenesse. Therefore blessed be his
'name world without end. Amen.'

To speak of this work of Ornithoparcus in general,
it abounds with a great variety of learning, and is
both methodical and sententious. That Douland
looked upon it as a valuable work may be inferred
from the pains he took to translate it, and his dedication of it to the lord treasurer, Robert Cecil,
earl of Salisbury.

It appears by the several dedications of his four
books of the Micrologus, that Ornithoparcus met
with much opposition from the ignorant and envious
among those of his own profession; of these he
speaks with great warmth in each of these epistles,
and generally concludes them with an earnest request
to those to whom they are addressed, that they would
defend and protect him and his works from the
malicious backbiters of the age.

STEFFANO VANNEO, director of the choir of the
church of St. Mark at Ancona, was the author of
a book in folio, intitled Recanetum de Musica aurea,
published at Rome in 1533. It was written originally in Italian, and was translated into Latin by
Vincentio Rossetto of Verona. The greater part of
it seems to be taken from Franchinus, though the
author has not confessed his obligation to him, or
indeed to any other writer on the subject.

GIOVANNI MARIA LANFRANCO, was the author of
Scintille di Musica, printed at Brescia in 1533, in
oblong quarto, a very learned and curious book.

It is well known that about this time the printers,
and even the booksellers, were men of learning;
one of this latter profession, named GEORGE RHAW,
and who kept a shop at Wittemberg, published in
1536, for the use of children, a little book, with this
title, Enchiridion utriusque Musicæ Practicæ Geor-
gio Rhaw, ex varijs Musicorum Libris, pro Pueris
in Schola Vitebergensi congestum. In the size,
manner of printing, and little typhographical ornaments contained in it, it very much resembles
the old editions of Lilly's grammar, and seems to
be a book well calculated to answer the end of its
publication.

One LAMPADIUS, a chanter of a church in Luneburg in 1537, published a book with this title,
Compendium Musices, tam figurati quam plani Cantus ad Formam Dialogi, in Usum ingenuæ Pubis
ex eruditissimis Musicorum scriptis accurate congestum, quale ante hac nunquam Visum, et jam
recens pnblicatum. Adjectis etiam Regulis Con-
cordantiarum et componendi Cantus artificio, sum-
matim omnia Musices præcepta pulcherrimis Exemplis illustrata, succincte et simpliciter complectens.

SEBALDUS HEYDEN, of Nuremberg, was the author
of a tract intitled Musicæ, id est, Artis Canendi.
It was published in 1537, and again in 1540, in
quarto; the last of the two editions is by much the
best. In this book the author has thus defined the
word Tactus, which in music signifies the division
of time by some external motion: 'Tactus est digi-
'timotus aut nutus, ad temporis tractatum, in vices
'æquales divisum, omnium notularum, ac pausarum
'quantitates coaptans.' An explanation that carries
the antiquity of this practice above two hundred
and thirty years back from the present time.*

NICOLAUS LISTENIUS, of Leipsic, in 1543 published
a treatise De Musica, in ten chapters, which he
dedicated to the eldest son of Joachim II. duke of
Brandenburg. It was republished in 1577, with the
addition of two chapters, at Nuremberg. Glareanus,
in his Dodecachordon, has given a Miserere, in three
parts, from this work of Listenius, which, whether

* This book is dedicated to Hieronymus Baumgartner, a great encourager of learning, and one of five merchants of Augsburg, who, as
Roger Ascham relates, were thought able to disburse as much ready
money as five of the greatest kings in Christendom.
The true spelling of this family name is Paumgartner; and it seems
that these brethren, or at least one of them, possessed the same princely
spirit as that which distinguished the Fuggers of the same city, who
were three in number, and are mentioned in the passage above-cited
from Ascham. Erasmus has drawn a noble character of one of the
Paumgartners, named John, in one of his Epistles, in which he takes
occasion to celebrate the liberality of the Fuggers also: and there is
extant a letter of John Paumgartner to Erasmus, filled with sentiments
of the highest friendship and benevolence. It is printed in the Appendix
to Dr. Jortin's life of Erasmus, pag. 471. John Paumgartner had a son
named John George, who seems to have inherited the liberal spirit of his
father, for he was desirous of making Erasmus some valuable present,
which the latter modestly declined, telling him in one of his Epistles,
that he had already received one of his father, a cup, a proper gift
to a Dutchman; but, says he, I am not able to drink Batavicè a la
Hollandoise. See Dr. Jortin's Life of Erasmus, vol. I. pag. 536.

it be a composition of his own, or of some other person, does not clearly appear.

The effects of these, and numberless other publications, but more especially the precepts for the composition of counterpoint delivered by Franchinus, were very soon discoverable in the great increase of practical musicians, and the artful contexture of their works. But although at this time the science was improving very fast in Italy, it seems that Germany and Switzerland were the forwardest in producing masters of the art of practical composition: of these some of the most eminent were Iodocus Pratensis, otherwise called Jusquin de Prez, Jacob Hobrecht, Adamus ab Fulda, Henry Isaac, Sixtus Dietrich Petrus Platensis, Gregory Meyer, Gerardus à Salice, Adamus Luyr, Joannes Richafort, Thomas Tzamen, Nicholas Craen, Anthony Brumel.

The translation of the works of the Greek harmonicians into a language generally understood throughout Europe, and the wonderful effects ascribed to the music of the ancients, excited a general endeavour towards the revival of the ancient modes; the consequence whereof was, that at the beginning of the sixteenth century, scarce a mass, a hymn, or a psalm was composed, but it was framed to one or other of them, as namely, the Dorian, the Lydian, the Phrygian, and the rest, and of these there are many examples now in print. This practice seems to have taken its rise in Germany; and the opinion that the music of the ancients was retrievable, was confirmed by the publication, in the year 1547, of a very curious book entitled ΔΟΔΕΚΑΧΟΡΔΟΝ, the work of Glareanus, of Basil, the editor of Boetius before mentioned. The design of this book is to establish the doctrine of Twelve modes, contrary to the opinion of Ptolemy, who allows of no more than there are species of the Diapason, and those are Seven. The general opinion is, that Glareanus has failed in the proof of his doctrine; he was nevertheless a man of very great erudition, and both he and his work are entitled to the attention of the learned, and merit to be noticed in a deduction of the history of a science, which if he did not improve, he passionately admired.

He was a native of Switzerland, his name HENRICUS LORITUS GLAREANUS. The time when he flourished was about the year 1540. Gerard Vossius, a very good judge, styles him a man of great and universal learning, and a better critic than some were willing to allow him. He was honoured with the poetic laurel and ring by the emperor Maximilian I. His preceptor in music was, as he himself declares, Joannes Cochlæus above-mentioned; and he acknowleges himself greatly beholden for his assistance in the prosecution of his studies, to Erasmus, with whom he maintained at Basil an intimate and honourable friendship. For taking occasion to mention a proverbial expression in the Adagia of Erasmus, wherein any sudden, abrupt, and unnatural transition from one thing to another is compared to ' the passing from the Dorian to the Phrygian mood,'* mentioned also by Franchinus, from whom possibly

Erasmus might have taken it, he acknowledges his obligation to them both, and speaks of his intimacy with the latter in these words : ' I am not ignorant ' of what many eminent men have written in this ' our age concerning this Adagium, two of whom ' however are chiefly esteemed by me, and shall never ' be named without some title of honour, Franchinus ' and Erasmus Roterodamus; the one was a mute ' master to me, but the other taught me by word of ' mouth; to both of them I acknowledge myself ' indebted in the greatest degree. Franchinus indeed ' I never saw, although I have heard that he was at ' Milan when I was there, which is about twenty-two ' years ago; but I was not then engaged in this ' work: however, in the succeeding years, that I may ' ingenuously confess the truth, the writings of that ' man were of great use to me, and gave me so much ' advantage, that I would read and read over again, ' and even devour the music of Boetius, which had ' not for a long time been touched, nay it was thought ' not to be understood by any one. As to Erasmus, ' I lived many years in familiarity with him, not ' indeed in the same house, but so near, that each ' might be with the other as often as we pleased, and ' converse on literary subjects, and those immense ' labours which we sustained together for the com- ' mon advantage and use of students; in which con- ' versations it was our practice to dispute and correct ' each other; I, as the junior, gave place to his age; ' and he as the senior bore with my humours, some- ' times chastising, but always encouraging me in my ' studies; and at last I ventured to appear before the ' public, and transmit my thoughts in writing; and ' whatsoever he had written in the course of twenty ' years he would always have me see before-hand; ' and really if my own affairs would have permitted ' it, I would always have been near him. I have ' been however present at several works: he did not ' take it amiss to be found fault with, as some would ' do now, provided it were done handsomely; nay he ' greatly desired to be admonished, and immediately ' returned thanks, and would even confer presents on ' the persons that suggested any correction in his ' writings. So great was the modesty of the man.'

But notwithstanding the prohibition implied in this adage, it seems that Iodocus Pratensis paid but little regard to it; nay Glareanus gives an instance of a composition of his, in which by passing immediately from the Dorian to the Phrygian mode, he seems to have set it at defiance.

A little farther on, in the same chapter, Glareanus relates that he first communicated to Erasmus the true sense of the above adage; but that the latter, drawing near his end, when he was revising the last edition, and having left Friburg, where Glareanus resided, to go to Basil, the paper which Glareanus had delivered to him containing his sentiments on the passage, was lost, and his exposition thereof neglected.

In another place of the Dodecachordon Glareanus gives an example of a composition in the Æolian mood, by Damianus à Goes, a Portuguese knight and nobleman, of whom a particular account will be shortly given. This person, who was a man of learn-

---

* The Dorian is said to be grave and sober; the Phrygian fierce and warlike.

ing, and had resided in most of the courts of Europe, came to Friburg, and dwelt some time with Glareanus, who upon his arrival there, desirous of introducing him to the acquaintance of this illustrious stranger, invited Erasmus to his house, where he continued some months in a sweet interchange of kind offices, which laid the foundation of a friendship between the three, which lasted to the end of their lives. In a letter now extant from Erasmus to the bishop of Paris, he recommends his friend Glareanus, on whom he bestows great commendations, to teach in France. It seems that Erasmus himself had received invitations to that purpose, but that he declined them. His letter in favour of Glareanus has this handsome conclusion : ' Sed heus tu, vacuis epistolis non est arces- ' sendus (Glareanus :) viaticum addatur oportet, velut ' arrhabo reliqui promissi. Vide quam familiariter ' tecum agam ; ceu tuæ sollicitudinis oblitus. Sed ita ' me tua corrupit humanitas, quæ hanc docuit impu- ' dentiam : quam aut totam ignoscas oportet, aut ' bonam certe partem tibi ipsi imputes.'

He died in the year 1563, and was buried in the church of the college of Basil, where there is the following sepulchral inscription to his memory :—

' Henricus Glareanus, poeta laureatus, gymnasii ' hujus ornamentum eximium, expleto feliciter su- ' premo die, componi hic ad spem futuræ resurrectionis ' providit, cujus manibus propter raram eruditionem, ' candoremque in profitendo, senatus reipublicæ lite- ' rariæ, gratitudinis et pietatis ergo, monumentum ' hoc æternæ memoriæ consecratum, posteritati ut ' extaret, erigi curavit. Excessit vita anno salutis ' MDLXIII. die xxviii mensis Martii, ætatis suæ ' LXXV '

CHAP. LXX.

The design of Glareanus in the Dodecachordon was evidently to establish the doctrine of Twelve modes, in which he seems not to have been warranted by any of the ancient Greek writers, some of whom make them to be more, others fewer than that number ; and after Ptolemy had condemned the practice of increasing the number of the modes by a hemitone, that is to say, by placing some of them at the distance of a hemitone from others ; and in short demonstrated that there could in nature be no more than there are species of the diapason, it seems that Glareanus had imposed upon himself a very difficult task.

In the eleventh chapter of his first book, premising that no part of music is so pleasant or worthy to be discussed as that relating to the modes, he admits that they are no other than the several species of the diapason, which latter do themselves arise out of the different species of diapente and diatessaron. He says that of the fourteen modes arising from the species of diapason, the writers of his time admit only eight, though thirteen have been used by some constantly, and by others occasionally. He adds that those who confine the number to eight, do not distinguish those eight by a true ratio, but by certain rules, which are not universal. He farther says that the moderns call the modes by the name of Tones,

and persist in the use of that appellation with such an invincible obstinacy, as obliges him to acquiesce in their error, which he says was adopted by Boetius himself, who, in the fourteenth chapter of his fourth book, says that there exist in the species of the diapason, the modes, which some call Tropes or Tones.

Chapter XVI. directs the method of infallibly distinguishing the musical consonances by the division of the monochord; and here the author takes occasion to lament, that for more than eighty years before his time, the sciences, and music in particular, had been greatly corrupted; and that many treatises on music had been given to the public by men who were not able to decline the very names or terms used in the science; a conduct which had sometimes excited his mirth, but oftener his indignation. Indeed for Guido, Berno, Theogerus the bishop, Vuillehelmus and Joannes, afterwards pope, he offers an excuse, by saying that they lived at a time when all the liberal sciences, together with correct language, lay more than asleep. Of Boetius he says, that no one taught music more learnedly or carefully : Franchinus he also commends for his skill and diligence; but he censures him for some grammatical inaccuracies, arising from his ignorance of the Greek language. He then proceeds according to the directions of Boetius, to explain the method of distinguishing the consonances by means of the monochord, for the division whereof he gives the following rules :—

' Boetius, the true and only artificer in this respect, ' in the last chapter of his fourth book teaches in what ' manner the ratios of the consonances may undoubt- ' edly be collected by a most easy and simple instru- ' ment, consisting of a chord stretched from a Magas ' to a Magas, at either end of the chord, each im- ' moveable, but with a moveable Magas placed be- ' tween them, to be shifted at pleasure. The instru- ' ment being thus disposed, if the intermediate space ' over which the chord is stretched, and which lies ' between the immoveable Magades, be divided into ' Three equal parts, and the moveable Magas be ' placed at either section, so that One part of the ' divided space will be left on one side of the Magas, ' and Two parts on the other, for thus the duple ratio ' will be preserved, the two parts of the chord being ' struck by a Plectrum, will sound the consonant dia- ' pason. But if the space between the immoveable ' Magades be divided into Four parts, and the move- ' able Magas be so placed, as that One part may be ' left on one side thereof, and Three on the other, ' then will the triple ratio be preserved; and the two ' parts of the chord being struck by a Plectrum will ' sound the consonant diapason cum diapente. More- ' over, if the same space be divided into Five parts, ' and One thereof be left on one side, and Four on ' the other, that so the ratio may be Quadruple, the ' same two parts of the chord will sound a Disdiapason, ' the greatest of all consonants, and which is in a ' quadruple ratio; and thus all the consonants may ' be had. Again, let the same division into Five ' parts remain, and let Three of those parts be left on ' one side, and two on the other ; in that case you ' will find the first consonant diapente in a super-

'particular genus, viz., in a Sesqualtera ratio. But
'if the space between the immoveable Magades be
'divided into Seven parts, and the moveable Magas
'leave Four of them on one side, and Three on the
'other, in order to have a Sesquitertia ratio, those
'two parts of the Chord will sound a diatessaron con-
'sonance. Lastly, if the whole space be divided into
'Seventeen parts, and Nine of them be left on one
'side, and Eight on the other of the moveable Magas,
'it will shew the tone, which is in the Sesquioctave
'ratio. But that these things may be more clearly
'understood, we will demonstrate them by letters, as
'he [Boetius] has done. Let A D be the regula, or
'table, upon which we intend to stretch the chord;
'the immoveable Magades, which the same Boetius
'calls hemispheres, are the two E and F, erected
'perpendicular to the Regula at B and C. Let the
'chord A E F D be stretched over these, and let K
'be the moveable Magas to be used within the space
'B C. If this be so placed, and the space be divided
'into three, so that one part may remain on one side,
'and two on the other; this chord by the application
'of a plectrum will sound a diapason, the queen of
'consonances; but if the space be divided into Four,
'and the chords on each side be as Three to One, the
'consonant diapason with a diapente will be produced.
'Moreover, if the space be divided into Five parts,
'Four against One will give a disdiapason, and Three
'to Two a diapente; and when the space is divided
'into Seven, Four against Three, produces a diates-
'saron; and lastly, when the space is divided into
'Seventeen, Nine to Eight, gives the tone : we here
'subjoin the type :—

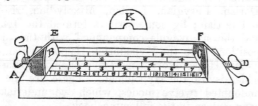

Chapter XXI. which is the last of the first book, is
a kind of introduction to the author's doctrine of the
Twelve modes, in which, speaking in his own person,
he delivers his sentiments in these words :—

'When I had put the last hand to this book,
'I obtained unexpectedly, by means of my excellent
'friend Bartholomæus Lybis, Franchinus's work
'De Harmonia Musicorum Instrumentorum, which,
'though I had eagerly sought after it many years,
'I could never procure. This I take to have been
'the last work of Franchinus, for he dedicated it in
'the year of Christ, 1518, to Joannes Grolerius of
'Lyons, who was treasurer of Milan to Francis king
'of France, having more than twenty years before
'that published a treatise of practical music. I was
'more overjoyed than I can express at the receipt
'of it; for I expected to have found certain passages
'of some authors, more especially Greek ones, cleared
'up by him, as they had given me a great deal of
'trouble for several years; and my hopes were
'greatly increased on reading the first chapter, where
'he says, that he had translated Bryennius, Bacchius,

'Aristides Quintilianus, and Ptolemy, from the Greek
'into the Latin language. I began to peruse him very
'carefully, and found in him his usual exactness and
'diligence; more especially in those things which
'Boetius treats of in the three genera of modulation
'by the five tetrachords, and in what related to the
'proportions and Proportionalities, for so they call
'them; but when I perceived that in his last book
'he had undertaken to discuss that abstruse subject
'the musical modes, I flattered myself with the hopes
'of finding Franchinus similar to himself in that
'part, and that he had produced somewhat worthy
'to be read from so many authors; but my expec-
'tations were not answered, and as far as I can con-
'jecture, he does not seem to have understood the
'words of Apuleius in his Florida,* lib. I. concern-
'ing Antigenides, or those of Marcianus Capella,
'Lucianus Athenæus, and Porphyrius; for he no
'where quotes those places which require explanation,
'which I greatly wonder at. He indeed several
'times quotes Plato, but not in those places where
'the reader is puzzled, such as that is in lib. iii.
'De Rep. concerning the authors of the six Modes.
'Truly, what Franchinus says in that book, except
'what is taken from Boetius, I may say without any
'error or spleen, for I much esteem the man, are
'words compiled by sedulous reading from various
'commentaries, but in no manner helping to clear up
'the matter. As that comparison of the four modes
'to four complexions, colours, and poetical feet, three
'other modes being banished undeservedly. I had
'much rather have had him ingenuously confess,
'either that he did not know the differences of those
'modes, or that they were Aristoxenean paradoxes,
'the opinions of which author were laughed at, re-
'jected, and exploded by Boetius and Ptolemy, men
'eminent in this art. Franchinus himself doubted as
'much about the eight modes as the common people
'did; for in this book, which is the last of his works,
'he does not dare even so much as to mention the
'Hypomixolydian, which he had named in his book
'entitled Practica, lib. I. chapters 8 and 14, confiding
'implicitly, as he himself confesses, in the opinions of
'others. But if it be not permitted to repeat the
'species of diapason, which objection he himself
'seems to make in his last work, then the Hyper-
'mixolydian will be no mode, since its diapason is
'wholly the Hypodorian. But Franchinus in this
'work leaving out the Hypomixolydian, which has
'the same diapason with the Dorian, and is our
'eighth, takes in the Hypermixolydian, that we may
'collect and confirm by his own authority the number
'of all the modes to be eight, according to the common
'opinion; but as there are in fact no more than seven
'species of the diapason, so there can be only seven
'modes, after that form which the church still retains,
'together with an eighth, which has a system inverse
'to that of the first mode. Franchinus says that to
'the seven modes of Boetius, viz. the Hypodorian,
'Hypophrygian, Hypolydian, Dorian, Phrygian,
'Lydian, and Mixolydian; and that of Ptolemy,

* Florida, the name of a book of Apuleius. Fabricius, Bibliothec.
Lat. tom. I. pag. 520.

'named the Hypermixolydian, Aristoxenus added 'these five, the Hypoiastian, the Hypoæolian, Iastian, 'Æolian, and Hyperiastian, and so made the number 'thirteen; but as five of these were, according to the 'authority of Bryennius to be rejected, and as he 'could not find out the name of the Hypermixolydian, 'not knowing that it was the same with the Hyperi-'astian of Aristoxenus, he has recourse to the Hyper-'mixolydian of Ptolemy, that the pretty octonary 'number of modes should not be lost: but the reader 'will hear our opinion concerning those things in its 'proper place. We shall now subjoin the words of 'Franchinus, that the reader may himself discern the 'opinion of this man concerning the modes; for after 'he has numbered up the species of the diapason that 'constitute the seven modes of Boetius and the eight 'of Ptolemy, he subjoins these words: " Posterity "has retained only these eight modes, because as "they return in a circle, they comprehend the intire "diatonic extension of an immutable and perfect "system of fifteen chords; wherefore they esteemed "the other five modes, viz., Hypoiastian, Hypoæolian, "Iastian, Æolian, and Hyperiastian as useless to the "sensible harmony of a full and perfect system, to "use the words of Bryennius; and as affording only "an idle demonstration of harmony. But Marcianus "numbers up indeed those fifteen modes, which Cas-"siodorus so ranged, that the constitutions of each "would differ by only the intension of a semitone: "but as every constitution, according to Aristoxenus, "makes up a diapason of twelve equisonant semi-"tones, those two acuter modes, the Hyperæolian and "Hyperlydian are rejected, seeing they do not com-"plete a diapason in the full system of fifteen chords, "and are found superfluous, for they go beyond the "disdiapason system by two semitones."

'Thus far Franchinus: in which discourse he 'plainly shews that he was not able to clear up the 'difficulties in which the doctrine of the modes is 'involved, all which arise, not so much from the sub-'ject itself, as from the many different appellations, 'for there are more than twenty, of these modes. 'We shall however follow the nomenclatura of Aris-'toxenus, which does not contradict us in what con-'cerns the modes, nor yet Boetius, although they do 'not agree in other things. Moreover, neither 'Franchinus nor Capella, in my opinion, understood 'Aristoxenus. The constitution of Cassiodorus is 'throughout repugnant to Boetius, yet, which I 'greatly wonder at, Franchinus did not dare to 'reprehend him, though he was a great asserter of 'the erudition of Boetius; and we do not think it 'convenient to refute him till we have laid the foun-'dation of our hypothesis, as we shall do hereafter. 'But in the mean time we admonish the reader that 'the number of names, though very many, does not 'change the nature of modes; nor can there really be 'more modes than there are species of the diapason, 'for whatsoever Harmonia has instituted concerning 'them, must fall under these seven species of the 'diapason; this is the issue and the sum total of the 'whole business. Wherefore the same Franchinus is 'not without reason accused of not having reflected

'on these things, when he has argued on others most 'shrewdly, and improved them with exact care. For 'the arithmetical and harmonical division in the 'species of the diapason were no secret to him, since 'he has taught them himself in his other works; but 'this also is worthy of reprehension, that agreeing 'with the common custom, he puts only four final 'keys in the seven modules of the diapason, rejecting 'the other three, when that of ♮ only ought to be 'rejected.

'But however, as Franchinus cites Marcianus 'Capella, and omits his words, I thought proper 'to subjoin them here, that the reader may judge 'for himself, and at the same time see how well, or 'rather how ill, Cassiodorus has adapted them to 'that form described by Franchinus. " There are, "says Marcianus Capella, fifteen tropes, but five of "them only are principals, to each of which two "others adhere, first, the Lydian, to which the "Hyperlydian and Hypolydian adhere; second, the "Iastian, to which are associated the Hypoiastian "and Hyperiastian; third, the Æolian with the "Hypoæolian; fourth, the Phrygian, with the Hy-"pophrygian and Hyperphrygian; fifth, the Dorian, "with the Hypodorian and Hyperdorian;" thus far 'Marcianus, who made five principals with two 'others agreeing with each, that they might al-'together make up the number fifteen. But we, as 'Aristoxenus has done, shall put six principals with 'each a plagal, that the number may be twelve, 'omitting the Hypermixolydian of Ptolemy, and the 'Hyperæolian and Hyperphrygian, which are after-'wards superadded. The six principals are the 'Dorian, Phrygian, Lydian, Mixolydian, Æolian, 'and Iastian; by some writers termed the Ionian; 'and the six plagals compounded with the prepo-'position Hypo, the Hypodorian, Hypophrygian, Hy-'lydian, Hypomixolydian, Hypoæolian, Hypoiastian, 'which is also the Hypoionian. These are the true 'undoubted twelve modes, which we undertake to 'comment on in the following book.

'Aristoxenus calls the Hypomixolydian the Hy-'periastian, in the manner of the rest of the modes 'compounded with Hyper; for if any one compounds 'those principals with the word Hyper, he will find 'six other modes, but they fall in with the others. 'Thus the Hyperiastian of Aristoxenus falls into the 'Hypomixolydian; and the Hypomixolydian of 'Ptolemy into the Hypodorian; in the same manner 'the Hypodorian into the Hypoæolian; the Hyper-'phrygian into the Hyperlydian; the Hyperlydian 'into the Hypoionian or Mixolydian; and the 'Hyperæolian into the Hypophrygian Hence it 'appears that many of the difficulties which attend 'the modes, arise from the multiplicity of their names, 'and not from the modes themselves.'

But notwithstanding this assertion of Glareanus, it is very clear that the doctrine of the modes was incumbered with other difficulties than what arose from the confusion of their names. For as to the number thirteen, which Aristoxenus assumed, and the fifteen of Marcianus Capella, they arise from a practice, which Ptolemy in the strongest terms condemns, namely, the augmenting the number of the modes by semitones, that is to say, by making many of the modes a semitone only distant from each other; departing from the order in which the seven species of diapason arise; but Glareanus, though a bigotted admirer of the ancients, has declined this method, and has borrowed his division of the modes from that of the ecclesiastical tones, introducing the arithmetical and harmonical division of each species of diapason, precisely in the same manner as St. Gregory had done by the four primitive tones instituted by St. Ambrose.*

This contrivance of Glareanus, which, to say no worse of it, has but little to recommend it, did not answer the end of vindicating the ancient practice; for the number of the modes thus adjusted, coincides neither with the thirteen modes of Aristoxenus, nor the fifteen of Marcianus Capella; in short, it gives but twelve, and that for this reason, the diapason from ♮ to ♮, is clearly incapable of an arithmetical division, by reason of the semidiapente between ♮ and F; and it is as clear that the diapason between F and f is incapable of an harmonical division, by reason of the excessive fourth between F and ♮, the consequence whereof is, that admitting five of the species to be capable of both divisions, and ♮ and F to be each capable of but one, the number of divisions

can be but twelve; † but these, in the opinion of the author, are so emphatically true and just, as to afford a reason for intitling his work Dodecachordon.

Glareanus has in several parts of his book admitted that the species of Diapason are in nature but seven, or, in other words, that in every progression of seven sounds in the diatonic series, the tones and semitones will arise in the same order as they do in one or other of those seven species; it therefore seems strange that he should endeavour to effect that which his own concession supposes to be impossible; but it seems he meant nothing more by this manifold distinction of modes than to assign to the final note of each a different pitch in the scale or system: in this he makes himself an advocate for the Musical doctrine, as it is called, of the ancients, which however mistaken has been shewn to be reconcileable to that other known by the name of the Harmonic doctrine of the same subject.

Not to pursue an enquiry into the nature of a subject which has long since eluded a minute investigation, and which neither Franchinus, nor this author, nor Doni, nor Dr. Wallis, nor indeed any of the most learned musicians of modern times, could ever yet penetrate; the following scheme, containing Glareanus's system of the twelve modes, is here exhibited, and is left to speak for itself:—

	Hypodorian.			Hypophrygian.			Hypolydian.			Dorian.			Phrygian.			Lydian.			Mixolydian.			Hypo-mix
		arith-met.	har-mocl.		arith-met.	har-mocl.		arith-met.	har-mocl.		arith-met.	har-mocl.		arith-met.	har-mocl.		arith-met.	har-mocl.		arith-met.	har-mocl.	
	First species of Diapason from A to a.	Second.	This is the Æolian mode of Aristoxenus. Ninth.	Second species of Diapason from E to b.	Fourth.	This division has no place in the Diatonic because of the tritone and semidiapente. Hyperæolian.	Third species of Diapason from C to c.	Old Sixth.	This by us called the fifth, by Aristoxenus the Iastian, and by others the Ioniar. Eleventh.	Fourth species of Diapason from D to d.	This by Aristoxenus is called the Hyperiastian, but is the Hypermixolydian. Eighth.	First.	Fifth species of Diapason from E to e.	This is the Hyperæolian mode of Aristoxenus. Tenth.	Third.	Sixth species of Diapason from F to f.	This division is improper for the Diatonic, because of the semidiapente and tritone. Hyperphrygian.	Old Fifth.	Seventh species of Diapason from G to g.	This by us is named the sixth, by Aristoxenus the Hypoiastian. Twelfth.	Seventh.	The eighth of Ptolemy being the same in its nature as the second. Disdiapason.

* The arithmetical division of the diapason is 6, 9, 12, the harmonical 6, 8, 12. See the reason of this distinction pag. 115 of this work.

† To this purpose Malcolm expresses himself very clearly and fully in a passage, which because it accounts for the distinction of the modes into the authentic and plagal, is here given in his own words:—
‘I find they [the modes] were generally characterized by the species of ‘8ve. after Ptolemy's manner, and therefore reckoned in all 7. But ‘afterwards they considered the harmonical and arithmetical divisions of

‘the 8ve, whereby it resolves into a 4th above a 5th, or a 5th above a 4th. ‘And from this they constituted twelve modes, making of each 8ve. two ‘different modes, according to this different division; but because there ‘are two of them that cannot be divided both ways, therefore there are ‘but twelve modes. To be more particular, consider, in the natural ‘system there are 7 different octaves proceeding from these 7 letters, a, ‘b, c, d, e, f, g; each of which has two middle chords, which divide it ‘harmonically and arithmetically, except f, which has not a true 4th,

But if the ancient modes required each a new tuning of the lyre, and that they did is expressly said by Ptolemy and others, there is great reason to believe the tones and semitones by every such tuning

'(because b is three tones above it, and a fourth is but two tones and
'a semitone) and b, which consequently wants the true 5th. (because
'f is only two tones and two semitones above it, and a true 5th contains
'3 tones and a semitone) therefore we have only five octaves that are
'divided both ways, viz. a, c. d, e, g; which make ten modes according
'to these different divisions, and the other two f and b make up the
'twelve. Those that are divided harmonically, *i. e.* with the 5ths lowest,
'were called authentic, and the other plagal modes. See the following
'scheme :—

MODES.
Plagal. Authentic.
8ve.　8ve.

4th　5th　6th

g — c — g — c
a — d — a — d
b — e — b — e
c — f — c — f
d — g — d — g
e — a — e — a

With respect to these distinctions, the following are the sentiments of the author now citing.—

'They considered that an 8ve, which wants a 4th or
'5th, is imperfect; these being the concords next to
'the 8ve. the song ought to touch these chords most
'frequently and remarkably; and because their con-
'cord is different, which makes the melody different,
'they establish by this two modes in every natural
'octave, that had a true 4th and 5th: then if the song
'was carried as far as the octave above, it was called
'a perfect mode; if less, as to the 4th or 5th, it was
'imperfect; if it moved both above and below, it was
'called a mixt mode: thus some authors speak about
'these modes. Others, considering how indispensable
'a chord the 5th is in every mode, they took for the
'final or key-note in the arithmetically divided octaves, not the lowest
'chord of that octave, but that very 4th; for example the octave g is
'arithmetically divided thus, g—c—g, c is a 4th above the lower g, and a
'5th below the upper g, this c therefore they made the final chord of the
'mode, which therefore properly speaking is c and not g; the only differ-
'ence then in this method, betwixt the authentic and plagal modes, is, that
'the authentic goes above its final to the octave, the other ascends a 5th,
'and descends a 4th, which indeed will be attended with different effects,
'but the mode is essentially the same, having the same final, to which
'all the notes refer. We must next consider wherein the modes of one
'species, as authentic or plagal, differ among themselves: this is either
'by their standing higher or lower in the scale, *i. e.* the different tension
'of the whole octave; or rather the different subdivision of the octave
'into its concinnous degrees. Let us consider then whether these dif-
'ferences are sufficient to produce so very different effects as have been
'ascribed to them; for example, one is said to be proper for mirth,
'another for sadness, a third proper to religion, another for tender and
'amorous subjects, and so on: whether we are to ascribe such effects
'merely to the constitution of the octave, without regard to other dif-
'ferences and ingredients in the composition of melody, I doubt any
'body now-a-days will be absurd enough to affirm; these have their
'proper differences, tis true, but which have so little influence, that by the
'various combinations of other causes, one of these modes may be used
'to different purposes. The greatest and most influencing difference is that
'of these octaves, which have the 3rd greater or lesser, making what is
'above called the sharp and flat key; but we are to notice, that of all the
'8ves, except c and a, none of them have all their essential chords in
'just proportion, unless we neglect the difference of tone greater and
'lesser, and also allow the semitone to stand next the fundamental in
'some flat keys (which may be useful, and is sometimes used) and when
'that is done, the octaves that have a flat 3rd will want the 6th greater,
'and the 7th greater, which are very necessary on some occasions, and
'therefore the artificial notes ♯ and ♭ are of absolute use to perfect the
'system. Again, if the modes depend upon the species of 8ves, how can
'they be more than 7? And as to the distinction of authentic and plagal,
'I have shewn that it is imaginary with respect to any essential dif-
'ference constituted hereby in the kind of the melody; for though the
'carrying the song above or below the final, may have a different effect,
'yet this is to be numbered among the other causes, and not ascribed to
'the constitution of the octaves. But it is particularly to be remarked,
'that those authors who give us examples in actual composition of their
'twelve modes, frequently take in the artificial notes ♯ and ♭, to perfect
'the melody of their key; and by this means depart from the con-
'stitution of the 8ve, as it stands in the fixt natural system. So we can
'find little certain and consistent in their way of speaking about these
'things; and their modes are all reducible to two, viz., the sharp and
'flat.' Treatise of Music, chap. xiv. sect. 5.

must have been dislocated; and in all probability for the purpose of preserving the order of nature, which, after all that has been said, will scarce allow of but two kinds of progression, namely, that in the diatonic series from A to a, and from C to c, the former the prototype of all flat, as the other is of all sharp keys. If this was the case, the only discrimination of the modes was their place in the system with respect to acuteness and gravity.

The partiality which Glareanus throughout his book discovers for the music of the ancients is thus to be accounted for. He was a man of considerable learning, and seems to have paid an implicit regard to the many relations of the wonderful effects of music, which Plutarch, Boetius, and many other writers have recorded; and no sooner were the writings of the ancient Greek harmonicians recovered and circulated through Europe, than he flattered himself with the hope of restoring that very practice of music to which such wonderful effects had been ascribed; and in this it seems he was not singular, for even the musicians of his time entertained the same hope. Franchinus by his publications had not only considerably improved the theory of the science, but had communicated to the world a great deal of that recondite learning, which is often more admired than understood; and although he had delivered the precepts of counterpoint, and thereby laid the foundation of a much nobler practice than the ancients could at any time boast of, many of his contemporaries forbore for a time to improve the advantages which he had put them in possession of, and vainly attempted to accommodate their works, which for the most part were compositions of the symphoniac kind, to a system which admitted of no such practice : that this was the case, is most evident from that great variety of compositions contained in the Dodecachordon, which, though they are the works of Iodocus Pratensis, Jacobus Hobrechth, Adamus ab Fulda, Petrus Platensis, Gerardus à Salice, Andreas Sylvanus, Gregorius Meyer, Johannes Mouton, Adamus Luyr, Antonius Brumel, Johannes Ockenheim, and many others, the far greater number contemporaries of Glareanus, are nevertheless asserted to be in the Dorian, the Lydian, the Phrygian, and other of the modes, and that with as much confidence as if the nature of the ancient modes had never been a subject of dispute. The following cantus for four voices, the work of an anonymous author, has great merit, and is given by Glareanus as an exemplar of the Dorian :—

AUCTOR INCERTUS.

Many of the compositions of this kind contained in the Dodecachordon are to be admired for the fineness of the harmony, and the artful contexture of the parts, but they smell of the lamp; and it is easy to see that they derive no advantage from an adherence to those rules which constitute the difference between one and the other of the ancient modes. The musicians of the succeeding age totally disregarded them, and laid the foundation of a practice independent of that which Glareanus had taken so much pains to establish, and which allowed of all that exercise for the invention, which in the composition of elegant music must ever be deemed necessary.

The XIIIth chapter of the second book has the following title, 'De Sono in Cælo duæ Opiniones, 'atque inibi Ciceronis Plinijque Loci excussi,' and contains his sentiments on that favourite opinion of the ancients, the music of the spheres, which the author has entered very deeply into, though he cites Aristotle to shew that the whole is a fiction, and thereby has suggested a very good reason for the omission of it in this place.

Chap. XXXIX. entitled 'De inveniendis Tenoribus ad Phonascos Admonitio,' contains advice touching the framing of tenors, of little worth or importance. To illustrate his precepts Glareanus has inserted three odes of Horace, with the music thereto, of his own composition, which he gives as exemplars of the Dorian, the Phrygian, and Ionian modes.

As to the musicians contemporary with Glareanus, and celebrated by him, short memorials of some of them are dispersed up and down his book; those of whom any interesting particulars are to be collected from other writers will be spoken of hereafter. But he has noticed two that fall not under this latter class, namely, Antonius Brumel and Henricus Isaac, as men of singular eminence: of the latter he thus speaks:—

'HENRICUS ISAAC, a German, is said to have 'learnedly composed innumerable pieces. This 'author chiefly affected the church style; and in his 'works may be perceived a natural force and majesty, 'in general superior to any thing in the compositions 'of this our age, though his style may be said to be 'somewhat rough. He delighted to dwell on one 'immovable note, the rest of the voices running as it 'were about it, and every where resounding as the 'wind is used to play when it puts the waves in 'motion about a rock. This Isaac was also famous 'in Italy, for Politian, a contemporary writer, cele-'brates him.' The following hymn is given by Glareanus as a specimen of his style and manner:—

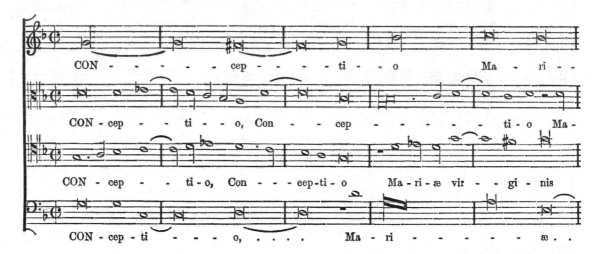

HENRICUS ISAAC.

Glareanus concludes this elaborate work with a very curious relation of Lewis XII. king of France, to this effect. It seems that that monarch had a very weak thin voice, but being very fond of music, he requested Iodocus Pratensis, the precentor of his choir, to frame a composition, in which he alone might sing a part. The precentor knowing the king to be absolutely ignorant of music, was at first astonished at this request, but after a little consideration promised that he would comply with it. Accordingly he set himself to study, and the next day, when the king after dinner, according to his wonted custom, called for some songs,* the precentor immediately produced the composition here subjoined, which being a canon contrived for two boys, might be sung without overpowering the weak voice of the king. The composer had so ordered it, that the king's part should be one holding note, in a pitch proper for a Contratenor, for that was the king's voice. Nor was he inattentive to other particulars, for he contrived his own part, which was the Bass, in such a manner, that every other note he sung was an octave to that of the king, which prevented his majesty from deviating from that single note which he was to intonate. The king was much pleased with the ingenuity of the contrivance, and rewarded the composer.

The following is the canon which Iodocus, or, as the French call him, Josquin or Jusquin, made upon this occasion :—

* The custom of having music at meals seems to have been almost universal in the palaces of kings and other great personages: Theodoric, king of the Goths, as appears from an epistle of his among those of Cassiodorus, understood and loved music; and Sidonius Apollinaris, in that epistle to his friend Agricola, wherein he gives the character of Theodoric, and describes his manner of living, speaks of the sounding of the hydraulic organ, and of those persons who were wont to play on the lyre and other instruments, for the entertainment of princes at their meals. Afterwards, and when in consequence of Guido's improvements, the practice of singing became more general, vocal music upon these occasions took place of instrumental, as appears by the above relation, and the following authentic memorial :—

In Ashmole's History of the Order of the Garter, pag. 404, is an engraving by Hollar after a curious limning on vellum, representing the manner of sitting at dinner of Ferdinand prince of Spain, on the day of his investiture with the habit and ensigns of the order. In this engraving the prince appears sitting under a canopy with the four commissioners of legation, two on each hand of him; on his left are servants attending, and on his right two men and a boy, each singing out of a music paper, and behind them three other persons, supposed to be also singing.

CHAP. LXXI.

Notwithstanding the great reputation of Glareanus, the above-mentioned work of his has not escaped the censures of some who seem to have understood the music of the ancients better than himself. The first of these is Giovanni Battista Doni, who in a very learned and entertaining work of his, intitled De Præstantia Musicæ Veteris,[†] accuses him of adopting the errors of modern musurgists, in a work designedly written to expose them; and laments that the author spent twenty years in composing a work entirely useless; and farther he reproves him for asserting that figurate music was arrived at perfection in his time, when it was notorious that it had not then been in use above a hundred years, and must in the nature of things have been susceptible of still farther improvement.

Salinas also, though he bears a very honourable testimony to his erudition, has pointed out some most egregious errors of Glareanus in the Dodecachordon, particularly one in the tenth chapter of his first book, where he asserts the semitone MI FA to be the lesser semitone, than which he says there cannot be any thing said more abhorrent to the judgment of sense and reason. He enumerates several other mistakes in this work, but insists most on his constitution of twelve modes, which he not only asserts are not taken according to the doctrine of the ancients, but adds that he did by no means understand the ancient modes; and for this opinion of his, Salinas gives as a reason the confession of Glareanus himself, that he had never read the three books of Ptolemy, nor those of Aristoxenus, nor Manuel Bryennius, nor indeed any of the ancient Greek authors.[‡]

After so severe a censure as this, it might seem like heaping disgrace on the memory of this author to declare the opinion of other writers with respect to his work; but there is a passage in the notes of Meibomius on Euclid, which it would be an injury to historical truth to suppress. It may be remembered that in a foregoing page Glareanus is said to have asserted that the word Tone was scarce used to signify Mode till the time of Boetius, and that the obstinacy of ignorant people had compelled him in the Dodecachordon to accept it in that sense. In answer to this Meibomius says, and indeed with great ingenuity demonstrates, that the term was used by the ancients, and Euclid in particular, long before the time of Boetius, and gives as a reason for it, that originally the modes were three, namely, the Dorian, the Phrygian, and the Lydian; that these, being a superoctave tone distant from each other in succession, acquired the name of Tones; and that this term, being once recognized, was applied to the other of the modes, even though some of them were removed from those that next preceded them by a less interval, namely a Semitone. The introduction of Meibomius to his argument is severe, but curious: 'A certain very learned Switzer, but an infant in 'ancient music, set himself in the front of those who 'maintain this opinion, one Glareanus, who, in lib. II. 'cap. ii. of his book, disputes thus,' &c.

To say the truth of the Dodecachordon, it is more to be regarded for the classical purity of its style, than for the matter contained in it; though with respect to the former, it is so very prolix, that it is very difficult to give the sense of the author in terms that would not disgust a modern reader; not to say that it abounds with egotisms and digressions, which detract from the merit of it even in this respect; but

---

* Anciently princes joined in the choral service, and actually sang the offices in surplices; this is said of Charlemagne, the emperor Otho III. and Henry II. and of Kunigunda, the consort of the latter, by Lustig, in his Musikkunde, pag. 259; and to this purpose Bourdelot relates the following story. Lewis IV. being at Tours with his court, about the year 940, some of his courtiers entered into the church of St. Martin at the time of singing the offices, and were much surprised to see there the count of Anjou, Foulque II. in the row of canons, singing the office as they did. The courtiers went and told the king that the count of Anjou was turned priest, and the king was diverted at the relation: at which the count was so disgusted, that on the next day he wrote the king a letter, wherein varying the well-known proverb, 'Rex illiteratus, 'asinus coronatus,' he made use of these words: 'Sçachez sire, qu'un 'roi sans musique est un ane couronné.' The author says that the English, during the troubles in France, had the education of this prince, and purposely brought him up in ignorance, but that notwithstanding he took the reproof in good part, and declared to his courtiers, that they that govern others should be more knowing than those whom they govern. Hist. Mus. et ses Effets, tom. I. pag. 205. An instance of a similar kind is related of Sir Thomas More, viz., that on Sundays, even when he was lord chancellor, he wore a surplice, and sung with the singers at the high-mass and Mattins in the church of Chelsey, which, says the relater, 'the duke of Norfolk on a time finding, sayd, God bodie, 'God bodie, my lord chauncelor a parish clarke! you disgrace the king and 'your office.' To which his lordship answered in the words of David, 'Vilior fiam in occulis meis.' Life of Sir Thomas More by his great-grandson Thomas More, Esq. pag. 179. The same story, with a little variation, is related in the life of Sir Thomas More, written by William Roper, and published by Hearne, pag. 29. *It appears that before the Reformation the laity were required to sing in divine service. Among the injunctions of Cardinal Pole published at the end of Hearne's edition of Robert de Avesbury, page 379, is the following:* "Item, that the churchwarden "of every parish where service was accustomed to be songe, shall exhort all "souche as can singe and have been accustomed to singe in the quire in the "time of schism or before, and now withdrawe themselves in singing or "serving God there, and yf anie souche refuse this to do, then the said "churchwardens to intimate the names of the same amonge other present- "ments to the ordinaire or his chancellor." *One of the common recreations in the family of Sir Thomas More was the music of voices, the viol and the organ: see his life by More, page 35—at page 91 he says, he caused his first wife, who was but young, to be taught all kinds of music, and that the second, though inclined to old age, he persuaded to play on the lute, viol, and other instruments, every day performing thereon her task.*

† Pag. 17.

‡ De Musica, lib. iv. cap. xxxi. pag. 223.

when we consider the substance of the work, and reflect on the very many erroneous opinions contained in it, the author's confessed ignorance of the sentiments of the ancients, more especially Ptolemy, with respect to the modes, and his endeavour to establish his hypothesis of twelve modes upon a foundation that has given way under him; when all this is considered, the authority of Glareanus will appear of very little weight in matters relating either to the music of the ancients, or that system which is the foundation of modern practice.

In another respect this work must be deemed a great curiosity, for it contains a number of compositions of some of the most eminent musicians of the sixteenth century, many whereof are of that kind of music, in which less regard is paid to the melody than to the harmony and curious contexture of the several parts, and in this view of them they are as perfect models as we may ever hope to see. And besides this, their intrinsic merit, they are to be esteemed on the score of their antiquity; for, excepting a few examples contained in the writings of Franchinus, they are the most ancient musical compositions in symphony any where extant in print.

But here it is to be noted, that the musical compositions of these times derive not the least merit from their being associated to words; nor does it appear that the authors of them had an idea of any power in music, concurrent with that of poetry, to move the passions. This appears in their choice of those hymns and portions of scripture to which musical notes are by them most frequently adapted, which, excepting the Miserere, De Profundis, Stabat Mater, Regina Cœli, and a few others, have nothing affecting in the sentiment or expression, but are merely narratory, and incapable, with all the aids of melody and harmony, to excite joy, devotion, pity, or, in short, any other of those affections of the mind which are confessedly under the dominion of music. To give a few instances of this kind; in the second book of the Dodecachordon is the Nicene Creed in the Æolian mode, as it is there called; and in the third is the genealogy of Christ, as it stands in the first chapter of St. Matthew's Gospel, set to music by Iodocus Pratensis, and given as an exemplar of the Hypophrygian. Doni has mentioned this latter as an evidence of barbarism, and the ignorance of the musicians of those times with respect to the power and efficacy of their own art. But this defect, namely, the want of energy in their compositions, was but the consequence of those rules which such writers as Glareanus had prescribed to them, and these were of such a kind as to exclude all diversity of style : no man could say this or that mass or hymn is the composition of Jusquin or Clement, of Gerard, of Andrew, or Gregory; they were all of the same tenor, and seemed as if cast in one mould. In short, in the composition of music to words, two things only were attended to, the correspondence of the notes, in respect to time, with the metre or cadence of the syllables, and the rules of harmony, as they referred to the several modes. Whoever is susceptible of the power of music, is able to judge how much it must have suffered by this servile attention to the

supposed practice of the ancients; and will clearly see that it must have suspended the exercise of the inventive faculty, and in short held the imagination in fetters.

From hence it appears that two things are to be objected to the compositions of the fifteenth, and the beginning of the sixteenth century; namely, a choice of words for the subjects of musical compositions, by which no passion of the human mind can be either excited or allayed, and the want of that variety, and those discriminating characteristics of style and manner, which are looked for in the compositions of different masters.

These defects in the music of which we are now speaking, are in some measure to be accounted for by the want of that union and connexion between music and poetry, which was effected by the invention of the musical drama ; in the conduct whereof the composers considered their art as subservient to that of the poet, and laboured at a correspondence of sentiment between their music and the words to which it was adapted : and hence we are to date the origin of pathetic music; and were the pathetic the only characteristic of fine music, we might pronounce of that of Iodocus Pratensis, Okenheim, and others their contemporaries, that it was very little worth, and should resolve those effects which were wrought by it into novelty, and the ignorance of its admirers.

But whoever is capable of contemplating the structure of a vocal composition in a variety of parts, will find abundant reason to admire many of those which Glareanus has been at the pains of preserving, and will discover in them fine modulation, a close contexture and interchange of parts, different kinds of motion judiciously contrasted; artful syncopations, and binding concords with discords sweetly prepared and resolved ; points that insensibly steal on the ear, and are dismissed at proper intervals ; and such a full harmony resulting from the whole, as leaves the ear nothing to expect or wish for : and of these excellencies Mr. Handel was so sensible, that he could never object to the compositions of this period any defect but the simplicity of the melody, the restraints on which have been shewn to arise from what were then deemed the fundamental precepts of musical composition.

It is easy to discover that the music here spoken of was calculated only for learned ears. Afterwards, when the number of those who loved music became greater than of them that understood it, the gratification of the former was consulted, passages were invented, and from these sprang up that kind of modulation called air, which it is as difficult to define, as to reduce to any rule : this the world were strangers to till they were taught it by the Italian masters, of the most eminent of whom, and the successive improvements made by them, an account will hereafter be given.

It may be remembered that in the account of Glareanus above given, very honourable mention is made of a learned and ingenious Portuguese, a common friend of him and Erasmus; the following is his story.

DAMIANUS A' GOËS, a Portuguese knight, distinguished in the sixteenth century for his learning and other accomplishments, was chamberlain to Emanuel king of Portugal, to whom, as also to his successor, he so recommended himself, that he was by them severally employed in negociations of great moment at foreign courts, particularly in France, Germany, and in the Low Countries, and in Poland. During the time of his abode in Italy he contracted a friendship with the Cardinals Bembo, Sadolet, and Madruce; and while he was resident in the Low Countries married Jane d' Hargen, of the house of Aremberg, with whom he led an easy, quiet, and pleasant life. He loved poetry and music, composed verses, sung well, and was in general estimation among the learned. Nor was he more celebrated for his learning and ingenuity than for his personal valour and skill in military affairs, which he testified in the defence of the city of Louvain in 1542, when it was besieged by the French. From this important service he was recalled into Portugal to write the history of that kingdom, but he lived not to finish it; for in the year 1596, being in his study, and, as it is imagined,

seized with a fit, he fell into the fire, and was found dead, and his body half consumed. Of his works there are extant, Legatio magni Indorum Imperatoris ad Emanuelem Lusitaniæ Regem, anno 1513. Fides, Religio, Moresque Æthiopum. Commentaria Rerum Gestarum in Indiâ à Lusitanio. The Histories of Emanuel and John II. kings of Portugal; and a Relation of the Siege of the City of Louvain. In the course of his travels he made a visit to Glareanus at Friburg, and there contracted a friendship with him and Erasmus, of which the former in his Dodecachordon speaks with great satisfaction. Erasmus acknowledges the receipt of a very handsome present from Damianus in one of his Epistles; and Damianus, in one to him, tells him that he should be glad to print his works at his own expence, and if he outlived him to write his life.* In music he was esteemed equal to the most eminent masters of his time. The following hymn of his composition is published in the Dodecachordon :—

* Jortin's Life of Erasmus, vol. I. pag. 537, 574.

DAMIANUS A' GÖES.

In the course of this work it has been found necessary to attend to the distinction between vocal and instrumental music. The preference which has ever been given to the former, and the slow progress of instrumental music in those ages when the mechanic arts, on which it greatly depends, were in their infancy, has determined the order in which each is to be treated, and will suggest a reason why the priority is given to that species, to the performance whereof the animal organs alone are adequate. Nor was it easy till the period at which we are now arrived, to give any such description of the instruments in general use, as might be depended on. The author of whom we are about to speak has prevented many difficulties that would have interrupted the course of this narration, by giving accurate delineations, which are now to be considered as the prototypes of most of the instruments now in use. Of him and his works the following is an account.

OTTOMARUS LUSCINIUS, a Benedictine monk, and a native of Strasburg, was the author of a treatise intitled Musurgia, seu Praxis Musicæ, published at Strasburg in 1536, in two parts, the first containing a description of the musical instruments in use in his time, and the other the rudiments of the science; to these are added two commentaries, containing the precepts of polyphonous music.* It is a small book, of an oblong quarto size, containing about a hundred pages, and abounds with curious particulars; the Musurgia is in the form of a dialogue, in which the interlocutors are Andreas Silvanus, Sebastianus Virdung, sive malis, to use his own expression, Bartholomeus Stoflerus, Ottomarus Luscinius. They meet by accident, and enter into conversation on music, in which Stoflerus, acknowledging the great skill of his friend in the science, desires to be instructed in its precepts, which the other readily consents to. The dialogue is somewhat awkwardly conducted, for though Stoflerus is supposed to be just arrived from a foreign country, and the meeting to be accidental, Luscinius is prepared to receive him with a great basket of musical instruments, which his friend seeing, desires to be made acquainted with its contents. The instruments are severally produced by Luscinius, and he complies with the request of his friend by a discourse, which is no other than a lecture on them. The merit of this book is greatly enhanced by the forms of the several instruments described in it, which are very accurately delineated, and are here also given. In the first class are the plectral instruments, exhibited in this and the following page :—

Of the above two instruments it is to be observed,

* Luscinius was a man of considerable learning, and an elegant writer. He translated the Symposiacs of Plutarch, and some of the Orations of Isocrates into Latin, and wrote Commentaries on the Holy Scriptures. Between him and Erasmus there was some misunderstanding, for the latter complains of Luscinius in one of his Epistles. Jortin's Life of Erasmus, vol. II. pag. 723.

that they are both in fact Spinnets, though the latter is by Luscinius termed a Virginal, which is but another name for a small oblong spinnet. Scaliger speaks of the Clavicitherium, which appellation seems to comprehend as well the one as the other of the above instruments, as being much more ancient than the triangular spinnet, or the harpsichord; and indeed the latter seem to be an improvement of the former.

The first of the three following instruments, called by Luscinius a Clavichord, and by others sometimes a Clarichord, is used by the nuns in convents; and that the practitioners on it may not disturb the sisters in the dormitory, the strings are muffled with small bits of fine woollen cloth.

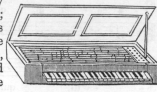

The Clavicimbalum, the next in position to it, is no other than the harpsichord, Clavicimbalum being the common Latin name for that instrument; the strings are here represented in a perpendicular situation; and there is good reason to suppose that the harpsichord was originally so constructed, notwithstanding that the upright harpsichord has of late been obtruded upon the world as a modern invention. There is a very accurate representation of an upright harpsichord in the Harmonici of Mersennus, viz., in the tract entitled De Instrumentis Harmonicis, lib. I. prop. xlii. and also in Kircher.

The last of the above three instruments is the Lyra Mendicorum, exhibited by Mersennus and Kircher; the strings are agitated by the friction of a wheel, which either is or should be rubbed with powder of rosin; all these he says have chords, which being touched with keys, make complete harmony.

There are others he says that require to be stopped at certain distances by the fingers, and of these he gives the following instrument, which he calls Lutina, and seems to be a small lute or mandolin, as an example :—

As to the above instrument, both the name and the size import that it is a diminutive of its species: that the lute was in use long before the time of Luscinius there is the clearest evidence in Chaucer and other ancient writers. In Dante is the following passage :—

'Io vidi un fatto à guisa di liuto,'

Inferno, Canto xxx.

to denote the figure of a person swoln with the dropsy. The Theorbo and Arch-lute are of more modern invention, and will be spoken of hereafter.†

† Salinas asserts that the instruments of the above class take the name of lute from their Halieutic or Boat-like form. De Musica, lib II. cap. xxi. It seems that the word Ἁλιευς [Alieus] is used by Homer and Plutarch; by the one as applying to a fisherman, by the other for a par-

Those stringed instruments, in which the vibration of the string is caused by the friction of a hair bow, as the following—

constitute, in the order observed by Luscinius, another class; the first of these instruments is a Monochord, for a reason, which it is very difficult to discover,  called the Trumpet Marine. The second, though of a very singular form, can be no other than the treble viol or the violin, for so Ludwig explains the term Geig;* and the third is clearly a species of the Chelys or bass viol. The elder Galilei is of opinion that this instrument was invented by the Italians, or rather in particular by the Neapolitans.†

In another class he places those instruments in which every chord produces a several sound, as do for example the annexed, the latter whereof is no other than a horizontal harp.

The instrument hereunder delineated corresponds exactly with the modern dulcimer; but Luscinius says it is little esteemed, because of the exceeding loudness of its sound. The name given by him to it is Hackbret, a word which in the German language signifies a Hackboard, i. e. a chopping board used by cooks,‡ to which it bears an exact resemblance. It is struck with two small sticks.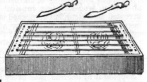

After having briefly mentioned these instruments,

ticular species of fish, vide Scap. Lex. Art. Αλς, and Leuto is the Italian word for a lute: the etymology is singular, and wants authority, and is the rather to be doubted, because Vincentio Galilei in the most express terms ascribes the invention of the lute to the English, and adds that in England lutes were made in great perfection, though some persons in his time gave the preference to those made in the neighbourhood of Brescia.

The same author observes that the lute is but little used in Germany, and gives this strange reason for it, that that country is so cold, that the inhabitants cannot stir out of their rooms, which are heated with stoves, for eight months in the year. By this it should seem that no person who does not go much abroad can be a proficient on the lute. He had never heard perhaps that Luther, who lived much in his study, played very finely on this instrument; and that upon his being summoned to render an account of his doctrines before the diet of Worms, in order to compose and calm his mind, he spent the greater part of the night preceding his appearance there, at his lute.

* Vide Jun. Etymol. Angl. Voce GIGGES. This word suggests the derivation of that other, JIGG, the name of an air or tune peculiarly adapted to the instruments of this class.

† Dial. dell Mus. pag. 147.

‡ Ludwig's German Lexicon.

Luscinius proceeds to describe those from which sound is produced by the means of air; those he says claim the first place that are acted upon by bellows, which force the air into them, and when filled, answer a touch of the finger with a musical sound. These instruments he adds, as they are more costly than others, so they exceed all others in harmony. He says that other instruments are for the use and pleasure of men, but that these are generally dedicated to the service of God.

Stoflerus upon this remarks, that the organ is almost every where made use of in divine service; and that our religious worship is no way inferior to that of the ancient Romans, which was always celebrated with music. As a proof whereof he says it is recorded that when Caius Junius, Publius Terentius, and Quintus Æmilius were consuls, the Tibicines employed in the public worship, being prohibited eating in the temple of Jove, went away in a body to the city of Tibur; the senate, growing impatient of their absence, besought the inhabitants of that city to give them up, and the Tibicines were summoned to appear in the senate-house, but they refused to obey. Upon this the Tiburtines had recourse to a stratagem; they invited them to a musical entertainment, and made them drunk, and while they were asleep threw them into a waggon and sent them to Rome, and on the morrow they found themselves in the midst of the Forum. The populace hearing of their arrival ran to meet them, and by their tears, and an assurance that they should be permitted to eat in the temple of Jove, prevailed on them to return to their duty.

This relation of Stoflerus leads him to ask the opinion of his friend upon this question, whether music has a tendency to corrupt the minds of those that apply themselves closely to the study of it, or not?

To this Luscinius answers, that no one was ever yet so senseless as to separate music from the other liberal arts, the great end whereof is to recommend integrity of life. He adds that the Pythagoreans deemed it one of the chief incentives to virtue; and that were any person of his time to make a catalogue of excellent musicians whom music itself had estranged from every vice, he would begin from Paul Hofhaimer, a man born in the Alps, not far from Saltsburg. But his character will be best given in the words of Luscinius himself, which are these: 'He has received 'great honours from the emperor Maximilian, whom 'he delights as often as he plays upon the organ. Nor 'is he more remarkable for skill in his profession, 'than for the extensiveness of his genius, and the 'greatness of his mind. Rome owes not more to 'Romulus or Camillus, than the musical world does 'to Paulus. To speak of his compositions, they are 'neither so long as to be tedious, nor does the brevity 'of them leave ought to be wished for: all is full and 'open, nothing jejune, or frigid, or languishing. His 'style is nor only learned but pleasant, florid, and 'amazingly copious, and withal correct, and this 'great man during thirty years, has suffered no one 'to exceed, or even equal him. In a word, what

'Quintilian says of Cicero I think is now come to
'pass ; and a person may judge of his own pro-
'ficiency in music according as he approves of the
'compositions of Paul, and labours day and night to
'imitate them.　This Paul has had many disciples,
'who are every where very honourably supported,
'and conduct our church in large cities and public
'places.　Of these there are several, whom I am
'very intimate with, and reverence for their great
'ingenuity and purity of manners, to wit, Johannes
'Buschner, at Constance, Joannes Kotter, Argentius
'of Bern, Conrade of Spires, Schachingerus of Padua,
'Bolfgangus of Vienna, Johannes Coloniensis, at the
'court of the duke of Saxony, and many others
'whom I pass over, as having no intimacy with
'them ; I think it is of great importance in delivering
'the precepts of any art to give an account of its
'several professors, that a learner may know whom
'he ought to imitate, and whose examples he should
'follow.'

After this eulogium on his friend Hofhaimer,
Luscinius proceeds in his description of the organ,
of which he says there are two kinds, the Portative
and the Positive, the first whereof, as its name imports, capable of being carried about like other
musical instruments, the other fixed as those are in
churches.　The figures of both are thus delineated
by Luscinius :—

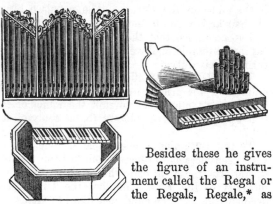

Besides these he gives
the figure of an instru-
ment called the Regal or
the Regals, Regale,* as

here represented :—

This it seems is a kind of diminutive portable
organ, and is at this day in common use in many
parts of Germany.　The second of the above figures
represents the instrument entire, the first the bellows
and wind-chest in a state of disunion from it.　In an
account of queen Elizabeth's annual expence, published
by Peck in his Desiderata Curiosa, vol. I. lib. II. page
12, among the musicians and players there occur
'Makers of instruments two,' which in a note on the
passage are said to be an organ-maker and a rigall-
maker, the former with a fee or salary of twenty, the
latter with one of ten pounds a year : and in the lists
of the establishment of his majesty's royal chapels
is an officer called Tuner of the Regals, whose business
at this day is to keep the organ of the royal chapel
in tune.

Having dispatched those instruments which are
rendered sonorous by means of wind collected and

'usus fuerit ante organa illa pneumatica quæ hodie usurpantur.' San-
sovinus, lib. VI. Descript. Venetiarum.　That is to say, in the church of
St. Raphael at Venice was to be seen the figure of a musical instrument
called a Rigabello, anciently used in churches instead of the organ.

Walther is more particular in his discription of the Regal : he makes
it to be a reed-work in an organ, with metal and also wooden pipes and
bellows adapted to it, so contrived, as that it may be taken out, and set
upon a chest or table.　He says that the name Regal is frequently given
to that stop in an organ called the Vox humana ; and in this sense Mersennus uses it in his Harmonie Universelle, liv. VI. Des Orgues, Prop.
VIII.　As touching the use of the Regal, the following is the account
which a very ingenious organ-maker, a German, now living in London,
gives of it.　'In Germany, and other parts of Europe, on Corpus Christi
'and other festivals, processions are made, in which a regal is borne
'through the streets on the shoulders of a man : wherever the procession
'stops the instrument is set down on a stool, and some one of the train
'steps forward and plays on it, he that carried it blowing the bellows.'
The same person says he once repaired a regal, so contrived as to shut up
and form a cushion, which when open discovered the pipes and keys on
one side, and the bellows and wind-chest on the other.　Walther adds to
his description of this instrument, from Michael Prætorius, that the
name of it is supposed to have arisen from the circumstance of its
having been presented by the inventor to some king.　'Regale, quasi
dignum rege.　Regium vel regale opus.'

These authorities, and the representation of it by Luscinius, seem
sufficient to prove that the regal is a pneumatic, and not a stringed
instrument.

But Mersennus relates that the Flemings invented an instrument, les
Regales de Bois, consisting of seventeen cylindrical pieces of wood,
decreasing gradually in length, so as to produce a succession of tones
and semitones in the diatonic series, which had keys, and was played
on as a spinnet, the hint whereof he says was taken from an instrument
in use among the Turks, consisting of twelve wooden cylinders, of
different lengths, strung together, which being suspended, and struck
with a stick having a ball at the end, produced music.　Harm. Universelle,
liv. III. pag. 175.

Ligon, in his History of Barbadoes, pag. 48, relates a pretty story of
an Indian, who having a musical ear, by the mere force of his genius
invented an instrument composed of wooden billets, yielding music, and
nearly corresponding with those above described, for speaking of the
music of the islanders he says, 'I found Macow [the negro] very apt for
'it of himselfe, and one day comming into the house (which none of the
'negroes use to doe, unless an officer as he was) he found me playing on
'a Theorbo, and singing to it, which he hearkened very attentively to ; and
'when I had done took the Theorbo in his hand, and strooke one string,
'stopping it by degrees upon every fret, and finding the notes to varie
'till it came to the body of the instrument, and that the neerer the body
'of the instrument he stopt, the smaller or higher the sound was, which
'he found was by the shortning the string ; considered with himselfe
'how he might make some triall of this experiment upon such an in-
'strument as he could come by, having no hope ever to have any instru-
'ment of this kind to practise on.　In a day or two after, walking in the
'plantine grove, to refresh me in that cool shade, and to delight myselfe
'with the sight of those plants, which are so beautifull, as though they
'left a fresh impression in me when I parted with them, yet upon a
'review something is discern'd in their beautie more then I remembered
'at parting, which caused me to make often repair thither ; I found this
'negroe (whose office it was to attend there, being the keeper of that
'grove,) sitting on the ground, and before him a piece of large timber,
'upon which he had laid cross six billets, and having a hand-saw and a
'hatchet by him, would cut the billets by little and little, till he had
'brought them to the tunes he would fit them to ; for the shorter they
'were the higher the notes, which he tried by knocking upon the ends of
'them with a stick which he had in his hand.　When I found him at it I
'took the stick out of his hand and tried the sound, finding the six billets
'to have six distinct notes one above another, which put me in a wonder
'how he of himselfe should without teaching doe so much.　I then
'shewed him the difference between flats and sharps, which he presently
'apprehended, as between FA and MI ; and he would have cut two more
'billets to those tunes, but I had then no time to see it done, and so left
'him to his own enquiries.　I say this much to let you see that some
'of these people are capable of learning arts.'

* REGALE, sorta di strumento simile all' organo, ma minore.　Altieri,
Dizion. Ital. ed Ingl.　Lord Bacon distinguishes between the regal and
the organ in a manner which shews them to be instruments of the same
class.　'The sounds that produce tones, are ever from such bodies as
'have their parts and pores equal, as are the nightingale pipes of regals
'or organs.'　Nat. Hist. Cent. II. Sect. 102.　But notwithstanding
these authorities, the appellative Regal has given great trouble to the
lexicographers, whose sentiments with regard to its significations are
here collected, and brought into one point of view.

Skinner, upon the authority of an old English dictionary, conjectures
the word Rigals, or Regals, to signify a stringed instrument, namely
a clavichord ; possibly founding his opinion on the nature of the office
of tuner of the regals, and not knowing that such wind instruments
as the organ need frequent tuning, as do the clavichord and other
stringed instruments.　It is highly probable that the word Regal is
a corruption of Rigabello, of which take the following explanation from
Sir Henry Spelman : 'In æde sancti Raphaelis Venetiis, instrumenti
'musici cujusdam forma extat, ei nomen Rigabello ; cujus in ecclesiis

forced into them by bellows, he speaks of such as are filled with air blown into them by the mouth; and of these he gives a great number, particularly the Schalmey, *i. e.* Chalameau, and Bombardt, flutes of various kinds, cornets, the Cornamusa, or bagpipe, and some other instruments, for which no other than German names can be found, all which are hereunder represented, according to their respective classes.

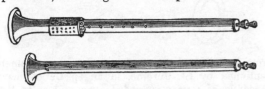

The second of the two instruments above delineated is the Schalmey, so called from Calamus a reed, which is a part of it; the other called Bombardt is the bass to the former; these instruments have been improved by the French into the Hautboy and Bassoon.

Next follow flutes of various sizes, all of which, bating the simplicity of their form, as being devoid of ornaments, seem to bear an exact resemblance to the flute à bec,* or, as it is called, the common English flute. Whether this instrument be of English invention or not, is hard to say. Galilei calls it Flauto dritto, in contradistinction to the Flauto traverso, and adds it was brought into Italy by the French. Notwithstanding which, Mersennus scruples not to term it the English flute, calling the other the Helvetian flute, and takes occasion to mention one John Price, an Englishman, as an excellent performer on it.† The word Flute is derived from Fluta, the Latin for a Lamprey or small eel taken in the Sicilian seas, having seven holes, the precise number of those in front of the flute, on each side, immediately below the gills. Luscinius has thus represented this species:—

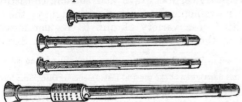

The largest instrument of the four is the bass flute.

These are succeeded by two other flutes, the first called the Schuuegel, the other the Zuuerchpfeiff; the former bears a resemblance to the traverse or German flute, though it is much slenderer and does not agree with it in number of holes:—

It seems that the invention of the traverse flute is not to be attributed either to the Germans or the Helvetians, notwithstanding that the elder Galilei and Mersennus ascribe it to the latter; the well-known antique statue of the piping faun seems to be a proof of the contrary; and there is now extant an engraving

on a very large scale published some years ago, of a tessellated pavement of a temple of Fortuna Virilis, erected by Sylla at Rome, in which is a representation of a young man playing on a traverse pipe, with an aperture to receive his breath, exactly corresponding with the German flute.

Of the Zuuerchpfeiff, the second of the above instruments, no satisfactory account can be given. Luscinius next exhibits the forms of four other wind instruments, namely, 1. The Ruspfeiff. 2. The Krumhorn. 3. The Gemsen horn. And 4. The Zincke:—

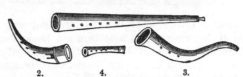

By the name of the first nothing more is meant than the black-pipe, Rus in the German language signifying Black, and Pfeiff a Pipe. The word Krumhorn is compounded of the adjective krum, *i. e.* crooked, and horn, and signifies a cornet or small shawm; and it is said that the stop in an organ called the Principal answers to it. Gems, in the German language, signifies the Shamoy or wild goat; and this appellation denotes the Gemsen horn. Zincken are the small branches on the head of a deer, and therefore it is to be supposed that the instrument here called the Zincke is little better than a child's toy, or in short a whistle.‡

Luscinius gives the Krumhorn in a more artificial form, that is to say, with the addition of a reed, or something like it, at one end, the other being contorted to nearly a semicircle, with regular perforations, as here:—

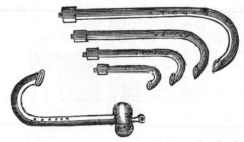

But for these, as also for the Platerspil, the lowest in position of the instruments above delineated, the bare representation of them must here suffice.

The Cornamusa, or Bagpipe, is in the German language very properly termed the Sackpfeiff, *i. e.* the Sack-pipe; its figure is thus given:—

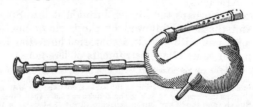

* Bec is an old Gaulish word, signifying the beak of a bird or fowl; but more especially a cock. Menage in articulo. The term Flute à bec must therefore signify the Beaked Flute, an epithet which appears upon comparing it with the traverse flute, to be very proper.
† Harmonic. De Instrumentis Harmonicis, lib. II. prop. ii. vi.

‡ The names and descriptions of these several instruments instruct us as to the nature and design of many stops in the organ, and what they are intended to imitate. To instance in the Krumhorn; the tone of it originally resembled that of a small cornet, though many ignorant

Luscinius next speaks of certain ductile tubes of brass, meaning thereby the trumpet species, though in strictness of speech the Tuba Ductilis signifies the Sacbut. Bross 226. The first he terms the Busaun, and is probably the sackbut or bass trumpet, and the second the Felt, *i. e.* the field or army trumpet :—

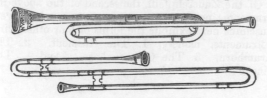

Vincentio Galilei says that the trumpet was invented at Nuremburg, an assertion not reconcileable to the general opinion of its antiquity. Brossard calls it the most noble of the ancient portative instruments; but it is highly probable that Galilei means the brazen trumpet; and that Brossard had a more general idea of it is evident from his making the word Tromba synonymous with Buccina, which means a trumpet made of the horn of an ox; and if so there is no great disagreement between the two authors.

The Claret which is next given by Luscinius, may mean the Clarion, an instrument of the same form, but smaller, and consequently of a more acute sound than the trumpet :—

The following instrument is by Luscinius called the Thurnerhorn, and is a kind of trumpet or clarion :—

From hence he descends to bells, and even to the anvil and hammers, by means whereof Pythagoras is said to have investigated the consonances. He then proceeds to treat of the pulsatile instruments, at the head whereof he places the common, or side, and kettle-drums. The drum is said by Le Clerc to be an Oriental invention; and he adds, that the Arabians,  or rather perhaps the Moors, brought it into Spain.

And these are followed by the bugle or hunting-horn,* a pot, with a stick, a contorted horn, the Jew's harp, and some other instruments of less note.

organ-makers have corrupted the word into Cremona, supposing it to be an imitation of the Cremona violin. The Gemsen horn and Busaun, corrupted into Buzain, answering to the sacbut, are to be found in many great organs in Germany, as is also the Zincke corruptly spelt Cink.

* BUGLE from the Saxon bugan, curvare, arcuare, signifies a thing bowed or bent. Vide Jun. Etymol. A basket-maker calls the curved handle or bale of a basket, a bugle.

It is probable that the hint of the stick and salt-box, Merry Andrew's

From hence he digresses to the Jewish instruments mentioned by St. Jerome, in an epistle of his to Dardanus, of a very awkward form, and as to their construction inexplicable.

The description of the musical instruments contained in this first book of the Musurgia leads Stoflerus into an enquiry into their use, the explanation whereof, the nature of the consonances, and the signification of the several characters, are the subject of the second book, which containing nothing remarkable, it is needless to abridge.

CHAP. LXXII.

NOTWITHSTANDING the great variety of instruments extant at the time when Luscinius wrote his Musurgia, there is very little reason to suppose that what we now call a concert of music, altogether instrumental, was then known. The first of this kind were symphoniac compositions, mostly for viols of different sizes, called Fantazias,† and these continued till about the middle of the seventeenth century, when they gave way to a much more elegant species of composition, the Sonata di Chiesa, and the Sonata di Camera; the first of these, as being adapted to church-service, was grave and solemn, consisting of slow movements, intermixed with fugues; the other admitted of a variety of airs to regular measures, such as the Allemade, the Courant, the Saraband,

instrument to divert the mob, was taken from the pot and stick above represented.

To this description of the musical instruments by Ottomarus Luscinius that contained in the Orbis Sensualium Pictus of Johannes Amos Comenius may be considered as a supplement, the brevity of which latter is amply atoned for by its perspicuity. Comenius's design in this little work was to instruct youth as well by sensible images, as the names of things; and under the article of Musical Instruments he has given the names and uses of thirty, with as precise a delineation of their respective forms as half a page of a small volume would allow of. The following character of this inestimable little book in the Sculptura of Mr. Evelyn exhibits but a faint representation of its excellence; speaking of the arts of sculpture, and their tendency to facilitate instruction, he says: 'What a specimen of this Jo. Amos Commenius in his Orbis 'Sensualium Pictus gives us in a Nomenclator of all the fundamental 'things and actions of men in the whole world, is public: and I do 'boldly affirm it to be a piece of such excellent use, as that the like was 'never extant; however it comes not yet to be perceived.' Sculptura, or the History of Chalcography, chap. V.

Comenius was a native of Moravia, and flourished in the middle of the last century. He came into England in the year 1641, upon an invitation to assist in a plan for a reformation in the method of instructing youth, but the troubles of the times drove him from hence to Sweden, where he was favourably entertained and patronized by count Oxenstiern. Bayle, art. COMENIUS, has given upon the whole an unfavourable account of him, representing him as an enthusiast in religion, and a friend of Madam Bourignon; neither of which particulars admitting them to be true, detract from the merit of his writings, nor indeed from his general character, which is that of a very learned, ingenious, and pious man. He died at Amsterdam in the year 1671, being then eighty years of age.

† In the Harm. Universelle of Mersennus, Des Instrumens à Vent. 277, is a Fantasia for cornets in five parts by the Sieur Henry le Jeune, but it seems to have been composed about the time that Fantazias began to be disused.

and others, of which there are numberless examples in the works of the Italian masters; these were succeeded by the concerto, which is nothing more than a sonata in four parts, with a reduplication of some of them, so as to make the whole number nominally seven.

The earliest intimation touching the origin of instrumental music in parts, is contained in a book written by Thomas à Sancta Maria, a Spanish Dominican, and published at Valladolid in 1570, intitled 'Arte de tanner fantasia para tecla, viguela y todo instrumendo de tres o quatro ordenes.' From hence, and because neither Franchinus, Glareanus, nor even Luscinius himself, have intimated to the contrary, it may be concluded that the instrumental music of their time was either solitary, or at most unisonous with the voice : and with respect to vocal harmony, it seems to have been so appropriated to the service of the church, as to leave it a question whether it was ever used at public festivities. It however continued not long under this restraint, for no sooner were the principles of counterpoint established and disseminated, as they were by the writings of Franchinus, Glareanus, and the other authors herein beforementioned, than harmony began to make its way into the palaces of princes and the houses of the nobility ; and of this the story above related of Lewis XII. and his Phonascus Iodocus Pratensis contains a proof ; and at this period the distinction between Clerical, or ecclesiastical, and Secular music seems to have taken its rise. At Rome the former was cultivated with a degree of assiduity proportioned to the zeal of the pontiffs, and the advantages which the science had derived from the lectures and writings of Franchinus : and in England it was studied with the same view, namely, the service of religion. The strictness of our own countrymen must indeed appear very remarkable in this respect, for if we judge from the compositions of the succession of English musicians, from John of Dunstable, who died in 1455, to Taverner, who flourished about 1525, it must seem that their attention was engrossed by the framing of masses, antiphons, and hymns ; no other than compositions of this kind being to be found in those collections of their works which are yet remaining, either in the public libraries or other repositories. It has already been related that the Germans, to whom may be added the inhabitants of the several parts of Switzerland, were among the first that cultivated the art of practical composition ; when this is recollected, it may induce an acquiescence in an opinion which otherwise might admit of a doubt, namely, that vocal concerts had their rise in the Low Countries, or rather in those parts of Flanders, which about the middle of the sixteenth century were under the dominion of the emperor of Germany. The fact is thus to be accounted for ; the crown of Spain had received a great accession of wealth and power by its conquests in America in the preceding century : and Charles V. king of Spain and emperor of Germany, favouring the disposition of the inhabitants of the Low Countries, which led them to trade and merchandise, not only made the city of Brussels the

place of residence for himself and his court, but by the encouragement he gave to traffic, and other means, so ordered it, that a considerable portion of his revenues centered in this part of his dominions as a bank from whence it was circulated through all Europe. The splendour and magnificence of his court, and the consequent encouragement of men of genius to settle there, drew together a number of men of the greatest eminence in all professions, but more especially musicians. Of some of the most famous of these particular mention is made by Lodovico Guicciardini, the nephew of the Italian historian of that name, in a work of his entitled 'Descrittione di tutti i Paesi Bassi,' printed at Antwerp in 1556 and in 1581. In this book the author speaks of the flourishing state of the Low Countries, the wealth of the inhabitants, and the perfection to which the arts had arrived there, in the enumeration whereof he speaks thus of music :
'Questi sono i veri maestri della musica, e quelli
'che l'hanno restaurata, e ridotta a perfettione,
'perche l'hanno tanto propria e naturale, che
'huomini e donne cantan' naturalmente a misura,
'con grandissima gratia e melodia, onde poi con-
'giunta l' arte alla natura, fanno e di voce, e di
'tutti gli strumenti quella pruova e harmonia, che
'si vede e ode, talche se ne truova sempre per tutto
'le Corti de Principi Christiani.'

The masters celebrated by this author as the great improvers of music are, Jusquin di Pres, Obrecht, Ockegem, Ricciafort, Adriano Willaert, Giovanni Mouton, Verdelot, Gomberto, Lupus lupi, Cortois, Crequilon, Clemente non Papa, and Cornelio Canis, who, he says, were all dead before the time of writing his book ; but he adds that they were succeeded by a great number of others, as namely, Cipriano di Rore, Gian le Coick, Filippo de Monti, Orlando di Lassus, Mancicourt, Jusquino Baston, Christiano Hollando, Giaches di Waert, Bonmarche, Severino Cornetto, Piero du Hot, Gherardo di Tornout, Huberto Waelrant, and Giachetto di Berckem, who were settled at Antwerp, and in other parts of Flanders, and were in the highest reputation for skill and ingenuity. This account given by Guicciardini of the flourishing state of music in the Low Countries is confirmed by Thuanus, who, in an eulogium on Orlando de Lasso, takes occasion to observe that in his time Belgium abounded with excellent musicians.

Besides that these men were favoured by their prince, they received considerable encouragement in the prosecution of their studies from the most opulent of the inhabitants, who at that time were both Merchants and Courtiers. Of the magnificence and liberality of which class of men such stories are related as must seem incredible to those who are not acquainted with the history of that period. Some idea may be formed of the grandeur and dignity of the mercantile character in the sixteenth century from the extensive commerce of Gresham and Sutton, our countrymen, the former of whom is said, by means of his correspondence and connexions, to have drained the bank of Genoa, and thereby retarded the Spanish invasion for two years ; and the other to have covered the sea with his ships.   Rembrandt's famous print of the gold-weigher encompassed with casks of coined gold, which he computes not by tale, but weight, suggests such an idea of enormous wealth, as makes the traders of the present time appear like pedlars; but the fact is, that the merchants in the ages preceding were but few in number, and that in consequence of their interest and intelligence, their knowledge in the living languages, and perhaps for other reasons, they had free access to princes, and held the rank of courtiers.*

The author above-cited, speaking of the city of Antwerp, the great mart of Europe, and of the numerous resort of merchants of all countries thither, takes occasion to speak of the Foccheri, or Fuggers, of Augsburg, three brothers of the same family, the eldest named Anthony, and the second Raimond, all merchants, whom he mentions as rivalling the highest nobility in Europe in riches, magnificence, and liberality.   Of the first a judgment may be formed from the journal of our Edward VI. printed in Burnet's History of the Reformation, wherein appear so many minutes of negociations with the Fuggers, for the loan of large sums of money, that he seems to have had more dependance on them than on his own treasury. In the journal above-mentioned the Foulacre is the term by which the copartnership or house of these three men is to be understood.   Sir John Hayward approaching somewhat nearer to the true orthography, calls it the Foulker.   From the minutes in the journal it appears that the rate of interest taken by them was ten in the hundred, which, according to Sir John Hayward's account, was four per cent. under the usual rate of interest at that time,† and that Thomas Gresham was the principal negotiator of these loans, in all which there appears to have been the most punctual and honourable dealing, as well on the part of the Fuggers, as of the king.‡

* Discrittione, pag. 42.
The evidence of this fact is contained in a very curious book, supposed to have been written in the twelfth century, by a Norwegian nobleman, in the Icelandic language, and from thence translated into Danish and Latin, with the title of Speculum Regale, and published at Soroe by Halfdan Einersen, a professor there, in 1768, in a quarto volume.   It is a system of policy adapted to the age in which it was originally composed, with a view to the four professions or occupations of the greatest importance to a state, that is to say, the merchant, the lawyer, the divine, and the husbandman or farmer.

Under the first head are contained the instructions of a father to his son, touching the means of advancing his fortunes, in which he exhorts him to betake himself to the profession of a merchant, and in order thereto, to acquire a competent skill in the mathematics, particularly arithmetic and astronomy; in the law, and in the Latin and Walloon languages, and to visit foreign countries.   He advises him also to be splendid in his apparel and equipage, magnificent in his entertainments, and to be careful that his table be 'covered with a clean cloth;' to be liberal in his expenses, and, above all, to appear frequently at courts, where, says he, merchants are considered as the Satellites of princes, to whom they are frequently appointed agents or procurators.   He also asserts that no one can become a Courtier unless he hath travelled as a Merchant to foreign countries.

It is a not little curious to observe how Guicciardini's account of the state of the Low Countries in his time, falls in with the sentiments of the author of the Speculum Regale, and that evidence of the truth of his assertions should subsist, notwithstanding the natural vicissitude of things, four hundred years after he wrote; for Guicciardini relates that the catholic king [Philip II.], the king of Portugal, and the queen of England disdained not to receive merchants into their company, but employed them in mercantile negociations, calling them their factors. He says that the catholic king had two, Gaspar Schetz and Gian Lopez; the king of Portugal one, Francesco Pesoa; and the queen of England one, namely, Messer Tommaso Grassano, cavaliere, i. e. Sir Thomas Gresham, a man much honoured, 'il quale parimente con sufficiente 'proccura, ha levato per lei di questa borsa grosse somme di denari e 'le va ricapitando nobilimente.' Descritt. pag. 170.

† Life and Raigne of king Edw. VI. quarto, pag. 154.

‡ Vide Collection of Records, &c. referred to in the second part of Burnet's Hist. Reform. pag. 25. 27. 46. 48. 53.

Roger Ascham, in a letter to a friend of his at Cambridge, dated 20 Jan. 1551, from Augsburg, says, 'There be five merchants in this town thought able 'to disburse as much ready money as five of the 'greatest kings in Christendom.   The emperor would 'have borrowed money of one of them, the merchant 'said he might spare "ten hundred thousand guil-"ders," and the emperor would have had eighteen; 'a guilder is 3s. 6d.   These merchants are three 'brethren Fuccurs, two brethren Bamgartner.§   One 'of the Fuccurs doth lodge, and hath done all the 'year, in his house the emperor, the king of the 'Romans, the prince of Spain, and the queen of 'Hungary, regent of Flanders, which is here, besides 'his family and children.   His house is covered with 'copper.'   Ascham's Works published by James Bennet, pag. 376.

Bayle says of these men that they had rendered themselves illustrious by their liberalities to men of letters: they made great offers to Erasmus, and presented him with a silver cup.

Luther takes notice of their amazing wealth, and says the Fuggers and the money-changers of Augsburg lent the emperor at one time eight and twenty tons of gold, and that one of them left eighty tons at his death.†

Bayle also celebrates the magnificence and generosity of these brethren, and tells the following story of them: 'The Fuggeri, celebrated German mer-'chants, to testify their gratitude to Charles V. who 'had done them the honour to lodge in their house 'when he passed through Augsburg, one day, amongst 'other acts of magnificence, laid upon the hearth a 'large bundle of cinamon, a merchandize then of 'great price, and lighted it with a note of hand of 'the emperor for a considerable sum which they had 'lent him.'¶

Farther, the riches of this family were so great as to be the subject of a proverb, which Cervantes himself puts in the mouth of his hero, for when Don Quixote is giving a fictitious account of his adventures in the cave of Montesinos, he relates that his mistress Dulcinea had sent a damsel to request of him the loan of six reals upon the pawn of her dimity petticoat, and that he dismissed the messenger with

§ Of the family of Bamgartner or Paumgartner an account is given pag. 314, in not.

‖ Colloquia Mensalia, pag. 86.

¶ It is probable that this story gave occasion to the following stanza in the old ballad of Whittington:—

'More his fame to advance,
'Thoufands he lent his king
'To maintain wars in France,
'Glory from thence to bring:
'And after at a feaft,
'Which he the king did make,
'He burnt the bonds all in jeft,
'And would no money take.

The author whereof, unwilling that his hero should be outdone by any foreign merchant, has engrafted this story into his narration, upon the bare supposition that under the like circumstances Whittington would have shewn as much loyalty and liberality as the Fugger, he being indeed a prodigy of wealth and munificence, and one of the many ancient citizens of London, whose good deeds have rendered them an honour to their country, and to human nature itself.   See an account of him in Stowe's Survey, tit. Honour of Citizens and Worthinesse of Men.

Sir Richard Whittington was thrice mayor of London, viz., in the years 1397, 1406, and 1419, but the ballad above-cited can hardly be more ancient than the time of queen Elizabeth.

four, which was all that he had, saying to her,* 'Sweetheart, tell your lady that I am grieved to my 'soul at her distresses, and wish I were a Fugger † 'to remedy them.'

The above facts imply liberality, and, to say the truth, a disposition not quite so commendable; but the nobleness and grandeur of their spirit was manifested in the erection of sumptuous edifices,‡ and by their patronage of learned and ingenious men in all professions; and the benefits thence arising were enjoyed by the scholars, the painters, sculptors, goldsmiths, engravers, and musicians of that day, in common with other artists. To what degree the musicians in particular were thought to merit encouragement, may in some measure be collected from the passage above referred to in Guicciardini; but their title to it will best appear from the account hereafter given of them, and the works by them severally published.

Guicciardini has taken frequent occasion to mention the pompous service in the great church of Antwerp, and in other churches of Flanders, celebrated with voices and instruments of various kinds. Compositions of this sort may well be supposed to have employed the masters residing there; but it was not in the study of these alone that they were engaged: concerts of instrumental music, as has already been mentioned, were then scarcely known; but vocal music in parts was not only the entertainment of persons of rank at public solemnities, but was so much the customary amusement at social meetings, and in private families, that every well-educated person of either sex was supposed capable of joining in it. Castiglione, who lived about this time, mentions this as one of the necessary accomplishments of his courtier, and requires of him to be able to sing his part at sight,§ which, when the nature of the vocal compositions then in practice is explained, will appear to have been no very difficult matter.

By that convivial kind of harmony above spoken of, is to be understood a musical composition of three or more parts for different voices, adapted to the words of some short but elegant poem, and known by the name of the Madrigal.‖ The Italian language

was at this time generally understood throughout Europe; its fitness for music entitled it to a preference above all others, and the sonnets of Petrarch, and other of the old Italian poets, to which in the preceding ages the barbarous melodies of the Provençal minstrels had been adapted, were looked on as the most eligible subjects for musical composition; and to render these delightful, the powers of melody and harmony were by some of the first class of masters mentioned by Guicciardini, very successfully employed.

It cannot be supposed that the first essays of this kind had much to recommend them besides the correctness of the harmony, which was just and natural, and yet these had their charms: Anne Boleyn, a lively and well accomplished young woman, and who had lived some years in France, doted on the compositions of Jusquin and Mouton, and had collections of them made for the private practice of herself and her maiden companions; but the best of these fell very far short of those of the succeeding age.

The excellence of this species of musical composition, the madrigal, may be inferred from this circumstance, that it kept its ground even long after the introduction of music on the theatres; for dramatic music, or what is now called the opera, had its rise about the year 1600, and it is well known that one of the finest works of Stradella, who was contemporary with our Purcell, is the madrigal for five voices, 'Clori son fido amante.'

Of some of the masters mentioned by Guicciardini, in the passage above-cited, there are particulars extant which may be thought worth relating; and first of Jusquin, so often mentioned by Glareanus and others of his time, by the name of IODOCUS PRATENSIS.

In that short account given of him by Walther, in his Lexicon, it is said that he was born in the Low Countries, but in what part thereof is not known, though his name Pratensis, bespeaks him a native of Prato, a town in Tuscany. He was a disciple of Johannes Ockegem, or Okenheim, and for his excellence in his art was appointed master of the chapel to Lewis XII. king of France. Salinas says he was universally allowed to be the best musician of his time. Glareanus is lavish in his commendation, and has given the following account of him: 'Iodocus 'Pratensis, or Jusquin de Prez, was the principal of 'the musicians of his time, and possessed of a degree 'of wit and ingenuity scarce ever before heard of. 'Some pleasant stories are related of him before he 'came to be known in the world, amongst many 'others the following may deserve a recital. Lewis 'XII. king of France had promised him some eccle-

* 'Amiga mia, à vuestra senora, que à mi me pesa en el alma de sus 'trabajos, y que quisièra sèr un Fucàr para remediarlos.' Don Quixote, part II. lib. VI. cap. xxiii.

† See Article "Fugger," Moreri's Dictionary edition, 1740.

‡ Beatus Rhenanus, in a letter to a friend, gives a description of the magnificent houses, or rather palaces, of Anthony and Raimond Fugger; and a late traveller speaks of a memorial of their opulence yet remaining, that is to say, a quarter in the city of Augsburg called the Fuggery, consisting of several streets and fair palaces built by them. Journey over Europe by A. D. Chancel, octavo, Lond. 1714, pag. 96.

§ Il Corteg. lib. II.

‖ It is very difficult to say from whence this word is derived. Kircher laboured in vain to find an etymology for it. The bishop of Avranches. Huet, in his treatise De l' Origine des Romans, supposes it to be a corruption of the word Martegaux, a name given to the ancient inhabitants of a particular district of Provence, who were probably the inventors of, or excelled in this particular species of musical composition. Had he known that there is in Spain a town named Madrigal, it is likely he would have deduced its origin from the Spaniards.

Doni, who is clear that the Madrigal came originally from the Provençals, is nevertheless at a great loss for the derivation of the word, and gives his reader the choice of two etymologies, the best of which seems to be the Italian word Mandra, a flock, a herd, a sheep-fold: and even against this it is objected that pastoral manners are not peculiar to this kind of poetical composition. Crescimbeni, in his Commentarj Intorno all' Istoria della volgare Poesia, vol. I. lib. ii. cap. 22, has taken up the enquiry, but leaves the matter nearly where he found it; and so indeed does Mattheson, who wrote some years after him. Better success

has attended the enquiries into the origin and history of this species of composition. Doni fixes the invention of it to the commencement of the fifteenth century. Trattato della Melodie, pag. 97. And Mattheson acquiesces in this opinion, and asserts that Anselmo de Parma, Marchetto de Padoana, Prosdocimus Beldimandis, and other musicians, who are but barely named by Franchinus, were the first composers of madrigals; and that Iodocus Pratensis, Joannes Mouton, Gombert, and others, brought this style to perfection. Volkomenon Capel-meister, pag. 79. In both these particulars Mattheson seems to be mistaken; for neither does it appear that these early musicians composed madrigals, nor were they brought to perfection by Iodocus and the rest named by him. Those that perfected this style were Orlando de Lasso, Philippo de Monte, Cypriano de Rore, among the Flemings, and of the Italians, Palestrina, Pomponio Nenna, and his disciple the admirable Carlo Gesualdo, prince of Venosa.

'siastical preferment; but the promise was forgot
' (as too often happens in kings' courts) Jusquin
' being much disturbed in mind, composed a Psalm
beginning " Memor esto verbi tui servo tuo," but
with such elegance and majesty, that when it was
carried to the king's chapel, and there justly performed, it excited universal admiration. The king,
who heard it, blushed for shame; and as it were did
not dare to defer the performance of his promise, but
' gave him the benefice. He then having experienced
' the liberality of this prince, composed another psalm
' by way of thanksgiving, beginning " Bonitatem fe-
' cisti cum servo tuo Domine." As to those two
' pieces of harmony, it may be observed how much
' more the hopes of reward incited his genius in the
' former, than the attainment of it did in the other.'

The Dodecachordon contains also some extracts
from a mass of his composing, intitled L'Homme
armé, which indeed is celebrated by Luscinius, Salinas, and many other authors. Besides these a great
number of his compositions are contained in the Dodecachordon, and among others, that in which, notwithstanding the adage of Erasmus above-mentioned,
he has ventured in a De Profundis for four voices to
pass from the Dorian to the Phrygian mode.

Notwithstanding the favour in which he stood with
Lewis XII. it seems that Jusquin in his latter days
experienced a sorrowful reverse of fortune. In the
Supplementi Musicali of Zarlino, pag. 314, is the following sonnet of Serasino Acquilano to that purpose:—

Giosquin non dir che'l ciel sia crudo ed empio,
 Che t'adornò de si soblime ingegno :
 Et s'alcun veste ben, lascia lo sdegno;
 Che di ciò gode alcun buffone, ò sempio.

Da quel ch'io ti dirò prendi l'essempio;
 L'argento e l'or, che da se stess' è degno,
 Si mostra nudo, è sol si veste il legno,
 Quando s'adorna alcun theatro ò tempio:
Il favor di costei vien presto manco,
 E mille volte il dì, sia pur giocondo,
 Si muta il stato lor di nero in bianco.
Mi chi hà virtù, gira à suo modo il mondo;
 Com' huom che nuota ed hà la zucca al fianco,
 Metti'l sott' acqua pur, non teme il fondo.

Walther, from the Athenæ Belgicæ of Swertius,
cites the following epitaph on him :—

O mors inevitabilis !
 Mors amara, mors crudelis
 Josquinum dum necasti
 Illum nobis abstulisti ;
 Qui suam per harmoniam
 Illustravit ecclesiam,
 Propterea dic tu musice:
 Requiescat in pace. Amen.

Castiglione relates a story which bespeaks the
high opinion entertained by the world of Jusquin's
character as a musician. He says that at a certain
time some verses were produced to the duchess of
Urbino as of the composition of Sannazaro, which
were applauded as excellent; but that as soon as it
was discovered that they were not really his, they
were condemned as worse than indifferent; so likewise says he a motet sung before the same duchess
met with little approbation till it was known to be of
the composition of Josquin de Prez.*

The following motett of Iodocus Pratensis, containing a canon of two in one, occurs in the Dodecachordon, and is here inserted as a specimen of his
style and abilities as a composer :—

* Il Corteg. lib. II.

IODOCUS PRATENSIS.

CHAP. LXXIII.

JACOBUS HOBRECHTH, a Fleming, is celebrated for his great skill and judgment, and is said by Glareanus to have been possessed of such a degree of strength and celerity of invention, as that he composed a whole mass, and a very excellent one, in a night's time, to the admiration of the learned. The same author asserts that all the monuments that are left of his composition have in them a wonderful majesty; and that he did not, like Jusquin, affect unusual passages, but gave his compositions to the public without disguise, trusting for the applause of his auditors to their own intrinsic merit.* He was preceptor in music to Erasmus.†

JOHANNES OCKEGEM, or as Glareanus calls him, Okenheim, was also a native of the Low Countries, and as he was the preceptor of Iodocus Pratensis, must be supposed to be somewhat more ancient than his disciple. Glareanus mentions a composition of his for thirty-six voices, which, though he had never seen it, he says, had the reputation of being admirable for its contrivance. In the composition of Fugue he is said to have been excellent; Glareanus says he affected to compose songs that might be sung in different modes, and recommends to the notice of his reader the following fugue for three voices, which, though said by him to be in the Epidiatessaron, or fourth below, is in truth in the Epidiapente or fifth below after a perfect time. It should seem by the different signatures at the head of each stave, that this was intended as an example of a cantus to be sung in different modes.

Ambrose Wilphlingsederus of Nuremberg was at the pains of resolving this intricate composition, and published it in his Erotemata Musices Practicæ printed in 1563. The canon and resolution are here given together :—

FUGA IN EPIDIAPENTE

RESOLUTION.

* Dodecachordon, pag. 456.   † Ibid.

JOHANNES OKENHEIM.

Antimo Liberati, a musician of the last century, and a singer in the pontifical chapel, says that, taking their example from the schools of those two great men Okenheim and Iodocus Pratensis, many foreign masters erected musical academies in different kingdoms and provinces, the first of whom was Gaudio Mell, a Fleming, who instituted at Rome a noble and excellent school for music, in which many pupils were instructed in the science, and among them Gio.

Pier Luigi Palestrina.* The truth of this relation, so far as it regards the name of Palestrina's preceptor, is very questionable, and will be the subject of a future enquiry.

About this time flourished ADRIANO WILLAERT, a native of Bruges; this person was intended for the profession of a lawyer, and studied in that faculty in the university of Paris, but an irresistible propensity

* Lettera scritta dal Sig. Antimo Liberati in risposta ad una del Sig. Ovidio Persapegi, Roma, 1685.

to music diverted his attention from the law, and engaged him deeply in the study of that science; upon his quitting Paris he went for improvement to Italy, and by the favour of pope Leo X. became, to use the style of Zarlino and other writers, 'Maestro 'di Cappella della serenissima Signoria di Venetia;'* by which appellation is to be understood master of the choir of the church of St. Mark. He seems to have been the inventor of compositions for two or more choirs, that is to say, those wherein the offices are sung alternately by several chorusses, the effect whereof is at this day sufficiently understood.† Artusi, Doni, Printz, and other writers speak of Willaert in general terms as a mere practical musician, a composer of motets, madrigals, and airs, among whom they however admit he holds the first rank; but Zarlino, who was his disciple, and consequently must have been intimately acquainted with him, relates that he was incessantly employed in making calculations and devising diagrams for demonstrating the principles of harmony, and, in short, represents him as the ablest theorist of the age. It is highly probable that this was his true character; and the particulars above related may in a great measure account for that extreme propensity which Zarlino throughout his voluminous works discovers for that branch of musical science. His master had made him sensible of its value, and had given a direction to the studies of his disciple, who in return has taken every occasion to celebrate his praises, and to transmit to posterity in the character of Adrian Willaert, an exemplar of a consummate musician.

There are extant of Willaert's composition, Psalmi Vespertini omnium Dierum Festorum per Annum, 4 Vocum, 1557; Motettæ 6 Vocum, published in 1542; Cantiones Musicæ, seu Motettæ, cum aliis ejusdem Cantionibus Italicis 4, 5, 6, et 7 Vocum; and Villanellæ Neapolitanæ 4 Vocum, published together in 1588, and other works.‡ He is sufficiently known to those who are conversant with the Italian writers on music, by the name of Messer Adriano.

A few of the most excellent of Willaert's motets are pointed out in the Istitutioni Harmoniche of Zarlino, terza parte, cap. lxvi. and are there celebrated as some of the finest compositions of that time. His doctrines and opinions respecting some of the most abstruse questions in music are delivered with great accuracy in the Dimostrationi of Zarlino. He was very much afflicted with the gout, but seems by Zarlino's account of him to have nevertheless retained the exercise of his mental faculties in all their vigour, and to have rendered himself singularly remarkable for his modesty, affability, and friendly disposition towards all who professed to love or understand music.§

The Dimostrationi of Zarlino, of which a particular account will in its place be given, are a series of dialogues tending to illustrate the Institutes of the same author. The interlocutors in these are Francesco Viola, an eminent musician and maestro di cappella to Alphonso duke of Ferrara; Claudio Merulo, organist of the great church at Parma; Adrian Willaert, and Zarlino himself. In the course of these dialogues many particulars occur from whence an adequate idea may be formed of Willaert, of whom Zarlino scruples not to say, as indeed do most that speak of him, that he was the first musician of his time.

The following motet is of his composition :—

* Walth. Lex. in Art. Zarl. Ragion. pag. 1. 8.   † Zarl. Istitut. 346. Documenti Armonici di Angelo Berardi, lib. I. pag. 78.
‡ Walth. Lex. in Art.   § Zarl. Dimostrationi passim.

ADRIANO WILLAERT.

CHAP. LXXIV.

JOHANNES MOUTON, a disciple of Adrian Willaert, was Maestro di Capella to Francis I. king of France,* and, by the testimony of his contemporaries, was one of the greatest musicians of the age he lived in. He composed many masses, which were highly approved by Leo X. A Miserere for four voices of his composition is to be found in the Dodecachordon of Glareanus, as is also the following hymn.

* This prince, as he was a great lover and encourager of learning and the liberal arts, was peculiarly fond of music. In the memoirs of Mr. De la Fôret, ambassador from Francis I. to Solyman II. emperor of the Turks, for concluding a treaty between those two princes, in the year 1543, it is related that the king designing to do a pleasure to his new ally, sent him a band of most accomplished musicians, making him, as he thought, a present worthy of his grandeur. Solyman received them very civilly, and was entertained by them with three different concerts at his palace, in presence of all his court; he shewed himself greatly pleased with the music, but having observed that it tended to enervate his mind, he judged by himself that it might make still a greater im-

pression upon that of his courtiers. He much applauded the musicians; nevertheless, as he was apprehensive that music might occasion, in consequence of its establishment, as much disorder in his empire as would be caused by a permission of the use of wine, he sent back the musicians with a handsome reward, after having ordered all their instruments to be broken, with a prohibition against their settling in his empire upon pain of death. Solyman thoroughly believed it to be a stroke of policy in Francis I., for he told the French ambassador that he imagined his master had sent him this amusement to divert him from the business of war, just as the Greeks sent the Persians the game of chess to slacken their military ardour. Histoire de la Musique et ses Effets, tom. I. pag. 212.

JOHANNES MOUTON.

THOMAS CREQUILON, a Fleming, was master of the chapel to the emperor Charles V. about the year 1556. He composed hymns for many voices, and some French songs in four, five, and six parts.

CLEMENS, otherwise JACOB CLEMENS NON PAPA, a Fleming, was one of the musicians of the emperor Charles V. and a composer of masses and other sacred offices. It seems that this prince, though not an avowed patron of the arts, as was his rival Francis I. was a lover of music. Ascham, in the letter above-cited, relates that being at Augsburg, he stood by the emperor's table, and that 'his chapel 'sung wonderful cunningly all the dinner-while.*

CYPRIAN DE RORE was born at Mechlin, but lived great part of his time in Italy. He composed many very fine madrigals to italian words. There is extant in the great church of Parma the following sepulchral inscription to his memory:—

Cypriano Roro, Flandro
artis musicæ
viro omnium peritissimo,
cujus nomen famaque
nec vetustate obrui
nec oblivione deleri poterit,
Herculis Ferrariens. Ducis II.
deinde Venetorum,
postremo
Octavi Farnesi Parmæ et Placentiæ
Ducis II. Chori Præfecto,
Ludovicus frater, fil. et hæredes
mœstissimi posuerunt.
Obiit anno M.D.LXV. ætatis XLIX.

The following madrigal is given as a specimen of his abilities in that style of musical composition:—

* The same author gives the following humorous account of the behaviour of the emperor at dinner: 'He had four courses, he had sod 'beef, very good roast mutton, baked hare; these be no service in 'England. The emperor hath a good face, a constant look; he fed well 'of a capon; I have had a better from mine hostess Barnes many times 'in my chamber. He and Ferdinando eat together, very handsomely 'carving themselves where they list, without any curiosity. The em- 'peror drank the best that ever I saw; he had his head in the glass five 'times as long as any of us, and never drank less than a good quart at 'once of Rhenish wine.' Ascham's Works, pag. 375.

CIPRIANO DE RORE.

PHILIPPUS DE MONTE, (*a Portrait,*) a native of Mons in Hainault, born in 1521, was master of the chapel to the emperor Maximilian II. a canon, and treasurer of the cathedral church of Cambray. In that church was a portrait of him, with the following distich under it :—

Cernimus excelsum, mente arte, et nomine Montem, Quo Musæ et Charites constituere domum.

The print given of him is taken from it, and is to be found in the Bibliotheca Chalcographica of Boissard. He composed, besides masses and motets, four books of madrigals, of which the following is one :—

FILIPPO DE MONTE.

ORLANDUS LASSUS, *(a Portrait,)* otherwise called Orlando de Lasso, was also a native of the city of Mons above-mentioned, a contemporary and intimate friend of Philippo de Monte. He, for the sweetness of his voice while he was a child, and his excellent compositions in his riper years, may be said to have been the delight of all Europe. Thuanus, in his history, gives the following account of him : 'Or-'landus Lassus, a man the most famous of any in our 'age for skill in the science of music, was born at 'Mons in Hainault; for this is the chief praise of 'Belgium, that it among other nations abounds in 'excellent teachers of the musical art. And he, 'while a boy, as is the fate of excellent singers, was, 'on account of the sweetness of his voice forced away, 'and for some time retained by Ferdinand Gonzaga in 'Sicily, in Milan, and at Naples. Afterwards, being 'grown up, he taught for the space of two years at 'Rome. After this he travelled to France and Italy 'with Julius Cæsar Brancatius, and at length returned 'into Flanders, and lived many years at Antwerp,

'from whence he was called away by Albert duke of 'Bavaria, and settled at that court, and there married. 'He was afterwards invited with offers of great 'rewards by Charles IX. king of France, to take 'upon him the office of his chapel-master, for that 'generous prince always retained a chosen one about 'him. In order to reap the benefit of this promotion, 'he set out with his family for France, but, before he 'could arrive there, was stopped by the news of the 'sudden death of Charles ; upon which he was re-'called to Bavaria by William the son and successor 'of Albert, to the same duty as he had before dis-'charged under his father : and having rendered 'himself most famous for his compositions both 'sacred and profane, in all languages, published in 'several cities for the space of twenty-five years, he 'died a mature death in the year 1595, on the third 'of June, having exceeded seventy-three years of 'age.

The account given by Thuanus does by no means agree either in respect to the time of his birth or

PHILIPPUS DE MONTE BELGA D.D.

MAX. II ET RODOLPH. II ROM. IMPP. CHORI MUSICI PRÆFCTUS.

METROPOL. ECCLESIÆ CAMERACENSIS CANONICUS ET THESAURARIUS.

ÆTATIS SUÆ LXXII A.D. MDXCIV.

ORLANDUS LASSUS

D. BAVAR. MUSICUS. MDLXIX.

decease, with the inscription on the monument of Orlando, which is as follows :

Orlandus Lassus, Bergæ, Hannoniæ urbe
natus anno MDXXX.
Musicus et Symphoniacus sui seculi facilè princeps :
Primâ ætate admodum pùer, ob miram vocis suavitatem
in canendo, aliquoties plagio sublatus :
Sub Ferdinando Gonzaga prorege Siciliæ, annis fermè
sex partim Mediolani, partim in Sicilia, inter symphoniacos
educatus.
Neapoli dein. per triennium, ac demùm Romæ amplius
biennium Musico præfectus Sacello longè celeberrimo.
Post peregrinationes Anglicanas et Gallicanas cum
Julio Cæsare Brancacio susceptas, Antverpiæ
totidem annis versatus.
Tandem Alberti et Gulielmi Ducis Bojorum, musicæ
Magister supremus per integrum vicennium.
A Maximiliano II. Cæs. nobilitatus : à summis imperii
Principibus, ac Proceribus summe honoratus.
Cantionibus Harmonicis tam sacris quam profanis omnium
linguarum in orbe universo celebratiss.
Obiit Monaci anno Sal. MDLXXXV. Æt. LV.

But there is reason to think that the inscription is erroneous, for there is extant a print of Orlando de Lasso engraved by Sadler, with a note thereon, purporting that he was sixty-one in 1593; but with this the epitaph agrees almost as badly as it does with Thuanus's relation. As to the great rewards which that generous prince, as Thuanus styles him, Charles IX. offered him upon condition of his accepting the direction of his choir, his majesty was induced to this act of beneficence by other motives than generosity : Thuanus did not care to tell them, but the reasons for his silence in this particular are long since ceased ; the fact is, that the king, who had consented to the massacre of the Hugonots in Paris, and who, forgetting the dignity of his station, himself had a hand in it,* was so disturbed in his mind with the reflection on that unparalleled act of inhumanity, that he was wont to have his sleep disturbed by nightly horrors, and was composed to rest by a symphony of singing boys : in short, to use the language of Job, 'he was scared with dreams and ' terrified through visions.' He was a passionate lover of music, and so well skilled in it, that, as Brantome relates, he was able to sing his part, and actually sung the tenor occasionally with his musicians :† and it was thought that such compositions as Orlando was ca-

pable of framing for that particular purpose,‡ might tend to alleviate that disorder in his mind, which bid defiance to all other remedies, in short, to heal a wounded conscience ; but he did not live to make the experiment.

The new Dictionnaire Historique Portatif, as does indeed the inscription on his monument, intimates that Orlando visited England, and contains the following singular epitaph on him :—

Etant enfant, j'ai chanté le dessus,
Adolescent, j'ai fait le contre-taille,
Homme parfait, j'ai raisonné la taille,
Mais maintenant je suis mis au bassus.
Prie, Passant, que l'esprit soit là sus.

Orlando de Lasso had two sons, who were also musicians, the one named Ferdinand, chapel-master to Maximilian duke of Bavaria ; the other Rudulph, organist to the same prince.   They collected the motetts of their father, and published them in a large folio volume with the following title, 'Magnum Opus ' musicum Orlandi de Lasso, Capellæ Bavaricæ quon- ' dam Magistri, complectens omnes Cantiones, quas ' Motetas vulgo vocant, tàm antea editas, quàm ' hactenas nondum publicatas, à 2 ac 12 voc. à ' Ferdinando Serenissimi Bavariæ Ducis Maximilian, ' Musicorum præfecto, et Rudulpho, eidem Principi ' ab Organis ; authoris Filiis summo Studio collectum, ' et impensis eorundem Typis mandatum. Monachii ' 1604.' These it is to be noted are sacred compositions ; but there are extant several collections of madrigals published by himself, which shew that he equally excelled in that other kind of vocal harmony.

The memory of Orlando de Lasso is greatly honoured by the notice which Thuanus has taken of him, for, excepting Zarlino, he is the only person of his profession whom that historian has condescended to mention. A great musician undoubtedly he was, and next to Palestrina, perhaps the most excellent of the sixteenth century. He was the first great improver of figurative music ; for, instead of adhering to that stiff formal rule of counterpoint, from which some of his predecessors seemed afraid to deviate, he gave way to the introduction of elegant points and responsive passages finely wrought ; and of these his excellencies there needs no other evidence than the following sweet madrigal of his composition :—

---

* Mezeray, and other of the historians of those times, mention, that in that shocking scene of horror and distress, his majesty, in great composure of mind, walked out of his palace with a loaded fowling-piece, which, with all the deliberation of a good marksman, he fired at those who fled from their pursuers.

† He founded the music-school of St. Innocent as a nursery for musicians.

‡ The Penitential Psalms, and some particular passages selected from the book of Job, which are extant, of Orlando's setting, seem to have been composed with this view.

ORLANDO DE LASSO.

CHAP. LXXV.

THE other masters mentioned by Guicciardini, namely, Gombert, Curtois, Cornelio Canis, Mancicourt, Jusquin Baston, Christian Holland, Giaches de Waert, Bonmarche, Severin Cornet, Piero du Hot, Gerard Turnhout, Hubert Waelrant, and Giachetto di Berckem, and the rest of those not particularly here characterised, were of somewhat less note; there are however extant some madrigals of Severin Cornct and Giaches de Waert, which shew them to have been eminently skilled in their profession.

From the foregoing deduction of the progress of music, it appears that the Flemings, more than any people in Europe, had contributed to bring it to a standard of purity and elegance; and that towards the latter end of the sixteenth century the Low Countries abounded with professors of the science, who in the art of practical composition seem to have exceeded the Italians themselves. The reason of this may be, that in consequence of the precepts which Franchinus had delivered, the latter, under the direction of the Roman pontiffs, were employed in the forming of a new style for the church service. It had been discovered that the clergy, and indeed the laity, were grown tired of the uniformity of the Cantus Gregorianus, and were desirous of introducing into the service a kind of music affording greater variety, and better calculated to engage the attention of the hearers.   Leo X. who was so fond of music that the love of it is reckoned in the number of his failings, was the first pope that endeavoured at this reformation; and he had carried it so far, that the Council of Trent, in the year 1562, took the state of church-music into consideration, and, to prevent the farther abuse of it, made a decree against Curious singing,* which however had not its effect till about the close of that century, when Palestrina introduced into the church that noble and majestic style which has rendered him the admiration of all succeeding ages.   After this the Italian masters fell in with the practice of the Flemings in the composition of madrigals and other forms of vocal harmony, in which a latitude was given to all the powers of invention, and in the exercise whereof it must be owned they discovered a wonderful degree of skill and judgment.

While these improvements were making abroad, it seems that in England also the science had made very considerable advances.   It is true that from the time of John of Dunstable, who lived about the year 1450, to Taverner, who flourished almost a century after, the musical offices for the church discover very little of that skill and invention which recommend those works of the old Symphonetæ contained in the Dodecachordon of Glareanus; but whether it was owing to the affection which it is known Henry VIII. bore to music, or to that propensity in the people of this nation to encourage it, which made Erasmus say that the English challenge the prerogative of having the most handsome women, and of being 'most accomplished in the skill of music of 'any people;' it is certain that the beginning of the sixteenth century produced in England a race of musicians not inferior to the best in foreign countries; and to this truth Morley, in pag. 151 of his Introduction, speaking of Farefax, Taverner, Shephard, Mundie, and others, has borne his testimony.

In the catalogue of Morley nothing like chronological order is observed, but in the following account of some of the persons mentioned, and of others omitted by him, the best arrangement is made of them that the scanty materials for that purpose would allow of.   To begin with Cornish.

WILLIAM CORNISH lived about the year 1500; bishop Tanner has an article for him, wherein he mentions that some of his musical compositions are to be found in a manuscript collection in the possession of Mr. Ralph Thoresby, and mentioned by him in his History of Leeds, pag. 517.   That manuscript has been searched, and it appearing that there were

two of the name, an elder and a younger, it is uncertain which of them was the author of the treatise between Trowthe and Enformacion, mentioned by Tanner to have been printed among the works of Skelton, and which has this title:—

In the Fleete made by me William Cornifhe, otherwife called *Nyfhewete*, chapelman with the moft famofe and noble king Henry the VII. his reyne the xix yere the moneth of July.   A treatife betwene Trouth and Informacion;

But as the poem, for such it is, contains a parable abounding with allusions to music and musical instruments, and is in many respects a curiosity, that part of it is here inserted.   It seems to be a complaint of Cornish himself against one that had falsely accused him, who is distinguished by the name of Informacion, as Cornish is by that of Musicke.

A parable betwen Informacion and Mufike.

The examples.

Mufike in his melody requireth true foundes,
Who fetteth a fong fhould geue him to armony;
Who kepeth true his tuenes may not paffe his fonds,
His alteracions and prolacions muft be pricked treuly,
For mufike is trew though minftrels maketh mayftry,
The harper careth nothing but reward for his fong,
Merily foundith his mouth when his tong goth all of wrong.

The *Harpe.*

A Harpe geueth founde as it is fette,
The harper may wreft it untunablye,
Yf he play wrong good tunes he doth lette,
Or by myftunyng the very trew armonye;
A harpe well playde on fhewyth fwete melody,
A harper with his wreft may tune the harpe wrong,
Myftuning of an inftrument fhal hurt a true fonge.

A *Songe.*

A fonge that is trewe and ful of fwetnes,
May be euyll fonge and tunyd amyfe,
The fonge of hymfelfe yet neuer the les
Is true and tunable, and fyng it as it is:
Then blame not the fong, but marke wel this,
He that hath fpit at another man's fonge,
Will do what he can to haue it fonge wronge.

A *Claricorde.*

The claricorde hath a tunely kynde,
As the wyre is wrefted hye and lowe,
So it tuenyth to the players mynde,
For as it is wrefted fo muft it nedes fhowe,
As by this refon ye may well know,
Any inftrument myftunyd fhall hurt a trew fong,
Yet blame not the claricord the wrefter doth wrong.

A *Trompet.*

A trompet blowen hye with to hard a blaft,
Shal caufe him to vary from the tunable kynde,
But he that bloweth to hard muft fuage at the laft,
And fayne to fall lower with a temperate wynde,
And then the trompet the true tune fhall fynde,
For an inftrument over wynded is tuned wrong,
Blame none but the blower, on him it is longe.

True *Counfell.*

Who plaieth on the harpe he fhould play trew,
Who fyngeth a fonge, let his voice be tunable,
Who wrefteth the claricorde myftunyng efchew,
Who bloweth a trompet let his wind be mefurable,
For inftruments in them felf be ferme and ftable,
And of trouth, wold trouth to every manes fonge,
Tune them then truly for in them is no wronge.

---

* This decree, which was made for correcting abuses in the celebration of the mass, prohibits, among other things, 'l' uso delle musiche nelle 'chiese con mistura di canto, o' suono lascivo, tutte le attioni secolari, 'colloquii profani, strepiti, gridori.'   i. e. The use of music in churches mixed with lascivious songs, all secular actions, profane speeches, noises and screeches.   Hist. del Concil. Trident, di Pietro Soave. Londra 1619, pag. 559.

Vincenzo Ruffo an eminent musician of the sixteenth century, and Maestro di Capella dal Duomo da Pistoria, composed and published at Venice in 1574, certain of the Psalms for five voices, and masses for six voices, with a note in the title of each, "that they were conformable to the decree of the Sacred Council of Trent;" and in the preface he relates, that his patron Cardinal Boromeo had willed him to observe the same as a rule in these several compositions.

Colours of Mufyke.

In Mufike I have learned iiij colours, as this,
Blake, ful blake, uerte,* and in lykewife redde,
By thefe colours many fubtill alteracions ther is,
That wil begile one tho in cuning he be wel fped,
With a prike of Indicion from a body that is dede,
He fhal try fo his nombre with fwetnes of his fong,
That the ear fhal be pleafed, and yet he al wrong.

The Practifer.

I pore man, unable of this fcience to fkyll,
Save litel practife I have by experience,
I mean but trouth and of good will,
To remembre the doers that ufeth fuch offence,
Not one fole, but generally in fentence,
By caufe I can fkyll of a little fonge,
To try the true corde to be knowen from the wrong.

Treuth.

Yet trouth was not drownde ne fanke,
But ftill dyd fleete aboue the water,
Informacion had played him fuch a pranke,
That with power the pore had loft his mater,
Bycaufe that trouthe began to clater,
Informacion hath taught hym to folfe his fonge,
Paciens parforce, content you with wronge.

Truth.

I affayde theis tunes me thought them not fwete,
The concordes were nothynge muficall,
I called Mafters of Mufike † cnnyng and difcrete;
And the firft pryncyple, whofe name was Tuballe,
Guido Boice, John de Murris, Vitryaco and them al,
I prayed them of helpe of this combrous fonge,
Priked with force and lettred with wronge.

True Anfwere.

They fayd I was horce I might not fynge,
My voice is to pore it is not awdyble,
Informacion is fo curyous in his chauntynge,
That to bere the trew plainfong, it is not pofible:
His proporcions be fo hard with fo highe a quatrible,
And the playn fong in the margyn fo craftely bound,
That the true tunes of Tuball cannot have the right founde.

Truthe.

Well quod trueth, yet ones I truft verely,
To have my voyce and fynge agayne,
And to flete out trueth and clarify truly,
And ete fuger candy adaye or twayne,
And then to the defke to fynge true and playn,
Informacion fhal not alwaye entune hys fong,
My parts fhal be true when his countreuers fhall be wrong.

Informacion.

Informacion hym enbolded of the monacorde,
From confonaunts to concordes he mufyd his mayftry,
I affayde the mufyke both knyght and lord,
But none would fpeke, the founde bord was to hye,
Then kept I the plain keyes the marred al my melody,
Enformacion drave a crotchet that paft al my fong
With proporcion parforce dreuen on to longe

Dialogue.

Sufferance came in to fyng a parte,
Go to, quod trouth, I pray you begyne,
Nay foft quod he, the gife of my parte
Is to reft a long reft or I fet in,
Nay by long reftyng ye fhal nothing wynne,
For informacion is fo crafty and fo hye in his fonge,
That yf ye fal to refting in fayth it will be wrong.

Treweth.

Informacion wil teche a doctor his game,
From fuperacute to the noble dyapafon,
I afayd to acute, and when I came
Enformacion was mete for a noble dyateffaron,
He fong by a Pothome ‡ that hath two kyndes in one,
With many fubtel femetunes moft met for this fong,
Pacience parforce, content you with wronge.

Trouth.

I kepe be rounde and he be fquare,
The one is bemole, and the other bequare,
If I myght make tryall as I could and dare,
I fhould fhow why thefe ij kynds do varye,
But God knowyth al, fo doth not kyng Harry,
For yf he dydde than chaunge fhold this iiij fong,
Pytye for patience, and confcience for wronge.
Neuyffwhete Parabolam.

The younger Cornish appears to have been a good musician. Two songs of his composition in the Thoresby manuscript above-mentioned, are inserted in the next succeeding book of this work.

JOHN TAVERNER, mentioned by Morley in his Catalogue, and also in his Introduction, pag. 151, and elsewhere, was organist of Boston in Lincolnshire, and of Cardinal, now Christ-Church college, in Oxford. It seems that he, together with John Frith the martyr, and sundry other persons, who left Cambridge with a view to preferment in this, which was Wolsey's new-founded college, held frequent conversations upon the abuses of religion which at that time had crept into the church; in short, they were Lutherans. And this being discovered, they were accused of heresy, and imprisoned in a deep cave under the college, used for the keeping of salt-fish, the stench whereof occasioned the death of some of them. John Fryer, one of these unfortunate persons, was committed prisoner to the master of the Savoy, where, as Wood says, 'he did much solace himself 'with playing on the lute, having good skill in 'music, for which reason a friend of his would 'needs commend him to the master; but the master 'answered, "take heed, for he that playeth is a devil, "because he is departed from the Catholic Faith."' He was however set at liberty, became a physician, and died a natural death at London.§ Frith had not so good fortune; he was convicted of heresy, and burnt in Smithfield, together with one Andrew Hewet, in 1533.‖

Taverner had not gone such lengths as Frith, Clerke, and some others of the fraternity; the suspicions against him were founded merely on his having hid some heretical books of the latter under the boards of the school where he taught, for which reason, and because of his eminence in his faculty, the cardinal excused him, saying he was but a musician, and so he escaped.¶

* This passage should be red, blake ful, blake voide, &c. for the reason given pag. 232 of this work.

† It is worthy of remark that the succeeding musicians to Hobrechth, Okenheim, Iodocus Pratensis, and others of the Flemish school, had the appellation of Master, and hence the term Master of Music, which till lately was the designation of a practical musician. This denomination seems to have been first given them towards the middle of the sixteenth century, for in the middle of it, when Glareanus wrote, they were termed Phonasci and Symphonetæ, Here they are called Masters of Music; and Guicciardini, in the passage lately cited from him, styles the musicians of Flanders 'Maestri della Musica.'

‡ *i. e.* APOTOME, the residue of three sesquioctave tones, after subtracting the diatessaron, consisting of two such tones, and the Pythagorean limma. See pag. 25 of this work.

§ Athen. Oxon. vol. II. pag. 124, Fasti, anno 1525.

‖ Fox's Acts and Monuments, vol. II. pag. 304, et seq.

¶ Fuller's Church History, Cent. XVI. Book V. pag. (171.) Fuller mistakes the Christian name of Taverner, calling him Richard.

JOHN TAVERNER.

Dr. Ward, in his Lives of the Gresham Professors, has brought forward to view a man of the name of John Taverner, who it seems was chosen music professor in the year 1610; and it is necessary, in order to prevent confusion between these two persons, who had the same christian and surname, to distinguish the one from the other; and especially as Ward has said but very little of the former of them, and in speaking of him has made use of an expression that oftener implies contempt than respect, 'There was 'one John Taverner of Boston, &c.'

The truth is, that this person is he whom all men mean when they speak of Taverner the musician; and as to the professor, he was the son of the famous Richard Taverner,* who in the year 1539, published a new edition of what is called Matthew's Bible, with corrections and alterations of his own; but it does not appear from the doctor's account of him that he had any better claim to the office of music professor than a testimonial from the university of Oxford, where he had studied, purporting that he was 'in his 'religion very sound, a due and diligent frequenter 'of prayers and sermons, and in his conversation 'very civil and honest,' with this general recommendation respecting his proficiency in music, 'that 'he had taken two degrees in that and other good 'arts.'

ROBERT FAIRFAX, of the Yorkshire family of that name, was a doctor in music of Cambridge, and was incorporated of Oxford in the year 1511. Bishop Tanner says he was of Bayford in the county of

* In the year 1552 this Richard Taverner, though a layman, there being then a scarcity of preachers, obtained of Edward VI. licence to preach in any part of his dominions, and preached before the king at court, wearing a velvet bonnet, a damask gown, and a gold chain; and in the reign of queen Elizabeth, being then high-sheriff of the county of Oxford, he appeared in the pulpit at St. Mary's, then of stone, with a sword and a gold chain about his neck, and made a sermon to the scholars, which had this hopeful beginning, 'Arriving at the mount of 'St. Mary's in the stoney stage, where I now stand, I have brought you 'some biscuits baked in the oven of charity, carefully conserved for the

'chickens of the church, the sparrows of the spirit, and the sweet 'swallows of salvation.' The story is told by Wood, and repeated by Dr. Ward, in his Lives of the Gresham Professors, with an intimation that such flowers of wit and eloquence were then in vogue. But the state of literature was not even then so very low as to afford an excuse for such nonsense, or to induce the readers of it to believe that Mr, Sheriff Taverner could be any other than a very shallow and conceited old gentleman.

Hertford, and that he died at St. Alban's, which is very probable, for he was either organist or chanter of the abbey church there, and lies buried therein. His coat-armour is depicted over the place of his interment, but has long been hid by the seat of the mayor of that town.* Some of his compositions, and the following among the rest, are in the manuscript of Mr. Thoresby above-mentioned :—

Doctor Fayrfax.

John Mason, in Morley's Catalogue called Sir John Mason, as being in orders,† took the degree of bachelor of music at Oxford in the year 1508, as appears by the Fasti Oxon. of Wood, who adds that he was much in esteem for his profession. He was a prebendary, and the treasurer of the cathedral church of Hereford, and died in 1547.

* In the Thoresby MS. it is the seat of the mayoress.

† The custom of prefixing the addition of Sir to the Christian-name of a clergyman was formerly usual in this country. Fuller, in his Church History, book VI. enumerates seven chauntries, part of a much larger number, in the old cathedral of St. Paul in the time of king Edward VI. with the names of the then incumbents, most of whom have the addition of Sir, upon which he remarks, and gives this reason why there were formerly more Sirs than Knights, 'Such priests as have the addition of Sir 'before their Christian-name were men not graduated in the university, 'being in orders, but not in degrees; whilst others entituled Masters had 'commenced in the arts.'

This ancient usage is alluded to in the following humorous catch :—
'Now I am married, Sir John I'll not curse,
'He joined us together for better for worse;
'But if I were single, I do tell you plain,
'I'd be well advis'd e'er I married again.'

CHAP. LXXVI.

John Dygon, as appears by a composition of his here inserted, was Prior of St. Austin's in Canterbury, and a very skilful musician. In the catalogue of the abbats of the monastery of St. Augustine, in Dr. Battely's Antiquities of Canterbury, part II. page 160, John Dygon is the sixty-eighth in number. It seems he was raised to this dignity from that of prior, for many instances of the kind occur in that list; and let it be remembered that the brethren of the monastery were of the Benedictine order. According to Dr. Battely, Dygon was elected abbat anno 1497, and died in 1509. In the Fasti Oxon. it is said that John Dygon, a Benedictine monk, was admitted to the degree of bachelor in music, anno 1512. This account agrees but ill with that given of Dygon of Canterbury, and yet the coincidence in both, of so many particulars as a christian and surname, and a religious and secular profession, will hardly admit of a supposition but that the persons severally spoken of were one and the same. The following Motet is the composition above referred to :—

JOHN DIGON, PRIOR OF SAINT AUSTIN'S, CANTERBURY.

WILLIAM CHELLE was admitted at Oxford to the degree of bachelor in music 19th July, 1526. He was a secular chaplain, a prebendary, and precentor of Hereford cathedral. Bishop Tanner mentions two tracts of his writing, the one intitled Musicæ Practicæ Compendium, the other De Proportionibus Musicis.

JOHN GUINNETH was a native of Wales, of very poor parentage, but supported in his studies by some beneficent clergyman, who allowed him an exhibition. In the year 1531, being then a secular priest, and having spent twenty years in the study and practice of music, and composed the responses for the whole year in division-song, and many masses and antiphons for the use of the church, he supplicated for the degree of doctor, and obtained it upon payment of twenty-pence, and in 1533 was presented to the rectory of St. Peter in West Chepe.* He wrote 'A Declaration of the State wherein Heretics do lead 'their Lives,' and other controversial tracts mentioned by Wood and Tanner.

JOHN SHEPHARD studied at Oxford twenty years, and obtained a bachelor's degree. In 1554 he supplicated for that of doctor, but it does not appear by the registers that he obtained it. Some of his compositions are extant in a book intitled 'Mornyng and 'Evening prayer and Communion, set forthe in foure 'partes, to be song in churches, both for men and 'children, wyth dyvers other godly prayers and An- 'thems, of sundry mens doynges. Imprinted at London 'by John Day, dwelling over Alderf-gate, beneath 'Saint Martins, 1565;' others in manuscript are among the archives in the music-school at Oxford.†

* Vide Athen. Oxon. vol. I. col. 102. Fasti, sub anno 1531.

† The music school at Oxford is the repository of a great number of books containing compositions of various kinds, many of them of great antiquity. That they are deposited in the music school rather than in the Bodleian or other libraries of the university, will be presently accounted for; but first it must be mentioned that one William Forrest, a priest in the reign of Henry VIII. well skilled in music and poetry, had made a copious collection of the best compositions then extant, and among them many of John Taverner of Boston, Marbeck of Windsor, Dr. Fairfax, the above-named Shephard, and many others. These came to the hands of William Heather or Heyther, one of the gentlemen of the royal chapel, and who in 1622 was admitted to the degree of doctor in music. This person, who died in 1627, founded the music lecture at Oxford, and for the use of the professor, who was required to read it in the music school, made a donation of the above collection, together with his own additions thereto.

JOHN SHEPHARD.

CHAP. LXXVII.

John Redford was organist and almoner of St. Paul's cathedral in the reign of Henry VIII., and, in virtue of the latter office, master of the boys there. Tusser, the author of the Five hundred Points of Husbandry, and his scholar, gives a character of him in the following stanza, taken from his life, written by himself in verse :—*

* * * * * *

By friendſhip's lot to Paul's I got,
So found I grace a certain ſpace
     Still to remaine
With Redford there, the like no where
For cunning ſuch and vertue much,
By whom ſome part of muſic's art
     So did I gaine.

John Thorne, a contemporary of Redford, and who has also a place in Morley's Catalogue, was of York, and most probably organist of that cathedral. The following motet may serve as a specimen of his abilities :—

JOHN THORNE, OF YORK.

GEORGE ETHERIDGE, in Latin Edrycus, born at Thame in Oxfordshire, was a scholar of Corpus Christi college in Oxford, anno 1534. He was admitted to a degree in physic, and, being excellently skilled in the Greek language, was appointed Regius professor thereof in that university about the year 1553; but having been in queen Mary's time a persecutor of the Protestants,* he was by her successor removed from that station, after which he betook himself to the practice of physic in the city of Oxford, by which, and the instruction of the sons of gentlemen of his own communion (for he strictly adhered to the Romish persuasion) in the rudiments of grammar, music, and logic, he acquired considerable wealth : one of his pupils was William Gifford, afterwards archbishop of Rheims. He was an excellent poet, and well skilled in the mathematics, as also in vocal and instrumental music, as appeared to Anthony Wood by some of his compositions, which it is probable he had seen, and the testimony of the more ancient writers. Leland, who was his familiar friend, thus celebrates his memory :

Scripsisti juvenis multâ cum laude libellos,
Qui Regi eximie perplacuere meo.

And Pits sums up his character in these words : ' Erat peritus mathematicus, musicus tum vocalis, ' tum instrumentalis, cum primis in Anglia confe- ' rendus, testudine tamen et lyra præ cæteris delecta- ' batur. Poëta elegantissimus. Versus enim Anglicos, ' Latinos, Græcos, Hæbreos accuratissime componere, ' et ad tactus lyricos concinnare pertissime solebat.'

RICHARD EDWARDS, a native of Somersetshire, was a scholar of Corpus Christi college, Oxon, and received his musical education under George Etheridge above-mentioned. At the foundation of Christ Church college by Henry VIII. in 1547, he was made senior student, being then twenty-four years of age. At the beginning of queen Elizabeth's reign he was made a gentleman of the chapel and master of the children. He was an excellent musician, and also a poet. Puttenham, in his Art of English Poesie, pag. 5, together with the earl of Oxford, celebrates ' Maister Edwardes ' of her Majestys chapel,' for comedy and interlude. A particular account of him is referred to a subsequent part of this work, in which the old English poets are enumerated and characterised. In this place he is spoken of as a musician only, and in that faculty he is said to have manifested his skill in many very excellent compositions.

ROBERT TESTWOOD, of Windsor, and JOHN MARBECK of the same place, a man to whom church-music is greatly indebted, he being the original composer of the music to the cathedral service in use at this day, will be spoken of hereafter; at present it may suffice to say, that in the reign of Henry VIII. they were both condemned to the stake for heresy, that the former suffered, and the latter escaped the same fate in regard of his great merit in his profession.

Besides the several English musicians above enumerated, there were many of great eminence of whom no memorials are now remaining, save those few of their compositions which escaped that general destruction of books and manuscripts which attended the dissolution of religious houses, and are now preserved in the libraries of cathedrals, those of the two universities, the colleges of Eton and Winchester, and the British Museum.† The following are the names of famous musicians who flourished before the Reformation, and have not a place in Morley's Catalogue printed at the end of his Introduction. John Charde, Richard Ede, Henry Parker, John Norman, Edmund Sheffield, William Newark, Sheryngham, Hamshere, Richard Davy, Edmund Turges, Sir Thomas Phelyppis, or Philips, Browne, Gilbert Banister, and Heydingham.

Morley's Catalogue may be supposed to contain the names of the principal musicians of his time, and of the age preceding ; but it is somewhat remarkable that he has neither in that, nor in any other part of his work, taken notice of our king HENRY VIII. as a composer of music. Erasmus relates that he composed offices for the church ; bishop Burnet has vouched his authority for asserting the same ; and there is an anthem of his for four voices, ' O Lord, ' the maker of all things,' in the books of the royal chapel, and in the collection of services and anthems lately published by Dr. Boyce, which every judge of music must allow to be excellent. It is true that in a collection of church-music, intitled ' The first book of ' selected Church Musick, collected by John Barnard, ' one of the minor canons of the cathedral church of ' St. Paul,' and published in the year 1641, this anthem is given to William Mundy, but the late Dr. Aldrich, after taking great pains to ascertain the author of it, pronounced it to be a genuine composition of Henry VIII.‡ The fact is, and there is additional evidence of it existing, not only that Henry understood music, but that he was deeply skilled in the art of practical composition; for in a collection of anthems, motets, and other church offices, in the hand-writing of one John Baldwin, of the choir of Windsor, a very good composer himself, which appears to have been completed in the year 1591, is the following composition for three voices, with these words, ' Henricus Octavus,' at the beginning, and these, ' Quod Rex Henricus Octavus,' at the end of the Cantus, or upper part :—

† Bale, who was a witness to it, gives the following relation of the havoc of books at that time, and the uses to which they were put :—
' A greate nombre of them whych purchased those superstycyouse ' mansyons, reserved of those librarye bokes, some to serve theyr iakes, ' some to scoure theyr candelstyckes, and some to rubbe their bootes. ' Some they solde to the grossers and sope-sellers, and some they sent ' over see to the bokebynders, not in small nombre, but at tymes whole ' shyppees full, to the wonderynge of the foren nacyons. Yea the ' unyversytees of thys realme are not all clere in this detestable fact. ' But cursed is that bellye whyche seketh to be fedde with suche ungodly ' gaynes, and so depelye shameth hys natural contreye. I knowe a ' merchaunt man whych shall at thys tyme be namelesse, that boughte ' the contentes of two noble lybraryes for xl. shyllynges pryce, a shame ' it is to be spoken. Thys stuffe hath he occupyed in the stede of graye ' paper by the space of more than these x yeares, and yet he hath store ' ynough for as many yeares to come. A prodygyuose example is this, ' and to be abhorred of all men which love their nacyon as they shoulde ' do.' Preface to The laboryouse Journey & Serche of Johan Leylande for Englande's Antiquities, with declaracyons enlarged : by Johan Bale, anno 1549.

‡ See the preface to Divine Harmony, or A new Collection of select Anthems used at her Majesty's Chappels Royal, Westminster Abbey, St. Paul's, Windsor, both Universities, Eton, and most Cathedrals in her Majesty's Dominions, octavo, 1712, which book, through an anonymous publication, was compiled by Dr. William Croft, as is attested by an intimate friend of his, a reverend and worthy clergyman now living.

* He assisted at the degradation of Ridley previous to the execution of the sentence on him, and recommended that he should be gagged, to prevent his speaking against his persecutors. Fox's Acts and Monuments, edit. 1641, vol. III. pag. 500. Fox calls him ' one Edrige, the ' reader then of the Greek lecture.'

HENRICUS OCTAVUS, ANGLIÆ REX.

And though such a degree of skill as is manifested in the above composition, may seem more than a king can well be supposed to have possessed, it is to be remembered, that being the younger of two brothers, and his chance of succeeding to the crown therefore precarious, he was intended by his father for the church, with a remote view to the archbishopric of Canterbury ; music was therefore a necessary part of his education.* *And the statutes of Trinity College, Cambridge, founded by Henry VIII., make part of the examination of candidates for fellowships to be ' Quid in Cantando possint;' indeed, all members were supposed capable of singing a part in choir service.*

As to the composition above given, the words are taken from the Canticum Canticorum, cap. vii. as rendered by the vulgate translation, and it may be presumed that the object of it was some female with whom the king was upon terms of great familiarity.†

It was doubtless owing to the affection which this prince entertained for music that his children also arrived at great proficiency in it. Edward VI. played on the lute, as appears from that expression in Cardan's account of him, ' Cheli pulsabat,' and indeed from his own Journal, where he mentions his playing on the lute to Monsieur le Mareschal St. Andrè, the French ambassador. Mary also played on the lute and on the virginal, as appears by a letter of queen Catherine her mother, wherein she exhorts her ' to use her virginals and lute, if she has ' any :' and as to Elizabeth, her proficiency on the virginal is attested by Sir James Melvil, who himself had once an opportunity of hearing her divert herself at that instrument. This affection in the children of Henry VIII. for music is but a trivial circumstance in the history of their lives, but it went a great way in determining the fate of choral service at several periods during the Reformation, when it became a matter of debate whether to retain or reject it, as will appear by the following deduction of particulars.

The clamours against choral service, arising from the negligent manner of performing it, were about this time very great, and the council of Trent in their deliberations with a view to the correction of abuses in the celebration of the mass, had passed some resolutions touching church music that gave weight to the objections of its enemies : as the Reformation advanced these increased ; those of the clergy who fell in with Wickliffe's notions of a reformation were for rejecting it as vain and unedifying ; the thirty-two commissioners appointed by

the statutes of 35 Henry VIII. and 3 and 4 Edward VI. to compile a body of ecclesiastical laws, it is true, allowed of singing ; but by the restraints that it is laid under in the Reformatio Legum Ecclesiasticarum, tit. De Divinis Officiis, cap. 5. it seems as if that assembly meant to banish figurate music out of the church, and by admitting only of that kind of singing in which all might join, to put cathedral and parochial service on a level.

In the reign of Mary no one presumed to vent his objections against choral singing : the Protestants were too much terrified by the persecutions to which their profession exposed them, to attend to the contents of the Romish ritual ; and when they were once persuaded that the worship of that church was idolatrous, it could not but be with them a matter of indifference whether the offices used in it were sung or said.

But the truth of the matter is, that those men who were best able to expose the errors and superstition of popery withdrew themselves, and in a state of exile conceived a plan of reformation and church discipline so truly spiritual, as seemed to render useless the means which some think necessary to excite in the minds of men those ideas of reverence and respect which should accompany every act of devotion. Actuated by their zeal against popery, they in short declared those rites and ceremonies to be sinful, which at most could be but indifferent, as namely, the habits anciently worn by the minister in the celebration of divine service, and the little less ancient practice of antiphonal singing ; and upon their arrival from Geneva and Francfort, at the accession of queen Elizabeth, the arguments against both were pushed with great vehemence in the course of the disciplinarian controversy.

This is a brief account of that opposition which threatened the banishment of the solemn choral service from our liturgy, and which, though made at different periods, was in every instance attended with the like ill success, as will appear from the following short review of the measures taken for its establishment and support.

For first, the disposition of Henry VIII. to retain the choral service may be inferred from the provisions in favour of minor canons, lay clerks, and choristers, not only in the refoundations by him of ancient cathedral and collegiate churches, but also in those modern erections of episcopal sees at Westminster, Oxford, Gloucester, Chester, Bristol, and Peterborough, which were made by him, and liberally endowed for the support and maintenance of singers in those cathedrals respectively.

Edward VI. manifested his affection for choral singing by his injunctions issued in the year 1547, wherein countenance is given to the singing of the litany, the priest being therein required to sing or plainly and distinctly to say the same. And in the first liturgy of the same king, the rubric allows of the singing of the 'Venite exultemus,' and other hymns, both at mattins and even-song, in a manner contradistinguished from that plain tune in which the lessons are thereby required to be read.

Farther, the statute of 2 and 3 Edward VI. for

---

* It has already been remarked that a competent skill in music was anciently necessary in the clerical profession : to the evidence of that fact formerly adduced may be added the following extract from a letter from Sir John Harrington to prince Henry, containing a character of Dr. John Still, bishop of Bath and Wells, in 1592. ' His breeding was ' from 'his childhood in good literature, and partly in musick, which was ' counted in those days a preparative to divinity ; neither could any be ' admitted to *primam tonsuram*, except he could first *bene le bene con bene* ' *can*, as they called it, which is to read well, to conster well, and to sing ' well, in which last he hath good judgment.' Vide Sir John Harrington's Brief View of the Church, and Nugæ Antiquæ, 12mo. Lond.1769, pag. 22.

† It was probably composed in his juvenile years, when it is known he had amours. One favourite of his he kept at Greenwich, her lodging was a tower in the park of the Old Palace ; the king was used when he visited her to go from Westminster in his barge, attended by Sir Andrew Flamock, his standard-bearer, a man of humour, who entertained him with jests and merry stories. The king, as the signal of his approach, was used to blow his horn at his entrance into the park. Puttenham's Arte of English Poesie, pag. 224.

uniformity of Service, contains a proviso that it shall be lawful to use Psalms or prayer taken out of the Bible, other than those directed by the new liturgy; which proviso let in the use of the metrical psalmody of the Calvinists, and also the anthem, so peculiar to cathedral service, and was recognized by the statute of 5 and 6 of Edward VI. made for confirming the second liturgy of the same king.

As to queen Elizabeth, she, by the forty-ninth of her injunctions, given in 1559, declares her sentiments of church music in terms that seem to point out a medium between the abuses of it, and the restraints under which it was intended to be laid by the Reformatio Legum Ecclesiasticarum. The statute of uni-formity made in the first year of her reign, establishes the second liturgy of Edward VI. with a very few alterations. The act of the legislature thus co-operating with her royal will, as declared by her injunctions, and indeed with the general sense of the nation, choral service received a twofold sanction, and was thenceforth received among the rites and ceremonies of the church of England.

From all which transactions it may be inferred that the retention of the solemn choral service in our church was in a great measure owing to that zeal for it in the princes under whom the Reformation was begun and perfected, which may be naturally supposed to have resulted from their love of music.

BOOK IX.   CHAP. LXXVIII.

THE foregoing deduction of the history of music in England, and the specimens of vocal compositions above given, respect chiefly the church-service, and bring us nearly to that period when the Romish ritual ceased to prescribe the mode of divine worship, and choral service in this country assumed a new form. The general havoc and devastation, the dispersion of conventual libraries, and the destruction of books and manuscripts, which followed the dissolution of monasteries, and the little care taken to preserve that which it was foreseen would shortly become of no use, will account for the difficulty of recovering any compositions of singular excellence previous to the time of the Reformation; and that any at all are remaining is owing to the zeal of those very few persons, who were prompted to collect them as evidences of the skill and ingenuity of our ancient church musicians.

From hence we may perceive that as far as concerns the music of the church, we are arrived at the commencement of a new era; and such in truth will it appear to be when we come to speak of the reformed liturgy, which though it was so calculated as to be susceptible of all those advantages that divine service is supposed to derive from music, can neither be said to be borrowed from that of the Romish church,* nor to resemble it so nearly as to offend any but such as deny the expediency, and even lawfulness of a liturgy in any form whatever.

These reasons render it necessary to postpone for a while the prosecution of the history of church-music in this our country, and to re-assume that of secular music; in the improvement whereof it is to be noted that we were at this time somewhat behind our neighbours; for till about the commencement of the sixteenth century, it does not appear that any one of the English masters had attempted to emulate the Flemings or the Italians in the composition of madrigals; for which reason the account of the introduction of that species of music into this kingdom must also be referred to a subsequent page.

In the interim it is to be observed that songs and ballads, with easy tunes adapted to them, must at all times have been the entertainment, not only of the common people, but of the better sort: These must have been of various kinds, as namely, satirical, humorous, moral, and not a few of them of the amorous kind. Hardly any of these with the music to them are at this day to be met with, and those few that are yet extant are only to be found in odd part books, written without bars, and with ligatures, in a character so obsolete, that all hope of recovering them, or of rendering to any tolerable degree intelligible, any of the common popular tunes in use before the middle of the sixteenth century, must be given up. The two that follow have nevertheless been recovered by means of a manuscript formerly in the collection of Mr. Ralph Thoresby, and mentioned in the catalogue of his Museum, at the end of his History of Leeds; they both appear to have been set by William Cornish, of the chapel royal, in the reign of Henry VII. The words of the first song were written by Skelton, and there is a direct allusion to them in a poem of his entitled the Crowne of Lawrell, printed among his works. The latter song is supposed to be a satire on those drunken Flemings who came into England with the princess Anne of Cleve, upon her marriage with king Henry VIII.

PART I.

A - H be-shrew you by my fay, these wan-ton clarks be nyce al - way, A - vent, a-

A - H beshrew you by my fay, A - vent, a-

These wan - ton clarks be nyce al - way, A-

---

* That the book of Common Prayer hath its original from the mass-book is expressly denied by Hamon L'Estrange, in his Alliance of Divine Offices, pag. 24; and the preface to queen Elizabeth's Liturgy refers to the ancient fathers for the original and ground thereof.

WILLIAM CORNYSHE, JUN.

WILLIAM CORNYSHE, JUN.

CHAP. LXXIX.

BETTER success has attended the attempts to recover the mere words of those songs and ballads which seem to have been the delight of past ages. By these which follow, we discover that with the young people of those times the passion of love operated in much the same manner as it does now; that our forefathers loved strong ale, and that the effects of it were discoverable in effusions of mirth and pleasantry, in a total oblivion of care, and a resolution to take no thought for the morrow.

If the coarseness of the raillery, or the profaneness, or indelicacy of expression observable in the two preceding, and in a few of the subsequent poems, should need an apology for inserting them, the best that can be made is, that they present to our view a true picture of the times.* Before the statute of James I. against profane cursing and swearing, the profanation of the name of God was so frequent in common discourse, that few looked on it as a crime. When Cox, bishop of Ely, hesitated about alienating a part of the episcopal estate in favour of Sir Christopher Hatton, queen Elizabeth disdained to expostulate with him, but swore by her Maker, in a letter yet extant under her own princely hand, to deprive him if he persisted in his refusal. In the earlier copies of our old English plays oaths make a part of the dialogue, and are printed at length : in the later editions these are expunged; an evidence that the national manners have in some respects improved in the course of a century.

As to the other objection, the indelicate style of love conversation, it may be imputed to the want of that refinement which the free and innocent intercourse of the sexes in the view of their elders and superiors necessarily induces, not to mention the improvements in literature, which furnish the means of regulating external demeanour, and teach us to distinguish the behaviour of a rustic from that of a gentleman.

In this respect, too, the manners of the present have greatly the advantage over those of past ages; at least the style of courtship, which is all that concerns the present question, is so much improved, that perhaps there are few gentlemen in this kingdom capable of writing to a mistress such letters as our king Henry VIII. in the ardour of his affection sent with presents of flesh, as he terms it, meaning thereby venison, to his beloved Anne Boleyn, a beautiful, modest, and well-bred young woman.

From the above particulars it may be inferred that the poetical compositions of the period here alluded to, wanted of that elegance which is now expected in every thing offered to the public view; and as a few of the following are destitute of such a recommendation, this circumstance would supply, were it necessary, the want of other evidence of their antiquity. The simplicity is no less remarkable than the style,

*A discretion has been exercised in reprinting this edition by omitting some passages which appeared absolutely due to the progress of good manners since Sir John Hawkins' time. Some persons may think that this might have been even more extensively exerted.

of the following dialogue, which seems to be very ancient :—

I.
Beware my lyttyll fynger, Syr, I you defire,
Ye wrynge my hand to fore,
I pray you do no more,
Alas therefor,
        Ye hurt my lyttyll fynger.

II.
Why fo do you fay ?
Ye be a wanton may,
I do but with you play,
        Beware my lyttyll fynger.

III.
Syr, no more of fuche fport,
For I have lyttyl comfort
Of your hyther refort
        To hurt my lyttyll fynger.

IV.
Forfoth goodly myfteris,
I am fory for your difeas :
Alack, what may you pleas ?
        Beware my lyttyll fynger.

V.
Forfoth ye be to blame,
I wis it will not frame,
Yt is to your grete fhame
        To hurt my lyttyll fynger.

VI.
Thys was agayn my wyll certayn,
Yet wold I haue that hole agayn,
For I am fory for your payn,
        Beware my lyttyll finger.

VII.
Seeing for the caufe ye be fory,
I wold be glad wyth you for to mary,
So that ye wold not ouer longe tarry
        To hele my lyttyll fynger.

VIII.
I fay wyth a joyfull hart agayne,
Of that I wold be full fayn,
And for your fake to take fume payne
        To hele your lyttyll fynger.

IX.
Then we be both agreed
I pray you by our wedding wede,
And then ye fhall haue lyttyll nede.
        To hele my lyttyll fynger.

X.
That I will by God's grace,
I fhall kyffe your minion face,
That yt fhall fhyne in euery place,
        And hele your lyttyll fynger.

XI.
Beware my lyttyll fynger,
Alas my lyttyll fynger,
And oh my lyttyll fynger,
Ah lady mercy ! ye hurt my lyttyll fynger.

Behold the sentiments which sloth, corpulence, and rags have a tendency to inspire, in the following stanzas :—

I.
I cannot eat
But lyttyl meat,
        My ftomack ys not good ;
But fure I think
That I can drynke
        With any that were a hode.
Though I go bare,
Take ye no care,
        I am nothing a cold ;

I ſtuff my ſkyn
So full within
　Of jolly good ale and old.
Back and ſydes go bare,
Both fote and hand go cold,
But belly God ſend thee good ale ynough,
　Whether it be new or ould.

II.

I loue no roſt,
But a nut-brown toſte,
　And a crab laid in the fire,
A little bread
Shall do me ſtead,
　Much bread I not deſire;
No froſt nor ſnow,
No winde I trow
　Can hurte me if I wolde,
I am ſo wrapt,
And throwly lapt,
　Of joly good ale and old.
　　Back and fides go bare, &c.

III.

And Tib my wife,
That as her life,
　Loueth well good ale to ſeek,
Full ofte drinkes ſhee,
Till ye may ſee
　The teares run down her cheeke;
Then doth ſhe trowle
To me the bowle,*
　Even as a mault-worm† ſhold;
And ſaith ſweet heart
I took my part
　Of this joly good ale and old,
　　Back and fides go bare, &c.

IV.

Now let them drink,
'Till they nod and wink,
　Euen as good fellows ſhould do,
They ſhal not miſſe
To haue the bliſſe
　Good ale doth bring men to:
And all poor ſouls,
That haue ſcowred boules,
　Or have them luſtely trolde,
God ſaue the liues
Of them and their wiues,
　Whether they be young or old.
　　Back and fides go bare, &c.‡

In the following the praiſes of meek Miſtreſs Margaret are celebrated by her lover:—

I.

Margaret meke,
Whom I now ſeke,
There is none like I dare well ſay;
　So manerly,
　So curteſly,
　So prately
She delis alway.

* TROWLE, or Trole the Bowl, was a common phrase in drinking, for passing the vessel about, as appears by the following beginning of an old catch:—

Trole trole the bowl to me,
And I will trole the same again to thee.

And in this other in Hilton's's collection:—

Tom Bouls, Tom Bouls,
Seest thou not how merrily this good ale trowles?

† MAULT-WORM is a humorous appellation for a lover of ale or strong drink.

‡ This song is to be found in the old comedy of Gammer Gurton's Needle, which was first printed in 1551, and is even now well known in many parts of England.

II.

That goodly las,
When ſhe me pas,
Alas I wote not where
　I go or ſtond,
　I thynk me bond,
　In ſe in lond
To comfort her.

III.

Her luſty chere,
Her eyes moſt clere,
I know no pere
In her beaute;
　Both Cate and Bes,
　Mawde and Anes,
　Sys is witneſs
Of her fetyſneſſe.

IV.

My Margaret
I cannot mete,
In feeld ne ſtrete,
Wofull am I;
　Leue loue this chance,
　Your chere avance,
　And let us dance
'Herk my Lady.'§

A lover sympathizes with his mistress, who is sick and ill at ease, in these lines:—

I.

Jhone is ſike and ill at eaſe,
I am full ſory for Jhone's diſeaſe;
Alak good Jhone what may you pleaſe?
I ſhall beare the coſt be ſwete ſent Denys.

II.

She is ſo pretty in euery degre,
Good lord who may a goodlyer be
In favoure and in facion lo will ye ſe,
But it were an angell of the Trinite.
　Alak good Jhone what may you pleſe?
　I ſhal beare the coſt be ſwete ſent Denys.

III.

Her countynaunce with her lynyacion,
To hym that wolde of ſuch recreacion,
That God hath ordent in his firſt formacion,
Myght wel be called conjuracion.
　Alak good Jhone what may you pleaſe?
　I ſhal beare the coſt be ſwete ſent Denys.

IV.

She is my lytell pretty one,
What ſhulde I ſay? my mynde is gone,
Yff ſhe and I were togethir alone,
I wis ſhe will not gyve me a bone,
　Alas good Jhone ſhall all my mone
　Be loſt ſo ſone? ‖

V.

I am a fole,
Leve this array,
　Another day
We ſhall both play,
When we are ſole.¶

The three following short poems exhibit a picture of the deepest amorous distress:—

Have I not cauſe to mourn, alas!
　Ever whiles that my lyfe do dure;
Lamenting thus my ſorrowful caſe
　In ſighes deepe without recure?
Now remembryng my hard aduenture,
Meruelloufly makyng my hart wo:
Alas! her lokes haue perſed me ſo!

§ Probably the name of some dance-tune now forgotten.
‖ i.e. treat me with contempt.
¶ Together or by ourselves.

Sad is her chere with color chryſtyne,
More fayrer of loke than fayer Elyn,
Eyes gray, clerer than columbyne,
Neuer a ſweter of nature femynyne ;
Goodly in port, O what a paſtyme and joy
Haue I when I behold her !

Wofully oppreſſed wyth ſorrow and payne,
　Wyth ſyghing my hart and body in diſtreſs,
Greuouſly tormented through diſdayne,
　Lackyng the company of my lady and myſtres,
　Whych to atayne is yet remedyles ;
But God of his grace ſurely me ſend
My ſorrows importunate joyfully to amend.

　Is it not ſure a dedly payne,
　　To you I ſay that louers be,
　When faythful harts muſt needs refrayn
　　The one the other for to ſee ?
　I you aſſure ye may truſt me,
　Of all the paynes that euer I knew,
　It is a payne that moſt I rewe.

The following trim stanzas exhibit the portrait of
a loyal lover :—

I.

As I lay ſlepynge,
In dremes fletynge,
Euer my ſwetyng
　Is in my mynd ;
She is ſo goodly,
With looks ſo louely,
That no man truly
　Such one can fynd.

II.

Her bewty ſo pure,
It doth under lure,
My pore hart full ſure
　In gouernance ;
Therfor now wyll I
Unto hyr apply,
And euer will cry
　For remembraunce.

III.

Her fayer eye perſyng,
My pore hart bledyng,
And I abydyng,
　In hope of mede ;
But thus have I long
Entunyd this ſonge,
Wyth paynes ful ſtronge,
　And cannot ſpede.

IV.

Alas wyll not ſhe
Now ſhew hyr pytye,
But thus wyll take me
　In ſuche dyſdayne ;
Methynketh I wys,
Unkynde that ſhe is,
That byndeth me thus,
　In ſuch hard payne.

V.

Though ſhe me bynde,
Yet ſhall ſhe not fynde
My pore hart unkynd,
　Do what ſhe can ;
For I wyll hyr pray,
Whiles I leue a day,
Me to take for aye,
　For hyr owne man.

The following is the expostulation of a lover disdained by his mistress, in a style of great simplicity :

I.

Complayn I may.
And right well ſay,
Loue goth aſtray,
　And waxeth wilde ;
For many a day
Loue was my pray,
It wyll away,
　I am begylde.

II.

I haue thankles
Spent my ſeruyce,
And can purches
　No grace at all ;
Wherefore doubtleſs,
Such a myſtres,
Dame Piteles,
　I may her call.

III.

For ſikerly,
The more that I
On her do try
　On me to thinke ;
The leſſe mercy
In her fynd I,
Alas I dye,
　My hart doth ſynke.

IV.

Fortune pardye,
Aſeineth me
Such cruelte,
　Wythouten gylt ;
Owght not to be,
I twis pitee,
O ſhame to ſee,
　A man ſo ſpilt.

V.

That I ſhuld ſpyll
For my good wyll,
I thynke gret ill,
　Agaynſt all ryght :
It is more ill,
She ſhuld me kyl.,
Whom I loue ſtyll,
　Wyth all my myght.

VI.

But to expreſſe
My heauynes,
Syth my ſeruyce
　Is thus forſake ;
All comfortles,
Wyth much dyſtres,
In wyldernes,
　I me betake.

VII.

And thus adewe,
Deth doth enſewe.
Wythout reſcue,
　Her　*　*　*
I trow a Jew
On me wold rew,
Knowing how trew
　That I have bene.

The two following are also of the amorous kind,
and are of equal antiquity with the rest :—

I.

Ah my ſwete ſwetyng ;
My lytyl prety ſwetyng,
My ſwetyng wyl I loue whereuer I go ;
She is ſo propre and pure,
Full ſtedfaſt, ſtabill and demure,
There is none ſuch ye may be ſure,
　As my ſwete ſweting.

II.

In all thys world as thynketh me,
Is none fo plefaunt to my eye,
That I am glad foo ofte to fee,
As my fwete fwetyng.

III.

When I behold my fwetyng fwete,
Her face, her hands, her minion fete,
They feeme to me there is none fo mete,
As my fwete fwetyng.

IV.

Aboue all other prayfe muft I,
And loue my pretty pygfnye
For none I fynd foo womanly
As my fwete fwetyng.

I.

What meaneft thou my fortune
From me fo faft to flye ·
Alas thou art importune
To worke thus cruelly.

II.

Thy wafte continually
Shall caufe me call and crye ;
Woo worth the tyme that I
To loue dyd fyrft apply.

The following is the dream of a lover, taken from Mr. Thoresby's MS. :—

Benedicite ! whate dremyd I this night ?
Methought the worlde was turnyd up fo down,
The fon the moone had loft ther force and lyght,
The fee alfo drowned both toure and towne :
Yet more meruell how that I harde the founde
Of onys uoyce faying bere in thy mind,
Thi lady hath forgoten to be kynd.

CHAP LXXX.

The two following short poems appear by the manuscript from which they were taken to have been composed about the time of Henry VIII. They were communicated by a very judicious antiquary lately deceased, whose opinion of them was that they were written either by, or in the person of Anne Boleyn ; a conjecture which her unfortunate history renders very probable :—

I.

Defiled is my name full fore,
Through cruel fpyte and falfe report,
That I may fay for euermore
Farewell, my joy ! adewe, comfort !

II.

For wrongfully ye judge of me,
Unto my fame a mortall wounde :
Say what ye lyft it wyll not be,
Ye feek for that cannot be found.

I.

O Death, rocke me on flepe,
Bringe me on quiet refte,
Let paffe my uerye giltlefs gofte,
Out of my carefull breft ;
Toll on the paffinge bell,
Ringe out the dolefull knell,
Let the founde my dethe tell,
For I muft dye,
There is no remedye,
For now I dye.

II.

My paynes who can expres ?
Alas ; they are fo ftronge
My dolor will not fuffer ftrength
My lyfe for to prolonge ;
Toll on, &c.

III.

Alone in prifon ftronge,
I wayle my deftenye ;
Wo worth this cruel hap that I
Should tafte this miferye.
Toll on, &c.

IV.

Farewell my pleafures paft,
Welcum my prefent payne,
I fele my torments fo increfe,
That lyfe cannot remayne.
Ceafe now the paffing bell,
Rong is my doleful knell,
For the found my deth doth tell,
Deth doth draw nye,
Sound my end dolefully,
For now I dye.

The following not inelegant stanzas seem to have been occasioned by the marriage of Margaret the daughter of Henry VII. to James IV. king of Scotland, in 1502 ; of whom it is related, that having taken arms against his own father, he imposed on himself the voluntary penance of continually wearing an iron chain about his waist :—

I.

O fayer, fayreft of euery fayre.
Princes mofte plefaunt and preclare.
The luftieft on lyue that bene,
Welcum of Scotland to be quene.

II.

Yong tender plant of pulchritude,
Defcendith of imperial blood,
Frefh fragrant flower of fayrehode fhene,
Welcum of Scotland to be quene.

III.

Sweet lufty imp of bewtie clere,
Mofte mighty kings dowghter dere,
Borne of a princes moft ferene,
Welcum of Scotland to be quene.

IV.

Welcum the rofe both red and whyte,
Welcum the flower of our delyte.
Our fpirit rejoicing from the fplene,
Welcum of Scotland to be quene.

The two following songs are more sententious ; the first is a sort of caveat against idle rumours :—

I.

Confidering this world, and th' increfe of vyce,
Stricken into dump, right much I mufed,
That no manner of man be he neuer fo wyfe,
From all forts thereof can be excufed.

II.

And one vyce there is, the more it is ufed
Mo inconueniens fhall grow day by day,
And that is this, let it be refufed
Geue no fure credens to euery herefay.

III.

Lyght womens thoughts wyll runne at large,
Whether the tayle be falfe or juft ;
Tydyngs of alehoufe or Grauefend barge,
Bere-baytings or barbers fhopes is not to truft.

IV.

An enemies tayle is fone diftruft,
 Ye fhall perceue it parfhall alway,
To all the forefayd refrayn we muft,
 To geue fure credens to euery herefay.

V.

Though herefay be trew, as perchaunce may fall,
 Yet fyx not thy credens to high,
And though the teller feem right fubftantial,
 And tell but herefay, why may he not lye?

VI.

Then betwyxt lyght credens and a tonge hafty,
 Surely the gyltlefs is caft away,
Condempnyng the abfent, that is unworthy
 So paffyth a lyfe from herefay to herefay.

VII.

Good Lord! how fome wyll wyth a loud uoyce,
 Tell a tale after the beft forte,
And fome herers how they will rejoyce,
 To here of theyr neybours ill report!

VIII.

As though it were a matter of comfort,
 Herein our charite doth dekay,
And fome maketh it but game and fport,
 To tell a lye after the herefay.

IX.

Tell a good tale of God or fome faynt,
 Or of fome mirakels lately done;
Some wyll beleue it hard and ftent,
 And take it after a full lyght facyon:

X.

We here fay Chrift fuffrid paffion,
 And man fhall reuert to earth and clay,
The rycheft or ftrongeft know not how foone,
 Beleue well now this, for true is that herefay.

This that follows is a dialogue between two lovers, in which there is great simplicity of style and sentiment, and a frankness discoverable on the lady's part not warranted by the manners of the present time:—

I.

[He] My harts luft and all my plefure,
 Is geuen where I may not take it agayne.
[She] Do you repent? [He] Nay I make you fure.
 [She] What is the caufe then you do complayne?

II.

[He] It plefyth my hart to fhew part of my payne,
 [She] To whom? [He] To you! [She] Plefe that wyl not me;
Be all thefe words to me, they be in vayn,
 Complayn where you may haue remedy.

III.

[He] I do complayn and find no releffe
 [She] Yea do you fo? I pray you tell me how.
[He] My lady lyft not my paynes to redreffe.
 [She] Say ye foth? [He] Yea, i make God a vowe.

IV.

[She] Who is your lady? [He] I put cafe you.
 [She] Who I? nay be fure it is not fo.
[He] In fayth ye be.   [She] Why do you fwere now?
 [He] In good fayth I loue you and no mo.

V.

[She] No mo but me? [He] No fo fay I.
 ]She] May I you truft? [He] Yea I make you fure.
[She] I fere nay.   [He] Yes, I fhall tell you why.
 [She] Tell on, lets here.   [He] Ye haue my hart in cure.

VI.

[She] Your hart? nay.   [He] Yes without mefure,
 I do you loue.   [She] I pray you fay not fo.
[He] In fayth I do.   [She] May I of you be fure?
 [He] Yea in good fayth.   [She] Then am I yours alfo.

By what kind of sophistry a lover may reason himself into a state of absolute indifference, the following ballad teaches:—

I.

Yf reafon did rule.
And witt kept fcoole,
Difcrecion fhoulde take place,
And heaue out heauines,
Which banifhed quietnes
And made hym hide his face.

II.

Sith time hath tried,
And truth hath fpied,
That fained faith is flatterie,
Why fhould difdaine
Thus ouer me raigne,
And hold me in captiuity?

III.

Why fhoulde caufe my harte to brafte,
 By fauoring foolifhe fantazie?
Why fhould difpare me all to teare,
 Why fhoulde I joyne with jelofie?

IV.

Why fhould I truft,
That neuer was jufte,
Or loue her that loues manye;
Or to lament
Time paft and fpente,
Whereof is no recouerie?

V.

For if that I
Should thus applye.
Myfelfe in all I can;
Truth to take place,
Where neuer truth was,
I weare a foolifhe man.

VI.

Sett foorth is by fcience,
Declare it doth experience,
By the frute to know the tree;
Then if a faininge flatterer,
To gaine a faithful louer,
It may in no wife be.

VII.

Therfore farewell flatterie,
Fained faith and jelofie,
Truth my tale fhall tell;
Reafon now fhall rule,
Witt fhall kepe the fcoole,
And bed you all farewell.

The arguments in favour of celibacy contained in the following song are neither new or very cogent; yet they are not destitute of humour:—

I.

The bachelor moft joyfullye,
 In pleafant plight doth paffe his daies,
Good fellowfhipp and companie
 He doth maintaine and kepe alwaie.

II.

With damfells braue he maye well goe,
The maried man cannot doe fo,
 If he be merie and toy with any,
 His wife will frowne, and words geue manye;
Her yellow hofe fhe ftrait will put on,
So that the married man dare not difpleafe his wife Joane.

There is somewhat subtle in the argument used by the author of the following stanzas against lending money, which in short is this, to preserve friendship, resist the emotions of it :——

I.
I had both monie and a frende,
　Of neither though no ſtore ;
lent my monie to my frende,
　And tooke his bonde therfore.

II.
I aſked my monie of my frende,
　But nawght ſave words I gott ;
I loſt my monie to kepe my frende,
　For ſewe hym would I not.

III.
But then if monie come,
　And frende againe weare founde,
I woulde lend no monie to my frende,
　Upon no kynde of bonde.

IV.
But after this for monie cometh
　A friend with pawne to paye,
But when the monie ſhould be had,
　My frende uſed ſuch delay,

V.
That neede of monie did me force,
　My frende his pawne to ſell,
And ſo I got my monie, but
　My frende clene from me fell.

VI.
Sith bonde for monie lent my frende,
　Nor pawne aſſurance is,
But that my monie or my frende
　Therbye I ever miſſe.

VII.
If God ſend monie and a frende,
　As I haue had before.
I will keepe my monie and ſave my frende.
　And playe the foole no more.

The examples above given are only of such songs and ballads as it is supposed were the entertainment of the common people about the year 1550, they are therefore not to be considered as evidences of the general state of poetry at that time, nor indeed at any given period of the preceding century ; for, not to mention Chaucer, who flourished somewhat before, and whose excellencies are known to every judge of English literature, the verses of Gower abound with beautiful images, and excellent moral precepts ; and those of the earl of Surrey, Sir Thomas Wyat, and a few others, their contemporaries, with the liveliest descriptions, and most elegant sentiments. One of the most excellent poems of the kind in the English language is the ballad of the Nut-brown Maid, published with a fine paraphrase by Prior, which, though the antiquity of it has by a few been questioned, was printed by Pinson, who lived about the year 1500, and probably was written some years before.

Many of the songs or popular ballads of this time appear to have been written by Skelton, and a few of them have been occasionally inserted in the course of this work ; as to his poems now extant, they are so peculiarly his own, so replete with scurrility, and, though abounding with humour, so coarse and indelicate, that they are not to be matched with any others of that time, and consequently reflect no disgrace on the age in which they were written.

Nothing can be more comical, nor nothing more uncleanly, if we except certain verses of Swift, than that poem of Skelton entitled the Tunnyng of Elynour Rummyng. This woman is said by him to have lived at Letherhead in Surrey, and to have sold ale, the brewing or tunning whereof is the subject of the poem. The humour of this ludicrous narrative consists in an enumeration of many sluttish circumstances that attended the brewing, and a description of several persons of both sexes, of various characters, as travellers, tinkers, servant-wenches, farmers' wives, and many others, whom the desire of Elynour's filthy beverage had drawn from different parts of the country ; of her ale they are so eager to drink, that many for want of money bring their household furniture, skillets, pots, meal, salt, garments, working-tools, wheel-barrows, spinning-wheels, and a hundred other things. This numerous resort produces drunkenness and a quarrel, and thus ends Skelton's poem the Tunnyng of Elynour Rummyng.

Of his talent for satire the same author has given an example in the following verses, which because they are characteristic of an ignorant singing-man, a contemporary of his, are here inserted at length :——

Skelton Laureate againſt a comely Coyſtrowne, that curiowſly chauntyd and carryſhly cowntred and madly in his Muſikes mokkyſhly made, agaynſt the ix Muſis of politike Poems and Poettys matriculat.

Of all nacyons under the Heuyn,
Theſe frantyke foolys I hate moſt of all,
For though they ſtumble in the ſynnes ſeuyn,
In peuyſhnes yet they ſnapper and fall,
Which men the vii deadly ſins call,
This peuyſh proud this prender geſt,
When he is well yet can he not reſt.

A ſwete ſuger lofe and ſowre bayards bun
Be ſumdele lyke in forme and ſhap,
The one for a duke the other for a dun ;
A maunchet for Morell thereon to ſnap,
His hart is to hy to haue any hap,
But for in his gamut carp that he can,
Lo Jak wold be a Jentylman.

With hey troly loly, lo whip here Jak,
Alumbek ſodyldym ſyllorym ben,
Curyowſly he can both counter and knak,
Of Martin Swart, and all hys mery men,
Lord how Perkyn is proud of his Pohen,
But aſk wher he ſyndyth among his monachords
An holy-water-clark a ruler of lordes.

He cannot fynd it in rule nor in ſpace,
He ſolfyth to haute, hys trybyll is to hy,
He braggyth of his byrth that borne was full bace,
Hys muſyk withoute meſure, to ſharp is his my,[*]
He trymmyth in his tenor to counter pardy,
His diſcant is beſy, it is without a mene,
To fat is his fantſy, his wyt is to lene.

He tumbryth on a lewde lewte, Roty bulle Joyſe,[†]
Rumbill downe, tumbill downe, hey go now now,
He fumblyth in his fyngering an ugly rude noiſe,
It ſeemyth the ſobbyng of an old ſow :
He wolde be made moch of and he wyſt how ;
Wele ſped in ſpyndels and tunyng of travellys,
A bungler, a brawler, a pyker of quarellys.

Comely he clappyth a payre of clauycordys,
He whyſtelyth ſo ſwetely he maketh me to ſwet,
His diſcant is daſhed full of diſcordes,
A red angry man but eaſy to intrete ;
An uſher of the hall fayn wold I get,
To pointe this proude page a place and a rome,
For Jak wold be a Jentilman that late was a grome.

---

* *i. e.* The syllable MI used in solmisation.
† The initial words of some old song.

Jak wold Jet and yet Jill fayd nay,
He counteth in his countenance to check with the beſt,
A malaperte medler that pryeth for his pray,
In a dyſh dare he ruſh to wrangill and to wreſt,
He findeth a proporcyon in his prycke ſonge,
To drynke at a draught a large and a long.

Nay jape not with him, he is no ſmall fole,
It is a folempne fyre and a folayne,
For lordes and ladyes lerne at his ſcole,
He techyth them ſo wyſely to folf and to fayne,
That neither they fing wel prike-fong nor plain,
This Doctor Dellias commenſyd in a cart,
A maſter, a mynſtrel, a fydler, a —.

What though ye can counter *Cuſtodi nos,*
As wel it becomith you a paryſh towne clarke
To fing *Supinitati dedit Ægros,*
Yet bere ye not to bold, to braule ne to bark,
At me that medeled nothing with youre wark,
Correct firſt thy felfe, walk and be nought,
Deme what you liſt thou knowiſt not my thought.

A prouerbe of old fay well or be ſtill,
Yc are to unhappy occafion to fynde,
Uppon me to clater or elfe to fay yll.
Now have I ſhewyd you part of your proud mind,
Take this in worth the beſt is behind.
Wryten at Croydon by Crowland in the clay,
On Candelmas euyn the Kalendas of May.

Mention has already been made of the service-books anciently used in the churches and chapels of this kingdom, by whom they were generally made, and of the enormous price they bore while copies of them could only be multiplied by writing. This, though a great inconvenience, was not the only one which music laboured under, for the characters used in musical notation were for a series of years fluctuating, so that they assumed a new form in every century, and can hardly be said to have arrived at any degree of stability till some years after the invention of printing; and it will surprise the reader to behold, as he may in the specimens of notation given (see Appendix, Nos. 45 to 55), the multifold variation of the musical characters between the eleventh century, when they were invented by Guido, and the fifteenth, when, with a few exceptions in the practice of the German printers, they were finally settled.

Upon these specimens it is to be remarked, that they exhibit a series of characters used for the purpose of musical notation from the eleventh century down to the fourteenth, as they are to be found in missals, graduals, antiphonaries, and other books of offices adapted to the Romish service. With regard to No. 48, 'Paupertate Spiritus,' the musical characters appear to be such as are said to have been in use previous to the invention of the stave by Guido, and from the smallness of the intervals it may be questioned whether the notes are intended to signify any thing more than certain inflections of the voice, so nearly approaching to monotony, that the utterance of them may rather be called reading than singing.

The example (No. 50) 'Eripe me Domine' is clearly in another method of notation, for the stave of Guido, and also the F cliff, are made use of in it. With regard to the characters on the lines and spaces, they are very different from those points, from the use

whereof in musical composition the term Contrapunto took its rise; and so little do they resemble the characters proper to the Cantus Mensurabilis, as described by Franco, De Handlo, and other writers on that subject, that it is not without great difficulty that they can be rendered intelligible. The author from whom this example is taken exhibits it as a specimen of the manner of notation in the twelfth century; it nevertheless appears to have continued in practice so low down as the sixteenth, for all the examples in the Margarita Philosophica of Gregory Reisch, printed in 1517, are in this character, as are also those in the Enchiridion of George Rhaw, the Compendium Musices of Lampadius, and other works of the like kind, published about the same time.

The specimen (No. 52) 'Verbum Patris' is of the thirteenth century, and as to the form of the characters, differs in some respects from the former; and here it may be remarked, that the F and C cliffs have each a place in the stave, and that the station of the former is marked by a pricked line. Other distinctions for the places of the cliffs, namely, by giving the lines a different colour or different degrees of thickness, were usual in the earlier times, and are taken notice of in an earlier part of this work.

The character in the specimen (No. 54) 'Vere dignum et justum' are supposed to denote the inflections of the voice in reading.

The plate No. 45 shews the different forms of the cliffs, and their gradual deviation from their respective roots at different periods.

The two next succeeding plates contain a comprehensive view of the musical notes in different ages, with their equivalents in modern characters.

The specimens are taken from the Lexicon Diplomaticum of Johannes Ludolphus Walther, published at Ulm in 1756; they appear to have been extracted from ancient service-books in manuscript, of which there are very many yet remaining in the public libraries of universities and other repositories in Europe.* The explanations in modern characters are the result of his own labour and learned industry, and furnish the means of rendering into modern characters those barbarous marks and signatures used by the monks in the notation of their music.

CHAP. LXXXI.

The invention of printing proved an effectual remedy for all the evils arising from the instability of musical notation, for besides that it eased the public in the article of expence, it introduced such a steady and regular practice as rendered the musical, an universal character.

The first essays towards music-printing were those examples which occur in the works of Franchinus, printed at Milan; but of these it may be observed, that the notes therein contained are not printed from letter-press types, with a character cut on each, but

* One of the finest of the kind, perhaps in the world, is the Liber Regalis, containing, among other things, the religious ceremonial of the coronation of Richard II. and his queen, with the musical notes to the offices. This curious MS. was originally intended for the use of the high-altar in Westminster-abbey, and is now in the library of that church.

in masses, or from blocks, with a variety of characters engraven thereon. The Germans improved upon this practice, and the art of printing music with letter-press types appears to have arrived at great perfection among them by the year 1500.

Mattheson, in his Volkomenen Capelmeister, pag. 58, relates that Jaques De Sanleques, a man who had arrived to play exquisitely on all instruments, without the least instruction, was the first who taught the art of making music-types, and the method of printing from them, in France; and that he died in the year 1660, at the age of forty-six, having precipitated his death by excessive study and application. This account of the introduction of musical printing types into France can never be true; for the Psalms and other works of Claude Le Jeune, which was published at Paris by Pierre Ballard before Sanleques was born, that is to say in 1603 and 1606, are a demonstration to the contrary; and, to judge from the exquisite beauty and elegance of the characters, and the many elegant ornaments and ingenious devices for the initial letters, it seems that the French had in this kind of printing greatly the advantage of their neighbours.

In England the progress of this art was comparatively slow, for in the Polychronicon * of Ranulph Higden, translated by Trevisa, and printed by Wynken de Worde, at Westminster in 1495, are the following musical characters, which Mr. Ames with good reason supposes to be the first of the kind printed in England :—

Grafton improved upon these characters in the book published by him in 1550, entitled, The Book of Common Prayer noted, which was composed by John Marbeck organist of Windsor, and contains the rudiments of our present cathedral service; these, in the opinion of the printer, stood so much in need of explanation, that he has inserted the following memorandum concerning them :—

‘ In this booke is conteyned fo much of the order of ‘ Common Prayer as is to be fung in churches, wherein ‘ are ufed only thefe iiii fortes of notes :—

‘ The firft note is a ftrene note, and is a breve; the ‘ fecond is a fquare note, and is a femybreve; the iii a ‘ pycke, and is a mynymme. And when there is a ‘ prycke by the fquare note, that prycke is halfe as

‘ muche as the note that goeth before it. The iiii is ‘ a clofe, and is only ufed at the end of a verfe.’

These characters were considerably improved by the industrious John Day, who in 1560 published the church-service in four and three parts, to be sung at the morning, communion, and evening prayer, and in 1562 the whole book of Psalms, collected into English metre by Sternhold, Hopkins, and others, with apt notes to sing them withal, and by Thomas Vautrollier, who in 1575 published the Cantiones of Tallis and Bird under a patent of queen Elizabeth to the authors, the first of the kind.† The succeeding music-printers to Vautrollier and Day were Thomas Este, who for some reasons not now to be guessed at, changed his name to Snodham,‡ John Windet, William Barley, and others, who were the assignees of Bird and Morley, under the patents respectively granted to them for the sole printing of music. These men followed the practice of the foreign printers, but made no improvement at all in the art, nor was any made till the time of John Playford, who lived in the reign of Charles II.

In what manner, and from what motives, music was first introduced into the church-service, has already been mentioned; and in the account given of that matter it has been shewn that the practice of antiphonal singing took its rise in the churches the East, namely, those of Antioch, Cesaræa, and Constantinople; that the Greek fathers, St. Basil and St. Chrysostom, were the original institutors of choral service in their respective churches; that St. Ambrose introduced it into his church at Milan; that from thence it passed to Rome, from whence it was propagated and established in France, Germany, Britain, and, in short, throughout the West: and, to speak more particularly, that Damasus ordained the alternate singing of the Psalms, together with the Gloria Patri, and Alleluja; in 384, Siricius, the anthem; in 507, Symmachus, the Gloria in Excelsis; that in 590 Gregory the Great reformed the Cantus Ambrosianus, and established that known by his name; and that about the year 660 Vitalianus completed the institution by joining to the melody of the voice the harmony of the organ.

From this deduction of the rise and progress of music in cathedral worship, it may seem that the introduction of music into the church was attended with little difficulty. But the case was far otherwise; fortunately for the science, the above-mentioned fathers were skilled in it, and their zeal co-operating with their authority, enabled them to procure it admittance into the church; but there were then, as there have been at all times, men, who either having no ear, were insensible to the effects of harmony, or who conceiving that all such adventitious aids to devotion were at least unnecessary, if not sinful, laboured with all their might to procure the exclusion of music of every kind from the church, and to restore the service to that original plainness and simplicity, which they conceived to be its perfection.

And first St. Austin, whose suffrage is even at this day cited in favour of choral music; although

* Those who do not know that the Polychronicon is a multifarious history of events without order or connexion, will wonder how these characters could find a place in it, but it is thus accounted for; the author relates the discovery of the consonances by Pythagoras, and to illustrate his narration gives a type of them in the form above described.

† Ames's Typographical Antiquities, pag. 335.   ‡ Ibid.

speaking of the introduction of antiphonal singing into the church of Milan, at which he was present, thus pathetically expresses himself : 'How abundantly ' did I weep before God to hear those hymns of thine ; ' being touched to the quick by the voices of thy ' sweet church song ! The voices flowed into my ears, ' and thy truth pleasingly distilled into my heart, ' which caused the affections of my devotion to over- ' flow, and my tears to run over, and happy did I ' find myself therein.'

Yet this very St. Austin having reason to suspect that he had mistaken the natural workings of his passions for the fervent operations of a vigorous devotion, censures himself severely for being so moved with sensual delight in divine worship, and heartily blesses God for being delivered from that snare. He withal declares that he often wished that the melodious singing of David's Psalter with so much art were moved from his and the church's ears ; and that he thought the method which he had often heard was observed by Athanasius, bishop of Alexandria, was the safest, who caused him that read the Psalm to use so little variation of the voice, that he seemed rather to pronounce than sing.* And elsewhere he declares that the same manner of sing-ing as was used in Alexandria prevailed throughout all Africa.†

St. Jerome, though a friend to magnificence in divine worship, seems to more than hint a dislike of artificial singing in the church, when he says, ' That ' we are not like tragedians to gargle the throat with ' sweet modulation, that our theatrical tunes and ' songs may be heard in the church, but we are to ' sing with reverence.'‡

Isidore of Sevil, though a writer on music, and as such mentioned in the account herein before given of writers on the science, says, that the singing of the primitive Christians was attended with so small a variation of the voice, that it differed very little from reading ; and as for that pompous manner of singing, which a little before his time had been in-troduced into the Western church, he says it was brought in for the sake of those who were carnal, and not on their account who were spiritual, that those who were not affected by words might be charmed by the sweetness of the harmony.§

Rabanus Maurus, another musical writer, and a disciple of the famous Alcuin, freely declares himself against the use of musical artifice and theatrical singing in the worship of God, and is only for such music as may move compunction, and be clearly understood by the hearers.||

Thomas Aquinas, universally reputed the ablest and most judicious of the schoolmen, declares against the use of instruments in divine worship, which, together with the pompous service of the choir, he intimates are Judaical. He says that ' musical in-' struments do more stir up the mind to delight, than ' frame it to a religious disposition.' He indeed allows that ' under the law such sensitive aids might ' be needful, as they were types or figures of some-

' thing else ; but that under the gospel dispensation ' he sees no reason or use for them.'¶

And, to come nearer our own times, Cornelius Agrippa, though a sceptic in most of the subjects which he has written on, declaims with great vehe-mence against cathedral music, which he says is ' so ' licentious, that the divine offices, holy mysteries, ' and prayers are chanted by a company of wanton ' musicians, hired with great sums of money, not to ' edify the understanding, but to tickle the ears of ' their auditory. The church,' he adds, ' is filled ' with noise and clamour, the boys whining the ' descant, while some bellow the tenor, and others ' bark the counterpoint ; others again squeak the ' treble, while others grunt the bass ; and they all ' contrive so, that though a great variety of sounds is ' heard, neither sentences, nor even words can be ' understood.' * *

Erasmus, who, as having been while a boy a chorister, might be reasonably supposed to entertain a prejudice rather in favour of music than against it, has a passage to this purpose : ' There is, says he, ' a kind of music brought into divine worship which ' hinders people from distinctly understanding a word ' that is said ; nor have the singers any leisure to ' mind what they sing ; nor can the vulgar hear any ' thing but an empty sound, which delightfully glides ' into their ears. What notions, says he, have they ' of Christ, who think he is pleased with such a noise ?'

And in another place he thus complains : ' We ' have brought a tedious and capricious kind of music ' into the house of God, a tumultuous noise of different ' voices, such as I think was never heard in the ' theatres either of the Greeks or Romans, for the ' keeping up whereof whole flocks of boys are main-' tained at a great expence, whose time is spent in ' learning such gibble-gabble, while they are taught ' nothing that is either good or useful. Whole ' troops of lazy lubbers are also maintained solely ' for the same purpose ; at such an expence is the ' church for a thing that is pestiferous.' Whereupon he expresses a wish ' that it were exactly calculated ' how many poor men might be relieved and main-' tained out of the salaries of these singers :' and con-cludes with a reflection on the English for their fondness of this kind for service.††

Zuinglius, notwithstanding he was a lover of music, speaking of the ecclesiastical chanting, says, that that ' and the roaring in the churches, scarce understood ' by the priests themselves, are a foolish and vain ' abuse, and a most pernicious hindrance to piety.'‡‡

But lest the suffrage of Zuinglius and Calvin, who speaks much in the same manner, should be thought exceptionable, it may not be amiss to produce that of cardinal Cajetan, who, though a great enemy to the reformers, agrees with them in declaring that it may be easily gathered from 1 Corinthians xiv. that it is much more agreeable to the apostle's mind that the sacred offices should be distinctly recited and intelligibly performed in the church, without musical

---

* Confess. lib. X. cap. 33.   † Epist. 119.   ‡ Epist. ad Rusticum.
§ De Eccl. Off. lib. I. cap. 5. || De Institut. Cleric. lib. II. cap. 48.

¶ In. 21. Qu. 91. a. 2. 4.
** De Vanitate et Incertudine Scientiarum, cap. 17.
†† Comment on 1. Corinth. xiv. 19.
‡‡ Zuinglii Act. Disp. pag. 106.

and artificial harmony, than so managed, as that with the noise of organs and the clamorous divisions, and absurd repetitions of affected singers, which seem as it were devised on purpose to darken the sense, the auditors should be so confounded as that no one should be able to understand what was sung.

Polydore Virgil, though an Italian, and of the Romish communion, writes to the same purpose: 'How, says he, the chanters make a noise in the 'church, and nothing is heard there but a voice; 'and others who are present rest satisfied with the 'consent of the cries, no way regarding the meaning 'of the words. And so it is, that among the multi-'tude all the esteem of divine worship seems to rely 'on the chanters, notwithstanding generally no men 'are lighter or more wicked.' And speaking of the choir service in general, he adds: 'I may say that 'this, and the ceremonies attending it, are for the 'most part brought into our worship from the old 'Heathens, who were wont to sacrifice with symphony, 'as Livy, lib. IX. witnesseth.'*

Lindanus, bishop of Ruremonde, speaking of the musicians and singers that had possessed the church after the Reformation, complains that their music is nothing but a theatrical confusion of sounds, tending rather to avert the minds of the hearers from what is good, than raise them to God; and declares that he had often been present, and as attentive as he could well be to what was sung, yet could he hardly understand any thing, the whole service was so filled with repetitions, and a confusion of different voices and tones and rude clamours. And thereupon he commends those who had expelled this sort of music out of their churches as a mere human device, and a profane hindrance of divine worship.†

To these censures of individuals some have added that implied in the decree of the council of Trent, made anno 1562, for correcting abuses in the celebration of the mass, not distinguishing between the use and the abuse of the subject in question.

Such are the authorities usually insisted on against the practice of antiphonal singing in cathedral churches, against which it might be objected, that the arguments, if such they may be called, of the several writers above-mentioned, seem less calculated to convince the reason than to inflame the passions of those who should attend to them; that allowing them all their weight, they conclude rather against the abuse of singing than the practice itself: and that all of those writers who have been thus free in their censures of church-music, were not so well skilled in the science as to be justifiable for pretending to give any opinion at all about it. Polydore Virgil has never yet been deemed a very respectable authority either for facts or opinions; and as to Cornelius Agrippa, the author of a book which the world have long stood in doubt whether to approve or condemn, choral singing might well seem confusion to him, who was so grossly ignorant in the science of music, as not to know the difference between the harmonical and metrical modes, and who has charged the

ancients with confusion in the modes of time, which were not invented till the middle of the eleventh century.‡

Against the objections of these men choral service has been defended by arguments drawn from the practice of the primitive church, and its tendency to edification; these are largely insisted on by Durandus, cardinal Bona, and others of the liturgical writers. As to the censure of the council of Trent, it regarded only the abuses of church-music; for it forbids only the use of music in churches mixed with lascivious songs, and certain indecencies in the performance of it which the singers had given into; § and as it was designed to bring it back to that standard of purity from which it had departed, it justified the decent and genuine use of it, and gave such authority to choral or antiphonal singing, that its lawfulness and expediency has long ceased to be a subject of controversy, except in the reformed churches; and in these a diversity of opinion still remains. The Calvinists content themselves with a plain metrical psalmody, but the Lutheran and episcopal churches have a solemn musical service. The original oppugners of that of the church of England were the primitive Puritans; the force of their objections to it is contained in the writings of their champion Thomas Cartwright, in the course of the disciplinarian controversy; and to these Hooker, in his Ecclesiastical Polity, has given what many persons think a satisfactory answer. The arguments of each are referred to in a subsequent part of this work.

However, these are merely speculative opinions, into which it were to little purpose to seek either for the causes that contributed to the establishment of choral music, or for the reasons that influenced those who opposed its admission, since in their determinations the bulk of mankind are actuated by considerations very remote from the reasonableness or propriety of any. The fact is, that the fathers above-mentioned, from a persuasion of its utility and agreeableness to the word of God, laboured to introduce it into the church; and it is no less certain, that chiefly on the score of its novelty it met with great opposition from the common people; for, not to mention the tumults which the introduction of it occasioned at Constantinople, and the concessions which St. Chrysostom thereupon made, it appears that when Gregory the Great, in 620, sent the Cantus Gregorianus into Britain by Austin the monk, the clergy were so little disposed to receive it, that the endeavours to establish it occasioned the slaughter of no fewer than twelve hundred of them at once; and it was not till fifty years after, when Vitalianus sent Theodore the Greek to fill up the vacant see of Canturbury, that the clergy of this island could be prevailed on either to celebrate the Paschal solemnity, the precise time for which was then a subject of great controversy, or to acquiesce in the admission of cathedral service in the manner required by the Romish ritual; nor did they then do it so willingly but that the pope about nine

---

* De Invent. Rerum. lib. VI. cap. ii.
† Lindan. Panopliæ, lib. V. cap. vii.

‡ Corn. Agrippa in loc. citat.
§ 'L' uso delle musiche nelle chiefe con mistura di canto, ò suono 'lascivo, tutte le attioni secolari, colloquii profani, strepiti, gridori.' Hist. del Concil. Trident. di Pietro Soave, Londra, 1619, pag. 559.

years after, found himself under the necessity of sending hither the principal singer of the church of St. Peter at Rome, who taught the Britons the Roman method of singing, so that the true era of cathedral music in this our land is to be fixed at about the year of our Lord 679.

But in France the business went on still less smoothly than in Britain, for which reason Adrian taking advantage of the obligation he had conferred on Charlemagne, by making him emperor of the West, stipulated with him for the introduction of the Cantus Gregorianus into the Gallic church : the account of this memorable transaction is thus given by Baronius. 'In the year 787 the emperor kept 'his Easter with pope Adrian at Rome ; and in 'those days of festivity there arose a great con-'tention between the French and Roman singers. 'The French pretended to sing more gravely and 'decently, the Romans more melodiously and arti-'ficially, and each mightily undervalued the other. 'The emperor yielded to the pope, and made his 'own servants submit ; and thereupon he took back 'with him Theodore and Benedict, two excellent 'Roman singers, to instruct his countrymen. The 'pope also presented him with the Roman antipho-'nary, which the emperor promised him should be 'generally used throughout his dominions ; and upon 'his return to France he placed one of these artists in 'the city of Metz, ordering that the singers should 'from all the cities in France resort hither to be 'taught by him the true method of singing and 'playing on the organ.'*

Thus the matter stood at about the end of the eighth century, by which time all actual opposition to cathedral music was pretty well calmed ; and, saving the objections above-cited, which seem rather to apply to the abuse of it than the practice itself, church-music may be said to have met with no interruption for upwards of seven centuries. On the contrary, during all that period the church of Rome, with a sedulous application continued its utmost endeavours to cultivate it. And from the time that Franchinus became a public professor of the science, the younger clergy betook themselves with great assiduity to the study of music, for which no adequate cause can be assigned other than that it was looked on as the ready road to ecclesiastical preferment.

Nor was it from those popes alone who were skilled in, or entertained a passion for the science, that music received protection ; others of them there were, who, influenced by considerations merely political, contributed to encourage it ; the dignity, the splendor, and magnificence of the Roman worship seemed to demand every assistance that the arts could afford. All the world knows how much of the perfection which painting has arrived at, is owing to the encouragement given by the church to its professors : Michael Angelo and Raphael were almost solely employed in adorning the church of St. Peter and the Vatican with sculptures and scripture-histories ; and from motives of a similar nature the greatest

* A circumstantial account of this event, as related by Durandus and cardinal Baronius, is given in book IV. chap. 30. of this work.

encouragements were given to musicians to devote their studies to that species of composition which is suited to the ends of divine worship ; and to the perfection of this kind of music the circumstances of the times were very fortunate : for notwithstanding the extreme licence taken by persons of rank and opulence at Rome, and indeed throughout all Italy, and that unbounded love of pleasure, which even in the fourteenth century had fixed the characteristic of Italian manners, it does appear that much of their enjoyment was derived from such public spectacles as to the other powers of fascination add music ; and that masquerades, feasting, and gallantry were with them the principal sources of sensual gratification. The musical drama, or what is now called the opera, was not then known ; the consequence whereof was, that the church not having then, as now, the stage for its competitor, had it in its power to attach the most eminent professors of the science to its service, and to render the studies of a whole faculty subservient to its purposes.

To this concurrence of circumstances, and a disposition in those whose duty led them to attend to the interests of religion, to which may be added that theoretical skill in the science, which Franchinus had by his public lectures disseminated throughout Italy, are owing the improvements which we find to have been made in the art of practical composition by the end of the sixteenth century. The prodigious havoc and destruction which was made in the conventual and other libraries, not only in England, at the dissolution of monasteries, but in France and Flanders also, in consequence of those commotions which the reformation of religion occasioned, have left us but few of those compositions from whence a comparison might be drawn between the church-music of the period now spoken of, and that of the more early ages ; but from the few fragments of the latter now remaining in manuscript, it appears to be of a very inartificial contexture, and totally void of those excellencies that distinguish the productions of succeeding times. Nor indeed could it possibly be otherwise while the precepts of the science inculcated nothing more than the doctrine of counterpoint and the nature of the canto fermo, a kind of harmony simple and unadorned, and in the performance scarcely above the capacities of those who in singing had no other guide than their ear and memory ; in short, a species of music that derived not the least advantage from any difference among themselves in respect of the length or duration of the notes, which all men know is an inexhaustible source of variety and delight.

But the assigning of different lengths to sounds, the invention of pauses, or rests, the establishment of metrical laws, and the regulating the motion of a great variety of parts by the tactus or beat, whereby an union of harmony and metre was effected, were improvements of great importance ; from these sprang the invention of fugue and canon, and those infinitely various combinations of tone and time which distinguish the canto figurato from the canto fermo, or ecclesiastical plain-song.

The principal motive to these improvements was undoubtedly the great encouragement given to students and professors of music by the court of Rome. Those writers, who, to palliate the vices of Leo X. insist on his love of learning, and the patronage afforded by him to the professors of all the finer arts, ascribe the perfection of music among the rest to his munificence; but in this they are mistaken; an emulation to promote music prevailed at this time throughout Europe, and the temporal princes were not less disposed to favour its improvement than even the pontiffs themselves; our own Henry VIII. not only sang, but was possessed of a degree of skill in the art of practical composition equal to that of many of its ablest professors, as appears by many of his works now extant. Francis the First of France reckoned Joannes Mouton, his chapel-master, and Crequilon, among the chief ornaments of his court; and the emperor Charles V. by his bounty to musicians had drawn many of the most celebrated then in Europe to settle in Germany and the Low Countries.

Such was the general state of the church-service in Europe in the age immediately preceding the Reformation, at the time whereof it is well known choral music underwent a very great change: the nature of this change, and the precise difference between the Romish and the other reformed churches in this respect will best appear by a comparison of their several offices; nevertheless a very cursory view of the Romish ritual, particularly of the missal, the gradual, and the antiphonary, will serve to shew that the greater part of the service of that church was sung to musical notes. In the Antwerp edition of the missal, printed MDLXXVIII. conformable to the decree of the council of Trent, the suffrages and responses are printed with notes, which are included within a stave of four red lines. The offices in usum Sarisburiensis, as they are termed, contained in the Missal, the Manual, the Processional, and other books, nay even those for the consecration of salt, of water, tapers, and ashes, are in like manner printed with musical notes. These it must be supposed, as they are for the most part extremely plain and simple, were intended for common and ordinary occasions; in short, they are that kind of plain-chant which is easily retained in the memory, and in which the whole of a congregation might without any dissonance or confusion join.

But the splendour and magnificence of the Romish worship is only to be judged of by the manner of celebrating divine service upon great festivals, and other solemn occasions, and that too in cathedrals and conventual churches, and in those abbies and monasteries where either the munificence of the state, or an ample endowment, afforded the means of sustaining the expense of a choir. In these cases the mass was sung by a numerous choir, composed of men and boys, sufficiently skilled in the practice of choral service, to music of a very elaborate and artificial contexture; in the composition whereof the strict rules of the tonal melody were dispensed with,

and the greatest latitude was allowed for the exercise of the powers of invention.

However, this mode of solemn service was not restrained to cathedral, collegiate, and conventual churches, it was practised also in the royal and universal chapels, and in the domestic chapels of the dignitaries of the church, and of the higher orders of nobility. Cavendish, in his life of cardinal Wolsey, relating the order and offices of his house and chapel, gives the following account of the latter:—

'Now I will declare unto you the officers of his 'chapel, and singing-men of the same. First, he 'had there a dean, a great divine, and a man of ex-'cellent learning; and a subdean, a repeatour of the 'quire, a gospeller and epistoller; of singing priests 'ten. A master of the children. The seculas of the 'chapel, being singing-men, twelve. Singing 'children ten, with one servant to wait upon the 'children. In the vestry a yeoman and two grooms; 'over and besides other retainers that came thither 'at principal feasts. And for the furniture of his 'chapel, it passeth my weak capacity to declare the 'number of the costly ornaments and rich jewells 'that were occupied in the same. For I have seen 'in procession about the hall forty-four rich copes, 'besides the rich candlesticks and other necessary 'ornaments to the furniture of the same.'*

Besides the higher dignitaries of the church, such as the archbishop of Canterbury, the bishops of Durham and Winchester, while those bishopricks were not held in commendam by the cardinal, and perhaps some others, whose station might require it, there were several among the principal nobility who seemed to emulate Wolsey in this particular, and had the solemn choral service performed in the chapels of their respective palaces and houses. One of these was the earl of Northumberland, whose great possessions and ample jurisdiction seem to have been adequate to, and to warrant every degree of magnificence under that of a king; for it appears that at the seat of the earl of Northumberland, contemporary with Wolsey, there was a chapel, in which, to judge from the number and qualifications of the persons retained for that purpose, it should seem that choral service was performed with the same degree of solemnity as in cathedral and conventual churches. The evidence of this fact is contained in an ancient manuscript of the Percy family, purporting to be the regulations and establishment of the household of Henry Algernon Percy, the fifth earl of Northumber-

---

* *The state and dignity in which Wolsey lived, seemed to require a retinue of secular musicians; and accordingly we find that he held a company of such attending him, which, upon some occasions, he lent to the King. To this purpose, Stow, in his Annals, p. 535, relates a fact which is here given in his own words:—* 'There was not only plenty of fine meats, but also much 'mirth and solace, as well in merry communication, as with the noise of my 'Lord's minstrels, who played there all that night so cunningly, that the 'King tooke therein great pleasure; insomuch that he desired my Lord to 'lend them unto him for the next night, and after supper their banquet 'finished, the ladies and gentlemen fell to daunsing, among whom, one 'Madame Fontaine, a maide, had the price. And thus passed they the 'most part of the night ere they departed. The next day the King tooke my 'Lord's minstrels, and rode to a nobleman's house where was some image to 'whom he vowed a pilgrimage, to performe his devotions. When he came 'there, which was in the night, hee daunsed and caused other to doe the same, 'after the sound of my Lord's minstrels, who played there all night, and 'never rested, so that whether it were with extreme labour of blowing, or 'with poyson (as some iudged) because they were commended by the King 'more than his owne, I cannot tell, but the player on the shalme (who was 'very excellent in that instrument) dyed within a day or two after!'

land, at his castles of Wresill and Lekingfield in Yorkshire, begun anno domini MDXII. By this it appears that the earl had his dean and subdean of the chapel, a gospeller and pistoler, gentlemen and children of the chapel, an organist, and, in short, the same officers and retainers as were employed in the royal and other chapels; and as to their number, it appears by the following entries in the manuscript above referred to:—

'Gentyllmen and Childeryn of the Chapell.

'Item. Gentyllmen and childryn of the chapell xiiij, 'viz., gentyllmen of the chapell viii, viz., ij bassys, ij 'tenors, and iiij countertenours—yoman or grome of the 'vestry j—childeryn of the chapell v, viz., ij tribills and 'iij meanys—xiiij.

'Gentilmen of the chapel ix, viz., the maister of the 'childre j—tenors ij—countertenors iiij—the pistoler j— 'and oone for the orgayns—childer of the chapell vj.'

The wages of the dean, the gentlemen, and the children of the chapel, are thus ascertained:—

'The dean of the chapel iiij l. if he have it in housholde 'and not by patentt.*

'Gentillmen of the chapel x, as to say two at x marc 'a pece—three at iiij l. a pece—two at v marc a pece— 'oone at xls.—and oone at xxs. viz.. ij bassys, ij tenors, 'and vj countertenors—childeryn of the chapel vj, after 'xxv s. the pece.

'The gentlemen ande childrin of my lordis chapell 'whiche be not appointid to uttend at no tyme, but oonely 'in exercising of Goddis service in the chappell daily at 'Mattins, Lady-Mass, Highe-Mass, Even-songe, and 'Complynge.

'Gentlemen of my lordis chappell.

'Furst, a bass. Item, a seconde bass, Item, the third 'bass. Item, a maister of the childer, a countertenour. 'Item, a second countertenour. Item, a third counter- 'tenour. Item, a iiijth countertenour. Item, a standing 'tenour. Item, a second standing tenour. Item, a 'iijd standing tenour. Item, a fourth standing tenour.

'Childrin of my lordis chappell.

'Item, the fyrst child a trible. Item, the ijd child a 'trible. Item, the iijd child a trible. Item, the iiijth 'child a second trible. Item, the vth child a second 'trible. Item, the vjth child a second trible.

'The noumbre of thois parsons as childrin of my lordis 'chappel vj.'

The wages or stipends severally assigned to the gentlemen and children of the above establishment have already been mentioned; provision was also made for their maintenance in this noble family, as appears by the following articles respecting their diet:—

'Braikfast in Lent for ij meas [mess] of gentilmen o' 'th' chapel, and a meas of childeryn, iij loofs of brede, 'a gallon dimid [half] of bere, and iij peces of salt fish 'or ells, iiiij white herryng to a meas—iij.'

And in another place their ordinary breakfast is directed to be—

'iij loif of houshold bred, a gallon dimid of bere, and 'iij peces of beif boylid.—j

'———— Braikfasts for ij meas of gentilmen o' th' chappel,

'and a meas of childer, iij loifs of houshold breid, a gallon 'dimid of bere, and a pece of salt-fische.

'Service for iiij mease of gentyllmen and childre of the 'chapell at suppar upon Tewisday in the Rogacion days, 'furst x gentylmen and vj childre of the chapel iiij meas.

'Service for gentylmen and childer o' th' chapell, to 'every meas a loof of bred, a pottell of bere, half a dysch 'of buttre, and a pece of saltt-fische, viij dyschis.' †

Besides these assignments, they had also liveries of white or wax-lights, of fagots, and of coals for fuel; provision was also made for the washing of Albes‡ and surplices for the gentlemen and children of the chapel, and also of altar-cloths: the times of washing them were regulated by the festivals that occur in the course of the year, and the rate of payment to the launderer was a penny for every three surplices. The whole expense of washing linen for the chapel as thus ascertained, was estimated at seventeen shillings and four pence a year, and the amount of the chapel-wages for a year was thirty-five pounds fifteen shillings.

'The orderynge of my lordes chapell in the queare at 'mattyngis, mass, and evynsonge. To stonde in ordure as 'hereafter followeth, syde for syde daily:—

'The deane side.	'The seconde side.
'The Deane.	'The Lady-masse priest.
'The subdeane.	'The gospeller.
'A basse.	'A basse.
'A tenor.	'A countertenor.
'A countertenor.	'A countertenor.
'A countertenor.	'A tenor.
'A countertenor.	'A countertenor.
	'A tenor.

† The regimen of diet prescribed by the book from which the above extracts are made, was, with a few variations extended to the whole family: the following regulations respect the breakfasts of the earl and the countess and their children during Lent:—

'Braikfast for my lorde and my lady.
'Furst, a loif of brede in trenchors, ij manchetts, a quart of bere, a 'quart of wyne, ij pecys of salt-fisch, vj baconn'd herryng, iiij white 'herryng, or a disch of sproits—j.
'Braikfaste for my lorde Percy and maister Thomas Percy.
'Item, half a loif of household brede, a manchet, a potell of bere, a 'dysch of butter, and a pece of salt-fish, a dysch of sproits, or iij white 'herrynge—j.
'Braikfaste for the nurcy for my lady Margaret and maister
'Ingerm Percy.
'Item. a manchet, a quarte of bere, a dysch of butter, a pece of salt- 'fisch, a dysch of sproitts, or iij white herryng—j.'
And, excepting the season of Lent and fish-days, the ordinary allow- ance for this part of the family throughout the year was as follows:
'Braikfastis of flesch days dayly thorowte the yere.
'Braikfastis for my lorde and my lady.
'Furst, a loof of brede in trenchors, ij manchetts, j quart of bere, a 'quart of wyne, half a chyne of muton, or ells a chyne of beef boiled—j.
'Braikfastis for my lorde Percy and Mr. Thomas Percy.
'Item halfe a loif of householde breide, a manchet, j potell of bere, a 'chekynge or ells iij mutton bonys boiled—j.
'Braikfasts for the nurcy for my lady Margaret and Mr. Yngram Percy.
'Item, a manchet, j quarte of bere, and iij mutton bonys boiled.'
The system of household œconomy established in this family must be supposed to correspond with the practice of the whole kingdom, and enables us to trace the progress of refinement, and in short, to form an estimate of national manners at two remote periods.

‡ The Alb is a white linen garment, and is frequently mistaken for the surplice, though the rubric at the end of the first liturgy of Edward VI. and also that before morning prayer in the second liturgy of the same king, has clearly distinguished between them; but as described by Durandus, Ration. Divin. Officior. lib. III. cap. iii. De Tunica, it is a garment made fit and close to the body, tied round the waist of the wearer with a girdle or sash. In the picture of the communion of St. Jerome by Dominichino, of which there is a fine print by Jacomo Frey, is the figure of a young man kneeling, with a book under his arm, having for his outer garment an alb. The Alb was anciently embroidered with various colours, and ornamented with fringe. See Bingham's Antiqui- ties, book XIII. chap. viii. § 2. Wheatley on the Common Prayer, chap. II. sect. 4.

'The ordurynge of my lordes chappell for the keapinge
'of our Ladyes mass thorowte the weike.

'Sonday.	'Monday.

'Master of the Childer a
  'countertenor.
    'A tenour.
    'A tenour.
    'A basse.
	'Master of the Childer a
	  'Countertenor.
	    'A countertenour.
	    'A counter-tenonr.
	    'A tenor.

'Twisday.	'Wedynsday

'Master of the childer a
  'countertenour.
    'A countertenour.
    'A countertenour.
    'A tenour.
	'Master of the childer a
	  'countertenor
	    'A countertenour.
	    'A tenour.
	    'A basse.

'Thursdaie.	'Fryday.

'Master of the childer a
  'countertenor.
    'A countertenoure.
    'A countertenoure.
    'A tenoure.
	'Master of the childer a
	  'countertenor.
	    'A countertenour.
	    'A countertenour.
	    'A basse.

'Satturday.	'Fryday.

'Master of the childer a
  'countertenor
    'A countertenor.
    'A countertenor.
    'A tenour.
	'And upon the saide
	'Friday th'ool chappell,
	'and evry day in the
	'weike when my lord
	'shall be present at the
	'saide masse.

'The ordurynge for keapinge weikly of the orgayns
'one after an outher as the namys of them hereafter
'followith weikly :—
'The maister of the childer, yf he be a player, the
'first weke.
'A countertenor that is a player the ijde weke.
'A tenor that is a player the thirde weike.
'A basse that is a player the iiijth weike.
'And every man that is a player to keep his cours
'weikly.'

CHAP. LXXXII.

It is probable that Wolsey looked upon this
establishment with a jealous eye. The earl might
be said to be his neighbour, at least he lived in the
cardinal's diocese of York, and such emulation of
pontifical magnificence in a layman could hardly be
brooked; be that as it may, it is certain that upon
the decease of the above-mentioned earl of Northumberland, the cardinal's intention was to deprive
his successor of the means of continuing the solemn
service in the family, by requiring of him the books
used in the chapel of his father: what pretext he
could frame for such a demand, or what reasons,
might induce the young earl to comply with it, it is not easy to
guess, but the books were delivered to him, and the
earl had no other resource than the hope of being
able one time or other to set up a chapel of his own,
which he expresses in a letter to one of his friends,
yet extant in the Northumberland family, a copy
whereof is given below.*

* 'Bedfellowe.
'After my most harté recomendacion : thys Monday the iijd off August
'I resevyd by my servaunt letters, from yowe beryng datt the xxth day
'off July, deleveryd unto hym the sayme day, at the king's town of
'Newcastell; wherin I do perseayff my lord cardenalls pleasour ys to
'have such boks as was in the chapell of my lat lord and fayther, (wos
'soll Jhesu pardon) to the accomplyshement off which at your desyer

From the foregoing account of the rise and progress
of choral music, it appears, that notwithstanding the
abuses that might naturally be supposed to arise from
an over zeal to improve and cultivate it, and in spite
of the arguments and objections from time to time
urged against it, as a practice tending rather to the
injury than the advantage of religion, it not only was
capable of maintaining its ground, but by the middle
of the sixteenth century was arrived at great perfection. It farther appears that the objections against
it, many of which were urged with a view to banish
music, or at least antiphonal singing, from the church-
service, produced an effect directly the contrary, and
were the cause of a reformation that conduced to its
establishment.

For it seems the objections against choral service
had acquired such weight, as to be thought a subject
worthy the deliberation of the council of Trent, in
which assembly it was urged as one of the abuses in
the celebration of the mass, that hymns, some of a
profane, and others of a lascivious nature, had crept
into the service, and had given great scandal to the
professors of religion. The abuses complained of
were severally debated in the council, and were reformed by that decree, under which the form of the
mass as now settled derives its authority.

It is easy to discern that by this decree choral
service acquired a sanction which before it wanted :
till the time of passing it the practice of singing in
churches rested solely on the arguments drawn from
the usage of the Jews, and the exhortations contained
in those passages in the epistles of St. Paul, which
are constantly cited to prove it lawful; but this act
of the council, which by professing to rectify abuses,

'I am confformable, notwithstanding I trust to be abell ons to set up a
'chapell off myne owne, but I pray God he may look better upon me
'than he doth. But methynk I have lost very moch ponderyng yt ys no
'better regardyd ; the occasion wheroff he shall perseayff.
'Fyrst, the long lyeng off my tressorer ; with hys very hasty and un-
'kynd words unto hym, not on my parte deservyd.
'Also the news of Mr. Manyng, the whych ys blon obroud over all
'Yorksher ; that neyther by the kyng nor by my lord cardenall I am
'regardyd ; and that he wyll tell me at my metyng with him, whan I com
'unto Yorksher ; whych shall be within thys month, God wyllyng ; but
'I ffer my words to Mr. Manyng shall despleas my lord, ffor I wyll
'be no ward.
'Also, bedfellow, the payns I tayk and have takyn sens my comyng
'hether are not better regardyd, but by a fflaterynge byshope off Carell
'[Carlisle] and that fals worm [William Worme undermentioned] shall
'be broth [brought] to the messery and carffulness that I am in ; and in
'such slanders, that now and my lord cardenall wold, he can not bryng
'me howth [out] thereoff.
              *   *   *   *
'I shall with all sped send up your lettrs with the books unto my lords
'grace, as to say, iiij antefffonars [antiphonars], such as I thynk wher nat
'seen a gret wyll ; v gralls [graduals] an ordeorly [ordinal], a manual,
'viij prossessioners [processionals], and ffor all the ressidew, they are
'not worth the sending nor ever was occupyed in my lords chapel. And
'also I shall wryt at this tyme as ye have wylled me.
'Yff my lords grace wyll be so good lord unto me as to gyff me lychens
'[lycence] to put Wyllm Worme within a castell of myn off Anwyk in
'assurty, unto the tyme he have accomptyed ffor more money recd than
'ever I recd, I shall gyff hys grace ij C. li. and a benyffis off a C worth
'unto his colleyg, with such other thyngs reserved as his [grace] shall
'desyre ; but unto such tyme as myne awdytors hayth takyn accompt off
'him : wher in, good bedfellow, do your best, ffor els he shall put us to
'send mysselff, as at owr metyng I shall show yow.
'And also gyff secuer credens unto this berer, whom I assur yow
'I have ffonddon a marvellous honest man as ever I ffownd in my lyff.
'In hast at my monestary off Hul-Park the iij day of August. In the
'owne hand off   Yours ever assured
              'To my bedfellow Arundell.   H. NORTHUMBERLAND.'

This earl of Northumberland was Henry Percy, the lover of Anne
Boleyn ; the person to whom the letter is addressed was Thomas Arundel,
one of the gentlemen of the privy-chamber to cardinal Wolsey. There is
another letter from the earl to the same person relating to Fountain's
Abbey in Yorkshire, in a curious work now publishing, Mr. Grose's Antiquities of England and Wales, Numb. XIII.

assumes and recognizes the practice, is as strong an assertion of its lawfulness and expediency as could have been contained in the most positive and explicit declaration.

This resolution of the council of Trent, an assembly, (if we may believe such writers as Pallavicini, and others of his communion,)the most august and awful that ever met for any purpose whatever, and acting, as they farther assert, under the immediate direction and influence of that spirit which Christ has said shall remain with his church, could hardly fail of exciting a most profound veneration for choral music in the members of the Romish church. Nor did it produce in the leaders of the Reformation that general aversion and abhorrence, which in many other instances they discovered against the determinations of that tribunal, in all human probability the last of the kind that the world will ever see : on the contrary, the Lutherans in a great measure adopted the Romish ritual, they too reformed the mass, and as to the choral service, they retained it, with as much of the splendour and magnificence attending it as their particular circumstances would allow of.

It must be confessed that the difference between the music of the Romish and reformed churches is in general very great ; but it is to be remarked that some of the reformed churches differ more widely from that of Rome than others. The church of England retains so much of the ancient antiphonal method of singing, as to afford one pretence at least for a separation from it ; and as to the Lutheran and Calvinistic churches, whatever may be their practice at this day, those persons greatly err who suppose that at the time of their establishment they were both equally averse to the ceremonies of that of Rome. In short, in the several histories of the Reformation we may discern a manifest difference between the conduct of Luther and Calvin with respect to the work they were jointly engaged in ; the latter of these made not only the doctrine but the discipline of the church of Rome a ground of his separation from it, and seemed to make a direct opposition to popery the measure of his reformation ; accordingly he formed a model of church government suited to the exigence of the times ; rejected ceremonies, and abolished the mass, antiphonal singing, and, in a word, all choral service, instead of which latter he instituted a plain metrical psalmody, such as is now in use in most of the reformed churches.

But Luther, though a man of a much more irascible temper than his fellow-labourer, and who had manifested through the whole of his opposition to it a dauntless intrepidity, was in many instances disposed to temporize with the church of Rome ; for upon a review of his conduct it will appear, first, that he opposed with the utmost vehemence the doctrine of indulgences ; that he asserted not only the possibility of salvation through faith alone, but maintained that good works without faith were mortal sins, and yet that he submitted these his opinions to the judgment of the Pope, protesting that he never meant to question his power or that of the church.

In the next place he denied the real presence of Christ in the eucharist, but yet he substituted in its place that mode of existence called consubstantiation, which if not transubtantiation, is not less difficult than that to conceive of. Again, although he denied that the mass is what the church of Rome declares it to be, a propitiatory sacrifice, and was sensible that, according to the primitive usage, it was to be celebrated in the vulgar tongue, that the people might understand it ; he in a great measure adopted the Romish ritual, and with a few variations permitted the celebration of it in the Latin. He allowed also the use of crucifixes, though without adoration, in devotion, and of auricular confession, and in general was less an enemy to the superstitious rites and ceremonies of the church of Rome than either Calvin, Zuinglius, or any other of the reformers.

The effect of this diversity of opinions and conduct are evident in the different rituals of the Lutheran and Calvinistic churches in Switzerland, France, and the Low Countries ; the Psalms of David were the only part of divine service allowed to be sung, and this too in a manner so simple and plain, as that the whole congregation might join in it. The Lutherans, on the contrary, affected in a great measure the pomp and magnificence of the Roman worship ; they adhered to the use of the organ and other instruments ; they had in many of their churches, particularly at Hamburg, Bremen, and Hesse Cassel, a precentor and choir of singers ; and as to their music, it was not much less curious and artificial in its contexture than that of the church of Rome, which had so long been a ground of objection.

Few or none of the authors who have written the history of the Reformation have been so particular as to exhibit a formulary of the Lutheran service. Dr. Ward, in his Lives of the Gresham Professors, says ' that the Lutherans seem to have gone much ' the same length in retaining the solemn service as ' the church of England, though with more instru- ' ments and variety of harmony.' But the truth of the matter is, that they went much farther, as appears by a book, which can be considered no otherwise than as their liturgy, printed about seven years after Luther's decease, in folio, with the following title, ' Psalmodia, hoc est, Cantica sacra veteris ecclesiæ selecta. Quo ordine, et melodiis per totius anni curriculum cantari usitate solent in templis de Deo, et de filio ejus JESU CHRISTO, de regno ipsius, doctrina, vita, passione, resurrectione, et ascensione, et de Spiritu Sancto. Item de sanctis, et eorum in Christum fide et cruce. Jam primum ad ecclesiarum, et scholarum usum diligenter collecta, et brevibus ac piis scholiis illustrata, per Lucam Lossium Luneburgensem.* Cum præfatione Philippi Melanthonis. Noribergæ Apud Gabrielem Hayn, Johan. Petrei generum, MDLIII.'

From this book it clearly appears that the Lutherans retained the mass, and sundry less exceptionable parts of the Romish service, as namely, the hymns and other ancient offices ; a few of the more modern

* A particular account of Lucas Lossius is given in a subsequent page of this work.

hymns are said to have been written by Luther himself, the rest are taken from the Roman antiphonary, gradual, and other ancient rituals; as to the music, it is by no means so strict as that to which the Romish offices are sung, nor does it seem in any degree framed according to the tonic laws; and it is highly probable that in the composition of it the ablest of the German musicians of the time were employed. Nay, there is reason to conjecture that even the musical notes to some of the hymns were composed by Luther himself, for that he was deeply skilled in the science is certain. Sleidan asserts that he paraphrased in the High German language, and set to a tune of his own composition, the forty-sixth Psalm,* 'Deus noster refugium.' Mr. Richardson the painter mentions a picture in the collection of the grand duke of Tuscany, painted by Giorgione, which he saw when he was abroad, of Luther playing on a harpsichord, his wife by him, and Bucer behind him, finely drawn and coloured.† And the late Mr. Handel was used to speak of a tradition, which all Germany acquiesced in, that Luther composed that well-known melody, which is given to the hundredth Psalm in the earliest editions of our English version, and continues to be sung to it even at this day.

And though this tune adapted to Psalm cxxxiv. occurs in Claude Le Jeune's book of psalm-tunes in four parts, published in 1613 by his sister Cécile Le Jeune, there is not the least pretence for saying that he composed the original tenor. Nay, the self-same melody is also the tenor-part of Psalm cxxxiv. in the Psalms of Goudimel, published in 1603, both these musicians professing only to adapt the three auxiliary parts of cantus, altus, and bassus, to the melodies as they found them.

If a judgment be made of the Lutheran service from the book now under consideration, it must be deemed to be little less solemn than that of the church of Rome; and from the great number of offices contained in it, all of which are required to be sung, and accordingly they are printed with the musical notes, it seems that the compilers of it were well aware of the efficacy of music in exciting devout affections in the minds of the people. The love which Luther entertained for, and his proficiency in music, has been already mentioned in the course of this work; but his sentiments touching the lawfulness of it in divine worship, and the advantages resulting to mankind, and to youth in particular, from the use of music both as a recreation and an incentive to piety, are contained in a book, known to the learned by the name of the Colloquia Mensalia of Dr. Martin Luther, the sixty-eighth chapter whereof is in these words :—

'Musick, said Luther, is one of the fairest and 'most glorious gifts of God, to which Satan is a 'bitter enemie; therewith many tribulations and 'evil cogitations are hunted away. It is one of the 'best arts; the notes give life to the text; it ex- 'pelleth melancholie, as we see on king Saul. Kings

'and princes ought to preserve and maintain musick, 'for great potentates and rulers ought to protect good 'and liberal arts and laws; and altho private people 'have lust thereunto, and love the same, yet their 'ability cannot preserve and maintain it. We read 'in the Bible that the good and godly kings main- 'tained and paid singers. Musick, said Luther, is the 'best solace for a sad and sorrowful minde, through 'which the heart is refreshed and settled again in 'peace, as is said by Virgil, " *Tu calamos inflare leves,* "*ego dicere versus:*" Sing thou the notes, I will sing 'the text. Musick is an half discipline and school- 'mistress, that maketh people more gentle and meek- 'minded, more modest and understanding. The base 'and evil fidlers and minstrels serve thereto, that we 'see and hear how fine an art musick is, for white can 'never be better known than when black is held 'against it. Anno 1538, the 17th of December, 'Luther invited the singers and musicians to a 'supper, where they sung fair and sweet Motetæ; ‡ 'then he said with admiration, seeing our Lord God 'in this life (which is but a mere *Cloaca*) shaketh 'out and presenteth unto us such precious gifts, what 'then will be done in the life everlasting, when every 'thing shall be made in the most compleat and 'delightfullest manner! but here is only *materia* '*prima*, the beginning. I always loved musick, 'said Luther. Who hath skill in this art, the 'same is of good kind, fitted for all things. We 'must of necessity maintain musick in schools; a 'school-master ought to have skill in musick, other- 'wise I would not regard him; neither should we 'ordain young fellows to the office of preaching, 'except before they have been well exercised and 'practised in the school of musick. Musick is a fair 'gift of God, and near allied to divinity; I would 'not for a great matter, said Luther, be destitute of 'the small skill in musick which I have. The youth 'ought to be brought up and accustomed in this art, 'for it maketh fine and expert people.— Singing, 'said Luther, is the best art and practice; it hath 'nothing to do with the affairs of this world; it is 'not for the law, neither are singers full of cares, but 'merry, they drive away sorrow and cares with sing- 'ing. I am glad, said Luther, that God hath bereaved 'the countrie clowns of such a great gift and comfort 'in that they neither hear nor regard music.— Luther 'once bad a harper play such a lesson as David 'played; I am persuaded, said he, if David now 'arose from the dead, so would he much admire how

---

* Comment. de Statu Religionis et Reipub. sub Carolo V. Cæsare, lib. XVI.

† Account of Statues, Bas Reliefs, Drawings, and Pictures in Italy, pag. 73.

‡ The MOTET is a species of vocal harmony appropriated to the service of the church. The etymology of the word is not easily to be ascertained; Menage derives it from Modus, to which it bears not the least affinity. Butler, à motu, because, says he, 'the church songs called motetæ move 'the hearts of the hearers, striking into them a devout and reverent 'regard of them for whose praise they were made.' On Musick, pag. 5, in notis. Morley seems to acquiesce in this etymology, but understands motion in a sense different from Butler, as appears by these his words : 'A motet is properlie a song made for the church, either upon some 'hymne or anthem, or such like; and that name I take to have been 'given to that kinde of musicke in opposition to the other, which they 'called Canto fermo, and we do commonlie call plain-song, for as nothing 'is more opposit to standing and firmness than motion, so did they give 'the motet that name of moving, because it is in a manner quight con- 'trarie to the other, which after some sort, and in respect of the other, 'standeth still.' Introd. part III. pag. 179.

Du Cange, voce MOTETUM, says that though this kind of composition is now confined to the church, it was originally of the most gay and lively nature; an opinion not inconsistent with the definition of the word.

' this art of musick is come to so great and an ex-
' celling height ; she never came higher than now
' she is.   How is it, said Luther, that in carnal
' things we have so many fine poems, but in spiritual
' matters we have such cold and rotten things ? and
' then he recited some German songs.   I hold this
' to be the cause, as St. Paul saith, I see another law
' resisting in my members ; these songs, added he,
' do not run in such sort as that of " *Vita ligno
' moritur*," which he much commended, and said
' that in the time of Gregory that and the like were
' composed, and were not before his time.   They
' were, said he, fine ministers and school-masters
' that made such verses and poems as those I spake
' of, and afterwards also preserved them.—Marie the
' loving mother of God hath more and fairer songs
' presented unto her by the Papists than her childe
' Jesus ; they are used in the Advent to sing a fair
' sequence " *Mittitur ad Virginem, &c.*"   St. Mary
' was more celebrated in grammar, music, and
' rhetoric than her childe Jesus.—Whoso contemneth
' music, as all seducers do, with them, said Luther,
' I am not content.   Next unto theology I give the
' place and highest honour to music, for thereby all an-
' ger is forgotten, the devil is driven away, unchastity,
' pride, and other blasphemies by music are expelled.
' We see also how David and all the saints brought
' their divine cogitations, their rhymes and songs
' into verse.   *Quia pacis tempore regnat musica,*
' *i. e.* In the time of peace music flourishes.' *

* The Colloquia Mensalia, a work curious in its kind, as it exhibits a
lively portrait of its author, will hardly now be thought so excellent
either for matter or form as to justify that veneration which we are told
was formerly paid to it : the subject of it is miscellaneous, and its form
that of a common place. In short, it answers to those collections which
at sundry times have appeared in the world with the titles of Scaligeriani,
Menagiani, Parrhasiana, &c. which every one knows are too much in the
style of common conversation to merit any great degree of esteem, and in
short are calculated rather for transient amusement than instruction.
But the publication of this book was attended with some such very
singular circumstances as entitle it in no small degree to the attention of
the curious.
    The sayings of Luther were first collected by Dr. Anthony Lauterbach,
and by him written in the German language. Afterwards they were disposed into common places by John Aurifaber, doctor in divinity. A
translation of the book was published at London in 1652, in folio, by one
Captain Henry Bell ; his motives for undertaking the work are contained
in a narrative prefixed to it, which is as follows :
' I, Captain Henrie Bell, do hereby declare both to the present age and
' posterity, that being employed beyond the seas in state affaires diverse
' years together, both by John James and also by the late king Charles, in
' Germany, I did hear and understand in all places great bewailing and
' lamentation made by reason of the destroying and burning of above
' fourscore thousand of Martin Luther's books, entitled his last divine
' discourses.
    ' For after such time as God stirred up the spirit of Martin Luther to
' detect the corruptions and abuses of popery, and to preach Christ, and
' clearly to set forth the simplicity of the gospel, many kings, princes, and
' states, imperial cities, and Hans-towns fell from the popish religion and
' became protestants, as their posterities still are, and remain to this
' very daie.
    ' And for the farther advancement of the great work of reformation
' then begun, the foresaid princes and 'the rest, did then order, that the
' said divine discourses of Luther should forthwith be printed, and that
' everie parish should have and receive one of the foresaid printed books
' into everie church throughout all their principalities and dominions, to
' be chained up for the common people to read therein.
    ' Upon which divine work or discourses the reformation begun before
' in Germanie was wonderfully promoted and encreased, and spread both
' here, in England, and other countries beside.
    ' But afterwards it so fell out, that the pope then living, viz. Gregory
' XIII. understanding what great hurt and prejudice he and his popish
' religion had already received by reason of the said Luther's divine dis-
' courses, and also fearing that the same might bring further contempt
' and mischief upon himself and upon the popish church, he therefore, to
' prevent the same, did fiercely stir up and instigate the emperor then in
' being, viz., Rudolphus II. to make an edict thorow the whole empire
' that all the foresaid printed books should be burned, and also that it
' should be death for any person to have or keep a copie thereof, but also
' to burn the same, which edict was speedily put in execution accordingly,
' insomuch that not one of all the said printed books, nor so much as any
' one copie of the same could be found out nor heard of in any place.

From the several passages above collected, which
it seems were taken from his own mouth as uttered
by him at sundry times, it must necessarily be concluded, not only that Luther was a passionate admirer of music, but that he was skilled in it, all
which considered, there is great reason to believe
that the ritual of his church was framed either by
himself or under his immediate direction.

It is more than probable that this institution of
a new form of choral service by the Lutherans, co-
operating with the censure of the council of Trent
against singing, as then practised in churches, produced that plain and noble style of choral harmony,
of which Palestrina is generally supposed to have
been the father.   This most admirable musician,
who was Maestro di Capella of the church of St.
Peter at Rome, with a degree of penetration and
sagacity peculiar to himself, in the early part of his
life discovered that the musicians his predecessors
had in a great measure corrupted the science ; he
therefore rejecting those strange proportions which

' Yet it pleased God that anno 1626 a German gentleman, named
' Casparus Van Sparr, with whom in the time of my staying in Germany
' about king James's business I became very familiarly known and
' acquainted, having occasion to build upon the old foundation of an
' house wherein his grandfather dwelt at that time when the said edict
' was published in Germany for the burning of the foresaid book, and
' digging deep into the ground under the said old foundation, one of the
' said original printed books was there happily found lying in a deep
' obscure hole, being wrapped in a strong linen cloth, which was waxed
' all over with bees wax, within and without, whereby the book was pre-
' served fair without any blemish.
    ' And at the same time Ferdinand II. being emperor in Germany, who
' was a severe enemy and persecutor of the protestant religion, the fore-
' said gentleman, and grand-childe to him that had hidden the said book
' in that obscure hole, fearing that if the said emperor should get know-
' ledge that one of the said books was yet forth comming, and in his
' custody, whereby not only himself might be brought into trouble, but
' also the book in danger to be destroyed as all the rest were so long
' before : and also calling me to minde and knowing that I had the High
' Dutch tongue very perfect, did send the said original book over hither
' into England unto me, and therewith did write unto me a letter, where-
' in he related the passages of the preserving and finding out of the
' said book.
    ' And also he earnestly moved me in his letter that for the advance-
' ment of God's glorie and of Christ's church, I would take the pains to
' translate the said book, to the end that that most excellent divine work
' of Luther might be brought again to light.
    ' Whereupon I took the said book before me, and many times began to
' translate the same, but alwaies I was hindred therein, beeing called
' upon about other business, insomuch that by no possible means I could
' remain by that work.   Then about six weeks after I had received the
' said book, it fell out that I being in bed with my wife one night between
' twelve and one of the clock, she beeing asleep, but myself yet awake,
' there appeared unto mee an ancient man standing at my bed side,
' arrayed all in white, having a long and broad white beard hanging down
' to his girdle-steed, who taking me by my right ear, spake these words
' following unto mee : "Sirrah, will not you take time to translate that
" book which is sent you out of Germany ? I will shortly provide for
" you both place and time to do it." And then he vanished away out
' of my sight.
    ' Whereupon being much thereby affrighted, I fell into an extreme
' sweat, insomuch that my wife awaking and finding me all over wet, she
' asked me what I ailed, I told her what I had seen and heard, but I
' never did heed nor regard visions nor dreams, and so the same fell soon
' out of my minde.
    ' Then about a fortnight after I had seen that vision, on a Sundaie
' I went to Whitehall to hear the sermon, after which ended I returned
' to my lodging, which was then in King-street at Westminster, and sit-
' ting down to dinner with my wife, two messengers were sent from the
' whole council board with a warrant to carry me to the keeper of the
' Gatehouse, Westminster, there to be safely kept until further order
' from the lords of the council, which was done without shewing me any
' cause at all wherefore I was committed. Upon which said warrant
' I was kept there ten whole years close prisoner, where I spent five
' years thereof about the translating of the said book, insomuch as I
' found the words very true which the old man in the foresaid vision
' did say unto me, "I will shortly provide for you both place and time to
" translate it."
    The author then proceeds to relate that by the interest of archbishop
Laud he was discharged from his confinement, with a present of forty
pounds in gold.
    By a note in his narrative it appears that the cause of his commitment
was that he was urgent with the lord treasurer for the payment of a long
arrear of debt due from the government to him.
    His translation of the Colloquia Mensalia was printed in pursuance of
an order of the House of Commons, made 24 February, 1646.

few were able to sing truly, and which when sung excited more of wonder than delight in the hearer, sedulously applied himself to the study of harmony, and by the use of such combinations as naturally suggest themselves to a nice and unprejudiced ear, formed a style so simple, so pathetic, and withal so truly sublime, that his compositions for the church are even at this day looked on as the models of harmonical perfection.

CHAP. LXXXIII.

The foregoing account of the rise and progress of church-music, or as it is most usually denominated, antiphonal singing, may in a great measure be said to include a history of the science itself so far downward as to the time of the Reformation; to what degree, and under what restraints it was admitted into the service of the reformed churches, will be the subject of future enquiry; in the interim, the order and course of this history require that the succession both of theoretic and practical musicians be continued from the period where it stopped, and that an account be given of that species of music which had its rise about the middle of the sixteenth century, namely, the dramatic kind, in which the Opera and Oratorio, as they are improperly called, are necessarily included.

Of the writers on music, the last hereinbefore mentioned is Peter Aron, a man more distinguished by his attachment to Bartholomew Ramis, the adversary of Franchinus, than by the merit of his own writings; he lived about the year 1545. The next writer of note was

Martinus Agricola, chanter of the church of Magdeburg, who flourished about this period, and was an eminent theoretic and practical musician. In the year 1528 he published a treatise, which he intitled **Teutsche Music;** and in the year following another, intitled Musica Instrumentalis; both these were written in German verse, and were printed for George Rhaw of Wittenberg, who though a bookseller, was himself also a writer on music, and as such, an account has been given of him in the course of this work.* In the latter of these works are the representations of most of the instruments in use in his time. He was the author also of a tract on figurate music, in twelve chapters, and of a little treatise De Proportionibus; and of another in Latin, intitled Rudimenta Musices, for the use of schools; but his great work is that intitled Melodiæ Scholasticæ sub Horarum Intervallis decantandæ, published at Magdeburg in 1612, and mentioned by Draudius in his Bibliotheca Classica Librorum Germanicorum. He was the author also of a tract intitled 'Scholia in Musicam Planam Wenceslai Philomatis de Nova Domo ex variis Musicorum Scriptis pro Magdeburgensis Scholæ Tybus, collecta,' in the preface to which he speaks thus of himself: 'Præterea, lector 'optime, cogitabis, me nequaquam potuisse singula 'artificiosissime tradere, quemadmodum alii excel-'lentes musici, quum ego nunquam certo aliquo

* Viz., book viii. chap. 69. page 314.

'præceptore in hac arte usus sim, sed tanquam 'musicus αὐτοφυης occulta quadam naturæ vi, qua 'me huc pertraxit, tum arduo labore atque domestico 'studio, id quod cuilibet perito facile est æstimare, 'Deo denique auspice, exiguum illud quod intelligo, 'sim assecutus, ut non omnino absolute, verùm tan-'quam aliquis vulgariter doctus, tantùm simplicissime, 'adeoque rudibus hujus artis pueris principia præ-'scribere, atque utcumque inculcare queam, non dis-'similis arbori, cui spontanea contigit è terra pul-'lulatio, quæ nunquam sua bonitate respondet alteri 'arbori, quæ nunc ab ipso hortulano, loco opportuno 'plantatur ac deinceps etiam quotidie fovetur ac 'irrigatur.' In the year 1545 he republished his Musica Instrumentalis, and dedicated it to George Rhaw, but so much was it varied from the former edition, that it can scarce be called the same work; and indeed the first edition was by the author's own confession so difficult to be understood, that few could read it to any advantage. In this latter edition, besides explaining the fundamentals of music, the author enters very largely into a description of the instruments in use in his time, as namely, the Flute, Krumhorn, Zink, Bombardt, Sackpipe, Swisspipe, and the Shalmey, with the management of the tongue and the finger in playing on them. He also treats of the violin and lute, and shows how the gripe, as he calls it, of each of these instruments is to be divided or measured; he speaks also of the division of the monochord, and of a temperature for the organ and harpsichord. Agricola died on the tenth day of June, 1556, and in 1561 the heirs of George Rhaw published a work of his intitled 'Duo Libri Musices 'continentes Compendium Artis, et illustria Exampla; 'scripti à Martino Agricola, Silesio soraviensi, in 'gratiam eorum, qui in Schola Magdeburgensi prima 'Elementa Artis discere incipiunt.'

The works of Agricola seem intended for the instruction of young beginners in the study of music; and though there is something whimsical in the thought of a scientific treatise composed in verse, it is probable that the author's view in it was the more forcibly to impress his instructions on the memory of those who were to profit by them. His Musica Instrumentalis seems to be a proper supplement to the Musurgia of Ottomarus Luscinius, and is perhaps the first book of directions for the performance on any musical instrument, ever published. Martinus Agricola is sometimes confounded with another Agricola, whose Christian-name was Rudolphus, a divine by profession, but an excellent practical musician, and an admirable performer on the lute and on the organ. Such as know how to distinguish between these two persons, call Rudolphus the elder Agricola, and well they may, for he was born in the year 1442, at Bafflen, a village in Friesland, two miles from Groningen, and dying in 1485 at Heidelberg, was buried in the Minorite church of that city, where is the following inscription to his memory :—

Invida clauserunt hoc marmore fata Rodulphum
　　Agricolam, Frisii spemque decusque soli.
Scilicet hoc uno meruit Germania, laudis
　　Quicquid habet Latium, Græcia quicquid habet.

CRISTOFORO MORALES

SPAGNUOLO,

CANTORE DELLA CAPPELLA PONTIFICIA.

MDXLIV.

HENRICUS FABER flourished about the year 1540. He wrote a Compendium Musicæ, which has been printed many times, and Compendiolum Musicæ pro Incipientibus, printed at Franckfort in 1548, and again at Norimberg in 1579. He was rector of the college or public school of Quedlinburg for many years, and died anno 1598: the magistrates of that place erected a monument for him, upon which is the following inscription :—

Clariss. et Doctiss. Viro, M. Heinr. Fabro, optimè de hac Scholâ merito monumentum hoc posuit Reipu. hujus Quedlinburg. Senatus.

Henrici ecce Fabri ora, Lector, omnis
Qui doctus bene liberalis artis,
Linguarumque trium probe peritus
Hanc rexit patriam Scholam tot annos,
Quot mensis numerat dies secundus,
Fide, dexteritate, laude tanta,
Quantam et postera prædicabit ætas,
Nunc pestis violentia solutus
Isto, quod pedibus teris, sepulcro
In Christo placidam capit quietem,
Vitam pollicito sereniorem.

27 Aug. obiit An. 1598. cum vixisset annos LV.

CHRISTOPHER MORALES (a Portrait), a native of Sevil, was a singer in the pontifical chapel under Paul III. in or about the year 1544, and an excellent composer. He was the author of two collections of masses, the one for five voices, published at Lyons in 1545, the other for four voices, published at Venice in 1563, and of a famous Magnificat on the eight tones, printed at Venice in 1562. Mention is also made of a motet of his, 'Lamentabatur Jacob,' usually sung in the pope's chapel on the fourth Sunday in Lent, which a very good judge* styles 'una maraviglia dell' arte.'† He

* Andrea Adami da Bolsena, nelle sue Osservazioni per ben regolare il Coro de 1 Cantori della Cappella Pontificia. Rom. 1711.

† Christopher Morales is the first of eminence that occurs in the scanty list of Spanish musicians. The slow progress of music in Spain may in some degree be accounted for by the prevalence of Moorish manners and customs for many centuries in that country. The Spanish guitar is no other than the Arabian Pandura a little improved; and it is notorious that most of the Spanish dances are of Moorish or Arabian original. With respect to the theory of music, it does not appear to have been at all cultivated in Spain before the time of Salinas, who was born in the year 1513, and it is possible that in this science, as well as in those of geometry and astronomy, in physics, and other branches of learning, the Arabians, and those descended from them might be the teachers of the Spaniards. There is now in the library of the Escurial an Arabic manuscript with this title, 'Abi Nasser Mohammed Ben Mohammed Alpharabi 'Musices Elementa, adjectis Notis Musicis et Instrumentorum Figuris 'plus triginta.' CMVI.'

As the date of this MS. and the age when the author lived are prior to the time of Guido Aretinus, we are very much at a loss to form a judgment of any system which could then prevail, other than that of the ancients, much less can we conceive of the forms of so great a variety of instruments as are said to be contained in it.

The author of this book is however sufficiently known. In the Nouveau Dictionnaire Historique Portatif, is the following article concerning him :—

'ALFARABIUS lived in the tenth century. He did not, like most 'learned men of his country, employ himself in the interpretation of the 'dreams of the Koran, but penetrated the deepest recesses of abstruse 'and useful science, and acquired the character of the greatest philoso-'pher among the Mussulmans. Nor was he more distinguished for his 'excellence in most branches of learning, than for his great skill in 'music, and his proficiency on various instruments. Some idea of the 'greatness of his talents may be formed from the following relation. 'Having made a pilgrimage to Mecca, and returning through Syria, he 'visited the court of the sultan Seifeddoulet. At his arrival he found 'the sultan surrounded by a great number of learned men, who were met 'to confer on scientific subjects, and joining in the conversation, argued 'with such depth of judgment and force of reasoning, as convinced all 'that heard him. As soon as the conversation was at an end, the sultan 'ordered in his musicians, and Alfarabius taking an instrument, joined 'in the performance. Waiting for a seasonable opportunity, he took an 'instrument in his hand of the lute or pandura kind, and touched it so 'delicately, that he drew the eyes and attention of all that were present. 'Being requested to vary his style, he drew out of his pocket a song, 'which he sang and accompanied with such spirit and vivacity, as pro-

composed also the Lamentations of Jeremiah for four, five, and six voices, printed at Venice in 1564. A Gloria Patri of his is preserved in the Musurgia of Kircher, lib. VII. cap. vii. sect. ii.

GREGORIUS FABER, professor of music in the university of Tubingen in the duchy of Wirtemberg, published at Basil, in 1553, Musices Practicæ Erotematum, libri II. a book of merit in its way. In it are contained many compositions of Jusquin de Pres, Anthony Brumel, Okeghem, and other musicians of that time.

ADRIAN PETIT COCLICUS, who styles himself a disciple of Jusquin de Pres, was the author of a tract intitled Compendium Musices, printed at Norimberg in 1552, in which the musicians mentioned by Glareanus, with many others of that time, are celebrated. The subjects principally treated of by him are thus enumerated in the title-page, De Modo ornato canendi —De Regula Contrapuncti—De Compositione. To oblige his readers, this author at the beginning of his book has exhibited his own portrait at full length, his age fifty-two. It would be very difficult to describe in words the horrible idea which this representation gives of him. With a head of an enormous bigness, features the coarsest that can be imagined, a beard reaching to his knees, and cloathed in a leather jerkin, he resembles a Samoed, or other human savage, more than a professor of the liberal sciences. But notwithstanding these singularities in the appearance of the author, his book has great merit.

LUIGI DENTICE, a gentleman of Naples, was the author of Due Dialoghi della Musica, published in 1552; the subjects whereof are chiefly the proportions and the modes of the ancients; in discoursing on these the author seems to have implicitly followed Boetius: there were two others of his name, musicians, who were also of Naples: the one named Fabricius is celebrated by Galilei in his Dialogue on ancient and modern Music, as a most exquisite performer on the lute. The other named Scipio is taken notice of in the Musical Lexicon of Walther. Adrian Le Roy, a bookseller of Paris, who in 1578 published Briefe et facile Instruction pour aprendre la Tablature à bien accorder, conduire, et disposer la Main

'voked the whole company to laughter; with another he drew from them 'a flood of tears; and with a third laid them all asleep. After these 'proofs of his extraordinary talents, the sultan of Syria requested of Alfa-'rabius to take up his residence in his court, but he excused himself, 'and departing homeward, was slain by robbers in a forest of Syria, in 'the year 954. Many of his works in MS. are yet in the public library at 'Leyden.'

It must be confessed that the foregoing account carries with it much of the appearance of fable: the following, contained in Mr. Ockley's translation of Abu Jaafar Ebn Tophail's Life of Hai Ebn Yokdhan, is of the two perhaps the nearest the truth :—

'ALPHARABIUS, without exception the greatest of all the Mahometan 'philosophers, reckoned by some very near equal to Aristotle himself. 'Maimonides in his epistle to Rabbi Samuel Aben Tybbon, commends 'him highly; and though he allows Avicenna a great share of learning 'and acumen, yet he prefers Alpharabius before him. Nay, Avicenna 'himself confesses that when he had read over Aristotle's Metaphysics 'forty times, and gotten them by heart, he never understood them 'till he happened upon Alpharabius's exposition of them. He wrote 'books of rhetoric, music, logic, and all parts of philosophy; and his 'writings have been much esteemed not only by Mahometans, but Jews 'and Christians too. He was a person of singular abstinence and conti-'nence, and a despiser of the things of this world. He is called Alphara-'bius from Farab, the place of his birth, which, according to Abulpheda, '(who reckons his longitude, not from the Fortunate Islands, but from 'the extremity of the western continent of Africa) has 88 deg. 30 min. of 'longitude, and 44 deg. of northern latitude. He died at Damascus in 'the year of the Hegira 339, that is about the year of Christ 950, when he 'was about fourscore years old.'

sur la Guiterne, speaks in that book of a certain tuning of the lute, which was practised by Fabrice Dentice the Italian, and others his followers, from whence it is to be inferred that he was a celebrated performer on that instrument.

But of the many writers of this time, no one seems to have a better claim to the attention of a curious enquirer than

Don NICOLA VICENTINO, a writer whom it has already been found necessary frequently to take notice of in the preceding pages of this work, inasmuch as there are few modern books on music in which he is not for some purpose or other mentioned. He, in the year 1555, published at Rome a book intitled 'L'Antica Musica ridotta alla moderna prattica, con 'la dichiaratione et con gli essempi de i tre generi, 'con le loro spetie. Et con l'inventione di uno nuovo 'stromento, nel quale si contiene tutta la perfetta 'musica, con molti segreti musicali.'

In this work of Vicentino is a very circumstantial account of Guido; and, if we except that contained in the MS. of Waltham Holy Cross, and a short memoir in the Annales Ecclesiastici of Baronius, it is perhaps the most ancient history of his improvements any where to be found; it is not however totally free from errors; for he attributes the contrivance of the hand to Guido, the very mention whereof does not once occur either in the Micrologus, the Epistle to his friend Michael, or in any other of his writings.

In the account he gives of the cliffs or keys, he asserts that the characters now used to denote them

are but so many corruptions of the letters F, C, G,* though he allows that the latter of the three continued in use long after the two former, of which there can be no doubt, since we find the letter used not only to denote the series of superacutes, but in Fantasies and other instrumental compositions it was constantly the signature of the treble or upper part, down to the end of the sixteenth century; the character now used for that purpose is manifestly derived from this which signifies gs, and was intended to signify the place of G SOL RE UT. He farther conjectures, that in order to distinguish the Hexachords, or, as others call them, the properties in singing, namely, in what cases b was to be sung by FA, and in what by MI, it was usual to affix two letters at the head of the stave, in the first case G and F, and in the last C and G.

The fourth chapter of the first book contains an account of John De Muris's invention of the eight notes, by which we are to understand those characters said to have been contrived by him to denote the time or duration of sounds, and of the subsequent improvements thereof; the whole is curious, but it is egregiously erroneous, as has been demonstrated.

He then proceeds to declare the nature of the consonances, and, with a confidence not unusual with the writers of that age, to attempt an explanation of that doctrine which had puzzled Boetius, and does not appear to have been clearly understood even by Ptolemy himself.

That Vicentino had studied music with great assiduity is not to be doubted, but it does not appear by his work that he had any knowledge of the ancients other than what he derived from Boetius, and those few of his own countrymen who had written on the subject. It was perhaps his ignorance of the ancients that led him into those absurdities with which he is charged by Doni and other writers in his attempts to render that part of the science familiar which must ever be considered as inscrutable; and as if the difficulty attending the doctrine of the genera were not enough, he has not only had the temerity to exhibit compositions of his own in each of the three severally, but has conjoined them in the same composition; for first, in the forty-eighth chapter of the third book is an example of the chromatic for four voices; in the fifty-first chapter of the same book is an example of the enarmonic for the same number; and in the fifty-fourth chapter is a composition also for four voices, in which the diatonic, the chromatic, and the enarmonic are all combined. These examples have a place in the preceding part of this work, and are there inserted to shew the infinite confusion arising from a commixture of the genera.

In the year 1551 Vicentino became engaged in a musical controversy, which terminated rather to his disadvantage: the occasion of it was accidental, but both the subject and the conduct of the dispute were curious, as will appear by the following narrative translated from the forty-third chapter of the fourth book of the work above-cited :—

'I, Don Nicola, being at Rome in the year of our 'Lord 1551, and being at a private academy where 'was singing, in our discourse on the subject of 'music, a dispute arose between the reverend Don 'Vincenzio Lusitanio and myself, chiefly to this effect. 'Don Vincenzio asserted that the music now in 'use was of the diatonic genus, and I on the contrary 'maintained that what we now practise is a com-'mixture of all the three genera, namely, the chromatic, 'the enarmonic, and the diatonic. I shall not mention 'the words that passed between us in the course of 'this dispute, but for brevity's sake proceed to tell 'that we laid a wager of two golden crowns, and 'chose two judges to determine the question, from 'whose sentence it was agreed between us there 'should be no appeal.

'Of these our judges the one was the reverend 'Messer Bartholomeo Escobedo, priest of the diocese 'of Segovia, the other was Messer Ghisilino Dan-'cherts, a clerk of the diocese of Liege, both singers 'in the chapel of his holiness ;† and in the presence 'of the most illustrious and most reverend lord 'Hyppolito da Este, Cardinal of Ferrara, my lord

---

* Kepler is of the same opinion, and has given an entertaining and probable relation of the gradual corruption of the cliffs in his Harmonices Mundi, the substance whereof is inserted in the account herein after given of him and his writings.

† Escobedo is celebrated by Salinas in these words : Cum Bartholomæo 'Escobedo viro in utraque musices parte exercitatissimo.' De Musica, lib. IV. cap. xxxii. pag. 228. And Ghisilino Dancherts is often mentioned in the preface to Andrea Adami's Osservazioni per ben regolare il Coro de i Cantori della Cappella Pontificia, by the name of Ghisilino d'Ankerts Puntatore, i. e. precentor of the college of singers of the pontifical chapel. The same author, in his Osservazioni above-mentioned, pag. 163, styles d'Ankerts 'ottimo contrapuntista di madrigali.'

'and master, and of many learned persons, and in
'the hearing of all the singers, this question was
'agitated in the chapel of his holiness, each of us, the
'parties, offering reasons and arguments in support
'of his opinion.

'It fortuned that at one sitting, for there were
'many, when the Cardinal of Ferrara was present,
'one of our judges, namely, Ghisilino, being pre-
'vented by business of his own, could not attend.
'I therefore on the same day sent him a letter, in-
'timating that in the presence of the Cardinal I had
'proved to Don Vincenzio that the music now in
'use was not simply the diatonic as he had asserted,
'but that the same was a mixture of the chromatic
'and enarmonic with the diatonic. Whether Don
'Vincenzio had any information that I had written
'thus to Ghisilino I know not, but he also wrote to
'him, and after a few days both the judges were
'unanimous, and gave sentence against me, as every
'one may see.

'This sentence in writing, signed by the above-
'named judges, they sent to the Cardinal of Ferrara,
'and the same was delivered to him in my presence
'by the hand of my adversary Don Vincenzio. My
'lord having read the sentence, told me I was con-
'demned, and immediately I paid the two golden
'crowns. I will not rehearse the complaints of the
'Cardinal to Don Vincenzio of the wrong the judges
'had done me, because I would rather have lost 100
'crowns than that occasion should have been given
'to such a prince to utter such words concerning me
'as he was necessitated to use in the hearing of such
'and so many witnesses as were then present. I
'will not enumerate the many requests that my
'adversary made to the Cardinal to deliver back the
'sentence of my unrighteous judges; I however
'obtained his permission to print it and publish it to
'the world, upon which Don Vincenzio redoubled
'his efforts to get out it of his hands, and for that
'purpose applied for many days to Monsignor Pre-
'posto de Troti, to whom the Cardinal had committed
'the care of the same.

'A few days after my lord and master returned to
'Ferrara, and after dwelling there for some time,
'was necessitated to go to Sienna, in which country
'at that time was a war; thither I also went, and
'dwelled a long time with much inquietude. After
'some stay there I returned to Ferrara, from whence
'I went with my lord and master to Rome, in which
'city by God's favour we now remain.

'I have said thus much, to the end that Don Vin-
'cenzio Lusitanio may not reprehend me if I have
'been slow in publishing the above sentence, which
'some time past I promised to do. The reasons
'why I have delayed it for four years are above
'related; I publish it now that every one may de-
'termine whether our differences were sufficiently
'understood by our judges, and whether their
'sentence was just or not. I publish also the rea-
'sons sent by me, and also those of Don Vincenzio,
'without any fraud, or the least augmentation or
'diminution, that all may read them.'

The following is a translation of a paper containing

the substance of Vincentino's argument, intitled 'Il
Tenore dell' Informatione manda Don Nicola à
M. Ghisilino per sua prova':—

'I have proved to M. Lusitanio, that the music
'which we now practise is not simply diatonic, as he
'says. I have declared to him the rules of the three
'genera, and shewn that the diatonic sings by the
'degrees of a tone, tone and semitone, which indeed
'he has confessed. Now every one knows that our
'present music proceeds by the incomposite ditone,
'as from UT to MI, and by the trihemitone UT FA,
'without any intermediate note, which method of
'leaping is I say according to the chromatic genus;
'and I farther say that the interval FA LA is of the
'enarmonic kind; and I say farther that the many
'intervals signified by these characters ♯ and ♭,
'which occur in our present music, shew it to partake
'of all the three genera, and not to be simply diatonic
'as M. Lusitanio asserts.'

The arguments on the other side of the question
are contained in a paper intitled 'Il tenore dell' Informatione mandò Don Vincentio Lusitanio à M.
Ghisilino per sua prova,' and translated is as follows:—

'Signor Ghisilino, I believe I have sufficiently
'proved before the Cardinal of Ferrara, and given
'him to understand what kind of music it is that is
'composed at this day, by three chapters of Boetius,
'that is to say, the eleventh and the twenty-first of
'the first book,* in which are these words: " In his
"omnibus, secundum diatonicum cantilene, procedit
"vox per semitonium, tonum, ac tonum in uno tetra-
"chordo. Rursus in alio tetrachordo, per semitonium,
"tonum, et tonum, ac deinceps. Ideoque vocatur
"diatonicum quasi quod per tonum ac per tonum
"progrediatur. Chroma autem (quod dicitur color,)
"quasi iam ab huiusmodi intentioni prima mutatio
"cantatur per semitonium et semitonium et tria
"semitonia. Toto enim diatessaron consonantia est
"duorum tonorum ac semitonii, sed non pleni.
"Tractum est autem hoc vocabulum ut diceretur
"chroma, à superficiebus, quæ cum permutantur in
"alium transeunt colorem. Enarmonium verò quod
"est maius coaptatum, est quod cantatur in omnibus
"tetracordis per diesin et diesin, et ditonum, &c."

'Being willing to prove by the above words the
'nature of the music in use at this day, it is to me
'very clear that it is of the diatonic kind, in that it
'proceeds through many tetrachords by semitone,
'tone and tone, whereas in the other genera, that is
'to say, the chromatic and enarmonic, no examples
'can be adduced from the modern practice of an
'entire progression by those intervals which severally
'constitute the chromatic and enarmonic; and I have
'shewn the nature of the diatonic from the fifth
'chapter of the fourth book of Boetius, beginning
" Nunc igitur diatonici generis descriptio facta est in
" eo, scilicet, modo qui est simplicior ac princeps
" quem Lidium nuncupamus."

'To this Don Nicola has objected that the melody
'above described is not the characteristic of the pure
'diatonic genus, because it admits of the semiditone

---

* This is a twofold mistake of Lusitanio: he has cited but two chapters of Boetius, and the eleventh of the first book contains nothing to
his purpose.

'and ditone, which are both chromatic and enar-
'monic intervals; to which I answered, that both
'these never arose in one and the same tetrachord,
'which is an observation that Boetius himself has
'made; and I said that Don Nicola was deficient in
'the knowledge of the true chromatic, which consists
'in a progression by semitone and semitone, as also
'of the enarmonic, proceeding by diesis and diesis.
'As to the ditone and semiditone, they are common
'to all the genera, and are taken into the diatonic, as
'agreeing with the order of natural progression: and
'though Don Nicola would insinuate that the ditone
'and semiditone are not proper to the diatonic, he
'does not scruple nevertheless to call the genus so
'characterized the diatonic genus, which I affirm it
'is. I desire you will communicate to your com-
'panion these reasons of mine, and, as you promised
'the Cardinal of Ferrara, pronounce sentence on
'Sunday next. Vincentinus Lusitan.'

Vicentino observes upon this paper, that the two
first chapters quoted by his adversary from Boetius
make against him, and prove that opinion to be true
which he, Vicentino, is contending for; and, in
short, that both the chromatic and enarmonic intervals, as defined by Boetius, were used in the
music in question, which consequently could not
with propriety be deemed the pure and simple
diatonic: he adds, that he will not arraign the
sentence of his judges, nor say that they understood
not the meaning of Boetius in the several chapters
above-cited from him, but proceeds to relate an instance of his adversary's generosity, which after all
that had passed must seem very extraordinary; his
words are these:—

'The courtesy of Don Vincentino has been such,
'that having gained my two golden crowns and a
'sentence in his favour, and thereby overcome me,
'he has a second time overcome me by speaking
'against the sentence of my condemnation, and
'against the judges who have done him this favour;
'and in so doing he has truly overcome and per-
'petually obliged me to him: and moreover he has
'published to the world, and proved in one chapter
'of his own, that the sentence against me was unjust;
'nay, he has printed and published the reasons con-
'tained in the paper written by me, and sent to Messer
'Ghisilino, our judge; and this he has done as he says
'to discharge his conscience, and because it seemed to
'him that he had stolen the two golden Scudi.*—
'God forgive all, and I forgive him, because he has be-
'haved like a good Christian; and to the end that every
'one may be convinced of the truth of what I now
'assert, I refer to a work of his intitled "Introduction
'"facilissima et novissima di canto fermo et figurato

* In this controversy two things occur that must strike an intelligent
reader with surprise: the one is that the two judges should concur in an
opinion so manifestly erroneous as that the system in question, which
was in truth no other than that now in use, was of the diatonic genus;
the other is the concession of Lusitanio that it partook of all the three
genera. The reader will recollect the sentiment of our countryman
Morley on this head, who, after diligently enquiring into the matter, pronounces of the music of the moderns that it is not fully, and in every
respect, the ancient diatonicum nor right chromaticum, but an imperfect
commixture of both; and, to shew that it does not partake of the enarmonic, he remarks that we have not in our scale the enarmonic diesis,
which is the half of the lesser semitone. Morley in the Annotations on
the first part of his Introduction. Vide Brossard, Dictionare de Musique.
Voce SYSTEMA, to the same purpose.

"contrapunto semplice, &c. Stampata in Roma in
"campo di Fiore per Antonio Blado, Impressore
"Aposto. L'anno del Signore M.D.LIII. à li xxv.
"di Settembre." At the end of this work he treats
'of the three genera of music in these words:—

"The genera or modes of musical progression are
"three, viz., the Diatonic, which proceeds by four
"sounds constituting the intervals of tone, tone, and
"semitone minor, the Chromatic, which proceeds by
"semitone, semitone major, and three semitones,
"making in all five semitones, according to the
"definition of Boetius in his twenty-first chapter;
"and according to his twenty-third chapter, by
"semitone minor, semitone major, and the interval
"of a minor third, RE FA, not RE MI FA, because RE
"FA is an incomposite, and RE MI FA is a composite
"interval. The Enarmonic proceeds by a diesis,
"diesis and third major in one interval, as UT MI,
"not UT RE MI; the mark for the semitone minor is
"this ♯, and that for the diesis is this x."

Vicentino remarks upon this chapter, that his
adversary has admitted in it that the leap of the
semiditone or minor third, RE FA or MI SOL, is of the
chromatic genus, which position he says he had
copied from Vicentino's paper given in to Messer
Ghisilino; he then cites Vincentio's explanation of
the enarmonic genus, where he characterizes the leap
of a ditone or major third by the syllables UT MI.
'This,' says Vicentino, 'my adversary learned from
'the above paper, to which I say he is also beholden
'in other instances, for whereas he has boldly said
'that I understand not the chromatic, I say as boldly
'that he would not have understood it but for the
'above paper of mine; because whoever shall con-
'front his printed treatise with that paper, will find
'that he has described the genera in the very words
'therein made use of; and his saying that he was
'able before he had seen it to give an example of
'chromatic music is not to be believed. Nay farther,
'in his paper to Messer Ghisilino he asserted that
'the ditone and semiditone are diatonic intervals, but
'in this treatise of his he maintains the direct con-
'trary, saying that RE FA is not of the diatonic, but
'of the chromatic genus. Here it is to be observed
'that the enarmonic ditone is UT MI, and not UT RE
'MI. In short,' continues Vicentino, 'it is evident
'that what my adversary has printed contradicts the
'reasons contained in his written paper. In short,
'I am ashamed that this work of Don Vincentio is
'made public, for besides that it is a condemnation
'as well of himself as our judges, it shews that he
'knows not how to make the harmony upon the
'enarmonic diesis. Nay he has given examples
'with false fifths and false thirds; and moreover,
'when he speaks of a minor semitone, gives MI FA,
'and FA MI as an example of it. And again, is of
'opinion that the semitones as we now sing or tune
'them, are semitones minor, whereas in truth they
'are semitones major, as FA MI or MI FA.'

Vicentino proceeds to make good his charge by
producing the following example from his adversary's
printed work, of false harmony:—

Alto con la quinta falsa　　soprano con la decima falsa.

Basso　　　　　　Tenore con le conson. false.

'It much grieves me,' says Vicentino, 'that I am
'obliged to produce this example of false harmony,
'but I am not the author of it, and have done it for
'my own vindication. It now remains to produce
'the sentence given against me, which I shall here do,
'truly copied from the original, subscribed by the
'judges, and attested in form :—

"Sententia.

"Christi nomine invocato, &c. Noi sopradetti
"Bartholomeo Esgobedo, et Ghisilino Dancharts, per
"questa nostra diffinitiva sententia et laude in pre-
"sentia della detta congregatione, et delli sopra detti
"Don Nicola, et Don Vincentio, presenti intelligenti,
"audienti, et per la detta sententia instanti. Pro-
"nontiamo sententiamo il predetto Don Nicola non
"haver in voce, ne in scritto provato sopra che sia
"fondata la sua intentione della sua proposta. Immo
"per quanto par in voce et in scriptis il detto Don
"Vincentio hà provato, che lui per uno competente-
"mente cognosce et intende di qual genere sia la
"compositione che hoggi communamente i compo-
"sitori compongono, et si canta ogni di, come ogniuno
"chiaramente disopra nelle loro informationi potrà
"vedere. Et per questo ill detto Don Nicola douer
"essere condennato, come lo condenniamo nella scom-
"messa fatta fra loro, come disopra. Et cosi noi
"Bartholomeo et Ghisilino soprascritti ci sotto scri-
"viamo di nostra mano propria. Datum Romæ in
"Palatia Apostolico, et Capella prædetta, Die vii.
"Junij. Anno suprascripto Pontificatus s. d. n. d.
"Julij. PP. iii. Anno secundo et laudamo.

　"Pronuntiavi ut supra. Ego Bartholomeus Esgo-
　"bedo, et de manu propria me subscripsi.

　"Pronuntiavi ut supra. Ego Ghisilinus Dancherts,
　"et manu propria me subscripsi.

　"Io Don Jacob Martelli faccio fede, come la sen-
"tentia et le due polize sopra notate sono fidelmente
"impresse et copiate dalla Copia della medesima
"sententia de i sopra detti Giudici.

　"Io Vincenzo Ferro confirmo quanto di sopra.

　"Io Stefano Bettini detti il Fornarino, confirmo
"quanto di sopra.

　"Io Antonio Barrè confirmo quanto di sopra."

It is to be suspected, as well from the publication
of the above sentence, as from the observations of
Vicentino on his adversary's book, that he is not in
earnest when he calls him a good Christian, and professes to forgive him; nor indeed does it appear by
his book, which has been consulted for the purpose,
that Vincenzio formally retracted the opinion maintained in the paper delivered in to Ghisilino; and
though the passages above cited from his treatise do
in effect amount to a confession that his former

opinion was erroneous, his publishing that work without taking notice of the injury Vicentino had sustained by the sentence against him, is an evidence of
great want of candour.

It seems that the principal design of Vicentino in
the publication of his book was to revive the practice
of the ancient genera, in order to which he invented
an instrument of the harpsichord kind, to which he
gave the name of Archicembalo, so constructed and
tuned, as to answer to the divison of the tetrachord
in each of the three genera: such a multiplicity and
confusion of chords as attended this invention, introduced a great variety of intervals, to which the ordinary division of the scale by tones and semitones was
not commensurate, he was therefore reduced to the
necessity of giving to this instrument no fewer than
six rows of keys, 'Sei ordini di tasti,' the powers of
which he has, though in very obscure terms, explained; and indeed the whole of the fifth and last
book of Vicentino's work is a dissertation on this
instrument.

CHAP. LXXXIV.

KIRCHER relates that Gio. Battista Doni, who lived
many years after Vicentino,[*] reduced the six Tasti
of his predecessor to three, and as it should seem,
without essentially interrupting that division of the
intervals to which the six Tasti were adapted.[†] In
another place of the Musurgia he says that the most
illustrious knight Petrus à Valle, in order to give an
example of the metabolic style, procured a triarmonic
instrument to be constructed under the direction of
Doni.[‡] This was Pietro Della Valle,[§] the famous
Italian traveller, who appears to have been intimate
with Doni, for the fourth discourse at the end of the
Annotazioni of Doni is dedicated to him; and Della
Valle in his book of travels takes occasion to mention
Doni in terms of great respect. The triarmonic instrument mentioned by Kircher is described by Doni
in the fifth of his discourses at the end of his Annotazioni.

In prosecution of these attempts to restore the
ancient genera, a most excellent musician, Galeazzo
Sabbatini of Mirandola, made a bold effort, and gave
a division of the Abacus or key-board, by means
whereof he proposed to exhibit all imaginable harmonies; but it seems that none of these divisions
were ever received into practice; they indeed may
be said to have given rise to several essays towards a

* This person was secretary to cardinal Barberini, afterwards a pope
Urban VIII. He wrote a treatise De Præstantia Musicæ veteris, another De Generi e di Mode' della Musica, and another, being annotations
on the latter. He possessed a considerable degree of musical erudition,
but appears to have been a bigot in his opinions. A full account of him
and his writings will be given in the course of this work.

† Musurg. tom. I. lib. VI. pag. 459.

‡ Musurg. tom. I. lib. VII. pag. 675.

§ Pietro della Valle was a Roman gentleman of great learning; he
spent twelve years in travelling over Turkey, Persia, India, and other
parts of the East. He married a young lady of Mesopotamia, named
Sitti Maani, who dying shortly after his marriage, he postponed her interment, carrying her remains about with him in his travels many years.
At length returning to Rome, he caused her to be buried with great pomp
in the church of Araceli, twenty-four cardinals attending the solemnity;
and the afflicted husband prepared to pronounce a funeral oration over
her body, began to deliver it, but was interrupted by his tears, and could
not proceed. The Roman poets of that time celebrated her death with
verses, and there is a book entitled Funerale di Sitti Maani della Valle,
celebrato in Roma nel 1627, e descritto da Girolamo Rocchi.

new temperament of the great system adapted to the diatonic genus, wherein it has been proposed to reduce the several keys to the greatest possible degree of equality in respect to the component intervals of the diapason. One Nicolaus Ramarinus, in the year 1640, invented a key-board, simple in its division, but changeable by means of registers.* By this invention he effected a division of the tone into nine commas; but neither was this contrivance adopted, for in general the primitive division of the key-board prevailed, and the arrangement of the tones and semitones in the organ and harpsichord, and other instruments of the like kind, is at this day precisely the same as when those instruments were first constructed.

The above-mentioned work of Vicentino is variously spoken of among musicians. Gio. Battista Doni, in his treatise De Generi e de' Modi della Musica, cap. I. pretends to point out many absurdities in his division of the tetrachord for the purpose of introducing the ancient genera into modern practice, and treats his invention of the Archicembalo with great contempt. But in his treatise De Præstantia Musicæ veteris, he is still more severe, and gives a character of Vicentino at length in the following speech, which he puts into the mouth of one of the interlocutors in that dialogue :—

'I suppose you have seen in a tract, which Donius 'has lately sent abroad, what depraved and absurd 'opinions, and altogether foreign to the truth, one 'Nicolaus Vicentinus has conceived concerning the 'nature, property, and use of the genera : he who, as if 'he had restored the music of the ancients in its prin-'cipal part, affected that specious, not to say arrogant, 'title or surname of Archimusicus, and boasting sang 'that the ancient music had just now lifted up its 'head above the deep darkness. Do not he and his 'followers seem to think that the nature and property 'of the enarmonic genus consists in having the har-'monical series, or what is called the perfect system, 'cut up into the smallest and most minute intervals? 'from whence arises that false and ridiculous opinion 'that the common Polyplectra are to be alone called 'diatonic, and that those which have their black keys 'divided in a twofold manner are chromatic, while 'those which are thicker divided, and consist of more 'frequent intervals, are to be termed enarmonic: they 'would not have fallen into this error if they had un-'derstood the ancient and natural harmonies in the 'writings of Aristoxenus and others. But if Vicen-'tinus had been somewhat better instructed in the 'rules of the science, and in the reading of the ancient 'authors, when he undertook the province of restor-'ing the ancient music, he would not have entered 'the sacred places of the Muses with unwashed feet, 'nor defeated that most ample praise he would have 'deserved for his honest intentions by unprosperous 'and vain attempts.—I have often wondered at the 'confidence of Vicentinus, who, although he could not 'but be sensible that he had but slender, or rather no 'learning and knowledge of antiquity, nevertheless 'did not hesitate to undertake so great a work. But 'I cease to wonder when I reflect on that Greek

'sentence, "Ignorance makes men bold, but learning "timid and slow."'

To say the truth, it does not appear from his book that Vicentino's knowledge of the science was derived from any higher source than the writings of Boetius; and with no better assistance than they could furnish, the restoration of the genera seems to have been a bold and presumptuous undertaking, and yet there have not been wanting musicians of latter times who have persisted in attempting to revive those kinds of music, which the ancients for very good reasons rejected; and there is to be found among the madrigals of Dominico Mazzochi, printed at Rome, one intitled Planctus Matris Euryali Diatonico-Chromatico-Enarmonico, that is to say, in all the three genera of the ancients, which is highly applauded by Kircher.

And with respect to Vicentino, so far are the writers on music in general from concurring with Doni in his censure of him, that some of the most considerable among them have been his encomiasts, and have celebrated both him and that invention or temperature of the Scala maxima to which his instrument the Archicembalo is adapted.

'The first among the moderns that attempted 'compositions in the three genera, was Nicolaus 'Vicentinus, who when he perceived that the 'division of the tetrachords, according to the three 'genera by Boetius, could not suit a polyphonous 'melothesia and our ratio of composition, devised 'another method, which he treats of at large in an 'entire book. There were not however some want-'ing, who being strenuous admirers and defenders of 'ancient music, cavilled at him wrongfully and un-'deservedly for having changed the genera, that had 'been wisely instituted by the ancients, and put in 'their stead I know not what spurious genera. But 'those who shall examine more closely into the 'affair will be obliged to confess that Vicentinus had 'very good reason for what he did, and that no other 'chromatic-enarmonic polyphonous melothesia could 'be made than as he taught.'†

And as touching that division of the octave by Vicentino, which Doni and others are said to have improved, the late Dr. Pepusch is clearly of opinion that it was perfectly agreeable to the doctrines of the ancients; for after remarking that Salinas had accurately determined the enarmonic, and that strictly speaking the fourth contains thirteen dieses, that is to say, each of the tones five, and the semitone major three; he adds that the true division of the octave is into thirty-one equal parts, which gives the celebrated temperature of Huygens, the most perfect of all, and concludes his sentiments on this subject with the following eulogium on Vicentino : 'The 'first of the moderns who mentioned such a division 'was Don Vincentino, in his book entitled, L'Antica 'Musica ridotta alla moderna Prattica, printed at 'Rome, 1555, folio. An instrument had been made 'according to this notion, which was condemned by 'Zarlino and Salinas without sufficient reason. But 'Mr. Huygens having more accurately examined the 'matter, found it to be the best temperature that

---

* Musurgia, tom. I. lib. VI. pag. 460, et seq.

† Musurgia, tom. I. lib. VII. pag. 660.

'could be contrived. Though neither this great
'mathematician, nor Zarlino, Salinas, nor even Don
'Vincentino, seem to have had a distinct notion of
'all these thirty-one intervals, nor of their names,
'nor of their necessity to the perfection of music.'*

HERMAN FINCK, chapel-master to the king of
Poland, in 1556, published in quarto a book with
this title 'Practica musica Hermanni Finckii, ex-
'empla variorum signorum, proportionum et canonum,
'judicium de tonis, ac quædam de arte suaviter et
'artificiose cantandi continens;' a good musical institute, but in no respect better than many others that
were published in Germany after the commencement
of the sixteenth century. The author, though a
chapel-master, seems to have been a protestant, for in
the beginning of his work he mentions Luther of
pious memory, and confirms the accounts of him that
say he loved and understood music.

AMBROSIUS WILPHLINGSEDERUS in 1563, published
at Norimberg, Erotemata Musices Practicæ, a curious
book, and abounding with a great variety of compositions of the most excellent masters; and in the
same year

LUCAS LOSSIUS, of Lunenburg, published a book
with this title, 'Erotemata Musicæ ex probatissimus
'quibus que hujus dulcissima artis scriptoribus ac-
'curate et breviter selecta et exemplis puerili in-
'stitutioni accomodis illustrata jam primum ad usum
'scholæ Lunenburgensis et aliarum puerilium in
'lucem edita, a Luca Lossio. Item melodiæ sex
'generum carminum usitatiorum in primis suaves in
'gratiam puerorum selectæ et editæ Noribergæ,
'M.D.LXIII.' and again in 1570, with additions by
Christopher Prætorius, a Silesian and chanter of the
church of St. John at Lunenburg. The title of this
book of Lossius does in a great measure bespeak its
contents: Lossius was a Lutheran divine, born at
Vacha in Hessia in the year 1508, and for above
fifty years rector of the college or public school at
Lunenburg, a celebrated instructor of youth, and very
well skilled in music. He died anno 1582. Two
years before his death, which happened anno 1582,
he composed the following epitaph on himself:—

> Hac placido Lucas requiescit Lossius urna.
>   Parte cinis terræ, qua levis ille fuit.
> Pars melior vivens cœli mens incolit arcem,
>   Inter, qui multos erudiere, viros.
> Qui pubi decies quinos atque amplius annos
>   Tradidit hic artes cum pietate bonas.
> Edidit et facili qui simplicitate libellos
>   Non paucos, Christi, Pieridumque scholis.
> Finibus Hassiacis nemorosis natus, et agris,
>   Vacham qua præter, clare Visurge, fluis.
> Hæc ubi cognoris, quo te via ducit euntem,
>   Lector abi, et felix vive, valeque diu.

It was this Lossius that published the Lutheran
Psalmodia, mentioned in a preceding page. It seems
by the numerous publications about this time of little
tracts, with such titles as these, Erotemata Musicæ,
Musicæ Isagoge, Compendium Musicæ, that the
protestants were desirous of emulating the Roman

* Letter from John Christoph. Pepusch, Mus. D. to Mr. Abraham de
Moivre, published in the Philosophical Transactions for the months of
Oct. Nov. and Dec. 1746, page 266 et seq.

catholics in their musical service, and that to that
end these books were written and circulated throughout Germany. They were in general printed in a
small portable size, and a book of this sort is to be
considered as a kind of musical accidence: that of
Wilphlingsederus, as also this of Lossius, are excellent in their way; the merit of them consists in
their brevity and perspicuity, and surely a better
method of institution cannot be conceived of than
this, whereby a child is taught a learned language,
and the rudiments of a liberal science, at the same
time.

These, and other books of the like kind, calculated
for the instruction of children in Cantu chorali et in
Cantu figurati vel mensurali, i. e. in plain-song and
in figurate or mensural music, are for the most part
in dialogue, in which the responses, according as required, are spoken in words or sung in notes. They
all contain a division or title De Clavibus signatis,
with a type of the cliffs as they are now called. Rhaw
gives it in this form :—

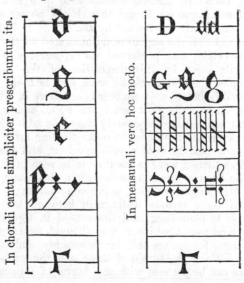

Et ponuntur omnes in lineali
situ, quædam tamen sunt magis
familiares, utpote F et C. g.
rariuscule. Γ vero et d d ra-
rissime utimur. Unde

Linea signatas sustentat scilicet omnes.

Et distant inter se mutuo per
diapentem.

F tamen γάμμα distinguat
septima quamvis.

And Wilphlingsederus thus :—

The Typus Clavium Signatarum of Lucas Lossius is in this form :—

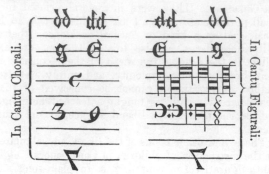

Lampadius, an author of the same class with those above-cited, and whose Compendium Musices is mentioned in a preceding page, gives the following character ♪ as the signature for G sol re ut in the series of superacutes; this is worthy of observation, for his Compendium was published in 1537, and it is the character in use at this day.

By the above types it appears that anciently five keys, or cliffs, as they are called, were made use of, whereas three are now found sufficient for all purposes. It may be said perhaps that Γ and dd were at no time necessary; but it seems that in order to imprint the place of the cliffs upon the memory of children, it was necessary in some way or other to tell them that the station of F was a seventh above Γ, and that the other cliffs were a diapente distant from each other; this Lossius does in the following verses :—

> Linea signatas claves complectitur omnes
> Mutuò distantes inter se per diapentem,
> F licet ab γαμμα distinguat septima tantum.

And Rhaw in these words :—

> Linea signatas sustentat scilicet omnes,
> Et distant inter se mutuo per diapentem.
> F tamen ab γαμμα distinguat septima quamvis.

It therefore became necessary to give Γ as the terminus à quo for F, and though the power of dd was sufficiently ascertained by the cliff g, it is to be observed that the signature dd answered to the rule above-cited, and preserved the appearance of regularity; for by this disposition of the cliff, C occupied the middle of the scale, and as there were two cliffs below, so were there two above it. Rhaw observes that the most usual are F, C, and g, and that Γ and dd are very rarely used; he adds, that it was anciently a practice to make the line for F of a red, and that for C of a yellow colour, and that instances thereof were in his time to be seen in ancient music books : this is a confirmation of a passage in the Micrologus of Guido to the same purpose.

All these writers distinguish between the cliffs proper to plain-song, and those used in figurate or mensural music, which it was thought necessary to do here, for unless this be thoroughly understood, very little of the music of these and the preceding times can be perused with any degree of satisfaction.

They also severally exhibit a Cantilena or actual praxis of the intervals by the voice, in order to impress them on the minds of children. The most ancient example of this kind known to be extant is a Cantilena for the practice of learners, inserted in a subsequent part of this work, said to have been framed by Guido himself; but for this assertion there seems to be no better authority than tradition, for it is not to be found in any of his writings. Those contained in the Enchiridion of George Rhaw, and the Compendium Musices of Lampadius, differ but very little from that of Guido above-mentioned.

Claudius Sebastianus published at Strasburg in 1563 a book intitled Bellum Musicale, inter Plani et Mensuralis Cantus Reges. A whimsical allegory, but a learned book.

Gioseffo Zarlino, of Chioggia,* a most celebrated theorist and practical musician, was born in the year 1540; from the greatness of his erudition there is reason to imagine that he was intended for some learned profession; this at least is certain, that it was by the recommendation of Adrian Willaert that he betook himself to the study of music, and Salinas asserts that he was a disciple of Willaert. Bayle styles him president and director of the chapel of the Signory of Venice, but the true designation of the office is maestro di capella of the church or temple of St. Mark. He composed the music for the rejoicings at Venice upon the defeat of the Turks at Lepanto, which was much applauded; notwithstanding which the world has chosen to consider him as a theorist rather than a practical composer, and in this they seem to have judged properly, for in the science of music he is indisputably one of the best writers of the modern times. He died at Venice in February 1599, as Thuanus relates, who has celebrated him among the learned men of that time.

In the catalogue of the library of Thuanus, mention is made of two books of Zarlino, the one intitled Dimostrationi Harmoniche, printed at Venice in the year 1571, and afterwards with additions in 1573; and the other printed in the same city in the year 1588, and intitled Sopplimenti Musicali; but the best edition of these and his other works is unquestionably that of 1589, in folio, printed at Venice with this title, Tutti l' Opere del R. M. Gioseffo Zarlino Da Chioggia. These consist of four volumes, the first is intitled Istitutioni Harmoniche, the second Dimostrationi Harmoniche in cinque Ragionamenti, the third Sopplimenti Musicali; the fourth volume is a collection of tracts on different subjects, which have no relation to music.

In the three first volumes of these his works, Zarlino, in a style, in the opinion of some very good judges of Italian literature, not inelegant, has entered into a large discourse on the theory and practice of music, and considered it under all the various forms in which it appears in the writings of the Greek harmonicians, and the writers of later times : as he appears to have been acquainted with the Greek language, there is little doubt but that he derived his intelligence from the genuine source; and as to

† An episcopal city in one of the isles of the gulph of Venice, in Latin Clodia, whence comes the Latin surname of Clodiensis given to Zarlino.

Boetius and the other Latin and Italian writers, he seems to be possessed of all the knowledge that their writings were capable of communicating.

As the substance of what is contained in the ancient writers has already been given in the course of this history, it is unnecessary to incumber it with a minute abridgment of so copious a work as that of Zarlino; and a general account of the contents of the Istitutioni, the Dimostrationi, and the Sopplimenti, with occasional remarks and observations on the several particulars contained in them, will suffice to shew the nature and tendency of Zarlino's writings, and exhibit a general view of the merit and abilities of their author.

The Istitutioni begins with a general eulogium on music, setting forth its excellence and use as applicable to civil and religious purposes; in his division of music into mundane and humane, Zarlino follows Boetius and other Latin writers. Of the number Six, he says that it comprehends many things of nature and art; and in a far more rational way than Bongus has done, he considers its properties so far only as they relate to music.

In his explanation of the several kinds of proportion of greater and lesser inequality, and of the difference between proportion and proportionality, he is very particular, and very learnedly and judiciously comments upon Boetius, who on this head is rather too concise.

The account of the ancient system given by him cannot be supposed to contain any new discoveries, all that can be said about it is to be found in the writings of the Greek harmonicians, and with these he seems to have been very well acquainted.

In his description of that species of the diatonic genus called the Syntonous, or intense of Ptolemy, in which the tetrachord is divided into tone major, tone minor, and a greater hemitone in the ratio of 16 to 15, he gives it the epithet of Natural, an expression which seems to bespeak that predilection in its favour, which he manifested in a formal dispute with Vincentio Galilei on the subject, in which he contended for its superior excellence in comparison with every other of the diatonic species, and succeeded.

Chap. xxv. of the second part of the Istitutioni is an explanation of an instrument called the Mesolabe, said to have been invented either by Archytas of Tarentum, or Eratosthenes, the use whereof is to distinguish, by means of mean proportionals, between the rational and irrational intervals, and to demonstrate the impossibility of an equal division of the superparticular ratios. This instrument was it seems a great favourite with Zarlino, for in the Sopplimenti, lib. IV. cap. 9. he enlarges on the utility of it, and complains of his disciples that they could not be prevailed on to study it with that degree of attention which it merited.

Chap. xxxix. contains a figure of the diapason, with a representation of the diatonic tetrachord, constituted of a greater semitone, in the ratio $\frac{16}{15}$ of a tone major $\frac{9}{8}$, and tone minor $\frac{10}{9}$; this is the division which Zarlino throughout his works contends for as the natural and only true one, and is called the

syntonous or intense diatonic of Ptolemy. The figure above-mentioned is thus delineated by Zarlino:—

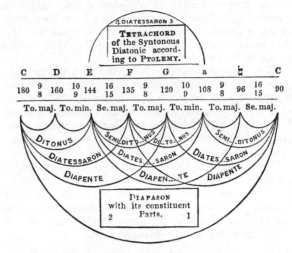

Chap. xlix. contains the author's sentiments of the ancient genera and their species, upon which he does not scruple to pronounce that the ancient division of them is vain and unprofitable.

The third part of the Istitutioni contains the elements of counterpoint, and directs how the several parts of a Cantilena are to be disposed. It contains also the precepts for the composition of fugue, whereon discoursing, the author makes frequent mention of Jusquin, Brumel, and other excellent composers; and celebrates, in terms of the highest respect, the excellencies of Adrian Willaert his master.

The fourth and last part of the Istitutioni treats of the modes or tones, that is to say, those of the ancients, and those other instituted by St. Ambrose and pope Gregory, and adapted to the service of the church. Zarlino's account of the former contains a great deal of that history which is justly suspected to be fabulous, as namely, that the Phrygian was invented by Marsyas; the Mixolydian by Sappho of Lesbos, the poetess; and the others by persons of whom scarce any memorials are extant. In this part of his work Zarlino very clearly explains the difference between the harmonical and arithmetical division of the diapason, from whence the two kinds of mode, the authentic and the plagal, are known to arise; but here with Glareanus he contends, notwithstanding the opinion of many others to the contrary, that the modes are necessarily twelve; he does not indeed profess to follow Glareanus in his division, but whether he has so done or not is a matter in which the science of music is at this time so little interested, that it scarce deserves the pains of an enquiry.

Chap. xxxii. of this last part contains some rules for accommodating the harmony of a cantilena to the words which are the subject of it. Rules indeed, if any can be prescribed for accommodating melody to words, might be of use, but between the harmony of sounds and the sentiments of poetry there seems to be no necessary relation.

The Dimostrationi Harmoniche are a series of discourses in dialogues, divided into five Ragionamenti.

The author relates that in the year 1562, his friend Adrian Willaert being then afflicted with the gout, he made him a visit, and found at his house Francesco Viola, chapel-master to Alfonso d'Este, duke of Ferrara, and Claudio Merulo, whom he styles a most sweet organist;* they begin a discourse on the subject of music, in which each delivers his sentiments with great freedom.

The subjects treated on in the first of the Ragionamenti are the proportions of greater and lesser inequality, and the measure of intervals. The whole of this dialogue may be said to be a commentary on Boetius; the thirty-ninth and last proposition contains a demonstration that six sesquioctave tones exceed the diapason.

The second and third of the Ragionamenti consist for the most part of demonstrations of the ratios of the consonances and the lesser intervals. In the second, Prop. xiv. is a diagram, an improvement on the Helicon of Ptolemy, whereby the ratios of the consonances are clearly demonstrated.

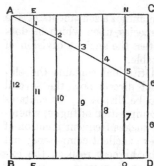

This parallelogram is divided into six parts by lines, which are bisected by a diagonal line proceeding from a point that divides the side C D equally, to the opposite angle. The side of the parellelogram A B is supposed to contain twelve parts; the bisection of the line C D is equal, that is to say it gives six parts on each side, but the bisection of the other lines is such, as gives the following harmonical proportions, amounting in number to no fewer than forty-five, as appears by this table :—

12 {
10 Semiditone
.9 Diatessaron
8 Diapente
6 Diapason
5 Diap. & semiditone
4 Diapason & diapente
3 Disdiapason
2 Disdiap. & diapente
1 Trisdiap. & diapente
}

10 {
9 Tone minor
8 Ditone
6 Hexachord major
5 Diapason
4 Diapason and ditone
3 Diapason and Hexachord major
2 Disdiapason & ditone
1 Trisdiap. and ditone
}

9 {
8 Tone major
6 Diapente
5 Heptachord minor
4 Diapason & tone maj.
3 Diapason & diapente
2 Disdiapason and tone major
1 Trisdiapason and tone major
}

8 {
6 Diatessaron
5 Hexachord minor
4 Diapason
3 Diapason and diatessaron
2 Disdiapason
1 Trisdiapason
}

6 {
5 Semiditone
4 Diapente
3 Diapason
2 Diapason & diapente
1 Disdiapason & semiditone
}

5 {
4 Ditone
3 Hexachord major
2 Diapason and ditone
1 Disdiapason & ditone
}

4 {
3 Diatessaron
2 Diapason
1 Disdiapason
}

3 {
2 Diapente
1 Diapason and diapente
}

2 1 Diapason

*CLAUDIO MERULO, or MERULA, of Correggio, was organist to the duke of Parma. He composed masses, psalms, and motets, and published Toccata d' Intavolatura d'Organo. In Roma, appresso Simone Vesovio, 1598, fol.

The divisions of the lines e f and n o, which give the proportions of 11 to 1, and 7 to 5, are irrational, and are therefore omitted in the table.

The fourth of the Ragionamenti directs the division of the monochord, and treats in general terms of the ancient system.

The fifth and last contains the sentiments of the author on the modes of the ancients, in which little is advanced that is not to be found elsewhere.

The Sopplimenti Musicali is dedicated to Pope Sixtus V.; the author styles it 'A declaration of the 'principal things contained in the two former volumes, 'and a formal defence of the author against the calum-'nies of his enemies.' The ground of the dispute between Zarlino and his adversaries was principally this, Zarlino through the whole of the two former volumes, in his discrimination of the five several species of the diatonic genus, rejects the ditonic diatonic of Ptolemy $\frac{256}{243} \frac{9}{8} \frac{9}{8}$, which indeed seems to be no other than the diatonic of Pythagoras himself, and prefers to it the intense or syntonous diatonic of Ptolemy, as it is called, $\frac{16}{15} \frac{9}{8} \frac{10}{9}$, as being the most natural to the ear. This is in truth the Diatonic of Didymus, for it was he that first distinguished between the greater and lesser tone, with this difference, that he places them in this order $\frac{16}{15} \frac{10}{9} \frac{9}{8}$, thereby giving to the lesser tone the first place in the tetrachord, whereas Ptolemy gives it the second; and in thus preferring the syntonous to the ditonic, Zarlino, as Dr. Wallis observes, was followed by Kepler, Mersennus, Des Cartes, and others.†

This, the Lutenists, who, as they were for the most part Aristoxeneans in practice, had adopted another tuning, opposed. They contended for a tetrachord of two equal tones and a semitone, but yet refused to abide a determination of the question by any other judgment than that of the ear.

At the head of these opponents of Zarlino stood Vincentio Galilei, a man of great learning and ingenuity, and who, though not a musician by profession, was deeply skilled in the science. He was besides a most exquisite performer on the lute, and a favourer of that division of Aristoxenus which is called the intense, and gave to the tetrachord a hemitone and two whole tones. This person, who had formerly been a disciple of Zarlino, published as it seems a short examen of the Istitutioni upon its first publication, intitled 'Discorso intorno all' Opere del Zarlino,' which he criticises with an unwarrantable degree of severity; but in a subsequent work, intitled 'Dialogo della musica antica et della moderna,' he takes great pains to prove that the preference which Zarlino had given to the syntonous species of the diatonic abovementioned, had no foundation in nature. The conduct of Galilei in this dispute is worthy of remark. He considers Zarlino as an innovator or corrupter of

† Dr. Wallis makes it a question whether or no Zarlino was the first that endeavoured to introduce the syntonous diatonic instead of the ditonic diatonic, but Galilei, in his Dialogue, pag. 112, expressly asserts that Lodovico Fogliano of Modena, and who published in 1529 a folio volume intitled Musica Theorica, of which an account has herein before been given, was the first who discovered that the diatonic of his time was not the ditonic, but the syntonous or intense diatonic. This, Zarlino, in the Sopplimenti, lib. III. cap. ii. seems to deny; but the truth of the matter is, that Fogliano, in the second section of his book, treats expressly 'De utilitate toni majoris et minoris,' which he would hardly have done, but with a view to establish that division of the tetrachord which Zarlino afterwards contended for.

music, and while he is treating him as such, he endeavours to make it believed, that he was the first among the moderns that attempted to introduce that species of the diatonic which admitted of dissimilar tones, but fearing lest instead of a corrupter he might in the opinion of some be deemed an improver of musical practice, he takes care to inform the world, and indeed expressly asserts, that Lodovico Fogliano, many years before Zarlino, found out and maintained that the diatonic even of that day was not the ditonic, but the syntonous diatonic of Ptolemy.

The Sopplimenti Musicali of Zarlino, lib. III. cap. 2, contains a defence of the author against this invidious charge of Galilei, whom he ironically styles his loving disciple, 'il mio discepolo amorevole.' As to the merits of the question between them, they seem to be determined in favour of Zarlino, for not only have Kepler, Mersennus, and Des Cartes adopted the division which he contended for,* but it is the only one practised at this day.

* As this assertion does at present stand on no better ground than a bare dictum of Dr. Wallis, in the appendix to his edition of Ptolemy, it may here be expected that in support of it the opinions of the authors above named should severally be adduced. To begin with Kepler. This author, who in his reasoning about music, affects a language peculiar to himself, after giving the preference to the division of the tetrachord $\frac{9}{8}\frac{10}{9}\frac{16}{15}$, speaks of two kinds of musical progression, the hard and the soft, which others characterize by the terms major and minor third. In the former of these, proceeding from the syllable UT, which is the progression referred to by all who speak of the disposition of the greater and lesser tone, he says that in the division of the tetrachord, nature herself informs us that the greater tone has the lower place, whereby he expresses his acquiescence in the opinion of Zarlino and his adherents upon the question in debate. Harmonices Mundi, lib. III. cap. vii.

As to Mersennus, who appears to have reviewed the controversy with great attention, he says that nature pays no regard to the conveniency of it, and that though the division of Aristoxenus may for particular reasons be preferred by those who play on the lute, it does by no means follow that it is upon the whole the most eligible; for, adds he, 'of all systems ' possible, that is the most natural and easy to sing, which follows ' the harmonical numbers, as is experienced when good voices sing seve- ' ral parts together, who could not do all that is marked in simple or ' diminished counterpoint commonly made use of, unless they observed ' the distinction of the greater and lesser tone, and that of the greater ' mean, and lesser semitone, and of several others elsewhere spoken of by ' him.' Harm. Univers. Des Instruments, liv. II. pag. 61. And in another place, ' that system which consists of a greater and lesser tone, ' and also of different semitones, and other just intervals both consonant ' and dissonant, is the best of all; and that this is the very nature of the ' song, the ear, the imagination, the instruments, and the understanding ' all confirm, provided experiments are made use of for an accurate ' enquiry into it.' Mersen. Harmonic. lib. V. De Dissonantiis, pag. 86.

The sentiments of Des Cartes on the question which of all others is the most eligible division of the diapason, are deducible from the chapter in his Compendium Musicæ, intitled De Gradibus sive Tonis musicis, wherein he asserts that the order to be observed in constituting the intervals contained in the diapason ought to be such, as that a semitone major shall have on each side next to it, a tone major and a tone minor. This disposition he illustrates by the following figure :—

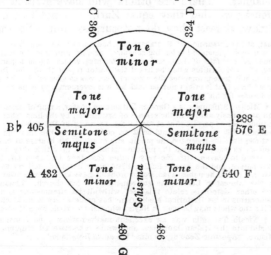

The Sopplimenti is of a miscellaneous nature, for it is a defence of many opinions advanced by the author in his former works. It contains also many particulars, many diagrams and mathematical problems, calculated to explain and illustrate his doctrines. In the fourth book he treats of the Genera and their species or colours, as they are called, and proposes a temperament adapted to the lute, whereby the diapason is divided by semitones into twelve equal parts. In the sixth book he treats of the ancient modes, which with Glareanus he makes to be twelve in number. In the eighth and last book he speaks of the organ, and describes one in the ancient city of Grado, the figure whereof is given in a preceding page of this work.

Many very curious particulars and little anecdotes of persons and things relating to music are interspersed in these three volumes of Zarlino's works, viz., the Istitutioni, Dimostrationi, and Sopplimenti, some of the most remarkable are these. Deer are delighted with the sound of music, and huntsmen by means thereof easily take them. Istit. II. pag. 11.†

Upon which it may be observed that A is assumed for the chord A, and the other letters for the corresponding chords in the scale. Between A and B♭ the ratio is $\frac{432}{405}$, which in smaller numbers is $\frac{16}{15}$, and between E and F $\frac{576}{540}$, also $\frac{16}{15}$, both of which are semitones major, $\frac{405}{360}$ is $\frac{9}{8}$, and $\frac{360}{324}$ is $\frac{10}{9}$, thus are produced the intervals contended for, $\frac{16}{15}\frac{9}{8}\frac{10}{9}$, which in the opinion of Zarlino and others constitute the syntonous or intense diatonic tetrachord of Ptolemy, and in that of Des Cartes is the most eligible division or temperament of that interval, and consequently of the diapason.

There is little doubt but that that division of the tetrachord which constitutes the syntonous or intense species of the diatonic genus is in theory the most eligible, and as far as regards vocal music, it may be equally well adapted to practice. But it seems that in such instruments as the organ, and others where the measure of intervals does not depend upon the performer, such a divison of the tetrachord as distinguishes between the greater and lesser tone is not admissible. Nay, were the concords themselves in such instruments to be uniformly tuned to the degree of perfection required by a nice ear, some of the consonant intervals would be so constituted as to approach very nearly to discord.

For this reason it is said that Zarlino could never prevail in his endeavours to establish a tuning of the organ correspondent to the division of the tetrachord in the syntonous diatonic; for Bontempi attests, that not only no organ in Italy or Europe was altered, or the tuning thereof in any degree varied, in consequence of his speculations, but that that of the chapel of St. Mark, where he presided, continued exactly in the state it had been left in by Claudio Monteverde, Giovanni Rovetta, and others his predecessors. Historia Musica di Bontempi, Parte prima, Corollario IV.

The difficulties arising from that surd quantity which in a course of numerical calculation arises in the division of the diapason, was but little noticed in vocal performance, for this reason, that the voice in singing accommodates itself to the ear, and with wonderful facility constitutes only grateful intervals, insensibly rejecting such as are dissonant. But in such instruments as the organ this quantity was for a long time found to be an unmanageable thing; a series of fifths all perfect through the scale was what the ear would not bear, and this consideration suggested the invention of what is called a Temperament, by which is to be understood a tuning, wherein by making the intervals irrational, more, in respect of harmony and coincidence of sound, is given to the dissonances than is taken from the consonances: the first essay of this kind is said by Polydore Virgil, De Rerum Inventoribus, lib. III. cap. xviii. to have been the invention of some very learned man in the science of music, but whose name, country, and even the age he lived in, are irrecoverably lost; it consisted in the intension of the diatessaron, and the remission of the diapente, and by necessary consequence made both the tones equal. Bontempi, 186. Salinas, lib. III. cap. xiii. has remarked upon this division that the equality of the tones implies the taking away of the comma; and in another place, that by this division the redundant commas in the diapason, which he makes to be three, are distributed throughout the diapason system. And this temperament is preserved by those tuners of the organ who make it a rule, and it is almost an universal one, to tune the thirds as sharp, and the fifths as flat, as the ear will bear them.

The reduction of the tones to an equality rendered each of them capable of a division into semitones, and gave rise to the invention of that called by the Italians Systema Participato, in which the diapason is divided into twelve semitones, whereby, in the opinion of some, the diatonic and chromatic genera are united, as indeed will seem to be the case upon a bare view of the keys of an organ or harpsichord.

† The author asserts this fact on the authority of Ælian, a writer of no great credit; nevertheless that these animals are susceptible of the power

—The human pulse is the measure of the beats in music. Ibid. 256.—Country people, and those that understand not music, naturally sing the diatonic

of music is not to be disputed, Plutarch, in the seventh book of his Symposiacs, says of deer and horses, that they are of all irrational creatures the most affected with harmony. Playford, in the preface to his Introduction to Music, says the same thing, and adds, 'Myself, as I 'travelled some years since near Royston, met a herd of stags, about 20, 'upon the road, following a bagpipe and violin, which when the music 'played they went forward, when it ceased they all stood still, and in this 'manner they were brought out of Yorkshire to Hampton Court.' And whoever will make the experiment, will find it in his power to draw to him and detain one of these creatures as long as he pleases by the sound of a violin or any instrument of that kind. Horses are also delighted with the sound of music.

'For do but note a wild and wanton herd,
'Or race of youthful and unhandled colts,
'Fetching mad bounds, bellowing and neighing loud,
'(Which is the hot condition of their blood)
'If they but hear perchance a trumpet sound,
'Or any air of music touch their ears,
'You shall perceive them make a mutual stand ;
'Their savage eyes turn'd to a modest gaze
'By the sweet power of music.'

SHAKESPEARE's Merchant of Venice, Act V. Scene I.

For this fact we have also the authority of the duke of Newcastle, who asserts it in his book of Horsemanship. Henry Stephens also relates that he once saw a lion at London, which would forsake his food to hear music. Pref. ad Herod.

Elephants are likewise said to be extremely susceptible of the power of music. Suetonius relates that the emperor Domitian had a troop of elephants disciplined to dance to the sound of music, and that one of them, who had been beaten for not having his lesson perfect, was discovered the night after in a meadow, practising it by himself. In the Melanges of Vigneul Marville, tom. III. is a humorous relation of the effects of music on a number of animals of different kinds, wherein it is said that a horse, a hind, a dog, and some little birds were very much affected by it, but that an ass, a cow, a cat, and a cock and hen were all insensible of its charms.

In the Histoire de la Musique, et de ses Effets, tom. I. pag. 321, is the following curious relation to this purpose :—

'Monsieur de ——, captain of the regiment of Navarre, was con-'fined six months in prison for having spoken too freely to Monsieur de 'Louvois, he begged leave of the Governor to grant him permission to 'send for his lute to soften his confinement. He was greatly astonished 'after four days to see at the time of his playing the mice come out of 'their holes, and the spiders descend from their webs, who came and 'formed a circle round him to hear him with attention. This at first so 'much surprised him, that he stood still without motion, when having 'ceased to play, all those insects retired quietly into their lodgings: 'such an assembly made the officer fall into reflections upon what the 'ancients have told us of Orpheus, Arion, and Amphion. He assured 'me that he remained six days without playing, having with difficulty 'recovered from his astonishment, not to mention a natural aversion he 'had for these sorts of insects, nevertheless he began afresh to give a 'concert to these animals, who seemed to come every day in greater 'numbers, as if they had invited others, so that in process of time he 'found a hundred of them about him. In order to rid himself of them, 'he desired one of the jailors to give him a cat, which he shut up some-'times in a cage when he chose to have this company, and let her loose 'when he had a mind to dismiss them, making it thus a kind of comedy 'that alleviated his imprisonment. I long doubted the truth of this story, 'but it was confirmed to me six months ago by M. P——, intendant of 'the duchess of V——, a man of merit and probity, who played upon 'several instruments to the utmost excellence. He told me that being 'at ——, he went up into his chamber to refresh himself after a walk, 'and took up a violin to amuse himself till supper-time, setting a light 'upon the table before him ; he had not played a quarter of an hour 'before he saw several spiders descend from the ceiling, who came and 'ranged themselves round about the table to hear him play, at which he 'was greatly surprised, but this did not interrupt him, being willing to 'see the end of so singular an occurrence. They remained upon the 'table very attentively until somebody came to tell him supper was 'ready, when having ceased to play, he told me these insects remounted 'to their webs, to which they would suffer no injury to be done. It was 'a diversion with which he often entertained himself out of curiosity.'

The same author says that he once saw, at the fair of St. Germain, rats dance in cadence upon a rope to the sound of instruments, standing up-right, each holding a little counterpoise, in the manner of rope-dancers. He says he also saw eight rats dance a figure-dance as truly as so many professed dancers ; and that a white rat from Lapland danced a saraband justly, and with all the gravity of a Spaniard.

Plutarch relates that a certain barber, who kept a shop in the Greek forum, had a magpye that imitated the sound of musical instruments, the cry of oxen, and could pronounce the words of men ; and that a certain rich man passing by, with trumpeters in his train, who, as was usual, stopped there and played for some time, the bird from that day became mute, to the wonder of every one. Many reasons were given for his silence, but the true one was he was meditating to imitate the sound of the trumpets, for first he was observed to practise silently and to him-self the tune they had played, at last he broke out, and sang it so truly and melodiously, that all were astonished who heard him.

Cælius Rhodiginus relates that he saw at Rome a parrot which Cardinal Ascanius had purchased for a hundred pieces of gold, that pronounced and clearly articulated, without hesitation or interruption, the words of the Apostle's Creed.

And lastly, Kircher relates, that when Basilius the emperor of the

octave with a third and sixth major. Ibid. 262.—Domenico da Pesaro, an excellent fabricator of harp-sichords, and other instrumenti da penna. Ibid. 171.—Boccace invented the Rima Ottava. Ibid. 381.—Jusquin considered the fourth as a consonance, and used it in two parts without any accompaniment. Ibid. 187.—Vincenzo Colombi, and Vincenzo Colonna of Italy, two organ-makers, inferior to none in the world. Ibid. 374.— Michael Stifelius, an excellent mathematician,* and Nicolò Tartaglia of Brescia,† attempted an equal division of the tone, but without success. Dimost. 146.—Adrian Willaert persuaded Zarlino to the study of music. Ibid. 12.— The Chromatists of Zarlino's time were in his opinion the enemies of good music. Ibid. 215.—Vincenzo Co-lombi, the famous organ-maker, made the author a monochord, diatonically divided, by semitone major, tone major, and tone minor. Ibid. 198.—Bede, who wrote on music, makes use of the terms Concentus and Discantus, from whence it is to be inferred that music in parts was known in his time. Soppli. 17. —Gioseffi Guammi of Lucca, an excellent organist and composer. Ibid. 18.

The fourth and last volume of Zarlino's work is on miscellaneous subjects. It contains a treatise on Patience, a discourse on the origin of the Capuchin Friars, and an answer to some doubts that had arisen touching the correction of the Julian calendar.

From the foregoing account of the works of Zar-lino it sufficiently appears that they are a fund of musical erudition ; and the estimation in which they are held by men of the greatest learning and skill in the science, may be judged of from the following character which John Albert Bannius has given of him and his writings. 'Joseph Zarlino of Chioggia 'was a great master of the theory of music. In his 'learned Institutions, Demonstrations, and Supple-'ments published in Italian at Venice, 1580, he has 'explained and improved the science with much 'greater success than any other author. He is some-'what prolix, but his learning amply compensates for 'that fault. John Maria Artusius Bononiensis re-'duced the precepts of Zarlino into a Compendium, 'and this again into tables. In these he sets forth the 'science of music in a short, clear, and perspicuous 'manner. There are others who have written on 'music, whether they equal Zarlino or not I do not 'know, at least they do not surpass him.—So that

East, at the persuasion of Santabarenus, had thrown his son Leo into prison on suspicion of his having conspired against him, the household lamented the fate of Leo, and sang mournful verses, these a parrot learned ; and Basilius when he heard the parrot repeat them, and in a melancholy tone pronounce the name of Leo, was so affected that he re-leased him, that it might not be said he was overcome by a parrot in tenderness for his son.

* Michael Stifelius was a German Lutheran minister, a man of learning, and particularly skilled in the science of arithmetic, by the help whereof he undertook to predict that at ten in the morning of the third day of October, 1533, the world would be at an end ; early in the morning of that day Stifelius ascended the pulpit, and exhorted his hearers to make themselves ready, for that the minute was at hand in which they were to ascend to heaven with the very clothes that they had then on; the hour passed, and the people finding themselves deceived, fell on their pastor, and had he not escaped, would probably have killed him; however, by the interest of Luther, he got reinstated in his church. Thuanus and other historians relate this fact with all its circumstances, and Camerarius in his Historical Meditations has made a very comical story of it : the whole may be seen in Bayle, who has an article for Stifelius.

† Nicolò Tartaglia was an excellent mathematician ; he translated Euclid into the Italian language, and wrote a treatise Di Numero et Misure. Apostolo Zeno styles him 'Un dotto Bresciano.'

'Zarlino alone will serve instead of the all the rest:
'without him the opinions of the ancients cannot be
'understood, nor a perfect knowledge of this science
'be easily attained.* But he does not come up to
'the perfection of the modern music. I have com-
'mended Zarlino above all the rest, not because the
'writings of other men on this subject are of no value,
'for they contain many excellent and learned in-
'structions, but because he is the best writer on this
'subject, and as many authors having given but an
'imperfect account of music, and this defect must be
'supplied by great study, industry, and various
'reading, I cannot recommend any one of them to
'those who study this art except Zarlino. Besides,
'few of them have at the same time thoroughly exa-
'mined and understood both the theoretical and
'practical part of music. Zarlino in my opinion has
'written on this subject with more learning and
'success than all the rest: and he is almost the only
'author who has succeeded in it. His Compendium,
'as it is drawn up by John Maria Artusius Bono-
'niensis, is an excellent method, and may be of
'singular use in the practice of musical composition.'†

Artusi is by this account of Bannius so connected
with Zarlino, that it becomes necessary to speak in
this place of him rather than of Vincentio Galilei,
the great opponent of the latter. The Compendium
above-mentioned was published at Venice in 1586,
and therefore must have been taken either from the
first or second edition of the Istitutioni. It is entitled 'L'Arte del Contraponto ridotta in tavole, dove
'brevemente si contiene i precetti à quest' arte ne-
'cessarii.' The author professes to follow the moderns, and particularly Zarlino, from whose work
above-mentioned he has extracted a variety of excellent rules. These are disposed in analytical order,
and are selected with such care and judgment, that
this Compendium, small as it is, for it makes but a
very thin folio, may be said to be one of the books
of the greatest use to a practical composer of any
now extant.

In 1589 Artusi published a second part of L'Arte
del Contraponto, intended, as the title-page declares,
to explain the nature and use of the dissonances; a
curious and valuable supplement to the former.

Artusi was an ecclesiastic, and a canon regular in
the congregation Del Salvatore at Bologna: a considerable time after the publication of his book entitled L'Arte del Contraponto, he published a treatise
Delle Imperfettioni della moderna Musica, in two
parts, with a view to correct some abuses in music
which had been introduced by modern writers and
composers; he was the author also of a little tract in
quarto, published in 1604, intitled 'Impresa del
'Molto R. M. Gioseffo Zarlino da Chioggia:' of
these an account will be given hereafter.

VINCENTIO GALILEI is next to be spoken of. He
was of Florence, and as it seems a man of rank, for
in the title-page of his books he styles himself
'Nobile Fiorentino,' and the father of the famous
Galileo Galilei, the mathematician. He had been
a disciple of Zarlino, and, by the help of his instructions, joined with an unwearied application to
the study of the ancients, became an excellent
speculative musician. Of the instruments in use
in his time, the lute and the harpsichord seem to
have held the preference; the latter of these was
chiefly the entertainment, as Zarlino relates, of the
ladies;‡ the practice of the former was cultivated
chiefly by the men. Galilei had an exquisite hand
on the lute, and his propensity to that instrument,
for very obvious reasons, led him to favour the
Aristoxenean principles, which Zarlino throughout
his works labours to explode. Galilei censured
many of the opinions of his master in a tract
intitled 'Discorso intorno all' Opere del Zarlino,'
which the latter has taken notice of in the second
volume of his works; but in 1581 he published a larger
work, intitled 'Dialogo della Musica antica e moderna,' written, as the title-page expresses it, 'in sua
Difesa contra Giuseppe Zarlino,' though the publication of this latter work was a formal attack on Zarlino, who is treated by his adversary with less respect
than seems to be due from a disciple to his master;
this Zarlino seems to have resented, for in the Sopplimenti he takes notice of the urbanity, as he calls it,
of the disciple to his preceptor, as an instance whereof he cites these words from the table to Galilei's
Dialogue, 'Gioseffo Zarlino si attribuisce per sue
'molte cose che non sono,' an expression not easily
to be reconciled with the commendation which in
many parts of this book he affects to bestow on Zarlino and his writings.

The division of the tetrachord which Galilei contended for, was that called the syntonous or intense
diatonic of Aristoxenus, which supposes the diatessaron to contain precisely two tones and a half,
according to the judgment of the ear. Ptolemy has
given it the ratio of 12, 24, 24, but Galilei failed in
his attempt to establish it; and the syntonous or
intense diatonic of Ptolemy is, as it is said, the only
division which the moderns have received into
practice.§

Galilei was also the author of a book intitled 'Il
'Fronimo, Dialogo sopra l'Arte del ben intavolare

---

* Notwithstanding this encomium on Zarlino, which at least implies
that he was well skilled in the ancients, there have not been wanting
those who have asserted that he never read them. Bontempi, speaking
of the modern system, in which most of the intervals are irrational, uses
these words, 'Egli non è ne il Sintono antico, ne il Sintono reformato da
'Tolemeo, come infelicemente sostenta il Zarlino, il quale, senza Greca
'litteratura, overo senza haver letto overo considerato la dottrina de'
'Greci, da l'essere ad un' altro sintono a modo suo, non constituito da
'padri della scientia.' Hist. Music, pag. 188.
    There can be little doubt but that Zarlino was acquainted with the
Greek language, seeing that his writings abound with quotations from
the Greek authors; but whether he had ever seen the Manual of Nicomachus, the Elements of Aristoxenus, the three books of Aristides Quintilianus De Musica, or the Harmonics of Ptolemy, with the Commentaries
of Porphyry and Manuel Bryennius thereon, may be questioned, since
Salinas, who wrote after him, intimates that in his time they were extant only in manuscript, and that by the favour of the Cardinal of
Burgos he procured transcripts of them from the library of St. Mark at
Venice.
    † Joan. Alberti Banni Dissertatio Epistolica de Musicæ-Natura. Lugd.
Bat. 1637, pag. 29. 57.

‡ Doni calls the harpsichord Clavichordium Matronale.

§ This is the sentiment of Dr. Wallis, as delivered by him in the
Appendix to his edition of Ptolemy, and is confirmed by Dr. Pepusch in
his letter to Mr. de Moivre, published in the Philosophical Transactions
for the year 1746; nevertheless it is said that since the invention of
a temperament the ancient distinctions of ditonic diatonic, intense diatonic, &c. have justly been laid aside. Vide Harmonics by Dr. Robert
Smith, 2d. edit. pag. 33, this is the more likely to be true, as the tuners
of instruments measure their intervals by the ear, and are therefore said
by Mersennus to be Aristoxeneans in practice.

'e rettamente suonare la Musica. In Venezia, 1583;' the design whereof is to explain that kind of musical notation practised by the composers for the lute, called the Tablature.* The Dialogo della Musica, notwithstanding the objections it is open to, is replete with curious learning, and seems to have been the effect of deep research into the writings of antiquity. Among other particulars contained in it are these. The Battuta, or beating of time, was not practised by the ancients, but was introduced by the Monks for the regulation of the choir, 101.—The monochord was invented by the Arabians, 133.— Diocles, and not Pythagoras, in the opinion of some, first discovered the musical proportions by the sound of an earthen vessel, 127.—Glareanus did not understand the modes of the ancient Greeks, 72.—Marcianus Capella, so far as relates to the modes, was an Aristoxenean, 56.—The music of the moderns is despised by the learned, and approved of only by the vulgar, 83.—The Romans derived their knowledge of music from the Greeks, 1.—At the close of this work he gives a probable account of the inventors of many of the instruments now in use, of which notice has herein before been taken. Speaking of the lute, he mentions a fact which an English reader will be glad to know, namely, that in his time the best were made in England. The style of Galilei is clear and nervous, but negligent. Nice judges say it is in some instances ungrammatical, nevertheless, to speak of his Dialogue on ancient and modern music, it abounds with instruction, and is in short an entertaining and valuable work.

CHAP. LXXXV.

Franciscus Salinas flourished about the middle of the sixteenth century; he was a native of Burgos in Spain, and the son of the questor or treasurer of that city; and though he laboured under the misfortune of incurable blindness, composed one of the most valuable books on music now extant in any language. His history is contained in the preface to his work published at Salamanca in 1577, and is so very curious, that it would be doing an injury to his memory to abridge it.

' From my very infancy I devoted myself to the 'study of music; for as I had sucked in blindness 'from the infected milk of my nurse, and there re-'maining not the least hope that I should ever re-'cover my sight, my parents could think of no em-'ployment so proper for me as that which was now 'suitable to my situation, as the learning necessary 'for it might be acquired by the sense of hearing, 'that other best servant of a soul endued with reason.

' I employed almost my whole time in singing and 'playing on the organ, and how much I succeeded 'therein I leave to the judgment of others; but this

* The Tablature is a method of notation adapted to the lute, and other instruments of the like kind, in which the chords are represented by a corresponding number of lines, and on these are marked the letters a, b, c, &c. which letters refer to the frets on the neck of the instrument. The time of the notes is signified by marks over the letters of a hooked form, that answer to the minim, crotchet, quaver, &c., this is the French tablature, but the Italians, and also the Spaniards, till of late years made use of figures instead of letters. Galilei's Dialogue teaches the tablature by figures, the other method is explained in a book written by Adrian le Roy of Paris, in 1578, the first of the kind ever published, of which a full account will hereafter be given.

'I dare affirm, that he who would perfectly under-'stand the doctrine of Aristoxenus, Ptolemy, and 'Boetius, and other famous musicians, should be long 'and much practised in this part of music, since every 'one of those has written concerning the first part of 'music which is called Harmonics, and belongs to the 'composition of instrumental harmony; and a man 'who is versed in the musical instruments which we 'make use of, will be able to judge more readily and 'perfectly of those things. But lest I should seem 'to say more of the studies of other men than of my 'own, be it known that while I was yet a boy there 'came into our country a young woman born of ho-'nest parents, and famous for her knowledge of the 'Latin language, who, as she was about to become a 'nun, had a vehement desire of learning to play on 'the organ, wherefore she became a sojourner in my 'father's house, and was taught music by me, and she 'in return taught me Latin, which perhaps I should 'never have learned from any other, because either 'that never came into my father's head, or because 'the generality of practical musicians persuaded him 'that letters would prevent or interrupt my learning 'of music; but I growing more eager for instruction 'from this little of learning that I had now got, pre-'vailed on my parents to send me to Salamanca, 'where for some years I applied myself closely to 'the study of the Greek language, as also to philo-'sophy and the arts, but the narrowness of my cir-'cumstances obliging me to leave that university, 'I went to the king's palace, where I was very kindly 'received by Petrus Sarmentus, archbishop of Com-'postella; and as he was afterwards taken into the 'number of cardinals, I went with him to Rome, 'more for the sake of learning than of enriching my-'self, where conversing with learned men, of whom 'there is always a great number there, I began to be 'ashamed of my ignorance in the art which I pro-'fessed, not being able to give any reason for those 'things I spoke of; and I at length perceived this 'saying of Vitruvius to be very true, and that it 'might be applied as well to music as architecture, 'viz., " Those who labour without learning, let them "be ever so well versed in the practice, can never "gain any credit from their labours; and those who "place their whole dependance on reasoning and "learning alone, seem to pursue the shadow and not "the thing; but those who are masters of both, like "men armed from head to foot, attain their ends with "greater facility and reputation." Wherefore when 'I found from Aristotle that the ratios of numbers 'were the exemplary causes of consonants and har-'monical intervals, and perceiving that neither all the 'consonants nor the lesser intervals were constituted 'according to their lawful ratio, I endeavoured to in-'vestigate the truth by the judgment both of reason 'and the senses, in which pursuit I was greatly 'assisted, not only by Boetius, whom every musician 'has in his mouth, but by several manuscript books 'of the ancient Greeks not yet translated into Latin, 'great plenty whereof I found there, but above all, 'three books of Claudius Ptolemæus (to whom whether 'music or astronomy be most indebted I cannot say)

' on harmonics, from the Vatican library, and of Por-
' phyrius's Comments thereon, constructed of great
' and valuable things collected from the reading of
' the ancients, which were procured for me by Car-
' dinal Carpensis ; also two books of Aristoxenus De
' Harmonicis Elementis, and also two books of Nico-
' machus, whom Boetius has followed, one book of
' Bacchius, and three books of Aristides, likewise
' three of Bryennius, which the Cardinal of Burgos
' caused to be transcribed at Venice from the library
' of St. Mark ; so that being made more learned by
' what they had well and truly said, and more cautious
' by what was otherwise, I was able to attain to an
' exact knowledge of this art, in the search and exa-
' mination whereof I spent upwards of thirty years,
' till at length, oppressed by many misfortunes, more
' especially by the death of the two cardinals and the
' viceroy of Naples, who all loved me more than they
' enriched me, and by the loss of three brothers, who
' were all slain, I determined to return to Spain, con-
' tent with what little I had, which might serve to
' supply me with a very slender maintenance ; and
' I also proposed to spend the small remainder of my
' life within my own walls in an honest poverty, and
' sing only to myself and the Muses :

' ' Nam nec divitibus contingunt gaudia solis,
' ' Nec vixit male, qui natus moriensque fefellit.

' But I imagine it seemed good to the greatest and
' best God that it should be otherwise, for he recalled
' me into Spain from Italy, where I had lived almost
' twenty years, not altogether in obscurity, and of all
' the other towns in Spain in which I might have
' practised the musical art with sufficient premiums,
' permitted me at length to return to Salamanca, after
' an absence of almost thirty years from the time
' I had left it, where a stipend sufficiently liberal was
' appointed for a professor of music capable of giving
' instructions both in the theory and practice. For
' Alphonsus king of Castile, the tenth of that name,
' and surnamed the Wise, who founded and endowed
' this professorship, knew that the science of music, no
' less than the other mathematical arts, in which he
' greatly excelled, ought to be taught ; and that not
' only the practical but the speculative part was ne-
' cessary for a musician. Wherefore he erected that
' school among the first and most ancient, and as a
' teacher was at that time wanted, and one was sought
' after who was capable of teaching both parts of music
' well, I came to Salamanca, that I might hear the
' professors of this art make their trials of skill there ;
' but when I had exhibited a specimen of my studies
' in music, I was adjudged qualified for that employ-
' ment, and obtained the chair, which was thereupon
' endowed with nearly double the usual stipend by the
' approbation of his majesty. Perhaps I have said
' more than is necessary concerning myself, but
' I mention these things that I might not be thought
' to attempt so great a work destitute of all assistance.'

To these particulars which Salinas has related of
himself and his fortunes, the following, grounded on
the testimony of others, may be added, viz., that being
an admirable performer on the organ and other instruments, he was in great esteem among persons of rank,

and particularly with Paul IV. then pope, by whose
favour he was created Abbat of St. Pancratio della
Rocca Salegna, in the kingdom of Naples. Thuanus
relates that he died in the month of February, 1590,
being seventy-seven years of age. Johannes Scri-
banius, a professor of the Greek language, his contemporary, wrote the following verses in praise of
him :—

Tiresiæ quondam cæco pensaverat auctor
    Naturæ damnum munere fatidico.
Luminis amissi jacturam cæcus Homerus
    Pignore divini sustinet ingenii.
Democritus visu cernens languescere mentis
    Vires, tunc oculos eruit ipse sibi.
His ita dum doctæ mentis constaret acumen,
    Corporis æquanimi damna tulere sui.
Unus at hic magnus pro multis ecce Salinas
    Orbatus visu, prestat utrumque simul.

The treatise De Musica of Salinas is divided into
seven books ; in the first he treats of proportion and
proportionality, between which two terms he distinguishes, making Proportion to signify the ratio
between two magnitudes, and Proportionality a certain analogy, habitude, or relation between proportions themselves. He says that as proportion cannot
be found in fewer than two numbers, so proportionality must consist at least of two proportions and
three numbers, whose mean divides them agreeably
to the nature of the proportionality. He says that
in the time of Boetius no fewer than ten different
kinds of proportionality were known and practised
by the arithmeticians, but that all that are necessary
in the speculative part of music are those three invented by Pythagoras, and mentioned by Aristotle
and Plato, namely, arithmetical, geometrical, and harmonical, concerning which severally he thus speaks :

' We call that an Arithmetical mean which is sepa-
' rated from either extreme by equal differences and
' unequal proportions ; by Differences we mean the
' quantities of the excesses which are respectively
' found between the numbers themselves, as in the
' proportion of 8 to 4 ; we say that 6 is an arith-
' metical mean because it is distant from each term
' by an equal difference, which is the number 2, but
' the proportions between the mean and the extreme
' terms are unequal, for 6 to 4 makes a sesquialtera,
' and 8 to 6 a sesquitertia, as plainly appears in these
' numbers, 4, 6, 8, in which the difference is the same
' between 6 and 4 as between 6 and 8, for each is
' equal to 2, whereas the proportions are unequal, as
' we have said. What is to be chiefly considered in
' this kind of proportionality by the musician is, that
' in it the greater proportions are found to be placed
' in the smaller numbers, and the lesser in the greater,
' as in this duple, 4 to 2, which when divided by the
' arithmetical mean 3, gives the sesquialtera and ses-
' quitertia, the greater of which proportions, the ses-
' quialtera, is found in the lesser numbers 3 to 2, and
' the lesser, the sesquitertia, in the greater numbers
' 4 to 3, as these numbers shew, 2, 3, 4. But the
' readiest method of finding an arithmetical mean is
' by adding the two extremes together, and the half
' of their sum when taken will be the mean required ;
' as in this same duple 4 to 2, the sum of whose terms

' is 6, and the half thereof 3, is the arithmetical mean
' between them. It is to be observed that if the num-
' ber arising from the sum of the two extremes be un-
' even (which is the case when one is even and the
' other uneven), and consequently the half thereof
' cannot be had, you must double the extremes, and
' then their sum will be an even number, and its half
' may be found; thus between 3 and 2, because their
' sum 5 is an uneven number, no arithmetical mean
' can be found in whole numbers, for they are distant
' from each other only by unity, which is indivisible,
' wherefore they must be doubled, to have 6 and 4,
' which being added together make 10, and the half
' thereof 5 will be the mean between them, and this
' is sufficient for the explanation of arithmetical pro-
' portionality.

' Geometrical proportionality is that in which the
' mean is distant from each extreme by equal propor-
' tions and unequal differences, as in the proportion
' 4 to 1, the geometrical mean will be 2, which is the
' duple of 1, as 4 is of 2, but the differences are un-
' equal, because 2 is distant from 1 by unity, and from
' 4 by 2, as these numbers shew :—

Geometrical division of the quadruple.

' This kind of mediation is not so often to be found
' as either of the others, because it can only be had in
' those numbers that are compounded of two equal
' ones, as the quadruple, the sum whereof is two
' duples, as is shewn in the above type, and the
' nonuple or ninefold, which consists of two triples,
' as 1, 3, 9, and in these, 9, 4, which include two
' sesquialteras, as appears in these numbers, 4, 6, 9,
' and in these numbers, 25, 9, which contain 2 super-
' bipartient 3, as these numbers shew, 9, 15, 25; and
' thus examples are frequently to be met with in all
' kinds of proportions except in such as are super-
' particular, for a superparticular proportion cannot
' be divided into two equal proportions in a certain
' determined number. This proportionality has this
' peculiar to it, that what in it is called the geometrical
' divisor or the mean, being multiplied into itself, will
' give the same product as arises from the multipli-
' cation of the two extremes into each other, as in this
' proportion, 9 to 4, whose geometrical mean is 6,
' that number bearing the same proportion to 4 as to
' 9, each being a sesquialtera to the mean 6, with un-
' equal differences, for 6 is distant from 4 by 2, and
' from 9 by 3. I say that 6 multiplied into itself will
' yield the same product 36 as is made by the multi-
' plication of 9 into 4; wherefore there is no readier
' method of finding out a geometrical mean than to
' multiply into each other the two numbers of such a
' proportion as we propose to divide geometrically,
' and then to find out some intermediate number,
' which being multiplied into itself, will produce the
' same sum as they did: thus if we would divide
' geometrically the proportion 16 to 9, we shall find

' the product of these two multiplied into each other
' to be 144, and as there cannot be any other number
' than 12 found, which being multiplied into itself
' will make that sum, that will be the geometrical
' divisor required, for it bears the same proportion to
' 9 as it does to 16, that is a sesquitertia. These
' things are esteemed requisite for musicians to con-
' sider, and I shall now only advertise the reader,
' that the numbers which express in the lowest terms
' any proportion that may be divided geometrically
' will be squares, for if the number can be divided
' into equal proportions, as the geometrical propor-
' tionality requires, it must necessarily be also com-
' pounded of two equal proportions, which compo-
' sition we have in another place called Doubling:
' now the doubling of any proportion is made by the
' squaring of the two numbers under which it was
' comprehended when single, wherefore those num-
' bers in which the proportion is found to be doubled
' must be squares.

' It now remains to speak of Harmonical Propor-
' tionality, which seems to have been so called as
' being adapted to harmony, for consonants are by
' musicians called harmonies, and answer to propor-
' tions divided by an harmonical mediation. The
' harmonical proportionality is that in which the
' mean, when compared to the extremes, observes
' neither the equality of differences as in the arith-
' metical mean, nor that of proportions, as the geo-
' metrical proportionality does, but is of such a nature,
' that whatsoever proportion the greater extreme bears
' to the lesser, the same will the excess of the greater
' extreme above the mean bear to the excess of the
' mean above the lesser extreme, as in this proportion,
' 6 to 3, in which the harmonic mean is 4, for the
' difference between 6 and 4, which is 2, bears the
' same proportion to the difference between 4 and 3,
' that is unity, as is found from 6 to 3, for they are
' each duple, as appears in these numbers :—

Differences of the mean and extremes.

Harmonical division of the duple.

' Plato in Timæus seems to have expressed this
' much more concisely and elegantly when he says
' the harmonic mean exceeds one extreme, and is also
' exceeded by the other by the same parts of those
' extremes respectively, as 8 between 6 and 12, for 8
' exceeds 6 by the third part of 6, and is exceeded
' by 12 by the third part of 12. It is to be observed
' that the harmonical proportionality is nothing else
' than the arithmetical inverted, for it is found to be
' divided into the same proportions, excepting that
' the greater proportions are found in the arithmetical
' division between the lesser numbers, but in the har-
' monical they are transferred to the greater numbers,
' while the lesser proportions (as must be the case)
' are found in the lesser numbers, and if possible
' remain in the same numbers in which they were
' before, as in this duple arithmetically divided, 2, 3, 4,

'which if we would have mediated harmonically, the
'sesquialtera proportion, which is between 3 and 2,
'must be transferred to greater numbers; and in
'order to leave the sesquitertia in the same as they
'were in, viz., 4 to 3, we must try whether 4 has a
'sesquialtera above it, which it will consequently
'have if it is encreased by its half 2, to produce the
'number 6, which is sesquialtera to 4, and the sesqui-
'tertia from 4 to 3 will be left as it was before; and
'thus the greater proportion is in the greater num-
'bers, and the lesser in the lesser, according to the
'property of harmonical proportionality, which these
'numbers shew :—

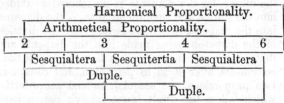

Harmonical Proportionality.			
Arithmetical Proportionality.			
2	3	4	6
Sesquialtera	Sesquitertia	Sesquialtera	
Duple.			
	Duple.		

'It now remains carefully to investigate the method
'of obtaining the harmonical mean, which will be
'easily found out if the arithmetical mean be first
'had, for where an arithmetical mean cannot be
'found, there also an harmonical mean cannot be had,
'since the harmonical proportionality, as we have
'said, is the arithmetical inverted. Having therefore,
'according to the method shewn above, found out the
'arithmetical mean, we must next enquire whether
'that has a number above it in the same proportion
'to it as subsisted between the numbers divided by
'the arithmetical mean, and if it has such a one, then
'that will be the mean which will divide the propor-
'tion harmonically, in which proportion that number
'which was the mean in the arithmetical proportion-
'ality will be the least extreme in the harmonical,
'and that which was the greatest extreme in the
'arithmetical, will be the harmonical mean, and the
'assumed number will be the greatest extreme; thus
'if we would harmonically divide this triple, 3 to 1,
'we must first find its arithmetical mean, which is 2,
'and then take the triple thereof, which is 6, and so
'the proportion which was arithmetically divided
'from 3 to 1, will be harmonically divided from
'6 to 2; and 3, which was the greatest extreme in
'the arithmetical, will be the mean in the harmonical,
'and 2, which was the arithmetical mean, will be the
'lesser extreme, and 6, the number assumed will be
'the greater, as may be perceived in these numbers:—

Triple arithmetically divided.			
Lesser extreme	Arithme- tical mean	Greater extreme	
1	2	3	6
	Lesser extreme	Harmoni- 'cal mean.	Greater extreme
	Triple harmonically divided.		

'But if no number can be found to bear the same
'proportion to the arithmetical mean as subsisted
'between these which it divided, the numbers must
'be doubled or tripled till such an one can be found;

'this, however, is not to be done rashly, but by some
'certain rule, for in multiples they are almost always
'found as in the duple and triple shewn before, and
'in the quadruple and quintuple in these numbers :—

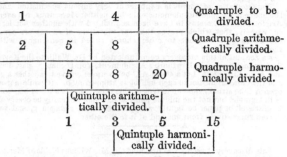

1	4		Quadruple to be divided.
2	5	8	Quadruple arithme- tically divided.
	5	8	20	Quadruple harmo- nically divided.

Quintuple arithme-
tically divided.
1   3   5   15
Quintuple harmoni-
cally divided.

'And examples of this kind are everywhere to be
'met with in almost all multiples. But in superpar-
'ticulars we must proceed by much more certain and
'constant rules; for as in finding an arithmetical
'mean in every superparticular proportion the num-
'bers must be doubled, so in finding an harmonical
'mean they must in the sesquialtera be doubled, in
'the sesquitertia tripled, in the sesquiquarta quadru-
'pled; and if this order be observed, the harmonical
'mean may be easily found in all superparticulars, as
'is manifest in these three examples :—

EXAMPLE I.

'2.   3. Sesquialtera to be divided.
'4. 5. 6. Sesquialtera divided arithmetically.
'8. 10. 12. The Numbers of the arithmetical pro-
'   'portionality doubled.
'   10. 12. 15. Sesquialtera harmonically divided.

EXAMPLE II.

'3.   4. Sesquitertia to be divided.
'6. 7. 8. Arithmetically divided.
'18. 21. 24. Numbers tripled.
'   21. 24. 28. Harmonically divided.

EXAMPLE III.

'4.   5. Sesquiquarta to be divided.
'8. 9. 10. Arithmetically divided.
'32. 36. 40. Numbers quadrupled.
'   36. 40. 45. Harmonically divided.'

Speaking of the Diapason, Salinas says though it
consists of eight sounds, it did not take its name from
the number 8, as the diapente does from 5, and the
diatessaron from 4, but it is called diapason, a word
signifying 'per omnes' or 'ex omnibus,' that is to say,
by all or from all the sounds, as Martianus Capella
asserts, and this with very good reason, for the diapason contains in it all the possible diversities of
sound, every other sound above or below the septenary, being but the replicate of some one included
in it.*

* The Unison, though in a sense somewhat different from that of
Martianus Capella in the above passage, may also be said to contain in
it, if not all the sounds, at least all the consonances in the septenary,
together with their replicates. To explain this matter, it is necessary to
observe that Aristotle in Prob. XVIII. of his 19th Sect. puts this question,
Why do the graver sounds include the acuter? and Mersennus, who has
taken upon him the solution of it, in the course of his investigation
asserts from experiments made by himself, that a chord being struck
when open, gives no fewer than five different sounds, namely the unison,
octave, 12th, 15th, and greater 17th, and, to a very nice ear, the greater 23d.

In the eighth and ninth chapters of his second book he contends against the modern musicians that the diatessaron is to be deemed a consonant ;* and in

Harmonic. De Instrum. Harm. lib. I. prop. xxxiii. Harm. Univers. lib. IV. pag. 209.

The Oscillation of chords is a subject of very curious speculation, and the above is a wonderful phenomenon ; but neither Mersennus, nor even Aristotle himself, seems to have been acquainted with another not less so, namely, that which proves that the vibrations of chords are communicated at a distance to other chords tuned in consonance with themselves.

An account of this discovery communicated by Dr. Wallis to the Royal Society may be seen in Lowthorp's Abridgment, Vol. I. chap. x. pag. 606, and is to this effect, Let a chord A C be an upper octave to another a g, and therefore an unison to each half of it stopped at b. If while a g is open A C be struck, the two halves of this other, that is a b and b g, will both tremble, but not the middle point at b, which will easily be observed if a little bit of paper be lightly wrapped about the string a g, and removed successively from one end of it to the other

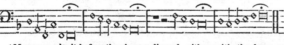

This discovery it seems was first made by Mr. William Noble of Merton college, and after him by Mr. Thomas Pigot of Wadham college. Long after that Monsieur Sauveur communicated it to the Royal Academy at Paris as his own discovery : but upon his being informed by some of the members present that Dr. Wallis had published it before, he immediately resigned all the honour thereof. There is an exquisite solution of these and other phenomena of sounds by Dr. Narcissus Marsh, in Dr. Plot's Natural History of Oxfordshire.

* Hardly any question has been more agitated by the modern musicians than this, whether the diatessaron be a concord or a discord ? The arguments to prove it the former are hardly anywhere so well enforced as in a very learned and ingenious book intitled The Principles of Music in Singing and Setting, with the twofold Use thereof. ecclesiastical and civil, by Charles Butler, of Magdalen college, Oxford, quarto, 1636, pag. 54, in not. and are to this purpose:—

' This concord is one of the three, so famous in all antiquity, with the ' symphony whereof the first musicians did content themselves ; and for ' the inventing of whose proportions, that most ancient and subtle ' philosopher Pythagoras has been ever since so much renowned among ' all posterity. The joint doctrine of these three concords, though it be ' as ancient as music itself, approved not only by Pythagoras, but also ' by Aristotle, Plato, Ptolemy, Euclid, and by Aristoxenus, Boetius, ' Franchinus, Glareanus, and all learned musicians ; yet some pregnant ' wits of later times, have made no bones to teach the contrary : and ' now, forsooth, this diatessaron, which for thousands of years hath been ' a special concord, without any the least impeachment or question, ' must needs upon the sudden be reckoned among the discords : and that ' not only authority, but reason also, and the very judgment of the ear, ' reclaiming. For he that listeth to try upon the organ or well-tuned ' virginal, shall find that of itself it doth well accord with the ground, ' and better than either of the other secondary concords [the sixth or im- ' perfect third] and with a sixth to yield as true a symphony as a third ' with a fifth : and more sweet than a third with a sixth : and with a sixth ' and an eighth, to sound fully and harmoniously in pleasing variety among ' other symphonies. So that although being no primary concord, it be ' not set to the base in a close ; yet is it good in other places, even im- ' mediately before the close, and that in slow time, as in this example:—

' Moreover, albeit before the close, a discord, either with the bass, or ' with an other part, be sometimes allowed (the note being but of short ' time, and a sweetening concord presently succeeding) yet in the close ' (where all parts meet together) in a long-timed note, not without some ' pause upon it (so that the ear doth especially attend it) there is never ' any discord at all : but all the upper notes are concords of one sort or ' other : and those as primary to the bass, so secondary among themselves. ' For example, where the close note of the bass is in GAM-UT (and con- ' sequently those of the other parts in B-MI, D-SOL-RE, and G-SOL-RE UT, ' or their eighths) B-MI being a perfect third to the bass, is an imperfect ' third to D-SOL-RE, and a sixth to G-SOL-RE-UT : and likewise D- ' SOL-RE being a fifth to GAM-UT, is a third imperfect to B-MI, and ' a fourth to G SOL-RE-UT. Seeing then that in closes, which are ' simply harmonious, no discord is admitted, but all notes concord ' among themselves ; it follows that a fourth as well as a sixth, or an ' imperfect third must be a concord : and seeing that a ground and his ' eighth are as it were all one, how can any man think that D SOL-RE, ' which is a fifth unto GAM-UT, and a fourth unto G-SOL-RE-UT [his eighth] ' should be the sweetest concord unto the one, and a discord unto the ' other ; and yet that B-MI, which is but a third unto the ground, should ' be a concord also to the eighth.

' And therefore that honourable sage [Lord Verulam] whose general ' knowledge and judgment in all kind of literature is generally applauded ' by the learned, rejecting their novel fancy that reject this ancient con- ' cord, professes himself to be of another mind. " The concords in " music," saith he, " between the unison and the diapason are the fifth : " which is the most perfect, the third next : and the sixth, which is more " harsh : and (as the ancients esteemed, and so do myself and some others) " the fourth, which they call diatessaron. Cent. II. Numb. 110. Among " those others, that singular musician (to whom the students of this " abstruse and mysterious faculty are more beholding, than to all that ever " have written thereof) Sethus Calvisius is one. His words are these : " Rejicitur hodiè à plerisque musicis ex numero consonantiarum, diates-

the following chapter he with admirable ingenuity shews that the ditone and semiditone, though perhaps the last or lowest in degree, are yet to be ranked among the consonances ; this he has almost made Ptolemy confess by the sense which he puts upon the sixth chapter of his first book, but his own arguments in favour of his position are the most worthy our attention, and they are comprised in the following passage :—

' Next after the diapente and diatessaron are formed ' by a division of the diapason, the ditone is easily to ' be found, and after that the semiditone, which in- ' terval is the difference whereby the diapente exceeds ' the ditone, for the diapente is no otherwise divided ' into the ditone and semiditone, than is the diapason ' into the diapente and diatessaron ; and the division ' of the diapason being made into the diapente and ' diatessaron, which are, as has been said, the next ' consonants after it as to perfection, and consist in ' two proportions, the sesquialtera and sesquitertia, ' which follow the duple immediately ; reason itself ' seems to demand that the diapente, which is the ' greater part of the diapason, should be rather di- ' vided than the diatessaron, which is the lesser part ; ' thus the diapente will be divided into the ditone and ' semiditone, as the sesquialtera ratio is into the ses- ' quiquarta and sesquiquinta ; for the terms of the ' sesquialtera ratio 2 and 3, because it cannot be di- ' vided in these, being doubled, there will arise 4 and ' 6, the arithmetical mean between which is 5, which ' is sesquiquarta to the lesser, and subsesquiquinta to ' the greater ; and though these two proportions do ' not immediately follow the sesquialtera as that does ' the duple, yet they divide it by a division which is ' the nearest to equality ; and in the same manner,

" saron, sed minùs rectè. Nam omnes musici veteres, tam Græci quàm " Latini, eam inter consonantias collocarunt : id quod monumenta " ipsorum testantur. Deindè quia conjuncta cum aliis intervallis, parit " consonantiam : ut si addatur ad diapente, fit diapason : si ad ditonon, " vel trihemitonion, fit sexta major aut minor. Nihil autem quod in " intervallis plurium proportionum consonat, per se dissonare potest. " Tertio, si chordæ in instrumentis musicis, exactè juxta proportiones " veras intendantur ; nulla dissonantia in diatessaron apparet ; sed ambo " soni uniformiter et cum suavitate quadam aures ingrediuntur : sic in " testudinibus chordæ graviores hoc intervallo inter se distant, et ratione " diatessaron intenduntur. Quarto, nulla cantilena plurium vocum " haberi potest, quæ careat hac consonantia. Nequaquam igitur est " rejicienda ; sed, propter usum, quem in Melopœia (si dextrè adhibeatur) " habet maximum, recipienda.' "

The several arguments contained in the above passage, with many others to the purpose, may be seen at large in a treatise written by Andreas Papius Gandensis, a man of excellent learning, and a good musician, entitled De Consonantiis seu pro Diatessaron. Antv. 1581.

But notwithstanding the authorities above-cited, it seems that those who scruple to call the diatessaron a consonant, have at least a colour of reason on their side ; for it is to be noted of the other consonants, namely, the diapason and diapente, that their replicates also are consonants, that is to say, the fifteenth is a consonant, as is also the twelfth, which is the diapason and diapente compounded, but the diapason and diatessaron compounded in the eleventh do not make a consonance. Dr. Wallis assigns as a reason for this, that its ratio $\frac{8}{3} = \frac{4}{3} \times 2$, or in words, 8 to 3, equal to 4 to 3 multiplied by 2, is neither a multiple nor a superparticular. Wall. Append. de Vet. Harm. 328. He adds with respect to the solitary or uncompounded fourth, that the reason for not admitting it in composition is not because it is not a consonant, but because whenever its diapason is taken with it, as it frequently must be, it as it were over-shadows or obscures it, and the fifth and not the fourth is the consonance heard. Ibid.

The observation of Dr. Wallis, that the Diapason cum Diatessaron is neither a multiple nor a superparticular, is grounded on a demonstration of Boetius in his treatise De Musica, lib. II. cap. xxvi. which see translated in the former part of this work, book III. cap. xxv. The title of the chapter in the original is ' Diatessaron ac Diapason non esse con- ' sonantiam, secundum Pythagoricos ;' and it is highly probable that this assertion, and the singular property of the diatessaron above noted, might give occasion to Des Cartes to say, as he does in his Compendium Musicæ, cap. IV. that the diatessaron is of all the consonances the most unhappy.

'though the ditone and semiditone do not imme-
'diately follow the diapente but the diatessaron, yet
'they divide it as the diapente and diatessaron divide
'the diapason, that is to say, in proportions the nearest
'to equality that may be, and the ditone, as being the
'greater part of the diapente, is found in the greater
'proportion, that is the sesquiquarta, and is therefore
'justly called by practical musicians the greater third.
'But the semiditone, which is the lesser part of the
'diapente, is in the sesquiquinta ratio, and is there-
'fore justly called the lesser third. The analogy of
'this new division is approved both by the senses
'and reason, and therefore its description must by no
'means be omitted.

Diapason $\begin{cases} \text{Diapente} \begin{cases} \text{Ditone} \\ \text{Semiditone} \end{cases} \\ \text{Diatessaron} \end{cases}$

'The same analogy is thus declared in numbers :—

	Duple divided.		Sesquialtera divided.	
Duple undivided	Sesquialtera undivided	Sesquitertia	Sesquiquarta undivided	Sesquiquinta
1	2	3	4	5	6
Diapason undivided	Diapente undivided	Diatessaron	Ditone undivided	Semiditone
	Diapason divided.		Diapente divided.	

Salinas adds, that men always did and always will
use the above consonances both in vocal and instrumental music, and not those of Pythagoras, some of
which were not only dissonant, but inconcinnous, as
the ditone 81 to 64, and the semiditone 32 to 27.
As to the ditone and semiditone investigated by him,
he says, as their proportions follow by a process of
harmonical numeration, that of the sesquitertia, they
must necessarily be consonants, and immediately follow the diatessaron. He concludes this chapter with
observing that Didymus seems to be the first of musicians that considered the ditone and semiditone as
answering to the sesquiquarta and sesquiquinta ratios,
and that the same may be gathered from those positions which Ptolemy has given in the second book,
chap. xiv. of his Harmonics.

CHAP. LXXXVI.

HAVING thus shewn the ditone and semiditone to
be consonances, with the method of producing them,
Salinas proceeds in the next subsequent chapters to
explain how the lesser intervals are produced, by
stating the several differences by which the greater
exceed the lesser. The method taken by him for
that purpose has been observed in a preceding chapter of his work, where the ratios of the several intervals are treated of, and therefore need not be here
repeated.

In the nineteenth chapter of the same second book is
contained a description of an instrument invented by
Salinas for demonstrating the ratios of the consonances, as also of the lesser intervals. He says that
this instrument is much more complete than the
Helicon of Ptolemy, described in the second book of
his Harmonics, for that in the Helicon are only five
consonants of the Pythagoreans, and the diapason
cum diatessaron, which Ptolemy himself added, and

of the dissonances, the tone major, and the diapason
cum tono majori, whereas he says in this instrument
the unison and seven consonants are found within
the diapason, five more within the disdiapason, and
two beyond it ; and of the dissonant intervals, not
only the greater tone, and diapason with the greater
tone, as in that, but also the lesser tone and greater
semitone ; so that, as he says, not one of the simple
intervals proper to the diatonic genus is undefined
by this invention of his, as may be seen in the explanation subjoined to the type thereof exhibited by
him, and which type is as follows :—

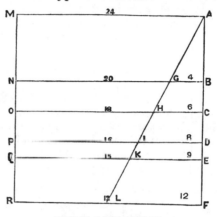

EXPLANATION.

'The side A F of this square is divided into many
'parts, first into two equally at the point c, then into
'three at the points B and D, and lastly into four, to
'give the point E, so that the whole line A F is triple
'of the part A B, duple of A C, sesquialtera to A D, and
'sesquitertia to A E. From these points are drawn the
'six parallel lines A M, B N, C O, D P, E Q, and F R, all
'of which, except the first, are, by a line drawn from
'the angle A, to the middle of the line F R, cut into
'two parts in the points G, H, I, K, L. If any one shall
'cause an instrument to be constructed of this form
'with chords, so that the stays which sustain the whole
'may fall in with the lines A F, and M R, and the chords
'with the other lines, and if a bridge be applied in the
'direction A, L, I say that all the consonants and the
'lesser intervals of the diatonic genus will be heard
'therein ; for as the sides of the similar triangles, which
'are opposite to equal angles, are proportional to each
'other by the fourth proposition of the sixth book of
'Euclid, therefore as the whole line A F is to its parts,
'so is the line F L to the sides that are parallel and
'opposite to it. Wherefore as the line A F of the
'triangle A, F, L, is constituted sesquitertia to A E of
'the triangle A E K, F L will also be sesquitertia to
'E K, and if the line F L be made to consist of twelve
'parts, the line E K will contain nine of them ; and
'by a like reasoning the lines D I will have 8, C H 6,
'and B G 4 ; and the upper line A M being double of F L,
'will contain 24. The remaining part of the lines
'beyond the bridge will contain as many parts as will
'complete the respective parts within the bridge to 24.
'So that G N will consist of 20, H O 18, I P 16, K Q 15,
'L R 12, and if every two of these numbers be com-
'pared together, the intervals which arise from strik-

'ing their respective chords will be perceived in
'this manner :—

'Unison 12 to 12.

'Greater semitone 16 to 15.

'Lesser tone 20 to 18.

'Greater tone twice, 9 to 8, 18 to 16.

'Semiditone twice, 18 to 15, 24 to 20.

'Ditone twice, 15 to 12, 20 to 16.

'Diatessaron five times, 8 to 6, 12 to 9, 16 to 12,
'20 to 15, 24 to 18.

'Diapente five times, 6 to 4, 9 to 6, 12 to 8, 18 to
'12, 24 to 16.

'Lesser hexachord twice, 24 to 15.

'Greater hexachord twice, 15 to 9, 20 to 12.

'Diapason five times, 8 to 4, 12 to 6, 16 to 8, 18
'to 9, 24 to 12.

'Some intervals repeated with the diapason.

'Diapason with the $\left\{\begin{array}{l}\text{Lesser tone 20 to 9.}\\ \text{Greater tone twice 9 to 4, 18 to 8.}\\ \text{Ditone twice, 20 to 8, 15 to 6.}\\ \text{Diatessaron twice, 16 to 6, 24 to 9.}\\ \text{Diapente thrice, 12 to 4, 18 to 6, 24 to 8.}\\ \text{Greater hexachord 20 to 6.}\end{array}\right.$

'Disdiapason twice, 16 to 4, 24 to 6.

'Some intervals repeated with a disdiapason.

'Disdiapason with the $\left\{\begin{array}{l}\text{Greater tone 18 to 4,}\\ \text{Ditone 20 to 4.}\\ \text{Diapente 24 to 4.}\end{array}\right.$

Upon this improvement of the Helicon of Ptolemy
Salinas himself remarks in the words following :—

'I thought proper thus minutely to explain all the
'parts of this instrument because of its great and
'wonderful excellence. But what I think seems
'most worthy of admiration in it is, that it consists
'in sextuple proportion, wherein are contained all the
'consonants and dissonants. And hereby the won-
'derful virtue of the senary number appears, since not
'only six simple consonants are found in the six first
'numbers, and in the six first simple proportions, and
'also in the six first which successively arise by mul-
'tiplication (so that we cannot either in the one or the
'other proceed farther to any other consonants or har-
'monical intervals) but also you may find consonants
'and dissonants constituted in all the six kinds of pro-
'portion, that is to say, in one of equality, and five of
'inequality, if you are minded to investigate their
'lawful proportions in numbers.' *

* The investigation of so great a number of consonant and dissonant
intervals as are above given by means of so simple an instrument or
diagram as this of Salinas, is a very delightful speculation. But it has
lately been discovered that from the famous theorem of Pythagoras, contained in the 47th Proposition of the first book of Euclid, the consonances
and dissonances may with no less a degree of certainty be demonstrated
than by the above method of Salinas. The author of this discovery was
Mr. John Harington, of the well-known family of that name, near Bath.
This gentleman made the important discovery above-mentioned, and in
the year 1693 communicated it to Mr. Newton, afterwards Sir Isaac, in a
letter, which, with the answer, are here inserted from a miscellany
entitled Nugæ Antiquæ, published in 1769:—

'Sir,—At your request I have sent you my scheme of the harmonic
'ratios adapted to the Pythagorean proposition, which seems better to
'express the modern improvements, as the ancients were not acquainted
'with the sesqualteral divisions, which appears strange. Ptolemy's
'Helicon does not express these intervals, so essential in the modern
'system, nor does the scheme of four triangles or three express so clearly
'as the squares of this proposition. What I was mentioning concerning
'the similitude of ratios as constituted in the sacred architecture, was
'my amusement at my leisure hours, but am not master enough to say
'much on these curious subjects. The given ratios in the dimensions of

In his demonstration that the ratio of a comma is
81 to 80, and that it is the difference between the tone
major and tone minor, he says that the comma is the

'Noah's ark, being 300, 50, and 30, do certainly fall in with what I ob-
'served; the reduction to their lowest terms comes out 6 to 1, which
'produces the quadruple sesqualteral ratio, and 5 to 3 is the inverse of
'6 to 5, which is one of the ratios resulting from the division of the ses-
'quialteral ratio; the extremes are as 10 to 1, which produce by reduction
'5 to 4, the other ratio produced by the division of the sesqualteral ratio.
'Thus are produced the four prime harmonical ratios, exclusive of the
'diapason or duple ratio. I have conjectured that the other most general
'established architectural ratios owe their beauty to their approximation
'to the harmonic ratios, and that the several forms of members are more
'or less agreeable to the eye, as they suggest the ideas of figures com-
'posed of such ratios. I tremble to suggest my crude notions to your
'judgment, but have the sanction of your own desire and kind promise
'of assistance to rectify my errors. I am sensible these matters have
'been touched upon before, but my attempts were to reduce matters to
'some farther certainty as to the simplicity and origin of the pleasures
'affecting our different senses, and try by comparison of those pleasures
'which affect one sense, from objects whose principles are known, as the
'ratios of sound, if other affections agreeable to other of our senses were
'owing to similar causes. You will pardon my presumption, as I am
'sensible neither my years nor my learning permit me to speak with
'propriety herein, but as you signified your pleasure of knowing what
'I was about, have thus ventured to communicate my undigested senti-
'ments, and am, Sir,   Your obedient servant,
'Wadham-college, May 22, 1693.   JOHN HARINGTON.'

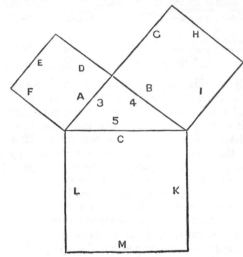

DEMONSTRATION.

KLMCC : KLMCB = 25 : 24 ♭ 2d		BA : CM = 7 : 10 ♭ 5th
CML : IBGH = 15 : 16 ♭ 2d		B : AD = 4 : 6 5th
CB : CM = 9 : 10 ♯ 2d		CB : CMB = 9 : 14 ♯ 5th
BG : BC = 8 : 9 ♯ 2d		C : BG = 5 : 8 ♭ 6th
BA : BG = 7 : 8 ♭♭ 3d		A : c ⚊ 3 : 5 ♯ 6th
AD : AB = 6 : 7 ♯♯ 2d		BGH : AB = 12 : 7 ♭♭ 7th
C : AD = 5 : 6 ♭ 3d		AB : B = 7 : 4 ♯♯ 6th
B : c = 4 : 5 ♯ 3d		CB : BGIH = 9 : 16 ♭ 7th
BA : CB = 7 : 9 ♭ 4th		C : CB = 5 : 9 ♭ 7th
A : B = 3 : 4 4th		BG : CML = 8 : 15 ♯ 7th
C : BA = 5 : 7 ♯ 4th		CMLK/CMLK BG : CMLKC = 48 : 25 ♯♯ 7th

The above demonstration is given in the author's own figures and
characters, but it seems in some instances to be rather inaccurately expressed; and perhaps it had been better if he had spoken thus: 25 to 24
semitone minus, 16 to 15 semitone majus, 10 to 9 tone minor, 8 to 9 tone
major, 6 to 5 third minor, 16 to 9 seventh minima, 9 to 5 seventh minor,
15 to 8 seventh major, 48 to 25 greatest, or sharp sharp seventh.

The following is the answer to Mr. Harington's letter:

'Sir,—By the hands of your friend, Mr. Consel, I was favoured with
'your demonstration of the harmonic ratios from the ordinances of the
'47th of Euclid. I think it very explicit, and more perfect than the
'Helicon of Ptolemy, as given by the learned Dr. Wallis. Your obser-
'vations hereon are very just, and afford me some hints, which when
'time allows I would pursue, and gladly assist you with any thing I can
'to encourage your curiosity and labours in these matters. I see you have
'reduced from this wonderful proposition the inharmonics, as well as the
'coincidences of agreement, all resulting from the given lines 3, 4, and 5.
'You observe that the multiples hereof furnish those ratios that afford
'pleasure to the eye in architectural designs. I have in former consider-
'ations examined these things, and wish my other employments would
'permit my further noticing thereon, as it deserves much our strict
'scrutiny, and tends to exemplify the simplicity in all the works of the

least of all the sensible intervals, and that he had experienced it to be so by his ear, in an instrument which he had caused to be made at Rome, in which both tones are heard, and their difference was plainly to be perceived, and he infers from a passage in Ptolemy, where he makes it indifferent whether the sesquioctave or sesquinonal tone have the acute place in the diatonic tetrachord, that the ear of Ptolemy was not nice enough to discern the difference between the greater and lesser tone.

Salinas observes, that besides the two semitones, the greater and lesser, into which the tone is divided, and which is the difference whereby the ditone exceeds the semiditone, there is a necessity for inserting into musical instruments, more especially the organ, another interval called the Diesis,* because without it there can be no modulating in that kind of music called by the Symphonetæ, Musica ficta,† in which there is occasion to make use of three diversities of b soft ; nor ought this, he says, to be deemed a new invention, for, which is curious and worthy of observation, he

'Creator; however, I shall not cease to give my thoughts towards this 'subject at my leisure. I beg you to pursue these ingenious speculations, 'as your genius seems to incline you to mathematical researches. You 'remark that the ideas of beauty in surveying objects arises from their 'respective approximations to the simple constructions, and that the 'pleasure is more or less as the approaches are nearer to the harmonic 'ratios. I believe you are right; portions of circles are more or less 'agreeable as the segments give the idea of the perfect figure from whence 'they are derived. Your examinations of the sides of polygons with 'rectangles certainly quadrate with the harmonic ratios; I doubt some 'of them do not, but then they are not such as give pleasure in the 'formation or use. These matters you must excuse my being exact in 'during your enquiries, till more leisure gives me room to say with 'more certainty hereon. I presume you have consulted Kepler, Mersenne, 'and other writers on the construction of figures. What you observe of 'the ancients not being acquainted with a division of the sesquialteral 'ratio is very right; it is very strange that geniuses of their great talents, 'especially in such mathematical considerations, should not consider that 'although the ratio of 3 to 2 was not divisible under that very denomi-'nation, yet its duple members 6 to 4 easily pointed out the ditone 4 to 5, 'and the minor tierce 6 to 5, which are the chief perfections of the diatonic 'system, and without which the ancient system was doubtless very im-'perfect. It appears strange that those whose nice scrutinies carried 'them so far as to produce the small limmas, should not have been more 'particular in examining the greater intervals, as they now appear so 'serviceable when thus divided. In fine, I am inclined to believe some 'general laws of the Creator prevailed with respect to the agreeable or 'unpleasing affections of all our senses; at least the supposition does not 'derogate from the wisdom or power of God, and seems highly consonant 'to the simplicity of the macrocosm in general. Whatever else your in-'genious inquiries may produce I shall attentively consider, but have 'such matters on my mind that I am unable to give you more satisfaction 'at this time; however, I beg your modesty will not be a means of pre-'venting my hearing from you as you proceed in these curious researches, 'and be assured of the best services in the power of
                        'Your humble servant,
'May 30, 1693.   'Is. NEWTON.'

* The author observes that the ancients gave a diesis to each of the three genera, that is to say, they called the least interval in each by that name. In short, the word diesis signifies properly a particle, and Macrobius uses it in that sense, and so explains it; but the diesis which Salinus is here for introducing, is that interval whereby the lesser semitone is exceeded by the greater, and is in the ratio of 128 to 125.

† Musica ficta, in English feigned music, is by Andreas Ornithoparcus thus defined : 'Musica ficta is that which the Greeks called Synemmenon, 'a song made beyond the regular compass of the scale; or it is a song 'full of conjunctions.' He means to say it is that kind of Cantus in which the tetrachord synemmenon is used, and which has for its final note or key some chord not included in the ordinary scale, as B ♭ or E ♭. See a type of it in the account herein-before given of Ornithoparcus, book VIII. chap. lxviii. pag. 308.
  It is pretty clear that at the time when Ornithoparcus wrote, that practice of dislocating the MI, which feigned music implies, was carried no farther than was necessary to constitute the keys B♭ and E♭, each with the major third. As to the latter, it is said to have been first made use of by Clemens non Papa, who lived about the year 1560; and it is worthy of observation, that that great variety of keys which is created by the multiplication both of the acute and grave signatures, except in the above instances, is a modern refinement. Compositions in these keys, for example, D with a major third, A with a major third, E with a major third, F♯ with a minor third, F with a minor third, and B natural with a minor third, are not to be traced much backwarder than to the middle of the last century, and probably owe their introduction to the improvements in the practice of the violin; else had they probably been included in the definition of Musica ficta by Ornithoparcus.

relates that the Italians have in their organs two dieses in every diapason, the one between a, diatonic, and g, chromatic, and another between d, diatonic, and c, chromatic ;‡ and that on many such organs as these he had often played, particularly on a very famous one at Florence, in the monastery of the Dominicans, called Santa Maria Novella.

In the subsequent chapters of this second book are a great number of scales and diagrams, contrived with wonderful ingenuity to explain and illustrate the several subjects treated of in the book.

In the third book he treats of the genera of the ancients, and that with so much learning and sagacity, that, as has already been noted, Dr. Pepusch scrupled not to declare to the world that the true enarmonic, the most intricate of the three, and which has been for many ages past supposed to be lost, is in this work of his accurately determined.

From his representation of the ancient genera, that is to say, of the enarmonic, the chromatic, and even some species of the diatonic, it most evidently appears that they consisted in certain divisions of the tetrachord, to which we at this day are strangers ; and it may farther be said that the intervals which divide both the chromatic and the enharmonic tetrachord, however rational they may be made to appear by an harmonical or numerical process of calculation, are to a modern ear so abhorrent as not to be borne without pain and aversion.

After what has been said in some preceding pages of this work touching the genera and their species, and from the testimony of some even of the Greek harmonicians herein-before adduced, it is clear beyond a doubt that both the enarmonic and chromatic genera are as it were by the general consent of mankind laid aside. It would therefore be to little purpose to follow Salinas through that labyrinth of reasoning by which he attempts to explain them ; such as are desirous of full information in this respect must be referred to his own work. In order, however, to gratify the curiosity of others, and to display the depth of knowledge with which this author investigates the doctrine of the ancient genera, it may not be amiss here to subjoin the following extracts, which contain the substance of his arguments in the discussion of this curious subject.

A Genus in music, according to this author, is a certain habitude or relation which the sounds that compose the diatessaron have to each other in modulation.

Having thus defined the term Genus, in the doing whereof he has apparently taken Ptolemy for his guide, he thus farther proceeds to deliver his sentiments of the genera at large :—

'The ancients were unanimously of opinion that 'the genera were determined rather by the division 'of the diatessaron, that being the least, than of any 'other system or consonance ; and this was not the 'sentiment of the Pythagoreans only, who held that 'there could be no consonance of a less measure than

‡ The passage in Salinas is as above, but it is to be suspected that the letter c is misprinted, and should have been e ; and if so, this improvement of the organ by the Italians corresponds exactly with what is to be observed in some organs in this country, that in the Temple church in particular, wherein are several keys for g♯ and a♭, and for d♯ and e♭, from the lowest to the highest in the range.

'two tones, but also of Aristoxenus himself, who,
'though he taught that the differences of the intervals
'were not commensurable by numbers and their pro-
'portions, but that the senses were the proper judges
'thereof, asserts in the first book of his Elements of
'Harmony, that no consonance can be found of a less
'content than that between the unison and its fourth;
'a position which, however, we have shown not to be
'strictly true, whether we appeal to the judgment of
'our senses or our reason. Not to enter into too scru-
'pulous a discussion of this matter, let it suffice to say,
'that for the purpose of defining the genera, all the
'ancients to a man have supposed a division of the
'diatessaron into four sounds or three intervals, from
'which method of division are constituted the three
'genera: the difference between each of these is gene-
'rally denoted by the epithets rarum, rare or thin ;
'spissum, thick or close set; and spississimum, thickest
'or closest set, according to the quantities of those
'lesser intervals by which they were severally di-
'vided : the primitive terms of distinction for the
'genera were those of Diatonica, Chroma, and Har-
'monia, though the writers of later times use those
'of Diatonicum, Chromaticum, and Enarmonium.
'The diatonicum was said to be rare because it pro-
'ceeds by a tone, tone and semitone, which are the
'greatest and most rare of the lesser intervals : and
'Ptolemy asserts that this genus was called the Dia-
'tonum because it abounded in tones. The Chro-
'maticum was that which proceeded by a trihemitone,
'a semitone and semitone ; and because the semitones
'are thicker or closer than the tones, this genus was said
'to be thicker and softer than the diatonum. The word
'Chroma, which in Greek signifies colour, was applied
'to it, as Boetius writes, as being expressive of its
'variation from the diatonum, or, as the Greeks say,
'because that as colour is intermediate between white
'and black, so also does the chromatic genus observe
'the medium between the rareness of the diatonum
'and the thickness of the harmonia. The Harmonia
'or Enarmonium proceeded by a ditone, a diesis, and
'diesis towards the grave, and because the dieses are
'thicker than the semitones, this genus, which is the
'thickest of the three, was termed the Enarmonium,
'as being the best coadapted, and the most absolute of
'them all.*

'Nor did the ancients proceed any farther in the
'constitution of the genera than is above related,
'because in it no harmonical interval less than that
'of a diesis is discoverable except the comma, which
'is common to all the three ; and though they may
'all seem to agree in dividing the diatessaron into
'three intervals in every genus, yet is there not one
'of those who have written on this subject that does
'not differ from the rest in determining the pro-
'portions of the several intervals that constitute it ;
'for Pythagoras, Archytas, Philolaus, Eratosthenes,
'and, in a word, all the writers on this branch of the
'science have assigned to it different ratios all equally
'repugnant to harmonical truth. Those who are de-
'sirous of more particular information, may consult
'Boetius, book III. chap. v. ; and Ptolemy, book II.

'towards the end. The most celebrated mode of
'generical division was undoubtedly that of Pytha-
'goras, which constituted the diatonic diatessaron of
'two tones, both in a sesquioctave ratio, and that in-
'terval which was wanting to complete it, but this
'we have nevertheless shewn to be erroneous in the
'eleventh chapter of the second book of this work,
'where we have treated of the ditone and greater
'semitone, seeing that both the ditone and lesser
'semitone or limma are both abhorrent to harmony,
'as is demonstrated by Ptolemy, and appears from
'reason itself. The division of Aristoxenus was es-
'teemed the next after this of Pythagoras, to which it
'was contrary in almost every thing, for Aristoxenus
'thought it agreeable in the diatonic genus to proceed
'not only by equal tones, but also in the chromatic
'to proceed by two equal semitones, and in the enar-
'monic by two equal dieses. A third division, that
'of Didymus and Ptolemy, made neither the tones
'nor semitones equal, but constituted a greater and
'lesser of each.†

'The genera can neither be more nor fewer than
'three, because that is the number of the lesser inter-
'vals whereby they are distinguished from each other.
'In the diatonic the least interval is the greater
'semitone ; in the chromatic the lesser ; and in the
'enarmonic the diesis ; and as the diesis is the least
'of all the intervals that can vary the genus, it
'follows that the enarmonic must be the thickest of
'them all ; and the reason why the diatessaron was
'chosen as the fittest of the consonances to adjust the
'several genera by, was not because, as the ancients
'assert, it was the smallest of the consonances, for
'that it certainly is not, but because all those inter-
'vals which arise from the first division of the lowest
'consonances, were found once in the diatessaron,
'such as the greater tone, the lesser tone, and the
'greater semitone ; for the greater and lesser tone
'arise from the first division of the ditone, and the
'greater tone and lesser semitone from the first
'division of the semiditone ; but if these were re-
'spectively added, the one to the former and the
'other to the latter, the complement would be a dia-
'tessaron consisting of three intervals and four sounds,
'wherefore the constitution of the genera is not to be
'found in any of those less systems than the dia-
'tessaron ; on the contrary, in the greater consonants,
'such as the diapente and diapason, we meet with
'a repetition of these three several intervals, for in
'the diapente the greater tone is found twice, and in
'the diapason three times, and the lesser tone and
'greater semitone are found twice in the diapason.'‡

Although Salinas has laboured to explain the
meaning of the terms spissum and non spissum,
which so frequently occur in the writings of the
ancients, and which are used to express a distinguishing property of the genera, he professes to use the
epithet spissum in a sense different from that in which
it was accepted by them : they called that constitution
spissum, or thick, where the acutest interval was
greater than the other two, as in the chromatic and
enarmonic ; and they called that non spissum, in

---

* Lib. III. cap. I. pag. 101.　　　　ᵇ. III. cap. i. pag. 102.　　　‡ Lib. III. cap. ii.

which the two grave ones taken together were greater than the acute, as in the diatonic. 'But we, says this author, 'maintain that genus not to be thick 'wherein the consonants are found intermediated 'with thinner and fewer intervals, of which sort is 'the diatonum, in which the consonants are inter-'sected by tones and a greater semitone, which are 'the thinnest of all the lesser intervals: the diatessaron, 'for example, is divided into three intervals; on the 'contrary, we say that that genus is thick in which 'all the consonants are intersected by thicker and 'more close intervals; such is the chromatic, which 'proceeds by a greater and lesser semitone, which 'are thicker intervals than tones, and in the com-'position of a perfect instrument divides the dia-'tessaron into six intervals and seven sounds, but 'according to that which we use, the division is 'into five intervals and six sounds, for the trihemi-'tone is not, as the ancients would have it, an inter-'val of this genus, seeing it is truly a consonant, and 'consonants are not the intervals of any genus.* 'But the thickest of the genera is the enarmonic, 'because it proceeds by lesser semitones and dieses, 'which are indivisible intervals; nor can the ditone 'be said to be an interval of this genus, although as 'well the ancient writers as those of later times assert 'it to be so, because it is a true and perfect consonant, 'and, like all the rest, requires to be filled up, where-'fore in this genus the diatessaron will have nine in-'tervals and ten sounds.

'The constitution of all the genera is not to be 'sought for in the division of the diatessaron, it is 'only in the diatonic that this method is to be taken, 'for the intervals by which it proceeds are not to be 'found in any lesser consonant. But to discover the 'constitution of the chromatic, we assert that the 'division of the greater tone is sufficient, because all 'the intervals by which this genus proceeds are to be 'found once therein. For the consideration of the 'enarmonic genus the greater semitone is sufficient, 'for in that are all the intervals to be found through 'which this genus proceeds; all this is the effect of 'the great and wonderful constitution of the har-'monical ratio. The diatessaron seems to have been 'assumed for displaying the diatonic genus, because 'it is the excess of the diapason above the diapente: 'the tone by which we explain the chromatic is the 'excess of the diapente above the diatessaron; and 'the greater semitone by which we declare the enar-'monic is the excess of the diatessaron above the 'ditone. Moreover it is necessary to know that the 'three genera stand in the relation to each other of 'good, better, and best; for as good can exist by 'itself, but better cannot be without good, so may 'the diatonic exist alone, and become the foundation 'of the others, as is seen in the Cythara, wherein are 'no semitones but the greater, in which this genus 'abounds, for the lesser semitones are proper to the 'chromatic.

* Here Salinas cautions his reader not to be disturbed that the Diates-saron, which takes its name from the number four, and is therefore understood to consist of so many sounds, should here be said to contain six intervals and seven sounds, for that circumstance, he says, is peculiar to the diatonic.

'But although the diatonic be the most natural, 'yet, as Boetius says, it is the hardest of the three, 'and to soften or abate of this hardness was the 'chromatic invented, and yet the chromatic could 'not have existed without the diatonic, it being 'nothing else than the diatonic thickened; and such 'does that constitution appear to be which we find 'in those instruments that are struck with black and 'white plectra. As to the enarmonic, it is clear that 'it cannot subsist by itself, and being a compound of 'the other two, it is the thickest, best compacted, 'and most perfect; and no one can believe that any 'modulation could be made in either the chromatic 'or enarmonic separated from the diatonic, seeing it 'is impossible to proceed without it through the 'chromatic or enarmonic intervals, and this is not 'only shown by Ptolemy, but it is evident both to 'sense and reason.' †

The notion which Salinas entertained of the genera was that the chromatic was the diatonic inspissated; and that the enarmonic was the chromatic inspissated, and in all his reasoning about them he supposes a necessity in nature for filling up those spaces or chasms, as he affects to consider them, which the difference between the greater and lesser intervals in the diatonic tetrachord seems to imply.

Of the several species of the diatonic, Salinas scruples not to prefer the syntonous or intense of Ptolemy, and says that if Plato had been sensible of its excellence, he would not have been so tormented as he was, at finding that the Pythagorean limma 256 to 243 was not superparticular, and therefore not in truth a proportion, but rather, as he is forced to term it, a portion, *i. e.* a particle or fraction.‡

CHAP. LXXXVII.

In the fifth chapter of his third book Salinas shews the method of constructing the type of the diatonic, which he does by such a division of the monochord as gives d d in the ratio of each to the other of 81 to 80, making thereby the one a tone minor, and the other a tone major above c; the former of these he calls d inferior, and the latter d superior, this dis-tinction he observes in the succeeding types of the chromatic and enarmonic; that of the diatonic is as follows:—

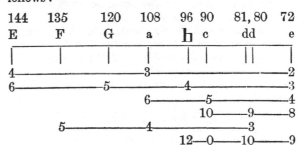

Of the Chromatic he says, chap. vi., that it arose from that division of the tone which was invented to soften the harshness of the tritonus between F and ♮; and in chap. vii. he directs, by the division of the

† Lib. III. cap. ii.   ‡ Lib. III. cap. iii. pag. 107.

monochord, the construction of the type of the chromatic genus.

As in the diatonic division he gives d inferior and d superior, so in this of the chromatic does he give F♯ inferior, and F♯ superior, and also b inferior and b superior, besides G♯, c♯, and e♭, distinguished by the short or different coloured plectra on the organ, harpsichord, and other instruments of the like kind.

The following is the type of the chromatic genus according to this author :—

2880	2700	2592	2560	2400	2304	2160	2025	2000	1920	1800	1728	1620	1600	1500	1440
E	F	♯	♯	G	♯	a	b	b	♮	c	♯	d	d	e♭	e
												27	0	25	24
				6				5				4			
20	0	18		0		16	15					3			
5				4											
				16	15	0	0			12					
18	0	16	15												

In the eighth chapter of the same book Salinas remarks that the characteristic of the chromatic is its least interval, which is a lesser semitone, and is therefore called the chromatic diesis, and is the difference whereby the lesser tone exceeds the greater semitone. The type above given is exhibited in the seventh chapter, with this remark, that in it the lesser semitone or chromatic diesis is found five times, that is to say, between F and F♯ inferior, G and G♯, b superior and ♮, c♯ and c, and e♭ and e.

In the same chapter he treats of the Enarmonic genus, which he says is the most perfect of all, as containing in it the other two; the following is the type of the enarmonic as given by him :

57600	55296	54000	51840	51200	50625	50000	48000	46080	45000	43200	41472	40960	40500	40000	38400	36864	36000	34560	33750	32400	32000	30720	30000	28800
E	♯	F	♯	♯	b	b	G	♯	a♭	a	♯	♯	b	b	♮	♯	c	♯	d♭	d	d	d♯	e♭	e
							6						5							4				
				5							4		0							3				
		15			0	0				12			0			10								
	6							5							4									
			5							4									3					
					12				0		0					9		8						
	16	15	0				12																	
				15	0	0				12						12		0		10				
6							5								4									

Upon which it is to be remarked, that the true enarmonic intervals are distinguished from the diatonic by a point placed over them.

As he had noted the chromatic by its diesis, which is the interval of a lesser semitone, so has he remarked that the characteristic of the enarmonic is the enarmonic diesis, which arises from a division of the greater semitone into a lesser semitone and a diesis, thus :—

GREATER SEMITONE.	
Chromatic Diesis.	Enarmonic Diesis.
120　　　　　125	128

Which lesser semitone, by the way, is no other than the chromatic diesis, and in its lowest numbers is 25 to 24. As to the enarmonic diesis, its ratio is above demonstrated to be 128 to 125, and it is the interval between F♯ inferior and G♭ inferior, that is to say, between the numbers 51840 and 50625, which are in the ratio of 128 to 125, for 51840 contains the number 405, 128 times, and 50625 contains the same number 405, 125 times. It is again found between a♯ inferior and b inferior, that is to say, between the numbers 41472 and 40500, for the former of these contains the number 324, 128 times, and the latter contains the same number 125 times. The enarmonic diesis is elsewhere to be found in the above division of the diapason in three instances, but the two above given are sufficient to make it known.

It was necessary to be thus particular in the representation of Salinas's system of the genera, more especially the enarmonic genus, because he himself appears to be so confident of his skill in this abstruse part of the musical science, that he scruples not to reprehend very roundly the Greek writers for mistakes about the genera; and speaking of his division of the enarmonic, he says, that if it be made as by him is directed, nothing in harmonics can be more absolutely just and perfect. It is positively asserted by Dr. Pepusch, in his letter to Mr. De Moivre, that Salinas has determined the enarmonic accurately: and it is more than probable that those are in the right who think so.

The diagrams made use of by Salinas to illustrate his doctrine of the genera, more especially the types, as he calls them, of each, are most astonishingly complicated, but very curious and satisfactory. It is to be remarked on this part of his work, that he meddles not with the colours or species of the genera. Of the diatonic, he has taken the syntonous or intense of Ptolemy; and in his description of the chromatic, he has given a representation which coincides with no one species of that genus, for it is neither the soft, the hemiolian, nor the toniac, but seems to be a division of his own. As to the enarmonic, it is well known that it admitted of no distinction into species.

That Salinas had any desire to restore the ancient genera is not to be inferred from the great labour he has bestowed in the explanation of them. He indeed seems to have been very solicitous to attemper some of the harsher intervals in the diatonic series, and for that purpose to have made an arrangement of the white and black plectra, as he calls them, a little differing from the ordinary one; and says that he had with him at Salamanca an instrument which he had caused to be made at Rome, wherein the tone between G and a is accurately divided. But the pains he has taken to ascertain the true division of the chromatic and enarmonic, seems to be resolvable into that eager desire of rendering the writings of the ancient Greeks intelligible, which he uniformly manifests in the course of his writings.

Seeing, then, that the world is in possession at last of the true enarmonic, it remains to be considered whether it must not at all times have been a matter rather of speculation than practice. Were we to think with the ancients, and adopt their reasoning about the spissum and non spissum, we should say that that series of harmonical progression which admitted of the smallest intervals, and left the fewest chasms in the system, approached the nearest to perfection; but this is a consideration merely speculative, and has as little to do with the sense of hearing as the external form of any given musical instrument with the hearing whereof we are delighted.

On the other hand, let any one make the experiment, and try the effect of such intervals as the enarmonic diesis, as above ascertained, on his ear, and he will hardly be persuaded that the genus to which it belongs could ever have been cordially embraced by the unprejudiced part of mankind.

To favour the opinion that it was never received into general practice, we have the testimony of some of the ancient writers themselves, who expressly say that on account of their intricacy both the chromatic and enarmonic grew very early to be disesteemed by the public ear, and gave way to that orderly progression the diatonic, which nature throughout her works seems to recognize as the only true and just succession of harmonical intervals.

In the thirteenth and subsequent chapters of his third book, Salinas treats of the temperament of the organ and other instruments. He says of the human voice that it is flexible, and being directed by that sense of harmony which is implanted in us, it chooses and constitutes that which is perfect, and preserves the consonants and the lesser intervals in their due proportions, no impediment intervening. Farther he says that it discriminates with the greatest exactness between the greater and the lesser tone, and that as the melody requires, it chooses either the one or the other; but in the organ and other instruments where the sounds are fixed, and are not determined by the touch of the performer, he says that the tones are of necessity equal, and that this equality is preserved by the distribution of the three commas, by which the three greater tones in the diapason exceed the lesser ones; so that by this distribution, the consonants and lesser intervals participate of that dissonance which in some part of the system or other is occasioned by the comma.

The system thus attempered is called by the Italians Systema Participato. It is mentioned in a preceding chapter of this work, and is described by Zarlino in his Istitutioni Harmoniche, part II. cap. xli. et seq.* Salinas says he himself when a youth at Rome, invented a Systema Participato, in nothing differing from that published by Zarlino, which he says is not to be wondered at, seeing that truth is but one and the same, and that it presents itself to all who rightly endeavour to investigate it.†

The fertility of Salinas's invention suggested to him various other temperaments, which he has described with his usual accuracy. After stating and comparing them, and giving the preference to the first, he proceeds in chap. xxvii. to show the bad constitution of a certain instrument begun to be constructed in Italy about forty years before the time of writing his book, that is to say, about the year 1537, concerning which he says that this instrument was called Archicymbalum, and that it divided each of the tones into five parts, giving to the greater semitone three, and to the lesser two; he says that this instrument was much esteemed, and was made use of by some musicians of great eminence. He says that as the diapason contains six tones and a diesis, it divided the octave into thirty-one parts;‡ but that they are dieses he absolutely denies. He then proceeds

* Bontempi has given a system of another form, which he calls Systema Participato, from its comprehending the diatonic and chromatic, but it seems to be no other than that now in practice, in which the diapason is divided into twelve semitones. Vide Bont. Hist. Mus. pag. 187.

† De Musica, lib. III. cap. xiv. Dr. Smith says that Salinas was the first inventor of a temperament, and that both he and Zarlino laid claim to the honour of the invention, and had a dispute about it. Harmonics, pag. 37, in a note. But this is hardly reconcileable with the declaration of Salinas above-mentioned, which seems to imply an inclination in him rather to waive than promote a dispute.

‡ Dr. Pepusch in his letter to Mr. De Moivre, herein before cited, says that this division of the octave into thirty-one parts was necessarily implied in the doctrine of the ancients; and that though the instrument above-mentioned was condemned both by Zarlino and Salinas, they condemned it without sufficient reason, for that Mr. Huygens having more accurately examined the matter, found it to be the best temperament that could be contrived.

to point out the defects of this instrument, and pronounces of it, that it was offensive to his ear, and was not constructed in any truly harmonical ratio.*

In the twenty-eighth and four subsequent chapters of his third book he takes occasion to speak of the lute, viol, and organ, and of certain temperaments the best adapted to each. In the former he says that although the viol by name is not to be met with in the writings of the ancients, yet Cassiodorus asserts that it is to be found described among their different kinds of Cythara; and he himself adds that in the works of Bede, an author sufficiently celebrated, it is expressly mentioned.

The eighth chapter of the fourth book contains

* There cannot be the least doubt but that the instrument above spoken of is the Archicembalo of Don Nicola Vicentino, though Salinas confesses himself at a loss to whom to ascribe the invention of it. Mersennus once thought it was invented by Fabius Columna. Harmonic, lib. VI. De Generibus et Modis, Prop. xiii. From these two particulars it may be inferred that neither Salinas nor he had ever seen Vicentino's book; but it seems that Mersennus was set right in his divison by the perusal of Salinas, and that he has made ample amends for his mistake by giving the thirty-one intervals with their ratios as here represented. As to the division of Fabius Columna, it was probably borrowed from this, but it was into thiry-nine sounds and thirty-eight intervals. and will be spoken of hereafter. Vide Mersenn. Harm. Univ. Des Genres de la Musique, Prop. x. xi.

32	C		144000
			lesser semitone
31	♮		138240
			diesis
30	♮		135000
			lesser semitone
29	·B		129600
			greater comma
28	B		128000
			lesser semitone
27	·λa		122880
			lesser comma
26	×a		121500
			greater comma
25	A		120000 [nimum†
			semitonium submi-
24	A		116640
			greater comma
23	·×g		115200
			lesser semitone
22	:×g		110592
			lesser comma
21	×g		109350
			greater comma
20	·G		108000
			lesser semitone
19	G		103680
			greater comma
18	·※g		102400
			lesser comma
17	×g		101250
			greater comma
16	·×f		100000 [nimum
			semitonium submi-
15	×f		97200
			greater comma
14	·F		96000
			lesser semitone
13	F		92160
			lesser comma
12	·※e		91125
			greater comma
11	×e		90000 [nimum
			semitonium submi-
10	·E		87480
			greater comma
9	E		86400
			lesser semitone
8	·※d		82944
			greater comma
7	·×d		81920
			lesser comma
6	×d		81000
			greater comma
5	·D		80000 [nimum
			semitonium submi-
4	D		77760
			greater comma
3	※d		76800
			lesser semitone
2	×a		73728
			diesis
1	C		72000

† To understand the nature of this interval, it is necessary to know that of semitones there are many kinds. Mersennus has enumerated them in his Latin work, liber V. De Dissonantiis, prop. xiii., but more particularly in his Harmonie Universelle, Des Dissonances, prop. ii. pag. 116: they appear to be the Semitonium maximum $\frac{27}{25}$, Semitonium majus $\frac{16}{15}$. Semitonium medium $\frac{135}{128}$, Semitonium Pythagoricum $\frac{256}{243}$, Semitonium minus $\frac{25}{24}$, Semitonium minimum $\frac{648}{625}$, and lastly, the Semitonium subminimum above given, which in its lowest, or radical numbers, will be found to be in the ratio of 250 to 243, for in 120000 the number 480 is found 250 times, and in 116640 it is found 243 times, in 100000 the number 400 is found 250 times, and in 97200 it is found 243 times : in 90000 the number 360 is found 250 times, and in 87480 it is found 243 times. Lastly, in 80000 the number 320 is found 250 times, and in 77760 it is found 243 times. It is to be noted that in the Harmonie Universelle, livre troisieme, pag. 167, and in that curious diagram preceding it, the number 87930 is mistaken for 87480. The Semitonium subminimum is an interval less than the chromatic diesis by a comma. Mersen. Harm., lib. V. prop. ix. Harm. Univ. Des Dissonances, prop. II. pag. 115.

among other things the doctrine of the modes, in the discussing whereof he seems to agree with Glareanus that they are in number twelve, and that they answer to the seven species of diapason harmonically and arithmetically divided; but as the third species proceeding from ♭ is incapable of an harmonical division as wanting a true fifth, and the seventh species proceeding from F is incapable of an arithmetical division as having an excessive fourth, the number of the modes, which would otherwise be fourteen, is reduced to twelve, which is the very position that Glareanus in his Dodecachordon endeavours to demonstrate.

In the tenth chapter is a diagram representing in a collateral view the tetrachords of the ancients conjoined with the hexachords of Guido Aretinus, and showing how the latter spring out of the former. Dr. Wallis has greatly improved upon this in the diagram by him inserted in his Appendix to Ptolemy, and which is given in a former part of this work, exhibiting a comparative view of the ancient Greek system with the scale of Guido.

In the twenty-second chapter he takes notice of the ancient division of the genera into species, but it seems that he did not approve of it, for in his own division of the genera he has rejected it, thereby making that species of each, whatever it be, which he has chosen for an exemplar, a genus of itself.

In the twenty-third chapter he undertakes to show the errors of Aristoxenus in a manner different from Ptolemy and Boetius; and in the five following chapters censures him, and even Ptolemy himself, with a degree of freedom which shews that though he entertained a reverence for the ancients, he was no bigot to their opinions, but assumed the liberty in many instances of thinking and judging for himself.

In the twenty-ninth chapter of the same fourth book he commends in general terms Jacobus Faber Stapulensis, though he seems to suspect that he had never read Ptolemy, nor any other of the Greek harmonicians, and says he does nothing more than demonstrate the propositions of Boetius.

The subsequent chapter contains his opinion of Franchinus and his writings, which he delivers in the following words:—

' Franchinus Gaffurius was a famous professor of ' theoretical and practical music, and published several ' works and wrote many things in both parts worthy ' to be known. He boasts that by his care, and at his ' expence, the three books of Ptolemy's Harmonics, ' the three of Aristides Quintilianus, and the three of ' Manuel Briennius, were translated from the Greek ' into the Latin. It is true he read those books, as he ' shows in his works, especially in that which he wrote ' concerning instrumental harmony, where he recites ' almost all their positions, but so confusedly, that he ' seems rather to have read them than understood them. ' But these Latin translations are not extant as far as ' I know, perhaps through the avarice of Franchinus ' himself, who had them made only for his own use, ' and did not give them to be printed, imagining that ' a time never would come when the musicians would

'understand the Greek language, and be able to read
'those authors in the originals. This man had a very
'good genius, but wanted judgment, for he recited, or
'rather reckoned up, the positions of these authors,
'but never examined them in order to find out which
'was true, or came nearest to the truth, but left them all
'untouched; and because Boetius was received by all,
'he dared not to contradict him; and though he seems
'in some instances to agree with Ptolemy, yet dares
'he not to assert which of the two he thought the
'best, but sometimes is drawn on this side, sometimes
'on that, so that nothing certain or fixed can be had
'from him: for sometimes, to favour Boetius and the
'Pythagoreans, he says in that book of music which
'he wrote in the Italian language, that he wondered
'at the inadvertency, as he calls it, of Ptolemy, who
'says that the diapason with the diatessaron is a con-
'sonant when it does not answer either to a multiple
'or superparticular proportion; and a little after, in
'the same book, he assumes the sesquiquarta and ses-
'quiquinta of Ptolemy, to constitute from them the
'greater and lesser third, contrary to Boetius and all
'the Pythagoreans.'

In the thirty-first chapter he delivers his sentiments
of Glareanus in these words :—

'Henricus Glareanus was a man excellently
'versed in all good arts, and has exhibited to the
'world several specimens of his learning, for he
'wrote a treatise on Geography, not less useful than
'concise and clear, which is read in many schools; he
'also made notes on the Odes of Horace, replete with
'all kind of erudition; and as to what concerns
'music, he taught it in three books, according to the
'rule of the ancient modes, as he himself thinks,
'which work he entitled Dodecachordon. In it he
'has gathered many examples both of the simple
'cantus and that of many forms, which at once give
'great pleasure and profit; and though he never
'wrote any thing of speculative music, yet he con-
'fesses in many places that he had applied himself
'too much to it, and that he had employed a great
'deal of time in the study thereof, especially in the
'reading of Boetius, which he manifestly shows in
'a preface really long enough, published with that
'work, in which he mentions that he corrected five
'books of the music of Boetius, which he says abounded
'with many errors, and illustrated it with several
'figures.'

In the thirty-second chapter he considers the
speculations of Ludovicus Follianus; and as to his
division of the diapason, he says it is the same with
that of Ptolemy, called the syntonous, intense, or
stretched diatonic, which he says Didymus invented
many years ago, with this difference, that Didymus
gave to the sesquinonal tone the first place in the
tetrachord, whereas Ptolemy gives it to the sesquioctave tone. He nevertheless says of the intense
diatonic in general, that it is a division of all others
the most correct and grateful to the ear. He says
that many of the ratios investigated by Follianus had
before his time been discovered by Bartholomeus
Ramis, a Spaniard, who is blamed by Franchinus for

differing from Boetius. Salinas says that he himself,
long before the treatise of Follianus had been read to
him, had made many of the discoveries therein contained, and that he had from time to time communicated them to Bartholomeus Escobedus, a man excellently versed in both parts of music, and his very
great friend, who told him there was a certain author
who had treated of all those things in the same
manner as he had thought on, and this author he
afterwards found to be Follianus. He blames
Follianus for using three semitones, which he calls
greater, lesser, and least, when no one else had
noticed more than two, and many but one; the
greater of the three is in the ratio $\frac{25}{27}$, the lesser $\frac{15}{16}$,
and the least $\frac{24}{25}$, the two last he says are well constituted, but the first he condemns as inconcinnous
and ungrateful to the ear.

He concludes his remarks on the writings of the
modern musicians with a character of Zarlino, of
whom he says that he was well skilled in both parts
of music, for that as to what regarded the practice,
he had been scholar to Adrian Willaert, the most
famous symphonist of his time, and succeeded him in
his school at Venice; and on the theory of the
science he wrote much better than those that went
before him.

The remaining three books of Salinas's work are
on the subject of the Rythmus, and are a copious
dissertation on the various kinds of metre used by
the Greek, the Roman, and, in honour of his own
country, the Spanish poets. In the course of his
enquiries touching their nature and use, he takes
frequent occasion to cite and commend St. Augustine,
who also wrote on the subject. The laws of metre
have an immediate reference to poetry; but Salinas
in a variety of instances shews that they are applicable
to music, and that the several kinds of air that occur
in the composition of music and of dances, such as
the Pavan, the Passamezzo, and others, consist in a
regular commixture and interchange of long and
short quantities.

For a character of this valuable work let it suffice
to say, that a greater degree of credit is due to it
than to almost any other of the kind, the production
of modern times, and that for this reason: the author
was a practical musician, that is to say an organist,
as well as a theorist, and throughout his book he
manifests a disposition the farthest removed that can
possibly be imagined from that credulity which betrayed Glareanus and some others into error; this
disposition led him to enquire into and examine very
minutely the doctrines of the Greek writers; and the
boldness with which he reprehends them does almost
persuade us that when he differs from them the truth
is on his side. This seems to be certain, and it is
wonderful to consider it, that notwithstanding the
ancients were divided in their notions of the genera,
and that the enarmonic genus was by much the most
difficult to comprehend of them all, Salinas, a man
deprived of the faculty of seeing, at the distance of
more than two thousand years after it had grown
into disuse, investigated and accurately defined it.

BOOK X.   CHAP. LXXXVIII.

THE musical characters hitherto spoken of, were calculated not only for vocal performance, but were applicable to every instrument in use after the time of inventing them, excepting the lute, which, for reasons best known to the performers on it, had a series of characters appropriated to that and others of the same class; when or by whom these characters were invented is not known. This kind of notation, which is by certain letters of the Roman alphabet, is called the Tablature, the first intimations of which are to be met with in the Musurgia of Ottomarus Luscinius. The Fronimo of Galilei is in the title-page called a Dialogue 'sopra l'Arte del bene in-'tavolare:' this kind of tablature differs from the other, the author, according to the manner of the Italians, as Mersennus says, making use of numbers instead of letters, and of straight or hooked lines instead of notes.*

Mersennus says that several skilful men had laboured to improve the Tablature, but yet insinuates that they affected to make a mystery of it, from whence he infers that diversity of notation between them. He adds that Adrian Le Roy is the only one who has in truth given to the world the precepts of the Tablature.† This man was a bookseller at Paris, and wrote the book which Mersennus above alludes to, with the title of 'Briefve et facile Instruction 'pour aprendre la Tablature à bien accorder, con-'duire, et disposer la Main sur la Guiterne,' which, together with another book of his of the same kind, intitled 'Instruction de partir toute Musique des huit 'divers Tons en Tablature de Luth,' were published about 1570, with a recommendatory preface by one Jacques Gohory, a musician, and a friend of the author.

This being the first book of the kind ever published, it was esteemed a great curiosity, and as such was immediately on its publication translated into sundry languages; that into the English has only the initials F. K. for the name of the translator, and was printed by John Kingston in 1574. The first of these books exhibits the lute in this form :—‡

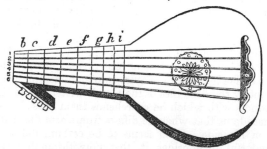

and represents by the following figure the posture for holding and playing on it :—

The lute which Le Roy treats of, is supposed to consist of six strings, or rather eleven, for that the five larger are doubled; and in the Tablature the stave of five lines answers to the five upper strings of the instrument, the lower or base string it seems being sufficiently denoted by its proximity to the fifth string, signified by the lowest line of the stave.

The frets come next to be explained : these are small strings tied about the neck of the lute at proper distances, eight in number, and figured by the letters b c d e f g h i;§ the letter a is omitted in the above series, forasmuch as wherever it is found the string is to be struck open. The general idea of the tablature therefore is this, the lines of the stave give the chords respectively, and the letters the points at which they are to be stopped, and consequently the notes of any given composition, the instrument being previously tuned for the purpose, as the precepts of the lute require.

As to the characters for time used in the tablature,

* De Instrumentis Harmonicis, lib. I. prop. xviii. pag. 24.

† Ibid.

‡ The above figure represents the lute in its original form, but the many improvements made in this instrument make it necessary to remark that the lute, simply constructed as this is, is called the French lute; the first improvement of it was the Theorbo or Cithara Bijuga, so called as having two necks, the second or longest whereof sustains the four last rows of chords, which give the deepest and gravest sounds; its use is to play thorough bass in the accompaniment of the voice. Brossard intimates that it was invented in France by the Sieur Hotteman, and thence introduced into Italy. But Kircher gives a different account

of the matter, saying that it received its name from a certain Neapolitan who first doubled the neck of the Testudo or lute, and added several chords to it. He says that the author of this improvement, with a kind of pun, gave to this instrument the name of Tiorba, from its near resemblance to a utensil so called, in which the glovers of Italy were wont, as in a mortar, to pound perfumes. Kircher adds, that Hieronymus Kapsperger, a noble German, was the first that brought the Theorbo into repute, and that in his time it had the preference of all other instruments. The strings of the Theorbo, properly so called, are single, nevertheless there are many who double the bass strings with an octave, and the small ones with an unison, in which case it assumes a new appellation, and is called the Arch-lute. Mersennus is extremely accurate in his description of the lute and the Theorbo, but he has not noted the diversity between the latter and the Arch-lute.

§ It seems that the use of the small letters of the alphabet in tablature was at first peculiar to the French. The Italians and other nations instead thereof making use of cyphers and other characters. Le Roy, pag. 64. But the French method, soon after the publication of Le Roy's book, became general.

they were of this form ⌐ ⌐ ⌐ answering to the minim, the crotchet, and the quaver, and placed over the stave in the manner represented in the subsequent example.

The other tract, intitled 'Instruction de partir 'toute Musique des huit divers Tons en Tablature 'de Luth,' directs the method of setting music al-

ready composed in proper notes in tablature for the lute ; and contains a great variety of examples chosen out of the works of Orlando de Lasso ;* the following, which is the first strain only of a song of his, beginning 'Quand mon Mary vient de dehors,' in four parts with the Tablature, may serve as a specimen of this kind of notation :—†

The ninth and last chapter of this latter book of Le Roy is on the subject of strings, concerning which there is much curious matter in Mersennus, as also a rule for trying them, and distinguishing between a true and a false string : but because this rule is

also to be found in Le Roy's book, and most probably was by Mersennus taken from thence, the whole of the chapter, which is very short, is here inserted.

'To put the laste hande to this worke, I will 'not omitte to give you to understande how to

* Gohory, in his preface to Le Roy's book, sums up the character of Orlando de Lasso in those words: 'Here then will I end, after I have 'advertised you that all the examples of this book be taken and chosen 'out of Orland de Lassis, of whom I will further witness, that he is this 'day, without danger of offence to any man, esteemed the most ex- 'cellent musitian of this time, as well in grave matters, as meane and 'more pleasaunt ; a thing given from above to fewe other, in which he 'hath attayned not only the perfection of melodie, but also a certaine grace 'of sound beyond all other, such as Appelles did accompt of Venus por- 'trature ; wherein he hath more than all other observed to fit the har- 'monie to the matter, expressing all partes of the passions thereof: being 'the first that hath eschewed bondes and common holdinges of the letter, 'by right placing of the sillabelles upon the notes, and observing the 'accent in French, and quantitie in Latine.'

† It seems that the method of notation by the tablature was also

adapted to the Viol de Gamba. In the second book of Songs or Ayres with Tablature, by John Dowland, printed in 1600, is a lesson in tabla- ture for the lute and bass viol, entitled Dowland's Adew for Master Oliver Cromwell ; and in a book printed in 1603, entitled The Schoole of Musicke, by Thomas Robinson, lutenist, is a song for the viol by tabla- ture. Nay, it was also used for the treble violin, and that so late as 1682 ; and, which is very remarkable, there were then two ways of tuning it, at the choice of the performer, by fifths and by eighths ; this appears in a book entitled Apollo's Banquet, containing Instructions and Variety of new tunes, Ayres, and Jiggs, for the treble Violin, the third edition published in that year by John Playford. Anthony Wood, who loved and understood music, also played on the violin ; and, as he himself re- lates, practised a still different method of tuning, viz., by fourths. Vide Life of Antony à Wood, at the end of Hearne's Caii Vindiciæ, and lately reprinted by itself.

'knowe stringes, whereof the best come to us out of
'Almaigne, on this side the town of Munic, and from
'Aquila in Italie; before we put them on the lute
'it is nedefull to prove them between the handes in
'maner as is sette forthe in the figures hereafter
'pictured, which shewe manifestlie on the finger and
'to the eye the difference from the true with the
'false; that is to wete, the true is knowen by this,
'that in strikyng hym betwene the fingers hee muste
'shewe to divide hymselfe juste in twoo, and that
'for so muche as shall reche from the bridge belowe
'to the toppe of the necke, because it maketh no
'matter for the rest of the stringes that goeth among
'the pinnes; notwithstandyng ye maie not be satis-
'fied in assaiyng the stringe holden only at that
'length, but that you must also prove hym in stryk-
'ing hym, treying holden at shorter lengthes to be
'well assured of his certaine goodness and perfection.
'Also the false strynge is knowen by the shew of
'many strynges, which it representeth when it is
'striken between the fingers; so muste you continewe
'the same triall in stryking the stryng till you
'perceive the tooken of the good to separate hym
'from the badde, accordyng to the figures followyng.'

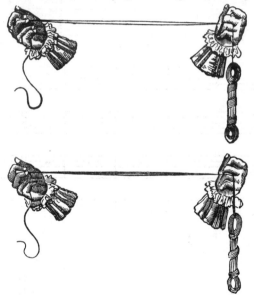

COSTANZO PORTA, a Franciscan friar, and a native
of Cremona, is highly celebrated among the musicians
of the sixteenth century. In the earlier part of his
life he was Maestro di Capella in the cathedral church
of Osimo as it is called, from the Latin Auximum,
a small city on the river Musone near Ancona, but
was afterwards advanced to the same station in the
church of Loretto. He was the author of that most
ingenious composition published first by Artusi in
his treatise 'Delle Imperfettioni della moderna
'Musica,' and inserted in the earlier part of this
work, and which is so contrived, as that besides that
the parts are inverted, it may be sung as well backward as forward. He is supposed to have died in
the year 1580, and has left behind him Motets for
five voices, printed at Venice in 1546, and other
works of the like kind, printed also there in 1566
and 1580. In an oration pronounced by Ansaldus

Cotta of Cremona in 1553, 'pro Instauratione Stu-
'diorum Cremonæ,' is the following eulogium on
'him: Constantius Porta non tam hujus urbis, quam
'Franciscanæ familiæ decus eximium, cujus in musica
'facultatem præstantiam plerisque cum Italiæ urbibus
'Roma potissimum, omnium regina gentium est ad-
'mirata.' Vide Arisii Cremonam literatam, pag. 453.
And elsewhere in the same oration he is styled
'Musicorum omnium præter invidiam facile princeps.'
Vide Draudii Bibl. Class. pag. 1693.

GIOVANNI PIERLUIGI DA PALESTRINA *(a Portrait)*
was, as his name imports, a native of the ancient
Præneste, now corruptly called Palestrina, and still
more corruptly Palestina.* He flourished in the
middle of the sixteenth century; and the year of his
birth is thus ascertained by Andrea Adami da Bolsena,
master of the pontifical chapel under Clement XI.
who professes to give the particulars of his life.
'The time of Palestrina's birth is not precisely to
'be ascertained, by reason that the records of the
'city of Palestrina, which may be supposed to con-
'tain the register of his birth, were destroyed at the
'sacking thereof by the duke d' Alva in 1557; but
'it appears by a book intitled Le grotte Vaticane,
'written by a person named Torrigio, that he was in
'the sixty-fifth year of his age when he died;' and
from other authentic evidences the same writer,
Adami, fixes the time of his death on the second
day of February 1594, from whence it may be computed that he must have been born some time in the
year 1529.†

The author who has enabled us thus satisfactorily
to settle the period of Palestrina's life, has been less
fortunate in ascertaining the name of his master.
He says that he was a scholar of Gaudio Mell,
Fiammengo, *i. e.* a Fleming, or native of Flanders;
this assertion is grounded on the testimony of Antimo
Liberati, a singer in the pontifical chapel, who has
given an account of Palestrina and his supposed
master in these words:—

'Among the many strangers who settled in Italy
'and Rome, the first who gave instructions for sing-
'ing and harmonic modulations was Gaudio Mell,
'Flandro, a man of great talents, and of a sweet
'flowing style, who instituted at Rome a noble and
'excellent school for music, where many pupils ren-
'dered themselves conspicuous in that science, but
'above all Gio. Pier Luigi Palestrina, who, as if
'distinguished by nature herself, surpassed all other

* The name Gianetto Palestina occurs in many collections of madrigals and other compositions published about this time; and in the Storia
della Musica of Padre Martini, pag. 198, is the following note: 'Giovanni
'Pier Luigi da Palestrina detto anche Gianetto da Palestrina come dal
'lib. I. intitolato Li Amorosi Ardori di diversi eccell. Musici a 5. raccolti
'da Cesare Corradi.'
The truth of this assertion, notwithstanding the authority on which it
is grounded, is at least questionable. In a collection of madrigals, intitled Medodia Olympica, published by Pietro Philippi in 1594, we meet
with the name Gio. Prenestini to the madrigals, 'Mori quasi il mio Core,'
and 'Veramente in amore;' and also with the name Gianetto Palestina
to 'Non son le vostri mani,' and 'O bella Ninfa.' And in a collection of
motets intitled 'Florilegium sacrarum cantionum quinque vocum pro
'diebus Dominicis et Festis totius anni e celeberrimis nostri temporis
'musicis,' printed by Petrus Phalesius of Antwerp in 1611, the name Jo.
Aloysius Prænestinus occurs in seven places, and that of Gianetto de
Palestina in four.
The argument hence arising is, that if both those names were intended
to denote the same person, the distinction between them would hardly
have been preserved in the instances above adduced in one and the same
publication.

† Vide Osservazioni per ben regolare il Coro della Cappella Pontificia,
fatte da Andrea Adami da Bolsena, pag. 169.

GIO. PIERLUIGI DA PALESTRINA,

COMPOSITORE DELLA CAPPELLA PONTIFICIA E

PRENCIPE DELLA MUSICA.

MDLXII.

rivals, and even his own masters. This great genius, 'guided by a peculiar faculty, the gift of God, adopted 'a style of harmony so elegant, so noble, so learned, 'so easy, and so pleasing both to the connoisseur and 'the ignorant, that in a mass composed on purpose, 'sung before pope Marcellus Cervinus and the sacred 'college of cardinals, he made that pontiff alter the 'intention he had of enforcing the bull of John 'XXII. which abolished entirely church-music under 'the penalty of excommunication. This ingenious 'man, by his astonishing skill and the divine melody 'of that mass, plainly convinced his holiness that 'those disagreeable jars between the music and the 'words so often heard in churches, were not owing 'to any defect in the art, but to the want of skill in 'the composers; and Paul IV. his successor, to whom 'he dedicated the mass entitled Missa Papæ Marcelli, 'appointed him perpetual composer and director in 'the pontifical chapel,* a dignity which has been 'vacant ever since his death.† This mass is now 'and ever will be performed, as long as there is 'a world, in the sacred temples at Rome, and in all 'other places where they have been so fortunate as 'to procure the compositions of a genius whose 'works breathe divine harmony, and enable us to 'sing in a style so truly sublime the praises of our 'Maker.'‡

Adami has adopted the facts contained in this relation, and acquiesced in the assertion that Gaudio Mell, a Fleming, was the master of a noble school at Rome, where the principles and practice of music were taught, and that Palestrina was his disciple.

It is to be feared that Liberati had no better authority for the particulars of his relation than bare report, for evidence is wanting that such a person as Gaudio Mell, a Fleming and musician, ever existed: his name does not occur in the list of Flemish musicians given by Guicciardini in his History of the Low Countries, nor in any of those collections of vocal music published by Pietro Phalesio, Hubert Waelrant, Andrew Pevernage, Pietro Philippi, Melchior Borchgrevinck, and others, between the years 1593 and 1620, nor in Printz's History of Music, nor in that of Bontempi, nor in the Musical Lexicon of John Godfrey Walther, which contains an accurate account of musicians from the time of Pythagoras down to the year 1732.

It may indeed be suspected that Liberati by Gaudio Mell might understand Goudimel, but his Christian name was Claude, for which reason he is by Monsieur Varillas confounded with Claude Le Jeune. Neither

* Paul IV. succeeded to the pontificate in 1560, and at that time Girolamo Maccabei was Maestro della Cappella Pontificia; and in 1567 he was succeeded by Egidio Valenti; these were both ecclesiastics, and not musicians, and the latter is styled 'Maestro del Collegio de Cantoria 'della Cappella Pontificia,' from whence it may be conjectured that this was an office that referred to the government of the college, and not to the performance of service in the chapel; so that by this appointment Palestrina seems to have been virtually Maestro di Cappella, as well of the pope's chapel as of the church of St. Peter, but that he did not choose to assume the title, it having been already appropriated to an officer of a different kind.

† This is a mistake of Antimo Liberati, and is noted by Adami, for Felice Anerio succeeded Palestrina in the office of Compositore da Cappella Pontificia immediately on his decease, as appears by a memorandum in a book of Ippolito Gamboce, Puntatore, i. e. register of the college, or as some say, an officer whose duty it is to appoint the functions for each day's service in the chapel. See the account of Felice Anerio hereafter given.

‡ Lettera scritta dal Sig. Antimo Liberati in risposta ad una del Sig. Ovidio Persapegi, 1688, pag. 22.

was Goudimel a Fleming, but a native of Franche Comté, as Bayle infers from certain verses which fix the place of his birth upon the Doux, a river that runs by Bezançon; and Franche Comté is not in Flanders, but in Burgundy.§

But besides that the master of Palestrina is said to have been a Fleming, there are other reasons for supposing that Goudimel was not the person. Goudimel was a protestant, and, as Thuanus relates, set the Psalms of David translated into métre by Clement Marot and Theodore Beza, to various and most pleasing tunes, which in his time were sung both publicly and privately by the protestants. He was massacred at Lyons, and not at Paris, as some assert, in 1572, and has a place and an eulogium in the protestant martyrology.||

After stating the above facts it must appear needless to insist on the improbability that Palestrina, whom we must suppose to have been born of parents of the Romish communion, should have ever been the disciple of a protestant, an intimate of Calvin, and a composer of the music to a translation of the Psalms into vernacular metre; and who, so far was he from having instituted a music-school at Rome, as is elsewhere asserted, does not appear by any of the accounts extant of him to have past the limits of his own country.

For these reasons it may be presumed that Liberati is mistaken in the name of Palestrina's master, who though in truth a Fleming, and of the name of Mell, seems to have been a different person from him whom he has dignified with that character. In a word, the current tradition is, and Dr. Pepusch himself acquiesced in it, that Palestrina was a disciple of Rinaldo del Mell [Renatus de Mell] a well-known composer in the sixteenth century, who is described by Printz and Walther as being a native of Flanders, and to have flourished about the year 1538, at which time Palestrina was nine years old, a proper age for instruction.

At the age of thirty-three, and in the year 1562, Palestrina was made Maestro di Cappella di S. Maria Maggiore, and in 1571 he was appointed to the same honourable office in the church of St. Peter at Rome, in the room of Giovanni Animuccia, which he held for the remainder of his life, honoured with the favour and protection of the succeeding popes, particularly Sixtus V.

Antimo Liberata relates that Palestrina, in conjunction with a very intimate friend and fellow-student [condiscepolo] of his, Gio. Maria Nanino by name, established a school at Rome, in which, notwithstanding his close attachment to his studies and the duties of his employment, the former often appeared assisting the students in their exercises, and deciding the differences which sometimes arose between the professors that frequented it.

In the course of his studies Palestrina discovered the error of the German and other musicians, who had in a great measure corrupted the practice of music by the introduction of intricate proportions, and set about framing a style for the church, grave, decent, and plain, and which, as it admitted of none

§ Vide Bayle in art. GOUDIMEL. || Ibid.

of those unnatural commixtures of dissimilar times, which were become the disgrace of music, left ample scope for invention. Influenced by that love of simplicity which is discoverable in all his works, he, in conjunction with Francesco Soriano, reduced the measures in the Cantus Ecclesiasticus to three, namely the Long, the Breve, and the Semibreve.*

Of many works which Palestrina composed, one

* Vide Il Canto Ecclesiastico da D. Marzio Erculeo. In Modano, 1686, pag. 3.

of the most capital is his Masses, published at Rome in 1572, in large folio, with this title, 'Joannis Petri 'Loysii Prænestini in Basilica S. Petri de urbe ca- 'pellæ magistri missarum, liber primus,' under which is a curious print from wood or metal after the design of some great painter, as must be inferred from the excellence of the drawing, representing the author making an offering of his book to the pope in the manner here exhibited :—

J. Hodgson, Sculp.

On the back of the title-page is a short commendatory epistle to Julius III. the then pope. Of these masses, which are five in number, and it is to be doubted whether Palestrina ever published any more in this form, four are for four voices, and one for five.   Many parts of each are composed in canon, and bespeak the learning and ingenuity of their author. The masses are printed in parts, on a coarse but very legible type, with Gothic initial letters curiously designed and executed.*

There are also extant of his composition Motets and Hymns for 4, 5, and 6 voices, printed in large folio, and published in 1589; some of these motets were also printed in a collection intitled 'Florilegium

'sacrarum cantionum quinque vocum pro diebus 'dominicis et festis totius anni, e celeberrimis nostri 'temporis musicis.'   This collection was given to the world in 1609 by Petrus Phalesius, a printer of Antwerp, who was a man of learning, and, as it should seem, a lover of music, for he published many other collections of music, and before his house had the sign of king David playing on the harp.   It is in the motets of Palestrina that we discover that grandeur and dignity of style, that artful modulation and sweet interchange of new and original harmonies, for which he is so justly celebrated; with respect to these excellencies let the following composition speak for him :—

* The art of printing music in letter-press or on metal types, was at this time arrived at great perfection, it was invented by one Ottavio de Petrucci of Fossombrone in Italy, who in the year 1515 and 1516 published the masses of Iodocus Pratensis. Osserv. da Andrea Adami, pag. 160. And in France it was improved by Pierre Ballard, as appears by the works of Claude le Jeune, published by him.

GIO. PIERLUIGI DA PALESTRINA.

Dr. Aldrich adapted English words, that is to say part of the sixty-third psalm, 'O God, thou art my God,' to the music of this motet, and it is frequently sung in our cathedrals as an anthem, as is also another of Palestrina, beginning 'Doctor Bonus,' to the words 'We have heard with our ears, O Lord,' these are remarkable instances of that faculty which Dr. Aldrich possessed of naturalizing as it were the compositions of the old Italian masters, and accommodating them to an English ear, by words perhaps as well suited to the music as those to which they were originally framed.

Bleau, in his Admiranda Italia, part II. pag. 312, relates that at the erection of the famous antique obelisk near the Vatican in 1586, Palestrina on the twenty-seventh day of September in that year, with eighteen choral singers, assisted in celebrating that stupendous work, which at this day does honour to the pontificate of Sixtus V.

Kircher, in the Musurgia, tom. I. lib. VII. cap. v. has given a Crucifixus of Palestrina, which he says is

deservedly the admiration of all musicians, as being the work of a most exquisite genius. Many of the masses of Palestrina are strict canon, a species of composition which he thoroughly understood, but his motets are in general fugues, in which it is hard to say whether the grandeur and sublimity of the point, or the close contexture of the harmony is most to be admired. As to the points or subjects of his fugues, though consisting in general of but few bars, nay, sometimes of no greater a number of notes than are usually contained in a bar, they were assumed as themes or subjects for other compositions, and this not by young students, but by masters of the first eminence. Numberless are the instances to be met with of compositions of this kind, but some of the most remarkable are contained in a work of Abbate Domenico dal Pane, a sopranist of the pontificial chapel, published in 1687, intitled ' Messe a quattro, ' cinque, sei, et otto voci, estratte da esquisiti motetti ' del Palestrina,' these are seven masses, of which seven motets of Palestrina, namely, Doctor bonus,

Domine quando veneris, Stella quam viderant Magi, O Beatum virum, Jubilate Deo, Canite tuba in Sion, Fratres ego enim accepi, are severally the theme.

The superior excellence of these compositions, it seems, excited in the contemporary musicians both admiration and envy. Johannes Hieronymus Kapsberger, a German, made an attempt on the reputation of Palestrina, which succeeded as it deserved. Kapsberger, who is represented by Doni as a man of great assurance and volubility of tongue, by the assistance of a friend procured admission to a certain bishop, to whom he insinuated that the compositions of Palestrina usually sung in the episcopal palace were rude and inelegant in respect to the melody and harmony, and that the repetition of the same words, but more especially of the same point or musical subject, in short, that which constitutes a fugue in one and the same cantus, detracted from the merit of the composition. The bishop, who seems to have been a weak man, listened with attention to a proposal of Kapsberger, which meant nothing less than the banishing from his chapel the music of Palestrina, and admitting that of his opponent in his stead; Kapsberger succeeded, and his music was given to the singers of the bishop's chapel; they at first refused, but were at length compelled to sing it, but they did

it in such a manner as soon induced him to desist from his attempt, and wisely decline a competition in which he had not the least chance of success. Kapsberger was a voluminous composer; he excelled all of his time in playing on the Theorbo, an instrument which he had greatly improved and brought into repute, and is represented by Kircher as a person of great abilities; the character he gives of him is, that he was an excellent performer on most instruments, a man noble by birth, and of great reputation for prudence and learning; in this he differs widely from Doni, but it seems that Kircher had received great assistance from Kapsberger while he was writing the Musurgia.

Palestrina seems to have devoted his whole attention to the duties of his station, for the improvement of the church style was the great object of his studies; nevertheless he composed a few madrigals, which have been preserved and are published.

In the year 1594 he published 'Madrigali Spirit-'uali a cinque voci,' dedicated to a patroness of his, the grand duchess of Tuscany; the style of these compositions is remarkably chaste and pathetic, the words are Italian, and purport to be hymns and penitential songs to the number of thirty.* The following is the ninth of them:—

* The dedication of the book is thus dated : ' Di Roma il primo giorno del anno 1594 ;' from whence it may be collected that this was his last work, and that it was published just a month before his decease, for he died on the second day of February in that year.

GIOVANNI MARIA NANINO

DA VALLERANO,

CANTORE DELLA CAPPELLA PONTIFICIA.

MDLXXVII.

GIO. PIERLUIGI DA PALESTRINA.

How long Palestrina enjoyed the honourable employment of Maestro di Capella in the church of St. Peter at Rome is above ascertained, by the year of his appointment and that of his death. His historian has in the way of his function mentioned some particulars relative to that event; he says that his funeral was attended not only by all the musicians of Rome, but by a multitude of the people, and was celebrated by three choirs, who sang a 'Libera me, Domine,' in five parts, of his own composition; that his body was interred in the church of St. Peter, before the altar of St. Simon and St. Jude, a privilege due to the merit of so great a man, inclosed in a sheet of lead, with this inscription, 'Petrus Aloysius Prænestinus Musicæ 'Princeps.' It is said that an original picture of him is yet extant in the archives of the pope's chapel, and it is probable that the portrait which Adami has given of him is taken from it. By this, which conveys the idea of a man remarkably mean in his appearance, it seems that his bodily endowments bore no proportion to those of his mind.

To enumerate the testimonies of authors in favour of Palestrina would be an endless task. John Baptist Doni before-mentioned, a profoundly learned musician, and whose partiality for the music of the ancients would hardly suffer him to admire that of the moderns, seems without hesitation to acquiesce in the general opinion that he was the greatest man in his time. Agostina Pisa, in a treatise intitled 'Battuta della Musica di-chiarata,' printed at Rome in 1611, pag. 87, calls him the honour of music, and prince of musicians. He elsewhere styles him 'Gian Pietro Aloisio Palestina 'luce et splendore della musica.' Giovanni Maria Bononcini also calls him 'Principe de musica,' as does Angelo Berardi, a very sensible and intelligent writer; this latter also styles him the father of music, and as such he is in general considered by all that take occasion to speak of him.

The following catalogue is exhibited for the use of such as may be desirous of collecting the works of this great man : 'Dodici libri di messe a 4, 5, 6, 8 voci, 'stamp. in Roma, ed. in Venct. 1554, 1567, 1570, '1572, 1582, 1585, 1590, 1591, 1594, 1599, 1600, '1601. Due libri d' Offertorii a 5, Ven. 1594. Due 'libri di Motetti a 4, Ven. 1571, 1606. Quattro libri 'di Motetti a 5, 6, 7, 8 voci, Ven. 1575, 1580, 1584, '1586. Magnificat 8 tonum, Romæ. 1591. Hymni 'totius anni 4 voc. Romæ et Ven. 1589. Due libri di 'madrig. a 4 voci, Ven. 1586, 1605. Due libri di 'madrig. a 5 voci, Ven. 1594. Litanie a 4, Ven. 1600.

CHAP. LXXXIX.

GIOVANNI MARIA NANINO, *(a Portrait,)* a condisciple or fellow-student of Palestrina, having been brought up under the same master, namely, Rinaldo del Mell, was a native of Vallerano, and in 1577 was appointed a singer in the pontifical chapel, where are preserved many excellent compositions of his. He became afterwards Maestro di Cappella di S. Maria Maggiore, and was probably the immediate successor of Palestrina in that office. Some very fine madrigals composed by him are to be found in the collections published by Andrew Pevernage, Pietro Phalesio, Hubert Waelrant, Pietro Philippi, and others, with the titles of Harmonia Celeste, Musica Divina, Symphonia Angelica, and Melodia Olympica. Padre Martini, in the catalogue of authors at the end of his Storia della Musica, tom. I., takes notice of two manuscripts of his that are extant, the one entitled ' Cen- ' tocinquantasette Contrapunte e Canoni a 2, 3, 4, 5, ' 6, 7, 8, 11 voci sopra del Canto fermo intitolato la ' Base di Costanzo Festa ;' the other, ' Trattato di ' Contrapunto con la Regola per far Contrapunto a ' mente di Gio. Maria, e Bernardino Nanino suo ' nipote.' Sebastian Raval, a Spaniard, and a cele- brated contrapuntist, was foiled by him in a compe- tition between them which was the abler composer.

It has already been mentioned that Nanino, in conjunction with his friend Palestrina, established at Rome a school for the study of music. Antimo Liberata, who relates this fact, intimates that this seminary was frequented by many eminent professors of the science, who resorted thither for improvement; and that Palestrina, besides taking his part in the in- struction of the youth, was a moderator in the dis- putes that sometimes arose among them. The same author adds, that among the many excellent musi- cians that were there educated, Bernardino Nanino, a younger brother of him of whom we are now speak- ing, was distinguished as a wonderful genius, and as having improved music by the introduction of a new and original style ; there is nevertheless nothing ex- tant of his composition but a work printed at Rome in 1620, entitled ' Salmi à 4 voci per le Domeniche, ' Solennita della Madonna ed Apostoli con doi Mag- ' nificat, uno à 4 e l' altro à 8 voci.' Antonio Cifra was also a disciple in this school.

FELICE ANERIO, (a Portrait,) a disciple of the elder Nanino, was the immediate successor of Pales- trina in the station of composer to the pontifical chapel.* He had the character of an excellent con- trapuntist ; many of his compositions are preserved in the library of the chapel, and there is extant a valuable collection of madrigals by him, printed at Antwerp in 1610.

RUGGIERO GIOVANELLI (a Portrait,) was master of the chapels of St. Lewis and St. Apollinare, and the immediate successor of Palestrina in the church of St. Peter at Rome ;† and also a singer in the pontifical chapel : a collection of madrigals by him, printed at Venice, is extant ; he composed also many masses, amongst which is one for eight voices, called ' Vestiva i colli,' taken from a madrigal with those initial words of Gianetto Palestrina, which is much celebrated.

In the year 1581 a book appeared in the world with this silly title, ' Il tesoro illuminato, di tutti i ' tuoni di Canto figurato, con alcuni bellissimi secreti ' non da altri più scritti : nuovamente composto dal ' R. P. frate illuminato Aijguino Bresciano, dell' or- ' dine serafico d' osservanza.' Notwithstanding the very emphatical title of this book, it contains very little worthy the attention of a curious reader. The author is lavish in the praises of Marchettus of Padua, and Spataro, and of his irrefragable master Peter Aron, whose name he never mentions without that extravagant epithet.

About this time lived PIETRO PONTIO of Parma ; he composed and published, about the year 1580, three books of masses. He was the author, also, of a book with the following title, ' Ragionamento di ' Musica del Rev. M. Don Pietro Pontio Parmegiano, ' ove si tratta de' pasaggi della consonantie e disso- ' nantie, buoni e non buoni ; e del modo di far Mot- ' tetti, Messe, Salmi, e altre compositioni ; d'alcuni ' avertimenti per il contrapuntista e compositore e ' altre cose pertinenti alla musica,' printed at Parma 1588, in quarto, a very entertaining dialogue, and re- plete with musical erudition.

HORATIO VECCHI of Modena was greatly celebrated for his vocal compositions at this time : our country- man Peacham was, as he himself relates, his disciple.‡

---

* The following account of his appointment, and the ceremonies at- tending it, is cited by Adami from the book of Ippolito Gamboci, the puntatore heretofore mentioned, with a remark that Antimo Liberata had little reason to say that Palestrina was the last composer to the chapel, seeing that Anerio succeeded him in that honourable employment.

' La mattina della Domenica delle palme venne in cappella il Sig. Luca ' Cavalcanti maestro di camera dell' illustriss. e reverendiss. Sig. Card. ' Aldrobandini, Nipote di N. S. papa Clemente VIII. e disse al collegio ' da parte del suddetto Sig. Cardinale, che sua santità aveva graziato ' Messer Felice Anerio del posto vacato per la morte di Pierluigi da ' Palestrina, e che lo aveva accettato per compositore della cappella, e che ' gia godeva la provisione, e però sua Signoria illustrissima pregava il ' collegio, che lo volesse accettare in detto posto, e che si contentassero ' tutti di far una fede di questa ammissione ; come fù fatto.'

† By this it should seem that the places which Palestrina held were at his decease divided ; for Felice Anerio is expressly said to have succeeded him as Compositore della Cappella, and here it is said that Giovanelli was appointed the successor to Palestrina in the church of St. Peter, of which Palestrina was Maestro di Cappella.

‡ This writer has, in his usual quaint manner, given a short character of Vecchi and his works, which, as he was a man of veracity and judg- ment, may be depended on. ' I bring you now mine owne master Horatio ' Vecchi of Modena, beside goodness of aire, most pleasing of all other ' for his conceipt and variety, wherewith all his works are singularly ' beautified, as well his madrigals of five and six parts, as those his can- ' zonets printed at Norimberge, wherein for tryall sing his " Vivo in ' fuoco amoroso Lucretia mia," where upon " Io catenato moro," with ' excellent judgment hee driveth a crotchet thorow many minims, causing ' it to resemble a chaine with the linkes ; againe in " S' io potesi raccor' ' " i mei sospiri," the breaking of the word Sospiri with crotchet and crot- ' chet rest in sighes ; and that " fa mi un canzone," &c. to make one ' sleep at noone with sundry other of like conceipt and pleasant invention.' Compleat Gentleman, 102.

The Compleat Gentleman was written by Henry Peacham, an author of some note in the reign of James I. It treats of nobility in general. ' Of the dignity and necessity of learning in princes and nobilitie. The ' dutie of parents in the education of their children. Of a gentleman's ' carriage in the universitie. Of stile in speaking and writing of history. ' Of cosmography. Of memorable observations in the survey of the ' earth. Of geometry. Of poetry. Of musicke. Of statues, and ' medalls, and antiquities. Of drawing and painting, with the lives of ' painters. Of sundry blazonnes both ancient and modern. Of armory, ' or blazing armes, with the antiquity of heralds. Of exercise of body. ' Of reputation and carriage. Of travaile. Of warre,' and of many other particulars, to which is added the Gentleman's Exercise, or an exquisite Practice for drawing all Manner of Beasts, making Colours, &c. quarto, 1634. This book abounds with a great number of curious particulars, and was in high estimation with the gentry even of the last age. Sir Charles Sedley, who had been guilty of a great offence against good manners, was indicted for it, and upon his trial being asked by the chief justice, Sir Robert Hyde, whether he had ever read the book called the Compleat Gentleman, Sir Charles answered, that saving his lordship he had read more books than himself. Athen. Oxon. Col. 1100.

Peacham seems to have been a travelling tutor, and was patronized by the Howard family. He was well acquainted with Douland the lutenist ; and, while abroad, was a scholar of Horatio Vecchi, as himself testi- fies in the above note, and probably the bearer of that letter from Luca Marenzio to Douland, mentioned in a subsequent account of that master, and inserted in the account hereafter given of Douland. Besides the Compleat Gentleman, Peacham published a Collection of Emblems, entitled Minerva Britanna, or a Garden of Heroical Devises, with moral reflections in verse, and a diverting little book entitled the Worth of a Penny. In his advanced age he was reduced to poverty, and subsisted by writing those little penny books which are the common amusement of children.

FELICE ANERIO

ROMANO,

COMPOSITORE DELLA CAPPELLA PONTIFICIA MDXCIV.

RUGGIERO GIOVANELLI DA VELLETRI, MAESTRO

DI CAPPELLA DI S. LUIGI, DI S. APOLLINARE E

CANT. DELLA CAPP. PONT. MDXCIX.

He composed Masses, Cantiones Sacræ, and one book of Madrigals, which are very fine ; but he delighted chiefly in Canzonets, of which he composed no fewer than seven sets.* Milton, who loved and understood music very well, seems to have entertained a fondness for the compositions of Horatio Vecchi ; for in his Life, written by his nephew Phillips, and prefixed to the English translation of his State Letters, it is said that when he was abroad upon his travels, he collected a chest or two of choice music-books of the best masters flourishing at that time in Italy, namely, Luca Marenzio, Monteverde, Horatio Vecchi, Cifra, the prince of Venosa, and others.

Eucharius Hoffman, con-rector of the public school at Stralsund, was the author of two tracts on music, the one entitled ' Musicæ practicæ præcepta,' the other ' Doctrina de tonis seu modis musicis,' both of which were very elegantly printed at Hamburg in 1584, and again in 1588. The first of these is of the same kind with those many books written about this time for the instruction of children in the elements of music, of which an account has hereinbefore been given ; like the rest of them it is written in dialogue. The author has defined the terms prolation, time, and mode, as they refer to mensural music, in a way that may be useful to those who would understand the Introduction to Practical Music of our countryman Morley ; for of prolation he says it is a rule by which is estimated the value of semibreves ; time he says considers the value of breves ; and mode, that of the long and the large. In his doctrine of the tones he seems to follow Glareanus.

Tomasso Lodovico da Victoria, a Spaniard, Maestro di Cappella of St. Apollinare, and afterwards a singer in the pontifical chapel, was an excellent composer. He published a set of Masses in 1583, dedicated to Philip II. king of Spain, and many other ecclesiastical works, one of the best whereof is that called La Messa de' Morti. Peacham says that he resided in the court of the duke of Bavaria about the year 1594 ; and that of his Latin songs the Seven Penitential Psalms are the best : he commends also certain compositions of his to French words, in which is a song beginning ' Susanna un jour.' He styles him a very rare and excellent author, adding that his vein is grave and sweet. Compleat Gentleman, 101, edit. 1661.

Luca Marenzio, a most admirable composer of motetts and madrigals, flourished about this time ; he was a native of Coccalia in the diocese of Brescia. Being born of poor parents, he was maintained and instructed in the rudiments of literature by Andrea Masetto, the arch-priest of the place ; but having a very fine voice, and discovering a strong propensity to music, he was placed under the tuition of Giovanni Contini, and became a most excellent composer, particularly of madrigals. He was first Maestro di

Cappella to Cardinal Luigi d' Este, and after that for many years organist of the pope's chapel. He was beloved by the whole court of Rome, and particularly favoured by Cardinal Cinthio Aldrobandini, nephew of Clement VIII. This circumstance, which is related by Adami, does not agree with the account of our countryman Peacham, who says that after he had been some time at Rome he entertained a criminal passion for a lady, a relation of the Pope, whose fine voice and exquisite hand on the lute had captivated him ; that he thereupon retired to Poland, where he was graciously received, and served many years, and that during his stay there the queen conceived a desire to see the lady who had been the occasion of his retreat, which being communicated to Marenzio, he went to Rome, with a resolution to covey her from thence into Poland, but arriving there, he found the resentment of the Pope so strong against him, that it broke his heart. Adami mentions his retreat to Poland, but omits the other circumstances ; and fixes the time of his death to the twenty-second day of August, 1599. Walther adds, that before his departure for Poland he received the honour of knighthood, but says not at whose hands ; and that on his arrival there he had an appointment of a thousand scudi per annum ; and, without taking notice of his amour, ascribes his quitting that country to his constitution, which was too tender to resist the cold. The following verses to his memory were written by Bernardino Stessonio, a Jesuit :—

Vocum opifex, numeris mulcere Marentius aures
   Callidus, et blandæ tendere fila Chelys,
Frigore lethæo victus jacet. Ite supremam
   In seriem mæsti funeris exequiæ ;
Et charis et biandi sensûs aurita voluptas.
   Et chorus, et fractæ turba canora lyræ :
Densæ humeris, udæ lachrymis, urgete sepulchrum,
   Quis scit, an hinc referat vox rediviva sonum ?
Sin tacet, ille choros alios instaurat in astris,
   Vos decet amisso conticuisse Deo.

Sebastian Raval, a Spaniard, and who published his first book of madrigals for five voices, in the dedication thereof styles him a divine composer. Peacham, who probably was acquainted with him, says he was a little black man. He corresponded with our countryman Douland the lutenist, as appears by a very polite letter of his writing, extant in the preface to Douland's First Booke of Songes or Ayres of four Partes, with Tableture for the Lute, and inserted in a subsequent part of this work.

The madrigals of Marenzio are celebrated for fine air and invention. Peacham says that the first, second, and third parts of his Thyrsis, ' Veggo dolce ' mio ben,' ' Chi fa hoggi il mio Sole,' and ' Cantava,' are songs the Muses themselves might not have been ashamed to have composed.† This that follows is also ranked among the best of his compositions :—

---

* The word Canzonet is derived from Canzone, which signifies in general a song, but more particularly a song in parts, with fuguing passages therein. The Canzonet is a composition of the kind, but shorter and less artificial in its contexture. Andrea Adami ascribes the invention of this species of musical composition to Alessandro Romano, surnamed Alessandro dalla Viola, from his exquisite hand on that instrument, and a singer in the pontifical chapel in the year 1560. Osserv. per ben. reg. il Coro de i Cant. della Cap. Pont. pag. 174.

† These are all adapted to English words, the first, ' Tirsi morir volea,' to a translation of the Italian ; the second, ' Veggo dolce mio ben,' to the words, ' Farewell cruel and unkind ; ' the third to ' What doth my pretty ' darling ? ' and the last to ' Sweet singing Amaryllis,' and are to be found in the Musica Transalpina, of which it is to be noted there are two parts, and in a collection of Italian madrigals with English words, published by Thomas Watson in 1589, as is also another mentioned by Peacham, ' I must depart all hapless,' translated from ' Io partiro.'

2 F   LUCA MARENZIO

Andreas Raselius, chanter in the college of Ratisbon, published at Norimberg, in 1589, 'Hexachordum, seu questiones musicæ practicæ.' This book is very methodically written, but contains little more than is to be found in others of the like kind, except some short examples of fugue from Orlando Lasso, Jusquin De Prez, and other authors, which in their way have great merit.

Caspar Krumbhorn was a native of Lignitz in Silesia, and was born on the twenty-eighth day of October, 1542. In the third year of his age he lost his sight by the small-pox, and became totally blind. His father dying soon after, his mother married one named Stimmler, which gave occasion to his being called Blind Stimmler. Krumbhorn had a brother named Bartholomew, who was considerably older than himself, and was pastor of Waldau; and he discovering in his younger brother, as he grew up, a strong propensity to music, placed him under the care of Knobeln, a famous musician and composer at Goldberg, of whom he learned to play first on the flute, next on the violin, and, last of all, on the harpsichord, on each of which instruments he became so excellent a performer, that he excited the admiration of all that heard him. The fame of these his excellencies, as also of his skill in composition, had reached the ears of Augustus, elector of Saxony; who invited him to Dresden, and having heard him perform, and also heard some of his compositions of many parts performed by himself and others; and being struck with so extraordinary a phenomenon as a young man deprived of the faculty of seeing, an excellent performer on various instruments, and deeply skilled in the art of practical composition, he endeavoured, by the offer of great rewards, to retain him in his service; but, preferring his own country to all others, Krumbhorn returned to Lignitz in the twenty-third year of his age, and was appointed organist of the church of St. Peter and Paul there, which station he occupied fifty-six years, during which space he had many times the direction of the musical college. He died on the eleventh day of June 1621, and was buried in the church of which he was organist, where on his tomb was engraven the following epitaph:—

Vis scire viator
Casparum Krumbhornium
Lign. Reip. civem honoratum,
qui
cum tertio ætatis anno variolar.
ex malignitate visu
privatus,
Musices dehinc scientia et praxi
admiranda
præclaram sibi nominis
Existimationem domi forisque
comparasset,
Conjugii optabilis felicitate,
Bonorum etiam Magnatum,
Dei imprimis gratia evectus
Singulari sortem moderatione
Ad ann. usque LXXIIX toleravit
Organic. munus apud Eccles. P. P.
Annos LVI. non sine industriæ
testimonio gessisset,
Pie demum beateque A. C. 1621.

11 Jun. in Dom. obdormivit.
Anna et Regina Filiæ, earumque
Mariti superstites
Parentem Socerumque B. M.
hoc sub lap. quem
Vivens sibi ipsimet destinaverat
honorifice condiderunt.
Nosti, quod voluit quicunque es,
Nosce te ipsum.

It is said that Krumbhorn was the author of many musical compositions, but it does not appear that any of them were ever printed.

Walther, in his Lexicon, has an article for Tobias Krumbhorn, organist at the court of George Rudolph, duke of Lignitz, and a great traveller, who died in the year 1617, aged thirty-one years. As Caspar and Tobias Krumbhorn were contemporaries, and of the same city, it is not improbable that they were relations at least, if not brothers; although nothing of the kind is mentioned in the accounts given by Walther of either of them.

CHAP. XC.

Balthazarini, surnamed Beaujoyeux, a celebrated Italian musician, lived under the reign of Henry III. of France. The Marshal de Brissac, Governor in Piedmont, sent this musician to the king with the band of Violins, of which he was chief. The Queen gave him the place of her valet-de-chambre, and Henry granted him the same post in his household. Balthazarini pleased the court as well by his skill in playing on the violin, as by his inventions of dances, music shows, and representations. It was he who composed in 1581 the ballet for the nuptials of the Duke de Joyeuse with Madlle. de Vaudermont, sister to the Queen, and the same was represented with extraordinary pomp; it has been printed under the title of the Queen's comic ballet made for the nuptials aforesaid.

Claude le Jeune, (*a Portrait,*) a native of Valenciennes, was a celebrated musician, and composer of the chamber to Henry IV. of France. He was the author of a work intitled Dodecachorde, being an exercise or praxis on the twelve modes of Glareanus; Mons. Bayle cites a passage from the Sieur D'Embry's Commentary on the French translation of the life of Apollonius Tyanæus, relating to this work, to this effect: 'I have some-'times heard the Sieur Claudin the younger say, 'who, without disrespect to any one, far exceeded 'all the musicians of the preceding ages, that an 'air, which he had composed with its parts, was 'sung at the solemnity of the late duke of Joyeuse's 'marriage in the time of Henry III. king of France 'and Poland, of happy memory, whom God absolve; 'which as it was sung, made a gentleman take his 'sword in hand, and swear aloud that it was im-'possible for him to forbear fighting with somebody. 'Whereupon they began to sing another air of the 'Subphrygian mode, which made him as peaceable as 'before; which I have had since confirmed by some 'that were present—such power and force have the

CLAUDE LE JEUNE

DE VALENCIENNE. MDXCVIII.

SIG. CAVALIERE

HERCOLE BOTTRIGARO. MDCII.

' modulation, motion, and management of the voice
' when joined together, upon the minds of men. To
' conclude this long annotation, if one would have an
' excellent experiment of these twelve modes, let him
' sing or hear sung, the Dodecachorde of Claudin the
' younger, of whom I have spoken above, and I assure
' myself he will find in it all those figures and va-
' riations managed with so much art, harmony, and
' skill, as to confess that nothing can be added to this
' master-piece but the praises that all the lovers of this
' science ought to bestow upon this rare and excellent
' man, who was capable of carrying music to the
' utmost degree of its perfection, if death had not
' frustrated the execution of his noble and profound
' designs upon this subject.'*

Claude le Jeune was also the author of a work entitled Meslanges, consisting of vocal compositions for
4, 5, 6, 8, and 10 voices, to Latin, Italian, and French
words, many of them in canon, printed in 1607. A
second part of this work was published in 1613, by
Louis Mardo, a relation of the author, and dedicated
to Mons. de la Planch, an advocate in the parliament
of Paris. But the most celebrated of his compositions
are his Psalms, which, being a Hugonot, he composed
to the words of the Version of Theodore Beza and
Clement Marot, and of these an account will hereafter be given.

Hercole Bottrigaro, (a Portrait,) a native of
Bologna, published, in 1593, ' Il Patrizio, overo de'
' tetracordi armonici di Aristosseno, parere et vera
' dimostratione.' The occasion of writing this book
was as follows : one Francesco Patricio, a man of
great learning,† had written a book intitled ' Della
' poetica, deca istoriale, deca disputata,' wherein,
discoursing on music, and of the Genera in particular, he gives the preference to that division of
the tetrachords which Euclid had adopted. Bottrigaro, who appears to have been an Aristoxenean,
enters into an examination of this work ; and not
without some severe reflections on his adversary,
contends for that division of the tetrachord in each
of the genera which distinguishes the system of Aristoxenus from that of Euclid.   This book, some few
years after its publication, Patricio being then dead,
was very severely criticised by Giovanni Maria Artusi,
of whom mention has already been made in the course
of this work, who, with a becoming zeal for the reputation of Patricio, undertook to vindicate him, as well
against Bottrigaro, as another writer named Annibale
Meloni, a musician of Bologna, the author of a book
intitled, ' Il Desiderio, overo de' concerti di varii
' strumenti musicali, Dialogo di Alemanni Benelli.'‡
But the most celebrated of Bottrigaro's works is that
intitled, ' Il Melone, discorso armonico del M. Ill.

* Bayle art. Goudimel, in not.

† Patricio was of Ossero in Dalmatia. In his youth he travelled much
in Asia ; then settled in the island of Cyprus, where he purchased a large
estate, but lost every thing when the Venetians lost that kingdom, so
that he was obliged to go to Italy, and there live on his wit. He read
Platonic philosophy in the university of Ferrara, and at last died at
Rome, much esteemed and caressed by all lovers of literature, though he
had advanced some opinions in the mathematical science, and about
Italian language, that were then, and still are, thought absurd. He was
an Academician of the Crusca, and one of the great defenders of Ariosto
against those that preferred Tasso to him. Baretti's Italian Library, 328.

‡ A fictitious name made up by the transposition of the letters of the
author's true name, as related at large in a subsequent part of this
work.

' Sig. Cavaliere Hercole Bottrigaro, ed. il Melone se-
' condo, considerazioni musicali del medesimo sopra
' un discorso di M. Gandolfo Sigonio intorno à' ma-
' drigali et à' libri dell' antica musica ridutta alla
' moderna prattica di D. Nicola Vicentino e nel
' fine esso Discorso del Sigonio.'   Ferrara, 1602.

In this book, which is professedly an examen of
that of Vicentino, the author relates at large the
controversy between him and Vicentio Lusitano.
He charges them both with vanity and inconsistency,
but seems to decide in favour of the former.   The
remark he makes on the conduct of Bartolomeo
Esgobedo and Ghislino D'Ancherts, is very judicious ;
for the sentence given by them, and published with
so much solemnity, assigns as the motive for condemning Vicentino, that he had not, either by words
or in writing, given the reasons of his opinion.   Bottrigaro's observation is this, seeing then that Vicentino had not declared the foundation of his opinion,
it was their duty as judges to have proceeded to an
enquiry whether it had any foundation or not, and,
agreeably to the result of this enquiry, to have given
sentence for or against him ; and for not pursuing
this method he sticks not to accuse them of partiality,
or rather ignorance of their duty, as the arbitrators
between two contending parties.

Bottrigaro appears to have been a man of rank ;
the letters to him, many of which he has thought it
necessary to print, bespeak as much.   Walther styles
him a count ; and his Il Melone, written in answer
to a letter of Annibale Meloni, is thus dated, ' Della
' mia à me diletteuole villa nel commune di S. Alberto.'
Notwithstanding this circumstance, and that he was
not a musician by profession, he appears to have been
very well skilled in the science.   It seems that he
entertained strong prejudices in favour of the ancient
music, and that he attempted, as Vicentino and others
had done, to introduce the chromatic genus into practice, but with no better success than had attended the
endeavours of others.   He corrected Gogavinus's Latin
version of Ptolemy in numberless instances, and that
to so good a purpose, that Dr. Wallis has in general
conformed to it in that translation of the same author,
which he gave to the world many years after.   He
also translated into Italian, Boetius De Musica, and
as much of Plutarch and Macrobius as relates to music ; besides this, he made annotations on Aristoxenus,
Franchinus, Spataro, Vicentino, Zarlino, and Galilei,
and, in short, on almost every musical treatise that he
could lay his hands on, as appears by the copies which
were once his own, and are now reposited in many
libraries in Italy.

It is to be lamented that the writings of Bottrigaro
are, for the most part, of the controversial kind, and
that the subjects of dispute between him and his adversaries tend so very little to the improvement of
music.   If we look into them we shall find him taking
part with Meloni against Patricio, and contending for
a practice which the ancients themselves had exploded ;
and in the dispute with Gandolfo Sigonio he does but
revive the controversy which had been so warmly
agitated between Vicentino and Vincentio Lusitano :
and though he seems to censure that determination of
the judges Bartolomeo Esgobedo and Ghisilino Dan-

cherts, by which the former was condemned, he leaves the question just as he found it.

Of Bottrigaro's works it is said that they contain greater proofs of his learning and skill in music than of his abilities as a writer, his style being remarkably inelegant; nevertheless he affected the character of a poet, and there is extant a collection of Poems by him, in octavo, printed in 1551. Walther represents him as an able mathematician, and a collector of rarities, and says that he was possessed of a cabinet, which the emperor Ferdinand II. had a great desire to purchase. He died in 1609.

We meet with the name of Ludovicus Brooman, an excellent musician, who flourished towards the end of the sixteenth century, and died at Brussels in 1597. Gerard Vossius has given him a place in his Catalogue, and he is elsewhere styled Musices Princeps. The misfortune of his being blind from his nativity might possibly contribute to exalt his character; for there are no compositions of his extant, at least in print. Some remarkable instances of blind persons who have been excellent in music, might lead to an opinion that the privation of that sense was favourable to the study of it: in the case of Salinas it seems to have been no impediment to the deepest research into the principle of the science. Caspar Krumbhorn of Lignitz, and Martini Presenti of Venice, are instances to the same purpose; the former of these being an excellent organist and a composer of church-music, and the latter a composer of vocal and instrumental music of almost all kinds; and both these persons were blind, the one from his infancy, and the other from his nativity; and it is well known that the famous Sebastian Bach and Handel, perhaps the two best organists in the world, retained the power both of study and practice many years after they were severally deprived of the sense of seeing.

Valerio Bona of Milan, published in 1595, 'Re-'gole del contraponto, et compositione brevemente 'raccolte da diuersi Auttori. Operetta molto facile 'et utile per i scolari principianti.' The author takes occasion to celebrate as men of consummate skill in music, Cyprian de Rore, Adrian Willaert, Orlando de Lasso, Christopher Morales, and Palestrina. The character of his book is, that it is remarkable for the goodness of its style and language. The author was an ecclesiastic, and a practical composer, as appears by a catalogue of his works in the Musical Lexicon of Walther; they consist of Motets, Masses, the Lamentations of Jeremiah, Madrigals, Canzonets, and other vocal compositions.

Lodovico Zacconi, an Augustine monk of Pesaro, and musician to the Duke of Bavaria, was the author of a valuable work in folio, printed at Venice in 1596, with the following title, ' Prattica di musica utile et ' necessaria si al compositore per comporre i canti suoi ' regolatamente, si anco al cantore per assicurarsi in ' tutti le cose cantabili.'

This book of Zacconi is justly esteemed one of the most valuable treatises on the subject of practical music extant. Morley appears to have been greatly indebted to the author of it, whom he calls Fryer Lowyes Zaccone, and cites frequently in his Introduction to Practical Music.

In the course of his work Zacconi seems to have declined all enquiry into the music of the ancient Greeks, and to have been very little solicitous about the investigation of ratios; his work seems to be calculated for the improvement of practical music, and therefore contains nothing relating to the theory of the science.

Zarlino's works seem to be intended for the use of philosophers, but this of Zacconi abounds with precepts applicable to practice, and suited to the capacities of singers and men of ordinary endowments. Among a great number of directions for the decent and orderly performance of choral service, he recommends a careful attention to the utterance of the vowels; which passage it seems Morley had an eye to when he complained, as he does in his Introduction, pag. 179, in these words: 'The matter is ' now come to that state, that though a song be never ' so well made, and never so aptly applied to the ' words, yet shall you hardly find singers to express ' it as it ought to be; for most of our churchmen, so ' they can cry louder in the quier than their fellowes, ' care for no more, whereas by the contrarie they ' ought to studie how to vowell and sing cleane, ' expressing their words with devotion and passion, ' whereby to draw the hearer, as it were in chaines of ' gold by the eares, to the consideration of holy things.'

In the sixty-seventh chapter of the first book Zacconi enumerates the necessary qualifications of a chapel-master.

In the thirty-eighth chapter of the second book he speaks of the mass of Jusquin De Prez, ' Le ' Homme armé,' mentioned by Glareanus, Salinas, Doni, and other writers, as one of the most excellent compositions of the time. This he does to introduce a mass of Palestrina with the same title, which he gives at length, with his own remarks thereon.

The third book is on the subject of proportion, which he has explained and illustrated by a variety of examples from the best authors.

At the end of the fourth and last book he enumerates the several musical instruments in use in his time, with the compass of notes proper to each; in his declaration whereof it is remarkable that he makes bb the limit of the superacutes, and the highest note in the scale for the violin, a particular from whence it is to be inferred that the practice of shifting the hand was unknown to him.

In the year 1622 Zacconi published a second part of his Prattica Musica, which Morley never saw, for he died in 1604. The author at this time was musician to Charles archduke of Austria, and also to William duke of Bavaria, his former patron. In this work he treats of the elements of music, and the principles of composition.

Speaking of the invention of the syllables by Guido Aretinus, he says that some of his time had objected that it was imperfect, inasmuch as it gave no syllable to the last note of the septenary, and thereby incumbered the system with what are called the mutations. And he mentions a musician, Don Anselmo Fiammengo, who had formerly been in the service of the duke of Bavaria, and, as Orlando de Lasso once told the author, made use of the syllable

HO in succession after that of LA for the purpose of getting rid of the mutations.*

Zacconi mentions also another musician, Don Adriano Bianchieri, of Bologna, who for b FA made use of the syllable BA, and for b MI the syllable BI, a distinction, that, as above is related, has been adopted by the Spaniards.

The rules for the composition of counterpoint, of fugue, and canon, in all their various forms laid down by Zacconi, are drawn from the writings of Zarlino, Artusi, and other the most celebrated Italian writers. In the course of the work he takes occasion to mention a conversation on music held in the presence of Zarlino in the year 1584, in which a character was given of the several musicians of that and the preceding age, and the respective attributes of each pointed out and assented to by the persons then present. To Costanzo Porta was ascribed great art, and a regular contexture in his compositions; to Alessandro Striggio, a vague but artificial modulation; and to Messer Adriano, by whom it is supposed was meant Adrian Willaert, great art, with a judicious disposition of parts: Morales, ho says, was allowed to have art, counterpoint, and good modulation; Orlando de Lasso, modulation, art, and good invention; and Palestrina, every excellence necessary to form a great musician.

In the thirty-second chapter of the second book he takes occasion to observe on the impiety of introducing madrigals and secular songs among the divine offices, the singing whereof is prohibited by the church as a mortal sin; from hence he takes occasion to applaud Palestrina for his conduct in this respect, who, he says, enriched the church with his own sweet compositions, in a style suited to public worship, calculated to promote the honour of God, and to excite devotion in the minds of the auditors.

CARLO GESUALDO, prince of Venosa, flourished about the latter end of the sixteenth century. Venosa was the Venusium of the Romans, and is now a principality of the kingdom of Naples, situate in that part of it called the Basilicate; it is famous for being the place where Horace was born; and little less so in the judgment of musicians on account of the person now about to be spoken of. He was, as Scipione Cerreto relates, the nephew of Cardinal Alfonso Gesualdo, archbishop of Naples, and received his instructions in music from Pomponio Nenna, a celebrated composer of madrigals. Blancanus, in his Chronologia Mathematicorum, speaks thus of him : 'The most noble Carolus Gesualdus, prince 'of Venusium, was the prince of musicians of our 'age; for he having recalled the Rythmi into 'music, introduced such a style of modulation, that 'other musicians yielded the preference to him; and 'all singers and players on stringed instruments, laying 'aside that of others, everywhere eagerly embraced his 'music.' Mersennus, Kircher, Doni, Berardi, and indeed the writers in all countries, give him the character of the most learned, ingenious, and artificial composer of madrigals, for it was that species of music alone which he studied, that ever appeared in the world. Blancanus also relates that he died in the year 1614.

Alessandro Tassoni, who celebrates him in the highest terms of commendation, adds to his character this remarkable particular, viz., that he imitated and improved that melancholy and plaintive kind of air which distinguishes the Scots melodies, and which was invented about the year 1420, by James the First, king of Scotland, and to this he ascribes the sweetness of his admirable compositions.†

There are extant no fewer than six books of madrigals for five, six, and more voices, of this excellent author; the first five were published in parts in 1585 by Simone Molinaro, a musician, and chapel-master of Genoa. The same person in the year 1613 published them, together with a sixth book in score, with this title, 'Partitura delli sci 'libri de' madrigali a cinque voci, dell' illustrissimo 'et excellentiss. Prencipe di Venosa D. Carlo 'Gesualdo. Fatica di Simone Molinaro, Maestro di 'Capella nel Duomo di Genoua. In Genoua, appresso 'Giuseppe Pavoni.' Folio.

It is very probable that the last of these publications was made under the direction of the author himself, and that it was intended for the use of students; the madrigals contained in it are upwards of one hundred in number: the sixth book was again published in parts at Venice in 1616. In a MS. in the music-school of Oxford, mention is made of two other collections of madrigals of the prince of Venosa, as namely, one by Scipio Stella in 1603, and another by Hector Gesualdo in 1604; but that by Molinaro above-mentioned, as it is in score, seems to be the most valuable collection of his works extant, and probably may include the whole of his compositions.

Doni speaking of the fourth madrigal in the sixth book, 'Resta di darma noia,' calls it 'quell' artificiosissimo Madrigali del principe;'‡ and indeed it well deserves that epithet; for being calculated to express sorrow, it abounds with chromatic, and even enarmonic intervals, indeed not easy to sing, but admirably adapted to the sentiments.

Kircher, in the Musurgia, tome I. pag. 599, mentions the following madrigal, being the first of the first book of Molinaro's edition, as a fine example of the amorous style.

---

* This objection has often been made to Guido's invention: Ericius Puteanus added, as a seventh, the syllable BI. Kepler speaks of a certain German who articulated the septenary by seven syllables, but reprehends him for it in terms that serve at least to show that the method of solmisation by the hexachords is to be preferred to that of the tetrachords, which prevailed some years in this country, and was practised by Dr. Wallis. The passage from Kepler is to this effect: 'But as there are 'three places of the semitone in the tetrachord, therefore that these 'syllables might not be too general, but rather that the semitone might 'always be denoted by MI, FA, or FA MI, there was a necessity for the 'addition of two other syllables, that in these UT, RE, MI, FA, the semi- 'tone might be in the highest place, but that in these RE, MI, FA, SOL, 'the semitone might be in the middle place; and, lastly, that in these, 'MI, FA, SOL, LA, the semitone might be in the lowest place; and this 'is a reason why the inventors of the scale made use of six syllables and 'not eight; therefore let the German see what advantage he has gained 'by the increase, when he made use of seven, instead of six syllables, 'BO, CE, DI, GA, LO, MA, NI; for if he thought it was necessary to make 'use of as many notes save one, as there are chords in an octave, in order 'to represent the identity of the octave by the first syllable BO, I pray 'you what deficiency was there in the letters a, b, c, d, e, f, g, which were 'long before made use of for that purpose?' Joann. Keplerus Harm. Mundi, lib. III. cap. x.

Notwithstanding this argument of Kepler, it is well known that the French to the six syllables of Guido add a seventh, namely, SI, of the introduction whereof by Le Maire an account is given in pag. 160 of this work.

† De' Pensieri diversi di Alessandro Tassoni, libro X. cap. xxiii.

‡ Gio. Batt. Doni, nelle sue Compendio del Trattato de' Generi e de' Modi della Musica. In Roma, 1635, quarto, pag. 16.

CARLO GESUALDO, PRENCIPE DI VENOSA.

And page 601 of the same tome of the Musurgia, he recommends the nineteenth madrigal of the third book, 'Dolcissimo sospiri,' as an example of sorrow.

Again, the same author, page 608 of the same tome of the Musurgia, recommends the twenty-second madrigal of the sixth book, 'Già piansi nel dolore,' as an example of joy and exultation.

The distinguishing excellences of the compositions of this admirable author are, fine contrivance, original harmony, and the sweetest modulation conceivable; and these he possessed in so eminent a degree, that one of the finest musicians that these later times

have known, Mr. Geminiani, has been often heard to declare that he laid the foundation of his studies in the works of the Prencipe di Venosa.

CHAP. XCI.

THE prince of Venosa is not the only person of rank who has distinguished himself by his skill in music. Kircher mentions an earl of Somerset as the inventor of a certain kind of Chelys or viol of eight chords, which contained all the secrets of music in an eminent degree, and ravished every hearer with admiration.   Musurg. tom. I. pag. 486.* And Walther says of Maurice, landgrave of Hesse Cassel, that he was an excellent composer of music.   Peacham speaks to the same purpose, and gives the following account of him:—

  'Above others who carryeth away the palme for 'excellency, not onely in musicke, but in whatsoever 'is to be wished in a brave prince, is the yet living 'MAURICE, LANDGRAVE OF HESSEN, of whose owne 'composition I have seene eight or ten severall setts 'of motets and solemne musicke, set purposely for his 'owne chappell,† where, for the great honour of 'some festivall, and many times for his recreation 'onely, he is his owne organist.   Besides he readily 'speaketh ten or twelve severall languages; he is so 'universall a scholler, that comming, as he doth often, 'to his university of Marpurge, what questions soever 'he meeteth with set up, as the manner is in the 'Germane and our universities, hee will ex tempore 'dispute an houre or two (even in bootes and spurres) 'upon them with their best professors.   I passe over 'his rare skill in chirurgery, he being generally 'accounted the best bone-setter in the country.   Who 'have seene his estate, his hospitality, his rich fur-'nished armory, his brave stable of great horses, his 'curtesie to all strangers, being men of quality and 'good parts, let them speake the rest.'‡   But to be more particular as to his skill in music.   Valentine Guckius began a work entitled 'Opera metrici sacri 'sanctorum, Dominicalium et feriarum,' but never finished it; this work was completed and published by Maurice, landgrave of Hesse, above-mentioned.

  GIOVANNI CROCE, of Venice, flourished at this time. He was chapel-master of St. Mark's, and very pro-bably the immediate successor of Zarlino.   Zacconi, in his 'Prattica di musica,' published in 1596, styles him vice-master of the chapel of St. Mark; from whence it is pretty certain that he must at first have been the substitute of Zarlino in that office.   Morley commends him highly; and Peacham says that for a full, lofty, and sprightly vein, he was second to none; he adds, that while he lived he was one of the most free and brave companions in the world. Nevertheless his compositions are all of a devout and serious kind, and of these, his Penitential Psalms, which have been printed with English words, are the best.

  SETHUS CALVISIUS, the son of a poor peasant named Jacob Kalwitz, of Gorschleb near Sachsenburg in Thuringia, was born on the twenty-first day of February, in the year 1556.   He received the ru-diments of learning in the public school of Francken-hausen, but, after three years stay, was removed to Magdeburg, from whence he was sent to the university of Leipsic, having no other means of support there than the contributions of some persons whom he had made his friends.   His pursuits in learning were various, for he is not more celebrated as a musician than a chronologer; but it is in the first capacity that he is here spoken of; and indeed he was deemed so able a proficient in music, that very early in his life he had the direction of the choir in the university church, and soon after became preceptor in music in the Schul - Pforte, or principal school in Upper-Saxony; ten years after which, he became chanter in the church of St. Thomas in the city of Leipsic, and fellow of the college there, in which stations he died on the twenty-third day of November, in the year 1617, or, as some write, 1615.   The greatness of his reputation procured him many invitations to settle in foreign universities, but he declined them all.   His musical writings are, 'Melopeiam, seu 'melodiæ condendæ rationem, quam vulgò musicam 'poeticam vocant,' printed at Erfurth in 1595, as Lipenius places it, or, according to others, in 1602. In 1611 he published his Opuscula Musica, and in the year after, his Compendium Musicum, a book for the instruction of beginners; but a method of sol-misation by the seven syllables, BO, CE, DI, GA, LO, MA, NI, having then lately been introduced, which he seemed greatly to approve, he republished it in the same year, with the title of 'Musicæ artis præcepta nova et facillima, &c.'   He also published 'Exer-'citationes musicas,' in number three.   In 1615 he composed the hundred and fiftieth Psalm in twelve parts, for three choirs, on the nuptials of Caspar Anckelman, a merchant of Hamburg, and caused it to be printed in folio at Leipsic.

  Of the Exercitationes, the first is on the modes of the ancients, and contains a catalogue of compositions by the old German, Flemish, and Italian masters in those several modes.

  The second of the Exercitationes is entitled 'De 'Initio et Progressu musices, et aliis quibusdam ad 'eam rem spectantibus.'   This appears to be the substance of lectures read by the author in the public school at Leipsic, and is a very learned, ingenious,

* We know of no earl of Somerset to whom the invention of any such musical instrument may be ascribed.   Edward Somerset, marquis of Worcester, the friend and favourite of king Charles I. was remarkable for his inventive faculty, which he endeavoured to manifest in a little book entitled 'A century of the names and scantlings of such inventions as at 'present I can call to mind to have tried and perfected [my former notes 'being lost];' first printed in 1663, and since among the Harleian tracts. Mr. Walpole has given an account of the contents of this book, not more humorous than just, in the following words: 'It is a very small piece, 'containing a dedication to Charles the Second, another to both houses 'of parliament, in which he affirms having, in the presence of Charles 'the First, performed many of the feats mentioned in his book; a table 'of contents, and the work itself, which is but a table of contents neither, 'being a list of an hundred projects, most of them impossibilities, but all 'of which he affirms having discovered the art of performing: some of 'the easiest seem to be, how to write with a single line; with a point; 'how to use all the senses indifferently for each other, as, to talk by 'colours, and to read by the taste; to make an unsinkable ship: how to 'do and to prevent the same thing; how to sail against wind and tide; how 'to form an universal character; how to converse by jangling bells out 'of tune; how to take towns or prevent their being taken; how to write 'in the dark; how to cheat with dice; and, in short, how to fly.   Of all 'these wonderful inventions the last but one seems the only one of which 'his lordship has left the secret.'   Catalogue of Royal and Noble Authors vol. I. pag. 242.

† These had been procured by Douland when he was abroad, and were shewn by him to Peacham at sundry times.   Peacham's Emblems, pag. 101, in not.

‡ Compl. Gent. edit. 1634, pag. 99.   It seems that formerly the cha-racter of this prince was well known, and his reputation very high in England, for till within these few years his head was the sign of a reputable public-house on the north side of the high eastern road leading to Mile-end from London; it represented a general in armour, and was underwrote Grave, i. e. Landgrave, Maurice; and upon repainting the sign, by corruption, Morris.

From this circumstance it should seem that he was a favourite with the English, who, though they might be strangers to his endowments, might esteem him for his firm attachment to the protestant religion, for the preservation whereof he formed a league in 1603, which produced a union of the protestant powers; but being overpowered by count Tilly in 1626, he was compelled to surrender his estates to his son William, and spend his days in retirement.   He died in 1632, and is not less cele-brated for his learning and piety, than for his many and various ac-complishments.   Heyl. Cosm. 419.

and entertaining composition. In it he takes notice of that invention of an anonymous Dutch musician for avoiding the mutations, by giving to the septenary the syllables BO, CE, DI, GA, LO, MA, NI, which, as has been mentioned in a preceding note, Kepler has taken notice of and reprehended. The two first parts of the Exercitationes were printed at Leipsic in 1600.

Calvisius in this discourse inclines to the opinion that polyphonous music was unknown to the ancient Greeks; and for fixing the era of its invention, observes that Bede makes use of the terms Concentus, Discantus, Organis, from which it is to be inferred that he was not able to carry it higher than the beginning of the eighth century, about which time Bede wrote.

The last of the Exercitationes, printed at Leipsic in 1611, contains a refutation of certain opinions of Hippolytus Hubmeier, poet-laureate to the emperor, and a public teacher at Gottingen, who it seems had written on music.

Our countryman Butler cites Calvisius in almost every page of his Principles of Music; and in one place in particular uses these words: ‘ Sethus Cal- ‘ visius, that singular musician, to whom the students ‘ of this abstruse and mysterious faculty are more be- ‘ holden than to all that have ever written thereon.’ His chronological writings are greatly esteemed; in them he had the good fortune to please Joseph Scaliger, who has given him great commendations: he wrote against the Gregorian calendar a work entitled ‘ Elenchus Calendarii Gregoriani, et duplex Calen- ‘ darii melioris formula,’ published at Frankfort in 1612, and lastly, Chronologia, printed at the same place in 1629.

GIOVANNI MARIA ARTUSI, an ecclesiastic of Bologna, of whom mention has already been made in the course of this work, was the author of an excellent treatise entitled ‘ L’Arte del Contraponto Ridotta in ‘ Tavole,’ published in 1586, of which an account has herein-before been given, and also of a discourse which he entitles ‘ L’Artusi, overo delle Imperfettioni ‘ della moderna Musica, Ragionamenti dui,’ printed at Venice in the year 1600.

The latter of these two treatises is a dialogue, which the author introduces with the following relation :—

‘ Upon the arrival of Margaret queen of Austria ‘ at Ferrara, in 1598, with a noble train, to celebrate ‘ a double marriage between herself and Philip III. ‘ of Spain, and between the archduke Albert and the ‘ infanta Isabella the king’s sister; soon after the ‘ nuptials they visited the monastery of St. Vito, ‘ where, for the entertainment of their royal guests, ‘ the nuns performed a concert, in which were heard ‘ cornets, trumpets, violins, bastard viols, double ‘ harps, lutes, flutes, harpsichords, and voices at the ‘ same time, with such sweetness of harmony, that ‘ the place seemed to be the mount of Parnassus, or ‘ Paradise itself.’

On this occasion two of the auditors, who happened to meet there, and were greatly pleased with the performance, enter into a conversation on the subject of music in general. It is needless to follow the in-

terlocutors through the whole of the dialogue, but it may be taken for granted that, notwithstanding the form it bears, it contains the sentiments of Artusi himself, who, after delivering some very obvious rules for the ordering of a musical performance, whether vocal or instrumental, such as the choice of place, of instruments, of voices, and lastly, of the compositions themselves, declares himself to the following purpose: and speaking first of the Cornet, he says that the tone of that instrument depends greatly upon the manner of tonguing it, concerning which practice he delivers many precepts, which at this time it would be of very little use to enumerate.

The cornet is an instrument now but little known, it having above a century ago given place to the hautboy; Artusi seems to have held it in high estimation; his sentiments of it will be best delivered in his own words, which are these :—

‘ To give the best tone, the performer on the cornet ‘ should endeavour to imitate the human voice; for ‘ no other instrument is so difficult to attain to ex- ‘ cellence on as this; the trumpet is sounded by the ‘ breath alone; the lute by the motion of the hands; ‘ the harpsichord and the harp may be attained by ‘ long practice; but the cornet requires the know- ‘ ledge of the different methods of tonguing, and the ‘ changes to be made therein according to the quality ‘ of the several notes; a proper opening of the lips ‘ joined to a ready finger attained by long habit; all ‘ these excellencies were possessed by Girolamo da ‘ Udine of Venice, and other eminent performers on ‘ that instrument who flourished formerly in Italy.’

In his observations on other instruments he speaks to this purpose: the different construction of instruments will occasion a diversity in their sounds; first, in respect of the matter of which they are formed; secondly, of the chords of some, and the pipes of others; and, thirdly, to speak of stringed instruments only, by reason of the manner in which the chords are struck. Under these several heads he makes the following remarks, viz., that the lute being a larger instrument than the guitar, the sound thereof is more diffused; as a proof whereof he says, that a string of the one being put on the other, will produce a change of tone derived from the effect of the different instrument; and that for the same reason, a gut string being put upon a harpsichord, the sound thereof is lost, or scarce heard. Farther, that a silver string will produce a sound more or less sweet, ac- cording to the quality and degree of the alloy with which the metal is attempered; and that if a string of Spanish gold, the alloy of which is harder than that of the Venetian, be put on a guitar, it will render a sweet, but a string of pure gold or silver an unpleasing sound. As to pipes, he says there can be no doubt but that leaden ones have a sweeter tone than those of tin or any harder metal. And as to the percussion of chords, he says that if a chord of metal or gut be struck with the finger, it must produce a sweeter sound than if struck by any thing else. These observations demonstrate the imperfections of instruments, though in general they are but little attended to.

Farther, the different tuning or temperature of

instruments is such, that oftentimes one interval is sounded for another; and frequently in the diatonic genus one performer will observe the syntonous division of Ptolemy, another that of Aristoxenus: and this also, says this author, is an evidence of the imperfection insisted on.

He cites from Ptolemy a passage, wherein it is asserted that in wind-instruments no certainty of sound can be depended on; and another from Aristoxenus to the same purpose, but more general, as applying to all instruments whatsoever.

From hence he takes occasion to consider the instruments of the moderns, and the temperaments of each species or class; the first he makes to consist of such as are tempered with the tones equal and the semitones unequal, as the organ, harpsichord, spinnet, monochord, and double harp. The instruments of the second class, under which he ranks such as are altered or attempered occasionally, are the human voice, trombone, trumpet, rebec, cornet, flute, and dulzain.* In the third class, consisting of instruments in which both the tones and semitones are equally divided, are placed the lute, viol, bastard viol, guitar, and lyre.

From this arrangement of instruments, and a comparative view of the temperaments proper to each, Artusi draws a conclusion, which, if not too refined, appears to be very judicious, namely, that in music in consonance the instruments of the first and third class ought never to be conjoined.

In the course of the dialogue Artusi puts into the mouth of one of the interlocutors this question, ' Had ' the ancients music in consonance, or not?' To this the answer is, ' I deny that the ancients had the ' knowledge of all those consonances that we make ' use of, as clearly may be read in Aristoxenus, lib. I. ' in Ptolemy, lib. I. cap. x. and in Euclid, who says, " Sunt consona diatessaron, diapente, diapason et " similia; dissona autem sunt ea quæ minora, quam " diatessaron, ut diesis, semitonium, tonus, sesqui- " tonus, et ditonus." From these authorities it must ' be believed that the ancients had not the imperfect ' consonances, the thirds, and sixths; or if they had ' any knowledge of them, they never used them, but ' reputed them discords.'

And touching the comparative excellence of the ancient and modern music, Artusi delivers his sentiments to this purpose:—

' The music of the ancients being more simple, ' caused a greater impression on the mind than can ' be effected by that of the moderns; which consisting ' in a variety of parts, whereof some are grave and ' others acute; some proceeding by a slow, others by

* The Dulzain, otherwise called the Dulcino, is a wind-instrument, used as a tenor to the hautboy. Brossard calls it the Quart Fagotto; and adds, that it is a small bassoon. That it is a kind of hautboy appears from a passage in Don Quixote. In the adventure of the puppet-show, the boy, who is the interpreter, desires the spectators to attend to the sound of the bells which rang in the steeples in the mosques of Sansuenna to spread the alarm of Melisendra's flight. Peter, the master of the show, is all the while behind ringing the bells, upon which Don Quixote calls out. ' Master Peter, you are very much mistaken in this ' business of the bells: for you are to know that among the Moors there ' are no bells, and that instead of them they make use of kettle-drums, ' and a kind of Dulzayns, like our Chirimias.' CHIRIMIA in the Spanish dictionaries is interpreted by the Latin Tibicen, inis; and Chirimias is by Jarvis properly enough translated Waits, that is to say hautboys; though, by a mistake arising from his want of skill in music, he has rendered the word Dulzàynas, Dulcimers.

' a quick motion, divides the attention, and keeps the ' mind in suspense: so that although it may be said ' that the music of the moderns consists in a richer ' and fuller harmony than that of the ancients, it is ' inferior to it in respect of the melody, and its power ' over the human mind.'

In the course of this dialogue, Artusi takes occasion to celebrate Cypriano De Rore, whom he styles a skilful composer, and the first that accommodated judiciously words to music, a practice which before his time was but very little understood by musicians.

Towards the end of the first of the Ragionamenti is a madrigal for two voices of Adriano Willaert, copied as Artusi testifies, from the writing of the author himself, and closing with the interval of a seventh, though to appearance the cadence is in the diapason.

To this madrigal is subjoined a letter printed from the original manuscript of Giovanni Spataro of Bologna, dated 9th September, 1524, purporting to be a criticism on it, wherein the author, after many honourable expressions in commendation of Messer Adriano and his works, censures him for having, by an unwarrantable kind of sophistry, made the madrigal in question, by the use of the flat signature, to appear different from what it really is.

Spataro's letter is replete with musical erudition. Artusi says that it came from a good school, and that the author was a most acute musician. It is followed by reflections of Artusi on what he calls Musica finta, in Latin Musica ficta, or feigned music, that is to say, that kind of music in which a change of the intervals is effected in various instances, by the use or application of the flat signature: Artusi seems to be no friend to this practice, and censures the multiplication of the transposed keys beyond certain limits.

He then proceeds to relate the dispute between Nicola Vicentino and Vincentio Lusitano in 1551. The latter maintaining that the then modern scale was purely diatonic, and the other asserting that the same consisted of a mixture of the chromatic and enarmonic genera; Artusi seems not to have attended to the concessions made by Vincentio Lusitano, which are so much the more worthy of note, as they were made after a determination in his favour, and nevertheless adopts his first opinion, and accordingly approves of the sentence against Vicentino by the judges in the controversy, Bartolomeo Esgobedo, and Ghisilino D'Ancherts.

CHAP. XCII.

In the second of the Ragionamenti are contained the censures of Artusi on a madrigal in five parts by an anonymous author, which, though it had been much applauded by the vulgar, is by him shown to be very faulty.

Speaking of the ancient modes, and of the designation of each of them by Euclid and Ptolemy, he remarks that these two writers differ in the order of the modes, though they agree both in the number and construction of them; for that in those of Ptolemy the tones and semitones in the ascending, succeed in the same order as those of Euclid do in the descending series.

Notwithstanding the several essays towards a temperature which are to be met with in the writings of Artusi, it is clear that he was not of the Aristoxenean sect of musicians; for of Aristoxenus himself he says that he is 'una discordante discordia,' and that among his followers there is infinite confusion.

He says that all the moderns are at variance with respect to the number, the order, and situation of the modes; and that neither Odo, Guido Aretinus, nor Jacobus Faber Stapulensis, seem to have understood the meaning of Boetius, which he ascribes to the many errors in the manuscript copies.

Artusi seems to agree with Glareanus in making the modes to be twelve in number, but he differs from him in his designation of them. By what artifice the modes are made to exceed the species of diapason, has already been mentioned; and, as to the difference between the modes of Glareanus and Artusi, the subject is so uninteresting, that it merits very little attention at this day.

Towards the close of this treatise, Artusi observes that every cantilena is mixed and composed of two modes, that is to say, the authentic and the plagal respectively in each of the several species of diapason; and that a cantilena, by being made to sing both backward and forward, may consist of four modes; and of this he gives an example in that enigmatical madrigal composed by Costanzo Porta, inserted in book V. chap. XLIV. of this work, saying that it is a fine and new invention.

In the year 1603, Artusi published a second part of this work, the occasion whereof is related in the preface, and is as follows: 'One Francesco Patricio, in 'the year 1586, had written a treatise intitled "Della "poetica deca historiale, deca disputata," wherein 'discoursing of music and poetry, he takes occasion 'to speak of the genera of the ancients, but in a way 'that in the opinion of some was liable to exception.'

This book was severely censured by Hercole Bottrigaro in a discourse entitled 'Il Patricio, overo de 'tetracordi armonici di Aristosseno, parere e vera 'demostratione dell' Illustre Signor Cavaliere Her-'cole Bottrigaro.' In Bologna, 1593, in quarto; and Patricio's book coming also to the hands of Annibale Meloni, a musician of Bologna,* he too published remarks on it entitled 'Il Desiderio di 'Alemanno Benelli,' a name formed by the transposition of the letters of the name Annibale Meloni; in it are some reflections, rather on the doctrines than the character of Francesco Patricio, wherefore he being dead, Artusi undertook to vindicate him from the calumnies of the one and the insinuations of the other of these his adversaries.

The conduct of Artusi in the management of this controversy is somewhat singular; for although the second part of the treatise Delle Imperfettioni, and more especially the Considerationi Musicali, printed at the end of it, are a defence of Patricio, and an examen of Bottrigaro's book, Il Patricio, in which many errors contained in it are pointed out, and

most strongly marked; yet to this very same Bottrigaro, the adversary of Patricio, and the aggressor in the dispute, does Artusi dedicate his book, and that in terms so equivocal, that it is not easy to discover that he means at once to flatter and revile him. In order to do this consistently, he very artfully affects to consider Bottrigaro's book Il Patricio as the work of an anonymous writer, calling him 'l'Auttor del parere;' and sticks not to say that in calumniating Patricio he does but bark at the moon.

Artusi's book, besides that it is a defence of Francesco Patricio, contains also an enquiry into the principles of some modern innovators in music: of these, one named Ottavio Ottusi, conceiving that the censures of Artusi were meant to reach himself, wrote a letter to Artusi, wherein he advances the following absurd positions, viz., that the discord of the seventh is sweeter to the ear than the octave; that the seventh may move up to the octave, and the fourth into the fifth; the third into the fourth, and the fifth into either of the sixths. This letter produced a controversy, which clearly appears to have terminated in favour of Artusi.

To this second part of the treatise 'Delle Imper-'fettioni della moderna musica,' are added 'Consi-'derationi musicali;' these contain the author's sentiments of Patricio and his work, as also the objections of his opponent. They are delivered with a becoming zeal for the honour of his memory, and in terms, which though they indicate a respect for the rank and station in life of Signor Cavaliere Hercole Battrigaro, sufficiently shew how far he ventured to differ from him in opinion.

Nor did Artusi rest the dispute here: Annibale Meloni, it seems, was his friend; Meloni had shewn him his book Il Desiderio, but Artusi excused himself from perusing it, as not being willing to forward a publication that in the least reflected on the doctrines delivered by Patricio: he nevertheless entertained a high opinion of its author, as appears by what he says of him in the preface to the second part of his book Delle Imperfettioni; and after its publication in 1594, some remaining copies coming to his hands, he republished it in 1601, with a preface, in which he intimates an opinion then generally prevalent that Battrigaro was the author of the book; and upon this he takes occasion to reproach him for arrogating to himself the merit of so excellent a work, and for not openly and publicly disclaiming all pretence to the honour of writing it.

The moderation of Artusi in his treatment of his adversary is very remarkable, for he blames him only for suffering an opinion to prevail that he was the author of Il Desiderio; but he might have carried the charge against him much farther; for Bottrigaro having got possession of the manuscript at a time when Annibale Meloni consulted him about it, he caused a copy to be made of it, and had the effrontery to publish it as his own; there is now extant an impression of it with this title 'Il Desiderio; overo de' 'concerti di vari stromenti musicali, dialogo di musica 'di Ercole Bottrigari.' In Bologna per il Bellagamba, 1590, in quarto.†

---

* Annibale Meloni was a man of considerable learning. Artusi, in the preface to his second part of the treatise Delle Imperfettioni, mentions a certain demonstration of some of the problems of Aristotle, and other works of his writing. For his profession we are to seek, though Bottrigaro styles him 'Molto Mag. M. Annibale Melone Decano de Musica ordinarii 'Illustriss. Signoria di Bologna.'

† N. Haym. Notizia de' libri rari nella lingua Italiana. Lond. 1726, octavo, pag. 269.

In the year 1604, Artusi published at Bologna a small tract in quarto, entitled ' Impresa del molto ' R. M. Gioseffo Zarlino da Chioggia.' It seems that Zarlino, some time before his decease, agreeably to the practice of many learned men in all faculties, had chosen for himself a device or impress adapted to his profession, and alluding to that method of reasoning which he had pursued in the course of his studies for demonstrating the harmonical ratios. This impress, which probably he might make the subject of an intaglio, or otherwise assume, was a cube, on which were drawn a variety of lines intersecting each other, and forming angles in harmonical ratios, with this motto above, ΟΥΔΕΝ ΧΩΡΙΣ ΕΜΟΥ, that is to say, ' Nothing without me,' and underneath this, ΑΕΙ Ο ΑΥΤΟΣ ' Always the same.'

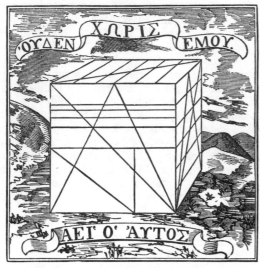

The diagrams inscribed on the three apparent sides of the above figure are such as Zarlino, in the course of his writings, had invented for the purpose of demonstrating the ratios of the consonances. Artusi's book is a commentary on the impress at large, with a formal declaration of the doctrines referred to by it; but from what has been said of the Helicon of Ptolemy, and the subsequent improvement of it, mentioned in the account herein-before given of Zarlino and his writings, the general import of these diagrams may be easily perceived.

The foregoing account of Bottrigaro and Artusi, and the controversy between them respecting Francesco Patricio, renders it necessary to speak of the treatise intitled Il Desiderio.

As to the book intitled Il Desiderio, it is a curious and entertaining dialogue on the concerts which at the time of writing it were the entertainment of persons of the first rank in the principal cities of Italy, particularly Venice and Ferrara. The interlocutors in it are Gratioso Desiderio, who, although the title of the book is taken from his name, seems to be a fictitious person, and the author himself under the name of Alemanno Benelli. In the course of the conversation, the principles of harmony, as delivered by the Greek and Italian writers, are investigated with great learning and ingenuity, with a view to establish a preference of the modern to the ancient

music. In support of his argument, the author recurs to that which is ostensibly the subject of his book, and speaks first of the concerts at Venice; next of those of the Academici Filarmonici at Verona; * and, lastly, of those performed in the ducal palace at Ferrara, of which he gives a particular description; for after taking notice of the grandeur and elegance of the apartments, and particularly of that splendid room in which the concert was accustomed to be given, he relates that the duke had in his service a great number of singers with fine voices, and excellent performers on various instruments, as well foreigners as Italians; and that the instruments made use of in concert were the cornet, trumpet, dulzain, flutes of various kinds, the viol, rebec, lute, cittern, harp, and harpsichord, and these to a considerable number.

After this general account of the instruments, the author mentions certain others which himself saw at the palace of the duke, and were there preserved, some for their antiquity, and others in respect of the singularity of their construction; among these he takes notice of a curious organ, formed to the resemblance of a screw, with pipes of box-wood all of one piece, like a flute; and a harpsichord invented by Don Nicola Vicentino surnamed Arcimusico, comprehending in the division of it the three harmonic genera. He adds that the multitude of chords in this astonishing instrument rendered it very difficult to tune, and more so to play; and that for this latter reason the most skilful performers would seldom care to meddle with it: nevertheless, he adds, that Luzzasco, the chief organist of his highness, who it is supposed must have understood and been familiar with the instrument, was able to play on it with wonderful skill. He says that this instrument by way of pre-eminence was called the Archicembalo; and that after the model of it two organs were built, the one at Rome, by the order of the Cardinal of Ferrara, and the other at Milan, under the direction of the inventor Don Nicola, in or about the year 1575, who died of the plague soon after it was finished.

The author relates that the duke of Ferrara had many Italian and foreign musicians retained in his service; and a very large collection of musical compositions, in print and in manuscript, and a great number of servants, whose employment it was to keep the books and instruments in order, and to tune the latter. The principal director of the musical

* The Accademia degli Filarmonici was instituted first at Vicenza. The time when cannot be precisely ascertained; but appears by an instrument of a public notary, yet extant, that so early as the year 1565 the Accademia degli Incatenati was incorporated with it, after which the members, upon their joint application to the magistracy of Verona, obtained a grant of a piece of ground, whereon a sumptuous edifice was erected; to this the nobility and gentry of the city were used to resort once a week, and entertain themselves with music: about the year 1732 a theatre was added to the great hall for the performance of operas. Walth. Lex. pag. 4.
The academy above-mentioned is supposed to be the most ancient of the kind of any in Italy, but since the institution of it others have been established, which, as they will be occasionally spoken of hereafter, it may not be improper to give an account of here. And 'first it is to be noted that in the year 1622 a society was established at Bologna by Girolamo Giacobbi, called the Accademia de' Filomusi; the symbol of this fraternity was a little hill with reeds or canes growing on it, the motto ' Vocis dul- ' cedine captant.' In 1633 another was instituted in the same city by Domenico Burnetti and Francesco Bertacchi, called the Accademia de' Musici Filachisi, having for its symbol a pair of kettle-drums, and for a motto ' Orbem demulcet attactu.' One of the two is yet subsisting, but it is uncertain which. Ibid.

performances was [Ippolito] Fiorino, maestro di cappella to his highness the duke.

Whenever a concert was to be performed at the duke's palace, circular letters were issued, requiring the attendance of the several performers, who were only such as had been previously approved of by the duke and Luzzasco; and after repeated rehearsals, was exhibited that musical entertainment, which, for order, exactness, and harmony, could not be equalled by any of the like kind in the world.

Meloni says that of the vocal music usually performed in this and other concerts in Italy, the canzones of the Flemish and French composers were some of the best. He speaks of a custom in Bologna, though it is common in most cities of Italy, Spain, and Portugal, viz., that of serenading or entertaining ladies and great personages with ambulatory concerts under their windows, and in the night; and, lastly, he celebrates for their skill in music, and exquisite performance on sundry instruments, the ladies of the duchess of Ferrara, and the nuns of St. Vito,* whom he resembles to the Graces.

CHAP. XCIII.

SCIPIONE CERRETO, *(a Portrait,)* a Neapolitan, was the author of a treatise entitled 'Della prattica 'musica vocale, et strumentale,' quarto, 1601. This, though it appears to be an elaborate work, and promises great instruction to such as delight in music, contains little more respecting the science than is to be found in Boetius, Franchinus, Zarlino, Zaccone, and other of the Italian writers. It appears by this author that in his time instrumental music was arrived at great perfection in Italy, and more particularly at Naples, for he gives a copious list of composers and excellent performers on the lute, the organ, the viol, the guitar, the trumpet, and the harp, who flourished in his time, and were either natives of, or resident in that city.

In the eighth chapter of his fourth book the author intimates that he himself was a performer on the lute;

and, besides giving directions for the holding and touching it, he explains with great perspicuity the tablature of the Italians adapted to the lute of eight chords; and first, he gives the characters for time, which are no other than those described by Adrian le Roy, and which have already been exhibited. And after that the tuning as here represented :—

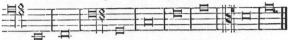

Then follows the succession of tones and semitones on each of the chords in this order :—

And after these, the tablature by figures according to the Italian manner, as here represented :—

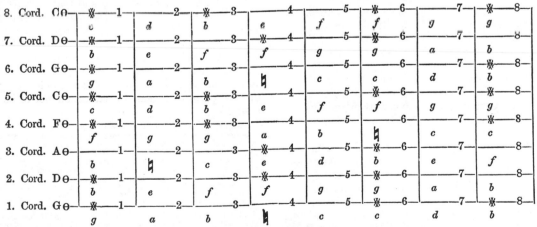

Cap. IX. of the same book treats of an instrument resembling a lute of seven chords, called by the author Bordelletto alla Taliana; and cap. X. of another of the same kind, called the Lira in Gamba, having eleven chords, with their several tunings, and of the tablature proper to each, in figures.

* These nuns are celebrated for their skill in music by Artusi, in the beginning of his discourse, 'Delle Imperfettioni della moderna musica.'

Cap. XI. treats of the Viola da Gamba, an instrument, as the author remarks, proper to accompany the voice in singing. It appears that the ancient method of notation for this instrument among the Italians was by figures. This kind of notation was practised both by the Italians and Spaniards, and differs from the French tablature, which is by the letters of the alphabet: who was the inventor of it we are yet to learn; Vincentio Galilei explained and improved it; but, notwithstanding this, it has long since given way to the French, perhaps as being more legible and less intricate.

This book of Cerreto abounds with curious particulars relating to music, but it has been remarked that the language and style of it are very indifferent.

Besides the several persons herein-before particularly enumerated, there flourished in this century many very eminent masters, of whom little more is known than their general characters, arising either from their compositions, or their skill and exquisite performance on the organ: among the former these are highly celebrated, Giovanni Cavaccio of Bergamo, maestro di cappella di S. Maria Maggiore; Jacques Arcadelt, a Frenchman, a disciple of Josquin, and maestro di cappella to the Cardinal of Lorrain; Johannes Knefel, a German, maestro di cappella to the elector Palatine; Ludovicus Senfelius, born at Zurich, maestro di cappella to the elector of Bavaria; Antonio Scandelli, maestro di cappella at Dresden; Gio. Maria Rossi, of Brescia; Nicolaus Rostius, a native of Weimar, and master of music in the court of the elector Palatine; Gio. Battista Pinelli, a Genoese by birth, and mastro di cappella at Dresden. As are also these :—

Agresta, Agostino.	Ingegneri, Marc. Ant.
Angelini, Orazio.	Laura, Dominico.
Animuccia, Paolo.	Leoni, Leon.
Baccusi, Hippolito.	Lucatello, Gio. Batt.
Bassani, Orazio.	Macque, Giov. de.
Bellasio, Paolo.	Mancini, Curtio.
Belli, Giulio.	Manenti, Giov. Pietro.
Bellhaver, Vincenzo.	Marsolo, Pietro Maria.
Bertani, Lelio.	Masorelli, Paolo.
Blotagrio, Guglielmo.	Massanio, Tiburtio.
Blasius, Ammon.	Molinaro, Simone.
Bonhomius, Petrus.	Moscaglia, Giov. Batt.
Casati, Girolamo.	Mosto, Gio. Batt.
Colombi, Gio. Bernardi.	Nasco, Giov.
Comis, Michele.	Nenna, Pomponio.
Conversi, Girolamo.	Nodari, Gio. Paolo.
Corregio, Claudio.	Nucetus, Flaminius.
Donati, Baldassare.	Palma, Gio. Vincenzo.
Duetto, Antonio.	Pace, Antonio.
Eremita, Giulio.	Pesenti, Benedetto.
Faignient, Noë.	Pevernagius, Andreas.
Farino, Francesco.	Pizzoni, Giov.
Fattorini, Gabriello.	Ponte, Giaches de.
Felis, Stefano.	Pordenone, Marc. Ant.
Ferretti, Giovanni.	Prætorius, Hieronymus.
Fonteijo, Gio.	Quartiero, Pietro Paolo.
Gabrieli, Andrea.	Quagliata, Paolo.
Gastoldi, Giacomo.	Reggio, Spirito.
Handl, Jacobus.	Rossi, Salomon.

Rubiconi, Chrysostom.	Turnhout, Giov.
Ruffo, Vincenzo.	Utendahl, Alessandro.
Sabino, Hippolito.	Valcampi, Curtio.
Santini, Marsilio.	Verdonck, Cornelius.
Scaletta, Orazio.	Vespa, Geronimo.
Scarabeus, Damianus.	Violante, Giov. Franc.
Spongia, Francesco.	Waelrant, Hubert.
Spontone, Alessandro.	Zoilo, Annibale.
Stabile, Annibale.	

Of organists, the following were some of the most eminent : Gioseffo Guammi, of Lucca; Ottavio Bariola, organist of Milan ; and Annibale Patavina, of Venice ; Johannes Leo Hasler, of Nuremberg ; Jacobus Paix, a native of Augsburg, and organist of Lawingen.

Of these it is to be observed that they were for the most part natives of Italy, Germany, and Flanders ; for it is strange to say, that, excepting England, those were almost the only countries in Europe in which music may be said to have made any considerable progress. Doni observes that Spain had in the course of a century produced only two men of eminence in music, namely, Christopher Morales and Franciscus Salinas ; and among the French scarce any musicians of note are mentioned besides Jusquin de Prez, Jean Mouton, Crequilon, and Claude le Jeune.* In England, Tye, Tallis, Bird, Bull, and Dowland, were highly esteemed ; and it is confidently asserted that in the general opinion they were equal to the best musicians of any country ; and the same is said of Peter Phillips, an Englishman, organist to the archduke and duchess of Austria, Albert and Isabella, governors of the Netherlands, residing at Brussels ; but of these, and other of our countrymen, mention will be made hereafter.

It has been already remarked, that during the last half of the sixteenth century, the madrigal was the species of vocal composition most practised and encouraged ; and as singing was the usual entertainment of the well-bred of both sexes, and had not then given place to cards and games of chance ; the demand for variety was so great as to excite an emulation in all that were qualified for it, to excel in this kind of composition ; and innumerable were the collections of madrigals which about this time were given to the world by their respective authors. They were generally published in an oblong quarto size, with both the notes and words printed in a good character on letter-press types, and without bars ; from such books as these it was held a disgrace for any person of rank or education not to be able to sing.†

* Jusquin de Prez is justly reckoned among the earliest of the French composers, but the science of counterpoint had been cultivated to some degree before his time ; one Guillaume Guerson of Longueville, a town in Upper Normandy, was the author of a treatise printed at Paris by Michael Thouloze, with this title, ' Utillissime musicales regule cunctis ' sũmopere necessarie plani cãtus sĩplisis cõtrapuncti rerũ factarũ tonorũ ' et artis accentuandi tam exẽplariter quam practicè.' [The Colophon after the word factarũ adds ' seu organorum.'] The book bears no date, but from the style and character of it, it is conjectured to be nearly as ancient as the time of Franchinus.

† Castiglione requires of his courtier that he be able to sing his part at sight. Bandello, in one of his novels, speaking of an accomplished young man, says, ' Era il detto Giouine molto costumato e vertuoso, ed oltra le ' buone lettere, si dilettaua mirabilmente de la musica, cantaua bene la ' sua parte e soura d' ogni strumento.' Novelle del Bandello, part II. Nov. xxv., and in Morley's Introduction, the reason given by Philomathes for applying to a master for instruction in music is as follows : Being at ' a banket of master Sophobulus, supper being ended, and musicke

SCIPIO CERRETUS MUSICUS PARTENOPEUS

ÆTATIS SUÆ LV

MDCI.

In consequence of this disposition in the public, such a profusion of vocal harmony was poured forth, as served rather to distract than oblige the votaries of the science ; and it became necessary to direct their choice by a judicious selection of such compositions as were most worthy of their regard : to this end, one Melchior Borchgrevinck, organist to the king of Denmark, published at Copenhagen, in the year 1606, a collection of madrigals for five voices, entitled ' Giardino novo bellissimo de varii fiori ' musicali scieltissimi,' in two parts, the latter whereof is dedicated to our king James I ; and about the same time, four persons, namely, Pietro Phalesio, a bookseller of Antwerp, and Andrea Pevernage, Hubert Waelrant, and Pietro Philippi above-named, three excellent musicians, in a kind of emulation severally published a collection of madrigals with the following titles, Musica Divina, Harmonia Celeste, Symphonia Angelica, Melodia Olympica, with this uniform declaration of their contents in these words, ' Nella ' quale si contengono i piu eccellenti madrigali che ' hoggidi si cantino.' They were printed for Phalesio, and sold at his shop, the sign of king David, in Antwerp.

These compositions were to words of Petrarch, Guarini, Tasso, Marino, Fulvio Testi, and other Italian poets ; and in the memory of such as understood and admired music, a favourite madrigal held the place of a popular song ; among other evidences to this purpose, a little poem of Sir Philip Sidney, printed with the sonnets at the end of his Arcadia, beginning ' Sleep baby mine,' may be reckoned as one, as it is directed to be sung to the tune of ' Basciami vita mia,' a fine madrigal of Noë Faignient, printed in the Musica Divina..

CHAP. XCIV.

Of English musicians, the first of note after the reformation of religion, and indeed of music itself, which had been greatly corrupted by the use of intricate measures, was JOHN MARBECK, of Windsor, a man to whom church-music has greater obligations than the world is sensible of ; for notwithstanding the vulgar opinion that Tallis composed it, it is certain that the cathedral musical service of the church of England was originally framed by Marbeck, and that the musical notes to the Preces, Suffrages, and Responses, as they are at this day sung in choral service, were of his composition.

The history of this man has entitled him to a place in the Martyrology of the zealous and laborious John Fox, and is as follows :—

About the year 1544, a number of persons at Windsor, who favoured the Reformation, had formed themselves into a society ; among them was Anthony Person, a priest, Robert Testwood, a singing-man in the choir of Windsor, a man in great estimation for his skill in music, and whose name occurs in Morley's Catalogue of eminent English musicians at the end

of his Introduction ; the above-named John Marbeck, who by a mistake of bishop Burnet is also called a singing-man, but in truth was organist of the chapel of St. George at Windsor,[*] and one Henry Filmer, a tradesman of the same town. Upon intimation given that these persons held frequent meetings, Gardiner, bishop of Winchester, procured a commission from the king to search suspected houses in the town for heretical books ;[†] upon which the four persons above-named were apprehended, and their books seized, among which were found some papers of notes on the Bible, and a Concordance in English, in the hand-writing of Marbeck. Upon his examination before the commissioners of the six articles touching these papers, he said, as to the notes, that he read much in order to understand the Scriptures ; and that whenever he met with any exposition thereof he extracted it, and noted the name of the author ;[‡] and as to the Concordance, that being a poor man, he could not afford to buy a copy of the English Bible, which had then lately been published with notes by Thomas Matthews ; and therefore had set himself to write one out, and was entering into the book of Joshua, when a friend of his, one Turner,[§] knowing his industry, suggested to him the writing of a Concordance in English, but he told him he knew not what that meant, upon which his friend explained the word to him, and furnished him with a Latin Concordance and an English Bible ; and having in his youth learned a little Latin, he, by the help of these, and comparing the English with the Latin, was enabled to draw out a Concordance, which he had brought as far as the letter L. This seemed to the commissioners who examined him a thing so strange, that they could not believe it. To convince them, Marbeck desired they would draw out any words under the letter M, and give him the Latin Concordance and English Bible, and in a day's time he had filled three sheets of paper with a continuation of his work, as far as the words given would enable him to do.[||] The ingenuity and industry of Marbeck were much applauded, even by his enemies ; and it was said by Dr. Oking, one of the commissioners who examined him, that he had been better employed than his accusers. However, neither his ingenuity nor industry could prevent his being brought to a trial for heresy, at the same time with the three other persons his friends and associates : Person and Filmer were indicted for irreverent expressions concerning the mass ; the charge against Marbeck was copying with his own hand an epistle of Calvin against it, which it seems was a crime within the statute of the well-known six articles, and they were all four found guilty and condemned to be burnt, which sentence was executed on all except Marbeck, the next day after the trial.[¶]

Testwood had discovered an intemperate zeal in dissuading people from pilgrimages, and had stricken off with a key, the nose of an alabaster image of the

Virgin Mary, which stood behind the high altar of St. George's chapel.* It is also related of him, that in the course of divine service one of the same chapel, named Robert Phillips,† singing, as his duty required, on one side of the choir, these words, ' O ' redemptrix et salvatrix,' was answered by Testwood singing on the other side, 'Non redemptrix nec ' salvatrix.'‡

For these offences, the four Windsor men, as they are called, were severally indicted, and by the verdict of a partial jury, composed of farmers under the college of Windsor, grounded on the testimony of witnesses, three of whom were afterwards convicted of perjury, in their evidence at the trial, they were all found guilty of heresy, and condemned to be burnt, which sentence was executed at Windsor on Person, Testwood, and Filmer the next day.§

It seems that the king, notwithstanding the severity of his temper, pitied the sufferings of these men, for at a time when he was hunting in Guildford park, seeing the sheriff and Sir Humfrey Foster, one of the commissioners that sat at the trial, together, he asked them how his laws were executed at Windsor, and upon their answering that they never sat on matter that went so much against their consciences as the trial of Person and his fellows, the king, turning his horse's head to depart, said 'Alas, poor innocents !'

But Marbeck being a man of a meek and harmless temper, and highly esteemed for his skill in music, was remitted to Gardiner, who was both his patron‖ and persecutor, in order either to his purgation, or a discovery of others who might have contracted the taint of heresy ; but under the greatest of all temptations he behaved with the utmost integrity and uprightness, and, refusing to make any discoveries to the hurt of others, he, through the intercession of Sir Humfrey Foster, obtained the king's pardon.

Having thus escaped martyrdom, he applied himself to the study of his profession, and, not having been required to make any public recantation, he indulged his own opinions in secret, without doing violence to his conscience, or giving offence to others, till the death of Henry VIII. which happened about two years after, when he found himself at liberty to make a public profession of his faith, as an evidence whereof he completed his Concordance, and published it in

1550 : he wrote also the following other books, 'The ' Lives of holy Saincts, Prophets, Patriarchs, and ' others,' quarto, 1574. ' A Book of Notes and ' Common Places with their Expositions, collected ' and gathered together out of the workes of divers ' singular writers,' quarto, 1581. ' The ripping up ' of the Pope's Fardel,' 1581. ' A Dialogue between ' Youth and Age ;' and other books.¶

The history of Marbeck's troubles is given at large by Fox, who notwithstanding he was acquainted with him, and had the relation of his sufferings from his own mouth, in the first edition of his Acts and Monuments, published in 1562, instead of a confessor, has made him a martyr, by asserting that he actually suffered in the flames at Windsor with Person and the other two ; which mistake, though he corrected it in the subsequent edition of his work,** exposed him to very severe censures from Cope, Parsons, and other Romish writers.††

The musical service thus framed by Marbeck, and, for aught that appears, without the least assistance from any of his profession, was published with this title, ' The Boke of Common Praier, noted.' The Colophon, ' Imprinted by Richard Grafton, printer ' to the kinges majestie, 1550, cum privilegio ad ' imprimendum solum,' with the name John Merbecke in the preceding page, to intimate that he was the author or composer of the musical notes, which are so very little different from those in use at this day, that this book may truly be considered as the foundation of the solemn musical service of the church of England.

A particular account of this curious work will be given hereafter, in the interim it is necessary to say that it was formed on the model of the Romish ritual ; as first, there was a general recitatory intonation for the Lord's Prayer, the Apostles' Creed, and such other parts of the service as were most proper to be read, in a certain key or pitch : to the introitus, supplications, suffrages, responses, prefaces, postcommunions, and other versicles, melodies were adapted of a grave and decent form, and nearly as much restrained as those of St. Ambrose or Gregory ; and these had a harmonical relation to the rest of the service, the dominant in each being in unison with the note of the key in which the whole was to be sung.

The abilities of Marbeck as a musician may be judged of by the following hymn of his composition.

---

* Acts and Monuments, edit. 1641, vol. II. pag. 543.

† Of this man, Fox says that he was so notable a singing-man, wherein he gloried, that wheresoever he came the longest song with most counterverses in it should be set up at his coming. His name, spelt Phelipp, occurs as a gentleman of the chapel in the lists of the chapel establishment both of Edward VI. and queen Mary.

‡ Acts and Monuments, vol. II. pag. 544.			§ Ibid. 543.

‖ It appears by sundry expressions of Gardiner to Marbeck, that he had an affection for him, possibly grounded on his great skill in his profession. Fox relates that at the third examination of Marbeck at Winchester-house, in Southwark, upon his appearance in the hall he found the bishop with a roll in his hand, and going toward the window, he called to him, and said, 'Marbeck, wilt thou cast away thyself?' upon his answering No, 'Yes,' replied the bishop, 'thou goest about it, for ' thou wilt utter nothing. What a devil made thee to meddle with the ' Scriptures? Thy vocation was another way, wherein thou hast a goodly ' gift, if thou diddest esteeme it.' 'Yes,' answered Marbeck, 'I do ' esteeme it, and have done my part therein according to that little know-' ledge that God hath given me.' ' And why the devil,' said the bishop, ' didst thou not hold thee there ?' And when Marbeck confessed that he had compiled the Concordance, and that without any help save of God, the bishop said, ' I do not discommend thy diligence, but what shouldest ' thou meddle with that thing which pertaineth not to thee ?' Acts and Monuments, edit. 1641, vol. II. pag. 548. These expressions, harsh as they were, seem to indicate a concern in Gardiner that Marbeck had brought himself into trouble.

¶ Vide Fasti, Oxon. anno 1550.

** Vol. II. printed in 1576, in which he says of Marbeck, ' he is yet not ' dead, but liveth, God be praised, and yet to this present singeth merrily, ' and playeth on the organs.'

†† To say the truth, Fox's zeal for the Protestant cause has very much hurt the credit of his history ; as a proof of his lightness of belief, take the following story, which lord chief justice Coke once told of him. Fox in his Martyrology had related of one Greenwood, of Suffolk, that he had been guilty of perjury, in testifying before the bishop of Norwich against a martyr during the persecution in the reign of queen Mary ; and that afterwards he went home to his house, and there by the judgment of God his bowels rotted out of his belly, as an exemplary punishment for his perjury. A priest, who had newly been made parson of the parish where Greenwood lived, and was but little acquainted with his parishioners, preaching against the sin of perjury, cited this story from Fox, mentioning Greenwood by name, who was then in the church listening attentively to the sermon ; the man, extremely scandalized by so foul an aspersion, brought his action against the parson, which was tried at the assizes before Anderson, who ruled that the action lay not, inasmuch as the words were not spoken with a malicious intent, but merely to exemplify the divine vengeance for so heinous a sin. Rolle's Abridgm. 87. Pl. 5.

JOHN MARBECK, ORGANIST OF WINDSORE.

CHAP. XCV.

CHRISTOPHER TYE, born at Westminster, and brought up in the royal chapel, was musical preceptor to prince Edward, and probably to the other children of Henry VIII. In the year 1545 he was admitted to the degree of doctor in music at Cambridge ; and in 1548 was incorporated a member of the university of Oxford ; in the reign of queen Elizabeth he was organist of the royal chapel, and a man of some literature. In music he was excellent ; and notwithstanding that Wood, speaking of his compositions, says they are antiquated, and not at all valued, there are very few compositions for the church of equal merit with his anthems.

In an old comedy or scenical history, whichever it is proper to call it, with the following whimsical title, 'When you see me you know me,' by Samuel Rowley, printed in 1613, wherein are represented in the manner of a drama, some of the remarkable events during the reign of Henry VIII., is a conversation between prince Edward and Dr. Tye on the subject of music, which for its curiosity is here inserted :—

' *Prince.* ———— Doctor Tye,
' Our musick's lecturer ? Pray draw near : indeed I
' Take much delight in ye.

' *Tye.* In musicke may your grace ever delight,
' Though not in me. Musicke is fit for kings,
' And not for those know not the chime of strings.

' *Prince.* Truely I love it, yet there are a sort
' Seeming more pure than wise, that will upbraid it,
' Calling it idle, vaine, and frivolous.

' *Tye.* Your grace hath said, indeed they do upbraid
' That tearme it so, and those that doe are such
' As in themselves no happy concords hold,
' All musicke jarres with them, but sounds of good ;
' But would your grace awhile be patient,
' In musicke's praise, thus will I better it :
' Musicke is heavenly, for in heaven is musicke,
' For there the seraphins do sing continually ;
' And when the best was born that ever was man,
' A quire of angels sang for joy of it ;
' What of celestial was reveald to man
' Was much of musicke : 'tis said the beasts did worship
' And sang before the deitie supernall ;
' The kingly prophet sang before the arke,
' And with his musicke charm'd the heart of Saul :
' And if the poet fail us not, my lord,
' The dulcet tongue of musicke made the stones
' To move, irrationall beasts and birds to dance.
' And last the trumpets' musicke shall awake the dead,
' And clothe their naked bones in coates of flesh,
' T' appeare in that high house of parliament,
' When those that gnash their teeth at musicke's sound,
' Shall make that place where musicke nere was found.

' *Prince.* Thou givest it perfect life, skilful doctor ;
' I thanke thee for the honour'd praise thou givest it,
' I pray thee let's heare it too.

' *Tye.* 'Tis ready for your grace. Give breath to
' Your loud-tun'd instruments.

         ' *Loud musicke.*

' *Prince.* 'Tis well : methinkes in this sound I prove
' A compleat age,
' As musicke, so is man govern'd by stops
' And by dividing notes, sometimes aloft,
' Sometimes below, and when he hath attaind

' His high and lofty pitch, breathed his sharpest and most
' Shrillest ayre ; yet at length 'tis gone,
' And fals downe flat to his conclusion.   [*Soft music.*]
' Another sweetnesse and harmonious sound,
' A milder straine, another kind agreement ;
' Yet 'mongst these many strings, be one untun'd,
' Or jarreth low or higher than his course,
' Nor keeping steddie meane amongst the rest,
' Corrupts them all, so doth bad man the best.

 ' *Tye.* Ynough, let voices now delight his princely eare.

    ' *A song.*

 ' *Prince.* ' Doctor I thank you, and commend your
' I oft have heard my father merrily speake   [cunning,
' In your high praise ; and thus his highnesse saith,
' England one God, one truth, one doctor hath
' For musickes art, and that is Doctor Tye,*
' Admired for skill in musick's harmony.

 ' *Tye.* Your grace doth honour me with kind acceptance,
' Yet one thing more I do beseech your excellence,
' To daine to patronize this homely worke,
' Which I unto your grace have dedicate.

 ' *Prince.*   What is the title ?

 ' *Tye.* The Actes of the holy Apostles turn'd into verse,
' Which I have set in several parts to sing :
' Worthy acts and worthily in you remembred.

 ' *Prince.*   I'll peruse them, and satisfy your paines.
' And have them sung within my father's chapel.†

* At the time when Farinelli was in England, viz., about the year 1735,
an exclamation of the like kind, and applied to that celebrated singer,
gave great offence ; he was singing in the opera, and as soon as he had
finished a favourite song, a lady from the boxes cried out aloud, ' One
' God, one Farinelli.' Mr. Hogarth has recorded this egregious instance of musical enthusiasm, in his Rake's Progress, plate II. by representing Farinelli as seated on a pedestal, before which is an altar, at
which a number of ladies are kneeling and offering to him, each a flaming
heart ; from the mouth of the foremost of these enraptured devotees
issues a label with the words ' One G—d, one Farinelli.'

† In another part of this old comedy Cranmer and Tye appear, and are
met by one young Browne (*supposed to be the son of Sir Anthony Browne,*
master of the horse to Henry VIII. and one of his executors) with the
prince's cloak and hat ; Cranmer enquires of him what has become of the
prince, and is told that he is at tennis with the marquis of Dorset.
Upon which follows this dialogue :—

Cranmer. Goe beare this youngster to the chappell straight,
And bid the maister of the children whippe him well,
The prince will not learne, Sir, and you shall smart for it.

Browne. O good my lord, I'll make him ply his booke to-morrow.

Cranmer. That shall not serve your turne. Away I say. [*Exit.*]
So Sir, this policie was well devised : since he was whipt thus
For the prince's faults
His grace hath got more knowledge in a moneth,
Than he attained in a yeare before ;
For still the fearful boy, to save his breech,
Doth hourely haunt him whereso'ere he goes.

Tye. 'Tis true my lord, and now the prince perceives it,
As loath to see him punish for his faults,
Plies it of purpose to redeeme the boy.

Upon which passage it is observable that there appears by an extract
from the Liber Niger, inserted in a preceding chapter, to have been in
the royal household two distinct masters, the one called Master of Song,
whose duty it was to teach the children of the chapel singing ; the other
a Master of the Grammar-school, who taught them also, and probably
other children in the palace, the rudiments of the Latin tongue ; and as
Browne does not appear to be a child of the chapel, it seems as if
Cranmer meant to send him for correction, not to the master of the
children properly so called, *i. e.* the master of song, but to the master of
the grammar-school.

It will doubtless seem very strange, seeing he had not been guilty of
any fault, that Browne should be whipt at all, but Cranmer's order may
be accounted for. The practice of whipping the royal children by proxy
had probably its rise in the education of prince Edward, and may be
traced down to the time when Charles the First was prince. *Besides*
Browne here mentioned, it appears that the prince had another proxy for
correction, namely, Barnaby Fitzpatrick, a very ingenious and accomplished youth, who became the founder of a noble family of that name
in Ireland. He is frequently mentioned in the journal of king Edward
VI. by the name of Mr. Barnaby ; and in Fuller's Worthies, Middlesex,
pag. 179, are several letters from the king to him when upon his travels,
containing directions for his conduct, and many expressions of affection
and concern for his welfare. Burnet, in his account of Mr. Murray of
the bed-chamber, Hist. of his own Times, vol. I. pag. 244, says he was
whipping-boy to king Charles I. In the Spectator, No. 313, is a story
somewhat to this purpose of Mr. Wake, father to the archbishop of that
name. A schoolfellow of his, whom he loved, had committed a fault,

The Acts of the Apostles, mentioned in the foregoing dialogue, were never completed, but the first
fourteen chapters thereof were in 1553 printed by
Wyllyam Seres, with the following quaint title :—

 ' The Actes of the Apostles, translated into Eng-
' lyshe metre, and dedicated to the kynges moste
' excellent maiestye by Christofer Tye, Doctor in
' musyke, and one of the gentylmen of hys graces
' moste honourable Chappell, wyth notes to eche
' Chapter, to synge and also to play upon the Lute,
' very necessarye for studentes after theyr studye, to
' fyle theyr wyttes, and alsoe for all Christians that
' cannot synge to reade the good and Godlye storyes
' of the lives of Christ hys Apostles.'

The dedication is ' To the vertuous and godlye
' learned prynce Edwarde the VI.' and is in stanzas
of alternate metre, of which the following may serve
as a specimen :—
   *   *   *   *   *   *

   ' Your grace may note fro tyme to tyme
    ' That some doth undertake
   ' Upon the Psalmes to write in ryme,
    ' The verse pleasaunt to make.

   ' And some doth take in hande to wryte
    ' Out of the booke of Kynges, ‡
   ' Because they se your grace delyte
    ' In suche like godlye thynges.

   ' And last of all, I youre poore man
    ' Whose doinges are full base,
   ' Yet glad to do the best I can,
    ' To geue unto your grace,

which Wake took upon himself, and was whipped for at Westminster
school. Mr. Wake was a cavalier, and had borne arms under Penruddock
and Grove in the West, and being taken prisoner, was indicted for high-
treason against the commonwealth, at Exeter, and after a short trial
convicted. It happened that the judge of assize who presided in court
was the very person for whom Mr. Wake had been whipt when a school-
boy, and recollecting his name and face, he asked him some questions,
the answers to which convinced him that he was about to pass sentence
on one to whom he was indebted for a very singular instance of friendship, the reflection on which inspired him with such a sense of gratitude,
that he rode immediately to London, and by his interest with the Protector procured his pardon. It is to Dr. Grey's edition of Hudibras, vol. I.
pag. 392, in not. that we are indebted for the name of the gentleman ;
and as Penruddock in the course of the trial takes occasion to mention
that he sees judge Nicholas upon the bench, there is very little doubt
but that he was the judge to whom the story refers. See the State Trials,
vol. II. pag. 260.

‡ Thomas Sternhold was the first that attempted a version of the
Psalms in English. He did to the number of about forty of them : the
rest in the printed collection used in churches were afterwards translated
by John Hopkins, William Whittingham, Thomas Norton, and others.
Sternhold's version was first published in the year 1549.

In the same year was published a version of the Penitential Psalms by
Sir Thomas Wyat, and in the year after ' Certayne Psalmes chosen out
' of the Psalter of David, and drawen furth into English meter by
' William Hunnis, servant to the ryght honorable Sir William Harberde,
' knight.' This William Hunnis was a gentleman of the chapel, temp.
Edward VI. and upon the death of Richard Edwards, in 1566, was appointed master of the children. He died June 6, 1597, and was succeeded
by Nathaniel, afterwards Dr. Giles. Cheque-book of the royal chapel.
Farther mention of him will be made hereafter.

In the year last above-mentioned, viz., 1550, were also published
' Certayn chapters taken out of the proverbes of Solomon, with other
' chapters of the holy scripture, and certayne Psalmes of David, translated
' into English metre by John Hall. Whych Proverbes of late were set
' forth, imprinted, and untruely entitled to be the doynges of Mayster
' Thomas Sternhold, late grome of the kynge's maiestes robes, as by thys
' copye it may be perceaved, MDL.' The chapters above-mentioned are
the sixth of the book of Wisdom called Sapientia ; the ninth of Ecclesiasticus, and the third of the second epistle of St. Paul to the Thessalo-
nians : the Psalms are Psalm xxi. xxiii. liii. lxiv. cxi. cxii. cxiii. and
cxliv.

The whole Psalter was translated into English metre by Dr. Matthew
Parker, afterwards archbishop of Canterbury, and printed by John Day
about the year 1560. The book is very little known, and is supposed to
have been printed only for presents. An account of it will be given
hereafter.

The passage to which this note refers has a plain allusion to these
parts of scripture thus rendered into metre, and to a version of part of
the book of Kings, which has escaped a diligent enquiry. In prosecution
of this design of turning select portions of scripture for the purpose of
singing them in churches, Dr. Tye versified some chapters of the Acts of
the Apostles, and set them to musical notes as above is related.

'Haue thought it good nowe to recyte
　'The ftories of the actes
'Euen of the twelve, as Luke doth wryte,
　'Of all their worthy factes.

*　　*　　*　　*　　*　　*

'Unto the text I do not ad,
　'Nor nothynge take awaye ;
'And though my ftyle be groffe and bad,
　'The truth perceyue you maye.

'And yf your grace fhall in good parte
　'My fymple worke fo take,
'My wyttes to this I will conuart
　'All vayne thynges to forfake.

'My callynge is another waye,
　'Your grace fhall herein fynde,
'By notes fet forthe to fynge or playe,
　'To recreate the mynde.

'And though they be not curious,
　'But for the letter mete,
'Ye fhall them fynde harmonious,
　'And eke pleafaunt and fwete.

'That fuch good thinges your grace might moue
　'Your lute when ye affaye,
'Inftede of fonges of wanton loue
　'Thefe ftories then to playe.*

'So fhall your grace pleafe God the Lorde,
　'In walkynge in his waye,
'His lawes and ftatutes to recorde
　'In your heart nyght and daye.

'And eke your realme fhall florifh ftyll,
　'No good thynge fhall decaye :
'Your fubjectes fhall with right good wyll
　'Thefe wordes recorde and faye,

"Thy lyfe, O kynge, to us doth fhyne
　"As Gods boke doth thee reache :
'Thou doft us fede with fuch doctrine
　"As Chrifte's elect dyd preache.

*　　*　　*　　*　　*　　*

Here follow the two initial stanzas of the four-teenth chapter of the version of the Acts of the Apostles, with the music by Dr. Tye. In the original the author has given the music in separate parts, but here it is in score.

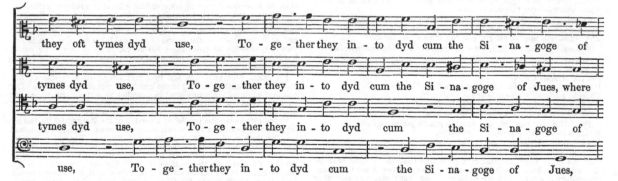

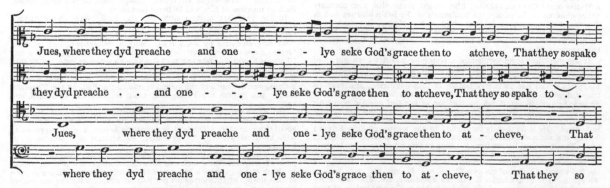

* This stanza, were other evidence wanting, would be a proof that the king played on the lute.

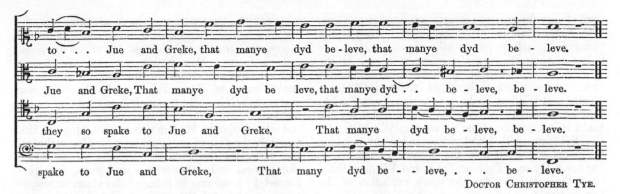

to ... Jue and Greke, that manye dyd be - leve, that manye dyd be - leve.

Jue and Greke, That manye dyd be leve, that manye dyd . . be - leve, be - leve.

they so spake to Jue and Greke, That manye dyd be - leve, be - leve.

spake to Jue and Greke, That many dyd be - - leve, . . . be - leve.

DOCTOR CHRISTOPHER TYE.

The Acts of the Apostles set to music by Dr. Tye, were sung in the chapel of Edward VI. and probably in other places where choral service was performed; but the success of them not answering the expectation of their author, he applied himself to another kind of study, the composing of music to words selected from the Psalms of David, in four, five, and more parts; to which species of harmony, for want of a better, the name of Anthem, a corruption of Antiphon, was given.

In Dr. Boyce's collection of cathedral music, lately published, vol. II. is an anthem of this great musician, 'I will exalt thee,' a most perfect model for composition in the church style, whether we regard the melody or the harmony, the expression or the contrivance, or, in a word, the general effect of the whole.

In the Ashmolean MS. fol. 189, is the following note in the hand-writing of Anthony Wood: 'Dr. 'Tye was a peevish and humoursome man, especially 'in his latter days, and sometimes playing on the 'organ in the chapel of Qu. Eliz. which contained 'much music, but little delight to the ear, she would 'send the verger to tell him that he played out of 'tune, whereupon he sent word that her ears were 'out of tune.' The same author adds that Dr. Tye restored church-music after it had been almost ruined by the dissolution of abbies.   Ibid.*

THOMAS TALLIS, one of the greatest musicians that this country ever bred, flourished about the middle of the sixteenth century.   He is said to have been organist of the royal chapel to king Henry VIII. king Edward VI. queen Mary, and queen Elizabeth; but the inscription on his grave-stone warrants no such assertion; and it is certain that in the reigns of Edward VI. and queen Mary he was simply a gentleman of the chapel, and served for seven pence halfpenny per diem: under Elizabeth' he and Bird were gentlemen of the chapel and organists.

The studies of Tallis seem to have been wholly devoted to the service of the church, for his name is not to be found to any musical compositions of songs, ballads, madrigals, or any of those lighter kinds of music framed with a view to private recreation.   Of the many disciples who had profited by his instruction, Bird seems to have possessed the greatest share of his affection, one proof whereof was a joint publication by them both of one of the noblest collections of hymns and other compositions for the service of the church that ever appeared in any age or country.

The work above alluded to was printed by Vautrollier in 1575, with the title of ' Cantiones 'quæ ab argumento sacræ vocantur quinque et sex 'partium, Autoribus Thoma Tallisio et Guilielmo 'Birdo, Anglis, serenissimæ reginæ majestati à 'priuato sacello generosis et organistis.'

This work was published under the protection of a patent of queen Elizabeth, the first of the kind that had ever been granted; and as the privileges contained in it are very singular, and serve to show what a share of royal favour they possessed, the substance thereof, as printed at the end of the book, is here inserted :—

'The extract and effect of the quenes maiesties 'letters patents to Thomas Tallis and William Birde, 'for the printing of musicke.

'Elizabeth by the grace of God quene of Eng-'lande, Fraunce, and Irelande, defender of the faith, '&c.   To all printers, bokesellers, and other officers, 'ministers, and subjects greting, Know ye, that we 'for the especiall affection and good wil that we have 'and beare to the science of musicke, and for the ad-'vauncement thereof, by our letters patents dated the 'xxii. of January in the xvii. yere of our raigne, 'have graunted full priviledge and licence unto our 'welbeloved servants Thomas Tallis and William 'Birde Gent. of our chappell, and to the overlyver 'of them, and to the assignes of them, and of the 'surviver of them, for xxi. yeares next ensuing, to 'imprint any and so many as they will of set songe 'or songes in partes, either English, Latine, French, 'Italian, or other tongues that may serve for musicke 'either in churche or chamber, or otherwise to be 'either plaid or soonge, And that they may rule and 'cause to be ruled by impression any paper to serve 'for printing or pricking of any songe or songes, 'and may sell and utter any printed bokes or papers 'of any songe or songes, or any bookes or quieres of 'such ruled paper, imprinted, Also we straightly by 'the same forbid all printers, booksellers, subjects 'and strangers, other then as is aforesaid, to do any 'the premisses, or to bring or cause to be brought

* This manuscript, containing brief notes and memoirs of famous musicians, is in the hand-writing of Antony Wood. In the Catalogue of the Manuscripts in the Ashmolean Museum, published by Mr. Huddesford in 1761, it is thus numbered and described: '8568. 106. Some 'materials toward a history of the lives and compositions of all English 'musicians; drawn up according to alphabetical order in 210 pages 'by A. W.'

'out of any forren realmes into any our dominions,
'any songe or songes made and printed in any forren
'countrie, to sell or put to sale, uppon paine of our
'high displeasure, And the offender in any of the
'premisses for every time to forfet to us our heires
'and successors fortie shillings, and to the said Thomas
'Tallis and William Birde, or to their assignes, and to
'the assignes of the surviver of thē, all and every the
'said bokes, papers, songe or songes, We have also
'by the same willed and commaunded our printers,
'maisters and wardens of the misterie of stacioners,
'to assist the said Thomas Tallis and William Birde
'and their assignes for the dewe execution of the
'premisses.'*

Ames, in his Typographical Antiquities, pag. 353, takes notice that the dedication of this book to queen Elizabeth is very remarkable; he does not say for what, but it is obvious that he means for its composition and style, which is most pure and elegant Latin. The epistle dedicatory it is more than probable was written by Richard Mulcaster, the master of Merchant Taylor's school, an excellent grammarian, and a man of the first degree of eminence in his profession. There are prefixed to the book some Latin commendatory verses, with his name to them, in which is the following compliment to queen Elizabeth upon her skill in music :—

'Regia majestas, ætatis gloria nostræ;
'Hanc in deliciis semper habere solet,
'Nec contenta graves aliorum audire labores
'Ipsa etiam egregie voce manuque canit.'†

In this work is contained that admirable composition of Tallis, 'O sacrum convivium,' better known to the world, indeed, by the initial words 'I 'call and cry,' which, with the whole of that anthem, were adapted to the notes of 'O sacrum convivium' by Dean Aldrich. Charles Butler, of Oxford, a man of great learning, and known to the world by his attempts to reform the English orthography, commends 'Absterge Domine,' the second of the Cantiones Sacræ of Tallis, in the highest terms, and makes use of the authority of it for several purposes.

It is commonly said that Tallis was organist to Henry VIII. and the three succeeding princes his descendants; but it may well be doubted whether any establishment of the kind was known till the beginning of the reign of queen Elizabeth, when Tallis and Bird were severally appointed organists of the royal chapel. And here it may be necessary to mention, as has been hinted before, that the ancient foundations of conventual, cathedral, and collegiate churches in this kingdom, although less ancient than the introduction of organs into the church service,

take not the least notice of such an officer as the organist, but are endowments uniformly in favour of canons, the greater and the less, lay vicars or clerks, and choristers. Nay farther, no provision for an organist appears either in the list of the choral establishment of Edward VI. or in that of queen Mary, though in both, trumpeters and players on the sackbut occur. Hence it may fairly be presumed, and Dr. Benjamin Rogers was of that opinion, that anciently the duty of the organist, as well in cathedral and collegiate churches and chapels, as in abbies, monasteries, and other religious houses, was performed by some one or other of the vicars choral, or other members of the choir; ‡ an evident proof of the flourishing state of music among us in those early times. In this view, and this only, can Tallis be considered as organist to Henry VIII. Edward VI. and queen Mary.

Notwithstanding that he was a diligent collector of musical antiquities, and a careful peruser of the works of other men, the compositions of Tallis, learned and elegant as they are, are so truly original, that he may justly be said to be the father of the cathedral style; and though a like appellation is given by the Italians to Palestrina, it is much to be questioned, considering the time when Tallis flourished, whether he could derive the least advantage from the improvements of that great man. It may therefore be conjectured that he laid the foundation of his studies in the works of the old cathedralists of this kingdom, and probably in those of the German musicians, who in his time had the pre-eminence of the Italians; and that he had an emulation to excel even these, may be presumed from the following particular. Johannes Okenheim, a native of the Low Countries, and a disciple of Iodocus Pratensis, had made a composition for no fewer than thirty-six voices, which Glareanus says was greatly admired. Tallis composed a motet in forty parts, the history of which stupendous composition, as far as it can now be traced, is as follows :—

It was originally composed, in the reign of queen Elizabeth, to the following words, 'Spem in alium 'nunquam habui præter in te Deus Israel, qui iras-'ceris, et propitius eris, et omnia peccata hominum, 'in tribulatione dimittis, Domine Deus, creator cœli 'et terræ, respice humilitatem nostram.' In the 'reign of the first or second Charles some person 'put to it certain English words, which are neither 'verse nor prose, nor even common sense; and it 'was probably sung on some public occasion; but 'the composition with the Latin words coming to 'the hands of Mr. Hawkins, formerly organist of the 'cathedral church of Ely, he presented it to Edward 'earl of Oxford. Diligent search has been made for 'it among the Harleian manuscripts in the British

---

* The power of the crown to grant such privileges as are contained in this and other patents of the like kind, is expressly denied by Sir Joseph Yates, in his argument in the great case of literary property, Millar v. Taylor, where speaking of the patent of Tallis and Bird, and also of that granted to Morley, he says they are arbitrary, gross, and absurd. *Question concerning literary property, published by Sir James Burrow, 4to. 1773, pag. 85. And it appears that Morley was questioned by the House of Commons three years after the granting it. Ames's Typogr. Antiq. 569.*

† *Thus translated in the Biogr. Brit., Art. John Bull, page 1007, in note :—*

'The Queen, the glory of our age and isle,
'With royal favor bids this science smile;
'Nor hears she only others' labor'd lays,
'But, artist-like herself both sings and plays.'

‡ In the statutes of St. Paul's cathedral, tit. DE GARTIONIBUS [i. e. of the grooms, from GARCIO, a poor servile lad, or boy-servant. COWEL.] it is said that the duty of these servants is, 'exculpent ecclesiam, com-'panas pulsant exsufflent organa, et omne aliud humile officium ex-'erceant in ecclesia ad imperium vergiferorum;' but though provision is thus made for blowing the organ, the statutes are silent as to who is to play it. For some years past there has been an organist of St. Paul's, with a salary, which, upon the appointment of Dr. Greene, was augmented with the revenue of a lay vicar's place.

Museum, but without effect. As to the music, it is adapted to voices of five different kinds, that is, tenor, counter-tenor, altus, or mean, and treble, eight of each; and though every musician knows that, in strictness of speech, in a musical composition there can in reality be but four parts, for where there are more, some must rest while others sing; yet this of Tallis is so contrived, that the melody of the four parts is so broken and divided as to produce the effect of as many parts as there are voices required to sing it.

It is somewhat difficult to account for the publication of the Cantiones Sacræ in the original Latin words at a time when it is well known that our liturgy was completely settled, and the whole of the church service was by law required to be performed in the English tongue. It is true that the first act of uniformity of Edward VI. allowed great latitude in singing, and left it in a great measure in the discretion of the clergy either to adopt the metrical psalmody of the Calvinists, or to persevere in the use of the solemn choral service; and accordingly we see them both practised at this day; but that the singing of anthems and hymns in the Latin tongue was permitted under the sanction of this licence, there is no authority for saying; and indeed, the original composition of music to the Latin service by Tallis and Bird, is not to be accounted for but upon a supposition, which there is nothing to contradict, that they were of the Romish persuasion, and that the Cantiones Sacræ were composed for the use of queen Mary's chapel: with respect to Tallis, it may be observed that his name occurs in a list of her establishment yet extant; and as to Bird, that besides his share in the above work, there are several masses of his composition in print, which favour the opinion that he was once of the same communion.

But notwithstanding his supposed attachment to the Romish religion, it seems that Tallis accommodated himself and his studies to those alterations in the form of public worship which succeeded the accession of Queen Elizabeth. With this view he set to music those several parts of the English liturgy, which at that time were deemed the most proper to be sung, namely, the two morning services, the one comprehending the Venite exultemus, Te Deum, and Benedictus; and the other, which is part of the Communion office, consisting of the Kyrie Eleison, Nicene Creed, and Sanctus; as also the evening service, containing the Magnificat and Nunc dimittis; all these are comprehended in that which is called Tallis's first service, as being the first of two composed by him.* He also set musical Notes to the Preces and Responses, and composed that litany, which, for its excellence, is sung on solemn occasions, in all places where the choral service is performed.

As to the Preces of Tallis in his first service, they are no other than those of Marbeck in his book of

* It may be remarked that neither the psalms, Jubilate Deo in the morning, nor Cantate Domino and Deus misereatur in the evening prayer, occur in the service of Tallis; the reason is, that in the first settlement of the choral service they were not included, the most ancient Jubilate being that of Dr. Giles, and the most ancient Deus misereatur that of Mr. Strogers, both printed in Barnard's Collection, hereafter mentioned. When the Cantate Domine was first taken it appears not.

Common Prayer noted: the responses are somewhat different, that is to say, in the tenor part, which is supposed to contain the melody; but Tallis has improved them by the addition of three parts, and thereby formed a judicious contrast between the supplications of the priest and the suffrages of the people, as represented by the choir.

The services of Tallis contain also chants for the Venite exultemus and the Creed of St. Athanasius; these are tunes that divide each verse of the psalm or hymn according to the pointing, to the end that the whole may be sung alternately by the choir, as distinguished by the two sides of the dean and the chanter. Two of these chants are published in Dr. Boyce's cathedral music, vol. I.*

* This method of singing, though it corresponds with that antiphonal singing which was introduced into the church about the year 350, by Flavianus and Diodorus, the one bishop of Antioch, the other of Tarsus, and is in truth that part of choral service which is best warranted by the practice of the primitive Christians, and the judgment of the fathers, is that which the Puritans mean when they inveigh against the practice of 'tossing the Psalms about like tennis-balls;' their sentiments are contained in that virulent libel, the first of those two Admonitions to the Parliament, the one written by Field, minister of Aldermary, London, the other by Thomas Cartwright, printed in the year 1572, wherein is the following bitter invective against the form of divine worship as then lately established: 'In all theyr order of service there is no edification 'according to the rule of the Apostle but confusion: they tosse the 'Psalmes in most places like tennice-balles. They pray that all men 'may be saved, and that they may be delivered from thundering and 'tempest, when no danger is nigh. That they sing Benedictus, Nunc 'Dimittis, and Magnificat, we know not to what purpose, except some 'of them were ready to die, or except they would celebrate the memory 'of the Virgine and John Baptist, &c. Thus they prophane the holy 'scriptures. The people, some standing, some walking, some talking, 'some reading, some praying by themselves, attend not to the minister. 'He againe posteth it over as fast as he can galloppe; for eyther he hath 'two places to serve, or else there are some games to be playde in the 'afternoone, as lying for the whetstone, heathenishe dauncing for the 'ring, a beare or a bull to be baited, or else jackanapes to ride on horse-'backe, or an interlude to be plaide; and if no place else can be gotten, 'this enterlude must be playde in the church, &c. Now the people sit, 'and now they stand up. When the Old Testament is read, or the 'lessons, they make no reverence, but when Gospel commeth then they 'al stand up, for why, they thinke that to be of greatest authoritie, and 'are ignorant that the Scriptures came from one spirite. When Jesus is 'named, then of goeth the cap, and downe goeth the knees, wyth such 'a scraping on the ground, that they cannot heare a good while after, so 'that the word is hindered; but when any other names of God are 'mentioned, they make no curtesie at all, as though the names of God 'were not equal, or as though all reverence ought to be given to the 'syllables. We speake not of ringing when mattens is done, and other 'abuses incident, bicause we shal be answered that by the boke they are 'not maintayned, only we desire to have a boke to reforme it. As for 'organes and curious singing, thoughe they be proper to Popyshe dennes, 'I meane to cathedrall churches; yet some others also must have them. 'The queenes chapell, and these churches (whych should be spectacles 'of Chrystian reformation) are rather patternes and presidentes to the 'people of all superstition.'

Hooker, Eccles. Pol. book V. sect. 33, has defended with great learning and jugment the practice of chanting or singing the Psalms by course, or side after side, against an objection of Cartwright, in another part of his works, to wit, that 'it is the more to be suspected, as the 'Devil hath gone about to get it authority;' nevertheless, so lately as the time of king William, endeavours were used to get it banished from the church, for in 1689, an ecclesiastical commission issued, and we are told that in execution thereof it was proposed, among other reformations of the church-service, to lay aside chanting in cathedrals. Vide, Calamy's Abridgment of Baxter's History of his Life and Times, Vol. I. p. 446-453. Hooker professes to wonder, as indeed any man would, how the Devil can be benefited by our singing of Psalms; and for singing the Benedictus and other hymns he thus apologizes: 'Of reading or singing 'Magnificat, Benedictus, and Nunc Dimittis oftener than the rest of the 'Psalms, the causes are no whit less reasonable; so that if the one may 'very well monthly, the other may as well even daily be iterated. They 'are songs which concern us so much more than the songs of David, 'as the Gospel toucheth us more than the law, the New Testament 'than the Old. And if the Psalms, for the exceliency of their use, 'deserve to be oftner repeated than they are, but that the multitude of 'them permitteth not any oftner repetition, what disorder is it, if 'these few Evangelical hymns, which are in no respect less worthy, and 'may be, by reason of their paucity, imprinted with much more ease in 'all men's memories, be for that cause every day rehearsed? In our own 'behalf it is convenient and orderly enough, that both they and we 'make day by day prayers and supplications the very same; Why not as 'fit and convenient to magnifie the name of God day by day with certain 'the very self-same Psalms of praise and thanksgiving: Either let 'them not allow the one, or else cease to reprove the other. For the 'ancient received use of intermingling hymns and psalms with divine 'readings, enough hath been written. And if any may fitly serve unto

The care of selecting from the Common Prayer the offices most proper to be sung, was a matter of some importance, especially as the Rubric contains no directions about it; for this reason it is supposed that the musical part of queen Elizabeth's liturgy was settled by Parker, archbishop of Canterbury, who, besides that he was a great divine, an excellent canon-lawyer and ritualist, and a general scholar, was also a skilful musician.* Besides the offices above-mentioned, constituting what are now termed the Morning, Communion, and Evening Services in four parts, with the preces, responses, and litany, that is to say, the versicles and suffrages, Tallis composed many anthems, as namely, 'O Lord, give 'thy holy spirit,' in four parts; 'With all our hearts,' 'Blessed be thy name,' 'Wipe away my sins,' and others in five parts, which are printed in a collection entitled 'The first Book of selected Church-music, 'collected out of divers approved authors by John 'Barnard, one of the minor canons of the cathedral 'church of St. Paul,' 1641.

Tallis died the twenty-third day of November, 1585, and was buried in the parish church of Greenwich in Kent. Strype, in his Continuation of Stow's Survey, published in 1720, says that in his circuit-walk round London he found in the chancel of that church, upon a stone before the rails, a brass plate thus inscribed in old letters :—

Enterred here doth ly a worthy wyght,
    Who for long tyme in mufick bore the bell :
His name to fhew, was Thomas Tallys hyght,
    In honeft uertuous lyff he dyd excell.

He feru'd long tyme in chappel with grete prayfe,
    Fower fouereygnes reygnes (a thing not often feene)
I mean kyng Henry and prynce Edward's dayes,
    Quene Mary, and Elizabeth our quene.

He maryed was, though children he had none,
    And lyu'd in loue ful thre and thirty yeres
Wyth loyal fpowfe, whos name yclept was Jone,
    Who here entomb'd, him company now bears.

As he dyd lyue, fo alfo did he dy,
    In myld and quyet fort, O happy man !
To God ful oft for mercy did he cry,
    Wherefore he lyues, let deth do what he can.

The stone on which this inscription was engraven was repaired by Dean Aldrich.†

The following motet of Tallis is the second in order of the Cantiones Sacræ published by him and Bird in 1575. The Miserere that here follows it, is the last composition in the same collection :—

'that purpose, how should it better have been devised, than that a com-
'petent number of the old being first read, these of the new should
'succeed in the place where now they are set? In which place notwith-
'standing, there is joined with Benedictus, the hundred Psalm; with
'Magnificat, the ninety-eight; the sixty-seventh with Nunc Dimittis;
'and in every of them the choice left free for the minister to use in-
'differently, the one for the other. Seeing, therefore, they pretend no
'quarrel at other Psalms which are in like manner appointed also to be
'daily read, Why do these so much offend and displease their taste?
'They are the first gratulations wherewith our Lord and Saviour was
'joyfully received at his entrance into the world, by such as in their
'hearts, arms, and very bowels, embraced him; being prophetical dis-
'coveries of Christ already present, whose future coming the other
'Psalm did but fore-signifie; they are against the obstinate incredulity
'of the Jews, the most luculent testimonies that Christian religion hath :
'yea, the only sacred hymns they are that Christianity hath peculiar unto
'itself; the other being songs too of praise and thanksgiving, but songs
'wherewith as we serve God, so the Jew likewise.' Eccles. Polity, bk. V.
sect. 40.

* Strype, in his life of this prelate, page 4, relates that in his youth he had been taught to sing by one Love, a priest, and also by one Manthorp, clerk of St. Stephen's in Norwich; and in his translation of the Psalms of David, a book but little known, and which he composed during his retreat from the persecution of queen Mary, are certain observations on the ecclesiastical tones, which shew him to have been deeply skilled in church-music.

† There was also in the old church of Greenwich an inscription on brass in memory of Richard Bowyer, gentleman of the chapel and master of the children under king Henry VIII. Edward VI. queen Mary, and queen Elizabeth. He died 26 July, 1561, and was succeeded by Richard Edwards, from Oxford.

There was also in the same church a stone, purporting that Ralph Dallans, organ-maker, deceased while he was making the organ, which was begun by him February, 1672, and finished by James White, his partner, who completed it, and erected the stone, 1673. But the old church being pulled down soon after the year 1720, in order to the re-building it, not the least trace of any of these memorials is now re-maining.

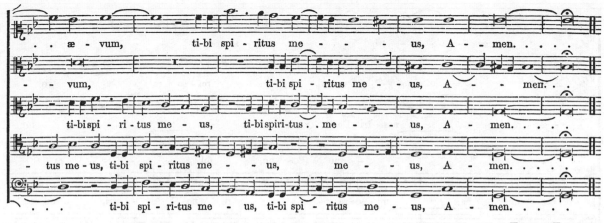

THOMAS TALLIS.

CANON.

THOMAS TALLIS.

The Miserere above exhibited is in its contexture extremely curious and artificial, as will appear by the following analysis of its parts :—

1 Superius primus - {	Duæ Partes in una, Canon in unisono.
2 Superius Secundus	Canon in unisono.
3 Discantus - - - {	Quatuor partes in una, Canon in unisono, crescit in duplo, Arsin et Thesin.
4 Contratenor - -	Canon in unisono.
5 Tenor - - - -	Voluntaria pars.
6 Bassus primus -	Canon in unisono.
7 Bassus secundus -	Canon in unisono.

RICHARD FARRANT, a fine old composer for the church, was a gentleman of the chapel royal in 1564, and after that master of the children of St. George's chapel at Windsor, with an allowance of 81*l*. 6*s*. 8*d*. per annum for their diet and teaching. He was also one of the clerks and one of the organists of the same chapel. Upon occasion of these latter appointments he resigned his place in the chapel royal, but in 1569 was called to it again, and held it till 1580, when Anthony Todd was appointed in his room. His places in the chapel at Windsor he enjoyed to the time of his death, which is supposed to have been in 1585, Nathaniel Giles, then a bachelor in music, being sworn into both of them on the first day of October in that year. His compositions are in a style remarkably devout and solemn; many of them are printed in Barnard's Collection of Church-music above-mentioned, and a few in Dr. Boyce's cathedral music.

ROBERT PARSONS, or, as his name is spelt by Morley, PERSONS, was organist of Westminster abbey. The following epitaph on him is in Camden's Remains.

Upon Master Parsons, Organist at Westminster.

Death passing by and hearing Parsons play,
Stood much amazed at his depth of skill,
And said 'This artist must with me away,'
For death bereaves us of the better still;
    But let the quire, while he keeps time, sing on,
    For Parsons rests, his service being done.

He was sworn of queen Elizabeth's chapel on the seventeenth day of October, 1563, and was drowned at Newark-upon-Trent on the twenty-fifth of January, 1569. Many of his compositions are extant in MS.

Butler, in his Principles of Music, page 91, speaks in terms of high commendation of the "In Nomines" of Parsons, and those also of Tye and Taverner.*

* The term In Nomine is a very obscure designation of a musical composition, for it may signify a fugue, in which the principal and the reply differ in the order of solmisation; such a fugue being called by musicians a Fugue in Nomine, as not being a fugue in strictness. Again, it may seem to mean some office in divine service, for in the Gradual of the Romish church the Introitus, In festos sanctissimi nominis Jesu, has this beginning, 'In nomine Jesu omne genu flectatur:' and this latter circumstance seems to be decisive of the question. But upon looking into an In Nomine of Master Taverner, in that venerable old book entitled 'Morning and Evening Praier and Communion set forth in 'fower partes, to be song in churches,' printed by John Day in 1565, it clearly appears that the term refers to the nineteenth Psalm, as it stands in the Vulgate, though it is the twentieth in our translation, and that by reason of the following verse in it, 'Lætabimur in salutari tuo: et in 'nomine Dei nostri magnificabimur.'

In the Life of Milton by his nephew Phillips, prefixed to the English translation of his State Letters, it is said that John Milton the father, who was so eminently skilled in music as to be ranked among the masters of the science in his time, composed an In Nomine, for which he received of a Polish prince a present of a gold chain and medal.

Parsons left behind him a son named John, who became master of the choristers in Westminster Abbey. In the year 1616, upon the recommendation of Dr. Mountain, the Dean, he was elected one of the parish clerks, and also organist of the Parish church of St. Margaret's, Westminster. See a subsequent part of this work.

CHAP. XCVI.

IN what manner the theory of music was anciently taught in the universities of this kingdom, especially that of Oxford, may in some measure be collected from the accounts given by Wood of the studies and exercises of candidates for degrees in that faculty. As to the practice of it, it is evident that for many years it was only to be acquired in monasteries, and in the schools of cathedral and collegiate churches. The music lecture in Oxford was not founded till the year 1626; and before that time, although there were endowments for the support of professors, and the reading of lectures in divinity and other faculties, we meet with no account of any thing of the kind respecting music.

It is probable that this consideration, and a view to the benefit that might accrue to students in music, in common with those intended for other professions, from public lectures, were the motives of that princely-spirited man, Sir Thomas Gresham, to the foundation of that college in London known by his name, which within these few years has ceased to exist; and the endowment for the maintenance of persons of sufficient ability to read public lectures in the faculties and sciences of divinity, astronomy, music, geometry, law, physic, and rhetoric.

To this end he by his will, bearing date the fifth of July, 1575, declares the uses of a conveyance made by him dated the twentieth day of May preceding, to his lady and certain other trustees therein named, that is to say : ' As to a moiety of his buildings in London ' called the Roiall Exchange, after the determination ' of the particular estates in the whole by the said ' conveyance limitted, to the maior and cominalty and ' cittezens of London and their successors, willing and ' disposing that they shall every year give and dis-' tribute to and for the sustentation, mayntenaunce, ' and findinge foure persons, from tyme to tyme to be ' chosen, nominated, and appointed by the said maior ' and cominalty and cittezens, and their successors, ' mete to rede the lectures of divynitye, astronomy, ' musicke, and geometry, within his then dwelling-' house in the parish of St. Hellynes in Bishopsgate-' streete, and St. Peeters the Pore, in the cittye of ' London, the somme of two hundred pounds of law-' full money of England, that is to say, to every of ' the said readers for the tyme beinge, the somme of ' fifty pounds yerely, for their sallaries and stipendes ' mete for four sufficiently learned to reade the said ' lectures, the same to be paid at two usual tearmes ' in the yere yerely, that is to say, at the feastes of ' th' annunciation of St. Mary the virgin, and of St. ' Mighell th' archangell, by even portions to be paid.'

And as concerning the other moiety which he had by his said will disposed to the wardens and cominalty of the mistery of the mercers of the cittye of London, the testator wills and disposes it to them and their successors that they shall 'yerely pay and 'distribute to and for the finding, sustentation, and 'mayntenaunce, of three persons mete to read the 'lectures of law, phisicke, and rethoricke, within his 'dwelling-house aforesaid, 150l., viz. 50l. to each of 'the said three persons.'

These endowments, by the terms of the will, were postponed during the life of lady Gresham. Sir Thomas died on the twenty-first day of November, 1579, and his lady on the third of November, 1596; upon which the provisions for the lectures took effect. In the beginning of the year succeeding the death of lady Gresham, the mayor, &c. of London, and the Mercers' Company, wrote to the universities of Oxford and Cambridge, requesting a nomination to them severally of persons properly qualified for professors, in consequence of which nomination three were chosen from each university; the seventh, that is to say, the music professor, Dr. John Bull, was appointed by the special recommendation of queen Elizabeth.

Having elected the professors, the city and the Mercers' Company next proceeded to settle the course and subjects of the lectures; and this was done by certain ordinances and agreements, bearing date the sixteenth day of January, 1597, between the mayor and commonalty and citizens of London on the first part, the wardens and commonalty of the mystery of Mercers of the same city of the second part, and the lecturers elected and appointed and placed in Gresham house on the third part.

It was for some time a matter of debate whether the lectures should be read in English or in Latin, or in both languages;* the reasons for reading them, or at least the divinity lecture, in English, are extant in Strype's edition of Stowe's Survey, but at length it was agreed that they should be read in both languages.

The ordinances above-mentioned may be seen at large in Strype's edition of Stowe, vol. II. Append. II. page 2, and also in the preface to Ward's Lives of the Gresham Professors: what concerns the music lecture is in these words :—

'The solemn musick lecture is to be read twice 'every week, in manner following, viz., the theorique 'part for half an hour, or thereabouts; and the prac- 'tique by concent of voice or of instruments, for the 'rest of the hour; whereof the first lecture to be in 'the Latin tongue, and the second in the English 'tongue. The days appointed for the solemn lectures 'of musick are Thursday and Saturday in the after- 'noons, between the hours of three and four; and 'because at this time Mr. Doctor Bull is recom- 'mended to the place by the queen's most excellent 'majesty, being not able to speak Latin, his lectures 'are permitted to be altogether in English so long as 'he shall continue the place of the music lecturer 'there.'

The ordinances above-mentioned appoint the days and hours for reading the several lectures; but these were not finally adjusted till the year 1631, when

* Book I. pag. 128, edit. 1720.

the reading was confined to the law terms, and that in the following order :—

Monday,	Divinity.
Tuesday,	Civil Law.
Wednesday,	Astronomy.
Thursday,	Geometry.
Friday,	Rhetoric.
Saturday,	{ Physic. Music. }

And this is the order now observed.†

WILLIAM BIRD, supposed to be the son of Thomas Bird, one of the gentlemen of the chapel in the reign of Edward VI.‡ was one of the children of the same; and, as it is asserted by Wood in the Ashmolean MS. was bred up under Tallis. There are some particulars relating to this eminent person that embarrass his history, and render it difficult to ascertain precisely either the time of his birth, or his age when he died, and consequently the period in which he flourished. That he was very young in the reign of Edward VI. may be concluded from the circumstance that he lived till the year 1623, at which time, supposing him to have been born in the first year of that prince's reign, viz. anno 1546, he must have been of the age of seventy-seven. And yet there are many of his compositions, particularly masses, extant, which must be supposed to have been made while the church service was in Latin, and bespeak him to have arrived at great excellence in his faculty before the final establishment of the liturgy under queen Elizabeth. The most probable conjecture that can be formed touching this particular seems to be, that he was a child of the chapel under Edward VI. and as his name does not occur in the chapel establishment of queen Mary, that he was either not in her service, or if he was, that he did not receive a stipend as Tallis and others did whose names are entered on the roll.

There can be very little doubt, considering the time when they lived, and the compositions by them published separately and in conjunction, but that both Tallis and Bird were of the Romish communion. It was not to be expected that in those times the servants of the chapel should be either divines or casuists, therefore it is not to be wondered at if Tallis in particular accommodated himself to those successive changes of the national religion which were made before the reformation was completed; or that he and Bird should afterwards fall in

† In the eighth year of the present king an act of parliament passed for carrying into execution an agreement of the city and the mercer's company with the commissioners of the excise revenue for the purchase of Gresham-college, and the ground and buildings thereunto belonging, and for vesting the same in the crown for the purpose of erecting and building an excise-office there, and for enabling the lecturers of the said college to marry, notwithstanding any restriction contained in the will of Sir Thomas Gresham, knight, deceased.

The bill was strongly opposed in the house of commons by the professors, with Dr. Pemberton, the physic professor, at their head; but a clause being inserted therein that gave him an additional sum of 50l. a year for his life, he was satisfied, as were the other professors with the sum of 50l. a year in lieu of their apartments in the college over and above their stipends, and that provision in the act that left them at liberty to marry. The city, and also the mercer's company were obliged to find and provide a proper and sufficient place or places for the professors to read in; and accordingly the lectures are now read in a room over the Royal Exchange.

‡ Besides being a gentleman of the chapel, it seems that he was clerk of the cheque. He died in 1561.

with that establishment which banished superstition and error from the church, and become good and sincere protestants.

Upon the accession of queen Elizabeth, and the resolutions taken by her to reform the choral service, Richard Bowyer, who had been master of the children under king Henry VIII. Edward VI. and queen Mary, was continued in that station; Dr. Tye, who seems to have been out of employ during the reign of queen Mary, and William Blitheman, were made organists, and Tallis continued a gentleman of the chapel royal. As to Bird, there seems to have been no provision made for him at court: on the contrary, he went to Lincoln, of which cathedral he had been chosen organist in 1563; nor does it appear that he had any employment in the chapel till the year 1569, when he was appointed a gentleman thereof in the room of Robert Parsons, who about a month before, by accident, was drowned at Newark-upon-Trent.* Upon his being elected into the chapel, Bird was permitted by the dean and chapter to execute his office of organist of Lincoln by a substitute named Butler, of whom there are no memorials remaining.

It appears that in 1575, Tallis and Bird were both gentlemen, and also organists of the royal chapel; but the time of their appointment to this latter office cannot now be ascertained

Wood, in his account of Morley, Fasti, anno 1588, says of Bird that he was skilled in the mathematics; and it there and elsewhere appears that Morley, who was his disciple, was taught by him as well mathematics as music.

These are all the particulars of his life that can now be recovered, excepting that he died on the fourth day of July in the year 1623, and that he had a son named Thomas, educated in his own profession, who in the year 1601 was the substitute of Dr. John Bull, and while he was travelling abroad for the recovery of his health, read the music lecture for him at Gresham college.

The compositions of Bird are many and various; those of his younger years were mostly for the service of the church, and favour strongly the supposition that he then adhered to the Romish communion; for with what reason can it be imagined that a protestant musician should, not to mention other Latin offices, compose masses? and of these there are three at least of Bird's actually in print, one for three, another for four, and another for five voices.

The work herein before spoken of, entitled 'Cantiones, quæ ab argumento sacræ vocantur, quinque et sex partium, Autoribus Thoma Tallisio et 'Guilielmo Birdo,' London 1575, oblong quarto, was composed by Bird, in conjunction with Tallis, and seems to be the earliest of his publications, though he must at that time have been somewhat advanced in years. He also composed a work of the same kind entitled 'Sacrarum Cantionum, quinque vocum,' printed in 1589, among which is that noble composition 'Civitas sancti tui,' which for many years past has

been sung in the church as an anthem to the words 'Bow thine ear, O Lord.'

Besides these he was the author of a work entitled 'Gradualia, ac Cantiones sacræ, quinis, quaternis 'trinisque vocibus concinnatæ. lib. primus. Authore 'Gulielmo Byrde, Organista regio Anglo.' Of this there are two editions, the latter published in 1610.

In the dedication of this work to Henry Howard, earl of Northampton, the author testifies his gratitude to that nobleman for the part he had taken in procuring for him and his fellows in the royal chapel an increase of salary. His words are these: 'Te suasore 'ac rogatore, serenissimus rex (exemplo post regis 'Edouardi tertii ætatem inaudito) me sociosq; meos, 'qui ipsius majestati in musicis deservimus, novis 'auxit beneficiis, et stipendiorum incrementis.†

The contents of this first book of the Gradualia are antiphons, hymns, and other offices, in the Latin tongue for the festivals, that is to say, In festo Purificationis, In festo omnium sanctorum, In festo corporis Christi, In festo nativitatis beatæ Mariæ Virginis, and others, probably composed during the reign of queen Mary.

Another collection of the like sort, and by the same author, was published by him in the same year 1610, with this title, 'Gradualia, seu cantionum 'sacrarum: quarum aliæ ad quatuor, aliæ vero ad 'quinque et sex voces editæ sunt.'

These, with the masses above-mentioned, after a careful enquiry, seem to be the whole of the compositions for the church, published by Bird himself; and, that he should think it proper to utter them in the reign of James the First, and at a time when the church had rejected these and numberless other offices of the like kind, which formerly made a part of divine service, can only be accounted for by that disposition which then prevailed in the public to receive and admire whatever had the sanction of his name.

Although it appears by these his works that Bird was in the strictest sense a church musician, he occasionally gave to the world compositions of a secular kind; and he seems to be the first among English musicians that ever made an essay in the composition of that elegant species of vocal harmony the madrigal. The La Verginella of Ariosto, which he set in that form for five voices, being the most ancient musical composition of the kind to be met with in the works of English authors.

To speak of his compositions for private entertainment, there are extant these that follow:—

'Songs of sundry natures, some of gravitie, and 'others of myrth, fit for all companies and voyces, 'printed in 1589.'

'Psalmes, sonets, and songs of sadness and pietie 'made into musicke of five parts, whereof some of

---

* This disaster befel Parsons January 25, 1569, and Bird was sworn in his room February 22, in the same year. Cheque Book.

† This passage has an allusion to a grant of James I. anno 1604, after a long and chargeable suit, with the furtherance of the earl of Northampton, and other honourable persons, whereby the stipends of the gentlemen of the chapel were increased from thirty to forty pounds per annum, and the allowance for the twelve children from sixpence to tenpence per diem, with a proportionable increase of salary to the serjeant, the two yeomen, and the groom of the vestry. A memorial of this grant is entered in the cheque-book of the chapel-royal, with an anathema upon whosoever shall take out the leaf. A copy of the whole verbatim is inserted in a subsequent page of this work.

'them going abroad among divers in untrue coppies,
'are here truly corrected ; and th' other being songs
'very rare and newly composed, are here published
'for the recreation of all such as delight in musicke,
'by William Byrd, one of the Gent. of the Queens
'Majesties royall chappell.'

The last of his works published by himself is
entitled ' Psalmes, Songs, and Sonets : some solemne,
'others joyfull, framed to the life of the words, fit
'for voyces or viols of 3, 4, 5, and 6 parts.' Lond.
1611.

Besides these he was the author of many compositions published in collections made by other
persons, namely, that entitled ' Parthenia, or the
'maiden-head of the first musick that ever was
'printed for the virginalls, composed by three
'famous masters, William Byrd, Dr. John Bull, and
'Orlando Gibbons, gentlemen of her majesties chappell,' in which are three lessons for that instrument
of his composition. In the printed collections of
services and anthems published at sundry times,
namely, those of Day and Barnard, are many composed by him, and still many more which exist only
in the manuscript books of the king's chapel, the
cathedral, and collegiate churches of this kingdom.

That he was an admirable organist there cannot
be the least doubt : a very good judge of music, who
was well acquainted with him, says that ' with fingers
'and with pen he had not his peer ;'* and we need
but advert to his compositions to judge of his style
and manner of playing on that noble instrument. If
he had, as the passage above-cited seems to indicate,
a free and voluble hand, we may reasonably conclude
that the exercise of it was sufficiently restrained and
corrected by his judgment ; and that his voluntaries
were enriched with varied motion, lofty fugues, artful
syncopations, original and unexpected cadences, and,
in short, all the ornaments of figurate descant, forming a style solemn, majestic, and devout.

His music for the virginals, or, as we should now
say, his lessons for the harpsichord, are of a cast
proper for the instrument ; and as we cannot but
suppose that he was able to play them himself,
bespeak in him a command of hand beyond what
will readily be conceived of by those who imagine,
as is the truth in many instances, that the powers of
execution, as well in instrumental as vocal music,
have been increasing for two centuries past even to
this day. In the collection entitled Parthenia above-
mentioned, the lessons of Bird are none of the easiest ;
but in a manuscript collection, consisting solely of
his own compositions, and presented by him to a
scholar of his, the lady Nevil, are some as difficult to
execute as any of modern times. In this collection
is that composition taken notice of by Dr. Ward in
his Life of Dr. Bull, entitled ' Have with you to
'Walsingham.'†

* See the verses of John Baldwin in a subsequent page.

† This lesson is mentioned by Dr. Ward, as being in a manuscript
volume in the library of Dr. Pepusch, the contents whereof he has
given at large ; in that collection it stands the first, and is called only
Walsingham. The Doctor in a note styles it ' As I went to Walsingham,'
and says, without vouching any authority, that this tune was first composed by Bird with twenty-two variations, and that afterwards thirty
others were added to it at different times by Dr. Bull.
Dr. Ward in this note seems to confound the lesson with the tune ; for

But, notwithstanding the number and variety of
Bird's compositions, the most permanent memorials
of his excellencies are his motets and anthems, to
which may be added a fine service in the key of D
with the minor third, the first composition in Dr.
Boyce's Cathedral Music, vol. III. and that well-
known canon of his ' Non nobis Domine,' concerning
which in this place it is necessary to be somewhat
particular.

There seems to be a dispute between us and the
Italians whether the canon ' Non nobis Domine'
be of the composition of our countryman Bird or of
Palestrina. That it has long been deposited in the
Vatican library, and there preserved with great
care, has been confidently asserted, and is generally
believed ; and that the opinion of the Italian musicians is that it was composed by Palestrina may be
collected from this, that it has lately been wrought
into a concerto in eight parts, and published at
Amsterdam in the name of Carlo Ricciotti, with a
note that the subject of the fugue of the concerto is
a canon of Palestrina ; and that subject is evidently
the canon above-mentioned in all its three parts.

Now though it is admitted that the canon ' Non
'nobis Domine' does not occur among any of the
works of Bird above enumerated, and that its first
publication was by John Hilton, at the end of his
collection of Catches, Rounds, and Canons, printed in
1652 ; yet there seems to be evidence more than
equipollent to what has yet been produced on the
other side of the question, that he and he only was
the author of it : in such a case as this, tradition

it is more than probable that it was composed upon the ground of a tune
to an old interlude or ballad in Pepy's collection mentioned by Dr. Percy
in his Reliques of ancient English Poetry, vol. II. pag. 91, and beginning thus :—

　　' As I went to Walsingham,
　　　' To the shrine with speede,
　　' Met I with a jolly palmer
　　　' In a pilgrime's weede.

　　" Now God you save you jolly palmer !
　　　" Welcome lady gay,
　　" Oft have I sued to thee for love,
　　　" Oft have I said you nay."

To confirm this opinion of the Doctor's mistake, it may be observed
that many of Bird's lessons were composed on old grounds or popular
tunes : to give an instance of one in particular, in Lady Nevil's book
above-mentioned is a lesson of Bird, entitled Sellenger's, i. e. St. Leger's
Round ; this Sellenger's Round was an old country dance, and was not
quite out of knowledge at the beginning of the present century, there
being persons now living who remember it. Morley mentions it in his
Introduction, pag. 118, and Taylor the water-poet, in his tract entitled ' The world runs on wheels.' And it is printed in a collection of
country-dances published by John Playford in 1679, the notes of it are as
follow :—

Bird's lesson called Sellenger's Round above mentioned, is apparently
a set of variations on the country-dance of the same name ; and it is
highly probable that the lesson ' As I went to Walsingham,' was also
a set of variations on the tune of some old ballad which had these for its
initial words.

must be deemed of some weight, it is hard to conceive that a falsehood of this kind could ever gain credit, and still harder that it should maintain its ground for nearly two centuries. Dr. Pepusch in his Treatise of Harmony has expressly ascribed it to Bird, and if he and the rest of the world concurred in believing it to be a composition of his, we at this day, without any substantial evidence to the contrary, can hardly be justified in doubting whether he or another was the author of it.

From the nature of his works it is easy to discover that Bird was a man of a grave and serious temper, the far greater part of them being for the church; and as to the rest, they are in general as he terms them, 'Psalmes and songs of sadnes and pietie.' Nevertheless he could upon occasion exercise his fancy on lighter subjects, but never in the composition to words of an indecent or profane import. Twice in his life it seems he made an essay of his talent for light music in the composition of the madrigals, 'La 'Verginella è simile un rosa' and 'This sweet and 'merry month of May:'* of the former of which Peacham says it is not to be mended by the best Italian of them all.

There is extant of Bird one, and one only essay in that kind of composition which tends to promote mirth and good fellowship by drinking and singing, namely, the Round or Catch. It is printed in Hilton's collection; the words are 'Come drink with 'me,' &c.

Morley relates that Bird and master Alfonso, [the elder Ferabosco] in a virtuous contention, as he terms it, in love betwixt themselves, made upon the plain-song of a Miserere each to the number of forty ways, and that they could have made infinite more at their pleasure. From which it is to be inferred that he was a man of an amiable disposition, and that between him and his competitor [Ferabosco] there was none of that envy which sometimes subsists between the professors of the same art, and which, as Morley insinuates, is chargeable on the times when they both lived.

The testimonies to the merits of this most excellent musician are almost as numerous as the authors, at least of this country, who have written on the science or practice of music since his time. In the cheque-book of the chapel-royal he is called the father of music; and in the commendatory verses before the second part of the Gradualia, 'Britannico 'musicæ parenti.' Morley styles him 'his loving 'master never without reverence to be named of 'musicians;' and Peacham asserts, that even by the judgment of France and Italy he was not excelled by the musicians of either of those countries. Speaking of his Cantiones sacræ and Gradualia, he says, what all must allow who shall peruse them, that they are angelical and divine; and of the madrigal La Ver-

ginella, and some other compositions in the same set, that they cannot be mended by the best Italian of them all.

Besides his salaries and other emoluments of his profession, it is to be supposed that Bird derived some advantages from the patent granted by queen Elizabeth to Tallis and him, for the sole printing of music and music-paper: Dr. Ward speaks of a book which he had seen with the letters T. E. for Thomas East, Est, or Este, for he spelt his name in all of these three ways, who printed music under that patent.

Tallis died in 1585, and the patent, by the terms of it, survived to Bird, who no doubt for a valuable consideration, permitted East to exercise the right of printing under the protection of it: and he in the title-page of most of his publications styles himself the assignee of William Byrd. This patent granted for twenty-one years expired in 1595; and afterwards another, containing a power to seize music books and music paper, was granted to Morley.

The music printed under this patent was in general given to the world in a very elegant form, for the initial letters of the several songs were finely ornamented with fanciful devices; every page had an ornamented border, and the notes, the heads whereof were in the form of a lozenge, were well cut, and to a remarkable degree legible.

Wood seems to have erred in ascribing to Bird an admired composition in forty parts, which he says is not extant. Compositions in forty parts are not very common; there is one of Tallis, of which an account has been given in a preceding page, and is probably the composition alluded to by Wood, who seems to have been guilty of a very excusable mistake of one eminent musician for another.

In a manuscript collection of motetts, madrigals, fantasias, and other musical compositions of sundry authors, in the hand-writing of one John Baldwine, a singing-man of Windsor, and a composer himself, made in the year 1591, are many of the motetts of Bird in score. The book is a singular curiosity, as well on account of its contents, as of certain verses at the end composed by Baldwine himself, in which the authors whose works he had been at the pains of collecting are severely characterised. The verses are very homely, but the eulogium on Bird is so laboured and bespeaks so loudly the estimation in which he was held, as well abroad as at home, that the insertion of the whole will hardly be thought to need an apology:—

Reede, here, behold and fee all that muficions bee :
What is inclofde herein, declare I will begine.

A ftore-houffe of treafure this booke may be faiede
   Of fonges moft excelente and the befte that is made,
Collected and chofen out of the beft autours
   Both ftranger and Englifh borne, whiche be the beft makers
And fkilfulft in muficke, the fcyence to fett foorthe
   As herein you fhall finde if you will fpeake the truthe.
There is here no badd fonge, but the beft can be hadd,
   The cheefeft from all men : yea there is not one badd,
And fuch fweet muficke as dothe much delite yeelde
   Bothe unto men at home and birds abroade in fielde.
The autors for to name I maye not here forgett,
   But will them now downe put and all in order fett.

---

* Taken from the Orlando Furioso, canto primo. The first of these madrigals is in five parts, and is printed at the end of the 'Psalmes, sonets, and songs of sadness and pietie;' a translation of the words fitted to the same notes, may be seen in a collection entitled 'Musica 'Transalpina;' the other madrigal is printed in a collection entitled 'The first sett of Italian madrigals Englished by Thomas Watson,' it is set both in five and six parts. In the title-page of the latter book the two latter madrigals are said to be composed after 'the Italian vaine at the request of the sayd Thomas Watson.'

I will begine with White, Shepper, Tye, and Tallis,
  Parſons, Gyles, Mundie th'oulde one of the queenes pallis,
Mundie yonge, th'oulde man's ſonne and like wyſe others moe ;
  There names would be to longe, therefore I let them goe ;
Yet muſt I ſpeake of moe euen of ſtraingers alſo,
  And firſte I muſt bringe in Alfonſo Feraboſco,
A ſtrainger borne he was in Italie as I here ;
  Italians ſaie of hime in ſkill he had no peere.
Luca Merenſio with others manie moe,
  As Philipp Demonte the emperour's man alſo ;
And Orlando by name and eeke Crequillion,
  Cipriano Rore : and alſo Andreon.
All famous in this arte, there is of that no doute :
  There workes no leſſe declare in euerie place aboute,
Yet let not ſtraingers bragg, nor they theſe ſoe commende ;
  For they maye now geve place and ſett themſelves behynd
An Engliſhe man, by name, Willm Birde for his ſkill
  Which I ſhould haue ſett firſt, for ſoe it was my will ;
Whoſe great ſkill and knowledge dothe excelle all at this tyme
  And far to ſtrange countries abroade his ſkill dothe ſhyne :
Famus men be abroade, and ſkilful in the arte,
  I do confeſſe the ſame and will not from it ſtarte ;
But in Ewropp is none like to our Engliſhe man,
  Which doth ſo farre exceede, as trulie I it ſcan,
As ye cannot finde out his equale in all thinges
  Throwghe out the worlde ſo wide, and ſo his fame now ringes.
With fingers and with penne he hathe not now his peere ;
  For in this world ſo wide is none can him come neere.
The rareſt man he is in muſicks worthy arte
  That now on earthe doth liue : I ſpeake it from my harte
Or heere to fore hath been or after him ſhall come :
  None ſuch I feare ſhall riſe that may be calde his ſonne.

O famus man ! of ſkill and judgemente greate profounde ;
  Lett heauen and earth ringe out thy worthye praiſe to ſownde ;
Ney lett thy ſkill it ſelfe thy worthie fame recorde
  To all poſteretie thy due deſert afforde ;
And lett them all which heere of thy greate ſkill then ſaie
  Fare well, fare well thou prince of muſicke now and aye ;
Fare well I ſay, fare well, fare well and here I end
  Fare well melodious Birde, fare well ſweet muſickes frende .
All theſe things do I ſpeake not for reward or bribe ;
  Nor yet to flatter him or ſett him upp in pride,
Nor for affeccion or ought might moue there towe,
  But euen the truth reporte and that make known to yowe.
Lo heere I end farewell, committinge all to God,
  Who kepe us in his grace and ſhilde us from his rodd.

Finis.——   Jo Baldwine.

The two following motets, the one printed in the second part of the Gradualia, and the other in the Cantiones Sacræ, are evidences of the skill and abilities of this admirable church musician.

Of the latter of these compositions it is to be remarked that it is in eight parts, that is to say, Superius primus et secundus, Contratenor primus et secundus, Tenor primus et secundus, and Bassus primus et secundus ; and that in the printed book each of these eight parts is in canon of two in one, rectè et retro. The whole is in the judgment of some of the ablest musicians at this day living, a most stupendous contrivance.

WILLIAM BIRD.

CANON RECTE ET RETRO.

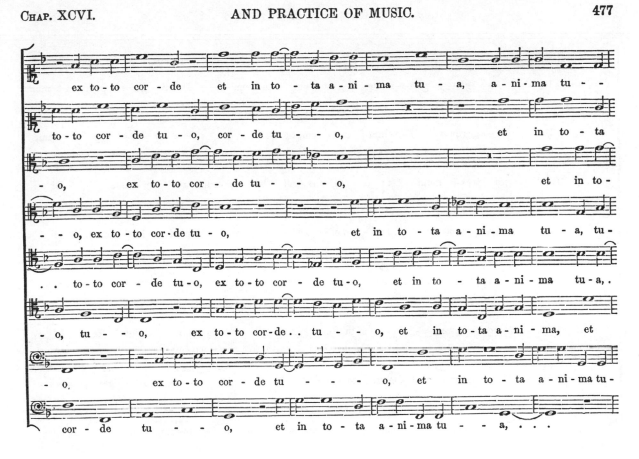

WILLIAM BIRD.

CHAP. XCVII.

ALFONSO FERABOSCO, as Dr. Wilson used to say, was born of Italian parents, at Greenwich in Kent. He never arrived to any academical honours in the faculty of music, nor does it appear that he had even any employment in the royal chapel, or about court;[*] nevertheless he is ranked among the first musicians of Elizabeth's time. Morley says that in a virtuous contention betwixt them, he and Bird made about forty waies, as he terms it, upon the plain-song of a certain Miserere; and Peacham speaks of another between the same persons, to wit, who of the two should best set the words of a certain ditty, 'The Nightingale so pleasant and so gay,' in which Ferabosco succeeded so well, that, in the judgment of Peacham, this composition, as also another of his, 'I saw my lady weeping,' for five voices, cannot be bettered for sweetness of air and depth of judgment.[†]

He had a son of the same Christian name, who for that reason is often mistaken for his father; he was the author of a book with this simple title, 'Ayres by Alfonso Ferabosco,' printed in folio, 1609, with the following commendatory verses by Ben Johnson :—

To my excellent friend Alfonso Ferrabosco.

To urge my lov'd Alfonso that bold fame
　Of building townes and making wild beasts tame
Which musique had ; or speak her known effects,
　That she removeth cares, sadness ejects,
Declineth anger, persuades clemency,
　Doth sweeten mirth and heighten pietie,

And is't a body often ill inclin'd,
　No less a soveraign cure then to the mind.
T' alledge that greatest men were not asham'd
　Of old, even by her practice to be fam'd,
To say, indeed, she were the soul of heaven,
　That the eight sphere, no less than planets seaven
Mov'd by her order, and the ninth more high,
　Including all were thence call'd harmony ;
I yet had utter'd nothing on thy part,
　When these were but the praises of the art,
But when I have saide the proofes of all these be
　Shed in thy songs, 'tis true, but short of thee.

Besides these verses, there are prefixed to the book the following :—

Musick's maister and the offspring
　Of rich musick's father,
Old Alfonso's image living,
　These fair flowers you gather
Scatter through the British soile ;
　Give thy fame free wing,
And gaine the merit of thy toyle.
　　We whose loves affect to praise thee,
　　Beyond thine own deserts can never raise thee.

　　　By T. Campion, Doctor in Physicke.[‡]

Besides the two above-mentioned, there was another named John, of the family of Ferabosco, a musician also, as appears by an evening service of his composing, in D, with the major third, well known in Canterbury and other cathedrals ; as one of the

---

[*] In Rymer's Fœdera Vol. 16, page 611, is a grant of an annuity of £50 a year to Alfonso Ferabosco, who is thus described, "one of the extraordinary grooms of our privy chamber." The grant is dated 22nd March, 1605, and is said to be made in regard of Ferabosco's attendance upon prince Henry, and instructing him in the art of music. The annuity is to be paid quarterly from the previous Christmas.

[†] Both printed in the Musica Transalpina, published by N. Yonge in 1588.

[‡] Of this Thomas Campion, Wood says, Fasti, vol. I. pag. 229, that he was an admired poet and musician ; there is extant of his an Art of Poesie in 12mo ; and it appears that he wrote the words of a masque represented in the banquetting-room at Whitehall on St. Stephen's night, 1614, on occasion of the marriage of Carr earl of Somerset and the lady Frances Howard, the divorced countess of Essex, the music to which was composed by Nicolas Laniere, John Cooper, or Coperario, as he affected to call himself, and others. One of that name, a Dr. Thomas Campion, supposed to be the same person, was the author of a book entitled 'A new way of making four parts in counterpoint,' and of another entitled 'The art of setting or composing music in parts ;' printed at the end of Playford's Introduction, the second edition, 1660, with annotations by Christopher Simpson.

same surname was formerly organist of Ely minster, it is not improbable but that the above person was he. A few years ago there was a Mostyn Ferabosco, a lieutenant in the royal navy, from which circumstance it is very probable that the family is yet in being.

WILLIAM BLITHEMAN, a gentleman of queen Elizabeth's chapel, and one of the organists of the same, is by Wood [Fasti, anno 1586,] celebrated as the excellent master of the famous Dr. John Bull. He died greatly lamented on Whitsunday, 1591, and was buried in the parish church of St. Nicholas Cole-Abbey, London. The following epitaph was engraven on a brass plate and fixed in the wall of the church, but being destroyed in the fire of London, it is now only to be found in Stow's Survey,* and is as follows :—

> Here Blitheman lies, a worthy wight,
> 　Who feared God aboue,
> A friend to all, a foe to none,
> 　Whom rich and poore did loue ;
> Of princes chappell gentleman
> 　Unto his dying day,
> Whom all tooke great delight to heare
> 　Him on the organs play ;
> Whose paſſing ſkill in muſickes art
> 　A ſcholar left behinde,
> John Bull by name, his maſters ueine
> 　Expreſſing in each kinde ;
> But nothing here continues long,
> 　Nor reſting place can haue,
> His ſoule departed hence to heauen,
> 　His body here in graue.

It seems that as a musician Blitheman's performance on the organ was his greatest excellence. Wood, who was likely to have known it, had he been a composer for the church, gives not the least hint to favour an opinion of the kind ; in short, he was a singular instance of a limited talent in the science of his profession.

JOHN BULL (a Portrait,) was born in Somersetshire, about the year 1563, and, as it is said, was of the Somerset family. He was educated under Blitheman before-named. In 1586 he was admitted at Oxford to the degree of bachelor of music, having practised in that faculty fourteen years ; and in 1592 was created doctor in the university of Cambridge. In 1591 he was appointed organist of the queen's chapel in the room of his master, Blitheman.

Bull was the first Gresham professor of music, and was appointed to that station upon the special recommendation of queen Elizabeth. However skilful he might be in his profession, it seems that he was not able to read his lectures in Latin ; and therefore, by a special provision in the ordinances respecting the Gresham professors, made anno 1597, it is declared, that because Dr. Bull is recommended to the place of music professor by the queen's most excellent majesty, being not able to speak Latin, his lectures are permitted to be altogether English, so long as he shall continue music professor there.†

In the year 1601, he went abroad for the recovery of his health, which at that time was declining ; and during his absence was permitted to substitute as his deputy a son of William Bird, named Thomas. He travelled incognito into France and Germany ; and Wood takes occasion to relate a story of him while abroad, which the reader shall have in his own words :—

'Dr. Bull hearing of a famous musician belonging 'to a certain cathedral at St. Omer's, he applied 'himself as a novice, to him, to learn something of 'his faculty, and to see and admire his works. This 'musician, after some discourse had passed between 'them, conducted Bull to a vestry or music-school 'joining to the cathedral, and shewed to him a 'lesson or song of forty parts, and then made a 'vaunting challenge to any person in the world to 'add one more part to them, supposing it to be so 'complete and full that it was impossible for any 'mortal man to correct or add to it ; Bull thereupon 'desiring the use of pen, ink, and ruled paper, such 'as we call musical paper, prayed the musician to 'lock him up in the said school for two or three 'hours ; which being done, not without great disdain 'by the musician, Bull in that time or less, added 'forty more parts to the said lesson or song. The 'musician thereupon being called in, he viewed it, 'tried it, and retried it ; at length he burst out into 'a great ecstasy, and swore by the great God that he 'that added those forty parts must either be the 'Devil or Dr. Bull, &c.‡ Whereupon Bull making 'himself known, the musician fell down and adored 'him. Afterwards continuing there and in those 'parts for a time, he became so much admired, that 'he was courted to accept of any place or preferment 'suitable to his profession, either within the do-'minions of the emperor, king of France, or Spain ; 'but the tidings of these transactions coming to the 'English court, queen Elizabeth commanded him 'home.' Fasti, anno 1586.

Dr. Ward, who has given the life of Dr. Bull in his Lives of the Gresham professors, relates that upon the decease of queen Elizabeth he became chief organist to king James,§ and had the honour of entertaining his majesty and prince Henry at Merchant Taylors' hall with his performance on the organ ; the relation is curious, and is as follows :—

'July the 16, 1607, his majesty and prince Henry, 'with many of the nobility, and other honourable 'persons, dined at Merchant Taylors' hall, it being 'the election-day of their master and wardens ; when 'the company's roll being offered to his majesty, he 'said he was already free of another company, but 'that the prince should grace them with the ac-'ceptance of his freedom, and that he would himself 'see when the garland was put on his head, which 'was done accordingly. During their stay they were 'entertained with a great variety of music, both 'voices and instruments, as likewise with several

---

* Stow, in the second, and probably in the first edition of his Survey, mentions that Blitheman, an excellent organist of the queen's chapel, lay buried there with an epitaph. In a subsequent edition, published in 1633, with additions, by A. M. [Anthony Munday] and others, the epitaph as above is inserted.

† In this instance it seems that the queen's affection for Bull got the better of her judgment, for not being able to speak Latin, it may be presumed that he was unable to read it ; and if so, he must have been ignorant of the very principles of the science, and consequently but very indifferently qualified to lecture on it even in English.

‡ An exclamation perhaps suggested by the recollection of that of Sir Thomas More, ' Aut tu es Erasmus, aut Diabolus.'

§ The fact is that he succeeded Tallis, and was sworn in his room, Jan. 1585 [Cheque book]. He was also in the service of prince Henry ; the name John Bull, doctor of music, stands the first in the list of the prince's musicians in 1611, with a salary of 40l. per annum. Append. to the Life of Henry Prince of Wales by Dr. Birch.

JOHN BULL

MUS . DOCT . CANTAB .

INSTAUR . OXON . MDXCII .

From an original Painting in the Music-School, Oxford.

'speeches. And while the king sat at dinner, Dr.
'Bull (who as Stow says) was free of that company,
'being in a cittizen's gowne, cappe, and hood, played
'most excellent melodie uppon a small payre of
'organs, placed there for that purpose onely.' The
author proceeds to relate that in 1613 Bull quitted
England, and went to reside in the Netherlands,*
where he was admitted into the service of the archduke. Wood† says that he died at Hamburg, or
rather, as others who remembered the man have
said, at Lubec.

A picture of Dr. Bull is yet remaining in the
music-school at Oxford. It is painted on a board,
and represents him in the habit of a bachelor of
music. On the left side of the head are the words
AN. AETATIS SVAE 26. 1589; and on the right
side an hour-glass, upon which is placed a human
skull, with a bone cross the mouth; round the four sides
of the frame is written the following homely distich :—

'The bull by force in field doth raigne,
'But Bull by skill good will doth gayne.'

The only works of Bull in print are lessons in the
collection entitled 'Parthenia, or the maiden-head of
'the first music that ever was printed for the virginals,'
of which mention has already been made. An
anthem of his, 'Deliver me, O God,' is to be found
in Barnard's Collection of Church-music.

Dr. Ward has given a long list of compositions of
Dr. Bull in manuscript in the collection of the late
Dr. Pepusch, by which it appears that he was equally
excellent in vocal and instrumental harmony. By
some of the lessons in the Parthenia it seems that he
was possessed of a power of execution on the harpsichord far beyond what is generally conceived of the
masters of that time. As to his lessons, they were,
in the estimation of Dr. Pepusch, not only for the
harmony and contrivance, but for air and modulation,
so excellent, that he scrupled not to prefer them to
those of Couperin, Scarlatti, and others of the modern
composers for the harpsichord.‡

BOOK XI.   CHAP. XCVIII.

John Dowland, the famous lutenist, was born in
1562, and admitted to his bachelor's degree together
with Morley. [Wood Fasti anno 1588.§] The

same author says that he was the rarest musician
that his age did behold, which, though he was

---

* Dr. Ward suggests as the reason for Bull's retirement, that the science began to sink in the reign of king James, which he infers from that want of court patronage which it seems induced the musicians of that day to dedicate their works to one another. There is some truth in this observation, but see the next note. Morley complains of the lack of Mecænates in his time, for notwithstanding the love which queen Elizabeth bore to music, the professors of it began to be neglected even in her reign. John Boswell, who in 1572 published a book entitled 'Workes of Armorie,' describing a coat-armour in which are organ-pipes, uses this exclamation, 'What say I, music one of the seven liberal 'sciences; it is almost banished the realme. If it were not the queenes 'majesty that did favour that excellente science, singing-men and 'choristers might go a begging, together with their master the player on 'the organes.'

As to singing-men in general, not to speak of the gentlemen of the royal chapel, who appear at all times to have been a set of decent orderly men, and many of them exquisite artists in their profession, they seem to have had but little claim to the protection of their betters. Dr. Knight, in his Life of Dean Colet, pag. 87, represents the choirmen about the time of the reformation as very disorderly fellows; as an instance whereof he relates that one at St. Paul's, and a priest too, in the time of divine service, flung a bottle down upon the heads of the congregation. And Cowley, in a poem of his entitled 'The Wish,' printed in his Sylva, has these lines :—

'From singing-men's religion, who are
'Always at church, just like the crows, 'cause there
'They build themselves a nest;
'From too much poetry, which shines
'With gold in nothing but its lines,
'Free, O ye pow'rs, my breast.'

Osborne, somewhere in his works, represents them as leud and dissolute fellows in his time; and Dr. Earle, who lived some years after Osborne, and, being a dignitary of the church, must be supposed acquainted with their manners, gives the following character of them, perhaps not less just than it is humorous :—

'The common singing-men are a bad society, and yet a company of 'good fellows, that roar deep in the quire, deeper in the tavern. They 'are the eight parts of speech which go to the Syntaxis of service, and 'are distinguished by their noises much like bells, for they make not a 'consort but a peal. Their pastime or recreation is prayers, their ex-'ercise drinking, yet herein so religiously addicted, that they serve God 'oftest when they are drunk. Their humanity is a leg to the Residencer, 'their learning, a chapter, for they learn it commonly before they read 'it; yet the old Hebrew names are little beholden to them, for they 'miscall them worse than one another. Though they never expound 'the scripture they handle it much, and pollute the Gospel with two 'things, their conversation and their thumbs. Upon worky-days they 'behave themselves at prayers as at their pots, for they swallow them 'down in an instant. Their gowns are laced commonly with streamings 'of ale, the superfluities of a cup or throat above measure. Their skill 'in melody makes them the better companions abroad, and their anthems 'abler to sing catches. Long lived for the most part they are not, 'especially the base, which they overflow their banks so oft to drown the 'organs. Briefly, if they escape arresting, they die constantly in God's 'service; and to take their death with more patience, they have wine

'and cakes at their funeral; and now they keep the church a great deal 'better, and help to fill it with their bones as before with their noise.' 'Microcosmography, or a piece of the world discovered in essays and characters,' printed without a name in 1633, but in a subsequent edition of 1732, ascribed to Dr. John Earle, successively bishop of Worcester and Salisbury.

James I. though it does not appear that he understood or loved music, yet was disposed to encourage it, for, after the example of Charles the Ninth of France, who had founded a musical academy, he by his letters patent incorporated the musicians of London, who are still a society and corporation, and bear for their arms Azure, a swan Argent within a tressure counterflure Or; and in a chief Gules, a rose between two lions, Or: and for their crest the sign called by astronomers the Orphean lyre. See the dedication to the Principles of Harmony by Charles Butler.

By this act of regal authority the only one of the liberal sciences that conferred the degree of Doctor, was itself degraded, and put upon a footing with the lowest of the mechanic arts; and under the protection of their charter the honourable fraternity of musicians of the city of London derive the sole and exclusive privilege of fiddling and trumpeting to the mayor and aldermen, and of scrambling for the fragments of a city feast.

† Bull had none of those reasons to complain of being slighted that others of his profession had. He was in the service of the chapel, and at the head of the prince's musicians; in the year 1604 his salary for the chapel duty had been augmented. The circumstance of his departure from England may be collected from the following entry, now to be seen in the cheque book, '1613, John Bull, doctor of music, went beyond the 'seas without license, and was admitted into the archduke's service, and 'entered into paie there about Mich. and Peter Hopkins a base from 'Paul's was sworn into his place the 27th of Dec. following: His wages 'from Mich. unto the daye of the swearing of the said Peter Hopkins 'was disposed of by the Deane of his majesty's chapel.' By this it should seem that Bull was not only one of the organists, but a gentleman of the chapel.

‡ This is a fact which several persons now living can attest, together with the following curious particuiars. The doctor had in his collection a book of lessons very richly bound, which had once been queen Elizabeth's; in this were contained many lessons of Bull, so very difficult, that hardly any master of the Doctor's time was able to play them. It is well known that Dr. Pepusch married the famous opera singer, Signora Margarita De L'Pine, who had a very fine hand on the harpsichord: as soon as they were married, the Doctor inspired her with the same sentiments of Bull as he himself had long entertained, and prevailed on her to practise his lessons, in which she succeeded so well, as to excite the curiosity of numbers to resort to his house at the corner of Bartlett's Buildings in Fetter-Lane, to hear her. There are no remaining evidences of her unwearied application in order to attain that degree of excellence which it is known she arrived at, but the book itself yet in being, which in some parts of it is so discoloured by continual use, as to distinguish with the utmost degree of certainty the very lessons with which she was most delighted. One of them took up twenty minutes to go through it.

§ Wood says he was one of the gentlemen of her majesty's chapel, but the truth of this assertion is doubtful; for he does not assume that title in any of his publications: on the contrary, he complains in the preface to his Pilgrime's Solace, that he never could attain to any though ever so mean a place.

doubtless an eminent composer, is not so true as that he was one of the most excellent lutenists of his time. Mention is made of him in a sonnet ascribed to Shakespeare, but how truly we cannot say. It is entitled Friendly Concord, and is as follows :—

'　If musicke and sweet poetry agree,
'　As they must needs (the sister and the brother),
'　Then must the love be great twixt thee and me,
'　Because thou lov'st the one and I the other ;
'　Dowland to thee is deer, whose heavenly touch
'　Upon the lute doth ravish human sense ;
'　Spenser to me whose deep conceit is such,
'　As passing all conceit, needs no defence ;
'　Thou lov'st to hear the sweet melodious sound
'　That Phœbus' lute (the queen of musick) makes,
'　And I in deep delight am chiefly drown'd,
'　When as himself to singing he betakes :
'　　One God is God of both, as poets faine ;
'　　One knight loves both, and both in thee remain.'*

Peacham, who was intimate with him, says that he had slipped many opportunities of advancing himself, in allusion to which his misfortune he gave him an emblem with this anagram,

JOHANNES DOVLANDUS
Annos ludendo hausi.

The emblem is a nightingale singing in the winter season on a leafless brier, with the following verses :—

'　Heere Philomel in silence sits alone,
'　In depth of winter, on the bared brier,
'　Whereas the rose had once her beautie showen,
'　Which lordes and ladies did so much desire :
'　　But fruitless now ; in winter's frost and snow
'　　It doth despis'd and unregarded grow.

'　So since (old frend) thy yeares have made thee white,
'　And thou for others hast consum'd thy spring,
'　How few regard thee, whome thou didst delight,
'　And farre and neere came once to heare thee sing !
'　　Ingratefull times, and worthless age of ours,
'　　That lets us pine when it hath cropt our flowers.'†

That Dowland missed many opportunities of advancing his fortunes may perhaps be justly attributed to a rambling disposition, which led him to travel abroad and neglect his duty in the chapel ; for that he lived much abroad appears from the prefaces to his works, published by him at sundry times, and these furnish the following particulars of his life.

In the year 1584 he travelled the chief parts of France ; thence he bent his course towards Germany, where he was kindly entertained by Henry Julio, duke of Brunswick, and the learned Maurice, land-grave of Hessen, the same of whom Peacham speaks, and commends as being himself an excellent musician. Here he became acquainted with Alessandro Orologio, a musician of great eminence in the service of the landgrave Maurice, and Gregorio Howet, lutenist to the duke of Brunswick. Having spent some months in Germany, he passed over the Alps into Italy, and saw Venice, Padua, Genoa, Ferrara, Florence, and divers other places. At Venice he became intimate with Giovanni Croce, who, as he relates, was at that time vice-master of the chapel of St. Mark. It does

not appear that he visited Rome, but he enjoyed the proffered amity of Luca Marenzio, and received from him sundry letters, one whereof was as follows :—

'　Multo magnifico Signior mio osservandissimo.
'　Per una lettera del Signior Maluezi ho inteso
'　quanto con cortese affetto si mostri desideroso di
'　essermi congiunto d' amicitia, deve infinitamente la
'　ringratio di questo suo buon' animo, offerendo
'　megli all' incontro se in alcuna cosa la posso servire,
'　poi che gli meriti delle sue infinite virtù, et qualità
'　meritano che ogni uno et me l' ammirino et osser-
'　vino, et per fine di questo le bascio le mani. Di
'　Roma à 13 di Luglio 1595. d. v. s. Affettionatissimo
'　servitore, Luca Marenzio.'

All these particulars are contained in a work of Dowland entitled 'The first booke of Songes or 'Ayres of foure Parts with Tablature for the Lute.' In a second book of Songs or Aires by Dowland for the lute or Orpherian, with the viol de gamba, printed in 1600, he styles himself lutenist to the king of Denmark ; to this book is prefixed a dedica-tion to the celebrated Lucy countess of Bedford, dated from Helsingnoure in Denmark the first of June, 1600.

In 1603 he published a third book of 'Songes or 'Aires to sing to the lute, Orpharion, or Violls.' Some time after this, but in what year is not mentioned, he published a work with this title 'Lachrimæ, or seaven Teares figured in seven pas-'sionate Pavans, with divers other Pavans, Galiards, 'and Almands, set forth for the Lute, Viols, or 'Violons, in five parts.'‡ This book is dedicated to Anne, the queen of king James the First, and sister of Christian IV. king of Denmark. In the epistle the author tells her that hastening his return to her brother and his master, he was by contrary winds and frost, forced back and compelled to winter in England, during his stay wherein, he had presumed to dedicate to her hands a work that was begun where she was born, and ended where she reigned.

In 1609 Dowland published a translation of the Micrologus of Andreas Ornithoparcus ; at this time it seems that Dowland had quitted the service of the king of Denmark, for he styles himself only lutenist, lute-player, and bachelor of music in both universities. In 1612 he published a book entitled 'A Pilgrime's 'Solace, wherein is contained musical harmony of 3, '4, and 5 parts to be sung and plaid with lute and 'viols.' In the title-page he styles himself lutenist to the Lord Walden.§ In the preface to this book

---

* From the Passionate Pilgrime of Shakespeare, first printed in 1609, and Poems written by Wil. Shakespeare, Gent. 12mo. 1640.

† Garden of Heroical Devices by Henry Peacham, pag. 74.

‡ This it seems was a celebrated work : it is alluded to in a comedy of Thomas Middleton, entitled 'No wit like a woman's,' in which a servant tells bad news, and is thus answered :—
'　Now thou plaiest Dowland's Lachrymæ to thy master.'

§ Wood is greatly mistaken in the account which he gives of Dowland, whom he supposes to have been taken into the service of the king of Denmark in 1606, whereas it is plain that he was his lutenist in 1600, and probably somewhat before ; again, there is not the least reason to suppose, as Wood does, that he died in Denmark, for he was in England in 1612, and lutenist to Lord Walden ; and it nowhere appears that after this he went abroad. He might, as he says, have a son named Robert trained up to the lute at the charge of Sir Thomas Monson, who it is well known was a great patron of music ; but that the Pilgrim's Solace was composed by him and not by his father, is not to be reconciled with the title, the dedication, or the preface to the book, which afford the best evidence of the fact that can be required. It may not be improper here to mention that the king of Denmark had begged Dowland of James, as he did afterwards Thomas Cutting, another celebrated lutenist, of his mistress the lady Arabella Stuart.

he says that he had received a kingly entertainment in a foreign climate, though he could not attain to any, though never so mean, place at home. He says that some part of his poor labours had been printed in eight most famous cities beyond the seas, viz., Paris, Antwerpe, Collein, Nuremburg, Frankfort, Liepsig, Amsterdam, and Hamburg, but that notwithstanding he had found strange entertainment since his return by the opposition of two sorts of people, the first simply Cantors or vocal singers, the second young men professors of the lute, against whom he vindicates himself. He adds that he is entered into the fiftieth year of his age, and because he wants both means, leisure, and encouragement, recommends to the more learned sort of musicians, who labour under no such difficulties, the defence of their lute-profession.

The preface of Dowland to this his translation of Ornithoparcus is dated from his house in Fetter-lane, 10th of April, 1609. This is the last of his publications, for it appears that he died in 1615.

PETER PHILLIPS, an Englishman by birth, better known to the world by the Italian name Pietro Philippi, was an exquisite composer of vocal music both sacred and profane. He styles himself Canonicus Sogniensis, i. e. a canon of Soigny, a city or town in Hainault, and was besides organist to the archduke and duchess of Austria, Albert and Isabella, governors of the Low countries. Peacham calls him our rare countryman, one of the greatest masters of music in Europe, adding, that he hath sent us over many excellent songs, as well motets as madrigals, and that he affecteth altogether the Italian vein. The works published by him, besides the collection of madrigals entitled Melodia Olympica, heretofore mentioned, are Madrigali à 8 voci, in 4to. an. 1599. Cantiones sacræ 5 vocum, in 4to. an. 1612. Gemmulæ sacræ 2 et 3 vocum, in 4to. an. 1613. Litaniæ B. M. V. in Ecclesia Loretana cani solitæ 4, 5, 9 vocum, in 4to. an. 1623. He is celebrated by Draudius in his Bibliotheca Classica.

His employments and the nature of his compositions for the church bespeak him to have been of the Romish communion. The Cantiones Sacræ are dedicated to the Virgin Mary in the following terms :—

'Gloriosissimæ Virgini Mariæ, Dei nostri parenti ' dignissimæ, cœli, terræque reginæ, angelorum, homi-'num, et omnium creaturarum visibilium, et in vi-'sibilium post Deum Dominæ : in honorem ejus sa-'cræ ædis Aspricollis, ubi ad D. O. M. gloriam, 'Christiani populi consolationem, et salutem ; Catho-'licæ, Apostolicæ, et Romanæ fidei confirmationem, 'et amplificationem ; cunctarum hæresum, et hære-'ticorum extirpationem, et confusionem, per poten-'tissimam ejus interventionem, frequentissima, di-'vinissima, et exploratissima patrantur miracula, hoc 'sacrarum cantionum opusculum Petrus Philippi cum 'omni humilitate offert, dicat consecratque.'

The following madrigal, printed in the Melodia Olympica, is of the composition of Peter Phillips :—

...mo - - ro e mo-ren - do, e mo-ren - do, e mo-ren - do

per voi ' mo - - ro e mo-ren - do, e mo-ren - do, mo-rend' in vi - ta.

voi mo - - ro, e .. mo-ren - do, e .. mo-ren - do, e mo-ren - do in

mo - - - ro, e mo-ren - do in vi-ta -

in vi-ta tor - no, in vi-ta torno, in vi-ta tor - - no.

...tor-no, .. e .. mo-rend' . in vi-ta tor - no, in vi - ta tor - no.

vi-ta tor - no, in vi-ta torn' - in vi-ta torn' in vi - ta tor - - no.

tor - no, in vi-ta tor - no, in vi-ta tor - no, in vi-ta tor - - no.

PIETRO PHILIPPI.

I.B.CIPRIANI PINX.   C.GRIGNION SCULP

GUIDO ARETINUS A BENEDICTINE MONK, HAVING REFORMED THE
SCALE OF MUSIC AND INVENTED A NEW METHOD OF NOTATION,
COMMUNICATES HIS IMPROVEMENTS TO POPE JOHN XX,
WHO INVITES HIM TO ROME AND BECOMES HIS DISCIPLE.

A
GENERAL HISTORY
of the
SCIENCE AND PRACTICE
of
MUSIC

by
SIR JOHN HAWKINS

With a New Introduction by
CHARLES CUDWORTH
Curator, Pendlebury Library of Music
University Music School, Cambridge, England

In Two Volumes

Volume II

DOVER PUBLICATIONS, INC.
NEW YORK　　　NEW YORK

Published in Canada by General Publishing
Company, Ltd., 30 Lesmill Road, Don Mills,
Toronto, Ontario.
Published in the United Kingdom by Constable
and Company, Ltd., 10 Orange Street, London
WC 2.

This new Dover edition, first published in 1963,
is an unabridged republication of the edition published by J. Alfred Novello in 1853.

In the 1853 edition, the portraits and other full-
page illustrations appeared as a separate volume; in
this Dover edition, all these illustrations are re-
produced in appropriate places within the two-volume
text.

This Dover edition also contains a new Introduc-
tion especially prepared for this edition by Charles
Cudworth, Curator, Pendlebury Library of Music,
University Music School, Cambridge, England.

Library of Congress Catalog Card Number: 63-4484

Manufactured in the United States of America

Dover Publications, Inc.
180 Varick Street
New York 14, N.Y.

List of Portraits in Volume Two

A
GENERAL HISTORY
OF THE
SCIENCE AND PRACTICE OF MUSIC.

CHAPTER XCIX.

THOMAS MORLEY, one of the gentlemen of queen Elizabeth's chapel, the author of a well known treatise on the subject of practical music, was a disciple of Bird, for whom he ever entertained the highest reverence. He obtained a bachelor's degree in 1588, and was sworn into his place in the chapel July 24, 1592; he was the author of Canzonets or little short songs to three voices, Lond. 1593. The first book of Madrigals to four voices, Lond. 1594. Canzonets or little short Airs to 5 or 6 voices, Lond. 1595. Madrigals to 5 voices, Lond. 1595. Introduction to Music, Lond. 1597. The first book of Aires or little short Songes to sing and play to the lute with the bass viol, Lond. 1600. And the first book of Canzonets to two voices, Lond. 1595, and 1619. He also composed divine services and anthems, the words of some whereof are printed in James Clifford's Collection of divine services and anthems usually sung in cathedrals.* A service for the burial of the dead of his composition, the first of the kind, to the words of our liturgy, is printed in Dr. Boyce's Cathedral Music, vol. I. He also collected and published madrigals, entitled the Triumphs of Oriana, to five and six voices, composed by divers authors, Lond. 1601, and a set or two of Italian madrigals to English words; but the most valuable of all his works is his Plaine and easie Introduction to practicall Musicke, so often referred to in the course of this work, and of which an account is here given.

This valuable work is divided into three parts, the first teaching to sing; the second treating of Descant, with the method of singing upon a plain-song; the other of composition in three and more parts. Each of the three parts of this book is a several and distinct dialogue, wherein a master, his scholar, and a person competently skilled in music, are the interlocutors; and in the course of their conversation so many little particulars occur relating to the manners of the times,

as render the perusal of the book in a great degree entertaining to those who are unacquainted with the subject of it; the truth of this observation will appear from the very introduction to the work, which is as follows:—

'POLYMATHES.
'PHILOMATHES.
'MASTER.

'POLYMATHES. Staye brother Philomathes, what haste? 'Whither go you so fast? PHILOMATH. To seek out an 'old friend of mine. POL. But before you goe I praie 'you repeat some of the discourses which you had yester-'night at Master Sophobulus his banket, for commonly he 'is not without both wise and learned guestes. PHI. It 'is true indeed, and yesternight there were a number of 'excellent schollers, both gentlemen and others: but all 'the propose which was then discoursed upon was 'musicke. POL. I trust you were contented to suffer 'others to speake of that matter. PHI. I would that 'had been the worst; for I was compelled to discover 'mine own ignorance, and confesse that I knewe nothing 'at all in it. POL. How so? PHI. Among the rest of 'the guestes by chance Master Amphron came thither 'also, who falling to discourse of musicke, was in an 'argument so quickly taken up and hotly pursued by 'Eudoxus and Calergus, two kinsmen of master Sopho-'bulus, as in his own art he was overthrowne, but he still 'sticking in his opinion, the two gentlemen requested me 'to examine his reasons and confute them, but I refusing, 'and pretending ignorance, the whole company con-'demned me of discurtesie, being fully persuaded that 'I had been as skilfull in that art as they took me to be 'learned in others; but supper being ended, and musicke 'bookes according to the custome, being brought to the 'table, the mistress of the house presented mee with a 'part, earnestly requesting me to sing, but when, after 'many excuses I protested unfeignedly that I could not, 'everie one began to wonder, yea some whispered to 'others, demanding how I was brought up: so that upon 'shame of mine own ignorance I goe nowe to seek out 'mine old friende master Gnorimus, to make myself his 'schollar. POL. I am glad you are at length come to 'be of that mind, though I wished it sooner, therefore 'goe, and I praie God send you such good successe as 'you would wish to yourself; as for me, I goe to heare 'some mathematical lectures, so that I thinke about one 'time wee may both meete at our lodging. PHI. Fare-

---

* This book is very frequently referred to by Wood. It is a collection of the words only, of the services and anthems then usually sung, printed in duodecimo, 1664. The compiler was a native of Oxford, a chorister of Magdalen college there, and afterwards a minor canon of St. Paul's, and reader in some church near Carter-lane, and also chaplain to the society of Serjeant's Inn in Fleet-street. Athen. Oxon.

'well, for I sit upon thornes till I be gone, therefore I
'will make haste; but, if I be not deceived, I see him
'whom I seeke sitting at yonder doore, out of doubt it is
'hee. And it should seeme he studieth upon some point
'of musicke, but I will drive him out of his dumpe.
'Good morrow, Sir. MASTER. And you also good
'Master Philomathes, I am glad to see you, seeing it is
'so long ago since I sawe you, that I thought you had
'either been dead, or then had vowed perpetually to
'keep your chamber and booke to which you were so
'much addicted. PHI. Indeed I have been well affected
'to my booke, but how have you done since first I saw
'you? MAST. My health since you saw mee hath been
'so badd as, if it had been the pleasure of him who made
'all things, to have taken me out of the world I should
'have been very well contented, and have wished it more
'than once: but what business hath driven you to this
'end of the town? PHI. My errand is to you, to make
'myself your scholler; and seeing I have found you at
'such convenient leisure, I am determined not to depart
'till I have one lesson in musicke. MAST. You tell mee
'a wonder, for I have heard you so much speake against
'that art, as to terme it a corrupter of good manners,
'and an allurement to vices, for which many of your com-
'panions termed you a Stoic. PHI. It is true, but I am
'fo far changed, as of a Stoic I would willingly make a
'Pythagorean; and for that I am impatient of delay I
'praie you begin even now. MAST. With a good will;
'but have you learned nothing at all in musicke before?
'PHI. Nothing. Therefore I pray you begin at the very
'beginning, and teach me as though I were a childe.
'MAST. I will do so, and therefore behold here is the
'scale of musicke which we terme the Gam.' [Giving
him the gamut with the syllables.]

The master then proceeds to instruct his scholar
in the rudiments of song, in the doing whereof he
delivers to him the precepts of the plain and mensurable cantus, illustrated with examples in notes, to
some whereof, for the greater facility of utterance,
he has joined the letters of the alphabet, and these
are introduced by a distich, and concluded by a
direction to begin again, as here is shown :—

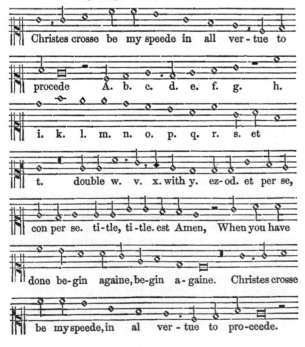

The second part of the Introduction of Morley is
a treatise of Descant, as it was then called; the
meaning of the term, and the nature of the practice,
are explained in the following colloquy :—

'MASTER. Whom do I see afar off, is it not my scholar
'Philomathes? out of doubt it is he, and therefore I will
'salute him. Good morrow, scholler. PHI. God give
'you good morrow and a hundredth, but I marvayle not
'a little to see you so early, not only stirring, but out of
'doors also. MAST. It is no marvayle to see a snayle
'after a rayne to creep out of his shell and wander all
'about seeking the moisture. PHI. I pray you talk not
'so darkely, but let me understand your comparysons
'playnley. MAST. Then in plaine tearmes being over
'wearied with studie, and taking the opportunity of the
'fayre morning, I came to this place to snatch a mouth-
'ful of this holsome ayre, which gently breathing upon
'these sweet-smelling flowers, and making a whispering
'noise amongst these tender leaves, delighteth with re-
'freshing, and refresheth with delight my over weary
'senses; but tell me, I pray you, the cause of your hither
'coming; have you not forgotten some part of that
'which I shewed you at our last being together. PHI.
'No verily, but the contrary, I am become such a singer
'as you would wonder to heare me. MAST. How came
'that to passe? PHI. Be silent, and I will shew you;

* The practice of annexing words of a frivolous import to notes, for
the assistance of novices in the art of singing, was no new thing; the
Monks were the authors of it, and many of the examples of Glareanus
himself are either Hebrew names or Latin nonsense, set to very good
music; but in the example before us, the distich

> Christ's cross be my spede
> In all vertue to procede,

has a meaning which it will be the business of this note to enquire after.

In the course of this work occasion has been taken to mention St.
Nicholas, and to shew that by those of the Romish communion he is
looked on as the patron of young scholars. In the homily against peril
of idolatry, which our church directed to be read for the instruction
of the people, is a very particular enumeration of those saints, who,
either from a supposed power to heal certain diseases, or to confer
peculiar graces, or, in short, some way or other to favour mankind, were
the most common objects of private supplication; the passage referred
to is as follows :—

'Every artificer and profession hath his special saint as a peculiar
'God. As for example, schollars have Saint Nicholas and Saint Gregory;
'Painters Saint Luke: neither lack soldiers their Mars, nor lovers their
'Venus amongst Christians. All diseases have their special Saints as
'Gods the curers of them. The pox Saint Roche, the falling evil St.
'Cornelis, the tooth ache St. Appollin, &c. Neither do beasts and cattel
'lack their gods with us, for Saint Loy is the horseleach [i. e. the horse-
'physician] and Saint Anthony the swineherd, &c. Where is God's
'providence and due honour in the mean season? * * * if we remember
'God sometimes, yet because we doubt of his ability or will, to help us,
'we join to him another helper, as he were a noun adjective, using these
'sayings: such as learn, God and Saint Nicholas be my speed: such as
'neese, God help and Saint John: to the horse, God and Saint Loy save
'thee, &c.'

From the above passage it appears that anciently 'God and Saint
'Nicholas be my spede,' was a customary ejaculation of young scholars;
and we can hardly suppose a more proper occasion for the use of it than
when infants of tender years are learning the rudiments of literature.
It is therefore not improbable that the distich

> 'Saint Nicholas be my spede
> 'In all vertue to procede,'

might be the introduction to the alphabet, and might be constantly repeated by the child previous to the beginning its lesson.

The alphabet is frequently termed the Criss Cross, that is to say
Christ's cross row, because of a cross constantly placed before the letter
A, which sign was anciently a direction to the child to cross itself before
it began its lesson, as it is now in the mass-book for the same action in
different parts of the service.

The use of the prayer to St. Nicholas may well be supposed to have
continued amongst us until the practice of praying to saints was condemned by our church as superstitious, which it was somewhat before
Morley's time; and after that, as our reformers had thought proper to
retain the use of the sign of the cross in some few instances, how
naturally did this variation suggest itself,

> Christ's cross be my spede
> In all virtue to procede.

which, as the reformation then stood, might well enough be deemed
a good Protestant prayer.

'I have a brother, a good scholar and a reasonable
'musition for singing, he at my first coming to you,
'conceived an opinion, I know not upon what reasons
'grounded, that I should never come to any meane
'knowledge in musicke, and therefore when he heard me
'practice alone he would continually mock me, indeed
'notwithstanding reason, for many times I would sing
'halfe a note too high, other while as much too lowe, so
'that he could not contain himself from laughing; yet now
'and then he would set me right, more to let me see that
'he could doe it, then that he ment any way to instruct
'me, which caused me so diligently to apply my prick-
'song booke, that in a manner I did no other thing but
'sing, practising to slip from one key to another, from
'flat to sharp, from sharp to flat, from any one place in
'the scale to another, so that there was no song so hard
'but I woulde venture upon it, no mood, nor proportion
'so strange but I would go through and sing perfectly
'before I left it; and in the end I came to such per-
'fection that I might have been my brother's maister, for
'although he had a little more practice to sing at first
'sight than I had, yet for the moods, ligatures, and other
'such things, I might set him to school. MAST. What
'then was the cause of your coming hither at this time?
'PHI. Desire to learne as before. MAST. What would
'you now learne. PHI. Beeing this last daye upon
'occasion of some businesse at one of my friends houses,
'we had some songs sung, afterwards falling to discourse
'of musicke and musitians, one of the company naming
'a friend of his owne, tearmed him the best Descanter
'that was to be found. Now, Sir, I am at this time come
'to knowe what Descant is, and to learne the same.
'MAST. I thought you had onely sought to know prickt
'song, whereby to recreate yourself, being wearye of
'other studies. PHI. Indeed when I came to you first
'I was of that minde, but the common proverb is in me
'verified, that much would have more; and seeing I have
'so far set foot in music, I doe not meane to goe backe
'till I have gone quite through all, therefore I pray you
'now, seeing the time and place fitteth so well, to dis-
'course with me what descant is, what parts, and how
'many it hath, and the rest. MAST. The heate in-
'creaseth, and that which you demand requireth longer
'discourse than you looke for, let us therefore go and sit
'in yonder shadie arbor to avoyde the vehementness of
'the sunne.—The name of Descant is usurped of the
'musitions in divers significations; some time they take
'it for the whole harmony of many voyces, others some-
'times for one of the voyces or partes, and that is when
'the whole song is not passing three voyces. Last of
'all, they take it for singing a part extempore upon
'a playne song, in which sense we commonly use it; so
'that when a man talketh of a descanter, it must be
'understood of one that can extempore sing a part upon
'a playne song. PHI. What is the meane to sing upon
'a playne song? MAST. To know the distances both
'of concords and discords. PHI. What is a concord?
'MAST. It is a mixt sound, compact of divers voyces, &c.'

Among the rules for extemporary descant, which
are in truth no other than the precepts of musical
composition, he explains the nature of that kind of
composition called two parts in one, which, as he
says, is when two parts are so made as that the
latter singeth every note and rest in the same length
and order as the leading part did sing before. From
hence he proceeds to declare the nature of canon
framed to a given plain-song; and of these he gives
sundry examples with the plain-song in various
situations, that is to say, sometimes above, sometimes
below, and at other times in the midst of the canon.

The third part of the Introduction treats of composing or setting of songs; and here the author
takes occasion to censure one master Boulde, an
ignorant pretender to music; and he does it in this
way, he supposes Philomathes by this time to have
profited so much by his master's instructions as to
have got the start of his brother Polymathes, and
that Polymathes, who is supposed to have learned
the little he knew of music of the above Master
Boulde, being sensible of this, is desirous of putting
himself under the tuition of his brother's master; the
master tenders him a plain-song, desiring him to
sing upon it a lesson of descant, which he does but
very indifferently, the faults in this and another
lesson or two which Polymathes sings, draws on
a discourse between him and his new master, wherein
he very humorously characterizes his former master,
Boulde.—'When,' says he, 'I learned descant of my
'maister Boulde, hee seeing me so toward and
'willing to learne, ever had me in his company; and
'because he continually carried a plaine song booke
'in his pocket, hee caused me to doe the like, and so
'walking in the fields he would sing the plainsong,
'and cause me to sing the descant, and when I sung
'not to his contentment he would shew me wherein
'I had erred; there was also another descanter,
'a companion of my maister's, who never came in
'my maister's company, though they were much
'conversant together, but they fell to contention,
'striving who should bring in the point soonest and
'make hardest proportions, so that they thought
'they had won great glory if they had brought in
'a point sooner or sung harder proportions the one
'than the other: but it was a worlde to heare them
'wrangle, everie one defending his owne for the best.
'What, saith the one, you keepe not time in your
'proportions; you sing them false, saith the other;
'what proportion is this, saith hee? Sesquipaltery,
'saith the other; nay, would the other say, you
'sing you know not what; it should seem you came
'lately from a barber's shop, where you had Gregory
'Walker* or a Coranta plaide in the new proportions
'by them lately found out, called Sesquiblinda and
'Sesqui-hearken after. So that if one unacquainted
'with musicke had stood in a corner and heard them,
'he would have sworne they had been out of their
'wittes, so earnestlie did they wrangle for a trifle.

* A note in the original. 'That name in derision they have given this
'quadrant Pavan because it walketh among barbers and fiddlers more
'common than any other.'

This note of the author requires explanation. In Morley's time and
for many years after, a lute or viol, or some such musical instrument,
was part of the furniture of a barber's shop, which was used then to be
frequented by persons above the ordinary level of the people, who
resorted to the barber either for the cure of wounds, or to undergo some
chirurgical operations, or, as it was then called, to be trimmed, a word
that signified either shaving or cutting and curling the hair; these, together with letting blood, were the ancient occupations of the barber-
surgeon. As to the other important branch of surgery, the setting of
fractured limbs, that was practised by another class of men called bone-
setters, of whom there are hardly any now remaining. Peacham, in his
account of Maurice landgrave of Hesse before cited, says he was generally
accounted the best bone-setter in his country, whence it appears that
this faculty was sometimes exercised by men of condition and benevolent
tempers. But to return to the barber: the musical instruments in his
shop were for the entertainment of waiting customers, and answered the
end of a newspaper. At this day those who wait for their turn at the
barber's, amuse themselves with reading the news of the day or week;
anciently they beguiled the time with playing on a musical instrument,
which custom gave occasion to Morley to say of the quadrant Pavan
mentioned by him, that it was so common that it walked amongst the
barbers.

'And in truth I myselfe thought sometimes that
'they would have gone to round buffets with the
'matter, for the descant bookes were made angels,*
'but yet fistes were no visitors of eares, and therefore
'all parted friends. But to say the verie truth, this
'Poliphemus had a very good sight, especially for
'treble descant, but very bad utterance, for that his
'voice was the worst that ever I had heard; and
'though of others he was esteemed verie good in that
'kinde, yet did none think better of him then hee
'did of himself; for if one had named and asked his
'opinion of the best composers living at this time,
'hee would say in a vaine glory of his own sufficiencie
'tush, tush, for these were his words, he is a proper
'man, but he is no descanter, there is no stuffe in
'him, I wil not give two pinnes for him except he
'hath descant.'

In the course of his directions for composing and
setting of songs, Morley takes occasion to censure
Alfonso Ferabosco and Giovanni Croce for taking
perfect concords of one kind in succession, a practice
which he loudly condemns, and says of Fairfax,
Taverner, Shepheard, Mundy, White, Parsons, and
Bird, that they never thought it greater sacrilege to
spurn against the image of a saint than to take two
perfect chords of one kind together.

Speaking of the several kinds of composition
practised in his time, Morley gives the first place to
the motet.†

Next to the motet he places the madrigal, for the
etymology of which word he says he can give no
'reason.‡ He says 'it is a kind of music made
'upon songs and sonnets, such as Petrarch and many
'other poets have excelled in, and that it is, next
'unto the motet the most artificial, and, to men of
'understanding, most delightful; and would not be
'so much disallowable if the poets who compose
'the ditties would abstain from some obscenities
'which all honest ears abhor, and from some such
'blasphemies as no man, at least who has any hope
'of salvation, can sing without trembling.' He then
enumerates the several kinds of composition and air
practised by the musicians of his time, mention
whereof will be made in a subsequent chapter.

It is to be remembered that the whole of this
work of Morley is in dialogue, and that by the
master, who is one of the interlocutors in it, he
means to represent himself, who having sufficiently
instructed his scholars dismisses them.

The dialogue being ended there follows what the
author calls the Peroratio, in which he discovers
much learning; in it he says that had it not been
for Boetius, the knowledge of music had not yet come
into our western part of the world, adding this as
a reason, 'The Greek tongue lying as it were dead
'under the barbarisme of the Gothes and Hunnes,
'and musicke buried in the bowels of the Greeke
'workes of Ptolomeus and Aristoxenus; the one of
'which as yet hath never come to light, but lies in

'written copies in some bibliothekes of Italie, the
'other hath beene set out in print, but the copies are
'everie where so scant and hard to come by, that
'many doubt if he have been set out or no.'

Next follow certain compositions of the author's
own, for three, four, and five voices, to Latin, Italian,
and English words, which have great merit.

The annotations at the end of the work are replete
with curious learning; in these Morley has not
spared to censure some ignorant pretenders to skill in
music, and, amongst the rest, the anonymous author
of a book entitled 'The Guide of the Path-Way to
'Music,' printed in 1596 in oblong quarto, for
William Barley, a great publisher of music books
about that time, of which he gives this character.
'Take away two or three scales which are filched
'out of Beurhusius,§ and fill up the three first pages
'of the booke, you shall not finde one side in all the
'booke without some grosse errour or other. For
'as he setteth down his dupla, so doth he all his
'proportions, giving true definitions and false ex-
'amples, the example still importing the contrarie
'to that which was said in the definition.‖ But
'this is the worlde; every one will take upon him
'to write and teach others, none having more need
'of teaching than himselfe. And as for him of
'whom we have spoken so much, one part of his
'booke he stole out of Beurhusius, another out of

§ FREDERIC BEURHUSIUS, con-rector of the college of Dortmund, an
Imperial town in the circle of Westphalia. He wrote an Erotemata
Musicæ, which was published about the year 1580.

‖ After this character of the book a particular account of its contents
will hardly be wished for; there are printed with it three books of
tablature, the first for the lute, the second for an instrument called the

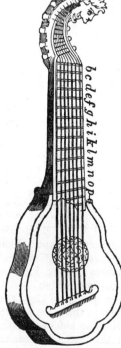

Orpharion, and the third for one called
the Bandore, concerning which two last
it may not be amiss here to speak, and
first of the Orpharion. It is of the following form, and is thus described by
the author:—
'The Orpharion is strung with more
'stringes than the lute, and also hath
'more frets or stops; and whereas the
'lute is struug with gut stringes, the
'Orpharion is strung with wire stringes,
'by reason of which manner of stringing,
'the Orpharion doth necessarilie require
'a more gentle and drawing stroke than
'the lute; I mean the fingers of the
'right hand must be easily drawn over
'the stringes, and not suddenly griped or
'sharpelie stroken as the lute is, for if
'yee should doo so, then the wire stringes
'would clash or jarre together the one
'against the other, which would be a
'cause that the sound would be harsh
'and unpleasant. Therefore it is meete
'that you observe the difference of the
'stroke. And concerning the frets or
'stoppes, the difference doth consist in
'the different number that is between
'them, for the lute hath no further
'than i, and the Orpharion hath to q;
'but it is seldom that any lesson for the
'Orpharion doth passe the stops of L or
'M, yet those that are cunning can at
'their pleasure make use of all the
'stops.'
Among the lessons contained in this
book for the Orpharion, there is one named
Bockington's Pound, which seems to be
no other than that tune now called Packington's Pound, and to which is adapted
one of the songs in the Beggar's Opera.
The original composer of it appears to be
one Francis Cutting.

As to the Bandore, the figure whereof is also given in the following
page, the author says it is easy to play on, and is both commendable and
fit, either in consort or alone. He adds that the manner of tuning doth
a little differ from the lute and orpharion, but he has forgotten to mention
whether the strings are of wire, like those of the orpharion, or of catgut

* *i. e.* they flew about their ears as if they had wings.

† See an explanation of this word in page 388 of this work, in a note.

‡ See the conjectures of various authors concerning it in page 335
of this work, in a note.

'Lossius, perverting the sense of Lossius his wordes, 'and giving examples flatte to the contrarie of that 'which Lossius saith. And the last part of his book 'treating of Descant he took verbatim out of an old 'written booke which I have: but it should seeme 'that whatsoever or whosoever he was that gave it 'to the presse, was not the author of it himselfe, 'else would he have set his name to it, or then he 'was ashamed of his labour.'

In the annotations on the second part of Morley's Introduction is the following curious note on the term Descant. 'Thoughe I dare not affirme that 'this part was in use with the musitions of the 'learned Ptolemæus, or yet of that of Boetius, yet 'may I with some reason say that it is more auncient 'than pricksong, and only by reason of the name, 'which is contrapunto, an Italian word devised since 'the Gothes did overrun Italy, and changed the 'Latine tongue into that barbarisme which they now 'use. As for the word itselfe, it was at that time fit 'enough to express the thing signified, because no 'diversity of notes being used, the musicians instead 'of notes did set down their musicke in plain prickes 'or points; but afterwards, that custom being altered 'by the diversitie of forms of notes, yet the name is 'retained amongst them in the former signification, 'though amongst us it be restrained from the gene-'rality to signifie that species or kind which of all 'others is the most simple and plaine; and instead 'of it we have usurped the name of descant. Also 'by continuance of time that name is also degene-'rated into another signification, and for it we use 'the word setting and composing: and to come to 'the matter which now we are to intreat of, the word 'descant signifieth in our tongue the forme of setting 'together of sundry voices or concords for producing 'harmony; and a musician if he heare a song sung 'and mislike it, he will say the descant is nought; 'but in this signification it is seldom used, and the 'common signification which it hath is the singing 'extempore upon a plain-song, in which sense there is 'none who hath tasted the first elements of musicke 'but understandeth it. When descant did begin, by 'whom, and where it was invented, is uncertaine; for 'it is a great controversie amongst the learned if it 'were known to the antiquitie or no. And divers 'do bring arguments to prove, and others to disprove 'the antiquity of it; and for disproving of it they 'say that in all the works of them who have written 'of musicke before Franchinus, there is no mention 'of any more parts than one, and that if any did 'singe to the harpe, which was their most usual 'instrument, they sung the same which they plaied. 'But those who would affirme that the ancients knew 'it, saie: That if they did not know it, to what end 'served all those long and tedious discourses and 'disputations of the consonantes, wherein the most 'part of their workes are consumed? But whether 'they knew it or not, this I will say, that they had 'it not in halfe that variety wherein we now have it, 'though we read of much more strange effects of 'their musicke than of ours.'[*]

At the end of this book is the following list of English musicians, the far greater part of whom appear to have flourished before the reformation. M. Pashe. Robert Jones. Jo. Dunstable. Leonel Power. Robert Orwel. M. Wilkinson. Jo. Gwin-neth. Robert Davis. M. Risby. D. Farfax. D. Kirby. Morgan Grig. Tho. Ashwell. M. Sturton. Jacket. Corbrand. Testwood. Ungle. Beech. Bramston. S. Jo. Mason. Ludford. Farding. Cornish. Pyggot. Taverner. Redford. Hodges. Selby. Thorne. Oclande. Averie. D. Tye. D. Cooper. D. Newton. M. Tallis. M. White. M. Persons. M. Byrde.

By the compositions of Fairfax, Cornish, Taverner, and Thorne, already given, a judgment may be formed of the state of Music in those days. It appears that many of the old English musicians were men of learning in other faculties, particularly in astronomy and physic, and what is strange, in logic. Thorne of York lies buried in the cathedral of that city, with the following inscription :—

Here lyeth Thorne, muſician moſt perfitt in his art,
In Logick's lore who did excell ; all vice who ſet apart:
Whoſe lief and converſation did all men's love allure,
And now doth reign above the ſkies in joys moſt firm and pure.
Who died Decemb. 7, 1573.

And in the same church is an inscription of the

like those of the lute. This instrument is said by Stowe in his Annals, pag. 869, to have been invented in the fourth year of Queen Elizabeth, by John Rose, citizen of London, living in Bridewell.

As to the instrument called the Or-pharion, above described, it is necessary to be observed that it cannot be the same with the Orphion, mentioned in the poems of Sir Aston Cockaine to have been invented by Thomas Pilkington, one of the queen's musicians, for Pilkington was one of the musicians of Henrietta, the consort of Charles I., and the Orpharion appears to be of greater antiquity.

Pilkington died about 1660, at Wolver-hampton, aged thirty-five, and lies there buried. Besides an epitaph, Sir Aston Cockaine wrote a poem to his memory, in which are the following quibbling lines :—

'Mastring all music that was known before,
'He did invent the Orphion, and gave more.
'Though he by playing had acquir'd high fame,
'He evermore escaped the gamester's name,
'Yet he at Gamut frequent was, and taught
'Many to play, till death set his Gam out.
'His flats were all harmonious ; not like theirs
'Whose ebbs in prose or verse abuse our ears.
'But to what end praise I his flats, since that
'He is grown one himself, and now lies flat !'

---

[*] It seems by the conclusion of this passage that Morley was but little acquainted with the effects of modern music, for there is extant a relation to this purpose that surpasses all accounts of the power of ancient music over the human mind. It is this: a musician of Ericus king of Denmark, surnamed the Good, who reigned about the year 1130, a hundred years after the time of Guido, having given out that he was able by his art to drive men into what affections he listed, even into anger and fury, and being required by the king to put his skill into practice, played so upon the harp that his auditors began first to be moved, and at last he set the king into such a frantic mood, that in a rage he fell upon his most trusty friends, and, for lack of weapon, slew some of them with his fist, which when he came to himself he did much lament. This story is recorded at large both by Krantzius and Saxo Grammaticus, and is cited by Butler in his treatise on the Principles of Music, pag. 7.

like import, celebrating the memory of another of his profession in these words :—

Muficus et logicus Wyrnal hic jacet ecce Johannes
Organa namque quafi fecerat ille loqui.

Thus humorously translated :—

Musician and logician both,
John Wyrnal lieth here;
Who made the organs erst to speak
As if, or as it were.

CHAP. C.

THE foregoing account may suffice to shew the design and method of Morley's Introduction to Music, a work for which all who love or practice the science are under the highest obligations to its author. John Caspar Trost, organist of the church of St. Martin at Halberstadt, a learned musician of the last century, translated it into the German language, and published it in folio, with the title of Musica Practica.

The particulars of Morley's life are no otherwise to be collected than from a few scattered notes concerning him in the Athenæ Oxonienses, and from his own work, throughout which he speaks the language of a sensible, a learned, and a pious man, a little soured in his temper by bodily infirmities, and more by the envy of some of his own profession, of which he complains in very feeling terms in the preface to almost every one of his publications. In that before his Introduction he speaks of the solitary life which he led, being compelled to keep at home, and that made him glad to find anything wherein to keep himself ex-

ercised for the benefit of his country : and in the course of his work he takes frequent occasion to mention the declining state of his health at the time of his writing it ; nevertheless he survived the publication of it some years, dying as it seems in the year 1604. Doni, in his 'Discorso sopra la perfettione de Melodia,' printed with his treatise 'De' Generi e de' modi,' pag. 111, styles him 'Tommaso Morley, erudito musico Inglese.'

As a practical composer he has doubtless shown great abilities ; he was an excellent harmonist, but did not possess the faculty of invention in any very eminent degree. His compositions seem to be the effect of close study and much labour, and have in them little of that sweet melody which are found in those of Bennet, Weelkes, Wilby, Bateson, and some others ; nor in point of invention and fine contrivance are they to be compared with those of either Bird or Tallis. He composed a solemn burial service, the first perhaps of the kind ever known in England, and which continued to be performed at the interment of persons of rank till it gave way to that of Purcell and Croft, which will hardly ever be excelled.

After the expiration of the patent granted to Tallis and Bird, it seems that Morley had interest enough to obtain of queen Elizabeth a new one of the same tenor, but with ampler powers.* It was granted to him 40 Eliz. Anno Dom. 1598. Under this patent William Barley printed most of the music books which were published during the time that it continued in force.

The style of Morley may be judged of by the following composition, which is the fourteenth of his madrigals to four voices, published in 1594 :—

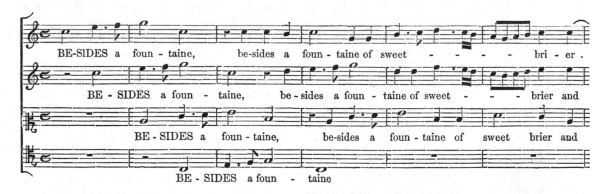

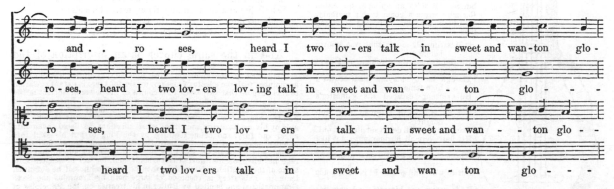

* *Vide ante page 456.*

he, sweet - ly come kisse me, then sweet - ly come kisse me, then sweet - ly kisse me and shew it.

- - ly come kisse me, then sweet - ly come kisse me, then sweet - ly come kisse me, then, and shew it.

it, quoth he, sweet - ly come kisse me, then sweet - ly come kisse me, then sweet - ly, and shew it.

he, sweet - ly come kisse me, then, and shew it.

THOMAS MORLEY.

CHAP. CI.

WILLIAM BATHE, a person scarce known to the world as a writer on music, was nevertheless the author of a book with this title : 'A brief intro-'duction to the true art of musicke, wherein are set 'downe exact and easie rules for such as seeke but to 'know the trueth, with arguments and their solutions, 'for such as seeke also to know the reason of the 'trueth : which rules be meanes whereby any by his 'owne industrie may shortly, easily, and regularly 'attaine to all such thinges as to this arte doe belong : 'to which otherwise any can hardly attaine without 'tedious difficult practice, by meanes of the irregular 'order now used in teaching, lately set forth by 'William Bathe, student at Oxenford. Imprinted 'at London by Abel Jeffes, dwelling in Sermon-lane 'neere Paules Chaine, anno 1584.' Small oblong quarto, black letter.

The authors of the Biographia Britannica, adding their own laborious researches to a few memorials in the Athen. Oxon. have given a much more satisfactory account than could be expected of this obscure person, for his name does not once occur in any treatise extant on the subject of music. The account they give of him is that he was born in Dublin anno 1564; that he was descended from a considerable family, who, what by rebellions, extravagance of heirs, and other misfortunes, were reduced to straight circumstances. They say of this William that he was of a sullen saturnine temper, and disturbed in his mind that his family was fallen from its ancient spendour; that he was educated under a Popish school-master, but removed to Oxford, where he studied several years with indefatigable industry, but in what college, or whether he ever attained to any academical honours, Wood himself could never learn. That growing weary of the heresy, as he usually called the protestant faith professed in England, he quitted the nation and his religion together, and in the year 1596 was initiated amongst the Jesuits. That having spent some time among the Jesuits in Flanders, he travelled into Italy, and completed his studies at Padua, from whence he passed into Spain, being appointed to govern the Irish seminary at Salamanca. That at length taking a journey to Madrid to transact some business of his order, he died there on the seventeenth day of June, 1614, and was buried in the Jesuits' convent of that city.

In the estimation of his brethren he was a man of learning ; and Wood says of him that he had a most ardent zeal for the gaining of souls ; and that though of a temper not very sociable, he was much esteemed by those of his own persuasion for his extraordinary virtues and good qualities. He was the author of several books, the titles whereof are given in the Biographia Britannica.

His Introduction to Music is dedicated to his uncle Gerald Fitzgerald, earl of Kildare, and that for reasons which seem to betray somewhat of that saturnine temper above ascribed to him, for in it he thus expresses himself, 'being rhetorically persuaded 'to graunt to the publishing thereof, I forbore to do it 'till I had considered two thinges, whereof the one 'was the worthinesse of the matter. The other, the 'feeding of the common affections. But for the 'worthinesse, I thought it not to be doubted, seeing 'heere one set forth a booke of a hundred mery 'tales ; * another of the battaile between the spider 'and the fly ;† another De Pugnis Porcorum ; 'another of a monster born at London the second 'of January, hedded lyke a horse and bodied lyke 'a man, with other such lyke fictions ; and thinking 'this matter then some of these to be more worthy. 'As for the other, wich is to feede the common 'affections of the patient learned, I doubt not but it 'may soon be ; but he that wil take in hand to serve 'to the purpose of every petty pratler, may as soone 'by sprinckling water suffice the drienes of the earth, 'as bring his purpose to passe.'

The preface was doubtless intended by the author to recommend his book to the reader's perusal, but he has chosen to bespeak his good opinion rather by decrying the ignorance of teachers, and the method of instruction practised by them, than by pointing out any peculiar excellencies in his own work. He says that many have consumed a whole year before they could come at the knowledge of song only, but that he had taught it in less space than a month.

But how highly soever the author might value his own work, he thought proper some years after the first publication to write it over again in such sort,

* The author here means a translation of Les Centes Nouvelles nou-velles, which is mentioned by Ames to have been printed about this time. The original was published in 1455, by Louis XI. of France, then dauphin, during his retreat from his father's court to that of the duke of Burgundy.
† The Parable of the Spider and the Fly, quarto, 1556, in old English verse, by John Heywood.

as hardly to retain a single paragraph of the former edition. This latter edition was printed by Thomas Este, without a date, with the title of 'A brief In-'troduction to the skill of song: concerning the 'practice, set forth by William Bathe, gentleman.'

And here again the author, according to his wonted custom, censures the musicians of his time, and magnifies the efficacy of his own rules; for mark the modesty of his preface :—

'Olde musitions laid downe for song, manifold 'and crabbed confuse tedious rules, as for example; 'though there be in all but six names, UT RE MI FA 'SOL LA, having amongst them an easie order, yet 'could not they by rule declare, whether of these 'should be attributed to everie note, unlesse they 'had first framed the long ladder or skale of gamut, 'to which some added, thinking the ladder too short; 'some hewed off a peece, thinking it too long. Then 'would they have the learner be as perfect in coming 'down backward, as in going up forward, lest in his 'practice he should fall and break his necke. Then 'must he learne GAMUT in rule, A RE in space, ♮ MI 'in rule, C FA UT in space, &c. Then must he 'know GAMUT, how many cleves, how many notes. 'A RE how many notes, &c. Then must he know '♮, quadrij, proper-chant, and b mul, RE in A RE, 'whereby UT in C FA UT, whereby MI in A LA MI RE, 'whereby, &c. And when all have done, after their 'long circumstances of time, whereby they should be 'often driven to millibi, for notes standing in diverse 'places of gamut have names that the place where 'they stand comprehend not. Touching all the 'prolixe circumstances and needlesse difficulties that 'they use, it loathes me greatly that heere I should 'write them : and much more would it grieve the 'reader to learne them. Also many things are used 'in song for which they give no rules at all, but 'committed them to dodge at it, harke to it, and 'harpe upon it.'

The precepts for singing contained in this book are divided into ante rules, and post rules; the ante rules respect Quantity, Time, and Tune; the post rules, Naming, Quantity, Time and Tune; and, from the manifold objections of the author to the usual method of teaching, a stranger would expect that these were not only better calculated for the purpose of instruction, but also discoveries of his own; but nothing like this appears: his rule of teaching is the scale with the six syllables, and the cliffs of Guido; the mutations, the stumbling-block of learners, he leaves as he found them; and, in short, it may be truly said that not one of the 'prolixe 'circumstances or needlesse difficulties' that others use in teaching, is by him removed, obviated, or lessened : nevertheless, as a proof of the efficacy of his rules, he produces the following instances :—

'In a moneth and leese I instructed a child about 'the age of eight yeares to sing a good number of 'songs, difficult crabbed songs, to sing at the first 'sight, to be so indifferent for all parts, alterations, 'cleves, flats and sharpes, that he could sing a part 'of that kinde of which he never learned any song, 'which child for strangeness was brought before the 'lord deputie of Ireland to be heard sing, for there

'were none of his age, though he were longer at it, 'nor any of his time (though he were elder) known 'before these rules to sing exactly.

'There was another who by dodging at it, heark-'ning to it, and harping upon it, could never be 'brought to tune sharps aright, who so soone as hee 'heard these rules set downe for the same, could tune 'them sufficiently well. I have taught diverse others 'by these rules in lesse than a moneth what myselfe 'by the olde, obtained not in more than two yeares. 'Diverse other proofes I might recite which heere 'as needlesse I doe omit, because the thing will shew 'itselfe. Diverse have repented in their age that 'they were not put to sing in their youth; but 'seeing that by these rules, a good skill may be had 'in a moneth, and the wayes learned in four or five 'dayes: none commeth too late to learne, and 'especially if this saying be true : That no man 'is so olde but thinketh he may live one yeere 'longer. As Aristotle in setting forth his pre-'dicaments saw many things requisite to be entreated 'of, and yet unfit to be mixed with his treatise ; he 'therefore made ante predicaments and post predica-'ments : so I for the same cause, desirous to abolish 'confusion, have added to my rules, ante rules and 'post rules. Vale.'

As to these rules, the best that can be said of them is that there is nothing like them to be met with in any writer on music, and of the perspicuity of his style let this, which is the first chapter of his post rules of song, as he calls them suffice for an example.

'The exceptions from the order of ascention and 'descention are diversely used according to the 'diversitie of place, and accordingly they are to 'be given, for each order in naming seemeth best to 'them that have been brought up withall.

'D is sometimes used in old songs as a cleve, and 'putteth UT down to the fifth place.

'In Italy as I understand, they change UT into 'SOL : in England they change RE into LA, when the 'next removing note before or after be under.'

The following is the third chapter of this ingenious author's post rules, and respects the singing of hard proportions :—

'In timing hard proportions that go odding, many 'take care only of the whole stroke, wholly kept 'without dividing it to the going up and then down 'agayne of the hand.

'Some keepe semibreefe time, as sufficient easie of 'itselfe, and do not divide it into minim time.'

'Three minim time is more difficult, and therefore 'some do divide it into minim time.'

But attend to a notable invention of this author for the measuring of time, and see what clear and in-telligible terms he has chosen to express his meaning.

'Take a stick of a certaine length, and a stone of 'a certaine weight, hold the stick standing upon an 'end of some table : see you have upon the stick 'divers marks : hold the stone up by the side of the 'stick, then as you let fall the stone, instantly begin to 'sing one note, and just with the noyse that it maketh 'upon the table, begin another note, and as long 'as thou holdest the first note, so long hold the rest, 'and let that note be thy cratchet or thy minim, &c.,

'as thou seest cause, and thus maist thou measure
'the verie time itselfe that thou keepest, and know
'whether thou hast altered it or not.'

*The account above given affords occasion to
mention a musician who lived about this time,
equally obscure, of the name of Whythorne, the
author of a book, of which the following (taking it
from the Tenor Part) is the title, and a very
quaint one it is: 'Tenor of songs for 5 voices,
'composed and made by Thomas Whythorne, gent.
'The which songs be of sundry sorts, that is to say,
'some long, some short, some hard, some easie to be
'songe, and some plesant or mery: so that accord-
'ing to the skill of the singers (not being musitians)
'and disposition or delite of the hearers they may
'here finde Songes for their contentation and
'liking.* ❧ *Now newly published A.D.* 1571,
'❧ *At the end of this book ye shall find an ad-
'vertisement concerning the use of the flats and
'sharps that are set with this musicke, also of the
'most needful faults to be amended that are escaped
'in the printing these five Books.'* *The book is of
an oblong form, printed in a neat black letter type
by old John Day. Whythorne's name does not
occur in any list of the musicians of this country,
and it is inferred that he attained to no degree of
eminence in his profession.*

JOHN MUNDY, organist, first of Eton college, and
afterwards of the free chapel of Windsor in queen
Elizabeth's reign, was educated under his father
William Mundy, one of the gentlemen of the chapel,
and an eminent composer. In 1586, at the same
time with Bull, Mundy the son was admitted to the
degree of bachelor of music at Oxford; and at the
distance of almost forty years after was created
doctor in the same faculty in that university. Wood
speaks of a William Mundy, who was a noted
musician, and hath composed several divine services
and anthems, the words of which may be seen in
Clifford's collection; this person was probably no
other than Mundy the father. John Mundy composed madrigals for five voices in the collection
entitled the Triumphs of Oriana, before spoken of,
and of which a particular account will be given
hereafter; was the author of a work entitled 'Songs
'and Psalmes composed into 3, 4, and 5 parts, for
'the use and delight of all such as either love or
'learne musicke,' printed in 1594. An excellent
musician undoubtedly he was, and, as far as can be
judged by the words he has chosen to exercise his
talent on, a religious and modest man, resembling in
this respect Bird. Wood says he gave way to fate
in 1630, and was buried in the cloister adjoining to
the chapel of St. George at Windsor.

CHAP. CII.

THOMAS WEELKES, organist of Winchester, and,
as it should seem, afterwards of Chichester, was the
author of Madrigals to 3, 4, 5, and 6 voices, printed
in 1597. He also published in 1598 'Ballatts and
'madrigals to five voices, with one to six voices;'
and in 1600 'Madrigals of six parts apt for the viols
'and voices.' Walther in his Lexicon mentions
that a monk of the name of Aranda published a
madrigal of Weelkes in a collection of his own
printed at Helmstadt in the year 1619. A madrigal
of his for six voices is published in the Triumphs of
Oriana. He also composed services and anthems,
which are well known and much esteemed. An anthem of his 'O Lord grant the king a long life,' is
printed in Barnard's collection.

There is extant also a work entitled 'Ayeres or
'phantasticke spirites for three voices, made and newly
'published by Thomas Weelkes gentleman of his
'majesties chapell, Bachelar of musicke, and Organest
'of the Cathedral church of Chichester.' Lond. 1608.

This collection contains also a song for six voices
entitled 'A remembrance of my friend M. Thomas
'Morley.'

The following most excellent madrigal of Weelkes
is the eleventh in the collection published by him
in 1597:—

THOMAS WEELKES.

By the Fasti Oxon. it appears that in 1602 William Weelkes of New College, Oxon. was admitted to the degree of bachelor; and Wood makes it a question whether the register of the university might not mistake the name of William, for that of Thomas Weelkes, which, considering the relation between New College and Winchester college, it is more than probable he did.

GILES FARNABY of Christ-Church college, Oxford, was in 1592 admitted bachelor of music. He was of Truro in Cornwall, and nearly related to Thomas Farnabie, the famous school master of Kent: there are extant of his composition, Canzonets to 4 voices, with a song of eight parts. Lond. 1598. A few of the Psalm-tunes in Ravenscroft's Collection, Lond. 1633, that is to say, the three additional parts to the tenor or plain-song, which is the ancient church tune, are of Farnaby's composition.

JOHN MILTON, the father of our celebrated epic poet, though not so by profession, was a musician, and a much more excellent one than perhaps will be imagined. He was born at Milton near Halton and Thame, in Oxfordshire, and, by the advice of a friend of the family, became a scrivener, and followed that business in a shop in Bread-street, London,* having for his sign the spread eagle, the device or coat-armour of the family. Under whom, or by what means he acquired a knowledge of music, the accounts that are given of him are silent, but that he was so eminently skilled in it as to be ranked among the first masters of his time there are proofs irrefragable.† *His son, in a Latin poem entitled "Ad Patrem," celebrates his skill in music; and in the following lines thereof, says of his father and himself, that the attributes of Phœbus, Music and Poetry, were divided between them :—*

'Ipse volens Phœbus se dispertire duobus
'Altera dona mihi, dedit altera dona parenti,
'Dividuum que Deum genitor que puerque tenemus.'

Among the Psalm-tunes composed into four parts by sundry authors, and published by Thomas Ravenscroft in 1633, there are many, particularly that common one called York tune, with the name John Milton; the tenor part of this tune is so well known, that within memory half the nurses in England were used to sing it by way of lullaby; and the chimes of many country churches have played it six or eight times in four and twenty hours from time immemorial. In the Triumphs of Oriana is a madrigal for five voices, composed by John Milton, and in a collection of musical airs and songs for voices and instruments entitled 'The Teares or 'lamentations of a sorrowful soule,' composed by Bird, Bull, Orlando Gibbons, Dowland, Ferabosco, Coperario, Weelkes, Wilbye, in short, by most of the great masters of the time, and set forth by Sir William Leighton, knight, one of the gentlemen pensioners in 1614, are several songs for five voices by John Milton, and among the rest, this :—

* The word scrivener anciently signified a mere copyist. Chaucer rebukes his amanuensis by the name of Adam Scrivenere. The writing of deeds and charters, making service-books, and copying manuscripts, was one of the employments of the regular clergy. After the dissolution of religious houses, the business of a scrivener became a lay profession; and 14 Jac. a company of scriveners was incorporated, about which time they betook themselves to the writing of wills, leases, and such other assurances as required but little skill in the law to prepare. It was at this time a reputable, and, if we may judge from the circumstances of the elder Milton, and the education which he gave his children, a lucrative profession; but after the fire of London the emoluments of it were greatly encreased by the multiplicity of business which that accident gave occasion to. Francis Kirkman the bookseller was put apprentice to a scrivener, and, in the account of his life, entitled The Unlucky Citizen, he relates that almost all the business of the city in making leases, mortgages, and assignments, and procuring money on securities of ground and houses, was transacted by these men, who hence assumed the name of money scriveners. The furniture of a scrivener's shop was a sort of pew for the master, desks for the apprentices, and a bench for the clients to sit on till their turn came to be dispatched. The following jest may serve to explain the manner in which this business was carried on: A country fellow passing along Cheapside, stopped to look in at a scrivener's shop, and seeing no wares exposed to sale, asked the apprentice, the only person in it, what they sold there? Loggerheads, answered the lad. By my troth, says the countryman, 'you must have 'a roaring trade then, for I see but one left in the shop.'

† We are told by Phillips, in his account of his uncle Milton, that he also was skilled in music. Mr. Fenton in his life of him adds that he played on the organ; and there can be but little reason to suppose, considering that he had his education in London, viz., in St. Paul's school, that he had his instruction in music from any other person than his father. From many passages in his poems it appears that Milton the younger had a deep sense of the power of harmony over the human mind. This in the Il Penseroso—

'But let my due feet never fail
'To walk the studious cloisters pale,
'And love the high embowed roof,
'With antique pillars massy proof,
'And storied windows richly dight,
'Casting a dim religious light.
'There let the pealing organ blow,
'To the full-voic'd choir below,
'In service high and anthems clear,
'As may with sweetness, through mine ear
'Dissolve me into extasies,
'And bring all Heav'n before mine eyes.'

shews that however he might object to choral service as a matter of discipline, he was not proof against that enthusiastic devotion which it has a tendency to excite. It may here be remarked that the lines above quoted present to the reader's imagination a view of an ancient Gothic cathedral, and call to his recollection such ideas as may be supposed to possess the mind during the performance of the solemn choral service; and it is probable that the poet became thus impressed in his youth by his frequent attendance at the cathedral of St. Paul, which was near his school, and in his father's neighbourhood, where the service was more solemn than it is now, and which cathedral, till it was destroyed by the fire of London, had perhaps the most venerable and awful appearance of any edifice of the kind in the world.

JOHN MILTON.

And lastly, it is said in the life of Milton the son, written by his nephew Edward Phillips, and prefixed to a translation of some of his Latin letters of state, printed in 1694, that Milton the father composed an In Nomine of no fewer than forty parts, for which he was rewarded by a Polish prince, to whom he presented it, with a golden medal and chain.*

CHAP. CIII.

JOHN COPERARIO, a celebrated artist on the viol da gamba, and a good composer for that instrument, and also for the lute, was in great reputation about the year 1600. He excelled in the composition of fantasias for viols in many parts; he taught music to the children of James the First; and under him prince Charles attained to a considerable degree of proficiency on the viol; some of his vocal compositions are to be found in Sir William Leighton's collection, mentioned in the preceding article, and of

* A golden medal and chain was the usual gratuity of princes to men of eminence in any of the faculties, more especially law, physic, poetry, and music. Orlando de Lasso is always represented in paintings and engravings with this ornament about his neck, as are Matthiolus, Baudius, Sennertus, Erycius Puteanus, and many others. It seems that the medal and chain once bestowed as a testimony of princely favour, was ever after a part of the dress of the person thus honoured, at least on public occasions. So lately as the beginning of the present century the emperor Joseph I. presented Antonio Lotti of Venice with a gold chain, as a compliment for dedicating to him a book of Duetti Terzetti, &c. of his composition, in which was contained the famous madrigal 'In una Siepe ombrosa.' Letters from the Academy of ancient Music at London to Signor Antonio Lotti of Venice, 1732.

his fantasias there are innumerable in manuscript. He, in conjunction with Nicholas Laniere and others, composed songs in a masque written by Dr. Thomas Campion, on occasion of the marriage of Carr earl of Somerset and the lady Frances Howard, the divorced countess of Essex, and presented in the banquetting-room at Whitehall on St. Stephen's night, 1614. Mr. Fenton, in his notes on Waller, on what authority he does not mention, says that Henry Lawes having been educated under him, introduced a softer mixture of Italian airs than before had been practised in our nation, from which, and from his giving him the appellation of Signor, he seems to intimate that he was an Italian: but the fact is that he was an Englishman, and named Cooper, who having spent much of his time in Italy, Italianized his name to Coperario, and was called so ever after. Coperario composed fantasias for viols to a great number, which are extant in manuscript only. His printed works are, the songs composed by him in conjunction with Laniere on occasion of the above-mentioned marriage, and these that follow:—

'Funeral Teares for the death of the Right
'Honorable the Earle of Devonshire, figured in
'seaven songes, whereof sixe are so set forth that
'the wordes may be exprest by a treble voice alone
'to the lute and base viol, or else that the meane
'part may be added, if any shall affect more fulnesse

'of parts. The seaventh is made in forme of a dia-
'logue, and cannot be sung without two voices.
'Invented by John Coperario. Pius piè   Fol.
Lond. 1606.

'Songs of Mourning, bewailing the untimely
'death of prince Henry, worded by Thomas Cam-
'pion, and set forth to bee sung with one voice to
'the lute or violl by John Coperario.' Fol. Lond. 1613.

ELWAY BEVIN, a man eminently skilled in the knowledge of practical composition, flourished towards the
end of queen Elizabeth's reign. He was of Welsh
extraction, and had been educated under Tallis, upon
whose recommendation it was that on the third day
of June, 1589, he was sworn in, gentleman extraordinary of the chapel, from whence he was expelled
in 1637, it being discovered that he adhered to the
Romish communion. He was also organist of Bristol
cathedral, but forfeited that employment at the same
time with his place in the chapel. Child, afterwards
doctor, was his scholar. It is worthy of remark that
although Wood has been very careful in recording
eminent musicians, as well those of Cambridge as of
Oxford, the name of Bevin does not once occur in
either the Athenæ or Fasti Oxonienses. One of the
reasons for his care in preserving the memory of men
of this faculty was that himself was a passionate lover
of music, and a performer, and Bevin's merits were
such as intitled him to an eulogium, so that it is
difficult to account for this omission. The above
memoir however will in some measure help to
supply it. He has composed sundry services, some
of which are printed in Barnard's collection, and
a few anthems.

Before Bevin's time the precepts for the composition
of canon were known to few. Tallis, Bird, Waterhouse,
and Farmer, were eminently skilled in this most abstruse part of musical practice. Every canon as given
to the public, was a kind of enigma. Compositions
of this kind were sometimes exhibited in the form of
a cross, sometimes in that of a circle : there is now
extant one resembling a horizontal sun-dial ; and the
resolution as it was called of a canon, which was the
resolving it into its elements, and reducing it into
score, was deemed a work of almost as great difficulty
as the original composition ; but Bevin, with a view
to the improvement of students, generously communicated the result of many years study and experience in a treatise which is highly commended by
all who have taken occasion to speak of it.

This book was published in quarto, 1631, and
dedicated to Goodman, bishop of Gloucester, with
the following title :—' A briefe and short instruction
'of the art of musicke, to teach how to make discant
'of all proportions that are in use : Very necessary
'for all such as are desirous to attain to knowledge
'in the art ; and may by practice, if they can sing,
'soone be able to compose three, four, and five parts,
'and also to compose all sorts of canons that are
'usuall, by these directions of two or three parts in
'one upon the plain-song.'

The rules contained in this book for composition in
general are very brief ; but for the composition of
canon there are in it a great variety of examples of

almost all the possible forms in which it is capable
of being constructed, even to the extent of sixty
parts. In the course of his work the author makes
use of only the following plain-song—

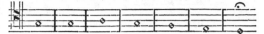

as the basis for the several examples of canon contained in his book, and it answers through a great
variety of canons, following at the stated distances of
a crochet, a minim, a semibreve, a breve, and three
minims, by augmentation and diminution, rectè et
retro and per arsin et thesin of three in one, four in
two, in the diatessaron and subdiatessaron, diapente
and subdiapente, and at various other intervals. But
what must be matter of amazement to every one
acquainted with the difficulties that attend this species
of composition is, that these few simple notes appear
virtually to contain in them all those harmonies which,
among a great variety of others, the following composition of this author is contrived to illustrate :—

CANON OF FIVE PARTS IN TWO, RECTE ET RETRO; ET PER ARSIN ET THESIN.

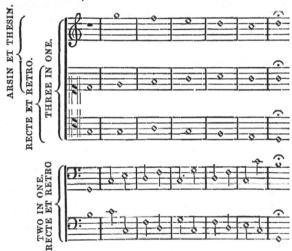

The author seems to have been a devout, but, in
some degree, a superstitious man, for speaking of
a canon of three parts in one, he makes use of these
words :—

'A Canon of three in one hath resemblance to the
'Holy Trinity, for as they are three distinct parts
'comprehended in one. The leading part hath
'reference to the Father, the following part to the
'Sonne, the third to the Holy Ghost.'

THOMAS BATESON, an excellent vocal composer,
was about the year 1600 organist of the cathedral
church of Chester. Wood says he was a person
esteemed very eminent in his profession, especially
after the publication of his English madrigals to
3, 4, 5, and 6 voices. About 1618 he became
organist and master of the children of the cathedral
church of the blessed Trinity in Dublin, and in the
university of that city it is supposed he obtained the
degree of bachelor of music. The following is one
of his madrigals for three voices :—

lie,   but when for them ...   they say they'll die,   they say they'll die,   be -

lie,   but when for them they   say ..   they'll die,   they say they'll die,   be - lieve them

lie,   but when for them they   say   they'll   die,   they say they'll die,   be - lieve

- lieve them not,   they do but lie,   be - lieve them   not, they do   but   lie,   be -

not,   they do   but   lie, but lie,   be - lieve   them   not, they do   but   lie,   be - lieve them

them   not,   they do but lie,   be - lieve them not,   they do   but   lie,   be -

- lieve   them   not,   they do   but   lie,   be - lieve ...   them not, they   do .. but   lie.

not,   they do but lie, .   . be - lieve   them not, they do but lie, they   do ...   but   lie.

- lieve them not,   they do   but lie, ...   they   do . . . .   but   lie.

THOMAS BATESON.

THOMAS TOMKINS was of a family that seems to have produced more musicians than any in England. His father was Thomas Tomkins, Chanter of the choir of Gloucester, who discovering in his son a propensity to music, put him under the care of Bird, by whose instructions he so profited, that for his merits he was made a gentleman of the chapel royal, and afterwards organist thereof: some years after this he became organist of the cathedral church at Worcester, and composed songs of 3, 4, 5, and 6 parts, printed at London without a date, but conjectured to have been published before the year 1600. He was also the author of a work in ten books, intitled 'Musica Deo sacra et Ecclesiæ Anglicanæ,' consisting of anthems, hymns, and other compositions adapted to the church service. The words of others of his compositions of this kind may be seen in the collection of James Clifford before mentioned. The same James Clifford had what Wood calls a set of vocal church-music of four and five parts in manuscript, composed by Thomas Tomkins, which he gave to the collection of music in the library of Magdalen college, Oxford. Some of the madrigals in the Triumphs of Oriana were composed by Thomas Tomkins, the subject of the present article. The time both of his birth and death are uncertain, as are also the particular times when his works were severally published; all that can be said touching the time when he flourished is, that he was a scholar of Bird, that he was admitted to his bachelor's degree in 1607, being then of Magdalen college, and that he

was living, as Wood relates,* after the grand rebellion broke out. He had a son named Nathaniel, a prebendary of Worcester, and several brethren, among whom were Giles, organist of the cathedral church of Salisbury; John, organist of St. Paul's cathedral, and a gentleman of the chapel ;† and Nicholas, one of the gentlemen of the privy-chamber to king Charles I., a person well skilled in the practice of music.

NICHOLAS LANIERE, LANIER, or LANEARE (*a Portrait*), for in all these ways is his name spelt, a musician of eminence in his time, though he lived and died in England, was born in Italy in the year 1568. He was a painter and an engraver, which two latter professions have entitled him to a place in the Anecdotes of Painting in England, published by Mr. Walpole, who has nevertheless considered him as a musician, and has given a brief but curious account of him.

During the reign of James I. the household musicians, those of the chapel, and many others of

* Fasti Oxon, vol. I. col. 176.

† In the old cathedral of St. Paul was the following inscription in 'memory of him :—Johannes Tomkins, Musicæ Baccalaureus, Organista 'sui temporis celeberrimus, postquam Capellæ regali, per annos duo- 'decim, huic autem Ecclesiæ per novemdecem sedulo inserviisset, ad 'cœlestem chorum migravit, Septembris 27, Anno Domini, 1638. 'Ætatis suæ 52. Cujus desiderium mœrens uxor hoc testatur Mar- 'more.' Dugd. Hist. St. Paul's Cath. edit. 1658. *Of this person Wood says, he was in high esteem for his admirable knowledge in the theoretical and practical part of his faculty. Among the poems of Phineas Fletcher, (the author of the " Purple Island,") is one in which, by the name of Thomalin he is celebrated, for the sweetness of his musical strains, with a tender reproof for his preferring court enjoyments to the pleasures of rural life; and it is highly probable that Fletcher meant to characterise him in the second, sixth, and last of his piscatory eclogues, in each of which Thomalin is interlocutor.*

eminence, whom the patronage of Elizabeth had produced, were neglected, and very little of the royal favour was extended to any besides Laniere and Coperario; and for this it will not be difficult to assign a reason: the one was an Italian by birth, and the other had lived in Italy till his style, and even his very name, were so Italianized, that he was in general taken for a native of that country: these men brought into England the Stylo Recitativo, as it is called in the masque mentioned by Mr. Walpole, and which had then lately been invented by Jacopo Peri, and Giulio Caccini, and improved by Claudio Monteverde.

The masque at Lord Hay's for the entertainment of the Baron de Tour, in Ben Johnson's works, was, as therein is mentioned, composed by Laniere solely; but at a solemnity of a different kind, the infamous nuptials of Carr earl of Somerset with the lady Frances Howard, the divorced countess of Essex, he and Coperario lent their joint assistance, for in a masque, written by Dr. Thomas Campion and performed in the banquetting room at Whitehall on St. Stephen's night, 1614, on occasion of that marriage, and printed in the same year, their names occur as the composers of the music. The masquers were the duke of Lenox, the earls of Pembroke, Dorset, Salisbury, Montgomery; the lords Walden, Scroope, North, and Hayes; Sir Thomas, Sir Henry, and Sir Charles Howard.

Many songs of Laniere are to be met with in collections published in the time of Charles I. but they seem to have little to recommend them.

An admirable portrait of himself, painted by his own hand, is yet in the music-school at Oxford, an engraving from which is inserted in the Appendix: at his right hand is a skull, in the mouth whereof is a label, containing a canon of his composition.

GEORGE FEREBE, master of arts of Magdalen college, Oxford, 1595, minister of Bishop's Cannings, Wilts, was a native of Gloucestershire, and well skilled in music. Wood, in the Fasti Oxon. vol. I. Col. 150, has given a curious account of him, which is here inserted in his own words:—'This person 'did instruct divers young men of his parish in the 'faculty of music, till they could either play or sing 'their parts. In the year 1613, Qu. Anne, the royal 'consort of K. James I. made her abode for some 'weeks in the city of Bath, purposely for the use of 'the waters there, in which time he composed a song 'of four parts, and instructed his scholars to sing it 'perfectly, as also to play a lesson or two which he 'had composed, upon their wind-instruments: on 'the 11th June, the same year, the queen in her 'return from Bath did intend to pass over the downes 'at Wensdyke, within the parish of Bishop's Cannings. 'Of which Ferebe having timely notice, dressed him- 'self in the habit of an old bard, and caused his 'scholars whom he had instructed, to be cloathed 'in shepherds' weeds. The queen having received 'notice of these people, she with her retinue made 'a stand at Wensdyke, whereupon these musicians 'drawing up to her, played a most admirable lesson 'on their wind-instruments; which being done, they

'sang their lesson of four parts with double voices, 'the beginning of which was this:—

'Shine, O thou sacred shepherds' star
'On silly shepherd swains, &c.

'which being well performed also, the bard concluded 'with an epilogue, to the great liking and content of 'the queen and her company. Afterwards he was 'sworn chaplain to his majesty, and was ever after 'much valued for his ingenuity.'

CHAP. CIV.

THE account herein before immediately given contains the succession of theoretic and practical musicians down to the end of the sixteenth century, at the commencement whereof, music, not to speak of that kind of it which was appropriated to divine service, from being the domestic recreation of private persons, and the entertainment of select companies, was introduced into the theatre, and made an auxiliary to dramatic performances. But before the history of this union and the subsequent progress of practical music can be given, it is necessary to review the past period, and ascertain the state of music in general at the close of it.

The compositions peculiar to the church, not to distinguish between one and the other of them, were, as has been related, the Mass, the Motet, the Anthem, and the Hymns for various occasions, such as the Stabat Mater, Salve Regina, A Solis ortu, Alma Redemptoris Mater, Ave Regina Cœlorum, and others to be found in the Romish Missal, the Antiphonary, and the Breviary; the only species of vocal harmony calculated for private amusement hitherto mentioned, were the Madrigal, the Canon, and the Catch or Round, all which required a plurality of voices; and of instrumental, the Fantazia for vio s and other instruments to a certain number. But besides these, the names of sundry other kinds of vocal and instrumental harmony and melody occur in Morley's Introduction, and other musical tracts, of which it is here proper to take notice; and first of the Canzone.

The Canzone is a composition somewhat resembling, but less elaborate than the madrigal. It admits of little fugues and points, and seldom exceeds three parts, though the name is sometimes given to a song for one voice. Cervantes, in Don Quizote, calls the song of Chrysostom a Canzone.

The word Canzonet is a diminutive of Canzone, and therefore means a little or short canzone or song in parts. Luca Marenzio, though he in general applied himself to more elaborate studies, Giovanni Feretti, and Horatio Vecchi, are said to have excelled in this species of composition.

The Villanella, the lightest and least artificial kind of air known in music, is a composition, as Morley says, made only for the ditty's sake, in which he adds, many perfect chords of one kind, nay even disallowances, may be taken at pleasure, suiting, as he says, a clownish music to a clownish matter. Among the sonnets of Sir Philip Sidney is one said to be written to the air of a Neapolitan villanella.

NICHOLAS LANIERE,

MASTER OF THE BAND OF MUSIC

TO HIS MAJESTY CHA. I.

From an original Painting in the Music-School, Oxford.

The Ballet is a tune to a ditty, and which may likewise be danced to. Morley speaks also of a kind of Ballets called Fa la's, some whereof, composed by Gastoldi, he says he had seen and it seems imitated, for there is a collection of songs of this kind by Morley in five parts.

Morley mentions many other kinds of air in practice in his time, as namely, the Pavan,* the Passamezzo, the Galliard, the Courant, the Jig, the Hornpipe, the Scottish Jig, and others. It must be noted that these were all dance-tunes, and that the difference between the one and others of them lay in the difference of measure and the number of bars of which the several strains were made to consist.

But of vocal music the madrigal appears to have been most in practice of any kind at this time, as well in England as in other countries; it was some years after this species of harmony was invented, that the English musicians applied themselves to the study of it, for Bird seems to have been the first composer of madrigals in this country; his first essay of the kind was upon two stanzas of the Orlando Furioso, 'La Verginella,' which he set for five voices, and was received with the utmost degree of approbation.

Hitherto a madrigal to any other than Italian words was a thing not known; and it seemed to be a doubt among musicians whether the words of English poetry could with any degree of propriety be made to consist with the madrigal style of musical composition, till 1583, when a certain gentleman, whose name is unknown, for his private delight, made an essay of this kind, by translating the words of some most celebrated Italian madrigals into English verse, so as thus translated they might be sung to the original notes. These came to the hands of one

Nicholas Yonge, who kept a house in London for the reception of foreign merchants and gentlemen, and he in the year 1588 published them, together with others of the same kind, with the following title :—' Musica Transalpina, Madrigales translated 'of four, five, and sixe parts, chosen out of divers 'excellent authors; with the first and second part of 'La Verginella, made by maister Bird upon two 'stanzas of Ariosto,† and brought to speak English 'with the rest, published by N. Yonge, in favour of 'such as take pleasure in music of voices.' ‡

In this collection are the first, second, and third parts of the Thyrsis of Luca Marenzio, as Peacham calls it, translated from ' Tirsi morir volea, 'Chi fa 'hoggi il mio sole,' of the same author, to ' What 'doth my pretty darling? The ' Susann' un jour,' of Orlando de Lasso, and the Nightingale of the elder Ferabosco, celebrated also by Peacham, with a number of other well chosen compositions from the best of the Italians. It was a work in great estimation; the picture of Dr. Heather, now in the music-school, Oxford, represents him with a book in

† These two stanzas are imitated from the Carmen Nuptiale of Catullus, and are as follow:—

'La Verginella è simile à la Rosa;
' Ch' in bel giardin sù la nativa spina,
' Mentre sola, e sicura si riposa,
' Nè greggè, nè pastor se l'avvicina;
' L'aura soave, e l'alba rugiadoso,
' L'acqua, la terra al suo favor s'inchina :
' Giovani vaghi, e donne inamorate,
' Amano haverne, e seni, e tempie ornate.

' Ma non si tosto dal maerno stelo
' Rimossa viene, e dal suo ceppo verde;
' Che, quanto havea da gli huomini, e dal cielo
' Favor, gratia, e bellezza, tutto perde:
' La vergine, che 'l fior; di che più zelo
' Che de begli occhi, e de la vita, havei de';
' Lascia altrui corre; il pregio c'hauea innanti;
' Perde nel cor di tutti gl' altri amanti.'

ORLANDO FURIOSO, Canto Primo.

The reader will at first sight discover that the air in the Beggar's Opera, ' Virgins are like the fair flower in its lustre,' is an imitation of the above stanzas.

‡ The history of this publication is contained in the dedication of the book to Gilbert lord Talbot, son and heir to George, earl of Shrewsbury, and is to this purpose:—

'Since I first began to keep house in this citie, it hath been no small 'comfort unto mee, that a great number of gentlemen and merchants of 'good accompt (as well of this realme as of forreine nations) have taken 'in good part such entertainment of pleasure as my poore abilitie was 'able to afford them, both by the exercise of musicke daily used in my 'house, and by furnishing them with bookes of that kinde, yeerely sent 'me out of Itaiy and other places, which being for the most part Italian 'songs, are for sweetness of aire verie well liked of all, but most in 'account with them that understand that language; as for the rest, they 'doe either not sing them at all, or at least with little delight. And 'albeit there be some English songs lately set forth by a great maister of 'musicke, which for skill and sweetness may content the most curious, 'yet because they are not many in number, men delighted with varietie 'have wished for more of the same sort. For whose cause chiefly 'I endevoured to get into my hands all such English songs as were 'praise-worthie, and amongst others I had the hap to find in the hands of 'some of my good friends, certaine Italian madrigales, translated most 'of them five yeeres agoe by a gentleman for his private delight (as not 'long before certaine Napolitans had been Englished by a very honour- 'able personage, a councellour of estate, whereof I have seen some, but 'never possessed any.) And finding the same to be singulerly well liked, 'not onely of those for whose cause I gathered them; but of many 'skilful gentlemen and other great musicians who affirmed the accent of 'the words to be well mainteined, the descant not hindred (though some 'fewe notes altred) and in everie place the due decorum kept: I was so 'bolde (beeing well acquainted with the gentleman) as to entreat the 'rest, who willingly gave me such as he had (for of some he kept no 'copies) and also some other more lately done at the request of his 'particular friends. Now when the same was seen to arise to a just 'number, sufficient to furnish a great set of bookes, diverse of my 'friendes aforesaid required with great instance to have them printed, 'whereunto I was as willing as the rest, but could never obtaine the 'gentleman's consent, though I sought it by many great meanes. For 'his answer was ever, that those trifles being but an idle man's exercise, 'of an idle subject written only for private recreation, would blush to be 'seen otherwise then by twilight, much more to be brought into the 'common view of all men.' He then relates that finding that they were 'about to be printed surreptitiously, he ventured to publish them himself.

* The Pavan, from Pavo a peacock, is a grave and majestic dance; the method of dancing it was anciently by gentlemen dressed with a cap and sword, by those of the long robe in their gowns, by princes in their mantles, and by ladies in gowns with long trains, the motion whereof in the dance resembled that of a peacock's tail. This dance is supposed to have been invented by the Spaniards; and its figure is given with the characters for the steps in the Orchesographia of Thoinot Arbeau. Every Pavan has its Galliard, a lighter kind of air made out of the former.

Of the Passamezzo little is to be said, except that it was a favourite air in the days of queen Elizabeth. Ligon, in his History of Barbadoes, mentions a Passamezzo Galliard which in the year 1647 a Padre in that island played to him on the lute, the very same he says with an air of that kind which in Shakespeare's Henry the Fourth was originally played to Sir John Falstaff and Doll Tearsheet by Sneak, the musician therein named. This little anecdote Ligon might have by tradition, but his conclusion that because it was played in a dramatic representation of the history of Henry the Fourth, it must be as ancient as his time, is very idle and injudicious.

The Courant, the Jig, the Hornpipe, and a variety of other airs, will be spoken of hereafter. As to Scottish jigs, and indeed Scottish tunes in general, all men know that the style and cast of them is unaccountably singular. The vulgar notion is that this singularity arises from a commixture of the primitive rude melody of that country with the more refined air of the Italians; and that David Rizzio, the minion of Mary, queen of Scots, was not only the author of this improvement, but that many of the most admired Scottish tunes yet in use are of his composition. This is highly improbable, seeing that none of the writers on music take the least notice of him as a composer. Buchanan says that he was sent for into Scotland to entertain the queen in the performance of madrigals, in which he sang the bass part. Melvil says the same, and adds that he had a fine hand on the lute. Besides all which it will hereafter be shewn that the Scottish music, so far from borrowing from it, has enriched the Italian with some peculiar graces.

Henry Peacham, the author of the Compleat Gentleman, in a humorous little tract of his intitled the Worth of a Penny, takes notice that northern or Scottish tunes were much in vogue in his time; for describing a man dejected in his mind for want of money, he says that he cannot stand still, but like one of the Tower wild beasts, is still walking from one end of his room to another, humming out some new northern tune or other. Pag. 14. And again, giving the character of one Godfrey Colton, a tailor in Cambridge, of whom he tells a pleasant story; he says he was a merry companion with his tabor and pipe, and sang all manner of northern songs before nobles and gentlemen, who much delighted in his company. Pag. 29.

his hand, on the cover whereof is written MUSICA TRANSALPINI.

In 1590 another collection of this kind was published with this title, 'The first set of Italian madri-'gals, Englished, not to the sense of the original 'dittie, but after the affection of the noate, by 'Thomas Watson gentleman. There are also heere 'inserted two excellent madrigalls of Master William 'Byrd's, composed after the Italian vaine at the request 'of the said Thomas Watson.'

This book contains, among others, those madrigals of Luca Marenzio which Peacham has pointed out as excellent, viz., 'Veggo dolce mio ben,' or 'Farewell 'cruel and unkind.' 'Cantava,' or 'Sweet singing 'Amaryllis.' Those of Bird, which he composed at the request of the publisher, are both to the same words, viz., 'This sweet and merry month of May,' the one in four, the other in six parts, and are a compliment to queen Elizabeth.

The success of these several publications excited, as it was very natural to expect it would do, an emulation in the English musicians to compose original madrigals in their own language, which were so well received, that from thenceforth those of the Italians began to be neglected.

The first collection of this kind seems to be that of Morley, published in 1594, entitled 'Madrigalls 'to foure voyces newly published, the first book.'

In 1597, N. Yonge above-mentioned, who then called himself Nicholas, published a second collection of translated madrigals with the title of Musica Transalpina, the second part.

In the same year GEORGE KIRBYE published a set of English madrigals for four, five, and six voices.

In 1597 also, Thomas Weelkes before named published 'Madrigals to three, four, five, and six voices;' and in 1598 'Ballets and Madrigals to five voyces, 'with one to six voyces.'

In 1598 Morley published with English words, 'Madrigals to five voyces, selected out of the best 'approved Italian authors.'

This collection contains madrigals of Alfonso Ferabosco, Battista Mosto, Giovanni Feretti, Ruggiero Giovanelli, Horatio Vecchi, Giulio Belli, Alessandro Orologio, Luca Márenzio, Hippolito Sabino, Peter Phillips, Stephano Venturi, and Giovanni di Macque, most of which are excellent in their kind, but no mention is made of the authors of the English words; it is therefore probable that they were written by Morley himself, who had a talent for poetry sufficient for the purpose. In the dedication of the book to Sir Gervis Clifton, is this remarkable aphorism, 'Whom God loveth not, they love not musique.'

In the same year, 1598, JOHN WILBYE, a teacher of music, and who dwelt in Austin Friars, London, published 'Madrigals to three, four, five, and six voices.' most of which are excellent; this which follows is the tenth, and is thought little inferior to the best compositions of the kind of the Italian masters :—

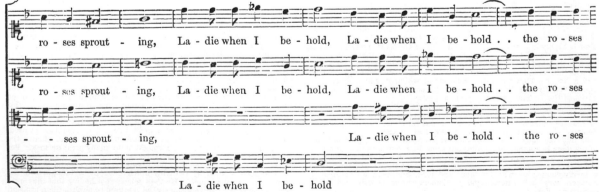

JOHN WILBYE.

The same Wilbye, in the year 1600, published 'A second set of Madrigals to 3, 4, 5, and 6 parts, 'apt both for viols and voices;' dedicated to the Lady Arabella Stuart.

CHAP. CV.

IN 1599 JOHN BENNET published 'Madrigals to 'four voyces, being his first works.' He also composed a madrigal in the Triumphs of Oriana, and some of the songs contained in a book written by Thomas Ravenscroft, and published in 1614, entitled 'A briefe discourse of the true but neglected 'use of charact'ring the degrees by their perfection, 'imperfection, and diminution in mensurable musicke, 'against the common practice and custom of these 'times.' In the preface to which book he is styled a gentleman 'admirable for all kind of composures either in art or ayre, simple or mixt.'

Excepting the above short eulogium, we meet with no particulars relating to this person. Wood does not so much as mention him, from which circumstance alone it may not only be inferred that he was not a graduate in either university, but also that he was little known to the world in his profession. In the dedication of his book of Madrigals to Ralph Asheton, Esq. receiver of the queen's duchy revenues in the counties Palatine of Lancaster and Chester, it is hinted that the author was indebted to that gentleman both for his patronage and his education; but under what masters he received it we are at a loss to find.

The madrigals composed by Bennet, and printed in the collection above-mentioned, are seventeen in number; this which follows is the tenth of them; they are finely studied, and abound with all the graces and elegancies of vocal harmony; and it may be said of the work in general, that it is an honour to our country, and in no respect inferior to any collection of the kind published by the Italian or other foreign musicians.:—

JOHN BENNET.

John Farmer, of whom mention has already been made, published in the same year, 1599, 'The first Sett of English Madrigals to four voices.' In the preface to this work the author professes to have so fully linked his music to number, as each give to other their true effect, which is to move delight; this virtue being, as he says, so singular in the Italians, as under that ensign only they hazard their honour.

The following madrigal is the first in the collection.

JOHN FARMER.

CHAP. CVI.

The names of other composers of madrigals occur about this time, or within a few years after, the chief of whom were, Henry Youll, John Ward, Michael Este, bachelor of music, and master of the choristers in the cathedral of Lichfield, and Orlando Gibbons. And here it may be remarked, that of the authors above enumerated, some only appear to have been graduates in one or other university, or beneficed musicians in some cathedral or collegiate church; as to the rest, the appellation assumed by them is simply that of practitioner in music. Youll and Farmer have no other adjunct to their respective names, and Bateson retained it till he acquired the degree of bachelor.

Besides the several collections of madrigals above mentioned, there is one, the title whereof is perpetually occurring in the Fasti Oxonienses. It is called the Triumphs of Oriana, and frequently in Wood's illiberal manner of expressing himself, the whole collection is called the Orianas. It seems by the work itself as if all the musicians of queen Elizabeth's time who were capable of composing, had endeavoured each to excel the other in setting a song, celebrating the beauty and virtues of their sovereign; for to the Triumphs of Oriana it appears that the following musicians contributed, namely, Michael Este, Daniel Norcome,* John Mundy, Ellis Gibbons,† John Bennet, John Hilton,‡ George Marston,§ Richard Carleton, John Holmes,‖ Richard Nicholson,¶ Thomas Tomkins, Michael Cavendish, William Cobbold, Thomas Morley, John Farmer, John Wilbye, Thomas Hunt, Thomas Weelkes, John Milton,** George Kirbye, Robert Jones,†† John Lisley, and Edward Johnson. This collection was published by Morley with the title of 'The Triumphs of Oriana, to five and six voices, composed by divers authors. Lond. 1601.'

The occasion of this collection is said to be this: the lord high admiral, Charles Howard earl of Nottingham, was the only person who in the last illness of Elizabeth could prevail on her to go into and remain in her bed;‡‡ and with a view to alleviate her concern for the execution of the earl of Essex, he gave for a prize-subject to the poets and musicians of the time, the beauty and accomplishments of his royal mistress, and by a liberal reward excited them severally to the composition of this work. This supposition is favoured by the circumstance of its being dedicated to the earl, and the time of its publication, which was in the very year that Essex was beheaded. There is some piece of secret history which we are yet to learn, that would enable us to account for the giving the queen this romantic name;

* A clerk or singing-man at Windsor. Temp. Jac. I.
† Ellis Gibbons, organist of Salisbury, and brother of the famous Orlando Gibbons, mentioned hereafter.
‡ Bachelor of music, and organist of the church of St. Margaret, Westminster.
§ Mentioned in Sir Anthony Weldon's Court and Character of King James, pag. 106.
‖ Organist of Salisbury. Temp. Eliz.
¶ The first professor of music at Oxford under Dr. Heather's endowment.
** The father of the poet.
†† A famous lutenist and composer for the lute
‡‡ Vide Hist. View of the Negociations between the Courts of England and France, by Dr. Birch, pag. 208. Biogr. Brit. vol. IV. pag. 2678.

probably she was fond of it. Camden relates that a Spanish ambassador had libelled her by the name of Amadis Oriana, and for his insolence was put under a guard. Vide Rapin, vol. II. pag. 88.§§

In the reign of James I. the practice of singing madrigals declined so fast, that few, if any, collections of them were published after the year 1620, the reason of which may be, that the entertainments of his court were for the most part masques and other theatrical representations, with which music, at least that kind of it which required much skill in the composition, had little to do. The merit of these entertainments consisted either in the quaintness of the device or fable, if it may be so called, the magnificence of the scenes, the artificial construction of the machinery, or in the splendid decorations of the theatre or place of exhibition; and it is well known that Jonson wasted much of his time in composing little interludes of this kind; and that Inigo Jones was condemned to the task of studying decorations for them, and exercising his luxuriant invention upon no better materials than pasteboard and canvas.

Of the madrigal it has already been said, that it is a species of vocal harmony very elegant in its structure, and adapted to such poetry as was fit to be sung or uttered in the hearing of the most polite and

§§ In the Triumphs of Oriana, madrigal VIII. is the following passage:—
'Thus Bonny Boots the birth-day celebrated
'Of her, his lady deerest,
'Fair Oriana which to his hart was nearest.'
And in Madrigal XXIV. this:—
'For Bonny Boots that so aloft could fetch it,
'Oh he is dead, and none of us can reach it.'
Again, in the first of Morley's canzonets of five and six voices, published in 1607, he is thus mentioned;—
'Fly love that art so sprightly,
'To Bonny Boots uprightly,
'And when in heaven thou meet him,
'Say that I kindly greet him,
'And that his Oriana
'True widow maid still followeth Diana.'
And again his name occurs in the ninth canzonet in the same collection:—
'Our Bonny Boots could toot it,
'Yea and foot it,
'Say lustie lads, who now shall Bonny Boot it?
Bonny Boots seems to be a nick-name for some famous singer, who, because of his excellent voice, or for some other reason, had permission to call the queen his lady; possibly the person meant might be one Mr. Hale, of whom mention is made by Sir William Segar, in his account of a solemn tilt or exercise of arms, held in the year 1590, before queen Elizabeth, in the Tilt-yard at Westminster, with emblematical representations and music, in which the above-mentioned Mr. Hale performed a part by singing the following song:—
'My golden locks time hath to silver turn'd
'(O time too swift, and swiftnes never ceasing)
'My youth 'gainst age, and age at youth hath spurn'd.
'But spurn'd in vaine; youth waineth by encreasing,
'Beauty, strength, youth, are flowers that fading beene,
'Duety, faith, love, are rootes and ever greene.
'My helmet now shall make an hive for bees,
'And lovers songs shall turn to holy psalmes,
'A man at armes must now sit on his knees,
'And feed on prayers that are old ages almes;
'And tho from court to cottage I depart,
'My saint is sure of mine unspotted hart.
'And when I sadly sit in homely cell,
'I'll teach my swaines this carrol for a song:
'Blest be the hearts that thinke my sovereigne well,
'Curs'd be the soules that thinke to doe her wrong.
'Goddesse, vouchsafe this aged man his right,
'To be your beadsman now, that was your knight.'
Sir William Segar says of this person that he was 'her majesties 'servant, a gentleman in that arte excellent, and for his voice both 'commendable and admirable.' Treatise on Honour Military and Civill, lib. III. cap. 54. And Sir Henry Wotton in his Parallel between the Earl of Essex and the Duke of Buckingham, says that a sonnet of the earl's was upon a certain occasion sung before the queen by one Hales, in whose voice she took some pleasure. Reliquæ Wottonianæ, 8vo. 1685, page 165.

well-bred persons. Songs in this form, for three, four, and more voices, were the entertainment of persons of rank and fashion, young gentlemen and ladies, and, in a word, of the better sort.

Other kinds of vocal harmony there were, in which the humour of the words was more regarded than the goodness of the metre, justness of thought, propriety of expression, or any other the requisites of good poetry. Short poems of this kind, suited to the humours of the vulgar, were set to music in the form of canon in the unison, generally in three, and sometimes in four, five, six, and so on to many more parts. Besides which, we meet about this time with little compositions for three and four voices, called, for what reason it is not easy to say, Freemen's Songs.* The sentiments contained in these poetical compositions were in general not very favourable to good manners, for if they were not satirical, they were in general, exhortations to riot, dissipation, or incentives to lewdness, to drinking, and smoking tobacco, in a vein of humour adapted to a tavern or an ale-house.

Many ancient songs of this kind, set in the form of canon in the unison, or, as it was otherwise called, round, or catch, where the words of one part fell in with those of the other, are yet extant, so finely suited with apt melody and delightful harmony, that the best musicians of later times have in vain endeavoured to equal them.

Much of the humours and manners of the people of this country at different periods, is to be collected from vulgar and favorite song ballads. These were of various kinds, namely, amorous ditties, of which specimens have already been given, rhyming histories, and popular stories, some founded in truth, others mere fiction. Of these a collection is extant in the library of Magdalen college, Cambridge, made by Samuel Pepys, Esq. secretary of the admiralty in the reigns of Charles and James II.; but the most curious of the kind is that lately given to the world by the Rev. Dr. Thomas Percy, entitled Reliques of ancient English Poetry, which is not more valuable for its contents, than for the essays contained in it on the subjects of the ancient English minstrels, ancient metrical romances, the origin of the English stage, and the metre of Pierce Plowman's Vision.

To this latter collection the inquisitive reader is referred for the history of this species of poetry during a period of nearly three hundred years. All that is necessary to remark in this place is, that excepting ancient songs and catches, some of which will hereafter be inserted, the ballads above-mentioned, with many others of the like kind, were the entertainment of the common people: they were till the beginning of this century, and for about ten years after, printed on the old black letter type; and were originally vended by persons who were capable of singing them to some well-known tune, who, in

London at least, did not wander about the streets for that purpose, but sold them in stalls.

Who was the author of the collection entitled Robinhood's Garland, no one has yet pretended to guess. As some of the songs have in them more of the spirit of poetry than others, it is probable it is the work of various hands; that it has from time to time been varied and adapted to the phrase of the times is certain.

The legend of Robinhood is of great antiquity, for in the Vision of Pierce Plowman, written by Robert Langland or Longland, a secular priest, and a fellow of Oriel college, and who flourished in the reign of Edward III. is this passage :—

> I cannot perfitly my Pater noster, as the prist it singeth,
> I can rimes of Robenhod and Randal of Chester,
> But of our Lorde or our Lady I lerne nothyng at all.

yet Ames takes no notice of any early impression of his songs. He mentions one only, entitled 'King Edward, Robinhood, and Little John,' printed by Caxton, or at least in his house, about the year 1500; the last edition of his Garland of any worth is that of 1719.

The history of this popular hero is but little known, and all the scattered fragments concerning him, could they be brought together, would fall far short of satisfying such an enquirer as none but real and well-authenticated facts will content. We must take his story as we find it. Stow in his Annals gives the following account of him :—

'In this time (about the year 1190, in the reign 'of Richard I.) were many robbers and outlawes, 'among which Robin Hood and little John, renowned 'theeves, continued in woods, despoyling and robb-'ing the goods of the rich. They killed none but 'such as would invade them; or by resistance for 'their own defence.

'The saide Robert entertained an hundred tall 'men and good archers, with such spoiles and thefts 'as he got, upon whom four hundred (were they ever 'so strong) durst not give the onset. He suffered 'no woman to be oppressed, violated, or otherwise 'molested : poore mens goods he spared, abundantlie 'relieving them with that which by theft he gat 'from abbies, and the houses of rich earles: whom 'Maior (the historian) blameth for his rapine and 'theft; but of all theeves he affirmeth him to be the 'prince and the most gentle theefe.' Annals, pag. 159.

Bishop Latimer, in his Sermons, tells the following story relating to him :—

'I came once myselfe to a place, riding on a journey 'homeward from London, and I sent word over 'night into the town that I would preach there in 'the morning, because it was holyday, and methought 'it was an holidayes worke; the church stoode in 'my way, and I took my horse and my company 'and went thither (I thought I should have found 'a great companye in the church) and when I came 'there the church doore was fast locked, I taryed 'there halfe an houre and more, and at last the key 'was found, and one of the parish comes to me and 'sayes Syr, this is a busie day with us. We cannot 'heare you, it is Robinhoodes daye. The parish are

---

* In a book entitled 'Deuteromelia: or the second part of Music's Melodie,' printed in 1609, are many of this kind. However difficult it may now be to account for this term, it was formerly well understood; for Urry, in his Glossary to Chaucer, Voce VERILAYE, from the French Virelaie, upon the authority of Blount, interprets it a roundelay, country ballad or FREEMAN's Song.

'gone abroad to gather for Robinhoode, I pray you
'let them not. I was fayne there to give place to
'Robinhoode: I thought my Rochet would have
'been regarded though I were not: but it would
'not serve, it was faine to give place to Robinhoodes
'men.' Sermon VI. before king Edward VI.
fol. 74. b.

Sir Edward Coke, in his third institute, pag. 197,
speaks of Robinhood, and says that men of his lawless profession were from him called Roberdsmen:
he says that this notable thief gave not only a name
to these kind of men, but that there is a bay in the
river of   in Yorkshire, called Robinhood's
bay. He farther adds, that the statute of Winchester,
13 Edward I. and another statute of 5 Edward III.
were made for the punishment of Roberdsmen and
other felons.

Drayton in his Polyolbion, song 26, thus characterizes him :—

'From wealthy abbots' chests, and churches abundant
       store,
'What oftentimes he took, he shar'd amongst the
       poore.
'No lordly Bishop came in lusty Robin's way,
'To him before he went, but for his pass must pay.
'The widow in distress he gratiously reliev'd,
'And remedied the wrongs of many a virgin griev'd.'

Hearne in his Glossary to Peter Langtoft, voce
trolo, inserts a manuscript note out of Wood, containing a passage cited from John Major, the Scottish
historian, to this purpose, that Robinhood was indeed
an arch-robber, but the gentellest thief that ever was;
and says he might have added, from the Harleian
MS. of John Fordun's Scottish Chronicle, that he
was, though a notorious robber, a man of great
devotion and charity.

He is frequently called Robert earl of Huntingdon;
and there is extant a dramatic history of his death
that gives him this title. There is also extant a
pedigree of his family, which shows that he had at
least some pretensions to the earldom. Nevertheless
the most ancient poems on him make no mention of
this title; and in a very old legend in verse, preserved in the archives of the public library of Cambridge, he is expressly asserted to have been simply
a yeoman.*

Dr. Stukeley, in his Palæographia Britannica, No. 11,
1746, has given an account of the descent of this
famous person, to this purpose; viz., that his true
name was Robert Fitz-Ooth, but that agreeably to
the practice in the north of England, the two last
letters of his name were contracted into d, whence he
was called Hood; that he was a man of rank, being
grandson of Ralph Fitz-Ooth, a Norman earl of
Kyme, whose name appears in the roll of Battell-
Abbey, and who came into England with William
Rufus.—That Robin Hood's maternal grandfather
was Gilbert de Gient, earl of Lincoln; his grandmother was the Lady Roisia de Vere, sister to the
earl of Oxford, and countess of Essex, from whom
the town of Royston, where she was buried, takes its
name. Robin Hood's father William was in those

times of feudal dependance, a ward of Robert earl of
Oxford, who by the king's order gave to him in
marriage the third daughter of lady Roisia.

Robinhood had for his coat-armour Gules, two
bends engrailed, Or. The tragedy above-mentioned
makes him to die by poison, but the vulgar tradition
is, that being compelled to apply to a nun for assistance in a disorder that required bleeding, she
performed the operation so that he died under it.

At Kirklees in Yorkshire, now the seat of the
Armitage family, but which was formerly a Benedictine nunnery, and probably the very place where
he received his death's wound, is a grave-stone near
the park, under which, as it is said, Robinhood lies
buried. There is an inscription on it, now not
legible; but Mr. Ralph Thoresby, in his Ducatus
Leodiensis from the papers of Dr. Gale, dean of York,
gives the following as his epitaph :—

> Hear, undernead dis laitl ftean,
> Laiz Robert, Earl of Huntingtun,
> Nea arcir ver az hie fa geude:
> An piple kauld im Robin Heud.
> Sic utlawz az hi, an iz men,
> Wil England never figh agen.
>   Obiit 24 kal. Dekembris, 1247.

Dr. Percy doubts the genuineness of this epitaph,
and with good reason, for the affected quaintness of
the spelling, and the even pace of the metre, are
certainly ground for suspicion.

The same author has given, from a manuscript of
his own, a ballad of Robinhood and Guy of Gisborne,
which was never before printed, and, as he says,
carries the marks of much greater antiquity than any
of the common popular songs on the subject.

The songs above-mentioned, although many of
them are totally devoid of historical truth, being in
short metrical legends, were yet interesting enough
to engage the attention of the people, for either the
subject was of some dignity, or the catastrophe
affecting, or the poetry was level to the common
apprehension; in short, they fell in with the popular
humour; and in this way only can we account for
their transmission through a succession of ages, and
their existence at the present time. Too con-
temptuously therefore does the author of the Art
of English Poesy speak of our ancient songs and
ballads, when, comparing them to those grave and
stately metres which he takes occasion to commend,
he calls them 'small and popular musickes, song by
'these *Cantabanqui* upon benches and barrels' heads,
'where they have none other audience then boys or
'countrey fellowes that passe by them in the streete,
'or else by blind harpers, or such like taverne min-
'strels that give a fit of mirth for a groat, and
'their matters being for the most part stories of
'old time, as the tale of Sir *Topas*, the reportes
'of *Bevis of Southampton, Guy of Warwicke,*
'*Adam Bel*, and *Clymme* of the *Clough*, and such
'other old romances or historicall rimes, made pur-
'posely for recreation of the common people at
'Christmasse diners and brideales, and in tavernes
'and alehouses, and such other places of base resort;
'also they be used in carols and rounds, and such

---

* **Vide Reliques of Ancient English Poetry, vol. I. pag. 81.**

'light or lascivious poemes, which are commonly
'more commodiously uttered by these buffons or
'vices in playes then by any other person.'

CHAP. CVII.

Such was the general state of music in England
at the close of the sixteenth century; as to our
poetry, it had been gradually refining from the time
of Chaucer, and was arrived to great perfection,
when it received some little check from the attempts
of a few fantastic writers to improve it by certain
rules, teaching men to become poets, or makers, as
they affected to call them, rules that left scarce any
room for the exercise of those faculties with which it
is, though perhaps a little hyperbolically, said a poet
is born; much of this affected cant about poets and
makers is observable in the writings of Roger
Ascham, the preceptor to the children of Henry
VIII. somewhat of it in Sir Philip Sidney's elegant
little tract 'The Defence of Poesie,' and in the Discoveries, as they are called, of Ben Jonson, and more
in a work entitled 'The Arte of English Poetry con-
'trived into three bookes, the first of poets and
'poesie, the second of proportion, the third of orna-
'ment.' London, quarto, 1589.*

The author of this book, though some have ascribed it to Sir Philip Sidney, is in general believed
to be one Webster Puttenham, a gentleman pensioner
of Queen Elizabeth, a man not altogether destitute
of learning, but whose notions of the perfection of
poetry are such, as no degree of learning can justify.
What the author has said in his first book of poets
and poesy is common enough, and scarcely worthy
of remark; but his second book, intitled of Proportion poetical, is founded upon such principles, and contains such rules for writing poetry as could never
have entered into the head of a man who had any
taste or relish of that art which he professes to teach.
His arguments in favour of proportion poetical are
these:—'It is said by mathematicians that all things
'stand by proportion, and by the doctors of our
'theology that God made the world by number,
'measure, and weight.' As to poetical proportion,
'he says, 'it holdeth of the musical, because poesie
'is a skill to speak and write harmonically; and
'verses or rhyme be a kind of musical utterance by

'reason of a certain congruitie in sounds pleasing to
'the ear, though not perchance so exquisitely as the
'harmonical concents of artificial musicke, consisting
'in strained tunes, as is the vocal musicke, or that
'of melodious instruments, as lutes, harps, regals,
'records, and such like.' And, adds he, 'this our
'proportion poetical resteth in five points, staffe,
'measure, concord, situation and figure.'

All these are treated of in their order: as to staffe
or stanza, he exhibits it in various forms, viz., as
consisting of few or many verses, for the framing
whereof the rules given by him are so mechanical,
that they leave very little room for the exercise of
fancy or invention.

As to proportion in figure, it is a thing so little
heeded in poetry, or rather indeed so little understood, that we are necessitated to adopt the explanation of it by the author, and make use of his
own words:—

'Your last proportion is that of figure, so called
'for that it yelds an ocular representation, your
'meeters being by good symmetrie reduced into
'certaine geometrical figures, whereby the maker
'is restrained to keepe him within his bounds, and
'sheweth not onely more art, but serveth also much
'better for briefness and subtiltie of device, and for
'the same respect are also fittest for the pretie
'amourets in court to entertaine their servants and
'the time withal, their delicate wits requiring some
'commendable exercise to keepe them from idlenesse.
'I find not of this proportion used by any of the
'Greeke or Latine poets, or in any vulgar writer,
'saving of that one forme which they cal Anacreons
'egge. But being in Italie conversant with a certaine
'gentleman who had long travelled the oriental parts
'of the world, and seen the courts of the great
'princes of China and Tartarie, I being very in-
'quisitive to knowe of the subtilties of those countreys,
'and especially in matter of learning, and of their
'vulgar poesie; he told me that they are in all their
'inventions most wittie, and have the use of poesie
'or riming, but do not delight so much as we do in
'long tedious descriptions, and therefore when they
'will utter any pretie conceit, they reduce it into
'metrical feet, and put it in form of a lozange or
'square, or such other figure, and so engraven in
'gold, silver, or ivorie, and sometimes with letters
'of ametist, rubie, emeralde, or topas, curiously
'cemented and peeced together, they send them in
'chaines, bracelets, collars, and girdles to their mis-
'tresses to weare for a remembrance; some fewe
'measures composed in this sort this gentleman gave
'me, which I translated word for word, and as near
'as I could, following both the phrase and the figure,
'which is somewhat hard to performe because of the
'restraint of the figure, from which ye may not
'digresse. At the beginning they wil seeme nothing
'pleasant to a English eare, but time and usage will
'make them acceptable inough, as it doth in all
'other newe guises, be it for wearing of apparell
'or otherwise.'

The geometrical figures recommended by him are
the lozenge, called Rombus, the fuzee or spindle

---

* Three years before this, was published a Discourse of English
Poetry, a small tract in quarto, written by William Webbe; this is a very
curious book, and contains in it a proposal for the reformation of English poetry, by establishing a prosodia of versification in imitation of the
Greeks and Latins. Sir Philip Sidney, Sir Edward Dyer, Spenser, and
some others laboured to subject our poetry to some such rules as are
here prescribed, but without effect. The author gives a general account
of the English poets from Gower down to his own time, and speaks in
terms of very high commendation of Anthony Munday, an earnest
traveller in this art, in whose name he says he had seen very excellent
works, especially upon nymphs and shepherds, well worthy to be viewed
and to be esteemed as very rare poetry. He celebrates also Dr. Phaer
and Dr. Twine, the translators of Virgil, and Arthur Golding for his
labour in Ovid's Metamorphoses, and Dr. Gabriel Harvey, the brother of
the physician, an admired Latin poet. He speaks of certain compositions after the manner of the acrostic, by W. Hunnis, and says that the
earl of Surrey translated some part of Virgil into English hexameters.
A fuller account of this curious book is given in the British Librarian of
Mr. Oldys, No. 11.

About the same time, viz., in 1584, was printed at Edinburgh in quarto,
'The Essayes of a prentise in the divine art of Poesie.' This prentise
was James the Sixth of Scotland, and of England the first. The book
contains Sonnets, the Uranie of Du Bartas translated into English verse,
a poem entitled Phœnix, a version of Psalm CIV. and 'Ane schort
'Treatise conteining some reulis and cautelis to be observit and eschewit
'in Scottis poesie.'

called Romboides, the triangle or tricquet, the square or quadrangle, the pillaster or cylinder, the spire or taper called Piramis, the rondel or sphere, the egge or figure ovall, the tricquet reversed, the tricquet displayed, the lozange reversed, the egg displayed, the lozange rabbated.

It is highly probable that the practice of composing verses resembling the form of eggs, altars, wings, and many other such quaint devices, now deservedly the subject of ridicule, had its foundation in the precepts contained in this book. The great proficients in this species of false wit were Withers, Quarles, Crashaw, Herbert, and some others, but they had but few followers; and notwithstanding the pains which Puttenham has taken to recommend it, the proportion of figure, as he terms it, has been little regarded.

The state of English poetry at this period is in general very well known to all that are conversant in English literature, but it may be thought necessary to be somewhat particular with respect to that species of it which is to be more immediately connected with music, and to give an account of a number of writers little known to the world, the authors of madrigals, sonnets, and other compositions for music, many whereof will be found to have great merit.

Puttenham has enumerated some of the most celebrated poets of his own time and of the age preceding, as namely, the earl of Surrey, Sir Thomas Wyat, Lord Vaux, Maister Chaloner, Maister Edward Dyer, N. Breton, George Gascoigne, Sir Philip Sidney, Sir Walter Ralcigh, and others; but there are many writers of this class whose names scarce ever occur but in collections of songs and short lyric poems, at this time very little known. One of the first of this kind extant is the 'Paradyse of daynty 'Devises,' printed in 1577, the greater part by Richard Edwards before mentioned,* others by

Lord Vaux, Edward Vere Earl of Oxford, William Hunnys, Thomas Churchyard, Lodowic Lloyd, Jasper Heywood, and others.

The first of these collections is in the title-page said to contain 'sundry pithy preceptes, learned 'counsels, and excellent inventions, right pleasant 'and profitable for all estates;' besides these there are divers songs, many of which have been set to music, and certain verses of Edwards's in commendation of music, beginning 'Where griping grief the hart would wound,' alluded to in Shakespeare's Romeo and Juliet, act IV. scene 5.

Another collection of the same kind was printed in the year 1614. with the title of England's Helicon, or the Muses Harmony, a collection of songs. The names of the authors are as follows: Sir Phil. Sidney, Edmund Spenser, Michael Drayton, Edmund Bolton, Robert Greene, Thomas Lodge, Nich. Breton, Shepheard Tonie, George Peele, Howard Earl of Surrey, Thomas Watson,† John Wooton, W. Shakespeare, Bar. Yong,‡ Richard Barnefield, Earle of Oxenford, Sir Edward Dyer, N. Yong,§ M. N. Howell, Christopher Marlow, William Browne,‖ Christ. Brooke.

The other collection, namely, England's Helicon, is altogether in that vein of Poetry which Sir Philip Sidney introduced amongst us, and is celebrated for its pastoral simplicity. In it are in truth many very fine compositions, most of which are set to music by the ablest masters of the time, and chiefly in the form of madrigals.

Most of the persons above named were, in comparison of our English classics, obscure writers; they are nevertheless recorded, with many curious particulars relating to them, by Winstanley, Langbaine, Phillips, and Wood, and their merits are such as entitle them to the regard of such as wish to form a true judgment of English literature.

To this class of poets succeeded another, who deviating from their predecessors, introduced into their compositions, allegory and all the subtleties of metaphysics, and even school theology; these were Sir John Davies, Phineas Fletcher, author of the Purple Island, Dr. Donne, and a few others; this style of writing furnished very little employment for the musical composers of this time: as it was affected and obscure, it was short-lived, and gave way to that natural, elegant, and easy vein of poetry, which Spenser, Daniel, Carew, and Waller introduced and

* Of Edwards as a musician mention has already been made, see page 362, but besides his excellency in the faculty of music, it seems that he possessed a considerable talent in poetry. Wood says he was a member of Lincoln's Inn, and gives a farther account of him in the Athen. Oxon. vol. I. col. 151, to this purpose, viz. that he was the author of two comedies, Damon and Pythias, and Palemon and Arcite, often acted at court before queen Elizabeth, and in the university of Oxford, in the hall, for he was of Christ-church college.—The queen was so delighted with the latter of these, that she sent for Edwards, and, after commending sundry passages in it, gave him many thanks, and a promise of a reward. This promise it seems she made good by appointing him first a gentleman of her chapel, and afterwards, upon the decease of Richard Bowyer, in 1561, master of the children. As a farther testimony of her favour, she formed the children of the royal chapel into a company of players, and granted to Edwards licence to superintend them. It is remarkable that the first regular establishment of a company of players was that of the children of Paul's in 1378; their theatre was the singing-school in or near the cathedral. The next was that of the parish-clerks of London at Skinner's-well; the next that of the children of the royal chapel above-mentioned; a few years after which another was established under the denomination of the children of the revels. These two companies of children last mentioned became very famous; all Lilly's plays, and many of Shakespeare's and Jonson's, were first acted by them; they were looked on with a jealous eye by the actors at the theatres; and Shakespeare alludes to the injudicious approbation of their performance in the following speeches of Rosencrantz and Hamlet:—

'—— There is an aiery of little children, little eyases [nestlings of 'an eagle or hawk] that cry out on the top of question, and are most 'tyrannically clapp'd for't: these are now the fashion; and so berattle 'the common stages (so they call them) that many wearing rapiers are 'afraid of goose-quills, and dare scarce come thither. HAM. What are 'they children? Who maintains them? How are they escoted? [paid] 'Will they pursue quality no longer than they can sing?' &c. HAMLET, act II. scene 2.

Among the children of queen Elizabeth's chapel was one named Sal. Pavey, who was it seems an excellent actor in the character of an old man. He died under the age of thirteen, and is celebrated by Ben Jonson in an epitaph printed with his epigrams.

Bishop Tanner, in his Bibliotheca, has an article for Edwards, in

which are mentioned some poems of his not printed in the Paradyse of daynty devises. He appears by the cheque book to have died on the last day of October, 1566.

WILLIAM HUNNIS, another of the authors above-mentioned, and who also wrote many of the poems printed in the Paradyse of daynty devises, and also translated some of David's Psalms into English metre, was likewise a musician and a gentleman of the chapel; his name occurs as such both in the list of Edward the Sixth's chapel establishment, and in that of queen Mary. He succeeded Edwards as master of the children, being appointed to that office on the fifteenth day of November, 1566, and died the sixth of June, 1597.

† Mentioned before as the publisher of the first Sett of Italian Madrigals Englished. From the circumstance of his having written poems printed in this collection, it is probable that he was the translator of the madrigals published by him.

‡ The translator of the Diana of George de Montemayor into English. Most of his poems in the England's Helicon are taken from this translation.

§ Nicholas Yong, before-mentioned as the publisher of the Musica Transalpina in two books.

‖ Author of Britannia's Pastorals. The rest may be met with in the Athenæ and Fasti Oxoniensis.

practised, and which lent to music as many graces as it borrowed from it.*

To the catalogue of English musicians herein before given, and continued down to the year 1600, the following additions may be made, of persons less noted for the number and variety of their publications, though perhaps not less excellent in their faculty, viz :—

RICHARD ALLISON, a private teacher of music in London, flourished in the reign of queen Elizabeth, and dwelt in Duke's Place near Aldgate. He was one of the ten authors that composed parts to the common Psalm tunes printed by Thomas Este in 1594, octavo. He also published the Psalms with this title ' The Psalmes of David in meter, the plaine ' song beeing the common tunne to be sung and plaid ' upon the Lute, Orpharyon, Citterne, or Base Viol, ' severally or altogether, the singing part to be ' either tenor or treble to the instrument, according ' to the nature of the voyce, or for foure voyces, with ' tenne short tunnes in the end, to which for the most ' part all the Psalmes may be usually sung, for the ' use of such as are of mean skill, and whose leysure ' least serveth to practise.' Fol. London, 1599.

HUGH ASTON, an organist in the time of Henry VIII. composed a Te Deum for five voices, now in the music-school, Oxon.

THOMAS ASHWELL, a cathedral musician, lived in the reigns of Henry VIII. Edward VI. and queen Mary ; some of his compositions are in the music-school, Oxon.

EDWARD BLANCKS, one of the composers of the Psalms in four parts, printed by Este, and mentioned above.

AVERY BURTON, a cathedral musician in the reign of Henry VIII. an anthem of his in five parts is in the music-school, Oxon.

RICHARD CARLETON, bachelor of music, and in priest's orders, was the author of Madrigals to five voices, printed in 1601. He was one of the composers of the Triumphs of Oriana.

BENJAMIN COSYN, a famous composer of lessons for the harpsichord, and probably an excellent performer on that instrument, flourished about this time. There are many of his lessons extant that seem in no respect inferior to those of Bull. The name WILLIAM COSIN occurs in the Ashmolean manuscript list of musicians of Anthony Wood, and he is therein said

to have been organist of the Charter-house before the wars. It is probable that these persons were the sons of JOHN COSYN, who in 1585 published the Psalms in music of five and six parts.

HUGH DAVIS, bachelor of music, of New college, and afterwards organist of Hereford cathedral, is celebrated for his skill in church music. He died in 1644.

JOHN FARRANT, organist of Salisbury, another JOHN FARRANT, organist of Christ's hospital within Newgate, London ; and DANIEL FARRANT, supposed to be the son of Richard Farrant before mentioned ; all flourished about the year 1600 ; the latter is said to have been one of the first of those musicians who set lessons lyra-way, as it is called, to the viol, in imitation of the old English lute and Bandore.

JOHN FLOYD, of Welch extraction, bachelor of music, and a gentleman of the chapel, temp. Hen. VIII. He made a pilgrimage to Jerusalem, returned and died in the king's chapel, and was buried in the Savoy church with this inscription : Johannes Floyd virtutis et religionis cultor. Obiit 3 Apr. 1523.

JOHN GILBERT, a bachelor of music of Oxon, 1510. JOHN GOODMAN, a noted composer, 1505. MATTHEW GOODWIN, 1585. WALTER HILTON, a Carthusian monk, and eminently skilled in music. He lived temp. Hen. VI. and wrote De Musica Ecclesiastica, lib. I. TOBIAS HUME, a soldier by profession, but an excellent performer on the Viol da Gamba ; he published in 1607, and dedicated to queen Anne, the consort of James I., a collection of songs entitled ' Captaine Hume's Poeticall Musicke, principally ' made for two basse violls, yet so contrived that it ' may be plaied 8 severall waies upon sundry in- ' struments with much facilitie.' MATTHEW JEFFRIES, ' a vicar choral of the cathedral of Wells, and bachelor ' of music of Oxon, 1593. JOHN KEEPER of Hart ' hall : he published select Psalms in four parts 1574. HENRY NOEL, a gentleman pensioner of queen Elizabeth, and much favoured by her, for his skill in music. FRANCIS PILKINGTON of Trinity college, Oxon, bachelor of music in 1595. HENRY PORTER of Christ-church college, Oxon. bachelor of music in 1600. RICHARD READ, bachelor of music in 1592. a composer of services. JOHN SILVESTER, bachelor of music in 1521, an eminent musician. ROBERT STEVENSON, created doctor in music, 1596. HENRY STONING, a noted musician, temp. Eliz.

BOOK XII.　CHAP. CVIII.

FROM the foregoing deduction of the history of music a judgment may be formed, as well of the practice and the uses to which it was at different periods applied, as of the improvements from time to time made in the science. In particular it may be observed, that in all ages, and in almost all countries, it made a part of religious worship. Among

the Heathens and Jews, music was employed in sacrifices ; and these authorities in the opinion of the primitive fathers were deemed sufficient to justify the introduction of it into the ritual of the Christian church. From the middle of the fourth century to this time, music has therefore in some way or other made a part in the public worship of every church which acknowledges Christ for its head.

As to secular music, it may be remarked to have consisted either in that kind of it which is suited to triumphs, to shows and public spectacles, rejoicings

---

* In this view of poetry the sonnets of Shakespeare and the Amoretti of Spenser, surpass every thing of the kind in the English language ; and it is to be wondered at that till about the year 1738, neither the one nor the other of them were ever set to music. A part of the Amoretti was then set, and published by Dr. Maurice Greene for a single voice, but the work did him little honour.

and festivities, or in that less vociferous kind, intended either for solitary practice or convivial recreation. In both of these the music was in general an auxiliar to poetry, or at least was made use of to enforce some sentiment, to awaken devotion, or inspire love. The principles of harmony were by this time sufficiently explored, and something like what we now call Air was discoverable in the melody of those times, the subsequent improvements in music respected chiefly, style, expression, and the power of exciting different passions by an artful combination and succession of corresponding sounds, and rendered it fit for a more intimate union and connection with poetry than had been known before; of which connection it is now time to speak.

It has already been shewn that the modern lyric poetry had its rise among the Provençals; and those who have undertaken to give the history of the theatre, seem more disposed to derive the origin of the principal theatrical entertainments now in use, from the same source, than from the more perfect models of ancient Greece and Rome. But here a distinction is to be made between tragedy and comedy on the one hand, and on the other those inferior species of dramatic poesy, namely, moralities, mysteries, mummeries, masques, serenatas, and above all the musical tragedy, or, as it has long been called, the Opera. The former of these have an undoubted claim to high antiquity, the latter it is conjectured had their rise in those times of ignorance and barbarism on which we look back with no other view than to estimate the degree of literary improvement in the course of a few centuries, and are in general of such a kind as scarce to merit a critical attention; the opera however will perhaps be thought so intimately connected with the subject of this work, as to require a very particular consideration.

The Italian writers have taken great pains to ascertain the origin of the musical drama or opera. Riccoboni in his 'Reflexions historiques et critiques sur les differens Théatres de l'Europe,' has collected their several opinions on the subject, and dates the public exhibition of operas from the year 1637, when, as he relates, the opera of Andromache was performed at the theatre of St. Cassan at Venice. This author seems to have made but a very indifferent use of the materials in his possession, and his account of the matter is very loose and unsatisfactory: it is to be observed that there is a diversity of opinions touching the origin of the musical drama, and he has adopted that which gives it the lowest degree of antiquity, the others carry it many years backwarder; these opinions shall severally be stated, and submitted to the reader's choice.*

First, it is said that the opera was invented by Johannes Sulpitius, surnamed Verulanus, a native of Veroli, a town in the Campania di Roma, and who flourished towards the end of the fifteenth century; this is asserted by Bayle in the article SULPITIUS, and his authority for it is Father Menestrier, who in his treatise 'Des Representations en Musique,' pag. 155, 156, has the following passage: 'Those remains of 'dramatic music which had been preserved in the 'church, served to restore it two hundred years ago; 'and Rome, (which had in a manner lost it, in order 'to bestow upon the recitation and declamation of 'actors, what the Grecians bestowed upon singing 'and harmony) brought it upon the stage towards 'the year 1480, as I learned from Sulpitius, in the 'epistle dedicatory prefixed to his notes upon Vitru-'vius,† which he presented to Cardinal Riari, great 'chamberlain of the church, and nephew of pope 'Sixtus IV. Sulpitius, praising the magnificence of 'the Cardinal, who had built many stately palaces in 'the neighbourhood of Rome, begs of him that he 'would erect public theatres for musical represen-'tations, of which Sulpitius calls him the restorer, 'having shewn at Rome a few years ago what had 'not been in use there for many ages. He tells the 'Cardinal in that epistle that Rome expects from 'him a theatre for such performances, because he has 'already given such an entertainment to the people 'upon a moveable theatre set up in a public place, 'and at other times in the castle of St. Angelo for 'the Pope's diversion, and in his palace for some 'Cardinals.'‡

Erythræus, in his Pinacotheca I. pag. 62, and Crescimbeni, ascribe the invention of the musical drama or opera to Emilio Cavaliere, who in the year 1590, exhibited in the palace of the grand duke at Florence, 'Il Satiro,' and 'La Disperazione di Fileno,' two dramas of the pastoral kind set to music.§ This relation, true as it may be, does not ascertain the original invention of the opera, which, according to

expences upon these occasions were out of the purse of the sovereign or republic, as has been often practised at Turin, Florence, Venice, &c.

In a postscript to the above-mentioned preface, Dryden retracts this opinion, and says that possibly the Italians went not so far as Spain for the invention of their operas; for that they might have taken the hint at home, and formed this drama by gathering up the shipwrecks of the Grecian and Roman theatres, which were adorned with music, scenes, dances, and machines, especially the Grecian. And in the preface itself he observes that though the opera is a modern invention, yet it is built on the foundation of the Ethnic worship.

† Bayle remarks that Menestrier is mistaken in this description of Sulpitius's edition of Vitruvius; it is true that he published it during the pontificate of pope Innocent VIII. that is 'to say, between 1484 and 1492, but without notes or various readings. Bayle, SULPITIUS, note A.

‡ 'Tu enim primus tragœdiæ quam nos juventutem excitandi gratiâ 'et AGERE et CANTARE primi hoc ævo docuimus (nam ejusmodi actionem 'jam multis sæculis Roma non viderat) in medio foro pulpitum ad 'quinque pedum altitudinem erectum pulcherrimè exornasti. Eam-'demque postquàm in Hadriani mole Divo Innocentio spectante est acta, 'rursùs intrà tuos penates tamquam in media Circi caveâ toto confessu, 'umbraculis tecto, admisso populo, et pluribus tui ordinis spectatoribus 'honorificè excepisti. Tu etiam primus picturatæ scenæ faciem, quùm 'Pomponiani comædiam agerent nostro sæculo ostendisti: quare à te 'theatrum novum tota urbs magnis votis expectat.'

It seems that the opera here spoken of, was set to music by Francesco Beverini, a learned musician who flourished in the pontificate of Sixtus IV. and that the subject of the drama was the conversion of St. Paul. It is remarkable that Sulpitius in his dedication styles himself only the reviver of this entertainment; by which expression he seems to intimate that it was in use among the ancients; and of that opinion Dryden appears at last to have been by the postscript to the preface to his Albion and Albanius before cited.

§ Crescimbeni, Commentarj. intorno all' Istoria della volgar Poesia, vol. I. lib. iv. page 234.

* Mr. Dryden, in the preface to his Albion and Albanius, confesses that he was not able by any search, to get any light either of the time when the opera began, or of the first author; but he professes, upon probable reasons, to believe that 'some Italians, having curiously observed 'the gallantries of the Spanish Moors at their Zambras, or royal feasts, '(where musick, songs, and dancing were in perfection; together with 'their machines at their running at the ring, and other solemnities) 'might have refined upon those Moresque amusements, and produced this 'pleasing kind of drama, by leaving out the warlike part, and forming a 'poetical design to introduce more naturally the machines, music and 'dances.' Then he proceeds to say, that however operas began, music has flourished principally in Italy; and that he believes their operas were first intended for the celebration of the marriages of their princes, or the magnificent triumphs of some general time of joy; and accordingly the

the above account, must have been in 1480, or, as Sulpitius intimates, still more early.

Notwithstanding these relations, it is insisted on by many that the musical drama or opera was invented by Ottavio Rinuccini, a native of Florence, a man of wit, handsome in person, polite, eloquent, and a very good poet.* He considerably enriched the Italian poetry with his verses, composed after the manner of Anacreon, and other pieces which were set to music and acted on the stage. His first composition of this kind was a pastoral called Daphne, which being but an essay or attempt to introduce this species of musical entertainment into practice, was performed only to a select and private audience; and the merit attributed to this peice encouraged him to write an opera called Eurydice.† The music both to the pastoral, Daphne, and the opera, Eurydice, was composed by Jacopo Peri, who on this occasion is said to have been the inventor of that well known species of composition, Recitative.‡ The Eurydice was represented on the theatre at Florence in the year 1600, upon occasion of the marriage of Mary de Medicis with Henry IV. of France. Rinuccini dedicated his opera to that queen, and in the following passage declares the sentiments he was taught to entertain of it by his friend Peri.

'It has been the opinion of many persons, most 'excellent queen, that the ancient Greeks and Romans 'sang their tragedies throughout on the stage, but 'so noble a manner of recitation has not that I know 'of been even attempted by any one till now; and 'this I thought was owing to the defect of the 'modern music, which is far inferior to the ancient; 'but Messer Jacopo Peri made me entirely alter my 'opinion, when upon hearing the intention of Messer 'Giacomo Corsi and myself, he so elegantly set to 'music the pastoral of Daphne, which I had com-'posed merely to make a trial of the power of vocal 'music in our age, it pleased to an incredible degree 'those few that heard it. From this I took courage: 'the same piece being put into better form and re-'presented anew in the house of Messer Peri, was 'not only favoured by all the nobility of the country,

'but heard and commended by the most serene grand 'duchess, and the most illustrious Cardinals dal 'Monte and Montalto. But the Eurydice has met 'with more favour and success, being set to music 'by the same Peri with wonderful art; and having 'been thought worthy to be represented on the stage, 'by the bounty and magnificence of the most serene 'grand duke, in the presence of your majesty, the 'cardinal legate, and so many princes and gentlemen 'of Italy and France; from whence, beginning to 'find how well musical representations of this kind 'were likely to be received, I resolved to publish 'these two, to the end that others of greater abilities 'than myself may be induced to carry on and im-'prove this kind of poetry to such a degree, that we 'may have no occasion to envy those ancient pieces 'which are so much celebrated by noble writers.'

Father Menestrier confirms the above account, adding thereto some farther particulars in the following passage :—

'Ottavio Rinuccini, a Florentine poet, having a 'particular talent at expressing in his verses all kinds 'of passions, found means to adapt music and singing 'to them so well, that they neither destroyed any 'part of the beauty of the verses, nor prevented the 'distinct understanding of the words, which is often 'hindered by an affected multiplicity of divisions. 'He consulted in this Giacomo Corsi, a gentleman of 'Florence, well skilled in music and polite literature, 'and both calling in Giacomo Cleri,§ and Giulio 'Caccini, excellent masters in music, they together 'composed a drama entitled Apollo and Daphne, 'which was represented in the house of Messer Corsi, 'in the presence of the grand duke and duchess of 'Tuscany, and the cardinals Monti and Montalto, 'with so much success that he was encouraged to 'compose another, namely, his Eurydice, and caused 'it to be exhibited soon after at the same place. 'Claudio de Monteverde, an excellent musician, com-'posed the music to the Ariadne on the model of 'these two; and being made chapel-master of St. 'Mark's in Venice, introduced into that city these 'representations, which are now become so famous 'by the magnificence of the theatres and dress, by 'the delicacy of voices, harmony of concerts, and the 'learned compositions of this Monteverde, Soriano, 'Giovanelli, Teosilo, and other great masters.'‖

Count Algarotti, from a preface of Peri to the Eurydice, has given a very succinct relation of the occasion and manner of this invention in the following words : 'When he [Peri] had applied himself to 'an investigation of that species of musical imitation 'which would the readiest lend itself to the theatric 'exhibitions, he directed his researches to discover

---

* He entertained a wild passion for Mary de Medicis, and followed her into France, where he notwithstanding succeeded so well in obtaining the favour of Henry IV. to whom she was married, that he made him one of the gentlemen of his bedchamber. It is said of him that he had a singular propensity to amorous pursuits, but that his inclination for the queen having been greatly mortified by her wisdom and virtue, he was affected with a salutary shame, became a penitent, and applied himself to exercises of devotion, which he continued during the remainder of his life. His poems were collected by his son Peter Francis Rinuccini, and were printed in Florence in 1624, with a dedication to Lewis XIII. An account of this person is given by Johannes Victor Roscius in his Pinacotheca II. pag. 61, published under the name of Janus Nicius Erythræus.

† Nicius Erythræus ascribes to him two other operas, Arethusa and Ariadne.

‡ This is the general opinion, and it is the more likely to be true, as Peri has almost in terms related the process of the invention. Nevertheless some writers, and particularly Kircher, have given the honour of it to Giulio Caccini, a contemporary musician with Peri; his words are: 'Julius Caccinus was the first that restored the ratio of the recitative 'style in singing, so much in use among the ancients' [Musurg. tom. I. pag. 510.] In this sentiment Kircher seems to be mistaken, though Peri himself, in his preface to the Eurydice, says that in the invention of it he imitated the practice of the ancient Greeks and Romans [Vide Crescimbeni, Commentarj intorno all' Istoria della volgar Poesia, vol. I. lib. IV. pag. 233,] for in those few ancient musical compositions now extant, there are no melodies to be found that can be said to bear the least resemblance to the modern recitative; neither is it to be inferred from what the ancient harmonicians have said of the Melopoieia, that they were in the least acquainted with the nature of that progression, which constitutes the difference between recitative and song.

§ This should be Jacopo Peri.

‖ Des Representat. en Musique, pag. 163, et seq.

That Kircher should ascribe to Caccini rather than Peri the invention of Recitative, can only be accounted for by this circumstance, that Menestrier's book was not published till thirty years after the writing of the Musurgia; and though he hints at Peri's preface to the Eurydice, it does not appear that he had ever seen it.

That they were both excellent musicians is not to be doubted; of Caccini very little is known, except that he was by birth a Roman. Peri was a Florentine, and is celebrated by Nicius Erythræus, in his Pinacotheca I. pag. 144; by Crescimbeni, in his Commentarj intorno all' Istoria della volgar Poesia, vol. I. pag. 233, and indeed by most writers that have taken occasion to mention him.

'the method of the ancient Greeks on similar oc-
'casions. He carefully remarked what Italian words
'were, and what were not capable of intonation; and
'was very exact in minuting down the several modes
'of pronunciation, and the proper accents to express
'grief, joy, and all the other affections of the human
'mind, with a view to make the base move in proper
'time, now with more energy, now with less, ac-
'cording to the nature of each. So scrupulous was
'he, that he attended to all the niceties and peculiari-
'ties of the Italian language, and frequently con-
'sulted with several gentlemen not less celebrated
'for the delicacy of their ears, than for their skill in
'the arts of music and poetry.

'The conclusion from this enquiry was, that the
'ground-work of the imitation proposed should be
'an harmony, following nature step by step, in a
'medium between common speaking and melody.
'Such were the studies of the musical composers in
'former times. They proceeded in the improvement
'of their art with the utmost care and attention, and
'the effect proved that they did not lose their time
'in the pursuit of unprofitable subtleties.'*

These are the accounts which the writers of greatest
authority give of the invention of the musical drama
or opera, as it is called;† and from this period it will
not be very difficult to trace its progress and farther
improvement.

In the extract herein before given from Menestrier,
it is said that the Ariadne of Rinuccini was set to
music by Claudio Monteverde; this is in the highest
degree probable, not only because Monteverde was
at that time in high reputation, being then Maestro
di Cappella to the republic of Venice;‡ but because
an opera of his entitled L'Orfeo, Favola in Musica,
is extant, which was represented at Mantua but a
very few years after the Eurydice, viz., in 1607,
corresponding most exactly with those set to music
by Peri; that is to say, it consists of airs and
chorusses, with an intermixture of recitative; answering to the description thereof in the passage above
cited from Algarotti, taken, as he asserts, from the
preface of Peri to the Eurydice.

This opera, for aught that can now be learned, was
the first ever printed with the music, and is supposed
to have been published soon after its representation.
A new edition of it was printed at Venice in 1615,
by Ricciardo Amadino.

The structure of this drama is so very unlike that
of the modern opera, as to render it a subject of
curious speculation; for first it is to be observed that
in the performance of it no accompaniment of a
whole orchestra was required; but the airs performed by the several singers were sustained by instruments of various kinds assigned to each character
respectively in the dramatis personæ, which stands
thus in the first page of the printed book:—

PERSONAGGI.	STROMENTI.
La Musica Prologo	Duoi Grauicembani
Orfeo	Duoi contrabassi de Viola
Eurydice	Dieci Viole da brazzo
Choro di Ninfe e Pastori	Un Arpa doppia
Speranza	Duoi Violini piccoli alla Francese
Caronte	Duoi Chitaroni
Chori di spiriti infernali	Duoi Organi di legno
Proserpina	Tre Bassi da gamba
Plutone	Quattro Tromboni
Apollo	Un Regale
Choro de pastori che	Duoi Cornetti
fecero la Moresca	Un Flautina alla vigesima seconda
nel fine.	Un Clarino con tre trombe sordine§

By the first personage is to be understood the
Genius of music, who sometimes speaks in that
character at large.

The overture, if it may be called by that name,
is a short prelude, eight bars of breve time in length,
in five parts, for a trumpet and other instruments,
and consists of two movements, the last whereof is
termed Ritornello, a word signifying the same with
symphony.

This composition, which the author calls a Toccato,
from toccare, to touch, is directed to be sounded

* Saggio sopra l'Opera in musica del Signor Conte Algarotti, pag. 27.

† Formerly a common appellation to denote it was, 'Opera con intermedii.' This appears by a passage in the life of Padre Paolo Sarpi,
wherein a relation is made of many attempts to murder that excellent
person, and of one in particular, wherein a friend of his, Padre Fulgentio,
was wounded, the assassins mistaking him for Father Paul. The relater
says that these murderers escaped, and adds that by a strange accident
they were not pursued so quickly as they might have been, for that that
evening was presented at the theatre of St. Luigi an Opera con intermedii,
which occasioned so great a concourse of people, that the murderers
found means to retreat.

‡ The Ariadne of Monteverde is celebrated by Gio. Battista Doni in
his treatise De Præstantia Musicæ veteris, pag. 67.

§ The names of the several instruments above-mentioned require some
particular explanation; and first it is to be observed, that the word
Grauicembani is misprinted, and should be Clavicembani, for the word
Clavicembano occurs frequently throughout the opera, and Grauicembani
never: as to Clavicembano, it is supposed to mean the same as Clavicembalo, the true Italian appellation for a harpsichord.

As to the Contrabassi de Viola, these are supposed to mean viols, of a
size between the tenor viol and violin.

The Viole da brazzo, of which it is to be observed there are ten required
in the performance of this opera, were clearly the arm-viol or tenor viol;
the term da brazzo being used in contradistinction to da gamba, which is
appropriated to that species of base viol which in the performance on it
is placed between the legs.

The Arpa doppia seems to be the double-strung harp, an instrument,
which though by some said to have been invented by the Welsh, and by
others by the Irish, was very well known at this time.

The Violini piccoli alla Francese must in strictness signify small
violins; and of these there are none now known but that contemptible
instrument called the Kit, which hardly any but dancing-masters are ever
known to touch; it is therefore probable that by Violini piccoli we are to
understand common treble violins; and this is the more likely, as violins
are no where else mentioned in the catalogue of instruments now under
consideration.

The noun Chitaroni is the nominative case plural of Chitarra, of which
the word Guitar is manifestly a corruption.

Organi di legno, of which two are here required, can signify nothing
but organs of wood, that is to say, organs with wooden pipes: for it is
well known that most organs are composed both of wooden and leaden
pipes.

The Bassi da gamba were clearly leg viols above described.

The Tromboni could be no other than trumpets, concerning which it
is unnecessary in this place to be particular.

The instrument against the name of Apollo, is Un Regale, a Regal,
which term has already been shown to mean a small portable organ, probably with pipes of metal.

The shepherds who sing the last chorus, dance also a Moresca; this it
seems they do to the instruments mentioned in the last three lines of the
above catalogue. The Cornet, though an instrument now out of use, is
very well described by Mersennus, Kircher, and other writers on music.
But the Flautino alla vigesima secondo, merits a very particular enquiry.

It is well known that of the flute Abec, which has already been described in this work, there are various sizes, smaller than that formerly
used in concerts, and which was therefore called the concert flute, and
that of these the lowest note, though nominally F, must in power
answer to that sound in the great system, to which it corresponds in a
regular course of succession upwards; for this reason that sized flute
whose lowest note F was an unison with the note f in the acutes, was
called an octave flute. Un Flautino alla vigesima secondo, by parity of
reason must therefore mean a treble octave flute, i. e. a flute whose
nominal F was by the smallness of the instrument removed three octaves,
measured by the interval of a twenty-second above its true and proper
situation in the scale. A flute thus small could not be much bigger than
the oaten reed so frequently mentioned by the pastoral poets.

The word Clarino, as Altieri renders it, is a small trumpet, perhaps an
octave higher than the noble instrument of that name.

The Trombe sordine were probably trumpets of a less shrill and piercing
sound than those of this day; but this is only conjecture.

three times 'Avanti il levar da la tela,' before the rising of the cloth or curtain.

To the overture succeeds the prologue, consisting of five speeches in recitative; it is spoken by the first of the personages named in the dramatis personæ, who represents the Genius of music, and sometimes speaks in that character at large, and at others in the person of a single performer, as thus, 'I su cetera d'or cantando soglio;' the purport of these speeches severally, is to declare the argument of the opera, to excite attention, and enjoin silence, not only on the audience, but on the birds, and even things inanimate, as in the following instance :—

    'Hor mentre i canti alterno hor lieti hor mesti,
    'Non si mova Augellin fra queste piante,
    'Ne s'oda in queste rive onda sonante
    'Et ogni auretta in suo camin s'arresti.'

The opera then begins with a speech in recitative by a shepherd, which is immediately succeeded by a chorus of five parts in counterpoint, directed to be sung to the sound of all the instruments. Other chorusses are directed to be sung to the sound of guitars, violins, and flutes, as particularly mentioned in the opera: solo airs there are none; but Recitatives, Chorusses, and Ritornellos, Terzetti, and Duetti, make up the whole of this opera, which concludes with what the author calls a Moresca; this is a composition in five parts, merely instrumental, and conjectured to be the tune of a dance a la Moresca, or after the fashion of the Moors, who it is well known long before this time settled in Spain, and introduced into that kingdom many customs which were adopted in other countries.

A specimen of recitative music, in the form in which it was originally conceived, cannot at this day but be deemed a curiosity; as must also an air in one of the first operas ever composed: for these reasons the following dialogue and duetto are inserted, taken from the fifth act of the Orfeo of Claudio Monteverde :—

APOLLO descende in una nuuola, cantando.

PERCH'a lo sdegno ed al do-lor in pre-da Co-si ti do-ni o fig — lio? Non è non è con-sig-lio? Di ge-ne-ro-so pet-to ser-vir al proprio'af-fet-to, Quinci biasmo e perig-lio; Già sou-ra star ti veg-gia, On-de mo-vo dal Ciel per dar-ti ai — ta, Hor tu m'ascol-ta, . . . en'haurai lo — de e-vi — ta.

ORFEO.

Pa-dre cor-te — se al maggior vo po'arri-vi Ch'a dis-pe-ra-to fi — ne, Con es-tre-mo do-lo — re, M'havean con-dot-to già sdegn' ed A- -mo-re ec-co-mi dunqu'at-ten-to a tue ra-gio-ni, Ce-les — te pa-dre hor cio' che vuoi m'im-po — ni.

APOLLO ed ORFEO ascende al cielo, cantando.

CLAUDIO MONTEVERDE.

Notwithstanding that this kind of melody is said by the inventors of it to correspond with the method of enunciation practised by the ancient Greeks and Romans, it may well be questioned whether the difference between the one and the other was not very great, for this reason, that the inflections of the voice in the modern recitative do not preserve a medium between speaking and singing, but approach too nearly towards the latter to produce the effects of oratory.

There is no final chorus of voices to the opera from whence the above extracts are made, but the representation concludes with a dance to the following tune :—

MORESCA

CLAUDIO MONTEVERDE.

CHAP. CIX.

THERE is very little doubt but that the Cantata Spirituale, or what we now call the Oratorio, took its rise from the Opera. Menestrier* attributes its origin to the Crusades, and says that the pilgrims returning from Jerusalem and the Holy Land, from St. James of Compostella, and other places to which pilgrimages were wont to be made, composed songs, reciting the life and death of the Son of God, and the mysteries of the Christian faith, and celebrating the achievements and constancy of saints and martyrs. This seems to be a mere conjecture of Menestrier; other writers render a much more probable account of the matter, and expressly say, that the Oratorio was an avowed imitation of the opera, with this difference only, that the foundation of it was ever some religious, or at least moral subject. Crescimbeni speaks of it in these terms :—

' The Oratorio, a poetical composition, formerly a ' commixture of the dramatic and narrative styles, ' but now entirely a musical drama, had its origin ' from San Filippo Neri,| who in his chapel, after ' sermons and other devotions, in order to allure ' young people to pious offices, and to detain them ' from earthly pleasure, had hymns, psalms, and ' such like prayers sung by one or more voices. ' These in process of time were published at Rome, ' and particularly in a book printed in 1585, with ' the title of Laudi Spirituali, stampate ad istanza ' de' RR. PP. della Congregazione dell' Oratorio ; ' and another in 1603, entitled Laudi Spirituali di ' diversi, solite cantarsi dopo sermoni da' PP. ' della Congregazione dell' Oratorio. Among these ' spiritual songs were dialogues ; and these entertain- ' ments becoming more frequent, and improving ' every year, were the occasion that in the seventeenth ' century oratorios were first invented, so called from ' the place of their origin.‡ It is not known who

' was the first that gave them this name, not even by ' the fathers of the Congregation, who have been ' asked about it. We are certain however that ' Oratorios could not begin before the middle of ' the above-mentioned century ; as we do not find ' any before the time of Francesco Balducci, who ' died about the year 1645, in whose collection of ' poems there are two, one entitled " La Fede, ove ' si spiega il Sagrifizio d' Abramo," the other " Il ' Trionfo sopra la Santissima Vergine ;" and although ' Giano Nicio Eritreo, who flourished even before ' 1640, speaking of Loreto Vettori, of Spoleto, an ' excellent musician and a good poet, says that on ' a certain night he heard him sing in the Oratory of ' the above-mentioned fathers, Magdalenæ sua de- ' flentis crimina, seque ad Christi pedes abjicientis, ' querimonia ; which lamentation might be in that ' kind of poetry we are just speaking of ; yet, as the ' author of it is unknown, and the time not certain ' when it was sung, we cannot say it preceded the ' Oratorios of Balducci.§

' These compositions in the beginning were a ' mixture of dramatic and narrative parts, for under ' the name of history, in those of Balducci or of Testo, ' as well as in all others, the poet has introduced the ' dramatis personæ ; but although Testo's manner ' has been followed even in our days, at present it ' is quite abolished, and the Oratorio is a drama ' throughout. Of these some are ideal, others para- ' bolical, and others with real persons, which are the ' most common, and others are mixed with both ' the above-mentioned kinds of persons : they are ' generally in two parts, and, being set to music, ' take up about two hours in the performance ; yet ' Malatesta Strinati, and Giulio Cesare Grazini, both ' men of letters, published two Oratorios, the former ' on St. Adrian, divided into three acts, the latter on ' St. George, into five. No change of place or length ' of time is observed in them, for being sung without ' acting, such circumstances are of no service. The ' metre of them is like that of the musical drama, ' that is to say, the lines rhymed at pleasure ; they ' are full of airs, and are truly very agreeable to hear ' when composed by good authors, such as Cardinal

* Des Represent. en Musique, pag. 153.

† St. Philip Neri was born at Florence in the year 1515. He was intended by his parents for a merchant, and to that end was sent to his uncle, who followed that employment, to be instructed therein, but he betook himself to study and exercises of devotion, and became an ecclesiastic. The congregation of the Fathers of the Oratory, founded by him, is an institution well known : in the first establishment of it he was assisted by Cæsar, afterwards Cardinal Baronius, who was his disciple. Baronius in his annals has borne an honourable testimony in his character and abilities, by styling him the original author and contriver of that great work. There is an account of St. Philip Neri in Ribadeneyra's Lives of the Saints, by means whereof, notwithstanding the many silly stories and palpable falsities related of him, it is easy to discover that he was both a devout and learned man.

‡ This though the true, is but an awkward etymology. The society

here spoken of, La Congregazione dei Padri dell Oratorio, evidently derives its name from the verb Orare, an oratory being a place of prayer: in this instance the appellative Oratorio is transferred from the place to the exercise ; a singular proof how inadequate the powers of language are to our ideas.

§ Jani Nicci Erythræi Pinac. altera lxviii. art. LORETUS VICTORIUS.

'Pier Matteo Petrucci, and Gio. Filippo Berninoa,
'prelate in the court of Rome, among the dead; and
'Cardinal Benedetto Pansilio, and Pietro Ottoboni,
'now living, who both in this, as well as in all kinds
'of poetry, are arrived at great excellency.

'But although Oratorios are at present so much in
'vogue, we have not lost entirely the manner of
'singing sacred things, for we hear some of them
'in those dialogues which are called Cantatas, and
'particularly in the summer, when the fathers of
'Vallicella perform their concerts in the garden of
'the monks of St. Onofrio. This custom is likewise
'followed with great splendour at particular times
'of the year by Cardinal Gio. Battista Spinola of
'St. Cecilia, who on Wednesdays has some very fine
'ones performed in his palace; for the most part the
'composition of Flaminio Piccioni, an eminent dra-
'matic poet. There is sung besides every year on
'Christmas eve in the pontiff's palace, a charming
'cantata, in the presence of the sacred college, for
'whom Giubileo da Pesaro, who died a few years
'ago, composed some very famous; as likewise Paolo
'Francesco Carli, a Florentine poet, not less cele-
'brated for his serious, than his comic productions: and
'this year the advocate Francesco Maria de Conti
'di Campello has favoured us with one, that for
'sweetness of versification, nobility of sentiment, and
'allusion to the present affairs of Italy, deserves to
'be highly commended.' *

To this account of Crescimbeni, Mons. Bourdelot
adds, that St. Philip Neri having prevailed upon the
most skilful poets and musicians to compose dialogues in Italian verse, upon the principal subjects
of the Holy Scripture, procured some of the finest
voices of Rome to sing, accompanied with all sorts
of instruments, and a band of music in the interludes.
—That these performances consisted of Monologues,
Dialogues, Duos, Trios, and Recitatives of four
voices; and that the subjects of some of them were
the conversation of the Samaritan woman with the
Son of God; of Job with his friends, expressing his
misery to them—The prodigal son received into his
father's house—Tobias with the angel, his father, and
wife—The angel Gabriel with the Virgin, and the
mystery of the incarnation.—That the novelty of
these religious dramas, and, above all, the exquisite
style of music in which they were composed, drew
together such a multitude of people as filled the
church boxes, and the money taken for admission
was applied in defraying the expences of the performance. Hence the origin of Oratorios as they
are now styled, or spiritual shows,† the practice

whereof is now become so general in Rome, that
hardly a day passes in which there are not one or
two such representations.‡

The deduction of the history of church-music,
herein before given, contains an account of the rise
and progress of antiphonal singing in the Greek and
Latin churches, the opposition it met with, the patronage given it by the Roman pontiffs at succeeding
periods, the form of the choral service exemplified
in the Cantus Gregorianus, with a general idea of
the musical offices directed by the ritual of the
church of Rome, as well on solemn as ordinary
occasions.

That the mode of religious worship, above described, prevailed in all the European churches till
the time of the Reformation, is not to be doubted:
the first deviation from it that we are now able to
trace, was that which followed the reformation by
Luther, who being himself a great proficient in, and
a passionate lover of music; and being sensible of its
use and importance in divine worship, in conjunction
with his friend Melancthon framed a ritual, little less
solemn, and calculated to engage the affections of the
people, than that of the church of Rome: and, to

---

† This is a mistake; spiritual shows, though not with music and recitative, are much more ancient than the time of St. Philip Neri. The fraternity del Gonfalone, as it is called, was founded in 1264; and in their statutes, printed in Rome in 1584, it is expressly declared that the principal end of this institution was, that the members of the fraternity should represent the passion of our Lord. It is true that this practice was abolished in the pontificate of Paul III. that is to say, about the year 1548; but we learn from Crescimbeni and other writers, that re-presentations of this kind were common in Italy, and the practice of great antiquity. Vasari, in his life of Buffalmacco the painter, gives an account of a feast that was solemnized on the river Arno in the year 1304, where a machine representing hell, was fixed on boats, and a sacred history acted, supposed to be that of Lazarus. Comment. int. all' Istor. della volg. Poesia, vol. I. lib. iv. pag. 241.
It is probable that this representation suggested to Pietro de Cosimo,

a Florentine painter, of whom Felibien has given an account, the idea of a spectacle, the most whimsical, and at the same time the most terrifying that imagination can conceive, which in the year 1510 he caused to be exhibited at Florence. Felibien's relation of it is to this purpose:
'Having taken a resolution to exhibit this extraordinary spectacle at the
'approaching Carnival, Cosimo shut himself up in a great hall, and there
'disposed so secretly every thing for the execution of his design, that no
'one had the least suspicion of what he was about. In the evening of
'a certain day in the Carnival season, there appeared in one of the chief
'streets of the city a chariot painted black, with white crosses and dead
'men's bones, drawn by six buffalos; and upon the end of the pole stood
'the figure of an angel with the attributes of Death, and holding a long
'trumpet in his hands, which he sounded in a shrill and mournful tone,
'as if to awaken and raise the dead: upon the top of the chariot sat
'a figure with a scythe in his hand, representing Death, having under his
'feet many graves, from which appeared, half way out, the bare bones of
'carcases. A great number of attendants, clothed in black and white,
'masked with Death's heads, marched before and behind the chariot,
'bearing torches, which enlightened it at distances so well chosen, that
'every thing seemed natural. There were heard as they marched,
'muffled trumpets, whose hoarse and doleful sound served as a signal for
'the procession to stop. Then the sepulchres were seen to open, out of
'which proceeded, as by a resurrection, bodies resembling skeletons, who
'sang, in a sad and melancholy tone, airs suitable to the subject, as
'Dolor pianto e Penitenza, and others composed with all that art and in-
'vention which the Italian music is capable of: while the procession
'stopped in the public places, the musicians sang with a continued and
'tremulous voice the psalm Miserere, accompanied with instruments
'covered with crape, to render their sounds more dismal. The chariot was
'followed by many persons habited like corpses, and mounted upon the
'leanest horses that could be found, spread with black housings, having
'white crosses and death's heads painted at the four corners. Each of
'the riders had four persons to attend him, habited in shrouds like the
'dead, each with a torch in one hand, and a standard of black taffety
'painted with white crosses, bones, and death's heads in the other. In
'short, all that horror can imagine most affecting at the resurrection of
'the dead, was represented in this masquerade, which was intended to
'represent the triumph of Death. A spectacle so sad and mournful struck
'a damp through Florence; and although in a time of festivity, made
'penitents of some, while others admiring the ingenious manner in which
'every thing was conducted, praised the whim of the inventor, and the
'execution of a concert so suitable to the occasion.'

Crescimbeni, Comm. int. all' Istor. della volg. Poesia, vol. I. lib. iv. pag. 243, speaking of those representations of sacred history, says that he had met with one, namely, Abraham and Isaac, written by Feo Belcari, and acted for the first time in the church of St. Mary Magdalen at Florence in 1449.

These representations, however well intended, failed of producing the end of their institution; Castelvetro says that in his time, and even at Rome, Christ's passion was so acted as to set the spectators a laughing. In France was a company of strollers, incorporated as it seems for the same purposes as the fraternity del Gonfalone, with whom Francis I. was much delighted; but the abuses committed by them were so nu-merous, that towards the end of his reign a process was commenced against them, and in four or five years after his decease they were banished France. Rymer, at the end of his Short View of Tragedy, has given a copy of the parliament roll, containing the process at length. He has also, because it contains a particular history of the stage, given an abridgment of it in English.

‡ Hist. de la Musique, et de ses Effets, tom. I. pag. 256.

say the truth, the whole of the liturgy, as settled by him, appears to be, if not a reasonable, at least a musical service. The evidence of this assertion is a book intitled 'Psalmodia, hoc est Cantica sacra veteris Ecclesiæ selecta,' printed at Norimberg in 1553, and at Wittemberg in 1561. The publisher of it was Lucas Lossius, rector of the college at Lunenberg,* who has also given his own Scholia thereon.

To speak of this work in particular, it is prefaced by an epistle from Melancthon to the editor, whom he acknowledges as his intimate friend. This is followed by a dedication of the book to the brethren Frederick and John, sons of the reigning king of Denmark. The work is divided into four books, and the offices therein severally contained appear by the titles of each as they follow thus in order:—

Liber primus, continens Antiphonas, Responsoria, Hymnos et Sequentias, quæ leguntur diebus Dominicis, et festis Christi.

Liber secundus, continens cantica veteris ecclesiæ, selecta de præcipiis festis sanctorum Jesu Christi.

Liber tertius, continens cantiones missæ, seu sacri, ut vocant, præter Introitus, quos suprà in Dominicis, et festis diebus invenies suo loco.

Liber quartus, Psalmi cum eorum antiphonis ferialibus, et intonationibus, additis scholiis et lectionis varietate ex Psalterio D. Georg. majoris.

Calvin, whose separation from the church of Rome was founded in an opposition as well to its discipline as its tenets, in his establishment of a church at Geneva, reduced the whole of divine service to prayer, preaching, and singing; and this latter was by him laid under great restraints, for none of the offices in the Romish service, namely, the Antiphon, Hymn, and Motet, with that artificial and elaborate music to which they were sung, were retained; but all of music that was adopted by him, consisted in that plain metrical psalmody now in general use among the reformed churches, and in the parochial churches of this country. Not but there is reason to believe that the practice of psalmody had the sanction of Luther himself.

The opinion which Luther entertains of music in general, and of the lawfulness of it in divine worship, appears by those extracts from his Colloquia Mensalia herein before given; and there is good reason to believe, not only that those sweet Motetæ, which his friends sang at supper with him, were the composition of German musicians, but that German musicians were also the authors or composers of many of those melodies to which the Psalms then were, and even now are, usually sung. Sleidan informs us that upon a certain occasion, mentioned by him in his History of the Reformation of the Church, Luther paraphrased in the High German language, and set to a tune of his own composing, the forty-sixth Psalm, 'Deus noster refugium.' It is certain that he was a performer on the lute; and in the work above cited he speaks of his skill in music as an acquisition that he would not exchange for a great matter. Besides this, there is a tradition among the German

Protestants that he was the author of many of the melodies to which the Psalms are now usually sung in their churches;† and Bayle expressly says that to sing a Psalm was, in the judgment of the orthodox of that day, to be a Lutheran. All this considered, it is more than probable, though history is silent in this respect, that the practice of psalmody had its rise in Germany. We are not however to conclude from hence that it was admitted into the churches of the reformed, or that it made part of their public worship in the life-time of Luther; it rather seems to have been confined to family worship, and considered as a source of spiritual consolation; and to this purpose the many devout ejaculations with which the Psalms of David abound, render it with a remarkable degree of propriety applicable.

In this situation stood the matter about a year before the death of Luther; no vulgate translation of the Psalter had as then appeared in the world, and there was little reason to expect one from any country where the reformation had not got firm footing, much less was there to think that any such work, in a country where the established religion was the Romish, could possibly receive the sanction of public authority. But it fell out otherwise; and, however paradoxical it may sound, the protestant churches were indebted for this indulgence to a body of men whose tenets indeed forbad any such hopes, namely the college of the Sorbonne at Paris.

It happened about the year 1543, that there lived in France, Clement Marot, a man moderately endowed with learning, but extremely improved by conversation with men of parts and ingenuity, who with great success had addicted himself to the study of poetry; he had acquired great reputation by certain imitations of Tibullus, Propertius, and Catullus, and had by an elegant translation of the first book of Ovid's Metamorphosis into the French language, established the character of a good poet. This man being inclined to Lutheranism, was persuaded by a friend to publish at Paris a French version of the first thirty of David's Psalms, which he did by permission of the doctors of the Sorbonne, wherein they declare that the book contained nothing contrary to the Christian faith; soon after he added twenty more, but before he could complete his design, which was to have translated the whole in like manner, he died, and a version of the rest in French metre also, was supplied by his friend Theodore Beza.

Sleidan, from whom the above account is in part taken, has bestowed this eulogium on Marot: 'I 'thought it not amiss to commend the name of so 'excellent an artist to other nations also; for in 'France he lives to all posterity; and most are of 'opinion that hardly any man will be able to equal 'him in that kind of writing; and that, as Cicero said 'of Cæsar, he makes wise men afraid to write. 'Others and more learned men than he, have handled 'the same subject, but have come far short of the 'beauty and elegancy of his poems.'

---

* See an account of this person, pag. 397 of this work.

† Mr. Handel has been many times heard to say that the melody of our hundredth Psalm, which by the way is that of the hundred and thirty-fourth both of Goudimel and Claude le Jeune's Psalms, and certain other Psalm-tunes, were of Luther's composition.

This it is to be noted is the character of Marot and his book, drawn by a Protestant historian. Another writer, but of a different persuasion, Famianus Strada, has given a less favourable account of both; and yet perhaps, allowing for that prejudice which he could not but entertain against the author of such an innovation as this of Marot undoubtedly was, it is such as will justify the character that Sleidan has given of him; that of Strada is as follows:—

'Among the grooms of the bed-chamber to Francis 'I. of France, there was one Clement Marot, born at 'Douve, a village in the earldom of Namur, a man 'nuturally eloquent, having a rare vein in French 'poetry, wherewith the king was much taken, who 'therefore kept him as a choice instrument of his 'learned pleasures. But as his wit was somewhat 'better than his conditions, from his acquaintance 'with the Lutherans he was suspected to have changed 'his religion; and therefore fearing the king would 'be offended, he fled to his majesty's sister at Bern, 'the old sanctuary for delinquents; a while after, the 'king was pacified and he returned to Paris, where 'he was advised by his friend Franciscus Vatablus, 'the Hebrew lecturer, to leave the trifling subjects 'he wrote upon, and study divine poesy. Thereupon 'he began to translate the Psalms of the Hebrew 'prophet into French stanzas, but so ignorantly and 'perversely,* as a man altogether unlearned, that 'the king, though he often sang his verses, yet, upon 'the just complaints of the doctors of the Sorbonne, 'and their severe censure past on them, commanded 'that nothing of Marot in that kind should be from 'thenceforth published. But being forbid by pro- 'clamation, as it often happens, the longing of the 'reader, and fame of the work was increased so, that 'new tunes were set to Marot's rhymes, and they 'were sung like profane ballads. He in the mean 'time growing bold by the applauses of the people, 'and not able to forbear bragging, for fear of punish- 'ment, ran to Geneva; and flying from thence for 'new crimes committed, and first having been well 'whipped for them, he died at Turin. The success 'of this translation of the Psalms moved Theodore 'Beza, a friend of Marot, and who wrote an elegy 'in French on his death, to add to the fifty which 'Marot had published, a version in French of the 'other hundred made by himself, so the whole book 'of David's psalms was finished; and to make it 'pleasing to the people, tunes were set to them by 'excellent composers, that chimed so sweetly, that 'every one desired to have the new psalter; but 'many errors in it against religion being detected, 'and the work therefore prohibited, as well because 'the sacred verses of the prophet were published in 'a vulgar tongue by profane persons, as that they 'were *dolo malo* bound up with Calvin's catechism 'at Geneva: these singing psalms, though abhorred 'and slighted by the Catholics, remained in high 'esteem with heretics; and the custom of singing 'the Geneva psalms in French at public meetings,

'upon the highway, and in shops, was thenceforth 'taken for the distinctive sign of a sectary.'†

To this account of Strada may be added from Bayle, that the first publication of thirty of the psalms was dedicated to Francis I., that it was so well received by the people, that copies could not be printed so fast as they were sold off; that they were not then set to music as they are now, to be sung in churches, but every one gave such a tune as he thought fit; 'Each of the princes and courtiers,' says this author, 'took a psalm for himself: Hen. II. loved this, "Ainsi qu'on oit le cerf bruire," which he sang in 'hunting; Madam de Valentinois took this, "Du "fond de ma pensée." The queen chose the psalm "Ne vueilles pas ô Sire," which she sang to a merry 'tune; Anthony king of Navarre took this, "Revenge "moy, pren le querelle," and sang it to the tune of a 'dance of Poitou. In the mean time, Marot, fearing 'lest he should be sent to prison, fled to Geneva, 'where he continued his version as far as fifty psalms. 'Beza put the remaining hundred into verse; and the 'psalms which he rhymed in imitation of Marot's, 'were received by all men with great applause.'

CHAP. CX.

No sooner was this version of the Psalms completed, than Calvin, who was then at the head of the church of Geneva, determined as it were to consecrate it, and introduce the practice of singing psalms amongst his people: for some time he stood in doubt whether to adopt the Lutheran choral form of singing in consonance, or to institute a plain unisonous melody in which all might join; at length he resolved on the latter, and to this end employed a musician, named Guillaume Franc, to set them to easy tunes of one part only, in which the musical composer succeeded so well, that the people became infatuated with the love of psalm-singing; at length, that is to say, in the year 1553, which was about seven after the version was completed, Calvin, to put the finishing hand to his design, divided the psalms into pauses or small portions, and appointed them to be sung in churches, and so made them a form of religious worship; soon after they were bound up with the Geneva Catechism, and from that time the Catholics, who had been accustomed to sing Marot's psalms in common with profane songs, were forbid the use of them under a severe penalty. The Protestants however continued the indiscriminate use of them at church; they considered the singing of psalms as an exercise of devotion; in the field it was an incentive to courage and manly fortitude, for in their frequent insurrections against their persecutors, a psalm sung by four or five thousand of them answered the end of the music of trumpets and other warlike instruments, and, in short, was among them the accustomed signal to battle.

To this purpose Strada mentions several notable instances that happened a few years after the publication of Marot's version; and first, speaking of the popular tumults in the Low Countries about the year

---

* Marot understood not the Hebrew language, but was furnished with a translation of the Psalms by Vatablus. Bayle, MAROT, in not.

† Strada de Bello Belgico, lib. III. Sir Rob. Stapylton's translation. Ex Florimond de Remond in Hist. Ortu. &c. Hæres. lib. viii.

1562, he relates that 'two French Calvinist preachers
'in the night, the one at Valenciennes, and the other
'at Tournay, openly before a great assembly in the
'market-place, delivered their new gospel, and when
'they had done were followed through the streets by
'the multitude, to the number of an hundred at Va-
'lenciennes, and six hundred at Tournay, singing
'David's Psalms in French.* And in another place
'he says that on the 21st of August, 1566, the
'heretics came into the great church at Antwerp with
'concealed weapons, as if they resolved, after some
'light skirmishes for a few days past, to come now to
'battle, and waiting till evensong was done, they
'shouted with an hideous cry Long live the Gheuses;†
'nay, they commanded the image of the blessed Virgin
'to repeat their acclamation, which if she refused to
'do, they madly swore they would beat and kill her;
'and though Johannes Immersellius, prætor of the
'town, with some apparitors, came and commanded
'them to keep the peace, yet he could not help it,
'but the people running away to get out of the tumult,
'the heretics shut the doors after them, and as con-
'querors possessed themselves of the church. Now
'when they saw all was theirs, hearing the clock strike
'the last hour of the day, and darkness giving them
'confidence, one of them, lest their wickedness should
'want formality, began to sing a Geneva psalm, and
'then, as if the trumpet had sounded a charge, the
'spirit moving them altogether, they fell upon the
'effigies of the mother of God, and upon the pictures
'of Christ and his saints, some tumbled down and
'trod upon them, others thrust swords into their
'sides, or chopped off their heads with axes, with so
'much concord and forecast in their sacrilege, that
'you would have thought every one had had his
'several work assigned him; for the very harlots,
'those common appurtenances to thieves and drunk-
'ards, catching up the wax candles from the altars,
'cast down the sacred plate, broke asunder the picture
'frames, defaced the painted walls; part setting up
'ladders, shattered the goodly organs, broke the win-
'dows flourished with a new kind of paint. Huge
'statues of saints that stood in the walls upon pedes-
'tals, they unfastened and hurled down, among which
'an ancient great crucifix, with the two thieves
'hanging on each hand of our Saviour, that stood
'right against the high altar, they pulled down with
'ropes and hewed it to pieces, but touched not the
'two thieves, as if they only worshipped them, and
'desired them to be their good lords. Nay they pre-
'sumed to break open the conservatory of the eccle-
'siastical bread, and putting in their polluted hands,
'to pull out the blessed body of our Lord. Those
'base offscourings of men trod upon the deity, adored
'and dreaded by the angels. The pixes and chalices
'which they found in the vestry they filled with wine
'prepared for the altar, and drank them off in de-
'rision; they greased their shoes with the chrisme or
'holy oil; and after the spoil of all these things, laughed
'and were very merry at the matter.' ‡

* De Bello Belgico, lib. III.

† A name which *signifies a Vagrant, or rather a Beggar, but having been applied to them by a nobleman, an enemy to their faction, they assumed it as a defiance of him. Vide Strada, sub anno 1556.*

‡ De Bello Belgico, lib. V.

Such were the effects produced by the introduction
of psalm-singing among those of the reformed religion; and no one can be at a loss for a reason why
those of the Romish communion have expressed
themselves with the utmost bitterness against the
practice of it. Bayle in the article Marot, has given
a letter from a gentleman who had served the queen
of Navarre, to Catherine de Medicis, subscribed Vil-
lemadon, dated in August 1590, containing an account
of the reception of the psalms which Marot met with at
court, but abounding with such severe and scurrilous
invectives against the Calvinistical psalmody, and
those who were the friends of it, that the omission of
it in this place will, it is hoped, find a ready excuse.

From the several relations herein-before given it
would be difficult to form any judgment either of the
merit of Marot's version or of its author, but Bayle
has summed up his character, and, after bestowing
high commendations on his Psalms, ranks him among
the best of the French poets.

Having said thus much of the poetry, it now remains
to speak of the music of Marot's psalms: the common
notion is that they were originally set by Lewis
Bourgeois and Claude Goudimel, which is only so
far true as it respects the setting of them in parts;
for it appears by an anecdote commuicated to Bayle
by a professor of Lausanne, and inserted in a note
on a passage of his life of Marot, that before this
they were sung to melodies of one part only in the
churches at Geneva, and that the composer of those
melodies was one Guillaume Franc; and to this fact
Beza himself testifies in a kind of certificate, signed
with his own hand, dated Nov. 2, 1552. Bayle's
correspondent farther adds, that he had in his possession a copy of the Geneva psalms, printed in 1564,
with the name Guillaume Franc to it, whereto is prefixed the licence of the magistrate, signed Gallatin,
and sealed with red wax, declaring Guillaume Franc
to be the author of the musical notes to which the
psalms in that impression are set.

It seems that Bourgeois composed music to only
eighty-three of the Psalms, which music was in four,
five, and six parts; these Psalms so set were printed
at Lyons in 1561. As to Goudimel, it is certain that
he set the whole in four and five parts, for the book
was printed at Paris in 1565, by Adrian Le Roy and
Robert Ballard. Nevertheless there is reason to
think that this or some other collection of Marot's
Psalms with the music, had made its appearance
earlier than 1565; and indeed express mention is
made of fifty of Marot's Psalms with the music,
printed at Strasburg with the liturgy in 1545; and
there is extant a preface to Marot's Psalms written by
Calvin himself, and dated June 10, 1543, wherein is
the following passage: 'All the psalms with their
'music were printed the first time at Geneva, with a
'preface concerning an agreement of the printers
'thereof, whereby they had engaged to appropriate a
'part of the profits arising from that and future im-
'pressions for the relief of the poor refugees at
'Geneva. §

§ Bayle, MAROT, in not. This agreement is alluded to by the deacons of the church of Geneva, who in a note after the preface to the Sermons of Calvin on Deuteronomy, published anno 1567, complain of the breach of it, insisting that those who printed the psalms every day, could not

The name Guillaume Franc is hardly known among musicians, however, as the original melodies have never been ascribed to any other author, credit may be given to the anecdote above-mentioned to have been communicated to Bayle concerning them. What those original melodies were will hereafter be considered. It is certain that the honour of first composing music in parts to the Geneva psalms is due to Bourgeois and Goudimel; of the former very little is to be learned, but the character and unfortunate history of the latter remain on record.

CLAUDE GOUDIMEL, a supposed native of Franche Comté, was of the reformed religion; and in the Histoire Universelle of Mons. D'Aubigné is mentioned, among other eminent persons, to have been murdered in the massacre of Paris on St. Bartholomew's day, anno 1572: the circumstances of his death, as there related, are, that he, together with Mons. Perot, a civilian, were thrown out of a window, dragged along the streets and cast into the river; but this account is erroneous in respect of the place of his death; for Thuanus, in that part of his history where he takes occasion to mention the massacre of Lyons, has these words: 'The same fate [death] 'attended Claudius Goudimel, an excellent musician 'of our time, who set the psalms of David, translated 'into metre by Clement Marot and Theodore Beza, 'to various and most pleasing tunes.' In the Protestant Martyrology mention is made of Goudimel in these words: 'Claudius Goudimel, an excellent 'musician, and whose memory will live for ever for 'having composed tunes to the greater part of David's 'psalms in French.'

With respect to Goudimel's work, the music in four parts to the psalms, it was first published in the year　　and has past a multitude of editions; one in 1602, printed at Delft, without any mention of Bourgeois, is intitled 'Les Pseaumes mis en rime 'Françoise. Par Clement Marot et Theodore de 'Beze; mis en musique à quatre parties par Claude 'Goudimel.' These psalms, for the greater facility in singing them, are of that species of musical composition called Counterpoint; but before his death Goudimel had meditated a noble work, viz., the psalms in five, six, seven, and eight parts, composed in the form of motets, with all the ornaments of fugue, and other inventions common to that kind of music; he had made a considerable progress in it, and, had not death prevented him, would quickly have completed the work.

The psalms of Marot and Beza were also set by another very eminent musician, Claude le Jeune, of whom an account has already been given.* He was a Protestant, a native of Valenciennes, and a favourite of Henry IV. of France. In the title-page of many of his works, published after his death, he is styled 'Phenix des musiciens;' and unquestionably he was in his art one of the greatest men of that day.

There are extant two collections of psalms with

the music of Claude le Jeune, both which appear to be posthumous publications; the one of these, most beautifully printed in separate books, of a small oblong form, at Paris, in 1613, and dedicated by his sister, Cecile le Jeune, to the Duke de Bouillon, contains the whole hundred and fifty psalms of Marot and Beza, with the music in four and five parts as it is said, but in truth the fifth part is frequently nothing more than a reduplication of some of the others in the octave above. A few of the psalms in this collection are plain counterpoint, the rest are of a more artificial contexture, but easy enough for the practice of persons moderately skilled in singing. There is extant also another collection, published at Paris in 1606, of a larger size than the former, entitled 'Pseaumes en vers mezurez, mis en Musique, 'A 2, 3, 4, 5, 6, 7, et 8 parties, par Claude le 'Jeune, natif de Valentienne, Compositeur de la 'musique de la chambre du Roy;' these are certain select psalms paraphrased by an unknown author, and as to the music, it abounds in all those ornaments of fugues, points, and varied motion, which distinguish the Canto figurato from the Canto fermo; so that thus set they might not improperly be styled Motets. This last collection of psalms was published by the author's sister, Cecile le Jeune, and dedicated by her to a friend and fellow-servant of her brother, one of the gentlemen of the chamber to Henry IV.

She also published in 1603, and dedicated to our king James I. a book entitled Le Printemps, containing compositions of her brother in three, four, five, six, seven, and eight parts, in the style of madrigals. By an advertisement prefixed to the book it seems that it was part of a work which the author had undertaken, and intended to adapt to the four seasons of the year. Another work of his was also published by the same Cecile le Jeune in 1606, intitled 'Octonaires de la vanité et inconstance du monde,' in three and four parts.

These two musicians, Goudimel and Claude le Jeune, are the most celebrated composers of music to the French psalms. But here it is necessary to remark, that though the common opinion is that they each composed the four parts, superius, contratenor, tenor, and bassus, of every tune, yet the tenor part, which at that time was of the most consequence, as it carried in it the air or melody of the whole composition, is common both to the tunes of Goudimel and le Jeune, and was in fact composed by another person, so that neither of them have done any thing more than given the harmony to a certain melody, which melody is in both authors one and the same.

It is very difficult to assign a reason for this conduct, unless we suppose that these melodies, to which the studies and labours of both these eminent men were but subservient, were on the score of their antiquity or excellence, in such estimation with the people, as to subject a modern musician that should reject them, to the imputation of envy or vanity; or, perhaps after all, and abstracted from every other claim to preference, the frequent use of them in the French protestant congregations might have occasioned such prejudices in their favour, as to render

---

with a good conscience do so without paying to their poor what was promised and agreed to be paid for their use before they were printed the first time.
* Book X. chap. xc. of this work.

any others actually inadmissible among them. In either case our curiosity leads us to enquire who was the author of those melodies which two of the most eminent musicians of France condescended thus to honour. In short, recollecting what Bayle has related about the original French psalm-tunes of one part, and laying the above circumstances together, there is little reason to doubt but that those original melodies which constitute the tenor part, and are therefore the ground-work of Goudimel and Claude le Jeune's psalm-tunes, were those very original tunes which the above-cited author has ascribed to Guillaume Franc.

The psalms thus set by Goudimel and Claude le Jeune, were introduced into the public service of the church, not only at Geneva, but in France, Flanders, and most other countries where the reformation had got footing, and the service was in the French language; and continued to be sung until the version became obsolete; the church of Geneva, the first that received, was the first that forsook it and made use of another, begun by Mons. Conrart, and finished by Mons. Bastide; but the French churches, which since the revocation of the edict of Nantes became settled in foreign countries, continued and still use the version of Marot and Beza, revised and altered from time to time through a great number of editions, so as to correspond with those innovations and refinements to which the French and most other living languages are liable.*

Of the German psalmody very little can be said. It is imagined that the High Dutch version of the psalms was made very soon after Luther's time by some of the ablest of their ministers; but as the language is not very fit for poetry, whether it be good or bad the world has shown very little curiosity to enquire. There are many excellent melodies sung in the German protestant congregations, which is no wonder, considering that that country has been famous for skilful musicians. They have a tradition among them that some of these melodies were composed by Luther himself; and as it is certain that he was skilled in music, that they were is highly probable.

CHAP. CXI.

It remains now to show what part the church of England acted with respect to church music, and to account for its existence at this day: and here it may be observed, that the great revolutions of religion and government generally take a tincture from the characters of those under whose authority or influence they are brought about. The affection of Leo X. to music, was propitious to the final establishment of choral service in the Romish church; and that it is yet retained in this kingdom, notwithstanding the reformation, and the many efforts of its enemies to banish it, may be ascribed to the like disposition in

the four last princes of the Tudor family. For to instance in Henry VIII. it is certain that he was not only a lover of music, but profoundly skilled in it as a science.[†]

It will appear farther, that all the children of Henry were skilled in music; with respect to his son Edward, we are told by Cardan that he 'Cheli 'pulsabat;' and in Edward's manuscript Journal, written with his own hand, now in the British Museum, and which is printed in Burnet's History of the Reformation, mention is made of his playing on the lute to the French embassador.[‡]

As to Mary, her affection for the choral service might probably arise from her attachment to the Romish religion, yet she too was skilled in the practice of music, as appears by a letter from her mother queen Catherine to her, wherein she recommends to her the use of the virginals or lute if she have any.[§]

The skill in music which Elizabeth possessed is clearly evinced by the following passage in Mclvil's Memoirs.[||] 'The same day, after dinner, my Lord 'of Hunsdean drew me up to a quiet gallery that 'I might hear some music, (but he said he durst not 'avow it) where I might hear the queen play upon 'the virginals. After I had hearkened a while I took 'by the tapestry that hung before the door of the 'chamber, and seeing her back was towards the door, 'I entered within the chamber, and stood a pretty 'space, hearing her play excellently well; but she 'left off immediately so soon as she turned her about 'and saw me. She appeared to be surprized to see 'me, and came forward, seeming to strike me with 'her hand, alledging she was not used to play before 'men, but when she was solitary to shun melancholy.'[¶] To this passage it may not be improper to add a little anecdote, which perhaps has never yet appeared in print, and may serve to shew either that she had, or affected to have it thought she had, a very nice ear. In her time the bells of the church of Shoreditch, a parish in the northern suburbs of London, were much esteemed for their melody; and in her journies from Hatfield to London, as soon as she approached the town, they constantly rang by way of congratulation. Upon these occasions she seldom failed to stop at a small distance short of the church, and amidst the prayers and acclamations of

---

† See the foregoing volume, book VIII. chap. lxxvii. In a letter from Sir John Harrington to the lord treasurer Burleigh, mention is made of certain old Monkish rhymes called 'The Blacke Saunctus, or Monkes Hymn to Saunte Satane.' The father of Sir John Harrington, who had married a natural daughter of Henry VIII. named Esther, and was very well skilled in music, having learned it, as the letter says, 'in the fellow-'ship of good Maister Tallis, set this hymn to music in a canon of three 'parts; and the author of the letter says that king Henry was used 'in 'plesaunt moode to sing it.' Nugæ Antiquæ, printed for W. Frederick at Bath, 8vo, 1769, pag. 132.

‡ '19 July [1551]. Mons. le Mareschal St. Andre supped with me; 'after supper saw a dozen courses, and after I came and made me ready. '20. The next morning he came to me to mine arraying, and saw my 'bedchamber, and went a hunting with hounds, and saw me shoot, and 'saw all my guards shoot together; he dined with me, heard me play on 'the lute, ride; came to me to my study, supped with me, and so 'departed to Richmond.' Collection of Records, &c. in the Appendix to Burn. Hist. Reform. part II. pag. 31.

§ Burnet Hist. Reform. part II. Appendix pag. 142.

|| Lond. 1752, pag. 99.

¶ It is also said that she played on an instrument strung with wire, called the Poliphant. Preface to Playford's Introduction to the Skill of Musick, edit. 1666.

---

* This must be understood with an exception, for in some churches both here and abroad, the French protestants sing a paraphrase of the Psalms, by Antoine Godeau. This person was successively Bishop of Grasse and Venice, and died in 1672. The Psalms thus paraphrased are set in four parts by Jacques de Goiry, and were first published in Amsterdam in 1691; some years after they were reprinted by Pearson for the use of the French churches in London.

the people, would listen attentively to and commend the music of the bells.

From these particulars it may reasonably be inferred, that the several princes to whom they relate were disposed to the retention of music in our solemn church service. It remains to shew on the other hand what were the sentiments of those who headed the reformation in England with respect to this part of divine service.

And first it appears that great complaints were made by many of the dignified clergy and others, of the intricacy and difficulty of the church music of those times. In consequence whereof it was once proposed that organs and curious singing should be removed from our churches.* Latimer, in his diocese of Worcester, went still farther, as appears by certain injunctions of his to the prior and convent of St. Mary, whereby he forbids in their service all manner of singing.†

By a statute of 27 Hen. VIII. cap. 15, power was given to the king to nominate two and thirty persons of his clergy and laity to examine all canons, constitutions, and ordinances provincial and synodical, and to compile a body of such ecclesiastical laws as should in future be observed throughout this realm. Nothing was done towards this necessary work during the life-time of Henry; but in the reign of his son the consideration of it was resumed, and a commission granted for the purpose to eight bishops, eight divines, eight civilians, and eight common lawyers. The deliberations of this assembly, composed of the ablest men in their several professions that the age afforded, terminated in a work, which though pr nted and exhibited to public view, is incomplete, and apparently defective in respect of authority, as wanting the royal sanction. It was published first in 1571, by Fox the Martyrologist, and by some other person, for very obvious reasons, in 1640, under the title of Reformatio Legum Ecclesiasticarum. Dr. Walter Haddon, a celebrated Latin scholar of that age, and Sir John Cheke, were employed in drawing it up, in the doing whereof they very happily imitated the style and form of the Roman civil law, as contained in the Pandects and Institutes of Justinian; but it seems the giving the work an elegant form was the whole of their merit, for virtually and in substance it was the work of Cranmer, who at that time was justly esteemed the ablest canonist in England.

Upon this work it may be observed that if ever choral music might be said to be in danger of being banished from our churches, the era of the compilation of the Reformatio Legum Ecclesiasticarum was of all others the time; and it may well be imagined that to those who were interested in the retention of the solemn church service, the years which were spent in framing that work, were a dreadful interval; however their fears were considerably abated when it was known that the thirty-two commissioners had not reprobated church music, but had barely condemned, by the name of figurate and operose music, that kind of singing which was

productive of confusion, and rendered unintelligible to the auditory those parts of the service which required their strictest attention; at the same time the rule prescribed by the commissioners requires that certain parts of the service be sung by the ministers and clerks in a plain, distinct, and audible manner; which in effect was nothing more than reducing choral service to that state of purity and simplicity from which it had deviated.‡

In the book of Homilies we meet with a passage, which, whether intended to justify or reprehend the use of music in divine worship, has been a matter of controversy: an objection is put into the mouth of a woman, supposed to be discoursing with her neighbour on the subject of the reformed church service, which she utters in the following words :—' Alas, ' goſſip, what ſhall we now do at church, ſince all the ' goodly ſights we were wont to have are gone; ſince we ' cannot hear the like piping, ſinging, chanting, and play-' ing upon the organs that we could before?' Upon which the preacher interposes, saying, ' But, dearly beloved, ' we ought greatly to rejoice and give God thanks that ' our churches are delivered out of all thoſe things which ' diſpleaſed God ſo ſore, and filthily defiled his holy houſe ' and his place of prayer.' §

Upon a review of the censures on church-music contained in the decree of the council of Trent, heretofore mentioned, and in the Reformatio Legum Ecclesiasticarum, it will for the most part be found that they were occasioned rather by the abuses that for a long time had attended it, than any persuasion in the reformers of the unlawfulness of the practice. It is true that those of the English clergy, who in the persecution under queen Mary had fled to Francfort, and there laid the foundation of nonconformity, affected to consider it as superstitious and idolatrous; but the less rigid of their brethren thought it had a tendency to edification, and was sufficiently warranted by scripture and the practice of the primitive church.

The rule laid down for church music in England, almost a thousand years ago, was ' Simplicem ' sanctámque Melodiam, secundum morem Ecclesiæ, ' sectentur;'‖ with a view to this the thirty-two commissioners laboured to prevent the corruption of a practice that had at least the sanction of antiquity on its side, and to remove from the church what they as justly as emphatically termed ' curious ' singing.'

---

* Burn. Hist. Reform. part III. pag. 302, 304.

† Burnet Hist. Reform. part II. Collection of Records, book II. numb. 23.

‡ 'In divinis capitibus recitandis, et Psalmis concinendis, ministri 'et clerici diligenter hoc cogitare debent, non solùm à se Deum laudari 'oportere, sed alios etiam hortatu et exemplo et observatione illorum 'ad eundem cultum adducendos esse. Quapropter partitè voces et dis-'tinctè pronuntient, et cantus sit illorum clarus et aptus, ut ad auditorum 'omnia sensum, et intelligentiam proveniant; itaque vibratam illam, 'et operosam musicam, quæ figurata dicitur, auferri placet, quæ sic in 'multitudinis auribus tumultuatur, ut sæpè linguam non possit ipsam 'loquentem intelligere. Tum auditores etiam ipsi sint in opere simul 'cum clericis et ministris certas divinorum officiorum particulas canentes, 'in quibus Psalmi primùm erunt, annumerabitur fidei symbolum, et gloria 'in excelsis, decem solemnia præcepta, cæteraque hujusmodi præcipua 'religionis capita, quæ maximum in communi fide nostra pondus habent: 'hiis enim piis divini cultus exercitationibus et invitamentis populus 'seipsum eriget, ac sensù quendam habebit orandi, quorum si nullæ nisi 'auscultandi partes sint, ita friget et jacet mens, ut nullam de rebus 'divinis vehementem et seriam cogitationem suscipere possit.' Reformatio Legum Ecclesiasticarum, tit. De Divinis Officiis, cap. 5.

§ Second part of the Homily of the Place and Time of Prayer, pag. 209.

‖ Spelman. Concil. vol. I. pag. 248.

There is an ambiguity in the expression 'curious singing' which might lead a stranger to the state of music at this period to suspect that it meant such a nicety, exactness, and volubility in the performance, as is at present required in the music of the theatre; but this seems not to have been the case. Morley, who is somewhat free in his censure of the choir singers of his time, acquits them of any such affected nicety in their singing as might lead men to say it was over curious: on the contrary, he represents their performance as slovenly to a great degree.* In short, the true object of those many censures which at different times were passed on choir service, was not curious singing, but intricate, elaborate, and unedifying music: *figurata* is the epithet by which it is characterised in the Reformatio Legum Ecclesiasticarum; now *Cantus figuratus* is a term used in contradistinction to *Cantus planus* or *Cantus firmus*, and means that kind of song which abounds with fugues, responsive passages, and a commixture of various and intricate proportions, which, whether extemporary or written, is by musicians termed descant, and of this kind of music a specimen will be found in Appendix, No. 57.†

CHAP. CXII.

The above particulars sufficiently explain the term Curious Singing, and shew that the music of the church was, at the time above spoken of, extremely elaborate and artificial in its contexture. It also appears that those who had the direction of choral service in the several churches and chapels in this kingdom, were to a great degree solicitous about the performance of it; and to the end that every choir should be furnished with a competent number of singers, more especially boys, writs or placards were issued, empowering the officers to whom they were directed, to impress the male children of poor persons in order to their being instructed in music, and qualified for choir service. Tusser, the author of the Five hundred Points of good Husbandry, and who was born in the reign of Henry VIII. relates that being a child, and having been sent by his father to a music school, as was the practice in those times, he was removed to Wallingford college, where he remained till he was seized by virtue of one of those placards, which at that time were issued out to

sundry men, empowering them to impress boys‡ for the service of the several choirs in this kingdom; and that at last he had the good fortune to be settled at St. Paul's, where he had Redford, a skilful musician, for his master. The poor child seems to have had a hard time of it, as appears by his account in these words :—

Stanza III.

It came to pas that born I was,
Of linage good and gentle blood,
In Effex laier in village faier
    That Rivenhall hight :
Which village lide by Banktree fide,
There fpend did I mine infancy ;
There then my name in honeft fame
    Remained in fight.

IV.

I yet but yoong, no fpeech of tong,
Nor tcares withall that often fall
From mothers eies when child out cries
    To part her fro ;
Could pitty make good father take,
But out I muft to fong be thruft ;
Say what I would, do what I could,
    His mind was fo.

V.

O painefull time ! for every crime
What toofed eares, like baited beares !
What bobbed lips, what yerkes, what nips,
    What hellifh toies !
What robes ! how bare ! what colledge fare !
What bread how ftale ! What penny ale !
Then Wallingford how wert thou abhor'd
    Of filly boies !

VI.

Thence for my voice, I muft (no choice)
Away of forfe like pofting horfe,
For fundrie men had placards then
    Such child to take ·
The better breft, the leffer reft §
To ferve the queere, now there now here ;
For time fo fpent I may repent,
    And forrow make.

VII.

But marke the chance, myfelf to vance.
By friendfhip's lot to Paule's I got ;
So found I grace a certain fpace
    Still to remaine
With Redford ‖ there, the like no where
For cunning fuch and vertue much,
By whom fome part of muficke art
    So did I gaine.

---

* Introd. to Practicall Music, pag. 179.

† Dr. Brown, on the authority of Gassendi, asserts that some time, he says not how long, after the invention of counterpart by Guido, according to the natural tendency of this improvement, all the world ran mad after an artificial variety of parts. Dissertation on the Union, &c. of Poetry and Music, pag. 209. In this he seems to have made a twofold mistake, for neither was Guido the inventor of counterpoint, nor was it after a variety of parts that the world were running mad; it was an affection for that curious and intricate music above spoken of that intoxicated the musicians, and which first the council of Trent, and afterwards the thirty-two commissioners, as above is related, endeavoured to reform. Nor is this author less unfortunate in his assertion that the Greeks that escaped from the taking of Constantinople brought a refined and enervate species of music into Italy from Greece. Ibid. Some ancient Greek manuscripts on music and other subjects were all they brought, and many of them have since been published ; that enervate species of music which he complains they brought to Rome, is no where taken notice of in history ; if by enervate he means elaborate, it is to be accounted for by supposing, that as the science improved, the musicians departed by degrees from that simplicity which distinguishes the songs of the Provençals, who, after all that can be said, were the fathers of the modern secular music, for as to ecclesiastical music, notwithstanding all that he has advanced, it was under the direction and management of the clergy.

‡ See a note of a commission, and also a letter directed to the master of the children of the chapel, Richard Gowre (query Bowyer mentioned infra page 542) Temp. Edward VI. in Strype's mem. eccles Vol. II., 538, 539, giving power to take up children for the king's use, and to serve in his chapel.

§ This expression is worthy of a critical observation :—
        'The better brest the lesser rest.'

In singing, the sound is originally produced by the action of the lungs ; which are so essential an organ in this respect, that to have a good breast was formerly a common periphrasis to denote a good singer. The Italians make use of the terms *Voce di Petto* and *Voce di Testa* to signify two kinds of voice, of which the first is the best. In Shakespeare's comedy of Twelfth Night, after the clown is asked to sing, Sir Andrew Aguecheek says :—
        'By my troth the fool has an excellent breast.'

And in the statutes of Stoke college in Suffolk, founded by Parker, archbishop of Canterbury, is a provision in these words : 'of which said 'queristers, after their breasts are changed [i. e. their voices broke] we 'will the most apt of wit and capacity be helpen with exhibition of forty 'shillings, &c.' Strype's Life of Parker, pag. 9.

‖ John Redford, organist and almoner of St. Paul's. See page 367 of this work.

VIII.

From l'aule's I went, to Eaton sent
To learn ſtreightwaies the latin phraies,
Where fiftie three ſtripes given to mee
　　At once I had
For fault but ſmall or none at all,
It came to pas thus beat I was;
　　See Udall* ſee the mercie of thee
　　To me poore lad.

Such was the general state of cathedral music about the middle of the fifteenth century; the reformation in religion, which took place at that period, produced great alterations, as well in the discipline as doctrine of the Christian church; these, so far as they respect the Lutheran ritual, have been already mentioned; and those that relate to the Calvanists are purposely referred to another place. It remains then to trace the rise and progress of that formulary which at present distinguishes the church of England from the other reformed churches. And first it is to be noted, that until about the year 1530, the liturgy, as well here as in other countries then in subjection to the see of Rome, agreeably to the Roman ritual, was said or sung in Latin. In the year 1536 the Creed, Pater noster, and Ten Commandments were by the king's command put into English; and this, as Fuller observes, was the farthest pace which the reformation stepped in the reign of king Henry VIII.†

In the year 1548, being the second of the reign of Edward VI. a liturgy wholly in English was composed by Cranmer, archbishop of Canterbury, and other eminent divines, confirmed by a statute 2 and 3 of the same king, that imposed a penalty on such as should deprave the same, or neglect the use thereof, and printed in the year 1549, with the title of the 'Book of Common Prayer, &c.' as being framed as well for the use of the people as the priest, and in which all are required to join in common. Against this liturgy some objections were taken by Calvin, Beza, Fagius, Peter Martyr, Bucer, and others, upon which a statute was made in the fifth and sixth years of the same king, enacting that it should be faithfully and godly perused, explained, and made perfect. This was accordingly done, and, with some variations, the liturgy was published in 1552.

* This Udall was Nicholas Udall, styled by Bale 'Elegantissimus 'omnium bonarum literarum magister, et earum felicissimus interpres;' and that master of Eton school whose severity made divers of his scholars run away from the school for fear of beating. Roger Ascham tells the story in the preface to his Scholemaster; and a specimen of Udall's elegance both in verse and prose may be seen in the appendix to Ascham's works in quarto, published by John Bennet, 1761.

The life of this poor man [Tusser] was a series of misfortune; from Eton he went to Trinity hall in Cambridge, but soon left the university, and at different times was resident in various parts of the kingdom, where he was successively a musician, school-master, serving-man, husbandman, grazier, and poet, but never throve in any of these several vocations. Fuller relates 'that he traded at large in oxen, sheep, dairies, 'and grain of all kinds, to no profit; that whether he bought or sold he 'lost; and that when a renter he impoverished himself, and never 'enriched his landlord:' all which seems to be too true by his own showing, and is a proof of the truth of that saying in holy scripture that the battle is not to the strong, nor the race to the swift.

As to the Five hundred Points of Husbandry, it is written in familiar verse, and abounds with many curious particulars that bespeak the manners, the customs, and modes of living in this country from the year 1520, to about half a century after; besides which it discovers such a degree of œconomical wisdom in the author, such a sedulous attention to the honest arts of thriving, such a general love of mankind, such a regard to justice, and a reverence for religion, that we do not only lament his misfortunes, but wonder at them, and are at a loss to account for his dying poor, who understood so well the method to become rich.

† Church Hist. in Britaine, book VII. pag. 386.

In the first year of the reign of queen Elizabeth it underwent a second, and in the first of James a third revisal; but the latter of these produced only a small alteration in the rubric, so that we may date the final settlement of the English liturgy from the year 1559, when it was printed by Grafton, with this title, 'The Booke of Common Prayer and 'Administration of the Sacraments, and other Rites 'and Ceremonies of the Church of England.'

But notwithstanding these several alterations and amendments of the ritual, it will be found that the solemn service of our church is nearly coeval with the liturgy itself; for the rubric, as it stands in the first common prayer of Edward VI. prescribes in terms the saying or *singing* of mattens and even-song; and in the ministration of the communion that the clerks shall *sing* in English for the office or Introite, as it is called, a psalm appointed for that day. And again it directs that the clerks shall sing one or many of the sentences therein mentioned, according to the length and shortness of the time that the people be offering. Again, the rubric to the same first common prayer of Edward VI. directs that on Wednesdays and Fridays the English litany shall be said or *sung* in all places after such form as is appointed by the king's majesty's injunctions. These, together with the several directions contained in the rubric above-cited, for singing the post communions, Gloria in excelsis, and other parts of the service, sufficiently prove that, notwithstanding the objections against choral music, and the practice of some of the reformed churches, the compilers of the liturgy, and indeed the king himself, as may be gathered from his injunctions, looked upon the solemn musical service as tending to edification, and were therefore determined to retain it. And this opinion seems to be adopted by the statute of 2 and 3 Edw. VI. cap. 1. which though it contains no formal obligation on the clergy or others to use or join in either vocal or instrumental music in the common prayer, yet does it clearly recognize the practice of singing, and that in such terms, as cannot but preclude all question about the lawfulness of it with those who admit the authority of parliament to determine the form and order of public worship, for the statute enacts that 'if any manner of parson, 'vicar, or other whatsoever minister that ought to 'sing or should *sing* or say Common Prayer, ac-'cording to the form then lately appointed, or shall 'refuse to use the same, or shall use any other form, 'he shall forfeit, &c.'

And section VII. of the same statute is a proviso that psalms or prayer taken out of the Bible may be used in due time, not letting or omitting thereby the service or any part thereof.‡ *This lets in the Jubilate, Magnificat, Nunc Dimittis, and Anthem, but not the Te Deum.*

The subsequent abolition of the mass, and the

‡ With respect to the manner of performing the solemn choral service at the beginning of the reign of Edward VI. we meet with the following note: 'On the eighteenth day of the moneth of September, 1547, the 'letany was sung in the English tongue in St. Paul's church between the 'quire and the high altar, the singers kneeling, half on the one side and 'half on the other. And the same day the epistle and gospel was also 'red at the high mass in the English tongue.' Heylin's History of the Reformation, pag. 42.

introduction of a new liturgy into the church, calculated to be either sung or said in churches, as it implied no less than a total repudiation of the ancient musical service, made it necessary for those who were concerned to maintain the dignity and splendour of divine worship to think of framing a new one. Many very excellent musicians were living about that time, but few of them had embraced the new religion, as it was called, and those of the old could not be expected immediately to assist in it. Dr. Tye, the king's preceptor in music, was a protestant, but he had undertaken, in emulation of Sternhold, to translate the Acts of the Apostles into English metre, and farther set them to music of four parts; notwithstanding all which, in less than two years after the compiling of king Edward's liturgy, a formule was composed, so perfect in its kind, that, with scarce any variation, it continues to be the rule for choral service even at this day.

The author of this valuable work was that John Marbeck or Merbecke, of whose persecution, grounded on a suspicion of heresy, an ample account has herein-before been given. This book was printed by Richard Grafton in 1550, and has this short title :—

The Booke of Common Praier noted.

At the bottom of the last leaf is the name **John Merbeke,** by which we are to understand that he was the author or composer of the musical notes: these, so far as the liturgy of Edward VI. and that of Elizabeth may be said to correspond, are very little different from those in use at this day, so that this book may truly be considered as the foundation of the solemn musical service of the church of England.

A particular account of this curious work is here intended to be given, but first it is necessary to observe that it is formed on the model of the Romish ritual; as first, it contains a general recitatory intonation for the Lord's Prayer, the Apostle's Creed, and such other parts of the service as are most proper to be read, in a certain key or pitch. To the Versicles, Responses, Introits, Kyries, Gloria in excelsis, Offertories, Prefaces, Sanctus, and Post-communions, melodies are adapted of a grave and decent form, and nearly as much restrained as those of St. Ambrose or Gregory; and these have a harmonical relation to the rest of the service, the dominant of each being in unison with the note of the key in which the whole was to be sung.

After a short explanation of the musical characters that occur in the book, follows the order of Mattins, beginning with the Lord's Prayer,* which, as it is not required by the rubric to be sung, is set to notes that bespeak nothing more than a succession of sounds of the same name and place in the scale, viz., C SOL FA UT, that being about the mean tone of a tenor voice. These notes are of various lengths, adapted to express the quantity of the syllables, which they do with great exactness.

For the reasons of this uniform kind of intonation

it is necessary to recur to the practice of the church at the time when choral or antiphonal singing was first introduced into it, when it will be found that almost the whole of the liturgy was sung; which being granted, the regularity of the service required that such parts of it as were the most proper for music, as namely, the Te Deum and other hymns, and also the evangelical songs, should be sung in one and the same key; it was therefore necessary that this key, which was to pervade and govern the whole service, should be fixed and ascertained, otherwise the clerks or singers might carry the melody beyond the reach of their voices. As the use of organs or other instruments in churches was not known in those early times, this could no otherwise be done than by giving to the prayers, the creeds, and other parts of the service not so proper to be sung as read, some general kind of intonation, by means whereof the dominant would be so impressed on the ears and in the memories of those that sung, as to prevent any deviation from the fundamental key; and accordingly it may be observed that in his book of the Common Praier noted, Marbeck has given to the Lord's Prayer an uniform intonation† in the key of C, saving a small inflexion of the final clause, which here and elsewhere he makes use of to keep the several parts of the service distinct, and prevent their running into each other. But this will be better understood by a perusal of the composition itself, which is as follows :—

MATTINS.

The QUERE *wyth the* PRIEST.

URE Fa-ther which arte in hea-ven, hal-low-ed, &c.

PRIEST.   O   Lorde   o - pen   thou   my   lippes.

ANSWER.   And   my   mouth   ſhal   ſhew   forth   thy   praiſe.

PRIEST.   GOD   make   ſpede   to   ſave   me.

ANSWER.   O   Lorde   make   haſt   to   helpe   me.

PRIEST.   Glo - ry   be   to   the Father and to the Sonne, and to the

* It is to be remarked that the sentences from scripture, one or more whereof the minister at his discretion is directed to recite; the exhortation, general confession, and absolution, with which the order of Common Prayer now begins, were no part of King Edward's liturgy, but were first inserted in that of Queen Elizabeth.

† It is true that that uniform kind of intonation above described, especially in the precatory parts of divine service, is liable to exception, as being void of that energy which some think proper in the utterance of prayer; yet when it is considered that the inflexions of the human voice are so various with respect to tone and cadence, that no two persons can in strictness be said to read alike, and that scarce any thing is more offensive to a nice and discerning ear than false emphasis or an affected pathos, it may well be questioned whether a grave and decent monotony is not upon the whole the best form of utterance, at least in public worship, as well for the other parts of the service required to be read, as the prayers.

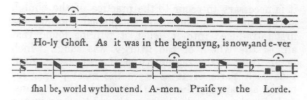

Ho-ly Ghoſt. As it was in the beginnyng, is now, and e-ver

ſhal be, world wythout end. A-men. Praiſe ye the Lorde.

The manner of intonating the psalms is directed to be the same as of the hymn Venite exultemus, the notes whereof are as follow :—

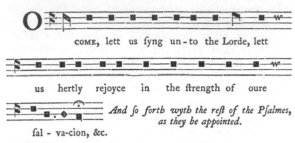

come, lett us ſyng un-to the Lorde, lett

us hertly rejoyce in the ſtrength of oure

And ſo forth wyth the reſt of the Pſalmes, as they be appointed.

ſal - va-cion, &c.

Next follows the Te Deum, which being a hymn of praise, deviates more from that tone of audible reading directed by the rubric than the preceding parts of the mattin-service. The Benedictus, which is directed to follow the second lesson, is noted in a different manner ; in short, it is set to a chanting tune, which is iterated as the several verses return. The same hymn, Benedictus, is set to other notes, but still in the form of a chant, and either of these, at the election of the priest, are allowed to be sung.*

Then follow the Kyrie and Christe Eleyson, and after them the Apostles' Creed and Lord's Prayer, both of which are intonated in C fa ut ; but in the intonation of the latter this particular is remarkable ; it is directed to be sung by the choir with the priest to the clause, 'And lead us not into temptation,' which the priest sings alone, and is answered by the choir in the last clause. The versicles,† responses, and collects follow immediately after ; the whole is thus intonated :—

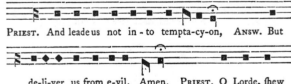

Priest. And leade us not in-to tempta-cy-on, Answ. But

de-li-ver us from e-vil. Amen. Priest. O Lorde, ſhew

* The practice of Chanting the Psalms, which doubtless is meant to imitate the ancient antiphonal singing instituted by Flavianus and Diodorus, is supposed to have had its rise at this time. In the English Psalter, to facilitate the practice of chanting, the text is constantly pointed in a manner no way reconcileable with the rules of Orthography, that is to say, with a colon as near the middle of the verse as possible, without the least regard had to the sense of it, as here, 'I am well 'pleased: that the Lord hath heard the voice of my prayer.' 'O how 'amiable are thy dwellings: thou Lord of hosts!' 'Behold now, 'praise the Lord: all the servants of the Lord.'

The Psalter referred to by the common prayer to be read in the daily service, is taken from the great Bible translated by Miles Coverdale and others ; and in the title page thereof the psalms are said to be pointed as they are to be sung or said in churches. In the great Bible the method of punctuation is that which the sense requires, but in the Psalter from queen Elizabeth's time downwards, the psalms are pointed in the manner above described. For the rule of chanting, before each verse of the psalm was thus divided, we are to seek.

† The versicles 'O Lord open thou my lips, &c.' and the responses are by the old church musicians improperly termed *Preces;* and the versicles 'The Lord be with you, &c.' with their answers, preceding the litany, *Responses.* Vide The first Book of selected Church-Music published by John Barnard, Lond. 1641, fol. 83. 91.

thy mercy up-on us, Answ. And graunt us thy ſalva-ci-on.

Priest. O Lorde ſave the kyng. Answ. And mercifully heare

us when we call up-on thee. Priest. Indue thy miniſters

with righteouſnes. Answ. And make thy cho-ſen peo-ple

joyfull. Priest. O Lorde ſave thy pe-ple, Answ. And

bleſſe thyne inheritaunce. Priest. Give peace in our tyme

O Lord ; Answ. Becauſe there is none other that fighteth

for us, but onely thou O God. Priest. O God make clene

our hertes within us, Answ. And take not thine Ho - ly

Spi-rit from us. Priest. The Lord be with you. Answ. And

wyth thy ſpirit. Priest. Let us pray. *After the Collect for the day, theſe that follow :—*

God, which arte auƈthor of peace and lover of concorde,

in know - ledge of whom ſtandeth our eternal life, whoſe ſervice is perfeƈte fredom : Defend us thy humble ſervauntes in all aſſaultes of our enemies, that we ſurely truſting in thy defence, maye not feare the power of any adverſaries : Through the might

of Je - ſu Chriſt oure Lorde. Answ. A - men.

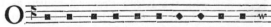

Lorde our heavenlye fa - ther, al - migh - tie

and everlyvyng God, which has ſafely brought us to the begynnyng of thys daye : defend us in the ſame wyth thy myghtye power, and graunt that this day we fall into no ſynne, neither runne into any kinde of daunger, but that all oure doynges may be ordred by thy governaunce, to do alwayes that is righteous in thy ſight :

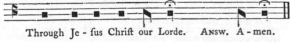

Through Je - ſus Chriſt our Lorde. Answ. A - men.

And thus, ſaith the book, endeth Mattyns.

CHAP. CXIII.

THE Even-song, as it stood in the first liturgy of Edward VI. is noted in like manner. The versicles and responses, which are here called suffrages, correspond very nearly with the form of singing them at this day.

The hymn Benedicite, and the Athanasian Creed, which are occasionally sung in the morning service, appear also in this work of Marbeck with music of his composing.

In the Communion service occurs, first the Introite, which is thus intonated :—

THE INTROITE.

At the Communion.

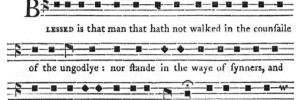

LESSED is that man that hath not walked in the counfaile

of the ungodlye : nor ftande in the waye of fynners, and

hath not fyt in the feate of the fcornefull, But his delight is, &c.

Then the Kyrie, intonated in the key of F FA UT :—

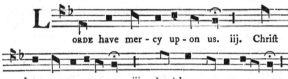

ORDE have mer - cy up-on us. iij. Chrift

have mer-cy up-on us. iij. Lord have mer-cy up-on us.

The Gloria in excelcis and Creed are composed as melodies, as are also the Offertories to the number of fifteen : The common and proper prefaces for Christmas, Easter, and Ascension days, and for Whit-Sundays and Trinity Sundays, follow next in order, and after them the Sanctus.*

SANCTUS.

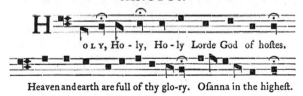

O L Y, Ho - ly, Ho - ly Lorde God of hoftes.

Heaven and earth are full of thy glo-ry. Ofanna in the higheft.

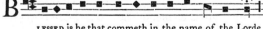

LESSED is he that commeth in the name of the Lorde :

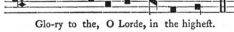

Glo-ry to the, O Lorde, in the higheft.

The prayer for the whole state of Christ's church, which has since been altered into a prayer for the whole state of Christ's church militant here on earth, with the last clause, is intonated in A RE, a fifth

---

* The SANCTUS is part of the communion office ; nevertheless in Cathedrals, on Sundays and high festivals it is constantly sung at the end of morning prayer, and before that part of the service which is read by the Episteller and Gospeller while they are making their approach to the communion table.

---

above D SOL RE, the final note of the Sanctus. Then follows a prayer for the blessing of the Holy Spirit on the elements, with the intonation of the last clause, versicles, and responses, the Lord's prayer, Agnus Dei, Post-communions, and a thanksgiving ; which several parts of the service are either wholly omitted, or greatly altered in the liturgy of Elizabeth. These are chiefly noted as melodies. Marbeck's book contains also an office at the burial of the dead, which differs greatly from that now in use.

The objections of particular persons, and the censure of the thirty-two commissioners in the Reformatio Legum Ecclesiasticarum against curious singing had made it necessary that the new service should be plain and edifying. In order that it should be so, this of Marbeck was framed according to the model of the Greek and Latin churches, and agreeable to that tonal melody, which the ancient fathers of the church have celebrated as completely adequate to all the ends of prayer, praise, thanksgiving, and every other mode of religious worship.

The interval between the framing the first liturgy of Edward VI. and the setting it to musical notes, was but a year at most. It appears that at this time, besides an establishment of household musicians, consisting of singers and players on sundry different instruments, there was also one of gentlemen and children of the royal chapel, which had subsisted in succession from the time of Edward IV. The following is a list of both, with the salaries or stipends of the several officers as it stood in the reign of Edward VI :—†

MUSITIONS and PLAYERS.

			£.	s.	d.
Trumpeters. Serjeante.	Benedict Browne	- - Fee	24	6	8
Trumpeters.	in No. 16, every of them having by the yere £24 6s. 8d. - -	- Fee	389	6	8
Luters.	Philip Van Welder - Peter Van Welder	- Fee	40	0	0
Harpers.	William Moore - Bernard de Ponte	- Fee - Fee	18 20	5 0	0 0
Singers.	Thomas Kent - Thomas Bowde -	- Fee - Fee	9 9	2 2	6 6
Rebeck.	John Severnecke	- Fee	24	6	8
Sagbutts in number 6, whereof	5 having £24 6s. 8d. by the yeere, and one at £36 10s. - -	- Fee	158	3	4
Vyalls in number 8, whereof	6 at £30 8s. 4d. the yeere, and one at £20, and another at £18 5s.	- Fee	220	15	0
Bagpiper.	Richard Woodward -	- Fee	12	3	4
Minstrelles in number 9, whereof	7 at £18 5s. a peece - 1 at £24 6s. 8d. - 1 at £3 6s. 8d. -	- Fee - Fee - Fee	127 24 3	15 6 6	0 8 8
Dromslades‡ in number 3, whereof	Robert Bruer, Master drummer Alexander Pencax - John Hodgkin -	Fee - Fee - Fee	18 18 18	5 5 5	0 0 5
Players on the flutes.	Oliver Rampons Pier Guye -	- Fee - Fee	18 34	5 8	0 4
Players on virginals	John Heywoode - Anthony de Chounte - Robert Bewman -	- Fee - Fee - Fee	50 30 12	0 8 3	0 4 4

† Vide extract from the Liber Niger Domus Regis at page 271, et seq.
‡ DRUMSLADE, idem quod DRUMMER, Minsh.

Musicians Straungers	{ the 4 brethren Venetians, viz., John, Anthonye Jasper, and Baptiste - } Fee	16	6	8
	Augustine Bassane - - Fee	36	10	0
	William Trosses - - Fee	38	0	0
	William Denivat - - Fee	38	0	0
Players of interludes in number 8	{ every of them at £3 6s. 8d. by yeere £26 13s. 4d. in Camera 7, £23 6d. 8d. in Sccio one £3 6s. 8d. - } Fee	26	13	4
Makers of instruments.	{ William Beton Organ-maker } - - Fee	20	0	0
	{ William Tresorer Regal-maker } - - Fee	10	0	0

Summa totalis　　　1732　5　0

Total number of persons　73

OFFICERS OF THE CHAPPELL.

		£	s.	d.				
Master of the children, Richard Bowyer	{ Fee - - -	40	0	0	}			
	Largesse to the children at high feasts -	9	13	4	} 65	13	4	
	Allowance for breakfast for the children	16	0	0	}			

Gentlemen of the chappell 32, every of them 7d. ob. a day.	Emery Tuckfield	John Kye			
	Nich. Archibald	John Angel			
	William Walker	William Huchins			
	R. Chamberleyn	Robert Phelipps			
	W. Gravesend	Thomas Birde			
	Richard Bowyer	Robert Perry			
	William Barber	Thomas Wayte			
	R. Richmounte	THOMAS TALLES	}	365	0 0
	Nicholas Mellowe	Thomas Wright			
	John Bendebow	Robert Stone			
	William Mawpley	J. SHEPHARDE			
	George Edwards	WIL. HYNNES or HUNNIS			
	Robert Morecock	Thomas Manne			
	R. Alyeworth	Roger Kenton			
	T. Palfreman	Lucas Caustell			
	RICHARD FARRANT	Edward Addams			

2 at 4d. ob. a day either of them	13	13	9	}		
5 at 4d. the daye every of them	30	8	4	} 46	2	1
Hugh Williams at 40s. a yeere	2	0	0	}		

Summa totalis　　　476　15　5

1732	5	0	Musicians	Number of persons 73
476	15	5	Officers of the Chappell	Number of persons 41
2209	0	5	Total of both	114

But all the labour and pains that had been bestowed in settling a ritual for the protestant service, were rendered vain; and the hopes that had been entertained of seeing the reformation of religion perfected, were defeated by the death of the king in 1553, and the succession to the throne of the lady Mary, from whose bigotry and natural gloominess of temper the protestants had every thing to fear. It is sufficiently known that this event was attended not only with an immediate recognition of the papal authority, but with the restoration of the Romish ritual, and that the zeal of this princess to undo all that had been done in the preceding reigns of her father and brother, was indefatigable. In particular she seems to have sedulously laboured the re-establishment of the Romish choral service, and directed the republication of a great number of Latin service-books,

among which were the Primer, Manual, Breviary and others, in Usum Sarum, which were reprinted at London by Grafton, Wayland, and other of the old printers, with the musical notes, for the use of her chapel.[*]

CHAP. CXIV.

The accession of Elizabeth to the throne in 1558, was followed by an act of parliament, entitled an Act for the uniformity of the common prayer and service in the church, and administration of the sacraments, which, after reciting that at the death of Edward VI. there remained one uniform order of common service and prayer, which had been set forth and authorized by an act of the parliament holden in the 5th and 6th years of his reign, and that the same had been repealed by an act of parliament in the first year of queen Mary, to the great decay of the due honour of God, and discomfort to the professors of the trueth of Christes religion, Doth enact 'That the said statute of repeal, and every thing 'therein contained, only concerning the saide booke 'and service, &c. shall be void. And that all 'ministers shall be bounden to say and use the 'Mattens, Evensong, celebration of the Lord's sup-'per, and administration of the sacraments in such 'order and form as is mentioned in the said booke 'so authorized by parliament in the fifth and sixth 'yere of the reigne of king Edward VI. with one 'alteration or addition of certaine lessens to be used 'on every Sunday in the yere, and the forme of the 'Letanie altered and corrected, and two sentences 'onely added in the deliverie of the sacrament to the 'communicants, and none other.'

By this statute the second liturgy of Edward VI with a few variations, was restored; but here we may note that correction of the litany which is referred to by the statute, for it indicates a temper less irascible than that which actuated the first reformers In the litany of Henry VIII. continued in both the liturgies of Edward, is contained the following prayer: 'From all sedition and privy con-'spiracy, *from the tyranny of the bishop of Rome* '*and all his detestable enormities*; from all false 'doctrine and heresy, from hardness of heart, and 'contempt of thy word and commandment. Good 'Lord deliver us;' taken, with a very small variation, from this in the litany of the Lutherans, 'Ut ab 'hostium tuorum, Turcæ, et Papæ blasphemiis, cæde 'et libidinibus clementer nos conservare digneris.'[†]

The correction above-mentioned consisted in the recision of so much of the prayer for deliverance from sedition, &c. as related to the bishop of Rome and all his detestable enormities, as they are termed, and the addition of the words rebellion and schism, which are now a part of the prayer.

It is said of Elizabeth, that being a lover of state

[*] It is worthy of remark, that notwithstanding the fundamental difference in religion and the form of public worship in the two reigns, it appears by a record now in the possession of the Antiquarian Society, that with the variety of only a very few names, the list of Mary's chapel establishment was the same with that above given of her brother Edward's.

[†] In Psalmod. sive cant. sacra. vet. Eccles. select. per Luc. Lossium Luneberg.

and magnificence, she was secretly a friend, though not to the doctrines,* yet to the pomp and splendor of the Romish religion, and consequently to the ancient form of worship; and from principles of policy she might wish that the difference between the reformed and the Romish service might be as little as possible ;† the effects of this disposition were visible in the reluctance with which she gave up the use of images and prayers for the dead, and the behaviour of those of the Romish communion, who made no scruple of attending the service of a church which had wrested the supremacy out of the hands of the pope.‡

At the beginning of her reign, those divines who had fled from the persecution under Mary, to Francfort, and other parts of Germany, and to Geneva, and had contracted a dislike to the discipline established in England, together with some of the principal courtiers, made some faint attempts towards a revival of the opposition to choral service; they insisted that the psalms of David in metre, set to plain and easy melodies, were sufficient for the purposes of edification; and for this they appealed to the authority of Calvin, and the practice of the churches under his direction. But the queen, and those to whom she had committed the care of revising the liturgy, thought that the foreign divines had already meddled more in these matters than

* Nevertheless she seems to have entertained some opinions, which none of the reformed churches would ever acquiesce in. When one of her chaplains, Mr. Alexander Nowel, dean of St. Paul's, had spoken less reverently in a sermon preached before her, of the sign of the cross than she liked, she called aloud to him from her closet window, commanding him to retire from that ungodly digression, and return to his text. And when one of her divines, on Good Friday, anno 1565, had preached a sermon in defence of the real presence, she openly gave him thanks for his pains and piety. Heylin's History of the Reformation, Eliz. pag. 124. It seems that when she gave that shrewd answer to a Popish priest, who pressed her very hard to declare her opinion touching the presence of Christ in the sacrament :—

    'Twas God the word that spake it,
      He took the bread and brake it;
    And what the word did make it;
      That I believe, and take it.

she had either not settled, or was too wise to declare, her opinion touching the doctrine of transubstantiation.

† It is certain she had a crucifix in her chapel. See a letter from Sandys, bishop of Worcester, to Peter Martyr, expressing his uneasiness at it. Burn. Reform. III. 289, 291, and Records to book VI. No. 61. Heylin says that it remained there for some years, till it was broken to pieces by Patch the fool, no wiser man daring to undertake such a desperate service, at the solicitation of Sir Francis Knolles, a near relation of the queen. Heylin's Hist. of the Reformation, Eliz. pag. 124. Neal goes much farther, and says 'that the altar was furnished with rich 'plate, with two gilt candlesticks, with lighted candles, and a massy 'crucifix in the midst, and that the service was sung not only with 'organs, but with the artificial music of cornets, sacbuts, &c. on solemn 'festivals. That the ceremonies observed by the knights of the garter 'in their adoration towards the alter, which had been abolished by 'Edward VI. and revived by queen Mary, were retained. That, in 'short, the service performed in the queen's chapel, and in sundry 'cathedrals, was so splendid and showy, that foreigners could not dis-'tinguish it from the Roman, except that it was performed in the 'English tongue.' By this method, he adds, most of the Popish laity were deceived into conformity, and came regularly to church for nine or ten years, till the pope, being out of all hopes of an accommodation, forbad them, by excommunicating the queen, and laying the whole kingdom under an interdict. Hist. of the Puritans, vol. I. page 156.

‡ This fact is rather invidiously mentioned by Neal in the passage cited from him in the preceding note; the authority for it is a letter from the queen to Sir Francis Walsyngham, dated 11. Aug. 1570, in which she says of the Roman Catholics, 'that they did ordinarily resort from 'the beginning of her reign in all open places to the churches, and to 'divine services in the church, without contradiction or shew of mis-'liking:' to the same purpose Sir Edward Coke, in a charge of his at Norwich assizes, asserted that for the first ten years of queen Elizabeth's reign the Roman Catholics came frequently to church; and in his speech against Garnet, and other conspirators, he affirmed this upon his own knowledge, giving an instance thereof in Bedingfield, Cornwallis, and several others of the Romish persuasion. Collier's Ecclesiast. Hist. vol. II. pag. 436.

became them; the common prayer of her brother had been once altered to please Calvin, Bucer, Fagius, and others of them, and she seemed determined to make no more concessions, at least to that side, and therefore insisted on the retention of the solemn church service.

The declaration of her will and pleasure in this respect is contained in the forty-ninth of those injunctions concerning the clergy and laity of this realm, which were published by her in the first year of her reign, A. D. 1559; they were printed first by Jugge and Cawood, and are to be found in Sparrow's Collection of Articles, Injunctions, and Canons, in quarto, 1684. That above referred to, entitled 'for 'continuance of syngynge in the church,' is in the words following :—

'Item, becaufe in dyvers collegiate, and alfo fome 'parifhe churches, there hath been lyvynges appoynted 'for the mayntenaunce of menne and chyldren, to ufe 'fyngynge in the churche, by meanes whereof the 'lawdable fcyence of muficke hath ben had in eftima-'tion, and preferved in knowledge: The queenes 'majeftie, neyther meanynge in any wife the decaye of 'any thynge that myght conveniently tende to the ufe 'and continuance of the faide fcience, neyther to have 'the fame in any parte fo abufed in the churche, that 'thereby the common prayer fhoulde be the worfe 'underftande of the hearers: Wylleth and commandeth 'that fyrft no alteration be made of fuch affignementes 'of lyvynge as heretofore hath been appointed to the 'ufe of fyngynge or muficke in the churche, but that 'the fame fo remayne. And that there bee a modefte 'and deyftynéte fong fo ufed in all partes of the com-'mon prayers in the churche, that the fame may be as 'playnely underftanded as yf it were read without 'fyngyng. And yet neverthelesse for the comforting 'of fuch as delite in muficke, it may be permytted that 'in the begynninge or in thend of common prayers, 'either at mornynge or evenynge, there may be funge 'an hymne or fuch lyke fonge, to the prayfe of Al-'mighty God, in the beft forte of melodye and muficke 'that may be convenienty devyfed, havynge refpeéte 'that the fentence of the hymme may bee underftanded 'and perceyved.'

And yet, notwithstanding this express declaration of the queen's pleasure with regard to continuance of singing in the church, about three years after the publishing these her injunctions, six articles, tending to a farther reformation of the liturgy, were presented to the lower house of convocation, the last whereof was that the use of organs be removed from churches; which, after great debate, were so near being carried, that the rejection of them was owing to a single vote, and that, too, by the proxy of an absent member.§ Bishop Burnet has given from Strype, but without a direction where they are to be found, the heads of another proposal for a reformation, wherein it is insisted that organs and curious singing should be removed.‖

In the resolution which queen Elizabeth maintained to continue the solemn musical service in the church,

§ Burn. Hist. Reform. part III. pag. 303.   ‖ Ibid. 304.

it is supposed she was confirmed by Parker, whom she had then lately promoted to the see of Canterbury, a man of great learning and abilities, and, as it happened, eminently skilled in music. Strype, in his life of this prelate, says he had been taught in his youth to sing by one Love, a priest, and also by one Manthorp, clerk of St. Stephen's in Norwich. In his retirement from the persecution under queen Mary he translated into English verse the whole book of the psalms of David. In the foundation of his college at Stoke in Suffolk is a provision for queristers. He had a considerable hand in revising the liturgy of queen Elizabeth. Some of the particulars above related afford ground for a conjecture that Parker's affection to music might co-operate with his zeal for the church, and induce him to join with Elizabeth in her endeavours to reform the choral service, and consequently that its re-establishment was in some degree owing to him.

By the passing of the act of uniformity of the first of Eliz. cap 2, the common prayer and communion service were restored by such words of reference to the usage in her brother Edward's time, as would well warrant the use of that music which Marbeck had adapted to them; for which reason, and because it had been printed under the sanction of royal authority, the Booke of Common Praier noted by John Marbecke, was considered as the general formula of choral service : and to the end that the whole should be uniform and consistent, it is directed by the rubric of Elizabeth's liturgy, that in such places where they do sing, those portions of scripture which constitute the lessons for the day, as also the epistles and gospels, shall be sung in a plain tune, after the manner of distinct reading; the meaning whereof seems to be, that they should be uttered in a kind of monotony, with a reference to the dominant or key-note of the service, which for the most part lay in C FA UT, that being nearly the mean tone of a tenor voice : and most of the printed collections of services give as well the intonation of the lessons, as the melodies of the hymns and evangelical songs.

The settlement of religion, and the perfecting of the reformation, as it was of the utmost importance to the peace of the kingdom, and coincided with the queen's opinion, so was it the first great object of her attention. She succeeded to the crown on the seventeenth day of November, in the year 1558; on the twenty-eighth of April, 1559, the bill for the uniformity of the common prayer passed into a law, and was to take effect on the twenty-fourth day of June then next. Hitherto the Romish office was permitted to continue, the Latin mass-book remained, and the priests celebrated divine service for the most part as they had done in the time of queen Mary, during which interval were great and earnest disputes between the Protestant and Romish clergy touching the English service-book. It seems that the queen was so eager to hear the reformed service, that she anticipated its restoration; for whereas the act required that it should take place throughout the kingdom on St. John the Baptist's day, service in English was performed in her chapel on Sunday, May

the second,* which was but four days after the use of it was enacted.

The liturgy of queen Elizabeth was printed in the first year of its establishment with this title, ' The ' Boke of common prayer and administration of the ' sacraments, and other rites and ceremonies of the ' church of England;' and the license contained in the rubrics, which declare that it may be said or sung, and direct that in choirs and places where they sing, the anthem shall follow certain parts of the service, is a plain intimation that this form of divine worship was calculated as well for choral as parochial service. The queen's injunctions, and also the act of uniformity, amounted to a tacit recognition of a solemn choral service; and under the authority of these, that of Marbeck was sung in the several choirs throughout the kingdom, but it was soon found that this formula, excellent as it was in its kind, was not adequate to all the purposes of framing it. In short, it was mere melody; the people, whose ears had been accustomed, as the homily above-cited expresses it, to piping, singing, chanting, and playing on the organs, could but ill brook the loss of those incentives to devotion; and in the comparison, which they could not but make between the pomp and splendour of the old form of worship, and the plainness and simplicity of the new, they were not a little disposed to prefer the former; the consideration whereof was probably the motive to the publication in the year 1560 of a musical service with this title, ' Certaine notes set forth in foure and ' three parts, to be song at the morning, communion, ' and evening praier, very necessarie for the church ' of Christe to be frequented and used : and unto them ' added divers godly praiers and psalmes in the like ' forme to the honor and praise of God. Imprinted ' at London, over Aldersgate, beneath S. Martins, by ' John Day, 1560.'

It does not appear by this book that any innovation was made in the service as formerly set to musical notes by Marbeck, and there is good reason to suppose that the supplications, responses, and method of intonating the Psalms, remained the same as he composed them. But it is to be remarked, that although the litany made a part of king Edward's first liturgy,† Marbeck had omitted or purposely forborne to set musical notes to it; and this is the rather to be wondered at, seeing that it was the ancient practice of the church, founded on the example of St. Gregory himself, to sing it; this omission however was soon supplied by the composer, whoever he was, of the

* Strype, in his Annals. vol. I. pag. 191, says the twelfth of May; but in this he must be mistaken, he having before, viz., pag. 77, said that the bill passed April the twenty-eighth. By a passage in the same volume of the Annals, page 134, it seems that the practice of singing psalms in churches had its rise a few months after, for he says ' On the   day of ' this month, September, [1559] began the true morning prayer at St. ' Antholin's, London, the bell beginning to ring at five, when a psalm ' was sung after the Geneva fashion, all the congregation, men, women, ' and boys singing together.'
Bishop Juel, in a letter written in March, 1560, seems to allude to this fact; his words are, ' the singing of psalms was begun in one church in ' London, and did quickly spread itself, not only through the city, but in ' the neighbouring places: sometimes at St. Paul's Cross there will be ' 6000 people singing together.' Vide Burnet Hist. Reform. part III. pag. 290. The foreign protestants had distinguished themselves by this practice some years before. Roger Ascham, in a letter from Augusta in Germany, dated 14 Maii, 1551, says ' three or four thousand, singing at a time in one church of that city is but a trifle.' Ascham's Works, published by James Bennet, 4to. pag. 382.
† See the twenty-second of king Edward's Injunctions.

litany in the book above described, and afterwards by Tallis, who composed the litany known by his name, which, by reason of its superior excellence, is the only one of many that have been made, that is used at this day. The great difference between Day's first book and that of Marbeck appears to be this. In Marbeck's the whole of the service was set to music of one single part, whereas in that published by Day, the offices in general were composed in four parts; the following is the order in which they stand, Venite exultemus, Te Deum laudamus, Benedictus Dominus, the Letanie, the Lorde's Praier; the Communion office, containing the Kyries after the commandments, Gloria in excelsis, Nicene Creed, Sanctus, the blessing of the minister upon the people.

The offices in the order of evening prayer set to music are only the Magnificat and Nunc dimittis.

Besides these, the book contains sundry prayers and anthems, composed also in four parts, in many of which this particular is remarkable, that the bass part is set for children.

The book also gives the names of many of those that composed the music; but it is to be observed that the litany has no name to it, neither does it in the least correspond with the litany of Tallis, so that we may suppose that he had not then set that office to music. Besides the name of Tallis, which occurs first at the end of the prayer ' Heare the voice and ' prayer of thy servants,' &c. we have these that follow. Thomas Cawston, M. [for Master] Johnson, Oakland, Shepard; and near the end of the book is inserted an In Nomine of Master Taverner, the bass part for children.

Five years after this, was published another collection of offices, with musical notes, with the following title, ' Mornyng and Evenyng prayer and Com-'munion set forthe in foure partes, to be song in ' churches, both for men and children, with dyvers ' other godly prayers and anthems of sundry men's ' doynges. Imprinted at London by John Day, 1565.'

The names of musicians that occur in this latter collection are Thomas Cawston, Heath, Robert Hasleton, Knight, Johnson, Tallis, Oakland, and Shepard.

Each of these works must be considered as a noble acquisition to the science of music; and had but the thought of printing them in score also occurred to those who directed the publication, the world had reaped the benefit of their good intentions even at this day; but being published as they are in separate parts, the consequence was that they could not long be kept together; and the books are now so dispersed, that it is a question whether a complete set of all the parts of either of these two collections is now to be found: and a farther misfortune is, that few persons are sufficiently skilled in music to see the evil of separating the parts of music books, or to attempt the retrieving them when once scattered abroad; on the contrary, many learned men have taken a single part for the whole of a musical work, and have thought themselves happy in the possession of a book of far less value than a mutilated statue. A single part of the Cantiones of Tallis and Bird, with the word Discantus at the top of the title-page, to dis-

tinguish it from the Superius, Medius, Bassus, and other parts, was in the possession of the late Dr. Ward, Gresham professor of rhetoric; and he, though one of the best grammarians of his time, mistook that for part of the title, and has given it accordingly. In like manner, Ames, a man of singular industry and intelligence in matters that relate to printing, having in his possession the Morning and Evening Prayer of 1565, above mentioned, has described it in his Typographical Antiquities by the title of the Common Prayer with musical notes Secundus Contratenor, never imagining that these two latter words were no part of the title, and that he had only one fourth part of a work which appeared to him to be complete.

Nevertheless the public were great gainers by the setting forth of the two collections of church-music above mentioned in print, one advantage whereof was, that the compositions therein contained were, by means of the press, secured against that corruption which inevitably attends the multiplication of copies of books by writing; and although it may be said of ancient manuscripts in general, that they are far more correctly and beautifully written than any since the invention of printing, it is easy to see that the increase of written copies must necessarily have been the propagation of error; and the fact is, that the ancient church-services, which before this time had been usually copied by monks and singing-men for the use of their respective churches, were, till they were corrected, and the text fixed by printed copies, so full of errors as to be scarce fit for use.

CHAP. CXV.

THUS was the solemn choral service established on a legal foundation, and the people not only acquiesced in it, but thought it a happy temperature between the extremes of superstition and fanaticism; but the disciplinarian controversy, which had its rise in the preceding reign, and had been set on foot at Francfort and Geneva, whither many able divines had fled to avoid persecution, was pushed with great vehemence by some, who insisted on a farther reformation in matters of religion than had as yet taken place; these were the men called Puritans, of whom the leader at that time was one Thomas Cartwright.

This man, a bachelor of Divinity, a fellow of Trinity college, Cambridge, and Lady Margaret's professor in that university, in his public lectures, read in the year 1570, had objected to the doctrine and discipline of the church. Against the tenets of Cartwright, Dr. Whitgift, afterwards archbishop of Canterbury, preached; Cartwright challenged the doctor to a public disputation, which the latter refused unless he had the queen's licence for it; he however offered a private conference with him in writing, which the other declining, Whitgift collected from his lectures some of the most exceptionable propositions, and sent them to the queen, upon which Cartwright was deprived of his fellowship, and expelled the university. He then went abroad, and became minister to the English merchants at

Antwerp, and afterwards at Middleburg; in his absence the Puritans had drawn up a book entitled An Admonition to the Parliament, containing an enumeration of their grievances, the authors whereof, two Puritan ministers, Mr. Field and Mr. Wilcox, were committed to Newgate; soon after this, Cartwright returned, and drew up a second admonition,* upon which a controversy ensued, wherein Cartwright maintained that the holy scriptures 'were not only 'a standard of doctrine, but of discipline and govern- 'ment, and that the church of Christ in all ages was 'to be regulated by them.'

Whitgift on the other hand asserted, that though the holy scriptures are a perfect rule of faith, they were not designed as a standard of church discipline or government; but that the forms of these are changeable, and may be accommodated to the civil government we live under: That the apostolical government was adapted to the church in its infancy, and under persecution, but was to be enlarged and altered as the church grew to maturity, and had the civil magistrate on its side.

In the course of this dispute, objections were made to the liturgy, and to the form and manner of cathe- dral service, particularly against 'the tossing the psalms from one side to the other,' a sarcastical expression which Cartwright frequently uses, with the intermingling of organs. Whitgift had defended this practice by the example of the primitive Chris- tians, and upon the general principle that the church had a power to decree rites and ceremonies agreeably to the twentieth article of the church of England; and here the dispute rested for some time;† but

it was afterwards revived by Walter Travers, the lecturer at the Temple, a friend of Cartwright; and a formal examination and refutation of his tenets was undertaken by the learned and excellent Hooker, who at that time was Master of the Temple.

In the Ecclesiastical Polity, the objections of Cartwright and his adherents against the doctrine and discipline of the established church, are occa- sionally inserted in the margin of the book, but, which seems a strange omission in the publishers of it, without any reference to the particular book of Cartwright, to which it was an answer, or any in- timation that he was the oppugner of Cartwright, other than the letters T. C. the initials of his Christian and surname, which are added to the several passages cited by Hooker.

The objections against singing in general, and also against antiphonal singing, are to this purpose: 'From whencesoever the practice [of antiphonal 'singing] came, it cannot be good, considering that 'when it is granted that it is lawfull for all the 'people to praise God by singing the Psalms of 'David, this ought not to be restrained to those few 'of the congregation who are retained in the service 'of the church for the sole purpose of singing; and 'where it is lawfull both with heart and voice to 'sing the whole psalm, there it is not meet that they 'should sing but the one half with their heart and 'voice, and the other with their heart only. For 'where they may both with heart and voice sing, 'there the heart is not enough; and therefore, besides 'the incommoding which cometh this way, in that 'being tossed after this sort, men cannot understand 'what is sung; those other two inconveniences come 'of this form of singing, and therefore it is banished 'in all reformed churches. And elsewhere, The 'singing of psalms by course, and side after side, 'although it be very ancient, yet it is not commendable,

* Fuller seems to be mistaken in his assertion that Cartwright drew up the first admonition; Neal ascribes it to the two persons above- named: both admonitions were rejected by the parliament; but the Puritans met with such favour from some of the members, that upon the dissolution of it, they presumed to erect a presbytery at Wands- worth in Surrey; this was in 1572, and from hence the origin of nonconformist or dissenting meeting-houses in this kingdom is to be computed. Vide Fuller's Church Hist. of Britain, Cent. XVI. book ix. pag. 103.

† It appears that Cartwright prosecuted this dispute many years after his return from abroad; and that in September, 1590, he was convened before the ecclesiastical commissioners; and for refusing to take the oath ex officio, was committed to the Fleet [Collier Eccl. Hist. vol. II. 626.] but was afterwards pardoned, and retired to an hospital at Warwick, of which he was master, and lived in friendship with the archbishop ever after. [Ib. 640.] Life of Hooker, 14. Nay, it is said that he changed his opinion, and sorely lamented the unnecessary troubles he had caused in the church by the schism which he had been the great fomenter of. Biogr. Brit. vol. VI. part II. pag. 4253. note KKK.

Contemporary with Cartwright was Robert Brown, a man descended of a good family in Rutlandshire, and a distant relation of the lord treasurer Burleigh; this man, though bred in Bennet college, Cambridge, entertaining a dislike to the doctrine and discipline of the established church, left England, and joined Cartwright's congregation at Middle- burg, and, being a man of bold temper and turbulent disposition, laboured with all his might to widen the breach that Cartwright had made between the Puritans and the church, and to multiply the reasons against conformity; to this end he contended that church government was antichristian, that the rites of the church of England were super- stitious, and its liturgy a mixture of popery and paganism: a summary of his doctrines, which are said to be the same in effect with those of the Donatists, is contained in a book printed by him at Middleburg, intitled a Treatise of Reformation, of which many copies were dispersed in England.

Returning hither soon after the publication of his book, Brown, together with one Richard Harrison, a country school-master, associated himself with some Dutchmen of the Anabaptist sect, and began a formal schism, in which he succeeded so well, that many separate congregations were set up in divers parts of the kingdom; at length his behaviour drew on him the censures of the church, which brought him to a partial recantation of his opinions, and procured him a benefice in Northampton- shire; but he soon after relapsed, and in an advanced age died in North- ampton gaol, to which prison he had been committed for a breach of the peace, not being able to find sureties for his keeping it. Fuller, who was acquainted with him, and had heard him preach, gives the following circumstantial relation of the causes and manner of his commitment and death.

'As for his death in the prison of Northampton many years after, in

'the reign of king Charles, anno 1630, it nothing related to those opinions 'he did, or his followers do maintain, for, as I am credibly informed, 'being by the constable of the parish, who chanced also to be his god- 'son, somewhat roughly and rudely required the payment of a rate, he 'hapned in passion to strike him. The constable not taking it patiently 'as a castigation from a god-father, but in anger, as an affront to his 'office, complained to Sir Rowland St. John, a neighbouring justice of 'the peace, and Brown is brought before him. The knight of himself 'was prone rather to pity and pardon than punish his passion, but 'Brown's behaviour was so stubborn, that he appeared obstinately 'ambitious of a prison, as desirous after long absence to renew his 'familiarity with his ancient acquaintance. His mittimus is made, and 'a cart with a feather-bed provided to carry him, he himself being too 'infirme (above eighty) to goe, too unweldie to ride, and no friend so 'favourable as to purchase for him a more comly conveyance. To North- 'ampton jayle he is sent, where soon after he sickned, died, and was 'buried in a neighbouring churchyard; and it is no hurt to wish that his 'bad opinions had been interred with him.' Church Hist. Cent. XVI. book ix. page 168.

The same author relates that he boasted he had been committed to thirty-two prisons, some of them so dark, that in them he was not able to see his hand at noon-day.

The opinions which Brown had propagated were those which dis- tinguished that religious sect, who after him were called Brownists. Not only Fuller and Collier, but Neal also represent him as a man of an idle and dissolute life, in no respect resembling either Cartwright or Travers, who dissented upon principle, and appear both, to have been very learned and pious men. These men were the first of those who opposed the liturgy, and were the occasion of those admirable arguments of Hooker in defence of church music, which here follow.

There is a passage in one of Howel's letters which seems to indicate that the tenets of Brown were grown very odious at the time when the former wrote, which for the singularity of it take in his own words:—

'Difference in opinion may work a disaffection in me, but not a detes- 'tation; I rather pitty than hate Turk or Infidell, for they are the same 'metall, and bear the same stamp as I do, though the inscriptions differ: 'if I hate any it is those schismatics that puzzle the sweet peace of our 'church, so that I could be content to see an Anabaptist go to hell on 'a Brownist's back.' Familiar Letters of James Howel, 1678, vol. I. sect. 6. Letter xxxii. To Sir Ed. B. Knt.

'and is so much the more to be suspected, for that
'the Devil hath gone about to get it so great
'authority, partly by deriving it from Ignatius time,
'and partly in making the world believe that this
'came from heaven, and that the angels were heard
'to sing after this sort, which as it is a mere fable,
'so is it confuted by historiographers, whereof some
'ascribe the beginning of this to Damasus, some other
'unto Flavianus and Diodorus.'

These are the principal arguments brought in
proof of the unlawfulness and impropriety of choral
antiphonal singing in the worship of God; in answer
to which it may be said, that its lawfulness, propriety,
and conduciveness to the ends of edification, have
been asserted by a great number of men, each as
fitly qualified to determine on a subject of this nature
as the ablest of their opponents. But the merits of
the controversy will best appear from that defence
of the practice in question contained in the Ecclesiastical Polity, of our countryman Hooker, who with
his usual temper, learning, eloquence, and sagacity, has
exhibited first a very fine eulogium on music itself,
and afterwards a defence of that particular application of it to divine service, which our national
church had recognized, and which it concerned him
to vindicate.

And first as to music in general, and its efficacy in
the exciting of devout affections, he uses these words:—

'Touching musical harmony, whether by instru-
'ment or by voice, it being but of high and low in
'sounds, a due proportionable disposition, such not-
'withstanding is the force thereof, and so pleasing
'effects it hath in that very part of man which is
'most divine, that some have been thereby induced
'to think that the soul itself by nature is, or hath in
'it harmony. A thing which delighteth all ages,
'and beseemeth all states; a thing as seasonable in
'grief as in joy; as decent, being added unto actions
'of greatest weight and solemnity, as being used
'when men most sequester themselves from action:
'the reason hereof is an admirable facility which
'music hath to express and represent to the mind
'more inwardly than any other sensible mean, the
'very standing, rising, and falling, the very steps
'and inflections every way, the turns and varieties of
'all passions whereunto the mind is subject; yea, so
'to imitate them, that whether it resemble unto us
'the same state wherein our minds already are, or
'a clean contrary, we are not more contentedly by
'the one confirmed, than changed and led away by
'the other. In harmony the very image and character
'even of virtue and vice is perceived, the mind de-
'lighted with their resemblances, and brought, by
'having them often iterated, into a love of the things
'themselves; for which cause there is nothing more
'contagious and pestilent than some kinds of har-
'mony, than some nothing more strong and potent
'unto good. And that there is such a difference of
'one kind from another we need no proof but our
'own experience, inasmuch as we are at the hearing
'of some more inclined unto sorrow and heaviness,
'of some more mollified and softened in mind; one
'kind apter to stay and settle us, another to move

'and stir our affections. There is that draweth to
'a marvellous grave and sober mediocrity; there is
'also that carrieth as it were into ecstasies, filling the
'mind with an heavenly joy, and for the time in
'a manner severing it from the body. So that al-
'though we lay altogether aside the consideration of
'ditty or matter, the very harmony of sounds being
'framed in due sort, and carried from the ear to
'the spiritual faculties of our souls, is, by a native
'puissance and efficacy, greatly available to bring to
'a perfect temper whatsoever is there troubled; apt
'as well to quicken the spirits, as to allay that which
'is too eager; sovereign against melancholy and
'despair; forceable to draw forth tears of devotion,
'if the mind be such as can yield them; able both to
'move and to moderate all affections. The prophet
'David having therefore singular knowledge, not in
'poetry alone, but in music also, judged them both
'to be things most necessary for the house of God,
'left behind him to that purpose a number of divinely
'indicted poems; and was farther the author of add-
'ing unto poetry, melody in public prayer, melody
'both vocal and instrumental for the raising up of
'men's hearts, and the sweetening of their affections
'towards God. In which considerations the church
'of Christ doth likewise at this present day retain it
'as an ornament to God's service, and an help to our
'own devotion. They which, under pretence of the
'law ceremonial abrogated, require the abrogation of
'instrumental music, approving nevertheless the use
'of vocal melody to remain, must shew some reason
'wherefore the one should be thought a legal cere-
'mony and not the other. In church music curiosity
'and ostentation of art, wanton, or light, or unsuitable
'harmony, such as only pleaseth the ear, and doth
'not naturally serve to the very kind and degree of
'those impressions, which the matter that goeth with
'it leaveth or is apt to leave in men's minds, doth
'rather blemish and disgrace that we do, than add
'either beauty or furtherance unto it. On the other
'side, these faults prevented the force and efficacy of
'the thing itself, when it drowneth not utterly, but
'fitly suiteth with matter altogether sounding to the
'praise of God, is in truth most admirable, and doth
'much edify, if not the understanding, because it
'teacheth not, yet surely the affection, because there-
'in it worketh much. They must have hearts very
'dry and tough, from whom the melody of the psalms
'doth not some time draw that wherein a mind re-
'ligiously affected, delighteth.' *

And to the objection against antiphonal singing,
'that the Devil hath gone about to get it authority,'
he thus answers:—

'Whosoever were the author, whatsoever the
'time, whencesoever the example of beginning this
'custome in the church of Christ; sith we are wont
'to suspect things only before tryal, and afterwards
'either to approve them as good, or if we find them
'evil, accordingly to judge of them; their counsel
'must need seem very unseasonable, who advise men
'now to suspect that wherewith the world hath had
'by their own account, twelve hundred years ac-

* Eccl. Polity, book V. sect. 38.

'quaintance and upwards; enough to take away
'suspicion and jealousie. Men know by this time,
'if ever they will know, whether it be good or evil
'which hath been so long retained. As for the
'Devil, which way it should greatly benefit him to
'have this manner of singing psalms accounted an
'invention of Ignatius, or an imitation of the angels
'of heaven, we do not well understand. But we
'very well see in them who thus plead, a wonderful
'celerity of discourse. For perceiving at the first,
'but only some cause of suspicion, and fear lest it
'should be evil, they are presently in one and the
'selfsame breath resolved that what beginning soever
'it had, there is no possibility it should be good.
'The potent arguments which did thus suddenly
'break in upon and overcome them, are First, that
'it is not unlawful for the people, all jointly to
'praise God in singing of psalms. Secondly, that
'they are not any where forbidden by the law of
'God to sing every verse of the whole psalm both
'with heart and voice quite and clean through-
'out. Thirdly, that it cannot be understood what is
'sung after our manner. Of which three, forasmuch
'as lawfulness to sing one way, proveth not another
'way inconvenient; the former two are true allega-
'tions, but they lack strength to accomplish their
'desire; the third so strong that it might persuade
'if the truth thereof were not doubtful. And shall
'this enforce us to banish a thing which all Christian
'churches in the world have received? a thing which
'so many ages have held: a thing which the most
'approved councils and laws have so oftentimes
'ratified; a thing which was never found to have
'any inconvenience in it; a thing which always
'heretofore the best men and wisest governours of
'God's people did think they never could commend
'enough; a thing which as Basil was persuaded did
'both strengthen the meditation of those holy words
'which are uttered in that sort, and serve also to
'make attentive, and to raise up the hearts of men;
'a thing whereunto God's people of old did resort
'with hope and thirst; that thereby, especially their
'souls might be edified; a thing which filleth the
'mind with comfort and heavenly delight, stirreth
'up fragrant desires and affections correspondent
'unto that which the words contain; allayeth all
'kind of base and earthly cogitations, banisheth and
'driveth away those evil secret suggestions which
'our invisible enemy is always apt to minister,
'watereth the heart to the end that it may fructify,
'maketh the virtuous, in trouble full of magnanimity
'and courage, serveth as a most approved remedy
'against all doleful and heavy accidents which be-
'fall men in this present life. To conclude, so
'fitly accordeth with the apostle's own exhortation,
"Speak to yourselves in psalms and hymns and
"spiritual songs, making melody and singing to the
"Lord in your hearts;" that surely there is more
'cause to fear lest the want thereof be a maim, than
'the use a blemish to the service of God.'*

As to the merits of this controversy, every one is
at liberty to judge; and if any shall doubt at the

* Eccl. Polity, book V. sect. 39.

lawfulness and expediency of choral music after considering the arguments on both sides, there is little
hope of their being reconciled to it till an abler advocate than Hooker shall arise in its defence.

The form and manner of divine service being thus
far adjusted, an establishment of a chapel seemed to
follow as a matter of course, the settlement whereof
was attended with but very little difficulty. As
those gentlemen of the chapel who had served under
Edward VI. continued in their stations notwithstanding the revival of the mass, so when the Romish
service was abrogated, and the English liturgy restored, they manifested a disposition to submit to
those who seemed to be better judges of religious
matters than themselves; and notwithstanding that
in the time of queen Mary all persons engaged in the
chapel service must, at least in appearance, have been
papists, we find not that any of them objected to the
reformed service: this at least is certain, that both
Tallis and Bird, the former of whom had set the
music to many Latin motets, and the latter made
sundry masses and other compositions for queen
Mary's chapel, continued in the service of Elizabeth,
the one till the time of his death, and the other
during the whole of her reign, and the greater part
of that of her successor, he dying in 1623.

For the state of queen Elizabeth's chapel we are
in a great measure to seek: it is certain that Tallis
and Bird were organists of it, and that Richard
Bowyer was upon her accession to the crown continued one of the gentlemen of her chapel, who
dying, Richard Edwards was appointed master of
the children. This person, who has been mentioned
in a former part of this work, was a native of
Somersetshire, and a scholar of Corpus Christi college in Oxford, under George Etheridge, and at the
time of its foundation was made senior student of
Christ Church college, being then twenty-four years
of age. Wood, in the Athen. Oxon. has given a
curious account of the representation of a comedy of
his writing, entitled Palemon and Arcite, before
queen Elizabeth, in the hall of Christ Church college,
and of the queen's behaviour on the occasion. Edwards died on the thirty-first day of October, 1596;
and the fifteenth of November in the same year
William Hunnis, a gentleman of the chapel, and who
had been in that station during the two preceding
reigns, was appointed his successor; this person died
on the sixth day of June, 1597, and was succeeded by
Dr. Nathaniel Giles, of whom an account will hereafter
be given.

CHAP. CXVI.

IT will now be thought time to enquire into the
rise and progress of psalmody in England; nor will
it be said that we were very remiss when it is known
how short the interval was, between the publication
of the French version and ours by Sternhold and
Hopkins, who as having been fellow-labourers in
this work of Reformation, are so yoked together,
that hardly any one mentions them asunder.

Thomas Sternhold is said to have been a native of
Hampshire. Where he received the rudiments of

literature is not known, but Wood says that he resided some time in the university of Oxford, and that he left it without the honour of a degree. By some interest that he had at court, he was preferred to the office of groom of the robes to Henry VIII. which he discharged so well, that he became a personal favourite of the king, who by his will left him a legacy of an hundred marks. Upon the decease of the king, Sternhold was continued in the same employment by his successor,; and having leisure to pursue his studies, he acquired some degree of esteem about the court for his vein in poetry and other trivial learning. He was a man of a very religious turn of mind, in his morals irreproachable, and an adherent to the principles of the reformation, and being offended with the amorous and immodest songs, which were then the usual entertainment of persons about the court, he undertook to translate the Psalms of David into English metre, but he died without completing the work. His will was proved the twelfth day of September, anno 1549; he is therein styled Groom of his Majesty's robes, and it thereby appears that he died seised of lands to a considerable value in Hampshire and in the county of Cornwall.

Fifty-one of the Psalms were all that Sternhold lived to versify and these were first printed by Edward Whitchurch, and published anno 1549, with the following title: 'All such Psalmes of David 'as Thomas Sternholde, late grome of the kinges 'majestyes robes did in his lyfe-tyme drawe into 'Englyshe metre.' The book is dedicated to king Edward VI. by the author, and was therefore probably prepared by him for the press. *In the dedication it is said that the king took pleasure in hearing these Psalms sung to him.* Wood is mistaken in saying that Sternhold caused musical notes to be set to his Psalms; they were published in 1549 and 1552, without notes; and the first edition of the Psalms with notes is that of 1562, mentioned hereafter.*

Ames takes notice of another work of the same author, entitled 'Certayne chapters of the Proverbs 'of Solomon drawen into metre;' this also was a posthumous publication, it being printed anno 1551, two years after Sternhold's decease.†

Contemporary with Sternhold was John Hopkins, originally a school-master, a man rather more esteemed for his poetical talents than his coadjutor: he turned

* It is worthy of remark that both in France and England the Psalms were first translated into vulgar metre by laymen, and, which is very singular, by courtiers. Marot was of the bed-chamber to Francis I. and Sternhold groom of the robes to Henry VIII and Edward VI; their respective translations were not completed by themselves, and yet they translated nearly an equal number of psalms, that is to say, Marot fifty, and Sternhold fifty-one.

† In the same year was published 'Certain Psalmes chosen out of the 'Psalmes of David, commonly called vii penytentiall Psalmes, drawen 'into Englyshe meter by Sir Thomas Wyat, Knyght, whereunto is added 'a prologe of the auctore before every Psalme, very pleasant and profett- 'able to the godly reader. Imprinted at London, in Paules churchyarde, 'at the sygne of the Starre, by Thomas Raynald and John Harryngton, 'cum previlegio ad imprimendum solum, MDXLIX. The last day of 'December.'
And in 1550, 'Certayne Psalmes chosen out of the Psalter of David, 'and drawen furth into Engiysh meter by William Hunnis, servant to 'the ryght honorable Syr William Harberde, knight. Newly collected 'and imprinted. Imprynted at London in Aldersgate strete, by the wydowe of John Herforde for John Harrington, the yeare of our Lord 'M D and L. Cum privilegio ad imprimendum solum.'

into metre fifty-eight of the Psalms, which are distinguished by the initial letters of his name. Bishop Tanner styles him, 'Poeta, ut ea ferebant tempora, eximius;' and at the end of the Latin commendatory verses prefixed to Fox's Acts and Monuments, are some stanzas of his that fully justify this character.

William Whittyngham had also a hand in this version of the Psalms; he was a man of great learning, and one of those English divines that resided abroad during the persecution under queen Mary; preferring the order and discipline of the Genevan church to that of Francfort, whither he first fled; he chose the latter city for the place of his abode, and became a favourite of Calvin, from whom he received ordination. He assisted in the translation of the Bible by Coverdale, Goodman and others, and translated into English metre those Psalms, in number only five, which in our version bear the initials of his name; among these is the hundred and nineteenth, which is full as long as twenty of the others. He also versified the Decalogue, and the prayer immediately after it, and very probably the Lord's Prayer, the Creed, and the hymn Veni Creator, all which follow the singing psalms in our version. He was afterwards, by the favour of Robert earl of Leicester, promoted to the deanery of Durham; and might, if he had made the best of his interest, have succeeded Sir William Cecil, afterwards Lord Burleigh, in the employment of secretary of state. Wood, who has raked together many particulars concerning him, relates that he caused the image of St. Cuthbert, in the cathedral church of Durham, to be broke to pieces, and that he defaced many ancient monuments in that church.‡

The letter N. is also prefixed to twenty-seven of the Psalms in our English version; this is intended to denote Thomas Norton, of Sharpenhoe in Bedfordshire, a barrister, and, in Wood's phrase, a forward and busy Calvinist in the beginning of queen Elizabeth's reign, a man then accounted eminent for his poetry and making of tragedies. Of his merit in which kind of writing he has left us no proofs excepting the three first acts of a tragedy, at first printed with the title of Ferrex and Porrex, but better known by that of Gorbuduc, which it now bears, the latter two acts whereof were written by Thomas Sackville, lord Buckhurst earl of Dorset, lord high treasurer in the reign of James I. and the founder of the present Dorset family. This performance is highly commended by Sir Philip Sidney in his Defence of Poesy, and is too well known to need a more particular character.

Robert Wisdome translated into metre the twenty-fifth psalm, and wrote also that prayer in metre at the end of our version, the first stanza whereof is:—

'Preserve us Lord by thy dear word,
'From Pope and Turk defend us Lord,
'Which both would thrust out of his throne
'Our Lord Jesus Christ thy deare son.'

For which he has been ridiculed by the facetious bishop Corbet and others, though Wood gives him the character of a good Latin and English poet for

‡ Athen. Oxon. col. 195.

his time. He adds, that he had been in exile in queen Mary's reign; that he was rector of Settrington in Yorkshire, and also archdeacon of Ely, and had been nominated to a bishoprick in Ireland, temp. Edward VI. and that he died 1568.

The 70, 104, 112, 113, 122, 125, and 134 Psalms are distinguished by the initials W. K. *These denote William Keshe, a Scotch divine. See Warton's History of English Poetry, Vol. III. pag. 418, in note. Psalm 136 has the letters T. C., but for the name of this person we are to seek.*

The first publication of a complete version of the Psalms was by John Day, in 1562, it bears this title: 'The whole booke of Psalmes, collected into 'English metre by T. Sternhold, J. Hopkins, and 'others, conferred with the Ebrue; with apt notes to sing them withall.'*

* Another version of the Psalms, and that a complete one, but very little known, is extant, the work of archbishop Parker during his exile. In the diary of that prelate printed from his own manuscript, in Strype's life of archbishop Parker is the following memorandum:—'And still this '6 Aug. [his birth day] An. Dom. 1557, I persist in the same constancy 'upholden by the grace and goodness of my Lord and Saviour Jesus 'Christ, by whose inspiration I have finished the book of Psalms turned 'into vulgar verse.'

Strype says, 'What became of the Psalms I know not;' nevertheless it seems that they were printed, and that with the following title:—'The 'whole Psalter translated into English Metre, which contayneth an 'hundreth and fifty Psalmes. "Quoniam omnis terre Deus: Psallite "sapienter—Psal. 47. Imprinted at London by John Daye, dwelling over "Aldersgate beneath S. Martyn's." without a date. In a copy of this book, very richly bound, which was bought at the sale of the late Mr. West's library, is a memorandum on a spare leaf in the hand-writing of Dr. White Kennet, bishop of Peterborough, purporting that the archbishop printed this book of Psalms, and that though he forbore to publish it with his name, he suffered his wife to present the book fairly bound to several of the nobility; Dr. Kennet therefore conjectures that the very book in which this memorandum is made, is one of the copies so presented; and gives for a reason that he himself presented a like copy to the wife of archbishop Wake, wherein Margaret Parker in her own name and hand dedicates the book to a noble lady. Signed Wh. Peterb.

After the preface, which is in metre, and directs the singing of the psalms distinctly and audibly, is a declaration of the virtue of psalms in metre, and the self-same directions from St. Athanasius for the choice of psalms for particular occasions, as are prefixed to the version of Sternhold and Hopkins, and the rest, and at the conclusion of each psalm is a collect. They are printed without music, save that at the end are eight tunes in four parts, Meane, Contratenor, Tenor, and Basse, which, agreeably to the practice of the Romish church, are composed in the eight ecclesiastical tones, the tenor being the plain-song. It is said by Strype that Parker in the course of his education had been instructed in the practice of singing by two several persons, the one named Love, a priest, the other one Manthorp, clerk of St. Stephen's in Norwich, of the harshness of both which masters he felt so much, that he could never forget it. His affection to music in his mature age may be inferred from the provision made by him in the foundation of a school in the college of Stoke, in the county of Suffolk, of which he was dean; in which the scholars, besides grammar, and other studies of humanity, were taught to sing and play on the organ and other instruments: and also from the statutes of the same college, framed by himself, the last whereof is in these words: 'Item, to be found in the college henceforth 'a number of queristers, to the number of eight or ten or more, as may 'be born conveniently of the stock, to have sufficient meat, drink, broth, 'and learning. Of which said queristers, after their breasts be changed, 'we will the most apt of wit and capacity be helpen with exhibition of 'forty shillings, four marks, or three pounds a-piece to be students in 'some college in Cambridge. The exhibition to be enjoyed but six years.'

And that he had some skill in music appears by the following characteristic of the ecclesiastical tones, prefixed to the eight tunes abovementioned.

The nature of the eyght tunes.

1. The first is meeke: devout to see,
2. The second sad: in majesty.
3. The third doth rage: and roughly brayth,
4. The fourth doth fawne: and flattry playth,
5. The fifth deligth: and laugheth the more,
6. The sixt bewayleth: it weepeth full sore,
7. The seventh tredeth stoute: in froward race
8. The eighte goeth milde: in modest pace.

The Tenor of these partes be for the people when they will syng alone, the other partes put for the greater queers, or to suche as will syng or play them privately.

It is conjectured that the Psalms thus translated, with tunes adapted to them, were intended by the author to be sung in cathedrals, for at the

Notwithstanding some of these persons are celebrated for their learning, it is to be presumed that they followed the method of Marot, and rendered the Hebrew into English through the medium of a prose translation: the original motive to this undertaking was not solely the introduction of psalm-singing into the English protestant churches; it had also for its object the exclusion of that ribaldry which was the entertainment of the common people, and the furnishing them with such songs as might not only tend to reform their manners, but inspire them with sentiments of devotion and godliness; and indeed nothing less than this can be inferred from that declaration of the design of setting them forth, contained in the title-page of our common version, and which has been continued in all the printed copies from the time of its first publication to this day: 'Set forth and allowed to be sung in churches 'of the people together, before and after evening 'prayer, as also before and after sermon; and more-'over in private houses, for their godly solace and 'comfort, laying apart all ungodly songs and ballads, 'which tend only to the nourishment of vice and 'corrupting of youth.'

There is good reason to believe that the design of the reformers of our church was in a great measure answered by the publication of the Psalms in this manner; to facilitate the use of them they were

time when they were turned into verse, the church were put to great shifts, the compositions to English words being at that time too few to furnish out a musical service; and this is the more probable from the directions given for singing many of them by the rectors and the quier alternately. Who we are to understand by the rectors it is hard to say, there being no such officer at this time in any cathedral in this kingdom. If the word were of the singular number it might be interpreted chanter. These directions seem to indicate that till some time after queen Elizabeth's accession, the form and method of choral service was not settled, nor that distinction made between the singers on the dean's side and that of the chanter, which at this day is observed in all cathedrals.

Archbishop Parker's version of the Psalms may be deemed a great typographical curiosity, inasmuch as it seems to have never been published, otherwise than by being presented to his friends, it is therefore not to be wondered that it never fell in the way either of Strype, who wrote his life, or of Mr. Ames, that diligent collector of typographical antiquities. As to the book itself, the merits of it may be judged of by the following version of Psalm xxiii. extracted from it:—

The Lord so good: who geveth me food
　　My shepeheard is and guide:
How can I want: or suffer scant
　　Whan he defendth my side.

To feede my neede: he will me lead,
　　In pastures greene and fat:
He forth brought me in libertie,
　　To waters delicate.

My soule and hart: he did convert,
　　To me he sheweth the path:
Of right wisenes: in holines,
　　His name such vertue hath.

Yea though I go: through Death hys wo
　　His vaale and shadow wyde:
I feare no dart: wyth me thou art,
　　With staff and rod to guide.

Thou shalt provyde: a table wyde,
　　For me agaynst theyr spite:
With oyle my head: thou hast bespred,
　　My cup is fully dight.

Thy goodnes yet: and mercy great,
　　Will kepe me all my dayes:
In house to dwell: in rest full well,
　　Wyth God I hope alwayes.

printed ' with apt notes to sing them withall ; '* and from thenceforth the practice of psalm-singing became the common exercise of such devout persons as attended to the exhortation of the apostle ; ' if any was ' afflicted, he prayed ; if merry, he sang psalms.'

To enquire into the merits of this our translation might seem an invidious task, were it not that the subject has employed the pens of some very good judges of English poesy, whose sentiments are collected in a subsequent page : it may here suffice to

* To the earlier impressions of the Psalms in metre was prefixed a treatise, said to be made by St. Athanasius, concerning the use and virtues of the Psalms, wherein, among many other, are the following directions for the choice of psalms for particular occasions and exigencies.

' If thou wouldst at any time describe a blessed man, who is he, and ' what thing maketh him so to be: thou hast the 1, 32, 41, 112, 128 ' psalmes.

' If that thou seest that evill men lay snares for thee, and therefore ' desirest God's eares to heare thy praiers, sing the 5 psalme.

' If so again thou wilt sing in giving thanks to God for the prosperous ' gathering of thy frutes, use the 8 psalme.

' If thou desirest to know who is a citizen of heaven, sing the 15 ' psalme.

' If thine enemies cluster against thee, and go about with their bloody ' hand to destroy thee, go not thou about by man's helpe to revenge it, ' for al mens judgments are not trustie, but require God to be judge, for ' he alone is judge, and say the 26, 35, 43 psalmes.

' If they presse more fiercelie on thee, though they be in numbers like ' an armed hoast, fear them not which thus reject thee, as though thou ' wert not annointed and elect by God, but sing the 27 psalme.

' If they be yet so impudent that they lay wait against thee, so that it ' is not lawfull for thee to have any vocation by them, regard them not, ' but sing to God the 48 psalme.

' If thou beholdest such as be baptized, and so delivered from the ' corruption of their birth, praise thou the bountifull grace of God, and ' sing the 32 psalme.

' If thou delightest to sing amongst many, call together righteous men of godlie life, and sing the 33 psalme.

' If thou seest how wicked men do much wickednesse, and that yet ' simple folke praise such, when thou wilt admonish any man not to ' follow them, to bee like unto them, because they shall be shortly rooted ' out and destroid : speake unto thyselfe and to others the 37 psalme.

' If thou wouldst call upon the blind world for their wrong confidence ' of their brute sacrifices, and shew them what sacrifice God most hath ' required of them, sing the 50 psalme.

' If thou hast suffered false accusation before the king, and seest the ' divel to triumph thereat, go aside and say the 52 psalme.

' If they which persecute thee with accusations would betray thee, as ' the Phariseis did Jesus, and as the aliens did David, discomfort not ' thyselfe therewith, but sing in good hope to God, the 54, 69, 57 psalmes.

' If thou wilt rebuke Painims and heretiks, for that they have not the ' knowledge of God in them, thou maist have an understanding to sing ' to God the 86, 115 psalmes.

' If thou art elect out of low degree, especially before others to some ' vocation to serve thy brethren, advance not thyselfe too high against ' them in thine own power, but give God his glorie who did chuse thee, ' and sing thou the 145 psalme.'

The effects of these directions may be judged of by the propensity of the people, manifested in sundry instances to the exercise of psalm-singing.

The Protestants who fled from the persecution of the duke de Alva in Flanders, were mostly woollen manufacturers. Upon their arrival in England they settled in Gloucestershire, Somersetshire, Wiltshire, and a few other counties, where they distinguished themselves by their love of Psalmody. ' Would I were a weaver,' says Sir John Falstaff, [in Henry IV. part I. the first edition] ' I could sing psalms or any thing.'

As the singing of psalms supposes some degree of skill in music, it was natural for those who were able to do it to reereate themselves with vocal music of another kind; and accordingly so early as the reign of James I. the people of these counties were, as they are at this day, expert in the singing of catches and songs in parts. Ben Jonson, in the Silent Woman, makes Cutberd tell Morose that the parson ' caught his ' cold by sitting up late, and singing catches with Clothworkers ;' and the old Gloucestershire three part song, ' The stones that built George Ridler's ' oven,' is well known in that and the adjacent counties.

And to speak of the common people in general, it may be remembered that the reading of the book of Martyrs, and the singing of psalms were the exercises of such persons of either sex, as being advanced in years, were desirous to be thought good christians ; and this not merely in country towns, villages and hamlets, where a general simplicity of manners, and perhaps the exhortations of the minister might be supposed to conduce to it, but in cities and great towns, and even in London itself; and the time is not yet out of the memory of a few persons now living, when a passenger on a Sunday evening from St. Paul's to Aldgate, would have heard the families in most of the houses in his way occupied in the singing of Psalms.

' In the year 1646, king Charles I. being in the hands of the Scots, ' a Scotch minister preached boldly before the king at Newcastle, and ' after this sermon called for the fifty-second psalm, which begins, " Why " dost thou tyrant boast thyself, thy wicked works to praise." His majesty ' thereupon stood up, and called for the fifty-sixth psalm, which begins, " Have mercy Lord on me I pray, for men would me devour." The ' people waived the minister's psalm, and sung that which the king called ' for.' Whitelocke's Memorials, 234.

say, that so far as it tends to fix the meaning of sundry words, now for no very good reasons become obsolete, or exhibits the state of English poetry at the period when it was composed, it is one of those valuable monuments of literary antiquity which none but the superficially learned would be content to want. But it seems these considerations were not of force sufficient to restrain those in authority from complying with that humour in mankind which disposes them to change, though from better to the worse ; and accordingly such alterations have at different times been made in the common metrical translations of the singing Psalms, as have frustrated the hopes of those who wished for one more elegant and less liable to exception.

Thus much may suffice for a general account of the introduction of psalmody into this kingdom, and the effects it wrought on the national manners ; the order and course of this history naturally lead to an enquiry concerning the melodies to which the Psalms are, and usually have been sung, no less particular than that already made with respect to the French psalm-tunes.

Sternhold's Psalms were first printed in the year 1549 ; and the whole version, as completed by Hopkins and others, in 1562, with this title : ' The ' whole booke of Psalmes collected into English ' metre by T. Sternhold, J. Hopkins, and others, ' conferred with the Ebrue, with apt notes to sing ' them withall.' By these apt notes we are to understand the tunes, to the number of about forty, which are to be found in that and many subsequent impressions, of one part only, and in general suited to the pitch and compass of a tenor voice, but most excellent indeed for the sweetness and gravity of their melody ; and because the number of tunes thus published was less than that of the Psalms, directions were given in cases where the metre and general import of the words allowed of it, to sing sundry of them to one tune.

The same method was observed in the several editions of the Psalms published during the reign of queen Elizabeth, particularly in those of the years 1564, and 1577, which it is to be remarked are not coeval with any of the editions of the Common Prayer, to which they are usually annexed, for which no better reason can here be assigned than that the singing psalms were never considered as part of the liturgy ; and the exclusive privilege of printing the Common Prayer was then, as it is now, enjoyed by different persons. Nor do we meet with any impression of the Psalms suited, either in the type or size of the volume, to either of the impressions of the liturgy of Edward the Sixth, published in 1549 and 1552. In short, it seems that the practice of publishing the singing psalms by way of appendix to the Book of Common Prayer, had its rise at the beginning of the reign of queen Elizabeth; for in 1562 that method was observed, and again in 1564 and 1577, but with such circumstances of diversity as require particular notice.

And first it is to be remarked that in 1576, though by a mistake of Jugge the printer, the year in the title-page is 1676, the liturgy was for the first time printed in a very small octavo size; to this are annexed Psalms of David in metre by Sternhold, Hopkins, and others, 'with apte notes to sing them withall,' imprinted by the famous John Daye, cum privilegio, 1577.

The publication of the Psalms in this manner supposed that the people, at least the better sort of them, could read; and by parity of reason it might be said that the addition of musical notes to the words implied an opinion in the publishers that they also could sing; but that they in fact did not think so at the time now spoken of, is most evident from the pains they were at in collecting together the general rudiments of song, which in the editions of 1564 and 1577, and in no other, together with the scale of music, are prefixed by way of introduction to the singing Psalms. Who it was in particular that drew up these rudiments, is as little known as the authors of the tunes themselves; they bear the title of 'A short Introduction into the Science of 'Musicke, made for such as are desirous to have the 'knowledge thereof for the singing of the Psalmes.'

As to the Introduction into the Science of Musicke, or, as it is called in the running title, 'The introduction to learn to sing,' it is not to be found in any of the impressions of the Common Prayer subsequent to that in 1577, which is the more to be wondered at, seeing the author, whoever he was, was so well persuaded of its efficacy as to assert, that 'by means 'thereof every man might in a few dayes, yea in 'a few houres, easily without all payne, and that also 'without all ayde or helpe of any other teacher, 'attain to a sufficient knowledge to singe any psalme 'contayned in the booke, or any other such playne 'and easy songes.' In which opinion the event shewed him to be grossly mistaken, as indeed, without the gift of prophesy, might have been foretold by any one who should have reflected on the labour and pains that are required to make any one a singer by notes to whom the elements of music are unknown; for in the year 1607 there came out an edition of the Psalms with the same tunes in musical notes as were contained in the former, with not only more particular directions for the sol-faing, but with the syllables actually interposed between the notes: this was in effect giving up all hope of instructing the people in the practice of singing, inasmuch as whatever they were enabled to do by means of this assistance, they did by rote.

Who was the publisher of this edition of 1607 does not appear; the title mentions only in general that it was imprinted for the company of stationers; the reasons for annexing the syllables to the notes are given at large in an anonymous preface to the reader, which is as follows :—

'Thou ſhalt underſtand (gentle reader) that I have '(for the helpe of thoſe that are deſirous to learne to 'ſing) cauſed a new print of note to be made, with 'letters to be joyned to every note, whereby thou 'maieſt know how to call every note by his right 'name, ſo that with a very little diligence (as thou art 'taught in the introduction printed heretofore in the 'Pſalmes) thou maieſt the more eaſily, by the viewing 'of theſe letters, come to the knowledge of perfect 'ſolfayeng : whereby thou maieſt ſing the Pſalmes the 'more ſpeedilie and eaſilie : the letters be theſe, U for 'Ut, R for Re, M for Mi, F for Fa, S for Sol, L for 'La. Thus where you ſee any letter joyned by the 'note, you may eaſilie call him by his right name, as 'by theſe two examples you may the better perceive :—

UT　RE　MI　FA　SOL　LA　LA　SOL　FA　MI　RE　UT

UT　RE　MI　FA　SOL　LA　FA　SOL　LA

LA　SOL　FA　LA　SOL　FA　MI　RE　UT

'Thus I commit thee unto him that liveth for ever, 'who grant that we ſing with our hearts unto the 'glorie of his holy name. Amen.'

And to exemplify the rule above given, every note of the several tunes contained in this edition has the adjunct of a letter to ascertain the sol-faing, as mentioned in the above preface.

After the publication of this edition in 1607, it seems that the company of stationers, or whoever else had the care of supplying the public with copies of the singing-psalmes, thought it best to leave the rude and unlearned to themselves, for in none of the subsequent impressions do we meet with either the introduction to music, or the anonymous preface, or, in a word, any directions for attaining to sing by notes.

CHAP. CXVII.

GREAT has been the diversity of opinions concerning the merit of this our old English translation. Wood, in the account given by him of Sternhold, says that so much of it as he wrote is truly admirable; and there are others, who reflecting on the general end of such a work, and the absolute necessity of adapting it to the capacities of the common people, have not hesitated to say that, bad as it may be in some respects, it would at this time be extremely difficult to make a translation that upon the whole should be better. Others have gone so far as to assert the poetical excellence of this version, and, taking advantage of some of those very sublime passages in the original, which are tolerably rendered, but which perhaps no translation could possibly spoil, have defied its enemies to equal it.* On the other hand, the general poverty of the style, the meanness of the images, and, above all, the awkwardness of the versification, have induced many serious persons to wish that we were fairly rid of a work, that in their opinion, tends less to promote religion than to disgrace that reformation of it, which is

* See a defence of the book of Psalms collected into English metre by Thomas Sternhold, John Hopkins, and others, &c. by bishop Beveridge. Lond. 1710.

justly esteemed one of the greatest blessings of this country.

Another, but a very different class of men from those above enumerated, the wits, as they style themselves, have been very liberal in their censure of the English version of the Psalms. Scarce ever are the names of Sternhold and Hopkins mentioned by any of them but for the purpose of ridicule. Fuller alone, of all witty men the best natured, and who never exercises his facetious talent to the injury of any one, has given an impartial character of them and their works, and recommended a revision of the whole translation against all attempts to introduce a better in its stead.* His advice was followed, though not till many years after his decease, for in an impression of the Psalms of Sternhold and Hopkins, printed in 1696, we find the version accommodated to the language of the times, by the substitution of well-known words and familiar modes of expression in the room of such as were become obsolete, or not intelligible to the generality of the common people. But as the poet, whoever he was, was at all events to mend the version, its conformity with the original, if peradventure he could read it, could be with him but a secondary consideration. Neither does it seem that he was enough acquainted with the English language to know that in the alteration of an old word for a new, the exchange is not always of the worse for the better. Hearne has given some shrewd instances of this kind in the Glossary to his Robert of Gloucester,† and very many more might be produced; however the first essay towards an emendation met with so little opposition from the people, that almost every succeeding impression of the Psalms was varied to the phrase of the day; and it is not impossible but that in time, and by imperceptible degrees, the whole version may be so innovated, as scarcely to retain a single stanza of the original, and yet be termed the work of its primitive authors.

A history of the several innovations in the metrical version of David's Psalms is not necessary in this place. It may suffice to remark, that in the first impression of the whole there is a variation from the text of Sternhold in the first stanza of the first psalm, which in the two editions of 1549 and 1552 reads thus :—

> The man is bleſt that hath not gone
> 　　By wicked rede aſtray,
> Ne ſat in chayre of peſtylence,
> 　　Nor walkte in ſynners waye.

And that the edition of 1562 stood unaltered till 1683, as appears by Guy's copy printed at Oxford in folio that year. In 1696 many different readings are found, the occasion whereof is said to be this ; about that time Mr. Nahum Tate and Dr. Nicholas Brady published a new version of part of the book of Psalms as a specimen of that version of the whole which was afterwards printed in 1696. In this essay of theirs they, in the opinion of many persons, had so much the advantage of Sternhold and Hopkins, that the company of stationers, who are possessed of the sole privilege of printing the Psalms, took the alarm, and found themselves under a necessity of meliorating the version of the latter, and for this purpose some person endued with the faculty of rhyming was employed by them in that very year 1696, to correct the versification as he should think proper ; and since that time it has been still farther varied, as appears by the edition of 1726, but with little regard to the Hebrew text, at the pleasure of the persons from time to time intrusted with the care of the publication.

The effects of these several essays towards a reformation of the singing psalms are visible in the version now in common use, which being a heterogeneous commixture of old and new words and phrases, is but little approved of by those who consider integrity of style as part of the merit of every literary composition, and the result is, that the primitive version is now become a subject of mere curiosity. The translation of the Psalms into metre was the work of men as well qualified for the undertaking as any that the times they lived in could furnish ; most of those which Norton versified, particularly psalms 109, 116, 139, 141, 145 ; and 104, 119, and 137 by Whittyngham, with a very small allowance for the times, must be deemed good, if not excellent poetry ; and if we compare the whole work with the productions of those days, it will seem that Fuller has not greatly erred in saying, that match these verses for their ages, they shall go abreast with the best poems of those times.

With respect to the version as it stands accommodated to the language of the present times, it may be said, that whatever is become of the sense, the versification is in some instances mended ; that the unmeaning monosyllable eke, a wretched contrivance to preserve an equality in the measure of different verses, is totally expunged ; that many truly obsolete words, such as *hest* for *command, mell* for *meddle, pight* for *pitched, Saw* for *Precept*, and many others that have gradually receded from their places in our language, are reprobated ; that many passages wherein the Divine Being and his actions are represented by images that derogate from his majesty, as where he is said to *bruise* the wicked with a *mace*, the weapon of a giant, are rendered less exceptionable than before ; and where he is expostulated with in ludicrous terms, as in the following passage :—

> Why dooſt withdraw thy hand aback,
> 　　And hide it in thy lappe,
> O pluck it out and be not ſlack
> 　　To give thy foes a rappe.‡

and this, which for its meanness is not to be defended :—

> For why their hearts were nothing bent
> 　　To him [*God*] nor to his trade.§

And where an expression of ridicule is too strongly pointed to justify the use of it in an address to God, as is this :—

> Confound them that apply,
> 　　And ſeeke to worke me ſhame,
> And at my harme do laugh, and cry
> 　　So, ſo, there goeth the game.‖

---

* Church Hist. of Britain, cent. XVI. book vii. pag. 406.

† Vocib. behet, rede.

‡ Psalm lxxiv. verse 12.　　§ Psalm lxxviii. verse 37.
‖ Psalm lxx. verse 3.

And where the rhymes are ill sorted like these :—

> Nor how he did commit their fruits
> Unto the caterpiller,
> And all the labour of their lands
> He gave to the grafhopper.*

And these others :—

> remembered } lord } remember }
> offended † } world ‡ } ever § }

In these several instances the present reading is to be preferred, but, after all, what a late author has said of certain of his own works, may with equal truth and propriety be applied to the language of the modern singing-psalms. 'It not only is such as 'in the present times is not uttered, but was never 'uttered in times past; and if I judge aright, will 'never be uttered in times future : it having too 'much of the language of old times to be fit for the 'present; too much of the present to have been fit 'for the old, and too much of both to be fit for any 'time to come.'

There is extant a metrical translation of the Psalms by James I. which was printed, together with the Common Prayer and Psalter, in 1636, upon the resolution taken by Charles I. to establish the liturgy in Scotland; some doubt has arisen whether this version was ever completed; but, unless credit be denied to the assertion of a king, the whole must be allowed to be the work of the reputed author, for in the printed copy, opposite the title-page is the following declaration concerning it :—

> 'Charles R.
>
> 'Having caused this translation of the Psalmes '(whereof our late dear father was author) to be 'perused, and it being found exactly and truly 'done, We do hereby authorize the same to 'be imprinted according to the patent granted 'thereupon, and do allow them to be sung in 'all the churches of our dominions, recommend-'ing them to all our good subjects for that effect.'

The Psalms have been either totally or partially versified by sundry persons, as namely, Sir Philip Sidney, Christopher Hatton, H. Dodd, Dr. Henry King, bishop of Chichester, Miles Smith, Dr. Samuel Woodford, John Milton, William Barton, Dr. Simon Ford, Sir Richard Blackmore, Dr. John Patrick, Mr. Addison, Mr. Archdeacon Daniel, Dr. Joseph Trapp, Dr. Walter Harte, Dr. Broome, and many others, learned and ingenious men, whose translations are either published separately, or lie dispersed in collections of a miscellaneous nature. There are also extant two paraphrases of the Psalms, the one by Mr. George Sandys, the other by Sir John Denham.

The foregoing account respects solely the poetry of the English Psalms, and from thence we are naturally led to an enquiry concerning the melodies to which they now are, and usually have been sung. Mention has already been made of certain of these, and that they were first published in the version of the Psalms by Sternhold and Hopkins, in the year 1562, by the name of apt notes to sing them withal, but as many of them have been altered and sophis-

* Psalm lxxviii. verse 46·
‡ Psalm lxxxiii. ver. ult.
† Psalm xiii. verse 1.
§ Psalm cxix. verse 49.

ticated, a few of them are here given as they stand in that edition, with the numbers of the psalms to which they are appropriated :—

PSALM I.

THE man is blest that hath not bent, to wicked rede his eare : Nor led his life as sinners do, nor sat in scorners chaire. But in the law of God the Lor d, doth set his whole delight : And in that lawe doth ex - er - cise himself both day and night.

PSALM XIV.

THERE is no God, as foolish men affirme in their mad moode : Their drifts are all corrupt and vayn, not one of them doth good. The Lord beheld from heaven high, the whole race of mankind : and saw not one that sought indeed, the liv-ing God to finde.

PSALM XVIII.

O God my strength and fortitude, of force I must love thee : Thou art my castle and defence in my ne-ces-si-tie. My God my rocke, in whome I trust, the worker of my wealth : My re-fuge, buckler, and my shield, The horne of all my health.

PSALM LXXII.

LORD, give thy judgments to the king, therein

instruct him well: And with his sonne, that princely

thing, Lord, let thy justice dwell. That he may governe

uprightly, and rule thy folke a-right; And so defend

through e - qui - ty, the poor that have no might.

PSALM CXXIV.

NOW Is-ra-el may say and that truely, If that

the Lord had not our cause maintayned, If that the

Lord had not our right susteined, When all the world

a-gainst us furiously, made their uprores, and sayd

we should all dye.

Besides the tunes to the psalms, there are others appropriated to the hymns and evangelical songs, such as Veni Creator, The humble Suit of a Sinner, Benedictus, Te Deum, The Song of the three Children, Magnificat, Nunc dimittis, Quicunque vult, or the Athanasian Creed, the Lamentation of a Sinner, the Lord's Prayer, the Decalogue, the Complaint of a Sinner, and Robert Wisdome's Prayer, 'Preserve us Lord by thy dear word;' all which are versified and have a place in our collection of singing psalms.

The want of bars, which are a late invention,* might make it somewhat difficult to sing these tunes in time, and the rather as no sign of the mood ever occurs at the head of the first stave; but in general the metre is a sufficient guide.

With respect to the authors of those original melodies, published in the more early impressions of the version of Sternhold and Hopkins, we are

---

* The use of bars is not to be traced higher than the time when the English translation of Adrian le Roy's book on the Tablature was published, viz., the year 1574; and it was some time after that, before the use of bars became general. To come nearer to the point, Barnard's Cathedral Music, printed in 1641, is without bars; but bars are to be found throughout the Ayres and Dialogues of Henry Lawes published in 1653, from whence it may be conjectured that we owe to Lawes this improvement.

somewhat to seek; it is probable that in so important a service as this seemed to be, the aid of the ablest professors of music was called in, and who were the most eminent of that time is easily known; but before we proceed to an enumeration of these, it is necessary to mention that some of the original melodies were indisputably the work of foreigners: the tunes to the hundredth, and to the eighty-first psalms are precisely the same with those that answer to the hundredth, and eighty-first in the psalms of Goudimel and of Claude le Jeune; and many of the rest are supposed to have come to us from the Low Countries. It is said that Dr. Pepusch was wont to assert that the hundredth psalm-tune was composed by Douland; but in this he was misunderstood, for he could hardly be ignorant of the fact just above-mentioned; nor that in some collections, particularly in that of Ravenscroft, printed in 1633, this is called the French hundredth psalm-tune; and therefore he might mean to say, not that the melody, but that the harmony was of Douland's composition, which is true. But if the insertion of this tune in the French collections be not of itself evidence, a comparison of the time when it first appeared in print in England, with that of Douland's birth, will go near to put an end to the question, and shew that he could hardly be the author of it. In the preface to a work entitled 'A Pilgrimes Solace,' published by Douland himself in 1612, he tells his reader that he is entered into the fiftieth year of his age, and consequently that he was born in 1563: now the tune in question appears in that collection of the singing-psalms above-mentioned to have been published in 1577, when he could not be much more than fourteen years old; and if, as there is reason to suppose, the tune is more ancient than 1577, the difference, whatever it be, will leave him still younger.

Of the musicians that flourished in this country about 1562, the year in which the English version of the Psalms with the musical notes first made its appearance, the principal were Dr. Christopher Tye, Marbeck, Tallis, Bird, Shephard, Parsons, and William Mundy, all men of eminent skill and abilities, and, at least for the time, adherents to the doctrines of the reformation.

There is no absolute certainty to be expected in this matter, but the reason above given is a ground for conjecture that these persons, or some of them, were the original composers of such of the melodies to the English version of the Psalms as were not taken from foreign collections; it now remains to speak of those persons who at different times composed the harmony to those melodies, and thereby fitted them for the performance of such as sung with the understanding.

The first, for aught that appears to the contrary, who attempted a work of this kind, seems to have been WILLIAM DAMON, of the queen's chapel, a man of eminence in his profession, and who as such has a place in the Bibliotheca of bishop Tanner. He it seems had been importuned by a friend to compose parts to the common church psalm-tunes; and having frequent occasion to resort to the house of this person, he so far complied with his request, as while he was there to compose one or more of the tunes at a time, till the whole was completed, intending thereby nothing more than to render them fit for the private use of him who had first moved him to the undertaking. Nevertheless this friend, without the privity of the author, thought fit to publish them with the following title :—' The Psalmes of David in Eng-' lish meter, with notes of foure partes set unto them ' by Guilielmo Daman for John Bull,* to the use of ' the godly Christians for recreating themselves, in-' stede of fond and unseemely ballades.' 1579.

It seems that neither the novelty of this work, nor the reputation of its author, which, if we may credit another and better friend of his than the former, was very great, were sufficient to recommend it : on the contrary, he had the mortification to see it neglected. For this reason he was induced to undertake the labour of recomposing parts, to the number of four, to the ancient church-melodies, as well those adapted to the hymns and spiritual songs, as the tunes to which the psalms were ordinarily sung. And this he completed in so excellent a manner, says the publisher, ' that by comparison of these and the ' former, the reader may by triall see that the auctor ' could not receive in his art such a note of disgrace ' by his friend's oversight before, but that now the ' same is taken away, and his worthy knowledge ' much more graced by this second travaile.' But the care of publishing the Psalms thus again composed, devolved to another friend of the author, William Swayne, who in the year 1591 gave them to the world, and dedicated them to the lord treasurer Burleigh. It is not impossible that either Damon himself, or his friend Swayne might buy up, or cause to be destroyed what copies of the former impression could be got at, for at this day the book is not to be found. This of 1591 bears the title of ' The former ' booke of the music of Mr. William Damon, late one ' of her Majesties musicians, conteyning all the tunes ' of David's Psalmes as they are ordinarily soung in ' the church, most excellently by him composed into ' 4 parts ; in which sett the tenor singeth the church-' tune. Published for the recreation of such as de-' lighte in musicke, by W. Swayne, Gent. Printed ' for T. Este, the assignè of W. Byrd, 1591.'

The same person also published at the same time with the same title, ' The second booke of the musicke ' of M. William Damon, containing all the tunes of ' David's Psalms, differing from the former in respect ' that the highest part singeth the church-tune.'

The tunes contained in each of these collections are neither more nor less than those in the earlier impressions of the Psalms, that is to say, exclusive of the hymns and spiritual songs, they are about forty in number ; the author has however managed, by the repetition of the words and notes, to make each tune near as long again as it stands in the original ; by which contrivance it should seem that he intended them rather for private practice than the service of the church ; which perhaps is the reason that none

* Called in the preface Citezen and Goldsmith of London : this person could not be Dr. Bull, who at this time was but sixteen years of age. Ward's Lives of Gresh. Prof. pag. 208, in not.

of them are to be found in any of those collections of the Psalms in parts composed by different authors, which began to appear about this time.

By the relation herein before given of the first publication of the Psalms in metre with musical notes, and the several melodies herein inserted, it appears that the original music to the English Psalms was of that unisonous kind, in which only a popular congregation are supposed able to join. But the science had received such considerable improvements about the beginning of the seventeenth century, and the people by that time were so much accustomed to symphoniac harmony, that a facility in singing was no longer a recommendation of church tunes.

At this time cathedral and collegiate churches, and above all, the royal chapels, were the principal seminaries of musicians. The simplicity and parsimony that distinguished the theatrical representations afforded no temptation to men of that profession to deviate from the original design of their education or employment, by lending their assistance to the stage ; the consequence hereof was, that for the most part they were men of a devout and serious turn of mind, with leisure to study, and a disposition to employ their skill in celebrating the praises of their Maker.

It was natural for men of this character to reflect that as much attention at least was due to the music of the church as had been shown to that of the chamber ; the latter had derived great advantages from the use of symphoniac harmony ; whereas the former had been at a stand for near half a century ; and though it might be a question with some, whether the singing of the Psalms in parts was not in effect an exclusion of the majority of every congregation in the kingdom from that part of divine service ; it is to be noted that neither the law nor the rubric of our liturgy gives any directions in what manner the Psalms of David are to be sung in divine service ; and that they had the example of foreign churches, particularly that of Geneva, between which and our own there was then a better understanding than is likely ever to be again, to authorize the practice.

In short, with a view to promote the practice of psalmody, as well in churches as in private houses, the most eminent musicians of queen Elizabeth's time undertook and completed a collection of the ancient church-tunes, composed in four parts, and in counterpoint. In the execution of which purpose it is plain that they had the example of Goudimel and Claude le Jeune in view ; and that their design was not an elaborate display of their own invention, in such an artificial commixture of parts, as should render these compositions the admiration of the profoundly learned in the science, but an addition of such plain and simple harmony to the common church-tunes, as might delight and edify those for whose benefit they were originally composed ; and hence arose the practice, which in many country churches prevails even at this day, of singing the Psalms, not by the whole of the congregation, but by a few select persons sufficiently skilled in music to sing each by himself, the part assigned him.

The names of those public-spirited persons who first undertook the work of composing the psalm-tunes in parts, is preserved in a collection, of which it is here meant to give more than a superficial account, as well on the score of its antiquity, as of its merit, namely, ' The whole booke of Psalmes, with their ' wonted tunes as they are sung in churches, com- ' posed into foure parts by X sondry authors; im- ' printed at London by Thomas Est, 1594.' These authors were John Douland, E. Blancks, E. Hooper, J. Farmer, R. Allison, G. Kirby, W. Cobbold, E. Johnson, and G. Farnaby, who in the title page are said to have ' so laboured in this worke that the ' unskilful by small practice may attaine to sing ' that part which is fittest for their voice.'*

The book is very neatly printed in the size and form of a small octavo, with a dedication by the printer Thomas Est, to Sir John Puckering, knight, lord keeper of the great seal of England, wherein we are told, ' that in the booke the church-tunes are ' carefully corrected, and other short tunes added, ' which are sung in London, and most places of this ' realme.'

The former publications consisting, as already has been mentioned, of the primitive melodies, and those to the amount of forty only, gave but one tune to divers psalms; this of Est appears to be as copious as need be wished, and to contain at least as many tunes as there are psalms, all of which are in four parts, in a pitch for and with the proper cliffs to denote the cantus, altus, tenor, and bass, as usual in such compositions. It is to be observed, that throughout the book the church-tune, as it is called, holds the place of the tenor; and as the structure of the compositions is plain counterpoint, the additional parts are merely auxiliary to that, which for very good reasons is and ought to be deemed the principal.

It may here be proper to remark, that although in these tunes the church-tune is strictly adhered to, so far as relates to the progression of the notes, yet here for the first time we meet with an innovation, by the substituting semitones for whole tones in almost every instance where the close is made by an ascent to the final note; or, in other words, in form- ing the cadence the authors have made use of the sharp seventh of the key; which is the more to be wondered at, because in vocal compositions of a much later date than this, we find the contrary practice to prevail; for though the coming at the close by a whole tone below be extremely offensive to a nice ear, and there seems to be a kind of necessity for the use of the acute signature to the note below the cadence, yet it seems that the ancient composers, who by the way made not so free with this character as their successors, particularly the composers of instru- mental music, left this matter to the singer, trusting that his ear would direct him in the utterance to prefer the half to the whole tone.

But these compositions, however excellent in

themselves, were not intended for those alone whose skill in the art would enable them to sing with pro- priety; they were, though elegant, simple; in short, suited to the capacities of the unlearned and the rude, who sung them then just as the unlearned and the rude of this day do.

If then it was found by experience that the com- mon ear was not a sufficient guide to the true singing of the ancient melodies, it was very natural for those who in the task they had undertaken of composing parts to them, were led to the revisal of the originals by the insertion of the character above-mentioned, to rectify an abuse in the exercise of psalm-singing, which the authors were not aware of, and consequently had not provided against.

About five years after the publication of the Psalms by Est, there appeared a collection in folio, entitled, ' The Psalmes of David in meter, the plaine song ' beinge the common tune to be sung and plaide upon ' the lute, orpharion, citterne, or base violl, severally ' or altogether, the singing part to be either tenor or ' treble to the instrument, according to the nature of ' the voyce; or for foure voyces, with tenne short ' tunes in the end, to which for the most part all the ' psalmes may be usually sung, for the use of such as ' are of mean skill, and whose leysure least serveth ' to practize. By Richard Allison, Gent. practitioner ' in the art of musicke, and are to be sold at his ' house in the Dukes place neere Aldgate. Printed ' by William Barley, the assignè of Thomas Morley, ' 1599, cum privilegio regiæ majestatis.'

The above book is dedicated ' to the right honour- ' able and most virtuous lady the lady Anne coun- ' tesse of Warwicke.' Immediately following the dedication are three copies of verses, the first by John Douland, bachelor of musicke; the second a sonnet by William Leighton, esquire, afterwards Sir William Leighton, and the third by John Welton, all in com- mendation of the author and his most excellent worke. This collection being intended chiefly for chamber practice, the four parts are so disposed in the page, as that four persons sitting round a table may sing out of the same book; and it is observable that the author has made the plain-song or church- tune the cantus part, which part being intended as well for the lute or cittern, as the voice, is given also in those characters called the tablature, which are peculiar to those instruments.

There are no original melodies in this collection: the author confining himself to the church-tunes, has taken those of the hymns and spiritual songs and psalms as they occur in the earlier editions of the version by Sternhold and Hopkins.

To this collection of Allison succeeded another in 1621, with the title of ' The whole book of Psalmes ' with the hymnes evangelicall and songs spirituall, ' composed into four parts by sundry authors, to such ' severall tunes as have beene and are usually sung ' in England, Scotland, Wales, Germany, Italy, ' France, and the Netherlands. By Thomas Ra- ' venscroft, Bachelor of Musicke,' in which is in- serted the following list of the names of the authors who composed the tunes of the psalms into four

---

* In the title-page Est is described as dwelling in Aldersgate-street, at the sign of the Black Horse. He therein styles himself the assignè of William Bird, who with Tallis, as before observed, had a joint patent from queen Elizabeth for the sole printing of music. Tallis died first, and this patent, the first of the kind, survived to Bird, who probably for a valuable consideration might assign it to Est.

parts: 'Thomas Tallis, John Douland, doctor of
'Musicke,* Thomas Morley, bachelor of Musicke,
'Giles Farnaby, bachelor of Musicke, Thomas Tom-
'kins, bachelor of Musicke, John Tomkins, bachelor
'of Musicke, Martin Pierson, bachelor of Musicke,
'William Parsons, Edmund Hooper, George Kirby,
'Edward Blancks, Richard Allison, John Farmer,
'Michael Cavendish, John Bennet, Robert Palmer,
'John Milton, Simon Stubbs, William Cranford,
'William Harrison, and Thomas Ravenscroft the
'compiler.'

In this collection, as in that of Est, the common
church-tune is the tenor part, which for distinction
sake, and to shew its pre-eminence over the rest, is
here in many instances called the tenor or plain-
song, and not unfrequently tenor or faburden.† Some
of the tunes in the former collection, as that to the
sixth psalm by George Kirby, that to the eighteenth
by William Cobbold, and that to the forty-first by
Edward Blancks, are continued in this; but the far
greater part are composed anew, and many tunes are
added, the melodies whereof are not to be found in
any other collection; and here we have the origin
of a practice respecting the names of our common
church tunes, that prevails among us to this day,
namely the distinguishing them by the name or
adjunct of a particular city, as Canterbury, York,
Rochester, and many others. It was much about
the time of the publication of this book that king
Charles I. was prevailed on by the clergy to attempt
the establishment of the liturgy in Scotland; and
perhaps it was with a view to humour the people
of that kingdom that some of these new-composed
tunes were called by the names of Dumferling,
Dundee, and Glasgow.

Among the new composed tunes in this collection,
that is to say such as have new or original melodies,
the composition of the author whose name they bear,
is that well-known one called York-tune, as also
another called Norwich-tune, to both whereof is
prefixed the name of John Milton; this person was
no other than the father of our great poet of that
name. The tune above spoken of called York-tune,
occurs in four several places in Ravenscroft's book,
for it is given to the twenty-seventh, sixty-sixth, and
one hundred and thirty-eighth psalms, and also to
a prayer to the Holy Ghost, among the spiritual
songs at the end of the book; but it is remarkable
that the author has chosen to vary the progression
of the notes of one of the parts in the repetition of the
tune; for the medius, as it stands to the words of
the one hundred and thirty-eighth psalm, and of the
prayer above-mentioned, is very different from the
same part applied to those of the twenty-seventh
and sixty-sixth.

Although the name of Tallis, to dignify the work,
stands at the head of the list of the persons who
composed the tunes in this collection, the only composition of his that occurs in it is a canon of two
parts in one, to the words 'Praise the Lord, O ye

'Gentiles;' and many of the tunes in Allison's collection are taken into this. Ravenscroft was a man
of great knowledge in his profession, and has discovered little less judgment in selecting the tunes than
the authors did in composing them.‡

Ravenscroft's book was again published in 1633,
and having passed many editions, it became the
manual of psalm-singers throughout the kingdom;
and though an incredible number of collections of
this kind have from time to time been published, the
compilations of those illiterate and conceited fellows
who call themselves singing-masters and lovers of
psalmody, and of divine music, yet even at this day
he is deemed a happy man in many places, who is
master of a genuine copy of Ravenscroft's psalms.

The design of publishing the Psalms in the manner above related was undoubtedly to preserve the
ancient church-tunes; but notwithstanding the care
that was taken in this respect, the same misfortune
attended them as had formerly befallen the ecclesiastical tones; and to this divers causes contributed,
for first, notwithstanding the pains that had been
taken by the publication of the Introduction into
the Science of Musike, prefixed to the earlier copies
of the Psalms in metre, to instruct the common
people in the practice of singing, these instructions
were in fact intelligible to very few except the minister and parish clerk, for we grossly mistake the
matter if we suppose that at that time of day many
of the congregation besides, could understand them.
In consequence of this general ignorance, the knowledge of music was not so disseminated among them
but that the poor and ruder sort fell into the usual
mistake of flat for sharp and sharp for flat.

Another cause that contributed to the corruption
and consequent disuse of the church tunes, was the
little care taken in the turbulent and distracted times
immediately following the accession of Charles I.
to appoint such persons for parish-clerks as were
capable of discharging the duty of the office. The
ninety-first of the canons, made in the year 1603,
had provided that parish-clerks should be sufficient
in reading and writing, and also of competent skill
in singing; but it is well known that instead of
rendering obedience to canons, those who at that
time were uppermost denied their efficacy. Nay, in
cases where a reason for the omission of a thing was
wanting, it was thought a good one to say that the
doing it was enjoined by the authority of the church.

The recognition of the office of a parish-clerk by
the church, and its relation to psalmody, naturally
lead us to enquire into the nature of that function,

---

* In the Fasti Oxon. it is noted that Douland was admitted to a
bachelor's degree at Oxford, 8 July 1588, but it does not appear that he
was ever created doctor.
† Of the term FABURDEN, see an explanation in page 256 of this work.

‡ It is in this collection of Ravenscroft that we first meet with the
tunes to which the Psalms are now most commonly sung in the parish
churches of this kingdom, for excepting those to the eighty-first,
hundredth, and hundred and nineteenth psalms, the ancient melodies
have given place to others of a newer and much inferior composition.
The names of these new tunes, to give them in alphabetical order,
are, Bath and Wells or Glastonbury, Bristol, Cambridge, Canterbury,
Chichester, Christ's hospital, Ely, Exeter, Gloucester, Hereford, Lincoln,
Litchfield and Coventry, London, Norwich, Oxford, Peterborough,
Rochester, Salisbury, Winchester, Windsor or Eaton, Worcester, Wol-
verhampton; and, to give what are styled northern tunes, in the same
order, they are Carlisle, Chester, Durham, Manchester, Southwell, and
York. The Scottish tunes are Abbey-tune, Duke's, Dumferling, Dundee,
Glasgow, Kings and Martyrs; and the Welch, St. Asaph, Bangor, St.
David's, Landaff, and Ludlow: so that the antiquity of these may be
traced back to the year 1621.

and the origin of the corporation of parish-clerks which has long existed in London.* Anciently parish-clerks were real clerks, but of the poorer sort; and of these every minister had at least one, to assist under him in the celebration of divine offices. By a constitution of Boniface archbishop of Canterbury, A. D. 1261, 45 Hen. III. it is ordained that the officer for the holy water shall be a poor clerk: and hence a poor clerk officiating under the minister is by the Canonists termed Aquæbajulus, a water-bearer. In the Register of archbishop Courtney the term occurs; and notwithstanding he was maintained by the parishioners, he was appointed to the office by the minister; and this right of appointment, founded on the custom of the realm, is there declared, and has in many instances been recognized by the common law. The offices in which the clerk was anciently exercised must be supposed to have respected the church-service, as the carrying and sprinkling holy water unquestionably did; and we are farther told that they were wont to attend great funerals, going before the hearse, and singing, with their surplices hanging on their arms, till they came to the church. Nevertheless we find that in the next century after making the above constitution, they were employed in ministring to the recreation, and, it may perhaps be said, in the instruction of the common people, by the exhibition of theatrical spectacles; and as touching these it seems here necessary to be somewhat particular

And first we are to know that in the infancy of the English drama, the people, instead of theatrical shows, were wont to be entertained with the re-presentation of scripture histories, or of some remarkable events taken from the legends of saints, martyrs, and confessors; and this fact is related by Fitz-Stephen, in his description of the city of London, printed in the later editions of Stow's Survey, in these words: 'Lundonia pro spectaculis theatralibus, 'pro ludis scenicis, ludos habet sanctiores, repre-'sentationes miraculorum, quæ sancti Confessores 'operati sunt, seu representationes Passionum, quibus 'claruit constantia Martyrum.'

The same author, speaking of the Wells near London, says that on the north side thereof is a well called Clarks-Well; and Stow, assigning the reason for this appellation, furnishes us with a curious fact relating to the parish-clerks of London, the subject of the present enquiry; his words are these: 'Clarks-'well took its name of the parish-clerks in London, 'who of old time were accustomed there yearly to 'assemble, and to play some large history of holy 'scripture for example, of later time, to wit, in the 'year 1390, the 14th of Richard the Second, I read 'that the parish-clerks in London on the 18th of 'July plaid Enterludes at Skinners-well near unto 'Clarks-well, which play continued three days to-'gether, the king, queen, and nobles being present. 'Also in the year 1409, the tenth of Henry the 'Fourth, they played a play at the Skinners-well,

'which lasted eight days, and was of matter from the 'creation of the world; there were to see the same 'most part of the nobles and gentiles in England.'†

It is to be remarked that Fitz-Stephen does not speak of the acting of histories as a new thing, for the passage occurs in his account of the sports and pastimes in common use among the people in his time; and therefore the antiquity of these spectacles may with good reason be extended as far back as to the time of the Conquest. Of this kind of drama there are no specimens extant so ancient as the re-presentation first above spoken of, but there are others in being, of somewhat less antiquity, from which we are enabled to form a judgment of their nature and tendency.

The anonymous author of a dialogue on old plays and old players, printed in the year 1699, speaks of a manuscript in the Cotton library, intitled in the printed catalogue 'A collection of Plays in old 'English Metre;'‡ and conjectures that this may be the very play which Stow says was acted by the parish-clerks in the reign of Henry IV. and took up eight days in the representation; and it must be confessed that the conjecture of the author above-mentioned seems to be well warranted. By the character and language of the book it seems to be upwards of three hundred years old: it begins with a general prologue, giving the arguments of forty pageants or gesticulations, which are as so many several acts or scenes representing all the histories of both Testaments, from the creation to the choosing of St. Matthias to be an apostle. The stories of the New Testament are more largely related, viz., the Annunciation, Nativity, Visitation, the Passion of our Lord, his Resurrection, and Ascension, and the choice of St. Matthias. After which is also represented the Assumption and Last Judgment. The style of these compositions is as simple and artless as can be supposed; nothing can be more so than the following dialogue :—

MARIA.

But hufband of a thyng pray you moft mekely,
I have knowing that your cofyn Ellfabeth with childe is,
That it pleafe yow to go to her haftyly:
If ought we myght comfort her it were to me blys.

JOSEPH.

A Goddys fake is fhe with child, fhe?
Than will hir hufband Zachary be mery;
In Montane they dwelle, far hencee fo mot yt be
In the city of Juda, I know it verily;
It is hence I trowe myles two a fifty,
We are like to be wery or we come of the fame;
I wole with a good wyll bleffyd wyff Mary
Now go we forth then in Goddys name, &c.

A little before the Resurrection.

Nunc dormient milites et veniet anima Christi de inferno, cum Adam et Eva, Abraham, John Baptist, et aliis.

---

† Survey of London, 4to. 1603, pag. 15.

‡ Sir William Dugdale, in his Antiquities of Warwickshire, pag. 116, cites it by the title of Ludus Coventriæ. The following is the title as it stands in the Catalogus Libror. Manuscript. Biblioth. Cotton, pag. 113. 'VIII. A Collection of Plays in old English Metre, *h. e.* Dramata sacra, 'in quibus exhibentur historiæ veteris et N. Testamenti introductis 'quasi in scenam personis illic memoratis, quas secum invicem collo-'quentes pro ingenio fingit Poeta videntur olim coram populo, sive ad 'instruendum sive ad placendum, à fratribus mendicantibus repræ-'sentata.'

ANIMA CHRISTI.

Come forth Adam and Eve with the,
And all my fryendes that herein be
In paradyfe come forth with me,
    In blyffe for to dwell :
The fende of hell that is your foo,
He fhall be wrappyd and woundyn in woo,
Fro wo to welth, now fhall ye go,
    With myrth ever mo to melle.

ADAM.

I thank the Lord of thy grete grace,
That now is forgiven my gret trefpace,
Now fhall we dwell yn blyffful place.

The last scene or pageant, which represents the day of Judgment, begins thus :—

MICHAEL.

Surgite, All men aryfe,
Venite ad judicium,
For now is fet the high juftice,
And hath affignyd the day of dome ;
Kepe you redyly to this grett affyfe,
Both grett and fmall, all and fum,
And of your anfwer you now advife,
What yow fhall fay when that yow come, &c.

Mysteries and moralites appear to have conftituted another species of the ancient drama ; the first seem to have been representations of the most interesting events in the gospel-history ; one of this kind, intitled Candlemas-Day, or the Killing of the Children of Israel, is among the Bodleian manuscripts, and was bequeathed to the university by Sir Kenelm Digby ; the name of its author was Jhan Parfre, and it appears to have been composed in the year 1512.

The subject of this drama is tragical, notwithstanding which there are in it several touches of that low humour, with which the common people are ever delighted ; for in it the poet has introduced a servant of Herod, whom he calls Watkyn the messenger. This fellow, who is represented as cruel, and at the same time a great coward, gives Herod to understand that three strangers, knights, as he calls them, had been to make coffins at Bethlehem ; upon which Herod swears he will be avenged upon Israel, and commands four of his soldiers to slay all the children they shall find within two years of age ; which Watkyn hearing, intreats of Herod first that he may be made a knight, and next that he may be permitted to join the soldiers, and assist them in the slaughter. This request being granted, a pause ensues, the reason whereof will be best understood by the following stage-direction : Here the knyghts walke abought the place till Mary and Jofeph be conveied into Egipt.

Mary and Joseph are then exhorted by an angel to fly, and they resolve on it. The speech of Joseph concludes thus :—

Mary, you to do pleafaunce without any let,
I fhall brynge forth your affe without more delay,
Ful foone Mary thereon ye fhall be fett,
And this litel child that in your wombe lay,
Take hym in your armys Mary I you pray,
And of your fwete mylke let him fowke inowe.
Mawger Herowd and his grett fray :
And as your fpoufe Mary I fhall go with you.
    This ferdell of gere I ley upon my bakke ;
Now I am redy to go from this cuntre,
All my fmale inftruments is put in my pakke.

Now go we hens, Mary it will no better be,
For drede of Herowd apaas I high me ;
Lo now is our geer truffed both more and leffe,
Mary for to plefe you with all humylite,
I fhall go before, and lede forth your affe.

           Et exeunt.

Then begins the slaughter, represented in the following dialogue :—

1 MILES.

Herke, ye wyffys, we be come your houfhold to vifite,
Though ye be never fo wrath nor wood,
With fharpe fwoords that redely wyll byte,
All your chyldren within to years age in our cruel mood
Thurghe out all Bethleem to kylle and fhed ther yong blood
As we be bound to the commaundement of the king,
Who that feith nay, we fhall make a flood
To renne in the ftretis by ther blood fhedyng.

2 MILES.

Therefor unto us make ye a delyverance
Of your yong children and that anon ;
Or ells be Mahounde we fhall geve a myfchaunce,
Our fharpe fwerds thurgh your bodies fhall goon.

WATKYN.

Therfor be ware for we wyll not leve oon
In all this cuntre that fhall us efcape,
I fhall rather flee them everych oon,
And make them to lye and mowe like an ape.

1 MULIER.

Fye on you traitors of cruel tormentrye,
Wiche with your fwerds of mortall violens——

2 MULIER.

Our young children that can no focoure but crie,
Wyll fle and devour in ther innocens.

3 MULIER.

Ye falfe traitors unto God ye do grete offens
To flee and morder yong children that in the cradell flumber ;

4 MULIER.

But we women fhall make ageyns you refiftens,
After our power your malyce to encomber.

WATKYN.

Peas you folyfhe quenys, wha fhuuld you defende,
Ageyns us armyd men in this apparaile ?
We be bold men and the kyng us ded fende,
Hedyr into this cuntre to holde with you battaile.

1 MULIER.

Fye upon thee coward : of thee I will not faile
To dubbe thee knyght with my rokke rounde,
Women be ferfe when thei lift to affaile,
Suche proude boyes to cafte to the grounde.

2 MULIER.

Avaunt, ye fkowtys, I defye you everych one,
For I wole bete you all myfelf alone.

       [*Watkyn hic occidet per se.*]

1 MULIER.

Alas, alas good cofynes, this is a forowfull peyn
To fe our dere children that be fo yong,
With thefe caytyves thus fodeynly to be flayn ;
A vengeaunce I afke on them all for this grett wrong.

2 MULIER.

And a very myfcheff mut come them amonge,
Wherefo ever thei be come or goon,
For thei have killed my yong fone John.

3 MULIER.

Goffippis, a fhamefull deth I afke upon Herowde our kyng,
That thus rygoroufly our chyldren hath flayn.

4. MULIER.

I pray God bryng hym to an ille endyng,
And in helle pytte to dwelle ever in peyn.

WATKYN.

What ye harlotts ? I have afpied certeyn
That ye be tratorys to my lord the kyng,
And therfor I am fure ye fhall have an ille endyng.

1 MULIER.

If ye abide, Watkyn, you and I fhall game
With my diftaffe that is fo rounde.

2 MULIER.

And yf I feas, thanne have I fhame,
Tyll thu be fellid down to the grounde.

3 MULIER.

And I may gete the within my bounde,
With this ftaffe I fhall make thee lame.

WATKYN.

Yee I come no more ther, be feynt Mahound,
For if I do, methynketh I fhall be made tame.

1 MULIER.

Abyde, Watkyn, I fhall make thee a knyght.

WATKYN.

Thu make me a knyght ! that were on the newe
But for fhame my trouthe I you plight,
I fhud bete your bak and fide tyll it were blewe,
But be my god Mahounde that is fo true,
My hert begynne to fayle and waxeth feynt,
Or ells be Mahounds blood ye fhuld it rue,
But ye fhall lofe your goods as traitors atteynt.

1 MULIER.

What thu jabell, canft not have do?
Thu and thi cumpany, fhall not depart,
Tyll of our diftavys ye have take part :
Therfor ley on goffippes with a mery hart,
And lett them not from us goo.

Here thei fhall bete Watkyn, and the knyghts fhall come to
refcue hym, and than thei go to Herowds hous.

Of Moralities, a fpecies of the drama differing from the former, there are many yet extant, the titles whereof may be seen in Ames's Typographical Antiquities ; the best known of them are one entitled Every Man, Lustie Juventus, and Hycke Scorner, an accurate analysis of which latter, Dr. Percy has given in his Reliques of ancient English Poetry, vol. I. pag. 130.

That such representations as these, namely, histories, mysteries, and moralities, were frequent, we may judge from the great number of them yet extant, and from the fondness which the people of this country have ever manifested for theatrical entertainments of all kinds ; and that the parish-clerks of all other persons should betake themselves to the profession of players, by exhibiting such as these to the public, will not be wondered at, when it is remembered that besides themselves, few of the laity, excepting the lawyers and physicians, were able to read ; and it might be for this reason that even the priests themselves undertook to personate a character in this kind of drama.

Of the fraternity of parish-clerks, Strype, in his edition of Stowe's Survey, book V. pag. 231, gives the following account : ' They were a guild or fra-' ternity first incorporated by K. Hen. III. known ' then by the name of the brotherhood of St. Nicholas, ' whose hall was near St. Helens by Bishopsgate ' street, within the gate, at the sign of the Angel, ' where the parish-clerks had seven alms-houses for ' poor clerks' widows, as Stow shews. Unto this ' fraternity men and women of the first quality, ' ecclesiastical and others, joined themselves, who ' as they were great lovers of church-music in ' general, so their beneficence unto parish-clerks ' in particular is abundantly evident, by some ancient ' manuscripts at their common hall in Great Wood ' street, wherein foot-steps of their great bounty ' appear by the large gifts and revenues given for ' the maintenance and encouragement of such as ' should devote themselves to the study and practice ' of this noble and divine science, in which the parish-' clerks did then excel, singing being their peculiar ' province.

' Some certain days in the year they had their ' public feasts, which they celebrated with singing ' and music, and then received into their society such ' persons as delighted in singing, and were studious ' of it. These their meetings and performances ' were in Guildhall college or chapel. Thus the ' 27th of September, 1560, on the eve thereof they ' had even-song, and on the morrow there was a ' communion ; and after they had retired to Car-' penter's-hall to dinner. And May 11, 1562, they ' kept their communion at the said Guildhall chapel, ' and received seven persons into their brotherhood, ' and then repaired to their own hall to dinner, and ' after dinner a goodly play of the children of West-' minster, with waits and regals and singing.

' King Charles I. renewed their charter, and con-' ferred upon them very ample privileges and im-' munities, and incorporated them by the style and ' title of the Master, Wardens, and Fellowship of ' Parish-Clerks, of the city and suburbs of London ' and the liberties thereof, the city of Westminster, ' the borough of Southwark, and the fifteen out-' parishes adjacent.'

BOOK XIII. CHAP. CXVIII.

The principles of music, and the precepts of musical composition, as taught in the several countries of Europe about the middle of the sixteenth century, were uniformly the same ; the same harmonies, the same modulations were practised in the compositions of the Flemish, the Italian, the German, the French, and the English musicians ; and nothing character-istic of the genius or humour of a particular country or province, as was once the case of the Moorish and Provençal music, was discernible in the songs of that period, except in those of the Scots and Irish, the former whereof are in a style so peculiar, as borrowing very little from art, and yet abounding in that sweetness of melody, which it is the business of art to cultivate and improve, that we are driven to seek for the origin of this kind of music elsewhere than in the writings of those authors who have treated on the subject in general terms.

To speak of the Scots music in the first place; the common opinion is that it has received a considerable degree of infusion from the Italians, for that David Ricci or Rizzio, a lutenist of Turin, in the year 1564, became a favourite of Mary queen of Scots, and was retained in her service as a musician; and finding the music of the country of such a kind as rendered it susceptible of great improvement, he set himself to polish and refine it; and adopting, as far as the rules of his art would allow, that desultory melody, which he found to be its characteristic, composed most of those tunes to which the Scots songs have for two centuries past, been commonly sung.

Against this opinion, which has nothing to support it but vulgar tradition, it may be urged that David Ricci was not a composer of any kind. The historians and others who speak of him represent him as a lutenist and a singer; and Sir James Melvil, who was personally acquainted with him, vouchsafes him no higher a character than that of a merry fellow, and a good musician. 'Her majesty,' says he, 'had 'three valets of her chamber, who sang three parts, 'and wanted a bass to sing the fourth part. There- 'fore they told her majesty of this man, as one fit 'to make the fourth in concert. Thus was he drawn 'in to sing sometimes with the rest; and afterward 'when her French secretary retired himself to France, 'this David obtained the same office.'*

Melvil, in the course of his Memoirs, relates that Ricci engrossed the favour of the queen; that he was suspected to be a pensioner of the pope; and that by the part he took in all public transactions, he gave rise to the troubles of Scotland, and precipitated the ruin of his mistress.

Buchanan is somewhat more particular; the account he gives is, that Ricci was born at Turin; that his father, an honest but poor man, got a mean livelihood by teaching young people the rudiments of music. That having no patrimony to leave them, he instructed his children of both sexes in music, and amongst the rest his son David, who being in the prime of his youth, and having a good voice, gave hopes of his succeeding in that profession. That with a view to advance his fortune, Ricci went to the court of the duke of Savoy, then at Nice; but meeting with no encouragement there, found means to get himself admitted into the train of the Count de Moretto, then upon the point of setting out on an embassy to Scotland. That the Count, soon after his arrival in Scotland, having no employment for Ricci, dismissed him. The musicians of Mary queen of Scots were chiefly such as she had brought with her from France, on the death of the king her husband; and with these, as Buchanan relates, Ricci ingratiated himself by singing and playing among them, till he was taken notice of by the queen, soon after which he was retained in her service as a singer. From this station, by means of flattery and the most abject arts of insinuation, he rose to the highest degree of favour and confidence; and being appointed her secretary for French affairs, became absorbed in the intrigues of the court, in the management whereof he behaved with such arrogance and contempt, even of his superiors, as rendered him odious to all about him.† The rest of his history is well known; he grew rich, and his insolence drawing on him the hatred of the Scottish nobility, he was on the ninth day of March, in the year 1566, dragged from the presence of the queen into an outer chamber of the palace, and there slain.

In such an employment as Ricci had, and with all that variety of business in which he must be supposed to have been engaged, actuated by an ambitious and intriguing spirit, that left him neither inclination nor opportunities for study, can it be thought that the reformation or improvement of the Scots music was his care, or indeed that the short interval of two years at most, afforded him leisure for any such undertaking? In fact, the origin of those melodies, which are the subject of the present enquiry, is to be derived from a higher source; and so far is it from being true, that the Scots music has been meliorated by the Italian, that the converse of the proposition may be assumed; and, however strange it may seem, an Italian writer of great reputation and authority has not hesitated to assert that some of the finest vocal music that his country can boast of, owes its merit in a great measure to its affinity with the Scots.

To account for that singularity of style which distinguishes the Scottish melodies, it may be necessary to recur to the account given by Giraldus Cambrensis of the music of the inhabitants of the northern parts of this kingdom, particularly near the Humber; and to advert to that passage in the ecclesiastical history of Bede, wherein he relates the arrival of John the Archchanter from Rome, his settlement among the Northumbrians; and the propensity of that people to music;‡ whose sequestered situation, and the little intercourse they must be supposed to have held with the adjacent countries, will account for the existence of a style in music truly original, and which might in process of time extend itself to the neighbouring kingdom.§

† Buchan. Rer. Scotic. Hist. lib. xvii.   ‡ See pag. 138 of this work.

§ The ancient Scotch tunes seem to consist of the pure diatonic intervals, without any intermixture of those chromatic notes, as they are called, which in the modern system divide the diapason into twelve semitones; and in favour of this notion it may be observed that the front row of a harpsichord will give a melody nearly resembling that of the Scots tunes. But the distinguishing characteristic of the Scots music is the frequent and uniform iteration of the concords, more especially the third on the accented part of the bar, to the almost total exclusion of the second and the seventh; of which latter interval it may be remarked, that it occurs seldom as a semitone, even where it precedes a cadence; perhaps because there are but few keys in which the final note is preceded by a natural semitone; and this consideration will also furnish the reason why the Scots tunes so frequently close in a leap from the key-note to the fifth above. The particulars above remarked are obvious in those two famous tunes Katherine Ogie and Cold and raw, which are unquestionably ancient, and in the true Scots style. *The construction of the old Scotch tunes is this, that almost every succeeding emphatical note is a third, a fifth, an octave, or, in short, some note that is in concord with the preceding note. Thirds are chiefly used; which are very pleasing concords. I use the word* emphatical *to distinguish those notes which have a stress laid on them in singing the tune, from the lighter connecting notes, that serve merely like grammar articles in common speech to tack the whole together.*

When we consider how these ancient *tunes were first performed, we shall see that such harmonical succession of sounds was natural and even necessary*

---

* Memoirs of Sir James Melvil of Halhill, 8vo. Lond. 1752, pag. 107.

How long it was that the popular melodies of Scotland continued to be propagated by tradition, it is not easy to ascertain, for it does not appear that that kingdom ever abounded with skilful musicians; however by the year 1400 the science had made such a progress there, that one of its princes, James Stuart, the first of his name, and the hundred and second in the list of their kings, attained to such a proficiency in it, as enabled him to write learnedly on music, and in his compositions and performance on a variety of instruments, to contend with the ablest masters of the time.

Bale and Dempster, and after them bishop Tanner, take notice of this prince in the accounts by them severally given of Scottish writers, and ascribe to him among other works, a treatise De Musica, and Cantilenas Scoticas.

Buchanan has drawn his character at full, and among many other distinguishing particulars, mentions that he was excellently skilled in music, more indeed, he adds, than was necessary or fitting for a king, for that there was no musical instrument on which he could not play so well, as to be able to contend with the greatest masters of the art in those days.*

The particulars of his story are related by all the Scottish historians, who, as do others, represent him as a prince of great endowments, being ignorant of no art worthy the knowledge of a gentleman; complete in all manly exercises, a good Latin scholar, an excellent poet, a wise legislator, a valiant captain, and, in a word, an accomplished gentleman and a great monarch. Notwithstanding which his amiable and resplendent qualities, a conspiracy was formed against him in the year 1436, by the earl of Athol, and others of his subjects, who broke into his chamber, he then being lodged in the Black Friars in Perth, and with many cruel wounds slew him in the forty-fourth year of his age, and the thirteenth of his reign.†

In the account given of James I. by bishop Tanner the brief mention of the Cantilenas Scoticas there

ascribed to him leaves it in some measure a question, whether he was the author of the words, or the music, of those Scots songs. That he was a poet is agreed by all; and Major, in his History de Gestis Scotorum, and bishop Nicholson,‡ mention a poem written by him on Joan daughter of the duchess of Clarence, afterwards his queen, and two songs of his writing, the latter of which is yet extant, and abounds with rural humour and pleasantry:§ but the evidence of his composing tunes or melodies is founded on the testimony of a well-known Italian author, Alessandro Tassoni, who in a book of his writing, entitled Pensieri diversi, printed at Venice in 1646, speaking of music, and first of the ancient Greek musicians, has this remarkable passage : 'We may reckon 'among the moderns, James, king of Scotland, who 'not only composed sacred poems set to music, but 'also of himself invented a new, melancholy, and 'plaintive kind of music, different from all other. 'In which he has since been imitated by Carlo 'Gesualdo, prince of Venosa, who in these our times 'has improved music with new and admirable com-'positions.'‖

That the Scots melodies at the time when they were originally composed were committed to writing there can be no doubt; but it is to be feared that there are no genuine copies of any of them now remaining, they having for a series of years been propagated by tradition, and till lately existed only in the memory of the inhabitants of that kingdom. Nevertheless they seem not to have been corrupted, nor to have received the least tincture from the music of other countries, but retain that sweetness, delicacy, and native simplicity for which they are distinguished and admired. Some curious persons have of late years made attempts to recover and reduce them to writing; and such of them as were sufficiently skilled in music, by conversation with the Highlanders, and the assistance of intelligent people, have been able to reduce a great number of ancient Scots melodies into musical notes.

There are many fine Scots airs in the collection of songs by the well-known Tom Durfey, entitled 'Pills to purge Melancholy,' published in the year 1720, which seem to have suffered very little by their passing through the hands of those English masters who were concerned in the correction of that book; but in the multiplicity of tunes in the Scots style that have been published in subsequent collections, it is very difficult to distinguish between the ancient and modern; those that pretend to be possessed of this discriminating faculty assert that the following, viz., Katherine Ogie, Muirland Willy,

*in their construction. They were composed to be played on the harp accompanied by the voice. The harp was strung with wire which gives a sound of long continuance, and had no contrivance like that in the modern harpsichord, by which the sound of the preceding could be stopped the moment a succeeding note began. To avoid actual discord it was therefore necessary that the succeeding emphatic note should be a chord with the preceding, as their sounds must exist at the same time. Hence arose that beauty in those tunes that has so long pleased, though men scarce know why. That they were originally composed for the harp, and of the most simple kind,—I mean a harp without any half notes, but those in the natural scale, and with no more than two octaves of strings from C to C,—I conjecture from another circumstance, which is, that not one of these tunes really ancient has a single artificial note in it; and that in tunes where it was not convenient for the voice to use the middle notes of the harp, and place the key in F, there the B, which if used should be a B ♭, is always omitted by passing over it with a third.

* ' In musicis curiosius erat instructus, quam regem vel deceat, vel 'expediat, nullum enim organum erat, ad psallendi usum, comparatum, 'quo non ille tam scite modulabatur, ut cum summis illius ætatis 'magistris contenderet.' Buch. Rer. Scotic. Hist. lib. x. sect. 57.
In the continuation of the Scotichronicon of Johannes de Fordun, [Scotichron. à Hearne, vol. IV. pag. 1323,] is a character of James I. to the same purpose, but more particular; and in Hector Boethius is an eulogium on him, which is here given in the dialect of the country, from the translation of that historian by Ballenden. ' He was weil lernit to 'fecht with the swerd, to just, to turnay, to worsyl, to syng and dance, 'was an expert medicinar, richt crafty in playing baith of lute and harp, 'and sindry othir instrumentis of musik. He was expert in gramer, 'oratry, and poetry, and maid sae flowand and sententious versis, apperit 'weil he was ane natural and borne poete.'
† Buch. Rer. Scot. Hist. lib. x. Holinshed's Hist. of Scotland, pag. 384.

‡ In his Scottish Historical Library, pag. 55.
§ Tanner includes these in his account of his works. Allan Ramsay, in his Ever-Green, and also in his own poems, has ascribed that humorous Scots poem, 'Christ's Kirk on the Green,' to James I. and in his notes on it has feigned some circumstances to give a colour to the opinion that he was the author of it; but bishop Tanner with much better reason, gives it to James V. who also was a poet.
‖ ' Noi ancora possiamo connumerar trà nostri Jacopo Rè di Scozia, 'che non pur cose sacre compose in canto, ma trovò da se stesso una 'nuova, musica lamentevole, e mesta, differente da tutte' l' altre. Nel 'che poi è stato imitato da Carlo Gesualdo, Prencipe di Venosa, che in 'questa nostra età hà illustrata anch' egli la musica con nuove mirabili 'invenzioni.' Lib. X. cap. xxiii. Angelo Berardi in his Miscellanea Musicale, pag 50, acquiesces in this relation, and, without citing his authority, gives it in the very words of Tassoni.

and Cold and Raw,* are of the highest antiquity, and that the Lass of Peatie's Mill, Tweed-side, Mary Scot, and Galloway Shiels, though perfectly in the Scots vein, bear the signatures of modern composition.†

Of the Irish music, as also of the Welch, alike remarkable with the Scotch for wildness and irregularity, but far inferior to it in sweetness of modulation, little is to be met with in the works of those who have written professedly on music. Sir James Ware has slightly mentioned it in his Antiquities of Ireland, and noted that the Irish harp is ever strung with brass wires. The little that has been said of the Welsh music is to be found in the Cambriæ Descriptio of Silvester Giraldus ;‡ and mention is made of the Irish music, as also of the Scotch, in the continuation of the Scotichronicon of Johannes De Fordun, lib. 16. cap. 29. The passage is curious, as it contains a comparison of the music of the three countries with each other, and is in these words :—

'In musicis instrumentis invenio commendabilem 'gentis istius diligenciam. In quibus, præ omni 'nacione quam vidimus, incomparabiliter instructa 'est. Non enim in hiis, ut in Britannicis, quibus 'assueti sumus, instrumentis tarda et morosa est 'modulacio, verum velox et præceps, suavis tamen 'et jocunda sonoritas, miraque in tanta tam præ- 'cipiti digitorum rapacitate musica proporcio et 'arte per omnia indempni, inter crispatos modulos 'organaque multipliciter intricata, tam suavi velo- 'citate, tam dispari paritate, tam discordi concordia 'consona redditur et completur melodia, seu Dia-

* This last air was wrought into a catch by John Hilton, which may be seen in his Collection of Catches, published in 1652. The initial words of it are 'Ise gæ with thee my Peggy.' This tune was greatly admired by queen Mary, the consort of king William ; and she once affronted Purcell by requesting to have it sung to her, he being present: the story is as follows. The queen having a mind one afternoon to be entertained with music, sent to Mr. Gostling, then one of the chapel, and afterwards subdean of St. Paul's, to Henry Purcell and Mrs. Arabella Hunt, who had a very fine voice, and an admirable hand on the lute, with a request to attend her ; they obeyed her commands ; Mr. Gostling and Mrs. Hunt sang several compositions of Purcell, who accompanied them on the harpsichord ; at length the queen beginning to grow tired, asked Mrs. Hunt if she could not sing the old Scots ballad ' Cold and Raw,' Mrs. Hunt answered yes, and sang it to her lute. Purcell was all the while sitting at the harpsichord unemployed, and not a little nettled at the queen's preference of a vulgar ballad to his music ; but seeing her majesty delighted with this tune, he determined that she should hear it upon another occasion : and accordingly in the next birth-day song, viz., that for the year 1692, he composed an air to the words, ' May her bright example chace Vice in troops out of the land,' the bass whereof is the tune to Cold and Raw ; it is printed in the second part of the Orpheus Britannicus, and is note for note the same with the Scots tune.

† About the year 1730, one Alexander Munroe, a native of Scotland, then residing at Paris, published a collection of the best Scotch tunes fitted to the German flute, with several divisions and variations, but the simplicity of the airs is lost in the attempts of the author to accommodate them to the style of Italian music.

In the year 1733, William Thompson published a collection of Scotch songs with the music, entitled Orpheus Caledonius ; the editor was not a musician, but a tradesman, and the publication is accordingly injudicious and very incorrect.

Three collections of Scots tunes were made by Mc Gibbon, a musician of Edinburgh, and published about twenty years ago with basses and variations ; and about the same time Mr. Francis Barsanti the father of Miss Barsanti, of Covent-Garden theatre, an Italian, and an excellent musician, who had been resident some years in Scotland, published a good collection of Scots tunes with basses of his own composition.

‡ It is said that the Welch music is derived from the Irish. In the Chronicle of Wales by Caradocus of Lhancarvan, is a relation to this purpose, viz., that Griffith Ap-Conan, king of North Wales, being by mother and grandmother an Irishman, and also born in Ireland, carried with him from thence divers cunning musicians into Wales, who devised in a manner all the instrumental music used there, as appears as well by the books written of the same, as also by the names of the tunes and measures used among them to this day. Vide Sir James Ware's Antiquities of Ireland, published by Walter Harris, Esq. chap. xxv. pag. 184.

'tessarone seu Diapente cordæ concrepent, semper 'tenera Bemol incipiunt, et in Bemol redeunt, ut 'cuncta sub jocunda sonoritatis dulcedine comple- 'antur, tam subtiliter modulos intrant et exeunt, sicque 'subtuso grossioris cordæ sonitu gracilium tinnitus 'licencius ludunt, latencius delectant, lasciviusque 'demulcent, ut pars artis maxima videatur arte velari, 'tamquam si lata ferat ars depressa pudorem. Hinc 'accidit, ut ea, quæ subtilius intuentibus, et artis 'archana decernentibus, internas et ineffabiles com- 'parent animi dilicias, ea non attendentibus, sed quasi 'videntibus non videndo, et audiendo non intelli- 'gentibus, aures pocius onerent quam delectant, et 'tam confuso et inordinato strepitu invitis audi- 'toribus fastidia parant tædiosa. Olim dicebatur, 'quod Scocia et Wallia Yberniam in modulis imitari 'æmula nitebantur disciplina. Hibernia quidem tan- 'tum duobus et delectatur instrumentis, cithara, 'viz. et tymphana, Scocia tribus, cythera, tympana 'et choro, Wallia, cythera, tibiis et choro. Æneis 'quoque utuntur cordis, non de intestinis vel corio 'factis. Multorum autem opinione hodie Scocia non 'tantum magistram æquiparavit Hiberniam, verum 'eciam in musica pericia longe jam prævalet et 'præcellit. Unde et ibi quasi fontem artis jam 'requirunt. Hæc ibi. Venerunt itaque periciores 'arte illa de Hibernia et Anglia, et de incom- 'parabili præcellencia et magisterio musicæ artis 'regiæ admirantes, eidem præ ceteris gradum attri- 'buunt superlativum. Ceterum quam diu hujus regni 'orbita volvitur, ejusdem prædicabilis practica, lau- 'dabilis rectoria, et præcellens policia accipient 'præconii incrementum.'

Towards the beginning of the seventeenth century, the principles of harmony being then generally known, and the art of composition arrived to great perfection, there appeared a great emulation among the masters throughout Europe in their endeavours towards the improvement of the science ; and to speak with precision on the subject, it seems that the competition was chiefly between the Italians and the Germans. The former of these, having Palestrina for their master, had carried church-music to the highest degree of perfection ; and in the composition of madrigals, for elegance of style, correctness of harmony, and in sweetness and variety of modulation, they were hardly equalled by the musicians of any country. Nevertheless it may be said that in some respects the Germans were their rivals, and, in the knowledge and use of the organ, their superiors. This people began very soon to discover the power and excellence of this noble instrument ; that it was particularly adapted to music in consonance ; that the sounds produced by it, not like those that answer to the touch of a string, were unlimited in their duration ; that all those various graces and elegancies with which the music of the moderns is enriched, such as fugues, imitative and responsive passages, various kinds of motion, and others, were no less capable of being uttered by the organ, than by a number of voices in concert ;§ and so excellent

§ Milton, who himself played on the organ, discovers a just sense of the nature and use of this noble instrument in that passage of his Tractate on education where he recommends, after bodily exercise, the recreating and composing the travailed spirits of his young disciples

were the Germans in this kind of performance on the organ, that towards the close of the fifteenth century, they seem almost to have exhausted its power; for in the year 1480, we are told that a German, named Bernhard, invented the pedal, thereby increasing the harmony of the instrument by the addition of a fundamental part.

But notwithstanding the competition above spoken of, it seems that as the principles of music were first disseminated throughout Europe by the Italians, so in all the subsequent improvements in practice they seemed to give the rule: to instance in a few particulars, the church style was originally formed by them; dramatic music had its rise in Italy; Recitative was invented by the Italians; that elegant species of vocal composition, the Cantata, was invented by Carissimi, an Italian; Thorough-bass was also of Italian origin. These considerations determine the order and course of the present narration, and will lead us, after doing justice to our own country, by extending the account of English musicians to about the close of the sixteenth century, to exhibit a given series, commencing at that period, of Italian musicians; interposing, as occasion offers, such eminent men of other countries as seem to be entitled to particular notice.

The history of music as hitherto deduced, is continued down to a period, at which the science may truly be said to have arrived at great perfection. Abroad it continued to be encouraged and to flourish; but in this country it was so little regarded, as to afford, at least to the professors of it, a ground of complaint that music was destitute of patronage, and rather declined: the king, James I. was a lover of learning and field recreations; and though he had some genius for poetry, he had little relish for either music or painting. Indeed, had his love of music been ever so great, his own country afforded scarce any means of improvement in it; for we read of no eminent Scottish musicians either before or since his time. It is true his mother, as she was a very finely accomplished woman, was an excellent proficient, and during the time she was in France had contracted a love for the Italian vocal music; and it is recorded that upon her return to Scotland she took into her service David Ricci, a native of Turin, who had a very fine bass voice, to assist in the performance of madrigals for her own private amusement: Ricci was slain in the presence of the queen at the time when she was with child of the prince, afterwards James I. after which there was perhaps scarce any person left in her dominions capable of the office of preceptor to a prince in the science of music.*

with the solemn and divine harmonies of music: 'Either while the 'skilful organist plies his *grave* and *fancied descant*, in *lofty fugues*, or 'the whole symphony with artful and unimaginable touches adorn and 'grace the well-studied chords of some choice composer.'

* Besides James I. of Scotland, we know of no person, a native of that country, who can with propriety be said to have been a musician; nevertheless it is to be observed that there is extant in the collection of the author of this work, a manuscript-treatise on music, written in the Scottish dialect, which appears to have been composed by some person eminently skilled in the science. It is of a folio size, and is entitled 'The Art of Music collectit out of all ancient Doctouris of Musick.' Pr. 'Qwhat is mensural musick?' It contains the rudiments of music, and the precepts of composition, with variety of examples, and a formula of the tones; from which circumstance it is to be conjectured that it was written before the time of the reformation in Scotland.

With respect to church-music, it is highly probable that James adhered to the metrical psalmody that had been instituted by Calvin, and adopted by many of the reformed churches; and of this his version of the Psalms may be looked upon as some sort of evidence; however upon his accession to the crown of England he was necessitated to recognize the form and mode of public worship established in this kingdom.

Notwithstanding the love which queen Elizabeth bore to music, and the affection which she manifested for the solemn choral service, it seems that the servants of her chapel experienced the effects of that parsimony, which it must be confessed was part of her character; they solicited for an increase of their wages; but neither the merits of Bull nor of Bird, both of whom she affected to admire, nor of Giles, or many other excellent musicians then in her service, were able to procure the least concession in their favour. Upon her decease they made the like application to her successor, having previously engaged some of the lords of the council to promote it. The event of their joint solicitation appears by an entry in the Cheque-book of the chapel-royal, of which the following is a transcript :—*

5 December, 1604.

The Lo. Charles Haward high admirall.

The Lo. Tho. Haward Lo. Chamberlaine

The Lo. Harrie Haward earle of Northampton

The Lo. Cecill vicount Cramborne

The Lo. Knowles treasurer of houshold

Be it remembered by all that shall succeed us, that in the year of our Lord God 1604, and in the second yeare of the reign of our most gracious sovereign Lord James, the first of that name, by the grace of God of Great Britaine, France, and Ireland, king. After a long and chargeable sute continued for increase of wages in the end, by the furtherance of certaine honourable persons named in the margent, commissioners, and by the special favour and help of the right worshipfull doctor Montague, deane of the chappel then beinge, and by the great paynes of Leonard Davies, subdeane, and of Nathaniel Gyles, then master of the children, with other auntients of the place, the king's most excellent majestie of his royall bountye and regard, pleased to add to the late intertainement of the chappell ten pounds per annum to every man: so increasinge there stipends from thirtie to fortie pounds per annum, and allso augmented the twelve childrens allowance from six pence to ten pence per diem. And to the sergeant of the vestrie, was then geven increase of xl. per annum, as to the gent. and the two yeomen and the groome of the vestrie, the increase of fower pence per diem as to the twelve children. His royall majestie ordayninge that these several increases should be payd to the members of the chapell and vestrie in the nature of bourd wages for ever. Now it was thought meete that seeinge the intertainement of the chappell was

* This is the augmentation alluded to by Bird in the dedication of his Gradualia, part I, to Henry Howard earl of Northampton, above styled Lo, Harrie Haward, earl of Northampton, *and is recorded amongst the instances of king James the First's bounty in Stow's Annals, page* 1037.

Cursed be the partie that taketh this leafe out of this book. Amen.

not augmented of many years by any his majesties progenitors kinges and quenes rainginge before his highnes, that therefore his kinglie bountie in augmenting the same (as is before shewed) should be recorded, to be had ever in remembrance, that thereby not onlye wee (men and children now lyveinge) but all those also which shall succeede us in the chappell shuld daylye see cause (in our most devoute prayers) humblye to beseech the devine majestie to bless his highnes, our gracious queen Ann, prince Henrie, and all and everye of that royal progenie with blessings both spirituall and temporall, and that from age to age, and everlastynglye. And let us all praye Amen, Amen.

The names of the Gent. lyveing at the time of this augmentation graunted :—

Leonard Davies, Subdean.
Barthol. Mason ⎫
Antho. Harrison ⎪
Robert Stuckey ⎬ Chaplaines
Steven Boughton ⎪
William Lawes ⎪
Antho. Kerbie ⎭
Doctor Bull, Organist
Nathaniel Gyles, Master of the Children
Thomas Sampson, Clerke of the Cheque
Robert Stone
Will. Byrde
Rychard Granwell
Crue Sharp
Edmund Browne
Tho. Woodson
Henrie Eveseede
Robert Allison
Jo. Stevens

Jo. Hewlett
Richard Plumley
Tho. Goolde
Peter Wright
Will. Lawrence
James Davies
Jo. Amerye
Jo. Baldwin
Francis Wyborow
Arthur Cocke
George Woodson
Jo. Woodson
Edmund Shirgoold
Edmund Hooper.

The Officers of the vestrie then were—
Ralphe Fletcher, Sergeant
Jo. Patten ⎫
Robert Lewis ⎬ Yeomen
Harrye Allred, Groome.

CHAP. CXIX.

The recreations of the court during the reign of James I. were altogether of the dramatic kind, consisting of masques and interludes, in the composing and performance whereof the gentlemen, and also the children of the chapel, were frequently employed. Most of these dramas were written by Ben Jonson,* some in the lifetime of Samuel Daniel, laureate or court poet; and others after Jonson, succeeded to that employment.†

* Speed's Chron. 725.
† The office of Poet Laureate is well known at this time. There are no records that ascertain the origin of the institution in this kingdom, though there are many that recognise it. The following is the best account that can here be given of it. As early as the reign of Henry III. who died in the year 1272, there was a court poet, a Frenchman, named Henry de Avranches, and otherwise 'Magistro Henrico Versificator,' Master Henry the Versifier, who from two several precepts, to be found in Madox's History of the Exchequer, is supposed to have had an assignment of a hundred shillings a year by way of salary or stipend. Vide Hist. of English Poetry by Mr. Thomas Warton, vol. I. pag. 47.
In the year 1341, Petrarch was crowned with laurel in the capitol by the senate of Rome. After that Frederic III. emperor of Germany, gave the laurel to Conradus Celtes; and ever since the Counts Palatine of the empire have claimed the privilege solemnly to invest poets with the bays.
Chaucer was contemporary with Petrarch, and is supposed to have become acquainted with him while abroad. Upon his return to England he assumed the title of Poet Laureat; and, anno 22 Rich. II. obtained a grant of an annual allowance of wine, as appears by the following docquet :—
'Vigesimo secundo anno Richardi secundi concessum Galfrido 'Chaucer unum dolium vini per annum durante vitâ, in portu 'civitatis London, per manus capitalis pincernæ nostri.' Vide Fuller's Worthies, 27.
John Kay, in his dedication of the Siege of Rhodes to Edward IV.

The children of James were well instructed in music, and particularly in dancing, for their improvement in which latter accomplishment the king appears to have been very solicitous. In a letter from him to his sons, dated Theobalds, April 1, 1623, now among the Harleian manuscripts in the British Museum, Numb. 6987. 24, he desires them to keep up their dancing privately, 'though they whistle and 'sing to one another for music.'

Prince Charles was a scholar of Coperario, and by him had been taught the Viol da gamba; and though Lilly the astrologer in his character of Charles I. contents himself with saying that the king was not unskilful in music, the fact is, that he had an excellent judgment in the science, and was besides an able performer on the above instrument.‡ As to prince Henry, it is highly probable that he had the same instructor with his brother: of his proficiency little is said in the accounts of his life; but that he was however a lover of music, and a patron of men of eminence in the science, may be inferred from the following extract from the list of his household establishment, as contained in the Appendix to the Life of Henry Prince of Wales, by Dr. Birch :—

MUSICIANS.

Dr. Bull	Mr. Ford	Valentine Sawyer
Mr. Lupo	Mr. Cutting	Matthew Johnson
Mr. Johnson	Mr. Stinte	Edward Wormall
Mr. Mynors	Mr. Hearne	Thomas Day
Mr. Jones	John Ashby	Sig. Angelo.

A brief declaration of what yearly pensions, and to whom his highness did grant the same, payable out of his highness's treasure from the time of his creation until the first day of November, 1612 :—

1611 June	£.		£.
To John Bull doctor of music	40	To John Ashby	30
		To Edward Wormall	20
To Robert Johnson	40	To Matthias Johnson	20
To Thomas Lupo	40	1611 March To Thomas Ford one of his highness's musicians, by way of increase to his former pension.	10
To John Mynors	40		
To Jonas Wrench	40		
To Thomas Day	40		
To Valentine Sawyer	40		
To Thomas Cutting§	40	August. To Jerom Hearne one of his highness's musicians.	20
To John Sturte	40		
To Thomas Ford	30		

subscribes himself his humble poet laureat; and Skelton, who lived in the reigns of Henry VII. and VIII. styles himself Skelton Laureate.
At the beginning of the reign of James I. Samuel Daniel was laureat; but though he was a man of abilities, Jonson was employed to write the court poems. Upon the death of Daniel, about the year 1619, Jonson was appointed his successor, who before this, viz., in February 1615, had obtained a grant of an annual pension of one hundred marks.
In the year 1630, by letters patent of Charles I. this pension was augmented to one hundred pounds per annum, with an additional grant of one terse of Canary Spanish wine, to be taken out of the king's store of wines yearly, and from time to time remaining at, or in the cellars within or belonging to his palace of Whitehall; and this continues to be the establishment in favour of the poet laureate.
Upon these grants of wine it may be observed that the first of the kind seems to be that in a pipe-roll Ann. 36 Hen. III. to Richard the king's harper, and Beatrice his wife, in these words: 'Et in uno dolio vini 'empto et dato Magistro Ricardo, Citharistæ regis xl. fol. per Br. Reg. 'Et in uno dolio empto et dato Beatrici uxori ejusdem Ricardi.'

‡ Playford, who had good opportunities of information, speaking of the skill in music of some of our princes, says, ' Nor was his late sacred 'majesty and blessed martyr king Charles the First, behind any of his 'predecessors in the love and promotion of this science, especially in the 'service of Almighty God, and with much zeal he would hear reverently 'performed, and often appointed the service and anthems himself, 'especially that sharp service composed by Dr William Child, being by 'his knowledge in music a competent judge therein; and would play his 'part exactly well on the bass-violl, especially of those incomparable 'fancies of Mr. Coperario to the organ.'

§ This Thomas Cutting was an excellent performer on the lute. In the year 1607 he was in the service of the Lady Arabella Stuart, when

Before the publication of Morley's Introduction the precepts of musical composition were known but to few, as existing only in manuscript treatises, which being looked upon as inestimable curiosities, were transmitted from hand to hand with great caution and diffidence; so that for the most part the general precepts of music, and that kind of oral instruction which was communicated in the schools belonging to cathedral churches, and other seminaries of music, were the only foundation for a course of musical study; and those who laboured to excel in the art of practical composition were necessitated either to extract rules from the works of others, or trust to their own powers in the invention of harmony and melody; and hence it appears that Morley's work could not but greatly facilitate and improve the practice of musical composition. The world had been but a few years in possession of Morley's Introduction before Thomas Ravenscroft, an author heretofore mentioned as the editor of the psalm-tunes in four parts, thought fit to publish a book of his writing with this title: ' A brief discourse of the true (but neglected) use of ' charact'ring the degrees by their Perfection, Imper-' fection, and Diminution in Measurable Musicke

Christian IV. king of Denmark, begged him of his mistress. The occasion was probably this: Christian loved the music of the lute, and having while in England heard Douland, he obtained permission to take him with him to Denmark; but Douland, after a few years stay at Copenhagen, imagining himself slighted, returned to England, and left the king without a lutenist; in this distress Christian applied to his sister Ann, the wife of James I. and she, and also her son prince Henry interceded with the Lady Arabella to part with her servant Cutting, and obtained her consent. It seems that Cutting stayed in Denmark but little more than four years, for he became a servant to Christian about March, 1607, and by the above list it appears that he was in the service of prince Henry in June, 1611. The following are the letters on the subject, the originals whereof are among the Harleian MSS. in the British Museum. See the Catalogue, No. 6986. 42, 43, 44.

Anna R.
Wellbeloved cousine Wee greete you hartlye well; Udo Gal, our deere brothers the king of Denmarks gentleman-servant, hath insisted with us for the licensing your servant thomas cottings to depart, but not without your permission, to our brother's service, and therefore we wryte these few lines to you, being assured your H. will make no difficultie to satisfie our pleasure and our deere brother's desires; and so geving you the assurance off our constant favours, with our wishes for the conteneuance or convalescence of your helth, expecting your returne, we commit your H. to the protection of God. From Whythall, 9 March 1607.

To our most honerable and wellbeloved
    cousine the Lady Arabella Stuart.

Madam, the queenes ma. hath commaunded me to signifie to your La. that shee would have Cutting your La. servant to send to the king of Denmark, because he desyred the queene that she would send him one that could play upon the lute, I pray your La. to send him back with ane answere as soon as your La. can. I desyre you to commend me to my lo. and my la. shrewsbury, and also not too think me any thing the worse scrivenere that I write so ill, but to suspend your judgement till you come hither, then you shall find me, as I was ever,
A Madame Arbelle   Your La. loving cousin
    ma Cousine.   and assured friend,
                                        Henry.

May it please your Highnesse,
I have received your Hs. letter whearin I am let to understand that the queene's majesty is pleased to command Cutting my servant for the king of Denmark: concerning the which your Highnesse requireth my answer to hir Majesty, the which I have accordingly returned by this bearer, referring him to hir Majesty's good pleasure and disposition. And although I may have some cause to be sorry to have lost the contentment of a good lute, yet must I confesse that I am right glad to have found any occasion whearby to expresse to her Majesty and your Highnesse the humble respect which I ow you, and the readinesse of my disposition to be conformed to your good pleasures: wherein I have placed a great part of the satisfaction which my heart can receive. I have according lo your Hs. direction signified unto my uncle and aunt of Shrewsbury your Hs. gratious vouchsafeing to remember them, who with all duty present theyr most humble thancks, and say they will ever pray for your Hs. most happy prosperity: and yet my uncle saith that he carrieth the same splene in his heart towards your Hs. that he hath ever done. And so praying to the Almighty for your Hs. felicity I humbly cease. From Sheffeild the 15th of March, 1607.
                            Your Hs. most humble and dutifull
To the Prince his Highnesse.   Arbella Stuart.

' against the common practice and custome of these ' times.' Quarto, 1614.*

The author of this book had been educated in St. Paul's choir, under Master Edward Pearce, and was not only a good musician, but a man of considerable learning in his faculty; the drift of it is to revive the use of those proportions, which, because of their intricacy, had long been discontinued. To justify this attempt, he cites the authority of Franchinus, Glareanus, and Morley; of which latter he says that he declared himself loth to break the common practice or received custom, yet if any would change that, he would be the first that would follow.

This declaration of Morley naturally leads to the question whether, even at the time of his writing his Introduction, any change for the better could have been possibly effected; since he himself has expressly said, that of the many authors who had written on mensurable music, and particularly on those branches of it, mood, time, and prolation, with their several varieties, hardly any two of them can be said to tell the same tale.

Upon the whole, proportion is a subject of more speculation; and as to practice, there seems to be no conceivable kind of proportion, but in the present method of notation may be signified or charactered without regarding those distinctions of perfection, imperfection, and diminution of mood, time, and prolation, which this author labours to revive.

To this discourse of Ravenscroft are added examples to illustrate his precepts, expressed in the harmony of four voices, concerning the ' Pleasure of ' five usual recreations: 1. Hunting; 2. Hawking; ' 3. Dancing; 4. Drinking; 5. Enamouring.' †

In the year 1603, Thomas Robinson published a book entitled ' The school of musicke, the perfect ' method of true fingering the Lute, Pandora, Or-' pharion, and Viol da Gamba.' It is a thin folio, and merits to be particularly noticed in this place. The style of it is remarkably quaint, and it is written, as the author expresses it, ' dialoguewise, betwixt a ' knight who has children to be taught, and Timo-' theus who should teach them.'

After a general eulogium on music, the author proceeds to his directions for playing on the lute, beginning with an explanation of that method of notation peculiar to it, called the Tablature, the precepts whereof seem to be nearly the same with those contained in the book of Adrian le Roy, an account whereof has herein before been given. These are succeeded by a collection of easy lessons for the lute,

* In this book it is asserted, on the authority of the' Præceptiones Musices Poeticæ seu de Compositione Cantus of Johannes Nucius,' that John Dunstable, of whom Morley takes notice, and who is also herein before mentioned, invented musical composition in parts; and that Franchinus de Colonia invented mensurable music. In this latter name Ravenscroft is mistaken, for it is to Franco, a scholastic or professor of Liege that the honour of this invention is due, though it is almost universally ascribed to Johannes de Muris. With regard to the antiquity of musical composition in parts, Morley had his doubts about it, and declares his inability to trace it much farther back than the time of Franchinus, who lived some years after Dunstable; and as to symphoniac music in general, there is no conclusive evidence that it existed before the time of Bede: and it is highly probable that it had its origin in that practice of extemporary descant described by Giraldus Cambrensis, and mentioned previously in this work.

† This Thomas Ravenscroft was also the author of a collection of songs entitled ' Melismata, Musical Phansies fitting the Court, Citie, ' and Countrey-Humours, to 3, 4, and 5 voyces,' published in the year 1611.

and these latter by what the author calls rules to instruct you to sing, and a few psalm-tunes set in Tablature for the viol da gamba. This book of Robinson may be deemed a curiosity, as it tends to explain a practice which the masters of the lute have ever shewn an unwillingness to divulge.

In the year 1609 was published a book with this title : ‘Pammelia, Musicks Miscellanie, or mixed ‘varietie of pleasant Roundelayes and delightful ‘Catches of 3. 4. 5. 6. 7. 8. 9. 10 parts in one. ‘None so ordinarie as musical, none so musical as not ‘to all very pleasing and acceptable. London, printed ‘by William Barley for R. B. and H. W. and are to ‘be sold at the Spread Eagle at the great North doore ‘of Paules.’ Quarto. It was again printed by Thomas Snodham, for Matthew Lownes and John Browne, in 1618.

This book, the oldest of the kind extant, fully answers its title, and contains a great number of fine vocal compositions of very great antiquity,* but, which is much to be lamented, without the names of the authors. Among the Rounds is the song mentioned in the character of Mr. William Hastings, written by the first earl of Shaftesbury, and printed in Peck’s Collection of curious Historical Pieces, No. xxxiii. concerning which it is first to be observed, that, among numberless other singularities, respecting the diet and manner of living of this person, it is in the character said that he never wanted a London Pudding, and always sang it in with ‘My pert eyes therein-a;’ absolute nonsense! which the song itself here given will set to rights :—

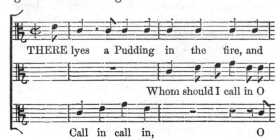

---

* The words to these compositions are for the most part on subjects of low humour, of which specimens are inserted in chap. LXVII., and here it may be observed that it was formerly a practice with the musicians to set the cries of London to music, retaining the very musical notes of them. In the collection entitled Pammelia, is a round to the cry of New oysters, Have you any wood to cleave? Orlando Gibbons set music of four parts to the Cries in his time, among which is one of a play to be acted by the scholars of our town; Morley set those of the Milliners’ Girls in the New Exchange in the Strand, built in the reign of James I., and pulled down about thirty years ago: and among others equally unknown to the present times, these occur: Italian Falling Bands, French Garters, Roman Gloves, Rabatos, a kind of ruffs, Sister’s, i.e., Nun’s Thread, Slick-stones, Poking-sticks, these were made taper, and were of use to open and separate the plaits of those great ruffs then in fashion. In a play called Tarquin and Lucrece, these cries occur, a Marking-stone, Bread and Meat for the poor Prisoners, Rock-Samphire.

A few rounds from this collection are inserted by way of example of canons in the unison, in chap. LXVII. of this work; these that follow are of the same kind of composition, but to words of a different import :—

a Hassoc for your Pew, or a Pesocke to thrust your feet in, Lanthorne and Candle-light, with many others.

The cries of London in the time of Charles II. differed greatly from those of the preceding reigns; that of a Merry new Song, in the set of Cries designed by Lauron, and engraved by Tempest, is a novelty, as the singing of ballads was then but lately become an itinerant profession. The ancient printed ballads have this colophon: ‘Printed by A. B., and ‘are to be sold at the stalls of the Ballad-singers;’ but Cromwell’s ordinance against strolling fiddlers, printed in Scobel’s collection, silenced these, and obliged the ballad-singers to shut up shop.

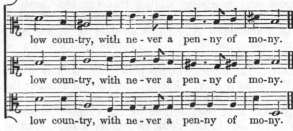

2. Here good fellow I drinke to thee,
    Pardonez moy je vouz en prie :
    To all good fellowes where ever they be.
    With never a penny of mony.

3. And he that will not pledge me in this,
    Pardonez moy je vouz en prie :
    Payes for the shot what ever it is,
    With never a penny of mony.

4. Charge it again boy, charge it againe,
    Pardonez moy je vouz en prie :
    As long as there is any incke in thy pen,
    With never a penny of mony.

CHAP. CXX.

OF musicians who flourished in or about the reign of James I. not heretofore particularly mentioned, the following is a list, including in it notes of their respective publications.

JOHN AMNER, bachelor of music, organist of the cathedral church of Ely, and master of the children. There are extant of his composition, Sacred Hymns, of three, four, five, and six parts, for voices and viols, quarto, Lond. 1615 ; and some anthems, the words whereof are in Clifford's collection.

JOHN ATTEY, gentleman and practitioner in music, was the author of a work entitled, ' The first Booke ' of Ayres of four parts with Tablature for the Lute, ' so made that all the parts may be plaide together ' with the lute, or one voyce with the lute and bass ' violl.' Fol. Lond. 1622.

JOHN BARTLETT, gentleman, and practitioner in the art of music, was the author of a work with this title, ' A Booke of Ayres with a triplicitie of musicke, ' whereof the first part is for the lute or Orpharion, ' and the viol da Gamba, and 4 parts to sing. The ' second is for trebles to sing to the lute and viole ; ' the third part is for the lute and one voyce, and the ' viole da Gamba.' Fol. Lond. 1606.

THOMAS BREWER, educated in Christ's Hospital London, and bred up to the practice of the viol, composed many excellent Fantasias for that instrument, and was the author of sundry rounds and catches, printed in Hilton's collection, as also of a celebrated song to the words ' Turn Amarillis to thy swain,' published in the earlier editions of Playford's Introduction, in two parts, and in his Musical Companion, printed in 1673, in three, and thereby spoiled, as some of the musicians of that day have not scrupled in print to assert.

THOMAS CAMPION was the author of two books of Airs, of two, three, and four parts. Wood, in the Fasti Oxon. vol. I. col. 229, styles him an admired

In the same year was published ' Deuteromelia, or ' the second part of Musick's Melodie, or melodious ' Musicke of pleasant Roundelaies, K. H. mirth or ' Freemens Songs,* and such delightful Catches, Qui ' canere potest canat, Catch that catch can. London, ' printed for Thomas Adams, dwelling in Paules ' church-yard, at the sign of the White Lyon, 1609.'

In this collection there are comparatively but few rounds or catches, it consisting chiefly of songs for three voices, in which all the stanzas are sung to the same tune like this, which is one of them :—

---

* Of this term, FREEMEN'S SONGS no other interpretation can here be given than that of Cotgrave in his Dictionary, where it is used to explain the words Verilay and Round ; and Verilay is elsewhere, by the same author, given as the signification of the word VAUDEVILLE, a country ballad or song, a Roundelay ; from Vaudevire, a Norman town, wherein Olivier Bassell, the first inventor of this kind of air, dwelt. For the meaning of the letters K. H. we are yet to seek.

poet and musician, adding that Camden mentions him together with Spenser, Sidney, and Drayton. In Ferabosco's Aires, published in 1609, are commendatory verses signed Thomas Campion Dr. of Physic; there are also prefixed to Coriate's Crudities certain Latin verses by the person, who is there styled Medicinæ Doctor. Farther, the entertainment at the nuptials of Carr with the lady Frances Howard, appears to have been written by Dr. Thomas Campion; there is also in the Bodleian library a book entitled 'Observations on the Art of English Poesy,' printed in 1602, by Thomas Campion, 12mo. Again, there is extant a work entitled 'Songs bewailing the un-'timely death of Prince Henry,' written by Dr. Thomas Campion, and set to the viol and lute by Coperario. Lond, 1613, folio. The same person was also the author of 'A new way of making fowre 'parts in Counterpoint by a most familiar and in-'fallible rule,' octavo, printed without a date, but dedicated to 'Charles, prince of Great Britaine.'* This tract, but under the title of the 'Art of Descant, 'or composing of Musick in parts, with annotations 'thereon by Mr. Christopher Simpson,' is published by way of Appendix to the earlier editions of Playford's Introduction. Wood mentions a Thomas Campion, of Cambridge, incorporated master of arts of Oxford, anno 1624, clearly a different person from him above-mentioned; but, which is strange, he does not so much as hint that Campion the poet and musician was a graduate in any faculty of either university.

WILLIAM CORKINE published 'Ayres to sing and 'play to the Lute and Basse Violl, with Pavins, 'Galliards, Almaines, and Corantes for the Lyra-'Violl. Fol. Lond. 1610.' In 1612 he published a second part of this work.

JOHN DANYEL, M.B. of Christ-Church, 1604. He was the author of 'Songs for the Lute, Viol, and Voice, 'in folio, Lond. 1606,' and is supposed to be the brother of Samuel Daniel, the poet laureate and historian, and the publisher of his works in 1623.

ROBERT DOWLAND, son of John, was the author of a work entitled 'A Musical Banquet,' folio, printed in 1610.

MICHAEL EST, bachelor of music, and master of the choristers of the cathedral church of Litchfield, was the author of sundry collections of Madrigals, and other vocal compositions, and of a madrigal of five parts, printed in the Triumphs of Oriana. His publications are much more numerous than those of any author of his time: one of them, entitled 'The sixt 'Set of Bookes, wherein are Anthemes for Versus, 'and Chorus of 5 and 6 parts; apt for Violls and 'Voices,' is dedicated to Williams, bishop of Lincoln, and lord keeper, with an acknowledgement of his beneficence in granting to the author an annuity for his life. It seems by the epistle that Est was an absolute stranger to the bishop, and that his lordship was

moved to this act of bounty by the hearing of some motetts of Est's composition. It is probable that this person was the son of that Thomas Est who first published the Psalms in parts, and other works, assuming in many of them the name of Snodham, and the brother of one John Est, a barber, famous for his skill on the Lyra-Viol.

JOHN EARSDEN, together with George Mason composed the music in a work entitled 'The Ayres that 'were sung and played at Brougham castle in West-'moreland, in the King's entertainment, given by the 'right honourable the Earle of Cumberland, and his 'right noble sonne the Lord Clifford.' Fol. Lond. 1618.

THOMAS FORD, the name of this person occurs in the list already given of Prince Henry's musicians, and also in certain letters patent purporting to be a grant of pensions or salaries to sundry of the king's musicians, 2 Car. I. herein after inserted. He was the author of a work entitled 'Musicke of sundre 'kindes, set forth in two books, the first whereof are 'Aires for 4 voices to the Lute, Orpherion, or Basse 'Viol, with a dialogue for two voices, and two basse-'viols in parts, tunde the lute-way. The second are 'Pavens, Galiards, Almaines, Toies, Jiggs, *Thumpes*,† 'and such like, for two basse Viols the liera way, so 'made as the greatest number may serve to play alone, 'very easy to be performed.' Fol. Lond. 1607. The same Thomas Ford was the author of some Canons or Rounds printed in John Hilton's collection.

EDMUND HOOPER, organist of Westminster Abbey, and a gentleman of the chapel royal, where he also did the duty of organist. He was one of the authors of the Psalms in four parts, published in 1594, and of sundry anthems in Barnard's Collection. He died July 14, 1621.

ROBERT JONES seems to have been a voluminous composer; two of the works published by him are severally entitled 'A musical Dreame, or the fourth 'book of Ayres; the first part for the Lute, two voices, 'and the Violl da Gamba; the second part is for the 'Lute, the Violl, and four voices to sing; the third 'part is for one voyce alone, or to the Lute the basse 'Viol, or to both if you please, whereof two are Italian 'ayres.' Fol. Lond. 1609. 'The Muses Gardin for 'delights, or the fift booke of Ayres onely for the 'Lute, the basse Violl, and the voyce.' Fol. Lond. 1611.

SIR WILLIAM LEIGHTON, Knight, one of the honorable band of gentlemen pensioners, published in 1614, 'The Tears or Lamentations of a sorrowful Soul, com-'posed with musical ayres and songs both for voices and divers instruments.' These are compositions by himself and other authors, of whom an account has already been given.

---

* The proof of that singular fact that Campion was a doctor in physic, and not, as some have imagined, a doctor in music, might be rested on the particulars above-mentioned; but the dedication to this tract fixes it beyond doubt: for the author, after declaring himself to be a physician by profession, apologizes for his offering 'a worke of musicke to his 'Highnesse by the example of Galen,' who he says became an expert musician, and would 'needes apply all the proportions of music to the uncertaine motions of the pulse.'

† The word *Dump*, besides sorrow and absence of mind, which are the two senses which Dr. Johnson gives of it in his Dictionary, has also another, which has escaped him, viz., a melancholy tune; or, as Mr. Steevens, in a note on a passage in Romeo and Juliet, act IV. scene v. conjectures, an old Italian dance; and considering the very licentious spelling of the time when this collection of Ford was printed, a suspicion might arise that the word *Thumpe* here noted was no other than the word *Dump*; but upon looking into the book, an air occurs, viz., the eleventh, wherein by a marginal note the performer on the lute is directed wherever he meets with one or two points under the letter a, which in the Tablature denotes an open string, to *thump* it with the first or second finger of the left hand: the use and effect of this strange practice is best known to the performers on the lute.

JOHN MAYNARD, a lutenist, was the author of a work with this title, 'The XII Wonders of the 'World, set and composed for the violl de gambo, 'the lute, and the voyce, to sing the verse, all three 'jointly, and none several; also lessons for the lute 'and base violl to play alone: with some lessons to 'play Lyra-wayes alone, or if you will to fill up the 'parts with another violl set lute-way, newly composed 'by John Maynard, lutenist at the famous schoole of St. 'Julian's in Hertfordshire.' Fol. Lond. 1611. These twelve wonders are so many songs exhibiting the characters of a courtier, a divine, a soldier, a lawyer, a physician, a merchant, a country gentleman, a bachelor, a married man, a wife, a widow, and a maid.

GEORGE MASON, see JOHN EARSDEN.

WILLIAM MEREDITH, organist of New College, Oxon. by Wood in his Hist. et Antiquit. Univ. Oxon. lib. II. pag. 157, styled 'Vir pius et facultate sua 'peritissimus,' is there said to have died anno 1637.

JOHN MUNDY, one of the organists of Queen Elizabeth's chapel, and also one of the organists of the free chapel of Windsor, was admitted to his bachelor's degree at Oxford in 1586, and to that of doctor in 1624. In the place of organist of Windsor he was the immediate successor of John Marbeck, of whose sufferings for religion, and providential escape from the flames, an account has herein before been given.* He was deeply skilled in the theory and practice of music, and published Songs and Psalms composed into three, four, and five parts, Lond. 1594; and was also the author of sundry anthems, the words whereof are printed in Clifford's Collection; and of a madrigal in the Triumphs of Oriana. He died anno 1630, and was buried in the cloister of St. George's chapel at Windsor.

WILLIAM MUNDY. Of this person Wood barely makes mention; he styles him one Will. Mundy, a noted musician, a composer of services and anthems, but no graduate. However it has been discovered that he was a composer as early as the year 1591, and was nevertheless the son of the former. In certain verses at the end of Baldwin's MS. cited in page 469 of this work containing the names of the several authors, whose compositions are therein inserted, are these lines:—

I will begine with White, Shepper, Tye, and Tallis,
Parfons, Gyles, Mundie th'oulde one of the queenes pallis
Mundie yonge, th'ould man's fon - - - - -

The old Mundy of the queen's palace was undoubtedly John, for in the Fasti, vol. I. col. 131, he is said to have been in 1586, or afterwards, one of the organists of her majesty's chapel; and Mundy the young is above expressly said to be the old man's son, and there are several compositions in Baldwin's MS. with the name Will. Mundie to them. The deduction from these particulars is, that William Mundy was the son of Dr. John Mundy, one of the

organists of queen Elizabeth's palace, or more properly of her royal chapel at Whitehall, and also organist of the chapel of St. George at Windsor. The name Will. Mundy is set to several anthems in Barnard's Collection, and, by a mistake, which Dr. Aldrich was at the pains of detecting, to that anthem of king Henry VIII. before mentioned, 'O God the 'maker of all things.'

MARTIN PIERSON or PEARSON, was master of the choristers at St. Paul's at the time when John Tomkins was organist there; he took his degree of bachelor in his faculty in 1613; and in 1630 published a work with this singular title, 'Mottects, or 'grave Chamber Musique, containing Songs of five 'parts of severall sorts, some ful, and some verse and 'chorus, but all fit for voyces and vials, with an 'organ part; which for want of organs may be per'formed on Virginals, Base-Lute, Bandora or Irish 'harpe. Also a mourning Song of sixe parts for the 'Death of the late Right Honorable Sir Fulke Grevil, 'Knight, composed according to the rules of art by 'M. P. batchelor of musique, 1630.' He died about the latter end of 1650, being then an inhabitant of the parish of St. Gregory, near the said cathedral, and was buried at St. Faith's church adjoining. He bequeathed to the poor of Marsh, in the parish of Dunnington, in the Isle of Ely, an hundred pounds, to be laid out in a purchase for their yearly use.

FRANCIS PILKINGTON, of Lincoln college, Oxford, was admitted a bachelor of music anno 1595. He was a famous lutenist, and one of the cathedral church of Christ in the city of Chester. Wood says he was father, or at least near of kin to Thomas Pilkington, one of the musicians of queen Henrietta Maria, celebrated in the poems of Sir Aston Cokaine. See page 493 of this work. He was the author of 'The 'first booke of Songs or Ayres of 4 parts, with 'Tablature for the lute or Orpherion, with the Violl 'da Gamba.' Fol. Lond. 1605.

PHILIP ROSSETER. This person was the author of a work entitled 'A booke of Ayres set foorth to be 'sang to the Lute, Orpherian, and base Violl, by 'Philip Rosseter, lutenist, and are to be sold at his 'house in Fleet-street, neere to the Grayhound.' Fol. Lond. 1601. In the preface to this book the author expresses in a humorous manner his dislike of those 'who to appeare the more deepe and singular in 'their judgment, will admit of no musicke but that 'which is long, intricate, bated with fugue, chained 'with sycopation, and where the nature of the word 'is precisely exprest in the note, like the old exploded 'action in comedies, when if they did pronounce 'Memini, they would point to the hinder part of 'their heads; if Video, put their finger in their eye.'

WILLIAM STONARD, organist of Christ-Church Oxon. and created doctor in music anno 1608. Besides certain anthems, the words whereof are in Clifford's Collection, he was the author of some compositions communicated by Walter Porter to Dr. John Wilson, music-professor at Oxford, to be reposed and kept for ever among the archives of the music-school. Dr. Stonard was a kinsman either of Dr. Wilson or Porter; but Wood's account of him is so am-

* Marbeck is conjectured to have died about the year 1585. He had a son named Roger, a canon of Christ-Church, Athen. Oxon. vol. I. col. 152, and provost of Oriel college, and the first standing or perpetual orator of the university, and who in 1573 was created doctor in physic, and afterwards was appointed first physician to queen Elizabeth. He died in 1605, and, as Wood conceives, was buried in the church of St. Giles without Cripplegate, London, in which parish he died. Fasti Oxon. vol. I. col. 109.

biguously worded, that this circumstance will apply to either.

NICHOLAS STROGERS, an organist temp. James I.; some services of his are to be found in Barnard's Collection.

JOHN WARD was the author of a service and an anthem in Barnard's Collection, and also of Madrigals to three, four, five, and six voices; and a song lamenting the death of Prince Henry, printed in 1613, and dedicated to Sir Henry Fanshaw, by whom he was highly favoured.

MATTHEW WHITE, of Christ-Church college, Oxon. accumulated doctor in music in 1629; the words of some anthems composed by him are in Clifford's Collection: there was also a Robert White, an eminent church musician, the composer of several anthems in Barnard's Collection. Morley celebrates one of this name, but whether he means either of these two persons, cannot be ascertained.

About the end of James the First's reign, to speak of the progress of it in this country, music received a new and very valuable acquisition in the foundation of a music lecture in the university of Oxford by Dr. WILLIAM HEYTHER;* *(a Portrait,)* the occasion was this: he was an intimate friend of the famous Camden, who having a few years before his decease determined to found a history-lecture in the same university, sent his friend Mr. Heyther with the deed of endowment properly executed to the vice-chancellor Dr. Piers; this was on the seventeenth day of May, 1622; and Mr. Heyther having for some years before applied himself to the study of music, and signified an intention to be honoured with a degree in that faculty, he, together with his friend Mr. Orlando Gibbons, were suffered to accumulate the degrees both of bachelor and doctor in music; and on that or the next day, viz., the eighteenth of May, 1622, they were both created doctors.†

It seems that there was at Oxford a professorship or music lecture founded by king Alfred, but how endowed does not at this distance of time clearly appear, and we find it continued till after the Restoration; for Anthony Wood, in his life, has given the succession of music-lecturers, as he terms them, from the

* His name of his own signature in the cheque-book is spelt HEYTHER, notwithstanding which it is frequently spelt Heather and that even by Camden himself.

† By the Fasti Oxon. vol. I. col. 221, it appears that Wood had searched in vain to find out whether Orlando Gibbons had been admitted to any degree in music or not; but the following letter from Dr. Piers to Camden, in the Collection of Epistles to and from Camden, published by Dr. Thomas Smith in 1691, pag. 329, is decisive of the question, and proves that Heyther and Gibbons were created doctors on the same day:—

CCLXIII.
G. Piersius. G. Camdeno.

'Worthy Sir,
'The university returns her humble thanks to you with this letter.
'We pray for your health and long life, that you may see the fruits of
'your bounty. We have made Mr. Heather a doctor in music; so that
'now he is no more Master, but Dr. Heather; the like honour for your
'sake we have conferred upon Mr. Orlando Gibbons, and made him
'a doctor too, to accompany Dr. Heather. We have paid Mr. Dr. Hea-
'ther's charges for his journey, and likewise given him the Oxford
'courtesie, a pair of gloves for himself, and another for his wife. Your
'honour is far above all these things. And so desiring the continuance
'of your loving favour to the university, and to me your servant, I take
'my leave.
'Oxon, 18 May   Yours ever to be commanded,
'1622.   'WILLIAM PIERS.'

'Mr. Whear shall make his oration this term; and I shall write
'to you from time to time what orders the university will com-
'mend unto your wisdom concerning your history-lecture.'

year 1661 to 1681; but by his list of their names it does not seem that any of them were musicians; and perhaps the reading of the old lecture was a matter of form, and calculated merely to preserve the station of music among the liberal sciences. As to that of Dr. Heyther, it was both theoretic and practical, as appears by the following account of the circumstances of its foundation, extracted from the books of the university:—

'This matter was first moved and proposed in a
'convocation held the 5th May, 1626, and afterwards
'agreed upon by the delegates, and published in the
'convocation-house, as approved by them, together
'with Dr. Heyther's orders about it the 16th of
'November the same yeare; by his deed, bearing
'date 20 Feb. 2.Cha. I. he gave to the university for
'ever an annuity or yearly rent charge of 16l. 6s. 8d.,
'issuing out of divers parcells of land, situate and
'being within the parish of Chislehurst in Kent,
'whereof 13l. 6s. 8d. is to be employed in the music-
'master's wages, out of which he is to repair the
'instruments and find strings; and the other 3l. is to
'be employed upon one that shall read the theory of
'music once every term, or oftner, and make an
'English music-lecture at the Act time. Unto which
'3l. Dr. Heyther requiring the ancient stipend of 40s.
'that was wont yearly to be given to the ordinary
'reader of music, to be added, or some other sum
'equivalent thereunto, the university thereupon agreed
'in a convocation that the old stipend of the morall
'philosophie reader, which was 45s., should be con-
'tinued to the music-reader, and so by that addition
'he hath 5l. 5s. yearly for his wages.'‡ The first professor under this endowment was Richard Nicholson, bachelor of music, and organist of Magdalen College.

The right of electing the professor is in the vice-chancellor, the dean of Christ-Church, the president of Magdalen College, the warden of New College, and the president of St. John's.

It further appears by the university books, that Dr. Heyther's professor was required to hold a musical praxis in the music-school every Thursday afternoon, between the hours of one and three, except during the time of Lent; to promote which he gave to the university an harpsicon, a chest of viols,§ and divers music-books both printed and written.

It is highly probable that Dr. Heyther was moved to this act of beneficence by Camden, who having been a chorister at Magdalen college, Oxford, may be supposed to have retained a love for music;|| and that Camden had a great ascendant over him, might be inferred from the intimate friendship that subsisted between them for many years. They had both employments that obliged them to a residence in Westminster; for Camden was master of Westminster

‡ This stipend was afterwards augmented by Nathaniel Lord Crew, bishop of Durham.

§ A CHEST or set of VIOLS consisted of six viols, which were generally two basses, two tenors, and two trebles, each with six strings; they were the instruments to which those compositions called Fantasias were adapted. A more particular description of a chest of viols will be given hereafter.

|| *By his Will published in the Appendix to Hearne's collection of Discourses written by eminent antiquaries, he gives six pounds to the singing men of the Collegiate Church of Westminster.*

WILLIAM HEYTHER

MUS. DOCT. OXON. MDCXXII.

From an original Painting in the Music-School, Oxford.

ORLANDO GIBBONS

MUS. DOCT. OXON. MDCXXII.

school, and Heyther a gentleman of the king's chapel. In town they lived in the same house; and when in 1609 a pestilential disease having reached the house next to Camden and himself, Camden was seized with it, he retired to the house of his friend Heyther at Chislehurst, and by the help of Dr. Gifford, his physician, was cured. But of the friendly regard which Camden entertained for Dr. Heyther, he gave ample testimony, by appointing him executor of his will; and in the deed executed by Camden on the nineteenth day of March, 1621-2, containing the endowment of his history-lecture at Oxford, the grant thereby made of the manor of Bexly in Kent, is subjected to a proviso that the profits of the said manor, estimated at 400l. a year, should be enjoyed by Mr. William Heyther, his heirs and executors, for the term of ninety-nine years, to commence from the death of Mr. Camden, he and they paying to the history professor 140l. per annum; at the expiration of which term the estate was to vest in the university. Biog. Brit. CAMDEN, 133, in note.

It has been doubted whether Heyther had any skill in music or not, but it appears that he was of the choir at Westminster, and that on the twenty-seventh day of March, 1615, he was sworn a gentleman of the royal chapel. Farther, it appears by the Fasti Oxon. that on the fifth day of July, 1622, a public disputation was proposed, but omitted to be held between him and Dr. Nathaniel Giles on the following questions: 1. Whether discords may be allowed in music? Affirm. 2. Whether any artificial instrument can so fully and truly express music as the natural voice? Negat. 3. Whether the practice be the more useful part of music, or the theory? Affirm.

That he had little or no skill in practical composition may fairly be inferred from a particular which Wood says he had been told by one or more eminent musicians, his contemporaries, viz., that the song of six or more parts, performed in the Act for Heyther, was composed by Orlando Gibbons.[*]

Dr. Heyther was born at Harmondsworth, in Middlesex; he died the latter end of July, 1627, and was buried on the first of August in the broad or south aisle, joining to the choir of Westminster abbey. He gave to the hospital in Tothill-Fields, Westminster, one hundred pounds, as appears by a list of benefactions to the parish of St. Margaret in that city, printed in the *New* View of London, pag. 339.

There is now in the music-school at Oxford a picture of Dr. Heyther in his gown and cap, with the book of madrigals, intitled Musica Transalpina, in his hand; from this picture the portrait of him is taken.

ORLANDO GIBBONS, *(a Portrait,)* a native of Cambridge, was, as Wood says, accounted one of the rarest musicians and organists of his time. On the thirty-first day of March, 1604, he was appointed organist of the chapels royal in the room of Arthur Cock: some of his lessons are to be found in the collection herein before spoken of, intitled Parthenia.

He published Madrigals of five parts for Voices and Viols. Lond. 1612.[†] But the most excellent of his works are his compositions for the church, namely, services and anthems, of which there are many extant in the cathedral books. One of the most celebrated of his anthems is his Hosanna, one of the most perfect models for composition in the church-style of any now existing; and indeed the general characteristic of his music is fine harmony, unaffected simplicity, and unspeakable grandeur. He also composed the tunes to the hymns and songs of the church, translated by George Withers, as appears by the dedication thereof to king James I.; they are melodies in two parts, and in their kind are excellent. It has been for some time a question whether Orlando Gibbons ever attained to either of those academical honours due to persons of eminence in his profession; but it appears most evidently by the letter inserted in the preceding article of Dr. Heyther, that on the seventeenth, *or at farthest the eighteenth* of May, 1622, he accumulated the degrees of bachelor and doctor in his faculty; as also that this honour was conferred on him for the sake of Camden, who was his intimate friend. In 1625, being commanded to Canterbury to attend the solemnity of the marriage of Charles I. and Henrietta of France, upon which occasion he had composed the music, he was seized with the small-pox, and died on Whit-Sunday in the same year, and was buried in the cathedral church of Canterbury; his widow Elizabeth erected a monument over his grave with the following inscription:—

'Orlando Gibbons Cantabrigiæ inter Musas et
'Musicam nato, sacræ R. Capellæ Organistæ, Sphæ-
'rarum Harmoniæ Digitorum: pulsu æmulo Can-
'tionum complurium quæque eum non canunt minus
'quam canuntur conditori; Viro integerrimo et cujus
'vita cum arte suavissimis moribus concordissimè
'certavit ad nupt. C. R. cum M. B. Dorobern. accito
'ictuque heu Sanguinis Crudo et crudeli fato extincto,
'choroque cœlesti transcripto die Pentecostes A. D. N.
'MDCXXV. Elizabetha conjux septemque ex eo
'liberorum parens, tanti vix doloris superstes, mæren-
'tissimo mærentissima. P. vixit A. M. D.'[‡]

Over his monument is a bust with the arms of Gibbons, viz., three scallops on a bend dexter, over a lion rampant.

Dr. Orlando Gibbons left a son named Christopher, an excellent organist, who will be spoken of hereafter.

He had two brothers, Edward and Ellis, the one organist of Bristol, the other of Salisbury. Edward was a bachelor of Cambridge, and incorporated at Oxon in 1592. Besides being organist of Bristol, he was priest-vicar, sub-chanter, and master of the choristers in that cathedral. He was sworn a gentleman of the chapel March 21, 1604, and was master to Matthew Lock. In the triumphs of Oriana are two

---

[*] A manuscript copy of the exercise for Dr. Heyther's degree has been found, with the name of Orlando Gibbons to it. It is an anthem for eight voices, taken from the forty-seventh Psalm, and appears to be the very same composition with the anthem of Orlando Gibbons to the words 'O clap your hands together, all ye people,' printed in Dr. Boyce's Cathedral Music, vol. II. pag. 59.

[†] *In the dedication of the book to Sir Christopher Hatton, the author says that they were composed in the house of his patron; and that Sir Christopher furnished the words. This person was a collateral descendant of the Lord Chancellor Hatton: he died 13th Sept. 1619, and lies interred in St. John Baptist's, otherwise Jolip's Chapel, in Westminster Abbey.*

[‡] The letters A. M. D. signify Annos, Menses, Dies, they were intended to have been placed at a distance from each other and to be filled up; but Mr. Dart, author of the antiquities of Canterbury Cathedral, has given a translation of the inscription, in which vixit A. M. D. is rendered 'he lived 1500.' Wood says he was not quite forty-five when he died.

madrigals the one in five, the other in six parts, composed by Ellis Gibbons. Wood styles him the admired organist of Salisbury. Of Edward it is said that in the time of the rebellion he assisted king Charles I. with the sum of one thousand pounds; for which instance of his loyalty he was afterwards very severely treated by those in power, who deprived him of a considerable estate, and thrust him and three grand-children out of his house, though he had then numbered more than fourscore years.

Nathaniel Giles was born in or near the city of Worcester, and took the degree of bachelor in 1585; he was one of the organists of St. George's chapel at Windsor, and master of the boys there. Upon the decease of William Hunnis, in 1597, he was appointed master of the children of the royal chapel, and was afterwards one of the organists of the chapel royal to king Charles I. He composed many excellent services and anthems. In 1607 he supplicated for the degree of doctor in his faculty, but for some unknown reason he declined performing the exercise for it till the year 1622, when he was admitted to it, at which time it was proposed that he should dispute with Dr. Heyther upon the certain questions, mentioned in the account above given of Dr. Heyther, but it does not appear that the disputation was ever held. Dr. Giles died January 24, 1633, aged seventy-five, and was buried in one of the aisles adjoining to St. George's Chapel at Windsor, under a stone with an inscription to his memory, leaving behind him the character of a man noted as well for his religious life and conversation, as his excellence in his faculty. He lived to see a son of his, named Nathaniel, a canon of Windsor and a prebendary of Worcester; and a daughter Margaret diposed of in marriage to Sir Herbert Croft, bishop of Hereford: she was living in the year 1695.

Upon the accession of Charles I. to the crown, Nicholas Laniere was appointed master of the king's music; and in Rymer's Fœdera, tom. XVIII. pag. 728, is the following grant in favour of him and other musicians, servants of the king:—

'Charles, by the grace of God, &c. To the 'treasurer and under-treasurer of our exchequer 'nowe being, and that hereafter for the tyme shall be, 'greetinge, Whereas wee have beene graciously 'pleased, in consideration of service done, and to be 'done unto us by sundrie of our musicians, to graunt 'unto them the severall annuities and yearly pensions 'hereafter following, (that is to say) to Nicholas 'Laniere master of our music two hundred poundes 'yearly for his wages, to Thomas Foord fourscore 'poundes yearly for his wages, that is, for the place 'which he formerly held, fortie poundes yearely, and 'for the place which John Ballard late deceased, held, 'and now bestowed upon him the said Thomas Foord 'fortie poundes yearly, to Robert Johnson yearely for 'wages fortie poundes and for stringes twentie poundes 'by the yeare, to Thomas Day yearely for his wages 'fortie poundes and for keeping a boy twenty-fower 'poundes by the yeare, also to Alfonso Ferabosco, 'Thomas Lupo, John Laurence, John Kelly, John 'Cogshall, Robert Taylor, Richard Deering, John

'Drewe, John Laniere, Edward Wormall, Angelo 'Notary, and Jonas Wrench, to everie of them fortie 'poundes a peece yearly for their wages, and to 'Alfonso Bales and Robert Marshe, to each of them 'twentie poundes a-peece yearely for their wages.

'Theis are therefore to will and command you, 'out of our treasure in the receipt of our exchequer, 'to cause payment to be made to our said musicians 'above-mentioned, and to every of them severally 'and respectively, the said severall annuities and 'allowances, as well presently upon the sight hereof 'for one whole year ended at the feast of th' Annun- 'ciation of the blessed Virgin Mary last past before 'the date hereof, as alsoe from the feast hitherto, and 'soe from tyme to tyme hereafter at the fower usuall 'feasts or termes of the yeare, (that is to say) at the 'feast of the Nativity of St. John the Baptist, St. 'Michael, th' Archangell, the birth of our Lord God, 'and th' Annunciation of the blessed Virgin Mary, 'by even and equall portions, during their naturall 'lives, and the lives of everie of them respectively, 'together with all fees, profitts, commodities, allow- 'ances and advantages whatsoever to the said places 'incident and belonging, in as large and ample man- 'ner as any of our musicians in the same places 'heretofore have had and enjoyed the same; and 'theis presents, or the inrollment thereof, shall be 'your sufficient warrant and dischardge in this be- 'halfe. In witnes whereof, &c.

Witnes ourself at Westminster, the eleventh day of July.

'Per breve de privato sigillo, &c.'

Charles Butler, a native of Wycomb in the county of Bucks, and a master of arts of Magdalen College, Oxford, published a book with this title, 'The Principles of Musik, in singing and setting: 'with the twofold use thereof, ecclesiasticall and 'civil.' quarto, Lond. 1636. The author of this book was a person of singular learning and ingenuity, which he manifested in sundry other works, enumerated by Wood in the Athen. Oxon. among the rest is an English grammar, published in 1633, in which he proposes a scheme of regular orthography, and makes use of characters, some borrowed from the Saxon, and others of his own invention, so singular, that we want types to exhibit them. And of this imagined improvement of his he appears to have been so fond, that all his tracts are printed in like manner with his grammar;* the consequence whereof has been an almost general disgust of all that he has written. His Principles of Music is however a very learned, curious, and entertaining book; and, by the help of the advertisement from the printer to the reader, prefixed to it, explaining the powers of the several characters made use of by him, may be read to great advantage, and may be considered as a judicious supplement to Morley's Introduction. Its contents are in the general as follows:—

Lib. I. cap. 1. Of the moodes: these the author makes to be five, following in this respect Cassiodorus, and ascribing to each a different character and effect;

* A specimen of his orthography is inserted in Dr. Johnson's grammar prefixed to his Dictionary.

their names are the Doric, Lydian, Æolic, Phrygian, and Ionic. Cap. 2. Of Singing; and herein of the number, names, tune, and time of the notes, with their external adjuncts. Cap. 3. Of Setting, and herein of the parts of a song, of melody, harmony, intervals, concords, and discords, with the consecution of each: Of Ornaments, that is to say, Syncope, fugue, and formality. Cap. 4. Of the two ways of setting, that is to say, in counterpoint and in discant.

Lib. II. cap. 1. Of instruments and of the voice. Of ditty-music, and of mixt music, in which instruments are associated with the voice. Cap. 2. Of the divine use of music. Of the continuance of church-music; of objections against it. Of the special uses of divine music, with an apostrophe to our Levites. Cap. 3. Of the allowance of civil music, with the special uses thereof, and of the objections against it. Epilogue.

This book abounds with a great variety of curious learning relating to music, selected from the best writers ancient and modern, among which latter the author appears to have held Sethus Calvisius in high estimation.

CHAP. CXXI.

Our church-music, through the industry of those who had set themselves to recover and collect the works of such musicians as flourished about the time of the Reformation; and the learning and ingenuity of those their successors who had laboured in producing new compositions, was by this time arrived at so high a degree of improvement, that it may be questioned, not only whether it was not then equal to that of any country; but whether it is if not even now, so near perfection, as to exclude the expectation of ever seeing it rivalled: and it is worthy of remark, that in the compositions of Tye, Tallis, Bird, Farrant, Gibbons, and some others, all that variety of melody, harmony, and fine modulation are discoverable, which ignorant people conceive to be the effect of modern refinement, for an instance whereof we need not seek any farther than to the anthem of Dr. Tye, 'I will exalt thee,' which a stranger to the music of our church would conceive to be a composition of the present day rather than of the sixteenth century. The same may be said of most of the compositions in the Cantiones Sacræ of Tallis and Bird, and the Cantiones Sacrarum and Gradualia of the latter, which abound with fugues of the finest contexture, and such descant, as, in the opinion of a very good judge, entitle them to the character of angelical and divine.

These considerations, aided by the disposition which Charles I. had manifested towards the church, and the favour shown by him to music and its professors, were doubtless the principal inducement to the publication in the year 1641, of a noble collection of church-music by one John Barnard, a minor canon of St. Paul's cathedral, the title whereof is as follows:—

'The first book of selected Church-music, consist-'ing of services and anthems, such as are now used 'in the cathedral collegiate churches of this kingdom,

'never before printed, whereby such books as were 'heretofore with much difficulty and charges tran-'scribed for the use of the quire, are now, to the 'saving of much labour and expence, published for 'the general good of all such as shall desire them 'either for publick or private exercise. Collected 'out of divers approved authors by John Barnard, 'one of the Minor Canons of the cathedral church 'of Saint Paul, London. London, printed by Edward 'Griffin, and are to be sold at the signe of the Three 'Lutes in Paul's alley. 1641.'

The contents of this book are services for morning and evening, and the communion, preces, and responses by Tallis, Strogers, Bevin, Bird, Orlando Gibbons, William Mundy, Parsons, Morley, Dr. Giles, Woodson; the Litany by Tallis, and anthems in four, five, and six parts, to a great number, by Tallis, Hooper, Farrant, Shepheard, Will. Mundy, Gibbons, Batten, Dr. Tye, Morley, Hooper, White, Dr. Giles, Parsons, Weelkes, Dr. Bull, and Ward: and here it may not be amiss to remark, that in this collection the anthem 'O God the maker of all things,' is ascribed to William Mundy, contrary to the opinion that has ever been entertained. It was probably this book that set Dr. Aldrich upon an inquiry after the fact, which terminated in a full conviction, founded upon evidence, that it is a composition of Henry VIII.

The book is dedicated to king Charles I. considering which, and the great expence and labour of such a publication, it might be conjectured that his majesty had liberally contributed towards it; but the contrary is so evident from a passage in the preface, where the author speaks of the charges of the work as an adventurous enterprize, that we are left at a loss which to commend most, his zeal, his industry, or the liberality of his spirit. For not to mention the labour and expence of collecting and copying such a number of musical compositions as fill a folio volume, not only the music, but the letter-press types appear to have been cast on purpose, the latter of which are in the character called by writing-masters, Secretary; with the initial letters in German text of a large size and finely ornamented.

A few years after the publication of Barnard's Collection, another was printed with this title, 'Musica 'Deo sacra et Ecclesiæ Anglicanæ, or music dedicated 'to the honour and service of God, and to the use 'of cathedrals and other churches of England, espe-'cially the chapel royal of king Charles I.' in ten books by Thomas Tomkins, bachelor of music, of whom an account has before been given.* This work consists of a great variety of services of different kinds, and anthems from three to ten parts, all of the author's own composition, many whereof are in great estimation.†

There was great reason to expect that the publications above-mentioned would have been followed

---

* See page 507 of this work.
† It is much to be lamented that the thought of printing them in score did not occur to the publishers of these several collections; the consequence is, that, by the loss of part of the book, they at this day can scarcely be said to exist. Some years ago diligent search was made for a complete set of Barnard's books, and in all the kingdom there was not one to be found; the least imperfect was that belonging to the choir of Hereford, but in this the boys' parts were defective.

by others of the like kind not less valuable ; but the Puritans, who had long been labouring to abolish the liturgy, had now got the reins of government into their hands, and all hopes of this kind were frustrated by an ordinance which passed the House of Lords January 4, 1644, repealing the statutes of Edward VI. and Elizabeth, for uniformity in the Common Prayer ; and ordaining that the book of Common Prayer should not from thenceforth be used in any church, chapel, or place of public worship within the kingdom of England or dominion of Wales ; but that the directory for public worship therein set forth, should be thenceforth used, pursued, and observed in all exercises of the public worship of God.*

The directory referred to by the above ordinance was drawn up by the assembly of divines at Westminster,† who were the standing council of the parliament in all matters concerning religion ; the preface represents the use of the liturgy or service-book as ' burdensome, and a great hindrance to the preach-
' ing of the word, and that ignorant and superstitious
' people had made an idol of common prayer, and,
' pleasing themselves in their presence at that service,
' and their lip-labour in bearing a part in it, had
' thereby hardened themselves in their ignorance and
' carelessness of saving knowledge and true piety.
' That the liturgy had been a great means, as on the
' one hand to make and increase an idle unedifying
' ministry, which contented itself with set forms made
' to their hands by others, without putting forth them-
' selves to exercise the gift of prayer, with which our
' Lord Jesus Christ pleaseth to furnish all his servants
' whom he calleth to that office ; so on the other side it
' had been, and ever would be, if continued, a matter
' of endless strife and contention in the church.'

For these and other reasons contained in the preface, which represent the hearing of the word as a much more important duty of religion than prayer or thanksgiving, the directory establishes a new form of divine worship, in which the singing of Psalms is all of music that is allowed ; concerning which the following are the rules :—

' It is the duty of Christians to praise God pub-
' lickly by singing of psalms, together in the congre-
' gation, and also privately in the family. In singing
' of psalms the voice is to be tuneably and gravely
' ordered ; but the chief care must be to sing with
' understanding and with grace in the heart, making
' melody unto the Lord. That the whole congre-
' gation may join herein, every one that can read is
' to have a psalm-book, and all others, not disabled
' by age or otherwise, are to be exhorted to learn to
' read. But for the present, where many in the con-
' gregation cannot read, it is convenient that the
' minister, or some fit person appointed by him and
' the other ruling officers, do read the psalm line by
' line before the singing thereof.'
*The objection of the Puritans to the use of in-
strumental Music in holy offices is, that it is both
Jewish and Popish : upon which it may be remarked
that the same may respectively be said of one at least*

*of the ten Commandments and of the Lord's Prayer ;
and Sir Edward Deering, who had the merit of
bringing into the House of Commons the Bill for
the abolition of Episcopacy, in the true spirit of
his party has asserted in print that one single groan
in the Spirit is worth the Diapason of all the Church
music in the world. See his Declaration and Petition to the House of Commons, Lond. 1644. The
Directory seems to have compounded the matter by
allowing the singing of Psalms, but has left it as
a question to be agitated in future, whether the use
of Organs in Divine worship be lawful or not ; accordingly upon the Restoration of the Liturgy and
the use of Organs in 1660, the Non-conformists declared against all instrumental music in Churches,
and gave occasion to the publication of a discourse
entitled ' The well-tuned Organ,' by one Joseph
Brookband, a Clergyman, 4to, 1660, wherein the
question is fully discussed and the Affirmative maintained. In 1679, Dr. Edward Wetenhall, then
Chanter of Christ Church, Dublin, and afterwards
Bishop of Kilmore and Ross, published a discourse
of Gifts and Offices, i. e. Prayer, Singing and
Preaching, in the worship of God, 8vo. wherein the
usage in the established church with respect to the
points in question is with great learning and judgment defended. In 1698, upon the erection of an
organ in the Parish Church of Tiverton, in the
County of Devon, a sermon was preached by one
Mr. Newte, which produced an anonymous answer
in 4to, 1698. This was followed by a discourse
concerning the rise and antiquity of Cathedral
Worship, in a letter to a friend first printed in
1699, and afterwards in a collection of Tracts on
the growth of Deism and other subjects, 8vo. 1709.
This discourse includes a very severe censure of the
practice in question ; but was suffered to remain
without animadversion. In 1700, the learned Mr.
Henry Dodwell published a treatise concerning the
lawfulness of music in holy offices, in an octavo
volume ; the preface written by the above Mr. Newte
is a formal reply to the answer to the sermon ; and
for upwards of four-score years this controversy,
which began between Cartright and Hooker, has
been at rest. Vide first note in chap. cxxv.*

Thus was the whole fabric of the liturgy subverted, and the study of that kind of harmony rendered useless, which had hitherto been looked upon as a great incentive to devotion. That there is a tendency in music to excite grave, and even devout, as well as lively and mirthful affections, no one can doubt who is not an absolute stranger to its efficacy ; and though it may perhaps be said that the effects of music are mechanical, and that there can be nothing pleasing to God in that devotion which follows the involuntary operation of sound on the human mind : this is more than can be proved ; and the scripture seems to intimate the contrary.

The abolition of the liturgy was attended not barely with a contempt of those places where it had been usually performed ; but by a positive exertion of that power which the then remaining reliques of the legislature had usurped, the Common Prayer had been declared by public authority to be a superstitious ritual. In the opinion of these men it therefore became necessary for the promotion of true religion that organs should be taken down ; that choral music-books should be torn and destroyed ; that painted glass windows should be broken ; that cathedral service should be totally abolished, and that those retainers to the church whose duty it had been to celebrate its more solemn service, should betake themselves to some employment less offensive to God than that of singing his praises.   In consequence of these, which were the predominant opinions of those times, collegiate and parochial churches were spoiled of their ornaments ; monuments were defaced ; sepulchral inscriptions engraven on brass were torn up ; libraries and repositories were ransacked for ancient musical service-books, and Latin or English, popish or protestant, they were deemed equally superstitious and ungodly, and as such were committed to the flames or otherwise destroyed, and, in short, such havoc and devastation made, as could only be equalled by that which attended the suppression of religious houses under Henry VIII.

The sentiments of these men, who, to express the meekness and inoffensiveness of their dispositions, had assumed the name of Puritans, with respect to the reverence due to places set apart for the purpose of religious worship, were such as freed them from all restraints of common decency : that there is no inherent holiness in the stones or timbers that compose a cathedral or other church ; and that the ceremony of consecration implies nothing more than an exemption of the place or thing which is the subject of it from vulgar and common use, is agreed by the sober and rational kind of mankind ; and on the minds of such the ceremonies attending the dedication of churches have operated accordingly ; but, as if there had been a merit in contradicting the common sense and opinion of the world, no sooner were these men vested with the power, than they found the means to level all distinctions of place and situation, and to pervert the temples of God to the vilest and most profane uses.

To instance in one particular ; the cathedral church of St. Paul was turned into horse-quarters for the soldiers of the parliament, saving the choir, which was separated by a brick wall from the nave, and converted into a preaching place, the entrance to which was at a door formerly a window on the north side eastwards.*   Hitherto many of the citizens and others were used to resort to hear Dr. Cornelius Burgess, who had an assignment of four hundred pounds a year out of the revenue of the church, as a reward for his sermons, which were usually made up of invectives against deans, chapters, and singing-men, against whom he seemed to entertain a great antipathy.†   The noble Corinthian portico at the west end, designed by Jones, was leased out to a man of a projecting head, who built in it a number of small shops, which were letten by him to haberdashers,

* Dugdale's Hist. of St. Paul's Cathedral, pag. 173
† Athen. Oxon. vol. II. col. 347.

glovers, semsters, as they were then called, or milliners, and other petty tradesmen, and obtained the name of St. Paul's Change.

Of musicians of eminence who flourished in the reign of king Charles I. the following are among the chief :—

RICHARD DEERING was descended from an ancient family of that name in Kent.   He was bred up in Italy, where he obtained the reputation of a most admirable musician.   On his return to England, he practised for some time, but being straightly importuned, he became organist to the monastery of English nuns at Brussels ; upon the marriage of king Charles I. he was appointed organist to his consort Henrietta Maria, in which station he continued till he was compelled to leave England : he took the degree of bachelor of music as a member of Christ-Church college, Oxon, in 1610 ; he has left of his composition ' Cantiones sacræ quinque vocum, ' cum basso continuo ad Organum.' Antwerp, 1597 ; and ' Cantica sacra ad melodiam madrigalium elabo- ' borata senis vocibus.' Antwerp, 1618.   He died in the communion of the church of Rome about the year 1657.

JOHN HINGSTON, a scholar of Orlando Gibbons,‡ was organist to Oliver Cromwell, who as it is said, had some affection for music and musicians.§   Hingston was first in the service of Charles I. but for a pension of one hundred pounds a year he went over to Cromwell, and instructed his daughters in music. He bred up under him two boys, whom he taught to sing with him Deering's Latin songs, which Cromwell greatly delighted to hear, and had often performed before him at the Cock-pit at Whitehall.   He had concerts at his own house, at which Cromwell would

‡ Anthony Wood, from whose manuscript in the Ashmolean Museum the above account is partly taken, was not able to fill up the blank which he left therein for the name of Hingston's master ; but a manuscript in the hand-writing of Hingston, now extant, ascertains it.   This relic is thus inscribed :—' My Masters Songs in score with some Fanta- ' zias of 6 parts of my own.'   The Fantazias stand first in the book, and are about six in number, some subscribed Jo. Hingston, Jan. 1640, and other dates ; the songs are subscribed Orlando Gibbons.   Hence it is to be inferred that Orlando Gibbons was the master of Hingston : and this supposition is corroborated by the following anecdote, communicated by one of Hingston's descendants now living, to wit, that the Christian name Orlando, for reasons which they have hitherto been ignorant of, has in several instances been given to the males of the family.   Note, that in the MS. above-mentioned one of Gibbons's songs has this memorandum, ' Made for Prince Charles to be sung with 5 voices to his wind ' instrument.'

§ There are many particulars related of Cromwell, which show that he was a lover of music : indeed Anthony Wood expressly asserts it in his life of himself, pag. 139, and as a proof of it relates the following story :— ' A. W. had some acquaintance with James Quin, M.A. one of the ' senior students of Christ Church, and had several times heard him ' sing with great admiration, His voice was a bass, and he had a great ' command of it ; t'was very strong, and exceeding trouling, but he ' wanted skill, and could scarce sing in consort.   He had been turn'd out ' of his student's place by the visitors, but being well acquainted with ' some great men of those times that loved musick, they introduced him ' into the company of Oliver Cromwell the protector, who loved a good ' voice and instrumental musick well.   He heard him sing with very ' great delight, liquor'd him with sack, and in conclusion said, " Mr. " Quin, you have done very well, what shall I do for you ? "   To which ' Quin made answer with great complements, of which he had command, ' with great grace, " That your Highness would be pleased to restore me " to my student's place ; " which he did accordingly, and so kept it to ' his dying day.'

Cromwell was also fond of the music of the organ, as appears from the following remarkable anecdote :—In the grand rebellion, when the organ at Magdalen college in Oxford among others was taken down, Cromwell ordered it to be carefully conveyed to Hampton-Court, where it was placed in the great gallery ; and one of Cromwell's favourite amusements was to be entertained with this instrument at leisure hours. It continued there till the Restoration, when it was returned to its original owners, and was the same that remained in the choir of that college till within these last thirty years.   Observations on the Fairy Queen of Spenser by Tho. Warton. Lond. 1772, vol. II. pag. 236, in not.

often be present. In one of these musical entertainments Sir Roger L'Estrange happened to be a performer, and Sir Roger not leaving the room upon Cromwell's coming into it, the Cavaliers gave him the name of Oliver's fiddler; but in a pamphlet entitled Truth and Loyalty vindicated, Lond. 1662, he clears himself from the imputation which this reproachful appellation was intended to fix on him, and relates the story in the words following :—

'Concerning the story of the fiddle, this I suppose 'might be the rise of it. Being in St. James's park, 'I heard an organ touched in a little low room of one 'Mr. Hinckson's; I went in, and found a private 'company of five or six persons : they desired me to 'take up a viole and bear a part, I did so, and that a 'part too, not much to advance the reputation of my 'cunning. By and by, without the least colour of a 'design or expectation, in comes Cromwell. He 'found us playing, and as I remember so he left us.'

Hingston was Dr. Blow's first master, though the inscription on Blow's monument takes no notice of it, but says that he was brought up under Dr. Christopher Gibbons. He had a nephew named Peter, educated under Purcell, and who was organist of Ipswich, and an eminent teacher of music there and in that neighbourhood. A picture of John Hingston is in the music-school, Oxon.

JOHN HILTON, *(a Portrait,)* a bachelor in music of the university of Cambridge, was organist of the church of St. Margaret, Westminster, and also clerk of that parish.* He was the author of a madrigal in five parts, printed in the Triumphs of Oriana. In 1627 he published Fa La's for three voices;† and in 1652, 'A choice Collection of Catches, Rounds, and Canons for 3 or 4 voyces,' containing some of the most excellent compositions of this kind any where extant, many of them by himself, the rest by the most eminent of his contemporaries.

There are extant in the choir-books of many cathedrals a morning and evening service of Hilton's composition, but they were never printed. He died in the time of the usurpation, and was buried in the cloister of the abbey-church of Westminster, with the solemnity of an anthem sung in the church before his corpse was brought out for interment; an honour which he well deserved, for, though not a voluminous composer, he was an ingenious and sound musician.

WILLIAM LAWES, the son of Thomas Lawes, a vicar-choral of the church of Salisbury, and a native of that city, having an early propensity to music, was, at the expence of Edward earl of Hertford,

educated under Coperario. He was first of the choir at Chichester, but was called from thence, and on the first day of January, 1602, was sworn a gentleman of the royal chapel. On the sixth day of May, 1611 he resigned his place in favour of one Ezekiel Wood, and became one of the private musicians to king Charles I. Fuller says he was respected and beloved of all such persons who cast any looks towards virtue and honour; and he seems to have been well worthy of their regard : his gratitude and loyalty to his master appear in this, that he took up arms for the king against the parliament, and though, to exempt him from danger, the general, Lord Gerrard, made him a commissary, yet the activity of his spirit disdained that security which was intended for him, and at the siege of Chester, in 1645, he lost his life by a casual shot. The king was so affected at his loss, that it is said he wore a particular mourning for him.‡

His compositions were for the most part Fantasias for viols and the organ. His brother Henry, in the preface to a joint work of theirs, hereunder mentioned, asserts that he composed above thirty several sorts of music for voices and instruments, and that there was not any instrument in use in his time but he composed so aptly to it as if he had only studied that. Many songs of his are to be met with in the collections of that day; several catches and rounds, and a few canons of his composition are published in Hilton's Collection, but the chief of his printed works are, 'Choice Psalms put into Musick for three voices,' with a thorough-bass, composed to the words of Mr. Sandys's paraphrase, by him in conjunction with his brother Henry, and published in 1648, with nine canons of William Lawes printed at the end of the thorough-bass book.

HENRY LAWES, *(a Portrait,)* the brother of the former. Of his education little is known, except that he was a scholar of Coperario. By the cheque-book of the chapel royal it appears that he was sworn in Pisteller on the first day of January, 1625, and on the third of November following a gentleman of the chapel; after that he was appointed clerk of the cheque, and of the private music to king Charles I. Lawes is celebrated for having first introduced the Italian style of music into this kingdom, upon no better pretence than a song of his, the subject whereof is the story of Theseus and Ariadne, being the first among his Ayres and Dialogues for one, two, and three voices, Lond. fol. 1653, wherein are some passages which a superficial reader might mistake for recitative. The book however deserves particular notice, for it is published with a preface by Lawes himself, and commendatory verses by Waller,

---

* These two offices may seem incompatible, but upon searching the Parish Books it is found. The antient usage of the Parish of St. Margaret was to elect two persons to the office of Parish Clerk, and one of them to that of Organist. Hilton was elected Parish Clerk and Organist in 1628, and in the account of the Churchwardens his salary as Clerk is charged at £6. 13s. 4d. or ten Marks a year: his salary for officiating in the latter capacity does not appear. It is supposed that his employment of Organist ceased in 1644; for in that year by an ordinance of Parliament, Organs were taken down; and the church seems to have been without one till after the Restoration, when Father Smith was employed to build that which is now in the above church, and was himself in 1676 elected Organist with a salary of £20. a year. It appears by the Parish Books, that, while the church was without an organ, it was the usage there to read, and not to sing the singing Psalms.

† Fa La's are short songs set to music, with a repetition of those syllables at the second and fourth line, and sometimes only at the end of every stanza. Morley composed many songs of this kind, but none equal to those of Hilton, which are remarkable for the goodness of the melody.

‡ The following quibbling lines were written on occasion of his death :—
On Mr. William Lawes, Musician, slain at the siege of West Chester.
    Concord is conquer'd; in this urn there lies
    The Master of great Music's Mysteries;
    And in it is a riddle like the cause,
    Will. Lawes was slain by those whose Wills were Laws.

Who was the author of them is hardly worth enquiry; but it may be noted, that among the commendatory verses prefixed to the second edition of Playford's Musical Companion, printed in 1673, are certain lines written by Thomas Jordan, wherein is this couplet—
    When by the fury of the good old cause,
    Will. Lawes was slain by such whose Wills were Laws.

This Thomas Jordan was a Dramatic Poet and a composer of city pageants : there is an article for him in Langbaine's account of the English Dramatic Poets, page 306.

JOHN HILTON

MUS.BACC.CANTAB. MDCXXVI.

From a Picture in the Music-School, Oxford.

HENRY LAWES SERVANT TO HIS MAJESTIE

KING CHA.I.IN HIS PUBLIC AND PRIVATE MUSIC.

Edward and John Phillips, the nephews of Milton, and other persons; besides, that the songs are, for the poetry, some of the best compositions of the kind in the English language; and, what is remarkable, many of them appear to have been written by young noblemen and gentlemen, of whose talents for poetry there are hardly any other evidences remaining; some of their names are as follow: Thomas earl of Winchelsea, William earl of Pembroke, John earl of Bristol, lord Broghill, Mr. Thomas Carey, a son of the earl of Monmouth, Mr. Henry Noel, son of lord Camden, Sir Charles Lucas, supposed to be he that together with Sir George Lisle was shot at Colchester after the surrender of the garrison; and Carew Raleigh, the son of Sir Walter Raleigh. In the preface to this book the author mentions his having formerly composed some airs to Italian and Spanish words; and speaking of the Italians, he acknowledges them in general to be the greatest masters of music: yet he contends that this nation had produced as able musicians as any in Europe. He censures the fondness of the age for songs sung in a language which the hearers do not understand: and to ridicule it, mentions a song of his own composition, printed at the end of the book, which is nothing else than an index containing the initial words of some old Italian songs or madrigals; and this index, which read together made a strange medley of nonsense, he says he set to a varied air, and gave out that it came from Italy, whereby it passed for an Italian song. In the title-page of this book is a very fine engraving of the author's head by Faithorne, a copy whereof, with the inscription under it, is inserted in the Portrait volume.

The first composition in this book is the Complaint of Ariadne, written by Mr. William Cartwright of Christ-Church college, Oxon. The music is neither recitative nor air, but is in so precise a medium between both, that a name is wanting for it. The song is in the key of C, with the minor third, and seems to abound with semitonic intervals, the use of which was scarcely known at that time. Whether it was this singular circumstance, or some other less obvious, that contributed to recommend it, cannot now be discovered, but the applauses that attended the publication of it exceed all belief.

In the year 1633, Henry Lawes, together with Simon Ives, were made choice of to compose the airs, lessons, and songs of a masque presented at Whitehall on Candlemas-night before the king and queen by the gentlemen of the four inns of court, under the direction of Noy the attorney-general, Mr. Edward Hyde, afterwards earl of Clarendon, Mr. Selden, Bulstrode Whitelocke,* and others. Of this ridi-

* Whitelocke made great pretensions to skill in music. In the manuscript memoirs of his life above-mentioned, he relates that 'with the 'assistance of Mr. Ives he composed an air, and called it Whitelocke's 'Coranto, which was first played publicly by the Black Friars music, 'then esteemed the best in London. That whenever he went to the 'playhouse there, the musicians would immediately upon his coming in 'play it. That the queen hearing it, would scarce believe it was com-'posed by an Englishman, because, as she said, it was fuller of life and 'spirit than the English airs, but that she honoured the Coranto and the 'maker of it with her majesty's royal commendation: and, lastly, that 'it grew to that request, that all the common musicians in this towne, 'and all over the kingdome, gott the composition of it, and played it 'publicly in all places for about thirty years after.' The reader may probably wish to peruse a dance tune the composition of a grave lawyer, one who was afterwards a commissioner of the great seal, and an ambassador, and which a queen of England vouchsafed thus to honour; and to gratify his curiosity it is here inserted by the favour of Dr. Morton of the British Museum, the possessor of the MS. from which it is taken:—

CORANTO.

LORD COMMISSIONER WHITELOCKE.

In the Journal of his embassy to Sweden, lately published from the above-mentioned MS. is this passage: 'Piementelle staying with 'Whitelocke above three howers, he was intertained with Whitelocke's 'musick; the rector chori was Mr. Ingelo, excellent in that and other 'faculties, and seven or eight of his gentlemen, well skilled both in 'vocall and instrumentall musicke; and Whitelocke himself sometimes 'in private did, beare his part with them, having bin in his younger dayes 'a master and composer of musick.' Vol. I. page 289.

In the account which gave occasion to this note it is said that Lawes

and Ives had each an hundred pounds for composing the music to the masque: the same adds that proportionable rewards were also given to four French gentlemen of the queen's chapel, who assisted in the representation. Whitelocke's words are these: 'I invited them one 'morning to a collation at St. Dunstan's taverne, in the great roome, the 'Oracle of Apollo, where each of them had his plate layd for him covered, 'and the napkin by it; and when they opened their plates, they found 'in each of them forty pieces of gould of their master's coyne for the 'first dish.'

culous scene of mummery Whitelocke has given an account in his Memorials, but one much longer and more particular in certain memoirs of his life extant in manuscript, wherein he relates that Lawes and Ives had each an hundred pounds for his trouble, and that the whole charge of the music came to about one thousand pounds. *The masque was written by Shirley, it is entitled the Triumph of Peace, and is printed in 4to. like his plays. William Lawes joined with his brother and Ives in the composition of the music.*

Henry Lawes also composed tunes to Mr. George Sandys's excellent paraphrase on the Psalms, published first in folio in the year 1638, and in 1676 in octavo. These tunes are different from those in the Psalms composed by Henry and William Lawes, and published in the year 1648; they are for a single voice with a bass, and were intended for private devotion: that to Psalm lxxii. is now, and beyond the memory of any now living, has been played by the chimes of the church of St. Lawrence Jewry, London, at the hours of four, eight, and twelve.

Milton's Comus was originally set by Henry Lawes and was first published by him in the year 1637, with a dedication to Lord Bracly, son and heir of the earl of Bridgewater.

Of the history of this elegant poem little more is known than that it was written for the entertainment of the noble earl mentioned in the title-page of it, and that it was represented as a masque by his children and others; but the fact is, that it is founded on a real story: for the earl of Bridgewater being president of Wales in the year 1634, had his residence at Ludlow-castle in Shropshire; lord Bracly and Mr. Egerton, his sons, and lady Alice Egerton, his daughter, passing through a place called the Hay-Wood forest, or Haywood in Herefordshire, were benighted, and the lady for some short time lost; this accident being related to their father upon their arrival at his castle, furnished a subject which Milton wrought into one of the finest poems of the kind in any language; and being a drama, it was represented on Michaelmas night, 1634, at Ludlow-castle, for the entertainment of the family and the neighbouring nobility and gentry. Lawes himself performing in it the character of the attendant spirit, who towards the middle of the drama appears to the brothers habited like a shepherd, and is by them called Thirsis.*

Lawes's music to Comus was never printed, and there is nothing in any of the printed copies of the poem, nor in the many accounts of Milton now extant, that tends to satisfy a curious enquirer as to the form in which it was set to music, whether in recitative, or otherwise; but by a MS. in his own hand-writing it appears that the two songs, 'Sweet 'Echo,' and 'Sabrina Fair,' together with three other passages in the poem, 'Back, shepherds, back,' 'To 'the ocean now I fly,' 'Now my task is smoothly 'done.' selected for the purpose, were the whole of the original music to Comus, and that the rest of it being blank verse, was uttered with action in a manner conformable to the rules of theatric representation. The first of these songs is here given. At the end of it a quaint alteration of the reading occurs, which none but a musician would have thought of :—

* See the dedication of the original printed in 1637, and in Dr. Newton's edition of Milton's poetical works.

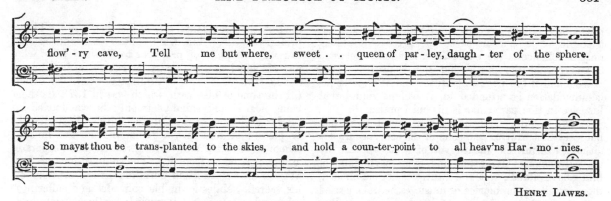

flow'-ry cave, Tell me but where, sweet .. queen of par-ley, daugh-ter of the sphere.

So mayst thou be trans-planted to the skies, and hold a coun-ter-point to all heav'ns Har-mo-nies.

HENRY LAWES.

Lawes taught music in the family of the earl of Bridgewater, the lady Alice Egerton was in particular his scholar;* he was intimate with Milton, as may be conjectured from that sonnet of the latter—

'Harry, whose tuneful and well-measured song.'

Peck says that Milton wrote his masque of Comus at the request of Lawes, who engaged to set it to music; this fact needs but little evidence; he fulfilled his engagement, adapting, as we may well suppose, the above song to the voice of the young lady whose part in the drama required that she should sing it.

The songs of Lawes to a very great number are to be found in the collections entitled 'Select musical 'Ayres and Dialogues,' by Dr. Wilson, Dr. Charles Colman, Lawes himself, and William Webb, fol. 1652; Ayres and Dialogues published by himself in 1653, and The Treasury of Music, 1669; and in various others printed about that time. Among them are most of the songs of Waller set by Lawes; and Mr. Waller has acknowledged his obligation to him for one in particular which he had set in the year 1635, in a poem wherein he celebrates his skill as a musician, concluding with these lines :—

'Let those which only warble long,
'And gargle in their throats a song,
'Content themselves with UT, RE, MI,
'Let words and sense be set by thee.'

Mr. Fenton, in a note on this poem, says that the best poets of that age were ambitious of having their verses composed by this incomparable artist, who having been educated under Signor Coperario, introduced a softer mixture of Italian airs than before had been practised in our nation.† This assertion has no better a foundation than the bare opinion of its author, and upon a slight examination will appear to be a mistake; Coperario was not an Italian, but an Englishman, who having visited Italy for improvement, returned to England, Italianized his name, and affected to be called Signor Giovanni Coperario,

instead of Mr. John Cooper. It appears by his compositions that he affected to imitate the style of the Italians, but that he introduced into our music any mixture of the Italian air, will hardly be granted by any that have perused his works. And as to Lawes, he has in the preface to his Ayres and Dialogues, intimated little less than a dislike of the Italian style, and in the last composition in that book done his utmost to ridicule it. The truth is, that not only in the time of Coperario, but in that of Lawes himself, the music of the English had scarce any air at all : and although in the much-applauded song of Lawes, his Ariadne, he has imitated the Italians by setting part of it in recitative ; there is nothing in the airs that distinguishes them from the songs of the time composed by English masters ; at least it must be confessed that they differ widely in style from those of Carissimi and Marc Antonio Cesti, who were the first that introduced into music that elegant succession of harmonic intervals which is understood by the term melody. This superiority of the Italian melody is to be ascribed to the invention of the opera, in which the airs are looked on as the most considerable part of the entertainment : it is but natural to suppose that when the stage was in possession of the finest voices of a country, every endeavour would be used to exhibit them to advantage ; and this could no way so effectually be done as by giving to the voice-parts such melodies as by their natural sweetness and elegant contrivance would most conduce to engage the attention of the judicious hearers.

But to return to Henry Lawes, he continued in the service of Charles I. no longer than till the breaking out of the rebellion ; after that he betook himself to the teaching of ladies to sing, and by his irreproachable life and gentlemanly deportment, contributed more than all the musicians of his time to raise the credit of his profession ; he however retained his place in the royal chapel, and composed the anthem for the coronation of Charles II. He died on the twenty-first day of October, 1662, and was buried in Westminster abbey.

If we were to judge of the merit of Lawes as a musician from the numerous testimonies of authors in his favour, we should rank him among the first that this country has produced ; but setting these aside, his title to fame will appear but ill-grounded. Notwithstanding he was a servant of the church, he contributed nothing to the increase of its stores : his

---

* She was also Countess of Carbery. See the Dedication to Lawes's Songs, 1653. Dr. Taylor preached her funeral sermon ; it is among his printed sermons. There is a song among the old collections entitled The Earl to the Countess of Carbery. Her sister Lady Mary married Lord Herbert of Cherbury. See the above Dedication, and Collins's Peerage—Egerton Duke of Bridgewater.

† Mr. Fenton, in the same note upon these lines of Waller, seems not to have understood the meaning of the two last. It was a custom with the musicians of those times to frame compositions, and those in many parts, to the syllables of Guido's hexachord, and many such are extant : Mr. Waller meant in the passage above-cited to reprehend this practice, and very emphatically says that while others content themselves with setting notes to syllables that have no meaning, Lawes employs his talent in adapting music to words replete with sentiment, like those of Mr. Waller.

talent lay chiefly in the composition of songs for a single voice, and in these the great and almost only excellence is the exact correspondence between the accent of the music and the quantities of the verse; and if the poems of Milton and Waller in his commendation be attended to, it will be found that his care in this particular is his chief praise.

It will readily be believed that music flourished but very little during the time of the usurpation; for although Cromwell was a lover of it, as appears by his patronage of Hingston, and other particulars of him above-noted; yet the liturgy being abolished, those excellent seminaries of music, cathedrals, ceased now to afford a subsistence to its professors, so that they were necessitated to seek a livelihood by teaching vocal and instrumental music in private families; and even here they met with but a cold reception, for the fanaticism of the times led many to think music an unchristian recreation, and that no singing but the singing of David's Psalms was to be tolerated in a church that pretended to be forming itself into the most perfect model of primitive sanctity.

Of the gentlemen of king Charles the First's chapel, a few had loyalty and resolution enough to become sharers in his fortunes; and among these were George Jefferies, his organist at Oxford in 1643, and Dr. John Wilson; of the latter Wood gives an account to this purpose :—

John Wilson (*a Portrait,*) was born at Feversham in Kent. He seemed to value himself on the place of his nativity, and was often used to remark for the honour of that county, that both Alphonso Ferabosco and John Jenkins were his countrymen; the former was born of Italian parents at Greenwich, and the latter at Maidstone; they both excelled in the composition of Fantasias for viols, and were greatly esteemed both here and abroad. He was first a gentleman of his majesty's chapel, and afterwards his servant in ordinary in the faculty of music; and was esteemed the best performer on the lute in England; and being a constant attendant on the king, frequently played to him, when the king would usually lean on his shoulder. He was created doctor at Oxford in 1644, but upon the surrender of the garrison of that city in 1646, he left the university, and was received into the family of Sir William Walter, of Sarsden in Oxfordshire, who with his lady, were great lovers of music. At length, upon the request of Mr. Thomas Barlow, lecturer of Church-Hill, the parish where Sir William Walter dwelt, to Dr. Owen, vice-chancellor of the university, he was constituted music-professor thereof anno 1656, and had a lodging assigned him in Baliol college, where being assisted by some of the royalists, he lived very comfortably, exciting in the university such a love of music as in a great measure accounts for that flourishing state in which it has long subsisted there, and for those numerous private meetings at Oxford, of which Anthony Wood, in his life of himself, has given an ample and interesting narrative. After the Restoration he became one of the private music to Charles II. and one of the gentlemen of his chapel, succeeding in the latter capacity Henry Lawes, who

died on the twenty-first day of October, 1662. These preferments drew him from Oxford, and induced him to resign his place of professor to Edward Low, who had officiated as his deputy, and to settle in a house at the Horse-ferry, at Westminster, where he dwelt till the time of his death, which was in 1673, he then being near seventy-nine years old : he was buried in the little cloister of St. Peter's church, Westminster. A picture of him is yet remaining in the music-school at Oxford, and the engraving (as in separate Volume) is taken from it. The compositions of Dr. Wilson are 'Psalterium Carolinum, the Devotions of 'his sacred Majestie in his solitudes and sufferings 'rendered in verse, set to musick for three voices and 'an organ or theorbo,' fol. 1657. 'Cheerful Airs or 'Ballads;' first composed for one single voice, and since 'set 'for three voices. Oxon. 1660.' 'Airs for a voice 'alone to a Theorbo or Bass Viol;' these are printed in a collection entitled 'Select Airs and Dialogues,' fol. 1653. 'Divine Services and anthems,' the words whereof are in James Clifford's Collection, Lond. 1663. He also composed music to sundry of the odes of Horace, and to some select passages in Ausonius, Claudian, Petronius Arbiter, and Statius, these were never published, but are extant in a manuscript volume curiously bound in blue Turkey leather, with silver clasps, which the doctor presented to the university with an injunction that no person should be permitted to peruse it till after his decease. It is now among the archives of the Bodleian library.

It appears that Dr. Wilson was a man of a facetious temper, and Wood has taken occasion from this circumstance to represent him as a great humourist, and a pretender to buffoonery : most people know that a humourist and a man of humour are two very different characters, but this distinction did not occur to Anthony. Henry Lawes has given a much more amiable, and probably a truer portrait of him in the following lines, part of a poem prefixed to the Psalterium Carolinum :—

'From long acquaintance and experience, I
'Could tell the world thy known integrity;
'Unto thy friend; thy true and honest heart,
'Ev'n mind, good nature, all but thy great art,
'Which I but dully understand.'

CHAP. CXXII.

Benjamin Rogers was the son of Peter Rogers of the chapel of St. George at Windsor; he was born at Windsor, and was first a chorister under the tuition of Dr. Nathaniel Giles, and afterwards a clerk or singing-man in that chapel : after that he became organist of Christ-Church, Dublin, and continued in that station till the rebellion in 1641, when being forced thence, he returned to Windsor, and again became a clerk in St. George's chapel; but the troubles of the times obliging him to quit that station, he subsisted by teaching music at Windsor, and on an annual allowance, which was made him in consideration of the loss of his place. In 1653, he composed Airs of four parts for Violins, which were presented to the archduke Leopold, afterwards

IOHN WILSON

MUS. DOCT. OXON.

MDCXLIV.

From an original Painting in the Music-School. Oxford.

emperor of Germany, and were often played before him to his great delight; he being himself an excellent musician.

Mr. Rogers was favoured in his studies by Dr. Nathaniel Ingelo, a fellow of Eton college, who in the year 1653 being appointed chaplain to lord commissioner Whitelocke, embassador to Sweden, took with him thither some compositions for instruments, which were oftentimes played before queen Christina, and greatly admired, not only by her majesty, but by the Italian musicians her servants.* Afterwards, viz., in the year 1658, the same Dr. Ingelo recommended his friend Rogers to the university of Cambridge, and having obtained a mandate from Cromwell for that purpose, he was admitted to the degree of bachelor in music of that university.

In the year 1662, October 21, Mr. Rogers was again appointed a clerk of St. George's chapel at Windsor, with an addition of half the salary of a clerk's place beside his own, and also an allowance of twenty shillings per month out of the salary of Dr. Child, in consideration of his performing the duty of organist whenever Child was absent; and about the same time he was appointed organist of Eton college.† All these places he held until a vacancy happening in Magdalen college, he was invited thither by his friend Dr. Thomas Pierce, and appointed organist there; and in 1669, upon the opening the new theatre, he was created doctor in music. In this station he continued till 1685, when being ejected, together with the fellows, by James II. the society of that house allowed him a yearly pension, to keep him, as Wood says, from the contempt of the world, adding, that in that condition he lived in his old age in a skirt of the city of Oxon. unregarded.

The works of Dr. Rogers enumerated by Wood are of small account, being only some compositions in a collection entitled 'Court Ayres, consisting of 'Pavans, Almagnes, Corants, and Sarabands of two 'parts,' by him, Dr. Child, and others, Lond. 1655, octavo, published by Playford; and some hymns and anthems for two voices in a collection entitled Cantica Sacra, Lond. 1674, and others in the Psalms and Hymns of four parts, published by Playford. But his services and anthems, of which there are many in our cathedral books, are now the most esteemed of his works, and are justly celebrated for sweetness of melody and correctness of harmony.

Wood concludes his account of him in these words: 'His compositions for instrumental music, whether 'in two, three, or four parts, have been highly valued, 'and were always 30 years ago or more, first called 'for, taken out and played, as well in the public 'Music-school, as in private chambers; and Dr. 'Wilson the professor, the greatest and most curious 'judge of music that ever was, usually wept when 'he heard them well performed, as being wrapt up

'in an extacy, or if you will, melted down, while 'others smiled, or had their hands and eyes lifted up 'at the excellency of them.'

Upon the restoration of Charles II. the city of London having invited the king, the dukes of York and Gloucester, and the two houses of parliament to a feast at Guildhall, Mr. Rogers was employed to compose the music; Dr. Ingelo upon this occasion wrote a poem entitled Hymnus Eucharisticus, beginning 'Exultate justi in Domino,' this Mr. Rogers set in four parts,‡ and on Thursday the fifth day of July 1660, it was publicly performed in the Guildhall, and Mr. Rogers was amply rewarded for his excellent composition.

JOHN JENKINS, a native of Maidstone in Kent, was one of the most celebrated composers of music for viols during the reigns of Charles the First and Second. He was patronized by   Deerham of Norfolk, Esq. and by Hamon L'Estrange of the same county, a man of very considerable erudition. In the family of this gentleman, Jenkins resided for a great part of his life, following at the same time the profession of a private teacher of music. His compositions are chiefly Fantasias for viols of five and six parts, which, as Wood asserts, were highly valued and admired, not only in England, but beyond seas. He set to music some part of a poem entitled Theophila, or Love's Sacrifice, written by Edward Benlowes, Esq., and printed at London, in folio, 1651; and many songs.

Notwithstanding that Jenkins was so excellent a master, and so skilful a composer for the viol, he seems to have contributed in some degree to the banishment of that instrument from concerts, and to the introduction of music for the violin in its stead. To say the truth, the Italian style in music had been making its way into this kingdom even from the beginning of the seventeenth century; and though Henry Lawes and some others affected to contemn it, it is well known that he and others were unawares betrayed into an imitation of it; Walter Porter published 'Airs and Madrigals with a Thorough-bass for the Organ, or Theorbo-lute, the Italian way;' even

---

* Whitelocke in the account of that embassy lately published, frequently mentions the applause given by the queen and her servants to what he calls his music, but he has forborne to mention to whom that applause was due, or even hinted that the author of it was Dr. Rogers. Whitelocke pretended to skill in music; he says that while he was in Sweden he had music in his family, and frequently performed a part. Vide page 579, in not. an air of his composition.

† Vide State Trials, Vol. IV., p. 274.

‡ Of this hymn, those stanzas which are daily sung by way of grace after meat at Magdalen college, Oxford, are part: they begin at 'Te Deum Patrem colimus.' Of the other compositions above spoken of, and of the reception they met with abroad, mention is made in a letter from Mr. Rogers to his intimate friend Anthony Wood, dated April 9, 1695, from his house in New-Inn, Hall-lane, Oxon., from which the following is an extract:—

'According to your desire when you were at my house last week, I 'have herewith made some addition to what I formerly gave you, viz.—

'That Dr. Nathaniel Ingelo going into Sweedland as chaplaine to the 'lord ambassador to Christina the queen, he did then present to the said 'queen two sets of musique which I had newly made, being four parts, 'viz., two treble violins, tenor, bass in Elami key, which were played 'often to her Majesty by the Italians, her musicians, to her great 'content.

'There are also several setts of his of two parts for the violins 'called Court-masquing Ayres, printed by John Playford, at the Inner 'Temple, in the year 1662, which were sent into Holland by the said John 'Playford, and played there by able masters to the States General at the 'conclusion of the treaty of peace, when the Lord Hollis went over am-'bassador there; which were so well liked off, that the noblemen and 'others at the playing thereof did drink the great rummer of wine to 'Minehere Rogers of England: this account I had of Mr. John Ferris 'of Magdalen college, who was there at that time, and one of the per-'formers thereof.'

The letter above written is signed Ben. Rogers, and directed to his worthy friend Anthony Wood, at his house over-against Merton College; the design of the letter is evidently to satisfy Wood in a request to have an account of the doctor's compositions; and therefore, notwithstanding the use of the pronoun his for mine, the compositions of two parts for violins abovementioned, must be understood to be the doctor's own, and as such they are mentioned in Wood's account of him in the Fasti Oxon vol. II. col. 174.

Dr. Child, whose excellence lay in the composition of church-music, disdained not to compose psalms after the Italian way, and Deering gave wholly into it, as appears by his Cantiones Sacræ, and his Cantica Sacra, the one published in 1597, the other in 1618. Others professed to follow the Italian vein, as it was called ; and to favour this disposition a collection of Italian airs was published about the beginning of king Charles the Second's reign, by one Girolamo Pignani, then resident in London, entitled ' Scelta di Canzo-' nétte Italiane de piu autori : dedicate a gli amatori ' della musica ;' after which the English composers, following the example of other countries, became the imitators of the Italians.

In compliance therefore with this general prepossession in favour of the Italian style, Jenkins composed twelve Sonatas for two violins and a bass, with a thorough-bass for the organ, printed at London about the year 1660, and at Amsterdam in 1664; and these were the first compositions of the kind by an Englishman. Jenkins lived to about the year 1680. He is mentioned in terms of great respect by Christopher Simpson, in his compendium of Practical Music ; and there is a recommendatory epistle of his writing, prefixed to the first edition of that work printed in 1667. Wood says he was a little man, but that he had a great soul.

Musicians of eminence in the reign of Charles I. besides those already noticed were :—

ADRIAN BATTEN, a singing-man of St. Paul's and a celebrated composer of services and anthems, of which there are many in Barnard's Collection ; as are also the words of many anthems composed by him in that of Clifford.

JOHN CAERWARDEN, a native of Hertfordshire, of the private music to king Charles I. a noted teacher on the viol but a harsh composer.

RICHARD COBB, organist to Charles I. till the rebellion, when he betook himself to the teaching of music.*

DR. CHARLES COLMAN, a gentleman of the private music to king Charles I. after the rebellion he taught in London, improving the lyra-way on the viol. Dr. Colman, together with Henry Lawes, Capt. Cook, and George Hudson, composed the music to an entertainment written by Sir William D'Avenant, intended as an imitation of the Italian opera, and performed during the time of the usurpation at Rutland-house in Charter-house-yard. Dr. Colman died in Fetter-lane, London.

WILLIAM CRANFORD, a singing man of St. Paul's, the author of many excellent rounds and catches in Hilton's and Playford's Collections. He composed that catch in particular to which Purcell afterwards put the words ' Let's lead good honest lives, &c.'

JOHN GAMBLE, apprentice to Ambrose Beyland, a noted musician, was afterwards musician at one of the play-houses ; from thence removed to be a cornet in the king's chapel. After that he became one in

* This name occurs in the Ashmolean manuscript ; but is probably mistaken for John Cobb, the composer of an elegy on William Lawes, printed among the Psalms of Henry and William Lawes, 4to. 1648, in which he is styled Organist of his Majesty's Chapel-Royal. Sundry catches and canons of his composition appear in Hilton's collection mentioned in page 578.

Charles the Second's band of violins, and composed for the theatre. He published ' Ayres and Dialogues to the Theorbo and bass Viol,' fol. Lond. 1659. Wood, in his account of this person. Fasti, vol. I. col. 285, conjectures that many of the songs in the above collection were written by the learned Thomas Stanley, Esq. the author of the History of Philosophy, and seemingly with good reason, for they resemble. in the conciseness and elegant turn of them, those poems of his printed in 1651, containing translations from Anacreon, Bion, Moschus, and others.

WILLIAM HOWES, born near Worcester, where he was bred up with the waits, became one of the choir of Windsor till the rebellion, when he. followed the king to Oxon. and was a singing man of Christ-Church ; he returned after the wars to Windsor, and had a soldier's pay allowed him to subsist on, till the restoration resettled him. in both places, he was afterwards a cornet in the king's chapel. He died at Windsor, and was buried in St. George's chapel yard.

GEORGE JEFFERIES, organist to Charles I. when he was at Oxon. 1643, servant to Lord Hatton of Kirby in Northamptonshire, where he had lands of his own, was succeeded in the king's chapel by Edward Low. His son Christopher Jefferies, a student of Christ-Church, played well on the organ.

RANDAL or RANDOLPH JEWIT, a scholar of Orlando Gibbons, and bachelor in music of the university of Dublin, was organist of Christ-Church Dublin, succeeding in that station Thomas Bateson, before spoken of. In 1639 he quitted it, and Benjamin, afterwards Dr. Rogers, was appointed in his room, upon which Jewit returned to England, and became organist of Winchester, where he died, having acquired great esteem for his skill in his profession.

EDWARD LOW, originally a chorister of Salisbury, afterwards organist of Christ-Church, Oxon. and professor of music, first as deputy to Dr. Wilson, and afterwards appointed to succeed him. He succeeded George Jefferies as organist of the chapel royal, he died at Oxford the eleventh of July, 1682, and lies buried in the Divinity chapel joining to Christ-Church there. He published in 1661 ' Short directions for the performance of Cathedral Service,' of which, as also of the author, there will be farther occasion to speak.

RICHARD NICHOLSON, organist of Magdalen college, Oxford, was admitted to the degree of bachelor in music of that university in 1595. He was the first professor of the musical praxis in Oxford under Dr. Heyther's endowment, being appointed anno 1626. He died in 1639, and was the author of many madrigals, and of one of five parts, printed in the Triumphs of Oriana.

ARTHUR PHILLIPS was made a clerk of New College, Oxford, at the age of seventeen ; after that he became organist of Magdalen college, took the degree of bachelor of music in that university, and upon the decease of Richard Nicholson, Dr. Heyther's professor, in 1639, was elected to succeed him. Upon the breaking out of the rebellion he went abroad, and after changing his religion for that of Rome, was retained by Henrietta Maria queen of England, then in France, as her organist, but being dismissed her service, he returned hither, and was entertained in the family of   Caryl, a gentleman of the Romish persuasion in Sussex. His vocal compositions of two and three parts are said to have great merit, but we know not that any of them are extant in print. Wood asserts that this person was nearly related to, if not descended from, the famous Peter Phillips, organist to the archduke and archduchess Albert and Isabel, of whom an account is herein before given.

WALTER PORTER, a gentleman of the chapel royal to Charles I. and master of the choristers at Westminster. He suffered in the time of the rebellion, and was patronized by Sir Edward Spencer: his works are 'Airs and Madrigals for two, three, four, 'and five voices, with a thorough-bass for the organ 'or Theorbo-lute, the Italian way,' printed in 1639; Hymns and Motets for two voices, 1657; and the Psalms of Mr. George Sandys composed into music for two voices, with a thorough-bass for the organ, printed about the year 1670.

THOMAS WARWICK, organist of the abbey-church of St. Peter's Westminster, and also one of the organists of the royal chapel. This person, as Tallis had done before him, composed a song of forty parts, which was performed before king Charles I. about the year 1635, by forty musicians, some the servants of his majesty, and others, of whom Benjamin, afterwards Dr. Rogers, was one. He was the father of the noted Sir Philip Warwick, secretary of the treasury in the reign of Charles II.

During that period, which commenced at the beginning, and terminated with the middle of the seventeenth century, the English seem to have possessed a style of their own; at least it may be said that till towards the year 1650 our music had received no stronger a tincture from that of Italy than must be supposed necessarily to result from the intercourse between the two countries; and this too was considerably restrained by those civil commotions which engaged the attention of all parties, and left men little leisure to enjoy the pleasures of repose, or to cultivate the arts of peace. Upon the restoration of the public tranquillity, the manners of this country assumed a new character; theatrical entertainments, which had long been interdicted, ceased to be looked on as sinful, and all the arts of refinement were practised to render them alluring to the public. To this end, instead of those obscure places, where tragedies and comedies had formerly been represented, such as the Curtain near Shoreditch,* the Magpye in Bishopsgate-street, and the Globe on the Bank-side, Black-Friars, theatres were erected with scenical decorations, and women were introduced as actors on the stage.

The state of dramatic music among us was at this time very low, as may well be inferred from

the compositions of Laneare, Coperario, Campion, and others to court masques in the reign of king James I. and from the music to Milton's Comus by Lawes; and yet each of these was in his time esteemed an excellent musician: this general disparity between ecclesiastical and secular music is thus to be accounted for: in this country there are not, as in Italy and elsewhere, any schools where the latter is cultivated; for, to say the truth, the only musical seminaries in England are cathedral and collegiate foundations; and it is but of late years that the knowledge of the science was to be attained by any other means than that course of education and study which was calculated to qualify young persons for choral service; it is notorious that the most eminent composers for the theatre for some years after the Restoration, namely, Lock, Purcell, and Eccles, had their education in the royal chapel; † and till the time of which we are now speaking, and indeed for some years after, he was held in very low estimation among musicians, who had not distinguished himself by his compositions of one kind or other for the church. From this propensity to the study of ecclesiastical music it naturally followed that the national style was grave and austere; for this reason, the blandishments of the Italian melody were looked on with aversion, and branded with the epithets of wanton and lascivious, and were represented as having a tendency to corrupt the manners of the people. It is very difficult to annex correspondent ideas to these words, as they respect music; we can only observe how the principle operated in the compositions of those masters who affected to be influenced by it; and here we shall find that it laid such restrictions on the powers of invention, that all discrimination of style ceased. In all the several collections of songs, airs, and dialogues published between the years 1600 and 1650, the words might, without the least injury to the sense, be set to any airs of a correspondent measure; and with regard to melody, he must have no ear that does not prefer a modern ballad tune to the best air among them.

The defects in point of melody under which the music of this country so long laboured, may justly be ascribed to the preference given to harmony; that is to say, to such compositions, namely, madrigals and fantasias for viols in five and six parts, as were the general entertainment of those who professed to be delighted with music; and these had charms sufficient to engage the attention not only of learned, but even of vulgar ears: The art of singing had never been cultivated in England with a view to the improvement of the voice, or the calling forth those powers of expression and execution, of which we at this time know it is capable; and as to solo-compositions for instruments, the introduction of such among us was at a period not much beyond the reach of the memory of persons yet living.

In Italy the state of music was far different; the

* At this theatre Ben Jonson was an actor; it was situated near the north-east corner of Upper Moorfields, and behind Hog-lane; the whole neighbourhood, for want of another name, is called the Curtain, which some have mistaken for the term Curtain used in fortification, imagining that some little fortress was formerly erected there, but it is taken from the sign of the theatre, which was a green curtain. Vide Athen. Oxon. vol. I. col. 608.

† This circumstance gave occasion to Tom Brown to say that the men of the musical profession hang between the church and the playhouse like Mahomet's tomb between the two loadstones. Works of Mr. Thomas Brown, vol. II. page 301, in a letter of Dr. Blow to Henry Purcell, in answer to one feigned to be written from among the dead.

invention of the opera had introduced a new species, differing from that of the church, in regard that it admitted of all those graces and ornaments, which, as they tended rather to gratify the sense than improve the affections, it had been the business of councils, and the care of bishops and pastors, to exclude from divine worship. In the musical entertainments of the theatres it was found that the melody of the human voice, delightful as it naturally is, was in males capable of improvement by an operation which the world is at this day well aware of; as also that in the performance on single instruments the degrees approaching towards perfection were innumerable, and were generally attained in a degree proportioned to the genius and industry of all who were candidates for the public favour.

The applauses, the rewards, and other encouragements given to distinguished performers, excited in others an emulation to excel; the effects whereof were in a very short time discerned. It was about the year 1590 that the opera is generally supposed to have had its rise; and by the year 1601, as Scipione Cerreto relates,* the number of performers celebrated for their skill in single instruments, such as the lute, the organ, viol d'arco, chittarra, viol da gamba, trumpet, cornet, and harp, in the city of Naples only, exceeded thirty.†

* Della Prattica Musica, pag. 157.

† In Coriat's Crudities the author mentions his hearing in the year 1608, at St. Mark's church at Venice, the music of a treble viol, so excellent that no man could surpass it. He also gives a description of a musical performance in the same city in honour of St. Roche, at which he was also present; and celebrates as well the skill and dexterity of many of the performers as the music itself, which he says was such as he would have gone an hundred miles to hear. The relation is as follows:—

'This feast consisted principally of musicke, which was both vocall 'and instrumentall, so good, so delectable, so rare, so admirable, so 'superexcellent, that it did even ravish und stupifie all those strangers 'that never heard the like. But how others were affected with it 'I know not; for mine owne part I can say this, that I was for the time 'even rapt up with St. Paul into the third heaven. Sometimes there 'sung sixteene or twenty men together, having their master or mode- 'rator to keepe them in order; and when they sung, the instrumentall 'musicians played also. Sometimes sixteene played together upon their 'instruments, ten sagbuts, foure cornets, and two violdegambaes of an 'extraordinary greatnesse; sometimes tenne, sixe sagbuts, and foure 'cornets; sometimes two, a cornet and a treble violl. Of those treble 'viols I heard three severall there, whereof each was so good, especially 'one that I observed above the rest, that I never heard the like before. 'Those that played upon the treble viols, sung and played together, and 'sometimes two singular fellowes played together upon Theorboes, to 'which they sung also, who yeelded admirable sweet musicke, but so 'still that they could scarce be heard but by those that were very neare 'them. These two Theorbists concluded that night's musicke, which 'continued three whole howers at the least. For they beganne about 'five of the clocke, and ended not before eight. Also it continued as 'long in the morning: at every time that every severall musicke played, 'the organs, whereof there are seven faire paire in that roome, standing 'al in a rowe together, plaid with them. Of the singers there were 'three or foure so excellent that I thinke few or none in Christendome 'do excell them, especially one, who had such a peerelesse and (as 'I may in a manner say) such a supernaturall voice for sweetnesse, 'that I thinke there was never a better singer in all the world, insomuch 'that he did not onely give the most pleasant contentment that could be 'imagined, to all the hearers, but also did as it were astonish and amaze 'them. I alwaies thought that he was an eunuch, which if he had beene, 'it had taken away some part of my admiration, because they do most 'commonly sing passing wel; but he was not, therefore it was much the 'more admirable. Againe it was the more worthy of admiration, because 'he was a middle-aged man, as about forty yeares old. For nature doth 'more commonly bestowe such a singularitie of voice upon boyes and 'striplings, then upon men of such yeares. Besides it was farre the 'more excellent, because it was nothing forced, strained, or affected, but 'came from him with the greatest facilitie that ever I heard. Truely 'I thinke that had a nightingale beene in the same roome, and contended 'with him for the superioritie, something perhaps he might excell him, 'because God hath granted that little birde such a priviledge for the 'sweetnesse of his voice, as to none other; but I thinke he could not 'much. To conclude, I attribute so much to this rare fellow for his 'singing, that I thinke the country where he was borne, may be as 'proude for breeding so singular a person as Smyrna was of her Homer, 'Verona of her Catullus, or Mantua of Virgil: but exceeding happy may

It was scarce possible but that a principle thus uniformly operating through a whole country, should be productive of great improvements in the science of melody, or that the style of Italy, where they were carrying on, should recommend itself to the neighbouring kingdoms; the Spaniards were the first that adopted it, the French were the next, and after them the Germans.

In England, for the reasons above given, it met at first with a cool reception, and Coperario, who went to Italy purposely for improvement, brought very little back but an Italian termination to his name. Lawes disclaimed all imitation of the Italians, though he was the first who attempted to introduce recitative amongst us, a style of music confessedly invented by Giulio Caccini, a musician of that country, Lawes's favourite song of Ariadne in Naxos is no other than a cantata, but how inferior it is to those of Cesti and others any one will determine who is able to make the comparison.

Other of our musicians who were less attached to what was called the old English style, thought it no diminution of their honour to adopt those improvements made by foreigners which fell in with that most obvious distinction of music into divine and secular, and which had before been recognized in this kingdom in compositions of Allemands, Corantos, Pavans, Passamezzos, and other airs borrowed from the practice of the Germans and the Italians. Even the grave Doctors Child and Rogers, both church-musicians, and Jenkins, who is said to have been the glory of his country, disdained not to compose in the Italian vein as it was called: the first of these published Court Ayres after the manner of the Italians, as did also Rogers, and Jenkins composed Sonatas for two violins and a bass, a species of music invented in Italy, and till the time of this author unknown in England. From the example of the e men ensued in this country a gradual change in the style of musical composition; that elaborate contexture of parts which distinguish the works of Tye, Tallis, Bird, and Gibbons, was no longer looked on as the criterion of good music, but all the little graces and refinements of melody were studied. To answer particular purposes, the strict rules of harmony were occasionally dispensed with; the transitions from key to key were not uniformly in the same order of succession; and in our melody, too purely diatonic, chromatic passages were introduced to aid the expression, and give scope for variety of modulation; in short, the people of this country, about the middle of the seventeenth century, began to entertain an idea of what in music is termed fine air, and seemed in earnest determined to cultivate it with as much zeal as their neighbours.

Nor are we to look on this propensity to innovation as arising from the love of novelty, or that caprice which often leads men to choose the worse for the better; the improvements in melody and harmony

'that citie, or towne, or person bee that possesseth this miracle of nature. 'These musicians had bestowed upon them by that company of Saint 'Roche an hundred duckats, which is twenty three pound six shillings 'eight pence starling. Thus much concerning the musicke of those 'famous feastes of Saint Lawrence, the Assumption of our Lady, and 'Saint Roche.' Coriat's Crudities, page 250.

are reciprocal, and both have a necessary tendency to introduce new combinations, and thereby produce variety.

CHAP. CXXIII.

THE efforts from time to time made by the Italians in the improvement of music, have been deduced to the year 1600; and its progress in other countries has been traced to the same period: it is necessary to observe the same course through the succeeding century, and by memoirs of the lives and works of the most eminent theoretic and practical musicians who flourished during that period, to relate the subsequent refinements, as well in the theory as the practice of the science.

BENEDETTO PALLAVACINO, a native of Cremona, and an eminent composer, was maestro di capella to the duke of Mantua about the year 1600. He is highly celebrated by Draudius, in his Bibliotheca Classica, pag. 1630. His works are chiefly madrigals for five and six voices, and in general are very fine.

DOMENICO PEDRO CERONE, a native of Bergamo, and maestro di capella of the royal chapel at Naples, was the author of a very voluminous work written in the Spanish language, and published at Naples in the year 1613, with this title, 'El Melopeo y Maestro. ' Tractado de musica theorica y pratica: en que se ' pone por extenso, lo que uno para hazerse perfecto ' musico ha menester saber: y por mayor facilidad, ' comodidad, y claridad del lector, esta repartido en ' xxii libros.'*

This book, perhaps the first of the kind ever written in the language of Spain, is a musical institute, and comprehends in it the substance of Boetius, Franchinus, Glareanus, Zarlino, Salinus, Artusi, Galilei, and, in short, of most of the writers on music who had gone before him. In it are treated of the dignity and excellency of music, of the necessary qualifications in a teacher of the science, and of the reciprocal duties of the master and disciple; in what cases correction may be administered to advantage, and of the reverence due from disciples to their masters: these, and a great number of other particulars still less to the immediate purpose of teaching music, and yet supported by a profusion of references to the scriptures, the fathers, and to the Greek and Latin classics, make up the first book.

The titles of the several books are as follow :—
Lib. i. De los Atavios, y Consonancias morales. Lib. ii. De las Curiosidades y antiguallas en Music. Lib. iii. Del Cantollano Gregoriano ò Ecclesiastico. Lib. iv. Del Tono para cantar las Orac. Epist. y Evang. Lib. v. De los Avisos necess. en Cantollano. Lib. vi. Del Canto metrico, mensural, ò de Organo. Lib. vii. De los Avisos necess. en canto de Organo. Lib. viii. De las glosas para glosar las obras. Lib. ix. Del Contrapunto comun y ordinario. Lib. x. De los Contrapuntos artificiosos y doctus. Lib. xi. De los movimientos mas observados en la Comp. Lib. xii. De los Avisos necessarios para la perf. Comp.

* It seems also to have been published in 1619 at Antwerp. Walth. 152.

Lib. xiii. De los Fragmentos Musicales. Lib. xiv. De los Canones, Fugas, y de los Contr. à la xij. &c. Lib. xv. De los Lugares comunes, Entradas y Clausulas, &c. Lib. xvi. De los Tonos en Canto de Organo. Lib. xvii. Del Modo, Tiempo, y Prolacion. Lib. xviii. Del valor de las notas en el Ternario. Lib. xix. De las Proporciones, y comp. de diversos Tiempos. Lib. xx. La declaracion de la Missa Lomme armè de Prenestina. Lib. xxi. De los Conciertos, e instrum. music y de su temple. Lib. xxii. De los Enigmas musicales.

In the fifty-third chapter of his first book Cerone enquires into the reasons why there are more professors of music in Italy than in Spain; and these he makes to be five, namely, 1. The diligence of the masters. 2. The patience of the scholars. 3. The general affection which the Italians entertain for music; and this he illustrates by an enumeration of sundry persons of the nobility in Italy who had distinguished themselves by their skill in music, and had been the authors of madrigals and other musical compositions, particularly the Count Nicolas De Arcos, the Count Ludovico Martinengo, the Count Marco Antonio Villachara, Geronimo Branchiforte Conde de Camerata, Carlo Gesualdo Principe de Venosa, Alexander Gonzaga, duke of Mantua, and Andrew Aquaviva, duke of Atri, the author of a learned treatise on music published in 1528. Under this head he takes occasion to celebrate the liberality of Philip III. the then reigning king of Spain towards musicians; as an instance whereof he says that of chapel-masters and organists under him, some had salaries of three hundred, and some of five hundred ducats a year. The fourth reason assigned by him is the great number of academies in Italy for the study of music, of which he says there are none in Spain, excepting one founded by Don Juan de' Borja, Major-domo to the empress Donna Maria de Austria, sister of Philip II. king of Spain. The fifth reason he makes to be the continual exercise of the Italian masters in the art of practical composition.

These reasons of Cerone sufficiently account for the small number of musicians which Spain has produced in a long series of years; but though it be said that during that interval between the time when St. Isidore, bishop of Sevil lived, and that of Salinas, we meet with no musician of eminence a native of Spain excepting Bartholomeus Ramis, the preceptor of Spataro, already mentioned, and Don Blas, i. e. Blasius Rosetta,† Christopher De Morales, and Thomas a Sancta Maria; nor indeed with any intimation of the state of the science in that country, yet at the time that Salinas published his treatise De Musica the Spaniards are remarked to have applied themselves to the study of the science with some degree of assiduity. The first musician of

† Rosetta was the author of a treatise published in 1529, entitled ' Rudimenta Musices, de triplici musices specie; de modo debite solvendi ' divinum pensum: et de auferendis nonullis abusibus in templo Dei.' Christopher Morales was an excellent composer of madrigals about the year mentioned before. Thomas a Sancta Maria was a native of Spain, being born at Madrid, and a Dominican monk; he lived a very few years before Salinas, and in the year 1565 published at Valladolid a work entitled 'Arte de tanner fantasia para tecla viguela y todo instrumendo de tres o quatro ordines.'

eminence among the Spaniards after, Salinas seems to have been Gonçalo Martinez, and after him Francesco de Montanos : this person was a portionist or pensioner and maestro di cappella in the church of Valladolid for the space of thirty-six years ; he was the author of a treatise entitled 'Arte de Musica theorica y practica,' published in 1592 ; and of another entitled 'Arte de Contollano,' published at Salamanca in 1610, to whom succeeded Sebastian Raval, a celebrated composer.

After this apology for the low state of music in his country, Cerone proceeds to explain the nature of the ancient system of music, making use of the several diagrams that occur in the works of Franchinus, Glareanus, Salinas, Zarlino, and other writers ; he then proceeds to teach the precepts of the Cantus Gregorianus, following herein that designation of the ecclesiastical tones, and the method of singing the offices which is to be found in the works of Franchinus. From these he proceeds to the practice of singing, and the Cantus Mensurabilis, next to the precepts of Counterpoint, or plain and figurate Descant, and then to fugue and canon.

Towards the end of this book he treats of the proportions in music, giving the substance of all that is said by other writers on that branch of the musical science.

In the twenty-first book he speaks of musical instruments, which he divides into three classes, namely, the pulsatile, which he calls Instrumentos de golpe, comprehending the Atambor, Symphonia, Gystro, Crotal, Ciembalo, Tintinabulo, Pandero, and Ataval. Under the head of wind-instruments he ranks the Chorus, Tibia or Flute, the Sambuca, Calamo, Sodelina or Gayta, the Syringa or Fistula, the Chirimia, Trompeta, Sacabuche, Corneta, Regal, Organo, Fagote, Cornamusa, Cornamuda, Dulçayna, and Doblado. Lastly, in the class of stringed instruments he places the Sistro comun, Psalterio, Accetabulo, Pandura, Dulcemiel, Rebequina or Rabel, Vihuela, Violon, Lyra, Cythara or Citola, Quitarra, Laud, Tyorba, Arpa, Monochordio, Clavichordio, Cymbalo, and Spineta. He speaks also of the temperature of the lute, and delivers the sentiments of the various writers on that controverted subject.

The twenty-second and last book is affectedly mysterious ; it consists of a great variety of musical enigmas as he calls them, that is to say, Canons in the forms of a cross, a key, and a sword, in allusion to the apostles Peter and Paul ; others that have a reference to the figure of a balance, a piece of Spanish coin, a speculum, a chess-board, and one resolvable by the throwing of dice.

It appears very clearly from this work of Cerone that the studies of the Spanish musicians had been uniformly directed towards the improvement of church-music ; and for this disposition there needs no other reason than that in Spain, music was a part of the national religion ; and how tenacious they were of that formulary which St. Gregory had instituted for the use of the Latin church, may be inferred from a fact related in a preceding part of this history, to wit, that a contest for its superiority

divided the kingdom, and was at length determined by the sword.

With this predilection in favour of ecclesiastical, it cannot be supposed that secular music could meet with much encouragement in Spain. In this huge volume, consisting of near twelve hundred pages, we meet with no compositions for instruments, all the examples exhibited by the author being either exercises on the ecclesiastical tones, or motets, or Ricercatas,* and such kind of compositions for the organ ; neither does he mention, as Scipione Ceretto, Mersennus, Kircher, and others have done, the names of any celebrated performers on the lute, the harp, the viol, or other instruments used in concerts.

The common musical divertisements of the Spaniards seem to have been borrowed from the Moors, who in a very early period had gained a footing in Spain, and given a deep tincture to the manners of the people ; these appear to be songs and dances to instruments confessedly invented by the Arabians, and from them derived to the Moors, such as the Pandore, the prototype of the lute ; and the Rebec, a fiddle with three strings, and to which most of the songs in Don Quixote are by Cervantes said to have been sung. As to their dances, excepting the Pavan, which whether it be of Spanish or Italian original is a matter of controversy, the most favourite among the Spaniards till lately have been the Chacone and Saraband† and that these were brought into Spain by the Moors, seems to be agreed by all that have written on music.

In the enumeration of instruments by Cerone mention is made of the guitar, Ital. Chittara, an appellation well known to be derived from the word Cithara. The form of the guitar is exhibited by Mersennus in his Harmonics, lib. I. De Instrumentis harmonicis, pag. 25, and is there represented as an instrument so very broad as to be almost circular ; the same author also gives the figure of an instrument longer in the body than the former, and narrower in the middle than at the extremities, somewhat resembling a viol, and this he calls the Cithara Hispanica or Spanish Guitar.‡

This instrument by numberless testimonies appears for some ages back to have been the common amusement of the Spanish gentlemen : Quevedo, an eminent Spanish writer of the last century, relates the adventures of a very accomplished gentleman, but a great humourist, one who in the day time constantly kept within doors, excluding the light of heaven from his apartments, and walked the streets of Madrid by

* RICERCATA, a term derived from the Italian verb Ricercare, to search or enquire into, signifies in the language of musicians, though improperly, a prelude or Fantasia for the organ, harpsichord, or Theorbo; they are generally extempore performances, and in strictness, when committed to writing, should, as should also voluntaries, be distinguished by some other appellation. Vide Dictionaire de Musique par Brossard.

† Besides the dances abovementioned there is one called the Fandango, which the Spaniards are at this time fond of even to madness, the air of it is very like the English hornpipe; it is danced by a man and woman, and consists in a variety of the most indecent gesticulations that can be conceived.

‡ About the year 1730 a teacher of the guitar, an Italian, arrived at London, and posted up in the Royal Exchange a bill inviting persons to become his scholars: it began thus: 'De delectabl music calit Chittara 'fit for te gantlman e ladis camera;' the bill had at the top of it the figure of the instrument miserably drawn, but agreeing with that in Mersennus. The poor man offered to teach at a very low rate, but met with none that could be prevailed on to learn of him.

night with his guitar, on which he had arrived at great perfection, imitating in this particular the practice of the young nobility and gentry of Spain, who followed it as the means of recommending themselves to the notice and favour of their mistresses.

For this instrument there are extant many collections of lessons composed by Spaniards and others. Mersennus mentions one published in 1626 by Ludovico de Briçenneo, entitled 'Tanner è Templar la 'Guitarra;' another written by Ambrosius Colonna of Milan, published in 1627, entitled 'Intavolatura 'di Cithara Spagnola,' containing many airs, viz., Passacalli tam simplices quam Passegiati, Chiacone, Zaravande, Folias, Spagnolette,* Pavagnilie Arie, Monache, Passe-mezzi, Romanescha, Corrente, Gagliarda, Toccata, Nizarda, Sinfonia, Balletto, Capricio, and Canzonette.

Romano Michieli, [Lat. Michaelius Romanus,] maestro di cappella in the church at Venice called Cathedrale de Concordia. He published at Venice a Compieta for six voices. This author is celebrated for his skill in the composition of canon, an example whereof in a canon for nine choirs or thirty-six voices is inserted in Kircher's Musurgia, tom. I. pag. 584. But his most celebrated work is a book entitled 'Musica vaga ed artificiosa,' published at Venice in 1615, in which the subject of canon is very learnedly discussed and explained by a variety of examples. In the preface to this book are contained memoirs of the most celebrated musicians living in Italy at the time of writing it.

Johann Woltz, organist of Heilbrun, an imperial town in the dukedom of Wirtemberg, and also a burgher thereof, was the publisher of a work printed at Basil in 1617, entitled 'Novam musices organices 'tabulaturam,' being a collection of motets and also fugues and canzones, gathered from the works of the most famous musicians and organists of Germany and Italy. In the dedication of this book to the magistrates of Heilbrun the author takes notice that he had been organist there forty years, and that his son had succeeded him. He was esteemed one of the most skilful organists of his time; nevertheless there are no compositions of his own extant, a circumstance much to be lamented.

Ludovico Viadana, maestro di cappella at first of the cathedral church of Fano, a small city situate in the gulph of Venice in the duchy of Urbino, and afterwards of the cathedral of Mantua, is celebrated for having about the year 1605 improved music by the invention of the figured or thorough-bass. Printz has given a relation of this fact in the following

terms: 'In the time of Viadana, Motets abounded 'with fugues, syncopations, the florid and broken 'counterpoint, and indeed every kind of affectation 'of learned contrivance; but as the composers seemed 'more to regard the harmony of the sounds than the 'sense of the words, adjusting first the one, and 'leaving the other to chance, such confusion and 'irregularity ensued, that no one could understand 'what he heard sung; which gave occasion for many 'judicious people to say, "Musicam esse inanem "sonorum strepitum.' Now this ingenious Italian 'organist and skilful composer, (who, as Christopher 'Demantius relates, was able to raise more admiration 'in the minds of the hearers with one touch upon 'the organ, than others with ten) perceiving this, he 'took occasion to invent monodies and concerts, in 'which the text, especially aided by a distinct pro- 'nunciation of the singer, may well and easily be 'understood. But as a fundamental bass was neces- 'sarily required for this purpose, he took occasion 'from that necessity to invent that compendious 'method of notation which we now call continued 'or thorough-bass.'

Draudius has mentioned several works of Viadana, among which are the following: 1. 'Opus musicum 'sacrorum Concentuum, qui et unica voce, nec non 'duabus, tribus, et quatuor vocibus variatis conci- 'nentur, una cum basso Cont. ad Organum applicato,' an. 1612. 2. 'Opera omnia sacrorum Concentuum, '1, 2, 3, et 4 vocum cum Basso continuo et generali, 'Organo applicato, novâque inventione pro omni 'genere et sorte Cantorum et Organistarum accom- 'modatâ. Adjunctâ insuper in Basso generali hujus 'novæ inventionis instructione et succinctâ expli- 'catione. Latine, Italice, et Germanice, an. 1613 '(item an. 1620).'†

Claudio Monteverde, maestro di cappella of the church of St. Mark at Venice,‡ was a famous composer of motets and madrigals, and flourished about the end of the sixteenth and the beginning of the last century. In the year 1600 he became engaged in a dispute with some of the ablest musicians of his time, occasioned by certain madrigals of his, in which the dissonances were taken in a manner not warranted by the practice of other musicians. The particulars of this controversy are related by Artusi in the second part of his treatise 'De Imperfettioni della moderna Musica.' Monteverde is celebrated for his skill in recitative, a style of music of which he may be said to have been one of the inventors; at least there are no examples of recitative more ancient than

---

* Of the several airs above enumerated a particular description will be given hereafter, at present it may not be improper to mention that the Chacone is supposed to have been invented by the Arabians, and the Saraband by the Moors; the Follia is so particularly of Spanish original, that in music-books it is frequently called Follia di Spagna. Grassineau has given a very silly description of it, styling it a particular sort of air called Fardinal's Ground, which mistake is thus to be accounted for: about the year 1690 there resided at the court of Hanover, in quality of concert-master, a musician named Farinelli. Corelli being then at Hanover, Farinelli gave him a ground to compose on; and the divisions by him made thereon, to the number of twenty-four, make the twelfth of his solos, termed Follia. Corelli had the practice of the Spanish musicians in his eye, the Follia di Spagna, being nothing else than a certain number of airs in different measures composed on a ground bass. Vivaldi also has composed a sonata consisting of divisions on the same ground, and called it Follia. See his Sonatas for two violins and a bass opera prima.

† It does not appear by the date of any of the above publications that Viadana invented thorough-bass so early as 1605. But as Printz has expressly asserted it, and his testimony has never yet been controverted, it would be too much at this distance of time to question it; nevertheless it may be remarked that within two years as early as the period above assigned, it was practised by another author, namely, Gregory Aichinger, a German, and a voluminous composer, who in 1607 published at Augsburg, 'Cantiones Ecclesiasticas a 3 et 4 voc. mit. 'einem G. B.' says the relator, i. e. with a general or thorough bass. Walth. 18.

Farther, it has been discovered that the practice of figuring basses was known before the beginning of the seventeenth century: in a work of our countryman Richard Deering, entitled 'Cantiones Sacræ quinque vocum,' published at Antwerp in 1597, the bass part is figured with a 6th wherever that concord occurs.

‡ Upon a comparison of times it seems probable that he was the immediate successor in that station of Zarlino, who himself succeeded Adrian Willaert.

are to be found in his opera of Orfeo, from which an extract is inserted in a subsequent part of this work; and indeed it may with truth be said that Monteverde was the father of the theatric style. It seems that before his advancement to the dignity of chapel-master of St. Mark's he was chapel-master to the duke of Mantua, for he is so styled in his fifth book of madrigals represented at Venice in the year 1612. Monteverde was one of the original members of the Accademia Filomusi, erected at Bologna in the year 1622. Some very fine madrigals of his composition are extant in the collections published by Pietro Phalesio and others, about the year 1600.

ANTONIO CIFRA, a Roman educated in the school heretofore mentioned to have been instituted by Palestrina and Nanino, for the instruction of youth in music; after he had finished his studies was taken into the service of the archduke Charles of Austria, brother of the emperor Ferdinand II. After that he became director of the music in the German college at Rome, and about the year 1614 was appointed maestro di cappella of the church of Loretto. He composed altogether for the church, and made a great number of masses and motets. Milton is said to have been very fond of his compositions, and to have collected them when he was in Italy.

PIETRO FRANCESCO VALENTINI, a Roman, and of a noble family, was educated under Palestrini and Gio. Maria Nanino, in the school instituted by them at Rome; he was an excellent theorist, and, notwithstanding the nobility of his birth, was necessitated to make music his profession, and even to play for hire. He was the author of many compositions of inestimable value, among the rest is the canon entitled 'Canon Polymorphus,' inserted in page 303 of this work, which may be sung two thousand ways; this composition was once in the possession of Antimo Liberati, who esteemed it as a very great curiosity; not knowing perhaps that the author had given it to Kircher, who published it in his Musurgia. Valentini was the author of a work published in 1645, entitled ' La Transformatione di Dafne, Favola morale con ' due intermedii; il primo contiene il ratto di Pro-' serpina, il secondo la cattività nella rete di Venere ' e Marte. La Metra Favola Græca versificata; con ' due intermedii; il primo rappresentante l'uccisione ' di Orfeo, ed il secondo Pitagora, che ritrova la ' Musica.'

PAOLO AGOSTINO, (a Portrait,) a disciple of the same school, was successively organist of Sancta Maria Trastevere, St. Laurence in Damaso, and lastly of St. Peter's at Rome. For invention he is said to have surpassed all his contemporaries. His compositions for four, six, and eight choirs are said to have been the admiration of all Rome. He died in 1629, aged thirty-six, and lies buried in the church of St. Michael in Rome. He left a daughter, married to Francesco Foggia, who will be spoken of hereafter.

GIROLAMO DIRUTA was a Franciscan friar, and the author of a work entitled ' Il Transilvano, Dialogo ' sopra il vero modo di sonar Organi ed Istromenti ' da penna,' printed at Venice in folio in the year

1625. The author styles himself Organista del Duomo di Chioggia. The design of this his work is to teach the method of playing on the organ and harpsichord. After explaining the scale of music and the characters used in the Cantus Mensurabilis, he remarks the distinction between the organ and the other instruments which are the subject of his discourse: the organ he observes is to be sounded gravely, and at the same time elegantly; other instruments used in concerts and in dancing he says are to be played on with spirit and vivacity. And here he drops a hint that the profane and lascivious music, forbidden to be used in the church by the decree of the council of Trent, consisted in airs resembling dance-tunes, i. e. 'Passemezzi, ed altre ' sonate da ballo.'

After some general directions respecting the position of the hand, and the application of the fingers to the instrument, he exhibits a variety of lessons or Toccatas upon the ecclesiastical tones, some by himself, and the rest by other masters, as namely, Claudio Merulo, Andrea Gabrieli, Luzzasco Luzzaschi, Paolo Quagliati, Gioseffo Guami, and others.

In the course of this dialogue the author takes occasion to mention in terms of the highest respect, Claudio Merulo and Andrea Gabrieli, who seem to have been joint organists of the church of St. Mark at the time of the first publication of this book.

In the year 1622 Diruta published a second part of the Transilvano; this is divided into four books, the first is said to be ' Sopra il vero modo de intavolare ciaschedun Canto.' The second teaches the rules of counterpoint, and the method of composing Fantasias, of which kind of music he gives a variety of examples, the composition of Luzzasco Luzzaschi, Gabriel Fattorini, and Adriano Bianchieri. The third part treats of the ecclesiastical tones, and of the method of transposing them, and other matters necessary to be known by every organist. The fourth book treats of the method of accompanying in choral service, with the use of the several registers or stops, as they are now called, of the organ.

MICHAEL PRÆTORIUS, a musician eminent both in the theory and practice, was a native of Creutzberg, a city, castle, and bailiwick on the river Wena in Thuringia, belonging to the duke of Saxe Eisenach, where he was born on the fifteenth day of February, 1571. Having made a great proficiency in music, he was appointed by Henry Julius, duke of Brunswick, chapel-master, and chamber-organist of his court, and also chamber or private secretary to Elizabeth his consort; after which, being an ecclesiastic by profession, he became prior of the Benedictine monastery of Ringelheim or Ringeln, situated between Goslar and Lichtenburg, in the bishopric of Hildesheim. In the year 1596 he was the forty-eighth of fifty-three organists who were appointed to make trial of an organ then lately erected in the castle-church of Groningen. He was also, but in what part of his life is not ascertained, chapel-master of the electoral court of Dresden; this appears by the superscription of a congratulatory ode in Latin, composed by John Steinmetz, prefixed to the first volume of the Syn-

PAOLO AGOSTINO

DA VALLERANO,

COMPOSITORE.

tagma Musicum of Prætorius. The musical compositions of Prætorius are very numerous, and consist of motetts, masses, hymns, and other offices in the church service. Besides these he composed a work, intended to consist of four volumes in quarto, but only three were printed, it is entitled Syntagma Musicum, and contains a deduction of the progress of ecclesiastical music from its origin to the author's own time, with a description of the several instruments in use at different periods. In the dedication of this work Prætorius complains of the many troubles and fatigues which he had undergone; and perhaps it is to be imputed to these that he left the work imperfect. He died at Wolfenbuttle on the fifteenth day of February, 1621, which day of the month was also that of his nativity, he having just completed the fiftieth year of his age.

HEINRICH SCHUTZ was born on the eighth day of October, 1585, at Kosteritz, a village on the river Elster in Voightland. His grandfather Albrecht Schutz, a privy-councellor, dying in 1591, at Weissenfeils, and leaving considerable possessions, Christopher his son removed with his family thither, and was elected a burgomaster of that city. In the year 1599, Heinrich having made a considerable proficiency in music, and having a very fine voice, was introduced to the Count Palatine Moritz at his court of Hesse Cassel, where having distinguished himself, he was by the direction of the Count instructed in languages and the arts. Having perfected himself in the rudiments of literature and the sciences, he in the year 1607, together with a brother of his, named George, and a son of his father's brother named Heinrich, went to the university of Marpurg, and prosecuted the study of the law. In the short space of two years Heinrich Schutz had made so good use of his time, that at the end of it he maintained a public disputation de Legatis, and gained great applause for his learning and acuteness. Soon after this his patron Count Moritz coming to Marpurg, Heinrich waited on him, and the Count discovering in him the same propensity to music that had first recommended him to his notice, proposed to him the leaving of the university in order to study music under Giovanni Gabrieli, a most celebrated musician at Venice, promising to bear his expences, and maintain him there. This offer of grace was no sooner made than accepted, Schutz went to Venice, and continued there till the death of his master in 1612. Having made a progress in his studies equal to any of his fellow disciples, he returned back to Hesse Cassel, and the Count Palatine settled on him a pension of two hundred guilders per annum; but not having determined to make music his profession, he betook himself again to the study of the law, which he pursued with great eagerness till the year 1615, when the elector of Saxony, John George, upon occasion of the baptism of the young prince Augustus his son, invited him to his court, and invested him with the dignity of director of his music, at the same time honouring him with a gold chain and medal. Being now settled in an honourable and lucrative employment, Schutz, on the first day of June, 1619, married Magdalen, a young woman

whom the original author of this account has distinguished by the description of Christian Wildeck of Saxony's land steward's book-keeper's daughter,* and by her had two daughters.

In the year 1625 Schutz became a widower; and in the year 1628, having a desire to revisit Italy, he obtained permission for that purpose. While he was abroad his father and also his wife's father died, the one in August, 1631, the other in October in the same year. During his abode at Venice, viz., in 1629, he published a collection of Latin motets with the title of Sagillarius.

Soon after his return to Dresden the electorate of Saxony became the seat of war; not choosing therefore to make that city his residence, Schutz, with the permission of the elector, in the year 1634 accepted an invitation of his Danish majesty to settle at Copenhagen; from thence in 1638 he removed to Brunswic Lunenburgh, and in 1642 returned to Denmark, where he was appointed director of the king's music. Towards the end of his life he became in a great measure deaf, after which misfortune he went very little abroad, betaking himself to the reading of the holy scriptures and the study of theology; yet he did not renounce the study of music, for in this his retirement he composed several very noble works, as namely, some of the Psalms, particularly the hundred and nineteenth, also the history of the Passion as recorded by three of the Evangelists. In his latter years he was afflicted with a diarrhœa, with which he struggled for a long time, till at length on the sixth day of November, 1672, a violent attack of that disorder put a period to his days, he being then eighty-seven years and twenty-nine days old, fifty-seven years whereof he had been chapel-master at the court of Saxony.

The works of Schutz are 𝕳𝖎𝖘𝖙𝖔𝖗𝖎𝖊 𝖉𝖊𝖗 𝕬𝖚𝖋𝖊𝖗𝖘𝖙𝖊=𝖇𝖚𝖓𝖌 𝕵𝖊𝖘𝖚 𝕮𝖍𝖗𝖎𝖘𝖙𝖎 in seven books, published at Dresden in 1623, 𝕶𝖑𝖊𝖎𝖓𝖊𝖓 𝖌𝖊𝖎𝖘𝖙𝖑𝖎𝖈𝖍𝖊𝖓 𝕮𝖔𝖓𝖈𝖊𝖗𝖙𝖊𝖓, for 1, 2, 3, 4, and 5 voices, Leipsig, 1636. Symphoniarum Sacrarum, the first part, published at Friburg in 1629, by George Hofman, a friend of the author, while he was abroad, dedicated to the elector John George. Symphoniarum Sacrarum the second part, published at Dresden by Johann Klemme, organist to the elector of Saxony, and Alexander Herings, organist of Bautzen in the year 1647, it is called his tenth work, and is by them dedicated to Christian V. king of Denmark. Symphoniarum Sacrarum, the third part, 1650. In the year 1661 all the works of Schutz were reprinted at Dresden by the express command of John George II. who committed the care of revising them to one Cornelius Becker.

JOHANN KLEMME, a celebrated organist and church musician, a Saxon by birth, was distinguished for his early proficiency in singing and knowledge of music by the elector of Saxony, Christian II. It seems that, agreeably to the custom of Germany and other countries, that prince was used to be entertained at his meals with vocal music, and that he had discovered in Klemme singular readiness and dexterity in the practice of descant: to encourage a genius so

* A Designatio Personæ almost as verbose as that with which the visitors of Don Saltero's Museum are amused, when they are shewn Pontius Pilate's wife's chamber-maid's sister's hat.

hopeful, he committed him to the tuition of the ablest masters in the court of Dresden, under whom he was instructed and maintained at the expence of the elector, for the space of six years, at the end of which his patron died. Fortunately for Klemme, John George the succeeding elector, entertained an equal affection for music with his predecessor, and having discovered in Klemme a strong propensity to improvement, he placed him for his farther instruction under Christian Erbach, a famous organist and composer at Augsburg, under whom he studied three years. At the expiration of this term Klemme returned to Dresden, and soon after was appointed master of the electoral chapel, and organist to the elector, by the recommendation of Schutz, who had held the former office fifty-seven years, and now resigned it on account of his age.

The works of Klemme are Fugues for the Organ, in number thirty-six, published at Dresden, 1631. He also in conjunction with Alexander Herings, organist of Bautzen, published in the year 1647, the second part of the Symphoniarum Sacrarum of Heinrich Schutz, and dedicated it to Christian V. king of Denmark, the first part of which work had been published at Friburg by some other friend of the author during his absence in the year 1629, with a dedication to the elector John George.

TARQUINIO MERULA, a cavalier, and also accademico filomuso in Bologna, was also maestro di cappella of the cathedral of Bergamo in the year 1639. His compositions are of various kinds, and consist as well of instrumental as vocal music; he published several collections of Masses and Psalms to be performed either with or without instruments: one of his works is entitled ' Canzoni overo sonate concertate per ' Chiesa e Camera, a 2, e 3 Stromenti, lib. 1, 2, 3, e 4.' Tarquinio Merula was one of those musicians who introduced instruments other than the organ, that is to say, viols and also violins, into the church in aid of choral singing; and, which is worth remarking, he appears by the work, the title whereof is above given at length, to have composed sonatas both for the church and the chamber as early as the year 1637, beyond which, in respect of antiquity, it will be found very difficult to carry the invention of this species of musical composition, since it is certain that for some years after that time, the only concert-music in practice either in France or England were

those fantasias for viols already described in the course of this work. Among the vocal compositions of Merula is one singularly humorous in its kind: it is the grammatical declension of the Latin pronoun hic, set to musical notes in the form of a fugue, or, as it is vulgarly called, a canon in the unison. It seems the office of chapel-master at Bergamo was not the first of Merula's preferments, for in a work of his entitled ' Concerti Spirituali, con alcune sonate à 2, 3, 4, e 5 voci,' printed at Venice in 1628, he is styled ' Organista nella Chiesa Collegiate di S. Agata, ' e Maestro di Cappella nella Cathedrale di Cremona.'

MARCO SCACCHI, a Roman by birth, and a celebrated musician, was maestro di cappella to Sigismund III. and Uladislaus IV. successively kings of Poland. Angelo Berardi, the author of the Miscellanie Musicali, Documenti Armonici, and other tracts on music, acknowledges that in the compilation of them he received great assistance from his friend Marco Scacchi. He was the author of a treatise published in 1643 with this title, ' Cribrum musicum ' ad triticum Siferticum, seu Examinatio succincta ' Psalmorum, quos non ita pridem Paulus Siferdus, ' Dantiscanus, in æde Parochiali ibidem Organædus, ' in lucem edidit, in quâ clarè et perspicuè multa ' explicantur, quæ summè necessaria ad artem melo-' poeticam esse solent, Autore Marco Scacchio, Ro-' mano, Regiæ Majestatis Poloniæ et Sueciæ Capellæ ' magistro. Venetiis apud Alexandrum Vincentium.'

In the year 1647 Scacchi published ' Cantilena ' V. voc. et lachrymæ sepulchrales,' containing a motet composed on occasion of the death of Johannes Stobæus; and certain canons entitled ' Canones sive ' Lachrimæ sepulchrales ad Tumulum Johannis ' Stobæi;' prefixed to the book is an eulogium celebrating the praises of Stobæus, of whom the author says that he was ' inter sui seculi musicos facilè ' princeps.' This person was a Prussian by birth, and chapel-master of the church of Koningsberg in Regal Prussia.

The musical compositions of Scacchi are greatly esteemed by the Italians for the exceeding closeness of their contexture, and that ingenious and artificial contrivance, which manifests itself to the curious observer. As a specimen of these his excellencies, Berardi, in the Documenti Armonici, has published two madrigals, the one in four, the other in five parts, the latter whereof is here inserted:—

-tes, au-di-en-tes non intel-li-gant, et au-di-en-tes non .. in-tel-li-gant.

et au-di-en-tes non in - telli-gant, non in-tel-li-gant, et au-di-en-tes non in-tel-li-gant.

non in-tel-ligant, et au-di-en-tes non ...... in-tel - li-gant.

non in-tel - li-gant, non in-tel-li-gant, et au-di-en-tes non in-tel-li-gant.

et au-di-en-tes non in-tel - li-gant.

MARCO SCACCHI.

GREGORIO ALLEGRI, *(a Portrait,)* a disciple of Gio. Maria Nanino, and a fellow student under him and Palestrina, with Bernardino Nanino, the nephew of Gio. Maria, Antonio Cifra, Pier Francesco Valentini, and Paolo Agostino, was a singer in the papal chapel, being admitted as such on the sixth day of December, 1629. He was besides, as a scholar of his, Antimo Liberati, relates, a celebrated contrapuntist. Andrea Adami, surnamed da Bolsena, who has given a brief account of him, says that he was but an indifferent singer ; but that he was distinguished for his benevolent disposition, which he manifested in his compassion for the poor, whom he daily relieved in crowds at his own door, and in daily visits to the prisons of Rome, and communications with those confined there, whose distresses he enquired into and relieved to the extent of his abilities. Allegri was a man of very devout temper: his works are chiefly for the service of the church ; nevertheless he sometimes composed for instruments :* among his compositions in the church style is a Miserere in five parts in the key of G, with the minor third, which by reason of its supposed excellence and pre-eminence over all others of the like kind, has for a series of years been not only reserved for the most solemn functions, but kept in the library of the pontifical chapel with a degree of care and reserve that none can account for.†

Andrea Adami, who might be a good singer, but was certainly a very poor writer, and, as may be collected from many passages in his book, less than a competent judge of the merits of musical composition, has given a character of this work in the following words : 'Among those excellent com-'posers who merit eternal praise, is Gregorio Allegri, 'who with few notes, but those well modulated, and 'better understood, has composed a Miserere, that 'on the same days in every year is sung, and is the 'wonder of our times, being conceived in such pro-'portions as ravish the soul of the hearer.'

The above eulogium, hyperbolical as it is, will be found to mean but little when it is considered that most men express delight and admiration, rapture and astonishment in the strongest terms that imagination can suggest. The Miserere of Allegri is in its structure simply counterpoint, a species of composition which it must be allowed does not call for the utmost exertions of genius, industry, or skill ; and it might be said that the burial service of Purcell and Blow may well stand in competition with it ; if not, the Miserere of Tallis, printed in the Cantiones Sacræ of him and Bird in the year 1575, in the opinion of a sober and impartial judge, will be deemed in every respect so excellent, as to suffer by the bare comparison of it with that of Allegri.

This person died on the eighteenth day of February, in the year 1652, and was buried near the chapel of St. Filippo in the Chiesa nuova, in the place of sepulture appropriated to the singers in the pope's chapel.

BARBARA STROZZI, otherwise STROZZA, a Venetian lady,‡ flourished towards the middle of the last century, and was the author of certain vocal compositions, containing an intermixture of air and recitative, which she published in 1653, with the title of 'Cantate, Ariette, e Duetti,' with an advertisement prefixed, intimating that she having invented this commixture, had given it to the public by way of trial ; but though the style of her airs is rather too simple to be pleasing, the experiment succeeded, and she is allowed to be the inventress of that elegant species of vocal composition the Cantata.

GIACOMO CARISSIMI, maestro di cappella of the church of St. Apollinare in the German college at Rome, is celebrated by Kircher and other writers as one of the most excellent of the Italian musicians. He is reputed to be the inventor of the Cantata, which is borrowed from the opera, but which in the

---

* A composition of his for two violins, a tenor and bass viol, is published in the Musurgia of Kircher, tom. I. pag. 487.

† The few copies of the Miserere of Allegri till lately extant are said to be incorrect, having been surreptitiously obtained, or written down by memory, and the chasms afterwards supplied : such it is said is that in the library of the Academy of Ancient Music, but one in every respect complete, and copied with the utmost care and exactness, was about three years ago presented as an inestimable curiosity by the present pope to an illustrious personage of this country.

The French church-musicians have a Miserere, which is highly valued among them, the production of their own country, composed by Allouette, of the church of Nôtre Dame in Paris, a celebrated composer of motets, and a disciple of Lully.

‡ This lady is not to be confounded with another of her own sex, Laurentia Strozzia, a Dominican nun of Florence, who lived near fifty years after her, and wrote on music. She was very learned, understood the Greek language, and wrote Latin Hymns, which were translated into French, and set to music by Jacques Mauduit, a French musician, celebrated by Mersennus in his Harmonie Universelle Des Instrumens de Percussion, page 63.

GREGORIO ALLEGRI

ROMANO

CANT. DELLA CAPP. PONT.

MDCXXIX.

preceding article is shewn to have been invented by Barbara Strozzi, a lady his contemporary, and in truth was only first applied by Carissimi to religious subjects, and by him introduced into the church : a remarkable composition of his in this kind is one on the last Judgment, which begins with a recitative to the words 'Suonare l'ultima tromba.' One of the most finished of his compositions is his Jephtha, a dialogue of the dramatic kind, and adapted to the church service ; it consists of recitatives, airs, and chorus, and for sweetness of melody, artful modulation, and original harmony, is justly esteemed one of the finest efforts of musical skill and genius that the world knows of. Kircher in his Musurgia, tom. I. page 603, speaks with rapture of this work, and after pointing out its beauties, gives the chorus of virgins 'Plorate filiæ Israel,' for six voices in score and at length.

Another work of Carissimi, of the same kind, and not less excellent than that abovementioned, is his Judicium Salomonis, to which may be added his dialogue between Heraclitus and Democritus, in which the affections of weeping and laughing are finely contrasted in the sweetest melodies that imagination ever suggested.*

To Carissimi is owing the perfection of the recitative style ; this species of music was invented by Jacopo Peri and Giulio Caccini, but reduced to practice, and greatly improved by Claudio Monteverde ; Carissimi excelled in imitating the inflections of the human voice, and in uniting the charms of music with the powers of oratory.

He was likewise the inventor of moving basses, in which he was imitated by a famous composer of Cantatas, Pier Simone Agostino, Colonna, Bassani, and lastly by Corelli. He was also among the first of those that introduced the accompaniment of violins and other instruments with the voices in the performance of motets, a practice which he took from the theatre, and was afterwards adopted by Colonna, Bassani, Lorenzani, and other Italians. A disciple of his, Marc Antonio Cesti, who will be spoken of in the next article, introduced the Cantata on the stage and into secular performances. Mattheson calls this a profanation, but with little reason, for the Cantata was never appropriated to church-service, and in its original design was calculated for private entertainment.

Kircher in the strongest expressions of gratitude acknowledges his having received great assistance from Carissimi in the compilation of the Musurgia, particularly in that part of it which treats of Recitative, in which style he asserts that Carissimi had not his equal.

Dr. Aldrich has adapted English words to many of Carissimi's motets ; one of them, 'I am well pleased,' is well known as an anthem, and is frequently sung in the cathedrals of this kingdom : and here it may be noted that the chorus in Mr. Handel's oratorio of Samson, 'Hear Jacob's God,' is taken from that in Jephtha 'Plorate filiæ Israel.'

Among the Harleian manuscripts is a volume of musical compositions, said by Mr. Humphrey Wanley, who drew up the Catalogue as far as No. 2407, to have been bought of himself, the first whereof is entitled 'Ferma, lascia, ch'io parli Sacrilego Ministro, 'Cantata di Giacomo Carissimi,' upon which is the following note : 'This Giacomo Carissimi 'was in his time the best composer of church-'music in all Italy. Most of his compositions were 'with great labour and expence collected by the late 'learned dean of Christ-Church, Dr. Henry Aldrich. 'However, some things of Carissimi I had the luck 'to light upon, which that great man could not 'procure in Italy, of which this Cantata was one. 'Carissimi living to be about ninety years old, com-'posed much, and died very rich as I have heard.'†

MARC ANTONIO CESTI was first a disciple of Carissimi, and afterwards a monk in the monastery of Arezzo in Tuscany. The emperor Ferdinand III. made him his maestro di cappella, notwithstanding which, and his religious profession, he composed but little for the church, for which he has been censured ; nay he composed for the theatre, operas to the number of five ; one entitled Orontea was performed at Venice about the year 1649, and another entitled La Dori some years after. His Cantatas, as has been mentioned in the article of Carissimi, were all of the secular kind, and the invention of the Cantata di Camera is therefore by some ascribed to him, while others contend that the honour of it is due to Carissimi his master ; neither of these opinions have any foundation in historical truth ; the Cantata, as above is related, was originally invented by Barbara Strozzi ; and there are some of her compositions now extant which bear the name of Cantatas, and are so in fact, as consisting of recitative and airs for the voice ; it is true that the evidences of art and skill in the contrivance of them are but few, however they are prior in respect of time to those of Carissimi and Cesti, and must therefore be looked on as the earliest compositions of the kind. One of the most celebrated Cantatas of Cesti is that to the words 'O cara Liberta ;' some of his airs are printed in a collection published in London about the year 1665 by Girolamo Pignani, entitled 'Scelta di Canzonette 'Italiane de piu Autori.' The following sprightly duet is also of his composition

CA-RA ca-ra'e dol - ce, ca - ra ca-ra'e dol - ce, ca - ra'e dol - ce Li - ber

CA-RA ca-ra'e dol - - ce Li-ber-ta, ca - ra'e, ca - ra'e dol - ce, ca - ra'e dol - ce -

* Pietro Torri, chapel-master of the church of Brussels in the year 1722, composed a duet on the same subject.   † Harleian Catalogue, No. 1265.

MARC ANTONIO CESTI.

ESTHER ELIZABETH VELKIERS may justly be thought to merit a place in a work of this kind, for her excellence in the faculty of music. She was a native of Geneva, and was born about the year 1640, but before she was a twelvemonth old, through the carelessness of a servant, was suffered to go so near a heated oven, that she was in an instant almost totally deprived of her sight. As she grew up, her father discovering in her a strong propensity to learning, taught her the use of letters by means of an alphabet cut in wood, and had her instructed in the Latin, German, French, and Italian languages. Being thus furnished, she applied herself to the study of the mathematics, natural and experimental philosophy, and lastly, theology; in all which sciences she acquired such a degree of knowledge as rendered her the wonder and admiration of the ablest professors. As a relief to her severer studies, she betook herself to music, the knowledge whereof she acquired with great facility. She had a good voice and a very fine hand, which she exercised on the harpsichord. She had scarce any remains of sight, but had nevertheless attained the power of writing a hand very legible. Nothing of her composition is remaining, nor any other memorials of her extraordinary genius and abilities, than are to be found in some of the German Lexicons, in which she is mentioned in terms of great respect.*

JOHANN CASPAR KERL, was a native of Saxony, and having in his early youth made great proficiency in music, was called to Vienna by the archduke Leopold, and appointed organist at his court, where discovering signs of an extraordinary genius, he was for his improvement committed to the care of Giovanni Valentini, maestro di cappella at the Imperial court, and after that sent to Rome for instruction under Carissimi : upon his return great offers were made him to enter into the service of the Elector Palatine, but he declined them, chusing rather to settle at Bavaria, where he became maestro di cappella to the elector Ferdinando Maria. His principal work is his ‘Modulatio Organica super Magnificat octo ‘Tonis Ecclesiasticis respondens,’ engraved and printed in folio at Munich in 1687. Kerl is justly esteemed one of the most skilful and able organists that the world ever produced. In a competition that he had with some Italian musicians at the court of the elector of Bavaria, he composed a piece for that instrument of wonderful contrivance, and which none but himself could execute.

The following is given as a specimen of Kerl's style of composition for the organ.

* Bishop Burnet in 1685, when abroad on his travels, saw and had long conversations with this extraordinary person.

CANZONA.

JOHANN CASPAR KERL.

FABIO COLONNA, of the illustrious family of that name at Rome, was a celebrated mathematician, naturalist, and speculative musician. He was born at Naples in the year 1567, and flourished at the beginning of the succeeding century. He acquired great reputation by his skill in botany, and by the publication at different times of three books of Plants with figures, and remarks on the writings of Theophrastus, Pliny, Dioscorides, and Matthiolus : he was a member of the society called Accademia Lyncæi, established by the Duke De Aqua Sparta ; the first of those institutions for the improvement of science and literature, which are now so numerous in Italy and other parts of Europe. In the year 1618 he published in the Italian language a work in three books, entitled 'Della Sambuca Lincea, overo dell' instrumento musico perfetto, which instrument he named Lincea, and also Pentecontachordon, as consisting of fifty strings.

In this work of Colonna is contained the division of the diapason, which many have confounded with that of Vicentino, and makes the octave to consist of thirty-two sounds or thirty-one intervals.

Salinas asserts, and as it seems Mersennus once thought, that the two systems of Vicentino and Colonna were one and the same, as they both divide the tone into five parts, three whereof are given to the greater semitone, and two to the lesser. Salinas's words are these : 'I should not pass over a certain 'instrument, which was begun to be fabricated in 'Italy about forty years since, and was by its in-'ventor, let him be who he will, called Archicymba-'lum, in which all the tones are found to be divided 'into five parts, three whereof are given to the greater 'semitone, and two to the lesser one.'

And Mersennus remarks that that division cannot be called a new one which began to be made ninety-seven years before the time of his, Mersennus's, writing, viz, in the year 1634 ; between which time, and the time when Salinas published his book, fifty years elapsed : wherefore says Mersennus, as Colonna is a very old man, and confesses that he received this invention from another, it agrees very well with what Salinas has remarked.*

But in the Harmonie Universelle, livre III. Des Genres de la Musique, Prop. XI. Mersennus exhibits Colonna's system, which has no one circumstance in common with that of Vicentino, excepting only the division of the tone into five parts, as appears by the following description :—

'Fabio makes use of a monochord of the length of 'seven feet between the two bridges, and divides it 'into 200 equal parts, by means of an iron wheel, 'of the size of a Julio, an Italian coin worth five 'pence, this wheel has forty teeth, and being placed

'in a collateral situation with the string, and rolled 'along, in fifty revolutions marks 200 points.

'As to the degrees of the different species of the 'Diatonic, which he endeavours to find in the division 'of the octave into thirty-eight intervals, they prove 'that the Greeks have groped in the dark for that 'which they might easily have found if they had 'followed nature.

'The design of Fabio is to prove that the tone 'ought to be divided into five parts, but this may 'be done, as we have elsewhere said, by a division 'of 19 parts.'†

A	1000	1000	
	1063 $\frac{14}{17}$	936 $\frac{3}{17}$	
G	1090 $\frac{10}{11}$	909 $\frac{1}{11}$	
	1111 $\frac{1}{9}$	888 $\frac{8}{9}$	
	1142 $\frac{6}{7}$	857 $\frac{1}{7}$	
♯f	1200	800	
F	1250	750	
E	1333 $\frac{1}{3}$	666 $\frac{2}{3}$	
	1538 $\frac{6}{13}$	461 $\frac{7}{13}$	
	1411 $\frac{13}{17}$	588 $\frac{4}{17}$	
	1428 $\frac{4}{7}$	571 $\frac{3}{7}$	
	1454 $\frac{6}{11}$	545 $\frac{5}{11}$	
D	1500	500	
♯c	1600	400	
	1739 $\frac{3}{23}$	260 $\frac{20}{23}$	
	1658 $\frac{18}{29}$	341 $\frac{11}{29}$	
C	1666 $\frac{2}{3}$	333 $\frac{1}{3}$	
	1684 $\frac{4}{9}$	315 $\frac{5}{9}$	
	1714 $\frac{2}{7}$	285 $\frac{5}{7}$	
♮	1777 $\frac{7}{9}$	222 $\frac{2}{9}$	
	1860 $\frac{20}{43}$	139 $\frac{23}{43}$	
	1811 $\frac{17}{53}$	188 $\frac{36}{53}$	
	1818 $\frac{2}{11}$	181 $\frac{9}{11}$	
	1828 $\frac{4}{7}$	171 $\frac{3}{7}$	
	1840 $\frac{2}{13}$	153 $\frac{11}{13}$	
	1882 $\frac{6}{17}$	117 $\frac{11}{17}$	
	1937 $\frac{59}{83}$	62 $\frac{24}{83}$	
	1900 $\frac{100}{101}$	99 $\frac{1}{101}$	
	1904 $\frac{16}{21}$	95 $\frac{5}{21}$	
	1910 $\frac{30}{67}$	89 $\frac{37}{67}$	
♯a	1920	80	
	1939 $\frac{13}{33}$	60 $\frac{20}{33}$	
	1963 $\frac{31}{163}$	36 $\frac{132}{163}$	
	1949 $\frac{47}{197}$	50 $\frac{150}{197}$	
	1951 $\frac{9}{41}$	48 $\frac{32}{41}$	
	1954 $\frac{20}{131}$	45 $\frac{11}{13}$	
	1959 $\frac{9}{49}$	40 $\frac{40}{49}$	
	1969 $\frac{3}{13}$	30 $\frac{10}{13}$	
A	2000		

'The table here ex-'hibited shews all the 'chords, and intervals in 'the octave of Fabio. Its 'two columns contain all 'the chords of the octave, 'and shew the different 'points of the monochord 'on which the bridge is 'to be placed, to find 'every degree and every 'interval, as well against 'the whole chord, as a-'gainst the residue ; and 'for this purpose the right 'hand column contains a 'number, which, together 'with its correspondent 'number on the left, com-'pletes the number 2000, 'representing the whole 'chord.

'For example, the num-'bers 1000 and 1000 at 'the top of each column, 'make up the number '2000 ; the numbers in 'the sixth place from the 'top, that is to say, 1200 'and 800 in like manner 'complete the number '2000 ; and the same 'thing will come to pass 'in all the rest of the num-'bers in the two columns, 'whose addition will al-'ways give the number '2000, the sum of the 'divisions contained in 'the whole chord.

'It is easy to know 'what every residue 'makes with the whole 'chord, or with the other

* Harmonici, lib. VI. De Generibus et Modis, Prop. xiii.

† Vide Harmon. lib. V. De Dissonantiis, Prop. xix.

'remaining part, that is to say, what every number
'of each column makes when compared with its
'opposite number, or with that of the whole chord,
'for example :—

'The sixth step of the first column, 1200, and the
'sixth of the second, 800, make the fifth, but 800
'with 2000, the greater tenth, and 1200 with 2000,
'the greater sixth. The rest of the relations are
'seen in this table, in which I have put the letters
'A, ♭, C, &c. that is A, RE, ♭ MI, C FA UT, and so
'on opposite the numbers answering to them. For
'example, the A with the ♭, or 2000 with $1777\frac{7}{9}$,
'makes the greater tone 9 to 8, for there is no
'number which makes the lesser tone, viz., 10 to 9
'with 2000, since 1800 is not there, which is to
'2000 as 9 to 10. Now I begin this system with
'our A RE, because it answers to the Proslambano-
'menos of the Greeks, and I put the other letters ♭
'MI, C FA UT, &c. with those feigned ones having
'this character ♯, ascending to the octave, A LA MI
'RE, opposite to the numbers which answer to these
'syllables, although you might begin from C UT, D
'RE, or any other syllable or harmonical letter.
'I really wonder that Colonna and others have
'laboured so much at the division of the octave
'without first ascertaining the true intervals that are
'necessary to be used in singing, for the C SOL UT FA
'at the bottom, marked 2000,* has no greater tone
'above it; the D LA RE SOL makes the greater tone;
'and he should have put the number 1750 to make
'the greater tone, without which it is not possible to
'obtain the justness of the consonants; he has also
'left out the B FA, that is 1125, which should make
'the greater semitone with A marked 1200, and the
'fourth with F marked 1500; he has no ♭ MI, which
'should make the fifth with E, or 1600, as does the
'number $1066\frac{2}{3}$. I omit several other harmonical
'intervals which cannot be found in his octave, both
'consonant and dissonant, but must observe that he
'has made the measures of his system so difficult,
'that out of the thirty-nine numbers there are only
'six that are not fractional, and these I could not
'reduce into less whole terms than those which are
'to be seen in the 12th proposition of the sixth book
'of the Harmonics, de Generibus et Modis, which
'are so prodigiously great, that there are but few who
'would not rather for ever quit all the pleasure of
'music than examine them, and proportion the chords
'of instruments to their intervals and ratios.

'But as the principal design of Colonna was to
'determine the several intervals by the monochord
'on every chord, and consequently to give a system
'which might serve for C SOL UT FA, or D LA RE SOL,
'E MI LA, F UT FA, G RE SOL UT, A MI LA RE, B FA,
'♭ MI, this invention should not be suffered to be
'buried in oblivion. The division of the tone into
'five equal parts is noted by four different characters
'called dieses; the first of these is made by two lines
'crossing each other obliquely, the second has four
'lines, the third six, and the fourth eight, as in this
'example :—

* The scheme of Colonna's system here referred to is that with the
numbers annexed.

'in which he puts the first diesis of the first note to
'the second, and so on, until he comes to the sixth
'note, which is a tone above the first, and a diesis
'above the fifth; and certainly if the tone could in
'reality be divided into five equal parts, the invention
'of these characters for distinguishing them is in-
'genious enough, because the number of crossing
'lines shews how many dieses we must ascend or
'descend in singing; for the first cross points out an
'ascent by one diesis, the second by two, &c.; and
'if the tone were capable of a division into eight
'commas, as some imagine, some such like characters
'might be made use of, or indeed the common
'numbers. But it is certain that the tone cannot be
'divided into five equal dieses by numbers, for as the
'diesis is the difference between the greater and
'lesser semitone, which last Colonna supposes equal
'to two dieses, it follows that all his divisions are
'false, for two dieses are greater than the lesser
'semitone $\frac{2591}{15625}$, as may be demonstrated by the
'rule of proportion, since the ratio of two dieses is
'16384 to 15625, and these two numbers are to one
'another as 25 $\frac{2591}{15625}$ to 24, when that of the lesser
'semitone is as 25 to 24.

'But this author seems not to have understood
'the perfect theory of music, because he takes no
'notice of the greater semitone, an essential interval
'in music, for the number, $1871\frac{1}{4}$ which makes that
'semitone with the first or greatest number of his
'monochord, that is to say, 2000, is not in his division,
'and had it been there, should have been placed
'between $1882\frac{6}{17}$ and $1840\frac{2}{13}$. And if the characters
'are truly marked, he puts the greater semitone
'2000 to $1882\frac{6}{17}$, and consequently makes it greater
'than it is.

'The following example will shew how he divides
'the octave by the chromatic and enarmonic degrees,
'opposite to which are placed the numbers of his
'monochord :—

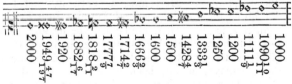

| 2000 | $1949\frac{47}{197}$ | 1920 | $1882\frac{6}{17}$ | $1818\frac{2}{11}$ | $1777\frac{7}{9}$ | $1714\frac{2}{7}$ | $1666\frac{2}{3}$ | 1600 | 1500 | $1428\frac{4}{7}$ | $1333\frac{1}{3}$ | 1250 | 1200 | $1111\frac{1}{9}$ | $1090\frac{10}{11}$ | 1000 |

'But the octave, divided as under into twelve
'equal semitones, answers all the ends of his division.

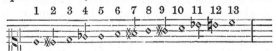

Mersennus has given so copious a description of
Colonna's system, that he has left very little to be
said on the subject, except that it has never been
adopted in any of the proposals for a temperature:
neither indeed has that of Vicentino, which he has
investigated with great ingenuity. On the contrary,
the above division of the octave into thirteen sounds
and twelve intervals, which is the same with that

mentioned in pag. 401 of this work, in not. and which Mersennus has particularly recommended in the Harmonie Universelle, liv. III. Des Genres de la Musique, Prop. XII. seems to prevail, as having hitherto resisted all attempts towards a farther improvement.

CHAP. CXXV.

MARIN MERSENNE, *(a Portrait,)* [Lat. Marinus Mersennus,] a most learned French writer, was born on the eighth day of September, 1588, at Oyse in the province of La Maine. He received his instruction in polite literature at the college of Flêche, but quitting that seminary, he went to Paris, and after having studied divinity some years in the college of the Sorbonne, entered himself among the Minims, and on the seventeenth day of July, 1611, received the habit. In September, 1612, he went to reside in the convent of that order at Paris, where he was ordained priest, and performed his first mass in October, 1613. Immediately upon his settlement he applied himself to the study of the Hebrew language under the direction of father John Bruno, a Scots Minim, and having acquired a competent degree of skill therein, he became a teacher of philosophy and theology in the convent of Nevers. In this station he continued till the year 1619, when he returned to Paris, determined to spend the remainder of his life in study and conversation, as indeed he did, making them his whole employment. In the pursuit of his studies he established and kept up a correspondence with most of the learned and ingenious men of his time. During his stay at la Flêche he had contracted a friendship with Des Cartes, which he manifested in many instances, of which the following may be reckoned as one. Being at Paris, and looked on as the friend of Des Cartes, he gave out that that philosopher was erecting a new system of physics upon the foundation of a Vacuum; but finding the public were indifferent to it, he immediately sent intelligence to Des Cartes that a Vacuum was not then the fashion, which made that philosopher change his system and adopt the old doctrine of a Plenum. The residence of Mersennus at Paris did not hinder him from making several journies into foreign countries, for he visited Holland in the middle of the year 1629, and Italy four times, viz., in 1639, 1641, 1644, 1646. In the month of July, 1648, and in the dog-days, having been to visit his friend Des Cartes, he returned home to his convent excessively heated; to allay his thirst he drank cold water, and soon after was seized with an illness which produced an abscess on his right side. His physicians imagining his disorder to be a kind of pleurisy, he was bled several times to no purpose; at last it was thought proper to open his side, and the operation was begun, but he expired in the midst of it on the first day of September, 1648, he being then about the age of sixty. He had directed the surgeons, in case of a miscarriage in the operation, to open his body, which they did, and found that they had made the incision two inches below the abscess.

The author of Mersennus's life, Hilarion de Coste, gives this farther character of him and his writings.

He was a man of universal learning, but excelled particularly in physics and the mathematics; on these subjects he published many books, and one in particular entitled ' Questiones celeberimæ in Genesim, ' cum accuratâ textûs explicatione : in quo volumine ' athæi et deistæ impugnantur, &c.' * Paris 1623 It abounds with long digressions, one on the subject of music, in which, and indeed in many other parts of his book, he takes occasion to censure the opinions of Robert Fludd, an Englishman, a doctor in physic, and a fellow of the college of physicians in London, but a crack-brained enthusiast, of whom, as he was a writer on music, an account will hereafter be given.

The character of Mersennus as a philosopher and a mathematician is well known in the learned world. To that disposition which led him to the most abstruse studies, he had joined a nice and judicious ear, and a passionate love of music, these gave a direction to his pursuits, and were productive of numberless experiments and calculations tending to demonstrate the principles of harmonics, and prove that they are independent on habit or fashion, custom or caprice, and, in short, have their foundation in nature, and the original frame and constitution of the universe.

In the year 1636 Mersennus, published at Paris, in a large folio volume, a work entitled Harmonie Universelle, in which he treats of the nature and properties of sound, of instruments of various kinds, of consonances and dissonances, of composition, of the human voice, and of the practice of singing, and a great variety of other particulars respecting music.

This book consists of a great number of separate and distinct treatises, with such signatures for the sheets and numbers for the pages as make them independent of each other. The consequence whereof is, that there are hardly any two copies to be met with that contain precisely the same number of tracts, or in which the tracts occur or follow in the same order, so that to cite or refer to the Harmonie Universelle is a matter of some difficulty. The titles of the tracts are as follow : De l'Utilité de l'Harmonie. De la Nature et des Proprietez du Son. Des Consonances. Des Dissonances. Des Instrumens. Des Instrumens à chordes. Des Instrumens à vent. Des Instrumens de Percussion. Des Orgues. Des Genres de la Musique. De la Composition. De la Voix. Des Chants. Du Mouvement des Corps. Des Mouvemens et du son des Chordes. De l'Art de bien chanter, and herein des Ordres de Sons, de l'Art d'embellir la Voix, les Recits, les Airs, ou les Chants. De la Rythmique.

As the substance of these several treatises is contained in the Latin work of Mersennus herein spoken of, it is not necessary to give any thing more than a general account of the Harmonie Universelle; nevertheless some material variations between the Latin and the French work will be noted as they occur.

In the year 1648, Mersennus published his Harmonie Universelle in Latin, with considerable addi-

---

* The title of the book as entered in the Bodleian Catalogue is Questiones et Explicatio in sex priora capita Genesews, quibus etiam ' Græcorum et Hebræorum Musica instauratur.' Par. 1623. It seems that the Harmonie Universelle and Harmonici, contain in substance the whole of what he has said in it relating to music.

MARIN MERSENNE

DE L'ORDRE DES PERES MINIMES

MDCXXXVI.

tions and improvements, with this title, 'Harmoni-
'corum libri xii. in quibus agitur de sonorum natura,
'causis, et effectibus : de consonantiis, dissonantiis,
'rationibus, generibus, modis, cantibus, compositione,
'orbisque totius harmonicis instrumentis.' This
work, though the title does not mention it, is divided
into two parts, the first containing eight, and the
second four books, thus distinguished : Lib. i. De
natura et proprietatibus sonorum. ii. De causis
sonorum, seu de corporibus sonum producentibus.
iii. De fidibus, nervis et chordis, atque metallis, ex
quibus fieri solent. iv. De sonis consonis, seu consonantiis. v. De musicæ dissonantiis, de rationibus,
et proportionibus; deque divisionibus consonantiarum.
vi. De speciebus consonantiarum, deque modis, et
generibus. vii. De cantibus, seu cantilenis, earumque
numero, partibus, et speciebus. viii. De compositione
musica, de canendi methodo, et de voce.

The several chapters of the second part are thus
entitled :—

Lib. i. De singulis instrumentis εντατοις seu
εγχορδοις hoc est nervaceis et fidicularibus. ii. De
instrumentis pneumaticis. iii. De organis, campanis,
tympanis, ac cæteris instrumentis κρουομενοις, seu que
percutiuntur. iv. De campanis, et aliis instrumentis
κρουομενοις seu percussionis, ut tympanis, cymbalis, &c.

The titles of these several books do in a great
measure bespeak the general contents of them severally; but the doctrines delivered by Mersennus
are founded on such a variety of experiments touching the nature and properties of sound, and of chords,
as well of metal as those which are made of the
intestines of beasts; and his reasoning on these
subjects is so very close, and withal so curious, that
nothing but the perusal of this part of his own
original work can afford satisfaction to an enquirer,
for which reason an abridgment of it is here forborne.

In the fourth and fifth books he treats of the
consonances and dissonances, shewing how they are
generated, and ascertaining with the utmost degree
of exactness the ratios of each; for an instance
whereof we need look no farther than his fifth book,
where he demonstrates that there are no fewer than
five different kinds of semitone, giving the ratios of
them severally.

His designation of the genera contained in his
sixth book, De Generibus et Modis, is inserted in
page 34 of this work. Previous to his explanation
of the modes, he exhibits a view of the scale of
Guido in a collateral position with that of the ancient
Greeks, making Proslambanomenos answer to A re,
and Nete hyperboleon to aa, la mi re. Of the
ancient modes he says very little, but hastens to
declare the nature of the modern, or as they are
otherwise termed the ecclesiastical tones, and these
with Glareanus he makes to be twelve. This book
contains also his examen and censure of the division
of the monochord by Fabio Colonna.

In his seventh book, De Cantibus, in order to
shew the wonderful variety in music, he exhibits
tables that demonstrate the several combinations or
possible arrangements of notes in the forming a Can-

tilena; and in these the varieties appear so multifarious, that the human mind can scarce contemplate
them without distraction; in short, to express the
number of combinations of which sixty-four sounds
are capable, as many figures are necessary as fill
a line of a folio page in a small type; and those
exhibited by Mersennus for this purpose are thus
rendered by him :—

'Ducenti viginti et unus vigintioctoiliones, 284
'vigintiseptemiliones, 59 vigintisexiliones, 310 vigin-
'tiquinqueiliones, 674 vigintiquatuoriliones, 795 vi-
'gintitresiliones, 878 vigintiduoiliones, 785 viginti
'et unusiliones, 453 vigintiliones, 858 novemdeci-
'miliones, 545 octodecimiliones, 553 septemdecimi-
'liones, 220 sexdecimiliones, 443 quindecimiliones,
'327 quatuordecimiliones, 118 tredecimiliones, 855
'duodecimiliones, 467 undecimiliones, 387 decimi-
'liones, 637 noviliones, 279 octiliones, 113 septi-
'liones, 59 sexiliones, 747 quintiliones, 33 quadri-
'liones, et sexcenti triliones.'*

In his book intitled De Instrumentis harmonicis,
Prop. II. he takes occasion to speak of the chords of
musical instruments, and of the substances of which
they are formed; and these he says are metal and
the intestines of sheep or any other animals. He
says that the thicker chords of the greater viols and of
lutes are made of thirty or forty single intestines,
and that the best of this kind are made in Rome
and some other cities in Italy, and this superiority
he says may be owing to the air, the water, or the
herbage on which the sheep of Italy feed : he adds
that chords may be also made of silk, flax, or other
materials, but that the animal chords are far the best.
Chords of metal he says are of gold, silver, copper,
brass, or iron, which being formed into cylinders, are
wrought into wires of an incredible fineness; these
cylinders he says are three, or four feet long, and by
the power of wheels, which require the strength of
two or three men to turn them, are drawn through
plates with steel holes, which are successively changed
for others in gradual diminution, till the cylinders
are reduced to slender wires.

To demonstrate the ductility of metals, particularly
silver and gold, he says that he tried a silver chord,
so very slender, that six hundred feet of it weighed
only an ounce, and found that it sustained a weight
of eight ounces before it broke; and that when it
was stretched by the same weight on a monochord
eighteen inches in length, it made in the space of
one second of time a hundred vibrations : as to gold,
he says that an ounce may be converted into sixteen
hundred leaves, each at least three inches square,
and that he remembered a gold-beater that by mere
dint of labour hammered out such a leaf of gold till
it covered a table like a table-cloth. He mentions
also the covering cylinders or chords of silver or
copper with gold, and demonstrates that an ounce of
gold being beaten into leaves, may be made to gild
a wire two hundred and sixty-six leagues long.

In Prop. VIII. of the same book, the author

* According to the computation of ringers, the time required to ring
all the possible changes on twelve bells is seventy-five years, ten months,
one week, and three days.

treats of the Cithara or Lute, and of the Theorbo, which he calls the Cithara bijuga, thus represented by him :—

After having explained the construction of these two several instruments, and shewn the tuning, and the method of playing on each, as also the mechanical operations of the workmen in making them, he directs the application of the hands and fingers, and describes the several little percussions or graces in the performance on the lute.

And here, to avoid confusion, it may be proper to note the difference between the above two instruments : the first is the primitive French lute improved by an additional number of strings from that represented in page 418 of this work. The other is the Theorbo or Cithara bijuga, so called from its having two necks, though we ought rather to say that it has two nuts, which severally determine the lengths of the two sets of strings. When the strings of the latter are doubled, as among the Italians they frequently are, the instrument is called Arcileuto, the Arch-lute. See page 418 of this work, in not. The use of it then is chiefly in thorough-bass. In the earlier editions of Corelli's Sonatas, particularly of the third opera, printed at Bologna in 1690, the principal bass part is entitled Violone, ò Arcileuto. In the Antwerp editions it is simply Violone, from whence it may be inferred that in Flanders the Arch-lute was but little, if at all, in use.

In Prop. XIII. he explains the tablature for the lute as well by figures as letters, illustrating the latter method in a subsequent proposition by a Cantilena of Mons. Boësset, master of the chamber-music to the king of France.

Prop. XIX. contains a description of another instrument of the lute-kind, which he calls the Pandura, of the following form :— and seems to be an improvement of the instrument

called the Bandore, invented by John Rose,* and spoken of in pag. 493 of this work.

* The right name of this person seems to have been Ross. He had a son, a famous viol-maker. Mace, in his Musick's Monument, pag. 245, says that one Bolles and Ross were two the best makers of viols in the world, and that he had known a bass-viol of the former valued at one hundred pounds.

In Prop. XX. are given the figure, concentus, and tablature of the Mandura or lesser lute, an instrument of this form ;—

In Prop. XXI. the following representation of the Cithara Hispanica, or Spanish Guitar.†

In Prop. XXII. are exhibited the form and concentus of the instrument called the Cistrum, thus delineated :—

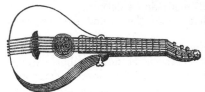

This instrument Mersennus says is but little used, and is held in great contempt in France, as indeed it has been till very lately in this country. The true English appellation for it is the Cittern, notwithstanding it is by ignorant people called the Guitar : the practice on it being very easy, it was formerly the common recreation and amusement of women and their visitors in houses of lewd resort. Many are the allusions to this instrument in the works of our old dramatic poets : whence it appears that the Cittern was formerly the symbol of a woman that lived by prostitution. Another proof of the low estimation in which it was formerly held in England is that it was the common amusement of waiting customers in barbers' shops.‡

Prop. XXIV. exhibits the form and use of an instrument resembling the Cittern in the body, but having a neck so long as to make the distance between the nut and the bridge six feet. The general

† According to the well-known maxim 'Additio probat minoritatem,' the appellation Cithara Hispanica, which we render the Spanish Guitar, supposes a guitar of some other country, but the case is not so, although a certain instrument now in fashion, and which is no other than the Cistrum or Cisteron of Mersennus, or the old cittern, is ignorantly termed a guitar. This confusion of terms is to be thus accounted for: almost every instrument of the lute-kind is in Latin called Cithara, and by the Italians Cetera, and sometimes Chittara; the Spaniards pronounce this latter word Guitarra, and sometimes, as in Cerone, Quitarra. So that upon the whole the simple appellative, Guitar, is a sufficient designation of the Cithara Hispanica or Spanish lute, which differs greatly from that of the French and Italians in its form, as may be seen by comparing their respective diagrams above exhibited.

‡ This fact is alluded to in Jonson's Comedy of the Alchemist, and also in his Silent Woman, in which Morose finding that instead of a mute wife he has got one that can talk, cries out of Cutberd, who had recommended her to him, 'That cursed barber ! I have married his Cittern that is common to all men.' It seems that formerly a barber's shop, instead of a newspaper to amuse those that waited for their turn, was furnished with a musical instrument, which was seldom any other than the Cittern, as being the most easy to play on of any, and therefore might be truly said to be common to all men : and when this is known, the allusion of the poet appears to be very just and natural ; as to the fact itself, it is ascertained in one of those many little books written by Crouch, the bookseller in the Poultry, and published with the initial letters R. B. for Robert Burton, entitled Winter Evening Entertainments, 12mo. 1687, it consists of ten pleasant relations, and fifty riddles in verse, each of which has a wooden cut before it ; Numb. XLIV. of these riddles is explained a barber ; the cut prefixed to it represents his shop with one person under his hands, and another sitting by and playing on a cittern This instrument grew into disuse about the beginning of this century. Dr. King, taking occasion to mention the barbers of his time, says that turning themselves to periwig making they had forgot their cittern and their music. Works of Dr. William King, Vol. 2, page 79.

name of it is the Colachon; but it is also called the Bichordon or Trichordon, accordingly as it is strung; the use of it is to play songs in two or three parts, which Mersennus says may be performed on it with all the varieties of fugues, Syncopes, and other ornaments of figurate music. He adds that the table or belly of this instrument may be of parchment or copper, or even of glass.

The several instruments above enumerated are of that genus which is characterized by the appellation of the Cithara, or as it is usually rendered, the Lute. Another class is included in the general denomination of the Barbiton, and of these there appear to be two species, the Violin and the Viol; these Mersennus particularly characterizes, but first he describes an instrument of a singular form, and a very diminutive size, which, for want of a better name, he calls the Lesser Barbiton;* this is a small violin invented for the use of the dancing-masters of France, of such a form and dimension, as to be capable of being carried in a case or sheath in the pocket. There are two forms of this instrument by him thus exhibited:—

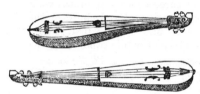

He then describes the violin properly so called; that is to say, the common treble violin, and from thence proceeds to the greater, called by the Italians the Violone, and of late years the Violoncello. He gives also a representation of the violin: to each of these instruments he assigns a tuning by fifths, but the ambit of the former differs from that of the modern Violoncello.

Mersennus speaks also of the tenor and contratenor violin, which he says differ only in magnitude from the treble violin. He adds that these instruments are severally strung with four chords, each acuter than the other in the progression upwards by a diapente.

Mersennus having treated thus largely of the violin species, and shewn what is to be understood by a concert of violins,† he proceeds to a description

of the viol species; and first he treats of the greater viol, which he says has six chords; the form of this instrument is thus represented by him:—

Speaking of that little pillar of wood placed under the belly of the viol and other instruments, which we call the sound-post, Mersennus makes it a question, why it is placed under the slenderest, rather than the thickest chord, which seems most to require a support, and recommends to the enquiry of ingenious persons the reason of this practice.‡

In Prop. xxii. Mersennus treats of an instrument which he calls the new, or rather the ancient lyre, but whether properly or not, almost any one is able to judge.

It is an instrument of a very singular kind as may be seen by the following representation of it:—

'pleasanter. If you have a mind to hear the upper part only, what can 'be more elegant than the playing of Constantinus? what more vehement 'than the enthusiasm of Bocanus? what more subtile and delicate than 'the little percussions or touches of Laxarinus and Foucardus? If the 'bass of Legerus be joined to the acute sounds of Constantinus, all the 'harmonical numbers will be compleated.'

At present we have no such instruments in use as the contratenor violin. It seems that soon after this arrangement it was found unnecessary, inasmuch as the part proper to it might with ease be performed on the violin, an instrument of a more sprightly sound than any other of the same species; and it may accordingly be observed, that in concertos, overtures, and other instrumental compositions of many parts, the second violin is in truth the countertenor part.

Mersennus has taken no notice of the instrument now used in concerts, called by the Italians and French the Violone, and by us in England the double bass; it seems that this appellation was formerly given to that instrument which we now call the Violoncello; as a proof whereof it may be remarked, that in the earlier editions of Corelli's Sonatas, particularly that of Opera III. printed at Bologna in 1690, that bass part which is not for the organ is entitled Violone, whereas in the latter, printed at Amsterdam by Estienne Roger, the same part is entitled Violoncello; hence it appears that the name Violone being transferred to the greatest bass of modern invention, there resulted a necessity of a new denomination for the ancient bass-violin, and none was thought so proper as that of Violoncello, which is clearly a diminutive of the former.

The Violone or double bass is by Brossard and others said to be double in its dimensions to the Violoncello, and consequently that its ambit is precisely an octave more grave; but this depends upon the number of strings, and the manner of tuning them, some performers using four strings, and others only three, and in the tuning of these there is a difference among them.

The true use of the Violone is to sustain the harmony, and in this application of it it has a noble effect; divided basses are improper for it, the strings not answering immediately to the percussion of the bow; these can only be executed with a good effect on the Violoncello, the sounds whereof are more articulate than distinct.

It is much to be doubted whether the countertenor violin ever came into England; Anthony Wood, in his Life, speaking of the band of Chas. II. makes no mention of the contratenor violin, the following is his description of it: 'Before the restoration of K. Ch. 2, and especially 'after, violins began to be out of fashion, and only violins used, as treble 'violin, tenor and bass violin; and the king, according to the French 'mode, would have 24 violins playing before him while he was at meals, 'as being more airie and brisk than viols.'

* In England this instrument is called a Kit, it is now made in the form of a violin; its length, measuring from the extremities, is about sixteen inches, and that of the bow about seventeen. Small as it is, its powers are co-extensive with those of the violin. Mr. Francis Pemberton, a dancing-master of London, lately deceased, was so excellent a master of the Kit, that he was able to play solos on it, exhibiting in his performance all the graces and elegancies of the violin, which is the more to be wondered at as he was a very corpulent man.

† We have here a perfect designation of a concert of violins, as contradistinguished from one of viols, usually called a chest of viols, by means whereof we are enabled to form an idea of that band of twenty-four violins established by Lewis XIV. which as Mons. Perrault and others assert, was the most famous of any in Europe.

The common opinion of this band is, that it consisted of four and twenty treble violins, thus ridiculously alluded to by Durfey in one of his songs,

'Four and twenty fiddlers all in a row.'

But the fact is that it was composed of Bass, Tenor, Contratenor, and Treble instruments, all of which were included under the general denomination of violins. Mersennus gives a very particular description of Lewis's band in the following passage:—'Whoever hears the 24 fidicinists 'of the king with six Barbitons to each part, namely, the bass, tenor, 'contratenor, and treble, perform all kinds of Cantilenas and tunes for 'dancing, must readily confess that there can be nothing sweeter and

‡ The figure here given represents the true form of the viol, but great confusion arises from the want of names whereby to describe the instruments of which we are now speaking; Mersennus could find no term to signify the Viol but the Barbiton and the Lyre; the former of these names he gives also to all the instruments included in the violin species; nay the Italians and others call a tenor violin Viola, and as to the Lyre, Galilei uses it for the lute, and by others of the Italian writers it is made to signify most other instruments of that class, but the true distinction between the viol and the violin species, arises from the difference of their form, and the number of their strings respectively, the viol, meaning that for concerts, of what size soever it be, having six strings, and the violin, whether it be the treble, the tenor, or the bass, having uniformly four.

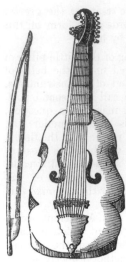

It is mounted with fifteen chords, sustained by a bridge which forms a segment of a very large circle, and of consequence is nearly flat: it is capable of performing a concentus of four, and even five parts. It seems that Mons. Bailif, a French musician, used this instrument in accompaniment to his voice. Mersennus' calls him the French Orpheus. The subject matter of Prop. xxxiii. is so very curious, that it will not admit of an abridgment. The proposition is entitled ' Explicare quamobrem ' nervus quilibet percussus ' plures simul sonos edat, qui ' faciunt inter se Diapason, Disdiapason, duodecimam, ' decimamseptimam,' &c. and is to this effect :—

' This proposition opens a wonderful phenomenon, ' and throws a light on the 8, 11, 12, 13, and other ' problems of Aristotle contained in his nineteenth ' section, in which he demands " Why do the graver " sounds include the acuter." And here it may be ' noted that Aristotle seems to have been ignorant ' that every chord produces five or more different ' sounds at the same instant, the strongest of which ' is called the natural sound of the chord, and alone ' is accustomed to be taken notice of, for the others ' are so feeble, that they are only perceptible by ' delicate ears. Some things therefore are here to be ' discussed, when some most certain and true experi- ' ments have been premised, the first of which is, ' that a chord of brass or metal produces as many ' sounds precisely as one made of gut; the second ' is that these several different sounds are more easily ' perceived in the thicker than the slenderer chords ' of instruments, for this reason, that the former ' are more acute; the third experiment teaches that ' not only the Diapason and Disdiapason, the latter ' of which is more clearly and distinctly perceived ' than the octave, but also the twelfth and greater ' seventeenth are always heard; and over and above ' these I have perceived the greater twenty-third, ' about the end of the natural sound.'* The fourth ex-

' periment convinces us that all these sounds are not ' perceived by some persons, although they imagine ' they have delicate and learned ears. The fifth ' shews that the sounds which make the twelfth and ' the seventeenth are more easily distinguished than ' the others, and that we very often imagine we ' perceive the diapente and the greater tenth, mis- ' taking for them their replicates, that is to say, the ' twelfth and seventeenth. Lastly, the sixth experi- ' ment teaches us that no chord produces a sound ' graver than its primary or natural sound.

' These things being premised, we are now to ' investigate the cause why the same chord should ' produce the sounds above-mentioned, and expressed ' in these lesser numbers, 1, 2, 3, 4, 5, for the dia- ' pason is as 1 to 2, the twelfth as 1 to 3, the Dis- ' diapason as 1 to 4, and the greater seventeenth as ' 1 to 5. These phenomena cannot be referred to ' any other causes than the different motions of the ' air; but it is very difficult to explain by what ' means the same chord or air is moved at the same ' time once, twice, thrice, four, and five times; for ' as it is struck but once, it is impossible that it can ' be moved twice or three times, &c. unless we allow ' that there is some motion of the chord or the air, ' greater than the rest, and of an equal tenor from ' the beginning to the end, while other intermediate

*The Diapason, Disdiapason, twelfth, greater seventeenth, and greater twenty-third here mentioned, are with respect to the octave or diapason, subordinate or secondary sounds: the four first arise from the respective vibrations of certain parts, ex. gr. a half, a fourth, a third, and a fifth of the chord, coinciding with the vibrations of the same chord in an harmonical ratio of 1 to 9. Mersennus at the close of the above proposition leaves it as a desideratum. Of these partial vibrations of a chord mention is made in some of the papers communicated to the Royal Society by Dr. Wallis and others, published in the Philosophical Transactions [Vide. page 407 in not. n et infra .] But Mons. Sauveur, of the Academy of Sciences at Paris, has pursued this discovery by a distinction of his own invention between harmonical and inharmonical sounds. According to him, harmonical sounds are such as make a determinate number of vibrations in the time that some other fundamental sound to which they are referred makes one vibration; and these are produced by the parts of chords which vibrate a certain number of times, while the whole chord vibrates once. By this circumstance the harmonical sounds are distinguished from the thirds major and minor, and fifth, where the relations of the vibrations are respectively 4 to 5, 5 to 6, 2 to 3. And whereas the ratios of sounds had before the time of Mons. Sauveur, been contemplated in the following series of numbers, 1 to 2, 2 to 3, 3 to 4, 4 to 5, measuring respectively the intervals of an octave, a fifth, a fourth, and a third major, he took the numbers in their natural order, 1, 2, 3, 4, 5, 6, &c. and found that as 1 to 2 is the ratio of the octave, 1 to 3 a twelfth, 1 to 4 a fifteenth or double octave, 1 to 5 a seven-

teenth major, 1 to 6 a nineteenth, meaning by the first number of these several ratios the whole of the chord, and by the second the parts thereof corresponding with such number; so while a general vibration of the whole chord was going on, other vibrations of the several parts thereof denoted by the above numbers exceeding the unit were making that produced subordinate sounds in consonance with their fundamental, and these he called harmonical sounds. Vide. Chamber's Dict. Voce Harmonical Sounds, and see the original tract of M. Sauveur in the History of the Academy of Sciences for the year 1701.

The parts of a bell, besides the general sound which is excited by the stroke of the clapper, do in like manner in certain proportions at the same time yield subordinate and acuter sounds in consonance therewith, which a nice ear will clearly distinguish. The same may be observed of that useful and most accurate instrument, the tuning fork as now constructed, the slightest percussion of which will bring out a variety of subordinate harmonical sounds; though here it must be remarked that the secondary sounds of bells are very frequently dissonant, as may be observed in the bell of almost any house clock; and in a peal of hand-bells tuned in respect of their primary sounds, with the utmost nicety, it has been discovered that being heard at such a distance as to render their secondary sounds predominant, viz., at that of fifty yards or thereabouts, these latter have been most offensively discordant. [Vide infra .] Of these subordinate or secondary sounds, more especially such as are produced from a chord or the tuning fork, the least acute which we hear is an octave with the whole sound, the next that follows is a twelfth, the next a seventeenth, till they grow too acute for the ear to perceive them. As to the greater twenty-third, it is an interval compounded of the Trisdiapason and tone, or in other words, the Triplicate of the second, and being therefore a Dissonant, is not to be accounted for upon the principles here laid down; and it may be observed that as it was the last sound of the five mentioned by him, that Mersennus was able to hear, it might possibly be the necessary result of languid and expiring vibrations, resembling as himself hints the departing smoke of a candle. Upon all which it is remarked that upon the percussion of a chord, no subordinate or secondary sound is produced that makes a fifth, or a third major or minor, with the fundamental or primary sound; nor in short, any that does not coincide in respect of its vibrations with every single vibration of the whole chord or sonorous body whatever it be.

The doctrine of subordinate sounds, so far as they are produced by the vibration of a chord, is by this discrimination clearly investigated, and we learn by it how far nature unassisted by art will go in the production of consonances; but on what principle those are founded that arise from the percussion of a bell, or the stroke of a tuning fork, on which the proportions of the subvibrating parts are unaiscoverable, and by consequence their proportions immensurable, remains yet to be discovered.

Mons. Sauveur asserts that the structure of the organ, by which he must be supposed to mean the combination of pipes therein, depends upon this so long-unknown principle; but we should rather say it is resolvable into it; in like manner as we must suppose the wedge of the pulley and the lever, which were in use before the principles on which they severally act were investigated; for in the construction of the organ, meaning thereby the Diapason or full concentus or symphony of the greater or lesser pipes, it was sufficient for the fabricators of that instrument to know, that they could not long be ignorant of it that the acuter sounds in the harmonical ratios above enumerated would coincide with, and also did, the fundamental or graver; and it remained for philosophers and speculative musicians to discover the physical causes of this wonderful coincidence.

'motions are made more frequent, almost in the same
'manner as, according to the Copernican system, the
'earth makes three hundred and sixty-five daily
'revolutions, while it makes only one round the sun.

'But it appears from experience that a chord of
'an hundred foot long, composed of any materials
'whatsoever, has not the two above-mentioned mo-
'tions, but only one, whereby it makes its courses
'backwards and forwards : wherefore the cause of
'this phenomenon is to be sought from other motions,
'unless it is to be imputed to the different surfaces
'of the chords, the upper one whereof might produce
'a graver, and the others that follow, as far as the
'centre of the chord, acuter sounds ; but as these
'surfaces constitute only one continued homogeneous
'body, as appears from chords made of pure gold or
'silver, and are therefore moved by the same action
'and vibrated backwards and forwards by the same
'number of courses, they cannot produce the different
'sounds, wherefore I imagine that the air which is
'first affected by the percussion of the chord, vibrates
'quicker than the chord itself, by its natural tension
'and aptitude for returning, and therefore produces
'an acuter sound, or rather that the same air being
'driven by the chord to the right side for example,
'returns at first with the same celerity, but is again
'repelled, and is agitated with a double velocity, and
'thus produces a Diapason with the primary and
'principal sound of the chord, which being still more
'agitated by the different returns of the chord, and
'returning more frequently itself, acquires a triple,
'quadruple, and quintuple celerity, and so generates
'the twelfth, fifteenth, and greater seventeenth. These
'first consonances must occur, nor can the air receive
'any other motions, as it should seem, before it is
'affected by them. But by what means it makes the
'twenty-third, or 1 to 9, let them who have leisure
'enquire, and I advise them to lend a most attentive
'ear to the chords, that they may be able to catch or
'perceive both the above sounds, and any others that
'may be produced.

'To this phenomenon of chords may be referred
'the different sounds produced at the same time by
'the greater bells, as is well known by every one ;
'and the leaps and intervals of the trumpet and litui,
'which imitate the sounds of the above-mentioned
'chords. Add to these the various sounds of glass
'vessels when their edges are pressed or rubbed by
'the finger, also the different figures and periods
'of smoke ascending from the flame of a candle ;
'and the pipes of organs which make two sounds at
'one time.'

Prop. XXXVI. contains a description of the instrument called by the author, Vielle, and by Kircher
Lyra Mendicorum ; a figure of this instrument is to
be seen in the Musurgia of Ottomarus Luscinius, and
in a preceding part of this work. Mersennus says
that the construction of it is little understood, by
reason that it is only used by blind men and other
beggars about the streets. He makes it to consist of
four chords, that is to say, two which pass along the
belly of the instrument, and are tuned in unison to
each other, but are an octave lower than the former

two. All the four strings are acted upon by a wheel
rubbed with powder of rosin, which does the office of
a bow. The middle strings are affected by certain
keys which stop them at different lengths, and produce
the tones while the others perform the part of a mono-
phonous bass, resembling the drone of a bagpipe.
Mersennus says that there were some in his time
who played so well on this contemptible instrument,
that they could make their hearers laugh, or dance,
or weep.

Mersennus next treats, viz. in Prop. xxxvii. of that
surprising instrument, the Trumpet Marine, here
delineated, con-
cerning which he
thus delivers his
sentiments :—

'The instrument commonly called the Marine
'Trumpet, either because it was invented by seamen,
'or because they make use of it instead of a trumpet,
'consists of three boards so joined and glued
'together, that they are broad at the lower end, and
'narrow towards the neck, so that it resembles a tri-
'lateral pyramid with a part cut off; a neck with
'a head is added to this pyramid in order to contain
'the peg that commands the chord ; near the greater
'end of the instrument is a stay, to which the chord
'is fastened by a knot under the belly, and detains it.
'To the left of the stay is the movable bridge which
'bears up the chord, and determines with the little
'bridge or nut at the smaller end, the harmonical
'length of the chord. The bow is necessary to strike
'the chord, and consists of silk, and a stick, as has
'been said in the discourse on the Barbitons.

'The most remarkable thing that occurs in this
'instrument is that little stud of ivory, bone, or other
'matter which is fastened into the left foot of the
'bridge, under which a square little piece of glass is
'placed, and fastened to the belly, that when it is
'agitated by the different strokes of the stud it may
'communicate a tremor to the sounds of the chord,
'and that by this means this instrument may imitate
'the military trumpet, for when the chord is rubbed
'by the bow, the left leg beats against the glass plate
'with repeated strokes, and impresses a peculiar
'quality or motion into the sounds of the chord, com-
'posed of the triple motion, namely of the stud, the
'chord, and the bow.

'The manner of using the trumpet marine is this,
'its head is turned towards the breast of the per-
'former, and leans thereon while he passes the bow
'across the chord, and lightly touches with the
'thumb or the fore-finger those parts of the chord
'which are marked by the divisions ; but the bow
'is to be drawn over the chord between the thumb
'which the chord is touched by, and the little bridge,
'not but that it might be drawn at any other place,
'but at that above directed it strikes the chord a
'great deal more easily and commodiously.

'Of the six divisions marked on the neck of the
'instrument, the first makes a fifth with the open
'chord, the second an octave, and so on for the rest,
'corresponding with the intervals of the military
'trumpet.'

Mersennus says that Glareanus has taken notice of the trumpet marine, and that he distinguishes it by the appellation of the Citharisticum; to which we may add, that there are many curious particulars both in the Dodecachordon of Glareanus, and the Harmonics of Mersennus, as also in the Harmonie Universelle of the latter, concerning this instrument.*

Prop. XXXIX. treats of the Spinnet, or, as Mersennus terms it, the Clavicymbalum; the figure which he has given of it resembles exactly the old English virginal, in shape a parallelogram, its width being to its depth in nearly the proportion of two to one; from whence it may be inferred that the triangular spinnet now in use is somewhat less ancient than the time of Mersennus. He makes it to consist of thirteen chords and keys, including twelve intervals; that being the number contained in an octave, divided according to the modern system into seven tones and five semitones. He says that the tuning of this instrument is by many persons held a great secret, nevertheless he reveals it by explaining

* In the Philosophical Transactions for 1692, is a discourse on the trumpet and trumpet marine by the Hon. Francis Roberts, and a copious extract from it in the Abridgment of Lowthorp and Jones, vol. I. pag. 607, wherein are many curious particulars concerning this instrument. As an introduction to his discourse the author observes of the military or common trumpet, that its ordinary compass is from double C FA UT to C SOL FA in alt, but that there are only some notes in that series which it will give; and farther that the 7th, 11th, 13th, and 14th notes in that progression, viz., B b, f, aa, and bb are out of tune.

To account for these defects he adverts to the trumpet marine, which though very unlike the common trumpet, has a wonderful agreement with it; as resembling it most exactly in sound, yielding the self same notes, and having the same defects.

He refers to the known experiment of two unison strings, and observes upon it that not only the unison will answer to the touch of a correspondent string, but also the 8th and 12th in this manner:—

If an unison be struck, it makes one entire vibration in the whole string, and the motion is most sensibly in the midst, for there the vibrations take the greatest scope.

If an 8th is struck it makes two vibrations, the point in the midst being in a manner quiescent, and the most sensible motion the middle of the two subdivisions.

If a 12th be struck it makes three vibrations, and the greatest motion at the midst of the three subdivisions, the points that divide the string into three equal parts being nearly at rest, so that in short the experiment holds when any note is struck which is an unison to half the string, and a 12th to the third part of it.

In this case (the vibrations of the equal parts of a string being synchronous) there is no contrariety in the motion to hinder each other, whereas it is otherwise if a note is unison to a part of a string that does not divide it equally, for then the vibrations of the remainder not suiting with those of the other parts, immediately make confusion in the whole.

Now, adds he, in the Trumpet Marine you do not stop close as in other instruments, but touch the string gently with your thumb, whereby there is a mutual concurrence of the upper and lower part of the string to produce the sound. This is sufficiently evident from this, that if any thing touches the string below the stop, the sound will be as effectually spoiled as if it were laid upon that part which is immediately struck with the bow. From hence therefore we may collect that the Trumpet Marine yields no musical sound but when the stop makes the upper part of the string an aliquot of the remainder, and consequently of the whole, otherwise, as we just now remarked, the vibrations of the parts will stop one another, and make a sound suitable to their motion altogether confused.

The author then demonstrates with great clearness that these aliquot parts are the very stops which produce the trumpet notes, and that the notes which the trumpet will not hit are dissonant, merely because they do not correspond with a division of the monochord into aliquot parts.

Having before premised that the trumpet and trumpet marine labour each under the same defects as the other, he applies this reasoning to the trumpet in these words:—

'Where the notes are produced only by the different force of the breath, 'it is reasonable to imagine that the strongest blast raises the sound by 'breaking the air within the tube, into the shortest vibrations, but that 'no musical sound will rise unless they are suited to some aliquot part, 'and so by reduplication exactly measure out the whole length of the 'instrument; for otherwise a remainder will cause the inconvenience 'before-mentioned to arise from conflicting vibrations; to which if we 'add that a pipe being shortened according to the proportions we even 'now discoursed of in a string, raises the sound in the same degrees, 'it renders the case of the trumpet just the same with the monochord.'

To these remarks of Mr. Roberts another not less curious and difficult to account for, may be added, viz., that the chord of the trumpet marine is precisely equal in length to the trumpet, supposing it to be one continued uninflected tube.

the method of tuning the spinnet, agreeable to the practice of the present times.

From the spinnet he proceeds in Prop. XL. to shew the construction of the Organocymbalum, in French called the Clavecin, and in English the harpsichord, an instrument too well known at this day to need a description. But it seems that in the time of Mersennus there were two kinds of harpsichord, the one of the French above spoken of, and the other of the Italians, called by him the Manichordium. Of this he treats at large in Prop. XLII.

In this instrument the diapason is said by the author to be divided according to the three genera; it resembles in shape the spinnet described by Mersennus, but is considerably larger, having fifty keys. He adds that the use of it is for the private practice of those who choose not to be heard; but he gives no reason for the difference between this and other instruments of the like kind in the division of the diapason.

He next proceeds to describe an instrument which he calls the Clavicytherium or harp with keys; this is no other than the upright harpsichord, which of late has been introduced into practice, and made to pass with the ignorant for a new invention.

Prop. XLIII. contains an explanation of the figure, parts, harmony, and use of the Chinor, Cinyra, or harp, which he exhibits in the form of a harp of our days. His description of this instrument is brief, and rather obscure, but in the Harmonie Universelle he is more particular, and delivers his sentiments of it to this effect: 'Many difficulties 'have been started relating to this instrument, among 'others whether the harp of David resembled this of 'ours; but as there are no vestiges of antiquity re-'maining, whereby we can conclude any thing about 'it, it must suffice to describe our own,' and this he does by a figure of it.

The verbal description which follows the figure of the instrument imports that this harp is triple strung, and that the chords are brass wire. The first row, and also the third, consist of twenty-nine chords, and are tuned in unison; the intermediate row consists of semitones, and contains a less number. In the Harmonie Universelle, which contains a much fuller description of the harp than the book now quoting, Mersennus speaks of a French musician, Mons. Flesle, who in his time touched the harp to such perfection, that many preferred it to the lute, over which he says it has this advantage, that all its chords are touched open, and besides, its accordature or tuning comes nearer to truth than that of the lute; and as to the imperfection complained of, that the vibrations of the chords sometimes continue so long as to create dissonance; he observes that a skilful performer may with his fingers stop the vibration of the chords at pleasure.

Prop. XLIV. contains an explanation of the figure, parts, concentus, and use of the Psalterium, together with a proposal of a mundane instrument. The instrument first above spoken of, as exhibited by Mersennus, is in truth no other than that common instrument known by the name of the Dulcimer.

The little rod or plectrum with which it is struck, is by him said to be made of the wood of the plumb, the pear, or the service-tree. He adds that two of these may be used at a time for the playing of Duos and Cantilenas in consonance.

The mundane instrument above-mentioned is more largely spoken of in the Harmonie Universelle; the figure of it is apparently taken from the Utriusque Cosmi Historia of Dr. Robert Fludd, a book of which a large account will hereafter be given. The conceit of a mundane instrument is certainly one of the wildest that madness ever formed; Mersennus says Γ answers to the earth, A to the water, ♭ to the air, and so on for the rest till G, which answers to the sun, supposed to be the centre of our system, and from thence in a progression of tones and semitones upwards to the heavens.

CHAP. CXVI.

The book of Mersennus entitled De Instrumentis Harmonicis is subdivided into two, the first whereof treats of nervaceous or stringed, and the second of pneumatic or wind instruments. In preface to this latter the author waives the consideration of the nature of wind, and refers to the Historia Ventorum of our countryman Lord Verulam.

In Prop. I. he describes an instrument resembling the Syringa of Pan, formed of reeds in different length con- 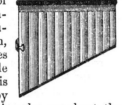 joined with wax. The instrument exhibited is of this form, and it consists of twelve tubes of tin, the lesser being subtriple in its ratio to the greater. This instrument he says is used by the braziers or tinkers of Paris, who go about the streets to mend kettles, and advertise the people of their approach by the sound of it.

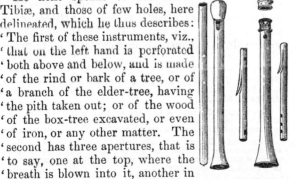

He next speaks of the lesser Tibiæ, and those of few holes, here delineated, which he thus describes: 'The first of these instruments, viz., 'that on the left hand is perforated 'both above and below, and is made 'of the rind or bark of a tree, or of 'a branch of the elder-tree, having 'the pith taken out; or of the wood 'of the box-tree excavated, or even 'of iron, or any other matter. The 'second has three apertures, that is 'to say, one at the top, where the 'breath is blown into it, another in 'front, below it, where the sound is made, and a third 'at the bottom where the wind goes out. The third 'and fifth figures represent pipes of reed or wheat-'straw, on which the shepherds play, wherefore the 'instrument is called "tenuis avena," "calamus agres-"tis," and "stipula," and those who play on the barley-'straw are called ραπαταυλαι because ραπατη is the 'same as καλαμις, as Salmasius on Solinus observes. 'But whether these pipes may be called Gingrinæ, 'a kind of short pipes of goose bones, that yield

'a small doleful sound, and those who play on them 'Gingritores; and whether they are said, jugere, to 'cry like a kite, I leave to the judgment of the 'critics, who also dispute whether the right and the 'left-hand pipes had the same number of holes, such 'as those we give in the sixth proposition, or whether 'they were unequal in the number of their holes. 'A very late translator of Vopiscus, concludes that 'they were unequal, and attributes more holes to the 'left tibia than to the right, that the former might 'sound more acute; and that the left or Tyrian, sung 'after, or followed, the right or Lydian in singing; 'and also that the Adelphi, Andria, and Heauton-'timorumenos of Terence were acted with these, and 'that in such manner as never to sing together. 'Moreover you may justly call the pipe which comes 'next in Prop. II. with three holes, the right-hand 'pipe, and the flajolet the left, if any person has 'a mind to sing the Cantus of Terence's comedies 'with these pipes; I shall however add that the left-'hand pipe, though not equal to it in the number of 'holes, was shorter than the right-hand one, in order 'to sound more acute; pipes of this kind are usually 'made after two manners, namely, with a little tongue 'placed in the middle of the reed, which appears in 'the third figure, so that while the mouth com-'prehends the little tongue, the left hand stops and 'opens with any finger the upper hole, as the right 'hand does the lower; or the tongue is cut in the 'upper part, as in the fifth figure, and then when the 'mouth blows therein the fingers of the right hand 'open and shut the holes to form the different sounds.

'There now remains the fourth pipe, which is 'commonly called the Eunuch. This sings rather by 'speaking than by blowing, for it returns a sound or 'voice of the same acumen with which it is prolated, 'and which is reflected with a bombus or humming 'sound like a drone, from a very thin or fine sheep-'skin or onion-peel, and acquires a new grace. This 'slender skin covers the orifice at the upper extremity, 'and like the head of a drum is stretched or strained 'on the pipe, and tied round with a thread, and the 'cap or cover, which is represented over it, and 'which has several holes in it, is put over it, but the 'sound comes freely out of the hole at the bottom. 'There are some persons who recite songs of four or 'more parts with these pipes. We must not omit 'that pipes of this kind may be made of the bones 'of mules or other animals well cleansed, or of those 'of birds, nay even of the middle stalk of an onion, 'of glass, wax, &c. and of these materials some have 'constructed organ-pipes.'

Prop. II. contains a description of the small flute, or pipe with three holes, with which the tabor or little drum is used in accompaniment. 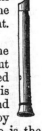 Its form is here delineated.

Upon this instrument Mersennus makes some curious observations, as that though it has but three holes, eighteen sounds may be produced from it. He says that the gravest sound is prolated when all the holes are stopped, and that the three next in succession are made by lifting up the fingers, so that the fourth note is the sound of the instrument when open. The other sounds, and which make up the number eighteen, he says are produced by stronger blasts of the breath, accommodated to the different degrees of acuteness required; and this variety of blowing is also observed in the other tibiæ and fistulæ, of which he afterwards speaks. Mersennus says he had heard an Englishman, John Price by name, by the sole variety of blowing on this instrument, ascend to the compass of a ter-diapason or twenty-second. He adds, that there are some things concerning this pipe which are wonderful. First, that after the graver sounds, g, a, b, c, which are produced by the least blast, the blowing a little stronger gives the fifth above: and yet it is impossible to produce from this instrument the three intermediate sounds which occur between the fourth note c, and the fifth gg, viz., d, e, f, that so the first octave might be perfect, as is the second: and this defect he says is peculiar to this instrument only. Secondly, that it leaps from its gravest sound to a diapason when the wind is a little increased, and again to a second diapason if the wind be increased to a greater degree.*

From the pipe with three holes, the associate of the tabor, Mersennus proceeds to what he calls the lesser tibia or Flajolet, here delineated.

Of this instrument Mersennus observes that it need not exceed the length of the little finger. He says that at the aperture near the top the impelled wind goes out, while the rest passes through the open holes and the lower orifice. He observes that the white circles marked on the instrument resembling a cypher, denote the holes on the back part of it, and that the uppermost of these is stopped by the thumb of the left hand, and the lowermost or fifth from the top, by the thumb of the right hand: the black circles represent the holes in the front of the instrument. He adds that in his time one Le Vacher was a celebrated performer on this instrument, and in his French work he intimates that he was also a maker of flajolets.

In the Harm. Univer. Des Instrumens à Vent, Prop. VII. Mersennus speaks more fully of the flajolet. He says that there are two ways of sounding this instrument; and all such as have the lumiere, i. e. the aperture under the tampion; the first is by simple blowing, the other by articulation and the action of the tongue; the former he says imitates the organ, the latter the voice: one is practised by villagers and apprentices, the other by masters.

The ambit of the flajolet, according to the scale exhibited by Mersennus, is two octaves from g SOL RE UT upwards. At the end of his description of the instrument, both in the Latin and French work, he gives a Vaudeville for flajolets in four parts† by

Henry le Jeune, who he says composed the examples for the other wind-instruments described in his book, as knowing very well their power and extent.

Prop. V. treats of the Fistula Dulcis, seu Anglica, called also the flute Abec; ‡ the figure of it is here represented. §

Of the two figures adjacent to the instrument at length, the uppermost shews the aperture for the passage of the wind between the tampion or plug and the beak; the other represents the end of the flute with a view of the beak and the tampion. This instrument has eight holes in the front, and one behind, which is stopped by the thumb; as to the lower or eighth hole, Mersennus remarks that there are two so numbered; for this reason, that the instrument may be played on either by right or left-handed persons, one or other of the two holes being stopped with wax.||

Mersennus observes that flutes are so adjusted by their different sizes as to form a concentus of treble, contratenor, tenor, and bass; and that the treble-flute is more acute than the contratenor by a ninth or a diapason, and a tone. The contratenor he makes to be a diapente more acute than the bass, as is also the tenor; for he supposes the contratenor and tenor to be tuned in unison, in the same manner as they are in several other harmonies of instruments.¶

In this, which is his Latin work, Mersennus does not mention the sizes of the several flutes, but in the Harmonie Universelle he is more particular, for he says that the length of the bass-flute is two feet and three quarters, that of the tenor one foot five inches, and the treble only eleven lines.**

From the scale or diagram for the flute exhibited by Mersennus, it appears that the ambit or compass of the instrument is a disdiapason or fifteen notes, and that the lowest note of the system for the treble-flute is C FA UT; but this system, as also those of the tenor and bass-flute, is adapted to what is called by him and other French writers, le petit Jeu; nevertheless there is a flute known by the name of the concert-flute, the lowest note whereof is F;†† indeed

---

* This observation applies to flutes of almost all kinds; in the flute Abec, by stopping the thumb hole, and certain others with the fingers, a sound is produced, but half stopping the thumb-hole without any other variation, gives an octave to such sound. The octaves to most of the sounds of the Fistula Germanica, or German flute, are produced only by a more forcible blast. This uniformity in the operations of nature, though it has never yet been accounted for, serves to shew how greatly the principles of harmony prevail in the material world.

† It is a kind of Gavot, having four bars in the first strain, and eight in the last. The air at the end of the fifth Sonata of the fourth Opera of Corelli answers precisely to this description. For the inventor of this kind of air, and the etymology of the word VAUDEVILLE, see page 569 of this work, in not.

‡ For the reason of this appellation see page 331 of this work, in not.

§ Flutes are mentioned in the works of St. Evremond with great encomiums on the French performers thereon, and in Sir George Etherege's Comedy of the 'Man of Mode.'

|| From hence it is evident that the practice of making the flute in pieces, that so the lower hole, by turning the piece about, might be accommodated to the hand, was not known when Mersennus wrote.

¶ Particularly the viol and violin, in neither of which species there is any distinction between the tenor and contratenor; perhaps in the concentus of flutes the contratenor part was given to the tenor, in that of the violin it is the second treble.

** This is a mistake of the author which we know not how to correct: a line is but a twelfth part of an inch.

†† The true concert flute is that above described; but there are also others introduced into concerts of violins of a less size, in which case the method was to write the flute part in a key correspondent to its pitch; this practice was introduced by one   Woodcock, a celebrated performer on this instrument, and by an ingenious young man, William Babell, organist of the church of Allhallows Bread-street, London, about the year 1710, both of whom published concertos for this instrument, in which the principal part was for a sixth flute, in which case the lowest note, though nominally F, was in power D, and consequently required a transposition of the flute-part a sixth higher, viz., into the key of D.

But these attempts failed to procure for the flute a reception into concerts of various instruments, for which reason one Thomas Stanesby, a very curious maker of flutes and other instruments of the like kind, about the year 1732, adverting to the scale of Mersennus, in which the lowest note is made to be C FA UT, invented what he called the new

ever since the introduction of the flute into concerts, the lowest note of the flute, of what size soever it be, has been called F, when in truth its pitch is determinable only by its correspondence in respect of acuteness or gravity with one or other of the chords in the Scala Maxima or great system.

Mersennus next proceeds to what he calls Fistulas regias, royal flutes,* or those of the Grand Jeu as he calls it; meaning thereby, as it is supposed, those that are tuned in unison with their respective notes in the Scala Maxima, respective forms whereof are thus represented by him :—

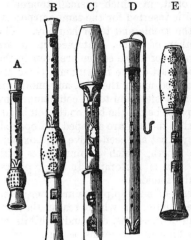

The Instruments here delineated are thus described by the author : The flute A, has a key, which by the pressure of the little finger opens the hole which is under it in the box. The fistula B, has three boxes, a greater and two lesser; the first of these is represented apart by C, that all the springs which are any way necessary to open and shut the holes may appear; below that part of the instrument, resembling in its form a barrel, are two keys which command two holes below them, and being pressed with the little finger, open either the one or the other of them. Beneath these are seen springs contained in the two lower boxes of the instrument B, but as they are too far distant from the hands, the little square pieces of brass which appear in the lower part of fig. C, are pressed down by the foot, in order to lift up the springs, as is seen in the tail of the lower spring, which being pushed down, lifts up the plate, and opens a great hole like a window, and nearly equal to the breadth of the fistula.

system, in which by making the flute of such a size as to be a fifth above concert pitch, the lowest note became C SOL FA UT ; by this contrivance the necessity of transposing the flute part was taken away ; for a flute of this size adjusted to the system above mentioned, became an octave to the violin.

To further this invention of Stanesby, one Lewis Merci, an excellent performer on the flute, a Frenchman by birth, but resident in London, published about the year 1735, six Solos for the flute, three whereof are said to be accommodated to Mr. Stanesby's new system, but the German flute was now become a favorite instrument, and Stanesby's ingenuity failed of its effect.

There were two persons, flute-makers, of the name of Stanesby, the father and the son, the Christian-name of both was Thomas ; they were both men of ingenuity, and exquisite workmen ; the father dwelt many years in Stonecutter-street leading from Shoe-lane to what is now the Fleet-market, and died about the year 1734 ; the son had apartments and his workshop over the Temple Exchange, in Fleet-street : he died in 1754, and lies buried in St. Pancras church-yard near London, where is a stone with the following incription to his memory :—' Here lies the body of the ' ingenious Thomas Stanesby, musical wind instrument maker ; esteemed ' the most eminent man in his profession of any in Europe. A facetious ' companion, a sincere friend ; upright and just in all his dealings ; ready ' to serve and relieve the distressed ; strictly adhering to his word, even ' upon the most trivial occasions, and regretted by all who had the hap- ' piness and pleasure of his acquaintance. Obiit, 2 Mart. 1754, ætat suæ, 62.'

* In the Harmonie Universelle, Des Instrumens, à Vent, Mersennus says that these flutes were a present from England to one of the kings of France, which perhaps is his reason for calling them royal flutes.

The figures D and E, represent a flute of the larger size in two separate pieces, the springs being concealed by the perforated box, which in fig. C, for the purpose of exhibiting the springs, must be supposed to be slipped up above the forked keys, the station whereof is above the box, as is seen in fig. B. The little tube with a curvature at each end, is inserted into the top of the instrument, and hooks into a hole of a piece of wood, which appears opposite the second hole in fig. B, that the mouth of the flute, which cannot be reached by the mouth of the performer, may be as it were transferred to the end of the tube opposite the second hole, fig. D. This contrivance is necessary only in flutes of the larger size, the bass especially, which are from seven to eight feet long.

After exhibiting a gavot of four parts as an example of a concentus for English flutes, Mersennus remarks that a performer on this instrument, at the same time that he plays an air, may sing a bass to it ; but without any articulation of the voice, for that the wind which proceeds from the mouth while singing is sufficient to give sound to the flute, and so a single person may perform a duo on this instrument.

Prop. VI. treats of the German flute, and also of the Helvetian flute or fife, each whereof is represented as having only seven holes, including that aperture which is blown into, from which it should seem that the eighth hole, or that which is now opened by means of a key, is a late improvement of this instrument.

Mersennus gives this figure† as an example of a treble-instrument, which he says ought to be one foot ten inches long, measuring from the bottom of the tampion, signified by the dotted circle, to the lower extremity : those for the other parts he observes should be longer, and also thicker. For example, he says that to produce the most grateful sounds of a concentus, or, as he otherwise expresses it in the Harm. Univer. Des Instrumens à Vent, Prop. IX. page 241, to make the octave or fifteenth, the flute should be twice or four times as long and as thick, as the treble-flute. He adds that flutes of this kind are made of such woods as are easily excavated, and will best polish, as namely, plumb-tree, cherry-tree, and box ; and that they may be made of ebony, crystal, and glass, and even of wax.

The system of this instrument is of a large extent, comprehending a disdiapason and diapente, or nineteen sounds ; Mersennus has given two scales, the one commencing from G, and the other from D, a fifth higher. The first of these scales it seems was adjusted by one Quiclet, Lat. Kicletus, a French cornetist, and the other by Le Vacher, already mentioned ; the method of stopping is apparently different in these two scales in many instances, that is to say, the same sound that is produced by the opening and shutting of certain holes in the diagram of Quiclet, is produced by the opening and shutting of others in that of Le Vacher ; and it is to be remarked that in the latter, no one sound of the instrument is directed

† It is to be observed that the instrument from which this figure was taken, was by accident become crooked, nevertheless Mersennus, in the Harm. Univer. Des Instrumens à Vent, pag. 241, says that he chose to give it thus deformed, it being one of the best flutes in the world.

to be produced by unstopping all the holes, from whence it appears that the present practice has its foundation in the example of Quiclet.

It is worthy of remark that neither of these persons had discovered that the diapason of any of the sounds in the first septenary was to be produced by a stronger blast of the breath; as is observed in the English flute, and at this day in the German flute; for to produce the notes in the second septenary, and so upwards, a different method of stopping is required than for their octaves below. This peculiarity, as also the reason why the ambit of this instrument is so much more extensive than that of other flutes, Mersennus recommends as a useful and entertaining subject of enquiry. *

In this proposition Mersennus treats also of the Tibia Helvetica, or Fife; this is in truth an instrument precisely of the same species with the former, but proportionably less in every respect; wherefore says the author, 'it sounds more acutely and vehe-'mently, which it ought to do, least the sound of it 'should be drowned by that of the drum.'

Speaking of a concentus for German flutes, Mersennus says that it can consist of only three parts, for that in a bass German flute the distance of the holes would be so great that no finger could command them, for which reason he says that in a concentus of four parts the bass is either the Sacbut or bassoon.

Propositions VII. and VIII. comprehend a description and explanation of the Hautboy, a treble-instrument, invented by the French, and of the instruments used in concentus with it, namely the Bassoon, Bombardt, Fagot, Courtaut, and Cervelat.

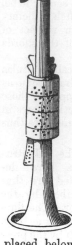

The hautboy described by Mersennus is by him given in two forms, viz., the treble and tenor; the first is the least, and has ten holes, the latter only seven, the lowest whereof is opened by a key.

In his description Mersennus notes a diversity between the holes for the fingers and those for the egress of the wind, therefore of the ten holes in the treble hautboy, nine only are to be reckoned harmonical; and of the eight in the tenor, which number includes that concealed under the box, and that on either side below it, the last serve only for the emission

of the wind, so that the number of harmonical holes is seven. Of the intermediate figures the upper shews the mouth-piece of the tenor called the Pirovette, in which the reed is inserted, in a larger size, the under is the box open and with the key exposed.

He gives also a representation of the bass-hautboy of the form in the margin. This instrument Mersennus says, is in length five feet, and being so long, is inspired by means of the tube at the top of it, in which a small tongue or reed is inserted for the same purpose as in the treble and tenor hautboy. The number of holes contained in it are eleven: of these seven are seen in the upper part of the instrument, three are contained under the box, and another is placed below it, in a situation to be commanded by that key which appears below the box on the left hand; the three holes within the box are stopped and opened, by three of the keys that are seen above the box, and that below by the fourth, which communicates with that below. The box is perforated in many places, to give egress to the sound.

Prop. VIII. treats of such pipes as are compacted together in a little bundle, for which reason they are called Fagots; and of Bassoons, &c. and exhibits an instrument of this kind in two forms, as also another called by the French the Courtaut. They are severally represented by the following figures:—

These figures are described by Mersennus in the order of their situation, the first has three keys, that on the left hand naked, the two on the right covered with boxes. The brazen tube has a mouth-piece at the extremity, by means whereof the instrument is inflated; the funnel at the top is moveable, and the instrument, though apparently consisting of two tubes, is in effect one, the two being bound together with hoops of brass, and the cavities of each stopped with a peg, as is seen in the under of the two short figures, in which are two white spots denoting two pegs that stop the cavities of the two tubes in such manner that the wind may not escape till it arrives at the upper hole under the funnel, except when either of the holes short of it is unstopped.

The second figure represents an instrument, called, by reason of its shortness, the Courtaut.† This Mersennus says is made of one cylindrical piece of wood, and has eleven holes. The upper of the two short figures shews that the Courtaut has two bores, which

---

* In the Harm. Univer, pag. 243, speaking of the flute, Mersennus says that in Sicily and elsewhere, there are persons who introduce into the mouth, and sound at one time, two and even three flutes of reed or cane; and he adds that if men had laboured as industriously and curiously to perfect instruments of this kind, as they have the organ, they might perhaps have found out some method of playing four or five parts with one and the same breath of the mouth; and if they were to take the pains to pierce them in such manner that the diatonic genus being on one side, as it is in effect, the chromatic and enarmonic might be on two other sides, and they might easily execute all that the Greeks knew with a bit of wood.

† Courtaut, from the adjective Court, short; the French dictionaries explain it a short bassoon. We have a verb, curtail, that signifies to shorten, and a noun, Curtail, interpreted a bass to the hautboy. Phillips.

are concealed under the moveable box into which the tube is inserted; the holes in those tampions called by Mersennus, Tetines, which project from each side of the instrument are for the fingers, and by being doubled are adapted for the use of either right or left-handed persons. The two light holes are on the opposite side of the instrument, the upper one is for the egress of the wind after all the rest are stopped. Mersennus adds that there are some persons, who by excavating a stick or walking-staff, have wrought it into an instrument of this latter kind, thereby making of it a kind of Bourdon, like those used by the pilgrims to the body of St. James at Compostella, for the purpose of recreating themselves on a walk.

For a description of the third instrument we must refer to the Harm. Universelle Des Instrumens à Vent, Prop. XXXII. where it is said to be the same with the first, but without the funnel.

The Bassoon, according to Mersennus, is an instrument exceeding in magnitude all others of the Fagot kind,* to which it is a bass, and therefore it is called the Bassoon; though there is another kind of bassoon which he calls the Cervelat, a word signifying a sausage; this strange instrument is inflated by means of a reed resembling that of a hautboy, but of a larger size. The instrument itself is but five inches in height, and yet is capable of producing a sound equally grave with one of forty inches in length. Within it are eight canals or ducts, answering to the number of holes in the lid or upper surface; these canals it seems have a communication with each other, and yet are affected by the stopping of those on the surface of the cylinder; some of them corresponding to one canal and others to others, in the same manner as if all were reduced into one continued tube.† The white circles denote the holes on the opposite side. The two bassoons are exhibited by Mersennus in this form:—

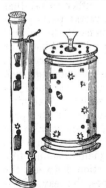

Prop. X. treats of the Tibia Pictavia or Hautbois de Poictou, a very slender hautboy; and also of the Cornamusa or bagpipe, consisting of a Bourdon or drone, a small pipe in which is inserted a wheaten straw, and another pipe called the Calumeau, with seven holes. These two pipes are inserted into the neck of a calf-skin bag, resembling in shape a chemist's retort, on the back whereof is fixed the drone above mentioned, as also a short pipe, through which the whole instrument is inflated by the mouth of the performer. There is no need to insert a figure of this instrument, as it differs but very little from the Scotch bagpipe.

* FAGOTTO is a word used by the Italians to signify a bassoon, but it appears above that it is common to that and all such other instruments as by being compacted together, resemble a fagot.

† Stanesby who was a diligent peruser both of Mersennus and Kircher, and in the making of instruments adhered as closely to the directions of the former as possible, constructed a short bassoon or Cervelat, such a one as is above described, for the late earl of Abercorn, then lord Paisley, and a disciple of Dr. Pepusch, but it did not answer expectation: by reason of its closeness the interior parts imbibed and retained the moisture of the breath the ducts dilated, and broke. In short the whole blew up.

Mersennus adds that in France the country people make use of this instrument on holidays, and in their songs and dances at weddings; nay, that they sing their vespers to it in churches where there are no organs. In the next proposition he describes an instrument of an elegant form and richly decorated, called the Musette, the bagpipe of the French.

In Prop. XIV. he describes the Italian bagpipe, called by him the Surdeline; this is a much larger and more complicated instrument than either of the former, and consists of many pipes and conduits for the conveyance of the wind, with keys for the opening of the holes by the pressure of the fingers: this instrument, as also the Musette, is inflated by means of bellows, which the performer blows with his arm, at the same time that he fingers the pipe.

CHAP. CXXVII.

MERSENNUS next proceeds to treat of those instruments which serve for ecclesiastical harmony; and first he describes the cornet. He says the use of it is to supply the acuter sounds, which he says in this instrument vibrate after the manner of lightning. The form of the Cornet in its various sizes is thus represented by him:—

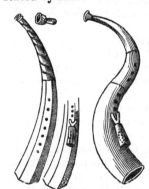

The first figure is of a treble cornet, the second shews the lower part of the tenor, the third is the bass, of the serpentine form, and is four or five feet in length. Mersennus says that the sounds of the cornet are vehement, but that those who are skilful, such as Quiclet, the royal cornetist, are able so to soften and modulate them, that nothing can be more sweet. He adds that the true and genuine bass of the cornet is the Serpent. Of this instrument Mersennus gives a particular description in Prop. XVI. And first he exhibits it in this form:—

The Serpent he says is thus contorted to render it commodious for carriage, its length being six feet and one inch. As it is usually made of a very brittle wood, namely nut-tree, and its thickness being but one line, or the twelfth of an inch; it is usually covered with leather, and also strengthened with sinews of oxen glewed round the first curve, which is the part by which it is held when transported from one place to another, though these precautions are unnecessary, when, as is frequently the case, this instrument is made of brass or silver.

Mersennus mentions some peculiar properties of this instrument, and, among others, that the sound of it is strong enough to drown twenty robust voices, being animated by the breath of a boy, and yet the sound of it may be attempered to the softness of the sweetest voice. Another peculiarity of this instrument is, that great as the distance between the third and fourth hole appears, yet whether the third hole be open or shut, the difference is but a tone.

After a description of the Hunting-horn, Mersennus proceeds in Prop. XVIII. to explain the figure, parts, system, tones, and use of that noble instrument the trumpet :* he says that the system of this instrument is wonderful, as indeed it appears to be from his description of it, in which he remarks that its first or lowest sound is C FA UT, and its next towards the acute, G SOL RE ; and that it cannot by any means whatever be made to utter the intermediate sounds RE MI FA. Again he says the third sound is C FA UT in the acute, making a diatessaron to the second. He endeavours in a long discourse to assign reasons for the defects in this instrument ; but they are better accounted for in a passage above-cited from a paper in the Philosophical Transactions, written by the Hon. Mr. Roberts, describing the trumpet marine.

But, notwithstanding these defects in the trumpet, Mersennus, in Prop. XX. speaking of a trumpet somewhat different from the former, intimates that they may in a great measure be overcome by practice ; and says that his imagination of the possibility of so doing is strongly encreased by certain letters by him received from Mons. Bourdelot, a most learned physician, resident at Rome, who therein asserts that a famous performer on the trumpet, Hieronymo Fantino by name, had actually produced from his instrument all the tones within its compass without intermission, joining them with those of the organ of St. Peter's church at Rome, Girolamo Frescobaldi, the organist of that church, playing on it at the same time. It is true, Mersennus says, that the trumpeters of the duke de Crequi, the French embassador, objected to these tones as inordinate, and indeed spurious ; but whether they are necessarily to be deemed so or not, or, in other words, whether a regular succession of intervals on the trumpet be repugnant to the order of nature or not, he recommends as a question well worthy of consideration.†

Prop. XXI. contains a description of the Tuba tractilis or Sacbut, so called from its being capable of being drawn out ; it is elsewhere said by Mersennus to be the true bass of the military trumpet, and indeed the similarity of sound in both seems to indicate no less.

In the concluding Proposition in this book, viz., that numbered XXII. he describes a Chinese instrument, which he says was sent him by an English gentleman named Hardy ; it consists of a large cane excavated and fixed to the necks of two Cucurbites, hollow and without bottoms ; along the surface of the cane, but a little distant from it, chords are strained by the means of pins ; he adds that the method of performing on this instrument is by iron plectra fastened to the ends of the fingers.

He also describes another instrument, which he says was sent to him from Rome by Giovanni Battista Doni, secretary to Cardinal Barberini. It was constructed of the half of an Indian fruit of the melon kind, cleared from its contents, and afterwards covered on the top with a serpent's skin like a kettle-drum : to this was affixed on the belly of the instrument a handle made of an Indian reed, about twice the length of the body. He describes also other Chinese and Indian instruments, equally barbarous and ill-constructed with those above-mentioned.

In the succeeding book, entitled De Organis, Campanis, Tympanis, ac cæteris Instrumentis κρουομενοις, seu quæ percutiuntur, Mersennus enters into a most minute investigation of the natures and properties of these several instruments, and with respect to the organ in particular, he is so very precise, that were the art of organ-building lost to the world, there is very little doubt but that it might be recovered by means of this book.

It is impossible so to abridge this elaborate and curious tract, as to render it of any use to the generality of readers, it must therefore suffice to say that it contains a description of the several parts of an organ, of the materials and dimensions of the several orders of pipes, with the division of the Abacus or key-board, and the temperament of the instrument.

Speaking of pipes, he distinguishes between such as are stopped at the ends and such as are open ; as also between pipes of wood and metal. Assigning the effects of these different materials in the production of tones of various kinds, he shews also the use of that tongue, which being inserted into the mouth of any pipe, causes it to yield a sound like that of a reed. As to the proportion between the length and circumference of pipes, he says it is a very difficult thing to ascertain, but that experience shews that the quadruple ratio is the cause of the best sound. This proportion is not taken from the diameter of the tube, but from the width of the plate, supposing it to be of metal, of which it is formed, which when reduced to a cylinder, bears a ratio of about 7 to 22 to its circumference. Nevertheless he says that in the first order of pipes the largest is sixteen feet in length ; he adds that he had seen pipes thirty-two feet long, but that it is not in the power of the ear to form a judgment of the sounds which these produce; and these pipes he resembles to chords of such an enormous length, as make but twelve returns and a half in the space of a second of time.

The difference of pipes in respect of the acumen and gravity of their sounds, depends upon their size, for the longer the pipe is, the slower are its vibrations, and consequently the graver is its sound; and, what is much to be wondered at, a pipe stopped at the end will produce a sound an octave lower than when open.*

From these particulars respecting the pipes of an organ, their ratios, and the sounds produced by them, Mersennus proceeds to explain the mechanism of this noble instrument by a verbal description of its several parts, and representations thereof in diagrams. Such a minute description as this was necessary in a work that professes no less than to teach the art of making the several instruments of which it treats. In a work such as is the present, the same degree of precision will hardly be required, especially as a very accurate description of the organ is contained in the Facteur d'Orgues, which makes part of the Descriptions des Arts et Métiers, now publishing at Paris; and a very satisfactory one is extant in the Principles of Mechanics of Mr. W. Emerson, Lond. quarto, 1758; nevertheless such a general description of the organ is here given as is consistent with the nature of the present work.

From what has already been said of the organ, it appears that it is to be considered in the several views of a machine and a musical instrument; the former of these belong to the science of mechanics, and such as are skilled therein may with wonder contemplate this noble effort of ingenuity and industry; such will be delighted to observe the means by which an instrument of this magnitude is inflated, and those contrivances of ducts and canals, whereby a due proportion of wind is distributed to thousands of pipes of different forms and magnitudes, and by what means it so communicated as to be in readiness to obey the touch of the finger, they will wonder at the variety of sound produced by pipes formed of the same materials differently constructed, and at the regular and artful arrangement of these for the purpose of occupying the whole of a given space; and lastly, they will be astonished at the general and universal concent of parts, which renders the whole of this stupendous machine obedient to the will of the performer.

In the consideration of the organ as a musical instrument, it is to be noted that the sounds produced by it are of various kinds, that is to say, some resemble those of the flute or pipe, allowing for the difference of shrillness and mellowness arising from different degrees of magnitude; others have a sound arising from the tremulous motion of the air re-

sembling the human voice, others imitate the clangor of the trumpet; and those orders of pipes, whether simple or compounded, that in the construction of the instrument are connected together or rendered subservient to one touch of the key, are called stops.

The simple stops are those in which only one pipe answers to the touch of the key, these are the Diapason, † Principal, Tierce, Twelfth, Fifteenth, Flute, Block-Flute, Trumpet, Clarion, Nazard, Vox-humana, Krumhorn, and some others. The compound stops are the Cornet, the Sesquialtera, Mixture, Furniture and sundry others; and are so called for that in them several pipes are made to speak at the touch of a single key, as in the Sesquialtera three, in the Cornet five, in the Mixture and in the Furniture three, four, or more; and the full organ or chorus is compounded of all.

Among pipes a distinction occurs, not only with respect to the materials of which they are formed,‡ but also between those in which the wind is cut by the tongue, which is visible in the aperture of pipes of that class, and others where the percussion is against a reed as it is called, though made of brass, inserted in the body of the pipe, and which answers to the Glottis or upper part of the human larynx; and of pipes thus constructed are composed the stops called the Vox-humana, Regal, Krumhorn, Trumpet, Clarion, Hautboy, and many others. The figures here exhibited represent these Glottides in different views, as also a pipe with the glottis affixed to it.

Fig. A shews the glottis of a trumpet-pipe in front; the wire is doubled at top, and one end thereof is bent down, and made to form a bar; the front of the glottis is of thin brass and very elastic; the bar pressing hard against this plate, being moved upwards or downwards by the wire, opens or closes the aperture, making the sound either flatter or sharper, and this is the method of tuning pipes of this kind. Fig. B is a side view of a glottis with the aperture. In Fig. C the pipe containing the glottis is mounted on a canal or duct, which being placed on the wind-chest, conveys the wind to the aperture, which cutting against the end of the spring, is the immediate cause of that reedy tone which distinguishes pipes of this class.

Of the pipes in an organ those called the Diapasons§ are to be considered as the basis or foundation; above these succeed in regular order other

---

* Mersennus in another place seems to contradict himself, saying that a covered pipe of the same height and breadth with an open one, does not produce a perfect diapason or octave, but one that is diminished by a semitone, and that the same when twice as wide makes an octave increased by a semitone. The organ-builders, in order to avoid this, make the breadth of the covered pipes sesquialtera to that of the open ones, in order to constitute a perfect octave.

† This is an improper term to signify a single order of pipes: the organ-makers are betrayed into the use of it by the consideration that it is the foundation of the harmony of the instrument, the pitch of all the other orders of pipes being accommodated to it. See the true sense of the word Diapason in a subsequent note.

‡ Pipes are made of either wood or metal, some have mouths like flutes, others have reeds; the smallest pipes are made of tin, or of tin and lead; the sound of wooden and leaden pipes is soft, short pipes are open and the long ones are stopped: the mouths of large square wooden pipes are stopped with valves of leather. Metal pipes have a little ear on each side of the mouth to tune them, by bending it a little in or out. Whatever note any open pipe sounds, when the mouth is stopped it will sound an octave higher, and a pipe twice its capacity will sound an octave lower.

§ These are of two kinds, the open and the stoped, the latter are of wood, and are so called from their being stopped with a tampion or plug of wood clothed with leather.

simple stops, tuned in harmonical intervals to the diapasons, as the tierce or third, the sesquialtera in the ratio of 3 to 2, or the fifth ; some in the octave, others in the tenth, which is the replicate of the third, the twelfth the replicate of the fifth, the bis-diapason, and so on to the twenty-second. By means of the Registers that command the several orders of pipes, the wind is either admitted into or excluded from them severally ; and we accordingly hear the cornet, the flute, or the trumpet, &c. at the will of the performer. When all the stops are drawn, and the registers open, the wind pervades the whole instrument, and we hear that full and complete harmony, that general and universal concent, which, as being per omnes, is what the ancient writers mean to express by the term Diapason.*

And here it is wonderful to consider that notwithstanding that surd quantity in the musical system, which renders it impossible precisely to adjust the intervals that compose the diatessaron, and which, as Boetius observes, makes the amount of six sesquioctave tones to exceed the diapason, by the commixture of pipes in the manner above-mentioned, all the irregularities hence arising are reconciled, and in effect annihilated.

Of the stops of an organ, the most usual are the Diapasons, the open and stopped, the Tierce, Sesquialtera, Flute, Cornet, Tenth, Twelfth, Fifteenth, Principal, Furniture, Mixture, Trumpet, Clarion, Hautboy, Larigot, Vox-humana, Krumhorn, and Nazard. The foreign organs, especially those of Germany, have many more, particularly that in the abbey church of Weingarten, a town in the Upper Palatinate, which has sixty-six, and contains no fewer than six thousand six hundred and sixty-six pipes.† The organ at Haerlem is said to have sixty stops, many of them but little known to the English workmen, among which are the Bourdon, Gemsen-horn, the Quintadena, Schalmey, Dulciana, Buzain, and Zink.‡

* The following passages in some of our best poets fully justify the above sense of these words :—

And 'twixt them both a quadrate was the base,
Proportion'd equally by seven and nine ;
Nine was the circle set in heaven's place,
All which compacted, made a goodly *Dyapase*.
            FAERIE QUEENE. book II. canto ix. stanza 22.

*   *   *   *   *   *

Jarr'd against nature's chime, and with harsh din
Broke the fair music that all creatures made
To their great Lord, whose love their motion sway'd
In perfect *Diapason* while they stood
In first obedience and their state of good.
            MILTON, at a solemn music.

Many a sweet rise, many as sweet a fall,
A full-mouth'd *Diapason* swallows all.   CRASHAW.

From harmony from heav'nly harmony
This universal frame began ;
   From harmony to harmony
Through all the compass of the notes it ran,
The *Diapason* closing full in man.
            DRYDEN, Song for St. Cecilia's day, 1687.

† Of this instrument, the most elegant and superb of any in the world, the figure, with a particular description, is given in the Facteur d'Orgues above-mentioned.

‡ The names, as also the etymologies of these appellations are but little understood, and many of them have so departed from their primitive significations, that they may be said to be arbitrary; to instance in the Tierce and Sesquialtera, the former can mean nothing but a third above the diapasons, and the latter must signify the interval expressed by that term which signifies the whole and its half, viz., the ratio of 3 to 2, or, in the language of musicians, the diapente or fifth ; whereas it has long been the practice to tune the Tierce a seventeenth, *i. e.* a double octave and a third, and to compound the Sesquialtera of the unison third and fifth.

Many of the above names bespeak their signification, others require

The German organs have also keys for the feet, called Pedals, an invention of a German, named Bernhard, about the year 1400. These command certain pipes, which, to encrease the harmony, are tuned below the diapasons.

Among the modern improvements of the organ the most remarkable are the Swell and the Tremblant, the former invented by an English artificer, consists in a number of pipes placed in a remote part of the instrument, and inclosed in a kind of box, which being gradually opened by the pressure of the foot, increases the sound as the wind does the sound of a peal of bells, or suppresses it in like manner by the contrary action. The Tremblant is a contrivance by means of a valve in the Port-vent or passage from the wind-chest, to check the wind, and admit it only by starts ; so that the notes seem to stammer, and the whole instrument to sob, in a manner very offensive to the ear. In the organ at the German chapel in the Savoy, is a Tremblant.

In cathedral churches where there are generally two organs, a large and a small, the latter the French distinguish by the epithet Positif, the reason whereof we are to seek, the term being only proper and belonging to organs fixed to a certain place, and is used in contradistinction to portatif, a term applied to those portable ones, which, like the Regal, may be carried about. We in England call it the choir, and by corruption the choir organ.

The foregoing account, intended to supersede the

to be explained ; the Larigot means a flajolet. The Krumhorn is an imitation of a pipe described by Ottomarus Luscinius, in his Musurgia, lib. I. pag. 20, and also in page 331 of this work, and is often corrupted into Cremona, from the notion that the sound of this stop resembles that of a Cremona violin.

The Nazard, or, as Mersennus terms it, the Nasutas, from its snuffling tone, resembles the singing of those who utter sounds seemingly through the nose.

The word Bourdon signifies the drone of a bagpipe ; the Latin word for it is Bombus, as also Bombyx. Hoffman. Lex. Univer. in Art. Mersennus in his Latin work uses the latter. At Manchester, and also at Coventry, is an organ with this stop.

The Gemsen-horn is a small pipe made of the horn of a quadruped called the Gems, a Shamoy or wild goat. Luscinius describes it, and the stop so named is an imitation of it. See page 331 of this work.

The appellation of Quintadena, corruptly spelt Quintadeena, quasi Quinta ad una, or five to one. This is the ratio of the greater seventeenth, which the word Quintadena was doubtless intended to bespeak, and the diapasons are the acute terms, consequently the pitch of this stop is a double octave and a third major below the diapasons. In the organ of Spitalfields church, made by Bridge, is a stop which he improperly, as it should seem, called a Quintadena, the pitch of it being only a fifth above the diapasons. However it is the only one of the kind in England.

The word Schalmey is derived from Chalumeau, and the latter from Calamus. The Schalmey is described by Luscinius, Musurgia, lib. I. pag. 19, and is a kind of hautboy, very long and slender. See the figure of it in page 331 of this work.

The Dulcian is probably an imitation of an instrument of Moorish original, called the Dulçana, a kind of tenor-hautboy, or, as Brossard describes it, a small bassoon. Mention is made of this instrument by Cerone, lib. XXI. cap. i. and by Cervantes in Don Quixote, ' Entre Moros—se usa un genero de Dulçaynas que paracen nuestras Chirimias.' See page 444 of this work, in not. Or it might signify a stop called the Dulciana, consisting of very long and narrow pipes in unison with the diapason, but that the latter is said to be a very recent invention.

The word Buzain is a corruption of Busaun, or, as it is now spelt, Posaune, which signifies a Sacbut or bass-trumpet, and the stop so named is an imitation of that instrument, which see represented in page 332 of this work.

The Zink, corruptly spelt Cink, is an imitation of the Zinken horn, a very small pipe, or rather a whistle, described and delineated from Luscinius, page 331 of this work. It is made of a small branch of a deer's horn.

The desire of variety in the stops of an organ has been indulged to a ridiculous degree. In the organ of Weingarten are stops intended to imitate the sound of bells, the voice of the cuckow, and the roaring of the sea. Other absurd fancies have intruded into this noble instrument, such as figures that beat time, alluded to by Dr. Donne in these lines :—

   ' As in some organs, puppets dance above,
   ' And bellows pant below, which them do move.'   Satire II.

necessity of giving at large Mersennus's description, may serve for a general idea of the organ. The early fabricators of this instrument are as little known as celebrated by their works; Zarlino mentions two persons at Rome, Vincenzo Colombi and Vincenzo Colonna, famous organ-makers in his time; but before them, viz., towards the end of the fifteenth century, there flourished Rudolphus Agricola, an admirable artist, who made the organ at Groningen.* Ralph Dallans, Bernard Smith, and Renatus Harris, are names well known in Germany, France, and England, as excellent organ-makers. Of these an account will hereafter be given. In the mean time it may be observed that there is no method of estimating the improvement of the manual arts so satisfactory as that of comparing the works of modern artificers with those of the ancient. The mechanism of an organ at this day proves it to be a wonderful machine, constructed with great ingenuity, and most elegantly wrought. The following figure represents an organ in the time of king Stephen, taken from a manuscript Psalter of Eadwine in the library of Trinity college, Cambridge. Insig. R. 17. 1.

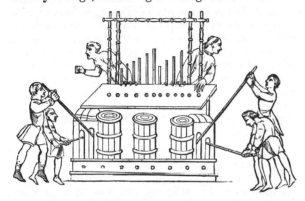

The eighth and last book of the harmonics treats of bells and other instruments of percussion, including therein drums of various kinds, as also Castanets, the Claquebois or regals of wood described page 330 of this work; and descending even to the Cymbalum Orale, or Jew's-harp.

With respect to bells, Mersennus treats of the different metals of which they are formed, of their figure, crassitude, and degrees of ponderosity as they respect each other in any given series. He describes also those peals of bells in the towers of many churches in Germany, called Carillons, on which, by the help of a contrivance of ropes fastened to the clappers, and collected together at the lower ex-

tremities, tunes are played at stated hours of the day. This kind of practice on bells is in effect tolling, and not ringing, an art which seems to be peculiar to England, which for this reason is termed the ringing island.

The ringing of bells is a curious exercise of the invention and memory; and though a recreation chiefly of the lower sort of people, is worthy of notice. The tolling a bell is nothing more than the producing a sound by a stroke of the clapper against the side of the bell, the bell itself being in a pendant position and at rest. In ringing, the bell, by means of a wheel and a rope, is elevated to a perpendicular; in its motion to this situation the clapper strikes forcibly on one side, and in its return downwards, on the other side of the bell, producing at each stroke a sound. The music of bells is altogether melody, but the pleasure arising from it consists in the variety of interchanges and the various succession and general predominance of the consonances in the sound produced.†

---

* RUDOLPHUS AGRICOLA was born at Bafflen in Friesland, two miles from Groningen. He was a learned divine, philosopher, poet, and musician, and also an excellent mechanic. *Those who would know more of him than can here be mentioned may consult Bayle in art. Blount's Censura Celebrium Auctorum, and Dr. Jortin's Life of Erasmus.* There are of his composition Songs in his native language to music in four parts: he is also said to have sung well, and to have had a fine hand on the lute. Melchior Adamus has celebrated him for his extensive learning and skill in music. That he made the organ at St. Martin's church is uniformly believed throughout the Netherlands upon better authority than bare tradition; Benthem, in his Hollandischen Kirch-und Schulen-Staat, expressly asserts it; and with him Walther agrees in the relation of the fact. The organ of Agricola is yet remaining in St. Martin's church: some additions have been made to it since his time, but they are no more to be considered as improvements, than the additions to the organs of Father Smith, which serve but as a foil to the unimproved part of the instrument.

† The invention of bells, that is to say, such as are hung in the towers or steeples of Christian churches, is by Polydore Virgil and others, ascribed to Paulinus bishop of Nola, a city of Campania, about the year 400; it is said that the names Nolæ and Campanæ, the one referring to the city, the other to the country, were for that reason given to them. In the time of Clothair II. king of France, and in the year 610, the army of that king was frighted from the siege of the city of Sens by ringing the bells of St. Stephen's church. Vincent, Spec. Hist. lib. XXIII. cap. ix. Bede relates that about the year 670, 'Audivit subito in aëre notum 'Campanæ sonum, quo ad orationes excitari vel convocari solebant.' Hist. Eccl. lib. IV. cap. xxiii. Ingulphus mentions that Turketulus, abbat of Croyland, who died about the year 870, gave a great bell to the church of that abbey, which he named Guthlac, and afterwards six others, viz., two which he called Bartholomew and Bettelin, two called Turketul and Tatwin, and two named Pega and Bega, all which rang together: the same author says, 'Non erat tunc tanta consonantia 'campanarum in totâ Angliâ.' Ingulph. Hist. fol. 889, edit. Franc. Not long after, Kinseus, archbishop of York, built a tower of stone to the church of St. John at Beverly, and placed therein two great bells, and at the same time provided that other churches in his diocese should be furnished with bells. J. Stubbs, Act. Pont. Eborc. fol. 1700. See more about bells in Spelman's Glossary, voce CAMPANA, and in Bingham's Antiquities of the Christian Church, book VIII. chap. vii. sect 15.

Mention is made by St. Aldhelm, and William of Malmesbury, of bells given by St. Dunstan to the churches in the West.

In the times of popery bells were baptised and anointed Oleo Chrismatis; they were exorcised and blessed by the bishop, from a belief that when these ceremonies were performed they had a power to drive the devil out of the air, to calm tempests, to extinguish fire, and to recreate even the dead. The ritual for these ceremonies is contained in the Roman pontifical; and it was usual in their baptism to give to bells the name of some saint. In Chauncy's History of Hertfordshire, page 383, is a relation of the baptism of a set of bells in Italy with great ceremony, a short time before the writing that book. The bells of the parish church of Winnington in Bedfordshire had their names cast about the verge of every one in particular, with these rhyming hexameters:—

Nomina Campanis hec indita sunt quoque nostris.
1. Hoc signum Petri pulsatur nomine Christi.
2. Nomen Magdalene campana sonat melode.
3. Sit nomen Domini benedictum semper in euum.
4. Musa Raphaelis sonat auribus Immanuelis.
5. Sum Rosa pulsata mundi que Maria vocata.
                                            Weev. Fun. Mon. 122.

By an old Chartulary, once in the possession of Weever the antiquary, it appears that the bells of the priory of Little Dunmow in Essex, were, anno 1501, new cast, and baptised by the following names:—

Prima in honore Sancti Michaelis Archangeli.
Secunda in honore S. Johannis Evangeliste.
Tertia in honore S. Johannis Baptiste.
Quarta in honore Assumptionis beate Marie.
Quinta in honore sancte Trinitatis, et omnium sanctorum.
                                            Fun. Mon. 633.

The bells of Osney abbey near Oxford were very famous; their several names were Douce, Clement, Austin, Hautecter [potius Hautcleri] Gabriel and John. Appendix to Hearne's Collection of Discourses by Antiquaries, Numb. XI.

Near Old Windsor is a public house vulgarly called the Bells of Bosely; this house was originally built for the accommodation of bargemen and others navigating the river Thames between London and Oxford. It has a sign of six bells, i. e. the bells of Osney.

In the Funeral Monuments of Weever, are the following particulars relating to bells:—

'Bells had frequently these inscriptions on them:—
'Funera plango, Fulgura frango, Sabbata pango,
'Excito lentos, Dissipo ventos, Paco cruentos. Page 122.

The Harmonie Universelle contains in substance the whole of the Harmonici, but is in some measure improved in the latter. There are nevertheless some tracts, and many curious particulars in the French which are not to be found in the Latin work. To instance, in Livre Septiesme, entitled Des Instrumens de Percussion; in this is an account of a French musician born in 1517, named Jacques Mauduit, and who, though not mentioned by any other writer on music, was styled Pere de la Musique. Mersennus gives him a most exalted character, and exhibits a Requiem in five parts of his composition.

BOOK XIV.   CHAP. CXXVIII.

JOHN KEPLER, a great astronomer and mathematician, was born at Wiel in the duchy of Wirtemberg, on the twenty-seventh of December, 1571. His father, Henry Kepler, was descended from a family

'In the Little Sanctuary at Westminster, king Edw. III. erected a 'Clochier, and placed therein three bells for the use of St. Stephen's 'chapel: about the biggest of them were cast in the metal these words:—

'King Edward made mee thirtie thousand weight and three, 'Take me down and wey mee, and more you shall fynd mee,

'But these bells being to be taken down in the raigne of king Hen. VIII. 'one writes underneath with a coale:—

'But Henry the eight, 'Will bait me of my weight.'   Ibid. 492.

This last distich alludes to a fact mentioned by Stow in his Survey of London ward of Farrindon Within, to wit, that near to St. Paul's school stood a Clochier, in which were four bells called Jesus bells, the greatest in all England, against which Sir Miles Partridge staked a hundred pounds, and won them of king Henry VIII. at a cast of dice.

It is said that the foundation of the Corsini family in Italy was laid by an ancestor of it, who, at the dissolution of religious houses, purchased the bells of abbey and other churches, and by the sale of them in other countries, acquired a very great estate.

Somerset the protector was a great spoiler of churches and chapels, and attempted to pull down the bells in all parish churches, and leave but one in a steeple, whereat the old commonally were offended and ready to rebel. Howe's Preface to his edition of Stow's Annals, edit. 1631.

The exportation of bell metal was temp. Hen. VIII. and Edw. VI., prohibited by statute and also by proclamation, from an apprehension that our enemies might cast it into great guns. Strype's Eccl. Mem. Vol. II. page 45.

It is said by some author that upon the surrender of a town, the first act of the besiegers is to seize the bells.

Nevertheless it appears that abroad there are bells of great magnitude. In the steeple of the great church at Roan in Normandy, is a bell with this inscription:—

Je suis George de Ambois, Qui trente cinque mille pois, Mes lui qui me pesera, Trente six mill me trovera.

I am George of Ambois, Thirtie five thousand in pois: But he that shall weigh me, Thirtie six thousand shall find me.   Ibid.

And it is a common tradition that the bells of King's college chapel, in the university of Cambridge, were taken by Henry V. from some church in France, after the battle of Agincourt. They were taken down some years ago, and sold to Phelps the bell-founder in White-Chapel, who melted them down.

The practice of ringing bells in change is said to be peculiar to this country, but the antiquity of it is not easily to be ascertained: there are in London several societies of ringers, particularly one known by the name of the College Youths; of this it is said Sir Matthew Hale, lord chief justice of the court of King's Bench, was, in his youthful days, a member; and in the life of this learned and upright judge, written by bishop Burnet, some facts are mentioned which favor this relation.

Mersennus has said nothing of the ringing of bells in changes; nor has Kircher done any thing more than calculate the possible combinations arising from a given number. In England the practice of ringing is reduced to a science, and peals have been composed which bear the names of the inventors. Some of the most celebrated peals now known were composed about fifty years ago by one Patrick; this man was a maker of barometers: in his advertisements he styled himself Torricellian Operator, from Torricelli, who invented instruments of this kind.

In the year 1684, one Abraham Rudhall, of the city of Gloucester, brought the art of bell-founding to great perfection. His descendants in succession have continued the business of casting bells; and by a list published by them, it appears that at Lady day, 1774, the family, in peals and odd bells, had cast to the amount of 3594. The peals of St. Dunstan's in the East, and St. Bride's, London, and St. Martin's in the Fields, Westminster, are in the number.

It seems that formerly the usual number of a peal of bells was five. Stow's Annals, 1003. In the year 1430, a sixth bell was added to the peal of five, in the Church of St. Michael's, Cornhill, after which it was accounted the best ring of bells for harmony and sweetness of tone in England. Stow's Survey, 4to., in Cornhill Ward.

It has been remarked, that the compleatest and most perfect ring of bells is a peal of six, in which whether ascending or descending the semitone holds the middle position, as it does in both the natural and the duram hexachord. In the molle hexachord the tritonus intervenes. Vide D. V. Holder's Treatise on the natural grounds of Harmony.

which had raised itself under the emperors by military desert, and was himself an officer of rank in the army, but, after a series of misfortunes, was reduced to the necessity of keeping a public house for the support of himself and his family. He died in 1590, leaving his son John in a very helpless and forlorn condition.

The necessitous circumstances of Kepler's father would not allow of his giving his children such an education as might tend to repair the ruined fortunes of the family: his son John, however, discovered an early propensity to learning, and found means, upon the death of his father, to put himself into a course of study in the university of Tubingen, where, after he had acquired a competent degree of knowledge in physics, he betook himself to the mathematics under the direction of Michael Moestlin, a famous professor there. In this branch of science Kepler made so rapid a progress, that in the year 1593 he was invited to teach the mathematics at Gratz in Styria. Being settled there, he applied himself wholly to the study of astronomy, and published his works from time to time.

In the year 1597 he married, and became involved in a vexatious contest for the recovery of his wife's fortune, and the year after was banished from Gratz on account of his religion, but was soon recalled; however, the growing troubles and the confusions of that place inclined him to think of a residence elsewhere; and as Tycho Brahe, having settled in Bohemia, and obtained from the emperor a great number of instruments for carrying on his pursuits in astronomy, had often solicited Kepler to come and abide with him, he left the university of Gratz, and removed into Bohemia with his family and library in the year 1600. Kepler in this journey was seized with a quartan ague, which continued seven or eight months; upon his recovery he set himself to assist Tycho Brahe with all his power, but there was but little cordiality between them: Kepler was offended at Tycho for the great reserve and caution with which he treated him, and for refusing to do some services to his family, which he had requested of him. Tycho Brahe died in 1601, but in the performance of the engagement which he had entered into with Kepler to induce him to settle at Prague, he had, on his arrival in that city, introduced him to the emperor Rudolphus, who received him very kindly, and made him his mathematician, upon condition that he should serve Tycho by making arithmetical calculations for him; in consideration thereof he was honoured with the title of mathematician to the emperor. Upon the decease of Tycho Brahe, Kepler received a command from the emperor to finish those tables begun by Tycho, which are known by the name of the Rudolphine tables, and he applied himself very vigorously to it; but such difficulties arose in a short time, partly from the nature of the work, and partly from the delay of the treasurers entrusted with the management and disposal of the fund appropriated for carrying it on, that they were not completed till the year 1627. Kepler complained that from the year 1602 he was looked upon by the treasurers with a very invidious eye; and that when in 1609 he had published a noble specimen of the work, and the emperor had given orders that, besides the expence of the edition, he should be immediately paid the arrears of his pension, which he said amounted to four thousand crowns, he in vain knocked at the doors of the Silesian and Imperial chambers, and it was not till two years after, that the generous orders of Rudolphus in his favour were obeyed. He met with no less discouragement from the financiers under the emperor Matthias than under Rudolphus, and therefore, after struggling with poverty for ten years at Prague, he began to think of removing thence, which the emperor hearing, stationed him at Lintz, and appointed him a salary from the states of Upper Austria, which was paid for sixteen years. In the year 1613 he went to the assembly at Ratisbon, to assist in the reformation of the Calendar, but returned to Lintz, where he continued to the year 1626.* In November in that year he went to Ulm, in order to publish the Rudolphine Tables; and afterwards in 1629, with the emperor's leave, settled at Sagan in Silesia, where he published the second part of his Ephemerides, for the first had been published at Lintz in the year 1617. In the year 1630 he went to Ratisbon to solicit the payment of the arrears of his pension, but being seized with a fever, which it is said he brought upon himself by too hard riding, he died there in November, in the fifty-ninth year of his age.

Before the time of Kepler the opinion of astronomers was, that the orbits of the heavenly bodies were circular, but in 1609 he shewed from the observations of Tycho Brahe, that the planet Mars described an ellipsis about the sun, placed in the lowermost focus, and collected the same to be the case of the rest.† He also discovered this great law observed by nature in the revolutions of the heavenly bodies, viz. that the squares of their periodical times are as the cubes of their mean distances.‡ Kepler is also said to have been the first investigator of the true cause of tides, as arising from the principle of gravitation, though Sir Isaac Newton so far improved upon his discoveries on that subject, as to make the doctrine in a manner his own.§

The most celebrated of Kepler's works are his Prodromus Dissertationum de Proportione Orbium cœlestium, and his Mysterium Cosmographicum, in which latter, as it is said, the sublime secret of the five regular bodies is laid open. Of this latter work the author thought so highly, that in a conversation with one of his friends, Thomas Lansius, he declared that if the electorate of Saxony were offered him on condition of his renouncing the honour of the discoveries contained therein, he would not accept it.

Besides these and many other books on astronomy and other mathematical subjects, Kepler was the author of a work entitled Harmonices Mundi, which he dedicated to our king James I., the third book whereof, as it is on the subject of musical harmony, it materially concerns us so far to take notice of, as to mention its general contents, and point out those singularities which distinguish it.

The third book of the Harmonices Mundi is on the subject of those proportions which we term harmonical, having for its title De Ortu proportionum harmonicarum, deque natura et differentiis rerum ad cantum pertinentium. The titles of the several chapters are as follow :—

Caput I. Ortus consonantiarum ex causis suis propriis. II. De septem chordæ sectionibus harmonicis, totidemque formis consonantiarum minorum. III. De medietatibus harmonicis; et trinitate consonantiæ. IV. Ortus et denominatio intervallorum usualium seu concinnorum. V. Secto et denominatio consonantiarum per sua intervalla usualia. VI. De cantus generibus, dûro et molli. VII. Proportio omnium octo sonorum usualium unius diapason. VIII. Abscissio semitoniorum, et ordo minimorum intervallorum in diapason. IX. De diagrammate, lineis, notis, literisque sonorum indicibus; de systemate, clavibus et scala musicâ. X. De tretrachordis et syllabis, UT, RE, MI, FA, SOL, LA. XI. De compositione systematum majorum. XII. De consonantiis adulterinis, ex compositione ortis. XIII. De cantu concinno simplici. XIV. De modus seu tonis. XV. Qui modi, quibus serviant affectibus. XVI. De cantu figurato seu per harmoniam.

In the introduction to this treatise Kepler observes that the antiquity of music may be inferred from the mention of the harp and organ in the book of Genesis;

---

* In a letter from Sir Henry Wotton to Lord Bacon is the following curious relation respecting Kepler, to whom Sir Henry, then being our ambassador to some one of the princes of Germany, had made a visit. 'I lay a night at Lintz, the metropolis of the Higher Austria, but then in 'very low estate, having been newly taken by the duke of Bavaria, who, 'blandiente fortunâ, was gone on to the late effects : there I found Kepler, 'a man famous in the sciences, as your Lordship knows, to whom I pur- 'pose to convey from hence one of your books, that he may see we have 'some of our own that can honour our king, as well as he hath done with 'his Harmonica. In this man's study I was much taken with the draught 'of a landskip on a piece of paper, methoughts masterly done; whereof 'inquiring the author, he bewrayed with a smile, it was himself; adding 'he had done it, Non tanquam Pictor, sed tanquam Mathematicus. This 'set me on fire: at last he told me how. He hath a little back tent (of 'what stuff is not much importing) which he can suddenly set up where 'he will in a field, and it is convertible (like a wind-mill) to all quarters 'at pleasure, capable of not much more than one man, as I conceive, and 'perhaps at no great ease; exactly close and dark, save at one hole, about 'an inch and a half in the diameter, to which he applies a long per- 'spective trunk, with a convex glass fitted to the said hole, and the 'concave taken out at the other end, which extendeth to about the 'middle of this erected tent, through which the visible radiations of all 'the objects without are intromitted, falling upon a paper, which is 'accommodated to receive them, and so he traceth them with his pen in 'their natural appearance, turning his little tent round by degrees till he 'hath designed the whole aspect of the field. This I have described to 'your Lordship, because I think there might be good use made of it for 'Chorograpy; for otherwise to make landskips by it were illiberal : though 'surely no painter can do them so precisely.' Reliquæ Wottonianæ, Lond. 1685, page 299.

It does not appear that Kepler claimed the honour of this invention, which, though Sir Henry Wotton seems not to have known it, is ascribed to Baptista Porta.

† See his Tabulæ Rudolphinæ, and Comment. de Stella Martis; as also Costard's History of Astronomy, pag. 173, 174. Kepler's problem, and the solution of it by Sir Isaac Newton, are inserted in Keill's Introduction to Astronomy. Lect. xxiii. xxiv.

‡ Maclaurin's Account of Sir Isaac Newton's Philosophical Discoveries, page 50.

§ Cost. Hist. of Astronomy, page 257.

and that from the similarity in the sound of the names and the attributes commonly ascribed to both, there is ground to conjecture that Jubal and Apollo were one and the same person; and that, for the same reasons, the like may be said of Tubal Cain and Vulcan. He then digresses to the contemplation of the Pythagorean Tetractys, and points out the mysterious properties of the number four.* He also takes notice that Ptolemy was the first that vindicated the sense of hearing against the Pythagoreans, and received among the concinnous intervals not only the diatessaron, diapente, and diapason, but also the sesquioctave for the greater, and the sesquinona for the lesser tone, and the sesquidecima for the semitone; and added not only other superparticulars that were approved of by the ear, as the sesquiquarta and sesquiquinta, but also introduced some of the superbipartients. By this means, he adds, Ptolemy indeed amended the Pythagorean speculation, as repugnant to the origin of harmonical proportions, but did not entirely reject it as false; yet he remarks that this same person, who had restored the judgment of the ears to its dignity, did however again desert it, he himself also insisting on and abiding by the contemplation of abstract numbers; wherefore he denied that the greater and lesser thirds and sixths are consonances, and admitted in their stead other proportions.

Chapter I. contains some of the principal axioms in Harmonics, upon which the author animadverts in a strain of philosophy that distinguishes his writings, to this purpose :—

'The speculation concerning these axioms is sub-'lime, Platonic, and analogous to the Christian faith, 'and regards metaphysics and the doctrine of the soul; 'for geometry, which has a relation to musical har-'mony, suggested to the divine mind in the creation 'of the world what was best, most beautiful, and 'nearest resembling God himself, and the images of 'God the creator, as are all spirits, souls, and minds 'which actuate bodies, and govern, move, increase, and 'preserve them. These by a certain instinct delight 'in the same proportions which God himself made 'use of in the formation of the universe, whether 'they are impressed on bodies and motions, or arise 'from a certain geometrical necessity of matter, divi-'sible in infinitum, or from motions excited by matter; 'and these harmonical proportions are said to consist 'not in Esse, but in Fieri. Nor do minds delight 'only in these proportions, but they also make use of 'the same as laws, to perfect or perform their offices, 'and to express these same proportions in the motions 'of bodies where it is allowable. Of this the follow-'ing books produce two most luculent examples, the 'one of God himself the Creator, who has regulated 'the motions of the heavens by harmonical propor-'tions; the other of that soul which we usually call 'the sublunary nature, which stirs up the meteors ac-'cording to the laws or prescripts of those proportions 'which occur in the radiations of the stars. A third 'example is that of the human soul, and the souls of 'beasts in some measure, for they delight in the har-'monical proportions of sounds, and are sad or dis-'pleased with such as are not harmonical; from which 'affections of the soul, the former are termed conso-'nances, and the latter dissonances; but if another 'harmonical proportion of voices and sounds, to wit, 'the metrical ratio of quantities long and short be also 'added, these affect the soul, and stir up the body to 'dancing or leaping, and the tongue to pronunciation, 'according to the same laws; to this workmen adapt 'the strokes of their hammers, and soldiers their pace. 'All things live when harmonies subsist, but deaden 'when they are disturbed.'

As touching the nature of harmony, and that determination which the senses make between concinnous and inconcinnous intervals, Kepler, as do indeed most other writers on the subject, resolves it into the coincidence of vibrations.

Chap. II. contains a series of proportions tending to shew that for producing the consonances, seven sections of a chord are all that can be admitted; in answer to which it need only be said that in the Sect o Canonis of Euclid and Aristides Quintilianus, the contrary is demonstrated.

In Chap. VI. the author declares his sentiments with respect to the hard and soft genera of Cantus; the first he says is called the soft cantus, because in it the intervals of the third and sixth from the lowest note are soft, and that the other is called the hard cantus for the contrary reason; upon which he remarks, that this distinction is recognized by God himself in the motions of the planets.

In Chap. VII. in which the author undertakes to demonstrate the natural order of the concinnous intervals contained in the octave, he asserts, without taking notice of the division of the diapason into tetrachords, that it seems most agreeable to nature that whenever we make choice of a section, the greater intervals should converge towards the grave sounds. In his section therefore he observes this order, greater tone 8, 9, lesser tone 9, 10, semitone 15, 16, which he says is sufficient to stand forth against the authorities of Ptolemy, Zarlino, and Galileo, who make the lesser tone the lowest in position.†

Chap. VIII. proposes a section of the monochord for the Testudo or lute, in which he censures that of Vincentio Galileo, declaring it to be an injudicious essay towards a temperament, and that the author was ignorant of the demonstrative quantity of sounds.

Chap. IX. treats of the modern method of notation by lines and the letters of the alphabet, and contains the author's opinion touching the origin of the cliffs,

---

* The Pythagoreans maintained that in the first of the five regular solids, viz., the Tetrahedron or Pyramid, the Tetractys is to be found, for that a point answers to unity, a line to the number two, a superficies to three, and solidity to four. Farther they say that the judicative power is fourfold, and consists in mind, science, opinion, and sense. In short, in physics, metaphysics, ethics, and theology, they made the number four an universal measure; and scrupled not to assert that the nature of God himself is typified by the Tetrad.

† Kepler, with all his acuteness, seems to have been bewildered in this abstruse speculation: indeed so far as not to be able to distinguish between the friends and the adversaries of his doctrine; for this very arrangement of the greater and lesser tone, that is to say the greater first, and the second next, constitutes the intense diatonic of Ptolemy, which had been received by Ludovico Fogliano, and recognized by Zarlino: nor were there any of the moderns, excepting Vincentio Galileo, who disputed it, and he contended for an equality of tones; notwithstanding which Kepler enumerates Galileo among the friends of Ptolemy, and, by a mistaken consequence, among the adversaries of himself. See Dr. Wallis's Appendix to Ptolemy, page 318; and see also page 401 of this work, in not.

which he with great ingenuity proves to be gradual deviations from the respective letters F C and G; he delivers his sentiments in these words :—

'Some things offer themselves to our observation 'concerning these letters; for first, all the letters are 'not written on the lines and spaces which their sta-'tions require, but only these, F G C, as often as there 'is a place for one of them on the line, B also when 'it has its sound in a space.

'Moreover the letter C has a different character, 'namely, the following ; I suppose that this arose 'from the distortion of the ancient letter C, for as the 'writers used broad-pointed pens, most of the notes 'were made square for dispatch in writing; nor could 'a round C be described with these pens: so that they 'made the C of three little lines, one slender, and the 'other two thick, in the room of the horns; the pen 'being drawn broadways thus , the fine little line, 'on account of their expeditious writing, was made 'longer, and was carried above and below beyond the 'horns thus ; but, in order to terminate the horns, 'they drew little lines parallel to the first thus , and 'at length these two lines were made one, and the 'whole character became of this form , but by the 'gaping of the quill it was frequently and at length 'generally made hollow or open thus .

'It may nevertheless be questioned whether or no 'the term musical scale might not suggest to the in-'ventors the character of a figure resembling a ladder, 'such as is used by the moderns, to denote the station 'of C in the scale.'

The conjectures of Kepler with regard to the origin of the character used to denote the tenor cliff are in-genious, but he seems to have failed in his attempt to account for the form of the character , which gives the F FA UT wherever it is placed; for first he sup-poses it to have been originally the small γ, and, secondly, that the two points behind it were intended to signify a reduplication of the note Γ; in this he certainly errs, for the station of the bass cliff on the fourth line is but a seventh from GAMUT, the replicate whereof is C SOL, RE, UT, and not F FA UT. It must be owned that for the origin of the above character we are greatly to seek, but it is highly probable that it is a corruption of the letter F; and that for this reason Guido, when he reformed the scale, found it necessary, in order to ascertain the denominations of the several chords contained in it, to affix some certain character to the lowest of them; for this purpose he made choice of the Greek Γ: succeeding musicians found it necessary in practice to ascertain the place of C SOL FA UT, which they did by the letter C; and the same motive induced them to point out also g SOL RE UT, by g, stationing it on the third line above that whereon C stood: a thought then suggested itself that a cliff on the third line below C, would give the whole a uniform appearance, by placing the cliffs in the middle of the scale, and making them equidistant from each other; and this was no sooner done by placing F three lines below C, than the whole character Γ on the first line of the

stave became useless; for the note GAMUT is as clearly determined by the station of F on the fourth line, as by its original character.

Touching the origin and use of the flat and sharp signatures, these are the sentiments of Kepler :—

'As to the first, b, its presence, whether it falls 'upon a line or a space, denotes the soft cantus, and 'its absence the hard; and by a certain abuse the letter b is used for the character of the semitone or syllable FA.

'When a semitone is extraordinarily constituted in 'the place of a tone, and the syllable MI in the place 'of the syllable FA, then the letter b, or the character 'derived from it, is prefixed to the note, for the 'ancients without doubt described it thus , but we 'instead thereof thus ♯ or ×, which, as Galileus 'imagines, should seem to say to the reader the same 'thing as the Greek word Diaschisma formerly did, 'for it evidently expresses a splitting, and points out 'to us the cutting of the semitones.'

Chap. X. contains a comparison of the hexachords of the moderns with the tetrachords of the ancient Greeks, very clearly demonstrating the superior ex-cellence of the hexachord system; and here by the way it is to be observed that he differs from Doctor Wallis and many other authors, who have expressed their wishes that Guido, instead of six, had taken seven syllables into this system: further he censures that German, whoever he was, that introduced the seven syllables BO, CE, DI, GA, LO, MA, NI.

Chap. XIII. the author speaks of the manner of singing, which he says the Turks and Hungarians are accustomed to, and resembles the noises of brute animals rather than the sounds of the human voice; but this kind of melody, rude as it is, he supposes not fortuitous, but to be derived from some instru-ment concinnously formed, which had led the whole nation into the use of such intervals in singing as nature abhors. To this purpose he relates that being at Prague, at the house of the Turkish ambassador, at a time when the accustomed prayers were sung by the priests, he observed one on his knees frequently striking the earth with his hand, who appeared to sing by rule, for that he did not in the least hesitate, though the intervals he sung were wonderfully un-accustomed, mangled, and abhorrent, which, that his reader may judge of them, he gives in the following notes :—

Touching that long-agitated question, whether the music of the ancient Greeks was solitary or in con-sonance, Kepler, chap. XVI, thus delivers his sen-timents :—

'Although the word Harmony was anciently used 'to signify a Cantus, yet we are not to understand 'by it a modulation by several voices in consonance: 'for that this is an invention of modern date, and 'was utterly unknown to the ancients, needs not to 'be proved.' He adds, 'It is indeed objected, that 'in the republic of Plato a tying together of the 'cantus by harmony is mentioned as if it had at that

'time been made use of;* but this passage is to be
understood of instruments, such as the Syringa, the
'Cornamusa, and Testudo, when one sound intonates
'in consonance with another.'

The author concludes his third book of the Harmonices Mundi with what he calls a political digression concerning the three kinds of mediation, taken in part from Bodinus, who appears to be no less fond than himself of such fanciful analogies.

As there are three forms of policy or civil government, namely, Democracy, Aristocracy, and Monarchy, he compares Democracy to arithmetical proportion, Aristocracy to the geometrical, and Monarchy to the harmonical. He farther remarks that as all the rules of governing are comprehended under justice, of which there are two kinds, viz., commutative justice, which is implied in the arithmetical equality, and distributive in the geometrical similitude,† so there is a third species of justice made up of both. He says that the poets, who feign the three daughters of Justice to be Equity, Law, and Peace, do as it were make them the tutelars severally of arithmetical, geometrical, and harmonical proportion: and that the laws concerning marriage afford an example of the three proportions, for says he 'If patricians marry patrician wives, and plebeians 'plebeian wives, then it is the geometrical similitude; 'where it is allowed to marry promiscuously, without 'any manner of restriction, then the arithmetical 'equality is found; but if, as in the case of factions, 'the poorest patricians are permitted to marry with 'the richer plebeians, then that gives the harmonical 'proportion as being convenient for both.'

Kepler pretends also to discover an analogy between the three kinds of proportion above enumerated, and the order observed in the arrangement of persons, distinguishing between senators and plebeians at feasts and at public shows. In the pursuit of this argument he insists on a variety of topics drawn from the Roman civil law, and pretends to trace resemblances which never did exist but in his own bewildered imagination.

He concludes this digression with a remark that Bodinus beautifully compares the arithmetical equality to the iron ruler Polycletus, which may be broken before it can be bent; the geometrical similitude to the leaden Lesbian ruler, which was accommodated to all angles; and the harmonical proportion to a wooden ruler which indeed may be bent, but immediately returns back.

Such singularities as are discoverable in the writings of Kepler, could hardly fail to draw on him the censures of those who were engaged in the same course of study with himself. Ismael Bullialdus says he abounds in fictions; and Martinus Schookius, who allows him to be an able astronomer and mathematician, says that where he affects to reason upon physical principles, no man talks more absurdly,‡ and expresses his concern that a man, in other respects so excellent, should disgrace the divine science of mathematics with his preposterous notions; for, says he, what could an old woman in a fever, dream more ridiculous than that the earth is a vast animal, which breathes out the winds through the holes of the mountains, as it were through a mouth and nostrils? Yet he writes expressly thus in his Harmonices Mundi, and attempts also seriously to prove that the earth has a sympathy with the heavens, and by a natural instinct perceives the position of the stars.

The absurdities of Kepler were such as have exposed him and his writings to the ridicule of many a less able mathematician than himself. Mr. Maclaurin has remarked that he was all his life in pursuit of fancied analogies; but he adds, that to this disposition we owe such discoveries as are more than sufficient to excuse his conceits.§ Upon which it may be observed, that had he made no greater discoveries in mathematics than he has done in music, it is highly probable that the conceits had remained, and the discoveries been forgotten.

CHAP. CXXIX.

ROBERT FLUD, Lat. de Fluctibus, a very famous philosopher and a writer on music, was the son of Sir Thomas Flud, knight, some time treasurer of war to queen Elizabeth in France and the Low Countries, and was born at Milgate, in the parish of Bearsted, in Kent, in the year 1574. He was admitted of St. John's college in the university of Oxford, in 1591, at the age of seventeen; and having taken both the degrees in arts, applied himself to the study of physic, and spent six years in travelling through France, Spain, Italy, and Germany, in most of which countries he not only became acquainted with several of the nobility, but even read lectures to them. After his return, in the year 1605, being in high repute for his knowledge in chemistry, he proceeded in the faculty of physic, took the degree of doctor, was admitted a fellow of the college of physicians, and practised in London. He was esteemed by many both as a philosopher and a physician, though it may be objected, that as he was of the fraternity of the Rosicrucians, as they are called, his philosophy was none of the soundest. His propensity to chemistry served also to mislead him, and induced him to refer to it not only the wonders of nature, but miracles, and even religious mysteries. His works,

---

* The passage here alluded to is that which gave rise to the controversy between Mons. Fraguier and Mons. Burette. See page 102, in not.

† *Great confusion appears among the writers on Ethics in their division of justice, and their definitions of its several species. Grotius as here, and also Puffendorf distinguishes it into distributive and commutative; and Gronovius, the Commentator on the former, assigns to distributive justice the geometrical, and to commutative the arithmetical Ratio. Vide Grotius de Jure Belli ac Dacis à Gronovis lib. I. cap. i. sect. 8. Puffendorf de Officio Hominis à Carmichael, lib. I. cap. ii, sect. 14. Dr. More dividing Justice into distributive and corrective, gives to the former the geometrical ratio 6, 2, 12, 4, and to the latter the arithmetical 5, 7, 9, 11. Enchirid Eth. lib. II. cap. 6, sect. 6. These analogies thus recognised are become scientific. Nevertheless the relation between qualities and quantities, moral actions and mathematical proportions, is not clearly discernible; the latter are measurable, the former not.*

‡ The singularity in Kepler's method of reasoning may be remarked in his endeavours to torture and strain the three kinds of proportion, that is to say, geometrical, arithmetical, and harmonical, to a resemblance of the three forms of civil policy, and the practice of the Romans in their marriages, and the order of seating the spectators of public shows and solemnities; and there are many other instances in the Harmonices Mundi, which, though they have escaped observation, are no less ridiculous, as where he says, speaking of the terms Αγωγη and Πλοκη, made use of by Euclid, that the Πλοκη wanders about the Αγωγη 'ut canis circa viatorem,' i. e. as a dog about a traveller.

§ Account of Sir Isaac Newton's Philosophical Discoveries, page 47.

which are very many, amounting to near twenty tracts, are in Latin; and it is said, that as he was a mystic in philosophy, and affected in his writings a turgid and obscure style, so was his discourse, particularly to his patients, so lofty and hyperbolical, that it resembled that of a mountebank more than of a grave physician, yet it is said that he practised with success, and what is more, that Selden held him in high estimation. Mosheim asserts that the reading his books turned the brain of Jacob Behmen; and at present it is their only praise, that for some time they were greatly admired and sought after by alchemists, astrologers, searchers after the philosophers' stone, and, in short, by all the madmen in the republic of letters both at home and abroad.

Some of his pieces were levelled against Kepler and Mersennus, and he had the honour of replies from both. He wrote two books against Mersennus, the first intitled, 'Sophiæ cum Moriœ certamen, in quo, 'lapis Lydius a falso structore, Fratre Marino Mer-'senno monacho, reprobatus, celeberrima voluminis 'sui Babylonici in Genesin figmenta accurate exa-'minat.' Franc. 1629, fol. The second, 'Summum 'bonorum quod est verum Magiæ Cabalæ, Alchymæ 'Fratrum Rosæ crucis verorum veræ subjectum, in 'dictarum scientiarum laudem, in insignis calumni-'atoris Fr. Mar. Mersenni dedecus publicatum per 'Joachim Frizium,' 1629, fol. Mersennus desiring Gassendus to give his judgment of these two books of Flud against him, that great man drew up an answer divided into three parts, the first of which sifts the principles of Flud's whimsical philosophy as they lie scattered throughout his works; the second is against 'Sophiæ cum Moriœ certamen, &c.' and the third against 'Summum bonorum, &c.' This answer, called Examen Fluddanæ Philosophiæ, is dated February 4, 1629, and is printed in the third volume of the works of Gassendus in folio. In the dedication to Mersennus is a passage in substance as follows, viz., 'Although I 'am far from thinking your antagonist a match for 'you, yet it must be owned that he is really a man of 'various knowledge, known to all the learned of the 'age, and whose voluminous works will shortly have 'a place in most libraries. And in the present dis-'pute will have one great advantage over you, namely, 'that whereas your philosophy is of a plain, open, 'intelligible kind, his, on the contrary, is so very ob-'scure and mysterious, that he can at any time conceal 'himself, and by diffusing a darkness round him, 'hinder you from discerning him, so far as to lay hold 'of him, much less to drag him forth to conviction.'

Dr. Flud died at his house in Coleman-street, London, in the year 1637, and was buried in the church of Bearsted, the place of his nativity. In the Athenæ Oxonienses is an account of him and a catalogue of his writings, but of the many books he wrote, the only one necessary to be taken notice of in this work is that entitled 'Utriusque Cosmi, Majoris scilicet et 'minoris, metaphysica, physica, atque technica histo-'ria in duo volumina, secundum Cosmi differentiam 'divisa. Tomus primus de Macrocosmi Historia in 'duos tractatus divisa.'* This work was printed at

* It seems that the second volume was never published.

Oppenheim, in a thick folio volume, and published in 1617. It abounds with plates and diagrams of the most fantastic kind, and though the author was beholden to a foreign press for its publication, is recommended to the patronage of his rightful sovereign James the First.

As to the work itself, the nature and tendency of it are unfolded in the following analytical distribution of its parts:—

Tractatus
{
Primus de {
Metaphysico Macrocosmi et Creaturarum illius ortu.
Physico Macrocosmi ingeneratione et corruptione progressu.
}
Secundus de arte naturæ simia in Macrocosmo producta et in eo nutrita et multiplicata, cujus filias præcipuas hîc anatomiâ vivâ recensuimus, nempe: {
Arithmeticam.
Musicam.
Geometriam.
Perspectivam.
Artem Pictoriam.
Artem Militarem.
Motus } Scientiam.
Temporis }
Cosmographiam.
Astrologiam.
Geomantiam.
}
}

The third book of the first tract is intitled De Musica Mundana. In this discourse the author supposes the world to be a musical instrument, and that the elements that compose it, assigning to each a certain place according to the laws of gravitation, together with the planets and the heavens, make up that instrument which he calls the Mundane Monochord, in the description whereof he thus expresses himself:

'We will take our beginning from the matter of 'the world, which I have made to resemble the chord 'of the monochord, whose great instrument is the 'Macrocosm itself, as a certain scale or ladder whereby 'the difference of the places lying between the centre 'and periphery of the mundane instrument is distin-'guished, and which difference of places we shall 'aptly compare to the musical intervals, as well the 'simple as the compound. Wherefore it is to be 'known that as the chord of an instrument in its 'progression from Γ is accustomed to be divided into 'intervals by metrical proportions, so likewise I have 'distributed both the matter and its form into degrees 'of quantity, and distinguished them by similar pro-'portions, constituting musical consonances; for if a 'monochord be supposed to extend from the summit 'of the empyrean heaven to the basis of the earth 'itself, we shall perceive that it may be divided into 'parts constituting consonances; and if the half part 'thereof were touched or struck, it would produce 'the consonant diapason in the same manner as the 'instrumental monochord.

'But it is to be considered that in this mundane 'monochord the consonances, and likewise the proper 'intervals, measuring them, cannot be otherwise de-'lineated than as we divide the instrumental mono-'chord into proportional parts; for the frigidity, and 'also the matter itself, of the earth, as to the thickness 'and weight thereof, naturally bears the same propor-'tion to the frigidity as the matter of the lowest 'region, in which there is only one fourth part of the 'natural light and heat, as 4 to 3, which is the ses-

'quitertia proportion; in which proportion a diates-
'saron consists, composed of three intervals, namely,
'water, air, and fire; for the earth in mundane music
'is the same thing as Γ in music, unity in arithmetic,
'or a point in geometry; it being as it were the term
'and sound from which the ratio of proportional
'matter is to be calculated. Water therefore occupies
'the place of one tone, and the air that of another
'interval more remote; and the sphere of fire, as it
'is only the summit of the region of the air, kindled
'or lighted up, possesses the place of a lesser semi-
'tone. But in as much as two portions of this matter
'are extended upwards as far as to the middle heaven,
'to resist the action of the supernatural heat; and the
'same number of parts of light, act downwards
'against these two portions of matter, these make up
'the composition of the sphere of the sun, and natu-
'rally give it the attribute of equality, and by that
'means the sesquialtera proportion is produced, in
'which three parts of the lower spirit or matter of
'the middle heaven are opposed to the two parts of
'the solar sphere, producing the consonant diapente:
'for such is the difference between the moon and the
'sun, as there are four intervals between the convexity
'of this heaven and the middle of the solar sphere,
'namely, those of the entire spheres of the moon,
'Mercury, and Venus, compared to full tones, and
'the half part of the solar sphere, which we have
'compared to the semitone. But as the consonant
'diapason is constituted of the diatessaron and dia-
'pente, therefore this consonant diapason must neces-
'sarily be there produced; and this is the most perfect
'consonance of matter, which can by no means acquire
'its perfection unless it fills up its appetite in the
'solar form. Moreover, this middle heaven, though
'its most perfect consonance ends in its heart, namely,
'the sun, and thence begins its motion to the formal
'diapason, yet it sounds out nothing else than the
'consonant diapente in its concavity, as well above its
'sphere of equality as below it; which consonant
'therefore suits better with this place than any of the
'other consonants, because it is less perfect, and is
'placed in the middle between the perfect and imper-
'fect: thus also this heaven, although it be perfect
'and free from corruption, is said to be less perfect
'with regard to the upper heaven, and obtains the
'middle situation between both heavens, namely, the
'perfect and imperfect.'

The definition which Boetius gives of mundane
music, so far as relates to the motion of the celestial
orbs, is founded in the Pythagorean notion of the
music of the spheres, and in this sense it has a literal
signification; but when he speaks of the composition
of the elements, the order of time, and the succession
of the seasons, and of the regularity, order, and harmony observable in the operations of nature, it is
evident he makes use of the term in a figurative sense.
In like manner do those who speak of human music,
moral music, and, as Kepler and others do, of political music; but this author not only supposes the
world to be a musical instrument, but proceeds without any data, to assign to the four elements and to the
planets, certain stations, and to portion out the heavens
themselves; and having distributed the several parts

of the creation according to the suggestions of his
own fancy, he pretends to discover in this distribution
certain ratios or proportions in strict analogy with
those of music, which he exhibits in the following
diagram:—

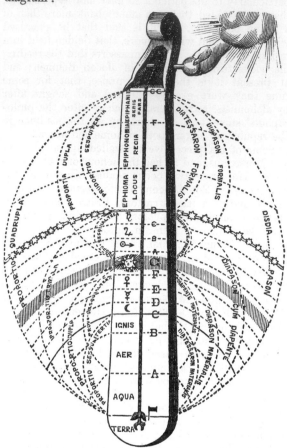

The mundane monochord thus adjusted and divided
into systems of diatessaron, diapente, and diapason,
is not to be considered as a subject of mere speculation; and it will be perceived that the author has not
been at the pains of stringing his instrument for nothing; for the soul or spirit of the world, according
to him, is a formal substance, striking on the chord
of the mundane instrument, which is a material substance, produces music: light therefore, says our
author, acts on the mundane instrument just as the
breath or spirit of a man acts on the air when he sings.

In Chap. IV. the author undertakes to demonstrate his whimsical hypothesis by the figure
of a pipe or flute in this form, from which he
says it appears that the true proportion of the
whole world may be collected; this boasted
demonstration is in the words following:—
'The pipe here spoken of is divided into three
'regions or parts, the two lower whereof have
'each three holes, denoting the beginning,
'middle, and end of each region; but the upper
'region, consisting of one great hole only, ex-
'presses the nature of the empyrean heaven,
'whose every part is of the same condition, or,
'as it were, most replete with the divine unity.
'But as this instrument is not moved by its

HIERONYMUS FRESCOBALDUS
FERRARIENSIS,
ORGANISTA ECCLESIÆ D.PETRI IN VATICANO.
ÆTAT. SUÆ XXXVI.

'own nature, nor sounds of itself without a moving
'soul, so neither can the world, or the part of the
'world move but by the immense mind or soul: as
'therefore the highest mind, God, is the summit of
'the whole machine, and as it were beyond the ex-
'treme superficies of the world, makes the joints of
'the world to exhibit his music, graver in the lower
'part, and acuter and clearer the nearer the parts
'approach to the summit itself; so likewise when
'the musician blows life and motion beyond the con-
'tent of the pipe, and in its summit, the farther the
'holes are from that blowing power, the more grave
'are the sounds that are produced; and the higher
'they ascend towards the point of inspiration, the
'more are they acute. And in the same manner as
'the great aperture near the top of the pipe gives as
'it were life and soul to the lower ones, so likewise
'the empyrean heaven gives soul to all the lower
'spheres. O how great and how heavenly is this
'contemplation in a subject seemingly so trivial,
'when it is diligently and profoundly considered by
'an intelligent mind!'

Were it possible to convey an idea in words of the
nature of that folly and absurdity which are discoverable in the writings of this enthusiast, the foregoing
extract from this work of his might be spared; but
his notions, as they elude all investigation, so cannot
they even be stated in any words but his own, and
this must be the apology for inserting them.

Tract II. part ii. of this work, agreeably to the
analysis above given of it, is on practical music. In
this he enters largely into the subject, and from the
manuscript of Waltham Holy Cross, which it is evident he had made use of, gives the whole doctrine of
the Cantus Mensurabilis, with the diagrams relating
to it, and among the rest that of the triangular shield,
exhibited in page 248 of this work, the invention
whereof he ascribes to one Robert Brunham, a monk.

He describes also the musical instruments of the
moderns, namely, the Barbiton or lute, the Orpharion
and Pandora; and under the pneumatic class, the
Regals, as also pipes of various kinds. Of the Sistrena or Cittern these are his words: 'Sistrena est
'instrumentum musicum ex quatuor chordis metallis
'duplis consistens, et tonsoribus commune;' most
exactly corresponding with what has been already
observed on this silly instrument, which is now become the recreation of ladies, and by the makers is
ignorantly termed the Guitar.

The rest of this tract, excepting those whimsical
devices, such as musical dials, musical windows, musical colonnades, and other extravagancies with which
the author has thought proper to decorate his work,
contains very little that deserves notice.

Upon the whole Flud appears to have been a man
of a disordered imagination, an enthusiast in theology
and philosophy: as such he is classed by Butler, with
Jacob Behmen and the wildest of the mystic writers:

'He Anthroposophus and Flud,
'And Jacob Behmen understood;'
                        HUDIBRAS, Part I. Canto i.
Notwithstanding which, Webster, in his Displaying

of supposed Witchcraft, asserts that he was a man
acquainted with all sorts of learning, and one of the
most Christian philosophers that ever wrote.

CHAP. CXXX.

GIROLAMO FRESCOBALDI *(a Portrait)*, a native of
Ferrara, was born in the year 1601, and at the age of
about twenty-three was organist of the church of St.
Peter at Rome. He is not less celebrated for his
compositions for the organ, than for his exquisite skill
in that instrument. He was the first of the Italians
that composed for the organ in fugue; and in this
species of composition, originally invented by the
Germans, he was without a rival.

Of many musicians it has been said, that they were
the fathers of a particular style, as that Palestrina
was the father of the church style, Monteverde of
the dramatic, and Carissimi of the chamber style: of
Frescobaldi it may as truly be said that he was the
father of that organ-style which has prevailed not
less in England than in other countries for more than
a hundred years past, and which consists in a prompt
and ready discussion of some premeditated subject in
a quicker succession of notes than is required in the
accompaniment of choral harmony. Exercises of
this kind on the organ are usually called Toccatas,
from the Italian Toccare, to touch; and for want of
a better word to express them, they are here in
England called Voluntaries. In the Romish service
they occur at frequent intervals, particularly at the
elevation, post communions, and during the offerings;*
and in that of our church, in the morning prayer,
after the psalms and after the Benediction, or, in other
words, between the first and second service; and in
the evening service after the psalms.†

In the year 1628, Bartolomeo Grassi, organist of
St. Maria in Acquirio in Rome, and who had been a
disciple of his, published a work of Frescobaldi entitled 'In partitura il primo libro delle canzoni a una
'due tre e quatro voci. Per sonare con ogni forte di
'stromenti.' At the end of the book is an advertisement from Grassi, in which he says that the compositions contained in it are in the grand gusto, and,
having been universally applauded, are to be looked
on as models of perfection. It seems from the title
of the work that these originally were vocal compositions, but that, for the improvement of the studious
in music, Grassi had published them in score, rejecting the words, and in this form they met with such a
favourable reception, that he expressly tells us he had
printed them three times.

The following composition is taken from a work of
Frescobaldi printed at Rome in 1637, entitled 'Il
'secondo libro di Toccata, Canzone, Versi d'Hinni,
'Magnificat, Gagliarde, Correnti et altre Partite d'In-
'tavolatura di Cimbalo et Organo,' and is the third
Canzone in that collection.

* A collection of this kind was published in the year 1716, by Domenico
Zipoli, organist of the Jesuits' church at Rome with this title, 'Sonate
'd'Intavolatura per Organo, e Cimbalo, parte prima, Toccata, Versi,
'Canzone, Offertorio, Elevazioni, Post-Communio, e Pastorale.'

† This order was settled at the Restoration. See The divine Services
and Anthems usually sung in his Majesties Chapel, and all Cathedrals,
&c. by James Clifford, Lond. 1664.

CANZONA.

GIROLAMO FRESCOBALDI.

René Des Cartes, the famous French philosopher and mathematician, the particulars of whose life and character are very well known, was the author of a treatise entitled Musicæ Compendium, written when he was very young, and in the year 1617, and, which is very extraordinary, while he was engaged in the profession of a soldier, and lay in garrison at Breda. The subject matter of this tract is distributed under the following heads : De numero vel tempore in sonis observando.   De sonorum diversitate circa acutum et grave.   De consonantiis.   De octavâ.   De quintâ.   De quartâ.   De ditono, tertiâ minore, etsextis.   De gradibus sive tonis musicis.   De dissonantiis.   De ratione componendi et modis.   De modis.

The above-mentioned tract, although comprehended in fifty-eight small quarto pages, contains a great number of very curious particulars relating to the science of music.* The observations of the author on the effects of various measures, as contained in the following passages, are new and judicious, and in the words of his translator are these :—

' We say in the generall that a slow measure doth ' excite in us gentle and sluggish motions, such as ' a kind of languor, sadnesse, fear, pride, and other ' heavy and dull passions : and a more nimble and ' swift measure doth proportionably excite more ' nimble and sprightly passions, such as joy, anger, ' courage, &c. the same may also be sayd of the ' double kind of percussion, viz., that a quadrate, or ' such as is perpetually resolved into equals, is slower ' and duller than a tertiate, or such as doth consist ' of three equal parts. The reason whereof is, because ' this doth more possesse and employ the sense, ' inasmuch as therein are more, namely 3, members ' to be adverted, while in the other are only 2.'

In his enumeration of the consonances, he, contrary to the sense of all other writers, from John De Muris down to Mersennus, excludes the unison, and for this very good reason, that ' therein is no difference of ' sounds as to acute and grave ; it bearing the same ' relation to consonances, as unity doth to numbers.

Of the two methods by which the diapason or octave is divided, the arithmetical and geometrical, the author, for the reasons contained in the sixth of his Prænotanda, prefers the former ; and for the purpose of adjusting the consonances, proposes the division of a chord, first into two equal parts, and afterwards into smaller proportions, according to this table :—

$\frac{1}{2}$ Eighth				
$\frac{1}{3}$ Twelfth	$\frac{2}{3}$ Fifth			
$\frac{1}{4}$ Fifteenth	$\frac{2}{4}$ Eighth	$\frac{3}{4}$ Fourth		
$\frac{1}{5}$ Seventeenth	$\frac{2}{5}$ Tenth Major	$\frac{3}{5}$ Sixth Major	$\frac{4}{5}$ Ditone	
$\frac{1}{6}$ Nineteenth	$\frac{2}{6}$ Twelfth	$\frac{3}{6}$ Eighth	$\frac{4}{6}$ Fifth	$\frac{5}{6}$ Third Minor

The advantages resulting from the geometrical division appear in the Systema Participato, mentioned by Bontempi, which consisted in the division of the diapason or octave into twelve equal semitones by eleven mean proportionals ; but Des Cartes rejects this division for reasons that are very far from satisfactory.

A translation of this book into English was, in 1653, published by a person of honour, viz., William Lord Brouncker, president of the Royal Society, and the first appointed to that office, with animadversions thereon, which show that his lordship was deeply skilled in the theory of the science ; and although he agrees with his author almost throughout the book, he asserts that the geometrical is to be preferred to the arithmetical division : and, as it is presumed, with a view to a farther improvement of the Systema Participato, he proposes a division of the diapason by sixteen mean proportionals into seventeen equal semitones ; the method of which division is exhibited by him in an algebraic process, and also in logarithms.

Andreas Hammerschmidt, a Bohemian, born in 1611, and organist, first of the church of St. Peter at Freyburg, and afterwards of that of St. John at Zittau, is celebrated for his assiduity in the cultivation and improvement of the church-style in Saxony, Thuringia, Lusatia, and other provinces in Germany.   Mattheson applauds in the highest terms that zeal for the glory of God, which he has manifested in his Motets for four, five, and six voices. He died in 1675 ; and in the inscription on his monument in the great church at Zittau, of which he was organist, he is styled the German Orpheus.

Johann Andreas Herbst [Lat. Autumnus,] was born at Nuremberg in the year 1588. In the year 1628 he was appointed chapel-master at Francfort on the Maine, and continued in that station till 1641, when he was called to the same office at Nuremburg. However, in 1650, he thought fit to return to Francfort, at the solicitation of the magistrates and others his friends ; and, being by them reinstated in his former dignity, he continued in that station till the time of his death, in the year 1660. He was excellently skilled in the theory of music ; and in the art of practical composition had few equals, and was besides, like most of the Germans, a sound and judicious organist. In the year 1643 he published in the German language a book entitled Musica Poetica ; and ten years after, a translation either from the Latin or the Italian, for it is extant in both languages, of the Arte prattica e poetica of Giov. Chiodino, in ten books. Herbst was also the author of a tract entitled ' Musica moderna prattica, overo ' maniere del buon canto,' printed at Francfort in 1658, in which he recommends the Italian manner of singing. His other works are a small tract on Thorough-bass, and a discourse on Counterpoint, containing directions for composing ' à mente non à penna.' Of his musical compositions, the only ones

* There are nevertheless some singularities in it, of which the following may serve as a specimen : ' This only thing seems to render the voice of ' man the most grateful of all other sounds, that it holds the greatest con- ' formity to our spirits. Thus also is the voice of a friend more grateful ' than that of an enemy, from a sympathy and dispathy of affections : by ' the same reason, perhaps, that it is conceived that a drum headed with ' a sheep's skin yields no sound though strucken, if another drum headed ' with a wolf's skin be beaten upon in the same room.'

extant in print are Meletemata sacra Davidis, and Suspiria S. Gregorii ad Christum, for three voices; these were printed in 1619, as was also a nameless composition of his for six voices. Vid. Draudii. Bibl. Class. pag. 1649.

JOHANN JACOB FROBERGER, a disciple of Frescobaldi, and organist to the emperor Ferdinand III. flourished about the year 1655. He was a most admirable performer on, and composer for the organ and harpsichord. Kircher, in the Musurgia, vol. I. page 466, has given a lesson of his upon UT, RE, MI, FA, SOL, LA, abounding with a great variety of fuguing passages that manifest his skill in the instrument. Mattheson ascribes to him the power of representing on the organ, by a certain imitative faculty, which he possessed in an eminent degree, even the histories of particular transactions; as an instance whereof he refers to an allemand of his where the passage of Count Thurn over the Rhine, and the danger he and his army were in, is very lively represented to the eye and ear by twenty-six cataracts or falls in notes, which it seems Froberger was the better able to do, he having been present with the Count at the time.* Mattheson takes notice that Froberger, in the composition of his lessons, made use of a stave of six lines for the right, and one of seven for the left hand; to which he might have added, that his master Frescobaldi used a stave of eight lines for the left hand.†

JOHANNES HIERONYMUS KAPSBERGER, a German of noble birth, celebrated by Kircher and others, was not more famous for the number and variety of his compositions, than for his exquisite skill and performance on almost all instruments, more particularly the Theorbo-lute, which appears to be a modern invention. The author of it was a Neapolitan musician, of whose name no account remains. As to the instrument, it is well known to be of the lute-kind; and as the improvements made in it wrought no essential change in its form, it might well have retained its primitive name; but the person, whoever he was, that improved it, by doubling the neck, and lengthening the chords, thought himself warranted in giving it the appellation of the Theorbo, for no better reason than its resemblance to an utensil, a kind of mortar used by glovers for the pounding of perfumes, and which is called Tiorba. The instrument thus improved seemed to rival the Clavicymbalum or harpsichord; Kapsberger laboured to recommend and bring it into practice, and in this he succeeded, for Kircher says that in his time it was deservedly preferred to all other instruments; no one being so adapted to the diatonic, chromatic, and enarmonic division. He assisted Kircher in the compilation of the Musurgia.

It appears by a list which Walther gives of his works, that Kapsberger was both a voluminous and a multifarious composer. Many of his compositions are for the lute in tablature, others for the church, as masses, litanies, and motets; others for the theatre, and some for public solemnities. Several of his vocal compositions are to poems and verses of Cardinal Maffeo Barberini, afterwards pope Urban VIII. and there is of his composition a work entitled 'Coro 'musicale in nuptiis D D. Thaddei Barberini et 'Annæ Columnæ,' printed at Rome in 1627, from which particulars it might be inferred that he stood in some degree of favour with the Barberini family. Nevertheless he is represented by Doni, who being so much with the cardinal, must have known Kapsberger very well, as a man of great assurance, which he manifested in his attempts to get banished from the church the compositions of Palestrina. The method he took to effect this purpose is related in page 427 of this work.

CHAP. CXXXI.

GERARDUS JOHANNES VOSSIUS, a native of a town in the neighbourhood of Heidelberg, a man of universal learning and great abilities, published at Amsterdam, in 1650, a work entitled De quatuor Artibus popularibus, in which is a chapter De Musice. Great erudition is manifested in this tract, and also in another of his entitled De universæ Mathesios Natura et Constitutione. The titles of the several chapters therein contained relating to music are as follow, viz., Cap. XIX. De musicæ contemplativæ objecto; ac duplici ejus κριτηρίῳ; et pro eo variantibus musicorum sectis. XX. De musices antiquitate; et quantum ea Pythagoræ debeat, et quis primus de musicis scripserit. Item alii aliquot veteres musices scriptores: sed qui injuriâ temporum deperierint. XXI. De utilitate musices. XXII. De musices partibus, generibus; ac præcipuis ejus, quos habemus, scriptoribus. LIX. De musicis Græcis priori hujus operis parte indictis. LX. De musicis Latinis antea omissis. In these tracts are contained a great variety of curious particulars relating to music and musicians, and such as have written on the science, in chronological succession, from the earliest times down to his own. In the course of his studies at Dort, which he began about the year 1590, he made a considerable progress in the science of music, for which he seems to have entertained a more than ordinary affection. An intimate friendship subsisted during the whole of his life between him and Erycius Puteanus, a fellow student with him at Dort, who being eminently skilled in the theory of music, is supposed to have assisted him in his researches into those authors who have treated on the subject. About the year 1600 he was chosen director of the college of Dort, being then but twenty-three years of age; and in 1614 he was appointed director of the theological college which the States of Holland had then lately founded in the

---

* It seems that many of the German musicians affected imitations of this kind. Dietrich Buxtehude of Lubeck, in six suits of lessons for the harpsichord, has attempted to exhibit the nature and motions of the planets: and Johann Kuhnau of Leipsic published six sonatas entitled *Biblische-Historien*, wherein, as Francis Lustig asserts, is a lively representation in notes of David manfully fighting with Goliah. Musikkunde, page 278.

† The studies of Frescobaldi and Froberger contributed greatly at this time to bring the harpsichord into general use, which before had been almost appropriated to the practice of ladies; as did also the exquisite workmanship of the Ruckers, harpsichord-makers of Antwerp, their contemporaries: there were three of the name and family, viz., the father, named Hans, and two sons, Andreas and Hans, who, for distinction sake, wrote his Christian name as the Germans do, Johann, and assumed for the initial of it, J. instead of H. The harpsichords of the Ruckers have long been valued for the fullness and sweetness of their tone, but are at this time less in use than formerly, on account of the narrowness of their compass, compared with the modern ones.

university of Leyden. Vossius, before this appointment, had attached himself to the profession of divinity, and had taken the side of Arminius at the famous synod of Dort, held in 1618. The principles which he avowed, and, above all, a history of the Pelagian Controversy, which he published in that year, recommended him to the favour of Laud, who being archbishop of Canterbury in 1629, procured for him of Charles I. a prebend in the church of Canterbury, with permission to hold it notwithstanding his residence at Leyden. Upon this promotion he came over to England to be installed; and having taken the degree of doctor of laws at Oxford, returned to Leyden, from whence he removed, in 1633, to Amsterdam, and became the first professor of history in the college then newly founded in that city. He died at Amsterdam anno 1649, aged seventy-two years.

GIOVANNI BATTISTA DONI, a Florentine by birth, and descended from a noble family, though not a musician by profession, is celebrated for his skill in the science. He was much favoured by Cardinal Barberini,* and, at his recommendation, was appointed secretary to the college of cardinals. Being a man of very extensive learning and great ingenuity, and finding the fatigues of his employment a great interruption to his studies, he quitted it, and retired to the city of his nativity, and ended his days there, being not much above fifty years of age. It appears by an account which Doni has given of himself and of his studies, that in his younger days he learned in France to play on the flageolet and the lute; and, in his more advanced age, to sing, to which end he made himself perfect in the practice of solmisation; that he also attained to some proficiency on the harpsichord; and, notwithstanding the little time he had to spare from his important occupation, he applied himself with an uncommon degree of assiduity to the study of the science of harmony, in the course whereof he, partly at his own, and partly at the expence of others, constructed a great number of instruments of his own invention.

In this account which he gives of himself, Doni professes to have directed his studies towards the restitution of the ancient practice, for which it must be confessed he seems to have entertained too great a fondness. He ascribes to the envy and malice of the world the ill reception that his labours met with, and intimates a resolution that he had taken of laying down his employment, and retiring to Florence, with a view to prosecute his studies, and keep up the remembrance of his family, which was become desolate by the immature death of two brothers.

In the Notitia Auctorum of Cardinal Bona is this character of Doni, ' De musica, modisque musicis ' antiquis et novis doctissime scripsit, doctius scrip-'turus si Græca eruditione præditus suisset.' And Meibomius, in the preface to his edition of the ancient

musicians, expressly says that he did not understand the Greek language.

In the year 1635 Doni published at Rome a discourse entitled ' Compendio del Trattato de' Generi ' e de' Modi della Musica, con un Discorso sopra la ' perfettione de' Concenti,' and dedicated it to his patron Cardinal Barberini. The following are the titles of the several chapters of the Compendium. Cap. I. Quanto mal' intesa sia hoggi la materia de' generi e de' modi. II. Quanto sia grande la diversità tra i modi antichi ed i moderni. III. Altre differenze tra i modi antichi ed i nostri. IV. Che per la restauratione de' generi, e de' modi gl' instrumenti d' archetto sono piu à proposito de gl' altri: e dell' origine dell' organo. V. Con quali mezzi i generi, e modi si possino anch' hoggi pratticare. VI. Come nelle viole suddette si debbono segnare le voci ed intavolarle. VII. Della vera differenza de' tuoni e modi; e dell' intavolatura, e connessione loro, con le giuste distanze. VIII. Quanto sia commoda et utile, la predetta divisione. IX. Altre considerationi intorno le dette viole. X. Della divisione de gl' organi ed altri instrumenti di tasti per l' uso de' generi e de' tuoni. XI. Della divisione harmonica de gl' instrumenti di tasti. XII. Dell' uso et utilità di questa divisione. XIII. Del modo d' accordare l' organo perfetto. XIV. Catalogo delle consonanze di ciascuna voce de' tre sistemi. XV. Sommario de' Capi più principali, che si contengono nell' opera intera.

This book is of a very miscellaneous nature; the avowed design of it is to shew that the music of the ancients is to be preferred to that of the moderns; and in the course of the argument many particulars occur worthy of notice. The author censures Vicentino for his arrogance and his vain attempt to introduce into practice the genera of the ancients, but commends Domenico Zampieri the painter, better known by the name of Dominichino, for a like attempt, and for the invention of a kind of viol much better calculated for that purpose than the archicembalo of Vicentino. He says that Hercole Bottrigaro understood the doctrine of the Genera better than any other of the moderns; and of Zarlino and Salinas, that the first was the prince of practical, as the other was of theoretic musicians.

Together with this treatise is printed a tract entitled Discorso sopra la Perfettione delle Melodie, at the beginning whereof the author treats of the madrigal-style in musical composition, and of those particulars that distinguish the Canto Figurato from the Canto Ecclesiastico; the invention of which last he says necessarily followed from the use of the organ. The passage is curious, and is as follows:—

' It is not difficult to trace the origin of this kind ' of music, for as organs in churches have been in use ' ever since the time of pope Vitalianus, to which ' instrument this kind of harmony, the Concenti ' Madrigaleschi, seems to belong, seeing that the ' voices may be lengthened at pleasure, and fugues, ' imitations, and such like artifices introduced as on ' the organ; it is very probable that the symphony ' peculiar to the organ might by degrees be transferred

---

* Cardinal Barberini, afterwards pope Urban VIII., as appears by many passages in his writings, was a lover of music. When Milton was at Rome he was introduced to him by Lucas Holstenius, the keeper of the Vatican library; and the Cardinal, at an entertainment of music performed at his own expence, received him at the door, and taking him by the hand, brought him into the assembly. Toland's Life of Milton, 8vo. 1761, page 13.

' to vocal performance, taking for a theme or subject
' some motet, anthem, or other sacred words, in a rude
' and awkward kind of counterpoint.   That this was
' the case I am very certain, having remarked that
' concenti of this kind were called Organa.   In a
' volume in the Vatican library marked No. 5120,
' containing, among others, sundry treatises on coun-
' terpoint, is one with this title :

" Sequitur Regula Organi."

' And a little after it is explained, according to the
' way of those times, Organum, Cantus factus et ordi-
' natus ad rectam mensuram, videlicit, quod unus
' punctus sit divisus ab alio : that is to say, that a
' note, for notes at that time were marked with points,
' whence proceeds the word Contrapunto, in one part
' should not correspond with a note in the other, nor
' be of the same measure.   Hence we may see that
' by Organum, in that age they meant the Contrapunto
' diminutivo,* which, according to Bede and more
' ancient writers, is better called Discantus; for where
' he says that music is practised " concentu, discantu,
" organis," I should think he means material organs,
' as he makes use of the plural number.   But when
' Guido, who lived between the time of Bede and that
' anonymous author, whom I am now citing, says, as
' he does in the Micrologus, chap. xviii. " Diaphonia,
" vocum disjunctio sonat, quam nos organum voca-
" mus ;" it seems he can mean nothing but that style
' of vocal composition in which diverse airs are given
' to the different parts, according to the meaning of
' the above-mentioned contrapuntist.   But, as we have
' presupposed with others, that this kind of music
' cannot be much more than two hundred years old,
' we may believe that Guido understood the term
' Contrapunto diminutivo in the sense which the
' Greek word Diaphonia, signifying Dissonance, seems
' to imply, and in which Franchinus uses the word
' Organizare.   This modern kind of concentus how-
' ever does not in reality consist in this, nor in the
' connection of several airs together, but in the sing-
' ing of musical words artfully ranged, and different
' passages at the same time, with many repetitions,
' fugues, and imitations, in such a manner, that in
' regard to the material part of the concentus, viz.,
' the sounds and consonances, one can hardly hear any
' thing more delightful.   But that which gives form
' and soul to music suffers remarkable imperfections,
' for by the utterance of many things together the
' attention of the hearer is disturbed, and then so
' many repetitions are frivolous and seem affected ;
' words also are curtailed, and the true pronunciation
' thereof spoiled.   I do not dispute whether this kind
' of music has been properly introduced, but this I
' know very well, that it has been in use only these
' few centuries ; for as in ancient times nothing but
' the plain and simple cantus was heard in churches,
' and that rather by connivance than under the sanc-
' tion of public authority ; so even now it is rather
' tolerated than approved of by the church in sacred
' subjects, in which it seems to have had its origin.'
He ascribes to Giulio Caccini the invention of

Recitative, and for the practice of it celebrates Giuseppe Cenci, detto Giuseppino, as he does Ludovico
Viadana for the invention of thorough-bass.

He censures the old German musicians for setting
to music such words as these, Liber Generationis Jesu
Christi Filii David, &c. as also the use of such forms
of speech as the following, which it seems were
common at Rome in his time, Le Vergini del Palestrina, Le Vergini dell' Asola, instead of Le Vergini
del Petrarca, modulate ò messe in musica dal Palestrina, dall' Asola, &c.   He says that the Canzones of
Petrarch, Guarini, Tasso, and Marino, as set to music
in the form of madrigals, are the finest of modern
vocal compositions : and he mentions the following
of Petrarch as peculiarly excellent, ' Italia mia,'
' Tirsi morir volea,' and ' Felice chi vi mira.'† He
intimates that for accompanying the human voice, the
Tibia is the fittest instrument ; and concludes with
the mention of an instrument invented by himself,
and called the Lyra Barberini, which participates of
the sweetness of both the harp and lute ; at the end
of this tract is a sonnet written by the author's patron,
Cardinal Barberini, who while the book was printing
was elected pope and assumed the name of Urban
VIII., set to music, at the instance of Doni, in four
parts, by Pietro Eredia ; and, as it is said, in the
ancient Dorian and Phrygian modes.

In the year 1640 Doni published his ' Annotazioni
' sopra il compendio de' generi, e de' modi della mu-
' sica,' and, together with these, sundry tracts and
discourses, that is to say, ' Trattato de' tuoni o modi
' veri,' inscribed to his friend Pietro della Valle.
' Trattato secondo de' tuoni, o harmonie de gl' antichi,
' Al rev. P. Leon Santi. Discorso primo dell' inutile
' osservanza de' tuoni, ò modi hodierni ; Al Signor
' Galeazzo Sabbatini a Bergamo. Discorso secondo,
' sopra le consonanze ; Al Padre Marino Mersenne a
' Parigi. Discorso terzo, sopra la divisione eguale
' attribuita ad Aristosseno ; Al Signor Piero de' Bardi
' de' Conti di Vernio à Firenze. Discorso quarto,
' sopra il Violone Panarmonico ; Al Signor Pietro
' della Valle. Discorso quinto, sopra il Violino
' Diarmonico ed la Tiorba a tre manichi, A' Signori
' Dominico e Virgilio Mazzocchi.' In this last discourse the author describes an instrument of his own
invention, resembling in shape the Spanish guitar,
but having three necks, each of them double, like the
Theorbo and Arch-lute ; the use of which instrument
is by a different temperature or disposition of the
frets on each of the three necks, to enable the performer to play at his election in either the Dorian, the
Phrygian, or the Hypolydian mode. ' Discorso sesto,
' sopra il Recitare in scena con l' accompagnamento
' d' Instrumenti musicali ; All' illustriss. et excel-
' lentiss. Signore il Sig. Don Camillo Colonna. Dis-
' corso settimo, della Ritmopeia de' versi Latini e
' della melodia de' Cori Tragichi ; Al Signor Gio.
' Jacomo Buccardi.' The annotations, and also the
tracts abound with curious particulars relating to the
music and musicians of the author's time.

* CONTRAPUNTUS DIMINUTUS is a term used by Kircher and others to
signify that kind of music where a given plain-song is broken or divided
into notes of a less value : it is the same with Contrapunctus floridus, an
example whereof is given in page 228 of this work.

† The second of these madrigals, set by Luca Marenzio for five voices,
is printed in the Harmonia Celeste, and, with the English words ' Thirsis
to die desired,' in the Musica Transalpina. It is divided into three parts,
and is one of those madrigals of Luca Marenzio which Peacham has
celebrated.

CHAP. CXXXII.

In the year 1647 Doni published a treatise entitled De Præstantia Musicæ veteris, in three books; this work is written in dialogue, and is a very learned disquisition on the subject of music, as well ancient as modern; the interlocutors are Charidorus, by whom is characterized the author himself; Philoponus, a man of learning, Polyaenus, a friend of both, and Eumolpus a singer.

In this curious and entertaining work the subject is discussed in the way of free conversation, wherein, although the author professes himself a strenuous advocate for the ancients, great latitude is given in the arguments of his opponents, and particularly of Philoponus, who is no less a favourer of the moderns. The argument insisted on in the course of this work is, that the musical faculty was treated of more skilfully by the ancient Greeks and by the Romans than at this day; and that in the construction and use of such instruments as the Cythara and Lyra, and pipes of all kinds, they were equal at least to the moderns; but in such as are made to sound by mutual percussions, as the Cymbala and Crotala, they far exceeded them.

The data required and granted for this purpose are, first, that almost all the more elegant arts and faculties, and among those that of music, grew obsolete, and at last entirely perished by the incursions and devastations of the Barbarians, who miserably over-ran and laid waste Greece and Italy, and all the provinces of the Roman empire. Secondly, that by so many plunderings, burnings, slaughters, and subversions, and changes of languages, manners, and institutions, the greatest part of the ancient books in all kinds of learning perished; so that not even the thousandth part escaped; and those that were saved were almost all maimed and defective, or loaded with errors, as they came down to us; and, as it always happens, the best were lost, and the more unworthy shared a better fate in this general shipwreck. Thirdly, that those who are to be called ancients, as far as relates to this subject of enquiry, are only such as flourished in Greece and Italy before these devastations; for those who lived between them and our forefathers, in whose time literature and music began again to flourish, are not properly to be called ancients, nor are they worth regarding.

As this treatise is written in dialogue, it is somewhat difficult so to connect the speeches of the several interlocutors, as to give them the form of an argument. The principal question agitated by them is simply this, Whether the music of the ancients or of the moderns is to be preferred: Doni, in the person of Charidorus, takes the part of the ancients; and Philoponus is a no less strenuous advocate for the moderns. Indeed the whole force of the argument rests in the speeches of these two persons, those of the other two being interposed merely for the sake of variety, and to enliven the conversation. For this reason it will perhaps be thought that the best method of abridging this tract will be by giving first the substance of Charidorus's argument in favour of the ancients, and opposing to it that of Philoponus in defence of the moderns, and this is the course we mean to pursue.

Charidorus asserts that as Pythagoras was the parent and founder of music, we are not to wonder that the most learned writers on the subject of harmonics were those of his school. Of these he says Archytas of Tarentum, Philolaus of Crotona, Hippasus Metapontinus, and Eubulides were the chief. He adds that the Platonics also, and many of the Peripatetics were great cultivators of the science of harmony; but that of the writings of these men there are no remains, excepting one little book, the nineteenth of the problems of Aristotle. Of the later philosophers he mentions Plutarch, who he says wrote a book on music, yet extant, full of things most worthy to be known. Of Aristoxenus he speaks with rapture, styling him the prince of musicians, and cites St. Jerome's opinion of him, that he was by far the most learned philosopher and mathematician of all the Greeks. He highly applauds Ptolemy of Pelusium, whose three books of Harmonics he says are full of excellent learning, but rather obscure, notwithstanding the noble commentaries of Porphyry on the first of them. With him he joins Aristides Quintilianus, Alypius, Bacchius, Gaudentius, Cleonides, Pappus Alexandrinus, Theo Smyrnæus, Diophantus, Adrastus, Diocles, Gemimus, Nichomachus, and others. He greatly commends the five books, De Musica, of Boetius as a very elegant, ingenious, and learned work. He says it was drawn from the manual of Nichomachus, and laments that the author did not live to complete it. As to the rest of the Latin writers, St. Augustin, Martianus Capella, Cassiodorus, and Bede, whom he reckons among the semi-ancients, he says their writings contain nothing either learned or notable; and that Varro, Apuleius, Albinus, and other Romans that laboured in this field, and whose works are since extinct, were more learned than any of them.

To the more ancient of the monkish writers on music, namely, Odo of Cluni, Berno the abbat, and Guido Aretinus, Notgerus, Hucbaldus, and some others, Charidorus allows some degree of merit; but of Franco of Cologne,* Philippus de Caserta, Marchettus Paduanus, Prosdocimus Beldimandus, Johannes de Muris, Anselmus Parmensis, and others of the old Italian writers, he says they did not even dream of what eloquence or polite learning was: nor does he scruple to censure even Franchinus himself for making use of the word Manerium instead of Modum, Tritechordium, Baritonantem, Altisonantem, and some others, as he does also Glareanus for the same reason.

He mentions also a certain modern author, but conceals his name, who in treating of the genera, asserts that the enarmonic genus is so called, for that it is as it were without harmony, ignorantly supposing the syllable *en* to be privative like *in*, as when we say ineptus insulsus, &c. and of another, who in a pretty large volume says that the diatonic was so

* Franco was of Liege, not of Cologne. See page 176 of this work.

called, because Dia in Greek signifies the number Six, and Tonicum resounding.

He censures severely Nicola Vicentino for his absurd opinions, and for arrogating to himself the title of Archimusicus; the passage is given at length, in page 396 of this work.

He says that Gaffarel, a most learned Frenchman, had commented on the music of the Jews; and praises the two books of Mersennus in French and in Latin, which he says the author sent him as a present; and adds that the same person translated Bacchius into French.

Then follows a curious account of a musical impostor, and of his attempt to introduce a new tuning of the organ in one of the principal churches in Rome, in these words: 'You remember that a certain 'ragged old man came into this city not long since, 'who knew nothing more than to play tolerably on 'the Polyplectrum, and yet would obtrude as a new 'and most useful invention that equality of the semi-'tones which is commonly, but unjustly attributed to 'the Aristoxeneans, and is falsely imagined to be 'found in the division of the keys of the organ, and 'that he attemperated his instrument accordingly. 'You know what crouds he gathered together, and 'what a noise he made, and when he had insinuated 'himself into the acquaintance of Chærilus, whom 'you know to be a most audacious and impudent man, 'that boasts of a certain counterfeit species of erudi-'tion, but chiefly of his proficiency in the study of 'poetry and music, in the circles and courts of princes, 'what think you he did? He extorted money from 'the French orator, whom he worked for on that 'foolish and tedious drama, which was exhibited on 'the birth-day of the Dauphin by the chorus of the 'Roman singers; and when the good singers were 'fretting and fuming, as resenting such roguery, and 'the best of them were so incensed, as to be ready to 'tear off their cassocks for being compelled to sing 'to such ill temperated organs, he at length, by 'prayers, promises, small gifts, and boasting speeches, 'drew the musurgists over to his opinion, and so 'softened, by frequent and gratuitous entertainments, 'that noble organist Psycogaurus, who presided over 'the music of the palace, that he was not ashamed, 'contrary to the faith of his own ears, to extol to the 'best of princes this invention: and he also reported 'abroad that the old man had been presented with a 'golden chain of a large price, that by this lie the 'imposter might gain credit among the unskilful. 'And that the farce might be the better carried on, 'the same person introduced to his friends this old 'man rather burdened than honoured with a chain of 'great weight, hired from some Jewish banker. But 'you will say that this is ridiculous: yet ought we 'rather to weep than laugh at it; for he had prevailed 'so far that the same prince, who, as chance would 'have it, was repairing at that time the choir and 'music-gallery in one of the chief and most ancient 'cathedrals in the city, gave orders for the reducing 'of the noble organ in the same to that dissonant 'species of temperature; and it actually had been 'executed had not our Donius prevented it.'

Doni then relates an attempt of Kapsberger to introduce his own music into the chapel of a certain bishop in prejudice to that of Palestrina, an account whereof has been given in the life of Palestrina, herein before inserted in this work.

After some very severe reflections on the conduct of Kapsberger, he proceeds to censure Fabio Colonna in these words: 'But lest I should seem to attack 'this our age too fiercely, hear what had liked to have 'happened in the Borghesian times.* Fabio Colonna, 'a man well known, and a diligent searcher into na-'ture, died lately at Naples; he, incited by an imma-'ture and depraved ambition, being at that time but 'a young man, published a certain book relating to 'theorical music, entitled Sambuca Lyncea; and I do 'not know that a more foolish or unlearned one has 'appeared for some time before; and there were not 'wanting some unskilful judges who persuaded pope 'Paul to send for this man from Naples, and allow 'him a large stipend for superintending the construc-'tion of an organ in the Vatican church, at a large 'expence, according to his own system; and the 'thing would have been done, had not that prince 'refused to be at the expence of it.'

Charidorus then breaks out into an eulogium on Olympus, the reputed inventor of the enarmonic genus, whose music he says was pathetic and divine. He then appeals to one of the interlocutors in these words: 'You best can judge, O Philoponus, whether 'this character be due to the symphonies of Iodocus 'and Johannes Mouton, and the rest of that class; 'for I am persuaded you are conversant in their 'works, remembering that I once saw a collection of 'Masses composed by them severally, and printed by 'the direction of pope Leo X. in curious types, lying 'on a table in your study.' Philoponus answers, 'There is really nothing of this kind to be found in 'them, yet the authors you mention were possessed 'of the faculty of harmony; and a marvellous felicity 'in modulating and digesting the consonances, afford-'ing great delight to the hearing; but the elocution 'is barbarous and inconcinnous; and as for moving 'the affections, they never so much as dreamt of it.'

Charidorus again recurs to the ancient musicians, of whom he gives a long account from Homer, Plato, Plutarch, Cicero, Quintilian, Seneca, Athenæus, and other writers. Speaking of the moderns, he celebrates Ercole as a skilful organist; but, as to the modern theorists, he says, that excepting Jacobus Faber Stapulensis, Salinas, Zarlino, Vincentio Galilei, Michael Prætorius, Mersennus, Bottrigaro, and some very few others, their works contain only trivial and common things, and what had been said a hundred times over. He adds that nobleness of birth and a liberal education in musicians conduce much to the elegance of their modulations; as a proof whereof he says, some have observed that the compositions of the prince of Venosa, and of Thomas Peccius, a patrician of Sienna in Tuscany,† had in them some-

* Paul V. who at that time was Pope, was of the Borghesian family, being son of Antonio Borghese of Sienna; he was elected anno 1605, and died in 1621. See Rycaut's Lives of the Popes, page 227.

† TOMASO PECCI, though but little known, is celebrated by Kircher as an excellent musician: there is extant of his composition a book of Madrigals, published at Venice in 1609.

what that was not vulgar nor plebeian, but that sounded elegant and magnificent.

Charidorus complains of the want of some severe law to repress that effeminate and light music which then prevailed; and says that that most wise pope Marcellus II. had determined to correct the licentiousness of the musicians according to the opinion of the holy council of Trent. But that he suffered himself to be imposed on by the cunning of one musician,* and the glory of such a work to be snatched out of his hands.

Book II. contains the argument of Philoponus, in which he undertakes to point out the defects of the ancient music, and to shew the superiority of the modern. To this end he infers that the ancients must have been unacquainted with music in consonance from this circumstance, that they never looked on the ditone and trihemitone, nor the greater and lesser sixth, as consonants; and in support of his opinion adduces the testimony of Zarlino and Galilei, both of whom say that, among the ancients, if at any time two singers were introduced, they did not sing together, but alternately. Philoponus next observes that the ancient musicians were ignorant of those graces and ornaments which we call Passaggios, and of those artful and ingenious contrivances, fugues, imitations, canons, and double counterpoints; and that the superiority of the modern music may be very justly gathered from the great plenty, variety, and excellence of instruments now in use, more especially the organ; whereas among the ancients the principal were the lyre and the cithara, which were mounted with very few chords.

As another proof of the superiority of the modern music, he mentions the extension of the scale by Guido Aretinus to the interval of a greater sixth beyond that of the Greeks, his invention of the syllables, and, lastly, the modern notation or method of writing down music.

Philoponus proceeds to celebrate the modern writers on music, namely, Salinas, Zarlino, and Galilei, as also the composers of songs both sacred and profane, that is to say, Adrian Willaert, Palestrina, Cristoforo Morales, Luca Marenzio, Pomponio Nenna, Tomaso Pecci, and the prince of Venosa, Cyprian de Rore, Felice Anerio, and Nanino, Filippo de Monte, and Orlando de Lasso. For the invention and improvement of Recitative he applauds Giulio Caccini, Jacopo Peri, and Claudio Monteverde; and for their singing, Suriano, and another named Theophilus; as also two very fine female singers, Hadriana Baroni, and her daughter Leonora, in these words 'If by chance we bring women into this 'contest, how great will be the injury to compare 'either Hadriana or her daughter Leonora† with the

'ancient Sappho? or if, besides the glory of well 'singing, you think a remarkable skill in music is 'necessary, there is Francesca, the daughter of Caccini, 'whom I have just now praised.'

He then celebrates Frescobaldi as an admirable performer on the organ, and others of his time for their excellence on other instruments; and remarks on the great concourse of people at the churches of Rome on festival days upon the rumour of some grand musical performance, especially when new motetti were to be sung.

Charidorus to these arguments of Philoponus replies; and first he asserts that although the ditone, trihemitone, and the two sixths were not known to the ancients as consonances; and for this he cites the testimony of Galilei, and Salinas, lib. II. cap. ii. page 60, who indeed says the same thing, but gives this awkward reason for not enumerating these intervals among the consonances, namely, that those who thought them such were unwilling to contradict

'omnes hic Romæ, quotquot ingenio et poëticæ facultatis laude præstant, 'carminibus, tum Etrusce tum Latinè scriptis, singulari ac prope divino 'mulieris illius canendi artificio tanquam faustos quosdam clamores et 'plausius edunt; legi, inquam, unum Lælii (Guidiccionis) epigramma, 'ita purum, ita elegans, ita argutum, ita venustum, prope ut dixerim, 'nihil me vidisse, in eo genere, elegantius neque politius.'

Fulvio Testi has also celebrated her in the following sonnet:—

Se l' Angioletto mia tremolo, e chiaro,
A le stelle, onde scese, il canto invia,
Ebbra del suono, in cui sè stessa obblia,
Col Ciel pensa la Terra irne del paro.

Ma se di sua Virtù non ponto ignaro
L' occhio accorda gli sguardi à l' armonia,
Trà il concento, e il fulgor dubbio è se sia
L' udir più dolce, ò il rimirar più caro.

Al divin lume, â le celesti note
De le potenze sue perde il vigore
L' alma, e dal cupo sen suelta si scote.

Deh, fammi cieco, ò fammi sordo, Amore:
Che distratto in più sensi (oimè) non pote
Capir tante dolcezze un picciol core.

Poesie Liriche del Conte D. Fulvio Testi, Ven. 1691, pag. 361.

Among the Latin poems of Milton are no fewer than three entitled ' Ad Leonoram Romæ canentem,' wherein this lady is celebrated for her singing, with an allusion to her mother's exquisite performance on the lute. Doni was acquainted with them both; and it may be supposed that they severally performed in the concerts at the Barberini palace. Mention has already been made of Milton's being introduced to one of these entertainments by the Cardinal himself; and it is more than probable that at this or some other of them he might have heard the mother play and the daughter sing.

A fine eulogium on this accomplished woman is contained in a Discourse on the Music of the Italians, printed with the life of Malherbe, and some other treatises at Paris, 1672, in 12mo, at the end of which are these words: ' This discourse was composed by Mr. Maugars, prior of ' St. Peter de Mac, the king's interpreter of the English language, and ' besides so famous a performer on the viol, that the king of Spain and ' several other sovereign princes of Europe have wished to hear him. ' The character given by this person of Leonora Baroni is as follows : " She is endowed with fine parts; she has a very good judgment to dis- " tinguish good from bad music; she understands it perfectly well; and " even composes, which makes her absolute mistress of what she sings, " and gives her the most exact pronunciation and expression of the " sense of her words. She does not pretend to beauty, neither is she " disagreeable, or a coquet. She sings with a bold and generous modesty, " and an agreeable gravity; her voice reaches a large compass of notes, " and is exact, loud, and harmonious; she softenes and raises it without " straining or making grimaces. Her raptures and sighs are not las- " civious; her looks have nothing impudent, nor does she transgress " a virgin modesty in her gestures. In passing from one key to another " she shews sometimes the divisions of the enharmonic and chromatic " kind with so much art and sweetness, that every body is ravished with " that fine and difficult method of singing. She has no need of any " person to assist her with a Theorbo or viol, one of which is necessary " to make her singing complete; for she plays perfectly well herself on " both those instruments. In short, I have had the good fortune to hear " her sing several times above thirty different airs, with second and " third stanzas composed by herself. I must not forget to tell you that " one day she did me the particular favour to sing with her mother and " her sister. Her mother played upon the lute, her sister upon " the harp, and herself upon the Theorbo. This concert, composed of " three fine voices, and of three different instruments, so powerfully " transported my senses, and threw me into such raptures, that I forgot " my mortality, and thought myself already among the angels enjoying " the felicity of the blessed.'" Bayle, Art. BARONI, in not.

---

* Who this cunning musician was we are at a loss to guess. It is said of Palestrina, that pope Marcellus II. being about to banish music out of the church, was induced to depart from a resolution which he had taken for that purpose by that fine mass of his composing, entitled Missa Papæ Marcelli. See page 421 of this work.

† ADRIANA of Mantua, for her beauty surnamed the Fair, and her daughter LEONORA BARONI: the latter of these two celebrated persons is by Bayle said to have been one of the finest singers in the world; a whole volume of poems in her praise is extant with this title, ' Applausi 'poëtica alle glorie della Signora Leonora Baroni. Nicius Erythræus,' in his Pinacotheca II. page 427, 12mo. Lips. 1712, alludes to this work, saying, ' Legi ego, in theatro Eleonoræ Baronæ, cantricis eximiæ, in quo

the doctrines of the Pythagoreans, who allowed of no other consonances than the diatessaron, diapente, and diapason ; yet upon this foundation he scruples not to assert, and that in terms the most positive, that the ancients were acquainted with and practised music in consonance.

He then enters into a long discourse on the Tibiæ of the ancients, the genera and their species, and other particulars of the ancient music. To what Philoponus had advanced in favour of Suriano and Theophilus, Charidorus answers that the complaint of Ariadne, written by Ottavio Rinuccini, and set to music by Claudio Monteverde, is more to be esteemed than any canon of either of them.

He commends that triumvirate, meaning, as it is supposed, Giulio Caccini, Jacopo Peri, and Claudio Monteverde, who revived the monodical or recitative style, but he adds, that what they did was not so much the effect of their own judgment and industry, as of the advice and assistance of the learned men then at Florence.

Of symphonetic music, the excellencies of which Philoponus had so strongly insisted on, Charidorus seems to entertain no very high opinion ; for he says that were the musicians in general to make their compositions as fine as those of Cypriano de Rore ; yet because the melody is required to be distributed through all the several parts, for if one part be highly finished, the rest will sing unhandsomely, the grace and beauty of the work will not shine forth. And as to that variety of motion and difference in the time of notes, and those sundry points and passages which constitute the difference between figurate and plain descant, he says that they produce nought but confusion, and that they render only an enervate kind of music ; and that as those who labour under a fever have an inordinate and inconstant pulse, so in this kind of harmony, the numbers being inordinate and confused, that energy which so greatly affects and delights our ears and minds is wanting, and the whole becomes a confused jargon of irregular measures.*

In the course of his reasoning Charidorus frequently cites Plato, Aristotle, Nichomachus, Aristides Quintilianus, Aristoxenus, Bacchius, Plutarch, Ptolemy, and others of the Greek writers on music ; and after collecting their sentiments, he opposes to them those of Guido Aretinus, Bartolomeo Ramis, Spataro, and Steffano Vanneo ; for as to Franco and Johannes De Muris, and the rest of that class, he says they are half ancient, and totally barbarous ; and adds, that among the ancients the very women were skilled in harmonics, for that Porphyry, in his Commentaries on the Harmonics of Ptolemy, mentions one Ptolemais, a certain woman, who treated accurately on the elements of the Pythagorean music. Speaking of the metrical part of music, he says that the ancients were very exact and curious in their phrase, and in their pronunciation, and examined the momenta of times, accents, letters, and syllables, but

that the moderns pay but little attention to these matters : yet he says that through the endeavours of the Florentine Academy, a more distinct and elegant pronunciation in the monodical cantus or recitative began to be esteemed. He adds, that recitative thus improved was introduced by a young man named Loretus, before-named, whom Nicola Doni, a relation of the author, very kindly entertained at his house for some years, and caused to be assisted in his musical studies.

Charidorus then bewails the fate of modern music, in that it is no longer as it was wont to be, the sister of poetry ; and observes that the ecclesiastical songs are deficient both in purity of phrase and elegance of sentiment : and as to harmony of numbers, he says it is not to be looked for, for that they are written in prose, in which so little regard is paid to concinnity or aptness of numbers, that there have not been wanting musicians who have set to music in parts, the genealogy of Jesus Christ, consisting wholly of Hebrew names.†

He then enters largely into the consideration of the Melopoeia and Rythmopoeia of the ancients, and next of the Progymnastica, or rudiments of music ; he says that the practice of singing was much more aptly and expeditiously taught by the ancient Greeks than by the modern Latins, with the help of the six syllables invented by Guido, or by the later Germans and French with that of seven : and he asserts, with the greatest degree of confidence, that the noviciate of the younger students in music would be much shortened were two of the six syllables of Guido cut off ; and as to the practice of solmisation, his sentiments are as follow : ' What that monk Aretinus ' boasts of his invention, saying that it greatly con- ' tributed to facilitate the learning of music, is ' partly true and partly false : it is true when com- ' pared with the ages next immediately before him, ' in which the ancient progymnastical syllables were ' out of use ; but false when compared with the prac- ' tice of the ancient Greeks and Romans, who made ' use of these four syllables, TA, TA, TE, TE ; and if, ' following their example, the system of Guido were ' reduced to the ancient measure, it would be far ' more commodious.'

In the third and last part, Doni, in the person of Charidorus, cites from Suetonius a passage wherein it is related of Nero, that in order to enable him to sing the better, he not only abstained from fruit and such kind of food as had a tendency to hurt his voice; but to improve it suffered a leaden plate to be fixed on his breast, and made use of vomits and clysters.‡

To this discipline of Nero, ridiculous as it was severe, and the servile condition of singers in ancient Greece and Rome, Charidorus opposes the licentious and disorderly lives of those of modern Italy, of whom he gives the following account :—

' In these our days the singers are generally of the

---

* This objection lays a ground for a suspicion that Doni was an incompetent judge of the merits of musical composition ; for who does not see, with respect to the power of moving the affections, the difference between mere melody and music in consonance, and the preference due to the latter ?

† Doni here alludes to a composition in Glareanus of Iodocus Pratensis, to the words of the first chapter of the Gospel of St. Matthew.

‡ The author gives not the least intimation to favour the notion that the practice of castration, with a view to the preservation of the voice, was in use among the ancients ; but he speaks of the practice of infibulation for a similar purpose, as mentioned by Juvenal, and refers to Celsus for a particular description of the method of performing the operation.

'lower class, yet are their masters unable to keep
'them under restraint; and their insolence is such as
'scarcely to be borne with. You see those nice
'eunuchs, who every one of them make more money
'than ten singing masters, how daintily they live,
'how much they boast of themselves, what little ac-
'count they make of other men, and that they even
'deride such as are learned. I say nothing of their
'morals, since what is seen by every body cannot be
'denied. When the princes Barberini have on certain
'festival days given to the public musical dramas,
'have you not seen some of them contesting with
'those lords, impudently thwarting them, and endea-
'vouring to get admitted whomsoever they pleased
'into the theatre? when tickets of admission were
'made out they have not been content with a few, but
'were ready to tear more out of the hands of such
'as were appointed to distribute them.'

He says that Vitruvius relates that he had been told by the son of Masinissa, king of Numidia, who made him a visit, and stayed some days at his house, that there was a certain place in Africa, Pliny calls it Zama, where were fountains of such a nature, that those who were born there and drank of the water had excellent voices for singing; and that he himself, at Luneburg, a city of Savoy, seated under the very Alps, had been at a fountain, the water whereof produced similar effects; and that coming there on a certain festival in the evening, he found some of the inhabitants singing praises to God with voices sweet and musical to a wonderful degree, and such as he conceives those of the singers in ancient Greece and Rome to have been.

He says that notwithstanding the great number of singers at Rome, there were in his time very few whose voices were perfect and sweet. He adds that the silence of the ancients in this particular implies that the practice of castration, for the purpose of meliorating the voice, was not in use among the ancient Greeks and Romans; but contradicts the vulgar opinion of its effect, insisting that the voices of women and boys are in general more sweet than those of eunuchs, the singing of whom together in large companies he resembles to the noise of a troop of wethers.

Philoponus having in his argument insisted largely on the exquisite performance of many modern musicians on various instruments, Charidorus replies that the best of them are not to be compared to those among the ancients, who played on the lyre and the tibia. He says that the English are allowed to excel on the flute; and that there are many in that kingdom good performers on the cornet, yet he cannot believe that the English artists are equal to the ancient players on the tibia, namely, Antigenides, Pronomus, and Timotheus.

Speaking of instruments, he says there are many particulars relating to the construction of them, which are unknown to the modern artificers, as namely, that the best strings are made when the north, and the worst when the south wind blows; and that the bellies of lutes and viols, and other instruments of the fidicinal kind, should be made of fir, cloven and not sawed, lest the fibres should be cut across in smoothing.*

He says it is no wonder that the tibiæ of the ancients excelled so greatly those of the moderns, seeing that the old Greeks and Romans were most diligent and curious about them; for they were constructed of box, the wood of the Lote-tree, of silver, and of the shank-bones of certain animals, that is to say, deer and asses, and of a Grecian reed, still in use among the nations of the East, excelling all the rest in sweetness, as he judges from having once heard an Englishman play on a pipe of this kind.

He greatly laments, that although Vitruvius has given a description of the ancient hydraulic organ, we, at this distance of time, are incapable of understanding the terms made use of by him for explaining it, and that the diagrams representing the several parts of it are lost. He adds, that the organ mentioned by Zarlino in his Sopplimenti, affords no argument to conclude that those of the ancients were not greatly superior to it.

He next proceeds to censure the musicians of his time for the licentiousness and levity of their compositions, in these words, 'Despising the most sweet 'motets of Prenestinus and Morales, and others which 'they call too old, and studying novelty, they daily 'obtrude their own symphonies, which they steal here 'and there, and afterwards tack together in a pitiful 'manner. Who taught them,' exclaims he, 'to adapt 'to a joyful modulation and concentus, that sad and 'mournful petition of Kyrie Eleison? Or, on the 'other hand, to make sad and mournful that clausula 'of Mary's song, the Gloria Patri, which is full of 'exultation? yet this they daily practise.'†

At the end of this treatise of Doni, De Præstantia Musicæ veteris, is a catalogue of the author's writings on the subject of music, amounting to no fewer than twenty-four tracts, reckoning many that were never published, and a few that he did not live to complete.

From the account above given of Doni it must appear that he was very deeply skilled in musical science, and that he had diligently perused as well the writings of the ancients as the moderns on the subject. Pietro della Valle, the famous traveller, who was intimately acquainted with him, bears a very honourable testimony to his character, for he says he had 'congiunta a gran bontà e integrità di costumi 'profondissima erudizione, con esatta notizia della 'lingua Greca, delle mattematiche, della teoria musi-'cale, della poesia, dell' istoria, e di ogni altra facoltà 'che a ciò possa giovare; con l' ajuto e comodità che 'ha avuto di vedere molti bei libri reconditi e non

* This remark, if attended to, will be found to amount to nothing; for the fibres of the wood are as much cut across by the smoothing or working the belly of such an instrument as by sawing.

† Both the objections implied in these queries are well founded, but the latter only of them will hold at this day; for the public ear is too depraved to bear pathetic music. As to the former objection, it arose from the practice of assimilating the music of the church to that of the theatre: and this abuse has so prevailed, that the Kyrie Eleison is now frequently set to a movement in jig-time. In a mass of Pergolesi, one of the most pathetic of modern composers, the Gloria Patri is a fugue in chorus, and the Amen a minuet. Graun's celebrated Te Deum is of a lighter cast than any opera of Lully, Bononcini, or Handel: in it that most solemn clause, 'Te ergo quæsumus, tuis famulis subveni, quos 'pretioso sanguine redemisti,' is set to a movement in triple time, in the lightest of all the keys, viz. E ♮ with the greater third, and with an accompaniment by a German flute. The church-music of Perez of Lisbon is for the most part in the same style.

'pubblicati alle stampe, massimamente autori antichi 'Greci nella Vaticana e in molt' altre librerie famose.'

This character of Doni, given by one who was intimate with him, and well knew the estimation he was held in at Rome, is in some measure confirmed by Meibomius, although he had no other foundation for his opinion than that intrinsic evidence of learning, industry, and ingenuity contained in the writings of Doni; for he says that none of the age he lived in had written with more learning or elegance than he had done; and that had he been better skilled in Greek literature, and known at least the first principles of the mathematics, he would have performed greater things. A few years ago the musical tracts of Doni were collected, and published in Italy, in two volumes folio, with a portrait of him.

CHAP. CXXXIII.

ATHANASIUS KIRCHER was born at Fulda in Germany, on the second day of May, 1601. At the age of seventeen he entered into the society of the Jesuits, and, after going through a regular course of study, during which he shewed most amazing parts and industry, he became a teacher of philosophy, mathematics, and the Hebrew and Syriac languages, in the university of Wirtzburg in Franconia. In the year 1631, when the Suedes entered Germany under Gustavus Adolphus, he retired into France, and settled in the Jesuits' college at Avignon, and remained there till 1635. He was then called to Rome to teach mathematics in the Roman college, which he did six years; afterwards he became professor of the Hebrew language in that city, and died there in the month of November, 1680, having written and published twenty-two volumes in folio, eleven in quarto, and three in octavo. The chief of his works are, the Musurgia Universalis. Primitiæ Gnomicæ Catoptricæ. Prodomus Copticus. Ars Magnetica. Thesaurus Linguæ Ægyptiacæ. Ars magna Lucis et Umbræ. Obeliscus Pamphilius. Oedipus Ægyptiacus, tom. IV. Itinerarium Extaticum. Obeliscus Ægyptiacus. Mundus subterraneus, tom. II. China Illustrata. Phonurgia nova. Kircher was more than ordinarily addicted to the study of hieroglyphical characters; and it is said that certain young scholars caused to be engraved some unmeaning fantastic characters or figures upon a shapeless piece of stone, and buried it in a place which was shortly to be dug up; upon digging the place the stone was found, and was by the scholars that had hid it, carried to Kircher as a most singular antique, who, quite in raptures, applied himself instantly to explain the hieroglyphics, and, as he conceived, made it intelligible.

As the Musurgia is dispersed throughout Europe, and is in the hands of many persons, a general view of it may suffice in this place. It is dedicated to Leopold, archduke of Austria, afterwards emperor of Germany, who was not only a patron of music, but an excellent performer on the harpsichord. Of its nature and contents an accurate judgment may be formed by the perusal of the following Synopsis prefixed to the first volume.

SYNOPSIS

MUSURGIÆ UNIVERSALIS,

IN X. LIBROS DIGESTÆ.

Quorum septem primi Tomo 1. Reliqui tres Tomo II. comprehenduntur.

Liber I.   Physiologicus, soni naturalis Genesin, naturam et proprietatem effectusque demonstrat.

Liber II.   Philologicus, soni artificialis, sive Musicæ primam institutionem propagationemque inquirit.

Liber III.   Arithmeticus, motuum harmonicorum scientiam per numeros et novam Musicam Algebraicam docet.

Liber IV.   Geometricus, intervallorum consono dissonorum originem per monochordi divisionem Geometricam, Algebraicam, Mechanicam, multiplici varietate ostendit.

Liber V.   Organicus, Instrumentorum omnis generis Musicorum structuram novis experimentis aperit.

Liber VI.   Melotheticus, componendarum omnis generis cantilenarum novam et demonstrativam methodum producit: continetque quicquid circa hoc negotium curiosum, rarum et arcanum desiderari potest.

Liber VII.   Diacriticus, comparationem veteris Musicæ cum moderna instituit, abusus detegit, cantus Ecclesiastici dignitatem commendat, methodumque aperit, qua ad patheticæ Musicæ perfectionem tandem perveniri possit.

Liber VIII.   Mirificus, novam artem Musarithmicam exhibet, qua quivis etiam Musicæ imperitus, ad perfectam componendi notitiam brevi tempore pertingere possit, continetque Musicam Combinatoriam, Poeticam, Rhetoricam, Panglossiam Musarithmicam omnibus linguis novo artificio adaptat.

Liber IX.   Magicus, reconditiora totius Musicæ arcana producit; continetque Physiologiam consoni et dissoni; Præterea Magiam Musico-medicam, Phonocampticam, sive perfectam de Echo, qua mensuranda, qua constituenda doctrinam, Novam Tuborum oticorum, sive auricularium, fabricam; item Statuarum, ac aliorum Instrumentorum Musicorum Autophonorum, seu per se sonantium, uti et sympathicorum structuram curiosis ac novis experientiis docet. Quibus adnectitur Cryptologia musica, qua occulti animi conceptus in distans per sonos manifestantur.

Liber X.   Analogicus, decachordon naturæ exhibet, quo Deum in 3 Mundorum Elementaris, Cœlestis, Archetypi fabrica ad Musicas proportiones respexisse per 10. gradus, veluti per 10. Naturæ Registra demonstratur.

Registrum 1.   Symphonismos Elementorum, sive Musicam Elementarem.

Registrum 2.   Cœlorum admirandam Symphoniam in motibus, influxibus effectibusque.

Registrum 3.   Lapidum, Plantarum, Animalium, in Physico, Medico, Chymico negotio.

Registrum 4.   Musicam Microcosmi cum Megacosmo, id est minoris cum majori mundo.

Registrum 5.   Musicam Sphigmicam, sive pulsuum in venis arterisque se manifestantem.

Registrum 6.   Musicam Ethicam in appetitu sensitivo et rationali elucescentem.

Registrum 7.   Musicam Politicam, Monarchicam, Aristocraticam, Democraticam, Oeconomicam.

Registrum 8.   Musicam Metaphysicam, sive Potentiarum interiorum ad Angelos et Deum comparatam.

Registrum 9.   Musicam Hierarchicam, sive Angelorum in 9 choros distributorum.

Registrum 10.   Musicam Archetypam, sive Dei cum universa natura concentum.

exhibet.

In the preface to the Musurgia the author relates that he had been assisted by many professors of the musical science in the compiling of his work, that is to say, by Antonio Maria Abbattini, chapel-master of St. John de Lateran and St. Lawrence in Damasus, and afterwards of St. Maria Maggiore, and to Pietro Heredia of Rome, in the ecclesiastic and motetic styles; by Pietro Francesco Valentini, and Francesco Picerli, in what relates to canon; by Hieronymus Kapsberger in the organic style; and by Giacomo Carissimi in the recitatives and the more abstruse parts of musical composition; and for this assistance he makes a grateful acknowledgment.

He apologizes for writing on music, himself not being a musician, by the example of the prince of Venosa, who, though not a musician by profession, was admirably skilled in the science, and was also an excellent composer: he adds, that neither Ptolemy nor Alphonsus were astronomers or musicians by profession, and yet the one wrote on Harmonics, and the other compiled Astronomical tables. For his own part, he says, that from his youth he had assiduously applied himself, not only to learning and the sciences, but to practical music, his skill in which can only be judged of by the contents of his work; nor is it, he says, the practice alone that he has laboured to cultivate, but he has treated largely of the theory, without which the knowledge acquired by practice will be, of little avail.

He takes notice that Mersennus had then lately given to the world a large volume entitled Harmonie Universelle, which he says is a most excellent work, but that it does not so much regard the practical musician as the philosopher.

Before we proceed to an account of this elaborate and entertaining work, it may be observed that even the title-page suggests a subject of enquiry sufficient to awaken curiosity, namely, the following emblematical device, which Kircher found engraven on an antique gem.

This figure of a lyre with one string broken, and a grasshopper or rather butterfly over it, alludes to a relation of Strabo to the following purpose. In Locris, one of the chief cities of Greece, dwelt Eunomus, an excellent musician; there lived also at the same time, in the neighbouring city of Rhegium, one of the same profession, named Aristonus, who had challenged Eunomus to a trial of skill in their art; Eunomus represented to his rival that nature was against him in this contest; for that on his side of the river Alax, which divides Locris from Rhegium, the grasshoppers sang, but that on the side where Aristonus dwelt they are silent: this did not discourage Aristonus; the contest began, and while Eunomus was playing, a string of his lyre broke, when presently a grasshopper leaping upon the instrument, supplied the melody of the broken chord, and enabled Eunomus to obtain the victory.*

* Heylin, in his Cosmography, edit. 1703, page 63, relating this story,

In Chap. II. of the same book Kircher gives the anatomy of the ear; and delineates, with seemingly great exactness, the organ of hearing in a man, a calf, a horse, a dog, a hare, a cat, a sheep, a goose, a mouse, and a hog.

From the organs of hearing he proceeds, Chap. XI. to describe the vocal organs in the human species, and in Chap. XIV. those of other animals and insects, particularly the frog and the grasshopper: he is very curious in his disquisitions touching the voice and the song of the nightingale, which he has endeavoured to render in notes borrowed from the musical scale.† In the same manner he has exhibited the crowing of the cock, the voice of the hen after laying, her clucking or call to her chickens, the note of the cuckow, and the call or cry of the quail.

In the same chapter he also takes notice, but without assenting to it, of that general opinion, that swans before death sing most sweetly, which besides that it is of very great antiquity, has the authority of Plato in its favour, and is upon relation delivered by Aldrovandus, concerning the swans on the river Thames near London. Notwithstanding which, from the difference in opinion of writers about it, who severally affirm that some swans sing not till they die, others that they sing, yet die not; and for other reasons, Sir Thomas Brown hesitates not to reject it as a vulgar error in these words: 'When therefore ' we consider the dissention of authors, the falsity of ' relations, the indisposition of the organs, and the ' immusical note of all we ever beheld or heard of; ' if generally taken, and comprehending all swans, or ' of all places, we cannot assent thereto. Surely he ' that is bit with a Tarantula shall never be cured by ' this musick;‡ and with the same hopes we expect ' to hear the harmony of the spheres.'§

In Book II. Kircher treats of the music of the Hebrews, and exhibits the forms of sundry of their instruments; from hence he proceeds to the music of the Greeks, of which in this place he gives but a very general and superficial account.

In Book III. he enters very deeply into the doctrine of Harmonics, first explaining the several kinds of proportion, and next demonstrating the ratios of the intervals. In Chap. VIII. of this book he exhibits the ancient Greek scale and that of Guido in a collateral situation, thereby demonstrating the coincidence of each with the other. This book contains also a system of musical arithmetic, drawn from the writings of Boetius and others, in which are contained rules for the addition, subtraction, multiplication, and division of intervals by means of characters adapted to the purpose.

says he does not insist on the belief of the reader, but he asserts that very good authors have said that on the Locrian side of the river Alax the grasshoppers do merrily sing; and that towards Rhegium they are always silent. He adds, that the story, whether true or false, is worthy to have been celebrated by the Muse of Strada in the person of the poet Claudian.

† The song of the nightingale, as given by Kircher, is very elaborate, and must have cost him much pains to get it into any form; it seems to correspond very well, with respect to the measure or time of the notes which constitute the several strains; but the division of our scale is too gross for the intervals, which are smaller than any to be found either there or in the more minute divisions of the ancients, the enarmonic not excepted.

‡ Sir Thomas Brown, though he rejected the fable of the singing of swans, gave credit to that other of the Tarantula

§ Enquiry into vulgar Errors, book III. chap xxvii.

This book contains also a very precise designation of the genera with their several colours or species, as they are found in the writings of the Greek harmonicians.

From the Genera Kircher proceeds to the modes of the ancients, which, with Ptolemy, he makes to be equal with the species of diapason; from hence he digresses to those of the moderns, which, with Glareanus, he makes to be twelve in number.

Book IV. is wholly on the division of the monochord, and directs the method of finding the intervals by various geometric and algebraic processes.

Book V. entitled De Symphoniurgia, contains directions for the composition of music in consonance, a practice, which, after a very laborious search and enquiry, he pronounces the ancient Greeks to have been absolutely ignorant of. To the examples of ancient notation, by points on the lines, and not the spaces of a stave, which he had found in the Dialogo della Musica of Vincentio Galilei, he adds another, which he had procured from a friend of his, the abbot of the monastery of Vallombrosa, consisting of a stave of two lines only, with points on each, and at different stations on the space; this example, which is inserted in a former part of this work,* he makes to be of greater antiquity than the improvement of the stave by Guido.

From this method of notation he says the term Counterpoint, so well understood at this day, is derived. And here Kircher takes occasion to mention John de Muris as the original inventor of the characters for notes of different lengths. Enough has been said in the course of this work in refutation of that popular error, and to prove that the invention is not to be ascribed to De Muris, but to Franco of Liege, who flourished in the same century with Guido.

In this book Kircher explains with sufficient exactness the nature of Counterpoint, both simple and figurate; as also of Fugue, by him termed Contrapuntus Fugatus; and delivers in general terms the precepts for composition in two, three, four, and more parts.

In the course of this book he gives various examples of the ecclesiastic and theatric styles, and celebrates for their skill in the former, Orlando de Lasso, Arcadelt, Iodocus Pratensis, Palestrina, Suriano, Nanino, Christopher Morales, Cifra, and many more; and for the madrigal-style the prince of Venosa, Horatio Vecchi, and others.

Towards the close of this book he speaks of that spurious kind of fugue called Fuga in Nomine; and not only explains the nature of canon, but gives examples of canons, wonderful in their contrivance, and mentions one that may be sung by twelve million two hundred thousand voices.

In Book VI. he treats of instrumental music, and of the various instruments in use among the moderns. Almost the whole of this book is taken from the Latin work of Mersennus, and it is but in few instances that Kircher differs from his author. At the end of this book, following the order of Mersennus,

* Page 158.

he treats of bells, and gives a particular description of the great bell at Erfurth; he says it was cast in the year 1497, by Gerard Wou de Campis, at the expence of the neighbouring princes and noblemen, and citizens of Erfurth; that it is in thickness a quarter and half quarter of an ell, its height is four ells three quarters, and its exterior periphery fourteen ells and a half, and its weight two hundred and fifty-two hundred.

Kircher says that it requires twenty-four men to ring or strike this bell, besides two others, who on each side shove forward the tongue or clapper,† and that the sound of it is plainly to be heard at the distance of three German leagues; he says that its fundamental note is D sol re, but that it gives also F fa ut, making a consonance of a minor third.‡

In Book VII. is a comparison between the ancient and modern music: with respect to the former the following are his sentiments:—

'The whole of the Greek monuments of the 'ancients that are extant are the writings of Aristides 'Quintilianus, Manuel Briennius, Plutarch, Aristotle, 'Callimachus, Aristoxenus, Alypius, Ptolemy, Euclid, 'Nichomachus, Boetius, Martianus Capella and some 'others, who flourished in the last age; several of 'whose Greek manuscripts are bound up together in 'one huge tome, in the library of the Roman college, 'where they are kept as a great treasure; and if you 'carefully compare all those authors together, as 'I have done, you will find nothing so different in 'any of them but what may be found in all the 'rest. For except the analogous, coelestial, humane, 'and divine music, they all, in the first place, dwell 'on the various composition, division, and mixture 'of the tetrachords and systems of the diapason: 'secondly, they all apply themselves with great care 'to the determination of the different tones or modes: 'and, thirdly, all their industry is employed in com-'pounding and determining the three genera, the 'diatonic, chromatic, and enarmonic; and in sub-'dividing the most minute intervals. Boetius seems 'to have snatched the palm from them all by his 'most exact and ingenious description; for he has 'so fully delivered the precepts of the ancient musi-'cians, so clearly explained what was obscure, and 'so dexterously supplied what was defective, and 'written so perfectly in that most learned work of 'his, that while he shews he let none of the ancient 'music be hid, he seems not only to have described, 'but also to have restored the music of the ancients,

† Kircher's expression in the original is, 'Ut plene exaudiatur, et 'sufficienter concutiatur à 24 hominibus compulsanda est, præter quos 'bini alii requiruntur, qui ex utroque latere linguam impellant;' and this suggests a doubt whether in fact this bell is ever rung at all or not; to ring a bell, in propriety of speech, is by means of the rope and the wheel to raise it on its axis, so as to bring it to a perpendicular situation, that is to say, with its rim upwards; the pull for this purpose gives a stroke of the clapper on one side of the bell, and its descent to its original pendent situation occasions another on the other side. The action of twenty-four men in Kircher's account is not clearly described, but that of the two men whose employment it is to shove the clapper against the side of the bell, does most plainly bespeak the act of tolling and not ringing, a practice which it is said to be peculiar to England, which for that reason, and the dexterity of its inhabitants in composing and ringing musical peals wherein the sounds interchange in regular order, is called the ringing island.

‡ Whoever is desirous of knowing more about bells, may consult Hieronymus Magius, De Tintinnabulis. Amstel. 1664, in which book are many curious particulars relating to them.

'by adding to the inventions of those that went 'before him several things discovered by himself; 'so that whatever is dispersed in all the rest, may 'be seen collected, encreased, and digested with 'exquisite care in Boetius.'

In this book he gives from Alypius some fragments of antiquity as specimens of the characters for the notation of music in use among the ancient Greeks; these are inserted in an earlier part of this work. Here also he takes occasion to describe the various kinds of dancing-air in practice in his time; as namely, the Galliard, Courant, Passamezzo, the Alle-

mand, and Saraband; of all which he gives examples, composed purposely by his friend Kapsberger.

This book is of a very miscellaneous nature; and it must here suffice to say, that besides a general enumeration of the most eminent musicians of the author's time, it contains a great variety of fine compositions selected from their works; among which are a madrigal of five parts, composed by the emperor Ferdinand III., and an air in four parts by Lewis XIII. king of France, which he found in Mersennus, and is here inserted:—

LEWIS XIII. KING OF FRANCE.

He mentions also that his Catholic majesty, the then king of Spain, had with great ingenuity composed certain litanies, but that he could not procure them time enough to insert in his work.*

The second volume begins with Book VIII. en-

titled De Musurgia Mirifica; in this are contained tables of the possible combinations of numbers as they respect the musical intervals; as also a very minute investigation of the rythmic art, in which the quantities which constitute the various kinds of metre in the Greek and Latin poetry are explained and illustrated by the characters used in musical notation; with some curious observations on the Hebrew, Syriac, and Arabic poetry, and also on that of the Samaritans, Armenians, and other Orientals.

In Book IX. is a chapter intitled De Sympathiæ et Antipathiæ sonorum ratione; the experiment therein described is wonderfully curious. It supposes five drinking-glasses of the same magnitude and capacity; the first filled with aqua vitæ, the second with wine, the third with aqua subtilis, and the fourth with some thick fluid, as sea-water or oil, and the fifth or

* The above air is inserted both in the Harmonici and Harmonie Universelle of Mersennus, and is by him termed a royal Cantilena: he gives it in two forms, viz., simply, as originally composed by the king, and with variations on the two first strains by the Sieur de la Barré, organist to the king and queen. These variations, consisting of diminutions to the amount of sixty-four notes to one measure or semibreve, are calculated for the harpsichord, and reduce the air to the form of a lesson. And here, to obviate a doubt of the possibility of depressing sixty-four keys in so short a time, Mersennus assures his reader that he had frequently seen Barré do it. He also celebrates another excellent performer, who, excepting Barré, he says had not his equal in the world, the younger Cappella, styled le Baron de Chaubonniere: the father of this person was living at the time when Mersennus wrote his book; he was then fourscore years of age, and had been clavicymbalist to Henry IV. The son told Mersennus that in his performance on the harpsichord he had been much more skilful and able than himself; and that he despaired of attaining to the same degree of perfection, or of ever meeting with his equal.

middle one with common water; in which case, if a finger be wetted and rubbed round the edge of the water-glass the following effects will be produced, viz., the aqua vitæ in the first glass will be prodigiously agitated, the wine in the second but gently shaken, the aqua subtilis in the third shaken in a less degree, and the sea-water or other fluid in the fourth scarcely at all. From this experiment it may be supposed the invention of music on glasses is derived. He then produces a great variety of instances of the wonderful effects wrought by music, beginning with the dispossession of Saul as recorded in sacred writ, which he endeavours to account for mechanically. In the same manner he reasons upon the fall of the walls of the city of Jericho at the sound of the trumpets of the priests; ascribing all to physical or mechanical causes; and, in short, arguing upon principles that tend to destroy in both instances the credit of the narration. But to prove that music has power as well to excite as to subdue evil affections, he by way of contrast to the case of Saul, cites from Olaus Magnus and Krantzius the story of Ericus king of Denmark, already related in page 493 of this work.

Seeing how particular Kircher is in his relation of the effects of music on the human mind, it can hardly be supposed he would omit to mention that instance of the wonderful efficacy of it in the cure of the frenzy, which is said to be occasioned by the bite of the Tarantula; and accordingly he describes the various symptoms that are brought on by the bite of that insect, and refers to histories where an absolute cure had been wrought by the sole power of music.*

* Kircher has illustrated his account of the Tarantula by histories of cases; and first he speaks of a girl, who being bitten by this insect, could only be cured by the music of a drum. He then proceeds to relate that a certain Spaniard, trusting to the efficacy of music in the cure of the frenzy occasioned by the bite of the Tarantula, submitted to be bitten on the hand by two of these creatures, of different colours, and possessed of different qualities; the venom was no sooner diffused about his body, than the symptoms of the disorder began to appear; upon which harpers, pipers, and other musicians were sent for, who by various kinds of music endeavoured to rouse him from that stupor into which he was fallen: but here it was observed that the bites of the two insects had produced contrary effects, for by one he was incited to dance, and by the other he was restrained therefrom: and in this conflict of nature the patient expired.

The same account of the Tarantula is given in the Phonurgia nova of Kircher, with the addition of a cut representing the insect in two positions, the patient in the action of dancing, together with the musical notes of the tune or air, by which in one instance the cure was effected.

In the Musurgia Kircher attempts mechanically to account for the cure of the bite of the Tarantula by music: he says of the poison, that it is sharp, gnawing, and bilious, and that it is received and incorporated into the medullary substance of the fibres. With respect to the music, he says that the sounds of chords have a power to rarify the air to a certain harmonical pitch; and that the air thus rarified, penetrating the pores of the patient's body, affects the muscles, arteries, and minute fibres, and incites him to dance, which exercise begets a perspiration, in which the poison evaporates.

Unsatisfactory as this theory appears, the belief of this strange phenomenon has prevailed among the ablest of modern physicians. Sir Thomas Brown, so far from disputing it, says that since many attest the fact from experience, and that the learned Kircherus hath positively averred it, and set down the songs and tunes solemnly used for the cure of the disease; and since some also affirm that the Tarantula itself will dance at the sound of music, he shall not at all question it. Enquiries into Vulgar Errors, book III. chap. xxviii.

Farther, that eminent Italian physician of the last century, Baglivi, a native of Apulia, the country where the Tarantula is produced, has written a dissertation ' De anatomia morsu et effectibus Tarantulæ.' In this he describes the region of Apulia, where the Tarantula is produced, with the anatomy and figure of the insect and its eggs, illustrated by an engraving; he mentions particularly the symptoms that follow from the bite, and the cure of the disease by music, with a variety of histories of cures thus wrought, many of them communicated by persons who were eye-witnesses of the process.

Ludovicus Valetta, a Celestine monk of Apulia, published at Naples in the year 1706, a treatise upon this Spider, in which he not only answers the objections of those who deny the whole thing, but gives,

The account which he, and indeed other writers, gives of the process, is in short this: the symptoms of the disorder appearing, which in general are violent sickness, difficulty of breathing, and universal faintness; a musician is brought, who tries a variety of airs, till at last he hits upon one that rouses the patient from his stupor, and urges him to dance, the violence of which exercise produces a proportionable agitation of the vital spirits, attended with a consequent degree of perspiration, the certain presage of a cure.

The remaining part of this book is a disquisition on Echos; and to this purpose the author relates from Cardan a pretty story, which does not shock our credulity like many others in his work; and is here given in the words of the relater: ' A certain friend

from his own knowledge, several instances of persons who had suffered this way, some of whom were of great families, and so far from being dissemblers, that they would at any rate, to avoid shame, have concealed the misfortune which had befallen them.

The honourable Mr. Robert Boyle, in his treatise of languid and unheeded Motions, speaking of the bite of the Tarantula, and the cure of the disease which follows it, by means of music, says that having himself had some doubts about the matter, he was, after strict enquiry, convinced that the relations in the main were true.

Lastly, Dr. Mead, in his Mechanical Account of Poisons, Lond. 1747. has given an essay on the Tarantula, containing the substance of the above relations, which he endeavours to confirm by his own reasoning thereon.

Notwithstanding the number and weight of these authorities, and the general acquiescence of learned and ingenious men in the opinion that the bite of the Tarantula is poisonous, and that the cure of the disorder occasioned by it is effected by music, we have reason to apprehend that the whole is a mistake.

In the Philosophical Transactions for the year 1672, page 4066, is an extract of a letter from Dr. Thomas Cornelio, a Neapolitan physician, to John Doddington, Esq. his majesty's resident at Venice, communicated by the latter, in which, speaking of his intention to send to Mr. Doddington some Tarantulas, he says, ' Mean while I shall not omit to impart ' to you what was related to me a few days since by a judicious and un-' prejudiced person; which is, that being in the country of Otranto, ' where those insects are in great numbers, there was a man, who thinking ' himself stung by a Tarantula shewed in his neck a small speck, about ' which in a very short time there arose some pimples full of a serous ' humour; and that in a few hours after that poor man was sorely ' afflicted with very violent symptoms, as syncopes, very great agitations, ' giddiness of the head, and vomiting; but that without any inclination ' at all to dance, and without all desire of having any musical instru-' ments, he miserably died within two days.

' The same person affirmed to me that all those who think themselves ' bitten by Tarantulas, except such as for evil ends feign themselves to ' be so, are for the most part young wanton girls, whom the Italian ' writer calls Dolce di Sale; who, by some particular indisposition falling ' into this melancholy madness, persuade themselves, according to the ' vulgar prejudice, to have been stung by a Tarantula. And I remember ' to have observed in Calabria some women, who, seized on by some such ' accidents, were counted to be possessed with the Devil, it being the ' common belief in that province that the greatest part of the evils which ' afflict mankind proceed from evil spirits.'

He mentions also a particular kind of tumour to which the people of Calabria are subject, called in their language Covela Mallgno; and which, if attended with certain symptoms, brings on death. He says that the common opinion of this distemper is, that it befalls those only who have eaten the flesh of animals that have died a natural death; which notion he affirms to be false, with a remark, that many strange effects we daily meet with, the true cause not being known, some one is assigned upon no better ground than vulgar prejudice, which he believes to be the only foundation for the common opinion touching the cause of that distemper, which appears in those that think themselves stung by the Tarantula.

Dr. Serao, an Italian physician, as it seems has written an ingenious book, in which he has effectually exploded this opinion as a popular error; and in the Philosophical Transactions, No. LX. for the year 1770, pag. 236, is a letter from Dominico Cirillo, M.D. professor of natural history in the university of Naples, wherein taking notice of Serao's book, he says that having had an opportunity of examining the effects of this animal in the province of Taranto, where it is found in great abundance, he finds that the surprizing cure of the bite of the Tarantula by music, has not the least truth in it; and that it is only an invention of the people, who want to get a little money by dancing when they say the Tarantism begins. He adds, ' I make no doubt but sometimes the ' heat of the climate contributes very much to warm their imaginations, ' and throw them into a delirium, which may be in some measure cured ' by music; but several experiments have been tried with the Tarantula, ' and neither men nor animals after the bite have had any other com-' plaint than a very trifling inflammation upon the part, like those pro-' duced by the bite of a scorpion, which go off by themselves without any ' danger at all. In Sicily, where the summer is still warmer than in any ' part of the kingdom of Naples, the Tarantula is never dangerous. And ' music is never employed for the cure of the pretended Tarantism.'

'of mine having set out on a journey, had a river to
'cross, and not knowing the ford, cried out *Oh*, to
'which an echo answered *Oh*; he imagining it to be
'a man, called out in Italian *Onde devo passar?* it
'answered *passa*; and when he asked *qui?* it replied
'*qui*; but as the waters formed a deep whirlpool
'there, and made a great noise, he was terrified, and
'again asked *Devo passar qui?* The echo returns
'*passa qui.* He repeated the same question often,
'and still had the same answer. Terrified with the
'fear of being obliged to swim in case he attempted
'to pass there, and it being a dark and tempestuous
'night, he concluded that his respondent was some
'evil spirit that wanted to entice him into the torrent,
'wherefore he returned, and relating the story to
'Cardan, was convinced by him that it was no demon,
'but the sport of nature.'

From this account of a natural, Kircher proceeds
to a description of an artificial echo, namely, that in
the Villa Simonetta near Milan; and of a building
at Pavia, mentioned by Cardan in his treatise De
Subtilitate, which would return a sound thirty times.
As also that at Syracuse, by some called the Prison,
and by others the Ear of Dionysius, described by
Mirabella in his Ichnography of Syracuse.

From Phonic and Acoustic buildings, Kircher
proceeds to a description of Phonotactic machines,
which by the rotation of a cylinder produce music
from bells, and organs constructed for the purpose;
and here he gives a very particular description of
what he calls a Cymbalarian machine, in the form of a
star, in the church of the monastery of Fulda, so contrived, as that by the motion of a cylinder round its
axis, music is produced from a number of small bells.

He next describes an instrument, contrived to resemble in the sound of it a concert of viols; it is in
fact a harpsichord with a circular belly, under which
is a wheel, one sixth part whereof rises above the
belly of the instrument. The strings, which are required to be of the intestines of animals, like those
of the harp, are strained into contact with the edge
of this wheel, which being rubbed with powder of
rosin, produces from each a sound like that of a viol.

In this chapter Kircher mentions a contrivance of
his own, an instrument which a few years ago was
obtruded upon the public as a new invention, and
called the harp of Æolus, of which he thus speaks.

'As the following instrument is new, so also is it
'easy to construct and pleasant, and is heard in my
'museum, to the great admiration of every one. It
'is silent as long as the window, in which it is placed,
'remains shut, but as soon as it is opened, behold an
'harmonious sound on the sudden arises that asto-
'nishes the hearers; for they are not able to perceive
'from whence the sound proceeds, nor yet what kind
'of instrument it is, for it resembles neither the sound
'of a stringed, nor yet of a pneumatic instrument,
'but partakes of both. The instrument is made of
'pine wood; it is five palms long, two broad, and
'one deep; it may contain
'fifteen or more chords, all
'equal, and composed of
'the intestines of animals,
'as appears in this figure.

'The instrument is A B C D, the pegs C A, the
'bridges I K and that at the other end parallel with
'it: the chords being put round the pegs, and ex-
'tended over the bridges, are fastened to keys at B V:
'the roses are F F F; and near S is a handle by
'which it may be suspended. The method of tuning
'it now remains, which is not, as in other instruments,
'by thirds, fourths, fifths, or eighths, but all the chords
'are to be tuned to an unison, or in octaves. It is
'very wonderful, and nearly paradoxical, that chords
'thus tuned should constitute different harmony. As
'this musical phenomenon has not as yet been ob-
'served by any one that I know of, I shall describe
'the instrument very minutely, to the end that it may
'be searched into more narrowly, and the effects pro-
'duced by it accounted for. But first I shall shew
'the conditions of the instrument, and where it
'ought to be fixed.

'The instrument is to be situated in a close place,
'yet so that the air may on either side have free
'access to it: in order to which it may be observed
'that the wind may be collected by various methods;
'first by canals that are made in the form of cones
'or shells, or else by valves; for example, let there
'be two valves, E F and
'B V C D, as in the
'figure below, so joined
'together in F and V
'D, that they may how-
'ever leave a passage for
'the wind into the space
'between the two parallel
'boards F R and V D.

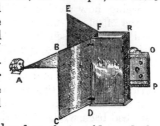

'Let the valves be placed on the outside, and the
'parallel boards on the inside of the room, at the
'back of which the instrument is to be fixed, at the
'chink S N, but so as to be turned against the chink
'in an oblique situation, that the wind being collected
'by the valves, and forced between the narrow part
'between the boards B V and E F, and going out
'through the chink, may strike all the chords of the
'instrument S O N P. When it is thus disposed
'you will perceive an harmony in the room in pro-
'portion as the wind is weaker or stronger; for
'from time to time all the chords having a tremulous
'motion impressed upon them, produce a corres-
'pondent variety of sounds, resembling a concentus
'of pipes or flutes, affecting the hearers with a strange
'pleasure.'*

In this book we also meet with a discourse on the
ancient hydraulic organ, which, from the description
of it by Vitruvius, Kircher laboured to construct;
but both his explanation, and the figure of the instrument, which he was at the pains of delineating,
and has given in the book, appear to be nothing
more than an exercise of that imagination, which
was ever at work and employed in solving difficulties.
Book X. is on the subject of Analogical music,

* It may here be remarked that many instruments, supposed to be of
very late invention, are to be found described in the writings of Mersennus and Kircher. The short bassoon, and the perpendicular harpsichord are instances to this purpose. The Lyrichord, as it is called, lately
constructed by Plenius, is evidently borrowed from an instrument
mentioned in a preceding page; and the harp of Æolus, so much celebrated as a modern discovery, is no other than the instrument here
described by Kircher.

as the author affects to term it, and tends to demonstrate the harmony of the four elements, and of the planetary system. He labours also to prove that the principles of harmony are discoverable in the proportions of our bodies, and in the passions and affections of the mind; and even in the seven sacraments of the Romish church. From these he proceeds to the consideration of political and metaphysical harmony; and, lastly, to that harmony, if any one can understand what it means, which subsists in the several orders of intellectual beings, and which is consummated in the union between God and the universe.

In the year 1673 Kircher published his Phonurgia Nova, a work in which he explains the nature, properties, powers, and effects of sound.

In the Phonurgia Nova, Sect. VI. Cap. i. the author gives a very circumstantial account of that useful instrument which we call the Speaking Trumpet, the invention whereof is generally ascribed to a native of this country, Sir Samuel Moreland,[*] but Kircher claims it as his own.

And first he relates that the motives for his attempt were drawn from that branch of the science of optics called catoptrics, and the structure of those tubes, by the help whereof curious men make observations on the sun; and that he conceived a possibility of magnifying sound by methods similar to those whereby bodies are, at least to our view, encreased beyond their true dimensions. How far his reasoning was just, or whether the sciences of optics and acoustics are founded on the same principles or not, it is not necessary here to enquire, but that he succeeded in his endeavours, and was the inventor of the instrument here spoken of, he does most positively assert.

He says, that in order to attain the end proposed, he made experiments with cylindrical, conic, and elliptic tubes, both simple and contorted, or twisted like a screw, but that he found that one of a cylindrical form succeeded best; and that this he improved by continuing it in length beyond that proportion which at first he thought sufficient for his purpose. His description of the instrument, and his relation of its effects are not a little curious, and are in these words:

* Of this instrument an account was published at London in the year 1671, wherein the author relates several experiments made by him with this instrument, the result thereof was, that a speaking trumpet constructed by him, being five feet six inches long, twenty-one inches diameter at the greater end, and two inches at the smaller, being tried at Deal castle, was heard at the distance of three miles, the wind blowing from the shore. Together with the book, which is a thin folio, entitled Tuba Stentoro-Phonica, printed for the famous Moses Pitt, bookseller in St. Paul's church-yard, was sold at his shop, the instrument itself, price 2l. 5s.

In the Philosohical Transactions, No. 141, for the year 1678, is a letter from Mr. J. Conyers, containing an account of what he calls a Reflecting Trumpet, consisting of two parts, the outermost a large concave pyramid, about a yard long, open at the base, and closed with a flat but concave head at the top, the figure then resembling a tall and very slender bell. Within this it is said a tube was fastened, which was continued from the top of the cone some inches below the base, and then returned at right angles. The letter says that this instrument was tried at Arundel-house in the Strand, where the meetings of the Royal Society were then held; and although the wind was contrary, and very strong, the sound thereof was distinctly heard across the garden of the said house, even to the other side of the Thames; whereby it appeared, that a reflecting trumpet made after this, or some like manner, of wood, tin, pewter, stone, earth, or of bell-metal, would carry the voice as far, if not farther, than the long one, invented by Mr. Samuel Moreland.

The same person attempted to improve the speaking-trumpet, by constructing it with three angular arches, instead of one reaching almost from one end to the other: but he found that little was gained by this variation of the instrument from its original form.

'There was a repository in my museum, in our 'college at Rome, parted from the rest of the building by a wall that had a gate in it; and at the end 'of the repository was a window of an oval form, 'looking into the college garden, which garden was 'about three hundred palms square. In this window 'I fixed a conic tube, composed of iron plates, 'twenty-two palms in length, the aperture whereof 'for speaking, exceeded not a quarter of a palm; 'the body of the tube was about one palm in diameter, 'but it was gradually encreased towards the further 'end to the diameter of three palms. The instrument thus constructed was placed in the window in 'a direction towards the garden.

'The Janitors or porters of our college had frequent occasions to speak to me, either to notify the 'approach of a stranger, or upon matters of a domestic concern; and as it was inconvenient for 'them to be continually coming to me, they called 'to me from the gate, and I, being in my chamber, 'heard them clearly and distinctly, and answered 'them through the tube, and was heard by them.'[†]

'To those who visited my museum, and were 'astonished to hear the effect of this instrument, 'I explained the contrivance of it; and it is scarce 'credible how many persons were drawn from distant 'cities to see and hear it.'

After having given this history of the invention of the Speaking-Trumpet, Kircher proceeds to refute the opinion that it was first discovered in England, in these words: 'I have here thought proper to 'communicate to the reader a description of this 'instrument, that he might not persuade himself that 'this was a new invention, brought out of England, 'but that it was exhibited by me in our college at 'Rome twenty-four years before the time when it is 'said to have been invented in England; and this 'many persons now living, both our own fathers, and 'also strangers, who deigned to visit my museum 'filled with rare curiosities, are able to testify.'[‡]

He then proceeds to relate that having been compelled to remove his museum to another part of the college called the Gallery, he made improvements in the tube, adapted to that place; and that he made a statue, the lips and eyes whereof, were made to move, and that by means of the tube, he uttered through it feigned and ludicrous consultations, with a view to shew the fallacy and imposture of ancient oracles.

He says that, with a desire of knowing the efficacy and power of the conic tube, he ascended the very high mountain of St. Eustachius, and took with him one of fifteen palms in length; and that in speaking through the same, he and his companions made themselves heard at different stations, two, three,

† This passage is very obscure in the original, and leaves it a question whether Kircher and the porters spoke through one or different instruments of the same kind; the latter is the most probable.

‡ To corroborate this assertion, sundry passages, extracted from the writings of other persons, are prefixed to the Phonurgia, as namely Jacobus Albanus Ghibbesius, Gaspar Schottus, and Franiscus Eschinardus; these import that the instrument called the Tuba Stentorophonica was invented by Kircher twenty years before the time when a description of it was published at London by Sir Samuel Moreland.

Kircher's museum was, as he intimates, a very curious one. A catalogue of it was published at Rome in the year 1709.

four, and five Italian miles distant from the place whence the sound was uttered; and that by means of the tube alone they called to the people of the neighbouring villages for necessaries, and were supplied; and farther, invited above two thousand of them, as by a voice from heaven, to ascend the mountain, and celebrate the feast of Pentecost, during which solemnity Kircher and his companions sung litanies through tubes of this kind constructed by him.

The works of Kircher are either on subjects of the most remote antiquity, or such as from their very nature seem to elude all enquiry; nevertheless, for his Musurgia Universalis, the world is under great obligations to him. In thus availing himself of the researches of other learned men, and also of all the assistance that he could possibly derive from an extensive correspondence, and the communications of persons the most eminent of his time in the theory and practice of music, he has exhibited such a fund of instruction and entertainment; such a diversity of curious particulars relating to the principles and gradual progress of the science, and such a number of curious anecdotes respecting the professors of his time, and the opinions entertained of their works, that we know not which to admire most, his ingenuity or industry.

But notwithstanding the merits of Kircher in these and other instances, the Musurgia soon after its publication was very severely censured by a man who had pursued the study of music with no small degree of assiduity, namely, Marcus Meibomius, of Amsterdam, of whom and his writings here follows an account.

CHAP. CXXXIV.

MARCUS MEIBOMIUS, a celebrated philologist and critic, was a native of Tonningen, in Holstein. In his advanced years he settled at Stockholm, and became a favourite of Christina, queen of Sweden. Having made a deep research into the works of the Greek writers on music, he contracted an enthusiastic fondness for the music of the ancients, and entertained an opinion not only of its superiority to that of the moderns, but that he was able to restore and introduce it into practice. The queen, who by frequent conversations with him had been made to entertain the same sentiments on the subject as himself, was easily prevailed on to listen to a proposal of his, which was to exhibit a performance of music, under his direction strictly conformable to the practice of the ancients; and, to crown all, he, who had but a bad voice, and had never in his youth been exercised in the practice of vocal music, was to sing in it. To this end instruments of various kinds were made at the expence of the queen, and under the directions of Meibomius; and public notice was given of a musical performance that was to captivate and astonish all that should be so happy as to hear it. On the appointed day Meibomius appeared, and addressing himself to sing, was heard with patience for a short time; but his performance and that of his auxiliaries was past enduring: neither the chromatic nor

the enarmonic genus suited the ears of his illiterate auditory, and the Lydian mood had lost its soothing power. In short, his hearers, unable to resist the impulses of nature, expressed their sense of the performance by general laughter.

Whatever were the feelings of the people, Meibomius was but little disposed to sympathize with them: their mirth was his disgrace, and he felt it but too sensibly: for seeing in the gallery Mons. Bourdelot the younger, a physician, and a rival of his in the queen's favour, he immediately imputed the behaviour of the people to some insinuations of his to the prejudice of the performance; and without being restrained by the presence of the queen, ran up to him, and struck him a blow on the neck; and, to avoid the consequences of his rashness, quitted the city before he could be called to account for it, and took up his residence at Copenhagen. In this latter city Meibomius was well received, and became a professor at Sora, a college in Denmark for the instruction of the nobility. Here he was honoured with the title of counsellor to the king; and soon after was called to Elsineur, and advanced to the dignity of Architeloni, or president of the board of maritime taxes or customs; but neglecting the duty of his employment, he was dismissed, and upon that occasion quitted Denmark. Soon after this he settled at Amsterdam, and became professor of history in the college there; but refusing to give private instruction to the son of a burgomaster of that city, alledging that he was not used to instruct boys but students, he was dismissed from that station. Upon this he quitted Amsterdam, and visited France and England, but afterwards returned to Amsterdam, and led a private life, and died in 1710 or 1711, having attained to a great age. He assisted in the publication of an edition of Vitruvius at Amsterdam, in 1643, wherein he has endeavoured to rectify such passages as related to music, and were misunderstood by former editors. But his great work was his edition of the seven Greek authors who had wrote on music, namely, Aristoxenus, Euclid, Nicomachus, Alypius, Gaudentius, Bacchius, and Aristides Quintilianus, of which it is here proposed to give a brief account. It was published at Amsterdam in the year 1652, and contains a general preface to the whole, and also a preface to each of the treatises as they occur, with a Latin translation of the Greek text, and copious notes, tending to reconcile various readings, and explain the meaning of the several authors. The work is dedicated to Christina, queen of Sweden, in an epistle that abounds with flattery, and is not more hyperbolical than pedantic; for, after enumerating her virtues, and celebrating her wisdom and learning, he says of her, 'tibi Hypatæ Diapason, Diapente, ac 'Diatessaron consonent.' In the general preface the author is very severe on the modern musurgists; and takes occasion to mention Kircher, whom he taxes with ignorance of Grecian literature. He then proceeds to relate that Vitruvius, in his treatise De Architectura, lib. V. cap. v. had promised a short but solid doctrine of harmonics, drawn from Aristoxenus, in order to determine the consonances of those echoing vessels which he proposed to place in the theatres of Rome; which doctrine, by a fate common to the works of ancient authors, came to the hands of Meibomius obscured with foul defects, and that he laboured for three years to restore it; but that Kircher, who also applied himself to the same laudable endeavour, has rendered the whole doctrine of Vitruvius erroneous. He farther censures Kircher for disregarding the niceties of grammar, and for the use of what he calls barbarous terms, such as Sesquitertias, Sesquiquartus, Sesquioctavus, instead of Supertertias, Superquartus, Superoctavus. He adds that the word Musurgia, the title of Kircher's work, and which he uses for Opus de Musica, is not warranted by the authority of any one Greek writer, but is repugnant to the analogy observed in the formation of compound words, and signifies a musical operation. Again he censures Kircher for this passage in the Musurgia, page 133, 'Aristoxenus semitonia putat 'esse dimidia tonorum. Hunc secutus Martianus 'Felix turpiori adhuc errore lapsus deprehenditur, 'qui non modo tonum in duas œquales, sed in 3 et 4 'dirimit atque secat partes.' 'What fouler error,' says Meibomius, 'could this man, Kircher, fall into, 'than to imagine that Martianus Capella, who was 'a mere copier of Aristides Quintilianus, and not 'a very exact one neither, should be the inventor of 'any thing new in music? Did Kircher,' exclaims Meibomius, 'ever read Aristoxenus, or any of the 'ancients? Did he ever read Boetius, who in express 'words attributes this division to Aristoxenus, in 'lib. V. cap. xv?' He proceeds to censure Kircher for his ignorance in the Greek language, as also for the many errors which he says are to be found in that plate in the Musurgia which exhibits the ancient Greek musical characters. And here Meibomius takes occasion to mention a visit which Ismael Bullialdus made him at Amsterdam, in the autumn previous to the publication of his book, and of the conversation between them: he says that Bullialdus informed him that Mersennus was then employed in translating Bacchius into the French language; and that upon Meibomius's shewing him many remarks which he had made on Bacchius, Claudentius, Euclid, and other ancient writers, Bullialdus generally acquiesced in his opinions. He remarks that Kircher, in the Musurgia, page 139, mentions Archytas, Didymus, Eratosthenes, and other authors, whose manuscripts he says he has in possession: 'I think,' says Meibomius, 'he must in this particular be 'mistaken; for, excepting their several divisions of 'the three genera, which are to be found at the end 'of Ptolemy's second book of Harmonics, there are 'no writings on music of either of these three persons 'recorded to be extant,' and he wishes that Kircher would publish them for the satisfaction of himself and others.* He says that the world is greatly mistaken in supposing that Guido enlarged the ancient system by the addition either of chords below or above it; for he asserts that they assumed a chord below Proslambanomenos, and afterwards rejected it, as producing a confused and undistinguishable

sound; but that Guido reassumed it, and marked it with the Greek letter Γ; and that the ancients proceeded farther in the acutes than Guido did, he says is evident from the tables of the three genera.

In this preface Meibomius takes occasion to introduce the Te Deum with ancient musical notes, concerning which he says there is no doubt but that this melody was used by St. Augustine and St. Ambrose, though perhaps it may have been corrupted in some measure since their time. At the close of this general preface he mentions that French translation of Bacchius by Mersennus, of which he had received information from Ismael Bullialdus, and says that immediately upon notice of it he sent to Paris for the book. He charges Mersennus with having omitted many difficult passages and mistaken others; and concludes, that if he had seen this translation before he had finished his notes on Bacchius, they would have been much fuller by his observations on the errors of Mersennus.

Besides the general preface of Meibomius, he has given one also to each of the Greek authors published by him: these chiefly relate to certain manuscripts of each, with which he was furnished by many learned men his contemporaries, whom he celebrates; among whom are Daniel Heinsius, Claudius Salmasius, and our countrymen Selden and Dr. Gerard Langbaine.

To his edition of the seven Greek authors Meibomius has added a treatise De Musica of Martianus Mineus Felix Capella, that is to say, lib. IX. of that author's work, entitled De Nuptiis Philologiæ et Mercurii. Martianus Capella has in some sort abridged Aristides Quintilianus; and it seemed right to Meibomius to give the work at large, and also the abridgement, with notes on each. The treatise De Nuptiis Philologiæ et Mercurii is in Latin; an account of it, as also of its author, is elsewhere given in this work. The edition published by Meibomius of the seven Greek authors, with a translation, and also of Martianus Capella with notes, was doubtless a very considerable acquisition to the science of music: the manuscripts of each of them had been brought into Europe by those learned Greeks who escaped at the sacking of Constantinople, and settling in Italy, became the revivers of learning; these were by accidents of various kinds dispersed; copies were made of them, which inevitably multiplied various readings; few persons knew where to find them; and they never having been brought together into one point of view, the very existence of some of the tracts which Meibomius has given to the world was a matter of doubt with the learned.

But notwithstanding the care and industry of Meibomius, manifested in the publication of this work, his manner of introducing it is justly reprehensible; for his general preface abounds with invectives against all who presumed to think less highly of the ancient music than himself, more especially Kircher. The Musurgia of Kircher is to be considered as an original work, very comprehensive in its extent, and formed from a great variety of materials; in the compilation of it, it must be supposed that the author attended more to the sub-

* This remark is justly founded, for the authors therein mentioned are enumerated among the Scriptores perditi.

ject matter of it than to the style : it appears therefore a very pedantic and froward behaviour in Meibomius to object to the Musurgia, which abounds with learning, and a great variety of curious and entertaining particulars, the want of that grammatical nicety and exactness, which few, except men of narrow and contracted minds, are apt to excel in.

But it is not of Kircher alone that Meibomius affects to speak in terms of contempt : Mersennus, who was possessed of more musical science than any man of his time, has hardly escaped his censure for errors pretended to be made by him in his translation of Bacchius ; nor has his friend Ismael Bullialdus met with better treatment in respect of his version of Theo. Smyrnæus. Indeed little less than such behaviour to those who differed from him was to be expected from a man so bigoted as Meibomius appears to have been, and whose irascible temper seems, by the relation contained in the account of his life, to have been incapable of restraint within the bounds of decency.

CHAP. CXXXV.

Pietro Mengoli, a musician and mathematician of Bologna, was the author of a work entitled Speculationi di Musica, printed at Bologna in the year 1670. In the proem to this book he gives an account of himself and the course of his studies to the following effect, viz., that he began to sing when he was ten years old ; and being arrived at the age of eighteen, applied himself very closely to the study of the theory of music ; and at the end of fourteen years, that is to say, in the year 1658, having, as he conceived, made very important discoveries, he undertook to read public lectures on music in several schools, wherein, besides his own doctrines, he endeavoured to explain those which Zarlino and Galileo had taught before him : That having instructed a gentleman, namely, Signor Ercole Zani, in the elements of music, this person directed a monochord to be made for the purpose of discovering the nature of consonance and dissonance, and the physical causes that render them severally grateful, or the contrary, 'o the sense of hearing ; but that in this enquiry they could never satisfy themselves, they having all along taken that for granted which they found to be wrong, namely, that concord arises from the frequent union of two sounds striking at the same instant the external drum of the ear : That Signor Ercole being however resolved to find out the truth, proposed what should have been thought of before, that is to say, to see and examine the organ of hearing ; they therefore applied to Gio. Galeazzo Manzi, a skilful anatomist, and a doctor of physic in the university of Bologna, who demonstrated to them that in the human ear there are three small bones bound together ; and that in the ear are contained not only one Tympanum, as other professors have thought, but two drums, the one, with respect to its situation in the ear, external, the other internal : and that the same person likewise shewed to them the cavity of the ear and its mouth ; and that after having made his

observations thereon, the author began to commit to writing his speculations, which he encreased afterwards by degrees, adding thereto whatever he thought necessary to the elucidation of his subject.

The proem to this work is succeeded by what the author terms the Natural History of music, in which are many curious particulars, the result of his anatomical researches ; the purport of it, as it is given in the Philosophical Transactions, is as follows :—

'A sound begins from the collision of two parts of 'the air, which separating, make a vacuum as to the 'air, in which vacuum two other parcels of air meet 'and strike each other ; and because the two first 'parcels of air incline to return to the centre of the 'collision, but cannot, because their room is taken 'up, they part from the centre by lines curved, and 'as it were recurring to their first place ; in the 'doing whereof they make a collision with those 'parts of the air, which have possessed themselves 'of their room, and thus the species of sound are mul-'tiplied and extended. These curved lines are more 'waving near the centre of the collision, as being 'more stretched long-ways than spirally, and less 'waving where they are farther from the centre ; in 'which latter lines the inclination to return towards 'the centre is prevalent above the impetus of receding 'from it ; so that at last they return back towards 'the centre. Thus of the species of sound there is 'filled a sphere of air, or such a part of a sphere of it, 'as this motion of the air can without impediment 'spread itself through. In the like manner two 'sounds from two centres, one within the sonorous 'sphere of the other, begin and are distributed 'through the small particles of the air, in such a 'manner, that some of the pulses are affected by one 'sound, and others, without confusion, by another ; 'and that the pulses of the acuter sound are swifter, 'and complete their pulses in a shorter time than 'those of a grave sound, which are slower and longer. 'The Aura or subtile matter in which these motions 'of the air are made, according to its comparable 'subtility, and that property it has of being altogether 'indifferent to any condition of bodies, and suited 'exactly to represent any motion, or stamp, or weight 'of other bodies, among which it is found ; this Aura 'does not impede, but assists the two motions pro-'duced by these two sorts of pulses, it being affected 'by all the intermediate motions. There may be 'also more sounds than two distributed through the 'particles of the air, yet not without some confusion ; 'and the more sounds there are, the more irregular 'will the distribution of the pulses be, especially near 'the centres themselves where the sounds begin. 'The ear is an organ by which a man placed in a 'sonorous sphere perceives and judges of sounds and 'their habitudes, whether of consonance or dissonance. 'This organ has three parts, the exterior, without 'the cavity of the ear, and visibly extant on the 'head ; the middlemost, which is the cavity itself ; 'and the innermost, which being within the cavity, 'is a bone, resembling in substance a spunge, in 'which is a cavern recurring to the hollow part of 'the ear, and shaped like a knot of ribbons ; and in

'all the holes of this spungy-like bone are found
'webs stretched out, that inclose the air. The
'middle part is closed up by two membranes, called
'drums, which are stretched over the cavity of the
'ear; and of these two the one is external, at the
'bottom of the exterior part of the air; and the
'other internal, upon the mouth of the cavern:
'between these drums are three small bones tied to
'one another, and to the drums, and fastened in two
'points to the sides of the cavity, and movable, so
'that if the outward drum be made to shake, the
'inward must shake also, and that twice as often.
'The inclination of these two drums is to move in
'duple proportion,* but the exigency of the instru-
'ment moves them differently from their inclinations:
'so that this is the sensitive organ in which the soul
'perceives what is acted there. Between these
'drums is no air,† properly so called, but only an
'Aura,‡ which seconding the inclinations of the
'drums to motion, and the motions themselves,
'preserves all the intermediate inclinations and
'motions; and the mind is able to contemplate the
'intermediate inclinations and motions of the Aura.
'If the ear be within a sonorous sphere, the particles
'of the air affected by the sound enter at the ex-
'ternal part of the ear one after another, passing in
'order through the spiral ways that are there to the
'bottom of the ear, and striking the drum, after
'which they issue out by other spiral ways, and give
'place to other particles of air. The external drum
'being struck once, shakes frequently, and, by means
'of these three little bones the internal drum answers
'to it in a double frequency; and the Aura in the
'cavern of the internal part of the ear, goes and
'comes alternately through its knot-like passage;
'spreading itself through the other ways of the
'spungy-like bone, and, being repercussed to the
'webs that inclose it, rebounds and multiplies the
'sound, until another parcel of air follows and strikes
'the drum, and causes the shaking as before. But
'if the ear be within two sonorous spheres, the
'affected pulses that cause the sound succeed the
'one the other, and by turns strike the outward
'drum; and, by the exigencies of the alternations,
'the ratios that are not expressible by numbers, are
'yet by the shakings of the drum rendered capable of
'being numbered.'

The above extracts contain in substance the
doctrines delivered in that part of the work now
under consideration, which the author calls his
Natural history of music; and these being premised, he gives a very particular description of the
ear, together with the phenomena of sound, and of
the hearing of sounds, especially two together, in
which description occur many new principles, by
him laid down as the chief foundation of the whole

work: after which he treats of musical intervals,
their perfections, and measure; explicating his doctrine by many theorems, giving withal definitions of
the several intervals, and taking particular notice of
six sorts of them, for which having found no names,
he has thought fit to borrow names from colours.
Next he discourses at large of the true numbers for
the musical intervals, shewing withal between what
numbers the species of each interval are most perfect.
Further he treats of musical chords; then of singing,
and of the modulations of tune; which latter he
distinguishes from singing in general, by observing
that modulation is a succession of sounds, impressing
itself so strongly upon the sense that we are able to
repeat it.

Besides this the author discourses amply of consonance, and of harmonical proportions; as also of
the passions of the soul, shewing how they are concerned in, and wrought upon by music; after which
he gives a table of the several musical chords suited
to the several affections, and concludes with a brief
discourse on the music of the moderns. §

JOHANN ROSENMULLER was a Saxon by birth, and
a joint professor of music with Tobias Michaelis in
the academy of St. Thomas at Leipsic, until, being
suspected of an unnatural vice, he was imprisoned;
but he found means to escape, and fled to Hamburg.
After some stay in that city he went to Italy, where
he was greatly esteemed for his skill and performance
on the organ, and published many compositions,
particularly Sonate da Camera à 5 Stromenti, and
a collection of airs of various kinds. At length he
became chapel-master in the great church at Wolfenbuttle, and died in the year 1685.

JOHANN THEIL, of Naumburg, was the son of
a tailor, and was born on the twenty-ninth day of
July, 1646. He received his first instructions in
music from 　　　　Scheffler, at that time the principal
musician of that city, and completed his studies in
the universities of Halle and Leipsic. From thence
he went to Weissenfels in Saxony; and under Schutz,
the chapel-master there, perfected himself in the art
of composition. Being thus qualified, he removed to
Stettin in Pomerania, and became a teacher of music;
and, among many others, had for his pupils Dietrich
Buxtehude, afterwards the famous organist of the
church of St. Mary in Lubec; and Zachau, the first
preceptor of Handel. In the year 1673 Thiel became
chapel-master at Gottorp; but being driven thence
by the wars, he went and settled at Hamburg, where
he continued for some years to teach the science of
music. In the year 1685 he accepted a call from the
magistracy of Wolfenbuttle to the office of chapel-
master, in the room of Rosenmuller, then lately

---

* Ital. Proportione dimidiati della doppia.

† Though the author will admit of no air properly so called between
the drums, yet he admits of air in the caverns, and within the Os
petrosum, the inward part of the ear, because the drums would have no
motion at all if there were nothing but Aura; forasmuch as this Aura,
though it may be moved by any other thing, yet it cannot be a means to
convey motion from one body to another: It is, says he, the internal
instrument of the mover that lodges there within, but not of any mover
that is without.

‡ AURA, a gentle gale or blast of wind, Altieri.

§ An account of this treatise of Mengoli is given in the Philosophical
Transactions, vol. VIII. No. C. page 6194, which, for the purpose of the
above article, has been compared with the original. At the close of the
account is this singular passage: 'Now whether this author has by all
'these speculations and pains given a perfect scale of music according
'to the true proportions of sounds (which is a great desideratum in
'music) we must leave to the judgment of the great masters, especially
'the judicious and extraordinary skilful musician Mr. John Birchensha,
'who it is still hoped, if he be competently encouraged and assisted, will
'in due time publish a complete system of music.' Of this man an
account will hereafter be given, as also of the boasting proposal here
alluded to, which, for want of encouragement, or perhaps other reasons,
was never fulfilled.

deceased, and held it for some years; after which he went into the service of Christian II. duke of Merseburg, and continued therein till the death of that prince. In the course of these his employments he made a great variety of compositions for the church, most excellent in their kind. For one mass of his, which was performed in the chapel of the Imperial court, he received at the hands of Heer Schmeltzer, a present of an hundred Rix-dollars. Many other presents he received from the emperor Leopold, and the queen of Prussia, both of whom entertained a great regard for him, and set a great value on his works. His compositions are chiefly masses, in some of which he professes to imitate the elegant and majestic style of Palestrina. He was also the author of a most valuable work, of which the following is the title at large. ' Novæ Sonatæ ' rarissimæ artis et suavitatis musicæ, partim 2 vocum, ' cum simplis et duplo inversis Fugis; partim 3 ' vocum, cum simplis, duplo et triplo inversis Fugis; ' partim 4 vocum, cum simplis, duplo et triplo et ' quadruplo inversis Fugis; partim 5 vocum, cum ' simplis, duplo, triplo, quadruplo aliasque variegatis ' inventionibus et artificiosis Syncopationibus. Summa ' 50 Sonatæ. Accedunt 50 Præludia 2, 3, 4 et 5 ' vocum, cum simplo, et duplo syncopato Contra- ' puncto. 50 Allem. et totidem Cour. 2, 3 et 4 ' vocum, cum brevibus Fugis similibusque aliis in- ' ventionibus suavissimis. 50 Ariæ et 50 Sarab. 2, ' 3 et 4 vocum, singularis gratissimæque suavitatis. ' 50 Ghique 2, 3, 4 et 5 vocum, cum simplicis et ' duplo variique generis inversis Fugis.'

From the clear evidence of deep learning and a prolific invention contained in these his works, Theil is justly ranked among the first of the German musicians. He had a son named Benedict Frederic, who had been a theorbist in the chapel of the duke of Wolfenbuttle, and afterwards became organist of the church of St. Wentzel in Naumburg, at whose house in that city Thiel died, in the year 1724, having attained the age of near fourscore, leaving behind him the character of a sound musician, and a virtuous and good man.

There was another famous musician contemporary with him above named, Andrew Theil, the author of a fine collection of lessons, entitled **Neuer Clabien Übung,** published in the year 1696, of whom notice is taken by Walther.

FRIEDRICH WILHELM ZACHAU, born at Leipsic in the month of November, 1663, was the son of a musician, and was by him instructed in the rudiments of music till he was of an age sufficient to entitle him to a reception into the public school at Leipsic, where he attained to a competent skill in the science, and became an excellent performer on the organ and other instruments. He finished his studies in music under Theil at Stettin, and in the year 1684 was called to the office of organist of the church of Our Lady, at Halle in Saxony, and continued therein till the day of his death, which was the fourteenth of August, 1721. He composed many pieces for the church, and some lessons for the clavier or harpsichord. His eminence in his faculty occasioned a great resort of young persons to him for instruction; and it is no small addition to his reputation that he was the master of Mr. Handel.

JOHANN PHILIP KRIEGER, the son of an eminent merchant of Nuremberg, born the twenty-sixth day of February, 1649, began to learn the clavier or harpsichord when he was but eight years of age, of Johann Drechsel who had been a disciple of Froberger. At the age of sixteen he was placed under the care of Johann Schroder of Copenhagen, organist of the church of St. Peter in that city: after five years continuance there, during which time he received considerable improvement under the royal chapel-master Forster, he went to Holland, and from thence to Bareith, where he became first chamber-organist to the Margrave, and afterwards chapel-master in that city. In the year 1672 he went to Italy, and at Rome considerably improved himself by the instructions of Abbatini, and Pasquini the famous performer on the harpsichord. On his return homewards he stayed some time at Naples, and took lessons from Rovetta, the organist of the church of St. Mark in that city. After a stay of some months he returned to Germany, determined to settle at Vienna, where he had no sooner arrived than he was invited by the emperor to court, who, after hearing him, presented him with a purse of ducats and a gold medal and chain: he continued in the service of the emperor some years, retaining, with the permission of the Margrave, his place of chapel-master of Bareith. Afterwards being invited to settle at Halle, he went thither, and at length became chapel-master to the elector of Saxony at the court of Weissenfels, which function he exercised near forty years, and died in the month of February, 1727.

The works of Krieger are of various kinds; they consist of Sonatas for the violin and viol da gamba, Field Music, or Overtures for trumpets and other sonorous instruments; Latin and German Psalms set to music; and, lastly, Songs in the several dramatic entertainments composed by him, entitled Flora, Cecrops, and Procris. Lessons of his for the harpsichord are also to be met with in manuscript, which have a masterly appearance; but it is no where said that he published any compositions for that instrument.

CHAP. CXXXVI.

JEAN BAPTISTE LULLY *(a Portrait)*, a celebrated musician, was born at Florence in the year 1634, of obscure parents; but discovering, even in his infancy, a propensity to music, a Cordelier, who had taken notice of him, undertook, for no other consideration than the hope of making him one day eminent in the science, to teach him the practice of the guitar, an instrument then much in use in most parts of Italy.

It happened that while Lully was under the tuition of this benevolent ecclesiastic, a French gentleman, the Chevalier Guise, then upon his travels, arrived at Florence; this person, upon his taking leave of Mademoiselle de Montpensier, a *cousin* of Lewis XIV.

JEAN BAPTISTE LULLY,

SECRETAIRE DU ROY ET SURINTEN-

DANT DE SA MUSIQUE.

at Paris, had been requested by her to find out some pretty little Italian, to be about her person in quality of a page ; and though the countenance of Lully did by no means answer to the instructions he had received, his vivacity and ready wit, and, above all, the proficiency which he had attained to on an instrument as much the favorite of the French as of the Italians, made him forget all other considerations ; and, trusting to these recommendations, he easily persuaded Lully, then about ten years of age, to follow him to Paris. Upon his arrival there, Lully met with but a cool reception from the lady for whose service he was intended. She liked not his appearance, which was mean and unpromising ; and, declining to retain him as a servant about her person, she assigned him a station which she thought best suited with his appearance, in her kitchen, and commanded the officers of her household to enter him in their books as her under-scullion.

Neither the disappointment which he had met with, nor the sordid employment to which he was destined, affected the spirit of Lully : in the moments of his leisure from the kitchen he used to scrape upon a scurvy fiddle, which the strong propensity that impelled him to music made him contrive to procure. A person about the court, the Count de Nogent, as it is said, happened to hear him, and informed the princess that her scullion had both talents and a hand. She thereupon employed a master to teach him the violin ; and Lully in a few months became so good a proficient, that he was sent for up to the chamber from whence his figure had before banished him ; and now behold him in the rank of musicians. But an unlucky accident, and his own indiscretion, occasioned his discharge from her service. The following stanza of Bardou will explain it :—

> Mon cœur outré de déplaisirs,
> Etroit si gros de ses soûpirs ;
> Voyant vôtre cœur si farouche :
> Que l'un d'eux se voyant réduit
> A ne pas sortir par la bouche,
> Sortit par un autre conduit.

A sigh of this nature, which had escaped his mistress in her private closet, was very plainly heard by Lully in his chamber, and he was foolish enough not only to mention it, but to set to music the verses above quoted, which had been scribbled on the occasion, and was very deservedly dismissed for his pains.

The lady did not follow her resentment, and Lully found means to get himself entered among the king's violins : some say that at first he was only their boy, that carried their instruments ; be that as it may, he plied his studies so closely, that in a little time he became able to compose ; and some of his airs being noticed by the king, he called for the author, and was so struck with his performance of them on the violin, on which instrument Lully was now become a master, that he created a new band, called Les petits Violons, and placed him at the head of it ; and under his direction it soon surpassed the famous band of twenty-four, till then the most celebrated in Europe. This was about the year 1660, at which

time the favorite entertainments at the French court, were representations of the dramatic kind, called Ballets ; these consisted of dancing, intermixed with action, and speaking in recitative ; and to many of them Lully composed the music.

Entertainments of this kind suited not those ideas of grandeur and magnificence that filled the mind of the king : an academy had been established at Venice for the performance of operas, and Lewis determined to have one in France that should if possible exceed it. Cardinal Mazarine encouraged this disposition ; accordingly in the year 1669 the king granted to the Abbé Perrin, master of the ceremonies to Philip duke of Orleans, a privilege for the purpose of conducting an opera, to be performed in the French language, but after the model of that at Venice.

Perrin had a talent for poetry ; he immediately engaged with Cambert, the organist of St Honoré ; this person had been sur-intendant de la musique to the queen mother, Ann of Austria, and the Marquis de Sourdeac, and was esteemed the best musician in France : the fruit of their joint labours was the opera of Pomone, which was performed in March, 1670, with universal applause ; but Lully having by this time gotten possession of the public, and indeed of the king's ear, and having been appointed Sur-intendant de la musique de la chambre du Roy, he soon found means to make the situation of Cambert so very uneasy, that he was glad for a consideration in money, backed with the injunctions of his sovereign to quit it, and Lully was immediately appointed to fill his place.* Upon this Lully associated himself with Quinault, who was appointed to write the operas : and being now become composer and joint director of the opera, he did not only detach himself from the former band, and instituted one of his own, but he determined on the building a new theatre near the Luxemburg palace, and in a short time accomplished it, agreeably to a design of Vigarini, an Italian architect.

The first musical performance in this newly erected theatre was in the month of November in the same year, 1670, of an entertainment consisting of a variety of detached pieces, included under the title of Le Combat de l'Amour et de Bacchus.

From the day that the king made him superintendent of his music Lully neglected the violin so much, that he even had not one in his house : whether it was vanity that made him put away from his sight

---

* Cambert retired to England in 1672, and was favoured by Charles II. he performed his Pomone here, but with indifferent success ; and died with grief, as it is said, in 1677. His death is thus accounted for by Bourdelot, 'Mais l'envie, qui est inséparable du mérite, lui abregea les 'jours. Les Anglois ne trouvent pas bon qu'un etrangér se mêle de 'leur plaire et de les instruire. Le pauvre garçon mourut là un peu 'plutôt qu'il ne seroit mort ailleurs.' Hist. de la Musique et de ses Effets, tom. III. pag. 164. A modest reflection in the mouth of a man whose country has produced fewer good musicians than any in Europe.

Perhaps one reason of the dislike of the English to Cambert's Pomone, was that the opera was a kind of entertainment to which they had not been accustomed ; another might be that the levity of the French musical drama is but ill suited to the taste of such as have a relish for harmony. The operas of Lully consist of recitatives, short airs, chiefly gavots, minuets, and courants, set to words ; and choruses in counterpoint, with entrées, and splendid dances, and a great variety of scenery ; and, in short, were such entertainments as none but a Frenchman could sit to hear, and it was never pretended that those of Cambert were at all better.

an instrument that could not but recall to his remembrance his employment in her highness's kitchen; or whether his attachment to his studies, and the duties of his station, and the obligation he was under to gratify the call for new compositions, induced him to free himself from his subjection to an instrument that requires assiduity and unremitted practice, it is difficult to determine: be this as it will, his performance on the violin, even in this state of desuetude, was so excellent as to attract the admiration of all who heard him; though it must be confessed, that after he was appointed to the direction of the opera, these were very few; his usual answer, even to such persons of rank about the court, as requested to hear from him an air on the violin, being, that he looked upon himself as engaged to acknowledge only one master, the Marshal de Grammont, who alone had the power to make him play from time to time upon it. This nobleman had a servant named La Lande, whom he afterwards made his valet, and who became one of the best performers on the violin of any in Europe; one day at the end of a meal the Marshal desired Lully to hear his valet, and give him a few instructions; La Lande came and played, and, without doubt, to the best of his power, but Lully, more attentive to his defects than his excellencies, whenever he erred would snatch the instrument out of his hand, and, under the notion of teaching him, would indulge the enthusiastic spirit that at the instant seized him, and play on it sometimes for three hours, and at length became so enraptured with the music, as to lay down the instrument with regret.*

On the other hand, to the guitar, a trifling instrument, Lully retained throughout his life such a propensity, that for his amusement he resorted to it voluntarily; and to perform on it, even before strangers, needed no incentive. The reason of this seeming perverseness of temper is thus accounted for: the guitar is an instrument of small estimation among persons skilled in music, the power of performing on it is attained without much difficulty; and, so far as regards the reputation of the performer, it is of small moment whether he plays very well on it; but the performance on the violin is a delicate and an arduous energy; this Lully knew, and he set too high a value on the reputation he had acquired when in constant practice, to risk the losing it.

In the year 1686 the king was seized with an indisposition that threatened his life, but, recovering from it, Lully was required to compose a Te Deum for the celebration of so providential an event; accordingly he did compose one, which is not more remarkable for its excellence than for the unhappy accident that attended the performance of it. He had neglected nothing in the composition of the music, and the preparations for the executing of it; and, the better to demonstrate his zeal, he himself beat the time: with the cane he used for this purpose he struck himself in the heat of action, a blow upon the end of his foot; this caused a small blister to arise thereon, which encreasing, Mons. Alliot, his

physician, advised him immediately to have his little toe cut off, and, after a delay of some days, the foot, and at length the whole limb: at this juncture an adventurer in physic presented himself, who hardily offered to cure the patient without an amputation. The family of Vendome, who loved Lully, promised this quack two thousand pistoles in case he should accomplish the cure; but this act of beneficence, and the efforts of the empiric, were in vain. Lully died on the twenty-second day of March, 1687, and was interred in the church of the discalceat Augustines at Paris, where a fine monument for him is yet remaining. His wife was the daughter of Michael Lambert, an excellent performer on the lute, and composer and Maître de la Musique de la Chambre du Roy. He had by her, living at his decease, three sons and three daughters.

A story is related of a conversation between Lully and his confessor in his last illness, which proves the archness of the one, and the folly of the other, to this purpose: for some years before the accident that occasioned his illness, Lully had been closely engaged in composing for the opera; the priest took occasion from hence to insinuate, that unless, as a testimony of his sincere repentance for all the errors of his past life he would throw the last of his compositions into the fire, he must expect no absolution. Lully at first would have excused himself, but after some opposition he acquiesced; and pointing to a drawer wherein the draft of Achilles and Polixene lay, it was taken out and burnt, and the confessor went away satisfied. Lully grew better, and was thought to be out of danger. One of the young princes, who loved Lully and his works, came to see him; and 'What, Baptiste,' says he to him, 'have you thrown your opera into 'the fire? you were a fool for giving credit thus to 'a dreaming Jansenist, and burning good music.' 'Hush, hush, my Lord,' answered Lully in a whisper, 'I knew very well what I was about, I have a fair 'copy of it.' Unhappily this ill-timed pleasure was followed by a relapse; the gangrene increased, and the prospect of inevitable death threw him into such pangs of remorse, that he submitted to be laid upon a heap of ashes, with a cord about his neck. In this situation he expressed a deep sense of his late transgression; and, being replaced in his bed, he, farther to expiate his offence, sung, to an air of his own composing, the following words:—

Il faut mourir pécheur il faut mourir.

With respect to his person, Lully was of a thicker and shorter make than his prints represent; in other respects they sufficiently resemble him. His countenance was lively and singular, but by no means noble; his complexion was black, eyes small, nose big, and mouth large and prominent; and his sight was so short, that he could hardly distinguish the features of those whom he conversed with. In his temper there was a mixture of dignity and gentleness; and it must be said to his praise that he behaved without pride or haughtiness to the lowest musician; and yet he had less of what is generally denominated politeness in his manner, than was to be expected from a man who had lived a

* Many stories of the like kind are related of Geminiani whose temper was such as renders them credible.

long time in a refined court. He had the gaiety of a Frenchman, with a little of the libertine, as far as regards wine and food, and no farther; for it was never known that he had any criminal connexion with women; but he was so far from being without a tincture of avarice, that in some instances it is said he was sordid; and that this disposition moved him to fall out with Fontaine, whom he contrived to curtail of his pay because he had inserted in an opera some words that Lully disliked. This at least must be allowed, that he knew the value of wealth, for it is said that he left behind him in ready money the sum of six hundred and thirty thousand livres.

The courtiers called Lully a miser, not because he did not often entertain them, but because he entertained them without profusion; the excuse he made was that of a man of sense: he declared that he would not imitate those who prepare costly banquets for noblemen, and are laughed at by them for their pains. He had a vivacity fertile in sallies of original wit, and told a story with admirable humour. These are the particulars of his life and general character, it now remains to speak of him as a musician.

At the time when Lully was placed at the head of the little band of violins, not half the musicians in France were able to play at sight: he was accounted an excellent master that could play thorough-bass on the harpsichord or theorbo in accompaniment to a scholar; and, with respect to composition, nothing can be conceived more inartificial than the sonatas and airs for violins of that time. The treble part contained the whole of the melody; the bass and the interior part were mere accompaniment, and the

whole was a gross and sullen counterpoint. The combinations of sounds then allowed of were too few to admit of sufficient variety; and the art of preparing and resolving discords was a secret too precious to be communicated. In every of these respects did Lully improve the music of France; farther in his overtures he introduced fugues, and in chorusses he first made use of the side and kettle-drum.

To speak of his style is a matter of some difficulty. He quitted Italy before he was old enough to receive any impressions either of melody or harmony, so that his cannot be said to be the style of the Italians; nor could it be that of the French, for at the time of his arrival at Paris there was among them no style at all; in short, his style was his own, original, self-formed, and derived from no other source than the copious fountain of his own invention.

After the account above given, it would be needless to mention that the compositions of Lully were chiefly operas, and other dramatic entertainments: these, though excellent in their kind, would give but little pleasure at this day, the airs being very short, formed of regular measures, and too frequently interrupted by the recitatives; the reason whereof is, that Lewis XIV. was very fond of dancing, and had no taste for any music but airs, in the composition whereof a stated and precise number of bars was the chief rule to be observed; of harmony, or fine melody, or of the relation between poetry and music, he seems to have had no conception.* The following composition, taken from his Roland, may serve as a specimen of the style of Lully's opera airs :—

ROLAND, cou - rez aux ar - mes, aux ar - - - mes, cou - rez aux ar - mes, Que la Glo - ire a de char - mes! Que la Glo -ire a de char - - mes! L'Amour de ses di - vins ap - pas Fait vivre au de la du tré - pas, L'Amour de ses di - vins ap - pas Fait

* In a contest between *Baptistin*, a scholar of Corelli, and one of the French band, an ordinary performer, Lewis preferred an air in Cadmus, an opera of Lully, and none of his best, to a solo, probably of Corelli, played by the former, saying, ' Voila mon goût, à moi: Voila mon goût.' Hist. Mus. et ses Effets, tom III. page 321. And it is said of Lully, that to comply with the taste of his master, he laboured as much in composing the dances as the airs of his operas. Ib. 209. *The person* *above-mentioned, a Florentine by birth, whether because of the smallness of his stature, or with reference to Lully, whose name was Baptiste, is by the French called le petit Baptiste. He was a scholar and the adopted son of Corelli, and is said to have first introduced the Violoncello into France. He composed three operas, Melagre, Mants la Fee, and Polydore; but is most celebrated for his cantatas; one whereof, viz., Democrite et Heraclite, the French hold in great estimation. He died so lately as the year* 1740.

vivre au de la du tré-pas. Roland, cou-rez aux ar-mes, aux ar—

—mes, cou-rez . . . . aux ar-mes; Que la Glo-ire a de charmes! Que la Glo-ire a de char - - mes!

JEAN BAPTISTE LULLY.

The merit of Lully is therefore to be judged of by his overtures, and works of a more serious nature than his operas. Some motets of his are extant, though not in print; and Mons. Perrault, in his account of Lully among the Eloges Historiques, mentions a Tenebræ* of his, which at the performance of that solemn service, of which it is a part, excited such an universal approbation, that, for the merit of having composed it, the king was prevailed on to appoint him Sur-Intendant of his music, and to confer on him some honours that seem to be little more than titular.†

His opera and other compositions for the theatre were from time to time printed in folio, in a fine character, as they were performed; the following is the list which the authors of the Nouveau Dictionnaire Historique-Portatif have given of them, viz., Cadmus, Alceste, Thesée, Atys, Psyche, Bellerophon, Proserpine, Persée, Phaëton, Amadis, Roland, Armide, these are tragedies in five acts. Les Fêtes de l' Amour et de Bacchus, Acis et Galathée, pastorals in three acts; Le Carnaval, a masque with entrées; Le Triomphe de l' Amour, a ballet with entrées; L' Idyle de la Paix, et L' Eglogue de Versailles, and Le Temple de la Paix, a ballet with entrées. He also composed the music to some of the comedies of Moliere, particularly l'Amour Médecin, Pourceaugnac, and Le Bourgeois Gentilhomme, in which latter he performed the part of the Mufti with great applause.

He composed also Symphonies for violins in three parts, but it does not appear that they were ever published. One observation more respecting this extraordinary person shall conclude the account of him. Lully may be said to be the inventor of that species of instrumental composition, the Overture; more particularly that spirited movement the Largo, which is the general introduction to the fugue;‡ for

though it may be said that the symphonies and preludes of Carissimi, Colonna, Bassani, and others, are in effect overtures, yet the difference between them and those of Lully is apparent; the former were compositions of the mild and placid kind, and stole upon the affections insensibly; the latter are animated, and full of that energy which compels attention.

CHAP. CXXXVII.

WOLFGANG CASPAR PRINTZ, was born the tenth day of October, 1664, at Weildthurn, a small city situate in the Upper Palatinate, on the frontiers of Bohemia, where his father was a principal magistrate, and a receiver of the public revenues, until, on account of his religion, he quitted that station, and removed to Vohenstraus, a small town in the territory of Furstenburg. Discovering an inclination to music, Printz was committed to the tuition of Wilhelm Stockel, a celebrated organist from Nuremburg, by whom he was taught the elements of the science, and the principles of composition. For his master on the Clavier or harpsichord and the violin he had Andrew Paul Vander Heyd, a Bohemian; and having finished his exercises under these persons, he frequented the school at Weyden from the year 1655 to the year 1659, having for his instructor on the harpsichord John Conrad Mertz, an organist, and a skilful composer; and on certain wind instruments John George Schober, after which he went to the university at Altdorff, where he continued till the year 1661.

Anno 1662, about Easter, having been recommended by Francesco Santi, a musician from Perugia, to Count Promnitz at Dresden, he was engaged in his service as music-director and court composer. With this nobleman, then a captain of foot in the Imperial service, he travelled through Silesia, Moravia, and Austria, and was with him at the encampment near Altenburg, in the month of June, 1663; from which, the Count being taken with a dangerous illness, Printz departed in October in the same year, and arrived at Sorau, a town in the circle of Upper Saxony.

Upon the decease of Count Promnitz, Printz was invited to the office of chanter in the church of a town named Triebel, where he married; but, after a year's

* An office in the Romish church, celebrated about four or five in the afternoon, on Maundy-Thursday, Good Friday, and other solemn days, to commemorate the darkness that overspread the face of the earth at the time of the crucifixion.

† In the titles of his operas he is styled Escuyer, Conseiller, Secretaire du Roy, Maison Couronne de France et de ses Finances; et Sur-Intendant de la Musique de sa Chambre.

‡ It is said that the overtures of Lully were in such esteem, that they are to be found prefixed to many manuscript copies of Italian operas; and Mattheson asserts that Mr. Handel in the composition of his overtures professed to imitate those of Lully. And indeed whoever will make the comparison, will find good reason to be of that opinion. Those to the operas of Theseus, Alexander, Muzio Scævola, and Ariodante are much in his cast; and this may be remarked of the fugues in the overtures of Lully, that they are generally in the time of six crotchets in a bar, equally divided by the Tactus or beat.

continuance in that employment, being called to the same office in the church at Sorau, he entered upon it at Whitsuntide, 1665. In the year 1682 he was appointed to the direction of the choir of the same church; and, as it is supposed, continued in that station till the time of his death.

The works of this author are many, and are enumerated by Walther in his Lexicon. Among them is a history of music, published at Dresden, in quarto, in the year 1690, with the title of **Historiche Beschreibung der edelen Sing-und kling-kunst,** of which it may be expected some account should here be given.

It is written in chronological order; the author begins his history with the invention of the harp and organ by Jubal, founding his relation on the authority of the holy scriptures, and those testimonies respecting the ancient Jewish musicians, which Kircher has collected from the rabbinical writers. He is very exact in his delineations of the Hebrew instruments, which for the most part are taken from Johannes Schütterus, the author of Collectaneis Philologicis. For want of better materials he adopts the fictions of the poets in the stories by them related of Orpheus, Amphion, and Arion. He relates the invention of the Mercurian Lyre from Nicomachus, Boetius, and other writers; and continues the succession of the Greek musicians in short extracts from a variety of authors, nearly down to the Christian æra. He then, from Eusebius, Theodoret, Sozomen, and other ecclesiastical writers, explains the practice of antiphonal singing introduced among the primitive Christians by Flavianus and Diodorus; and, from other authorities, the final establishment of church music by St. Ambrose and St. Gregory. He speaks of the invention of the organ, and the introduction of that instrument into the church-service by pope Vitalianus; and celebrates Bede and Rabanus Maurus among the most eminent musicians of their time.

He dates the invention of music in consonance from the year 940, and with great formality of circumstance ascribes it to St. Dunstan, archbishop of Canterbury. The following is a translation of the author's own words:—'In the year of Christ '940, Dunstan, otherwise Dunstaphus, an English-'man, being very young, betook himself to the study 'of music, and thereby became of immortal memory. 'He was the first that composed songs in different 'parts, namely, Bass, Tenor, Discant, and Vagant or 'Alt.' A little farther on in his work he is some-what more particular. He says that in the time of Dunstan the method of notation was by points placed on lines, of which method he gives a specimen, the same with that herein before inserted, page 158, from Galilei. He says that at this time the music of the church was very simple, and that Dunstan was the first that found out the harmony of four different voices, though he proceeded no farther in it than the Contrapunctus Simplex. But that it was not till some years after this invention that the practice of singing in consonance became general.*

* Printz professes to have taken the above account of the invention of music in consonance from one or both of the authors cited by him,

The rest of this book contains a brief deduction of the history of the science, and a particular enumeration of such persons as have excelled in it, down to his own time; concluding with an account of himself and his studies, from which the foregoing particulars of his life are taken. Printz appears to have been a very able man in his profession, and to have bestowed great pains in the compilation of this work, the brevity of which is its only fault. Walther says the author had written it also in Latin, but that he did not live to publish it in that language.

Mattheson, in his **Forschendes Orchestre,** page 242, relates that during the last illness of Printz he wrote a book entitled De Instrumentis in toto Orbe musicis; and Walther adds that he died on his birth-day, viz., the tenth of October, in the year 1717.

Johann Christopher Denner is celebrated for his exquisite skill and ingenuity in the construction of flutes, and other instruments of the like kind; he was born at Leipsic on the thirteenth day of August, 1655; and at the age of eight years was taken to Nuremburg, in which city his father, a common turner in wood, had then lately chose to settle with his family. After a very few years stay there, the younger Denner, having been instructed like other boys of his age, in the rudiments of music, betook himself to his father's trade, and in particular to the fabrication of flutes, hautboys, and other wind instruments, which, by the help of a nice ear, added to the skill he had acquired in music, and the proficiency he had attained to in playing on them, he tuned so exquisitely, that his instruments were sought for from all parts. He is said to have greatly improved the Chalumeau, an instrument resembling the hautboy, and described by Mersennus

namely, David Chytræus, and Conrad Dieterich; nevertheless Walther, who appears to have been very well acquainted with Printz's writings, seems to give very little credit to this relation; for he cites a book written by Salomon Van Til, entitled 'Sing-Dicht-und Spiel-Kunst,' page 125, wherein it is said that the invention of music in consonance is of an older date than the time of St. Dunstan, though he admits that Dunstan might have introduced it among his countrymen.

The truth of the above relation is at this day so little questioned, that the modern writers on music seem generally agreed to acquiesce in it. Francis Lustig of Groningen and Marpourg of Berlin, have expressly asserted that St. Dunstan was the inventor of Counterpoint, the one in a treatise entitled 'Musik Kunde,' the other in a book printed in quarto at Berlin in 1766, entitled Traité de la Fugue et du Contrepoint, part II. sect. 7. But upon a careful enquiry after the evidence of the fact, there appears none to support it; on the contrary, the relation involves in it a series of the grossest blunders, as shall here be demonstrated.

In the year 1613, one Johannes Nucius, an ecclesiastic of Gorlitz in Lusatia, published a book with the title of Musices Poeticæ, sive de Compositioni Cantus Præceptiones absolutissimæ, wherein, on what authority we know not, he asserts that John of Dunstable, of whom an account is given page 274 of this work, was the inventor of musical composition. His words are an answer to the question, 'Quem dicimus 'Poeticum Musicum?' and are these: 'Qui non solum præcepta musicæ 'apprimè intelligit, et juxta ea rectè ac benè modulatur, sed qui proprij 'ingenij penetralia tentans, novas cantilenas cudit et flexibiles sonos pio 'verborum pondere textibus aptat. Talem artificem Glareanus Sym-'phonetæ appellatione insignit. Sicut Phonasci nomine cantorem 'insinuat. Porrò tales artifices clarverunt, primum circa annum Christi '1400 aut certè paulò post. Dunastapli Anglus à quo primum figuralem 'musicam inventam tradunt.' Mus. Poet. cap. I.

It is extremely difficult to find out any sense in which the above relation can be said to be true; for if by the term Figuralem musicam we are to understand, as all men do, the Cantus figuratus or mensurable music, it is certain that that was in use some centuries before the time of John of Dunstable: if it be taken for music in consonance, the invention of that, though at this time it is impossible to fix precisely the æra of it, is at least as ancient as the time of Bede, who makes use of the word Discantus. See page 188.

But taking the relation of Nucius for true, it refers to John of Dunstable, who flourished about the year 1400, whereas his invention or improvement, whatever it was, is by Printz, Lustig, and Marpourg, the two last of whom are now living, ascribed to Dunstan, died about the year 1000.

and Kircher; and to have been the original inventor of another instrument, which neither of them do so much as mention, namely, the Clarinet. He died on the twentieth day of April, 1707, leaving behind him two sons, who followed the business of their father, and, like him, were excellent performers on most of the instruments they professed to make.*

A son of one of these Denners betook himself to painting, and became remarkable for the singularity of his style. His studies were only heads, and those in general of old persons; his colouring was very fine, and his portraits were so close a copy, that he represented the defects and decays of nature, and even the ravages of disease in the human countenance. His pictures were so elaborate, and of consequence his price so high, that few, without the hope of a more favourable likeness than it was his practice to paint, would choose to sit to him. About the year 1745 a portrait of his, the head of an old man, was exhibited to public view in London, at the rate of half a crown each person, and many resorted to see it. Notwithstanding his ill success, a disciple of Denner, one Van Smissen, ventured to pursue the same course of study, and practised the same style of painting. Trusting to the propensity which, as he had been told, the English have to favour foreigners, he came over to England, and took lodgings in St. Martin's Lane, London; his paintings on canvas were like enamel, but he had no idea of grace or elegance; and meeting with but little encouragement, after a short stay he left this country.

Alessandro Stradella, one of the great Italian musicians in his time, flourished about the middle of the seventeenth century; he was both a very fine singer and an exquisite performer on the harp, an instrument in which he greatly delighted; over and above which qualifications, he possessed a talent for vocal composition, sufficient alone to have rendered him famous to all posterity. He was for some time composer to the opera at Venice, under an appointment of the magistrates of that republic, and frequently sang on the stage, cantatas and other of his own compositions, accompanying himself on the harp.

His character as a musician was so high at Venice, that all who were desirous of excelling in the science were solicitous to become his pupils. Among the many whom he had the instruction of, was one, a young lady of a noble family of Rome, named Hortensia, who, notwithstanding her illustrious descent, submitted to live in a criminal intimacy with a Venetian nobleman. The frequent access of Stradella to this lady, and the many opportunities he had of being alone with her, produced in them both such an affection for each other, that they agreed to go off together for Rome. In consequence of this resolution they embarked in a very fine night, and by the favour of the wind affected their escape.

Upon the discovery of the lady's flight, the Venetian

---

* It is somewhat remarkable that many excellent performers on such wind instruments as the flute and hautboy, have also been makers of them. Denner, Le Vacher, and Quiclet, so much celebrated by Mersennus, are instances of this; to whom may be added Meuschel of Nuremburg, a maker of trumpets.

had recourse to the usual method in that country of obtaining satisfaction for real or supposed injuries; he dispatched two assassins, with instructions to murder both Stradella and the lady, giving them a sum of money in hand, and a promise of a larger if they succeeded in the attempt. Being arrived at Naples, the assassins received intelligence that those whom they were in pursuit of were at Rome, where the lady passed for the wife of Stradella. Upon this they determined to execute their commission, wrote to their employer, requesting letters of recommendation to the Venetian embassador at Rome, in order to secure an asylum for them to fly to, as soon as the deed should be perpetrated.

Upon the receipt of letters for this purpose, the assassins made the best of their way towards Rome; and being arrived there, they learned that on the morrow, at five in the evening, Stradella was to give an oratorio in the church of San Giovanni Laterano. They failed not to be present at the performance, and had concerted to follow Stradella and his mistress out of the church, and, seizing a convenient opportunity, to make the blow. The performance was now begun, and these men had nothing to do but to watch the motions of Stradella, and attend to the music, which they had scarce begun to hear, before the suggestions of humanity began to operate upon their minds; they were seized with remorse, and reflected with horror on the thought of depriving of his life a man capable of giving to his auditors such pleasure as they had but just then felt. In short, they desisted from their purpose, and determined, instead of taking away his life, to exert their endeavours for the preservation of it; they waited for his coming out of the church, and courteously addressed him and the lady, who was by his side, first returning him thanks for the pleasure they had received at hearing his music, and informed them both of the errand they had been sent upon; expatiating upon the irresistible charms, which of savages had made them men, and had rendered it impossible for them to effect their execrable purpose; and concluded with their earnest advice that Stradella and the lady should both depart from Rome the next day, themselves promising to deceive their employer, and forego the remainder part of their reward, by making him believe that Stradella and his lady had quitted Rome on the morning of their arrival.

Having thus escaped the malice of their enemy, the two lovers took an immediate resolution to fly for safety to Turin, and soon arrived there. The assassins being returned to Venice, reported to their employer that Stradella and Hortensia had fled from Rome, and taken shelter in the city of Turin, a place where the laws were very severe, and which, excepting the houses of embassadors, afforded no protection for murderers; they represented to him the difficulty of getting these two persons assassinated, and, for their own parts, notwithstanding their engagements, declined the enterprize. This disappointment, instead of allaying, served but to sharpen the resentment of the Venetian: he had found means to attach to his interest the father of Hortensia, and by various arguments, to inspire him with a resolution to become the murderer of his own daughter. With this old man, no less malevolent and vindictive than himself, the Venetian associated two ruffians, and dispatched them all three to Turin, fully inspired with a resolution of stabbing Stradella and the old man's daughter wherever they found them. The Venetian also furnished them with letters from Mons. l'Abbé de Estrades, then embassador of France at Venice, addressed to the marquis of Villars, the French embassador at Turin. The purport of these letters was a recommendation of the bearers of them, who were therein represented to be merchants, to the protection of the embassador, if at any time they should stand in need of it.

The duchess of Savoy was at that time regent; and she having been informed of the arrival of Stradella and Hortensia, and the occasion of their precipitate flight from Rome; and knowing the vindictive temper of the Venetians, placed the lady in a convent, and retained Stradella in her palace as her principal musician. In a situation of such security as this seemed to be, Stradella's fears for the safety of himself and his mistress began to abate, till one evening, walking for the air upon the ramparts of the city, he was set upon by the three assassins abovementioned, that is to say, the father of Hortensia, and the two ruffians, who each gave him a stab with a dagger in the breast, and immediately betook themselves to the house of the French embassador as to a sanctuary.

The attack on Stradella having been made in the sight of numbers of people, who were walking in the same place, occasioned an uproar in the city, which soon reached the ears of the duchess: she ordered the gates to be shut, and diligent search to be made for the three assassins; and being informed that they had taken refuge in the house of the French embassador, she went to demand them. The embassador insisting on the privileges which those of his function claimed from the law of nations, refused to deliver them up; he nevertheless wrote to the Abbé de Estrades to know the reason of the attack upon Stradella, and was informed by the Abbé that he had been surprized into a recommendation of the three men by one of the most powerful of the Venetian nobility. In the interim Stradella was cured of his wounds, and the marquis de Villars, to make short of the question about privilege, and the rights of embassadors, suffered the assassins to escape.

From this time, finding himself disappointed of his revenge, but not the least abated in his ardour to accomplish it, this implacable Venetian contented himself with setting spies to watch the motions of Stradella. A year was elapsed after the cure of his wounds; no fresh disturbance had been given to him, and he thought himself secure from any further attempts on his life. The duchess regent, who was concerned for the honour of her sex, and the happiness of two persons who had suffered so much, and seemed to have been born for each other, joined the hands of Stradella and his beloved Hortensia, and they were married. After the ceremony Stradella and his wife having a desire to visit the port of Genoa, went thither with a resolution to return to Turin: the assassins having intelligence of their departure, followed them close at their heels. Stradella and his wife it is true reached Genoa, but the morning after their arrival these three execrable villains, rushed into their chamber, and stabbed each to the heart. The murderers had taken care to secure a bark which lay in the port; to this they retreated, and made their escape from justice, and were never heard of more.

Mr. Wanley, who in the Catalogue of the Harleian manuscripts, No. 1272, has given a short account of Stradella, says that the lover of this lady, whom he calls the baroness or countess, was the heir of either the Cornaro or Colonna family; and that after the murder of Stradella, which he says was in the year 1670, she was sent for to France by the then king; and that she had been heard to sing both in Italy and France by a friend of Mr. Wanley, Mr. Berenclow, who said she was a perfect mistress of the best manner, for which, with her, he only admired Cornelio Galli, and the two eunuchs, Tosi and Sifacio.[*]

The truth of this relation is very questionable: in the above account, taken from a French writer, Mons. Bourdelot, author of the Histoire de la Musique et de ses Effets, it is said that, in full gratification of the malice of their enemy, both Stradella and the lady were murdered. There was about that time a lady, but a German, as it is supposed; a fine singer, who sang in the operas abroad, and even at London,[†] known by no other name than the Baroness; and it is not improbable that Mr. Barenclow might be deceived into an opinion that she was the relict of Stradella.

The same person says that when the report of Stradella's assassination reached the ears of Purcell, and he was informed jealousy was the motive to it, he lamented his fate exceedingly; and, in regard of his great merit as a musician, said he could have forgiven him any injury in that kind; which, adds

---

[*] This Mr. Berenclow was a musician of some eminence in queen Anne's reign, and the son of a Dr. Bernard Martin Berenclow, of whom Mr. Wanley, in the Harleian Catalogue, No. 1265. 19, gives the following account: 'Dr. Berenclow was born in the duchy of Holstein near 'Toninghen; his mother was a Berchem, a family sufficiently eminent 'both in the Upper and Nether Germany. He married Katherine, one 'of the daughters of Mr. Laneir, clerk of the closet to king Charles the 'First. He was professor of physic in the university of Padua, and 'practised with success and reputation in Italy, France, Germany, 'Holland, Flanders, and England. And, notwithstanding his frequent 'journies and removals, died rich in ready money, jewels, plate, pictures, 'drawings, &c. of great price and curiosity; which his widow, notwith- 'standing (by true pains-taking) made a shift to overcome, and utterly 'squander away in about five years after his decease.'

Cornelio Galli was a native of Lucca, and one of the gentlemen of the chapel to Catherina, the consort of Charles II. He is said to have first introduced a fine manner of singing into England. Vide Harleian Catalogue, No. 1264.

Pier-Francesco Tosi was an Italian by birth, but travelled much, and resided at different times at most of the courts in Europe. He was in England in the several reigns of king James, king William, and king George I. and was patronized by the earl of Peterborough. He lived to the age of fourscore; and, besides sundry elegant cantatas, was the author of a tract entitled 'Opinioni de' Cantori antiche e moderna, o sieno 'Osservazioni sopra il Canto figurato,' printed at Bologna in 1723, which Mr. Galliard translated into English, and published in 1743.

Sifacio. The true name of this person is unknown: this, which he was generally called by, was given him on occasion of his performing the part of Syphax in an Italian opera. He was in England, and a singer in the chapel of king James II., but, returning to Italy, was assassinated.

[†] She performed the part of Lavinia in the opera of Camilla, represented at Drury-Lane theatre in 1706, and that of Eurilla, in the Triumph of Love, at the Hay-market, some time after.

the relator, 'those who remember how lovingly 'Mr. Purcell lived with his wife, or rather what a 'loving wife she proved to him, may understand 'without farther explication.'

It may be questioned whether any of the compositions of Stradella were ever published; Walther has given no catalogue of them, nor has any been met with in the accounts of him by other writers. Many of his pieces in manuscript are in the library of the Academy of ancient Music, particularly an oratorio entitled San Giovanni Battista, and sundry madrigals, among which is a very fine one for five voices, to the words 'Clori son fido amante,' &c.

BOOK XV.   CHAP. CXXXVIII.

Gio. Andrea Angelini Bontempi, a native of Perugia, was the author of a work entitled Historia Musica. He it seems was a practical musician; and, in the earlier part of his life, was chapel-master to the elector of Saxony. He was a man eminently learned in his profession, as appears by a tract of his writing, entitled Nova quatuor Vocibus componendi methodus, printed at Dresden in 1660; but the work by which he is best known is his History of Music, printed in folio at Perugia in 1695.

This book is divided into three parts, which are thus entitled, Della Teorica, Della Pratica antica, Della Pratica moderna, from whence it may be conjectured, that, in the judgment of the author, there could be no theory of the moderns properly so called. Each of these three titles is subdivided into two parts, so as to render it difficult to cite the book otherwise than by the pages.

Discoursing on music at large at the beginning of his work, Bontempi takes notice of that analytical division of it by Aristides Quintilianus in his first book, and mentioned in a preceding page of this work; but this division Bontempi seems here to reject, preferring the scholastic division into mundane, humane, political, rythmical, metrical, and harmonical music. The former however he seems to have adopted, merely in compliance with the method of the Latin and Italian writers, for he hastens to the latter branch of his subdivision. On the subject of rythmical or metrical music he is very elaborate; and, with a view to reduce the precepts delivered by him into practice, he exhibits an oratorio written by himself, founded on the history of the life and martyrdom of St. Emilianus, bishop of Trevi, the poetry whereof is conformable to those metrical rules which the author endeavours to recommend. The History of Music begins with the title Musica Harmonica; and, after giving different etymologies of the word Music, Bontempi, from Boetius, Polydore Virgil, Alstedius, and other writers, ascribes to a variety of personages, deities, semideities, heroes and others, the invention of the several instruments in use among the ancients.

The invention of the lyre by Mercury, the improvement of it by Terpander, with the formation of the Systema maxima by Pythagoras, are faithfully related by this author from Nicomachus, and other ancient writers; but here he fails not to mention that egregious mistake in the relation of the discovery of the consonances by means of hammers of different weights, which we have before noted; and having it seems seen the detection of this error in the writings of Galileo Galilei, he, prompted by curiosity, as he himself relates, made an experiment of chords distended by weights in the ratios of 12, 9, 8, 6, which, instead of consonances, produced irrational intervals.*

After having treated largely on the music of the Greeks, and given the substance of what the several writers have said on the subject, he gives a very decisive opinion that the ancients were strangers to music in consonance, notwithstanding the assertion of Vincentio Galilei and others to the contrary.†

In the second division of his first part Bontempi continues to discourse on the theory of the ancients, in his explanation whereof he follows the division of Aristides Quintilianus, making music to consist of seven parts, that is to say, 1. sounds, 2. intervals, 3. the genera, 4. systems, 5. the tones or modes, 6. the mutations, 7. the melopoeia.‡

In the first subdivision of the second part, Della Pratica antica, he endeavours to explain the practice of the ancients by a commentary on some select passages of Aristoxenus relating to the measure of intervals, and the constitution of the genera, and their colours or species.

He then takes occasion to celebrate Virgilio Mazzochi, maestro di cappella of the church of St. Pietro in Vaticano, and professor in the college or school instituted at Rome for the education of youth for the service of the papal chapel; and gives an account of their exercises and method of study. He says that one hour in a day is spent in the practice of difficult passages; another in the Trillo or shake; another in singing in the presence of the master, and before a looking-glass, in order to prevent bad habits, and distortions of the features, and to regulate the actions of the muscles; and that these are the exercises of the morning. In the afternoon he says a small portion of time is employed in the study of the theory of music; that one hour is given to the framing of counterpoints on a Canto fermo; that another is spent in hearing from the master, and committing to writing the precepts of counterpoint at large, or practical composition; and another in reading, as in the morning; and that the remainder of the day is devoted to the practice of the Clavicembalo, and the framing some composition, for instance, a psalm, a motet, a canzonet, or a song, best suited to the genius of the students. On those

* Page 54.

† Che gli Antichi cantassero in consonanza, come vuole il Galilei nel suo Discorso intorno all' Opere del Zarlino, è una favola de' Moderni, che senza Greca letteratura, camina unitamente con l' altre.

‡ Page 83.

days on which they are permitted to go out of the college, he says the scholars are wont to sing at a certain place without the Porta Angelica, near the Mount of Marius, where is an echo, which, as it is pretended, returns the sound of their voices in such a manner as to enable them to discover their defects in singing. At other times, says he, they resorted to the churches in Rome, and either assisted in the service, or attended to the performance of those excellent singers and musicians who flourished during the pontificate of Urban VIII. After which they returned to the school or college, and, making exercises on what they had heard, communicated them and their observations to their master, who in return, in lectures delivered and explained to them the precepts of science and practice.*

He then proceeds to exhibit from Franchinus, or, as he calls him, Gaffaro, and Vanneo, the constitution of the four ecclesiastical tones of St. Ambrose, which he shews to be derived from the Dorian, Phrygian, Lydian, and Mixolydian modes of the ancient Greeks. After which he proceeds to relate that St. Gregory increased the number of the ecclesiastical tones to eight, by adding thereto four others, derived as he says, from the Hypodorian, Hypophrygian, Hypolydian, and Hypermixolydian, distinguishing the eight ecclesiastical tones into authentic and plagal.†

In the first subdivision of the third part, Della Pratica Moderna, he considers the practice of the moderns, founding it on the reformation of the scale by Guido Aretinus; of whose invention of a method of determining the place of the semitones in the diapason, by the use and application of the syllables, he has given a just account.‡

The syllables of Guido, as they were invented solely for the purpose of assisting the voice in the discrimination between the tones and semitones, determine nothing as to the ratios or measures of those intervals; and it is obvious that a succession of tones precisely equal with the semitones, interposed in their natural order, had been productive of those inconveniences, arising from a surd quantity in the constitution of the diatessaron, which it had been the endeavour of many writers to palliate, and which had given rise to that controversy between Zarlino and Galilei, whether the ditonic diatonic of Ptolemy, or rather of Pythagoras, or the intense or syntonous diatonic of the former was to be preferred.

To remedy this inconvenience, a system had been invented which divided the octave into thirteen sounds or chords, and twelve intervals, that is to say, semitones, of which Bontempi speaks to the following purpose: 'This was that sublime and 'memorable operation, which so improved the noble 'science of counterpoint; for a very skilful man, 'whose name, and even the age he lived in, is not 'known, having found that the diatessaron and dia-'pente would admit of a small variation without offence to the ear, he reformed those intervals. 'Besides this he first interposed in the middle of 'each tetrachord the Spesso Cromatico; § and after-

* Page 170.　† Page 172.　‡ 182, et seq.

§ By the Spesso Cromatico Bontempi means the chromatic or double diesis, or, in other words, the lesser semitone, consisting of four commas,

'wards, at other distances, an interval never known 'before in the orders of tetrachords, marked thus ✗, 'or thus b, according as the modulation was either 'of the sharp or flat kind; thus he formed a system 'of sounds, separated from each other by the interval 'of a semitone, and thereby united the chromatic 'with the diatonic genus, and of the two formed one.'‖

Bontempi has said that the name of the author of this last and great improvement of the musical system, as also the age in which he lived, are unknown, and refers to Polydore Virgil, lib. III. cap. xviii. Polydore Virgil's book De Inventoribus Rerum, contains little more respecting music than a brief account of the invention of it, and of a few instruments, such as the harp, the organ, and the lyre; and it seemed strange that he who has mentioned in particular no one system, should take notice of the improvement of any; his work has therefore been recurred to, and all that he says on the subject is found to be contained in the following words: 'Multa insuper novissimis temporibus instrumenta 'musica inventa sunt, quorum autores jam in ob-'livionem venerunt. Ex quibus propter suavitatem 'concentus omni admirationi et laude digna sunt 'illa, quæ organa nuncupant, valde quidem ab illis 'dissimilia, quæ David Judæorum rex fecerat, qui-'bus Levitæ sacros hymnos concinerent, sicut nos 'his pariter canimus. Item alia id genus sunt, 'quæ monochordia clavicymbala varieq; nominantur,

denoted by a double cross, which is the common sharp signature. Vide Brossard Dict. de Musique, DIESIS.

‖ Page 186.

Brossard has given an account of this improvement, which, as it is much more full and satisfactory than that of Bontempi, is here inserted :—

'It being found that there was a chord placed between the Mese and 'Paramese of the ancients, or our A and B, which divided the interval of 'a tone, that was between them, into two semitones: it was thought 'that chords also might be added, as well between those that were at the 'like distance from each other, i. e. had a tone between them; the 'author of this improvement therefore not only inserted the B mol, as 'in Guido's system, but also the chromatic chords of the ancient scale, 'that is those which divide the tones major of each tetrachord into 'semitones; and this he did by raising the lowest chord a semitone, by 'means of a double diesis ✗, which was placed immediately before the 'note so to be raised, or on the same degree with it after the cliff: again, 'it having been found that the tones minor terminating the tetrachords 'upwards, were no less capable of such division, he, by the help of the 'chromatic chords, divided them also ; so that the octave then became 'composed of thirteen sounds and twelve intervals, eight whereof are 'diatonic or natural, distinguished by white notes thus ○, and five 'chromatic thus, by black ones ◆; and the diesis prefixed.' Dict. de Musique, voce SYSTEMA.

Brossard elsewhere observes, that in the several systems of the diatonic genus for which he refers to Bontempi, page 93, the tetrachord is composed of three intervals, that is to say, semitone, tone major, and tone minor; and that Ptolemy and Didymus, among all their reformations, taking it for granted that the tone minor was indivisible into semitones, interposed but one chromatic sound in the tetrachord, thereby dividing the tone major into semitones, the one major and the other minor, leaving the tone minor as they found it. But he says that it having afterwards been found necessary to divide the tone minor in like manner, and also to extend the diatessaron and contract the diapente; a very learned man, whose name is not mentioned in history, perceiving that the ear was not displeased if the fifth was a little diminished, that is, if it was not quite of so great an extent, found out an admirable temperament, which rendered the second tone of the fourth equal to the first, by giving the fourth a little greater extent than it naturally had from its mathematical form of 3, 4, which tone consequently admitted one chromatic chord, that divided it into two semitones. This system is called by the Italians Systema Temperato. He observes that by means of this addition of the chromatic chord the octave becomes divisible into twelve semitones, without any chasm in or between the two tetrachords that compose it; and also that thereby two of the genera, that is to say, the chromatic and diatonic, are brought into one system, which, for that reason, is by Bontempi and other of the Italian writers, called Systema Participato. Vide Brossard, voce TEMPERAMENTO.

' eorum, tamen æque inventores magno quidem suæ
' gloriæ damno in nocte densissima delitescunt.' *

In the second subdivision of the third part, della
Practica Moderna, Bontempi deduces the practice of
counterpoint from the time of its supposed invention
by Guido down to the time of Johannes de Muris,
who lived about three hundred years after. Implicitly relying on Gaffurius, Vanneo, and Kircher, he
ascribes to De Muris the invention of the Cantus
Mensurabilis, and says that it was adopted and improved by Prosdocimus, Tintor, Franco, Caserta,
Anselmo da Parma, and other contrapuntists. He says
that in the original invention of counterpoint the
sounds in consonance were distinguished in writing,
by an opposition of note against note, but that by
the introduction of the Cantus Mensurabilis, which
was signified by certain characters, of dissimilar
forms, that which was originally termed counterpoint
assumed the name of Canto figurato.†

In treating on the science of counterpoint, this
author, following the method of the Italians, divides
it into five parts, namely, 1. the figures or characters
used to denote the sounds and their measures; 2. the
degrees of mode, time, and prolation, signified by
their respective characters; 3. the proportions; 4.
Contrapunto semplice; 5. Contrapunto florido.‡ In
the discussion of each of these he is very accurate;
and in his discourse on the last two heads delivers
the precepts for the composition of a cantilena in
consonance both in the Contrapunto florido and the
Contrapunto semplice, according to the practice of
his time.

In the course of his work he celebrates two of his
countrymen, namely, Lemme Rossi§ and Baldassare
Ferri, both of Perugia; the former of these had
written a treatise on music, from which Bontempi
has given many copious extracts; the latter was
a singer, of whom he gives a great character.

The Historia Musica of Bontempi is a work of some
merit; but, to speak ingenuously, it seems little
calculated for instruction; the author appears to have
read a great deal on the subject of music; nevertheless it is apparent in many instances that the
knowledge he had attained was not derived from
the genuine source. That he had perused the Greek
writers in the edition of Meibomius cannot be doubted,
for he cites the book, though he has not adopted all
the prejudices of the editor. But his great fault is
a too ready acquiescence in the authorities of Franchinus, Steffano Vanneo, and Kircher in matters
respecting the theory and practice of music among
the moderns, under which comprehensive term he
properly enough includes not only Guido, the inventor
of the modern system, but St. Gregory and St.
Ambrose, who, from the modes of the ancients,
instituted for the purpose of religious worship, that

formula of vocal melody comprized in the eight
ecclesiastical tones. In a discourse on this important
branch of musical history, it was requisite that the
author should have recurred to original materials,
such as are to be found in public repositories, not to
say in Italy only, but in almost every city and
university in Europe: the neglect of this method
has led Bontempi to adopt the errors of former
writers, who seem to have founded their reports on
mere popular tradition, and to become the propagator
of many errors, which, as a historian, it was his duty
to detect and explode. To enumerate instances of
this kind is an invidious office, but those contained in
his relation of the invention of music in consonance
by Guido, and of the Cantus Mensurabilis by Johannes de Muris, are of such importance, that they
merit particular notice. With respect to the former
assertion, there is not the least authority for it either
in the Micrologus or the Argumentum novi Cantus
inveniendi of Guido, or in his epistle to his friend
Michael of Pomposa; and, from the superficial account
which he gives of Guido and his improvements, there
is reason to think that Bontempi had never perused
any of his writings; and as to the Cantus Mensurabilis, no one can read the relation of its invention
by Franco of Liege, as given by the learned Benedictines, the publishers of the Histoire Literaire de
la France, but must conclude that the names De
Muris, Prosdocimus, Tintor, Franco, Caserta, and
Anselmo da Parma, are cited by rote from the
margin of the Practica Musicæ of Franchinus, or
rather from the Systema Musica of his compatriot
Lemme Rossi, whose name occurs in almost every
page of his work. Indeed it is easy to discover
where the materials of this author failed him; for
while he had the Latin version of the Greek writers
on music lying before him, he was able to give an
account of the original constitution of the lyre of
Mercury, and of the names of the several persons
who at different times increased the number of
chords of which it consisted, from four to seven,
as also of the subsequent extention of the system to
fifteen chords, with other improvements; but no
sooner does he dismiss these materials, than his
narration is interrupted, and a chasm ensues, which
he attempts to supply by citations from Alstedius
and other chronological writers, the bare recorders
of memorable events; and from materials so scanty
as these we are not to wonder if he found himself
unable to furnish many particulars respecting that
history, the deduction whereof is the object of his
work.

The invention of the several musical instruments
in use among the moderns, and the successive improvements made in them at different periods, is
surely a very essential part of musical history; and
it would be but a weak answer to any one who
should object that Bontempi is silent on this head,
to say that a great deal to the purpose is to be found
in the Musurgia of Ottomarus Luscinius, the Dialogo
della Musica of Vincentio Galilei, in the writings of
Mersennus, the Musurgia of Kircher, and in the
History of Music of Wolfgang Caspar Printz. And

---

* Polyd. Virgil. De Invent. Rer. Lib. VIII. Basil. apud Johan.
Froben. 1521.

† Page 199.   ‡ 205.

§ Lemme Rossi was an eminent mathematician and philosopher, and
professor of the Greek language in the university or academy of Perugia.
He appears to have been deeply skilled in the theory of music by the work
above alluded to, which was published at Perugia in the year 1666,
and is entitled 'Systema Musica, overo Musica speculativa, dove si
' spiegano i più celebri di tutti trè generi.'

FRANCESCO FOGGIA ROMANO,

COMPOSITORE .

ANTIMO LIBERATI MUSICO NELLA CAPPELLA PONTIFICIA

MAESTRO DI CAPPELLA NELLA CHIESA DELLA SANTISSIMA

TRINITA DE PELLEGRINI, E MAESTRO DI CAPPELLA ED ORGANISTA

NELLA CHIESA DI S. MARIA DELL ANIMA DELLA NATIONE TUETONICA.

here it may be remarked, that an unjustifiable partiality for the country where the author was born distinguishes this work; for, among the moderns whom he has taken occasion to mention, the name of any musician not an Italian, scarcely occurs. In a word, the information contained in the Historia Musica of Bontempi is just sufficient to awaken that curiosity which it is the end of history to gratify. In those who are ignorant of the subject it may excite approbation; but that it falls short of affording satisfaction to a learned and curious enquirer, every one of that character must feel when he reads it.

LORENZO PENNA, of Bologna, a Carmelite monk, and a professor of music, was the author of a work entitled Albori Musicale, printed at Bologna in 1672, divided into three parts, the first treating of the elements or principles of the Canto Figurato; the second on Counterpoint; and in the third, of the precepts or rules, to use the author's own expression, 'per suonare l'Organo sopra la parte.'

In this book, which is one of the best of those many on the subject written by Italians, and published after the year 1600, the scale of Guido with the use of the syllables* and the cliffs, and the nature of the mutations are explained in a very concise and intelligible manner, as are also the characters used in the Cantus Mensurabilis. Of the rules for counterpoint laid down by this author, little can be said other than that they are perfectly consistent with the laws of harmony. In the course of his directions for the composition of counterpoint, examples in notes are contained, teaching the student the use and application of various passages, with cautions for avoiding such as the rules of harmony prohibit.

Under the head of Contrapunto Fugato his directions are very concise and perspicuous. Of Canon he gives a variety of examples, both in Partito and in Corpo, with rules for the composition of canon in the unison, the second, the third major and minor, and so on to the diapason.

The third part is in effect a treatise on thoroughbass or the art of accompanyment, and is drawn from the works of Luzzasco Luzzaschi, Claudio Merula, Frescobaldi, and other celebrated organists of Italy.

The second part of the Albori Musicale was published at Venice in the year 1678, but whether by the author or some one else does not appear. The publication of one part only of the three which the Albori Musicale contains, is perhaps to be accounted for by the circumstance of its utility to students in the musical faculty, an intimation whereof is given by the words 'Per li Studiosi,' in the title-page of the second impression.

FRANCESCO FOGGIA *(a Portrait)*, is celebrated as one of the most eminent of the Italian musicians of the last century. He was born about the year 1604, and was a disciple, and also the son-in-law of Paolo Agostino, as having married his daughter. Very early in his life, being distinguished for his skill in ecclesiastical harmony, he was appointed maestro di cappella of the church of San Giovanni Laterano in

Rome. Kircher, in the Musurgia, lib. VII. cap. vi. page 614, has spoken of him in terms of high commendation. He was living in the year 1684, the year in which Antimo Liberati published his letter in answer to one of Ovidio Persapegi, in which is the following character of him—'essendo il sostegno, 'e 'l padre della musica, e della vera harmonia 'ecclesiastica, come nelle stampe hà saputo far vedere, 'e sentire tanta varietà di stile, ed in tutti far cog- 'noscere il grande, l' erudito, il nobile, il polito, il 'facile, ed il dilettevole, tanto al sapiente, quanto all' 'ignorante; tutte cose, che difficilmente si trovano 'in un solo huomo, che dovrebbe esser' imitato da 'tutti i seguaci di buon gusto della musica, come io 'hò cercato di fare colla mio debolezza, essendo stato 'sempre invaghito, innamorato di quella nobilissima 'maniera di concertare.'

ANDREAS LORENTE, of Alcala, organist of the principal church there, published in the year 1673, a work in folio in the Spanish language, entitled El Porque de la Musica, in four books, the first containing the elements of plainsong; the second treating of consonance and the Cantus Mensurabilis, the third of counterpoint, and the fourth of the composition of music. This book, of which the late Mr. Geminiani was used to say it had not its fellow in any of the modern languages, is questionless a very learned work; it is in truth a musical institute, and may be said to contain all that is necessary for a practical composer to know. From the method of solmisation directed by this author, it is evident that the Spaniards, as well as the French and others, have for some time past solfaed by heptachords; or in other words, they have added a syllable to the six of Guido. It has been already said that the French use SI after LA; Lorente directs to sing BI in the same place. In the course of the work are interspersed a great number of compositions of his own and other authors, from three to five parts; that is to say, hymns and offices for the church, and some motets, which shew great skill and invention.

GIO. PAOLO COLONNA, maestro di cappella nella Basilica di S. Petronio in Bologna, Accademico Filaschisi, e Filarmonico, flourished at this time. His compositions, which are very numerous, are altogether for the church, consisting of Motets, Litanies, Masses, Psalms, and Offices for the dead, many whereof he published at Bologna, between the years 1681 and 1694. Like the motets of Carissimi, Bassani, and other of the church-musicians of the last century, his are usually with instrumental parts. His style is at once pathetic and sublime; and in the composition of church-music he stands among the first of the Italians.

CHAP. CXXXIX.

ANTIMO LIBERATI, *(a Portrait)*, when a youth, served in the Imperial chapel of Ferdinand III. and his brother Leopold. Afterwards he became a singer in the pontifical chapel, and maestro di cappella, and organist of the church della Santissima Trinità de' Pellegrini; and, lastly, maestro di cappella and

---

* This author makes use of the syllable DO instead of UT, and speaks of it as a modern practice in his time.

organist of the church di Santi Maria dell' Anima della Natione Teutonica at Rome. In this quality he wrote a letter dated the fifteenth of October, 1684, with the following title : ' Lettera scritta dal Sig. Antimo Liberati in risposta ad una del Sig. Ovidio Persapegi,' the occasion whereof was as follows : about the middle of the year 1684 the place of maestro di cappella of the metropolitical church of Milan being vacant, Persapegi, by the direction, as it is presumed, of those who had the appointment to that office, wrote to Liberati for his opinion touching the pretensions of five persons, who at that time were candidates for it. Who they were does not appear by the answer of Liberati ; nor is it certain that Persapegi's letter is extant in print.*

After discussing the merits of the several compositions tendered by the candidates as evidence of their abilities, he proceeds to trace the rise and progress of music from the time of Pythagoras downwards, taking particular notice of Guido's invention, and the completion of it by Johannes de Muris. Among the less ancient practical musicians he celebrates Johannes Okenheim, the disciple of Iodocus Pratensis He mentions, from Glareanus, the circumstance of his having made a composition for thirty-six voices or nine choirs, to obviate an opinion of some professors of his time, that music for so many voices was a modern invention. Besides this he asserts that fugue, canon, and double counterpoint were invented by the same Okenheim.

He says that from these two great men, Iodocus Pratensis and Johannes Okenheim, sprang many excellent masters, who erected musical academies in different kingdoms and provinces ; that many of them settled in Italy and in Rome ; and that the first who gave public instructions for singing and harmonic modulation was Gaudio Mell, Flandro, a man of great talents, and of a sweet flowing style, who opened at Rome a noble and excellent school for music, where many pupils distinguished themselves in that science, but, above all, Gio. Pierluigi Palestrina,† who, as if marked by nature herself, he says surpassed all other rivals, and even his own master. With him he joins Gio. Maria Nanino, the intimate friend of Palestrina, and conrector with him in the musical school by them established at Rome. Among many eminent musicians educated in this seminary, he mentions Bernardino Nanino, the youngest brother of Gio. Maria Nanino, Antonio Cifra, Pier Francesco Valentini, Gregorio Allegri, and Paolo Agostino, of whom he gives a very high character. Of Allegri he says that he wrote for

the pontifical chapel, where he was a singer, and that from him he, Liberati, received his instructions in music. Of Agostino he says that in music he surpassed all of his time, and that he died in the flower of his youth ; and that from him sprang Francesco Foggia, then living, and eighty years of age. He mentions also another disciple of Agostino, Vincenzo Ugolino, famous for his skill in teaching, and for having been the master of Lorenzo Ratti and Horatio Benevoli, who for many years was maestro di cappella nella Basilica di San Pietro.

Liberati says that at the time of writing his letter there were living three disciples of Horatio Benevoli, of whom the oldest was himself ; the next in age Ercole Bernabei, who succeeded Benevoli at St. Peter's, and went afterwards to Bavaria, invited thither by the elector ; the youngest he says was Giovanni Vincenti, for many years maestro di cappella della Santa Casa di Loretto, but who then lived in perfect ease, enjoying his patrimony, and the fruits of his studies.

Angelo Berardi, a canon of the collegiate church of St. Angelo di Viterbo, was the author of many musical tracts, and, amongst the rest, one entitled Documenti Armonici, in the composing whereof he was assisted, as himself confesses, by Marco Scacchi, chapel-master to the king of Poland. It was printed at Bologna in 1687, and is divided into three books, containing the precepts for the composition of counterpoint, fugue, and canon, illustrated by a great variety of examples, among which are sundry compositions of Adrian Willaert, Iodocus Pratensis, and others, well deserving the attention of the curious.

In the year 1689, Berardi published, at Bologna, Miscellanea Musicale, in three parts ; the first is a collection from Boetius, Zarlino, Kircher, and other writers, containing, it must be confessed, few particulars relating to the state of music at different times, that are not to be found in every treatise on the subject that has been written within these last hundred years.

He takes occasion to enumerate many princes who have been distinguished, as well for their skill in music, as their affection for it ; and, among the rest, James I. king of Scotland, concerning whom he cites verbatim from Alessandro Tassoni the passage inserted in the account herein before given of that prince, and his improvement of the Scots music.

In the second part he relates the invention of the syllables,‡ and the reformation of the scale by Guido, as also the institution of the Cantus Mensurabilis by John de Muris ; but, as he professes to follow Vincentino, it is no wonder that his account is erroneous in many particulars.

The third part contains a variety of examples of

---

* Walther speaks of the letter of Liberati as a great curiosity. It seems he was never able to get a sight of it, and therefore was content with an extract of it, with which he was furnished by a friend of his, Gottfried Heinrich Stoltzels, chapel-master to the duke of Saxe Gotha, and from it has inserted the character of Francesco Foggia in its place. Better success has attended the researches of the author of this work, who thinks himself warranted in saying that the letter, which is now lying before him, abounds with very many curious particulars of musical history, which it would have been scarcely possible to supply from any other materials ; and of this opinion it seems was Andrea Adami, who, in his Osservazioni per ben regolare il Coro de i Cantori della Cappella Pontificia, has followed Liberati very closely, and even adopted some of his mistakes.

† See a detection of this error in the account of Palestrina, given in page 419, et seq.

‡ Brossard relates that Berardi very ingeniously comprised the syllables of Guido in the following line :—

UT RElevet MIserum FAtum SOLitosque LAbores.

But it does not appear in this place, nor is it to be found in any of the tracts above spoken of ; but it may be remarked that the sign of the printer at Bologna who published Corelli's Opera terza, is a violin with this verse round it.

counterpoint, and a series of exercises on the twelve tones.

In 1693, Berardi being then maestro di cappella of the church di Santa Maria in Trastevere, published at Bologna ' Il Perche Musicale overo Staffetta Armonica ;' and, in 1706, Arcani Musicali ; and these, according to Walther, are all his works.

The writings of this author abound with particulars worthy the attention of a student in music. He appears to have been an ingenious, and certainly was a modest man, for, although a canon, and maestro di cappella of a cathedral, he governed himself according to the directions of his friend Marco Scacchi, and submitted his works to his inspection ; and of his friendly disposition towards those of his own profession a judgement may be formed from the tract entitled Il Perche Musicale, which is divided into sections, many of which are dedicated to contemporary musicians in terms of great esteem and affection.

IsAAC Vossius, a man of considerable parts and learning, was the son of Gerard John Vossius, already spoken of. He was born at Leyden in the year 1618, and, having his father for his instructor, soon became distinguished for his proficiency in academical learning, and was honoured with the favour of Christina, queen of Sweden, who corresponded with him by letters, and invited him to her court, and was taught by him the Greek language ; but, about the year 1652, having incautiously intended a design to write against Salmasius, who at that time stood very high in her favour, the queen withdrew her regard from Vossius, and dismissed him from any further attendance on her.

After the death of his father, Isaac Vossius was by the university of Leyden complimented with the offer of the history professor's chair, but thought proper to decline it. In the year 1670 he came into England, and was created doctor of laws in the university of Oxford. In 1673 king Charles II. appointed him a canon of Windsor, and assigned him lodgings in the castle, where he died in 1688, leaving behind him a library, which for a private one, was then supposed to be the best in the world.

Of his works, which are not near so numerous, nor indeed so valuable as those of his father, the most popular is his treatise ' De Poematum cantu et ' viribus Rythmi,' printed at Oxford in 1673, of which here follows an account :—

It begins with a remark that music is of two kinds, that is to say, it is either naked and simple, consisting of mere sounds, or of sounds joined to words ; and that although many think them to be poets who are able to sing verses, because anciently poets were also musicians, he held a different opinion, because poets were not the only singers of poems ; the distinction between the two being that those who made verses were called poets, and those that sung them singers, or, by a more honourable name, musicians. He says that the primitive verses wanted feet, and were therefore ungraceful, but that metre and rythmus were afterwards invented, which are as it were the very soul of poetry, and of these he

speaks to the following purpose. The beauty and elegance of verse consist in an apt disposition of different numbers and their symmetry. The Greeks first observed that it was not sufficient that the verses should run with an equal number of syllables, without a ratio of time, and therefore divided the syllables into long, short, and ambiguous : afterwards finding that those verses did not move concinnously which wanted members, they distributed the syllables into classes, and composed feet of two, three, or more, that the motion of the cantus and verses might be distinguished by measures and intervals. But as it was not sufficient for the members to be moved unless they had motions suited to the affections which they were designed to express, they invented feet of different times and modes, by which they represented in so lively a manner, not only the conspicuous motions of the body, but the dispositions of the mind, that there was scarce any thing existing that they could not express in their cantus and numbers.

After a brief enumeration of the various kinds of metrical feet, he proceeds in his observations on the force and efficacy of that particular arrangement and interchange of quantities, which he calls the Rythmus, ascribing to that only those wonderful effects which are said to have been wrought by the music of the ancients. He says that the ancient manner of reciting verses differed but little from the practice of scanning ; though he admits a difference between the cantus of singing, and recitation or common speech ; in the latter whereof he says it was ever esteemed a fault for the voice to ascend higher than the Diapente. He adds, that among the ancient musicians there was a threefold method of prolation, namely, continuous, diastemical or distinguished by intervals ; and another in a medium between both ; and that Aristides Quintilianus, Martianus Capella, and Boetius uniformly assigned the latter to the recitation of verses ; on the contrary, he says Dionysius Halicarnassæus and Nichomachus make no distinction between the voice of recitation and common speech.

To manifest his contempt of modern music and musicians, he cites, from Saxo Grammaticus, the relation of the effects of music on Ericus king of Denmark, already mentioned in the course of this history, but insists it is a fable borrowed from the story of Alexander and Timotheus. He says that the power of exciting the affections by music has ceased above these thousand years, that is to say, from the time that the knowledge and use of the rythmus was lost ; and that now, when music is much more flourishing than it was at the time when Ericus lived, no musician would dare attempt what his citharedist is said to have effected.

After observing that there is a rythmus in the arterial pulse, and bestowing a few commendations on Galen for his diligent enquiries on that subject in his book ' De Natura et Differentiis Pulsuum,' he asserts that the Chinese, as they excel the Europeans in many things, so do they in the medicinal art ; for that without enquiring of their patients whether their head, their stomach, their shoulders, or any other part of their body gives them pain, they feel both pulses at the same instant, and, without ever failing, pronounce the nature of the disorder with which the patient is afflicted.

Upon that controverted question, namely, whether the ancients were acquainted with music in consonance or not, the author, with his usual temerity, delivers these as his sentiments :—

' Some have arrived to such a pitch of folly as to ' assert in their writings that the Concentus of several ' voices was utterly unknown to the ancients ; and ' that what they called Symphony, was nothing more ' than the Concentus sung alternately. Can any ' person be so ignorant of Greek and Latin, as not ' to see that even the terms Harmony, Symphony, ' and Concentus testify the contrary ? Who can ' there be so foolish as to think that the chorusses of ' singers and troops of symphonists under a Choro- ' didasculus, did not sing together but alternately ? ' Surely if this had been the case, Seneca must have ' lied when he spoke thus in Epistle 84. "Non " vides, quam multorum vocibus chorus constet ? " Unus tamen ex omnibus sonus redditur. Aliqua " illic acuta est, aliqua gravis, aliqua media. Ac- " cedunt veris feminæ, interponuntur tibiæ. Singu- " lorum ibi latent voces, omnium apparent." * What ' need I bring down Plato, Aristotle, Cicero, and ' an infinite number of others, who all with one ' unanimous consent teach us, that harmony or con- ' centus was made when several voices, differing in ' the acumen and gravity of sound, were equally ' mingled together ? I make no mention of the ' manifold concentus of the tibiæ, or the harmonical ' fullness of the hydraulic organ, being ashamed to ' dwell any longer on a thing that is so manifest.'

He says that the patrons of this age infer the ignorance of the ancients with respect to music in consonance, from this circumstance, to wit, that they did not reckon the ditone, and trihemitone, or semi-ditone, nor either of the two sixths, namely, the greater and the less, among the consonants ; but that this argument is no better than that other adduced to prove that the modern music is more complete than the ancient, namely, that the system of the ancients contained only fifteen chords, which is less by a hexachord than that of Guido ; but he says that many of the improvements ascribed to Guido are erroneously attributed to him ; for that in the framing of the scale he did but follow the example of the organs and harps of his time, which consisted respectively of twenty pipes or strings, as a writer more ancient than Guido by some ages testifies.

The application of the syllables UT, RE, MI, &c. he makes to be an invention of no worth ; never-theless he says that the Egyptians prolated their musical sounds by the vowels, which he conceives to be the more convenient practice ; and that the very Barbarians distinguished their sounds by such like syllables or diminutive words, long before the time of Guido.†

The arguments of the imperfection of the ancient music, arising from the form of their instruments, he endeavours, but in vain, to refute ; and hastens to a description of the ancient hydraulic organ, the representation whereof, as given by him, seems to be but a creature of his own imagination. After describing this instrument, he censures Kepler for affirming that the ancient organists were no better than the modern Utricularii, or mendicant bag-pipers: an appellation which he says more properly belongs to the modern organists. As to the cantus of the tibia blown on by the mouth, he thinks it may be truly said that the modern performers know no more of it than the ancient shepherds ; and that, if we except the Chinese, who alone excel in this kind of music, we shall find none in this age that can please even a moderate ear.

Speaking of the ratios of chords, and of pipes, he refutes an error of the elder Galileo, in his dialogues De Motu, which it seems had been adopted by Mersennus and Des Cartes, namely, that, cæteris paribus, the thinner chords yield the acuter sounds; the contrary whereof he affirms to be the fact.

After having treated very copiously on the Tibiæ of the ancients, and, without the least evidence from history, discriminated them into species, some as peculiar to the Phrygian, others to the Dorian, and others to the Ionian mood, he proceeds to con-sider the instruments of the moderns, as namely, the Harp, the Testudo or lute, the Barbiton or viol, and the Pandura or violin, the invention of all which he ascribes to Barbarians, for this notable reason, that the necks of these several instruments are divided by those transverse chords which we term frets ; whereas no such appear in the instru-ments of the ancients. He adds, that these Com-pendia are evidences of ignorance in the modern musicians ; and, lamenting the deplorable state of music in his time, professes to question whether since that of Charlemagne, the science has not sustained a loss more than equal to all the improve-ments of the moderns.

He censures very severely those Plasmata or divisions, which he says distinguish the modern music ; and adds, that both the Italian and French singers abound in flexions ; but that the Italians use the longer, and are therefore laughed at by the French, who, to do them justice, he says, observe the rythmus, which is the reason that in many of their songs we meet with concinnous and very elegant motions. He commends the Italians and Spaniards for their distinct articulation in singing.

After such a laboured encomium on the rythmus of the ancients as this of Vossius appears to be, it cannot be expected but that he should treat the invention of the Cantus Mensurabilis, its substitute, with the greatest contempt ; and accordingly he

---

* ' Do you not see how many voices the chorus consists of ? yet there ' is but one sound rendered by them all ; some voices are acute, some ' grave, and some in the medium ; women are joined with the men, and ' the tibiæ are interposed. In this case the voice of either person is not ' to be distinguished, but those of all may be heard.'

† It is evident from this passage that Vossius was ignorant of the use of the syllables. All men are sensible that musical sounds are most easily prolated by vowels associated with consonants, but none but a person skilled to some degree in music knows that it was for the purpose of ascertaining the stations of the two semitones in the diapason that the syllables of Guido were taken.

has delivered his sentiments of it in the following terms : 'To comprehend many things in a few 'words, all the notes of which modern music con-'sists are, the Maxima, Longa, Breve, Semibreve, 'Minim, Semiminim, Fusa, and Semifusa, which 'as they are barbarous names, so are they also 'barbarous and foolish inventions. If we have 'a mind that the cantus should be elegant and con-'cinnous, it should be ordered so that every syllable 'should answer to a correspondent syllable. But 'as there are no syllables which are not either long 'or short, and of these, as I have often said before, 'the short consists only of one time, and the long 'of two; so also should there be no more nor no 'fewer notes introduced than two sorts, to agree 'with the minim and semiminim, as they are com-'monly called; for who is there that ever dreamt 'of syllables of eight, or sixteen, or thirty-two 'tones, or of others so short, that no speech can 'possibly express them; who does not laugh at the 'sound of one syllable prolated so slowly, that two 'or three heroic verses may be most commodiously 'uttered in the same time? Away therefore with 'these elgancies; and, if we have any love for 'music, let us follow the example of the ancients 'in this as in other things; for if we restore the 'Rythmus, joined to a distinct pronunciation of the 'words, so that the ancient form and beauty of 'music may return, all these common ornaments of 'the modern cantus, I mean the small flexions, 'teretismata or iterations, fugues, syncopes, and 'other such foolish artifices, will vanish as shades 'and clouds on the appearance of the sun.'*

In the course of this work, which is nothing better than an unintelligible rhapsody, the author is very lavish in his censures of the ignorance and folly of other writers on the subject of music; and there are many who think that his enthusiasm and extreme bigotry have justly rendered him liable to the imputation of the latter; for the proof whereof the following most curious passage is selected from page 62 of his work, and submitted to the reflection of the impartial reader. 'Many people take delight 'in the rubbing of their limbs, and combing of their 'hair; but these exercises would delight much 'more, if the servants at the baths and of the 'barbers were so skilful in this art, that they could 'express any measures with their fingers. I re-'member that more than once I have fallen into the 'hands of men of this sort, who could imitate any 'measure of songs in combing the hair, so as some-'times to express very intelligibly Iambics, Trochees, 'Dactyls, &c. from whence there arose to me no 'small delight.'†

In a word, the above-mentioned treatise abounds with evidence of that gross credulity for which the

author was remarkable ;‡ nor is this the only weak-ness with which he is justly charged; his partiality for the ancients, his bold and hasty conclusions, his affected contempt of all modern improvements in science, his insolent treatment of such as differed from him in opinion, and, above all, his vanity, have placed him in the foremost rank of literary coxcombs. As to his work, it may upon the whole be said to be a very futile and unsatisfactory disquisition.

Giovanni Maria Bononcini, a disciple of Gio. Paolo Colonna, maestro di cappella in the church of San Petronio in Bologna, was a celebrated composer, and the author of a treatise printed at the same place in the year 1673, entitled 'Musico prattico, 'che brevemente dimostra il modo di giungere alla 'perfetta cognizione di tutte quelle cose, che con-'corrono alla composizione de i Canti, e di ciò ch' 'all' Arte del Contrapunto si ricerca.'

In the compilation of this treatise the author appears to have availed himself of the writings and compositions of the most celebrated Italian musicians, as well theorists as practical composers, of whom he gives a numerous list at the beginning of his book. About the year 1695 he published a second part, which was translated into the German language, and printed at Stutgard in the year 1701. The subject matter of these two books is, first, an intro-duction to the science of music, and next the pre-cepts of musical composition; the author appears to be eminently skilled in the science, but his work contains scarce any thing but may be found in the writings of others who had treated the subject before him : and indeed his censure is so justly applicable to the Italian writers from the time of Franchinus downward, that the bare mention of their works of this kind must suffice in our future memoirs of them.

Of his musical compositions there are extant 'Cantate per Camera à voce sola,' dedicated to Francesco II. d'Este, reigning duke of Modena, printed at Bologna in 1677. In the dedication to this work he promises in a short time to publish Madrigals for five voices, on the twelve modes, with the title of Composizione da Tavolino,§ but whether

* Page 128.

† 'Gaudent complures membrorum frictione et pectinatione capillorum, 'verum hæc ipsa multò magis juvant si balnearii et tonsores adeo in 'arte sua fuerint periti, ut quosvis etiam numeros suis possint explicare 'digitis. Non semel recordor me in ejusmodi incidisse manus, qui 'quorumvis etiam canticorum motus suis imitarentur pectinibus, ita ut 'nonnunquam iambos vel trochæos, alias dactylos vel anapæstos, non-'nunquam amphibraches aut pæonas quam scitissime experimerent, 'unde haud modica oriebatur delectatio.'

‡ His credulity, and also the singularity of his character, will appear from the following particulars, which Mons. des Maizeaux has recorded of him in his Life of St. Evremont. He says that Vossius understood most of the languages in Europe, without being able to speak one of them well; that he was intimately acquainted with the genius and customs of antiquity, but an utter stranger to the manners of his own times. That he published books to prove that the Septuagint version was divinely inspired, yet discovered in conversation, and by his behaviour in his last moments, that he believed no revelation at all: that in other respects he was the weakest and most credulous man alive, being ever ready to credit any extraordinary and wonderful re-lation, though ever so fabulous or ill-grounded. St. Evremont was used to spend the summers with the court at Windsor; he knew, and fre-quently conversed with Vossius; the above is his character of him, and Des Maizeaux has added to it many more particulars respecting Vossius to the same purpose.

Mons. Renaudot in his Dissertations added to the Anciennes Relations des Indes et de la Chine, relates that Vossius, having had frequent con-ferences with Father Martini, while he was in Holland, superintending the printing of his Atlas Chinois, made no scruple of believing all which that father told him concerning the wonderful things in China; and that he did not stop where Martini stopped, but proceeded farther, even to infer as a certain fact the antiquity of the Chinese accounts above that of the books of Moses. King Charles II. who knew his nature and character well, used to call him the strangest man in the world, for 'there is nothing,' the king would say, 'which he refuses to believe, 'except the Bible.' It is said that Lord Shaftesbury alludes to this in-consistent character of Vossius in his advice to an Author. Vide Characteristics, vol. I. page 345.

§ By this term we are to understand such vocal compositions as are usually sung by divers persons in a chamber, or sitting at a table : in the

he ever published them or not we are unable to say. 'Sinfonie a 5, 6, 7, a 8 Instromenti, con alcune à 'una e due Trombe, servendo ancora per Violini,' dedicated to his master Gio. Paolo Colonna, Bologna 1685. 'Sinfonie à tre Instromenti, col Basso per l' 'Organo.' Bologna 1686. Both these collections are in fact Sonate da Chiesa, and, like the first and third operas of Corelli, consist of slow movements, with fugues of various measures intermixed. Masses for eight voices, dedicated to Orazio Maria Bonfioli, abbat of the church di S. Giovanni in Monte, of which the author was maestro di cappella.

There were three other eminent musicians of the name of Bononcini, the sons of the above person; the one named Antonio resided at Modena; his name is to be found subscribed to a recommendatory epistle prefixed to Marcello's Psalms, printed at Venice in 1723. Gio. Battista, another of them, settled at Vienna, was composer to the emperor in 1703. Giovanni Bononcini is supposed to have been the younger of the three brothers; he also is one of those many eminent musicians who joined in the recommendation of Marcello's Psalms. He spent some years of his life in England; and, having been for a time composer to the opera at London, and the rival of Mr. Handel, a farther account of him will be given hereafter.

CLAUDE FRANCOIS MENESTRIER, a French Jesuit, wrote and published at Paris, in the year 1681, a treatise entitled 'Des Representations en Musique anciennes et modernes.' In this book, among a great variety of curious particulars, is contained a brief enquiry into the music of the Hebrews, in which the author cites the testimony of Origen to prove that the Song of Solomon is a poem of the dramatic kind, viz., an epithalamium on occasion of the nuptials of that prince, and was a representation in music, and enforces the argument with his own observations on the poem itself. He asserts that dramatic music was introduced into France in the time of the crusades, by the pilgrims, who returning from the Holy Land, formed themselves as it were into choirs, and exhibited spectacles of devotion, accompanied with music and songs, in which were declared the achievements and sufferings of saints and martyrs, with suitable elogies. Menestrier is very circumstantial in this relation; and, notwithstanding what is said in page 529 of this work, there seems, upon a review of the passage, no reason to doubt the truth of it; and his information is the more worthy of note, for that it leads us to a practice, which it is highly probable suggested to St. Philip Neri the introduction into Italy of the oratorio or sacred drama, of which it is generally said he was the inventor.

He relates that in the year 1647, Cardinal Mazarine being desirous of introducing into France the divertisements of Italy, procured a company of comedians to represent at the Palais Royal the drama of Orpheus and Eurydice, in Italian verse, with the music. And that in 1669 Lewis XIV.

Miscellanea Musicale of Angelo Berardi, parte prima, page 41, is the following passage: 'Lo stile da camera si divide, e si considera sotto tre 'stili. I. Madrigali da tavolino. II. Madrigali concertati con il basso 'continuo. III. Cantilene concertate con varie sorti di strumenti.'

having concluded the treaty of the Pyrennées, and thereby given peace to Europe, and being at leisure to cultivate the arts, he, by the advice of the Cardinal, established academies of painting, sculpture, architecture, philosophy, and mathematics; and by his letters patent of the twenty-eighth of June, 1669, granted liberty to the Sieur Perrin to establish at Paris, and in other cities, academies of music for the public performance of musical dramas agreeable to the practice in Italy, Germany, and England. He says that under this patent Perrin continued for a few years to exhibit entertainments of this kind, but that afterwards the same was revoked, and another granted to Lully in the following terms :—

'LOUIS par la grace de Dieu, Roi de France et de 'Navarre, à tous presens et à venir, salut. Les 'Sciences et les Arts étant les ornemens les plus 'considèrables des Etats, nous n'avons point eu de 'plus agreables divertissemens depuis que nous avons 'donné la paix à nos peuples, que de les faire revivre, 'en appellant prés de nous tous ceux qui se sont 'acquis la reputation d'y exceller, non seulement 'dans l'étenduë de nôtre Royaume; mais aussi dans 'les Pays étrangers : et pour les obliger d'avantage 'de s'y perfectionner, nous les avons honorés des 'marques de nôtre estime, et de nôtre bienveillance : 'et comme entre les Arts Liberaux, la Musique y 'tient un des premiers rangs, nous aurions dans le 'dessein de la faire reussir avec tous ces avantages, 'par nos Lettres patentes du 28 Juin, 1669, accordé 'au Sieur Perrin une permission d'établir en nôtre 'bonne Ville de Paris, et autres de nôtre Royaume, 'des Academies de Musique pour chanter en public 'de pieces de Theatre, comme il se pratique en 'Italie, en Allemagne, et en Angleterre. Mais ayant 'été depuis informé que les peines et les soins que 'ledit Perrin a pris pour cét établissement, n'ont pû 'seconder pleinement nôtre intention et élever la 'Musique au point que nous nous l'étions promis; 'nous avons crû pour mieux réüssir qu'il étoit à 'propos d'en donner la conduite à une personne, 'dont l'experience, et la capacité nous fussent connuës, 'et qui eût assez de suffisance pour fournir des éleves 'tant pour bien chanter, et actionner sur le Theatre, 'qu'à dresser des bandes de Violons, Flûtes, et 'autres instrumens. A ces Causes bien informez de 'l'intelligence, et grande connoissance que s'est acquis 'nôtre cher et bien-amé Jean Baptiste Lully, au fait 'de la Musique, dont il nous a donné, et donne 'journellement de tres-agreables preuves depuis 'plusieurs années, qu'il s'est attaché à nôtre service, 'qui nous ont convié de l'honorer de la charge de 'Surintendant, et Compositeur de la Musique de 'nôtre chambre; Nous avons au dit Sieur Lully, 'permis et accordé, permettons et accordons par ces 'presentes, signées de nôtre main d'établir une 'Academie Royale de Musique dans nôtre bonne 'Ville de Paris, qui sera composée de tel nombre, 'et qualité de personnes qu'il avisera bon être, que 'nous choisirons et arréterons, sur le rapport qu'il 'nous en fera pour faire des representations devant 'nous, quand il nous plaira, des pieces de Musique 'que seront composées, tant en vers François qu'au-

'tre langues ètrangeres, pareilles, aux Academies 'd'Italie, &c.'

This book farther contains many curious accounts of public spectacles, dramatic and musical representations in sundry courts of Europe, upon occasion of the marriages and births of princes, and other solemnities.

Menestrier also published, in 1682, a tract entitled 'Des Ballets anciens et modernes selon les Regles du Theatre.' The general contents whereof are inserted in the Act. Erudit. Lipsiæ. The author died on the twenty-first day of January, 1705.

Johann Pachelbel, a celebrated organist and composer of music, was born at Nuremburg on the first day of September, 1653. Discovering in his early youth a strong inclination to liberal studies, particularly music, he was provided by his parents with the ablest instructors that could be procured. His master for the harpsichord was Heinrich Schemmern, of Nuremberg, under whose tuition he remained for a few years; after which he went to Altdorff, meaning there to have finished his studies, but, finding himself straitened in his circumstances, having obtained permission of absence for one year, he, for the sake of a better subsistence, and greater improvement, removed to the Gymnasium Poeticum in Regensburg, where he remained three years, prosecuting his studies particularly in music, with so much diligence, that the fame of his proficiency spread throughout Germany. Upon his quitting Regensburg he went to Vienna, and became vicar to the organist of the church of St. Stephen in that city. This situation, though attended with but little profit, was very agreeable to him, as it procured him the acquaintance and friendship of the famous Johann Caspar Kerl then chapel-master at Vienna. In 1675, Pachelbel had a call to Eisenach, which he readily accepted, and upon his arrival was preferred to the dignity of court organist. In 1678 he removed to Erfurth, and for twelve years was eminently distinguished in that city. In 1690 he was invited to Stutgard, but that city being threatened with an invasion of the French, he quitted it soon after his arrival, and settled at Gotha. In 1695, George Caspar Wecker, who had been for many years organist of Nuremburg, died, and Pachelbel received an invitation to succeed him, which he readily embraced, being desirous of a settlement in his native country; and in that station he continued till the day of his death, which was the third of March, 1706, or, as Walther rather thinks, about Candlemas, 1705. Pachelbel is celebrated as one of the most excellent of those German Organists, of whom Kerl is accounted the father. He laboured in the improvement of the grand and full style on the organ, and was no less solicitous to perfect the vocal music of the church. The works published by him are but few, being only four Funeral Hymns, composed at Erfurth in the time of the pestilence that then raged there, and published at the same place; and seven Sonatas for two violins and a bass, and Airs with variations, both printed at Nuremberg.

Joachim Meyer was a doctor of laws, and professor in the university of Gottingen, where, in the year 1686, he was also appointed professor of music, and Cantor Figuralis. These employments he held for the space of about ten years, when retaining to himself the bare title of professor of music, he relinquished the practice of it, and gave lectures on history and public law. Upon the death of Justus Dranszfeld he became rector of the college, but at the end of three years quitted that honorable station on account of his age and infirmities, when, as the reward of his great merit, he was permitted to receive and enjoy all his salaries and emoluments, with the addition of a pension. He nevertheless continued to reside in his college, and, being esteemed one of the ablest lawyers of his time, was frequently called on to assist at consultations with the members of the state, and those of that profession, till the year 1732, in which he died. In the year 1726 he published a tract entitled 'Unvorgreifffiche Gedancken uber die Neuliche ingeriffene Theatrilifche-kirchen-MUSIC,' in which he very feverely censures sundry of his contemporaries, who, by the levity of their compositions, had confounded the ecclesiastic with the theatric style.

Johann Kuhnau, the son of a fisherman of Geysingen, a town near Altenberg, on the borders of Bohemia, four miles distant from Dresden, was an eminently learned and skilful musician. In the year 1684 he was organist of the church of St. Thomas at Leipsic; and, while he was in that station wrote a dissertation De Juribus circa Musicos Ecclesiasticos, and afterwards defended it against the censures of his adversaries. In 1689 he published lessons for the harpsichord in two volumes, and, in 1696, seven Sonatas, entitled Clavier-Fruchte, that is to say, fruits of the Clavier; and, in 1700, six sonatas entitled Biblifche Hiftorien;* and, in the same year, to silence the clamours of some ignorant men of his profession, who envying his merit and reputation, had libelled him, he wrote a small tract, which he entitled the Musical Quacksalver. In the same year, 1700, Kuhnau was appointed Director Musices of the university of Leipsic, in which station he died on the fifth day of June, 1722, in the sixty-third year of his age, and was succeeded in that honourable post by John Sebastian Bach. Ernest Wilhelm Hertzog, a German count palatine, and a magistrate of Merseburg, has celebrated the memory of Kuhnau in a discourse entitled 'Memoria 'beate defuncti directoris chori musices Lipsiensis, 'Dn. Johannis Kuhnau, polyhistoris musici, et 'reliqua, summopere incluti, &c.' printed at Leipsic in 1722, and therein extols him for his skill 'in 'Theologiâ, in Jure, in Oratoriâ, in Poësi, in 'Algebrâ et Mathesi, in Linguis exoticis, et in Re 'Musicâ.' He left behind him two manuscripts in Latin, which have never yet been published, the one entitled 'Tractatus de Monochordo, seu Musica 'antiqua ac hodierna, occasione Tetrachordi, non ad

* A modern author, Francis Lustig, of Groningen, in a treatise entitled 'Inleiding tot de Musykkunde,' takes notice of this work, and says that in it is a lively representation, in musical notes, of David manfully combating Goliah.

'Systema tantum, sed et Melopœiam accommodati,
'cum prævio Præludio e penu Matheseos puræ
'depromto, ac lectorem ad intelligenda, quæ in hoc
'opere tractantur, præparante.' The other manuscript abovementioned is entitled 'Disputatio de
Triade Harmonicâ.'

JOHANN KROPFFGANTZ was the son of a burgomaster of a small town in Germany named Arnshaug,
who was himself a good musician and lutenist.
He was born in the year 1668, at Neustadt on the
Orla in Osterland. At nine years of age he began
to play on the lute; and, having been removed to
Leipsic for farther instruction, he, at the age of
twelve, became a great proficient on that instrument. Being intended by his father for the profession of a merchant, and not a musician, Kropffgantz laid aside his instrument, and applied himself
to business, and, in a course of years, became
a merchant at Breslau. After some years continuance in trade, he was moved by an irresistible
desire to betake himself again to music; and took
lessons in the theory, and also in the practice, on
his favourite instrument, from the ablest masters,
namely, Schuchart and Moley, who was then lately
returned from Paris, and others no less eminent.
He continued in this course for twenty-five years,
till, having the misfortune to dislocate his right
hand, he had nothing left to employ him but the
study of the theory of music, which he pursued
with great ardour. The time of his death is uncertain; he left three children, viz., two sons and
a daughter, who were all excellent performers on
the lute; the latter, named Johanna Eleonora, was
born on the fifth of November, 1710; and it was
for many years a kind of fashion for the nobility
and strangers, whose occasions drew them to Breslau,
to visit her, and be entertained with her fine
performance.

GABRIEL NIVERS was one of the four organists of
the chapel of Lewis XIV. and also organist of the
church of St. Sulpice, at Paris; he was the author
of a very learned and curious tract, entitled Dissertation sur le Chant Gregorien, published at Paris
in 1683.* The occasion of writing this book was,
that the Cantus Gregorianus, in the course of so
many years as had elapsed since its original institution, had been greatly corrupted. Nivers
undertook to restore it to its original purity, in
order to which he had recourse to anicent manuscripts, and particularly those numerous tracts on
the modes or tones from the time of Guido and
Berno the abbot, down to the end of the fifteenth

century, of which mention has been made in the
course of this history; and in this laborious task
Nivers succeeded so well, that he restored the
church-music of France to its original purity and
simplicity; and, agreeably to his corrections, the
antiphonary of the Gallican church was republished
by the express command of the king himself.

The Dissertation sur le Chant Gregorien is a
small octavo volume, divided into eighteen chapters,
entitled as follows :—

Chapitre I. De l'origine, et de l'excellence du
Chant Gregorien. Chap. II. Du l'utilité du Chant
de l'Eglise, et de ses effets. Chap. III. Contre les
Heretiques et tous ceux qui blasment le Chant de
l'Eglise. Chap. IV. Que le Chant Gregorien ou
Romain, ayant esté communiqué, et s'estant répandu
dans toutes les Eglises des Diocèses et des Ordres
Religieux, a esté changé et corrompu en plusieurs
parties. Chap. V. Que le Chant Romain, ou le
Chant Gregorien mesme à Rome, a esté corrompu
en quelques parties, quoy que neantmoins il y soit
resté le plus pur et le plus correct de tous. Chap.
VI. De la facilité qu'il y avoit de corrompre le
Chant Gregorien, et de la necessité qu'il y a de le
corriger. Chap. VII. Des abus qui se sont glissez
dans la maniere de chanter le Pleinchant. Chap.
VIII. Des abus commis au Chant Gregorien dans
plusieurs parties de l'Office divin, contre les Regles
de la science, prouvez par les termes de l'Epistre
de saint Bernard, conformément aux mesmes Regles.
Chap. IX. Du nombre, des figures, et de l'usage des
Caracteres du Pleinchant. Chap. X. De la quantité
des Notes. Chap. XI. Du commencement de l'Office
divin. Chap. XII. Des Antiennes. Où il est traité
a fond des huit Tons de l'Eglise. Chap. XIII. Des
Pseaumes. Où il est traité a fond de leurs Ter-
minaisons differentes et specifiques selon les huit
Tons du Chant Gregorien. Chap. XIV. Des Capi-
tules et des Respons. Chap. XV. Des Hymnes.
Chap. XVI. Des Cantiques. Chap. XVII. Des
autres Parties de l'Office divin. Chap. dernier.
Que le Chant Gregorien est le plus authentique, et
le plus considerable de tous les Chants Eccle-
siastiques.

At the end of the Dissertation are the forms of
the offices, with the musical notes adjusted according
to the rules laid down by the authors. These are
entitled ' Formulæ Cantus ordinarii Officii divini,'
they direct the intonation of the prayers, the books
of the prophets, the epistles, the gospels, the
versicles, the office for the dead, and other parts
of divine service; and are followed by a short
discourse, entitled ' Tractatus de modis canendi
Psalmos et Cantica, secundum octo Cantûs Gregoriani tonos,' including a formula of the eight
tones, entitled Tabula Tonorum. After these follow
six litanies, the Stabat Mater, sundry anthems to
the Virgin Mary, and a prayer for the king, all
with musical notes.

The author of this book appears to have been
well skilled in ecclesiastical history, and to have
read to good purpose the writings of Amalarius
Fortunatus, St. Bernard, Durandus, Cardinal Bona,

---

* Before this time, but at what particular period is not ascertained,
a French ecclesiastic, named Jumillac, published a tract entitled ' La
Science et Pratique du Pleinchant,' esteemed the best of its kind. Hist.
Mus. tom. IV. page 80. In 1678 an author named Gerolamo Cantone,
Maestro de' Novizi, e Vicario nel Convento di Francesco di Torino,
published a tract entitled 'Armonia Gregoriana,' containing the rudiments
of the Cantus Ecclesiasticus. In 1682 was published a work entitled
' Cantore addotrinato,' by Matteo Coferati, the preface to which is a
discourse ' dell' origine e progressi del Canto Ecclesiastico,' written by
Francesco Cionacci, a priest of Florence. In 1686 was published at
Milan, 'Il Canto Ecclesiastico,' by Marzio Erculeo, in which, besides the
necessary instructions for the Cantus Ecclesiasticus, are contained the
forms of the most solemn functions in the Romish service. But the
most copious treatise on the subject is one with the title of ' Istruzioni
Corali, by Domenico Scorpione, maestro di cappella, e del Canto nel
Sagro Seminario di Benevento,' printed at Benevento in 1702.

MATTEO SIMONELLI ROMANO,

CANT. DELLA CAPP. PONT.

MDCLXII.

and other of the Roman ritualists. In short, the Dissertation sur le Chant Gregorien is a most entertaining and valuable work, and is the best history of church-music any where extant.

In the year 1697 Nivers published at Amsterdam, Traité de la Composition de Musique. This work was printed with a Dutch translation by Estienne Roger, and is dedicated to a merchant at Amsterdam, named Abraham Maubach. In the general catalogue of books printed at Paris, published in the year 1729, quarto, the two following articles are ascribed to Nivers, Le premier Livre des Motets, and Le premier Livre des Pieces d'Orgue.

CHAP. CXL.

Matteo Simonelli, (a Portrait), was a singer in the pontifical chapel in the year 1662, and was, in the language of the Italian writers, a grand contrapuntist; for which reason, as also for his excellency in the church style, of which he gave proofs in a variety of compositions for the most solemn of the pontifical functions, he was styled the Palestrina of his time. Nor was he more celebrated for learning and skill in his profession, than for his assiduity and success in teaching the science and practice of music to others. He was the instructor of a great number of pupils, and had the honour to be the first master to Corelli. It does not appear that any compositions of his were ever published, but his works are preserved with great care in the college of the pontifical singers at Rome.

Giovanni Legrenzi was organist of the church of Santa Maria Maggiore in Bergamo, afterwards maestro di cappella in the church della Spirito Santo in Ferrara: and in his latter years maestro di cappella of the church of St. Mark at Venice. The works of this author consist of Masses, Motets, Sonate per Chiesa and da Camera, Psalms, Litanies, and Cantatas. His opera XIV. is entitled ' Echi ' di Riverenza di Cantate, e Canzoni a gli Applausi ' festeggianti ne gli Himenei delle Altezze Sereniss. ' di Maria Anna Arciduchessa d' Austria, e Gio. ' Guglielmo Prencipe Co. Palatino del Reno, &c.' ' being twenty-four Cantatas, à voce sola, published at Bologna in 1678. The last of his publications is his Opera XVII. entitled ' Motetti Sacri à Voce sola con tre Stromenti,' published in 1692. Legrenzi was the master of Antonio Lotti, of Venice, his successor in the chapel of St. Mark; and also of Michael Angelo Gasparini, a brother, as it is supposed, of Francesco Gasparini, both of whom resided in the house of Legrenzi in the year 1686, for the purpose of receiving his instructions.

Giovanni Battista Bassani, maestro di cappella of the cathedral church of Bologna, was a very voluminous composer of music, having given to the world no fewer than thirty-one different works. He is equally celebrated both as a composer for the church and for concerts, and was besides a celebrated performer on the violin, and, as it is said, taught Corelli on that instrument. His compositions consist of Masses, Psalms, Motets with instrumental parts, and Sonatas for violins; his fifth opera in particular, containing twelve Sonatas for two violins and a bass, is much esteemed; it is written in a style wonderfully grave and pathetic, and abounds with evidences of great learning and fine invention. The first and third operas of Corelli are apparently formed after the model of this work.

Bassani was one of the first who composed motets for a single voice, with accompaniments of violins; a practice which is liable to objection, as it assimilates church-music too nearly to that of the chamber: and of his solo-motets it must be confessed that they differ in style but little from opera airs and cantatas; two operas of them, viz., the eighth and the thirteenth, were printed in London, by Pearson, above fifty years ago, with the title of Harmonia Festiva: many of the masters here gave them to their scholars as lessons; and there are ladies now living, who had Mr. Robinson, the late organist of Westminster abbey, for their master, who yet sing to the harpsichord those two favourite airs of Bassani, Quid Arma, quid Bella, and ' Alligeri Amores.'

Ercole Bernabei, a Roman by birth, and a disciple of Horatio Benevoli, succeeded Kerl as chapelmaster to the elector of Bavaria, Ferdinando Maria. After that he was called to the same office in the church of San Luigi de' Francesi in Rome; and at length, upon the decease of Benevoli, maestro di cappella of the pontifical chapel. He was the master of Steffani, and died about the year 1690. In the year 1669 he published at Rome a fine collection of Madrigals for three and four voices. At his decease, viz., in 1691, a collection of Motets, composed by Bernabei, was published at Munich, and, some years after, another at Amsterdam.

Agostino Steffani was born about the year 1650, at Castello Franco, a small frontier town in the territory of Venice.* Of his family or descent nothing certain is known; nor is there any further ground for conjecture, than his having in his infancy been a singer in some neighbouring cathedral church or chapel; a circumstance, from which we may at least conclude that his parents were not distinguished for their rank in life.

His want of the advantages of birth and fortune was however amply recompensed by those extraordinary talents that nature had endowed him with, among which an excellent voice was perhaps not the least. He had not served above two years in the choir, when a nobleman of Germany, who had been at Venice to be present at the diversions of the carnival, happened upon some public occasion to hear him sing, and was so pleased with his voice and appearance, that, upon application to the chapelmaster, he procured his discharge from the choir, and took him to Bavaria, the place of his residence. At the expence of this beneficent person was Steffani maintained, and instructed in all the branches of useful and ornamental learning: the direction of his

---

* Walther says he was born at Leipsic, though his name seems to indicate that he was an Italian; but Mr. Handel, who knew him intimately, and furnished most of the particulars contained in his memoir, gave the author the above account of the place of his nativity.

musical studies in particular was committed to Signor Ercole Bernabei, then chapel-master to the elector of Bavaria, and one of the most considerable masters of his time. What proficiency he made under him will best appear from his works; and what opinion of his merit his tutor entertained, may be inferred from that strict friendship, which for many years subsisted between them. It is needless, as Steffani was a native of Italy, to say that he was of the Romish persuasion; however it must not be omitted, that, in compliance with the request of his munificent patron, who was desirous of making the learned education he had bestowed on him the means of some further advantage, our author at the proper age received ordination, and soon afterwards became entitled to an appellation, by which indeed he is now most commonly distinguished, viz. that of Abbate or Abbot.

In the course of his studies he had composed several Masses, Motets, Hymns, Kyries, Magnificats, and other essays in the church-style, which he thought proper now to exhibit, and they were occasionally performed in the chapel at Munich, so greatly to his reputation, that Ernestus Augustus, duke of Brunswic, the father of king George I. though a protestant prince, being a passionate lover of music, invited him to the court of Hanover, and, it is said, conferred on him the employment of master of his chapel,* and committed to his care the management of the opera, an entertainment which had then but lately found its way into Germany. The latter trust, however agreeable it might be to his inclination, was the occasion of great uneasiness to him; for, whether it was owing to the ignorance or petulance of the persons employed to sing, it was sometimes with great difficulty that they could be prevailed on to study their parts, so as to do justice to the composer; and even when their condescension was greatest in this respect, so many feuds and jealousies were continually arising among them, as frequently disappointed an illustrious audience of their entertainment. This particular is in some degree verified by what is related of the elector's son, the late king Geo. I. who, upon some such occasion as this, prevailed on our author to resign his charge for a short time to him, imagining perhaps that his rank and quality might give him a better title to command this set of people, than even the great merit of their manager; but he was soon convinced of the difficulty of the undertaking, for in a few days he quitted it, and left them to themselves, declaring that he could with much more ease command an army of fifty thousand men, than manage a company of opera singers.

The earlier compositions of Steffani were for the church, and consisted of Masses and Motets; but, being settled in Germany, he applied himself wholly to the study of secular music, and composed sundry operas, as namely, Alexander the Great, Orlando, Enrico, Alcides, Alcibiades, Atalanta, Il Trionfo

del Fato, and Le Rivali Concordi, which being translated from the Italian into the German language, were performed at Hamburg between the years 1694 and 1700. He also composed a few madrigals in five parts; a very fine one of his, 'Gettano il 'Re,' is frequently performed in the Academy of ancient Music, as is also one of his motets, 'Qui 'diligit Mariam,' the scores whereof were presents from himself to the society. A short duet, and an air from some of his operas were introduced into the English opera of Thomyris Queen of Scythia, performed at Drury-lane theatre in 1708, and adapted severally to the words, 'Prithee leave me,' and 'Farewell love.'

But the most celebrated of all his works are his duets, composed for two voices, with no other accompaniment than a bass calculated simply to sustain the harmony without increasing in effect the number of parts. It is probable that he might apply his studies so much to this species of composition, in compliance with the taste of the ladies about the court; for it is observable that the poetry of them is altogether of the amatory kind;† and it appears by little memorandums in several copies, that many of his duets were composed at the request of divers ladies of distinction; and that some of them were made for their own private practice and amusement. Who the particular persons were we are at a loss to discover, as they are distinguished only by initial letters, denoting their quality, except in the instance of the two duets beginning 'Inquieto mio cor,' and 'Che volete,' these appearing to have been made for and sung by her highness the electress of Brandenburg.‡

Of these compositions it is their least praise that Mr. Handel professed but to imitate them, in twelve duets which he composed for the practice of the late queen Caroline. Mattheson remarks of Steffani's duets, that they are imitations in the unison and octave, and for the most part they are so. By this circumstance they stand eminently distinguished from those desultory compositions that bear the name of duets, in which the air, whatever it be, is deserted before it has well reached the ear; as also from those other, in which the accompaniment is no better than the insipid harmony of thirds and sixths.§

The characteristic of these compositions is fine and elegant melody, original and varied modulation,

---

† The words of these poems were composed by the Marquis de Ariberti, Sig. Conte Palmieri, Abbate Guidi, hereafter mentioned in the life of Corelli, Sig. Averara, and Abbate Hortensio Mauro: this last named person wrote also the words for twelve duets, which Mr. Handel composed for the practice of the late queen Caroline when she was princess of Wales, who greatly admired this kind of composition.

‡ This must have been the admired lady Sophia Charlotta, only daughter of the aforesaid duke of Brunswic, and sister to the late king, and the person whom Corelli has honoured with the patronage of his Opera quinta. In the year 1684 she was married to Frederic III. marquis of Brandenburg, by whom she had issue the father of the present king of Prussia.

§ *Frederick prince of Wales had a collection of Steffani's duets in ten or twelve volumes in small oblong quarto, finely written, and the initia* letters ornamented. It was probably made for the princess Sophia or the elector her son (George I.) and contained about one hundred duets. This collection, excepting two volumes that were left behind by accident, the prince gave to the lady of Signor Capello, ambassador from the Republic of Venice, about the year 1744.*

and a contexture of parts so close, that in some instances canon itself is scarcely stricter; and, which is very remarkable, this connection is maintained with such art as not to affect the air materially, or superinduce the necessity of varying it in order to accommodate it to the harmony. But as these compositions exceed the power of verbal d-scription, the following must testify to their merits:

ABBATE STEFFANI.

It may be remembered that in the account herein before given of Antimo Liberati, mention is made of a letter from him to Ovidio Persapegi. In this letter the author seems to adopt the notions respecting music, of Sextus Empiricus, in his treatise adversus Mathematicos, and of Cornelius Agrippa, in his discourse de Incertitudine et Vanitate Scientiarum, and affects to doubt whether the principles of music have any foundation in nature or not, or, in short, whether the pleasure arising from the contemplation of musical harmony is not resolvable into mere fancy, and a previous disposition of the mind to approve it. To obviate this silly notion, Steffani, in the year 1695, published a series of letters with this title, 'Quanta certezza abbia da suoi principii la musica,' which Andreas Werckmeister, a most excellent musician, and organist of the church of St. Martin at Halberstadt, translated and published at Quedlinburg, in the year 1700. Mattheson, in his Orchestra, page 300, 302, mentions two persons, namely, John Balhorn and   Weigweiser, as the authors of observations on these letters of Steffani; but, according to Mattheson's account, neither of them was either able to read the original, or in the translation to distinguish between the sense of the author, as delivered in the text, and the opinions of the translator, contained in the notes.

The musical talents of our author, however extraordinary, were far from being the only distinguishing part of his character: he had great natural endowments, and these he had considerably improved by study, and the conversation of learned and polite men. Nor did he confine his pursuits merely to those branches of learning that are immediately connected with his profession; but he applied himself to the study of the constitution and interests of the empire, by which he became enabled to act in a sphere that very few of his profession were ever known to attain—politics and the business of the public. It is therefore not to be wondered at that he was frequently employed in negociations to foreign courts, or that he should on such occasions be honoured with all the marks of distinction usually paid to public ministers. Among other transactions, he had a considerable share in concerting with the courts of Vienna and Ratisbon the scheme for erecting the duchy of Brunswic Lunenberg into an electorate; a step which the critical situation of affairs in the year 1692 rendered necessary to the preservation of a proper balance between the interests of the house of Austria and its adversaries, who, by the accession of the Newburg family to the electorate of the Rhine, were now thought to be too formidable. This important service could not fail of recommending him to the friends of the Austrian family; accordingly the elector, as a testimony of his regard, assigned him a pension of fifteen hundred rix-dollars per annum; and the pope, Innocent XI., promoted him to the bishopric of Spiga.* Though as the advantages resulting from this event could but very remotely, if at all, affect the interests of the Roman

* SPIGA is situate in Anatolia or Asia Minor, and is one of those nominal bishoprics which are said to be in partibus infidelium. Anciently it was a city of great eminence, and called Cyzicus. Vide Heyl. Cosmogr. page 610, Edit. 1703.

catholics in the empire, some have been induced to think that this signal instance of favour shown by the pontiff himself must have been the reward of a negociation more favourable to their cause, viz., the procuring liberty for those of that persuasion to erect a church at Hanover, and publicly to exercise their religion there; a privilege which, till the time Steffani solicited for it, had been denied them, and which at this juncture it was not thought prudent any longer to refuse.

He was now considered as a statesman, and was besides a dignitary of the church; and having a character to sustain, with which he imagined the public profession of his art not properly consistent, he forebore the setting his name to his future compositions, and adopted that of his secretary or copyist, Gregorio Piua. Influenced perhaps by the same motives, in the year 1708 he resigned his employment of chapel-master in favour of Mr. Handel.

About the year 1724 the Academy of ancient Music in London was become so famous as to attract the notice of foreigners; and Steffani, as a testimony of his regard for so laudable an institution, having presented that society with many of his own valuable compositions, the Academy, in return for so great a favour, unanimously elected him their president,* and received from him a very polite letter, acknowledging the honour done him.

In the year 1729, an inclination to see his relations and the place of his nativity, determined him to take a journey into Italy, from whence, after he had staid a winter, and visited the most eminent masters then living, he returned to Hanover. He had not remained long in that city, before some occasion called him to Francfort, and soon after his arrival he became sensible of the decay of his health; being of a constitution which the slightest disorder would affect, and consequently little able to endure the infirmities incident to old age, after an indisposition of a few days he died.

When he was last in Italy, he resided chiefly at the palace of Cardinal Ottoboni, with whom it had long been a custom on Monday in every week to have performances of concerts; or of operas, oratorios, and other grand compositions: on these occasions, in the absence of a principal singer, it has many times fallen to the lot of Steffani to be a performer; and it is said by some, whose good fortune it has been to be present at such an accident, that when he sang he was just loud enough to be heard, but that this defect in his voice was amply recompensed by his manner, in the chasteness and elegance of which he had few equals. As to his person, he was less than the ordinary size of men, of a tender constitution of body, which he had not a little impaired by intense study and application. His deportment is said to have been grave, but tempered with a sweetness and affability that

rendered his conversation very engaging; he was perfectly skilled in all the external forms of polite behaviour, and, which is somewhat unusual, continued to observe and practise them at the age of fourscore.

Besides the letters above-mentioned, there are extant in print the following works of Steffani, viz., Psalmodia Vespert. 8. Voc. Romæ, 1674; a collection of Motets entitled Sacer Janus Quadrifrons, 3. Voc. Monachii, 1685; and a collection of Airs taken from his operas: the latter is not to be regarded as a genuine publication, though of Estienne Roger of Amsterdam, for the title bears not his Christian name, and his surname is mis-spelt Stephani; besides this, the title is 'Sonate da Camera, à tre, due Violini, alto Viola e Basso,' but the book itself is in truth no other than a collection of overtures, symphonies, entrés, dance-tunes, and airs for instruments, in which kind of composition it is well known Steffani did not excel.†

CHAP. CXLI.

ANDREAS WERCKMEISTER, the son of a brewer at Bennickenstein, a small town in Thuringia, was born on the thirtieth day of November, in the year 1645. He was instructed for two years in music by his father's brother, Christian Werckmeister, organist at Bennungen; but in the month of August, 1660, he was removed to a school at Nordthausen, where he staid for two years. From thence he went to Quidlenburg, in the college whereof another brother of his father, Victor Werckmeister, was cantor, and having greatly improved himself in the study and practice of music, received an invitation from the council of Hasselfelde, a city on the river Hartz, in the principality of Blankenburg, to become their organist, which he accepted. While he was in this employment he had a like call to Ellrich, but was prevented from complying with it by the duke Rudolphus Augustus, who desired to keep him in the district of Blankenburg. However, being invited, in the year 1674, to Elbingerod, by the offer of the employments of organist, and also recorder of that town, he was permitted to accept them. In the year 1696 he was appointed organist of the church of St. Martin at Halberstadt, in which station he died on the twenty-sixth day of October, 1706. In a sermon, preached at his funeral by John Melchior Gotzens, and printed in 1707, it is mentioned that he was Royal Prussian Inspector of the organs in the principality of Halberstadt. Mr. Handel, who was well acquainted with him, was used to speak of him in terms of great respect; and he was doubtless a learned and very skilful musician: his works are, **Orgel=Probe**, printed in 1681; Musicæ Mathematicæ Hodegum curiosum, 1687; Sonatas for a Violin, with a thorough-bass, 1689; **Musicalische** Temperatur, 1691; a Treatise in German on the use and abuse of music, printed

---

* 'Huic ut annumerentur Societati, petiisse non dedignati sunt primi 'Ordinis Viri, Musicæ studio dediti, Praxeosque periti; inter quos 'semper meminisse juvabit Abbatem Steffani, Spigæ Episcopum, qui 'dum nomen suum nostris Tabulis inscribi rogavit, Præses unanimi 'omnium consensu est electus.' Letters from the Academy of Ancient Music at London to Signor Antonio Lotti of Venice, with his Answers and Testimonies, Lond. 1732.

† Dr. Cooke has twelve motets of Steffani for three voices, as has also Professor Aylward. They are manuscript, and are probably these. Among them are two that are exquisitely fine—'Qui pacem amatis' and 'Cingit floribus.'

in the same year, Hypomnemata Musica, 1697; **Erweiterte Orgel=Probe**, 1698; Cribrum Musicum, 1700; a translation of Steffani's Letters above-mentioned with notes, 1700; Reflections on Thorough-bass, in German, without a date; Harmonologiam Musicam, 1702; Organum Gruningense Redivivum, 1705; **Musicalische** Paradoxal Discurse, published the year after his decease.

SEBASTIAN DE BROSSARD, an eminent French musician, in the former part of his life had been prebendary and chapel-master of the cathedral church of Strasburg, but afterwards became grand chaplain, and also Maître de Chapelle in the cathedral of Meaux. There is extant of his a work entitled ' Prodromus Musi-'calis, ou Elevations et Motets à Voix seule, avec une Basse-continue.' The first edition printed in the second in 1702. ' Elevations et Motets à 'ii et iii Voix, et à Voix seule, deux dessus de 'Violon, ou deux Flûtes avec la Bass-continuë,' 1698, being the second part of the Prodromus Musicalis. He was the author also of a very useful book, entitled ' Dictionaire de Musique, contenant une explica-'tion des termes Grecs, Latins, Italians, et François 'les plus usitez dans la Musique,' printed at Amsterdam, in folio, in 1703, and afterwards at the same place in octavo, without a date. At the end of this book is a catalogue of authors, ancient and modern, to the amount of nine hundred who have written on music, divided into classes, wherein are interspersed many curious observations of the author relating to the history of music. By Mr. Boivin's Catalogue general des Livres de Musique for the year 1729, it appears that Brossard was the author of two sets of motets, as also of nine Leçons de Tenebres therein mentioned.

It seems that these several publications were at a time when the author was far advanced in years; for Walther takes notice that in the Mercure Galante he is mentioned as an abbé and componist so early as the year 1678.

PAOLO LORENZANI, a Roman by birth, and a pupil of Horatio Benevoli, was maestro di cappella, first in the Jesuits' church at Rome, and afterwards in the cathedral of Messina in Sicily; from whence he was invited by Lewis XIV. to Paris, where he was greatly caressed by the king and all the nobility. He composed and published at Paris a collection of very fine motets. In the year 1679, the king sent him to Italy to engage singers for his chapel; and it is said that he returned with five, who had scarce their equals in Europe.

ARCANGELO CORELLI (*a Portrait*), a native of Fusignano, a town situated near Imola, in the territory of Bologna, was born in the month of February, 1653. His first instructor in music was Matteo Simonelli, a singer in the pontifical chapel, mentioned in a preceding article, by whom he was taught the rudiments of the science, and the art of practical composition; but the genius of Corelli leading him to prefer secular to ecclesiastical music, he afterwards became a disciple of Giovanni Battista Bassani, who, although maestro di cappella of the church of Bologna, was celebrated for his excellence in that species of

composition which Corelli most delighted in, and made it the study of his life to cultivate.

We may reasonably suppose that to facilitate his studies Corelli had been taught the Clavicembalo and organ; nevertheless he entertained an early propensity to the violin, and, as he advanced in years, laboured incessantly in the practice of that instrument. About the year 1672 his curiosity led him to visit Paris, probably with a view to attend the improvements which were making in music under the influence of Cardinal Mazarine, and in consequence of the establishment of a Royal Academy; but, notwithstanding the character which he brought with him, he was driven back to Rome by Lully, whose jealous temper could not brook so formidable a rival as this illustrious Italian. In the year 1680 he visited Germany, and met with a reception suitable to his merit from most of the German princes, particularly the elector of Bavaria, in whose service he was retained, and continued for some time. After about five years stay abroad, he returned again to Rome, and there pursued his studies with great assiduity.

In the year 1686, our king James II. being disposed to cultivate a good understanding with pope Innocent XI., sent the earl of Castlemain, with a numerous train, his embassador to the court of Rome. Upon this occasion Christina, who had then lately resigned the crown of Sweden, and taken up her abode at Rome, entertained the city with a musical drama of the allegoric kind, written by Alessandro Guidi of Verona, a fine Italian poet, and set to music by Bernardi Pasquini.[*]

The proficiency of Corelli on his favourite instrument, the violin, was so great, that the fame of it reached throughout Europe; and Mattheson has not scrupled to say that he was the first performer on it in the world; and Gasparini styles him ' Virtuosis-'simo di violino, e vero Orfeo de nostri tempi.'[†] It does not, however, appear that he had attained to a power of execution in any degree comparable to that of later professors; and it may well be supposed that the just and rational notions which he entertained of the instrument, and of the end and design of music in general, aided by his own good sense, restrained him from those extravagances, which have no other tendency than to disgust the judicious, and excite the admiration of the ignorant. The style of his performance was learned, elegant, and pathetic, and his tone firm and even: Mr. Geminiani, who was well

* It is printed in the Poems of Guidi, octavo, Verona, 1726, with this title, ' Accademia per Musica fatta in Roma nel real Palazzo della ' Maestà di Cristina Regina di Suezia per Festiggiare l'assonzione al ' trono di Jacopo Re d' Inghilterra. In occasione della solenne Am-' basciata mandata da S. M. Britannica alla Santita di nostro Signore ' Innocenzo XI.

' Personnaggi.
' Londra, Tamigi, Fama, Genio Dommante, Genio Ribelle, Cori di ' Cento Musici.'
And at the bottom of the page is the following note: ' Bernardo ' Pasquini, Compositore della Musica, Arcangelo Corelli Capo degl' ' Istromenti d' arco, in numero di Centocinquanta.'

† L'Armonico Prattico al Cembalo, cap. vii. This appellation seems to have been generally given him, and is recognized in the following verses under the prints of him:
' Liquisse Infernas jam credimus Orphea Sedes
' Et terras habitare, hujus sub imagine formæ
' Divinus patet ipse Orpheus, dum numine dignâ
' Arte modos fingit, vel chordas mulcet, utramque
' Agnoscit laudem, meritosque Britannus honores.'

ARCANGELUS CORELLIUS

DE FUSIGNANO,

DICTUS BONONIENSIS.

acquainted with and had studied it, was used to resemble it to a sweet trumpet. A person who had heard him perform says that whilst he was playing on the violin, it was usual for his countenance to be distorted, his eyes to become as red as fire, and his eyeballs to roll as in an agony.

About the year 1690 the opera was in great perfection at Rome; Pasquini was the great dramatic composer: Mattheson infers the excellence of this entertainment from this circumstance, that Pasquini, Corelli, and Gaetani were performers in the Roman orchestra at the same time, the first being at the harpsichord, the second at the head of the band, and the latter performing on the lute.

While he was thus engaged at Rome, Corelli was highly favoured by that great patron of poetry and music, Cardinal Ottoboni. Crescembini says that he regulated the musical academy held at the palace of his eminence every Monday afternoon. Here it was that Mr. Handel became acquainted with him; and in this academy a Serenata of Mr. Handel, entitled Il Trionfo del Tempo, was performed, the overture to which was in a style so new and singular, that Corelli was confounded in his first attempt to play it.*

The merits of Corelli as a performer were sufficient to attract the patronage of the great, and to silence, as indeed they did, all competition; but the remembrance of these is at this day absorbed in the contemplation of his excellencies as a musician at large, as the author of new and original harmonies, and the father of a style not less noble and grand, than elegant and pathetic.

The works of Corelli are solely compositions for instruments, and consist of six operas,† entitled as follows :—

Suonate a trè due Violini, e Violone, col Basso per l' Organo Opera prima.

Sonate da Camera a trè, doi Violini, e Violone, ò Cimbalo. Opera Seconda.

Suonate a trè, doi Violini, e Violone, ò Arcileuto col Basso per l' Organo. Opera Terza.

Suonate da Camera a trè, doi Violini, e Violone ò Cimbalo. Opera Quarta.

Sonate à Violino e Violone ò Cembalo. Opera Quinta, Parte Prima : Parte Seconda, Preludii, Allemande, Correnti, Gighe, Sarabande Gavotte, e Follia.

This work was first published at Rome, with a dedication by the author to Sophia Charlotta, electress of Brandenburg, dated the first day of January, 1700.

Concerti Grossi con duoi Violini e Violoncello di Concertino obligati e duoi altri Violoni, Viola e Basso di Concerto Grosso ad arbitrio che si potranno radoppiare.‡

The four operas of Sonatas were published, as they were completed, at different times; the first edition of the first opera has escaped a diligent search, but those of the second, third, and fourth have been recovered : the second Opera, printed at Rome in 1685, is dedicated to Cardinal Panfilio; the third, printed at Bologna in 1690, to Francis II. duke of Modena; the fourth, also printed at Bologna, in 1694, to Cardinal Ottoboni, in whose palace at Rome the author then resided ' col spetioso carattere d' attuale servitore' of his eminence, as the dedication expresses it. These early editions, and also the subsequent ones published at Antwerp, were printed on the old lozenge-headed note, with the quavers and semiquavers disjoined from each other, forming a very obscure and illegible character.§

About the year 1720 Estienne Roger of Amsterdam printed a fine edition of the four Operas of Sonatas, stamped on copper, in the same character with the rest of his numerous publications.

Of the Concertos, the first is that beautiful one printed at Amsterdam for Estienne Roger and Michael Charles Le Cene, with a frontispiece before it, designed by Francesco Trevisani, of a muse playing on and singing to the lute.‖ The dedication of this work to John William, Prince Palatine of the Rhine, bears date at Rome the third day of December, 1712.

During the residence of Corelli at Rome, besides those of his own country, many persons were ambitious of becoming his disciples, and learning the practice on the violin from the greatest master of that instrument the world had then heard of. Of these it is said the late Lord Edgecumbe was one; and that the fine mezzotinto print of Corelli by Smith, was scraped from a picture painted by Mr. Hugh Howard at Rome for that nobleman.¶

* This Serenata, translated into English, and entitled The 'Triumph of Time and Truth,' was performed at London in 1751. The overture is in the printed collection of Mr. Handel's overtures, and it is conjectured, that the first movement was what appeared difficult to Corelli.

† There are two collections of Sonatas, printed at Amsterdam, not included in the above enumeration, the one entitled 'Sonate a trè, doi 'Violini e Basso per il Cimbalo, si crede che Siano State Composte di 'Arcangelo Corelli avanti le sue altre Opere, Opera Settima. Stampate 'à Spesa di Michele Carlo Le Cene;' the other 'Sonate a trè, due Violini 'col Basso per l' Organo di Arcangelo Corelli di Fusignano, Ouvrage 'posthume,' published by Estienne Roger and the above Le Cene. Of the authenticity of the posthumous work there is not the least evidence; and as to the Opera Settima, there is the fullest to prove it the work of another. In short, these Sonatas, in the title-page whereof the reader is told that they are believed to have been composed by Arcangelo Corelli before his other works, are no other than nine of twelve Sonatas for two violins and a bass, composed by a countryman of ours resident in Italy, and which were published with this title, 'Sonate a trè, doi Violini 'Violone, ó Arcileuto col Basso per l'Organo. Dedicate all' Altezza 'Serenissima di Ferdinando III. Gran Prencipe di Toscana. Da Gio- 'vanni Ravenscroft, alias Rederi, Inglese, Opera Prima. In Roma, per 'il Mascardi, 1695.

There is extant also in the book entitled the Division Violin, part II. a Solo in the key of G, with the lesser third, said to be of Corelli, but it wants authority.

‡ Of this species of musical composition we are told that Giuseppe Torelli, of Bologna, was the inventor.

§ Of the Antwerp editions the following only have come to hand, Opera Prima Nuovamente Ristampata. In Anversa Stampato in Casa di Henrico Aertssens al Monte Parnasso, anno 1688. Opera Terza Nuovamente Ristampata, by the same person, 1691. But such was the parsimony of the printers of these subsequent editions, that the dedications are omitted, which might have ascertained the time of the first publication of each Opera, and possibly furnished some particulars respecting the author, as that to the original edition of the fourth does, whereby we are informed that Corelli was a domestic of Cardinal Ottoboni, that the work which it precedes was composed in his palace, and that the pieces contained in it were frequently performed in the academy there held.

The Italian and Flemish editions were so little fit for use, that the demand for Corelli's works being very great in England, many persons acquired a subsistence by copying in writing the Sonatas of Corelli in a legible character; in particular Mr. Thomas Shuttleworth, a teacher of music, and who was living in Spitalfields in the year 1738, by his industry in this practice was enabled to bring up a numerous family.

‖ For want of attention in the engraver, the print is the reverse of the painting, and the muse is made to finger the instrument with her left hand.

¶ This picture was painted between 1697 and 1700, for in that interval it appears that Mr. Howard was abroad. Anecdotes of Painting in England by Mr. Horace Walpole, vol. III. page 144. That Corelli sat to Mr. Howard for it is certain, for in the print after it is this inscription: 'H. Howard ad vivum pinxit.' Mr. Howard was no very extraordinary painter, but being an Englishman, and the English being celebrated for

Corelli died at Rome about six weeks after the publication of his Opera Sesta, that is to say, on the eighteenth day of January, 1713, and was buried in the church of the Rotunda, otherwise called the Pantheon, in the first chapel on the left hand of the entrance. Over the place of his interment is a sepulchral monument to his honour, with a marble bust thereon, erected at the expense of Philip William, Count Palatine of the Rhine, under the care and direction of Cardinal Ottoboni.* The following is the inscription thereon :—

D. O. M.
ARCANGELO CORELLIO A FUSIGNANO
PHILIPPI WILLELMI COMITIS PALATINI RHENI
S. R. I. PRINCIPIS AC ELECTORIS
BENEFICENTIA
MARCHIONIS DE LADENSBURG
QUOD EXIMIIS ANIMI DOTIBUS
ET INCOMPARABILI IN MUSICIS MODULIS PERITIA
SUMMIS PONTIFICIBUS APPRIME CARUS
ITALIÆ ATQUE EXTERIS NATIONIBUS ADMIRATIONI FUERIT
INDULGENTE CLEMENTE XI. P. O. M.
PETRUS CARDINALIS OTTOBONUS S. R. E. VIC. CAN.
ET GALLIARUM PROTECTOR
LIIRISTE CELEBERRIMO
INTER FAMILIARES SUOS JAM DIU ADSCITO
EJUS NOMEN IMMORTALITATI COMMENDATURUS
M. P. C.
VIXIT ANNOS LIX. MENS. X. DIES XX.
OBIIT IV. ID. JANUARII ANNO SAL. MDCCXIII.

For many years after his decease, this excellent musician was commemorated by a solemn musical performance in the Pantheon, on the anniversary of his death. In the year 1730 an eminent master, now living, was present at that solemnity, who relates that at it the third and the eighth of his Concertos were performed by a numerous band, among whom were many who had been the pupils of the author. He adds, that these two pieces were performed in a slow, distinct, and firm manner, without graces, and just as they are wrote ; and from hence concludes that this was the manner in which they were played by the author himself.

He died possessed of a sum of money equal to about six thousand pounds sterling. He was a passionate admirer of pictures,† and lived in an uninterupted friendship with Carlo Cignani and Carlo

portrait-painting, it is imagined that he left behind him one other picture of Corelli, painted by himself, or at least a copy of the former; for the bust on the monument of Corelli in the Rotunda at Rome, does in every respect most exactly correspond with the mezzotino print of Smith.

* It is commonly said here that the Jig in the fifth Sonate in the Opera Quinta, is engraven on Corelli's monument ; but it is in the following sense only that this assertion is true. The bust represents him, as the print does, with a music-paper in his hand, on which are engraven certain musical-notes, which, upon a near inspection, appear to be a few bars of that fine air.

† It may serve as an argument to prove the affinity of the sister arts of music and painting, that the love of each to an equal degree has in many instances centered in the same person. Mr. Handel, though not a collector, was a lover of pictures, and for many years before his death frequented, for the purpose of viewing them, all collections exposed to sale : Geminiani, in the latter years of his life, was absorbed in the love of painting, and once declared to the author of this work, that he loved it better than music. Nicholas Laniere, though celebrated as one of the first musicians in his time, has rendered his character so ambiguous by his excellence in painting, that both faculties claim him ; and in Mr. Walpole's Anecdotes he stands ranked among the painters, and with very good reason ; his own portrait in the music-school at Oxford, painted by himself, being a masterly work. On the other hand, there are instances of painters who have been no less excellent in the practice of music, as were Leonardo da Vinci, Domenichino, and Sir Godfrey Kneller ; Guido Reni, and our countryman Mr. Samuel Cooper were famous for their skill and performance on the lute.

Maratti : these two eminent painters were rivals for his favour, and for a series of years presented him at times with pictures, as well of other masters as of their own painting. The consequence hereof was, that Corelli became possessed of a large and valuable collection of original paintings, all which, together with the sum above-mentioned, he bequeathed to his dear friend and patron, Cardinal Ottoboni, who, reserving the pictures to himself, generously distributed the rest of the effects among the relations of the testator.

Corelli is said to have been remarkable for the mildness of his temper and the modesty of his deportment; the lineaments of his countenance, as represented in his portrait, seem to bespeak as much ; nevertheless he was not insensible to the respect due to his skill and exquisite performance. Cibber, in the Apology for his Life, page 340, relates that when he was playing a solo at Cardinal Ottoboni's, he discovered the Cardinal and another person engaged in discourse, upon which he laid down his instrument ; and being asked the reason, gave for answer, that he feared the music interrupted conversation. He was censured by some who were acquainted with him for his parsimony, upon no better ground than the accustomed plainness of his garb, and his disinclination to the use of a coach or other carriage. Mr. Handel had remarked these two little particulars in his conduct, and would sometimes, when he spoke of him, add, but without a view to depreciate his character, that his ordinary dress was black, and his outer garment a plain blue cloak.

That he was a man of humour and pleasantry may be inferred from the following story, related by Walther, in his account of Nicolas Adam Strunck, violonist to Ernestus Augustus, elector of Hanover. This person being at Rome, upon his arrival made it his business to see Corelli ; upon their first interview Strunck gave him to understand that he was a musician ; 'What is your instrument?' asked Corelli ; 'I can play,' answered Strunck, 'upon the 'harpsichord, and a little on the violin, and should 'esteem myself extremely happy might I hear your 'performance on this latter instrument, on which I 'am informed you excel.' Corelli very politely condescended to this request of a stranger ; he played a solo, Strunck accompanied him on the harpsichord, and afterwads played a Toccata, with which Corelli was so much taken, that he laid down his instrument to admire him. When Strunck had done at the harpsichord, he took up the violin, and began to touch it in a very careless manner, upon which Corelli remarked that he had a very good bow-hand, and wanted noting but practice to become a master of the instrument ; at this instant Strunck put the violin out of tune, and, applying it to its place, played on it with such dexterity, attempering the dissonances occasioned by the mis-tuning of the instrument with such amazing skill and dexterity, that Corelli cried out in broken German, 'I am called 'Arcangelo, a name that in the language of my 'country signifies an Archangel ; but let me tell 'you, that you, Sir, are an Arch-devil.'

Our observations on the works of Corelli may properly enough be classed under two heads, that is to say, their general history, and their peculiar character; as to the first, it is confidently asserted that they were composed with great deliberation; that they were revised and corrected from time to time; and, finally, submitted to the inspection of the most skilful musicians of the author's time. Of the Sonatas it may be remarked that the first and third Operas consist of fugues and slow movements, without any intermixture of airs; these are termed Sonate da Chiesa, in contradistinction to those in the second and fourth operas, which are styled da Camera: the former, we are told by Mattheson, were usually played in the churches abroad after divine service; and the whole four operas for many years furnished the second music before the play at both the theatres in London. The fifth opera consists of those solo-sonatas which the author himself was accustomed to perform on special occasions; there is one edition of them in two distinct parts, viz. one for the violin, and the other for the violoncello or harpsichord; and another with the graces to the adagio movements, which some have suspected to be spurious, but they are in one of the Amsterdam editions; and to obviate a doubt of their genuineness, the publisher, Estienne Roger, has, in one of his printed catalogues, signified that the original copy of them, as also some letters of the author on the subject, were open to the inspection of the curious at his shop. The last of the twelve is a set of divisions, twenty-four in number, on a favourite air, known in England by the name of Farinelli's Ground,* and is called by Corelli, Follia. The twelfth Sonata of Vivaldi's Opera Prima is a praxis on the same melody.

So much for the general history of his works; as to their peculiar character, it may be said that to enumerate the various excellencies of this great master would require a particular examen of his several compositions; of his Sonatas Mattheson remarks, that there is more art and contrivance in them than in his Overtures, i. e. his Concertos; but in this he certainly is mistaken. The first opera is but an essay towards that perfection to which he afterwards arrived; there is but little art and less invention in it; the third, eighth, and ninth Sonatas therein contained are almost the only ones in practice. The second opera carries with it the evidences of a genius matured by exercise; the second, the fifth, the eighth, and the eleventh Sonatas are both learned and elegant. The third opera is the most elaborate of the four, as abounding in fugues. The first, the fourth, the sixth, and the ninth Sonatas of this opera are the most distinguished; the latter has drawn tears from many an eye; but the whole is so excellent, that, exclusive of mere fancy, there is scarce any motive for preference. The fourth opera is, in its kind, equal to the former two; the second and eleventh Sonatas excite a melancholy, soothing and of the most pathetic kind. The third, sixth,

and tenth are gay and lively in an eminent degree; they do not provoke mirth, but they inspire cheerfulness, gaiety, and every species of good humour short of it. Of his Solos, the second, the third, the fifth, and the sixth are admirable; as are the ninth, the tenth, and, for the elegant sweetness of the second movement, the eleventh. A very good musician, Giorgio Antoniotti, has remarked of the fugue in the first, that the melody of the subject is but indifferent,† but every one must own that the subject itself is well sustained.

The sixth opera, though composed at a time when the faculties of the author might be supposed to have been on the decline, affords the strongest proof of the contrary; nothing can exceed in dignity and majesty the opening of the first Concerto, nor, for its plaintive sweetness, the whole of the third. And he must have no ears, nor feeling of the power of harmony, or the effects of modulation, who can listen to the eighth without rapture. ‡

The compositions of Corelli are celebrated for the harmony resulting from the union of all the parts; but the fineness of the airs is another distinguishing characteristic of them: the Allemand in the tenth Solo is as remarkable for spirit and force, as that in the eleventh is for its enchanting delicacy: his jigs are in a style peculiarly his own; and that in the fifth Solo was never equalled. In the Gavot-movements in the second and fourth operas, the melody is distributed with great judgment among the several parts. In his minuets alone he seems to fail; Bononcini, Mr. Handel, and Giuseppe Martini have excelled him in this kind of air.

It is said there is in every nation a style both in speaking and writing, which never becomes obsolete; a certain mode of phraseology, so consonant and congenial to the analogy and principles of its respective language, as to remain settled and unaltered.§ This, but with much greater latitude, may be said of music; and accordingly it may be observed of the compositions of Corelli, not only that they are equally intelligible to the learned and unlearned, but that the impressions made by them have been found to be as durable as general. His music is the language of nature; and for a series of years all that heard it became sensible of its effects; of this there cannot be a stronger proof than that, amidst all the innovations which the love of change had introduced, it continued to be performed, and was heard with delight in churches, in theatres, at public solemnities and festivities in all the cities of Europe for near forty years. Men remembered, and would refer to passages in it as to a classic author; and even at this day the masters of the science, of whom it must be observed, that though their studies are regulated by the taste of the public, yet have they a taste of their own, do not hesitate to pronounce of the compositions of Corelli, that, of fine harmony and elegant modulation, they are the most perfect exemplars.

---

* This ground was composed by   Farinelli, uncle of the famous singer Carlo Broschi Farinelli, and componist, violinist, and concert-master at Hanover about the year 1684. He was ennobled by the king of Denmark, and was by king George I. appointed his resident at Venice.

† In a treatise entitled L'Arte Armonica, published at London in 1760, page 95.

‡ This concerto was composed on occasion of a solemnity peculiar to the Romish church, the celebration of the Nativity; the printed copies having this advertisement, ' Fatto per la Notte di Natale.'

§ Dr. Sam. Johnson's preface to his edition of Shakespeare.

The natural and familiar style of Corelli's music, and that simplicity which is one of its characteristics, betrayed many into an opinion that it was easily to be imitated; and whoever considers that from harmonies such as his are, a rule or canon might be drawn that would give to any music, composed in conformity to it, a similar appearance, would entertain the same notion; but the experiment has been made, and has failed. Ravenscroft professed to imitate Corelli in those Sonatas which Roger published. and hoped to make the world believe were some of the earliest of his works. The airs indeed of Albinoni, Torelli, Giuseppe Valentini, and Mascitti, especially the Allemands, Courants, and Jigs, seem to have been cast in Corelli's mould; but an Englishman, named James Sherard, an apothecary by profession,* composed two operas of Sonatas, which an ordinary judge, not knowing that they were the work of another, might mistake for compositions of this great master.

ALESSANDRO SCARLATTI of Naples, and a Cavaliero, a most voluminous composer, is celebrated as having perfected the theatric style. It is said that he composed near a hundred operas; and oratorios, serenatas, and cantatas to an incredible number; and farther, that his invention was so fertile, and his application so intense, that his copyist was not able to write so fast as he composed. Of his numerous compositions we know of but two works in print, viz. 'Cantate à una e due Voci,' and 'Motetti à una, 'due, tre, e quattro Voci con Violini.'† He is said to have first introduced into his airs accompaniments for the violin, and symphonies, which both enrich the melody and give relief to the singer. He had a son named Domenico, who was formerly chapel-master in some church of Rome, but in the year 1728 was taken into the service of the king of Portugal, who it is said, upon his arrival at Lisbon, to defray the expense of his journey, presented him with two thousand dollars, since which time he has applied himself to the composition of lessons for the harpsichord, of which there are a great number in print.

TOMASO ALBINONI, a Venetian, was originally a maker of cards, but having an early propensity to music, and having been taught the violin in his youth, he became not only an excellent performer on that instrument, but also an eminent composer. The titles of such of his works as are in print may be seen in the Dutch Catalogues; they consist solely of music for instruments, viz. Concertos and Sonatas for Violins, and Cantate da Camera, and a Collection of Airs, entitled 'Balletti à tre, due Violini e Vio- 'loncello col Basso da Tomaso Albinoni, Dilettante 'Veneto, Opera terza,' which were sundry times printed, and at length became so familiar in England, that many of the common fiddlers were able to play them. In the year 1690 we find him associated with Gasparini, mentioned in the next article, in the composition of an opera called Engelberta, performed at the theatre di San Cassiano at Venice. Albinoni was living about the year 1725, and was known to a person who furnished the above facts concerning him.

FRANCESCO GASPARINI, born at Lucca about the year 1650, Accademico filarmonico, and director of the choir in the hospital della Pietà at Venice, was one of the finest vocal composers of the last century. He excelled equally in the composition of chamber and theatrical music, his Cantatas being esteemed among the finest of the kind ever published; and his operas, of which he composed a great number, are scarcely exceeded by those of Scarlatti. An opera of his, entitled Merope, was performed in Italy, not so long ago as to be beyond the remembrance of a very able musician lately deceased, who relates that he was present at the representation of it, and that one recitative without instruments, sung by Merope and her son, produced a general effusion of tears from a crowded assemby of auditors. He joined with Albinoni in the composition of an opera entitled Engelberta, mentioned in the preceding article, and was living at Rome in the year 1723, as appears by a letter of his writing, prefixed to the Psalms of Marcello, in answer to one of the author. The works of Gasparini in print are, Cantate da Camera à Voce sola, printed at Lucca in 1697; and a treatise, published at Venice in 1708, entitled L'Armonico Prattico al Cimbalo, regole per ben suonare il basso.

It is needless to observe upon the foregoing deduction of facts, that music was arrived at a great degree of perfection towards the end of last century; and it must appear from the accounts already given in the course of this work, of eminent professors in different ages, and of various countries, that the science owes much of the perfection to which it has been brought to the Italians and Germans. In what degree the English contributed to its improvement, can only be judged of by their works, and the suffrages of those writers, and, among others, Erasmus, who have borne testimony to the general disposition of the people of this country to favour the practice of it; to which may be added one farther testimony, viz., the declaration of Lewis XIV. in his grant to Lully, before inserted, wherein he recites that he had granted to Perrin licence to establish academies of music, in which should be sung theatrical dramas, 'comme il se pratique en Italie, en 'Allemagne, et en Angleterre;' from whence it seems that, in the opinion of the French in the year 1669, the dramatic music of the English was of such a kind as to be at least worthy of imitation, and that by a people who were endeavouring to form a taste after the purest models of perfection.

This consideration, as also another, to wit, that

---

* This person lived in Crutched-Friars, London; he was the brother of Dr. Sherard the botanist, author of the Hortus Elthamensis. The Sonatas of Sherard were printed at Amsterdam, and published by Estienne Roger.

† An opera of his, entitled 'Pyrrhus and Demetrius,' was translated into English, and, with some additional airs and an overture, by Nicolini Haym, was performed at the Haymarket theatre in 1708, and printed with both the Italian and English words. The original opera was performed with universal applause at Rome, Naples, and other places, and is said to be the finest in its kind of all Scarlatti's works.

In the English opera the airs of Haym are distinguished from those of Scarlatti by their superior excellence; and also by this circumstance, that the latter have the Italian printed under the English words. The air 'Vieni o Sonno,' is celebrated as divine; and that of 'Veder parmi un ombra nera,' as also another not printed, are, in the opinion of a very good judge, who was living at the time of the performance, two of the most masterly airs that were ever composed for the theatre. See a Comparison between the French and Italian Music and Operas, translated from the French, with remarks. Page 15, in not. and page 75.

the succession of English musicians has, in this work, hitherto been continued down no further than to about the middle of the last century, makes it necessary to recur some years backward, and to take a view of the state of music in that gloomy period, during which a sullen abstinence from innocent and elegant delights was looked upon as conducive to the glory of God and the interests of religion; and this naturally leads us to the history of the theatre, which will be found to involve in it, at least for a considerable number of years, the history of music also.

CHAP. CXLII.

THE intelligent reader need not be told, that during the time of the usurpation stage plays were an abomination; the first writer who endeavoured to possess the world with the belief that theatrical entertainments were inconsistent with the purity of the christian religion, was one Stephen Gosson, rector of St. Botolph's without Bishopsgate, a man of wit and learning, who himself had written some few things for the stage, but falling in with the principles of the puritans, he changed the course of his studies, and became a bitter enemy to plays, players, and pipers, by whom he means musicians in general, as appears by a little book published by him 1579, entitled ' The School of Abuse, containing ' a pleasant invective against poets, pipers, plaiers, ' jesters, and such like catterpillers, of a common ' welth; setting up the flagge of defiance to their ' mischievous exercise, and overthrowing their bul-' warkes by prophane writers, natural reason, and ' common experience.'

Gosson's book, notwithstanding the severity of the satire, is in truth what he calls it, a pleasant in-vective, for it abounds with wit and humour, and exhibits a very lively picture of the manners of the age in which it was written. The author soon after published a small tract, entitled, ' Plays confuted in ' five Actions. proving, that they are not to be ' suffered in a christian common weale; by the ' waye, both the cavils of Thomas Lodge,* and the ' Play of Playes, written in their defence, and other ' objections of players frendes are truely set downe, ' and directly aunswered,' wherein are several severe reflections, as well on musicians, as on the authors and frequenters of stage entertainments.

The quarrel which Gosson had commenced against plays and players, was prosecuted with all the male-volence that fanaticism could suggest, by that hot-brained zealot William Prynne, in his book entitled ' Histrio-Mastix, the Players Scourge, or Actors ' Tragædie, in which it is pretended to be evidenced, ' that stage playes, (the very pompes of the divell, ' which we renounce in baptisme, if we believe the ' fathers) are sinful, heathenish, lewde, ungodly ' spectacles, and most pernicious corruptions; con-' demned in all ages as intolerable mischiefes to ' churches, to republickes, to the manners, mindes, ' and soules of men. And that the profession of

' play-poets, of stage players, together with the ' penning, acting, and frequenting of stage players ' are unlawfull, infamous, and misbecoming christians. ' All pretences to the contrary are here likewise fully ' answered, and the unlawfulnes of acting or beholding ' academicall enterludes briefly discussed, besides ' sundry other particulars concerning dancing, dicing, ' health-drinking, &c.'†

The prosecution of Prynne for publishing this book and the consequences of it, are well known to every person conversant with English history; but the effects it wrought upon the minds of the people in general, were such as put a total stop to stage exhibitions of every kind. The public could but ill brook the total interdiction of dramatic represen-tations, which, under proper regulations might, and indeed have been rendered subservient to the pur-poses of morality; and the dissatisfaction that was expressed on this occasion suggested to Sir William Davenant, the thought of an entertainment resembling the Italian opera, in which he was encouraged by no less a person than the famous Sir John Maynard, Serjeant at Law, and several citizens. That this entertainment was in the Italian language, though Wood calls it an Italian opera, is much to be doubted; but whatever it was, it was performed at Rutland House, in Charterhouse-yard or Square, on the 23rd day of May, 1656.‡ It is highly probable, it was no other than that drama published among Sir William Davenant's Works, page 341, entitled, ' the First day's Entertainment at Rutland House, ' declamations and music, after the manner of the ' ancients,' and if so, it had not the least claim to the title of an opera. It consists of several orations in prose, intermixed with vocal and instrumental music, which in a note at the end, we are told, was composed by Dr. Charles Coleman, Mr. Henry Lawes, and Mr. George Hudson.

Wood says, that this opera, as he calls it, was afterwards translated to the Cockpit in Drury-lane, and delighting the eye and ear extremely well, was much frequented for many years.

But notwithstanding these attempts in its favour, the forbidding the use of the liturgy, and the re-straints on the stage, amounted in effect, to a pro-scription of music from the metropolis, and drove the professors of it to seek protection where they were most likely to find it. It will easily be conceived, that the prohibition of cathedral service left a great number of musicians, as namely, organists, minor canons, lay-clerks, and other persons attendant on choirs, without employment; and the gloomy and sullen temper of the times, together with the fre-quent hostilities that were carried on in different parts of the kingdom, during the usurpation, had driven music to a great degree out of private families. The only place which these men could, as to an asylum, resort, was to Oxford, whither the King

---

* Dr. Lodge, the author of sundry pastoral poems in England's Helicon, and other elegant compositions.

† It is pretended that Prynne meant by this book, to libel Queen Henrietta Maria, the consort of Charles I. who, about the time of its publication, had acted a part in a pastoral at Somerset House; but Whitelock asserts, that it was published six weeks before that pastoral was acted. See his Memorials and Athen. Oxon. 434.

‡ Athen. Oxon. vol. II. col. 412.

had retired ; there went with him thither, Dr. Wilson, one of the Gentlemen of his chapel, and he had an organist with him named George Jeffries ; these and a few others, with the assistance of the University people, made a stand against the persecution of the times ; choral service was performed there after a very homely fashion, and concerts of vocal and instrumental music were sometimes had in the rooms of the Gentlemen of the University for the entertainment of each other. But this lasted only till the surrender of the garrison in 1646, when the King was obliged to leave the place ; however, the spirit that had been excited in favour of music during his residence there, and the continuance of Dr. Wilson in the University, who was professor, and a man of a cheerful disposition, contributed to an association of Gentlemen of the University, with the musicians of the place, and these together established a weekly concert. The place of greatest resort for this purpose was the house of one William Ellis, formerly organist of Eton College, and, at the time now spoken of, organist of St. John's. Of this meeting, and of the persons who frequented it Wood gives a very particular account in his life, published by Hearne, at the end of his edition of Caii Vindiciæ Antiq. Acad. Oxon. 1730, and again at Oxford in 1772 ; and in the manuscript of his in the Ashmolean Museum, mentioned in vol. III. page 258, in not. is the following memoir relating to it :—

'After Cathedrals and Organs were put down in 'the grand Rebellion, he [Ellis] kept up a weekly 'Meeting in his house opposite to that Place where 'the Theatre was afterwards built, which kept him 'and his wife in a comfortable Condition. The 'Meeting was much frequented and many Masters 'of Musick were there, and such that had belonged 'to Choirs, being out of all Employ, and therefore 'the Meeting, as all other Musick Meetings, did 'flourish ; and Musick, especially vocal, being dis-'countenanced by the Presbyterians and indepen-'dents, because it favoured much the Cathedrals and 'Episcopacy, it was the more used. But when 'King Charles was restored and Episcopacy and 'Cathedrals with it, then did the Meetings decay, 'especially for this Reason, because the Masters of 'Musick were called away to Cathedrals and Col-'legiate Choirs.'

Of the meeting itself the following is Wood's account in his own words :—*

* Wood may be credited in whatever he relates touching music, for he was passionately fond of it ; and was besides, a good proficient on the violin, as appears by the following extract from his life, page 70, edit. 1772 :—

'This yeare [1651] A. W. began to exercise his natural and insatiable 'Genie he had to Musick. He exercised his Hand on the Violin, and 'having a good eare to take any tune at first hearing, he could quickly 'draw it out from the Violin, but not with the same tuning of Strings 'that others used. He wanted Understanding, Friends, and Money, to 'pick him out a good Master, otherwise he might have equal'd in that 'Instrument, and in singing, any person then in the Universitie. He had 'some companions that were musical, but they wanted instruction as 'well as he.'

Elsewhere [page 74] he says, 'that being taken ill he retired to Cassing-'ton, and there learn't to ring on the six Bells, then newly put up; and 'having had from his most tender years, an extraordinary ravishing 'Delight in Musick, he practised privately there, without the help of an 'Instructer, to play on the Violin. It was then that he set and tuned 'his strings in Fourths, and not in Fifths, according to the manner: 'And having a good eare, and being ready to sing any Tune upon hearing

'By this time, [viz. anno 1656,] A. W. had some 'genuine skill in Musick, and frequented the 'Weekly Meetings of Musitians in the house of 'Will. Ellis, late Organist of S. John's Coll. situat 'and being in a House, opposite to that place 'whereon the Theater was built. The usual Com-'pany that met and performed their parts were (1) 'Joh. Cock, M. A. Fellow of New Coll. by the 'Authority of the Visitors. He afterwards became 'Rector of Heyford-Wareyne neare Bister,† and 'marrying with one of the Woodwards of Wood-'stock, lived an uncomfortable Life with her. (2) 'Joh. Jones, M. A. Fellow of the said Coll. by the 'same Authority. (3) George Croke, M. A. Fellow 'of the said Coll. also by the same Authority. He 'was afterwards drown'd, with Brome, son of Brome 'Whorwood of Halton near Oxon. in their passage 'from Hampshire to the Isle of Wight, 5. Sept. 1657. '(4) Joh. Friend, M. A. Fellow also of the said 'House, and by the same Authority. He died in 'the Country, an. 1658. (5) George Stradling, 'M. A. Fellow of Alls. Coll. an admirable Lutinist, 'and much respected by Wilson the Professor. '(6) Ralph Sheldon, Gent. a Rom. Catholick of 'Steple-Barton in Oxfordshire, at this time living in 'Halywell neare Oxon. admired for his smooth and 'admirable way in playing on the Viol. He died 'in the City of Westminster....165 , and was 'buried in the Chancel of the Church of S. Martin in 'the Fields. (7) Thom. Wren, a yonger son of 'Matthew Wren, Bishop of Ely, a Sojourner now in 'the House of Franc. Bowman, Bookseller, living 'in S. Marie's parish in Oxon. (8) Tho James, 'M. A. of Magd. Coll. would be among them, but 'seldome played. He had a weekly Meeting in 'his Chamber at the Coll. practised much on the

'it once or twice, he would play them all in short time with the said 'way of Tuning, which was never knowne before.'

In the year 1653 he put himself under the tuition of a master, of whom, and his proficiency under him, he gives the following account :—

'After he [A. W.] had spent the Summer at Cassington in a lonish 'and retir'd condition, he return'd to Oxon, and being advised by some 'persons, he entertain'd a Master of Musick to teach him the usual way 'of playing on the Violin, that is, by having every String tuned 5 notes 'lower than the other going before. The Master was Charles Griffith, 'one of the Musitians belonging to the City of Oxon. whom he thought 'then to be a most excellent Artist; but when A. W. improv'd himself 'in that Instrument, he found him not so. He gave him 2s. 6d. entrance, 'and 10s. quarterly. This person after he had extreamly wondered how 'he could play so many Tunes as he did by Fourths, without a Director 'or Guide, he then tuned his Violin by Fifths, and gave him Instructions 'how to proceed, leaving then a Lesson with him to practice against his 'next coming. Ibid. 76.

'Whereas A. W. had before learned to play on the Violin by the In-'struction of Charles Griffith, and afterwards of Jo. Parker, one of the 'Universitie Musitians, he was now advis'd to entertaine one Will. 'James, a Dancing-Master, by some accounted excellent for that Instru-'ment; and the rather, because it is said, that he had obtained his 'knowledge in Dancing and Musick in France. He spent in all half 'a yeare with him, and gained some improvement from him; yet at 'length he found him not a compleat Master of his facultie, as Griffith 'and Parker were not: and, to say the Truth, there was yet no compleat 'Master in Oxon. for that Instrument, because it had not been hitherto 'used in Consort among Gentlemen, only by common Musitians, who 'played but two Parts. The Gentlemen in privat Meetings, which A. W. 'frequented, play'd three, four and five Parts with Viols, as Treble-Viol, 'Tenor, Counter-Tenor and Bass, with an organ, Virginal, or Harpsicon 'joyn'd with them: and they esteemed a Violin to be an Instrument 'only belonging to a common Fidler, and could not endure that it should 'come among them, for feare of making their Meetings to be vaine and 'fidling. But before the Restoration of K. Ch. 2. and especially after, 'Viols began to be out of fashion, and only Violins used, as Treble-'Violin, tenor and Bass-Violin; and the King, according to the French 'Mode, would have 24 Violins playing before him, while he was at Meales 'as being more airie and brisk than Viols.' Ibid. 96.

† Wood is very licentious in his spelling: the place here meant is Bicester, a market-town in Oxfordshire.

'Theorbo Lute; and Gervace Westcote being often
'with him as an Instructor, A. W. would sometimes
'go to their Meeting and play with them.

'The Musick Masters, who were now in Oxon.
'and frequented the said meeting, were (1) Will.
'Ellis, Bach. of Musick, owner of the House
'wherein the Meeting was. He alwaies play'd his
'part either on the Organ or Virginal. (2) Dr.
'Joh. Wilson, the public Professor, the best at the
'Lute in all England. He sometimes play'd on
'the Lute, but mostly presided at the Concert. (3)
'———— Curteys, a Lutinist, lately ejected from
'some Choire or Cath. Church. After his Majes-
'tie's Restoration he became Gent. or singing-man
'of Ch. Church in Oxon. (4) Tho. Jackson, a
'Bass-Violist; afterwards one of the Choire of S.
'John's Coll. in Oxon. (5) Edw. Low, Organist
'lately of Ch. Church. He play'd only on the
'Organ; so when he performed his part Mr. Ellis
'would take up a Counter-Tenor Viol, and play, if
'any person were wanting to performe that part.
'(6) Gervace Littleton *alias* Westcot, or Westcot
'*alias* Littleton,* a Violist. He was afterwards a
'singing man of S. John's Coll. (7) Will. Glexney,
'who had belonged to a Choire before the Warr.
'He was afterwards a Gent. or singing-man of
'Ch. Ch. He play'd well upon the Bass-Viol, and
'sometimes sung his part. He died 6 Nov. 1692,
'aged 79 or thereabouts. (8) ———— Proctor, a
'yong man and a new Commer. He died soon
'after. * * * * John Parker, one of the Uni-
'versitie Musitians, would be sometimes among
'them, but Mr. Low, a proud man, could not
'endure any common Musitian to come to the
'Meeting, much less to play among them. Among
'these I must put Joh. Haselwood an Apothecary,
'a starch'd formal Clisterpipe, who usually play'd
'on the Bass-Viol, and sometimes on the Counter-
'Tenor. He was very conceited of his Skil (tho he
'had but little of it) and therefore would be ever
'and anon ready to take up a Viol before his betters:
'which being observed by all, they usually call'd
'him *Handlewood.* * * * *

'———— Proctor died in Halywell, and was
'buried in the middle of the church there. He
'had been bred up by M. Joh. Jenkyns, the Mir-
'rour and Wonder of his Age for Music, was ex-
'cellent for the Lyra-Viol and Division-Viol, good
'at the Treble-Viol and Treble-Violin, and all
'comprehended in a man of three or 4 and twentie
'yeares of age. He was much admired at the
'Meetings, and exceedingly pitied by all the faculty
'for his loss.'†

* The grandfather of Littleton, the famous lawyer and judge, temp.
Edw. IV. Thomas de Littleton, took his name from the place of his
birth. He had issue a daughter Elizabeth, his only child, who was
married to Thomas Westcote, Esq. but, as Lord Coke observes, ' she
'being fair, and of a noble spirit, and having large possessions and
'inheritance, resolved to continue the honour of her name; and there-
'fore prudently, whilst it was in her power, provided by Westcote's assent
'before marriage that her issue inheritable should be called by the name
'of de Littleton.' Pref. to Lord Coke's first Institute. And accordingly
Littleton is by Gamden, in his Britannia, named Thomas Littleton alias
Westcote. The person above-mentioned was doubtless a descendant of
this family; and hence it appears how long it was before the Littletons
renounced their paternal, in favour of their maternal name, as deeming
the latter the more honourable.

† Life of Anthony à Wood, Oxf. 1772, page 88, et seq.

The state of music in Oxford, the only part of the
kingdom in which during this melancholy period it
could be said to receive any countenance, is farther
related by Wood in the following passages contained
in his life of himself :—

'In the latter end of this yeare, 1657, Davis
'Mell, the most eminent Violinist of London,‡ being
'in Oxon. Peter Pett, Will. Bull, Ken. Digby, and
'others of Allsoules, as also A. W. did give him a
'very handsome entertainment in the Taverne cal'd
'*The Salutation* in S. Marie's parish Oxon. own'd
'by Tho. Wood, son of - - - - Wood of Oxon.
'sometimes servant to the father of A. W. The
'Company did look upon Mr. Mell to have a pro-
'digious hand on the Violin, and they thought that
'no person, as all in London did, could goe beyond
'him. But when Tho. Baltzar, an Outlander, came
'to Oxon. in the next yeare, they had other thoughts
'of Mr. Mell, who tho he play'd farr sweeter than
'Baltzar, yet Baltzar's hand was more quick, and
'could run it insensibly to the end of the Finger-
'board.§

'1658. A. W. entertain'd two eminent Musitians
'of London, named Joh. Gamble and Tho. Pratt,
'after they had entertain'd him with most excellent
'Musick at the Meeting House of Will. Ellis.
'Gamble had obtained a great name among the
'Musitians of Oxon. for his book before publish'd,
'entit. *Ayres and Dialogues to be sung to the
'Theorbo-Lute or Bass-Viol;*‖ the other for se-
'veral compositions; which they played in their
'consorts.

'Tho. Baltzar, a Lubecker borne, and the most
'famous Artist for the Violin that the World had
'yet produced, was now in Oxon. and this day
'A. W. was with him and Mr. Ed. Low, lately
'Organist of Ch. Church, at the Meeting-House of
'Will. Ellis. A. W. did then and there, to his very
'great astonishment, heare him play on the Violin.
'He then saw him run up his Fingers to the end of
'the Finger-board of the Violin, and run them
'back insensibly, and all with alacrity and in very
'good tune, which he nor any in England saw the
'like before. A. W. entertain'd him and Mr. Low
'with what the House could then afford, and after-
'wards he invited them to the Tavern; but they
'being engag'd to goe to other Company, he could
'no more heare him play or see him play at that
'time. Afterwards he came to one of the weekly
'Meetings at Mr. Ellis's house, and he played to the
'wonder of all the auditory: and exercising his
'Fingers and Instrument several wayes to the
'utmost of his power, Wilson thereupon the public
'Professor (the greatest Judg of Musick that ever

‡ Of this person mention is made in the Miscellanies of John Aubrey,
Esq. under the article Miranda. He is there styled the famous Violinist
and Clock maker. The story related by Aubrey is, that a child of his,
crookbacked, was cured by the touching or rubbing of a dead hand. In
the diary of Wood he is called ' Davie or Davis Mell the eminent Violinist
'and Clockmaker.' Life of Wood 1772, pag. 108, in note.

§ Ibid. page 108.

‖ Gamble was one of the playhouse musicians, and of king Charles
the Second's band: he was a man of considerable note in his time. The
words of the above Ayres and Dialogues are supposed to have been
written by Mr. Stanley, author of the History of Philosophy. Vide ante,
page 584.

'was) did, after his humoursome way, stoop downe
'to Baltzar's Feet, to see whether he had a Huff *
'on, that is to say, to see whether he was a Devil or
'not, because he acted beyond the parts of a man.†

'About that time it was, that Dr. Joh. Wilkins,
'Warden of Wadham Coll. the greatest Curioso of
'his time, invited him and some of the Musitians to
'his Lodgings in that Coll. purposely to have a
'consort, and to see and heare him play. The In-
'struments and Books were carried thither, but
'none could be perswaded there to play against
'him in Consort on the Violin. At length the
'Company perceiving A. W. standing behind in a
'corner neare the dore, they haled him in among
'them, and play, forsooth, he must against him.
'Whereupon he being not able to avoid it, he took
'up a Violin, and behaved himself as poor Troylus
'did against Achilles. He was abash'd at it, yet
'honour he got by playing with and against such a
'grand Master as Baltzar was. Mr. Davis Mell
'was accounted hitherto the best for the Violin in
'England, as I have before told you; but after
'Baltzar came into England, and shew'd his most
'wonderful parts on that instrument, Mell was not
'so admired; yet he play'd sweeter, was a well-bred
'Gentleman, and not given to excessive drinking
'as Baltzar was.‡

'All the time that A. W. could spare from his
'beloved Studies of English History, Antiquities,
'Heraldry and Genealogies, he spent in the most
'delightful facultie of Musick, either instrumental

'or vocal: and if he had missed the weekly
'Meetings in the House of Will. Ellis, he could not
'well enjoy himself all the week after. All or
'most of the Company, when he frequented that
'Meeting, the names of them are set downe under
'the yeare 1656. As for those that came in after,
'and were now performers, and with whome A. W.
'frequently playd, were these: (1) Charles Perot,
'M. A. Fellow of Oriel Coll. a well bred Gent.
'and a person of a sweet nature. (2) Christop.
'Harrison, M. A. Fellow of Queen's Coll. a maggot-
'headed person and humourous. He was afterwards
'Parson of Burgh under Staynsmore in Cumberland,
'where he died in the Winter time *an.* 1694. (3)
'Kenelm Digby, Fellow of Alls. Coll. He was
'afterwards LL.Dr. and dying in the said Coll. on
'Munday night Nov. 5. *an.* 1688, was buried in the
'Chappel there. He was a Violinist, and the two
'former Violists. (4) Will. Bull, Mr. of Arts,
'Bach. of Phys. and Fellow of Alls. Coll. for the
'Violin and Viol. He died 15 Jul. 1661. aged 28
'yeares, and was buried in the Chappel there. (5)
'Joh. Vincent, M. A. Fellow of the said Coll.
'a Violist. He went afterwards to the Inns of
'Court, and was a Barrester. (6) Sylvanus Taylor,
'somtimes Com. of Wadh. Coll. afterwards Fellow
'of Allsoules, and Violist and Songster. He went
'afterwards to Ireland, and died at Dublin in the
'beginning of Nov. 1672. His elder brother, capt.
'Silas Taylor, was a Composer of Music, playd and
'sung his part;§ and when his occasions brought

---

* *i. e.* a hoof.   † Life of Wood, page 111.

‡ Life of Wood, 112.
The account given by Wood of Baltzar may seem a little exaggerated;
and, so far as regards his performance, we must take it upon the credit

of the relator; but were it to be judged of by the style and manner of his
compositions, of which there are some in print, it must have been
admirable. The following Allemand of his is taken from the Division-
Violin, part II. published in 1693, and is the first air of the book:—

ALLEMAND.

THOMAS BALTZAR.

---

§ Of the elder of these two young men, Silas Domville or D'omville
alias Taylor, there is an account in the Athen. Oxon. vol. II. col. 623.
He was, by the testimony of Wood, a man of learning and ingenuity,
and well versed in the history and antiquities of this country, as appears
by a history of Gavelkind written by him, and published in 1663, 4to.
He was also well skilled in music. Wood says that he composed two or
more anthems, which being sung in his majesty's chapel, and well per-

formed, his majesty was pleased to tell the author he liked them. A
composition of his in two parts is printed in Playford's Collection of
Court Ayres, &c. He set to music Cowley's translation of an ode of
Anacreon, 'The thirsty earth,' &c. for two voices: it is printed in Playford's 'Musical Companion,' edit. 1673, page 78, and wrote also rules for
the composition of music, which were never published; a manuscript
copy thereof is in the collection of the author of this work. At the

' him to Oxon, he would be at the Musical Meetings,
' and play and sing his part there. (7) Hen. Langley,
' M. A. and Gent. Com. of Wadh. Coll. a Violist and
' Songster. He was afterwards a worthy Knight,
' lived at Abbey-Foriat neare Shrewsbury, where he
' died in 1680. (8) Samuel Woodford, a Commoner
' and M. A. of the said Coll. a Violist.* He was
' afterwards a celebrated Poet, beneficed in Hamp-
' shire, and Prebendary of Winchester. (9) Franc.
' Parry, M. A. Fellow of Corp. Ch. Coll. a Violist
' and Songster. He was afterwards a Traveller, and
' belonged to the Excise Office. (10) Christop.
' Coward, M. A. Fellow of C. C. Coll. He was
' afterwards Rector of Dicheat in his native County
' of Somersetshire, proceeded D. of D. at Oxon. in
' 1694. (11) Charles Bridgeman, M. A. of Queen's
' Coll. and of Kin to Sr. Orlando Bridgeman. He
' was afterwards Archdeacon of Richmond. He died
' 26 Nov. 1678, and was buried in the Chap. belong-
' ing to that Coll. (12) Nathan. Crew, M. A. Fellow
' of Linc. Coll. a Violinist and Violist, but alwaies
' played out of Tune, as having no good eare. He
' was afterwards, thro several Preferments, Bishop of
' Durham. (13) Matthew Hutton, M. A. Fellow of
' Brasnose Coll. an excellent Violist. Afterwards
' Rector of Aynoe in Northamptonshire. (14) Thom.
' Ken of New Coll. a Junior.† He would be some-
' times among them, and sing his part. (15) Christop.
' Jeffryes, a junior Student of Ch. Church, excellent
' at the Organ and Virginals or Harpsichord, having
' been trained up to those Instruments by his Father
' Georg Jeffryes, Steward to the Lord Hatton of
' Kirbie in Northamptonshire, and Organist to K.
' Ch. I. at Oxon. (16) Rich. Rhodes, another junior
' Student of Ch. Church,‡ a confident Westmonas-
' terian, a Violinist to hold between his Knees.

' These did frequent the Weekly Meetings, and
' by the help of publick Masters of Musick, who
' were mixed with them, they were much improv'd.
' Narcissus Marsh, M. A. and Fellow of Exeter

' Coll.§ would come sometimes among them, but
' seldome play'd, because he had a weekly Meeting
' in his Chamber in the said Coll. where Masters of
' Musick would come, and some of the Company
' before mention'd. When he became Principal of
' S. Alban's hall, he translated the Meeting thither,
' and there it continued when that Meeting in Mr.
' Ellis's house was given over, and so it continued
' till he went into Ireland, and became Mr. of Trin.
' Coll. at Dublin. He was afterwards Archb. of
' Tuam in Ireland.

' After his Majestie's Restoration, when then the
' Masters of Musick were restored to their several
' places that they before had lost, or else if they
' had lost none, they had gotten then preferment, the
' weekly Meetings at Mr. Ellis's house began to
' decay, because they were held up only by Scholars,
' who wanted Directors and Instructors, &c. so that
' in a few yeares after, the Meeting in that house
' being totally layd aside, the chief Meeting was at
' Mr. (then Dr.) Marshe's Chamber, at Exeter Coll.
' and afterwards at S. Alban's hall, as before I have
' told you.

' Besides the Weekly Meetings at Mr. Ellis's
' house, which were first on Thursday, then on Tues-
' day, there were Meetings of the Scholastical Musi-
' cians every Friday Night, in the Winter time, in
' some Colleges: as in the Chamber of Hen. Langley,
' or of Samuel Woodford in Wadham Coll. in the
' Chamber of Christop. Harrison in Queen's Coll. in
' that of Charles Perot in Oriel, in another at New
' Coll. &c. to all which some Masters of Musick
' would commonly retire, as Will. Flexney, Tho.
' Jackson, Gervas Westcote, &c. but these Meetings
' were not continued above 2 or 3 yeares, and I think
' they did not go beyond the yeare 1662.'

CHAP. CXLIII.

PRYNNE, who in his Histrio-Mastix has made
stage-plays the principal object of his satire, is not
less bitter in his censure of music, especially vocal.
He asserts that one unlawful concomitant of stage-
plays is amorous, obscene, lascivious, lust-provok-
ing songs, and poems, which he says were once so
odious in our church, that in the articles to be
enquired of in visitations, set forth in the first
yeere of queene Elizabeth's raigne, Art. 54, churchwardens were enjoined to enquire ' whether any
' minstrels or any other persons did use to sing or
' say any songs or ditties that be vile and uncleane.'
And as to instrumental music, he cites Clemens
Alexandrinus to prove that ' cymbals and dulcimers
' are instruments of fraud; that pipes and flutes
' are to be abandoned from a sober feast; and that
' chromaticall harmonies are to be left to impudent
' malapertnesse in wine, to whorish musicke crowned
' with flowers:' with a deal of such nonsense.

In these bitter invectives Prynne does but speak
the language of the sectaries of his time. Gosson

instance of his father he took part with the usurpers, and became a
captain under colonel Edward Massey, and after that a sequestrator for
the county of Hereford, but exercised his power with so much humanity
and courtesy, that he was beloved of all the king's friends.

* Afterwards DD. Upon his leaving the university he went to the
Inner Temple, and was chamber-fellow with Thomas Flatman the poet.
He paraphrased the Psalms and the Canticles; the former is commended
by Mr. Richard Baxter, and was also the author of a few original poems.
See more of him in Athen. Oxon. vol. II. col. 1098.

† Afterwards bishop of Bath and Wells, and one of the seven bishops
that were sent to the Tower. His conscience not permitting him to
take the oaths at the revolution, he was deprived, and spent the remainder
of his days in retirement. He was so eminently distinguished for piety
and benevolence, that Dryden is said to have intended for him that
character of a good parson, which he has imitated from Chaucer. During
his retreat bishop Ken amused himself with poetry: many of his compositions were published, together with his life, in 1713, by a relation of
his, William Hawkins of the Middle Temple, Esq., and in the Harmonia
Sacra, book II. is an Evening Hymn, written by him and set to music
by Jeremiah Clark.

‡ ' Richard Rhodes, a Gentleman's Son of London, was educated in
' Westminster School, transplanted thence to Ch. Ch. and soon after was
' made Student thereof, being then well grounded in Grammar and in
' the Practical Part of Music. He wrote and composed Flora's Vagaries,
' a Comedy, which, after it had been publickly acted by the Students of
' Ch. Ch. in their common Refectory on the 8th of Jan. 1663, and at the
' Theatre Royal by his Maj. Servants, was made publick at London 1670,
' and afterwards in 1677. This person, who only took one Degree in
' Arts, [at which time he made certain Compositions in Musick of two
' or more Parts, but not as I conceive, extant] went afterwards into
' France, and took, as I have heard, a Degree in Physick at Mountpelier.
' But being troubled with a rambling Head, must needs take a Journey
' into Spain, where, at Madrid, he died, and was buried in 1668.' Athen.
Oxon. vol. II. col. 419.

§ Of this person there is a fuller account in Athen. Oxon. vol. II.
col. 960. Among other things there mentioned he is said to have
written ' An introductory Essay to the Doctrine of Sounds,' printed in
the Philosophical Transactions, and of which an account will herein after
be given.

and Stubs talk in the same strain: the latter calls those, baudy pipers and thundering drummers and assistants in the Devil's Daunce, who play to the Lord of Misrule and his company in country towns and villages upon festivals.* The consequence of the hatred excited by these and other writers against the recreations of the people, were an almost total interdiction of stage-plays and other theatrical entertainments,† and such a general reprobation of music, as in a great measure banished it from the metropolis, and drove it, as has been related, to Oxford, where it met with that protection and encouragement which has ever been shown it by men of liberal and ingenious minds.

The necessary connection between dramatic entertainments and music we have hitherto forborne to speak of; reserving the subject for this place. That this connection is nearly as ancient as the drama itself few need be told, it being well known that the scenic representations, as well of the Greeks as Romans, were accompanied with music, both vocal and instrumental. In the old English Moralities, which were dramas of a religious kind, songs were introduced in the course of the representation; thus in the old morality intitled Lusty Juventus, written in the reign of Edward VI. a song is introduced. In the comedy of Gammer Gurton's Needle, the most ancient in our language, the second act begins with a song, which, though it has been greatly corrupted, is at this time not unknown in many parts of England.‡ In the comedy of King Cambises musicians play at the banquet. In the tragedy of Ferrex and Porrex, otherwise called Gorboduc, written about the year 1556, the order of the dumb show before each act requires severally the music of violins, cornets, flutes, hautboys, and of drums and flutes together. In the Statiro-Mastix or the Untrussing of the humourous Poet, by Thomas Dekker, in the advertisement ad Lectorem it is intimated to have been customary for the trumpet to sound thrice before the beginning of a play. In the Return from Parnassus, act V. begins with a concert. In the pleasant comedy called Wily beguiled, nymphs and satyrs enter singing; and in a word, the plays of Shakespeare, Beaumont and Fletcher, Jonson, and others written before the time of the usurpation, afford such abundant evidence of the union of music with theatrical representations, as proves little less than that they are necessarily co-existent, and that the banishment of the one from the stage was a proscription of the other.

The Restoration was followed by a total change in the national manners; that disgust which the rigour of the preceding times had excited, drove the people into the opposite extreme of licentiousness; so that in their recreations and divertisements they were

* Anatomie of Abuses, page 107.

† There was nevertheless a sort of connivance at these entertainments in favour of friends, and to a limited degree; as in the instance of Sir William Davenant's entertainment at Rutland house, which was patronised by Serjeant Maynard, and of a licence granted in 1659 to Rhodes the bookseller for acting plays at the Cockpit in Drury-lane; but the restraints under which the stage was laid were such, that Whitelocke thought it a bold action of Sir William Davenant to print his entertainment. Vide Whitel. Mem. of Engl. Affairs sub anno 1656.

‡ See it in page 373.

hardly to be kept within the bounds of moderation the theatres, which in the reign of king James I. to speak of London only, were seventeen in number,§

§ The author of the preface to Dodsley's collection of old Plays, has given the following enumeration of as many of them as he was able to recover.

'St. Paul's singing-school, the Globe on the Bankside, Southwark, the 'Swan and the Hope there; the Fortune between Whitecross-street and 'Golden-lane, which Maitland tell us was the first playhouse erected in 'London; the Red Bull in St. John's Street, the Cross-Keys in Grace-'church-street, Juns, the Theatre, the Curtain, the Nursery in Barbican, 'one in Black-Friers, one in White-Friers, one in Salisbury Court, and 'the Cockpit, and the Phœnix in Drury-Lane.'

The same person seems to think that, having continued his account of the English theatre down to the year 1629, it becomes immediately connected with that given by Cibber in his life, which commences a little after the restoration. But in his history there is a chasm, which no one has thought of supplying, so that we can have but a very confused notion of the number and situation of the playhouses in the time of Charles I. But by the help of a pamphlet, now become very scarce, entitled 'Roscius 'Anglicanus or a Historical Review of the Stage,' written by Downes, who at first was an actor in, and afterwards prompter to that which was called the Duke's theatre, we are enabled to connect the two accounts, to correct many mistakes in our theatrical history, which we have hitherto passed unnoticed, and to bring the whole of it into one point of view.

This author relates 'that in the reign of king Charles I. there were 'six playhouses allow'd in town: the Black-Friars Company, his 'Majesty's Servants; the Bull in St. John's Street; another in Salisbury 'Court; another call'd the Fortune; another at the Globe; and the sixth 'at the Cockpit in Drury Lane; all which continu'd acting till the 'beginning of the said Civil Wars. The scattered remnant of several 'of those houses, upon King Charles's Restoration, fram'd a Company, 'who acted again at the Bull, and built them a new house in Gibbons 'Tennis Court in Clare market, in which two places they continu'd acting 'all 1660, 1661, 1662, and part of 1663. In this time they built them a 'new Theatre in Drury Lane; Mr. Thomas Killegrew gaining a Patent 'from the King in order to create them the King's Servants; and from 'that time they call'd themselves his Majesty's Company of Comedians 'in Drury Lane.'

Touching Drury-lane theatre, it may be observed that it was permitted in the time of the usurpation, for Downes in his pamphlet, page 17, says, 'in the year 1659 General Monk marching then his army out of Scotland 'to London, Mr. Rhodes a Bookseller being Wardrobe-keeper formerly '(as I am inform'd) to king Charles the first's Company of Comedians 'in Black Friars, getting a License from the then Governing State, fitted 'up a House then for Acting called the Cock-pit in Drury Lane, and in 'a short time compleated his Company.'

Cibber, in his Apology for his Life, 4to. page 53, 54, says that the patent for Drury-lane was granted to Sir William Davenant, and that another was granted to Henry Killigrew, Esq. for that company of players which was called the Duke's Company, and acted at the Duke's theatre in Dorset Garden. In this he is egregiously mistaken, Sir William Davenant never had any concern in the theatre at Drury-lane, nor had Killigrew any with the Duke's company, who acted first in Lincoln's Inn fields, and afterwards in Dorset Garden. He farther informs us, page 240, that the new theatre in Drury-lane was designed by Sir Christopher Wren. The description he gives of it is such, as joined with our own feelings, must make us regret those alterations in that edifice which the thirst of gain has from time to time suggested to the managers.

Downes mentions that the theatre in Drury-lane opened on Thursday in Easter week, being the eighth day of April, 1663, with the comedy of the Humorous Lieutenant.

The theatre in Drury-lane was called the King's theatre: of that called the Duke's, the following is the history. King Charles I. by his letters patent, bearing date the twenty-sixth day of March, in the fifteenth year of his reign, grants to Sir William Davenant, his heirs and assigns, licence to erect upon a parcel of ground behind the Three Kings ordinary in Fleet-street, in the parish of St. Dunstan in the West, or St. Bride's, London, or in any other place to be assigned him by the Earl Marshall, a theatre or playhouse, forty yards square at the most, wherein plays, musical entertainments, scenes, or other the like presentments may be presented. The patent is extant in Rymer's Fœdera, tom. XX. page 377.

It does not appear that any theatre was erected by Sir William Davenant on the spot described in the above licence; it seems that he engaged with Betterton, who had been an apprentice to Rhodes the bookseller above-mentioned, and was afterwards a player under him, and also with the rest of Rhodes's company, to build one elsewhere. Sir William having thus formed a company of actors, obtained from Charles II. licence to erect a new theatre in Lincoln's Inn fields. Downes says that by this patent Betterton, who was then but twenty-two years of age, and the rest of Rhodes's company were created the King's Servants, and were sworn by the earl of Manchester, then lord chamberlain, to serve his royal highness the duke of York at the theatre in Lincoln's Inn fields. Rosc. Angl. 19.

While this theatre was building, Sir William Davenant wrote the Siege of Rhodes, in two parts, and that excellent comedy the Wits, which were rehearsed at Apothecary's Hall; and upon opening the house in 1662, these were the first plays acted there. Rosc. Angl. 20.

After a few years continuance at Lincoln's Inn fields, Sir William Davenant erected a magnificent theatre in Dorset Garden, in a situation between Salisbury Court, and the Thames, and determined to remove thither with the players under him. But he died in 1668, probably before it was compleated, and his interest in the patent devolved to his widow, lady Davenant, and Mr. Betterton.

Cibber says that the actors both at the King's and the Duke's theatre were, it is true, reduced to two, namely, the King's in Drury-lane, and the Duke of York's in Dorset Garden, but these latter exceeded the former in splendour and magnificence so greatly, that the difference between the one and the other in these respects was immeasurable. The old playhouses were either a large room in a noted alehouse, or a slight erection in a garden or place behind an alehouse; the pit unfloored, in which the spectators either stood, or were badly accommodated with benches to sit on; the music was seldom better than that of a few wretched fiddles, hautboys, or cornets; and to soothe those affections which tragedy is calculated to excite, that of flutes was also made use of: but the music of these several classes of instruments when associated being in the unison, the performance was far different from what we understand by concert and symphony; and upon the whole mean and despicable.

The modern playhouses above-mentioned were truly and emphatically styled theatres, as being constructed with great art, adorned with painting and sculpture, and in all respects adapted to the purposes of scenic representation. In the entertainments there exhibited music was required as a

were masters of their art. In each there were also women; Downes says that four of Sir William Davenant's women actresses were boarded at his own house. Rosc. Angl. 20.

This passage in Downes's narrative ascertains the time when female actors first appeared on the stage. In the infancy of the English theatre it was held indecent for women thus to expose themselves, and, to avoid the scandal thence arising, it was the custom for young men dressed in female habits to perform the parts of women; but this was exclaimed against by puritan writers, particularly Prynne, who in his ' Histrio-Mastix,' page 169, cites St. Chrysostom and other of the fathers to prove that the dressing up a youth to represent the person of a tender virgin, is a most abominable act. So that at this time the former was looked upon as the lesser evil. This gave occasion to Sir William Davenant to solicit for permission to employ females; and accordingly in his patent was the following clause: 'And whereas the women's parts in plays have ' hitherto been acted by men in the habits of women, at which some have ' taken offence, we do permit and give leave, for the time to come, that ' all women's parts be acted by women.'

Cibber relates that in the contest between the two companies for the public favour, that of the king had the advantage; and that therefore, these are his words, 'Sir William Davenant, master of the Duke's ' Company, to make head against their success, was forc'd to add spectacle ' and musick to action; and to introduce a new species of plays, since ' called Dramatick Operas, of which kind there are the Tempest, Psyche, ' Circe, and others, all set off with the most expensive decorations of ' scenes and habits, with the best voices and dancers.' Life of Cibber, 57.

It is to be feared that in this relation Cibber, without recurring to authentic memorials, trusted altogether to the reports of others; for not one of the plays above-mentioned were represented under the direction, or even during the life-time of Sir William. The fact stands thus: Sir William died in 1668; the theatre in Dorset Garden was opened on the ninth day of November, 1671, with the comedy of Saint Martin Marr-all. In 1673 was represented the Tempest, made into an opera by Shadwell, and set to music by Matthew Lock. In February in the same year came forth the opera of Psyche, also written by Shadwell, and set to music by Lock and Sign. Baptist Draghi; and in 1676 was performed Circe, an opera, written by Dr. Charles Davenant, a son of Sir William, and set to music by Mr. John Banister.

These representations are related to have been made at a prodigious expense, in music, dancing, machinery, scenes, and other decorations, and were intended to rival those of the French stage; and some of the best French dancers, namely, L' Abbeè, Balon, and Mademoiselle Subligny, performed at them. At length, in the year 1682, according to Downes, but, as Cibber says, in 1684, the Duke's company not being able to subsist, united with the King's, and both were incorporated by the name of the King's Company of Comedians.

For about ten years that at Drury-lane was the only theatre in London. But Mr. Betterton obtained a licence from king William to erect a theatre within the walls of the tennis court in Lincoln's-Inn fields, and, by the help of a liberal subscription of the nobility and gentry, opened it in 1695, with a new comedy of Mr. Congreve, viz. Love for Love. Cibber's Life, 113, 114.

The theatre in Lincoln's-Inn fields was rebuilt by William Collier, Esq. a lawyer, and member for Truro in Cornwall, and in 1714 opened with the comedy of the Recruiting Officer. The subsequent history of the two theatres, as also the erection of that in the Haymarket, now the Opera-house, are related at large by Cibber in the Apology for his Life.

The patent for Lincoln's Inn fields theatre came afterwards into the hands of Mr. Christopher Rich, whose son, the late Mr. John Rich, built the present theatre in Covent-Garden. Mr. Shepherd was the architect who designed it.

necessary relief, as well to the actors as the audience, between the acts: compositions for this purpose were called Act-tunes, and were performed in concert; instruments were also required for the dances and the accompaniment of songs. Hence it was that, upon the revival of stage-entertainments, music became attached to the theatres, which from this time, no less than, formerly the church had been, became the nurseries of musicians; insomuch, that to say of a performer on any instrument that he was a playhouse musician, or of a song, that it was a playhouse song, or a playhouse tune, was to speak of each respectively in terms of the highest commendation.

It must be confessed that this exaltation of the stage did not immediately follow the restoration: a work of greater importance engaged the attention of all serious men, to wit, the restoration of the liturgy, and the revival of that form of religious worship which had been settled at the reformation, and which by the ordinance that abolished the use of it, and by the preface to the directory substituted in its place, had been stigmatized as vain, superstitious, and idolatrous. In what manner this great purpose was effected, and in particular the methods which were taken to restore cathedral service, will hereafter be related, as will also the prosecution of that design, which has been hinted at in the relation herein before given of an entertainment at Rutland-house, intended by the author, Sir William Davenant, as an imitation of the opera, and the subsequent progress of music in its connection with the drama; but first it will be necessary, by way of explanation of Wood's account of the state of music at Oxford during a period of near twenty years, to describe particularly those concerts which were so well attended, and afforded such entertainment to the members of the university.

CHAP. CXLIV.

WHAT is to be understood by a concert of viols, such as Wood speaks of, is now hardly known: we are therefore necessitated to recur to a book published by old John Playford in the year 1683, entitled ' An Introduction to the Skill of Music, the tenth ' edition, for a description of the bass, the tenor, and ' the treble viol, with the respective tunings of each;' and from thence we learn that the bass-viol had six strings, the first called the treble; the second the small mean; the third the great mean; the fourth the counter-tenor; the fifth the tenor or gamut string, and the sixth the bass: and that the tuning these was as follows, viz. the first or treble string, D LA SOL RE; the second, A LA MI RE; the third, E LA MI; the fourth, C FA UT; the fifth, GAMUT; and the sixth double D SOL RE.

The Tenor-viol, which also had six strings, was tuned to the same intervals, the sixth or greatest string answering to GAMUT on the bass, and the first to G SOL RE UT on the treble viol, which had its tuning precisely an octave higher than the bass-viol.*

* We have here a perfect designation of the order and tuning of a set of viols, and this will explain what is meant by a chest of viols, which generally consisted of six in number, and were used for playing Fantazias

The bass-viol was originally a concert instrument, and used in the performance of Fantazias from two to six parts, but it was frequently played on alone, or as an accompaniment to the voice, in the manner of the lute. In the first case it was called the Concert-viol, in the other the Viol da gamba. It was fretted with more or fewer frets, according to the use to which it was employed; when used in concert, four were generally sufficient, but when alone, or to accompany the voice, seven were requisite.

Concerning compositions of many parts adapted to viols, of which there are many, it is to be observed, that when the practice of singing madrigals began to decline, and gentlemen and others began to excel in their performance on the viol, the musicians of the time conceived the thought of substituting instrumental music in the place of vocal; and for this purpose some of the most excellent masters of that instrument, namely Douland, the younger Ferabosco, Coperario, Jenkins, Dr. Wilson, and many others, betook themselves to the framing compositions called Fantazias, which were generally in six parts, answering to the number of viols in a set or chest, as it is called in the advertisement in the preceding note, and abounded in fugues, little responsive passages, and all those other elegancies observable in the structure and contrivance of the madrigal. In what manner a set of these instruments was tuned for the purpose of performing in concert, has been already mentioned. It now remains to speak of the Bass-viol or Viol da Gamba.

To the instructions respecting the bass, the tenor, and the treble viol contained in the second book of Playford's Introduction, are added brief directions for the treble violin, the tenor violin, and the bass violin, which, as they are each strung with four strings, appear clearly a species separate and distinct from the viol. And here it is to be noted,

in six parts. To this purpose old Thomas Mace of Cambridge speaks, in that singularly humorous book of his writing, 'Musick's Monument.' page 245. 'Your best provision (and most compleat) will be a good 'chest of viols, six in number (viz.) 2 Basses, 2 tenors, and 2 trebles, all 'truly and proportionably suited. Of such there are no better in the 'world than those of Aldred, Jay, Smith, yet the highest in esteem are 'Bolles and Ross (one bass of Bolles's I have known valued at 100l.) 'these were old, but we have now very excellent workmen, who (no 'doubt) can work as well.'

In a collection of airs, entitled 'Tripla Concordia, published in 1667 'by John Carr, living at the Middle Temple gate in Fleet Street,' is the following advertisement :—

'There is two Chests of Viols to be sold, one made by Mr. John Ross, 'who formerly lived in Bridewell, containing two trebles, three tenors, 'and one bass: the chest was made in the year 1298.

'The other being made by Mr. Henry Smith, who formerly lived over-'against Hatton-house in Holbourn, containing two trebles, two tenors, 'two basses. The chest was made in the year 1633. Both chests are 'very curious work.'

The John Ross mentioned in the above advertisement, was the son of the person mentioned in the Annals of Stowe by the name of John Rose, to have invented 4to. Eliz. the instrument called the Bandora. See page 493, in not.

Concerts of viols were the usual entertainments after the practice of singing madrigals grew into disuse: and these latter were so totally excluded by the introduction of the violin, that, at the beginning of this century, Dr. Tudway of Cambridge was but just able to give a description of a chest of viols, as appears by the following extract from a letter to his son, written for the purpose of instructing him in music :—

'A chest of viols was a large hutch, with several apartments and 'partitions in it; each partition was lined with green bays, to keep the 'instruments from being injured by the weather; every instrument was 'sized in bigness according to the part played upon it; the least size 'played the treble part, the tenor and all other parts were played by a 'larger sized viol; the bass by the largest size. They had six strings 'each, and the necks of their instruments were fretted. Note, I believe 'upon the treble-viol was not higher than G or A in alt, which is nothing 'now.'

that the bass-violin, which is also described by Playford, and had the tuning of its first or highest string, in G sol re ut, its second in C fa ut, and its third in FF fa ut, and its fourth in BB mi, appears clearly to have been an instrument different from the Violoncello, now the associate of the treble and tenor violin in concerts, into which it was first introduced by the Italians. But we are now speaking of the viol species; and of this it is to be observed, that the method of notation proper to it was by the characters common to both vocal and instrumental music, but that about the time of king James I. the notation for the lute called the tablature, was by Coperario transferred to the Bass-viol. The tablature as adapted to the Bass-viol consisted in a stave of six lines, representing the six strings of the instrument, with letters of an antique form, signifying the place of the tones and semitones on each string. The first of these methods was calculated for the performance on the viol in concert. the compositions for that instrument called Fantazias being uniformly written in the notes of the Gamut. The Lyra-way,* as it was called, was adapted to the tablature, and by that method the viol was rendered capable, without a variation of the characters, of performing lute lessons.

In either way the instrument, consisting of six strings, was tuned according to the following directions of Playford : 'The treble, being raised as high 'as it will conveniently bear, is called D la sol re; 'then tune your second four notes lower, and it is 'A la mi re; the third four notes lower, is E la mi; 'the fourth three notes lower is C fa ut; the fifth 'four notes lower is Gamut; and the sixth four 'notes lower than the fifth, is double D sol re.'† The instrument being fretted with five frets for the first or treble string, and four for each of the others, the progression on each string will be as follows :—

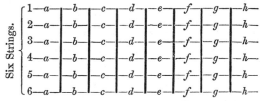

Open First Second Third Fourth Fifth Sixth 7th Fret.

The frets which cross the stave in the above example, together with the letters adjoining to them, determine the station of the tones and semitones on each string; thus, to instance in the first string, *a* stands for D, which has the sound for the string open or unstopped; *b* for D , *c* for E, *d* for F, *e* for F♯, *f* for G, *g* for G♯, and *h* for A; and this explanation will apply to the other strings on the instrument. As to the frets, they were nothing more than pieces of very small catgut string dipped in warm glue and tied round the neck of the instru-

* Playford calls the method of playing on the Bass-viol by the Tablature the Lyra-way, and the instrument played on in this manner the Lyra-viol. Introduction to the Skill of Musick, page 96, 87, edit. 1683.

† The six lines above, as they answer to the strings of the instrument, have not the least relation to the stave of Guido; the letters and not the lines represent the notes in succession; and as to the characters to denote their several lengths, they are referred to above.

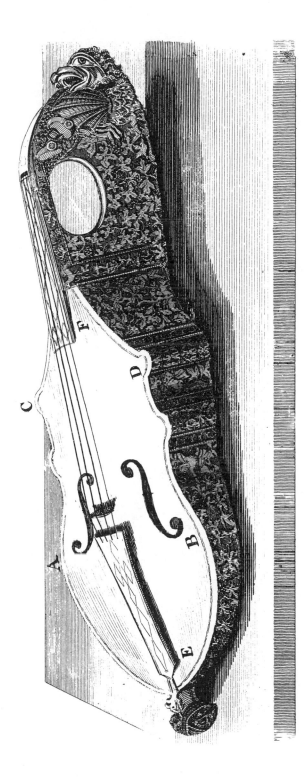

ment, at proper distances; and in stopping them it was required that the extremity of the finger should be behind, but in immediate contact with the fret.

The notation by the tablature determines nothing as to the time or value of notes, and therefore requires the aid of other characters for this purpose; those in use when the viol was in greatest esteem were such as were originally adapted to the tablature for the lute, and are described in page 419. But afterwards they were changed to those characters that are used in the notation according to the Gamut.*

It has already been mentioned that the practice of singing madrigals, which had prevailed for many years throughout Europe, gave way to concerts of viols, such as are above described; but the languor of these performances, which consisted of Fantazias of five and six parts, was not compensated by that sweet and delicate tone which distinguishes the viol species; the violin, though it had long been in the hands of the vulgar,† and had been so degraded that the appellation of Fiddler was a term of reproach, was found to be an instrument capable of great improvement; and the softness and delicacy of the violin tone, and the occasional force and energy of the instrument itself, were such recommendations of it as determined the Italian masters, about the beginning of the seventeenth century, to introduce it into practice.

The treble violin, the tenor violin, and the violoncello, have a necessary connection with each other, and form a species of fidicinal instruments distinct from that of the viol: the introduction of these into concerts is therefore to be considered as a new era in musical history, and may justify a retrospect to the circumstances that preceded and contributed to this event.

What kind of an instrument the ancient violin or fiddle mentioned by Chaucer was, we are at a loss at this distance of time to discover; but what the fiddle was about the year 1530, appears by the figure of it in the Musurgia of Ottomarus Luscinius, hereinbefore exhibited. Notwithstanding this certainty, there is good reason to suppose that towards the end of the sixteenth centry the shape of it was rather vague and undetermined, for at a sale by auction of the late duke of Dorset's effects, a violin was bought, appearing to have been made in the year 1578, which, though of a very singular form, and encumbered with a profusion of carving, was essentially the very same instrument with the four-

stringed violin, as appears by the following representation of it :—‡

To the above engraving, taken immediately from the instrument itself, a verbal description of it will be deemed but a necessary adjunct.

The dimensions of the instrument are as follow. From the extremity of the tail-pin to the dragon's head, two feet. From A to B seven inches and a half. From C to D six inches. Length of the belly thirteen inches. Thickness at E one inch, at F four and a half. Over the pins is a silver gilt plate, that turns upon a hinge, and opens from the nut downwards; thereon are engraved the arms of England, and under them, encircled by a garter with the usual motto, the bear and ragged staff,§ and an earl's coronet at top; in the tail-pin is inserted a gilt silver stud, to which the tail-piece is looped, with a lion's face curiously wrought on the top; this is secured by a nut, which screws to it on the under side of the instrument, whereon are engraven these letters and figures I P supposed to signify the year when it was made, and the initials of the maker's name. The subject of the carving on the deepest part, and on the side above presented to view, is a man with an axe, standing on the ground, and working upon some fallen branches of an oak tree: on the opposite part are represented hogs under an oak tree, and a man beating down acorns; the rest of the carving is foliage; the whole is in alto relievo. Under the carving is a foil of tinsel or silver gilt. The back of the instrument is not curved, but forms a very obtuse angle; and from the bottom of the back, extending to the back of the dragon's head, the carving, which is very bold, consists of oak foliage.

Notwithstanding the exquisite workmanship of it, the instrument produces but a close and sluggish tone, which considering the profusion of ornament, and the quantity of wood with which it is incumbered, is not to be wondered at.

But, notwithstanding the diversities in the shape of the violin at different periods, that the modern violin had assumed the form which it now bears, almost as early as the beginning of the seventeenth century, is indisputable, for of the violins of Cremona, so long celebrated for the beauty of their shape and fineness of tone,‖ there are great numbers that

---

* These have been considerably improved both in England and Holland since their first invention, for originally the quavers and semiquavers, though ever so numerous in succession, were all distinct; but about the year 1660 Playford invented what he called the new tyed note, wherein by one or two strokes continued from the bottom of each note to the next, the quavers and semiquavers were formed into compages of four or six, as the time required, a contrivance that rendered the musical characters much more legible than before. The Dutch followed this example soon after the English had set it; and afterwards the French, and after them the Germans; but so lately as the year 1724, when Marcello's Psalms were published in a splendid edition at Venice, the Italians printed after the old manner, and so did the Spaniards till within these very few years.

† Dr. Tudway, in his letter to his son, says that within his remembrance it was scarce ever used but at wakes and fairs, and that those who played on it travelled about the country with their instrument in a cloak-bag.

‡ *A larger plate of this instrument will be found in the Supplementary Volume of Portraits.*

§ The bear and ragged staff was the cognizance of the Nevils earls of Warwick. Robert Dudley, earl of Leicester, who derived his pedigree from them, took it for his crest. See Fuller's Worthies in Warwickshire, 118. This agrees with a tradition concerning it, that the instrument was originally queen Elizabeth's, and that she gave it to her favourite the earl of Leicester, which is not improbable, seeing that her arms are also upon it.

‖ There were three persons of the name of Amati, natives of Cremona, and makers of violins, that is to say, Andrew, Jerome, and Antony his

appear to have been made before year 1620, and yet it does not appear that the violin was used in concert till some years after.

Scipione Cerreto, in his treatise De Prattica musicale, enumerates the many excellent composers and performers on various instruments living at Naples in the year 1601; and it is worthy of note that among the latter are mentioned only Sonatori excellenti del Liuto, d'Organo, di Viola d'arco, di Chittara a sette chorde, di Lira in gamba, di Tromboni, di Ciaramelle e Cornetti, and dell' Arpa à due ordini, from whence it may be inferred that at that time the violin in Italy, as in England and other countries, was an instrument of little account, and deemed fit only for the entertainment of the vulgar; nevertheless we find that in a very few years after it rose so high as to be admitted into the theatre: indeed it may be said to be coeval with the opera itself. It has already been mentioned that the most ancient opera in print is the Orfeo of Claudio Monteverde, represented at Mantua in 1607, and published at Venice in 1615; to this is prefixed the personages of the drama, and the names and numbers of the instruments used in the performance; and among the latter occur duoi Violini piccoli alla Francese: now the diminutive, piccoli, supposes an instrument of the same species, of a larger size than itself, i. e. a violin; but this it seems was not admitted into the performance, perhaps for this reason, that the Viola da brazzo, i. e. the treble viol, held its place: and if it be asked what then was the use of the Violino piccoli? it may be answered, perhaps for a particular accompaniment, the imitation of the singing of birds for instance; or for a like purpose as the Flauto alla vigessima seconda, viz. a treble octave flute. However it is certain that at the beginning of the sixteenth century the practice of the violin was cultivated in Italy with uncommon assiduity; so that in a few years after it became the principal of concert instruments. From Italy it passed into France, and from thence into England. At first it was used in accompaniment with the voice, and was confined to the theatre; but the good effects of it, in giving to the melody a force and expression which was wanting in the sound of the voice, and extending the limits of the harmony in the chorus, recommended it also to the church.

The motetts and hymns that made a part of divine service, had hitherto been composed for voices, with no other accompaniment than that of the organ; and this kind of music, which corresponds with the practice of the primitive church, is still retained in the pope's chapel; but no sooner were the advantages discovered that resulted from the union of voices and instruments, than all the objections arising from the seeming profanation of the temples of God, by admitting into them such instruments as had hitherto been appropriated to theatrical representations, vanished.

This innovation gave rise to a new church-style, in which the principal end of the composer was rather to display the excellencies of either some fine singer or instrumental performer, than to inspire the auditory with those sentiments which should accompany divine worship. For examples of this kind we need look no farther than the motets of Carissimi, Colonna, and Bassani, in which the solo vocal parts are wrought up to the highest degree of perfection; and the instrumental accompaniments abound with divisions calculated to shew the powers of execution in the performers.

Whether vocal music gains more than it loses by being associated with such instruments as it is usually joined with, may admit of a question: it is universally agreed, that of all music that of the human voice is the sweetest; and it may be remarked, that in a chorus of voices and instruments the sounds never coalesce or blend together in such a manner, as not to be distinguishable by the ear into two species; while in a chorus of voices alone, well sorted, and perfectly in tune, the aggregate of the whole is that full and complete union and consent, which we understand by the word Harmony, as applied to music. On the other hand it may be said that what is wanting in harmony is made up by the additional force and energy which is given to vocal music by its union with that of instruments; but it is worthy of consideration whether music, the end whereof is to inspire devotion, stands in need of such aids, or rather indeed whether such aids have not a tendency to defeat its end.

This at least is certain, that the theatric and ecclesiastic styles are discriminated by the very nature and tendency of each, and that the confusion of the one with the other has for upwards of a century been considered by the ablest defenders of choral service as one of the great abuses of music.

CHAP. CXLV.

It is now time to speak of the revival of choral service upon the restoration of king Charles the Second. At this time no more than nine of the bishops of the church of England were living; these immediately on the king's return took possession of their respective bishoprics; and such sees as were vacant were immediately filled up, either by translations or new appointments. The sequestered clergy severally entered upon the livings which they had been ejected from, and dispossessed the incumbents whom they found there. Heads and fellows of colleges were also reinstated, and the government and discipline of the church were reduced to the legal form.

No sooner was the liturgy re-established, than

sons, and Nicolas, the son of the latter. Andrew flourished about the year 1600.
    Besides these there were two persons of the name of Stradivarius of Cremona, admirable artisans; the latter was living at the beginning of this century: his signature was 'Antonius Stradivarius Cremonensis Faciebat Anno   A†S.'
    Andrew Guarnier, also of Cremona, signed thus, 'Andreas Guarnerius, 'fecit Cremonæ sub titulo Sancta Teresæ, 1680.'
    The violins of Cremona are exceeded only by those of Stainer, a German, whose instruments are remarkable for a full and piercing tone; his signature is as follows:—
    'Jacobus Stainer, In Absam propè Oenipontum 1647.' Oenipons is the Latin name of Insprunck in Germany, the chief city of Tyrol.
    Matthew Albani, also a Tyrolese, signed thus 'Matthias Albanus fecit in Tyrol Bulsani 1654.'

the bishops and clergy became sensible of the necessity of reviving the choral service; but here they were greatly at a loss. By an ordinance made in the year 1644, organs in churches and chapels had been commanded to be taken down;* and the fury of the rabble was not less remarkable in their demolition, than in that impious zeal which prompted them to despoil churches of their ornaments, and, as far as it was in their power, by the destruction of funeral monuments, to efface from the remembrance of mankind those virtues of the illustrious dead, which it is the end of monuments and sepulchral inscriptions to perpetuate.

Organs being thus destroyed, and the use of them forbidden in England, the makers of those instruments were necessitated to seek elsewhere than in the church for employment; many went abroad, and others betook themselves to such other occupations for a livelihood, as were nearest related to their own; they became joiners and carpenters, and mixed unnoticed with such as had been bred up to those trades; so that, excepting Dallans, Loosemore of Exeter, Thamar of Peterborough, and Preston of York, there was at the time of the restoration scarce an organ-maker that could be called a workman in the kingdom. Some organs had been taken down, and sold to private persons, and others had been but partially destroyed; these, upon the emergency that called for them, were produced, and the artificers above named were set to work to fit them up for use; Dallans indeed was employed to build a new organ for the chapel of St. George at Windsor, but, whether it was through haste to get it finished, or some other cause, it turned out, though a beautiful structure, but an indifferent instrument.

The next step towards the revival of cathedral service, was the appointment of skilful persons for organists and teachers of music in the several choirs of the kingdom; a few musicians of eminence, who had served in the former capacity under the patronage of Charles I. namely Child, Christopher Gibbons, Rogers, Wilson, Low, and others, though advanced in years, were yet living; these were sought out and promoted; the four first named were created doctors, and Child, Gibbons, and Low were appointed organists of the royal chapel; Gibbons was also made master of the children there, and organist of Westminster Abbey. Rogers, who had formerly been organist of Magdalen college at Oxford, was preferred to Eton; Wilson had a place both in the chapel and

in Westminster choir; and Albertus Bryne was made organist of St. Paul's.

By this method of appointment the choirs were provided with able masters; but great difficulties, arising from the late confusion of the times, and the long intermission of choral service, lay behind. Cathedral churches, from the time of the suppression of monasteries, had been the only seminaries for the instruction of youth in the principles of music; and as not only the revenues appropriated for this purpose were sequestered, but the very institution itself was declared to be superstitious, parents were deprived both of the means and the motives to qualify their children for choral duty, so that boys were wanting to perform those parts of the service which required treble voices. Nay, to such streights were they driven, that for a twelvemonth after the restoration the clergy were forced to supply the want of boys by cornets,† and men who had feigned voices. Besides this, those of riper years, whose duty it had been to perform choir service, namely, the minor canons and lay-clerks of the several cathedrals, had upon their ejection betaken themselves to other employments; some went into the king's army, others taught the lute and virginals; and others psalmody, to those whose principles restrained them from the use of any other music in religious worship.

In consequence hereof, and of that inaptitude which follows the disuse of any faculty, when the church-service was revived, there were very few to be found who could perform it; for which reason the universities, particularly that of Oxford, were very sedulous in their endeavours to promote the study of practical music: and, to render the church-service familiar, a book, written by Edward Low, was printed at Oxford in 1661, entitled 'Some short directions for the performance of Cathedral Service.' This Edward Low‡ came from Salisbury, having been brought up under John Holmes, the organist of that cathedral. In the year 1630 he

---

* The words of the ordinance are 'all organs, and the frames or cases 'wherein they stand, in all churches and chappels [i. e. cathedral, 'collegiate, or parish churches or chappels] shall be taken away and 'utterly defaced, and none other hereafter set up in their places.' Scobell's Collection of Arts, 1651, page 181. Bishop Sanderson, in one of his sermons, says, that the Puritans objected to the use of instrumental music in divine worship, deeming it unlawful: this opinion was adopted by the Nonconformists at the Restoration, and in general seems to be still retained by them. At the close of the last century, upon occasion of erecting an organ in a parish church at Tiverton, in the county of Devon, a sermon was preached by one Mr. Newte, which was remarked on in an anonymous pamphlet, entitled 'a letter to a friend in the country concerning the use of instrumental music in the worship of God, 4to. 1698. To this letter the preacher replied in the preface to a treatise by the learned Mr. Dodwell on the lawfulness of instrumental music in holy offices, 8vo. 1700. The preface and the tract that follows it contain a full and decisive vindication of the practice in question, and so far prevailed with some of the more moderate of the Dissenters, that Dr. Edmund Calamy was once heard to say that in his Meeting Place in Long Ditch, Westminster, he should have no objection to the erection of an organ.

† These instruments had been introduced into the choral service before, for in the Statutes of Canterbury Cathedral, provision is made for players on sackbuts and cornets. And the same appears by the following passage in the Life of Archbishop Whitgift, as given in the Biographia Britannica, page 4255, respecting the service at Canterbury Cathedral. 'There happily 'landed an intelligencer from Rome, who wondered to see an Archbishop or 'Clergyman in England so reverenced and attended, and being present also 'the Sunday following at service at the Cathedral in Canterbury, where 'seeing his grace attended with his gentlemen and servants, as also the Dean, 'Prebendaries, and Preachers, in their Surplices and scarlet hoods, and 'hearing the solemn music, with the voices and organs, cornets and sackbuts, 'he was struck with amazement and admiration, and declared that they 'were led in great blindness at Rome by our own nation, who made the 'people there believe, that there was not in England either Archbishop or 'Bishop, or Cathedral or any church or Ecclesiastical government; but that 'all was pulled down to the ground, and that the people heard their Minister 'in woods and fields, among trees and brute beasts; but for his own part he 'protested that, unless it were in the Pope's chapel, he never saw a more 'solemn sight, or heard a more heavenly sound.' And we are told that at the churching of the queen, after the birth of lady Mary, daughter of James I. in the Royal Chapel sundry Anthems were sung with organ, cornets, sackbuts, and other excellent instruments of music. Vide Stow's Annals, 864. Lastly Charles I. when at Oxford, had service at the Cathedral with organs, sackbuts, recorders, cornets, &c. From a tract entitled 'The well tuned Organ,' by Joseph Brookband, 4to, 1660.

‡ Of this person mention has already been made. Vide ante pag. 584 et 681, and Wood in his life takes frequent occasion to speak of him. Soon after the restoration he was appointed one of the organists of the chapel royal. He died on the eleventh of July, 1682, and was buried at the upper end of the divinity chapel, on the north side of the cathedral of Christ Church, near to the body of Alice, his sometime wife, daughter of Sir John Peyton the younger, of Doddington in the Isle of Ely, Knight. Fasti, vol. I. coll. 178. Henry Purcell succeeded him in the place of organist of the royal chapel, July 14, 1682, as appears by the Cheque-Book.

succeeded Dr. Stonard as organist of Christ Church, Oxford. He was also for some years deputy music professor for Dr. Wilson, but, upon Wilson's leaving the university, was appointed professor in his own right. Wood says that though not a graduate, he was esteemed a very judicious man in his profession. Fasti, vol. I. col. 178. The book above-mentioned was again published in duodecimo, anno 1664, under the title of 'A Review of some short directions for performance of Cathedral Service,' with a dedication to Dr. Walter Jones, subdean of the chapel royal, and a preface, addressed to all gentlemen that are true lovers of cathedral service, wherein he informs them, which is strictly true, that the versicles, responses, and single tunes of the reading psalms then in use, and which he has published, are exactly the same that were used in the time of Edward VI., for which he refers to another copy, printed anno 1550, which can be no other than the book entitled 'The Booke of Common Praier noted,' by John Marbeck, of which an account has herein before been given.

As the formulary contained in this book of Low is adapted to the liturgy established in the reign of queen Elizabeth, and continued, with a few inconsiderable variations, to this time, it necessarily follows that it must differ in many respects from that of Marbeck, which was adapted to the common prayer of Ewd. VI. To enumerate all the particulars in which they differ will hardly be thought necessary; it may suffice to say that the versicles and responses are very nearly the same in each: besides these, the author has inserted a variety of chanting tunes for the Psalms, Venite exultemus, &c. some of which it is conjectured were composed by Dr. Child, of Windsor, as is also a Te Deum of four parts in counterpoint, there also given. The litany seems to be that of Tallis in four parts:* it is followed by a burial service in four parts of Mr. Robert Parsons, and a Veni Creator, the author unknown, which concludes the book.

The places of organist and master of the children in the several cathedrals were no sooner filled up with able men, than those on whom they were bestowed, as also the gentlemen of the king's chapel, laboured incessantly in the composition of services and anthems; thereby endeavouring to make up the loss which church-music had sustained in the preceding period of near twenty years, so that in the short space of two years a great number of each were composed by them, as appears by James Clifford's Collection of divine Services and Anthems usually sung in his Majesties Chappell, and in all the Cathedrals and Collegiate Choires of England and Ireland. Lond. 1664, duod.

This James Clifford was a native of Oxford, being born in the parish of St. Mary Magdalen there. He was educated in Magdalen college school, and became a chorister of that college, but took no degree in the university of Oxford. After the restoration he was a minor canon of St. Paul's cathedral, and reader in some church near Carter-

It is Tallis only in part.

lane; and after that chaplain to the honourable society of Serjeants-Inn in Fleet-street, London.† He died about the year 1700, leaving a widow, who survived him some years; she dwelt in Wardrobe-court, in Great Carter-lane, London, and had a daughter, who taught a school of little children.‡ Besides the above collection, he published a Catechism, and a preparation Sermon; and these seem to be the whole of his writings.

To the collection of Services and Anthems above-mentioned is a dedication to Dr. Walter Jones, subdean of the chapel royal, and two prefaces, the one whereof seems to have been published with an earlier edition of the book, the other containing chanting tunes for the Venite, Te Deum, Benedicite, Jubilate, Magnificat, Cantate Domino, Nunc Dimittis, Deus Misereatur, the Psalms, and Quicunque vult.. After these follow 'Brief directions for the 'understanding of that part of the divine service 'performed with the organ in St. Paul's cathedral 'on Sundayes, &c.' The particulars most worthy of regard among these directions are the following: 'After the Psalms, a voluntary upon the organ 'alone.' 'After the third collect "O Lord our "heavenly father, &c." is sung the first anthem.' 'After the blessing "The grace of our Lord Jesus "Christ, &c" a voluntary alone upon the organ.§ In the second or communion service nothing remarkable occurs; but after the sermon follows another anthem, which concludes the morning service.

At evening service, 'After the psalms a voluntary 'alone by the organ.' After the third collect, "Lighten our darkness, &c." is sung the first, and "after the sermon the last anthem.'

At the end of the book is a short address to the reader, in which it is intimated that the best musicians of later times had found it expedient to reduce the six syllables used in solmisation to four, by permutation of UT, RE, into SOL, LA. At the end of this postscript the author professes to exhibit a table, containing, as he terms it, 'that very basis or foun-'dation of music which had long before been com-'piled for the instruction of youth in the rudiments 'of musick, by that most worthy and excellent 'author thereof, Ralph Winterton, Dr. of Physick 'and Regius Professor of the same in the university 'of Cambridge, in his own words and methode;' 'but, by some unaccountable mistake, this table or basis, whatever it be, is omitted in all the copies of the book that have come to our hands, and instead thereof is inserted 'A Psalm of Thanksgiving to be 'sung by the Children of Christ's Hospital on 'Monday and Tuesday in Easter holydaies at St.

† Athen. Oxon. vol. II. col. 1019.

‡ These particulars were communicated by a person now living, who was one of the daughter's little pupils, and, though turned of fourscore, retains a remembrance of his person.

§ This was the usage in cathedrals for many years, but in some, particularly St. Paul's and Canterbury, and at Westminster, the practice has been, and still is, instead of a voluntary, to sing the Sanctus to solemn music in the interval between morning prayer, concluding with the Benediction, and the second or communion service, which is certainly a change for the better. In the Temple church, which by the way is neither a cathedral nor parochial church, a voluntary is introduced in this part of the service, but at no other in London.

'Maries Spittle, for their founders and benefactors,
' composed to Music by Thomas Brewer.'

This book, as it contains not the music, but only the words of the services and anthems in use at the time of its publication, is so far at least valuable, as it serves to show what was the stock of music which the church set out upon at the restoration, as also who were the composers of greatest eminence in that and the preceding time. The names that occur in this collection are, William Bird, Thomas Tallis, Thomas Weelks, Richard Farrant, Edmund Hooper, William Mundy, John Shepherd, Orlando Gibbons, Adrian Batten, Dr. Tye, Robert White, Dr. Giles, Robert Parsons, Thomas Morley, John Ward, John Hilton, Dr. Bull, Richard Price, Albertus Bryne, organist of St. Paul's cathedral; Michael East, Henry Lawes, Henry Smith, Mr. Cob, Henry Molle, Mr. Johnson, Thomas Tomkyns, Christ. Gibbons, Lawrence Fisher, Mr. Stonard, Henry Loosemore, Mr. Jeffries, Randolph Jewett, Mr. Bennett, Mr. Wilkinson, Mr. Gibbs, John Amner, John Holmes, Mr. Coste, Mr. Cranford, Dr. Wilson, Richard Gibbs, organist of Christ Church in Norwich; Mr. Wigthorpe, Leonard Woodson, Richard Hutchinson, Mr. Rogers, Martin Peerson, Mr. Mudde, John Heath, Dr. Child, Edward Smith, Peter Stringer, organist of Chester cathedral; Richard Hinde, Richard Portman, George Mason, John Hingestone, Richard Carre, Giles Tomkins, William Lawes, Edward Low, Pelham Humfrey, John Blow, and Robert Smith, the three latter children of his majesty's chapel; Henry Cook, Esq., master of the children, and one of the gentlemen of his majesty's chapel royal; Matthew Lock, Esq. Sir William Leighton, Robert Jones, Alphonso Ferabosco.

The number of workmen in England being found too few to answer the demand for organs, it was thought expedient to make offers of encouragement for foreigners to come and settle here; these brought over from Germany Mr. Bernard Schmidt and Harris; the former of these, for his excellence in his art, and the following particulars respecting him, deserves to live in the remembrance of all such as are friends to it.

Bernard Schmidt, (*a Portrait*), or, as we pronounce the name, Smith, was a native of German, but of what city or province in particular is not known. Upon the invitations of foreign workmen to settle here, he came into England, and brought with him two nephews, the one named Gerard, the other Bernard; and, to distinguish him from these, the elder had the appellation of Father Smith. Immediately upon their arrival Smith was employed to build an organ for the royal chapel at Whitehall, but, as it was built in great haste, it did not answer the expectations of those who were judges of his abilities. He had been but a few months here before Harris arrived from France, bringing with him a son named Renatus, who had been brought up in the business of organ-making under him; they met with little encouragement, for Dallans and Smith had all the business of the kingdom; but

upon the decease of Dallans in 1672,* a competition arose between these two foreigners, which was attended with some remarkable circumstances. The elder Harris was in no degree a match for Smith, but his son Renatus was a young man of ingenuity and spirit, and succeeded so well in his endeavours to rival Smith, that at length he got the better of him.

The contest between Smith and the younger Harris was carried on with great spirit; each had his friends and supporters, and the point of preference between them was hardly determined by that exquisite piece of workmanship of Smith, the organ now standing in the Temple church; of the building thereof the following is the history, as related by a person who was living at the time, and intimately acquainted with both Smith and Harris.

'Upon the decease of Mr. Dallans and the elder
' Harris, Mr. Renatus Harris and Father Smith
' became great rivals in their employment, and
' several tryals of skill there were betwixt them on
' several occasions; but the famous contest between
' these two artists was at the Temple church, where
' a new organ was going to be erected towards the
' latter end of K. Charles the second's time: both
' made friends for that employment; but as the
' society could not agree about who should be the
' man, the Master of the Temple and the Benchers
' proposed they both should set up an organ on each
' side of the church, which in about half a year or
' three quarters of a year was done accordingly;
' Dr. Blow and Mr. Purcell, who was then in his
' prime, shewed and played Father Smith's organ on
' appointed days to a numerous audience; and, till
' the other was heard, every body believed that
' Father Smith certainly would carry it.

'Mr. Harris brought Mr. Lully,† organist to
' Queen Catherine, a very eminent master, to touch
' his organ, which brought Mr. Harris's organ into
' that vogue; they thus continued vying with one
' another near a twelvemonth.

'Then Mr. Harris challenged Father Smith to
' make additional stops against a set time; these
' were the Vox-humane, the Cremona or Violin
' stop, the double Courtel or bass Flute, with some
' others I may have forgot.

'These stops, as being newly invented, gave great
' delight and satisfaction to the numerous audience;
' and were so well imitated on both sides, that it
' was hard to judge the advantage to either. At last
' it was left to my Lord Chief Justice Jeffries, who
' was of that house, and he put an end to the con-
' troversy by pitching upon Father Smith's organ;
' so Mr. Harris's organ was taken away without loss
' of reputation,‡ and Mr. Smith's remains to this

---

* An inscription on a stone in the old church of Greenwich ascertained nearly the time of his death; Strype gives it in these words: ' Ralph ' Dallans, Organ-maker, deceased while he was making this organ; ' begun by him Feb. 1672. James White his partner finished it, and ' erected this stone 1673.' Circuit Walk. Greenwich. The organ at New College, Oxford, as also that in the music-school there, were made by Dallans.

† Qy. *Draghi, whose christian name Baptist, might mislead Dr. Tudway, the author of this account,*

‡ Harris's organ was afterwards purchased for the cathedral of Christ Church at Dublin, and set up there: but about twenty years ago Mr.

'day.* * * * * Now began the setting up of organs 'in the chiefest parishes of the city of London, where 'for the most part Mr. Harris had the advantage of 'Father Smith, making I believe two to his one; 'among them some are reckoned very eminent, viz. 'the organ at Saint Bride's, Saint Lawrence near 'Guildhall, Saint Mary Ax, &c. *

Notwithstanding the success of Harris, Smith was considered as an able and ingenious workman; and, in consequence of this character, he was employed to build an organ for the cathedral of St. Paul;† *in which undertaking he narrowly escaped being a great sufferer, for on the 27th day of February, 1699, a fire broke out in a little room, at the west end of the North aisle of the church, enclosed for the organ builder's men, which communicating itself towards the organ, had probably consumed the same and endangered at least one side of the choir; but it was timely extinguished, though not without damage to two of the pillars and some of the fine carving by Gibbons. Vide New View of London, 457. The vulgar report was, that the Plumbers or some others employed in soldering or repairing the metal pipes, had been negligent of their fire; but the true cause of the accident was never discovered.* The organs made by Smith, though in respect of the workmanship they are far short of those of Harris, and even of Dallans, are justly admired, and for the fineness of their tone have never yet been equalled.

The name of Smith occurs in the lists of the chapel establishment from 1703 to 1709, inclusive, as organ-maker to the chapel, and also to queen Anne. He had a daughter, married to Christopher Schrider, a workman of his, who about the year 1710 succeeded him in his places.‡

The organ of St. Paul's, erected soon after the

year 1700, had established the character of Smith as an artist; whether Harris had been his competitor for building an instrument for that church, as he had been before at the Temple, does not now appear; but in the Spectator, No. 552, for December 3, 1712, is a recommendation of a proposal of Mr. Renatus Harris, organ-builder, in these words: 'The am-'bition of this artificer is to errect an organ in St. 'Paul's cathedral, over the west door, at the entrance 'into the body of the church, which in art and 'magnificence shall transcend any work of that kind 'ever before invented. The proposal in perspicuous 'language sets forth the honour and advantage such 'a performance wou'd be to the British name, as 'well that it would apply the power of sounds in 'a manner more amazingly forcible than perhaps 'has yet been known, and I am sure to an end 'much more worthy. Had the vast sums which 'have been laid out upon operas without skill or 'conduct, and to no other purpose but to suspend or 'vitiate our understandings, been disposed this way, 'we should now perhaps have an engine so formed, 'as to strike the minds of half a people at once in 'a place of worship with a forgetfulness of present 'care and calamity, and a hope of endless rapture, 'joy, and Hallelujah hereafter.'

In the latter part of his life Renatus Harris retired to Bristol, and, following his business there, made sundry organs for the churches in that city, and in the adjacent parishes, as also for churches in the neighbouring counties. He had a son named John, bred up under him, who followed the business of organ-making, and made a great number of very fine instruments.§ In the Mercurius Musicus for September and October, 1700, is a song inscribed 'Set by Mr. René Harris.'

CHAP. CXLVI.

IMMEDIATELY upon the restoration the utmost endeavours were exerted for the establishment of a

---

Byfield was sent for from England to repair it, which he objected to, and prevailed on the chapter to have a new one made by himself, he allowing for the old one in exchange. When he had got it he would have treated with the parishioners of Lynn in Norfolk for the sale of it; but they disdaining the offer of a second-hand instrument, refused to purchase it, and employed Snetzler to build them a new one, for which they paid him 700l. Byfied dying, his widow sold Harris's organ to the parish of Wolverhampton for 500l. and there it remains at this day. One of two eminent masters now living, who were requested by the churchwardens of Wolverhampton to give their opinions of this instrument, declares it to be the best modern organ he ever touched.

Mr. Francis Piggot was the first organist of the Temple church. This person had been an organist extraordinary of the chapel royal, but, upon the decase of Dr. Child, was appointed to succeed him as organist in ordinary, and was sworn in accordingly, 10 Apr. 1697. He died in 1704, and was succeeded at the Temple by his son, who died about the year 1736. As the church is common to both the societies of the Inner and Middle Temple, there have for many years past been two organists of it.

* Dr. Tudway's letter to his son above cited.

† He also made the organ for the theatre, and Christ Church. and for the church of St. Mary at Oxford; and at London he made that of St. Mary at Hill, St. Clement Danes, and of St. Margaret's Westminster. That at the theatre was taken down, and removed to the church of St. Peter in the East at Oxford, and a new one, made by Byfield and Green, erected in its stead.

‡ On this person there is the following humorous Epitaph in print:—

> Here rests the musical Kit Schrider,
> Who organs built when he did bide here;
> With nicest ear he tuned 'em up;
> But Death has put the cruel stop:
> Tho' breath to others he convey'd,
> Breathless, alas! himself is laid,
> May he who us such keys has given,
> Meet with St. Peter's Keys of Heaven!
> His Cornet, twelfth, and Diapason
> Could not with air supply, he weasoned;
> Bass, Tenor, Treble, Unison,
> The loss of tuneful Kit bemoan.
>
> Webb's Collection of Epitaphs, vol. II. page 76.

§ The subsequent history of organ-makers and of organ-making in this country lies in so short a compass, that it may briefly be continued down from the time when Dr. Tudway's account ends, to nearly the present.

Smith's nephews, Gerard and Bernard, worked chiefly in the country, as did also one Swarbrick, bred up under the elder Harris, and one Turner of Cambridge; their employment was more in the repairing of old than the building of new organs. About the year 1700, one Jordan, a distiller, who had never been instructed in the business, but had a mechanical turn, and was an ingenious man, betook himself to the making of organs, and succeeded beyond expectation. He had a son named Abraham, whom he instructed in the same business; he made the organ for the chapel of the Duke of Chandois at Canons near Edgware, and many organs for parish churches. Byfield and Bridge were two excellent workmen; the former made the organ for Greenwich hospital, and the latter that noble instrument in the church of Spitalfields, for which he had only 600l. These are all now dead. In the latter part of their lives, to prevent their underworking each other, there was a coalition between them; so that whoever was the nominal artificer of any instrument, the profits accruing from the making of it were divided among them all.

Contemporary with these men was one Morse of Barnet, an apothecary by profession, who would needs be a maker of organs. He made an organ for the church of St. Matthew Friday-street, and another for that of St. James Clerkenwell; they were both wretched instruments, and were taken down in a very few years after they were set up. One Griffin a barber in Fenchurch-street, also pretended to make organs: he dealt with a few parishes in London in a very singular way: in consideration of an annuity granted to him for his life, he built for the contracting parish an organ, and engaged to pay a person for playing it as long as the annuity should be payable: encouraged by his success in three or four instances of the kind, this man stood for Gresham professor of music against a person well skilled in the science, and, being a common-council man, and the electors also common-council men of London, he was chosen.

BERNARD SMITH

ORGAN — MAKER.

From a Picture in the Music-School, Oxford.

choir in the royal chapel : three organists were appointed, namely, Dr. Child, Dr. Christopher Gibbons, and Mr. Edward Low. These had also other places ; for Child was organist of Windsor, Gibbons of Westminster Abbey, and Mr. Low of Christ church, Oxford ; and, as they attended by monthly rotation, their foreign places were rendered tenable with those at the chapel. Henry Cook was made master of the children : this person had been bred up in the king's chapel, but quitted it at the commencement of the rebellion, and went into the king's army. In the year 1642 he obtained a captain's commission, and ever after was called Captain Cook. Not his loyalty alone, but that and his skill in music recommended him to the favour of Charles II. A hymn of his composing in four parts was performed instead of the litany, in the chapel of St. George at Windsor, by order of the sovereign and knights of the garter, on the seventeenth day of April, 1661.

The establishment of the chapel of king Charles II. appears by the following entry in the Chequebook :—

'The names of the Subdean, Gentlemen, and others of his 'Majesty's Chapel Royal, at the time of the Coronation of 'King Charles the Second.

April 23d, being St. George's Day, 1661.

Dr. Walter Jones, Subdean.

Roger Nightingale
Ralph Amner
Philip Tinker
John Sayer
Durant Hunt
George Low
Henry Smith
William Tucker   } Ministers.

Edward Lowe
William Child   } Organists.
Christ. Gibbons

Henry Cook, Master of the Children.

Henry Lawes, Clerk of the Cheque.

Thomas Piers
Thomas Hazzard   } Gents.
John Harding

William Howes
Thomas Blagrave
Gregory Thorndell
Edward Bradock
Henry Purcell
James Cobb
Nathaniel Watkins
John Cave
Alphonso Marsh
Raphael Courteville
Edward Coleman
Thomas Purcell
Henry Frost
John Goodgroom
George Betenham
Matthew Pennell   } Gents.

Thomas Haynes, Serjeant of the Vestry.
William Williams, Yeoman.
George Whitaker, Yeoman.
Augustine Cleveland, Groom.

'At which time every gentleman of the chapel in orders 'had allowed to him for a gown five yards of fine scarlet; and 'the rest of the gentlemen, being laymen, had allowed unto 'each of them foure yards of the like scarlet.'

The stock of music which they set out upon consisted chiefly of the anthems and services contained in Barnard's collection, and such others in manuscript as could be recovered and made perfect : these lasted about three or four years ; but the king perceiving a genius in many of the young people of the chapel, encouraged them to compose themselves ; and many of this first set, even while they were children of the chapel, composed anthems and services which would do honour to a mature age. These were sung to violins, cornets, and sacbuts, the performers on which were placed in the organ-loft ; and, by the king's special order, had Symphonies and Ritornellos adapted to those instruments.

The salaries of the gentlemen of the chapel had

been augmented both by James I. and Charles I., and in the year 1663 Charles II., by a privy-seal, farther augmented them to seventy pounds a year, and granted to Mr. Cook and his successors in office thirty pounds a year, for the diet, lodging, washing, and teaching each of the children of the chapel royal. A copy of this grant is entered in the cheque-book ; in the margin thereof is a memorandum purporting that it was obtained at the solicitation of Mr. Cook.*

The encouragement given to church music by king Charles II. had an effect upon all the choirs in the kingdom. In cathedrals that were amply endowed, as St. Paul's for instance, in which a maintenance is assigned for minor canons and lay singers, the performance was little inferior to that of the royal chapel :† in other cathedrals, where the revenues were so small as to reduce the members of the church to the necessity of taking mechanics and illiterate persons to assist in the choral service, it was proportionably inferior. But the most obvious effect of it was a variation in the church style. It

* Charles the Second had some knowledge of music ; he understood the notes, and sang, to use the expression of one who had often sung with him, a plump bass ; but it no where appears that he considered music in any other view than as an incentive to mirth. In a letter of his to Henry Bennet, afterwards earl of Arlington, dated from Bruges, August 18, 1655, he says, 'Pray get me pricked down as many new 'Corrants and Sarrabands and other little dances as you can, and bring 'them with you, for I have got a small fidler that does not play ill on 'the fiddle.' See the account of the preservation of King Charles II. after the battle of Worcester, page 150.

And in another letter to the same person, dated Sept. 1, 1656, he says 'You will find by my last, that though I am furnished with one small 'fidler, yet I would have another to keep him company ; and if you can 'get either he you mention, or another that plays well, I would have you 'do it.' Ibid. page 168.

His taste for music seems to have been such as disposed him to prefer a solo song to a composition in parts ; though it must be confessed that the pleasure he took in hearing Mr. Gostling sing, is a proof that he knew how to estimate a fine voice. This gentleman came from Canterbury, and in 1678 was sworn a gentleman extraordinary, and in a few days afterwards, a vacancy then happening by the death of Mr. William Tucker above mentioned, a gentleman in ordinary of the royal chapel. He was afterwards subdean of St. Paul's, and his memory yet lives in that cathedral. Purcell made sundry compositions purposely for him, and, among others, one, of which the following is the history :—

The king had given orders for building a yacht, which, as soon as it was finished, he named the Fubbs, in honour of the Duchess of Portsmouth, who we may suppose was in her person rather full and plump. The sculptors and painters apply this epithet to children, and say for instance of the boys of Fiammengo, that they are fubby. Soon after the vessel was launched the king made a party to sail in this yacht down the river, and round the Kentish coast ; and, to keep up the mirth and good humor of the company, Mr. Gostling was requested to be of the number. They had got as low as the North Foreland, when a violent storm arose, in which the king and the duke of York were necessitated, in order to preserve the vessel, to hand the sails, and work like common seamen ; by good providence however they escaped to land : but the distress they were in made an impression on the mind of Mr. Gostling, which was never effaced. Struck with a just sense of the deliverance, and the horror of the scene which he had but lately viewed, upon his return to London he selected from the psalms those passages which declare the wonders and terrors of the deep, and gave them to Purcell to compose as an anthem, which he did, adapting it so peculiarly to the compass of Mr. Gostling's voice, which was a deep bass, that hardly any person but himself was then, or has since been able to sing it ; but the king did not live to hear it : this anthem, though never printed, is well known. It is taken from the 107th psalm ; the first two verses of the anthem are the 23rd and 24th of the psalm. 'They that go down to the sea in ships, 'and occupy business in great waters. These men see the works of the 'Lord, and his wonders in the deep.'

King Charles II. could sing the tenor part of an easy song ; he would oftentimes sing with Mr. Gostling ; the duke of York accompanying them on the guitar.

† About this time it was very common for persons of rank to resort in the afternoon to St. Paul's to hear the service, and particularly the anthem ; and to attend a lady thither was esteemed as much an act of politeness, as it would be now to lead her into the opera. In the life of Mary Moders, the famous pretended German princess, who was executed in the year 1673, for a capital felony in stealing plate, and who had been married to many husbands, it is related that whilst Mr. Carleton, one of them, was courting her, and in the infancy of their acquaintance, he invited her to honour him with her company to St. Paul's to hear the organ, and certain excellent hymns and anthems performed by rare voices.

has already been remarked, that the services and anthems contained in Barnard's collections were the stock which the church set out upon at the restoration; these were grown familiar after a few years' practice; the king was in the flower of his age, and the natural gaiety of his disposition rendered him averse to the style of our best church music; in short, he had not solidity of mind, nor skill sufficient to contemplate the majesty and dignity, nor taste enough to relish that most exquisite harmony, which distinguish the compositions of Tye, of Tallis, Bird, Farrant, Gibbons, and many others. This was soon discovered by the young people of the chapel, and gave such a direction to their studies, as terminated in the commencement of what may very truly and emphatically be called a new style of church music.*

Amongst those that affected to compose in the light style of church music, Mr. Pelham Humphrey,† Mr. Blow, and Mr. Michael Wise were the chief; these were children of the chapel, educated under Captain Cook; they were all three young men of genius, and were not more distinguished for the novelty and originality of their style, than for their skill in the principles of harmony.

The restoration of monarchy, and the re-establishment of ecclesiastical discipline, induced many devout persons to attempt a revival also of that knowledge which is necessary to the decent and orderly performance of parochial music or psalmody; and to that end John Playford published a new edition of his 'Introduction to the Skill of Musick,' originally printed during the usurpation, viz., in 1655, which was followed by a collection entitled 'Psalms and 'Hymns in solemn musick, in foure parts, on the 'common tunes to the psalms in metre used in parish 'churches. Also six hymns for one voice to the 'organ,' by the same John Playford; printed by W. Godbid, and dedicated to Sancroft, dean of St. Paul's. Fol. 1671.

In the preface to this work, which carries with it an air of seriousness that distinguishes the writings of this honest old man, the testimony of some of the fathers and the example of the primitive church are adduced in favour of the practice of psalm-singing. The author cites a passage from Comenius, which shows that in his time the Bohemians, besides the Psalms of David, had no fewer than seven hundred hymns in use. He then gives a short history of the custom of singing psalms; and, speaking of our old version, and the reception it met with, says it was made by men whose piety exceeded their poetry, but that, such as it was, it was ranked with the best English poesy at that time; that the Psalms, translated into English metre, and having apt tunes set to them, were at first used and sung only for devotion in private families, but that soon after by permission

they were brought into churches; that for many years this part of divine service was skilfully and devoutly performed with delight and comfort by many honest and religious people, and is still continued in our churches, but not with that reverence and estimation as formerly, some not affecting the translation, others not liking the music, both which he confesses need reforming; that those many tunes formerly used to these psalms, for excellency of form, solemn air, and suitableness to the matter of the Psalms, are not inferior to any tunes used in foreign churches, but that the best and almost all the choice tunes are lost and out of use in our churches; the reason whereof he gives in these words:—'In and about this great 'city, in above one hundred parishes, there is but 'few parish-clerks to be found that have either 'ear or understanding to set one of these tunes 'musically as it ought to be; it having been a custom 'during the late wars, and since, to chuse men into 'such places more for their poverty than skill and 'ability, whereby this part of God's service hath 'been so ridiculously performed in most places, that 'it is now brought into scorn and derision by many 'people.'

For these reasons he professes, through the assistance of Almighty God, to have undertaken the publication of this work, and therein to have selected all the best and choicest tunes, to the number of forty-seven, to which, with a bass he has composed two contratenors, making four parts, all which are fitted to men's voices.

Playford appears to have been no admirer of the old version of the Psalms, and therefore he has selected from a translation by Dr. Henry King, bishop of Chichester, and from another by one Mr. Miles Smith, and also from the poems of Mr. George Herbert, such psalms and hymns, as for elegance of style, smoothness of language, and suitableness to the tunes, he thinks excel those contained in the former.

There are few positions in this preface of Playford but what will be readily assented to, except that which relates to the loss of the best and almost all the choice tunes anciently used in our churches; for, though in a great measure out of use, they exist even at this day in the collections of Este, Ravenscroft, Allison, and other authors, as has been shewn.

The same Playford soon after published in octavo, 'The whole Book of Psalms: with the usual Hymns 'and Spiritual Songs. Together with the ancient 'and proper Tunes sung in Churches, with some 'of later use. Composed in three parts, Cantus, 'Medius, and Bassus, in a more plain and useful 'method than hath been formerly published.' In this collection the author, varying from the rule observed by him in the former, has given the church-tune to the cantus part, and has contrived the medius so as not to rise above the cantus, to the end that the air of the church-tune should predominate; farther he has placed the two upper parts in the G SOL RE UT cliff, an innovation which it is easier to make than defend.

We meet here with a great variety of tunes now

* The particular instances of innovation were solo anthems and movements in courant time, which is a dancing measure, and which the king had acquired a great fondness for while he was in France.

† Of Humphrey it is said in particular that his proficiency in music, and the presages of his becoming a great man in his profession, gave great uneasiness to his master, Captain Cook. In the Ashmolean Manuscript, mentioned in page 455, it is said by the author, Anthony Wood, of Cook that he was the best musician of his time, till Pell. Humphries came up, after which says the MS. he died in discontent.

in common use, which are not contained in Ravenscroft, namely, St. James's, London New, St. Mary's, and others called Proper Tunes, which, for ought that appears to the contrary, we may conclude were composed by Playford himself.

From the reasons deducible from the above account of his works, Playford is looked upon as the father of modern psalmody; but, notwithstanding his labours, it does not appear that the practice has much improved since his time; one cause whereof may possibly be the use of the organ in parish churches, which within this last century has increased to so great a degree, that in most of the cities and great towns in the kingdom it is a sign of great poverty in a parish for a church to be without one. The consequence whereof is, that the conduct of this part of the service devolves to the organist: he plays the thorough-bass, or, in other words, the whole harmony of the tune, while the clerk and the congregation sing the tenor, which they remember and sing by ear only, in which kind of performance not the least skill in music is necessary.*

Besides what are to be found in the collections before enumerated, there are extant many other musical compositions to the words of David's Psalms, either closely or paraphrastically rendered, which lie dispersed in the works of the musicians who flourished about the latter end of the sixteenth, and the beginning of the last century: to mention a few instances, a collection entitled Certaine Pſalmes ſelect out of the Pſalmes of David, and drawen into Englyſhe Metre, with notes to everie Pſalme in foure partes to ſynge, was published by Francis Seager, 12mo. 1553. John Keeper, of Hart Hall, Oxon. published in 1574, 'Select Psalms of David set to musicke of foure 'parts;' and in 1585 one John Cosin published the Psalms in musicke of five and six parts.

In 1594 Dr. John Mundy, organist of the chapel of Windsor,† published 'Songs and Psalmes com- 'posed into 3 and 4 parts for the use and delight of 'all such who either love or learne musicke.' As to the songs, they are to every intent madrigals; and for the psalms, some are prose, as they stand in the old Bible translation, the rest are of the version of Sternhold and Hopkins, to the amount of about twenty in the whole.

Some years after, a person, of whom nothing more than the initials of his name, R. H. is known, published a translation of an Italian paraphrase of the seven penitential psalms, written by Francesco Bembo, with the music of Giovanni Croce, Maestro di Cappella of the church of St. Mark at Venice, a celebrated composer of that time,‡ and whom

Morley mentions as such in his Introduction. The title of the book is 'Musica Sacra to six voyces, 'composed in the Italian tongue by Giovanni Croce, 'new Englished,' printed by Este in 1608. The motives of the publication of this book, which are said to be the excellence of the songs, and the promotion of piety, are given at large in the dedication of the work 'to the vertuous lovers of musicke.'

These compositions are in a style greatly superior to those contained in the former collections, which, as they were intended solely for popular use, were, as has been mentioned, of that species of musical composition distinguished by the name of Counterpoint: On the contrary, these of Mundy and Cosin, and more eminently those of Byrd are descant, and that of a very artificial contexture.

The paraphrase of the Psalms by George Sandys was, and that very deservedly, in great estimation about the beginning of the last century; and this induced the two brothers, Henry and William Lawes, the great musicians of that day, to set many of them to music. Sandys's Psalms are also set to music for two voices, with a thorough-bass, by Mr. Walter Porter.

A paraphrase of some select psalms by Sir John Denham, Mr. Addison, and others, was set to music for a single voice with instrumental parts, by Mr. Andrew Roner, a teacher of music in London, and published about the year 1730.

CHAP. CXLVII.

THE practice of music had suffered no less than the profession of it during the usurpation. King Charles I. soon after his accession, had shewn a disposition to encourage the liberal arts, and particularly music, as appears by his charter granted to Nicholas Laniere and others, herein before inserted.§ He had also in the eleventh year of his reign granted a charter to divers persons, the most eminent musicians, incorporating them by the style of Marshall, Wardens, and Cominalty of the Arte and Science of Musick in Westminster, in the County of Middlesex, and invested them with sundry extraordinary powers and privileges, which charter was by the same king confirmed in the fourteenth year of his reign.

This charter had lain dormant from the time of granting it to the restoration, that is to say, above twenty-five years, but immediately after that event, the persons named in it, or such of them as were then living, determined to rescue music from the disgrace into which it had fallen, and exert their authority for the improvement of the science and the interest of its professors.

The history of this company lies in a short compass; the minutes of their transactions are extant among the Harleian manuscripts, in a book formerly Mr. Wanley's, numbered in the catalogue 1911. As there is no entry in this book of the charter, recourse has been had to the patent-roll, in the chapel of the Rolls: the purport whereof is as follows:—

---

* In country parishes, where the people have not the aid of an instrument to guide them, such young men and women as nature has endowed with an ear and a tolerable voice, are induced to learn to sing by book as they call it; and in this they are generally assisted by some poor ignorant man, whom the poring over Ravenscroft and Playford has made to believe that he is as able a proficient in psalmody as either of those authors. Such men as these assume the title of singing-masters and lovers of divine music, and are the authors of those collections which are extant in the world, and are distinguished by the titles of 'David's 'Harp new strung and tuned,' 'The Harmony of Sion,' 'The Psalm- 'singer's Companion,' and others of the like kind, to an incredible number.

† Mentioned page 571 of this work.

‡ See an account of him in page 442.

§ Page 574 of this work.

The charter bears date 15 Jul. 11 Car. and recites that king Edw. 'IV. by his letters patent under the 'greate seale of his realme of England, bearing date 'the foure and twentieth day of Aprill, in the nynth 'yeare of his raigne, did for him and his heires give 'and graunt licence unto Walter Haliday* Marshall

* Sic Orig. The Christian name of Marshall is Robert, as appears by the charter itself, which as a singular curiosity is here inserted from Rymer's Fœdera, tom. XI.

'*Pro Fraternitate Ministrallorum Regis.*
'Rex Omnibus, ad quos &c. Salutem.
'Sciatis quòd, ex Querelosa Insinuatione, Dilectorum Nobis, *Walteri*
'*Haliday* Marescalli, *Johannis Cliff, Roberti Marshall, Thomæ Grene,*
'*Thomæ Calthorn, Willielmi Cliff, Willielmi Christean,* Et *Willielmi*
'*Eyneysham,* Ministrallorum nostrorum accepimus qualiter nonnulli,
'rudes Agricolæ et Artifices diversarum Misterarum Regni nostri Angliæ,
'finxerunt se fore Ministrallos,
'Quorum aliqui Liberatam nostram, eis minimè datam, portarent,
'Seipsos etiam fingentes esse Ministrallos nostros proprios,
'Cujus quidem Liberatæ ac dictæ Artis sive Occupationis Ministral-
'lorum colore, in diversis Partibus Regni Nostri prædicti, grandes
'Pecuniarum Exactiones de Ligeis nostris deceptivè colligunt et re-
'cipiunt,
'Et licet Ipsi in Arte sive Occupatione illa minimè Intelligentes sive
'Experti existant, et diversis Artibus et Operationibus Diebus Ferialibus
'sive Profestis utuntur, et Victum suum inde sufficienter Percipiant, de
'Loco tamen ad Locum in Diebus Festivalibus discurrunt, et Proficua
'illa totaliter percipiunt, e quibus Ministralli nostri prædicti, et cæteri
'Ministralli nostri pro tempore existentes, in Arte sive Occupatione
'prædicta sufficienter Eruditi et Instructi, nullisque aliis Laboribus,
'Occupationibus, sive Misteriis utentes, vivere deberent,
'Nedùm in Artis sive Occupationis illius nimiam Verecundiam, ac
'ipsorum Ministrallorum nostrorum, eadem Arte sive Occupatione ut
'prædictum est utentium, Deteriorationem multiplicem et manifestam,
'verùm etiam in Populi nostri in hujusmodi Agricultura sua et aliter
'Dampnum ut accepimus non modicum et Gravamen,
'Unde iidem Ministralli nostri Nobis humilimè supplicârunt ut **Nos**
'eis de Remedio congruo in hac parte ex Gratia nostra speciali providere
'dignaremur,
'Nos, Præmissa considerantes ac Supplicationi suæ rationabili in ea
'parte favorabiliter inclinati, de Gratia nostra prædicta, ac ex certa
'Scientia et mero Motu nostris, *Concessimus* et *Licentiam dedimus,* ac
'per Præsentes *Concedimus* et *Licentiam damus,* pro Nobis, et Hæredibus
'nostris, quantum in Nobis est, præfatis, *Waltero Haliday* Marescallo, *Jo-*
'*hanni Cliff Roberto Marshalle, Thomæ Grene, Thomæ Calthorn, Willielmo*
'*Christean,* Et *Willielmo Eneysham,* Ministrallis nostris quòd Ipsi, ad
'Laudem et Honorem Dei, et ut specialiùs exorare teneantur pro salubri
'Statu nostro et Præcarissimæ Consortis nostræ *Elizabethæ Reginæ*
'Angliæ dùm agimus in humanis, et pro Animabus nostris cùm ab hac
'luce migraverimus, necnon pro Anima Carissimi Domini et Patris
'nostri *Richardi* nuper *Ducis Eborum,* et Animabus inclitorum Pro-
'genitorum nostrorum, et omnium Fidelium Defunctorum, tàm in
'Capella beatæ Mariæ Virginis infra Ecclesiam Cathedralem Sancti
'Pauli Londoniæ, quàm in Libera Capella nostra Regia Sancti Anthonii
'in eadem Civitate nostra Londoniæ, quandam FRATERNITATEM sive
'GILDAM perpetuam (quam, ut accepimus, Fratres et Sorores Fraterni-
'tatis Ministrallorum Regni nostri prædicti, retroactis temporibus,
'Inierunt, Erexerunt, et Ordinârunt) Stabilire, Continuare, et Augmen-
'tare, ac quascúmque Personas, tàm Homines, quàm Mulieres, eis
'grato animo Adhærentes, in FRATRES et SORORES FRATERNITATIS
'sive GILDÆ *prædictæ* Recipere, Admittere, et Acceptare possent et
'valeant,
'Et quòd Marescallus et Ministralli nostri prædicti per Se sint et esse
'debeant, Jure et Nomine UNUM CORPUS et UNA COMMUNITAS PER-
'PETUA, ac Habiles et Capaces in Lege, Habeantque Successionem
'perpetuam,
'*Et quod* tàm Ministralli prædicti, qui nunc sunt, quàm cæteri
'Ministralli nostri et Hæredum nostrorum qui exnunc erunt imper-
'petuum, ad eorum libitum Nominare possint, Eligere, Ordinare, et
'successivè Constituere de Seipsis UNUM MARESCALLUM habilem et
'idoneum, pro Termino Vitæ suæ in Officio illo permansurum, ac etiam
'quolibet Anno DUOS CUSTODES *ad Fraternitatem sive Gildam prædictam*
'*Regendum et Gubernandum.*
'*Et, ulterius, Volumus* et per Præsentes *Concedimus,* pro Supportatione
'et Augmentatione *Fraternitatis sive Gildæ prædictæ,* quòd nullus
'Ministrallus Regni nostri prædicti, quamvis in hujusmodi Arte sive
'Occupatione sufficienter Eruditus existat, eadem Arte sive Occupatione
'infra Regnum nostrum prædictum de cætero, nisi de *Fraternitate sive*
'*Gilda prædicta* sit et ad eandem Admissus fuerit et cum cæteris Con-
'fratribus ejusdem contribuerit, aliquo modo utatur, nec eam palàm seu
'publicè excerceat (ita tamen quòd nullus prædictorum Ministrallorum,
'sic ut prædicitur admittendorum, solvat pro hujusmodi Ingressu sive
'Admissione ultra *Tres Solidos et Quatuor Denarios*) et, si secus fecerit,
'seu quoquo modo contravenerit, per præfatos Marescallum et Mini-
'strallos nostros et Hæredum nostrorum prædictorum, pro tempore
'existentes, juxta eorum Discretiones Amercietur,
'Et quòd prædicti *Marescallus et Ministralli* nostri, ac *Custodes* et
'*Successores* sui *Congregationes et Communicationes licitas* et honestas de
'Seipsis, ac *Statuta et Ordinationes licita* pro salubri Gubernatione et
'Commodo *Fraternitatis sive Gildæ prædictæ,* quotiens et quando opus
'fuerit, licitè et impunè Incipere, Facere, et Ordinare valeant,
'*Et, si* aliquis hujusmodi Ministrallorum nostrorum vel Hæredum
'nostrorum prædictorum Decesserit vel Obierit, seu ob Demerita vel
'Offensas sua, aut aliâ Causâ quacúmque, a Servitio nostro prædicto
'Exoneratus, Amotus, sive Depositus fuerit, adtunc *Marescallus et*

'and John Cliff, and others, then minstrells† of the
'said king, that they by themselves should be in
'deed and name one body and cominalty, perpetual
'and capable in the lawe, and should have perpetual
'succession; and that as well the minstrells of the

'*cæteri Ministralli nostri,* et Hæredum nostrorum pro tempore exis-
'tentes, alium Ministrallorum idoneum et in Arte sive Occupatione illa
'Expertum sufficienter et Eruditum, ubicùmque loco infra Regnum
'nostrum prædictum tàm infra Libertates quàm extra eum inveniri
'contigerit (Comitatu Cestriæ Excepto) Vice et Loco hujusmodi sic
'Descendentis Exonerati, Amoti, sive Depositi, ex parte nostra Eligere,
'Nominare, et in unum Ministrallorum nostrorum et Hæredum nos-
'trorum penes Nos Retinendum Habilitare, ac ad Vadia nostra, nostro
'Regio Assensu superinde habito, Admittere et Acceptare possint et
'valeant.
'*Et, insuper, Volumus* et per Præsentes *Concedimus* præfatis Mare-
'scallo et Ministrallis nostris, quòd Ipsi et Successores sui de cætero
'Potestatem habeant et Facultatem Inquirendi, omnibus viis modis et
'mediis rationabilibus et legitimis quibus meliùs sciverint, per totum
'Regnum nostrum prædictum, tàm infra Libertates quàm extra (dicto
'Comitatu Cestriæ Excepto) de omnibus et singulis hujusmodi Personis
'fingentibus se fore Ministrallos, et dictam Liberatam nostram surreptivè
'portantibus, ac Arte sive Occupatione illâ, ut prædictum est, indebité
'et minus justè utentibus, seu eandem exercentibus, aut *de Fraternitate*
'*sive Gilda prædicta* non existentibus, et de omnibus aliis Articulis et
'Circumstantiis Præmissa qualitercúmque concernentibus,
'Ac ad omnes et singulas hujusmodi Personas, prædictam Artem et
'Occupationem Ministrallorum Excercentes, de tempore in tempus,
'quotiens necesse fuerit, tàm infra Libertates quàm extra (dicto Comitatu
'Cestriæ ut præmittitur Excepto) Supervidendum, Scrutandum, Re-
'gendum, et Gubernandum, et earum quamlibet, ob Offensas et Defectus
'suos in Præmissis factos, justè et debitè Corrigendum et Puniendum,
'Ac quæcùmque Amerciamenta, Fines, Forisfacturas, et Deperdita
'(si quæ prætextu hujusmodi Inquisitionis Supervisûs seu Scrutinii,
'ratione Præmissorum, super quascúmque Personas, se ut præfertur
'Ministrallos fingentes, seu aliter Delinquentes, debitè et probabiliter
'invenerint Adjudicata, Assessa, sive Afferata) ad Usum et Proficuum
'*Fraternitatis prædictæ,* pro continua et perpetua Sustentatione certarum
'Candelarum cerearum, vulgariter nuncupatarum *Tapers,* ad Sumptus
'ejusdem Fraternitatis in Capellis prædictis ad præsens existentium de
'cætero existere contingentium, Levandum, Applicandum, et Dis-
'ponendum,
'*Habenda et Occupanda, Excercenda et Gaudenda,* omnia et singula
'prædicta Inquisitionem, Scrutinium, Supervisum, Regimen, Guber-
'nationem, Correctionem, Punitionem, ac cætera Præmissa modis et
'formis supradictis, præfatis *Waltero, Johanni, Roberto, Thomæ Grene,*
'*Thomæ Calthorn, Willielmo Cliff, Willielmo Cristean,* et *Willielmo*
'*Eynesham,* Ministrallis nostris, et Successoribus suis Ministrallis
'nostris et Hæredum nostrorum prædictorum imperpetuùm, sine
'Occasione, Impedimento, Impetitione, Molestatione, Perturbatione,
'seu Calumnia Nostri, vel Hæredum nostrorum, Justiciariorum, Es-
'cætorum, Vicecomitum, aut aliorum Ballivorum seu Ministrorum
'nostrorum, vel Hæredum nostrorum et aliorum quorumcúmque,
'Et hoc absque Fine vel Feodo Magno seu Parvo, in Hanaperio
'Cancellariæ nostræ seu alibi, ad usum nostrum seu Nomine nostro,
'pro Præmissis faciendis aut solvendis,
'*Eo* quòd expressa mentio de vero Valore seu Certitudine Præ-
'missorum, sive eorum alicujus, in Præsentibus minimè facta existit,
'aut aliquo Statuto, Actu, sive Ordinatione in contrarium factis, editis,
'seu provisis, non obstantibus.
'In cujus &c.
'Teste Rege apud *Westmonasterium* Vicesimo quarto die Aprilis.
'*Per Breve de Privato Sigillo et de Data, &c.*'
The above Walter Haliday, Robert Marshall, and John Cliff, together
with one William Wykes, had it seems been minstrels of the king's predecessor Hen. VI. and were impowered by him to impress minstrels
'in solatium regis,' as the writ expresses it. This singular precept
appears in Rymer's Fœdera, tom. XI. page 375, and is in this form:—

'*De Ministrallis propter Salarium Regis providendis.*
'Rex, dilectis sibi, *Waltero Halyday, Roberto Marshall, Willielmo*
'*Wykes,* et *Johanni Clyffe,* Salutem.
'Sciatis quòd Nos, considerantes qualiter quidem Ministralli nostri
'jam tardè Viam universæ Carnis sunt ingressi, aliisque, loco ipsorum,
'propter Salatium nostrum de necesse indigentes, Affignavimus vos,
'conjunctim et divisim, ad quosdam Pueros, Membris Naturalibus
'Elegantes, in Arte Ministrellatûs instructos, ubicùnque inveniri po-
'terint, tàm infra Libertates, quàm extra, Capiendum, et in Servitio
'nostro ad Vadia nostra Ponendum, &c.'
It is highly probable that the placards for impressing children for the
service of the choir, mentioned by Tusser, and under which he himself
was taken from his father's house, [See page 537,] were founded on the
authority of this precedent.

† *It appears by this charter, as also by the list of the household establishment
of Edw. IV. see page 271, that in the reign of that prince Circa 1461,
Minstrel was the common appellation of one that played on any musical
instrument; and we find that such persons continued to be so denominated
down to the time of the latest English translation of the Bible. In the 2nd
book of Kings, Chapter III. verse 15, it is related that the prophet
Elisha upon a certain occasion called for a minstrel to compose his mind
and fit it for divine inspiration. And 9 Matt. 22 we read that when
Jesus came into the ruler's house in order to raise his daughter then dead,
and about to be carried to her funeral, he saw the Minstrels. Men of this
profession have been for many years past, and now are called Musicians,
a term which, as Boetius has clearly shewn, belongs to the higher order of
speculatists in the science.*

' said king, which then were, as other minstrells of
' the said king, and his heires which should be
' afterwards, might at their pleasure name, chuse,
' ordeine, and successively constitute from amongst
' themselves, one Marshall, able and fitt to remaine
' in that office during his life, and alsoe twoe wardens
' every yeare, to governe the said fraternity and guild.'

It also recites that ' certeine persons, suggesting
' themselves to be freemen of a pretended society
' of minstrells in the cittie of London, in prejudice
' of the liberties and priviledges aforesaid in the said
' recited letters patents mencioned and intended to
' the minstrells and musicians of the said king and
' his heires, did by untrue suggestions procure of
' and from king James of ever blessed memory,
' letters patent under his greate seale of England,
' bearing date the eight day of July, in the second
' yeare of his raigne, to incorporate them by the
' name of master, wardens, and cominalty of the arte
' or science of the musicians of London. And,
' amongst divers other priviledges, to graunt unto
' them the survey, scrutiny, correction, and govern-
' ment of all and singular the musicians and minstrells
' within the said cittie of London, suburbs, liberties
' and precincts of the said cittie, or within three
' miles of the same cittie. By colour whereof they
' endeavoured to exclude the musicians and minstrells
' enterteyned into the king's service, and all others
' expert and learned in the said art and science of
' musick, from teaching and practising the same
' within the said cittie, and three miles thereof,
' that would not subject themselves unto theire said
' pretended fraternity, or purchase their appro-
' bation thereunto, although greate part of them
' were altogether unskilfull in the said art and science
' of musick.'

It farther recites that ' at the prosecution of
' Nicholas Lanier, Thomas Ford, Jerome Lanier,
' Clement Lanier, Andrewe Lanier, Thomas Day,
' John Cogshall, Anthony Roberts, Daniell Farrant,
' John Lanier, Alfonso Ferabosco, Henry Ferabosco,
' Edward Wormall, and John Drewe, musicians en-
' terteyned in the king's service, a Scire Facias had
' bin brought in the king's name against the said
' pretended master, wardens, and cominalty of the
' art or science of the musicians of London, in the
' high court of chauncery, for the cancelling and
' making voide of the said letters patent; and that
' judgement at theire said prosecution had been had
' and given by the said court accordingly, and the
' said letters patent vacated and cancelled thereupon.'

The king, therefore, ' for and in consideration of
' the good and faithfull service which his said mu-
' sicians had done and performed unto him, and in
' pursuance of the intent and meaninge of the said
' king Edward the Fourth, in his said recited letters
' patent mentioned, of his speciall grace, certeine
' knowledge, and meere motion, DOTH for him, his
' heires, and successors, will, ordeine, constitute,
' declare, and graunt that the said Nicholas Lanier,
' Thomas Ford, Jerome Lanier, Clement Lanier,
' Andrewe Lanier, Thomas Day, John Cogshall,
' Anthony Roberts, Daniel Farrant, John Lanier,

' Alfonso Ferabosco, Henry Ferabosco. Edward
' Wormall, John Drewe, John Stephens, Thomas
' Tompkins, Ezechiell Wade, Roger Nightingall,
' Walter Porter, John Frost senior, John Frost
' junior, Ralph Amner, Henry Lawes, John Tom-
' kins, William Lanier, Jeronimo Bassano, Robert
' Baker, Anthony Bassano, William Gregory, Robert
' Parker, John Mason, Christopher Bell, John
' Adson, Frauncis Farmelowe, Thomas Mell, Moun-
' sieur Gaultier,* Nicholas Du Vall, John Kelly,
' Giles Tomkins, Robert Taylor, William Lawes,
' John Wilson, Phillip Squire, Morrice Webster,
' Stephen Noe, John Woodington, Davis Mell,†
' Thomas Lupo, Daniell Johnson, and Theophilus
' Lupo, his said musicians, and all such persons as
' are, or shall be the musicians of him, his heires,
' and successors, shall from thenceforth for ever, by
' force and vertue of the said graunt, be a body cor-
' porate and politique, in deed, fact, and name, by
' the name of Marshall, Wardens, and Cominalty of
' the arte and science of musick, in Westminster in
' the county of Middlesex, and by the same name
' have perpetual succession, and be capable in the
' law to impleade and be impleaded : And that they
' have a common seale.'

The charter goes on to appoint Nicholas Lanier
the first marshal for life, Thomas Ford and Jerome
Lanier first wardens until Midsummer day next
ensuing the date of the patent, and Clement Lanier.
Andrew Lanier, Thomas Day, John Cogshall,
Anthony Roberts, Daniel Farant, John Lanier,
Alfonso Ferabosco, Henry Ferabosco, Edward
Wormall, and John Drewe to be the first assistants, and continue in the same office for their
natural lives, with power to elect a marshal, warden,
and assistants in future.

The other powers granted by this charter are,
that the corporation shall meet in or near the city of
Westminster from time to time. That they make
bye-laws and impose fines on such as transgress
them, which fines they shall have to their own use,
after which is a clause in these words :—

' And for the better government and ordering of
' all such person or persons as doe or shall at any
' time hereafter, professe and exercise the said art
' and science of musique within our said realme of
' England, our county palatine of Chester only ex-
' cepted,‡ Wee doe hereby, for us, our heires, and
' successors, further will, give, and graunt unto the
' said marshall, wardens, and cominalty of the said
' art and science of musique in Westmister, in the
' county of Middlesex, and theire successors, that the
' said marshall, wardens, and assistants, and theire
' successors, or the greater part of them, for the tyme
' being, for ever hereafter, shall have the survey,
' scrutinie, correction, and government of all and
' singuler the musicians within our said kingdome of

---

* JACQUES GOUTER. a Frenchman. and a celebrated lutenist. There
is extant a very fine etching of him, of which see an account in Granger's
Biogr. Hist. vol. I. page 538. The author of that work is mistaken in
saying that he is represented holding two lutes in his left hand, for the
instrument he holds is a theorbo, which has two necks, and is therefore
termed Cithara bijuga.

† The famous violinist mentioned page 681.

‡ For the reason of this exception see page 191, et seq.

'England, the said county palatine of Chester onely 'excepted. And wee doe for us, our heires, and suc-'cessors, give and graunt unto the said marshall, 'wardens, and cominalty of the art and science of 'musique, in Westminster in the county of Mid-'dlesex, and their successors, that it shall and may 'be lawfull to and for the said marshall, wardens, 'and cominalty, and every person and persons that 'shall be at any tyme hereafter admitted to be a 'member of theire said fraternity and corporation, or 'shall be, upon due examination and tryall had of 'theire sufficiency and skill in the said art or science, 'allowed thereunto by the said marshall, wardens, 'and assistants, or the greater part of them, to use, 'exercise, and practise the said arte and science of 'musique in and within the cittie of London, and 'suburbs and liberties thereof, or elsewhere soever 'within our said kingdome of England, our said 'county palatine of Chester onely excepted, any act, 'ordinance, or constitution of common council of the 'said citty of London, or any other matter or thing 'whatsoever to the contrary thereof in any wise not-'withstanding.'

In pursuance of the powers above granted, the corporation hired a room in the house of one Mr. Ganley, situated in Durham-yard, in the Strand, and within the city and liberty of Westminster. Their first meeting was on the twenty-second day of Oc-tober, 1661, Nicholas Laniere then being marshal, from which day they proceeded to make orders, of which the following are the most remarkable :—

'1662. Jan. 20. Ordered that Edward Sadler, for 'his insufficiency in the art of musique, be from 'henceforward silenced and disabled from the exer-'cise of any kinde in publique houses or meetings.'

Some orders signed 'Hen. Cooke, Dep. Marshall.'

'Feb. 3. Richard Graham, appointed their soli-'citor at law.'

19. It appears they licensed teachers of music.

'1663. Nov. 24. Symon Hopper resigns his 'office of assistant, John Banister elected in his 'room.

'Jan. 13. Ordered that Matthew Lock, Christopher 'Gibbons, Dr. Cha. Colman, and William Gregory, 'do come to the chamber at Durham-yard on Tuesday 'next, at two of the clock in the afternoon, and 'bring each of them ten pounds, or show cause to the 'contrary.

'March 1. Ordered that there be a petition pre-'sented to the king's majestie for the renewing of 'their former patent.

'1664. May 13. Ordered that Henry Cooke, 'George Hudson, John Hingston, and John Lilly 'do meete fower of the musique of the cittie of 'London, to treat upon such matters and things as 'concern the good of the said corporation.

'June 14. Proceedings at law ordered against all 'such persons that make any benefit or advantage of 'musique in England and Wales, and that do not 'obey the grant under the great seale to the cor-'poration.

'June 21. Ordered that John Hill, Francis 'Dudeny, John Dunstan, James Saunders, and

'others, now waites of the cittie of Westminster, do 'appear before this corporation at Mr. Ganley his 'house in Durham-yard, in the county of Middlesex, 'on Tuesday next at 10 of the clock in the morning, 'as they tender obedience to his majesties letters 'patent in that behalf graunted.

'July 2. Ordered that Richard Hudson, the clerk 'of the corporation, doe summon all the common 'minstrells from tyme to tyme to come before the 'corporation.

'July 9. Thomas Purcell chosen an assistant in 'the room of Dr. Charles Colman, deceased.

'Same day. Ordered that all his majesties mu-'sique do give their attendance at the chamber at 'Durham-yard for practise of musique, when the 'master of the musique shall appoint them, upon for-'feiture of 5l. each neglect.

'1670. Jan. 21. Pelham Humphrey chosen an 'assistant.

1670. *From Monday, August 22, to Thursday, August 25. Whereas His Sacred Majesty hath been pleased, after the example of his Royal An-cestors, to incorporate the Musitians of England for its encouragement of that excellent science, and the said corporation to have power over all that pro-fess the same, and to allow and make free all such as they shall think fit: This is to give notice to all persons concerned in Musique that the Corporation sits the Saturday in every week at their Hall in Durham-yard in the Strand, in pursuance of the trust and authority to them committed by His Most Gracious Majesty, and that they have granted several deputations into several counties to execute the same.—London Gazette, No. 498, page 173.*

'1672. June. 24. Henry Cooke, Esq. being mar-'shall of the corporation of musique in Westminster, 'in the county of Middlesex, resigns by reason of 'sicknesse, and Thomas Purcell appointed in his 'room. Signed, John Hingeston, deputy marshal, 'and by the wardens and assistants.

'July 18. John Blow chosen assistant.

'1675. Dec. 17. Mr. Nicholas Staggins chosen an assistant, and admitted deputy marshal.'

The meetings of the corporation after this time appear by the entries in their minute-book to have been very few; the last was at the Three Tuns tavern, on the second day of July, 1679, when John Moss was chosen an assistant in the room of John Lilly. It seems that they were incapable, otherwise than by their own particular studies, of affecting any thing for the improvement of the science, and that they held it the wisest course to leave the matter as they found it. By a note of Mr. Wanley on this manuscript in the Harleian Catalogue, it appears that at the time of making it the corporation was extinct.*

* There can be no doubt that this corporation is extinct, and there is good ground to suppose that the London company of musicians are in a condition but little better; their charter appearing to have been obtained by untrue suggestions, and to have been vacated by a judgment of the court of chancery. The law it is true recognizes as corporations those fraternities that subsist by prescription, but it requires as a con-dition to this title that their exercise of corporate functions shall have been from time immemorial; but as to that of London, its origin may be traced to the time of Ja. I. which in a legal sense is within time of memory.

A very remarkable particular occurs in Strype's Continuation of Stowe's

BOOK XVI.　CHAP. CXLVIII.

Meetings of such as delighted in the practice of music began now to multiply, and that at Oxford, which had subsisted at a time when it was almost the only entertainment of the kind in the kingdom, flourished at this time more than ever. In that general joy, which the restoration of public tranquility had produced, an association was formed of many of the principal members of the university, heads of houses, fellows, and others, in order to promote the study and practice of vocal and instrumental harmony in the university. The occasion and circumstances of this laudable design can only now be made appear by a list of the contributors to it, now extant in the music-school, and also by a written table, exhibiting an account of the expenditure of divers sums of money, which had been given to promote it, these are as follow :—

I.

The list of those noble and worthy benefactors who have contributed to the refurnishing the publique Musick Schoole in this university with a new organ, harpsecon, all sortes of the best authors in manuscript for vocall and instrumentall music, and other necessaryes to carry on the practicall music in that place. All the old instruments and bookes left by the founder, being either lost, broken, or imbeasled in the time of rebellion and usurpation. This collection began in the yeare 1665. and was carryed on in part of the two following yeares, and then ceased by reason of the first Dutch warr, but now compleated in this yeare 1675.

Noblemen in 1665.		Dr. Gardner, Chr. Ch.	- £2
Ld. Annesley gave -	- £5	Dr. Allestrey, Chr. Ch.	- 2
Sr. Seamour Shirley -	- 5	Dr. Mayne - - -	- 2
Mr. Crew now Bp. -	- 3	Dr. Mew, Bp. - -	- 2
Drs. in 1665.		Dr. Yates, Prin. Braz.	- 2
Dr. Blandford, vice chanc.	3	Dr. Jenkins, Princ. Jes.	- 1
Dr. Fell, Deane Chr. Ch.	4	Masters in 1665.	
Dr. Merredeth, All. S.	- 3	Mr. Houghton, Braz.	- 1
Dr. Woodward, N. Coll.	3	Mr. R. Hill, Chr. Ch.	- 1
Dr. Dolbin, now Bp. -	- 2	Mr. R. South, Chr. Ch.	- 1
Dr. Dickenson - -	- 2	Mr. H. Bagshaw, Chr. Ch.	1
Dr. Pierce, Pre. Mag. -	- 2	Mr. Martin, Chr. Ch.	- 1
Dr. Barlow, now Bp. -	- 2	Mr. Coward, Cp. Christi	- 1

Mr. Sterry, Merton -	- £1	Mr. T. Spratt, Wad.	- £1
Mr. Denton, Queens	10s.	Noblemen in 1675.	
Mr. Parry, Cor. Christi	- £1	Sr. J. Parsons, Chr. Ch. -	2
Mr. J. Price, St. Johns	10s.	Sr. J. Chichester, Exeter	2
Mr. J. Price, New Coll.	- £1	Sr. C. Yelverton - -	3
Mr. T. Tomkins, All. S.	1	Sr. T. Isham - - -	3
Mr. J. Tomkins, Bal.	- 1	Drs. in 1675.	
Mr. Hutton, Braz.	- 1	Dr. Bathurst, Vice chanc.	3
Mr. Lowe, New Coll	- 1	Dr. Lockey, Chr. Ch.	- 2
Mr. Thomas, New Coll.	10s.	Dr. Wallis - - -	- 1
Mr. Hawkins, Bal. -	- £1	Dr. Smith - - -	- 2
Mr. Fairfax, Mag. -	- 1	Masters in 1675.	
Strangers in 1665.		Mr. Bernard, St. Johns	- 1
Bp. H. King - -	- 5	Mr. Thornton, Wad.	- 1
Dr. Franklin - -	- 1	Mr. Old, Chr. Ch. -	-
Mr. Hannes - -	- 1	Mr. Aldrich, Chr. Ch.	-
Mr. Tinker - -	10s.	Strangers in 1675.	
Mr. Sayer - -	10s.	Mr. C. Harris - -	- 2
Mr. Hodges - -	10s.	G. Lowe, Esq. - -	- 2
Mr. Stratford, Trin. -	- £1	J. Lowen - -,	£1. 10s.

II.

The account of instruments, books, and other necessaries bought for the use of the music school, with money contributed for that use from those noble and worthy benefactors nominated on the other side, as also what instruments, books, &c., have been given by others.

	£	s.	d.
1 upright organ with 4 stopps, made by Ralph Dallans, for which he received 48l. (abating 10l. for the materials of the old organ) and for painting and gilding to Mr. Taylor painter in Oxford 3l. 10s. in all -	51	10	0
Sets of choice books for instrumental music, ii. whereof are the composition of Mr. John Jenkins, for 2. 3. 4. 5 and 6 parts for the organ and harpsecon, and 6 sets more composed by Mr. Lawes, Coprario, Mr. Brewer, and Orlando Gibbons, all bought of Mr. Wood, which cost - - - -	22	0	0
2 violins with their bowes and cases, bought of Mr. Comer in the Strand ; cost 12l. 10s. and are at 2nd hand, * * * * which was Mr. Bull's of All Soulds cost 2l. 10s. In all	15	0	0
1 set of books, the composition of Mr. Baltzar (commonly called the Swede) for violins, viol, and harpsicon ; as also the compositions of Dr. Christopher Gibbons, his famous Ayres and Galliards for violins, viol, and organ, both sets together cost -	5	0	0
7 desks to lay the books on for the instruments and organ, bought of John Wild at 2s. a piece - - - - -	0	14	0
To Mr. Taylor the painter for the long picture in the music schoole of our Saviour and the woman of Samaria - - -	3	0	0
By charge in procuring the several pictures of those great masters in the facultie of music, carriage of them hither, frames to some of them, boarding all of them behinde to secure them from the dampe wall, &c. - -	10	0	0
The several disbursements then in the year 1667 was and deducting what was allowed for the materials of the old organ, there rests - - - - -	101	4	0

Mr. Henry Lawes, Gent. of his majesty's chappell royal and of his private music, gave to this school a rare Theorbo for singing to, valued at * * * with the earl of Bridgewater's crest in brass just under the fingerboard, with its case, as also a set of * * *

Survey of London ; that author, under the head of Temporal Government, exhibits the arms of the several companies of London, with a short history of them severally, beginning with the day and year of their incorporation. In the instance of the Musicians, book V. chap. xxv. he gives the arms of that company, but says not a word of the corporation itself. This omission he endeavours to supply in the second appendix to his work, page 16, by a letter from Mr. Mauduit, Windsor herald, containing an account of some incorporations not expressed in the Survey. In this letter Mr. Mauduit, speaking of the company of Musicians, says 'that the time of their incorporation was refused by the clerk of the company to be given.' He however supposes that they were incorporated by James I. by the name of Master, Wardens, and Commonalty. Of their arms he says that they were granted them by patent by William Camden Clarencieux, An. 1614.

The reason for this refusal may be collected from the recitals in the preamble to the above patent, but it is not so easy to account for the exercise of those powers which the London company of musicians even at this day claim, particularly that by which they exclude from performances within the city such musicians as are not free of their company. A remarkable instance of this kind happened in the year 1737. One Povey, a whimsical man, and known to the world by his having been the original projector of the Penny-post office, engaged a number of musicians, some from the opera, to play at a weekly concert, for which he obtained subscriptions, to be held in a great room in an old house in a court in St. Martin's le Grand. The first night of performance was the Saturday after the interment of queen Caroline ; the bills and advertisements announced that an oration would be delivered, deploring the death of that princess, but in the midst of the performance such of the musicians as were known to be foreigners were arrested at the suit of the company of musicians of London ; a proceeding, which had it been contested, could scarcely have been warranted, seeing that St. Martin's le Grand is not part of the city of London, but a liberty of Westminster.

Dr. Will. Child, Gent. of his majesty's chappell royal, and organist of the free chapp. at Windsor, gave his own picture from * * * * taffaty curtain * * * * the whole charge amounting to   -   -   -   6 9 6

The paper containing the above accounts being pasted on a wainscot board, has been so much injured by the damp, that no more of the writing is legible.

This at Oxford was the first subscription concert of which any account is to be met with: indeed it seems to have been the only association of the sort in the kingdom; the reason of this might be, that the pretenders to the love of music were not then so numerous as they have been of late years. A concert was formerly a serious entertainment, at which such only as had a real and genuine affection for music assembled, for the purpose of enjoying the pleasures of harmony, and contemplating the effects of it in a silent approbation : such as had no ear for music, and these are by far the majority of the human species, were then ingenuous enough to confess it, and that a concert was an entertainment that afforded them no kind of pleasure ; and we may accordingly suppose that concerts were the entertainment of such select companies only, and that at the houses of persons of distinction, the avowed patrons of the science of harmony, and its professors.

The first assembly of the kind deserving the name of a concert in London, was established under circumstances that tended rather to degrade than recommend such an entertainment, as being set on foot by a person of the lowest class among men in this country, in a suburb of the town, difficult of access, unfit for the resort of persons of fashion, and in a room that afforded them scarce decent accommodations when they had escaped the dangers of getting at it. In short, it was in the dwelling of one Thomas Britton, a man whose livelihood was selling about the streets small coal, which he carried in a sack on his back, that a periodical performance of music in parts was first exhibited, and that gratis too, to the inhabitants of this metropolis. The house of this man was situate in Aylesbury-street, leading from Clerkenwell-green to St. John's-street ; the room of performance was over his small-coal shop, and, strange to tell, from the year 1678, when he first began to entertain the public, to the time of his death in 1714, Tom Britton's concert was the weekly resort of the old, the young, the gay and the fair of all ranks, including the highest order of nobility.

The history of this extraordinary person will find a place in a subsequent part of this work, where an account will be given of sundry persons eminent in music, from whose assistance his concert derived its reputation; that it is here mentioned will scarce need any other apology, than that the order of narration seemed to require it.

For the common and ordinary sort of people there were entertainments suited to their notions of music ; these consisted of concerts in the unison, if they may be so called, of fiddles, of hautboys, trumpets, &c.; these were performed in booths at fairs held in and about London, but more frequently in certain places

called music-houses, of which there many in the time of Charles II.* The first of this kind was one known by the sign of the Mitre, situate near the west end of St. Paul's ; the name of the master of this house was Robert Hubert, *alias* Forges. This man, besides being a lover of music, was a collector of natural curiosities, as appears by the following title of a pamphlet published in duodecimo, anno 1664, 'A Catalogue of ' the many natural rarities, with great industry, cost, ' and thirty years travel into foreign countries, col-' lected by Robert Hubert, *alias* Forges, Gent. and ' sworn servant to his majesty, and daily to be seen ' at the place called the Musick-House at the Mitre, ' near the west end of St. Paul's church.†

Another place for entertainment of the like kind was the music-house at Stepney, situated in the row of houses fronting the west end of Stepney church ; it had for a sign the head of Charles II. and was the resort of seafaring people and others. In a great room of this house was an organ‡ and a band of fiddles and hautboys, to the music whereof it was no unusual thing for parties, and sometimes single persons, and those not of the very inferior sort, to dance.

Ward, in his London Spy, Part XIV. has given a particular description of a music-house which he visited in the course of his ramble, surpassing all of the kind in or about London. Its situation was in Wapping, but in what part of that suburb we are not told. The sign was that of the Mitre, and by the account which this author gives of it, the house, which was both a tavern and a music-house, was a very spacious and expensive building. He says that the music-room was a most stately apartment, and that no gilding, carving, painting, or good contrivance were wanting in the decoration of it ; the seats, he says, were like the pews in a church, and the upper end being divided by a rail, appeared to him more like a chancel than a music-loft. Of the music he gives but a general account, saying only that it consisted of violins, hautboys, and an organ.

---

* Edward Ward, in his London Spy, Part XI. page 255, mentions these, as also the music-houses and music-booths in Bartholomew fair, which, as he relates, were very numerous so late as about the year 1700 ; but it seems that upon his visit to the fair, he liked this kind of music so little, that he professes he had rather have heard an old barber ring Whittington's bells upon a cittern, than all that these houses afforded. London Spy, Part XI. page 255.

† In a manuscript of the late Mr. Oldys, being a collection relating to the city of London and its history, mention is made of this pamphlet with the following note. 'I have been informed by Sir Hans Sloane ' that this collection, or a great part of it, was purchased by him into his ' noble museum of the like curiosities, which now with his library is ' removed from his late house by Bloomsbury-square to his larger house ' at Chelsea.'

It is conjectured that this house was situated in London-house Yard, at the north-west end of St. Paul's church, and on the very spot where now stands the house known by the sign of the Goose and Gridiron ; for the tradition is that it was once a music-house. It seems that the successor of Hubert was no lover of music, but a man of humour, and it is said that in ridicule of the meetings formerly held there, he chose for his sign a goose stroking the bars of a gridiron with his foot, and called it the Swan and Harp.

‡ *It seems that in the usurpation, when the Liturgy and the use of organs in divine service was abolished, these instruments, being removed from the churches, were set up in such houses as that above described, and to this purpose the anonymous author, a Frenchman, of a character of England, translated by Mr. Evelyn, and published with an answer 24to 1659 has these words: 'they have translated the organs out of their churches and set ' them up in Taverns chanting their dithyrambics and bestial Bacchanalias ' to the tune of those instruments which were wont to assist them in the ' celebration of God's praises,' page 30.*

§ *Probably in Shadwell. On the South side of that street, is a place called Music house-court, New View of London 57. See it in the Plan of St. John's, Wapping, and St. Paul's, Shadwell. Strype's Stow. Book IV. page 47.*

The house being a tavern, was accommodated as well to the purpose of drinking as music; it contained many costly rooms, with whimsical paintings on the wainscotting. The kitchen was railed in to prevent the access to the fire of those who had nothing to do at it, and overhead was what this author calls an harmonious choir of canary birds singing.

The owner of this house had, according to Ward's account, used every method in his power to invite guests to it; and, under certain circumstances, appeared to be not less solicitous for their safety than their entertainment; for he had contrived a room under ground, in which persons were permitted to drink on Sundays, even during the time of divine service, and elude the search of the churchwardens.*

Another music-house, and which subsists even at this day, but in a different form, was that of Sadler's Wells, concerning which a pamphlet was published in the year 1684, with this title, 'A true and exact account of 'Sadler's Wells lately found at Islington, treating of 'its natures and vertues; together with an enumera-'tion of the chief diseases which it is good for, and 'against which it may be used, and the manner and 'order of taking it, published for the good of the 'publick by T. G., Doctor in Physick.'†

The music performed at these houses of entertainment was such as, notwithstanding the number of instruments, could scarcely entitle it to the name of a concert. For the most part it was that of violins, hautboys, or trumpets, without any diversity of parts, and consequently in the unison; or if at any time a bass instrument was added, it was only for the purpose of playing the ground-bass to those divisions on old ballad or country-dance tunes which at that time were the only music that pleased the common people. Some of the most admired of these were then known, and are still remembered by the following names:—John Dory;‡ Paul's Steeple; Old

Simon the King; Farinel's Ground;§ Tollet's Ground; Roger of Coverly; John come kiss me, a tune inserted in the earlier editions of Playford's Introduction;‖ Johnny cock thy Beaver, a tune to the song in D'Urfey's Pills to Purge Melancholy, 'To Horse brave Boys,' &c.; Packington's, quasi Bockington's Pound; Green Sleeves, which is the tune to the air in the Beggar's Opera, 'Though laws are made for every degree'; The Old Cebell, composed by Signor Baptist Draghi, and printed with a song to it in dialogue, sung in an opera called the Kingdom of the Birds, written by D'Urfey, and printed in the first volume of his Pills to purge Melancholy; a sweet air composed by Mr. Solomon Eccles, with divisions, printed as a country-dance tune, and called Bellamira, in the 'Dancing Master,' published by Henry Playford in 1701, page 149.

Besides these there occasionally came into practice divers song and dance-tunes that had been received with applause at the theatres, and which by way of eminence were called play-house tunes, such as Genius of England, Madam Subligny's minuet, the Louvre, and many others. The principal composers of this kind of music not already named, were Mr. John Reading,¶ John Banister, Godfrey Finger,** Mr. Bullimore, John Lenton, Christopher Simpson, Matthew Lock, Henry and John Eccles, Raphael Courteville, and other less eminent musicians.

This, as far as it can be now traced, was the state of popular music about the end of the last century. Of the gradual refinements in the practice of it at large, and of the introduction of the opera into this kingdom, the following is the history :—

The restoration of king Charles II. must be considered as a remarkable epoch in the history of music in two respects; first as the re-establishment of choral service, and the commencement of a new style in church-music is to be dated from thence; and, secondly, as it gave a new form to that kind of music, which, in contradistinction to that of the church, is usually termed secular music. The instruments commonly used in this latter appear to have been the lute, the harp, the fiddle, cornets, pipes of various kinds, and, lastly, viols, the latter of which were at length so adjusted with respect to size and tuning, that a concert of viols became a technical term in music.

Hitherto in England the viol had never been con-

* Within the time of memory it was customary for the churchwardens in London and the suburbs, to perambulate their parishes on Sundays, during the time of divine service, and search the taverns and alehouses; and if they found any persons drinking therein, to turn them out, and deal with the keepers of such houses according to law.

† The author says the water of this well was before the reformation very much famed for several extraordinary cures performed thereby, and was thereupon accounted sacred, and called Holywell. The priests belonging to the priory of Clerkenwell using to attend there, made the people believe that the virtues of the water proceeded from the efficacy of their prayers. But upon the reformation the well was stopped up, upon a supposition that the frequenting of it was altogether superstitious; and so by degrees it grew out of remembrance, and was wholly lost, until found out by the labourers which Mr. Sadler, who had newly built the musick-house there, and, being surveyor of the highways, had employed to dig gravel in his garden, in the midst whereof they found it stopped up, and covered with a carved arch of stone, in the year 1683. It is here also said to be of a ferruginous taste, somewhat like that of Tunbridge, but not so strong of the steel. It is recommended for opening all obstructions, and also for purging and sweetening of the blood, &c. And Dr. Morton had that summer advised several of his patients to drink it, as the owner also was to brew his beer with it.

After the decease of Mr. Sadler above mentioned, one Francis Forcer, a musician, and the composer of many songs printed in the 'Theater of Music,' published by Henry Playford and John Carr in the years 1685, 1686, and 1687, became the occupier of the Wells and music-house. His successor therein was a son of his, who had been bred up to the law, and, as some said, a barrister; he was the first that exhibited there the diversions of rope-dancing, tumbling, &c. He was a very gentlemanly man, remarkably tall and athletic, and died in an advanced age, about the year 1730, at the Wells, which for many years had been the place of his residence.

‡ The song of John Dory, with the tune to it, is printed in the Deuteromelia, or the second part of 'Musick's Melodie,' 1609. The legend of this person is, that being a sea-captain, or perhaps a pirate, he engaged to the king of France to bring the crew of an English ship bound as captives to Paris, and that accordingly he attempted to make prize of an English vessel, but was himself taken prisoner. The song

of John Dory, and the tune to it were a long time popular in England: in the comedy of the Chances, written by Beaumont and Fletcher, Antonio, a humorous old man, receives a wound, which he will not suffer to be dressed but upon condition that the song of John Dory be sung the while.

§ Mentioned page 677 of this work, to have been composed by Farinelli of Hanover, and to have been made the subject of Corelli's twelfth Solo.

‖ This was a very favourite tune: in the first part of the Division Violin there are two sets of divisions on it, the one by Mr. Davis Mell, the other by Baltzar the Lubecker, of whom Anthony Wood speaks so highly in his life. Most of the tunes above mentioned, together with many others of great antiquity, in a style peculiar to this country, are inserted in an appendix to this work.

¶ A scholar of Dr. Blow; organist of Hackney, and afterwards of St. Dunstan in the West, and St. Mary Woolnoth. He published a book of anthems by subscription, and died but a few years ago.

** A native of Olmutz in Moravia, and of the chapel to James II. He composed several Operas of Sonatas for violins, and also for flutes, the titles whereof are in the Catalogue of Estienne Roger. Lenton, the two named Eccles, and Banister, were of the band to king William; Banister was his first violin; of him, as also of Simpson and Lock, mention will be made hereafter.

sidered as an instrument proper for a concert, or indeed of any other use than as an incentive to dancing, and that kind of mirth which was anciently the concomitant of religious festivity, particularly at Christmas, in the celebration whereof fiddlers were deemed so necessary, that in the houses of the nobility they were retained by small stipends, as also cloaks and badges, with the cognizance or arms of the family, like certain other domestic servants.* From the houses of great men to wakes, fairs, and other assemblies of the common people, the transition of these vagrant artists was natural. Bishop Earle has given a very humorous character of a common fiddler, which exhibits this particular of ancient local manners in a strong point of view.†

* This usage is mentioned in the Dialogue on old Plays and Players, and is alluded to in an old comedy entitled ' Ram-Alley,' or Merry Tricks, written by Lodowic Barrey, and printed in 1611, in which Sir Oliver Small-shanks says to the fiddlers that attend him,

' This yeare you shall have my protection,
' And yet not buy your liverie coates yourselves.'

The retainer of these servants, like watermen at this day, might possibly leave them at liberty, as occasion offered, to seek a livelihood elsewhere than in the families to which they properly belonged; and they might nevertheless be itinerants in some degree, as may be collected from the following speech in the old play of the Return from Parnassus or the Scourge of Simony, to a company of fiddlers, who desire to be paid for their music:

' Faith fellow fiddlers, here is no silver found in this place; no not
' so much as the usual Christmas entertainment of musicians,
' a black jacke of beer, and a Christmas pye.'

† ' A poor fiddler is a man and fiddle out of case, and he in worse case ' than his fiddle. One that rubs two sticks together (as the Indians ' strike fire) and rubs a poor living out of it; partly from this, and partly ' from your charity, which is more in the hearing than giving him, for ' he sells nothing dearer than to be gone. He is just so many strings ' above a beggar, though he have but two; and yet he begs too, only ' not in the downright for God's sake, but with a shrugging God bless ' you, and his face is more pin'd than the blind man's. Hunger is the ' greatest pain he takes, except a broken head sometimes, and the ' labouring John Dory. Otherwise his life is so many fits of mirth, and ' 'tis some mirth to see him. A good feast shall draw him five miles by ' the nose, and you shall track him again by the scent. His other ' pilgrimages are fairs and good houses, where his devotion is great to ' the Christmas, and no man loves good times better. He is in league ' with the tapsters for the worshipful of the inn, whom he torments next ' morning with his art, and has their names more perfect than their ' men. A new song is better to him than a new jacket, especially if ' baudy, which he calls merry, and hates naturally the Puritan, as an ' enemy to his mirth. A country wedding and Whitson ale are the two ' main places he domineers in, where he goes for a musician, and over- ' looks the bagpipe. The rest of him is drunk and in the stocks.'

In the times of puritanical reformation, the profession of a common fiddler was odious; Butler has spoken the sentiments of the party in the invectives of Hudibras against Crowdero and his profession; and by the way the following lines in his poem,

' He and that engine of vile noise,
' On which illegally he plays,
' Shall dictum factum both be brought
' To condign punishment as they ought.'

are a plain allusion to an ordinance made in 1658, in which is the fol- lowing clause:—

' And be it further enacted by the authority aforesaid, that if any ' person or persons, commonly called fiddlers or minstrels, shall at any ' time after the said first day of July, [1657] be taken playing, fiddling, ' and making musick in any inn, ale-house, or tavern, or shall be taken ' proffering themselves, or desiring, or intreating any person or persons ' to hear them play, or make musick in any of the places aforesaid, that ' every such person and persons so taken, shall be adjudged, and are ' hereby adjudged and declared to be rogues, vagabonds, and sturdy ' beggers, and shall be proceeded against and punished as rogues, ' vagabonds, and sturdy beggers within the said statute, any law, statute, ' or usage to the contrary thereof in any wise notwithstanding.'

Of Whitson-ales, mentioned in the above character, as also of Church- ales, little is now known besides the name. In the Anatomie of Abuses by Philip Stubs, a book already cited, is the following description of both:—

' In certaine towns where drunken Bacchus beares swaie, against ' Christmas and Easter, Whitsunday, or some other time, the church- ' wardens, (for so they call them) of every parish, with the consent ' of the whole parish, provide halfe a score or twenty quarters of mault, ' whereof some they buy of the church stocke, and some is given them ' of the parishoners themselves; every one conferring somewhat according ' to his ability: which mault being made into strong ale or beere, is set ' to sale eyther in the church, or in some other place assigned to that ' purpose. Then when this Nippitatum, this Huffecappe (as they call ' it) and this Nectar of life is set abroach, well is he that can get the ' soonest to it, and spend the most at it, for he that sitteth the closest

But farther to show in how small estimation the violin was formerly held in this country: it appears that at the time when Anthony Wood was a young man, viz., about the year 1650, that the tuning of it was scarcely settled; for in the account by him given of his learning to play on that instrument, he says that he tuned it by fourths, and the notation was borrowed from the tablature of the lute, which had then lately been transferred to the viol da gamba. But the king, soon after his return to England, having heard Baltzar's exquisite per- formance on the violin, took him into his service, and placed him at the head of a band of violins, but he dying in 1663, was succeeded by Mr. John Banister, who had been bred up under his father, one of the waits, as they are called, of the parish of St. Giles in the Fields, near London; this person was sent by Charles II. to France for improvement, but soon after his return was dismissed the king's service for saying that the English violins were better than the French.‡

' to it, and spendes the most at it, hee is counted the Godliest man of all ' the rest, and most in God's favour, because it is spent upon his church ' forsooth: but who either for want cannot, or otherwise for feare of God's ' wrath will not, stick to it, he is counted one destitute both of vertue ' and godlinesse. In so much as you shall have many poore men make ' hard shift for money to spende thereat. And good reason for being put ' into this Corban, they are perswaded it is meritorious and a good ' service to God. In this kinde of practise they continue sixe weekes, ' a quarter of a yeare, yea halfe a yeare together, swilling and gulling ' night and day, til they be as drunke as swine and as mad as March ' hares.'

The above passage may serve for an explanation of the word BRIDALE, which differs from BRIDAL, a nuptial festival, and may possibly signify the distribution of drink to a neighbourhood upon occasion of a nuptial solemnity.

The same author says, that to justify these disorderly practises, it is pretended that the money received at these assemblies is expended by the churchwardens, &c. in the repair of their respective churches and chapels, and that with it they buy ' bookes for service,' Cuppes for the ' celebration of the Sacrament, Surplesses for Sir John, and other ' necessaries, and maintaine other extraordinarie charges in their ' parishes besides.'

See a description of Church-ales, as also an apology for them in Carew's Survey of Cornwall, 68 et seq.

From the Antiquarian Repertory.
Customs of Church Ale. From a MS. in the library of Thomas Astle, Esq. Inter MSS. Dodsworth in Bib. Bod. Vol. 158, p. 97.
This is the agreement betwixt the inhabitants of the towns and parishes of Elvaston, Thurlaston, and Ambaston of the one part, and the inhabitants of the town of Okebrook within the said parish of Elvaston, in Com. Derby, on the other part, by John, Abbot of the Dale, Ralph Saucheverell, Esq., John Bradshaw, and Henry Tithel, Gent., Witnesseth, that the inhabitants, as well of the said parish of Elvaston, as of the said town of Okebrook, shall brew four ales, and every ale of one quarter of malt, and at their own costs and charges, betwixt this and the feast of St. John Baptist next coming— And that every inhabitant of the said town of Okebrook shall be at the several ales, and every husband and his wife shall pay twopence, every cot- tager one penny, and all the inhabitants of Elvaston, Thurlaston, and Am- baston shall have and receive all the profits and advantages coming of the said ales to the use and behoof of the said church of Elvaston; and the in- habitants of the said towns of Elvaston, Thurlaston, and Ambaston, shall brew eight ales betwixt this and the feast of St. John the Baptist, at the which ales, and every one of them, the inhabitants of Okebrook shall come and pay as before rehearsed; and if he be away at one ale, to pay at the t'oder ale for both, or else to send his money. And the inhabitants of Oke- brook shall carry all manner of tymber being in the dale wood now felled, that the said prestchyrch of the said towns of Elvaston, Thurlaston, and Ambaston shall occupye to the use and profit of the said church.
N. B. This appears to have been the old method of paying money for the repair of country churches.

Custom of Bride Ale.
From the Court Rolls of Hales-owen Borough in Com. Salop, in the hands of Thomas Lyttleton, Lord of the said Borough, de Anno. 15 Eliz. R.
Item, a payne is made, that no person or persons that shall brewe any weddyn ale to sell, shall not brewe above twelve strike of malt at the most, and that the said persons so married shall not keep nor have above eight messe of persons at his dinner within the burrowe: and before his brydall daye he shall keep no unlawfull games in hys house, nor out of hys house, on pain of 20 shillings.
Communicated by Thomas Astle, Esq.

‡ It seems that he had good reason for saying so, for at the time when Lully was placed at the head of a band of violins, created on purpose for him by Lewis XIV. and called Les petits Violons, in contradistinction to that of twenty-four, not half the musicians in France were able to play at sight.

By means of this circumstance, and the several particulars before enumerated, respecting the taste of Charles II. for music, we are enabled to trace with some degree of certainty the introduction of the violin species of instruments into this kingdom, and to ascertain the time when concerts, consisting of two treble violins, a tenor, and a bass violin or violoncello, came into practice;* that they had their origin in Italy can scarce admit of a question; and it is no less certain that they were adopted by the French; though it is not easy to conceive the use of a band wherein were twenty-four performers on the same instrument; nor indeed how so many could be employed to advantage in any such concerts as were known at that time.

Indeed the idea of a performance, where the instruments for the bass and intermediate parts were in number so disproportionate to the treble, seems to be absurd; and there is reason to suspect that the song 'four and twenty fiddlers all on a row,' in D'Urfey's Pills to purge Melancholy, was written in ridicule of that band of twenty-four violins, which, as the French writers assert, was the most celebrated of any in Europe.†

During the residence of Charles at the court of France, he became enamoured of French manners and French music; and upon his return to England, in imitation of that of Lewis, he established a band of violins, and placed at the head of it, at first Baltzar the Lubecker, and after him Banister, who, for a reason above assigned, was removed from the direction of it.

Besides the person that presided over the violins, who can hardly be supposed to have been any other than he that played the principal violin part, there was also a master or director of the king's music; the person who first occupied this station was Nicholas Laniere, as appears by a grant of Charles I. herein before inserted. Upon the death of Laniere, who lived some years after the restoration, Matthew Lock was appointed to that office, with the same allowance of 200l. a year; but about the year 1673, Cambert, a French musician, who had been master of music to the queen mother Ann of Austria, and the Marquis de Sourdeac, and also joint manager of the opera at Paris, came into England, and by Charles II. was made superintendent of his music.

Cambert, though he died in 1677, lived here long enough to exhibit an opera of his composition, entitled Pomone, which had been received at Paris with general applause, and to introduce into concerts

the violins, and those other instruments of that species, the tenor violin and violoncello, the characteristic whereof is that they have uniformly four strings tuned in fifths. To these were adapted compositions of a new structure, namely, Sonatas, the invention of some of the most eminent performers on the violin among the Italians; these were of two kinds, viz., Sonate da Chiesa, and Sonate da Camera; the first consisted of slow solemn movements, intermixed with fugues; the other of preludes and airs of various forms, as Allemands, Courants, Sarabands, Gavots, and Jigs.

But here a distinction is to be noted between the airs abovementioned, and those of the age preceding, and this will require a particular specification of each.

The word Air is rather a modern term in music; it had its original among the Italian masters; Lord Bacon makes use of it in his essay on Beauty, saying that the sweetest airs in music are made by a kind of felicity, and not by rule. These were the Passamezzo, the Pavan, the Galliard, the Allemand, the Coranto, the Jig, and some others, which may be termed old airs.

The Passamezzo, from passer to walk, and mezzo the middle or half, is a slow dance, little differing from the action of walking. As a Galliard‡ consists of five paces or bars in the first strain, and is therefore called a Cinque Pace; the Passamezzo, which is a diminutive of the Galliard, has just half that number, and from that peculiarity takes its name.

The Pavan is by some writers said to be an air invented in Padua. This is founded on no better authority than mere etymological conjecture; the word is derived from the Latin Pavo, a peacock, and signifies a kind of dance, performed in such a manner, and with such circumstances of dignity and stateliness, as show the propriety of the appellation. §

The Galliard is a lively air in triple time;

* Of the French concerts there are few memorials remaining, other than some scattered passages in Mersennus, cited or referred to in the course of this work. In this kingdom the music for concerts of violins, before the invention of the Sonata, consisted altogether of airs in three, and sometimes four parts. Of these sundry collections were published by Playford, and others: some of the most celebrated of them were those entitled 'Court Ayres, Pavins, Almains, Corants, and Sarabands,' by Dr. Child, Dr. Coleman, Dr. Rogers, Will. Lawes, Jenkins, and others, published by Playford in 1656, 'Tripla Concordia, or a Choice Collection 'of new Airs in three parts for treble and Basse Violins,' by Matthew Lock, Robert Smith, William Hall, John Banister, Robert King, and Francis Forcer: printed for John Carr, 1977, obl. quarto; and a collection of airs by Matthew Lock, called his little Consort.

† Notwithstanding this establishment and the pains that Lewis XIV. took to introduce the opera into France, it is to be doubted whether the scenery, the decorations, and, above all, the dances, were not the principal object of his regard in these splendid representations: and it is said of Lully, that to gratify his master he laboured as much in composing the dances as the airs of the opera. Hist. de la Musique et de ses Effets, tom. III. page 321.

‡ In lessons for the harsichord and virginal the airs were made to follow in a certain order, that is to say, the slowest or most grave first, and the rest in succession, according as they deviated from that character, by which rule the Jig generally stood last. In general the Galliard followed the Pavan, the first being a grave, the other a sprightly air; but this rule was not without exception. In a manuscript collection of lessons composed by Bird, formerly belonging to a lady Neville, who it is supposed was a scholar of his, is a lesson of a very extraordinary kind, as it seems intended to give the history of a military engagement. The following are the names of the several airs in order as they occur. 'The 'Marche before the battell, The Souldiers Sommons, The Marche of 'foot-men, The Marche of horse-men: Now folowethe the Trumpets, 'The Bagpipe and the Drone, the Flute and the Drome, the Marche to 'the Fighte, Here the battells be joyned, The Retreate, Now folowethe 'a Galliarde for the victory.' There is also in the same collection a lesson called the Carman's Whistle.

The airs composed about the time of queen Elizabeth, however excellent in their kind, seem to have derived their reputation from their being the tunes of dances actually performed at court, or at public assemblies for the purpose of feasting and recreation. In a work entitled 'Lachrymæ or Seaven Teares figured in seaven passionate Pavans with 'divers other Pavans, Galiards, and Almands by John Dowland,' the several airs are distinguished by appellations which seem to indicate their being the favourites of particular persons, as in these instances: 'M. John Langton's Pavan, the King of Denmark's Galiard, the Earl of 'Essex Galiard, Sir John Souch his Galiard, M. Henry Noell his Galiard, 'M. Giles Hoby his Galiard, M. Nicho. Gryffith his Galiard, M. Thomas 'Collier his Galiard with two trebles, Captaine Piper his Galiard, M. 'Bucton his Galiard, Mr. Nichols Almand, Mr. George Whitehead his 'Almand.'

Of this fact it is some sort of proof that the airs above enumerated are in the title-page of the book said to be set forth for the lute, viols, or violins; and it is certain that in Dowland's time the latter of these instruments was appropriated to the practice of dancing. Farther it is expressly said by Christopher Simpson, in his Compendium of Practical Music, page 143, that fancies and symphonies excepted, instrumental music in its several kinds was derived from the various measures in dancing.

§ See page 215 of this work.

Brassard intimates that it is the same with the Romanesca, a favourite dance with the Italians.

The ALLEMAND, ALMAND, or ALMAIN, as its name imports, is an air originally invented by the Germans; it is of a grave and serious cast, yet full of spirit and energy, arising from the compass of notes which it takes in; the measure of it is duple time of four crotchets in a bar; the air consists of two strains, with a repetition of each; and those that define it with exactness say that it ought to begin with an odd quaver or semiquaver, or with three semiquavers. Walther says that in this species of instrumental composition, especially the Allemand for the dance, the Germans excel all other nations; but this assertion seems rather too bold; the Allemands of the Italian masters, particularly Corelli, Albinoni, and Geminiani, being inferior to none that we know of: that in the tenth solo of Corelli may be looked upon as one of the most perfect models for this kind of air.

The CORANTO, Courant, Fr. Corrente, Ital. Currens saltatio, Lat., is a melody or air consisting of three crotchets in a bar, but moving by quavers, in the measure of $\frac{3}{4}$, with two strains or reprises, each beginning with an odd quaver. Walther, who describes it, assigns to it no determinate number of bars; nor is there any precise rule that we know of for the measure of it, save that the number of bars, whatever it be, is the multiple of 8. Of dance-tunes it is said to be the most solemn.

The SARABAND is an air of great antiquity; the Spaniards write it Zarabanda, and this orthography seems to confirm the opinion of those who derive it from the Moors, saying that they brought it into Spain, and that from thence it was diffused throughout Europe.*

The CHACONE, a less common air than any of those above enumerated, is said by some, who take it for granted that the word is derived from the Italian cieco, blind, to be the invention of some blind musician; but others assert that, like the Saraband, it is of Moorish original; and those who would carry it still higher, suggest that the word is derived from the Persian Schach, which signifies a king; and that Chacone might signify a royal dance: from the Persians, say these, it might pass to the Saracens, and from them to the Moors. The characteristic of the Chacone is a bass or ground, consisting of four measures, of that kind of triple wherein three crotchets make the bar, and the repetitions thereof with variations in the several parts from the beginning to the end of the air, which, in respect of its length, has no limit but the discretion of the composer. The whole of the twelfth Sonata of the second opera of Corelli is a Chacone.

There is another air in music called by the Italians the PASSACAGLIO, and by the French Passacaille, which, like the Chacone, consists in a variety of divisions on a given ground bass; the only essential difference between the one and the other of the two is, that the Chacone is ever in the major, and the Passacaille in the minor third of the key. In Mr. Handel's lessons for the harpsichord, Suite Septieme is an air of the sort last above described.

The JIGG is supposed by some to have been invented by the English, but its derivation from the Teutonic GIEG, or, as Junius writes it, GHIJGHE, a fiddle, is rather against this opinion. Mattheson speaks of the Jigs of this country as having in general a pointed note at the beginning of every bar; but for this distinction there seems not to be the least authority. The same author seems to think that originally the Jig was a dance tune, and of English invention: nevertheless it has been adopted by most nations in Europe; for not only in England, but in Italy, Germany, and France it appears to have been a favourite species of air. Its characteristic is duple time, thus marked, $\frac{6}{8}$ or $\frac{12}{8}$. The air itself consists of two strains, undetermined as to the number of bars †

To speak now of the airs of the moderns, and first of the Gavot.

The Gavot, so far as regards the general practice of it, is hardly to be traced further backwards than to the time of Lully, that is to say about the year 1670. Huet says that the appellation is derived from the Gavots, a people inhabiting a mountainous district in France called Gap.‡ It signifies a dance-tune in duple time, consisting of two strains, the first whereof contains four bars, and the latter eight, and sometimes twelve, each beginning with two crotchets, or the half of a bar, with a rise of the hand in beating, and ending also with two crotchets that begin the last bar. Walther says it is required that the first strain of a Gavot should have its cadence in the third or fifth of the key, for that if it be in the key-note itself, it is not a Gavot but a Rondeau; and in this opinion both Brossard and Mattheson concur.§

The invention of the MINUET, Fr. Menuet, seems generally to be ascribed to the French, and particularly to the inhabitants of the province of Poictou; the word is said by Menage and Furetiere to be de-

---

* Within the memory of persons now living, a Saraband danced by a Moor was constantly a part of the entertainment at a puppet shew; this particular may be considered as an additional circumstance in proof that this dance is of Moorish original. See page 216.

† The Jigs of Corelli abound with fine melody: that in the sixth of his Solos is celebrated throughout Europe. In the fourth of Mr. Handel's Concertos for the organ is an example of a jig movement interwoven with one in andante time, and the contrast has a remarkably fine effect.

‡ 'GAVOTE. Sorte de danse. M. Huet, dans son Traité curieux de 'l' Origine des Romans, page 124. *Les Martegales et Madrigaux ont pris* 'leur nom des MARTEGAUX, *peuples montagnards de Provence; de même* 'que les Gavots, *peuples montagnards du pays de Gap, ont donné le nom* 'à cette danse que nous appellons Gavote. *Cette ètymologie me paroît* 'très véritable.' M. Menage, article GAVOTE.

§ The Gavots of Corelli, Albinoni, Vivaldi, and others of the Italians, correspond with these rules as far as they relate to the measure, the number of bars in each strain, and the cadences; but in respect to the initial notes of the air, they deviate from it; for they sometimes begin with a whole bar, as that in the first Sonata of the second Opera of Corelli, and the fifth of his fourth Opera, and yet they are termed Gavots, as are also those airs of the Gavot-kind in the tenth of his Solos, and the ninth of his Concertos, each whereof begins with an odd quaver. As to those airs which are said to be tempo di Gavotta, such as that in his ninth Solo, and those in the fifth and eighth of his second, and the third and tenth of his fourth Opera, they are not Gavots, but movements in the time of the Gavot, with a general imitation of the air.

After all, the Gavot, strictly so called, is an air that disgusts by its formality; those Gavots only have a pleasing effect in which the middle and final closes are suspended by a varied and eloquent modulation, of which the Gavot in the overture of Semele, and the last movement in the third of Mr. Handel's Concertos for the organ, are remarkable instances.

rived from the French Menuë or Menue, small or little, and in strictness signifies a small pace. The melody of this dance consists of two strains, which, as being repeated, are called reprises, each having eight or more bars, but never an odd number. The measure is three crotchets in a bar, marked thus, $\frac{3}{4}$, though it is commonly performed in this time, $\frac{3}{8}$. Walther speaks of a minuet in Lully's opera of Roland, each strain of which contains ten bars, the sectional number being 5, which renders it very difficult to dance.

The PASPY, Fr. Passe-pied, from passer to walk, and pied a foot, is a very brisk French dance, the measure $\frac{3}{8}$, and often $\frac{6}{8}$. It has three or more strains or reprises, the first consisting of eight bars. It is said to have been invented in Bretagne, and is in effect a quick minuet.

The BOUREE is supposed to come from Auvergne in France; it seldom occurs but in compositions of French masters; its time is duple, consisting of twice four measures in the first strain, and twice eight in the second.

The SICILIANA is an air probably invented in Sicily, of a slow movement, thus characterised, $\frac{12}{8}$; it consists of two strains, the first of four, and the second of eight bars or measures.

The LOUVRE is a mere dance-tune; the term is not general, but is applied singly to a French air, called L'amiable Vainqueur, of which Lewis XIV. was extremely fond; the French dancing masters composed a dance to it, which is well known in England.

That the HORNPIPE was invented by the English seems to be generally agreed: that it was not unusual to give to certain airs the names of the instruments on which they were commonly played, may be instanced in the word Geig, which with a little variation is made to signify both a fiddle and the air called a Jig, and properly adapted to it. Indeed we have no such instrument as the hornpipe, but in Wales it is so common that even the shepherd-boys play on it. In the Welsh language it has the name of the Pib-corn, i. e. the Hornpipe; and it is so called as consisting of a wooden pipe, with holes at stated distances, and a horn at each end, the one to collect the wind blown into it by the mouth, and the other to carry off the sounds as modulated by the performer. A very learned and curious antiquary, the Hon. Daines Barrington, has lately communicated to the world a description, as also the form of this rustic instrument, and with no small appearance of probability conjectures that it originally gave the name to the air called the Hornpipe.*

The measure of the Hornpipe is triple time of six crotchets in a bar, four whereof are to be beat

with a down, and two with an up hand. There occurs in the opera of Dioclesian, set to Music by Purcell, a dance called the CANARIES: of this, and also another called TRENCHMORE, it is extremely difficult to render a satisfactory account. The first is alluded to by Shakespeare in the following passage :—

  ' *Moth.* Master, will you win your love with a French ' brawl? †
  ' *Arm.* How meanst thou? brawling in French?
  ' *Moth.* No, my compleat master : but to jig off a tune ' at the tongue's end, *canary* to it with your feet, humour ' it with turning up your eyelids,' &c.
      LOVE'S LABOUR LOST, Act III. Scene 1.

As to the air itself, it appears by the example in the opera of Dioclesian to be a very sprightly movement of two reprises or strains, with eight bars in each. The time three quavers in a bar, the first pointed. That it is of English invention, like the country-dance, may be inferred from this circumstance, that none of the foreign names that distinguish one kind of air from another correspond in the least with this. Nay, farther, the appellation is adopted by Couperin, a Frenchman, who among his lessons has an air which he entitles Canaries.

Of the dance called Trenchmore frequent mention is made by our old dramatic writers: thus in the Island Princess of Beaumont and Fletcher, Act V. one of the townsmen says—

  ' All the windows i' th' town dance a new *Trenchmore*.

In the Table talk of Selden, tit. KING OF ENGLAND, is the following humorous passage :—

  ' The court of England is much alter'd. At ' a solemn dancing, first you had the grave measures, ' then the Corantoes and the Galliards, and this kept ' up with ceremony ; and at length to Trenchmore, ' and the Cushion dance : Then all the company ' dances, lord and groom, lady and kitchen-maid, no ' distinction. So in our court in queen Elizabeth's ' time, gravity and state were kept up. In king ' James's time things were pretty well. But in king ' Charles's time there has been nothing but Trench-'more and the Cushion-dance, omnium gatherum, ' tolly polly, hoite come toite.'

And in the comedy of the Rehearsal, the Earth, Sun, and Moon are made to dance the Hey to the tune of Trenchmore : from all which it may be inferred that the Trenchmore was also a lively movement ‡

The COUNTRY-DANCE is also said to have had its origin with us. Indeed Mr. Weaver, one of the best teachers of dancing in the kingdom of the last age, and who appears to have been well acquainted with the history of his art, has asserted it in express terms. He says that the country-dance is the peculiar growth of this nation, though it is now transplanted into almost all the courts of Europe, and it is become in the most august assemblies one of the favourite diversions. §

---

* See the Archæologia of the Antiquarian Society, vol. III. page 33. That there was anciently a musical instrument called the Hornpipe is evident from the following passage in Chaucer, in which it is mentioned with the flute :—

    Controve he would, and foule faile
    With Hornpipes of Cornwaile.
    In floites made he discordaunce,
    And in his musike with mischaunce
    He would feine, &c.
      ROMAUNT OF THE ROSE, Fo. 135. b. edit. 1561.

† *i. e.* the dance called the Brawl or Brauls, mentioned page 215.

‡ In the Dancing Master, or Directions for dancing Country-dances, with the tunes to each dance. published by Henry Playford in 1698, page 44, is a tune entitled ' Trenchmore,' inserted in the Appendix to this work.

§ Essay towards a History of Dancing by John Weaver. Lond. 8vo. 1712, page 170.
For the composition of country-dance tunes no rule is laid down by

We meet also among the compositions of the English masters of the violin who lived in the time of Charles II. with an air called the CEBELL, an appellation for which no etymology, nor indeed any explanation, is attempted by any of our lexicographers: for this reason we are necessitated to resort for satisfaction to those few exemplars of this kind of air now remaining, and by these it appears to have been an air in duple time of four bars or measures, only repeated in division at the will of the composer, but with this remarkable circumstance, that the several strains are alternately in the grave and the acute series of notes in the musical scale.*

That elegant species of composition the Sonata, had its rise about the middle of the seventeenth century: who were the original inventors of it is not certainly known, but doubtless those that excelled most in it were Bassani and Corelli. The first essay towards the introduction of the Sonata into England was a collection of Sonatas for two violins and a bass, by Mr. John Jenkins; these it is true were in three parts only; and compositions of this kind must be said to have been wanting in that variety of harmony which is produced by a concert of six viols; but this defect was soon remedied by giving to the violoncello one bass part, and to the organ, harpsichord, or arch-lute another; and, lastly, by the invention of the Concerto Grosso, consisting of two choruses, with an intermediate part, so necessary in all symphoniac music, for the tenor violin. It is said that we are indebted for this great improvement in instrumental music to Giuseppe Torelli, and from about the year 1700, until almost the present time, the designation of a full concert for violins has been, two principal and two second violins, a tenor violin, and a violoncello, with a thorough-bass for the harpsichord, and of consequence the viol species of instruments has grown into disuse.

The lute, notwithstanding the great improvements which the French had made of it, as well by varying its form as by increasing the number of chords, thereby rendering it in some respects the rival of the harpsichord, was nevertheless now declining in the estimation of the world. Waller suggests as a reason for it, an opinion, which, although it is controverted by Mace and other masters, had very probably its foundation in truth: it was suspected that the practice of the lute had a tendency to bring on deformity in ladies and persons of delicate habits,† an evil which was not to be feared from the erect and graceful posture required in playing on the harpsichord. But whoever considers the structure of the lute, the labour of stringing it, and the attention requisite to keep it in order, over and above the incessant practice necessary to acquire a fine hand on it, need not look far for reasons why it has given place to the harpsichord, of all musical instruments ever invented the most easy.

CHAP. CXLIX.

THE Italian opera having undergone a gradual refinement, was now arrived at great perfection, and, notwithstanding the early prejudices of the French against Italian music, had found its way to Paris. Lewis XIV. in the year 1669, had established the Academie Royal de Musique; Corneille, Quinault, and other the best poets of France, composed the drama of many operas, and first Cambert, and afterwards Lully, set them to music. The public taste, and the posture of affairs in this country, were not then so favourable to theatrical representations of this kind, as to enable us to emulate our neighbours in the exhibition of them: some faint attempts of imitation had indeed been made by the introduction of vocal and instrumental music into some of our plays, as particularly Macbeth and the Tempest, composed by Matthew Lock, in which were a few airs and choruses, distributed at proper intervals through the five acts, with a few short recitatives; but for want of a proper fable, of machinery, and other requisites, and, above all, a continued recitative to connect and introduce the airs, these representations could hardly be said to bear more than a very faint resemblance of the Italian opera properly so called.

The above two plays of Macbeth and the Tempest, altered from Shakespeare, the one by Sir William Davenant, and the other by Shadwell, were performed at the theatre in Lincoln's-Inn fields; the latter was wrought into the form of an opera; the applause with which they were severally received gave encouragement to Shadwell to compose a drama named Psyche, which, though he would have it thought he took it from Apuleius, is in a great measure a translation of the Psyche of Quinault, which was set to music by Lully in 1672, in the manner of the Italian opera. Lock had succeeded beyond expectation in the music to Macbeth and the Tempest, and he, together with Gio. Battista Draghi, composed the music to this opera of Psyche. The following advertisement in the preface of Shadwell to Psyche will show the part which each of them took, as also what other persons assisted in the work.

'All the instrumental music (which is not min-'gled with the vocal) was composed by that great 'master, Signior Gio. Battista Draghi, master of the

---

any of the writers on music, perhaps for this reason, that there is in music no kind of time whatever but may be measured by those motions and gesticulations common in dancing; and in fact there are few song-tunes of any account within these last hundred years that have not become also country-dances. Simpson in his Compendium of 'Practical Musick,' page 144, says of country-dances, and indeed of some other airs, that they are so easy to compose, that he has known some 'who by 'a natural aptness, and by the accustomed hearing of them, would make 'such like, being untaught, although they had not so much skill in 'music as to be able to write them down in notes.'

* Examples of this species of air occur in the Division Violin, a book which has already been mentioned. But the most celebrated of any that we know of, is that called the Old Cebell, which some very old persons now living remember to have been one of the most popular tunes at the beginning of this century. It is printed as a song with words to it in D'Urfey's Pills to purge Melancholy, vol. I. page 139; the author of it is there said to be Sig. Baptist, by whom some have understood Lully, whose christian names were Jean Baptiste, but the person meant is Sig. Giovanni Battista Draghi, of whom an account will hereafter be given.

† See in his works the letter following that to Lady Lucy Sidney. Mace in answer to the objection, which it seems was a common one, asserts that in his whole time he never knew any person that grew awry by the practice of the lute. Musick's Monument, page 46.

'Italian music to the king. The dances were made
' by the most famous master of France, Monsieur St.
' Andrée. The scenes were painted by the ingenious
' artist, Mr. Stephenson. In those things that con-
' cern the ornament or decoration of the play, the
' great industry and care of Mr. Betterton ought to
' be remembered, at whose desire I wrote upon this
' subject.'

This opera was performed at the theatre in Dorset
Garden in February, 1673 ; Downes, the prompter,
says that the scenes, machines, cloths, and other
necessaries and decorations, cost upwards of 800l.
He adds that it was performed eight days together,
but did not prove so beneficial to the undertakers as
the Tempest.

In the year 1677, Charles Davenant, the elder son
of Sir William Davenant,* wrote an opera entitled
Circe, the music to which was composed by Mr.
John Banister ; it was performed at Lincolns-Inn
fields theatre, and was well received.

In 1685, the year in which king Charles II. died,
Mr. Dryden wrote an allegorical drama, or, as he
calls it, an opera, entitled Albion and Albanius ; it
was set to music by Monsieur Louis Grabu, a French
musician, and performed at the theatre in Dorset
Garden : it appears by the preface to have been
written during the life-time of the king, but was not
represented till some months after his decease. As
this opera is printed among the dramatic works of
Mr. Dryden, with a preface, in which the composer
of the music is complimented to the prejudice of
Purcell, and the rest of the English musicians, it
may here suffice to say that it is a satire against
sedition, with a view to the conduct of the earl of
Shaftesbury,† who then, though in a declining state
of health, headed the opposition to the court measures. It abounds with ridiculous pageantry, such
as Juno drawn by peacocks, and the representation
of a rainbow, or some such meteor, which had then
lately been seen in the heavens, and was exhibited
at an expense that far exceeded the amount of the
money taken for admittance. Downes says it was
performed on a very unlucky day, viz., that on which
the duke of Monmouth landed in the west ; and he
intimates that the consternation into which the
kingdom was thrown by this event was a reason

---

why it was performed but six times, and was in
general ill received.‡

After an interval of about five years, Mr. Betterton
made another attempt to introduce the opera on the
English stage. To that end he prevailed on Mr.
Dryden to write King Arthur, which having in it a
great deal of machinery and dancing, and being
finely set to music by Purcell, succeeded very well,
and encouraged him to alter the Prophetess of
Beaumont and Fletcher into the resemblance of an
opera ; and this he did by retrenching some of the
seeming superfluities, and introducing therein musical interludes and songs to a great number, all
which, together with the dances, which were composed by Mr. Priest, were set to music by Purcell,
and was performed with great applause. The same
method was practised with the Midsummer Night's
Dream of Shakespeare, which was altered into a
drama called the Fairy Queen. To this also Mr.
Priest composed the dances, and Purcell the music.

Of these entertainments it is observed that they
were in truth only plays with songs intermixed with
the scenes, and that there could be no pretence for
calling them operas, other than because chorusses and
dances were introduced in them after the manner of
the French.

CHRISTOPHER SIMPSON (*a Portrait*), was a musician
of considerable eminence, and flourished about this
time. He was greatly celebrated for his skill on the
viol, and was the author of two treatises, of which an
account will shortly be given. Of his birth or education we find nothing recorded ; nor are there any
particulars extant of him, save that in his younger

---

* This gentleman was first an actor on the stage in Dorset-Garden,
under his mother Lady D'avenant, Mr. Betterton, and Mr. Harris, and
removed with them to the theatre in Lincoln's-Inn-fields. He afterwards took the degree of Doctor of Laws, and obtained the post in the
Custom-house of inspector general of the exports and imports. He was
extremely well skilled in political arithmetic, and matters relating to the
revenue, and wrote many valuable tracts on those subjects.

† This appears by a device of machinery thus described : ' Fame rises
' out of the middle of the stage, standing on a globe, on which is the
' arms of England: the globe rests on a pedestal: on the front of the
' pedestal is drawn a man with a long, lean, pale face, with fiends' wings,
' and snakes twisted round his body : he is encompassed by several
' phanatical rebellious heads, who suck poison from him, which runs
' out of a tap in his side.'

The wit of this satire at this day stands in some need of an explanation.
The earl of Shaftesbury was afflicted with a dropsy, and had frequent
recourse to the expedient of tapping ; and such was the malevolence of
his enemies, that although they had their choice of numberless particulars by which he might have been distinguished, that of the tap
appeared to them the most eligible. Some time before his death it was
a fashion in taverns to have wine brought to guests, and set upon table
in a wooden or silver vessel shaped like a tun, with a cock to it, and this
was called a Shaftesbury.

---

‡ The following humorous ballad was written in ridicule of this drama,
and in particular of Grabu's music to it :—

From Father Hopkins, whose vein did inspire,
   Bayes sends this raree-show to publick view ;
Prentices, fops, and their footmen admire him,
   Thanks patron, painter, and Monsieur *Grabu*.

Each actor on the stage his luck bewailing,
   Finds that his loss is infallibly true ;
Smith, Nokes, and *Leigh* in a Feaver with railing,
   Curse poet, painter, and Monsieur *Grabu*.

Betterton, Betterton, thy decorations,
   And the machines were well written we knew ;
But all the words were such stuff we want patience,
   And little better is Monsieur *Grabu*.

D— me, says *Underhill,* I'm out of two hundred,
   Hoping that rainbows and peacocks would do ;
Who thought infallible Tom could have blunder'd,
   A plague upon him and Monsieur *Grabu*.

Lane, thou hast no applause for thy capers,
   Tho' all without thee would make a man spew ;
And a month hence will not pay for the tapers,
   Spite of Jack Laureat and Monsieur *Grabu*.

Bayes, thou wouldst have thy skill thought universal,
   Tho' thy dull ear be to musick untrue ;
Then whilst we strive to confute the Rehearsal,
   Prithee learn thrashing of Monsieur *Grabu*.

With thy dull prefaces still wouldst thou treat us,
   Striving to make thy dull bauble look fair ;
So the horn'd herd of the city do cheat us,
   Still most commending the worst of their ware.

Leave making operas and writing Lyricks,
   'Till thou hast ears and canst alter thy strain ;
Stick to thy talent of bold Panegyricks,
   And still remember the breathing the vein.

Yet if thou thinkest the town will extol 'em,
   Print thy dull notes, but be thrifty and wise ;
Instead of angels subscrib'd for the volume,
   Take a round shilling, and thank my advice.

In imitating thee this may be charming,
   Gleaning from Laureats is no shame at all ;
And let this song be sung next performing,
   Else ten to one but the prices will fall.

days he was a soldier in the army raised by William Cavendish, duke of Newcastle, for the service of Charles I. against the parliament; that he was of the Romish communion, and patronised by Sir Robert Bolles, of Leicestershire, whose son, a student in Gray's Inn, Simpson taught on the viol. He dwelt some years in Turnstile, Holborn, and finished his life there. In the year 1665, Simpson published in a thin folio volume a book entitled Chelys Minuritionum; in English, the Division Viol, printed in columns, viz. in Latin, with an English translation; Editio secunda, dedicated to Sir John Bolles, son and heir of Sir Robert Bolles above mentioned.

In the dedication of this second edition, the author, among the reasons which he gives for recommending the former edition to the patronage of this young gentleman's father, represents his circumstances in these terms:—' All the motives that could enter into ' a dedication of that nature did oblige me to it. ' First, as he was a most eminent patron of music and ' musicians; secondly, as he was not only a lover of ' music, but a great performer in it, and that the ' treatise had its conception, birth, and accomplish- 'ment under his roof in your minority; lastly, as he ' was my peculiar patron, affording me a cheerful ' maintenance, when the iniquity of the times had ' reduced me, with many others in that common ca- ' lamity, to a condition of needing it.'* In the same epistle dedicatory he scruples not to say of this young gentleman, Sir John Bolles, that the book recommended to his patronage, as it was written for his instruction, so had it made him not only the greatest artist, but the ablest judge of the contents of it of any person in Europe, being a gentleman, and no professor of the science; and in support of this assertion he refers to a paper of verses printed at Rome, occasioned as he says by the rare expressions on the viol of this his pupil and patron at a music meeting, in which were present ' not only divers grandees of ' that court and city, with some embassadors of ' foreign states, but also the great musicians of Rome, ' all admiring his knowledge of music, and his excel- ' lence upon that instrument.'†

* It should seem by this that Simpson had been of some choir, and that at the usurpation he was turned out of his place, for that was the common calamity which befel the musicians of that time.

† The verses above mentioned are these that follow:—

Eximiæ Nobilitati, Doctrinæ, Virtuti, cum summa Musices harmonia consono adolescenti, illustrissimo Domino, D Joanni Bolles, Anglo, Roberti Baronet. Hæredi Filio. Mirificam suavitatem ejusdem et argutiam in tangenda Britannica Chely, quam vulgò dicunt Violam Majorem stupori Romæ fuisse.

ODE.
Jacobi Albani Ghibbesii, Med. Doct. ac in Romana Sapientia Eloq. Prof. Primarii.

Res suas dicam sibi habere Phœbo,
Te modis aures retinente nostras:
Quale solamen Samius negârit
Doctor Olympo.

Quantus Alcides animos triumphas,
Gallico major! trahat ille vulgus:
Roma Te vidit stupefacta primos
Ducere patres:

Roma tormentum fidium insecuta
Dulce, concentus licèt ipsa mater.
Allobrox miræ Venetusque plausit
Nuntius arti.

Vividum claro, celebrémque alumno
Laudo Simpsonum: vaga fama quantum
Thessali cultu juvenis magistrum
Distulit orbi.

The epistle containing this remarkable anecdote concludes with an intimation, somewhat obscurely worded, that the Latin translation of the book was made by Mr. William Marsh, some time a scholar of the author, for the purpose of making it intelligible to foreigners.

The book has the like imprimatur with others published about that time; but the licenser, Sir Roger L'Estrange, has superadded to his allowance a preface recommending it in terms that import much more than a compliment to his friend the author, as Sir Roger was a very fine performer on the instrument which is the subject of it.

As to the book itself, the design of it is to render familiar a practice which the performers on the Viol da Gamba, about the time of its publication, were emulous to excel in, namely, the making extemporary divisions on a ground-bass; but as this was not to be done at random, and required some previous skill in the principles of harmony, the author undertakes to unfold them in his treatise.

It is divided into three parts: the first contains instructions at large for the performance on the instrument; the second teaches the use of the concords and discords, and is in truth a compendium of descant; the third part contains the method of ordering division to a ground, a practice which the author thus explains:—

' Diminution or division to a ground, is the break- 'ing either of the bass or of any higher part that ' is applicable thereto. The manner of expressing it ' is thus:—

' A ground, subject, or bass, call it what you ' please, is prick'd down in two several papers; one ' for him who is to play the ground upon an organ, ' harpsichord, or what other instrument may be apt ' for that purpose; the other for him that plays upon ' the viol, who having the said ground before his ' eyes as his theme or subject, plays such variety of ' descant or division in concordance thereto as his ' skill and present invention do then suggest unto ' him. In this manner of play, which is the perfec- 'tion of the viol or any other instrument, if it be ' exactly performed, a man may show the excellency ' both of his hand and invention, to the delight and ' admiration of those that hear him.

' But this you will say is a perfection that few ' attain unto, depending much upon the quickness of ' invention as well as quickness of hand. I answer ' it is a perfection which some excellent hands ' have not attained unto, as wanting those helps ' which should lead them to it; the supply of which ' want is the business we here endeavour.'

Hactenùs plectrum, citharamque vates
Noverint; Arcu Violaque freti
Concinent posthac: nequè Thressa certet
Chorda Britannæ.

O virûm felix, et opima rerum
Albion, sedes placitura Musis!
O poli sidus mihi, quò remotam
Dirigo puppim!

à Museo nostro, Kal. April 1661. Monumentum, et pignus amoris.

Of this Dr. Gibbes there is an account in the Fasti Oxon. vol. II, col 192, by which it appears that he was born of English parents at Roan in Normandy; that he became poet laureat to the emperor Leopold, and was by diploma declared doctor in physic of the university of Oxford. He died anno 1676, and was buried in the Pantheon at Rome.

CHRISTOPHORI SIMPSON EFFIGIES.

MDCLXVII.

After giving sundry examples of grounds, with the method of breaking or dividing them, the author proceeds to treat of descant division, which he thus defines :—

'Descant division is that which makes a different 'concording part unto the ground. It differs from 'the former in these particulars : That breaks the 'notes of the ground; This descants upon them : 'That takes the liberty to wander sometimes be-'neath the ground; This, as in its proper sphere, 'moves still above it; That meets every succeeding 'note of the ground in the unison or octave ; This in 'any of the concords. But in the main business of 'division they are much the same; for all division, 'whether descant or breaking the bass, is but a 'transition from note to note, or from one concord 'to another, either by degrees or leaps, with an ad-'mixture of such discords as are allowed in com-'position.'

However difficult the practice may seem of making a division extempore upon a given ground, preserving the melody without transgressing the rules of harmony, this author speaks of two viols playing together in division, and for this exercise he gives the following rules :—

'First let the ground be prick'd down in three 'several papers, one for him who plays upon the 'organ or harpsichord, the other two for them 'that play upon the two viols ; which for order and 'brevity we will distinguish by three letters, viz., A 'for organist, B for the first bass, and C for the 'second.

'Each of these having the same ground before 'him, they may all three begin together, A and B 'playing the ground, and C descanting to it in slow 'notes, or such as may suit the beginning of the 'musick. This done, let C play the ground, and B 'descant to it, as the other had done before, but with 'some little variation. If the ground consists of two 'strains, the like may be done in the second ; one 'viol still playing the ground, whilest the other 'descants or divides upon it.

'The ground thus play'd over, C may begin 'again, and play a strain of quicker division ; which 'ended, let B answer the same with another, some-'thing like it but of a little more lofty ayre ; for the 'better performance whereof, if there be any dif-'ference in the hands or inventions, I would have the 'better invention lead, but the more able hand still 'follow, that the musick may not seem to flaccess or 'lessen, but rather increase in the performance.

'When the viols have thus, as it were vied and 'revied one to the other, A, if he have the ability 'of hand, may, upon a sign given him, put in his 'strain of division ; the two viols playing one of 'them the ground, and the other slow descant to it ; 'A, having finished his strain, a reply thereto may 'be made, first by one viol and then by the other.

'Having answered one another in that same man-'ner so long as they think fit, the two viols may 'divide a strain both together. In which doing, let 'B break the ground, by moving into the octave up-'ward or downward, and returning from thence 'either to his own note, or to meet the next note in 'the unison or octave ; by this means C knowing B's 'motion, he knows also to avoid running into the 'same, and therefore will move into the third or fifth, 'or sixth where it is required, meeting each succeed-'ing note in some one of the said concords, until he 'come to the close : where he may, after he has divi-'ded the binding, meet the close note in the octave ; 'which directions well observed, two viols may move 'in extemporary division a whole strain together, 'without any remarkable clashing in the consecution 'of fifths or eighths.

'When they have proceeded thus far, C may begin 'some point of division, of the length of a breve or 'semibreve, naming the same word, that B may know 'his intentions ; which ended, let B answer the same 'upon the succeeding note or notes, to the like quan-'tity of time ; taking it in that manner one after 'another, so long as they please. This done they 'may betake themselves to some other point, a new 'variety.

'This contest in breves, semibreves, or minims, 'being ended, they may give the signe to A, if as I 'said he have the ability of hand, that he may begin 'his point, as they had done one to another, which 'point may be answered by the viols, either singly or 'jointly ; if jointly it must be done according to the 'former instructions of dividing together, playing 'still slow notes, and soft whilest the organist di-'vides ; for that part which divides should always be 'heard lowdest.

'When this is done both viols may play another 'strain together, either in quick or slow notes, which 'they please ; and if the music be not yet spun out to a 'sufficient length, they may begin to play triplas 'and proportions answering each other, in whole 'strains or parcels, and after that join together in a 'thundering strain of quick division, with which they 'may conclude ; or else with a strain of slow and 'sweet notes, according as may best sute the circum-'stance of time and place.' *

To illustrate the practice which it is the design of the book to recommend, Simpson has inserted, by way of appendix to it, sundry grounds with divi-sions on them, composed by himself, and among others the following :—

* The practice of extemporary descant, either by the voice or with an instrument, is now unknown in music. Of vocal descant Morley has given his sentiments at large in the following words :—
'Singing extempore upon a plainsong is indeede a peece of cunning, 'and very necessarie to be perfectly practised of him who meaneth to be 'a composer, for bringing of a quick sight ; yet it is a great absurditie so 'to seeke for a sight, as to make it the end of our studie, applying it to 'no other use ; for as a knife or other instrument not being applied to 'the end for which it was devised (as to cut) is unprofitable, and of no 'use ; even so is descant, which being used as a helpe to bring readie 'sight in setting of parts, is profitable ; but not being applied to that 'ende, is of itselfe like a puffe of wind, which being past cometh not 'againe, which hath beene the reason that the excellent musitians have 'discontinued it, although it be unprofitable to compose without it, but 'they rather employ their time in making of songes, which remain for 'the posterity then to sing descant, which is no longer known then the 'singer's mouth is open expressing it, and for the most part cannot be 'twise repeated in one manner.' Introduction to Practical Music, page 121.
The same reflections must arise upon the practice of extemporary descant by instruments. As to the descant of viols, we know no more of it than is contained in this elaborate treatise ; and for aught that appears to the contrary, it began and ended with this author.

DIVISION ON A GROUND.

CHRISTOPHER SIMPSON.

In 1667 Simpson published A Compendium of practical Musick, in 5 parts, containing 1. The rudiments of Song. 2. The principles of composition. 3. The use of discord. 4. The form of figurate Descant. 5. The contrivance of Canon.

This book is dedicated to William Duke of Newcastle, the author of the celebrated treatise on Horsemanship, who was also a great lover of music, and is strongly recommended by two prefatory epistles, the one of Mathew Lock, and the other by John Jenkins.

The first part contains little more than is to be found in every book that professes to teach the precepts of singing.

The second teaches the principles of composition, and treats of Counterpoint, Intervals, and Concords, with their use and application; of the key or tone, and of the closes or cadences belonging to the key. By the directions here given it appears, as indeed it does in those of Dr. Campion, that the ancient practice in the composition of music in parts was to frame the bass part first.

He begins his rules for composition with directions how to frame a bass, and how to join a treble to a bass, after which he proceeds to composition of three parts, concerning which his directions are as follow:—

'First, you are to set the notes of this part in 'concords different from those of the treble. 2. 'When the treble is a 5th to the bass, I would have 'you make use either of a 3d. or an 8th for the other 'part; and not to use a 6th therewith, untill I have 'shewed you how, and where a 5th and a 6th may 'be joyned together. 3. You are to avoid 8ths in 'this inner part likewise, so much as you can with 'convenience. For though we use 5ths as much as 'imperfects, yet we seldom make use of 8ths in three 'parts. The reason why we avoid 8ths in two or 'three parts is, that imperfect concords afford more 'variety upon accompt of their majors and minors: 'besides imperfects do not cloy the ear so much as 'perfects do.

'Composition of four parts. If you design your 'composition for four parts, I would then have you 'join your Altus as near as you can to the treble; 'which is easily done by taking those concords note 'after note which are next under the treble, in 'manner as follows.

'Make the altus and the treble end in the same

'tune; which in my opinion is better than to have
'the treble end in the sharp 3d. above; the key of
'the composition being flat, and the sharp third more
'proper for an inner part at conclusion.'

For the adding a fourth part, viz. a tenor, he
gives the following rules: 'First, that this part
'which is to be added be set in concords, different
'from the other two upper parts; that is to say, if
'those be a 5th and 3d, let this be an 8th; by which
'you may conceive the rest.

'Secondly, I would have you join this tenor as
'near the Altus as the different concords do permit;
'for the harmony is better when the three upper
'parts are joined close together.

'Thirdly, you are to avoid two 8ths or two 5ths
'rising or falling together, as well amongst the
'upper parts, as betwixt any one part and the bass;
'of which there is less danger by placing the parts
'in different concords.'

From hence the author proceeds to compositions
in five, six, seven and eight parts, and to compositions for two choirs each.

The third part of the book teaches the use of
the discords, and shows the nature of Syncopation,
and relation inharmonical. Here he takes notice of
the three scales of music, the diatonic, the chromatic,
and the enharmonic, of which he gives a concise
but clear definition.

He inclines to the opinion that the modern scale,
in which the octave is divided into twelve semitones,
is in fact a commixture of the diatonic and the chromatic, touching which he delivers these his sentiments :—

' Now as to my opinion concerning our common
'scale of musick, taking it with its commixture of
'the chromatick, I think it lies not in the wit of man
'to frame a better as to all intents and purposes for
'practical musick. And as for those little dissonances,
'for so I call them for want of a better word to ex-
'press them, the fault is not in the scale, whose
'office and design is no more than to denote the dis-
'tances of the concords and discords, according to
'the lines and spaces of which it doth consist, and
'to show by what degree of tones and semitones a
'voice may rise or fall :

'For in vocal musick those dissonances are not
'perceived, neither do they occur in instruments
'which have no frets, as violins and wind instru-
'ments, where the sound is modulated by the touch
'of the finger; but in such only as have fixed stops
'or frets, which being placed and fitted for the
'most usual keyes in the scale, seem out of order
'when we change to keys less usual; and that as I
'said doth happen by reason of the inequality of
'tones and semitones, especially of the latter.'

The fourth part teaches the form of figurate descant, and treats first, in a very concise but perspicuous manner, of the ancient modes or tones. In
his directions for figurate descant the author shews
how they are made to pass through each other, and
speaks of the consecution of fourths and fifths, thirds
and sixths. He next explains the nature of fugue
in general, and gives directions for constructing a
fugue per arsin et thesin, and also of a double fugue.

He next treats of music composed for voices;
upon which he observes that it is to be preferred to
that of instruments, and for this opinion refers to
the testimony of Des Cartes, who in the beginning
of his Compendium asserts that, of all sounds, that of
the human voice is the most grateful.

Of the different kinds of vocal music in use in his
time he thus speaks :—

' Of vocal music made for the solace and civil de-
'light of man, there are many different kinds, as
'namely, Madrigals, in which fugues and all other
'flowers of figurate musick are most frequent.

'Of these you may see many sets of 3, 4, 5, and
'6 parts, published both by English and Italian
'authors. Next the dramatic or recitative musick,
'which as yet is something a stranger to us here in
'England. Then Cansonets, Vilanellas, Airs of all
'sorts, or what else poetry hath contrived to be set
'and sung in musick. Lastly Canons and Catches,
'which are commonly set to words; the first to such
'as be grave and serious, the latter to words designed
'for mirth and recreation.'

For accommodating notes to words he gives the
following rules :—

' When you compose musick to words, your chief
'endeavour must be that your notes do aptly ex-
'press the sense and humour of them. If they be
'grave and serious, let your musick be such also :
'if light, pleasant, or lively, your musick likewise
'must be suitable to them. Any passion of love,
'sorrow, anguish, or the like is aptly expressed by
'chromatick notes and bindings. Anger, courage,
'revenge, &c. require a more strenuous and stirring
'movement. Cruel, bitter, harsh, may be expressed
'with a discord; which nevertheless must be brought
'off according to the rules of composition. High,
'above, heaven, ascend; as likewise their contraries,
'low, deep, down, hell, descend, may be expressed
'by the example of the hand, which points upward
'when we speak of the one, and downward when we
'mention the other; the contrary to which would be
'absurd. You must also have respect to the points
'of your ditty, not using any remarkable pause or
'rest, untill the words come to a full point or pe-
'riod : Neither may any rest, how short soever, be
'interposed in the middle of a word; but a sigh or
'sob is properly imitated by a crochet or quaver
'rest.

' Lastly you ought not to apply several notes, nor
'indeed any long note, to a short syllable, nor a
'short note to a syllable that is long. Neither do I
'fancy the setting of many notes to any one syllable,
'though much in fashion in former times, but I would
'have your musick to be such, that the words may
'be plainly understood.'

He next speaks of music designed for instruments;
and this he says abounds no less than vocal music
with points, fugues, and all other figures of descant.
He describes the several kinds of instrumental music
in use at the time of writing his book, in these
words :—

' Of this kind the chief and most excellent for art
'and contrivance, are fancies of 6, 5, 4, and 3 parts
'intended commonly for viols. In this sort of

'musick the composer, being not limited to words,
'doth employ all his art and invention solely about
'the bringing in, and carrying on of these fugues.

'When he has tried all the several ways which he
'thinks fit to be used therein, he takes some other
'point and does the like with it; or else for variety
'introduces some chromatick notes with bindings
'and intermixtures of discords; or falls into some
'lighter humour, like a madrigal, or what else his
'fancy shall lead him to: but still concluding with
'something that hath art and excellency in it.

'Of this sort you may see many compositions
'made heretofore in England by Alfonso Ferabosco,
'Coperario, Lupo, White, Ward, Mico, Dr. Colman,
'and many more now deceased. Also by Mr.
'Jenkins, Mr. Lock, and divers other excellent men,
'doctors and bachelors in musick yet living.

'This kind of musick, the more is the pity, is now
'much neglected, by reason of the scarcity of audi-
'tors that understand it: their ears being better
'acquainted and more delighted with light and airy
'music.

'The next in dignity after a fancy is a Pavan,
'which some derive from Padua in Italy; at first
'ordained for a grave and stately manner of dancing,
'as most instrumental musicks were in their several
'kinds, fancies and symphonies excepted, but now
'grown up to a height of composition made only to
'delight the ear.

'A Pavan, be it of 2, 3, 4, 5, or 6 parts, doth
'commonly consist of three strains, each strain being
'played twice over. Now as to any peice of music
'that consists of strains take these following obser-
'vations.

'All musick concludes in the key of his compo-
'sition, which is known by the bass, as hath been
'shown; this key hath always other keys proper to
'it for middle closes. If your Pavan or what else,
'be of three straines, the first strain may end in the
'key of the composition as the last doth; but the
'middle strain must always end in the key of a
'middle close.

'Sometimes the first strain does end in a middle
'close, and then the middle strain must end in some
'other middle close; for two strains following imme-
'diately one another, ought not to end in the same
'key. Therefore when there are but two strains let
'the first end in a middle close, that both strains
'may not end alike.'

The fifth and last part is on the subject of Canon,
a species of composition in which the author says
divers of our countrymen have been excellent; and
here he takes notice of Mr. Elway Bevin, who he says
professes fair in the title-page of his book, and gives
us many examples of excellent and intricate canons
of divers sorts, but not one word of instruction how
to make such like.

He then proceeds to explain the method of composing canon in two or three parts, as also canon in
the unison; syncopated or driving canon; canon a
note higher or lower; canon rising or falling a note
each repetition; retrogade canon, or canon recte et
retro; double descant, in which the parts are so
contrived that the treble may be the bass, and the
bass the treble: and canon on a given plain song,
with examples of each.

Lastly, he gives directions for the composition
of Catch or Round, by some called Canon in the
Unison.

Simpson was also the author of Annotations on
Dr. Campion's little tract on Composition, mentioned
page 560 of this work, and which is reprinted in
some of the earlier editions of Playford's Introduction, particularly that of 1660, but omitted in
the latter ones, to make room for a tract entitled
'An Introduction to the Art of Descant,' probably
written by Playford himself, but augmented by
Purcell.

CHAP. CL.

EDMUND CHILMEAD, an excellent Greek and Latin
scholar, and mathematician, was also well skilled in
the theory and practice of music, and was the author
of a tract entitled 'De Musicâ antiquâ Græcâ,'
printed in 1672, at the end of the Oxford edition of
Aratus, as also of annotations on three Odes of
Dionysius, there also published,[*] with the ancient
Greek musical characters.

This person was born at Stow in the Wold in
Gloucestershire, and became one of the clerks of
Magdalen college. About the year 1632 he was
one of the petty canons or chaplains of Christ Church;
but being ejected by the Parliament visitors in 1648,
he came to London, and, being in great necessity,
took lodgings in the house of that Thomas Este, a
musician, and also a printer of music, of whom
mention is made in a preceding part of this work;
this man dwelt at the sign of the Black Horse in
Aldersgate-street, and having in his house a large
room, Chilmead made use of it for a weekly music
meeting, deriving from the profits thereof the means
of a slender subsistence.

Being an excellent Greek scholar, Chilmead was
employed to draw up the Catalogus Manuscriptorum
Græcorum in Bibliotheca Bodleiana. In the catalogue
which Wood gives of his works, he mentions a
treatise 'De Sonis,' which does not appear to have
ever been published. The rest of his works seem
to have been chiefly translations, amongst which is
that well-known book of Jacques Gaffarel, entitled
'Curiosités inovies sur la Sculpture Talismanique
'des Persans,' and in the translation 'Unheard of
'Curiosities,' &c. He died in the year 1653, in the
forty-third year of his age, having for some years
received relief in his necessities from Edward Byshe,
Esq. Garter King at Arms, and Sir Henry Holbrook,
knight, the translator of Procopius. He was interred
in the church of St. Botolph without Aldersgate,
but no inscription to his memory is there to be
found.[†]

Together with the Oxford edition of Aratus is
published the ΚΑΤΑΣΤΕΡΙΣΜΟΙ of Eratosthenes,
whose division of the genera is to be seen among

* See page 32, in a note.
† Vide Athen. Oxon. vol. I. col. 169.

CHRISTOPHER GIBBONS

MUS . DOCT . OXON . MDCLXIV .

From an original Painting in the Music-School, Oxford .

WILLIAM CHILD

MUS. DOCT. OXON. MDCLXIII.

From an original Painting in the Music-School Oxford

others of the ancient Greek writers in the Harmonics of Ptolemy.

The editor of this book, seeming to consider it as a fragment necessary to be preserved, has given from Ptolemy this division; and, to render it in some degree intelligible, annexes three odes of Dionysius, which Dr. Bernard, a fellow of St. John's college, had found in Ireland among the papers of Archbishop Usher, with the annotations of Chilmead thereon; as also a short treatise, ' De Musicâ antiquâ Græcâ,' by the same person. This tract contains a designation of the ancient genera agreeable to the sentiments of Boetius, with a general enumeration of the modes; after which follow the odes, with the Greek musical characters, which Chilmead has rendered in the notes of Guido's scale; and at the end of the book is inserted a fragment of an ode of Pindar, with the ancient musical characters and modern notes, found by Kircher in the library of the monastery of St. Salvator in Sicily, and inserted in the Musurgia, and also in a preceding part of this work.*

WILLIAM TUCKER was a gentleman of the chapel royal in the reign of king Charles II. and junior priest there at the time of the coronation, and also a minor canon in the collegiate church of St. Peter at Westminster. He was a good church musician, and composed sundry anthems, the most celebrated whereof are ' Praise the Lord O ye servants,' ' This ' is the day that the Lord hath made,' and ' Unto ' thee O Lord.' He died on the twenty-eighth day of February, 1678, and was succeeded in his place by the Rev. John Gostling, A. M. from Canterbury.

WILLIAM GREGORY, also a gentleman of the chapel royal in the same reign, was a composer of anthems, of which those of best note are ' Out of the deep ' have I called,' and ' O Lord thou hast cast us out.' In the music-school Oxon. is a portrait of him.

CHRISTOPHER GIBBONS, (a Portrait), the son of the celebrated Dr. Orlando Gibbons, was bred up from a child to music, under his uncle Ellis Gibbons, organist of Bristol; he had been favoured by Charles I. and was of his chapel. At the restoration he was appointed principal organist of the king's chapel, organist in private to his majesty, and organist of Westminster-abbey. In the year 1664 he was licensed to proceed Doctor in music of the university of Oxford in virtue of a letter from the king in his behalf, in which is a recital of his merits in these words, ' the bearer Christopher Gibbons, one of our ' organists of our chappell royal, hath from his youth ' served our royal father and ourself, and hath so ' well improved himself in music, as well in our ' judgment, as in the judgment of all men skilled in ' that science, as that he may worthily receive the ' honour and degree of doctor therein.' He completed his degree in an act celebrated in the church of St. Mary at Oxford on the eleventh day of July in the year above-mentioned.†

Dr. Christopher Gibbons was, as Dr. Tudway

* It is there said that the Oxford edition of Aratus was published by Chilmead, but upon better information it is conjectured that Dr. Aldrich was the editor of it.

† Fasti Oxon. vol. II. col. 158.

asserts, more celebrated for his skill and performance on the organ than for his compositions; nevertheless there are many anthems of his extant, though we know of none that have ever been printed. Those of most note are ' God be merciful unto us,' ' Help ' me O Lord,' ' Lord I am not high-minded,' and ' Teach me O Lord.' It is said that he had a principal hand in a book entitled ' Cantica Sacra,' containing Hymns and Anthems for two voices to the organ, both Latin and English. Lond. 1674, fol. He died in the parish of St. Margaret, Westminster, on the twentieth day of October, anno 1676.‡

ALBERTUS BRYNE was a scholar of John Tomkins, and his successor as organist of St. Paul's cathedral, being appointed to that office immediately upon the restoration. He was an eminent church-musician, and a composer of services and anthems, and as such his name occurs in Clifford's Collection. He died in the reign of Charles II. and was buried in the cloister of Westminster Abbey, but there is no inscription to be found there to ascertain precisely the time of his death, or the place of his interment.

WILLIAM CHILD, (a Portrait), a native of Bristol, was educated in music under Elway Bevin, organist of the cathedral of that city. In the year 1631, being then of Christ Church college Oxford, he took his degree of bachelor in that university; and in 1636 was appointed one of the organists of the chapel of St. George at Windsor, in the room of Dr. John Mundy, and soon after one of the organists of the royal chapel at Whitehall. After the restoration he was appointed to the office of chanter of the king's chapel, and became of the private music to Charles II. In 1663 he obtained licence to proceed Doctor in his faculty, and on the thirteenth day of July in the same year completed his degree at an act celebrated in St. Mary's church, Oxon. Dr. Child died in the year 1696, having attained the age of ninety years, and was succeeded in his place of organist of the king's chapel by Mr. Francis Piggot.

His works are ' Psalms of three voices, &c. with ' a continual bass either for the Organ or Theorbo, ' composed after the Italian way,' Lond. 1639. Catches and Canons, published in Hilton's collection entitled ' Catch that Catch can.' Divine Anthems and compositions to several pieces of poetry, some of which were written by Dr. Thomas Pierce of Oxford. Some compositions of two parts, printed in a book entitled ' Court Ayres,' mentioned in a preceding page. The engraving is taken from a whole length picture of him now in the music-school Oxon. (See Portrait volume).

‡ Wood says that Dr. Christopher Gibbons was master of the singing-boys belonging to Charles the Second's chapel; but in this he seems to be mistaken. By the Cheque-book it appears that Capt. Cook, who had been appointed to that office at the restoration, died in 1672, and that he was succeeded in it by Humphrey. It farther appears by a subsequent entry in the same book, that Humphrey died in July 1674, and that in his place as master of the children came Mr. John Blow. Gibbons died in 1676, and it is well known that Blow held the place till the time of his death, which was in 1708. Farther, the entry of Gibbons's death in the Cheque-book, styles him only organist of the chapel, from all which it must be concluded that Gibbons was never master of the children. The only remaining difficulty arises from the inscription on Dr. Blow's monument, in which it is said that he was a scholar of Dr. Christopher Gibbons. This assertion may either be founded on the mistaken authority of Wood, or it may mean that he was taught the principles of music at large, or the practice of the organ by Dr. Gibbons.

He composed many services and anthems, none of which appear to have been printed, except his service in E with the lesser third, and that famous one in D with the greater third, and three fine anthems; and those only in Dr. Boyce's Cathedral Music. His style was in general so remarkably natural and familiar that it sometimes gave offence to those whose duty it was to sing his compositions. Being at Windsor, he called the choir to a practice of a service that he had newly composed, which the choirmen found so easy in the performance, that they made a jest of it. This fact is said to have occasioned his composing his famous service in D♯, which in some parts of it is remarkably intricate and difficult,* but upon the whole is delightfully fine. Playford, in the preface to his Introduction, edit. 1683, says that king Charles I. often appointed the service and anthems himself, especially that sharp service composed by Dr. William Child.

The memory of Dr. Child is celebrated for an act of beneficence that was hardly to be expected from one in his station of life: it seems that he was so ill paid for his services at Windsor, that a long arrear of his salary had incurred, which he could not get discharged: after many fruitless applications to the dean and chapter, he told them that if they would pay him the sum in arrear he would new pave the choir of their chapel for them: they paid him his money, and the doctor performed his promise; neither they, nor the knights companions of the most noble order of the garter interposing to prevent it, or signifying the least inclination to share with a servant and dependant of theirs in the honour of so munificent an act.

He lies interred in the chapel of St. George at Windsor: the following is the inscription on his gravestone:—

' Here lies the body of William Child, doctor in music,
' and one of the organists of the chapel royal at White-
' hall, and of his majesty's free chapel at Windsor 65
' years. He was born in Bristol, and died here the 23d
' of March 1696-7 in the 91st year of his age. He paved
'.the body of the choir.

' Go, happy soul, and in the seats above
' Sing endless hymns of thy great Maker's love.
' How fit in heavenly songs to bear thy part,
' Before well practic'd in the sacred art;
' Whilst hearing us, sometimes the choire divine,
' Will sure descend, and in our consort join;
' So much the music, thou to us hast given,
' Has made our earth to represent their heaven.'

He gave twenty pounds towards building the town-hall at Windsor, and fifty pounds to the corporation, to be disposed of in charitable uses at their discretion.

JOHN BANISTER was the son of one of that low class of musicians called the Waits, of the parish of St. Giles near London; but having been taught by his father the rudiments of music, he became in a short time such a proficient on the violin, that by king Charles II. he was sent to France for im-

provement, and upon his return was made one of his band; but having taken occasion to tell the king that the English performers on that instrument were superior to those of France, he was dismissed from his service. He set to music the opera of Circe, written by Dr. Davenant, and performed in the year 1676, at the theatre in Dorset Garden; as also sundry songs printed in the collections of his time. He died on the third day of October, 1679, and lies buried in the cloister of Westminster Abbey, as appears by an inscription on a marble stone in the wall of the west ambulatory thereof, yet remaining legible. He left a son of both his names, a fine performer on the violin, of whom an account will be given hereafter.

MATTHEW LOCK (a Portrait), was originally a chorister in the cathedral church of Exeter, while William Wake was organist there: he was afterwards a scholar of Edward Gibbons, and became so eminent that he was employed to compose the music for the public entry of King Charles II. Although bred in a cathedral, he seems to have affected the style of the theatre, and to have taken up dramatic music where Henry Lawes left it. Downes says he composed the music to the tragedy of Macbeth, as altered by Sir William Davenant. Nevertheless, there are extant of his many compositions that are evidence of his great skill and ingenuity in the church style, as, namely, two anthems, 'Not unto us, O Lord,' and 'Turn thy face from my sins;' and one for five voices, in Dr. Boyce's collection, 'Lord, let me know my end.' He appears to have been a man of a querulous disposition, and therefore it is not to be wondered at that he had enemies. Being composer in ordinary to the king, he composed for the chapel a morning service, in which the prayer after each of the ten commandments had a different setting; this was deemed an inexcusable innovation, and on the first day of April, 1666, at the performance of it before the king, the service met with some obstruction, most probably from the singers.

The censures which this small deviation from the ancient practice had drawn on him, and the disgrace he had suffered in the attempt to gratify the royal ear with a composition that must have cost him some study, reduced Lock to the necessity of publishing the whole service; and it came abroad in score, printed on a single sheet, with the following vindication of it and its author by way of preface:—

' Modern Church Musick pre-accused, censured,
' and obstructed in its performance before his
' majesty, April 1, 1666. Vindicated by the
' author, Matt. Lock, composer in ordinary to
' his majesty.

' He is a slender observer of humane action, who
' finds not pride generally accompanied with igno-
' rance and malice, what habit soever it wares. In
' my case zeal was its vizor, and innovation the
' crime. The fact, changing the custome of the
' church, by varying that which was ever sung in
' one tune, and occasioning confusion in the service
' by its ill performance. As to the latter part of the
' charge, I must confess I have been none of the

* Dr. Tudway says that from this circumstance it was in his time questioned whether Dr. Child was really the author of it; but this doubt has long subsided.

J. Caldwall sculp.

MATTHEW LOCK,

COMPOSER IN ORDINARY TO HIS MAJESTY

CHA. II.

From a Picture in the Music School Oxford.

fortunatest that way; but whether upon design or 'ignorance of some of the performers it so happen'd, 'I shall neither examine nor judge, (they are of age 'to understand the value of their own reputation, 'and whom they serve): nor is it my business to 'find eyes, ears, or honesty to any, or answer for 'other men's faults: but, that such defects should 'take their rise from the difficulty or novelty of the 'composition, I utterly deny; the whole, being a 'kind of counterpoint, and no one change, from the 'beginning to the end, but what naturally flows 'from, and returns to its proper center, the Kay. 'And for the former, the contrary is so notoriously 'manifest, that all relating to the church know that 'that part of the liturgy assigned for musick, was 'never but variously compos'd by all that under- 'took it: witness the excellent compositions of Mr. 'Tallis, Byrd, Gibbons, (and other their and our co- 'temporaries) on the Te Deum, Commandments, 'Preces, Psalms Magnificat, &c. in use to this day, 'both in his majesties chappel, and the cathedralls in 'this nation. And to speak rationally, should it be 'otherwise, art would be no more art, composers 'useless, and science pinion'd for destruction. If 'therefore, in imitation of them, I have according 'to art, and the nature of the words, contrived and 'varied this little composition; and, as to the true 'manner of speaking, conducted it in the mid-way 'between the two extremes of gravity and levity; 'I hope I may without ostentation affirm myself 'guiltless, and return the crime from whence it 'came: Æsop's maunger. And here might I fairly 'take notice of a thing lately crawl'd into the world, 'under the notion of composition, which in the 'height of its performance is both out of time, out 'of tune, and yet all to the same tune, had I the 'itch of retaliation; but since the accuser has been 'pleased to passe a publick censure on the tender of 'my duty, I shall only at present take the freedom '(though it was never intended for a publick view) 'in this manner to expose it; that all capable of 'judging, may see, there's neither heresie, nor schism, 'nor any thing of difficulty as to performance either 'in the matter or form of it. In fine, this vindica- 'tion offers at no more, than denying those to be 'judges in science, who are ignorant of its principles.'

The singularity of this service consisted in this, that whereas it had been the practice to make the Preces to all the commandments except the last, in the same notes, here they are all different; in other respects there is nothing singular in the composition: it is in the key of F, with the major third, and all counterpoint, except the Nicene Creed, which is what the musicians term Canto figurato.

About the year 1672 Lock became engaged in a controversy with one Thomas Salmon, the occasion of which was as follows: this man was a master of arts of Trinity college, Oxford, and at length rector of Mepsall in Bedfordshire, and had written a book entitled 'An essay to the advancement of music, by 'casting away the perplexity of different cliffs, and 'uniting all sorts of music, lute, viol, violins, organ, 'harpsichord, voice, &c. in one universal character:'

in which he substitutes in the place of the usual cliffs, the letters B for the bass, M for the mean or middle part, and Tr. for the treble, proposing thereby to facilitate the practice both of vocal and instrumental music.

This in a general view of it is the design of the book, but with the help of an abridgment of it, by one who seems to have taken great pains to under- stand the design of the author, we are enabled to give a summary of his proposal in the following few lines:—

'Mr. Salmon reflecting on the inconveniences 'attending the use of the cliffs, and also how useful 'it would be that all music should be reduced to one 'constant cliff, whereby the same writing of any 'piece of musick would equally serve to direct the 'voice and all instruments; a thing one should 'think to be of very great use: he proposes in his 'Essay to the Advancement of Musick, what he calls 'an universal character, which I shall explain in a 'few words. In the first place he would have the 'lowest line of every particular system constantly 'called g, and the other lines and spaces to be 'named according to the order of the seven letters; 'and because these positions of the letters are 'supposed invariable, therefore he thinks there is 'no need to mark any of them; but then, secondly, 'that the relations of several parts of a composition 'may be distinctly known, he marks the treble with 'the letter T at the beginning of the system, the 'mean with M, and the bass with B; and the gs 'that are on the lowest line of each of these systems, 'he supposes to be octaves to each other in order. 'And then for referring these systems to their 'corresponding places in the general system, the 'treble g, which determines all the rest, must be 'supposed in the same place as the treble cliff of the 'common method; but this difference is remarkable, 'that tho' the g of the treble and bass systems are 'both on lines in the general system, yet the mean 'g, which is on a line of the particular system, is on 'a space in the general one; because in the pro- 'gression of the scale, the same letter, as g, is 'alternately upon a line and a space; therefore the 'mean system is not a continuation of any of the 'other two, so as you could proceed in order out of 'the one into the other by degrees, from line to 'space, because the g of the mean is here on a line, 'which is necessarily upon a space in the scale; and 'therefore in referring the mean system to its proper 'relative place in the scale, all its lines correspond 'to spaces of the other, and contrarily; but there 'is no matter of that if the parts be so written 'separately, as their relations be distinctly known, 'and the practice made more easy; and when we 'would reduce them all to one general system, it is 'enough we know that the lines of the mean part 'must be changed into spaces, and its spaces into 'lines. Thirdly, if the notes of any part go above 'or below its system, we may set them as formerly 'on short lines drawn on purpose: but if there are 'many notes together above or below, Mr. Salmon 'proposes to reduce them within the system, by

'placing them on the lines and spaces of the same
'name, and prefixing the name of the octave to
'which they belong. To understand this better,
'consider he has chosen three distinct octaves fol-
'lowing one another; and because one octave needs
'but four lines, therefore he would have no more in
'the particular system; and then each of the three
'particular systems expressing a distinct octave of
'the scale, which he calls the proper octaves of these
'several parts, if the song run into another octave
'above or below, it is plain; the notes that are out
'of the octave peculiar to the system, as it stands by
'a general rule marked T, or M, or B, may be set
'on the same lines and spaces; if the octave they
'belong to be distinctly marked, the notes may be
'very easily found, by taking them an octave higher
'or lower than the notes of the same name in the
'proper octave of the system. For example, if the
'treble part runs into the middle or bass octave, we
'prefix to these notes the letter M or B, and set
'them on the same lines and spaces, for all the three
'systems have in this hypothesis the notes of the
'same name in the same correspondent places; if
'the mean run into the treble or bass octaves, prefix
'the signs T or M. And lastly, because the parts
'may comprehend more than three octaves, therefore
'the treble may run higher than an octave, and the
'bass lower; in such cases the higher octave for the
'treble may be marked T t, and the lower for the
'bass B b. But if any body thinks there be any
'considerable difficulty in this method, which yet
'I am of opinion would be far less than the changing
'of cliffs in the common way, the notes may be con-
'tinued upward and downward upon new lines and
'spaces, occasionally drawn in the ordinary manner.
'And tho' there may be many notes far out of the
'system above or below, yet what is the inconveniency
'of this? Is the reducing the notes within 5 lines,
'and saving a little paper, an adequate reward for
'the trouble and time spent in learning to perform
'readily from different cliffs?

'As to the treble and bass, the alteration by this
'new method is very small; for in the common posi-
'tion of the bass cliff the lowest line is already g,
'and for the treble it is but removing the g from the
'second line, its ordinary position, to the first line;
'the greatest innovation is in the parts that are set
'with the c cliff.'

These are the sentiments of Malcolm touching
Salmon's proposal for rejecting the cliffs from the
scale of music; but it must be presumed that he had
never perused the arguments of Lock and Playford
against it, in which it is demonstrated to be im-
practicable.

Salmon's book, for what reason it is hard to guess,
was not published by the author himself, but by
John Birchensha, a noted musician in his time, who
recommends it in a preface of his own writing. If
Salmon had understoood more of music than it
appears he did, he never would have thought the
knowledge of the cliffs so difficult to attain, nor
would he have attempted, by the establishment of a
new and universal character, to have rendered unin-

telligible to succeeding generations the many inestimable compositions extant in his time: notwithstanding this, there is in his manner of writing such
an air of pertness and self-sufficiency, as was enough
to provoke a man of Lock's temper; and accordingly
he published in the same year a book entitled 'Observations upon a late book entitled an Essay, &c.,'
which, as Wood says, lying dead upon the booksellers's hands, had another title prefixed to it, viz.,
'The present practice of music vindicated against
'the exceptions and new way of attaining music,
'lately published by Tho. Salmon,' to which, continues Wood, was added a very scurrilous, abusive,
and buffooning thing entitled 'Duellum Musicum,
'written by John Phillips, and a letter from John
'Playford to Mr. Thomas Salmon, by way of confu-
'tation of his essay.' Lond. 1673, 8vo.*

As to the observations of Lock, above mentioned
to have lain dead on the bookseller's hands, the book
is now grown so scarce, that after twenty years'
inquiry not one copy has been to be found; nevertheless, the merits of this controversy may be judged
of from Lock's 'Present Practice of Music Vindicated,' and Playford's letter at the end of it, in
both which it is demonstrated that Salmon's scheme
would introduce more difficulties in music than it
would remove, and that in some instances it cannot
possibly be applied to practice. And as to Wood's
censure of the Observations that they are scurrilous
and abusive, it may be said that if they are more
scurrilous and abusive than the answer to it, entitled 'A Vindication of an Essay to the advancement of musick from Mr. Lock's observations,' they
must in truth be a great curiosity.†

* Athen. Oxon. vol. II. col. 1075.

† Salmon was also the author of a treatise entitled 'A proposal to per-
'form Musick in perfect and mathematical Proportions,' Lond. 4to 1688,
divided into three chapters.
In Chap. I. the author, after lamenting 'that fatal period when the
'North swarmed with barbarous multitudes, who came down like a
'mighty torrent, and subdued the best nations of the world, which were
'forced to become rude and illiterate, because their new masters and
'inhabitants were such,' observes that 'amidst these calamities it is no
'wonder that music perished.' 'All learning,' says he, 'lay in the dust,
'especially that which was proper in the times of peace.' But he tells us
'that this darkness was not perpetual, for that the ages at last cleared up,
'and from the ruins of antiquity brought forth some broken pieces, which
'were by degrees set together, and by this time of day are arrived near
'their ancient glory. Guido has been refining above six hundred years.'
He then, in a style equally vulgar and affected with the passage above
cited, felicitates the world on the publication of the ancient Greek
writers on music by Meibomius, and of Ptolemy by Dr. Wallis; and also
of those two fragments of ancient Greek music published with Chilmead's
notes, at the end of the Oxford edition of Aratus.
Chap. II. contains some few observations on the practice of music in
the author's time, with a remark that for the last twenty years before
the time of writing this book, the internal constitution of the octave had
been twofold, that is to say, either with the greater third, sixth, and
seventh, or a lesser third, sixth, and seventh; which progressions
severally constitute the flat and sharp keys, of the one whereof he makes
that of A to be the prototype, as that of C is the other.
Chap. III. contains an account of his tables of proportion. It seems
that the divisions therein contained are adapted to the practice of the
viol; for he gives his reader the choice of any one of several strings for
the two divisions of the octave recommended by him. The whole of his
proposal terminates in a contrivance of changeable finger-boards, differently fretted according to the key, by means whereof, those dissonances, which in some keys arise and are discoverable in the organ
and harpsichord, when perfectly tuned, are palliated.
It is difficult to discover in what sense proportions thus adjusted can
be termed mathematical. All men know that it has been the labour of
mathematicians for many ages to effect an equal division of the octave,
and that all their endeavours for that purpose have been baffled by that
surd quantity which has remained in every mode of division that the
wit of man has hitherto suggested; it may therefore be inferred that no
proportions strictly mathematical can be found by which a division, such
as the author pretends to have discovered, can be effected.
After all, this proposal is not mathematical, but simply practical
and as all the inconveniences that this author proposes to remove by the
use of changeable finger-boards for the viol arise, from the frets, so by

Wood is greatly mistaken in the account by him given of this dispute; for the observations of Lock on Salmon's book, and 'The present Practice of Music Vindicated,' by the same author, with the 'Duellum Musicum' of Phillips, and the letter from Playford, are two separate and distinct publications. The following is the true history and order of the controversy:—

I. Essay to the advancement of music by Thomas Salmon.

II. Observations thereon by Matthew Lock.

III. A vindication of an Essay to the advancement of Music from Mr. Matthew Lock's observations inquiring into the real nature and most convenient practice of that Science, by Thomas Salmon, M.A. of Trin. Coll. Oxon.

This vindication is in the form of a letter to Dr. John Wallis, Savilian professor of geometry in the university of Oxford, and begins with thanks for a letter from that person to the author, testifying his approbation of the essay, and an acknowledgment of the honour done him by the Royal Society, who in their Transactions, No. 80, published in February, 1671-2, had upon their judgments recommended it to public practice.

These several tracts were all published in the year 1672. In the following year came forth

IV. The present practice of music vindicated, with the Duellum Musicum and Playford's letter, which closes the dispute.

The subject-matter of this controversy is not now so important as to require a minute detail of the arguments; it may suffice to say, that with a studied affectation of wit and humour, it abounds with the most abusive scurrility that ever disgraced controversy.

Wood, who seems to have entertained an unjustifiable partiality for Salmon and his proposal, intimates that he had the best of the argument; but the contrary may be presumed from the total silence of Salmon, after the last publication against him by Lock and his associates, and from the opinion of the public, who have never acquiesced in the proposal to reject the cliffs, from a well-grounded persuasion that the substituting of letters in their places would introduce rather than prevent confusion; so that the method of notation contended for by Lock continues to be practised, without the least variation, to this day; and Mr. Thomas Salmon, together with his essay to the advancement of music, by casting away the cliffs, and uniting all sorts of music in one universal character, are now very deservedly forgotten.

Mention has been made in a preceding page of

the introduction of the opera into this kingdom, and of the opera of Psyche, written by Shadwell, and composed by Lock; this entertainment seems to have been well received by the public, for in 1675 he published it in score, together with the music in the Tempest, before mentioned, with a preface in his usual style, and a dedication to James duke of Monmouth.

It appears by Lock's preface that the instrumental music, before and between the acts, of Psyche, was composed by Sig. Giovanni Battista Draghi, a musician in the service of queen Catherine, and who is mentioned in the next succeeding article.

The world is indebted to Lock for the first rules ever published in this kingdom on the subject of continued or thorough-bass; a collection of these he has given to the world in a book entitled Melothesia, Lond. oblong quarto, 1673. It is dedicated to Roger L'Estrange, Esq., afterwards Sir Roger L'Estrange, a man eminently skilled in music, and an encourager of its professors, and contains, besides the rules, some lessons for the harpsichord and organ by himself and other masters. He was also the author of a collection of airs entitled 'A little Consort of three parts for Viols or Violins,' printed in 1657, and of the music to sundry songs printed in the Treasury of Music, the Theater of Music, and other collections of songs. In the latter of these is a dialogue, 'When death shall part us from these kids,' which he set to music, and, together with Dr. Blow's 'Go, perjured man,' was ranked amongst the best vocal compositions of the time.

Lock was very intimate with Silas Taylor, the author of a History of Gavelkind, who himself was a good musician,* as also an antiquary. Their acquaintance commenced through Lock's wife, who was of the same county with Taylor, viz. Hereford: her maiden name was Gammons. It is to be presumed that at the time when he composed his morning service he was of the chapel royal, and consequently a protestant; but it is certain that he went over to the Romish communion, and became organist to queen Catherine of Portugal, the consort of Charles II. and that he died a papist in 1677.†

GIOVANNI BATTISTA DRAGHI was an Italian by birth, and was probably a brother of Antonio Draghi, maestro di capella at Vienna, and of Carlo Draghi, organist to the emperor Leopold. He is supposed to have been one of those musicians who came into England with Mary d'Este, princess of Modena, the consort of James II. He was a very fine performer on the harpsichord, and composed and published in England lessons for that instrument. He joined with Lock in composing the music to the opera of Psyche, and upon his decease in 1677, succeeded him in the place of organist to the queen.‡

the removal of the frets the inconveniences are removed: and we find by experience that persons having a good ear, and nature only for their guide, do in all cases divide the octave most accurately.

At the end of the proposal is a letter of Dr. Wallis to the author, approving in general of his design, but attended with some such shrewd remarks on it, as tend to show that Salmon was far from equal to the task he had undertaken. At the close of the remarks is a very curious passage, containing an assertion of Dr. Wallis, that there are manifest places in Ptolemy that the frets, $\mu\alpha\gamma\alpha\delta\iota\alpha$, of the ancients were moveable, not in tuning only, but even in playing, which is a strong argument against the opinion that in the ancient modes the tones and semitones followed in succession as they arise in the scale, and that of seven modes or keys, five are lost; so that only two, viz. A and C, are remaining.

* An anthem of his, 'God is our hope and strength,' is well known among the church musicians.

† It is probable that his residence was at Somerset-house, the palace of the queen dowager, for his last publication is dated from his lodgings in the Strand.

‡ The queen was permitted the exercise of her own religion; and it is probable that in some part of Whitehall she might have a chapel, in which mass was celebrated, with an organ, and something like a choir. This is certain, that when, upon the death of Charles II. she went to reside at the palace of Somerset-house, she had an ecclesiastical establishment, which included in it an organist and three chapel-boys, as appears

Although Draghi was an Italian, and there are many compositions of his extant, particularly a Madrigal among the Harleian manuscripts in the British museum, 'Qual spaventosa Tromba,' which are altogether in the Italian style, he seems during his long residence in this country to have, to a remarkable degree, assimilated his style to that of the old English masters, as appears by an anthem of his, 'This is the day that the Lord hath made,' and more evidently in sundry old ballad airs and dance-tunes composed by him, the melodies whereof are singularly excellent.

During the reigns of Charles II. and James II. Draghi seemed to be a favourite court musician. Mr. Wanley, a faithful narrator of facts, and who, being a musical man, might possibly have been personally acquainted with him, says that Draghi was music-master to our most excellent queen Anne;* meaning, it is presumed, that the queen, when young, and of a suitable age, had been taught music by this person, as was probably her sister, the princess Mary.

Towards the latter end of his life he composed the music to an opera written by D'Urfey, 'The Wonders in the Sun, or the Kingdom of Birds.' This whimsical drama was performed at the Queen's Theatre in the Hay-market, in the month of July, 1706. It is said that the songs in this opera, of which there are a great number, were written by several of the most eminent wits of the age, who lent the author their assistance; and it is probable that for this reason he dedicated it to the Kit Kat Club. Among others that seem to be the production of a genius superior to D'Urfey, is that excellent song known by the name of the 'Dame of Honour.' This song was set by Draghi, and it is difficult to say which is most to be admired, the song for the sentiments, or the air for the sweetness of its melody. There are also in it the famous tune called the 'Old Cebell;' as also another very fine one to the words 'Tell me, Jenny, tell me roundly;' and, lastly, a tune which, some years after the exhibition of the opera, became a country-dance, and in the printed collections of country-dance tunes is called the Czar.

Downes, the prompter, says of this opera that the singers in it were Mr. Cook, Mr. Laroon, Mr. Lawrence, Mr. Hudson, and others, and the dancers, Mons. De Bargues, Mons. L'Abbé's brother, Mr. Fairbank, Mr. Elford,† and others; and that it lasted only six days, not answering half the expense of it.

We meet in the printed collections many songs with the name Signor Baptist to them; this subscription means uniformly Baptist Draghi, and not Baptist Lully, as some have supposed.

PELHAM HUMPHREY was one of the first set of children after the restoration, and educated, together with Blow and Wise, under Captain Cook. He was admitted a gentleman of the chapel Jan. 23, 1666, and distinguished himself so greatly in the composition of anthems as to excite the envy of his master, who, it is confidently asserted, died of discontent at seeing paid to him that applause which was but due to his merit.‡ Cook died on the thirteenth day of July, 1672, and on the thirtieth of the same month Humphrey was appointed master of the children in his room. This honourable station he held but a short time, for he died at Windsor on the fourteenth day of July, 1674, in the twenty-seventh year of his age, and was succeeded as master of the children by his condisciple Blow. He lies interred in the east ambulatory, reaching from north to south of the cloister of Westminster Abbey. On his gravestone was the following inscription, but it is now effaced:—

HERE LIETH INTERRED THE BODY OF
PELHAM HUMPHREY,
WHO DIED THE XIVTH OF JULY, ANN. DOM. MDCLXXIV,
AND IN THE XXVIITH YEAR OF HIS AGE.

In Dr. Boyce's Collection of Cathedral Music are two very fine anthems of Humphrey, 'O Lord my God,' and 'Have mercy upon me.' In conjunction with Dr. Blow and Dr. Turner he composed the anthem 'I will alway give thanks.' He also composed tunes to many of the songs in the Theater of Music, the Treasury of Music, and other collections in his time, particularly that to the song 'When Aurelia first I courted,' which was the favourite of those times; and another to a song said to have been written by king Charles II. 'I pass all my hours in an old shady grove,' printed with the music in the appendix to this work.

PIETRO REGGIO, a native of Genoa, was of the private music to Christina, queen of Sweden, and was greatly celebrated for his performance on the lute.§ Upon the queen's resignation of the crown he came to England, and choosing Oxford for the place of his residence, in the year 1677 published there a little tract entitled 'A Treatise to sing well any Song

---

by the following list in Chamberlayne's present state of England, printed in 1694.

Lord Almoner, Cardinal Howard of Norfolk; Mr. Paulo de Almeyda, Mr. Emanuel Diaz, Almoners; Confessor, Father Christopher de Rozario; Father Huddlestone, and Father Michael Ferreyra, Chaplains; three Portugal Franciscan Friars, called Arrabidoes, and a lay brother; Mr. James Martin, Mr. Nicholas Kennedy, Mr. William Hollyman, Chapelboys; Mr. John Battista Draghi, Organist; Mr. Timothy de Faria, Mr. James Read, Mr. Anthony Fernandez, Virgers.

Queen Catherine's chapel at Somerset-house was remaining till the year 1733, when it was destroyed to make room for the Prince of Orange, when he came over to marry the Princess Anne. A gentleman, who remembers it, says that adjoining to it was a bed-chamber, with a small window, contrived that the queen when in bed might see the elevation of the Host. *The window was at the top above the bedstead, so that she might hear the service but could see nothing. I have been in that room.* —Horace Walpole.

* Queen Anne played on the harpsichord. She had a spinnet, the loudest and perhaps the finest that ever was heard, of which she was very fond. She gave directions that at her decease this instrument should go to the master of the children of the chapel royal for the time being, and descend to his successors in office: accordingly it went first to Dr. Croft, and is now in the hands of Dr. Nares, master of the children of the royal chapel.

† Mr. Richard Elford was educated in the choir of Lincoln, and was afterwards of the choir at Durham, but coming to London, he became a singer on the stage. His person being, as Dr. Tudway relates, awkward and clumsy, and his action disgusting, he quitted the theatre, and was admitted a gentleman of the chapel royal, and to the places of a lay-vicar in St. Paul's cathedral and Westminster abbey. His voice was a fine countertenor. As a gentleman of the chapel he had an addition of an hundred pounds a year to his salary. Mr. Weldon's six Solo Anthems, published with the title of 'Divine Harmony,' were composed on purpose for him; and in the preface the author celebrates Mr. Elford for his fine performance of them. He had a brother, also a singer, who by the interest of Dean Swift was preferred to a place in one of the cathedrals in Dublin.

‡ Captain Henry Cook was made master of the children at the restoration. He was esteemed the best musician of his time to sing to the lute, till Pelham Humphries came up, after which he died with discontent. Ashmolean MS. art. COOK.

§ Whitelock, when embassador at Stockholm, heard him sing and accompany himself on the Theorbo, with great applause. Ashmolean MS.

whatsoever.' He also set to music for a single voice, with a thorough-bass, those love-verses of Cowley called the Mistress.

After some years residence in Oxford, he removed to London, and died in the parish of St. Giles in the Fields, on the twenty-third day of July, 1685. The following inscription to his memory was remaining till about the year 1735, when the church was pulled down in order to be rebuilt :—

PETRUS REGGIO
CUJUS CORPUS EX ADVERSO JACET
NATUS GENUÆ DIVINAM MUSICÆ
SCIENTIAM A CLARISSIMIS IN SUA
PATRIA ATQUE A DEO IN TOTO
ORBE MAGISTRIS EXCULTAM
AB IPSO ULTERIUS ORNATAM
EX ITALIA ET COELO DICERES TRANSALPES
IN HISPANIAM GERMANIAM
SUECIAM ET GALLIAM
DEINDE IN ANGLIAM TRANSTULIT
POSTREMO AD COELESTES CHOROS
SECUM EVEXIT
DIE XXIII JULII MDCLXXXV.

MICHAEL WISE, a most sweet and elegant composer, born in Wiltshire, was one of the first set of children of the royal chapel after the restoration : he became organist and master of the choristers in the cathedral church of Salisbury in 1668; and on the sixth of January, 1675, was appointed a gentleman of the chapel royal in the room of Raphael Courtville, deceased. On the twenty-seventh of January, 1686, he was preferred to be almoner and master of the choristers of St. Paul's. He was much favoured by Charles II. and being appointed to attend him in a progress which he once made, claimed as the king's organist pro tempore, to play the organ at whatsoever church the king stopped at : it is said that at one church he presumed to begin his voluntary before the preacher had finished his sermon; a very unwarrantable and indecent exertion of his right, how well soever founded. It is possible that some such indiscreet behaviour as this might draw on him the king's displeasure ; for upon his decease he was under a suspension, and at the coronation of James II. Edward Morton officiated in his room.

He composed several very fine anthems, namely, 'Awake up my glory,' 'Prepare ye the way of the Lord,' 'Awake, put on thy strength,' and some others. He also composed that well-known two-part song, 'Old Chiron thus preached to his pupil Achilles,' and some Catches, printed in the Musical Companion, which are excellent in their kind. He was a man of great pleasantry, but ended his days unfortunately; for being with his wife at Salisbury in the month of August, 1687, some words arose between him and her, upon which he went out of the house in a passion, and, it being towards midnight, he was stopped by the watch, with whom he began a quarrel, in which he received a blow on the head with a bill, which fractured his skull and killed him.

The advantages were very great which music derived from the studies of these men : they improved and refined upon the old church-style, and formed a new one, which was at once both elegant and solemn ;

and from the many excellent compositions of the musicians of king Charles the Second's reign now extant, it may be questioned whether the principles of harmony, or the science of practical composition, were ever better understood than in his time; the composers for the church appearing to have been possessed of every degree of knowledge necessary to the perfection of the art. Other improvements, it is true, lay behind, but these regarded the philosophy of sound in general, and in the division of the science of physics are comprehended under the term Phonics.

The first, at least among modern philosophers, that have treated on the generation and propagation of sound is Lord Verulam, who in his Natural History, Century II. has given a great variety of very curious experiments touching music in general, and in particular touching the nullity and entity of sounds. II. The production, conservation, and dilation of sounds. III. The magnitude and exility and damps of sounds. IV. Of the loudness or softness of sounds, and their carriage at longer or shorter distance. V. Touching the communication of sounds, &c.

The Royal Society, which was instituted at London immediately after the restoration, for the improvement of natural knowledge, seems to have prosecuted this branch of it with no small degree of ardour, as appears by a great variety of papers on the subject of sound, its nature, properties, and affections, from time to time published in the Philosophical Transactions. Besides which there are extant a great variety of tracts on this subject, written by the members of that society, and published separately, some of the most distinguished of which are, 'A Philosophical Essay on Music,' published in quarto, 1677, without the name of the author, but which it is certain was written by Sir Francis North, Lord Chief Justice of the Court of Common Pleas, and afterwards Lord Keeper of the Great Seal;* a translation of ' Des Cartes de Musica,' by a person of honour, Henry Lord Brouncker, president of the Royal Society, with learned notes by the translator; an ' Introductory Essay to the Doctrine of Sound, containing some proposals for the improvement of Acousticks,' by Narcissus, bishop of Ferns and Leighlin ; and a ' Discourse on the natural Grounds and Principles of Harmony,' by William Holder, D.D. London, octavo, 1694.

A short abstract from two of the discourses above mentioned will suffice to show the nature and tendency of each. Of the others mention is elsewhere made in the course of this work.

The general purport of the treatise written by Sir Francis North is as follows :—

It begins with an inquiry into the cause of sounds : in order thereto the author states those phenomena of sound which he thinks most considerable, as, first, that it may be produced in the Toricellian vacuity. 2. That it causes motion in solid bodies. 3. That it is diminished by the interposition of solid bodies; and 4. If the bodies interposed are very

* This is expressly asserted in the Life of the Lord Keeper North, written by his brother, the Hon. Roger North, Esq. page 297.

thick, its passage is wholly obstructed. 5. That it seems to come to the ear in straight lines, when the object is so situated that it cannot come in straight lines to the ear. 6. That when there is a wind, the sphere is enlarged on that part on which the wind blows, and diminished on the contrary part. 8 That it arrives not to the ear in an instant, but considerably slower than sight. 9. That it comes as quick against the wind as with it, though not so loud, nor so far.

Hence he raises the following hypothesis; he supposes the air we breathe in to be a mixture of divers minute bodies, of different sorts and sizes, though all of them are so small as to escape our senses: the grosser of them he makes elastical, and to be resisted by solid bodies, altogether impervious to them: the smaller parts he supposes to pass through solid bodies, though not with that ease; but that upon a sudden and violent start of them they shock the parts of solid bodies that stand in their way, and also the grosser parts of the air. Lastly, he supposes there may be another degree of most subtle ethereal parts, with which the interstices of these and all other bodies are replete, which find a free passage everywhere, and are capable of no compression, and consequently are the medium and cause of the immediate communication of sound.

Now, of these three, he esteems the middle sort to be the medium and cause of sound, and supposes that at any time when the grosser air is driven off any space, and leaves it to be possessed by these and other more subtle bodies, and returns by its elasticity to its former place, then are these parts extruded with violence, as from the centre of that space, and communicate their motion as far as the sound is heard: or that where any solid body is moved with a sudden and violent motion, these parts must be affected thereby; for as these parts are so much resisted by solid bodies as to shock them, so on the contrary they must needs be moved by a sudden starting of solid bodies.

So that, according to him, sound may be caused by the trembling of solid bodies, without the presence of gross air; and also by the restitution of gross air, when it has been divided by any sudden force, as by the end of a whip, having all the motion of a whip contracted in it, and by a sudden turn throwing off the air; or by ascension, as in thunder and guns; or by any impression of force, carrying it where other air cannot so forcibly follow, as upon compressing of air in a bladder till it breaks, or in a potgun, a sudden crack will be caused.

Having laid down this hypothesis, and left his reader to apply it to the before-mentioned phenomena, he proceeds to discourse of music itself, and labours to show how this action that causes sound is performed by the several instruments of music.

His definition of a tone is adapted to his hypothesis, and will be thought somewhat singular: 'A tone,' says he, 'is the repetition of cracks or pulses 'in equal spaces of time, so quick, that the interstices 'or intervals are not perceptible to sense.'

He observes that the compass of music extends from such tones, whose intervals are so great, that the several pulses are distinguishable by sense, to those whose interstices are so very small, that they are not commensurate with any other.

Speaking of the production of tones, and of the assistances to sound by instruments, he says that wherever a body stands upon a spring that vibrates in equal terms, such a body put in motion will produce a tone, which will be more grave or acute according to the velocity of the returns; and that therefore strings vibrating have a tone according to the bigness or tension of them; and bells that vibrate by cross ovals produce notes according to the bigness of them, or the thickness of their sides; and so do all other bodies, whose superficies being displaced by force, result or come back by a spring that carries them beyond their first station. And here he observes that it is easy to comprehend how every pulse upon such vibrations causes sound; for that the gross air is thrown off by the violence of the motion, which continues some moment of time after the return of the vibrating body; whereupon some space must be left to that subtle matter, which upon the result of the air starts as from a centre, which action being the same as that which our author supposes to be the cause of sound, is repeated upon every vibration.

But finding it more difficult to show how tones are made by a pipe, where there are no visible vibrations, he considers the frame of a pipe, and the motion of the air in it, and thereby attempts to find the cause of the tone of a pipe, and the pulse that gives it sound.

His doctrine on this head is delivered in these words: 'To shew how the pulses are caused, 'whereby the included air is put into this motion, it 'is necessary to observe the frame of a pipe, which 'chiefly consists in having a long slit, through which 'the air is blown in a thin film against, or very near, 'a solid edge that is at some distance opposite to it, 'in such manner that the intermediate space is 'covered by the stream of air. This film of air on 'the one side is exposed to the outward air, and on 'the inside is defended from it by the sides of the 'pipe, within which the air inclosed in the pipe 'stagnates, whilst the outward air is by the blast 'put into a vortical motion.

'The vortical motion or eddy on the outside is so 'strong, that there not being a balance to that force 'on the inside, the film of air gives way, and 'the eddy bears into the pipe, but is immediately 'overcome by the blast, which prevails until the 'eddy overcomes it again; and so there is a crossing 'of streams by turns and pulses, which causes the 'voice of the pipe, the gross air of one stream being 'thrown off by the interposition of the other.

'These vicissitudes or terms will answer the tone 'of the pipe according to the gage of its cavity: for 'the spring of the included air helps towards the 'restitution of the blast and eddy in their turns, 'which causes those turns to comply with the tone of 'the pipe; and therefore the same blast will cause 'several tones, if the gage or measure of the included 'air be changed by apertures in the side of the pipe.

'But there must be some proportion between the

'mouth, so I call that part of the pipe where the
'voice is, and the gage of the pipe; for though the
'pulses will be brought to comply with the tone of
'the pipe in any reasonable degree, yet when there
'is great disparity it will not do so; as if the pipe be
'too long for the proportion of the diameter, the
'pulses at the mouth cannot be brought to so slow
'terms as to answer the vibrations of the included
'air; therefore the pipe will not speak unless it can
'break into some higher note. If the slimy stream
'of air be too thick, the pipe will not speak, because
'the eddy cannot break through; if the opposite
'edge be too remote, the stream cannot entirely cover
'the aperture, for it mixes with the outward air,
'and is more confused the further it is from the vent
'or passage, whereby some outward air may have
'communication to make an opposite eddy on the
'inside of the stream. For the same reason, if there
'be the least aperture in the region of the mouth of
'the pipe, it will not speak at all.

'Hence it is that the voice of organ pipes is so
'tender and nice: but shrill whistles depend not
'upon this ground; for they are made in any small
'cavity, where the blast is so applyed that the erum-
'pent air must cross it, whether the stream be thick
'or thin. Therefore the bore of a key, a piece of
'nut-shell, or any other cavity will make a whistle,
'whose tone will be according to the quantity of the
'included air; for the less that is, the harder it is to
'be compressed, and the quicker and stronger it
'must break forth.

'Another kind of whistle is, when a hollow body
'with a small cavity is perforated by opposite holes,
'a blast either way will cause a tone, which seems
'to be made in this manner.

'The air that is violently drawn or thrust through
'these holes, is straitned at the passage by the swift-
'ness of the motion, and within the cavity is some-
'what enlarged, and consequently its force is directed,
'and it presses beyond the compass of the opposite
'aperture, whereupon it bears of all sides into the
'cavity; hereby the air within the cavity is com-
'pressed until it breaks forth by crossing the stream,
'which being done by vicissitudes, causes a tone:
'this kind of action, as I imagine, is performed when
'men whistle with their lips.

'In some pipes the pulses are caused by springs,
'as the Regal stop of an organ, which is commonly
'tuned by shortening the spring, whereby it becomes
'stronger, but the note will be changed by the alter-
'ation of the cavity; and therefore to make them
'steddy, some that stand upon very weak springs
'have pavilions set to them.

'A rustick instance may be given of the compliance
'of a spring, in taking such vibrations as are pro-
'portionable to the cavity; it is a Jews-harp, or
'Jews-trump, the tongue whereof has natural vibra-
'tions according to the strength and length of the
'of the spring, and so is fitted to one particular tone;
'but countrymen framing their breath and their
'mouth to several notes make a shift to express a
'tune by it.

'In a shawm or hautboy the quill at the mouth is

'a kind of spring, but so weak and indifferent, that it
'complies with any measure*, and therefore the tone
'will be according to the apertures of the pipe.

'The fluttering and jarring of discording sounds,
'which I did before observe, is so regular, and
'the sounds take their turns with equal interstices,
'which makes the joining of them produce a harsher
'sound than either had before; whereby organ-
'makers imitate the hautboy or trumpet without any
'spring or quill, by joining discording pipes.†

'In a Sacbut the lips of a man do the same office as a
'quill does in a Shawm or hautboy; when the inclu-
'ded air is lengthened, the tone varies; nevertheless
'they can produce several notes that are in chord to
'the tone of the instrument by strengthening the blast
'without lengthening the cavity: and in a trumpet
'which is the same kind of instrument, only not
'capable of being lengthened, they can sound a whole
'tune, which is by the artificial ordering the blast
'at the mouth, whereby the sound breaks into such
'notes as are to be used.'

Having thus shown how tones are produced by
instruments of music, the author proceeds to take
notice of other assistances which instruments give to
sound, in these words:—

'In violins and harpsicords the tones are made
'wholly by the vibrating strings, but the frame of
'the instrument adds much to the sound; for such
'strings vibrating upon a flat rough board, would
'yield but a faint and pitiful sound.

'The help that instruments give to the sound, is
'by reason that their sides tremble and comply with
'any sound, and strike the air in the same measure
'that the vibrations of the music are, and so consi-
'derably increase the sound.

'This trembling is chiefly occasioned by the con-
'tinuity of the sides of the instrument with the
'vibrating string; therefore if the bridge of a violin
'be loaded with lead, the sound will be damp; and
'if there be not a stick called the sound post to
'promote the continuity between the back and belly
'of the instrument, the sound will not be brisk and
'sprightly.

'Such a continuity to the nerve of hearing will
'cause a sense of sound to a man that hath stopped
'his ears, if he will hold a stick that touches the
'sounding instrument between his teeth.‡

'The sound of itself, without such continuity,
'would occasion some trembling; but this is not
'considerable in respect of the other, though it be all
'the assistance that the structure of a chamber can
'give to musick, except what is by way of echo.

* *Sig. Orig.* but Quere if not pressure?
† In this sentiment the author is mistaken: discordant pipes are made use of by the organ-makers to imitate the kettle-drum; and the best for this purpose are F♯ and GAMUT, but the hautboy and trumpet are imitable only by reed pipes of the same form as those instruments respectively, that is to say, having the greater end spreading with a curve like a bell, in a greater or less degree.
‡ Thomas Mace, a writer of whom there will shortly be occasion to speak, and a lutenist, having almost lost his hearing, invented a double lute, which he contrived to make the loudest instrument of the lute kind he had ever heard; nevertheless he was not able to hear all that he played on it, except by means of such a contrivance as is above suggested. In short, as he relates, he heard by the help of his teeth, which when he played he was wont to lay close to the edge of the instrument, where the lace is fixed, and thereby derived, as he expresses it, with thankfulness to God, one of the principal refreshments and contentments that he enjoyed in this world. Musick's Monument, page 203.

'This tremble of the instruments changes with 'every new sound; the spring of the sides of the in- 'strument standing indifferent to take any measure, 'receives a new impression; but a vibrating string 'can take no measure but according to its tension.

'Therefore instruments that have nothing to stop 'the sounding strings, make an intolerable jangle to 'one that stands near, as bells to one that is in 'the steeple, and hears the continuing sound of 'dissonant tones; such is the Dulcimer: but the harp- 'sichord, that hath rags upon the jacks, by which 'the vibration of the string is staid, gives no distur- 'bance by the sonorousness of the instrument, for 'that continues not the sound after the vibrations 'determined, and another tone struck, but changes 'and complies with the new sound.'

Next he treats of the varying and breaking of tones into other tones, both in strings and in pipes. In his discourse on this part of music there occur divers pertinent observations concerning the motions of pendulums, the nature of the trumpet marine, and of the true trumpet, and of the sacbut. And having shown that sound causes a motion, not only of solid bodies, but of the grosser parts of the air, within the sphere of it, he considers that if the air which is moved by being inclosed, stands upon such a degree of resistance to compression, that it hath a spring vibrating in the same measure with the sound that puts it into motion, there will be the same effect as when two strings are tuned in unison; that is, the motion will be so augmented by succeeding regular pulses, that the inclosed air may be brought to ring, and produce a tone. And here he takes notice of the advice of Vitruvius in his Architecture, importing that in the structure of a theatre there should be vases or hollow pots of several sizes, to answer all the notes of music, placed upon the stage; in such a manner that the voice of them which sing upon the stage may be augmented by the ringing of them; Vitruvius mentioning divers ancient theatres where such were, in some of brass, in some of earth.

After this he proceeds to consider the nature of the keys in music, and of a single tune, which he says consists in the succeeding notes having a due relation to the preceding, and carrying their proper emphasis by length, loudness, and repetition, with variety that may be agreeable to the hearer. Next he treats of Schisms, and the scale of music, showing that the latter is not set out by any determinate quantities of whole notes or half notes, though the de- grees are commonly so called; but that the degrees of the musical scale are fixed by the ear in these places where the pulses of the tones are coincident, without any regard to the quantity; and here he endeavours, by a division of the monochord, corresponding as it seems very nearly with that of Lord Brouncker, in his translation of Des Cartes, to show how all notes come into the scale by their relation and dignity; whence he thinks it is obvious why, for easiness of instruction and convenience, the scale of degrees of music is made as musicians now exhibit it.

He next proceeds to the consideration of music consisting of several parts, which, as he expresses it, is made up of harmony, formality, and conformity.

Lastly, he speaks of time, or the measure of music, the due observation whereof he says is grateful, for the reasons given by him for the formality of a single tune, because the subsequent strokes are measured by the memory of the former; and if they comprehend them, or are comprehended by them, it is alike pleasant, for that the mind cannot choose but com- pare the one with the other, and observe when the strokes are coincident with the memory of the former. Wherefore he says it is that the less the intervals are, the more grateful the measure; because it is easily and exactly represented by the memory; whereas a long space of time, that cannot be compre- hended in one thought, is not retained in the memory in its exact measure, nor can abide the comparison, the time past being always shortened by so much as it is removed from the time present.

He concludes his discourse with two observations, first, that it plainly appears how music comes to be so copious, for, considering the species of keys, the number of them, the variety of chords, the allowable mixture of discords, and the diversity of measure, it is not to be wondered at, that it should, like language, afford every age and nation, nay, every person, particular styles and modes. Secondly, it appears that tones or modes of music in ancient time could not be of other kinds than they are now, since there can be no other in nature; whereof the great effects it then had, if truly related, must be imputed to the rarity of it, and the barbarity of the people, who are not transported with anything after it becomes common to them.

A farther account of this scarce and curious tract is given in that singular book The Life of the Lord Keeper Guilford, written by the honourable Roger North,* a brother of his lordship, which, as it

* This person wrote also the lives of his two brothers, the honourable Sir Dudley North, Knight, commissioner of the customs, and afterwards of the treasury to Charles II. and the hon. and rev. Dr. John North, master of Trinity college in Cambridge; as also an Examen or Enquiry into the Credit and Veracity of the compleat History of England, com- piled by Bishop Kennet, 4to. 1740. The Life of the Lord Keeper is a curious book, as it contains the history of Westminster Hall, with a great variety of entertaining particulars of the most eminent practisers from the year 1650 to 1680; but the style of it, like that of the author's other writings, is exceedingly quaint and affected. Nor are his opinions of men and things, particularly of law and justice, less singular, as will presently be shown.

Sir Dudley North was a Turkey merchant, and, being one of the English factory at Constantinople, had the management of a great number of lawsuits; how he managed them, and what were the sentiments of his brother touching his conduct, and particularly of the obligation of an oath, the following passage will show:—

'Another scheme of our merchants law conduct was touching proofs. 'The Turkish law rigidly holds every person to prove all the facts of his 'case by two Turkish witnesses, which makes the dealing, with a view 'of dispute, extremely difficult; for which reason the merchants usually 'take writing; but that hath its infirmity also, for the witnesses are 'required to prove not only the writing, which with us is enough, but 'they must prove every fact contained in it to be true, or else the evidence 'is insufficient. It fell out sometimes that when he had a righteous 'cause, the adversary was knavish, and would not own the fact, and he 'had not regular and true witnesses to prove it; he made no scruple in 'such case to use false ones; and certain Turks that had belonged to the 'factory, and knew the integrity of their dealings, would little scruple to 'attest facts to which they were not privy, and were paid for it. I have 'heard the merchant say he had known that at trials Turks standing by 'unconcerned, have stept forwards to help a dead lift (as they tell of 'a famous witnessing attorney, who used to say at his trial, 'Doth it 'stick? give me the book),' as these expect to be paid, and the merchants 'fail not to send them the premio, else they may cause great incon- 'veniences. Nay, a merchant there will directly hire a Turk to swear the 'fact, of which he knows nothing, which the Turk doth out of faith he 'hath in the merchant's veracity; and the merchant is very safe in it, for 'without two Turks to testify, he cannot be accused of subornation. This 'is not as here accounted a villainous subornation, but an ease under an 'oppression, and a lawful means of coming into a just right. The 'Christian oath is not in the case, so there is no profanation: and (upon 'the whole) the morality of the action seems to depend on the pure

contains a summary of the doctrines laid down in
the Philosophical Essay of Music, as also some
particulars relating to his lordship's musical studies,
is here inserted in the words of the author:—

'Now to illustrate his lordship's inclination to
ingenious arts, and sciences, I have two subjects to
'enlarge upon. 1. Musick. 2. Picture. As for his
'musick, I have already mentioned his exquisite
'hand upon the Lyra and Bass-Viol, and the use he
'made of it to relieve his solitude in his chamber.
'He had a desire to use also the Theorbo and violin.
'He scarce attempted the former, but supplied the
'use of it by the touch of his Lyra Viol upon his
'knee, and so gained a solitary consort with his
'voice.* He attempted the violin, being ambitious
'of the prime part in consort, but soon found that
'he began such a difficult art too late; and his profit
'also said nay to it, for he had not time for that kind
'of practice. It was great pity he had not naturally
'a better voice, for he delighted in nothing more
'than in the exercise of that he had, which had
'small virtue but in the tuneableness and skill. He
'sang anything at first sight, as one that reads in a
'new book, which many, even singing-masters,
'cannot do. He was a great proller of songs, espe-
'cially duets, for in them his brother could accom-
'pany him; and the Italian songs to a thorough-bass
'were choice purchases, and if he liked them he
'commonly wrote them out with his own hand;
'and I can affirm that he transcribed a book of
'Italian songs into a volume of the largest quarto,
'and thicker than a Common Prayer Book. And this
'was done about the time he had received the Great
'Seal; for if he would discharge his mind of
'anxieties, he often took the book of Songs, and
'wrote one or two of them out; and as he went
'along he observed well the composition and ele-
'gancies, as if he not only wrote but heard them,
'which was great pleasure to him.

'His lordship had not been long master of the
'viol, and a sure consortier, but he turn'd composer,
'and from raw beginnings advanced so far as to
'complete divers concertos of two and three parts,
'which at his grandfather's house, were perform'd
'with masters in company, and that was no small
'joy and encouragement to him. But it was not to
'be expected he should surmount the style and mode
'of the great musick-master Mr. Jenkins, then in

'justice and right, and not upon the regularity (in a Christian sense) of
'the means. The Turks in their country are obliged, as we are here, by
'the rules of common justice. But it is to be supposed that being here,
'they would not regard our forms, but would get their right if they
'might by infringing them all. So we in that country are obliged in
'common honesty to observe even their law of right and equity, but have
'no reason to regard their forms; and the compassing a right by any means
'contrary to them all, is not unreasonable. But to apprehend these
'diversities one must have a strong power of thought, to abstract the
'prejudices of our domestic education, and plant ourselves in a way of
'negotiating in heathen remote countries.
'Our merchant found by experience that in a direct fact a false
'witness was a surer card than a true one; for if the judge has a mind
'to baffle a testimony, an harmless honest witness, that doth not know
'his play, cannot so well stand his many captious questions as a false
'witness used to the trade will do, for he hath been exercised, and is
'prepared for such handling, and can clear himself when the other will
'be confounded; therefore if there be true witness, circumstances may
'be such as shall make the false ones more eligible.' Life of the Hon.
Sir Dudley North, page 46.
    * The nature of the Lyra-Viol, and the practice of the Viol Lyra way
are fully explained in the account herein after given of John Playford.

'use where he came. And, after his capacity reach'd
'higher, he had no time to be so diverted. Yet
'while he was Chief Justice, he took a fancy to set
'to musick, in three parts, a Canzon of Guarini,
'beginning thus, "Cor mio del," &c. In that he
'aimed to compass what he thought a great per-
'fection in consort-musick, ordering the parts so
'that every one shall carry the same air, and how-
'ever leading or following, the melody in each part
'is nearly the same, which is in composing no
'easy task.

'Not many years before his lordship was preferred
'to the Great Seal, he fell upon a pleasing specula-
'tion of the real mechanism whereby sounds are dis-
'tinguished into harmony and discord, or disposed
'to please or displease our sense of hearing. Every
'one is sensible of those effects, but scarce any know
'why, or by what means they are produced. He
'found that tones and accords might be anatomised,
'and by apt schemes be presented to the eye as well
'as to the ear, and so musick be demonstrated in
'effigie. After he had digested his notions, and
'continued his schemes, he drew up a short tract,
'which he entitled A Philosophical Essay of Musick,
'not with the form and exactness of a solemn writer,
'but as the sense of a man of business, who minds
'the kernel and not the shell. This was printed by
'Mr. Martin, printer to the Royal Society, in 1677.
'The piece sold well, and in a few years it was out
'of print, and ever since is scarce to be met with but
'in private hands. If I may give a short account of
'his lordships's notion, it is but this: all musical
'sounds consist of tones, for irregular noises are
'foreign to the subject. Every tone consists of dis-
'tinct pulses or strokes in equal time, which being
'indistinguishably swift, seem continual. Swifter
'pulses are, accordingly, in sound sharper, and the
'slower flatter. When diverse run together, if the
'pulses are timed in certain proportions to each
'other, which produce coincidences at regular and
'constant periods, those may be harmonious, else dis-
'cord. And in the practice of musick, the stated
'accords fall in these proportions of pulsation, viz.
'$\frac{2}{1}, \frac{3}{2}, \frac{4}{3}, \frac{5}{4}, \frac{6}{5}$. Hence flow the common denomina-
'tions of 8th, 5th, 4th, 3d, 2d; and these are produced
'upon a monochord by abscission of these parts,
'$\frac{1}{2}, \frac{1}{3}, \frac{1}{4}, \frac{1}{5}, \frac{1}{6}$. Of all which the fuller demonstration
'is a task beyond what is here intended.

'But to accomplish an ocular representation of
'these pulses, his lordship made a foundation upon
'paper by a perpetual order of parallel lines, and
'those were to signify the flux of time equably.
'And when a pulse happened, it was marked by
'a point upon one of those lines, and if continued
'so as to sound a base tone, it was marked upon
'every eighth line; and that might be termed the
'Base. And then an upper part, which pulsed as
'$\frac{2}{1}$, or octave, was marked, beginning with the first
'of the base, upon every fourth line, which is twice
'as swift: and so all the other harmonious pro-
'portions, which shewed their coincidences, as well
'with the base as with one another. And there
'was also shewed a beautiful and uniform aspect in

'the composition of these accords when drawn
'together. This as to Times. The ordinary col-
'lation of sounds is commonly made by numbers,
'which, not referred to a real cause or foundation
'in nature, may be just, but withal very obscure,
'and imparting of no knowledge. Witness the
'mathematicians musical proportions. His lordship
'did not decline numbers, but derived them from
'plain truths. He found 360 the aptest for those
'subdivisions that musick required, and, applying
'that to an open string or monochord, each musical
'tone, found by abscission of a part of the string, is
'expressible by those numbers so reduced in pro-
'portion. As $\frac{1}{2}$ of the string pinched off is as $\frac{2}{1}$, or
'180, an octave; and $\frac{1}{3}$ as $\frac{3}{2}$ 240; and so of the
'rest down to the tone or second, which cuts off $\frac{1}{9}$,
'and the semitone a $\frac{1}{16}$, &c.'* Life of Lord Keeper
Guilford, page 296.

The discourse of Dr. Marsh is of a different kind,
and treats altogether of the philosophy of sound,
without intermeddling with either the theory or
practice of music. Of the author mention has been
made in a preceding page. From the account given
of him by Wood it appears that he was well skilled
in the practical part of music; and that while he
was a fellow of Exeter college, and principal of
Alban-hall, he had a weekly meeting or concert of
instrumental, and sometimes vocal music at his
lodgings: and to the account of his subsequent
preferments given by Wood, may be added, that
from the archiepiscopal see of Cashell he was translated to that of Dublin, and from thence to that of
Armagh, and that he died in 1713.

In his discourse on Acousticks the Doctor treats
very largely on Vision, and the improvements thereof by means of glasses and tubes of various kinds,
and from the principles laid down in the preceding
part of his discourse, he concludes that considerable
improvements may also be made in Acousticks,
which improvements he distributes into two classes,
viz. improvements of hearing as to its object, which
is sound, and the improvements of the organ of
hearing, and the medium through which sound is
propagated. Under these two several heads he
treats at large of the imitation of the voices of
sundry animals, as quails and cats; and of those
sounds which are produced by the collision of solid
bodies; of the speaking-trumpet, and of reflected
audition by echoes, which he says is capable of great
improvement, one whereof he thus describes :—

* The author of this book was himself well acquainted with the
principles of music, and entertained some doubts on the division of the
monochord, of which he could find no solution in the method of division
proposed by his brother in the essay above cited. Among the papers of
Dr. Pepusch was found the following quære in his own hand-writing, as
also the answer to it in the hand-writing of the Doctor.

Quære. The sound arising by the abscission of $\frac{8}{9}$ths is a tone, and
more remote from perfection of consonance than that of $\frac{7}{8}$ths; why then
is the former accepted in music, and not the latter, which is abhorred?
Dic et eris Apollo.

Answer. Considering only the numbers, it is true that $\frac{7}{8}$ is nearer to
concordance than $\frac{8}{9}$, but as they are both discords, $\frac{8}{9}$ is allowed, having
a natural and immediate relation to the concords, which $\frac{7}{8}$ having not,
is absolutely rejected. For the same reason, all relations compounded of
the numbers 2, 3, 5, are musical, all others $\frac{7}{8}$, $\frac{11}{10}$, $\frac{13}{12}$, &c. are contrary to it.

'As speculas may be so placed, that reflecting one
'upon or into the other, either directly or obliquely,
'one object shall appear as many: after the same
'manner ecchoing bodies may be so contrived and
'placed, as that reflecting the sound from one to
'another, either directly and mutually, or obliquely
'and by succession, out of one sound shall many
'echoes be begotten, which in the first case will be
'altogether, and somewhat involved and swallowed
'up by each other, and thereby confused, as a face
'in a looking-glass obverted; in the other they will
'be separate, distinct, and succeeding one another,
'as most multiple ecchoes do.
'Moreover a multiple eccho may be made by so
'placing the ecchoing bodies at unequal distances,
'that they reflect all one way, and not one on the
'other, by which means a manifold successive sound
'will be heard, not without astonishment; one clap
'of the hand like many; one Hah! like laughter;
'one single word like many of the same tone and
'accent, and one viol like many of the same kind,
'imitating each other.†
'Furthermore, as Speculas may be so ordered,
'that by reflection they will make one single object
'appear many; as one single man to seem many
'men differing in shape and complexion, or a com-
'pany of men; so may ecchoing bodies also be
'ordered, that from any one sound given they shall
'produce as many ecchoes, different both as to their
'tone and intension; the grounds whereof have
'elsewhere been laid down in a treatise concerning
'the sympathy of lute-string.
'By this means a musical room might be so con-
'trived, that not only one instrument play'd in it
'shall seem as many of the same sort and size, but
'even a concert of somewhat different ones, only by
'placing certain ecchoing bodies, so that any note
'played shall be return'd by them in third, fifth,
'and eighth.'

There is very little doubt but that the writings of
Mersennus and Kircher, and probably the various
discoveries of Lord Bacon, and the hints suggested
by him in his Natural History, gave this direction
to the studies of philosophical men of this time. It
seems that the Academy Del Cimento had for some
time been making experiments on the philosophy
of sound, many of which are referred to in the
Transactions of the Royal Society: the result of
these appears with great advantage in a very learned
treatise written by Padre Daniello Bartoli, of the
Society of Jesus, printed at Rome in the year 1679,
entitled 'Del Suono de Tremori Armonici e dell'
udito.' The pursuits of the Royal Society of
London were directed to the same object: in the
Philosophical Transactions are sundry papers on the
nature and properties of sound, and others expressly
on the subject of music, among which is one entitled
'The Theory of music reduced to arithmetical and
'geometrical proportions, by Thomas Salmon.'

† It is the opinion of some that the sound of words may be imprisoned
and let loose so as to articulate. Of this persuasion the papists endeavour
to avail themselves when they produce, as they are said to do, a most
precious relic, the Hah! of Joseph the husband of the blessed Virgin,
uttered by him when fetching a stroke with his axe, hermetically sealed, in a
glass viol. Vide Bp. Wilkin's Secret and Swift Messenger, Chap. XVII.

This paper seems to contain in substance that proposal to perform music in perfect and mathematical proportions, of which mention has been made in the preceding account of this person, and refers to a musical experiment said to have been made before the society, for the purpose, as it seems, of trying the truth of his proportions. The nature of this experiment will best appear from the author's own words, which are these :—

'To prove the foregoing propositions, two viols 'were mathematically set out, with a particular fret 'for each string, that every stop might be in a per-'fect exactness : upon these a sonata was perform'd 'by Mr. Frederick and Mr. Christian Stefkins; 'whereby it appeared that the theory was certain, 'since all the stops were owned by them to be per-'fect. And that they might be proved agreeable to 'what the best ear and the best hand perform in 'modern practice, the famous Italian, Signor Gas-'parini,* plaid another sonata upon the violin in 'consort with them, wherein the most compleat har-'mony was heard.'

The result of this experiment was a conviction, at least of the author, that the harmony resulting from his division was the most complete that ever had been heard, and that by it the true theory of music was demonstrated, and the practice of it brought to the greatest perfection. Vide Philosoph. Trans. No. 302, page 2072. Jones's Abridgm. vol. IV. part II. page 469.

John Abell, one of the chapel in the reign of King Charles II. was celebrated for a fine counter-tenor voice, and for his skill on the lute. The king admired his singing, and had formed a resolution to send him, together with one of his chapel, Mr. Gostling, to the Carnival at Venice, in order to show the Italians what good voices were produced in England ; but the latter signifying an unwilling-ness to go, the king desisted from his purpose. He continued in the chapel till the time of the revolu-tion, when he was discharged as being a papist. Upon this he went abroad, and distinguished himself by singing in public in Holland, at Hamburg, and other places, where acquiring considerable sums of money, he lived profusely, and affected the expense of a man of quality, moving about in an equipage of his own, though at intervals he was so reduced as to be obliged to travel, with his lute slung at his back, through whole provinces. In rambling he got as far as Poland ; and upon his arrival at Warsaw, the king having notice of it, sent for him to his court. Abell made some slight excuse to evade going, but upon being told that he had everything to fear from the king's resentment, he made an apology, and re-ceived a command to attend the king next day. Upon his arrival at the palace, he was seated in a chair in the middle of a spacious hall, and imme-diately drawn up to a great height ; presently the king with his attendants appeared in a gallery oppo-

site to him, and at the same instant a number of wild bears were turned in ; the king bade him then choose whether he would sing or be let down among the bears : Abell chose the former, and declared afterwards that he never sang so well in his life. This fact is alluded to in a letter from Pomigny de Auvergne to Mr. Abell of London, singing-master, among the letters from the dead to the living in the works of Mr. Thomas Brown, vol. II. page 189.†

Mattheson, in his Vollkommenen Cappellmeister, takes notice of Abell, and says that he sang in Hol-land, and at Hamburg, with great applause. He adds that he was possessed of some secrets, by which he preserved the natural tone of his voice to an ex-treme old age.

About the latter end of Queen Ann's reign Abell was at Cambridge with his lute, but he met there with poor encouragement. How long he lived after-wards is not known, but the account of his death was communicated to the gentleman who furnished many of the above particulars by one, who, having known him in his prosperity, assisted him in his old age, and was at the expense of his funeral.

After having rambled abroad for many years, it seems that Abell returned to England, for in 1701 he published at London a Collection of Songs in several languages, with a dedication to King William, wherein he expresses a grateful sense of his majesty's favours abroad, and more especially of his great cle-mency in permitting his return to his native country. In this collection is a song of Prior, ' Reading ends in melancholy,' published among his posthumous works, and there said to have been set by Mr. Abell. Mention is made in the Catalogue of Estienne Roger of Amsterdam, of a work of Abell, entitled ' Les Airs d'Abell pour le Concert du Duole ;' and in the ' Pills to purge Melancholy,' vol. IV. are two songs, set by Abell to very elegant tunes.

CHAP. CLI.

John Birchensha was probably a native of Ireland ; at least it is certain that he resided at Dublin in the family of the Earl of Kildare, till the rebellion in the year 1641 drove him from thence hither : he was remarkable for being a very genteel man in his person and behaviour ; he lived in London many years after the restoration, and taught the viol. Shadwell, in his comedy of the Humourists, act III. puts this speech into the mouth of a brisk fantastical coxcomb, 'That's an excellent Corant ; really I must ' confess that Grabu is a pretty hopeful man ; but ' Birkenshaw is a rare fellow, give him his due ; for ' he can teach men to compose that are deaf, dumb, ' and blind.'   [*walks about combing his peruke.*‡

---

* Francesco Gasparini, of whom an account is given in page 678 of this work. The two persons of the name of Stefkins were of the king's band in 1694, as appears by Chamberlayne's present State of England, published in that year, and were the sons of Theodore Stefkins, a very fine performer on the lute, celebrated by Salmon in his essay to the Advancement of Music.

† In this letter are many intimations that Abell was a man of intrigue; there are in it also allusions to some facts not particularly mentioned, as that the king of France presented him with a valuable diamond for singing before him, which was stolen from him by an Irishman ; and that he received a sum of money from the Elector of Bavaria for some particular purpose, and went off with it ; and in Abell's answer he is made to confess the fact, by his apology that it was but spoiling the Egyptians. In another letter of the same person from Henry Purcell to Dr. Blow, Abell is celebrated as a fine singer. Brown's Works vol. II. page 297.

‡ Combing the peruke, at the time when men of fashion wore large wigs, was even at public places an act of gallantry. The combs for this

The last sentence of the above speech has an allusion to a proposal of his, hereunder mentioned, for printing by subscription a work entitled Syntagma Musicæ. He published in 1664, Templum Musicum, or the Musical Synopsis of Johannes Henricus Alstedius,* and a small tract in one sheet, entitled Rules and Directions for composing in Parts.

In the Philosophical Transactions for the year 1672, page 5153, is the following pompous advertisement respecting a book which Birchensha was about to publish. 'There is a book preparing for the press ' entituled Syntagma Musicæ, in which the eminent ' author, John Birchensha, Esq. treats of music ' philosophically, mathematically, and practically. ' And because the charge of bringing this book to ' the press will be very great, especially the several ' cuts therein, with their printing off, amounting by ' computation to more than 500l. besides other great ' expenses for the impression of the said book, divers ' persons, for the encouragement of the said author ' have advanced several sums of money, who for ' every 20s. so advanced are to receive one of the ' said books fairly bound up; the author engaging ' himself under his hand and seal to deliver to each ' of the subscribers and advancers of so much money ' one of the said books, at or before the 24th March, ' 1674. In which excellent work there will be :—

' 1st. A discovery of the reasons and causes of ' musical sounds and harmony. A complete scale ' of music never before perfected. The proportions ' of all consonant and dissonant sounds useful in ' music, demonstrated by entire numbers, which the ' author says hath not been done by any. The ' different opinions of musical authors reconciled. ' Of sounds generated and diffused in their medium. ' Of their difference to the organ of hearing; together ' with their reception there, and wonderful effects. ' Of the matter, form, quantity, and quality of musical ' bodies or sounds: that musical sounds are originally ' in the radix or unison; and of their fluxion out of ' it. Of the general and special kinds, differences, ' properties, and accidents of sounds. Of the truth ' and falsehood of sounds.

' 2. Of the mathematical principles of music. ' Of the whole and parts of the scale of music. ' Of sounds equal and unequal. Of the numeration,

' addition, subtraction, multiplication, and division ' of musical sounds. Of musical proportions and ' their various species. What a musical body or ' sound mathematically considered, viz. as numerable, ' is. Of musical medieties, scilicet, arithmetical, ' geometrical, and harmonical; together with eight ' other musical medieties, of which no mention is ' made by any musical author. Of the radixes of ' musical numbers; and that by their powers all ' those numbers, and no other, which demonstrate ' the proportions of sounds do arise. Of music ' diatonic, chromatic, and enharmonic. Of the prin- ' cipals of a musical magnitude : What and how ' manifold they are; how they are conjoin'd. Of ' the contact, section, congruity, and adscription of ' a musical body. Of the commensurability thereof. ' In what respect a musical sound may be said to be ' infinite, and how to bound that infinity.

' 3. Of musical systems, characters, voice or ' key. Of the transposition of keys. Of the mu- ' tations of musical voice. Of musical pauses and ' periods. Of the denomination of notes. Of the ' moods and intervals. Of pure and florid counter- ' point. Of figurate music. Of fugues, canons, ' double descant, syncope, of the mensuration of ' sounds called time; the reason thereof. Of choral ' musick both Roman and English. Of the rythmical ' part of music. Of solmization, and the reason ' thereof.

' 4. The abstruse and difficult terms of this science ' are explained. The unnecessary and mystical sub- ' tleties into which the causes both of the theory ' and practice of music were reduced, to the great ' obscuring this art, are omitted : the principles of ' philosophy, mathematicks, grammar, rhetoric, and ' poetry are applied to musical sounds, and illustrated ' by them; the generation of such sounds is discoursed ' of, and particularly demonstrated.

' 5. An easy way is by this author invented for ' making airy tunes of all sorts by a certain rule, ' which most men think impossible to be done; and ' the composing of two, three, four, five, six, and ' seven parts, which by the learner may be performed ' in a few months, viz. in two months he may exqui- ' sitely, and with all the elegancies of music, compose ' two parts; in three months three parts, and so ' forward, as he affirms many persons of honour and ' worth have often experienced, which otherwise ' cannot be done in so many years.

' 6. Whatsoever is grounded upon the several ' hypotheses and postulata in this book, is clearly ' demonstrated by tables, diagrams, systems,' &c.

This book was either never published, or is become very scarce; for after a very careful search, and much inquiry, a copy of it has not been found.

Birchensha was also the publisher of that book written by Thomas Salmon, which gave rise to the controversy between the author and Matthew Lock, of which an account has already been given. The preface to it is subscribed John Birchensha.

THOMAS MACE (a Portrait), a practitioner on the lute, one of the clerks of Trinity college, Cambridge, stands distinguished among the writers on music by

---

purpose were of a very large size, of ivory or tortoise-shell curiously chased and ornamented, and were carried in the pocket as constantly as the snuff-box: at court, on the mall, and in the boxes, gentlemen conversed and combed their perukes. There is now in being a fine picture by the elder Laroon, of John duke of Marlborough at his levee, in which his grace is represented dressed in a scarlet suit, with large white satin cuffs, and a very long white peruke, which he combs while his valet, who stands behind him, adjusts the curls after the comb has passed through them.

* ALSTEDIUS was a German divine of the reformed religion, and one of the most voluminous writers of the last century. He was for many years professor of theology and philosophy at Herborn, in the county of Nassau, and after that at Alba-Julia in Transylvania; and was one of the divines that assisted at the synod of Dort. He laboured for the greatest part of his life to reduce the several branches of science into systematical order, in which, according to the opinion of most men, he succeeded well. Nevertheless it must be said of the Templum Musicum that it is so formal as to resemble a logical more than a musical treatise. Of the many works which he was the author of, his encyclopœdia and his Thesaurus Chronologicus are deemed the most valuable. He was a Millenarian, and published in 1627 a treatise De Mille Annis, wherein he taught that the faithful shall reign with Jesus Christ upon earth a thousand years, at the end whereof would be the general resurrection and last judgment; and he asserted that this reign would commence in the year 1694. He died at Alba-Julia in the year 1638, being fifty years of age.

EFFIGIES THO: MACE TRIN.

COL. CANTABR. CLERICI

ÆTAT. SUÆ LXIII.

a work entitled ' Musick's Monument, or a Remem-
' brancer of the best practical Musick both divine
' and civil, that has ever been known to have been
' in the world,' folio, 1676.

This person was born in the year 1613: under
whom he was educated, or by what means he became
possessed of so much skill in the science of music,
as to be able to furnish out matter for a folio volume,
he has no where informed us : nevertheless his book
contains so many particulars respecting himself, and
so many traits of an original and singular character,
that a very good judgment may be formed both of
his temper and ability. With regard to the first, he
appears to have been an enthusiastic lover of his
art ; of a very devout and serious turn of mind, and
cheerful and good-humoured under the infirmities
of age, and the pressure of misfortunes. As to the
latter, his knowledge of music seems to have been
confined to the practice of his own instrument, and
so much of the principles of the science, as enabled
him to compose for it; but for his style in writing
he certainly never had his fellow.

As to the book itself, a singular vein of humour
runs through it, which is far from being disgusting,
as it exhibits a lively portraiture of a good-natured,
gossiping old man, and this may serve as an apology
for giving his sentiments in many instances in his
own phrase.

The four first chapters of his first book are an
eulogium on psalmody and parochial music ; the
fifth contains a recommendation of the organ for that
purpose ; and the sixth, with its title, is as follows :—

' How to procure an Organist.

' The certain way I will propose shall be this,
' viz., first, I will suppose you have a parish clark,
' and such an one as is able to set and lead a psalm,
' although it be never so indifferently.

' Now this being granted, I may say that I will,
' or any musick master will, or many more inferiours,
' as virginal players, or many organ makers, or
' the like ; I say any of those will teach such a
' parish clark how to pulse or strike most of our
' common psalm-tunes, usually sung in our churches,
' for a trifle, viz. 20, 30, or 40 shillings, and so well
' that he need never bestow more cost to perform
' that duty sufficiently during his life.

' This I believe no judicious person in the art will
' doubt of. And then, when this clark is thus well
' accomplished, he will be so doated upon by all the
' pretty ingenuous children and young men in the
' parish, that scarcely any of them but will be begging
' now and then a shilling or two of their parents to
' give the clark, that he may teach them to pulse a
' psalm-tune ; the which any such child or youth
' will be able to do in a week or fortnight's time
' very well.

' And then again, each youth will be as ambitious
' to pulse that psalm-tune in publick to the congre-
' gation, and no doubt but shall do it sufficiently well.

' And thus by little and little the parish in a short
' time will swarm or abound with organists, and
' sufficient enough for that service.

' For you must know, and I intreate you to be-

' lieve me, that seriously it is one of the most easie
' pieces of performances in all instrumental musick,
' to pulse one of our psalm-tunes truly and well after
' a very little shewing upon an organ.

' The clark likewise will quickly get in his money
' by this means.

' And I suppose no parent will grutch it him, but
' rather rejoyce in it.

' Thus you may perceive how very easily and cer-
' tainly these two great difficulties may be overcome,
' and with nothing so much as a willing mind.

' Therefore be but willingly resolved, and the
' work will soon be done.

' And now again methinks I see some of you
' tossing up your caps, and crying aloud, " We will
" have an organ, and an organist too; for 'tis but
" laying out a little dirty money, and how can we
" lay it out better than in that service we offer up
" unto God ? and who should we bestow it upon, if
" not upon him and his service ?"

' This is a very right and an absolute good resolve,
' persist in it and you will do well, and doubtless
' find much content and satisfaction in your so doing.

' For there lies linked to this an unknown and un-
' apprehended great good benefit, which would re-
' dound certainly to all or most young children, who
' by this means would in their minorities be so
' sweetly tinctured or seasoned, as I may say, or
' brought into a kind of familiarity or acquaintance
' with the harmless innocent delights of such pure
' and undefilable practices, as that it would be a great
' means to win them to the love of virtue, and to
' disdain, contemn, and slight those common, gross,
' ill practices which most children are incident to
' fall into in their ordinary and accustomed pursuits.'

But lest his arguments in favour of the general
use of the organ should fail, this author shows in
Chap. VIII. how psalms may be performed in
churches without that instrument; his method is
this :—

' Wheresoever you send your children to the
' grammar-school, indent so with the master, that
' your children shall be taught one hour every day
' to sing, or one half day in every week at least,
' either by himself, or by some music-master whom
' he shall procure ; and no doubt but if you will pay
' for it the business may be effected.

' For there are divers who are able to teach to
' sing, and many more would quickly be, if such a
' general course were determined upon throughout
' the nation.

' There would scarcely be a schoolmaster but
' would or might be easily able himself to do the
' business once in a quarter or half a year ; and
' in a short time every senior boy in the school will
' be able to do it sufficiently well.

' And this is the most certain, easie, and substantial way that can possibly be advis'd unto.

' And thus, as before I told, how that your organists
' would grow up amongst you as your corn grew in
' the fields ; so now, if such a course as this would
' be taken, will your quiresters increase even into
' swarms like your bees in your gardens ; by which

'means the next generation will be plentifully able
'to follow St. Paul's counsel, namely, to teach and
'admonish one another in psalms, and hymns and
'spiritual songs, and so sing with a grace in their
'hearts and voices unto the Lord, and to the setting
'forth of his glorious praise.'

Chap. X. the author mentions the time and place
when and where was heard, as he professes to believe,
the most remarkable and excellent singing of psalms
known or remembered in these latter ages; in his
judgment far excelling all other either private or
public cathedral musick, and infinitely beyond all
verbal expression or conceiving.

'The time when was in the year 1644, the place
'where, was in the cathedral church of the royal
'city York.* * * * The occasion of it was the great
'and close siege which was then laid to the city,
'and strictly maintain'd for eleven weeks space, by
'three very notable and considerable great armies,
'viz. the Scotch, the Northern, and the Southern;
'whose three generals were these, for the Scotch,
'the old Earl Leven, viz. David Lessley, alias
'Lashley; for the Northern, the old Ferdinando
'Lord Fairfax; for the Southern, the Earl of
'Manchester: and whose three chief commanders
'next themselves were, for the Scotch, Lieutenant
'General ————; for the Northern, Sir Thomas
'now Lord Fairfax; and for the Southern, Oliver
'Cromwell, afterwards Lord Protector.

'By this occasion there were shut up within that
'city abundance of people of the best rank and
'quality, viz. lords, knights, and gentlemen of the
'countries round about, besides the soldiers and
'citizens, who all or most of them came constantly
'every Sunday to hear publick prayers and sermon
'in that spacious church.

'And indeed their number was so exceeding great,
'that the church was, I may say, even cramming or
'squeezing full.

'Now here you must take notice, that they had
'then a custom in that church, which I hear not in
'any other cathedral, which was, that always before
'the sermon the whole congregation sang a psalm,
'together with the quire and the organ: and you
'must also know, that there was then a most ex-
'cellent, large, plump, lusty, full-speaking organ,
'which cost, as I am credibly informed, a thousand
'pounds.

'This organ I say, when the psalm was set before
'the sermon, being let out into all its fullness of stops,
'together with the quire began the psalm.

'But when that vast concording unity of the
'whole congregational-chorus, came, as I may say,
'thundering in, even so as it made the very ground
'shake under us; Oh the unutterable ravishing
'soul's delight! in the which I was so transported
'and wrapt up in high contemplations, that there was
'no room left in my whole man, viz., body, soul,
'and spirit, for any thing below divine and heavenly
'raptures: nor could there possibly be any thing on
'earth to which that very singing might be truly
'compared, except the right apprehensions or con-
'ceivings of that glorious and miraculous quire, re-

'corded in the scriptures at the dedication of the
'temple, of which you may read in the 2 Chron.
'ch. 5, to the end; but more particularly eminent
'in the two last verses of that chapter, where king
'Solomon, the wisest of men, had congregated the
'most glorious quire that ever was known of in all
'the world: and at their singing of psalms, praises,
'or thanksgivings, the glory of the Lord came
'down amongst them, as there you may read.* * *
'But still further that I may endeavour to make
'this something more lively apprehended, or under-
'stood to be a real true thing.

'It would be considered that if at any time or
'place such a congregated number could perform
'such an outward service to the Almighty, with
'true, ardent, inward devotion, fervency, and affec-
'tionate zeal, in expectation to have it accepted by
'him; doubtless it ought to be believed that it
'might be and was done there and then.

'Because that at that time the desperateness and
'dismaidness of their danger could not but draw
'them into it, in regard the enemy was so very
'near and fierce upon them, especially on that side
'the city where the church stood; who had planted
'their great guns so mischievously against the
'church, and with which constantly in prayers time
'they would not fail to make their hellish dis-
'turbance, by shooting against and battering the
'church, insomuch that some times a canon bullet
'has come in at the windows, and bounced about
'from pillar to pillar, even like some furious fiend
'or evil spirit, backwards and forwards, and all
'manner of side ways, as it has happened to meet
'with square or round opposition amongst the
'pillars, in its returns or rebounds, untill its force
'has been quite spent.

'And here is one thing most eminently remarkable,
'and well worth noting, which was, that in all the
'whole time of the siege there was not any one
'person, that I could hear of, did in the church re-
'ceive the least harm by any of their devilish cannon
'shot; and I verily believe that there were con-
'stantly many more than a thousand persons at that
'service every Sunday during the whole time of
'that siege.'

In Chapters XI. and XII. this author treats of
cathedral music, and after asserting that we have in
this nation a large collection of compositions for
the church, so magnificently lofty and sublime, as
never to be excelled by art or industry, he laments
the paucity of clerks in the several choirs of this
kingdom, and the inability of many of them; and
assigns as a principal reason for the decline of
cathedral service, that the lay clerks are necessitated
to be barbers, shoemakers, tailors, and smiths, and
to follow other still inferior occupations, having no
better a provision than the ancient statutable wages;
the hardship of which restraint he says himself had
been an experimental witness of during more than
fifty years' service in the church; and upon this
occasion he tells a story to the following purpose,
of which he says he was both an eye and ear witness:
a singing man, a kind of pot-wit, very little skilled

in music, had undertaken in his choir to sing a solo anthem, but was not able to go through with it : as the dean was going out, and the clerk was putting off his surplice, the dean rebuked him sharply for his inability ; upon which with a most stern, angry countenance, and a vehement rattling voice, such as made the church ring, shaking his head at him, he answered the dean, 'Sir, I'd have you know that 'I sing after the rate of so much a year,' naming his wages, 'and except ye mend my wages, I am re-'solved never to sing better whilst I live.'

The second part of this work treats of the lute, and professes to lay open all the secrets of that instrument, which till the author's time were known only to masters ; and to this their closeness, and extreme shyness in revealing the secrets of the lute, he attributes it that the instrument is so little understood. On this occasion he complains of the French, who he says are generally accounted great masters, for that they would seldom or never write their lessons as they played them, much less reveal any thing that might tend to the understanding of the art of the instrument, so that there have seldom been at any time above one or two excellent or rare artists in this kind.

In the second chapter he endeavours to refute the common objections against the lute, such as that it is the hardest instrument in the world ; that it will take up the time of an apprenticeship to play well upon it ; that it makes young people grow awry ; that one had as good keep a horse as a lute for cost ; that it is a woman's instrument ; and that it is out of fashion. Under the objection of difficulty he takes notice that it is chiefly grounded on the number of strings on the lute, which he makes to be twelve, only six whereof are used in grasping or stopping ; the other six, being basses, and are struck open with the thumb : and the easiness of hitting them, he demonstrates by what he calls an apt comparison ; for he supposes a table with six or seven ranks of strings, such, he says, as many country people have at the end of some cupboards, fastened on with nails at each end, with small stones or sticks to cause them to rise and sound from the wood : he says that an ingenious child might strike these six or seven strings in order, resembling the bells, and then out of order, in changes ; and to these ranks of strings on the country people's cupboards does he resemble the six ranks of the lute-basses. The objection that the lute is a costly instrument, he answers by an affirmation that all his life long he never took more than five shillings the quarter to maintain a lute with strings, nor for the first stringing more than ten shillings.

Chap. III. contains directions how to know and choose a good lute ; the author says that the lutes most esteemed in his time were those made by Laux Maller, two whereof he says he had seen, pitiful, old, battered, cracked things, valued at one hundred pounds a-piece ; one of these he says was shown him by Goutier, the famous lutenist,* which the king had paid that sum for : the other he says was

* JACQUES GOUTER, vide page 697 of this work.

the property of Mr. Edward Jones, one of Goutier's scholars, who being minded to dispose of it, made a bargain with a merchant that desired to have it with him in his travels, that on his return he should either pay Mr. Jones a hundred pound as the price of it, or twenty pound for his use of it in the journey.

After a multiplicity of directions for ordering the lute, and particularly for taking off the belly, which he says is generally necessary once in a year or two, he proceeds in Chap. VI. to give directions for stringing the lute, and describes very minutely the various kinds of strings, and for the choice of a true length gives the following direction, which he calls a pretty curiosity :—

'First draw out a length or more, then take the 'end, and measure the length it must be of within 'an inch or two, for it will stretch so much at least 'in the winding up ; and hold that length in both 'hands, extended to a reasonable stiffness ; then 'with one of your fingers strike it, giving it so 'much liberty in slackness as you may see it vibrate, 'or open itself ; which, if it be true, it will appear 'to the eye just as if there were two strings ; but 'if it shews more than two it is false, and will sound 'unpleasantly upon your instrument ; nor will it ever 'be well in tune, either stopt or open, but snarle.'†

Chap. IX. contains an explanation of that kind of notation called the Tablature, in which each of the six strings of the lute are represented by a line, and the several frets or stops by the letters a, b c, d, e, f, g, h, y,‡ k, the letter a ever signifying the open string in all positions.§

With the same precision and singularity of style he describes the characters for the time of notes, calling the semibreve the master note ; and for the more easy division of it, calling that a groat, the minim two pence, the crotchet a penny, the quaver a half penny, and the semiquaver a farthing. From thence he proceeds to directions for the fingering, as also for the graces, one whereof, by him called the nerve-shake, he says he was not able to make well, and that for a reason, which with his usual pleasantry he gives in these words :—

'Some there are, and many I have met with, who 'have such a natural agility in their nerves, and 'aptitude to that performance, that before they could 'do anything else to purpose, they would make 'a shake rarely well. And some again can scarcely 'ever gain a good shake, by reason of the unaptness 'of their nerves to that action, but yet otherwise 'come to play very well.

'I for my own part have had occasion to break 'both my arms, by reason of which I cannot make

† This direction is given by Adrian Le Roy in his instructions for the lute. See page 420 of this work, and is adopted both by Mersennus and Kircher. Indeed this experiment is the only known test of a true string, and for that reason is practised by such as are curious at this day.

‡ y is used by him in preference to i, as being a more conspicuous character.

§ Of the notation by the tablature frequent mention has been made in the course of this work ; from the nature of it, it is obvious that it has not the least relation to the musical characters properly so called ; and the fact is, that many persons have been good performers on the lute, and at the same time totally ignorant of the notes of the Gamut, and yet there are masters of the lute who play by them ; and this is supposed in those compositions of Corelli's in particular, where the thorough-bass is said to be for the organ, harpsichord, or arch-lute.

'the nerve-shake well nor strong; yet by a certain 'motion of my arm, I have gained such a contentive 'shake, that sometimes my scholars will ask me how 'they shall do to get the like? I have then no 'better answer for them than to tell them they must 'first break their arm as I have done, and so possibly 'after that, by practice they may get my manner 'of shake.'

Among a variety of lessons of the author's composition, inserted in this his work, is one which he calls his Mistress, as having been composed a short time before his marriage, and at the instant when, being alone, he was meditating on his intended wife. It is written in tablature, but is here rendered in the characters of musical notation :—

Thomas Mace.

The occasion of his composing it, and the reasons for giving it the name of his Mistress, are related in the following singular history :—

'You must first know that it is a lesson, though 'old yet I never knew it disrelished by any; nor is 'there any one lesson in this book of that age as it 'is; yet I do esteem it in its kind, with the best 'lesson in the book, for several good reasons which 'I shall here set down.

'It is, this very winter, just 40 years since I made 'it; and yet it is new, because all like it; and 'then, when I was past being a suitor to my best 'beloved, dearest, and sweetest living mistress, but 'not married, yet contriving the best and readiest 'way towards it: and thus it was.

'That very night, in which I was thus agitated 'in my mind concerning her, my living mistress, 'she being in Yorkshire, and myself at Cambridge, 'close shut up in my chamber, still and quiet, about '10 or 11 a clock at night, musing and writing 'letters to her, her mother, and some other friends; 'in summing up and determining the whole matter 'concerning our marriage: You may conceive I 'might have very intent thoughts all that time, and 'might meet with some difficulties; for as yet I had 'not gained her mother's consent, so that in my 'writings I was sometimes put to my studyings. 'At which times, my lute lying upon my table, 'I sometimes took it up, and walked about my 'chamber, letting my fancy drive which way it 'would, for I studied nothing at that time as to 'musick; yet my secret genius or fancy prompted 'my fingers do what I could into this very humour, 'so that every time I walked and took up my lute 'in the interim betwixt writing and studying, this 'ayre would needs offer itself unto me continually; 'insomuch that at the last, liking it well, and lest 'it should be lost, I took paper and set it down, 'taking no further notice of it at that time; but 'afterwards it passed abroad for a very pleasant and 'delightful ayre amongst all; yet I gave it no name 'till a long time after, nor taking more notice of it 'in any particular kind, than of any other my com- 'posures of that nature.

'But after I was married, and had brought my

'wife home to Cambridge, it so fell out that one 'rainy morning I stay'd within, and in my chamber, 'my wife and I were all alone; she intent upon her 'needle-works, and I playing upon my lute at the 'table by her. She sat very still and quiet, listning 'to all I played without a word a long time, till at 'last I happened to play this lesson, which so soon 'as I had once play'd, she earnestly desired me to 'play it again; for, said she, that shall be called 'my lesson.

'From which words so spoken with emphasis and 'accent, it presently came into my remembrance the 'time when, and the occasion of its being produced, 'and returned her this answer, viz., That it may very 'properly be called your lesson, for when I composed 'it you were wholly in my fancy, and the chief 'object and ruler of my thoughts; telling her how 'and when it was made; and therefore ever after 'I thus called it my Mistress; and most of my 'scholars since call it Mrs. Mace to this day.'

This relation is followed by a kind of commentary on the lesson itself in these words :—

'First, observe the two first bars of it, which will 'give you the fugue, which fugue is maintained quite 'through the whole lesson.

'Secondly, observe the form and shape of the 'whole lesson, which consists of two uniform and 'equal strains, both strains having the same number 'of bars.

'Thirdly, observe the humour of it, which you 'may perceive by the marks and directions is not 'common.

'These three terms or things ought to be con- 'sidered in all compositions and performances of 'this nature, viz., ayres or the like.

'The fugue is lively, ayrey, neat, curious, and 'sweet like my mistress.

'The form is uniform, comely, substantial, grave, 'and lovely like my mistress.

'The humour is singularly spruce, amiable, plea- 'sant, obliging, and innocent like my mistress.'

He afterwards composed a second part of this 'lesson, so contrived, as to be, as he calls it, a Consort- 'lesson to the former, to be played upon another 'equal lute, or as a lone lesson.

THOMAS MACE.

Touching the performance of which, he gives a direction, purporting that when the second part is played with the first, the performer is to rest the two last notes of the fourth bar, and the three first notes of the fifth.

The remainder of the second part consists of directions for the composition of lessons for the lute, as namely, Preludes, Fancies, and Voluntaries, Pavans, Almains, Galliards, Corantos, Sarabands, Tattle de Moys,* Chacones, Toys or Jigs, Common tunes,† and Grounds, with examples of each; and concludes with a comparison between two tunings of the lute, the one called by him the flat tuning, and the other the new tuning, though he says it was in his time at least forty years old: the latter of these he endeavours by a variety of examples to prove is the best, and concludes his argument with this assertion, 'The flat tuning is a most perfect, full, 'plump, brisk, noble, heroic tuning; free and copious, 'fit, aptly and liberally to express any thing in any 'of the 7 keys; but that new tuning is far short of 'these accommodations, and is obviously subject to 'several inconveniences.'

The third part treats of the viol, and of music in general; and here he takes occasion to lament the abuse of music in the disproportionate numbers of bass and treble instruments in the concerts of his time, in which he says it was not unusual to have but one small weak-sounding bass-viol, and two or three violins, scolding violins, as he calls them; nay he says that he has frequently heard twenty or more violins at a sumptuous meeting, and scarce half so many basses, which latter he says should in reason be the greater number.

Of the concerts which he had been accustomed to hear in his youth, and before the violin became a concert instrument, he never speaks but in such

terms of rapture, as shew him to have been thoroughly susceptible of the charms of music. The following is his description of them, and refers to about the beginning of the last century :—

'In my younger time we had musick most ex-'cellently choice and most eminently rare, both 'for its excellency in composition, rare fancy, and 'sprightly ayre; as also for its proper and fit per-'formances; even such, as if your young tender ears 'and fantasies, were but truly tinctured therewith, 'and especially if it possibly could but be cry'd up 'for the mode or new fashion, you would embrace 'for some divine thing.

'And lest it should be quite forgot, for want of 'sober times, I will set down, as a remembrancer 'and well-wisher to posterity, and an honourer of 'the memory of those most eminent worthy masters 'and authors, who some of them being now de-'ceased, yet some living, the manner of such musick 'as I make mention of, as also the nature of it.

'We had for our grave musick Fancies of 3, 4, 5, 'and 6 parts to the organs, interposed, now and then, 'with some Pavins, Allmaines, solemn and sweet 'delightful ayres, all which were, as it were, so many 'pathetical stories, rhetorical and sublime discourses, 'subtil and acute argumentations, so suitable and 'agreeing to the inward, secret, and intellectual 'faculties of the soul and mind, that to set them forth 'according to their true praise, there are no words suf-'ficient in language; yet what I can best speak of them 'shall be only to say, that they have been to myself, 'and many others, as divine raptures, powerfully cap-'tivating all our unruly faculties and affections for the 'time, and disposing us to solidity, gravity, and a 'good temper, making us capable of heavenly and 'divine influences.

''Tis great pity few believe thus much; but far 'greater that so few know it.

'The authors of such like compositions have been 'divers famous Englishmen and Italians, some of 'which for their very great eminency and worth in 'that particular faculty, I will name here, viz., Mr.

* This is the name of an air invented by himself, much like a Saraband, but having as he expresses it, more of conceit in it, and speaking in a manner those very words.

† These tunes he says are such as the boys and common people sing about the streets, many whereof were then as the common song-tunes have since been, most excellent.

'Alfonso Ferabosco, Mr. John Ward, Mr. Lupo, Mr.
'White, Mr. Richard Deering, Mr, William Lawes,
'Mr. John Jenkins, Mr. Christopher Simpson, Mr.
'Coperario, and one Monteverde, a famous Italian
'author; besides divers and very many others, who
'in their late time were all substantial, able, and pro-
'found composing masters in this art, and have left
'their works behind them, as fit monuments and
'patterns for sober and wise posterity, worthy to be
'imitated and practised: 'tis great pity they are so
'soon forgot and neglected, as I perceive they are
'amongst many.

'And these things were performed upon so many
'equal and truly-siz'd viols, and so exactly strung,
'tuned, and played upon, as no one part was any
'impediment to the other; but still, as the composi-
'tion required, by intervals, each part amplified and
'heightened the other, the organ evenly, softly, and
'sweetly according to all.

'We had, beyond all this, a custom at our meet-
'ings, that commonly after such instrumental music
'was over, we did conclude all with some vocal
'music to the organ, or, for want of that, to the
'Theorboe.

'The best which we ever did esteem, were those
'things which were most solemn and divine, some of
'which I will for their eminency name, viz. Mr.
'Deering's Gloria Patri, and other of his Latin songs,
'now lately collected and printed by Mr. Playford,
'a very laudable and thank-worthy work, besides
'many other of the like nature, Latin and English,
'by most of the above-named authors and others,
'wonderfully rare, sublime, and divine beyond all
'expression.

'But when we would be most ayrey, jocond,
'lively, and spruce, then we had choice and singular
'consorts, either for 2, 3, or 4 parts, but not to the
'organ, as many, now a days, improperly and unad-
'visedly perform such like consorts with, but to the
'harpsicon; yet more properly and much better to
'the pedal, an instrument of a late invention, con-
'trived, as I have been inform'd, by one Mr. John
'Hayward of London, a most excellent kind of in-
'strument for a consort, and far beyond all harpsicons
'or organs that I yet ever heard of, I mean either
'for consort or single use; but the organ far beyond
'it for those other performances before mentioned.'

Of the pedal above mentioned he gives a brief description, which seems to indicate that it was a kind
of harpsichord with stops to be governed by the
feet. He says that the pedal was not commonly
used or known, because few could make of them
well, and fewer would go to the price of them, twenty
pounds being the ordinary price of one, but that the
great patron of music in his time, Sir Robert Bolles,
whom in the university he had the happiness to
initiate in the high art of music, had two of them,
the one at thirty pounds, and the other at fifty pounds.

He then proceeds to give directions for procuring
and maintaining the best music imaginable, and exhibits first the plan of a music-room contrived by
himself for concerts, with galleries for auditors,
capable of holding two hundred persons. Among
the instruments proper for a great concert to be
performed in this room, he recommends a table-
organ, as being far more reasonable and proper than
an upright organ. He says that two table organs
were in being at the time when he wrote his book,
that they were of his own contrivance, and were
for his own use, as to the maintaining of public
concerts, &c. and that he did design to erect such
a music-room as he has described, but that it
pleased God to disappoint and discourage him,
chiefly by the loss of his hearing, and the consequent emptiness of his purse; but concludes his
account with an advertisement, that although it had
been his unhappiness to be compelled to part with
these instruments, yet that one of them was then to
be sold, and that if any person would send to him
about it, he would find it a very, very, jewel. He
next recommends as the properest instruments for
a concert, a chest of viols, a description whereof,
as the term is at this day scarcely understood, is here
given in his own words:—

'Your best provision and most compleat will be
'a good chest of viols, six in number, viz., two
'basses, two tenors, and two trebles, all truly and
'proportionably suited.

'Of such there are no better in the world than
'those of Aldred, Jay, Smith, yet the highest in
'esteem are Bolles and Ross; one bass of Bolles
'I have known valued at 100*l*. These were old,
'but we have now very excellent good workmen,
'who no doubt can work as well as those, if they
'be so well paid for their work as they were; yet
'we chiefly value old instruments before new; for
'by experience they are found to be far the best.
'****** But if you cannot procure an intire
'chest of viols, suitable, &c. endeavour to pick up
'here or there so many excellent good odd ones, as
'near suiting you as you can, every way, viz., both
'for shape, wood, colour, &c. but especially for size.

'And to be exact in that, take this certain rule,
'viz. let your bass be large: Then your trebles
'must be just as short again in the string, viz., from
'bridge to nut, as are your basses, because they
'stand eight notes higher than the basses, therefore
'as short again; for the middle of every string is
'an eighth. The tenors in the string just so long
'as from the bridge to F fret, because they stand
'a fourth higher than your basses, therefore so long.

'Let this suffice to put you into a compleat order
'for viols either way; only note, that the best place
'for the bridge is to stand just in the three quarter
'dividing of the open cuts below, though most,
'most erroneously suffer them much to stand too
'high, which is a fault.

'After all this you may add to your press a pair
'of violins, to be in readiness for any extraordinary
'jolly or jocund consort occasion; but never use
'them but with this proviso, viz., be sure you make
'an equal provision for them, by the addition and
'strength of basses, so that they may not out-cry
'the rest of the musick, the basses especially; to
'which end it will be requisite you store your press
'with a pair of lusty, full-sized Theorboes, always

'to strike in with your consorts or vocal musick, to
'which that instrument is most naturally proper.

'And now to make your store more amply com-
'pleat, add to these three full-sized Lyra-viols, there
'being most admirable things made, by our very best
'masters for that sort of musick, both consort-wise,
'and peculiarly for two or three Lyres.

'Let them be lusty, smart-speaking viols; because
'that in consort they often retort against the treble,
'imitating, and often standing instead of that part,
'viz., a second treble.

'They will serve likewise for Division-viols very
'properly.

'And being thus stored, you have a ready enter-
'tainment for the greatest prince in the world.'

He next proceeds to give directions for the practice of the viol, together with a few lessons by way
of example; and concludes with a chapter on music
in general, but which contains nothing more than
some reflections of the author on the mysteries of
music, which he says have a tendency to strengthen
faith, and are a security against the sin of atheism.

Mace does not appear to have held any considerable rank among musicians, nor is he celebrated
either as a composer or practitioner on the lute;
nevertheless his book is a proof that he was an
excellent judge of the instrument, and contains such
a variety of directions for the ordering and management thereof, as also for the performance on it, as
renders it a work of great utility. In it are many
curious observations respecting the choice of stringed
instruments, the various kinds of wood of which
they are made, the method of preserving them, and
the preference due to the several kinds of strings imported hither from Rome, Venice, Pistoja, Lyons,
and other places. In another view of it his work
must be deemed a great curiosity, as containing in it
a full and accurate description of that kind of notation called the Tablature, of the truth and accuracy
whereof proof has been made by persons ignorant of
the lute, in the translation of some of his lessons
into the characters of musical notation. The singularity of his style, remarkable for a profusion of
epithets and words of his own invention, and tauto-
logy without end, is apt to disgust such as attend less
to the matter than the manner of his book; but on
others it has a different effect, as it exhibits, without
the least reserve, all the particulars of the author's
character,* which the reader will easily discern was
not less amiable than singular.

The engraving given of Mace (see Portrait
Volume) is taken from one of Faithorne, prefixed to
his book, the inscription under which bespeaks him
to have been sixty-three years of age in 1676. How
long he lived afterwards is not known. It seems
that he had children, for in his book he speaks of

his youngest son named John, who, with scarce any
assistance from his father, had attained to great proficiency on the lute by reading his book.†

CHAP. CLII.

JOHN PLAYFORD (a Portrait), born in the year
1613, was a stationer and seller of musical instruments, music-books, and music-paper. What his
education had been is not known, but that he had
attained to a considerable proficiency in the practice
of music and musical composition is certain. In the
Ashmolean Manuscript it is said he was clerk of the
church belonging to the Temple, and that he dwelt
near the Inner Temple gate. This latter assertion
is erroneous in two respects, for in the first place
many of the title-pages of books published by him
describe his shop as situated in the Temple near the
church-door; and it may be thence conjectured that
it was at the foot of the steps, either on the right
hand or on the left, descending from the Inner
Temple-lane to the cloisters. As to his dwelling,
it was in Arundel-street in the Strand.

In the year 1655 he published an introduction to
the skill of music, which appears to be extracted from
Morley's Introduction, Butler's Principles of Music,
and other books on the subject of music; it is divided into three books, the first containing the
principles of music, with directions for singing; the
second, instructions for the bass, treble, and tenor
viol, and also for the treble violin, with lessons for
each; and the third the art of descant, or composing
of music in parts.

Wood says that in the drawing up of this book
Playford had the assistance of Charles Pidgeon of
Grays-Inn; and that Dr. Benjamin Rogers also
assisted him in many of his vocal compositions, of
which there are many extant. Be this as it may,
the Introduction of Playford, as it was written in
a plain and easy style, succeeded so well, that in
the year 1683 was published a tenth edition of it,
considerably improved and enlarged by the author
and his friends. This is the edition referred to
here and elsewhere in this work, its character being
that it is fuller than some editions, and more correct
than any.

The explanation given by this author of the scale
of music, and of the several kinds of time, are no
other than are to be found in most books on the
subject; but what he says of the graces proper in
singing is entire new matter, and is taken from
a tract with this title: 'A brief discourse of the
'Italian manner of singing, wherein is set down the
'use of those graces in singing, as the Trill and
'Gruppo, used in Italy, and now in England;
'written some years since by an English gentleman
'who had lived long in Italy, and, being returned,
'taught the same here.'‡

---

* The most remarkable of these are that affected precision with which
he constantly delivers himself, and his eager desire to communicate to
others, even to the most hidden secrets, all the knowledge he was
possessed of. In the relation he gives of the occasion of composing that
lesson of his called Mrs. Mace, and the tenderness and affection with
which he speaks of her who had been his wife more than forty years,
who does not see the portrait of a virtuous and kind-hearted man? To
which we may add, that the book throughout breathes a spirit of devotion; and, agreeably to his sentiments of music, is a kind of proof that
his temper was improved by the exercise of his profession.

† Page 45. To this instance of the efficacy of his book in teaching
the practice of the lute, it may here be added, that the late Mr. John
Immyns, lutenist to the chapel royal, had the like experience of it.
This person, who had practised on sundry instruments for many years,
and was able to sing his part at sight, at the age of forty took to the lute,
and by the help of Mace's book alone, became enabled to play thorough-
bass, and also easy lessons on it, and by practice had rendered the
tablature as familiar to him as the notes of the scale.

‡ Who was the author of this discourse is not known. He says of

Of the graces here treated on, the Trill, or plain shake, and the Gruppo are the chief: the first is defined to be a shake upon one note only, in the making whereof the scholar is directed to sing the first of these examples :—

Trill.

Co — — — — — — — — — — re

Gruppo.

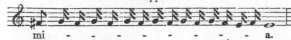

mi — — — — — — — — — . — a.

beginning with the first crotchet, and beating every note with the throat upon the vowel o to the last breath. The Gruppo as defined by this author, appears to be no other than the shake now practised, and which consists in the alternate prolation of two tones in juxta position to each other, with a close on the note immediately beneath the lower of them. The second of the above examples is intended to explain it. The first of these graces, called the Trill, or plain shake, is farther described in the following note of Playford relating to it :—

'Our author having briefly set forth this chief or 'most usual grace in singing called the Trill, which, 'as he saith very right, is by a beating in the throat 'on the vowel o; some observe that it is rather the 'shaking of the Uvula or palate on the throat in 'one sound upon a note: for the attaining of this 'the most sure and ready way is by imitation of 'those who are perfect in the same; yet I have 'heard of some that have attained it after this manner, 'in singing a plain-song of six notes up and six 'down, they have in the midst of every note beat or 'shaked with their finger upon their throat, which 'by often practice came to do the same notes exactly 'without. It was also my chance to be in company 'with some gentlemen at a musical practice, which 'sung their parts very well, and used this grace, 'called the Trill, very exactly. I desired to know 'their tutor, they told me I was their tutor, for they 'never had any other but this my Introduction. 'That, I answered, could direct them but in the 'theory, they must needs have a better help in the 'practice, especially in attaining to sing the Trill 'so well. One of them made this reply, which 'made me smile; I used, said he, at my first learn-'ing the Trill to imitate the breaking of a sound in 'the throat, which men use when they lure their 'hawks, as he-he-he-he, which he used slow at first, 'and after more swift on several notes, higher and 'lower in sound, till he became perfect therein.

'The Trill being the most usual grace, is usually 'made in closes or cadences, and when on a long 'note exclamation or passion is expressed, there the

'Trill is made in the latter part of such note; but 'most usually upon binding notes, and such as pre-'cede the closing note. To those who once attain 'to the perfect use of the Trill, other graces will be-'come easie.*'

Of the other graces in singing mentioned by this author, the exclamation is the chief, and which is nothing more than an increase of the voice to some degree of loudness at the extremity of an ascending passage.

After sundry examples of short songs for the practice of learners, and a few of the most common psalm tunes, follows the order of performing the divine service in cathedrals and collegiate chapels, taken from Edward Low's treatise on that subject, of which an account has already been given. The second book consists of an introduction to the playing on the bass viol or viol da gamba, as also on the other instruments of that species, namely, the treble and tenor viol; this is followed by a like introduction to the treble violin, including the tuning of the tenor or bass violin. What the author has said respecting the first of these two classes of instruments has been given in a preceding page, and the following extracts from his book will show the system of the latter, as also the manner of teaching the violin in the author's time.

It has already been related that the notation by the tablature had been transferred from the lute to the viol. This method had been found so easy and convenient for those who were content to be small proficients, that it was applied also to the violin, and may be understood by the following scale and example of a tune called Parthenia, set in that manner :—

The First or Treble.   The Second or small Mean.

The Third or great Mean.   The Fourth String or Bass.

himself that he had been taught that noble manner of singing which he professes to teach others, by the famous Scipione del Palla in Italy; and that he had heard the same frequently practised there by the most famous singers, men and women. He speaks also of airs of his composition, which, as also this discourse, were by him intended for publication. Playford, in his Introduction, edit. 1666, says that the publication of it by the author was prevented by his death, but that the manuscript fortunately coming to his hands, he was by some of the most eminent masters encouraged to print it.

* Notwithstanding all that is above said of it, the trill must appear to be somewhat very different from a grace or ornament in singing; nay, that the practice of it approaches to a defect; for it is nothing less than an intermitted prolation of a single tone. As to the Gruppo or shake, properly so called, it is the chief grace, as well in instrumental as vocal performance; nevertheless it is not once mentioned by Morley or Butler, or any of the old English writers on music, and seems to have been unknown among us at the time when Playford wrote; which is much to be wondered at, seeing that it had been practised in Italy long before, as appears by Doni's treatise ' De Præstantia Musicæ veteris,' page 59, where Philoponus, one of the interlocutors, speaking of the graces and elegancies of modern music, makes use of these words : ' Hinc fre-'quentes argutissimorum ac prædulcium melismatum usurpationes; et 'Compismorum in clausulis jucundissimus usus.' The directions above given point out very properly where the shake may be used, but they were little heeded in England till the practice of the opera singers had taught us the true use of it. Those who can recollect Mr Phillip Hart,

JOHANNIS PLAYFORD EFFIGIES.

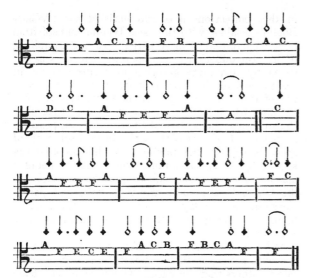

Which tune, according to the rule before given, respecting the lute and the viol, viz., that if a crotchet be over any letter, the following letters are to be crotchets also till the note be changed, and the like of other notes, is thus to be rendered in the characters of musical notation :—

Parthenia.

The third part of Playford's Introduction consists of rules for composing music in parts; but this has been varied from time to time in the several editions, as occasion offered. In that of 1660, the third part consisted solely of Dr. Campion's tract entitled 'The art of Descant, or composing music in parts, with the annotations of Christopher Simpson;' but in that of 1683 Campion's tract is rejected, and instead thereof we have 'A brief Introduction to the art of Descant, or composing music in parts,' without the name of the author, and probably written by Playford himself. In the subsequent editions, particularly that of 1713, this is continued, but with very considerable additions, said to have been made by Mr. Henry Purcell.

Playford appears to have possessed the friendship of most of the eminent musicians of his time, and in consequence thereof was the publisher of a very great number of music-books between the years 1650 and 1685. He was a good judge of music, had some skill in composition, and was very industrious in his vocation, contributing not a little to the improve-

ment of the art of printing music from letter-press types, by the use of what he calls in some of his publications the new tied note, of the invention whereof it may not be improper here to take some notice.*

The musical characters formerly in use in this kingdom were wrought from metal types : the notes were distinct from each other, and the quavers and semi-quavers were signified by single and double tails, without any mark of colligation or connection whatever. In the Melothesia of Matthew Lock, published by John Carr in 1673, the quaver and semi-quaver are joined by single and double tails. But it is to be noted that the music in that work is printed from copper-plates; from hence it is supposed Playford took the hint, and transferred the practice to letter-press types.

Of the numerous publications of Playford, the collection of Catches by John Hilton, entitled 'Catch that Catch can,' printed in 1652, seems to be the first. Playford was then clerk of the Temple church, and the book was sold at his shop near the church-door. In 1667 it was published with the additional title of the Musical Companion, with very considerable additions; and a second part, containing Dialogues, Glees, Ayres, and Ballads for two, three, and four voices. This edition was dedicated to Charles Pigeon, Esq. and other members of a music society and meeting in the Old Jewry, London. Before it are recommendatory verses in Latin and English, by the said Pigeon, who appears to have been a member of the society of Gray's Inn. In 1673 the Musical companion was published with still farther additions; and in 1687 a second book; and after that a few additional sheets without a title, but called the third part. The catches, rounds, and canons in this collection were composed by Hilton himself, Henry and William Lawes, Holmes, Nelham, Cranford, Ellis, Brewer, Webb, Jenkins, Dr. Child, Ives, Dr. Wilson, Ford, Dr. Rogers, Captain Cooke, Lock, and others, the most eminent musicians of that time; and it is not too much to say that they are the best of the kind extant.†

* In page 380 of this work, it is remarked that the first musical types used in this country appear in Higden's Polychronicon, printed by Wynkyn de Word, in the year 1495 : and their introduction being thus ascertained, it may be thought necessary to continue the history of music printing, at least in this country, down to that period to which we have brought the history of the science itself : and here it is to be noted that after Wynkyn de Word, Grafton appears to have used musical types, and after him old John Day of Aldersgate; but in queen Elizabeth's reign letters patent were obtained by Tallis and Bird, granting to them and their assigns the sole privilege of printing music: neither Tallis nor Bird were printers in fact, but they employed to print their Cantiones, in 1575, Thomas Vautrollier of Black Friars, and after him Thomas East, Est, or Este, who about the year 1600 changed his surname to Snodham.

In the year 1598 a patent, with ampler powers than were contained in the former, was granted to Thomas Morley, author of the Introduction; after the expiration of which it seems the business of music printing lay under no restraints, but was exercised by the printers in common, that is to say, by John Windet, William Barley, William Godbid, and many others, for various booksellers and publishers till the time of the restoration, soon after which the sellers of musical instruments took to the business of selling music books also.

† In this collection is a Three Part Song, 'The Glories of our Birth and State,' set by Edward Coleman, which was formerly much sung at Oxford and elsewhere, by the friends of king Charles I. as being thought to allude to his unhappy catastrophe. It was reputed to have been written on that occasion by Butler; and as such is printed among his Posthumous Works in three little volumes. Further to recommend it, the last stanza has very much the appearance of a version of a passage in the Eikon Basilike Sect. 15. Yet after all, the whole of it was written, and probably before

organist of the church of St. Mary Undershaft, and Mr. Bernard Gates, master of the children of the chapel royal, must have remarked in the playing of one and the singing of the other, such a frequent iteration of the shake, as destroyed the melody : and that even the last set of boys educated by the latter, sang in the manner their great grandfathers must be supposed to have done.

Another publication of Playford merits also particular notice in this place, as it explains a practice to which we at this day are strangers. The book here meant is entitled 'Musick's Recreation on the Viol Lyra-way,' concerning which the following advertisement is given in the preface :—

'The Lero or Lyra-Viol is so called from the 'Latin word Lyra, which signifies a harp, alluding 'to the various tuning under the name of Harp-way, '&c. This way of playing on the viol is but of late 'invention; an imitation of the old English lute or 'bandora, whose lessons were prickt down by certain 'letters of the alphabet, upon six lines or rules; 'which six lines did allude to the six course of 'strings upon those instruments, as they do now 'unto the six single strings upon the viol. The first 'authors of inventing and setting lessons this way to 'the viol were Mr. Daniel Farrant, Mr. Alphonso 'Ferabosco, and Mr. John Coperario, alias Cooper, 'who composed lessons not only to play alone, but 'for two or three Lyra-viols together in consort; 'and since it hath been much improved by the 'excellent inventions and skill of famous masters, 'viz., Mr. William Lawes, Dr. Colman, Mr. Jenkins, 'Mr. Ives, Mr. Hudson, Mr. Withie, Mr. Bates, Mr. 'Lillie, Mr. Gregory, Mr. Mosse, Mr. Wilson, and 'others.'

Playford says the Lyra-viol has six strings, as also frets or stops to the number of seven, on the neck of the instrument, to which are assigned seven letters of the alphabet, viz., **b, c, d, e, f, g, h,** the letter **a** answering to the open string wherever it occurs. It seems that there were sundry methods of tuning the Lyra-viol, which were severally adopted by the masters of the instrument, the most usual whereof were those termed harp-way sharp and harp-way flat, high harp-way sharp and high harp-way flat, and of these the book contains examples.

The two methods of notation for the viol and other stringed instruments, by the letters and by the notes, are severally distinguished by the terms Lyra-way and Gamut-way, with this exception, that the literal notation for the lute is ever called the Tablature; concerning which, as also the notation by letters in general, it may be observed that they do not imply the least degree of skill in the system or scale of music, and are therefore a very inartificial practice; the same may be said of the old method of notation for the flute and flageolet by dots, of which, as a matter of curiosity, an account will hereafter be given.

Playford's skill in music was not so great as to entitle him to the appellation of a master. He knew nothing of the theory of the science, but was very well versed in the practice, and understood the rules of composition well enough to write good harmony; of this he has given proofs in a great number of songs in two, three, and four parts, printed in the Musical companion, as also in his Psalms and Hymns in solemn Music, in four parts, printed in folio,[*] and

in that collection in octavo entitled the 'Whole Book of Psalms, with the usual Hymns and spiritual Songs, composed in three parts.' In the compiling of his Introduction it is apparent that he was assisted by men more knowing than himself; for in the preface to the later editions of it, particularly that of 1666, are sundry curious particulars relating to music which indicate a greater degree of learning than a man in his station of life could be supposed to be possessed of. Doubtless the book itself was of great benefit to the public, as it disseminated the knowledge of music among the common people; many learned to sing, and to play on the viol and the fiddle, in a homely way it is true, and parish clerks in the country acquired a competent skill in psalmody, having no other instructor than Playford's Introduction.

With such talents as Playford was possessed of, and with a temper that disposed him to communicate to others that knowledge which could not have been attained without much labour; and being besides an honest and friendly man, it is not to be wondered at that he lived upon terms of friendship with the most eminent professors of music his contemporaries, or that he should have acquired, as he appears to have done, almost a monopoly in the publication of music-books. He lived to near the age of fourscore. His memory is celebrated in two or three short poems on his death, and in an elegy by Nahum Tate, the then poet laureat, *which was set to music by Henry Purcell, and published in* 1687.

Playford had a son named John, a printer of music, and a younger named Henry, who followed the business of his father, at first in the shop near the door of the Temple-church, but afterwards in the Temple Exchange, Fleet-street. His dwelling-house was that which had been his father's in Arundel-street in the Strand. The music books advertised by him were but few in number compared with those published by his father. Among them were the Orpheus Britannicus, and the ten Sonatas, and the airs of Purcell. The printers employed by him were John Heptinstall and William Pearson; the latter greatly improved the art of printing music on metal types; he dwelt in Aldersgate-street, near the end of Long-lane, and was living after the year 1735.

Henry Playford published in 1701 what he called the second book of the 'Pleasant musical Companion, 'being a choice collection of Catches for three and 'four Voices; published chiefly for the encourage-'ment of the musical societies, which will be speedily 'set up in all the chief cities and towns in England.' The design of this publication is more fully explained in the preface to the book, particularly in the following passage :—

'And that he [the publisher] may be beneficial to 'the publick in forwarding a commendable society, 'as well as the sale of his book, he has prevailed with 'his acquaintance and others in this city to enter

---

the Eikon Basilike, as a solemn funeral song in a play of Shirley's, entitled 'The Contention of Ajax and Ulysses.' Vide Percy's Reliques of Ancient English Poetry, vol. I. page 270.

[*] It is worth remarking, that in the preface to this book it is said that the ancient practice in the singing of psalms in church was for the clerk to repeat each line; probably because at the first introduction of the psalms into our service, great numbers of the common people were unable to read.

'into several clubs weekly, at taverns of convenient
'distance from each other, having each house a par-
'ticular master of musick belonging to the society
'established in it, who may instruct those, if desir'd,
'who shall be unskilled, in bearing a part in the
'several catches contained in this book, as well as
'others; and shall perfect those who have already
'had some insight in things of this nature, that they
'shall be capable of entertaining the societies they
'belong to abroad. In order to this he has provided
'several articles to be drawn, printed, and put in
'handsome frames, to be put up in each respective
'room the societies shall meet in, and be observed
'as so many standing rules, which each respective
'society is to go by; and he questions not but the
'several cities, towns, corporations, &c. in the king-
'doms of Great Britain and Ireland, as well as foreign
'plantations, will follow the example of the well-
'wishers to vocal and instrumental musick in this
'famous city, by establishing such weekly meetings
'as may render his undertaking as generally received
'as it is useful. And if any body or bodies of gentle-
'men are willing to enter into or compose such
'societies, they may send to him, where they may
'be furnished with books and articles.'

This project was recommended in certain verses
written by Tom Brown, and dated from Mr. Steward's,
at the Hole in the Wall in Baldwin's Gardens,
inscribed to his friend Mr. Playford on his book of
Catches, and his setting up a weekly club for the
encouragement of music and good fellowship. It
had some success in promoting the practice of catch-
singing in and about London, and also at Oxford;
but it does not appear that in other parts of the
kingdom any such musical clubs or societies were
formed, as it was the drift of the proposal to
recommend.

It is conjectured that Henry Playford survived
his father but few years, for we meet with no publication by him after the year 1710, about which
time Mr. John Young was become a man of note in
the business of selling musical instruments and music
books. The shop of this person was at the corner
of London-House-yard in St. Paul's church-yard,
and was much frequented by the choir-men of St.
Paul's. Edward Ward, in his London Spy, says
that there was perpetual fiddling in it to draw in
customers, and that the door used to be crowded
with hearers; this Mr. John Young was the father
of a musical family, and of Mr. Talbot Young, a fine
performer on the violin, the founder of the Castle
concert in Paternoster-row, of whom there will be
occasion to speak hereafter.

CHAP. CLIII.

THE flute appears to be an instrument of great
antiquity in this kingdom; it is frequently mentioned
by Chaucer; and it seems by the description of it
in Mersennus, that there was a species of it, which
by himself and other foreigners was termed the
English Flute, 'Fistula dulcis seu Anglica.'* The

* See page 608 of this work.

proper and most discriminating appellation for it is
that of the Flute à bec, or beaked flute;† nevertheless we meet with ancient books of instructions
for the instrument, wherein it is termed, but very
improperly, as it is conceived, the Recorder. Milton
could never mean that they were one and the same
instrument, when in the same line he mentions

'Flutes and soft Recorders.'

Among bird-fanciers the word record is used as
a verb to signify the first essays of a bird in singing;‡
and it is well known that Bullfinches and other birds
are taught to sing by a flajolet. Lord Bacon, in his
Natural History, Cent. III. Sect. 221, speaks of
Recorders and Flutes at the same instant, and says
that the Recorder hath a less bore and a greater,
above and below; and elsewhere, Cent. II. Sect.
187, he speaks of it as having six holes, in which
respect it answers to the Tibia minor or flajolet of
Mersennus. From all which particulars it should
seem that the Flute and the Recorder were different
instruments, and that the latter in propriety of
speech was no other than the flajolet.§

Nevertheless the terms are confounded; and in
a book of instructions and lessons for the flute, so
old that the notation is by dots, the instructions
for the instrument are entitled directions for the
Recorder.

We are now to speak of the method of notation
by dots, which will easily be understood by such as
have ever had occasion to look into the books published for the instruction of learners on the flute,
German flute, or hautboy, for it consists simply of
a stave of eight lines, answering to the number of
holes on the instrument, whereon dots are placed to
signify when the holes are to be stopped, the uppermost line answering to the thumb-hole; so that dots
on all the eight lines bespeak the note F, and dots
on all the lines but the lowest, G; and so of the
rest: and as to the time, it was signified by such
characters as were used for the same purpose in the
tablature for the lute. The like way of playing by
dots was used for the flajolet, as appears by a book
entitled 'The Pleasant Companion, or new Lessons
'and Instructions for the Flagelet by Thomas
'Greeting, Gent.' printed for John Playford in 1675.

The last publication of this kind was a book
called The New Flute Master, printed in 1704, in
which are sundry preludes by Mr. John Banister,
the grandson of that Banister mentioned before to
have been sent to France by king Charles II. for
improvement on the violin; in this the learner is

† See an explanation of this term page 331, in note.

‡ Nevertheless the pastoral poets use it for the singing of birds in
general, as in these instances:—

Sweet Philomel, the bird,
    That hath the heavenly throat,
Doth now alas! not once affoord,
    Recording of a noate.
            N. BRETON, in ENGLAND'S HELICON.

Now birds *record* new harmonie,
    And trees do whistle melodies;
Now every thing that nature breeds,
    Doth clad itself in pleasant weedes.
            THO. WATSON, in the same collection.

§ *Thirlby, bishop of Westminster, while a scholar of Trinity Hall,
Cambridge, had a chamber under that of Bilney the martyr; at which time
he used often to play on his recorder for his diversions, and then good
Bilney would go to his prayers. Strype's Eccles. Mem. Vol. II. 464.*

3 B

furnished with directions for playing either Dot-way or Gamut-way, for these were the terms of distinction, and is left to his choice of either.

After what has been said of the tablature, and of the notation by dots, it must appear that the playing at sight after either of these methods was scarcely practicable, and that the rejection of them both is but a consequence of the great improvements of music within this last century.

From the account herein before given of the progress of music, it appears that through every stage of improvement, besides that it was the profession of persons educated to the practice of it, it was the recreation of gentlemen: among the latter, those of a more grave and serious turn betook themselves to the practice of the lute and viol da gamba,* resorting to it as a relief from study, and as an incentive to sober mirth. Others, less sensible of the charms of harmony and melody, looked upon music as a mere accomplishment, and were content to excel only on those instruments on which a moderate degree of proficiency might be attained with little labour and application; and these seem to have been the Flute à bec and the Flageolet: the latter of these was for the most part the amusement of boys; it was also used for the purpose of teaching birds, more particularly bullfinches, to sing easy tunes; for which reason one of the books of instructions for the flageolet now extant, is entitled The Bird-fancier's Delight; but the flute, especially of the larger size, was a more solemn instrument, and was taken to by the fine gentlemen of the time, whose characters were formed after that model of good breeding exhibited in the French court towards the end of the last century.

Cibber, in the Apology for his Life, page 214, has with great propriety marked the character of the beaux of his time, who he says were of a quite different cast from the modern stamp, and had more of the stateliness of the peacock in their mein, than which now seems to be their highest emulation, the pert air of a lapwing; to which remark we may add, that the character of a gentleman, in the vulgar apprehension, consisted then in the assemblage of such external qualifications, as served to recommend him to the favour of those who looked no farther than the mere outside; among which some small skill in music was thought as necessary as the accomplishment of dancing.

As the French mode of behaving and conversing had been adopted here, so were in some degree their recreations and amusements. From the time of making that present of English flutes to the king of France, which Mersennus speaks of, the flute became a favourite instrument among the French, and many gentlemen were notable proficients on it; and though the instrument had passed from England to France, the general practice of it by persons of fashion was then derived from thence to us.† That

the flute was formerly the instrument of a gentleman may be inferred from the following circumstance: in that species of graphical representation called Still Life, we observe a collection of implements and utensils thrown in disorder on a table, exhibiting a group of various forms, contrasted with each other, at the will of the artist. He that shall carefully attend to pictures of this kind, will seldom fail to find a lute, and also a flute, frequently with a book of lessons for one or the other instrument; but if this particular fail to prove that the flute was the recreation of gentlemen, what shall be said to a portrait of one of our poets, who died above fifty years ago, drawn when he was about twenty, wherein he is represented in a full trimmed blue suit, with scarlet stockings rolled above his knees, a large white peruke, and playing on a flute near half an ell in length; or to this, which is the frontispiece to a book of instructions and lessons for this instrument, published about the year 1700.

And to come nearer to our own times, it may be remembered by many now living, that a flute was the pocket companion of many who wished to be thought fine gentlemen. The use of it was to entertain ladies, and such as had a liking for no better music than a song-tune, or such little airs as were then composed for that instrument; and he that could play a solo of Schickhard of Hamburg, or Robert Valentine of Rome, was held a complete master of the instrument. A description of the mutual compliments that attended a request to one of these accomplished gentlemen to perform, or a recital of the forms of entreaty or excuse, with a relation of the apologies, the bows, the congees that passed upon such an occasion, might furnish matter for a diverting scene in a comedy; but here it

---

* In the will of Sir Henry Wotton, printed in his remains, is a bequest of his viol da gamba to one of his friends. Sir John Bolles, Sir Francis North, and Sir Roger L'Estrange, as above related, were excellent performers on this instrument.

† *The flageolet had also its admirers: in that most ingenious and entertaining book, Dr. More's divine Dialogues, Hylobares one of the interlocutors, at intervals during the conversation, entertains his friends with the music of the Flageolet, as does another of them, Bathynous, on the Theorbo. On this latter instrument we are told the author himself was a performer, and that the power of the music thereof, aided by his own rapturous thoughts, was frequently so great as forced him to desist. See his Life by the Rev. Mr. Richard Ward, and the Biog. Brit. Art.* MORE [Henry.]

may suffice to say, that in the present state of manners, nothing of the kind is to be found amongst us.*

As the French had set us the example for the practice of the flute à bec, so did they for the German or traverse flute, an instrument of little less antiquity. The Sieur Hotteterre le Romain of Paris was the first that published instructions for it; and these were considerably improved in a treatise entitled 'Methode pour apprendre aisèment à joüer de la Flute traversiere,' by Mons. Corrette: the former of these books was published about the year 1710; and from that time the practice of the flute à bec descended to young apprentices of tradesmen, and was the amusement of their winter evenings; the German or traverse flute still retains some degree of estimation among gentlemen, whose ears are not nice enough to inform them that it is never in tune.†

Nicholas Staggins, a man bred under his father, a common musician in London, had interest enough to procure himself the place of composer to Charles II. and afterwards to be master of the band of music to William III. In the year 1664, more by the favour of Dr. James, the vice-chancellor, than any desert of his own, he attained to the degree of doctor in music. His exercise should have been a vocal composition in five or six parts, and also one for instruments, but the former, as being the more difficult work, was dispensed with. The partiality shown to this man seems to have occasioned great murmurings, and to silence them the following advertisement was published in the Gazette for the year 1664, No. 1945:—'Cambridge, July 6. Dr. Nicholas Staggins, 'who was some time since admitted to the degree of 'Dr. of music, being desirous to perform his exercise 'upon the first public opportunity for the said 'degree, has quitted himself so much to the satisfac- 'tion of the whole university this commencement, 'that by a solemn vote they have constituted and 'appointed him to be a public professor of music 'there.'

At Cambridge is no endowment for a music professor, so that the appointment here mentioned must have been merely honorary; however, in virtue of it Dr. Tudway succeeded to the title upon the death of Dr. Staggins, and it has been continued down to the present time.

In a collection entitled 'Choice Ayres, Songs, and 'Dialogues to sing to the Theorbo-Lute or Bass- 'Viol,' published in 1675, is a song composed by Dr. Staggins, to the words 'While Alexis;' and in Playford's Dancing Master is a country-dance tune called Dr. Staggins's Jig; a few other such compositions may possibly be found, but it does not appear that he ever composed anthems or services, or

indeed any works that could render him justly eminent in his faculty.

John Wallis, an eminent divine and mathematician, was born at Ashford in Kent on the twenty-third day of November, 1616. From a grammar-school at Felsted in Essex he went to Emanuel college in Cambridge, and became a fellow of Queen's college before a vacancy happened in his own. About the year 1640 he was admitted to holy orders, and, leaving the university, became domestic chaplain to Sir Richard Darly of Yorkshire, and the Lady Vere, the dowager of Lord Horatio Vere. In 1664, he was chosen one of the scribes or secretaries to the assembly of divines at Westminster. Having made a considerable progress in mathematics and natural philosophy, he was in 1649 appointed Savalian professor of geometry at Oxford; upon which occasion he entered himself at Exeter college, and was admitted to the degree of master of arts, and in 1654 to that of doctor of divinity: soon after which, upon the decease of Dr. Gerrard Langbaine, he was appointed Custos Archivorum of the university.

In his younger years he invented the art of deciphering, and by his great penetration and ingenuity discovered and established those principles which have been the rule of its professors ever since, and have entitled him to the appellation of the father of the art. His singular readiness in developing the sense of secret writing, drew upon him the suspicion of having deciphered the letters of Charles I. taken at the battle of Naseby; but he fully cleared himself in a letter to Dr. Fell, bishop of Oxford, dated April 8, 1685, an extract whereof is published in the preface to Hearne's edition of Peter Langtoft's Chronicle.

Dr. Wallis was one of those persons whose private meetings for the improvement of philosophy by experiments, gave occasion to the institution of the Royal Society; and after its establishment he was a constant attendant, and frequent correspondent of the society, communicating from time to time his discoveries in various branches of natural philosophy and the mathematics, as appears by his publications in the Philosophical Transactions.

The learning of Dr. Wallis was not less deep than extensive. A singular degree of acuteness and penetration is discoverable in all his writings, which are too multifarious to be here particularized; and the rather as a copious account of them is given in his life in the Biographia Britannica. Those which it concerns us here to take notice of, are his edition of Ptolemy, with the appendix entitled 'De veterum 'harmonia ad hodiernam comparata;'‡ as also 'Por- 'phyrii in Harmonica Ptolemæi Commentarius, ex 'cod. MSS. Græce et Latine editus;' and 'Manuelis 'Bryennii harmonica ex cod. MSS.,' which are contained in the third and last volume of his works in folio, printed at Oxford in 1669. These pieces of ancient harmonics, with those before published by

---

* This account will not seem exaggerated to those who remember such old gentlemen as had been the scholars of Banister, Woodcock, Baston, and other masters of the flute.

† This is an objection that lies in common against all perforated pipes; the best that the makers of them can do is to tune them to some one key, as the hautboy to C, the German flute to D, and the flute à bec to F; and to effect this truly, is a matter of no small difficulty. The flutes of the latter kind of the younger Stanesby approach the nearest of any to perfection; but those of Bressan, though excellent in their tone, are all too flat in the upper octave. For these reasons some are induced to think, notwithstanding what we daily hear of a fine embouchure, and a brilliant finger, terms equally nonsensical applied, as they are, to the German flute, that the utmost degree of proficiency on any of these instruments is scarcely worth the labour of attaining it.

‡ The reduction of the ancient system of music to the modern, which makes the Greek scale, as far as it goes, correspond with that of Guido, though an arduous undertaking, Dr. Wallis has happily effected in his appendix to Ptolemy; and in his notes on that work he has gone very near to demonstrate an exact correspondence between the modes of the ancients and keys of the moderns.

Meibomius, complete the whole of what the ancient Greek writers have left upon that subject.

Dr. Wallis was also the author of sundry papers printed in the Philosophical Transactions, particularly A Discourse on the Trembling of consonant Strings;[*] another on the division of the monochord;[†] another on the imperfection of the organ;[‡] and a fourth on the strange effects reported of music in former times.[§]

Many particulars of the life of this great man are related in a letter from him to Dr. Thomas Smith, printed in the preface to Hearne's edition of Peter Langtoft's Chronicle; at the end of which letter is a very serious vindication of himself from the calumnies of his enemies. What is related of him in the Athen. Oxon. is little to be regarded, for it is evident that Wood hated him for no other reason than the moderate principles which he professed, and which show Dr. Wallis to have been a much wiser man than himself.

He died on the twenty-eighth day of October, 1703, in the eighty-eighth year of his age, and was buried in the church of St. Mary at Oxford, in which is a handsome monument to his memory.

CHAP. CLIV.

JOHN BLOW (a Portrait), a native of North Collingham, in the county of Nottingham, was one of the first set of children after the restoration, being bred up under Captain Henry Cook. He was also a pupil of Hingeston, and after that of Dr. Christopher Gibbons. On the sixteenth day of March, 1673, he was sworn one of the gentlemen of the chapel in the room of Roger Hill; and in July, 1674, upon the decease of Mr. Pelham Humphrey, was appointed master of the children of the chapel. In 1685 he was made one of his majesty's private music, and composer to his majesty, a title which Matthew Lock had enjoyed before him, but which seems to have been at that time merely honorary. He was also almoner and master of the choristers of the cathedral church of St. Paul, being appointed to those places upon the death of Michael Wise, in 1687, who had been admitted but in the January preceding; but he resigned them in 1693, in favour of his scholar Jeremiah Clark. Blow was not a graduate of either university; but archbishop Sancroft, in virtue of his own authority in that respect, conferred on him the degree of doctor in music. Upon the decease of Purcell in 1695, he became organist of Westminster-Abbey. In the year 1699 he was appointed composer to his majesty, with a salary of forty pounds a year, under an establishment, of which the following is the history. After the revolution, and while king William was in Flanders, the summer residence of queen Mary was at Hampton Court. Dr. Tillotson was then dean of St. Paul's and the reverend Mr.

Gostling sub-dean, and also a gentleman of the chapel. The dean would frequently take Mr. Gostling in his chariot thither to attend the chapel duty; and in one of those journeys, the dean talking of church music, mentioned it as a common observation, that ours fell short of what it had been in the preceding reign, and that the queen herself had spoken of it to him. Mr. Gostling's answer was, that Dr. Blow and Mr. Purcell were capable of composing at least as good anthems as most of those which had been so much admired, and a little encouragement would make that appear. The dean mentioned this to her majesty, who approved of the thought, and said they should be appointed accordingly, with a salary of 40l. per annum,[‖] adding that it would be expected that each should produce a new anthem on the first Sunday of his month of waiting.[¶]

This conversation, according to the account above given, which was communicated by the son of Mr. Gostling now living, was had in the life-time of Purcell, that is to say, before the year 1695, but it did not take effect till four years after, and then only as to one composer,[**] as appears by the following entry in the Cheque-book :—

> ' 1699. Upon a new establishment of a com-
> ' poser's place for the chapel royal, Dr. John
> ' Blow was admitted into it by a warrant
> ' from the right reverend dean, and sworn in
> ' by me 　　　' RALPH BATTELL, Subdean.'

Blow was a composer of anthems while a chapel-boy, as appears by Clifford's collection, in which are several subscribed ' John Blow, one of the children of his majesty's chapel;' and on the score of his merit was distinguished by Charles II. The king admired very much a little duet of Carissimi to the words ' Dite o Cieli,' and asked of Blow if he could imitate it. Blow modestly answered he would try, and composed in the same measure, and the same key of D with a minor third, that fine song, ' Go perjured man.'[††] That the reader may be able to draw a comparison between the two compositions, that of the Italian is here inserted. Blow's is known to every Englishman conversant in music.

[‖] These salaries have since been augmented to 73l. per annum, and thereby made equal to those of the gentlemen of the chapel.

[¶] Dr. Tillotson's interest with queen Mary, which was very great, is thus to be accounted for. Upon her marriage, the prince of Orange and she were hurried out of town so fast (there being a secret design to invite them to an entertainment in the city which the court did not like), that they had scarce time to make provision for their journey. Being come to Canterbury, they repaired to an inn, where, through haste, they came very meanly provided. Upon application by Mr. Bentinck, who attended them, to borrow money of the corporation, the mayor and his brethren, after great deliberation, were afraid to lend them any. Dr. Tillotson, then dean of Canterbury, hearing of this, immediately got together his own, and what other plate and money he could borrow, and went to the inn of Mr. Bentinck with the offer of what he had. This was highly acceptable to the prince and princess, and the dean was carried to wait upon them. By this lucky accident he began that acquaintance and correspondence with the prince and Mr. Bentinck, which advanced him afterwards to the archbishoprick. Echar's Hist. of Eng. Appendix, page 11. Rapin, vol. II. page 683. This fact is related by Dr. Birch in his life of archbishop Tillotson, page 49, with this additional circumstance, that it is drawn from a manuscript account taken from the archbishop's own mouth.

[**] There was no appointment of a second composer till 1715, when Mr. John Weldon was admitted and sworn into that place.

[††] He afterwards composed another, little inferior, also printed in the Amphion Angelicus, to the words ' Go perjured maid.'

---

[*] Philos. Trans. No. 134, pag. 839, Mar. anno 1677.

[†] Ibid. No. 238, pag. 80, Mar. anno 1698.

[‡] Ibid. No. 242, pag. 249, July, anno 1698.

[§] No. 243, pag. 297, Aug. anno 1698. Lowthorp and Jones's Abridgm. edit. 1732, chap. x. pag. 606, et seq.

GIACOMO CARISSIMI.

The song of 'Go perjured man' was first published singly, and some years after in the fourth and last book of the Theater of Music, printed for Henry Playford in 1687. It was again published with the addition of instrumental parts, in the Amphion Anglicus of Dr. Blow, *but in none of the copies are the words sense. The song is to be found in a book for the extreme scarcity of which no reason can be assigned, other than that it was never thought* worthy of a second impression. *It is a Collection of Poems much in the cast of those of Cleveland, and is entitled 'Hesperides,' by Robert Herrie, 8vo. 1648. The words, such as they are, are as under.**

* Go, perjur'd man, and if thou e'er return
To see the small remainder of my Urn,
When thou shalt laugh at my religious dust,
And ask where's now the colour, form, and trust
Of woman's beauty? and with hand more rude
Rifle the flowers which the virgins strew'd,
Know, I have pray'd to fury, that the wind
May blow my ashes up and strike thee blind.

The Orpheus Britannicus of Purcell had been published by his widow soon after his decease, and contained in it some of that author's finest songs: the favourable reception it met with was a motive with Blow to the publication, in the year 1700, of a work of the same kind, entitled 'Amphion Anglicus, 'containing compositions for one, two, three, and 'four voices, with accompanyments of instrumental 'music and a thorough-bass figured for the organ, 'harpsichord, or theorbo-lute.'

This book was dedicated to the princess Anne of Denmark; in the epistle the author gives her royal highness to understand that he was preparing to publish his church services and divine compositions, but he lived not to carry his design into effect. To the Amphion Anglicus are prefixed commendatory verses by sundry persons, many of whom had been his scholars, as namely, Jeremiah Clark, organist of St. Paul's cathedral; William Croft, organist of St. Anne, Soho, and John Barret, music-master to the boys in Christ's hospital, and organist of St. Mary at Hill. Among them is an ode addressed to the author by one Mr. Herbert, in a note on which it is said that an anthem of Bird, in golden notes, is preserved in the Vatican library; and in the second stanza are the following lines respecting Blow :—

' His Gloria Patri long ago reach'd Rome,
' Sung and rever'd too in St. Peter's dome;
' A canon will outlive her jubilees to come.'

The canon here meant is that fine one to which the Gloria Patri in Dr. Blow's Gamut service is set.* That it should be sung in St. Peter's church at Rome may seem strange, but the fact is thus accounted for: Dr. Ralph Battell, subdean of the royal chapel, and a prebendary of Worcester, being at Rome in the reign of James II. was much with Cardinal Howard, then protector of the English nation, as Cardinal Albani is now, and being upon his return to England, the Cardinal requested of him some of our church-music, particularly the compositions of Blow and Purcell, which he said he had been told were very fine; the doctor answered he should readily oblige his eminence, and desired to know how he should send them; the Cardinal replied in William Penn's packet.† And there can be little doubt but that so

* The whole service is printed in the first volume of Dr. Boyce's Cathedral Music, page 263, and the Canon alone, in the editions of Playford's Introduction after the year 1700.

† This was the famous William Penn, the Quaker, who from the favour shown him by James II. and other circumstances, was strongly suspected to be a concealed papist. The imputation he affected to consider as greatly injurious to his character; and accordingly entered into a very serious debate with the archbishop Tillotson on the subject, which he did not give over till by his letters he had fully convinced him that the charge was groundless. If the above anecdote does not stagger the faith of those who have read Penn's Letters, it is possible the following story may :—
The same Dr. Battell being a prebendary of Worcester, was, as his duty required, annually resident there for a certain portion of the year; the gaoler of the city was a man of such a character, as procured him admittance into the best company. By this person, Dr. Battell was told that he had once in his custody a Romish priest, who lamenting the troubles of James the Second's reign, told his keeper that the misfortunes of that prince were chiefly owing to Father Petre and *Father* Penn. Dr. Battell recollecting that Penn was frequently with Sherlock, then dean of St. Paul's, was determined to sift him about it; accordingly he applied to Dr. Sherlock, with whom he was well acquainted, and told him the story; the Doctor said that Mr. Penn dined with him once a week, and that he should be glad to be satisfied touching the truth or falsehood of the insinuation; that he would mention it to Penn, and engage Dr. Battell to meet him at the deanery and state the fact as he had heard it; but Penn evaded an appointment and from that time forbore his visits to Dr. Sherlock.

excellent a composition as that above mentioned was in the number of those sent.

Of the work itself little is to be said; in the songs for two, three, and four voices, the harmony is such as it became so great a master to write; but in the article of expression, in melody, and in all the graces and elegancies of this species of vocal composition, it is evidently defective.

Dr. Blow set to music an Ode for St. Cecilia's day, 1684, the words by Mr. Oldham, published together with one of Purcell on the same occasion, performed in the preceding year. He also composed and published a collection of lessons for the harpsichord or spinnet, and an ode on the death of Purcell, written by Mr. Dryden. There are also extant of his composition sundry hymns printed in the Harmonia Sacra, and a great number of Catches in the latter editions of the Musical Companion.

This great musician died in the year 1708, and lies buried in the north aisle of Westminster Abbey. On his monument is the canon above mentioned, engraven on a book under the following inscription : —

Here lieth the body
Of John Blow, Doctor in Musick,
Who was organist, composer, and
Master of the children of the chapel
Royal for the space of 35 years,
In the reigns of
K. Cha. II. K. Ja. II.
K. Wm. and Q. Mary, and
Her present majesty Q. Anne,
And also organist of this collegiate church,
About 15 years.
He was scholar to the excellent musician
Dr. Christopher Gibbons,
And master to the famous Mr. H. Purcell,
and most of the eminent masters in musick since.
He died Oct. 1, 1708, in the 60th year of his age.
His own musical compositions,
Especially his church musick,
Are a far nobler monument
To his memory,
Than any other can be raised
For him.

He married Elizabeth, the only daughter of Edward Braddock, one of the gentlemen, and clerk of the cheque, of the royal chapel, one of the choir, and master of the children of Westminster Abbey. She died in childbed on the twenty-ninth day of October, 1683, aged thirty. By her he had four children, viz., a son, named John, and three daughters, Elizabeth, married to William Edgeworth, Esq. Catherine, and Mary. John died on the second day of June, 1695, aged fifteen; he lies buried in the north ambulatory of the cloister of Westminster Abbey, next to his mother, with an inscription, purporting that he was a youth of great towardness and extraordinary hopes. Elizabeth died on the second day of December, 1719; Catherine the nineteenth of May 1730, and Mary the nineteenth of November 1738.

Dr. Blow was a very handsome man in his person, and remarkable for a gravity and decency in his deportment suited to his station, though he seems by some of his compositions to have been not altogether insensible to the delights of a convivial hour

JOHN BLOW MUS. DOCT. MDCC.

VERA EFFIGIES

HENRICI PURCELL.

ÆTAT. SUÆ XXIV.

He was a man of blameless morals, and of a bene-volent temper; but was not so insensible of his own worth, as to be totally free from the imputation of pride. Such as would form a true estimate of his character as a musician, must have recourse to his compositions for the church, which are very many; and to them we are very judiciously referred by the author of his epitaph; for it is not in his songs, a few excepted, that we find much to admire; the reason whereof may be that his studies had been uniformly directed to the expression in musical language of the most sublime sentiments. Not-withstanding the encomiums contained in the verses prefixed to the Amphion Anglicus, the publication of that work drew on Blow the censures of Dr. Tudway and others of his friends, some of whom ascribed it to no better a motive than a desire to emulate Purcell; though whoever shall compare it with the Orpheus Britannicus, must be convinced that in point of merit the difference between the two is immeasureable. For this reason the friends of Dr. Blow's memory may wish that this collection of songs had never been published, but for their con-solation let them turn to those heavenly compositions, his services and anthems, particularly his services in E la mi and A re, his Gamut service above mentioned, and the anthems 'God is our hope and 'strength,' 'O God, wherefore art thou absent,' and 'I beheld and lo a great multitude,'* printed in Dr. Boyce's Cathedral Music, which afford abundant reason to say of Dr. Blow, that among church musi-cians he has few equals, and scarce any superior.

CHAP. CLV.

Henry Purcell (a Portrait), was the son of Henry Purcell,† and the nephew of Thomas Purcell, both gentlemen of the chapel at the restoration of Charles II.‡ The former died on the eleventh day of August, 1664,§ his son being then but six years old; the latter survived, and continued in his station till the day of his death, which was the thirty-first of July, 1682.‖ At the time of the decease of the elder Henry, Capt. Cook was master of the children of the chapel, and having been appointed to that charge immediately upon the restoration, had edu-cated one set of children, who for distinction sake are called the first set of chapel children after that

---

* Touching the last of the above-mentioned anthems there is an anecdote, which, as it was communicated by Mr. Weeley of the king's chapel, who had been a scholar of Blow, we may venture to give as authentic. In the reign of king James II. an anthem of some Italian composer had been introduced into the chapel, which the king liking very much, asked Blow if he could make one as good; Blow answered he could, and engaged to do it by the next Sunday, when he produced the anthem 'I beheld,' &c. When the service was over the king sent Father Petre to acquaint Blow that he was much pleased with it. 'But,' added Petre, 'I myself think it too long:' 'That,' answered Blow, 'is 'the opinion of but one fool, and I heed it not.' The Jesuit was so nettled at this expression of contempt, that he meditated revenge, and wrought so with the king, that Blow was put under a suspension, which however he was freed from by the Revolution, which took place very shortly after.

† Ashmol. MS.

‡ Vide page 693, the list of the gentlemen and officers of the chapel at the time of the coronation of king Charles II. being St. George's day, 1661. Thomas Purcell was the author of that fine chant printed in Dr. Boyce's collection, vol. I. page 289, No. II. called the Burial Chant.

§ Ashmol. MS.   ‖ Cheque Book.

event. Among these were Blow, Wise, Pelham Humphrey, and others.

Purcell was one of the second set, and is said to have been educated under Blow; but considering that Purcell was born in 1658, and that Blow was not appointed master of the children till sixteen years after, it can hardly be thought that Blow was his first instructor. It may with a great appearance of probability be supposed that Purcell was at first a scholar of Cook, who came in at the restoration, and died in 1672; and the rather as it is certain that he was a scholar of Humphrey, who was Cook's imme-diate successor. To reconcile these several facts with the inscription on Blow's monument, in which it is expressly said that Blow was Purcell's master, the only way is to suppose that Purcell, upon quit-ting the chapel, might, for the purpose of completing his studies, become the pupil of Blow, and thereby give occasion to what is generally reported touching the relation between them of master and scholar.

Being very diligent and attentive to the instruc-tions of his teachers, Purcell became an early profi-cient in the science of musical composition, and was able to write correct harmony at an age, when to be qualified for the performance of choral service is all that can be expected. And here it may be noted that among the first set of children of the chapel after the restoration, were several, who while they were in that station were the composers of anthems; and Purcell, who was of the second set, gave proofs of his genius by the composition of several of those anthems of his, which are now sung in the church.

Upon the decease of Dr. Christopher Gibbons in the year 1676, Purcell, being then but eighteen years of age, was appointed organist of the collegiate church of Saint Peter at Westminster; and in the year 1682, upon the decease of Mr. Edward Low, he became his successor as one of the organists of the chapels royal. *In the beginning of the year 1689 he became engaged in a dispute with Dr. Sprat, the then Dean, and the Chapter of Westminster, the occasion whereof was this. It seems that at the coronation of king William and queen Mary, he had received and claimed as his right, the money taken for admission into the organ loft of persons desirous of being near spectators of that ceremony, which for the following reasons must be supposed to have amounted to a considerable sum; the profit arising to the owner of one of the houses at the west end of the Abbey, where only the procession could be viewed, amounted at the last coronation to five hundred pounds. The organ in Purcell's time was on the north side of the choir, and was much nearer the altar than now, so that spectators from thence might behold the whole of that august ceremony.*

A sum like that which this must be presumed to have been was worth contending for, and if Purcell had the authority of precedent for his support, he was right in retaining it as a perquisite arising from his office; but his masters thought otherwise, and insisted on it as their due, for in an old chapter book I find the following entry: '18 April, 1689,

'*Mr. Purcell, the organ blower, to pay to Mr.*
'*Needham such money as was received by him for*
'*places in the organ loft, and in default thereof his*
'*place to be declared null and void, and that his*
'*stipend or sallary be detained in the Treasurer's*
'*hands until further orders.*' *Upon which it may*
be observed that the penning of it is an evidence of
great ignorance or malice, in that it describes him
by the appellation of organ blower who was organist
of their own church, and in truth the most excellent
musician of his time.

What the issue of this contest was does nowhere
appear.   It may be supposed either that he refunded
the money or compounded the matter with the Dean
and Chapter, it being certain that he continued to
execute his office for some years after.

It has been remarked by one who was intimately
acquainted with him, that Purcell in his earlier
compositions gave into that style which King Charles
II. affected : this is true so far as it respects the
melody of his compositions, and for so doing he had
the authority of Wise and Humphrey ; though, to
say the truth, the taste of the king, and the example
of these his predecessors did but coincide with his
own ideas of music.   There is a vulgar tradition
that Mary D'Este of Modena, the consort of king
James II., upon her arrival in England brought with
her a band of musicians of her own country, and that
Purcell, by acquaintance and conversation with them,
and sometimes joining with them in performance,
contracted an affection for the Italian style ; but for
this assertion there is no foundation, for before this
time he had looked very carefully into the works of
the Italian masters, more especially Carissimi, Cesti,
Colonna, Gratiani, Bassani, and Stradella, of which
latter he could never speak without rapture.

There is but very little doubt that the study of the
works of these excellent masters was the motive with
Purcell for introducing into his compositions a more
elegant and pathetic melody than had been known in
England ; of the good effects whereof he was so soon
well persuaded, that in the year 1683 he published
twelve Sonatas for two violins and a bass, for the organ
or harpsichord, in the preface to which he gives the following as his sentiments of the Italian music :—* * *
'*For its author he has faithfully endeavoured a just*
'*imitation of the most famed Italian masters, prin-*
'*cipally to bring the seriousness and gravity of that*
'*sort of musick into vogue and reputation among our*
'*countrymen, whose humour 'tis time now should*
'*begin to loath the levity and balladry of our neigh-*
'*bours.   The attempt he confesses to be bold and*
'*daring ; there being pens and artists of more emi-*
'*nent abilities, much better qualified for the imploy-*
'*ment than his or himself, which he well hopes*
'*these his weak endeavours will in due time provoke*
'*and enflame to a more accurate undertaking.   He*
'*is not ashamed to own his unskilfulness in the*
'*Italian language, but that is the unhappiness of his*
'*education, which cannot justly be counted his fault ;*
'*however he thinks he may warrantably affirm that*
'*he is not mistaken in the power of the Italian notes,*
'*or elegancy of their compositions.*'

From the structure of these compositions of Purcell.

it is not improbable that the sonatas of Bassani, and
perhaps of some other of the Italians, were the
models after which he formed them : for as to Corelli,
it is not clear that any of his works were got abroad
so early as the year 1683.   Be that as it may, the
sonatas of Purcell have manifestly the cast of Italian
compositions ; each begins with an adagio movement :
then follows what we should call a fugue, but which
the author terms a canzone ; then a slow movement,
and last of all an air.   Before the work is a very
fine print of the author, his age twenty-four, without
the name of either painter or engraver, but so little
like that prefixed to the Orpheus Britannicus, after
a painting of Closterman, at thirty-seven, that they
hardly seem to be representations of the same person.

It should seem that this work of Purcell met
with encouragement, for afterwards he composed ten
Sonatas, in four parts, among which is one in F FA
UT, that for its excellence has acquired the appellation of the Golden Sonata.   These were not published till after his decease, and will therefore be
spoken of hereafter.

As Purcell had received his education in the
school of a choir, the natural bent of his studies was
towards church music : services he seemed to
neglect, and to addict himself to the composition of
anthems, a kind of music which in his time the
church stood greatly in need of.

And here it is proper to mention an anthem of
his, '*Blessed are they that fear the Lord,*' as being
composed on a very extraordinary occasion.   Upon
the supposed pregnancy of king James the Second's
queen in 1687, a proclamation was issued for a thanksgiving to be observed on the fifteenth day of January,
in London and twelve miles round ; and on the
twenty-ninth day of the same month throughout
England, for joy of this event ; and Purcell, being
then one of the organists of the royal chapel, was
commanded to compose an anthem, and he did it
accordingly for four voices with instruments.   The
original score in his own hand-writing is yet extant.

The anthem '*They that go down to the sea in*
'*ships,*' was composed at the request of the Rev.
Mr. Subdean Gostling, who being at sea with the
king and the duke of York in the Fubbs yacht, and
in great danger of being cast away, providentially
escaped.*

Among the letters of Tom Brown from the dead
to the living, is one from Dr. Blow to Henry
Purcell, in which it is humorously observed, that
persons of their profession are subject to an equal
attraction of the church and the playhouse, and are
therefore in a situation resembling that of the tomb
of Mahomet,† which is said to be suspended between
heaven and earth.   This remark of Brown does so
truly apply to Purcell, that it is more than probable
his particular situation gave occasion to it ; for he
was scarcely known to the world before he became,
in the exercise of his calling, so equally divided
between both the church and the theatre, that
neither the church, the tragic, nor the comic muse
could call him her own.

* For the particulars of this deliverance, vide ante, page 693, in not.
† Works of Mr. Thomas Brown, vol. II. page 301.

In the pamphlet, so often referred to in the course of this work, entitled ' Roscius Anglicanus,' or an ' Historical View of the Stage,' written by Downes the prompter, and published in 1708, we have an account of several plays and entertainments, the music whereof is by that writer said to have been composed by Purcell. It does not appear that he had any particular attachment to the stage, but a occasional essay in dramatic music drew him into it. One Mr. Josias Priest, a celebrated dancing-master, and a composer of stage dances, kept a boarding school for young gentlewomen in Leicester-fields ;* and the nature of his profession inclining him to dramatic representations, he got Tate to write, and Purcell to set to music, a little drama called Dido and Æneas ;† Purcell was then of the age of nineteen, but the music of this opera had so little appearance of a puerile essay, that there was scarce a musician in England who would not have thought it an honour to have been the author of it. The exhibition of this little piece by the young gentlewomen of the school to a select audience of their parents and friends was attended with general applause, no small part whereof was considered as the due of Purcell.

At this time Banister and Lock were the stage composers ; the former had set the music to Dr. D'avenant's opera of Circe, and the latter to Macbeth ; but the fame of Dido and Æneas directed the eyes of the managers towards Purcell, and Purcell was easily prevailed on by Mr. Priest to enter into their service. He composed the music to a variety of plays mentioned in Downes's account, of which the following is an abstract :—

Theodosius or the Force of Love, written by Nat. Lee, the music by Mr. Henry Purcell, being the first he ever composed for the stage. King Arthur, an opera written by Dryden, the musical part set by Mr. Henry Purcell, and the dances composed by Mr. Josiah‡ Priest. The Prophetess, an opera written by Mr. Betterton, the vocal and instrumental music by Mr. Henry Purcell, and the dances by Mr. Priest. The Fairy Queen, an opera altered from the Midsummer Night's Dream of Shakespeare, the music by Mr. Purcell, the dances by Mr. Priest.

These are all the plays to which, according to Downes's account, Purcell composed the music. But it appears by the Orpheus Britannicus that he made the music to very many others, namely, Timon of Athens, Bonduca, the Libertine, Œdipus, the Tempest, as altered from Shakespeare by Dryden and Sir William Davenant ; and composed many of the songs in that most absurd of all dramatic representations, the History of Don Quixote, in three parts, by Tom D'Urfey ; farther, that collection of Airs composed for the Theatre, published by his widow in 1697, contains the overtures and airs to the following operas and plays : Dioclesian,§ King Arthur,

Fairy Queen, the Indian Queen, the Married Beau,|| Old Bachelor, Amphitryon, and Double Dealer, comedies ; and to the Princess of Persia,¶ the Gordian Knot untied,** Abdelazor, or the Moor's Revenge,†† and Bonduca,‡‡ tragedies, and the Virtuous Wife, a comedy.§§

The opera of Dioclesian in score was published by Purcell himself in the year 1691, with a dedication to Charles duke of Somerset, in which he observes that ' Music is yet but in its nonage, a forward ' child, which gives hope of what he may be hereafter ' in England, when the masters of it shall find more ' encouragement ;' and ' that it is now learning ' Italian, which is its best master, and studying ' a little of the French air, to give it somewhat more ' of gaiety and fashion.'

In the year 1684 Purcell published ' A musical ' entertainment performed on November 22, 1683, it ' being the festival of St. Cecilia, a great patroness of ' Music.'

The rest of Purcell's compositions in print are chiefly posthumous publications by his widow, and consist of ' A Collection of Ayres composed for the Theatre, and upon other occasions, 1697.' The ten Sonatas above mentioned, the ninth whereof is that which for its excellence is called the Golden Sonata in F FA UT, printed also in 1697. Lessons for the Harpsichord, Orpheus Britannicus, in two books, a work not more known than admired, sundry hymns and four anthems in the Harmonia Sacra, and part of the solemn burial service, which was completed by Dr. Croft, and is printed at the end of his book of anthems. The compositions above mentioned, as also a great number of songs and airs, rounds and catches, and even dance-tunes, set by him, are a proof of Purcell's extensive genius ; but neither the allurements of the stage, nor his love of mirth and good-fellowship, of which he seems to have been very fond, were strong enough to divert his attention from the service of the church.

The Te Deum and Jubilate of Purcell are well known to all persons conversant in cathedral music. The general opinion has long been that he composed these offices for the musical performance at St. Paul's for the benefit of the sons of the clergy,|||| grounded perhaps on the uniform practice of performing them on that occasion until about the year 1713, when they gave way to the Te Deum and

|| By Crowne.   ¶ By Elkanah Settle.   ** The author unknown.
†† By Mrs. Behn.   ‡‡ By Beaumont and Fletcher.   §§ By D'Urfey.

|||| Of this benevolent institution the history is as follows. In the time of the usurpation a sermon was preached at St. Paul's, Nov. 8, 1658, to the sons of ministers solemnly assembled, by George Hall, minister at St. Botolph Aldersgate, *son of the famous bishop Hall, and afterwards bishop of Chester.* It is supposed that the design of this discourse was to promote charitable contributions in favour of the sons of the clergy, since the corporation created for that purpose date their origin from the time above-mentioned. Whether before the restoration sermons of this kind were annual we know not, but afterwards a charter was granted, bearing date the first day of July, 1678, whereby a body politic and corporate was constituted by the name of the Governors of the Charity for the Relief of the poor Widows and Children of Clergymen, with licence to possess any estate not exceeding the yearly value of 2000*l.* Afterwards, upon the accession of Dr. Thomas Turner's gift, which amounted to about 18,000*l.* the governors, Dec. 16, 1714, obtained an augmentation of the said grant, by a licence to possess the yearly value of 3000*l.* over and above all charges and reprises, as also over and above the said 2000*l.* per annum. To promote the design of this institution, a sermon was preached at the anniversary meeting of the sons of clergymen in the church of St. Mary le Bow on the seventh day of November,

* He removed in 1680 to the great school-house at Chelsea, formerly Mr. Portman's, Vide Gazette, Numb. 1567.

† The song in the Orpheus Britannicus ' Ah ! Belinda,' is one of the airs in it. In the original opera the initial words are ' Ah ! my Anna.'

‡ Sic Orig.

§ Called also the Prophetess ; it was not written by Betterton, but was altered by him from Beaumont and Fletcher.

Jubilate of Mr. Handel, which had been composed for the thanksgiving on the peace of Utrecht, but the fact is otherwise, as will be shown.

Soon after the restoration of Charles II., when the civil commotions that had long disturbed the peace of this realm were at an end, the people gave into those recreations and amusements which had been so severely interdicted during the usurpation. Plays were not only permitted to be acted, but all the arts of scenical representation were employed to render them the objects of delight, and musical associations were formed at Oxford, and in other parts of the kingdom.

The first voluntary association of gentlemen in London, for the purpose of musical recreation, and which could properly be called a concert, seems to have been that at the house of Britton, the small-coal man, established about the year 1678, an acount whereof, as also of concerts given by masters, and which were uniformly notified in the London Gazette, will hereafter be given; but the lovers of music residing in this metropolis had a solemn annual meeting at Stationers' Hall on the twenty-second day of November, being the anniversary of the martyrdom of St. Cecilia,* from the time of re-

building that edifice after the fire of London. The performances on occasion of this solemnity being intended to celebrate the memory of one who, for reasons hard to discover, is looked on as the tutelar saint and patroness of music, had every possible advantage that the times afforded to recommend them: not only the most eminent masters in the science contributed their performance, but the gentlemen of the king's chapel, and of the choirs of St. Paul's and Westminster, lent their assistance, and the festival was announced in the London Gazette :† *and to give it a greater sanction, a sermon was annually for some years preached at the Church of St. Bride, Fleet-street.*

For the celebration of this solemnity Purcell composed his Te Deum and Jubilate, and also the most curious painting of the saint, as also a stately monument, with a cumbent statue of her with her face downwards.

St. Cecilia is usually painted playing either on the organ or on the harp, singing as Chaucer relates thus :—

> And whiles that the organs made melodie,
> To God alone thus in her herte fong fhe,
> O Lorde my foul and eke my body gie
> Unwemmed left I confounded be.

Over and above this account there is a tradition of St. Cecilia, that she excelled in music, and that the angel, who was thus enamoured of her, was drawn down from the celestial mansions by the charms of her melody; this has been deemed authority sufficient for making her the patroness of music and musicians.

The legend of St. Cecilia has given frequent occasion to painters and sculptors to exercise their genius in representations of her, playing on the organ, and sometimes on the harp. Raphael has painted her singing with a regal in her hands; and Domenichino and Mignard singing and playing on the harp. And in the vault under the choir of St. Paul's cathedral, against one of the middle columns on the south side, is a fine white marble monument for Miss Wren, the daughter of Sir Christopher, wherein that young lady is represented on a bass relief, the work of Bird, in the character of St. Cecilia playing on the organ, a boy angel sustaining her book, under which are the following inscriptions :—

'M. S.

'Desideratissimæ Virginis Janæ Wren Clariss. Dom. Christophori 'Wren Filæ unicæ, Paternæ indolis literis deditæ, piæ, benevolæ, 'domisidæ, Arte Musica peritissimæ.

'Here lies the body of Miss. Jane Wren, only daughter of Sir 'Christopher Wren, Kt. by Dame Jane his wife, daughter of William 'Lord Fiz-William, Baron of Lifford in the kingdom of Ireland. Ob. 29 'Decemb. anno 1702, Ætat. 26.'

In this vault lies interred also Dr. Holder, who will be spoken of hereafter. As few are acquainted with this place of sepulture, this opportunity is taken to mention that in a book entitled ' A new View of London,' in two volumes octavo, 1708, it is said to be probably one of the most capacious, and every way curious vaults in the world.

A few words more touching the above-mentioned book are here added for the information of the curious reader, and will conclude what it is feared may by some be thought a tedious note.

It was written by Mr. Edward Hatton, surveyor to one of the Fire-offices in London, and the author of Comes Comercii, an Index to Interest and useful books. The duty of the author's employment obliged him to make surveys of houses in all parts of the city, and in the discharge thereof he took every opportunity of remarking what appeared to him most worthy of note. His View of London contains the names of squares, streets, lanes, &c., and a description of all public edifices; among these are the churches, which, he being very well skilled in architecture, are no where else so accurately described; and although in the book the monumental inscriptions are sometimes erroneously given, no one can see it, as he may almost every day, exposed to sale on stalls, but must regret that a work of such entertainment and utility is held so cheap.

† Of the several poems written on occasion of this solemnity, Dryden's Alexander's Feast has unquestionably the preference; though it has been remarked that the two concluding lines have the turn of an epigram. Without pretending to determine on their respective merits, here follows a list of as many others of them as are to be found in Dryden's Miscellany.

A Song for St. Cecilia's day, 1687. By Mr. Dryden, part IV. page 331. Set to music by Mr. Handel many years after it was written.

A Song for St. Cecilia's day, 1690. Written by Tho. Shadwell, Esq., composed by Mr. King, part IV. page 93.

An Ode for St. Cecilia's day, 1690, part VI. page 130.

An Ode for St. Cecilia's day, 1693, written by Mr. Tho. Yalden, and composed by Mr. Daniel Purcell, part IV. page 35.

A Hymn to Harmony, written in honour of St. Cecilia's day, 1701, by Mr. Congreve, set to music by Mr. John Eccles, master of her majesty's music, part IV. page 308.

A Song for St. Cecilia's day at Oxford. By Mr. Addison, part IV. page 20.

Besides these there is extant an Ode for St. Cecilia's day, 1708, by Mr. Pope, printed among his works.

1678, by Dr. Thomas Sprat, afterwards bishop of Rochester, in which, upon a reference to it, it appears that these solemnities had been usual before they were encouraged by a royal establishment.

The sermons continued to be preached at Bow church till the year 1697, when Dr. George Stanhope preached his sermon for the benefit of this charity at the cathedral church of St. Paul, at which time, as it is imagined, the thought was first suggested of a grand musical performance, as a joint motive to devotion and pity, with the eloquence of the preacher.

The annual feast of the sons of the clergy appears to be prior to their incorporation. In the London Gazette of November 22, 1677, is an advertisement of the annual feast of the sons of the clergy, to be held at Merchant Taylors' hall, on Thursday the twenty-ninth day of November then next.

Since the year 1697 there has been constantly an annual sermon, and also a grand musical service at the cathedral church of St. Paul to promote the ends of this charity; the most eminent divines of our church have in succession been the preachers, and the musical performance has received all the advantages that could possibly be derived from the assistance of the ablest of the faculty. For many years past it has been the practice of the stewards of the corporation to have at St. Paul's on the Tuesday preceding the day of the sermon, what is called a rehearsal of the performance, as also a collection for the charity.

* St. Cecilia, among Christians, is esteemed the patroness of music, for the reasons whereof we must refer to her history, as delivered by the notaries of the Roman church, and from them transcribed into the Golden Legend, and other books of the like kind. The story says that she was a Roman lady, born of noble parents, about the year 225. That notwithstanding she had been converted to Christianity, her parents married her to a young Roman nobleman named Valerianus, a pagan, who going to bed to her on the wedding night, *as the custom is,* says the book, was given to understand by his spouse that she was nightly visited by an angel, and that he must forbear to approach her, otherwise the angel would destroy him. Valerianus somewhat troubled at these words, desired he might see his rival the angel, but his spouse told him that was impossible, unless he would be baptised and become a Christian, which he consented to: after which returning to his wife, he found her in her closet at prayer, and by her side, in the shape of a beautiful young man, the angel cloathed with brightness. After some conversation with the angel, Valerianus told him that he had a brother named Tiburtius, whom he greatly wished to see a partaker of the grace which he himself had received; the angel told him that his desire was granted, and that shortly they should both be crowned with martyrdom. Upon this the angel vanished, but soon after showed himself as good as his word; Tiburtius was converted, and both he and his brother Valerianus were beheaded; Cecilia was offered her life upon condition that she would sacrifice to the deities of the Romans, but she refused, upon which she was thrown into a cauldron of boiling water, and scalded to death; though others say that she was stifled in a dry bath, *i. e.* an inclosure from whence the air was excluded, having a slow fire underneath it; which kind of death was sometimes inflicted among the Romans upon women of quality who were criminals. See the second Nonne's Tale in Chaucer, the Golden Legend, printed by Caxton, and the Lives of Saints by Peter Ribadeneyra, Priest of the Society of Jesus. Printed at St. Omer's in 1699.

Upon the spot where her house stood is a church, said to have been built by pope Urban I. who administered baptism to her husband and his brother; it is the church of St. Cecilia in Trastevere. Within is a musical entertainment performed for St. Cecilia's day above mentioned; the lattter was published, together with a second musical entertainment of Dr. Blow for the same anniversary, in the following year. The former was printed under the direction of Mrs. Purcell, but on so coarse a type, and with such evidences of inattention, as have subjected those who had the care of the publication to censure.*

The several works above-mentioned were composed with great labour and study, and with a view to the establishment of a lasting reputation; but there are others that is to say, hymns, in the Harmonia Sacra,† and single songs and ballad tunes to a very great number, in the printed collections of his time, which alone shew the excellencies of Purcell in vocal composition; even his rounds and catches, many whereof were composed and sung almost at the same instant, have all the merit which can be ascribed to that species of harmony. And here it may not be improper to mention an anecdote respecting one of them, which the communication of a friend to this work has enabled the author to give. The reverend Mr. Subdean Gostling played on the viol da gamba, and loved not the instrument more than Purcell hated it. They were very intimate, as must be supposed, and lived together upon terms of friendship; nevertheless, to vex Mr. Gostling, Purcell got some one to write the following mock eulogium on the viol,‡ which he set in the form of a round for three voices.

> Of all the instruments that are,
> None with the viol can compare :
> Mark how the strings their order keep,
> With a whet whet whet and a sweep sweep sweep;
> But above all this still abounds,
> With a zingle zingle zing, and a zit zan zounds.

Though the unsettled state of public affairs at the time when he lived, obliged almost every man to attach himself to one or other of the two contending parties, Purcell might have availed himself of that exemption which men of his peaceable· profession have always a right to insist on, but he seemed not disposed to claim it. In James the Second's time he sang down the Whigs, and in that of William, the Tories. It is true he did not, like William Lawes, sacrifice his life to the interests of a master who loved and had promoted him, but he possessed a kind of transitory allegiance; and when the former had attained to sovereignty, besides those gratuitous effusions of loyalty which his relation to the court disposed him to, could as easily celebrate the praises of William as James.

> 'His billet at the fire was found,
> 'Whoever was depos'd or crown'd.'

This indifference is in some degree to be accounted for by that mirth and good humour, which seem to have been habitual to him; and this perhaps is the best excuse that can be made for those connexions and intimacies with Brown and others, which show him not to have been very nice in the choice of his company. Brown spent his life in taverns and ale-houses; the Hole in the Wall in Baldwin's Gardens§ was the citadel in which he baffled the assaults of creditors and bailiffs, at the same time that he attracted thither such as thought his wit atoned for his profligacy. Purcell seems to have been of that number, and to merit censure for having prostituted his invention, by adapting music to some of the most wretched ribaldry that was ever obtruded on the world for humour. The house of Owen Swan, a vintner‖ in Bartholomew-lane, humorously called Cobweb-hall, was also a place of great resort with the musical wits of that day; as also a house in Wych-street, behind the New Church in the Strand, within time of memory known by a sign of Purcell's head, a half length; the dress a brown full-bottomed wig, and a green night-gown, very finely executed. the name of the person who last kept it as a tavern was Kennedy, a good performer on the bassoon, and formerly in the opera band.

But notwithstanding the intimacies above mentioned, he had connections that were honourable. The author of the Life of the Lord Keeper North, speaking of his lordship's skill in the science, and the delight he took in the practice of music, says that at his house in Queen-street his lordship had a concert, of which Mr. Purcell had the direction; and at that time of day concerts were so rare, that it required the assistance of no less than a master to keep four or five performers together : his scholars were the sons and daughters of the nobility and principal gentry in the kingdom, a circumstance which alone bespeaks the nature of his connexions, and the rank he held in his profession.

Of his performance on the organ we are able to say but little, there being no memorials remaining that can tend to gratify our curiosity in this respect, save a humorous rebus in Latin metre, written by one Mr. Tomlinson, and here inserted; in which it is intimated that he was not less admired for his performance than his compositions. The verses above alluded to were set to music in the form of a catch by Mr. Senton; they were first printed in

§ *A pretended privileged place.* See *Northhook.*

‖ In the Pleasant Musical Companion, printed in 1726, is a catch on this person, the words whereof are written by himself. A gentleman now living, who knew him, relates that the sign of his house was the Black Swan, and that he was parish-clerk of St. Michael's in Cornhill ; that failing in his trade as a vintner in his latter years, he removed to a small house in St. Michael's-alley, and took to the selling of tobacco, trusting to the friendship of a numerous acquaintance ; and that on his tobacco papers were the following lines composed by himself :—

> The dying Swan in sad and moving strains,
> Of his near end and hapless fate complains,
> In pity then your kind assistance give,
> Smoke of Swan's best, that the poor bird may live.

A like exhortation to lend assistance to this poor old man, is contained in the following epigram, written by one of his friends :—

> The aged Swan, opprest with time and cares,
> With Indian sweets his funeral prepares ;
> Light up the pile, thus he'll ascend the skies,
> And, Phœnix like, from his own ashes rise.

* Vide Preface to Dr. Croft's Anthems.

† The Harmonia Sacra is a collection in two books, of divine hymns and dialogues, set to music by Lock, Humphrey, Blow, Purcell, and others. The third edition, printed in 1714, is by far the best. In it are four anthems by Purcell, and three by Croft, Blow, and Clark. To the second book are verses addressed to Blow and Purcell by Dr. Sacheverell. Tate collected the words, and published them in a small volume without the music.

‡ It was first printed in the second book of the 'Pleasant Musical Companion,' published in 1701, and has been continued in most of the subsequent collections of Catches.

the second book of the Pleasant Musical Companion, published in 1701, and are as follow :—

> Galli marita, par tritico seges,
> Praenomen est ejus, dat chromati leges ;
> Intrat cognomen blanditiis Cati,
> Exit eremi in Ædibus stati,
> Expertum effectum omnes admirentur.
> Quid merent Poetæ ? ut bene calcentur.

Thus translated and set to music :—

> A mate to a cock, and corn tall as wheat,
> Is his Christian name who in musick's compleat :
> His surname begins with the grace of a cat,
> And concludes with the house of a hermit ; note that.
> His skill and performance each auditor wins,
> But the poet deserves a good kick on the shins.

Purcell died on the twenty-first day of November, 1695.* There is a tradition that his death was occasioned by a cold which he caught in the night, waiting for admittance into his own house. It is said that he used to keep late hours, and that his wife had given orders to his servants not to let him in after midnight : unfortunately he came home heated with wine from the tavern at an hour later than that prescribed him, and through the inclemency of the air contracted a disorder of which he died. If this be true, it reflects but little honour on Madam Purcell, for so she is styled in the advertisements of his works ; and but ill agrees with those expressions of grief for her dear lamented husband, which she makes use of to Lady *Elizabeth* Howard in the dedication of the Orpheus Britannicus.† It seems probable that the disease of which he died was rather a lingering than an acute one, perhaps a consumption ; and that, for some time at least, it had no way affected the powers of his mind, since one of the most celebrated of his compositions, the song ' From rosy bowers,' is in the printed book said to have been the last of his works, and to have been set during that sickness which put a period to his days. He was interred in Westminster Abbey. On a tablet fixed to a pillar, before which formerly stood the organ,‡ placed there by his patroness the Lady Elizabeth Howard, is an inscription, which has been celebrated for its elegance, and is as follows :—

> ' Here lyes
> ' HENRY PURCELL, Esq. ;
> ' Who left this life,
> ' And is gone to that blessed place,
> ' Where only his harmony
> ' can be exceeded.
> ' Obiit 21mo. die Novembris,
> ' Anno Ætatis suæ 37mo,
> ' Annoq ; Domini 1695.'

Lady *Elizabeth* Howard had been a scholar of Purcell ; she was the eldest daughter of Thomas earl of Berkshire, and the wife of Dryden, who is plainly alluded to in the dedication of the Orpheus Britannicus. Many of his best compositions were made for her entertainment, and were recommended by her own performance. Purcell had set the music to King Arthur, and many other of Dryden's dramatic works. Dryden wrote an ode on his death which Dr. Blow set to music ; and Lady *Elizabeth* erected the tablet. From all these particulars the inference is not unnatural that Dryden was the author of the above inscription. On a flat stone over his grave was the following epitaph, now totally effaced :—

> Plaudite, felices superi, tanto hospite ; nostris
>   Præfuerat, vestris additur ille choris :
> Invida nec vobis Purcellum terra reposcat,
>   Questa decus seêli, deliciasque breves.
> Tam cito decessisse, modos cui singula debet
>   Musa, prophana suos religiosa suos.
> Vivit Io et vivat, dum vicina organa spirant,
>   Dumque colet numeris turba canora Deûm.

Thus translated :—

> Applaud so great a guest celestial pow'rs,
> Who now resides with you, but once was ours ;
> Yet let invidious earth no more reclaim
> Her short-liv'd fav'rite and her chiefest fame ;
> Complaining that so prematurely dy'd
> Good-nature's pleasure and devotion's pride.
> Dy'd ? no he lives while yonder organs sound,
> And sacred echos to the choir rebound.

The dwelling-house of Purcell was in a lane in Westminster, beyond the abbey, called St. Anne's lane, situated on the south side of Tothill-street, between Peter's-street and the east end of Orchard-street.§ It is presumed that he married young ; at least it is certain that he was a housekeeper at the age of twenty-five, for his first Sonatas, published in 1683, are in the London Gazette of June 11, in that year, advertised to be sold at his house above mentioned.

Of the circumstances of his family we have no kind of intimation, other than the acknowledgement of his widow to Lady Howard that her generosity had extended itself to his posterity, and that the favours she had entailed upon them were the most valuable part of their inheritance : from hence we may conclude that he had children living at the time

---

* Dr. Boyce, in the account of Purcell prefixed to his Cathedral Music, vol. II. says that he resigned his place of organist of Westminster-Abbey in 1693 ; but in this particular he seems to have been misinformed ; upon searching the treasurer's accounts for 1694, Purcell appears to have been then organist. Farther he is a subscribing witness to an agreement dated 20th July, 1694, between the dean and chapter of Westminster and Father Smith for repairing the abbey organ, and is therein called organist of the said church. The treasurer's accounts for 1695 are not to be found ; nor can any entry be found in the books or accounts of the abbey that will determine the question whether Purcell resigned or died in the office ; but upon the evidence above stated the latter is the more eligible supposition. As organist of the chapel royal he was succeeded by Mr. Francis Piggot, organist of the Temple ; and as organist of Westminster Abbey by Dr. Blow, who was his senior, and had been his master.

† Mr. Wanley in the Harleian Catalogue, No. 1272, giving an account of Stradella, says that when Purcell, who had only seen two or three of his compositions, heard that he was assassinated, and upon what account, he lamented him exceedingly ; nay, so far as to declare that he could have forgiven him an injury in that kind ; and then adds this reflection of his own, ' which those who remember how lovingly Mr. Purcell lived ' with his wife (or rather what a loving wife she proved to him) may ' understand without farther explication.'

‡ The customary place of interment for an organist is under the organ of his church. In Purcell's time, and long after, the organ of Westminster Abbey stood on the north side of the choir, and this was anciently the station of the organ in all churches. In Hollar's fine view of the inside of old St. Paul's in Sir William Dugdale's history of that cathedral, the organ is so situated, as it is at this day at Canterbury and the king's chapel. The reason of it was that the organist should not be obliged to turn his back to the altar. But this punctilio is now disregarded, and, which is extraordinary, even at the embassador's chapel in Lincoln's-Inn fields, where the organ stands at the west end, as in most churches in this kingdom.

§ There is a sort of curiosity in some readers which it is possible may be gratified by the following note. Dr. Heyther lived at Westminster in the same house with Camden. Dr. Christopher Gibbons in New-street, betwixt the Ambry [Almonry] and Orchard-street, Westminster. In the Gazette for July 6, 1671, he advertises the loss of a silver tankard from thence. Dr. Blow's house was in the Broad Sanctuary, Westminster : Jeremy Clark's dwelling was in St. Paul's churchyard, where now the Chapter-house stands.

of his decease, and that they were but ill provided for.* Of these we have been able to trace one only, viz., a son named Edward, who was bred to music, and in July 1726 was elected organist of the church of St. Margaret, Westminster.† He was also organist of the church of St. Clement, Eastcheap, London, and dying in the year 1740, was succeeded in that place by his son Henry, who had been bred up in the king's chapel under Mr. Gates. This Henry became also organist of the church of St. Edmund the King, London, and afterwards of that of St. John, Hackney. He died about twenty-five years ago. His father was a good organist, but himself a very indifferent one. Henry Purcell had two brothers, the one named Edward, whose history is contained in a monumental inscription on his grave-stone in the chancel of the church of Wightham, near Oxford, and here inserted ‡ The other was Daniel, a musician, who will be the subject of the next article.

The premature death of Purcell was a great afflic-tion to the lovers of his art. His friends, in conjunc-tion with his widow, for whom and his family he had not been able to make any great provision, were anxious to raise a monument of his fame. To that end they selected, chiefly from his compositions for the theatre, such songs as had met with a favourable reception, and by the help of a subscription of twenty shillings each person, published in the year 1698 that well-known work the Orpheus Britannicus, with a dedication to the author's good friend and patroness the above-mentioned Lady Howard, and commenda-tory verses by his brother Daniel, Mr. J. Talbot, fellow of Trinity college, Cambridge, Henry Hall, organist of Hereford, and other persons.§

It is conceived that the Orpheus Britannicus suffered not a little from the impatience of those who were contributors to the expense of it; for had due time been allowed, there would have been found among the author's compositions, particularly his music for plays, a great number of songs, for the omission whereof no reason but that above can be assigned. To go no farther, in the Tempest are many recita-tives and songs equally good with the best in the Orpheus Britannicus; and if this should be doubted, let the following, taken from that drama, and which has never yet been printed, speak for itself:—

ÆOLUS, you must ap-pear, my great commands to hear, rough . . . Æ-o-lus ap-

1mo. & 2ndo.

-pear.

While these pass o'er the

---

* His will, dated the first day of November, 1695, recites that at the time of making it he was very *ill in constitution*, but of sound mind. In it no particular mention is made of his estate or effects, or of his children: it is in short a general devise to his loving wife Frances, and an appointment of her his executrix, and was proved by her in the prerogative court of the archbishop of Canterbury, on the seventh day of December, 1695.

† Upon an inspection of the parish books for the purpose of ascertain-ing this fact, it appears that the organ of this church was built by Father Smith in 1676, and that himself was the first organist there, and played for a salary.

‡ 'Here lyeth the body of EDWARD PURCELL, eldest son of Mr. 'PURCELL, gentleman of the royal chapel, and brother to Mr. HENRY 'PURCELL, so much renowned for his skill in musick. He was 'gentleman-usher to king Charles the 2nd. and lieutenant in Col. 'Trelawney's regiment of foot, in which for his many gallant actions in 'the wars of Ireland and Flanders, he was gradually advanced to the

'honour of lieutenant-colonel. He assisted Sir GEORGE ROOK in the 'taking of Gibraltar, and the prince of HESSE in the memorable 'defence of it. He followed that prince to Barcelona, was at the taking 'of Mount-joy, where that brave prince was killed; and continued to 'signalize his courage in the siege and taking of the city in the year '1705. He enjoyed the glory of his great services till the much 'lamented death of his late mistress queen ANNE, when, decayed with 'age, and broken with misfortunes, he retired to the house of the Right 'Hon. Montague earl of Abingdon, and died June 20th, 1717. Aged 64.

§ A second edition of the Orpheus Britannicus was published in 1702, in a better character than the former, and with the addition of above thirty songs; to make room for which some in the first edition are omitted. The additional songs were communicated by the Rev. Mr. George Lluellyn. This person had been a page of the back stairs in the reign of Charles II., and at court became acquainted with Purcell. Afterwards he entered into holy orders, and had a living near Shrewsbury.

HENRY PURCELL.

In the year 1702 was published a second edition of the Orpheus Britannicus, and also a second book; the editor of this latter was Henry Playford. It is dedicated to Charles Lord Halifax, and contains songs in the Fairy Queen, the Indian Queen, birthday songs,* and other occasional compositions, together with that noble song, 'Genius of England.' This latter composition, which has an accompaniment for a trumpet, and is said to have been sung by Mr. Freeman and Mrs. Cibber, leads us to remark that Purcell was the first who composed songs with symphonies for that instrument; and that it is to be inferred from the many instances in the Orpheus Britannicus of songs so accompanied, that he had a great fondness for it, which is thus to be accounted for :—

In the royal household is an establishment of a sergeant and office of trumpets, consisting of the sergeant and sixteen trumpets in ordinary. The origin of this office may be traced back to the time of Edw. VI., when Benedict Browne was sergeant-trumpeter, with a salary of £24 6s. 8d. per ann. (see page 541 of this work.) The salary was afterwards augmented to £100, and so continues; but even thus increased, it bears but a small proportion to the perquisites or fees of office, some of which arise from creations of nobility, and even from the patents by which sheriffs are appointed.

In Purcell's time the serjeant was Matthias Shore. This man had a brother named William, a trumpeter, and also a son named John, who by his great ingenuity and application had extended the power of that noble instrument, too little esteemed at this day, beyond the reach of imagination, for he produced from it a tone as sweet as that of a hautboy. Matthias Shore had also a daughter, a very beautiful and amiable young woman, whom Purcell taught to sing and play on the harpsichord. Cibber was well acquainted with John Shore, and being one day on a visit to him at his house, happened to hear his sister at her harpsichord, and was so charmed with

* Among these is the song 'May her blest example chase,' the bass whereof is the melody of the old ballad 'Cold and raw.' For the history of this composition vide ante page 564, in note.

her that he became her lover and married her. Cibber was then not quite twenty-two years of age, and, as himself confesses,† had no other income than twenty pounds a year allowed him by his father, and twenty shillings a week from the theatre,‡ which could scarce amount to above thirty pounds a year more. The marriage having been contracted against the consent of the lady's father, she and her husband were by him left to shift for themselves; upon which she took to the stage; and in a part in Don Quixote, together with Mr. Freeman, sang the song above-mentioned, her brother performing the symphony on the trumpet.

CHAP. CLVI.

To entertain an adequate idea of the merits of Purcell, we must view him in the different lights of

† Of this family the following is the farther history. William Shore succeeded Matthias, and survived him but a few years. By a note in Strype, [St. Martin's in the Fields, page 73,] it appears that he was buried in the old church of that parish. Old Mr. Shore was afterwards so far reconciled to his daughter, Mrs. Cibber, that he gave her a small fortune; the rest of what he was possessed of, he laid out in building a house on the bank of the Thames, which was called Shore's Folly, and has been demolished several years. John Shore the son succeeded his uncle in the office of Serjeant Trumpeter; and by the lists of the royal household it appears that in 1711 he had a place in the queen's band. At the public entry of king George I., in 1714, he rode as Serjeant Trumpeter in cavalcade, bearing his mace; and on the eighth day of August, 1715, upon a new establishment of gentlemen and additional performers in the king's chapel, was sworn and admitted to the place of lutenist therein. He was a man of humor and pleasantry, and was the original inventor of the tuning-fork, an instrument which he constantly carried about him, and used to tune his lute by, and which whenever he produced it gave occasion to a pun. At a concert he would say, 'I have 'not about me a pitch-pipe, but I have what will do as well to tune by, 'a pitch fork.' Some of his contemporaries in office, now living, give him the character of a well-bred gentleman, extremely courteous and obliging to all. It is said that he had the misfortune to split his lip in sounding the trumpet, and was ever after unable to perform on that instrument, and also to be engaged in contentious suits for the ascertaining of his fees; and that his bad success in some of them, disordered his understanding, insomuch that meeting one day with Dr. Croft in the Park, he would needs fight him. He died in the year 1753, and was succeeded in his place of Serjeant Trumpeter by Mr. Valentine Snow, and in that of lutenist to the chapel by Mr. John Immyns. His sister, Mrs. Cibber, was very much afflicted with an asthma, and died about the year 1730. These particulars respecting Cibber's marriage, and his wife's father, are related by his daughter, Mrs. Charlotte Charke, in a narrative of her life, published in 1755. *Mr. Snow died about ten years ago, and is the subject of the following humorous epitaph:*—

    Thaw every breast, melt every eye with woe,
    Here's dissolution by the hand of death;
    To dirt, to water's turn'd the fairest Snow,
    O! the king's Trumpeter has lost his breath.
                Webb's Collection of Epitaphs Vol. II. page 4.

‡ Apology for his Life, quarto, page 107.

a composer for the church, the theatre, and the chamber. He was not fond of services, and, excepting that sublime composition, his Te Deum and Jubilate, his services in B♭, and what is called his second or Benedicite service, in the same key, we know of no work of his of this kind extant. Anthems afforded more exercise for his invention, and in these his excellencies are beyond the reach of description: that of his to the words 'O give thanks,' is esteemed the most capital of them; but there are others, namely, 'O God thou art my God,' 'O God thou hast cast us 'out,' 'O Lord God of hosts,' 'Behold I bring you 'glad tidings,' 'Be merciful unto me O God,'* and 'My song shall be alway of the loving kindness of 'the Lord,' a solo anthem, composed on purpose for Mr. Gostling; which are in a style so truly pathetic and devout, that they can never be heard without rapture by those who are sensible of the powers of harmony: and so finely were his harmonies and melodies adapted to the general sense of mankind, that all who heard were enamoured of them. Brown in one of his Letters mentions that the cathedrals were crowded whenever an anthem of Purcell was expected to be sung.

Of his compositions for the theatre we are enabled to form some judgement, from those parts of them that are published in the Orpheus Britannicus; of these the music to King Arthur seems to have been the most admired: the frost scene in that drama, and the very artful commixture of semitones therein, contrived to imitate that shivering which is the effect of extreme cold, have been celebrated by the pen of Mr. Charles Gildon, in his Laws of Poetry; but doubtless the most perfect of his works of this sort are the music to the Tempest, the Indian Queen, and Œdipus. The former of these plays, in compliance with the very corrupt taste of the times, was altered by Sir William D'avenant and Dryden from Shakespeare, who, as if they had formed their judgment of dramatic poesy rather on the precepts of Mons. Quintinye, than of Aristotle, and thought that the exact regularity observed in the planning of the gardens of that day, afforded a good rule for the conduct of the drama, chose that the characters of Caliban and Miranda should each have a counterpart, and accordingly have given us a Sycorax, a female savage; and Hyppolito, a man that never saw a woman.

It is said that Dryden wrote his Alexander's Feast with a view to its being set by Purcell, but that Purcell declined the task, as thinking it beyond the power of music to express sentiments so superlatively energetic as that ode abounds with. The truth of this assertion may well be questioned, seeing that he composed the Te Deum, and scrupled not to set to music some of the most sublime passages in the Psalms, the Prophecy of Isaiah, and other parts of holy scripture; not to mention that Mr. Thomas Clayton, he that set Mr. Addison's opera of Rosamond, who was the last in the lowest class of musicians, saw nothing in Alexander's Feast to deter him from setting and performing it at the great room in

Villiers-street, York-buildings, in 1711, Sir Richard Steele and he being then engaged in an undertaking to perform concerts at that place for their mutual benefit.† But Clayton's composition met with the contempt it deserved; and the injury done by him to this admirable poem was amply repaired by Mr. Handel.

As to the chamber-music of Purcell, it admits of a division into vocal and instrumental; the first class includes songs for one two and three voices; those for a single voice, though originally composed for the stage, were in truth Cantatas, and perhaps they are the truest models of perfection in that kind extant; among the principal of these are ' From rosy bowers,' sung by Mrs. Cross in the character of Altisidora, in the third part of Don Quixote; and that other 'From silent shades;' to which we may add the incantation in the Indian Queen, 'Ye 'twice ten hundred deities,' with the song that follows it, 'Seek not to know what must not be revealed;' and that bass song sung by Cardenio in Don Quixote, 'Let the dreadful engines of eternal will.'‡ Nor can less with justice be said of his songs for two voices, particularly 'Sing all ye Muses,' 'When 'Myra sings,' 'Fair Chloe my breast so alarms,' and others: as to his dialogues 'Since times are 'so bad,' and 'Now the maids and the men,' they are songs of humour, and in a style so peculiarly his own, that we know not to what test of comparison they can be brought, or how to judge of them, otherwise than by their own intrinsic excellence.

Other compositions of his there are of a class different from those above mentioned, as ballads and catches, of which he made many. The air 'What 'shall I do to show how much I love her,' in the opera of Dioclesian; 'If love's a sweet passion,' in the Fairy Queen;§ and another printed in Comes Amoris, book IV. song I. to the words 'No, no, 'poor suff'ring heart,' are ballads, and perhaps the finest of the kind ever made. Of Catches it may be said that they are no more the test of a musician's abilities than an epigram is of a poet's; nevertheless each has its peculiar merit: and of the catches of Purcell it may be said, that they have every excellence that can recommend that species of vocal harmony.

As Purcell is chiefly celebrated for his vocal compositions, it may perhaps be conceived that in the

---

† Life of Mr. John Hughes prefixed to his poems.

‡ Of the two compositions last above mentioned we are able here to give the judgment of foreigners. When the Italian musicians, who came hither with the princess of Modena, king James the Second's queen, became acquainted with our language, they discovered great beauties in Purcell's recitative; and it is said on very good authority, that the notes to the words in the song, 'Seek not to know, &c.,

'Enquire not then who shall from bonds be freed,
'Who 'tis shall wear a crown, and who shall bleed,'
charmed them to astonishment.

And touching the other, a reverend divine, a member of a cathedral choir, a great lover and an excellent judge of music, communicates the following anecdote. 'A very eminent master in London told me that a 'disciple of his, who went by his advice to Italy for improvement of his 'studies in music, at his first visit to him after his return mentioned his 'having heard Purcell talked of as a great composer, and desired his 'opinion of him; for an answer the master sat down to the harpsichord, 'and performed this song. The young gentleman was so struck when 'he heard the passage "Can nothing warm me," that he did not know 'how to express his admiration, but by crying out he had never heard 'music before.'

§ Printed among his Ayres, page 12.

original performance of them they derived considerable advantages, and that the singers, like the actors of that day, had abilities superior to those of the present; but this, as far as the inquiry can be traced, was not the fact: before the introduction of the Italian opera into England the use of the vocal organs was but little understood; and as to what is called a fine manner, the best singers were as much strangers to it as they were to the shake, and those many nameless graces and elegances in singing now so familiar to us; for which reason it is that we see in many of Purcell's songs the graces written at length, and made a part of the composition. From all which it may be inferred that the merit of the singers in and about this time rested chiefly in that perfection which is common to all ages, a fine voice. Those among them who seem to have been most liberally endowed with this gift, were, of men, Mr. James Bowen, Mr. Harris, Mr. Freeman, and Mr. Pate, all actors and singers at the theatres;* and Mr. Damascene, Mr. Woodson, Mr. Turner, and Mr. Bouchier, gentlemen of the chapel;† and of women, Mrs. Mary Davis, Miss Shore, afterwards Mrs. Cibber, Mrs. Cross, Miss Campion, and Mrs. Anne Bracegirdle.‡

* None of the men abovementioned are greatly celebrated as singers, their chief praise being that they were excellent actors, especially Harris, who is highly spoken of by Downes.

† The gentlemen of the chapel about this time were used occasionally to assist in musical performances on the stage, but queen Anne, thinking the practice indecent, forbad it.

‡ Mrs. Davis was one of those female actresses who boarded with Sir William D'avenant in his house. Downes relates that she acted the part of Celania, a shepherdess, in a play called the Rivals, said to have been written by him; and in it sang, in the character of a shepherdess mad for love, the following song:—

My lodging it is on the cold ground,
    and very hard is my fare;
But that which troubles me most is
    the unkindness of my dear;
Yet still I cry, O turn love,
    and I prethee love turn to me,
For thou art the man that I long for,
    and alack what remedy!

I'll crown thee with a garland of straw then,
    and I'll marry thee with a rush ring,
My frozen hopes shall thaw then,
    and merrily we will sing;
O turn to me my dear love,
    and I prethee love turn to me,
For thou art the man that alone canst
    procure my liberty.

But if thou wilt harden thy heart still,
    and be deaf to my pittyful moan,
Then I must endure the smart still,
    and tumble in straw all alone;
Yet still I cry, O turn love,
    and I prethee love turn to me,
For thou art the man that alone art
    the cause of my misery.

Which king Charles the Second hearing, he was so pleased that he took her off the stage, and had a daughter by her, who was named Mary Tudor, and was married to Francis lord Ratcliffe, afterwards earl of Derwentwater. Mrs. Davis was also a fine dancer; she danced with Mr. Priest an Entrée in a masque in the last act of Dryden's comedy of Feigned Innocence, or Sir Martin Mar-all, and was greatly applauded. Of Miss Shore mention has already been made. Mrs. Cross was a celebrated actress, especially in those characters in which singing was required. She acted the part of Altisidora in the third part of Don Quixote, and in that character sang the song 'From rosy bowers.' The history of Mrs. Bracegirdle is well known. She it seems had a fine voice, and acted the part of Marcella in the second part of Don Quixote, and in it sang the song 'I burn, I burn,' set to music by Mr. John Eccles. In the Orpheus Britannicus is a song in which she is celebrated for her performance of this character. Miss Campion was a young woman of low extraction, unhappy in a beautiful person and a fine voice. William the first duke of Devonshire took her off the stage, and made her his mistress. She died in May 1706, in the nineteenth year of her age; and the duke, who was then in his sixty-sixth, buried her in the church of Latimers, the seat of his family in the county of Bucks. In the chancel of that church he erected a monument for her, on which is a Latin inscription, importing that she was wise above her years, bountiful to the poor, even beyond her abilities; and at the playhouse, where she sometime acted, modest

His music for instruments consists of overtures, act-tunes, and dance-tunes composed for the theatre, and the two sets of Sonatas for violins, of the publication whereof mention is above made. These compositions are greatly superior to any of the kind published before his time; and if they fall short of his other works, the failure is to be attributed to the state of instrumental music in his time, which was hardly above mediocrity. For although Ferabosco, Coperario, and Jenkins, in their compositions for viols had carried the music for those instruments in concert to great perfection, upon the introduction of the violin into this kingdom these were disregarded, and the English musicians, namely, Rogers, Porter, Child, Lock, and others, set themselves to compose little airs in three and four parts for violins and a bass. Jenkins indeed composed a set of Sonatas for those instruments, and so did Godfrey Finger some years after; but of these works the chief merit was their novelty.

Neither does it appear that in Italy the improvements in instrumental had kept an equal pace with those of vocal music. In a general view of the state of instrumental music towards the end of the last century, it will appear to have been wanting in spirit and force: in the melody and harmony it was too purely diatonic; and, in regard to the contexture of parts, too nearly approaching to counterpoint. In France Lully invented that energetic style which distinguishes his overtures, and which Handel himself disdained not to adopt; and in Italy Corelli introduced a variety of chromatic, or at least semitonic combinations and passages, which, besides that they had the charm of novelty to recommend them, gave a greater latitude to his modulation, and allowed a wider scope for invention: nor was the structure of his compositions less original than delightful; fugues well sustained, and answering at the properest intervals through all the parts; fine syncopations, and elegant transitions from key to key; basses, with the sweetest harmony in the very melody; these are the characteristics of Corelli's compositions, but these Purcell lived rather too early to profit by. Doubtless, therefore, Lully and Corelli are to be looked on as the first great improvers of that kind of instrumental harmony which for full half a century

and untainted; that, being taken with a hectic fever, with a firm confidence and christian piety she submitted to her fate, and that William duke of Devonshire upon her beloved remains had erected that tomb as sacred to her memory. Dr. White Kennet, afterwards bishop of Peterborough, preached the funeral sermon of this noble personage, and published memoirs of his family, representing him in both, as also in his complete History of England, as no less distinguished by his virtues than his titles, the chief reason whereof, seems to be that the duke styled himself a hater of tyrants, and was a great instrument in the Revolution. Notwithstanding which, a general indignation rose in the minds of all sober and good men against the duke and his panegyrist, the one for the shameless insult on virtue and good manners, contained in the above inscription, the other for his no less shameless prostitution of his eloquence, in an endeavour to confound the distinctions between moral good and evil, and represent as worthy of imitation a character, which in one very essential particular is justly to be abhorred. It is said that the duke repented of his past life, and it is to be hoped, though there is no evidence of it, that in the number of his errors his conduct in the above instance was included.

To the account already extant of Mrs. Bracegirdle it may be added, that in the latter part of her life she dwelt in the family of Francis Chute, Esq., one of his majesty's learned counsel, his house being then in Norfolk-street in the Strand. She died on the twelfth day of September, 1748, in the eighty-fifth year of her age, and lies buried in the east ambulatory of the cloister of Westminster Abbey, under a black marble stone, the inscription on which is all, except her name, effaced.

has been practised and admired throughout Europe. The works of the latter of these were not published until a few years before Purcell's death, so that unless we suppose that he had seen them in manuscript, it may be questioned whether they ever came to his hands;* and therefore who those famed Italian masters were whom he professes to have imitated in the composition of his first sonatas, we are at a loss to discover.

And yet there are those who think that, in respect of instrumental composition, the difference between Purcell and Corelli is less than it may seem. Of the Golden Sonata the reputation is not yet extinct; there are some now living who can scarce speak of it without rapture : and Dr. Tudway of Cambridge, in that letter of his to his son, which has so often been quoted in the course of this work, has not scrupled to say of it that it equals if not exceeds any of Corelli's sonatas. Which sentiment, whether it be just or not, the reader may determine by the help of the score here inserted :—

SONATA.

* In the London Gazette, Numb. 3116, for September 23, 1695, is the following advertisement : 'Twelve Sonatas (newly come over from Rome) 'in 3 parts, composed by Signeur Archangelo Corelli, and dedicated to 'his Highness the Elector of Bavaria, this present year 1694, are to be 'had fairly prick'd from the true original, at Mr. Ralph Agutter's, Musical 'Instrument Maker, over-against York-Buildings in the Strand, London.' Upon the face of this advertisement it may be questioned whether the book to which it refers was then printed or not, but it is pretty clear from the expression 'prick'd from the true original,' which means the notation of music by writing, in contradistinction to printing, that the copy above mentioned was a manuscript one. And it is certain that for some years, that is to say, till about 1710, when the elder Walsh first printed them on pewter plates, the Sonatas of Corelli were circulated through this kingdom in manuscript copies.

HENRY PURCELL.

Whatever encomiums may have been bestowed elsewhere, as namely, on Coperario, Lawes, Laneare, and others, it is certain that we owe to Purcell the introduction amongst us of what we call fine air, in contradistinction to that narrow, contracted melody, which appears in the compositions of his predecessors: the first effort of this kind was the Ariadne of Henry Lawes, between which and the 'Rosy bowers' of Purcell the difference in point of merit is immeasurable. It has already been mentioned, and Purcell has expressly said, that in his compositions he imitated the style of the Italians;* and there is good ground to suppose he sedulously contemplated the works of Carissimi and Stradella: how far he profited by their example, and to what degree of perfection he improved vocal music in this countr , those only know who are competently skilled in this divine science, and have studied his works with that care and attention which they will ever be found to merit.

DANIEL PURCELL was a brother of the former, and from him derived most of that little reputation which as a musician he possessed. It does not appear that he was educated in any choir, or that he stood in any degree of relation to the church other than that of organist; so that unless we suppose him to have been a scholar of his brother, we are at a loss to guess who was his instructor in the science. He was for some time organist of Magdalen college, Oxford, and afterwards of St. Andrew's Church in Holborn.† He was one of the candidates for a prize payable out of the sum of 200l. raised by some of the nobility, to be distributed amongst musicians. The design of this act of bounty will be best explained by the following advertisement respecting it, published in the London Gazette, No. 3585, for March 21, 1699:—'Several persons of quality having ' for the encouragement of musick advanced 200 ' guineas, to be distributed in 4 prizes, the first of ' 100, the second of 50, the third of 30, and the ' fourth of 20 guineas, to such masters as shall

---

* The very explicit declarations to this purpose in the dedication of his first sonatas. and of his opera of Dioclesian, are enough to silence for ever those, who, knowing nothing either of him or his works, assert that the music of Purcell is different from the Italian, and entirely English.

† The occasion of his coming to London was as follows: Dr. Sacheverell, who had been a friend of his brother Henry, having been presented to the living of St. Andrew Holborn, found an organ in the church, of Harris's building, which, having never been paid for, had from the time of its erection in 1699, been shut up. The doctor upon his coming to the living, by a collection from the parishioners, raised money to pay for it, but the title to the place of organist was litigious, the right of election being in question between the rector, the vestry, and the parish at large: Nevertheless he invited Daniel Purcell to London, and he accepted it; but in February, 1717, the vestry, which in that parish is a select one, thought proper to elect Mr. Maurice Greene, afterwards Dr. Greene, in preference to Purcell, who submitted to stand as a candidate. In the year following Greene was made organist of St. Paul's, and Daniel Purcell being then dead, his nephew Edward was a candidate for the place, but it was conferred on Mr. John Isum, who died in June 1726.

'be adjudged to compose the best; this is therefore
'to give notice, that those who intend to put in for
'the prizes are to repair to Jacob Tonson at Grays-
'Inn-gate, before Easter next day, where they may
'be further informed.'

It is conjectured that the earl of Halifax was
a liberal contributor to the fund out of which these
sums were proposed to be paid.* The poem given
out as the subject of the musical composition was
the Judgment of Paris, written by Mr. Congreve.
Weldon, Eccles, and Daniell Purcell were three of
the competitors;† the two former obtained prizes,
and we may suppose that the latter was in some
degree successful, seeing that he was at the expense
of publishing his work in score.

Daniel Purcell composed also the music to an
opera entitled Brutus of Alba, or Augusta's Triumph,
written by George Powell, the Comedian, and performed in 1697 at the theatre in Dorset-garden. A
collection of single songs from this opera, with the
music, is in print. He composed also songs for
plays to a very great number; sundry of them, but
without the basses, are in the Pills to purge Melancholy. In general they have but little to recommend them, and Daniel Purcell is at this day better
known by his puns, with which the jest-books
abound, than by his musical compositions.

CHAP. CLVII.

WILLIAM HOLDER *(a Portrait)*, doctor in divinity, a canon of Ely, a residentiary of St. Paul's,
and subdean of the chapel royal, a person of great
learning and sagacity, was the author of a treatise of
the natural grounds and Principles of Harmony,
octavo, 1694; as also a tract entitled the Elements of
Speech, and a discourse concerning time, with application of the natural day, lunar month, and solar
year. He is said to have taught the use of speech
to a young gentleman, Mr. Alexander Popham, born
deaf and dumb, by a method which he relates in an
apendix to his Elements of Speech; but it seems
that Mr. Popham was afterwards sent to Dr. Wallis,
who had done the same thing by another young
person; and upon Mr. Popham's being made able to
speak, Dr. Wallis claimed the merit of it in a paper
published in the Philosophical Transactions, which
Dr. Holder answered.‖ The wife of Dr. Holder,
Susanna, the sister of Sir Christopher Wren, was not
less famous than her husband for cures of another
kind, it being related of her in the inscription on
her sepulchral monument that 'in compassion to the
'poor she applied herself to the knowledge of me-
'dicinal remedies, wherein God gave so great a
'blessing, that thousands were happily healed by
'her, and no one ever miscarried; and that king
'Charles the Second, queen Catherine, and very
'many of the court had also experience of her suc-
'cessful hand.§

* This is hinted at in the dedication of the second book of the Orpheus Britannicus.

† Jerry Clark being asked why he did not compose for the prize, gave for answer that the nobility were to be the judges, leaving the querist to make the inference.

‡ Fasti Oxon. vol. II. col. 139.

§ This inscription seems to allude to a cure which corresponds with

It will appear by the account hereafter given of
Dr. Holder's treatise on harmony, that he was very
deeply skilled in the theory, and well acquainted
with the practice of music. In the chapel and the
cathedrals where his duty required him to attend,
he was a strict disciplinarian, and, for being very
exact in the performance of choral service, and frequently reprimanding the choir-men for their negligence in it, Michael Wise was used to call him Mr.
Snub-dean. He died at his house in Amen-corner,
in London, on the twenty-fourth day of January,
1696, aged eighty-two, and lies buried in the vault
under the choir of St. Paul's cathedral, with a marble
monument, on which is the following inscription:—

'H. S. E.

'Gulielmus Holder, S. T. P. Sacelli Regalis Sub-
'decanus Sereniss. Regiæ Majestati Subeleemosi-
'narius Ecclesiæ Sti Pauli et Eliens. Canonicus,
'Societatis Regiæ Lond. Sodalis, &c. Amplis quidem
'Titulis donatus amplissimis dignus. Vir per ele-
'gantis et amœni ingenii Scientias Industriâ suâ
'illustravit, Liberalitate promovit, egregie eruditus
'Theologicis, Mathematicis, et Arte Musica, Me-
'moriam excolite posteri et â Lucubrationibus suis
'editis Loquelæ Principia agnoscite et Harmoniæ.
'Obiit 24 Jan. 1697.'

The treatise of the natural grounds and principles
of harmony is divided into chapters. In the first
the author treats of sound in general, how it is produced and propagated.

Chap. II. is on the subject of sound harmonic, the
first and great principle whereof is shewn to be,
that the tune of a note, to speak in our vulgar phrase,
is constituted by the measure and proportion of
vibrations of the sonorous body, that is to say, of
the velocity of those vibrations in their recourses,
whether the same be a chord, a bell, a pipe, or the
animal larynx. After explaining with great perspicuity Galileo's doctrine of pendulums, he supposes
for his purpose the chord of a musical instrument
to resemble a double pendulum moving upon two
centres, the nut and the bridge, and vibrating with
the greatest range in the middle of its length.

Chap. IV. He makes a concord to consist in the
coincidence of the vibrations of the chords of two
instruments, and speaks to this purpose:—If the
vibrations correspond in every course and recourse,
the concord produced will be the unison, if the ratio
of the vibrations be as 2 to 1, in which case they
will unite alternately, viz., at every course, crossing
at the recourse, the concord will be the octave. If
the vibrations be in the ratio of 3 to 2, their sounds
will consort in a fifth, uniting after every second,
i. e. at every other or third course; and if as 4 to
3, in a diatessaron or fourth, uniting after every
third recourse, viz., at every fourth course, and so
of the other consonances according to their respective
ratios.

the following anecdote. Mrs. Holder was recommended to Charles II. to cure a sore finger that he had; the king put himself under her care, and while she was dressing it, the serjeant surgeon came in, and enquiring what she was about, the king gave him his finger; the surgeon upon looking at it, said 'Oh, this sore is nothing:' 'I know very well (said 'the king) it is nothing, but I know as well that of it you would have 'made something, which was what I meant to prevent, by committing 'myself to the care of this good lady.'

GUILIELMUS HOLDER S.T.P. SACELLI REGALIS SUBDECANUS SERENISSIMI

REGIÆ MAJESTATI SUBELEEMOSYNARIUS ECCLESIARIUM

SANCTI PAULI ET ELIENSIS CANONICUS SOCIETATIS REGIÆ

LONDINENSIS SODALIS MDCLXXXIII.

MRS. ARABELLA HUNT.

In Chap. V. he treats of the three sorts of proportion, namely, arithmetical, geometrical, and that mixed proportion resulting from the former two, called harmonical proportion. Under the head of geometrical proportion, the author considers the three species of multiplex, superparticular, and superpartient, already explained in the course of this work, and gives the rules for finding the habitudes of rations or proportions, as also a medium or mediety between the terms of any ration, by addition, subtraction, multiplication, and division of rations, forming thereby a praxis of musical arithmetic.

In Chap. VI. entitled of Discords and Degrees, the author digresses to the music of the ancients, touching which he seems to acquiesce in the opinion of Kircher and Gassendus, that the Greeks never used concert music, i. e. of different parts at once, but only solitary, for one single voice or instrument; which music he says by the elaborate curiosity and nicety of contrivance of degrees, and by measures, rather than by harmonious consonancy and by long studied performance, was more proper to make great impressions upon the fancy, and operate accordingly as some historians relate. Whereas, adds he, ours more sedately affects the understanding and judgment, from the judicious contrivance and happy composition of melodious consort. He concludes this sentiment with an assertion that the diatonic genus of music is founded in the natural grounds of harmony; but not so, or not so regularly, the chromatic or enarmonic kinds, of which nevertheless he gives an accurate designation, concluding with a scheme from Alypius of the characters used in the notation of the ancient Greek music, with their several powers.

In the conclusion of this work he gives as a reason why some persons do not love music, a discovery of the famous Dr. Willis, to wit, that there is a certain nerve in the brain which some persons have and some have not.

The above-mentioned treatise of Dr. Holder is written with remarkable accuracy; there is in it no confusion of terms; all that it teaches is made clear and conspicuous, and the doctrines contained in it are such as every musician ought to be master of; and much more of the theory of music he need not know.

It appears that besides a profound knowledge in the theory of music, Dr. Holder was possessed of an eminent degree of skill in the science of practical composition. In a noble collection of church-music, in the hand-writing of Dr. Thomas Tudway, now in the British Museum, of which an account will hereafter be given, is an anthem for three voices in the key of C with the greater third, to the words 'Praise our God ye people,' by Dr. William Holder.

MRS. ARABELLA HUNT, (a Portrait), celebrated for her beauty, but more for a fine voice and an exquisite hand on the lute, lived at this time, and was the person for whom many of the songs of Blow and Purcell were composed. She taught the princess Anne of Denmark to sing; and was much favoured by queen Mary, who, for the sake of having Mrs.

Hunt near her, bestowed on her an employment about her person, and would frequently be entertained in private with her performance, even of common popular songs.* A gentleman now living, the son of one who used frequently to sing with her, remembers to have heard his father say, that Mrs. Hunt's voice was like the pipe of a bullfinch. She was unfortunate in her marriage : nevertheless she lived irreproachably, and maintained the character of a modest and virtuous woman ; the reputation whereof, together with her accomplishments, rendered her a welcome visitant in the best families in the kingdom. In the summer season she was much at the house of Mr. Rooth, at Epsom. This gentleman had married the dowager of the second earl of Donegal, and being very fond of music, had frequent concerts there. In a letter from Mr. Rooth to Mr. John Hughes, the author of the Siege of Damascus, he tells him that Mrs. Hunt is at his house, and waits to see him, and hopes he will bring Signor Corelli with him.†

Mrs Hunt died on the twenty-sixth day of December, 1705. Mr. Congreve has celebrated her in an ode entitled 'On Mrs. Arabella Hunt singing,' and in the following lines, written after her decease, under the picture of her by Kneller :—

Were there on earth another voice like thine,
Another hand so blest with skill divine,
The late afflicted world some hopes might have
And harmony retrieve thee from the grave.

In the foregoing account respecting the English church musicians, frequent occasion has occurred to mention their appointments to places in the royal chapel. The term royal chapel means in general the chapel in each of the royal palaces, but in common speech it is taken for that of Whitehall. This makes it necessary to relate a melancholy accident that happened near the end of the last century, which was followed by a translation of the royal residence, and may in some sort be considered as a new era in the history of church-music.

The palace of Whitehall was originally built by Cardinal Wolsey. On his attainder it became forfeited to the crown, and was the town residence of our princes from Henry VIII. down to William and Mary : it was a spacious building, in a style somewhat resembling Christ Church college, Oxford, and the chapel was a spacious and magnificent room. On the fifth day of January, 1698, by the carelessness, as it is said, of some of the servants in the laundry, the whole of it was consumed,‡ and the king and queen necessitated to take up their residence at St.

* Vide ante, page 564, in note, the story of her singing, at the queen's request, the old ballad of 'Cold and raw,' and Purcell's revenge on the queen for it.

† Meaning the Sonatas of Corelli, then but lately published.

‡ This edifice narrowly escaped a total demolition by fire on the ninth day of April, 1691. The circumstances are thus related in a letter from Mr. Pulteney to Sir W. Colt, cited in the Continuation of Rapin's History of England, vol. I. page 171. 'It began about eight o'clock at night, by 'the negligence of a maid servant, who (to save the pains of cutting a 'candle from a pound) burnt one off, and threw the rest down carelessly 'before the flame was out, at the lower end of the stone gallery, in those 'lodgings which were the duchess of Portsmouth's, and burnt very vio- 'lently till four the next morning, during which time almost all the stone 'gallery and buildings behind it, as far as the Thames, were consumed, 'and one or two men killed by the buildings that were blown up.

James's, where there was neither room sufficient to receive, nor accommodations for, half the household.*

Concerning the palace of St. James, it is said by Stow, Newcourt, and others, that it was formerly, even before the time of the Conquest, an hospital founded by the citizens of London for fourteen sisters, maidens that were leprous, living chastely and honestly in divine service.

' This hospital was surrendered to king Hen. VIII. ' in 23 of his reign, being then valued at 100l. per ' ann. The sisters being compounded with, were al- ' lowed pensions for term of their lives, and the king

' built there a goodly mannor, annexing thereunto a ' park, inclosed about with a wall of brick, now ' called St. James's Park, which hath been of late ' years (to wit) soon after the restauration, very much ' improved and beautified with a canal, ponds, and ' curious walks between rows of trees, by king ' Charles II. and since that very much enlarged, and ' the whole encompassed round with a brick wall by ' the same king, and serves indifferently to the two ' palaces of St. James and White-hall.' Newcourt's Repertorium, vol. I. page 662. Stow's Survey, edit. 1633, page 495.

BOOK XVII.

IN tracing the progress of music in this country, it is found that the compositions of our most celebrated masters were calculated either for the service of the church, for theatric entertainment, or for private chamber practice. Those persons who understood or professed to love music had their meetings in divers

CHAP. CLVIII.

parts of the kingdom for the practice of vocal and instrumental music; but till the establishment of those weekly musical meetings at Oxford of which an account has herein before been given, we meet with no voluntary associations for musical recreation, till some time after the restoration. The first of the kind in London had its rise in a very obscure part of the town, viz., at Clerkenwell, in such a place, and under such circumstances, as tended more to disgrace than recommend such an institution. In short it was in the house, or rather hovel of one Thomas Britton, a man who for a livelihood sold small-coal about the streets, that this meeting was held, the first of the kind in London, as beginning in the year 1678, and the only one that corresponded with the idea of a concert.

An account of this extraordinary man, and of the meetings at his house, is referred to a future page. His concert is here mentioned as that which gave rise to other meetings for a similar purpose, of which there were many towards the end of the last century.

In the interim it is proposed to speak of those musical performances with which the people in general were entertained at places of public resort, distinguishing between such as were calculated for the recreation of the vulgar, and those which for their elegance come under the denomination of concerts. The first of these were no other than the musical entertainments given to the people in Music-houses, already spoken of, the performers in which consisted of fiddlers and others, hired by the master of the house; such as in the night season were wont to parade the city and suburbs under the denomination of the Waits.† The music of these men could scarcely be called a concert, for this obvious reason, that it had no variety of parts, nor commixture of different instruments: half a dozen of fiddlers would scrape Sellenger's Round, or John come kiss me, or Old Simon the King with divisions, till themselves and their audience were tired, after which as many players on the hautboy would in the most harsh and discordant tones grate forth Green Sleves, Yellow Stockings, Gillian of Croydon, or some such common dance-tune, and the people thought it fine music.

But a concert, properly so called, was a sober re-

---

* The places of the royal residence from time to time are very indistinctly noted by our historians, the inquiry into them is a subject of some curiosity, and not unworthy the attention of an antiquary: the most ancient that we know of was the palace of Edward the Confessor, adjoining to the monastery of Westminster, the site whereof is now called Old Palace yard. In this was the Aula Regia, in which were holden the courts of justice. William Rufus built Westminster-hall, as it is said, to rid his house of so great and troublesome assemblies; and it is further said that he meditated building near it a new palace, which design of his gave name to New Palace-yard. Nevertheless the succeeding kings down to Henry VIII. continued to dwell in the old palace.

Whitehall was originally built by Hubert de Burgh, earl of Kent, and justiciary of England, and afterwards became the inn or town residence of the archbishops of York. Wolsey re-edified it, but being convicted of a premunire, anno 1529, it was, 21 Henry VIII. by Sir Thomas More, lord chancellor, the duke of Norfolk, and certain other great officers, recovered to them and their heirs for the use of the king against the cardinal, by the name of York-place, and they by charter delivered and confirmed the same to the king, which charter, dated 7 Feb. 21 Hen. VIII. is now extant among the records at Westminster. Strype, book VI. page 5.

After this, Henry VIII. removed his dwelling from the old palace near the monastery of St. Peter Westminster to Whitehall, and that because the old palace was then, and had been a long time before, in utter ruin and decay, as it is expressed in an act of parliament, 28 Hen. VIII. cap. 12, and that the king had lately obtained this Whitehall, which is styled in the same act, ' One great mansion, place and house, being parcel of ' the possessions of the archbishoprick of York, situate in the town of ' Westminster, not much distant from the same ancient palace; and that ' he had lately upon the soil of the said mansion, place and house, and ' upon the ground thereunto belonging, most sumptuously and curiously ' builded and edified many and distinct beautiful, costly, and pleasant ' lodgings, buildings, and mansions, for his grace's singular pleasure, ' comfort, and commodity, to the honour of his highness and his realm. ' And thereunto adjoining had made a park, walled and environed with ' brick and stone; and there devised and ordained many and singular ' commodious things, pleasures, and other necessaries, apt and convenient ' to appertain to so noble a prince for his pastime and solace.'

By the said act the whole limits of the royal palace are set out and described, namely, ' That all the said soil, ground, mansion, and buildings, ' and the park, and also the soil of the ancient palace, should be from ' thenceforth the king's whole palace at Westminster, and so be taken, ' deemed, and reputed, and to be called and named the king's palace at ' Westminster for ever. And that the said palace should extend, and be ' as well within the soil and places before limited and appointed, as also ' in all the street or way leading from Charing Cross unto the Sanctuary- ' gate at Westminster; and to all the houses, buildings, lands, and ' tenements on both sides of the same street or way from the said Cross ' unto Westminster-hall, between the water of the Thames on the east ' part, and the said park-wall on the west part, and so through all the ' limits of the old palace.'

Before this time, besides the old palace at Westminster, our princes had sundry places of residence, as namely the Tower, the Old Jewry, where Henry VI. dwelt; Baynard's Castle, the habitation of Henry VII. Tower Royal, of Rich. II. and Stephen; the Wardrobe in Carter-lane, of Rich. III. Hen. VII. lived also at Bridewell, and Elizabeth at White-hall, and also at Somerset House. Of their summer palaces, namely Windsor, Hampton-Court, Shene, Greenwich, Eltham, and others, frequent mention is made in history.

In the reign of James I. Inigo Jones made a design for a new palace at Whitehall, but the only part of it ever built was the Banqueting-house as it now appears. One Cavendish Weedon, a member of Lincoln's-Inn, of whom farther mention will be made hereafter, published a proposal for rebuilding it in seven years, at an expence not exceeding 600,000l. as also a scheme for raising the money. Vide Strype's Continuation of Stow's Survey of London, book VI. page 6.

---

† It was the ancient custom for the waits to parade the streets nightly during the winter. Now they go about a few nights only before Christmas to furnish a pretence for asking money at the return of that festival.

recreation; persons were drawn to it, not by an affectation of admiring what they could not taste, but by a genuine pleasure which they took in the entertainment. For the gratification of such, the masters of music exerted their utmost endeavours; and some of the greatest eminence among them were not above entertaining the public with musical performances, either at their own houses, or in places more commodious; receiving for their own use the money paid on admission. And to these performances the lovers of music were invited by advertisements in the London Gazette, the form and manner whereof will appear by the following extracts.

Numb. 742. Dec. 30, 1672. 'These are to give 'notice, that at Mr. John Banister's house (now called 'the Musick-school) over against the George tavern 'in White Fryers, this present Monday, will be mu- 'sick performed by excellent masters, beginning 'precisely at 4 of the clock in the afternoon, and 'every afternoon for the future, precisely at the same 'hour.'

Numb. 958. Jan. 25, 1674. Mr. John Banister advertises that he is removed to Shandois-street, Covent Garden, and there intends entertainment as formerly on Tuesday then next, and every evening for the future, Sundays only excepted.

Numb. 961. Feb. 4, 1674. 'A rare concert of 'four Trumpets Marine, never heard of before in 'England. If any persons desire to come and hear 'it, they may repair to the Fleece tavern near St. 'James's, about two of the clock in the afternoon, 'every day in the week except Sundays. Every 'concert shall continue one hour, and so begin again. 'The best places are one shilling, and the other 'sixpence.'

Numb. 1154. Dec. 11, 1676. 'On Thursday 'next, the 14th instant, at the Academy in Little 'Lincoln's-Inn-fields, will begin the first part of the 'Parley of Instruments, composed by Mr. John 'Banister, and perform'd by eminent masters, at six 'o'clock, and to continue nightly, as shall by bill or 'otherwise be notifi'd. The tickets are to be deli- 'ver'd out from one of the clock till five every day, 'and not after.'

Numb. 1356. Nov. 18, 1678. 'On Thursday 'next, the 22d of this instant November, at the 'Musick-school in Essex-buildings, over-against St. 'Clement's church in the Strand,* will be continued 'a consort of vocal and instrumental musick, be- 'ginning at five of the clock every evening, composed 'by Mr. John Banister.'

Banister died in the year 1679, as has been already related; he left a son named John, a fine performer on the violin, who was one of king William's band, and played the first violin at Drury-lane theatre when operas were first performed there, and will be spoken of hereafter.

Numb. 2088. Nov. 23, 1685. An advertisement of the publication of several Sonatas, composed after the Italian way, for one and two bass-viols, with a thorough-bass, by Mr. August Keenell, and of their

being to be performed on Thursday evenings at the dancing-school in Walbrook, next door to the Bell inn; and on Saturday evenings at the dancing-school in York-buildings, at which places will be also some performance on the Baritone by the said Mr. August Keenell.

About this time we also find that concerts were performed in Bow-street, Covent Garden, for in the Gazette, Numb. 2496, Oct. 14, 1689, is an advertisement that the concerts that were held in Bow-street and York-buildings were then joined together, and would for the future be performed in York Buildings.

Numb. 2533. Feb. 20, 1689. The music meeting that was lately held in Villiers-street, York-build- ings,† is advertised to be removed into Exeter Change in the Strand; but in a subsequent advertisement of March 10, in the same year, it is said to be removed back to Villiers-street.

Numb. 2599. Oct. 9, 1690. 'Mr. Franck's con- 'sort of vocal and instrumental musick will be 'performed to-morrow, being the 10th instant, at the '2 Golden Balls, at the upper end of Bow-street, 'Covent-Garden, at 7 in the evening; and next 'Wednesday at the Outroper's* office in the Royal 'Exchange, and will be continued all the ensuing 'winter.'

Numb. 2637. Feb. 19, 1690. 'The consort of 'musick lately in Bow-street is removed next 'Bedford-gate in Charles-street, Covent Garden, 'where a room is newly built for that purpose, and 'by command is to begin on Friday next the 20th 'instant, where it is afterwards to be continued 'every Thursday, beginning between 7 and 8 in the 'evening.'

Numb. 2651. April 9, 1691. 'The consort of 'vocal and instrumental musick, lately held in York- 'Buildings, will be performed again at the same 'place and hour as formerly, on Monday next, 'being Easter Monday, by the command, and for 'the entertainment of Her Royal Highness the 'Princess of Denmark.'

Numb. 2654. April 20, 1691. 'The concert of 'vocal and instrumental music in Charles-street, 'Covent Garden, by their Majesties' authority will 'be performed on Tuesday next, the 23d instant, 'and so continue every Thursday by command.'

Numb. 2746. March 6, 1691. 'A concert of 'musick, with several new voices, to be performed

---

* Viz., in the great house a few doors down on the right hand, now occupied by Mr. Paterson, the auctioneer.

† In Villiers-street, York-buildings, was formerly a great room used for concerts and other public exhibitions. In the Spectator are sundry advertisements from thence. About the year 1711 Sir Richard Steele and Clayton were engaged in a concert performed there; and since their time it has been used for the like purposes. The house of which it was part was on the right hand side of the street, near the bottom, and adjoining to what is now called the water-office, but within these few years it was pulled down, and two small houses have been built on the site of it.

‡ For the etymology of the appellative Outroper we are to seek; but the following clause in the charter granted by Charles II. to the citizens of London, will go near to explain the meaning of it. 'Also we will, 'and for us our heirs and successors do erect and create in and through 'the said city, &c. a certain office called Outroper or common cryer, to 'and for the selling of houshold stuff, apparel, leases of houses, jewels, 'goods, chattels, and other things of all persons who shall be willing 'that the said officers shall make sale of the same things by public and 'open clamour, commonly called Outcry, and sale in some common and 'open place or places in the said city, &c.' And in the London Gazette, Numb. 2404, is an order of the Mayor and Aldermen of London for re- viving the said office of Outroper, for the benefit of the orphans to whom the chamber of London is indebted, and that Thomas Puckle be admitted thereto: And that the West Pawn of the Royal Exchange be the place for such sales.

'on the 10th instant at the Vendu in Charles-street,
'Covent Garden.' *

Numb. 2834. Jan. 9, 1692. 'The Italian lady,
'(that is lately come over that is so famous for her
'singing) has been reported that she will sing no
'more in the concert in York-buildings : This is to
'give notice that next Tuesday, being the 10th in-
'stant, she will sing in the concert in York Buildings,
'and so continue during this season.'

Numb. 2838. Jan. 23, 1692. 'These are to give
'notice that the musick meeting, in which the Italian
'woman sings, will be held every Tuesday in York-
'buildings, and Thursdays in Freeman's-yard, in
'Cornhill, near the Royal Exchange.

Numb. 2858. April 3, 1693. 'On next Thurs-
'day, being the 6th of April, will begin Signor
'Tose's † consort of musick, in Charles-street, Covent-
'garden, about eight of the clock in the evening.

Numb. 2917. Oct. 26, 1693. 'Signor Tosi's con-
'sort of musick will begin on Monday, the 30th
'instant, in York-buildings, at eight in the evening,
'to continue weekly all the winter.'

Numb. 2926. Nov. 27, 1693. 'In Charles-street,
'in Covent-garden, on Thursday next, the 30th in-
'stant, will begin Mr. Franck's consort of musick,
'and so continue every Thursday night, beginning
'exactly at eight of the clock.'

Numb. 2943. Jan. 25, 1693. 'At the consort-
'room in York-buildings, on this present Thursday,
'at the usual hour, will be performed Mr. Purcell's
'Song, composed for St. Cecilia's Day in the year
'1692, together with some other compositions of his,
'both vocal and instrumental, for the entertainment
'of his Highness Prince Lewis of Baden.'

Numb. 2945. Feb. 1, 1693. 'At the consort in
'York-buildings, on Monday next, the 5th instant,
'will be performed Mr. Finger's St. Cecilia's Song,
'intermixed with a variety of new musick, at the or-
'dinary rates.'

Numb. 2982. June 11, 1694. 'On Thursday
'will be a new consort of musick in Charlest-street,
'Covent-garden, where a gentlewoman sings that
'hath one of the best voices in England, not before
'heard in publick, to be continued every Thursday
'for a month.'

Numb. 3027. Nov. 15, 1694. 'A consort of
'musick, composed by Mr. Grabue,‡ will be per-
'formed on Saturday next at Mr. Smith's, in Charles-
'street, Covent-garden, between the hours of seven
'and eight.'

Numb. 3030. Nov. 26, 1694. 'The consort of
'musick in Charles-street, Covent-garden, will
'begin again next Thursday, with the addition of
'two new voices, one a young gentlewoman of 12
'years of age, the room being put in good condition,
'and there to continue this season.'

Numb. 3250. Jan. 1696. 'The musick that was
'performed of St. Cecilia's Day, composed by Signor
'Nicola,§ will be performed on Thursday night in
'York-buildings, being the 7th instant.'

Numb. 3286. May 10, 1697. 'On Thursday
'next, being the 13th instant, will be performed in
'York-buildings an entertainment of vocal and in-
'strumental musick, composed by Dr. Staggins.'

Numb. 3356. Jan. 10, 1697. 'In York-buildings,
'this present Monday, the 10th instant, at the re-
'quest of several persons of quality, will be a con-
'sort of vocal and instrumental music never per-
'formed there before, beginning at the usual hour,
'for the benefit of Mr. King and Mr. Banister.' ‖

Numb. 3366. Feb. 14, 1697. 'An entertainment
'of new musick, composed on the peace by Mr. Van
'[Vaughan] Richardson, organist of Winchester
'cathedral, will be performed on Wednesday next,
'at 8 at night, in York-buildings.'

Numb. 3374. March 14, 1697. 'Wednesday
'next, being the 16th instant, will be performed in
'York-buildings a consort of new musick, for the
'benefit of Dr. Blow and Mr. Paisible, beginning at 8.'

Numb. 3377. March 24, 1698. 'Monday next,
'the 28th instant, will be performed in York-build-
'ings, a new consort of musick by the chiefest masters
'in England, where Signior Rampony, an Italian
'musician belonging to the prince of Vaudemont, at
'the request of several persons of quality, will for
'once sing in the same in Italian and French.   Half
'a guinea entrance.'

Numb. 3388. May 2, 1698. 'Wednesday next,
'the 4th of May, will be performed, in York-build-
'ings, the Song which was sung before her royal
'highness on her birth-day last.   With other va-
'riety of new vocal and instrumental musick, com-
'posed by Dr. Turner,¶ and for his benefit.'

Numb. 3390. May 9, 1698. 'On Tuesday next,
'the 10th instant, will be performed in York-build-
'ings an entertainment of vocal and instrumental
'musick, being St. Cecilia's Song, composed by Dr.
'Blow, and several other new songs, for the benefit
'of Mr. Bowman and Mr. Snow.'

Numb. 3396. May 30, 1698. 'This present
'Monday, being the 30th of May, Mr. Nicola's con-
'sort of vocal and instrumental musick will be per-
'formed in York-buildings.'

Numb. 3454. December 19, 1698. 'On Friday
'next will be performed, in York-buildings, a new
'entertainment of vocal musick by Signeur Fidelio,
'beginning exactly at 7 at night.'

Numb. 3458. Jan. 2, 1698. 'On Wednesday next
'will be performed in York-buildings Mr. Daniel
'Purcell's musick made for last St. Cecilia's feast, for
'the benefit of Mr. Howell and Mr. Shore, with an
'addition of new vocal and instrumental musick, be-
'ginning at 7 at night.'

It appears also that concerts were occasionally
performed at the theatre in Drury-lane.   In Dryden's

---

* The Vendu, by an advertisement in the preceding Gazette, appears
to have been a place for the sale of paintings, and to have been situate
next Bedford-gate in Charles-street.

† PIER-FRANCESCO TOSI, a fine singer, mentioned in page 653,
in note, and of whom occasion will be taken to speak hereafter.   It may
be remarked that the spelling in all these advertisements is very
incorrect, and the notification in the most awkward terms.

‡ The person who set to music Dryden's Albion and Albanius.   See
page 707, in note.

§ Supposed to be Nicola Matteis, the author of two collections of airs
for the violin.

‖ The younger Banister: the elder died about eight years before.

¶ Of the royal chapel: he lived far into the present century, and is
therefore referred to a subsequent page.

Miscellany, part III. page 151, are verses thus entitled, ' Epilogue to the ladies, spoken by Mr. Wilks ' at the musick-meeting in Drury-lane, where the ' English woman* sings. Written by Mr. Man- ' waring, upon occasion of their both singing before ' the queen and K. of Spain at Windsor.†'

About this time a man of a projecting head, one Cavendish Weedon, a member of Lincoln's Inn, had formed a design of an establishment for the relief of poor decayed gentlemen, and for erecting a school for the education of youth in religion, music, and accounts. To this end he had a performance of divine music at Stationers' Hall, January the 31st, 1701, for the entertainment of the lords spiritual and temporal, and the honourable House of Commons. This performance consisted of an oration written by himself, two poems by Nahum Tate, and three anthems, one composed by Dr. Blow, the two others by Dr. Turner. The words of the whole are extant in a quarto pamphlet printed at the time.

He had also another performance of the same kind, and for the same purpose, at Stationers' Hall, in the month of May, 1702: the oration was written by Jeremy Collier; the music was an anthem and a Te Deum, both composed by Dr. Blow.

Besides this benevolent design, the author entertained another, in which he seems to have been desirous of emulating Amphion, and by the power of harmony to erect public edifices. To this end he projected a musical service of voices and instruments, to be performed in Lincoln's Inn chapel every Sunday at eleven o'clock, except during Lent and the vacation, under the direction of Dr. Edward Maynard, by subscription, the proposals for which were engraved on a folio sheet, and on two others the plan of Lincoln's Inn-fields, with the figures of the twelve apostles, and water-works at each corner, to be supplied from Hampstead water, and the model of St. Mary's chapel, to be erected in the centre *for praise*, as he terms it, after a design of Sir Christopher Wren, engraved by Sturt in 1698.‡

Strype, in his continuation of Stowe's Survey, book IV. page 74, mentions a proposal of the same person which, whether it be included in the above or was another does not there appear, for building the Six Clerks' office, and other Chancery offices at the east side of Lincoln's Inn garden.

CHAP. CLIX.

Henry Aldrich, *(a Portrait)*, an eminent scholar and divine, the son of Henry Aldrich of Westminster, Gent., was born there in the year 1647, and educated in the college school in that city under the famous Dr. Richard Busby. In 1662 he was admitted of Christ Church college, Oxon. and having been elected

a student under that foundation, took the degree of master of arts April 3, 1669. Entering soon after into holy orders, he distinguished himself by his great proficiency in various branches of divine and human learning, and became a famous tutor in his college. On the fifteenth of February, 1681, he was installed a canon of Christ Church, and the second of May following accumulated the degrees of bachelor and doctor in divinity. In the controversy with the papists during the reign of king James II. he bore a considerable part, and thereby rendered his merit so conspicuous, that when at the revolution Massey the popish dean of Christ Church fled beyond sea, his deanery was conferred on Dr. Aldrich, who was therein established the seventeenth of June, 1689. In this eminent station he presided with a dignity peculiar to his person and character, behaving with great integrity and uprightness, attending to the interests of his college, and the welfare of those under his care, and promoting to the utmost of his abilities learning, religion, and virtue.

The learning of Dr Aldrich, and his skill in polite literature were evinced by his numerous publications, particularly of many of the Greek classics, one whereof he generally published every year as a gift to the students of his house. He also wrote a system of logic for the use of a pupil of his, and printed it; but he possessed so great skill in architexture and music, that his excellence in either would alone have made him famous to posterity. The three sides of the quadrangle of Christ Church college, Oxford, called Peck-water square, were designed by him, as was also the elegant chapel of Trinity college, and the church of All Saints in the High-street, to the erection whereof Dr. Ratcliff, at his solicitation, was a liberal contributor.

Amidst a variety of honourable pursuits, and the cares which the government of his college subjected him to, Dr. Aldrich found leisure to study and cultivate music, particularly that branch of it which related both to his profession and his office. To this end he made a noble collection of church-music, consisting of the works of Palestrina, Carissimi, Victoria, and other Italian composers for the church, and by adapting with great skill and judgment English words to many of their motets, enriched the stores of our church, and in some degree made their works our own.§

With a view to the advancement of music, and the honour of its professors, Dr. Aldrich had formed a design of writing a history of the science, which, had he lived to complete it, would have superseded the necessity of any such work as the present. The materials from which he proposed to compile it are yet extant in the library of his own college. Upon a very careful perusal of them it seems that he had noted down everything he had met with touching music and musicians, but that no part of them had been wrought into any kind of form.

---

* Supposed to be Mrs. Tofts.

† Of the arrival of this prince mention is made in Salmon's Chronological Historian in the following passage. ' Dec. 23, [1703] King Charles ' III. arrived at Spithead. The duke of Somerset, master of the horse, ' brought him a letter from her majesty, and invited him to Windsor, ' where he arrived the 29th, and on the 31st returned with the duke of ' Somerset to his seat at Petworth in Sussex. He set sail for Portugal ' the 5th of January, but being put back by contrary winds, it was the ' 27th of February before he arrived at Lisbon.'

‡ Anecdotes of British Topography, page 312.

§ Instances of this kind are the anthems ' I am well pleased,' from Carissimi, and ' O God king of glory,' from Palestrina. To improve himself in the practice of composition, he was very industrious in putting into score the works of others. The author of this work has in his collection four books of the madrigals of the Prencipe di Venosa, copied by the late Mr. John Immyns from a score in the hand-writing of Dr Aldrich.

The abilities of Dr. Aldrich as a musician rank him among the greatest masters of the science: he composed many services for the church, which are well known, as are also his anthems, to the number of near twenty.

In the Pleasant Musical Companion, printed in 1726, are two catches of Dr. Aldrich, the one, 'Hark the bonny Christ-church bells,' the other entitled 'A Smoking Catch, to be sung by four men smoking their pipes, not more difficult to sing than diverting to hear.'*

That he was a lover of mirth and pleasantry may be inferred from the above and numberless other particulars related of him. The following stanzas of his composition are a version of a well known song, and evidence of a singular vein of humour, which he possessed in an eminent degree :—

Miles et navigator,
Sartor, et ærator,
Jamdudum litigabant,
De pulchrâ quam amabant,
    Nomen cui est Joanna.

Jam tempus consummatum,
Ex quo determinatum,
Se non vexatum iri,
Præ desiderio viri,
    Nec pernoctare solam.

Miles dejerabat,
Hanc prædâ plus amabat,
Ostendens cicatrices,
Quas æstimat felices,
    Dum vindicavit eam.

Sartor ait ne sis dura,
Mihi longa est mensura,
Instat æris fabricator,
Ut olla sarciatur,
    Rimaque obstipetur.

Dum hi tres altercantur,
Nauta vigilantur,
Et calide moratur,
Dum prælium ordiatur,
    Ut agat suam rem.

Perinde ac speratur,
Deinceps compugnatur,
Et sæviente bello,
Transfixit eam telo
    Quod vulneravit cor.

The publication of Lord Clarendon's History of the Rebellion was committed to the care of Dr. Aldrich jointly with Dr. Sprat, bishop of Rochester, and upon no better testimony than the hearsay evidence of a zealous patriot, Mr. John Oldmixon, they were charged with having altered and interpolated that noble work.

In 1702 Dr. Aldrich was chosen prolocutor of the convocation ; and on the fourteenth day of December, 1710, to the unspeakable grief of the whole university, he died at his college of Christ Church, being then in the sixty-third year of his age. He continued in a state of celibacy all his lifetime, and as he rose in the world, disposed of his income in works of hospitality and charity, and in the encouragement of learning. Notwithstanding that modesty and humility for which he was remarkable, and which he manifested by withholding his name from his numerous learned publications, he exerted a firm and steady conduct in the government of his college. Pursuant to his directions before his death, he was buried in the cathedral of Oxford, near the place where bishop Fell lies, and without any memorial of him, other than that character which he had justly acquired, of a deep scholar, a polite gentleman, a good churchman, and a devout Christian.

* Dr. Aldrich's excessive love of smoking was an entertaining topic of discourse in the university, concerning which the following story among others passed current. A young student of the college once finding some difficulty to bring a young gentleman his chum into the belief of it, laid him a wager that the dean was smoking at that instant, viz., about ten o'clock in the morning. Away therefore went the student to the deanery, where being admitted to the dean in his study, he related the occasion of his visit. To which the dean replied in perfect good humour, 'You see you have lost your wager, for I'm not smoking but 'filling my pipe.' The catch above mentioned was made to be sung by the dean, Mr. Sampson Estwick, then of Christ church, and afterwards of St. Paul's, and two other smoking friends. Of this Mr. Estwick, who is plainly pointed out by the words in the above catch 'I prithee 'Sam fill,' an account will be given in the next ensuing article.

The smoking catch gave occasion to another on snuff, which for the singular humour of it is here inserted. Tom Brown wrote the words, and Robert Bradley, a composer of songs in the collections of that time, set them to the following notes :—

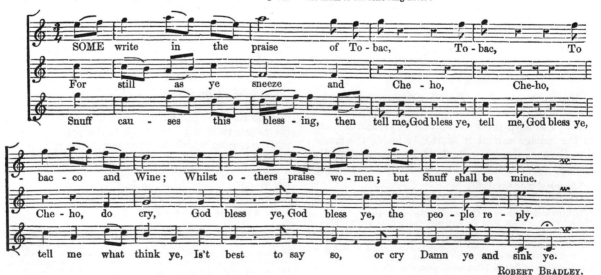

SOME write in the praise of To-bac, To-bac, To-bac-co and Wine; Whilst o-thers praise wo-men; but Snuff shall be mine.

For still as ye sneeze and Che-ho, Che-ho, Che-ho, do cry, God bless ye, God bless ye, the peo-ple re-ply.

Snuff cau-ses this bless-ing, then tell me, God bless ye, tell me, God bless ye, tell me what think ye, Is't best to say so, or cry Damn ye and sink ye.

Robert Bradley.

HENRICUS ALDRICH S.T.P.

ECCLESIÆ CHRISTI OXON. DECANUS.

SAMPSON ESTWICK was one of the first set of children after the restoration, and educated under Captain Henry Cook. From the king's chapel he went to Oxford, and entering into holy orders, became a chaplain of Christ Church, where he was honoured with the friendship of Dr. Aldrich, his intimacy with whom may be inferred from the famous smoking catch mentioned in the preceding article. Upon the decease of Dr. Aldrich he came to London, and was appointed one of the minor canons, and afterwards a cardinal of St. Paul's.* After he had been some time in the choir, he was presented to the rectory of St. Michael, Queenhithe, London. Nevertheless he continued to perform choral duty till near the time of his decease, when he was a little short of ninety years of age. In the former part of his life, viz., soon after his settlement in London, he was a candidate for Gresham professor of music, but without success. He died in the month of February, 1739. In a character given of him in one of the public papers, he is styled a gentleman universally beloved for his exemplary piety and orthodox principles.

This venerable servant of the church still survives in the remembrance of many persons now living. Bending beneath the weight of years, but preserving his faculties, and even his voice, which was a deep bass, till the last, he constantly attended his duty at St. Paul's, habited in a surplice, and with his bald head covered with a black satin coif, with grey hair round the edge of it, exhibited a figure the most awful that can well be conceived. Some compositions of his are extant, but not in print.

Besides the several English musicians who lived after the restoration, of whom an account has been given in the foregoing pages, there were many others of whom few memorials are now remaining; these may be classed under three heads, namely, composers whose works exist only in manuscript; performers on particular instruments, whose merits could not long survive themselves; and gentlemen of the chapel, distinguished by remarkable circumstances. Of these it is here thought proper to give an account, commencing about the middle, and continued down to the end of the last century.

SAMUEL AKEROYD, of the Yorkshire family of that name. He composed many songs in the Theater of Music, a collection of Songs in four books, published in the years 1685, 1686, and 1687.

THOMAS BALTZAR. This person is mentioned in a preceding page; he was born at Lubec, and was esteemed the finest performer on the violin of his time. He came into England in the year 1658,

and lived about two years in the house of Sir Anthony Cope, of Hanwell, in Oxfordshire. In the memoranda of Anthony Wood concerning musicians, it is said that Baltzar commenced bachelor of music at Cambridge, which is rather improbable, seeing that he resided chiefly at Oxford; but to ascertain the fact, recourse has been had to the register of the university of Cambridge, and in a list of graduates in music, extracted from thence, his name does not appear. He was the great competitor of Davis Mell, who, though a clock maker by trade, was, till Baltzar came hither, allowed to be the finest performer on the violin in England; and after his arrival he divided with him the public applause, it being agreed that Mell exceeded in the fineness of his tone and the sweetness of his manner, and Baltzar in the power of execution and command of the instrument. Moreover, it is said of the latter that he first taught the English the practice of shifting, and the use of the upper part of the finger-board. Baltzar was given to intemperance, and is said to have shortened his days by excessive drinking: he was buried in the cloister of Westminster-abbey on the twenty-seventh day of July, 1663, as appears by the register of that church.†

JOHN BISHOP was a scholar of Daniel Rosingrave, organist of Salisbury Cathedral, and a lay singer in King's college chapel, Cambridge, but removing thence, he became organist of the cathedral and college of Winchester. He published a collection of airs for two flutes, entitled Harmonia Lenis, and composed some things for the church.

THOMAS BLAGRAVE, a gentleman of the chapel of Charles II., and a performer on the cornet there,‡ was of the Berkshire family of that name; a few songs of his are printed in ' Select Ayres and Dialogues,' folio. 1669. His picture is in the music school, Oxford.

RICHARD BRIND, educated in St. Paul's choir, and afterwards organist of that cathedral, and Dr. Greene's master. He composed two thanksgiving anthems, now scarcely known.

WILLIAM CÆSAR, alias SMEGERGILL, composed sundry songs, printed in Playford's Musical Companion, the Treasury of Music, published in 1669, and other collections of that time.

JULIUS CÆSAR, a physician of Rochester, descended from an ancient family of that city, was well skilled in music. Two catches of his composition are published in the Pleasant Musical Companion, 1726, and are inferior to none in that collection.

EDWARD COLMAN, son of Dr. Charles Colman, a

---

* 'The church of Saint Paul had before the time of the Conqueror 'two Cardinalls, which office still continues. They are chosen by the 'deane and chapter out of the number of the twelve petty canons, and 'are called Cardinales chori; their office is to take notice of the absence 'or neglect of the quire, and weekely to render accompt thereof to the 'deane and chapter. These two Cardinalls doe minister ecclesiasticall 'sacraments to the ministers of the church and their seruants, as well to 'the healthfull as to the sieke. They heare confessions, and appoint 'comfortable penance: and lastly, they commit the dead to some conue- 'nient sepulture. These Cardinals haue the best preheminence in the 'quire above all next to the Subdeane, and the best stalls.' Weever's Funeral Monuments, page 384; and see the Statutes of St. Paul's in the Appendix to Dugdale's History of that Cathedrall, tit. De Cardinalibus chori.—*Vide Fuller's Worthies, Chapter 4, Page 13.*

† Ashmol. MS.

‡ Upon the revival of choral service, in the royal chapel especially, they were necessitated, for want of treble voices, to make use of cornets; [See page 689]: and on particular occasions sacbuts and other instruments were also employed. Besides this, as Dr. Tudway relates, king Charles II. commanded such as composed for the chapel to make also Symphonies and Ritornellos to many of the anthems in use, which were performed by a band of instruments placed in the organ-loft. The knowledge of this fact will in some measure account for the places in the procession at the coronation, which performers on these instruments have sometimes had. At that of James II. and also that of Geo. I. walked two of the king's musicians in scarlet mantles, playing each on a sacbut, and another, clad in like manner, playing on a double curtal or bassoon. The organ-blower had also a place in the two processions above mentioned, having on him a short red coat, with a badge on his left breast, viz., a nightingale of silver, gilt, sitting on a sprig.

singing master in London, and also a teacher of the lute and viol.*

JOHN COURTEVILLE was the author of sundry songs printed in the Theater of Music.

RAPHAEL COURTEVILLE was a gentleman of the chapel in the reign of Charles II., and the first organist of the church of St. James, Westminster, and is supposed to have been the brother of him mentioned above. He composed Sonatas for two flutes, and sundry songs printed in the collections of his time. A son of his, named also Raphael, succeeded him as organist of St. James's. The latter of these was the reputed author of the Gazetteer, a paper written in defence of Sir Robert Walpole's administration, and was by the writers on the side of opposition stigmatized with the name of Court-evil.†

ALEXANDER DAMASCENE, one of the gentlemen of the chapel royal in the reign of William and Mary, composed sundry songs published in the Theater of Music.

THOMAS DEAN, organist of Warwick and Coventry. Some airs of his composition are printed in the Division-Violin. He flourished at the beginning of this century, and accumulated the degrees of bachelor and doctor in his faculty of the university of Oxford in 1731.

JOHN EST, a barber. It has been before observed that the profession of music had some sort of connexion with the trade of a barber, and that a cittern was part of the furniture of a barber's shop.‡ This man was first a small proficient on that instrumen, but afterwards took to the Lyra-viol, and became so famous a performer on it as to give occasion to the following verses, which are here inserted, not for their goodness, but because they are evidence of a fact that has been frequently asserted in the course of this work :—

> In former time 't hath been upbrayded thus,
> That barber's musick was most barbarous,
> For that the cittern was confin'd unto
> The Ladies Fall, or John come kiss me now,
> Green Sleeves, and Pudding Pyes, with Nell's delight,
> Winning of Bolloigne, Essex' last good night.§
> 　But, since reduc'd to this conformity,
> And company became society,
> Each barber writes himself, in strictest rules,
> Master, or bachelor i' th' musick schools,
> How they the mere musitians do out-go,
> These one, but they have two strings to their bow.
> Barber musitians who are excellent,
> As well at chest, as the case instrument,
> Henceforth each steward shall invite his guest
> Unto the barber's and musitian's feast,
> Where sit ye merry, whilst we joy to see
> Art thus embrac'd by ingenuity.

* Formerly there were in London many masters who taught the practice of singing by the syllables: the profession is alluded to in some of the comedies written about the time of Charles II. But singing follows so naturally the smallest degree of proficiency on any instrument, that the learning of both is unnecessary; and in fact those that teach the harpsichord are now the only singing-masters, that we know of, except a few illiterate professors, who travel about the country, and teach psalmody by the notes, at such rates as the lower sort of people are able to pay.

† In a weekly paper, now deservedly forgotten, entitled the Westminster Journal, Numb. 54, for Saturday, December 4, 1742, is a fictitious letter subscribed, 'Ralph Courtevil, Organ-blower, Essayist, and 'Historiographer.'

‡ A song to this purpose in the 'Pills to purge Melancholy.'

§ Popular tunes so called.

THOMAS FARMER, originally one of the waits in London, was nevertheless admitted to the degree of bachelor in music of the university of Cambridge in 1684. He composed many songs printed in the collections of his time, and particularly in the 'Theater of Music' and the 'Treasury of Music,' and was the author of two very fine collections of airs, the one entitled 'A Consort of Music in 'four parts, containing thirty-three lessons, beginning 'with an overture,' and another 'A second Consort 'of Music in four parts, containing eleven lessons, 'beginning with a Ground,' both printed in oblong quarto, the one in 1686, the other in 1690. In the Orpheus Britannicus is an elegy on his death, written by Tate and set by Purcell, by which it appears that he died young. His dwelling house was in Martlet-court in Bow-street, Covent-garden.

DANIEL FARRANT, supposed to be a son of Richard Farrant, mentioned page 522, of this work, was one of the first of those musicians who set lessons lyraway for the viol, in imitation of the old English lute and Bandore.

JOHN GOODGROOME, bred a chorister at Windsor, a gentleman of the chapel in the reigns of Charles II. and William and Mary, composed songs, printed in the 'Treasury of Music.' One of the same name, probably his son, was about fifty years ago organist of the church of St. Peter in Cornhill, London.

RICHARD GOODSON, bachelor in music, organist of New college and Christ Church, Oxford, elected professor in that university the nineteenth of July, 1682. He lies buried in the chapel adjoining to the choir of Christ Church, on the south side thereof, under a stone, on which is the following inscription :—

> 'H. S. E.
> 'Richardus Goodson,
> 'Hujus Ecclesiæ organista,
> 'Hujus Academ. Mus. Prælector
> 'Utriq; Deliciæ et Decus.
> 'Ob. Jan. 13, 1717-8.'

He was succeeded as professor and organist of Christ Church by his son Richard Goodson, who was also a bachelor in music, and the first organist of Newbery. He died Jan. 9, 1740-1, and lies buried near his father.

WILLIAM HALL, one of the royal band, temp. Gul. & Mar. composed sundry airs published in a collection entitled Tripla Concordia. He died in 1700, and lies buried in the church-yard of Richmond in Surrey. On his grave-stone he is styled William Hall, a superior violin.

CHAP. CLX.

HENRY HALL, born about the year 1655, the son of Capt. Henry Hall, of New Windsor, was educated in the royal chapel, and had for his last master Dr. Blow. His first promotion was to the place of organist of Exeter. After that he became organist of Hereford, and also a vicar choral in the same church. He died March 30, 1707, and lies buried under a stone inscribed to his memory in the cloister of the college of the vicars of Hereford cathedral. He had a son of both his names, who was a vicar and also organist of Hereford, and dying Jan. 22 1713, was buried near his father in the above mentioned cloister. The similar situation of these two persons, and the small difference of six years between the time of the death of both father and son, make it somewhat difficult to distinguish them, and this difficulty is increased by the additional circumstance that each had a talent of poetry. The elder was a sound musician, and composed sundry anthems, well known to those who are conversant in church-music. He also wrote commendatory verses to both books of the Orpheus Britannicus : in those to the first, are these lines, which bespeak him to have been a fellow-disciple with Purcell under Blow, and consequently the elder of the two.

' Hail ! and for ever hail harmonious shade !
' I lov'd thee living, and admire thee dead.
' Apollo's harp at once our souls did strike,
' We learnt together, but not learnt alike :
' Though equal care our master might bestow,
' Yet only Purcell e'er shall equal Blow :
' For thou, by heaven for wondrous things design'd,
' Left'st thy companion lagging far behind.'

Prefixed to the Amphion Anglicus are commendatory verses, subscribed Henry Hall, organist of Hereford, addressed to his esteemed friend Dr. Blow upon publishing his book of Songs, upon which it may be observed that as they are written in a very familiar style, and contain not the least intimation that the relation of master and scholar ever subsisted between them, it is to be inferred that these were written by the younger Hall. The following are the concluding lines of this address :—

' Thus while you spread your fame, at home I sit,
' Amov'd by fate, from melody and wit,
' The British bard on harp a Treban* plays,
' With grated ears I saunter out my days ;
' Shore's most harmonious tube ne'er strikes my ear,†
' Nought of the bard besides his fame I hear :
' No chanting at St. Paul's regales my senses,
' I'm only vers'd in Usum Herefordensis.
' But if by chance some charming piece I view,
' By all caress'd because put forth by you ;
' As when of old, a knight long lost in love,
' Whose Phillis neither brine nor blood cou'd move,
' Throws down his lance, and lays his armour by,
' And falls from errantry to clegy :
' But if some mighty hero's fame he hears,
' That like a torrent all before him bears,
' In haste he mounts his trusty steed again,
' And led by glory, scow'rs along the plain ;
' So I with equal ardour seize my flute,
' And string again my long neglected lute.'

The above lines are far from being destitute of merit, but there are verses of the same author that have gained him rank among our poets. A ballad of his on the Jubilee in 1700 found its way into a collection in two volumes, printed by Lintot, and called Pope's Miscellany, as containing in it Windsor

Forest, the Rape of the Lock, Eloisa to Abelard, and other of his best poems ; and in a collection entitled the Grove, consisting of original poems and translations by Walsh, Donne, Dryden, Butler, Suckling, and others, published in 1721,‡ are as many of Hall's poems as probably could be found. Among them is that well-known ballad beginning ' All in the land of cyder,' and these verses that follow, addressed to Mr. R. C., who every year sent him a Dun a little before St. Paul's day :—

' If rhime for rhino could atone,
' Or wit stave off an ardent dun,
' If words in sweetest numbers chose,
' Would but wipe off our tickling prose,
' How blest a life would poets lead,
' And, ah ! how punctual you'd be paid !
' But since the greatest stroke of wit,
' Will not compound the meanest debt,
' Nor fifty feet in Congreve's muse
' Tick with old Tranter § for two shoes ;
' Nor all the rhymes great Dryden wrote,
' Prevail to trust him for a coat ;
' Know, Robin, I design you money,
' To face the fair now falling on you. ||
' But of the Saints both great and small,
' There's none torments me like Saint Paul,
' Who yearly persecutes the poor,
' As he did Christians heretofore :
' For still about that holy tide,
' When folk to fair of Bristol ride,
' More dunning bills to me are brought,
' Than e'er the Saint epistles wrote.
' But here the difference is, we see,
' He wrote to Heathens, they to me.
' Nor can I blame their cleanly calling,
' So often from their faith for falling,
' Since many a one thro' sly deceivers
' Have been undone by being believers.
   ' But, Robin, this is not your case,
' Whom heav'n some coin has giv'n, and grace ;
' Who gruff when sober, bright when mellow,
' Art in the main a pretty fellow.'

In the same collection are the following lines of his on the Vigo expedition :—

' Whilst this bumper stands by me brim full of cydero,
' A fig for king Philip and Portocarrero ;
' With the smoke of my pipe thus all my cares vanish,
' Whilst, with their own silver, we purchase the Spanish,¶
' And since the whole Flota is taken or sunk, boys,
' We'll be, as becomes us, exceedingly drunk, boys.'

Most of the musical compositions with the name Henry Hall are to be ascribed to the elder of the two of that name, for it is not clear that the younger was the author of any ; and indeed it seems that his character of a musician is lost in that of a poet.

STEPHEN JEFFRIES, *a pupil of Michael Wise, in 1680, being then but twenty years of age, was elected organist of Gloucester Cathedral, which office he held thirty-four years. He composed that fine melody which the chimes of the above-mentioned church continue to play to this day, and which, for*

---

* The Treban, called also the warrior's song, is a tune of great antiquity among the inhabitants of Wales : the words to it are in stanzas of three lines, each of seven syllables. The Treban of South Wales, called Treban morganisg, has the same character, but is conjectured to be less ancient. Ex. Rel. Mr. Edw. Jones, the harper and publisher of a late Collection of Welch Poetry and Music.
† The trumpet of Serjeant Shore, who is mentioned page 752 of this work.

‡ In this collection are sundry poems, written by   Kenrick, a doctor both in divinity and physic. He wrote for Purcell those two songs in the Orpheus Britannicus, ' When Teucer from his father fled,' and ' Nestor who did to thrice man's age attain,' which are printed in the collection abovementioned.
§ A shoemaker. || Bristol fair.
¶ Spanish tobacco : In Dr. Aldrich's smoking catch the concluding words are ' a pipe of Spanish.'

*the singular contrivance of it, deserves remark—for it is to be observed that the bells thereof are eight in number, descending by a major sixth and third from d to D, and that the clock bell is a minor third lower than the tenor bell, viz., B♮. The tune, which is a very solemn one, is so contrived as to take in every bell in the peal, and, by an artful evasion of the semitone below D, which there is no bell to answer, to make the clock bell the final note, thereby constituting a series of tones and semitones proper to the key of B. The notes of this singular melody are given below.**

This person died in 1712, and lies buried in the east ambulatory of the cloister adjoining to his church, as appears by an inscription on his gravestone.

The choirmen of Gloucester relate that, to cure him of a habit of staying late at the tavern, his wife drest up a fellow in a winding-sheet, with directions to meet him with a lanthorn and candle in the cloisters through which he was to pass on his way home; but that, on attempting to terrify him, Jeffries expressed his wonder only by saying, ' I thought all you spirits had been abed before this time.'

That Jeffries was a man of singular character we have another proof in the following story related of him. A singer from a distant church, with a good voice, had been requested and undertook to sing a solo anthem in Gloucester Cathedral, and for that purpose took his station at the elbow of the organist in the organ-loft. Jeffries, who found him trip in the performance, instead of palliating his mistake and setting him right, immediately rose from his seat, and leaning over the gallery, called out aloud to the choir and the whole congregation, ' He can't sing it.'

WILLIAM HINE *succeeded to the place of organist of Gloucester Cathedral upon the decease of Stephen Jeffries in 1712. He joined with one of the Halls in that composition which is known by the name of Hall and Hine's Service, and was so much esteemed for skill in his faculty and his gentlemanly qualities, that his salary was, by the dean and chapter of his church, increased twenty pounds a year. He was the musical preceptor of Mr. Richard Church, late organist of Christ Church, Oxford, and also of Dr. William Hayes, late professor of music in that university. He died at the age of forty-three, in August, 1730.*

WILLIAM INGLOTT, organist of the cathedral church of Norwich, should have have had a place in a preceding page, as having lived at the beginning of the last century; nevertheless, rather than omit it, a memoir of him is here inserted. He lies buried in the above-mentioned cathedral, and, by an inscription to his memory, seems to have been in his

day a famous organist, at least Dr. Croft may be supposed to have thought so when he repaired his monument, on which are the following lines :—

' Here William Inglott organist doth rest,
' Whose art in musick this cathedral blest,
' For descant most, for voluntary all,
' He past on organ, song and virginall :
' He left this life at age of sixty-seven,
' And here 'mongst angells all sings first in heav'n,
' His fame flies far, his name shall never die,
' See art and age here crown his memorie.

' Non digitis Inglotte tuis terrestria tangis ;
' Tangis nunc digitis organa celsa poli.
             ' Anno Dom. 1621.

' Buried the last day   This erected the 15th day
' of December 1621.   of June 1622.

' Ne forma hujusce monumenti injuriâ
' Temporum penè deleti, dispereat, exculpi
' Ornavit Gul. Croft, Reg. Capellæ in
' Arte Musicâ Discipul. Præfectus.'

SIMON IVES was a lay vicar in the cathedral of St. Paul, till driven from thence by the usurpation, when he became a singing-master and a teacher in private families. He and Henry Lawes were made choice of to compose the airs, lessons, and songs of the masque presented by the four inns of court before king Charles I. and his queen at Whitehall, on Candlemas night 1633.† Many catches and rounds of Ives are to be found in Hilton's collection, and in Playford's Musical Companion, as are also single songs among the Ayres and Dialogues published in his time. He died in the parish of Christ Church, London, 1662. Whitelock in his Memorials gives him the character of an excellent musician and a worthy man.

WILLIAM KING, organist of New College, Oxford, set to music Cowley's Mistress, and published it with this title, ' Poems of Mr. Cowley and others ' composed into songs and ayres, with a thorough-' basse to the Theorbo, Harpsecon, or Base-violl.' fol. Oxford 1668.

ROBERT KING, bachelor in music, of Cambridge, 1696, one of the band of William and Mary. He composed sundry airs printed in the Tripla Concordia ; and set to music many songs printed in the Theater of Music.

JOHN LENTON, one of the band of king William and queen Mary, was a master of the flute. He composed and published, in conjunction with Mr. Tollet, hereafter mentioned, a work entitled ' A con-' sort of musick in three parts.' Some catches of his composition are printed in the Pleasant Musical Companion. *He was also author of a tract, entitled ' the Gentleman's Diversion, or the violin explained,' oblong 4to, no date: at the end are sundry fine airs by himself and other masters of his time. A second edition of it with an appendix, but without the airs, was published in 1702, under the title of ' The ' useful instructor on the violin.' In the directions for ordering the bow and instrument, the learner is cautioned, as well against holding the latter under the chin, as against a most unaccountable practice,*

---

* *The tune as it is set to the proper key of the bells, by Mr. Abraham Rudhall, bell founder, in Gloucester.*

† See page 479 of this work.

viz., the holding it so low as the girdle; which he says some do in imitation of the Italians: so that we must conclude he means that the violin should rest on the breast of the performer. It is also remarkable that in neither of the editions of the book is there any mention, nay the least hint about shifting, and that the scale therein exhibited reaches but to C on the second line above the stave; a proof of the comparatively small degree of proficiency to which the masters of the instrument were at that period arrived; and yet at the end of his book the author says, that this nation was never so well provided with able performers, as at the time of its publication.

Henry Loosemore, bachelor in music of Cambridge, 1640, and organist first of King's college, Cambridge, and afterwards of the cathedral of Exeter. He composed services and anthems. One of this name, a lay singer or organist of Exeter cathedral, is said to have built the organ which was erected in that church at the restoration.

George Loosemore, bachelor in music of Trinity college, Cambridge.

Alphonsus Marsh was a gentleman of the chapel in the reign of Charles II. Sundry songs of his composition, as also of a song of his, of both his names, are extant, in the 'Treasury of Musick,' and other collections of that time.

John Newton, doctor in divinity, and rector of Ross in Herefordshire, a person of great learning and skill in the mathematics, was the author of the 'English Academy, or a brief Introduction to the 'seven liberal Arts,' in which music, as one of them, is largely treated of. It was published in octavo, anno 1667. Vide Athen. Oxon. col. 632.

Roger Nightingale, a clergyman, and one of the chapel at the restoration, was then an old man. He had been of the chapel to Charles I. and, even before the commencement of that king's reign, distinguished as a singer. He dwelt with Williams, bishop of Lincoln, at Bugden in Huntingdonshire, the episcopal seat; and when that prelate was translated to York, he took Nightingale with him to Cawood-castle, and, as a mark of his favour, gave him a lease worth £500 to be sold.*

Francis Piggot, bachelor in music of the university of Cambridge, 1698, and first organist of the Temple church. He succeeded Purcell as one of the organists of the royal chapel. An anthem of his, 'I was glad,' is extant in many cathedrals. He had a son, who succeeded him as organist of the Temple, and was also organist of Windsor chapel, but coming into a large fortune upon the decease of a relation, Dr. John Pelling, rector of St. Anne, Westminster, he retired to Windsor, and either resigned his places, or did his duty by deputies.

John Reading, a scholar of Dr. Blow, was a lay vicar, and also master of the children in the cathedral church of Lincoln. Removing from thence, he became organist of the parish church of St. John,

Hackney, and afterwards St. Dunstan in the West, and St. Mary Woolnoth, London. He published a collection of anthems of his composition with this strange title, 'By subscription a Book of new An-'thems, containing a Hundred Plates fairly en-'graven, with a Thorough Bass figured for the 'Organ or Harpsichord with proper Retornels. By 'John Reading, Organist of St. John's, Hackney; 'educated in the Chapple Royal, under the late 'famous Dr. John Blow. Price 10 Shillings.' He died a few years ago, in a very advanced age.

Vaughan Richardson, a scholar of Dr. Blow, and organist of the cathedral of Winchester. He published, in the year 1706, A Collection of Songs for one two, and three voices, accompanied with instruments, and composed sundry anthems, which are well known in most cathedrals.

Daniel Rosingrave, educated in the chapel royal, and a fellow-disciple of Purcell, became organist of Salisbury, and afterwards of St. Patrick's, Dublin. He had two sons musicians, one of whom, named Thomas, having been sent by his father into Italy to study, in the year 1710, returning to England, was elected organist of the parish church of St. George, Hanover-square; the other remained in Ireland, and was his father's successor.

Theodore Stefkins, one of the finest performers on the lute in his time, and as such he is celebrated by Salmon in his Essay to the Advancement of Music. There were two other persons of this name, Frederic and Christian, sons of the former, who were of the band of William and Mary; the latter was living in 1711.

William Thatcher, born at Dublin, and bred there under Randal Jewit, came into England and taught on the virginals before and after the restoration. He died in London about 1678.

Thomas Tollet. This person composed that well-known ground known by his name, and published directions to play on the French flageolet. In conjunction with John Lenton, mentioned above, he composed and published, about the year 1694, a work entitled A Consort of Musick in three parts. A daughter of his was a dancer at Goodman's-fields playhouse about the year 1728, when that theatre was first opened.

To these may be added the following names of famous organists, celebrated performers on particular instruments, and composers of music of various kinds, who flourished during the above period.

Isaac Blackwell. This person composed songs, printed in a collection entitled 'Choice Ayres, Songs, and Dialogues to sing to the Theorbo-lute and Bass-viol,' fol. 1675. There are some compositions of his for the church in the books of the royal chapel, and in those of Westminster Abbey. Bowman, organist of Trinity college, Cambridge. James Cooper, organist of the cathedral of Norwich, and there buried. Cotton, also organist of the same cathedral, and there buried. William Davis, one of the choir, and master of the children of the cathedral of Worcester. Edward and John Dyer, dancing masters by profession, but both excellent musicians:

---

* Bishop Williams was very beneficent to musicians. Happening to hear some compositions of Michael Est, to whom he was quite a stranger, he settled an annuity on him for his life, moved by no other consideration than his merit in his profession. See page 560 of this work.

they lived about the time of the restoration, and had their dwelling in Shoe-lane, London. JAMES HART, a gentleman of the chapel in the reign of king William and queen Mary. JAMES HAWKINS, the father and son, the one organist of the cathedral of Ely, the other that of Peterborough. WILLIAM HINE, organist of Gloucester. GEORGE HOLMES, organist of Lincoln. BENJAMIN LAMB, organist of Eton college, and verger of the chapel of St. George at Windsor: he composed many anthems. JOHN MOSS, composer of sundry songs in the Treasury of Music. NORRIS, master of the children of the same cathedral of Lincoln. PAISIBLE, a famous master of the flute, and a composer for that instrument. THOMAS PLEASANTS, organist of the cathedral of Norwich, and there buried. CHARLES QUARLES, bachelor in music of Cambridge, 1698, and organist of Trinity college there. JOHN ROGERS, servant to Charles II., a famous lutenist, lived near Aldersgate, and died about the year 1663. ANTHONY WAKELEY, organist of the cathedral of Salisbury. JOHN WALTER, organist of the collegiate church at Windsor. THOMAS WANLESS, bachelor in Music of Cambridge, 1698, and organist of York cathedral. THOMAS WILLIAMS, organist of St. John's college, Cambridge.

GIUSEPPE TORELLI, a native of Verona, academico filarmonico di Bologna, and a famous performer on the violin, was concert master at Anspach about the year 1703. After that he removed to Bologna, and became maestro di capella in the church of San Petronio in that city. He composed and published sundry collections of airs and Sonatas for violins, but the most considerable of his works is his eighth opera, published at Bologna by his brother, Felice Torelli, after the death of the author, viz., in 1709, entitled 'Concerti grossi con una pastorale, per il santissimo natale,' consisting of twelve concertos, 'à due violini concertini, due violini ripieni, viola e cembalo.' He is said to have been the inventor of that noble species of instrumental composition the Concerto grosso.

ZACCARIA TEVO, a native of Saccha, a city in Sicily, a Franciscan monk, bachelor in divinity, and a professor or master of music in Venice, published in the year 1706, in quarto, a work entitled Il Musico Tesore, containing in substance the whole of what has been written on the subject by Boetius, Franchinus, Galilei, Mersennus, Kircher, and, in short, almost every other author on the subject of music. As the works of these have been mentioned in order as their names have occurred, there seems to be but little occasion for a more particular account of Tevo's book than the following Index, containing the heads of the several chapters, will furnish. Nevertheless it may be remarked, that he is so liberal in his quotations from the Margarita Philosophica of Gregory Reisch,* that almost the whole of the tract on music therein contained is inserted in the Musico Tesore of Tevo:—

PARTE PRIMA.

Cap 1. Del Titolo dell' Opera; 2. Della Definitione, e Divisione della Musica; 3. Della Musica

* See the account of this book in page 306 of this work.

Mondana; 4. Della Musica Humana; 5. Della Musica Armonica; 6. Della Musica Metrica, e Ritmica; 7. Della Musica Organica; 8. Della Musica Piana, e Mesurata; 9. Della Musica Teorica, & Inspettiva; 10. Della Musica Prattica, & Attiva; 11. Dell' Inventione della Musica; 12. Della Propagatione della Musica; 13. Qual fosse l'Antica Musica; 14. Quanto fosse rozza l'Antica Musica; 15. Degl' effetti della Musica; 16. Dell' inventione del Cantar in consonanza; 17. Del detrimento della Musica; 18. A che fine si deve imparare la Musica; 19. Qual sii il vero Musico; 20. Della difesa della Musica, e Cantar moderno.

PARTE SECONDA.

Cap. 1. Delle Voci, e suoni in Commune; 2. Della definitione delle Voci, e suoni; 3. Della formatione della Voce; 4. Della varietà delle Voci, e suoni; 5. Della formatione, e propagatione de suoni nell' Aria; 6. Come vengono comprese le voci, e suoni dal senso dell' udito; 7. Dell' inventione delle Figure Musicali; 8. Del Tuono, e Semituono; 9. Che cosa sii Musico intervallo; 10. Delli Tetracordi, e Generi della Musica; 11. Del Sistema Greco, & antico, sua inventione, e divisione; 12. Del Sistema di Guido Aretino; 13. Del Sistema principato comparato alle quattro Parti, & alla tastatura dell' Organo; 14. Della Melopeia; 15. Della proprietà del Canto; 16. Delle quattro parti Musicali, e loro natura; 17. Delle Mutationi; 18. Della Battuta; 19. Degl' Essempii di qualsivoglia Battuta; 20. Degl' Affetti causati dalla modulatione delle Parti.

PARTE TERZA.

Cap. 1. Che sii contrapunto, consonanza, dissonanza, numero sonoro; 2. Delle consonanze, de dissonanze in particolare, e loro formatione in ordine Pratico; 3. Della consideratione del Numero in ordine Armonico; 4. Delle proportioni in ordine Armonico; 5. Delle dimostrationi delle consonanze, e dissonanze in ordine Teorico; 6. Del modo di formare li Passaggi; 7. Che non si possino fare due conzonanze perfette del medesimo genere; 8. Delli passaggi del Unisono; 9. Delli passaggi della terza maggiore, e minore; 10. Delli passaggi della Quinta; 11. Delli passaggi della Sesta maggiore, e minore; 12. Delli passaggi dell' Ottava; 13. Delle dissonanze in commune; 14. Delli passaggi della Seconda; 15. Delli passaggi della Quarta; 16 Delli passaggi della quarta superflua, e della Quinta diminuta; 17. Delli passaggi della Settima; 18. Delle Legature, e delle Sincope; 19. Delle due dissonanze, e delle due Negre; 20. Di alcune osservationi per le parte di mezzo.

PARTE QUARTA.

Cap. 1. Di alcune regole generali del Contrapunto; 2. Delle spetie del Contrapunto; 3. Modo di formare l'Armonial Testura a due, e più voci per Contrapunto semplice; 4. Delli Tuoni, ò Modi Armoniali secondo gl' Antichi; 5. Delli Tuoni, ò Modi Armoniali secondo li Moderni; 6. Del modo di formare il Contrapunto a due, e più voci, e delle sue cadenze; 7. Delle regole per la formatione del Contrapunto sopra il Basso; 8. Delle Cadenze degli otto Tuoni delli Moderni; 9. Della natura, e proprietà delli Tuoni; 10. Del Contrapunto Fugato in genere; 11. Della Fuga in particolare, e delle sue Specie; 12. Delle Imitationi; 13. Delli Duo, e Fughe per tutti li Tuoni; 14. Delli Canoni; 15. Della formatione di più soggetti; 16. Delli Contrapunti doppii; 17. Del modo di rivoltare le Parti, e Soggetti; 18. Del modo di formare le Compositioni con Voci, Instrumenti; 19. Della Musica Finta, e Trasportatione delli Tuoni; 20 & Ultimo. Congedo dell' Auttore al suo Musico Testore.

It has already been remarked of the several treatises on music by Italian authors, from the time of Franchinus downwards, that the latter have for the most part been but repetitions of the former; and this might be objected to Tevo's book; but when it is considered that, notwithstanding the copiousness of the subject, it is concise, and at the same time perspicuous, it may well be considered as a valuable abridgment, abounding with a great variety of learning and useful instruction.

CHAP. CLXI.

PIETRO TORRI, an Italian by birth, was, in the younger part of his life, chamber musician to the Margrave of Bareith; after that he became chapel master of the great church at Brussels. It is said that he was a disciple of Steffani, which is probable, seeing that his compositions are chiefly duets and close imitations of the style of that master. One of the most celebrated of his compositions of this kind is a duet entitled Heraclitus and Democritus, in which the affections of laughing and weeping are contrasted and expressed with singular art and ingenuity. He died about the year 1722. The fame of his excellence was very great throughout all Flanders; and it is said that in queen Anne's time, while we were at war with the French, his house being in some danger, the duke of Marlborough gave particular orders that it should be protected from violence; in gratitude for which instance of generosity, he presented the duke with a manuscript, containing some of the most valuable of his compositions, which are yet remaining in the family library.

About the beginning of the present century music flourished greatly under the patronage of the emperor Leopold, who was himself not only a judge, but a great master of the science; as an evidence whereof there are yet extant many compositions made by him for the service of his own chapel. He was a great friend of Kircher, as also to Thiel of Naumburg, mentioned in a former part of this work. To the latter he made many presents in reward of his excellent compositions.

The anonymous author of the life of this prince, published at London in 1708, in the character which he gives of him, speaks particularly to his affection for music, and represents the personal indignities to which his love of it sometimes exposed him, in the following passage :—

'This person was versed in most of the specula-' tive sciences, and understood musick to perfection, ' and had several pieces of his own composing sung in ' his own chapel, and therefore he had several mu-' sicians, especially Italians, about him, who showed ' themselves very insolent upon divers occasions, and ' more than once refused to sing in the face of the ' emperor himself and his court, upon pretence their ' salaries were not well paid them; and this, upon a ' representation to his Imperial majesty, what punish-' ment they deserved, gave him occasion jestingly to ' answer, that these fellows, when they are deprived ' of their virility, might at the same time lose part of ' their brains. The impertinence of these eunuchs ' may be judged of by the behaviour of one of them ' a little before the emperor's death. This person ' crouding into the chapel where he had at that time ' no part of the music, and pressing upon a foreign ' knight to make way for him, which the other was ' not forward to do, the eunuch angrily said to him, " Ego sum Antonius M. Musicus sacræ Cæsareæ " majestatis."

The principal musicians in the court of the emperor Leopold were, his chapel-master Fux, and his vice chapel-masters Caldara and Ziani, all three very great men, but differently endowed, the first being a theorist, the others mere practical musicians. Here follows an account of them severally :—

JOHANN JOSEPH FUX was a native of Stiria, a province of Germany in the circle of Austria. In 1707 he published at Nuremberg a work of his composition, entitled ' Concentum musico-instrumentale in 7 partitas divisum,' and also composed an opera called Eliza, for the birth of the empress Elizabeth Christiana, which was printed at Amsterdam by Le Cene. But he is better known to the world by his ' Gradus ' ad Parnassum, sive manuductio ad compositionem ' musicæ regularem, methodo novâ ac certâ, nondum ' antè tam exacto ordine in lucem edita,' printed in the year 1725, and dedicated to the emperor Charles VI., who defrayed the whole expense of the publication. This work is printed in a folio volume, divided into two books, and merits particular notice.

In the preface he gives as reasons for writing his book, that many learned men have written on the speculative part of music, but few on the practice,* and that the precepts of these latter are not sufficiently clear. For these reasons, he says, and farther, because many young students of his acquaintance had testified an ardent desire of knowledge in the science, but were not able to attain it for want of proper instructors, he at first gave lectures to such, and continued so to do for near thirty years, during which time he had served three emperors of the Romans. At length, recollecting that sentiment of Plato recorded by Cicero, viz., that we were not born for ourselves, but for our country, our parents, and our friends, he determined to give his labours to the world, and now offers them to the public, with an apology for the work, that he was frequently interrupted in the progress of it by sick-

* In this assertion Fux is grossly mistaken: Franchinus, Zarlino, Zaccone, Artusi, Berardi, the elder Bononcini, Gasparini, and many others, whom we have enumerated, have written expressly on the subject of practical music.

ness, and the necessary attendance in the discharge of his function.

The first book is altogether speculative, its principal subject being number, with the proportions and differences thereof. The proportions that respect music the author makes to be five, namely, multiple, superparticular, superpartient, multiple-superparticular, and multiple-superpartient.

The division of proportion he says is threefold, namely, into arithmetical, harmonical, and geometrical, of all which an explanation has been given in the foregoing part of this work. He next describes the several operations for the multiplication, addition, and subtraction of ratios; applying the rules laid down by him to the discovery of the ratios of the several intervals contained in the octave.

Towards the conclusion of this book the author observes that the genera of the ancient Greeks were three; but that the moderns had restrained them to two, namely, the diatonic and chromatic, the commixture of which he says he does not disapprove: but he most earnestly dissuades the musicians of his time against the use of the mixed genus in the composition of church-music, having as he says, by long practice and experience found that the diatonic alone is most suitable to this style.

The second book is written in the form of a dialogue, the interlocutors in which are Aloysius a master, and Joseph a disciple. The author's reason for assuming those names is to be found in the preface, where he says that by Aloysius he means Præstinus or Palestrina, to whom he owns himself indebted for all his knowledge in music, and whose memory he professes to reverence with the most pious regard; wherefore we are to understand by Joseph, Fux himself, whose Christian names were John Joseph.

In this conversation the author, in the person of Aloysius, delivers the precepts of musical composition, beginning with simple counterpoint, i. e. that which consists in the opposition of note to note, with various examples of compositions on a plain-song in two and three parts. From thence he proceeds to the other kinds, explaining as he goes along the use of the dissonances. From simple he proceeds to florid counterpoint, the doctrine of which he illustrates by a variety of exercises in four parts on a given plain-song.

Having delivered and illustrated by examples the precepts of counterpoint, the author goes on to explain the doctrine of fugue, which denomination he contends is applicable only to those compositions, where a certain point is proposed by one part, and answered by another, in intervals precisely the same, that is to say, such as may be proved by the solmisation. This obliges him to lay down the order in which the tones and semitones succeed each other in the several modes or keys, and terminates in a very obvious distinction between fugues properly so called, in which the points in the several parts sol-fa alike, and those other where the solmisation is different; these latter, though to the eye

they may appear fugues, being in fact no other than imitations.*

This explanation of the nature of fugue in general, is succeeded by rules for the composition of fugues in two, three, and four parts, and of double counterpoint, a kind of composition so constructed, as that the parts are converted the one into the other; that is to say, the upper becoming the under, and è converso; with many other varieties incident to this species, such as diminution, inversion, and retrograde progression.

At the end of this discourse on fugue, Aloysius reprehends very severely the singers in his time for those licentious variations which it was the practice with them to make.

Discoursing on the modes, he cites a passage from Plato in his Timæus, to show that the music of the ancient Greeks was originally very deficient in respect of the number of the intervals. He says that the ancient modes borrowed their names from those countries in which they were respectively invented or most in use, but that the true distinction between them arises from the different succession of the tones and semitones in each, from the unison to the octave. In short, he supposes the modes and the species of diapason to be correlative, and making the latter to be six in number, viz., D, E, F, G, A, C, he pronounces that, notwithstanding other authors reckon more, the modes are in fact only six.†

But here it is to be noted, that he admits of the distinction of the modes into authentic and plagal, the first of which two classes consists in the harmonical, the other in the arithmetical division of the diapason; and had he admitted B as a species of diapason, he would, agreeably to the sentiments of Glareanus, Zarlino, Artusi, and most of the succeeding writers, have brought out twelve modes, that is to say, six authentic, and six plagal; instead of which latter he gives but five, namely, C, D, E, G, A, passing over F, as incapable of an arithmetical division, by reason of the tritone arising at b. So that upon the whole he makes but eleven modes, agreeing in this particular with no one author that has written on the subject of music.

For the distinction between the authentic and plagal modes he cites the opinion of Zarlino, who says that the beginnings and endings, or closes, are the same in both, and that the sole difference between them consists in the nature of the modulation, which in the authentic modes is in the acute, and in the plagal in the grave part.

Having before assumed that there are but six species of diapason or octave, and having justly remarked that the distinction of authentic and plagal respects chiefly the ecclesiastical tones, he proceeds to point out, by means of the flat and sharp signatures, several successions of tones and semitones, which he says are transpositions from the several modes: a needless labour as it seems, seeing that the use

* This distinction is very accurately noted in Dr. Pepusch's Short Introduction to Harmony.

† The species of diatessaron are three, and of diapente four; and these added together form seven species of diapason. See page 130 of this work; and Wallisii Append. in Ptolemæi Harmonicis, 4to. page 310, 311.

of six modes, in the sense in which the term is strictly understood, is unknown to the moderns, who look upon the word as synonymous with the word key; and of these there seem to be in nature but two, viz., those whose respective finals are A and C,* the one having its third minor, and the other major; and into one or other of these all that variety of keys, included under the denomination of Musica ficta, or, as the Italians call it, Musica finta, that is to say, feigned music, are demonstrably resolvable.

Towards the conclusion of his work he treats of the ecclesiastical style, which he says is of two kinds, to wit, that of the chapel, and that proper for a full choir. With respect to the former he observes that in the primitive times the divine offices were sung without the aid of instruments; and that the same practice prevails in many cathedral churches, and also in the court of the emperor during the time of Lent. But that notwithstanding the primitive practice, the organ, and a variety of other instruments were introduced into the chapel service, and continued to be used, with the exceptions above noted, in his time. He recommends in the composition of music for the service of the chapel, the pure diatonic genus, without any mixture of the chromatic, and celebrates Palestrina as the prince of composers in the chapel style, referring to a motet of his, 'Ad te 'Domine levavi animam meam,' as a composition admirably adapted to the sense of the words, and in other respects most excellent.

After this he gives some directions for compositions for the chapel, wherein the organ and other instruments are employed. In these he says the restrictions are fewer than in the former; and adds, that the first and second violin parts should ever be in the unison with the cantus, as the trumpets are with the altus and tenor.

Of the mixed style, or that which is proper for a full choir, he says but little, and proceeds to the recitative style, for composing in which he gives a few general rules; and is most particular in pointing out those rests and clausules which best correspond with the points or stops in written speech, namely, the comma, semicolon, colon, and period; as also with the notes of interrogation and admiration, and with these he concludes his discourse.

Upon a careful survey of this work of Fux, it may be said to be sui generis, for it is of a class a little superior to those many introductions to music, heretofore mentioned to have been written for the instruction of children, and published in Germany above two centuries ago, under the titles of Enchiridion Musicæ, Musicæ Isagoge, Erotemata Musicæ, Compendium Musices,† &c. and greatly below those more elaborate works that treat of the science at large.

Antonio Caldara, one of the vice-chapel-masters of the emperor Leopold, under Fux, is celebrated for the sublimity of his style, which he has manifested in two oratorios of his composition, the one

entitled Giuseppe, performed in the year 1722; the other 'Il Ré del dolore, in Giesu Cristo Signor 'nostro, coronato di spine.' He published two operas of sonatas for two violins and a bass, printed at Amsterdam, and 'Cantate da Camera à voce sola,' printed at Venice.

Mark Antonio Ziani, the other vice-chapel-master of the Emperor Leopold, composed sundry operas and oratorios, which, being extant only in manuscript, are no where to be found but in the collections of the curious, though there are sonatas of his extant, printed by Roger. The three persons above named are spoken of in terms of great respect in a collection of Letters from the Academy of Ancient Music at London to Sig. Antonio Lotti of Venice, with his answers and testimonies, published at London 1732.

Antonio Lotti was organist of the ducal chapel of St. Mark at Venice. In the year 1705 he published at Venice, and dedicated to the emperor Joseph, a work entitled 'Duetti Terzetti e Madrigali.' In this collection is a madrigal for five voices, inscribed 'La Vita Caduca,' beginning 'In una Siepe ombrosa.' The history of this composition is attended with some peculiar circumstances: the words of it were written by Abbate Pariati, and the music to it composed at his request: in return for some compositions of Ziani, Lotti sent to that master a copy of this madrigal, which he caused to be sung before the emperor Leopold, who highly approved of it; upon which Lotti determined to publish his Duetti Terzetti, &c., and dedicated it to the emperor; but he dying before it was finished, he dedicated it to the emperor Joseph, who honoured him with a present customary on those occasions, a gold chain and medal.

Many years after the publication of the book, this madrigal was produced in manuscript in the Academy of Ancient Music at London, as a composition of Giovanni Bononcini, then resident here. But it being known to some of the members that it had been published among other of Lotti's works, Bononcini's title to it was disputed; and he refusing to clear up the matter, an appeal was made to the author himself, he being then living, which terminated in the utter confusion of Bononcini and his adherents. The particulars of this controversy will be given in a subsequent page, among other transactions of the Academy of Ancient Music.

Excepting the above work, we know of no compositions of Lotti in print, but there are very many in manuscript, which shew him to have been a very fine composer of church-music. He married Signora Santini, a celebrated singer, who had appeared in most of the courts in Germany. Lotti was living at Venice in the year 1731, as appears by his correspondence with the Academy above mentioned.

Francesco Conti, a celebrated theorbist, was, upon the decease of Ziani, appointed vice-chapel-master to the emperor of Germany. He composed an opera entitled 'Archelao Rè di Cappadocia,' the words whereof were written by Abbate Pariati, as also

* Vide ante, page 60 of this work, et seq.

† See page 397 of this work, et seq.

the opera of Clotilda, performed at London in the year 1709.

The misfortunes of this person, arising from an inconsiderate indulgence of his resentment, have excited compassion in some, who would otherwise perhaps have envied the reputation and honours which he enjoyed. In the year 1730, upon some provocation given him by a secular priest at Vienna, he revenged the insult by blows, and was sentenced to a most severe punishment. The particulars of his sentence are contained in the following extract of a letter from Ratisbon, dated October 19, 1730.

‘ Vienna, Sept. 10. The Imperial composer, ‘ Franc. Conti, in pursuance of a decree of a church- ‘ ban pronounced against him, was sentenced to ‘ stand at the door of the cathedral church of St. ‘ Stephen. His Imperial majesty indeed, with his ‘ usual clemency, reduced the standing three times ‘ to once only; but as he behaved so ill the first ‘ time of standing in the presence of many hundred ‘ people, he was ordered to stand again at the said ‘ door the 17th of Sept. for the second time, in ‘ a long hair coat, called a coat of penitence, between ‘ twelve peace-officers, forming a circle about him, ‘ with a black lighted torch in his hand, for an hour, ‘ which he is to do again on the 24th. His allowance ‘ is bread and water, so long as he is in the hands of ‘ the spiritual court, and as soon as he shall be ‘ delivered to the temporal he will be fined to pay ‘ 1000 florins to the clergyman he struck, and all ‘ the costs and damages besides, and to be imprisoned ‘ four years, and afterwards banished for ever from ‘ the Austrian dominions, because he behaved so ‘ rude and scandalously the first time of his standing ‘ before the church door.

‘ The following epigram was made on this occa- sion :—

‘ Non ea musa bona est nec musica, composuisti
‘ Quam Conti, tactus nam fuit ille gravis;
‘ Et bassus nimium crassus neque consona clavis:
‘ Perpetuo nigras hic geris ergo notas.’

It evidently appears by the foregoing account of the progress of music, that among the moderns the great improvements both in science and practice were made by the Italians; and that these were in general adopted by the Germans, the French, the English, and indeed almost every other nation in Europe. The French, even so early as the time of Charlemagne, appear to have been extremely averse to innovations, at least in their church-music; since that they have been very backward in adopting the improvements of their neighbours; and it was not till about the middle of the last century that music flourished in any considerable degree among them. But soon after that time, in consequence of the studies of Mersennus, and the practice of Lully, a style was formed in France, which by other countries was thought worthy of imitation.

Of Cambert and Lully, Nivers and Brossard, an account has already been given. Here follow memoirs of such other French musicians as are most dis- tinguished for skill either in the theory or practice of the science.

CHAP. CLXII.

HENRI DUMONT, chapel-master to Louis XIV. is celebrated by the French writers as a masterly performer on the organ. He was born in the diocese of Leige in 1610, and was the first French musician that introduced thorough-bass into his compositions. There are extant some of his motets, which are in great estimation; as also five grand masses, called royal masses, which are still performed in some of the convents in Paris, and in many provincial churches of France. Dumont died at Paris in the year 1684.

MICHEL LAMBERT was born in 1610, at Vivonne, a small village of Poitou. He had an exquisite hand on the lute, and sang to it with peculiar grace and elegance. His merit alone preferred him to the office of master of the king's chamber music; upon which he became so eminent, that persons of the highest rank became his pupils, and resorted to his house, in which he held a kind of musical academy. Lambert is reckoned the first who gave his country- men a just notion of the graces of vocal music. His compositions however are of but small account, consisting only of some little motetts, music for the Leçons de Ténebres, and a collection containing sundry airs of one, two, three, and four parts, with a thorough-bass. Lambert had a daughter, who was the wife of Lully. He died at Paris in the year 1690.*

GAUTHIER, surnamed the Elder, was also an admired French lutenist. He, together with a cousin of his, Pierre Gauthier, mentioned in the next article, published a collection entitled ‘ Livre ‘ de tableau des pieces de Luth sur différens modes.’ The authors have added some rules for playing on this instrument. The principal piece of the elder Gauthier are those lessons of his entitled l'Immor- telle, la Nonpareille, le Tombeau de Mezangeau. There was also a Denis Gauthier, who composed lessons much admired by performers on the lute, of which the most esteemed are those entitled l'Homicide, le Canon, and le Tombeau de Lenclos.

PIERRE GAUTHIER, a musician of Ciotat, in Provence, was director of an opera company, which exhibited by turns at Marseilles, Montpellier, and Lyons. He embarked at the Port de Cette, and perished in the vessel, at the age of fifty-five, in 1697. There is extant of his composition a collection of duos and trios, which is much esteemed.

LOULIE', a French musician, was the author of an ingenious and useful book, published in 1698 by Estienne Roger of Amsterdam, entitled ‘ Elements ou Principes de Musique mis dans un nouvel ordre,’ in which, after teaching the method of solmisation according to the French manner, in which the syllable SI is assumed for the last note of the septenary, he explains the nature of trans- position, and suggests the method of reducing music in any of the keys denoted by either the acute or grave signatures into the original or radical keys,

* In Sir George Etherege's comedy of the Man of Mode, Sir Fopling says, ‘ I learned to sing at Paris, of Lambert, the greatest master in the ‘ world, but I have his own fault, a weak voice.’

from which they are respectively transpositions; which practice is explained at large in Chapter XII of this work. A discovery the more worthy of notice, as some pains have been taken to conceal it.*

In the course of his work the author lays down an easy rule for the division of the monochord, and assigns the proportions of the natural sounds in the octave, distinguishing between the greater and lesser tone. Towards the end of the book is a description of an instrument called by him the Chronometer, contrived for the measuring of time by means of a pendulum. The form of the instrument, as exhibited by him, is that of an Ionic pilaster, and is thus described by Malcolm in his Treatise of Music, page 407 :—

'The Chronometer consists of a large ruler or 'board six foot or seventy-two inches long, to be 'set on end; it is divided into its inches, and the 'numbers set so as to count upwards; and at every 'division there is a small round hole, through whose 'center the line of division runs. At the top of 'this ruler, about an inch above the division 72, 'and perpendicular to the ruler, is inserted a small 'piece of wood, in the upper side of which there is 'a groove, hollowed along from the end that stands 'out to that which is fixt in the ruler, and near 'each end of it a hole is made : through these holes 'a pendulum chord is drawn, which runs in the 'groove; at that end of the chord that comes 'through the hole furthest from the ruler the ball 'is hung, and at the other end there is a small 'wooden pin, which can be put in any of the holes 'of the ruler; when the pin is in the upmost hole 'at 72, then the pendulum from the top to the center 'of the ball, must be exactly seventy-two inches; 'and therefore whatever hole of the ruler it is put 'in, the pendulum will be just so many inches as 'that figure at the hole denotes. The manner of 'using the machine is this; the composer lengthens 'or shortens his pendulum till one vibration be 'equal to the designed length of his bar, and then 'the pin stands at a certain division, which marks 'the length of the pendulum; and this number 'being set with the clef at the beginning of the 'song, is a direction to others how to use the 'chronometer in measuring the time according to 'the composer's design; for with the number is set 'the note, crotchet or minim, whose value he would 'have the vibration to be; which in brisk duple 'time is best a minim or half a bar, or even a whole 'bar, when that is but a minim; and in slow time 'a crotchet. In triple time it would do well to be 'the third part, or half or fourth part of a bar; and 'in the simple triples that are allegro, let it be a

'whole bar. And if in every time that is allegro, 'the vibration is applied to a whole or half bar, 'practice will teach us to subdivide it justly and 'equally. And mind that to make this machine of 'universal use, some canonical measure of the divi-'sions must be agreed upon, that the figure may 'give a certain direction for the length of the 'pendulum.'

JEAN BAPTISTE MOREAU, a musician of Angers, was led by his musical talents to try his fortune in Paris; and having succeeded in a bold attempt to get unperceived into the closet of Madame the Dauphiness Victoire de Baviere, who was fond of music, he had the assurance to pull her by the sleeve, and ask permission to sing to her a little air of his own composing; the dauphiness, laughing, permitted him; he sang without being disconcerted, and the princess was pleased. The story came to the king, and he desiring to see him, Moreau was introduced to his majesty in the apartment of Madame Maintenon, and sang several airs, with which the king was so well pleased, that he immediately ordered him to compose a musical entertainment, which was performed at Marli two months after, and applauded by the whole court. He was also engaged to compose the interludes for the tragedies of Esther, Athalie, Jonathas, and several other pieces for the house of St. Cyr. His chief excellence consisted in his giving the full force of expression to all kinds of words and subjects assigned him. The poet Lainez, with whom he was intimate, furnished him with songs and little cantatas, which he set to music, but none of them are published.

MARC ANTOINE CHARPENTIER was superintendant of the music of the duke of Orleans, and his instructor in the art of musical composition. He has left several operas, one of which, viz., his Medèe, was in its time highly celebrated. He composed another called Philomele, which was thrice represented in the Palais Royal. The duke of Orleans, who had composed part of it, would not suffer it to be published. Charpentier died at Paris in 1704.

LOUIS LULLY, and JEAN LOUIS LULLY, sons of Jean Baptist Lully, were also musicians. They composed in conjunction the music to the opera of Zephire et Flore, written by Michel du Boullai, secretary to the grand prior of Vendôme, and represented in the Academie Royal on the twenty-second day of March, 1688. They also set the opera of Orpheus, written by the same person, and an opera called Alcide.

PASCAL COLASSE, chapel-master to Louis XIV., was born at Paris 1636. He was a pupil of Lully and took him for his model in all his compositions, as the following lines testify :—

Colasse de Lulli craignit de s'écarter,
Il le pilla, dit-on, cherchant à l'imiter.

But it is said that whether he imitated Lully or not, his opera of Thetis and Peleus will always be esteemed an excellent production. There are besides of his composition, motets and songs. Colasse destroyed both his fortune and health in an infatuated

---

* In Dr. Pepusch's Short Introduction to Harmony is a whole chapter on the subject of transposition, referring to a plate with a diagram of six keys, viz., three with the minor, and three with the major third, with the flats and sharps in order as they arise. Over this is a stave of lines which he calls the slider, with the letters signifying the cliffs placed thereon. To enable the student to reduce any transposition to its original key, he is directed to cut off the slider, and apply it to the diagram, which process will terminate in the annihilation of the flat and sharp signatures, and shew the original key from whence the transposition is made. For the reason of the whole the student is to seek; but the secret is revealed by Loulié in the twenty-ninth page of his book above mentioned.

pursuit of the Philosopher's Stone, and died at Versailles in the year 1709.

N. ALLOUETTE, conductor of the music in the church of Notre Dame at Paris, is known for his motets and a very fine Miserere. Lully was his master.

GUILLAUME MINORET was one of the four masters of, or composers to the chapel of Louis XIV.[*] He composed many motets, which, though greatly admired, have never yet been printed. Those in greatest esteem are 'Quemadmodum desiderat,' 'Lauda Jerusalem Dominum,' 'Venite exultemus,' 'Nisi Dominus ædificaverit domum.' Minoret died in the year 1716 or 1717, in a very advanced age.

ANDRÉ CAMPRA, born at Aix in Provence in 1660, was at first a chorister in the cathedral of that city, having for his instructor in music William Poitevin, a preacher to that church. Soon after his leaving the choir he became distinguished by his motets, which were performed in churches and private concerts, and so well received that they procured him the rank of director of the music in the Jesuits' church at Paris, and some other preferment in that metropolis. His genius having been too much confined while restrained to the narrow limits of a motet, he set himself to compose for the stage, and made the music to sundry operas. His progress in this new course of study was answerable to his industry, and by following the manner of Lully he acquired a degree of excellence but little inferior. His Europe Galante, Carnaval de Venise, and Fêtes Venitiennes; his Ages, his Fragmen de Lully, which are ballets, his operas of Hesione, Alcide, Telephé, Camille, and Tancrede, were greatly applauded, and are still admired. The grace and vivacity of his airs, the sweetness of his melody, and, above all, his strict attention to the sense of the words, render his compositions truly estimable.

JEAN GILLES, of Tarascon, in Provence, was director of the music, or chapel-master in the church of St. Stephen in Thoulouse. He possessed the Christian virtue of charity in so great a degree, and had such a disposition to relieve the distresses of others, as tended to the impoverishment of himself. He was a singer in the choir of the cathedral of Aix, and a fellow-pupil, with the celebrated Campra, of William Poitevin, mentioned in the preceding article. Gilles's abilities soon became so conspicuous, that Bertier, bishop of Rieux, who particularly esteemed him, solicited for him the place of chapel-master in the church of St. Stephen in Thoulouse; but the chapter had already conferred it on Farinelli,[†] who, on being told that Gilles was a candidate for it,

sought out his competitor, and obliged him to acquiesce in his resignation of the office—an instance of generosity equally honourable to both. There are of Gilles many fine motets; several of them have been performed in the Concert Spirituel at Paris with great applause, particularly his 'Diligam te.' But his capital work, however, is a Messe des Morts, in which, at the first time of performing it, he sang himself.

MICHEL RICHARD DE LALANDE, born at Paris in the year 1657, was the fifteenth child of his parents, and discovering in his infancy a strong propensity to music, he was entered a chorister in the church of St. German l'Auxerrois, and was there distinguished for the fineness of his voice. At the age of puberty his voice left him, but before that time, by diligent application, and frequently spending whole nights in practice, he attained to great perfection on various instruments, and on the violin in particular he played with great facility and judgment. Being thus qualified, he applied to Lully, requesting to be taken into the opera, but being rejected, he broke his instrument, and renounced the use of it for ever.[‡] After this discouragement he betook himself to the organ and harpsichord, and was soon solicited to accept of several churches, but at length was chosen by the duke de Noailles to instruct his eldest daughter. This nobleman, who never suffered any opportunity to escape him of bearing testimony to the merit of Lalande, embraced an occasion of recommending him to Louis XIV., and did it with so much honest warmth that the king chose him to instruct his daughters, Mademoiselle de Blois and Mademoiselle de Nantes, on the harpsichord. He frequently composed in obedience to the orders, and sometimes even in the presence of Louis, little musical pieces, and so much was the king delighted with him that he loaded him with favours. He enjoyed in succession the two offices of music-master of the king's chamber, the two of composer, that of superintendent of music and the four offices of the royal chapel. His motets. which were always performed before Louis XIV. and Louis XV. with great applause, have been collected and published in two volumes in folio. The Cantate, the Dixit, and the Miserere, are principally admired. He died at Versailles in 1726.

J. THEOBALDE, called THEOBALDO GATTI, was born at Florence. It is said of him, that, being charmed with the music of Lully, which had reached him even in his native country, he went to Paris to compliment that celebrated musician, and in all his compositions studied to emulate him, and at length discovered himself to be a meritorious pupil of that great man, by two operas which he caused to be represented in the Royal Academy of Paris, viz., Coronis, a pastoral in three acts, the words by Mons. Baugé; and Scylla, a tragedy in five. He died at Paris in the year 1727, at an advanced age, having for fifty years been a performer on the bass viol in the orchestra of the opera, and was interred in the church of St. Eustache.

---

[*] The others were Colosse, Lalande, and Coupillet. They were all chosen upon great deliberation, for upon the death of Dumont in 1680, or thereabouts, the king finding instead of two composers for his chapel would have four; and to that end he directed circular letters to be sent into all the provinces of France, inviting musicians to Versailles, in order to give proof of their abilities. Le Seur was a candidate for one of the places, but lost it by his unhappy setting of two words in a motett, and Coupillet succeeded by fraud; for after he was elected it was discovered that the composition by which he obtained the place was not his own, but the work of Desmarets, a young man then unknown, but who afterwards became one of the first musicians in France.

[†] This might possibly be that Farinelli already spoken of as concert-master or director of the music in the electoral palace of Hanover, and whom Mattheson in his Vollkommenen Capellmeister expressly asserts to have been the uncle of Carlo Broschi Farinelli, the famous singer in the opera at the Haymarket.

[‡] *He had been valet to the Marshal de Grammont, and by him was introduced to Lully. See page 648 of this work.*

JEAN FRANCOIS LALOUETTE, a disciple of Lully, successively conducted the music in the churches of St. Germain l'Auxerrois and Notre Dame. He composed many motets for a full choir, which are much admired; but none of his compositions have been published, except some motets for the principal anniversary festivals, for one, two, and three voices, with a thorough bass. He died at Paris in 1728, at the age of 75.

MARIN MARAIS, born at Paris in 1656, made so rapid a progress in the art of playing on the viol, that Sainte-Colombe, his master, at the end of six months would give him no farther instructions. He carried the art of playing on this instrument to the highest pitch of perfection, and was appointed one of the chamber music to the king. Marais was the first that thought of adding to the viol three strings of brass wire to deepen the tone. He composed several pieces for the viol, and sundry operas, namely, Alcide, Ariane, Bacchus, Alcione, and Semelé, the most celebrated of which is the Alcione. There is a tempest in it particularly admired, and which produces an astonishing effect; a rumbling and doleful sound joining with the sharp notes of a flute and other instruments, presents to the ear all the horrors of a tempestuous ocean and the whistling of the wildest winds. His works bear the pregnant marks of a fertile genius, united to an exquisite taste and judgment. This celebrated musician died in 1728, in the Fauxbourg S. Marceau, and lies buried in the church of St. Hyppolite. He has left behind him of his composition three collections of pieces for the bass viol.*

ELIZABETH CLAUDE JACQUETTE DE LA GUERRE, a female musician, the daughter of Marin de la Guerre, organist of the chapel of St. Gervais in Paris, was born in that city in 1669, and instructed in the practice of the harpsichord and the art of composition by her father. She was a very fine performer, and would sing and accompany herself with so rich and exquisite a flow of harmony as captivated all that heard her. She was also an excellent composer, and, in short, possessed such a degree of skill, as well in the science as the practice of music, that but few of her sex have equalled her. An opera of her composition, entitled Cephale et Procris, was represented in the Royal Academy of Paris in the year 1694, and is extant in print. She died in the year 1729, and lies buried in the church of St. Eustache in Paris.

SALOMON, a native of Provence, was admitted into the band of the chapel royal to play on the bass viol, an instrument on which he excelled. This man, who was very plain and simple in his appearance, seemed to possess no other talent than that of playing with exactness and precision; yet he composed an opera entitled Medée et Jason, which was performed in the Royal Academy in 1713 with great applause, and is in print. At the first night of

* Catalogue de la Musique, imprimée à Amsterdam chez Etienne Roger, page 42.

the representation he went disguised into the crowd, and was a silent witness of the praises and censures passed upon the piece. Salomon died at Versailles in the year 1731, being seventy years of age.

JEAN LOUIS MARCHAND was a native of Lyons, and an organist of some church in that city; when, being very young, he would needs go to Paris, and strolling as by accident into the chapel of the college of St. Louis le Grand, a few minutes before service was to begin, he obtained permission to play the organ; and so well did he acquit himself, that the Jesuits taking pains to find him out, retained him amongst them, and provided him with every requisite to perfect himself in his art. Marchand would never give up his office in that college, though he was tempted to it by advantageous offers. He died at Paris in 1732, aged sixty-three, and left of his composition two books of lessons for the harpsichord, which are greatly admired.

FRANCOIS COUPERIN, organist of the chapel to Louis XIV. and his successor, the late king, and also of his chamber-music, in which he had the charge of the harpsichord, was a very fine composer for this latter instrument.

The family of Couperin has produced a succession of persons eminent in music; the following is a brief account of it. There were three brothers of the name of Louis, Francis, and Charles, natives of Chaume, a little town in Brie. Louis, the eldest, was become eminent for his performance on the organ, and in consequence thereof obtained the place of organist of the king's chapel. In reward of his merit a post was created for him, namely, that of Dessus-de-viole. He died about the year 1665, at the age of thirty-five, and has left of his composition three suites of lessons for the harpsichord, in manuscript, which are to be found only in the collections of the curious.

Francis, the second of the three brothers, was a master of the harpsichord, but no composer: he practised and taught his scholars the lessons of his brother. At the age of seventy he had the misfortune to be overturned in a carriage in one of the streets of Paris, and lost his life by the accident. He had a daughter named Louisa, who sang and played on the harpsichord with admirable grace and skill, and who, notwithstanding her sex, was in the number of the king's musicians, and in that capacity received an annual pension or salary. She died in the year 1728, at about the age of fifty-two.

Charles, the youngest, was a celebrated organist: he died in 1669, leaving one son, namely, Francis Couperin, above spoken of, and who was indeed the glory of the family, being, perhaps, the finest composer for the harpsichord that the French have to boast of. The lessons for this instrument, published by himself, make four volumes in folio; among them is one entitled 'Les Goûts réunis, ou l'Apothéose de Lulli et de Corelli,' and the following allemande, which may serve as a specimen of his style:—

FRANCOIS COUPERIN.

The foregoing air is entitled 'Les Idées Heureuses,' agreeably to the practice of the French composers of lessons for the harpsichord. See the article　Gauthier, ante page 776.

This Couperin, whom we must call the younger Francis, died in 1733, aged sixty-five, leaving two daughters, equally celebrated for their performance on that which appears to have been the favourite instrument of the family; the one a nun in the abbey of Maubuisson; the other is the successor of her father in the charge of the harpsichord in the king's chamber, an employment which, except in this instance, was never known to have been conferred on any but men.

CHAP. CLXIII.

THE establishment of the Royal Academy at Paris contributed greatly to the improvement of the French music, but it failed of answering the ultimate end of its institution. It appears to have been the design of Cardinal Mazarine and Louis XIV. to introduce a style in France corresponding with that of the Italians: but for reasons arising from the temper and genius of the people, or perhaps some other inscrutable causes, it gradually deflected from its original, and in the space of a few years assumed a character so different from that of the Italian music, that it afforded ground for a dispute which of the two was entitled to the preference, and gave rise to a controversy which is scarcely yet at an end. It began as follows:—

In the year 1704 was published a small tract entitled 'Paralele des Italiens et des François, en ce qui regarde la Musique et les Opera,' in which the pretensions of each are thus stated:—

On the part of the French it is asserted, that the French operas are, in respect of the poetry, regular coherent compositions, perfectly consistent with the laws of the drama; and as to the music, that the French have the advantage of bass voices, so proper in the character of gods, kings, and heroes; that the French opera derives still farther advantages from the chorusses and dances; that the French masters excel those of Italy in their performance on the violin, the hautboy, and the flute;* the latter of whom, says this author, have taught the instrument to lament in so affecting a manner in the mournful airs, and to sigh so amorously in those that are tender, that all are moved by them. Besides these advantages he mentions others on the side of the French, as, namely, their habits and their dances; he says that the Combatans and the Cyclopes in Perseus, the Trembleurs and the Forgerons in Isis, and the Songes Funestes in Atys, all operas of Lully, as well in respect of the airs as of the stops adapted thereto by Beauchamp, are originals in their kind. And lastly, that the conduct and economy of a French opera is through the whole so admirable, that no person of common understanding will deny that it affords a more lively representation than the Italian, and that a mere spectator cannot but be much better pleased in France than Italy.

* Here the author celebrates as fine performers on the flute, Philbert, Philidor, Descoteaux, and les Hoteterres.

In behalf of the Italian music the author observes, that the language itself, abounding with vowels that are all sonorous, whereas above half the French vowels are mute, or at least are seldom pronounced, is more naturally adapted to music than that of the French. That in their respective compositions the invention of the Italians appears to be inexhaustible; that of the French narrow and constrained. That the French in their airs affect the soft, the easy, and the flowing; but the Italians pass boldly from sharp to flat, and from flat to sharp, venturing on the most irregular dissonances, and the boldest cadences; so that their airs resemble the compositions of no other nation in the world: and that a like boldness is discoverable in the Italian singers, who, having been taught from their cradles to sing at all times, and in all places, sing the most irregular passages with the same assurance as they would the most orderly, uttering everything with a confidence that secures them success. He says that the Italians are more susceptible of the passions than the French, and by consequence express them more strongly in their music; as an instance whereof the author refers to a symphony in a performance at the Oratory of St. Jerome at Rome, on St. Martin's day, in the year 1697, upon these two words, 'mille saette,' of which he speaks to this purpose. 'The air consisted of 'disjoined notes, like those in a jig, which gave the 'soul a lively impression of an arrow; and that 'wrought so effectually on the imagination, that 'every violin appeared to be a bow, and their bows 'were like so many flying arrows darting their 'pointed heads upon every part of the symphony.' From simple airs the author proceeds to the consideration of compositions in several parts, in which he says the Italians have greatly the advantage; for that whereas in the French music the melody of the upper part is only regarded, in the Italian it is so equally good in all the parts, that we know not which to prefer. He concludes his remarks on the general comparison of the French and Italian music, with an observation that Lully was an Italian; and that he excelled all the musicians in France, even in the opinion of the French themselves; and that therefore, to establish an equality between the two nations, an instance ought to be produced of a French musician who has in the like degree excelled those of Italy; but this he says is impossible. He adds that Italy produced Luigi, Carissimi, Melani, and Legrenzi, and after them Scarlatti, Bononcini, Corelli, and Bassani, who were living at the time of his writing, and charmed all Europe with their excellent productions.

From this general comparison the author proceeds to one more particular, viz., that of the French with the Italian opera. He confesses that the French recitative is to be preferred to the Italian, which he says is close and simple, with very little inflection of the voice, and therefore too nearly approaches common speech; but he says that accompanying their recitatives with such fine harmony as the Italians use, is a practice not to be met with in any other part of the world whatsoever. Having mentioned in the foregoing part of his discourse the advantage which the music of France derives from the number of bass voices with which that country abounds, he observes that this is small in comparison with the benefit which the opera in Italy receives from the castrati, who are there very numerous; and on the comparative excellence of these over women, in respect of the sweetness, flexibility, and energy of the voice, he expatiates very largely, adding, that whereas the voices of women seldom continue in perfection above twelve years, those of castrati will continue for forty : he adds, that the latter are fitter in general to represent female characters than even women themselves, for that they usually look handsomer on the stage; as an instance whereof he mentions Ferini, who performed the part of Sybaris, in the opera of Themistocles at Rome, in 1685. He says that all the towns in Italy abound with actors of both sexes; and that himself once saw at Rome a man who understood music well; and who, though he was neither a musician nor a comedian by profession, but a procurator or solicitor, that had left his business in the carnival time to perform a part in the opera,* acquitted himself as an actor as well as either the French Harlequin or Raisin could have done upon such occasion.

He says that the Italians have the same advantage over the French in respect of their instruments and the performers, as of their singers and their voices. That their violins are much larger strung, and their bows longer.† That the arch-lutes of the Italians are as large again as the theorboes of the French, as are also their bass-viols. That in Italy, youths of fourteen or fifteen play at sight over the shoulders of perhaps two or three persons standing between them and the book, such symphonies as would puzzle the best French masters, and this correctly, without having the time measured to them; whereas nothing of the kind is to be seen at Paris. But the reason he gives for the exquisite performance in the Italian bands is, that the greatest masters are not above appearing in them. 'I have,' says this author, 'seen Corelli, Pasquini, and Gaetani play all together 'in the same opera at Rome; and they are allowed 'to be the greatest masters in the world on the 'violin, the harpsichord, and Theorbo or Arch-lute; 'and as such they are generally paid 3 or 400 'pistoles a-piece for a month or six weeks at most; 'whereas in France the profession of music is 'despised.'

He concludes his comparison with a description of some very extraordinary representations on the Italian stage, of which he says he was an eye-witness; which description is here given in the words of a very judicious person,‡ the translator of the book into English. 'To conclude all, the Italian 'decorations and machines are much better than 'ours; their boxes are more magnificent; the open-'ing of the stage higher, and more capacious; our 'painting, compared to theirs, is no better than 'daubing; you will find among their decorations 'statutes of marble and alabaster, that may vie with 'the most celebrated antiques in Rome; palaces, 'colonnades, galleries, and sketches of architecture, 'superior in grandeur and magnificence to all the 'buildings in the world; pieces of perspective that 'deceive the judgment as well as the eye, even of 'those that are curious in the art; prospects of 'a prodigious extent, in spaces not thirty feet deep; 'nay, they often represent on the stage the lofty 'edifices of the ancient Romans, of which only the 'remains are now to be seen; such as the Colossus 'which I saw in the Roman college in the year 1698,§ 'in the same perfection in which it stood in the reign 'of Vespasian its founder; so that these decorations 'are not only entertaining but instructive.

'As for their machines, I cannot think it in the 'power of human wit to carry the invention farther. 'In the year 1697 I saw an opera at Turin, wherein 'Orpheus‖ was to charm the wild beasts by the 'power of his voice: of these there were all sorts 'introduced on the stage; nothing could be more 'natural, or better designed; an ape among the 'rest played an hundred pranks, the most diverting 'in the world, leaping on the backs of the other 'animals, scratching their heads, and entertaining 'the spectators with the rest of his monkey-tricks. 'I saw once at Venice an elephant discovered on 'the stage, when, in an instant, that great machine 'disappeared, and an army was seen in its place; 'the soldiers having, by the disposition of their 'shields, given so true a representation of it, as if 'it had been a real living elephant.

'The ghost of a woman, surrounded with guards, 'was introduced on the theatre of Capranica at Rome 'in the year 1698; this phantom extending her arms, 'and unfolding her cloaths, was, with one motion, 'transformed into a perfect palace, with its front, its 'wings, its body, and court-yard, all formed by 'magical architecture; the guards striking their 'halberds on the stage, were immediately turned 'into so many water-works, cascades, and trees, 'that formed a charming garden before the palace. 'Nothing can be more quick than were those changes, 'nothing more ingenious or surprising: and, in 'truth, the greatest wits in Italy frequently amuse

* The name of the person here alluded to was Paciani, a man well known at Rome at the latter end of the last century; his performances on the theatre were gratuitous, and the mere result of his fondness for the profession of an actor.

† The bow of the violin has been gradually increasing in length for these last seventy years; it is now about twenty-eight inches. In the year 1720, a bow of twenty-four inches was, on account of its length, called a Sonata bow; the common bow was shorter; and by the account above given the French bow must have been shorter still.

‡ Supposed to be Mr. Galliard.

§ 'The Colossus the author mentions was painted by father Andrea 'Pozzo the Jesuit, who, as well for his painting in the church of St. 'Ignatius belonging to his order, and other pieces, but especially for his 'book of perspective, in folio, printed at Rome, is worthily esteemed as 'the first man in that kind, by all those that have any skill in that 'science.'
The intelligent reader needs hardly be told that both in the passage above, and in this note, the translator has mistaken his author in rendering the word Colisée Colossus, instead of Coliseum, the name of the amphitheatre of Vespasian, the ruins whereof are yet to be seen at Rome.

‖ This opera of Orpheus was afterwards performed at Rome, but not succeeding, the undertakers were obliged to have recourse to the opera of Roderigo, which they had presented just before. This opera of Roderigo was composed by Francesco Gasparini, and was universally applauded. Both these were performed on the theatre della Pace, and the principal parts were done by Biscione, Maurino, and Valentino, he who afterwards sang in the opera in London.

' themselves with inventions of this nature: people
' of the first quality entertain the publick with such
' spectacles as these, without any prospect of gain
' to themselves.* Signor Cavaliero Acciaioli, brother
' to the cardinal of that name, had the direction
' of those on the theatre Capranica in the year 1698.
' This is the sum of what can be offered on behalf
' of the French or Italian musick by way of parallel.
' I have but one thing more to add in favour of the
' operas in Italy, which will confirm all that has
' been already said to their advantage; which is,
' that though they have neither chorusses nor other
' diversions in use with us, their entertainments last
' five or six hours together,† and yet the audience is
' never tired; whereas after one of our representations,
' which does not hold above half so long at most,
' there are very few spectators but what grow suffi-
' ciently weary, and think they have had more than
' enough.'

The author of this discourse, though he affected
concealment, was soon after its publication discovered
to be the Abbé Raguenet, a native of Rouen, the
author of 'Les Monumens de Rome, ou description

* On this passage the English translator of the Parallel makes the
following note. ' Besides the machines mentioned by the author in this
' place, we saw several others at Rome of the same Cavaliero Acciaioli's
' contrivance, as la Frescatane on the theatre of Torre di Nona, the
' Colonnato of Lapis Lazuli, the funeral in Penelope, and many
' more equally surprizing. Upon the theatre of Capranica the same
' artist contrived Il Gigante, &c. But the most famous of all on that
' theatre was the Intermede of Hell, in the opera of Nerone Infante,
' which I will endeavour to describe with as much brevity as I am able,
' it being impossible to express it in such words as it deserves. At the
' sound of a horrid symphony, consisting of Corni, Serpentoni, and Regali,
' part of the floor of the stage opened and discovered a scene underneath,
' representing several caves full of infernal spirits, that flew about in
' a prodigious number, discharging fire and smoak at their nostrils and
' their mouths: at some distance likewise was observed a great number
' of damned spirits, labouring under their several torments; and in
' another side was discovered a river of Lethe with Charon's boat, on
' board of which was Mercury, Cupid, and the soul of one who had lately
' died for love. Upon their landing a prodigious monster appeared,
' whose mouth opening, to the great horror of the spectators covered
' the front wings, and the remaining part of the stage: within his jaws
' were discovered a throne composed of fire, and a multitude of monstrous
' serpents, on which Pluto sate, with a crown of fire on his head, and
' habited in other royal ornaments of the same nature. The singer that
' performed this part was one of those deep basses which, in the author's
' opinion are so rarely found in Italy. After Cupid had demanded justice
' of Pluto upon those old women, who in the preceding intermede, had
' cut his wings for making Agrippina, Nero's mother, in love; and several
' other passages belonging to this intermede, the mouth of the monster
' closed, at which instant Cupid endeavouring to fly off was arrested by
' a little devil, who seized on his foot; upon which Cupid giving himself
' a little turn shot the devil with one of his darts; whereupon the devil
' was transformed into a curling smoke that disappeared by degrees, and
' Cupid escaped. After this the great monster expanding his wings
' began to move very slowly towards the audience; under his body
' appeared great multitudes of devils, who formed themselves into a
' ballet, and plunged one after another into the opening of the floor before
' mentioned; out of which a prodigous quantity of fire and smoke was
' discharged. After this the great monster being got as far as the
' musick-room, and whilst all the spectators were intent upon what was
' doing, and began to fear he would come into the pit, he was in an in-
' stant transformed into an innumerable multitude of broad white
' butterflies, which flew all into the pit, and so low that some of them
' touched the hats of several of the spectators; at which some seemed
' diverted, and others not a little terrified, till by degrees they lodged
' themselves on different parts of the theatre, and at length disappeared.
' During this circumstance, which sufficiently employed the eyes of the
' spectators, the stage was refitted, and the scene changed into a beautiful
' garden, with which the third act begun. This representation was so
' extraordinary in its nature, so exactly performed, and so universally
' admired and applauded, that great numbers of foreigners came to
' Rome on purpose to behold it; and confessed when they had seen it,
' that it far exceeded the expectations fame had given them of it. And
' it must be confessed it gave the spectators a more perfect instructive
' idea of hell, than 'tis possible for the most artful flowing fancy to de-
' lineate. So that the author was not mistaken when he said that these
' sorts of entertainments are no less instructive than agreeable.'

† The Italian operas do not usually last five or six hours, as this author
imagines, the longest being not above four: it is true that sometimes at
Vienna the late emperor Leopold would have operas of the length the
author mentions, provided they were good, being a great admirer of the
Italian music: besides he composed himself, and played on the harpsichord to perfection.

' des plus beaux ouvrages de Peinture, de Sculpture,
' et d'Architecture de Rome, avec des observations.'
Paris, 1700 et 1702; 'L'Histoire d'Olivier Cromwel,'
and other works; upon which Mons. Jean-Laurent
le Cerf de la Vieuville de Freneuse, undertook
a refutation of the Parallel in three dialogues,
entitled ' Comparaison de la Musique Italienne, et
' de la Musique François.' Brux. 1704.

The Comparaison consists of three dialogues, in
which the several passages in the Parallel that tend
either to the praise of the Italian or the censure of
the French music, are made to undergo a severe
examination.   In the comparison between the
musicians of the two countries, Charpentier and
Colasse are opposed to Luigi, i. e. Palestrina, and
Carissimi; Lully is placed above all competition,
and Bassani and Corelli below it. Of the compositions of the latter, he says that they are harsh
and irregular, abounding with dissonances; that he
has seen a piece of Corelli in which were fourteen
fourths together, and that in the eleventh sonata of
his fourth opera the reader may discern twenty-six
sixths in succession.

After a long eulogium on Lully, in which the
most celebrated airs in his operas are pointed
out, the author takes notice of a passage in the
Parallel, in which the voices of the Italian castrati
are compared to those of nightingales; and of another
that follows it, wherein it is asserted, that from the
particular circumstances that distinguish persons of
this kind, they are better actors of female characters
than even women themselves. To refute an assertion so wild as this, requires no great force of
argument; nevertheless this author takes great
pains to render it ridiculous, and has succeeded in
the attempt.

To his instance of the Roman procurator, who left
his employment in carnival time, and became an
actor on the public stage, he opposes the example of
Mons. Destouches, whose profession it seems was that
of a soldier, un mousquetaire, notwithstanding which,
for his pleasure he studied music, and was the composer of many fine operas.

To that passage in the Parallel, in which the
author asserts that he has seen at Rome, Corelli,
Pasquini, and Gaetani perform together in the same
opera, he answers, that at Paris the great masters do
the same; and that Rebel, Theobald, and La Barre
were wont to appear in the orchestra, whenever
a performance of theirs required their attendance;
and notwithstanding that exquisite piece of machinery
devised by the Cavalier Acciaioli, mentioned in the
Parallel, he says that the French are more ingenious
than the Italians in representations of this kind; and
that in the decorations of the theatre they excel all
other nations. And for this assertion, as also for the
superiority of the French machinery, he appeals to
the testimony of Misson and St. Evremont, who both
say something to the same purpose.

At the end of the dialogues is a letter from the
author to an anonymous friend, dated 3 April, 1704,
to the same effect with the rest of the work.

It appears that the Abbé Raguenet replied to the

Comparaison, and that Le Cerf defended it in an answer and two other pieces, which were reprinted some years after the first publication of them, and are extant in an edition of the Histoire de la Musique et de ses effets, printed in the year 1725. Thus the controversy ended as between the parties; but a French physician named Andri, who about the time wrote in the Journal de Sçavans, after commending the first of Le Cerf's publications, turned into ridicule the two last; upon which Le Cerf being greatly irritated, published a pamphlet entitled 'L'Art de décrier ce qu'on n'entend point; ou le Médecin Musicien.' The piece was full as bitter as its title seemed to indicate, and it seems that its bitterness was its most remarkable characteristic; for Fontaine, upon reading of it, pronounced, that if any one deserved to be called a complete fool, it was Le Cerf: But to qualify this severe censure, the Abbé Trublet, from whom this anecdote is taken, says that folly does not imply a total privation of reason and penetration; and that Le Cerf had a great share of both; but that his great defect was that want of common sense, which will sometime expose a man to the ridicule of his inferiors in understanding.

The succession of eminent English musicians from that period at which we were constrained to interrupt it by the above account, is as follows.

CHAP. CLXIV.

JEREMIAH CLARK was educated in the royal chapel, under Dr. Blow, who entertained so great a friendship for him, as to resign in his favour the place of master of the children and almoner of St. Paul's; and Clark was appointed his successor in 1693, and shortly after he became organist of that cathedral. In July, 1700, he and his fellow-pupil were appointed gentlemen extraordinary of the royal chapel; and in 1704 they were jointly admitted to a place of organist thereof in the room of Mr. Francis Piggot. Clark had the misfortune to entertain a hopeless passion for a very beautiful lady in a station of life far above him; his despair of success threw him into a deep melancholy: in short, he grew weary of his life, and on the first day of December, 1707, shot himself.*

The compositions of Clark are few: his anthems are remarkably pathetic, at the same time that they preserve the dignity and majesty of the church

style; the most celebrated of them are, 'I will love 'thee,' printed in the second book of the Harmonia Sacra; 'Bow down thine ear,' and 'Praise the Lord, 'O Jerusalem.'

The only works of Clark published by himself are lessons for the harpsichord, and sundry songs, which are to be found in the collections of that day, particularly in the Pills to purge Melancholy; but they are there printed without the basses. He also composed for D'Urfey's comedy of the Fond Husband or the Plotting Sisters, that sweet ballad air, 'The bonny grey-eyed morn,' which Mr. Gay has introduced into the Beggars Opera, and is sung to the words, ''Tis woman that seduces all mankind.'

JOHN WELDON, a native of Chichester, had his instruction in music under John Walter, organist of Eton college, and afterwards under Henry Purcell. From Eton he went to Oxford, and was made organist of New College. On the sixth day of January, 1701, he was appointed a gentleman extraordinary of the royal chapel; and in 1708 succeeded Dr. Blow as organist thereof. In 1715, upon the establishment of a second composer's place, Weldon was admitted to it:† He had been but a short time in this station before he gave a specimen of his abilities in the composition of the Communion-office, that is to say, the Prefaces, Sanctus, and Gloria in excelsis; and also sundry anthems, agreeably to the condition of his appointment.

At the same time that Weldon was organist of the royal chapel, he was also organist of the church of St. Bride, London; and king George I. having presented the parish of St. Martin in the Fields with an organ, Mr. Weldon, perhaps in compliment to the king, was chosen organist.‡

The studies of Weldon were for the most part in church music; and we do not find that, like Lock and Purcell, and many others of his profession, he ever

---

* He was determined upon this method of putting an end to his life by an event, which, strange as it may seem, is attested by the late Mr. Samuel Weeley, one of the lay-vicars of St. Paul's, who was very intimate with him, and had heard him relate it. Being at the house of a friend in the country, he took an abrupt resolution to return to London: his friend having observed in his behaviour marks of great dejection, furnished him with a horse and a servant. Riding along the road, a fit of melancholy seized him, upon which he alighted, and giving the servant his horse to hold, went into a field, in a corner whereof was a pond, and also trees; and began a debate with himself whether he should then end his days by hanging or drowning. Not being able to resolve on either, he thought of making what he looked upon as chance, the umpire, and drew out of his pocket a piece of money, and tossing it into the air, it came down on its edge and stuck in the clay: though the determination answered not his wish, it was far from ambiguous, as it seemed to forbid both methods of destruction; and would have given unspeakable comfort to a mind less disordered than his was. Being thus interrupted in his purpose, he returned, and mounting his horse, rode on to London, and in a short time after shot himself. He dwelt in a house in St. Paul's church-yard, situate on the place where the Chapter-house now stands: old Mr. Reading, mentioned in page 771 of this work, was passing by at the instant the pistol went off, and entering the house found his friend in the agonies of death.

† Upon the accession of George I. to the crown, that prince, who was a lover of music, carried into execution the proposal of Dr. Tillotson, mentioned in the foregoing account of Blow, for an establishment of two composers for the chapel; and made some other regulations for the improvement of the service: these appear by the following entries in the Cheque-book of the chapel royal:—
'1715. His majesty having been graciously pleased to add four gentle-'men of the chapel to the old establishment, viz., Mr. Morley, Mr. 'George Carleton, Mr. Tho. Baker, and Mr. Samuel Chittle, and by 'virtue of four several warrants from the right rev. father in God, John, 'lord bishop of London, dean of his majesty's chapel royal, I have 'sworn and admitted the aforesaid gentlemen, gentlemen in ordinary of 'his majesty's chapel royal, to enjoy the same together with all privileges 'and advantages thereunto belonging. Witness my hand this 8th day 'of August, 1715.
'Dan. Williams, clerk　　　　　　　　'J. DOLBEN, Subdean.'
'of the Cheque.

'Aug. 8, 1715. That besides the four additional gentlemen of the 'chapel above-mentioned, there was added in king George's establishment 'as follows, viz.:—
'A second composer in ordinary, which place Mr. John Weldon was 'sworn and admitted into.
'A lutenist, which place Mr. John Shore was sworn and admitted into.
'A violist, which place Mr. Francisco Goodsens was sworn and ad-'mitted into.
'All these three were sworn and admitted into their respective places 'by me.
'Witness, Dan. Williams.'　　　　　　　'J. DOLBEN, Subdean.'
'There was likewise inserted in the aforesaid establishment an allowance 'to Dr. William Croft, as master of the children, of eighty pounds per 'annum, for teaching the children to read, write, and accompts, and for 'teaching them to play on the organ and compose music.'
'J. DOLBEN, Subdean.'

‡ The reason that moved the king to this act of munificence was a very singular one; the parish had chosen him their churchwarden, and he executed the office for two months, but at the end thereof, as he well might, he grew tired of it, and presented the parish with that noble instrument which is now in the church.

composed for the theatre, except that in competition with two other masters, namely, Daniel Purcell, John Eccles, and one Franck, or Franco, mentioned in page 763 of this work, and perhaps many others, he set to music Mr. Congreve's masque, the Judgment of Paris. The motive to this undertaking was an advertisement in the London Gazette, offering rewards out of a fund of two hundred guineas advanced by sundry persons of quality, to be distributed in prizes to such masters as should be adjudged to compose the best.* The largest was adjudged to Weldon, and the next to Eccles.

Some songs of Weldon's composition are to be found in a book entitled Mercurius Musicus, and other collections; the following is yet remembered as a favourite air in its time:—

* See the advertisement, page 759 of this work.

help . me Art, ... why should I . . . de - ny . . my heart? If a lo - ver

will . . . pur - sue, like the wi - sest let me do, I will

fit . . him if he's true, if he's false . I'll fit . . him too.

JOHN WELDON.

At the time when Weldon became first of the chapel, Mr. Elford was a singer there, and was celebrated for a very fine counter-tenor voice. Weldon composed for him sundry solo anthems, six of which he published, with a preface acknowledging the advantages they derived from his fine performance. These have their merit, but they fall very far short of his full anthems, particularly those to the words, 'In thee, O Lord,' 'Hear my crying,' of which it is hard to say whether the melody or the harmony of each be its greatest excellence.

Weldon was a very sweet and elegant composer of church music: He died in the year 1736, and lies buried in the church-yard of St. Paul, Covent-garden. His successor in his places in the royal chapel is one whose merits will ever endear him to the lovers and judges of harmony, and particularly of cathedral music, Dr. William Boyce.

JOHN ECCLES was the son of Solomon Eccles, a master of the violin, and the author of sundry grounds with divisions thereon, published in the second part of the Division Violin, printed at London, in 1693, oblong quarto. He was instructed by his father in music, and became a composer for the theatre, of act-tunes, dance-tunes, and such incidental songs as frequently occur in the modern comedies, a collection whereof he published, and dedicated to queen Anne. He composed the music to a tragedy entitled Rinaldo and Armida, written by Dennis, and performed in 1699, in which is a song for a single voice, 'The 'jolly breeze,' which for the florid divisions in it was by many greatly admired. Eccles set to music an

ode for St. Cecilia's Day, written by Mr. Congreve, and performed on the anniversary festival of that saint in 1701; as also his masque entitled the Judgment of Paris, for one of the prizes mentioned in the preceding article; and obtained the second, which was of fifty guineas. His music to the Judgment of Paris is published.

In the collection above mentioned are many excellent songs, particularly one for three voices, 'Inspire us, Genius of the day,' and another, also for three voices, 'Wine does wonders every day,' sung in a comedy entitled Justice Busy, which has long been a favourite with the Gloucestershire singers of catches, and other small proficients in vocal harmony. In it are also contained a very spirited song for two voices, sung in the play of Henry V. to the words 'Fill all your glasses;' and a solo song, which with sundry others the author composed for D'Urfey's play of Don Quixote, the rest being set by Purcell. That of Eccles above mentioned is a mad song, sung by Mrs. Bracegirdle, in the character of Marcella, the words whereof are 'I burn, my brain consumes 'to ashes.' In the Orpheus Britannicus is a song occasioned by Mrs. Bracegirdle's singing 'I burn,' &c.; there are also some pretty tunes of his composing to songs in the Pills to purge Melancholy, published by D'Urfey. Eccles composed the tune to the song 'A soldier and a sailor,' * in Mr. Congreve's comedy of Love for Love, with a bass peculiarly adapted to the manner of singing it as directed by the play; which never having been printed, is here inserted.

* The words of this song are those translated by Dean Aldrich, ' Miles et navigator,' vide page 766 of this work.

JOHN ECCLES.

About the year 1698, upon the decease of Dr. Staggins, Eccles was appointed master of the queen's band; but in the latter part of his life he was known to the musical world only by the New Year and Birth-day Odes, which it was his duty to compose, having retired to Kingston in Surrey for the convenience of angling, a recreation of which he was very fond.

There were three brothers of the name of Eccles, all musicians, viz., the above named John Henry, a violin player in the king of France's band, and the author of twelve excellent solos for that instrument, printed at Paris in 1720, and Thomas,* who was one of those itinerant musicians, perhaps the

last of them, who in winter evenings were used to go about to taverns, and for the sake of a slender subsistence expose themselves to the insults of those who were not inclined to hear them; there are none of this class of mendicant artists now remaining, but in the time of the usurpation they were so numerous, that an ordinance was made declaring them vagrants.†

From the above account of English musicians in

---

* This person was living about thirty years ago. A good judge of music, who had heard him play, gives the following account of him and his performance. 'It was about the month of November, in the year '1735, that I with some friends were met to spend the evening at a 'tavern in the city, when this man, in a mean but decent garb, was in-'troduced to us by the waiter; immediately upon opening the door 'I heard the twang of one of his strings from under his coat, which was 'accompanied with the question, "Gentlemen will you please to hear '"any music?" Our curiosity, and the modesty of the man's deportment, 'inclined us to say yes; and music he gave us, such as I had never heard 'before, nor shall again under the same circumstances: with as fine and 'delicate a hand as I ever heard, he played the whole fifth and ninth 'solo of Corelli, two songs of Mr. Handel, Del minnaciar in Otho, and 'Spero si mio caro bene, in Admetus; in short, his performance was 'such as would command the attention of the nicest ear, and left us his 'auditors much at a loss to guess what it was that constrained him to 'seek his living in a way so disreputable: he made no secret of his 'name; he said he was the youngest of three brothers, and that Henry, 'the middle one, had been his master, and was then in the service of the 'king of France: we were very little disposed to credit the account he 'gave us of his brother's situation in France, but the collection of solos 'above-mentioned to have been published by him at Paris, puts it out of 'question.' Upon inquiry some time after, it appeared that he was idle, and given to drinking. He lodged in the Butcher-row near Temple bar, and was well known to the musicians of his time, who thought themselves disgraced by this practice of his, for which they have a term of reproach not very intelligible; they call it going a-busking. By the Leges Conviviales of the academy of Ben Jonson, held in the Apollo Room, at the Devil Tavern, Temple bar, such persons as these were forbidden admittance into that assembly.

Fidiun, nisi accersitus, non venito.

Let no saucy fiddler dare to intrude unless he is sent for to vary our bliss. Vide second part of Miscellany Poems, published by Mr. Dryden, 12mo. 1716, page 148-150.

---

† Vide ante, page 702, in a note.

To the practice of having music in taverns and inns there are numberless allusions in our old English writers. In bishop Earle's character of a poor fiddler, inserted in the note above referred to, we are told that he made it his business to get the names of the worshipful of the inn, in order that he might salute them by their names at their rising in the morning: but it seems that formerly there were to the greater inns, musicians who might be said to be in some sort retainers to the house. Fynes Moryson has given a hint of this in his Itinerary, part III. page 151, in a passage, the whole whereof, as it exhibits a view of the manners of his time, is here inserted. 'As soone as a passenger comes to an Inne, 'the servants run to him, and one takes his horse and walkes him till he 'be cold, then rubs him, and gives him meate, yet I must say that they 'are not much to be trusted in this last point, without the eye of the 'Master or his Servant to oversee them. Another servant gives the 'passenger his private chamber, and kindles his fier, the third pulls of 'his bootes, and makes them cleane. Then the Host or Hostesse visits 'him, and if he will eate with the Host, or at a common Table with 'others, his meale will cost him sixpence, or in some places but foure 'pence, (yet this course is less honourable and not used by Gentlemen): 'but if he will eate in his chamber, he commands what meate he will 'according to his appetite, and as much as he thinkes fit for him and his 'company, yea, the kitchen is open to him, to command the meat to 'be dressed as he best likes; and when he sits at the Table, Host or 'Hostesse will accompany him, or if they have many Guests, will at least 'visit him, taking it for curtesie to be bid sit downe: while he eates, if 'he have company especially, he shall be offered musicke, which he may 'freely take or refuse, and if he be solitary, the Musitians will give him 'the good day with Musicke in the morning. It is the custome and no 'way disgracefull to set up part of supper for his breakfast: in the 'evening or in the morning after breakefast, (for the common sort use 'not to dine, but ride from breakfast to supper time, yet comming early 'to the Inne for better resting of their Horses) he shall have a reckoning 'in writing, and if it seeme unreasonable, the Host will satisfie him, 'either for the due price, or by abaiting part, especially if the servant 'deceive him any way, which one of experience will soone find. I will 'now onely adde that a Gentleman and his Man shall spend as much, as 'if he were accompanied with another Gentleman and his Man, and if 'Gentlemen will in such sort joyne together, to eate at one Table, the 'expenses will be much diminished. Lastly, a Man cannot more freely 'command at home in his owne House, then he may doe in his Inne, 'and at parting if he give some few pence to the Chamberlin and Ostler, 'they wish him a happy journey.'

succession, it is necessary here to digress to make way for the relation of a discovery, the result of a series of experiments made by Sir Isaac Newton, tending to demonstrate what has often been asserted in the course of this work, viz., that the principles of harmony are discoverable in so great a variety of instances, that they seem to pervade the universe. Many arguments in favour of this opinion are deducible from geometry, as particularly from the Helicon of Ptolemy, the famous theorem of Archimedes,* and that other of Pythagoras, contained in the 47th Proposition of the first book of Euclid, with the observations thereon by Mr. Harrington and Sir Isaac Newton, mentioned previously. But, which was little to be expected, farther demonstration of this general principle results from the analogy between colours and sounds. This noble discovery we owe to the sagacity of Sir Isaac Newton, whose relation of it is here given in his own words:—

'When I had caused the rectilinear line sides AF, 'GM, of the spectrum of colours made by the prism 'to be distinctly defined, as in the fifth experiment 'of the first book is described, there were found in 'it all the homogeneal colours in the same order 'and situation one among another as in the spectrum 'of simple light, described in the fourth experiment 'of that book. For the circles of which the spec-'trum of compound light P T is composed, and 'which in the middle parts of the spectrum inter-'fere and are intermixt with one another, are not 'intermixt in their outmost parts where they touch 'those rectilinear sides A F and G M. And therefore 'in those rectilinear sides when distinctly defined, 'there is no new colour generated by refraction. 'I observed also, that if any where between the 'two outmost circles T M F and P G A a right line, 'as $\gamma \delta$, was cross to the spectrum, so as at both ends 'to fall perpendicularly upon its rectilinear sides, 'there appeared one and the same colour and degree 'of colour from one end of this line to the other. 'I delineated therefore in a paper the perimeter of 'the spectrum F A P G M T, and in trying the third 'experiment of the first book, I held the paper so 'that the spectrum might fall upon this delineated 'figure, and agree with it exactly, whilst an assistant, 'whose eyes for distinguishing colours were more 'critical than mine, did by right lines $\alpha\beta$, $\gamma\delta$, $\epsilon\zeta$, '&c. drawn cross the spectrum, note the confines 'of the colours, that is of the red M $\alpha \beta$ F of the 'orange $\alpha \gamma \delta \beta$, of the yellow $\gamma \epsilon \zeta \delta$, of the green '$\epsilon \eta \theta \zeta$, of the blue $\eta \iota \kappa \theta$, of the indigo $\iota \lambda \mu \kappa$, and 'of the violet λ G A μ. And this operation being 'divers times repeated both in the same and in 'several papers, I found that the observations agreed 'well enough with one another, and that the rec-'tilinear sides M G and F A were by the said cross

* Of this theorem of Archimedes mention is made in page 10, in a note. It seems he thought the discovery of such importance to man-kind, that he caused a diagram thereof to be engraven on his sepulchre. Cicero, in the Tusculan Disputations, book V. sect. 23, glories in his having discovered at Syracuse, without one of the city gates, the sepulchre of Archimedes covered with brambles and thorns, and says that he knew it by the figure of a cylinder and a sphere carved on the stone.

'lines divided after the manner of a musical chord. 'Let G M be produced to X, that M X may be 'equal to G M, and conceive G X, λ X, ι X, η X, 'ϵ X, γ X, a X, M X, to be in proportion to one 'another, as the numbers 1, $\frac{8}{9}$, $\frac{5}{6}$, $\frac{3}{4}$, $\frac{2}{3}$, $\frac{3}{5}$, $\frac{9}{16}$, $\frac{1}{2}$, and 'so to represent the chords of the key, and of a tone 'a third minor, a fourth, a fifth, a sixth major, 'a seventh, and an eighth above that key: And 'the intervals M a, $a \gamma$, $\gamma \epsilon$, $\epsilon \eta$, $\eta \iota$, $\iota \lambda$. and λ G, will 'be the spaces which the several colours (red, 'orange, yellow, green, blue, indico, violet) take 'up.' Sir Isaac Newton's Optics, book I. part II. prop. iii. prob. i. exper. vii.

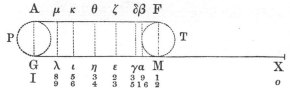

From the relation of this curious and important discovery in the theory, we proceed to relate the farther progress of music in such particulars as respect the practice.

The concert of Britton, the small-coal man at Clerkenwell, continued to flourish till the end of the century in which it was established, and onward into the next, completing a period of more than forty years, when his death put an end to it. Many particulars relating to the life and character of this extraordinary man, are to be met with in books published about and after the time when he lived: but the most authentic account of him, so far as it goes, is contained in Hearne's Appendix to his Hemingi Chartularii Ecclesiæ Wygorniensis, page 665, which, as it was drawn up by one that was well acquainted with him, and he a man of the most scrupulous accuracy, is entitled to the highest degree of credit. Some pains have been taken by searches, and inquiries of persons in his neigh-bourhood, and of others who remember him, to collect those suppletory anecdotes which here follow Hearne's account of him, and furnish a copious memoir of this extraordinary person.

CHAP. CLXV.

'Mr. Thomas Britton, *(a Portrait)*, the famous 'Musical Small-Coal Man, was born at or near 'Higham Ferrers in Northamptonshire. From 'thence he went to London, where he bound himself 'Apprentice to a Small-Coal Man in St. John 'Baptist's Street. After he had served his full 'time of seven Years, his Master gave him a Sum 'of Money not to set up. Upon this Tom went in-'to Northamptonshire again, and, after he had spent 'his Money, he returned again to London, set up 'the Small-Coal Trade (notwithstanding his Master 'was still living) and, withal, he took a Stable, and 'turned it into a House, which stood the next Door 'to the little Gate of St. John's of Jerusalem next 'Clarken-Well-Green. Some time after he had 'settled here, he became acquainted with Dr. Ga-

THOMAS BRITTON

SMALL · COAL · MAN.

'renciers, his near Neighbour, by which means he
'became an excellent Chymist, and perhaps, he
'performed such Things in that Profession, as had
'never been done before, with little Cost and Charge,
'by the help of a moving Elaboratory, that was
'contrived and built by himself, which was much
'admired by all of that Faculty, that happened to
'see it; insomuch that a certain Gentleman of Wales
'was so much taken with it, that he was at the
'Expense of carrying him down into that Country,
'on purpose to build him such another, which Tom
'performed to the Gentleman's very great satis-
'faction, and for the same he received of him a very
'handsome and generous Gratuity. Besides his
'great skill in Chymistry, he was as famous for his
'knowledge in the Theory of Musick; in the Practick
'Part of which Faculty he was likewise very con-
'siderable. He was so much addicted to it, that
'he pricked with his own Hand (very neatly and
'accurately) and left behind him a valuable Col-
'lection of Musick, mostly pricked by himself, which
'was sold upon his Death for near an hundred
'Pounds. Not to mention the excellent Collection
'of printed Books, that he also left behind him,
'both of Chymistry and Musick. Besides these
'Books that he left behind him, he had, some Years
'before his Death, sold by Auction a noble Col-
'lection of Books, most of them in the Rosacrucian
'Faculty (of which he was a great Admirer) whereof
'there is a printed Catalogue extant (as there is of
'those that were sold after his Death) which I have
'often looked over with no small surprize and
'wonder, and particularly for the great Number of
'MSS. in the before mentioned Faculties that are
'specifyed in it. He had, moreover, a considerable
'Collection of Musical instruments, which were sold
'for fourscore Pounds upon his Death, which hap-
'pened in September 1714, being upwards of three-
'score Years of Age, and lyes buried in the Church-
'Yard of Clarken-Well, without Monument or
'Inscription, being attended to his Grave, in a very
'solemn and decent manner, by a great Concourse
'of People, especially of such as frequented the
'Musical Club, that was kept up for many Years
'at his own Charges (he being a Man of a very
'generous and liberal Spirit) at his own little Cell.
'He appears by the Print of him (done since his
'Death) to have been a Man of an ingenious Coun-
'tenance and of a sprightly Temper. It also re-
'presents him as a comely Person, as indeed he was,
'and, withal, there is a modesty expressed in it
'every way agreeable to him. Under it are these
'Verses, which may serve instead of an Epitaph:—

'   Tho' mean thy Rank, yet in thy humble Cell
'   Did gentle Peace and Arts unpurchas'd dwell;
'   Well pleas'd Apollo thither led his Train,
'   And Musick warbled in her sweetest Strain.
'   Cyllenius so, as Fables tell, and Jove
'   Came willing Guests to poor Philemon's Grove.
'   Let useless Pomp behold, and blush to find
'   So low a Station, such a liberal Mind.*

* These verses were written by Mr. John Hughes, who was a frequent
performer on the violin at Britton's concert: they are printed in the first
volume of his Poems, published in 1735; and are also under one of two
mezzotinto prints of Britton.

'In short, he was an extraordinary and very valuable
'Man, much admired by the Gentry, even those of
'the best Quality, and by all others of the more
'inferiour Rank, that had any manner of Regard
'for Probity, Sagacity, Diligence, and Humility.
'I say Humility, because, tho' he was so much fam'd
'for his Knowledge, and might, therefore, have lived
'very reputably without his Trade, yet he continued
'it to his Death, not thinking it to be at all beneath
'him. Mr. Bagford and he used frequently to con-
'verse together, and when they met they seldom
'parted very soon. Their Conversation was often
'about old MSS. and the Havock made of them.
'They both agreed to retrieve what Fragments of
'Antiquity they could, and, upon that occasion, they
'would frequently divert themselves in talking of
'old Chronicles, which both loved to read, tho'
'among our more late Chronicles, printed in English,
'Isaackson's was what they chiefly preferr'd for
'a general knowledge of Things, a Book which
'was much esteem'd also by those two eminent
'Chronologers, Bp. Lloyd and Mr. Dodwell. By
'the way, I cannot but observe, that Isaackson's
'Chronicle is really, for the most part, Bp. Andrews's,
'Isaackson being Amanuensis to the Bishop.'

Hearne seems to have understood but very little
of music, and we are therefore not to wonder that
his curiosity extended not to an inquiry into the
order and economy of that musical club, as he calls
it, which he says Britton for many years kept up in
his own little cell. The truth is, that it was nothing
less than a musical concert; and so much the more
does it merit our attention, as it was the first meeting
of the kind, and the undoubted parent of some of the
most celebrated concerts in London. The time when
Britton lived is not so remote, but that there are
some now living who are able to give an account of
this extraordinary institution, of the principal persons that performed at his concert, and of the company that frequented it: many of these have been
sought out and conversed with, for the purpose of
collecting all that could be known of him: inquiries
have been made in his neighbourhood, of particulars
touching his life, his character, and general deportment; and the result of these will furnish out such
a supplement to what has been said of this extraordinary man in print, as can hardly fail to gratify the
curiosity of such as take pleasure in this kind of
information.

Of the origin of Britton's concert we have an
account written by a near neighbour of his, one who
dwelt in the same parish, and indeed but a small distance from him, namely, the facetious Mr. Edward
Ward, the author of the London Spy, and many
doggrel poems, coarse, it is true, but not devoid of
humour and pleasantry. Ward at that time kept
a public-house in Clerkenwell, and there sold ale of
his own brewing. From thence he removed to a
house in an alley on the west side of Moorfields,
between the place called Little Moorfields and the
end of Chiswell-street, and sold the same kind of
liquor His house, as we are given to understand by
the notes on the Dunciad, was for a time the great

resort of high churchmen. In a book of his writing, entitled Satirical Reflections on Clubs, he has bestowed a whole chapter on the small-coal man's club: from the account therein given we learn that 'this club was first begun, or at least confirmed, by 'Sir Roger L'Estrange, a very musical gentleman, 'and who had a tolerable perfection on the bass viol.' Ward says that 'the attachment of Sir Roger and 'other ingenious gentlemen, lovers of the Muses, to 'Britton, arose from the profound regard that he had 'in general to all manner of literature: that the pru- 'dence of his deportment to his betters procured him 'great respect, and that men of the best wit, as well 'as some of the best quality, honoured his musical 'society with their company: that Britton was so 'much distinguished, that when passing the streets 'in his blue linen frock, and with his sack of small- 'coal on his back, he was frequently accosted with 'such expressions as these, "There goes the famous "small-coal man, who is a lover of learning, a per- "former in music, and a companion for gentlemen." Ward adds, and speaks of it as of his own knowledge, and indeed the fact is indisputable, that he had made a very good collection of ancient and modern music by the best masters; that he also had collected a very handsome library, which he had publicly disposed of to a very considerable advantage; and that he had remaining by him many valuable curiosities. He farther says that, at the first institution of it, his concert was performed at his own house, but that some time after he took a convenient room out of the next to it. What sort of a house Britton's own was, and the spot where it stood, shall now be related.

It was situated on the south side of Aylesbury-street, which extends from Clerkenwell-green to St. John's-street, and was the corner house of that passage leading by the old Jerusalem tavern, under the gateway of the priory, into St. John's-square;* on the ground floor was a repository for small-coal; over that was the concert-room, which was very long and narrow, and had a ceiling so low, that a tall man could but just stand upright in it. The stairs to this room were on the outside of the house, and could scarce be ascended without crawling. The house itself was very old and low-built, and in every respect so mean, as to be a fit habitation for only a very poor man. Notwithstanding all, this mansion, despicable as it may seem, attracted to it as polite an audience as ever the opera did; and a lady of the first rank in this kingdom, the duchess of Queensbury, now living, one of the most celebrated beauties of her time, may yet remember that in the pleasure which she manifested at hearing Mr. Britton's concert, she seemed to have forgotten the difficulty with which she ascended the steps that led to it.

Britton was in his person a short, thickset man, with a very honest, ingenuous countenance. There are two pictures of him extant, both painted by his friend Mr. Woolaston, and from both there are mezzotinto prints; one of the pictures is now in the British Museum, the occasion of painting it, as related by Mr. Woolaston himself, to the author of

* It has long since been pulled down and rebuilt: at this time is an alehouse, known by the sign of the Bull's Head.

this work, was as follows: Britton had been out one morning, and having nearly emptied his sack in a shorter time than he expected, had a mind to see his friend Mr. Woolaston; but having always been used to consider himself in two capacities, viz., as one who subsisted by a very mean occupation, and as a companion for persons in a station of life above him, he could not, consistently, with this distinction, dressed as he then was, make a visit; he therefore in his way home varied his usual round, and passing through Warwick-lane, determined to cry small-coal so near Mr. Woolaston's door as to stand a chance of being invited in by him. Accordingly he had no sooner turned into Warwick-court, and cried small-coal in his usual tone,† than Mr. Woolaston, who had never heard him there before, flung up the sash and beckoned him in. After some conversation Mr. Woolaston intimated a desire to paint his picture, which Britton modestly yielding to, Mr. Woolaston then, and at a few subsequent sittings, painted him in his blue frock, and with his small-coal measure in his hand, as he appears in the picture at the Museum. A mezzotinto print was taken from this picture, for which Mr. Hughes wrote those lines inserted in page 789; and this is the print which Hearne speaks of. But there was another picture of him painted by the same person, upon what occasion is not known: from that a mezzotinto print was also taken, which being very scarce, has been made use of for the engraving of Britton inserted in this work: in this he is represented tuning a harpsichord, a violin hanging on the side of the room, and shelves of books before him. Under the print are the following lines :—

Tho' doom'd to small-coal, yet to arts ally'd,
Rich without wealth, and famous without pride;
Musick's best patron, judge of books and men,
Belov'd and honour'd by Apollo's train;
In Greece or Rome sure never did appear
So bright a genius in so dark a sphere;
More of the man had artfully been sav'd,
Had Kneller painted and had Vertue grav'd.

The above verses were scribbled by Prior with a view to recommend Vertue, then a young man, and patronised by Edward earl of Oxford, though they are little less than a sarcasm on Woolaston and Johnson, who scraped the plate. It is suspected that the insignificant adverb *artfully* was inserted by a mistake of the transcriber, and that it originally stood *probably*.

CHAP. CLXVI.

THE account above given of Britton will naturally awaken a curiosity to know of what kind was the music with which his audience was entertained, and who were the persons that performed in his concert: an answer the first of these queries may be collected from the catalogue of his music, which follows this account of him; to the latter an answer is at hand: Dr. Pepusch, and frequently Mr. Handel, played the harpsichord, Mr. Banister, and also Mr. Henry

† *The goodness of his ear directed him to the use of the most perfect of all musical intervals, the diapason; his cry being, as some relate that remember it:—*

Small coal.

Needler, of the Excise-office, and other capital performers for that time, the first violin; Mr. John Hughes, author of the Siege of Damascus, Mr. Woolaston, the painter, Mr. Philip Hart, Mr. Henry Symonds, Mr. Abiell Whichello, and Mr. Obadiah Shuttleworth, a fine player on the violin, some constantly, and others frequently, performed there. That fine performer Mr. Matthew Dubourg was then but a child, but the first solo that ever he played in public, and which probably was one of Corelli's, he played at Britton's concert, standing upon a joint-stool; but so terribly was the poor child awed at the sight of so splendid an assembly, that he was near falling to the ground.* It has been questioned whether Britton had any skill in music or not; but those who remember him say that he could tune a harpsichord, and that he frequently played the viol da gamba in his own concert.

Britton's skill in ancient books and manuscripts is mentioned by Hearne; and indeed in the preface to his edition of Robert of Gloucester he refers to a curious manuscript copy of that historian in Britton's possession. The means used by him and other collectors of ancient books and manuscripts about that time, as related by one of that class lately deceased, were as follow, and these include an intimation of Britton's pursuits and connexions :—

About the beginning of this century a passion for collecting old books and manuscripts reigned among the nobility. The chief of those who sought after them were Edward earl of Oxford, the earls of Pembroke, Sunderland, and Winchelsea, and the duke of Devonshire. These persons in the winter season, on Saturdays, the Parliament not sitting on that day, were used to resort to the city, and dividing themselves, took several routes, some to Little Britain, some to Moorfields, and others to different parts of the town, inhabited by booksellers; there they would inquire in the several shops as they passed along for old books and manuscripts, and some time before noon would assemble at the shop of one Christopher Bateman, a bookseller, at the corner of Ave Maria-lane, in Paternoster-row; and here they

* Mr. Walpole, in his account of Woolaston the painter, Anecdotes of Painting, vol. III., has taken occasion to mention some particulars of Britton, which he says he received from the son of Mr. Woolaston, who, as well as his father, was a member of Britton's musical club : it is there said that Britton found the instruments, that the subscription was ten shillings a year, and that they had coffee at a penny a dish.
It seems by this passage that Britton had departed from his original institution, for at first no coffee was drunk there, nor would he receive, in any way whatever, any gratuity from his guests : on the contrary, he was offended whenever it was offered him. This is the account of a very ancient person now living, a frequent performer at Britton's concert; and it seems to be confirmed by the following stanza of a song written by Ward in praise of Britton, printed at the end of his description of the small-coal man's club above cited :—

> Upon Thursdays repair
> To my palace, and there
> Hobble up stair by stair,
> But I pray ye take care
> That you break not your shins by a stumble :
>
> And without e'er a souse
> Paid to me or my spouse,
> Sit as still as a mouse
> At the top of the house,
> And there you shall hear how we fumble.

And it is farther confirmed by a manuscript diary of Mr. Thomas Rowe, the husband of the famous Mrs. Elizabeth Rowe, and the author of some supplemental lives to Plutarch, in which there is this memorandum, 'Thomas Britton, the musical small-coal man, had con-'certs at his house in Clerkenwell forty-six years, to which he admitted 'gentlemen gratis. He died October, 1714.'

were frequently met by Mr. Bagford and other persons engaged in the same pursuits, and a conversation always commenced on the subject of their inquiries. Bagford informed them where anything curious was to be seen or purchased, and they in return obliged him with a sight of what they from time to time collected. While they were engaged in this conversation, and as near as could be to the hour of twelve by St. Paul's clock, Britton, who by that time had finished his round, arrived clad in his blue frock, and pitching his sack of small-coal on the bulk of Mr. Bateman's shop window, would go in and join them ; and after a conversation which generally lasted about an hour, the noblemen above mentioned adjourned to the Mourning Bush at Aldersgate,† where they dined and spent the remainder of the day.

The singularity of his character, the course of his studies, and the collections he made, induced suspicions that Britton was not the man he seemed to be : and what Mr. Walpole says as to this particular is very true; some thought his musical assembly only a cover for seditious meetings, others for magical purposes, and that Britton himself was taken for an atheist, a presbyterian, a Jesuit; but these were ill-grounded conjectures, for he was a plain, simple, honest man, perfectly innoffensive, and highly esteemed by all who knew him, and, notwithstanding the meanness of his occupation, was called Mr. Britton.

The circumstances of this man's death are not less remarkable than those of his life. There dwelt in Britton's time, near Clerkenwell-close, a man named Robe, who frequently played at his concert, and who, being in the commission of the peace for the county of Middlesex, was usually called Justice Robe; at the same time one Samuel Honeyman, a blacksmith by trade, and who lived in Bear-street, near Leicester-square, became very famous for a faculty which he possessed of speaking as if his voice proceeded from some distant part of the house where he stood; in short, he was one of those men called Ventriloqui, i. e., those that speak as it were from their bellies, and are taken notice of by Reginald Scott in his Discovery of Witchcraft, page 111, for which reason he was called the Talking Smith. The pranks played by this man, if collected, would fill a volume.‡ During the time that Dr. Sacheverell was under censure, and had a great resort of friends to his house, near the church in Holborn, he had the confidence to get himself admitted, by pretending that he came from a couple who wished to be married by the doctor. He stayed not long in the room, but made so good use of his time, that the doctor, who was a large man, and one of the stoutest and most athletic then living, was

† A bush was anciently the sign of a tavern, as may be inferred from the proverb ' Good wine needs no bush.' This was succeeded by a thing intended to resemble a bush, consisting of three or four tier of hoops fastened one above another ; with vine leaves and grapes richly carved and gilt, and a Bacchus bestriding a tun at top. The owner of this house, at the time when king Charles I. was beheaded, was so affected upon that event, that he put his bush in mourning by painting it black.
‡ The following one is related by Dr. Shaw in his edition of the Philosophical Works of Lord Bacon, Vol. III. page 112, in nota. 'Tis said that he once counterfeited a man's voice coming out of a large cask, in a cart loaded with empty casks, as it was going along the streets, to the great astonishment and perplexity of the carman.

almost terrified into fits. Dr. Derham, of Upminster, that sagacious enquirer into the works of nature, had a great curiosity to see Honeyman, but the person he employed to bring about the meeting, and who communicated this anecdote, contrived always to disappoint him, knowing full well that, had it taken effect, it must have terminated in the disgrace of the doctor, whose reputation as a divine and a philosopher he thought a subject too serious to be sported with.

This man, Robe was foolish and wicked enough to introduce, unknown, to Britton, for the sole purpose of terrifying him, and he succeeded in it: Honeyman, without moving his lips, or seeming to speak, announced, as from afar off, the death of poor Britton within a few hours, with an intimation that the only way to avert his doom was for him to fall on his knees immediately and say the Lord's Prayer. The poor man did as he was bid, went home and took to his bed, and in a few days died, leaving his friend Mr. Robe to enjoy the fruits of his mirth.

Hearne says that his death happened in September, 1714. Upon searching the parish-books, it is found that he was buried on the first day of October following.

Britton's wife survived her husband   He left little behind him besides his books, his collection of manuscript and printed music, and musical instruments. The former of these were sold by auction at Tom's coffee-house, Ludgate-hill.   Sir Hans Sloane was a purchaser of sundry articles, and catalogues of them are in the hands of many collectors of such things as matters of curiosity.   His music-books were also sold in the month of December, in the year of his death, by a printed catalogue, of which the following is a copy:—

' A CATALOGUE of extraordinary musical instruments made
' by the most eminent workmen both at home and abroad.
' Also divers valuable compositions, ancient and modern,
' by the best masters in Europe; a great many of which
' are finely engrav'd, neatly bound, and the whole care-
' fully preserv'd in admirable order; being the entire
' collection of Mr. Thomas Britton of Clerkenwell, small-
' coal man, lately deceased, who at his own charge
' kept up so excellent a consort forty odd years at his
' dwelling-house, that the best masters were at all times
' proud to exert themselves therein; and persons of the
' highest quality desirous of honouring his humble cottage
' with their presence and attention: but death having
' snatched away this most valuable man that ever enjoyed
' so harmonious a life in so low a station, his music books
' and instruments, for the benefit of his widow, are to be
' sold by auction on Monday, Tuesday, and Wednesday,
' the 6th, 7th, and 8th Decemb. at Mr. Ward's, house in
' Red Bull-Yard, in Clerkenwell, near Mr. Britton's,
' where Catalogues are to be had gratis; also at most
' Music-shops about town.   Conditions of sale as usual.

' 1.   Two sets of books, one of three, and one of four parts,
' by divers authors. 2. Two sets of ditto in 4 parts by Jen-
' kins, Lock, Lawes, &c. 3. Two sets ditto by Robert Smith,
' Brewer, and other authors. 4. Two sets ditto by Mr. Richard
' Cobb, and other authors. 5. Two Lyra consorts by Loose-
' more, Wilson, &c. 6. Three sets of books by Baptist, &c.
' 7. Two sets ditto by old Mr. Banister, Akeroyd, &c. 8. Two
' sets of books by Mr. Paisible, Grabu, &c. 9. Three ditto,
' two by Mr. Courteville and one by Mr. Banister. 10. Two
' ditto, four parts, by Chr. Simpson and Mr Wilson. 11. Two
' ditto, Jenkins's Pearl consort and Dr. Rogers. 12. Two
' ditto of Lyra consorts by Jenkins and Wilson. 13. Three
' ditto by Jenkins, Simpson, and Cuts. 14. Nicola's 1st, 2nd,

' 3d, and 4th books, original plates, with second trebles and
' tenors. 15. Three sets of three parts by Dr. Gibbons and
' other authors. 16. Two ditto of four parts by Mr. Eccles.
' Mr. Courteville, and Dr. Coleman. 17. Three printed operas
' by Vitali, Grossi, and one by divers authors, Italian. 18.
' Two sets in three parts by Jenkins, Mr. Paisible, &c. 19.
' Four sets ditto by Vitali, &c. 20. Corelli's Opera Quarta,
' and Ravenscroft's Ayres. 21. 25 Sonatas by Corelli, Bassani,
' &c. Italian writing. 22. Ditto. 23. 16 Concertos by Carlo
' Catrilio, Carlo Ambrosio, Corelli ditto. 24. 25 Sonatas by
' Melani, Bassani, Ambrosio, &c. 25. Mr. H. Purcell's
' musick in Dioclesian with trumpets, Mr. Finger. 9 books
' with ditto. 26. Trumpet pieces in 4 and 5 parts by Dr.
' Pepusch, &c. 27. Two sets of books ayres by Mr. Eccles,
' Barret, Bassani, Gabrielli. 28. Desnier's Overtures, Ayres,
' &c. engraved and neatly bound, another set by divers. 29.
' Fantasies, &c. by Ferabosco, &c. 30. Ayres in 2, 3, and 4
' parts by Lenton, Tollet, Jenkins, &c. 31. 13 Sonatas of 2,
' 3, and 4 parts by Corelli, Italian writing. 32. Five books of
' Pavans, Ayres, &c. neatly bound. 33. Four sets of Ayres
' of 3 and 4 parts by Jenkins, &c. 34. Three sets of Lyra
' books by Wilson and Simpson. 35. Two sets of books by
' Mr. Jenkins in 3 parts. 36. Three sets ditto by Vitali, R.
' Smith, &c. 3 parts. 37. Three sets ditto by Mr. Courteville,
' Finger, Grabu, &c. 4 parts. 38. Six sets ditto by Mr. H.
' Purcell, Mr. Paisible, Mr. Demoivre, &c. Duos for flutes and
' violins. 39. Three sets ditto by Sign. Baptist, Lock, &c.
' 3 parts. 40. One set ditto of Gillier of his last and best
' works. 41. 12 Sonatas by Batt. Gigli for the marriage of
' the Duke of Tuscany. 42. Simpson's Division Violist in
' English, neatly bound. 43. Simpson's ditto in English
' and Latin, ditto. 44. Three sets by Orl. Gibbons, Mons. la
' Voles, and Lock, 3 parts. 45. Six sets of books of Redding's
' Lyra, 2 violins, &c. and divers authors. 46. A set of
' Sonatas in three parts with two basses. 47. Mr Sherard's
' Opera prima on the best large paper, and finely bound and
' lettered. 48. A set of Grabu in 5 parts, and a set of Vitali
' in 6 parts. 49. Two sets of Sonatas by Carlo Manelli and
' Cav. Tarq. Merula. 50. Three sets by Vitali, Uccellini,
' and Adson, printed in 5 parts. 51. 17 Sonatas by Mr.
' Finger. two of them with a high violin. 52. Canzonette for
' 3 and 4 voices, with a harpsichord and lute part. 53. Mace's
' Musick's Monument. 54. 12 Sonatas by Fiorenzo a Kempis
' for a violin, and viol da gamba and bass. 55. A set of
' Sonatas by Baltzar for a lyra violin, treble violin, and bass.
' 56. 2 sets ditto by Coperario, Lupo, Dr. Gibbons, &c. and
' Fancies, 3 parts, also a set by Baptist. 57. 2 sets ditto by
' Vitali, and 1 set by Hernels, 3 parts. 58. 12 Sonatas by
' Mr. Novel finely engraved and on good paper. 59. 2 sets
' of fancies of 3 and 4 parts by Ferabosco, Lupo, and other
' excellent authors. 60. Mr. Finger's printed Sonatas, 2 first
' violins and 2 basses. 61. 3 sets ditto by Vitali, Opera 14,
' and Lock, &c. 62. The opera of Isis, and a set of 5 parts
' by several authors. 63. A collection of many divisions, &c.
' by Baltzar, Mell, &c. 64. Concertos by P. Romolo and
' Nicola. 65. Overtures and tunes, 4 parts, by Mr. Paisible,
' Mr. Courteville, &c. 66. 3 sets of ditto and fancies by
' Jenkins, Gibbons. 67. 12 Solos by Torelli for a violin and
' bass, and 10 Solos by Corelli. 68. 16 Solos by Corelli, Dr.
' Croft, &c. some for flutes and some for violins. 69. 4 sets
' by Lock, and Young's Sonatas, Farmer's Ayres, &c. 70.
' 18 Sonatas by Dr. Pepusch, Carlo Ruggiero. 71. 3 sets of
' books of Sonatas by divers authors 72. Krieger's 12 Sonatas.
' 73. 3. sets of Sonatas, and one set by Lawes, 5 and 6 parts,
' and 2 sets by Birchenshaw. 74. 4 sets of Sonatas and Ayres
' by divers authors. 75. Caldara's 1st and 2d operas. 76.
' Mr. H. Purcell's 2 operas of Sonatas, and Bassani's opera 5ta
' printed. 77. Bassani's opera quinta, and a set of sonatas.
' 78. 4 sets of books for 2 violins by Finger, Courteville, &c.
' 79. Merula and Bleyer's sonatas, 3 parts. 80. Grassi's
' sonatas of 3, 4, and 5 parts. 81. Walter's Solos finely
' engrav'd and neatly bound. 82. Mr. H. Purcell's Overtures
' and Ayres in his Operas, Tragedies and Comedies, 8 books,
' printed in Holland. 83. Ditto fairly printed here. 84.
' Bassani's best Sonatas well wrote. 85. A large and good
' collection of Ayres in 3 and 4 parts, by the best modern
' masters. 86. Nicolini Cosmi's solo book neatly bound. 87.

'Corelli's solo book, Dutch print. 88. Ditto. 89. Senallio's
'Solos finely engrav'd. 90. Danrieu's Solos ditto. 91. Biber's
'Sonatas, 5 parts. 92. Lock's Fancies, 4 parts : Cobb's 3 parts,
'Vitali 3 parts, &c. 93. 6 Concertos for trumpets, hautboys,
'and Mr. Eccles's Coronation of Q. Anne. 94. Hely's Sonatas
'for 3 viols, and ditto by several authors. 95 to 98. Corelli's
'Opera terza finely wrote. 98. Corelli Opera terza in sheets.
'99. Corelli Opera prima. 100. Playhouse tunes of 3 and
'4 parts. 101. 12 Concertos and Sonatas, 10 of them by
'Dr. Pepusch. 102. 12 Concertos by Dr. Pepusch, young
'Mr. Babel, Vivaldi. 103. Albinoni's Concertos, Dutch print.
'104. Biber's Solo book finely engrav'd. 105. A curious
'collection of Concertos by Dr. Pepusch, &c. 106. Mr. Corbet's
'3d and 4th Operas, Mr. Williams's 6 Sonatas, and Mr.
'Finger's 9 Sonatas. 107. Mr. Keller's Sonatas for Trumpets,
'Flutes, Hautboys, &c. Dutch print. 108. Pez Opera prima
'engrav'd in Holland. 109. 3 sets of books in 3 parts. 110.
'9 sets ditto of tunes. 111. 7 sets ditto for 4, 5, 6, 7, 8, and
'10 instruments. 112. 5 sets ditto for violins, lyra viols, with
'basses by Jenkins. 113 to 115. 6 sets ditto of 2 and 3 parts.
'116. Lawes's Royal Consort, Jenkins, Simpson, &c. 4 parts.
'117 to 120. Sets of books, viz. Jenkin's Pearl Consort, and
'most by him, and other in 3 and 4 parts. 121 to 124. Sets
'of books of fancies, &c. 2 and 3 parts by Jenkins, &c. 125.
'8 sets ditto of lyra pieces, most by Jenkins, in 2, 3, 4, and 5
'parts. 126. 5 sets ditto of 3 parts, most by Jenkins. 127.
'6 sets ditto for the organ by Bird, Bull, Gibbons, &c. 128.
'A great collection of divisions on grounds. 129. 6 sets of
'Duos by Veracini and other authors. 130. 9 books of in-
'structions for the Psalmody, Flute and Mock-trumpet. 131.
'15 ditto for the Lute, Guitar, Citharen, &c. 132. 2 sets by
'Becker, Rosenmuller, in 2, 3, 4, and 5 parts. 133. 5 sets for
'2 viols and violins by Jenkins, Simpson, &c. 134. 8 sets for
'Lyra viols and other instruments by Jenkins, &c. 135.
'Bononcini's Ayres, and a great collection with them. 136.
'5 sets Pavans, Fancies, &c. by Jenkins, Mico, &c. in 4 and
'5 parts. 137. 5 books of instructions and lessons for the
'harpsichord. 138. 2 sets of books of Concertos &c. by Dr.
'Pepusch, &c. 139. 8 Concertos, Italian writing, for Trum-
'pets, &c. divers authors. 140. 2 sets for three lyra viols,
'and one set for a lyra viol, violin and bass, Jenkins. 141.
'Des Cartes, Butler, Bath, &c. 6 books of the theory of
'Musick. 142. Cazzati's Sonatas and pieces for lyra viols,
'and Sonatas, Ayres, &c. 143. Sonatas for 3 flutes, and
'several Solos and Sonatas for flutes and violins, Dr. Pepusch,
'&c. 144. Country dances with the basses, and other books.
'145. 2 books finely bound, most plain paper. 146. Several
'excellent Sonatas, with a great parcel of other music. 147.
'Romolo's 2 Choirs in 6 books, Uccellini and Becker's So-
'natas. 148. Corelli's first, second, and third operas printed.
'149. Plain paper of several sizes. 150. 3 sets of books, most
'plain paper. 151. 12 Sonatas by an unknown author. 152.
'Morley's Introduction. 153. Ditto. 154. Lawes's Treasury
'of Music. 155. Butler's Principles of Music. 156. 6 books
'full of Opera Overtures, Sonatas, &c. of the best authors.
'157. 6 books of Trumpet Sonatas and Tunes for 2 flutes and
'2 hautboys. 158. 6 books Overture of Hercules, and a Con-
'certo of Corelli. 159. 5 books of Morgan's best Overtures,
'Cibels, and tunes, and some by Mr. Clark. 160. Simpson's
'Months and Seasons ; a bundle of cases for books ; odd
'books and papers.

'VOCAL MUSICK.

'1. Divine Companion, Canons, Catches, Godeaus French
'Psalms, &c. 2. Nine books of the theory of musick by
'divers authors. 3. The first and second sets of Madrigals
'of that excellent author John Wilbye. 4. The Gentleman's
'Journal for almost three years, with songs at the end. 5.
'3 Different Catch Books by Mr. Purcell and the best masters.
'6. Anthems in 4, 5, and 6 parts in English and Latin, in 6
'books neatly bound. 7. The Treasury of Musick in 5 books,
'by H. Purcell, &c. neatly bound. 8. Orpheus Britannicus,
'the 2 volumes in one book, well bound. 9. Several little
'books of Songs. 10. Orpheus Britannicus, the first book,
'with new additions. 11. Amphion Angelicus by Dr. Blow,
'for 1, 2, 3, and 4 voices, to a thorow bass. 12. The opera
'Pyrrhus and Demetrius with the Symphonies. 13. The
'opera of Antiochus with the Symphonies. 14. The opera of

'Hydaspes with the Symphonies. 15. A great collection of
'ancient and modern songs, some by Bassani, &c. 16.
'Bassani's Motetts, Opera 8 with Symphonies. 17. Ditto
'Opera 13. 18. Pietro Reggio's Song book. 19. The operas
'of Camilla and Thomyris with Symphonies. 20. Several
'Catch-books. 21. The opera of Clotilda with Symphonies.
'22. The opera of Almahide ditto. 23. Dr. Pepusch's
'Cantatas. 24 to 25. A great collection of Song-books by
'divers authors. 26. Services and anthems by Tallis, Bird,
'Gibbons, &c. the part for the organ. 27. The 2 Harmonia
'Sacras by Mr. H. Purcell. 28. A very large collection of
'sheet songs. 29. A collection of song books. 30. Nine
'song books by divers authors. 31. Bird's Psalms in 5 parts,
'and Lawes's Psalms in 3 parts, and 9 Canons of 3 and 4.
'32. Several divine pieces in 3 and 4 parts, and Child's
'Psalms. 33. Seven song-books, &c. 34. One set for 2 and
'3 voices : and one set for 5 voices by Dr. Gibbons. 35. 2
'sets of books for 2, 3, 4, and 5 voices, by Dumont, Jones, &c.
'36. Six sets of books, most of Dowland, for many parts.
'37. 5 books of Playford's Psalms in 4 parts, folio, proper for
'a shopkeeper. 38 An old book finely wrote of Latin church
'musick. 39. Several books and sets of songs. 40. Lawes's
'Psalms, and several ditto. 41. Four new Psalm books.
'42. 2 Harmonia Sacras, first part.

'SCORES.

'1. Mr. Jenkins, Dr. Gibbons, and another author, 3 books.
'2. Mr. Purcell's Cecilia, Lock's opera of Psyche, and 15
'sheets. 3. By Baptist Lully, Lock, Smith, &c. 4. Songs
'for 2 and 3 voices by Dr. Wilson. 5. Albion and Albanius
'by Mr. Grabu. 6. Mr. Purcell's Te Deum and Jubilate.
'7. Mr. Purcell's opera of Dioclesian. 8. Ditto. 9. A large
'book of Sonatas. 10. A noble book by Gasparini and the
'best Italian authors, 168 folios. 11. Ditto by Melani and
'the best Italian authors, 166 folios.

'INSTRUMENTS.

'1. A fine Guittar in a case. 2. A good Dulcimer. 3. Five
'instruments in the shape of fish. 4. A curious ivory Kitt
'and bow in a case. 5. A good Violin by Ditton. 6. Another
'very good one. 7. One said to be a Cremona. 8. An ex-
'traordinary Rayman.* 9. Ditto. 10. Ditto. 11. Ditto.
'12. One very beautiful one by Claud, Pleray of Paris, as
'good as a Cremona. 13. One ditto. 14. Another very
'good one. 15. Another ditto. 16. A very good one for a
'high violin. 17. Another ditto. 18. An excellent tenor.
'19. Another ditto by Mr. Lewis. 20. A fine viol by Mr.
'Baker of Oxford. 21. Another excellent one, bellied by Mr.
'Norman.† 22. Another, said to be the neatest that Jay
'ever made. 23. A fine bass violin, new neck'd and bellied
'by Mr. Norman. 24. Another rare good one by Mr. Lewis.
'25. A good harpsichord by Philip Jones. 26. A Rucker's
'Virginal, thought to be the best in Europe. 27. An Organ
'of five stops, exactly consort pitch, fit for a room, and with
'some adornments may serve for any chapel, being a very
'good one.

'N. B. There is not one book or instrument here men-
'tioned that was not his own : and as it will be the best sale
'that hath been made in its kind, so it shall be the fairest. All
'persons that are strangers to pay 5s. in the pound for what
'they buy, and to take away all by Friday night following.

'There are a great many books that Mr. Britton had
'collected in most parts of learning, the whole consisting of
'14 or 1500 books, which will shortly be sold at his late
'dwelling house. But the manner and method of sale is not
'yet concluded on.'

CHAP. CLXVII.

BEFORE we proceed to give an account of sundry
concerts and musical meetings which may be said to
have taken their rise from that of Britton, it will be
necessary to mention one of a very different kind, as

---

* Jacob Rayman dwelt in Bell-yard, Southwark, about the year 1650.
The tenor violins made by him are greatly valued.

† Barah Norman was one of the last of the celebrated makers of viols
in England : he lived in Bishopsgate, and afterwards in St. Paul's church-
yard. He had two daughters, who were actresses of the lower class at
the theatre in Goodman's-fields.

being conducted at a great expense, namely, that of the duchess of Mazarine, who came into England in the reign of Charles II., and for a series of years contrived by various methods to make her house the resort of all that had any pretensions to wit, gallantry, or politeness. To understand the nature of the entertainment above mentioned a sketch of this lady's history will hardly be thought improper.

HORTENSIA MANCINI was one of the four daughters of Lorenzo Mancini by Jeronima Mazarine, sister of Cardinal Mazarine. She had been in France from the time that she was six years of age, and improving in wit and beauty, attracted the regard of the whole court. King Charles II. saw her at Paris, and more than once demanded her in marriage; but the cardinal, seeing no prospect of his restoration, refused his consent, though he lived to repent it, and in 1661 married her to the duke de la Meilleraie, with whom she lived about four years without reproach; but, upon a disagreement with him, she left him, possessed of the fortune which the cardinal had bequeathed to her, amounting to twenty millions of livres; and in 1675, having been invited hither with a view to supplant the duchess of Portsmouth in the king's affections, she came into England, where she was scarce arrived before the king settled on her an annual pension of four thousand pounds; and there was little doubt but she would have answered the end of her being sent for, but in the following year the prince of Monaco arriving here, she was so negligent of her business as to engage in an amour with him, which coming to the king's ear, he withdrew her pension, and was hardly prevailed on to restore it. She had other intrigues upon her hands at different times, which are not to be wondered at, seeing that she was even in her youth, or rather infancy, so great a libertine as not to have the least tincture of religion. In the memoirs of her life, written by the Abbé de St. Real, but under her own immediate direction, it is related that the cardinal her uncle was much displeased with her, and her sister Madame de Bouillon, for their want of devotion; and that once complaining to them that they did not hear mass every day, he told them that they had neither piety nor honour; adding this exhortation, which deserves to be remembered to his credit, 'At least, if you will not hear mass for God's sake, do it for the world's.'

But the want of religious principle in this lady seems, in the opinion of her panegyrists, especially Mons. St. Evremond, to have been amply atoned for by her wit and beauty. This person, who had a considerable hand in the laudable business of bringing her hither, might almost be said to have resided in her house (*Lindsay House*), which was at Chelsea; and, if we may believe the accounts that are given of her manner of living, was a kind of academy, and daily frequented by the principal nobility, and persons distinguished for wit and genius, where, in the style of free conversation, were discussed subjects of the deepest speculation, such as philosophy and religion, as also history, poetry, criticism on dramatic and other ingenious compositions, and the niceties of

the French language. And that nothing might be wanting to increase the attractions of this bower of bliss, the game of basset was introduced, and an obscure man, named Morin permitted to keep a bank in it;* and concerts were given there, in which St. Everemond himself set the music: indeed, if we come to inquire into his share of the musical composition, his attempts in this way must appear ridiculous; for we are told, though he composed tunes to his own verses. and particularly to sundry Idyls, Prologues, and other pieces of his writing, yet that as to overtures, chorusses, and symphonies, he left them to some able musician, who we elsewhere learn was Mr. Plaisible, the famous composer for the flute, already spoken of in this work.

St. Evremond, though an old man, was blind to the follies, and even vices of this woman, whom we may style the modern Cleopatra, and has disgraced himself by the fulsome praises of her with which his works abound. He wrote the words to most of the vocal compositions performed at her house, and generally presided at the performance. The duchess died in 1699, aged fifty-two.

The musical representations at the duchess of Mazarine's were chiefly dramatic, and are celebrated for their magnificence. The singers in them were women from the theatres, whose names have been mentioned in the preceding part of this work, and the instrumental performers the most eminent masters of the time. It is supposed that the design of introducing the Italian opera into England was first concerted in this assembly: the death of the duchess retarded but for a few years the carrying of it into execution, for in 1707 the opera of Arsinoe, consisting of English words adapted to Italian airs by Mr. Thomas Clayton, was performed at Drury-lane theatre; and a succession of entertainments of this kind terminated in the establishment of an opera properly so called, in which the drama was written in the Italian language, and the music in the Italian style of composition. This important era in the history of music, as it respects England, will be noticed in a succeeding page: in the interim it is found necessary to continue the account of eminent church musicians who flourished in this period.

The encouragement given to church music by the establishment of two composers for the chapel, had excited but little emulation in the young men to distinguish themselves in this kind of study, so that after the decease of Blow there were but few that addicted themselves to the composition of anthems, and of these the most considerable were Tudway, Croft, Creighton, Dr. Turner, Heseltine, Godwin, King, and Greene.

THOMAS TUDWAY received his education in music in the chapel royal, under Dr. Blow, being one of

---

* *In a song of Sir George Etherege's on Basset, is this stanza :—*

　　Let equipage and dress despair,
　　Since Bassett has come in;
　　For nothing can oblige the fair,
　　Like Money and Morin.

Morin is also mentioned in Bruyere's Characters. Sidney earl of Godolphin told Sir Robert Walpole that he had played at the duchess of Mazarine's, and that, in consideration of her poverty, it was customary to leave a guinea under the carpet on the table.

those called the second set of chapel children, and a fellow-disciple of Turner, Purcell, and Estwick. On the twenty-second day of April, 1664, he was admitted to sing a tenor in the chapel at Windsor. After that, viz., in 1671, he went to Cambridge, to which university he was invited by the offer of the place of organist of King's College chapel, and in 1681 was admitted to the degree of bachelor in his faculty. In the year 1705 queen Anne made a visit to the university of Cambridge, upon which occasion he composed an anthem, ' Thou, O God, hast heard my vows,' which he performed as an exercise for the degree of doctor in music, and was created accordingly, and honoured with the title of public professor of music in that university.* He also composed an anthem, ' Is it true that God will dwell with men on earth ?' on occasion of her Majesty's first going to her royal chapel at Windsor ; and for these compositions, and perhaps some others on similar occasions, he obtained permission to style himself composer and organist extraordinary to queen Anne.

A few songs and catches are the whole of Dr. Tudway's works in print ; nevertheless it appears that he was a man studious in his profession, and a composer of anthems to a considerable number. He had a son, intended by him, as it seems, for his own profession ; for his information and use the doctor drew up, in the form of a letter, such an account of music and musicians as his memory enabled him to furnish. Many very curious particulars are related in it, and some facts which but for him must have been buried in oblivion ; among which are the contest between father Smith and Harris about the making of the Temple organ, and the decision of it by Jefferies, afterwards Lord Chancellor—a fact scarcely known to any person living except such as have perused the letter.

His intimacy with Purcell, who had been his school-fellow, furnished him with the means of forming a true judgment, as well of his character as his abilities, and he has borne a very honourable testimony to both in the following passage :—' I knew ' him perfectly well ; he had a most commendable ' ambition of exceeding every one of his time, and ' he succeeded in it without contradiction, there ' being none in England, nor anywhere else that ' I know of, that could come in competition with him ' for compositions of all kinds. Towards the latter ' end of his life he was prevailed with to compose ' for the English stage ; there was nothing that ever ' had appeared in England like the representations ' he made of all kinds, whether for pomp or solem- ' nity ; in his grand chorus, &c., or that exquisite ' piece called the freezing piece of music ; in repre- ' senting a mad couple, or country swains making ' love, or indeed any other kind of musick whatever. ' But these are trifles in comparison of the solemn ' pieces he made for the church, in which I will ' name but one, and that is his Te Deum. &c., with ' instruments, a composition for skill and invention

' beyond what was ever attempted in England before ' his time.'

In his sentiments touching music, as delivered in his letter, Dr. Tudway is somewhat singular, inasmuch as he manifests an almost uniform dislike to the practice of fuguing in vocal music, alledging as a reason that it obscures the sense of the words, which is either the case or not, according as the point is managed. Certain it is, that the practice of the ablest masters, both before and since his time, is against him ; and it is perhaps owing to this singularity of opinion that the best of his compositions do not rise above mediocrity, and that scarce any of them are in use at this day.

In the latter part of his life Dr. Tudway was mostly resident in London. Having a general acquaintance with music, and being personally intimate with the most eminent of the profession, he was employed by Edward, earl of Oxford, in collecting for him musical compositions, chiefly of the Italians, and in making a collection of the most valuable services and anthems, the work of our own countrymen. Of these he scored with his own hand as many as filled seven thick quarto volumes, which are now deposited in the British Museum, and answer to Numb. 7337, et seq. in the printed catalogue of that collection.

The favour shown him by Lord Oxford, together with his merit in his profession, procured him admittance into a club, consisting of Prior, Sir James Thornhill, Christian the seal engraver, Bridgman the gardener, and other ingenious artists, which used to meet at Lord Oxford's once a week. Sir James Thornhill drew all their portraits in pencil, and amongst the rest that of Dr. Tudway playing on the harpsichord, and Prior scribbled verses under the drawings. These portraits were in the collection of Mr. West, the late president of the Royal Society.

In the music-school at Oxford is a painting of Dr. Tudway, with the anthem performed on the queen's coming to Cambridge in his hand. The picture was a present from the late Dr. Rawlinson. Dr. Tudway is yet remembered at Cambridge for his singular style in conversation, and for that, like Daniel Purcell, he could scarce ever speak without a pun.

Samuel Marshall, *a young man of a promising genius and amiable character, merits a place among the church musicians of this time. He was a scholar of Blow, and organist of St. Catherine Cree Church, London. An anthem, ' Behold how good and joyful,' in the key of C with the greater third, extant only in manuscript, and a few Songs, printed with his name, are all of his compositions that at this day are known : among them is one for two voices, ' Earth's Treasure', which being sung at a concert at Stationers' Hall, was received with great applause. It was reprinted about twenty years ago, but without a name, in a collection entitled The Essex Harmony. He died in 1714, at the age of twenty-seven, and lies buried under the organ of his church. Over the place of his interment is a marble tablet, erected by the Rev. Mr. Prat, at that time minister of St. Botolph's, Aldgate, with an encomiastic inscription too long to be here inserted, but which is given at length in Strype's edition of Stow's Survey, Book II. Page 63.*

WILLIAM CROFT *(a Portrait)*, a native of Nether Eatington, in the county of Warwick, was educated in the royal chapel under Dr. Blow; and upon the erection of an organ in the parish church of St. Anne, Westminster, was elected organist of that church. In 1700 he was admitted a gentleman extraordinary of the chapel royal, and in 1704 was appointed joint-organist of the same with Jeremiah Clark, upon whose decease in 1707 he obtained the whole place. In the year 1708 he succeeded Dr. Blow as master of the children and composer to the chapel royal, as also in his place of organist of the collegiate church of St. Peter, Westminster.

In the year 1711 he resigned his place of organist of St. Anne, Westminster, in favour of Mr. John Isham, who was elected in his room, and in the following year published, but without his name, 'Divine 'Harmony, or a new Collection of select Anthems 'used at her Majesty's Chapels Royal, Westminster Abbey, St. Paul's, &c.' This collection, like that of Clifford, so often mentioned in the course of this work, contains only the words and not the music of the several anthems selected. Before it is a preface, containing a brief account of church music, and an encomium on Tallis and Bird, the former of whom is therein said to have been famous all over Europe. And here the author takes occasion to mention, that although the first anthem in the collection, 'O Lord, the maker of all things,' had been printed with the name of Munday to it, yet that Dr. Aldrich had restored it to its proper author, king Hen. VIII.

In 1713 Croft was created doctor in music in the university of Oxford. His exercise for that degree was an English and also a Latin ode, written by Mr. Joseph Trapp, afterwards Dr. Trapp, which were performed by gentlemen of the chapel, and others from London, in the theatre, on Monday, 13 July, 1713. Both the odes with the music were afterwards curiously engraved in score, and published with the title of Musicus Apparatus Academicus.

In the same year an addition was made to the old establishment of the royal chapel of four gentlemen, a second composer, a lutenist, and a violist, in which was inserted an allowance to Dr. William Croft, as master of the children, of eighty pounds per annum, for teaching the children to read, write, and accompts, and for teaching them to play on the organ and to compose music.

In the year 1724 Dr. Croft published by subscription a noble work of his composition, entitled 'Musica 'Sacra, or select Anthems in score,' in two volumes, the first containing the burial service, which Purcell had begun, but lived not to complete. In the preface the author observes of this work that it is the first essay in music-printing of the kind, it being in score, engraven and stamped on plates; and that for

want of some such contrivance, the music formerly printed in England had been very incorrectly published; as an instance whereof he mentions the Te Deum and Jubilate of Purcell, in which he says the faults and omissions are so gross, as not to be amended but by some skilful hand.

He professes himself ignorant of the state of church music before the reformation, as the same does not appear from any memorials or entries thereof in books remaining in any of our cathedral churches, from whence it is to be inferred that he had never seen or heard of that formula of choral service the Boke of Common Praier noted, composed by John Marbeck, of which, and also of the author, an account has already been given.

He celebrates, in terms of high commendation, for skill and a fine voice, Mr. Elford, of whom he says, ' he was a bright example of this kind, exceeding all ' as far as is known, that ever went before him, and ' fit to be imitated by all that come after him; he ' being in a peculiar manner eminent for his giving ' a due energy and proper emphasis to the words of ' his music.'

The anthems contained in this collection are in that grand and solemn style of composition which should ever distinguish music appropriated to the service of the church. Many of the anthems were made on the most joyful occasions, that is to say, thanksgivings for victories obtained over our enemies during a war in which the interests of all Europe were concerned: upon the celebration of which solemnities it was usual for queen Anne to go in state to St. Paul's Cathedral.* Others are no less worthy to be admired for that majestic and sublime style in which they are written, and of which the following, viz. 'O Lord rebuke me not,' 'Praise the 'Lord, O my soul,' 'God is gone up,' and 'O Lord 'thou hast searched me out,' are shining examples.

Dr. Croft died in August 1727, of an illness occasioned by his attendance on his duty at the coronation of the late king George II. A monument was erected for him at the expence of one of his most intimate friends and great admirers, Humphrey Wyrley Birch, Esq., a gentleman of good estate, and a lawyer by profession,† whereon is inscribed the following character of him:—

---

* As 'I will always give thanks,' for the victory Oudenarde; 'Sing 'unto the Lord,' for the success of our arms in the year 1708. Many other anthems were composed by Dr. Croft and others on the like occasions, which are not in print. *See Bayley's Collection of Anthems.*

† This person was remarkable for the singularity of his character. He was a man of abilities in his profession: he was of counsel for Woolston in the prosecution against him for his blasphemous publications against the miracles of our blessed Saviour, and made for him as good a defence as so bad a cause would admit of. He was possessed of a good estate, and therefore at liberty to gratify his passion for music, which was a very strange one, for he chiefly affected that which had a tendency to draw tears. Of all compositions he most admired the funeral service by Purcell and Croft, and would leave the circuit and ride many miles to Westminster Abbey to hear it. At the funeral of queen Caroline, for the greater convenience of hearing it, he, with another lawyer, who was afterwards a judge, though neither of them could sing a note, walked among the choirmen of the abbey, each clad in a surplice, with a music paper in one hand and a taper in the other. Dr. Croft was a countryman of Mr. Wyrley Birch, which circumstance, together with his great merit in his profession, was Mr. Birch's inducement to the above-mentioned act of munificence, the erection of a monument for him.

GULIELMUS CROFT MUS. DOCT.

NATUS APUD EATINGTON INFERIOREM

IN AGRO WARWICENSI.

Hic juxta Sepultus est
GULIELMUS CROFT
Musicæ Doctor,
Regiiq; Sacelli et hujusce Ecclesiæ Collegiatæ
Organista.
Harmoniam,
A præclarissimo Modulandi Artifice,
Cui alterum jam claudit latus,
Feliciter derivavit;
Suisq; celebratis Operibus,
Quæ Deo consecravit plurima,
Studiose provexit;
Nec Solennitate tantùm Numerorum,
Sed et Ingenii, et Morum, et Vultûs etiam Suavitate,
Egregiè commendavit.
Inter Mortalia
Per quinquaginta fere Annos
Cum summo versatus Candore,
(Nec ullo Humanitatis Offici conspectior
Quàm erga suos quotquot instituerit Alumnos
Amicitiâ et charitate verè Paternâ)
XIV Die Augusti, A. D. M.DCC. XXVII.
Ad Cœlitum demigravit Chorum,
Præsentior Angelorum Concentibus
Suum adstiturus HALLELUJAH.

Expergiscere, mea GLORIA;
Expergiscere, Nablium et cithara;
Expergiscar ego multo mane.

Thus translated: 'Near this place lies interred 'William Croft, doctor in music, organist of the 'royal chapel and this collegiate church. His 'harmony he happily derived from that excellent 'artist in modulation who lies on the other side of 'him.* In his celebrated works, which for the 'most part he consecrated to God, he made a dili- 'gent progress; nor was it by the solemnity of the 'numbers alone, but by the force of his ingenuity, 'and the sweetness of his manners, and even his 'countenance, that he excellently recommended 'them. Having resided among mortals for fifty 'years, behaving with the utmost candour (not 'more conspicuous for any other office of humanity 'than a friendship and love truly paternal towards 'all whom he had instructed), he departed to the 'heavenly choir on the fourteenth day of August, '1727, that, being near, he might add his own 'Hallelujah to the concert of angels. Awake up 'my glory, awake psaltery and harp, I myself will 'awake right early.'†

Dr. Croft was a grave and decent man, and being a sincere lover of his art, devoted himself to the study and practice of it. The bent of his genius led him to church music; nevertheless he composed and published six sets of tunes for two violins and a bass, which in his youth he made for several plays. He also composed and published six Sonatas for two flutes, and six Solos for a flute and a bass. The flute, as we have already observed, being formerly a favourite instrument in this kingdom.

There are also extant in print songs of his composition to a considerable number, and some in manuscript, that have never yet appeared; among the latter is that well-known song of Dr. Byrom, 'My time O ye Muses,'‡ first published in the Spectator, No. 603, to which Dr. Croft made the following tender and pathetic air:—

* Dr. Blow.   † Psalm lvii. verse 9.

‡ The lady the subject of the above ballad, was the eldest daughter of the famous Dr. Richard Bentley, and a university beauty at the time when the author was at college; she was married to Dr. Richard Cumberland, late bishop of Kilmore, a son of Dr. Cumberland, bishop of Peterborough, the author of that noble antidote against the poison of Hobbes's philosophy, 'De Legibus Naturæ Disquisitio Philosophica,' and died a few months ago.

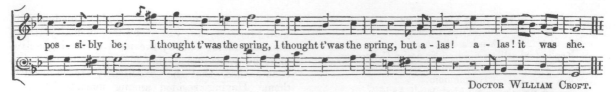

pos - si- bly be; I thought t'was the spring, I thought t'was the spring, but a - las! a - las! it was she.

DOCTOR WILLIAM CROFT.

BOOK XVIII.　CHAP. CLXVIII.

ROBERT CREIGHTON, doctor in divinity, was the son of Dr. Robert Creighton of Trinity college, Cambridge, who was afterwards bishop of Bath and Wells, and attended Charles II. during his exile. In his youth he had been taught the rudiments of music, and entering into holy orders, he sedulously applied himself to the study of church music; he attained to such a degree of proficiency therein, as entitled him to a rank among the ablest masters of his time. In the year 1674 he was appointed a canon residentary, and also chanter of the cathedral church of Wells; and, being an unambitious man, and in a situation that afforded him opportunities of indulging his passion for music, he made sundry compositions for the use of his church, some of which are remaining in the books thereof. He died at Wells in the year 1736, having attained the age of ninety-seven. Dr. Boyce has given to the world an anthem for four voices, 'I will arise and go to 'my father,' composed by Dr. Creighton, which no one can peruse without regretting that it is so short.

WILLIAM TURNER, one of the second set of chapel children, and a disciple of Blow; when he was grown up, his voice broke into a fine countertenor, a circumstance which procured him an easy admittance into the royal chapel, of which he was sworn a gentleman on the eleventh day of October, 1669, and afterwards was appointed a vicar choral in the cathedral church of St. Paul, and a lay vicar of the collegiate church of St. Peter at Westminster. In the year 1696 he commenced doctor of his faculty in the university of Cambridge.

In the choir-books of the royal chapel, and of many cathedrals, is an anthem, 'I will alway give thanks,' called the club anthem, as having been composed by Humphrey, Blow, and Turner, in conjunction, and intended by them as a memorial of the strict friendship that subsisted between them.

Dr. Turner died at the age of eighty-eight, on the thirteenth day of January, 1740, and was buried in the cloister of Westminster Abbey, in the same grave and at the same time with his wife Elizabeth, whose death happened but four days before his own. They had been married but a few years short of seventy, and in their relation exhibited to the world an illustrious example of conjugal virtue and felicity. The daughter and only child of these two excellent persons was married to Mr. John Robinson, organist of Westminster Abbey, and also of two parish churches in London, namely, St. Lawrence Jewry, and St. Magnus, and of her further mention will be made hereafter. She had a good voice, and sang in the opera of Narcissus, performed at the Haymarket in 1720.*

JOHN GOLDWIN was a disciple of Dr. William Child, and on the 12th day of April, 1697, succeeded him as organist of the free chapel of St. George at Windsor. In the year 1703 he was appointed master of the choristers there; in both which stations he continued till the day of his death, which was the 7th of November, 1719. Of the many anthems of his composition, Dr. Boyce has selected one for four voices, 'I have set God alway before me,' which, in respect of the modulation, answers precisely to the character which the doctor has given of the music of Goldwin, viz., that it is singular and agreeable.

CHARLES KING, bred up in the choir of St. Paul's, under Dr. Blow, was at first a supernumerary singer in that cathedral for the small stipend of 14l. a year. In the year 1704 he was admitted to the degree of bachelor in music in the university of Oxford, and, upon the death of Jeremiah Clark, whose sister was his first wife, was appointed Almoner and master of the children of St. Paul's, continuing to sing for his original stipend, until 31 Oct. 1730, when he was admitted a vicar choral of that cathedral, according to the customs and statutes thereof. Besides his places in the cathedral, he was permitted to hold one in a parish church in the city, being organist of St. Bennet Fink, London: in which several stations he continued till the time of his death, which happened on the seventeenth day of March, 1745. With his second wife he had a fortune of seven or eight thousand pounds, which was left her by the widow of Mr. Primatt the chemist, who lived in Smithfield, and also in that house at Hampton which is now Mr. Garrick's. But, notwithstanding this accession of wealth, he left his family in but indifferent circumstances. King composed some anthems, and also services to a great number, and thereby gave occasion to Dr. Greene to say, and indeed he was very fond of saying it, as he thought it a witty sentiment, that 'Mr. King was a very serviceable man.' As a musician he is but little esteemed; his compositions are uniformly restrained within the bounds of mediocrity; they are well known, as being frequently performed, yet no one cares to censure or commend them, and they leave the mind just as they found it. Some who were intimate with him say he was not devoid of genius, but averse to study; which character seems to agree with that general indolence and apathy which were visible in his look

* In the Memoranda of Anthony Wood mention is made of a William Turner, the son of a cook of Pembroke college, Oxon. who had been bred a chorister in Christ-church under Mr. Low, and was afterwards a singing-man in that cathedral: this might be Dr. Turner; and upon searching the books of the parish of St. Margaret, Westminster, it appears that on the sixth day of April, 1708, Henry Turner was elected organist of that church in the room of Bernard Smith, being recommended by Mr. John Robinson: probably, therefore, this Henry Turner was a brother of the doctor.

and behaviour at church, where he seemed to be as little affected by the service as the organ-blower.

John Isham, or, as his name is sometimes corruptly spelt, Isum, though little known in the musical world, was a man of abilities in his profession. Where he received his instruction in music is not known. He was the deputy of Dr. Croft for several years, and was one of the many persons who went from London to Oxford to assist in the performance of his exercise for his doctor's degree. It appears that Mr. Isham, together with William Morley, a gentleman of the royal chapel, were admitted to the degree of bachelor in music at the same time that Croft commenced doctor. In the year 1711 Dr. Croft resigned the place of organist of St. Anne's, Westminster, and by his interest in the parish Isham was elected in his stead.

Isham had no cathedral employment, nor any place in the royal chapel; for which, considering his merit in his profession, no better reason can be suggested, than that perhaps he had not the recommendation of a good voice; at least this is the only way in which we are able to account for his being so frequently a candidate for the place of organist to several churches in and about London. To that of St. Anne, Westminster, he was chosen on the twenty-second day of January, 1711. On the third day of April, 1718, he was elected organist of St. Andrew, Holborn, with a salary of fifty pounds a year; upon which occasion Dr. Pelling, the rector of St. Anne's, moved in vestry that he might be permitted to retain his place in that church, which motion being rejected, Isham quitted the place; and a vacancy at St. Margaret's, Westminster, happening soon after, he stood for organist of that church, and was elected.

He died about the month of June, 1726, having, with very little encouragement to such studies, made sundry valuable compositions for the use of the church. The words of two anthems composed by him, viz., 'Unto thee, O Lord,' and 'O sing unto the Lord a new song,' are in the collection heretofore mentioned to have been made by Dr. Croft, and published in 1712. He joined with William Morley, above mentioned, in the publication of a collection of songs composed by them both, among which is the following one for two voices:—

all . . . her charms are such, we think her some-thing so di - vine, we can - not

all . . . . her charms are such, we think her some-thing so di - vine, we can - - not

gaze, ... not gaze, ... we can - not, can - - not gaze too much.

gaze, ... not gaze, ... we can - not, can - - not gaze too much.

JOHN ISHAM.

DANIEL HENSTRIDGE, organist of the cathedral church of Canterbury about the year 1710, composed sundry anthems. The words of some of them are in the collection entitled Divine Harmony, herein before mentioned to have been published by Dr. Croft in 1712.

JAMES HESLETINE, a disciple of Blow, was organist of the cathedral church of Durham, and also of the collegiate church of St. Catherine, near the Tower, the duty of which latter office he executed by deputy. He was an excellent cathedral musician, and composed a great number of anthems, a few whereof, namely, 'Behold how good and joyful,' and some others, are to be found in the choir books of many of the cathedrals of this kingdom; others, to a great number, he caused to be copied into the books of his own cathedral; but having, as he conceived, been slighted, or otherwise illtreated by the dean and chapter, he in revenge tore out of the church-books all his compositions that were there to be found. He died in an advanced age about twenty years ago.

MAURICE GREENE was the son of a London clergyman, viz., Mr. Thomas Greene, vicar of St. Olave Jewry, and nephew of John Greene, serjeant at law. He was brought up in St. Paul's choir under Mr. King, and upon the breaking of his voice was taken apprentice by Mr. Richard Brind, then organist of that cathedral. Being an ingenious and studious young man, he was very soon distinguished, as well for his skill in musical composition, as for an elegant and original style in performing on the organ. About the year 1716, his uncle then being a member of Sergeant's-Inn, which is situate in the parish of St. Dunstan in the West, London, had interest enough to procure for his nephew, though under twenty years of age, the place of organist of that parish church. In February, 1717, Daniel Purcell, organist of St. Andrew's, Holborn, being then lately dead, and the parish having agreed to make the salary fifty pounds a year, Greene stood for the place, and carried it; but the year following Brind dying, Greene was by the dean and chapter of St. Paul's appointed his successor; and upon this his preferment he quitted both his places. The dean of St. Paul's at this time was Dr. Godolphin, a musical man, and a friend of Greene, and he by his influence with the chapter procured, in augmen-

tation of the ancient appointment or salary of the organist, the addition of a lay vicar's stipend.

In the year 1730 Mr. Greene was created doctor in music of the university of Cambridge, and at the same time was honoured with the title of public professor of music in that university, in the room of Tudway, who it is supposed died some short time before. As there will be farther occasion to speak of Dr. Greene, the conclusion of this memoir concerning him is postponed.

Frequent occasion has been taken, in the course of this work, to mention Estienne Roger, and Michael Charles Le Cene, two booksellers of Amsterdam. These persons were the greatest publishers of music in Europe; and as they greatly improved the method of printing music on copper plates, are entitled to particular notice. And here it must be observed that the practice now spoken of is supposed to have begun at Rome about the time of Frescobaldi, whose second book of Toccatas was printed there in the year 1637, on copper plates engraven. The practice was adopted by the Germans and the French. The English also gave into it, as appears by a collection of lessons by Dr. Bull, Bird, and others, entitled 'Parthenia, or the Maidenhead of the first Music 'that ever was printed for the Virginals.' Notwithstanding these instances, it appears in general that music continued in most countries to be printed on letter-press types; and, to speak of England only, it prevailed so greatly here, that but for the single songs engraven by one Thomas Cross,* who dwelt in Catherine-wheel-court near Holborn, or as it was also called, Snow-hill Conduit, and published from time to time, about the beginning of this century, to a great number, we should scarce have known that any other method of printing music existed among us.

Playford, whose shop, during the space of near half a century, was the resort of all musicians and practitioners in and about London, seems actually to have been himself a printer of music, at least for a great part of his life. His printing-house was in Little Britain,† and there he bred up to the business

<hr/>

* This person is mentioned by Harry Hall in some verses of his prefixed to the second part of the Orpheus Britannicus; and in his verses addressed to Dr. Blow upon the publication of his Amphion Anglicus is this humorous distich :—
    ' While at the shops we daily dangling view
    ' False concord by Tom Cross engraven true.'

† In the London Gazette, Numb. 2136, of 6 May, 1686, is an advertise-

his elder son named John, who printed several books published by his brother Henry. His successors in that business have been mentioned in 'page 736 of this work, and there are a few persons who follow it at this time.

As to printing on copper plates, it had in many respects the advantage of letter-press; the great objection was the expence of it, but this the Dutch artificers found means to reduce; for they contrived by some method, which to others is yet a secret, so to soften the copper, as to render it susceptible of an impression from the stroke of a hammer on a punch, the point whereof had the form of a musical note. The success of this invention is only to be judged of by the numerous articles contained in the Dutch catalogues of music published between the year 1700 and the present time, which seem to indicate little less than that the authors of this discovery had a monopoly of that business.

The difficulty in getting music from abroad, and the high duty on the importation of it, were motives to an attempt of a somewhat similar kind in England. Two persons, namely John Walsh and John Hare, engaged together about the year 1710, to print music on stamped pewter plates. The one had a shop in Catherine-street in the Strand, the other kept a shop, the sign of the Viol, in St. Paul's church-yard,* and another in Freeman's-yard, or court, in Cornhill. They imported from time to time music from Holland, and reprinting it here, circulated it throughout the kingdom to their very great emolument. They were both very illiterate men, neither of them was able to form a title-page according to the rules of grammar, and they seemed both to be too penurious to employ others for the purpose. Their publications were in numberless instances a disgrace to the science and its professors; but they got money, and no one complained.

There lived about this time one Richard Mears, a maker of musical instruments, an ingenious but whimsical man; he had been bred up under his father to that business,† and seeing the slovenly manner in which music was published by Walsh and Hare, and being desirous to participate in so gainful a trade, he became their rival, and proposed to himself and the public to print in a fairer character than pewter would admit of, and to sell his books at a

price little above what they were sold for by the others.

In prosecution of this design he procured of Mattheson, of Hamburgh, who had married an English woman, and was besides secretary to the British resident in that city, the manuscript of two collections of lessons composed by him. These he caused to be engraven on copper in a handsome character, and printed in a thin folio volume. Some years after, Mr. Handel, having composed for the practice of the princess Anne sundry suits of lessons for the harpsichord, made a collection of them, and gave it to Mears to print; but, properly speaking, it was published by the author's amanuensis, Christopher Smith, who then lived at the sign of the Hand and Music-book in Coventry-street, the upper end of the Haymarket. Mears also printed Mr. Handel's opera of Radamistus, and Coriolanus, composed by Attilio. The next undertaking of Mears was an edition of the works of Corelli; for the four operas of Sonatas he had the assistance of a subscription; the work he completed in an elegant manner, but Walsh and Hare damped the sale of it by lowering the price of an edition published by them some years before. Nevertheless Mears continued to go on. He printed the Opera quinta of Corelli in the same character, and undertook to print his Concertos; but in this work he failed; only the first and second violin parts were engraven, the others were stamped, and that in a worse character than had been made use of by Walsh and his colleague.

After a variety of projects, Mears found himself unable to stand his ground; he quitted his shop in St. Paul's church-yard, and some years after set up in Birchin-lane; he continued there about two years, and then removed to London-house-yard in St. Paul's church-yard, where he died about the year 1743, leaving a son of Walsh in possession of almost the whole trade of the kingdom.

There were two other persons, namely J. Cluer and Benjamin Creake, co-partners; the former dwelt in Bow church-yard, and besides being a printer, was a vender of quack medicines; the latter lived in Jermyn-street. These men undertook to stamp music, and printed many of Handel's operas, that is to say, Admetus, Siroe, Scipio, Rodelinda, Julius Cæsar, Tamerlane, Alexander, and some others, but generally in a character singularly coarse and difficult to read. Thomas Cross, junior, a son of him above mentioned, stamped the plates of Geminiani's Solos, and a few other publications, but in a very homely and illegible character, of which he was so little conscious that he set his name to everything he did, even to single songs. William Smith, who had been an apprentice of Walsh, and lived at the sign of Corelli's head, opposite Norfolk-street, in the Strand, and Benjamin Cooke, in New-street, Covent-garden, were printers of music: the former was chiefly employed by such authors as Festing and a few others, who published their works themselves, and had a type of his own, remarkably steady and uniform.

But the last and great improver of the art of

ment for the sale of Playford's printing-house and utensils. The industry of this man, and the pains he took to get an honest livelihood for himself and his family, are very remarkable; and it seems he had a wife who came not behind him in that virtue. At the end of one of his publications in 1679, is an advertisement purporting 'that at Islington, over-against 'the church, Mrs. Playford then kept a boarding-school, where young 'gentlewomen might be instructed in all manner of curious works, as 'also reading, writing, musick, dancing, and the French tongue.'

* In St. Paul's church-yard were formerly many shops where music and musical instruments were sold, for which at this time no better reason can be given, than that the service at that cathedral drew together twice a day all the lovers of music in London; not to mention that the choirmen were wont to assemble there, where they were met by their friends and acquaintance. The rebuilding of the church was but little interruption to these meetings; for though the church was not finished till 1710, divine service was performed in it as soon as the choir was completed, which was in 1697, *for on the second day of December in that year the same was opened, and a solemn thaksgiving celebrated therein on occasion of the peace of Ryswic.*

† The elder Mears kept a shop for the sale of musical instruments opposite the Catherine-wheel inn without Bishopsgate; and in the London Gazette, Numb. 2433, for March 7, 1688, advertised from thence lutes and viols fretted according to Mr. Salmon's proposal, of which an account is given, page 716, in a note, and also page 724.

stamping music in England was one Phillips, a Welchman, who might be said to have stolen it from one Fortier, a Frenchman, and a watchmaker, who stamped some of the parts of Martini's first opera of Concertos, and a few other things. This man, Phillips, by repeated essays arrived at the methods of making types of all the characters used in music. With these he stamped music on pewter plates, and taught the whole art to his wife and son. In other respects he improved the practice of stamping to so great a degree, that music is scarce anywhere so well printed as in England.

About ten years ago one Fougt, a native of Lapland, arrived here, and taking a shop in St. Martin's-lane, obtained a patent for the sole printing of music on letter-press types of his own founding, which were very neat. This patent, had it been contested at law, would undoubtedly have been adjudged void, as the invention was not a new one. He published several collections of lessons and sonatas under it, but the music sellers in London copied his publications on pewter plates, and by underselling, drove him out of the kingdom.

CHAP. CLXIX.

ANDREA ADAMI (*a Portrait*), surnamed da Bolsena, Maestro della Cappella Pontificia, was the author of a book entitled ' Osservationi per ben re-' golare il Coro de i Cantori della Cappella Pontificia, ' tanto nelle Funzioni ordinarie, che straordinairie,' printed at Rome in 1711, 4to; containing, first, a formula of the several functions performed as well on solemn as on ordinary occasions in the pontifical chapel; and, secondly, a brief account of the principal musicians and singers, members of the college of the same chapel.

The preface to this work is a history of the college above mentioned. It begins with an enumeration of the suffrages of the fathers in favour of church music,* in substance as follows :—

'After the death of our Saviour, the singing of ' psalms and hymns was introduced into the church ' by the apostles themselves, according to the docu-' ments of their Master. During the reigns of the ' Roman emperors, in all the eastern and western ' temples, the ecclesiastical functions were performed ' in Canto figurato, till St. Athanasius introduced ' into the church of Alexandria the Canto piano.

'St. Augustine, in his Confessions, lib. ix. Con-' fess. 7, assures us, as does also Dominicus Macrus, ' in his Lexicon,† that St. Ambrose introduced into ' his church at Milan the Canto soave e figurato, in ' imitation of that of the Greek church, commonly ' called χρωματιζομενος. About a century after, that ' is to say, in 460, pope St. Hilary introduced at ' Rome the true Cantus Ecclesiasticus, and founded ' an academy for singers. This is also said by ' Macrus in his Lexicon, but Johannes Diaconus,

'with more probality, ascribes it to St. Gregory ' the Great.

'In the year 590, St. Gregory reformed the ' Cantus Ecclesiasticus, and instituted the Cantus ' Gregorianus, which is still used in the pontifical ' chapel. This great man instituted also a school for ' singers, from which the college of pontifical singers ' now existing derives its origin, and appointed sala-' ries and proper habitations for all the performers. ' St. Gregory took upon himself to preside in the ' school thus founded and endowed by him; after his ' decease one of the most skilful scholars was elected ' Primicerius Scholæ Cantorum, answering to the ' πρωτωψάλτης or λαοσυνακτης in the Greek church.

'Upon the decease of St. Gregory music lost its ' principal support, and declined greatly, until ' Vitalianus, in 683, Leo II., the Sicilian, and ' chiefly venerable Bede, revived and restored it. ' Notwithstanding these eminent men, church music ' fell again into disuse, not less by the incursions of ' barbarians than by the little attention paid to it at ' that time. And although Guido Aretinus, Josquin ' del Prato, and Christopher Morales, a Spaniard, ' supported it in the eleventh and sixteenth centu-' ries by many inventions and improvements, the ' true spirit of it was lost at the time of Marcellus ' II., when Palestrina manifested to that pontiff and ' the world the great powers of sacred music.

'The sacred college, however, maintained itself ' always with great decorum and splendour, even ' when the holy see was transferred to Avignon; but ' it flourished greatly upon the return of Gregory ' IX. to Rome.

'The singers in the pontifical chapel have ever ' been held in great veneration and esteem, even by ' monarchs. Pope Agatho sent John, the principal ' singer in the church of St. Peter, and abbot of the ' monastery of St. Martin, to England, to inquire ' into the state of the catholic religion; and at a ' synod convened by Theodore, archbishop of Can-' terbury, he assisted as the pope's legate.

'All this may be seen at large in the Ecclesiastical ' History of Bede, lib. IV., cap. xviii., where it is ' related that the aforesaid John taught the English ' to sing after the Roman and Gregorian manner, ' and that he died at Tours, and was buried there on ' his return to Italy. The pontifical singers were in ' such estimation, that for particular purposes they ' were the delegates of the pope himself. By a bull ' of Clement IV. it appears that one of the singers of ' the chapel was sent by that pope to Lando, bishop ' of Anagni.

'Mabillon, in his Museo Italico, tom. II., shows ' the pre-eminence due to the college of singers, and ' relates that on a certain occasion, in reading the ' mattin lecture before the pope, on Candlemas-day, ' the singers were preferred to the canons, and that ' the primicerius, or first singer, bore the pontiff's ' mantle: that on Easter-day they received the ' ceremony of the Pax before the subdean and acoly-' thites, and all other inferior orders. Besides that, ' the pope on that day used to administer to them ' the cup, &c., with many other ceremonies.'

---

* Next to the exhortations in St. Paul's Epistles to St. James and to the Colossians to sing psalms and spiritual songs, the following passage in the Confessions of St. Augustine, lib. x. cap. 33, is most frequently adduced in favour of church music. ' Verumtamen cum reminiscor ' lacrymas meas, quas fudi ad cantus ecclesiæ tuæ in primordiis re-' cuperatæ fidei meæ; et nunc ipso, quod moveor non cantu, sed rebus, ' quæ cantantur, (cum liquidâ voce, et convenientissimâ modulatione ' cantantur,) magnam instituti hujus utilitatem rursus agnosco.'

† Hierolexicon, sive Dictionarium sacrum, in quo Ecclesiasticæ voces, &c. elucidantur. Rom. 1677.

ANDREA ADAMI DA BOLSENA CITTADINO ORIGINARIO

VENEZIANO BENEFIZIATO DI S. M. MAGGIORE E

MAGISTRO DELLA CAPPELLA PONTIFICIA.

Adami observes that these marks of distinction declare the good opinion and esteem which the holy see entertained of the singers in the pontifical chapel in former ages. He adds, that when the French singers who accompanied Charlemagne to Rome contended with the sacred college for pre-eminence in music, that emperor could not help deciding in favour of the Roman singers, saying that the rivulets should not be larger than the fountains, and requested Adrian I. to send two Roman singers to France, to teach throughout the kingdom the true Cantus Gregorianus. For this he cites Cardinal Bona, lib. 1. cap. xxv.

In after times it was the uniform endeavour of the Roman pontiffs to procure the ablest singers for the service of the papal chapel, to which end they frequently made instances to secular princes to send to Rome the most celebrated singers in their dominions ; as a proof whereof he inserts the following letter from Leo X. to the marquis of Mantua :—

'Quoniam ad sacra conficienda, precesque divinas 'celebrandas cantore mihi opus est, qui graviori 'voce concinat. Velim, si tibi incommodum non est, 'ut ad me Michælum Lucensem cantorem tuum 'mittas, ut eo nostris in sacris, atque templo, quod 'est omnium celeberrimum, atque sanctissimum, com-'munemque totius orbis terrarum suavitatem et læti-'tiam contineat, uti possim. Datum 3 Kal. Augusti 'anno 2. Romæ.'

He proceeds, 'Many are the privileges and immu-'nities granted to singers of the pontifical chapel ; 'but unhappily few of the instruments by which 'they were granted escaped the flames in the de-'plorable sack of Rome in the pontificate of Clement 'VII. There are existing, however, in the archives 'of the Vatican, and of the castle of St. Angelo, 'a brief of Honorius III., a bull of Clement IV., and 'another of Eugenius IV., in which the singers 'are mentioned with great distinction ; and in one 'of Eugenius IV. they are styled the pope's 'companions, and the constant attendants on his 'person. Calixtus III., Pius II., and Sixtus IV. 'ratify and confirm the said brief and bulls. Inno-'cent VIII. forbids all lawyers, notaries, or attorneys 'taking any fee of the pontifical singers, and em-'powers the bishop maestro di capella to present 'the singers of the chapel to the benefices of the de-'ceased members, that they may perpetually remain 'in the possession of the sacred college. This pri-'vilege was confirmed by Alexander VI. and Julius 'II., and Leo X. ordained that every cardinal that 'says mass in the pontifical chapel should pay four 'ducats to the singers, instead of the usual collation, 'and every bishop or prelate attendant two ducats, 'and granted them many perquisites at a cardinal's 'funeral. Clement VII. and Paul III. enacted several 'laws in favour of the singers. Farther, Julius III. 'declared the college of singers equal in every re-'spect to that of the apostolic writers, and limited it 'to the number of twenty-four.

'Sixtus V. endowed the sacred singers with the 'revenues of the monastery of Santa Maria in Cris-'piano, in the diocese of Taranto of Saint Salvador's 'church in Perugia, and of Santa Maria in Felonica, 'in the diocese of Mantua. He reduced their 'number to twenty-one, and appointed a cardinal for 'their patron and judge in all causes. He also pro-'vided for the old and infirm members by a grant of 'the same allowances as they enjoyed when in actual 'service of the chapel ; but Gregory IV. repealed all 'these bulls of Sixtus V. and made an aggregate 'fund for the college, by which the singers enjoy 'a handsome stipend to this day, with all their former 'privileges and immunities.'

Who was the first maestro di cappella Signor Adami thinks it is impossible to ascertain ; he how-ever says, that originally the maestro was always a bishop ; and this appears by the succession of maestri di cappella, which he gives from the year 1507 to 1574.

He mentions also a Cardinal, Protettore del Col-legio de Cantori della Cappella Pontificia, the first of whom he says was Decio Azzolino, in the pon-tificate of Sixtus V. and continues the succession down to his own time, concluding with Cardinal Pietro Ottoboni, elected 27 Nov. 1700.

The foregoing particulars are contained in the preface to Adami's book ; the book itself exhibits an inside view of the pontifical chapel, otherwise called La Cappella Sistina, as having been built by pope Sixtus IV., *and will be found in the supple-mentary Volume with the Portraits.* After which follows a description of the several functions per-formed in that chapel, as well upon ordinary as solemn occasions ; from which it appears that by the usage of the chapel, motets, and other offices of sundry masters by name are appropriated to peculiar days : thus for instance, Alla Messa dell' Epifania, is sung a motet of Palestrina, 'Surge illuminare 'Jerusalem.' Nella terza Domenica di Quaresima, a motet of Cristoforo Morales, 'Lamentabatur Jacob ;' and on Wednesday and Friday in the Holy Week the Miserere of Allegri, referring to the books of the chapel where the several compositions are to be found.

The several functions described by Adami are performed agreeably to the ancient usage of the Romish church : that in which the Nativity is celebrated seems to be of the dramatic kind, and accounts for that note prefixed to the eighth concerto of Corelli, 'Fatto per la Notte di Natale.' The function itself is thus described : 'Primo Vespero 'di Natale. Il regolamento di questa funzione di-'pende dal sapere, se il Papa nel seguente giorno 'di Natale vuol celebrare egli stesso la messa, perchè 'in tal caso il vespero và ordinato nella stessa guisa 'di quello di S. Pietro, quando che nò, come quello 'di tutt' i Santi.

'Terminato il vespero, restano nel Palazzo Apos-'tolico quelli eminentissimi Cardinali, che nella se-'guente notte vogliono assistere al mattutino, ed 'alla messa, alla quali li ministri del detto Palazzo, 'a spese della reverenda camera danno una lautissima 'cena, con un apparecchio nobile di varj trionfi, che 'rappresentano i fatti della Natività del nostro Re-'dentore. Prima della cena è costume dare ancora

' alli detti eminentissimi un virtuoso divertimento
' di musica, con una cantata volgare sopra la Nati-
' vità del Bambino Gesù, la quale si dee regolare
' dal nostro Signor Maestro di Cappella, e però pre-
' ventivamente dovrà egli portarsi da Monsignor
' Maggiordomo, a cui spetta la direzone di tutta
' questa funzione, per intender da esso l'elezione
' tanto del poeta, quanto del compositore della musica;
' e poi dovrà scieglier i migliori cantori del nostro
' collegio per cantarla; e dopo terminata, unito alli
' cantori, e egli stromenti dovrà portarsi al luogo
' destinato per la cena, che ancora essi suol dare la
' reverenda camera apostolica.'

The second part contains a description of the
extraordinary functions, namely these that follow:—
Nella Creazione del nuovo Pontefice. Nella
Consagrazione del nuovo Pontefice. Nella Consagrazione che fa il Papa di qualche Vescovo. Nella
Coronazione del nuovo Pontefice. Nel Possesso del
nuovo Pontefice. Nell' Anniversario della Creazione del Pontefice. Nell' Anniversario della Coronazione del Pontefice. Nel Consistoro pubblico.
Nell' aprire la Porta Santa. Nel serrare la Porta
Santa. Nella Canonizazione de' Santi. Nel Batte-
simo di qualche Ebreo. Nelle Processioni straor-
dinarie per Giubilei, o Indulgenze. Nell' Essequie
de' Sommi Pontefici. Settima Essequie. Decimo
Giorno. Nell' Anniversario del Sommo Pontefice
Defonto. Nell' Essequie degli Eminentissimi Car-
dinali Defonti. Nell' Essequie d'un nostro Compagno
Defonto, ed altri Anniversarj della Cappella. Nell'
Anniversario di Marazzoli, e de' nostri Compagni
Defonti a S. Gregorio. Nelle Cappelle Cardinalizie
di San Tomasso d'Aquino, e San Bonaventura. Nella
Festa della Annunziata. Per S. Marta Festa di
Palazzo alla sua Chiesa vicino a S. Pietro.

The remainder of the book consists of an account
of the pontifical singers from the time of Paul III.
to that of the then reigning pope, Clement XI.
extracted from the books of the chapel, and other
authentic memorials, with sundry historical particulars relating to such of them as were celebrated
for their compositions. The following is the substance of this account, so far as it regards the most
eminent of them :—

' Many are the singers who distinguish themselves
' in the pontifical chapel since the first institution
' thereof; amongst them was Jacopo Pratense, who
' flourished in the sixteenth century, and was ad-
' mitted a singer in the said chapel under Sixtus IV.
' His name is engraven in the choir of the Vatican
' palace. His works, consisting of Masses, were
' published at Fossombrone, in three volumes, in
' the years 1515 and 1516, by Ottavio de Petrucci,
' the first inventor of printing music.

' Giacomo Arcadelt, maestro di cappella to Cardinal
' di Lorena, was esteemed one of the first of his
' time of the composers of madrigals, five books
' whereof composed by him were printed at Venice;
' one of the finest among them is that celebrated
' one, " Il bianco e dolce Cigno cantando muore."

' In 1544, under Paul III. was admitted into the
' sacred college, Christoforo Morales of Sevil.' The

particulars respecting this person, as also Palestrina,
are already inserted in this work.

' In this century, under Pius IV. flourished Ales-
' sandro Romano. He was for his skill in playing
' on the viol called Alessandro della Viola. He was
' the inventor of Canzonets for four and five voices.
' Upon leaving the chapel he changed his name to
' that of Julius Cæsar, and embraced the monastic
' life in the Olivetan congregation.

' About the year 1562 the reverend Father Fran-
' cesco Soto da Langa, by birth a Spaniard, and
' a soprano singer, began to display his musical
' talents. He was of the congregation of St. Philip
' Neri, and the thirteenth priest in succession after
' that saint; and founded a nunnery at Rome in
' honour of St. Teresa. He died in 1619, aged 85.

' Arcangelo Crivelli Bergamasco, a tenor, admitted
' in 1583, published divers works highly esteemed,
' and particularly a book of Masses. Many of his
' compositions are sung in the apostolic chapel.

' In 1631 the reverend father Girolamo Rosini da
' Perugia, a soprano, was esteemed for his voice and
' fine manner of singing. He stood candidate for
' a place of singer in the pontifical chapel; and
' although heard and approved of by Clement VIII.
' the Spanish singers contrived to get him excluded,
' for no other reason than that he was not of their
' country,* and elected in his stead a man very much
' his inferior. At which repulse being highly mor-
' tified he took the habit of St. Francis, and became
' a brother in a convent of Capuchins. But the
' pontiff being informed of the injustice done him,
' severely reprimanded the Spanish singers, and re-
' called the Perugian, annulling the solemn vow he
' had taken upon his entering into the monastic life.
' He was received afterwards into the congregation
' of St. Philip Neri in 1606, eleven years after the
' death of that saint; and, being a man of exemplary
' goodness, was favoured by all the popes to the
' time of his death.

' Teofilo Gargano da Gallese, a contralto, was
' admitted in 1601. He left a legacy to maintain
' four students, natives of this country, to enable
' them to prosecute the study of music at Rome, and
' died in 1648.

' Vincenzo de Grandis da Monte Albotto, a con-
' tralto, was admitted in 1605, under Paul V. and
' published many works, particularly a set of Psalms,
' printed by Philip Kespeol.

' In 1610 the reverend Martino Lamotta, a Sicilian,
' and a tenor; in 1612, Giovanni Domenico Poliaschi,
' a Roman tenor; and in 1613 Francesco Severi
' Perugino, a soprano, were severally admitted; the
' two latter distinguished themselves by their several
' compositions dedicated to Cardinal Borghesi in
' 1618 and 1615.

' The reverend Santi Naldino, a Roman contralto,
' is mentioned in 1617. He was a Silvestrine monk,
' and a good composer, as may be seen by his printed
' Motets. He died in 1666, and was buried in S.
' Stefano del Cacco, as appears by a monument in

---

* It seems that till his time no native Italian had ever been a soprano
singer in the chapel.

' the said church, where there is a fine canon of his
' composition.

' Under Gregory XV. 1662, was admitted as a
' soprano, Cavalier Loreto Vittori da Spoleti, an
' excellent composer of airs and cantatas. He set
' to music the favorite drama of Galatea, which
' was received with uncommon applause, and printed
' with a dedication to Cardinal Barberini. He was
' buried in the church of Santa Maria sopra Minerva,
' where is a monument for him.

' In 1628, under Urban VIII. the reverend
' Odoardo Ceccarelli da Mevania was admitted a
' tenor; he was a man of letters, and collected
' several rules about our constitution for the use of
' the Puntatore; and was famous for setting music
' to Latin words.

' In 1639, Stefano Landi, a Roman contralto, a
' beneficiary clerk of St. Peter's, published the first
' book of Masses for four and five voices.

' In 1636 the reverend Filippo Vitali, a Florentine
' tenor, and an excellent church composer, was ad-
' mitted. He published Hymns and Psalms.

' In 1637 Marco Marazzoli, a tenor. He composed
' several oratorios, which were much applauded,
' and the same had been many times performed in
' the Chiesa Nuova, in the hearing of Adami himself.
' He was an excellent player on the harp, and has
' left many compositions behind him.

' In 1642 Marco Savioni, a Roman contralto. He
' published several chamber-compositions in parts,
' and sundry other works very much esteemed by
' the judges of harmony.

' Under pope Innocent X. in 1645, was admitted
' Bonaventura Argenti Perugino, a soprano. He
' was highly favoured by cardinal Pio Mori. For
' defraying the expences of finishing the church of
' St. Mary Vallicella, he bequeathed six thousand
' crowns to the fathers of the Oratory, and they out
' of gratitude buried him in their own vault.

' The reverend Domenico del Pane, a Roman
' soprano, was admitted into the college in 1654;
' an excellent composer in the grand style. He left
' many valuable compositions.*

' And under Alexander VII. the reverend father
' Antonio Ceati, a Florentine, and a tenor, was ad-
' mitted into the college 1 Jan. 1660.' A memoir
of this person has a place in page 595 of this work.
Adami says that he excelled both in the chamber
and the theatric styles; and that he composed an
opera, La Dori, reckoned a masterpiece in its kind.

In the course of this work are contained accounts
of the following persons, members of the college
of pontifical singers, viz., Christopher Morales,
Palestrina, Gio. Maria Nanino, Felice Anerio, Luca
Marenzio, Ruggiero Giovanelli, Tomasso Lodovico
da Vittoria, Antimo Liberati, and Matteo Simonelli.
The substance of these severally is herein before
inserted in the article respecting each person.

* Of these one of the most celebrated is a work entitled ' Messe dell'
' Abbate Domenico dal Pane, Soprano della Cappella Pontificia, à quattro,
' cinque, sei, ed otto Voci, estratte da exquisiti Mottetti del Palestrina.
' In Roma, 1687.' This is a collection of masses made on the following motets of Palestrina, ' Doctor bonus,' from which the anthem ' We have heard
with our ears' is taken, and ' Domine quando veneris,' à 4 voci. ' Stella
' quam viderant Magi,' ' O Beatum Virum,' and ' Jubilat Deo,' à 5 voci,
' Canite Tuba in Sion,' and ' Fratres ego enim accepi,' à 6 voci.

The design of Adami is evidently to exalt into
importance the college of pontifical singers. A work
of this kind afforded the author a fair opportunity
of deducing the history of choral singing and church
music, from the time of its first introduction, through
a variety of periods, in some whereof it was in
danger of an almost total repudiation: The materials for such an historical account are very copious,
and lie dispersed in the writings of the ecclesiastical
historians, ritualists, and the Corpus Juris Canonici;
and, above all, in the Lexicon of Dominicus Macrus,
cited by him; besides what was to be extracted
from Bulls, Breviates, and other pontifical instruments, containing grants in their favour. It seems
that Adami was aware of the information that these
would afford, for he has cited Durandus, Cardinal
Bona, and other writers on the subject; but his
extracts from them are very brief and unsatisfactory.
The account of the contest between the Roman and
French singers in the time of Charlemagne, though
related by Baronius and the French chroniclers,
with a variety of curious particulars, Adami has
but slightly mentioned; which is the more to be
wondered at, seeing that the issue of the contest was
a triumph of the Roman over the Gallican ritual.

The description of the several functions performed
in the pontifical chapel we may suppose to be very
accurate; and we learn from it that many compositions of great antiquity, and which are in the
collections of the curious in this kingdom, are still
held in high estimation.

The lives of such of the pontifical singers as he
has thought proper to distinguish, are simple narra-
tions of uninteresting facts; they can no way be
considered as portraits of the persons whom they
are intended to represent; and they are greatly
deficient in respect of those reflections, which a paucity of events renders necessary in biographical
writings; so that, upon the whole, Adami's work is
little more than an obituary, or at best a register;
and if we allow it to be a correct one, we give it
all due praise.

CHAP. CLXX.

The Italian music had for near fifty years been
making its way in this country, and at the beginning
of this century many persons of distinction, and gentlemen, had attained to great proficiency in the performance on the viol da gamba, the violin, and the
flute. In the year 1710 a number of those, in conjunction with some of the most eminent masters of
the time, formed a plan of an academy for the study
and practice of vocal and instrumental harmony, to
be held at the Crown and Anchor tavern, opposite
St. Clement's church, in the Strand, in which was a
spacious room, in every respect proper for musical
performances. The principal persons engaged in
this laudable design were Mr. Henry Needler, a gentleman who held a considerable post in the excise;
Mr. John Christopher Pepusch, Mr. John Ernest
Galliard, a fine performer on the hautboy, and a very
elegant composer; Mr. Bernard Gates, of the queen's

chapel; and many other persons, whose names at this distance of time are not to be recovered.

The foundation of this society was laid in a library, consisting of the most celebrated compositions, as well in manuscript as in print, that could be procured either at home or abroad; these were a voluntary donation from several of the members of the society. With the assistance of the gentlemen of the chapel royal, and the choir of St. Paul's, and the boys belonging to each, and the small contribution of half a guinea a member, the academy set out, and greatly to the improvement of themselves, and the delight of such as heard their performances, this institution continued to flourish till the year 1728, when an accident happened that went very near to destroy them, of which, and other particulars of their history, a relation will be given hereafter.

Mr. HENRY NEEDLER (a Portrait), was the grandson of a gentleman in the army, Colonel Needler, a royalist, who served under General Monk about the time of the restoration, and a brother's son of Mr. Henry Needler of the Navy-office, a collection of whose poems was published in 1724. His father was a good performer on the violin, and instructed him in the practice of that instrument; but having attained in a short time to a considerable proficiency on it, he was committed to the care of Purcell, by whom he was instructed in the principles of harmony. After that he became a pupil of Mr. John Banister, who played the first violin at Drury-lane theatre, and was esteemed one of the best performers in his time.

Being an excellent penman and arithmetician, before he had attained the age of twenty-five he was promoted to the place of Accountant-general of the Excise, the duties of which he discharged with the utmost care and fidelity. Notwithstanding that multiplicity of business in which his office involved him, and the close attendance which it obliged him to, having acquired in his youth a habit of industry and application, he found means to prosecute his musical studies, and to form connections of the best kind. At that time there were weekly concerts at the houses of the duke of Rutland, the earls of Burlington and Essex, lord Percival, father of the late earl of Egmont, and others of the nobility, at which Mr. Needler was always a welcome visitant as a gentleman performer. The soundness of his judgment and the goodness of his taste led him to admire the music of Corelli, and it is said that no person of his time was equal to him in the performance of it, and he stands distinguished by this remarkable circumstance, that he was the first person that ever played the concertos of Corelli in England, and that upon the following occasion. He was used to frequent a weekly concert at the house of Mr. John Loeillet, in Hart-street, Covent-garden. There lived at that time opposite Southampton-street, in the Strand, where Mr. Elmsley now resides, Mr. Prevost, a bookseller, who dealt largely to Holland. It happened that one day he had received a large consignment of books from Amsterdam, and among them the concertos of Corelli, which had just then been published; upon looking at them he thought

of Mr. Needler, and immediately went with them to his house in Clement's-lane, behind St. Clement's church in the Strand, but being informed that Mr. Needler was then at the concert at Mr. Loeillet's, he went with them thither. Mr. Needler was transported with the sight of such a treasure; the books were immediately laid out, and he and the rest of the performers played the whole twelve concertos through, without rising from their seats.*

Mr. Needler was one of that association which gave rise to the establishment of the Academy of Ancient Music, and being a zealous friend to the institution, attended constantly on the nights of performance, and played the principal violin part. The toils of business he alleviated by the study of music, and in his leisure hours employed himself in putting into score the works of the most celebrated Italian masters, with a view to improve himself, and enrich the stores of the academy.

He dwelt for the greatest part of his life in an old-fashioned house in Clement's-lane, behind St. Clement's church, in the Strand, and was there frequently visited by Mr. Handel, and other the most eminent masters of his time. He married late, and having no children, nor any worldly pursuits to engage him, other than the discharge of the duties of his office, in which he was very punctual, he indulged himself in his love of music to such a degree, as to forego all other pleasures for the sake of it; and the delight he took in it seemed to have such an effect upon his mind, as to induce in him a habit of cheerfulness and good-humour. When he was at the Academy he seemed to be at home; strangers that came as visitors were introduced to him at their first entrance: he did the honours of the society in a manner becoming a gentleman, and was in his deportment courteous and obliging to all.

He was a very fine and delicate performer on the violin, and, till he was advanced in years, when his arm grew stiff, was equal, in point of execution, to the performance of any composition that was not too difficult to be good for anything, and in the performance of Corelli's music, in particular, he was not exceeded by any master of his time.

* Besides Mr. Needler, other gentlemen, not of the profession of music, have been distinguished for their skill and performance. Mr. Valentine Oldys, an apothecary in Black-Friars, was the author of several compositions in Court Ayres, published in 1655. Lord Keeper North, when young, was one of the greatest violists of his time, and afterwards became a good composer, and an excellent theorist. Dr. Nathaniel Crew, afterwards lord Crew, bishop of Durham, when at Oxford played his part in concert on the viol da gamba. The family of the Harringtons, descendants of Sir John Harrington, has produced several both theoretic and practical musicians. Sir Roger L'Estrange was an excellent violist. Mr. Sherard, an apothecary in Crutched-Friars, played finely on the violin, and composed two operas of Sonatas. Dr. Cæsar, a physician of an ancient family at Rochester, many of whose ancestors are interred in that cathedral, composed two excellent Catches, printed in the Pleasant Musical Companion, published in 1726. Col. Blathwayt, whose picture when a boy, painted by Kneller, hangs in the music-school, Oxford, was a prodigy on the harpsichord at fourteen. He had been taught that instrument abroad by Alessandro Scarlatti. Dr. Arbuthnot composed an anthem: the words of it 'As pants the hart,' are in a collection printed in 1712. without a name, but made by Dr. Croft, who wrote the preface to the book. In the collection of services and anthems made by Dr. Tudway for the earl of Oxford, in seven volumes, now in the British Museum, is a Te Deum and Jubilate composed by the hon. and rev. Mr. Edward Finch, afterwards dean of York, temp. Anne. Mr. Bendall Martyn, secretary to the commisioners of the Excise, played on the violin, and composed fourteen Sonatas for that instrument which were published upon his decease about fifteen years ago. And lastly, Capt. Marcellus Laroon, the son of old Laroon the painter, played on the violoncello, and composed Solos for that instrument. This gentleman died at Oxford in 1772

HENRY NEEDLER ESQ;

This ingenious and amiable man died on the eighth day of August, 1760, aged seventy-five, and was buried at Frinsbury, near Rochester.*

During the time that Britton's concert subsisted, it was resorted to by the most eminent masters, who gave their performance gratis. Upon the absence of such performers as Banister, Corbett, or such others as usually played the principal violin, that part was taken by Mr. Woolaston, the portrait painter, of whom mention has been made before. He was a sound performer on that instrument, as also on the flute. Being but an indifferent painter, he, upon Britton's decease, with a view to the increase of his acquaintance, and consequently his business, gave a concert on Wednesday evenings at his house in Warwick-court, in Warwick-lane, Newgate-street, which was frequented by the best families in the city, especially Dissenters, till the establishment of the concert at the Castle tavern in Paternoster-row, of which there will shortly be occasion to speak. In the interim it is necessary to take notice that upon the breaking up of Britton's concert, the persons that frequented it formed themselves into little societies, that met at taverns in different parts of the town for the purpose of musical recreation. One of these was at the Angel and Crown tavern in White-chapel, where the performance was both vocal and instrumental: the persons that frequented it were Mr. Peter Prelleur, then a writing-master in Spital-fields, but who played on the harpsichord, and after-wards made music his profession, and by study and application became such a proficient in it as to be ranked among the first masters of his time. Mr. John Gilbert, a mathematical instrument maker, and clerk to a Dissenters' meeting in Eastcheap, and Mr. John Stephens, a carpenter in Goodman's-fields, two persons with good voices, and who had been used to sing Purcell's songs, were also of the number. Others of Britton's friends accepted a hospitable in-vitation to the house of Mr. William Caslon, the letter founder. This person had been bred to the business of engraving letters on gun-barrels, and served his apprenticeship in the Minories; but, being an ingenious man, he betook himself to the business of letter-founding, and by diligence and unwearied application, not only freed us from the necessity of importing printing types from Holland, but in the beauty and elegance of those made by him surpassed the best productions of foreign artificers.

Mr. Caslon meeting with encouragement suitable to his deserts, settled in Ironmonger-row, in Old-street, and being a great lover of music, had fre-quent concerts at his house, which were resorted to by many eminent masters: to these he used to invite his friends, and those of his old acquaintance, the companions of his youth. He afterwards removed to a large house in Chiswell-street, and had an organ in his concert-room: after that he had stated monthly concerts, which for the convenience of his friends, and that they might walk home in safety when the performance was over, were on that Thursday in the month which was nearest the full moon, from which circumstance his guests were wont humorously to call themselves Lunatics. The performers at Mr. Caslon's concert were Mr. Woolaston, and oftentimes Mr. Charles Froud, organist of Cripplegate church, to whom, whenever he came, Mr. Woolaston gave place, and played the second violin; Mr. William De Santhuns, who had been an organist in the country, and succeeded Mr. Prelleur as organist of Spitalfields; Mr. Samuel Jeacock, a baker at the corner of Berkeley-street in Red Lion-street, Clerk-enwell, and many others, who occasionally resorted thither. The performance consisted mostly of Corelli's music, intermixed with the overtures of the old English and Italian operas, namely, Clotilda, Hydaspes, Camilla, and others, and the more modern ones of Mr. Handel. In the intervals of the per-formance the guests refreshed themselves at a side-board, which was amply furnished; and, when it was over, sitting down to a bottle of wine, and a decanter of excellent ale, of Mr. Caslon's own brew-ing, they concluded the evening's entertainment with a song or two of Purcell's sung to the harpsichord, or a few catches, and about twelve retired.

These and a few others for the same purpose were select meetings, but there were also about this time, though but very few in comparison with the present, public concerts, to which all were admitted that brought either tickets or money. Performances of this kind had been exhibited from about the year 1700, at the great room in York-buildings and other places, but these were discontinued about the year 1720, and Stationers' Hall in the city, and the Devil tavern at Temple-bar, were the places from whence concerts were most frequently advertised. The method of announcing them was by advertisement in the papers, and bills posted up, in which the names of the principal singers were generally inserted. There was one Mr. Charles Young, organist of the church of Allhallows, Barking, who had three daughters, namely, Cecilia, Esther, and Isabella;† the first of these had an excellent voice, and was a good singer; at the concert here spoken of she was generally the first performer; and as few people then resorted to concerts but such as were real lovers of music, three or four performances of this kind in a winter were found to be as many as the town would bear; and these were in a great measure dis-continued upon the establishment, in 1724, of the Castle concert in Paternoster-row, of which the fol-lowing is the history:—

There dwelt at the west corner of London-house-yard, in St. Paul's church-yard, at the sign of the Dolphin and Crown, one John Young, a maker of violins and other musical instruments; this man had a son whose Christian name was Talbot, who had been brought up with Greene in St. Paul's choir, and had attained to great proficiency on the violin, as Greene had on the harpsichord. The merits of the two Youngs, father and son, are cele-brated in the following quibbling verses, which were set to music in the form of a catch, printed in the Pleasant Musical Companion, published in 1726:—

---

* On Tuesday se'nnight died, at Dorking in Surrey, Mrs. Hester Needler, relict of Henry Needler Esq. in the 91st year of her age; a lady greatly beloved by all who knew her, for her benevolent disposition.—St. James' Chronicle, June 5, 1783.

† Afterwards Mrs. Arne and Mrs. Lampe.

You scrapers that want a good fiddle well strung,
You must go to the man that is old while he's young,
But if this same fiddle you fain would play bold,
You must go to his son, who'll be young when he's old.
There's old Young and young Young, both men of renown,
Old sells and young plays the best fiddle in town,
Young and old live together, and may they live long,
Young to play an old fiddle, old to sell a new song.

This young man, Talbot Young, together with Greene and several persons, had weekly meetings at his father's house for the practice of music. The fame of this performance spread far and wide, and in a few winters the resort of gentlemen performers was greater than the house would admit of; a small subscription was set on foot, and they removed to the Queen's Head tavern in Paternoster-row. Here they were joined by Mr. Woolaston and his friends, and also by a Mr. Franchville, a fine performer on the viol da gamba. And after a few winters, being grown rich enough to hire additional performers, they removed in the year 1724, to the Castle in Paternoster-row, which was adorned with a picture of Mr. Young painted by Woolaston.

The Castle concert continuing to flourish for many years, auditors as well as performers were admitted subscribers, and tickets were delivered out to the members in rotation for the admission of ladies. Their fund enabling them, they hired second-rate singers from the opera; and many young persons of professions and trades that depended upon a numerous acquaintance, were induced by motives of interest to become members of the Castle concert.

Mr. Young continued to perform in this society till the declining state of his health obliged him to quit it; after which time Prospero Castrucci, and other eminent performers in succession continued to lead the band. About the year 1744, at the instance of an alderman of London, now deservedly forgotten, the subscription was raised from two guineas to five, for the purpose of performing oratorios. From the Castle this society removed to Haberdashers' hall, where they continued for fifteen or sixteen years; from thence they removed to the King's Arms in Cornhill, where they now remain.

Upon the plan of the Castle concert another society was formed at the Swan tavern, now the King's Arms, in Exchange Alley, Cornhill. The master of the house, one Barton, had been a dancing-master, and loved music; the great room in his house was one of the best for the purpose of any in London; a great number of merchants and opulent citizens raised a subscription for a concert about the year 1728: Mr. Obadiah Shuttleworth played the first violin; after him Mr. John Clegg, then Mr. Abraham Brown, and after him Mr. Michael Christian Festing. This society flourished for about twelve years, but it broke into factions, which were put an end to by the melancholy accident of a fire, which, on the evening of a performance, on the twenty-fourth day of March, 1748, consumed the books and instruments, and among the latter a fine organ made by Byfield, and laid the house and adjacent buildings in ashes.

CHAP. CLXXI.

It is now necessary, in order to lay a foundation for an account of the introduction of the Italian opera into this kingdom, to recur to the beginning of the century, and, having mentioned Scarlatti, Gasparini, Bononcini, Conti, and some other composers in the theatric style, to take notice of some of the most eminent instrumental performers of the time, as also of a few of the most applauded singers of both sexes.

At this time there were many performers in Italy, who for their excellence on various instruments were celebrated throughout Europe; namely, for the harpsichord, BERNARDO PASQUINI, and his scholar BERNARDO GAFFI, as also ALESSANDRO SCARLATTI; these were settled at Rome. At Venice were POLLAROLI, and a son of Scarlatti, called SCARLATTINO, the wonder of his time. For the violin at Rome Corelli was without a rival: next to him his scholar MATTEO and ANTONIO MONTENARI were most esteemed. At Florence MARTINO BITTI was reckoned the most famous, and at Venice ALBINONI; at Naples GIOVANNI CARLO CAITO and PEDRILLO, as also GIOVANNI ANTONIO GUIDO; and above all, CARLO AMBROSIO LUNATI, of Milan, surnamed Il Gobbo della Regina, who with Sifacio, a famous singer, was here in England in the reign of James II.

For the violoncello BUONONCINI was indisputably the first; at Turin, FIORE; at Bologna, GIUSEPPE JACHINI; and at Rome, PIPPO AMADIO were in the highest degree of reputation.

On the theorbo, TEDESCHINO of Florence was esteemed a most capital performer; but he was afterwards excelled by Conti, he who was in England in the year 1708, and had a hand in the opera of Clotilda.

Contemporary with Corelli and Pasquini at Rome was GAETANO, an admirable master on the theorbo, who died very young. These three persons were performers at the same time in the opera at Rome. PETRUCCIO and DOMENICO SARRI of Naples were at the same time celebrated for their performance on that instrument; and GALLETTI on the cornet was deemed the greatest performer in the world.

Of singers, he that was known by the name of SIFACIO, from his having appeared in the character of Syphax in some opera abroad, was reckoned the first. He had been in England a singer in the chapel of James II., but, after a short stay, returned to Italy; and about the year 1699, in his passage from Bologna to Ferrara, was murdered; he had a very fine voice, and was remarkable for a very chaste and pure manner of singing, and fine expression.

LUIGINO, a singer in the chapel of the emperor Joseph, was also in high repute. He died in 1707, and had been a scholar of Pistocchi, who, as having by the introduction of a chaste, elegant, and pathetic style, greatly improved the practice of vocal music among the Italians, was of such eminence, that he merits to be particularly noticed.

FRANCESCO ANTONIO PISTOCCHI had a very fine

soprano voice, which by a dissolute life he lost, together with a fortune which he had acquired by the exercise of it. In this distress he was reduced to the necessity of becoming a copyist, in which employment, by his attention and assiduity, he arrived at such a degree of skill in music, as to be able himself to compose. In the course of a few years he discovered that his voice was returning; and having experienced great misery while he was deprived of that faculty, he practised incessantly till it settled into a fine contralto. With this valuable acquisition he determined to travel, and accordingly visited most of the courts in Europe; and from a variety of manners in singing formed that elegant style, which the more modern refinements in singing render it difficult to conceive of. The encouragement he met with, and the offer of the employment of chapel-master to the Margrave of Anspach, with a handsome stipend, induced him to settle at that court, where in the possession of a newly acquired fortune he continued many years. At length he returned to Italy, and retired to a convent, in which he died about the year 1690.

There is extant of Pistocchi's composition, a collection of cantatas, duets, and songs, entitled 'Scherzi-Musicali,' dedicated to Frederic III., Margrave of Brandenburg Anspach, published by Estienne Roger of Amsterdam; at the end are two airs, one to French the other to German words; in the former he professes to have imitated the style of Lully, in the latter that of the German composers.

There were about the beginning of this century many other fine singers, but by some it is said that the excellences of them all were united in Nicolini Grimaldi, called Signor Nicolini di Napoli, who, not more for his singing than his personal merit, had been dignified with the title of Cavaliero di San Marco.

This person came into England in the year 1708, and made his first appearance in the opera of Camilla. Mr Galliard, in a note in his translation of Tosi's Opinioni de' Cantori, says that he was both a fine actor and a good singer. Mr. Addison in the Spectator, No. 405, has given him the same character, and complimented him on the generous approbation he had given to an English opera, Calypso and Telemachus, written by Mr. Hughes, and set by Mr. Galliard, when the other Italians were in a confederacy to ruin it. Nicolini seems to have enjoyed the friendship both of Steele and Addison. He entertained an affection for them and their writings, and was inclined to study the English language, for the pleasure of reading the Tatler.* He was in England at two or three different periods: upon his quitting it the first time it was supposed he meant not to return; and the assurance thereof gave occasion to the following verses, published in Steele's Miscellany, which bespeaks the general sentiments of the English with regard to the Italian opera and singers:—

Begone, our nation's pleasure and reproach!
Britain no more with idle trills debauch,

* Letters from several eminent persons deceased, including the Correspondence of John Hughes, Esq. vol. I. page 60.

Back to thy own unmanly Venice sail,
Where luxury and loose desires prevail;
There thy emasculating voice employ,
And raise the triumphs of the wanton boy.
Long, ah! too long the soft enchantment reign'd,
Seduc'd the wise, and ev'n the brave enchain'd;
Hence with thy curst deluding song! away!
Shall British freedom thus become thy prey;
Freedom which we so dearly used to prize,
We scorn'd to yield it—but to British eyes.
   Assist ye gales, with expeditious care,
Waft this prepost'rous idol of the fair;
Consent ye fair, and let the trifler go,
Nor bribe with wishes adverse winds to blow:
Nonsense grew pleasing by his syren arts,
And stole from Shakespeare's self our easy hearts.†

VALENTINI was a singer on the opera stage in London at the same time with Nicolini. He had been a scholar of Pistocchi, and was, in the opinion of Mr. Galliard, though not so powerful in voice or action as Nicolini, much more chaste in his singing.

Of the female singers the following were in the first degree of eminence at the end of the last century, and at the beginning of this.

SIGNORA GIORGINA, a great favourite of Christina queen of Sweden, as also of the vice-queen of Naples, to whom she was first lady of honour, and by whose interest she was ennobled with the dignity of a marchioness of Spain.

MARGARITINA SAN NICOLA, she was the principal singer in the court of Dresden, and was highly favoured by the elector of Saxony. In Italy Signora POLLACINI and Signora MARCHESINA; as also those other females, BOMBACE, MIGNATTA, BARBARUCCI, DIAMANTINA, and CECCA, were highly celebrated.

SIGNORA SANTINI sang in several of the courts of Germany with great applause; afterwards she went to Venice, where Sig. Antonio Lotti, the famous chapel-master of St. Mark's, married her.

FRANCESCA VANINI BOSCHI and her husband were in England in 1710, and sang in Mr. Handel's opera of Rinaldo: she continued here only one season, at the end whereof she went to Venice, leaving her husband behind her: She was at this time in years, and her voice upon the decline. Signor Giuseppe Boschi had a fine bass voice. He sang here in the opera of Hydaspes after his wife left England. Mr. Handel composed songs on purpose for him, and among many others, those two fine ones, 'Del min-'nacciar in vento,' in Otho, and 'Deh Cupido,' in Rodelinda.

There was also a woman, who had sung in many of the courts of Europe, yet was known by no other appellation than that of the Baroness. Some have supposed her to be the unfortunate relict of Stradella, see page 653 of this work, but this is a mistake. She was a German, a very fine singer, and, being in

† It seems that he was used to frequent Bath, and that he sang in public there. In Tony Aston's song entitled 'The Bath Medley,' is the following line:—

'Here's half a guinea to hear Nicolini!'
Mus. Misc. Vol. III. page 162.
And among Durfey's songs is one entitled 'The Bath Teazers,' with this stanza:—

'Then comes Nicolini to teaze them the more,
'Subscribe your two guineas to make up fourscore.
'I never performed at so low rate before.'
Pills to Purge Melancholy, Vol. VI. page 283.

England, sang in the operas of Camilla, the Triumph of Love, and Pyrrhus and Demetrius.

From the account herein before given of the progress of music in this country after the Restoration, it evidently appears that the taste of the English was accommodating itself to that of the Italians, not to say of the French, who in this respect were then as little worthy of imitation as they are now. Cibber, in the Apology for his Life, says, that about the beginning of this century the Italian opera began to steal into England; and that the new theatre in the Haymarket opened with a translated opera to Italian music called the Triumph of Love. That this account is erroneous in many respects will presently be shewn: it is true that entertainments of a similar kind to the opera were known among us soon after the Restoration; but these were in strictness no more than musical dramas; tragedies with interludes set to music, such as the Tempest, Oedipus, the Indian Queen, Timon of Athens, Dioclesian, and some others by Purcell, Circe by Banister, and Psyche by Matthew Lock. These for a series of years were performed at the theatre in Drury-lane, designed by Sir Christopher Wren, and furnished with all the conveniencies and accommodations requisite in a building of that kind. But the first opera, truly and properly so called, exhibited on the English stage, was that of Arsinoe, set to music by Mr. Thomas Clayton, and performed at Drury-lane theatre in 1707. The merit of this work, as also of its author, may be judged of by the following memoir, and the account hereafter given of his Rosamond :—

THOMAS CLAYTON was one of the royal band of music in the reign of king William and queen Mary; there are two of the name of Clayton in the list of the royal band in Chamberlayne's present State of England, published in 1694, the one William, the other Thomas. The one of them is mentioned in Shadwell's comedy of Bury Fair, act III. scene 1. in this speech: '——They sing Charon, O gentle 'Charon, and Come my Daphne [two famous old 'dialogues] better than Singleton and Clayton did.' The latter, a man of no account in his profession, travelled into Italy with a view to improvement; and returning from thence into England, possessed people with an high opinion of his abilities, insomuch that men were persuaded into a belief that by means of Mr. Clayton's assistance the rusticity of the English music would no longer be its characteristic, and that, due encouragement being given to him, it would in a short time emulate that of the Italians themselves. This is an artifice that has been practised more than once in this kingdom, but never with such success as in this instance. With the hope of great advantages, Clayton associated to him two persons, namely, Signor Nicolino Haym and Mr. Charles Dieupart, both of them good musicians, and either of them, in respect of abilities, far his superior. Clayton had brought with him a collection of Italian airs, which he set a high value on; these he mangled and sophisticated, and adapting them to the words of an English drama, *written for the purpose by Motteux*, and entitled Arsinoe

Queen of Cyprus, called it an opera, composed by himself. There will be farther occasion to speak of this man; in the interim it may be observed that Mr. Addison says that Arsinoe was the first opera that gave us a taste of the Italian music; and as he intimates that it met with great success, and afterwards suffered Clayton to set his opera of Rosamond, it may be inferred that he thought it a fine composition : But a better judge than himself* pronounces of it, that excepting Rosamond, it is one of the most execrable performances that ever disgraced the stage.

In the year 1706 Sir John Vanbrugh designed, and, with the help of a subscription, erected a theatre in the Haymarket, and opened it with a pastoral entertainment entitled the Loves of Ergasto,† set to music after the manner of the Italian opera, that is to say, in recitative, with airs intermixed, by a German musician, who had studied in Italy, and called himself Signor Giacomo Greber. This man brought with him from Tuscany Signora Margarita de l'Epine, and gave occasion to her being called Greber's Peg. This entertainment, though but ill received, was succeeded by another of the same kind, the Temple of Love, composed by Signor Saggioni, a Venetian, and a performer on the double bass, which pleased as little as the former.

The bad success of these entertainments at the Haymarket induced the managers of Drury-lane theatre to attempt, in good earnest, the exhibition of an Italian opera; they fixed upon that of Camilla, *the words whereof were written by Silvio Stampiglia, a Roman by birth, and poet to his Cæsarean Majesty, and the music* composed by Bononcini, then resident in the court of the emperor. To accommodate the singers of our own country, many of the recitatives and airs were translated into English; the conduct of the whole was referred to Nicolino Haym, who was himself an able musician; Valentini performed the part of Turnus; and, notwithstanding the glaring absurdity of so motley a performance, it is said that the opera of Camilla never met with so good a reception abroad as it did here.

To Camilla succeeded Rosamond, an entertainment of which the town had for some considerable time conceived a longing expectation, as well from the character of Mr. Addison as the supposed abilities of the musical composer. The names of the singers and the cast of the parts were as follow :—

Queen Eleanor,	Mrs. Tofts.
Page,	Mr. Holcombe.
Sir Trusty,	Mr. Leveridge.
Grideline,	Mrs. Linsey.
Rosamond,	Signora Maria Gallia.
King Henry,	Mr. Hughs.
War,	Mr. Lawrence.
Peace,	Miss Reading.

* The translator of the Abbé Raguenet's Parallel of the French and Italian Musick and Operas, in his Critical Discourse on Operas and Musick in England, printed at the end thereof. Supposed to be Mr. Galliard.

† *A prologue written by Dr. Garth was spoken on the occasion, in which is this line—*
        ' *By beauty founded and by wit designed,*'
Alluding to lady Sunderland who laid the first stone, and Sir John Vanbrugh the architect.

A criticism on this most wretched performance is more than it deserves, but, to account for the bad reception it met with, it is necessary to mention that the music preponderating against the elegance and humour of the poetry, and the reputation of its author, bore it down the third night of representation.

To begin with the overture; it is in three parts, and in the key of D with the greater third; the first movement pretends to a great deal of spirit, but is mere noise. The two violin parts are simple counterpoint, and move in thirds almost throughout; and the last movement intended for an air is the most insipid ever heard. As to the songs, they have neither air nor expression. There is one that sings thus:—

O the pleasing, pleasing, pleasing, pleasing, pleasing anguish.

An ingenious and sensible writer, mentioned in a preceding note, who was present at the performance, says of Rosamond that it is a confused chaos of music, and that its only merit is its shortness. The overture and the succeeding duetto are given as a specimen of the work:—

THOMAS CLAYTON.

THOMAS CLAYTON.

We meet, in a critical discourse on operas and music in England, published by way of appendix to an English translation of the Abbé Raguenet's Parallel between the French and Italians in regard to their Music, with the mention of a person by the name of the Swiss Count; this was John James Heidegger, by birth a Fleming, as is supposed, who arriving in England in 1708, undertook the conduct of the opera in the Haymarket, and continued it with various success till about 1730, by which he acquired a large fortune, which he lived to enjoy for twenty years after. What were his pretensions to the title ascribed to him is not known; he was a man of a projecting head, possessed of such talents as enabled him to gratify those whose chief pursuits were pleasure, which he exercised in the introduction of masquerades into this country.*

This man, who is represented as in necessitous circumstances at the time of his arrival in England, had the address to procure a subscription, with which he was enabled to furnish out the opera of Thomyris, which, like the former was in English; the music, however, was Italian, that is to say, airs selected from sundry of the foreign operas by Bononcini, Scarlatti, Steffani, Gasparini, and Albinoni. It was performed at the Queen's Theatre in the Haymarket in 1709.

Most of the songs in Thomyris were excellent, those by Bononcini especially; Valentini, Margarita, and Mrs. Tofts sang in it; and Heidegger by this performance alone was a gainer of five hundred guineas.† The following is one of the songs composed by Bononcini, and was sung by Mrs. Tofts:—

* In a collection of letters of several eminent persons deceased, including the correspondence of Mr. John Hughes, vol. III., is a humorous dedication of his Vision of Charon or the Ferry-boat, printed in his works, to the Swiss Count [Heidegger.]

† Camilla and Thomyris were revived at Lincoln's-Inn fields in 1726, but the taste of the town was improved, and they did not succeed.

GIOVANNI BONONCINI.

CHAP. CLXXII.

THE good success of Thomyris was an inducement with Valentini soon after to undertake an exhibition at the same theatre of a pastoral called the Triumph of Love. This pastoral was written by Cardinal Ottoboni, and set to music by Carlo Cesarini Giovanni, surnamed del Violone, and Francesco Gasparini, and was intended to introduce a kind of drama, wherein certain little wooden figures were the actors, which by means of springs, contrived by two famous mechanics, the Count St. Martini and the Cavalier Acciaioli, were made to move with surprising grace and agility : the expense of this singular exhibition may in some measure be guessed at, when it is known that each of these little figures cost the cardinal an hundred pistoles. The music to this entertainment Valentini found means to procure, and having got it, he contrived to get it set to English words ; he rejected almost all the recitatives, to make room for a great number of noisy airs and chorusses, with dances after the French manner, and endeavoured to suit the performance, which was calculated for chamber amusement, to the opera stage ; but the bad success that attended the representation convinced him of his error, and determined him to confine himself to his profession of a singer, and never more act as a manager.

In the winter of 1709 the opera of Pyrrhus and Demetrius, written by Owen Mac Sweney and set to music of Alessandro Scarlatti, was performed at the Haymarket theatre. Haym fitted the music to the words, and added many airs of his own composition, one whereof is inserted in the account hereafter given of him. It was received with general applause, and, in the opinion of very good judges, was held to be superior even to Camilla.

Clotilda, represented also in 1709, was the next opera that appeared. This was made up by Heidegger; the airs were of Bononcini, Scarlatti, and Signor Francesco Conti, already spoken of, who made the overture. To these succeeded the opera of Almahide, consisting of songs both in Italian and English, adapted to Italian airs; the latter were sung by Dogget the comedian. And with these the town were in general pleased till the arrival of Mr. Handel in England, whose coming announced the production of operas, such as were performed at the theatres in Italy; that is to say, the drama being in the Italian language, and the music in the modern Italian style.

At this time Mr. Aaron Hill was in the direction of the Haymarket theatre. Mr. Handel, then a very young man, had received pressing invitations from some of the principal nobility to come and settle in England; to these he yielded, and arrived in the year 1710. Mr. Hill received him with open arms; he immediately concerted with him the plan of an opera entitled Rinaldo, and in a very short time wrought it into form; in short, he wrote the whole drama, and got it translated into Italian by a Signor Rossi, and Mr. Handel set it; an extract from the preface is inserted in the Spectator, No. 5, in which we are told that Mr. Handel composed this opera in a fortnight. It is needless to point out the beauties of this excellent composition, as the overture and the airs are in print; the applause it met with was greater than had been given to any musical performance in this kingdom: in a word, it established Mr. Handel's character on a firm and solid basis.

The success of Rinaldo was in some measure injurious to the interests of those whose employment it had been to furnish out operas by collections from various Italian masters, and torturing music to a sense that it was never intended to bear; for in the Spectator, No. 258, for 26 Dec. 1711, and in another of the same papers, No. 278, Clayton, Haym, and Charles Dieupart, in a letter signed by them all, complain of their dismission, and solicit the public to favour a musical performance for their joint benefit at the house of Mr. Clayton in York-buildings.*

The principal performers before this time were Valentini and Nicolini, Signora Margarita de l'Epine, and Mrs. Tofts, singers: in the band of instrumental performers were Dieupart above-mentioned, Mr. Pepusch, and Mr. Leoillet, masters of the harpsichord; Mr. John Banister, a son of him of that

name, formerly mentioned; Mr. William Corbet, and Signor Claudio, violin masters; Haym for the violoncello, and Saggioni for the double bass. The alteration that immediately followed Mr. Handel's coming to the Haymarket is no otherwise noticed than by the above letter, notwithstanding which, and the applause given to Rinaldo, other operas of the like kind with the former, particularly in 1712, Hydaspes, composed by Francesco Mancini, was represented at the Haymarket: the decorations of this opera were very splendid; the scenes were painted by Morco Ricci, and the words of the songs were all Italian.

From this time the opera was conducted in a manner less liable to exception than at first; and to this reformation it is probable the ridicule of Mr. Addison, and the censures of critics less humorously disposed than himself, might not a little contribute; for though in Rinaldo we are told that sparrows were introduced,† and in Hydaspes a lion, which part was performed by a man, and gave occasion to some of the most diverting papers in the Spectator,‡ we hear no more of these absurdities after the performance of Hydaspes, and the opera was freed from all objections, save only those to which the entertainment itself was at all times obnoxious.

To understand the force of Mr. Addison's satire, if it merits to be called by so harsh a name, it is necessary for us to take a view of the opera at the time of its first introduction among us. Of the nature of this entertainment in general, a judgment may be formed from the account herein before given of the invention of recitative by the Italians, of the musical representations of the same people, and of the establishment of the Royal Academy of Paris; as also from the memoirs of eminent French musicians, inserted in the preceding pages of this work; but of the English Italian opera no mortal can form a judgment, that is not acquainted with the circumstances of its introduction among us, or has not with a critical eye perused the several productions, which in the short space of four or five years at most, were obtruded on the world under that denomination. To take them in their order, Arsinoe consisted of English words fitted to Italian music, originally adapted to Italian poetry, of which the English does not so much as pretend to be a translation; no wonder then if the hearers sought in vain for that correspondence between the sound and the sense, which in the opinion of some make so considerable a part of the merit of vocal composition. The case was the same in Camilla, Thomyris, Pyrrhus and Demetrius, and the rest, with this difference, that for the sake of those singers, who, as being foreigners, were strangers to our language, many of the songs were sung in the original Italian, to which a great part of the audience must at least at that time be

† Spectator, No. 5.

‡ The humour of these papers is so strong and pointed, that it is said the Pope, on reading them, laughed till his sides shook. Mr. Addison, perhaps from the bad success of Rosamond, was led to think that only nonsense was fit to be set to music; and this error is farther to be accounted for by that want of taste, not to say of skill, in music, which he manifests in his preference of the French to the Italian composers, and in his general sentiments of music and musicians, in which he is ever wrong.

* In the preface to the poems of Mr. John Hughes is a letter from Sir Richard Steele, in the name of himself and Mr. Clayton, requesting him to alter Dryden's Alexander's Feast for music, in order to its being performed in York-buildings. He complied, and Clayton had the courage to attempt it, but failed, as Mr. Hughes relates in a letter to Sir Richard Steele, mentioned in the preface above cited. It is printed as altered, in Mr. Hughes's poems, and was performed in 1711.

supposed to be utter strangers. But this was not all ; in the adapting English words to the Italian airs, not one circumstance was adverted to, except that of a correspondence, in respect of measure and cadence, between the words and the music ; sentiment and sense were held unnecessary, and these being neglected, what must the poetry have been but such nonsense as the following ?

> So sweet an air, so high a mien
> 　Was never seen.　　　ARSINOE.

> For thy ferry boat Charon I thank thee,
> But thrust me not out for I come in a hurry.　Ibid.

> Since you from death thus save me,
> 　I'll live for you alone ,
> The life you freely gave me,
> 　That life is not my own.　　CAMILLA.

> Charming fair,
> 　For thee I languish,
> 　　But bless the hand that gave the blow ;
> 　With equal anguish
> Each swain despairs,
> And when she appears
> 　　Streams forget to flow.　　Ibid.

> My delight, my dear, my princess,
> With desire I lose my senses,
> I before you feel with fury,
> 　My blood hurry
> 　　Through every vein,
> 　　　At my heart
> 　　I feel a smart,
> Dying thus who can complain.

> I had vow'd to play the rover,
> Fool with love or give it over,
> But who can though grave and wise,
> 'Scape those dimples, lips, and eyes,
> 　Then to bless you
> 　I'll caress you,
> 　　Press you,
> 　　Kiss you,
> 　And caress you,
> Till like me you cry 'tis vain,
> O my dear to frown and feign,
> Dying thus who can complain.　　THOMYRIS.

> Away you rover,
> For shame give over,
> So bold a lover
> 　Never will pass ;
> You press and thunder
> To bring us under,
> Then all you plunder,
> 　And leave the place.
> Though you are for storming,
> And think you are charming,
> Your faint performing
> 　We read in your face.　　Ibid.

> 　No more trial,
> 　Nor denial,
> 　Be more kind,
> And tell your mind ;
> 　　So tost,
> 　　So crost,
> 　　I'm sad,
> 　　I'm mad,
> No more then hide your good nature
> 　Thou dear creature ;

> 　Baulk no longer,
> 　Love nor hunger,
> 　Both grow stronger
> When they're younger ;
> 　　But pall,
> 　　And fall
> 　　At last,
> If long we fast.　　LOVE'S TRIUMPH.*

It must be confessed that, as musical compositions, such of the operas as were compiled from the works of Italian masters had great merit. As to Camilla, though wholly the work of Bononcini, it was but a puerile essay, the author being scarce eighteen when he set it, and seems to have been greatly over-rated ; the airs are so very short, that they admit of no variety. The first air, 'I was born of royal race,' is but fourteen bars in length, and is no sooner heard than the idea of it is effaced by a succeeding one in a different key. In Thomyris, and Pyrrhus and Demetrius this fault seems to have been avoided ; besides which the airs appear to have been selected with great care from the works of a variety of great masters, such as Scarlatti, Bononcini, Cesarini, Gasparini, and others ; and where these have failed, as they do in the latter, the defect has been ably supplied by Haym : so that upon the whole those entertainments were not destitute of merit, but it was of such a kind as no audience composed of persons promiscuously assembled, some with an ear for music, and others without, could be supposed capable of discerning ; and this circumstance co-operating with the others abovementioned, seems to lead to the true reason why the opera was less favourably received here than in Italy and France. In these and many of the subsequent operas some of the principal female singers were natives of this country, and among them Mrs. Barbier and Mrs. Anastasia Robinson, afterwards countess of Peterborough, were the most celebrated. Mrs. Tofts, of whom we shall presently have occasion to speak, sang in Arsinoe, the first opera performed in England, but she quitted the stage in a short time ; the others continued to perform long after the opera had been supplied with Italian women : in her voice and manner she so far surpassed the rest of the English women, as to be able to divide the applause of the town with Margarita ; but between any other of our countrywomen and the Italians we hear of no competition ; the reason whereof may perhaps be, that, in respect of their performance, the Italian women had so much the advantage over the English, that the latter could not but consider themselves as their scholars. The most celebrated English women singers about the end of the last century, were Mrs. Davis, Mrs. Cross, Mrs.

---

* *Love's Triumph, from whence the above air is taken, is a different drama from the Triumph of Love mentioned in page 810 of this work; it was written by Motteux, as were also the operas of Arsinoe, Thomyris, the Temple of Love, and most of the musical dramas and interludes that preceded the introduction of the Italian opera on the English stage. This man kept what in his time was called an India shop, in Leadenhall-street, which was then much frequented by the old duchess of Marlborough, and other ladies of queen Anne's court ; and sold tea, fans, screens, Japan cabinets, silks, and other commodities imported by the India Company : it was also the staple of city news, and in the opinion of many a place of intrigue. The numerous publications of Motteux have entitled him to a rank among the English dramatic poets ; but of them he must be said to have been one of the most vulgar. He died in 1717-18, and was interred in the parish church of St. Andrew Undershaft, London.*

Cibber, Mrs. Bracegirdle, and Miss Campion,* all of whom have been already spoken of; but it is easy to discover that their perfections were confined to perhaps a beautiful person, graceful and easy action, and a fine voice, the gift of nature, and that owed little of its fascinating power to the improvements of art; if this fact should be doubted, let any one look into the songs of that day, particularly those of Purcell, where he will find the graces written at length, a manifest proof that in the performance of them little was meant to be trusted to the singer.

The two following ladies, as they contributed by their performance to establish the Italian opera in this country, merit our notice :—

Mrs. Tofts, although a native of this country, is celebrated as a singer little inferior, either for her voice or her manner, to the best Italian women. Cibber, who was well acquainted with her, speaks thus of her in the Apology for his Life, page 226. 'Mrs. Tofts, who took her first grounds of musick 'here in her own country, before the Italian taste 'had so highly prevail'd, was then but an adept in 'it: yet, whatever defect the fashionably skilful 'might find in her manner, she had, in the general 'sense of her spectators, charms that few of the most 'learned singers ever arrive at. The beauty of her 'fine proportioned figure, and the exquisitely sweet, 'silver tone of her voice, with that peculiar, rapid 'swiftness of her throat, were perfections not to be 'imitated by art or labour.' She sang in the operas of Arsinoe, Camilla, Rosamond, Thomyris, and Love's Triumph.

The author of the following epigram, supposed to be Mr. Pope, at the same time that he celebrates her beauty and fine singing, has taken care to contrast these her excellencies with two vices, which, supposing him to speak truth, must have considerably abated the power of her charms.

So bright is thy beauty, so charming thy song,
As had drawn both the beasts and their Orpheus along;
But such is thy avarice, and such is thy pride,
That the beasts must have starv'd, and the poet have died.

In the opera of Camilla she performed the part of Camilla; and it is conjectured that the dignity which she was obliged to assume in that character, had an effect upon her mind; for in the Tatler, No. 20, for Thursday, May 26, 1709, there is this plain intimation that her brain was turned: 'The unfortunate 'Camilla has had the ill-luck to break before her 'voice, and to disappear at a time when her beauty 'was in the height of its bloom. This lady enter'd 'so thoroughly into the great characters she acted, 'that when she had finished her part, she could not 'think of retrenching her equipage, but would appear 'in her own lodgings with the same magnificence 'that she did upon the stage. This greatness of soul 'has reduced that unhappy princess to an involuntary 'retirement, where she now passes her time among 'the woods and forests, thinking on the crowns and

'scepters she has lost, often humming over in her 'solitude,

'   'I was born of royal race,
'   'Yet must wander in disgrace.†

'But for fear of being overheard, and her quality known, she usually sings it in Italian.

'   'Nacqui al regno, nacqui al trono,
'   'E pur sono
'   'Sventurata.'

It seems that this disorder had taken deep root in her mind: nevertheless, by the help of medicines and other proper remedies, she was restored to the use of her reason.

In the meridian of her beauty, and possessed of a large sum of money, which she had acquired by singing, Mrs. Tofts quitted the stage, and was married to Mr. Joseph Smith, a gentleman, who being appointed consul for the English nation at Venice, she went thither with him. Mr. Smith was a great collector of books, and patron of the arts; he procured engravings to be made from pictures and designs of Amiconi, Marco Ricci, Piazetta, and other masters. He lived in great state and magnificence; but the disorder of his wife returning, she dwelt sequestered from the world in a remote part of the house, and had a large garden to range in, in which she would frequently walk, singing and giving way to that innocent frenzy which had seized her in the earlier part of her life. She was living about the year 1735. Mr. Smith died about five years ago, and left a numerous and valuable collection of books, which was brought over into England, and sold by auction by Mr. Baker of York-street.

Francesca Margarita de L'Epine, a native of Tuscany, and also a celebrated singer, performed in some of the first of the Italian operas that were represented in England. She came hither with one Greber, a German, but who had studied some few years in Italy,‡ and appeared first in a musical entertainment of his composition, called the Loves of Ergasto, but better known by the name of Greber's Pastoral.§ The most memorable circumstance relating to it is that it was performed in the year 1706, at the opening of the Haymarket theatre, and was the first entertainment of any kind there exhibited.

From the connection between Margarita and Greber, she became distinguished by the invidious appellation of Greber's Peg. After it was ended she commenced a new one with Daniel, earl of Nottingham, which, in an imitation of an ode of Horace, 'Ne sit ancillæ tibi amor pudori,' by Mr. Rowe, is thus alluded to:—

Did not base Greber's Peg inflame
The sober earl of Nottingham,
Of sober Sire descended?
That, careless of his soul and fame,
To playhouses he nightly came,
And left church undefended.||

† A song of her's in Camilla, the first in the opera.

‡ Vide ante, page 810.

§ In the Catalogue de la Musique of Estienne Roger, page 20, is the following article: 'Six Sonates à une Flûte et une Basse continué, com-'posées par Messrs. Greber et Fede.'

|| The earl had written against Whiston on the doctrine of the Trinity.

* Miss Campion sang in the Island Princess, as altered by Motteux, together with Mr. Magnus's boy, as he is called, a dialogue beginning 'Must I a girl for ever be?' set by Jerry Clark. She also sang at the theatre, and at the concert in York-buildings, many songs set by Weldon purposely for her.

And there is extant the following shrewd epigram relating to her, written by lord Halifax :—

On Orpheus and Signora Francesca Margarita.*

Hail, tuneful pair ! say by what wondrous charms,
One scap'd from Hell, and one from Greber's arms ?
When the soft Thracian touch'd the trembling strings,
The winds were hush'd, and curl'd their airy wings ;
And when the tawny Tuscan † raised her strain,
Rook furls the sails, and dares it on the main.
Treaties unfinish'd in the office sleep,
And Shovell yawns for orders on the deep.
Thus equal charms and equal conquests claim, ⎫
To him high woods, and bending timber came, ⎬
To her shrub-hedges, and tall Nottingham. ⎭

Margarita sang in many of the earlier operas, particularly Thomyris, in which she did the part of the queen ; and in Love's Triumph, in which she performed the character of Olinda. In Mr. Hughes's opera of Calypso and Telemachus she appeared in the character of Calypso. She also sang in concerts at York-buildings and Stationers'-hall, and once in the hall of the Middle Temple, in a musical performance at the Christmas revels of that society. She continued to sing on the stage, and occasionally at concerts and other public entertainments, till about the year 1718, when having, as Downes relates, got, at a modest computation, above ten thousand guineas, she retired, and was married to Mr. afterwards Dr. Pepusch.

The two singers abovementioned were rivals for the public favour, and it seems divided pretty equally the applause of the town. The following verses of Mr. John Hughes are a proof of this fact, and point out who of the principal nobility were at the head of the two parties that severally patronized them :—

Music has learn'd the discords of the state,
And concerts jar with Whig and Tory hate.
Here Somerset and Devonshire attend
The British Tofts, and every note commend ,
To native merit just, and pleas'd to see
We've Roman arts, from Roman bondage free.
There fam'd L'Epine does equal skill employ,
While list'ning peers crowd to th' ecstatic joy :
Bedford to hear her song his dice forsakes,
And Nottingham is raptur'd when she shakes :
Lull'd statesmen melt away their drowsy cares
Of England's safety in Italian airs.
Who would not send each year blank passes o'er,
Rather than keep such strangers from our shore.

Mrs. Barbier, a native of England, was also celebrated among the female singers at the beginning of this century. Her first appearance was in the opera of Almahide, represented in the year 1711, upon which occasion she is said to have discovered a more than ordinary concern, that recommended her no less than her agreeable voice and just performance.‡ She sang in many of the subsequent operas, and in that of Calypso and Telemachus, represented at the Haymarket in 1712. She also performed the part of Daphne in Mr. Hughes's masque of Apollo and Daphne, set to music by Dr.

* Collection of the works of celebrated authors, published by Tonson in three volumes duodecimo.
† This epithet of tawny is very characteristic of her, for she was remarkably swarthy, and in general so destitute of personal charms, that Dr. Pepusch, who afterwards married her, seldom called her by any other name than Hecate, which she answered to very readily.
‡ See a letter in the Spectator, No. 231.

Pepusch, and performed at Drury-lane theatre in 1716. Notwithstanding her attachment to the stage, she remained under the protection of her parents, residing at her father's house till the year 1717, when, being no longer able to resist the solicitations of one that pretended love to her, she left it, and gave occasion to Mr. Hughes to write the following verses :—

O yes !—hear, all ye beaux and wits,
Musicians, poets, 'squires, and cits,
All, who in town or country dwell,
Say, can you tale or tidings tell
Of Tortorella's hasty flight ?
Why in new groves she takes delight,
And if in concert, or alone,
The cooing murmurer makes her moan ?
Now learn the marks by which you may
Trace out and stop the lovely stray !
Some wit, more folly, and no care,
Thoughtless her conduct, free her air ;
Gay, scornful, sober, indiscreet,
In whom all contradictions meet ;
Civil, affronting, peevish, easy,
Form'd both to charm you and displease you ;
Much want of judgment, none of pride,
Modish her dress, her hoop full wide ;
Brown skin, her eyes of sable hue,
Angel, when pleas'd, when vex'd a shrew.
Genteel her motion, when she walks,
Sweetly she sings, and loudly talks ;
Knows all the world, and its affairs,
Who goes to court, to plays, to prayers,
Who keeps, who marries, fails, or thrives,
Leads honest, or dishonest lives ;
What money match'd each youth or maid,
And who was at each masquerade ;
Of all fine things in this fine town,
She's only to herself unknown.
By this description, if you meet her,
With lowly bows and homage greet her ;
And if you bring the vagrant beauty
Back to her mother and her duty,
Ask for reward a lover's bliss,
And (if she'll let you) take a kiss ;
Or more, if more you wish and may, ⎫
Try if at church the words she'll say, ⎬
Then make her, if you can—" obey." ⎭

After this elopement Mrs. Barbier returned to the stage, and attaching herself to Mr. Rich, sang in most of his pantomime operas ; and, upon the revival of Camilla and Thomyris at Lincoln's-Inn fields in 1726, sang in both of them. Her last appearance on the stage was in the pantomime of Perseus and Andromeda, composed by Rich, in conjunction with Mr. Thurmond, a dancing-master, and represented about the year 1729. In a note on the above poem, which is printed among the letters of Mr. Hughes, herein before cited, it is said that the late John, earl of Corke, who knew her well, expressed his opinion of her as follows : ' She never could rest long in a ' place ; her affectations increased with her years. I ' remember her in the parts of Turnus and Orontes, ' when the operas of Camilla and Thomyris were ' represented at Lincoln's-Inn fields. She loved ' change so well, that she liked to change her sex.' There is an affectation of wit in this puerile sentiment that renders it totally unintelligible.

CHAP. CLXXIII.

THE opera was an entertainment calculated for the better sort of people in this country: to say the truth, the practice of singing had never till lately been cultivated with any great assiduity among us; and the best that is said of any of our most celebrated vocal performers from the time of Mr. Hales, in queen Elizabeth's, down to the end of queen Anne's reign, is that they were severally endowed with the gift of a fine voice, but as to grace and elegance, or what is called a manner in singing, their panegyrists are silent. In Italy we hear of schools of singers, wherein different styles were cultivated, by which the students of each were as much discriminated as were the disciples of the several schools of painters, the Roman, the Florentine, the Venetian, the Lombard, and the Flemish. In England we have none such; no wonder then if the generality of the people had but little relish for those refinements which the Italian opera was productive of. Those who had a natural taste for music, were content with the plain harmony of vocal composition; or, to speak of vocal performance, with such singing as the playhouses afforded, which consisted for the most part in occasional songs set to music by English masters; with these the stage was competently supplied, and the success of them was a perpetual incentive to poets of an inferior class, and the musicians, to furnish the public with compositions of the like kind. The subjects of these were generally love and rural gallantry, or the delights of the bottle: in short, their general tendency was to promote mirth, to alleviate the toils of labour, and superinduce a temporary oblivion of care. Among the poets of this class, the authors of popular songs, one stands so eminently distinguished as to claim a regard from all lovers of vocal melody, and merit that eulogium which is given him in the ensuing article.

THOMAS D'URFEY (a Portrait), was a native of Devonshire, and bred to the profession of the law, which he forsook under a persuasion, which some poets, and even players, have been very ready to entertain as an excuse for idleness, and an indisposition to sober reflection, viz., that the law is a study so dull, that no man of genius can submit to it. With the full confidence in the powers of a mind thus liberally formed, D'Urfey enlisted himself in the service of the stage, and became an author of tragedies, comedies, and operas, of which he wrote near thirty. The success of his dramatic productions far exceeded their deserts; for whether we consider the language, the sentiments, or the morals of his plays, they are in all these respects so exceptionable, as to be below criticism, and to leave him in possession of that character only which he seemed most to affect, to wit, that of a pleasant companion. The time when D'Urfey lived was very favourable to men of his facetious, and, we may say, licentious turn of manners: he came into the world a few years after the Restoration, when all was joy and merriment, and when to be able to drink and to sing were reckoned estimable qualities; D'Urfey could do both; and, superadded to these

gifts, he had a talent of poetry, which he could adapt to any occasion: he wrote songs, and, though unskilled in music, and labouring under the impediment of stammering in his speech, having a tolerable voice, sang them himself frequently at public feasts and meetings, and not seldom in the presence of king Charles II., who, laying aside all state and reserve, would lean on his shoulder and look over the paper.* The compositions of D'Urfey are so many, and so singularly humorous, that they elude all description, save that they are in general mirthful in the highest degree; so that such of them as were not liable to exception, on account of their indelicacy, became favourites with the whole kingdom. Mr. Addison, in a paper in the Guardian, No. 67, after exhibiting a lively portrait of D'Urfey, whom he is pleased to call his old friend and contemporary, speaking to the ladies his disciples, says that he had often made their grandmothers merry; and that his sonnets had perhaps lulled asleep many a toast among the ladies then living, when she lay in her cradle. And in No. 82 of the same paper is a notification to the reader that a play of D'Urfey's, the Plotting Sisters, which had been honoured with the presence of king Charles the Second three of its first five nights, was then shortly to be acted for his benefit, concluding with a recommendation of it as a pleasant entertainment. But nothing distinguishes his songs more than the uncouthness and irregularity of the metre in which they are written; the modern Pindaric odes, which are humorously resembled to a comb with the teeth broken by frequent use, are nothing to them. Besides that he was able to set English words to Italian airs, as in the instance of ' Blouzabella my buxom doxy,' which he made to an air of Bononcini, beginning ' Pastorella che trà le selve,' he had the art of jumbling long and short quantities so dexterously together, that they counteracted each other, so that order resulted from confusion. Of this happy talent he has given us various specimens, in adapting songs to tunes composed in such measures as scarce any instrument but the drum would express; and, to be even with the musicians for giving him so much trouble, he composed songs in metres so broken and intricate, that few could be found that were able to suit them with musical notes. It is said that he once challenged Purcell to set to music such a song as he would write, and gave him that well-known ballad ' One long Whitsun holiday,' which cost the latter more pains to fit with a tune than the composition of his Te Deum.

Three volumes, consisting mostly of songs written by D'Urfey, were by him published early in this century, with the title of ' Laugh and be fat, or Pills to Purge Melancholy;' but in the year 1719, he, with the assistance of a numerous subscription of lords, ladies, and gentry, as he styles them, republished them, with the addition of three volumes, including a great number of Orations, Poems, Pro-

* See Pills to Purge Melancholy, vol. I. page 246, the song ' Remember ' ye Whigs what was formerly done,' which is thus entitled, ' Advice to ' the City, a famous song: set to a tune of Signor Opdar, so remarkable, ' that I had the honour to sing it with king Charles at Windsor, he ' holding one part of the paper with me.'

F. Gouge pinx:

C. Grignion sculp.

THOMAS DURFEY

POETA LYRICUS.

logues, and Epilogues written by him, and gave the whole collection the title of ' Wit and Mirth, or Pills to Purge Melancholy ; being a Collection of the best merry Ballads and Songs, old and new, fitted to all Humours ; having each their proper Tune for either Voice or Instrument.'

In this collection, besides a great number of singularly humorous songs, are many that bespeak the political sentiments of their author ; Tom, at least in the early part of his life, was a Tory by principle, and never let slip an opportunity of representing his adversaries the Whigs as a set of sneaking rascals. Mr. Addison says that the song of ' Joy to great Cæsar,' gave them such a blow as they were never able to recover during the reign of King Charles II.* This song is set to a tune called Farinel's Ground, of which we have had occasion to speak in a preceding page ; divisions were made upon it by some English master ; it became a favourite tune, and D'Urfey set words to it, in which he execrates the Papists, and their attempts to disturb the peace of the kingdom. Farinelli was a papist, a circumstance which gave occasion for that shrewd remark of Mr. Addison, that his friend Tom had made use of Italian tunes and sonatas for promoting the protestant interest, and turned a considerable part of the pope's music against himself. The paper in which these and other passages, equally humorous, respecting D'Urfey and his compositions are contained, was written by Mr. Addison with a view to fill the house at a play, the Plotting Sisters, acted for his benefit on the fifteenth day of June, 1713, concluding with a character of him :—

' As my friend, after the manner of the Old ' Lyricks, accompanies his works with his own voice, ' he has been the delight of the most polite com- ' panies and conversations from the beginning of ' king Charles the Second's reign to our present ' times. Many an honest gentleman has got a repu- ' tation in his country by pretending to have been in ' company with Tom D'Urfey.

' I might here mention several other merits in my ' friend, as his enriching our language with a multi- ' tude of rhimes, and bringing words together, that ' without his good offices would never have been ac- ' quainted with one another so long as it had been a ' tongue. But I must not omit that my old friend ' angles for a trout the best of any man in England. ' May-flies come in late this season, or I myself ' should before now have had a trout of his hooking.

' After what I have said, and much more that I ' might say on this subject, I question not but the ' world will think that my old friend ought not to ' pass the remainder of his life in a cage like a ' singing-bird, but enjoy all that Pindarick liberty ' which is suitable to a man of his genius. He has ' made the world merry, and I hope they will make ' him easy so long as he stays among us. This ' I will take upon me to say, they cannot do a kind- ' ness to a more diverting companion, or a more ' chearful, honest, and good-natured man.' †

D'Urfey was a great frequenter of places of public

* Guardian, No. 67.　　　† Ibid.

resort, and, among the rest, Epsom, where in his time many of the best fashion were induced to pass a few weeks in the summer for the sake of the waters ; being there one season, a quarrel commenced between him and a person named Bell, a musician, and a duel ensued, which was the occasion of some mirth at the place. It seems that neither of the combatants had much stomach for fighting ; and a wit of the time maliciously compared this rencounter with the famous single combat of Clinias and Dametas in Sir Philip Sidney's Arcadia, in the following verses :—

' I sing of a duel in Epsom befel
' 'Twixt fa sol la D'Urfey and sol la mi Bell :
' But why do I mention the scribbling brother,
' For naming the one you may guess at the other ?
' Betwixt them there happen'd a horrible clutter,
' Bell set up the loud pipes, and D'Urfey did sputter
' " Draw, Bell wert thou dragon, I'll spoil thy soft note ; "
' " Thy squealing," said t'other, " for, I'll cut thy throat."
' With a scratch on the finger the duel's dispatch'd,
' Thy Clinias (O Sidney) was never so match'd.'
　　　　　　Ex. MS. Harl. No. 7319, page 625.

Of D'Urfey it may be said as of Falstaff, that he not only had wit himself, but was also the cause of it in other men. In the Miscellanies of Pope and Swift are some humorous verses, occasioned by an &c. at the end of his name, in the title to one of his plays, and also a prologue designed for his last play : and in the fourth volume of the works of Tom Brown are three stanzas on him, wherein for presuming to call his ballads Lyric Odes, this judgment is denounced against him :—

' Horace shall pluck thee by the nose,
' And Pindar beat thy brains out.'

This merry fellow died, in a very advanced age, on the twenty-sixth day of February, 1723, and lies buried in the church-yard of St. James's, Westminster.

CHAP. CLXXIV.

Nicola Francesco Haym, by birth a Roman, was settled at London as a professor of music, and engaged with Clayton and Dieupart in an attempt to establish an Italian opera here. It does not appear that he had any hand in the opera of Arsinoe, represented at Drury-lane theatre in 1707 ; that doughty performance being a collection of Italian airs adapted to English words by Clayton himself ; but in the opera of Camilla, performed at the same place in the year following, he lent his assistance, by fitting the airs to English words, and otherwise rendering it a proper entertainment for an English audience. He did the same by Pyrrhus and Demetrius, and added to it an overture, and sundry songs of his own composition, which rank with the best in the work. He continued thus employed, sharing with his colleagues the profits arising from these and other representations of the like kind, till the year 1710, when Mr. Handel arrived in England, and performed the opera of Rinaldo at the Haymarket. The superior merit of Rinaldo over every representation of this nature, that till then had been exhibited on the English stage, had such an effect as to silence all the attempts of Clayton and his associates to entertain the town with dramatic music; and of this they heavily complain in a joint letter, printed in the Spectator, No. 258, for Wednesday, December 26, 1711, and also in another, printed in No. 278 of the same paper, for January 8, in the following year, wherein they claim the merit of having introduced Italian music into England, and solicit the encouragement of the public to a musical entertainment for their joint benefit at the house of Mr. Clayton, in York-buildings. For the success of this application we are to seek; and we only know with certainty that Clayton precipitated into contempt;* that

Haym had little to do with the opera, or indeed with music, after the year 1712; and that Dieupart, who was a very fine performer on the violin, enlisted himself into the opera band, and became a teacher of the harpsichord.

The merit of Haym as a musician entitled him to better encouragement than he seems to have met with. He published two operas of Sonatas for two violins and a bass, which shew him to have been an able master; and his talent for dramatic music may be judged of by the following air in Pyrrhus and Demetrius, composed by him, and sung by Mrs. Tofts:—

* Mr. Tickell, in his life of Mr. Addison, speaking of the opera of Rosamond, says, 'that as the Italian taste prevailed, the musick was 'thought sufficiently inexcusable because it was the composition of an 'Englishman.' This it is for men to talk of what they do not understand; and it is for the sake of refuting this injudicious charge, that the overture, and also a duet in this opera, are inserted in a preceding part of this work; to those two compositions the intelligent reader is referred, and upon perusal of them is left to judge for himself, whether for the failure of Rosamond a better reason might not be assigned, than that the music to it was composed by an Englishman.

Must I behold those charms,   must I behold those charms   doom'd to another's arms while, I

. . . am dy-ing; doom'd to another's arms, while I . . am dy-ing;   while I am dy - - ing. Da Capo.

4   ♯   ♯   ♯   6   6   4   ♯   NICOLINO HAYM.

Haym was a man of learning, and is to be regarded in other respects than as a mere musician; he was well skilled in medals, and published a work entitled 'Il Tesoro delle Medaglie antiche,' in two volumes in quarto, Italian and English. He also wrote La Merope and La Demodice, two tragedies, and published a fine edition of the Gierusalemme Liberata of Tasso, in two volumes in quarto, with cuts; and was the compiler of a very useful book to the lovers of Italian literature, entitled 'Notizia de' Libri rari Italiani.'

This person published also, about the year 1730, proposals for printing by subscription the whole history of music in two volumes in quarto, which he had written in Italian, and was to have been translated into English; but it is to be presumed that he met with small encouragement, seeing that the work was never published, so that of the nature of it we can only judge by the proposals, in which the author first declares his intention in these words :—

'The author's design is, I. to render his subject 'intelligible and agreeable to all readers, even to 'those that do not understand music. II. From 'ancient writers, antique statues, bass relievos, and 'medals, to collect whatever is most material to 'ancient music : To give an account of its origin, 'and the esteem in which it was in the several 'periods of time : The lives of their musicians, 'and the use they made of music in their games, 'sacrifices, &c , with some explications of the ancient 'fables concerning it. III. The progress and decay 'of the said science in the different ages down to 'the present time. IV. The introduction of operas 'into several parts of Europe, and particularly into 'England; with an accurate account of their pro-'gress and success. V. The lives of all the eminent 'masters and professors of this art in all times, with 'their effigies.'

This is the substance of the printed proposals circulated among the author's friends; but besides these the following table, showing the order of the work, has come to hand :—

'Contents of the History of Musick in two Volumes.

'Volume I. Book I. Begins from the earliest 'antiquity to the restoring of Music in the Temple 'after the captivity of the Jews; to which is 'annexed an account of twenty gods of the Gen-'tiles, who were all musicians, and the most 'remarkable medals concerning them.

'Book II. The introduction of music into Greece 'in the time of Cadmus, down to the siege of Troy; 'wherein mention in also made of 44 persons who 'exercised music and poetry in those ages; together 'with all the monuments relating to them that are 'now extant.

'Book III. From the siege of Troy to the first 'Olympiad, with an account of forty persons who 'flourished during that period; and the effigies 'of such of them as have been transmitted to pos-'terity. In these three books several ancient fables, 'necessary for the illustration of this history, are 'explained.

'Book IV. From the first Olympiad to Alexander 'the Great, containing the history of 84 musicians, 'with several other particulars relating to the science 'they professed; as also their effigies, and other 'antique monuments as above. N.B. To this period 'the reader will have a complete history of poetry 'as well as music, it being proved that all poets 'were hitherto musicians also.

'Book V. From Alexander the Great to the 'emperor Alexander Severus, when the music of 'the Gentiles ends; containing the fall of ancient 'music, and an account of 40 other musicians as 'before; to which is annexed 50 apophthegms of 'ancient musicians.

'Book VI. Treats of all those solemnities, &c. 'in which music was employed by the ancients, 'as sacrifices, wars, triumphs, nuptials, banquets, 'tragedies, comedies, pantomimic entertainments, 'dancings, funerals, festivals, and games, all proved 'and illustrated by medals, gems, bass reliefs, and 'other antique monuments.

'Book VII. Treats of the several instruments 'used by the ancients in a manner altogether new, 'and much clearer than has been done hitherto; 'with such of their instruments, as could be deli-'neated from antiquities now existing, engraved on 'copper. The whole making the most complete 'collection of that kind yet published.

'Book VIII. Includes a curious enquiry into 'ancient music in the several periods of time, with 'its excellency; wherein the ancient musicians ex-'celled the moderns; and also those particulars in 'which the latter surpassed them; and concludes 'with judging the palm to the ancient music.

'Vol. II. Book I. Begins from Christ, with the 'institution of music in the Christian churches; and 'comprehends also the invention of the notes now

'used, and harmony; their introduction into all
'parts of Europe; with the institution of doctors
'of music in England; and several other curious
'matters that occurred during the space of 1550
'years.

'Book II. An account of the greatest masters in
'all parts of Europe during the fifty years following,
'with several other particulars.

'Book III. Beginning with the xvii. century,
'gives an accurate account of the invention of
'operas in imitation of the Greeks, with several
'important particulars; and a series of masters to
'anno 1650.

'Book IV. Another series of masters for the
'succeeding 25 years; the introduction of operas
'and other kind of music into different parts of
'Europe.

'Book V. The continuation as before for the next
'25 years.

'Book VI. Beginning at 1700, with an account
'of the introduction of Italian operas into England,
'and the progress they have since made; the founding
'of the royal academy, and several other curious
'matters.

'Book VII. Some account of the principal masters
'now living, and the present state of music in all
'parts of Europe.

'Book VIII. A curious dissertation or enquiry
'in what manner music may be carried to a greater
'perfection than it hath hitherto attained to.'

Haym met with but small encouragement for this
undertaking, as appears by a printed copy of the
proposals and plan, with a list of subscribers in his
own hand-writing, scarce amounting to forty in
number; for this reason he dropped the design, and,
abandoning the profession of music, betook himself
to another, viz., that of a collector of pictures; and
in that capacity was employed by Sir Richard Walpole, Dr. Mead, and other persons. Besides his
talent in music, which was no inconsiderable one,
he possessed the faculty of poetry: in a collection
of Mr. Galliard's compositions, in his own hand-
writing, are two Italian Cantatas written by Haym.
He was also the author of Etearco, an opera represented at the Haymarket in the year 1711.

Charles Dieupart, a Frenchman by birth, and
a fine performer on the violin, and also on the
harpsichord, together with Clayton and Haym promoted the introduction of the Italian opera into
England, and greatly assisted the former in bringing
on the stage the first opera ever performed here,
namely Arsinoe, represented at the theatre in Drury-
lane in 1707. At the performance of that and the
subsequent operas of Camilla, and Pyrrhus and
Demetrius, he played the harpsichord, and Haym
the violoncello. Upon Mr. Handel's first arrival in
England in the year 1710, and the representation of
Rinaldo at the Haymarket theatre, it was received
with such applause, that the managers of the opera
at Drury-lane were discouraged from any farther
attempts of that kind; the consequence thereof was
that Clayton, Haym, and Dieupart were necessitated
to solicit the encouragement of the town in behalf

of a concert, which they proposed jointly to carry
on at Clayton's house in York-buildings, in which
was a large room, where concerts had been usually
performed before. Their proposals for this undertaking are contained in two letters printed in the
Spectator, Numb. 258 and 278.

This association continued but a short time, for
in 1711 we find him engaged with Sir Richard
Steele in the performance of concerts there.* Haym
went to the Haymarket, and became a performer in
the opera band, and farther assisted in bringing on
that stage sundry musical performances. Dieupart
betook himself wholly to teaching the harpsichord,
and in the capacity of a master of that instrument,
had admission into some of the best families in the
kingdom. In the latter part of his life he grew
negligent, and frequented concerts performed at
ale-houses, in obscure parts of the town, and distinguished himself not more there, than he would
have done in an assembly of the best judges, by his
neat and elegant manner of playing the solos of
Corelli. He died far advanced in years, and in very
necessitated circumstances, about the year 1740.
There are extant of Dieupart's composition, 'Six
'Suittes de Clavessin, divisées en Ouvertures, Alle-
'mandes, Courantes, Sarabandes, Gavottes, Minuets,
'Rondeaux, et Gigues, composées et mises en Con-
'cert pour un Violin et Flûte, avec une Basse de
'Viole et un Archilut.'

Godfrey Keller was a celebrated master of the
harpsichord about this time. He, together with
Finger, published Sonatas in five parts for flutes
and hautboys, and was the author of Six Sonatas
for violins, trumpets, hautboys and flutes. The
titles at large of these two several publications may
be seen in the Dutch catalogue. At present Keller
is known only by a work which he had prepared
for the press, but was prevented from publishing by
an immature death: it was however printed a short
time after by John Cullen, at the Buck, between the
two Temple-gates, in Fleet-street, with the title of
'A compleat Method for attaining to play a Tho-
'rough-Bass upon either Organ, Harpsichord, or
'Theorbo-Lute, by the late famous Mr. Godfry
'Keller, with Variety of proper Lessons and Fugues,
'explaining the several Rules throughout the whole
'Work; and a Scale for tuneing the Harpsichord
'or Spinnet, all taken from his own copies, which
'he did design to print.'

It was afterwards reprinted by Pearson of Aldersgate-street, as an Appendix to Dr. Holder's Treatise
of the natural Grounds and Principles of Harmony,
to which it must be owned it is but an awkward
supplement, as being altogether practical. Matthew
Lock's Melothesia is the first book on the subject of
thorough-bass published in England, this of Keller
is the next; since his time there have been others
without number.

William Corbett, one of the king's band, was
a celebrated performer on the violin, and leader of
the first opera orchestra at the Haymarket, at the
time when Arsinoe was performed there. Of this

person there are some particulars worth noting. He was a good composer, and a great collector of music and musical instruments. When the Italian opera, properly so called, was established at London, that is to say in the year 1710, when Rinaldo was performed at the Haymarket, a new set of instrumental performers were introduced; and Corbett, though in the service of the king, was permitted to go abroad. Accordingly he went to Italy, and resided at Rome many years, during which time he made a valuable collection of music and musical instruments. Those who, as being acquainted with his circumstances, were otherwise at a loss to account for his being able to lay out such sums as he was observed to do in the purchase of books and instruments, confidently asserted that besides his salary he had an allowance from the government, and that his business at Rome was to watch the motions of the Pretender.

In his younger days, and before he left England, he had published two or three sets of Sonatas for violins and flutes, twelve Concertos for all instruments, and sundry sets of tunes made for plays; but upon his return, about the year 1740, he brought over with him a great quantity of music of his composing during his residence abroad, from the publication of which here he hoped to derive considerable advantage: accordingly he published proposals for printing by subscription his Opera VIII. a work which he entitled 'Concertos or Universal 'Bizzarries, composed on all the new Gustos during 'many years residence in Italy,' in three books, containing thirty-five Concertos of seven parts, in which the styles of the various kingdoms in Europe, and of divers cities and provinces in Italy are professed to be imitated; that is to say, to give a few of them, the several styles of Milan, Rome, Naples, Florence, Bologna, Brescia, Tyrol, England, Ireland, Scotland, Flanders, Hungary, Denmark, Muscovy, &c. The proposal was ridiculous; for in music, composed according to the principles generally known and received, there can be no such discrimination of style as will enable the hearer to distinguish the music of one country, much less one city, from another. However the author was determined to try the experiment; and to make the proposal to go down, he advertised that any person of quality willing to encourage the publication of these compositions, should, upon notice, be waited on by the author and a band of performers, in order, as he phrases it, 'that they might hear the idea of them.' With little or no encouragement Corbett proceeded to publish this his work; but, not being able to vend the many copies of it which he had caused to be printed, they in a short time became waste paper, and lay exposed on booksellers' stalls.

Corbett died at an advanced age in the year 1748. By his will he bequeathed the best of his musical instruments, by the description of his 'Serys 'or Gallery of Cremonys and Stainers,' mentioned in an inventory, part of the will,* to the managers, as he calls them, of Gresham college, with a view

as it seems that they should remain for inspection under certain rules. He also bequeathed 10l. a year to a female servant to show these instruments; and directed that the rest of his personal estate should be sold 'for the establishment of the rules of 'Gresham college;'† and farther gave to the same college many sets of the concertos composed by him, with directions that four copies should be presented every year to foreigners that were good performers. How far this whimsical disposition was complied with we know not,‡ but in a short time after the testator's decease, there was a sale by auction of his instruments at Mercer's-hall, where many curious violins were knocked down at prices far beneath their value. His collection of music-books and manuscripts was also sold by auction at his house in Silver-street, near Pulteney-street, Golden-square.

JOHN LOEILLET, a relation, as it is supposed, of John Baptist Loeillet, of Ghent, a famous master of the flute, and the author of four operas of Solos for that instrument, was a celebrated master of the harpsichord, and a performer in the opera band at the same time with Corbett and the others above mentioned. He was a man well respected by those of his profession; and dwelling in a house in Hart-street, Covent-garden, in which was a large room, had a weekly concert there, which was frequented chiefly by gentlemen performers, who gratified him very handsomely for his assistance in conducting it. It was at this concert that the concertos of Corelli were first performed in England, the particular circumstances whereof are related in the account herein before given of Mr. Henry Needler.

Loeillet was a teacher of the harpsichord, and an excellent composer for that instrument. *He was also celebrated for his performance on the hautboy.* There is extant among his printed lessons a minuet in the key of A, with the minor third, which was a great favourite with the ladies of the last age. The vulgar pronunciation of Loeillet's name led the world into a mistake, so that it was universally ascribed to Jean Baptiste Lully, and few are sensible of the error. In the latter part of his life he dwelt in New North-street, near Red Lion-square. He died about the year 1728, having by his industry acquired a fortune of 16,000l. The works published by him, and printed for Walsh, are six suits of lessons for the harpsichord, six Sonatas for variety of instruments, viz., flutes, hautboys, German flutes, and violins, Opera prima. Twelve Sonatas for violins, German flutes, and common flutes, Opera secunda. Twelve Solos for a German flute, common flute, and violin, Opera terza.

CHAP. CLXXV.

PIER FRANCESCO TOSI was an Italian singer greatly celebrated in his time. Having resided in most of the courts of Europe, and being an attentive hearer of others, and a person of reflection, he attained to

---

* In the inventory one of the violins is said to have been formerly Corelli's.

† *i. e.* the rules by him prescribed, touching the custody of the instruments, and the use to be made of them.

‡ Repeated applications have been made to the clerk of the Mercer's Company for information in this respect, but to no purpose.

such a degree of skill and judgment in the practice of singing, as enabled him to compose a treatise on the subject, which he published at Bologna in the year 1723, with this title, 'Opinioni de' Cantori 'antichi e moderni, o sieno Osservazioni sopra il 'Canto Figurato di Pier Francesco Tosi, Academico 'Filarmonico,' and dedicated to the earl of Peterborough.

Tosi not only visited England, but had made London his residence from the latter end of king William's reign to the end of that of George I. except during such short intervals as either business, or the desire of seeing his friends and relations called him hence : nevertheless it does not appear that he ever sang in the opera here, which is the more to be wondered at, seeing that he had concerts for his benefit.* During his abode in England he was greatly favoured by the principal nobility ; and upon lord Peterborough's return from Spain, and final settlement in England, was much at his house at Parson's-green, where he had opportunities of conversing with Mrs. Anastasia Robinson, then a singer in the opera, afterwards countess of Peterborough.

The treatise of Tosi above mentioned is altogether practical, and contains a great number of particulars respecting the management of the voice, and the method of singing with grace and elegance. Moreover, it contains short memoirs and general characters of the most celebrated singers, male and female, of the author's time. Of Pistocchi in particular he speaks in terms of high commendation, and scruples not to say that he excelled not only those of his own, but of all former times. Mr. Galliard, in the year 1743, published a translation into English of this book, with notes thereon; but by adhering too closely to the original, and adopting those rhapsodical expressions of the author, which, though they suit well enough with the Italian language, disgust an English reader, he has rather degraded than recommended the art which it is the design of the book to teach.

Tosi was, it seems, not only a very fine singer, but also a composer. Mr. Galliard relates, that after his voice had left him he composed sundry cantatas of an exquisite taste, especially in the recitatives, wherein he says the author excels, in the pathetic and expression, all others. To Galliard's translation is a prefatory discourse, containing a brief account of the author, wherein it is said that he died soon after the late king's accession to the crown, having attained above the age of fourscore.

JOHN BANISTER (a Portrait), was the son of that Banister mentioned before to have been sent into France by king Charles II. for his improvement on the violin. The father died in the year 1679, and the son, who had been educated under him, played the first violin at Drury-lane theatre, as well when the opera was performed there, as ordinarily. He too was a composer, and made several Grounds, with

divisions thereon, published in the Division Violin ; and in the London Gazette, Numb. 2712, for November 5, 1691, is an advertisement of a collection of music, composed by Godfrey Finger and himself, to be sold at Banister's house in Brownlow-street, Drury-lane. That he was a man eminent in his profession may be inferred from the mezzotinto of him by Smith, from which the engraving is taken. Banister continued at the head of the band at Drury-lane till about the year 1720, when he was succeeded by Carbonelli. He died in or about the year 1725. A son of his taught the flute, and was it seems a celebrated performer ; for in Brightland's English Grammar, published about the year 1710, this sentence is given as an example, to show that the particle *at* is frequently used for *on* or *upon*,

'Banister is good at the flute.'

He was famous for playing on two flutes at once.

THOMAS ROSEINGRAVE was the son of Daniel Roseingrave already spoken of,† who, having been organist of Salisbury, went to Ireland, and in the year 1698 was appointed organist, and also one of the vicars choral of the cathedral church of St. Patrick in Dublin. He had two sons, whom he brought up to music, the one named Thomas, the other Ralph ; Thomas, of whom we are about to speak, being a young man of a promising genius, was favoured by the chapter of St. Patrick with a pension, to enable him to travel for improvement ; and accordingly he went to Rome in the year 1710, where he became acquainted with Alessandro Scarlatti, and his son Domenico, with whom he contracted a friendship, which subsisted for many years.

How long Roseingrave continued abroad is not certainly known, but in 1720 he had some concern in the management of the opera at the Haymarket : for in that year he brought upon the stage the opera of Narcissus, written by Rolli, and set to music by Domenico Scarlatti, with additional songs composed by Roseingrave himself. A short time after this representation the management of the opera got into other hands, and Roseingrave became a teacher of music, in the principles whereof he was looked upon to be profoundly skilled ; notwithstanding which, his style both of playing and composing was harsh and disgusting, manifesting great learning, but void of elegance and variety. About the year 1725, an organ having been erected in the new church of St. George, Hanover-square, Roseingrave offered himself for the place. The parish being determined to choose the person best qualified, required that each of the candidates should give a specimen of his abilities by a performance, of which Mr. Handel and Geminiani were requested to be judges ; the test of which was by them settled to be a point or subject of a fugue, which the performer was to conduct at his pleasure : this kind of trial was so suited to the talents of Roseingrave, that he far exceeded his competitors, and obtained the place, with a salary of fifty pounds a year. With few other motives than the love of his art, Roseingrave pursued the study of music with

---

* Vide ante, page 764, an advertisement in the Gazette for April 3, 1693, of a concert for Signor Tosi's benefit in Charles-street, Covent-Garden ; and another in the Gazette for October 26, in the same year, purporting that Signor Tosi's concert would be performed weekly during the winter in York-buildings.

† Vide ante, page 771.

Mr. JOHN BANNISTER.

intense application, but so greatly to the injury of his mental faculties, that he refused to teach even persons of the first quality. He was an enthusiastic admirer of Palestrina, and the furniture of his bed-chamber was scraps of paper, containing select passages from the works of that author. His brother Ralph having been bred to music, their father, in the year 1718, obtained permission of the dean and chapter of St. Patrick's to resign his place of or-ganist in favour of him; and in April, 1719, Ralph Roseingrave was elected in his room. This person died in October, 1747, and left a son, William Roseingrave, Esq., who is now living in Dublin, and enjoys several considerable employments under the government in Ireland.

Thomas Roseingrave died about the year 1750, having subsisted for some years chiefly on the bounty of his nephew above mentioned. Some time before his death he published a collection of lessons of his friend Domenico Scarlatti, in which is a composition or two of his own. His other works in print are, Additional Songs to the opera of Narcissus, Volun-taries and Fugues for the organ and harpsichord, to the number of fifteen; and twelve Solos for the German flute, with a thorough-bass for the harpsi-chord. He was a frequent visitant of the reverend Mr. Woodeson, master of the free-school at Kingston-upon-Thames, and would often leave his bed in the night to go to the harpsichord. Mr. Woodeson wrote an epitaph for him, which Roseingrave was so pleased with that he set it to music. It was an elegant composition, but is irrecoverably lost.

JOHN BARRETT was music-master to the boys in Christ's hospital, London,* and organist of the church of St. Mary-at-Hill. He was a skilful musician, and made the tunes to songs in sundry plays; excelling most of his time in the composition of songs and ballad airs. In the Pills to Purge Melancholy are many songs composed by him. He was the author of that sweet air to the song of 'Ianthe the lovely,' made on queen Anne and prince George of Denmark, to which tune a song is adapted in the Beggar's Opera, 'When he holds up his hand.' Some verses of Barrett, prefixed to the Amphion Anglicus, bespeak him to have been a pupil of Blow.

LEWIS RAMONDON was a singer in sundry of the English Italian operas. His first appearance was in that of Arsinoe. In Camilla he performed the part of Metius, and in Pyrrhus and Demetrius that of Cleartes. He had attained to some skill in music, and composed the tunes to some songs in a collection published in 1716, entitled the 'Merry Musician, or 'a Cure for the Spleen,' among which is a hymn upon the execution of two criminals, beginning 'All you 'that must take a leap in the dark.' It is there printed with only the song part, but there are other copies with the bass, which shew it to be a perpetual

fugue, or composition in canon. Gay, in the Beggar's Opera, has adapted a song to this fine tune.

PHILIP HART, supposed to be the son of Mr. James Hart, one of king William's band, and whose name frequently occurs in the Treasury of Music, and other collections of that time, was organist of the church of St. Andrew Undershaft, and also of St. Michael's, Cornhill, which latter place he quitted upon a disagreement with the churchwardens, who were so mean as to contend that during a repair of the organ, which took up a year, his salary should cease, and was elected organist to the neighbouring church of St. Dionis Backchurch. He was a sound musician, but entertained little relish for those re-finements in music which followed the introduction of the Italian opera into this country, for which rea-son he was the idol of the citizens, especially such of them as were old enough to remember Blow and Purcell. He was a grave and decent man, remark-able for his affability and gentlemanly deportment. There are extant of his composition a collection of Fugues for the organ, and the Morning Hymn from the fifth book of the Paradise Lost, which latter work he published in March, 1728-9. Mr. Galliard had set this hymn, and published it by subscription in 1728; and it is said that Mr. Hart meant to emu-late him by a composition to the same words; but if he did, he failed in the attempt, for Mr. Galliard's hymn is a fine and elegant composition, admired at this day, whereas that of Mr. Hart is forgotten. He died about the year 1750, at a very advanced age.

GEORGE MONRO was an organist, and a competitor with Roseingrave for the place at St. George's, Hanover-square: failing in this application, he be-came organist of the church of St. Peter, in Cornhill. He played the harpsichord at Goodman's-fields the-atre from the time when it was first opened, in 1729, till his death, which happened in a year or two after-wards. Monro had a happy talent in composing song tunes and ballad airs, of which he made many that were greatly admired. Sundry of them are printed in the Musical Miscellany, an elegant collec-tion of songs with the music, in six volumes, printed and published by Watts in the year 1731.

GEORGE HAYDEN was organist of the church of St. Mary Magdalen, Bermondsey; he composed and published, about the year 1723, three Cantatas, the first whereof was sung by one Bat, or Bartholomew Platt, a favourite singer with the vulgar, in a pan-tomime called Harlequin Director, performed at Sadler's Wells; the first words of it are 'A cypress grove, whose melancholy shade,' a composition which would have done honour to some of the ablest masters of the time. He also composed a song called New Mad Tom, beginning 'In my triumphant chariot hurl'd,' which the same Bat. Platt was used to sing at Sadler's Wells, dressed in the character of a madman,† to the great delight of all who mistook roaring for singing. There is also extant of Hayden's composition a pretty song in two parts, 'As I saw

---

* In this Hospital, anno. 3 Jac. a free singing school was founded and endowed by Robert Dow, whose many charitable donations are recorded by Stow in his Survey, edit. Strype, book II. page 18-19, book V. page 62; wherein, as in the college at Dulwich founded by Allen the Player, the children were to be taught prick-song. These, as far as can be recollected, are the only endowments of the kind since the Reformation. At Dulwich the boys are taught the musical notes, and are able to chant; but at Christ's Hospital they sing only psalm tunes, and those by ear.

† Songs of this kind, such as Tom of Bedlam, and others set by Lawes, of which there are perhaps more in the English than any other language, were frequently sung in character. In Shadwell's comedy of Bury Fair, act III. scene I. Sir Humphrey Noddy says of a fellow, one of the Thetford music, that he acts Tom of Bedlam to a miracle.

fair Chlora walk alone,' which is well known to the proficients in vocal harmony.

VANBRUGH composed and published two elegant collections of songs, some of which became great favourites. Of this person very little, not even his Christian name, is known: though by the title-page of the second book it appears that the author's house was next door to the Black Lion, near Serjeants'-Inn, Fleet-street.

MAGNUS, organist of the church of St. Giles-in-the-Fields, was esteemed a great master of harmony, and had a style which none could imitate. In his voluntaries on the organ he despised the use of single stops, and attained to so great a command of the instrument as to be able to conduct four parts in fugue. Excessive study and application brought on a disorder in his mind, and he died a young man.

WILLIAM BABELL, organist of the church of All-hallows, Bread-street, and of his majesty's private music, was the son of a musician, who played the bassoon at Drury-lane theatre till he was eighty years of age. He was instructed by his father in the rudiments of music, and *by Dr. Pepusch in the practice of Composition;* and taking to the harpsichord, he became an admirable proficient. Coming into the world about the time when the opera began to get footing in England, he made it his study to emulate the Italians. His first essay in composition was to make the favourite airs in the operas of Pyrrhus and Demetrius, Hydaspes, and some others, into lessons for the harpsichord. After that he did the same by Mr. Handel's opera of Rinaldo, and succeeded so well in the attempt, as to make from it a book of lessons, which few could play but himself, and which has long been deservedly celebrated. He also composed twelve Solos for a violin or haut-boy, twelve Solos for a German flute or hautboy, six Concertos for small flutes and violins, and some other works, enumerated in Walsh's catalogue. Babell died *at about the age of thirty three, on the twenty-third of September, 1723, at Canonbury House, Islington, and was buried in the Church of which he was Organist.* It seems the fame of Babell's abilities had reached Hamburgh, for Mattheson says he was a pupil of Handel; but in this he is mistaken, for Handel disdained to teach his art to any but princes.

ROBERT WOODCOCK, a famous performer on the flute, composed twelve concertos, so contrived, as that flutes of various sizes, having the parts transposed, might play in concert with the other instruments[*]. He had a brother named Thomas, who kept a coffee-house at Hereford, an excellent performer on the violin, and played the solos of Corelli with exquisite neatness and elegance. In that country his merits were not known, for his employment was playing country-dances, and his recreation angling. He died about the year 1750.

JOHN SHEELES was a harpsichord master, and the author of two collections of lessons for that in-

[*] When the flute was an instrument in vogue this was a very common practice. Corelli's concertos had been in like manner fitted for flutes by Schickard of Hamburgh, a great performer on, and composer for, that instrument.

strument. He, together with Mr. Monro, before mentioned, Mr. Whichello, who will be spoken of hereafter, and Mr. Galliard, were great contributors to the Musical Miscellany, a collection of songs published in the year 1731, and mentioned in a preceding article.

CHAP. CLXXVI.

OBADIAH SHUTTLEWORTH, organist of the church of St. Michael, Cornhill, London, was elected to that place upon Mr. Hart's quitting it, and a few years after was appointed one of the organists of the Temple church. He was the son of old Mr. Shuttleworth of Spitalfields, the father of a musical family, and who had acquired a little fortune, partly by teaching the harpsichord, and partly by copying Corelli's music before it was printed in England. There were three sons of this family, and also a daughter. The father had frequent concerts at his house for the entertainment of a few select friends, in which the sons played the violin, the daughter the harpsichord, and the old gentleman the viol da gamba. Obadiah in particular played the violin to such a degree of perfection, as gave him a rank among the first masters of his time. He played the first violin at the Swan concert in Cornhill, from the first institution of that society till the time of his death, which was about the year 1735. He was besides a very good composer, and made twelve Concertos, and sundry Sonatas for violins, of which some of his friends were favoured with manuscript copies. Nothing of his composition is extant in print, except two Concertos made from the first and eleventh Solos of Corelli. Of his two brothers, the one was a clerk in the South-Sea-house, a very gay man; the other had a place in some other of the public offices, and was as remarkably grave; they were both excellent performers on the violin, and used to be at all concerts in the city. Obadiah Shuttleworth was celebrated for his fine finger on the organ, and drew numbers to hear him, especially at the Temple church, where he would frequently play near an hour after evening service.

HENRY SYMONDS, one of the king's band of musicians, and organist of the church of St. Martin, Ludgate, and also of the chapel of St. John, at the end of James-street, near Bedford-row, was a cele-brated master of the harpsichord in his time. He published Six suites of lessons for the harpsichord, in the dedication whereof to the duchess of Marl-borough he intimates that they had been seen and approved by Bononcini. He died about the year 1730.

ABIELL WHICHELLO had been for some years deputy to Mr. Hart, who being a pluralist, had need of an assistant; after that he became organist of the church of St. Edmund the King, and taught the harpsichord in some of the best families in the city. He composed many songs, which have been sepa-rately printed, and a collection of lessons for the harpsichord or spinnet, containing Almands, Courants, Sarabands, Airs, Minuets, and Jigs. He was one of those masters that used to frequent the concert of Britton the small-coal man, and became there acquainted with Mr. John Hughes, for whose memory he was used to profess a sincere regard. He died about the year 1745.

John Robinson, organist of Westminster-abbey, and also of the parish churches of St. Laurence Jewry, and St. Magnus, London; educated in the royal chapel under Blow, was a very florid and elegant performer on the organ, insomuch that crowds resorted to hear him. His wife was the daughter of Dr. William Turner, already spoken of in this work, who as it seems, sang in the opera of Narcissus; and to distinguish her from Mrs. Anastasia Robinson, a singer in the same opera, was called Mrs. Turner Robinson. He had a daughter, who sang for Mr. Handel in Hercules, and some other of his oratorios. Being a very active and industrious man, and highly celebrated as a master of the harpsichord, he was in full employment for many years of his life; and had a greater number of scholars than any one of his time. He died at an advanced age in the year 1762. There is a good print of him sitting at a harpsichord, engraved by Vertue.

Richard Leveridge, a young man possessed of a deep and firm bass voice, became a very early retainer to the theatres. In Dryden's tragedy of the Indian Queen he performed the part of Ismeron, a conjurer, and in it sang that fine song 'Ye twice ten hundred deities,' composed by Purcell on purpose for him. He also sang in the opera of Arsinoe, composed by Clayton; and afterwards in Camilla, Rosamond, Thomyris, and Love's Triumph. When the opera came to be entirely Italian, the bass parts were sung by singers of that country, of whom Boschi was one of the first; and Leveridge became a singer in Lincoln's-Inn fields playhouse, under Rich, where he made himself very useful by performing such characters as Pluto, Faustus, Merlin, or, in short, any part in which a long beard was necessary, in the pantomimes and other exhibitions of that kind, of which Rich was the contriver. Mr. Galliard, who made the music to the best of these entertainments, composed many songs purposely for him, and one in particular in the Necromancer, or Harlequin Dr. Faustus, which Leveridge valued himself much upon singing, 'Arise ye subtle forms that sport.' He had a talent both for poetical and musical composition; the first he manifested by sundry songs of the jovial kind, made to well-known airs; the latter by the songs in the play of the Island Princess, altered by Motteux, which have great merit, and various others. Though he had been a performer in the opera at the same time with Nicolino and Valentini, he had no notion of grace or elegance in singing; it was all strength and compass; and at one time, viz., in the year 1730, he thought his voice so good, that he offered, for a wager of a hundred guineas, to sing a bass song with any man in England.

About the year 1726, he opened a coffee-house in Tavistock-street, Covent-Garden, and published a collection of his songs in two pocket volumes, neatly engraved. In Rowe's edition of Shakespeare the music in the second act of Macbeth is said to be set by Leveridge; and perhaps we are to understand that the rest of the songs in that tragedy were also set by him: but whether that editor did not mistake the musick of Matthew Lock for Leveridge, may deserve enquiry. Being a man of rather coarse manners, and able to drink a great deal, he was by some thought a good companion. The humour of his songs, and indeed of his conversation, consisted in exhortation to despise riches and the means of attaining them; to drown care by drinking; to enjoy the present hour, and to set reflection and death at defiance.* With such a disposition as this, Leveridge could not fail to be a welcome visitor at all clubs and assemblies, where the avowed purpose of meeting was an oblivion of care; and being ever ready to contribute to the promotion of social mirth, he made himself many friends, from whose bounty he derived all the comforts that in an extreme old age he was capable of enjoying. A physician in the city procured from a number of persons an annual contribution for his support, which he continued to receive till about seven years ago, when he died, having nearly attained the age of ninety.

Henry Carey (a Portrait), was a man of facetious temper, resembling Leveridge in many respects. He was a musician by profession, and one of the lower order of poets; his first preceptor in music was Olaus Westeinson Linnert, a German; he received some farther instructions from Roseingrave; and, lastly, was in some sort a disciple of Geminiani.† But with all the advantages he might be supposed to have derived from these instructors, the extent of his abilities seems to have been the composition of a ballad air, or at most a little cantata, to which he was just able to set a bass. Being thus slenderly accomplished in his art, his chief employment was teaching at boarding-schools, and among people of middling rank in private families. Though he had but little skill in music, he had a prolific invention, and very early in his life distinguished himself by the composition of songs, being the author both of the words and the music: one of these, beginning 'Of all the girls that are so smart,' he set to an air so very pretty, and withal so original, that it was sung by everybody. The subject of it is the love of an apprentice for a young girl in the lowest station of life, and, as the author relates, was founded on a real incident; and, mean as the subject

* Sentiments of this kind are predominant in almost all his songs, but in no one of them are they more closely compacted than in the following:—

Should I die by the force of good wine,
'Tis my will that a tun be my shrine;
And for the age to come
Engrave this story on my tomb:—
Here lies a body once so brave,
Who with drinking made his grave.
Since thus to die will purchase fame,
And raise an everlasting name,
　Drink, drink away,
　Drink, drink away;
And there let's be nobly interr'd;
　Let misers and slaves
　Pop into their graves,
And rot in a dirty church-yard.

† See his Poems, edit. 1729, pages 118, 111, 113.

may appear, Carey relates that Mr. Addison was pleased with that natural ease and simplicity of sentiment which distinguishes the ballad, and more than once vouchsafed to commend it.

With a small stock of reputation thus acquired, Carey continued to exercise his talent in poetry and music. He published, in the year 1720, a little collection of poems, and, in 1732, six Cantatas, written and composed by himself; he also composed sundry songs for modern comedies, particularly those in the Provoked Husband, and thereby commenced a relation to the theatres; soon after which he wrote a farce called the Contrivances, in which were several little songs to very pretty airs of his own composition : he also made two or three little dramas for Goodman's-fields theatre, which were very favourably received. In 1729 he published, by subscription, his poems much enlarged, with the addition of one entitled 'Namby Pamby;' the occasion of it was as follows : Ambrose Phillips being in Ireland at the time when lord Carteret was lord lieutenant of Ireland, wrote a poem on his daughter, lady Georgina, now the dowager lady Cowper, then in the cradle; in such a kind of measure, and with such infantine sentiments, as were a fair subject for ridicule : Carey laid hold of this, and wrote a poem, in which all the songs of children at play are wittily introduced, and called it by a name by which children might be supposed to call the author, whose name was Ambrose, Namby Pamby. Carey's talent lay in humour and unmalevolent satire; in ridicule of the rant and bombast of modern tragedies he wrote one, to which he gave the strange title of Chrononhotonthologos, acted, in 1734, at the Little Theatre in the Haymarket, of which it is the least praise to say that no one can read it and preserve a serious countenance; he also wrote a farce called the Honest Yorkshireman; two interludes, the one called Nancy, or the Parting Lovers, the other Thomas and Sally; and two serious operas, viz., Amelia, set to music by Mr. John Frederick Lampe; and Teraminta, set by Mr. John Christopher Smith.

Carey was an Englishman, and entertained an excusable partiality for his country and countrymen; in consequence whereof he had an unsurmountable aversion to the Italian opera and the singers in it; which throughout his poems, and in some of his musical compositions, he has taken care to express. Farther, in pursuance of a hint in a little book called 'The Touchstone, or historical, critical, poli-'tical, philosophical, and theological Essays on the 'reigning diversions of the town.' duod. 1728, written by the late Mr. James Ralph, he wrote a burlesque opera on the subject of the Dragon of Wantley, and gave it to a friend of his, the above mentioned Mr. John Frederick Lampe, a native of Saxony, but who had been some years in England, to set to music; Lampe undertook it, and did such justice to the work, that it may be said to be the truest burlesque of the Italian opera that was ever represented, at least in this country. Carey wrote a sequel to it, entitled the Dragoness, which Lampe also set, and is in no respect inferior to the Dragon of Wantley.

As the qualities that Carey was endowed with

were such as rendered him an entertaining companion, it is no wonder that he should be, as he frequently was, in straits. He had experienced the bounty of his friends by their readiness to assist him with little subscriptions to the works by him from time to time published. Encouraged by these, he republished, in 1740, all the songs he had ever composed, in a collection entitled 'The Musical 'Century, in one hundred English Ballads on various 'subjects and occasions, adapted to several characters 'and incidents in human life, and calculated for 'innocent conversation, mirth, and instruction.' In 1743 he published his dramatic works in a small quarto volume, and as well to this as his collection of songs, was favoured with a numerous subscription.

With all his mirth and good humour, Carey seems to have been at times deeply affected with the malevolence of some of his own profession, who, for reasons that no one can guess at, were his enemies : It is true that in some of his poems he manifests a contempt for them, but it is easy to discover that it is dissembled. Unable to resist the shafts of envy, and labouring under the pressure of his circumstances, about the year 1744, in a fit of desperation he laid violent hands on himself, and at his house in Warner-street, Coldbath fields, put a period to a life which had been led without reproach.

As a musician Carey seems to have been one of the first of the lowest rank; and as a poet, the last of that class of which D'Urfey was the first, with this difference, that in all the songs and poems written by him on wine, love, and such kind of subjects, he seems to have manifested an inviolable regard for decency and good manners.

HENRY HOLCOMBE was a singer in the opera at its first introduction into this country. In that of Camillo he performed the part of Prenesto; and being very young at the time, is in the printed copy of the music called the boy. In Rosamond he did the page, and is called by his name. He continued not long after a singer on the stage, but took to the profession of a harpsichord master, and taught in the families of some of the chief citizens of London. One, and but one song of his composition, 'Happy hours all hours excelling,' is printed in the Musical Miscellany, the words whereof were written by Dr. Wright, a dissenting teacher, minister to a congregation in Carter-lane. Mr. Holcombe also set to music the song of Arno's Vale, written by Charles earl of Middlesex, afterwards duke of Dorset, and addressed to a favourite of his, Signora Muscovita, a singer, on occasion of the death, in the year 1737, of John Gaston, the last duke of Tuscany of the house of Medici. It is printed in a collection of twelve songs set by Mr. Holcombe, and published by himself a few years before his death, which happened about the year 1750.

CHAP. CLXXVII.

JOHN ERNEST GALLIARD was the son of a perruquier, and a native of Zell; he was born in or about the year 1687, and received his instructions in the practice of musical composition from Farinelli, the

J.Worsdale pinx.   C.Grignion sculp.

HARRY CAREY.

director of the concerts at Hanover, and of Steffani,* who was resident there in another capacity. After he had finished his studies he applied himself to the practice of the hautboy and the flute, which latter instrument was then the recreation of well-bred gentlemen, and was taken into the service of prince George of Denmark, who appointed him one of his chamber music. Upon the marriage of the prince with the lady, afterwards queen Anne, Galliard came over to England; at that time Baptist Draghi, who had been her master, was chapel-master to the queen dowager Catherine, the relict of Charles II., at Somerset House, but upon her death this place became a sinecure, and Draghi dying soon after her, it was bestowed on Mr. Galliard.

It appears by his own manuscript collection of his works, in which he has carefully noted down the times and occasions of his several compositions, that Mr. Galliard was much about the court; and many of them are there said to have been made at Richmond and Windsor, the places of the royal residence. He composed a Te Deum and Jubilate, and three anthems performed at St. Paul's and at the royal chapel at St. James's, upon thanksgiving for victories obtained in the course of the war;† and was in general esteemed an elegant and judicious composer.

The merits of Mr. Galliard, together with his interest at court, afforded reason at one time to suppose that he would have had the direction of the musical performances in this kingdom; but he was not able to stand in competition with either Bononcini or Handel, and wisely declined it. Nevertheless, in compliance with the request of his friend Mr. John Hughes, he set to music his opera of Calypso and Telemachus, which in the year 1712 was performed at the Haymarket theatre; the singers were Signora Margarita, Signora Manina, Mrs. Barbier, Mrs. Pearson, and Mr. Leveridge. Notwithstanding the goodness both of the poetry and the music, and that Nicolini himself had the generosity to applaud it, the friends of the Italian opera formed a resolution to condemn it; so that it was represented under the greatest discouragements; but some years afterwards it was revived with better success at Lincoln's Inn fields.

As Mr. Galliard led a retired and studious life, and had little intercourse with the musical world, there will be but little occasion to mention him hereafter, wherefore the particulars relating to him are here collected in one point of view.

From the time of Mr Handel's final settlement in this kingdom, he was occasionally the author of many elegant compositions, particularly six Cantatas, five of them written by Mr. John Hughes, and the sixth by Mr. Congreve; to the first impression of this work is a preface, containing sundry curious

particulars respecting this species of musical composition; three other Cantatas written by Mr. Hughes, and printed in his works; six Solos for the flute, with a thorough-bass; six Solos for the violoncello or bassoon, composed at the request of one Kennedy, a fine player on the bassoon, and by him often performed in public. He also set to music, and published by subscription in 1728, the Morning Hymn of Adam and Eve, taken from the fifth book of Paradise lost; and in 1742 published a translation of Tosi's 'Opinioni de' Cantori antichi e moderni,' with the title of 'Observations on the Florid Song, or Sentiments on the ancient and modern singers.' Of the merits of this translation mention is made in the account hereinbefore given of Pier Francesco Tosi.‡

But his principal employment for a series of years was composing for the stage. He set to music an opera of one act, called Pan and Syrinx, written by Mr. Lewis Theobald, and performed at Lincoln's Inn fields in 1717; and in virtue of his engagements with Mr. Rich, was doomed to the task of composing the music to such entertainments as that gentleman from time to time thought proper to set before the public at his theatre in Lincoln's Inn fields, and afterwards at that of Covent-garden, consisting of a strange conjunction of opera and pantomime, the highest and lowest species of dramatic representation. Those of Mr. Galliard's composition, as far as can now be collected, were Jupiter and Europa; the Necromancer, or Harlequin Dr. Faustus; the Loves of Pluto and Proserpine, with the Birth of Harlequin; Apollo and Daphne, or the Burgomaster tricked. One of the last of his works of this kind was the music to an entertainment called the Royal Chace, or Merlin's Cave, in which is that famous song 'With early horn,' by the singing whereof, for some hundred nights, Mr. Beard first recommended himself to the public. He also composed the music for the tragedy of Œdipus, which had before been set by Purcell. This was never printed, but is in the library of the Academy of Ancient Music. Mr. Galliard was a great contributor by songs of his composition to the Musical Miscellany, in six volumes, printed by Watts, and mentioned in a preceding page. He also published, about 1740, in a separate volume, twelve songs composed by him at sundry times.

A letter from Mr. Galliard to Mr. John Hughes is printed in the preface to Mr. Hughes's Poems in two volumes, duodecimo, published in the year 1735.

About the year 1745 he had a concert for his benefit at Lincoln's Inn fields theatre, in which were

---

* See the printed catalogue of his music, in which, lot 65 of the manuscripts, is thus described: 'Mr. Galliard's first lessons for com- 'position under the tuition of Sig. Farinelli and Abbate Steffani, at the 'age of 15 or 16, in 1702;' and in a manuscript collection of many of his compositions is a Sonata for a hautboy and two bassoons, with this note in his own hand-writing, 'Jaij fait cet Air a Hannover, que Jaij Joué a 'la Serenade de Monsieur Farinelli ce 22me Juin, 1704.'

† The words of these severally are, 'I will magnify thee, O Lord,' 'O Lord God of hosts,' and 'I am well pleased.'

‡ Mr. Galliard, though a foreigner, had attained to such a degree of proficiency in the English language, as to be able to write it correctly; but he was not enough acquainted with the niceties of it to know that we have no term that answers to the appellative Canto figurato, and consequently that that of the florid song could convey to an Englishman scarce any other idea than of the song of a bird, the nightingale for instance, and it happened accordingly that upon the publication of his translation men wondered what was meant by the term. Mr. Galliard has illustrated his author by notes of his own, which are curious and entertaining; and it is upon the use of certain phrases and peculiar modes of expression, common to the translation of the Abbé Raguenet's Parallel, published in 1709, with the title of 'A comparison between the 'French and Italian Musick and Operas, with Remarks,' and this of Tosi's book, that we found a conjecture that Mr. Galliard was the translator of both, and also the author of 'A Critical Discourse upon 'Operas in England, and a means proposed for their improvement,' printed at the end of the translation of the Parallel.

performed the chorusses to Sheffield duke of Buckingham's two tragedies of Brutus and Julius Cæsar,
set to music by Mr. Galliard, and an instrumental
piece for twenty-four bassoons and four double basses.

Mr. Galliard died in the beginning of the year
1749, leaving behind him a small but very curious
collection of music, containing, among other things,
a great number of scores of valuable compositions in
his own hand-writing, which has been inspected for
the purpose of compiling this article; and an Italian

opera of his composition, not quite completed, entitled
'Oreste e Pilade, overo la Forza dell' Amicizia.'
This collection, together with his instruments, was
sold by auction at Mr. Prestage's, a few months after
his decease.

The following duet in the hymn of Adam and
Eve is inserted as a specimen of that natural and
elegant style which distinguishes the compositions
of this ingenious master :—

JOHN ERNEST GALLIARD.

JOHN CHRISTOPHER PEPUSCH (*a Portrait*), one of the greatest theoretic musicians of the modern times, was born at Berlin about the year 1667. His father, a minister of a protestant congregation in that city, discovering in him an early propensity to music, employed at the same time two different masters to instruct him, the one in the theory, the other in the practice of the science; the former of these was

Klingenberg, the son of Gottlieb Klingenberg, componist and organist of the churches of St. James and St. John, at Stettin in Pomerania, the latter, one Grosse, a Saxon, and an exceedingly fine performer on the organ.*

Under the care of these two masters Pepusch continued but the short space of one year, the strait circumstances of his father not affording him the means of farther instruction; but labouring incessantly at his studies, he profited so greatly under them, that he acquired an early reputation for his skill and performance; for at the age of fourteen he was sent for to court, and by accompanying one of the ladies who sang before the queen, so recommended himself, that he was immediately appointed to teach the prince, the father of the present king of Prussia, on the harpsichord, and that very day gave him a lesson.

Encouraged by a patronage so honorable, Pepusch prosecuted his studies with unremitted diligence; nor were his pursuits confined to that kind of knowledge, which is sufficient for a practical composer. He had an inquisitive disposition, that led him to investigate the principles of his art; and being competently skilled in the learned languages, he applied himself to the study of the ancient Greek writers, and acquired the character of a deep theorist in music. He continued at Berlin a professor of Music, and in the service of the court, till about the thirtieth year of his age, when, being in the royal palace, he became an eye-witness of a transaction which determined him to quit the country of his nativity. An officer in the service of his Prussian majesty had at a levee made use of some expression which so exasperated the king, that he ordered the offender into immediate custody, and, without a trial, or any other judicial proceeding, his head was struck off. Mr. Pepusch, who was present, conceived the life of every subject so precarious in a country where in the punishment of offences the forms of public justice were dispensed with, that he determined to abandon it, and put himself under the protection of a government founded on better principles.

In pursuance of this resolution he quitted Berlin, and arriving in England about the year 1700, was retained as a performer at Drury-lane. It is probable that he assisted in fitting the operas for the stage that were performed there, for in that of Thomyris is an additional song of his composition, to the words 'How blest is a soldier.'

While he was thus employed, he forbore not to prosecute his private studies, and these led him to an enquiry into the music of the ancients, and the perusal of the Greek writers, in which he persisted so inflexibly, that he arrived at a greater knowledge of the ancient system, than perhaps any theorist since the time of Salinas; and at length entertained an opinion that the science, instead of improving, had for many years been degenerating, and that what is now known of it, either in principle or practice, bears little proportion to that which is lost. Nevertheless this persuasion wrought not so upon his mind, as to prevent him from the exercise of his inventive faculty, nor of directing his studies to that kind of composition which was best suited to gratify the public ear, as appears by the works published by him at different times.

It is well known that at the beginning of this century the state of dramatic music was very low; and of the opera in particular, that it was scarce able to stand its ground against the ridicule of Mr. Addison, and other writers in the Spectator. Nevertheless there were so many who affected to discover charms in the Italian music, particularly that novel species of it, Recitative, as gave great encouragement to the composers of the time to study it: trusting to this disposition in its favour, Mr. Pepusch set to music six Cantatas for a voice and instruments, the words whereof were written by Mr. John Hughes; and afterwards six others by different authors. The several compositions contained in these two collections are evidently in the style of the Italian opera, as consisting of airs intermixed with recitative; and he must be but very moderately skilled in music who cannot discover between them and the cantatas of Alessandro Scarlatti a very near resemblance. They were received with as much applause as the novelty of this kind of music could well entitle them to; but the remembrance of this work exists only in the cantata 'See from the silent grove,' which is yet heard with delight.

The abilities of Pepusch as a practical composer were not likely to become a source of wealth to him; his music was correct, but it wanted variety of modulation; besides which Mr. Handel had gotten possession of the public ear, and the whole kingdom were forming their taste for harmony and melody by the standard of his compositions. Pepusch, who soon became sensible of this, wisely betook himself to another course, and became a teacher of music, not the practice of any particular instrument, but music in the strict sense of the word, that is to say, the principles of harmony and the science of practical composition; and this not to children or novices, but in very many instances to professors of music themselves.

In the year 1713, at the same time with Croft, Mr. Pepusch was admitted to the degree of doctor in music in the university of Oxford,† and continued

* Probably Severus Grosse of Hildesheim, a bishopric in the circle of Lower Saxony. He was organist of the cathedral church at Groningen, a town situate in the principality of Halberstadt.

† To assist in the performance of the exercise for his degree, he took from London many of the performers from the theatres, and had concerts in the city for his benefit, which was censured as a very unacademical practice, and unwarranted by any precedent. His conduct in this respect

to prosecute his studies with great assiduity. Having taken upon himself to teach the rudiments of music, and the art of composition, he reverted to the system of Guido, and revived the practice of solmisation by the hexachords, which for almost a century had been disused in favour of a method far less certain and perfect, viz., that in which only the syllables SOL, LA, MI, FA, were used.*

His manner of inculcating the precepts of musical composition, and the method he took with his pupils to form their style, was somewhat singular. From the time that the works of Corelli first became known to the public, he entertained a most exalted opinion of their merit; and conceiving that they contained the perfection of melody and harmony, he formed a kind of musical code, consisting of rules extracted from the works of this his favourite author; and the exercises which he enjoined his disciples were divisions on, and harmonies adapted to, basses selected from his works.

In the course of his studies Dr. Pepusch had discovered the error of those, who seemed to resolve the efficacy of music and its influence on the human mind solely into novelty; he saw with concern persons who made pretensions to great skill in the science, treat with indifference and contempt the music of the preceding century; and being himself persuaded of its superior excellence, he laboured to retrieve and exhibit it to public view. To this end, about the year 1710, he concerted with some of the most eminent masters then living, and a number of gentlemen distinguished for their performance on various instruments, the plan of an academy for the practice of ancient vocal and instrumental music. The origin of this institution has already been spoken of; the farther history of it is reserved for another part of this work.

About the year 1712, the duke of Chandois having built himself a house near Edgware in Middlesex, which he named Cannons, in pursuance of a plan which he had formed of living in a state of regal magnificence,† determined on having divine service

performed in his chapel, with all the aids that could be derived from vocal and instrumental music. To this end he retained some of the most celebrated performers of both kinds, and engaged the greatest masters of the time to compose anthems and services with instrumental accompaniments, after the manner of those performed in the churches of Italy. It is well known that Mr. Handel's anthems, to the number of near twenty, were made for the duke's chapel. It is also certain that the morning and evening services performed there were for the most part the compositions of Dr. Pepusch; many of these, among which is a very fine Magnificat, as also some anthems composed by him at the request of the duke, are now in the library of the Academy of Ancient Music, and are occasionally performed in that society.

About the year 1722 Signora Margarita de l'Pine having quitted the stage with a large sum of money, Dr. Pepusch married her, and went to reside in Boswell-court, Carey-street. Her mother also lived with him. The house where they dwelt was sufficiently noted by a parrot, which was used to be set out at the window, and had been taught to sing the air 'Non e si vago e bello,' in Julius Cæsar. The farther particulars respecting Dr. Pepusch are referred to a future page.

---

being contrasted with that of Croft, whose exercise was performed by singers from the chapel royal, and who declined all pecuniary emoluments on the occasion, gave great offence to the university.

* Touching the syllables used in solmisation, it may not be amiss to remark that they were originally six, UT, RE, MI, FA, SOL, LA. See page 155, et seq. The Italians finding the syllable UT rather difficult to pronounce, rejected it, and instead of it, made use of DO; and we find it adopted in the Armonia Gregoriana of Gerolamo Cantone, published in 1678. Some years before this, that is to say, upon the Restoration, when the masters throughout this kingdom were employed in training up children for cathedral service, which had been abolished in the time of the usurpation, they, as thinking it more easy, introduced a practice of solfaing by the tetrachords, using only the syllables, SOL, LA, MI, FA; which method Dr. Wallis has followed in the several examples by him given in his Appendix to Ptolemy; but it having been found in some respects less true and certain than the former, Dr. Pepusch revived the practice of solmisation by the hexachords; which at first appeared so difficult, that few could be prevailed on to learn it. Stanesby the flutemaker, a very ingenious man, in the year 1736, declared that besides Dr. Pepusch he never met with but one person who could solfa by the hexachords, namely Mr. John Grano, the author of sundry Trumpettunes, and a celebrated performer on that instrument. *Mr. Bernard Gates, master of the chapel children, first introduced the practice into his school,* and since that time the boys of St. Paul's choir have been taught to do it with great facility.

† The very short period that intervened between the time of the

erection and demolition of that fabric, Cannons, affords an example of the instability of human grandeur that history can hardly parallel.

James Bridges, duke of Chandois, was paymaster of the forces during queen Anne's war; and having accumulated an immense sum of money, determined on the building of two magnificent houses, the one for a town, the other for a country residence: for the situation of the former he made choice of Cavendish-square, but proceeded no farther in that design than the building of two pavilions, which are the two houses at the extremities of the north side of that quadrangle, and may be distinguished by the similarity of their form, and the roofs, which are somewhat singular. For the site of his country house, the place he fixed on was a little west of Brentford, about half a mile north of the great road, and on the right hand side of the lane where lord Holderness's house now stands; and there are yet remaining the stone piers for the gates, and some other erections, which mark the very spot fixed on; but upon some disagreement with Charles, duke of Somerset, who did not choose that in his manor of Sion a mansion should be erected that was likely to vie with Sion-house itself, the duke of Chandois changed his intention, and went to Edgware in the county of Middlesex, from which place he had married his duchess, and there erected that splendid edifice, which for a few years was known by the name of Cannons. Three architects were employed in the design of it, namely Gibbs, James of Greenwich, and one Sheppard, who had been a plaisterer, but having built in and about Grosvenor-square with some success, professed himself an architect, and designed Goodman's-fields theatre, and after that Covent-Garden. The fabric, the costly furniture, and the mode of living at this place, subjected the owner of it to the censure of Mr. Pope, who has been pretty free in pronouncing, that, unless for vain expence and inelegant profusion, the duke had no taste at all; he might have included in the exception his grace's taste for music, of which he gave the best proofs; but panegyric and satire sort but ill together. It may be said that Mr. Pope in one of his letters to Mr. Aaron Hill, has denied that his Epistle on Taste is a satire on the duke of Chandois; but how far he may be credited, they only can judge who are able to point out, who but his Grace is meant by Lord Timon. Mr. Pope had the comfort to see the cause of his uneasiness removed in the change of the duke's circumstances, occasioned by the misfortunes of the year 1720, which in a short time obscured the splendour of Cannons; and had he lived to the year 1747, he might have enjoyed the pleasure of seeing this magnificent structure, which cost 200,000l. erecting and furnishing, sold at such a price, as afforded the purchaser a temptation to pull it down, and dispose of the materials in lots, one of which, namely, the marble staircase, was bought by the late earl of Chesterfield for his house near Hyde park, and is now there.

Of the order and economy of his Grace's expenditure it is not so difficult to judge, as of the proportion which it bore to his fortune; this however is certain, that when the plan of living at Cannons was originally concerted, the utmost abilities of human prudence were exerted to guard against profusion. One of the ablest accomptants in England, Mr. Watts, master of the academy in Little Tower-street, was employed by the duke to draw a plan which ascertained, and by inspection declared, the total of a year's, a month's, a week's, and even a day's expenditure. The scheme was engraved on a very large copper plate; and those who have seen impressions from it, pronounce it a very extraordinary effort of economical wisdom.

JOHANNES CHRISTOPHORUS PEPUSCH.

MUS. DOCT. OXON.

BOOK XIX.   CHAP. CLXXVIII.

In the year 1715 was published 'Histoire de la 'Musique, et de ses Effets, depuis son Origine jusqu' 'à présent.' The editor of this work was Bonnet, paymaster of the salaries of the lords of the parliament of Paris, who finding among the manuscripts of his uncle the Abbé Bourdelot, and also among those of his own brother Bonnet Bourdelot, physician to the king of France, certain memoirs on the subject of music, was induced to publish them.* The first edition of the book, and which was printed in 1705, seems to contain only so much as was written by the Abbé, but a later, printed in 1715, and at Amsterdam in 1725,† extends it to four volumes, and comprehends the papers of Bonnet Bourdelot.

The author begins his history with an account of the invention of the lyre by Mercury, and the establishment of a system by Pythagoras, founded on a division of the monochord. The relation which he gives is taken chiefly from Boetius, and needs not here to be repeated. In tracing the subsequent improvements by Gregory the Great, Guido Aretinus, and De Muris, he agrees in general with other writers.

It is to be observed that this work is written in a very desultory manner, by no means containing a regular deduction of the history of the science: all the use thereof that will be here made of it, will be to give from it such particulars respecting music as are worth noticing, and are not to be found elsewhere, and of these there are many.

In delivering the sentiments of the ancient philosophers, poets, and musicians, touching the use of music, and its effects on the passions, the author takes occasion to mention the marriage of our Henry VIII. with Anne Boleyn, who, he says, and cites Mezeray for his purpose, could sing and dance too well to be wise or staid, of which the king was well convinced when he discovered an intrigue between her and Mark Smeton, one of her musicians.‡ He cites from the memoirs of the Abbé Victorio Siry, a relation that queen Elizabeth of England, in the hour of her departure, ordered her musicians into her chamber, and died hearing them: and says that he had been informed by a friend of his, one of the attendants on the prince of Orange, afterwards king William III. that in the year 1688, the prince being then at the Hague, and, as it may be supposed, deeply engaged in reflections on the critical situation of his affairs at that time, had three choice musicians to play to him whenever he was disposed to be melancholy or over thoughtful.

Another instance, and that a very affecting one, of the power of music to assuage grief, he cites from the life of the emperor Justinian to this effect:

Ricimer, king of the Vandals,§ having been defeated in a great battle by Belisarius, was constrained to fly to the mountains, and was there with his army invested by him. Overwhelmed with grief, he made to the general this moving request: 'Send me,' says he, 'a loaf of bread, lest I perish with hunger; 'a spunge to dry up my tears; and a musical instru- 'ment to console me under my afflictions.'

Other particulars respecting music in general occur in this order. The ancient chronicles of France mention that Cherebert, king of Paris, about the year 562, married successively two of the maids of honour of his queen Ingoberge; their names were Meroflede and Marcouefe, his inducement to it being that they were both fine singers.‖ Dagobert, king of France, in the year 630 divorced his queen Gomatrude upon pretence of barrenness, and married Nantilde, a nun, and a fine singer. William, duke of Normandy, in his expedition to England had singers at the head of his army. Francis I. king of France had music both for his chamber and his chapel: the musicians of his chapel followed him to Milan, and, jointly with those of pope Leo X. sang high mass, in the year 1515, at Bologna. Great numbers of Italian musicians followed Catherine de Medicis into France, upon her marriage with Henry II. and raised an emulation among the French, which contributed greatly to the improvement of their music. In the reign of Charles IX. king of France, Jean-Antoine de Baïf established an academy of music in his house, to which the king resorted once a week, and assisted at it in his own person, as did also his successor Henry III. till the civil wars of France obliged Baïf to break up the academy. At this time Eustache du Carroys, a native of Beauvais, was chapel-master to Charles IX. who dying, he was continued in his employment by his successor.¶ In the year 1580, Baltzarina, an Italian, afterwards called Beaujoyeux, came into France with a band of violins, and was made first valet-de-chambre to the queen. He was esteemed the finest performer on the violin then in Europe. Lewis XIII. of France is said to have composed a book of airs.** In 1630 a musician named Du Manoir, a fine performer on the violin, was by letters patent appointed King of the violins, with power to licence performers on that instrument in all the provinces in France. In 1684, cardinal Mazarine having sent for musicians from Italy, entertained the court at the Louvre with a representation of an Italian opera; the subject of it was the amours of Hercules: Lully composed the Entrées, and thereby gave proofs

---

* Of the authors that cite this book, some, not adverting to the circumstances of its publication, refer to it as the work of Bonnet, who was in truth but the editor.

† I have it 1743.

‡ Of this supposed intrigue Burnet has given the circumstances, which amount to no more than that Smeton was used to play on the virginals to the queen; that one day standing in a window of her apartments, very pensive, she asked him why he was so sad; he said it was no matter. She answered, 'You must not expect I should speak to you as if you 'were a nobleman, since you are an inferior person.' 'No, no, Madam,' says he, 'a look suffices me.' Vide Burn. Hist. Reform. vol. I. page 199.

§ The author seems to have mistaken this name for Gilimer, one of the nephews of Genseric, king of the Vandals, who claimed to be successor to his uncle. Justinian engaged in a war with him in behalf of Yldericus, another nephew of Genseric, and a competitor for his crown, and drove Gilimer into the mountains of Numidia. Of such a person as Ricimer we meet with no mention in the history of those times.

‖ Cherebert had by his queen Ingoberge, a daughter, named Bertha, who was married to Ethelbert, king of Kent, and greatly favoured the arrival of Austin the monk, when he came to teach the christian religion

¶ Some compositions of his are to be found both in the French and the Latin work of Mersennus.

** This may be true, for see an air of his composition in page 638.

of his genius for music. In 1660 Lambert, master of the king's music, brought singing to perfection in France, by introducing the shake, and other graces, to which the French till his time were strangers. In 1669 the king granted to Cambert his letters patent for an opera, he having a short time before set to music a pastoral of Perrin, which was represented at Vincennes with great applause. The dialogues in the operas performed under the direction of Cambert, were composed by Lambert, Martin, Pordigal, Boisset, and himself, and were the models after which the French recitative was formed. Lewis XIV. understood music in perfection; he was also the best dancer in his court; cardinal Mazarine sent to Italy for a master to teach him the guitar, and in eighteen months the king excelled his master. All the foreign embassadors at the court of France allowed that the music of the king's chapel, as also of his chamber, excelled that of any prince in Europe. Few nations have a greater passion for music than the Spaniards; there are few of them that do not play on the guitar, and with this instrument at night they serenade their mistresses. At Madrid, and in other cities of Spain, it is common to meet in the streets, young men equipped with a guitar and a dark lanthorn, who taking their station under the windows, sing, and accompany themselves on their instrument; and there is scarce an artificer or labourer in any of the cities or principal towns, who when his work is over does not go to some of the public places and entertain himself with his guitar: nevertheless few Spaniards are composers of music; their operas are Italian, and the performers come chiefly from Milan, Naples, or Venice. Upon the marriage of the king of Spain, Charles II. with Mademoiselle d'Orleans, sundry operas of Lully were represented at Madrid, but the Spaniards were but little pleased with them. The emperor Charles V. was a great lover and judge of music. Guerrino, the best musician in all Spain, composed motets, and, with a licence which some great masters have at times used, had made free with the compositions of others; this the emperor discovered, although none of the musicians of his court were able to do it. The court of Vienna was the last that admitted the Italian music: upon the marriage of the emperor Leopold in the year 1660, an Italian opera was represented; the subject was the story of Orpheus and Eurydice; and since that time the emperor's musicians have been Italians. The marquis Santinella, an excellent musician, composed five or six Italian operas, one whereof was represented at the emperor's own expence, and was therefore entitled Opera Regia. Scarlatti composed an opera for the birth-day of the electoral prince of Bavaria; the subject of it was 'The Triumph of Bavaria over 'Heresy.' The English are said to owe their music to the French, for in 1668 Cambert left France, and went into England, and at London performed his opera of Pomone; but although he was favoured by the king, he was envied by the English musicians, envy being inseparable from merit. Some Englishmen had composed music to operas in their own language, but these not succeeding, the Italian opera has taken place in that kingdom. Some years ago certain French musicians attempted an opera at London, which was well received by the audience; but the English musicians being determined to interrupt the performance, began a quarrel, in which five or six were killed on one side or the other, and the survivors of the French musicians went back to their own country.* In England are concerts at all the places resorted to for the benefit of mineral waters. The king of England's band of music is either good or otherwise, accordingly as he cares for the expence of it. That of James II. was very indifferent, for this reason, that the king chose rather to employ his superfluous money in charity than in music.

These and other particulars contained in the first tome of this work, make the whole of the history of music, as given by the author; the remainder of it has not the least pretence to that character, it being a miscellaneous collection of dissertations, dialogues, discourses, and reflections on the subject of music, without the least regard to the order and course of historical narration. Many of those it is to be suspected are not the work of the author, seeing that the second tome begins with and contains the whole of the 'Comparaison de la Musique Italienne et de 'la Musique Françoise,' written by Mons. de la Viéuville de Freneuse, in answer to the 'Paralele 'des Italiens et des François,' &c., and mentioned in a preceding page of this work.

The first of these detached pieces, and which makes the twelfth chapter of the first tome of the 'Histoire de la Musique et de ses Effets,' is entitled 'Dissertation sur le bon Goût de la Musique d' Italie, de la Musique Françoise, et sur les Opera.' It begins with a remark that the admirers of the Italian music are a small sect of demi-sçavans in the art, notwithstanding they are persons of condition, and that they absolutely condemn the French music as insipid. But that there is another party more deeply skilled in the science, who are faithful to their country, and cannot without indignation suffer that the French music should be despised; and these look upon the Italian music as wild, capricious, and contrary to the rules of art. Between these two parties the author professes to be a moderator: of his impartiality a judgment may be formed from the following sentiments. The harmony of the Italian musicians is learned, especially in their Cantatas and Sonatas; but the style of the French is more natural: besides that, the French performers exceed the Italians in point of execution. The music of the Italians is like Gothic architecture, abounding with ornaments that obscure the work. The Italians express all the passions alike; their symphonies are but echoes of the song. They change the key too frequently, and repeat the same passages too often. Their Cantatas are fit only for the chamber,

* Of this quarrel no mention is made in any of the accounts extant of the English drama, nor any traces of it to be met with in any of the newspapers of the time, which we allow to comprehend all that interval between the first publication of the Gazette in king Charles the Second's reign and the year 1715, when the book now citing was first published.

and their Sonatas of two parts should be played by one violin only. Their thorough-basses doubled and chorded, and their Arpeggios are calculated to deceive the ignorant; and they are like dust thrown into the eyes of men to prevent their seeing; with a deal more to the same purpose. He says that the Abbé de la Louette made certain compositions for a concert at Rome, performed at the palace of the princess Colonna in 1689, which were so difficult to execute, that the famous Francisci was twice out in playing them; from hence he says it appears that the Italian performers are not infallible when they attempt to play or sing at sight.

In the thirteenth and last chapter of the 'Histoire 'de la Musique et de ses Effets,' that is to say, the history of music properly so called, the author treats of the sensibility of some animals, and of the effects of music upon many of them. He says that, being in Holland in the year 1688, he went to see a villa of Milord Portland, and was struck with the sight of a very handsome gallery in his great stable. 'At 'first,' says he, 'I concluded it was for the grooms to 'lye in, but the master of the horse told me that it 'was to give a concert to the horses once a week to 'chear them, which they did, and the horses seemed 'to be greatly delighted therewith.' He says that naturalists observe that hinds are so ravished with the sound of a fine voice, that they will lie down and hearken to it with the more attention; and that some of them are so enraptured with music, as to suffer themselves frequently to be taken without resistance.* It is not uncommon, he adds, to see nightingales, at the time of their making love, assemble themselves in a wood when they hear the sound of instruments or the singing of a fine voice, which they will answer by warbling with so much violence, as often to fall down expiring at the feet of the performer; and as a proof of this fact, he relates that in the month of May the people of Paris go to play in the gardens of the Tuilleries upon lutes and guitars, and that the nightingales and linnets there will perch upon the necks of the instruments, and listen with great attention and delight.

The second tome begins with and contains the whole of the Comparaison de la Musique Italienne et de la Musique Françoise, with a letter of the author to one of his friends on the same subject.

The third tome contains a letter to a lady on the subject of music and the French opera, with some songs adapted to well-known airs in the French operas, and a pastoral drama entitled L'Innocente. This is followed by several dialogues on music in general, containing many curious particulars respecting the French musicians, more particularly Lully, of which a due use has been made in the memoir herein before inserted of that musician.

In tome IV. the author re-assumes the style of history, interspersing a variety of observations upon church music, on the qualifications of a master of music, and on music in general; and relates that Henry II. of France sang with the chanters of his chapel, as did also Charles IX., who, as Brantome asserts, sang his part very well; and for an encouragement to the study and practice of church music, founded the school of St. Innocent. He adds that Henry III. also sang, and that both he and his predecessor, Henry II., were composers of music.

The rest of this tome is taken up with an examen of the Italians and French with respect to the music of each. And herein the author takes occasion to observe on the liberty which some of the Italian musicians have assumed in the composition of motets, to alter the words of the vulgate translation; and of this he gives as an instance a motet of Carissimi, 'Peccavi Domine,' &c., in which he severely censures him for the use of the word Culpas, though he allows the motet to be a beautiful one. Again he remarks that the Italian musicians seldom regard the expression of the words; as an instance whereof he refers to the Judicium Salomonis of this author, upon which he observes, that the setting of the word Discernere, in the prayer of Solomon, is shocking, as containing a melody in which all the chords are taken, which he condemns as a puerile effort. Nevertheless, he commends very highly other parts of this composition, particularly the chidings of the two mothers; and, above all, the dignity and majesty with which Solomon is made to pronounce his decree. The author adds, that this composition is the finest of Carissimi's works that he had ever seen, and that he looks upon this musician as the least unworthy adversary whom the Italians have to oppose Lully.

He observes that, for want of attention, the expression of a particular word in music may become ridiculous, and may even be a burlesque of the sentiment. And to this purpose he relates the following story: 'In 1680 or 82, when Dumont 'died, and Robert retired, instead of the two masters 'of music which the king had at his chapel, he 'chose to have four; and to the end that these 'places should be filled by musicians that were 'worthy of them, he sent into the provinces a 'circular letter, by which all the masters at cathe-'drals were invited to Versailles, in order to give 'proofs of their several abilities. Among many 'that offered themselves was Le Sueur, chapel-'master of the church of Notre Dame at Rouen, 'a man of a happy and fruitful genius, one who 'had a very good knowledge of the Latin tongue, 'and merited this post as well as any. As he had 'no great patrons, he endeavoured to recommend 'himself by the performance of a studied com-'position, previous to that which was to be the test 'of his abilities: to that end he prepared a piece 'to be sung one day at the king's mass: it was the 'seventieth psalm, "Qui habitat in adjutorio," &c.† 'an admirable one, and equal to the text; and the 'king and all his court heard it with great attention. 'At the seventh verse, "Cadent a latere tuo," &c., 'Le Sueur had represented the falling, signified by

---

* That horses are sensible of the effects of music is remarked by the duke of Newcastle in his treatise of Horsemanship; and that deer are rendered tame by it, is no less confidently asserted: Playford relates that he saw a herd of stags, twenty in number, who were drawn by the sound of a bagpipe and a violin, from Yorkshire to Hampton-Court. See page 402, in note.

† This is a mistake of the author, the psalm is the ninetieth in the Vulgate, and the ninety-first in our translation.

'the word Cadent, by a chorus in fugue, which made
'a rumbling through seven or eight notes descending;
'and when the deep basses had run over the noisy
'octave, resting upon the last note, there was no
'auditor but must be supposed, according to Le Sueur,
'whom this invention had charmed, to have repre-
'sented to himself the idea of a man rolling down
'stairs, and falling with great violence to the bottom.
'This description struck but too much one of the
'courtiers, who, upon hearing the rumblings of the
'fugue, at one of those Ca-a-a-dents, cried out,
"There is somebody down that will never get up
"again." This pleasantry disturbed the gravity and
'the silence of the whole assembly. The king
'laughed at it, and the rest appeared to wait only
'for permission to second him. A long uninterrupted
'hearty laugh ensued, at the end whereof the king
'made a sign with his hand, and the music went on.
'At the tenth verse, " Et flagellum non appropin-
"quabit," &c., poor Le Sueur, whose misfortune was
'that of not having exalted himself above those
'puerilities, had set a new fugue upon the word
'Flagellum, in notes that represented the lashing of
'scourges, and that in so lively a manner, that a
'hearer must have thought himself in the midst of
'fifty Capuchins, who were whipping each other with
'all their might. " Alas!" cried another courtier,
'tired with this hurly burly, " these people have
'been scourging each other so long, that they must
"be all in blood." The king was again taken with
'a fit of laughter, which soon became general. The
'piece was finished, and Le Sueur was in hopes that
'the exceptionable passages in it would have been
'forgot. The time of trial drawing on, the candi-
'dates were shut up in a house, and for five or six
'days maintained at the king's expence, but under a
'strict command that none of them should be per-
'mitted to communicate with any person. Each
'tried his utmost efforts upon a psalm appointed for
'the competition, which was the thirty-first, " Beati
"quorum remissæ sunt," &c. But as soon as those
'of the chapel began to sing the work of Le Sueur,
'instead of attending to the beauties of the compo-
'sition, the courtiers recalling to mind the idea of the
'two obnoxious passages in his former master-piece,
'and the jests passed thereupon, cried out, " This is
"the Ca-a-a-dent," and a general laughter ensued.
'The consequence was, that Colasse, La Lande,
'Minoret, and Coupillet were chosen; the three first
'worthy without a doubt, of this post, the last not;*
'and Le Sueur returned home melancholy to his
'house, to execute in the choir of his church an
'excellent " Beati quorum," which no one would
'hear at Versailles, though it received a thousand
'applauses at Rouen. This adventure, which Le
'Sueur after recounted with a very lively resentment
'against the court, had nevertheless so well cured
'him of trifling and false expression, that he passed
'over almost to the opposite extreme. He threw all
'his old music into the fire, fine and pleasing as it
'was; and, during the remainder of his life, com-
'posed new upon every occasion, sober even to
'dryness.'

* For a reason that will be given hereafter.

Throughout his book the author takes every occasion that offers to censure the practice of fugue;
and, taking advantage of the story above related, he
says that although in their church-music, and in their
opera, fugues are the delight of the Italians, they are
tiresome, and in church-music improper; for that
there are few passages in scripture which allow us to
repeat them so many times as the fugue would demand. It is even difficult, adds he, for one to find
words in the church-service with which these frequent repetitions can agree. As to double fugues,
which are made to differ at the same time, good sense
requires that they should be sung by two choirs.

He says of the profane music of France, that it
was originally too intricate and elaborate; but that
Lully reformed it, and left a shining example of that
medium, which ought ever to be preserved between
the extremes of simplicity and refinement. Yet he
observes that the music of Dumont, who flourished
before Lully, though his motets were not printed till
1688, is of an extreme simplicity. He farther says
of this author, that it was he who brought in, or at
least established in France, the use of continued
basses; and that the art and high skill which appear
in the more modern compositions, have not rendered
those of Dumont contemptible, but that they are yet
bought; their respective graces are yet felt; and his
dialogue between an angel and a sinner, ' Peccator
'ubi es?' is still heard with pleasure.

He says that Desmarets, author of the fine opera,
Æneas and Dido, ought to be reckoned among the
church musicians, it being certain that he composed
all that music which Coupillet caused to be performed:
as a proof whereof he relates the following fact.
'After Coupillet had been named for the king's cha-
'pel, merely because Madam the Dauphiness, whom
'Mons. Bossuet had solicited, desired it; he soon
'became sensible of his inability to discharge the
'duties of it, and had recourse to Desmarets, a young
'man then needy and unknown. A bargain was
'made between them, and during ten or a dozen
'years Coupillet held his employment with reputation
'and esteem, till upon breach of the agreement on
'the part of Coupillet, Desmarets made a discovery
'of the secret, and Coupillet retired.'

Towards the close of this work we meet with a
tract, that appears to be an answer to a reply of the
Abbé Raguenet to the Comparaison de la Musique
Italienne et de la Musique Françoise; and by this
author's recognition of the Comparaison, we know it
to be the work of Mons. de la Viéuville de Freneuse.
In this answer it appears that the applauses which in
the Parellel are given to the Italians, more particularly Corelli and Bononcini, had greatly irritated him,
and even bereft him of every source of argument,
excepting personal reflection. Of Corelli he does
but repeat the censures contained in the Comparaison,
but Bononcini is made the subject of a distinct tract,
entitled ' Eclaircissement sur Buononcini.' In this
senseless libel, for it deserves no better a name, the
author enters into an examination of the duets and
cantatas of Bononcini, which he says have no other
fault than that they cannot be sung; which impossi-

bility he makes to arise from the use of fugues, counter-fugues, and intervals but little used, most of them false and irregular ; objections, he says, which are equally to be made against the compositions both of Corelli and Bononcini. He then proceeds to examine a Cantata of Bononcini, as he has done a Sonata of Corelli, that he may equally satisfy, as he professes to do, the friends of these two heroes in different kinds of music. To this end he remarks on a cantata of Bononcini, ' Arde il mio petto amante ;' for the choice whereof he gives this notable reason, that it is very short, and therefore one of the best of the many which that author had composed : and after a great number of idle objections to the expression of the poet's sentiments, the conduct of the melody and harmony, and the use of the tritone in the recitatives, he expresses his sentiments in the following modest terms : ' Ces jolis traits de Corelli et de ' Buononcini, dont vous êtes enchantez, choquent, ' renversent toutes les régles et de la musique et du ' bon sens: on vous défie de trouver quoi que ce soit ' de pareil dans Boesset, Lambert, Camus, dans tous ' les ouvrages de Lulli, et dans les ouvrages de ' Campra, de Desmarets, de M. des Touches, qui ont ' eu du succès ; toute la France, les gens de la cour, ' les connoisseurs ont jusqu'ici méprisé, abhorré de si ' fausses beautez.'

He concludes his invective with an assertion, that, let his adversary, with all his skill in music, choose any sonata of Corelli, or cantata of Bononcini, and correct it at his pleasure, he will not be able to accommodate it to the taste of a Frenchman ; which assertion may be very true, and no reflection on the merit of either of these two persons.

And lastly, to express his contempt, he exhorts the people, as it seems is the custom in Italy, to throw apples, medlars, and oranges at the heads of such musicians as those whom he has so freely censured in the passage above quoted.

Traits du peuple en corroux, pommes, nefles, oranges,
Sifflets de toute espèce et de toute grandeur,
　　Volez sur ce compositeur,
　　　Célebréz ses louanges.

No one that reflects on this controversy can wonder that nothing decisive is produced by it, seeing that in questions of this kind, those of one party generally reason upon principles which are denied by the other. In such a case there can be no appeal but to the general sense of mankind, which has long determined the question, and given to the Italian music that preference, which upon principles universally admitted, is allowed to be its due.

CHAP. CLXXIX.

Baron de Astorga was eminently skilled in music, and a celebrated composer. Of his history little is known, save that he was a Sicilian by birth, and was at the court of Vienna at the beginning of this century, where he was greatly favoured by the emperor Leopold, from whence it is presumed he went to Spain,* and had that title conferred upon him, which,

* Astorga is a city in the province of Leon in Spain, and a bishop's see.

for want of his family name, is the only known designation of him. He was at Lisbon some time, and after that at Leghorn, where being exceedingly caressed by the English merchants there, he was induced to visit England, and passed a winter or two in London, from whence he went to Bohemia ; and at Breslaw, in the year 1726, composed a pastoral entitled Daphne, which was performed there with great applause. He excelled altogether in vocal composition ; his cantatas in particular are by the Italians esteemed above all others. He never travelled without a great number of them, and, though very short-sighted, was used to sing them, accompanying himself on the harpsichord. The anonymous author of Remarks on Mr. Avison's Essay on Musical Expression, says that the Cantatas of the Baron d'Astorga have in general too much of that extravagant gusto, which he condemns, at the same time that he celebrates a Stabat Mater of his as a composition to which he says he scarcely ever met with an equal. This hymn, he adds, had lately been performed at Oxford with universal approbation. The Academy of Ancient Music are in possession of it, and it now frequently makes a part of their entertainment on Thursday evenings.

Antonio Vivaldi *(a Portrait),* Maestro de' Concerti del Pio Ospitale della Pieta in Venetia, and Maestro di Capella dà Camera to Philip, landgrave of Hesse Darmstadt, was a celebrated composer for the violin, as also a great master of that instrument. He composed Solos, Sonatas, and Concertos to a great number ; but his principal works are his third and eighth operas ; the latter of these consists of two books of concertos, entitled ' Il Cimento dell Armonia e dell' Inventione ;' but the common name of them is the Seasons. The plan of this work must appear very ridiculous ; for the four first concertos are a pretended paraphrase, in musical notes, of so many sonnets on the four seasons, wherein the author endeavours, by the force of harmony, and particular modifications of air and measure, to excite ideas correspondent with the sentiments of the several poems. The subsequent compositions have a similar tendency, but are less restrained ; whether it be that the attempt was new and singular, or that these compositions are distinguished for their peculiar force and energy, certain it is that the Opera VIII. is the most applauded of Vivaldi's works. Indeed the peculiar characteristic of Vivaldi's music, speaking of his Concertos—for as to his Solos and Sonatas they are tame enough—is, that it is wild and irregular ; and in some instances it seems to have been his study that it should be so ; some of his compositions are expressly entitled Extravaganzas, as transgressing the bounds of melody and modulation ; as does also that concerto of his in which the notes of the cuckoo's song are frittered into such minute divisions as in the author's time few but himself could express on any instrument whatsoever. From this character of his compositions it will necessarily be inferred that the harmony of them, and the artful contexture of the parts, is their least merit ; but against this conclusion there are a few exceptions ;

the eleventh of his first twelve Concertos being, in the opinion of the judicious author of Remarks on Mr. Avison's Essay on Musical Expression, a very solid and masterly composition, and an evidence that the author was possessed of a greater degree of skill and learning than his works in general discover. For these his singularities, no better reason can be given than this: Corelli, who lived a few years before him, had introduced a style which all the composers of Italy affected to imitate: as Corelli formed it, it was chaste, sober, and elegant, but with his imitators it degenerated into dulness; this Vivaldi seemed to be aware of, and for the sake of variety, gave into a style which had little but novelty to recommend it.*

The account herein before given of the progress of music in England respects solely this island, where only it had been cultivated as a liberal science. Mention has occasionally been made of the state of music in Wales, in Ireland, and in Scotland; and a particular account has been given of the origin of those melodies which distinguish the music of this latter kingdom from that of every other country. In the principality of Wales, and the kingdom of Ireland, it appears that music derived very little assistance from those precepts which it had been the endeavour of learned and ingenious men to disseminate throughout Europe; the consequence whereof has been, that, submitting to no regulation but the simple dictates of nature, the music of those countries has for many centuries remained the same; and can hardly be said to have received the least degree of improvement.

In Scotland the case has been somewhat different: a manuscript is now extant,† written in the Scottish dialect, entitled 'The art of Music collectit out of 'all ancient Doctouris of Music,' wherein all the modern improvements respecting the composition of music in parts are adopted; and the precepts of Franchinus, Zarlino, and other eminent writers, are enforced by arguments drawn from the principles of the science, and the practice of those countries where it had been first improved, and has continued to flourish in the greatest degree. The study of the mathematics has in these later years been cultivated in Scotland; and at the beginning of this century some faint essays were made in that country towards an investigation of the principles of music: the result of these we are strangers to; but of the success of the pursuit in general we are enabled to form a judgment by means of a learned and valuable work, entitled 'A Treatise of Music, speculative, 'practical, and historical, by ALEXANDER MALCOLM,' printed at Edinburgh in 1721, of which it is here proposed to give an account.

This book contains fourteen chapters, subdivided into sections.

Chap. I. contains an account of the object and end of music, and the nature of the science. In the definition and division of it under this head, the author considers the nature of sound, a word he says that stands for every perception that comes immediately by the ear; and which he explains to be the effect of the mutual collision, and consequent tremulous motions in bodies, communicated to the circumambient fluid of the air, and propagated through it to the organs of hearing. He then enquires into the various affections of sound, so far as they respect music, of which he makes a two-fold division, that is to say, into

I. The knowledge of the Materia Musica.

II. The art of Composition.

Chap. II. treats of tune, or the relation of acuteness and gravity in sounds. The author says that sounds are produced in chords by their vibratory motions, which, though they are not the immediate cause of sound, yet they influence those insensible motions that immediately produce it; and, for any reason we have to doubt of it, are always proportional to them; and therefore he infers that we may measure sounds as justly in these as we could do in the other, if they fell under our measures; but as the sensible vibrations of whole chords cannot be measured in the act of producing sound, the proportions of vibrations of different chords must be sought in another way, that is to say, by chords of different tensions, or grossness, or lengths, being in all other respects equal. And for the effect of these differences he cites Vincentio Galilei, who asserts that there are three ways by which we may make the sound of a chord acuter, viz., by shortening it, by a greater tension, and by making it smaller, cæteris paribus. By shortening it, the ratio of an octave is 1 : 2; by tension it is 1 : 4; and by lessening the thickness it is also 1 : 4; meaning in the last case when the tones are measured by the weights of the chord.

The vibrations of chords in either of the cases above put, in order to ascertain the degrees of acuteness and gravity, are insensible; and being by necessary consequence immeasurable, can only be judged by analogy. In order however to form some conclusion about them, the author cites from Dr. Holder's treatise, the following passage; on which he says the whole theory of his natural grounds and principles of harmony is founded. 'The first 'and great principle upon which the nature of har- 'monical sounds is to be found out and discovered 'is this: That the tune of a note (to speak in our 'vulgar phrase) is constituted by the measure and 'proportions of vibrations of the sonorous body; 'I mean of the velocity of these vibrations in their 'recourses; for the frequenter these vibrations are, 'the more acute is the tune: the slower and fewer 'they are in the same space of time, by so much 'more grave is the tune. So that any given note of 'a tune is made by one certain measure of velocity 'of vibrations, viz., such a certain number of courses 'and recourses, e. g. of a chord or string in such 'a certain space of time, doth constitute such a de- 'terminate tune.'

* The Opera terza of Vivaldi, containing twelve Concertos for violins, was reprinted in England, and published by Walsh and Hare, with the following title, which is here inserted as a proof of the assertion in page '801 of this work, that they were both illiterate men; 'Vivaldi's most 'celebrated Concertos in all their parts for violins and other instruments, 'with a Thorough-Bass for the Harpsichord, Compos'd by Antonia 'Vivaldi, Opera terza.'

† Penes Authorem.

EFFIGIES ANTONII VIVALDI

Upon this passage Malcolm observes, that though we want experiments to prove that the difference of the numbers of vibrations in a given time is the true cause on the part of the object of our perceiving a difference of tune, yet we find by experience and reason both, that the differences of tunes are inseparably connected with the number of vibrations; and therefore these, or the lengths of chords to which they are proportional, may be taken for the true measure of different tunes.

Chap. III. contains an enquiry into the nature of concord and discord. The several effects of these on the mind are too obvious to need any remark; but the causes of those different sensations of pleasure and distaste severally excited by them, he resolves into the will of God, as other philosophers do the principle of gravitation. Yet upon what he calls the secondary reason of things, arising from the law or rule of that order which the divine wisdom has established, he proceeds to investigate the ratios of the several intervals of the diapason, distinguishing them into concords and discords: and concludes this chapter with a relation of some remarkable phœnomena respecting concord and discord; such as the mutual vibration of consonant strings; the breaking of a drinking-glass by the sound of the human voice adjusted to the tune of it, and gradually encreased to the greatest possible degree of loudness;* and to these, which are the effects of concord, he adds an instance of a different kind, that is to say, of an effect produced by discordant sounds: the relation is taken from Dr. Holder, a person of sound judgment in music, and of unquestionable veracity, and is well worthy of attention.

' Being in an arched sounding room near a shrill ' bell of a house-clock, when the alarm struck I ' whistled to it, which I did with ease in the same ' tune with the bell; but endeavouring to whistle ' a note higher or lower, the sound of the bell and ' its cross motions were so predominant, that my ' breath and lips were checked so, that I could not ' whistle at all, nor make any sound of it in that ' discordant tune. After, I sounded a shrill whistling ' pipe, which was out of tune to the bell, and their ' motions so clashed that they seemed to sound like ' switching one another in the air.'†

Chap. IV. is on the subject of harmonical arithmetic, and contains an explanation of the nature of arithmetical, geometrical, and harmonical proportion, with rules for the addition, subtraction, multiplication, and division of ratios and intervals.

Chap. V. contains the uses and application of the preceding theory, explaining the nature of the original concords, and also of the compound concords.

Chap. VI. explains the geometrical part of music, and the method of dividing right lines, so as their sections or parts one with another, or with the whole, shall contain any given interval of sound.

Chap. VII. treats of harmony, and explains the

* It is said that Mr. Francis Hughes, a gentleman of the royal chapel in the reign of king George I. who had a very strong counter-tenor voice, could with ease break a drinking-glass in this manner.

† Treatise of the Natural Grounds and Principles of Harmony, page 34.

nature and variety of it, as it depends upon the various combinations of concording sounds.

Chap. VIII. treats of concinnous intervals, and the scale of music, and herein are shewn the necessity and use of discords, and their original dependence on the concords. Farther it explains the use of degrees in the construction of the scale of music.

Chap. IX. treats of the mode or key in music, and of the office of the scale of music.

Chap. X. treats of the defects of instruments, and of the remedy thereof in general, by the means of sharps and flats.

In order to shew these defects he exhibits in the first place the series of tones and semitones in the Systema Maxima, taking it from C, and extending it to cc, as hereunder given; upon which it is to be observed that the colon between two letters is the sign of a greater tone, 8 : 9; a semicolon the sign of a lesser tone, 9 : 10; and a point the sign of a semitone, 15 : 16; supposing the letters to represent the several notes of an instrument tuned according to the relations marked by those tones and semitones.

C : D; E . F : G; A : B . c : d; e . f : g; a : b . cc.

Upon which he makes the following observation: ' Here we have the diatonick series with the 3d ' and 6th greater proceeding from C; and therefore ' if only this series is expressed, some songs com- ' posed with a flat melody, i. e. whose key has a ' lesser 3d, &c. could not be performed on the organ ' or harpsichord, because no one of the octaves of ' this series has all the natural intervals of the ' diatonick series, with a 3d lesser.'

To remedy these and other defects of instruments whose intervals depend not upon the will of the performer, but are determined by the tuning, he says a scale of semitones was invented, which he exhibits in this form:—

c. c♯. d. d♯. e. f. f♯. g. g♯. a. b. ♮ cc.

$\frac{15}{16}$ $\frac{128}{135}$ $\frac{15}{16}$ $\frac{24}{25}$ $\frac{15}{16}$ $\frac{128}{135}$ $\frac{15}{16}$ $\frac{15}{16}$ $\frac{24}{25}$ $\frac{15}{16}$ $\frac{128}{135}$ $\frac{15}{16}$

And upon it he observes that it contains the diatonic series in the key C, with both the greater and lesser third, with their accompaniments in all their just proportions; and that it corrects the errors of the tritone between F and ♮, and the defective fifth between ♮ and F.

This division corresponds in theory with the Systema Participato mentioned by Bontempi, and spoken of in page 415, and elsewhere in the course of this work.

Malcolm also gives a second division of the octave into semitones in the following form:—

c. c♯. d. d♯. e. f. f♯. g. g♯. a. b. ♮ cc.

$\frac{16}{17}$ $\frac{17}{18}$ $\frac{18}{19}$ $\frac{19}{20}$ $\frac{15}{16}$ $\frac{16}{17}$ $\frac{17}{18}$ $\frac{18}{19}$ $\frac{19}{20}$ $\frac{16}{17}$ $\frac{17}{18}$ $\frac{15}{16}$

being that invented by Mr. Thomas Salmon, and inserted in the Philosophical Transactions; upon which Malcolm observes, that having calculated the ratios thereof, he found more of them false than in the preceding scale, but that their errors were considerably fewer; so that upon the whole the merits of both seem to be nearly equal.

This chapter of Malcolm's book contains many curious observations upon the necessity of a temperature, arising from that surd quantity, which for many centuries, even from the time of Boetius, it has been the study of musicians to dispose of. The author concludes with a general approbation of the semitonic division, and of the present practice in tuning the organ and harpsichord, corresponding as nearly to it as the judgment of the ear will enable men. As to the pretences of the nicer kind of musicians, he demonstrates that they tend to introduce more errors than those under which the present system labours.

Chap. XI. describes the method and art of writing music, and shews how the differences in tune are represented. Under this head the author explains the nature and use of the cliffs; as also the nature of transposition, both by a change of the cliff and of the key or mode. He also explains the practice of solmisation, and makes some remarks on the names of notes. Lastly he enters into an examination of Salmon's proposal for reducing all music to one cliff, as delivered in his Essay to the Advancement of Music. This proposal Malcolm not only approves of, but expresses himself with no little acrimony against that ignorance and superstition which haunts little minds, and the pride and vanity of the possessors of the art; all which he says have concurred in the rejection of so beneficial an invention.

Chap. XII. treats of the time or duration of sounds in music, and herein, 1. Of time in general, and its subdivision into absolute and relative; and particularly of the names, signs, and proportions in relative measures of notes as to time. 2. Of absolute time, and the various modes or constitution of parts of a piece of melody, on which the different airs in music depend; and particularly of the distinction of common and triple time; and the description of the Chronometer for measuring it. 3. Concerning rests and pauses of time, with some other necessary remarks in writing music.

The Chronometer mentioned in this chapter is an invention of Mons. Loulie, a French musician, and is described in the account herein before given of him, and of a book of his writing, entitled 'Elemens ou Principes de Musique.'

Chap. XIII. contains the general rules and principles of harmonic composition.

The whole of this chapter, as Malcolm acknowledges in the introduction to his work, was communicated to him by a friend, whom he is forbidden to name. The rules are such as are to be found in almost every book on the subject of musical composition.

The account given in Chap. XIV. of the ancient music, is, considering the brevity of it, very entertaining and satisfactory. Speaking of the tones or modes, he says there are four different senses in which the term is accepted, that is to say, it is used to signify, 1. A single sound, as when we say the lyre had seven tones. 2. A certain interval, as for example, the difference between the diatessaron and diapente. 3. The tension of the voice, as when we say one sings with an acute or a grave voice.* 4. A certain system, as when they say the Doric or Lydian mode or tone.

In the consideration of this latter sense of the word Mode, he observes that Boetius has given a very ambiguous definition of the term; for, to give the remark in his own words, Malcolm says he first tells us 'that the modes depend on the seven 'different species of the diapason, which are also 'called Tropi; and these, says he, are 'Con'stitutiones in totis vocum ordinibus vel gravitate 'vel acumine differentes.' Again he says, 'Con'stitutio est plenum veluti modulationis corpus, ex 'consonantiarum conjunctione consistens, quale est 'Diapason, &c. Has igitur constitutiones, si quis 'totas faciat acutiores, vel in gravius totas remittat 'secundum supradictas Diapason consonantiæ species, 'efficiet modes septem.' This is indeed a very 'ambiguous determination, for if they depend on 'the species of 8ves, to what purpose is the last 'clause? and if they differ only by the tenor or 'place of the whole 8ve, i. e. as it is taken at a 'higher or lower pitch, what need the species of '8ves be at all brought in? His meaning perhaps 'is only to signify that the different orders or 'species of 8ves lie in different places, i. e. higher 'and lower in the scale. Ptolemy makes them the 'same with the species of diapason; but at the 'same time he speaks of their being at certain 'distances from one another.'

Upon this seeming ambiguity it may be remarked, that the two definitions of a mode or tone above cited from Boetius, are reconcileable with each other; for the proof whereof we refer to a dissertation on this subject by Sir Francis Haskins Eyles Stiles, published in the Philosophical Transactions, vol. LI. part ii. for the year 1760, and abridged in book II. chap. 11, 12, of this work.

In a short history of the improvements in music, which makes part of the fourteenth chapter, the author takes particular notice of the reformation of the ancient scale by Guido, and adopts the sentiments of some very ingenious man, who scruples not to say of his contrivance of six syllables to denote the position of the two semitones in the diatonic series of an octave, that it is 'Crux tenellorum ingeniorum.'†

In the comparison between the ancient and modern music, contained in this chapter, this author says that the latter has the preference; and upon that controverted question, whether the ancients were acquainted with music in consonance or not, he cites

* Acuteness and gravity are affections of sound: and note of tone, that both the grave and acute pipes of any given stop in an organ, the vox humana and cornet, for instance, have, comparing pipe with pipe, the same tone, or rather that peculiarity of sound which distinguishes the voice of one person from another, or the sound of the cornet from another instrument.

† This censure is grounded on the opinion of some very ingenious man, whom Malcolm has not thought fit to name, and probably never heard of. Great pains have been taken to find out the author of it, but to no purpose. All that can be said of it is, that it occurs in Brossard's Dictionaire de Musique, voce SYSTEME, as the sentiment of an illustrious writer of the last age. Dr. Pepusch has given it an answer in his Treatise of Harmony, edit. 1731, page 70.

a variety of passages from Aristotle, Seneca, and Cassiodorus, to the purpose, and scruples not to determine in the negative.

From this general view of its contents, it must appear that the work above mentioned is replete with musical erudition. Extensive as the subject is, the author has contrived to bring under consideration all the essential parts of the science. His knowledge of the mathematics has enabled him to discuss, with great clearness and perspicuity, the doctrine of ratios, and other abstract speculations, in the language of a philosopher and a scholar. In a word, it is a work from which a student may derive great advantage, and may be justly deemed one of the most valuable treatises on the subject of theoretical and practical music to be found in any of the modern languages.

CHAP. CLXXX.

JOHN FRANCIS DE LA FOND, a singing-master, and a teacher of the principal instruments, and also of the Latin and French tongues, published in 1725, at London, an octavo volume, entitled ' A new ' System of Music both theoretical and practical, ' and yet not mathematical,' wherein he undertakes to make the practice of music easier by three quarters, and to teach a new and easier method than any yet known of figuring and playing thorough, or, as he affects to call it, compound bass.

The first of these ends he attempts to effect by an indiscriminate charge of folly and absurdity on all that had written on music before him, and an assertion that mathematics have little or nothing to do with music ; the second by an argument tending to prove, what no one ever yet denied, to wit, that in the semitonic scale, which divides the octave into tones and semitones, there are twelve intervals. His proposition of teaching thorough-bass consists not in the rejection of the figures with which it is necessarily encumbered, but in the assigning to them severally, powers different from what they now possess ; it is conceived in the following terms : ' Nature teaches us to call the first or unison, the ' unison ; the flat 2nd the 2nd ; the sharp 2nd the ' 3rd, the flat 3rd the 4th ; the sharp third the 5th, ' the 4th the 6th, the flat 5th the 7th, the natural ' 5th the 8th, the sharp 5th or flat 6th the 9th, the ' sharp 6th the 10th, the flat 7th the 11th, the sharp ' 7th the 12th ; the 8th, which according to their ' notions should be either natural, flat, or sharp, or ' sometimes one of them, and sometimes another ; ' the 8th I say is the 13th, the flat 9th the 14th, ' and the sharp 9th the 15th, all which I mark thus, ' 1, 2, 3, 4, 5, 6, 7, 8, 9, o, u, d, t, q, Q, using ' letters for the five last, not only for the sake of ' keeping to one figure only, but because those letters ' are the initials of the proper names of those con- ' cords ; and I make the last a capital, to distinguish ' it from the last but one. The concords I think ' proper to call by the Latin names, as being more ' musical than the English ones. And these terms ' I write here at length for the sake of the Non- ' Latinists ; Unison or Prime, Second, Terce, Quart,

' Quint, Sexte, Septime, Octave, None, Decime, ' Undecime, Duodecime, Tredecime, Quatuordecime, ' and Quindecime. Nor can this be thought a great ' innovation, for three of those names are received ' already.

' All these denominations are plain, self-consistent, ' and free from the very shadow of ambiguity. The ' scholar, counting his concords from the bass note, ' as is now done, and minding his plain figures, ' without troubling himself about the naturalness, ' flatness, or sharpness of any note, will at once find ' all his concords, let the mode be soft or gay, or ' the piece run over all their flats and sharps.'*

To illustrate this whimsical scheme of notation, the author gives an example in the sixth Sonata of the fourth opera of Corelli, figured according to the above directions.

Another improvement of music suggested by this author, and which he means to refer to the first head, of an easier practice, is the rejection of the cliffs, for which innovation the following is his modest apology :—' At my first setting out, I have ' complained of a veil that has for many ages hung ' before the noble science of music. This complaint ' I have repeated since ; but this is the place where ' it ought to be repeated with the most passionate ' tone. For indeed the business of clefs is the thickest ' part of that thick veil. This veil, or rather this ' worst part of it, is so much the more intolerable, ' as it seems to have been wilfully made. We have ' seen that the authors of the seven pretended notes, ' &c. have probably been misled into that absurd ' notion by their idle remark that the voice naturally ' sings eight notes. But I think it impossible to ' assign any cause of mistake in the introducing of ' the clefs into the tablature.'† His proposal for getting rid of the cliffs is in truth a notable one, and is nothing more than that we should suppose the three parts of a musical composition to be comprehended within the compass of one cliff, viz., the treble, in which case, to use his own words, ' I call ' the note upon the second line G, (as it is now ' called in the trebles) not only in the treble, but ' likewise in the tenor and the bass * * * In short, ' I reduce both the tenor and the bass to the treble, ' because there are a great many more trebles played ' than there are tenors and basses, both put together.'‡

With regard to his system, as he calls it, so far as it tends to establish a division of the octave into twelve notes, omitting the blunder of notes for intervals,§ it is not his own, but is the systema participato, mentioned by Bontempi, explained in the foregoing part of this work, and referred to at the bottom of the page. His method of figuring thorough-bass is less intelligible than that now in use ; and as to his proposal for rejecting the cliffs,

* Page 113, et seq.

† Page 40. The Tablature is that method of notation in which the sounds are signified by the letters of the alphabet, and not by the musical notes : here the author substituted the term in the place of the word Scale, and adds one instance more to the many others that occur in his book, of his ignorance of the subject he is writing on.

‡ The Systema participato, or semitonic scale, divides the octave into thirteen sounds or notes, comprehending twelve intervals of a semitone each. See page 401 of this work, in note, 415, in note, 455, in note.

§ Page 146.

there is no end to the confusion which it has a tendency to introduce; nor can any one without the cliffs be capable of understanding the nature and office of the scale of music. And, after all, the arguments urged in favour of these several innovations, are none of them of weight sufficient to justify them, seeing, that with all the difficulties imputed to it, the modern system of notation is a language that we find by experience

' Girls may read, and boys may understand.' Pope.

But allowing it to be otherwise, it might admit of a question what would be gained by an innovation that would render the compositions of all former musicians as generally unintelligible as is at this day a Saxon manuscript.

To enumerate all the arrogant assertions in favour of his own notions, and the contemptuous expressions with respect to the discoveries and improvements of others, that occur in the course of this work, would be in effect to transcribe the whole of a book now deservedly consigned to oblivion.

In the year 1724, the lovers of music were gratified with a work, the only one of the kind, and which, for the circumstances attending it, may be considered as the grandest and most splendid of any musical publication at this day extant; the title of it, to give it at length, is as follows: ' Estro ' poetico-armonico Parafrasi sopra li primi venti- ' cinque Salmi. Poesia di Girolamo Ascanio Gius- ' tiniani, Musica di Benedetto Marcello, Patrizi ' Veneti.' This work, consisting of no fewer than eight volumes in folio, has the recommendation of some of the most eminent musicians of the time in all the several countries of Europe; and these accompany not only the first, but each of the several volumes, in such sort, that it appears to have been the occasion of a correspondence, in which some of the most eminent poets and musicians were engaged, ultimately tending to celebrate the work and its author. The letters that passed on this occasion, and are prefixed to the several volumes, abound with a variety of curious particulars respecting music, and have the signatures of the following persons, viz., Domenico Lazzarini, Francesco Gasparini, Antonio Bononcini, Francesco Conti, Francesco Rosellini, Carlo Baliani, Francesca-Antonio Calegari, Giovanni Bononcini, Tommaso Carapella, Domenico Sarri, John Mattheson, Steffano Andrea Fiorè, Giuseppe Bencini, Geminiano Jacomelli, and George Philip Telemann. Thus much must serve for a general character of the work, a particular account of it is referred to a memoir of the author, which it is here proposed to give.

Benedetto Marcello, a noble Venetian, was born on the twenty-fourth day of July, 1686. His father, Agostino Marcello, was a senator of Venice; his mother, Paolino, was of the honourable family of Cappello, being the daughter of Girolamo Cappello, and the aunt of Pietro Andrea Cappello, ambassador from the state of Venice to the court of Spain, Vienna, and Rome, and who also was resident in England in that capacity about the year 1743, and afterwards.

The male issue of these two persons were Alessandro, a son next to him whose Christian name is unknown, and the above mentioned Benedetto Marcello. The elder of them addicted himself to the study of natural philosophy and the mathematical sciences, as also music, in which he attained to great proficiency; his younger brother Benedetto had been well instructed in classical literature, and having gone through a regular course of education under proper masters, was committed to the tuition of his elder brother, and by him taken into his house, with a view to his farther improvement in philosophy and the liberal arts.

Alessandro Marcello dwelt at Venice; he had a musical academy in his house, holden regularly on a certain day in every week, in which were frequently performed his own compositions. Being a man of rank, and eminent for his great endowments, his house was the resort of all strangers that came to visit the city. It happened at a certain time that the princes of Brunswic were there, who being invited to a musical performance in the academy above mentioned, took particular notice of Benedetto, at that time very young, and among other questions, asked him, in the hearing of his brother, what were the studies that most engaged his attention; ' O,' said his brother, ' he is a very ' useful little fellow to me, for he fetches my books ' and papers; the fittest employment for such a one ' as he is.' The boy was nettled at this answer, which reflected as much upon his supposed want of genius, as his youth, he therefore resolved to apply himself to music and poetry; which his brother seeing, committed him to the care of Francesco Gasparini, to be instructed in the principles of music;[*] for poetry he had other assistances, and at length became a great proficient in both arts.

In the year 1716, the birth of the first son of the emperor Charles VI. was celebrated at Vienna with great magnificence; and upon this occasion a Serenata, composed by Benedetto Marcello, was performed there with great applause. In the year 1718, he published a little collection of Sonnets under the title of ' Driante, Sacreo Pastor Arcade,' which he dedicated to the celebrated Giovanni Mario Crescimbeni of Macerata, by his assumed name of Alfesibeo Cario, one of the founders of the Academy of Arcadians, into which Benedetto, from his great reputation, had been some time before elected.[†]

In the year 1722, he published an elegant little work, intitled ' Teatro alla moda,' of which there have been many editions. The judgment which the Marquis Scipio Maffei has given of this excellent performance, which is in the gay, lively, and facetious style, may be seen in the third volume of his Literary Observations, page 308, of the Verona edition, printed in 1738, and in the letters of Apostolo Zeno, both of them to the honour of the author.

Benedetto Marcello also published a collection of

---

[*] See a letter of this person prefixed to the first volume of Marcello's Psalms, wherein he mentions that Marcello prosecuted his studies under him.

[†] Vide Le Vite degli Arcade Illustri, in the Istoria della Volgar Poesia of Crescimbeni, printed at Venice in 1730, vol. VI. page 378.

Sonnets intitled 'Sonetti a Dio,' with various other compositions on sacred subjects, of which there were two numerous impressions in a short time. This work he published as a forerunner of a greater, which he did not live to finish. To prepare himself for this learned and sublime undertaking, he employed some years in the study of theology and the holy fathers.

As to his musical compositions, they were many and various; two Cantatas of his, the one intitled 'Il Timoteo,' the other 'La Cassandra,' are celebrated by Signor Abbate Conti, in a letter to Girolamo Ascanio Giustiniani, to this effect: 'Dryden, 'a celebrated English poet, in an ode for music in- 'troduces Timotheus, who singing to Alexander, one 'while of wars and victories, another of tenderness 'and love; then of the slain in battle, and their 'ghosts, and of other subjects which move terror or 'pity, raises in him by turns all the softest and most 'furious passions. I was so pleased with the new- 'ness of this thought, that so long ago as when 'I was in France, I translated the ode out of English 'into Italian verse, changing the lyric form of the 'poem into the dramatic, by introducing the chorus 'and two persons, one of whom explains the subject 'of the song, the other is Timotheus himself, who 'sings. Benedetto Marcello being pleased with the 'poem, set it to music in the form of a Cantata, dis- 'playing therein the fruitfulness, and at the same 'time the depth of his art. Afterwards he desired 'to have the whole variety of passions expressed in 'Timotheus, brought into a poem by means of some 'other fable or story, in which one person only should 'speak; and recollecting that first Euripides, and 'afterwards Lycophron, had introduced Cassandra to 'foretell the misfortunes that should befall, in the 'one case the Greeks, in the other the Trojans, 'I undertook to imitate them; and to give magnifi- 'cence and beauty to the imaginations of poetry, 'I put into the mouth of Cassandra, in the form of 'a prophecy, the most remarkable events celebrated 'by Homer in the Iliad. Marcello was pleased with 'the invention, and adorned it with all those colours 'of harmony which are most interesting, surprising, 'and delightful; and I think I say everything when 'I compare the music of the Cassandra, making due 'allowance for the deficiency of the subject, to that 'of the Psalms paraphrased by your excellence, and 'sung with so much applause at Venice, Vienna, 'and Padua.'

Marcello made also a composition for a mass, which is highly celebrated, and was performed for the first time in the church of Santa Maria della Celestia, on occasion of Donna Alessandra Maria Marcello, his brother's daughter, taking the veil in that monastery. He also set to music the Lamentations of Jeremiah, the Miserere, and the Salve: these, with many other sacred compositions, he gave to the clergy of the church of Santa Sophia, and was at the pains of in- structing them in the manner in which they were to be performed.

For many years Marcello was a constant member of a musical academy held at the house of Agostino Coletti, organist of the church of the Holy Apostles, in which he always sat at the harpsichord; and by his authority, which every one acquiesced in, directed and regulated the whole performance.

In the year 1724 came out the first four volumes of the Paraphrase of the Psalms by Giustiniani, in Italian, set to music for one, two, and three voices, by Benedetto Marcello; and in the two subsequent years four more, including in the whole the first fifty of the Psalms. Before the work is a prefatory ad- dress of the poet and the musical composer, explaining the nature and tendency of the work, wherein they observe that it is the first of its kind, and is intro- duced into the world without the advantage of any precedent that might have directed the method and disposition of it. Of the Paraphrase they say, that, although embellished with the ornaments of poetry, it is rather literal than allegorical; and that where the poet has ventured to dilate upon the text, he has followed those interpreters, who have most closely adhered to the letter. Farther, it is said that the verse is without rhyme, and of various metres; in which latter respect it corresponds with that of the Psalms as they stand in the Hebrew text, to which, notwithstanding that the Paraphrase is chiefly founded on the Vulgate translation, as also to the Septuagint version, the poet has in some instances had recourse.

In what regards the music, we must suppose the preface to speak the sentiments of Marcello himself. And herein he observes, that as the subject requires that the words and sentiments be clearly and pro- perly expressed, the music for the most part is composed for two voices only. It was, he says, for this reason, and to move the passions and affections the more forcibly, that the music of the ancients, as namely the Hebrews, the Phœnicians, and Greeks, was altogether unisonous; but in these our days, and now that our ears are accustomed to the harmony of many parts, an attempt to approach too nearly to the happy and simple melody of the ancients, might prove no less difficult than dangerous. It was therefore, he says, judged not improper to compose these Psalms, as he had done, for two, and sometimes for three and four parts; but, after all, the author confesses that this kind of composition, which is ra- ther to be called an ingenious counterpoint, than natural melody, is more likely to please the learned reader, who peruses it in writing, than the ordinary hearer; as well by reason of the perpetual conflict of fugues and imitations in the different parts, as from the multiplicity of mixed consonances which accom- pany them, in order to fill and complete the chorus; and which in fact are not real consonances, according to the undeniable geometric and arithmetic experi- ments of the ancient Greek philosophers, who in the investigation of what is to be admired in this science, have discovered great skill.

On the other hand this author remarks, that during a long series of years, new laws have been given both to the theory and practice of music, to which it is necessary to render obedience.

From this observation the author digresses to the

music of the ancient Greeks, which he commends for its simplicity; ascribing to it more power to affect the passions than that of the moderns with all its laboured and artificial ornaments. For this, as also for other reasons, Marcello professes that in his work he has not always affected the modern style, though he would not take upon him to reform it; yet he owns that he has sometimes transgressed against the rules of it, in order to attain to the true simplicity and manly gravity which characterizes that of the ancients.

After lamenting the debasement of music, by its association with vain and trivial poetry; and the abuse of the science, not only in the theatre, but in places of sacred worship, the author professes that his design is to restore it to its primitive dignity. And that to that end he has chosen for his subject the Psalms of David, which, though by him composed for the most part for two voices, he says may and ought to be sung by a great number, agreeably to the practice recorded in the holy scriptures, which speak of psalms and hymns sung by many companies or chorusses.

He gives his reader to understand that he has introduced in the course of his work several of the most ancient and best known intonations of the Hebrews, which are still sung by the Jews, and are a species of music peculiar to that people. These, which for want of a better word, we are necessitated to call Chants, he says he has sometimes accompanied according to the artificial practice of the moderns, as he has done by certain Cantilenas of the ancient Greeks; the latter, he says, he has interpreted with the utmost diligence; and, by the help of those two ancient philosophers, Alypius and Gaudentius, has reduced them to modern practice.

To those mysterious and emphatic sentences, in which the royal prophet has denounced the terrors of divine justice, he says he has thought it not inexpedient to adapt a peculiar kind of music, that is to say, a modulation in the Madrigalesc style, with a commixture of the diatonic and chromatic genera. And in this respect he compares his present labours to those of a pilot, who in a wide and tempestuous ocean avails himself of every wind that may conduct him to his port, yet in a long and dangerous voyage is constrained to vary his course.

A few brief directions for the performance of the several compositions, and a modest apology for the defects in the work, conclude this preface, which, though written under the influence of strong prejudices, is an ingenious and learned dissertation on the subjects of poetry and music.

In the year 1726 this great work was completed by the publication of four volumes more, containing a paraphrase of the second twenty-five psalms; and as an evidence of the author's skill in that kind of composition, in which some of the most eminent musicians have endeavoured to excel, viz., Canon, he has, at the end of the last volume, given one of a very elaborate contexture.

For the character of this work we must refer to the letters and testimonies of those eminent musicians and other persons above named, who have joined in the recommendation of it in their several addresses to the author. Mattheson of Hamburg, in a letter to him, prefixed to the sixth volume, says that the music to some of the Psalms had been adapted to words in the German language, and had been performed with great applause in the cathedral of that city. And we are farther told, that for the satisfaction of hearing these compositions, the Russians had made a translation of the Italian paraphrase into their own language, associating to it the original music of Marcello,* and that some sheets of the work had been transmitted to the author in his lifetime. At Rome these compositions were held in the highest estimation by all who professed either to understand or love music: at the palace of Cardinal Ottoboni was a musical academy holden on Monday in every week, in which Corelli performed; at this musical assembly one of the psalms of Marcello made constantly a part of the entertainment; and for the purpose of performing them there, the author composed to them instrumental parts.† When the news of Marcello's death arrived at Rome, his eminence, as a public testimony of affection for his memory, ordered that on a day appointed for the usual assembly, there should be a solemn musical performance. The room was hung with black; the performers and all present were in deep mourning; Father Santo Canal, a Jesuit, made the oration; and the most eminent of the learned of that time rehearsed their respective compositions upon the occasion in various languages, in the presence of the many considerable personages there assembled. Nor has this country been wanting in respect for the abilities of this great man; Mr. Charles Avison, organist in Newcastle, had celebrated this work in an Essay on Musical Expression, and had given out proposals for publishing by subscription an edition of it revised by himself; but it seems that the execution of this design devolved to another person, Mr. John Garth, of Durham, who was at the pains of adapting to the music of Marcello suitable words from our own prose translation of the Psalms, with a view to their being performed as anthems in cathedrals; and with the assistance of a numerous subscription, the work was completed and published in eight folio volumes.

From the foregoing account of his studies and pursuits it might be supposed that Marcello had wholly devoted himself to a life of ease and retirement; but in this opinion it seems we should be mistaken, for we find that he held several honourable posts in the state, and as a magistrate was ever ready to contribute his share of attention and labour towards the support of that government under which he lived. He was for many years a judge in one of the councils of forty: from thence he was removed to the charge of Proveditor of Pola. Afterwards he was appointed to the office of chamberlain or treasurer of the city of Brescia, where he gained the affection and esteem of all orders of men, and, above

---

* Life of Marcello prefixed to the English Psalms adapted to the music of Marcello.

† A copy of these was in the collection of the late Mr. Smith, the English consul at Venice, and was sold as part of his library by Messieurs Baker and Leigh, booksellers, in York street, Covent-Garden.

all, of his eminence Cardinal Quirini, who encouraged frequent visits from him in the most familiar manner; and had once a week a literary conference with him.

Marcello died at Brescia in the year 1739. He was buried in the church of the fathers, Minor Observants of St. Joseph of Brescia, with a degree of funeral pomp suited to his rank. On his tombstone of marble, in the middle of the church, is engraved the following inscription:—

BENEDICTO MARCELLO PATRITIO VENETO
SAPIENTISSIMO PHILOLOGO POETÆ MUSICES PRINCIPI
QUESTORI BRIXIENSI UXOR MOESTISSIMA
POSUIT
ANNO MDCCXXXIX VIII KALENDAS AUGUSTI
VIXIT ANNOS LII MENSES XI DIES XXVIII.

While he was at Brescia he wrote a very elegant poem, which he entitled Volo Pindarico Eroi-comico, in which, feigning himself to be carried with a sudden flight to the coffee-house in the square of St. Felice at Venice, which he used to frequent, to meet the many friends he had there, he describes, in a pleasing and lively strain of humour, the peculiar manners and characters of them severally; and then gives them the like information of his own way of life at Brescia, and of the most respectable of those persons whose friendship he there enjoyed.

He left in manuscript some admonitions in prose to his nephew, Lorenzo Alessandro, a son of his brother Alessandro, a young man of great genius and learning: these consist of counsels and precepts that bespeak as well the piety as the wisdom of their author; twenty-five cantos of the poem above-mentioned; a treatise of proportions; another of the musical system; another of the harmonical concords; and a great number of poetical compositions, the manuscripts whereof are in the possession of his above-mentioned nephew.

Of the noble family of Marcello mention is made by all the historians of Venice, and in the oldest chronicles in manuscript. Battista Nani celebrates Lorenzo Marcello, captain of the Venetian Galleasses, who in an engagement at sea, with the fleet of Amurath IV. had his arm broken, and was afterwards by the senate raised to a post of great honour. Among the moderns Casimire, Frescoth, Bruzen, La Martiniere, in his Geographical Dictionary, under the article Venice; and Marco Foscarini, in his excellent treatise of the Italian literature, speak of this family in terms of the greatest respect.

To the foregoing account of the works of Marcello may be added from the Dutch catalogues, VI. Sonate a violoncello solo e basso continuo, opera prima. XII. Sonate a flauto solo e basso continuo, opera seconda; and VI. Sonate a tre, due violoncelli o due viole da gamba, e violoncello o basso continuo, called opera seconda.

Mr Avison, as well in certain remarks on the Psalms of Marcello, prefixed to the English version adapted to his music, as in the proposals for the publication thereof, printed at the end of the second edition of his Essay on Musical Expression, has represented this work as a most perfect exemplar of the grand, the beautiful, and the pathetic in music; with sundry other epithets, not less proper, as applied to music, than fanciful: notwithstanding which, and the numerous testimonies of authors, that accompany the original work, there have not been wanting in this country men of sober judgment, and of great eminence for skill in the science of practical composition, who object to the Psalms of Marcello, that the levity of these compositions in general renders the work a fitter entertainment for the chamber, than an exercise for church service.* That they abound in the evidences of a fertile invention, improved to a high degree by study, all must allow; but whoever shall contemplate that style in music, which in the purest ages has been looked upon as the best adapted to excite devout affections, and understands what in musical speech is meant by the epithets, sublime and pathetic, will be apt to entertain a doubt whether these can with greater propriety be applied to them than to many less celebrated compositions.

The following specimen of Marcello's style is selected from the forty-second of his Psalms:—

* See Remarks on Mr. Avison's Essay on Musical Expression, Lond. 1743, pag. 113, et seq. The author of these Remarks, in proof of his assertion, has referred to the eighth of Marcello's Psalms, than which a more injudicious association of sound and sentiment can hardly be found: in this poem the psalmist celebrates the power and goodness of God, as manifested in his works of creation and providence; and to one of the most sublime sentiments contained in it, the musical composer has adapted an air in minuet time, the lightest that can be conceived. This psalm, which as it stands in the English version, begins, 'O Lord our governor, how excellent is thy name in all the world!' is now frequently sung as an anthem; and there are persons that will give a boy half a guinea to sing it, who can scarce lend their attention to Gibbons's 'Hosanna,' or Purcell's 'O give thanks.'

BENEDETTO MARCELLO.

FRANCESCO GEMINIANI.

CHAP. CLXXXI.

FRANCESCO GEMINIANI (*a Portrait*), a native of Lucca, was born about the year 1680. He received his first instructions in music from Alessandro Scarlatti, and after that became a pupil of Carlo Ambrosio Lunati, surnamed Il Gobbo,* a most celebrated performer on the violin; after which he became a disciple of Corelli, and under him finished his studies on that instrument.

In the year 1714 he came to England, where in a short time he so recommended himself by his exquisite performance, that all who professed to understand or love music, were captivated at the hearing him; and among the nobility were many who severally laid claim to the honour of being his patrons; but the person to whom he seemed the most closely to attach himself was the Baron Kilmansegge, chamberlain to king George I. as elector of Hanover, and a favourite of that prince. In the year 1716 he published and dedicated to that nobleman twelve Sonatas, a Violino Violone e Cembalo: the first six with fugues and double stops, as they are vulgarly called; the last with airs of various measures, such as Allemandes, Courants, and Jigs.

The publication of this work had such an effect, that men were at a loss to determine which was the greatest excellence of Geminiani, his performance or his skill and fine style in composition; and, with a due attention to his interest, there is no saying to what degree he might have availed himself of that favour, which his merits had found in this country: this at least is certain, that the publication of his book impressed his patron with such a sense of his abilities, as moved him to endeavour to procure for him a more beneficial patronage than his own; to this end he mentioned Geminiani to the king as an exquisite performer, and the author of a work, which at the same time he produced, and the king had no sooner looked over, than he expressed a desire to hear some of the compositions contained in it performed by the author. The baron immediately communicated the king's pleasure to Geminiani, who, though he was gladly disposed to obey such a command, intimated to the Baron a wish that he might be accompanied on the harpsichord by Mr. Handel, which being signified to the king, both masters had notice to attend at St. James's, and Geminiani acquitted himself in a manner worthy of the expectations that had been formed of him.

It is much to be doubted whether the talents of Geminiani were of such a kind as qualified him to give a direction to the national taste; his compositions, elegant and ornate as they were, carried in them no evidences of that extensive genius which is required in dramatic music; nor did he make the least effort to show that he was possessed of the talent of associating music with poetry, or of adapting corresponding sounds to sentiments: the consequence hereof was, that he was necessitated to rely on the patronage of his friends among the nobility,

Vide ante, page 808.

and to depend for subsistence upon presents, and the profits which accrued to him by teaching, upon terms which himself was permitted to make.

A situation like this must appear little better than humiliating, to one that considers the ease and affluence, and, comparatively speaking, independent situation of Corelli, who through his whole life seems to have enjoyed the blessings of ease, affluence, and fame. Corelli for some years led the orchestra in the opera at Rome; we find not that Geminiani occupied a similar situation at London, nor that he was at any time of his life a public performer: it may therefore be a wonder what were his means of subsistence during his long stay in this country. All that can be said to this purpose is, that he had very many bountiful patrons and pupils, as many in number as he could possibly attend.

The relation between the arts of music and painting is so near, that in numberless instances, those who have excelled in one have been admirers of the other. Geminiani was an enthusiast in painting, and the versatility of his temper was such, that, to gratify this passion, he not only suspended his studies, and neglected the exercise of his talents, but involved himself in straits and difficulties, which a small degree of prudence would have taught him to avoid. To gratify his taste, he bought pictures; and, to supply his wants, he sold them; the necessary consequence of this kind of traffic was loss, and its concomitant, necessity.

In the distress, which by this imprudent conduct he had brought on himself, Geminiani was necessitated, for the security of his person, to avail himself of that protection which the nobility of this country have power to extend in favour of their servants. The late earl of Essex was a lover of music, and had been taught the violin by Geminiani, who at times had been resident in his lordship's family; upon this ground the earl was prevailed on to inroll the name of Geminiani in the list of those servants of his whom he meant to screen from the process of the law.

The notification of the security which Geminiani had thus obtained was not so general as to answer the design of it. A creditor for a small sum of money arrested him, and threw him into the prison of the Marshalsea, from whence, upon an application to his protector, he was, however, in a very short time discharged.†

A series of conduct such as that of Geminiani was, the neglecting the improvement of those advantages which would have resulted from his great abilities in his profession; his contracting of debts, and neglect in payment of them, seem to indicate as well a want of principle as discretion: nevertheless that he was in an eminent degree possessed of the former, will appear from the following anecdote.

The place of master and composer of the state music in Ireland had been occupied for several years

† Immediately upon his confinement he sent, by one Forest, an attorney, a letter to a gentleman in lord Essex's family, who, upon shewing it to his lordship, was directed to go to the prison and claim Geminiani as the servant of the earl of Essex, which he did, and the prisoner was accordingly discharged. This fact, together with many others above-mentioned, was communicated by the person to whom the letter was sent.

by John Sigismund Cousser, a German musician of great eminence, who will be spoken of hereafter. This person died in the year 1727; and notice of his decease coming to the earl of Essex, he, by means of lord Percival, obtained of the minister, Sir Robert Walpole, a promise of the place; which he had no sooner got, than lord Essex immediately sent for Geminiani, and told him that his difficulties were now at an end, for that he had provided for him an honourable employment, suited to his profession and abilities, and which would afford him an ample provision for life; but upon enquiry into the conditions of the office, Geminiani found that it was not tenable by one of the Romish communion, he therefore declined accepting it, assigning as a reason that he was a member of the catholic church; and that though he had never made great pretensions to religion, the thought of renouncing that faith in which he had been baptized, for the sake of worldly advantage, was what he could in no way answer to his conscience. Upon this refusal on the part of Geminiani, the place was bestowed on Mr. Matthew Dubourg, a young man who had been one of his pupils, and was a celebrated performer on the violin.

Some years had now elapsed since the publication of his Solos, and as well with a view to advantage, as in compliance with his inclinations, he set himself to compose parts to the first part of the Opera quinta of Corelli, or, in other words, to make Concertos of the first six of his Solos. This work he completed, and, with the help of a subscription, at the head of which were the names of the royal family, he published it in the year 1726. A short time after, he made the remaining six of Corelli's Solos also into Concertos; but these having no fugues, and consisting altogether of airs, afforded him but little scope for the exercise of his skill, and met with but an indifferent reception.

He also made Concertos of six of Corelli's Sonatas, that is to say, the ninth in the first opera, and the first, third, fourth, ninth, and tenth of the third. This seems to have been a hasty publication, and is hardly now remembered. In the year 1732 he published what he styled his Opera second, that is to say, VI. Concerti grossi con due Violini, Violoncello, e Viola di Concertino Obligati, e due altri Violini, e basso di Concerto grosso ad arbitrio, with a dedication to Henrietta, duchess of Marlborough. The first of these compositions is celebrated for the fine minuet with which it closes; the first idea of the Concerto was the following Solo, which the author had composed many years before, and has never yet appeared in print:—

FRANCESCO GEMINIANI.

The publication of this work was soon followed by another of the same kind, that is to say, his Opera terza, consisting of six Concertos for violins, the last whereof is looked upon as one of the finest compositions of the kind in the world.

Geminiani was now in the highest degree of estimation as a composer for instruments; for, to say the truth, he was in this branch of music without a rival; but his circumstances were very little mended by the profits that resulted from these several publications. The manuscript of his Opera seconda had been surreptitiously obtained by Walsh, who was about to print it, but thinking it would be the better for the corrections of the author, he gave him the alternative of correcting it, or submitting it to appear in the world with such faults as would have reflected indelible disgrace on the author.

An offer of this kind was nothing less than an insult, and as such Geminiani received it. He therefore not only rejected it with scorn, but instituted a process in the court of chancery for an injunction against the sale of the book, but Walsh compounded the matter, and the work was published under the inspection of the author.

The Opera terza he parted with for a sum of money to Walsh, who printed it, and in an advertisement has given the lovers of music to understand that he came honestly by the copy.

As Geminiani lived to a great age, and published at different times many other of his compositions, the farther particulars of his life are referred to a subsequent part of this work.

The refinements that resulted from the association of music with the drama, were successively adopted by the English and the French; by the former at the restoration of Charles II., and by the latter in the year 1669, when Lewis XIV. established the Royal Academy of Music at Paris. Germany at that time abounded with excellent musicians, viz., deep theorists, and men profoundly skilled in the principles of harmony, and the practice of musical composition; but, excepting the organists of that country, and they must be acknowledged to have been at all times excellent, we hear of few that were distinguished for their performance on any particular instrument; and of still fewer of either sex that were celebrated as fine singers; and it seems that without those adventitious aids, which in other countries were thought necessary to the support of music, that is to say, the blandishments of an effeminate and enervated melody, and the splendour of scenic decoration, in Germany both the science and the practice continued to flourish for many ages in the simple purity of nature, and under regulations so austere, as seemed to bid defiance to innovations of any kind.

It happened, notwithstanding, that the emperor Leopold, being a great lover of music, began to discover an early propensity to the style of the Italians: the recitative of Carissimi exhibited to him a species of composition, in which the powers of eloquence derived new force by the association to speech, of sounds that corresponded to the sense, and were of all others the most melodious. As soon therefore as a cessation from the toils of war gave him leisure to cultivate the arts of peace, he set himself to introduce the Italian music into Germany; accordingly we find that he had Italian composers in his court; that he gave pensions and rewards to the most excellent of them, as namely, Caldara, Ziani, Lotti, Bononcini, and others; that he had also representations of Italian operas, and that some of the most celebrated singers performed in them, and requited his patronage and bounty with their usual ingratitude and insolence.

Nor was it alone at Vienna that Italian music and the opera were thus introduced and encouraged; the same passion influenced other princes of Germany, and in other cities, namely, Berlin, Hanover, and Hamburg, we find that the Italian musicians were greatly caressed; that the works of some of the most eminent of them, that is to say, Pistocchi, Corelli, Vivaldi, and many others, are dedicated to German princes; that operas were represented in the principal cities in Germany, some whereof were written in the German language; and, lastly, that the German musicians themselves became composers of operas.

From these circumstances we are enabled to ascertain the origin of dramatic music in Germany, and having fixed it, it becomes necessary to give an account of some of the most celebrated composers in the theatric style, natives of that country, including one who chose this kingdom for his residence, and whose loss will long be deplored by its inhabitants.

CHAP. CLXXXII.

Johann Sigismund Cousser, born about the year 1657, was the son of an eminent musician of Presburg, in Hungary; and being initiated by his father in the rudiments of music, and also in the practice of composition, he travelled for improvement into France, and at Paris became a favourite of Lully, and was by him assisted in the prosecution of his studies. After a stay of six years in Paris, Cousser visited Germany, where he was so well received, that in two cities, viz., Wolffenbuttel and Stutgard, he was successively chosen chapel-master; but, being of a roving disposition, he quitted the latter charge, and went to settle at Hamburg, where being chosen director of the opera, he, about the year 1693, introduced the Italian method of singing, to which the Germans had till that time been strangers. About the year 1700 he took a resolution to visit Italy, and made two journies thither in the space of five years. Upon his last return to Germany, failing of that encouragement which he thought due to his merit, he quitted that country, and came to England, and, settling in London, became a private teacher of music; by which profession, and also by the profits arising from an annual public concert, he was enabled to support himself in a decent manner. In the year 1710 he went to Ireland, and obtained an employment in the cathedral church of Dublin, which, though our ecclesiastical constitution knows no such officer, he looked upon as equivalent to that of chapel-master in foreign countries. After some continuance in that city, his merits recommended him to the place of master of the king's band of music in Ireland, which he held till the time of his death. From the time of his first settlement in Ireland, Cousser applied himself to the study of the theory of music, with a view, as it is said, to his attainment of the degree of doctor in that faculty of the university of Dublin. His works in print are Erindo, an opera, 1693; Porus, and Pyramus and Thisbe, 1694; Scipio Africanus, 1695; and Jason, 1697. These several operas had been performed at Hamburg. There was also published at Nuremberg, in 1700, a work of Cousser, entitled 'Apollon enjoüe, con-'tenant six Overtures de Theatre, accompagnées de 'plusieurs airs;' and in the same year an opera entitled Ariadne; as also a collection of airs from it, entitled Helicon-ische Musen-Lust. He was re-sident in London at the time of the death of Mrs. Arabella Hunt, and set to music an ode written on that occasion by one William Meres, Esq. beginning 'Long have I fear'd that you, my sable muse.'

The last of his publications was, A Serenade represented on the Birth-day of Geo. I. at the castle of Dublin, the 28th of May, 1724, in the title whereof he styles himself 'master of the musick 'attending his Majesty's state in Ireland, and chapel-'master of Trinity-college, Dublin.'

Cousser died at Dublin in the year 1727; and, having recommended himself to the people of that city by his great abilities in his profession, and the general tenor of his deportment, his loss was greatly lamented. His successor in the office of master of the king's band was Mr. Matthew Dubourg, a pupil of Geminiani, and a celebrated performer on the violin.

REINHARD KEISER was a native of Saxe-Weissen-fels, and chapel-master to the duke of Mecklenburg. He was a most voluminous writer, and is said to have exceeded Scarlatti in the number of operas composed by him; which may probably be true, for in the preface to an opera of his, published at Hamburg in 1725, that work is said to be the hundred and seventh opera of his composing. The operas of Keiser were written in the German lan-guage, the music was nevertheless in the style of the Italians; they were performed at Hamburg, and many of them were by the author himself published in that city. He had the direction of the opera at Hamburg from the time when it was first established, till, being a man of gaiety and expence, he was necessitated to quit it; after which the composers for that theatre were successively Steffani, Mattheson, and Mr. Handel. From Hamburg, Keiser went to Copenhagen; and, in 1722, being royal chapel-master in that city, he composed an opera for the king of Denmark's birth-day, entitled Ulysses. An imperfect catalogue of his works, containing an account of such only of them as are printed, is given by Walther in the article KEISER; they consist of Operas, Oratorios, Hymns, and Cantatas, amounting to an incredible number.

Keiser is ranked with Scarlatti and other the most eminent musicians who flourished at the begin-ning of this century; and although his compositions could derive but little advantage from the poetry with which his music was associated, such was the native ease and elegance of his style, and such his command over the passions of his hearers, that all became susceptible of their effects.

DIETRICH BUXTEHUDE, son of Johann Buxtehude, organist of St. Olaus at Elsineur, was a disciple of John Thiel, and organist of the church of St. Mary at Lubec. Mattheson, in his Vollkommenen Capellmeister, page 130, celebrates him as a famous organist and composer, and speaks of six Suites of Lessons for the harpsichord of his, in which the nature of the planets is represented or delineated. With these are printed a choral com-position to German words, being a lamentation on the death of his father. In 1696 he published two operas of Sonatas a Violino, Viola da Gamba, e Cembalo.

JOHANN MATTHESON, a native of Hamburg, was born the twenty-eighth day of September, 1681. In the seventh year of his age he was by his parents placed under the care of different masters, and was by them instructed in the rudiments of learning and the principles of music, in which science he improved so fast, that at the age of nine he was able to sing to the organ at Hamburg, compositions of his own. At the same time that he pursued the study of music he made himself master of the modern languages, and applied himself to attain a knowledge of the civil law; to which purpose he became a diligent attendant on the public lectures successively read by two eminent doctors in that faculty. At the age of eighteen he composed an opera, and in it performed the principal part. In 1703 an offer was made him of the place of organist of the church at Lubec, but, not liking the conditions of the appointment, which were that he should submit to the yoke of marriage with a young woman whom the magistrats had chosen for him,* he thought proper to decline it. In 1704 he visited Holland, and was invited to accept the place of organist at Harlem, with a salary of fifteen hundred florins a year; but he declined it, choosing to return to his own country, where he became secretary to Sir Cyril Wych, resident at Hamburg for the English court. In this station he made himself master of the English tongue, and, without abandoning the study of music, took up a resolution to quit the opera stage, on which he had been a singer for fifteen years. In 1709 he married Catherine, a daughter of Mr. Jennings, a clergyman, nearly related to the admiral Sir John Jennings.

In the course of his employment as secretary to the resident, he was intrusted with several important

* This expedient to get rid of a burgher's daughter, by yoking her with the town organist, suggests to remembrance a practice nearly similar to it in this country. The road from Putney to Richmond lies through common fields, at the entrance whereof are sundry gates, at each of which a poor man is stationed, who upon opening the gate for passengers, is generally rewarded with a halfpenny. The appointment of these persons is by the parish officers, who, considering that the profits thus arising are more than adequate to the wants of a poor man, annex to their grant a condition that the person appointed shall marry a poor woman out of their workhouse, and rid the parish of the expense of maintaining her.

negotiations, and made frequent journies to Leipsic, Bremen, and divers parts of Saxony, from which he reaped considerable advantages. Upon the death of Sir Cyril Wych, in the year 1712, the care of the English affairs in the circle of Lower Saxony devolved upon Mattheson, and he occupied the office of resident till the son of the late minister was appointed to it. Upon the accession of king George I. to the crown of England, he composed a memorable Serenata; and in the year 1715 obtained the reversion of the office of chapel-master in the cathedral of Hamburg, with certain other preferments annexed to it. During all this time he continued his station of secretary to the British resident; and, upon many occasions of his absence, he discharged in his own proper person the functions of the minister. Amidst that multiplicity of business which necessarily sprang from such a situation, Mattheson found means to prosecute his musical studies; he composed music for the church and for the theatre, and was ever present at the performance of it: he practised the harpsichord at his own apartments incessantly, and on that instrument, if not on the organ, was unquestionably one of the first performers of his time. He wrote and translated books to an incredible number, and this without an exclusive attachment to any particular object; and the versatility of his temper cannot be more strongly marked than by observing that he composed church-music and operas, wrote treatises on music, and upon the longitude; and translated from the English into the German language, the Chevalier Ramsay's Travels of Cyrus, and the History of Moll Flanders, written by Daniel de Foe. Of his musical treatises his Orchestre, his Critica Musica, his **Musicalische** Patriot, and his **Vollkommenen Capellmeister,** are the best known. His writings in general abound with intelligence communicated in a desultory manner, and are an evidence that the author possessed more learning than judgment.

Mattheson was very well acquainted with Handel. Before the latter came to settle in England they were in some sort rivals, and solicited with equal ardour the favour of the public. Mattheson relates that he had often vied with him on the organ both at Hamburg and Lubec. The terms upon which these two great men lived when they were together, must appear very strange. Handel approved so highly of the compositions of Mattheson, particularly his lessons, that he was used to play them for his private amusement;* and Mattheson had so great a regard for Handel, that he at one time entertained thoughts of writing his life. In the years 1735 and 1737 he published a work entitled **Die wol-klingende Fin-**

ger=**Sprache,** *i. e.* 'The well-sounding Finger 'Language,' consisting of twelve fugues for the organ, on two and three subjects, and dedicated it to Handel, who, upon the publication of it, wrote him a letter, in which is the following passage:—

'——à present je viens de receivoir votre dernier 'lettre avec votre ouvrage, je vous en remercie 'Monsieur, et je vous assure que j'ai toute l'estime 'pour votre merite.—L'ouvrage est digne de l'atten-'tion des connoisseurs,—et quant a moi je vous rends 'justice.'

And yet these two men were in one moment of their lives at so great enmity, that each had the other opposed to the point of his sword. In short, they, upon a dispute about the feat at the harpsichord at the performance of one of Mattheson's operas, fought a duel in the market-place of Hamburg, which a mere accident prevented from being mortal to one or both of them. Mattheson died at Hamburg in the year 1764. At the beginning of the sixth volume of Marcello's Psalms, is a letter of his to the author, in the Italian language, dated Hamburg, 6 Oct. 1725, with this subscription, 'Giovanni Mattheson di 'S. A. R. il Duca d' Holstein, Secretario Britannico. 'Canonico minore della Chiesa d'Amburgo, e 'Direttore della Musica Catedrale.'

JOHANN BERNHARD BACH, eldest son of Giles Bach, senior musician to the senate of Erfurth, was born November 23, 1676, and was at first organist in the merchants' church there. Afterwards he went to reside at Magdeburg, and in the year 1703 to Eisenach, where he became chamber-musician to the duke.

JOHANN CHRISTOPHER BACH, of the same family, was organist at Eisenach, and continued in that function thirty-eight years. He died in the year 1703, leaving behind him three sons, all musicians, namely, JOHANN NICOLAUS, organist at Jena in the year 1695, and a celebrated maker of harpsichords. JOHANN CHRISTOPHER, who resided first at Erfurth, afterwards at Hamburgh, and after that at Rotterdam and London, in which cities his profession was teaching; and JOHANN FREDERICK, organist of the church of St. Blase at Muhlhausen.

JOHANN MICHAEL BACH, brother of the above-mentioned John Christopher Bach, of Eisenach, was organist, and also town-clerk of Gehren, a market-town and bailiwick near the forest of Thuringia. He has composed a great many church pieces, concertos, and harpsichord lessons, of which none have ever yet been printed.

JOHANN SEBASTIAN BACH, son of John Ambrose Bach, formerly musician to the court and senate of Eisenach, and a near relation of him last named, was born in that city on the twenty-first day of March, 1685. He was initiated in the practice of the harpsichord by his eldest brother John Christopher Bach, organist and professor of music in the school of Ohrdruff; and in 1703 was appointed first organist of the new church at Arnstadt, which station he quitted in 1707, for the place of organist of the church of St. Blase at Muhlhausen. Here also he stayed but a short time, for in 1708 he went to settle

* Mattheson had sent over to England, in order to their being published here, two collections of lessons for the harpsichord, and they were accordingly engraved on copper, and printed for Richard Meares, in St. Paul's church-yard, and published in the year 1714. Handel was at this time in London, and in the afternoon was used to frequent St. Paul's church for the sake of hearing the service, and of playing on the organ after it was over; from whence he and some of the gentlemen of the choir would frequently adjourn to the Queen's Arms tavern in St. Paul's church-yard, where was a harpsichord: it happened one afternoon, when they were thus met together, Mr. Weely, a gentleman of the choir, came in and informed them that Mr. Mattheson's lessons were then to be had at Mr. Meares's shop; upon which Mr. Handel ordered them immediately to be sent for, and upon their being brought, played them all over without rising from the instrument.

at Weimar, and became chamber-musician, and also court-organist to the duke; and in 1714 was appointed concert-master to that prince. In 1717 he was preferred to the office of chapel-master to the prince of Anhalt Cothen; and in 1723, upon the decease of Kuhnau, to that of music-director at Leipsic; and about the same time was appointed chapel-master to the duke of Weissenfells. Amongst a great variety of excellent compositions for the harpsichord, he published, in 1726, a collection of lessons entitled **Clabier=Ubung,** or Practice for the Harpsichord. He composed a double fugue in three subjects, in one of which he introduces his name.*

This person was celebrated for his skill in the composition of canon, as also for his performance on the organ, especially in the use of the pedals. Mattheson says that on this instrument he was even superior to Handel. His son, Mr. John Christian Bach, now in London, who has furnished some of the anecdotes contained in this article, relates that there are many printed accounts of his father extant in the German language; as also that he had a trial of skill with Marchand, the famous French organist, and foiled him. The particulars of this contest are

as follow: Marchand being at Dresden, and having shewn himself superior to the best organists of France and Italy, made a formal notification that he was ready to play extempore with any German who was willing to engage with him. Upon which the king of Poland sent to Weimar for John Sebastian Bach, who accepting the challenge of Marchand, obtained, in the judgment of all the hearers, a complete victory over him.

John Sebastian Bach died about the year 1749, leaving four sons, who, as if it had been intended that a genius for music should be hereditary in the family, are all excellent musicians: the eldest, Frederic William, is at this time organist of Dresden: the second, Charles Philip Emanuel, is now an organist and music-director at Hamburg; the third, John Frederic Christian, is in the service of the Count de la Lippe; and the fourth, John Christian, after having studied some years in Italy, has chosen London for the place of his residence; and in his profession has the honour to receive the commands of our amiable queen.†

The following composition of John Sebastian Bach is among his lessons above mentioned. :—

ARIA.

---

* Walther relates that he had observed that the notes B♭, A, C, and ♮ are melodious in their order; the last is by the Germans signified by the letter ♮: taking, therefore, this succession of notes for a point or subject, he wrought it into a fugue, as above is mentioned. Mr. John Christian Bach being applied to for an explanation of this obscure passage in Walther's memoir of his father, gave this account of it, and in the presence of the author of this work, wrote down the point of the fugue.

† Her majesty's master of the harpsichord upon her arrival in England was Mr. Kelway, an Englishman; as is also the dancing-master of the present queen of France, a circumstance so singular as to merit remembrance. At Layton Stone, in Essex, dwells an eminent dancing-master, Mr.   Jay; a few years ago he had an apprentice, the son of a neighbour, a diligent and ingenious lad, and who was generally called by the familiar appellation of Harry Bishop. A person of distinction, who had a seat near Layton Stone, had taken notice of him, and conceiving him to be a youth of great hopes, sent him for improvement to Paris, and in a short time he excelled the most celebrated masters there; and, such are his abilities in a profession in which the French are generally allowed to exceed all Europe, that the queen of France is at this time the scholar of Mr. Bishop, an Englishman, and at the royal palace of Versailles receives from him a stated number of lessons in every week.

JOHANN SEBASTIAN BACH.

CHAP. CLXXXIII.

GEORGE PHILIPP TELEMANN was born at Magde-burg on the fourteenth day of March, 1681. His father was a minister of the Lutheran church, who dying in the infancy of this his son, left him to the care of his mother. As the child grew up he dis-covered a strong propensity to music, which his mother endeavoured to get the better of, intending him for the university; but she finding that her son, who had been taught the rudiments of music, as other children in the German schools usually are, was determined to pursue the study of it, gave way to his inclination. As a proof of the early abilities of Telemann, it is said that he composed motets, and other pieces for the church service, in his infancy; and that by the time he was twelve years of age, he had composed almost the whole of an opera.

Having taken a resolution to yield to this inclination of her son, and seeing the progress he had already made in music, the mother of Telemann was easily prevailed on by the friends of the family to encourage him in this course of study; accordingly she placed him first in the school of Zellerfelde, and after four years stay there, removed him to the Gymnasium at Hildesheim, where he perfected his studies in litera-ture; and in music made such great improvements that he was appointed director of the church-music in the monastery of the Godchardins, and in the per-formance thereof was indulged with the liberty of employing musicians of the Lutheran persuasion.

This was but the beginning of his fame; soon after a wider field opened for him to exhibit his un-common talents in, for in the year 1701, being sent to Leipsic to study the law, he was appointed to the direction of the operas, and was also chosen first music-director and organist in the new church.

Anno 1704 he became chapel-master to the count of Promniz, which post, in 1709, he exchanged for that of secretary and chapel-master to the duke of Eisenach. In 1712 he was chosen chapel-master to the Carmelite monastery at Francfort-on-the-Mayne. Shortly after he obtained the music direction in St. Catherine's church, and was appointed chapel-master at the court of Saxe Gotha.

In the year 1721, the city of Hamburg, desirous of having such an extraordinary man amongst them, prevailed on him to accept the place of director of their music, as also of the office of chanter in the church of St. John. He had hardly been a year at Hamburg, when an offer was made him of the post of music-director at Leipsic, which by the decease of Kuhnau was then lately become vacant; but being so well settled, he declined accepting it, and it was thereupon conferred on John Sebastian Bach. All this time Telemann continued in the service of the duke of Eisenach, who found him sufficient employ-ment, not only in the way of his profession, but in his post of secretary, to which he had formerly appointed him. The few leisure hours which these his employments left him, he devoted to the service of the Margrave of Bareith, to whom for some years he had presented his compositions, and who had appointed him his chapel-master. However all these numerous avocations could not detain him from pur-suing a design, which for many years he had enter-tained, of seeing Paris; and accordingly about Michaelmas, 1738, he made a journey thither; and as his fame had reached that country, he met upon his arrival there with all the distinguishing marks of esteem due to his character. After a stay of about six months at Paris he returned to Hamburg, where he spent the remainder of his days. The time of his death is variously reported, but the better opinion is that it was about the year 1767.

Telemann was a very voluminous composer, and the greatest church musician in Germany. Handel, speaking of his uncommon skill and readiness, was used to say that he could write a church piece of eight parts with the same expedition as another would write a letter. Telemann was twice married; by both his wives he had ten children, of whom it is remarkable that none of them ever discovered the least genius for music; six of them were living at the time of his decease. To testify his regard for the city of Leipsic, to which he was indebted for his first preferments, he founded a music school there, which still exists. His successor in the office of music-director at Hamburg is the celebrated Charles Philip Emanuel Bach, mentioned in the preceding article.

JOHANN GOTTFRIED WALTHER was one of a family that from the time of Luther downwards, had pro-duced many excellent musicians. The person here spoken of flourished in the present century, and was organist of the church of St. Peter and Paul in the city of Weimar, and is by Mattheson, in his 𝕍ollkommenen Capellmeister, ranked among the most famous organists and composers for the organ of his time.

Of his musical compositions little is here to be

said, the titles of none of them occurring in any of the catalogues, whence information of this kind has been derived in the course of this work; but the friends of music have the highest obligation to him, as the author of a laborious and most valuable book compiled by him, and published at Leipsic in 1732, entitled 𝕸𝖚𝖘𝖎𝖈𝖆𝖑𝖎𝖘𝖈𝖍𝖊𝖘 Lexicon, oder 𝕸𝖚𝖘𝖎𝖈𝖆𝖑𝖎𝖘𝖈𝖍𝖊 𝕭𝖎𝖇𝖑𝖎𝖔𝖙𝖍𝖊𝖈, in a large octavo volume, containing not only an explanation, in the manner of Brossard, of all the terms used in music, but memoirs of musicians in all ages and all countries, from the first institutors of the science down to his own time. Of the exactness and precision with which this work is executed, a clearer proof cannot be given, than that there is scarce a musician of any eminence, or a parish organist at all celebrated for his performance in this our country, for whom he has not an article.

The book is written in the German language; and no one that is sensible of the copious fund of knowledge contained in it, and the great variety of information it is capable of affording, but must regret that it is not extant in every language in Europe.

The Lexicon of Walther, unlike the History of Music of Printz, contains no account of the author himself, and therefore we are to seek for the particulars of his life. Considering the great variety of learning, and the evidence of long and laborious research displayed in this his work, we cannot suppose him a young man at the time of its publication, and that being now forty-three years ago, it is probable that he has long been at rest from his labours.

GEORGE FREDERIC HANDEL (a Portrait), or, if we would recur to the original spelling of his name, HENDEL, was a native of Halle, a city in the circle of Upper Saxony, and born on the twenty-fourth day of February, 1684. His mother was the second wife of his father, then a man advanced in years, being upwards of sixty; a physician, and also a surgeon in that city.

From the time that Handel began to speak he was able to sing, or at least to articulate musical sounds; and as he grew up, his father, who almost from the time of his birth had determined him for the profession of the law, was very much concerned to find in the child such a strong propensity to music, as was at one time or other likely to thwart his endeavours for his welfare. To prevent the effects of this growing inclination, he banished from his house all musical instruments, and by every method in his power endeavoured to check it. As yet Handel, an infant under seven years of age, having never been sent, as most of the German children are, to the public schools, where they learn music as they do grammar, had no idea of the notes or the method of playing on any instrument: he had, perhaps, seen a harpsichord or clavichord, and, with the innocent curiosity of a child, may be supposed to have pressed down a key, which producing a sound, affected him with pleasure; be this as it may, by the exercise of that cunning, which is discoverable very early in children, Handel found means to get a little clavichord conveyed into a room at the top of his father's house, to which he constantly resorted as soon as the family retired to rest; and, astonishing to say! without any rules to direct his finger, or any instructor than his own ear, he found means to produce from the instrument both melody and harmony.

The father of Handel had a son by his former wife, who was valet de chambre to the duke of Saxe-Weissenfells, and by the time that Handel had nearly attained the age of seven years, he had determined on a journey to see him: his intention was to have gone alone, but Handel having a strong desire to see his half-brother, pressed to be taken with him; his father refused, and accordingly set out by himself; the boy, however, contrived to watch when the chaise set off, and followed it with such resolution and spirit, as to overtake it; and begging with tears to be taken up, the tenderness of a father prevailed, and Handel was made a companion in the journey. Being arrived at the court of the duke, Handel being suffered to go about the apartments, could not resist the temptation to sit down to a harpsichord wherever he met with one. One morning he found means, when the service was just over, to steal to the organ in the duke's chapel, and began to touch it before the people were departed; the duke himself was not gone, and hearing the organ touched in an unusual manner, upon his return to his apartments enquired of his valet what stranger was at it, and was answered his brother; the duke immediately commanded him to be sent for, as also his father: it is needless to repeat the conversation between them, for it terminated in a resolution in the father to yield to the impulse of nature, and give up his son to the profession of music; and accordingly on his return to Halle he placed him under the care of Frederick William Zachau, a sound musician, and organist of the cathedral church of that city.* After having taught him the principles of the science, Zachau put into the hands of his young pupil the works of the greatest among the Italian and German composers, and, without directing his attention to any of them, left him to form a style of his own. Handel had now been under the tuition of Zachau about two years, during which time he had frequently supplied his place, and performed the cathedral duty; the exercises which he had been accustomed to were the composition of fugues and airs upon points or subjects delivered to him from time to time by his master.† At the age of nine he actually composed motets for the service of the church, and continued to make one every week for three years, with scarce any intermission. By the time he was arrived at the age of thirteen, Handel began to look upon Halle as a place not likely to afford him opportunities of much farther improvement; he determined

---

* See an account of him in page 646 of this work.

† This in Germany is the mode of exercise for young proficients in music, and is also the test of a master. When an organist was to be chosen for the new church of St. George, Hanover-square, Mr. Handel, who lived in the parish, Geminiani, Dr. Pepusch, and Dr. Croft, were the judges to determine of the pretensions of the candidates; they gave them each the same subject for a fugue; and Roseingrave, who acquitted himself the best in the discussion of it, was elected.

GEORGE FREDERIC HANDEL.

to visit Berlin, and arriving in that city in the year 1698, found the opera there in a flourishing condition, under the direction of Bononcini and Attilio; the former of these, a most admirable musician, was yet a haughty and insolent man; the other, his inferior, was of a modest and placid disposition, a proof whereof he gave in the affection shewn by him to this young stranger, whom he would frequently set upon his knee, and listen to with delight while he played on the harpsichord.

Handel had been but a short time at Berlin before the king, the grandfather of the present king of Prussia, took notice of him, and signified to him an intention to send him to Italy; but by the advice of his friends, Handel declined the offer, and returned home to Halle; soon after which he had the misfortune to be deprived of his father. Being by this accident less attached to the city of his nativity than before, Handel began to think of another place of residence. There was at that time an opera at Hamburg, little inferior to that at Berlin: Steffani had composed for it, and Conradina and Mattheson were the principal singers; the former of these was the daughter of a barber at Dresden, named Conradine, but, according to custom, she had given her name an Italian termination.* Mattheson was an indifferent singer, but he was a very good composer, and played finely on the harpsichord and organ.

CHAP. CLXXXIV.

Upon Handel's arrival at Hamburg he found the opera under the direction of a great master, Reinhard Keiser, a native of Weissenfels, and chapel-master to the duke of Mecklenburgh, who being a man of gaiety and expense, was reduced to the necessity of absconding, to avoid the demands of his creditors. Upon occasion of his absence, the person who had played the second harpsichord thought he had a good title to the first, and accordingly placed himself at it; but Handel, who had hitherto played the violin in the orchestra, and, as it is said, only a Ripieno part, with a promptitude which his inexperience of the world will hardly excuse, put in his claim to Keiser's place, and urged his ability to fill it. The arguments of Handel were seconded by the clamours of a numerous audience, who constrained the substitute of Keiser to yield to his competitor. For the name of this person we are to seek; it is said he was a German; he was deeply affected with the indignity that had been shown him: his honour had sustained an injury, but he comforted himself with the thought that it was in his power to repair it by killing his adversary, a youth but rising to manhood, and who had never worn, nor knew the use of a weapon; and at a time, too, when none were near to assist him. Accordingly one evening, when the opera was over, this assassin followed Handel out of the orchestra, and at a convenient place made a pass at him with his sword; and, had it not been for the

* She was both a fine singer and an excellent actress. She sang in the opera at Berlin in 1708, and in 1711 was married to Count Gruzewska.

score of the opera which Handel was taking home with him, and had placed in his bosom, under his coat, there is little doubt but that the thrust would have proved mortal.

The absence of Keiser, the merits of Handel, and the baseness of this attempt to deprive him of life, operated so strongly, that those who had the management of the opera looked upon Handel as the only fit person to compose for it: he was then somewhat above fourteen years of age, and being furnished with a drama, he in a very few weeks brought upon the stage his first opera, named Almeria, which was performed thirty nights without intermission.

Handel having continued at Hamburgh about three years, during which time he composed and performed two other operas, namely, Florinda and Nerone, resolved to visit Italy. The prince of Tuscany, brother to the grand duke John Gaston de Medicis, had been present at the performance of the operas of Almeria and Florinda, and had given Handel an invitation to Florence; as soon, therefore, as he found himself in a situation to accept it, he went thither, and composed the opera of Roderigo, being then in his eighteenth year, for which he was honoured by the grand duke with a present of one hundred sequins and a service of plate. The prince's mistress, Vittoria, sang the principal part in it, and, if fame says true, conceived such a passion for Handel, as, if he had been disposed to encourage it, might have proved the ruin of them both. After about a year's stay at Florence, Handel went to Venice, and there composed the opera of Agrippina, which was performed twenty-seven nights successively; from thence he went to Rome, where being introduced to Cardinal Ottoboni, he became acquainted with Corelli and Alessandro Scarlatti; the first of these had apartments in the cardinal's palace, and played the first violin in a concert which the cardinal had there on Monday in every week. From Rome he went to Naples, and after some stay there, having seen as much of Italy as he thought necessary, he determined to return to Germany. He had no particular attachment to any city, but having never seen Hanover, he bent his way thither. Upon his arrival he found Steffani in possession of the place of musician to the court; he might perhaps be styled chapel-master, a title which the foreign musicians are very ambitious of; but he could not be so in fact, for the service in the electoral chapel was according to the Lutheran ritual, and Steffani was a dignitary in the Romish church. The reception which Handel met with from Steffani was such as made a lasting impression upon his mind. The following is the manner in which he related it to the author of this work:—'When I first arrived at 'Hanover I was a young man, under twenty; I was 'acquainted with the merits of Steffani, and he had 'heard of me. I understood somewhat of music, 'and,' putting forth both his broad hands, and extending his fingers, 'could play pretty well on the 'organ; he received me with great kindness, and 'took an early opportunity to introduce me to the 'princess Sophia and the elector's son, giving them 'to understand that I was what he was pleased to 'call a virtuoso in music; he obliged me with in-'structions for my conduct and behaviour during my 'residence at Hanover; and being called from the 'city to attend to matters of a public concern, he left 'me in possession of that favour and patronage 'which himself had enjoyed for a series of years.'

The connection between the court of Hanover and that of London at this time was growing every day more close, and Handel, prompted perhaps by curiosity to see a city which was likely one time or other to become the place of his residence, determined to visit London. At the time that he was preparing for his departure, a nobleman at the court of Hanover, Baron Kilmansegge, was actually soliciting with the electer the grant of a pension to Handel of fifteen hundred crowns per annum, which he having obtained, Handel hesitated to accept, being conscious of the resolution he had taken to visit England. Upon this objection the Baron consulted his highness's pleasure, and Handel was then acquainted that he should not be disappointed in his design by the acceptance of the pension proposed, for that he had permission to be absent for a twelvemonth or more, if he chose it, and to go whithersoever he pleased. On these easy conditions he thankfully accepted the electer's bounty. Before he left Germany he made a visit to his mother at Halle, whom he found labouring under the accumulated burthen of old age and blindness; he visited also his preceptor Zachau, and some other of his friends; and passing through Dusseldorp to Holland, embarked for England, and arrived at London in the winter of the year 1710.

The state of the opera in England at this time has already been spoken of; Mr. Aaron Hill was concerned in the management of it; he gave to Rossi, an Italian poet, the story of Rinaldo from Tasso's Gierusalemme; and Rossi having wrought it into the form of an opera, Mr. Handel set the music to it, and Hill published it with an English translation.

As to the poem itself, it is neither better nor worse than most compositions of the kind; Mr. Addison, in the Spectator, No. 5, is very arch on it, and has extracted from the preface the following curious passage: 'Eccoti, benigno Lettore, un Parto 'di poche Sere, che se ben nato di Notte, non e' 'però aborto di Tenebre, mà si farà conoscere 'Figliolo d' Apollo con qualche Raggio di Par-'nasso;' that is, 'Behold, gentle reader, the birth of a 'few Evenings, which though it be the offspring of 'the Night, is not the abortive of darkness, but will 'make itself known to be the son of Apollo, with a 'certain ray of Parnassus.' The following is the author's apology for the imperfections of the work :— 'Gradisci, ti prego, discreto lettore, questa mia 'rapida fatica, e se non merita le tue lodi, almeno 'non privarla del tuo compatimento, chi dirò più 'tosto giustizia per un tempo così ristretto, poiche il 'Signor Hendel, Orfeo del nostro secolo, nel porla 'in musica, a pena mi diede tempo di scrivere; e 'viddi con mio grand stupore, in due sole settimane 'armonizata al maggior grado di perfezzione un 'opera intiera.' Mr. Handel is said to have com-

posed the opera of Rinaldo in the short space of a fortnight; in it is an air, 'Cara sposa,' sung by Nicolini, which the author would frequently say was one of the best he ever made. The success of this opera was greater than can be imagined; Walsh got fifteen hundred pounds by the printing it.

After this specimen of his abilities, the lovers of music here used every motive to prevail on Handel to make London the place of his residence; but, after a twelvemonth's stay in England, he determined to return to Hanover. He took leave of the queen, and, upon expressing his sense of the obligations which he had to the English nation, and her majesty in particular, she made him some valuable presents, and intimated a wish to see him again. Upon his return to Hanover he composed for the electoral princess, Caroline, afterwards queen of England, twelve chamber duets, in imitation, as he professed, of those of Steffani, but in a style less simple, and in other respects different from those of that author. The words of these compositions abound with all the beauties of poetry, and were written by Abbate Hortensio Mauro.

After two years stay at Hanover, Mr. Handel obtained leave of the elector to revisit England, upon condition of his returning within a reasonable time. He arrived at London about the latter end of the year 1712, at which time the negociations of the peace of Utrecht were in great forwardness. In the following year the treaty was concluded; a public thanksgiving was ordered for the occasion, and Mr. Handel received from the queen a command to compose a Te Deum and Jubilate, which were performed at St. Paul's cathedral, her majesty herself attending the service. The queen died in 1714, and the elector of Hanover immediately came over. On his arrival here, he had two grounds of resentment against Handel, the one the breach of his engagement to return to Hanover after a reasonable stay here; the other his having lent the assistance of his art towards the celebrating as happy and glorious, an event which by many was looked upon as detrimental to the interests, not only of this kingdom, but of all the protestant powers of Europe. To avert the king's displeasure, baron Kilmansegge contrived an expedient, which nothing but his sincere friendship for Handel could have suggested; the Baron formed a party, who were to take the pleasure of a fine summer's day on the Thames, and the king condescended to be of it: Handel had an intimation of the design, and was advised by the baron to prepare music for the occasion; and he composed for it that work, consisting of an overture and a variety of airs and other movements, which we know by the name of the Water Music. It was performed in a barge, attendant on that in which the king and his company were, and Handel himself conducted it. The king being little at a loss to guess who was the composer of music so grand and original as this appeared to be, anticipated the relation that Mr. Handel was the author of it. From this time the baron waited with impatience for an intimation from the king of his desire to see Handel; at length an opportunity offered, which he with the utmost eagerness embraced; Geminiani had been in England a short time, during which he had published and dedicated to baron Kilmansegge his Opera prima, consisting of those twelve Solos for the violin, which will be admired as long as the love of melody shall exist, and the king was desirous of hearing them performed by the author, who was the greatest master of the instrument then living; Geminiani was extremely pleased with the thought of being heard, but was fearful of being accompanied on the harpsichord by some performer, who might fail to do justice both to the compositions and the performance of them: in short, he suggested to the baron a wish that Mr. Handel might be the person appointed to meet him in the king's apartment; and upon mentioning it to his majesty, the baron was told that Handel would be admitted for the purpose, and he attended accordingly; and upon expressing his desire to atone for his former misbehaviour, by the utmost efforts of duty and gratitude, he was reinstated in the king's favour; and soon after, as a token of it, received a grant of a pension of 200l. a year, over and above one for the same sum which had been settled on him by queen Anne.

Being now determined to make England the country of his residence, Handel began to yield to the invitations of such persons of rank and fortune as were desirous of his acquaintance, and accepted an invitation from one Mr. Andrews, of Barn-Elms, in Surrey, but who had also a town residence, to apartments in his house. After some months stay with Mr. Andrews, Handel received a pressing invitation from the earl of Burlington, whose love of music was equal to his skill in architecture and his passion for other liberal studies, to make his house in Piccadilly the place of his abode. Into this hospitable mansion was Handel received, and left at liberty to follow the dictates of his genius and invention, assisting frequently at evening concerts, in which his own music made the most considerable part. The course of his studies during three years residence at Burlington-house, was very regular and uniform: his mornings were employed in study, and at dinner he sat down with men of the first eminence for genius and abilities of any in the kingdom. Here he frequently met Pope, Gay, Dr. Arbuthnot,* and others of that class: the latter was able to converse with him on his art, but Pope understood not, neither had he the least ear or relish for music; and he was honest enough to confess it. When Handel had no particular engagements, he frequently went in the afternoon to St. Paul's church, where Mr. Greene, though he was not then organist, was very assiduous in his civilities to him: by him he was introduced to, and made acquainted with the principal performers in the choir. The truth is, that Handel was very fond of St. Paul's organ, built by father Smith, and which was then almost a new instrument; Brind was then the organist, and no very celebrated per-

former: the tone of the instrument delighted Handel; and a little intreaty was at any time sufficient to prevail on him to touch it, but after he had ascended the organ-loft, it was with reluctance that he left it; and he has been known, after evening service, to play to an audience as great as ever filled the choir. After his performance was over it was his practice to adjourn with the principal persons of the choir to the Queen's Arms tavern in St. Paul's church-yard, where was a great room, with a harpsichord in it; and oftentimes an evening was there spent in music and musical conversation.†

After three years residence at Burlington-house, during which time he composed three operas, namely, Amadis, Theseus, and Pastor Fido, Mr. Handel received a pressing invitation from the duke of Chandois to undertake the direction of the chapel at his superb mansion, Cannons. Pepusch had had for some years the direction of it, and had composed services and anthems for it to a great number; but, like most other of his compositions, they were merely correct harmony, without either melody or energy; and it suited but ill with the duke's ideas of magnificence, and the immense expence he had been at in building such a house, and furnishing his chapel, to have any other than the greatest musician in the kingdom for his chapel-master. We may suppose that the offers made to induce Handel to exchange the patronage of one nobleman for another, and to enter into engagements that rendered him somewhat less than master of himself and his time, were proportioned as well to the munificence of his new patron as his own merits: whatever they were, he complied with the invitation, and in the year 1718 went to reside with the duke at Cannons, where he was no sooner settled, than he sat himself to compose a suite of anthems for the duke's chapel. In the course of these his studies, he seems to have disdained all imitation, and to have looked with contempt on those pure and elegant models for the church style, the motets of Palestrina, Allegri, and Foggia, and for that of the chamber the Cantatas of Cesti and Pier Simone Agostino; for these he thought, and would sometimes say, were stiff, and void of that sweetness of melody, which he looked upon to be essential as well to choral as theatrical music; much less would he vouchsafe an imitation of those milder beauties which shine so conspicuously in the anthems of the English composers for the church, namely, Tallis, Bird, Gibbons, and others; or, to come near to his own time, those of Wise, Humphrey, Blow, and Purcell: in short, such was the sublimity of his genius, and the copiousness of his invention, that he was persuaded of his ability to form a style of his own: he made the experiment, and it succeeded.

The establishment of the chapel at Cannons consisted in a sufficient number of voices of various pitches, including those of boys, for the performance of any composition merely vocal; but, in imitation

---

* Dr. Arbuthnot was not only a passionate lover of music, but was well skilled in the science: an anthem of his composition, ' As pants the hart,' is to be found in the books of the chapel royal. See Divine Harmony, or a new Collection of select Anthems. Lond. octavo, 1712.

† At one of these meetings, word being brought that Mattheson's lesson's which had been engraved and printed in London, were just come from the press, the book was immediately sent for, and Handel, without hesitation, played it through.

of the practice in the chapels of foreign countries, the duke retained a band of the best instrumental performers ; the anthems composed by Mr. Handel were made for voices and instruments, and in number are supposed to be little short of twenty : as they have never been printed, it may be some satisfaction to the curious to be told that in the library of the Academy of Ancient Music in London, are the following : ' O praise the Lord,' ' As pants the ' hart,' ' O sing unto the Lord,' ' Have mercy upon ' me,' ' O come let us sing,' ' I will magnify thee,' ' The Lord is my light,' ' My song shall be alway,' ' In the Lord put I my trust,' ' The king shall ' rejoice,' and ' Let God arise.'

The Academy have also an anthem of his, ' Sing ' unto God,' performed at the marriage of Frederic, prince of Wales.

He also composed for the duke of Chandois, his serenata of Acis and Galatea, the words whereof are said to have been written by Mr. Gay. Handel while at Naples had composed and performed a serenata entitled Acide e Galatea ; and it is probable that he might have adapted many parts of the original composition to the English words ; however this particular is to be remarked in the Acis and Galatea, that the fine chorus, ' Behold the monster Poly-' pheme,' so much admired for expressing horror and affright, is taken from one of his duets, in which the self-same notes are set to words of a very different import.

During the last year of his residence with the duke of Chandois, the principal nobility and gentry of the kingdom formed themselves into a musical academy for the performance of operas at the theatre in the Haymarket, to be composed by Mr. Handel, and performed under his direction. To this end a subscription was raised, amounting to 50,000l. The king subscribed 1000l., and permitted the society thus formed to be dignified with the title of the Royal Academy. It consisted of a governor, deputy governor, and twenty directors, whose names were as follow : Thomas, duke of Newcastle, governor ; lord Bingley, deputy governor ; directors, the dukes of Portland and Queensberry, the earls of Burlington, Stair, and Waldegrave, lord Chetwynd, lord Stanhope, James Bruce, Esq., colonel Blathwayt,* Thomas Coke, of Norfolk, Esq., Conyers D'Arcy, Esq., brigadier-general Dormer, Bryan Fairfax, Esq., colonel O'Hara, George Harrison, Esq., brigadier-general Hunter, William Pulteney, Esq., Sir John Vanbrugh, major-general Wade, and Francis Whitworth, Esq.

Handel being thus engaged, found it necessary to seek abroad for the best singers that could be procured. Accordingly he went to Dresden ; and, having secured Senesino and Signora Margarita Durastanti, returned with them to England. It has been asserted that at this time Bononcini and Attilio were in possession of the opera stage ; but this can no otherwise be true, than that the compositions of those two masters, or rather operas made up of

songs selected from Italian operas composed by them, were represented here : that this was the case with respect to Bononcini, is most evident from what has already been related touching the operas of Camilla and Thomyris. Besides which it may be observed that Bononcini came first to reside in London upon the invitation of the Academy ; and the first entire opera of his, named Astartus, was performed in the year 1720, and Coriolanus, the first of Attilio, in 1723. The fact seems to stand thus : Bononcini, though he had never been in England, had a strong party among the nobility ; and at the institution of the Royal Academy it seems to have been the design of the directors that the entertainment should have all the advantages that could be derived from the studies of men of equal abilities, but different talents, and accordingly Bononcini was included in the resolutions, and Attilio engaged about three or four years after.

CHAP. CLXXXV.

Giovanni Bononcini (a Portrait), or as he affected to spell his name, Buononcini, was one of the sons of Giovanni Maria Bononcini, of whom an account has already been given,† and a native of Modena. After having finished his musical studies, probably under his father, who, to judge from the works published by him, particularly a treatise entitled Musico Prattico, must have been an able instructor ; he went to Vienna, and having a very fine hand on the violoncello, was entered in the band of the emperor Leopold, and retained with a very large salary. At this time Alessandro Scarlatti had gained great reputation by the operas which he had composed ; and Bononcini, desirous to emulate him, though but eighteen years of age, composed one entitled Camilla, which was performed at Vienna, and also at divers of the Italian theatres, with greater applause than had ever been given to any work of the kind.

The introduction of the Italian opera into England, and the feeble attempts of Mr. Clayton to recommend it, have already been mentioned ; Mr. Haym, convinced of the merit of Camilla, and of the possibility of adapting it to the taste of an English audience but little sensible of the charms of Italian melody, contrived to fit it with English words ; and, notwithstanding the disadvantages arising from this conjunction, it is said to have been received no less favourably here than abroad. This was about the year 1707 ; and so deep was the impression which the music of Bononcini had made upon the minds of the people here, that till the year 1710, the managers found themselves reduced to a kind of necessity of introducing into every opera they exhibited, more than an equal proportion of Bononcini's airs, selected from a variety of works, which by that time he had composed. In the year above-mentioned Mr. Handel arrived in England, and soon after gave to the English the opera of Rinaldo, and thereby laid the foundation for that

---

* This gentleman, an officer in the army, had when a child been a pupil of Alessandro Scarlatti. His proficiency on the harpsichord at twelve years of age astonished every one. There is a picture of him by Kneller, painted when he was about that age, in the music school, Oxon.

† Page 661.

GIOVANNI BUONONCINI

DA MODENA,

COMPOSITORE

fame which he afterwards acquired, and so long enjoyed in this country, and indeed throughout Europe; but his connections at Hanover did not allow of his making London his residence, wherefore, after a twelvemonth's stay here, he returned.

The nobility and gentry, who were now become sensible of the charms of dramatic music, began to associate in its behalf, and themselves became conductors of the opera. Mr. Handel returned again to England; but having entered into engagements with the earl of Burlington and the duke of Chandois, he was for some years but an occasional composer of operas: as soon as these were determined, the foundation of a royal academy was laid in the manner above related; Bononcini was then at Rome, and, as he himself expressly asserts, was called from thence to the service of the Royal Academy.* About three years after, Attilio was also sent for from Bologna, and, in virtue of their engagements with the directors, and during an interval of about seven years, they composed and exhibited the following operas; that is to say, Bononcini composed the operas of Astartus, Crispus, Griselda, Pharnaces, Erminia, Calphurnia, and Astyanax; and Attilio, those of Coriolanus, Vespasian, Artaxerxes, Darius, and Lucius Verus.

It was hardly possible that men possessed of talents so different as were those of Handel and Bononcini, should be equally admired and patronized by the same persons. The style of Bononcini was tender, elegant, and pathetic; Handel's possessed all these qualities, and numberless others, and his invention was inexhaustible. For some or other of these considerations, and perhaps others of a very different kind, two parties were formed among the nobility, the one professing to patronize Handel, and the other Bononcini: as to Attilio, he was an ingenious and modest man, and was therefore left to make his way as he could. Handel was honoured with the favour of the electoral family; and this might be one, among other reasons, that induced the Marlborough family, as it stood affected at that time, to take his rival under their protection; and yet, so strange and capricious are the motives of party opposition, Handel was espoused by the Tories, and Bononcini by the Whigs. Upon the death of John, duke of Marlborough, in 1722, Bononcini was employed by the family to compose an anthem, which was performed at his interment in Henry the Seventh's chapel, Westminster-abbey, and published in score;† and soon after the countess of Godolphin, who upon the decease of her father, by a peculiar limitation of that title, was now become duchess of Marlborough, took him into her family, and settled on him a pension of five hundred pounds a year.‡ Her dwelling was in the Stable-

yard near St. James's palace, in the house lately inhabited by her husband, the earl of Godolphin; and there she had concerts twice a week, in which the music was solely the composition of this her favourite master, and the principal singers in the opera performed in it.

In this easy and honourable situation, Bononcini had leisure and opportunity to pursue his studies; here he composed most of his operas, as also twelve Sonatas or Chamber Airs for two violins and a bass, printed in the year 1732.

That subscription of the nobility and gentry which has been already mentioned, and which laid the foundation of what was called the Royal Academy of Music, was calculated with a view to the improvement of the science; but, unluckily for Bononcini, the views of this association were chiefly directed towards Handel, and accordingly he was the first retained in their service, and this notwithstanding that Bononcini had for his friend the governor of the academy, the late duke of Newcastle, who had married the daughter of the countess of Godolphin, his patroness.

The academy was no sooner established, than a contest began between the friends of Handel on the one part, and those of Bononcini on the other, which was brought to a crisis by the performance of the opera of Muzio Scævola, of which Handel, Bononcini, and Attilio composed each an act: the judgment of the public in favour of Handel, put an end to the competition, and left him without a rival for the public favour. This dispute, although it determined the point of precedence between Handel and Bononcini, did not operate in the total exclusion of the latter from the academy. He continued to perform operas there till the year 1727; after which he retired, and pursued a life of study and ease in that noble family which had so long afforded him protection; but, being a man of a haughty and imperious temper, he at length rendered himself unworthy of this honourable patronage; and finding that he had ruined his fortunes in the Marlborough family, and by a singular instance of folly and disingenuity, forfeited the esteem of his friends in the musical world, he associated himself with a common sharper; and, finding England no abiding place for them, took leave of it altogether. The motives to this retreat, so far as respected Bononcini, were as follow:—

The Academy of ancient Music, of the establishment whereof an account has been given in a preceding page, continued to flourish, and was become the resort of the most eminent masters, as well foreigners as natives, of the time, and Bononcini himself was a member of it. About the beginning of the year 1731, one of the members had received from Venice a book intitled 'Duetti, Terzetti and 'Madrigali, Consecrati alla Sacra Cesarea Real 'Maestà di Gioseppe I. Imperatore: Da Antonio 'Lotti Veneto, Organista della Ducale di San Marco, 'Venezia, 1705;' and, having looked it over, he appointed the eighteenth madrigal in the book, beginning 'In una siepe ombrosa,' to be sung in the

---

* In the dedication of his Cantatas to king George I.

† The initial sentence of it is as follows: 'When Saul was king over 'Israel, thou wast he that leddest out and broughtest in Israel.' This composition, though a fine one, is not uniformly excellent; but allowances must be made for the short interval to which the author was confined.

‡ This circumstance is mentioned by Rolli in the notes on his translation of the comedy of the Conscious Lovers, and is confirmed by a lady of high rank, the daughter of the duchess, now living, who communicated many of the particulars contained in this memoir.

course of the next evening's performance, which was done accordingly: this madrigal had about four years before, by Dr. Greene, been produced in manuscript as a composition of Signor Giovanni Bononcini, who was then in England, and one of their members; and he, hearing that it was now performed as the work of another author, writes a letter to the Academy, wherein he makes grievous complaints, accuses the pretended author of plagiarism, and affirms that he himself composed it thirty years before, exactly as it is printed in the book, at the command of the emperor Leopold; for a proof of which assertion he appeals to the archives of that emperor. This obliged the Academy to write by their secretary to Signor Lotti, who in his answer assures them that he was the author of the madrigal in question, and had formerly given a copy of it to Sig. Ziani, chapel-master to the emperor Leopold, before whom it had been performed; and that it seemed incredible to him that Signor Bononcini should, in the 'gayeté de coeur,' as he expresses himself, adopt his defects for his own. This letter was delivered into Bononcini's own hands; but he not thinking fit to answer it, the Academy wrote again to Venice, and procured from Lotti an instrument under the seal of a public notary, wherein, after an invocation of the name of the eternal God, it is certified that four of the most eminent masters of Venice,* and an officer of the emperor, had appeared before him, and, having voluntarily taken their oath, 'tacto pectore, et tactis Scripturis,' had deposed that they knew the madrigal, 'In una siepe ombrosa,' to be the work of the above-named Signor Antonio Lotti; some of them having seen it composing in the rough draught; others having sung it, and others having heard it practised before it went to the press. Besides this certificate, there were at the same time transmitted to London divers attestations of persons of undoubted credit living at Vienna, one of whom was the Abbate Pariati, author of the words of the above madrigal, to the same effect. These letters, for the satisfaction of the public, were soon after printed, and thus this remarkable contest ended.†

The consequence of this dispute was very fatal to the interests of Bononcini; it was thought a very dishonest thing in him to assume, and that in terms so positive and express, the merit of a composition, which he could not but know was the work of another; to palliate this, it is said that the score of the madrigal delivered in to be sung at the Academy was not subscribed with the name of Bononcini, as others of his compositions had invariably been; and to this fact a gentleman of undoubted veracity, now living, speaks with great certainty, who was present at the performance, and perused the manuscript of the score; but whether the letters above referred to

are not evidence of his claim, and also of the injustice of it, will hardly bear a question.‡

Notwithstanding the variety and strength of the evidence against Bononcini, it does not appear that he ever retracted his claim to the madrigal in question, or apologized for his behaviour in any one instance during the contest, but with a sullen kind of pride left his adversaries to pursue their own measures; all which conduct must seem unaccountable to such as are acquainted with his great abilities; and the more so, as there are extant sundry compositions of his of this very kind, that is to say, madrigals for five voices, not only equal to this of Lotti, but to any that we know of.

From this time the reputation of Bononcini began to sink in the world; and, what was worse, he found that his disgrace began to operate upon his interest in the Marlborough family; indeed his behaviour in it had at no time been such as suited with that generous protection which it had invariably afforded him, for he was haughty and capricious, and was for ever telling such stories of himself as were incredible. From a propensity, that must seem unaccountable, he affected to be thought a much older man than he was; and in the year 1730, when every circumstance in his person and countenance bespoke the contrary, he scrupled not to assert that he was on the verge of fourscore. About the year 1733 his affairs were come to a crisis in England: there was at that time about the town a man, who with scarce any other recommendation than fine clothes, and a great stock of impudence, appeared at court, and assumed the title of Count Ughi; it is said that he was a friar, but his pretence here was that he was an Italian nobleman, and a natural son of our king James II. Being a man of parts, and well accomplished, he on the footing of relation, such as it was, gained an easy admission to the duchess of Buckingham, and became so much her favourite, that those who were not aware of the supposed consanguinity between them, hesitated not to say she meant to make him her husband.

This fellow, among various other artifices, pretended to be possessed of the secret of making gold, and Bononcini, who had never in his life known the want of it, was foolish enough to believe him. In short, he was prevailed on to leave the hospitable roof under which he had so long been sheltered, and became a sharer in the fortunes of this egregious impostor; they quitted the kingdom together, but it is probable that this connexion lasted not long, and that Bononcini was constrained to recur for a livelihood to the exercise of his profession; for a few years after his leaving England, he was at Paris, and composed for the royal chapel there, a motet, in which was a solo, with an accompaniment for the

---

* Their names and titles were as follow, viz., the most reverend Antonio Bifi, maestro di capella of the most serene republic of Venice; Girolamo Melari, musician of the ducal chapel of St. Mark; Claudio Severo Frangioni, also musician of the said ducal chapel; the reverend Sig. D. Clemente Leopoldo de Tarsis et Ottavio, late chamberlain of the Golden Key to his Imperial majesty, hereditary postmaster general of the empire at Venice, and Giorgio Gentili, first violin of the said ducal chapel.

† Vide Letters from the Academy of ancient Music at London, to Signor Antonio Lotti of Venice, with his Answers and Testimonies, octavo, Lond. 1732.

‡ Dr. Greene, who had introduced the madrigal in question into the Academy, notwithstanding the evidence to the contrary, was one of the last to believe that it was a composition of any other than his friend Bononcini; but finding himself almost singular in this opinion, he withdrew from the society, carrying with him the boys of St. Paul's; and, calling to his assistance Mr. Festling, the first violin of the king's band, he established a concert at the Devil tavern, Temple Bar, which being performed in the great room called the Apollo, was named the Apollo Society; and the joke upon this occasion among the academicians was, that Dr. Greene was gone to the Devil.

violoncello, which he himself performed in the presence of the late king of France. This composition was printed at Paris.

Upon the conclusion of the peace of Aix la Chapelle, Bononcini was sent for to Vienna by the emperor of Germany, and composed the music for that occasion, and was rewarded with a present of eight hundred ducats. This was in the year 1748; and soon after the rejoicings for the peace were over, he, together with Monticelli, a singer who had appeared in the opera at London, set out for Venice, the one having been engaged as composer, the other as principal singer there. Mr. Carrington, the messenger, was at Vienna at the same time, and saw them both set off in the same post-chaise.

CHAP. CLXXXVI.

The merits of Bononcini as a musician were very great; and it must be thought no diminution of his character to say that he had no superior but Handel; though, as the talents which each possessed were very different in kind, it is almost a question whether any comparison can justly be made between them. Handel's excellence consisted in the grandeur and sublimity of his conceptions, of which he gave the first proofs in his Te Deum and Jubilate; Bononcini's genius was adapted to the expression of tender and pathetic sentiments. His melodies, the richest and sweetest that we know of, are in a style peculiarly his own; his harmonies are original, and at the same time natural: in his recitatives, those manifold inflexions of the voice, which accompany common speech, with the several interjections, exclamations, and pauses proper thereto, are marked with great exactness and propriety.

Whoever reflects on the divisions and animosities occasioned by the competition between the two great masters, Handel and Bononcini, must wonder at the infatuation of the parties that severally espoused them, in that they were not able to discern in the compositions of both, beauties, of different kinds it is true, but such as every soul susceptible of the charms of music must feel and acknowledge. This animosity may seem to have been owing to the determination of an over-refined judgment; but such as have a true idea of the ridiculous character of an opera connoisseur, or are sensible of the extravagant length to which the affectation of a musical taste will carry silly people of both sexes, will justly impute it to ignorance, and an utter inability to form any judgment or well grounded opinion about the matter.

But where was the reason for competition? Is it not with music as in poetry and painting, where the different degrees of merit are not estimated by an approximation to any one particular style or manner as a standard, and where different styles are allowed to possess peculiar powers of delighting? And, to apply the question to the present case, why was it to be assumed as a principle, that to an ear capable of being affected with the sublimity and dignity of Handel's music, the sweetness and elegance of

Bononcini's must necessarily be intolerable? and, vice versa. Milton and Spenser were not contemporaries; but had they been so, could the admirers of one have had any reason for denying praise to the other? In this view of the controversy, the conduct of the parties who severally espoused Handel and Bononcini can be resolved only into egregious folly and invincible prejudice; and that mutual animosity, which men, when they are least in the right, are most disposed to entertain.

The long residence of Handel in this country, the great number of his compositions, and the frequent performance of them, enable us to form a competent judgment of his abilities; but the merits of Bononcini are little known and less attended to. Such as form their opinion of him by his early operas, such as Camilla, and those others from which the airs in Thomyris were taken, will greatly err in the estimation of his talents, these being but puerile essays, while he was under twenty years of age. The works of his riper years carry in them the evidences of a mature judgment; and though his characteristic be elegance, softness, and a fine, easy, flowing fancy, there are compositions of his extant in manuscript, particularly a mass for eight voices, with instruments, a Laudate Pueri, and sundry madrigals for five voices, from which we must conclude that his learning and skill were not inferior to those powers of invention, which in an eminent degree he was allowed to possess.

A person now living, and at the head of the profession of music, and who perfectly remembers Bononcini, inclines to the opinion, that, notwithstanding the suspicions to the contrary, the reports which he made of his very advanced age were founded in truth; and calculates that in the year 1748 he could be but little short of a hundred. He says that his merit in his profession may be inferred from that respect and deference with which he was treated by the singers in the opera, particularly Senesino; as also by the principal instrumental performers, Carbonelli, the elder Castrucci, and Giuseppe San Martini.[*] A letter of Bononcini, dated from London, in the year 1725, is printed in the fifth volume of Marcello's Psalms, and contains a commendation of that work and its author.

The works of Bononcini published in England are, Cantate e Duetti, dedicati alla sacra Maestà di Giorgio Re della Gran Bretagna, &c. Londra, 1721.[†] The subscription to this book was two guineas: It was honoured with the names of many of the principal nobility, who were very liberal to the author; the duke and duchess of Queensberry subscribed each for twenty-five books; and the countess of Sunderland alone for fifty-five; and many others for ten and five; and it is computed that this work produced the author near a thousand guineas. The operas of Astartus and Griselda, Divertimenti da Camera pel Violino o Flauto, dedicati all' eccellenza del Duca di Rutland, &c. Londra, 1722. The

* Of these severally an account will hereafter be given.

† Some copies of the book are abroad, with a title-page expressing barely the name of the book and of the author, and with no dedication.

funeral anthem for John, duke of Marlborough, and Twelve Sonatas for the Chamber, for two violins and a bass, dedicated to the duchess of Marlborough, London, 1732. Of these publications the first seems to be the chief; and was the produce of those leisure hours of study, when, without being goaded by the call of the public, he was at liberty to wait the returns of his fancy, and to take advantage of those moments in which he found the powers of his genius and invention at the highest. Certain it is that the Cantatas and Duets contained in the above collection have long been held in high esti-

mation by all good judges of music; and it is some proof thereof, that the preludes to them, consisting of airs for two violins and a bass, till within about the last twelve years, were alternately, with Corelli's Sonatas, the second music before the play at one or other of the theatres.

The following air of Bononcini, taken from his opera of Astyanax, was, at the time when that opera was performed, greatly admired for the sweetness of the air, and the originality of the accompaniment; it was never printed, and may be esteemed a curiosity :—

lor a lacrimar chio mi contento, chio mi con - ten - to, con piu dolore a lacrimar chio mi conten - to,

chio mi con - ten - to   Deh las - cia o

GIOVANNI BONONCINI.

ATTILIO ARIOSTI (*a Portrait*), an ecclesiastic, and therefore usually called in England and elsewhere Padre Attilio,* was a native of Bologna, and chapel-master to the electress of Brandenburg. In the year 1700, on the anniversary of the nuptials of Frederic, hereditary prince of Hesse Cassel, with the electoral princess of Brandenburg, Louisa Dorothea Sophia, being the first day of June, he performed at Lutzenburg, a villa of the princess at a small distance from Berlin, a ballet, and on the sixth of the same month, an opera, both of his composition, which were received with great applause. In the former he affected to imitate the style of Lully; but in the latter, following the dictates of his own genius and invention, he exceeded the highest expectations. The title of the opera was Atys, in which a shepherd of that name is represented in the extremity of rage and despair, to which passions Attilio had adapted a composition called Sinfonia Infernale, the modulation whereof was so singular, and withal so masterly, that the audience were alternately affected with terror and pity, in an exact correspondence with the sentiments of the poet and the design of the repre-

* It is said that he was a Dominican friar, but that he had a dispensation from the pope that exempted him from the rule of his order, and left him at liberty to follow a secular profession.

sentation. He also composed a musical drama entitled 'Amor tra Nemici,' which was performed on the birth-day of the emperor Joseph in that year. The words of this drama were printed for the perusal of the audience during the time of performance; and it is from the title-page of this publication only, that the fact of his being an ecclesiastic is ascertained; for as to his profession, it was altogether secular, and he never pretended to the exercise of any ecclesiastical function. Attilio was a celebrated performer on the violoncello; but he was most distinguished for his performance on an instrument, of which if he was not the inventor, he was the great improver, namely, the Viol d'Amore, for which he made many compositions. The residence of Attilio at Berlin in the year 1698, the time when Handel, then but a child, arrived at that city, gave him an opportunity of knowing him, and laid the foundation of a friendship, which, notwithstanding a competition of interests, subsisted for many years after. The occasion of his leaving Berlin was an invitation from the directors of the opera here to come and settle at London; upon his arrival he joined with Bononcini: the consequences of that association are related in the account herein

ATTILIUS ARIOSTI BONONIENSIS.

before given of his colleague and his rival Handel, and leaves little to be said of him farther than regards his works, and his general character as a musician.

Of sundry operas composed by Attilio, only Coriolanus and Lucius Verus are in print, though many of the airs in others of them are to be found in collections published by Walsh. Of his operas Coriolanus was best received, and is the most celebrated; the prison scene in particular is wrought up to the highest degree of perfection that music is capable of, and is said to have drawn tears from the audience at every representation: one of the Newgate scenes in the Beggar's Opera is apparently a parody on it, and Mr. Gay seems to intimate no less in his preface.

The success of Mr. Handel in the composition of operas, and the applause with which his productions were received, not only silenced all competition against him, but drove his opponents to the necessity of relinquishing their claim to the public favour. Bononcini, upon his ceasing to compose for the opera, found a comfortable retreat, and a sovereign remedy for the pangs of disappointed ambition, in the Marlborough family; the lot of Attilio was less happy, and we know of no patronage extended to him. Pressed by the necessity which followed from his want of encouragement, he not so properly solicited as begged, a subscription from the nobility and gentry to a book of Cantatas, in which he purposed to display the utmost of his abilities. Before this time Bononcini had made the like attempt in a proposal to publish his Duettos and Cantatas; the subscription to the work was two guineas; and he succeeded so well, that the profits of the publication were estimated at near a thousand guineas. Attilio, in the hope of like success, applied himself to such as he thought his friends, and, as well where he failed of a promise, as where he obtained one, he inrolled the name of the person applied to, in his list of subscribers, and his book was published with the strange title of ' Alla Maestà di Giorgio Rè della Gran Britagna, &c., &c., &c.,' and only the initials of his name to the dedication. The work consists of six Cantatas, the words whereof are conjectured to have been written by Paolo Rolli; and a collection of lessons for the Viol d'Amore. The compositions of both kinds contained in it abound with evidences of a fertile invention, and great skill in the art of modulation and the principles of harmony; and upon the whole, may be said to have merited a better reception than the public vouchsafed to give them. After the publication of this book Attilio took leave of England.

CHAP. CLXXXVII.

THE account which it is proposed to give of the opera, and of those contentions among the singers, that, in the subsequent history of it will be found to have greatly embarrassed the directors. and divided the supporters of it into parties, will convince every one who reads it, that the profession of an opera singer was become of great importance; and that the caresses of princes and other great personages, who were slaves to their pleasures, had contributed to make them insolent; and this consideration makes it necessary to recur some years backwards, and take a view of the profession in its infancy, and to assign the causes that contributed to aggrandize it.

The profession of a public singer was not unknown to the ancient Romans; but among that people those that followed it were in general the slaves or domestic servants of the Patricians. In after-times it was followed for a livelihood by persons of both sexes, and with the greatest emolument by males, who in their infancy had undergone an operation, which seldom fails to improve the vocal organs. Of the general character and behaviour of this latter class of singers, we have no clear intimation till about the year 1647, when Doni published his treatise De Præstantia Musicæ veteris, in which he gives many instances of their arrogant and licentious behaviour to their superiors, and their general disposition to luxury and extravagance. Of the women the above writer says little but what is to their honour; two the most celebrated female singers of his time, Hadriana Baroni, and Leonora her daughter, he represents as virtuous and modest women.

The same author informs us, that in his time singers with remarkably fine voices were hired at great rates to sing at the public theatres; but so servile in his estimation does the profession seem to appear, that he has forborne, except in the instances above mentioned, to distinguish even the most celebrated of them by their names. In proportion as theatric music improved, these people became more and more conspicuous; but not till the close of the last century were any of the singers in the Italian opera known by their names; the first that can be readily recalled to memory is Sifacio, who, after having sung abroad for many years with great applause, came into England, and was a singer in the chapel of James II., soon after whom appeared Francesco Antonio Pistocchi, who, to borrow a term from the painters, was the founder of a school, which has produced some of the most celebrated singers in these latter ages. The school of Pistocchi is called the School of Bologna; but it seems that there was also one more ancient, called the School of Tuscany; and to this seminary Milton seems to allude in the following lines, part of a sonnet inscribed to Mr. Lawrence :—

What neat repast shall feast us, light and choice,
  Of Attic taste, with wine; whence we may rise
To hear the lute well toucht, or artful voice
  Warble immortal notes and Tuscan air ?

Mr. Martinelli, in two letters by him written to an English nobleman, on the origin of the Italian opera,* would insinuate that the style of the Tuscan school, even down to the beginning of the present century, retained much of that natural simplicity and austerity which characterized the songs of the church; and that Sifacio,† and La Tilla, both natives of

* Lettere Familiari e Critiche di Vincenzio Martinelli. Londra, 1758.

† This was a name of distinction given to him on his performing the character of Syphax in an opera, and in consequence thereof his true name was forgotten.

Tuscany, and of this ancient school, determined the epocha of this grave and simple music; and farther that Pistocchi corrupted it. His character of this person is, 'that he sang at first upon the theatre, but 'being obliged, because of his disagreeable voice and 'ungraceful figure, to quit the stage, he turned priest, 'and undertook to teach an art which he was judged 'unable to practice with success.'

To this opinion of Mr. Martinelli, so far as it respects Pistocchi, we have to oppose that of a much better judge, namely, Mr. Galliard, who gives the following account of him, viz., 'That he refined the 'manner of singing in Italy, which was then a little 'crude; and that his merit in this is acknowledged 'by all his countrymen, and contradicted by none: 'that when he first appeared to the world, and a 'youth, he had a very fine treble voice, but by a 'dissolute life lost it: that after some years he re-'covered a little glimpse of voice, which by time 'and practice turned into a fine contralto; that he 'took care of it, and, travelling all Europe over, 'where hearing different manners and tastes, he 'appropriated them to himself, and formed that 'agreeable mixture which he produced in Italy, 'where he was imitated and admired.' Mr. Galliard concludes this character of Pistocchi with the mention of a remark, which he seems to acquiesce in, viz., that though several of his disciples shewed the improvement they had from him, yet others made an ill use of it, having not a little contributed to the introduction of the modern taste.

To proceed with the school of Bologna. Mr. Martinelli adds, the most celebrated scholars of Pistocchi were Bernacchi* and Pasi, both of Bologna, and his countrymen; the former he says has acquired the applause of a few enthusiasts, who are fond of difficulties, by his skill and ingenuity in running over the most hard passages of music in the short space of an Arietta; but that he was never so successful as to please the generality, because he often neglected the sentiment which he had to express, in order to give a loose to his fancy; besides, he adds, his voice was little pleasing, and his figure wanted consequence. On the contrary, he says, that Pasi retained none of the lessons of his master but what were necessary in order to set off a voice, which, though weak, was exceedingly agreeable; a circumstance, that, joined to an advantageous figure, procured him in a short time the reputation of the most perfect singer that had appeared upon the stage. The same author mentions Porpora as the instructor of Farinelli and other celebrated singers, and who, as he taught his pupils a manner of singing till then unknown, is, as well as Bernacchi, considered as the founder of a school which will be mentioned in a future page.†

While the proposal for an academy was under consideration, and to accelerate the carrying of it into execution, Mr. Handel set himself to compose the opera of Radamistus, and caused it to be represented at the Haymarket theatre in the winter of the year 1720. The applause with which it was received cannot be better related than in the words of the anonymous author of Memoirs of the Life of Mr. Handel, published in the year 1760, which are as follow: 'If persons who are now living, and who 'were present at that performance, may be credited, 'the applause it received was almost as extravagant 'as his Agrippina had excited; the crowds and 'tumults of the house at Venice were hardly equal 'to those at London. In so splendid and fashionable 'an assembly of ladies, to the excellence of their 'taste we must impute it, there was no shadow of 'form or ceremony, scarce indeed any appearance of 'order or regularity, politeness or decency: many, 'who had forced their way into the house with an 'impetuosity but ill suited to their rank and sex, 'actually fainted through the excessive heat and 'closeness of it; several gentlemen were turned 'back who had offered forty shillings for a seat in 'the gallery, after having despaired of getting any 'in the pit or boxes.'

The performance of the opera of Radamistus had impressed upon the friends of Handel, and indeed upon the public in general, a deep sense of his abilities. It received great advantages from the performance; for Senesino sang in it that admirable air, 'Ombra Cara,' and Durastanti others; but, to remove all suspicion that the applause of the public was paid to the representation, and not to the intrinsic merit of the work, Handel published it himself, having previously obtained a licence under the sign manual, dated 14 June, 1720, for securing to him the property in that, and such other of his works as he should afterwards publish.‡

Whoever peruses the opera of Radamistus, will find abundant reason to acquiesce in the high opinion that was entertained of it. The airs in it are all excellent, but those of chief note are, 'Deh fuggi un 'traditore,' 'Son contenta di muore,' 'Doppo torbide 'procelle,' 'Ombra Cara,' 'Spero placare,' 'La sorte 'il ciel amor,' and 'Vanne sorella ingrata.'§ The performance and the publication jointly operated in bringing the interests of the three rivals to a crisis. Neither was disposed to yield, and the friends of each concurred in a proposal that Handel, Bononcini, and Attilio should in conjunction compose an opera, that is to say, each of them an act, as also an overture: the opera was Mutius Scævola; Bononcini set the first act, Attilio the second, and Handel the third; the songs and the overture in the first and third are in print, and we are enabled to make a comparison

---

* Antonio Bernacchi: one of that name sang at London in the opera of Lotharius, represented in the year 1729, but with little applause, though he was allowed to be a great master.

† The cant of all professions is disgusting, and that of the musical connoisseurs most so, as it is ever dictated by ignorance and affectation. Nevertheless as the term school, as applied to musical performance, may be thought technical, we choose rather to adopt it than express it by a periphrasis.

‡ It was in the title-page said to be published by the author, and printed and sold by Richard Meares, musical instrument maker, and music printer, in St. Paul's church-yard, and by Christopher Smith, at the Hand and Music book in Coventry street, near the Haymarket, and nowhere else in England.

§ There is in this opera a short air, 'Cara Sposa,' in the key of A, with the greater third, which is to be distinguished from one with the same beginning in the opera of Rinaldo in E, with the lesser third, which is a studied composition, for this reason that Mr. Handel looked upon the two airs, 'Cara Sposa,' and 'Ombra Cara,' as the two finest he ever made, and declared this his opinion to the author of this work.

between Handel and Bononcini, but of Attilio's part of the work we can say nothing.

The issue of this contest determined the point of precedence between Handel and his competitors: his act in Mutius Scævola was pronounced superior to the others, and Bononcini's next in merit. This victory however was not productive of those consequences that some might hope for; it did not reduce the adversaries of Handel to the necessity of a precipitate retreat, nor even leave the conqueror in possession of the field of battle, for both Bononcini and Attilio continued to compose for the opera after the dispute; and indeed the finest compositions of each, as namely, Astartus, Crispus, Griselda, Pharnaces, Calphurnia, Erminia, Astyanax, by the former; and Coriolanus, Vespasian, Artaxerxes, Darius, and Lucius Verus, by the latter, were composed and performed with the applause severally due to them, between the years 1721 and 1727.*

Of the singers in the Royal Academy two only have as yet been particularly mentioned, that is to say, Senesino and Durastanti; and these had the greatest share in the performance. There were others however of such distinguished merit, as to deserve to be noticed, as namely, Signor Gaetano Berenstadt, whom Mr. Handel had brought from Dresden with the two former, and Boschi, for whom were composed those two celebrated bass songs, 'Del minacciar del 'vento,' in Otho, and 'Deh Cupido,' in Rodelinda; and when these went off, their places were supplied by Pacini, Borosini, Baldi, Antenori, Palmieri, and others. Of female singers there were also some whose merits were too considerable to be forgotten: there were two of the same name, viz., Robinson, though no way related to each other; one of them, Mrs. Anastasia Robinson, afterwards countess of Peterborough, will be spoken of hereafter; the other was the daughter of Dr. William Turner, and the wife of Mr. John Robinson, organist of Westminster-abbey, already mentioned; for which reason, and to distinguish her from the former, she was called Mrs. Turner Robinson.† Soon after the establishment of the Royal Academy, Mr. Handel had engaged Signora Cuzzoni, who sang with unrivalled applause till the year 1726, when Signora Faustina came hither, and became a competitor with her for the public favour, and succeeded so well in her endeavours to obtain it, as to divide the musical world into two parties, not less violent in their enmity to each other than any that we read of in history.

An account of the dispute between these two famous singers, equally excellent, but in different ways, will be reserved for a future page. In the interim it is to be remarked, that the establishment of the opera gave a new turn to the sentiments and manners of the young nobility and gentry of this kingdom: most of these were great frequenters of the opera; they professed to admire the music, and next to that the language in which they were written;

many of them became the scholars of the instrumental performers, and by them were taught the practice of the violin, the violoncello, and the harpsichord. Others, who were ambitious of being able to converse with the singers, especially with the females; to utter with a grace the exclamations used to testify applause, and to be expert in the use of all the cant phrases which musical connoisseurs affect, set themselves to learn the Italian language; and in proportion to their progress in it were more or less busy behind the scenes, and in other respects troublesome and impertinent.

Who was the first writer in England of Italian operas is now only known in the instance of Etearcus, written by Haym, and represented in 1711; unless it can be supposed that Rossi, the author of Rinaldo, had been sufficiently encouraged to a second attempt of that kind; however, at the time of the establishment of the Academy the directors took care to engage in their service one whose abilities as a poet were never questioned, namely, Paolo Antonio Rolli. This person was a Florentine by birth, and, notwithstanding his pretensions to an honourable descent, was, as it is asserted by a gentleman who knew him in England, originally of a very mean occupation, that is to say, a maker of vermicelli; in plain English a pastry-cook; but having a talent for poetry, he cultivated it with great assiduity; and in some little songs, cantatas, and occasional poems, by him published from time to time, gave proofs of his genius. He came into England about the year 1718, and wrote for the managers the opera of Narcissus; Rolli wrote also Mutius Scævola, Numitor, Floridante, Astartus, Griselda, and Crispus,‡ and, in short, most of the operas exhibited under the direction of the Royal Academy: Elpidia, represented in 1725, was written by Apostolo Zeno. Finding in the English that frequented the opera a propensity to the study of the Italian language, Rolli became a teacher of it to those who were able to make him such gratifications, as men possessed with a high sense of their own merits are wont to require. Being a man of assiduity, he applied himself to the publication of valuable books written in his own language, as namely, the Decameron of Boccace, the Satires of Ariosto, the Opere burlesche of Francesco Berni, Giovanni della Cafa, and other Italian poets, and the translation of Lucretius by Alessandro Marchetti. For the improvement of his scholars he also translated into Italian two of Sir Richard Steele's comedies, viz., the Conscious Lovers and the Funeral, and also the Paradise Lost of Milton; upon which it is to be remarked, that, being of the Romish communion, he has left out the Limbo of Vanity, and that some of the copies were printed on blue paper. In the year 1744 he quitted England, and retired, as it is said,

---

* Elpidia and Elisa were performed in the year 1725, but by whom they were composed is not known.

† She is so called in the opera of Narcissus, composed by Domenico, the son of Alessandro Scarlatti, with additional songs by Roseingrave, and performed at the theatre in the Haymarket in 1720.

‡ The subject of the opera of Griselda is the well known story of the marquis of Saluzzo and Griselda, related by Boccace, and is the Clerk of Oxford's tale in Chaucer. See vol. II. page 29. It is known to the vulgar by an old ballad entitled 'Patient Grisel,' beginning 'A noble marquis as he did ride a hunting.' It seems that at the time of performing the operas of Griselda and Crispus, their comparative merits were the subject of a dispute that divided the ladies into parties, one whereof preferred the former, the other the latter. This difference of opinion is taken notice of by Sir Richard Steele in his comedy of the Conscious Lovers, Act II.

to the enjoyment of a patrimonial estate in the Campania of Rome, assuming the title of a Roman senator.

Besides the singers, the instrumental performers in the opera deserve some notice ; Corbett played the first violin at the time when they were first introduced : to him succeeded Claudio, an Italian, a sound and judicious performer ; but when the en-tertainment was put upon a new and better footing, Carbonelli was placed at the head of the orchestra. He continued in that station about seven years, and was succeeded by Pietro Castrucci. Mr. Galliard played the first hautboy, and Kenny, mentioned before in the life of Purcell by the mistaken name of Kennedy, the bassoon.

BOOK XX.   CHAP. CLXXXVIII.

Mr. Handel continued to fulfil his engagements with the directors, until the year 1726, when, having composed a new opera, entitled Alessandro, and engaged a new singer, namely Signora Faustina, he laid the foundation of a dispute, that terminated in the ruin of the whole undertaking.

But before we proceed to relate the circumstances of this event, it may be observed that it seemed to be no more than the necessary consequence of that extravagant applause which the opera audience had shewn itself ever ready to bestow on their favourites among the singers. Senesino was one of the first that discovered this benevolent propensity in the English, and he laboured by a vigorous exertion of all his powers, to cultivate and improve that good opinion which had been conceived of him on his first appearance among us; and it was not long before he began to feel his own importance. Handel was not a proud man, but he was capricious : in his comparison of the merits of a composer and those of a singer, he estimated the latter at a very low rate, and affected to treat Senesino with a degree of indifference that the other could but ill brook; in short, they were upon very ill terms almost from the time of their first coming together ; but in a year or two after Faustina's arrival, the flame of civil discord burst forth, and all was disorder and confusion. The two women were soon sensible, from the applause bestowed upon Senesino, that the favour of an English audience was worth courting; and in proportion as it appeared desirable, each of them began to grow jealous of the other : Senesino had no rival, but each of the women was possessed of talents sufficient to engage a very strong party. To render the history of this contest intelligible will require a short digression.

Mrs. Anastasia Robinson (*a Portrait*) was descended from a good family in the county of Leicester ; her father was brought up to the profession of a portrait painter, and having, to perfect himself in his studies, travelled to Rome, he returned to England, and settling in London, married a woman of some fortune, by whom he had *two daughters, Anastasia, the subject of the present article, and another named Margaret. In the infancy of these his children, Mr. Robinson had the misfortune to lose his wife; and needing the assistance of a female to bring them up and manage the concerns of his family, he married a young gentlewoman of the name of Lane.* Soon after this Mr. Robinson contracted a disorder in his eyes, which terminated in the loss of his sight, and deprived him of the means of supporting himself and his family by the exercise of his pencil. Under the heavy pressure of this calamity, he and his wife reflecting on their inability to make a provision for them, resolved to bring up both the children to a profession : Anastasia, the elder, having discovered in her childhood an ear for music, was designed by them for a singer; and other motives, equally cogent at the time, determined them to make of Peggy a miniature painter. The story of this younger daughter is but short, and is, against the order of precedence, here inserted, to prevent a digression in that which is more to our purpose, the the history of her sister.

The second Mrs. Robinson was possessed of a small income, part whereof, under the direction of her husband, was appropriated to the instruction of the two children in the professions they were severally intended for ; but all the endeavours of the parents in favour of the younger were in vain; she slighted her studies, and, deviating into her sister's track, would learn nothing but music : yielding, therefore, to this strong propensity, Mr. Robinson placed her under Bononcini, and afterwards sent her to Paris, where, being committed to the tuition of Rameau, and having a most delicate ear, and great powers of execution, she attained to such a degree of perfection in singing as set her upon a level with the most celebrated performers of the time ; but having a natural bashfulness, which she could never overcome, and being besides lower in stature than the lowest of her sex, she could never be prevailed on to become a public singer; *yet with these disadvantages she was not destitute of attractions: a gentleman of the army, Colonel Bowles, liked and married her.* On the other hand, Anastasia, who had been committed to the care of Dr. Croft, but was rather less indebted to nature for the gift of a voice than her sister, prosecuted her studies with the utmost n-dustry. With the assistance of her father she became such a mistress of the Italian language, that she was able to converse in it, and to repeat with the utmost propriety passages from the poets. To remedy some defects in her singing, to mend if possible her shake, which was not altogether correct, and, above all, to make the Italian modulation familiar to her, the assistance of Sandoni, a celebrated teacher,[*] was called in ; but all that could be done by him, and the lady called the Baroness, a singer in

[*] Pier Giuseppe Sandoni ; he published, and dedicated to the countess of Pembroke, a work of his entitled ' Cantate da Camera e Sonate per il Cembalo.'

MRS. ANASTASIA ROBINSON.

AFTERWARDS COUNTESS OF PETERBOROUGH.

FRANCESCO BERNARDO SENESINO.

the opera, then greatly caressed, in these respects was but little; she had a fine voice, and an extensive compass, but she wanted a nice and discriminating ear to make her a perfect singer. Her first public appearance was in the concerts performed at that time in York-buildings, and at other places, in which she sang, and generally accompanied herself on the harpsichord. Her father had carefully attended to her education, and had exerted his utmost efforts in the improvement of her mind; the advantages she derived from these instances of his affection, added to her own good sense and amiable qualities, consisting in a strictly virtuous disposition, a conduct full of respect to her superiors, and an undissembled courtesy and affability to others, mixed with a cheerfulness that diffused itself to all around her, were visible in the reception she met with from the public, which was of such a kind as seemed to ensure her success in whatever she undertook. Encouraged by the favour of the public to his daughter, and more especially by the countenance and bounty of some persons of high rank of her own sex, Mr. Robinson took a house in Golden-square, and had concerts, and also conversations on certain days in every week, which were the resort of all who had any pretensions to politeness. *A lady of very high rank now living (the Duchess Dowager of Portland), who honoured Mrs. Anastasia Robinson with her patronage, and was very intimate with her, has condescended to furnish some of the above anecdotes respecting her and her family, which she concludes with saying that it was to support her afflicted father that she became a singer in the opera, and, speaking of her mental endowments, gives her this exalted character:—* ' Mrs. Robinson was most perfectly well bred and ' admirably accomplished, and, in short, one of the ' most virtuous and best of women, but never very ' handsome.' *The same person says that Mr. Robinson had by his second wife a daughter, who was married to Mr. George Arbuthnot, a wine merchant, a brother of Dr. Arbuthnot, the physician and friend of Mr. Pope.*

At the time when Mrs. Tofts and Margarita retired from the stage, scarce any female singers worth hearing were left; Mrs. Lindsey, Mrs. Cross, Signora Isabella Girardeau, and the Baroness above mentioned, are the only names that we meet with, except the two former, and Signora Maria Gallia, who sang the part of Rosamond in Mr. Addison's opera of that name, between the time of the first introduction of the opera and the year 1718. Under these favourable circumstances, and the several others above enumerated, Mrs. Robinson was prevailed on to appear on the opera stage. The first opera she sang in was that of Narcissus, mentioned in a preceding page to have been composed by Domenico Scarlatti, and brought on the stage by Roseingrave; in this she sang the part of Echo with great applause. In the succeeding operas of Mutius Scævola, Crispus, Griselda, Otho, Floridante, Flavius, Julius Cæsar, Pharnaces, Coriolanus, and Vespasian, she also sang, and, together with Cuzzoni and Senesino, contributed greatly to the support of the entertainment. Her

salary was a thousand pounds, and her emoluments, arising from benefits and presents of various kinds, were estimated at nearly as much more. She continued to sing in the opera till the year 1723, at the end whereof she retired from the stage, in consequence, as it is supposed, of her marriage with the earl of Peterborough; for she at that time went to reside at his house at Parson's Green, and appeared there the mistress of his family; and the marriage was announced some years after in the public papers, in terms that imported it to be a transaction some years precedent to the time of notifying it, which was not till the year 1735. During this critical interval, in which the earl, for the same reasons that restrained him from publishing his marriage, studiously avoided the styling her his countess, she was visited by persons of the highest rank, under a full persuasion, founded on the general tenor of her life and conduct, that she could be no other than the mistress of the mansion in which she did the family honours, and that she had a legal title to a rank which, for prudential reasons, she was content to decline. This nobleman had a seat called Bevis Mount, situate near Southampton. By a letter from the earl to Mr. Pope, written about the year 1728, it appears that Mrs. Robinson then lived with him, for she is there mentioned by the appellation of the Farmeress of Bevis; and in others from the same person, of a later date, are sundry expressions alluding to the severities which at stated seasons she practised on herself, and plainly indicating that she was of the Romish communion.*

In this exalted station of life she forgot not her obligations to Bononcini; he had improved her manner of singing, and in most of his operas, particularly Crispus and Griselda, had composed songs peculiarly adapted to her powers of execution; for him she obtained the pension of five hundred pounds a year, granted him by the duchess of Marlborough; and for his friend Greene she procured the places of

---

* Works of Alexander Pope, Esq. Lond. 1739, vol. VI. page 210, et seq. It is conjectured that all her family were of the same persuasion; at least it is certain that Mr. Robinson's second wife was, and that her brother Mr. Lane, resided in the family of the earl of Peterborough, from the time of his marriage with Mrs. Robinson, in the avowed character of a Romish ecclesiastic.

The general character of the above-mentioned nobleman, who is equally celebrated for his bravery and his parts, is well known; he wrote those exquisitely neat and elegant lines in Pope and Swift's Miscellany, beginning ' I said to my heart between sleeping and waking;' four letters in Pope's collection, and a few other things of small account, mentioned in Mr. Walpole's Catalogue of Royal and Noble Authors; but Mrs. Howard, afterwards countess of Suffolk, the subject of the above verses, had seen and read in the manuscript three volumes of his lordship's memoirs, which it is feared are irrecoverably lost. That lady, who knew him very well, used to relate a story, which she had from his own mouth, so singular, that the mention of it here may merit an excuse. Lord Peterborough, when a young man, and about the time of the Revolution, had a passion for a lady who was fond of birds; she had seen and heard a fine canary bird at a coffee-house near Charing-cross, and entreated him to get it for her; the owner of it was a widow, and lord Peterborough offered to buy it at a great price, which she refused: finding there was no other way of coming at the bird, he determined to change it; and getting one of the same colour, with nearly the same marks, but which happened to be a hen, went to the house; the mistress of it usually sat in a room behind the bar, to which he had easy access; contriving to send her out of the way, he effected his purpose; and upon her return took his leave. He continued to frequent the house to avoid suspicion, but forbore saying any thing of the bird till about two years after; when taking occasion to speak of it, he said to the woman, ' I would have bought that bird of you, and you refused my money for it, ' I dare say you are by this time sorry for it.' ' Indeed, Sir,' answered the woman, ' I am not, nor would I now take any sum for him, for would ' you believe it? from the time that our good king was forced to go ' abroad and leave us, the dear creature has not sung a note.'

organist and composer to the royal chapel, vacant by the decease of her master, Dr. Croft.

The earl was very far advanced in years at the time when he married Mrs. Robinson; in 1735, being advised to go to Lisbon for the recovery of his health, he went thither, and on the twenty-fifth day of October, in the same year, died at the advanced age of seventy-seven. The countess surviving him, continued to reside at Bevis Mount till the year 1750, when she also died.

During the residence of Mrs. Robinson at Parson's Green she had a kind of a musical academy there, in which Bononcini, Martini, Tosi, Greene, and others of that party, were frequent performers. His lordship had also frequent dining parties, whom he entertained with music, and, what was little less delightful, the recital of his adventures during his long residence abroad, particularly while he commanded in Spain. In that kingdom, while he was upon journies he was frequently in danger of perishing for want of food; and when he could get it, was so often constrained to dress it himself, that he became a good cook; and, such was the force of habit, that, till disabled by age, his dinner was constantly of his own dressing. Those who have dined with him at Parson's Green say that he had a dress for the purpose, like that of a tavern cook; and that he used to retire from his company an hour before dinner time; and, having despatched his culinary affairs, would return properly dressed, and take his place among them.

CHAP. CLXXXIX.

FRANCESCO BERNARDO SENESINO (*a Portrait*), a native of Sienna, as his surname imports, was a singer in the opera at Dresden in the year 1719, at the same time with Signora Margarita Durastanti. In consequence of his engagement with the directors of the academy, Mr. Handel went to Dresden, and entered into a contract with both these persons, as also with Berenstadt, to sing in the opera at London, the former at a salary of fifteen hundred pounds for the season. Senesino had a very fine even-toned voice, but of rather a narrow compass; some called it a mezzo soprano, others a contralto; it was nevertheless wonderfully flexible: besides this he was a graceful actor, and in the pronunciation of recitative had not his fellow in Europe. His first appearance was in the opera of Mutius Scævola, represented in the year 1721.

It has been already mentioned, that notwithstanding Senesino was so excellent and useful a singer, as to be in a great measure the support of the opera, Handel and he agreed but ill together; and that a short time after the arrival of Faustina, the disputes among the singers rose to such a height, as threatened the ruin of the opera. Handel suspected that the example of Senesino had given encouragement to that refractory spirit which he found rising in the two contending females; and being determined to strike at the root of the evil, he proposed to the directors to discard Senesino; but they refusing to consent, Handel refused also to compose for him any

longer, or indeed to have any farther concern with him. A year or two afterwards the academy broke up, after having flourished for more than nine years.

The academy being thus dissolved, some of the nobility raised a new subscription for an opera at Lincoln's-Inn fields, in which Porpora was engaged to compose, and Senesino to sing. The success of this undertaking will be the subject of a future page; Senesino continued in the service of the nobility, singing at Lincoln's-Inn fields theatre, and afterwards at the Haymarket, which Handel had quitted, till about the year 1735, when, having acquired the sum of fifteen thousand pounds, he retired to Sienna, the place of his nativity, and built a handsome house, which, upon his decease, he bequeathed, together with the whole of his fortune, to his relations.

Signora MARGARITA DURASTANTI was engaged by Mr. Handel at the same time with Senesino, and came with him into England. She sang in the operas composed by Handel, Bononcini, and Attilio, till the year 1723. For the reason of her quitting England we are to seek, unless we may suppose that the applause bestowed on Cuzzoni, who appeared on the stage for two or three winters with her, was more than she could bear. However, she made a handsome retreat, and, as it seems, took a formal leave of the English nation by singing on the stage a song written for her in haste by Mr. Pope, at the earnest request of the earl of Peterborough, which, together with a burlesque of it by Dr. Arbuthnot, were lately printed in some of the public papers from a volume of poems among the Harleian manuscripts in the British Museum. Both poems are here inserted:—

Generous, gay, and gallant nation,
　Bold in arms, and bright in arts;
Land secure from all invasion,
　All but Cupid's gentle darts!
From your charms, oh who would run?
Who would leave you for the sun?

　Happy soil, adieu, adieu!
Let old charmers yield to new.
　In arms, in arts, be still more shining;
All your joys be still encreasing;
　All your tastes be still refining;
All your jars for ever ceasing:
　But let old charmers yield to new
　Happy soil, adieu, adieu!

Puppies, whom I now am leaving,
　Merry sometimes, always mad,
Who lavish most, when debts are craving,
　On fool, and farce, and masquerade!
Who would not from such bubbles run,
And leave such blessings for the sun?

　Happy soil, and simple crew!
　Let old sharpers yield to new;
All your tastes be still refining;
All your nonsense still more shining:
Blest in some Berenstadt or Boschi,
He more aukward, he more husky;
And never want, when these are lost t'us,
Another Heidegger and Faustus.
　Happy soil, and simple crew!
　Let old sharpers yield to new?
　Bubbles all, adieu, adieu!

FRANCESCA CUZZONI SANDONI,

DA PARMA.

SIGNORA FAUSTINA.

Francesca Cuzzoni Sandoni *(a Portrait)*, a native of Modena, became a singer in the opera at London soon after the arrival of Senesino; for it appears that she sang in the opera of Otho, which was performed in the year 1722. She continued to sing the principal songs till the year 1726, when Faustina arrived, and becoming a competitor with her for the public favour, gave rise to a contest, which more properly belongs to the next article.

Signora Faustina* *(a Portrait)*, a Venetian by birth, and a young woman with a handsome face, and of a pleasing form, had sung abroad with such applause, that, as it is said, persons labouring under the tortures of the gout left their beds, and resorted to the theatres to hear her; and at Florence, in particular, medals in honour of her were struck. It was thought that the accession of such a distinguished singer would tend greatly to the advantage of the opera in England; accordingly, in the year 1726, she was engaged, and appeared first in the opera of Alexander. In the powers of execution, and a distinct manner of singing quick passages, she exceeded Cuzzoni: the merit of her rival consisted in a fine-toned voice, and a power of expression that frequently melted the audience into tears. For the circumstances of this famous dispute recourse has been had to some persons of distinguished rank, leaders of the two parties which it gave rise to; and as all animosity between them is now subsided, the relation of each appears to be such as may safely be relied on.

Till the time of Faustina's arrival, Cuzzoni as a female singer was in full possession of the public favour; the songs which Mr. Handel gave her were composed with the utmost solicitude to display her talents to advantage, as appears by the songs 'Affanni del pensier,' in Otho, 'Da tanti affanni 'oppressa,' 'Sen vola lo sparvier,' and 'E per monti 'e per piano,' in Admetus, and others. She had driven Durastanti out of the kingdom; Mrs. Robinson quitted the stage about the same time, so that for three seasons she remained without a rival. The consciousness of her great abilities, and the stubborn resistance of Senesino to Handel, had no small effect on the behaviour of Cuzzoni: she too could at times be refractory; for some slight objection that she had to the song 'Falsa imagine,' in Otho, she at the practice of it refused to sing it; when Mr. Handel referring to other instances of her stubbornness, took her round the waist, and swore, if she persisted, to throw her out of the window. It was high time therefore to look out for means of quieting this rebellious spirit, and, to effect his purpose, nothing seemed to bid so fair as the engagement of Faustina.

As Handel had taken the pains to compose songs peculiarly adapted to the powers and excellencies of Cuzzoni, he was not less solicitous to display those of Faustina; accordingly he made for her the air, 'Alla sua gabbia d'oro,' in Alexander, in the performance whereof she emulated the liquid articula-

tion of the nightingale, and charmed the unprejudiced part of her hearers into ecstasy; as also ' Vedeste 'mai sul prato,' in Siroe, 'Gelosia spietato alletto,' in Admetus, and many others. *Riccoboni asserts that she invented, but we should rather say introduced, a new manner of singing, and it seems so by the songs composed for her, which abound with long and rapid divisions, such as none but a voice like hers could execute.*

From the account above given of Cuzzoni and Faustina, it appears that they were possessed of very different talents. The design of the directors in producing them both on the same stage, was to form a pleasing contrast between the powers of expression and execution, that of Handel was to get rid of Cuzzoni; but the town no sooner became sensible of the perfections which each was possessed of, than they began to compare them in their own minds, and endeavour to determine to whom of the two the greatest tribute of theatrical applause was due. Some ladies of the first quality entered very deeply into the merits of this competition; a numerous party engaged to support Cuzzoni, and another not less formidable associated on the side of Faustina. Thus encouraged, the behaviour of the rivals to each other was attended with all the circumstances of malevolence that jealousy, hatred, and malice could suggest; private slander and public abuse were deemed weapons too innoxious in this warfare, blows were made use of in the prosecution of it, and, shame to tell! the two Signoras fought. The countess of Pembroke† headed the Cuzzoni party, and carried her animosity to such lengths, as gave occasion to the following epigram :—

Upon Lady Pembroke's promoting the catcalling of Faustina.

Old poets sing that beasts did dance
    Whenever Orpheus play'd,
So to Faustina's charming voice
    Wise Pembroke's asses bray'd.

The chief supporters of Cuzzoni among the men are pointed out in the following epigram, which with that above given is extracted from a volume of poems among the Harleian manuscripts now in the British Museum, Numb. 7316, pages 394, 319.

Epigram on the Miracles wrought by Cuzzoni.

Boast not how Orpheus charm'd the rocks,
And set a dancing stones and stocks,
    And tygers' rage appeas'd;
All this Cuzzoni has surpass'd,
Sir Wilfred ‡ seems to have a taste,
    And Smith § and Gage ‖ are pleas'd.

Faustina's friends among the ladies were Dorothy, countess of Burlington, and Charlotte, lady Delawar; the men in general were on her side, as being by far a more agreeable woman than Cuzzoni.¶

---

† Mary Howe, third wife of earl Thomas.

‡ Sir Wilfred Lawson, Bart.   § Simon Smith, Esq.   ‖ Sir William Gage, Bart, all subscribers to the Royal Academy.

¶ *In the contest between Faustina and Cuzzoni, Sir Robert Walpole took part with the former, as being the least assuming of the two. His Lady, that the latter might not be borne down by his influence countenanced Cuzzoni; and on Sundays when he was gone to Chelsea would invite them to dinner. She was at first distrest to adjust the precedence between them at her table, but their concessions to each other were mutual.*

---

* *Riccoboni in his account of the theatres in Europe, gives her two surnames, calling her Faustina Bardoni Asse. The latter, it is supposed, is meant for that which she acquired by her marriage with Hasse. Vide infra 874.*

The directors, greatly troubled with the dispute, and foreseeing the probable consequences of it, fell upon an odd expedient to determine it. The time for a new contract with each of these singers was at hand, and they agreed among themselves to give as a salary to Faustina one guinea a year more than to her rival. Lady Pembroke and some others, the friends of Cuzzoni, hearing this, made her swear upon the holy gospels never to take less than Faustina, and the directors continuing firm in their resolution not to give her quite so much, Cuzzoni found herself ensnared by her oath into the necessity of quitting the kingdom. The following lines were written by Ambrose Phillips on her departure :—

> Little syren of the stage,
> Charmer of an idle age,
> Empty warbler, breathing lyre,
> Wanton gale of fond desire ;
> Bane of every manly art,
> Sweet enfeebler of the heart ;
> O ! too pleasing is thy strain,
> Hence to southern climes again :
> Tuneful mischief, vocal spell,
> To this island bid farewell ;
> Leave us as we ought to be,
> Leave the Britons rough and free.

About the year 1748 she was engaged to sing at the Haymarket, and appeared in the opera of Mitridate, composed by Terradellas, but, being far advanced in years, she gave but little satisfaction. She returned to Italy at the end of the season, and, as we have been informed, was living about five years ago in a very mean condition, subsisting by the making of buttons. *That she was of a turbulent and obstinate temper may be inferred from a circumstance noted in a preceding page, and that she was ungrateful and insolent is little less certain, if credit be due to the author of the 'Essai sur la 'Musique,' printed at Paris, in four tomes, quarto, who relates that she begged of an English nobleman a suit of lace, but not liking it when sent to her, she threw it into the fire. After her leaving England she was for some time in Holland, where being imprisoned for debt, she was occasionally indulged by her keeper with permission to sing at the theatre, one of his servants attending to conduct her back. By these means she was enabled to pay her debts. Upon her enlargement she went to Bologna, and there, having experienced the miseries of extreme poverty, died.*

A better fate attended Faustina. She remained in England a short time after Cuzzoni, and in 1728 sang in the operas of Admetus and Siroe ; but, upon the disagreement between Handel and the directors of the opera, which terminated in the dissolution of the Royal Academy, she too left England, and went to Dresden, where she was married to Hasse, a musician of some eminence there, and is now living at Vienna.

CHAP. CXC.

THE singing of Senesino, Cuzzoni, and Faustina had captivated the hearers of them to such a degree, that they forgot the advantages which the human voice derives from its association with instruments,

so that they could have been well content with mere vocal performance during the whole of the evening's entertainment. The cry was that these persons were very liberally paid, and that the public had not singing enough for their money ; and from a few instances, such as occur in the song 'Lusinghe 'piu care,' in Alexander, 'Luci care,' in Admetus, and some others, in which the song part seems to be overcharged with symphony, it was complained of that compositions thus constructed were not so properly songs as sonatas. In favour of this notion an anonymous pamphlet was published in the year 1728, entitled 'Avviso ai Compositori, ed ai Can-'tanti,' with an English translation ; the design of it was to rectify the errors, real or supposed, in the composition of opera songs, but without any such particular instances as might lead to a suspicion that it was written to serve the interests of either of those masters who had for some time divided the opinion of the public ; in the general drift of it it seems calculated to add as much as possible to the importance of the singers, and to banish from the stage those aids of instrumental performance, which serve as reliefs to the vocal, and enable the singer to display his talent to greater advantage.

To this purpose the author expresses himself in these words : 'Another irregularity is that of en-'cumbering and overcharging the composition with 'too many symphonies. This custom has so much 'grown upon us within these late years, that 'if a stop be not put to it, the singer will be made 'to give place to the instruments, and the orchestra 'will be more regarded than the voices. It cannot 'be denied, that if symphonies are well intermixed 'with the songs, it will have a very good effect, 'especially if the composer rightly understands how 'to make use of them, and is a complete master ; but 'then he must take particular care that they do not 'make his composition any ways confused, and must 'guard himself against running into excess in the use 'of them, remembering that most useful saying 'of Terence, "Ne quid nimis."'

At the time when the opera was in its most flourishing state, that is to say, in the year 1727, was brought on the stage the Beggar's Opera, written by Mr. John Gay. Dean Swift says that this comedy exposeth with great justice that unnatural taste for Italian music among us,[*] which is wholly unsuitable to our northern climate. But there is nothing to warrant this assertion, unless Macheath's appearing in Newgate in fetters can be supposed a ridicule of the prison scene in Coriolanus, which had been represented at the Haymarket a few years before :[†] it was in truth a satire, and that so

---

[*] Intelligencer, No. 3, in Swift's works, printed by Faulkner, vol. I. page 284.

[†] The truest burlesque of the Italian opera is a mean subject, affording a mock hero, wrought into the form of a drama, in a style of bombast, set in recitative, with airs intermixed, in which long divisions are made on insignificant words. In a book entitled the Touchstone, or Historical, Critical, Political, Philosophical, and Theological Essays on the reigning Diversions of the Town, written by Mr. James Ralph ; the Dragon of Wantley, Robinhood and Little John, the London Prentice, Tom Thumb, and Chevy Chase, are proposed as subjects for a mock opera : the plan recommended by this writer was pursued by the facetious Henry Carey, who wrote the Dragon of Wantley, and got it set by Lampe, a Saxon, who was here some years ago, and composed for Covent Garden theatre ; and by the author of Tom Thumb, taken from Fielding's Tragedy of

general, as to include in it all stations and characters, and, in short, every class of men whose rank or situation of life was above that of the author. The motive for writing this piece, and for the many acrimonious expressions and bitter invectives against statesmen, lawyers, priests, and others, contained in it, was the disappointment of Mr. Gay in his application for preferment at court. He had been brought up to the trade of a mercer, but did not choose to follow it; for, having a genius for poetry, he became acquainted with Pope and Swift, who might probably tell him that he was a man of genius, and that such men had a right to places and preferments; and that from the time of the Revolution it had been a matter of contention between the leaders of the Whig and Tory parties, which should provide best for the writers of verses on either side respectively.* The poor man took their advice, and wrote his Fables for the use and instruction of the duke of Cumberland, then a child. He also wrote a tragedy called the Captives, which he was permitted to read to queen Caroline, and which was acted at Lincoln's-Inn fields, in 1720, with tolerable success. As a reward of these his merits, and upon the solicitation of some persons of high rank about the court, an offer was made him of the place of gentleman-usher to the princess Louisa, which he rejected with contempt, and, in the greatness of his soul, preferred to it a life of ease, and servile dependence on the bounty of his friends and the caprice of the town.

The Beggar's Opera had a run of sixty-three nights, during which the operas of Richard I. and Admetus were performing at the Haymarket, and, as it is said, but to thin audiences. The malevolence of the people, and the resentment which they had been taught to entertain against that conduct of administration, which they were equally unqualified to approve or condemn, were amply gratified by the representation of it; but the public were little aware of the injury they were doing to society, by giving countenance to an entertainment, which has been productive of more mischief to this country than any would believe at the time; for, not to

mention that the tendency of it, by inculcating that persons in authority are uniformly actuated by the same motives as thieves and robbers, is to destroy all confidence in ministers, and respect for magistrates, and to lessen that reverence, which, even in the worst state of government, is due to the laws and to public authority, a character is exhibited to view, of a libertine endowed with bravery, generosity, and the qualities of a gentleman, subsisting by the profession of highway robbery, which he defends by examples drawn from the practice of men of all professions. In this view Macheath is as much a hero as the principal agent in an epic poem; but lest this character should not be sufficiently fascinating to young minds, he is farther represented as having attained to some degree of wealth, to keep good company, that is to say, gamesters of fashion; to be a favourite with the women, and so successful in his amours, that one is with child by him, and another he marries. In short, his whole life is represented as an uninterrupted pursuit of criminal gratifications, in which he has the good fortune to succeed, and in the end to escape with impunity. Nevertheless the vox populi was in favour of this immoral drama; and Dr. Herring, the late archbishop of Canterbury, for presuming to censure it in a sermon delivered before the honourable society of Lincoln's-Inn, while he was preaching there, was by Dean Swift stigmatized with the appellation of a stupid, injudicious, and prostitute divine.†

The effects of the Beggar's Opera on the minds of the people have fulfilled the prognostications of many that it would prove injurious to society. Rapine and violence have been gradually increasing ever since its first representation: the rights of property, and the obligation of the laws that guard it, are disputed upon principle. Every man's house is now become what the law calls it, his castle, or at least it may be said that, like a castle, it requires to be a place of defence; young men, apprentices, clerks in public offices, and others, disdaining the arts of honest industry, and captivated with the charms of idleness and criminal pleasure, now betake themselves to the road, affect politeness in the very act of robbery, and in the end become victims to the justice of their country: and men of discernment, who have been at the pains of tracing this evil to its source, have found that not a few of those, who, during these last fifty years have paid to the law the forfeit of their lives, have in the course of their pursuits been emulous to imitate the manners and general character of Macheath.

It has been already mentioned that the consequence of the dispute between the nobility and Mr. Handel, and the determination of the former to support Senesino, was the utter dissolution of the academy; but the nobility raised a new subscription for an opera to be represented at the theatre in Lin-

Tragedies, and made into an opera, and set to music, but with less success than the former. The Beggar's Opera is nothing like either of these; the dialogue is common speech, and the airs are old ballad-tunes and country-dances; and yet it is said, but without any foundation in truth, that it contributed more to bring the Italian opera into contempt, than the invectives of the poets and the friends of the drama, and the writings of Dennis, who had been labouring all his life to convince the world of the absurdity of this exotic entertainment.

* In the writings of Swift, particularly in his letters, there occur many such sentiments. In consequence of an opinion that men possessed of a talent for poetry were best qualified for public employment, Mr. Addison was made secretary of state, Prior was secretary to the English plenipotentiaries at the Hague, after under-secretary of state, and, lastly, a lord of trade; and Congreve, Stepney, Steele, and others, had seats at some of the public boards; the error of this opinion was evinced in the case of Mr. Addison, who, with all those talents for which he is justly celebrated, not only made a very mean figure in the office of secretary of state, but shewed himself to be as little fit for active life, as an excess of timidity, even to sheepishness, could render a man. Though a minister, he attempted to speak in the house of commons, but was not able to do it, and was very deservedly removed to make room for one that could. Dr. Mandeville, the author of the Fable of the Bees, who, though of very bad principle, was a man of understanding, and that knew the world, was very frequently with the lord chief justice Parker, afterwards earl of Macclesfield, whom Mr. Addison visited, and expressed to the chief justice a desire to meet him; his lordship brought them together, and, after an evening's conversation, asked the doctor what was his opinion of Mr. Addison; 'I think,' answered the Doctor, 'he is a parson in a ' tye-wig.'

† Intelligencer, No. 3, Dublin edition of Swift's works, vol. I. page 284. This paper is a laboured defence of the Beggar's Opera, addressed to the people of Ireland; and the sentiments therein delivered do very well consist with the character of a man, of whom it may with justice be said, that scarce any one of his profession, whose writings are of an equal bulk with those of Swift, has, as an author, contributed less than he to the promotion of religion, virtue, or the general interests of mankind.

coln's-Inn fields, and established a direction of twelve of their own body, who in the conduct thereof resolved to act without the control of such as should be retained to assist in it, whether composers or singers, although of these latter Senesino was one, and indeed the chief. Seeing this formidable association, Handel had nothing left but to enter into an agreement with Heidegger, who, though old, was yet living, for carrying on an opera in conjunction, for the short term of three years, at the Haymarket. Upon the conclusion of this agreement, Handel found himself under a necessity of going to Italy for the purpose of engaging singers. After a short stay abroad, he returned with Fabri, and another Castrato; Strada, surnamed del Po, and Bertoli; the two last were women, and the former of them a very fine singer. He also engaged a German named Reimschneider, a bass singer, and some other persons of less account. The winter after his arrival Handel began his contest with the nobility by the representation of his opera of Lotharius, on the sixteenth of November, 1729. This was succeeded by Parthenope, with which he closed the season.

Handel continued at the Haymarket till the expiration of the term for which he stood engaged with Heidegger, during which he composed and performed successively the operas of Porus, Sosarmes, Orlando, and Ætius: at the end thereof he, together with old Mr. Smith, went abroad in quest of singers. In Italy he heard Farinelli, a young man of astonishing talents, and also Carestini, and, which is very strange, preferring the latter, he engaged with him, and returned to England. With this assistance he ventured to undertake an opera at the Haymarket on his own bottom.

During all this time the adversaries of Handel went on with but little better success; they performed a variety of operas, composed by sundry authors whose names are now forgotten, but to audiences that were seldom numerous enough to defray the ordinary expenses of the representation. At length they entered into engagements with Porpora, a musician who had distinguished himself abroad, and Farinelli, and took possession of the Haymarket theatre, which Handel at the end of the season had abandoned. Of the success of this new association there will be farther occasion to speak: at present it may suffice to say, that, having two such singers as Farinelli and Senesino at their command, the nobility had greatly the advantage, and for one season at least were great gainers. It is true they were losers in the end, for Cibber, who was living at the time, and kept a watchful eye on the theatres, asserts that Farinelli during his stay here had been known to sing to an audience of five and thirty pounds.*

CARLO BROSCHI FARINELLI (a Portrait), was the nephew of that Farinelli whom we have before mentioned to have been concert-master or director of the elector's music at Hanover. He was born at Naples, in the year 1705, and derived great advantage from the instructions of Porpora. He had sung at Rome and at Bologna, at the latter of which cities he had

* Apology for his Life, page 243.

heard Bernacchi; and also at Venice; when the fame of his great talents reaching England, he was engaged to sing in the opera at London, and in the year 1734 came over hither. His arrival in this country was in the newspapers announced to the public as an event worthy of notoriety. As soon as he was enough recovered from the fatigue of his journey, he was introduced to the king at St. James's, and had the honour to sing to him, the princess royal, afterwards princess of Orange, accompanying him on the harpsichord. At the same time with Farinelli arrived in England Porpora, who had been his instructor, and was the companion of his fortunes, and Giacomo Amiconi, the painter.† These three persons seem to have been united together in the bonds of a strict friendship and a communion of interests: at the same time that the nobility under the new subscription engaged with Farinelli, they also agreed with Porpora as a composer for the opera, and with Amiconi to paint the scenes. The operas in which Farinelli sang, were, Ariadne and Polifemo, set by Porpora, and Artaxerxes, by Hasse, who had acquired some reputation in Germany by his compositions for the theatre. He sang also in the oratorio of David, composed by Porpora, and in an opera entitled Demetrius, by Pescetti, both performed at the Haymarket. The world had never seen two such singers upon the same stage as Senesino and Farinelli; the former was a just and graceful actor, and in the opinion of very good judges had the superiority of Farinelli in respect of the tone of his voice; but the latter had so much the advantage in other respects, that few hesitated to pronounce him the greatest singer in the world; this opinion was grounded on the amazing compass of his voice, exceeding that of women, or any of his own class; his shake was just, and sweet beyond expression; and in the management of his voice, and the clear articulation of divisions and quick passages, he passed all description. Such perfections as these were enough for one singer to possess, and indeed they were so evident, and their effects so forcible on the minds of his hearers, that few were disposed to reflect that his person was tall and slender to excess, and by consequence his mien and action ungraceful.

Upon what terms Farinelli was engaged to sing

† Amiconi found employment here as a portrait, and also a history painter. In the former capacity it was the fashion among the friends of the opera and the musical connoisseurs to sit to him; in the latter he exercised his talent in the painting of halls and staircases; and this, notwithstanding that Kent, who, because he was a bad painter himself, had, as an architect, in his construction of stair-cases driven that kind of painting out of the kingdom, Amiconi painted the staircase of Powis-house in Ormond-street with the story of Judith and Holofernes, in three compartments; and the hall in the house at More-park in Hertfordshire, with that of Jupiter and Iö. Of this house the following is a brief history: in 1617 it was granted by the crown to the earl of Bedford, and he by a deed, declaring the uses of a fine, limited the inheritance thereof to himself for life, remainder to Lucy his wife and her heirs. See Chauncy's Historical Antiquities of Hertfordshire, page 479. This Lucy was the famous countess of Bedford, celebrated by Sir Toby Matthews, Dr. Donne, and other writers of those times; and she it is said laid out the gardens in such a manner as induced Sir William Temple, in his Essay on Gardening, to say it was the perfectest figure of a garden he ever saw. Many years after the decease of the countess of Bedford, the duke of Ormond became the owner of More-park; and, after his attainder, Mr. Stiles; who employed Amiconi to paint the hall: the succeeding proprietor of this mansion was lord Anson, and the present, Sir Laurence Dundas. The fondness of Sir William Temple for this place, induced him to give the name of it to his seat near Farnham in Surrey. Hence has arisen a mistaken notion that the More-park mentioned in his Essay on Gardening was in Surrey.

CARLO BROSCHI,

DETTO FARINELLI.

here, is not known to a degree of certainty; his salary however, be it what it might, bore but a small proportion to the annual amount of his profits, which, by a benefit, and rich presents of various kinds, were estimated at five thousand pounds a year. The excessive fondness which the nobility discovered for this person, the caresses they bestowed on, and the presents they made him indicated little less than infatuation; their bounty was prodigality, and their applause adoration.*

That unmanly propensity in persons of high rank to promote and encourage this last refinement of modern luxury which they manifested in these and various other instances, was loudly complained of as derogating from the national character. It was urged that the reputation of this country abroad was founded on the disposition of the people to arms, and their love of letters; and that we were adopting the manners of a people who have long since ceased to be distinguished for either. Indeed it was ridiculous to see a whole people in such a state of fascination as they were in at this time; many pretended to be charmed with the singing of Farinelli, who had not the least ear for music; and who could not, if they had been left to themselves, have distinguished between him and an inferior singer. However the experiment of a few years was sufficient to convince the world of this truth at least, that two operas at a time were more than this metropolis could support; and determined Farinelli to try his success in another country. The particulars of his retreat will be mentioned in a subsequent page. Mr. Martinelli has given the following short character of him, which naturally leads us to give an account of his master Porpora, and also of Hasse, the joint composer with him for the opera, during the residence of Farinelli in London. 'He had a voice proportioned to his 'gigantic stature, extending beyond the ordinary 'compass near an octave, in notes equally clear and 'sonorous. At the same time he possessed such 'a degree of knowledge in the science of music, as 'he might be supposed to have derived from the in-'structions of the skilful Porpora, bestowed on a 'diligent and favourite pupil: with unexampled 'agility and freedom did he traverse the paths which 'Bernacchi had trod with success, till he became the 'idol of the Italians, and at length of the harmonic 'world.'†

* Mr. Hogarth, in his Rake's Progress, has ridiculed this folly with great humour; in the second plate of that work he represents his rake at his levee in a circle, consisting of a bravo, a jockey, a dancing-master, a fencing-master, a gardener, and other dependents. In a corner of the room sits an opera composer at a harpsichord, with a long roll hanging from the back of his chair, on which is the following inscription: 'A list 'of the rich presents Signor Farinelli the Italian singer condescended to 'accept of the English nobility and gentry for one night's performance in 'the opera of Artaxerxes. A pair of diamond knee-buckles, presented 'by   a diamond ring by   A bank-note enclosed 'in a rich gold case by   A gold snuff box chased with the 'story of Orpheus charming the brutes, by T. Rakewell, Esq. 100l. '200l. 100l.' Many of the above presents were actually made to Farinelli during his stay among us, and were mentioned in the daily papers. On the floor lies a picture representing Farinelli seated on a pedestal, with an altar before him, on which are several flaming hearts; near which stand a number of people with their arms extended, offering him presents: at the foot of the altar is one lady kneeling, tendering her heart, from whose mouth a label issues, inscribed 'One God, one Farinelli;' alluding to a lady of distinction, who being charmed with a particular passage in one of his songs, uttered aloud from the boxes that impious exclamation.

† Lettere familiare e critiche, Carte 361.

CHAP. CXCI.

Nicolo Porpora is celebrated among the modern musicians, not less as the instructor of some of the most applauded singers, than as a musical composer of the dramatic class. In the early part of his life he was in the service of Augustus, king of Poland, but quitting it, he made a temporary residence in sundry of the German courts, and afterwards in the principal cities of Italy. At Naples he became acquainted with Farinelli, who was then very young, and having a very promising voice, was endeavouring to acquire that style and manner of singing, which it is said Antonio Bernacchi of Bologna took from Pistocchi, and which gave rise to the denomination of the Bernacchi school. Porpora seeing this, and being desirous of correcting those extravagancies which Bernacchi had introduced into vocal practice, he laboured to form a style of greater simplicity, such as was calculated rather to affect than to astonish the hearers. As to Farinelli in particular, he set himself with all his might to improve those great talents which he had discovered in him, and in the end made him the finest singer that had then or has ever since been heard. A degree of success, alike proportioned to their several abilities, had he in the tuition of Salimbelli, Caffarelli, and Mingotti, all of whom were the pupils of Porpora.

The attachments of Porpora to Farinelli were of such a friendly kind, as determined him to become, if not a sharer in his fortunes, at least a witness of that applause which was bestowed on him whithersoever he went: with this view he was the companion of his travels; and it may well be supposed that the English nobility, when they engaged Farinelli to sing here, considered Porpora as so intimately connected with him, that an attempt to separate them would go near to render a treaty for that purpose abortive; accordingly they were both engaged and arrived in England together.

The operas of Porpora, as musical compositions, had little to recommend them: that of Ariadne was looked upon as inferior to the Ariadne of Handel, in which, excepting the minuet at the end of the overture, there is scarce a good air. Dr. Arbuthnot however, in a humorous pamphlet written on occasion of the disputes about the opera, entitled Harmony in an Uproar, calls that of Handel the Nightingale, the other the Cuckoo.‡

In the year 1735 Porpora published and dedicated to Frederic, prince of Wales, who had taken part with him in the dispute with Handel, Twelve Italian Cantatas, which at this day are greatly esteemed. He also published Six Sonatas for two violins and a bass; these compositions are mere symphonies, and, having in them very little of design or contrivance, are now scarcely remembered.

Giovanni Adolfo Hasse was born near Hamburg, and received his first instructions in music in that city. At the age of eighteen he composed an opera entitled Antigono; but, being desirous of farther improvement, he went to Naples, and for a short time

‡ Miscellaneous works of the late Dr. Arbuthnot, vol. II. page 21.

was under the tuition of Porpora, but afterwards became a disciple of Alessandro Scarlatti. Upon his return to Germany he became maestro di cappella to the elector of Saxony, and at Dresden composed operas, some in the German, and others in the Italian language. In the composition of operas he was esteemed abroad the first of the German masters; and the fame of his abilities reaching England at the time of the rupture between Handel and the English nobility, he was employed by them, and composed the opera of Artaxerxes, written by Metastasio, and some others, which were represented here, and received great advantage from the performance of Farinelli. He married Faustina soon after her return from England: it does not appear that he was ever here himself; it seems he was strongly pressed at the time above-mentioned to come to London, but Mr. Handel being then living, he declined the invitation, not choosing to become a competitor with one so greatly his superior.

The abilities of Hasse seem to have been greatly over-rated by some of our countrymen who have taken occasion to mention him. Six Cantatas for a voice, with an accompaniment for the harpsichord, a Salve Regina for a single voice with instruments, a single concerto for French horns, and other instruments, and a few airs selected from his operas performed here, are all of his compositions that have been published in England; and these are so far from affording evidence of any extraordinary talent, that they are a full justification of the author of the Remarks on Mr. Avison's Essay on Musical Expression, who has not hesitated to assert that the distinguishing characteristic of Hasse's compositions is effeminacy.

The contest between Handel and the nobility was carried on with so much disadvantage to the former, that he found himself under the necessity of quitting the Haymarket theatre at the time when his opponents were wishing to get possession of it; and in the issue each party shifted its ground by an exchange of situations. The nobility removed with Farinelli, Senesino, and Montagnana, a bass singer, who had sung for Handel in Sosarmes and other of his operas; and Handel, with Strada, Bertoli, and Waltz, a bass singer, who had been his cook, went to Lincoln's-Inn fields. Here he continued but for a short time; for, finding himself unable singly to continue the opposition, he removed to Covent Garden, and entered into some engagements with Rich, the particulars of which are not known; save that in discharge of a debt that he had contracted with him in consequence thereof, he some years after set to music an English opera entitled Alceste, written by Dr. Smollett, and for which Rich was at great expence in a set of scenes painted by Servandoni; but it was never performed. Handel afterwards adapted this music to Dryden's Song for St. Cecilia's Day, 1687, printed in the fourth part of his Miscellaneous Poems, and performed it together with Alexander's Feast.

Such as are not acquainted with the personal character of Handel, will wonder at his seeming temerity, in continuing so long an opposition which tended but to impoverish him; but he was a man of a firm and intrepid spirit, no way a slave to the passion of avarice, and would have gone greater lengths than he did, rather than submit to those whom he had ever looked on as his inferiors: but though his ill success for a series of years had not affected his spirit, there is reason to believe that his genius was in some degree damped by it; for whereas of his earlier operas, that is to say, those composed by him between the years 1710 and 1728, the merits are so great, that few are able to say which is to be preferred; those composed after that period have so little to recommend them, that few would take them for the work of the same author. In the former class are Radamistus, Otho, Tamerlane, Rodelinda, Alexander, and Admetus, in either of which scarcely an indifferent air occurs; whereas in Parthenope, Porus, Sosarmes, Orlando, Ætius, Ariadne, and the rest down to 1736, it is a matter of some difficulty to find a good one.

The nobility were no sooner settled at the Haymarket, than Farinelli appeared in the meridian of his glory: all the world resorted thither, even aldermen and other citizens, with their wives and daughters, to so great a degree, that in the city it became a proverbial expression, that those who had not heard Farinelli sing and Foster preach, were not qualified to appear in genteel company.*

But it fared far otherwise with Handel, who, after his engagement with Rich, performed to almost empty houses; and, after a contest, which lasted about three years, during which time he was obliged to draw out of the funds almost the whole of what in his prosperous days he had there invested, he gave out; and discovered to the world that in this dreadful conflict he had not only suffered in his fortune but his health.† To get rid of that dejection

* Mr. James Foster was a dissenting minister of the Anabaptist denomination. In the Old Jewry, during the winter season, on Sunday evenings, he preached a lecture, in which with great clearness and strength of reasoning he enforced the obligations of religion and virtue, chiefly from principles in which all mankind are agreed. The Freethinkers, as they are called, took him for a Deist, and his audiences were somewhat the larger for them; but they were greatly mistaken: on the contrary he was a devout and sincere Christian, as the author of this work can testify, who lived many years with him on terms of strict friendship; and gave ample proof of his faith in an excellent answer to a worthless book, Christianity as old as the Creation; and contributed to put to confusion its more worthless author, Dr. Matthew Tindal. Pope was acquainted with Foster, and, having frequently resorted to the Old Jewry purposely to hear him, complimented him with the following lines:—

Let modest Foster, if he will, excel
Ten metropolitans in preaching well.
Epilogue to the Satires, Dialogue I.

Lord Bolingbroke expressed to Mr. Pope a great desire to know Foster, and an appointment was made for a meeting of all the three; but an accident prevented it. Most of the sermons preached at the Old Jewry lecture are extant in four volumes, published by the author himself: they were also preached to a congregation of which he was pastor, in a place situated between Red-cross street and Barbican; but such was the fashion of the time, and such were the different effects of the same discourses at different places, that few but his own congregation resorted to the one, and people, at the risk of their limbs, struggled to get in at the other. In consideration of his great merit, and the estimation in which he was held throughout this kingdom, the university of Aberdeen honoured him with the degree of doctor in divinity. In the year 1746 he was requested to assist in preparing lord Kilmarnock for a submission to that sentence, which, for having been active in the rebellion of 1745, he was doomed to suffer. Dr. Foster complied with this request, and was necessitated to be a spectator of his end; the unspeakable anguish of mind which he felt upon this occasion, and the frequent reflection on all the circumstances of the execution, made such a deep impression on him, as could never be effaced; his mental faculties forsook him, and on the fifth day of November, in the year 1753, he died.

† Upon occasion of this his distress, Strada and others of the singers were content to accept of bonds for the payment of their arrears, and left the kingdom upon Mr. Handel's assurances that they should be discharged; and he paid a due regard to his engagement by remitting them the money

of mind, which his repeated disappointments had brought on him, he was advised to the use of the waters at Tunbridge, and a regimen calculated to assist their operation ; but his disorder was so deeply rooted, that by several particulars in his behaviour, which it would give the reader no pleasure to be informed of, he discovered that his mental powers were affected ; and, to complete his distress, one of those hands, which had frequently administered such delight to others, was now become useless to himself ; in a word, the palsy had seized his right arm, and the whole of the limb was by a sudden stroke rendered incapable of performing its natural functions.

Medicines having been found ineffectual to remove his disorder, he was prevailed on, but with great difficulty, to resort to Aix la Chapelle ; accordingly he went thither, and submitted to such sweats, excited by the vapour baths there, as astonished every one. After a few essays of this kind, during which his spirits seemed to rise rather than sink under an excessive perspiration, his disorder left him ; and in a few hours after the last operation he went to the great church of the city, and got to the organ, on which he played in such a manner that men imputed his cure to a miracle. Having received so much benefit from the baths, he prudently determined to stay at Aix la Chapelle, till the end of six weeks from the time of his arrival there, and at the end thereof returned to London in perfect health.

Farinelli, during the interval of a few winters, had accumulated great wealth, but it arose chiefly from presents, and crowded houses at his benefits ; and as he had experienced what it was to sing to an audience of thirty-five pounds, he began to suspect that his harvest in this country, which, as Mattheson terms it, was a golden one, was pretty well over, and began to think of trying his success in another : he had visited France in the year 1736, and finding at his return to London but little encouragement to engage at the opera, he finally quitted England the following summer, and on the ninth of July, 1737, appeared at Versailles, hoping to derive great advantages from the solemnities which were expected to attend the approaching birth of the duke of Anjou ; but in this he was disappointed.

It happened about this time that the king of Spain laboured under a melancholy disorder, for which no relief could be suggested but music ; his queen contrived to entertain him with frequent concerts : to make these as delightful to him as possible, she sent for Farinelli, and upon his arrival at Madrid attached him to the service of that court by a pension of 1400 piastres, or 3150*l.* per annum, and a coach and equipage maintained at the king's expense. Over and above his salary, considerable presents were made him ; the king gave him his picture set with diamonds, valued at 5000 dollars : the queen presented him with a gold snuff-box, with two large diamonds on the lid ; and the prince of Asturias gave him a diamond button and loop of great value. Upon the death of Philip V., Farinelli was continued in his station by his successor, Ferdinand VI., and in 1750 was honoured with the cross of Calatrava,

the badge of an order of knighthood in Spain of great antiquity. He continued, with the assistance of the best composers and singers, and of Metastasio and Amiconi the painter, which latter had followed him into Spain, to conduct the opera till about the year 1761, when he took a resolution to return to Italy ; accordingly he went thither, and had an audience of Benedict XIV., to whom, upon his recounting the riches and honours that had been showered down upon him here and in Spain, the pope made this remark : ' In other words you mean ' to say, that you found abroad what you left here.'

His pension from the court of Spain being still continued to him, Farinelli chose the neighbourhood of Bologna for his residence ; and in a house of his own building, near that city, he is now living in ease and great affluence.

It is now necessary to recur to a former period, and in an orderly course of narration to relate such other particulars respecting the subject of this history, as were necessarily postponed to make way for the above account of Mr. Handel.

Greene, who already has been mentioned as an ingenious young man, was got to be organist of St. Paul's ; and having, upon the decease of Dr. Croft, in 1727, been appointed organist and composer to the royal chapel in his room, was thereby placed at the head of his profession in England. He courted the friendship of Mr. Handel with a degree of assiduity, that, to say the truth, bordered upon servility ; and in his visits to him at Burlington-house, and at the duke of Chandois's, was rather more frequent than welcome. At length Mr. Handel discovering that he was paying the same court to his rival, Bononcini, as to himself, would have nothing more to say to him, and gave orders to be denied whenever Greene came to visit him.

Some particulars respecting Greene and his first appearance in the world have been given towards the commencement of Book XVIII. The busy part he acted at this time, his attachment to Bononcini, and his opposition to Mr. Handel, make it necessary in this place to resume his history.

In the year 1730 he took the degree of doctor in music in the university of Cambridge : his exercise for it was Mr. Pope's ode for St. Cecilia's day, which he set very finely to music.* It was performed with great applause ; and, as an additional testimony to

* Mr. Pope, to answer Greene's purpose, condescended to make considerable alterations in this poem, and at his request to insert in it one entire new stanza, viz., the third. As he thereby rendered it greatly different from the ode originally published, and as with the variations it has never yet appeared in print, it is here given as a curiosity :—

ODE for St. Cecilia's Day,
As altered by Mr. Pope for Dr. Greene.
I.
Descend ye Nine ! descend and sing ;
The breathing instruments inspire ;
Wake into voice each silent string,
And sweep the sounding lyre !
In a sadly pleasing strain
Let the warbling lute complain :
In more lengthen'd notes and slow,
The deep, majestic, solemn organs blow,
Hark ! the numbers soft and clear,
Gently steal upon the ear ;
Now louder they sound,
'Till the roofs all around
The shrill echos rebound :
'Till, by degrees, remote and small,
The strains decay,
And melt away
In a dying, dying fall.

his merit, he was honoured with the title of professor of music in the university of Cambridge.

The following duett, taken from the doctor's own manuscript, was part of the performance :—

II.
By music minds an equal temper know,
    Nor swell too high, nor sink too low.
If in the breast tumultous joys arise,
Music her soft, assuasive voice applies ;
    Or when the soul is sunk in cares,
    Exalts her with enlivening airs.
Warriors she fires by sprightly sounds ;
Pours balm into the lover's wounds :
Passions no more the soul engage,
Ev'n factions hear away their rage.

III.
Amphion thus bade wild dissension cease,
And soften'd mortals learn'd the arts of peace.
    Amphion taught contending kings,
        From various discords to create
        The music of a well-tun'd state ;
    Nor slack nor strain the tender string
        Those usual touches to impart,
        That strike the subject's answ'ring heart,
And the soft silent harmony that springs
From sacred union and consent of things.

IV.
But when our country's cause provokes to arms,
How martial music every bosom warms !
    When the first vessel dar'd the seas
        The Thracian rais'd his strain,
    And Argo saw her kindred trees
    Descend from Pelion to the main.
    Transported demi-gods stood round,
    And men grew heroes at the sound,
        Inflam'd with glory's charms !
    Each chief his sev'nfold shield display'd,
    And half unsheath'd the shining blade :
    And seas, and rocks, and skies rebound
        To arms, to arms, to arms !

V.
But when thro' all th' infernal bounds,
Which flaming Phlegeton surrounds,
Sad Orpheus sought his consort lost :
    The adamantine gates were barr'd,
    And nought was seen and nought was heard
Around the dreary coast ;
        But dreadful gleams,
        Dismal screams,
        Fires that glow,
        Shrieks of woe,
        Sullen moans,
        Hollow groans,
        And cries of tortur'd ghosts !
But hark ! he strikes the golden lyre ;
And see ! the tortur'd ghosts respire,

See, shady forms advance !
    And the pale spectres dance !
The Furies sink upon their iron beds,
And snakes uncurl'd hang list'ning round their heads.

VI.
By the streams that ever flow,
By the fragrant winds that blow
    O'er th' Elysian flow'rs ;
By those happy souls that dwell
In yellow meads of Asphodel,
    Or Amaranthine bow'rs,
By the heroes' armed shades,
Glitt'ring thro' the gloomy glades,
By the youths that dy'd for love,
Wand'ring in the myrtle grove,
Restore, restore Eurydice to life,
Oh take the husband, or return the wife !

VII.
He sang, and hell consented
    To hear the poet's pray'r ;
Stern Proserpine relented,
    And gave him back the fair.
        Thus song could prevail
        O'er death and o'er hell,
A conquest how hard and how glorious ?
        Tho' fate had fast bound her
        With Styx nine times round her,
Yet music and love were victorious.

The earlier writers on music, and even Kircher, a modern, have in their division of music distinguished it into mundane, humane, and political. And Cicero, de Repub. lib. II. says that what in music is termed harmony is in the government of a city styled concord: of the latter of these distinctions it may be observed that Shakespeare has shown himself not a little fond of it, as in Henry V. act 1, scene 2.—
> *For government though high and low and lower,*
> *Put into parts doth keep in one consent,*
> *Congruing in a full and natural close*
> *Like music.*

And again in Troilus and Cressida, Act 1, Scene 3.—
> *Take but degree away, untune that string,*
> *And hark what discord follows.*

The same fanciful notion we find recognised in the third stanza of the above ode. Milton also seems to allude to it in this passage :—
> ———— *orders and degrees*
> *Jar not with liberty, but well consist.*
> > *Par. Lost, Book V. line 792.*

It may be thought not unworthy of remark, that in the two passages first above cited, and also in Mr. Pope's Ode, the word consent *is mistaken for* concent, *from the Latin* concentus, *a concert of music.*

take the husband or re-turn, re-turn the wife.   By the streams that e-ver

Oh take the husband or re-turn, re-turn the wife.

flow, By the fragrant winds that blow   O'er th'e-lysian flow'rs,   o'er th'e-lysian flow'rs;

By those happy souls who dwell in yellow meads of As-pho-del   or Ama-ran-thine

By the heroes' armed shades glitt'ring thro' the gloomy

bow'rs,   or A-ma-ranthine bow'rs.

glades,　　　　　　　　Restore Eu-ry-di-ce to life,　　Oh take the

By the youths that dy'd for love Wand'ring in the myrtle grove, Restore Eu-ry - di-ce to life, Oh . . take the

husband or return, return the wife,　　　　Restore Eu-ry - di-ce to life,　　Oh take the

husband or re-turn, return the wife,　　　Restore Eu-ry - di -ce to life, Oh . . take the

husband or return, re-turn the wife,　　oh take the husband or return, return the wife, return the wife.

husband or re - turn, return the wife,　　oh take the husband or return, return the wife, return the wife.

DOCTOR MAURICE GREENE.

In the disputes between Handel and Bononcini, Greene had acted with such duplicity, as induced the former to renounce all intercourse with him; and from that time no one was so industrious as he in decrying the compositions of Handel, or applauding those of his rival. He was a member of the Academy of ancient Music, and, with a view to exalt the character of Bononcini, produced in the year 1728 the madrigal 'In una siepe ombrosa,' which gave rise to a dispute that terminated in the disgrace of his friend. Not able to endure the slights of those who had marked and remembered his pertinacious behaviour in this business, Dr. Greene left the academy, and drew off with him the boys of St. Paul's cathedral, and some other persons, his immediate dependents; and fixing on the great room called the Apollo at the Devil tavern, for the performance of a concert, under his sole management, gave occasion to a saying not so witty as sarcastical, viz., that Dr. Greene was gone to the Devil.

Dr. Greene was happy in the friendship of Bishop Hoadley and his family: he set to music sundry elegant pastoral poems, namely, Florimel, Phœbe, and others, written, as it is said, by Dr. John Hoadley, a son of that prelate. He had also an interest with the late duke of Newcastle, probably through the duchess, who had frequent musical parties at Newcastle-house, at which Greene used to assist; and whose mother, Henrietta, duchess of Marlborough, was the patroness of Bononcini, with whom, as has been related, Greene had contracted a close intimacy. With such connexions as these, Greene stood fair for the highest preferments in his profession, and he attained them; for, upon the decease of Dr. Croft, through the interest of the countess of Peterborough, he succeeded to his places of organist and composer to the royal chapel; and, upon that of Eccles, about 1735, was appointed master of the royal band.

Greene had given some early specimens of his abilities in the composition of a set of lessons for the harpsichord, which he probably meant to publish; but a copy having been surreptitiously obtained by one Daniel Wright, a seller of music and musical instruments, near Furnival's Inn, who never printed any thing that he did not steal, they were published by him in so very incorrect a manner, that the doctor was necessitated to declare that they were not his compositions; and Wright, no less falsely than impudently, asserted in the public papers that they were. Notwithstanding that he was an excellent organist, and not only perfectly understood the nature of the instrument, but was a great master of fugue, he affected in his voluntaries that kind of practice on single stops, the cornet and the vox-humana for instance, which puts the instrument almost on a level with the harpsichord; a voluntary of this kind being in fact little more than a solo for a single instrument, with the accompaniment of a bass; and in this view Greene may be looked on as the father of modern organists. This kind of performance, as it is calculated to catch the ears of the vulgar, who are ever more delighted with

melody, or what is called air, than harmony, was beneath one, whose abilities were such, that Mattheson, a man but little disposed to flattery, and who was himself one of the first organists in Europe, has not scrupled to rank him among the best of his time.

CHAP. CXCII

THE conduct of Pepusch was very different from that of Greene. Upon Mr. Handel's arrival in England, he acquiesced in the opinion of his superior merit, and chose a track for himself in which he was sure to meet with no obstruction, and in which none could disturb him without going out of their way to do it. He had been retained by the duke of Chandois, and assisted as composer to his chapel, till he gave place to Handel; after that he professed the teaching of the principles of musical science, and continued so to do till about the year 1724, when a temptation offered of advancing himself, which he was prevailed on to yield to: few persons conversant in literary history are unacquainted with the character and benevolent spirit of Dr. George Berkeley, the late excellent bishop of Cloyne; or that this gentleman, upon his promotion to the deanery of Londonderry, formed a plan for the propagation of religion and learning in America, in which was included a scheme for erecting a college in the Summer Islands, otherwise called the Isles of Bermudas. With a view to carry this project into execution, Dr. Berkeley obtained permission to found and endow such a college, and also engaged divers persons of distinguished eminence in the several professions and faculties to accompany him, and become professors in his intended college; of these Dr. Pepusch was one. He and his associates embarked for the place of the intended settlement, but the ship was wrecked, and the undertaking frustrated; immediately after which such difficulties arose as put a final end to the design.

Being returned to England, Dr. Pepusch married Signora Margarita de l'Epine, and went to reside in Boswell-court, Carey-street, taking, together with his wife, her mother, a woman as remarkably short as her daughter was tall. The fortune which Margarita had acquired was estimated at ten thousand pounds, and the possession thereof enabled the doctor to live in a style of elegance which till his marriage he had been a stranger to: this change in his circumstances was no interruption to his studies; he loved music, and he pursued the knowledge of it with ardour. He, at the instance of Gay and Rich, undertook to compose, or rather correct, the music to the Beggar's Opera. Every one knows that the music to this drama consists solely of ballad tunes and country dances; it was, nevertheless, necessary to settle the airs for performance, and also to compose basses to such as needed them. This the doctor did, prefixing to the opera an overture, which was printed in the first, and has been continued in every succeeding edition of the work.

The reputation of the doctor was now at a great

height; he had perused with great attention those several ancient treatises on harmonics which Meibomius had given to the world about the middle of the last century, and that of Ptolemy, published by Dr. Wallis with his own learned appendix. In the perusal of these authors, the difficulties which occurred to him were in a great measure removed by his friend Mr. Abraham de Moivre, an excellent mathematician, who assisted him in making calculations for demonstrating those principles which are the foundation of harmonic science; and in consequence of these his studies, Pepusch was esteemed one of the best theoretic musicians of his time.

About the year 1730 he took a house in Fetterlane, the next door but one to the south corner of the passage leading from thence into Bartlett's-buildings, and fitted up a large room in it for the reception of his books and manuscripts, which were very many, and had been collected by him with great labour and expense. His wife had long quitted the opera stage, and, though rather advanced in years, retained her hand on the harpsichord, and was in truth a fine performer. The doctor had in his library a book which had formerly been queen Elizabeth's, containing a great number of lessons for the harpsichord, composed by Dr. Bull; of the merit of these pieces he entertained a very high opinion; and though they were much more difficult to execute than can be well conceived by those who reflect on their antiquity, yet by a regular course of practice she attained to such perfection in playing them, that great was the resort of persons to hear her. He had one only son, whom he determined to qualify for his own profession, a child of very promising parts; the doctor laboured incessantly in his education, but he lived not to attain the age of thirteen.

Among the many that resorted to him for instruction, lord Paisley, afterwards earl of Abercorn, was one; and to him the doctor had communicated lessons in writing for his private study, with no other obligation not to impart them to the world than is implied in the mutual relation of teacher and disciple; which it seems was so ill understood, that in the year 1730 the substance of the doctor's lessons was by his pupil given to the world with the following title: 'A short treatise on harmony, containing the chief 'rules for composing in two, three, and four parts, 'dedicated to all lovers of music. By an admirer of 'this noble and agreeable science.'

The publisher of this little book had studiously avoided inserting in the book any of those examples in musical notes which the precepts contained in it made it necessary to refer to, for which omission he makes a kind of apology.

The doctor affected to speak of the publication of this book as injurious both to his character and interest; however it did not long, if at all, interrupt the friendship between lord Paisley and him. For proof of the fact that his lordship and the doctor were upon very good terms after the publishing the short treatise on harmony, recourse has been had to the doctor's papers, among which has been found a diary in his own hand-writing, containing an account

of the daily occurrences in his life for a series of years, and, among others, a relation of a visit he made to lord Paisley at his seat at Witham in Essex, in the summer of the year 1733, and of his entertainment during a week's stay there; which may serve to show, either that the surreptitious publication of the book was not the act of his lordship, or that the lapse of less than three years had effaced from his remembrance all sense of injury resulting from it.

The book, as published in the manner above related, was of very little use to the world. It wanted the illustration of examples, and was in other respects obscure and most affectedly perplexed; besides all which, it was written in a style the meanest that can be conceived: the motto in the title-page was that trite passage of Horace, 'Si quid novisti rectius istis,' &c., and the sentence intended to supply the omission of the author's name, contains in it the flattest anti-climax that ever disgraced a literary production.

The doctor spoke the English language but indifferently, and wrote it worse than many foreigners do that have long resided in this country; and it may be doubted whether the lessons which he used to give his pupils were ever digested into the form of a treatise; but seeing that the book could not be recalled, and that he was looked upon by the world as responsible for the subject matter of it, he thought it prudent to adopt it; and accordingly in the year 1731 published a genuine edition, retaining the language of the former, but considerably altered and enlarged, and also illustrated with those examples in notes, which were in truth an essential part of it. The precepts delivered, and the laws of harmonical combination contained in this book, are such only as are warranted by the practice of modern composers; and the rules of transition from key to key are evidently extracted from the works of Corelli; but the most valuable part of the book is the chapter treating of solmisation, which practice is explained with the utmost precision and perspicuity.* In forming the diagrams, it is said that the doctor was assisted by Brooke Taylor, LL.D., author of a well-known treatise on Perspective, who, besides being an excellent mathematician, was eminently skilled in the theory of music.

It has already been mentioned that Pepusch was one of the founders of the Academy of ancient Music. That society, with his assistance, continued to flourish until the year 1734, when, upon some disgust taken by Mr. Gates, master of the children of the royal chapel, it was deprived of the assistance which it was wont to receive from them, and left without boys to sing the soprano parts.† After trying for one winter what could be done without

---

* That of the hexachords, with directions for the mutations by the arrows and daggers, is a great stroke of invention. But the table adjoining to it, for reducing a composition in a transposed key to its natural one, by the help of the slider, is a disingenuous artifice, and calculated rather to blind than enlighten those whom the author professes to teach. Had he, as Loulie has done in his Elements ou Principes de Musique, given the rule to call the last sharp, in the case of sharp keys, B, and the last flat in the flat keys F; and sol-fa upwards and downwards accordingly, the wretched contrivance of a slider to be cut off, and which being lost, would render the table useless and the book imperfect, would have been unnecessary. See page 59, in note.

† Dr. Greene, upon the dispute about the author of the madrigal, 'In 'una siepe ombrosa,' three years before, had retired, and taken with him the boys of St. Paul's choir

treble voices, and finding that their endeavours amounted to nothing, the managers determined to enlarge the plan, and make the Academy a seminary for the instruction of youth in the principles of music and the laws of harmony. Invitations to parents, and offers of such an education for their children as would fit them as well for trades and businesses as the profession of music, were given by advertisements in the public papers; these brought in a great number of children, and such of them as were likely to be made useful were retained.* Upon this occasion Dr. Pepusch generously undertook the care of their instruction, for a stipend greatly disproportionate to his merit, though the largest the circumstances of the Academy could afford, and succeeded so well in his endeavours, that many of those his pupils became afterwards eminent professors in the science.

The above memoir of Dr. Pepusch continues the history of the Academy down to about the year 1735, when the managers had recourse to the expedient of educating boys for their purpose, and that of admitting auditor members, both which answered their ends; and upon that footing, excepting the difference of an increased subscription, the society subsists at this day.

The Academy made it their constant care to keep up a correspondence with the most eminent masters and professors of music in foreign countries; and Steffani having desired to be admitted a member of their society, and having from time to time presented them with compositions of great value, bearing the name of Gregorio Piua, his secretary or copyist, but which were in truth his own, they unanimously chose him their president; and, upon occasion of the dispute about the madrigal 'In una siepe ombrosa,' mentioned in the foregoing memoir of Bononcini; they entered into a correspondence with Signor Antonio Lotti. with which he thought himself so honoured, that he presented them with a madrigal and a mass of his composition, and they in return sent him, as a specimen of the English music, two motets, the one ' Domine quis habitabit,' for five

voices, by Tallis, the other · Tribulationes Civitatum,† also for five voices, by Bird, both which were thankfully accepted.

As an institution designed for the improvement of music, the Academy was generally visited by foreigners of the greatest eminence in the faculty. Many of the opera singers and celebrated masters on particular instruments, by the performance of favourite airs in the operas, and solos calculated to display their various excellencies, contributed to the variety of the evening's entertainment. Tosi frequently sang here; and Bononcini, who was a member, played solos on the violoncello, on which he ever chose to be accompanied by Waber on the lute. Geminiani was a frequent visitor of the Academy, and would often honour it with the performance of his own compositions previous to their publication.

And here it may not be improper to mention an anecdote in musical history, which reflects some credit on this institution. In the interval between the secession of Dr. Greene and Mr. Gates, viz., in the month of February, 1732, when the conflict between Mr. Handel and the nobility had rendered the situation of the former almost desperate, the Academy being in possession of a copy of the oratorio of Esther, originally composed for the duke of Chandois by Mr. Handel, performed it by their own members and the children of the chapel royal; and the applause with which it was there received, suggested to the author the thought of performing it himself, and of exhibiting in future during the Lent season, that species of musical entertainment. So that to this accident it may be said to be in a great measure owing, that the public for a series of years past have not only been delighted with hearing, but are now in possession of, some of the most valuable compositions of that great master.

The advantages that resulted to music from the exercises of the Academy were evident, in that they tended to the establishment of a true and just notion of the science; they checked the wanderings of fancy, and restrained the love of novelty within due bounds; they enabled the students and performers to contemplate and compare styles; to form an idea of classical purity and elegance; and, in short, to fix the standard of a judicious and rational taste. One of the principal ends of the institution was a retrospect to those excellent compositions of former ages, which its very name implies; and in the prosecution thereof were brought forth to public view, the works of very many authors, whose names, though celebrated with all the applauses of panegyric, had else been consigned to oblivion : nor was this all; the spirit that directed the pursuits of this society diffused itself, and gave rise to another, of which here follows an account.

Mr. John Immyns, an attorney by profession, was a member of the Academy, but, meeting with misfortunes, he was occasionally a copyist to the society, and amanuensis to Dr. Pepusch; he had a strong

---

* Among the children who were thus taken into the service of the Academy, was one whose promising genius and early attainments in music render him worthy of notice in this place. His name was Isaac Peirson; his father, a poor man, and master of the charity-school of the parish of St. Giles without Cripplegate, dwelt in the school-house in Redcross-street, and being, as he was used to style himself, a lover of divine music, or, in other words a singer of psalm-tunes after the fashion of those who look upon Playford as one of the greatest among musicians, he gladly laid hold of the opportunity which then offered, and got his son, about seven years old, admitted into the Academy. A very few months tuition of the doctor enabled him to sing his part; and in less than a twelvemonth he had attained to great proficiency on the organ, though his fingers were so weak that he was incapable of making a true shake, and instead thereof was necessitated to make use of a tremulous motion of two keys at once, which he did so well, that the discord arising from it passed unnoticed. In the instruction of this child the doctor took uncommon pains, and shewed great affection, making him the associate of his own son in his studies. He endeavoured to inculcate in him the true organ-style, and succeeded so well, that his pupil, before he was full nine years of age, rejecting the use of set voluntaries, began upon his own stock, and played the full organ extempore, with the learning and judgment of an experienced master. The circumstances of his parents co-operating with his irresistible propensity, determined him to music as a profession; he was therefore taught the violin, and soon became able to execute the most difficult of Geminiani's concertos with great facility. With these attainments, singularly great for one of his years, and a temper of mind in every respect amiable, he gave to his parents and friends the most promising assurances of his becoming a great musician; but his death defeated their hopes before he had quite attained the age of twelve years.

† The first of these is not in print; the latter is the twenty-fourth motett in the Sacræ Cantiones of Bird, printed by Tho. Este in 1589.

counter-tenor voice, which, being not very flexible, served well enough for the performance of madrigals. Of this species of music he in a short time became so fond, that in the year 1741 he formed the plan of a little club, called the Madrigal Society; and got together a few persons who had spent their lives in the practice of psalmody; and who, with a little pains, and the help of the ordinary solmisation, which many of them were very expert in, became soon able to sing, almost at sight, a part in an English, or even an Italian madrigal. They were mostly mechanics; some, weavers from Spitalfields, others of various trades and occupations; they met at first at the Twelve Bells, an alehouse in Bride-lane, Fleet-street, and Immyns was both their president and instructor; their subscription was five shillings and sixpence a quarter, which defrayed their expenses in books and music paper, and afforded them the refreshments of porter and tobacco. After four or five years continuance at the Twelve Bells, the society removed to the Founders' Arms in Lothbury; and from thence, after a short stay, to the Twelve Bells again, and after that to the Queen's Arms in Newgate-street, a house that had been formerly a tavern, but was now an alehouse. In it was a room large enough for the reception of the society, who were about five-and-twenty in number, with a convenient recess for a large press that contained their library. The meetings of the society were on Wednesday evening in every week; their performance consisted of Italian and English madrigals in three, four, and five parts; and, being assisted by three or four boys from the choir of St. Paul's, they sang compositions of this kind, as also catches, rounds, and canons, though not elegantly, with a degree of correctness that did justice to the harmony; and, to vary the entertainment, Immyns would sometimes read, by way of lecture, a chapter of Zarlino translated by himself.

The persons that composed this little academy were men not less distinguished by their love of vocal harmony, than the harmless simplicity of their tempers, and their friendly disposition towards each other. Immyns was a man of a very singular character; and as he was one of the most passionate admirers of music of his time, merits to be taken particular notice of. He had a cracked counter-tenor voice, and played upon the flute, the viol da gamba, the violin, and the harpsichord, but on none of them well: in his younger days he was a great beau, and had been guilty of some indiscretions, which proved an effectual bar to success in his profession, and reduced him to the necessity of becoming a clerk to an attorney in the city. The change in his circumstances had not the least tendency to damp his spirits; he wrote all day at the desk, and frequently spent most part of the night in copying music, which he did with amazing expedition and correctness. At the age of forty he would needs learn the lute, and by the sole help of Mace's book, acquired a competent knowledge of the instrument; but, beginning so late, was never able to attain to any great degree of proficiency on it: having a

family, he lived for some years in extreme poverty, the reflection on which did not trouble him so much as it did his friends; Mr. George Shelvocke, secretary to the general post office, was one of the number, and, upon the decease of Mr. Serjeant Shore, by his interest obtained for Immyns the place of lutenist of the royal chapel, the salary whereof is about forty pounds a year. The taste of Immyns was altogether for old music, which he had been taught to admire by Dr. Pepusch; and this he indulged to such a degree, that he looked upon Mr. Handel and Bononcini as the great corrupters of the science. With these prejudices, it is no wonder that he entertained a relish for madrigals, and music of the driest style: Vincentio Ruffo, Orlando de Lasso, Luca Marenzio, Horatio Vecchi, and, above all, the prince of Venosa, were his great favourites. He was very diligent in collecting their works, and studied them with incredible assiduity; nevertheless he was but meanly skilled in the theory of the science, considering the opportunities which his intimacy with Dr. Pepusch afforded him. He was the founder, and chief support of the Madrigal Society, and, being a man of great good-humour and pleasantry, was much beloved by those that frequented it. In the latter part of his life he began to feel himself in tolerable circumstances, but the infirmities of old age coming on him apace, he died of an asthma at his house in Cold-Bath-fields on the fifteenth day of April, 1764.

Mr. Samuel Jeacocke, another member of this fraternity, was a man not less remarkable for singularities of another kind: this man was a baker by trade, and the brother of Mr. Caleb Jeacocke, now living, and who for many years was president of the Robin Hood disputing society. The shop of Samuel was at the south-west corner of Berkeley-street, in Red-lion street, Clerkenwell. He played on several instruments, but mostly the tenor-violin; and at the Madrigal Society usually sang the bass part. In the choice of his instruments he was very nice, and when a fiddle or a violoncello did not please him, would, to mend the tone of it, bake it for a week in a bed of saw-dust. He was one of the best ringers and the best swimmer of his time; and, even when advanced in years, was very expert in other manly exercises; he was a plain, honest, good-humoured man, and an inoffensive and cheerful companion, and, to the grief of many, died about the year 1748.

The Madrigal Society still subsists, but in a manner very different from its original institution; they meet at a tavern in the city, but under such circumstances, as render its permanency very precarious.

CHAP. CXCIII.

The music with which the public in general had been formerly entertained, was chiefly that of the theatre, and such as was occasionally performed at concerts; but, in proportion to the increase of wealth in the metropolis, the manners of the people began to relax; the places of public entertainment increased in number, and to these music seemed to be essential. It is curious to reflect on the parsimony of our ancestors in all their recreations and amusements; the playhouses afforded them entertainment during the winter season, and the length of the summer days afforded leisure for a walk in the gardens of the inns of court, the park, or to the adjacent villages. Besides these there were several Mulberry-gardens about the town; and places at the extremities of it distinguished by the name of Spring Gardens and the World's End: some of these were frequented by the better sort of persons of both sexes, for purposes that may be guessed at.

The World's End is mentioned in Congreve's comedy of Love for Love, in a scene where Mrs. Foresight rallies Mrs. Frail for having been seen with a man in a hackney-coach: there is a place so called between Chelsea and Fulham,* another a little beyond Stepney, and another opposite St. George's Fields, in the road to Newington. The reason of this appellation is, that the houses of this sort were generally the last in the neighbourhood; the sign was usually a man and a woman walking together, with the following distich underwrote:—

I'll go with my friend
To the World's End.

A kind of intimation what sort of company were most welcome there.†

Barn-Elms and Vauxhall were also places of great resort for water parties; of the latter of these the history is but little known; all we can learn of it is, that the house so called was formerly the habitation of Sir Samuel Moreland. Aubrey, in his Antiquities of Surrey, gives this account of it: 'At Vauxhall 'Sir Samuel Moreland built a fine room, anno 1667, 'the inside all of looking-glass, and fountains very 'pleasant to behold, which is much visited by 'strangers; it stands in the middle of the garden, '—— foot square, —— high, covered with Cornish 'slate; on the point whereof he placed a Punchinello, 'very well carved, which held a dial, but the winds have demolished it.' Vol. I. page 12.

The house seems to have been rebuilt since the time that Sir Samuel Moreland dwelt in it. About the year 1730, Mr. Jonathan Tyers became the occupier of it; and, there being a large garden belonging to it, planted with a great number of stately trees, and laid out in shady walks, it obtained the name of Spring Gardens; and the house being converted into a tavern, or place of entertainment, it was much frequented by the votaries of pleasure. Mr. Tyers opened it with an advertisement of

a Ridotto al Fresco, a term which the people of this country had till that time been strangers to. These entertainments were several times repeated in the course of the summer, and numbers resorted to partake of them; and this encouraged the proprietor to make his garden a place of musical entertainment for every evening during the summer season; to this end he was at great expence in decorating the gardens with paintings; he engaged a band of excellent musicians; he issued silver tickets for admission at a guinea each; and, receiving great encouragement, he set up an organ in the orchestra, and in a conspicuous part of the garden erected a fine statue of Mr. Handel, the work of Mr. Roubiliac.

The success of this undertaking was an encouragement to another of a similar kind; a number of persons purchased the house and gardens of the late earl of Ranelagh; they erected a spacious building of timber, of a circular form, and within it an organ, and an orchestra capable of holding a numerous band of performers: the entertainment of the auditors during the performance is either walking round the room, or refreshing themselves with tea and coffee in the recesses thereof, which are conveniently adapted to that purpose. Mr. Festing, during his life-time, led the band; the performance here, as at Vauxhall, is instrumental, intermixed with songs and ballad airs, calculated rather to please the vulgar, than gratify those of a better taste.

The account given of Mr. Handel in the preceding pages, has been continued down to the year 1736, at which time the restoration of his health, which had suffered greatly in the contest with the nobility, engrossed his whole attention. Having happily got the better of that disorder, which boded little less than a privation of his mental faculties, he returned to England, and at Covent-Garden made an effort to regain the public favour by the performance of the operas of Atalanta, ‡ Justin, Arminius, and Berenice; these succeeded but ill; and the indifference of the town towards him may be judged of by the fruitless endeavours of his friends to render the publication of the above compositions beneficial to him, evidenced by a subscription to them severally, that hardly defrayed the expence of printing.

In the composition of the two subsequent operas of Faramond and Alexander Severus, performed in 1737, he was indemnified against all risk of loss by an engagement with the late duke of Dorset, then earl of Middlesex, in virtue whereof he composed them both, and was paid by his lordship the sum of one thousand pounds. Three other operas, namely Xerxes, Hymen, and Deidamia, of his composition, were represented between the years 1737 and 1740, after which Handel gave another direction to his studies, better suited, as he himself used to declare, to the circumstances of a man advancing in years, than that of adapting music to such vain and trivial poetry as the musical drama is generally made to consist of. This resolution led him to reflect on

---

* The sign of the house at this time is the globe of the world in that state of conflagration which is to put an end to its existence; a pun in painting as singular as the title of a well known song, 'The Cobbler's End.'

† *Spring Garden, and the Mulberry Garden, are mentioned as places of Intrigue in Sir George Etherege's Comedy of 'She would if she could;' and in a comedy of Sir Charles Sedley's, entitled 'The Mulberry Garden,' the scene is in the Mulberry Garden, near St. James's. At the time when the above were places of public resort, there was an edifice built of timber and divided into sundry rooms with a platform and balustrade at top, which floated on the Thames above London Bridge, and was called the Folly; a view of it, anchored opposite Somerset House, is given in Strype's Stow, book IV. page 105; and the humours of it are described by Ward in his London Spy. At first it was resorted to for refreshment by persons of fashion; and queen Mary with some of her courtiers had once the curiosity to visit it. But it sank into a receptacle for companies of loose and disorderly people, for the purposes of drinking and promiscuous dancing; and at length becoming scandalous, the building was suffered to decay, and the materials thereof became fire-wood.*

‡ Originally performed on occasion of the marriage of the prince of Orange with our princess royal.

that kind of representation, the Concerto Spirituale, so frequent in the Romish countries, and which, by the name of the Oratorio, is nearly of as great antiquity as the opera itself, and determined him to the choice of sacred subjects for the exercise of his genius.   He was well acquainted with the Holy Scriptures, and was sensible that the sublime sentiments with which they abound would give opportunities of displaying his greatest talents : he had made the experiment in the anthems which he had composed for the duke of Chandois, and in four others performed at the coronation of the late king ; and as to the risk that an entertainment so little known in this country as the oratorio would be disrelished, of that too he was able to form some judgment, for in the year 1733, upon occasion of the solemnization of a public act in the university of Oxford, he performed the oratorio of Athaliah, and the profits thereof were so considerable as in some degree to repair the damage his fortunes had sustained in that dreadful conflict in which he was then engaged.

Other considerations suggested to him the almost certain benefit of such an undertaking : the performance of a sacred drama would consist with the solemnity of the Lent season, during which stage representations in this as in other Christian countries are in general forbidden ; but, above all, this served to recommend it, that it could be conducted at a small expence : no costly scenery was required, nor dresses for the performers, other than a suit of black, with which all persons that appeared in public were supposed to be provided.*   Instead of airs that required the delicacy of Cuzzoni, or the volubility of Faustina to execute, he hoped to please by songs, the beauties whereof were within the comprehension of less fastidious hearers than in general frequent the opera, namely, such as were adapted to a tenor voice, from the natural firmness and inflexibility whereof little more is ever expected than an articulate utterance of the words, and a just expression of the melody ; and he was happy in the assistance of a singer† possessed of these and many other valuable qualities.   He knew also that he could attach to him the real lovers and judges of music by those original beauties, which he was able to display in the composition of fugue and chorus ;‡ and these being once gained, the taste of the town was likely to fall in, as it frequently does, with the opinion of those who are best qualified to give a direction to it.   To such a performance the talents of a second-rate singer, and persons used to choir service were adequate. Signora Francesina, and afterwards Signora Frasi, and some others in succession, were engaged on terms comparatively easy ; and the chapel royal and

the choir of St. Paul's furnished boys and chorus singers sufficient in abilities and number to answer his purpose.

The former performances of the oratorios of Athaliah, Deborah, and Esther, were but essays towards the introduction of this kind of entertainment ; and it is upon very good authority asserted, that Mr. Handel was induced to this attempt by the performance of Esther at the academy of ancient Music in the month of February, 1731, which was so greatly applauded, that in the following year, in the Lent season, he performed it, as also Deborah, at Covent Garden theatre.   Upon this occasion he also gratified the public with a species of music of which he may be said to be the inventor, namely, the organ-concerto.   Few but his intimate friends were sensible that on this instrument he had scarce his equal in the world ; and he could not but be conscious that he possessed a style of performing on it that at least had the charm of novelty to recommend it.   From the third of his Sonatas for two violins or hautboys, which he had composed some years before, he had made an overture to Esther ; and of the last movement in the same composition, inserting in it sundry solo passages adapted to the instrument, and adding to it a prelude and an air singularly elegant, he now formed a concerto, the beauties whereof he displayed by his own masterly performance.   It must be confessed that this was not that true organ-style which a profound judge of music would admire, and of which Handel had shewn himself a complete master in the voluntaries and fugues for the organ published by him ; but the full harmony of the instrumental parts in this composition, contrasted with those eloquent solo passages interspersed in it, protracting the cadences, and detaining the ear in a delightful suspense, had a wonderful effect.

Having thus made an experiment of the disposition of the town towards these entertainments, Handel determined to rest his future fortunes on the success of them ; accordingly, on his return to London from Aix la Chapelle, he set to music Mr. Dryden's ode for St. Cecilia's Day, entitled Alexander's Feast, and therein introduced a trio, which he had formerly set to the words ' Quel fior che al alba ride,' which, with the addition of another part, he adapted so well to the chorus ' Let old Timotheus yield the prize,' that most men took it for an original composition.   The success of this performance determined him in his resolution to addict himself for the future to this species of composition, and accordingly he persisted in it, with a few occasional deviations, for the remainder of his life.   And finding that his own performance on the organ never failed to command the attention of his hearers, he set himself to compose, or rather make up, concertos for that instrument,§

---

* It is a trivial circumstance to remark upon, but it serves to shew a great change of manners, and the little regard to the decencies of religion in this country of liberty : neither the singers in the oratorio, nor their hearers, make any distinction in their dress between Lent and a season of festivity.

† Mr. Beard.

‡ The chorusses of Mr. Handel's oratorios are of a cast very different from those in his operas ; the latter are simply counterpoint, and are destitute of all art and contrivance ; the former answer to the sublime in poetry ; they are of his own invention, and are the very basis of his reputation.

§ Of his first six organ concertos, only the first and fourth are original compositions ; both the second and third are taken from his Sonatas ; the fifth was a lesson for the harp, composed for the younger Powel, a fine performer on that instrument ; and the sixth is a solo for the flute, as is apparent from the compass of it, and was made for the practice of a gentleman, one of Handel's friends.   The second set of organ concertos is evidently made out of his grand concertos.

There were two persons of the name of Powel, father and son, who played finely on the harp ; the elder was patronized by the duke of Portland, and when that nobleman was appointed governor of Jamaica,

and uniformly interposed one in the course of the evening's performance.

The applause bestowed on the oratorios of Handel, was at least equal to that of the best of his operas; but, such was the taste of the town, that he was constrained to give these entertainments a dramatic form; for he was used to say, that, to an English audience, music joined to poetry was not an entertainment for an evening, and that something that had the appearance of a plot or fable was necessary to keep their attention awake. Perhaps he might be mistaken in this opinion; and the success of Israel in Egypt, L'Allegro ed Il Penseroso, and Messiah, seem to indicate the contrary; nevertheless it determined his conduct with respect to these entertainments, and frequently induced him to have recourse to some small poet for his assistance in forming a drama, which, without regard to sentiment or language, or indeed any thing but the conduct of the drama, was to be the mere vehicle of his music; and such, for instance, are the oratorios of Esther, Saul, Susanna, and many others. Some of the pretended admirers of music were for carrying the illusion still farther, and offered many reasons, such as they were, in favour of a real representation of the history which was the subject of the entertainment; and would have had, to give one instance as an example of the rest, Jacob and Joseph and his brethren personated on the stage, with all the aids of action and scenic decoration. In some of his performances, included under the general denomination of oratorios, such as Alexander's Feast, Israel in Egypt, and L'Allegro ed Il Penseroso, and others equally unsusceptible of a dramatic form, the idea of personal representation would have been absurd, and therefore the audience acquiesced in that disposition of words and sentiments, which in the judgment of the musical composer was best calculated to display the powers of his art; and these never appeared to so great advantage as when he made use of passages selected from Holy Writ for the subjects of his compositions; of this there needs no other evidence than his Israel in Egypt and the Messiah, concerning which latter work there are some particulars, which for his honour deserve to be remembered. It was performed for the first time at Covent Garden in the

went with him thither. The younger stayed in England, and Mr. Handel being desirous to make him known, composed for him the lesson abovementioned, and introduced it in one or two of his oratorios: as also the song in Esther, 'Tune your harps to cheerful strains,' which has an accompaniment the harp.

Besides the Powels there was at the same time in London a performer on the harp, who merits to be had in remembrance: his name was Jones, a Welchman, and blind; the old duchess of Marlborough would have retained him with a pension, but he would not endure confinement, and was engaged by one Evans, who kept a home-brewed ale house of great resort, the sign of the Hercules Pillars, opposite Clifford's-Inn passage in Fleet-street, and performed in a great room up-stairs during the winter season. He played extempore voluntaries, the fugues in the Sonatas and Concertos of Corelli, as also most of his Solos, and many of Mr. Handel's opera songs with exquisite neatness and elegance. He also played on the violin, and on that instrument imitated so exactly the irregular intonation, mixed with sobs and pauses, of a quaker's sermon, that none could hear him and refrain from immoderate laughter. The man of the house dying, his widow took Cuper's Garden, in Surrey, opposite Somerset-house, and erected therein an orchestra and an organ, intending it as a place of entertainment for the summer evenings, like Vauxhall, with the addition of fireworks. It subsisted for four or five summers, but, failing at length, Jones, who was supported by her all the time, was turned adrift, and, about the year 1738, died. He was buried in Lambeth church-yard, and his funeral, which was celebrated with a dead march, was attended by a great number of the musical people.

year 1741, by the name of a Sacred Oratorio. As it consisted chiefly of chorus, and the airs contained in it were greatly inferior to most in his operas and former oratorios, it was but coldly received by the audience; the consciousness whereof, and a suspicion that the public were growing indifferent towards these entertainments, determined him to try the temper of the people of Ireland; accordingly he went to Dublin in the year 1741, and gave a performance of the Messiah for the benefit of the prisoners in that city. He returned to London in the year 1741-2, and performed an oratorio, consisting of passages selected from the Samson Agonistes of Milton, which was received with such applause, as seemed to insure him success in his future attempts of that kind.

About this time he published by subscription twelve grand Concertos. To this undertaking Handel was probably encouraged by the good success of a former publication of the like kind, namely, Six Concertos composed on occasion of the marriage of the prince of Orange with the princess royal, and distinguished by the name of his Hautboy Concertos, which being made up of fugues taken from his lessons, and from six fugues for the organ, composed by him as studies, had great merit. But as to these twelve Concertos, they appear to have been made in a hurry, and in the issue fell very short of answering the expectations that were formed of them, and inclined men to think that the composition of music merely instrumental, and of many parts, was not Handel's greatest excellence.

In the succeeding year he had a slight return of that disorder which had driven him to seek relief from the baths of Aix-la-Chapelle; and, to add to this misfortune, an opposition to him and his entertainment was set on foot by some persons of distinction, who by card assemblies, and other amusements, at that time not usual in the Lent season, endeavoured to make his audiences as thin as possible. The effects of this association he felt for a season or two, in the course whereof he frequently performed to houses that would not pay his expenses; but at length a change of sentiment in the public began to manifest itself; the Messiah was received with universal applause, and has ever since been considered as one of the most sublime of his compositions. In gratitude for the favour shown him by the public, and actuated by motives of benevolence, he performed the Messiah for the benefit of an institution, which then stood in need of every assistance, the Foundling-hospital; and this he not only continued to do for several years, but, by presenting the charity with a copy of the score and parts of this composition, gave them such a title to it as seemed to import an exclusive right to the performance of it. This act of bounty was so ill understood by some of the governors of that foundation, that they formed a resolution for an application to parliament to establish their supposed right; in short, to prohibit, under penalties, the performance of the Messiah by any others than Mr. Handel and themselves. To facilitate the passing of a law for the purpose, Mr. Handel's concurrence was asked, but he was so little sensible of the propriety of it, that upon the bare mention of it he broke out into a furious passion, which he vented in the following terms : ' For vat sal de Foundlings put mein oratorio ' in de Parlement ? Te Teuffel ! mein musik sal not ' go to de Parlement.'

The retreat of Handel to Ireland, and the favourable reception he met with at Dublin, awakened the people of this country to a sense of his merit, and was a kind of reproach on those who had necessitated him to seek protection in that kingdom ; so that his return hither was felicitated with every testimony of esteem and respect, and the strongest assurances of future encouragement. His Messiah was frequently performed to such audiences, as he could no otherwise accommodate than by erecting seats on the stage, to such a number as scarcely left room for the performers. In this prosperous state did his affairs go on, till he was afflicted with the misfortune of blindness, which, great as it was, did not totally incapacitate him from study, or the power of entertaining the public. The circumstances of this misfortune, as also of his death, are reserved for that which is meant to be the last period of the memoir here given of him.

CHAP. CXCIV.

STEFANO CARBONELLI had studied the practice of the violin under Corelli ; and coming hither from Rome, was received into the family of the duke of Rutland, a great patron of music. During his residence with this nobleman, he published and dedicated to him twelve Solos for a violin and a bass of his composition, which he frequently played in public with great applause. Upon the institution of the Royal Academy, Carbonelli was placed at the head of the opera band, and soon became so celebrated for his excellent hand, as to give Sir Richard Steele, in his comedy of the Conscious Lovers, occasion of making him a very handsome compliment. The manner of it was this ; Carbonelli led the orchestra at the Haymarket in the year 1721, when Bononcini's opera of Griselda was performed there ; and in a discourse between Young Bevil and Indiana, the lady is made to commend that opera, particularly the air in it, ' Dolce Sogno ;' upon which a conversation ensues on the subject of the opera in general, which is interrupted by a servant, who enters and informs his master that Signor Carbonelli waits his commands in the next room ; upon this Bevil tells the lady that she had mentioned the day before, her desire to hear him ; accordingly he is introduced, and plays a solo.* About the year 1725, Carbonelli quitted the opera-house, and went to Drury-lane theatre, where he led, and frequently played select pieces between the acts. His successor at the opera-house was Pietro Castrucci. After continuing a few years at Drury-lane, Carbonelli quitted his station there in favour of Mr. Richard Jones, and attached

himself to Mr. Handel at the time when he began to perform oratorios. For a series of years he played at the rehearsal and performance at St. Paul's for the benefit of the sons of the clergy.

At his first coming into England, Carbonelli professed himself to be of the Romish persuasion, but after his arrival he became a protestant, and married the daughter of Mr. Warren, parish-clerk of St. James's, Westminster. In the latter part of his life he in some measure declined the profession of music, and betook himself to that of a merchant, and an importer of wines from France and Germany. By the interest of a powerful friend he obtained the place of one of the purveyors of wine to the king ; and died in that employment in the year 1772.

Among the performers on the violin at the time when the Italian opera was first introduced into England, were some whose names are now scarcely remembered ; of these Signor Claudio, a native of Lucca, was the chief : he played the second violin at the Haymarket many years ; and was the author of six Solos for that instrument, published a few years before his death, that is to say, in or about 1740. Others there were of greater eminence, of whom here follows an account.

PIETRO CASTRUCCI, by birth a Roman, was an excellent performer on the violin. He succeeded Corbett as first violin at the opera-house, and led the opera for many years ; but growing old, Handel had a mind to place a young man, named John Clegg, a scholar of Dubourg, at the head of his orchestra ; Castrucci being in very necessitous circumstances, and not in the least conscious of any failure in his hand, was unwilling to quit his post ; upon which Handel, in order to convince him of his inability to fill it, composed a concerto, in which the second concertino was so contrived, as to require an equal degree of execution with the first ; † this he gave to Clegg, who in the performance of it gave such proofs of his superiority, as reduced Castrucci to the necessity of yielding the palm to his rival. Oppressed with years, he immediately sank into oblivion, and at the age of eighty, upon the merit of his past services, became a supplicant to the public for a benefit, at which he performed a solo, and soon after died. He published two sets of Solos for a violin, with a thorough-bass, and twelve Concertos for violins, which, though hardly known, have great merit. He had a brother, younger than himself, named Prospero, who for some years led the concert at the Castle tavern in Paternoster-row, and was author of six Solos for a violin and a bass ; but as a musician he was in no respect equal to Pietro.

Clegg succeeded to the favour of Handel, and under his patronage enjoyed the applause of the town. This person had been a pupil of Dubourg in Ireland, and travelling with lord Ferrers to Italy, so greatly improved himself, that at his return he excelled in the leading of a concert, all in England : the strength of his tone, and the most rapid and distinct execution that had ever been heard in this country, were the

---

* Rolli, who translated the Conscious Lovers into Italian in the year 1724, has a note on this passage, indicating that Carbonelli was then in the service of the duke of Rutland.

† It is printed in the fourth collection of Concertos, entitled Select Harmony, published by Walsh.

qualities that recommended him. His intense application and incessant practice had such an effect on his mind, that he became a lunatic, and was confined in the hospital of Bedlam. During his continuance there, he was at times permitted the use of his instrument, and drew crowds to hear him.

Richard Charke was a performer on the violin, and, succeeding as first violin in the band at Drury-lane one who was called Dicky Jones, attained to some degree of eminence. He married Charlotte, the youngest daughter of Colley Cibber, and by his ill usage of her gave occasion to those reflections on him contained in a narrative of her most extraordinary life, written by herself, and published in 1755. Charke was famous for playing the eleventh of Carbonelli's Solos in A♯. Being a loose extravagant fellow, and deeply involved in debt, he was necessitated to quit this country : Jamaica was his asylum, and he died there in the prime of his age. He was the first that composed medley-overtures, which are overtures made up of passages taken from well-known airs and common popular tunes ; and among three or four that are extant, his is reckoned the best : this, and a hornpipe that bears his name, are the only compositions of Charke extant.

Matthew Dubourg was a scholar of Geminiani, and by him was taught the practice of the violin. Upon the death of Cousser, in the year 1728, Geminiani having declined the offer of his place of master and composer of the state music in Ireland, it was conferred on Dubourg. As the duties of this employment did not require his constant residence in that kingdom, he passed much of his time in England, and had the honour to be the instructor in music of the late prince of Wales and the duke of Cumberland. There is nothing of his composition extant that we know of, excepting a set of variations on a minuet of Geminiani, to which the song, ' Gently touch the warbling lyre,' is adapted, and these have never yet been printed ; nay it does not appear that he ever composed solos for his own practice, contenting himself with performing those of Corelli and his master Geminiani.*

Dubourg's performance on the violin was very bold and rapid ; greatly different from that of Geminiani, which was tender and pathetic ; and these qualities it seems he was able to communicate, for Clegg his disciple possessed them in as great perfection as himself. He had many admirers, and among them was Mrs. Martin : this woman was a native of Holland, and the widow of a Dutch burgomaster, but having married an Englishman, and being possessed of a large fortune, she came to reside in London, and dwelt in the house in Sherborn-lane, formerly Sir Gilbert Heathcote's, where during the winter season she had frequent concerts, which were resorted to by citizens of the first rank, and at times by sundry of the nobility. A picture of Dubourg, painted when he was a boy, was a conspicuous object in Mrs. Martin's concert-room, which was very large

* Dubourg must have had some instructor before he became a pupil of Geminiani ; he played a solo, standing upon a joint-stool at Britton's concert : Britton died in 1714, and Geminiani arrived in England in the same year.

and splendid, two sides of it being lined with looking-glass. He died on the third day of July, 1767, aged sixty-four, and lies buried in the church-yard of Paddington, under a monumental stone, whereon is the following inscription :—

> Tho' sweet as Orpheus thou could'st bring
> Soft pleadings from the trembling string,
> Uncharm'd the king of terror stands,
> Nor owns the magic of thy hands.

Michael Christian Festing, a master of the violin, and a very elegant composer for that instrument, was at first a scholar of Dicky Jones, above-mentioned, the successor of Carbonelli at Drury-lane theatre ; but was perfected in his musical studies by Geminiani, under whom he acquired such a degree of skill, as, cultivated by his own natural genius, enabled him, at least so far as regards composition for the violin, to form a style original as it was elegant. Being a man of understanding and knowledge of the world, he found means throughout his life to form such connexions, and to attach to him such patrons of music among the nobility, as were his constant support. He also derived considerable advantage from the friendship of Dr. Greene ; and, being of the royal band, led the performance in the odes of his composing performed at court. He played the first violin in what was called the Philharmonic Society, consisting of noblemen and gentlemen performers, who met on Wednesday nights during the winter season, at the Crown and Anchor tavern in the Strand ; and upon the building of the rotunda in the garden of Ranelagh house at Chelsea, besides that he led the band, he had the sole conduct of the musical performances there. By his interest and indefatigable industry he contributed greatly to the establishment and increase of the fund for the support of decayed musicians and their families, and for some years discharged gratis the duty of secretary to that institution. He had a brother named John, who played on the hautboy, and was a teacher of the German flute, for which latter instrument he had more scholars than any master in London ; *and whose success in this his profession affords a very remarkable instance of what industry and economy are capable of effecting in the exercise of it ; for he died in the year 1772 possessed of the sum of £8000, acquired chiefly by teaching.*

The works of Festing in print were all published by himself, that is to say, he took subscriptions for them, and was not beholden for the circulation of them through the kingdom to the keepers of music-shops ; the consequence whereof is, that they are less known than the compositions of any other master of his time. He died in the year 1752, leaving a son, a clergyman, who married the daughter of Dr. Greene. His goods, books, and instruments were sold at his house in Warwick-street near Golden-square, in the month of September, in the year above-mentioned.

As a performer on the violin, Festing was inferior to many of his time ; but as a composer, particularly of solos for that instrument, the nature and genius whereof he perfectly understood, he had but few equals.

LEWIS MERCY or MERCI, an Englishman by birth, though his name imports him to have been of French extraction,* was a celebrated performer on the flute abec, and an excellent composer for that instrument. He published six Solos, with a preface, containing a very brief history of the scale, and of Guido's reformation of it, taken from Brossard : and after that his Opera seconda, containing also six solos for the same instrument. Mercy lived at the time when the flute was becoming an unfashionable recreation for gentlemen, and the German flute was growing into favour ; he therefore concerted with the younger Stanesby, the wind-instrument-maker, the scheme of a new system, and of making the flute a concert instrument, without an actual transposition, by changing the denomination of the lower note from F to C, by which contrivance a flute of the fifth size was precisely an octave above the other treble instruments. He published twelve Solos, the first six whereof are said to be for the Traverse-flute, Violin, or English Flute, according to Mr. Stanesby's new system, with a preface in recommendation of it, in which he refers to Mersennus, de Instrumentis Harmonicis, and asserts that Stanesby's is in truth the ancient system of the flute ; and so upon a reference to the book it appears to be.† He also makes a comparison between the flute abec and the German flute, and asserts that the former of the two is the best in tune, and in other respects to be preferred. But all the endeavours of Stanesby and Mercy to restore this instrument seem to have failed of their end. Mercy lived in Orange-court in Castle-street near Leicester-fields, and advertised that his works were there to be had. His solos for the flute may be ranked among the best compositions for that instrument extant.

JONATHAN MARTIN had his education in the royal chapel under Dr. Croft, and soon after his decease was committed to the tuition of Roseingrave, then organist of St. George's, Hanover-square; and having under him attained to a great proficiency on the organ, and, with other assistances, qualified himself for choral duty, he became the deputy of Weldon as organist of the chapel ; and, upon his decease in the year 1736, his places of organist and composer to the chapel becoming vacant, Martin was appointed to one, and Dr. William Boyce to the other. Martin had the misfortune to labour under a pulmonic indisposition that suffered him to enjoy his preferment but a short time. In the year 1737, and a few months before his decease, he had a concert for his benefit at Stationers'-hall, at which were present almost every person in London that pretended to any skill in music, and where, though he had scarcely strength to sit upright, by two voluntaries on the organ he gave such proofs of a fine invention and a masterly hand, as astonished all his hearers. His manual performance was his greatest excellence,

there being nothing of his composition extant, save the song in Tamerlane, 'To thee O gentle sleep,' which ever since his decease has been sung to his music at the performance of that tragedy. Martin lies buried in the cloister of Westminster-abbey, but without a stone to point out the place of his interment.‡

JOHN HUMPHRIES, a young man of promising parts, and a good performer on the violin, published, before he was twenty, Six Solos for that instrument ; a puerile effort of a genius that was approaching to maturity. His success in that publication encouraged him to farther attempts, and in the year 1728 he published by subscription twelve Sonatas for two violins and a bass, of a very original cast, in respect that they are in a style somewhat above that of the common popular airs and country-dance tunes, the delight of the vulgar, and greatly beneath what might be expected from the studies of a person at all acquainted with the graces and elegancies of the Italians in their compositions for instruments. To this it must be attributed that the sonatas of Humphries were the common practice of such small proficients in harmony, as in his time were used to recreate themselves with music at alehouse clubs, and places of vulgar resort in the villages adjacent to London : of these there were formerly many, in which six-pence at most was the price of admission.§

Humphries died about the year 1730. Cooke, of New-street, Covent-Garden, a seller of music, published twelve Concertos of Humphries, precisely in the same cast with his sonatas.

JOHN RAVENSCROFT was one of the waits, as they are called, of the Tower Hamlets, and in the band of Goodman's Fields play-house was a Ripieno violin, notwithstanding which, he was a performer good enough to lead in any such concerts as those above described ; and, to say the truth, was able to do justice to a concerto of Corelli, or an overture of Handel. He was much sought after to play at balls and dancing parties ; and was singularly excellent in the playing of hornpipes, in which he had a manner that none could imitate. It seems that this was a kind of music which of all others he most affected ; so that by mere dint of a fancy accommodated to these little essays, he was enabled to compose airs of this kind equal to those of the ablest masters ; and yet so little was he acquainted with the rules of composition, that for suiting them with basses he was indebted to others. As a singular instance of the powers of a limited genius, the following are selected from a collection of hornpipes published by Ravenscroft :—

---

* He seems to have been fearful of being mistaken for a Frenchman, for in the title-page of one of his publications he styles himself ' di Nazione Inglesa.'

† See page 608, in note.

‡ A very elegant inscription was composed by Mr. Vincent Bourne, and intended for a tablet over the spot of his interment; but as yet it is extant only in his poems, of which there are sundry editions. Together with Martin and very near his grave, was buried Charles Stroud, a disciple of Dr. Croft, a young man of great hopes, known by an anthem of his composition, "Hear my prayer O God."

§ To such readers as are interested in the knowledge of low manners, it may be some gratification to mention that there were concerts of this kind at the following places: the Blacksmith's Arms on Lambeth hill, behind St. Paul's; the Cock and Lion in St. Michael's alley, Cornhill ; the Coachmakers' Arms in Windmill-street, Piccadilly : at sundry alehouses in Spitalfields, frequented by journeymen weavers ; and at Lambeth Wells, and the Unicorn at Hoxton. The keepers of these houses were generally men that loved music.

JOHN RAVENSCROFT.

Ravenscroft was a very corpulent man, a circumstance which made the neatness of his performance the more remarkable. He died about the year 1745.

GIUSEPPE SAN MARTINI was a native of Milan. He was a performer on the hautboy, an instrument invented by the French, and of small account, till by his exquisite performance, and a tone which he had the art of giving it, he brought it into reputation. Martini arrived in England about the year 1729, and was favoured by Bononcini, Greene, and others of that party, as also by Frederic, prince of Wales, who was his great patron. When Greene went to Cambridge to take his degree, Martini attended him, and performed in the exercise for it; and had there a concert for his benefit, which produced him a considerable sum. He was an admirable composer; and, for instrumental music, may, without injury to either, be classed with Corelli and Geminiani. His first compositions were Sonatas for two flutes, and others for German flutes : these are scarcely known, but the greatness of his talents is manifested in six Concertos and twelve Sonatas, published by himself, the latter dedicated to the late princess of Wales. The first of these works was published in the year 1738, when the concertos of Corelli and Geminiani, and the overtures of Mr. Handel were become familiar, there being scarce any concert in which the compositions of these two masters did not make a considerable part of the evening's entertainment; and, with respect to those of Corelli, this had been the case for almost thirty years. Martini had therefore a ground to hope that the charm of novelty would recommend these his compositions to the public favour; but he was disappointed in the expectations he had formed of the immediate sale of the whole impression of his book, and in an evil hour destroyed not only a great number of the copies, but also the plates from which they were wrought. The work being thus rendered scarce, Johnson, of Cheapside, was tempted to republish it; and it was so well received, that the author soon found reason to repent his rashness, and was encouraged to prepare for the press eight overtures, and six grand concertos for violins, &c., but just as he had completed them he died; however they were published by Johnson after his decease, with an advertisement in the title-page, that the work was engraved for the author in his life-time, and was by him intended to be published by subscription. The overtures in this collection are called Opera decima, and the concertos, Opera XI.* Walsh also published eight overtures in eight parts, and six grand concertos for violins, &c., by Martini, which, notwithstanding they are a posthumous publication, carry with them undoubted evidence of their genuineness.

The merits of Martini as a composer of music in many parts, were unquestionably very great. He had a fertile invention, and gave into a style of modulation less restrained by rule than that of his predecessors, and by consequence affording greater scope for his fancy. Those who ascribe his deviation from known and established rules to the want of musical erudition, are grossly mistaken: he was thoroughly skilled in the principles of harmony; and his singularities can therefore only be ascribed to that boldness and self-possession which are ever the concomitants of genius; and in most of the licences he has taken, it may be observed that he is in a great measure warranted by the precepts, and indeed by the example, of Geminiani.

He performed on the hautboy in the opera till the time that Bononcini left it; after that he played at the Castle concert, and occasionally at others; but being patronized by Frederic, prince of Wales, he was at length received into his family upon the footing of a domestic, and appointed master or director of the chamber music to his royal highness.

In the course of this employment he composed a great number of Sonatas for the practice of the chamber; and, upon the birth of the princess of Brunswick, set to music a drama written on occasion of that event. He also composed a musical solemnity, which was publicly performed at the chapel of the Bavarian minister. In the honourable and easy station above-mentioned, Martini continued till about the year 1740, when he died.

As a performer on the hautboy, Martini was undoubtedly the greatest that the world had ever known. Before his time the tone of the instrument was rank, and, in the hands of the ablest proficients, harsh and grating to the ear; by great study and application, and by some peculiar management of the reed, he contrived to produce such a tone as approached the nearest to that of the human voice of any we know of.† It may well be supposed that he was not backward in communicating the improvements which he had made on this his favourite instrument, since a pupil of his, Mr. Thomas Vincent, is known to have possessed most of his excellencies in a very eminent degree; and we farther observe that the performers on the hautboy at this time are greatly superior to any that can be remembered before the arrival of Martini in England.

JOHN FREDERIC LAMPE was, as he affected to style himself, sometime a student of music at Helmstadt in Saxony; and arriving in England about the year 1725, obtained employment in the opera band. About the year 1730 he was engaged by Rich, of Covent Garden theatre, to compose the music to his pantomimes, and other entertainments performed there. Carey, who had received from him some instructions, had a high opinion of his abilities, and got him to set to music his burlesque opera of the Dragon of Wantley, as also the sequel to it, entitled Margery, and in his printed dramatic works, the Dragoness, in both which he has happily ridiculed the extravagancies of the modern Italian music, and the affected manner of the opera singers. In 1737 he published, in a quarto volume, 'A plain and ' compendious method of teaching Thorough-bass ' after the most rational manner, with proper rules ' for practice,' and dedicated it to Col. Blathwayt, assigning as a reason for so doing, his elegant taste and sound knowledge of music. There are extant many single songs composed by Lampe at sundry times, some of which are printed in the Musical Miscellany, in six volumes, published by Watts. He set to music, in a burlesque style exactly suited to the words, a Cantata of Swift, beginning 'In ' harmony would you excel,' printed at the end of the eighth volume of Faulkner's edition of Swift's works.‡ His wife was Isabella, one of the daughters of

* The intermediate publications of Martini between his first concertos and the Opera decima, are erroneously numbered; the sonatas are his Opera terza, the rest are sonatas and solos for German flutes, and are of small account.

† About the year 1735 an advertisement appeared in the public papers, offering a reward of ten guineas for a hautboy-reed that had been lost. It was conjectured to be Martini's, and favoured the opinion that he had some secret in preparing or meliorating the reeds of his instrument, though none could account for the offer of a reward so greatly disproportionable to the utmost conceivable value of the thing lost. It seems that the reed was found, and brought to the owner, but in such a condition as rendered it useless.

‡ It was originally printed for Johnson, in Cheapside, with the title of 'The Force of Music and Poetry, a Pindaric Ode,' and, though an anonymous publication, is undoubtedly the work of Lampe.

Mr. Charles Young, who, together with her sister Esther, sang in the Dragon of Wantley. Lampe died in London about twenty years ago.

Francesco Barsanti, a native of Lucca, born about the year 1690, studied the civil law in the university of Padua; but, after a short stay there, chose music for his profession. Accordingly he put himself under the tuition of some of the ablest masters in Italy, and having attained to a considerable degree of proficiency in the science of practical composition, took a resolution to settle in England, and came hither with Geminiani, who was also a Luccese, in the year 1714. He was a good performer on the hautboy, and also on the flute; in the former capacity he found employment in the opera band; and in the latter derived considerable advantages by teaching. He published, with a dedication to the earl of Burlington, Six Solos for a flute, with a thorough-bass, and afterwards Six Solos for a German flute and a bass. He also made into sonatas for two violins and a bass, the first six solos of Geminiani. He continued many years a performer at the opera-house; at length, reflecting that there was a prospect of advantage for one of his profession in Scotland, he went thither; and, with greater truth than the same is asserted of David Rizzo, may be said to have meliorated the music of that country, by collecting and making basses to a great number of the most popular Scots tunes.

About the year 1750 Barsanti returned to England, but, being advanced in years, he was glad to be taken into the opera band as a performer on the tenor violin; and in the summer season into that of Vauxhall: at this time he published twelve Concertos for violins, and, shortly after, Sei Antifone, in which he endeavoured to imitate the style of Palestrina, and the old composers of motets; but from these publications so little profit resulted, that, towards the end of his life, the industry and œconomy of an excellent wife, whom he had married in Scotland, and the studies and labours of a daughter, whom he had qualified for the profession of a singer, but is now an actress at Covent-Garden, were his chief support.*

Peter Prelleur, a person of French extraction, was, in the very early part of his life, a writing-master in Spitalfields; but, having a genius for music, and having been taught the harpsichord, he studied the science with great assiduity, and at length took to music as a profession. About the year 1728 he was elected organist of St. Alban, Wood-street, London; and a short time after, upon the decease of Monro, was taken into the band at the theatre in Goodman's-fields, and there played the harpsichord, till that house was suppressed by the operation of the statute of the tenth of the late king, cap. 28, whereby the acting of plays is restrained to the city of Westminster, and the places of his majesty's residence. His skill in music enabled

* This circumstance in the character of Miss Barsanti, as also her dutiful regard for her surviving parent, are well known; and, to the honour of the present age, it is here mentioned, that the public are not more disposed to applaud her theatrical merit, than to distinguish by their favour so illustrious an example of filial duty and affection.

him to compose the dances, as also interludes of various kinds, for which there is ever a demand at a theatre, and in these his merits were apparent.

About the year 1730 he was employed by Cluer and Dicey, music-printers in Bow church-yard, to compile an Introduction to Singing, as also instructions for the practice of most instruments; this work he completed, and added thereto a brief history of the science, extracted chiefly from Bontempi, containing sundry curious particulars.

About the year 1735, the parish of Christ-Church, Middlesex, had come to a resolution to erect an organ in their church, which is situated in Spitalfields, and Prelleur having many friends in that quarter, made an early interest for the place of organist, but was opposed by a young man who lived in that neighbourhood: the contest was carried on with such spirit by both parties, as was scarce ever known, but in popular elections to some great office. A scurrilous pamphlet was published by his competitor in support of his pretensions, and the inhabitants of the parish were set at enmity; but, notwithstanding all his endeavours and artifices, Prelleur was elected.

Upon the suppression of Goodman's-fields theatre, a place of entertainment was opened in the neighbourhood of it, of a similar kind with Sadler's Wells, and though there was no pretence of a well near it, it was called Goodman's-fields Wells: with the proprietor of this place Prelleur engaged, and during a few seasons that it was suffered, he composed the songs and dances, and also a little interlude, called Baucis and Philemon, in which there is a good overture, and a few pretty songs.

John James, a celebrated organist, was for some years only a deputy, at a salary of about eight pounds a year; but after that was elected to the place of organist of St. Olave, Southwark, which he quitted about the year 1738 for that of St. George, Middlesex. In his performance he was distinguished by the singularity of his style, which was learned and sublime. He paid very little attention to his interest, and was so totally devoid of all solicitude to advance himself in his profession, as to prefer the company and conversation of the lowest of mankind to that of the most celebrated of his own profession. To the wonder of all that knew him, his love of an art, that has a general tendency to improve the mind, had not the least influence on his manners, which were to so great a degree sordid and brutal, that his associates were butchers and bailiffs, and his recreations dog-fighting and bull-baiting. In a perfect consistence with the character he most affected, which was that of a blackguard, he indulged an inclination to spirituous liquors of the coarsest kind, such as are the ordinary means of ebriety in the lowest of the people; and this kind of intemperance he would indulge even while attending his duty at church.

The sole merit of James was his extempore performance; he composed a few voluntaries, which are in the hands of every deputy-organist in London. Three or four songs of his setting are all of his works that are known to be in print. He died about the year 1745; his funeral was attended by great numbers of the musical profession, and was celebrated by the performance of a dead march composed by himself. He left behind him a son, baptized by the name of Handel, who now rows a sculler on the Thames.

CHAP. CXCV.

THE progress of music in Italy had been very rapid for more than a century, and it was thought that both the science and practice had received nearly the last degree of improvement in the studies of Corelli: it was no small argument in favour of this opinion, that for some years after his decease, such an uniformity of style prevailed, especially in the instrumental compositions of the time, as seemed to indicate that the topics of invention were exhausted. The succeeding race of musicians however gave proofs of the contrary, and, emancipating music from that state of bondage which imitation ever implies, by the introduction of new combinations they added to the fund of harmony, and laid the foundation of a new style.

To bring the proof of this assertion home to ourselves, we need do no more than consult the compositions of Geminiani, and the later Italian musicians, namely, Pergolesi, Tartini, Vinci, Leo, Galuppi, and others which are recent in the memory of persons now living. To enumerate all of this class is unnecessary, but the two first are of such distinguished eminence as to merit a memorial.

GIOVANNI BATTISTA PERGOLESI was born at Naples about the year 1718; and at an age when he could be scarce supposed to have finished his studies, introduced a style of vocal composition, which, for its singular sweetness and power over the affections, has hitherto been inimitable. Those who have analysed his works resolve that original strain of modulation, which characterizes them, into a liberal use of the semitonic intervals, and a studious rejection of passages or musical phrases ready formed, which being adopted by succeeding writers, render a composition little better than a cento. Pergolesi died at the age of twenty two, just as he had finished the last verse of a Stabat Mater, by which he will ever be remembered: his premature death, and the great reputation he had so suddenly acquired, furnished ground for a suspicion that, to remove him out of the way, his rivals for fame had recourse to poison; but others, better informed, attribute his death to a severe attack of a pleurisy that baffled all attempts to save him. His Cantatas, published at Rome in 1738; two comic interludes, the one entitled La Serva Padrona, the other Il Maestro di Musica, a Salve Regina, and his famous Stabat Mater, the last printed in England, are all of his works that have been published.* There are in print twelve Sonatas for violins that bear his name; but evidence that they are genuine is wanting.

* In the library of the Academy of ancient Music are the following compositions of Pergolesi in manuscript: Two Masses, one for two choirs; A Salve Regina Domine adjuvandum, Confitebor, Laudate Pueri, and a Miserere.

GIUSEPPE TARTINI, of Padua, the last great improver of the practice of the violin, and a most sweet and judicious composer for that instrument, was born in the year 1692, at Pirano, a sea-port town in Istria, a province in the Venetian territory. When he was very young he entertained a passion for a young woman, who being in circumstances inferior to those of his own family, was by his friends thought an improper match for him; and all arguments to induce him to divert his affection proving ineffectual, his father confined him to his room; and, to engage his attention, furnished him with books and musical instruments, in the use whereof he profited so greatly, that when some time after he had got the better of his passion, and determined to make music his profession, being committed to the care of proper instructors, he gave the most promising hopes of becoming, both of the theory and practice, a complete master.

Having effaced from his mind the image of that mistress who had been the innocent cause of his restraint, he settled his affections on another, whom he married; but the object of his choice being but slenderly endowed with those mental qualities that are essential to conjugal happiness, and having no children, nor a prospect of any, he still found himself in a state of solitude, from which he could find no relief but in the pursuit of his studies.

In remarking the improvements that have been made in the practice of instruments, it may be noted, that the later performers have begun, as it were, where their predecessors left off; and that the powers of execution have been amazingly increased of late years: this is no other way to be accounted for, than upon the supposition that those particular energies which constitute perfection on any instrument, have been carefully noted down, and made to serve as common places for succeeding practisers. That Tartini was very assiduous in his remarks of this kind, is manifest from the nature of his performance, which was regulated by such principles as lead to perfection by the shortest road; of his success in these his observations in particular, one example shall suffice.

All men acquainted with music are sensible that the instruments of the fidicinal kind, which are those that are acted upon by a bow, are the most difficult of practice, and that the difference as well in respect of tone, and the powers of execution between one performer and another, is very great; but few have observed that this difference does almost solely arise from the action of the wrist of the right-hand, which being made to hang loose, will shoot the bow at right angles across the strings, and return it in the same line, producing a free and mellow tone, and giving power to execute the quickest passages; when this is not attended to, the shoulder becomes the centre of motion: the bow forms a curve in its passage, the weight of the arm prevents the vibration of the instrument, and by consequence damps the tone, and easy passages become difficult.

Tartini seems to have been the first that discovered this secret in the performance on the violin, and he made it a leading principle in the instruction of his pupils, who invariably adhere to it, and are the best performers in the world.

The perfection to which Tartini had attained on his favourite instrument, was alone sufficient to have established his character as a master, but, following the example of Zarlino, he made the theory of his art his study. Of sundry treatises that he wrote, the most celebrated is one entitled 'Trattata di 'Musica secondo la vera Scienza dell' Armonia,' printed at Padua in 1754, wherein from that well-known phenomenon mentioned by Mersennus and Dr. Wallis, that a chord, besides the sound to which it is tuned, will produce its twelfth, seventh, and, as the former asserts, its twenty-second also, he deduces sundry observations, tending to explain the scale, and, in the opinion of some, to correct sundry of the intervals of which it is composed.

An attempt to explain the doctrines contained in this tract, which all allow to be very obscurely written, was lately made in a book entitled Principles and Power of Harmony, printed in 1771, upon which it may be observed, that wherever the commentator can catch a glimpse of the author's meaning, he is very diffuse in his illustrations ; but in others, where the sense is too deep for his powers of investigation, and those occur but too frequently, he, to do him justice, candidly acknowledges the difficulty, or else he offers an explanation that fails of its end. Whoever peruses the preface and introduction to the Principles and Power of Harmony, would expect to find the book a commentary on Tartini's treatise, but instead thereof it is for the most part a collection of miscellaneous observations, made in the course of a transient view of some very able writers on music, whose sense the author has not so often illustrated as mistaken.*

To explain the doctrines delivered in his book, Tartini has recourse to numerical and algebraical calculations, in which he discovers that he was but meanly skilled in even the first of those sciences.

* For instance, he asserts in Sect. 59 of his book, that the harp was formerly the favourite instrument of our ancestors ; and Sect. 62, cites sundry passages from Spenser, Shakespeare, Milton, and others, in support of his opinion : that it was so with the Britons, and also with the Saxons, no one can doubt ; but that it was ever in practice among the English, we are not warranted to say, much less that it was a favourite instrument in the time of any of these writers whose testimony is adduced for the purpose. What compositions have we extant for the harp, or who among the English musicians are celebrated for their performance on it ? The truth is, that harp, like lyre, is a poetical term for a string musical instrument ; and in the sense in which these appellatives are used, each is as vague and indefinite as the other. Sect. 85, he says that Tartini has not been more successful in his endeavours to discover the true enarmonic than others. Perhaps he has been less so, for, in the opinion of Dr. Pepusch, Salinas and others have determined this genus of ancient music accurately : see his letter to Mr. Abraham De Moivre in the Philosophical Transactions, Numb. 481, page 266. And again, neither Tartini, nor his expositor, in their elucidation of the ancient modes, seem to have been aware of a passage in Ptolemy, and taken notice of by Dr. Wallis, viz., that they answered to the seven species of diapason, but that in each a particular tuning of the lyre was necessary, which could not be effected without a dislocation of the semitones. When he says, as he does in Sect. 9, that the discoveries contained in the first chapter of Tartini's book are fully sufficient to account for every thing practised or practicable in art, we think he has asserted too much. And when in his Appendix he gives to the Kamschatcans as good a right to decide against the possibility of foretelling an eclipse, or of representing all the elements of speech by about twenty-four marks, as the moderns have to doubt of the effects of ancient music, he seems rather to rave than reason. These strictures on a book, which, by an ostentatious display of deep and various reading, has raised in some a high opinion of his merit, would have been spared, had not the errors contained in it called for animadversion, and the exceeding confidence and self-sufficiency of the author for reprehension.

He seems clearly to declare his opinion that the ancient Greeks were unacquainted with music in consonance, in the following passage : 'La loro 'armonia era formata non come la nostra di note 'equitemporance, ma di note successive.'† And in the frequent comparisons which he occasionally makes between the ancient and modern music, generally decides in favour of the latter. To show at least that, in respect of its influence on the passions, the modern is not inferior to the ancient music, he relates that in an opera represented at Ancona in the year 1714, he heard a passage of recitative, with no other accompaniment than that of the bass, which made himself and the others that heard it change colour, and caused a sensible commotion in their minds ; he says that this effect was produced by notes that expressed indignation so forcibly, that they seemed to freeze the blood ; and that it was uniformly the same in a representation thirteen times of the drama.

The residence of Tartini during almost the whole of his life was at Padua, to which city he was attached by the employment of director of the music in the great church of St. Anthony ; thither resorted to him for instruction in music, but chiefly in the practice of the violin, great numbers of young men from various countries. In the early part of his life he published ' Sonate a Violino e Violoncello o Cim-'balo, Opera prima,' with a dedication to Sig. Girolamo Giustiniani, the celebrated paraphrast of those Psalms which Marcello set to music, and are spoken of in the memoir herein before given of him : these, as also his Opera seconda, being six Sonatas or Solos for the same instrument, and another work of his, entitled 'XVIII. Concerti a 5 Stromenti,' are all published by Le Cene of Amsterdam, and shew him to have been as able a composer as he was a theorist.

Towards the end of his life he was afflicted with the palsy. The time of his death is not precisely ascertained in any of the accounts extant that speak of him, but is supposed to be about the beginning of the year 1770.

Among the Germans the successive improvements in music, and the variations of style may be traced in the compositions of Buxtehude, Mattheson, Telemann, Bach, and Handel. The French continued for many years at a stand : Lully had formed a style, which in their opinion was incapable of improvement ; Couperin convinced them of the contrary. Of the true organ-style they had no conception, till Marchand and D'Andrieu displayed the powers of that instrument. Their symphonies and other compositions for violins were of a light and shadowy cast, destitute of invention and contrivance ; and as to theory, the study of it had been discontinued in France from the time of Mersennus and Des Cartes, who, in the general opinion of the musicians of that country, had nearly exhausted the subject. Of these errors they were however at length convinced by the studies of Le Clair and Rameau ; the first introduced among them a style of instrumental composition, in

† Trattato, pag. 143.

which the suggestions of a wild and irregular fancy were made to give place to a solid and substantial harmony, that spoke to the understanding : and the latter, by a deep investigation of the principles of harmony, and a variety of experiments and numerical calculations, taught them that much remained to be known. Of these eminent professors, as also of some others who flourished in France in the age immediately preceding the present, the following memoirs are extant.

NICOLAS BERNIER was born at Mante on the Seine, in the year 1664. By his merit in his profession he attained to be conductor of the music in the chapel of St. Stephen, and afterwards in that of the king. The regent duke of Orleans admired his works, and patronized their author. This prince having given him a motet of his own composition to examine, and, being impatient for his observations thereon, went to the house of Bernier, and, entering his study, found the Abbé de la Croix there, criticising his piece, while the musician himself was in another room, carousing and singing with a company of his friends. The duke broke in upon and interrupted their mirth, with a reprimand of Bernier for his inattention to the task assigned him. This musician died at Paris in 1734. His five books of Cantatas and Songs for one and two voices, the words of which were written by Rousseau and Fuselier, have procured him great reputation. There are besides of his composition ' Les Nuits de Sceaux,' and many motets, which are still in great esteem.

MICHEL MONTECLAIR was born, in the year 1666, at Andelot, a town of Bassigny, about ten miles from Chaumont. He took his surname from an old castle near the place of his birth. He was at first a teacher of music at Paris ; after that he was taken into the Royal Academy there ; and is said to have first introduced the Violone or double bass into the orchestra of the opera. He died near St. Dennis in 1737. There are extant of his works ' Méthode ' pour apprendre la Musique,' ' Principes pour le ' Violon,' ' Trios de Violons,' Cantatas, Motets, and one Messe de Requiem. He also composed the music to an entertainment entitled ' Les Fêtes de ' l' Eté,' and to the celebrated opera of Jepthé, written by Pellegrin, and represented at Paris in the year 1732.

JEAN-JOSEPH MOURET, born at Avignon in 1682, became remarkable from the age of twenty for his excellent musical compositions : his sense, wit, and taste for music rendered him a favourite with the great ; the duchess of Maine employed him to compose music for the festivals so much celebrated under the name of the Nuits de Sceaux. Ragonde, or la Soirée de Village, represented at the opera-house in Paris with great applause, was one of those entertainments. The levity of Mouret's compositions, and the sprightliness of his airs, were the great recommendations of his music. Towards the close of his life he became subject to some mental disorders, and met with other misfortunes, which hastened his end. Of these the most considerable was the loss of an income of five thousand livres a year, which arose

from the places of director of the Concert Spirituel, Superintendent of the music of the duchess of Maine, and musical composer to the Italian comedy. Mouret died at Charenton near Paris in the year 1738. He composed sundry operas, ballets, and other musical representations, namely, ' Les Fêtes ' de Thalie,' ' Les Amours des Dieux,' ' Le Triomphe ' des Sens,' ' Les Graces,' opera-ballets ; and Ariane, and Pirithous, tragedies, the one represented in 1717, the other in 1723. He also composed three books of songs of various kinds, and other works of less account.

JEAN-FRANÇOIS DANDRIEU, a celebrated musician, was born in the year 1684. He was a masterly performer on the organ and harpsichord, nor were his compositions less excellent. He resembled the celebrated Couperin both in style and execution. Dandrieu died at Paris in 1740, leaving of his works, three volumes of pieces for the harpsichord, and one of pieces for the organ, ' avec un suite de Noels,'* all which are greatly esteemed.

HENRI DESMARETS, born at Paris in the year 1662, was page de la musique to the king, and enjoyed a pension of nine hundred livres a year. Being on a journey to Senlis, he became enamoured with the daughter of the President of Elections, and, without the knowledge of her friends, married her. The father of the young woman instituted a process against Desmarets for seducing and carrying off his daughter ; in consequence of which, by a sentence du Châtelet, he was condemned to death. Desmarets fled into Spain, and from thence to Lorrain ; but, at length succeeding in his solicitations to the parliament for a pardon, he returned to Paris, and became a composer to the opera. When he was a young man he composed those motets which go under the name of Coupillet ;† but the most celebrated of his works are his operas of Didon and Iphigénie in Tauride, represented at Paris in the year 1704, with some alterations of Campra. Desmarets died at Luneville in the year 1741.

CHARLES-HUBERT GERVAIS was intendant of the band of the regent duke of Orleans, and afterwards master of the chapel royal. He died at Paris in the year 1744, aged seventy-two. He composed three operas, namely Meduse, represented in 1702 ; Hypermnestre, in 1716 ; and Les Amours de Protée, in 1720. These, with sundry Motets, and a collection of Cantatas of his composition, are in print.

ANDRE-CARDINAL DESTOUCHES was born at Paris in the year 1672. He accompanied Father Tachard, a Jesuit, in a voyage to Siam, with an intention to enter himself of that society on his return. On his arrival however at Paris, he changed his mind, and betook himself to the profession of a soldier ; but, being passionately fond of music, he quitted the military profession, and became an eminent composer of operas. His first essay of this kind was the opera of Issé, represented at Paris in 1708, with which the king was so pleased, that he gave him a purse of two hundred Louis d'Ors, adding that he meant by

---

* Carols or Songs celebrating the nativity of our Saviour.
† Vide ante, page 836.

that present only to attach him to his service; for that, excepting the operas of Lully, he had never heard any that delighted him so much as this of Issé. It is said with great confidence that at the time he composed this opera, Destouches had not the least knowledge of the rules of composition, but that nevertheless a happy coincidence of words and expression rendered the recitative part of it peculiarly excellent.* To encourage him in his new profession, the king made him superintendent of his band, and inspector-general of the Royal Academy; upon which Destouches set himself to study the rules of his art, but it was observed that the restrictions which these laid him under, served but to check the flights of his genius, and had a bad effect upon his future compositions, which were the operas, or, as the French call them, the tragedies of Amadis de Grece, Marthesie, Omphale, Télémaque, and Sémiramis, and sundry Ballets, all which were represented in the Royal Academy, but with far less applause than was bestowed on his first production, the opera of Issé. Destouches died in the year 1749 in the employments above-mentioned, having for many years been favoured by the royal bounty with a pension of four thousand livres per annum.

Louis-Nicolas Clerambault was a native of Paris, and, being a favourite of Louis XIV., was by him appointed director of the private concerts of Madam de Maintenon, and organist of St. Cyr. There are extant of his composition five books of Cantatas, in which there is one entitled Orphée, that is greatly admired; and there are also attributed to him sundry Motets, and other vocal compositions for particular festivals, that shew him to have been a man of considerable abilities in his profession. He died at Paris in the year 1749.

Joseph-Nicolas-Pancrace Royer, a native of Savoy, came to reside at Paris about the year 1725, and there acquired much reputation for his manner of singing, and his excellent performance on the organ and harpsichord. Being a well-bred man, and of an amiable character, he formed such connections as led him into the way of preferment at court. By the interest of his friends there, and his own merit, he obtained a reversionary grant of the place of music-master to the royal family of France, and came into the possession of it in the year 1746. In the following year he was appointed director of the Concert Spirituel. In 1754 he was appointed composer of the music for the king's chamber, and inspector-general of the opera. He lived not long to enjoy these lucrative employments, for he died on the eleventh of January, 1755, in the fiftieth year of his age. Royer composed the following operas, viz., Pyrrhus, Zaïde, Le Pouvoir de l'Amour, Amalsis, and Prométhée, and many lessons for the harpsichord, of which only one collection has as yet been published.

Francois-Colin de Blamont was born at Versailles in the year 1690, and, for his merit in his profession, was made a chevalier of the order of St. Michael. He was a composer for the opera, and enjoyed the places of superintendent of the king's music, and master of that of his chamber. The operas composed by him are Didon, and Les Fêtes Grecques et Romaines. He died in the year 1760.

Jean-Marie Le Clair was born at Lyons in 1697. His father was a musician, and with his instructions, and the assistance of able masters, he became a fine performer on the violin. He travelled abroad some years for improvement, and seemed disposed to settle in Holland; but, upon an invitation from the duke de Grammont, who had been his pupil, he went to Paris, and was favoured by him with a handsome pension. By the recommendation of this nobleman, and his own masterly performance, Le Clair attained to the place of symphonist to Louis XV. in which he laboured incessantly to improve the practice of the violin among his countrymen. With this view he composed and published in the year 1723, a collection of Solos for the violin; and soon after that another of the same kind, in both which the author has displayed a perfect knowledge of the instrument, and the powers of a rich and well-regulated fancy.

The character and demeanour of Le Clair were such as attracted the esteem of all that knew him; and, as he affected a retired and contemplative life, he had little reason to fear the shafts of envy: nevertheless it seems that he fell a sacrifice to his own fame, for, without having given offence to any one, being abroad in the streets of Paris, in the evening of the twenty-second day of October, 1764, and returning to his own home, he was assassinated. Besides the two collections of Solos above-mentioned, Le Clair was the author of Six Sonatas for two Violins and a bass, Oeuvre IV. which have this singular circumstance to distinguish them, that in the title-page they are said to be engraved by his wife, 'Gravée par Madam son Epouse.'† Le Clair is celebrated for the spirit and energy of his manual performance, and these compositions are in some sort a proof of it. At least it may be said, that, for grandeur and dignity of style, there are no instrumental compositions of the French musicians, not even of Lully himself, that merit to be compared with them. It is true that they are difficult to be executed, and this for some time was a general objection to the compositions of Le Clair; but the French musicians, like those of other countries, have improved on the violin, and this difficulty has long since vanished. The other works of Le Clair in print are two books of Duos, two of Trios, two of Concertos, two under the title of Récréations, and the opera of Sylla and Glaucus.

Jean-Philippe Rameau was born at Dijon on the twenty-fifth of September, 1683. After having learned the rudiments of music, his taste for the art led him while young to leave his native country, and wander about with the performers of a strolling opera. At the age of eighteen he composed a

---

* This is a most unaccountable relation; all that can be said in defence of it is, that it is taken from the Nouveau Dictionnaire Historique, originally written by Mons. l'Advocat, and improved on by a set of men who had opportunities of the best information.

† He is in the title-page styled Mons. Le Clair l'aîné, from which adjunct it is conjectured that he was the elder of two brothers of the same profession.

musical entertainment, which was represented at Avignon, and was received with as much applause as can be thought due to so puerile an essay : but as this applause was less than the author hoped for, he removed from thence, and, after travelling through a part of Italy and France, corrected his ideas of music by the practice of the harpsichord; on which instrument, by incessant application, he attained a degree of proficiency little inferior to that which distinguished the famous Marchand. In the course of his travels he stopped at Dijon, and performed on the organ of the Holy Chapel; he did the same at Clermont, and played on the organ of that cathedral; in both places to large audiences, composed of the members of the church, and other good judges of music. The reputation which he by these means acquired, brought Marchand to hear him, who upon that occasion is said to have made use of this expression, ' Rameau a plus de main que moi, mais ' j'ai plus de tête que lui.' Upon hearing this, Rameau, with a view to satisfy himself touching the merits of Marchand's pretensions, went to Paris, where he had no sooner heard him than he became sensible of his own inferiority, and with great candour and modesty professed himself an humble hearer of Marchand, expressing at the same time an ardent desire to become his pupil. Marchand generously condescended to his request, and laboured to the utmost of his power in the improvement of a genius so capable of cultivation. Rameau, by a course of severe study, had in a great measure united the perfections of Marchand with his own; and upon the strength of these he became a candidate for the place of organist of the church of St. Paul in Paris; but failing to obtain it, he had almost determined to decline that branch of his profession, but was prevented by the offer of the place of organist of the cathedral church of Clermont in Auvergne, which he accepted. In this retirement he studied with the utmost assiduity the theory of his art. His investigations in the course of this pursuit gave birth to his ' Traité de l'Harmonie,' printed at Paris in 1722; and to his ' Nouveau ' Systeme de Musique Theorique,' printed at the same place in 1726. But the work for which Rameau is most celebrated is his ' Démonstration du Principe ' de l'Harmonie,' Paris 1750, in which, as his countrymen say, he has shewn that the whole depends upon one single and clear principle, viz., the fundamental bass : and in this respect he is by them compared to Newton, who by the single principle of gravitation was able to assign reasons for some of the most remarkable phenomena in physics; for this reason they scruple not to style Rameau the Newton of Harmony.

With such extraordinary talents as these, and a style in musical composition far surpassing, in the opinion of some, that of the greatest among the French musicians, it had been a national reproach had Rameau been suffered to remain organist of a country cathedral. He was called to Paris, and appointed to the management of the opera; in which employment it was his care to procure the ablest performers of all kinds that could be found, and to furnish from the inexhaustible stores of his own invention, compositions worthy of so great a genius. His music was of an original cast, and the performers complained at first that it could not be executed; but he asserted the contrary, and evinced it by experiment. By practice he acquired a great facility in composing, so that he was never at a loss to adapt sounds to sentiments. It was a saying of Quinault, ' that the poet was the musician's servant;' but Rameau would say, ' Qu'on me donne la Gazette ' d'Hollande et je la mettrai en musique.' The king, to reward his extraordinary merit, conferred upon him the ribbon of the order of St. Michael; and a little before his death raised him to the rank of the noblesse. Rameau was a man of pure morals, and lived happily with a wife whom he tenderly loved : there was much simplicity in his character; and his temper, though not so philosophic as to render him altogether inirascible, was upon the whole mild and placid, and in the offices of friendship and humanity no man went beyond him.

This philosophical artist died at Paris on the twelfth day of September, in the year 1764. His exequies were celebrated by a musical solemnity in the church of the Oratory in the street of St. Honoré, the place of his sepulture, in which several extracts from his own compositions were introduced. Besides the tracts above-mentioned, there are extant of Rameau's writing the following : ' Generation Har- ' monique,' Paris, 1737 ; and ' Nouvelles Reflexions ' sur la Démonstration,' &c. His musical compositions consist of sundry collections of lessons for the harpsichord, and his operas, the names whereof are as follow : Hyppolite et Aricie, les Indes Galantes, Castor et Pollux, les Fêtes d'Hébé, Dardanus, Platée, les Fêtes de Polhimnie, le Temple de la Gloire, les Fêtes de l'Himen, Zaïs, Pigmalion, Naïs, Zoroastre, la Guirlande, Acante et Céphise, Daphnis et Eglé, Lisis et Délie, les Sybarites, la Naissance d'Osiris, Anacréon, les Surprises de l'Amour, and les Paladins.

As a theorist, the character of Rameau stands very high ; and as a testimony to his merit in this particular, it is here mentioned as a fact, that Mr. Handel was ever used to speak of him in terms of great respect. As a musical composer his character remains to be settled ; while one set of men celebrate his works for the grace and spirit of them, others object to them that they are either stiff and laboured, or light and trifling even to puerility. Should the latter be the true characteristic of them, it would be no wonder, since a fine style of composition is by no means the necessary consequence of profound skill in the principles of harmony. The poetic faculty does not keep pace with our improvements in the niceties of grammar or the laws of prosody ; and the compositions of those deep theorists, Zarlino and Pepusch, do not rise above mediocrity. As to the French music in general, the merit of it has at different periods been a subject of controversy ; many think that in the art of musical composition the French are an age behind the rest of Europe : and many more are of opinion that, having deviated from the path of nature, they may be two before they find their way back again.

Besides the above persons who were practical musicians, there were many among the French who are distinguished for general skill in the principles of the science ; Pere Antoine Parran, a Jesuit, who flourished about the middle of the last century, is reckoned one of their best writers on the subject of music at large. He published at Paris, in the year 1646, ' Traité de la Musique Theorique et Practique, ' contenant les Preceptes de la Composition.' Some years after Claude Perrault, the architect, and for his great skill therein called the French Vitruvius, published a ' Dissertation de la Musique des ' Anciens,' wherein he denies that the ancients were acquainted with music in consonance. In later times the Abbé Raguenet distinguished himself by his Parallel between the French and Italian Music, and Mons. de la Viéville de Freneuse by his answer to it. Of both these tracts an account has already been given : the latter of these persons is also known by the name of Jean-Laurent le Cerf; he was keeper of the seals of the parliament of Normandy, and died in 1707. There are several dissertations of his writing in the Journals de Trevoux. The Abbé Chateauneuf in 1725 published a ' Dialogue sur la ' Musique des Anciens ;' others there are who have obliged the world by occasional discourses and dissertations on the subject of music in the Memoirs of the Academy of Inscriptions, printed at the Hague in duodecimo, with the title of ' Memoires de Litera- ' ture tirés des Régistres de l'Académie Royal des ' Inscriptions et Belles-Lettres.' The papers respecting music in this collection most worthy of notice, are those that tend to obviate a doubt that had been raised of the genuineness of Plutarch's Dialogue on Music ; and to settle a question the most embarrassing of all that have arisen on the subject of music, that is to say, whether the ancients were acquainted with, or ignorant of, the practice of music in consonance, polyphonous music, simultaneous harmony, or whatever else is to be understood by the term, music in parts.

The controversy touching Plutarch's Dialogue, as it arose from an inconsiderate remark of Amyot the French translator of his works, made above a hundred years ago, and which no one till of late had thought worthy of a refutation, was terminated by Mons. Jean-Pierre Burette, a physician of Paris, and member of the Academy of Inscriptions, in favour of the piece in question ; but those who disputed its authority, founding their objections upon the circumstance that the mention of music in consonance does not once occur in it, the determination of the question, as to the authenticity of the book, had no other effect than to bring on another of a greater latitude. They who contended that the dialogue was spurious, assumed that the ancients were acquainted with music in consonance ; and it was necessary for them to get rid of a book which was negative evidence of the contrary ; but the authority of it being once

established, their adversaries made good use of their advantage, and insisted that the silence of such an author as Plutarch as to any such practice, was a very strong argument in favour of the contrary opinion.

It is not necessary here to repeat what was urged in the course of this dispute, or to recapitulate those arguments respecting the question itself which are stated in an earlier part of this work. It may suffice to say, that Mons. Fraguier, a member of the academy, was the champion of the ancients, and Mons. Burette of the moderns, and that the latter in his ' Dissertation sur la Symphonie des Anciens,' published in the Memoirs abovementioned, tom. V. page 151, gained a complete victory.*

Two other French writers, namely, the fathers Bougeant and Cerceau, have in the principal question taken the side of Burette, as appears by the papers of theirs published in the Journals de Trevoux for April and Oct. 1725, and Jan. and Feb. 1729. In a word this question, to use a phrase of Chaucer, has been ' bolted to the bran ;' and there is very little probability remaining that any argument in favour of the affirmative can in future be adduced that has not been refuted.

CHAP. CXCVI.

The termination of the dispute between Handel and his adversaries, as it left him in the quiet possession of that empire, in which it seems to have been his fixed resolution never to admit a rival, though it totally extinguished emulation, was in general favourable to music. Covent-Garden theatre was an excellent seminary ; and by the performance of the oratorio there, the practice of music was greatly improved throughout the kingdom. As to its precepts, the general opinion was that they needed no farther cultivation : Dr. Pepusch had prescribed to the students in harmony a set of rules, which no one was hardy enough to transgress ; the consequence thereof was a disgusting uniformity of style in the musical productions of the time ; while these were adhered to, fancy laboured under the severest restrictions, and all improvement in the science of composition was at a stand.

That we are at this time in a state of emancipation from the bondage of laws imposed without authority, is owing to a new investigation of the principles of harmony, and the studies of a class of musicians, of whom Geminiani seems to have been the chief ; and this consideration makes it necessary to resume the account of him, and to relate, among other particulars, the efforts made by him towards the improvement of the science of harmony.

It is observable upon the works of Geminiani, that his modulations are not only original, but that

---

* Burette seems to have been less sensible of the force of his own reasoning, than many of his readers ; for after he had refuted his adversary, he was provoked to resume the controversy, and made some few concessions, that tended to weaken his former arguments ; particularly, that besides the unison and octave, the ancients made use of the third in consonance ; the latter of which facts has never yet been proved. On the contrary, it is strongly insisted that they never used either the third or sixth, no such practice being mentioned, or even hinted at, in any of the old Greek writers.

his harmonies consist of such combinations as were never introduced into music till his time : the rules of transition from one key to another, which are laid down by those who have written on the composition of music, he not only disregarded, but objected to as an unnecessary restraint on the powers of invention. He has been frequently heard to say, that the cadences in the fifth, the third, and the sixth of the key which occur in the works of Corelli, were rendered too familiar to the ear by the frequent repetition of them : and it seems to have been the study of his life, by a liberal use of the semitonic intervals, to increase the number of harmonic combinations ; and into melody to introduce a greater variety than it was otherwise capable of.

In a full persuasion of the advantages that must result to music from the study of variety, he compiled an harmonical code, consisting of a great number of passages composed by himself, connected with and referring to others in a series almost infinite ; and published proposals for printing it, with the title of Guida Armonica, but it was not till several years after that it appeared in the world.

In the year 1739 he published his Opera quarta, consisting of twelve Sonatas for a violin and a bass ; and also a new edition of his Opera prima, with considerable additions and improvements ; and soon after, what he called ‘A Treatise on good Taste ;’ and also ‘Rules for playing in Taste ;’ a cant phrase much in use with the musical connoisseurs. These two publications contained, besides examples of such graces as himself was used to practice on the violin, variations on some well-known airs, such as that of Purcell in the opera of Dioclesian, ‘What shall I do ‘to shew how much I love her,’ and some select Scots tunes.

About this time he also published the ‘Art of ‘playing on the Violin,’ containing the most minute directions for holding the instrument, and for the use of the bow, the graces, the various shifts of the hand,* and a great variety of examples adapted to the rules.

About the year 1740 he published and dedicated to the Academy of ancient Music his Opera settima, consisting of six Concertos for violins. This work carries with it the evidence of great labour and study, but it is greatly inferior to his former works of the like kind.

In the month of April, 1742, came forth his long expected work, with the title of ‘Guida Armonica ‘o Dizionario Armonico,’ with a preface, wherein, after giving due commendation to Lully, Corelli, and Bononcini, as having been the first improvers of instrumental music, he endeavours to obviate an opinion that the vast foundations of universal harmony can be established upon the narrow and confined modulation of those authors, and remarks on the uniformity of modulation, apparent in the com-

positions that have appeared in different parts of Europe for forty years back.

The publication of this book was attended with circumstances that seemed but little to favour its reception ; some suspected that the author's chief view in the publication of it was the getting money to supply his necessities ; many had been made to believe that the author professed by it no less than to teach the art of musical composition to persons totally ignorant of the science, and of consequence ridiculed the attempt ; and there were very few that were able to comprehend either the motives to, or the tendency of, the work.

In one of those excursions which Geminiani was frequently making during his residence in England, that is to say, to Italy, France, Holland, and other countries, he visited at Paris a learned and ingenious Jesuit, Pere Castel, a man well skilled in music ; † to whom he shewed his manuscript, and explained the nature and design of it : and with a view to obviate the prejudices that had been entertained against it, this person published in the Journal des Sçavans a dissertation on the Guida Armonica, which Geminiani upon his return hither got translated into English, and published in a pamphlet of about thirty pages.

The author of this dissertation says, that, upon a careful examination of the Guida Armonica, he found that any person able to read and write might by the help thereof become able to compose true, good, and well-modulated music, with proper figures to denote the accompaniment ; and that the execution of this contrivance was as simple and infallible as the plan of it was wonderful ; and that it is in reality a set of musical integers ready to be connected into a body.

The facility of this practice appearing at first suspicious, Pere Castel says he took the liberty of opposing it to the author as an objection to his scheme, comparing it to the German organ, which being turned by the most unskilful person, will nevertheless make excellent music. He also compared it in his own mind with an invention of Johannes Trithemius, abbat of Spanheim, who flourished about the year 1490, and wrote a treatise entitled Steganographia, the third book whereof professes to teach a man ignorant of letters, only knowing his mother-

---

* There is reason to suppose that the practice of shifting on the violin was greatly improved by Geminiani ; Baltzar the Lubecker introduced it into England in the time of Charles I. ; but with him, and subsequent performers, it answered no other purpose than extending the compass of the instrument to D : the half shift, contrived to avoid the disgusting clangor of an open string, and enable the performer to shake with the third instead of the little finger, is but of late invention.

† Louis-Bertrand Castel was born at Montpelier in 1688, and entered into the society of the Jesuits in 1703. About the end of the year 1720 he removed from Thoulouse to Paris, where he became known to the world by his treatise on Gravitation, published in two volumes in duodecimo in 1727. According to his hypothesis, all things depend upon two principles, the gravity of bodies and the action of spirits ; by means of the former all things tend to rest, while motion proceeds from the latter principle. This system was attacked by the Abbé de St. Pierre, and the dispute was carried on between them for some time with a considerable degree of vivacity. His second work was a concise system of universal mathematics, in one volume quarto, which met with general applause, and procured him an admission into the Royal Society at London. In the course of his pursuits he had discovered a certain analogy between the laws of colours and sound. Upon this principle he proceeded to construct an instrument called by him the Clavecin Oculaire, which by a proper mixture and just succession of the different colours, should be the means of exciting in the mind of the spectator a pleasure similar to that derived from harmony. This attempt, visionary as it was, produced some useful discoveries. The other writings of Castel are of little importance, and are chiefly contained in the Memoires de Trevoux. His style is lively and full of affected refinements, but desultory and incorrect. He died in the year 1757, aged sixty-three.

tongue, in the space of two hours to read, and understand Latin, and write it ornately and eloquently.* But Castel says he thinks that in neither instance the comparison will hold; and finally recommends the Guida Armonica to the students in music in the following terms:

' Mr. Geminiani's book is then a useful work, and ' that even to the masters themselves, since it contains ' all the musical passages, whether regular, or of the ' class of licences and exceptions, that may be, or ' have already been employed by the greatest masters, ' with guides and references that serve to link them ' together in all the various manners in which they ' can be connected. In a word, it is a musical ma-' nual, a library, a repertory; a kind of dictionary, ' though not an alphabetical one, in which is always ' to be found a musical phrase or periphrasis fit to ' be adapted, even with elegance and variety, to any ' other already formed. By it we are enabled to ' determine whether a phrase, a passage, a succession ' of harmony, a certain progression of modulation, ' which the composer is desirous of taking, be regular ' and allowable or not; whether it has its proper ' arithmetical figures, or is preceded by, and followed ' with, proper consonances; in short, what are the ' most eligible and elegant modes of passage from ' one series or compages of sounds to another, and of

' returning again to those from which the deviation ' was made.'

Castel's dissertation is throughout, an eulogium on the Guida Armonica; he was well skilled in music, but by no means a competent judge of musical composition. Such as had made it their study, were unanimously of opinion that it contains very little that was not known before, and is besides so very obscure as to be of small use to any one. The publication of the Guida Armonica was followed by that of a supplement, with examples showing its use.[†]

Of his performance it is very difficult to convey an idea, there being no master of the violin at this day living with whom he can with any propriety be compared, Jackson excepted, who possesses many of his excellencies, but never came near him in point of tone. It must therefore suffice to say that he had none of the fire and spirit of the modern violinists, but that all the graces and elegancies of melody, all the powers that can engage attention, or that render the passions of the hearer subservient to the will of the artist, were united in his performance. The following solo of Corelli, written as Geminiani used to play it, and copied from a manuscript in his own hand-writing, is here inserted as the best specimen that can be given of the style and manner of his execution.

Preludio. Largo.

CORELLI & GEMINIANI.

CHAP. CXCVII.

THE old musicians who were living at the time when Geminiani published his Guida Armonica, stood aghast at the licences which it allowed, and predicted little less from the work than the utter ruin of the musical science. Not choosing to deviate from the good and wholesome rules which they had been taught in choirs, and had extracted from the compositions of those who were looked on as the classics in harmony, they shook their heads, and hung their harps upon the willows. Pepusch had little at heart but the welfare of his favourite academy, and the investigation of the ancient Rythmus ; and for this and the like studies a favourable opportunity had presented itself in the year 1737, by a vacancy in the place of organist of the Charter-house, occasioned by the death of Mr. Thomas Love. The duchess of Leeds had been his scholar, and at her recommendation he was elected. To apartments assigned him in this venerable mansion, the Doctor, together with his wife, retired. In the year 1739 the place of Gresham professor of music becoming vacant, he solicited to succeed to it ; but finding that his being a married man was a disqualification, he forbore offering himself as a candidate, and one Mr. Thomas Brome was elected.*

About the year 1740 the Doctor's wife died, and he having before lost his son, an only child, had scarce any source of delight left, other than the prosecution of his studies, and the teaching a few favourite pupils, who attended him at his apartments. Here he drew up that account of the ancient genera which was read before the Royal Society, and is published in the Philosophical Transactions for the months of October, November, and December, in the year 1746, the substance whereof is given in an earlier part of this work ; and soon after the publication thereof he was elected a fellow of the Royal Society. During his residence in the Charterhouse, notwithstanding his advanced age, he prosecuted his studies with unwearied application : his evening amusements were the game of chess, and the conversation of a few select friends, of whom Mr. John Immyns, the lutenist, mentioned in a preceding page ; Mr. Travers, one of the organists of the royal chapel, and also organist of St. Paul, Covent-Garden ; and Mr. Ephraim Kelner, of the band at Drury-lane theatre, were the most intimate. To the latter two of these persons the Doctor had some obligations ; and shortly before his death he made a disposition which entitled them to his effects, and particularly his valuable library, whenever it

* The right of electing the Gresham music professor is in the mayor and commonalty and citizens of London, and it is curious to reflect on their conduct in the execution of this trust. The first professor, Dr. Bull, was a man eminent in his faculty, but, out of thirteen persons his successors, only two had the least pretence to skill in the science. Dr. Robert Shippen, principal of Brazen-nose college, and rector of Whitechapel, was professor for some time, till he resigned in favour of his brother Edward, a physician, who was elected in his room ; and both the brothers made no secret of declaring that they understood not a note of music. Concerning the election of Dr. Robert Shippen there goes the following story. His competitor it seems was a person every way qualified for the place : it happened some time after his disappointment that the place of astronomy professor became vacant, and the electors conscious of the injury they had done him in rejecting his application for the music professorship, determined to repair it, and accordingly made him an offer of the astronomy lecture : but he assigned his reasons for declining it in a bitter sarcasm : ' Gentlemen,' says he, ' I am much obliged ' to you for your offer, but I cannot consistent either with my conscience ' or my reputation accept it, for I understand astronomy as little as ' Dr. Shippen does music.' The other persons whose names appear in the list of professors, were men who had received an academical education, and might be supposed able to compose a lecture on music fit to be heard ; but those who have of late years been elected to the office, grounded their pretensions solely on their being freemen of London ; the last professor was a barber, and the predecessor of him an engraver ; hopeful teachers of a liberal science !

should happen. He died in the month of July, in the year 1752, and was buried in the chapel of the Charter-house. By a voluntary subscription of some of his friends, a tablet was erected near the place of his interment, on which is the following memorial of him :—

Near this Place lye the Remains
of
John Christopher Pepusch,
Doctor of Music in the University of Oxford.
He was born at Berlin,
And resided at London, highly esteemed above Fifty Years,
Distinguished as a most learned Master
And Patron of his Profession.
In the Year 1737 he retired to the private Employment
of
Organist to this House,
Where he departed this life,
July 20, 1752, Aged 85.
The Academy of Ancient Music, established in 1710,
Of which he was one of the Original Founders,
And to which he bequeathed a valuable Collection of Music,
In grateful Respect to his Memory
Caused this monument to be erected,
1767.

The history of his library, which contained in it the most valuable treatises on music in various languages that are any where extant, either in manuscript or in print ; as also a noble collection of musical compositions, is attended with some singular circumstances. Immediately upon his decease, in virtue of the disposition which he had previously made of his effects, Travers and Kelner took possession of them, and divided his library into moieties. Travers survived the Doctor but a short time, and his part of it came to the hands of his representative, an old woman ; and after that to a person, who dying, it was sold by auction in July, 1766, and produced a very inconsiderable sum of money. Kelner, who had long assisted the Doctor as his amanuensis, was a man of learning, and a sound musician. He lodged in a house in Martlet-court in Russel-street, Covent-Garden ; having no relations, he gave a man named Cooper, who had been his copyist, and had done him many good offices, reason to hope for a share of the little he should leave at his decease ; but, dying without making any written disposition of his effects, the woman of the house in which they were, laid hands on his instruments, books, and manuscripts, and insisted on keeping them as she had the possession, and there was no legatee or representative to claim them. It was in vain for Cooper to urge the friendly intention of Kelner to him, or, which was the truth, that he had assisted him with money at sundry times, and was therefore a creditor : the right of possession, and the vulgar maxim that it is eleven points of the law, was insisted on, and his claim set at defiance. The man upon this felt his spirit rise, and, taking the advice of a lawyer, applied for and obtained letters of administration as a creditor of the deceased ; commenced a suit in Chancery against the woman, and in a few days time got into his possession the books and manuscripts to the amount of two cart loads ; part of which were disposed of

by private contract ; the rest were sold by auction at Patersons's in Essex-street, on Saturday the twenty-sixth of March, 1763. In this sale were two very curious articles, the one an Antiphonary, which, by a memorandum in an outer leaf of it, appeared to have been found, with almost a cargo of Romish service-books, on board a Spanish man of war, taken at the defeat of the Armada in 1588 ; the other a manuscript very richly bound, that formerly was queen Elizabeth's, most probably written for her own practice, in a fine character, and containing a collection of lessons by Dr. Bull ; the book had been pretty well thumbed by Signora Margarita, who had for many years played out of it, but was otherwise in good preservation.

The manuscript papers of the Doctor, that is to say, his studies for a long course of years, came to the hands of the author of this work, who is sorry to say, that, after a very careful selection and diligent perusal of them, they appear to contain hardly any thing that can tend to the improvement of music, or the gratification of public curiosity. The Doctor for many years before his decease, from a persuasion, which seems to have been uppermost in his mind, that part of the science had been lost,[*] had endeavoured to recover the ancient genera ; and it appears by a passage in his diary abovementioned, that he was upon that pursuit while on his visit to lord Paisley ; but we see the whole of what he was able to effect towards it in his letter on that subject printed in the Philosophical Transactions.[†] Towards the end of his life he had adopted the silly notions of Isaac Vossius respecting the rythmus, and endeavoured to introduce into music somewhat that should correspond with the practice of the ancients ; but in this too he failed, for out of a vast number of essays which appear in his own hand-writing, nothing conclusive or satisfactory is deducible. The same may in a great measure be said of his numerous arithmetical calculations of ratios, of which he appears to have been too fond : had he considered how little Salinas, Mersennus, Kircher, and Dr. Wallis have left unsaid on this part of musical science, he might possibly have turned his thoughts another way.

At the time when Pepusch came to settle in England, he found the practice of music in a very low state ; very few but professors being able to play in concert : with a view to the improvement of it he published twenty-four airs for two violins in all the varieties of measure that music is capable of : these seem to be but an introduction to Corelli's Sonatas, which were then deemed much too hard to be put into the hands of learners.[‡] To assist the students in music he published the Sonatas and Concertos of Corelli in score.

Pepusch was a voluminous composer, as appears

---

* Vide Treatise on Harmony, first edit. page 24.

† *This paper, the doctor not being able to write English, was drawn up by Mr. George Lewis Scott, author of the Supplement to Chambers' Dictionary, in two volumes. He was a Barrister of the Inner Temple, and, being a man of science, assisted in the education of his present Majesty (Geo. III.) ; for which he was rewarded with the post of one of the Commissioners of the Excise. He died about the year 1778.*

‡ In the title-page they are expressly said to be for the improvement of Practitioners in Concert.

by the Catalogue of Roger and Le Cene. Little of his music is printed in England; the Airs above mentioned, twenty-four Solos for a violin and a bass, two collections of Cantatas, and a few songs, are all that we know of. His manuscript compositions to a great number he directed to be given to the Academy of Ancient Music, and they remain in the library of that society. He was a learned, but a dry composer, and was apparently deficient in the powers of invention. His cantata 'See from the silent 'grove,' is the only one of all he ever published that has any pretence to elegance. Of his manuscript compositions we know of only one that rises above mediocrity, viz., 'Rejoice in the Lord, O ye righteous,' a full anthem, and in this all the various excellencies of harmony and melody are united.

The contests, which had long divided the votaries of harmony into factions, had in some measure subsided upon the retreat of Cuzzoni and the departure of Bononcini; but the ill success of the opera after the dissolution of the Royal Academy, and the shipwreck of some fortunes engaged in the support of it, induced the people to turn their eyes towards Mr. Handel, and to look on him as the only person from whom, in the way of musical performance, they were to expect any solid and rational entertainment. Greene was sensible of this; and there being in England no competitor of Mr. Handel to whom he could attach himself, he pursued his own track, and endeavoured as a cathedral musician to exalt his character to the utmost. With this view he published in score forty anthems, in a style of composition that furnishes occasion for some remarks. But first it is to be noted that the original formation of the church style, as applied to the English reformed service, was immediately consequent on the establishment of the first liturgy of Edward VI., and in the compositions of Marbeck, Tallis, Bird, Fairfax, Taverner, Shepherd, Redford, and many others, we have the clearest evidence that the whole of our reformed church musical service was borrowed from that which was in use in the age immediately preceding the above-mentioned establishment. To speak more fully to the purpose, the book of Common Prayer noted, is formed on the model of the Roman ritual; and the services and anthems of the authors above named answer to those motets which then were, and at this day are used in the Romish service. This latter is so precisely the fact, that most of the music to the English anthems which bear the name of Tallis and Bird, will upon comparison be found to have been originally set to Latin words in the form of motets, and composed by them for the service of the chapel of Hen. VIII. and Mary; but upon the final settlement of the liturgy at the beginning of queen Elizabeth's reign, the authors thought they could not do better than to adapt the same music to English words, and accordingly these compositions now bear the form of anthems.

The style of these great men was adopted by Tye, Bull, Morley, Gibbons, and Tomkins, and continued to be the standard of church-music till the Restoration, when the king, who, during his abode in France,

had entertained a liking for the music of that country, signified a desire that that of his chapel might partake of the imaginary excellencies of the French music as much as possible.* The chapel composers, though they had no mind to take the French for their masters, relaxed somewhat of the ancient severity of church composition, and in the anthems of Humphrey, Blow, Purcell, Wise, Weldon, and most others, we find a richer vein of melody than in those of their predecessors, but no such resemblance of the French church-music as the king wished for. Most men were of opinion that by this union of melody and harmony our church-music was carried to its utmost degree of perfection; and consequently that in any future variations, the loss on one hand would be equal to the gain on the other. But Greene, who had carefully attended to all those refinements in melody which the opera had introduced, was of opinion that they led to a farther improvement of our church-music; accordingly he formed a style, neat and elegant it is true, but greatly deficient in that dignity and solemnity which are essential in compositions for the church. And this we may call the third, and at present the last, improved style of cathedral music.

The other works of Greene are single songs to a great number, a few Cantatas, Canons, and Catches, published in separate and detached collections; Overtures to his dramatic pastorals, mentioned in a preceding page, and to other of his compositions; the Amoretti of Spenser, that is to say, certain Sonnets selected from the work so called, and a collection of lessons for the harpsichord.

Greene was a man of understanding, and in the exercise of his profession was careful to form connections of the best kind. By his personal civilities to Mrs. Anastasia Robinson, he so recommended himself to her, that when she became countess of Peterborough she procured for him the places of organist and composer to the royal chapel in the room of Dr. Croft.

His wife was a young woman of the name of Dillingham; she, together with her sister, who was married to the Rev. Mr. George Carleton, subdean of the royal chapel,† kept a milliner's shop in Paternoster-row, and had about five hundred pounds when Greene married her. He had but little besides to begin the world with, nevertheless, by industry and œconomy he was enabled to bring up a family of children, and make considerable savings. His uncle, Serjeant Greene, was a single man, and left a natural son of the name of John, who was bred to the bar, and was for some years steward of the manor of Hackney; the Serjeant had by his will devised to him an estate in Essex of about seven hundred pounds a year, called Bois-Hall. This person died about the year 1750, having left by his will to Dr. Greene the whole of his estate.

* Charles II. was but little acquainted with the English church-music, and it is probable that upon his return to England he might conceive a dislike of it. Lock set the music for his public entry, and Capt. Cooke that for his coronation, as Sir Richard Baker asserts : the latter was but a dry composer.

† These two sisters were cousins of the wife of Mr. Charles King, almoner of St. Paul's, and she was a sister of Jerry Clark.

In the state of affluence to which Dr. Greene was raised by this event, he meditated on the corruptions of our church-music, occasioned by the multiplication of copies, and the ignorance and carelessness of transcribers; and resolved to correct, and also secure it against such injuries for the future; accordingly he began with collating a great number of copies of services and anthems, and reducing them into score. By the year 1755, he had made a considerable progress in the work; but his health failing him, he made his will, and remitted the farther prosecution of it to one that had been his disciple, his friend Dr. William Boyce, who, in a manner worthy of himself, completed the work, and thereby gave to the public a collection that has not its fellow in the world. Dr. Greene died on the first day of September, 1755, leaving behind him only one child, a daughter, married to the Rev. Dr. Michael Festing, rector of Wyke Regis, in the county of Dorset, and a son of Mr. Michael Christian Festing, an eminent composer for the violin, and performer on that instrument, mentioned in a preceding chapter of this work.

JOHN TRAVERS received his education in music in the chapel of St. George at Windsor; and, being a favourite boy of Dr. Henry Godolphin, dean of St. Paul's and provost of Eton college, was by him put apprentice to Greene; and about the year 1725 became organist of St. Paul's church, Covent-Garden, and after that of Fulham. Upon the decease of Jonathan Martin in 1737, Travers was appointed organist of the royal chapel; soon after which, upon some disgust, he quitted his place at Fulham. Travers was a sound musician; he commenced an early acquaintance with Dr. Pepusch, and received some assistance from him in the course of his studies, which by a sedulous application he was very careful to improve. In the chapel books are sundry anthems of his composition; but as a composer he is best known to the world by eighteen Canzonets, being verses and songs chiefly taken from the posthumous works of Prior, which he set for two and three voices, in a style as elegant as it is original. Besides these he published the whole book of Psalms for one, two, three, four, and five voices, with a thorough-bass for the harpsichord. He died in the year 1758, and as organist of the royal chapel was succeeded by Dr. William Boyce.

We are now arrived at that which may be considered as the last period of Mr. Handel's life, commencing at that happy conjunction of events, which left him without a competitor, and disposed the public to receive with the utmost approbation whatever he should in future produce for their entertainment.

The oratorio of Sampson, performed in 1743, was followed in the succeeding year by Semele, written by Mr. Congreve, which, though not a sacred composition, but an opera founded on a poetical fiction, was suffered to be performed in that season, during which theatrical representations are forbidden. He had now given a permanent direction to his studies, and composed in succession the entertainments of Susanna, Belshazzar, Hercules, the Occasional Ora-

torio, Judas Maccabæus, Joseph, Alexander Balus, Joshua, Solomon, Theodora,* the Choice of Hercules, Jephtha, and an entertainment called the Triumph of Time and Truth,† most of which were received with general applause. In these he took an ample scope for the exercise of that which was his greatest talent, the sublime in music, and this he displayed to the astonishment of every one in the chorusses to these entertainments.

In the beginning of the year 1751 he was alarmed by a disorder in his eyes, which, upon consulting with *Mr. Samuel Sharp, Surgeon of Guy's Hospital,* he was told was an incipient Gutta serena. From the moment this opinion of his case was communicated to him, his spirits forsook him; and that fortitude which had supported him under afflictions of another kind, deserted him *upon being told* that a freedom from pain in the visual organs was all that he had to hope, for the remainder of his days. In this forlorn state, reflecting on his inability to conduct his entertainments, he called to his aid Mr. Smith, a son of him who had for many years been his copyist and faithful friend; and with this assistance oratorios continued to be performed even to that Lent season in which he died, and this with no other abatement in his own performance than the accompaniment by the harpsichord; the rich vein of his fancy ever supplying him with subjects for extempore voluntaries on the organ, and his hand retaining the power of executing whatever his invention suggested.

The loss of his sight, and the prospect of his approaching dissolution, wrought a great change in his temper and general behaviour. He was a man of blameless morals, and throughout his life manifested a deep sense of religion. In conversation he would frequently declare the pleasure he felt in setting the Scriptures to music; and how much the contemplating the many sublime passages in the Psalms had contributed to his edification; and now that he found himself near his end, these sentiments were improved into solid and rational piety, attended with a calm and even temper of mind. For the last two or three years of his life he was used to attend divine service in his own parish church of St. George, Hanover-square, where, during the prayers, the eyes that at this instant are employed in a faint portrait of his excellencies, have seen him on his knees, expressing by his looks and gesticulations the utmost fervour of devotion.

Towards the beginning of the year 1758 he began to find himself decline apace; and that general debility which was coming on him was rendered still more alarming by a total loss of appetite. When that symptom appeared he considered his recovery as hopeless, and resigning himself to his fate, expired on the fourteenth day of April, 1759. He was buried in Westminster-abbey, the dean, Dr. Pearce, bishop of Rochester, assisted by the choir, performing the funeral solemnity. Over the place of his interment is a monument, designed and

---

* Founded on the story of the martyrdom of Theodora and Didymus, related by Mr. Boyle in a little book with that title.

† Mostly taken from Il Trionfo del Tempo, composed by Handel at Rome, and there performed.

executed by Roubiliac, representing him at full length, in an erect posture, with a music paper in his hand, inscribed ' I know that my Redeemer liveth,' with the notes to which those words are set in his Messiah. He died worth about twenty thousand pounds, almost the whole whereof he bequeathed to his relations abroad.

Such as were but little acquainted with Handel are unable to characterize him otherwise than by his excellencies in his art, and certain foibles in his behaviour, which he was never studious to conceal : accordingly we are told that he had a great appetite, and that when he was provoked he would break out into profane expressions. These are facts that cannot be denied ; but there are sundry particulars that tend to mark his character but little known, and which may possibly be remembered, when those that serve only to shew that he was subject to human passions are forgotten. In his religion he was of the Lutheran profession ; in which he was not such a bigot as to decline a general conformity with that of the country which he had chosen for his residence, at the same time that he entertained very serious notions touching its importance. These he would frequently express in his remarks on the constitution of the English government ; and he would often speak of it as one of the great felicities of his life that he was settled in a country where no man suffers any molestation or inconvenience on account of his religious principles.

His attainments in literature cannot be supposed to have been very great, seeing that the studies of his profession absorbed him ; and the prodigious number of his compositions will account for a much greater portion of time than any man could well be supposed able to spare from sleep and the necessary recruits of nature ; and yet he was well acquainted with the Latin and Italian languages ; the latter he had rendered so familiar to him, that few natives seemed to understand it better. Of the English also he had such a degree of knowledge, as to be susceptible of the beauties of our best poets ; so that in the multiplicity of his compositions to English words, he very seldom stood in need of assistance in the explanation of a passage for the purpose of suiting the sense with correspondent sounds. The style of his discourse was very singular ; he pronounced the English as the Germans do, but his phrase was exotic, and partook of the idiom of the different countries in which he had resided, a circumstance that rendered his conversation exceedingly entertaining.*

* Among other particulars in his character, that rendered his conversation very pleasing, one was a talent that enabled him to tell a story with all the circumstances that tend to enliven it. Being one Sunday at court, he was seen engaged with the late Dr. Thomas, bishop of Lincoln : their discourse was in the German language ; and as soon as it was over, and they were parted, a friend of Mr. Handel went up to him, and remarked on the facility with which the bishop spoke high Dutch ; upon which Mr. Handel answered, that, having been chaplain to the English factory at Hamburg, he had made himself master of it ; and that therefore whenever the king went to visit his German dominions, he chose that Dr. Thomas should attend him thither ; and this, says Mr. Handel, brings to my mind a pleasant story, which I will now tell you, and accordingly he related it to this effect. In one of the king's visits to Hanover, the Doctor walking upon deck, a squall of wind blew his hat overboard ; this loss made some diversion among the sailors, and the rumour of it coming to the king's ears, he, the next time they met,

The course of his life was regular and uniform. For some years after his arrival in England his time was divided between study and practice, that is to say, in composing for the opera, and in conducting concerts at the duke of Rutland's, the earl of Burlington's, and the houses of others of the nobility who were patrons of music, and his friends. There were also frequent concerts for the royal family at the queen's library in the Green-Park, in which the princess royal, the duke of Rutland, lord Cowper, and other persons of distinction performed ; of these Handel had the direction.† As these connections dissolved, he gradually retreated into a state of privacy and retirement, and showed no solicitude to form new ones. His dwelling was on the south side of Brooke-street, near Hanover-square, in a house now in the occupation of Sir James Wright, four doors from Bond-street, and two from the passage to the stable-yard. His stated income was six hundred pounds a year, arising from pensions ; that is to say, one of two hundred pounds, granted him by queen Anne, another of two hundred pounds granted by Geo. I., and another of the same amount, for teaching the princesses. The rest was precarious ; for some time it depended upon his engagements with the directors of the Academy, and afterwards upon the profits arising from the musical performances carried on by him on his own account. However, he had at all times the prudence to regulate his expence by his income. At the time of his contest with the nobility he had ten thousand pounds in the funds, and of this he sold out the last shilling, and lived upon his pensions, which, by an interest that he had with the minister, were punctually paid him.‡ Some years after, when he found himself in a state of affluence, and the produce of his oratorios amounted to more than two thousand pounds a season, he continued his wonted course of living, which was equally distant from the extremes of parsimony and profusion. In the latter part of his life he forbore yielding to a temptation, which few in such circumstances as he was then in would, in these times be able to resist, that of keeping a carriage. Indeed, when his sight failed him, he was necessitated occasionally to hire a chariot and horses, especially in his visits to the city for the purpose of investing his money, which he constantly disposed of at the end of the Lent season, under the direction of Mr. Gael Morris, a broker of the first eminence, whom he used to meet and confer with at Garraway's or Batson's coffee-house.

His social affections were not very strong ; and to this it may be imputed that he spent his whole life in a state of celibacy ; that he had no female

affected to condole him upon it ; upon which the Doctor seemed to make light of the accident, by remarking that it was in his majesty's power to repair the loss of his hat by a covering for the head of another kind. The king conceiving that he meant a mitre, answered him only with a smile ; but soon after his return to England nominated him to the vacant see of *St. Asaph, from whence before consecration he was translated to Lincoln, and after that to Salisbury.*

† It is here to be remarked that the king, the queen, and the princesses were the constant patrons of Handel : at the breaking up of the Royal Academy, they continued to favour him, but the prince of Wales took part with the nobility.

‡ *Sir Edward Walpole told me he assisted him in this particular.*

attachment of another kind may be ascribed to a better reason. His intimate friends were but few; those that seemed to possess most of his confidence were Goupy, the painter, and one Hunter, a scarlet-dyer at Old Ford, near Bow, who pretended a taste for music, and at a great expense had copies made for him of all the music of Handel that he could procure. He had others in the city; but he seemed to think that the honour of his acquaintance was a reward sufficient for the kindness they expressed for him.

A temper and conduct like this, was in every view of it favourable to his pursuits; no impertinent visits, no idle engagements to card parties, or other expedients to kill time, were suffered to interrupt the course of his studies. His invention was for ever teeming with new ideas, and his impatience to be delivered of them kept him closely employed. He had a favourite Rucker harpsichord, the keys whereof, by incessant practice, were hollowed like the bowl of a spoon. He wrote very fast, but with a degree of impatience proportioned to the eagerness that possesses men of genius, of seeing their conceptions reduced into form. And here it may not be impertinent to observe, what every person conversant in his works will be inclined to believe, viz. that his style was original and self-formed; and were evidence of the fact wanting, it is capable of proof by his own testimony, for in a conversation with a very intelligent person now living, on the course of his studies, Mr. Handel declared that, after he became master of the rudiments of his art, he forbore to study the works of others, and ever made it a rule to follow the suggestions of his own fancy.

Like many others of his profession, he had a great love for painting; and, till his sight failed him, among the few amusements he gave into, the going to view collections of pictures upon sale was the chief.

He was in his person a large made and very portly man. His gait, which was ever sauntering, was rather ungraceful, as it had in it somewhat of that rocking motion, which distinguishes those whose legs are bowed. His features were finely marked, and the general cast of his countenance placid, bespeaking dignity attempered with benevolence, and every quality of the heart that has a tendency to beget confidence and insure esteem. Few of the pictures extant of him are to any tolerable degree likenesses, except one painted abroad, from a print whereof the engraving given of him in this work is taken : in the print of him by Houbraken, the features are too prominent; and in the mezzotinto after Hudson there is a harshness of aspect to which his countenance was a stranger; the most perfect resemblance of him is the statue on his monument, and in that the true lineaments of his face are apparent.

As to his performance on the organ, the powers of speech are so limited, that it is almost a vain attempt to describe it otherwise than by its effects. A fine and delicate touch, a volant finger, and a ready delivery of passages the most difficult, are the praise of inferior artists : they were not noticed in Handel, whose excellencies were of a far superior

kind; and his amazing command of the instrument, the fullness of his harmony, the grandeur and dignity of his style, the copiousness of his imagination, and the fertility of his invention were qualities that absorbed every inferior attainment. When he gave a concerto, his method in general was to introduce it with a voluntary movement on the diapasons, which stole on the ear in a slow and solemn progression; the harmony close wrought, and as full as could possibly be expressed; the passages concatenated with stupendous art, the whole at the same time being perfectly intelligible, and carrying the appearance of great simplicity. This kind of prelude was succeeded by the concerto itself, which he executed with a degree of spirit and firmness that no one ever pretended to equal.

Such in general was the manner of his performance; but who shall describe its effects on his enraptured auditory? Silence, the truest applause, succeeded the instant that he addressed himself to the instrument, and that so profound, that it checked respiration, and seemed to controul the functions of nature, while the magic of his touch kept the attention of his hearers awake only to those enchanting sounds to which it gave utterance.

Wonderful as it may seem, this command over the human passions is the known attribute of music; and by effects like these the poets have ever described it, always supposing in the hearers a mind susceptible of its charms. But how are we to account for the influence of that harmony, of which we are now speaking, on those who, so far as regards music, may be said to have no passions, no affections on which it could operate? In all theatrical representations a part only of the audience are judges of the merit of what they see and hear, the rest are drawn together by motives in which neither taste nor judgment have any share : and, with respect to music, it is notorious that the greater number of mankind are destitute, though not of hearing, yet of that sense, which, superadded to the hearing, renders us susceptible of the harmony of musical sounds ;* and in times when music was less fashionable than

* Swift remarks of poetry, eloquence, and music, that it is certain that very few have a taste or judgment of the excellencies of the two former; and that if a man succeed in either, it is upon the authority of those few judges that lend their taste to the bulk of readers that have none of their own. And farther, that there are as few good judges in music, and that among those that crowd the operas, nine in ten go thither merely out of curiosity, fashion, or affectation. Intelligencer, No. 3, Faulkner's edition of Swift's works, vol. I. page 278. To these observations we may add, that of all who profess to admire the works of our great dramatic poet, and who talk of nature as if they were privy to her secrets, and judges of her operations upon occasions that do not present themselves in a long course of life to one in a million, few can be supposed to have more than a general sense of the author's meaning; the style of the dialogue being familiar only to those who are well skilled in the English language; these people, in the phrase of Swift, borrow the taste of others, and applaud the sentiment and the action as they are taught, being left to themselves, they are insensible to all that passes, and secretly prefer a ballad opera to the noblest productions of genius.

As to music, there are instances of persons who have entertained a love of the other polite arts, and yet have had no taste for this; and of others with whom it was an object of aversion. Pope once expressed his sentiments of music to a person now living in these words: 'My 'friend Dr. Arbuthnot speaks strongly of the effect that music has on 'his mind, and I believe him; but I own myself incapable of any pleasure 'from it.' The author of a well-known law-book, entitled 'The Office of 'an Executor,' by Thomas Wentworth, but in fact written by Sir John Dodderidge, a judge of the court of King's Bench, temp. Jac. I., prefers a cry of hounds to any other music. Dr. Ralph Bathurst is by Mr. Warton, in his life of him, page 201, said to have had a strong aversion to music; and among the peculiarities of the famous John Philip Barretier, it is in particular noted by Dr. Johnson, in his life of that extraordinary young man, that he could not bear music.

it is now, many of both sexes were ingenuous enough to confess that they wanted this sense, by saying, 'I have no ear for music.' Persons such as these, who, had they been left to themselves, would have interrupted the hearing of others by their talking, were by the performance of Handel not only charmed into silence, but were generally the loudest in their acclamations. This, though it could not be said to be genuine applause, was a much stronger proof of the power of harmony, than the like effect on an audience composed only of judges and rational admirers of his art.

There seems to be no necessary connection between those faculties that constitute a composer of music, and the powers of instrumental performance; on the contrary, the union of them in the same person, seems as extraordinary as if a poet should be able to write a fine hand; nevertheless in the person of Handel all the perfections of the musical art seemed to concenter. He had never been a master of the violin, and had discontinued the practice of it from the time he took to the harpsichord at Hamburg; yet, whenever he had a mind to try the effect of any of his compositions for that instrument, his manner of touching it was such as the ablest masters would have been glad to imitate. But what is more extraordinary, without a voice he was an excellent singer of such music as required more of the pathos of melody than a quick and voluble expression. In a conversation with the author of this work, he once gave a proof that a fine voice is not the principal requisite in vocal performance; the discourse was upon psalmody, when Mr. Handel asserted that some of the finest melodies used in the German churches were composed by Luther, particularly that which in England is sung to the hundredth psalm, and another, which himself sang at the time, and thereby gave occasion to this remark. At a concert at the house of lady Rich he was prevailed on to sing a slow song, which he did in such a manner, that Farinelli, who was present, could hardly be persuaded to sing after him.

The works of Handel come next to be considered; they have been judiciously classed by the author of his life, published in 1760, but are so multifarious, that they elude all but general criticism. This may be remarked of his compositions, that the disparity among them is no way to be accounted for but upon the supposition that he wrote to two sorts of persons, the judicious and the vulgar; and this solicitude to please both seems to have been pretty nearly equal: the former he meant to delight by such airs as the following, viz.: 'Cara Sposa,' in Rinaldo, 'Ombra Cara,' in Radamistus, 'Affanni del pensier,' in Otho, 'Da tempeste,' in Julius Cæsar, 'Di notte il Pellegrino,' in Richard I., and 'Spera si,' in Admetus;* and the latter to fascinate by such as

* Of this air the late Mr. John Lockman relates the following story, assuring his reader that himself was an eye-witness of it, viz., That being at the house of Mr. Lee, a gentleman in Cheshire, whose daughter was a very fine performer on the harpsichord, he saw a pigeon, which, whenever the young lady played this song, and this only, would fly from an adjacent dove-house to the window in the parlour, where she sat, and listen to it with the most pleasing emotions, and the instant the song was over would return to the dove-house. Some Reflexions concerning Operas, &c. prefixed to Roselinda, a Musical Drama by Mr. Lockman, 4to. 1740.

'Si caro,' in Admetus, 'See the conquering hero comes,' in Joshua, 'Powerful Guardians,' and 'Come ever smiling Liberty,' in Judas Maccabæus, and very many others.†

At the same time that he laboured to please his hearers, he seems not to have been unmindful of his own gratification; and if it be said, and of necessity it must be admitted, that many of his compositions were formed in haste,‡ and without any attention to those critical moments, in which the powers of genius are at their spring tide, it is no less true that there are others which must be supposed to have been produced under the influence of the strongest enthusiasm, when the brightest illuminations irradiated his fancy, and he himself felt all that rapture which he meant to excite in others.

In the first and highest class of Handel's works no competent judge of their merits would hesitate to rank his first Te Deum, and the Jubilate, his coronation and other anthems, the Dettingen Te Deum, as it is called, and the chorusses in his oratorios. In many of these compositions, especially those chorusses in his anthems in which the praises of God are celebrated, the power of his harmony is beyond conception; there is one in the anthem 'O come let us sing unto the Lord,' to the words 'Rejoice in the Lord O ye righteous,' in which nothing less is suggested to the imagination of the hearer than all the powers of the universe associated in the worship of its creator. On the other hand, the music to those passages in the Psalms and in his Oratorios which breathe a spirit of humiliation and contrition, is to the last degree soothing and pathetic; and, unassociated with the words, could scarce fail to excite sentiments corresponding with those of the poetry.§

† Most of the songs in the opera of Ariadne are calculated to please the many; and for this deviation from his general conduct, Mr. Handel gave to one of his friends as a reason, that he meant by it to recover the favour of the nobility, whom he was sensible he had displeased in some of his most elaborate compositions for the stage; but this attempt failed of its end, except that the minuet at the end of the Overture became the most popular air ever known: from those who professed a taste for music the admiration of it descended to the lowest of the people, insomuch that for some years after its publication it was played by the common fiddlers about the streets. The modulation of this air seems to suit but ill with unlearned ears, there being in it some transitions to which they are but little accustomed; but the circumstance that struck the vulgar was its great compass, extending to two octaves, and this they took for a peculiar excellence.

‡ In the composition of the funeral anthem for queen Caroline he gave an amazing proof of the fecundity of his invention. It was on a Wednesday that he received orders from the king to compose it, the words having been previously selected for the purpose, and approved. On the Saturday se'nnight after it was rehearsed in the morning, and on the evening of the same day it was performed at the solemnity in the chapel of king Hen. VII. The entertainment L'Allegro ed il Penseroso, and a senseless adjunct to it, Il Moderato, were begun and completed in fifteen days.

§ To point out the various excellencies in the choruses of Handel would be an endless task. In general it may be observed that they are fugues, in which the grandest subjects are introduced, and conducted with such art as only himself possessed: some are in the solemn style of the church, as that at the end of the first act in Saul; others have the natural and easy elegance of madrigals, as 'Then shall they know that he whose name Jehovah is,' in Samson; some again are full of exultation, as that in the anthem 'Have mercy upon me,' 'Thou shalt make me to hear of joy and gladness;' and that other in Israel in Egypt, 'I will sing unto the Lord;' and these in the Messiah, 'For unto us a child is born,' and 'For the Lord God omnipotent reigneth;' and, lastly, there are others in a style peculiar to himself, and calculated to excite terror, as these, 'He gave them hailstones for rain,' 'But the waters overwhelmed their enemies,' and 'Thy right hand O Lord hath dashed in pieces the enemy,' in Israel in Egypt. And though it may be said that Handel, agreeably to the practice of his countrymen, has too much affected imitation, particularly in the latter of the above-mentioned productions, by passages broken in the time to express the hopping of frogs, and others calculated to resemble the buzzing of swarms of flies; and that in Joshua he has endeavoured, by the harmony of one long-extended

In the composition of music merely instrumental it seems that Handel regarded nothing more than the general effect. Of all his productions of this class, scarce any appear to have been real studies, his lessons and fugues for the organ always excepted. His overtures, excellent as they are, were composed as fast as he could write; and the most elaborate of them seldom cost him more than a morning's labour. His concertos for violins are in general wanting in that which is the chief excellence of instrumental music in many parts, harmony and fine modulation: in these respects they will stand no comparison with the concertos of Corelli, Geminiani, and Martini; they seem to indicate that the author attended to little else than the melody of the extreme parts, and that he trusted for their success to the effect that results from the clash of many instruments; and to this only it can be imputed that in the tenor parts of his concertos there are none of those fine binding passages that occur in the music of the authors above-mentioned, and that in general they are destitute of art and contrivance.

His duets and his lessons are of a far more elaborate texture; the former, as also two trios, were composed for the practice of queen Caroline, and are professed imitations of those of Steffani, but their merits are of a different kind; they are thirteen in number, and, although they are all excellent, a preference seems to be due to 'Che vai 'pensando,' 'Conservate raddoppiate avvivate amante 'cori,' 'Tacete ohime tacete,' and 'Tanti strali al 'sen mi scocchi.'*

The lessons of Handel for the harpsichord were composed for the practice of the princess Anne, and consist of suites of airs, with fugues intermixed; the latter perhaps are more proper for the organ, and, because they require a masterly hand, are but little practised. Of the airs, the Allemandes in the third, fifth, and eighth sets are, for the sweetness of the melody, and the rich vein of fancy that runs through them, inimitable; as are the fugues in the second, fourth, and sixth, for the closeness of the harmony, and skilful iteration of their respective subjects. In short, without the hazard of contradiction, or the necessity of an exception, it may be asserted of these compositions, that they are the most masterly productions of the kind that we know of in the world.

The character of an author is but the necessary result of his works, and as the compositions of Handel are many and various, it is but justice to point out such of them as seem the most likely to be the foundation of his future fame. Many of the

note, to impress upon the imagination of his hearers the idea of the great luminary of the universe arrested in its course, or, in other words, to make them hear the sun stand still, it may be said that they abound with examples of the true sublime in music, and that they far surpass in majesty and dignity the productions of every other dead or living author.

* These compositions have never been printed, and are in the hands of only the curious. We may suppose that the author set a value on them, he having borrowed largely from them in his subsequent compositions: for instance, the overture to Judas Maccabeus is taken from the last movement in the first of the Duets; the chorus in Acis and Galatea, 'Behold the monster Polypheme,' from another; and the chorus in Alexander's Feast, 'Let old Timotheus yield the prize,' and that in Il Penseroso, 'These pleasures melancholy give,' from one of the Trios.

excellencies, which as a musician recommended him to the favour and patronage of the public during a residence of fifty years in this country, he might perhaps possess in common with a few of the most eminent of his contemporaries; but, till they were taught the contrary by Handel, none were aware of that dignity and grandeur of sentiment which music is capable of conveying, or that there is a sublime in music as there is in poetry. This is a discovery which we owe to the genius and inventive faculty of this great man; and there is little reason to doubt that the many examples of this kind with which his works abound, will continue to engage the admiration of judicious hearers as long as the love of harmony shall exist.

CHARLES AVISON, organist of Newcastle, and a disciple of Geminiani, was the author of an Essay on Musical Expression, published in the year 1752, in which are some judicious reflections on music in general, but his division of the modern authors into classes is rather fanciful than just. Throughout his book he celebrates Marcello and Geminiani; the latter frequently in prejudice to Mr. Handel, of whose music he vouchsafes no better a character than that 'we often find in it the noblest harmonies, 'and these enlivened with such a variety of modu- 'lation, as could hardly be expected from one who 'had supplied the town with musical entertainments 'of every kind for thirty years together.'

In the year 1753 came out Remarks on Mr. Avison's Essay on Musical Expression, the author whereof first points out sundry errors against the rules of composition in the works of Avison; and, inferring from thence that he was but meanly skilled in the subject of his book, he proceeds to examine it, and, to say the truth, seldom fails to prove his adversary in the wrong. In the same year Avison republished his Essay, with a reply to the author of the Remarks, and a letter, containing a number of loose particulars relating to music, collected in a course of various reading, unquestionably written by Dr. Jortin.

It has already been mentioned that Avison promoted and assisted in the publication of Marcello's music to the Psalms adapted to English words. Of his own composition there are extant five collections of Concertos for violins, forty-four in number, and two sets of Sonatas for the harpsichord and two violins, a species of composition little known in England till his time. The music of Avison is light and elegant, but it wants originality, a necessary consequence of his too close attachment to the style of Geminiani, which in a few particulars only he was able to imitate.

In the year 1748 an attempt towards the farther improvement of music was made by Robert Smith, master of Trinity college, Cambridge, in a book entitled Harmonics, or the Philosophy of Sounds, published in that year, and again in 1758, much improved and augmented; the principal end whereof is a temperament of the scale by calculations of those beats or pulses that attend the vibration of a chord, and which the author gives us to understand are not so minute as to elude the judgment of the ear. It seems that in the second edition of this book the author was assisted by Mr. Harrison, the clockmaker, who by some experiments on the monochord, and certain calculations made by him of the proportion which the circumference of a circle bears to its diameter, had discovered the means of a more correct tuning than at present is known. It is far from being clear that any benefit can result to music from that division of the octave which Dr. Smith recommends; but this is certain, that his book is so obscurely written, that few who have read it can be found who will venture to say they understand it. We are told that Mr. Harrison's sentiments on the division of the monochord are digested into a treatise written by him, entitled ' A short but full account of ' the grounds and foundation of music, particularly ' of the real existence of the natural notes of melody,' and that there is reason to hope for its publication.*

In the year 1762, a society for the improvement of vocal harmony was established by a great number of the nobility and gentlemen, met for that purpose at the Thatched-house tavern in St. James's-street, Westminster, by the name of the Catch Club. As an incentive to the students in music, they gave prize medals to such as were adjudged to excel in the compositions of canons and catches; and rewards of the same kind have with the same view been annually dispensed by them ever since.† These encouragements have contributed greatly to extend the narrow limits of the old harmony; and it is now only to be wished that the plan of this laudable society were adapted to the encouragement of a species of composition too little esteemed in our days, viz., Madrigals, which afford ample scope for the exercise of skill, and all the powers of invention; and for social practice are for many reasons to be preferred to every other kind of vocal harmony.

Of those great musicians who flourished in England at the beginning of this century, Geminiani was the only one living at this time; and, to resume the account herein before given of him and his works, it must be observed, that as he had never attempted dramatic composition of any kind, he drew to him but a small share of the public attention, that being in general awake only to such entertainments as the theatres afford. The consequence whereof was, that the sense of his merits existed only among those who had attained a competent skill in the practice of instrumental harmony to judge of them, and to these his publications were ever acceptable.

In a life so unsettled as that of Geminiani was, spent in different countries, and employed in pursuits that had no connection with his art, and only served to divert his attention from it, we must suppose the number of his friends to be very great, and that they were equally possessed of inclination and abilities to assist him, to account for the means of his support. That in the former part of his life he ex-

perienced the liberality of some persons of distinction is a fact pretty well ascertained; but he was not possessed of the art of forming beneficial connections, on the contrary, he would sometimes decline them;‡ so that as he advanced in years he had the mortification to experience the increase of his wants, and a diminution in the means of supplying them. In general his publications did, in respect of pecuniary advantage, in no degree compensate for his many years' labour and study employed in them, for which reason he had recourse to an expedient for obtaining a sum of money which he had never tried before, viz., a performance by way of benefit at one of the theatres; to this end, in the year 1748, he advertised a Concerto Spirituale, to be performed at Drury-lane theatre, chiefly of compositions of Italian masters of great eminence, but whose names were scarcely known in England.

Geminiani was an utter stranger to the business of an orchestra, and had no idea of the labour and pains that were necessary in the instruction of singers for the performance of music to which they were strangers, nor of the frequent practices which are required previous to an exhibition of this kind. The consequence whereof was, that the singers whom he had engaged for the Concerto Spirituale not being perfect in their parts, the performance miscarried. The particular circumstances that attended this undertaking were these; the advertisements had drawn together a number of persons, sufficient to make what is called a very good house; the curtain drew up, and discovered a numerous band, with Geminiani at their head: by way of overture was performed a concerto of his in a key of D with the minor third, printed in a collection of Concertos published by Walsh, with the title of Select Harmony, in which is a fugue in triple time, perhaps one of the finest compositions of the kind ever heard; then followed a very grand chorus, which, being performed by persons accustomed to sing in Mr. Handel's oratorios, had justice done to it; but when the women, to whom were given the solo airs and duets, rose to sing, they were not able to go on, and the whole band, after a few bars, were necessitated to stop. The audience, instead of expressing resentment in the usual way, seemed to compassionate the distress of Geminiani, and to consider him as a man who had almost survived his faculties, but whose merits were too great to justify their slight of even an endeavour to entertain them: they sat very silent till the books were changed, when the performance was continued with compositions of the author's own, that is to say, sundry of the concertos in his second and third operas, and a solo or two, which notwithstanding his advanced age, he performed in a manner that yet lives in the remembrance of many of the auditors.

The profits which arose from this entertainment enabled Geminiani to gratify that inclination for rambling which he had ever been a slave to; he

---

* Biographia Britannica, Appendix to the Supplement, page 229.

† The device is a tripod with a lyre, an ewer, and a cup thereon, encircled with a chaplet, Apollo and Bacchus as supporters sitting by it. The motto, taken from a canon of Dr. Hayes, is

LET'S DRINK AND LET'S SING TOGETHER.

‡ The late prince of Wales greatly admired the compositions of Geminiani, and at the same time that he retained Martini in his service, would have bestowed on him a pension of a hundred pounds a year, but the latter affecting an aversion to a life of dependence, declined the offer.

went to France, and took up his residence at Paris. He had formerly experienced the neatness and accuracy of the French artists in the engraving of music; and reflecting that his concertos had never been printed in a manner agreeable to his wishes, he determined to publish them himself, and also to give to the world what had long been earnestly wished for, a score of them. Accordingly he set himself to revise his second and third operas; but here the desire of making improvements, and a passion for refinement betrayed him into errors, for, besides the insertion of a variety of new passages, which did but ill sort with the general design of the several compositions into which they were engrafted, he entirely new modelled some of them, giving in many instances those passages to the second violin which had originally been composed for the tenor. Besides this he frequently made repeats of particular movements, and those so intricately ordered, as to render them very difficult of performance.

He stayed long enough at Paris to get engraven the plates both for the score and the parts of the two operas of concertos; and about the year 1755 returned to England, and took lodgings at the Grange-Inn, in Carey-street,* and advertised them for sale. About the same time he published what he called the Enchanted Forest, an instrumental composition, grounded on a very singular notion, which he had long entertained, namely, that between music and the discursive faculty there is a near and natural resemblance;† and this he was used to illustrate by a comparison between those musical compositions in which a certain point is assumed in one part, and answered in the other with frequent iterations, and the form and manner of oral conversation. With a view to reduce this notion to practice, Geminiani has endeavoured to represent to the imagination of his hearers the succession of events in that beautiful episode contained in the thirteenth canto of Tasso's Jerusalem, where, by the arts of Ismeno, a pagan magician, a forest is enchanted, and each tree informed with a living spirit, to prevent its being cut down for the purpose of making battering-rams and other engines for carrying on the siege of Jerusalem.

The Enchanted Forest was succeeded by the publication of two numbers of a work entitled 'The 'Harmonical Miscellany, containing sundry modula-'tions on a bass, calculated for the improvement of 'students in music, and the practice of the violin and 'harpsichord.' The author intended to have continued this work by periodical publications, but meeting with little encouragement, he desisted from his purpose.

Notwithstanding the fine talents which as a musician Geminiani possessed, it must be remarked that the powers of his fancy seem to have been limited. His melodies were to the last degree elegant, his modulation original and multifarious, and in their general cast his compositions were tender and pathetic; and it is to the want of an active and teeming imagination that we are to attribute the publication of his works in various forms. Perhaps it was this that moved him to compose his first opera of solos into sonatas for two violins and a bass, notwithstanding that the latter six of them had been made into Sonatas by Barsanti many years before; and also to make into concertos sundry of the solos in his opera quarta. In the same spirit of improvement he employed the latter years of his life in varying and new moulding his former works, particularly he made two books of lessons for the harpsichord, consisting chiefly of airs from his solos; and it was not always that he altered them for the better. Besides those compositions of his which were published by himself, or under his immediate inspection, there are others of Geminiani in print, of which little notice has ever been taken, particularly the concerto above mentioned; as also two others in a collection published by Walsh, with the title of Select Harmony. And in a collection of solos, published by the same person, with the names of Geminiani and Castrucci, are three solos undoubtedly of the former, two whereof are nowhere else to be found.

In the year 1761 he went over to Ireland, and was kindly entertained there by Mr. Matthew Dubourg, who had been his pupil, and was then master of the king's band in Ireland. This person through the course of his life had ever been disposed to render him friendly offices; and it was but a short time after the arrival of Geminiani at Dublin that his humanity was called upon to perform for him the last. It seems that Geminiani had spent many years in compiling an elaborate treatise on

---

* A person who had the curiosity to see him, and went thither to purchase the book, gives this account of him: 'I found him in a room 'at the top of the house half filled with pictures, and in his waistcoat. 'Upon my telling him that I wanted the score and parts of both operas 'of his concertos, he asked me if I loved pictures; and upon my answer-'ing in the affirmative, he said that he loved painting better than music, 'and with great labour drew from among the many that stood upon the 'floor round the room, two, the one the story of Tobit cured of his 'blindness, by Michael Angelo Caravaggio; the other a Venus, by 'Correggio. These pictures, said Geminiani, I bought at Paris, the 'latter was in the collection of the duke of Orleans; they are inestimable, 'and I mean to leave them to my relations: many men are able to 'bequeath to their relations great sums of money, I shall leave to mine 'what is more valuable than money, two pictures that are scarcely to 'be matched in the world.' After some farther conversation, in which it was very difficult to get him to say any thing on the subject of music, the vistor withdrew, leaving Geminiani to enjoy that pleasure which seemed to be the result of frenzy.

† Lord Bacon means somewhat to this purpose in the following passages: 'There be in music certain figures or tropes, almost agreeing 'with the figures of rhetoric. * * * The reports and fugues have an 'agreement with the figures in rhetoric of repetition and traduction.' Nat. Hist. Cent. II. Sect. 113. Upon this sentiment Martinelli has raised a fanciful hypothesis, which seems to have been the motive with Geminiani to this undertaking, and is here given in his own words: 'Le 'sonate d'ogni strumento non fanno che imitare un discorso, rappre-'sentante qualche passione. Il sonatore giudizioso procura sempre di 'scegliere quei tuoni che sono più grati all' orecchio di chi ascolta. Quei 'tuoni delle voci della infanzia acerbi striduli e disgustevoli sono quelli, 'i quali devono maggiormente evitarsi, e i bambini ne i loro vagiti non 'rappresentano che espressioni di quel dolore, al quale quella tenera età 'o per le percussioni troppo violenti dell' aria, o per qualche altro 'accidente gli tiene continuamente soggetti. I sonatori specialmente di 'violino, se avvessero in vista questa considerazione, si guarderebbono 'con molta cura da quei tanti sopracuti de i quali per il loro ingrate e 'insignificanti bravure continuamente si servono. Per le cose allegre l' 'età della gioventù è la più propria, che vale a dire il moderato soprano 'e il contralto, siccome per le amorose, le quali convengono anco al 'tenore, ma con più moderazione. Un discorso serio si sa ordinaria-'mente dalle persone più adulte, e questo il tenore, il baritono e il 'basso lo possono esprimere propriamente. In un concerto dove si 'figura che tutte le voci concorrano in un modesimo discorso, gli accuti 'che figurano le voci più giovanni, devono entrar più di rado, siccome 'rappresentanti persone, alle quali è dalla modestia permesso di parler 'più di rado. Di questa filosofia pare che il Corelli più d' ogni altro si 'sia servito perguida ne' suoi componimenti, avendo fatto suo maggior 'negozio delle voci di mezzo, e quindi usati i bassi come regolatori della 'zinfonia, o sia del suo discorso musicale.' Lettere familiare e critiche di Vincenzio Martinelli, Londra, 1758, page 379.

music, which he intended for publication; but, soon after his arrival at Dublin, by the treachery of a female servant, who it is said was recommended to him for no other purpose than that she might steal it, it was conveyed out of his chamber, and could never after be recovered. The greatness of this loss, and his inability to repair it, made a deep impression on his mind, and, as it is conjectured, precipitated his end; at least he survived it but a short time, the seventeenth of September, 1762, being the last day of his life, *which had been prolonged to the age of* 96. The following list comprises the whole of his publications, except two or three articles of small account:—Twelve Solos for a violin, Opera prima; Six Concertos in seven parts, Opera seconda; Six Concertos in seven parts, Opera terza; Twelve solos for a violin, Opera quarta; Six Solos for a violoncello, Opera quinta; the same made into Solos for a violin; Six Concertos from his Opera quarta; Six Concertos in eight parts, Opera settima; Rules for playing in Taste; a Treatise on good Taste; the Art of playing the Violin; Twelve Sonatas from his first Solos, Opera undecima; Ripieno parts to ditto; Lessons for the Harpsichord; Guida Armonica; Supplement to ditto; the Art of Accompaniment, two books; his two first operas of Concertos in score; and the Enchanted Forest.

These cursory remarks on the compositions of Geminiani may suffice for a description of his style and manner. Of his Solos the Opera prima is esteemed the best. Of his Concertos, some are excellent, others of them scarce pass the bound of mediocrity. The sixth of the third opera not only surpasses all the rest, but, in the opinion of the best judges of harmony, is the finest instrumental composition of the kind extant.

CONCLUSION.

IN the original plan of the foregoing work, it was for reasons, which have yet their weight with the author, determined to continue it no farther than to that period at which it is made to end. It nevertheless appears necessary, on a transient view of the present state of music, to remark on the degree of perfection at which it is at this time arrived; and from such appearances as the general manners of the times, and the uniform disposition of mankind in favour of novelty, to point out, as far as effects can be deduced from causes, the probable changes which hereafter it will be made to undergo; as also those improvements which seem to be but the consequence of that skill in the science to which we have attained.

That we are in possession of a more enlarged theory than that of the ancients will hardly be denied, if the arguments contained in this work, and the opinions and testimonies of the gravest authors are allowed to have any weight; and that we should excel them in our practice seems to be but a necessary consequence; at least the order and course of things, which are ever towards perfection, warrant us in thinking so. Whatever checks are given to the progress of science, or the improvement of manual arts, are accidental and temporary; they do but resemble those natural obstacles that impede the course of a rivulet, which for a short time may occasion a small deviation of its current, but at length are made to yield to its force.

In the comparison of the modern with the ancient music it must evidently appear that that of the present day has the advantage, whether we consider it in theory or practice: the system itself as it is founded in nature, will admit of no variation; consonance and dissonance are the subjects of immutable laws, which when investigated become a rule for all succeeding improvements. Whatever difference is to be found between the modern and ancient musical system, has arisen either from the rejection of those parts of it which the ancients themselves were willing enough to give up, and which as it were by universal consent, have been suffered to grow into disuse; or such additions to it as reason and experience have at different periods enabled men to make. To instance in a few particulars; the enarmonic and chromatic genera, with all the species or colours of the latter, are no longer recognized as essential parts of music; but the diatonic, attempered as it is with a mixture of chromatic intervals, is found to answer the purpose of all three; and the extension of the scale beyond the limits of the bisdiapason is no more than the extended compass of the modern instruments of all kinds naturally leads to. As to the philosophy of sound, or the doctrine of phonics, it appears that the ancients were almost strangers to it: this is a branch of speculative music; and as it results from the modern discoveries in physics, the moderns only are entitled to the merit of its investigation.

With respect to the relations of the marvellous effects of the ancient music, this remark should ever be uppermost in the minds of such as are inclined to credit them, viz., that men are ever disposed to speak of that which administers delight to them in the strongest terms of applause. At this day we extol the excellencies of a favourite singer, or a celebrated performer on an instrument, in all the hyperbolical terms that fancy can suggest; and these we often think too weak to express those genuine feelings of our own which we mean to communicate to others.

It has been asserted by a set of fanciful reasoners, that there is in the course of things a general and perpetual declination from that state of perfection in which the author of nature originally constituted the world; and, to instance in a few particulars, that men are neither so virtuous, so wise, so ingenious, so active, so strong, so big in stature, or so long lived, as they were even long after the transgression of our first parents, and the subsequent contraction of the period of human life : but no one has ever yet insinuated that the vocal organs have participated in this general calamity ; or that those mechanic arts to which we owe the invention and perfection of the various kinds of musical instruments, are in a less flourishing state than heretofore : till the contrary can be made appear, it may therefore be fairly presumed that in this respect the moderns have sustained no loss.

Farther, if a comparison be made between the instruments of the ancients and those of the moderns, the advantage will be found to be on the side of the latter : the ancient instruments, excepting those of the pulsatile kind, which in strictness are not to be considered as a musical species, as producing no variety of harmonical intervals, are comprehended under two classes, namely, the Lyre and the Tibia ; the former, under all its various modifications, appears to have been extremely deficient in many of those circumstances that contribute to the melioration of sound, and which are common to the meanest instruments of the fidicinal kind ; and, notwithstanding all that is said by Bartholinus and others, of the ancient tibia, and the extravagant elogies which we so frequently meet with of the ancient tibicines, we know very well that the tibia was a pipe greatly inferior to the flutes of modern times, which are incapable of being constructed so as not to be out of tune in the judgment of a nice and critical ear ; and to these no miraculous effects have ever yet been ascribed. To these two classes of instruments of the ancient Greeks, the Romans are said to have added another, viz., the hydraulic organ, for the use whereof we are as much to seek, as we are for a true idea of its structure and constituent parts.

It is true that the instruments in use among the moderns, in the general division of them, like those of the ancients, are comprehended under the tensile and inflatile kinds ; but numberless are the species into which these again are severally divided ; to which it may be added, that they have been improving for at least these five hundred years. And now to begin the comparison ; the instruments of the viol kind are so constructed as to reverberate and prolong that sound, which, when produced from the Lyre, must be supposed to have been wasted in the open air ; the modern flutes, as far as can be judged by a comparison of them with the graphical representations of the ancient Tibiæ, have greatly the advantage ; and as to pipes of other kinds, such as the Hautboy, the Bassoon, the Chalumeau, and others, these, as having the adjunct of a reed, constitute a species new and original, and are an invention unknown to the ancients.

To the hydraulic organ, said to have been invented by Ctesibus of Alexandria, we have to oppose the modern pneumatic organ ; not that rude machine of Saxon construction, a representation whereof is given in page 615 of this work, but such as that noble instrument used in divine worship among us, that of St. Paul's or the Temple church for instance.

Upon a view of the ancient and modern practice of music, and a comparison of one with the other, grounded on the above facts, we cannot but wonder at the credulity of those who give the preference to the former, and lament, as Sir William Temple in good earnest does, that the science of music is wholly lost in the world.[*]

But this is not the whole of the argument : as far as we can yet learn, it is to the moderns that we owe the invention of music in consonance ; and were it otherwise, and it could be said that we derive it from the Greeks, the multiplication of harmonical combinations must be supposed to be gradual, and is therefore to be ascribed to the moderns ; a circumstance that must necessarily give to the music of any period an advantage over that of the age preceding it. Nor is this kind of improvement any thing more than what necessarily results from practice and experience. In the sciences the accumulated discoveries of one age are a foundation for improvement in the next : and in the manual arts it may be said, that those who begin to learn them, in their noviciate often attain that degree of perfection at which their teachers stopped.[†]

This is the natural course and order of things ; but how far it is liable to be checked and interrupted may deserve consideration. With respect to music it may be observed, that much of its efficacy is by the vulgar admirers of it attributed to mere novelty ; and as these are a very numerous party, it becomes the interest of those who administer to their delight to gratify them, even against the conviction of their own judgments, and to the injury of the art. If novelty will ensure approbation, what artist will labour at intrinsic excellence, or submit his most arduous studies to the censure of those who neither regard, or indeed are able to judge of their merits ?[‡]

To this disposition we may impute the gradual declination from the practice and example of the ablest proficients in harmony, discoverable in the

---

[*] In his Essay upon the ancient and modern Learning.

[†] This observation will be found to be true in many and various instances : as it respects music, it may suffice to say that the young women of this age are finer performers on the harpsichord than the masters of the last ; and that there are now many better proficients on the violin under twenty, than there were of double their age fifty years ago.

[‡] That some persons do not love music is a known fact ; and Dr. Willis, the great physician and anatomist, has endeavoured to account for it by his observations on the structure of the human ear ; and that the majority of those who frequent musical entertainments have no sense of harmony is no less certain. The want of this sense is no ground for reproach, but the affectation of it in those to whom nature has denied it, is a proper subject for ridicule. If it be asked what is the test of a musical ear, the answer is, a general delight in the harmony of sounds. As to those to whom harmony is offensive, and who yet affect a taste for music, their own declarations are often evidence against them, and in general they will be found to be,

    Such as having no defect in their vocal organs, are unable to articulate even a short series of musical sounds.

    Such as at a musical performance express an uneasiness at the variety and seeming intricacy of the harmony, by a wish that all the instruments played the same tune.

    Such as think the quickest music the best, and call that spirit and fire which is but noise and clamour.

    Such as by the delight they take in the music of French horns, clarinets, and other noisy instruments, discover that the associated ideas of hunting, and the pleasures of the chase are uppermost in their minds.

    Such as think a concert a proper concomitant of a feast.

    Such, as having no scruple to it on the score of their religious profession, complain of cathedral music as being dull and heavy.

    And lastly, such as at the hearing an adagio movement, or any composition of the pathetic kind, the eighth concerto of Corelli. for instance, complain of an inclination to sleep.

compositions of the present day, which, as they abound in noise and clamour, are totally void of energy. Music of this kind, constructed without art or elegance, awakens no passion : the general uproar of a modern symphony or overture neither engages attention, nor interrupts conversation ; and many persons, in the total absence of thought, flatter themselves that they are merry. To assist this propensity, and as much as possible to banish reflection, the composers of music seem now to act against a fundamental precept of their art, which teaches that variety and novelty are ever to be studied, by reprobating, as they uniformly do, the use of all the keys with the minor third, upon a pretence that they tend to excite melancholy ideas ;* and by rejecting those grave and solemn measures, which, besides that they correspond with the most delightful of our sensations, form a contrast with those of a different kind. Is this to promote variety, or rather is it not contracting the sources of it ? Nor is the structure of their compositions such as can admit of any other than an interchange of little frittered passages and common-place phrases, difficult to execute, and for the most part so rapid in the utterance, that they elude the judgment of the ear ; and, without affecting any one passion, or exciting the least curiosity concerning the composer, leave us to wonder at the art of the performer, and to contemplate the languid effects of misapplied industry.

There can be no better test of the comparative merits of the music of the present day, and that which it has taken place of, than the different effects of each. The impression of the former was deep and is lasting : the compositions of Corelli, Handel, Geminiani, yet live in our memories ; and those of Purcell, though familiarized by the lapse of near a century, still retain their charms ; but who now remembers, or rather does not affect to forget the music that pleased him last year ? Musical publications no longer find a place in our libraries ; and we are as little solicitous for their fate as for the preservation of almanacs or pamphlets.

That music was intended merely to excite that affection of the mind which we understand by the word mirth, is a notion most illiberal, and worthy only of those vulgar hearers who adopt it. On the contrary, that it is an inexhaustible source of entertainment, or, as Milton finely expresses it, 'of sacred ' and home-felt delight,' is known to all that are skilled in its precepts or susceptible of its charms. The passions of grief and joy, and every affection of the human mind, are equally subservient to its call ; but rational admirers of the science experience its effects in that tranquillity and complacency which it

is calculated to superinduce, and in numberless sensations too delicate for expression.

It is obvious to men of understanding and reflection, that at different periods false notions have prevailed, not only in matters of science, where truth can only be investigated by the improved powers of reason, but in those arts wherein that discriminating faculty, that nameless sense, which, for want of a more proper term to define it by, we call taste, is the sole arbiter. In painting, architecture, and gardening, this truth is most apparent : the love of beauty, symmetry, and elegance, has at times given way to a passion for their contraries ; fashion has interposed in subjects with which fashion has nothing to do : nevertheless it may be observed, that while opinion has been veering round to every point, the principles of these arts, as they are founded in nature and experience, have ever remained in a state of permanency.

To apply this reasoning to the subject before us : we have seen the time when music of a kind the least intelligible has been the most approved. Our forefathers of the last century were witnesses to the union of elegance with harmony, and we of this day behold their separation : let us enquire into the reason of this change.

The prevalence of a corrupt taste in music seems to be but the necessary result of that state of civil policy which enables, and that disposition which urges men to assume the character of judges of what they do not understand. The love of pleasure is the offspring of affluence, and, in proportion as riches abound, not to be susceptible of fashionable pleasures is to be the subject of reproach ; to avoid which men are led to dissemble, and to affect tastes and propensities that they do not possess ; and when the ignorant become the majority, what wonder is it that, instead of borrowing from the judgment of others, they set up opinions of their own ; or that those artists, who live but by the favour of the public, should accommodate their studies to their interests, and endeavour to gratify the many rather than the judicious few ?

But, notwithstanding these evils, it does not appear that the science itself has sustained any loss ; on the contrary, it is certain that the art of combining musical sounds is in general better understood at this time than ever. We may therefore indulge a hope that the sober reflection on the nature of harmony, and its immediate reference to those principles on which all our ideas of beauty, symmetry, order and magnificence are founded ; on the infinitely various modifications of which it is capable ; its influence on the human affections ; and, above all, those nameless delights which the imaginative faculty receives from the artful disposition and succession of concordant sounds, will terminate in a thorough conviction of the vanity and emptiness of that music with which we now are pleased, and produce a change in the public taste, that, whenever it takes place, can hardly fail to be for the better.

* There is nothing more certain than that those who reason in this manner are ignorant of the structure of the human mind, which is never more delighted than with those images that incline us most to contemplation. Else why do the poets so strenuously labour to awaken the tender passions ? Why are the ravings of Lear, or the sorrows of Hamlet made the subjects of public speculation ? Such as approve only of mirthful music, to be consistent should proclaim aloud their utter aversion to all theatric representations except comedy, farce, and pantomime, and leave the nobler works of genius for the entertainment of better judges.

APPENDIX.

No. 1.—Verses supposed to be a complaint of Anne Boleyn, from an ancient MS; the music by Robert Johnson from another.

No. 1.

un - to my fame a mor - tal wounde, un - to my fame a mor - tal, mor - tal

fame a mor - tal wounde, a mor - tal wounde, un - to my fame a mor - tal

wounde, un - to my fame a mor - tal wounde, un - to my fame a mor - tal wounde,

un - to my fame a mor - tal wounde, a mor - tal wounde, un - to my fame a mor -

wounde, say what ye list it will not be, it will not be, say what ye

wounde, say what ye list, say what ye list, say what ye list it will not

say what ye list, say what ye list it will . . . not be, say what ye list, say what ye

- - - tal wounde. say what ye list it will not be, it will not be,

list it will not be, say what ye list it will not be, ye seek for that can - not be founde .

be, say what ye list it will not be, ye seek for that can - not be founde,

list it will not be, say what ye list it will not be, ye seek for that cannot be founde, ye seek . . for that can -

say what ye list it will not be, ye seek for that cannot cannot be founde, ye seek for that can -

. . . ye seek . . . . . for that can - not be founde, De - fyl - ed is my name.

ye seek for that can - not be founde can - not be founde,

- not be founde, ye seek . . for that can - not be founde, ... Do - fyl -

- not, can - not be founde, ye seek for that can - - not be founde, be founde, de - fyl - ed,

ROBERT JOHNSON.

No. 2.—The Black Sanctus, a song so called, set to music as a canon in the sub-diatessaron and diapason. Concerning which the following account is given in a letter of Sir John Harington to the lord treasurer Burleigh, printed in the Nugæ Antiquæ, vol. I. page 132. 'In an old booke of my 'father's I read a merrie verse, which for lack of my own, I send by Mr. Bellot, to divert your lordshippe, when as you say weighty pain and weightier 'matters will yield to quips and merriment. This verse is called The Blacke Sauntus, or Monkes Hymn to Saunte Satane, made when kynge Henrie 'had spoylede their synginge. My father was wont to say that kynge Henrie was used in pleasaunte moode to singe this verse ; and my father, who 'had his good countenance, and a goodlie office in his courte, and also his goodlie Esther [This Esther was a natural daughter of the kyng's, to whom 'he gave as a dower the lands belonging to the Bathe priory, or a part thereof] to wife, did sometyme receive the honour of hearing his own songe, 'for he made the tune which my man Combe hath sent herewith ; having been much skilled in musicke, which was pleasing to the kynge, and which 'he learnt in the followship of good Maister Tallis, when a young man.'

No. 2.

O Tu qui dans o - ra - cu - la, Scin - dis co - tem no - va - cu - la, Da nos - tra &c.

O Tu . . qui dans o - ra - cu - la, Scin - dis cotem no - va - cu - la, Da &c.

O Tu . . qui dans o - - ra - cu - la, Scin - - dis cotem no - va - cu - la, Da &c.

JOHN HARINGTON.

'O tu qui dans oracula, scindis cotem novacula,
'Da nostra ut tabernacula, lingua canant vernacula,
'Opima post jentacula, hujusmodi miracula,
'Sit semper plenum poculum, habentes plenum loculum,
'Tu serva nos ut specula, per longa et læta sæcula,
'Ut clerus ut plebecula, nec nocte nec de cula,
'Curent de ulla recula, sed intuentes specula,
'Dura vitemus spicula, jacentes cum amicula,
'Quæ garrit ut cornicula, seu tristis seu ridicula,
'Tum porrigamus oscula, tum colligamus floscula,
'Ornemus ut cœnaculum, et totum habitaculum,
'Tum culy post spiraculum, spectemus hoc spectaculum.'

The foregoing lines are undoubtedly corrupt in 'more than one place, [In the sixth and twelfth lines perhaps we should read *de pecula* instead of *de cula*, and *culo* in the place of *culy*], but as they are singularly humorous, and nearly resemble the facetious rhymes of Walter de Mapes, archdeacon of Oxford, who lived in the time of Hen. II., and as Camden says, filled England with his merriments, the following translation has been attempted under all the disadvantages that must arise from the obscurity of an original so difficult to be understood :—

O thou who utt'ring mystic notes,
The whetstone cut'st with razor,
In mother-tongue permit our throats,
Henceforth to sing and say, Sir!

To rich, material breakfasts join
These miracles more funny—
Fill all our cups with lasting wine,
Our bags with lasting money!

To us a guardian tow'r remain,
Through ages long and jolly;
Nor give our house a moment's pain
From thought's intrusive folly!

Ne'er let our eyes for losses mourn,
Nor pore on aught but glasses;
And sooth the cares that still return,
By toying with our lasses;

Who loud as tatling magpies prate,
Alternate laugh and lour;
Then kiss we round each wanton mate,
And crop each vernal flow'r.

To deck our rooms, and chiefly that
Where supper's charms invite;
Then close in chimney-corner squat,
To see so blest a sight!

No. 3.—A song set to music by William Bird in the form of a madrigal for three voices. Concerning the words of this song, it has long been a received tradition, among musical people, that they were written on some particular occasion by king Henry VIII; and in the Nugæ Antiquæ, vol. II. page 248, is a letter from Sir John Harington to prince Henry, written in 1609, wherein the fact is ascertained by the following passage: 'I will now venture to send to your readinge a special verse of king Henrie the eight, when he conceived love for Anna Bulleign. And 'hereof I entertain no doubt of the author, for if I had no better reason than the rhyme, it were sufficient to think that no other than suche a king 'coud write suche a sonnet; but of this my father oft gave me good assurance. who was in his houshold.' *Notwithstanding this assertion it can never be assented to as a fact, for the whole of the song is to be found in the legend of Jane Shore, written by Thomas Churchyard, and forms a complete Stanza of that poem. It is reprinted in Mr. Cooper's Muses' Library, page 18.* 'This sonnet was sung to the Lady Anne at his commaundment; and here followeth:—'   "The eagle's force, &c."

The music is unquestionably Bird's, for the song as given in this Appendix stands the first among the songs in a work published by himself in 1611, entitled 'Psalmes, Songs, and Sonnets: some solemne, others joyful, framed to the life of the words: fit for Voyces or Viols of 3, 4, 5, and 6 parts.'

No. 3.

THE ea-gle's force sub-dues eache byrd that .. flyes; what me - tal
THE ea-gle's force sub-dues eache byrd that flyes, eache byrd that flyes; what me -
THE ea-gle's force sub-dues eache byrd that flyes; what me - tal

can re-sist, re - sist the flam - inge fyre? dothe not the sunne da - -
tal can re-syst the flam - inge fyre? dothe not the sunne da - zle the clear - - este
can re-syst the flam - - inge fyre? dothe not the sunne da - zle the clear - este

zle the clear-este eyes, the cleareste eyes, the clear - este eyes and melte the ice, and make
eyes, the cleareste eyes, the clear - - este eyes, and melte the ice, and
eyes, da - - zle the clear - - este eyes, and melte the ice, and

.. the froste re - - tyre, re - - tyre? who can with - stand a puissant
make the froste re - tyre, re - tyre? who can withstand a puissant King's de-sire, ..
make the froste re - tyre, .. re - tyre? who can withstand a puissant King's de - sire, a

the wisest are with Prin - ces made but fools, the wisest are with Prin - ces made but

Princes made but fools, are with Prin - ces made but fools, the wisest are with Prin - ces

Princes made . . . but fools, the wisest are with Prin - ces made with fools, the

fools, made but fools, the wisest are with Prin - ces made but fools, the wisest are . . with Princes made but fools.

made but fools, the wisest are with Prin - ces made but fools, the wisest are with Princes made but fools.

wisest are with Prin - ces made but fools, made but fools, made but fools.

WILLIAM BIRD.

No. 4.—A Song written by Richard Edwards, a gentleman of queen Elizabeth's chapel, and afterwards master of the children there, printed in the Paradyse of daynty Devises, and alluded to in the play of Romeo and Juliet; the music from an ancient manuscript.

No. 4.

WHERE gri - ping grief the hart would wound, and dol-ful domps the mind op - presse,

WHERE gri - ping grief the hart would wound, and dol-ful domps the mind op - presse,

WHERE gri - ping grief the hart would wound, and dol-ful domps the mind op - presse,

WHERE gri - ping grief the hart would wound, and dol-ful domps the mind op - presse,

there Mu-sick with . . her sil - ver sound is wont with spede to give re - - dresse;

there Mu-sick with her sil - ver sound is wont with spede to give re - dresse;

there Mu-sick with her sil - ver sound is wont with spede to give re - dresse;

there Mu-sick with her sil - ver sound is wont with spede to give re - dresse;

of trou-bled minds, for e - ve-ry sore, swete Mu - sick hath a salve in store.

of trou-bled minds, for ev' - ry sore, swete Mu - sick hath a salve in . . store.

of trou-bled minds, for e - ve-ry sore, swete Mu - sick hath a salve in store.

of trou-bled minds, for ev' - ry sore, swete Mu - sick hath a salve in store.

In joy it maks our mirth abound,
    In grief it chers our heavy sprights,
The carefull head releaf hath found,
    By Musick's pleasant swete delights;
Our senses, what should I saie more,
    Are subject unto Musick's lore.

The Gods by Musick hath their prayse,
    The soule therin doth joye;
For as the Romaine poets saie,

In seas whom pirats would destroye,
A dolphin sav'd from death moste sharpe,
Arion playing on his harpe.

Oh heavenly gift, that turnes the minde,
    Like as the sterne doth rule the ship,
Of musick whom the Gods assignde,
    To comfort man whom cares would nip,
Sith thou both man and beast doest move,
    What wise man then will thee reprove

No. 5.—Another written by Francis Kindlemarsh, from the Paradyse of daynty Devises; the music by the above Richard Edwards
from the same MS.

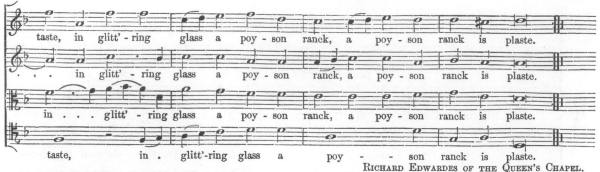

taste, in glitt'-ring glass a poy-son ranck, a poy-son ranck is plaste.

. . . in glitt'-ring glass a poy-son ranck, a poy-son ranck is plaste.

in . . . glitt'-ring glass a poy-son ranck, a poy-son ranck is plaste.

taste, in . glitt'-ring glass a poy- -son ranck is plaste.

RICHARD EDWARDES OF THE QUEEN'S CHAPEL.

So pleasant woordes, without performing deedes,
May well be deemed to spring of Darnel seedes.
The freendly deede is it, that quickly tryes
Where trusty faith and freendly meaning lyes.
That state therefore most happy seems to be,
Where woordes and deedes most faithfully agree.

My freend yf thou wilt keepe thy honest name
Fly from the blotte of barking slaunder's blame.
Let not in woord thy promise be more large,
Then thou in deede are wyllyng to discharge.
Abhorred is that false dissembling broode,
That seemes to beare two faces in one hoode.
To say a thing, and not to meane the same,
Wyll turne at length to losse of thy good name.
Wherefore, my freend, let double dealing goe,
In steade whereof let perfect plaineness flowe.
Doo thou no more in idle woordes exceede,
Then thou intendes to doo in very deede.

So goode report shall spread thy woorthy prayse
For being just in woord and deede alwayes.

You worldly wightes, that worldly dooers are,
Before you let your woord slip foorth too farre,
Consyder well, what inconvenience springes
By breach of promise made in lawfull thinges.
First God mislikes where such deceit dooth swarme;
Next it redoundeth unto thy neighbour's harme;
And last of all, which is not least of all,
For such offence thy conscience suffer shall.
As barren groundes bringe foorth but rotten weedes,
From barren woordes so fruitlesse chaffe proceedes;
As saverie flowres doo spring in fertill ground,
So trusty freendes by tryed freendes are found.
To shunne therefore the woorst that may ensue,
Let deedes alway approve thy sayinges true.

No. 6.—Another from the Paradyse of daynty Devises, written by William Hunnis of the queen's chapel, the successor of Edwards as master of the children, and set to music by Thomas Tallis; from the same MS.

No. 6.

LIKE as the dole-full dove delights a-lone to be, and doth re-fuse the bloumed

LIKE as the dole-full dove delights a-lone to be, and doth re-fuse the bloumed

LIKE as the dole-full dove delights a-lone to be, and doth re-fuse the bloumed

LIKE as the dole-full dove delights a-lone to be, and doth re-fuse the bloumed

branch, chusing the leve-les tre, where-on wail-ing his chaunce with bit-ter teares be-sprent, doth with his

branch, chusing the leve-les tre, where-on wail-ing his chaunce with bit-ter teares be-sprent, doth with his

branch, chusing the leve-les tre, where-on wail-ing his chaunce with bit-ter teares be-sprent, doth with his

branch, chusing the leve-les tre, where-on wail-ing his chaunce with bit-ter teares be-sprent, doth with his

bill his ten-der brest oft persse and . . . all to rent; whose gre-vous gro-nings, tho' whose grips of

bill his ten-der brest oft persse and all to rent; whose gre-vous gro-nings, tho' whose grips of

bill his ten-der brest oft persse and all to . . . rent; whose gre-vous gro-nings, tho' whose grips of

bill his ten-der brest oft persse and all to . . rent; whose gre-vous gro-nings, tho' whose grips of

pi - ning paine,   whose gast - ly lookes, whose blood-ly strems out flow - ing from each vaine, whose fall - ing

pi - ning paine,   whose gast - ly lookes, whose blood-ly strems out flow - ing from each vaine, whose fall - ing

pi - ning paine,   whose gast - ly lookes, whose bloodly strems out flow - ing from each vaine, whose fall - ing

pi - ning paine,   whose gast - ly lookes, whose blood-ly strems out flow - ing from each vaine, whose fall - ing

from the tree, whose pan-ting on the ground, ex - am-ples be of mine es - tate tho' there a - pere no wound.

from the tree, whose pan-ting on the ground, ex - am-ples be of mine es - tate tho' there a - pere no wound.

from the tree, whose pan-ting on the ground, ex - am-ples be of mine es - tate tho' there a - pere no wound.

from the tree, whose pan-ting on the ground, ex - am-ples be of mine es-tate tho' there a - pere no wound.

THOMAS TALLIS.

No. 7.—A Tale from the same collection, written by the above Richard Edwards; the music from the same MS.

No. 7.

IN   go - ing to my na - - ked bedde,   as

IN go - ing to my na - ked bedde,   na - ked bedde,   as   one that

IN   go - ing to my na - - - ked bedde, as   one that would have

IN   go - ing to my   na - - - ked bedde,

one that would have slept,   I heard a   wife   sing   to   her   child that long be - fore had wept.

would have slept,   I heard a   wife sing to her   child   that   long be - fore   had   wept.

slept, I heard a   wife sing to her   child   that   long   be - fore . . . had wept.

I heard a   wife   sing   to her   child   that   long be - fore   had   wept.

She sigh-ed sore and sang full sweete to bring   the babe to   rest,   that would not cease but

She sigh-ed sore and sang full sweete to bring   the babe to   rest,   that would not cease but

She sigh-ed sore and sang full sweete to bring   the babe to   rest, that would not cease but cri - ed

She sigh-ed sore and sang full sweete to bring   the babe to   rest,   that would not cease but

Then took I paper, penne and ynke,
  This proverbe for to write,
In regester for to remaine
  Of such a worthie wight :
As she proceeded thus in song
  Unto her little bratte,
Muche matter uttered she of waight,
  In place whereas she satte,
And proved plaine there was no beast,
  Nor creature bearing life,
Could well be knowne to live in love,
  Without discorde and strife :
Then kissed shee her little babe,
  And sware by God above,
The falling out of faithfull frends
  Renuing is of love.

She saied that neither king ne prince,
  Ne lord could live aright,
Untill their puissance they did prove,
  Their manhode and their might.
When manhode shal be matched so
  That feare can take no place,
Then wearie works makes warriours
  Eche other to embrace,
And leave their forse that failed them,
  Which did consume the rout,
That might before have lived their tyme,
  And their fulle nature out :
Then did she sing as one that thought
  No man could her reprove,
The falling out of faithfull frends
  Renuing is of love.

She said she sawe no fishe ne foule,
　Nor beast within her haunt,
That mett a straunger in their kinde,
　But could geve it a taunt:
Since fleshe might not indure,
　But rest must wrathe succede,
And forse who fight to fall to play,
　In pasture where they feede.
So noble nature can well ende
　The works she hath begone,
And bridle well that will not cease
　Her tragedy in some;
Thus in her songe she oft reherst,
　As did her well behove,
The falling out of faithfull frends
　Renuing is of love.

I marvaile much pardy quoth she,
　For to beholde the route,
To see man, woman, boy and beast
　To tosse the world about:
Some knele, some crouch, some beck, some chek,
　And some can smothly smile,
And some embrace others in arme,
　And there thinke many a wile.
Some stande aloufe at cap and knee,
　Some humble and some stoute,
Yet are they never frends indeede,
　Untill they once fall out;
Thus ended she her song and saied
　Before she did remove,
The falling out of faithfull frends
　Renuing is of love.

No. 8.—An Anthem composed by John Redford, of St. Paul's, temp. Hen. VIII.

JOHN REDFORD.

No. 9.—A Meane composed by William Blitheman, Dr. Bull's master.

WILLIAM BLITHEMAN.

No. 10.—A Poynte.

JOHN SHEPHARD.

No. 11.—A Voluntary.

MASTER ALLWOODE.

No. 12.—The first stanza of the Hymnus Eucharisticus of Dr. Nath. Ingelo, set to music by Dr. Benjamin Rogers, of Oxford, and sung by way of grace after dinner in the hall of Magdalen college.

No. 12.

TE De-um Pa-trem col—i-mus, Te lau-di-bus pro-se—qui-mur;

TE De-um Pa-trem col—i-mus, Te lau-di-bus pro-se—qui-mur;

TE De-um Pa-trem col-i-mus, Te lau-di-bus pro-se——qui-mur;

TE De-um Pa-trem col-i-mus, Te lau-di-bus pro-se-qui——mur;

Qui Cor-pus ci-bo re-fi——cis cœ-les-ti men-tem gra-ti-a.

Qui Cor-pus ci-bo re-fi——cis cœ-les-ti men-tem gra-ti-a.

Qui Cor-pus ci-bo re-fi——cis cœ-les-ti men-tem gra-ti-a.

Qui Cor-pus ci-bo re-fi——cis cœ-les-ti men-tem gra-ti-a.

DOCTOR BENJAMIN ROGERS.

Nos. 13 and 14.—Two very ancient country-dance tunes, viz.: The Shaking of the Shetes, mentioned by Taylor the water-poet, in his character of a bawd ; and Trenchmore, mentioned in the Island Princess of Beaumont and Fletcher, and in the Table-talk of Selden.

No. 15.—Paul's Steeple.

No. 16.—Old Simon the King. *This is the tune to an old Song, which see in Pills to purge Melancholy, vol. III, page 144. It is conjectured that the subject of it was Simon Wadloe, who kept the Devil Tavern at the time when Ben Jonson's Club, called the Apollo Club, met there. In the verses over the door of the Apollo Room was this couplet :—*

> " *Hang up all the poor hop drinkers,*
>   *Cries Old Sim, the King of Skinkers.*"

A Skinker is one that serves drink.—Johns. Dict.   In Camden's remains is the following epitaph on this person :—

> *Apollo et cohors Musarum,*
> *Bacchus vini et uvarum,*
> *Ceres pro pane et cerevisia*
> *Adeste omnes cum tristitia.*
> *Düque Deæque lamentate cuncti,*
> *Simonis Vadloe funera defuncti*
> *Sub signo malo bene vixit mimbile*
> *Si ad cœlus recessit, gratias Diabole.*

As to the Song, there is in it nothing characteristic of the man, but it attributes to him the following two strings of Aphorisms ; each of them forming that kind of argument which the Logicians call a Sontes :

> Drink will make a man drunk,   Drinking will make a man quaff,
> And drunk will make a man dry,   Quaffing will make a man sing,
> Dry will make a man sick,   Singing will make a man laugh,
> And sick will make a man die,   And laughing long life will bring,
>   Says Old Simon the King.   Says Old Simon the King.

No. 17.—Tollet's Ground.

THOMAS TOLLET.

No. 18.—John, come kiss me.

No. 19.—Roger of Coverly.

No. 20.—Cold and raw. [An old tune, which makes part of a canon in the unison, by John Hilton, and printed in his Collection of Catches, Rounds, and Canons, published in 1652. It takes the above name from the initial words of an old ballad, which is set to it, and was a favourite tune of queen Mary, the consort of William III. See page 564 of this work, in note.]

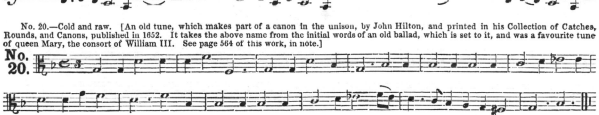

No. 21.—Green Sleeves.

No. 22.—The Old Cebell.

GIO. BATT. DRAGHI.

No. 23.—Bellamira, a favourite Ground.

SOLOMON ECCLES.

No. 24.—Farinel's Ground.

No. 25.—Johnny, cock thy beaver.

No. 26.—Hedge-lane, a dance-tune.

JOHN BANISTER.

No. 27.—Mademoiselle Subligny's Minuet. This person, *whose Christian name was Thérèse, was a Dancer in the Opera at Paris in the year 1704, with a pension of 800 livres. Betterton, upon the decline of his company at Lincoln's Inn Theatre, at an extraordinary rate got her over hither, as also at different times Mons. L'Abbé, and Mons. Balon. She danced for a season or two with great applause, and returned to her own country.—Vide Histoire du Theatre de L'Academie Royale de Musique en France, page 94. Life of Colley Cibber, page 180.* Before the arrival of these persons, French dancing was unknown on the English stage.

No. 28.—Ballad of John Dory, with the tune; a round for three voices.

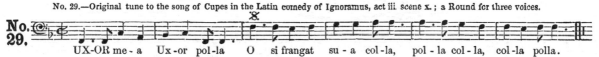

No. 28.

AS it fell on a ho-li-day, as it fell on a ho-li-day and up-on a ho-ly-

-tide a, and up-on a ho-ly-tide a, and up-on a ho-ly-tide a;

John Dory bought him an ambling nag
  to Paris for to ride a.

And when John Dory to Paris was come,
  a little before the gate a;
John Dory was fitted, the porter was witted,
  To let him in thereat a.

The first man that John Dory did meet
  Was good king John of France a;
John Dory con'd well of his courtesie,
  but fell down in a trance a.

A pardon, a pardon, my liege and my king,
  For my merie men and for me a;
And all the churles in merie England
  I'le bring them all bound to thee a.

Sir Nichol was then a Cornish man,
  a little beside Bohyde a;
And he mann'd forth a good blacke barke,
  with fiftie good oares on a side a.

Run up my boy unto the maine top,
  and looke what thou canst spy a:
Who, ho; a goodly ship I do see,
  I trow it be John Dory a.

They hoist their sailes both top and top,
  the mizen and all was tried a;
And every man stood to his lot,
  what ever should betide a.

The roring canons then were plide,
  and dub a dub went the drumme a;
Tho braying trumpets lowdlie cride
  to 'courage both all and some a.

The grapling hooks were brought at length,
  the browne bill and the sword a;
John Dory at length, for all his strength,
  was clapt fast under board a.

No. 29.—Original tune to the song of Cupes in the Latin comedy of Ignoramus, act iii. scene x.; a Round for three voices.

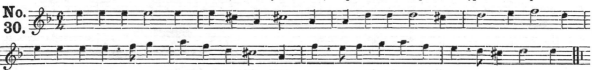

No. 29.

UX-OR me-a Ux-or pol-la   O si frangat su-a col-la,   pol-la col-la,   col-la polla.

No. 30.—The tune to the old ballad of Cock Lorrel, written by Ben Jonson, and printed in his masque of the Gypsies metamorphosed.

No. 30.

No. 31.—An old ballad tune to which D'Urfey has adapted a song with the words at the end of every stanza, 'Hey boys up go we.'

No. 31.

No. 32.—A song, said in an old copy to be written by king Charles II., set by Mr. Pelham Humphrey, master of the children of his chapel.

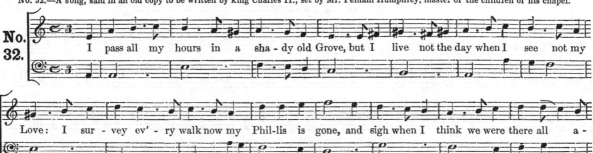

No. 32.

I pass all my hours in a sha-dy old Grove, but I live not the day when I see not my

Love: I sur-vey ev'-ry walk now my Phil-lis is gone, and sigh when I think we were there all a-

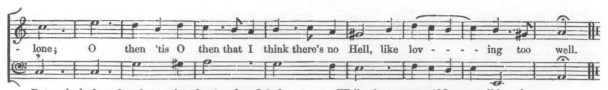

-lone;   O   then 'tis O   then that I think there's no Hell, like lov - - - - ing too   well.

But each shade and each conscious bow'r, when I find
Where I once have been happy, and she has been kind ;
When I see the print left of her shape in the green,
And imagin the pleasure may yet come agen ;
　　O then 'tis I think no joys are above
　　　　The pleasures of love.

While alone to myself I repeat all her charms,
She I love may be lockt in another man's arms,
She may laugh at my cares, and so false she may be,
To say all the kind things she before said to me ;
　　O then 'tis O then that I think there's no hell
　　　　Like loving too well.

But when I consider the truth of her heart,
Such an innocent passion, so kind without art,
I fear I have wrong'd her, and hope she may be
So full of true love to be jealous of me :
　　And then 'tis I think that no joys are above
　　　　The pleasures of love.

No. 33.—The tune to the Fandango, a favourite dance of the Spaniards.

No. 33.

No. 34.—A tune for a rope-dance in a singular style, by Mr. John Eccles.

No. 34.

JOHN ECCLES.

A COLLECTION OF

FAC-SIMILES, &c.

OF

ANCIENT MANUSCRIPTS,

FORMING

APPENDIX, Nos. 35 to 57.

COLLECTION OF
FAC-SIMILES &c.

FROM

ANCIENT MANUSCRIPTS.

Nº 37 see page 18. (For Appendix 35 & 36 see following page so placed in order that both may be seen at one view.)

Musical Fragment from Pindar, and its transcript in modern notation.

No. 35. (see page 18.) Table of Greek Musical Characters.

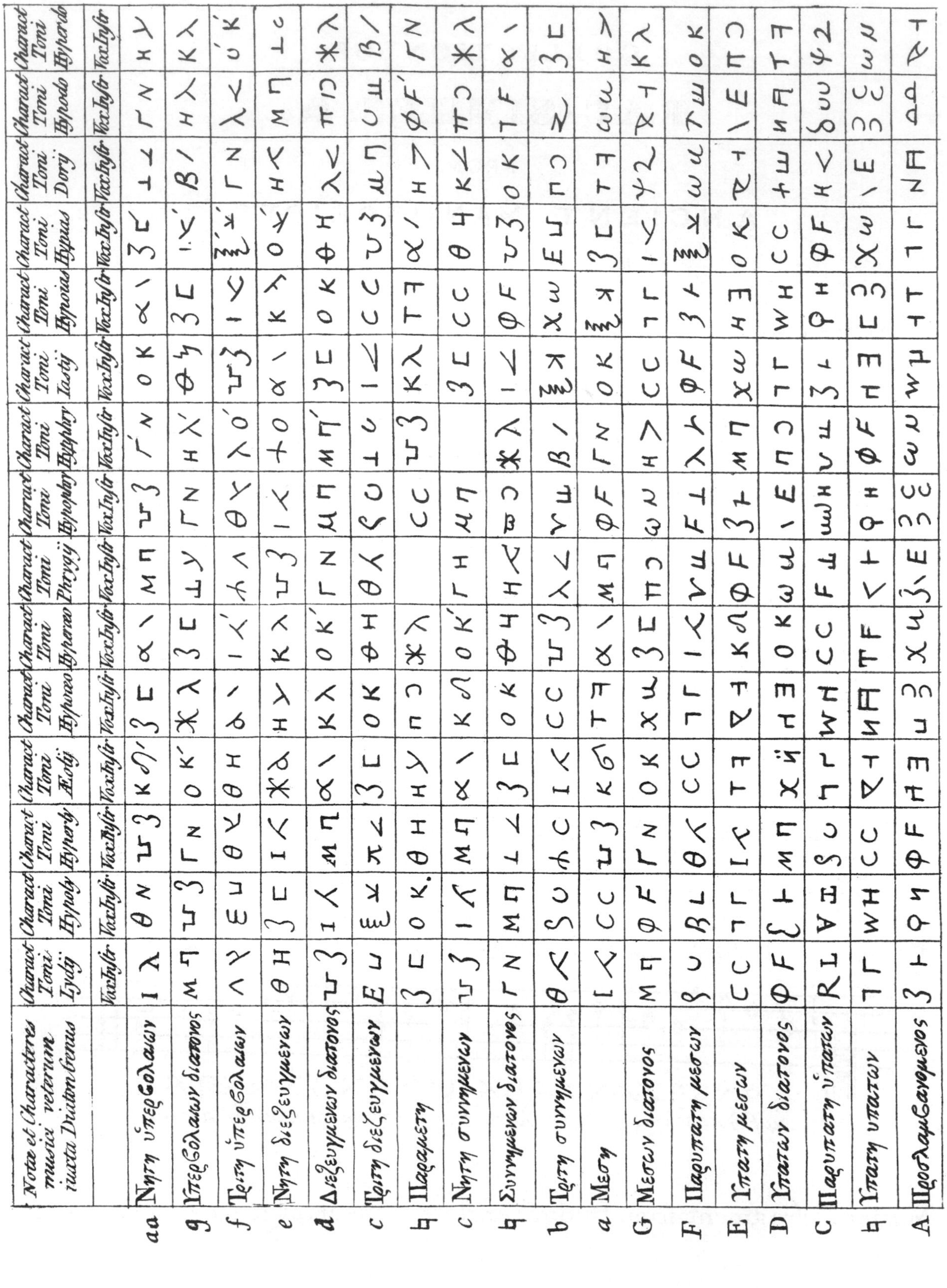

Notae et Characteres musici veterum iuxta Diaton. Genus
Charact. Toni Lydij
Charact. Toni Hypolyd
Charact. Toni Hyperlyd
Charact. Toni Æolij
Charact. Toni Hypoæo
Charact. Toni Hyperæo
Charact. Toni Phrygij
Charact. Toni Hypophry
Charact. Toni Hyperphry
Charact. Toni Iastij
Charact. Toni Hypoias
Charact. Toni Hyperias
Charact. Toni Dorij
Charact. Toni Hypodo
Charact. Toni Hyperdo
Vox Instr.
aa Νητη ὑπερβολαιων
g Ὑπερβολαιων διατονος
f Τριτη ὑπερβολαιων
e Νητη διεζευγμενων
d Διεζευγμενων διατονος
c Τριτη διεζευγμενων
♮ Παραμεση
c Νητη συνημμενων
♮ Συνημμενων διατονος
b Τριτη συνημμενων
a Μεση
G Μεσων διατονος
F Παρυπατη μεσων
E Ὑπατη μεσων
D Ὑπατων διατονος
C Παρυπατη ὑπατων
♮ Ὑπατη ὑπατων
A Προσλαμβανομενος

No. 36. (see page 18.)   Table of Greek Musical Characters.

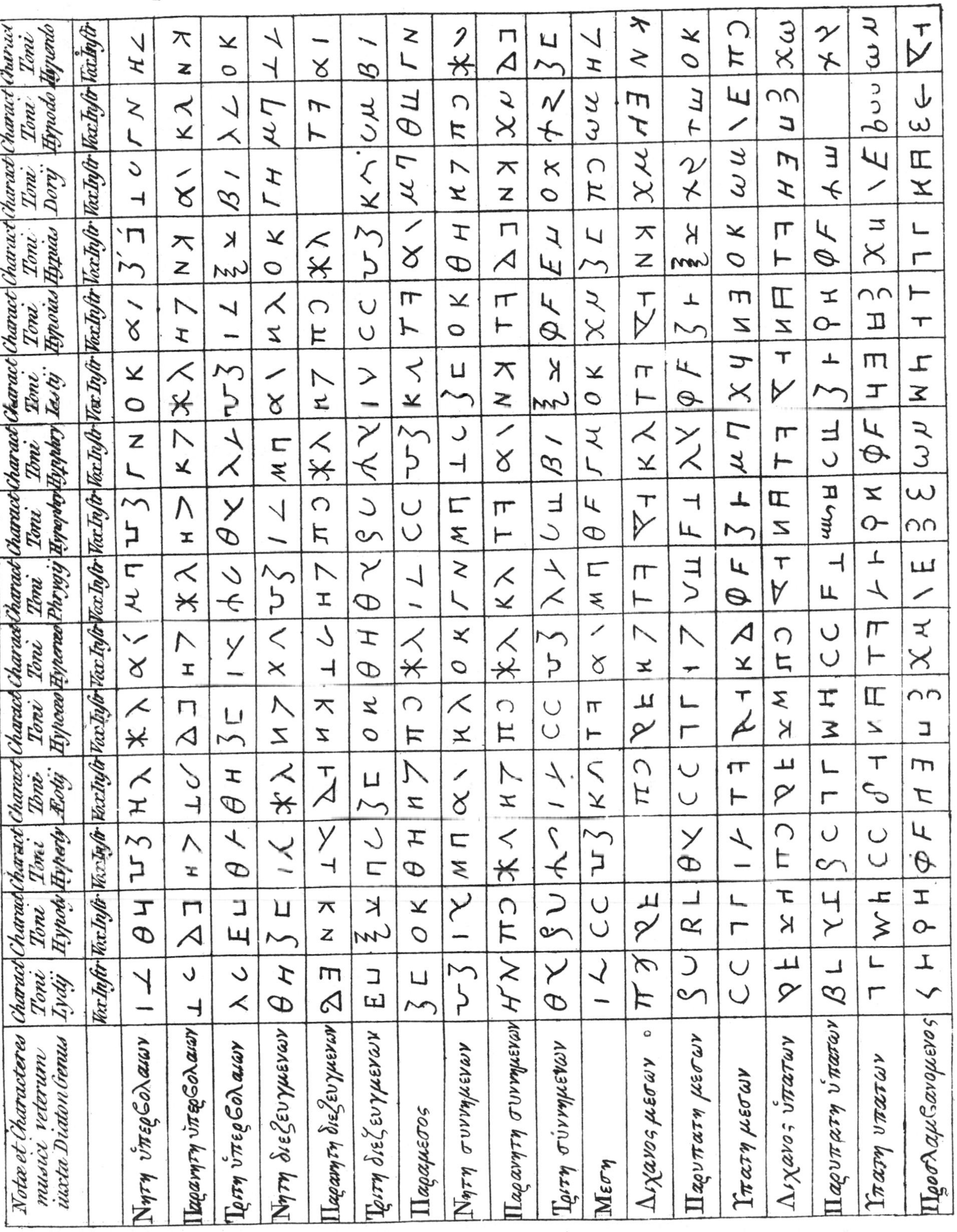

The table consists of handwritten Greek musical notation characters arranged in columns headed by the tonoi. The column headings read:

Notae et Characteres musici veterum iuxta Diaton Genus	Charact. Toni. Lydij	Charact. Toni. Hypolyd	Charact. Toni. Æoly	Charact. Toni. Hyperæo Phrygij	Charact. Toni. Hypophry	Charact. Toni. Iastij	Charact. Toni. Hypoias	Charact. Toni. Hypias	Charact. Toni. Dory	Charact. Toni. Hypodo	Charact. Toni. Hypermo

Row labels (leftmost column, Greek note-names):

- Νήτη ὑπερβολαιων
- Παρανήτη ὑπερβολαιων
- Τρίτη ὑπερβολαιων
- Νήτη διεζευγμενων
- Παρανήτη διεζευγμενων
- Τρίτη διεζευγμενων
- Παραμεσος
- Νήτη συνημμενων
- Παρανήτη συνημμενων
- Τρίτη συνημμενων
- Μέση
- Λιχανος μεσων
- Παρυπατη μεσων
- Ὑπατη μεσων
- Λιχανος ὑπατων
- Παρυπατη ὑπατων
- Ὑπατη ὑπατων
- Προσλαμβανομενος

Appendix N.º 37. will be found on the previous page.

No. 38 (see page 144.)

Greek Musical Notation from a Manuscript of the eleventh century.

No 39. see page 146.

Initial page from a
Greek ritual, found
in Buda.

No 40. see page 146.

Final page of a
Greek ritual
found at Buda.

Nº 41. (see page 169 in note)

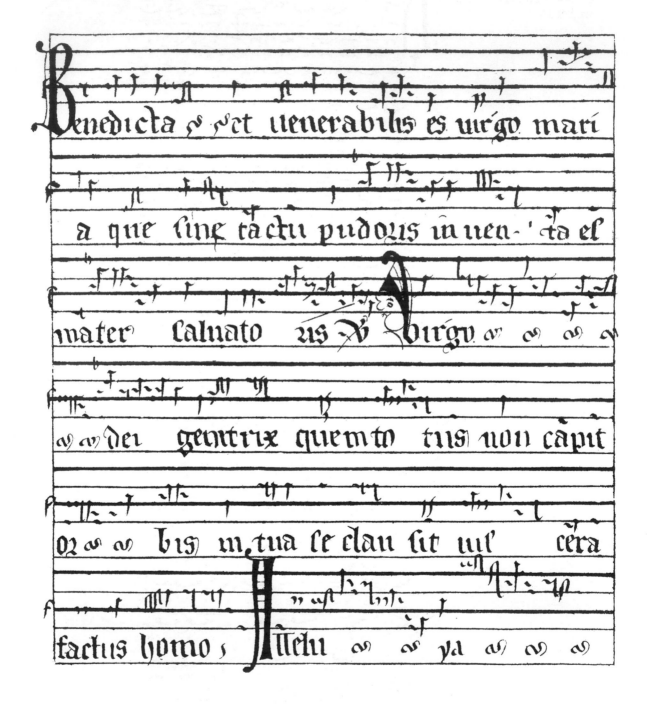

Specimen of Manuscript with thick lines to point out the place of the C & F cleff.

Nº 42 see page 169

Specimen from
Martini.

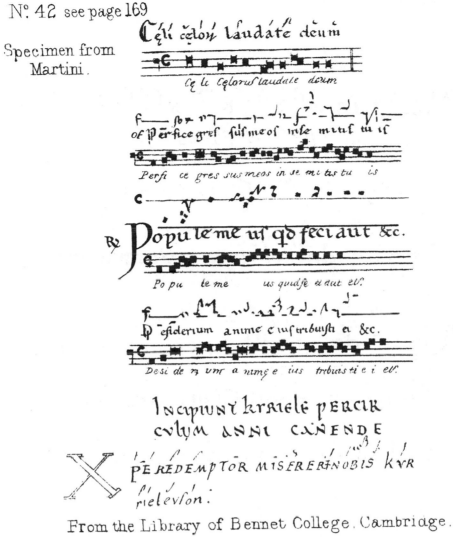

From the Library of Bennet College, Cambridge.

Nº 43 see page 182

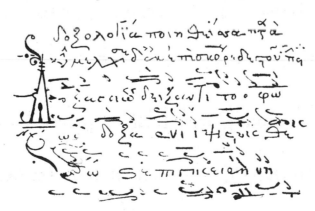

Greek Hymn from the Library of Jesus College, Oxon.

Nº 44 see page 181.

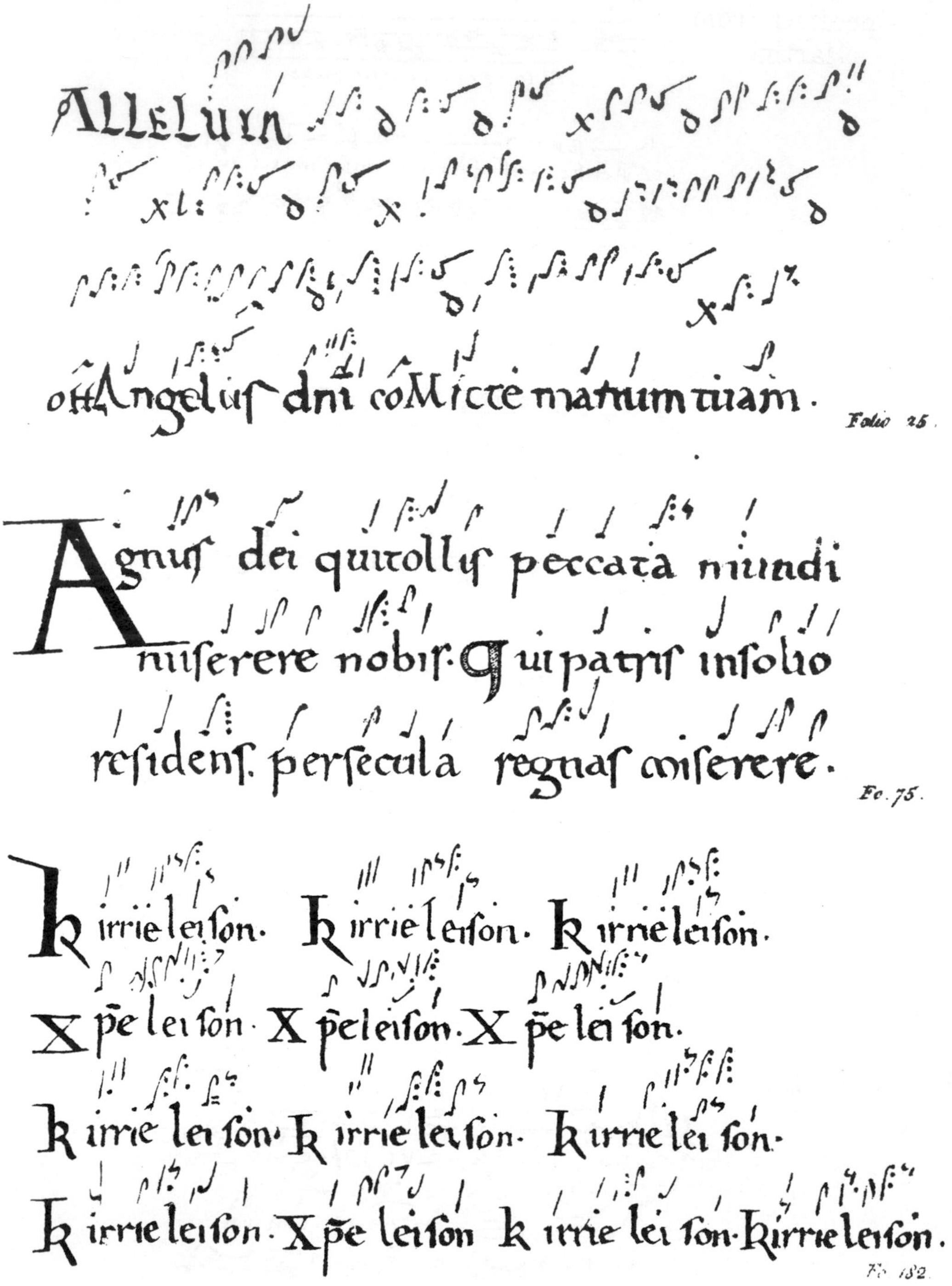

ALLeLuiA

 offAngeluſ dni coMicte matrum tuam .

Folio 25.

Agnuſ dei quitollıſ peccata niundi

miſerere nobıſ. Qui patrıſ infolio

reſidenſ. perfecula regnaſ miſerere .

Fo. 75.

Kirrieleiſon. Kirrieleiſon. Kirrieleiſon.

Xpe leiſon . Xpeleiſon. Xpe leiſon.

Kirrie leiſon. Kirrie leiſon. Kirrie lei ſon.

Kirrieleiſon. Xpe leiſon Kirrie lei ſon. Kirrieleiſon.

Fo. 132.

Manuscript by various hands from Bodleian Library Oxford

Claues medii canticorum aeui.

N.º 45.
See Page 379.

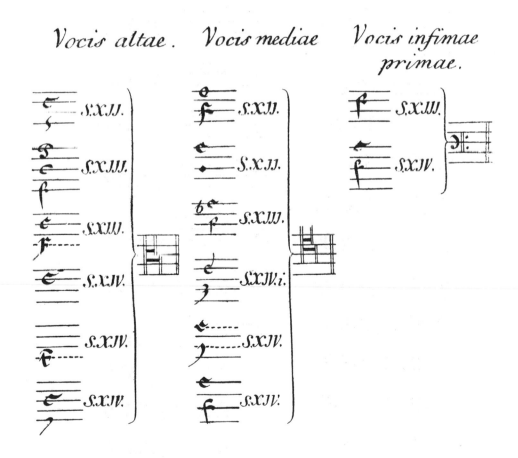

Musical Cleffs in use from the eleventh to the fourteenth Century.

No. 46. *Notae Musicae.*

See page 379.

Musical Characters in use from the eleventh to the fourteenth

No. 47.   *Notae Musicae.*
See page 379.

Century, with their equivalents in modern notation.

No. 48. see Page 379

Manuscript with Notation previous to the invention of the Staff.

Nº 49. see page 379.

Responsorium. In paupertā - te spi - ri tus serui ens Chri sto Suit
ber - - tus super ter ram pauper cum pau - pere in his
quae sur - sum sunt di - ues cum di uite, vbi cor fi xum
habuit in coe - - - - - lo thesauri a - - - - - - - - -
- - uit Ae - - - - - uia Versiculus. Auribus audiendi audi - ens
dicentem Jesum , vbi est thesaurus tu - us ibi est et cor tu um.
Vbi cor fi - xum.

*Sed expugnatis non longo post tempore Boructuatrus agente antiquorum Saxonum dispersi
sunt quilibet hi qui uerbum receperant. Ipse antistes cum quibusdam Pippinum petiit, qui interpellante
Brithtrude coniuge sua, dedit ei locum mansionis in insula Hreni quae lingua illorum uocatur in
littore. In qua ipse constructo monasterio quod hactenus possident heredes eius aliquandiu con -
tinentissimam gessit uitam, ibique clausit ultimum diem.*

Responsorium. Laudemus Do - - - mi num in be a ti an -
tisti - tis Suitber - ti me - ri tis glo - - - ri o - sus ad -
se pul chrum e - ius aegri ue - - - ni unt et sa nan - - -
- tur. Ae - -
uia. Versiculus. Vere mira bilis De us, qui assi du is be u
tum Suitbertum miraculis coru - scare fa - cis Ad se pul
chrum. Gloria patri. Justum deduxit Dominus. Laudes. Serue
bone et fi delis. quia in pauca fu isti fi delis. supra mul - ta
te constituam, in - tra in gaudi um Domini De - i tui.
Ae - uia - - - - - - - -

The equivalent of the opposite page in modern characters

Nº 50. see page 379.

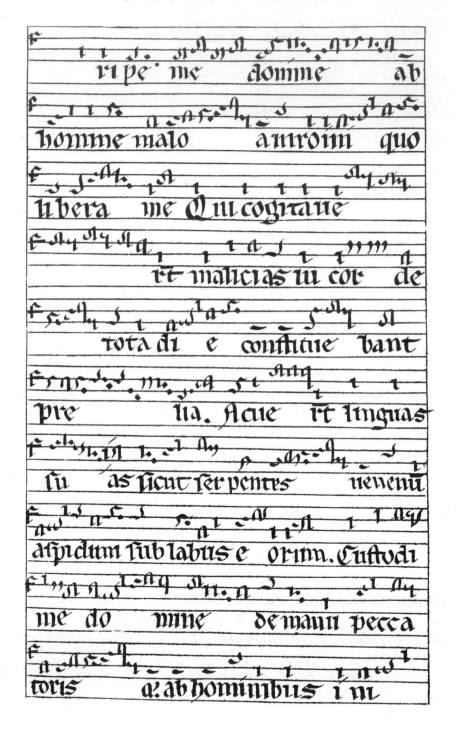

Notation said to be of the Twelfth Century.

N.° 51. see page 379.

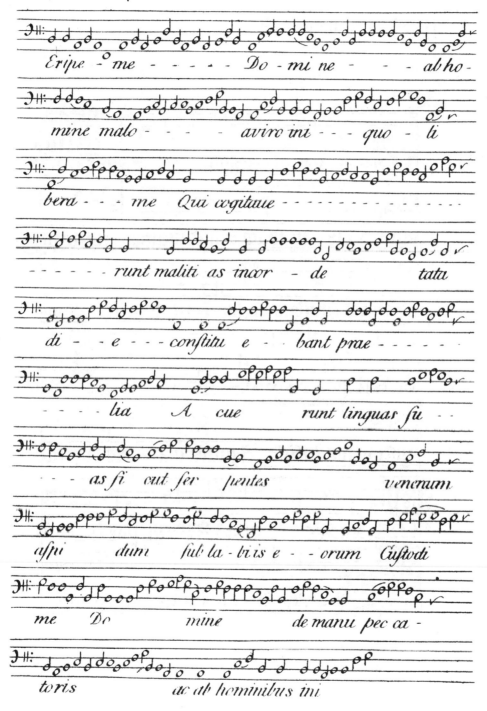

The equivalent of the opposite page in modern notation

N.º 52. see page 379.

Notation said to be of the Thirteenth Century.

N° 53. see page 379.

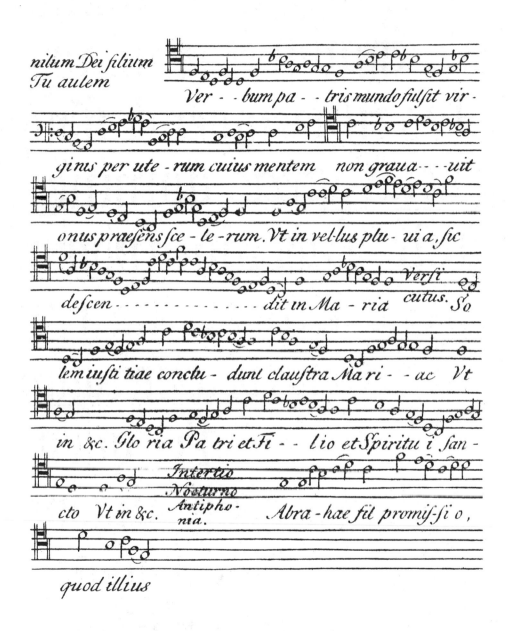

The equivalent of the opposite page in modern notation

Nº 54 see page 379.

Uere dignium et iustum
est. equum et salutare.
Nos tibi semper et ubiq;
gracias agere. domine
sancte pater omnipotens
eterne deus. Quia per
incarnati uerbi misterium
                              Per quem
maiestatem tuam laudant
angeli. adorant dominati
ones. tremunt potestates.
Celi celorumq; uirtutes ac

beata seraphyn socia exul
tatione concelebrant.
Cum quibus et nostras uo
ces ut admitti iubeas depre
camur. supplici confessione
dicentes. Sanctus. s. s.

N.º 55.

Vere dignum et iustum est. ae-quum et sa-luta-
re. Nos tibi semper et vbi-que grati-as agere, domine
sancte pater omni potens aeterne De-us. Quia per in
carna-ti uerbi mi-ste-rium . . . . Per quem
maiestatem tuam laudant ange-li, ado- - rant dominati-o-
nes, tre-munt po-testa-tes, Coeli coelorum-que uirtutes ac
beatae Se-ra-phim so-cia exulta-ti-o-ne conce-lebrant.
Cum qui-bus et nostras uoces vt ad-mitti iubeas de-pre-
ca-mur. sup-plici confessi-o-ne di-cen-tes: San- -ctus,
sanctus, s. s.

N.° 56. see page 160.

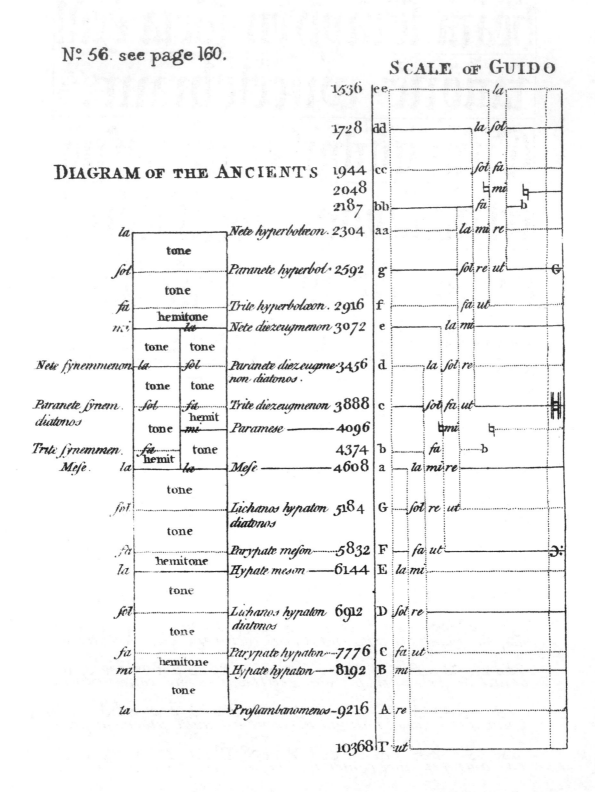

Nᵒ 57 see page 537.

A Lesson of Descant of thirtie eighte Proportions of sundrie kindes made by Master Giles, Master of the children at Windsor.

MISERERE

DOCTOR NATHANIEL GILES.

GENERAL INDEX.

N.B. Pages 1 to 486 are in Vol. I.—Pages 487 to end are in Vol. II.

INDEX

TO

MUSICAL ILLUSTRATIONS.

INDEX

TO

DIAGRAMS, WOODCUTS, AND MISCELLANEOUS ILLUSTRATIONS.

N.B. Pages 1 to 486 are in Vol. I.—Pages 487 to end are in Vol. II.

TABLE OF PARALLEL BOOKS, CHAPTERS, AND PAGES,

To render the New Index available for such Persons as possess the QUARTO EDITION.

TABLE OF PARALLEL BOOKS, CHAPTERS, AND PAGES.